W9-ABI-139

The
CHELSEA HOUSE LIBRARY
of LITERARY CRITICISM

The

CHELSEA HOUSE LIBRARY
of LITERARY CRITICISM

The

MAJOR AUTHORS EDITION
of the
NEW MOULTON'S LIBRARY *of* LITERARY CRITICISM
Volume 3

Caroline—Late Georgian

General Editor

HAROLD BLOOM

1988
CHELSEA HOUSE PUBLISHERS
NEW YORK
NEW HAVEN   PHILADELPHIA

EDITOR
S. T. Joshi

ASSOCIATE EDITOR
Jack Bishop

EDITORIAL COORDINATOR
Karyn Gullen Browne

COPY CHIEF
Richard Fumosa

EDITORIAL STAFF
Marie Claire Cebrian
Anthony C. Coulter
Stephen L. Mudd

PICTURE RESEARCH
Karen Herman

DESIGN
Susan Lusk

Printed and bound in the United States of
America.

3   5   7   9   8   6   4   2

Library of Congress Cataloging in Publication
Data

The Major Authors Edition of the New
   Moulton's library of literary criticism.
   (The Chelsea House library of literary criti-
   cism)
   Includes bibliographies.
   Contents: v. 1. Medieval—Late Renais-
sance.—   —v. 3. Caroline—Late Georgian.
1. English literature—History and criticism—
Collected works.   2. American literature—His-
tory   and   criticism—Collected   works.   I.
Bloom, Harold.   II. Series: New Moulton's
library of literary criticism.
PR85.M33   1985   820'.9   84-27426
ISBN 0-87754-815-3 (v. 1)
         0-87754-817-X (v. 3)

CONTENTS

Andrew Marvell 1253
John Bunyan 1281
John Dryden 1305
Daniel Defoe 1365
Alexander Pope 1401
Jonathan Swift 1457
Henry Fielding 1507
Laurence Sterne 1549
Thomas Gray 1585
Tobias Smollett 1611
Oliver Goldsmith 1647
David Hume 1679
Samuel Johnson 1707
Edward Gibbon 1765
Robert Burns 1797
Richard Brinsley Sheridan 1841

Additional Reading 1867

The Index to this series, *The Major Authors Edition*, appears in Volume 6.

ANDREW MARVELL

ANDREW MARVELL

1621–1678

Andrew Marvell was born on March 31, 1621, near Hull, in Yorkshire. His father, a clergyman with Calvinist leanings, was Master of the Almshouse at Hull. Marvell was educated at the Hull Grammar School and Trinity College, Cambridge, from which he graduated with a B.A. in 1639. After his mother's death in 1638 and his father's in 1640, Marvell left England to travel on the Continent. Little is known of the ten years that followed; he was abroad from 1642 to 1646, possibly as a tutor in France.

In 1650 he became tutor to Lord Fairfax's daughter, and it was about Fairfax's home that he wrote one of his best-known poems, "Upon Appleton House." Marvell remained at Nun Appleton for two years, and it is from that period that much of his lyric poetry seems to date.

While his sympathies appear to have been with the Royalists during his years with Fairfax, who was himself in exile because of his monarchist leanings, Marvell later came to admire Cromwell. The admiration was mutual, and in 1653 Marvell became tutor to William Dutton, a ward of Cromwell's. In 1657 he was appointed assistant to John Thurloe, Secretary of State, a position for which Milton had recommended him in 1652. He became the Member of Parliament for Hull in 1659 and served in that capacity, apart from a brief interruption, until his death. Milton's championing of Marvell was repaid in kind in 1660, when Marvell defended him against charges of regicide. From 1662 until his death Marvell published various satires, including *The Rehearsall Transpros'd* in two parts in 1672 and 1673. He died on August 18, 1678, in London and is buried at St. Giles-in-the-Fields. His *Miscellaneous Poems*, containing most of his poems, was purportedly published by his housekeeper, claiming to be his widow, in 1681; it appears, however, that Marvell never married.

Personal

He had not been long there (at Cambridge), before his Studys were interrupted by this remarkable Accident. Some *Jesuits*, with whom he was then conversant, seeing in him a Genius beyond his Years, thought of Nothing less than gaining a Proselyte. And doubtless their Hopes extended farther. They knew, if that Point was once obtained, he might in Time be a great Instrument towards carrying on their Cause. They used all the Arguments they could to seduce him away, which at last they did. After some Months his Father found him in a *Bookseller*'s Shop in *London* and prevailed with him to return to the College.—JOHN NORTON, Letter to Reverend Marvell (c. Jan. 1640)

My Lord,

But that it would be an interruption to the publick, wherein your studies are perpetually imployd, I should now & then venture to supply this my enforced absence with a line or two, though it were my onely busines, & that would be noe slight one, to make my due acknowledgments of your many favours; which I both doe at this time & ever shall; & have this farder which I thought my parte to let you know of, that there will be with you to morrow upon some occasion of busines a Gentleman whose name is Mr. Marvile; a man whom both by report, & the converse I have had with him, of singular desert for the State to make use of; who alsoe offers himselfe, if there be any imployment for him. His father was the Minister of Hull & he hath spent foure yeares abroad in Holland, France, Italy, & Spaine, to very good purpose, as I beleeve, & the gaineing of those 4 languages; besides he is a scholler & well read in the latin & Greeke authors, & noe doubt of an approved conversation; for he com's now lately out of the house of the Lord Fairefax who was Generall, where he was intrusted to give some instructions in the Languages to the Lady his Daughter. If upon the death of Mr. Wakerley

the Councell shall thinke that I shall need any assistant in the performance of my place (though for my part I find noe encumberance of that which belongs to me, except it be in point of attendance at Conferences with Ambassadors, which I must confesse, in my Condition I am not fit for) it would be hard for them to find a Man soe fit every way for that purpose as this Gentleman, one who I beleeve in a short time would be able to doe them as good service as Mr. Ascan.—JOHN MILTON, Letter to Lord Bradshaw (Feb. 21, 1652/3)

He was of middling stature, pretty strong sett, roundish faced, cherry cheek't, hazell eie, browne haire. He was in his conversation very modest, and of very few words: and though he loved wine he would never drinke hard in company, and was wont to say that, he would not play the goodfellow in any man's company in whose hands he would not trust his life. He had not a generall acquaintance.

In the time of Oliver the Protector he was Latin Secretarie. He was a great master of the Latin tongue; an excellent poet in Latin or English: for Latin verses there was no man could come into competition with him.

I remember I have heard him say that the Earle of Rochester was the only man in England that had the true veine of Satyre.

His native towne of Hull loved him so well that they elected him for their representative in Parliament, and gave him an honourable pension to maintaine him.

He kept bottles of wine at his lodgeing, and many times he would drinke liberally by himselfe to refresh his spirits, and exalt his Muse. (I remember I have been told that the learned Goclenius (an High-German) was wont to keep bottells of good Rhenish-wine in his studie, and, when his spirits wasted, he would drinke a good Rummer of it.)

Obiit Londini, Aug. 18. 1678; and is buried in St. Giles church in-the-fields about the middle of the south aisle. Some suspect that he was poysoned by the Jesuites, but I cannot be positive.—JOHN AUBREY, "Andrew Marvell," *Brief Lives*, 1669–96

The way having been made ready after this fashion, at the beginning of the next fit [the fourth, that is, of tertian ague] a great febrifuge was administered, that is to say, a draught of Venice treacle, etc. By the doctor's orders the patient was covered up close with blankets, or rather buried under them; and composed himself to sleep and sweat, in order to escape the cold shivers that ordinarily accompany the onset of the ague-fit. Seized with the profoundest sleep and sweating profusely, in the short space of twenty-four hours after the last fit he died comatose [*Apopleptice*]. Thus the patient died who, had a single ounce of Peruvian bark been properly administered, might easily have escaped, in twenty four hours, from the jaws of death and the grave. This is what I, burning with anger, informed the doctor when he told me this story without any sense of shame.—RICHARD MORTON, *Pyretologia*, 1692

Amongst these lewd Revilers, the lewdest was one whose name was *Marvel*. As he had liv'd in all manner of wickedness from his youth, so being of a singular impudence and petulancy of nature, he exercised the province of a Satyrist ⟨. . .⟩ Being abandon'd by his father, and expell'd the University, ⟨. . .⟩ A vagabond, ragged, hungry Poetaster, ⟨. . .⟩ At length, by the interest of *Milton*, to whom he was somewhat agreeable for his ill-natur'd wit, he was made Undersecretary to *Cromwell's* Secretary. ⟨. . .⟩ But the King being restor'd, this wretched man falling into his former poverty, did, for the sake of a livelihood, procure himself to be chosen Member of Parliament for a Borough, in which his father had exercis'd the office of a Presbyterian teacher. ⟨. . .⟩ In all Parliaments he was an enemy to the King's affairs. ⟨. . .⟩ But out of the House, when he could do it with impunity, he vented Himself with the greater bitterness, and daily spewed infamous libels out of his filthy mouth against the King himself. ⟨. . .⟩ But this *Bustuarius*, or fencer, never fought with more fury, than near his own grave, in a book written a little before his death, to which he gave this title, *An Account of the Growth of Popery, and Arbitrary Government in England.*—SAMUEL PARKER, *History of His Own Time*, 1727

General

Is this the Land, where, in those worst of times,
The hardy Poet rais'd his honest rimes
To dread rebuke, and bade controulment speak
In guilty blushes on the villain's cheek,
Bade Pow'r turn pale, kept mighty rogues in awe,
And made them fear the Muse, who fear'd not Law?
   —CHARLES CHURCHILL, "The Author," 1763

His pen was always properly directed, and had some effect upon such as were under no check or restraint from any laws human or divine. He hated corruption more than he dreaded poverty; and was so far from being venal, that he could not be bribed by the king into silence, when he scarce knew how to procure a dinner. His satires give us a higher idea of his patriotism, parts, and learning, than of his skill as a poet.—JAMES GRANGER, *Biographical History of England*, 1769–1824

By his writings Marvell obtained the character of the wittiest man of his time, and doubtless was of great service to the cause he espoused, which had in general been defended rather by serious argument than by ridicule. He occasionally threw out a number of poetical effusions of the humorous and satirical kind, in which he did not spare majesty itself. These are careless and loose in their composition, and frequently pass the

bounds of decorum; but they were well calculated for effect as party pieces, and became very popular. He exercised his wit still more copiously in prose. In 1672, Dr. Sam. Parker, afterwards bishop of Oxford, a flaming and intolerant high churchman, published a work of bishop Bramhall's, to which he added a preface of his own, maintaining the most extravagant positions concerning the rights of sovereigns over the consciences of their subjects. This piece Marvell attacked in the same year in a work which he entitled *The Rehearsal Transprosed*. With a profusion of witty sarcasm, it contains much solid argument, and may be reckoned one of the ablest exposures of the maxims of religious tyranny. Parker wrote an answer, to which Marvell replied; and the reverend champion did not choose to carry the controversy further.—JOHN AIKIN, *General Biography; or Lives of the Most Eminent Persons*, 1799–1815

Marvell abounds with conceits and false thoughts, but some of the descriptive touches are picturesque and beautiful. His description of a gently rising eminence is more picturesque, although not so elegantly and justly expressed, as the same subject is in Denham. ⟨. . .⟩ Sometimes Marvell observes little circumstances of rural nature with the eye and feeling of a true poet:

Then as I careless on the bed
Of *gelid strawberries* do tread,
And through the hazels thick, espy,
The hatching throstle's shining eye.

The last circumstance is new, highly poetical, and could only have been described by one who was a real lover of nature, and a witness of her beauties in her most solitary retirement. It is the observation of such *circumstances* which can alone form an accurate descriptive rural poet. In this province of his art Pope therefore must evidently fail, as he could not describe what his physical infirmities prevented his observing. For the same reason Johnson, as a critic, was not a proper judge of this sort of poetry.—WILLIAM LISLE BOWLES, "Introduction" to *The Works of Alexander Pope, Esq.*, 1806

The humour and eloquence of Marvell's prose tracts were admired and probably imitated by Swift. In playful exuberance of figure he sometimes resembles Burke. For consistency of principles, it is not so easy to find his parallel. His few poetical pieces betray some adherence to the school of conceit, but there is much in it that comes from the heart warm, pure, and affectionate.—THOMAS CAMPBELL, *Specimens of the British Poets*, 1819

His poems possess many of the finest elements of popularity; a rich profusion of fancy which almost dazzles the mind as bright colours dazzle the eye; an earnestness and heartiness which do not always,—do not often belong to these flowery fancies, but which when found in their company add to them inexpressible vitality and savor; and a frequent felicity of phrase, which, when once read, fixes itself in the memory, and *will* not be forgotten. ⟨. . .⟩ His mind was a bright garden, such a garden as he has described so finely, and that a few gaudy weeds should mingle with the healthier plants does but serve to prove the fertility of the soil.—MARY RUSSELL MITFORD, *Recollections of a Literary Life*, 1851, pp. 532–33

Fundamentally, the Poetry of Marvell is genuine as a bird's singing, or the singing of the brook on its gleaming way under the leafage. There is the breath and fragrance of inviolate Nature in every page of the *Poems of the Country* and *Poems of Imagination and Love*, and in *Poems of Friendship* and State Poems such THINKING and aspiration as were worthy of their greatest themes; and I am here remembering, and wish it to be remembered, that John Milton and Oliver Cromwell and Blake are celebrated by him.—ALEXANDER B. GROSART, "Memorial-Introduction" to *The Complete Poems of Andrew Marvell*, 1872, p. lxvi

Marvell holds a unique place in the seventeenth century. He stands at the parting of the ways, between the extravagancies of the lyrical Jacobeans on the one hand, and the new formalism initiated by Waller on the other. He is not unaffected by either influence. The modish handling of the decasyllable couplet is very marked here and there. You have it, for instance, in the poem on Blake:

> Bold Stayner leads; this fleet's designed by fate
> To give him laurel, as the last did plate.

And elsewhere, of course, he has conceits which cry aloud in their flagrancy. But his real affinities are with a greater than Waller or Suckling. Milton in those days "was like a star, and dwelt apart"; but of all who "called him friend," Marvell is the one who can claim the most of spiritual kinship. The very circumstances of their lives are curiously similar. Each left poetry for statecraft and polemic: for Milton the flowering time came late; for Marvell, never. And their poetic temper is one: it is the music of Puritanism,—the Puritanism of Spenser and Sidney, not uncultivated, not ungracious, not unsensuous even, but always with the same dominant note in it, of moral strength and moral purity. Marvell is a Puritan; but his spirit has not entered the prison-house, nor had the key turned on it there. He is a poet still, such as there have been few in any age. The lyric gift of Herrick he has not, nor Donne's incomparable subtlety and intensity of emotion; but for imaginative power, for decent melody, for that self-restraint of phrase which is the fair half of art, he must certainly hold high rank among his fellows. The clear sign of this self-restraint is his mastery over the octosyllable couplet, metre which in less skilful hands so readily becomes diffuse and wearisome.

Marvell writes love poems, but he is not essentially a love poet. He sings beautifully to Juliana and Chlora, but they themselves are only accidents in his song. His real passion—a most uncommon one in the seventeenth century—is for nature, exactly as we moderns mean nature, the great spiritual influence which deepens and widens life for us. How should the intoxication of meadow, and woodland, and garden, be better expressed than in these two lines—

> Stumbling on melons, as I pass,
> Insnared with flowers, I fall on grass.

unless indeed it be here—

> I am the mower Damon, known
> Through all the meadows I have mown,
> On me the morn her dew distils
> Before her darling daffodils;
> And if at noon my toil me heat,
> The sun himself licks off my sweat;
> While, going home, the evening sweet
> In cowslip water bathes my feet.

These mower-idylls, never found in the anthologies, are among the most characteristic of Marvell's shorter poems. I cannot forbear to quote two stanzas from "The Mower to the Glowworms":

> Ye living lamps, by whose dear light
> The nightingale doth sit so late,
> And studying all the summer night,
> Her matchless songs doth meditate.

> Ye country comets, that portend
> Nor war, nor prince's funeral,
> Shining unto no higher end
> Than to presage the grass's fall.

Observe how Marvell makes of the nightingale a conscious artist, a winged *dira*. Elsewhere he speaks of her as sitting among the "squatted thorns," in order "to sing the trials of her voice."

I must needs see in Marvell something of a nature-philosophy strangely anticipative of George Meredith. For the one, as for the other, complete absorption in nature, the unreserved abandonment of self to the skyey influences, is the really true and sanative wisdom. Marvell describes his soul, freed of the body's vesture, perched like a bird upon the garden boughs—

> Annihiliting all that's made
> To a green thought in a green shade.

The same idea is to be found in the lines "Upon Appleton House," a poem which will repay careful study from all who wish to get at the secret of Marvell's genius. It shows him at his best—and at his worst, in the protracted conceit, whereby a garden, its flowers and its bees, are likened to a fort with a garrison. And here I am minded to enter a plea against the indiscriminate condemnation of conceits in poetry. After all, a conceit is only an analogy, a comparison, a revealing of likeness in things dissimilar, and therefore of the very essence of poetic imagination. Often it illumines, and where it fails it is not because it is a conceit, but because it is a bad conceit; because the thing compared is not beautiful in itself, or because the comparison is not flashed upon you, but worked out with such tedious elaboration as to be "merely fantastical." Many of Marvell's conceits are, in effect, bad; the well-known poem, "On a Drop of Dew," redeemed though it is by the last line and a half, affords a terrible example. But others are shining successes. Here is one, set in a haunting melody, as of Browning:

> Gentler times for love are meant:
> Who for parting pleasures strain,
> Gather roses in the rain,
> Wet themselves and spoil their scent.

Next to green fields, Marvell is perhaps happiest in treating of death. His is the mixed mode of the Christian scholar, not all unpaganised, a lover of heaven, but a lover of the earthly life too. There is the epitaph on a nameless lady, with its splendid close:

> Modest as morn, as mid-day bright,
> Gentle as evening, cool as night:
> 'Tis true: but all too weakly said;
> 'Twas more significant. She's dead.

There is the outburst on the death of the poet's hero, the greater Portector:

> O human glory vain! O Death! O wings!
> O worthless world! O transitory things!

And to crown all, there are these lines, which remind me, for their felicities, their quaintness, and the organ-note in them, of the *Hydriotaphia*:

> But at my back I always hear
> Time's winged chariot hurrying near.
> And yonder all before us lie
> Deserts of vast eternity.
> Thy beauty shall no more be found,
> Nor, in thy marble vault, shall sound
> My echoing song; then worms shall try
> Thy long-preserved virginity,
> And your quaint honour turn to dust,

And into ashes all my lust:
The grave's a fine and private place,
But none, I think, do there embrace.

I have left myself no room to speak of the Satires. They are not a subject to dwell upon with pleasure. One sees that they were inevitable, that a man of Marvell's strenuous moral fibre, in all the corruption of the Restoration court, could not but break forth into savage invective; yet one regrets them, as one regrets the *Defensio* and *Eikonoklastes*.—EDMUND K. CHAMBERS, *Academy*, Sept. 17, 1892, pp. 230–31

One of the most original poets of the Stuart period, the new tentative features of the age in poetry, again, are clearly marked. The lyrical work belonging to his early life has often passages of imaginative quality, equally strong and delicate. If we exclude Milton, no one of that time touches sweeter or nobler lyrical notes; but he is singularly unequal; he flies high, but is not long on the wing. The characteristic Elizabethan smoothness of unbroken melody was now failing; the fanciful style of Donne, the seventeenth century *concetti*, seized on Marvell too strongly, and replaced in him the earlier mythological landscape characteristic of the Renaissance.—FRANCIS TURNER PALGRAVE, *Landscape in Poetry*, 1896, p. 154

Works

We copy a portion of Marvell's "Maiden lamenting for her Fawn"—which we prefer not only as a specimen of the elder poets, but in itself as a beautiful poem abounding in pathos, exquisitely delicate imagination and truthfulness, to anything of its species:

It is a wondrous thing how fleet
'T was on those little silver feet,
With what a pretty skipping grace
It oft would challenge me the race,
And when 't had left me far away,
'T would stay, and run again, and stay;
For it was nimbler much than hinds,
And trod as if on the four winds.
I have a garden of my own,
But so with roses overgrown,
And lilies that you would it guess
To be a little wilderness;
And all the spring-time of the year
It only loved to be there.
Among the beds of lilies I
Have sought it where it should lie,
Yet could not till itself would rise
Find it, although before mine eyes.
For in the flaxen lilies shade,
It like a bank of lilies laid;
Upon the roses it would feed
Until its lips even seemed to bleed,
And then to me 't would boldly trip,
And print those roses on my lip,
But all its chief delight was still
With roses thus itself to fill,
And its pure virgin limbs to fold
In whitest sheets of lilies cold.
Had it lived long it would have been
Lilies without, roses within.

How truthful an air of lamentation hangs here upon every syllable! It pervades all. It comes over the sweet melody of the words—over the gentleness and grace which we fancy in the little maiden herself—even over the half-playful, half-petulant air with which she lingers on the beauties and good qualities of her favorite—like the cool shadow of a summer cloud over a bed of lilies and violets, "and all sweet flowers." The whole is redolent with poetry of a very lofty order. Every line is an idea—conveying either the beauty and playfulness of the fawn, or the artlessness of the maiden, or her love, or her admiration, or her grief, or the fragrance and warmth and *appropriateness* of the little nest-like bed of lilies and roses which the fawn devoured as it lay upon them, and could scarcely be distinguished from them by the once happy little damsel who went to seek her pet with an arch and rosy smile on her face. Consider the great variety of truthful and delicate thought in the few lines we have quoted—the *wonder* of the maiden at the fleetness of her favorite—the "little silver feet"—the fawn challenging his mistress to a race with "a pretty skipping grace," running on before, and then, with head turned back, awaiting her approach only to fly from it again—can we not distinctly perceive all these things? How exceedingly vigorous, too, is the line,

And trod as if on the four winds!—

a vigor fully apparent only when we keep in mind the artless character of the speaker and the four feet of the favorite—one for each wind. Then consider the garden of "my own," so over grown—entangled—with roses and lilies, as to be "a little wilderness"—the fawn, loving to be there, and there "only"—the maiden seeking it "where it *should* lie"—and not being able to distinguish it from the flowers until "itself would rise"—the lying among the lilies "like a bank of lilies"—the loving to "fill itself with roses,"

And its pure virgin limbs to fold
In whitest sheets of lilies cold,

and these things being its "chief" delights—and then the pre-eminent beauty and naturalness of the concluding lines—whose very hyperbole only renders them more true to nature when we consider the innocence, the artlessness, the enthusiasm, the passionate grief, and more passionate admiration of the bereaved child—

Had it lived long, it would have been
Lilies without—roses within.
—EDGAR ALLAN POE, "Old English Poetry" (1845), *Complete Works*, ed. James A. Harrison, Vol. 12, pp. 143–46

Andrew Marvel, a thoughtful and graceful poet, a masterly prose-writer and controversialist, a wit of the first water, and, above all, an incorruptible patriot, is thought to have had no mean hand in putting an end to the dynasty of the Stuarts. His wit helped to render them ridiculous, and his integrity added weight to the sting. The enmity, indeed, of such a man was in itself a reproach to them; for Marvel, though bred on the Puritan side, was no Puritan himself, nor a foe to any kind of reasonable and respectable government. He had served Cromwell with his friend Milton, as Latin Secretary, but would have aided Charles the Second as willingly, in his place in Parliament, had the king been an honest man instead of a pensioner of France. The story of his refusing a *carte blanche* from the king's treasurer, and then sending out to borrow a guinea, would be too well known to need allusion to it in a book like the present, if it did not contain a specimen of a sort of practical wit.

Marvel being pressed by the royal emissary to state what would satisfy his expectations, and finding that there was no other mode of persuading him that he had none, called in his servant to testify to his dining three days in succession upon one piece of mutton.

Even the wise and refined Marvel, however, was not free

from the coarseness of his age; and hence I find the same provoking difficulty as in the case of his predecessors, with regard to extracts from the poetical portion of his satire. With the prose I should not have been at a loss. But the moment these wits of old time began rhyming, they seem to have thought themselves bound to give the same after-dinner license to their fancy, as when they were called upon for a song. To read the noble ode on "Cromwell," in which such a generous compliment is paid to Charles the First,—the devout and beautiful one entitled "Bermuda," and the sweet overflowing fancies put into the mouth of the "Nymph lamenting the loss of her Faun,"—and then to follow up their perusal with some, nay most of the lampoons that were so formidable to Charles and his brother, you would hardly think it possible for the same man to have written both, if examples were not too numerous to the contrary. Fortunately for the reputation of Marvel's wit, with those who chose to become acquainted with it, he wrote a great deal better in prose than in verse, and the prose does not take the license of the verse.—LEIGH HUNT, *Wit and Humour*, 1846

Marvell's "Horation Ode," the most truly classic in our language, is worthy of its theme. The same poet's Elegy, in parts noble, and everywhere humanly tender, is worth more than all Carlyle's biography as a witness to the gentler qualities of the hero, and of the deep affection that stalwart nature could inspire in hearts of truly masculine temper.—JAMES RUSSELL LOWELL, "Dryden" (1868), *Among My Books*, 1870, p. 19

By way of flourishing my Eyes, I have been looking into Andrew Marvell, an old favourite of mine—who led the way for Dryden in Verse, and Swift in Prose, and was a much better fellow than the last, at any rate.

Two of his lines in the Poem on "Appleton House," with its Gardens, Grounds, etc., run:

> But most the *Hewel's* wonders are
> Who here has the Holtseltster's care.

The "Hewel" being evidently the Woodpecker, who, by tapping the Trees, etc., does the work of one who measures and gauges Timber; here, rightly or wrongly, called "Holtseltster." "Holt" one knows: but what is "seltster"? I do not find either this word or "Hewel" in Bailey or Halliwell. But "Hewel" may be a form of "Yaffil," which I read in some Paper that Tennyson had used for the Woodpecker in his Last Tournament.

This reminded me that Tennyson once said to me—some thirty years ago, or more—in talking of Marvell's "Coy Mistress," where it breaks in—

> But at my back I always hear
> Time's winged Chariot hurrying near, etc.

"*That* strikes me as Sublime—I can hardly tell why." Of course, this partly depends on its place in the Poem.—EDWARD FITZGERALD, Letter to W. A. Wright (Jan. 20, 1872)

As a poet Marvell is very unequal. He has depth of feeling, descriptive power, melody; his study of the classics could not fail to teach him form; sometimes we find in him an airy and tender grace which remind us of the lighter manner of Milton. but art with him was only an occasional recreation, not a regular pursuit; he is often slovenly, sometimes intolerably diffuse, especially when he is seduced by the facility of the octosyllabic couplet. He was also eminently afflicted with the gift of 'wit' or ingenuity, much prized in his day. His conceits vie with those of Donne or Cowley. He is capable of saying of the Halcyon:—

> The viscous air where'er she fly
> Follows and sucks her azure dye;
> The jellying stream compacts below,
> If it might fix her shadow so.

And of Maria—

> Maria such and so doth hush
> The world and through the evening rush.
> No new-born comet such a train
> Draws through the sky nor star new-slain.
> For straight those giddy rockets fail
> Which from the putrid earth exhale,
> But by her flames in heaven tried
> Nature is wholly vitrified.

'The Garden' is an English version of a poem written in Latin by Marvell himself. It may have gained by being cast originally in a classical mould, which would repel prolixity and extravagant conceits. In it Marvell has been said to approach Shelley: assuredly he shows a depth of poetic feeling wonderful in a political gladiator. The thoughts that dwell in 'a green shade' have never been more charmingly expressed.

'A Drop of Dew', like 'The Garden', was composed first in Latin. It is a conceit, but a pretty conceit, gracefully as well as ingeniously worked out, and forms a good example of the contrast between the philosophic poetry of those days, a play of intellectual fancy, and its more spiritual and emotional counterpart in our own time. The concluding lines, with their stroke of 'wit' about the manna are a sad fall.

'The Bermudas' was no doubt suggested by the history of the Oxenbridges. It is the 'holy and cheerful note' of a little band of exiles for conscience sake wafted by Providence in their 'small boat' to a home in a land of beauty.

'Young Love' is well known, and its merits speak for themselves. It is marred by the intrusion in the third and fourth stanzas of the fiercer and coarser passion.

The 'Horatian Ode on Cromwell's Return from Ireland' cannot be positively proved to be the work of Marvell. Yet we can hardly doubt that he was its author. The point of view and the sentiment, combining admiration of Cromwell with respect and pity for Charles, are exactly his: the classical form would be natural to him; and so would the philosophical conceit which disfigures the eleventh stanza. The epithet *indefatigable* applied to Cromwell recurs in a poem which is undoubtedly his; and so does the emphatic expression of belief that the hero could have been happier in private life, and that he sacrificed himself to the State in taking the supreme command. The compression and severity of style are not characteristic of Marvell; but they would be imposed on him in this case by his model. If the ode is really his, to take it from him would be to do him great wrong. It is one of the noblest in the English language, and worthily presents the figures and events of the great tragedy as they would impress themselves on the mind of an ideal spectator, at once feeling and dispassionate. The spirit of Revolution is described with a touch in the lines

> Though Justice against Fate complain
> And plead the ancient rights in vain
> (But those do hold or break
> As men are strong or weak).

Better than anything else in our language this poem gives an idea of a grand Horatian measure, as well as of the diction and spirit of an Horatian ode.

Of the lines 'On Milton's *Paradise Lost*' some are vigorous; but they are chiefly interesting from having been written by one who had anxiously watched Milton's genius at work.

Marvell's amatory poems are cold; probably he was

passionless. His pastorals are in the false classical style, and of little value. 'Clorinda and Damon' is about the best of them, and about the best of that is

> Near this a fountain's liquid bell
> Tinkles within the concave shell.

The Satires in their day were much admired and feared: they are now for the most part unreadable. The subjects of satire as a rule are ephemeral; but a great satirist like Juvenal or Dryden preserves his flies in the amber of his general sentiment. In Marvell's satires there is no amber: they are mere heaps of dead flies. Honest indignation against iniquity and lewdness in high places no doubt is there; but so are the meanness of Restoration politics and the dirtiness of Restoration thought. The curious may look at 'The Character of Holland,' the jokes in which are as good or as bad as ever, though the cannon of Monk and De Ruyter have ceased to roar; and in 'Britannia and Raleigh' the passage of which giving ironical advice to Charles II is a specimen of the banter which was deemed Marvell's peculiar gift, and in which Swift and Junius were his pupils.

Like Milton, Marvell wrote a number of Latin poems. One of them had the honour of being ascribed to Milton.
—GOLDWIN SMITH, "Andrew Marvell," *The English Poets*, ed. Thomas Humphry Ward, 1880, Vol. 2, pp. 382–84

'He earned the glorious name,' says a biographer of Andrew Marvell (editing an issue of that poet's works, which certainly has its faults), 'of the British Aristides.' The portly dullness of the mind that could make such a phrase, and, having made, award it, is not, in fairness, to affect a reader's thought of Marvell himself nor even of his time. Under correction, I should think that the award was not made in his own age; he did but live on the eye of the day that cumbered its mouth with phrases of such foolish burden and made literature stiff with them. He, doubtless, has moments of mediocre pomp, but even then it is Milton that he touches, and not anything more common; and he surely never even heard a threat of the pass that the English tongue should come to but a little later on.

Andrew Marvell's political rectitude, it is true, seems to have been of a robustious kind; but his poetry, at its rare best, has a 'wild civility', which might puzzle the triumph of him, whoever he was, who made a success of this phrase of the 'British Aristides'. Nay, it is difficult not to think that Marvell too, who was 'of middling stature, roundish-faced, cherry-cheeked', a healthy and active rather than a spiritual Aristides, might himself have been somewhat taken by surprise at the encounters of so subtle a muse. He, as a garden-poet, expected the accustomed Muse to lurk about the fountain-heads, within the caves, and by the walks and the statues of the gods, keeping the tryst of a seventeenth-century convention in which there were certainly no surprises. And for fear of the commonplaces of those visits Marvell sometimes outdoes the whole company of garden-poets in the difficult labours of the fancy. The reader treads with him a 'maze' most resolutely intricate, and is more than once obliged to turn back having been too much puzzled on the way to a small, visible, plain, and obvious goal of thought.

And yet this poet two or three times did meet a Muse he had hardly looked for among the trodden paths; a spiritual creature had been waiting behind a laurel or an apple tree. You find him coming away from such a divine ambush a wilder and a simpler man. All his garden had been made ready for poetry, and poetry was indeed there, but in unexpected hiding and in a strange form, looking rather like a fugitive, shy of the poet

who was conscious of having her rules by heart, yet sweetly willing to be seen, for all her haste.

For it is only in those well-known poems, 'The Garden', translated from his own Latin, and 'The Nymph Complaining for the Death of Her Fawn', in that less familiar piece 'The Mower against Gardens', in 'The Picture of T.C. in a Prospect of Flowers', with a few very brief passages in the course of duller verses, that Marvell comes into veritable possession of his own more interior powers—at least in the series of his garden lyrics. The political poems, needless to say, have an excellence of a different character and a higher degree. They have so much authentic dignity that 'the glorious name of the British Aristides' really seems duller when it is conferred as the earnings of the 'Horatian Ode upon Cromwell's Return from Ireland' than when it inappropriately clings to Andrew Marvell, cherry-cheeked, caught in the tendrils of his vines and melons. He shall be, therefore, the British Aristides in those moments of midsummer solitude; at least, the heavy phrase shall then have the smile it never sought.

Marvell can be tedious in these gardens—tedious with every ingenuity, refinement, and assiduity of invention. When he intends to flatter the owner of the *Hill and Grove at Billborow*, he is most deliberately silly, not as the eighteenth century was silly, but with a peculiar innocence. Unconsciousness there was not, assuredly; but the aritificial phrases of Marvell had never been used by a Philistine; the artifices are freshly absurd, the cowardice before the plain face of commonplace is not vulgar, there is an evident simple pleasure in the successful evasion of simplicity, and all the anxiety of the poet comes to a happy issue before our eyes. He commends the Billborow hill because 'the stiffest compass could not strike' a more symmetrical and equal semi-circle than its form presents, and he rebukes the absent mountains because they deform the earth and affright the heavens. This hill, he says, with a little better fancy, only 'strives to raise the plain'. Lord Fairfax of the soil are dedicated, and whose own merit they illustrate, is then said to be admirable for the modesty whereby, having a hill, he has also a clump of trees on the top, wherein to sequester the honours of eminence. It is not too much to say that the whole of this poem is untouched by poetry.

So is almost that equally ingenious piece, 'Appleton House', addressed to the same friend. It chanced that Appleton House was small, and out of this plain little fact the British Aristides contrives to turn a sedulous series of compliments with fair success and with a most guileless face. What natural humility in the householder who builds in proportion to his body, and is contented like the tortoise and the bird! Further on, however, it appears that the admired house had been a convent, and that to the dispossessed nuns was due the praise of proportion; they do not get it, in any form, from Marvell. A pretty passage follows, on the wasting of gardens, and a lament over the passing away of some earlier England. ⟨. . .⟩ But nothing here is of the really fine quality of 'The Picture of T.C.', or 'The Garden', or 'The Nymph Complaining for the Death of Her Fawn'.

In these three the presence of a furtive irony of the gentlest kind is the sure sign that they came of the visitings of the unlooked-for muse aforesaid. Marvell rallies his own 'Nymph', rallies his own soul for her clapping of silver wings in the solitude of summer trees; and more sweetly does he pretend to offer to the little girl 'T.C.' the prophetic homage of the habitual poets. ⟨. . .⟩

The noble phrase of the 'Horatian Ode' is not recovered again high or low throughout Marvell's book, if we except one single splendid and surpassing passage from 'The Definition of Love'. The hopeless lover speaks:

> Magnanimous despair alone
> Could show me so divine a thing.

'To his Coy Mistress' is the only piece, not already named, altogether fine enough for an anthology. The Satires are, of course, out of reach for their inordinate length. The celebrated Satire on Holland certainly makes the utmost of the fun to be easily found in the physical facts of the country whose people 'with mad labour fished the land to shore'. The Satire on *Flecknoe* makes the utmost of another joke we know of—that of famine. Flecknoe, it will be remembered, was a poet, and poor; but the joke of his bad verses was hardly needed, so fine does Marvell find that of his hunger. Perhaps there is no age of English satire that does not give forth the sound of that laughter unknown to savages—that craven laughter.—ALICE MEYNELL, "Andrew Marvell," *Pall Mall Gazette*, July 14, 1897

HENRY RODGERS
From "Andrew Marvell"

Edinburgh Review, January 1844, pp. 90–104

The characteristic attribute of Marvell's genius was unquestionably wit, in all the varieties of which—brief sententious sarcasm, fierce invective, light raillery, grave irony, and broad laughing humour—he seems to have been by nature almost equally fitted to excel. To say that he *has* equally excelled in all would be untrue, though striking examples of each might easily be selected from his writings. The activity with which his mind suggests ludicrous images and analogies is astonishing; he often absolutely startles us by the remoteness and oddity of the sources from which they are supplied, and by the unexpected ingenuity and felicity of his repartees.

His *forte*, however, appears to be a grave ironical banter, which he often pursues at such a length that there seems no limit to his fertility of invention. In his endless accumulation of ludicrous images and allusions, the untiring exhaustive ridicule with which he will play upon the same topics, he is unique; yet this peculiarity not seldom leads him to drain the generous wine even to the dregs—to spoil a series of felicitous ralleries by some far-fetched conceit or unpardonable extravagance.

But though Marvell was so great a master of wit, and especially of that caustic species which is appropriate to satirists, we will venture to say that he was singularly free from many of the faults which distinguish that irritable brotherhood. Unsparing and merciless as his ridicule is, contemptuous and ludicrous as are the lights in which he exhibits his opponent; nay, further, though is invectives are not only often terribly severe, but (in compliance with the spirit of the age) often grossly coarse and personal, it is still impossible to detect a single particle of malignity. His general tone is that of broad laughing banter, or of the most cutting invective; but he appears equally devoid of malevolence in both. In the one, he seems amusing himself with opponents too contemptible to move his anger; in the other, to lay on with the stern imperturbable gravity of one who is performing the unpleasant but necessary functions of a public executioner. This freedom from the usual faults of satirists may be traced to several causes; partly to the *bonhommie* which, with all his talents for satire, was a peculiar characteristic of the man, and which rendered him as little disposed to take offence, and as placable when it

was offered, as any man of his time; partly to the integrity of his nature, which, while it prompted him to champion any cause in which justice had been outraged or innocence wronged, effectually preserved from the wanton exercise of his wit for the gratification of malevolence; partly, perhaps principally, to the fact, that both the above qualities restricted him to encounters in which he had personally no concern. If he carried a keen sword, it was a most peaceable and gentlemanly weapon; it never left the scabbard except on the highest provocation, and even then, only on behalf of others, His magnanimity, self-control, and good temper, restrained him from avenging any insult offered to himself; his chivalrous love of justice instantly roused all the lion within him on behalf of the injured and oppressed. It is perhaps well for Marvell's fame that his quarrels were not personal: had they been so, it is hardly probable that such powers of sarcasm and irony should have been so little associated with bitterness of temper.

This freedom from malignity is highly honourable to him. In too many cases it must be confessed that wit has been sadly dissociated from amiability and generosity. It is true, indeed, that there is no necessary connexion between that quality of mind and the malevolent passions, as numberless illustrious examples sufficiently prove. But where wit is conjoined with malevolence, the latter more effectually displays itself; and even where there is originally no such conjunction, wit is almost always combined with that constitutional irritability of genius which is so readily gratifies, and which, by gratifying, it transforms into something worse. Half the tendencies of our nature pass into habits only from the facilities which encourage their development. We will venture to say, that there is not a tithe of the quarrels in the world that there used to be when all men were accustomed to wear arms; and we may rest assured, that many a waspish temper has become so, principally from being in possession of the weapon of satire. Not seldom, too, it must with sorrow be admitted, the most exquisite sense of the ridiculous has been strangely combined with a morbid, gloomy, saturnine temperament, which looks on all things with a jaundiced imagination, and surveys human infirmities and foibles with feelings not more remote from those of compassionate benevolence than of good-humoured mirth. Happy when, as in the case of Cowper, the influence of a benign heart and unfeigned humility, prevents this tendency from degenerating into universal malevolence. There are few things more shockingly incongruous than the ghastly union of wit and misanthropy. Wit should be ever of open brow, joyous, and frank-hearted. Even the severest satire may be delicious reading, when penned with the *bonhommie* of Horace, or of Addison, or the equanimity of Plato, or of Pascal. Without pretending these immortal writers, we firmly believe he had as much kindly feeling as any of them. Unhappily the two by no means go together; there may be the utmost refinement without a particle of good-nature; and a great deal of good-nature without any refinement. It were easy to name writers, who with the most exquisite grace of diction can as little disguise the malice of their nature, as Marvell, with all his coarseness, can make us doubt his benevolence. Through the veil of their language (of beautiful texture, but too transparent) we see chagrin poorly simulating mirth; anger struggling to appear contempt, and failing; scorn writhing itself into an aspect of ironical courtesy, but with grim distortion in the attempt; and sarcasms urged by the impulses which, under different circumstances, and in another country, would have prompted to the use of the stiletto.

It is impossible, indeed, not to regret the coarseness, often amounting to buffoonery, of Marvell's wit; though, from the consideration just urged, we regard it with the more forbear-ance. Other palliations have been adverted to, derived from the character of his adversaries, the haste with which he wrote, and the spirit of the age. The last is the strongest. The tomahawk and the scalping-knife were not yet discreditable weapons, or thrown aside as fit only for savage warfare; and it is even probable, that many of the things which we should regard as gross insults would then pass as pardonable jests. It is difficult for us, of course, to imagine that callousness which scarcely regards any thing as an insult but what is enforced by the *argumentum baculinum*. Between the feelings of our forefa-thers and our own, there seems to have been as great a difference as between those of the farmer and the clergyman, so ludicrously described by Cowper, in his 'Yearly Distress':

> O, why are farmers made so coarse,
>   Or clergy made so fine?
> A kick that scarce would move a horse,
>   May kill a sound divine.

The haste with which Marvell wrote must also be pleaded as an excuse for the inequalities of his works. It was not the age in which authors elaborated and polished with care, or sub-mitted with a good grace to the *limæ labor;* and if it had been, Marvell allowed himself no leisure for the task. The second part of the *Rehearsal*, for example, was published in the same year in which Parker's *Reproof* appeared. We must profess our belief, that no small portion of his writings stand in great need of this apology. Exhibiting, as they do, amazing vigour and fertility, the wit is by no means always of the first order.

We must not quit the subject of his wit, without presenting the reader with some few of his pleasantries; premising that they form but a very small part of those which we had marked in the perusal of his works; and that, whatever their merit, it were easy to find others far superior to them, if we could afford space for long citations.

Ironically bewailing the calamitous effects of printing, our author exclaims—'O Printing! how hast thou disturbed the peace of mankind? Lead, when moulded into bullets, is not so mortal as when founded into letters. There was a mistake, sure, in the story of Cadmus; and the serpents' teeth which he sowed, were nothing else but the letters which he invented.' Parker having declared, in relation to some object of his scurrility, that he had written, 'not to impair his esteem,' but 'to correct his scribbling humour;' Marvell says—'Our author is as courteous as lightning, and can melt the sword without ever hurting the scabbard.' After alleging that his opponent often has a byplay of malignity even when bestowing commen-dations, he remarks—'The author's end was only railing. He could never have induced himself to praise one man but in order to rail on another. He never oils his hone but that he may whet his razor, and that not to shave but to cut men's throats.' On Parker's absurd and bombastic exaggeration of the merits and achievements of Bishop Bramhall, Marvell wittily says— 'Any worthy man may pass through the world unquestioned and safe, with a moderate recommendation; but when he is thus set off and bedaubed with rhetoric, and embroidered so thick that you cannot discern the ground, it awakens naturally (and not altogether unjustly) interest, curiosity, and envy. For all men pretend a share in reputation, and love not to see it engrossed and monopolized; and are subject to enquire (as of great estates suddenly got) whether he came by all this honestly, or *of what credit the person is that tells the story?* And the same hath happened as to this bishop . . . Men seeing him furbished up in so martial accoutrements, like another Odo, Bishop of Baieux, and having never before heard of his

prowess, begin to reflect what giants he defeated, and what damsels he rescued . . . After all our author's bombast, when we have searched all over, we find ourselves bilked in our expectation; and he hath created the Bishop, like a St. Christopher in the Popish churches, as big as ten porters, and yet only employed to sweat under the burden of an infant.' Of the paroxysms of rage with which Parker refers to one of his adversaries, whom he distinguishes by his initials, Marvell says—'As oft as he does but name those two first letters, he is, like the island of Fayal, on fire in threescore and ten places;' and affirms; 'that if he were of that fellow's diet here about town, that epicurizes on burning coals, drinks healths in scalding brimstone, scranches the glasses for his dessert, and draws his breath through glowing tobacco-pipes, he could not show more flame than he always does upon that subject.' Parker, in a passage of unequalled absurdity, having repre-sented Geneva as on the south side of the lake Leman, Marvell ingeniously represents the blunder as the subject of discussion in a private company, where various droll solutions are proposed, and where he, with exquisite irony, pretends to take Parker's part. 'I,' says Marvell, 'that was still on the doubtful and excusing part, said, that to give the right situation of a town, it was necessary first to know in what position the gentleman's head then was when he made his observation, and that might cause a great diversity—as much as this came to.' Having charged his adversary with needlessly obtruding upon the world some petty matters which concerned only himself, from an exaggerated idea of is own importance, Marvell drolly says—'When a man is once possessed with this fanatic kind of spirit, he imagines if a shoulder do but itch that the world has galled it with leaning on it so long, and therefore he wisely shrugs to remove the globe to the other. If he chance but to sneeze, he salutes himself, and courteously prays that the foundations of the earth be not shaken. And even so the author of the *Ecclesiastical Polity*, ever since he crept up to be but the weathercock of a steeple, trembles and creaks at every puff of wind that blows him about, as if the Church of England were falling, and the state tottered.' After ludicrously describing the effect of the first part of the *Rehearsal* in exacerbating all his opponent's evil passions, he remarks—'He seems not to fit at present for the 'archdeacon's seat, as to take his place below in the church amongst the *energumeni.*' Parker had charged him with a sort of plagiarism for having quoted so many passages out of his book. On this Marvell observes—'It has, I believe, indeed angered him, as it has been no small trouble to me; but how can I help it? I wish he would be pleased to teach me an art (for, if any man in the world, he hath it) to answer a book without turning over the leaves, or without citing passages. In the mean time, if to transcribe so much out of him must render a man, as he therefore styles me, a "scandalous plagiary," I must plead guilty; but by the same law, whoever shall either be witness or prosecutor in behalf of the King, for treasonable words, may be indicted for a highwayman.' Parker having viewed some extravaganza of Marvell's riotous wit as if worthy of serious comment, the latter says—'Whereas I only threw it out like an empty cask to amuse him, knowing that I had a whale to deal with, and lest he should overset me; he runs away with it as a very serious business, and so moyles himself with tumbling and tossing it, that he is in danger of melting his spermaceti. A cork, I see, will serve without a hook; and, instead of a harping-iron, this grave and ponderous creature may, like eels, be taken and pulled up only with bobbing.' After exposing in a strain of uncommon eloquence the wickedness and folly of suspending the peace of the nation on so frivolous a matter as 'ceremonial,' he says 'For a prince to adventure all upon such a cause, is like Duke Charles of Burgundy, who fought three battles for an imposition upon sheep-skins;' and 'for a clergyman to offer at persecution upon this ceremonial account, is (as is related of one of the Popes) to justify his indignation for his peacock, by the example of God's anger for eating the forbidden fruit.' He justifies his severity towards Parker in a very ludicrous way—'No man needs letters of marque against one that is an open pirate of other men's credit. I remember within our own time one Simons, who robbed always on the bricolle—that is to say, never interrupted the *passengers*, but still set upon the *thieves themselves*, after, like Sir John Falstaff, they were gorged with a booty; and by this way—so ingenious that it was scarce criminal—he lived secure and unmolested all his days, with the reputation of a judge rather than of a highwayman.' The sentences we have cited are all taken from the *Rehearsal*. We had marked many more from his 'Divine in Mode,' and other writings, but have no space for them.

But he who supposes Marvell to have been nothing but a wit, simply on account of the predominance of that quality, will do him injustice. It is the common lot of such men, in whom some one faculty is found on a great scale, to fail of part of the admiration due to other endowments; possessed in more moderate degree, indeed, but still in a degree far from ordinary. We are subject to the same illusion in gazing on mountain scenery. Fixing our eye on some solitary peak, which towers far above the rest, the groups of surrounding hills look positively diminutive, though they may, in fact, be all of great magnitude.

This illusion is further fostered by another circumstance in the case of great wits. As the object of wit is to amuse, the owl-like gravity of thousands of common readers, would decide that wit and wisdom must dwell apart, and that the humorous writer must necessarily be a trifling one. For similar reasons, they look with sage suspicion on every signal display, either of fancy or passion; think a splendid illustration nothing but the ambuscade of a fallacy, and strong emotion as tantamount to a confession of unsound judgment. As Archbishop Whately has well remarked, such men having been warned that 'ridicule is not the test of truth,' and that 'wisdom and wit are not the same thing, distrust every thing that can possibly be regarded as witty; not having judgment to perceive the combination, when it occurs, of wit and sound reasoning. The ivy wreath completely conceals from their view the point of the *thyrsus*.'

The fact is, that all Marvell's endowments were on a large scale, though his wit greatly predominated. His judgment was remarkably clear and sound, his logic by no means contemptible, his sagacity in practical matters great, his talents for business apparently of the first order, and his industry indefatigable. His wit, would, if sufficiently cultivated, have made him a poet considerably above mediocrity: though chiefly alive to the ludicrous, he was by no means insensible to the beautiful. We cannot, indeed, bestow all the praise on his Poems which some of his critics have assigned them. They are very plentifully disfigured by the conceits and quaintnesses of the age, and as frequently want grace of expression and harmony of numbers. Of the compositions which Captain Thompsons's indiscriminate admiration would fain have affiliated to his Muse, the two best are proved—one not to be his, and the other of doubtful origin. The former, beginning—

When Israel, freed from Pharoah's hand,

is a well-known composition of Dr. Watts; the other, the ballad of 'William and Margaret,' is of dubious authorship. Though probably of earlier date than the age of Mallet, its reputed

author—the reasons which Captain Thompson gives for assigning it to Marvell, are altogether unsatisfactory. Still, there are unquestionably many of his genuine poems which indicate a rich, though ill-cultivated fancy; and in some few stanzas there is no little grace of expression. The little piece on the Pilgrim Fathers, entitled the 'Emigrants,' the fanciful 'Dialogue between 'Body and Soul,' the 'Dialogue between the Resolved Soul and Created Pleasure,' and the 'Coronet,' all contain lines of much elegance and sweetness. It is in his satirical poems, that, as might be expected from the character of his mind, his fancy appears most vigorous; though these are largely disfigured by the characteristic defects of the age, and many, it must be confessed, are entirely without merit. With two or three lines from his ludicrous satire on Holland, we cannot refrain from amusing the reader. Some of the strokes of humour are irresistibly ridiculous:

> Holland, that scarce deserves the name of land,
> As but the off-scouring of the British sand;
> And so much earth as was contributed
> By English pilots when they heav'd the lead;
> Or what by th' ocean's slow alluvion fell,
> Of shipwreck'd cockle and the muscle-shell;
> This indigested vomit of the sea
> Fell to the Dutch by just propriety.
> Glad then, as miners who have found the ore,
> They, with mad labour fish'd the land to shore;
> And dived as desperately for each piece
> Of earth, as if it had been of ambergris;
> Collecting anxiously small loads of clay,
> Less than what building swallows bear away;
> For as with pigmies, who best kills the crane,
> Among the hungry he that treasures grain,
> Among the blind the one-eyed blinkard reigns,
> So rules among the drowned be that drains,
> Not who first see the rising sun commands:
> But who could first discern the rising lands.
> Who best could know to pump an earth so leak,
> Him they their lord, and country's father, speak.

His Latin poems are amongst his best. The composition often shows no contemptible skill in that language; and here and there the diction and versification are such as would not have absolutely disgraced his great coadjutor, Milton. In all the higher poetic qualities, there can of course be no comparison between them.

With such a mind we as we have ascribed to him—and we think his works fully justify what we have said—with such aptitudes for business, soundness of judgment, powers of reasoning, and readiness of sarcasm, one might have anticipated that he would have taken some rank as an orator. Nature, it is certain, had bestowed upon him some of the most important intellectual endowments of one. It is true, indeed, that with his principles and opinions he would have found himself strangely embarrassed in addressing any parliament in the days of Charles II., and stood but a moderate chance of obtaining a candid hearing. But we have no proof that he ever made the trial. His parliamentary career in this respect resembled that of a much greater man—Addison, who, with wit even superior to his own, and with much more elegance, if not more strength of mind, failed signally as a speaker.

Marvell's learning must have been very extensive. His education was superior; and, as we have seen from the testimony of Milton, his industry had made him master, during his long sojourn on the Continent, of several continental languages. It is certain also, that he continued to be a student all his days; his works bear ample evidence of his wide and miscellaneous reading. He appears to have been well versed in most branches of literature, though he makes no pedantic display of erudition, and in this respect is favourably distinguished from many of his contemporaries; yet he cites his authors with the familiarity of a thorough scholar. In the department of history he appears to have been particularly well read; and derives his witty illustrations from such remote and obscure sources, that Parker did not hesitate to avow his belief that he had sometimes drawn on his invention for them. In his Reply, Marvell justifes himself in all the alleged instances, and takes occasion to show that his opponent's learning is as hollow as all his other pretensions.

The style of Marvell is very unequal. Though often rude and unpolished, it abounds in negligent felicities, presents us with frequent specimens of vigorous idiomatic English, and now and then attains no mean degree of elegance. It bears the stamp of the revolution which was then passing on the language; it is a medium between the involved and periodic structure so common during the former half of the century, and which is ill adapted to a language possessing so few infections as ours, and that simplicity and harmony which were not fully attained till the age of Addison. There is a very large infusion of short sentences, and the structure in general is as unlike that of his great colleague's prose as can be imaged. Many of Marvell's pages flow with so much ease and grace, as to be not unworthy of a later period. To that great revolution in style to which we have just alluded, he must in no slight degree have contributed; for, little as his works are known or read now, the most noted of them were once universally popular, and perused with pleasure, as Burnet testifies, by every body, 'from the king to the tradesman.'

Numerous examples show, that it is almost impossible for even the rarest talents to confer permanent popularity on books which turn on topics of temporary interest, however absorbing at the time. If Pascal's transcendant genius has been unable to rescue even the *Lettres Provinciales* from partial oblivion, it is not to be expected that Marvell should have done more for the *Rehearsal Transprosed*. Swift, it is true, about half a century later, has been pleased, while expressing this opinion, to make an exception in favour of Marvell. 'There is indeed,' says he, 'an exception, when any great genius thinks it worth his while to expose a foolish piece; so we still read Marvell's answer to Parker with pleasure, though the book it answers be sunk long ago.' But this statement is scarcely applicable now. It is true that the 'Rehearsal' is occasionally read by the curious; but it is by the resolutely curious alone.

Yet assuredly he has not lived in vain who has successfully endeavoured to abate the nuisances of his own time, or to put down some insolent abettor of vice and corruption. Nor is it possible in a world like this, in which there is such continuity of causes and effects—where one generation transmits its good and its evil to the next, and the consequences of each revolution in principles, opinions, or tastes, are propagated along the whole line of humanity—to estimate either the degree or perpetuity of the benefits conferred by the complete success of works even of transient interest. By modifying the age in which he lives, a man may indirectly modify the character of many generations to come. His works may be forgotten while their effects survive.

Marvell's history affords a signal instance of the benefits which may be derived from well-directed satire. There are cases in which it may be a valuable auxiliary to decency, virtue, and religion, where argument and persuasion both fail. Many, indeed, doubt both the legitimacy of the weapon itself, and the success with which it can be employed. But facts are

against them. To hope that it can ever supply the place of religion as a radical cure for vice or immorality, would be chimerical; but there are many pernicious customs, violations of propriety, ridiculous, yet tolerated, follies, which religion can scarcely touch without endangering her dignity. To assail them is one of the most legitimate offices of satire; nor have we the slightest doubt that the 'Spectator' did more to abate many of the prevailing follies and pernicious customs of the age, than a thousand homilies. This, however, may be admitted, and yet it may be said that it does not reach the case of Marvell and Parker. Society, it may be argued, will bear the exposure of its own evils with great equanimity, and perhaps profit by it—no individual being pointed at, and each being left to digest his own lesson, under the pleasant conviction that it was designed principally for his neighbours. As corporations will perpetrate actions of which each individual member would be ashamed; so corporations will listen to charges which every individual member would regard as insults. But no man, it is said, is likely to be reclaimed from error or vice by being made the object of merciless ridicule. All this we believe most true. But then it is not to be forgotten, that it may not be the satirist's object to reclaim the individual—he may have little hope of that; it may be for the sake of those whom he maligns and injures. When the exorcist takes Satan in hand, it is not because he is an Origenist, and 'believes in the conversion of the devil,' but in pity to the supposed victims of his malignity. It is much the same when a man like Marvell undertakes to satirize a man like Parker. Even such a man may be abashed and confounded, though he cannot be reclaimed; and if so, the satirist gains his object, and society gets the benefit. Experience fully shows us that there are many men who will be restrained by ridicule long after they are lost to virtue, and that they are accessible to shame when they are utterly inaccessible to argument.

This was just the good that Marvell effected. He made Parker, it is true, more furious; but he diverted, if he could not turn the tide of popular feeling; and thus prevented mischief. Parker, and others like him, were doing all they could to inflame angry passions, to revive the most extravagant pretensions of tyranny, and to preach up another crusade against the Nonconformists. Marvell's books were a conductor to the dangerous fluid; if there was any explosion at all, it was an explosion of merriment. 'He had all the laughers on his side,' says Burnet. In Charles II.'s reign, there were few who belonged to any other class; and then, as now, men found it impossible to laugh and be angry at the same time. It is our firm belief, that Marvell did more to humble Parker, and neutralize the influence of his party, by the *Rehearsal Transprosed*, than he could have done by writing half a dozen folios of polemical divinity; just as Pascal did more to unmask the Jesuits and damage their cause by his *Provincial Letters*, than had been effected by all the efforts of all their other opponents put together.

But admirable as were Marvell's intellectual endowments, it is his moral worth, after all, which constitutes his principal claim on the admiration of posterity, and which sheds a redeeming lustre on one of the darkest pages of the English annals. Inflexible integrity was the basis of it—integrity by which he has not unworthily earned the glorious name of the 'British Aristides.' With talents and acquirements which might have justified him in aspiring to almost any office, if he could have disburdened himself of his conscience; with wit which, in that frivolous age, was a surer passport to fame than any amount either of intellect or virtue, and which, as we have seen, mollified even the monarch himself in spite of his prejudices; Marvell preferred poverty and independence to riches and servility. He had learned the lesson, practised by few in that age, of being content with little—so that he preserved his conscience. He could be poor, but he could not be mean; could starve, but could not cringe. By economizing in the articles of pride and ambition, he could afford to keep what their votaries were compelled to retrench, the necessaries, or rather the luxuries, of integrity and a good conscience. Neither menaces, nor caresses, nor bribes, nor poverty, nor distress, could induce him to abandon his integrity; or even to take an office in which it might be tempted or endangered. He only who has arrived at this pitch of magnanimity, has an adequate security for his public virtue. He who cannot subsist upon a little; who has not learned to be content with such things as he has, and even to be content with almost nothing; who has not learned to familiarize his thoughts to poverty, much more readily than he can familiarize them to dishonour, is not yet free from peril. Andrew Marvell, as his whole course proves, had done this. But we shall not do full justice to his public integrity, if we do not bear in mind the corruption of the age in which he lived; the manifold apostasies amidst which he retained his conscience; and the effect which such wide-spread profligacy must have had in making thousands almost sceptical as to whether there were such a thing as public virtue at all. Such a relaxation in the code of speculative morals, is one of the worst results of general profligacy in practice. But Andrew Marvell was not to be deluded; and amidst corruption perfectly unparalleled, he still continued untainted. We are accustomed to hear of his virtue as a truly Roman virtue, and so it was; but it was something more. Only the best pages of Roman history can supply a parallel: there was no Cincinnatus in those ages of her shame which alone can be compared with those of Charles II. It were easier to find a Cincinnatus during the era of the English Commonwealth, than an Andrew Marvell in the age of Commodus.

The integrity and patriotism which distingusihed him in his relations to the Court, also marked all his public conduct. He was evidently most scrupulously honest and faithful in the discharge of his duty to his constituents; and, as we have seen almost punctilious in guarding against any thing which could tarnish his fair fame, or defile his conscience. On reviewing the whole of his public conduct, we may well say that he attained his wish, expressed in the lines which he has written in imitation of a chorus in the *Thyestes* of Seneca:

> Climb at *court* for me that will—
> Tottering favour's pinnacle;
> All I seek is to lie still.
> Settled in some secret nest,
> In calm leisure let me rest,
> And far off the public stage,
> Pass away my silent age.
> Thus, when without noise, unknown,
> I have lived out all my span,
> I shall die without a groan,
> An old honest countryman.

He seems to have been as amiable in his private as he was estimable in his public character. So far as any documents throw light upon the subject, the same integrity appears to have belonged to both. He is described as of a very reserved and quiet temper; but, like Addison, (whom in this respect as in some few others he resembled,) exceedingly facetious and lively amongst his intimate friends. His disinterested championship of others, is no less a proof of his sympathy with the oppressed than of his abhorrence of oppression; and many pleasing traits of amiability occur in his private correspondence, as well as in his writings. On the whole, we think that

Marvell's epitaph, strong as the terms of panegyric are, records little more than the truth; and that it was not in the vain spirit of boasting, but in the honest consciousness of virtue and integrity, and that he himself concludes a letter to one of his correspondents in the words—

> Disce, puer, virtutem ex me, verumque laborem;
> Fortunam ex aliis.

JOHN ORMSBY
From "Andrew Marvell"
Cornhill Magazine, July 1869, pp. 21–40

When Marvell's name occurs in any work on English literature or any collection of old English poetry, the mention is generally followed by the remark that as a poet he has not received full justice. In his lifetime he does not appear to have ranked as a poet at all, but that was because he himself laid no claim to the rank. The only productions of his in verse that appeared in print during his life were three or four commendatory pieces prefixed to works of friends after the friendly fashion of the time, and some political satires which were necessarily anonymous and unacknowledged. If with posterity he has not held his due place among the minor poets of his time, one cause, undoubtedly, is that he already occupies, in another character, a higher position in the eyes of the world. The "mind's eye" is so far like that of the body, that it finds a difficulty in seeing at once more than one side of any object, and having settled itself to one point of view, it is slow to take up any other. It was Marvell's fate to stand out before the eyes of succeeding generations as an example of purity and integrity in a corrupt age, and the brightness of his virtues has in some degree outshone the lustre of his genius. Had he been less brilliant as a patriot, he would have been more conspicuous as a poet.

It would be unjust, however, to represent Marvell as an altogether neglected poet. Up to the present time five editions of his poems have appeared, a number which implies a greater posthumous popularity than any of his contemporaries obtained.—Milton, Butler, and Dryden excepted. The first, dated 1681, three years after his death, is clearly a mere bookseller's speculation, published without the authority or sanction of his family or friends, and without the editorial supervision of any one in any way qualified by acquaintance with the author or with his works. The surreptitious character of the collection is shown by the impudent address to the "ingenious reader," pretending to come from one "Mary Marvell," who certifies that the contents are printed according to the exact copies in the handwriting of her "late dear husband," found after his death among his other papers. Marvell was never married; and Cooke, the editor of the next edition of his works, gives us to understand that his papers were sold by the woman in whose house he lodged. The volume is a thin folio of 126 pages, which,—at least in every copy we have seen,—are made by an ingenious fault in the pagination to appear 140 in number. It is, however, fairly printed, and is embellished with a portrait somewhat in the manner of Faithorne, though without the finish characteristic of his work. Marvell's violent satires on the court and the court-party are, of course, excluded. Eight years afterwards, when the revolution was an accomplished fact, these, which up to that time had circulated only in manuscript, or else in clandestine printed tracts, came out with the author's name attached in that curious collection, the *Poems on Affairs of State*, so necessary to every one who wishes to study the history, politics, manners, or scandals of the reigns of the two last Stuarts. In 1726 Curll published a very neat duodecimo edition in two parts: the first containing very nearly the contents of the folio; the second, the political satires, some pieces of Latin and Greek verse, and a selection from Marvell's letters. This was edited, with some care, by Thomas Cooke, who claims to have corrected the errors of the folio, and to have been careful to exclude some pieces which there, and also in the *Poems on Affairs of State*, have been wrongly attributed to the author. He has, however, reproduced everything in the folio except a dozen Latin verses on the Louvre, and every one of the pieces ascribed to Marvell in the *State Poems*, two of which are certainly not by his hand. The two we refer to are *Oceana and Britannia*, and *Hodge's Vision from the Monument*, both of which contain allusions to events that occurred after Marvell's death, especially events in connection with the so-called Popish plot, the execution of Coleman, Wakeman's trial, and the browbeating of the witnesses by Scroggs and Jones. The plot was disclosed on the 12th of August, 1678, and Marvell died four days afterwards, its first victim in the opinon of many at the time; for the suddenness of his death, and the absence of any perceptible cause, were held to be conclusive evidence of poison. The suspicion had no foundation in fact, but at such a time it was not unnatural. Marvell was a marked man as a foremost champion of Protestantism, and an uncompromising enemy of the Popish party which had, or was supposed to have, its hopes set upon the Duke of York; and no name was more likely than his to hold a high place on a roll of obnoxious Protestants to be removed on the earliest opportunity—a document the existence of which was firmly believed in by a large majority. The satires in question belong so nearly to Marvell's time, and, though wanting in the wit, pungency, and earnestness which mark all his writings of the same sort, bear such a general resemblance to his pieces in style and manner, that the error is, perhaps, somewhat excusable. It deserves notice, however, as it is one which has been repeated in every subsequent edition. In 1772, Davies, the friend of Johnson and Boswell, published an exact reprint of Cooke's edition and in 1776 Captain Edward Thompson produced his edition of the works of Marvell in prose and verse in three imposing-looking quarto volumes. This is, in some respects, the most valuable, in others the most worthless of all. Captain Thompson's only qualification for the task he undertook was an enthusiastic admiration for the personal character of his author. His zeal was abundant; it would be more correct to say superabundant; but in judgment, literary taste, and a comprehension of the duties of an editor he was entirely deficient. He had the assistance of a collection of documents previously made with a view to a complete edition of Marvell's works, among which was a manuscript book partly in Marvell's hadnwriting, containing, with other pieces, the well-known version of the 19th Psalm,—

The spacious firmament on high;

that of the 114th Psalm—

When Israel freed from Pharaoh's hand;

the hymn beginning with

When all thy mercies, O my God,
My rising soul surveys;

and also the ballad of *William and Margaret*. It is not made to appear that these pieces were in Marvell's writing, but the discovery of them in a book which was once in Marvell's possession and contained pieces in his writing, was, to Captain

Thompson's mind, full and sufficient proof that they were his productions. As the claim thus set up has been recently reasserted, at least as regards the first-mentioned piece, by an authority so well qualified to give an opinion on literary questions as the *Athenæum*, it is necessary to state the case somewhat at length. We need scarcely remind the reader that the three first pieces of poetry appeared originally in the *Spectator*, and that the second of them was, a few years later, acknowledged and published as his own by Dr. Watts. Now it is incredible that a man of Dr. Watts's character, a man too so scrupulous in acknowledging the most trifling obligations to other writers, could have purloined an entire poem in so barefaced a manner. The other two have been always attributed to Addison. They belong to a series of "pieces of divine poetry," to use the *Spectator's* favourite description, which appeared from time to time in the Saturday numbers written by Addison. We have the *Spectator's* word for it that they are all by the same author. "I shall never," he says in No. 461, "publish verse on that day (Saturday) but what was written by the same hand." Therefore, if we are to believe both Captain Thompson and the *Spectator*, not only these two but also the version of the 23rd Psalm, in No. 441

The Lord my pasture shall prepare,
And lead me with a Shepherd's care;

and the verses in Nos. 489 and 513, beginning with

How are thy servants blest, O Lord!

and—

When rising from the bed of death—

are all the productions of Marvell. This is an attempt to prove too much. It in effect charges Addison, or the *Spectator*, with appropriating, not a fugitive piece, but a collection of pieces by an author of whom something at least must have been known to those who had obtained access to his writings. The *Athenæum* considers that the language of Addison in the essays in which these pieces are introduced favours the idea that he was not their author. We confess to holding an entirely opposite opinion: that the manner in which Addison introduced these pieces would be, to call it by the very mildest term, disingenuous, if he himself were not the author of them. That he was the author, however, we have, apart from probabilities and internal evidence, the statement of Pope. "He had," says Pope, as reported in *Spence's Anecdotes*, "a design of translating all the Psalms for the use of churches. Five or six of them that he did translate were published in the *Spectators*." Two only of the five can be strictly called translations; but it is, of course, to these five pieces that Pope alludes. As regards the ballad of *William and Margaret* the case is simpler. It made its first appearance in print in 1724, in Aaron Hill's *Plain Dealer*, and also in the collection called *The Hive*, and was afterwards owned and printed by Mallet among his poems, with some slight alterations, and the explanation that it had been suggested to him by the fragment of the old ballad quoted in Fletcher's *Knight of the Burning Pestle*. Plagiarism has, as Dr. Johnson says, "been boldly charged but never proved" against Mallet in this matter; but, whoever the writer may have been, to any one conversant with old poetry it will be plain that he was a writer of the eighteenth and not of the seventeenth century. The same may be said of another ballad in *The Hive* collection, *The Despairing Shepherd*, which is also claimed for Marvell by Captain Thompson; and indeed, notwithstanding the opinion of the *Athenæum*, we think the poems printed in the *Spectator* bear unmistakably the stamp of the same age. It is necessary to go into these particulars because the claims set up for Marvell must stand or fall together. In vulgar parlance they "row in the same boat," and if one sinks all sink. Against those claims there is the improbability of three men, Addison, Watts, and Mallet, all lighting upon the same mine of unpublished manuscript, and each pilfering and publishing as his own what suited him best. As we said before, Captain Thompson effectually disproves his case by attempting to prove too much. There is also the improbability of all of these pieces escaping the notice of a reasonably painstaking editor like Cooke, who was, besides, in communication with and assisted by members and friends of Marvell's family. All these poems had been already many times printed and published at the time when Cooke's edition appeared, and it is, to say the least, extremely unlikely that persons interested in Marvell's name, and in posession of evidence to prove his title to them, should have allowed them to pass unchallenged. From the account, too, which Captain Thompson gives of the manuscript book in which he found these pieces, it would seem that its existence and contents could scarcely have been unknown to Cooke. Captain Thompson had it from Mr. Raikes, who had it from Mr. Nettleton, who was the son of Marvell's niece, and Marvell's two nieces are specially thanked by Cooke for having furnished him with manuscripts and materials for his memoir and edition. Against all this we have nothing but the personal conviction of an uncritical sea-captain. There is nothing to show that the book was anything more than a kind of poetical album, originally, it is possible, the property of Marvell, but into which successive possessors copied such pieces as struck their taste or fancy.

To Captain Thompson, however, we owe the addition of three pieces undoubtedly Marvell's, which were probably considered too eulogistic of Cromwell and the Commonwealth to be inserted in the edition of 1681: the poem on Cromwell's Government—the genuineness of which is vouched for by Marvell's old enemy. Bishop Parker,—that on the "Death of His late Highness the Protector," and the "Horatian Ode upon Cromwell's Return from Ireland," in which occur those noble lines on the death of Charles I. so often quoted. Upon these, and the collection of Marvell's prose tracts and letters, the merits of this edition rest, for the editor took no pains to correct the errors or supply the deficiencies of his predecessors, and merely flung together, without any attempt at order, method, or examination, all the materials he could lay his hands upon.

The last edition we have to mention is one published in Boston (U.S.) in 1857, a very elegant reprint of that of Cooke, supplemented by the additional poems given by Captain Thompson.

It will be seen, from this statement of the case, that Marvell has not been treated with that utter neglect which the expressions made use of by some of his admirers would seem to imply. None of his contemporaries except those we have named,—neither Cowley nor Waller nor Denham, so famous in their own day, and still so conspicuous on the roll of English poets,—have in modern times received so much attention from editors or publishers. They, however, in a manner discounted their fame. They secured great popularity while they lived, and left extant a sufficient number of editions of their works to supply the demands of posterity for a considerable period. Still, though not overlooked, Marvell cannot be said to have been generally recognized as one of the poets until the present century. That Dr. Johnson should have not thought him worthy of a place beside men whose lives and works are so ardently desired as those of Stepney, King, Duke, Yalden, Sprat, and Smith, is not indeed surprising. Marvell's earlier poetry is not of a kind at all likely to find favour in the eyes of a critic of Johnson's mould, and in manner as well as

in matter, his political pieces are not well calculated to conciliate a Jacobite, high churchman, and strict moralist. He who could not forgive Milton could scarcely be expected to acknowledge Marvell. But it is not a little strange that his poetry should have been so generally excluded from the various collections and miscellanies of the last century, and his name so seldom mentioned by any of its writers. When Churchill alludes to him, it is of his "spotless virtue" he speaks; and Mason,—as far as we remember, the only one who seems aware of the fact that he was a poet,—commends him for deserting poetry for politics.

Another impediment to Marvell's fame as a poet is the undeniable coarseness of some of his political satires. His works come to us weighted with matter in the highest degree offensive to modern taste. This, however, was not the fault of the man but of the age he lived in, and it is one from which few of the writers of his time are free. For a satirist, indeed, it was scarcely possible to avoid it. Disregard of decency in conduct was the crying evil of the time; and in such cases the homœopathic principle of *similia similibus curantur* has always been the one that has been acted upon. Party warfare, too, in those days was a rough struggle untempered by the courtesies and amenities which have been by degrees introduced into the strategy of modern politics. It was rather a *mêlée* fought out with any weapons that came to hand, than an organized and systematic contest waged at long range with arms of precision, and between large bodies of combatants. The periodical press was then barely in its infancy, and for attack and defence men had to trust rather to individual efforts than to the co-operation of numbers. For Marvell, besides, there is an excuse which cannot be pleaded for most of the other satirists of his day. His satires were intended for use simply, not for show. Dryden, like a skilled artificer, prided himself on the artistic finish of the weapon he forged: but Marvell plucked a cudgel from the nearest hedgerow, careless if it became fuel after it had served his purpose. It was meant to hurt, and it hurt all the more for those rough knots and excrescences so unsightly in our eyes. ⟨. . .⟩

As a poet he is generally classed among the poets of Charles the Second's reign; but in reality he belongs to an earlier age, and has nothing whatever in common with Waller, Sedley, Dorset, or Rochester. He is, in fact, no more one of the Restoration poets than Milton. His true place is with the men of the preceding period,—with Herrick, Habingdon, Suckling, Lovelace, and Wither, to each of whom occasional resemblances may be traced in his poetry. But the poet that influenced him most, probably, was Donne. When Marvell was a student at Cambridge the influence of Donne's poetry was at its height, and it acted in the same way as the influence of Spenser in the preceding generation, of Cowley some thirty years later, and of Byron and Tennyson in modern times. Donne was the accepted poet with the young men, the orchestra-leader from whom they took their time and tone, and whose style, consciously or unconsciously, they assimilated. Marvell's earliest poem is an illustration of this. His satire on "Flecknoe, an English Priest at Rome," might easily pass for one of Donne's, so thoroughly has he caught not only the manner and rugged vigorous versification of Donne's satires, but also his very turns of thought, and the passion for elaborate conceits, recondite analogies, and out-of-the-way similitudes with which his poetry is so strongly imbued.

Few of the poets of the time of Charles I. and the Commonwealth escaped the infection of this, the metaphysical school of poetry, as Dryden somewhat awkwardly called it, which Donne is generally accused of having founded. In truth, neither he in England, nor Marini in Italy, nor Gongora in Spain, can be properly said to have founded a school. They were simply the most prominent masters of a certain style or method of writing, which came into fashion from causes independent of the example or teaching of any man, and affected prose as well as poetry. Its essential characteristic may be described as wit run to seed, or rather, perhaps, an unnatural growth of wit produced by the very richness and high cultivation of the literature of the period; for in each case the phenomenon made its appearance in, or immediately after, a period eminently rich in literature, that of Shakspeare, of Tasso, or of Cervantes and Lope de Vega. Metaphysical poets, Marinisti, or Conceptistas, all wrote under the same inspiration—a desire of being distinguished for wit and fancy at a time when wit and fancy were especially held in honour; a nervous dread of being thought trite, unoriginal, and commonplace, if they should be found treading in the footsteps of others; and a sort of suspicion that the legitimate fields of imagination were already worked out, and that now nothing was left to the poet but to fall back upon ingenuity. Traces of the prevailing fashion are to be met with frequently in Marvell's poems; and that they are not more abundant is probably owing to the fact that he wrote simply to please himself, "for his own hand," and not with any ambition of one day claiming a place among the poets. But in this respect there is a difference between his earlier and later verses. For instance, his "Nymph complaining for the Death of her Fawn," written, it would seem, before the close of the civil war, graceful, simple, and tender as the lines are, is not free from those *tours de force* of fancy which disfigure so much of the poetry of that day. Even the lowest, the mere verbal form of this forced wit, breaks out, e.g.:

> But Sylvio soon had me beguiled.
> This waxéd tame; while he grew wild,
> And, quite regardless of my smart,
> Left me his *fawn*, but took his *heart*.

On the other hand, the poem on the "Bermudas," produced, we may fairly presume, several years later, when Marvell was in daily communication with John Oxenbridge,—one of those very exiles to the Bermudas whose feelings the poem is supposed to express,—is as direct, natural, and unaffected as a poem of Wordsworth's could be. Both of these pieces have been of late frequently printed in collections of old poetry and works on English literature, especially the last, which a critic whose taste and judgment no one will dispute, has called "a gem of melody, picturesqueness, and sentiment, nearly without a flaw." They are therefore, probably, too familiar already to the majority of our readers to justify quotation here, however tempting they may be as specimens of Marvell at his best; and we shall take, instead, a few illustrations from less-known poems. In the verses addressed "To his Coy Mistress," the extravagant fancy, that in the graver sort of poetry is a blemish, becomes an ornament, employed as it is to push a kind of *argumentum ad absurdum* to the farthest possible limits, and its effect is heightened by the exquisite assumption of gravity in the opening lines,—

> Had we but world enough and time,
> This coyness, lady, were no crime.
> We would sit down, and think which way
> To walk, and pass our long love's day.
> Thou by the Indian Ganges' side
> Should'st rubies find: I by the tide
> Of Humber would complain. I would
> Love you ten years before the flood:
> And you should, if you please, refuse
> Till the conversion of the Jews.

> My vegetable love should grow
> Vaster than empires, and more slow.
> An hundred years should go to praise
> Thine eyes, and on thy forehead gaze:
> Two hundred to adore each breast;
> But thirty thousand to the rest.
> An age at least to every part,—
> And the last age should show your heart.
> For, lady, you deserve this state:
> Nor would I love at lower rate.
>   But at my back I always hear
> Time's winged chariot hurrying near:
> And yonder all before us lie
> Deserts of vast eternity.

The conclusion, therefore, is to the same effect as Herrick's advice, "Then be not coy, but use your time."

>   Now, therefore, while the youthful hue
> Sits on thy skin like morning dew,
> Let us roll at our strength and all
> Our sweetness up into one ball,
> And tear our pleasures with rough strife
> Thorough the iron gates of life.
> Thus, though we cannot make our sun
> Stand still, yet we will make him run.

The little poem of which we have here quoted the greater part is characteristic of Marvell in many ways, but more especially of that peculiarity of his which has been before alluded to, his trick—if anything so obviously natural and spontaneous can be called a trick—of passing suddenly from a light, bantering, trivial tone, to one of deep feeling, and even, as in the instance just quoted, of solemnity. Nothing in Suckling, or Carew, or any other of the poets to whom love-making in verse was a pastime, is more gay, folâtre, careless, and at the same time, profoundly obsequious, than the first part; but lightly and playfully as the subject is treated, it suggests thoughts that lead to a graver and more impassioned strain. A few pages further on we find a poem which is in truth only a conceit expanded into a poem, but which in its very flimsiness shows a rare lightness of hand, and neatness of execution. It is a sort of miniature idyll cast in, the amœbean form, and entitled "Ametas and Thestylis making Hay-ropes."

> *Ametas:* Think'st thou that this love can stand,
>   Whilst thou still dost say me nay?
>   Love unpaid does soon disband:
>   Love binds love, as hay binds hay.
> *Thestylis:* Thinks't thou that this rope would twine,
>   If we both should turn one way?
>   Where both parties so combine,
>   Neither love will twist nor hay.
> *Ametas:* Thus you vain excuses find,
>   Which yourself and us delay;
>   And love ties a woman's mind
>   Looser than with ropes of hay.
> *Thestylis:* What you cannot constant hope
>   Must be taken as you may.
> *Ametas:* Then let's both lay by our rope,
>   And go kiss within the hay.

Nothing could be more designedly trifling than this, and yet what a finished elegance there is about it. It is not the highest art, perhaps, but there is a certain antique grace in the workmanship that reminds one, somehow, of a cameo or an old engraved gem. Charles Lamb, with his own peculiar felicity of expression, has hit off the precise phrase when he speaks of "a witty delicacy," as the prevailing quality in Marvell's poetry. If he did sin, as it must be confessed he did occasionally, in forcing wit beyond its legitimate bounds, he made amends for the offence by the graceful turn he gave to a conceit. To take an instance from the lines "To a Fair Singer": poets have again and again tasked their ingenuity to compliment ladies who are fortunate enough to add skill in music to their other charms, but we doubt if it has been ever done with greater elegance than here:

> I could have fled from one but singly fair;
>   My disentangled soul itself might save,
> Breaking the curléd trammels of her hair;
>   But how should I avoid to be her slave,
> Whose subtle art invisibly can wreathe
> My fetters of the very air I breathe?

The taste for subtleties, ingenuities, and prettinesses, which here and there breaks out in Marvell's verse, is, however, his only artificiality. He had, what was very rare among his contemporaries, a genuine love and reverence for nature. Most of the poets of his day seem to treat nature in a somewhat patronizing spirit, as a good sort of institution, deserving of support, especially from poets, as being useful for supplying illustrations, comparisons, and descriptions available for poetic purposes. They, we suspect, regarded it very much as the cook does the shrubbery, from which he gets the holly and laurel leaves to garnish his dishes. Marvell is one of the few men of that time who appear to have delighted in nature for its own sake, and not merely for its capabilities in the way of furnishing ideas. He enjoyed it thoroughly and thankfully, and in the poems written during his residence with Lord Fairfax at Nun-Appleton, he shows a keen sense of pleasure in natural beauty and scenery, and, what was even rarer in those days, close observation and study of nature. The longest, that upon Appleton House, for an adequate specimen of which we have not sufficient space, is an ample proof of this, and from beginning to end "breathes"—to use a phrase of Washington Irving's—"the very soul of a rural voluptuary." One of his most graceful little poems, evidently belonging to this time, is a protest against the artificial gardening then coming into fashion, of which he says:

> 'Tis all enforced; the fountain and the grot,
>   While the sweet fields do lie forgot:
> Where willing nature does to all dispense
>   A wild and fragrant innocence:
> And fauns and fairies do the meadows till,
>   More by their presence than their skill.
> Their statues polished by some ancient hand,
>   May to adorn the gardens stand:
> But, howsoe'er the figures do excel,
>   The Gods themselves do with us dwell.

The specimens we have quoted are rather one-sided, exhibiting Marvell's poetry only in its lighter and more elegant phase. In justice to his powers, we must give a few lines as an example of his graver and loftier verse. The following passage is from the conclusion of his poem "Upon the Death of his late Highness the Lord Protector":

> Not much unlike the sacred oak which shoots
> To heaven its branches, and through earth its roots,
> Whose spacious boughs are hung with trophies round,
> And honour'd wreaths have oft the victor crown'd;
> When angry Jove darts lightning through the air
> At mortals' sins, nor his own plant will spare,
> It groans, and bruises all below, that stood
> So many years the shelter of the wood,
> The tree, erewhile foreshorten'd to our view,
> When fall'n shows taller yet than as it grew.

So shall his praise to after times increase,
When truth shall be allowed and faction cease,
And his own shadows with him fall; the eye
Detracts from objects than itself more high;
But when Death takes them from that envied state,
Seeing how little, we confess how great.

There is one more point to be considered in connection with Marvell's place among the minor poets of the seventeenth century. To Butler is generally given the credit of having turned the extravagance of idea peculiar to the so-called metaphysical school of poetry to good purpose, by enlisting it in the service of burlesque, as he did in *Hudibras*. But Marvell has a certain claim to a share of the credit, such as it is. His delightful vagary in verse called "A Character of Holland" was written, as the latter portion clearly shows, at the time of the great burst of national exultation at the victory obtained by Blake, supported by Dean and Monk, over the Dutch under Van Tromp, off Portland, in February, 1653, and, therefore, probably some time before *Hudibras*, the first part of which did not appear till 1663. But to whichever the merit of priority may belong, Marvell certainly struck the same note as Butler, and if not with the same success, at least with sufficient success to give him a high place among the poets of wit and humour. To take, for example, his description of the genesis of Holland:

> Glad then, as miners who have found the ore,
> They, with mad labour, fished the land to shore;
> And div'd as desperately for each piece
> Of earth, as if't had been of ambergris;
> Collecting anxiously small loads of clay,
> Less than what building swallows bear away;
> Or than those pills which sordid beetles roll,
> Transfusing into them their dunghill soul.
> How they did rivet, with gigantic piles,
> Thorough the centre their new catched miles;
> And to the stake a struggling country bound,
> Where barking waves still bait the forced ground;
> Building their watery Babel far more high
> To reach the sea, than those to scale the sky.

Here, as in Butler's happiest passages, we have the ludicrous exaggerations chasing each other like waves, and each as it rises seeming to overtop the absurdity of its predecessor.

Marvell's poetry cannot rank with the very highest in our language, but it unquestionably has high and varied qualities. It makes little pretension to depth or sublimity, but it abounds in wit and humour, true feeling, melody, and a certain scholarly elegance and delicate fancy. The late Mr. Tupling, the most erudite of London bibliopoles, used to add to the description of a copy of Marvell's poems in one of his quaint annotated catalogues of old books, "Few know how great the poetry here is." "Great" is not exactly the word; but it is at least genuine.

EDMUND GOSSE
From "The Reaction"
From Shakespeare to Pope
1885, pp. 211–21

I have ⟨. . .⟩ to present the greatest and the most interesting of the poets who wrote during the Commonwealth in opposition to Waller and his followers. The name of Andrew Marvell is illustrious wherever political purity is valued, wherever intellectual liberty is defended. To dwell upon the qualities of a character so candid, and upon the virtues of so single-minded a patriot, may seem out of place in a disquisition on the rise of classical poetry in England, but this patriot, this exquisite citizen, was a poet also, and a poet worthy of his civic reputation. Nor was there anything inconsistent in the fact that a man whose hands were pure in an age of universal corruption, and who put the interests of the people first when public virtue had scarcely been discovered, should be a romantic idealist when he came to put his innermost thoughts down in metre. Marvell is nothing if not consistent, and we find the same brain and heart engaged with rustic visions at Nunappleton and with the anger of statecraft at Westminster. ⟨. . .⟩

The world is seldom told at what stray and occasional moments, how hurriedly, and again how seldom, a poet's inspiration flows. It may well be that the music lies frozen at a young man's heart until some peculiar condition in his circumstances, a chain of emotions called forth by some peaceful and novel situation, melts it into sudden poetry. In a few months, perhaps, the conditions change, the mind is released from its tension, and he has written in that short time most of what is to introduce him to posterity as a poet. In ages of general political disorder, and of civic and personal insecurity, this must particularly be the case. We know for how long a time the muse of Milton was silenced by public and private anxieties, and we should be ignorant of one great section of his genius, of his romantic and melodious power in lyrical writing, if it had not been for his retirement at Horton. What Horton was to Milton, Nunappleton was to Marvell, it made a lyrical poet of him.

This series of verses was carefully preserved by his widow, and given to the world, with other of his pieces, in a small folio, in 1681. A fine copy of this rare book is one of the most dainty and desirable of all English publications from the Restoration to the end of the century. It is not quite complete, and notably the celebrated Horatian Ode on Oliver Cromwell is not included in it,—Mrs Marvell did not trouble herself with any poems but those which she possessed in her husband's handwriting,—but it is still the most luxurious shape in which Marvell's poems can be read. The Nunappleton pieces are strewed over it without any attempt at arrangement, and the one which holds the key to the rest is printed last. This is a long poem in praise of the house, written in eight-line stanzas of octo-syllabic verse, and extending to nearly eight hundred lines. Any student who wishes to understand Marvell must read this long and difficult piece with care. He will soon see that he has to deal with what Dr. Johnson called a "metaphysical," and what I have ventured to call a "Marinist" poet of the most extreme order.

Marvell is the last of the school of Donne, and in several respects he comes nearer to the master than any of his precursors. Certain conceits of Donne's, for instance that one about the lover and the pair of compasses, are often quoted as examples of a monstrous class. We get to think of Donne as exclusively the forger of tawdry false jewellery such as this, "rime's sturdy cripple," as Coleridge ingeniously calls him. But Donne was also the writer of lines and passages that speak so directly to the heart and to the senses that those who have come under their spell feel a sort of shyness in quoting them; they are so personal that to discuss them seems an indiscretion. Something of the same odd reserve seems due in the reader of some of Shakespeare's *Sonnets*, of some of Coleridge's shorter poems. I cannot, myself, bear to hear poetry of this intimate kind analyzed or even touched by unsympathetic people. This is a feeling which may not be praiseworthy in the student, but it is a proof of extraordinary felicity, mingled with sincerity, in

the style of the writer so discussed or touched. There can be no doubt that Donne possesses this quality, denied perhaps to all his scholars, until revealed again, in a certain measure, in Marvell. The note, however, is not so sharply struck in him as in Donne; there is more suavity and grace. The conceits are perhaps as wild. Here is one:

> Love wisely had of long foreseen
> That he must once grow old,
> And therefore stored a magazine,
> To save him from the cold.
> He kept the several cells replete
> With nitre thrice refined,
> The naphtha's and the sulphur's heat,
> And all that burns the mind.

This terrible magazine, which is fortified by a double gate, and which would have enflamed the whole of nature if one spark had fallen into it, turns out to be—the heart of Celia. Again, whole stanzas in the Nunappleton poem are taken up with a description of the garden as a military camp, through which the bee beats his drum, while the flowers are soldiers, who fire off volleys of perfume, and stand at parade, under their various colours, in stately regiments all day long:

> But when the vigilant patrol
> Of stars walks round about the pole,
> Their leaves that to their stalks are curled,
> Seem to their staves the ensigns furled.
> Then in some flower's belovèd hut
> Each bee as sentinel is shut,
> And sleeps so too, but if once stirr'd
> She runs you thro' or asks the word.

This is pretty and harmless, but perhaps just because it errs so gently against the canons of style, we ask ourselves how so seriously-minded a man as Marvell could run on in such a childish way. There is a good deal in Marvell that is of this species of wit, graceful and coloured, but almost infantile. Waller and Denham had taught English people to outgrow these childish toys of fancy, and if there had been nothing more than this in Marvell, we should not be regarding him as a serious element in the reaction. But there is a great deal more, and allowing the conceits to be taken for granted, we may inquire into the character of what is best in his lyrics.

In the long Nunappleton poem, then, and in that celebrated piece which is printed now in most collections of English poetry, "The Garden," we find a personal sympathy with nature, and particularly with vegetation, which was quite a novel thing, and which found no second exponent until Wordsworth came forward with his still wider and more philosophical commerce with the inanimate world. For flowers, trees, and grasses, Marvell expresses a sort of personal passion. They stand between him and humanity, they are to him "forms more real than living man." He calls upon the woodlands of Nunappleton to save him from the noisy world:

> Bind me, ye woodbines, in your twines,
> Curl me about, ye gadding vines,
> And oh! so close your circles lace
> That I may never leave this place.

Again he says:

> How safe, methinks, and strong, behind
> These trees have I encamped my mind,

and he repeats this sentiment of the security of natural solitude again and again. His style, when he can put his conceits behind him, is extremly sharp and delicate, with a distinction of phrase that is quite unknown to most of his contemporaries. To praise "The Garden" or "Bermudas" would be an impertinence; but I think few readers know what charming and unique poetry lies hid in the series of poems in which Marvell writes as a Mower, with a fantastical regret for the flowers and grasses that he cuts down. He says:

> I am the mower Damon, known
> Through all the meadows I have mown,
> On me the morn her dew distils
> Before her darling daffodils.

He declares a profound passion for a possible Juliana, but it is really the wood-moths gleaming on the bark, the vigilant heron in its nest at the top of the ash-tree, the garish eye of the new-hatched throstle staring through the hazels, that hold his poetical affections. He is the last of the English romantic poets for several generations, and no one of them all, early or late, has regarded nature with a quicker or more loving attention than he. He is an alien indeed among the men of periwigs and ruffles.

A. C. BENSON
"Andrew Marvell" (1892)
Essays
1896, pp. 68–95

Few poets are of sufficiently tough and impenetrable fibre to be able with impunity to mix with public affairs. Even though the spring of their inspiration be like the fountain in the garden of grace, "drawn from the brain of the purple mountain that stands in the distance yonder," that stream is apt to become sullied at the very source by the envious contact of the world. Poets conscious of their vocation have generally striven sedulously, by sequestering their lives somewhat austerely from the current of affairs, to cultivate the tranquillity and freshness on which the purity of their utterance depends. If it be hard to hear sermons and remain a Christian, it is harder to mix much with men and remain an idealist. And if this be true of commerce in its various forms, law, medicine, and even education, it seems to be still more fatally true of politics. Of course the temptation of politics to a philosophical mind is very great. To be at the centre of the machine, to be able perhaps to translate a high thought into a practical measure; to be able to make some closer reconciliation between law and morality, as the vertical sun draws the shadow nearer to the feet,—all this to a generous mind has an attraction almost supreme.

And yet the strain is so great that few survive it. Sophocles was more than once elected general, and is reported to have kept his colleagues in good humour by the charm of his conversation through a short but disagreeable campaign. Dante was an ardent and uncompromising revolutionary. Goethe and Lamartine were statesmen. Among our own poets, the lives of Spenser and Addison might perhaps be quoted as fairly successful compromises; but of the poets of the first rank Milton is the only one who deliberately abandoned poetry for half a lifetime, that he might take an active part in public life.

It is perhaps to Milton's example, and probably to his advice, that we owe the loss of a great English poet. It seems to have been, if not at Milton's instigation, at any rate by his direct aid, that Andrew Marvell was introduced to public life. The acquaintance began at Rome; but Marvell was introduced into Milton's intimate society, as his assistant secretary, at a most impressionable age. He had written poetry, dealing like "L'Allegro" and "Il Penseroso" mainly with country subjects,

and was inclined no doubt to hang on the words of the older poet as on an oracle of light and truth. We can imagine him piecing out his aspirations and day-dreams, while the poet of sterner stuff, yet of all men least insensible to the delights of congenial society, points out to him the more excellent way, bidding him to abjure Amaryllis for a time. He has style, despatches will give it precision; knowledge of men and life will confirm and mature his mind; the true poet must win a stubborn virility if he is to gain the world. The younger and more delicate mind complies; and we lose a great poet, Milton gains an assistant secretary, and the age a somewhat gross satirist.

At a time like this, when with a sense of sadness we can point to more than one indifferent politician who might have been a capable writer, and so very many indifferent writers who could have been spared to swell the ranks of politicians, we may well take the lesson of Andrew Marvell to heart.

The passion for the country which breathes through his earlier poems, the free air which ruffles the page, the summer languors, the formal garden seen through the casements of the cool house, the close scrutiny of woodland sounds, such as the harsh laughter of the woodpecker, the shrill insistence of the grasshopper's dry note, the luscious content of the drowsy, croaking frogs, the musical sweep of the scythe through the falling swathe; all these are the work of no town-bred scholar like Milton, whose country poems are rather visions seen through the eyes of other poets, or written as a man might transcribe the vague and inaccurate emotions of a landscape drawn by some old uncertain hand and dimmed by smoke and time. Of course Milton's "Il Penseroso" and "L'Allegro" have far more value even as country poems than hundreds of more literal transcripts. From a literary point of view indeed the juxtapositions of half a dozen epithets alone would prove the genius of the writer. But there are no sharp outlines; the scholar pauses in his walk to peer across the watered flat, or raises his eyes from his book to see the quiver of leaves upon the sunlit wall; he notes an effect it may be; but his images do not come like treasures lavished from a secret storehouse of memory.

With Andrew Marvell it is different, though we will show by instances that even his observation was sometimes at fault. Where or when this passion came to him we cannot tell; whether in the great walled garden at the back of the old school-house at Hull, where his boyish years were spent; at Cambridge, where the oozy streams lapped and green fens crawled almost into the heart of the town, where snipe were shot and wild-duck snared on the site of some of its now populous streets; at Meldreth perhaps, where doubtless some antique kindred lingered at the old manor-house that still bears his patronymic, "the Marvells."—Wherever it was,—and such tastes are rarely formed in later years—the delicate observation of the minute philosopher, side by side with the art of intimate expression, grew and bloomed.

We see a trace of that learning nature, the trailing dependence of the uneasy will of which we have already spoken, in a story of his early years. The keen-eyed boy, with his fresh colour and waving brown hair, was thrown on the tumultuous world of Cambridge, it seems, before he was thirteen years of age, a strange medley no doubt,—its rough publicity alone saving it, as with a dash of healthy freshness, from the effeminacy and sentimentalism apt to breed in more sheltered societies. The details of the story vary; but the boy certainly fell into the hands of Jesuits, who finally induced him to abscond to one of their retreats in London, where over a bookseller's shop, after a long and weary search, his father found him and persuaded him to return. Laborious Dr. Grosart has extracted from the Hull Records a most curious letter relating to this incident, in which a man whose son has been inveigled away in similar circumstances, asks for advice from Andrew Marvell's father.

Such an escapade belongs to a mind that must have been ardent and daring beyond its fellows; but it also shows a somewhat shifting foundation, an imagination easily dazzled, and a pliability of will that cost us, we may believe, a poet. After Cambridge came some years of travel, which afforded material for some of his poems, such as the satire on Holland, of which the cleverness is still apparent, though its elaborate coarseness and pedantic humour make it poor pasture to feed the mind upon.

But the period to which we owe almost all the true gold among his poems, is the two years which he spent at Nunappleton House, 1650–1652, as tutor to the daughter of the great Lord Fairfax, the little Lady Mary Fairfax, then twelve years old. Marvell was at this time twenty-nine; and that exquisite relation which may exist between a grown man, pure in heart, and a young girl, when disparity of fortune and circumstance forbids all thought of marriage, seems to have been the mainspring of his song. Such a relation is half tenderness which dissembles its passion, and half worship which laughs itself away in easy phrases. The lyric "Young Love," which indubitably though not confessedly refers to Mary Fairfax, is one of the sweetest poems of pure feeling in the language.

> Common beauties stay fifteen;
>   Such as yours should swifter move,
> Whose fair blossoms are too green
>   Yet for lust, but not for love.
>
> Love as much the snowy lamb,
>   Or the wanton kid, doth prize
> As the lusty bull or ram,
>   For his morning sacrifice.
>
> Now then love me; Time may take
>   Thee before thy time away;
> Of this need we'll virtue make,
>   And learn love before we may.

It is delightful in this connection to think of the signet-ring with the device of a fawn,—which he used in early life and may still be seen on his papers,—as a gift of his little pupil, earned doubtless by his poem on the Dying Fawn, which is certainly an episode of Lady Mary's childhood.

In this group of early poems, which are worth all the rest of Marvell's work put together, several strains predominate. In the first place there is a close observation of Nature, even a grotesque transcription, with which we are too often accustomed only to credit later writers. For instance, in "Damon the Mower" he writes:

> The grasshopper its pipe gives o'er,
> And hamstringed frogs can dance no more;
> But in the brook the green frog wades,
> And grasshoppers seek out the shades.

The second line of this we take to refer to the condition to which frogs are sometimes reduced in a season of extreme drought, when the pools are dry. Marvell must have seen a frog with his thighs drawn and contracted from lack of moisture making his way slowly through the grass in search of a refreshing swamp; this is certainly minute observation, as the phenomenon is a rare one. Again, such a delicate couplet as,

> And through the hazels thick espy
> The hatching throstle's shining eye,

is not the work of a scholar who walks a country road, but of a man who will push his way into the copses in early spring, and

has watched with delight the timorous eye and the upturned beak of the thrush sunk in her nest. Or again, speaking of the dwindled summer stream running so perilously clear after weeks of drought that the fish are languid:

> The stupid fishes hand, as plain
>   As flies in crystal overta'en,

Or of the hayfield roughly mown, into which the herd has been turned to graze:

> And what below the scythe increast,
>   Is pinched yet nearer by the beast.

The mower's work, begun and ended with the dews, in all its charming monotony, seems to have had a peculiar attraction for Marvell; he recurs to it in more than one poem.

> I am the mower Damon, known
> Through all the meadows I have mown:
> On me the morn her dew distils
> Before her darling daffodils.

And again, of the mowers,

> Who seem like Israelites to be
> Walking on foot through a green sea,
> To them the grassy deeps divide
> And crowd a lane to either side.

The aspects of the country on which he dwells with deepest pleasure—and here lies the charm—are not those of Nature in her sublimer or more elated moods, but the gentler and more pastoral elements, that are apt to pass unnoticed at the time by all but the true lovers of the quiet country side, and crowd in upon the mind when surfeited by the wilder glories of peak and precipice, or where tropical luxuriance side by side with tropical aridity blinds and depresses the sense, with the feeling that made Browning cry from Florence,

> Oh, to be in England, now that April's there!

Marvell's lines, "On the Hill and Grove at Billborow," are an instance of this; there is a certain fantastic craving after antithesis and strangeness, it is true, but the spirit underlies the lines. The poem however must be read in its entirety to gain the exact impression.

Again, for simple felicity, what could be more airily drawn than the following from "The Garden"?—

> Here at the fountain's sliding foot,
> Or at some fruit-tree's mossy root,
> Casting the body's vest aside,
> My soul into the boughs doth glide,
> There like a bird it sits and sings,
> Then whets and claps its silver wings.

Or this, from the Song to celebrate the marriage of Lord Fauconberg and the Lady Mary Cromwell, of the undisturbed dead of night?—

> The astrologer's own eyes are set,
> And even wolves the sheep forget;
> Only this shepherd, late and soon,
> Upon this hill outwakes the moon.
> Hark! how he sings with sad delight
> Through the clear and silent night.

Other poems, such as the "Ode on the Drop of Dew" and the "Nymph Complaining for the Death of her Fawn," too long to be quoted here, are penetrated with the same essence.

At the same time it must be confessed that Marvell's imagery is sometimes at fault—it would be strange if it were not so; he falls now and then, the wonder is how rarely, to a mere literary conceit. Thus the mower Damon sees himself reflected in his scythe; the fawn feeds on roses till its lip "seems to bleed," not with a possibly lurking thorn, but with the hue of its pasturage. With Hobbinol and Tomalin for the names of swain and nymph unreality is apt to grow. When the garden is compared to a fortress and its scents to a salvo of artillery—

> Well shot, ye firemen! O how sweet
> And round your equal fires do meet—

and,

> Then in some flower's beloved hut
> Each bee as sentinel is shut,
> And sleeps so, too—but if once stirred,
> She runs you through, nor asks the word—

here, in spite of a certain curious felicity, we are in the region of false tradition and rococo expression. The poem of "Eyes and Tears," again (so whimsically admired by Archbishop Trench), is little more than a string of conceits; and when in "Mourning" we hear that

> She courts herself in amorous rain,
> Herself both Danae and the shower;

when we are introduced to Indian divers who plunge in the tears and can find no bottom, we think of Macaulay's "Tears of Sensibility," and Crashaw's fearful lines on the Magdalene's eyes—

> Two walking baths, two weeping motions,
> Portable and compendious oceans.

Nevertheless Marvell's poems are singularly free as a rule from this strain of affectation. He has none of the morbidity that often passes for refinement. The free air, the wood-paths, the full heat of the summer sun—this is his scenery; we are not brought into contact with the bones beneath the rose-bush, the splintered sun-dial, and the stagnant pool. His pulses throb with ardent life, and have none of the "inexplicable faintness" of a deathlier school. What would not Crashaw have had to say of the "Nuns of Appleton" if he had been so unfortunate as to have lighted on them? But Marvell writes:

> Our orient breaths perfumed are
> With incense of incessant prayer,
> And holy water of our tears
> Most strangely our complexion clears;
> Not tears of Grief, but such as those
> With which calm Pleasure overflows.

And passing by a sweet and natural transition to his little pupil, the young Recluse of Nunappleton—

> I see the angels, in a crown,
> On you the lilies showering down,
> And, round about you, glory breaks,
> That something more than human speaks

The poems contain within themselves the germ of the later growth of satire in the shape of caustic touches of humour, as well as a certain austere philosophy that is apt to peer behind the superficial veil of circumstance, yet without dreary introspection. There is a "Dialogue between Soul and Body," which deals with the duality of human nature which has been the despair of all philosophers and the painful axiom of all religious teachers. Marvell makes the Soul say;

> Constrained not only to endure
> Diseases, but what's worse, the cure,
> And ready oft the port to gain,
> Am shipwrecked into health again.

In the same connection in "The Coronet," an allegory of the Ideal and the Real, he says:

> Alas! I find the serpent old,
> Twining in his speckled breast,
> About the flowers disguised doth fold,
> With wreaths of fame and interest.

Much of Marvell's philosophy however has not the same vitality, born of personal struggle and discomfiture, but is a mere echo of stoical and pagan views of life and its vanities drawn from Horace and Seneca, who seem to have been his favourite authors. Such a sentiment as the following, from "Appleton House"—

> But he, superfluously spread,
> Demands more room alive than dead;
> What need of all this marble crust,
> To impart the wanton mole of dust?—

and from "The Coy Mistress"—

> The grave's a fine and private place,
> But none, methinks, do there embrace—

are mere pagan commonplaces, however daintily expressed.

But there is a poem, an idyll in the form of a dialogue between Clorinda and Damon, which seems to contain an original philosophical motive. Idylls in the strict sense of the word are not remarkable for including a moral; or if they do include one it may be said that it is generally bad, and is apt to defend the enjoyment of an hour against the conscience of centuries; but in "Clorinda and Damon," the woman is the tempter, and Damon is obdurate. She invites him to her cave, and describes its pleasures.

> *Clo.:* . . . . A fountain's liquid bell
> Tinkles within the concave shell.
> *Da.:* Might a soul bathe there and be clean,
> Or slake its drought?
> *Clo.:* What is't you mean?
> *Da.:* Clorinda, pastures, caves, and springs,
> These once had been enticing things.
> *Clo.:* And what late change?—
> *Da.:* The other day
> Pan met me.
> *Clo.:* What did great Pan say?
> *Da.:* Words that transcend poor shepherds' skill.

This poem seems a distinct attempt to make of the sickly furniture of the idyll a vehicle for the teaching of religious truth. Is it fanciful to read in it a poetical rendering of the doctrine of conversion, the change that may come to a careless and sensuous nature by being suddenly brought face to face with the Divine light? It might even refer to some religious experience of Marvell's own: Milton's "mighty Pan," typifying the Redeemer, is in all probability the original.

The work then on which Marvell's fame chiefly subsists—with the exception of one poem which belongs to a different class, and will be discussed later, the Horatian Ode—may be said to belong to the regions of nature and feeling, and to have anticipated in a remarkable degree the minute observation of natural phenomena characteristic of a modern school, even to a certain straining after unusual, almost bizarre effects. The writers of that date, indeed, as Green points out, seem to have become suddenly and unaccountably modern, a fact which we are apt to overlook owing to the frigid reaction of the school of Pope. Whatever the faults of Marvell's poems may be, and they are patent to all, they have a strain of originality. He does not seem to imitate, he does not even follow the lines of other poets; never,—except in a scattered instance or two, where there is a faint echo of Milton,—does he recall or suggest that he has a master.

At the same time the lyrics are so short and slight that any criticism upon them is apt to take the form of a wish that the same hand had written more, and grown old in his art. There is a monotony, for instance, about their subjects, like the song of a bird, recurring again and again to the same phrase; there is an uncertainty, an incompleteness not so much of expression as of arrangement, a tendency to diverge and digress in an unconcerned and vagabond fashion. There are stanzas, even long passages, which a lover of proportion such as Gray (who excised one of the most beautiful stanzas of the Elegy because it made too long a parenthesis) would never have spared. It is the work of a young man trying his wings, and though perhaps not flying quite directly and professionally to his end, reveling in the new-found powers with a delicious ecstasy which excuses what is vague and prolix; especially when over all is shed that subtle, precious quality which makes a sketch from one hand so unutterably more interesting than a finished picture from another,—which will arrest with a few commonplace phrases, lightly touched by certain players, the attention which has wandered throughout a whole sonata.

The strength of Marvell's style lies in its unexpectedness. You are arrested by what has been well called a "pre-destined" epithet, not a mere otiose addition, but a word which turns a noun into a picture; the "hook-shouldered" hill "to abrupter greatness thrust," "the sugar's uncorrupting oil," "the vigilant patrol of stars," "the squatted thorns," "the oranges like golden lamps in a green night," "the garden's fragrant innocence,"— these are but a few random instances of a tendency that meets you in every poem. Marvell had in fact the qualities of a consummate artist, and only needed to repress his luxuriance and to confine his expansiveness. In his own words,

> Height with a certain grace doth bend,
> But low things clownishly ascend.

Before passing on to discuss the satires I may be allowed to say a few words on a class of poems largely represented in Marvell's works, which may be generally called Panegyric.

Quite alone among these—indeed, it can be classed with no other poem in the language—stands the Horatian Ode on Cromwell's return from Ireland. Mr. Lowell said of it that as a testimony to Cromwell's character it was worth more than all Carlyle's biographies; he might without exaggeration have said as much of its literary qualities. It has force with grace, originality with charm, in almost every stanza. Perhaps the first quality that would strike a reader of it for the first time is its quaintness; but further study creates no reaction against this in the mind—the usual sequel to poems which depend on quaintness for effect. But when Mr. Lowell goes on to say that the poem shows the difference between grief that thinks of its object and grief that thinks of its rhymes (referring to Dryden), he is not so happy. The pre-eminent quality of the poem is its art; and its singular charm is the fact that it succeeds, in spite of being artificial, in moving and touching the springs of feeling in an extraordinary degree. It is a unique piece in the collection, the one instance where Marvell's undoubted genius burned steadily through a whole poem. Here he flies *penna metuente solvi*. It is in completeness more than in quality that it is superior to all his other work, but in quality too it has that lurking divinity that cannot be analysed or imitated.

> 'Tis madness to resist or blame
> The force of angry heaven's flame,
>   And if we would speak true,
>   Much to the man is due
> Who from his private gardens, where
> He lived reservèd and austere,
>   (As though his highest plot
>   To plant the bergamot,)
> Could by industrious valour climb
> To ruin the great work of Time,
>   And cast the kingdoms old
>   Into another mould.

This is the apotheosis of tyrants; it is the bloom of republicanism just flowering into despotism. But the Ode is no party utterance; the often-quoted lines on the death of Charles, in their grave yet passionate dignity, might have been written by the most ardent of Royalists, and have often done service on their side. But, indeed, the whole Ode is above party, and looks clearly into the heart and motives of man. It moves from end to end with the solemn beat of its singular metre, its majestic cadences, without self-consciousness or sentiment, austere, but not frigid.

Marvell's other panegyrics are but little known, though the awkward and ugly lines on Milton have passed into anthologies, owing to their magnificent exordium, "When I beheld the poet blind yet old." But no one can pretend that such lines as these are anything but prosaic and ridiculous to the last degree—

> Thou hast not missed one thought that could be fit,
> And all that was improper dost omit;
>
> At once delight and horror on us seize,
> Thou sing'st with so much gravity and ease—

though the unfortunate alteration in the meaning of the word *improper* makes them now seem even more ridiculous than they are. The poems on the "First Anniversary of the Government of the Lord Protector," on the "Death of the Lord Protector," and on "Richard Cromwell," are melancholy reading though they have some sonorous lines.

> And as the angel of our Commonweal
> Troubling the waters, yearly mak'st them heal,

may pass as an epigram. But that a man of penetrating judgment and independence of opinion should descend to a vein of odious genealogical compliment, and speak of the succeeding of

> Rainbow to storm, Richard to Oliver,

and add that

> A Cromwell in an hour a prince will grow,

by way of apology for the obvious deficiencies of his new Protector, makes us very melancholy indeed. Flattery is of course a slough in which many poets have wallowed; and a little grovelling was held to be even more commendable in poets in that earlier age; but we see the pinion beginning to droop, and the bright eye growing sickly and dull. Milton's poisonous advice is already at work.

But we must pass through a more humiliating epoch still. The poet of spicy gardens and sequestered fields seen through the haze of dawn is gone, not like the Scholar Gipsy to the high lonely wood or the deserted lasher, but has stepped down to jostle with the foulest and most venal of mankind. He becomes a satirist, and a satirist of the coarsest kind. His pages are crowded with filthy pictures and revolting images; the leaves cannot be turned over so quickly but some lewd epithet or vile realism prints itself on the eye. His apologists have said that it is nothing but the overflowing indignation of a noble mind when confronted with the hideous vices of a corrupt court and nation; that this deep-seated wrath is but an indication of the fervid idealistic nature of the man; that the generous fire that warmed in the poems, consumed in the satires; that the true moralist does not condone but condemn. To this we would answer that it is just conceivable that a satirist may be primarily occupied by an immense moral indignation, and no doubt that indignation must bear a certain part in all satires; but it is not the attitude of a hopeful or generous soul. The satirist is after all only destructive; he has not learned the lesson that the only cure for old vices is new enthusiasms. Nor if a satirist is betrayed into the grossest and most unnecessary realism can we acquit him entirely of all enjoyment of his subject. It is impossible to treat of vice in the intimate and detailed manner in which Marvell treats of it without having, if no practical acquaintance with your subject, at least a considerable conventional acquaintance with it, and a large literary knowledge of the handling of similar topics; and when one critic goes so far as to call Marvell an essentially pure-minded man, or words to that effect, we think he would find a contradiction on almost every page of the satires.

They were undoubtedly popular. Charles II. was greatly amused by them; and their reputation lasted as late as Swift, who spoke of Marvell's genius as pre-eminently indicated by the fact that though the controversies were forgotten, the satires still held the mind. He started with a natural equipment. That he was humorous his earlier poems show, as when for instance he makes Daphne say to Chloe:

Rather I away will pine
In a manly stubbornness,
Than be fatted up express,
For the cannibal to dine.

And he shows, too, in his earlier poems, much of the weightier and more dignified art of statement that makes the true satirist's work often read better in quotations than entire; as for instance—

Wilt thou all the glory have,
That war or peace commend?
Half the world shall be thy slave,
The other half thy friend.

But belonging as they do to the period of melancholy decadence of Marvell's art, we are not inclined to go at any length into the question of the satires. We see genius struggling like Laocoon in the grasp of a power whose virulence he did not measure, and to whom sooner or later the increasing languor must yield. Of course there are notable passages scattered throughout them. In "Last Instructions to a Painter," the passage beginning, "Paint last the king, and a dead shade of night," where Charles II. sees in a vision the shapes of Charles I. and Henry VIII. threatening him with the consequences of unsympathetic despotism and the pursuit of sensual passion, has a tragic horror and dignity of a peculiar kind; and the following specimen from "The Character of Holland" gives on the whole a good specimen of the strength and weakness of the author:

Holland, that scarce deserves the name of land,
As but the off-scouring of the British sand,
And so much earth as was contributed
By English pilots when they heaved the lead,
Or what by the Ocean's slow alluvion fell
Of shipwrecked cockle and the mussel-shell,
This undigested vomit of the sea,
Fell to the Dutch by just propriety.

Clever beyond question; every couplet is an undeniable epigram, lucid, well-digested, elaborate; pointed, yet finikin withal,—it is easy to find a string of epithets for it. But to what purpose is this waste? To see this felicity spent on such slight and intemperate work is bitterness itself; such writing has, it must be confessed, every qualification for pleasing except the power to please.

Of the remainder of Marvell's life, there is little more to be said. He was private tutor at Eton to a Master Dutton, a relative of Cromwell's, and wrote a delightful letter about him to the Protector; but the serious business of his later life was Parliament. Of his political consistency we cannot form a high

idea. He seems, as we should expect him to have been, a Royalist at heart and by sympathy all along; "'Tis God-like good," he wrote, "to save a falling king." Yet he was not ashamed to accept Cromwell as the angel of the Commonweal, and to write in fulsome praise of Protector Richard; and his bond of union with the extreme Puritans was his intense hatred of prelacy and bishops which is constantly coming up. In "The Loyal Scot" he writes:

The friendly loadstone has not more combined,
Than Bishops cramped the commerce of mankind.

And in "The Bermudas" he classes the fury of the elements with "Prelates' rage" as the natural enemies of the human race. Such was not the intermeddling in affairs that Milton had recommended. To fiddle, while Rome burnt, upon the almost divine attributes of her successive rulers, this was not the austere storage of song which Milton himself practised.

Andrew Marvell was for many years member for Hull, with his expenses paid by the Corporation. His immense, minute, and elaborate correspondence with his constituents, in which he gave an exact account of the progress of public business, remains to do him credit as a sagacious and conscientious man. But it cannot be certainly imputed to any higher motive than to stand well with his employers. He was provided with the means of livelihood, he was in a position of trust and dignity, and he may well be excused for wishing to retain it. In spite of certain mysterious absences on the Continent, and a long period during which he absented himself from the House in the suite of an embassy to Russia, he preserved the confidence of his constituents for eighteen years, and died at his post. He spoke but little in the House, and his reported speeches add but little to his reputation. One curious incident is related in the Journals. In going to his place he stumbled over Sir Philip Harcourt's foot, and an interchange of blows in a humorous and friendly fashion with hand and hat, took place. At the close of the sitting the Speaker animadverted on this, Marvell being absent; and a brief debate took place the next day on the subject, Marvell speaking with some warmth of the Speaker's grave interference with what appears to have been nothing more than a piece of childish horse-play. "What passed (said Mr. Marvell) was through great acquaintance and familiarity between us. He never gave him an affront nor intended him any. But the Speaker cast a severe reflection upon him yesterday when he was out of the House, and he hopes that as the Speaker keeps us in order, he will keep himself in order for the future."

For one thing Marvell deserves high credit; in a corrupt age, he kept his hands clean, refusing even when hard pressed for money a gift of £1000 proffered him by Danby, the Lord-Treasurer, "in his garret," as a kind of retainer on the royal side. In Hartley Coleridge's life of Marvell this is told in a silly, theatrical way, unworthy and not even characteristic of the man. "Marvell," he says, "looking at the paper (an order on the Treasury which had been slipped into his hand) calls after the Treasurer, 'My lord, I request another moment.' They went up again to the garret; and Jack the servant-boy was called. 'Jack, child, what had I for dinner yesterday?' 'Don't you remember, sir? You had the little shoulder of mutton that you ordered me to bring from a woman in the market.' 'Very right, child. What have I for dinner to-day?' 'Don't you know, sir, that you bid me lay by the blade-bone to broil?' ''Tis so; very right, child; go away.' 'My lord, do you hear that? Andrew Marvell's dinner is provided. There's your piece of paper; I want it not. I know the sort of kindness you intended. I live here to serve my constituents; the Ministry may seek men for their purpose,—I

am not one.'" But with the exception of perhaps the concluding words, there is no reason to think the story authentic,
though the fact is unquestioned.

Over Prince Rupert, Marvell seems to have had a great
influence, so much so that, when the Prince spoke in public,
it was commonly said: "He has been with his tutor."

Marvell died suddenly in 1678, not without suspicion of
poisoning; but it seems to have been rather due to the
treatment he underwent at the hands of an old-fashioned
practitioner, who had a prejudice against the use of Peruvian
bark which would probably have saved Marvell's life. Upon his
death a widow starts into existence, Mary Marvell by name, so
unexpectedly and with such a total absence of previous
allusion, that it has been doubted whether her marriage was
not all a fiction. But Dr. Grosart points out that she would
never have administered his estate had there been any reason to
doubt the validity of her claims; and it was under her auspices
that the Poems were first given to the world a few years after his
death, in a folio which is now a rare and coveted book.

Of his Prose Works it is needful to say but little; they may
be characterised as prose satires for the most part, or political
pamphlets, "The Rehearsal Transposed" and "The Divine in
Mode" are peculiarly distasteful examples of a kind of controversy then much in vogue. They are answers to publications,
and to the ordinary reader contrive to be elaborate without
being artistic, personal without being humorous, and digressive without being entertaining; in short, they combine the
characteristics of tedium, dulness, and scurrility to a perfectly
phenomenal degree. As compared with the poems themselves,
the prose works fill many volumes; and any reader of ordinary
perseverance has ample opportunities of convincing himself of
Andrew Marvell's powers of expression, his high-spirited beginning, the delicate ideals, the sequestered ambitions of his
youth, and their lamentable decline.

It is a perilous investment to aspire to be a poet,—
periculosæ plenum opus aleæ. If you succeed, to have the
world, present and to come, at your feet, to win the reluctant
admiration even of the Philistine; to snuff the incense of
adoration on the one hand, and on the other to feel yourself a
member of the choir invisible, the sweet and solemn company
of poets; to own within yourself the ministry of hope and
height. And one step below success, to be laughed at or softly
pitied as the dreamer of ineffectual dreams, the strummer of
impotent music; to be despised alike by the successful and the
unsuccessful; the world if you win,—worse than nothing if you
fail.

Mediocribus esse poetis
Non di, non homines, non concessere columnæ.

There is no such thing as respectable mediocrity among poets.
Be supreme or contemptible.

And yet we cannot but grieve when we see a poet over
whose feet the stream has flowed, turn back from the brink and
make the great denial; whether from the secret consciousness of
aridity, the drying of the fount of song, or from the imperious
temptations of the busy, ordinary world we cannot say.
Somehow we have lost our poet. It seems that,

Just for a handful of silver he left us,
Just for a ribbon to stick in his coat.

And the singer of an April mood, who might have bloomed
year after year in young and ardent hearts, is buried in the dust
of politics, in the valley of dead bones.

H. C. BEECHING
"The Lyrical Poems of Andrew Marvell"
National Review, July 1901, pp. 747–59

Any one who wished to defend the thesis that our own
generation, however it may fall below its predecessors in
outstanding poetical genius, is markedly their superior in
poetical taste, might find matter for his argument in the recent
rise into fame of the lyrical verse of Marvell. It may be
interesting to trace the progress of this growth of appreciation.

In 1681, three years after Marvell's death, a well printed
folio was brought out by his widow containing all his poetry
that existed in manuscript, except the political pieces, which,
as the Stuarts were still upon the throne, could not be
published with safety. Of this book no second edition was
called for. In 1726 a literary hack, one Thomas Cooke, who
translated Hesiod, and for attacking Pope was rewarded with
immortality:

From these the world will judge of men and books,
Not from the Burnets, Oldmixons, and Cookes,

issued an edition of Marvell's poems including the political
satires, and rests Marvell's fame almost exclusively on political
grounds. "My design," he says, "in this is to draw a pattern for
all freeborn *Englishmen*, in the life of a worthy Patriot, whose
every Action has truely merited to him, with *Aristides*, the
surname of the *Just*." How little capable Cooke was of
appreciating any of the distinctive qualities of Marvell's verse
may be judged from the poems he singles out for special praise.
"If we have any which may be properly said to come finished
from his Hands, they are these, "On Milton's Paradise Lost,"
"On Blood's Stealing the Crown," and "A Dialogue between
Two Horses.""

Just fifty years after Cooke's pretty little edition, there
appeared another in three great quarto volumes by an editor as
little competent to appreciate Marvell's peculiar charm as his
predecessor; though he, like Cooke, was a poet in his way. This
was Edward Thompson, a captain in the Royal Navy, who was
interested in the fame of Marvell, from being himself a native
of Hull, and also on the political side, from his friendship with
Wilkes. Thompson puts on his title-page some lines from his
namesake of *The Seasons*, "Hail, Independence, Hail," &c.;
and dedicates his volumes to the Mayor and Aldermen of Hull
as the "Friends of Liberty and England"; professing that his
labour was undertaken to show his esteem for "a person who
had been a general friend to mankind, a public one to his
country, and a partial and strenuous one to the town of Hull."
Thompson's gifts as a critic may be estimated from his
assigning to Marvell not only Addison's hymn, "The Spacious
Firmament on High," which at least is in Marvell's metre, if
not in his manner, but also Mallet's "William and Margaret,"
a poem that could not have been written before Allan Ramsay's
publications had revived interest in the old Scots ballads.
Thompson had found these poems with others in a manuscript
book, some part of which he declared to be in Marvell's
handwriting; and of this fact he would have been a very
competent judge from his familiarity with the many letters of
Marvell written to his constituents at Hull, which he printed in
his edition. From this invaluable autograph he set up his text.
"Afterwards, as rare things will, it vanished." But it restored to
the world the poem by which Marvell is generally known, "An
Horatian Ode upon Cromwell's Return from Ireland." I must
not speak here about Captain Thompson, but I may perhaps be
allowed to say I have come to regard his volumes with much

more interest since reading in the *Cornhill Magazine* for May 1868 some extracts from a manuscript journal of his kept in the year 1783–5. The only entry there precisely bearing on our subject is the following, under date 1784, "A nephew of Emma's [his mistress] was named by me Andrew Marvell; when he comes to reason, the name may inspire him to be virtuous." This would show, if more evidence were needed, that it was mainly on the political side that Marvell interested the Captain. His own poetical effusions were chiefly squibs and epigrams, and what he well called "Meretricious Miscellanies." The list of subscribers to Thompson's volumes tells the same tale. It includes the Duke of G——, the Marquis of Granby, the Earl of Shelburne and other Whig peers, the Lord Mayor of London (Sawbridge), and a dozen Members of Parliament, among them Burke, and such stalwarts as Wilkes and Oliver. It includes, more remarkably, the notorious Rigby, who was said by the wits to have bequeathed by his will "near half a million of public money." Learning is represented by that stout republican, Thomas Hollis, and by Daines Barrington the antiquary and naturalist, and correspondent of White of Selborne, who, according to Charles Lamb, was so much the friend of gardens that he paid the gardener at the Temple twenty shillings to poison the sparrows. But literature has only a few names. There is the Rev. Prebendary Mason, his friend the eccentric Dr. Glynn, who once wrote a prize poem, Mrs. Macaulay, and Mr. William Woty. Samuel Johnson, LL.D., is conspicuous by absence. The theatre (for Captain Thompson was himself something of a playwright) contributes David Garrick, Esq., Samuel Foote, Esq., and Mr. Colman; and among other personal friends of the editor is the notorious John Stevenson Hall, better known as Hall Stevenson. This worthy and the Duke of Cumberland (Henry Augustus), who heads the list, may have been attracted by the indelicacy of the satires, hardly by anything else.

Eleven years after Thompson's edition of Marvell, appeared that very interesting book, ominous of the dawn of a new era, *Select Beauties of Ancient English Poetry*, by Henry Headley, A.B., an enthusiastic young clergyman with genuine taste for the seventeenth-century poets. He revived the memory of Drayton and Daniel, whom he praises with discrimination, quoting from the former the now famous sonnet, "Since there's no help, come let us kiss and part"; and he has a good word to say for Drummond, Browne, Carew and Crashaw; but Marvell is not mentioned. Four years later, however, Marvell makes his appearance in George Ellis's *Specimens of the Early English Poets*, where he is spoken of as "an accomplished man who, though *principally* distinguished by his inflexible patriotism, was generally and justly admired for his learning, his acuteness in controversial writing, his wit, *and* his poetical talents." Ellis represents him by extracts from "Daphnis and Chloe," and "Young Love," which is much as if the author of the "Ancient Mariner" and "Kubla Khan" should be represented by the song "If I had but two little wings." I do not recall any reference to Marvell in Coleridge; and Wordsworth quotes him only as a patriot:

> The later Sidney, Marvell, Harrington,
> Young Vane, and others who called Milton friend.

It was Charles Lamb who made the discovery of Marvell's merit as a lyrical poet. In his essay upon the Old Benchers of the Inner Temple, printed in the *London Magazine* for September 1821, he quotes, *apropos* of the Temple sun-dial, four stanzas from "The Garden," and says of them that they "are full, as all his serious poetry was, of a witty delicacy." The phrase has become classical, as it deserves. The most popular anthology of the last half of the century has been Mr. Palgrave's *Golden Treasury of Songs and Lyrics*, and this shows, in its later editions, a curious and interesting growth in appreciation of Marvell. When the first edition appeared, in 1861, it contained three poems of his, "The Horatian Ode," "The Garden," and "The Bermudas." In 1883 there was added an extract from "The Nymph complaining for the Death of her Fawn," with a note saying "Perhaps no poem in this collection is more delicately fancied, more exquisitely finished"; and in 1891 room was found for "The Picture of Little T. C. in a Prospect of Flowers." With five poems in so small and picked a collection, Marvell's popular reputation as a lyric poet may be reckoned to have culminated.

Marvell was born in 1621, the son of a celebrated preacher who was also master of the Grammar School of Hull, where the boy was educated. He proceeded to Cambridge, took his degree, and then travelled in Holland, France, Italy, and Spain. When he returned to England he was engaged by Lord Fairfax as tutor to his daughter Mary, and it is to the time that he spent in retirement in Fairfax's house at Nun Appleton in Yorkshire, perhaps from 1650 to 1653, that we owe the best of his lyrical works. Before this he had written one or two things in rhymed couplets, a preface to Lovelace's *Lucasta* a copy of verses on Lord Hastings' death, full of wit, and with lines here and there that haunt the memory, like—

> Go stand between the morning and the flowers;

and in 1650 was composed the Horatian Ode; but whether any of the lyrics in octosyllables are of an earlier date than these cannot be determined. It will be best, then, to waive all question of chronological precedence, and look at the poems in groups according to their subject. But a word may first be said about the poet's models. He had two; we might call them his good and bad angels. They were John Milton, whose volume of lyrics appeared in 1645, and John Donne, whose poems were not printed during his lifetime, but were widely circulated in manuscript. Donne, one of the most remarkable among seventeenth-century Englishmen of genius, had one of the greatest poetical virtues and two of the greatest poetical vices. His virtue was passion, intensity; his vices were a too cavalier indifference to accent, and a love of quaint and extravagant conceits. Marvell is the pupil of his intensity, and to a certain degree of his extravagance; but he was saved from his careless writing by the study of Milton. The best example of Marvell's work in the manner of Donne is the lyric entitled "The Fair Singer." The breathless haste of the rhythm, and the absence of any pause except at the end of the lines, are studied after that master; so is the ingenuity of the idea. The first line of the poem, "To make a final conquest of all me," is Donne pure and simple. But even in this poem there is a regularity of measure which betrays the influence of the other school, that of Ben Jonson and Milton:

> I could have fled from one but singly fair;
>   My disentangled soul itself might save,
> Breaking the curled trammels of her hair;
>   But how should I avoid to be her slave
> Whose subtle art invisibly can wreathe
> My fetters of the very air I breathe!

Of the fantastic and forced images that Marvell copied from Donne it will suffice to offer a single example. In the "Dialogue between the Soul and the Body" he makes the body say:

> O who shall me deliver whole
> From bonds of this tyrannic soul,

Which stretched upright impales me so
That mine own precipice I go!

The poem called "Eyes and Tears," which is full of the same sort of thing, is, I suspect, an exercise, the inspiration of which may be traced to the appearance of Crashaw's poem of "The Weeper" in his volume of 1646. As a rule, Marvell's humour saved him from the worst banalities of this school; as a rule, also, he keeps his fantastic *tours de force* for semi-humorous passages, and often uses these, by way of contrast, to heighten the outburst of passion that follows. Thus, in the poem "Upon Appleton House," he compares Fairfax's garden to a fort:

See how the flowers, as at parade,
Under their colours stand displayed;
Each regiment in order grows,
That of the tulip, pink, and rose.
But when the vigilant patrol
Of stars walks round about the pole,
The leaves that to the stalks are curled
Seem to their staves the ensigns furled.
Then in some flower's beloved hut,
Each bee, as sentinel, is shut,
And sleeps so too; but if once stirred,
She runs you through, nor asks the word.

And then, while the reader is still smiling, he finds himself in the midst of a passionate apostrophe to England:

Oh, thou, that dear and happy isle,
The garden of the world erewhile,
Thou Paradise of the four seas
Which Heaven planted us to please;
But, to exclude the world, did guard
With watery, if not flaming, sword,—
What luckless apple did we taste
To make us mortal, and thee waste?

The influence of Milton may be traced in the fine sense of form generally, and, in particular, in the use of the octo-syllabic couplet. Occasionally we seem to hear an echo of Milton's airy grace, as in the couplet:

Near this a fountain's liquid bell
Tinkles within the concave shell.

But this is only occasional. Marvell is much more rigid in his rhythms than Milton, and he never attained to Milton's simplicity. That he had read him with care is evident; and there are a few direct reminiscences in the "First Anniversary," such as the phrase "beaked promontories," and the lines—

the dragon's tail
Swindges the volumes of its horrid flail,

and

Unto the kingdom blest of peace and love.

A more interesting reminiscence is the line in "The Garden"—

Waves in its plumes the various light,

which is certainly an echo of the difficult line in "Il Penseroso,"

Waves at his wings in aery stream,

though it throws no light upon its interpretation. But too much must not be made of these imitations. After all, Milton was Milton, and Marvell was Marvell; and what survives to charm us in Marvell is what he gives us of his own. Let me briefly summarise some of the elements in this charm.

The first quality to strike a reader who takes up Marvell's book is his extraordinary terseness. Look, for example, at the poem with which the only good modern edition, that of Mr.

G. A. Aitken, opens, "Appleton House." The poet wishes to praise the house for not being too big, like most country-houses of the time, and this is how he does it:

Within this sober frame expect
Work of no foreign architect,
That unto caves the quarries drew,
And forests did to pastures hew.

If this were "transprosed," it would have to run something as follows: "Our boasted Italian architects make houses so huge that by drawing the stone for them they hollow out quarries into caves, and cut down whole forests for timber so that they become pastures." As a part of the same skill it is remarkable in how few strokes he can paint a picture. In this same poem, describing a copse, he says:

Dark all without it knits; within
It opens passable and thin,

which gives exactly the difference of impression from without and upon entering. A second notable quality in Marvell's verse is its sensuousness, its wide and deep enjoyment of the world of sense. "The Garden," which everybody knows, may stand as the best example of this quality—

Stumbling on melons as I pass
Ensnared with flowers, I fall on grass.

Marvell is the laureate of grass, and of greenery. A third excellent quality is his humour, to which I have already referred, sometimes showing itself as intellectual wit, or as irony or sarcasm. Still keeping to "Appleton House," one may notice the ingenuity of the suggestion of Fairfax's generosity—

A stately frontispiece of *poor*
Adorns without the open door,

or the deprecation of over-large houses:

What need of all this marble crust
To impark the wanton mole of dust;
That thinks by breadth the world to unite,
Tho' the first builders failed in height.

Once or twice the humour runs to coarseness when it allies itself with the bitter Puritanism of the time, as in the picture of the nuns defending their house:

Some to the breach against their foes
Their wooden saints in vain oppose;
Another bolder stands at push,
With their old holy-water brush.

But most characteristic of all the qualities of Marvell's verse is what Lamb well spoke of as his "witty delicacy"—his delicate invention. The shining and unapproachable instances of this delicacy are "The Nymph complaining for the death of her Fawn" and "The picture of little T.C." The former of these pieces is often hyperbolic in fancy, but the hyperbole fits the pastoral remoteness of the setting; the second needs not even this apology. It is a masterpiece in a *genre* where masterpieces are rare, though attempts are not infrequent. Prior, Waller, and Sedley have tried the theme with a certain success, but their pieces lack the romantic note. "The Picture of Little T.C." has this to perfection; it has not a weak line in it, and moves through its five stanzas, each more exquisite than the last, to its admirably mock-serious close:

Meantime, whilst every verdant thing
Itself does at thy beauty charm,
Reform the errors of the spring;
Make that the tulips may have share
Of sweetness, seeing they are fair;
And roses of their thorns disarm;
But most procure
That violets may a longer age endure.

But O, young beauty of the woods,
Whom Nature courts with fruit and flowers,
Gather the flowers, but spare the buds;
Lest Flora, angry at thy crime
To kill her infants in their prime,
Do quickly make the example yours;
      And ere we see,
Nip in the blossom all our hopes and thee.

One other quality of Marvell's lyrical writing remains to be noticed, which is somewhat difficult to fix with a name, unless we call it *gusto*. We imagine him smiling to himself as he writes, smiling at his own fancies, or his own sensuousness, or happy turns. He wrote, we are sure, for his own pleasure quite as much as for ours. I remember the remark being made to me that "The Bermudas," for a religious poem, went pretty far in the way of self-indulgence. And so it does. Lastly, it cannot fail to be noted that Marvell was an artist, with an artist's love of making experiments. Perhaps he never attained perfect facility, but he is never amateurish.

Among the various groups into which is lyrical poetry divides itself, the least satisfactory is that whose theme is love. Marvell's love-poetry has, with the exception of one piece, as little passion as Cowley's, while it is as full of conceits. "The Unfortunate Lover" is probably the worst love-poem ever written by a man of genius. "The Definition of Love" is merely a study after Donne's "Valediction." Cleverer and more original, and somewhat more successful, is "The Gallery." The two opposite sides of one long picture-gallery into which the chambers of his heart have been thrown by breaking down partitions are supposed to be covered with portraits of his lady. On the one side she is drawn in such characters as Aurora and Venus; on the other as an enchanter and a murderess.

Marvell was the friend of Milton, and one conjectures that, like his respected friend, he also may have had theories as to the true relation of these sexes which interfered with the spontaneous expression of feeling. There is, nevertheless, one poem in which passion is allowed to take its most natural path, although even in it one feels that the poet is expressing the passion of the human race rather than his own individual feeling; and the passion being, as often in Marvell, masked and heightened by his wit, the effect is singularly striking; indeed, as a love-poem "To his Coy Mistress" is unique. It could never be the most popular of Marvell's poems, but for sheer power I should be disposed to rank it higher than anything he ever wrote. He begins with hyperbolical protestations to his mistress of the slow and solemn state with which their wooing should be conducted, if only time and space were their servants and not their masters.

Had we but world enough and time,
This coyness, lady, were no crime.
We would sit down and think which way
To walk, and pass our long love's day.
Thou by the Indian Ganges' side
Should'st rubies find: I by the tide
Of Humber would complain. I would
Love you ten years before the flood,
And you should, if you please, refuse
Till the conversion of the Jews

Each beauty also of face and feature should have its special and age-long praise—

But at my back I always hear
Time's winged chariot hurrying near;
And yonder all before us lie
Deserts of vast eternity. . . .

The grave's a fine and private place,
But none I think do there embrace.

A second division of Marvell's lyric poetry has for its subject religion. The most curious of the religious poems are the pastorals "Clorinda and Damon," and "Thyrsis and Dorinda." Despite their obvious artificiality I must confess that these poems give me pleasure, perhaps because religious poetry is apt to be shapeless, and these, in point of form, are admirable. It is matter for regret that in the first of the two Marvell should have made the nymph sensual and the swain pious; but the friend of Milton, as I have already suggested, probably shared his low views of the female sex. And then the conversion of the lady is sudden and leaves something to desire in its motive. In "Thyrsis and Dorinda" the two young things talk together so sweetly of Elysium that they drink opium in order to lose no time in getting there. More genuine in feeling, and more religious in the ordinary sense of the word, are two dialogues: one between the "Resolved Soul and Created Pleasure," the other between "Soul and Body." The form of the first is noteworthy. The octosyllabic stanzas are alternately unshortened and shortened, the Soul speaking in serious iambics and Pleasure in dancing trochees; and the allurements of sense rise in a well-conceived scale from mere softness through art up to the pleasures of knowledge. The dialogue between Soul and Body is a brilliant duel, each party accusing the other of his proper woes; and except for the one terrible line I quoted above, the poem is an excellent piece of writing. But religious passion sounds a higher and less artificial strain in a pair of odes, the one "On a Drop of Dew," in which the soul is compared to the dewdrop upon a leaf, which reflects heaven and is reluctant to coalesce with its environment; the other called "The Coronet," an apology for religious poetry on the ground that because it admits art it leaves room for the artist's pride. "The Coronet" is interesting as a study in Herbert's manner, and contains one line of exquisite modesty:

Through every garden, every mead,
I gather flowers (my fruits are only flowers).

But the ode "On a Drop of Dew" is by far the finer. The ideas are evolved after the manner of Donne, but the rhythm is slower and more contemplative:

See, how the orient dew,
Shed from the bosom of the morn
    Into the blowing roses,
(Yet careless of its mansion new
For the clear region where 'twas born,)
    Round in itself incloses;
And in its little globe's extent
Frames, as it can, its native element;
How it the purple flower does slight,
    Scarce touching where it lies;
    But, gazing back upon the skies,
Shines with a mournful light
    (Like its own tear),
Because so long divided from the sphere.
Restless it rolls and unsecure,
Trembling lest it grow impure,
Till the warm sun pity its pain
And to the skies exhale it back again.
    So the soul, that drop, that ray
    Of the clear fountain of eternal day,
(Could it within the human flower be seen)
    Remembering still its former height
Shuns the sweet leaves and blossoms green,
    And recollecting its own light
Does, in its pure and circling thoughts, express

> The greater heaven in an heaven less.
> In how coy a figure wound
> Every way it turns away,
> So the world excluding round
> Yet receiving in the day.

A third and final division of Marvell's lyrics would comprise his poems upon nature; and here we have Marvell at his best, because here he lets his passion inspire him. Except in Shakespeare, who includes "all thoughts, all passions, all desires" we have but little passion for nature between Chaucer and Marvell; but in Marvell the love for natural beauty is not short of passion. Of course his love is not for wild nature—a feeling which only dates from Gray and Wordsworth—but for the ordinary country scenes:

> Fragrant gardens, shady woods,
> Deep meadows and transparent floods;

and for these he brings the eye of a genuine lover and, what is more, of a patient observer. The lines upon "Appleton House" are full of observation. He speaks of the "shining eye" of the "hatching throstle," and has a fine imaginative description of the woodpecker:

> He walks still upright from the root
> Measuring the timber with his foot,
> And all the way, to keep it clean,
> Doth from the bark the wood-moths glean;
> He with his beak examines well
> Which fit to stand and which to fell;
> The good he numbers up and hacks
> As if he marked them with the axe;
> But where he, tinkling with his beak,
> Does find the hollow oak to speak,
> That for his building he designs
> And through the tainted sides he mines.

In his poem called "The Garden" Marvell has sung a palinode that for richness of phrasing in its sheer sensuous love of garden delights is perhaps unmatchable. At the same time the most devout lover of gardens must agree with Marvell that even in a garden the pleasures of the mind are greater than those of the sense. The poet's thought, as he lies in the shade, can create a garden for himself far more splendid and also imperishable; as indeed, in this poem, it has done:

> Meanwhile the mind from pleasure less
> Withdraws into its happiness;
> The mind, that ocean where each kind
> Does straight its own resemblance find;
> Yet it creates, transcending these,
> Far other worlds and other seas,
> Annihilating all that's made,
> To a green thought in a green shade.
> Here at the fountain's sliding foot,
> Or at some fruit-tree's mossy root,
> Casting the body's vest aside
> My soul into the boughs does glide:
> There like a bird it sits and sings,
> Then whets and combs its silver wings,
> And, till prepared for further flight,
> Waves in its plumes the various light.

Next to "The Garden" as a descriptive poem must rank the "Bermudas." Marvell's "Bermudas" are not "still vexed" like Shakespeare's but an earthly Paradise. His interest in these islands arose from meeting at Eton, while he was there as tutor to a ward of Cromwell's, a certain John Oxenbridge, who had been one of the exiles thither for conscience sake. The poem is built upon the same plan as "The Garden"; first, the sen-

suous delights are described as no one but Marvell could describe them:

> He hangs in shades the orange bright
> Like golden lamps in a green night,
> And does in the pomegranate close
> Jewels more rich than Ormuz shows;
> He makes the figs our mouths to meet
> And throws the melons at our feet
> But apples [i.e., pine-apples] plants of such a price
> No tree could ever bear them twice.

And then he passes on, though in this case it must be allowed with much less effect, to the spiritual advantages of the place. We may note in passing that Mr. Palgrave in his "Golden Treasury" has taken the extraordinary liberty of altering the arrangement of some of the early lines, perhaps through not understanding their construction as they stand. In the folio and all the early editions the lines run as follows:

> What should we do but sing His praise
> That led us through the watery maze,
> Unto an isle so long unknown
> And yet far kinder than our own?
> Where He the huge sea-monsters wracks
> That lift the deep upon their backs,
> He lands *us* on a grassy stage
> Safe from the storms and prelates' rage.

Mr. Palgrave prints lines 5 and 6 before lines 3 and 4, thereby breaking up the arrangement of the line into quatrains, apparently not seeing that "where" is equivalent to "whereas," and that the safety of the exiles is contrasted with the wrecking of the sea-monsters. But to have introduced Marvell's verse to so wide a public should atone to the poet's *manes* for such an injury; especially as the Puck which sits ever upon the pen of commentators has already avenged it by making Mr. Palgrave append to the poem the following note: "Emigrants supposed to be driven *towards America* by the government of Charles I." There is no hint in the poem that the "small boat" was bringing the emigrants across the Atlantic, or that they were describing the newly-discovered islands by the gift of prophecy.

Of the patriotic verse, which in its own way is full of interest, it is impossible to speak in this paper; except of the one poem which can claim to be a lyric, the "Horatian ode upon Cromwell's return from Ireland." As was said above, this ode was first published in Captain Thomson's edition, and so must take its stand as Marvell's only by the weight of internal evidence. But that evidence is conspicuous in every line. The poem runs on in a somewhat meandering and self-indulgent course, like all Marvell's longer poems. But many details are recognisably in Marvell's vein. The stroke of cleverness about King Charles's head being as lucky as that which was found when they were digging the foundations of Rome, and the fun he pokes at the Scotch and Irish are certainly Marvell. So is the view taken that Cromwell made a great sacrifice in renouncing a private life, which we get also in Marvell's prose; so is the touch about Cromwell's garden:

> where
> He lived reserved and austere,
> (As if his highest plot
> To plant the bergamot.)

So also is the remarkable detachment from political prejudice, of which the verses prefixed to the cavalier poet Lovelace's *Lucasta*, about the same date, afford another instance, a detachment that would have been impossible for the author of "Lycidas." Even now, in an age which boasts of its tolerant spirit, it gives one a shock to remember that the stanzas about

Charles, which present the very image of the cavalier saint and martyr, come in a poem to the honour and glory of the man to whom he owed his death:

> He nothing common did, or mean
> Upon that memorable scene,
> > But with his keener eye
> > The axe's edge did try;
> Nor called the gods with vulgar spite
> To vindicate his helpless right;
> > But bowed his comely head
> > Down, as upon a bed.

These two stanzas are now the only part of the ode that is remembered, and with justice; for the rest of the poem, although in form and spirit it is Horatian, yet it has little of the *curiosa felicitas* of Horace's diction to make it memorable. But in these two stanzas the diction has attained to the happiness of consummated simplicity. They recall the two stanzas at the close of the fifth ode in the third book in which Horace draws a picture of the martyred Regulus:

> Atque sciebat, quæ sibi barbarus
> Tortor pararet: non aliter tamen
> > Dimovit obstantes propinquos,
> > Et populum reditus morantem,
> Quam si clientum longa negotia
> Dijudicata lite relinqueret,
> > Tendens Venafranos in agros
> > Aut Lacedæmonium Tarentum.

JOHN BUNYAN

JOHN BUNYAN

1628–1688

John Bunyan, the son of Thomas Bunyan, who was either a brazier or a traveling tinker, was born at Elstow, near Bedford, in November 1628. He studied at the village school and read various religious works on his own. In 1644 his mother and younger sister died, and his father remarried; later that year he was drafted into the parliamentary army, in which Bunyan encountered many religious radicals who stimulated his own spiritual development.

Some time after his discharge in 1647 Bunyan married his first wife, who introduced him to two religious works which impressed him deeply—Dent's *Plain Man's Pathway to Heaven* and Bayly's *Practice of Piety*. In 1655 he joined the Nonconformist church in Bedford led by John Gifford, which admitted all who professed "faith in Christ and holiness of life," and quickly became an effective preacher, traveling from place to place in Bedfordshire. In response to attacks by the Quakers he wrote *Some Gospel Truths Opened* (1656), *A Vindication* (1657), and *A Few Sighs from Hell* (1658). Around 1659 Bunyan married for a second time, his first wife having died in 1656.

After the Restoration in 1660 Bunyan, who refused to submit to the Church of England, was imprisoned for twelve years. During the first six years or so he wrote nine books, chief among them the autobiographical *Grace Abounding to the Chief of Sinners* (1666). *The Holy City or the New Jerusalem* appeared in 1665, and in 1672 he published *A Confession of My Faith*. After his release in 1672 he was appointed pastor at his old church, but was again imprisoned briefly in 1676, during which time he probably finished the first part of the allegorical *Pilgrim's Progress*, his principal work. This first part was published in 1678; the complete work appeared in 1684. Bunyan's other important works are *The Life and Death of Mr. Badman* (1680), which is almost a novel in form, and the allegorical *Holy War* (1682), probably inspired by his experiences serving in the parliamentary army. After his release from prison in 1675 Bunyan continued to preach without further harassment until his death on August 31, 1688.

Personal

What hath the devil, or his agents, gotten by putting our great gospel minister Bunyan, in prison? For in prison he wrote many excellent books, that have published to the world his great grace, and great truth, and great judgment, and great ingenuity; and to instance in one, the *Pilgrim's Progress*, he hath suited to the life of a traveller so exactly and pleasantly, and to the life of a Christian, that this very book, besides the rest, hath done the superstitious sort of men more good than if he had been let alone at his meeting at Bedford, to preach the gospel to his own auditory.—CHARLES DOE, *The Struggler: Life and Actions of John Bunyan*, 1692

He was not only well furnished with the helps and endowments of nature beyond ordinary, but eminent in the graces and gifts of the Spirit and fruits of holiness. He was a true lover of all that love our Lord Jesus and did often bewail the different and distinguishing appellations that are among the godly, saying, he did believe a time would come when they should be all buried. His carriage was condescending, affable and meek to all; yet bold and couragious for Christ's and the gospel's sake. He was much struck at in the late times of persecution and his sufferings were great, under all which he behaved himself like Christ's soldier, being far from any sinful compliance to save himself, but did chearfully bear the cross of Christ. As a minister of Christ he was laborious in his work of preaching, diligent in his preparation for it and faithful in dispensing the word, not sparing reproof for outward circumstances whether in the pulpit or no, yet ready to succour the tempted; a son of consolation to the broken-hearted, yet a son of thunder to secure and dead sinners. ⟨. . .⟩ His remembrance is sweet and refreshing to many and so will continue: For the righteous shall be had in everlasting remembrance.—JOHN WILSON, "Epistle to the Reader," *Bunyan's Works*, 1692

I heard Mr. Bagford (some time before he dyed) say that he walked once into the Country, on purpose to see the study of John Bunnyan. When he came, John rec'd him very civilly and courteously, but his study consisted only of a Bible and a parcell of Books (the *Pilgrim's Progress* chiefly) written by himself, all lying on a Shelf or Shelves.—THOMAS HEARNE, *Reliquiae Hearnianae*, April 7, 1723

General

One of the greatest poets that ever lived—we mean John Bunyan, homely as may be the associations connected with the inspired tinker's name—has left some most pertinent instances in his writings of the sway exercised by the imagination over the external senses. In describing the dark internal conflicts which convulsed him, during one stage of his religious experience, he says:—"I lifted up my head, and methought I saw as if the sun that shineth in the heavens did *grudge* to give me light; as if the very stones in the street, and tiles upon the houses, did band themselves against me." This is as perfect poetry as ever was written.—EDWIN P. WHIPPLE, "Wordsworth" (1844), *Essays and Reviews*, 1850, Vol. 1, p. 229

The special interest of Bunyan's writings, in our point of view, consists in the number and variety of the pictures of popular Puritanism that they contain. His allegories teem with such pictures. He is the great artist of the spiritual life of Puritanism. He had himself lived through almost every phase of its pious excitement; his deep, sensitive nature responded to all its chords of emotion; and his vividly creative imagination enabled him to seize and reproduce its varied experiences in concrete representations, which have perpetuated them far more lastingly than any analysis or description could have done. And not only what he himself had felt and known, but what he had seen—all the diverse aspects of the religious and the irreligious life around him—stamped themselves as pictures on his mind, and reappear in his writings. The field from which he drew his artistic materials was strictly limited. It was only its relation to religion—to his own form of it, in fact—that made any aspect of life interesting to him; but within his range, there is no artist has produced so many clearly-marked individualities of portraiture.

So perfect in many respects is Bunyan's art,—so fertile and easy his creative faculty,—that we are apt to overlook the extent to which he borrowed directly from the real life around him. The more, however, we study the *Pilgrim's Progress* and the *Holy War*, in connection with his own history and times, the more will we see reason to believe that their numerous characters directly and broadly reflect both the outer and inner characteristics of the religious world familiar to him. ⟨. . .⟩

The idea and forms of a trial had strongly impressed themselves on Bunyan's mind. It had been one of the most familiar and imposing scenes of his own life, and so had become fixed upon his memory, and a part of his imaginative furniture. It is depicted at great length in the *Holy War*, as well as in the *Pilgrim's Progress*. This shows the homely limits, but at the same time the strength and vivacity, of his fancy. He drew from his own narrow experience—but his art made the dim pictures of his memory all alive with the fitting touches of reality.

This realistic character of Bunyan's allegories is of special interest to us now. We are carried back to Bedford and the Midland Counties in the seventeenth century, and we mingle with the men and women that lived and did their work there. It is in many respects a beautiful and affecting picture that we contemplate. A religion which could produce men like Greatheart, and old Honest, and Christian himself, and Faithful, and Hopeful—and of which the gentle and tenderhearted Mercy was a fair expression,—had certainly features both of magnanimity and of beauty. There is a simple earnestness and a pure-minded loveliness in Bunyan's highest creations that are very touching. Puritanism lives in his pages—spiritually and socially—in forms and in colouring which must ever command the sympathy and enlist the love of all good Christians.

But his pages no less show its narrowness and deficiencies. Life—even spiritual life—is broader than Bunyan saw it and painted it. It is not so easily and sharply defined—it cannot be so superficially sorted and classified. It is more deep, complex, and subtle—more involved, more mixed. There may have been good in Talkative, with all his emptiness and love for the ale-bench—and Mrs. Timorous, and even By-ends, might have something said for them. Nowhere, in reality, is the good so good, or the bad so bad, as Puritan evangelical piety is apt to conceive and represent them. There is work to be done in the city of Destruction as well as in fleeing from it. The Meadow with the sparkling river, and the Enchanted Ground, are not mere snares to lure and hurt us. There is room for leisure and literature, and poetry and art even, as we travel to Mount Zion. There is a meeting-point for all these elements of human culture, and the "one thing needful"—without which all culture is dead—though Bunyan and Puritanism failed to see it.—JOHN TULLOCH, *English Puritanism and Its Leaders*, 1861, pp. 477–88

Bunyan's ruling faculty was imagination, and he possessed it in perilous excess. In his *Grace Abounding*—certainly one of the most curious and striking of autobiographical sketches—we see how it domineered over him, and made him for a time a dweller on the shores of Tophet. It brought all his past sins

before him—his dancing, his bell-ringing, his Sabbath-breaking, his profane oaths—with more than their warranted terrors, and they disturbed his quiet as the ghost of Banquo disturbed the quiet of Macbeth. And when contrition brought peace and a new mode of life, it created for him the Delectable Mountains peopled with amiable shepherds; it made blaze for him the Celestial City, and made audible the melodious voices of its inhabitants. When he secured spiritual peace, his prevailing mood of mind became a certain devout fancifulness, and his long confinement—for he wrote the greater proportion of his books in prison—made the exercise of this fancifulness a more than ordinary relief.

> When the body is up-mew'd,
> Then the fancy furthest flies.

Bunyan dreamed his dream, and supported his own spirit; he made tagged thread-laces and supported his wife and family,—and so the years wore on. He was a profoundly religious man; but when his religion had become habitual and terrorless, he handed it over to Fancy, that she might play with it. And just as the ancient pagan heard Pan's pipe in the thicket, saw the hamadryad issue from the tree "like music from an instrument," caught in the fountain the momentary gleam of a naiad's limbs and face, he saw spiritual meanings in the aspects of external nature and in the ongoings of domestic life; found something to pierce the conscience in the lark quivering in mid-air above its nest; and discovered the illustration of a doctrine in the pot simmering upon the cottage fire. In every material object he saw a spiritual similitude. He was a religious Æsop, with a fable for everything that might occur. *The Pilgrim's Progress* is a long similitude, but in its course it contains many minor similitudes—as, for instance, in the objects shewn to Christian at the house of the Interpreter. This devout playfulness, with a constant eye for the practical application; this sermonising in disguise; this masquerading with a serious brow beneath the vizor, which is sure to be shewn at the proper time, is a mood in which Bunyan loved to indulge, and in which he is almost always successful. In the present little book of *Divine Emblems* he gives free rein to his fantasy; he finds texts in the most unlikely places, and from these texts he extracts the most unexpected sermons. He displays art and ingenuity; and the meanings he deduces from the objects with which he works are for the most part pertinent and natural. There is a further charm in the book, in that it is written in verse. Bunyan's muse is clad in russet, wears shoes and stockings, has a country accent, and walks along the level Bedfordshire roads. If as a poet he is homely and idiomatic, he is always natural, straightforward, and sincere. His lines are unpolished, but they have pith and sinew, like the talk of a shrewd peasant. In the *Emblems* there are many touches of pure poetry, shewing that in his mind there was a vein of silver which, under favourable circumstances, might have been worked to rich issues; and everywhere there is an admirable homely pregnancy and fulness of meaning. He has the strong thought, and the knack of the skilled workman to drive, by a single blow, the nail home to the head.—ALEXANDER SMITH, "Preface" to *Divine Emblems*, c. 1867, pp. viii–xi

The vast superiority of Bunyan over Spenser lies in the fact that we help make his allegory out of our own experience. Instead of striving to embody abstract passions and temptations, he has given us his own in all their pathetic simplicity. He is the Ulysses of his own prose-epic. This is the secret of his power and his charm, that, while the representation of what *may* happen to all men comes home to none of us in particular, the story of any one man's real experience finds its startling parallel in that of every one of us. The very homeliness of Bunyan's names and the everydayness of his scenery, too, put us off our guard, and we soon find ourselves on as easy a footing with his allegorical beings as we might be with Adam or Socrates in a dream. Indeed, he has prepared us for such incongruities by telling us at setting out that the story was of a dream. The long nights of Bedford jail had so intensified his imagination, and made the figures with which it peopled his solitude so real to him, that the creatures of his mind become *things*, as clear to the memory as if we had seen them. But Spenser's are too often mere names, with no bodies to back them, entered on the Muses' muster-roll by the specious trick of personification. There is, likewise, in Bunyan, a childlike simplicity and taking-for-granted which win our confidence. His Giant Despair, for example, is by no means the Ossianic figure into which artists who mistake the vague for the sublime have misconceived it. He is the ogre of the fairy-tales, with his malicious wife; and he comes forth to us from those regions of early faith and wonder as something beforehand accepted by the imagination. These figures of Bunyan's are already familiar inmates of the mind, and, if there be any sublimity in him, it is the daring frankness of his verisimilitude.—JAMES RUSSELL LOWELL, "Spenser" (1875), *Works*, Riverside ed., Vol. 4, pp. 322–23

The work of John Bunyan hardly finds its proper place in a history of prose fiction; he regarded it as anything but fictitious. Moreover, in form and outline it bears something the same relation to the novel proper that the "Morality" bears to the drama proper. Yet how rich are his works, not only the *Pilgrim's Progress* (1678), but the *Holy War* (1682), and the *Life and Death of Mr. Badman* (1680), in literary, as well as practical and moral lessons, in demonstrations whereby the novelists might profit to learn character-painting, admirable narrative, and the attainment of the illusion of reality. Where was the professed writer of fiction in the seventeenth century who could enthral the reader's imagination by his two opening sentences, and hold him spellbound to the end? This is how the *Pilgrim's Progress* begins:—

"As I walked through the wilderness of this world I lighted on a certain place where there was a den, and I laid me down in that place to sleep, and as I slept I dreamed a dream. I dreamed, and behold I saw a man, a man clothed in rags, standing with his face from his own home, with a book in his hand, and a great burden upon his back."

This is more than pathetic allegory, it is perfect narrative and vivid picture; that one descriptive phrase, of masterly restraint, "standing with his face from his own home," which contains Bunyan's thought upon two worlds, at once stirs the hearts of those who read beneath it, and secures the eager interest of children in the expectance of coming adventures.

It was well for literature that Bunyan learnt his style from the English Bible, and not from Mlle. de Scudéry. His abstractions are more living than the portraits of other writers. The bathos that was reached by the heroic romance when it laboured under the additional weight of allegory may be well seen in the *Bentivolio and Urania* (1660) of Nathaniel Ingelo, D.D., wherein the heroic model was employed to set forth the pursuit by Bentivolio, or Good Will, of his mistress Urania or Heavenly Wisdom. In the fourth edition of this romance (1682), "the obscure words throughout the book are interpreted in the margin, which makes this much more delightful to read than the former editions." Some one, therefore, must have read it, let it pass for a book; it marks for

the historian of literature the lowest depth to which English romance-writing sank. Its unillumined profundity swarms with low forms of life; polysyllabic abstractions crowd its pages, and deposit their explanatory spawn upon its margin; "the very deep did rot."

The abstractions of Bunyan, on the other hand, are hardly abstractions; they breathe and move in the atmosphere and light of his imagination. Giant Pope and Giant Pagan, Pliable and Mr. Worldly Wiseman, Faithful and Christian himself are additions to the portrait gallery of English fiction. In the *Life and Death of Mr. Badman* the author gives a singularly minute and realistic biography of a tradesman in a provincial English town, who leads a sordid and successful life, and dies "like a chrisom child, quietly and without fear." The grim and awful reality of the whole sketch is enhanced by numberless matter-of-fact touches, and by the writer's simplicity and freedom from all extravagance. Here is no double-dyed villainy, but a perfectly consistent hard and ugly life, such as Bunyan had more than once observed, perhaps in Bedford, only projected by him, by implication rather than by direct contrast, against the white background of eternity.—WALTER RALEIGH, *The English Novel*, 1894, pp. 115–18

"He had a sharp quick eye, accomplished with an excellent discerning of persons, being of good judgment and quick wit." So writes Bunyan's first biographer. "I never went to school to Aristotle or Plato, but was brought up in my father's house in a very mean condition among a company of poor countrymen." So writes Bunyan in his religious autobiography *Grace Abounding to the Chief of Sinners*. And these two sentences give us more than half the explanation of the charm of Bunyan's writing; for that charm lies, first of all, in the *excellent discerning of persons*, the quick comprehension of the various mixtures of simple and radical virtues and vices, of which his "poor countrymen" were composed, and then in the vivid homely phrases in which the sketches were made. It is more especially the first of these great qualities, the discernment of spirits, which gives permanence to the permanent residue of Bunyan's vast literary production; for while in all his writing there is abundant evidence of brain-power, and his skill in marshalling texts to defend his dogmatic positions is admirable, yet this general cleverness would not have raised him above the rank of the popular preacher whose performances in the next generation cumber the book-stalls, had it not been for that drop of precious elixir which nature infused into his eyes at birth, as into those of such different people as Geoffrey Chaucer and Jane Austen. It is this which divides Bunyan from one in other respects so like him as George Fox. Both were children of the people, both were intensely religious, both were given to hearing voices in their ears speaking the words of God or of Satan, both for their faith were "in prisons oft"; but the discriminating eye, and the sense of humour which accompanies it, were lacking to Fox, as his *Journal* makes abundantly conspicuous.

One outcome of this gift of vivid realisation was of course the corresponding vigour of the characters in the allegories; it is a commonplace to acknowledge that Mr. By-ends, Mr. Talkative, and the rest are as familiar to us as people we have met in real life. They were no doubt drawn from the quick, and the descriptive touches are put in with a sure pencil so that they live to us. Examples will be found on nearly every page, but the epithet "gentlemanlike" by which he describes the attitude of Demas, is one of the simplest and most effective. And how happy he is in the names of persons and places, "Mr. Worldly Wiseman," "Sir Having Greedy," "Mrs.

Bats-eyes," "Mr. Facing-both-ways," "A young woman her name was Dull," "Vanity Fair," "The Slough of Despond," "Flesh Lane" (where Forget-good dwelt) "right opposite to the Church." His vocabulary as a rule is homely enough, but it is copious, and it is always justly and accurately employed. In the preface to *Grace Abounding* Bunyan says, "I could have stepped into a style much higher than this in which I have here discoursed, and could have adorned all things more than here I have seemed to do, but I dare not. I may not play in the relating of them, but be plain and simple, and lay down the thing as it was." The accurate delineation which in that book he gives of "the thing as it was," in that case the growth of his religious feelings and ideas, depends upon his vivid perception, and this again enables him to clothe his experiences in adequate and nervous language; and so too when the thing he has to represent is some neighbour whom he knows, or some coinage of his fancy, the fit words are equally at command. Had the poor tinker's son been sent to grammar-school or university, this natural freedom of style, though probably from his preacher's habit it could never have been pestered in such a pinfold as Milton affected, yet it could not but have grown more abstract, and perhaps have made him a more lively Howe; as it was, the words and phrases and images remained racy of the soil. Here are some sentences from the *Holy War*: "Nor did the silly Mansoul stick or boggle at all at this most monstrous engagement, but as if it had been a sprat in the mouth of a whale, they swallowed it without any chewing." "He had for his malapertness one of his legs broken, and he that did it wished it had been his neck." "At this they were all of them struck into their dumps." "When Mr. Cerberus and Mr. Profane did meet they were presently as great as beggars"; and there are a hundred other quaint expressions for which it would be hard to find a parallel in religious literature, such as "quat and close," "in the very nick and first trip," "ticking and toying," "put to my plunge." The same freshness may be noted in such phrases as "a tongue bravely *hung*," "*to clap up* in prison," "gird them up from the ground, and let them not lag with dust and dirt," "he saw something like a lion, and it came *a great padding pace* after," "I saw the clouds *rack* at an unusual rate." Free scope is given for such lively turns of phrase by the large use of dialogue.

Bunyan's literary education was based upon two books, Foxe's *Acts and Monuments*, and the Genevan version of the Bible. The former supplied him with the model of a homely and yet forcible mode of writing, and to this example we probably owe it that Bunyan was contented to write in the vernacular. He borrowed from it further the practice of using the margin for notes and comments, very desirable appendages to an allegory. Occasionally some of his are pungent summaries of the text, and some are exclamations; e.g.: "Hopeful swaggers," "Christian snibbeth his fellows," "O brave Talkative!" "O good riddance!" "O sweet prince!" "That's false, Satan!" again, "Mark this!" "Take heed, Mansoul!" "Look to it, Mansoul!" the last of these repeated very effectively at each period in the infernal Conclave. The Bible Bunyan must have known by heart; its phraseology and imagery he made so thoroughly his own, that many passages of description are simply a cento of quotations; elsewhere he intermingles them with those of his own day without any sense of incongruity. At times to us the incongruity is sufficiently manifest, as when Mercy falls down before the Keeper of the Gate, and says "Let my Lord accept of the sacrifice which I now offer Him *with the calves of my lips*"; at times also his extreme familiarity with the text seems to have led him to quote more than he meant, as in the close of the Preface to the *Holy War*.

> If thou wouldst know
> My riddle, *and would with my heifer plow*,
> It lies there in the window.

But such singularities are but trifles in comparison with the magnificent use he made of the book generally. Two passages in *Grace Abounding* show the passionate intuition he brought to the sacred text: "When I have considered also the truth of his resurrection and have remembered that word, *Touch me not Mary*, etc., I have seen as if he leaped at the grave's mouth for joy that he was risen again." "At this time also I saw more in those words *Heirs of God*, than ever I shall be able to express while I live in this world. *Heirs of God!* God himself is the portion of the saints. This I saw and wondered at, but cannot tell you what I saw." As a consequence of this penetrating appreciation he was able to vivify not only the events of the narrative, but the images and the very metaphors, which were thus erected into the machinery of his allegories.

Outside the Bible he had nothing to draw upon but his own observation, and this, while if afforded a sufficient variety of persons, left him little choice in the matter of scenery. He was born and bred, as Kingsley says "in the monotonous Midland," and so, while his meadows and streams and sloughs are described graphically (though sometimes idealised as, e.g. the meadow by the River of God, which was "curiously beautified with lilies"), his hills and the *ferior natura* have no verisimilitude; in one place he allows himself to speak of "a wide field full of dark mountains"; in another of Emmanuel "leaping over the mountains," a phrase which a verse in Canticles (ii.8) may account for, but will not justify. But where his eye has once rested upon the object the descriptions are very lively.

"By this time they were got to the enchanted ground, where the air naturally tended to make one drowsy. And that place was all grown over with briars and thorns. The way also was here very wearisome through dirt and slabbiness. Nor was there on all this ground so much as one inn or victualling-house, therein to refresh the feebler sort. Here therefore was grunting, and puffing, and sighing; while one tumbleth over a bush, another sticks fast in the dirt, and the children, some of them lost their shoes in the mire. While one cries out, I am down, and another, Ho, where are you? and a third, The bushes have got such fast hold on me I think I cannot get away from them."—H. C. BEECHING, "John Bunyan," *English Prose*, ed. Henry Craik, 1894, Vol. 3, pp. 73–77

Works

GRACE ABOUNDING

What genuine superstition is exemplified in that bandying of texts and half texts, and demi-semi texts, just as memory happened to suggest them, or chance brought them before Bunyan's mind! His tract, entitled, *Grace abounding to the Chief of Sinners*, is a study for a philosopher. Is it not, however, an historical error to call the Puritans dissenters? Before St. Bartholomew's day, they were essentially a part of the church, and had as determined opinions in favour of a church establishment as the bishops themselves.—SAMUEL TAYLOR COLERIDGE, *Table Talk*, June 10, 1830

We have just been reading, with no slight degree of interest, that simple but wonderful piece of autobiography, entitled *Grace Abounding to the Chief of Sinners*, from the pen of the author of *Pilgrim's Progress*. It is the record of a journey more terrible than that of the ideal Pilgrim; "truth stranger than fiction;" the painful upward struggling of a spirit from the blackness of despair and blasphemy, into the high, pure air of

Hope and Faith. More earnest words were never written. It is the entire unveiling of a human heart; the tearing off of the fig-leaf covering of its sin. The voice which speaks to us from these old pages seems not so much that of a denizen of the world in which we live, as of a soul at the last solemn confessional. Shorn of all ornament, simple and direct as the contrition and prayer of childhood, when for the first time the Spectre of Sin stands by its bedside, the style is that of a man dead to self-gratification, careless of the world's opinion, and only desirous to convey to others, in all truthfulness and sincerity, the lesson of his inward trials, temptations, sins, weaknesses, and dangers; and to give glory to Him who had mercifully led him through all, and enabled him, like his own Pilgrim, to leave behind the Valley of the Shadow of Death, the snares of the Enchanted Ground, and the terrors of Doubting Castle, and to reach the land of Beulah, where the air was sweet and pleasant, and the birds sang and the flowers sprang up around him, and the Shining Ones walked in the brightness of the not distant Heaven. In the introductory pages he says: "I could have dipped into a style higher than this in which I have discoursed, and could have adorned all things more than here I have seemed to do; but I dared not. God did not play in tempting me; neither did I play when I sunk, as it were, into a bottomless pit, when the pangs of hell took hold on me; wherefore, I may not play in relating of them, but be plain and simple, and lay down the thing as it was."

This book, as well as *Pilgrim's Progress*, was written in Bedford prison, and was designed especially for the comfort and edification of his "children, whom God had counted him worthy to beget in faith by his ministry." In his introduction he tells them, that, although taken from them, and tied up, "sticking, as it were, between the teeth of the lions of the wilderness," he once again, as before, from the top of Shemer and Hermon, so now, from the lion's den and the mountain of leopards, would look after them with fatherly care and desires for their everlasting welfare. "If," said he, "you have sinned against light; if you are tempted to blaspheme; if you are drowned in despair; if you think God fights against you; or if Heaven is hidden from your eyes, remember it was so with your father. But out of all the Lord delivered me."

He gives no dates; he affords scarcely a clue to his localities; of the man, as he worked, and ate, and drank, and lodged, of his neighbors and contemporaries, of all he saw and heard of the world about him, we have only an occasional glimpse, here and there, in his narrative. It is the story of his inward life only that he relates. What had time and place to do with one who trembled always with the awful consciousness of an immortal nature, and about whom fell alternately the shadows of hell and the splendors of heaven? We gather, indeed, from his record, that he was not an idle on-looker in the time of England's great struggle for freedom, but a soldier of the Parliament, in his young years, among the praying sworders and psalm-singing pikemen, the Greathearts and Holdfasts whom he has immortalized in his allegory; but the only allusion which he makes to this portion of his experience is by way of illustration of the goodness of God in preserving him on occasions of peril.—JOHN GREENLEAF WHITTIER, "John Bunyan," *Old Portraits and Modern Sketches*, 1849

There are few more interesting narratives than the little work entitled, *Grace Abounding to the Chief of Sinners; or, The Life of John Bunyan. Written by himself.* Any one will be the better for studying this book; and he may perhaps discover a page in human nature with which he has been hitherto unacquainted, and depths which have not been revealed to him; for there he

will find the faithful account of a true servant of God, who lived wholly in the thoughts of another world, first having the consciousness of sin, then of forgiveness; one who passed from darkness to light, or rather, was always passing from one to the other until he attained to his final rest. He describes himself as continually in an agony of terror and hope and joy, tortured as on a rack for whole days together, having fetters of brass on his legs; falling suddenly into great guilt and despair, like a bird who is shot from the top of a tree, until he at last wings his way heavenward. Sometimes he will tell you of the wounds inflicted upon him by misapplied passages of Scripture, and then of other passages by which the wounds were healed, and he obtained peace again. Then he will compare himself to a child fallen into a mill-pit, which, though it could make some shift to scramble and sprawl in the water, yet, because it could find neither hold for hand or foot, at last must die in this condition. But the time would fail me to tell of all the images under which the author of the *Pilgrim's Progress* describes the dealings of God with his soul.—BENJAMIN JOWETT, "John Bunyan and Benedict Spinoza" (1871), *Sermons Biographical and Miscellaneous*, ed. W. H. Fremantle, 1899, pp. 48–49

THE PILGRIM'S PROGRESS

When at the first I took my Pen in hand,
Thus for to write; I did not understand
That I at all should make a little Book
In such a mode; Nay, I had undertook
To make another, which when almost done,
Before I was aware, I this begun.

And thus it was: I writing of the Way
And Race of Saints in this our Gospel-Day,
Fell suddenly into an Allegory
About their Journey, and the way to Glory,
In more than twenty things, which I set down;
This done, I twenty more had in my Crown,
And they again began to multiply,
Like sparks that from the coals of Fire do flie.
Nay then, thought I, if that you breed so fast,
I'll put you by your selves, lest you at last
Should prove *ad infinitum*, and eat out
The Book that I already am about.

Well, so I did; but yet I did not think
To shew to all the World my Pen and Ink
In such a mode; I only thought to make
I knew not what: nor did I undertake
Thereby to please my Neighbour; no not I,
I did it mine own self to gratifie.

Neither did I but vacant seasons spend
In this my Scribble; Nor did I intend
But to divert my self in doing this,
From worser thoughts, which make me do amiss.

Thus I set Pen to Paper with delight,
And quickly had my thoughts in black and white.
For having now my Method by the end;
Still as I pull'd, it came; and so I penn'd
It down, until it came at last to be
For length and breadth the bigness which you see.

Well, when I had thus put mine ends together,
I shew'd them others, that I might see whether
They would condemn them, or them justifie:
And some said, let them live; some, let them die:
Some said, *John*, print it; others said, Not so:
Some said, It might do good; others said, No.

Now was I in a straight, and did not see
Which was the best thing to be done by me:
At last I thought, Since you are thus divided,
I print it will, and so the case decided.

For, thought I; Some I see would have it done,
Though others in that Channel do not run;
To prove then who advised for the best,
Thus I thought fit to put it to the test.
   I further thought, if now I did deny
Those that would have it thus, to gratifie,
I did not know, but hinder them I might,
Of that which would to them be great delight.
   For those that were not for its coming forth;
I said to them, Offend you I am loth;
Yet since your Brethren pleased with it be,
Forbear to judge, till you do further see.
   If that thou wilt not read, let it alone;
Some love the meat, some love to pick the bone:
Yea, that I might them better palliate,
I did too with them thus Expostulate.

  . . .

   And now, before I do put up my Pen,
I'le shew the profit of my Book, and then
Commit both thee, and it unto that hand
That pulls the strong down, and makes weak ones
     stand.
   This Book it chaulketh out before thine eyes,
The man that seeks the everlasting Prize:
It shews you whence he comes, whither he goes,
What he leaves undone; also what he does:
It also shews you how he runs, and runs,
Till he unto the Gate of Glory comes.
   It shews too, who sets out for life amain,
As if the lasting Crown they would attain:
Here also you may see the reason why
They loose their labour, and like fools do die.
   This Book will make a Travailer of thee,
If by its Counsel thou wilt ruled be;
It will direct thee to the Holy Land,
If thou wilt its Directions understand:
Yea, it will make the sloathful, active be;
The Blind also, delightful things to see.
   Art thou for something rare, and profitable?
Wouldest thou see a Truth within a Fable?
Art thou forgetful? wouldest thou remember
From *New-years-day* to the last of *December?*
Then read my fancies, they will stick like Burs,
And may be to the Helpless, Comforters.
   This Book is writ in such a Dialect,
As may the minds of listless men affect:
It seems a Novelty, and yet contains
Nothing but sound and honest Gospel-strains.
   Wouldst thou divert thy self from Melancholly?
Would'st thou be pleasant, yet be far from folly?
Would'st thou read Riddles, and their Explanation,
Or else be drownded in thy Contemplation?
Dost thou love picking-meat? or would'st thou see
A man i' th Clouds, and hear him speak to thee?
Would'st thou be in a Dream, and yet not sleep?
Or would'st thou in a moment Laugh and Weep?
Wouldest thou loose thy self, and catch no harm?
And find thy self again without a charm?
Would'st read thy self, and read thou know'st not
     what
And yet know whether thou art blest or not,
By reading the same lines? O then come hither,
And lay my Book, thy Head and Heart together.
      —JOHN BUNYAN, "The Author's Apology for His
      Book," *The Pilgrim's Progress*, 1678

Some gentlemen, abounding in their university erudition, are
apt to fill their sermons with philosophical terms, and notions
of the metaphysical or abstracted kind; which generally have
one advantage, to be equally understood by the wise, the
vulgar, and the preacher himself. I have been better entertained, and more informed, by a few pages in the *Pilgrim's
Progress*, than by a long discourse upon the will and the
intellect, and simple or complex ideas.—JONATHAN SWIFT,
"Letter to a Young Clergyman," 1720

I know there are readers in the world, as well as many other
good people in it, who are no readers at all,—who find
themselves ill at ease, unless they are let into the whole secret
from first to last, of every thing which concerns you.
   It is in pure compliance with this humour of theirs, and
from a backwardness in my nature to disappoint any one soul
living, that I have been so very particular already. As my life
and opinions are likely to make some noise in the world, and,
if I conjecture right, will take in all ranks, professions, and
denominations of men whatever,—be no less read than the
Pilgrim's Progress itself—and, in the end, prove the very thing
which *Montaigne* dreaded his essays should turn out, that is, a
book for a parlour-window; I find it necessary to consult every
one a little in his turn; and therefore must beg pardon for going
on a little further in the same way: For which cause, right glad
I am, that I have begun the history of myself in the way I have
done; and that I am able to go on tracing every thing in it, as
Horace says, *ab Ovo.*—LAURENCE STERNE, *The Life and
Opinions of Tristram Shandy*, 1759, Vol. 1, Ch. 4

   O thou whom, borne on fancy's eager wing
   Back to the season of life's happy spring,
   I pleased remember, and, while memory yet
   Holds fast her office here, can ne'er forget;
   Ingenious dreamer, in whose well-told tale
   Sweet fiction and sweet truth alike prevail;
   Whose humorous vein, strong sense, and simple
     style
   May teach the gayest, make the gravest smile;
   Witty, and well employed, and, like thy Lord,
   Speaking in parables His slighted word;
   I name thee not lest so despised a name
   Should move a sneer at thy deservèd fame,
   Yet, e'en in transitory life's late day
   That mingles all my brown with sober gray,
   Revere the man whose PILGRIM marks the road
   And guides the PROGRESS of the soul to God.
     —WILLIAM COWPER, *Tirocinium; or, A Review of
     Schools*, 1784

Johnson praised Bunyan highly. 'His *Pilgrim's Progress* has
great merit, both for invention, imagination, and the conduct
of the story; and it has had the best evidence of its merit, the
general and continued approbation of mankind. Few books, I
believe, have had a more extensive sale. It is remarkable, that
it begins very much like the poem of Dante; yet there was no
translation of Dante when Bunyan wrote. There is no reason to
think that he had read Spenser.'—JAMES BOSWELL, *Life of
Johnson*, 1791

A splendid edition of Bunyan's *Pilgrim*—why, the thought is
enough to turn one's moral stomach. His cockle hat and staff
transformed to a smart cockd beaver and a jemmy cane, his
amice gray to the last Regent Street cut, and his painful
Palmer's pace to the modern swagger. Stop thy friend's
sacriligious hand. Nothing can be done for B. but to reprint the
old cuts in as homely but good a style as possible. The Vanity
Fair, and the pilgrims there—the silly soothness in his setting
out countenance—the Christian idiocy (in a good sense) of his
admiration of the Shepherds on the Delectable Mountains—

the Lions so truly Allegorical and remote from any similitude to Pidcock's. The great head (the author's) capacious of dreams and similitudes dreaming in the dungeon. Perhaps you don't know *my* edition, what I had when a child: if you do, can you bear new designs from—Martin, enameled into copper or silver plate by—Heath, accompanied with verses from Mrs. Heman's pen O how unlike his own—

> Wouldst thou divert thyself from melancholy?
> Wouldst thou be pleasant, yet be far from folly?
> Wouldst thou read riddles and their explanation?
> Or else be drowned in thy contemplation?
> Dost thou love picking meat? or wouldst thou see
> A man i' th' clouds, and hear him speak to thee?
> Wouldst thou be in a dream, and yet not sleep?
> Or wouldst thou in a moment laugh and weep?
> Or wouldst thou lose thyself, and catch no harm,
> And find thyself again without a charm?
> Wouldst read *thyself*, and read thou knowst not what,
> And yet know whether thou art blest or not
> By reading the same lines? O then come hither,
> And lay my book, thy head and heart together.
>
> (John Bunyan.)

Shew me such poetry in any of the 15 forthcoming combinations of show and emptiness, yclept Annuals. Let me whisper in your ear that wholesome sacramental bread is not more nutritious than papistical wafer stuff, than these (to head and heart) exceed the visual frippery of Mitford's Salamander God, baking himself up to the work of creation in a solar oven, not yet by the terms of the context itself existing. Blake's ravings made genteel.—CHARLES LAMB, Letter to Bernard Barton (Oct. 11, 1828)

I know of no book, the Bible excepted, as above all comparison, which I, according to my judgment and experience, could so safely recommend as teaching and enforcing the whole saving truth according to the mind that was in Christ Jesus, as the *Pilgrim's Progress*. It is, in my conviction, incomparably the best *Summa Theologiae Evangelicae* ever produced by a writer not miraculously inspired.

It disappointed, nay surprised me, to find Robert Southey express himself so coldly respecting the style and diction of the *Pilgrim's Progress*. I can find nothing homely in it but a few phrases and single words. The conversation between Faithful and Talkative is a model of unaffected dignity and rhythmical flow.—SAMUEL TAYLOR COLERIDGE, "Notes on the *Pilgrim's Progress*" (1830), *Literary Remains*, ed. Henry Nelson Coleridge, 1836, Vol. 3, pp. 391–92

His is a homespun style, not a manufactured one; and what a difference is there between its homeliness and the flippant vulgarity of the Roger L'Estrange and Tom Brown school! If it is not a well of English undefiled, to which the poet as well as the philologer must repair if they would drink of the living waters, it is a clear stream of current English, the vernacular speech of his age; sometimes, indeed, in its rusticity and coarseness, but always in its plainness and its strength. To this natural style Bunyan is in some degree beholden for his general popularity; his language is everywhere level to the most ignorant reader and to the meanest capacity; there is a homely reality about it; a nursery tale is not more intelligible, in its manner of narration, to a child.—ROBERT SOUTHEY, "Preface" to *The Pilgrim's Progress*, 1830

It is not, however, the words and manner of the *Pilgrim's Progress* alone which have raised that singular allegory to so high a rank among our general readers. The form and style of composition is safely referred to the highest authority—

> Who spake in parables, I dare not say,
> But sure *He* knew it was a pleasing way.

And, without dwelling on the precedent suggested by the poet, we may observe how often the allegory, or parable, has gained, without suspicion, those passes of the human heart which were vigilantly guarded against the direct force of truth by self-interest, prejudice, or pride. When the prophet approached the sinful monarch with the intention of reproving his murder and adultery, a direct annunciation of his purpose might have awakened the king to wrath, instead of that penitence to which it was the will of heaven that he should be invited. But David listened unsuspectingly to the parable of the ewe-lamb; and it was not till the awful words—'Thou art the man'—were uttered, that he found the crime which he had so readily condemned was, in fact, the type of that which he had himself committed. In this respect, the comparing the parable with the real facts which it intimates, is like the practice of the artists to examine the reflection of their paintings in a mirror, that they may get clear of false lights and shadows, and judge of their compositions more accurately by seeing them presented under a change of light and circumstances. But, besides the moral uses of this species of composition, it has much in it to exercise those faculties of the human mind which it is most agreeable to keep in motion. Our judgment is engaged in weighing and measuring the points of similarity between the reality and the metaphor as these evolve themselves, and fancy is no less amused by the unexpected, surprising, and, we may even say, the witty turns of thought, through means of which associations are produced between things which, in themselves, seemed diametrically opposed and irreconcileable, but which the allegorist has contrived should nevertheless illustrate each other. In some cases, the parable possesses the interest of the riddle itself; the examination and solution of which are so interesting to the human intellect, that the history and religious doctrines of ancient nations were often at once preserved and disguised in the form of such ænigmata.

In a style of composition, rendered thus venerable by its antiquity, and still more so by the purposes to which it has been applied, John Bunyan, however uneducated, was a distinguished master. For our part, we are inclined to allow him, in the simplicity of his story, and his very shrewdness, and, if the reader pleases, homely bluntness of style, a superiority over the great poet to whom he has been compared by D'Israeli,—which, considering both writers as allegorists, may, in some respect, counterbalance the advantages of a mind fraught with education, a head full of poetic flight and grace—in a word, the various, the unutterable distinction between the friend of Sidney and of Raleigh, the fascinating poet of fairy land, and our obscure tinker of Elstow, the self-erected holder-forth to the anabaptists of Bedford. Either has told a tale expressive of the progress of religion and morality—Spenser's under the guise of a romance of chivalry, while that of Bunyan recalls the outline of a popular fairy tale, with its machinery of giants, dwarfs, and enchanters. So far they resemble each other; and if the later writer must allow the earlier the advantage of a richer imagination, and a taste incalculably more cultivated, the uneducated man of the people may, in return, claim over Spenser the superiority due to a more simple and better concocted plan, from which he has suffered no temptation to lead him astray.—SIR WALTER SCOTT, "Southey's Life of John Bunyan," *Quarterly Review*, Oct. 1830, pp. 485–86

⟨. . .⟩ John Bunyan may pass for the father of our novelists. His success in a line of composition like the spiritual romance or allegory, which seems to have been frigid and unreadable in the few instances where it had been attempted, is doubtless enhanced by his want of all learning and his low station in life. He was therefore rarely, if ever, an imitator; he was never enchained by rules. Bunyan possessed in a remarkable degree the power of representation; his inventive faculty was considerable, but the other is his distinguishing excellence. He saw, and makes us see, what he describes; he is circumstantial without prolixity, and in the variety and frequent change of his incidents, never loses sight of the unity of his allegorical fable. His invention was enriched, and rather his choice determined, by one rule he had laid down to himself, the adaptation of all the incidental language of Scripture to his own use. There is scarce a circumstance or metaphor in the Old Testament which does not find a place, bodily and literally, in the story of the *Pilgrim's Progress*; and this peculiar artifice has made his own imagination appear more creative than it really is. In the conduct of the romance no rigorous attention to the propriety of the allegory seems to have been uniformly preserved. Vanity Fair, or the cave of the two giants, might, for anything we see, have been placed elsewhere; but it is by this neglect of exact parallelism that he better keeps up the reality of the pilgrimage, and takes off the coldness of mere allegory. It is also to be remembered that we read this book at an age when the spiritual meaning is either little perceived or little regarded. In his language, nevertheless, Bunyan sometimes mingles the signification too much with the fable; we might be perplexed between the imaginary and the real Christian; but the liveliness of narration soon brings us back, or did at least when we were young, to the fields of fancy. Yet the *Pilgrim's Progress*, like some other books, has of late been a little overrated; its excellence is great, but it is not of the highest rank, and we should be careful not to break down the landmarks of fame, by placing the John Bunyans and the Daniel De Foes among the Dii Majores of our worship.—HENRY HALLAM, *Introduction to the Literature of Europe*, 1837–39, Pt. 4, Ch. 7, Par. 57

To get beautiful allegories, a perfect poetic symbol, was not the want of men; but to know what they were to believe about this Universe, what course they were to steer in it; what, in this mysterious Life of theirs, they had to hope and to fear, to do and to forbear doing. The *Pilgrim's Progress* is an Allegory, and a beautiful, just and serious one: but consider whether Bunyan's Allegory could have *preceded* the Faith it symbolises! The Faith had to be already there, standing believed by everybody;—of which the Allegory could *then* become a shadow; and, with all its seriousness, we may say a *sportful* shadow, a mere play of the Fancy, in comparison with that awful Fact and scientific certainty, which it poetically strives to emblem. The Allegory is the product of the certainty, not the producer of it; not in Bunyan's nor in any other case.—THOMAS CARLYLE, "The Hero as Divinity," *On Heroes, Hero-Worship and the Heroic in History*, 1841

The fame of Bunyan during his life, and during the century which followed his death, was indeed great, but was almost entirely confined to religious families of the middle and lower classes. Very seldom was he during that time mentioned with respect by any writer of great literary eminence. Young coupled his prose with the poetry of the wretched D'Urfey. In the Spiritual Quixote, the adventures of Christian are ranked with those of Jack the Giant-Killer and John Hickathrift. Cowper ventured to praise the great allegorist, but did not venture to name him. It is a significant circumstance that, till a recent period, all the numerous editions of the *Pilgrim's Progress* were evidently meant for the cottage and the servants' hall. The

paper, the printing, the plates, were all of the meanest description. In general, when the educated minority and the common people differ about the merit of a book, the opinion of the educated minority finally prevails. The *Pilgrim's Progress* is perhaps the only book about which, after the lapse of a hundred years, the educated minority has come over to the opinion of the common people.

The attempts which have been made to improve and to imitate this book are not to be numbered. It has been done into verse: it has been done into modern English. *The Pilgrimage of Tender Conscience*, the *Pilgrimage of Good Intent*, *The Pilgrimage of Seek Truth*, *The Pilgrimage of Theophilus*, *The Infant Pilgrim*, *The Hindoo Pilgrim*, are among the many feeble copies of the great original. But the peculiar glory of Bunyan is that those who most hated his doctrines have tried to borrow the help of his genius. A Catholic version of his parable may be seen with the head of the Virgin in the title page. On the other hand, those Antinomians for whom his Calvinism is not strong enough may study the pilgrimage of Hephzibah, in which nothing will be found which can be construed into an admission of free agency and universal redemption. But the most extraordinary of all the acts of Vandalism by which a fine work of art was ever defaced was committed so late as the year 1853. It was determined to transform the *Pilgrim's Progress* into a Tractarian book. The task was not easy: for it was necessary to make the two sacraments the most prominent objects in the allegory; and of all Christian theologians, avowed Quakers excepted, Bunyan was the one in whose system the sacraments held the least prominent place. However, the Wicket Gate became a type of Baptism, and the House Beautiful of the Eucharist. The effect of this change is such as assuredly the ingenious person who made it never contemplated. For, as not a single pilgrim passes through the Wicket Gate in infancy, and as Faithful hurries past the House Beautiful without stopping, the lesson, which the fable in its altered shape teaches, is that none but adults ought to be baptized, and that the Eucharist may safely be neglected. Nobody would have discovered from the original *Pilgrim's Progress* that the author was not a Pædobaptist. To turn his book into a book against Pædobaptism was an achievement reserved for an Anglo-Catholic divine. Such blunders must necessarily be committed by every man who mutilates parts of a great work, without taking a comprehensive view of the whole.—THOMAS BABINGTON MACAULAY, "John Bunyan" (1854), *Critical, Historical, and Miscellaneous Essays*, 1860, Vol. 6, pp. 148–50

Out of that old notion of the Christian life as a pilgrimage, which had existed in hundreds of minds before till it had become a commonplace, there grew and grew in Bunyan's mind the whole visual allegory of his book—from the Wicked-gate seen afar over the fields under the Shining Light, on, by the straight undeviating road itself, with all its sights and perils, and through the Enchanted Ground and the pleasant land of Beulah, to the black and bridgeless river by whose waters is the passage to the glimmering realms, and the brightness of the Heavenly City.—DAVID MASSON, *British Novelists and Their Styles*, 1859, p. 74

In the *Pilgrim's Progress* we have his best self—as superior to his own inferior self as to his contemporaries. It is one of the peculiar delights of that charming volume that when we open it all questions of Conformity or Nonconformity, of Baptists or Pædobaptists, even of Catholic and Protestant, are left far behind. It is one of the few books which acts as a religious bond to the whole of English Christendom. It is, perhaps, with six others, and equally with any of those six, the book which, after the English Bible, has contributed to the common religious culture of the Anglo-Saxon race. It is one of the few books, perhaps almost the only English book, which has succeeded in identifying religious instruction with entertainment and amusement both of old and young. It is one of the few books which has struck a chord which vibrates alike amongst the humblest peasants and amongst the most fastidious critics.

Let us pause for an instant to reflect how great a boon is conferred upon a nation by one such uniting element. How deeply extended is the power of sympathy, and the force of argument, when the preacher or the teacher knows that he can enforce his appeal by a name which, like that of an apostle or evangelist, comes home as with canonical weight to every one who hears him; by figures of speech which need only be touched in order to elicit an electric spark of understanding and satisfaction. And when we ask wherein this power consists, let me name three points.

First, it is because the *Pilgrim's Progress*, as I have already indicated, is entirely catholic—that is, universal in its expression and its thoughts. I do not mean to say—it would be an exaggeration—that it contains no sentiments distasteful to this or that section of Christians, that it has not a certain tinge of the Calvinist or the Puritan. But what is remarkable is that this peculiar colour is so very slight. We know what was Bunyan's own passionate desire on this point. "I would be," he says, "as I hope I am, 'a Christian,' but as for those factious titles of Anabaptists, Independent, Presbyterian, or the like, I conclude that they come neither from Jerusalem nor Antioch, but from hell or Babylon." It was this universal charity that he expressed in his last sermon, "Dost thou see a soul that has the image of God in him? Love him, love him. This man and I must go to heaven one day. Love one another and do good for one another." It was this discriminating forbearance that he expressed in his account of the Interpreter's Garden. "Behold," he says, "the flowers are diverse in stature, in quality, in colour, in smell, and in virtue; and some are better than some; also where the gardener has set them there they stand and quarrel not with one another." There is no compromise in his words, there is no faltering in his convictions; but his love and admiration are reserved on the whole for that which all good men love, and his detestation on the whole is reserved for that which all good men detest. And if I may for a moment enter into detail, even in the very forms of his narrative, we find something as universal as his doctrine. Protestant, Puritan, Calvinist as he was, yet he did not fear to take the framework of his story and the figures of his drama, from the old mediæval Church, and the illustrations in which the modern editions of his book abound give us the pilgrim with his pilgrim's hat, the wayside cross, the crusading knight with his red-cross shield, the winged angels at the Celestial Gate, as naturally and as gracefully as though it had been a story from the "Golden Legend," or from the favourite romance of his early boyhood, "Sir Bevis of Southampton." Such a combination of Protestant ideas with Catholic forms had never been seen before, perhaps never since; it is in itself a union of Christendom in the best sense, to which neither Catholic nor Protestant, neither Churchman nor Nonconformist can possibly demur. The form, the substance, the tendency of the *Pilgrim's Progress* in these respects may be called latitudinarian, but it is a latitudinarianism which was an indispensable condition for its influence throughout the world. By it, as has been well said by an admirable living authority learned in all the learning of the Nonconformists, John Bunyan became the teacher, not of any particular sect, but of the universal Church.

Secondly, this wonderful book, with all its freedom, is never profane; with all its devotion, is rarely fanatical; with all its homeliness, is never vulgar. In other words, it is a work of pure art and true genius, and wherever these are we mount at once into a freer and loftier air. Bunyan was in this sense the Burns of England. On the tinker of Bedfordshire, as on the ploughman of Ayrshire, the heavenly fire had been breathed which transformed the common clay, and made him a poet, a philosopher—may we not say a gentleman and a nobleman in spite of himself. "If you were to polish the style," says Coleridge, "you would destroy the reality of the vision." He dared (and it was, for one of his straitened school and scanty culture, an act of immense daring) to communicate his religious teaching in the form of fiction, dream, poetry. It is one of the most striking proofs of the superiority of literature over polemics, of poetry over prose, as a messenger of heavenly truth. "I have been better entertained and more informed," says Dean Swift, "by a few pages of the *Pilgrim's Progress*, than by a long discourse on the will and the intellect." "I have," says Arnold, "always been struck by its piety. I am now equally struck, and even more, by its profound wisdom." It might, perhaps, have been thought that Bunyan, with his rough and imperfect education, must have erred—as it may be he has sometimes erred—in defective appreciation of virtues and weaknesses not his own; but one prevailing characteristic of his work is the breadth and depth of his intellectual insight. For the sincere tremors of poor Mrs. Muchafraid he has as good a word of consolation as he has for the ardent aspirations of Faithful and Hopeful. For the dogmatic nonsense of Talkative he has a word of rebuke as strong as he has for the gloomy dungeons of Doubting Castle; and for the treasures of the past he has a feeling as tender and as pervasive as if he had been brought up in the cloisters of Oxford or Westminster Abbey.—A. P. STANLEY, "John Bunyan," *Macmillan's Magazine*, July 1874, pp. 276–77

The images of the *Pilgrim's Progress* are the images of prophet and evangelist; it borrows for its tenderer outbursts the very verse of the Song of Songs and pictures the Heavenly City in the words of the Apocalypse. But so completely has the Bible become Bunyan's life that one feels its phrases as the natural expression of his thoughts. He has lived in the Bible till its words have become his own. He has lived among its visions and voices of heaven till all sense of possible unreality has died away. He tells his tale with such a perfect naturalness that allegories become living things, that the Slough of Despond and Doubting Castle are as real to us as places we see every day, that we know Mr. Legality and Mr. Wordly Wiseman as if we had met them in the street. It is in this amazing reality of impersonation that Bunyan's imaginative genius specially displays itself. But this is far from being his only excellence. In its range, in its directness, in its simple grace, in the ease with which it changes from lively dialogue to dramatic action, from simple pathos to passionate earnestness, in the subtle and delicate fancy which often suffuses its childlike words, in its playful humour, its bold character-painting, in the even and balanced power which passes without effort from the Valley of the Shadow of Death to the land "where the Shining Ones commonly walked because it was on the borders of heaven," in its sunny kindliness unbroken by one bitter word, the *Pilgrim's Progress* is among the noblest of English poems. For if Puritanism had first discovered the poetry which contact with the spiritual world awakes in the meanest souls Bunyan was the first of the Puritans who revealed this poetry to the outer world. The journey of Christian from the City of Destruction to the Heavenly City is simply a record of the life of such a Puritan as Bunyan himself seen through an imaginative haze of spiritual idealism in which its commonest incidents are heightened and glorified. He is himself the pilgrim who flies from the City of Destruction, who climbs the hill Difficulty, who faces Apollyon, who sees his loved ones cross the river of Death towards the Heavenly City, and how, because "the hill on which the City was framed was higher than the clouds, they therefore went up through the region of the air, sweetly talking as they went."—JOHN RICHARD GREEN, *History of the English People*, 1877–80, Bk. 8, Ch. 2

The people are living now—all the people: the noisy bullying judges, as of the French Revolutionary Courts, or the Hanging Courts after Monmouth's war; the demure, grave Puritan girls; and Matthew, who had the gripes; and lazy, feckless Ignorance, who came to so ill an end, poor fellow; and sturdy Old Honest, and timid Mr. Fearing; not single persons, but dozens, arise on the memory.

They come, as fresh, as vivid, as if they were out of Scott or Molière; the Tinker is as great a master of character and fiction as the greatest, almost; his style is pure, and plain, and sound, full of old idioms, and even of something like old slang. But even his slang is classical.

Bunyan is everybody's author. The very Catholics have their own edition of the *Pilgrim:* they have cut out Giant Pope, but have been too good-natured to insert Giant Protestant in his place. Unheralded, unannounced, though not uncriticised (they accused the Tinker of being a plagiarist, of course), Bunyan outshone the Court wits, the learned, the poets of the Restoration, and even the great theologians.—ANDREW LANG, "John Bunyan," *Essays in Little*, 1891, p. 188

Put your Shakespearian hero and coward, Henry V and Pistol or Parolles, beside Mr Valiant and Mr Fearing, and you have a sudden revelation of the abyss that lies between the fashionable author who could see nothing in the world but personal aims and the tragedy of their disappointment or the comedy of their incongruity, and the field preacher who achieved virtue and courage by identifying himself with the purpose of the world as he understood it. The contrast is enormous: Bunyan's coward stirs your blood more than Shakespear's hero, who actually leaves you cold and secretly hostile. You suddenly see that Shakespear, with all his flashes and divinations, never understood virtue and courage, never conceived how any man who was not a fool could, like Bunyan's hero, look back from the brink of the river of death over the strife and labor of his pilgrimage, and say "yet I do not repent me"; or, with the panache of a millionaire, bequeath "my sword to him that shall succeed me in my pilgrimage, and my courage and skill to him that can get it." This is the true joy in life, the being used for a purpose recognized by yourself as a mighty one; the being thoroughly worn out before you are thrown on the scrap heap; the being a force of Nature instead of a feverish selfish little clod of ailments and grievances complaining that the world will not devote itself to making you happy. And also the only real tragedy in life is the being used by personally minded men for purposes which you recognize to be base. All the rest is at worst mere misfortune or mortality: this alone is misery, slavery, hell on earth; and the revolt against it is the only force that offers a man's work to the poor artist, whom our personally minded rich people would so willingly employ as pandar, buffoon, beauty monger, sentimentalizer and the like.—GEORGE BERNARD SHAW, "Epistle Dedicatory" to *Man and Superman*, 1903

THE HOLY WAR

The style of *Pilgrim's Progress* is the very perfection of what the style of such a book should be—homely and yet distinguished, exquisitely simple, yet tuned to music at all its finer moments. The allegory is successful above all other allegories in literature. The abstractions which people it, even when they are mentioned only in one or two lines, never fail to live and stand out vividly as human beings.

Admirers of *The Holy War* have tried to assert as much for that longer and more laborious work. But popular taste has rightly determined that there should be a thousand readers of the first story to ten of the second. There are very fine passages in *The Holy War*; the opening, especially all the first siege of Mansoul, is superbly conceived and executed. But the personages which are introduced are too incongruous, the intrigues of Shaddei and the resistance of Diabolus are too incredible, the contest is too one-sided from the first, to interest us as we are interested in the human adventures of Christian. Bunyan seems powerless to close *The Holy War*, and before he is able to persuade himself to drop the threads, the whole skein of the allegory is hopelessly entangled.—EDMUND GOSSE, *A History of Eighteenth Century Literature*, 1888, p. 85

There can, in fact, be little doubt that the idea is consciously derived from *Paradise Lost*. In both the banished fiends cast about for some means of retaliating upon their omnipotent foe; in Milton their attack is levelled against the Garden of Eden, in Bunyan against the soul of man. All human attributes, virtuous or vicious, are allegorized with graphic liveliness, but at length one wearies of the crowd of abstractions; and where strength was most necessary, Bunyan is weak. Emanuel is not godlike, and Diabolus is not terrible. The book is perhaps chiefly interesting as an index to the great progress effected since Bunyan's time in spirituality as regards men's religious conceptions, and in freedom and enlightenment as concerns the things of earth. No one would now depict the offended majesty of Heaven as so like the offended majesty of the Stuarts; or deem that the revolters' offence could be mitigated by the abjectness of their submission; or try criminals with such unfairness; or lecture them upon conviction with such lack of judicial decorum. Bunyan's own spirit seems narrower than of old; among the traitors upon whom Emanuel's ministers execute justice he includes not only No-truth and Pitiless, but also Election-doubter and Vocation-doubter, who represent the majority of the members of the Church of England. The whole tone, in truth, is such as might be expected from one nurtured upon the Old rather than the New Testament, and who had never conceived any doubts of the justice of the Israelites' dealings with the Canaanites. The literary power, nevertheless, is unabated; much ingenuity is shown in keeping up the interest of the story; and there is the old gift of vitalizing abstractions by uncompromising realism of treatment.
—RICHARD GARNETT, *The Age of Dryden*, 1895, p. 239

⟨. . .⟩ if we read Bunyan's alleogry as a setting forth of the struggle between the powers of good and evil for Man as a social being we shall find that the ideas of the Melchiorite Anabaptists concerning the world around him were his. Man, according to the teaching of the *Holy War*, was created for the delight and glory of God, and as a society to live eternally under His government—a society which could, therefore, in the classical sense, be spoken of as "a city"—"a city whose builder and founder was God, and at whose creation the sons of God sang with joy." This human city, listening to the devil, fell, and became his captive and slave; many efforts were made for its deliverance, but this could only be done by its own rightful prince, who himself comes and redeems it. But, though redeemed from its captivity to Diabolus, Mansoul was still a city divided against itself, for a great number of its inhabitants were Diabolonians by nature, apparently foreigners naturalised under Diabolus. These Diabolonians work together for the restoration of the power of their master, and succeed in getting their fellow citizens so to trust in the prosperous condition of affairs that they grow indifferent to their true prince, and careless concerning the stealthy progress of his adversary. When this process has gone on long enough to create a breach between Mansoul and its prince, Diabolus commences to besiege the city, and, making a partially successful assault, the Diabolonian forces enter, and Mansoul becomes, in Bunyan's forcible language, "a den of dragons, an emblem of hell, and a place of total darkness." The castle, however, still remains in the hands of the captains of Immanuel, and they keep up the fight until the prince himself at last suddenly returns to Mansoul, utterly routs Diabolus and his army, and once again re-establishes His kingdom in the city. This summary of Bunyan's allegory is equally a summary of what the Münster or Melchiorite Anabaptists in their book, *The Restitution*, conceived to be the history of Christendom.

And Bunyan, while entering into the Anabaptist idea of that history, shared the Anabaptist spirit. For not only does he describe the inhabitants of this city as composed of two sorts of men, Diabolonians and servants of Shaddai, but the spirit in which the latter treat the former in the hour of triumph is exactly that with which the Book of the Restitution and the Book of Vengeance sought to animate true Israelites against Babylonians. ⟨. . .⟩

The singular similarity both in the drama and in the spirit of the history and of the allegory cannot be explained, so far as I can see, except by supposing that Bunyan had heard and assimilated the story of the Anabaptist Kingdom of Münster, and had heard it, not through distorted histories, but by the living voice of tradition. And if it be admitted that the struggle of which Münster became the centre was the archetype of Bunyan's *Holy War*, then we not only get an interesting literary fact, but, what is more important, a vivid light on the mind of the religious common people of England during a period when this country was as virile in its character as at any period in its history.—RICHARD HEATH, "The Archetype of *The Holy War*," *Contemporary Review*, July 1897, pp. 111–18

THOMAS BABINGTON MACAULAY
From "John Bunyan" (1830)
Critical, Historical, and Miscellaneous Essays
1860, Volume 2, pp. 252–67

The characteristic peculiarity of the *Pilgrim's Progress* is that it is the only work of its kind which possesses a strong human interest. Other allegories only amuse the fancy. The allegory of Bunyan has been read by many thousands with tears. There are some good allegories in Johnson's works, and some of still higher merit by Addison. In these performances there is, perhaps, as much wit and ingenuity as in the *Pilgrim's Progress*. But the pleasure which is produced by the Vision of Mirza, the Vision of Theodore, the genealogy of Wit, or the contest between Rest and Labour, is exactly similar to the pleasure which we derive from one of Cowley's odes or from a canto of *Hudibras*. It is a pleasure which belongs wholly to the understanding, and in which the feelings have no part whatever. Nay, even Spenser himself, though assuredly one of the greatest poets that ever lived, could not succeed in the attempt to make allegory interesting. It was in vain that he lavished the riches of his mind on the House of Pride and the House of Temperance. One unpardonable fault, the fault of tediousness, pervades the whole of the *Fairy Queen*. We become sick of cardinal virtues and deadly sins, and long for the society of plain men and women. Of the persons who read the first canto, not one in ten reaches the end of the first book, and not one in a hundred perseveres to the end of the poem. Very few and very weary are those who are in at the death of the Blatant Beast. If the last six books, which are said to have been destroyed in Ireland, had been preserved, we doubt whether any heart less stout than that of a commentator would have held out to the end.

It is not so with the *Pilgrim's Progress*. That wonderful book, while it obtains admiration from the most fastidious critics, is loved by those who are too simple to admire it. Dr. Johnson, all whose studies were desultory, and who hated, as he said, to read books through, made an exception in favour of the *Pilgrim's Progress*. That work was one of the two or three works which he wished longer. It was by no common merit that the illiterate sectary extracted praise like this from the most pedantic of critics and the most bigoted of Tories. In the wildest parts of Scotland the *Pilgrim's Progress* is the delight of the peasantry. In every nursery the *Pilgrim's Progress* is a greater favourite than *Jack the Giant-killer*. Every reader knows the straight and narrow path as well as he knows a road in which he has gone backward and forward a hundred times. This is the highest miracle of genius, that things which are not should be as though they were, that the imaginations of one mind should become the personal recollections of another. And this miracle the tinker has wrought. There is no ascent, no declivity, no resting-place, no turn-stile, with which we are not perfectly acquainted. The wicket gate, and the desolate swamp which separates it from the City of Destruction, the long line of road, as straight as a rule can make it, the Interpreter's house and all its fair shows, the prisoner in the iron cage, the palace, at the doors of which armed men kept guard, and on the battlements of which walked persons clothed all in gold, the cross and the sepulchre, the steep hill and the pleasant arbour, the stately front of the House Beautiful by the wayside, the chained lions crouching in the porch, the low green valley of Humiliation, rich with grass and covered with flocks, all are as well known to us as the sights of our own street. Then we come to the narrow place where Apollyon strode right across the whole breadth of the way, to stop the journey of Christian, and where afterwards the pillar was set up to testify how bravely the pilgrim had fought the good fight. As we advance, the valley becomes deeper and deeper. The shade of the precipices on both sides falls blacker and blacker. The clouds gather overhead. Doleful voices, the clanking of chains, and the rushing of many feet to and fro, are heard through the darkness. The way, hardly discernible in gloom, runs close by the mouth of the burning pit, which sends forth its flame, its noisome smoke, and its hideous shapes, to terrify the adventurer. Thence he goes on, amidst the snares and pitfalls, with the mangled bodies of those who have perished lying in the ditch by his side. At the end of the long dark valley he passes the dens in which the old giants dwelt, amidst the bones of those whom they had slain.

Then the road passes straight on through a waste moor, till at length the towers of a distant city appear before the traveller; and soon he is in the midst of the innumerable multitudes of Vanity Fair. There are the jugglers and the apes, the shops and the puppetshows. There are Italian Row, and French Row, and

Spanish Row, and Britain Row, with their crowds of buyers, sellers, and loungers, jabbering all the languages of the earth.

Thence we go on by the little hill of the silver mine, and through the meadow of lilies, along the bank of that pleasant river which is bordered on both sides by fruit-trees. On the left branches off the path leading to the horrible castle, the court-yard of which is paved with the skulls of pilgrims; and right onward are the sheepfolds and orchards of the Delectable Mountains.

From the Delectable Mountains, the way lies through the fogs and briers of the Enchanted Ground, with here and there a bed of soft cushions spread under a green arbour. And beyond is the land of Beulah, where the flowers, the grapes, and the songs of birds never cease, and where the sun shines night and day. Thence are plainly seen the golden pavements and streets of pearl, on the other side of that black and cold river over which there is no bridge.

All the stages of the journey, all the forms which cross or overtake the pilgrims, giants, and hobgoblins, ill-favoured ones, and shining ones, the tall, comely, swarthy Madame Bubble, with her great purse by her side, and her fingers playing with the money, the black man in the bright vesture, Mr. Worldly Wiseman and my Lord Hategood, Mr. Talkative, and Mrs. Timorous, all are actually existing beings to us. We follow the travellers through their allegorical progress with interest not inferior to that with which we follow Elizabeth from Siberia to Moscow, or Jeanie Deans from Edinburgh to London. Bunyan is almost the only writer who ever gave to the abstract the interest of the concrete. In the works of many celebrated authors, men are mere personifications. We have not a jealous man, but jealousy; not a traitor, but perfidy; not a patriot, but patriotism. The mind of Bunyan, on the contrary, was so imaginative that personifications, when he dealt with them, became men. A dialogue between two qualities, in his dream, has more dramatic effect than a dialogue between two human beings in most plays. In this respect the genius of Bunyan bore a great resemblance to that of a man who had very little else in common with him, Percy Bysshe Shelley.

⟨. . .⟩ The *Pilgrim's Progress* undoubtedly is not a perfect allegory. The types are often inconsistent with each other; and sometimes the allegorical disguise is altogether thrown off. The river, for example, is emblematic of death; and we are told that every human being must pass through the river. But Faithful does not pass through it. He is martyred, not in shadow, but in reality, at Vanity Fair. Hopeful talks to Christian about Essau's birthright and about his own convictions of sin as Bunyan might have talked with one of his own congregation. The damsels at the House Beautiful catechize Christiana's boys, as any good ladies might catechize any boys at a Sunday School. But we do not believe that any man, whatever might be his genius, and whatever his good luck, could long continue a figurative history without falling into many inconsistencies. We are sure that inconsistencies, scarcely less gross than the worst into which Bunyan has fallen, may be found in the shortest and most elaborate allegories of the *Spectator* and the *Rambler*. The *Tale of a Tub* and the *History of John Bull* swarm with similar errors, if the name of error can be properly applied to that which is unavoidable. It is not easy to make a simile go on all-fours. But we believe that no human ingenuity could produce such a centipede as a long allegory in which the correspondence between the outward sign and the thing signified should be exactly preserved. Certainly no writer, ancient or modern, has yet achieved the adventure. The best thing, on the whole, that an allegorist can do, is to present to

his readers a succession of analogies, each of which may separately be striking and happy, without looking very nicely to see whether they harmonize with each other. This Bunyan has done; and, though a minute scrutiny may detect inconsistencies in every page of his Tale, the general effect which the Tale produces on all persons, learned and unlearned, proves that he has done well. The passages which it is most difficult to defend are those in which he altogether drops the allegory, and puts into the mouth of his pilgrims religious ejaculations and disquisitions, better suited to his own pulpit at Bedford or Reading than to the Enchanted Ground or to the Interpreter's Garden. Yet even these passages, though we will not undertake to defend them against the objections of critics, we feel that we could ill spare. We feel that the story owes much of its charm to these occasional glimpses of solemn and affecting subjects, which will not be hidden, which force themselves through the veil, and appear before us in their native aspect. The effect is not unlike that which is said to have been produced on the ancient stage, when the eyes of the actor were seen flaming through his mask, and giving life and expression to what would else have been an inanimate and uninteresting disguise.

It is very amusing and very instructive to compare the *Pilgrim's Progress* with the *Grace Abounding*. The latter work is indeed one of the most remarkable pieces of autobiography in the world. It is a full and open confession of the fancies which passed through the mind of an illiterate man, whose affections were warm, whose nerves were irritable, whose imagination was ungovernable, and who was under the influence of the strongest religious excitement. In whatever age Bunyan had lived, the history of his feelings would, in all probability, have been very curious. But the time in which his lot was cast was the time of a great stirring of the human mind. A tremendous burst of public feeling, produced by the tyranny of the hierarchy, menaced the old ecclesiastical institutions with destruction. To the gloomy regularity of one intolerant Church had succeeded the license of innumerable sects, drunk with the sweet and heady must of their new liberty. Fanaticism, engendered by persecution, and destined to engender persecution in turn, spread rapidly through society. Even the strongest and most commanding minds were not proof against this strange taint. Any time might have produced George Fox and James Naylor. But to one time alone belong the frantic delusions of such a statesman as Vane, and the hysterical tears of such a soldier as Cromwell.

The history of Bunyan is the history of a most excitable mind in an age of excitement. By most of his biographers he has been treated with gross injustice. They have understood in a popular sense all those strong terms of self-condemnation which he employed in a theological sense. They have, therefore, represented him as an abandoned wretch reclaimed by means almost miraculous, or, to use their favourite metaphor, "as a brand plucked from the burning." Mr. Ivimey calls him the depraved Bunyan and the wicked tinker of Elstow. Surely Mr. Ivimey ought to have been too familiar with the bitter accusations which the most pious people are in the habit of bringing against themselves, to understand literally all the strong expressions which are to be found in the *Grace Abounding*. It is quite clear, as Mr. Southey most justly remarks, that Bunyan never was a vicious man. He married very early; and he solemnly declares that he was strictly faithful to his wife. He does not appear to have been a drunkard. He owns, indeed, that, when a boy, he never spoke without an oath. But a single admonition cured him of this bad habit for life; and the cure must have been wrought early; for at eighteen he was in the army of the Parliament; and, if he had carried the vice of profaneness into that service, he would doubtless have received something more than an admonition from Serjeant Bind-their-kings-in-chains, or Captain Hew-Agag-in-pieces-before-the-Lord. Bell-ringing and playing at hockey on Sundays seem to have been the worst vices of this depraved tinker. They would have passed for virtues with Archbishop Laud. It is quite clear that, from a very early age, Bunyan was a man of a strict life and of a tender conscience. "He had been," says Mr. Southey, "a blackguard." Even this we think too hard a censure. Bunyan was not, we admit, so fine a gentleman as Lord Digby; but he was a blackguard no otherwise than as every labouring man that ever lived has been a blackguard. Indeed Mr. Southey acknowledges this. "Such he might have been expected to be by his birth, breeding, and vocation. Scarcely indeed, by possibility, could he have been otherwise." A man whose manners and sentiments are decidedly below those of his class deserves to be called a blackguard. But it is surely unfair to apply so strong a word of reproach to one who is only what the great mass of every community must inevitably be.

Those horrible internal conflicts which Bunyan has described with so much power of language prove, not that he was a worse man than his neighbours, but that his mind was constantly occupied by religious considerations, that his fervour exceeded his knowledge, and that his imagination exercised despotic power over his body and mind. He heard voices from heaven. He saw strange visions of distant hills, pleasant and sunny as his own Delectable Mountains. From those abodes he was shut out, and placed in a dark and horrible wilderness, where he wandered through ice and snow, striving to make his way into the happy region of light. At one time he was seized with an inclination to work miracles. At another time he thought himself actually possessed by the devil. He could distinguish the blasphemous whispers. He felt his infernal enemy pulling at his clothes behind him. He spurned with his feet and struck with his hands at the destroyer. Sometimes he was tempted to sell his part in the salvation of mankind. Sometimes a violent impulse urged him to start up from his food, to fall on his knees, and to break forth into prayer. At length he fancied that he had committed the unpardonable sin. His agony convulsed his robust frame. He was, he says, as if his breastbone would split; and this he took for a sign that he was destined to burst asunder like Judas. The agitation of his nerves made all his movements tremulous; and this trembling, he supposed, was a visible mark of his reprobation, like that which had been set on Cain. At one time, indeed, an encouraging voice seemed to rush in at the window, like the noise of wind, but very pleasant, and commanded, as he says, a great calm in his soul. At another time, a word of comfort "was spoke loud unto him; it showed a great word; it seemed to be writ in great letters." But these intervals of ease were short. His state, during two years and a half, was generally the most horrible that the human mind can imagine. "I walked," says he, with his own peculiar eloquence, "to a neighbouring town; and sat down upon a settle in the street, and fell into a very deep pause about the most fearful state my sin had brought me to; and, after long musing, I lifted up my head; but methought I saw as if the sun that shineth in the heavens did grudge to give me light; and as if the very stones in the street, and tiles upon the houses, did band themselves against me. Methought that they all combined together to banish me out of the world. I was abhorred of them, and unfit to dwell among them, because I had sinned against the Saviour. Oh, how happy now was every creature over I! for they stood fast, and kept their station. But I was gone and lost." Scarcely any madhouse could produce an instance of delusion so strong, or of misery so acute.

It was through this Valley of the Shadow of Death, overhung by darkness, peopled with devils, resounding with blasphemy and lamentation, and passing amidst quagmires, snares, and pitfalls, close by the very mouth of hell, that Bunyan journeyed to that bright and fruitful land of Beulah, in which he sojourned during the latter period of his pilgrimage. The only trace which his cruel sufferings and temptations seem to have left behind them was an affectionate compassion for those who were still in the state in which he had once been. Religion has scarcely ever worn a form so calm and soothing as in his allegory. The feeling which predominates through the whole book is a feeling of tenderness for weak, timid, and harassed minds. The character of Mr. Fearing, of Mr. Feeble-Mind, of Mr. Despondency and his daughter Miss Much-afraid, the account of poor Littlefaith who was robbed by the three thieves, of his spending money, the description of Christian's terror in the dungeons of Giant Despair and in his passage through the river, all clearly show how strong a sympathy Bunyan felt, after his own mind had become clear and cheerful, for persons afflicted with religious melancholy.

Mr. Southey, who has no love for the Calvinists, admits that, if Calvinism had never worn a blacker appearance than in Bunyan's works, it would never have become a term of reproach. In fact, those works of Bunyan with which we are acquainted are by no means more Calvinistic than the articles and homilies of the Church of England. The moderation of his opinions on the subject of predestination gave offence to some zealous persons. We have seen an absurd allegory, the heroine of which is named Hephzibah, written by some raving supralapsarian preacher who was dissatisfied with the mild theology of the *Pilgrim's Progress*. In this foolish book, if we recollect rightly, the Interpreter is called the Enlightener, and the House Beautiful is Castle Strength. Mr. Southey tells us that the Catholics had also their *Pilgrim's Progress*, without a Giant Pope, in which the Interpreter is the Director, and the House Beautiful Grace's Hall. It is surely a remarkable proof of the power of Bunyan's genius, that two religious parties, both of which regarded his opinions as heterodox, should have had recourse to him for assistance.

There are, we think, some characters and scenes in the *Pilgrim's Progress*, which can be fully comprehended and enjoyed only by persons familiar with the history of the times through which Bunyan lived. The character of Mr. Great-heart, the guide, is an example. His fighting is, of course, allegorical; but the allegory is not strictly preserved. He delivers a sermon on imputed righteousness to his companions; and, soon after, he gives battle to Giant Grim, who had taken upon him to back the lions. He expounds the fifty-third chapter of Isaiah to the household and guests of Gaius; and then he sallies out to attack Slaygood, who was of the nature of flesh-eaters, in his den. These are inconsistencies; but they are inconsistencies which add, we think, to the interest of the narrative. We have not the least doubt that Bunyan had in view some stout old Greatheart of Naseby and Worcester, who prayed with his men before he drilled them, who knew the spiritual state of every dragoon in his troop, and who, with the praises of God in his mouth, and a two-edged sword in his hand, had turned to flight, on many fields of battle, the swearing, drunken bravoes of Rupert and Lunsford.

Every age produces such men as By-ends. But the middle of the seventeenth century was eminently prolific of such men. Mr. Southey thinks that the satire was aimed at some particular individual; and this seems by no means improbable. At all events, Bunyan must have known many of those hypocrites who followed religion only when religion walked in silver slippers, when the sun shone, and when the people applauded. Indeed he might have easily found all the kindred of By-ends among the public men of his time. He might have found among the peers my Lord Turn-about, my Lord Time-server, and my Lord Fair-speech; in the House of Commons, Mr. Smooth-man, Mr. Anything, and Mr. Facing-both-ways; nor would "the parson of the parish, Mr. Two-tongues," have been wanting. The town of Bedford probably contained more than one politician who, after contriving to raise an estate by seeking the Lord during the reign of the saints, contrived to keep what he had got by persecuting the saints during the reign of the strumpets, and more than one priest who, during repeated changes in the discipline and doctrines of the church, had remained constant to nothing but his benefice.

One of the most remarkable passages in the *Pilgrim's Progress* is that in which the proceedings against Faithful are described. It is impossible to doubt that Bunyan intended to satirise the mode in which state trials were conducted under Charles the Second. The license given to the witnesses for the prosecution, the shameless partiality and ferocious insolence of the judge, the precipitancy and the blind rancour of the jury, remind us of those odious mummeries which, from the Restoration to the Revolution, were merely forms preliminary to hanging, drawing, and quartering. Lord Hategood performs the office of counsel for the prisoners as well as Scroggs himself could have performed it.

> *Judge*: Thou runagate, heretic, and traitor, hast thou heard what these honest gentlemen have witnessed against thee?
> *Faithful*: May I speak a few words in my own defence?
> *Judge*: Sirrah, sirrah! thou deservest to live no longer, but to be slain immediately upon the place; yet, that all men may see our gentleness to thee, let us hear what thou, vile runagate, hast to say.

No person who knows the state trials can be at a loss for parallel cases. Indeed, write what Bunyan would, the baseness and cruelty of the lawyers of those times "sinned up to it still," and even went beyond it. The imaginary trial of Faithful, before a jury composed of personified vices, was just and merciful, when compared with the real trial of Alice Lisle before that tribunal where all the vices sat in the person of Jefferies.

The style of Bunyan is delightful to every reader, and invaluable as a study to every person who wishes to obtain a wide command over the English language. The vocabulary is the vocabulary of the common people. There is not an expression, if we except a few technical terms of theology, which would puzzle the rudest peasant. We have observed several pages which do not contain a single word of more than two syllables. Yet no writer has said more exactly what he meant to say. For magnificence, for pathos, for vehement exhortation, for subtle disquisition, for every purpose of the poet, the orator, and the divine, this homely dialect, the dialect of plain working men, was perfectly sufficient. There is no book in our literature on which we would so readily stake the fame of the old unpolluted English language, no book which shows so well how rich that language is in its own proper wealth, and how little it has been improved by all that it has borrowed.

Cowper said, forty or fifty years ago, that he dared not name John Bunyan in his verse, for fear of moving a sneer. To our refined forefathers, we suppose, Lord Roscommon's *Essay on Translated Verse*, and the Duke of Buckinghamshire's *Essay on Poetry*, appeared to be compositions infinitely superior to

the allegory of the preaching tinker. We live in better times; and we are not afraid to say, that, though there were many clever men in England during the latter half of the seventeenth century, there were only two minds which possessed the imaginative faculty in a very eminent degree. One of those minds produced the *Paradise Lost*, the other the *Pilgrim's Progress*.

GEORGE BARRELL CHEEVER
From "Southey's Life of Bunyan"
North American Review, April 1833, pp. 453–65

Bunyan's imagination was powerful enough, in connexion with his belief in God's superintending Providence, to array his inward trials with a sensible shape, and external events with a light reflected from his own experience; hopes and fears were friends and enemies; acting in concert with these, all things he met with in the world were friends or enemies likewise, according as they aided or opposed his spiritual life. He acted always under one character, the Christian Soldier, realizing, in his own conflicts and conquests, the Progress of his own Pilgrim. Therefore his book is a perfect Reality in oneness as a whole, and in every page a book not of imaginations and shadows, but of Realities experienced. To those who have never set out on this pilgrimage, nor encountered its dangers, it is interesting, as would be a book powerfully written of travels in an unknown, romantic land. Regarded as a work of original genius simply, without taking into view its spiritual meaning, it is a wonder to all, and cannot cease to be. Though a book of personification and allegory, it enchants the simplest child, as powerfully, almost, as the story of Aladdin and his Lamp, or the adventures of Sindbad the Sailor, or the history of Robinson Crusoe himself. It is interesting to all, who have any taste for poetical beauty, in the same manner as Spenser's *Fairy Queen*, or we might mention, expecially, for the similar absorbing interest we take in all that happens to the hero, Homer's *Odyssey*.

Yet its interest for the imagination is in reality the smallest part of its power; and it will be pleasing to the imagination, just in proportion as the mind of the reader has been accustomed to interpret the things of this life by their connexion with another, and by the light that comes from that world to this. A reader who has not formed this habit, nor ever felt that he is a stranger and pilgrim in a world of temptations and snares, can see but half the beauty of such poetry as fills this work, because it cannot make its appeal to his own experience; for him there is nothing within, that tells more certainly than any process of judgment or criticism, the truth and sweetness of the picture; there is no reflection of its images, nor interpretation of its meaning, in his own soul. The Christian, the actual Pilgrim, reads it with another eye. It comes to his heart. It is like a painting meant to be exhibited by firelight: the common reader sees it by day. To the Christian, it is a glorious transparency; and the light that shines through it, and gives its incidents such life, its colors such depth, and the whole scene such a surpassing glory, is light from Eternity, the meaning of Heaven.

We repeat it, therefore, as a truth which to us seems very evident, that the true beauty of the allegory in the *Pilgrim's Progress* can only be felt by a religious mind. No one, indeed, can avoid admiring it. The honest nature in the characters, their homely truth, the simplicity and good sense of the conversations, the beauty of the incidents, the sweetness of the scenery through which the reader is conducted, the purity of the language,

The humorous vein, strong sense, and simple style,
To teach the gayest, make the gravest smile,

all these things to the eye of the merest critic are beautiful, and he who loves to read Shakespeare will admire them, and on common ground. But such a reader, in respect to the veiled beauty of the allegory, is like a deaf man, to whom you speak of the sweetness of musical sounds. Of the faithfulness with which Bunyan has depicted the inward trials of the Christian conflict, of the depth and power of the appeal which that book makes to the Christian's heart, of the accuracy and beauty of the map therein drawn of the dealings of the Spirit of God in leading the sinner from the City of Destruction to Mount Zion above, he knows and can conceive nothing. It is like Milton's daughters reading aloud from his Hebrew Bible to the blind poet, while they could only pronounce the words, but were ignorant of the sacred meaning, nor could divine the nature of the inspiration it excited in his soul. Little can such a reader see

Of all that power
Of prospect, whereof many thousands tell.

⟨. . .⟩ Of the best part of our language, Bunyan was a master: he became so in the study of the Bible. It was his book of all learning; for years he studied it as for his life. No bewildered mariner, in a crazy bark, on an unknown sea, amidst sunken reefs and dangerous shallows, ever pondered his chart with half the earnestness. It was as if life or death depended on every time he opened it, and every line he read. 'The Scriptures were wonderful things' to him. The fear of 'those sentences that stood against me, as sometimes I thought they every one did,—made me with careful heart and watchful eye, with great fearfulness, to turn over every leaf, and with much diligence, mixed with trembling, to consider every sentence with its natural force and latitude.' Now would he 'leap into the bosom of that promise, that yet he feared did shut its heart against him. Now also I would labor to take the word as God hath laid it down, without restraining the natural force of one syllable thereof. Oh! what did I now see in that blessed sixth of John, "and him that comes to me, I will in no wise cast out."—Oh, many a pull hath my heart had with Satan for that blessed sixth of John!—A word! a word! to lean a weary soul upon, that it might not sink forever! 't was that I hunted for! Yea, often, when I have been making to the promise, I have seen as if the Lord would refuse my soul forever: I was often as if I had run upon the pikes, and as if the Lord had thrust at me, to keep me from him, as with a flaming sword!'

Here is the secret of his knowledge of the Bible; and his intense study of the Bible is the secret of the purity of his English style. The fervor of the Poet's soul, acting through the medium of such a language as he learned from our common translation of the Scriptures, has produced some of the most admirable specimens in existence of the homely power and familiar beauty of the English tongue. There are passages even in the *Grace Abounding*, which, for homely fervidness and power of expression, might be placed side by side with any thing in the most admired authors, and not suffer in the comparison. As long as the Bible, in its present translation, is the property of all who read English, while the *Pilgrim's Progress* is the book of the people, and the merit of Shakspeare rightly appreciated, we need not fear any great corruption in the English tongue. ⟨. . .⟩

The poetry of the Bible was not less the source of Bunyan's poetical power, than the study of the whole Scriptures was the source of his simplicity and purity of style. His heart was not only made new by the spirit of the Bible, but his whole intellectual being was penetrated and transfigured by its influence. He brought the spirit and power, gathered from so long and exclusive a communion with the prophets and apostles, to the composition of every page of the *Pilgrim's Progress*. To the habit of mind thus induced, and the workings of an imagination thus disciplined, may be traced the simplicity of all his imagery, and the power of his personifications. The spirit of his work is Hebrew; we may trace the mingled influence both of David and Isaiah in the character of his genius; and as to the images in the sacred poets, he is lavish in the use of them in the most natural and unconscious manner possible; his mind was imbued with them. He is indeed the only poet, whose genius was nourished entirely by the Bible. ⟨. . .⟩

A great characteristic of original genius, perhaps its greatest proof, and one which Bunyan possessed in common with Shakspeare, is its spontaneous exertion; the evidence of having written without labor, and without the consciousness of doing any thing remarkable, or the ambitious aim of performing a great work. The thought 'how will this please?' has no power as a motive, nor is it ever suggested to such minds: the greatest efforts of genius seem as natural to it, as it is for common men to breathe. In this view Bunyan's work comes nearer to the poetry of the Hebrews in its character, than any other human composition. He wrote from the impulse of his genius, sanctified and illuminated by a heavenly influence; and its movements were as artless, as the movements of a little child left to play upon the green by itself; as if, indeed, he had exerted no voluntary supervision whatever over its exercise. Every thing is as natural and unconstrained, as if there had been no other breather in this world but himself, no being to whose inspection the work he was producing could ever possibly be exhibited, and no rule or model with which it could ever be compared.

We can imagine this suffering Christian and unconscious poet, in the gloom of his prison, solacing his mind with its own visions as they came in one after another, like heavenly pictures to his imagination. They were so pleasant, that he could not but give them reality, and when he found how they accumulated, then first did the *ideal* of his *Pilgrim's Progress* rise before his view. Then did he, with the pervading, informing, and transfusing power of genius, melt the materials and mould them into shape. He put the pictures into one grand allegory, with the meaning of Heaven shining over the whole, and a separate interest and beauty in every separate part. It is an allegory conducted with such symmetry and faithfulness, that it never tires in its examination, but discloses continually new meaning to the mind, and speaks to the heart of the Pilgrim volumes of mingled encouragement, warning and instruction.

We know of no other work, in which we take a deeper sympathetic interest in all the circumstances of danger, trial, or happiness, befalling the hero. The honesty, integrity, openheartedness, humor, simplicity, and deep sensibility of Christian's character, make us love him: nor is there a character depicted in all English literature, that stands out to the mind in bolder truth and originality. There is a wonderful charm and truth to nature, in Christian's manifest growth in grace and wisdom. What a different being is Christian on the Delectable Mountains, or in the land Beulah, and Christian when he first set out on his Pilgrimage! And yet, he is always the same being; we recognise him at once. The change is not of the original features of his character, but a change into the character of the 'Lord of the Way,' a gradual imbuing with his spirit, a change, in Paul's expressive language, 'from glory to glory into the same image.' In proportion as he arrives nearer the Celestial City, he shines brighter, his character unfolds in greater richness, he commands more veneration from us, without losing any of our affection. As we witness his steadily increasing lustre, we think of that beautiful Scripture image, 'the path of the just is as a shining light, that shineth brighter and brighter unto the Perfect Day.' From being an unwary Pilgrim, just setting out, with all the rags of the City of Destruction about him, and the burden of guilt bending him down, he becomes that delightful character, an experienced Christian; with the robe given him by the Shining Ones shining brighter and brighter, and the roll of assurance becoming clearer, and faith growing stronger, and courage more confirmed and steady, and in broader and broader light Heaven reflected from his countenance. We go with him in his Pilgrimage all the way. We enter the Interpreter's House; we see all the rarities which the Lord of the Way keeps there for the entertainment of the Pilgrims; we turn aside from the rough path to go in the soft meadow; we are overtaken by the storm; we fall into Giant Despair's Castle, we are there from Wednesday noon till Saturday night;—there never was a poem, into which we entered so wholly, and with all the heart, and in such fervent love and believing assurance.

All this admirable accuracy and beauty Bunyan wrought seemingly without design. It was not so much an exertion, a labor of his mind, as the promptings and wanderings at will of his unconscious genius. He never thought of doing all this, but he did it. He was a child under the power and guidance of his genius, and with a child's admiration he would look upon the creations, which his own imagination presented to his mind. Thus Bunyan went on, painting that narrow way, and the exquisite scenery each side of it, and the many characters crossing, appearing, and passing at a distance, and Christian and Hopeful on their way, and making every part of the picture, as he proceeded, harmonize with the whole, and yet add anew to its meaning, and all with as much quiet unconscious ease and simplicity, as an infant would put together its baby-house of cards, or as the frost on a winter's night would draw a picture on the window.

HIPPOLYTE TAINE
From *History of English Literature*
tr. H. Van Laun
1871, Book 2, Chapter 5

After the Bible, the book most widely read in England is the *Pilgrim's Progress*, by John Bunyan. The reason is, that the basis of Protestantism is the doctrine of salvation by grace, and that no writer has equalled Bunyan in making this doctrine understood.

To treat well of supernatural impressions, one must have been subject to them. Bunyan had that kind of imagination which produces them. Powerful as that of an artist, but more vehement, this imagination worked in the man without his co-operation, and besieged him with visions which he had neither willed nor foreseen. From that moment there was in him as it were a second self, dominating the first, grand and terrible, whose apparitions were sudden, its motions unknown, which redoubled or crushed his faculties, prostrated or transported him, bathed him in the sweat of anguish, ravished him with trances of joy, and which by its force, strangeness,

independence, impressed upon him the presence and the action of a foreign and superior master. Bunyan, like Saint Theresa, was from infancy 'greatly troubled with the thoughts of the fearful torments of hell-fire,' sad in the midst of pleasures, believing himself damned, and so despairing, that he wished he was a devil, 'supposing they were only tormentors; that if it must needs be that I went thither, I might be rather a tormentor, than be tormented myself.' There already was the assault of exact and bodily images. Under their influence reflexion ceased, and the man was suddenly spurred into action. The first movement carried him with closed eyes, as down a steep slope, into mad resolutions. One day, 'being in the field, with my companions, it chanced that an adder passed over the highway: so I, having a stick, struck her over the back; and having stunned her, I forced open her mouth with my stick, and plucked her sting out with my fingers, by which act, had not God been merciful to me, I might, by my desperateness, have brought myself to my end.' In his first approaches to conversion he was extreme in his emotions, and penetrated to the heart by the sight of physical objects, 'adoring' priest, service, altar, vestment. 'This conceit grew so strong upon my spirit, that had I but seen a priest (though never so sordid and debauched in his life), I should find my spirit fall under him, reverence him, and knit unto him; yea, I thought, for the love I did bear unto them (supposing they were the ministers of God), I could have laid down at their feet, and having been trampled upon by them; their name, their garb, and work did so intoxicate and bewitch me.' Already his ideas clung to him with that irresistible hold which constitutes monomania; no matter how absurd they were, they ruled him, not by their truth, but by their presence. The thought of an impossible danger terrified him as much as the sight of an imminent peril. As a man hung over an abyss by a sound rope, he forgot that the rope was sound, and vertigo seized upon him. After the fashion of English villagers, he loved bell-ringing: when he became a Puritan, he considered the amusement profane, and gave it up; yet, impelled by his desire, he would go into the belfry and watch the ringers. 'But quickly after, I began to think, "How if one of the bells should fall?" Then I chose to stand under a main beam, that lay overthwart the steeple, from side to side, thinking here I might stand sure: but then I thought again, should the bell fall with a swing, it might first hit the wall, and then rebounding upon me, might kill me for all this beam. This made me stand in the steeple-door; and now, thought I, I am safe enough, for if a bell should then fall, I can slip out behind these thick walls, and so be preserved notwithstanding. So after this I would yet go to see them ring, but would not go any farther than the steeple-door; but then it came into my head, "How if the steeple itself should fall?" And this thought (it may, for aught I know, when I stood and looked on) did continually so shake my mind, that I durst not stand at the steeple-door any longer, but was forced to flee, for fear the steeple should fall upon my head.' Frequently the mere conception of a sin became for him a temptation so involuntary and so strong, that he felt upon him the sharp claw of the devil. The fixed idea swelled in his head like a painful abscess, full of sensitiveness and of his life's blood. 'Now no sin would serve but that: if it were to be committed by speaking of such a word, then I have been as if my mouth would have spoken that word whether I would or no; and in so strong a measure was the temptation upon me, that often I have been ready to clap my hands under my chin, to hold my mouth from opening; at other times, to leap with my head downward into some muckhill hole, to keep my mouth from speaking.' Later, in the middle of a sermon which he was preaching, he was assailed by blasphemous thoughts: the word came to his lips, and all his power of resistance was barely able to restrain the muscle excited by the tyrannous brain.

Once the minister of the parish was preaching against the sin of dancing, oaths, and games, when he was struck with the idea that the sermon was for him, and returned home full of trouble. But he ate; his stomach being charged, discharged his brain, and his remorse was dispersed. Like a true child, entirely absorbed by the emotion of the moment, he was transported, jumped out, and ran to the sports. He had thrown his ball, and was about to begin again, when a voice from heaven suddenly pierced his soul. '"Wilt thou leave thy sins and go to heaven, or have thy sins and go to hell?" At this I was put to an exceeding maze; wherefore, leaving my cat upon the ground, I looked up to heaven, and was as if I had with the eyes of my understanding, seen the Lord Jesus look down upon me, as being very hotly displeased with me, and as if He did severely threaten me with some grievous punishment for these and other ungodly practices.' Suddenly reflecting that his sins were very great, and that he would certainly be damned whatever he did, he resolved to enjoy himself in the meantime, and to sin as much as he could in his life. He took up his ball again, recommenced the game with ardour, and swore louder and oftener than ever. A month afterwards, being reproved by a woman, 'I was silenced, and put to secret shame, and that too, as I thought, before the God of heaven: wherefore, while I stood there, hanging down my head, I wished that I might be a little child again, and that my father might learn me to speak without this wicked way of swearing; for, thought I, I am so accustomed to it, that it is in vain to think of a reformation, for that could never be. But how it came to pass I know not, I did from this time forward so leave my swearing, that it was a great wonder to myself to observe it; and whereas before I knew not how to speak unless I put an oath before, and another behind, to make my words have authority, now I could without it speak better, and with more pleasantness, than ever I could before.' These sudden alternations, these vehement resolutions, this unlooked-for renewing of heart, are the products of an involuntary and impassioned imagination, which by its hallucinations, its mastery, its fixed ideas, its mad ideas, prepares the way for a poet, and announces one inspired.

In him circumstances develop character; his kind of life develops his kind of mind. He was born in the lowest and most despised rank, a tinker's son, himself a wandering tinker, with a wife as poor as himself, so that they had not a spoon or a dish between them. He had been taught in childhood to read and write, but he had since 'almost wholly lost what he had learned.' Education draws out and disciplines a man; fills him with varied and rational ideas; prevents him from sinking into monomania or being excited by transport; gives him determinate thoughts instead of eccentric fancies, pliable opinions for fixed convictions; replaces impetuous images by calm reasonings, sudden resolves by the results of reflection; furnishes us with the wisdom and ideas of others; gives us conscience and self-command. Suppress this reason and this discipline, and consider the poor working man at his work; his head works while his hands work, not ably, with methods acquired from any logic he might have mustered, but with dark emotions, beneath a disorderly flow of confused images. Morning and evening, the hammer which he uses in his trade, drives in with its deafening sounds the same thought perpetually returning and self-communing. A troubled, obstinate vision floats before him in the brightness of the hammered and quivering metal. In the red furnace where the iron is bubbling, in the clang of the hammered brass, in the black corners where the damp shadow

creeps he sees the flame and darkness of hell, and the rattling of eternal chains. Next day he sees the same image, the day after, the whole week, month, year. His brow wrinkles, his eyes grow sad, and his wife hears him groan in the night-time. She remembers that she has two volumes in an old bag, *The Plain Man's Pathway to Heaven* and *The Practice of Piety*; she spells them out to console him; and the impressive thoughtfulness, already sublime, made more so by the slowness with which it is read, sinks like an oracle into his subdued faith. The braziers of the devils—the golden harps of heaven—the bleeding Christ on the cross,—each of these deep-rooted ideas sprouts poisonously or wholesomely in his diseased brain, spreads, pushes out and springs higher with a ramification of fresh visions, so crowded, that in his encumbered mind he has no further place nor air for more conceptions. Will he rest when he sets forth in the winter on his tramp? During his long solitary wanderings, over wild heaths, in cursed and haunted bogs, always abandoned to his own thoughts, the inevitable idea pursues him. These neglected roads where he sticks in the mud, these sluggish rivers which he crosses on the cranky ferry-boat, these threatening whispers of the woods at night, where in perilous places the livid moon shadows out ambushed forms,—all that he sees and hears falls into an involuntary poem around the one absorbing idea; thus it changes into a vast body of sensible legends, and multiplies its power as it multiplies its details. Having become a dissenter, Bunyan is shut up for twelve years, having no other amusement but the *Book of Martyrs* and the Bible, in one of those infectious prisons where the Puritans rotted under the Restoration. There he is, still alone, thrown back upon himself by the monotony of his dungeon, besieged by the terrors of the Old Testament, by the vengeful outpourings or denunciations of the prophets, by the thunder-striking words of Paul, by the spectacle of trances and of martyrs, face to face with God, now in despair, now consoled, troubled with involuntary images and unlooked-for emotions, seeing alternately devil and angels, the actor and the witness of an internal drama whose vicissitudes he is able to relate. He writes them: it is his book. You see now the condition of this inflamed brain. Poor in ideas, full of images, given up to a fixed and single thought, plunged into this thought by his mechanical pursuit, by his prison and his readings, by his knowledge and his ignorance, circumstances, like nature, make him a visionary and an artist, furnish him with supernatural impressions and sensible images, teaching him the history of grace and the means of expressing it.

⟨. . .⟩ under his simplicity you will find power, and in his puerility the vision. These allegories are hallucinations as clear, complete, and sound as ordinary perceptions. No one but Spenser is so lucid. Imaginary objects rise of themselves within him. He has no trouble in calling them up or forming them. They agree in all their details with all the details of the precept which they represent, as a pliant veil fits the body which it covers. He distinguishes and arranges all the parts of the landscape—here the river, on the right the castle, a flag on its left turret, the setting sun three feet lower, an oval cloud in the front part of the sky—with the preciseness of a carpenter. We fancy in reading him that we are looking at the old maps of the time, in which the striking features of the angular cities are marked on the copperplate by a tool as certain as a pair of compasses. Dialogues flow from his pen as in a dream. He does not seem to be thinking; we should even say that he was not himself there. Events and speeches seem to grow and dispose themselves within him, independently of his will. Nothing, as a rule, is colder than the characters in an allegory; his are living. Looking upon these details, so small and familiar, illusion gains upon us. Giant Despair, a simple abstraction, becomes as real in his hands as an English gaoler or farmer. He is heard talking by night in bed with his wife Diffidence, who gives him good advice, because here, as in other households, the strong and brutal animal is the least cunning of the two:—

> Then she counselled him that when he arose in the morning he should (take the two prisoners and) beat them without mercy. So when he arose, he getteth him a grievous Crab-tree Cudgel, and goes down into the Dungeon to them, and there first falls to rating of them as if they were dogs, although they gave him never a word of distaste. Then he falls upon them, and beats them fearfully, in such sort, that they were not able to help themselves, or to turn them upon the floor.

This stick, chosen with a forester's experience, this instinct of rating first and storming to get oneself into trim for knocking down, are traits which attest the sincerity of the narrator, and succeed in persuading the reader. Bunyan has the freedom, the tone, the ease, and the clearness of Homer; he is as close to Homer as an Anabaptist tinker could be to an heroic singer, a creator of gods.

I err; he is nearer. Before the sentiment of the sublime, inequalities are levelled. The depth of emotion raises peasant and poet to the same eminence; and here also, allegory stands the peasant in stead. It alone, in the absence of ecstasy, can paint heaven; for it does not pretend to paint it: expressing it by a figure, it declares it invisible, as a glowing sun at which we cannot look full, and whose image we observe in a mirror or a stream. The ineffable world thus retains all its mystery; warned by the allegory, we imagine splendours beyond all which it presents to us; we feel behind the beauties which are opened to us, the infinite which is concealed; and the ideal city, vanishing as soon as it appears, ceases to resemble the big Whitehall imagined for Jehovah by Milton.

GEORGE EDWARD WOODBERRY
"Three Men of Piety: I. Bunyan"
Studies in Letters and Life
1890, pp. 209–19

The word genius is often used to conceal a puzzle which the critic, through defects of analytic power or sympathetic insight, is unable to solve; but perhaps this short and easy method was never more feebly resorted to than when a writer, with a strong prejudice in favor of sweetness and light, described Bunyan as a "Philistine of genius." In this designation there is much darkness and some acerbity. The wonderful thing about this man was not so much his gifts as the strange combination of them. There must be, of course, something extraordinary in any common man who becomes a leader in the higher life of the race. The history of the Church, however, is starred with the names of the ignorant and the humble who, since the fishermen were called from their nets by Galilee, have been chosen to be shepherds of the flock and evangelists of the faith. Bunyan was visited with the experience of Protestant Christendom, of which the successive terms are an outraged conscience, an offended God, and a miraculous pardon, and when he came to his peace he spread the glad news, acceptably to the pious, and convincingly to the impenitent; but tens of thousands of Christian lands have

passed through that same strait gate, and hundreds of them have discovered that they possessed the gift of tongues. Had Bunyan done no more his sermons would have turned to yellow dust long ago, and his memory would be treasured only by a sect, for, eloquent as he was, he was not one of the missionaries who are world-famous. He wrote a book; and it turned out that this book of an uneducated man was a great literary classic. Had he written an epic it would have seemed less marvelous, because there is a popular superstitition that nature makes poets, but in prose does not enter into competition with the common school. Bunyan wrote verses, it is true, and the man who set the delectable mountains on the rim of earth had the magical sight; but just as surely his doggerel shows that he had not the singing voice. He was a master of prose, and wrote a book that neighbors the Bible in our religious homes.

Two things are, of course, indispensable to a boy of genius,—imagination and the gift of expression. Now Bunyan was fond of representing himself as very wicked in youth; and so he was, from his own point of view. The worst he can say for himself is, that he lied and swore, without malice or injury to others, but because he had a talent for tales and oaths. It is not trifling to remark that his powers of invention and forcible Saxon speech appear to have found their first channel in this sort of mental activity. The possible openings for the development of genius in the tinker's cottage at Bedford were few. It is plain that the mind of the young man was one of intense life, and, in the lack of guidance and knowledge, wandered at random or turned to feed upon itself. The only intellectual or moral ideas that came to him were conveyed from the Bible, mostly through the medium of the parish church in the years of the Puritan ascendency. The commonplace that the Bible affords a good education, especially on the imaginative and moral sides, is true, and the theology that attaches to it has developed strong intellects; it was, in the end, the total book-culture of Bunyan,—all that he knew of that vast and various world. But in the primary classes it is not a simple text-book of life, especially for a boy of genius who is all sense, all spirit. Bunyan in after years did not regret his first lessons; he preached that children should be taught the terrors of the law. Certainly his own mind laid hold of the easily apprehended images of threatened vengeance, and was filled with vague alarm and driven to a torturing scrutiny of his own spirit. The experience of conversion repeats in the individual the religious history of the race in the same order in which it is developed in the evolution of Biblical thought itself, and Bunyan's case was not substantially different from that of others, Puritan or Catholic, to whom there is no Calvary without a Sinai. The peculiarity lay in the soil into which this fiery seed was sown. His imagination ceased its childish fabling and became visionary; he saw, as the eye sometimes will, his mind-pictures, and this the more readily because his uneducated mind was accustomed to move through concrete ideas, and hence would be characterized by a high visualizing power. That this was a marked trait of his mental habit is shown by the fact that all his stories about himself are localized in a distinctly remembered place.

At this stage his mind approached the danger-line of religious madness: his descriptions of his moods, of his despairs, and of his struggles with fancies, whose importance to his intellectual life arose from the fewness of his ideas and the limited field of their play, show that he had no power over his thoughts, that he had not learned to use his will in thinking. This objectivity of his religious experience and his powerlessness before it, which have been recorded of other intense lives likewise, gave him a strong sense of the reality of spiritual things; and when he at last had laid his doubts and come into the calm, he kept this conviction to such a degree that earthly matters, even when religion was largely interested in politics, seemed of no consequence: this world was the dream, and the next world the truth. To our days the account of this conversion seems to indicate a lack of sanity, a spirit touched with the fever that ends in fanaticism; but we may be sure that to his hearers there was nothing incredible in it, nothing that could not be paralleled out of what they had known in themsleves or heard from their neighbors. So, early in life, the plot of his career was brought to its crisis. In this faith in the reality of eternal things his mind reached its growth, and afterward knew no change.

But with this sure hold on the spirit and its high concerns there went a perfect realism. Bunyan was the opposite of a mystic. His common sense in his sermons of advice is extraordinarily close-packed and hard, and exhibits acute observation of the ways of human nature in practical life. He wrote once what was almost a novel, a history of one Mr. Badman, which is probably truer to contemporary life than the adventures of Jonathan Wild in the next century. If he did not weaken his eyesight over books, he sharpened it on men and women. All his volumes abound with anecdotes and incidents which he had evidently seen in the town streets or by the roadside, and with phrases and proverbial sayings close to the soil. Not the least agreeable of the signs of this realism, this sight for the bare fact in sense alone, are those descriptions of the country, of the birds, and flowers, and fields, and the simple cheerfulness of them to the country-born boy, which strew his pages from cover to cover. So, when he came to write his great book, he united in a perfectly natural way, and without forethought, the reality of a journey on earth with that of the search for heaven. The success with which, in a literary work, truth is fused with fact, is a measure of genius. It is, perhaps, more striking in this case because the work is an allegory, which is usually so drearily pale a kind of composition. The characters and action of the *Pilgrim's Progress*, on the contrary, are a transcript of life, so vivid that it cannot wear out. It is not more realistic, however, than other portions of Bunyan's voluminous writings, in which one may get an idea of English provinicial character of high historical value and human interest. How close, how truthful to his surroundings he was as a literary workman, is brought home with great force, though perhaps unconsciously, by the view which his biography gives of Bedford things and people.

From it one may reconstruct the religious state of the poor people of the Lincoln diocese in Bunyan's time, and bring very near the look of the lowly life which was the original soil of English dissent and the field of the tinker-preacher's labors. In reading terse extracts from the old documents—"short and simple annals of the poor," truly—of prayers in the barn and fines in the court-house, of levies on workmen's tools and old women's chattels, of these families of "the meanest sort," as the Bishop's schedule calls them, whose petty share of poverty was confiscated for the security of a Stuart throne and an Anglican prayer-book,—in reading of these things, a chapter of the history of the English people comes out which has been too closely written over with the wit and frolic of Charles's court; and the query as to what became of the Commonwealth when Cromwell died does not seem so wholly unanswerable as the silence of standard history on the point would indicate.

After all, one is almost inclined to say that no man ever owed more than Bunyan to his limitations. Within his bounds, he used all his spiritual and earthly experience, and, aided by a native gift of imagination and of fluency in the people's speech, blended them, and poured the full fountain of his life through his books. Had his youth included other powerful elements of emotion and knowledge besides his conversion, had theology, or learning, or wider duties removed him somewhat more from the life of his neighbors and friends and the folk of the diocese, of which he was jestingly called the "bishop," he might have found so complete self-expression a more difficult task. As it was, he told all he had to tell,—told the highest truth in the commonest words and made it current. It is curious to observe that he exhibits no consciousness that he is writing a great work; he speaks of a rush of thought and fancy, and an attractiveness in the subject, but he does not seem to think that he is doing more than adding another to the two-score publications he has already sent out. It is noticeable, too, that he did not meditate upon it for years beforehand, nor spend more than a few months in its composition. Some passages were added at a later time, but as a whole it was a spontaneous and rapid composition. The reason is that he was ripe for it. Without knowing it, he had been working up to this crowning book, both in thought, treatment, and style, through many years of sincere and straightforward, face-to-face conversation with men and women whom he was endeavoring to guide in the way which he had traveled. *Pilgrim's Progress* has been called the last book that was written without the fear of the reviewer; it is of more consequence that it is one of the few works that have been composed without ambition.

Bunyan's memory is singularly agreeable. Personally he was free from the defects of assumption, dogmatism, and spiritual pride, which entered largely into the religious character of his epoch, and his sensitive conscience seems to have kept him humble after he had won a name. The two great elements of his work—the homely quality and the Christian quality—were deep-seated in his nature, and give him charm. In an age of sectaries he was not a narrow bigot, and did not stickle for meaningless things; and in a time of political strife, growing out of religious differences, and though himself a sufferer by twelve years' imprisonment in early manhood, he did not confuse heaven with any fantastic monarchy or commonwealth of Christ in London, nor show any rancor or revengeful spirit as a subject. It is worth remembering that out of Puritanism, which is regarded as a narrow creed and life, came the only book since the Reformation which has been acceptable to the whole of Christendom, and is still regarded as the substantial truth of the Christian life in all the churches that preach it under any creed of orthodoxy. The life of the man who could evolve such a story must have been very simply typical of the Christian life itself. "A Philistine of genius"—is there no light nor sweetness in this?

EDWARD DOWDEN
From "John Bunyan"
Puritan and Anglican
1901, pp. 232–36, 253–69

I

To consider Bunyan merely as a representative of English Puritanism or Nonconformity in the second half of the seventeenth century would be to do an injustice to his genius and his work. Had he interpreted only what was peculiar to a special period and a particular phase of religious thought and feeling, what he has written might still be valuable as a document for historical students, but it could not be a living power with successive generations of readers of every class and in almost every region of the globe. What gives vitality to the *Pilgrim's Progress* is not its Puritanism as such, but rather its Christian spirit and more than this its profound humanity. Yet the *Pilgrim's Progress* is a characteristic product of Puritan faith and feeling; and to bring this fact home to ourselves we have only to imagine what Bunyan would have been if all his life had been passed as that of a member of the Anglican communion; or, rather, we have to put the question to ourselves—"Would an Anglican Bunyan have been possible?" If we desire to see a typical representative of Anglican piety in Bunyan's century we may find such a representative in George Herbert. It is a beautiful type of religious temper, ardent within appointed bounds, spiritual, and finding in forms and ceremonies an aid to spiritual life, exalted without extravagance, regardful not only of holiness but of the visible beauty of holiness, delicate, pure, not driven to passionate extremes, not the prey of intolerable terrors and blissful raptures; a type of piety as it lives and moves in an organised and cultivated community, with a high tradition, and making use of all those adjuncts to the inward life which are afforded by habit and rite and emblem, those regular means of relieving and systematising the emotions, those calculated channels and aqueducts which irrigate and refresh the soul. Gracious flower in the garden of the Master, we are not unmindful of its comeliness or its fragrance.

In such a community there is reasonable scope for the play of individual feeling; yet individual feeling is directed and controlled by a general method and order. In the smaller religious communities a public opinion exists, which is stricter in reference to conduct, and may even result in a close and tyrannous surveillance; but in the drama of the private passions of religion there is often an intenser energy; religion is less of a complex, organised institution, and more of a personal unique experience; the relations of the soul to God are less determined in appointed ways; hence wilder aberrations become possible; but also there may be an incandescence of the inward life, unallayed in its glow, a flame of devout passion which touches heights and depths beyond what can be safely approached in forms suited for the general and habitual uses of religion. In a great and comprehensive community a place is found for such nobly intemperate souls in some special Order, which converts the *enfant perdu* of piety into the leader of a forlorn hope.

All that is best and most characteristic in Bunyan's writings proceeds from that inward drama, in which the actors were three—God, Satan, and a solitary human soul. If external influences from events or men affected his spirit, they came as nuncios or messengers from God or from the Evil One. Institutions, churches, ordinances, rites, ceremonies, could help him little, or not at all. The journey from the City of Destruction to the Celestial City must be undertaken on a special summons by each man for himself alone; if a companion join him on the way, it lightens the trials of the road; but of the companions each one is an individual pilgrim, who has started on a great personal adventure, and who as he enters the dark river must undergo his particular experiences of hope or fear. Yet through what is most personal in each of us we come upon the common soul; let any man record faithfully his most private experiences in any of the great affairs of life, and his words awaken in other souls innumerable echoes; the deepest community is found not in institutions, or corporations, or Churches, but in the secrets of the solitary heart. And because Bunyan, rich as his nature was in our common humanity, put into his writings the central facts of his personal life, his books are not for himself alone, but for all men of like passions, who must each tread for himself the same arduous way.

Must tread the same way; but not necessarily in the same manner. Bunyan's religious history, recorded in his wonderful autobiography *Grace Abounding to the Chief of Sinners*, may be repeated age after age in its essentials, for it is the history of a soul struggling from darkness to light, from confusion to clearness, from self-division to unity, from weakness to strength, from wretchedness to peace and joy; but if truths of the seventeenth century remain truths in the nineteenth, they operate under different conditions; they mingle with new elements in our minds; they require new adjustments; they must be translated into modern speech. And who will say that in the religious passion of an Englishman of the mid-years of the seventeenth century the parallax of truth was not considerable? who will assert that gross mists arising from his own brain did not cloud and distort the light? If the deep realities of Puritanism remain—its seriousness, its ardour, its plea for the loins girt and the lamp lit—yet its exact modes of thought and feeling, which did their work and have been replaced by others, can no more be revived than its exact forms of speech. *Grace Abounding* may truly be described as an awakening book, and the moment we are really awake we perceive that if we are to attempt a solution of the problems and a conquest of the difficulties which beset us, we must apply ourselves to the task with Bunyan's resolution indeed, but not with Bunyan's intelligence.

The writings of John Bunyan fill some thousands of large and closely printed pages. The strength of his heart and mind are adequately felt in four works—his religious autobiography, *Grace Abounding*, the *Pilgrim's Progress*, the *Holy War*, and the *Life and Death of Mr Badman*. Among these four there is a marked inequality; the *Holy War* is an allegory rather manufactured,—manufactured with admirable skill—than inspired; the *Life and Death of Mr Badman* is a religious tract of portentous size put into the form of a narrative. These are remarkable books; but the one is an ingenious construction; the other is a study of the vices of middle class English life in Bunyan's day, turned to purposes of warning and edification. Neither of them is an immediate living experience; neither of them is an inspired vision. But these are the words that describe aright the other two books which form the most vital part of Bunyan's work. *Grace Abounding* is a fragment of life; we touch, in reading it, a quivering human heart; the *Pilgrim's Progress* is a vision of a man of genius, the *Divina Commedia* of Puritanism.

III

⟨. . .⟩ The *Pilgrim's Progress* is a gallery of portraits, admirably discriminated, and as convincing in their self-verification as those of Holbein. His personages live for us as few figures outside the drama of Shakespeare live. They are not, like the humourists of Ben Jonson's plays, constructed by heaping a load of observations on a series of ethical abstractions; they are of a reasonable soul and human flesh subsisting. We are on terms of intimate acquaintance with each of them; with Talkative, the son of one Say-well, who dwelt in Prating-row,—wherever the notional apprehension of things is taken for the real apprehension, there is that discoursing wit to-day; with By-ends, always zealous when a good cause goes in silver slippers, a gentleman of excellent quality, though his grandfather was but a waterman, looking one way and rowing another;

with that brisk lad Ignorance, who came into the path by a little crooked lane leading from the country of Conceit; there is a narrow gate in science and in art as well as in religion, which the kinsfolk of Bunyan's Ignorance decline to enter; with Mrs Lightmind, who yesterday at Madam Wanton's was as merry as the maids—surely she is cousin to the brothers Jolly and Griggish, who came to an ill fate at the hands of my Lord Willbewill, and so ended their ticking and toying with my Lord's daughters; with Mr Brisk, who, since Mercy was of a fair countenance and therefore the more alluring, offered her his love, but was dashed when she explained that her needlework was meant to clothe the naked, and decided on reconsideration that she was indeed a pretty lass, but troubled with ill conditions; with that old pilgrim Father Honest, a cock of the right kind, for he had said the truth; with Mr Fearing, one of the most troublesome of pilgrims, a chicken-hearted man, yet having the root of the matter in him, and who at last almost dryshod crossed the river, when it was at its lowest ebb; with Mr Feeble-mind, who must needs be carried up the Hill Difficulty by one of the Interpreter's servants, yet bravely resolved to run when he could, to go when he could not run, and to creep when he could not go; with Mr Ready-to-halt, who, despite the crutch, footed it well in view of the dead giant's head, hand in hand with Despondency's daughter Much-afraid, both answering the music handsomely; with Madam Bubble, that tall comely dame, somewhat swarthy of complexion, speaking very smoothly, and giving you a smile at the end of a sentence, while still she kept fingering her money as if it were her heart's delight; with Mr Valiant-for-truth, Mr Standfast, who crossing the river in a great calm, like the saintly John Wesley, when he was half-way in, stood for a while and talked to his companions; with the dozen enlightened jurymen of Vanity-Fair, and many another. Yet these are but examples from the drawings of the Holbein of spiritual England.

One book of Bunyan's is, indeed, a detailed study of English middle-class life and of its vulgar vices. Recent criticism has assigned to *The Life and Death of Mr Badman* a higher place in literature than it deserves; but it presents one side of its author's mind more fully than any other of his writings. Having published the first part of the *Pilgrim's Progress*, and enjoyed the surprise of its extraordinary success, Bunyan seems to have thought of presenting a counterpart in the story of one who had travelled another road than that of Christian, the road leading not to the Celestial City, but to the gates of hell. The book is not a vision or a dream; it lacks the beautiful ideality of the *Pilgrim's Progress*, which has made that allegory of universal interest. It has, on the other hand, something of Hogarth's naturalism and something of Hogarth's enforcement of morality by means of the tomahawk; it is the tale of an Idle Apprentice; it is a bourgeois Rake's Progress. The narrative, thrown into the form of dailogue, is interrupted by discourses on the several species of sin practised by that rascally provincial tradesman, the hero, with many examples drawn from real life of God's judgments against sinners.

The book had its origin not in Bunyan's personal experiences, idealised and purified by the imagination, but in his observations of the evil that lay around him. Even as a child Badman was a highly promising pupil of the destroyer—addicted to lying, a pilferer, abandoned (like young Richard Baxter) to the joy of robbing orchards, a blackmouthed wretch who cursed and swore, a boy who could not endure the Lord's Day, swarming, indeed, with sins as a beggar is with vermin. When his good father would rebuke him, what would young Badman do but stand gloating, hanging down his head in a sullen pouching manner, while he secretly wished for the old man's death? As an apprentice he read beastly romances and books full of ribaldry, slept in church, or stared at pretty faces and whispered and giggled during sermon, being thus grown to a prodigious height of wickedness. His knavish fingers found their way to his master's cash-box, and soon his first apprenticeship closed disgracefully in flight. After a second apprenticeship, during which a base-born child was laid to his charge, Badman set up in business, but through dissipation, high-living, idleness, and evil company quickly came to the end of the money obtained from his over-indulgent father. To retrieve his fortunes he sought out a maid who had a good portion, and as she was godly, he made religion his stalking-horse; but after marriage he hanged his religion upon the hedge, oppressed his unhappy wife, squandered her coin upon his drabs, and towards morning would come home as drunk as a swine. He reached a yet lower depth of degradation, when he turned informer, obtaining a wretched hire by betrayal to the authorities of the nonconformist religious assemblies. Running up credit and paying five shillings in the pound—the neatest way of thieving—Badman in time gained hatfuls of money. He knew all tricks of the trade—the art of deceitful weights and measures, that of mingling commodities so that what was bad might go off, and he was skilled in misreckoning men in their accounts. So he goes, with hardly an interruption, from bad to worse. During a dangerous fit of sickness, indeed, consequent on the breaking of his leg in a drunken bout, he thought of death and hell-fire, and altered his carriage to his wife, who was now his duck and dear; but his repentance was worth no more than the howling of a dog. The broken-hearted wife dies, and Badman is tricked into marriage with a woman as wicked as himself. At last dropsy and consumption seize their victim; he lies upon his bed given up to hardness and stupidity of spirit. "Pray how was he," asks Attentive, "at his death? was death strong upon him? or did he die with ease, quietly?" The last and severest earthly judgment of God is not an agony of remorse; it is apathy. He died "as quietly as a lamb." And with this terrible word Bunyan's book concludes.

Such a narrative as this could not connect itself with work of an order so different as the *Pilgrim's Progress*. The two inventions move on different planes. The *Pilgrim's Progress* is the poetry of Bunyan's soul; the *Life and Death of Mr Badman* is the prose of his moral observation of the world. Successive generations may in general be trusted to preserve the heirlooms of literature. *Mr Badman* is not one of these; but it deserves the attention of a student of Bunyan, and the attention of a student of Bunyan's age.

IV

The great allegories of human life commonly make choice between two modes of representation; they describe life as a journey or they describe life as a warfare. The *Divine Comedy* is a journey through the realms of eternal life and death; the *Vision of Piers Plowman* is a pilgrimage in search of the highest good; the *Faerie Queene* is a series of knightly crusades against the powers of evil. In his two allegories Bunyan has presented both conceptions; the *Pilgrim's Progress* is a journey from the City of Destruction to the Celestial City; the *Holy War* tells of the assault upon the town of Mansoul by Diabolus, his conquest by fraud and force, the recapture of the town for Shaddai, its lawful possessor, by Prince Emmanuel, its invasion and partial ruin by the enemy, and the final victory of righteousness.

In one respect, and in that alone, can Bunyan's later

allegory the *Holy War* be said to surpass the *Pilgrim's Progress*—it is more ingenious in the adaptation of its details. The design was not fortunate; there is no central personage having the parts and passions of a man; the town, with its walls, and gates, and citadel, is an inanimate abstraction—a generalisation of humanity, not a living and breathing human creature. The multitude of its inhabitants, the multitude of their foes and of their friends, parcel out the powers of good and evil in the soul into fragments and atoms. No single figure interests us supremely; not one lives in the popular memory. We hardly feel on closer terms of familiarity with Captain Credence, or Captain Goodhope, or Captain Patience, than with the five points of Calvinistic controversy. In the *Pilgrim's Progress* womanhood is presented side by side with manhood; even in the first Part gracious female forms appear; in the *Holy War* counsellors and warriors leave no place for women; half of our human society is unrepresented. The pilgrimage of Christian is an individual experience idealised in art; it is the *Wahrheit und Dichtung* of Bunyan's spiritual life; the allegory of Mansoul is a piece of universal history; it is the work of Bunyan the preacher, who, having taken his side in the warfare of good and evil, was interested in a great cause. But the epic of a cause requires as its representative a champion exposed to the vicissitudes of fortune and in the end falling or triumphant. Bunyan's Emmanuel is too much of a *deus ex machina*; his beleaguered city is an abstraction of humanity; the epic is one without a hero. Bunyan's ingenuity in detail astonishes and fatigues the reader; poetry is replaced by wit in the form of allegory. One episode, indeed, rises to the height of Bunyan's nobler work, but it is difficult to find a second of equal merit. The town of Mansoul has been conquered by Emmanuel, who has not yet made his entrance and remains in the fields. The guilty inhabitants, freed from the tyranny of their oppressors, are still uncertain of the temper of their deliverer. The prisoners, with ropes about their necks, go forth to stand before the Prince; trembling and amazed they hear his doom of mercy; "the grace, the benefit, the pardon, was sudden, glorious, and so big that they were not able, without staggering, to stand up under it." The joy of Bunyan's own heart, when he could have spoken of God's love and mercy to the very crows sitting on the furrows, returned upon him: "They went down to the camp in black, but they came back to the town in white; they went down to the camp in ropes, they came back in chains of gold; they went down to the camp in fetters, but came back with their steps enlarged under them; they went also to the camp looking for death, but they came back from thence with assurance of life; they went down to the camp with heavy hearts, but came back again with pipe and tabor playing before them. So, as soon as they were come to Eye-gate, the poor and tottering town of Mansoul adventured to give a shout; and they gave such a shout as made the captains in the Prince's army leap at the sound thereof." ⟨. . .⟩

Bunyan's biographer, Dr Brown, conjectured that the *Pilgrim's Progress* was begun not during his long imprisonment of twelve years in the county gaol of Bedford, but during a later and shorter imprisonment of 1675–76 in the town prison and toll-house on Bedford Bridge. Mr Thorpe's discovery of the warrant of 1674 confirmed Dr Brown's happy conjecture.[1] Bunyan was engaged upon another book—perhaps *The Strait Gate*—as he himself informs us, when he "fell suddenly into an allegory"; the vision seemed hourly to grow by virtue of its own vitality. When he had set down twenty things, twenty more were in his head; ideas and images rose into his consciousness "like sparks that from the coals of fire do fly;" lest they should distract him wholly from the book on which he

had deliberately resolved, he found that he must make a place for them, he must bestow them in a fit receptacle. The *Pilgrim's Progress*, he declares, was not written to instruct his neighbours but to gratify himself; that is to say, it was the work of a devout artist, like those mediæval craftsmen who carved a capital or illuminated a missal, and being such a work, done for his own contentment, with no laboured didactic purpose, it is the one book of Bunyan's which has delighted every generation, and edified, while it delighted, more than all the rest. Dr Brown supposes that the portion of the book written in prison closes where Christian and Hopeful part from the shepherds on the Delectable Mountains. At that point a break in the narrative is indicated—"So I awoke from my dream;" it is resumed with the words—"And I slept and dreamed again, and saw the same two pilgrims going down the mountains along the highway towards the city." Already from the top of an high hill called "Clear," the Celestial City was in view; dangers there were still to be encountered; but to have reached that high hill and to have seen something like the gate, and some of the glory of the place, was an attainment and an incentive. There Bunyan could pause.

The second part—the pilgrimage of Christiana—was written several years later. Another Christian on the same journey could only have repeated in essentials the adventures of the first with artificial variations, and the book must have been a feebler version of the original narrative. But women and children desire the Celestial City as well as men. It has been suggested that in Christiana we have an idealised portrait of Bunyan's second wife, Elizabeth, who in the Swan Chamber pleaded his cause before Sir Matthew Hale, while Mercy may perhaps have been created from memories of the wife of his youth. The second part is doubtless inferior to the first in its intensity and directness; it was less a record of Bunyan's personal experiences. The terrors of the way are softened; its consolations, if not more exquisite, are more freely distributed—"and one smiled, and another smiled, and they all smiled for joy that Christiana was become a pilgrim." There is no moment in the women's pilgrimage so dreadful as that when Christian in the Valley of the Shadow of Death took the voice of the wicked one, suggesting many grievous blasphemies, for his own utterance. Roaring giants armed with clubs are less appalling than the soft-footed and whispering fiend; and Great-heart is at hand, convoying his weak ones, a conductor sufficiently skilled in the art of decapitating giants or piercing them under the fifth rib.

Yet we could ill spare the second part of the *Pilgrim's Progress*. Mr Froude was surely in error when he called it a feeble reverberation of the first; on the contrary, it is the best of all after-pieces. And the manly tenderness of Bunyan's heart finds expression here as it does nowhere else. He honours Christiana for her courage; he leans lovingly over Mercy—a little tripping maid who followed God. Beelzebub shoots no arrows at the women as they stand knocking at the gates; it is bad enough that a dog (and a great one too) should make a heavy barking against them; while they knock the Master gives them a wonderful innocent smile. If the two ill-favoured ones cause them alarm, the Reliever is presently at hand. The Interpreter, with a "sweet-heart" and a "dear-heart" to encourage Mercy, shows them things easy to understand, His garden where was great variety of flowers, the robin with a spider in his mouth, the hen walking in a fourfold method towards her chickens—a simplified text of an Evangelical Æsop's fables. When arrayed in fine linen, white and clean, the women, fair as the moon, had more than joy in their beautiful garments; they seemed to be a terror one to the other, for in their marvellous humility "they could not see that glory each on herself which they could see in each other." They are comforted in departing with a bottle of wine, some parched corn, together with a couple of pomegranates—delightful fare for pilgrims. Before descending to the Valley of Humiliation they hear the birds singing their curious melodious notes, which had been learnt, as might happen with pious birds, from Sternhold's version of the Psalms. The valley, beautified with lilies, was for them as fruitful a place as any the crow flies over, and there it was that they espied the fresh-favoured shepherd-boy feeding his father's sheep, who sang of the blessedness of a lowly spirit, and wore more of that herb called heart's-ease in his bosom than he that is clad in silk and velvet. Even in going through the Valley of the Shadow they had daylight. They heard the celebration of their sex from the lips of the good Gaius; they had a medical adviser as well as a beloved spiritual conductor; they had the happiness of being interested in several weddings; and instead of lying in the dungeon, nasty and stinking, of Despair, they enjoyed a pious dance around the giant's head; the shepherds decorated them with such bracelets and earrings as Delectable Mountains afford; and it was the men of Bunyan's earlier pilgrimage—so courteous is he—not the adorned women, of the later, who were taken in the flatterer's net. The token sent to Christiana that she should make haste to cross the river was an arrow with a point sharpened with love; and even Despondency's daughter, Much-afraid, went through the waters singing—singing of some incomprehensible consolation, for none on the hither side could comprehend what she said.

Yet the dangers of the way are many and great. Until Paradise is entered wary walking must be the pilgrim's rule. From the moment when Christian abandons the doomed city to the moment when he touches the heavenward riverbank, he is exposed to peril; at every point of the road vigilance is needed; the wayfarer's loins must be ever girt; he must at every instant be addressed to quit him like a man. At the first step Christian is plunged into the Slough of Despond; he escapes from it only to be sent astray by Mr Worldly-wiseman and to endure the terrors of the mount; the refreshment at the Interpreter's house is followed by the ascent of the Hill Difficulty, where in an arbour the pilgrim slumbers and lets his roll fall from his hand; the lions, whose chains are unseen, test his courage as he approaches the House Beautiful; thence he descends into the valley where he encounters Apollyon; the Valley of Humiliation leads to the more dreadful Valley of the Shadow of Death, having on the right hand a very deep ditch and on the left a dangerous quag, where in the darkness Christian hears doleful voices and mysterious rushings to and fro; even the second part of the valley is full of perils, being set with snares, traps, gins, and nets, and abounding in deep holes and desperate shelvings; after the valley comes the wilderness; and after the wilderness the town of Vanity-Fair, where one pilgrim endures the cage and the other seals his witnessing with a martyr's death; escaped from Vanity-Fair, Christian enters into discourse with By-ends, and is tempted by Demas to explore the fatal silver-mine; a little farther on is By-path meadow—"one temptation," comments the marginal note, "does make way for another"—where, sleeping, the wanderers fall into the hands of Giant Despair. Even from the Delectable Mountains terrible things are viewed, men dashed to pieces at the bottom of the hill Error; men, seen from the hill Caution,

walking up and down among the tombs, and stumbling because they are blind; and, yet more awful, the door in the side of an hill, by-way to hell that hypocrites go in at. The Celestial City is now visible through a perspective-glass, but it is with warnings in their ears that Christian and Hopeful part from the shepherds; of a sudden they are snared by the Flatterer's net; delivered and scourged by the Shining One, they go for a while softly along the right way, but presently Atheist is at their side, and when he turns from them they have reached the Inchanted ground; the pious converse by which they resist the invasion of sleep is interrupted by the volubility of young Ignorance; at length they have arrived at the country of Beulah, where every day the flowers appear in the earth and the voice of the turtle is heard in the land. But still the river lies before them, a river that is very deep; they set foot in the water; all the waves and billows go over Christian's head, and he is troubled with apparitions of hobgoblins and evil spirits. Only when the heavenly shore is attained are all dangers at an end; the City, indeed, is set upon an hill, but up that hill the pilgrims go with ease, for they have left behind them their mortal garments, and the rest is glorious joy which neither tongue nor pen can express. Yet the final word of Bunyan is one of solemn warning. Ignorance, who had crossed the river in the boat of one Vain Hope, a ferryman, finds no entrance into the golden city; he is bound hand and foot, and thrust through a door that is in the side of the hill: "Then saw I that there is a way to Hell even from the gates of Heaven, as well as from the City of Destruction. So I awoke, and behold it was a dream."

A dream of terrors, but also of consolations, hope, and joy; more than a dream, the veritable history of a human soul, lifted into a higher reality by the power of imagination. Bunyan's material was given to him by a series of agonising personal experiences, which seemed at times to border on insanity, and by a great deliverance wrought in his own heart.[2] Nothing is more remarkable than the mastery with which his imagination controls and pacifies and purifies his memories of pain and rapture; the humblest realities coalesce with spiritual passions that belong to eternity as much as to time. Every thing verifies itself as actual, yet the total effect is ideal. And thus the book acquired an universal import, and may serve as a manual of the inner life even for persons whom Bunyan, with his Puritan theology, would have classed among heathen men and infidels. All his powers co-operated harmoniously in creating this book—his religious ardour, his human tenderness, his sense of beauty, nourished by the Scriptures, his strong common sense, even his gift of humour. Through his deep seriousness play the lighter faculties. The whole man presses into this small volume. The purport of what he writes in its most general significance is no other than that exhortation of all great spiritual teachers—to live for what is best and highest and most real, and to live for these with the loins girt and the lamp lit—"Viriliter age, exspectans Dominum" *quit ye like men.*

Notes

1. See Mr. Thorpe's article "How I Found the Bunyan Warrant," *Gentleman's Magazine*, February, 1890.
2. Mr. Heath, in articles contributed to the *Contemporary Review*, October 1896 and July 1897, endeavours to trace much in Bunyan's designs in the *Pilgrim's Progress* and the *Holy War* to Anabaptist tradition and history.

JOHN DRYDEN

JOHN DRYDEN

1631–1700

John Dryden, poet, dramatist, and critic, was born on August 9, 1631, into a Puritan family at Aldwinkle, Northamptonshire, and was educated at Westminster School (1646–50) and at Trinity College, Cambridge (1650–54). Dryden inherited a small estate from his father, but supported himself mainly through his writing. His first major poem was the *Heroique Stanza's* (1658), which mourned the death of Cromwell; with the coming of the Restoration he switched allegiances and wrote *Astraea Redux* (1660) and *To His Sacred Majesty* (1661) in celebration of the king's return. Dryden also addressed poems to, among others, the Earl of Clarendon ("To My Lord Chancellor," 1662), and to Sir Robert Howard, a Royalist, whose sister Lady Elizabeth he married in 1663. Dryden's attempts at self-advancement through calculated choices of subject and flattering dedication provoked Samuel Johnson to remark that Dryden "no longer retains shame in himself, nor supposes it in his patrons"; Johnson nonetheless acknowledged his poetic excellence. Dryden's most ambitious early work, a long poem in quatrains entitled *Annus Mirabilis*, was published in 1667; it is a celebration of the kingdom's strength and prosperity. In the following year he became Poet Laureate, and in 1670 he was named Historiographer Royal.

From the Restoration until the 1680s most of Dryden's writing was for the theatre, for which he wrote comedies, rhymed heroic plays, and tragicomedies. Among numerous works special mention should be made of the comedies *Secret Love* (1667), *The Conquest of Granada* (in two parts, 1670), and *Marriage à la Mode* (1672), and of several plays written in a heroic style: *Tyrannick Love* (1669), *Aureng-Zebe* (1676), and *All for Love* (1678). All these plays reveal his considerable interest in political and philosophical matters. Dryden also wrote a great deal of criticism, mostly defending his own literary practices; his first major critical work was *Of Dramatick Poesie* (1668), which was followed by many other essays, published separately and as prefaces to his plays; all are models of English prose style.

In 1681 Dryden published *Absalom and Achitophel*, an immensely popular work which displayed his considerable talents as a satirist. The targets of this satire were Lord Shaftesbury and the Duke of Monmouth, who sought to block the accession to the throne of James, Duke of York; Dryden's portrayal of these two men turned public opinion against them. Dryden then entered into a rivalry with Thomas Shadwell, whom he satirized in *Mac Flecknoe* (1682) and in *The Second Part of Absalom and Achitophel* (1682), co-written with Nahum Tate. Dryden himself was burlesqued in *The Rehearsal* (1671), which had several authors, including the Duke of Buckingham and possibly Samuel Butler; in 1679 he was attacked and severely beaten, for unknown reasons.

Dryden turned to religious controversy in 1682 with the publication of *Religio Laici*, written in defense of Anglicanism. Following the accession of James II, however, he converted to Catholicism and wrote the pro-Catholic *Hind and the Panther* (1687), a long poem written in the form of an allegorical fable. Dryden also continued to be active in the theatre. The romantic *Don Sebastian* (produced in 1690) and *Amphitryon*, a comedy (produced 1690, written several years earlier), are particularly outstanding among the plays from this later period. Towards the end of his life Dryden undertook a series of translations, mostly of classical works, including the whole of Vergil (published as *The Works of Virgil* in 1693) and some of Homer, Ovid, Horace, Theocritus, Lucretius, and others; his culminating achievement in this area was *Fables Ancient and Modern* (1700), which contains translations of Ovid, Boccaccio, and Chaucer. Dryden died in London on May 1, 1700.

Personal

You know I am no flatterer, and therefore will excuse me when I tell you I cannot endure you should arrogate a thing to yourself you have not the least pretence to. Is it not enough that you excel in so many eminent virtues but you must be a putting in for a vice which all the world knows is properly my province? If you persist in your claim to laziness you will be thought as affected in it as Montaigne is, when he complains of the want of memory. What soul has ever been more active than your own? what country, nay what corner of the earth has it not travelled into? whose bosom has it not dived into and informed itself there so perfectly of all the secrets of man's heart that only the Great Being, whose image it bears, knows them better? I, whose every action of *my* life is a witness of my idleness, little thought that you, who have raised so many immortal monuments of your industry, durst have set up to be my rival. But to punish you I will distinguish: you have no share in that noble laziness of mind which all I write make⟨s⟩ out my just title to, but as for that of the body I can let you come in for a snack without any jealousy. I am apt to think you have bated something of your mettle since you and I were rivals in other matters, though I hope you have not yet obtained the perfection I have heard Sir Charles Sidley brag of: which is, that when a short youth runs quick through every vein and puts him in mind of his ancient prowess, he thinks it not worth while to bestow motion on his *et caetera muscle*. ⟨. . .⟩

I was so pleased with reading your letter that I was vexed at the last proof you gave me of your laziness, the not finding it in your heart to turn over the paper. In that you have had the better of me; but I will always renounce that darling sin, rather than omit anything which may give you an assurance of my being faithfully yours, &c.—SIR GEORGE ETHEREGE, Letter to John Dryden (c. March 1686/7)

For I confess my chief endeavours are to delight the age in which I live. If the humour of this be for low comedy, small accidents, and raillery, I will force my genius to obey it, though with more reputation I could write in verse. I know I am not so fitted by nature to write comedy: I want that gaiety of humour which is required to it. My conversation is slow and dull; my humour saturnine and reserved: in short, I am none of those who endeavour to break jests in company, or make repartees. So that those who decry my comedies do me no injury, except it be in point of profit: reputation in them is the last thing to which I shall pretend.—JOHN DRYDEN, A *Defence of An Essay of Dramatick Poesy*, 1668

Sir:

 Tho I have never been ambitious of being obliged by many men, yet I am very much pleasd with the being so by Mr. Dryden. Not out of vanity in having my inconsiderable name placed (by so great a man) in the front of one of his Works ⟨the translation of Virgil's *Georgics*⟩, but because it gives the World a testimony of his freindship to me. I confess that I have alwayes esteem'd you the Homer of this Age, and I am sure that you have one advantage far above him, for he never shin'd much but in the darke, I mean till he was dead, and you have had that glory the greatest part of your life. But I do not pretend to offer the incence of prase, to him who is the best teacher of others how to give it; my intention being onely at this time to express some part of my resentments for the unvaluable Present that you have made me; and to desire your acceptance (by this bearer) of a small mark of those respects which shall ever be payd you by your most humble servant.—EARL OF CHESTERFIELD, Letter to John Dryden (Aug. 10, 1697)

 A sleepy eye he shows, and no sweet feature,
 Yet was indeed a favourite of nature.
 Endow'd and graced with an exalted mind,
 With store of wit, and that of every kind.
 Juvenal's tartness, Horace's sweet air,
 With Virgil's force, in him concenter'd were.
 But though the painter's art can never show it,
 That his exemplar was so great a poet,
 Yet are the lines and tints so subtly wrought,
 You may perceive he was a man of thought.
 Closterman, 'tis confess'd, has drawn him well,
 But short of Absalom and Achitophel.
   —UNSIGNED, *Epigrams on the Paintings of the Most Eminent Masters*, 1700

I come now from Mr. *Dryden's* Funeral, where we had an Ode in *Horace* Sung, instead of *David's* Psalms; whence you may find, that we don't think a Poet worth Christian Burial; the Pomp of the Ceremony was a kind of Rhapsody, and fitter, I think, for *Hudibras* than him; because the Cavalcade was mostly Burlesque; but he was an extraordinary Man, and bury'd after an extraordinary Fashion; for I do believe there was never such another Burial seen; the Oration indeed was great and ingenious, worthy the Subject, and like the Author, whose Prescriptions can restore the Living, and his Pen embalm the Dead. And so much for Mr. *Dryden*, whose Burial was the same with his Life; Variety, and not of a Piece. The Quality and Mob, Farce and Heroicks; the Sublime and Rediculе mixt in a Piece, great *Cleopatra* in a Hackney Coach.—GEORGE FARQUHAR, Letter (1700), *Love and Business in a Collection of Occasionary Verse and Epistolary Prose*, 1701

 Here lyes John Dryden, who had Enemies three,
 Old Nick, Sr. Dick and Jeremy.
 The Fustian Knight was forced to yield,
 The other two maintained the Field:
 But had our Poet's Life been holier
 He had knick't both Devil and the Collier.
   —THOMAS HEARNE, "Epitaph upon Mr. John Dryden," *Reliquiae Hearnianae*, Nov. 5, 1707

He was of a nature exceedingly humane and compassionate; easily forgiving injuries, and capable of a prompt and sincere reconciliation with them who had offended him.

 Such a temperament is the only solid foundation of all moral virtues and sociable endowments. His friendship, where he professed it, went much beyond his professions; and I have been told of strong and generous instances of it by the persons themselves who received them, though his hereditary income was little more than a bare competency.

 As his reading had been very extensive, so was he very happy in a memory, tenacious of everything that he had read. He was not more possessed of knowledge than he was communicative of it. But then his communication of it was by no means pedantic, or imposed upon the conversation; but just such, and went so far, as, by the natural turns of the discourse in which he was engaged, it was necessarily promoted or required. He was extreme ready and gentle in his correction of the errors of any writer, who thought fit to consult him; and full as ready and patient to admit of the reprehension of others, in respect of his own oversight or mistakes. He was of very easy, I may say, of very pleasing access; but something slow, and, as it were, diffident in his advances to others. He had something in his nature, that abhorred intrusion into any society whatsoever. Indeed, it is to be regretted, that he was rather blamable in the other extreme; for, by that means, he was personally less known, and, consequently, his character might become liable both to misapprehensions and misrepresentations.

 To the best of my knowledge and observation, he was, of all the men that ever I knew, one of the most modest, and the most easily to be discountenanced in his approaches either to his superiors or his equals.—WILLIAM CONGREVE, Dedication to *The Dramatick Works of John Dryden, Esq.*, 1717

Mr. John Dryden, the Great Poët, was buried in Westminster Abbey, among the old Poëts, in May, 1700, being carried from the College of Physicians, where an Oration was pronounced by the famous Dr. Garth, in which he did not mention one Word of Jesus Xt, but made an Oration as an Apostrophe to the Great God Apollo, to influence the Minds of the Auditors with a wise, but, without doubt, Poëtical Understanding; and, as a Conclusion, instead of a Psalm of David, repeated the 30th Ode of the 3rd Book of Horace's Odes, beginning, *Exegi Monumentum*, &c. He made a great many Blunders in the Pronunciation.—THOMAS HEARNE, *Reliquiae Hearnianae*, Nov. 6, 1726

As we have sometimes great Composers of Musick who cannot sing, we have as frequently great Writers that cannot read; and though without the nicest Ear no Man can be Master of Poetical Numbers, yet the best Ear in the World will not always enable him to pronounce them. Of this Truth *Dryden*, our first great Master of Verse and Harmony, was a strong Instance: When he brought his Play of *Amphytrion* to the Stage, I heard him give it his first Reading to the Actors, in which, though it is true he deliver'd the plain Sense of every Period, yet the whole was in so cold, so flat, and unaffecting a manner, that I am afraid of not being believ'd when I affirm it.—COLLEY CIBBER, *An Apology for the Life of Mr. Colley Cibber*, 1739

Dryden lived in Gerrard Street, and used most commonly to write in the ground-room next the street.

Dryden was not a very genteel man, he was intimate with none but poetical men.—He was said to be a very good man, by all that knew him; he was plump as Mr. Pitt; of a fresh colour, and a down look, and not very conversible.

Dryden had three or four sons; John, Erasmus, Charles, and perhaps another. One of them was a priest, and another a captain in the Pope's guards.—He left his family estate, which was about one hundred and twenty pounds a year, to Charles.—The Historiographer's and Poet Laureate's places were worth about three hundred pounds a year to him.

Dryden cleared every way about twelve hundred pounds by his Virgil; and had sixpence each line for his Fables.—For some time he wrote a play, at least every year; but in those days ten broad pieces was the usual highest price for a play: and if they got fifty pounds more in the acting, it was reckoned very well.—His Virgil was one of the first books that had any thing of a subscription; (and even that was a good deal on account of the prints, which were from Ogilby's plates touched up:) as the Tatlers were the first great subscription.

It was Dryden who made Will's Coffee-house the great resort for the wits of his time. After his death, Addison transferred it to Button's; who had been a servant of his: they were opposite each other, in Russell Street, Covent Garden. —ALEXANDER POPE (1742–43), cited in Joseph Spence, *Anecdotes, Observations and Characters of Books and Men*, ed. S. W. Singer, 1820

Dryden was as disgraceful to the office ⟨of poet laureate⟩, from his character, as the poorest scribbler could have been from his verses. The office itself has always humbled the professor hitherto (even in an age when kings were somebody), if he were a poor writer by making him more conspicuous, and if he were a good one by setting him at war with the little fry of his own profession, for there are poets little enough to envy even a poet-laureat.—THOMAS GRAY, Letter to William Mason (Dec. 19, 1757)

The modesty which made him so slow to advance, and so easy to be repulsed, was certainly no suspicion of deficient merit, or unconsciousness of his own value: he appears to have known, in its whole extent, the dignity of his own character, and to have set a very high value on his own powers and performances. He probably did not offer his conversation, because he expected it to be solicited; and he retired from a cold reception, not submissive but indignant, with such reverence of his own greatness as made him unwilling to expose it to neglect or violation.

His modesty was by no means inconsistent with ostentatiousness: he is diligent enough to remind the world of his merit, and expresses with very little scruple his high opinion of his own powers; but his self-commendations are read without scorn or indignation; we allow his claims, and love his frankness.

Tradition, however, has not allowed that his confidence in himself exempted him from jealousy of others. He is accused of envy and insidiousness; and is particularly charged with inciting Creech to translate Horace, that he might lose the reputation which Lucretius had given him.

Of this charge we immediately discover that it is merely conjectural; the purpose was such as no man would confess; and a crime that admits no proof, why should we believe?

He has been described as magisterially presiding over the younger writers, and assuming the distribution of poetical fame; but he who excels has a right to teach, and he whose

judgement is incontestable may, without usurpation, examine and decide.

Congreve represents him as ready to advise and instruct; but there is reason to believe that his communication was rather useful than entertaining. He declares of himself that he was saturnine, and not one of those whose spritely sayings diverted company; and one of his censurers makes him say,

> Nor wine nor love could ever see me gay;
> To writing bred, I knew not what to say.

There are men whose powers operate only at leisure and in retirement, and whose intellectual vigour deserts them in conversation; whom merriment confuses, and objection disconcerts, whose bashfulness restrains their exertion, and suffers them not to speak till the time of speaking is past; or whose attention to their own character makes them unwilling to utter at hazard what has not been considered, and cannot be recalled.

Of Dryden's sluggishness in conversation it is vain to search or to guess the cause. He certainly wanted neither sentiments nor language; his intellectual treasures were great, though they were locked up from his own use. *His thoughts, when he wrote, flowed in upon him so fast, that his only care was which to chuse, and which to reject.* Such rapidity of composition naturally promises a flow of talk, yet we must be content to believe what an enemy says of him, when he likewise says it of himself. But whatever was his character as a companion, it appears that he lived in familiarity with the highest persons of his time. It is related by Carte of the duke of Ormond, that he used often to pass a night with Dryden, and those with whom Dryden consorted: who they were, Carte has not told; but certainly the convivial table at which Ormond sat was not surrounded with a plebeian society. He was indeed reproached with boasting of his familiarity with the great; and Horace will support him in the opinion, that to please superiors is not the lowest kind of merit.

The merit of pleasing must, however, be estimated by the means. Favour is not always gained by good actions or laudable qualities. Caresses and preferments are often bestowed on the auxiliaries of vice, the procurers of pleasure, or the flatterers of vanity. Dryden has never been charged with any personal agency unworthy of a good character: he abetted vice and vanity only with his pen. One of his enemies has accused him of lewdness in his conversation; but if accusation without proof be credited, who shall be innocent?

His works afford too many examples of dissolute licentiousness, and abject adulation; but they were probably, like his merriment, artificial and constrained; the effects of study and meditation, and his trade rather than his pleasure.

Of the mind that can trade in corruption, and can deliberately pollute itself with ideal wickedness for the sake of spreading the contagion in society, I wish not to conceal or excuse the depravity.—Such degradation of the dignity of genius, such abuse of superlative abilities, cannot be contemplated but with grief and indignation. What consolation can be had, Dryden has afforded, by living to repent, and to testify his repentance.—SAMUEL JOHNSON, "Dryden," *Lives of the English Poets*, 1779–81

General

Well mightst thou scorn thy Readers to allure
With tinkling Rhime, of thy own Sense secure;
While the *Town-Bays* writes all the while and spells,
And like a Pack-Horse tires without his Bells.
    —ANDREW MARVELL, "On Mr. *Milton's* Paradise lost," 1674

John Dryden, Poet-Laureat, and Historiographer to his present Majesty, with whom such hath been the approbation and acceptance his poetry hath received, especially what he hath written of dramatic, with wonderful success to the Theatre Royal: viz. Comedies, several abounding with no vulgar wit and ingenuity; as *The Maiden Queen*;—*The Wild Gallant*;—*The Mock Astrologer*;—*Marriage à-la-mode*;—*The Amorous Old Woman*;—*The Assignation*;—*Tyrannic Love*; and *Amboyna*; Tragedies; besides historical dramas; viz. *The Indian Emperor*; and two Parts of *The Conquest of Granada*; in which if he have indulged a little too much in the French way of continual rhyme, and interlarding of history with ascititious love and honour, I am apt to impute it rather to his complying with the modified and gallantish humour of the times, than to his own well examined judgment.—EDWARD PHILLIPS, *Theatrum Poetarum Anglicanorum*, 1675

> Well Sir, 'tis granted, I said Dryden's Rhimes,
> Were stoln, unequal, nay dull many times:
> What foolish Patron, is there found of his,
> So blindly partial, to deny me this?
> But that his Plays, Embroider'd up and downe,
> With Witt, and Learning, justly pleas'd the Towne,
> In the same paper, I as freely owne:
> Yet haveing this allow'd, the heavy Masse,
> That stuffs up his loose Volumes must not passe:
> For by that Rule, I might as well admit,
> Crownes tedious Scenes, for Poetry, and Witt.
>   . . .
>   Dryden, in vaine, try'd this nice way of Witt,
> For he, to be a tearing Blade thought fit,
> But when he wou'd be sharp, he still was blunt,
> To friske his frollique fancy, hed cry Cunt;
> Wou'd give the Ladyes, a dry Bawdy bob,
> And thus he got the name of Poet Squab:
> But to be just, twill to his praise be found,
> His Excellencies, more than faults abound.
> Nor dare I from his Sacred Temples teare,
> That Lawrell, which he best deserves to weare.
> But does not Dryden find ev'n Johnson dull?
> Fletcher, and Beaumont, uncorrect, and full
> Of Lewd lines as he calls em? Shakespeares Stile
> Stiffe, and Affected? To his owne the while
> Allowing all the justnesse that his Pride,
> Soe Arrogantly, had to these denyd?
> And may not I, have leave Impartially
> To search, and Censure, Drydens workes, and try,
> If those grosse faults, his Choyce Pen does Commit
> Proceed from want of Judgment, or of Witt.
> Of if his lumpish fancy does refuse,
> Spirit, and grace to his loose slatterne Muse?
> Five Hundred Verses, ev'ry Morning writ,
> Proves you noe more a Poet, than a Witt.
> —JOHN WILMOT, EARL OF ROCHESTER, "An Allusion to Horace: The 10th Satyr of the 1st Book," 1678

I know you gentlemen of Will's coffee-house will be glad to hear some news of Mr. Dryden. I must tell you, then, that we have had the devil and all of combustions and quarrels here in hell since that famous bard's arrival among us. The Grecians, the Romans, the Italians, the Spaniards, the French, but especially the Dutch authors, have been upon his back; Homer was the first that attacked him for justifying Almanzor's idle rants and monstrous actions, by the precedent of Achilles. The two poets, after a little squabbling, were without much difficulty persuaded to let their two heroes fight out the quarrel for

them, but the nimble-heeled Grecian soon got the whip-hand of the furious Almanzor, and made him beg pardon. Horace too, grumbled a little in his gizzard at him for affirming Juvenal to be a better satirist than himself, but upon second thoughts thought it not worth his while to contest the point with him. Once it happened, that Mr. Bays came into our room when Petronius Arbiter was diverting us with a very fine nouvelle. Mons. Fontaine, Sir Philip Sidney, Mr. Waller, my late lord Rochester, with Sir Charles Sedley, composed part of this illustrious audience; when Mr. Dryden unluckily spoiled all by asking the latter, what the facetious gentleman's name was, that talked so agreeably? 'How,' says Sir Charles Sedley, 'hadst thou the impudence, in the preface before thy English Juevenal, to say that so soon as the pretended Belgrade supplement of Petronius's fragments came into England, thou couldst tell, upon reading but two lines of that edition, whether it was genuine or no; and here hast thou heard the noble author himself talk above an hour by the clock, and couldst not find him out?' Upon this the old bard retired in some disorder.

But what happened to him a day or two after, was more mortifying. Chaucer meets him in one of our coffee-houses, and after the usual ceremonies were over between two strangers of their wit and learning, thus accosts him. 'Sir,' cries Chaucer, 'you have done me a wonderful honour to furbish up some of my old musty tales, and bestow modern garniture upon them, and I look upon myself much obliged to you for so undeserved a favour; however, Sir, I must take the freedom to tell you, that you over-strained matters a little, when you likened me to Ovid, as to our wit and manner of versification.' 'Why, Sir,' says Mr. Dryden, 'I maintain it, and who then dares be so saucy as to oppose me?' 'But under favour, Sir,' cries the other, 'I think I should know Ovid pretty well, having now conversed with him almost three hundred years, and the devil's in it if I don't know my own talent; and therefore, tho' you pass a mighty compliment upon me in drawing this parallel between us, yet I tell you there is no more resemblance between us, as to our manner of writing, than there is between a jolly well-complexioned Englishman and a black-haired, thin-gutted Italian.' 'Lord, Sir,' says Dryden to him, 'I tell you that you're mistaken, and your two styles are as like one another as two Exchequer-tallies.' 'But I, who should know it better,' says Chaucer, 'tell you the contrary.' 'And I,' says Mr. Bays, 'who know these things better than you, and all the men in the world, will stand by what I have affirmed,' and upon that gave him the lie.

Rhadamanthus, who is one of Pluto's oldest judges, and a severe regulator of good manners and conversation, immediately sent for our friend John to appear in Court; and after he had severely reprimanded him for using such insufferable language upon no provocation, 'for your punishment,' says he, 'I command you to get Sir Richard Blackmore's translation of Job by heart, and to repeat ten pages of it to our friend the author of the *Rehearsal* every morning.' Poor Bays desired his lordship to mitigate so rash a sentence, and by way of commutation frankly offered to drink so many quarts of liquid sulphur every morning. 'No,' says my lord judge, 'tho' they commute penances in Doctors-Commons, yet we are not such rogues to commute them in hell, and so I expect to be obeyed.'—TOM BROWN, "Last Letter from Seignior Giuseppe Hanesio," *Letters from the Living Dead*, 1687

> How long, great poet, shall thy sacred lays
> Provoke our wonder, and transcend our praise?
> Can neither injuries of time, or age,
> Damp thy poetick heat, and quench thy rage?
> Not so thy Ovid in his exile wrote,

Grief chill'd his breast, and check'd his rising
        thought;
Pensive and sad, his drooping muse betrays
The Roman genius in its last decays.
    Prevailing warmth has still thy mind possest,
And second youth is kindled in thy breast;
Thou mak'st the beauties of the Romans known,
And England boasts of riches not her own;
Thy lines have heighten'd Virgil's majesty,
And Horace wonders at himself in thee.
Thou teachest Persius to inform our isle
In smoother numbers, and a clearer stile;
And Juvenal, instructed in thy page,
Edges his satyr, and improves his rage.
Thy copy casts a fairer light on all,
And still outshines the bright original.
    Now Ovid boasts th' advantage of thy song,
And tells his story in the British tongue;
Thy charming verse, and fair translations, show
How thy own laurel first began to grow;
How wild Lycaon chang'd by angry gods,
And frighted at himself, ran howling through the
        woods.
    O mayst thou still the noble task prolong,
Nor age, nor sickness interrupt thy song:
Then may we wondering read, how human limbs
Have water'd kingdoms, and dissolv'd in streams;
Of those rich fruits that on the fertile mould
Turn'd yellow by degrees, and ripen'd into gold:
How some in feathers, or a ragged hide,
Have liv'd a second life, and different natures try'd.
Then will thy Ovid, thus transform'd, reveal
A nobler change than he himself can tell.
        —JOSEPH ADDISON, "To Mr. Dryden," 1693

'Tis true, that when the coarse and worthless dross
Is purg'd away, there will be mighty loss;
Ev'n Congreve, Southern, manly Wycherley,
When thus refin'd, will grievous sufferers be;
Into the melting pot when Dryden comes,
What horrid stench will rise, what noisome fumes!
How will he shrink, when all his lewd allay,
And wicked mixture, shall be purg'd away!
        —SIR RICHARD BLACKMORE, A *Satyr against
        Wit*, 1700

When I had the good Fortune to meet you in the City, it was
with Concern that I heard from you of the Attempt to lessen
the Reputation of Mr. *Dryden*; and 'tis with Indignation that I
have since learnt that that Attempt has chiefly been carried on
by small Poets, who ungratefully strive to eclipse the Glory of
a great Man, from whom alone they derive their own faint
Lustre. But that Eclipse will be as Momentary as that of the
Sun was lately. The Reputation of Mr. *Dryden* will soon break
out again in its full Splendor, and theirs will disappear. It was
upon hearing of this Attempt that I reflected with some
Amazement, that I should have got the Reputation of an
ill-natur'd Man, by exposing the Absurdities of living Authors;
and Authors for the most part of great Mediocrity, tho' I have
always done it openly and fairly, and upon just and personal
Provocations; and that these should basely arraign the Reputation of a great Man deceas'd, who now can make no Answer
for himself, and upon whom they fawn'd while living, and
should yet escape uncensur'd. But when I heard that that
Attempt was in favour of little Pope, that diminutive of
Parnassus and of humanity, 'tis impossible to express to what a
height my Indignation and Disdain were rais'd. Good God!

was there ever any Nation in which (I will not say a false Taste,
for we never had a true one, but in which) a wrong Sense and
a fatal Delusion so generally prevail'd! For have not too many
of us lately appear'd to contemn every thing that is great and
glorious, and to praise and exalt every thing that is base and
infamous? Have not too many of us shewn to all the World, by
a manifest execrable Choice, that they prefer Weakness to
Power, Folly to Wisdom, Poverty to Wealth, Fury and
Madness to Moderation, Infamy to Glory, Submission to
Victory, Slavery to Liberty, Idolatry to Religion, the Duke of
O⟨rmond⟩ to the D. of M⟨arlborough⟩ the empty Pretender to
the Royal *George* our only rightful King, and the little Mr.
Pope to the illustrious Mr. *Dryden*? If I appear a little too
warm, I hope you will excuse my Affection for the Memory,
and my Zeal for the Reputation of my departed Friend, whom
I infinitely esteem'd when living for the Solidity of his
Thought, for the Spring, the Warmth, and the beautiful Turn
of it; for the Power, and Variety, and Fulness of his Harmony;
for the Purity, the Perspicuity, the Energy of his Expression;
and (whenever the following great Qualities are requir'd) for
the Pomp and Solemnity and Majesty of his Style. But Pope is
the very reverse of all this: he scarce ever thought once solidly,
but is an empty eternall babbler: and as his thoughts almost
always are false or trifling, his expression is too often obscure,
ambiguous, and uncleanly. He has indeed a smooth verse and
a rhyming jingle, but he has noe power or variety of harmony;
but always the same dull cadence, and a continuall bagpipe
drone. Mr. Dryden's expressions are always worthy of his
thoughts: but Pope never speaks nor thinks at all; or, which is
all one, his language is frequently as barbarous, as his thoughts
are false.

This I have ventured to say, in spight of popular errour.
But popular errour can be of noe significancy either to you or
me, who have seen Mr. Settle in higher reputation than Mr.
Pope is at present. And they who live thirty years hence, will
find Mr. Pope in the same classe in which Mr. Settle is now;
unlesse the former makes strange improvements. Good sense is
the sole foundation of good writing; and noe authour who
wants solidity, can ever long endure. This I have ventur'd to
say in spight of popular errour; and this is in my power, when
ever I please, to prove to all the world.

You may now see, Sir, by this Letter, how little most Men
know one another, who converse daily together. How many
were there in Mr. *Dryden's* Life-time, who endeavour'd to
make him believe, that I should be the foremost, if I surviv'd
him, of all his Acquaintance to arraign his Memory; whereas
I am he of all his Acquaintance, who, tho' I flatter'd him least
while living, having been contented to do him Justice both
behind his Back and before his Enemies Face, am now the
foremost to assert his Merit, and to vindicate his Glory.

If Mr. *Dryden* has Faults, (as where is the Mortal who has
none?) I by searching for them perhaps could find them. But
whatever the mistaken World may think, I am always willing to
be pleas'd, nay, am always greedy of Pleasure as any *Epicurean*
living; and whenever I am naturally touch'd, I give my self up
to the first Impression, and never look for Faults. But whenever
a cried-up Author, upon the first reading him, does not make
a pleasing Impression on me; I am apt to seek for the Reason
of it, that I may know if the Fault is in him or in me. Wherever
Genius runs thro' a Work, I forgive its Faults, and wherever
that is wanting no Beauties can touch me. Being struck by Mr.
Dryden's Genius, I have no Eyes for his Errors; and I have no
Eyes for his Enemies Beauties, because I am not struck by their
Genius.—JOHN DENNIS, Letter to Jacob Tonson (June 4,
1715)

As to his writings, I shall not take upon me to speak of them: For to say little of them would not be to do them right; and to say all that I ought to say, would be to be very voluminous. But I may venture to say, in general terms, that no man hath written in our language so much, and so various matter, and in so various manners so well. Another thing I may say very peculiar to him, which is, that his parts did not decline with his years, but that he was an improving writer to his last, even to near seventy years of age, improving even in fire and imagination, as well as in judgment; witness his "Ode on St. Cecilia's Day," and his *Fables*, his latest performances.

He was equally excellent in verse and in prose. His prose had all the clearness imaginable, together with all the nobleness of expression; all the graces and ornaments proper and peculiar to it, without deviating into the language or diction of poetry. I make this observation, only to distinguish his style from that of many poetical writers, who, meaning to write harmoniously in prose, do, in truth, often write mere blank verse.

I have heard him frequently own with pleasure, that if he had any talent for English prose, it was owing to his having often read the writings of the great Archbishop Tillotson.

His versification and his numbers he could learn of nobody; for he first possessed those talents in perfection in our tongue. And they, who have best succeeded in them since his time, have been indebted to his example; and the more they have been able to imitate him, the better have they succeeded.

As his style in prose is always specifically different from his style in poetry, so, on the other hand, in his poems, his diction is, wherever his subject requires it, so sublimely and so truly poetical, that its essence, like that of pure gold, cannot be destroyed. Take his verses and divest them of their rhymes, disjoint them in their numbers, transpose their expressions, make what arrangement and disposition you please of his words, yet shall there eternally be poetry, and something which will be found incapable of being resolved into absolute prose; an incontestable characteristic of a truly poetical genius.

I will say but one word more in general of his writings, which is, that what he has done in any one species, or distinct kind, would have been sufficient to have acquired him a great name. If he had written nothing but his prefaces, or nothing but his songs or his prologues, each of them would have entitled him to the preference and distinction of excelling in his kind.—WILLIAM CONGREVE, Dedication to *The Dramatick Works of John Dryden, Esq.*, 1717

I cannot pass by that admirable English poet, without endeavouring to make his country sensible of the obligations they have to his Muse. Whether they consider the flowing grace of his versification; the vigorous sallies of his fancy; or the peculiar delicacy of his periods; they will discover excellencies never to be enough admired. If they trace him from the first productions of his youth to the last performances of his age, they will find, that as the tyranny of rhyme never imposed on the perspicuity of the sense; so a languid sense never wanted to be set off by the harmony of rhyme. And as his earlier works wanted no maturity; so this latter wanted no force, or spirit. The falling off of his hair had no other consequence, than to make his laurels be seen the more.

As a translator he was just; as an inventor he was rich. His versions of some parts of Lucretius, Horace, Homer, and Virgil throughout, gave him a just pretence to that compliment which was made to monsieur d'Ablancourt, a celebrated French translator; "It is uncertain who have the greatest obligations to him, the dead or the living."

With all these wondrous talents, he was libelled in his life-time by the very men who had no other excellencies, but as they were his imitators. Where he was allowed to have sentiments superior to all others, they charged him with theft: but how did he steal? no otherwise than like those that steal beggars' children, only to clothe them the better.

It is to be lamented, that gentlemen still continue this unfair behaviour, and treat one another every day with most injurious libels. The Muses should be ladies of a chaste and fair behaviour: when they are otherwise, they are Furies. It is certain that Parnassus is at best but a barren mountain, and its inhabitants contrive to make it more so by their unneighbourly deportment; the authors are the only corporation that endeavour at the ruin of their own society. Every day may convince them, how much a rich fool is respected above a poor wit. The only talents in esteem at present are those of Exchange-Alley; one tally is worth a grove of bays; and it is of much more consequence to be well read in the tables of interest, and the rise and fall of stocks, than in the revolutions of empires.

Mr. Dryden is still a sad and shameful instance of this truth: the man that could make kings immortal, and raise triumphant arches to heroes, now wants a poor square foot of stone, to show where the ashes of one of the greatest poets, that ever was upon Earth, are deposited.—SIR SAMUEL GARTH, "Preface" to *Ovid's Metamorphoses*, 1717

Dryden, though my near relation, is one I have often blamed as well as pitied. He was poor, and in great haste to finish his plays, because by them he chiefly supported his family, and this made him so very uncorrect; he likewise brought in the Alexandrine verse at the end of the triplets.—JONATHAN SWIFT, Letter to Thomas Beach (April 12, 1735)

> We conquer'd France, but felt our captive's charms;
> Her Arts victorious triumph'd o'er our Arms:
> Britain to soft refinements less a foe,
> Wit grew polite, and Numbers learn'd to flow.
> Waller was smooth; but Dryden taught to join
> The varying verse, the full resounding line,
> The long majestic march, and energy divine.
>
> Tho' still some traces of our rustic vein
> And splay-foot verse, remain'd, and will remain.
> Late, very late, correctness grew our care,
> When the tir'd nation breath'd from civil war.
> Exact Racine, and Corneille's noble fire
> Show'd us that France had something to admire.
> Not but the Tragic spirit was our own,
> And full in Shakespear, fair in Otway shone:
> But Otway fail'd to polish or refine,
> And fluent Shakespear scarce effac'd a line.
> Ev'n copious Dryden, wanted, or forgot,
> The last and greatest Art, the Art to blot.
> —ALEXANDER POPE, *Imitations of Horace*, 1737, *Ep.* II. i. 263–81

⟨. . .⟩ Immoralities of the Stage had by an avow'd Indulgence been creeping into it ever since King *Charles* his Time; nothing that was loose could then be too low for it: The *London Cuckolds*, the most rank Play that ever succeeded, was then in the highest Court-Favour: In this almost general Corruption, *Dryden*, whose Plays were more fam'd for their Wit than their Chastity, led the way.—COLLEY CIBBER, *An Apology for the Life of Mr. Colley Cibber*, 1739

I learned versification wholly from Dryden's works; who had improved it much beyond any of our former poets; and would, probably, have brought it to its perfection, had not he been unhappily obliged to write so often in haste.

Dryden always uses proper language; lively, natural, and fitted to the subject. It is scarce ever too high, or too low: never, perhaps, except in his plays.—ALEXANDER POPE (1742–43), cited in Joseph Spence, *Anecdotes, Observations and Characters of Books and Men*, ed. S. W. Singer, 1820

Most of the celebrated writers of this age remain monuments of genius, perverted by indecency and bad taste; and none more than Dryden, both by reason of the greatness of his talents and the gross abuse which he made of them. His plays, excepting a few scenes, are utterly disfigured by vice or folly, or both. His translations appear too much the offspring of haste and hunger: even his fables are ill-chosen tales, conveyed in an incorrect, though spirited versification. Yet amidst this great number of loose productions, the refuse of our language, there are found some small pieces, his "Ode to St. Cecilia," the greater part of *Absalom and Achitophel*, and a few more, which discover so great genius, such richness of expression, such pomp and variety of numbers, that they leave us equally full of regret and indignation, on account of the inferiority or rather great absurdity of his other writings.—DAVID HUME, *History of England*, 1754–62

> Behold, where Dryden's less presumptuous car,
> Wide o'er the fields of Glory bear
> Two Coursers of ethereal race,
> With necks in thunder cloath'd, and long-resound-
>   ing pace.
> —THOMAS GRAY, *The Progress of Poesy*, 1757

Dryden, destitute of Shakespeare's genius, had almost as much learning as Jonson, and, for the buskin, quite as little taste. He was a stranger to the pathos; and by numbers, expression, sentiment, and every other dramatic cheat, strove to make amends for it; as if a saint could make amends for the want of conscience, a soldier for the want of valor, or a vestal of modesty. The noble nature of tragedy disclaims an equivalent: like virtue, it demands the heart; and Dryden had none to give. Let epic poets think; the tragedian's point is rather to feel: such distant things are a tragedian and a poet, that the latter, indulged, destroys the former. Look on Barnwell and Essex, and see how, as to these distant characters, Dryden excels and is excelled. But the strongest demonstration of his no-taste for the buskin are his tragedies fringed with rime; which, in epic poetry, is a sore disease, in the tragic, absolute death. To Dryden's enormity, Pope's was a light offence. As lacemen are foes to mourning, these two authors, rich in rime, were no great friends to those solemn ornaments which the nature of their works required.

"Must rime, then," say you, "be banished?" I wish the nature of our language could bear its entire expulsion; but our lesser poetry stands in need of a toleration for it: it raises that, but it sinks the great; as spangles adorn children, but expose men. Prince Henry bespangled all over in his eyelet-hole suit with glittering pins, and an Achilles, or an Almanzor, in this Gothic array, are very much on a level, as to the majesty of the poet and the prince. Dryden had a great, but a general, capacity; and as for a general genius, there is no such thing in nature. A genius implies the rays of the mind concentered, and determined to some particular point: when they are scattered widely, they act feebly and strike not with sufficient force to fire or dissolve the heart. As what comes from the writer's heart reaches ours; so what comes from his head sets our brains at work and our hearts at ease. It makes a circle of thoughtful critics, not of distressed patients; and a passive audience is what

tragedy requires. Applause is not to be given, but extorted; and the silent lapse of a single tear does the writer more honor than the rattling thunder of a thousand hands. Applauding hands and dry eyes (which during Dryden's theatrical reign often met) are a satire on the writer's talent and the spectator's taste. When by such judges the laurel is blindly given, and by such a poet proudly received, they resemble an intoxicated host and his tasteless guests over some sparkling adulteration, commending their champagne. But Dryden has his glory, though not on the stage. What an inimitable original is his ode! A small one, indeed, but of the first lustre, and without a flaw; and, amid the brightest boasts of antiquity, it may find a foil.—EDWARD YOUNG, *Conjectures on Original Composition*, 1759

Dryden, though a great and indisputed genius, had the same cast as Lestrange. Even his plays discover him to be a party-man, and the same principle infects his stile in subjects of the lightest nature; but the English tongue, as it stands at present, is greatly his debtor. He first gave it regular harmony, and discovered its latent powers. It was his pen that formed the Congreves, the Priors, and the Addisons, who succeeded him; and had it not been for Dryden, we never should have known a Pope, at least in the meridian lustre he now displays. But Dryden's excellencies, as a writer, were not confined to poetry alone. There is in his prose writings an ease and elegance that have never yet been so well united in works of taste or criticism.—OLIVER GOLDSMITH, "An Account of the Augustan Age in England," *The Bee*, No. 8 (Nov. 24, 1759)

> Here let me bend, great DRYDEN, at thy shrine,
> Thou dearest name to all the tuneful nine.
> What if some dull lines in cold order creep,
> And with his theme the poet seems to sleep?
> Still when his subject rises proud to view,
> With equal strength the poet rises too.
> With strong invention, noblest vigour fraught,
> Thought still springs up and rises out of thought;
> Numbers, ennobling numbers in their course,
> In varied sweetness flow, in varied force;
> The pow'rs of Genius, and of Judgment join,
> And the Whole Art of Poetry is Thine.
> —CHARLES CHURCHILL, *The Apology*, 1761, ll.
>   376–87

> POOR SIGISMUNDA! what a Fate is thine!
> DRYDEN, the great High Priest of all the Nine,
> Reviv'd thy name, gave what a Muse could give,
> And in his Numbers bad thy Mem'ry live;
> Gave thee those soft sensations, which might move
> And warm the coldest Anchorite to Love;
> Gave thee that Virtue, which could curb desire,
> Refine and Consecrate Love's headstrong fire;
> Gave thee those griefs, which made the Stoic feel,
> And call'd compassion forth from hearts of steel;
> Gave thee that firmness, which our Sex may shame,
> And made Man bow to Woman's juster claim,
> So that our tears, which from Compassion flow,
> Seem to debase thy dignity of woe.
> But O, how much unlike! how fall'n! how chang'd!
> How much from Nature, and herself estrang'd!
> How totally depriv'd of all the pow'rs
> To shew her feelings, and awaken our's,
> Doth SIGISMUNDA now devoted stand,
> The helpless victim of a Dauber's hand!
> —CHARLES CHURCHILL, *An Epistle to William*
>   *Hogarth*, 1763, ll. 487–506

Dryden was the father of true English poetry, and the most universal of all poets. This universality has been objected to him as a fault; but it was the unhappy effect of penury and dependance. He was not at liberty to pursue his own inclination; but was frequently obliged to prostitute his pen to such persons and things as a man of his talents must have despised. He was the great improver of our language and versification. The chains of our English bards were formerly heard to rattle only; in the age of Waller and Dryden, they became harmonious. He has failed in most of his dramatic writings, of which the prologues, epilogues, and prefaces, are generally more valuable than the pieces to which they are affixed. But even in this branch of poetry, he has written enough to perpetuate his fame; as his *All for Love*, his *Spanish Friar*, and *Don Sebastian*, can never be forgotten. There was a native fire in this great poet, which poverty could not damp, nor old age extinguish. On the contrary, he was still improving as a writer, while he was declining as a man; and was far advanced in years when he wrote his "Alexander's Feast," which is confessedly at the head of modern lyrics, and in the true spirit of the ancients. Great injury has been done him, in taking an estimate of his character from the meanest of his productions. It would be just as uncandid, to determine the merit of Kneller, from the vilest of his paintings.—JAMES GRANGER, *Biographical History of England*, 1769–1824

We have a language far more energic, and more sonorous too than the French. Shakespeare could do what he would with it in its unpolished state. Milton gave it pomp from the Greek, and softness from the Italian; Waller now and then, here and there, gave it the elegance of the French. Dryden poured music into it; Prior gave it ease, and Gray used it masterly for either elegy or terror.—HORACE WALPOLE, Letter to Robert Jephson (c. Feb. 1775)

There is no modern writer, whose style is more distinguishable. Energy and ease are its chief characters. The former is owing to a happy choice of expressions, equally emphatical and plain: the latter to a laudable partiality in favour of the idioms and radical words of the English tongue; the *native* riches and *peculiar* genius whereof are perhaps more apparent in him, than in any other of our poets. In Dryden's more correct pieces, we meet with no affectation of words of Greek or Latin etymology, no cumbersome pomp of epithets, no drawling circumlocutions, no idle glare of images, no blunderings round about a meaning: his English is pure and simple, nervous and clear, to a degree which Pope has never exceeded, and not always equalled. Yet, as I have elsewhere remarked, his attachment to the vernacular idiom, as well as the fashion of his age, often betrays him into a vulgarity, and even meanness, of expression, which is particularly observable in his translations of Virgil and Homer, and in those parts of his writings where he aims at pathos or sublimity. In fact, Dryden's genius did not lead him to the sublime or pathetic. Good strokes of both may be found in him; but they are momentary, and seem to be accidental. He is too witty for the one, and too familiar for the other. That he had no adequate relish for the majesty of *Paradise Lost*, is evident to those who have compared his opera called *The State of Innocence* with that immortal poem; and that his taste for the true pathetic was imperfect, too manifestly appears from the general tenor of his Translations, as well as Tragedies. His Virgil abounds in lines and couplets of the most perfect beauty; but these are mixed with others of a different stamp: nor can they who judge of the original by this translation, ever receive any tolerable idea of that uniform magnificence of sound and language, that exquisite choice of words and figures, and that sweet pathos of expression and of sentiment, which characterise the Mantuan Poet.—In delin-

eating the more familiar scenes of life, in clothing plain moral doctrines with easy and graceful versification, in the various departments of Comic Satire, and in the spirit and melody of his Lyric poems, Dryden is inferior to none of those who went before him. He exceeds his master Chaucer in the first: in the three last, he rivals Horace; the style of whose epistles he has happily imitated in his *Religio's Laici*, and other didactic pieces; and the harmony and elegance of whose odes he has proved that he could have equalled, if he had thought proper to cultivate that branch of the poetic art. Indeed, whether we consider his peculiar significancy of expression, or the purity of his style; the sweetness of his lyric, or the ease and perspicuity of his moral poems; the sportive severity of his satire, or his talents in wit and humour; Dryden, in point of *genius* (I do not say *taste*), seems to bear a closer affinity to Horace, than to any other ancient or modern author. For energy of words, vivacity of description, and apposite variety of numbers, his "Feast of Alexander" is superior to any ode of Horace or Pindar now extant.

Dryden's verse, though often faulty, has a grace and a spirit peculiar to itself. That of Pope is more correct, and perhaps upon the whole more harmonious; but it is in general more languid, and less diversified. Pope's numbers are sweet but elaborate; and our sense of their energy is in some degree interrupted by our attention to the art displayed in their contexture: Dryden's are natural and free; and, while they communicate their own sprightly motion to the spirits of the reader, hurry him along with a gentle and pleasing violence, without giving him time either to animadvert on their faults, or to analyse their beauties. Pope excels in solemnity of sound; Dryden, in an easy melody, and boundless variety of rhythm. In this last respect he is perhaps superior to all other English poets, Milton himself not excepted. Till Dryden appeared, none of our writers in rhyme of the last century approached in any measure to the harmony of Fairfax and Spenser. Of Waller it can only be said, that he is not harsh; of Denham and Cowley, if a few couplets were struck out of their works, we could not say so much. But in Dryden's hands, the English rhyming couplet assumed a new form; and seems hardly susceptible of any further improvement. One of the greatest poets of this century, the late and much lamented Mr. Gray of Cambridge, modestly declared to me, that if there was in his own numbers any thing that deserved approbation, he had learned it all from Dryden.

Critics have often stated a comparison between Dryden and Pope, as poets of the same order, and who differed only in *degree* of merit. But, in my opinion, the merit of the one differs considerably in *kind* from that of the other. Both were happy in a sound judgment and most comprehensive mind. Wit, and humour, and learning too, they seem to have possessed in equal measure; or, if Dryden may be thought to have gone deeper in the sciences, Pope must be allowed to have been the greater adept in the arts. The diversities in point of correctness and delicacy, which arose from their different ways of life, I do not now insist upon. But, setting those aside, if Dryden sounds any claim of preference on the originality of his manner, we shall venture to affirm, that Pope may sound a similar claim, and with equal justice, on the perfection of his taste; and that, if the critical writings of the first are more voluminous, those of the second are more judicious; if Dryden's inventions are more diversified, those of Pope are more regular, and more important. Pope's style may be thought to have less simplicity, less vivacity, and less of the purity of the mother-tongue; but is at the same time more uniformly elevated, and less debased by vulgarism, than that of his great master:—and the superior variety that animates the numbers of the latter, will perhaps be found to be compensated by the steadier and more majestic modulation of the former. Thus far their merits would appear to be pretty equally balanced.—But if the opinion of those critics be true, who hold that the highest regions of Parnassus are appropriated to pathos and sublimity, Dryden must after all confess, that he has never ascended so far as his illustrious imitator: there being nothing in the writings of the first so pathetic as the "Epistle of Eloisa," or the "Elegy on the Unfortunate Lady"; nor so uniformly sublime as the *Essay on Man*, or the *Pastoral of the Messiah*. This last is indeed but a selection and imitation of choice passages; but it bespeaks a power of imitation, and a taste in selection, that Dryden does not seem to have possessed. To all which may I not be permitted to add, what I think I could prove, that the pathos of Homer is frequently improved by Pope, and that of Virgil very frequently debased by Dryden?—JAMES BEATTIE, "An Essay on Poetry and Music," 1776

But I admire Dryden most, who has succeeded by mere dint of genius, and in spite of a laziness and carelessness almost peculiar to himself. His faults are numberless, but so are his beauties. His faults are those of a great man, and his beauties are such (at least sometimes), as Pope, with all his touching and retouching, could never equal.—WILLIAM COWPER, Letter to William Unwin (Jan. 5, 1782)

> Then comes a bard,
> Worn out and pennyless, and poet still
> Though bent with years, and in impetuous rhyme
> Pours out his unexhausted song. What muse
> So flexible, so generous as thine,
> Immortal Dryden. From her copious fount
> Large draughts he took, and unbeseeming song
> Inebriated sang. Who does not grieve,
> To hear the foul and insolent rebuke
> Of angry satire from a bard so rare?
> To trace the lubricous and oily course
> Of abject adulation, the lewd line
> Of shameless vice, from page to page, and find
> The judgment brib'd, the heart unprincipled,
> And only loyal at th' expence of truth,
> Of justice, and of virtue?
> —JAMES HURDIS, *The Village Curate*, 1788

I was much pleased to hear of your engagement with Dryden: not that he is, as a *Poet*, any great favourite of mine: I admire his talents and Genius greatly, but his is not a poetical Genius: the only qualities I can find in Dryden that are *essentially* poetical are a certain ardour and impetuosity of mind with an excellent ear: it may seem strange that I do not add to this, great command of language: *that* he certainly has and of such language also as it is most desirable that a Poet should possess, or rather should not be without; but it is not language that is in the high sense of the word poetical, being neither of the imagination or the passions; I mean of the amiable the ennobling or intense passions; I do not mean to say that there is nothing of this in Dryden, but as little, I think, as is possible, considering how much he has written. You will easily understand my meaning when I refer to his versification of Palamon and Arcite as contrasted with the language of Chaucer. Dryden had neither a tender heart nor a lofty sense of moral dignity: where his language is poetically impassioned it is mostly upon unpleasing subjects; such as the follies, vice, and crimes of classes of men or of individuals. That his cannot be the language of the imagination must have necessarily followed from this, that there is not a single image from Nature in the whole body of his works; and in his translation from Vergil whenever Vergil can be fairly said to have had his *eye* upon his object, Dryden always spoils the passage.—WILLIAM WORDSWORTH, Letter to Sir Walter Scott (Nov. 7, 1805)

I have a very high admiration of the talents both of Dryden and Pope, and ultimately, as from all good writers of whatever kind, their Country will be benefited greatly by their labours. But thus far I think their writings have done more harm than good.—WILLIAM WORDSWORTH, Letter to Sir Walter Scott (Jan. 18, 1808)

Dryden and Pope are the great masters of the artificial style of poetry in our language, as the poets of whom I have already treated, Chaucer, Spenser, Shakspeare, and Milton, were of the natural; and though this artificial style is generally and very justly acknowledged to be inferior to the other, yet those who stand at the head of that class, ought, perhaps, to rank higher than those who occupy an inferior place in a superior class. They have a clear and independent claim upon our gratitude, as having produced a kind and degree of excellence which existed equally nowhere else. What has been done well by some later writers of the highest style of poetry, is included in, and obscured by a greater degree of power and genius in those before them: what has been done best by poets of an entirely distinct turn of mind, stands by itself, and tells for its whole amount. Young, for instance, Gray, or Akenside, only follow in the train of Milton and Shakspeare: Pope and Dryden walk by their side, though of an unequal stature, and are entitled to a first place in the lists of fame. This seems to be not only the reason of the thing, but the common sense of mankind, who, without any regular process of reflection, judge of the merit of a work, not more by its inherent and absolute worth, than by its originality and capacity of gratifying a different faculty of the mind, or a different class of readers; for it should be recollected, that there may be readers (as well as poets) not of the highest class, though very good sort of people, and not altogether to be despised. ⟨. . .⟩

Dryden was a better prose-writer, and a bolder and more varied versifier than Pope. He was a more vigorous thinker, a more correct and logical declaimer, and had more of what may be called strength of mind than Pope; but he had not the same refinement and delicacy of feeling. Dryden's eloquence and spirit were possessed in a higher degree by others, and in nearly the same degree by Pope himself; but that by which Pope was distinguished, was an essence which he alone possessed, and of incomparable value on that sole account. Dryden's Epistles are excellent, but inferior to Pope's, though they appear (particularly the admirable one to Congreve) to have been the model on which the latter formed his. His Satires are better than Pope's. His *Absalom and Achitophel* is superior, both in force of invective and discrimination of character, to any thing of Pope's in the same way. The character of Achitophel is very fine; and breathes, if not a sincere love for virtue, a strong spirit of indignation against vice.

Mac Flecknoe is the origin of the idea of the *Dunciad*; but it is less elaborately constructed, less feeble, and less heavy. The difference between Pope's satirical portraits and Dryden's, appears to be this in a good measure, that Dryden seems to grapple with his antagonists, and to describe real persons; Pope seems to refine upon them in his own mind, and to make them out just what he pleases, till they are not real characters, but the mere driveling effusions of his spleen and malice. Pope describes the thing, and then goes on describing his own description till he loses himself in verbal repetitions. Dryden recurs to the object often, takes fresh sittings of nature, and

1313

gives us new strokes of character as well as of his pencil. *The Hind and Panther* is an allegory as well as a satire; and so far it tells less home; the battery is not so point-blank. But otherwise it has more genius, vehemence, and strength of description than any other of Dryden's works, not excepting the *Absalom and Achitophel*. It also contains the finest examples of varied and sounding versification. ⟨. . .⟩

The *Annus Mirabilis* is a tedious performance; it is a tissue of far-fetched, heavy, lumbering conceits, and in the worst style of what has been denominated metaphysical poetry. His Odes in general are of the same stamp; they are the hard-strained offspring of a meagre, meretricious fancy. The famous 'Ode on St. Cecilia' deserves its reputation; for, as piece of poetical mechanism to be set to music, or recited in alternate strophe and antistrophe, with classical allusions, and flowing verse, nothing can be better. It is equally fit to be said or sung; it is not equally good to read. It is lyrical, without being epic or dramatic. For instance, the description of Bacchus,

> The jolly god in triumph comes,
> Sound the trumpets, beat the drums;
> Flush'd with a purple grace,
> He shews his honest face—

does not answer, as it ought, to our idea of the God, returning from the conquest of India, with satyrs and wild beasts, that he had tamed, following in his train; crowned with vine leaves, and riding in a chariot drawn by leopards—such as we have seen him painted by Titian or Rubens! Lyrical poetry, of all others, bears the nearest resemblance to painting: it deals in hieroglyphics and passing figures, which depend for effect, not on the working out, but on the selection. It is the dance and pantomime of poetry. In variety and rapidity of movement, the 'Alexander's Feast' has all that can be required in this respect; it only wants loftiness and truth of character.

Dryden's plays are better than Pope could have written; for though he does not go out of himself by the force of imagination, he goes out of himself by the force of common-places and rhetorical dialogue. On the other hand, they are not so good as Shakspeare's; but he has left the best character of Shakspeare that has ever been written.

His alterations from Chaucer and Boccaccio shew a greater knowledge of the taste of his readers and power of pleasing them, than acquaintance with the genius of his authors. He ekes out the lameness of the verse in the former, and breaks the force of the passion in both. The Tancred and Sigismunda is the only general exception, in which, I think, he has fully retained, if not improved upon, the impassioned declamation of the original. The Honoria has none of the bewildered, dreary, preternatural effect of Boccaccio's story. Nor has the Flower and the Leaf any thing of the enchanting simplicity and concentrated feeling of Chaucer's romantic fiction. Dryden, however, sometimes seemed to indulge himself as well as his readers, as in keeping entire that noble line in Palamon's address to Venus:

> Thou gladder of the mount of Cithæron!

His Tales have been, upon the whole, the most popular of his works; and I should think that a translation of some of the other serious tales in Boccaccio and Chaucer, as that of Isabella, the Falcon, of Constance, the Prioress's Tale, and others, if executed with taste and spirit, could not fail to succeed in the present day.—WILLIAM HAZLITT, *Lectures on the English Poets*, 1818

He is a writer of manly and elastic character. His strong judgement gave force as well as direction to a flexible fancy; and his harmony is generally the echo of solid thoughts. But he is not gifted with intense or lofty sensibility; on the contrary, the grosser any idea is the happier he seems to expatiate upon it. The transports of the heart, and the deep and varied delineations of the passions, are strangers to its poetry. He could describe character in the abstract, but could not embody it in the drama, for he entered into character more clear perception than fervid sympathy. This great high-priest of all the nine was not a confessor to the finer secrets of the human breast. Had the subject of Eloisa fallen into his hands, he would have left but a coarse draught of her passion.—THOMAS CAMPBELL, *An Essay on English Poetry*, 1819

Dryden's genius was of that sort which catches fire by its own motion; his chariot wheels *get* hot by driving fast.—SAMUEL TAYLOR COLERIDGE, *Table Talk*, Nov. 1, 1833

> Our course by Milton's light was sped,
> And Shakspeare shining overhead:
> Chatting on deck was Dryden too,
> The Bacon of the rhyming crew,
> None ever crost our mystic sea,
> More richly stored with thought than he;
> Tho' never tender nor sublime,
> He struggles with and conquers Time.
> —WALTER SAVAGE LANDOR, "To Wordsworth," 1834

Davenant indeed and Denham may be reckoned the models of Dryden, so far as this can be said of a man of original genius, and one far superior to theirs. The distinguishing characteristic of Dryden, it has been said by Scott, was the power of reasoning and expressing the result in appropriate language. This indeed was the characteristic of the two whom we have named, and so far as Dryden has displayed it, which he eminently has done, he bears a resemblance to them. But it is insufficient praise for this great poet. His rapidity of conception and readiness of expression are higher qualities. He never loiters about a single thought or image, never labours about the turn of a phrase. The impression upon our minds that he wrote with exceeding ease is irresistible, and I do not know that we have any evidence to repel it. The admiration of Dryden gains upon us, if I may speak from my own experience, with advancing years, as we become more sensible of the difficulty of his style, and of the comparative facility of that which is merely imaginative.—HENRY HALLAM, *Introduction to the Literature of Europe*, 1837–39, Pt. 4, Ch. 5, Par. 38

And then came "glorious John," with the whole fourth era in his arms;—and eloquent above the sons of men, to talk down, thunder down poetry as if it were an exhalation. Do we speak as if he were not a poet? nay, but we speak of the character of his influences; nay, but he was a poet—an excellent poet—in marble: and Phidias, with the sculpturesque ideal separated from his working tool, might have carved him. He was a poet without passion, just as Cowley was: but, then, Cowley lived by fancy, and that would have been poor living for John Dryden. Unlike Cowley, too, he had an earnestness which of itself was influential. He was inspired in his understanding and his senses only; but to the point of disenchanting the world most marvellously. He had a large soul for a man, containing sundry Queen Anne's men, one within another, like quartetto tables; but it was not a large soul for a poet, and it entertained the universe by potato-patches. He established finally the reign of the literati for the reign of the poets—and the critics clapped their hands. He established finally the despotism of the final emphasis—and no one dared, in affecting criticism, to speak any more at all against a tinkling cymbal. And so, in distinctive succession to poetry and inspiration, began the new system of harmony "as by law established;" and so he translated Virgil not only into English but into Dryden; and so he was kind enough to translate Chaucer too, as an example,—made him a much finer speaker, and not, according to our doxy, so good a versifier—and cured the readers of the old *Knight's Tale* of sundry of their tears; and so he reasoned powerfully in verse—and threw into verse, besides, the whole force of his strong sensual being; and so he wrote what has been called from generation to generation, down to the threshold of our days, "the best ode in the English language." To complete which successes, he thrust our nature with a fork; and for a long time, and in spite of Horace's prophecy, she never came back again. Do we deny our gratitude and his glory to glorious John because we speak thus? In nowise would we do it. He was a man greatly endowed; and our language and our literature remain, in certain respects, the greater for his greatness—more practical, more rapid, and with an air of mixed freedom and adroitness which we welcome as an addition to the various powers of either. With regard to his influence—and he was most influential upon POETRY—we have spoken; and have the whole of the opening era from which to prove.—ELIZABETH BARRETT BROWNING, *The Book of the Poets* (1842), *Life, Letters and Essays of Elizabeth Barrett Browning*, 1863

If Dryden had been cast in a somewhat finer mould, and added sentiment to his other qualifications, he would have been almost as great a poet in the world of nature, as he was in that of art and the town. He had force, expression, scholarship, geniality, admirable good sense, musical enthusiasm. The rhymed heroic couplet in his hands continues still to be the finest in the language. But his perceptions were more acute than subtle; more sensual, by far, than spiritual. The delicacy of them had no proportion to the strength. He prized the flower, but had little sense of the fragrance; was gross as well as generous in his intellectual diet; and if it had not been genuine and hearty, would have shown an almost impudent delight in doing justice to the least refined of Nature's impressions. His Venus was not the Celestial. He would as soon have described the coarsest flower, as a rose; sooner, if it was large and luxuriant. ⟨. . .⟩ Agreeably to this character of his genius, Dryden's wit is less airy than masculine; less quick to move than eloquent when roused; less productive of pleasure and love than admiration and a sense of his mastery. His satire, if not so learned and universal as Butler's, is aimed more at the individual and his public standing, and therefore comes more home to us.—LEIGH HUNT, *Wit and Humour*, 1846

> Then Dryden came, a mind of giant mould,
> Like the north wind, impetuous, keen, and cold;
> Born to effect what Waller but essay'd,
> In rank and file his numbers he array'd,
> Compact as troops exact in battle's trade.
> Firm by constraint, and regularly strong,
> His vigorous lines resistless march along,
> By martial music order'd and inspired,
> Like glowing wheels by their own motion fired.
> So as a nation long inured to arms,
> And stirring strains, fierce pleasures, brisk alarms,
> Disdains a calm, and can no longer bear
> A soft, a pensive, or a solemn air;
> Thus Dryden taught the English to despise
> The simply sweet, long-lingering melodies
> That lovely Spenser and his thoughtful peers
> Had warbled erst to rapt attentive ears.
> E'en Milton's billowy ocean of high sound,

> Delighted little, though it might astound;
> The restless crowd impatient turn'd away,
> And sought a shorter, shriller, lighter lay.
>   Yet Dryden nobly earn'd the poet's name,
> And won new honours from the gift of fame.
> His life was long, and when his head was grey,
> His fortune broken, and usurp'd his bay,
> His dauntless genius own'd no cold dismay;
> Nor in repining notes of vain regret
> He made his crack'd pipe pitifully fret.
> But when cashier'd and laid upon the shelf,
> To shame the court excell'd his former self,
> Who meant to clip, but imp'd his moulted wings,
> And cured him of his ancient itch of praising kings.
> He sat gigantic on the shore of time,
> And watch'd the ingress of encroaching slime,
> Nor dream'd how much of evil or of good
> Might work amid the far unfathom'd flood.
>   —HARTLEY COLERIDGE, "Dryden," *Sketches of the English Poets*, 1849

Dryden, a true littérateur, simply reflects his epoch; the revolution he was intent upon, and which we are especially bound to consider, was that of English verse composition. While Newton was balancing the earth, and Locke weighing the intellect, Dryden was measuring syllables. While Penn and Locke were venturing experiments in government, he was making them in prosody. Political movements and agitations—the plot and the new plot—dissolutions and elections—falls of ministries and impeachments and deaths were to him chiefly of interest because he must mould the subject of his verse accordingly. To please the King as laureate he is in duty bound; and to serve his cause with rhyme to the purpose. Also prose.

Yet what side *should* a littérateur of real excellence take if not that of the King and the court? who certainly had the best taste, were the most judicious critics as well as the most likely paymasters. Settle and Shadwell might suit the Aldermen and the Exclusionists, who knew no better. And nothing, I imagine, more completely suited Dryden, more exactly met his feelings, and gave freer scope to his talents, than the revolution in literature which the new King and court sought to naturalise in England. To guide the process of that change and to elevate a matter of mere passing court fashion into a permanent reformation of English literature; to dignify a mere slipslop aversion of pedantry by converting it into an appreciation of elegance and propriety of writing—this was his vocation. He devoted himself to it for forty years with infinite zeal and perseverance, laborious study, and patient carefulness. And certainly with some considerable success.

During the whole of the next century I suppose it was considered that our language first was written, so to speak, by him. For models of composition no one was recommended anterior to him. In English poetry he is for them the earliest name. Into Johnson's collection Cowley and Butler, and one or two others coëval with Dryden, are admitted, but not Spenser. So too in prose it is only in our time that people have begun to talk of Jeremy Taylor and Milton as legitimate standards of English prose composition. Dryden was supposed to have commenced in the two kinds of writing what Pope and Addison made perfect. For style Shakespeare was dangerous and Hooker pernicious reading; Ben Jonson's wit was ponderous and the wisdom of Bacon pedantic; the mirth of Fletcher was rude and vulgar, the elegance of Sidney formal and factitious.

Maxims of this kind prevailed from the days of Dryden to

those of Byron and Scott. There are circles where they are still current, and there are possibilities of their again finding a more general acceptation. I incline to believe that there is a great deal of truth in them. Our language before the Restoration certainly was for the most part bookish, academical, and stiff. You perceive that our writers have first learnt to compose in Latin; and you feel as if they were now doing so in English. Their composition is not a harmonious development of spoken words, but a copy of written words. We are set to study ornate and learned periods; but we are not charmed by finding our ordinary everyday speech rounded into grace and smoothed into polish, chastened to simplicity and brevity without losing its expressiveness, and raised into dignity and force without ceasing to be familiar; saying once for all what we in our rambling talk try over and over in vain to say; and saying it simply and fully, exactly and perfectly.

This scholastic and constrained manner of men who had read more than they talked, and had (of necessity) read more Latin than English; of men who passed from the study to the pulpit, and from the pulpit back to the study—this elevated and elaborated diction of learned and religious men was doomed at the Restoration. Its learning was pedantry, and its elevation pretence. It was no way suited to the wants of the court, nor the wishes of the people. It was not likely that the courtiers would impede the free motions of their limbs with the folds of the cumbrous theological vesture; and the nation in general was rather weary of being preached to. The royalist party, crowding back from French banishment, brought their French tastes and distastes. James I. loved Latin and even Greek, but Charles II. liked French better even than English. In one of Dryden's plays is a famous scene, in which he ridicules the fashionable jargon of the day, which seems to have been a sort of slipshod English, continually helped out with the newest French phrases.

Dryden then has the merit of converting this corruption and dissolution of our old language into a new birth and renovation. And not only must we thank him for making the best of the inevitable circumstances and tendencies of the time, but also praise him absolutely for definitely improving our language. It is true that he sacrificed a great deal of the old beauty of English writing, but that sacrifice was inevitable; he retained all that it was practicable to save, and he added at the same time all the new excellence of which the time was capable.

You may call it, if you please, a democratic movement in the language. It was easier henceforth both to write and to read. To understand written English, it was not necessary first to understand Latin; and yet written English was little less instructive than it had been, or if it was less elevating, it was on the other hand more refining.

For the first time, you may say, people found themselves reading words easy at once and graceful; fluent, yet dignified; familiar, yet full of meaning. To have organised the dissolving and separating elements of our tongue into a new and living instrument, perfectly adapted to the requirements and more than meeting the desires and aspirations of the age, this is our author's praise. But it is not fully expressed until you add that this same instrument was found, with no very material modification, sufficient for the wants and purposes of the English people for more than a century. The new diction conquered, which the old one had never done, Scotland and Ireland, and called out American England into articulation. Hume and Robertson learnt it; Allan Ramsay and Burns studied it; Grattan spoke it; Franklin wrote it. You will observe that our most popular works in prose belong to it. So do our greatest

orators. A new taste and a new feeling for the classics grew up with it. It translated, to the satisfaction of its time, Homer and Virgil.

Our present tongue, so far as it differs from this, cannot profess to have done nearly so much. Homer and Virgil no longer content us in Pope and Dryden, but we have not been able to get anything to content us. The English diction of the nineteenth century has no Burke or Chatham to boast of, nor any Hume or Johnson.

There may be some superiority in matter. We have had a good deal of new experience, both in study and in action—new books and new events have come before us. But we have not yet in England, I imagine, had any one to give us a manner suitable to our new matter. There has been a kind of dissolution of English, but no one writer has come to re-unite and re-vivify the escaping components. We have something new to say, but do not know how to say it. The language has been popularised, but has not yet vindicated itself from being vulgarised. A democratic revolution is effecting itself in it, without that aristocratic reconstruction which pertains to every good democratic revolution. Everybody can write, and nobody writes well. We can all speak, and none of us know how. We have forgotten or rejected the old diction of our grandfathers, and shall leave, it seems likely, no new diction for our grandchildren. With some difficulty we make each other understand what we mean, but, unassisted by personal explanations and comment, it is to be feared our mere words will not go far. Our grandfathers read and wrote books: our fathers reviews: and we newspapers; will our children and grandchildren read our old newspapers? Have we any one who speaks for our day as justly and appropriately as Dryden did for his? Have we anything that will stand wear and tear, and will be as bright and un-obsolete a hundred and fifty years hence, as 'Alexander's Feast' is to-day?—ARTHUR HUGH CLOUGH, "On the Formulation of Classical English" (c. 1852), *Prose Remains*, 1888, pp. 325–29

If Dryden is a skilled politician, a trained controversialist, well armed with arguments, knowing all the ins and outs of discussion, versed in the history of men and parties, this pamphleteering aptitude, practical and English, confines him to the low region of every day and personal combats, far from the lofty philosophy and speculative freedom which give endurance and greatness to the classical style of his French contemporaries. In this age, in England, all discussion was fundamentally narrow. Except the terrible Hobbes, they all lack grand originality. Dryden, like the rest, is confined to the arguments and insults of sect and fashion. Their ideas were as small as their hatred was strong; no general doctrine opened up beyond the tumult of the strife a poetical vista; texts, traditions, a sad train of rigid reasoning, such were their arms; prejudice and passion swayed both parties. This is why the subject-matter fell below the art of writing. Dryden had no personal philosophy to develop; he does but versify themes given to him by others. In this sterility art soon is reduced to the clothing of foreign ideas, and the writer becomes an antiquarian or a translator. In fact, the greatest part of Dryden's poems are imitations, adaptations, or copies. He translated Persius, Virgil, part of Horace, Theocritus, Juvenal, Lucretius, and Homer, and put into modern English several tales of Boccaccio and Chaucer. These translations then appeared to be as great works as original compositions. When he took the *Æneid* in hand, the nation, as Johnson tells us, appeared to think its honor interested in the issue. Addison furnished him with the arguments of every book, and an essay on the *Georgics*; others supplied him with editions and notes; great lords vied with one another in offering him hospitality; subscriptions flowed in. They said that the English Virgil was to give England the Virgil of Rome. This work was long considered his highest glory. Even so at Rome, under Cicero, in the early dearth of national poetry, the translators of Greek works were as highly praised as the original authors.

This sterility of invention alters or depresses the taste. For taste is an instinctive system, and leads us by internal maxims, which we ignore. The mind, guided by it perceives connections, shuns discordances, enjoys or suffers, chooses or rejects, according to general conceptions which master it, but are not visible. These removed, we see the tact, which they engendered, disappear; the writer is clumsy, because philosophy fails him. Such is the imperfection of the stories handled by Dryden, from Boccaccio and Chaucer. Dryden does not see that fairy tales or tales of chivalry only suit a poetry in its infancy; that ingenious subjects require an artless style; that the talk of Renard and Chanticleer, the adventures of Palamon and Arcite, the transformations, tournaments, apparitions, need the astonished carelessness and the graceful gossip of old Chaucer. Vigorous periods, reflective antitheses, here oppress these amiable ghosts; classical phrases embarrass them in their too stringent embrace; they are lost to our sight; to find them again, we must go to their first parent, quit the too harsh light of a learned and manly age; we cannot pursue them fairly except in their first style in the dawn of credulous thought, under the mist which plays about their vague forms, with all the blushes and smile of morning. Moreover, when Dryden comes on the scene, he crushes the delicacies of his master, hauling in tirades or reasonings, blotting out sincere and self-abandoning tenderness. What a difference between his account of Arcite's death and Chaucer's! How wretched are all his fine words, his gallantry, his symmetrical phrases, his cold regrets, compared to the cries of sorrow, the true outpouring, the deep love in Chaucer! But the worst fault is that almost everywhere he is a copyist, and retains the faults like a literal translator, with eyes glued on the work, powerless to comprehend and recast it, more a rhymester than a poet. When La Fontaine put Æsop or Boccaccio into verse, he breathed a new spirit into them; he took their matter only: the new soul, which constitutes the value of his work, is his, and only his; and this soul befits the work. In place of the Ciceronian periods of Boccaccio, we find slim, little lines, full of delicate raillery, dainty voluptuousness, feigned frankness, which relish the forbidden fruit because it is fruit, and because it is forbidden. The tragic departs, the relics of the middle-ages are a thousand leagues away; there remains nothing but the jeering gayety, Gallic and racy, as of a critic and an epicurean. In Dryden, incongruities abound; and our author is so little shocked by them, that he imports them elsewhere, in his theological poems, representing the Roman Catholic Church, for instance, as a hind, and the heresies by various animals, who dispute at as great length and as learnedly as Oxford graduates. I like him no better in his Epistles; as a rule, they are but flatteries, almost always awkward, often mythological, interspersed with somewhat vulgar sentences. "I have studied Horace," he says, "and hope the style of his Epistles is not ill imitated here." Do not imagine it to be true. Horace's Epistles, though in verse, are genuine letters, brisk, unequal in movement, always unstudied, natural. Nothing is further from Dryden than this original and sociable spirit, philosophical and lewd, the most refined and the most nervous of epicureans, a kinsman (at eighteen centuries' distance) of Alfred de Musset and Voltaire. Like Horace, an author must be a thinker and a man of the world to write agreeable morality, and Dryden was no more than his contemporaries a thinker of a man of the world.—HIPPOLYTE TAINE, *History of English Literature*, tr. H. Van Laun, 1871, Bk. 3, Ch. 2

To the plays of Dryden we must not look for the enduring part of his writings. Versatile, vigorous, and inventive as they are, they nevertheless lack wit and genuine pathos, and they are disfigured by bombast, and a coarseness of the crudest, not satisfactorily explained by the prevailing profligacy of the time, or excused by the tardy regrets of the poet's maturer years. Few of them survived the age of their writer. It is in his satires, translations, fables, and prologues, where he gives full play to his matchless mastery over heroics, that his successes are most signal. As a satirist he was probably unequalled, whether for command of language, management of metre, or the power of reasoning in verse.—AUSTIN DOBSON, *Handbook of English Literature*, 1874

The importance of Dryden from a historical point of view can scarcely be overestimated. Probably no writer ever left so deep an impression on the literature of his country. For nearly a hundred years the greater part both of our poetry and of our criticism was profoundly affected by his influence. He stood indeed in pretty much the same relation to *belles lettres* as Bacon had stood to philosophy. He was the exponent, if not the initiator, of new ideas, the prophet of a new dispensation. At once summing up and concentrating what had found scattered and somewhat uncertain expression in the earlier representatives of the critical school, he gave it precision, power, vogue, and authority. Neither Waller nor Denham, neither Davenant nor Cowley, singly or collectively, would have been able permanently to affect the course and character of our literature. But Dryden appeared, and an epoch was made. Temper, tone, colour, style—all became changed. A transformed society had found its literary interpreter and teacher—an age not merely unpropitious but inimical to poetry had found its poet. Dryden taught our literature to adapt itself to an altered world. He struck the keynote of the new strains; he marshalled the order of the new procession. Of the poets and men of letters most characteristic of the eighteenth century he was the acknowledged master. He directed them to the classics of ancient Rome and modern France for their models in composition and for their canons of criticism, and both by example and by precept he made those models and canons predominantly influential. It would be no exaggeration to say that if we except *The Rape of the Lock* and *Windsor Forest*, Pope not only followed implicitly in the footsteps of Dryden, but was indebted to him for the archetypes, or at least the suggestions, of every kind of poetry attempted by him. He once observed that he could select from Dryden's works better specimens of every mode of poetry than any other English writer could supply; and the remark is significant. Indeed, Dryden was to Pope what Homer and Apollonius, Theocritus and Nicander, were to Virgil. On criticism his influence was almost equally extensive. Till the appearance of the subtler and more philosophical disquisitions of Hurd, Kames, and Harris, he contributed more than any single writer to give the ply and the tone to the criticism of the eighteenth century, to prescribe its limits, to determine its scope, not so much directly by virtue of his own authority as a legislator, as indirectly by introducing, interpreting, and popularising the critics of antiquity and of modern France. Johnson has observed, and observed with reference to Dryden, that a writer who obtains his full purpose loses himself in his own lustre. It is certainly doing Dryden no more than justice to say that Addison and the periodical writers in their capacity as critics, that Pope in his prefaces and dissertations, that Goldsmith in his critical papers, and that Johnson himself in his great work are satellites in the system of which he was the original and central luminary. Of modern English prose, of the prose, that is to say, which exchanged the old synthetic and rhetorical scheme of structure and colour for that happier temper of ease and dignity, of grace and variety, familiar to us in the style of such writers as Addison, Bolingbroke, and Chesterfield, he was the first to furnish a perfect model.

The judgment of our forefathers which assigned to Dryden the third or fourth place among English poets will not be corroborated by modern criticism. It would, indeed, be easy to frame, and to frame with unexceptionable correctness, a definition of poetry which should exclude, or nearly exclude, him from the right to be numbered among poets at all. Of imagination in the sensuous acceptation of the term he had little, in the higher acceptation of the term nothing. And if his genius is, to borrow an expression from Plato, without the power of the wing, it is almost equally deficient in most of those other qualities which constitute the essential distinction between poetry and rhetoric. It was neither finely touched nor finely tempered. It had little sense of the beautiful, of the pathetic, of the sublime, though it could juggle with their counterfeits. To say with Wordsworth that there is not a single image from Nature to be found in the whole body of his poetry would be to say what is not true; but it is true that such images are rare. The predominating power in Dryden was a robust, vigorous, and logical intellect, intensely active and extraordinarily versatile. In addition to this he possessed, or, to speak more properly, acquired, a singularly fine ear for the rhythm of verse, and a plastic mastery over our language, such as few even of the Classics of our poetry have attained. What these powers could effect they effected to the full. They placed him in the front rank of rhetorical poets. They enabled him to rival Lucretius in didactic poetry, Lucan in epic, and Juvenal in satire. If they could not supply what Nature had denied him, they supplied its semblance. There is in Dryden's poetry, and especially in his lyrical poetry, a vehemence and energy, a rapidity of movement and a fertility and vividness of imagery, which it is sometimes difficult to distinguish from the expression of that emotional and spiritual exaltation which constitutes genuine enthusiasm. But genuine enthusiasm is not there. "Alexander's Feast" is a consummate example both of metrical skill and of what a combination of all the qualities which enter into the composition of rhetorical masterpieces can effect. But it is nothing more. The moment we compare it, say, with Pindar's first Pythian Ode, its relation to true poetry becomes at once apparent. It is the same when he attempts the pathetic and when he attempts the sublime. For the first he substitutes—as in the Elegy on Oldham, the "Ode on Mrs. Anne Killigrew," "Eleonora," and the lines on Ossory in *Absalom and Achitophel*—elaborate eloquence; for the second, if he does not collapse in bombast, magnificence and pomp.

But when all deductions are made, how much must the most scrupulous criticism still leave to Dryden. As long as our literature endures, his genial energy, his happy unstinted talent, his incomparable power of style, can never fail to fascinate. It may be said with simple truth that what is best in his work is in our language the best of its kind. His only rival in satire is Pope; but the satires of Pope stand in the same relation to *Absalom and Achitophel*, *The Medal*, and *Mac-Flecknoe*, as the *Æneid* stands to the *Iliad*. Some of the most eminent of our poets have essayed to make rhymed verse the vehicle for argumentative discussion; but what have we

which can for a moment be placed beside the *Religio Laici* and *The Hind and the Panther*? His Epistles again, the Epistles, for example, to Roscommon, to Congreve, to his cousin, to Kneller, to the Duchess of Ormond, are the perfection of this species of composition. His Prologues and Epilogues are models of what such pieces should be. If his lyrics have not the finer qualities of poetry, and jar on us now with the note of falsetto and now with the note of vulgarity, the first "Ode on Saint Cecilia's Day," "Alexander's Feast," the "Ode on Mrs. Anne Killigrew," and the Horatian Paraphrase are superb achievements. No one, indeed, can contemplate without wonder the manifold energy of that vigorous and plastic genius, which added to our literature so much which is excellent and so much which is admirable, and which elicited from one of the most fastidious of poets and critics the rapturous exhortation—to read Dryden—"and be blind to all his faults!"—JOHN CHURTON COLLINS, "John Dryden" (1878), *Essays and Studies*, 1895, pp. 85–90

The poet's portrait is preserved in the Hall of Trinity College, Cambridge, and shows a face of so much masculine sanity and gentleness as predisposes us to credit all the good, and disregard all the evil, which could be propounded of its original. The features are well-set and comely, and the whole countenance has the breadth of intellectual and personal self-possession—large resources largely and beneficially utilized.

Robustness is the great characteristic of Dryden's poetry; he is often excessive, but it is the excess of faculty, not of endeavour. Whatever he does is done with solidity and superiority: he dominates his subject and his reader, and effects this by the direct unlaboured expression of himself. Animated and resolute conception finds its precise and ample equivalent in nervous diction. The Roman writers nourished his style, which took in his hands such sturdy and full-bodied dimensions as to constitute, though without any extraordinary originality to start with, the nucleus of a new school; the Roman writers far rather than those of the Romance tongues of modern Europe, so prolific in their influence upon preceding British literature. It was doubtless with surprise no less than zealous delight that in his old age Dryden discovered for himself the magic of Chaucer, as in his youth the unapproached profusion and profundity of Shakespeare. His greatest power, hardly exercised until he had reached the maturity of his age, was in satire—satire into which he poured the whole energy of his temperament, even more than the brilliancy of his mind, and which represents chiefly vehement invective, as distinct from the sting and scintillation of epigram or lampoon. The abounding sweep and resilient strength of his versification form another of his prime excellences; and he may almost be said to have remoulded the English heroic measure—puffing it out to excess, it should fairly be admitted, with triple rhymes and rolling Alexandrines. His were essentially a mind and a hand which grasped and used their materials—educing from them the utmost for his own purposes, and leaving them to his successors drained and flaccid for further service.—WILLIAM MICHAEL ROSSETTI, "John Dryden," *Lives of Famous Poets*, 1878, pp. 106–7

Are Dryden and Pope poetical classics? Is the historic estimate, which represents them as such, and which has been so long established that it cannot easily give way, the real estimate? Wordsworth and Coleridge, as is well known, denied it; but the authority of Wordsworth and Coleridge does not weigh much with the young generation, and there are many signs to show that the eighteenth century and its judgments are coming into favour again. Are the favourite poets of the eighteenth century classics?

It is impossible within my present limits to discuss the question fully. And what man of letters would not shrink from seeming to dispose dictatorially of the claims of two men who are, at any rate, such masters in letters as Dryden and Pope; two men of such admirable talent, both of them, and one of them, Dryden, a man, on all sides, of such energetic and genial power? And yet, if we are to gain the full benefit from poetry, we must have the real estimate of it. I cast about for some mode of arriving, in the present case, at such an estimate without offence. And perhaps the best way is to begin, as it is easy to begin, with cordial praise.

When we find Chapman, the Elizabethan translator of Homer, expressing himself in his preface thus: 'Though truth in her very nakedness sits in so deep a pit, that from Gades to Aurora and Ganges few eyes can sound her, I hope yet those few here will so discover and confirm, that, the date being out of her darkness in this morning of our poet, he shall now gird his temples with the sun,'—we pronounce that such a prose is intolerable. When we find Milton writing: 'And long it was not after, when I was confirmed in this opinion, that he, who would not be frustrate of his hope to write well hereafter in laudable things, ought himself to be a true poem,'—we pronounce that such a prose has its own grandeur, but that it is obsolete and inconvenient. But when we find Dryden telling us: 'What Virgil wrote in the vigour of his age, in plenty and at ease, I have undertaken to translate in my declining years; struggling with wants, oppressed with sickness, curbed in my genius, liable to be misconstrued in all I write,'—then we exclaim that here at last we have the true English prose, a prose such as we would all gladly use if only we knew how. Yet Dryden was Milton's contemporary.—MATTHEW ARNOLD, "Introduction" to *The English Poets*, ed. Thomas Humphry Ward, 1880, Vol. 1, pp. xxxvii–xxxviii

In one of his own last letters he states that his life-object had been to improve the language, and especially the poetry. He had accomplished it. With our different estimate of the value of old English literature, we cannot, indeed, adopt Johnson's famous metaphor, and say that "he found English of brick and left it of marble." The comparison of *Hamlet* and *Macbeth* to "brick," with *Don Sebastian* and the *Spanish Friar* for "marble," would be absurd. But in truth the terms of the comparison are inappropriate. English as Dryden found it—and it must be remembered that he found it not the English of Shakspeare and Bacon, not even the English of such survivals as Milton and Taylor, but the English of persons like Cowley, Davenant, and their likes—was not wholly marble or wholly brick. No such metaphor can conveniently describe it. It was rather an instrument or machine which had in times past turned out splendid work, but work comparatively limited in kind, and liable to constant flaws and imperfections of more or less magnitude. In the hands of the men who had lately worked it, the good work had been far less in quantity and inferior in quality; the faults and flaws had been great and numerous. Dryden so altered the instrument and its working that, at its best, it produced a less splendid result than before, and became less suited for some of the highest applications, but at the same time became available for a far greater variety of ordinary purposes, was far surer in its working, without extraordinary genius on the part of the worker, and was almost secure against the grosser imperfections. The forty years' work which is at once the record and the example of this accomplishment is itself full of faults and blemishes, but they are always committed in the effort to improve. Dryden is always striving, and consciously striving, to find better literary forms, a better vocabulary, better metres, better constructions, better style. He may in no one branch have attained the entire and flawless perfection which distinguishes Pope as far as he goes; but the range of Dryden is to the range of Pope as that of a forest to a shrubbery, and in this case priority is everything, and the priority is on the side of Dryden. He is not our greatest poet; far from it. But there is one point in which the superlative may safely be applied to him. Considering what he started with, what he accomplished, and what advantages he left to his successors, he must be pronounced, without exception, the greatest craftsman in English letters, and as such he ought to be regarded with peculiar veneration by all who, in however humble a capacity, are connected with the craft.

This general estimate, as well as much of the detailed criticism on which it is based, and which will be found in the preceding chapters, will no doubt seem exaggerated to not a few persons, to the judgment of some at least of whom I should be sorry that it should seem so. The truth is, that while the criticism of poetry is in such a disorderly state as it is at present in regard to general principles, it cannot be expected that there should be any agreement between individual practitioners of it on individual points. So long as any one holds a definition of poetry which regards it wholly or chiefly from the point of view of its subject-matter, wide differences are unavoidable. But if we hold what I venture to think the only Catholic faith with regard to it, that it consists not in a selection of subjects, but in a method of treatment, then it seems to me that all difficulty vanishes. We get out of the hopeless and sterile controversies as to whether Shelley was a greater poet than Dryden, or Dryden a greater poet than Shelley. For my part, I yield to no man living in rational admiration for either, but I decline altogether to assign marks to each in a competitive examination. There are, as it seems to me, many mansions in poetry, and the great poets live apart in them. What constitutes a great poet is supremacy in his own line of poetical expression. Such supremacy must of course be shown in work of sufficient bulk and variety, on the principle that one swallow does not make a summer. We cannot call Lovelace a great poet, or Barnabe Barnes; perhaps we cannot give the name to Collins or to Gray. We must be satisfied that the poet has his faculty of expression well at command, not merely that it sometimes visits him in a casual manner; and we must know that he can apply it in a sufficient number of different ways. But when we see that he can under these conditions exhibit pretty constantly the poetical *differentia*, the power of making the common uncommon by the use of articulate language in metrical arrangement so as to excite indefinite suggestions of beauty, then he must be acknowledged a master.

When we want to see whether a man is a great poet or not, let us take him in his commonplaces, and see what he does with them. Here are four lines which are among the last that Dryden wrote; they occur in the address to the Duchess of Ormond, who was, it must be remembered, by birth Lady Margaret Somerset:

O daughter of the rose, whose cheeks unite
The differing titles of the red and white,
Who heaven's alternate beauty well display,
The blush of morning and the milky way.

The ideas contained in these lines are as old, beyond all doubt, as the practice of love-making between persons of the Caucasian type of physiognomy, and the images in which those ideas are expressed are in themselves as well worn as the stones of the Pyramids. But I maintain that any poetical critic worth his salt could, without knowing who wrote them, but merely from the arrangement of the words, the rhythm and cadence of the line, and the manner in which the images are presented, write "This is a poet, and probably a great poet," across them, and that he would be right in doing so. When such a critic, in reading the works of the author of these lines, finds that the same touch is, if not invariably, almost always present; that in the handling of the most unpromising themes, the *mots rayonnants*, the *mots de lumière* are never lacking; that the suggested images of beauty never fail for long together; then he is justified in striking out the "probably," and writing "This is a great poet." If he tries to go farther, and to range his great poets in order of merit, he will almost certainly fail. He cannot count up the beauties in one, and then the beauties in the other, and strike the balance accordingly. He can only say, "There is the faculty of producing those beauties; it is exercised under such conditions, and with such results, that there is no doubt of its being a native and resident faculty, not a mere casual inspiration of the moment; and this being so, I pronounce the man a poet, and a great one." This can be said of Dryden, as it can be said of Shelley, or Spenser, or Keats, to name only the great English poets who are most dissimilar to him in subject and in style. All beyond this is treacherous speculation. The critic quits the assistance of a plain and catholic theory of poetry, and develops all sorts of private judgments, and not improbably private crotchets. The ideas which this poet works on are more congenial to his ideas than the ideas which that poet works on; the dialect of one is softer to his ear than the dialect of another; very frequently some characteristic which has not the remotest connexion with his poetical merits or demerits makes the scale turn. Of only one poet can it be safely said that he is greater than the other great poets, for the reason that in Dryden's own words he is larger and more comprehensive than any of them. But with the exception of Shakspeare, the greatest poets in different styles are, in the eyes of a sound poetical criticism, very much on an equality. Dryden's peculiar gift, in which no poet of any language has surpassed him, is the faculty of treating any subject which he does treat poetically. His range is enormous, and wherever it is deficient, it is possible to see that external circumstances had to do with the apparent limitation. That the author of the tremendous satire of the political pieces should be the author of the exquisite lyrics scattered about the plays; that the special pleader of *Religio Laici* should be the tale-teller of Palamon and Arcite, are things which, the more carefully I study other poets and their comparatively limited perfection, astonish me the more. My natural man may like *Kubla Khan*, or the "Ode on a Grecian Urn," or the "Ode on Intimations of Immortality," or "O World! O Life! O Time!" with an intenser liking than that which it feels for anything of Dryden's. But that arises from the pure accident that I was born in the first half of the nineteenth century, and Dryden in the first half of the seventeenth. The whirligig of time has altered and is altering this relation between poet and reader in every generation. But what it cannot alter is the fact that the poetical virtue which is present in Dryden is the same poetical virtue that is present in Lucretius and in Æschylus, in Shelley and in Spenser, in Heine and in Hugo.—GEORGE SAINTSBURY, *Dryden*, 1881, pp. 187–92

For my case I shd. also remark that we turned up a difference of taste and judgment, if you remember, about Dryden. I can scarcely think of you not admiring Dryden without, I may say, exasperation. And my style tends always more towards Dryden.

What is there in Dryden? Much, but above all this: he is the most masculine of our poets; his style and his rhythms lay the strongest stress of all our literature on the naked thew and sinew of the English language, the praise that with certain qualifications one would give in Greek to Demosthenes, to be the greatest master of bare Greek.—GERARD MANLEY HOPKINS, Letter to Robert Bridges (Nov. 6, 1887)

The absence of a truly catholic taste, and the survival of an exclusive devotion to the romantic ideals of the early part of the present century, must, I suppose, be the cause of a tendency, on the part of some of those who have replied to me, to question the right of Dryden and Pope to appear on my list of great poets. It appears that Dryden is very poorly thought of at Crawfordsville, Indiana, and even at busier centres of American taste he is reported as being not much of a power. "Dryden is not read in America," says one of my critics, with jaunty confidence. They say that we in England are sometimes harsh in our estimates of America; but I confess I do not know the Englishman bold enough to have charged America with the shocking want of taste which these children of her own have so lightly volunteered to attribute to her. Dryden not read in America! It makes one wonder what *is* read. Probably Miss Amélie Rives?

But to be serious, I can conceive nothing more sinister for the future of English literature than that to any great extent, or among any influential circle of reading and writing men, the majesty and sinewy force of the most masculine of all the English poets should be despised and rejected. Something of a temper less hurried than that of the man who runs and reads is no doubt required for the appreciation of that somewhat heavy-footed and sombre giant of tragic and of narrative song, John Dryden, warring with dunces, marching with sunken head—"a down look," as Pope described it—through the unappreciative flat places of our second Charles and James. Prosaic at times he is, slow, fatigued, unstimulating; but, at his best, how full of the true sublime, how uplifted by the wind of tragic passion, how stirred to the depths by the noblest intellectual and moral enthusiasm! For my own part, there are moments and moods in which nothing satisfies my ear and my brain as do the great accents of Dryden, while he marches down the page, with his elephants and his standards and his kettledrums, "in the full vintage of his flowing honours."

There must be something effeminate and feeble in the nervous system of a generation which cannot bear this grandiose music, this virile tramp of Dryden's soldiers and camp-followers; something singularly dull and timid in a spirit that rejects this robust intellectual companion. And, with all his russet suit of homespun, Dryden is imbued to the core with the truest and richest blood of poetry. His vehemence is positively Homeric; we would not give *Mac Flecknoe* in exchange even for the lost *Margites*. He possesses in a high degree all the qualities which we have marked as needed for the attribution of greatness. He is original to that extent that mainly by his efforts the entire stream of English poetry was diverted for a century and a half into an unfamiliar channel; he has an executive skill eminently his own, and is able to amaze us to-day after so many subsequent triumphs of verse-power; he has distinction such as an emperor might envy; and after all the poets of the eighteenth century have, as Mr. Lowell says, had their hands in his pockets, his best lines are as fresh and as magical as ever.—EDMUND GOSSE, "What Is a Great Poet?" (1889), *Questions at Issue*, 1893, pp. 101–3

Works

DRAMAS

I don't think Dryden so bad a dramatic writer as you seem to do. There are as many things finely said in his plays, as almost by any body. Beside his three best, (*All for Love, Don Sebastian,* and the *Spanish Fryar,*) there are others that are good: as, *Sir Martin Mar-all, Limberham,* and *The Conquest of Mexico.* His *Wild Gallant* was written while he was a boy, and is very bad.—All his plays are printed in the order they were written.—ALEXANDER POPE (1734–36), cited in Joseph Spence, *Anecdotes, Observations and Characters of Books and Men,* ed. S. W. Singer, 1820

This man, from his influence in fixing the laws of versification and poetical language, especially in rhyme, has acquired a reputation altogether disproportionate to his true merit. We shall not here inquire whether his translations of the Latin poets are not manneristical paraphrases, whether his political allegories (now that party interest is dead) can be read without the greatest weariness; but confine ourselves to his plays, which considered relatively to his great reputation, are incredibly bad. Dryden had a gift of flowing and easy versification; the knowledge which he possessed was considerable, but undigested; and all this was coupled with the talent of giving a certain appearance of novelty to what however was borrowed from all quarters; his serviceable muse was the resource of an irregular life. He had besides an immeasurable vanity; he frequently disguises it under humble prologues; on other occasions he speaks out boldly and confidently, avowing his opinion that he has done better than Shakspeare, Fletcher, and Jonson (whom he places nearly on the same level); all the merit of this he is, however, willing to ascribe to the refinement and advances of the age. The age indeed! as if that of Elizabeth compared with the one in which Dryden lived, were not in every respect "Hyperion to a Satyr!" Dryden played also the part of the critic: he furnished his pieces richly with prefaces and treatises on dramatic poetry, in which he chatters most confusedly about the genius of Shakspeare and Fletcher, and about the entirely opposite example of Corneille; of the original boldness of the British stage, and of the rules of Aristotle and Horace.—He imagined that he had invented a new species, namely the Heroic Drama; as if Tragedy had not from its very nature been always heroical! If we are, however, to seek for a heroic drama which is not peculiarly tragic, we shall find it among the Spaniards, who had long possessed it in the greatest perfection. From the uncommon facility of rhyming which Dryden possessed, it cost him little labour to compose the most of his serious pieces entirely in rhyme. With the English, the rhymed verse of ten syllables supplies the place of the Alexandrine; it has more freedom in its pauses, but on the other hand it wants the alternation of male and female rhymes; it proceeds in pairs exactly like the French Alexandrine, and in point of syllabic measure it is still more uniformly symmetrical. It therefore unavoidably communicates a great stiffness to the dialogue. The manner of the older English poets before them, who generally used blank verse, and only occasionally introduced rhymes, was infinitely preferable. But, since then, on the other hand, rhyme has come to be too exclusively rejected.—AUGUST WILHELM SCHLEGEL, *Lectures on Dramatic Art and Literature,* 1809, tr. John Black

Dryden's comedies have all the point that there is in ribaldry, and all the humour that there is in extravagance. I am sorry I can say nothing better of them. He was not at home in this kind of writing, of which he was himself conscious. His play was *horse-play.* His wit (what there is of it) is ingenious and scholar-like, rather than natural and dramatic. Thus Burr, in the *Wild Gallant,* says to Failer, 'She shall sooner cut an atom than part us.'—His plots are pure *voluntaries* in absurdity, that bend and shift to his purpose without any previous notice or reason, and are governed by final causes. *Sir Martin Mar-all,* which was taken from the Duchess of Newcastle, is the best of his plays, and the origin of the *Busy Body.*—WILLIAM HAZLITT, *Lectures on the English Comic Writers,* 1818

Dryden's plays have not come down to us, except in the collection of his printed works. The last of them that was on the list of regular acting plays was *Don Sebastian.* The *Mask of Arthur and Emmeline* was the other day revived at one of our theatres, without much success. *Alexander the Great* is by Lee, who wrote some things in conjunction with Dryden, and who had far more power and passion of an irregular and turbulent kind, bordering upon constitutional morbidity, and who might have done better things (as we see from his *Œdipus*) had not his genius been perverted and rendered worse than abortive by carrying the vicious manner of his age to the greatest excess. Dryden's plays are perhaps the fairest specimen of what this manner was. I do not know how to describe it better than by saying that it is one continued and exaggerated common-place. All the characters are put into a swaggering attitude of dignity, and tricked out in the pomp of ostentatious drapery. The images are extravagant, yet not far-fetched; they are outrageous caricatures of obvious thoughts: the language oscillates between bombast and bathos: the characters are noisy pretenders to virtue, and shallow boasters in vice; the versification is laboured and monotonous, quite unlike the admirably free and flowing rhyme of his satires, in which he felt the true inspiration of his subject, and could find modulated sounds to express it. Dryden had no dramatic genius either in tragedy or comedy. In his plays he mistakes blasphemy for sublimity, and ribaldry for wit. He had so little notion of his own powers, that he has put Milton's *Paradise Lost* into dramatic rhyme to make Adam look like a fine gentleman; and has added a double love-plot to the *Tempest,* to 'relieve the killing languor and over-laboured lassitude' of that solitude of the imagination, in which Shakespear had left the inhabitants of his Enchanted Island.—WILLIAM HAZLITT, *Lectures on the Dramatic Literature of the Age of Elizabeth,* 1820

⟨. . .⟩ no candid admirer of Dryden's in some respects almost incomparable genius can truthfully plead on his behalf, that manhood and old age, which mellowed his literary powers, at the same time refined his literary morality as a dramatist. The brilliant style of his *Amphitryon* can no more conceal his defiance of the principles of good manners than the crudity of his *Wild Gallant* can excuse it. He was no more able than were the puniest of his rivals or would-be rivals, to resist the temptation of painting vice of a particular kind in attractive colours, and his defence of the leniency with which at times he deals out dramatic justice to his vicious characters in comedy is as shallow as he must have known it to be.

But while only a perverse misinterpretation of the claims of genius will excuse in a great writer what it blames in a small, it would be an altogether oblique view of Dryden as a dramatist which should treat a defect shared by him with many others as a distinctive characteristic of his dramatic productions. As a dramatist he exhibits qualities raising him above the level of any of his competitors—though less conspicuously so than in one or two other branches of literature illustrated by his genius. The flexibility of that genius—all the more notably, inasmuch as his first dramatic composition dates from the thirty-first year of his life—enabled him in both tragedy and comedy to excel all, or very nearly all, his contemporaries. In the former, after a more or less tentative effort of a mixed character, he threw himself in with the current of a mistaken innovation, to which nothing but his example—not even his own brilliant theoretical sophistries—could have secured the vitality it exhibited. But for the brilliancy of style which he lavished upon them, heroic plays would have remained unremembered by posterity, when, with his abandonment of the species, it had ceased to keep a hold over the age which had given birth to it. In these plays, and even in his later efforts in the tragic drama, he never passed beyond the limits of those themes to which the tragedy of the age had gradually restricted itself; although while binding himself to a more rigid method of construction, he had come to recognise in characterisation the highest task and the surest test of dramatic power. Love and honour were the pivots upon which the mimic world of his tragedies turned, even where, as in a solitary instance, another motive (that of religious devotion) is admitted to an apparent share in the action. In the delineation of these passions he never passed beyond his 'heroic' conceptions of their genesis, and of the laws of their being: but within these limits he was master of his themes. Lee may perhaps be held to have occasionally approached him in his fervent representations of heroic honour and love—but at how considerable an interval may be best seen from the works which they composed jointly—while in the reproduction of the most pathetic moments of amorous sentiment he was probably surpassed by Otway. In his use of far-fetched expedients for the provocation of terror he knew no bounds, often confounding the extraordinary with the powerful, and momentary sensation with enduring effect. His diction was often even more excessive than his action; but the former was the product of a real natural force, which it is difficult to withstand even on the printed page, and which must have been irresistible when aided by the art of Betterton's 'well-govern'd voice' and manner, and by the efforts of the eminent actors and actresses with whom he was associated. The unequalled impetus of Dryden's tragic eloquence was freely acknowledged by the most resolute of his adversaries. For comedy, on the other hand, Dryden at times expressed a dislike resembling contempt, at times declared himself by nature unfitted. 'I want,' he said, 'that gaiety of humour which is required to it;' and 'even in his own partial judgment' he held that some of his contemporaries had outdone him in this branch of the drama. He was, I think, doubly mistaken. Beginning with a reproduction of those Spanish plots which pleased the age, but which in truth amount only to delusive perversions of the real excellences of dramatic construction, he rarely took the trouble to construct a good plot, though he was manifestly capable of such an achievement. That he was unequal to the conception of comic character would (even if he had never written a comedy) be a charge too ludicrous to need refutation; that he succeeded in its dramatic presentation has been sufficiently shown by the examples noticed in the preceding pages, ranging from the excellent high comedy of *Secret Love* to the equally excellent low comedy of *The Spanish Friar*. It is surely strange criticism which considers a third-rate writer like Crowne to have surpassed Dryden in comedy: in truth, there was no rival whom he needed to fear, and only one—his adversary Shadwell—who surpassed him in fertility, though falling far behind him in finish, of dramatic characterisation. The prose dialogue of comedy he had at his command whenever he chose to exert his powers in this direction; here, as in the dialogue of rimed tragedy, he was without a peer, till the vigour of Wycherley and the brilliant wit

of Congreve announced the advent of a new generation of comic dramatists. No one was more ready to welcome them than Dryden, one of the kindliest befrienders of younger talent whom the world of letters has ever known. While recognising the merits of Wycherley as well as those of Etherege and Southerne in terms generously chosen, he addresses Congreve in a strain which breathes, together with magnanimous delight in the merits of his successor, the conscious pride of a legitimate sovereign:

> Well had I been deposed if you had reign'd!
> The father had descended for the son,
> For only you are lineal to the throne.

The sway which he thus resigned he had exercised with an authority neither unchallenged nor well guarded by himself. But, taking his dramatic works for all in all, his pre-eminence seems indisputable; and the Restoration drama in the stricter sense of the term will be best understood and best appreciated by those who consistently regard Dryden as its central figure. He reflects both the faults and the vices of that drama with sufficient distinctness to teach us what to shun; of its merits and its excellences few are wanting in its foremost representative, or shine elsewhere with so dazzling a brilliancy as that which is the unrivalled distinction of this great master of style. —ADOLPHUS WILLIAM WARD, *A History of English Dramatic Literature* (1875), 1899, Vol. 3, pp. 387–90

In that valuable and admirable treatise, *An Essay of Dramatic Poesy*, 1668, published when he had already produced five of his dramatic experiments, Dryden very clearly and unflinchingly lays down the law about theatrical composition. Plays are for the future to be "regular"—that is to say, they are to respect the unities of time, place, and action; "no theatre in the world has anything so absurd as the English tragi-comedy," and this is to be rigorously abandoned; a great simplicity of plot, a broad and definite catastrophe, an observation of the laws of stage decorum, these are to mark the English theatre in future, as they already are the ornament of the French. After all this, we are startled to discover Dryden turning against his new allies, praising the English irregularity, finding fault with Corneille, and finally unravelling his whole critical web with a charming admission: "I admire the pattern of elaborate writing, but—I love Shakespeare." The fact is that the great spirit of Dryden, here at the practical outset of his career, was torn between two aims. He saw that English poetry was exhausted, disillusioned, bankrupt, and that nothing short of a complete revolution would revive it; he saw that the Latin civilisation was opening its arms, and that England was falling into them, fascinated like a bird by a snake (and Dryden also was fascinated and could not resist); yet, all the time, he was hankering after the lost poetry, and wishing that a compromise could be made between Shakespeare and Aristotle, Fletcher and Molière. So, with all his effort to create "heroic drama" in England, no really well-constructed piece, no closely wrought and highly polished *Cinna* was to reward Dryden for his cultivation of the unities.—EDMUND GOSSE, *A Short History of Modern English Literature*, 1897, pp. 177–78

THE CONQUEST OF GRANADA

Conquest of Granada, by the *Spaniards*, in two Parts, acted at the Theatre-Royal, printed in quarto *Lond.* 1678. and dedicated to his Royal Highness the Duke. These Plays I have seen acted with great Applause, which so pufft up our Author with vanity, that he could not refrain from abusing his Predecessors, not only in the Postscript already mention'd; but even in a detracting Epilogue to the second Part, which I shall leave to the Readers perusal. I have already hinted, that not only the *Episodes*, and main Plot, but even the Characters are all borrow'd from *French* and *Spanish* Romances, as *Almahide*, *Grand Cyrus*, *Ibrahim*, and *Gusman*: so that Mr. *Dryden* may be said to have made a Rod for himself, in the following Lines;

> And may those drudges of the Stage, whose Fate
> Is damn'd dull Farce more dully to Translate,
> Fall under that Excise the State thinks fit
> To set on all *French* Wares, whose worst is Wit.
> *French* Farce worn out at home, is sent abroad;
> And patcht up here is made our English Mode.

How much Mr. *Dryden* has borrow'd from the *French* in this Play, cannot be comprehended in the compass to which I confine my self; and therefore I shall only mention some of the most remarkable Passages which are stollen. I am therefore in the first place to begin with the Persons represented: The Character of *Almanzor* is chiefly taken from *Ponce de Leon* in *Almahide*; from *Ozmin* in *Gusman*, and *Artahan* in *Cleopatra*. His other Characters of *Boabdelin, Almahide, Ferdinand* and *Isabella*, Duke of *Arcos, Ozmin, Hamet, Gomel*, &c. are taken from *Almahide*. The Characters of *Ozmin* and *Benzaida*, are borrow'd from *Ibrahim*, in the Story of *Ozmin* and *Alibech*, and *Lyndaraxa*, are copied from Prince *Ariantes, Agathirsis*, and *Elibesis*; See *Grand Cyrus*, Part IX. Book I.

I am now to give some Instances that may make good my Assertion, That Mr. *Dryden* has borrow'd most of his Thoughts, as well as his Characters from those Authors above-mention'd, tho' he has new cloath'd them in Rime. In the beginning of the First Act, he has borrow'd the Description of his *Bull-feast*, from *Guzman's Juego de Toros & Cannas*: See the Story of *Ozmin* and *Daraxa*, part I. pag. 82. and 85. The Description of the Factions *pag*. 4 is borrow'd from *Almahide* p. I. The next four Lines spoken by the King is taken from Prince *Mussa's* advice in *Almahide*, p. 6. The King's Speech in going between the Factions, *pag* 5. is borrow'd from *Almahide*, Part 3. Book 3. p. 63. The Description of the Quarrel between *Tarifa* and *Ozmin*, is founded on *Abindarrays* his Speech in *Alm*. p. 2. The Rise of the Families, *p*. 6. from the same. *Almanzor's* killing *Gomel*, from *Alm*. p. 64. His quelling the Factions, from *Alm*. p. 64, 65. In the Second Act, *Almanzor's* Victory, and his taking the Duke of *Arcos* Prisoner, *p*, 12. is copied from *Almahide*, p. 65. The Scene between *Abdalla* and *Lyndaraxa*, p. 13. is stollen from *Alm*. p. 62. and from the Story of *Elibesis* in *Cyrus*, Part 9. Book I. p. 20. *Zulema's* Plea for *Abdalla's* right to the Crown, *p*. 17. is copied from *Alm*. p. 62. His tempting him to Rebellion, from *Cyrus* in the place above-mention'd. In the Third Act, *Almanzor's* going over to *Abdalla*, on the Kings refusal to grant the Duke of *Arcos* his Liberty, *pag*. 18. is taken from *Alm*. p. 55. &c. The Alarm after the *Zambra* Dance from the same page. The first meeting of *Almanzor* and *Almahide*, p. 27. from *Alm*. p. 69. Of *Abdalla* and *Almanzor*, p. 30. from *Alm*. p. 71. The Controversy between *Almanzor* and *Zulema*, p. 31. from the same Column. In the Fourth Act, *Almanzor's* going over to *Boabdelin's* Party, *p*. 34. is taken from *Alm*. p. 72. *Abdelmelech* his coming to visit *Lyndaraxa* in Disguise, *p*. 35. is stollen from the former Story of *Elibesis* in *Cyrus*, p. 25. &c. *Abdalla* visiting her, being Royally attended with Guards, *p*. 39. from the same, p. 67. *Almanzor's* freeing *Almahide* from *Abdalla's* Captivity, *p*. 45. is copied from *Alm*. p. 73. The beginning of the Fifth Act, *viz*. The Scene between *Abdalla*, and *Lyndaraxa*, under the Walls of the *Albayzin*, immediately after his Defeat, *p*. 48. is stollen from *Cyrus* in the Story aforesaid, *p*. 61. His flying to the Christians, *p*. 50. from *Alm*. p. 72. *Ozmin* and *Benzaida's* flight, *p*. 62. from *Ibrahim*, p. 8.

I might proceed through the Second Part, did I not fear the Reader to be already as tir'd as my self. I shall therefore only acquaint him, that most of that Play is borrow'd as well as the former: So that had our Author stollen from others, in none of his Labours, yet these Plays alone argue him guilty of the highest Confidence, that durst presume to arraign the Ancient English Poets as Plagiaries, in a Postscript to two Plays, whose Foundation and Language are in a great measure stollen from the Beginning to the End. I would therefore defire Mr. *Dryden* henceforth to ponder upon the following Epigram, which seems to give him better Advice.

> Cum fueris Censor, primum te crimine purga,
>   Nec tua te damnent facta nefanda reum.
> Ne'tua contemnas aliena negotia curans;
>   An tibi te quisquam junctior esse potest.

There are several Authors that have given an Account of this famous Action, as *Mariana*, L. 25. G. 18. *Mayerne Tarquet*, L. 23. *Thuanus*, L. 48. *Guicciardine*, L. 12. *Luc. Marinxus Sic*. L. 20. *Car. Verardus. Domingo Baltanas*, &c. —GERARD LANGBAINE, *An Account of the English Dramatick Poets*, 1691

In the conduct of the story there is much brilliancy of event. The reader, or spectator, is never allowed to repose on the scene before him; and although the changes of fortune are too rapid to be either probable, or altogether pleasing, yet they arrest the attention by their splendour and importance, and interest us in spite of our more sober judgment. The introduction of the ghost of Almanzor's mother seems to have been intended to show how the hero could support even an interview with an inhabitant of the other world. At least, the professed purpose of her coming might have been safely trusted to the virtue of Almahide, and her power over her lover. It afforded an opportunity, however, to throw in some fine poetry, of which Dryden has not failed to avail himself. Were it not a peculiar attribute of the heroic drama, it might be mentioned as a defect, that during the seige of the last possession of the Spanish Moors, by an enemy hated for his religion, and for his success, the principle of patriotism is hardly once alluded to through the whole piece. The fate, or the wishes, of Almahide, Lyndaraxa, and Benzayda, are all that interest the Moorish warriors around them, as if the Christian was not thundering at their gates, to exterminate at once their nation and religion. Indeed, so essentially necessary are the encouragements of beauty to military achievement, that we find Queen Isabella ordering to the field of battle a *corps de reserve* of her maids of honour, to animate the fighting warriors with their smiles, and counteract the powerful charms of the Moorish damsels. Nor is it an inferior fault, that, although the characters are called Moors, there is scarce any expression, or allusion, which can fix the reader's attention upon their locality, except an occasional interjection to Allah or Mahomet.

If, however, the reader can abstract his mind from the qualities now deemed essential to a play, and consider the *Conquest of Granada* as a piece of romantic poetry, there are few compositions in the English language, which convey a more lively and favourable display of the magnificence of fable, of language, and of action, proper to that style of composition. Amid the splendid ornaments of the structure we lose sight of occasional disproportion and incongruity; and, at an early age particularly, there are few poems which make a more deep impression upon the imagination than the *Conquest of Granada*.—SIR WALTER SCOTT, *The Works of John Dryden*, 1808

The first tragedies of Dryden were what was called heroic, and written in rhyme; an innovation which, of course, must be ascribed to the influence of the French theatre. They have occasionally much vigour of sentiment and much beautiful poetry, with a versification sweet even to lusciousness. The *Conquest of Granada* is, on account of its extravagance, the most celebrated of these plays; but it is inferior to the *Indian Emperor*, from which it would be easy to select passages of perfect elegance. It is singular that although the rhythm of dramatic verse is commonly permitted to be the most lax of any, Dryden has in this play availed himself of none of his wonted privileges. He regularly closes the sense with the couplet, and falls into a smoothness of cadence which, though exquisitely mellifluous, is perhaps too uniform. In the *Conquest of Granada* the versification is rather more broken. —HENRY HALLAM, *Introduction to the Literature of Europe*, 1837–39, Pt. 4, Ch. 6, Par. 42

The Conquest of Granada by the Spaniards has been generally, and justly, regarded as the most prominent type of the 'heroic plays' of this age. Its historical background and part of its plot were borrowed by Dryden from Madeleine de Scudéry's romance of *Almahide*; but besides deriving certain turns in action and dialogue from the Spanish work on which the French authoress founded her story, he has interwoven with it, as already Langbaine pointed out, portions of the stories of *Le Grand Cyrus* and of *Ibrahim ou L'Illustre Bassa*. Furthermore, Dryden confesses, in his lofty way, that of the chief character of the play, Almanzor, he had derived 'the first image from the Achilles of Homer, the next from Tasso's Rinaldo (who was a copy of the former), and the third from the Artaban of Monsieur Calpranède, who had imitated both. He is,' the English poet complacently adds, 'on a grand scale (not like the heroes of French romance)'—and in truth, one ventures to think, would have created no wholly pleasant sensation in the *salons* where those romances were indigenous. Without pretending to decide the question whether 'the most probable of the actions' of this hero are not impossible, we shall readily allow that the spirit of the dialogue of this play is from first to last nothing short of amazing. If a vast quantity of rant is requisite to give expression to the 'over-boiling' courage of Almanzor, and if the conception of his pride and valour are alike hyper-Achillean—so that altogether he was a fit model for the caricature of Drawcansir in *The Rehearsal*—yet many of the turns of diction are extraordinarily vigorous, and the force of the impetus which enables the author to sustain the character through ten acts is simply without a parallel. The extravagance of the conception is, however, such as to render the entire character at times almost grotesque, while the bombast of particular passages renders them ludicrous so soon as we pause to examine into their meaning. Of the other characters the best is Almahide—a picture of real female dignity, against which the passion of love contends in vain. The ambitious Lyndaxara, on the other hand, seems to me drawn without power. The remaining personages are in themselves uninteresting; but the entire play is written with such marvellous spirit that, hurried along by its resistless current, the reader has no breath left with which to protest his weariness.—ADOLPHUS WILLIAM WARD, *A History of English Dramatic Literature* (1875), 1899, Vol. 3, pp. 360–61

AURENG-ZEBE

Dryden's last and most perfect tragedy in rime was *Aurengzebe*. In this play, the passions are strongly depicted, the characters well discriminated, and the diction more familiar and dramatic, than in any of his preceding pieces. Hart and Mohun

greatly distinguished themselves in the characters of Aurengzebe and the old Emperor. Mrs. Marshall was admired in Nourmahul; and Kynaston has been much extolled, by Cibber, for his happy expression of the arrogant and savage fierceness in Morat.—'Booth, in some part of this character,' says the same critical historian, 'was too tame, from an apprehension of raising the mirth of the audience improperly.'—THOMAS DAVIES, *Dramatic Miscellanies*, 1784, Vol. 3, p. 93

In the tragedy of *Aureng-Zebe*, acted and printed 1676, Dryden once more, and for the last time, produced a rimed heroic play. In the Dedication to Mulgrave (Buckinghamshire), he professes himself weary of low comedy, to which, as has been seen, motives of convenience had induced him to return, and desirous, if he 'must be condemned to rhyme,' of 'some ease in his change of punishment.' He wishes to be 'no more the Sisyphus of the stage'; in other words, he at that time entertained the thought (which he failed to carry into execution) of composing an epic poem. And in the justly celebrated Prologue to this play, he gives frank expression to his weariness 'of his long-loved mistress, Rhyme'; as it were throws up his weapon in confessing that

> Passion's too fierce to be in fetters bound,
> And nature flies him like enchanted ground;

and, while protesting that his present is his most successful effort in the 'correct' style, avows, with a sincerity which all but atones, not only for this boast, but for the unbecoming arrogance of the Epilogue to *The Conquest of Granada*, that

> Spite of all his pride, a secret shame
> Invades his breast at Shakespeare's sacred name:
> Awed when he hears his god-like Romans rage,
> He, in a just despair, would quit the stage;
> And to an age less polished, more unskilled,
> Does, with disdain, the foremost honours yield.

The magnanimity which lies at the root of such a confession is one of the rarest, as it is one of the most delightful, of qualities in an eminent man of letters; nor has there ever been an English author of whom this quality is more characteristic than it is of Dryden in whose case it may well be allowed to cover a multitude of errors. The tragedy *Aureng-Zebe* has been diversely judged; on the whole, however, it must be held both for better and for worse to fall short of Dryden's supreme achievement among his heroic plays, *The Conquest of Granada*. If the diction of the later play has less of vehement force, it is on the other hand varied by passages more subtly impressive; and the verse itself is less monotonously true to the self-established pattern. The historical theme is treated with considerable freedom, for Aureng-Zebe (Great Mogul from 1660 to 1707) was a living prince; but although the master of India was not altogether unacquainted with the course of English affairs, and came into very direct contact with English enterprise in his own latitudes, his name can scarcely have come home more closely to Englishmen at large than that of Mithridates, the subject of a tragedy by Racine, to which the author of *Aureng-Zebe* was assuredly no stranger. (A single scene in this play was borrowed by Dryden from the *Grand Cyrus*.) The absence of all supernatural machinery is noticeable as a further indication of the change which was preparing itself in the author's theories of dramatic composition and effect. —ADOLPHUS WILLIAM WARD, *A History of English Dramatic Literature* (1875), 1899, Vol. 3, pp. 370–72

It is in some respects a very noble play, free from the rants, the preposterous bustle, and the still more preposterous length of the *Conquest of Granada*, while possessing most of the merits of that singular work in an eminent degree. Even Dryden hardly ever went farther in cunning of verse than in some of the passages of *Aurengzebe*, such as that well-known one which seems to take up an echo of *Macbeth*:

> When I consider life, 'tis all a cheat.
> Yet, fooled with hope, men favour the deceit,
> Trust on, and think to-morrow will repay.
> To-morrow's falser than the former day,
> Lies worse, and while it says, we shall be blest
> With some new joys, cuts off what we possest.
> Strange cozenage! none would live past years again,
> Yet all hope pleasure in what yet remain,
> And from the dregs of life think to receive
> What the first sprightly running could not give.
> I'm tired with waiting for this chemic gold
> Which fools us young and beggars us when old.

There is a good deal of moralizing of this melancholy kind in the play, the characters of which are drawn with a serious completeness not previously attempted by the author. It is perhaps the only one of Dryden's which, with very little alteration, might be acted, at least as a curiosity, at the present day. It is remarkable that the structure of the verse in the play itself would have led to the conclusion that Dryden was about to abandon rhyme. There is in *Aurengzebe* a great tendency towards *enjambement*; and as soon as this tendency gets the upper hand, a recurrence to blank verse is, in English dramatic writing, tolerably certain. For the intonation of English is not, like the intonation of French, such that rhyme is an absolute necessity to distinguish verse from prose; and where this necessity does not exist, rhyme must always appear to an intelligent critic a more or less impertinent intrusion in dramatic poetry. Indeed, the main thing which had for a time converted Dryden and others to the use of the couplet in drama was a curious notion that blank verse was too easy for long and dignified compositions. It was thought by others that the secret of it had been lost, and that the choice was practically between bad blank verse and good rhyme.—GEORGE SAINTSBURY, *Dryden*, 1881, pp. 56–57

ALL FOR LOVE

This is the only play, if we may believe the author, that he wrote for himself. It is a pity, however, his favorite play is not original, for all the beauty is derived at least from SHAKESPEAR, and this circumstance has obliged the world to acknowledge that it is very nearly a complete tragedy. To shew, however, with what caution genius ought to be suppressed and curtailed, in furbishing up this play from SHAKESPEAR, the polish has displaced many of the beauties, and whatever it has gained in harmony and regularity it has lost in fire and nature. DRYDEN in this tragedy has professed to have imitated SHAKESPEAR, but he has done more, he has actually quoted him, not only out of this play but out of others; but every body knows the distinction; the merit of both are admirable, yet one truth is invincible. DRYDEN could never have shewn so much skill as a lapidary if SHAKESPEAR had not furnished the diamond. —CHARLES DIBDIN, *A Complete History of the Stage*, 1795, Vol. 4, pp. 169–70

Having given Dryden the praise of superior address in managing the story, I fear he must be pronounced in most other respects inferior to his grand prototype. Antony, the principal character in both plays, is incomparably grander in that of Shakespeare. The majesty and generosity of the military hero is happily expressed by both poets; but the awful ruin of grandeur, undermined by passion, and tottering to its fall, is far more striking in the Antony of Shakespeare. ⟨. . .⟩ In the Cleopatra of Dryden, there is greatly less spirit and originality than in Shakespeare's. The preparation of the latter for death has a grandeur which puts to shame the same scene in Dryden, and serves to support the interest during the whole fifth act, although Antony has died in the conclusion of the fourth. No circumstance can more highly evince the power of Shakespeare's genius, in spite of his irregularities; since the conclusion in Dryden, where both lovers die in the same scene, and after a reconciliation, is infinitely more artful, and better adapted to theatrical effect.—SIR WALTER SCOTT, *The Works of John Dryden*, 1808

All for Love may be almost described as a trial of strength not only against Shakspere, upon whose *Antony and Cleopatra* Dryden's tragedy may be fairly said to be to some extent based, but against many of the chief wits of the nation before and after Shakspere. Dryden's complacency in the result is not wholly unjustified. In a sense, his tragedy is original; the character of Antony is drawn with considerable skill; the dominion which passion is capable of acquiring over a human being is, I think, exhibited quite as effectively as it is in Shakspere—but Dryden's Antony lacks elevation. His Cleopatra is comparatively uninteresting. The writing maintains a high level throughout; and the scene to which, as just noted, the author directs special attention is undoubtedly admirable. The construction of the play is close and effective; and its general tone is sufficiently moderated, without becoming open to the charge of tameness. Within certain limits, there assuredly never was a more flexible genius than Dryden's. The tasks which he set himself, without actually failing in their performance, are many and extraordinary; in the present instance he cannot be said to rival Shakspere on his own ground, but he follows him on it without making himself guilty of servile imitation or breaking down from lack of original force. *All for Love* has been not unjustly designated by an eminent critic as 'Dryden's finest play.' —ADOLPHUS WILLIAM WARD, *A History of English Dramatic Literature* (1875), 1899, Vol. 3, pp. 372–73

Antony and Cleopatra and *All for Love*, when they are contrasted, only show by the contrast the difference of kind, not the difference of degree, between their writers. The heroic conception has here, in all probability, as favourable exposition given to it as it is capable of, and it must be admitted that it makes a not unfavourable show even without the "dull sweets of rhyme" to drug the audience into good humour with it. The famous scene between Antony and Ventidius divides with the equally famous scene in *Don Sebastian* between Sebastian and Dorax the palm among Dryden's dramatic efforts. But as a whole the play is, I think, superior to *Don Sebastian*. The blank verse, too, is particularly interesting, because it was almost its author's first attempt at that *crux*; and because, for at least thirty years, hardly any tolerable blank verse—omitting of course Milton's—had been written by any one. The model is excellent, and it speaks Dryden's unerring literary sense, that, fresh as he was from the study of *Paradise Lost*, and great as was his admiration for its author, he does not for a moment attempt to confuse the epic and the tragic modes of the style. *All for Love* was, and deserved to be, successful.—GEORGE SAINTSBURY, *Dryden*, 1881, pp. 58–59

THE SPANISH FRIAR

When I first designed this play, I found, or thought I found, somewhat so moving in the serious part of it, and so pleasant in the comic, as might deserve a more than ordinary care in both. Accordingly, I used the best of my endeavour, in the management of two plots, so very different from each other, that it was not perhaps the talent of every writer to have made them of a piece. Neither have I attempted other plays of the same nature, in my opinion, with the same judgment; though with like success. And though many poets may suspect themselves for the fondness and partiality of parents to their youngest children, yet I hope I may stand exempted from this rule, because I know myself too well to be ever satisfied with my own conceptions, which have seldom reached to those ideas that I had within me; and consequently, I presume I may have liberty to judge when I write more or less pardonably, as an ordinary marksman may know certainly when he shoots less wide at what he aims. Besides, the care and pains I have bestowed on this, beyond my other tragi-comedies, may reasonably make the world conclude that either I can do nothing tolerably, or that this poem is not much amiss. Few good pictures have been finished at one sitting; neither can a true just play, which is to bear the test of ages, be produced at a heat, or by the force of fancy, without the maturity of judgment. For my own part, I have both so just a diffidence of myself, and so great a reverence for my audience, that I dare venture nothing without a strict examination; and am as much ashamed to put a loose indigested play upon the public as I should be to offer brass money in a payment. For though it should be taken (as it is too often on the stage), yet it will be found in the second telling; and a judicious reader will discover in his closet that trashy stuff whose glittering deceived him in the action. I have often heard the stationer sighing in his shop, and wishing for those hands to take off his melancholy bargain which clapped its performance on the stage. In a playhouse, everything contributes to impose upon the judgment: the lights, the scenes, the habits, and, above all, the grace of action, which is commonly the best where there is the most need of it, surprise the audience, and cast a mist upon their understandings; not unlike the cunning of a juggler, who is always staring us in the face, and overwhelming us with gibberish, only that he may gain the opportunity of making the cleaner conveyance of his trick. But these false beauties of the stage are no more lasting than a rainbow; when the actor ceases to shine upon them, when he gilds them no longer with his reflection, they vanish in a twinkling.—JOHN DRYDEN, Dedication to *The Spanish Friar*, 1681

The *Spanish Friar* has been praised for what Johnson calls the 'happy coincidence and coalition of the two plots.' It is difficult to understand what can be mean by a compliment which seems either ironical or ignorant. Nothing can be more remote from the truth. The artifice of combining two distinct stories on the stage is, we may suppose, either to interweave the incidents of one into those of the other, or at least so to connect some characters with each intrigue, as to make the spectator fancy them less distinct than they are. Thus in the *Merchant of Venice*, the courtship of Bassanio and Portia is happily connected with the main plot of Antonio and Shylock by two circumstances: it is to set Bassanio forward in his suit that the fatal bond is first given; and it is by Portia's address that its forfeiture is explained away. The same play affords an instance of another kind of underplot, that of Lorenzo and Jessica, which is more episodical, and might perhaps be removed without any material loss to the fable; though even this serves to account for, we do not say to palliate, the vindictive exasperation of the Jew. But to which of these do the comic scenes in the *Spanish Friar* bear most resemblance? Certainly to the latter. They consist entirely of an intrigue which

Lorenzo, a young officer, carries on with a rich usurer's wife; but there is not, even by accident, any relation between his adventures and the love and murder which go forward in the palace. The *Spanish Friar*, so far as it is a comedy, is reckoned the best performance of Dryden in that line. Father Dominic is very amusing, and has been copied very freely by succeeding dramatists, especially in the Duenna. But Dryden has no great abundance of wit in this or any of his comedies. His jests are practical, and he seems to have written more for the eye than the ear. It may be noted as a proof of this, that his stage directions are unusually full. In point of diction, the *Spanish Friar* in its tragic scenes, and *All for Love*, are certainly the best plays of Dryden. They are the least infected with his great fault, bombast, and should perhaps be read over and over by those who would learn the true tone of English tragedy. In dignity, in animation, in striking images and figures, there are few or none that excel them; the power indeed of impressing sympathy, or commanding tears, was seldom placed by nature within the reach of Dryden.—HENRY HALLAM, *Introduction to the Literature of Europe*, 1837–39, Pt. 4, Ch. 6, Par. 44

For that branch of the drama indeed, which he held in inferior regard, his brilliant literary endowment still more than sufficed. The comic portion of the tragi-comedy of *The Spanish Friar, or The Double Discovery* (acted 1681) is generally acknowledged to be one of Dryden's happiest dramatic efforts. Of the two well-combined plots the comic one bears a partial resemblance to that of Fletcher's *The Spanish Curate*; the Friar himself, however, is by no means a copy of the Curate, but rather a fat rascal of incontestable originality. This part of the action is carried on with extraordinary spirit, and its central figure is one of the most humorous creations of our later drama, which may be enjoyed without a discussion of its bearing upon the biographical question of Dryden's religious opinions or sentiments. As for the serious plot, though interesting and not ineffective, it has the great blemish of representing the heroine (Leonora) as morally guilty of a crime and thus unworthy of sympathy. The writing of this play in both its serious and comic portions is throughout admirable. Dryden was by this time master of an easy but dignified movement in his blank-verse; and the merits of his comic prose dialogue, as exemplified by this play, have not to my knowledge been at any time surpassed.—ADOLPHUS WILLIAM WARD, *A History of English Dramatic Literature* (1875), 1899, Vol. 3, pp. 376–77

DON SEBASTIAN

"Comedy," says Horace, "sometimes raises her voice;" and Tragedy may likewise on proper occasions abate her dignity; but as the comick personages can only depart from their familiarity of style, when the more violent passions are put in motion, the heroes and queens of tragedy should never descend to trifle, but in the hours of ease, and intermissions of danger. Yet in the tragedy of *Don Sebastian*, when the King of Portugal is in the hands of his enemy, and having just drawn the lot, by which he is condemned to die, breaks out into a wild boast that his dust shall take possession of Africk, the dialogue proceeds thus between the captive and his conqueror:

Muley Moluch: What shall I do to conquer thee?
Seb.: Impossible!
   Souls know no conquerors.
M. Mol.: I'll ⌐hew thee for a monster thro' my Afric.
Seb.: No, t⌐ ⌐canst only shew me for a man:
   Afric is stored with monsters; man's a prodigy
   Thy subjects have not seen.
M. Mol.: Thou talk'st as if

Still at the head of battle.
Seb.: Thou mistak'st,
    For there I would not talk.
Benducar, the Minister: Sure he would sleep.

This conversation, with the sly remark of the minister, can only be found not to be comick, because it wants the probability necessary to representations of common life, and degenerates too much towards buffoonery and farce.—SAMUEL JOHNSON, *The Rambler*, No. 125 (May 28, 1751)

Don Sebastian has been weighed, with reference to its tragic merits, against *All for Love*; and one or other is universally allowed to be the first of Dryden's dramatic performances. To the youth of both sexes the latter presents the most pleasing subject of emotion; but to those whom age has rendered incredulous upon the romantic effects of love, and who do not fear to look into the recesses of the human heart, when agitated by darker and more stubborn passions, *Don Sebastian* offers a far superior source of gratification.

To point out the blemishes of so beautiful a tragedy is a painful, though a necessary, task. The style, here and there, exhibits marks of a reviving taste for those frantic bursts of passion which our author has himself termed the "Delilahs of the theatre." The first speech of Sebastian has been often noticed as an extravagant rant, more worthy of Maximin or Almanzor, than of a character drawn by our author in his advanced years and chastened taste—

I beg no pity for this mouldering clay;
For if you give it burial, there it takes
Possession of your earth:
If burnt and scatter'd in the air, the winds,
That strew my dust, diffuse my royalty,
And spread me o'er your clime; for where one atom
Of mine shall light, know, there Sebastian reigns.

The reader's discernment will discover some similar extravagancies in the language of Almeyda and the Emperor.

It is a separate objection, that the manners of the age and country are not adhered to. Sebastian, by disposition a crusading knight-errant, devoted to religion and chivalry, becomes, in the hands of Dryden, merely a gallant soldier and high-spirited prince, such as existed in the poet's own days. But, what is worse, the manners of Mahometans are shockingly violated. Who ever heard of human sacrifices, or of any sacrifices, being offered up to Mahomet; and when were his followers able to use the classical and learned allusions which occur through the dialogue!—SIR WALTER SCOTT, *The Works of John Dryden*, 1808

Don Sebastian is as imperfect as all plays must be in which a single personage is thrown forward in too strong relief for the rest. The language is full of that rant which characterised Dryden's earlier tragedies, and to which a natural predilection seems, after some interval, to have brought him back. Sebastian himself may seem to have been intended as a contrast to Muley Moloch; but if the author had any rule to distinguish the blustering of the hero from that of the tyrant, he has not left the use of it in his reader's hands. The plot of this tragedy is ill conducted, especially in the fifth act. Perhaps the delicacy of the present age may have been too fastidious in excluding altogether from the drama this class of fables; because they may often excite great interest, give scope to impassioned poetry, and are admirably calculated for the ἀναγνώρισις, or discovery, which is so much dwelt upon by the critics; nor can the story of Œdipus, which had furnished one of the finest and most artful tragedies ever written, be well thought an improper subject even for representation. But they require, of all others,

to be dexterously managed; they may make the main distress of a tragedy, but not an episode in it. Our feelings revolt at seeing, as in *Don Sebastian*, an incestuous passion brought forward as the make-weight of a plot, to eke out a fifth act, and to dispose of those characters whose fortune the main story has not quite wound up.—HENRY HALLAM, *Introduction to the Literature of Europe*, 1837–39, Pt. 4, Ch. 5, Par. 43

After the Revolution of 1688 Dryden produced but few plays. Of these the tragedy of *Don Sebastian* (acted 1690), which is in blank-verse and prose, has received very high praise, and Scott repeatedly pronounces it Dryden's dramatic masterpiece. In one respect it certainly deserves special acknowledgment. Dryden has here, in accordance with the views developed in his last critical essay on the drama, carefully and powerfully developed two tragic characters—Sebastian and Dorax. Particular passages in the play, moreover, are indisputably very fine; but as a whole it is, as the author frankly confesses, obnoxious to the charge of lengthiness, especially in the quasi-comic parts, where a thin staple of humour is long drawn-out. Moreover the plot—in which the author grafts upon a story already familiar to the English drama an invention of his own, which has no organic connexion with the opening situation— is intolerably harrowing; and the dramatic solution attempted, although morally satisfactory, is too artificial to content our sense of probability. And while there is much that is powerful in the progress, as depicted in the play, of the fatal passion of the hero and heroine, the tone, though not the conception, of the close lacks elevation. In general, however, the style of this tragedy, notwithstanding an ingredient of rant in its earlier part, is strong as well as attractive; and in the serious portions of the action Dryden repeatedly rises to an unusual height of dramatic effect.—ADOLPHUS WILLIAM WARD, *A History of English Dramatic Literature* (1875), 1899, Vol. 3, p. 383

KING ARTHUR

I went to *King Arthur* on Saturday, and was tired to death, both of the nonsense of the piece and the execrable performance, the singers being still worse than the actors. The scenes are little better (though Garrick boasts of rivalling the French opera), except a pretty bridge, and a Gothic church with windows of painted glass. This scene, which should be a barbarous temple of Woden, is a perfect cathedral, and the devil officiates at a kind of high mass! I never saw greater absurdities.—HORACE WALPOLE, Letter to Henry Seymour Conway (Dec. 25, 1770)

He tells us (in the preface to *Albion and Albanius*), that "this opera was only intended as a prologue to a play of the nature of the *Tempest*; which is a tragedy mixed with opera, or a drama written in blank verse, adorned with scenes, machines, songs, and dances; so that the fable of it is all spoken and acted by the best of the comedians; the other part of the entertainment to be performed by the same singers and dancers who are introduced in this present opera."

The tragedy here alluded to was *King Arthur*, which was not performed till about the year 1690; by which time the fame and productions of Purcell had convinced Dryden, that it was not necessary to import composers from France for the support of what were then called *operas* in England. Further notice has been taken of this musical drama in speaking of our great countryman's productions for the theatre, as well as those of the church and chamber. As to the eloge bestowed by Dryden on M. Grabut, some of it, I fear, must be placed to the account of flattery to his royal master Charles II. as well as to this artist, who had been set over the King's band at the decease of Cambert; which not being very agreeable to the Antigallicans of this country, or, indeed, to unprejudiced judges of Music, while we were in possession of a native composer whose genius was equal to that of the greatest musicians of Europe; though from his situation, short life, and the barbarous state of secular Music, during the period in which he flourished, his genius was less cultivated than that of many great professors of later times.

By Dramatic Opera, Dryden, and writers of his time, mean a drama that is declaimed or spoken, and in which songs and symphonies are introduced; differing from real operas, where there is no speaking, and where the narrative part and dialogue is set to recitative.—CHARLES BURNEY, A *General History of Music*, 1776–89, Bk. 4, Ch. 5

> The mightiest chiefs of British song
> Scorn'd not such legends to prolong:
> They gleam through Spenser's elfin dream,
> And mix in Milton's heavenly theme;
> And Dryden, in immortal strain,
> Had raised the Table Round again,
> But that a ribald King and Court
> Bade him toil on, to make them sport;
> Demanded for their niggard pay,
> Fit for their souls, a looser lay,
> Licentious satire, song, and play;
> The world defrauded of the high design,
> Profaned the God-given strength, and marr'd the
>   lofty line.
>   —SIR WALTER SCOTT, "Introduction" to
>   *Marmion*, 1808

King Arthur, or The British Worthy was performed and printed in 1691, and with the aid of Purcell's music, proved very successful. It possesses a certain interest from the fact that its subject was one which both Milton and Dryden intended to treat as an epos. But the historical—or quasi-historical—theme is treated very flimsily in the 'dramatic opera' which the later of the two great poets actually produced; and the main interest of the piece, such as it is, turns on the rival passions of Arthur and the heathen King of Kent for the blind Emmeline. Her blindness is treated with a mixture of naïveté and something quite the reverse; and this attempt in a direction in which few dramatists have ventured with success, is only noteworthy as a proof that no art in the poet—or, it may be added, in the actor—can render tolerable on the stage the analysis of a physical infirmity. This particular infirmity may indeed occasionally be represented with great and legitimate effect; but an endeavour to analyse it appertains to a sphere different from that of the drama. The conception of Philidel, the fallen but repentant angel, seems Dryden's own. For the rest, *King Arthur*, according to its kind, contains a good deal of magical business—not altogether original. The political significance of this opera is small; the tag concerning the future is intentionally short and unhopeful; the poet, though a certain buoyancy of spirit was to the last an essential element in his nature, was now an avowed malcontent.—ADOLPHUS WILLIAM WARD, A *History of English Dramatic Literature* (1875), 1899, Vol. 3, pp. 382–83

THE HIND AND THE PANTHER

Mr. Wynne has sent me the *Hind and Panther*, by which I find John Dryden has a noble ambition to restore poetry to its ancient dignity in wrapping up the mysteries of religion in verse. What a shame it is to me to see him a saint and remain still the same devil. I must blame the goodness of my constitution which cannot be much altered since my mind is not much changed from what it was at the gravel pits. I saw a play about ten years ago called the *Eunuch*, so heavy a lump the players durst not charge themselves with the dead weight, but it seems Sir Charles Sedley has animated the mighty mass and now it treads the stage lightly. He had always more wit than was enough for one man, and therefore does well to continue his charity to one who wants it. Dryden finds his *Macflecknoe* does no good; I wish better success with his *Hind and Panther*.—SIR GEORGE ETHEREGE, Letter to Lord Middleton (June 23/July 3, 1687)

The verse in which these doctrines, polemical and political, are delivered, is among the finest specimens of the English heroic stanza. The introductory verses, in particular, are lofty and dignified in the highest degree: as are those in which the splendour and majesty of the Church of Rome are set forth, in all the glowing colours of rich imagery and magnificent language. But the same praise extends to the versification of the whole poem. It never falls, never becomes rugged; rises with the dignified strain of the poetry; sinks into quaint familiarity, where sarcasm and humour are employed; and winds through all the mazes of theological argument without becoming either obscure or prosaic.—SIR WALTER SCOTT, *The Works of John Dryden*, 1808

The argumentative talents of Dryden appear, more or less, in the greater part of his poetry; reason in rhyme was his peculiar delight, to which he seems to escape from the mere excursions of fancy. And it is remarkable that he reasons better and more closely in poetry than in prose. His productions more exclusively reasoning are the *Religio Laici* and the *Hind and Panther*. The latter is every way an extraordinary poem. It was written in the hey-day of exultation, by a recent proselyte to a winning side, as he dreamed it to be, by one who never spared a weaker foe, nor repressed his triumph with a dignified moderation. A year was hardly to elapse before he exchanged this fulness of pride for an old age of disappointment and poverty. Yet then too his genius was unquenched, and even his satire was not less severe.

The first lines in the *Hind and Panther* are justly reputed among the most musical in our language; and perhaps we observe their rhythm the better because it does not gain much by the sense; for the allegory and the fable are seen, even in this commencement, to be awkwardly blended. Yet, notwithstanding their evident incoherence, which sometimes leads to the verge of absurdity, and the facility they give to ridicule, I am not sure that Dryden was wrong in choosing this singular fiction. It was his aim to bring forward an old argument in as novel a style as he could; a dialogue between a priest and a parson would have made but a dull poem, even if it had contained some of the excellent paragraphs we read in the *Hind and Panther*. It is the grotesqueness and originality of the fable that give this poem its peculiar zest, of which no reader, I conceive, is insensible; and it is also by this means that Dryden has contrived to relieve his reasoning by short but beautiful touches of description, such as the sudden stream of light from heaven which announces the victory of Sedgmoor near the end of the second book.

The wit in the *Hind and Panther* is sharp, ready, and pleasant, the reasoning is sometimes admirably close and strong; it is the energy of Bossuet in verse. I do not know that the main argument of the Roman church could be better stated; all that has been well said for tradition and authority, all that serves to expose the inconsistencies of a vacillating

Protestantism, is in the Hind's mouth. It is such an answer as a candid man should admit to any doubts of Dryden's sincerity. He who could argue as powerfully as the Hind may well be allowed to have thought himself in the right. Yet he could not forget a few bold thoughts of his more sceptical days, and such is his bias to sarcasm that he cannot restrain himself from reflections on kings and priests when he is most contending for them.—HENRY HALLAM, *Introduction to the Literature of Europe*, 1837–39, Pt. 4, Ch. 5, Pars. 41–43

He retired for a time from the bustle of coffeehouses and theatres to a quiet retreat in Huntingdonshire, and there composed, with unwonted care and labor, his celebrated poem on the points in dispute between the Churches of Rome and England. The Church of Rome he represented under the similitude of a milk-white hind, ever in peril of death, yet fated not to die. The beasts of the field were bent on her destruction. The quaking hare, indeed, observed a timorous neutrality; but the Socinian fox, the Presbyterian wolf, the Independent bear, the Anabaptist boar, glared fiercely at the spotless creature. Yet she could venture to drink with them at the common watering-place under the protection of her friend, the kingly lion. The Church of England was typified by the panther, spotted indeed, but beautiful, too beautiful for a beast of prey. The hind and the panther, equally hated by the ferocious population of the forest, conferred apart on their common danger. They then proceeded to discuss the points on which they differed, and, while wagging their tails and licking their jaws, held a long dialogue touching the real presence, the authority of Popes and Councils, the penal laws, the Test Act, Oates's perjuries, Butler's unrequited services to the Cavalier party, Stillingfleet's pamphlets, and Burnet's broad shoulders and fortunate matrimonial speculations.

The absurdity of this plan is obvious. In truth the allegory could not be preserved unbroken through ten lines together. No art of execution could redeem the faults of such a design. Yet the Fable of the *Hind and Panther* is undoubtedly the most valuable addition which was made to English literature during the short and troubled reign of James the Second. In none of Dryden's works can be found passages more pathetic and magnificent, greater ductility and energy of language, or a more pleasing and various music.—THOMAS BABINGTON MACAULAY, *History of England*, 1848–59

ALEXANDER'S FEAST

In the meane time I am writeing a Song for St Cecilia's feast, who you know is the Patroness of Musique. This is troublesome, & no way beneficiall: but I could not deny the Stewards of the feast, who came in a body to me, to desire that kindness; one of them being Mr Bridgman, whose parents are your Mothers friends.—JOHN DRYDEN, Letter to His Sons (Sept. 3, 1697)

This ode has been more applauded, perhaps, than it has been felt; however, it is a very fine one, and gives its beauties rather at a third or fourth than at a first perusal.—OLIVER GOLDSMITH, *The Beauties of English Poetry*, 1767

From Pindar we learn that sudden transitions, bold and abrupt metaphors, a regular cadence, and a warm and impetuous glow of thought and language,

> Thoughts that breathe, and words that burn,

are essentials of the higher mode of lyric writing. I place a regular cadence among these requisites in spite of Dryden's wonderful ode; which is of itself worth all that Pindar has written, as a large diamond is worth a vast heap of gold,

because that master-piece is a dithyrambic poem, not a lyric one. And that as well for its want of regularity, as for its subject, which, being perfectly convivial as its title speaks, falls with much propriety into that class which the ancients called dithyrambic, and which were most commonly sacred to Bacchus.—JOHN PINKERTON (as "Robert Heron"), "Letter V: On the Spirit of Lyric Poetry," *Letters of Literature*, 1785, p. 34

Dryden's "Alexander's Feast" is a magnificent composition, and has high poetical beauties; but to a refined judgment there is something intrinsically unpoetical in the end to which it is devoted, the praises of revel and sensuality. It corresponds to a process of clever reasoning erected on an untrue foundation—the one is a fallacy, the other is out of taste.—JOHN HENRY NEWMAN, "Poetry, with Reference to Aristotle's *Poetics*" (1828), *Essays Critical and Historical*, 1871

TRANSLATION OF VIRGIL

On the left wing of the horse, Vergil appeared, in shining armour completely fitted to his body; he was mounted on a dapple grey steed, the slowness of whose pace was an effect of the highest mettle and vigour. He cast his eye on the adverse wing with a desire to find an object worthy of his valour, when, behold! upon a sorrel gelding of a monstrous size, appeared a foe issuing from among the thickest of the enemy's squadrons: but his speed was less than his noise, for his horse, old and lean, spent the dregs of his strength in a high trot, which though it made slow advances, yet caused a loud clashing of his armour, terrible to hear. The two cavaliers had now approached within the throw of a lance, when the stranger desired a parley, and lifting up the vizard of his helmet, a face hardly appeared from within, which, after a pause, was known for that of the renowned Dryden. The brave Ancient suddenly started as one possessed with surprise and disappointment together, for the helmet was nine times too large for the head, which appeared situate far in the hinder part, even like the lady in a lobster, or like a mouse under a canopy of state, or like a shrivelled beau from within the pent-house of a modern periwig, and the voice was suited to the visage, sounding weak and remote. Dryden, in a long harangue, soothed up the good Ancient; called him father; and by a large deduction of genealogies made it plainly appear that they were nearly related. Then he humbly proposed an exchange of armour, as a lasting mark of hospitality between them. Vergil consented, for the goddess Diffidence came unseen and cast a mist before his eyes, though his was of gold, and cost a hundred beeves, the other's but of rusty iron. However, this glittering armour became the Modern yet worse than his own. Then they agreed to exchange horses, but when it came to the trial, Dryden was afraid and utterly unable to mount.—JONATHAN SWIFT, *The Battel of the Books*, 1704

It is a great Loss to the Poetical World that Mr. *Dryden* did not live to translate the *Iliad*. He has left us only the first Book and a small Part of the sixth; in which if he has in some Places not truly interpreted the Sense, or preserved the Antiquities, it ought to be excused on account of the Haste he was obliged to write in. He seems to have had too much Regard to *Chapman*, whose Words he sometimes copies, and has unhappily follow'd him in Passages where he wanders from the Original. However had he translated the whole Work, I would no more have attempted *Homer* after him than *Virgil*, his Version of whom (notwithstanding some human Errors) is the most noble and spirited Translation I know in any Language. But the Fate of great Genius's is like that of great Ministers, tho' they are confessedly the first in the Commonwealth of Letters, they must be envy'd and calumniated only for being at the Head of it.—ALEXANDER POPE, "Preface" to *The Iliad of Homer*, 1715

Dryden's Virgil has delighted me. I do not know whether the critics will agree with me, but the *Georgics* are to me by far the best of Virgil. It is indeed a species of writing entirely new to me, and has filled my head with a thousand fancies of emulation: but, alas! when I read the *Georgics*, and then survey my own powers, 'tis like the idea of a Shetland pony, drawn up by the side of a thorough-bred hunter, to start for the plate. I own I am disappointed in the *Æneid*. Faultless correctness may please, and does highly please, the lettered critic; but to that awful character I have not the most distant pretensions. I do not know whether I do not hazard my pretensions to be a critic of any kind, when I say that I think Virgil, in many instances, a servile copier of Homer. If I had the *Odyssey* by me, I could parallel many passages where Virgil has evidently copied, but by no means improved, Homer. Nor can I think there is anything of this owing to the translators; for, from everything I have seen of Dryden, I think him, in genius and fluency of language, Pope's master.—ROBERT BURNS, Letter to Mrs. Dunlop (May 4, 1788)

His Virgil is, in my apprehension, the least successful of his chief works. Lines of consummate excellence are frequently shot, like threads of gold, through the web; but the general texture is of an ordinary material. Dryden was little fitted for a translator of Virgil: his mind was more rapid and vehement than that of his original, but by far less elegant and judicious. This translation seems to have been made in haste; it is more negligent than any of his own poetry; and the style is often almost studiously, and, as it were, spitefully vulgar.—HENRY HALLAM, *Introduction to the Literature of Europe*, 1837–39, Pt. 4, Ch. 5, Par. 46

Dryden's style in poetry is sufficiently unlike that which finds most favour in the present day: but it cannot be said to be obsolete. And though in its minuter shades it affords rather a contrast than a parallel to Virgil's, they have at all events the common quality of being really poetical; that inner identity which far outweighs a thousand points of external similarity, supposing these to be attainable.—JOHN CONINGTON, "Preface" to *The Aeneid of Virgil*, 1867

SATIRES

Nearly at the same period, after some momentary gleams and strong flashes in the horizon, Satire arose in England. When I name DRYDEN, I comprehend every varied excellence of *our* poetry. In harmony, strength, modulation, rhythm, energy, he first displayed the full power of the English language. My business with him at present, is only as a Satirist. I will be brief: I speak to the intelligent. He was the first poet who brought to perfection, what I would term, "the Allegory of Satires." Fables indeed, and apologues, and romances, have always been the most ancient modes of reproof and censure. It was the peculiar happiness of Dryden to give an eternal sense and interest to subjects which are transitory. He placed his scene on the ground of actual history. The reader of every age has an interest in the delineation of characters and names, which have been familiar to him from his earliest years. He is already prepared, and feels a predilection for the subject. This accommodation of ancient characters to existing persons has a peculiar force in the age to which it is addressed; and posterity reads with delight a poem founded on pristine story, and illustrated by the records of modern times. Dryden's power of

Satire has been generally acknowledged in his *Mac-Flecknoe*; but his master-piece is that wonderful and unequalled performance, *Absalom and Achitophel*. He presents to us an heroic subject in heroic numbers, a well constructed allegory, and a forcible appeal to our best feelings and passions. He paints the horrors of anarchy, sedition, rebellion, and democracy, with the pencil of Dante, or of Michael Angelo; and he gives the speeches of his heroes with the strength, propriety, and correctness of Virgil. It is Satire in its highest form: but it is Satire addressed to the few. It is not adapted to the general effect of this species of poetry. In my opinion, Dryden has not the style and manner of Horace, or Juvenal, or Persius, or Boileau. Pope called him *"unhappy,"* from the looseness of the age in which he lived. He has enthusiasm, majesty, seriousness, severity, gravity, strength of conception, and boldness of imagery. But sprightliness, gaiety, and easy badinage, an occasional playfulness, so necessary to the general effect of satirical poetry, were all wanting to him. Perhaps the genius was too sublime. He could not, or he would not, descend to the minutiæ which are often required, the anecdotes, and the passing traits of the time. His satire had an original character. It was the strain of Archilochus sounding from the lyre of Alcæus.—THOMAS JAMES MATHIAS, *The Pursuits of Literature*, 1794

It is as a satirist and pleader in verse that Dryden is best known, and as both he is in some respects unrivalled. His satire is not so sly as Chaucer's, but it is distinguished by the same good-nature. There is no malice in it. I shall not enter into his literary quarrels further than to say that he seems to me, on the whole, to have been forbearing, which is the more striking as he tells us repeatedly that he was naturally vindictive. It was he who called revenge "the darling attribute of heaven." "I complain not of their lampoons and libels, though I have been the public mark for many years. I am vindictive enough to have repelled force by force, if I could imagine that any of them had ever reached me." It was this feeling of easy superiority, I suspect, that made him the mark for so much jealous vituperation. Scott is wrong in attributing his onslaught upon Settle to jealousy because one of the latter's plays had been performed at Court,—an honor never paid to any of Dryden's. I have found nothing like a trace of jealousy in that large and benignant nature. In his vindication of the *Duke of Guise*, he says, with honest confidence in himself: "Nay, I durst almost refer myself to some of the angry poets on the other side, whether I have not rather countenanced and assisted their beginnings than hindered them from rising." He seems to have been really as indifferent to the attacks on himself as Pope pretended to be. In the same vindication he says of the *Rehearsal*, the only one of them that had any wit in it, and it has a great deal: "Much less am I concerned at the noble name of Bayes; that's a brat so like his own father that he cannot be mistaken for any other body. They might as reasonably have called Tom Sternhold Virgil, and the resemblance would have held as well." In his *Essay on Satire* he says: "And yet we know that in Christian charity all offences are to be forgiven as we expect the like pardon for those we daily commit against Almighty God. And this consideration has often made me tremble when I was saying our Lord's Prayer; for the plain condition of the forgiveness which we beg is the pardoning of others the offences which they have done to us; for which reason I have many times avoided the commission of that fault, even when I have been notoriously provoked." And in another passage he says, with his usual wisdom: "Good sense and good-nature are never separated, though the ignorant world has thought otherwise. Good-nature, by which I mean beneficence and candor, is the product of right reason, which of necessity will give allowance to the failings of others, by considering that there is nothing perfect in mankind." In the same *Essay* he gives his own receipt for satire: "How easy it is to call rogue and villain, and that wittily! but how hard to make a man appear a fool, a blockhead, or a knave, without using any of those opprobrious terms! . . .This is the mystery of that noble trade. . . . Neither is it true that this fineness of raillery is offensive: a witty man is tickled while he is hurt in this manner, and a fool feels it not. . . . There is a vast difference between the slovenly butchering of a man and the fineness of a stroke that separates the head from the body, and leaves it standing in its place. A man may be capable, as Jack Ketch's wife said of his servant, of a plain piece of work, of a bare hanging; but to make a malefactor die sweetly was only belonging to her husband. I wish I could apply it to myself, if the reader would be kind enough to think it belongs to me. The character of Zimri in my *Absalom* is, in my opinion, worth the whole poem. It is not bloody, but it is ridiculous enough, and he for whom it was intended was too witty to resent it as an injury. . . . I avoided the mention of great crimes, and applied myself to the representing of blind sides and little extravagances, to which, the wittier a man is, he is generally the more obnoxious.

Dryden thought his genius led him that way. In his elegy on the satirist Oldham, whom Hallam, without reading him, I suspect, ranks next to Dryden, he says:—

> For sure our souls were near allied, and thine
> Cast in the same poetic mould with mine;
> One common note in either lyre did strike,
> And knaves and fools we both abhorred alike.

His practice is not always so delicate as his theory; but if he was sometimes rough, he never took a base advantage. He knocks his antagonist down, and there an end. Pope seems to have nursed his grudge, and then, watching his chance, to have squirted vitriol from behind a corner, rather glad than otherwise if it fell on the women of those he hated or envied. And if Dryden is never dastardly, as Pope often was, so also he never wrote anything so maliciously depreciatory as Pope's unprovoked attack on Addison. Dryden's satire is often coarse, but where it is coarsest, it is commonly in defence of himself against attacks that were themselves brutal. Then, to be sure, he snatches the first ready cudgel, as in Shadwell's case, though even then there is something of the good-humor of conscious strength. Pope's provocation was too often the mere opportunity to say a biting thing, where he could do it safely. If his victim showed fight, he tried to smooth things over, as with Dennis. Dryden could forget that he had ever had a quarrel, but he never slunk away from any, least of all from one provoked by himself. Pope's satire is too much occupied with the externals of manners, habits, personal defects, and peculiarities. Dryden goes right to the rooted character of the man, to the weaknesses of his nature, as where he says of Burnet:—

> Prompt to assail, and careless of defence,
> Invulnerable in his impudence,
> He dares the world, and, eager of a name,
> He thrusts about and *justles into fame.*
> So fond of loud report that, not to miss
> Of being known (his last and utmost bliss),
> *He rather would be known for what he is.*

It would be hard to find in Pope such compression of meaning as in the first, or such penetrative sarcasm as in the second of the passages I have underscored. Dryden's satire is still quoted

for its comprehensiveness of application, Pope's rather for the elegance of its finish and the point of its phrase than for any deeper qualities. I do not remember that Dryden ever makes poverty a reproach. He was above it, alike by generosity of birth and mind. Pope is always the *parvenu*, always giving himself the airs of a fine gentleman, and, like Horace Walpole and Byron, affecting superiority to professional literature. Dryden, like Lessing, was a hack-writer, and was proud, as an honest man has a right to be, of being able to get his bread by his brains. He lived in Grub Street all his life, and never dreamed that where a man of genius lived was not the best quarter of the town. "Tell his Majesty," said sturdy old Jonson, "that his soul lives in an alley."—JAMES RUSSELL LOWELL, "Dryden" (1868), *Among My Books*, 1870, pp. 67–71

ABSALOM AND ACHITOPHEL

Tis not my intention to make an Apology for my Poem: Some will think it needs no Excuse; and others will receive none. The Design, I am sure, is honest: but he who draws his Pen for one Party, must expect to make Enemies of the other. For, *Wit* and *Fool*, are Consequents of *Whig* and *Tory*: And every man is a Knave or an Ass to the contrary side. There's a Treasury of Merits in the *Phanatick Church*, as well as in the *Papist*; and a Pennyworth to be had of Saintship, Honesty, and Poetry, for the Leud, the Factious, and the Blockheads: But the longest Chapter in *Deuteronomy*, has not Curses enow for an Anti-*Bromingham*. My Comfort is, their manifest Prejudice to my Cause, will render their Judgment of less Authority against me. Yet if a *Poem* have a *Genius*, it will force its own reception in the World. For there's a sweetness in good Verse, which Tickles even while it Hurts: And, no man can be heartily angry with him, who pleases him against his will. The Commendation of Adversaries, is the greatest Triumph of a Writer; because it never comes unless Extorted. But I can be satisfied on more easy termes: If I happen to please the more Moderate sort, I shall be sure of an honest Party; and, in all probability, of the best Judges; for, the least Concern'd, are commonly the least Corrupt: And, I confess, I have laid in for those, by rebating the *Satyre*, (where Justice would allow it) from carrying too sharp an Edge. They, who can Criticize so weakly, as to imagine I have done my Worst, may be Convinc'd, at their own Cost, that I can write Severely, with more ease, than I can Gently. I have but laught at some mens Follies, when I coud have declaim'd against their Vices; and, other mens Vertues I have commended, as freely as I have tax'd their Crimes. And now, if you are a Malitious *Reader*, I expect you should return upon me, that I affect to be thought more Impartial than I am. But, if men are not to be judg'd by their Professions, God forgive you *Common-wealths-men*, for professing so plausibly for the Government. You cannot be so Unconscionable, as to charge me for not Subscribing of my Name; for that woud reflect too grosly upon your own Party, who never dare, though they have the advantage of a Jury to secure them. If you like not my *Poem*, the fault may, possibly, be in my Writing: (though 'tis hard for an Authour to judge against himself;) But, more probably, 'tis in your Morals, which cannot bear the truth of it. The Violent, on both sides, will condemn the Character of *Absalom*, as either too favourably, or too hardly drawn. But, they are not the Violent, whom I desire to please. The fault, on the right hand, is to Extenuate, Palliate and Indulge; and, to confess freely, I have endeavour'd to commit it. Besides the respect which I owe his Birth, I have a greater for his Heroique Vertues; and, *David* himself, coud not be more tender of the Young-man's Life, than I woud be of his

Reputation. But, since the most excellent Natures are always the most easy; and, as being such, are the soonest perverted by ill Counsels, especially when baited with Fame and Glory; 'tis no more a wonder that he withstood not the temptations of *Achitophel*, than it was for *Adam*, not to have resisted the two Devils; the Serpent, and the Woman. The conclusion of the Story, I purposely forbore to prosecute; because, I coud not obtain from my self, to shew *Absalom* Unfortunate. The Frame of it, was cut out, but for a Picture to the Wast; and, if the Draught be so far true, 'tis as much as I design'd.

Were I the Inventour, who am only the Historian, I shoud certainly conclude the Piece, with the Reconcilement of *Absalom* to *David*. And, who knows but this may come to pass? Things were not brought to an Extremity where I left the Story: There seems, yet, to be room left for a Composure; hereafter, there may only be for pity. I have not, so much as an uncharitable Wish against *Achitophel*; but, am content to be Accus'd of a good natur'd Errour; and, to hope with *Origen*, that the Devil himself may, at last, be sav'd: For which reason, in this *Poem*, he is neither brought to set his House in order, nor to dispose of his Person afterwards, as he in Wisedom shall think fit. God is infinitely merciful; and his Vicegerent is only not so, because he is not Infinite.

The true end of *Satyre*, is the amendment of Vices by correction. And he who writes Honestly, is no more an Enemy to the Offendour, than the Physician to the Patient, when he prescribes harsh Remedies to an inveterate Disease: for those, are only in order to prevent the Chyrurgeon's work of an *Ense rescindendum*, which I wish not to my very Enemies. To conclude all, If the Body Politique have any Analogy to the Natural, in my weak judgment, an *Act of Oblivion* were as necessary in a Hot, Distemper'd State, as an *Opiate* woud be in a Raging Fever.—JOHN DRYDEN, "To the Reader," *Absalom and Achitophel*, 1681

In the next Place, if we look into Human Nature, we shall find that the Mind is never so much pleased, as when she exerts her self in any Action that gives her an Idea of her own Perfections and Abilities. This natural Pride and Ambition of the Soul is very much gratified in the reading of a Fable; for in Writings of this Kind, the Reader comes in for half of the Performance; Every thing appears to him like a Discovery of his own; he is busied all the while in applying Characters and Circumstances, and is in this respect both a Reader and a Composer. It is no wonder therefore that on such Occasions, when the Mind is thus pleased with it self, and amused with its own Discoveries, that it is highly delighted with the Writing which is the Occasion of it. For this Reason the *Absalom* and *Achitophel* was one of the most popular Poems that ever appeared in *English*. The Poetry is indeed very fine, but had it been much finer it would not have so much pleased, without a Plan which gave the Reader an Opportunity of exerting his own Talents. —JOSEPH ADDISON, *The Spectator*, No. 512 (Oct. 17, 1712)

Take Dryden's Achitophel and Zimri,—Shaftesbury and Buckingham; every line adds to or modifies the character, which is, as it were, a building up to the very last verse; whereas in Pope's Timon, &c., the first two or three couplets contain all the pith of the character, and the twenty or thirty lines that follow are so much evidence or proof of overt acts of jealousy, or pride, or whatever it may be that is satirized.—SAMUEL TAYLOR COLERIDGE, *Table Talk*, Aug. 6, 1832

His *Absalom and Achitophel*, the greatest satire of modern times, had amazed the town, had made its way with unprecedented rapidity even into rural districts, and had, wherever it appeared, bitterly annoyed the Exclusionists, and raised the courage of the Tories. But we must not, in the admiration which we naturally feel for noble diction and versification, forget the great distinctions of good and evil. The spirit by which Dryden and several of his compeers were at this time animated against the Whigs deserves to be called fiendish. The servile judges and sheriffs of those evil days could not shed blood as fast as the poets cried out for it. Calls for more victims, hideous jests on hanging, bitter taunts on those who, having stood by the King in the hour of danger, now advised him to deal mercifully and generously by his vanquished enemies, were publicly recited on the stage, and, that nothing might be wanting to the guilt and the shame, were recited by women, who, having long been taught to discard all modesty, were now taught to discard all compassion.—THOMAS BABINGTON MACAULAY, *History of England*, 1848–59

Dryden like the royalists generally believed that the arrest of Shaftesbury had alone saved England from civil war, and from that worst of civil wars where a son fights against his father's throne. In his *Absalom and Achitophel* the poet told the story of the threatened strife under the thin veil of the revolt against David. Charles was the Hebrew king, Monmouth was Absalom, Shaftesbury was the wily Achitophel who drew him into revolt. The *Absalom* was a satire, and it was the first great English satire, for the satires of Marston and Hall were already forgotten. It is in ages indeed like the Restoration that satire naturally comes to the front. In the reaction after a time of high ideals and lofty efforts the sense of contrast between the aims and the powers of man, between his hopes and their fulfilment, takes form whether in the kindly pitifulness of humour or in the bitter revulsion of satire. And mingled with this in Dryden was an honest indignation at the hypocrisy around him. The men he attacks are not real men but actors. Buckingham and Shaftesbury, the infidel leader of the Independents and the deistical leader of the Presbyterians, were alike playing a part. But the largeness and fairness of his temper saved Dryden's satire from the vicious malignity of that of Pope. He has an artistic love of picturesque contrast, he has a great writer's pride in the consciousness of power. But he has no love of giving pain for the mere pain's sake, and he has a hatred of unfairness. Even in his contempt for the man he is just to Buckingham, and his anger does not blind him to the great qualities of Shaftesbury.—JOHN RICHARD GREEN, *History of the English People*, 1877–80

MAC FLECKNOE

The severity of this satire, and the excellence of its versification, give it a distinguished rank in this species of composition. At present, an ordinary reader would scarcely suppose that Shadwell, who is here meant by Mac Flecknoe, was worth being chastised; and that Dryden, descending to such game, was like an eagle stooping to catch flies. The truth however is, Shadwell at one time held divided reputation with this great poet. Every age produces its fashionable dunces, who, by following the transient topic or humour of the day, supply talkative ignorance with materials for conversation.—OLIVER GOLDSMITH, *The Beauties of English Poetry*, 1767

Mac-Flecknoe must be allowed to be one of the keenest satires in the English language. It is what Dryden has elsewhere termed a Varronian satire; that is, as he seems to use the phrase, one in which the author is not contented with general sarcasm upon the object of attack, but where he has woven his piece into a sort of imaginary story, or scene, in which he introduces the person whom he ridicules as a principal actor.

The position in which Dryden has placed Shadwell is the most mortifying to literary vanity which can possibly be imagined, and is hardly excelled by the device of Pope in *The Dunciad*, who has obviously followed the steps of his predecessor. Flecknoe, who seems to have been universally acknowledged as the very lowest of all poetasters, and whose name had passed into a proverb for doggerel verse and stupid prose, is represented as devolving upon Shadwell that pre-eminence over the realms of Dulness which he had himself possessed without a rival. The spot chosen for this devolution of empire is the Barbican, an obscure suburb, in which it would seem that there were temporary theatrical representations of the lowest order, among other receptacles of vulgar dissipation, for the amusement of the very lowest of the vulgar. Here the ceremony of Shadwell's coronation is supposed to be performing with an inaugural oration by Flecknoe, his predecessor, in which all his pretensions to wit and to literary fame are sarcastically enumerated, and confuted by a counter-statement of his claims to distinction by pre-eminent and unrivalled stupidity. In this satire the shafts of the poet are directed with an aim acutely malignant. The inference drawn concerning Shadwell's talents is general and absolute; but in the proof, Dryden appeals with triumph to those parts only of his literary character which are obviously vulnerable. He reckons up, among his titles to the throne of Flecknoe, his desperate and unsuccessful attempts at lyrical composition in the opera of *Psyche*; the clumsy and coarse limning of those whom he designed to figure as fine gentlemen in his comedies; the false and florid taste of his dedications; his presumptuous imitation of Jonson in composition, and his absurd resemblance to him in person. But the satirist industriously keeps out of view those points in which he internally felt some inferiority to the object of his wrath. He mentions nothing that could recall to the reader's recollection that insight into human life, that acquaintance with the foibles and absurdities displayed in individual pursuits, that bold though coarse delineation of character, which gave fame to Shadwell's comedies in the last century, and renders them amusing even at the present day. This discrimination is an excellent proof of the exquisite address with which Dryden wielded the satirical weapon, and managed the feelings of his readers. We never find him attempting a desperate or impossible task; at least in a way which seems, in the moment of perusal, desperate or impossible. He never wastes his powder against the impregnable part of a fortress, but directs all his battery against some weaker spot, where a breach may be rendered practicable. In short, by convincing his reader that he is right in the examples which he quotes, he puts the question at issue upon the ground most disadvantageous for his antagonist, and renders it very difficult for one who has been proved a dunce in one instance to establish his credit in any other.
—SIR WALTER SCOTT, *The Works of John Dryden*, 1808

In *Mac Flecknoe*, his satire on his rival Shadwell, we must allow for the inferiority of the subject, which could not bring out so much of Dryden's higher powers of mind; but scarcely one of his poems is more perfect. Johnson, who admired Dryden almost as much as he could any one, has yet, from his proneness to critical censure, very much exaggerated the poet's defects. 'His faults of negligence are beyond recital. Such is the unevenness of his compositions, that ten lines are seldom found together without something of which the reader is ashamed.' This might be true, or more nearly true, of other poets of the seventeenth century. Ten good consecutive lines will, perhaps, rarely be found, except in Denham, Davenant, and Waller. But it seems a great exaggeration as to Dryden. I would particularly instance *Mac Flecknoe* as a poem of about

four hundred lines, in which no one will be condemned as weak or negligent, though three or four are rather too ribaldrous for our taste. There are also passages, much exceeding ten lines, in *Absalom and Achitophel*, as well as in the later works, the *Fables*, which excite in the reader none of the shame for the poet's carelessness, with which Johnson has furnished him.—HENRY HALLAM, *Introduction to the Literature of Europe*, 1837–39, Pt. 4, Ch. 5, Par. 40

PROSE

But if you think this Trade too base,
(Which seldom is the Dunce's Case)
Put on the Critick's Brow, and sit
At *Wills* the puny Judge of Wit.
A Nod, a Shrug, a scornful Smile,
With Caution us'd, may serve a-while.
Proceed no further in your Part,
Before you learn the Terms of Art:
(For you may easy be too far gone,
In all our modern Criticks Jargon.)
Then talk with more authentick Face,
Of *Unities, in Time and Place.*
Get Scraps of *Horace* from your Friends,
And have them at your Fingers Ends.
Learn *Aristotle's* Rules by Rote,
And at all Hazards boldly quote:
Judicious *Rymer* oft review:
Wise *Dennis*, and profound *Bossu.*
Read all the *Prefaces* of *Dryden*,
For these our Criticks must confide in,
(Tho' meerly writ at first for filing
To raise the Volume's Price, a Shilling.)
—JONATHAN SWIFT, "On Poetry: A Rapsody,"
1733

The restoration of King Charles II. seems to be the æra of the formation of our present Style. Lord Clarendon was one of the first who laid aside those frequent inversions which prevailed among writers of the former age. After him, Sir William Temple polished the language still more. But the author, who, by the number and reputation of his works, formed it more than any one, into its present state, is Dryden. Dryden began to write at the Restoration, and continued long an author both in poetry and prose. He had made the language his study; and though he wrote hastily, and often incorrectly, and his Style is not free from faults, yet there is a richness in his diction, a copiousness, ease, and variety in his expression, which has not been surpassed by any who have come after him.—HUGH BLAIR, *Lectures on Rhetoric and Belles Lettres*, 1783, Lecture 18

It would be superfluous to echo the praise of Dryden's prose style, which is in every one's mouth. Perhaps it may not be equally so, to suggest a limitation of it. Its excellence is an ease and apparent negligence of praise, which shows, as it were, a powerful mind on *en deshabille*, and free from the fetters of study. This is well fitted to the nature of Dryden's prose, consisting either of dedications, which are real letters, or of prefaces, which are a sort of letters, to the public. Both of these, by their nature, announce somewhat of more promise, upon which we expect the labour of the author to have been employed, and readily forgive a lively negligence in those accessory parts which seem to be written without effort. But we cannot think the style of Dryden adapted to an historical, much less to a didactic work. We should, indeed, strongly recommend the study of it to those engaged, in such compositions, so far, as to relieve, in some degree, by its variety and copiousness of English idiom, that stiffness and monotony, which habits of precise and laborious thinking, especially upon abstract subjects, are very apt to engender. But no man, we suspect, could write altogether like Dryden, without falling into that vague way of expression, and those loose immethodical transitions, which gave in fact the charm of ease and variety to his language. These, however, must not be bought at too high a price; change of measure may delight the fancy, but an equable sustained cadence will be found more effectual in keeping the attention steady through continued reasoning. We have said thus much, because Dryden's style is sometimes unfairly contrasted with that of writers, by whom his could not have been judiciously adopted; by those, in short, who meant to teach, which he scarce ever does, rather than to please, in which he seldom fails.—HENRY HALLAM, "Scott's Edition of Dryden," *Edinburgh Review*, Oct. 1808, pp. 133–34

In prose as in other branches of literature, however, the greatest name throughout the last forty years of the century is that of John Dryden. If he is never quite so exquisite as Temple, or even perhaps as Evelyn, at their best, it is that he had much more to say than they have, and less need to study his manner of saying it. He is the manliest, the most straightforward, the most authoritative prose-writer of the age, and, in his long career of more than thirty years, he surveyed and laid out the whole estate of modern English prose. He was not born with a style. His speech came to him slowly, laboriously, and it was by slow degrees that he threw off the cumbersome robes of his forerunners. Mr. Matthew Arnold has said that "the needful qualities for a fit prose are regularity, uniformity, precision, balance"; these are the very qualities which we meet with in Dryden, and to a like extent in no one before him, when once we have proceeded far enough in his career. It is easy, moreover, to trace his progress, for his prose-works are mainly prefixed or appended to his better known poetical or dramatic productions, and thus more exactly dated than the miscellanies of most of his contemporaries. ⟨. . .⟩

Dryden reached the zenith of his powers as a prose-writer a little after his supremacy as a poet was finally acknowledged. He quitted the peaceful fields of literary criticism in two pamphlets of surpassing vigour, the "Epistle to the Whigs" (prefixed to *The Medal*), 1682, and *The Vindication of the Duke of Guise* (1683). Of these the first displays him as having followed Halifax into political pamphleteering, the latter is sheer polemic. In the first occurs that happy taunt, "If God has not blessed you with the talent of rhyming, make use of my poor stock, and welcome; let your verses run upon my feet; and for the utmost refuge of notorious blockheads, reduced to the last extremity of sense, turn my own lines upon me, and in utter despair of your own satire, make me satirise myself." The second contains the famous pious wish that Shadwell, being "only born for drinking, would let both poetry and prose alone." *The Vindication* was published separately, and was more like a book than any prose-writing which Dryden had hitherto produced. In 1684 he translated Louis Maimbourg's laborious *History of the League*, and added a postscript of fifty pages of his own. He wrote or translated other bulky works of a semi-historical, semi-controversial character, and produced, almost to the day of his death, miscellaneous writings far too numerous to be here named in detail. Last, but not least, among them comes the noble preface to the *Fables* of 1700.

It is almost entirely as a critic that Dryden has left his mark upon English prose. His brief prefaces introduced into our literature an element which it had lacked before, although Hobbes had made one or two efforts in the same direction. Dryden is the earliest of our literary critics, and where his knowledge is not defective he remains still one of the most

sympathetic. He owed much to the French in the manner of his analysis, and something in particular to Corneille, who had prefixed prose "examens" to his plays. But Dryden is far more systematic than the French critics of his day, and his gradual revolt against Gallic taste gave him a strength and independence of judgment such as were not to be found in Paris. His delivery is very genial and agreeable, and he has nothing of the unpleasant dictatorial manner of Temple, besides having much more thorough mastery over his subject. He is apparently inconsistent, because of his candour, and because his intellect and taste were developing all through his long career. ⟨. . .⟩ Erudition, in the pedantic sense, was never his forte, but his praise is that he treated literature as a living plant, with a past and a future, not as a mere desert of dead logs. He released us on the one hand from ignorance and indifferentism, and on the other hand from an empirical philosophy of letters. He is not only a fine dramatist and a very lofty poet, but a great pioneer in prose criticism also.—EDMUND GOSSE, *A History of Eighteenth Century Literature*, 1888, pp. 90–94

As Dryden was now first in poetry, so he was in prose. No one can understand the poetry of this time, in its relation to the past, to the future, and to France, who does not read the Critical Essays prefixed to his dramas, "On the Historical Poem," on dramatic rhyme, on "Heroic Plays," on the classical writers, and his *Essay on Dramatic Poetry*. He is in these essays, not only the leader of modern literary criticism, but the leader of that modern prose in which the style is easy, unaffected, moulded to the subject, and in which the proper words are put in the proper places. Dryden was a great originator.—STOPFORD A. BROOKE, *English Literature*, 1896, pp. 177–78

Dryden's prose, which is intended for the greatest number, which is meant to be popular, loses nothing of its value by being compared with his contemporaries, though it may be found to be not altogether exceptional nor new in character. Dryden himself, according to Congreve's well-known evidence, acknowledged Tillotson as his master in the art of familiar discourse; and there were others; before all, there was Cowley, whose style obtains from Dr. Johnson little less than the praise given to the Essays of Dryden for their lightness, grace, and ease. There were also the French authors. However much the influence of France may have been abused by historians as an explanation of the new fashions of literature at the accession of Charles II, there is no reason why it should be disallowed or refused its due in accounting for the changes of taste. French criticism, French talk about literature, had already found the right kind of expression thirty years and more before the *Essay of Dramatic Poesy*. The ancestors of Dryden's prose are to be traced in Chapelain's Preface to the *Adone* of Marino, in Mesnardière's *Poëtique*, in the Dialogues and Essays of Sarrasin, in the Prefaces of Scudéry, in the Discourses and *Examens* of Corneille. In all these different authors, and in others, there was to be found, with different faculties, the same common quality of clearness in exposition and argument, which even without genius may be pleasing, and with genius is the most valuable auxiliary, as in the essays of Dryden and Corneille. What criticism might be without the example of the French is shown in the Preface to *Samson Agonistes*. In date it is some years later than Dryden's *Essay*; in temper it belongs to the Italy of a hundred years before; it is like one of the solemn sermons before an Italian learned society, in which the doctrine of Poetry used to be expounded more gravely than any text of St. Thomas. The difference between an Italian and a French education in their influence on prose may be seen by comparing Milton and Chapelain, authors much alike in ambition, self-respect, and solemnity of mind; in everything but poetical genius and the circumstances of their lives. Milton writing his opinions about Tragic Poetry writes like an Italian contemporary of Tasso, with grave magnificence; Chapelain, by nature no less grave, and as much inclined as Milton to walk with the gait of 'the magnanimous man,' is obliged by his associates to let his dignity go and to speak like other people. Between the scholar who was also a wit—Ménage—and the man of the world who was also a student—Sarrasin—there was no more room for declamation than there is in a reading party in summer. Chapelain the pedant has written a dialogue with Ménage and Sarrasin the wits taking part in it, and it is as easy and pleasant as the writing of the wits themselves, as fresh as anything of Dryden's; a defence of Lancelot and the library of Don Quixote, a delightful apology for Romance, by the great champion of literary authority, the patron if not the inventor of the Unities. It is no small part of the attraction of Dryden's *Essays* that they bring their readers into acquaintance with that new world of France in the age of Louis XIII, when all the world and the Dramatic Unities were young, when Corneille at the Hôtel de Bourgogne scarcely knew himself as yet for anything different from Hardy, when Scaramouche and Jodelet were getting things ready for Molière, and when the cloak and sword of Madrid, and the Castilian Point of Honour, were mingled in the visions of the dramatic poet with an idea of some unattained perfection, a sort of inaudible dramatic music, a harmony partly moral, partly imaginative, which should constitute the absolutely faultless play. It is from this world, so adventurous yet so decorous, so strangely mixed of 'Gothic' traditions and pedantic authority, Spanish comedies and classical learning, and through all of it the zest and interest of a society which sees a long day before it and much to be won, that the spirit of Dryden's *Essays* is in great measure derived.

Much also is native to them in England; they inherit from Ben Jonson's *Discoveries* as well as from the Discourses of Corneille. But it is from the language and the manners of Corneille and his fellows that the *Essays* of Dryden have caught their style and accent.

There is little that is peculiarly French in the details of Dryden's prose. In a well-known passage of *Marriage à la Mode*, Act iii. sc. I, there is a satire on the importation of French phrases and their use in the warfare of conversation. 'They began at *sottises* and ended *en ridicule*'; they include *foible, chagrin, grimace, embarrasse, double entendre, equivoque, eclaircissement, suitte, beveue, façon, penchant, coup d' etourdy, languissant.* Dryden does not allow himself to be led very far on this way in his own practice. In the Dedication of the *Rival Ladies* he protests against the abuse of foreign terms, and in the Preface to the *Second Miscellany* he even seems to note the word *diction* as not completely naturalized. But Dryden was not the man to make any fanatical opposition to a prevailing fashion, and he uses French words as they come convenient.

If there is anything old-fashioned in his style it is perhaps that liking for conceits which fortunately never disappears from his verse nor from his prose. He is indeed more temperate than the men *moribus antiquis*, such as Butler must be reckoned in spite of Butler's affection for lucidity and good sense. But there are many places where Dryden seems to be writing for a sentence or two in the manner of Butler or Cleveland.—W. P. KER, "Introduction" to *Essays of John Dryden*, 1900, pp. xxvii–xxx

----

THOMAS SHADWELL
From *The Medal of John Bayes:*
A Satyr against Folly and Knavery
1682

How long shall I endure, without reply,
To hear this *Bayes*,[1] this Hackney-rayler lie?
The fool uncudgell'd, for one Libel swells,
Where not his Wit, but Sawciness excels;
Whilst with foul Words and Names which he lets
    flie,
He quite defiles the *Satyr's* Dignity.
For Libel and true *Satyr* different be;
This must have *Truth*, and *Salt*, with *Modesty*.
Sparing the Persons, this does tax the Crimes,
Gall's not great Men, but Vices of the Times,
With Witty and Sharp, not blunt and bitter rimes.
Methinks the Ghost of *Horace* there I see,
Lashing this *Cherry-cheek'd Dunce* of Fifty three;
Who, at that age, so boldly durst profane,
With base hir'd Libel, the free *Satyr's* Vein.
Thou stil'st it Satyr, to call Names, Rogue, Whore,
Traytor, and Rebel, and a thousand more.
An Oyster-wench is sure thy *Muse* of late,
And all thy *Helicon's* at *Billingsgate*.
A Libellers vile name then may'st thou gain,
And moderately the Writing part maintain,
None can so well the beating part sustain.
Though with thy Sword, thou art the last of Men,
Thou art a damn'd *Boroski* with thy Pen.
As far from *Satyr* does thy Talent lye,
As far from being cheerful, or good company.
For thou art *Saturnine*,[2] thou dost confess;
A civil word thy Dulness to express.
An old gelt Mastiff has more mirth than thou,
When thou a kind of paltry Mirth would'st show.
Good humour thou so awkwardly put'st on,
It sits like Modish Clothes upon a Clown;
While that of Gentlemen is brisk and high,
When Wine and Wit about the room does flie.
Thou never mak'st, but art a standing Jest;
Thy Mirth by foolish Bawdry is exprest;
And so debauch'd, so fulsome, and so odd,
As—
Let's Bugger one another now by G-d.
(When ask'd how they should spend the
    Afternoon,
This was the smart reply[3] of the Heroick Clown.)
He boasts of Vice (which he did ne'r commit)
Calls himself *Whoremaster*, and *Sodomite*;
Commends *Reeve's* Arse, and says she Buggers
    well,
And silly Lyes of vitious pranks does tell.
This is a Sample of his Mirth and Wit,
Which he for the best Company thinks fit.
In a rich Soyl, the sprightly Horse y' have seen,
Run, leap, and wanton o're the flow'ry green,
Praunce, and curvet, with pleasure to the sight;
But it could never any eyes delight,
To see the frisking frolicks of a Cow;
And such another merry thing art Thou.
In Verse, thou hast a knack, with words to chime,
And had'st a kind of Excellence in Rime:
With Rimes like leading-strings, thou walk'dst; but
    those
Lay'd by, at every step thou brok'st thy Nose.

How low thy Farce! and thy blank Verse how
    mean!
How poor, how naked did appear each Scene!
Even thou didst blush at thy insipid stuff,
And laid thy dulness on poor harmless Snuff.
No Comick Scene, or humour hast thou wrought;
Thou 'st quibling Bawdy, and ill breeding taught;
But Rime's sad downfal has thy ruine brought.
No Piece did ever from thy self begin;
Thou can'st no web, from thine own bowels, spin.
Were from thy Works cull'd out what thou 'st
    purloin'd,
Even D—fey would excel what's left behind.
Should all thy borrow'd plumes we from thee tear,
How truly Poet Squab[4] would'st thou appear!
Thou call'st thy self, and Fools call thee, in Rime,
The goodly Prince of Poets, of thy time;
And Sov'raign power thou dost usurp, John Bayes,
And from all Poets thou a Tax dost raise.
Thou plunder'st all, t' advance thy mighty Name,
Look'st big, and triumph'st with thy borrow'd fame.
But art (while swelling thus thou think'st th' art
    Chief)
A servile Imitator and a Thief.[5]
All written Wit thou seizest on as prize;
But that will not thy ravenous mind suffice;
Though men from thee their inward thoughts
    conceal,
Yet thou the words out of their mouths wilt steal.
How little owe we to your Native store,
Who all you write have heard or read before?
Except your Libels, and there's something new;
For none were ere so impudent as you.
Some Scoundrel Poetasters yet there be,
Fools that Burlesque the name of Loyalty,
Who by reviling Patriots, think to be
From louziness and hunger ever free:
But will (for all their hopes of swelling bags)
Return to Primitive nastiness and rags.
These are blind Fools: thou hadst some kind of sight,
Thou sinn'st against thy Conscience and the Light.
After the drubs[6] thou didst of late compound,
And sold for th' weight in Gold each bruise and
    wound,
Clear was thy sight, and none declaim'd then more
'Gainst Popish Plots, and Arbitrary Power.
The Ministers thou bluntly wouldst assail,
And it was dangerous to hear thee rail.
(Oh may not England stupid be like thee!
Heaven grant it may not feel before it see.)
Now he recants, and on that beating thrives;
Thus Poet Laureats, and Russian Wives,
Do strangely upon beating mend their Lives.
But how comes Bayes to flag and grovel so?
Sure your new Lords are in their payments slow.
Thou deserv'st whipping thou 'rt so dull, this time,
Thou 'st turn'd the Observator into Rime.
But thou suppliest the want of Wit and Sense,
With most malitious Lies, and Impudence.
At Cambridge first your scurrilous Vein began,
When sawcily you traduc'd a Nobleman,[7]
Who for that Crime rebuk'd you on the head,
And you had been Expell'd had you not fled.
The next step of Advancement you began,
Was being Clerk to Nolls Lord Chamberlain,
A Sequestrator and Committee-man.
There all your wholesome Morals you suckt in,
And got your Gentile Gayety and Meen.

Your Loyalty you learn'd in Cromwels Court,
Where first your Muse did make her great effort.
On him you first shew'd your Poetick strain,
And prais'd his opening the Basilick Vein.[8]
And were that possible to come agen,
Thou on that side wouldst draw thy slavish Pen.
But he being dead, who should the slave prefer,
He turn'd a Journey-man t' a Bookseller;[9]
Writ Prefaces to Books for Meat and Drink,
And as he paid, he would both write and think.
Then by th' assistance of a Noble Knight,[10]
Th' hadst plenty, ease, and liberty to write.
First like a Gentleman he made thee live;
And on his Bounty thou dist amply thrive.
But soon thy Native swelling Venom rose,
And thou didst him, who gave thee Bread, expose.
'Gainst him a scandalous Preface didst thou write,
Which thou didst soon expunge, rather than fight.
(When turn'd away by him in some small time)
You in the Peoples ears began to chime,
And please the Town with your successful Rime.
When the best Patroness of Wit and Stage,
The Joy, the Pride, the wonder of the Age,
Sweet Annabel the good, great, witty, fair;
(Of all this Northern Court, the brightest Star)
Did on thee, Bayes, her sacred beams dispence,
Who could do ill under such influence?
She the whole Court brought over to thy side,
And favour flow'd upon thee like a Tide.
To her thou soon prov'dst an ungrateful Knave;[11]
So good was she, not only she forgave,
But did oblige anew, the faithless Slave.
And all the Gratitude he can afford,
Is basely to traduce her Princely Lord.
A Heroe worthy of a God-like Race,
Great in his Mind, and charming in his Face,
Who conquers Hearts, with unaffected Grace.
His mighty Vertues are too large for Verse,
Gentle as billing Doves, as angry Lions fierce:
His Strength and Beauty so united are,
Nature design'd him Chief, in Love and War.
All Lovers Victories he did excel,
Succeeding with the beautious Annabel.
Early in Arms his glorious course began,
Which never Heroe yet so swiftly ran.
Wherever danger shew'd its dreadful face,
By never-dying acts, h' adorn'd his Royal Race.
Sure the three Edwards Souls beheld with Joy,
How much thou outdidst Man, when little more
    than Boy.
And all the Princely Heroes of thy Line,
Rejoyc'd to see so much of their great Blood in thine.
So good and so diffusive is his Mind,
So loving too, and lov'd by Humane kind,
He was for vast and general good design'd.
In 's height of Greatness he all eyes did glad,
And never Man departed from him sad.
Sweet and obliging, easie of access,
Wise in his Judging, courteous in address.
Ore all the Passions he bears so much sway,
No Stoick taught 'em better to obey.
And, in his Suffering part, he shines more bright,
Than he appear'd in all that gaudy light;
Now, now, methinks he makes the bravest show,
And ne're was greater Heroe than he 's now.
For publick good, who wealth and power forsakes,
Over himself a glorious Conquest makes.
Religion, Prince, and Laws to him are dear;

And in defence of all, he dares appear.
'Tis he must stand like *Scæva* in the breach,
'Gainst what ill Ministers do, and furious Parsons
    preach.
Were 't not for him, how soon some *Popish* Knife
Might rob us of his *Royal* Fathers Life!
We to their fear of thee that blessing owe:
In such a Son, happy Great King art thou,
Who can defend, or can revenge thee so.
Next, for thy Medal, *Bayes*, which does revile
The wisest *Patriot* of our drooping Isle,
Who *Loyally* did serve his Exil'd *Prince*,
And with the ablest Councel blest him since;
None more than he did stop *Tyrannick* Power,
Or, in that *Crisis*, did contribute more,
To his Just Rights our Monarch to restore;
And still by wise advice, and Loyal Arts,
Would have secur'd him in his Subjects Hearts.
You own the Mischiefs, sprung from that Intrigue,
Which fatally dissolv'd the *Tripple-League.*
Each of *your Idol mock-Triumv'rate knows,*
Our *Patriot* strongly did that Breach oppose.
Nor did this Lord a *Dover*-Journey go,
From thence our tears, the Ilium *of our woe.*[12]
Had he that Interest follow'd, how could he
By those that serv'd it then discarded be?
The *French* and *Papists* well his Merits know;
Were he a friend, they'd not pursu'd him so:
From both he would our beset King preserve,
For which he does Eternal wreaths deserve.
His Life they first, and now his Fame would take,
For Crimes they forge, and secret Plots they make.
They by hir'd Witnesses the first pursue,
The latter by vile Scriblers hir'd like you.
Thy Infamy will blush at no disgrace,
(With such a harden'd Conscience, and a Face)
Thou only want'st an *Evidences* place.
When th' *Isle* was drown'd in a Lethargick sleep,
Our vigilant *Heroe* still a watch did keep.

. . .

Go, *Abject Bayes!* and act thy slavish part;
Fawn on those *Popish Knaves*, whose Knave thou art:
'Tis not ill writing, or worse Policy,
That can enslave a Nation, so long free.

. . .

Now farewel wretched Mercenary *Bayes*,
Who the *King* Libell'd, and did *Cromwel* praise.
Farewel, abandon'd Rascal! only fit
To be abus'd by thy own scurrilous Wit.
Which thou wouldst do, and for a Moderate Sum,
Answer thy Medal, and thy *Absolom.*
Thy piteous Hackney-Pen shall never fright us,
Thou 'rt dwindl'd down to *Hodge*, and *Heraclitus.*
Go, *Ignoramus* cry, and *Forty One*,
And by *Sams Parsons*[13] be thou prais'd alone,
Pied thing! half Wit! half Fool! and for a Knave,
Few Men, than this, a better mixture have:
But thou canst add to that, Coward and Slave.

Notes

1. *His Name in the* Rehearsal.
2. *In his* Drammatick Essay.
3. *At Windsor, in the company of several persons of Quality, Sir* G⟨eorge⟩ E⟨therege⟩ *being present.*
4. *The Name given him by the Earl of* Rochester.
5. *Oh imitatores servum pecus!*
6. *In* Rose-Alley.
7. *A* Lords Son, *and all* Noblemens Sons, *are called Noblemen there.*

8. *See his Poem upon* Oliver.—*And wisely he essay's to stanch the Blood by breathing of a Vein.*
9. Mr. Herringman, *who kept him in his House for that purpose.*
10. Sir R⟨obert⟩ H⟨oward⟩ *who kept him generously at his own House.*
11. *When he had thrice broken his Word, Oath, and Bargain with Sir* William Davenant, *he wrote a Letter to this great Lady to pass her word for him to Sir* William, *who would not take his own; which she did. . . .*
12. Bayes *his own expression,* Medal.
13. *A* coffee-house *where the Inferiour Crape-gown-men [clergy] meet with their Guide* Roger ⟨L'Estrange⟩ *to invent Lies for the farther carrying on the Popish-Plot.*

SAMUEL JOHNSON
From "Dryden"
Lives of the English Poets
1779–81

Dryden may be properly considered as the father of English criticism, as the writer who first taught us to determine upon principles the merit of composition. Of our former poets, the greatest dramatist wrote without rules, conducted through life and nature by a genius that rarely misled, and rarely deserted him. Of the rest, those who knew the laws of propriety had neglected to teach them.

Two *Arts of English Poetry* were written in the days of Elizabeth by Webb and Puttenham, from which something might be learned, and a few hints had been given by Jonson and Cowley; but Dryden's *Essay on Dramatick Poetry* was the first regular and valuable treatise on the art of writing.

He who, having formed his opinions in the present age of English literature, turns back to peruse this dialogue, will not perhaps find much increase of knowledge, or much novelty of instruction; but he is to remember that critical principles were then in the hands of a few, who had gathered them partly from the Ancients, and partly from the Italians and French. The structure of dramatick poems was then not generally understood. Audiences applauded by instinct, and poets perhaps often pleased by chance.

A writer who obtains his full purpose loses himself in his own lustre. Of an opinion which is no longer doubted, the evidence ceases to be examined. Of an art universally practised, the first teacher is forgotten. Learning once made popular is no longer learning; it has the appearance of something which we have bestowed upon ourselves, as the dew appears to rise from the field which it refreshes.

To judge rightly of an author, we must transport ourselves to his time, and examine what were the wants of his contemporaries, and what were his means of supplying them. That which is easy at one time was difficult at another. Dryden at least imported his science, and gave his country what it wanted before; or rather, he imported only the materials, and manufactured them by his own skill.

The dialogue on the Drama was one of his first essays of criticism, written when he was yet a timorous candidate for reputation, and therefore laboured with that diligence which he might allow himself somewhat to remit, when his name gave sanction to his positions, and his awe of the public was abated, partly by custom, and partly by success. It will not be easy to find, in all the opulence of our language, a treatise so artfully variegated with successive representations of opposite probabilities, so enlivened with imagery, so brightened with illustrations. His portraits of the English dramatists are wrought with great spirit and diligence. The account of Shakespeare may stand as a perpetual model of encomiastick criticism; exact without minuteness, and lofty without exaggeration. The praise lavished by Longinus, on the attention of the heroes of Marathon, by Demosthenes, fades away before it. In a few lines is exhibited a character, so extensive in its comprehension, and so curious in its limitations, that nothing can be added, diminished, or reformed; nor can the editors and admirers of Shakespeare, in all their emulation of reverence, boast of much more than of having diffused and paraphrased this epitome of excellence, of having changed Dryden's gold for baser metal, of lower value though of greater bulk.

In this, and in all his other essays on the same subject, the criticism of Dryden is the criticism of a poet; not a dull collection of theorems, nor a rude detection of faults, which perhaps the censor was not able to have committed; but a gay and vigorous dissertation, where delight is mingled with instruction, and where the author proves his right of judgement, by his power of performance.

The different manner and effect with which critical knowledge may be conveyed, was perhaps never more clearly exemplified than in the performances of Rymer and Dryden. It was said of a dispute between two mathematicians, 'malim cum Scaligero errare, quam cum Clavio recte sapere'; that *it was more eligible to go wrong with one than right with the other*. A tendency of the same kind every mind must feel at the perusal of Dryden's prefaces and Rymer's discourses. With Dryden we are wandering in quest of Truth; whom we find, if we find her at all, dressed in the graces of elegance, and if we miss her, the labour of the pursuit rewards itself; we are led only through fragrance and flowers: Rymer, without taking a nearer, takes a rougher way; every step is to be made through thorns and brambles; and Truth, if we meet her, appears repulsive by her mien, and ungraceful by her habit. Dryden's criticism has the majesty of a queen; Rymer's has the ferocity of a tyrant.

As he had studied with great diligence the art of poetry, and enlarged or rectified his notions, by experience perpetually increasing, he had his mind stored with principles and observations; he poured out his knowledge with little labour; for of labour, notwithstanding the multiplicity of his productions, there is sufficient reason to suspect that he was not a lover. To write *con amore*, with fondness for the employment, with perpetual touches and retouches, with unwillingness to take leave of his own idea, and an unwearied pursuit of unattainable perfection, was, I think, no part of his character.

His criticism may be considered as general or occasional. In his general precepts, which depend upon the nature of things, and the structure of the human mind, he may doubtless be safely recommended to the confidence of the reader; but his occasional and particular positions were sometimes interested, sometimes negligent, and sometimes capricious. It is not without reason that Trapp, speaking of the praises which he bestows on Palamon and Arcite, says, 'Novimus judicium Drydeni de poemate quodam *Chauceri*, pulchro sane illo, et admodum laudando, nimirum quod non modo vere epicum sit, sed Iliada etiam atque Aeneada aequet, imo superet. Sed novimus eodem tempore viri illius maximi non semper accuratissimas esse censuras, nec ad severissimam critices normam exactas: illo judice id plerumque optimum est, quod nunc prae manibus habet, & in quo nunc occupatur.'

He is therefore by no means constant to himself. His defence and desertion of dramatick rhyme is generally known. *Spence*, in his remarks on Pope's *Odyssey*, produces what he thinks an unconquerable quotation from Dryden's preface to the *Eneid*, in favour of translating an epick poem into blank verse; but he forgets that when his author attempted the *Iliad*, some years afterwards, he departed from his own decision, and translated into rhyme.

When he has any objection to obviate, or any license to defend, he is not very scrupulous about what he asserts, nor very cautious, if the present purpose be served, not to entangle himself in his own sophistries. But when all arts are exhausted, like other hunted animals, he sometimes stands at bay; when he cannot disown the grossness of one of his plays, he declares that he knows not any law that prescribes morality to a comick poet.

His remarks on ancient or modern writers are not always to be trusted. His parallel of the versification of Ovid with that of Claudian has been very justly censured by *Sewel*. His comparison of the first line of Virgil with the first of Statius is not happier. Virgil, he says, is soft and gentle, and would have thought Statius mad if he had heard him thundering out

Quae superimposito moles geminata colosso.

Statius perhaps heats himself, as he proceeds, to exaggerations somewhat hyperbolical; but undoubtedly Virgil would have been too hasty, if he had condemned him to straw for one sounding line. Dryden wanted an instance, and the first that occurred was imprest into the service.

What he wishes to say, he says at hazard; he cited *Gorbuduc*, which he had never seen; gives a false account of *Chapman's* versification; and discovers, in the preface to his Fables, that he translated the first book of the *Iliad*, without knowing what was in the second.

It will be difficult to prove that Dryden ever made any great advances in literature. As having distinguished himself at Westminster under the tuition of Busby, who advanced his scholars to a height of knowledge very rarely attained in grammar-schools, he resided afterwards at Cambridge, it is not to be supposed, that his skill in the ancient languages was deficient, compared with that of common students; but his scholastick acquisitions seem not proportionate to his opportunities and abilities. He could not, like Milton or Cowley, have made his name illustrious merely by his learning. He mentions but few books, and those such as lie in the beaten track of regular study; from which if ever he departs, he is in danger of losing himself in unknown regions.

In his Dialogue on the Drama, he pronounces with great confidence that the Latin tragedy of *Medea* is not Ovid's, because it is not sufficiently interesting and pathetick. He might have determined the question upon purer evidence; for it is quoted by Quintilian as the work of Seneca; and the only line which remains of Ovid's play, for one line is left us, is not there to be found. There was therefore no need of the gravity of conjecture, or the discussion of plot or sentiment, to find what was already known upon higher authority than such discussions can ever reach.

His literature, though not always free from ostentation, will be commonly found either obvious, and made his own by the art of dressing it; or superficial, which, by what he gives, shews what he wanted; or erroneous, hastily collected, and negligently scattered.

Yet it cannot be said that his genius is ever unprovided of matter, or that his fancy languishes in penury of ideas. His works abound with knowledge, and sparkle with illustrations. There is scarcely any science or faculty that does not supply him with occasional images and lucky similitudes; every page discovers a mind very widely acquainted both with art and nature, and in full possession of great stores of intellectual wealth. Of him that knows much, it is natural to suppose that he has read with diligence; yet I rather believe that the knowledge of Dryden was gleaned from accidental intelligence and various conversation, by a quick apprehension, a judicious selection, and a happy memory, a keen appetite of knowledge, and a powerful digestion; by vigilance that permitted nothing to pass without notice, and a habit of reflection that suffered nothing useful to be lost. A mind like Dryden's, always curious, always active, to which every understanding was proud to be associated, and of which every one solicited the regard, by an ambitious display of himself, had a more pleasant, perhaps a nearer way, to knowledge than by the silent progress of solitary reading. I do not suppose that he despised books, or intentionally neglected them; but that he was carried out, by the impetuosity of his genius, to more vivid and speedy instructors; and that his studies were rather desultory and fortuitous than constant and systematical.

It must be confessed that he scarcely ever appears to want book-learning but when he mentions books; and to him may be transferred the praise which he gives his master Charles.

> His conversation, wit, and parts,
> His knowledge in the noblest useful arts,
>   Were such, dead authors could not give,
>   But habitudes of those that live;
> Who, lighting him, did greater lights receive:
>   He drain'd from all, and all they knew,
>   His apprehension quick, his judgement true:
> That the most learn'd with shame confess
> His knowledge more, his reading only less.

Of all this, however, if the proof be demanded, I will not undertake to give it; the atoms of probability, of which my opinion has been formed, lie scattered over all his works; and by him who thinks the question worth his notice, his works must be perused with very close attention.

Criticism, either didactick or defensive, occupies almost all his prose, except those pages which he has devoted to his patrons; but none of his prefaces were ever thought tedious. They have not the formality of a settled style, in which the first half of the sentence betrays the other. The clauses are never balanced, nor the periods modelled; every word seems to drop by chance, though it falls into its proper place. Nothing is cold or languid; the whole is airy, animated, and vigorous; what is little, is gay; what is great, is splendid. He may be thought to mention himself too frequently; but while he forces himself upon our esteem, we cannot refuse him to stand high in his own. Every thing is excused by the play of images and the spriteliness of expression. Though all is easy, nothing is feeble; though all seems careless, there is nothing harsh; and though, since his earlier works, more than a century has passed, they have nothing yet uncouth or obsolete.

He who writes much will not easily escape a manner, such a recurrence of particular modes as may be easily noted. Dryden is always *another and the same*, he does not exhibit a second time the same elegances in the same form, nor appears to have any art other than that of expressing with clearness what he thinks with vigour. His style could not easily be imitated, either seriously or ludicrously; for, being always equable and always varied, it has no prominent or discriminative characters. The beauty who is totally free from disproportion of parts and features, cannot be ridiculed by an overcharged resemblance.

From his prose, however, Dryden derives only his accidental and secondary praise; the veneration with which his name is pronounced by every cultivator of English literature, is paid to him as he refined the language, improved the sentiments, and tuned the numbers of English poetry.

After about half a century of forced thoughts, and rugged metre, some advances towards nature and harmony had been already made by Waller and Denham; they had shewn that long discourses in rhyme grew more pleasing when they were broken into couplets, and that verse consisted not only in the number but the arrangement of syllables.

But though they did much, who can deny that they left much to do? Their works were not many, nor were their minds of very ample comprehension. More examples of more modes of composition were necessary for the establishment of regularity, and the introduction of propriety in word and thought.

Every language of a learned nation necessarily divides itself into diction scholastick and popular, grave and familiar, elegant and gross; and from a nice distinction of these different parts, arises a great part of the beauty of style. But if we except a few minds, the favourites of nature, to whom their own original rectitude was in the place of rules, this delicacy of selection was little known to our authors; our speech lay before them in a heap of confusion, and every man took for every purpose what chance might offer him.

There was therefore before the time of Dryden no poetical diction, no system of words at once refined from the grossness of domestick use, and free from the harshness of terms appropriated to particular arts. Words too familiar, or too remote, defeat the purpose of a poet. From those sounds which we hear on small or on coarse occasions, we do not easily receive strong impressions, or delightful images; and words to which we are nearly strangers, whenever they occur, draw that attention on themselves which they should transmit to things.

Those happy combinations of words which distinguished poetry from prose, had been rarely attempted; we had few elegances or flowers of speech, the roses had not yet been plucked from the bramble, or different colours had not yet been joined to enliven one another.

It may be doubted whether Waller and Denham could have overborne the prejudices which had long prevailed, and which even then were sheltered by the protection of Cowley. The new versification, as it was called, may be considered as owing its establishment to Dryden; from whose time it is apparent that English poetry has had no tendency to relapse to its former savageness.

The affluence and comprehension of our language is very illustriously displayed in our poetical translations of Ancient Writers; a work which the French seem to relinquish in despair, and which we were long unable to perform with dexterity. Ben Jonson thought it necessary to copy Horace almost word by word; Feltham, his contemporary and adversary, considers it as indispensably requisite in a translation to give line for line. It is said that Sandys, whom Dryden calls the best versifier of the last age, has struggled hard to comprise every book of his English Metamorphoses in the same number of verses with the original. Holyday had nothing in view but to shew that he understood his author, with so little regard to the grandeur of his diction, or the volubility of his numbers, that his metres can hardly be called verses; they cannot be read without reluctance, nor will the labour always be rewarded by understanding them. Cowley saw that such *copyers* were a *servile race*; he asserted his liberty, and spread his wings so boldly that he left his authors. It was reserved for Dryden to fix the limits of poetical liberty, and give us just rules and examples of translation.

When languages are formed upon different principles, it is impossible that the same modes of expression should always be elegant in both. While they run on together; the closest translation may be considered as the best; but when they divaricate, each must take its natural course. Where correspondence cannot be obtained, it is necessary to be content with something equivalent. *Translation therefore*, says Dryden, *is not so loose as paraphrase, nor so close as metaphrase.*

All polished languages have different styles; the concise, the diffuse, the lofty, and the humble. In the proper choice of style consists the resemblance which Dryden principally exacts from the translator. He is to exhibit his author's thoughts in such a dress of diction as the author would have given them, had his language been English: rugged magnificence is not to be softened: hyperbolical ostentation is not to be repressed, nor sententious affectation to have its points blunted. A translator is to be like his author: it is not his business to excel him.

The reasonableness of these rules seems sufficient for their vindication; and the effects produced by observing them were so happy, that I know not whether they were ever opposed but by Sir Edward Sherburne, a man whose learning was greater than his powers of poetry; and who, being better qualified to give the meaning than the spirit of Seneca, has introduced his version of three tragedies by a defence of close translation. The authority of Horace, which the new translators cited in defence of their practice, he has, by a judicious explanation, taken fairly from them; but reason wants not Horace to support it.

It seldom happens that all the necessary causes concur to any great effect: will is wanting to power, or power to will, or both are impeded by external obstructions. The exigences in which Dryden was condemned to pass his life, are reasonably supposed to have blasted his genius, to have driven out his works in a state of immaturity, and to have intercepted the full-blown elegance which longer growth would have supplied.

Poverty, like other rigid powers, is sometimes too hastily accused. If the excellence of Dryden's works was lessened by his indigence, their number was increased; and I know not how it will be proved, that if he had written less he would have written better; or that indeed he would have undergone the toil of an author, if he had not been solicited by something more pressing than the love of praise.

But as is said by his Sebastian,

What had been, is unknown; what is, appears.

We know that Dryden's several productions were so many successive expedients for his support; his plays were therefore often borrowed, and his poems were almost all occasional.

In an occasional performance no height of excellence can be expected from any mind, however fertile in itself, and however stored with acquisitions. He whose work is general and arbitrary, has the choice of his matter, and takes that which his inclination and his studies have best qualified him to display and decorate. He is at liberty to delay his publication, till he has satisfied his friends and himself; till he has reformed his first thoughts by subsequent examination; and polished away those faults which the precipitance of ardent composition is likely to leave behind it. Virgil is related to have poured out a great number of lines in the morning, and to have passed the day in reducing them to fewer.

The occasional poet is circumscribed by the narrowness of his subject. Whatever can happen to man has happened so often, that little remains for fancy or invention. We have been all born; we have most of us been married; and so many have died before us, that our deaths can supply but few materials for a poet. In the fate of princes the publick has an interest; and what happens to them of good or evil, the poets have always considered as business for the Muse. But after so many inauguratory gratulations, nuptial hymns, and funeral dirges,

he must be highly favoured by nature, or by fortune, who says any thing not said before. Even war and conquest, however splendid, suggest no new images; the triumphal chariot of a victorious monarch can be decked only with those ornaments that have graced his predecessors.

Not only matter but time is wanting. The poem must not be delayed till the occasion is forgotten. The lucky moments of animated imagination cannot be attended; elegances and illustrations cannot be multiplied by gradual accumulation: the composition must be dispatched while conversation is yet busy, and admiration fresh; and haste is to be made, lest some other event should lay hold upon mankind.

Occasional compositions may however secure to a writer the praise both of learning and facility; for they cannot be the effect of long study, and must be furnished immediately from the treasures of the mind.

The death of Cromwell was the first publick event which called forth Dryden's poetical powers. His heroick stanzas have beauties and defects; the thoughts are vigorous, and though not always proper, shew a mind replete with ideas; the numbers are smooth, and the diction, if not altogether correct, is elegant and easy.

Davenant was perhaps at this time his favourite author, though *Gondibert* never appears to have been popular: and from Davenant he learned to please his ear with the stanza of four lines alternately rhymed. ⟨. . .⟩

Rhyme has been so long banished from the theatre, that we know not its effect upon the passions of an audience; but it has this convenience, that sentences stand more independent on each other, and striking passages are therefore easily selected and retained. Thus the description of Night in the *Indian Emperor*, and the rise and fall of empire in the *Conquest of Granada*, are more frequently repeated than any lines in *All for Love*, or *Don Sebastian*.

To search his plays for vigorous sallies, and sententious elegances, or to fix the dates of any little pieces which he wrote by chance, or by solicitation, were labour too tedious and minute.

His dramatick labours did not so wholly absorb his thoughts, but that he promulgated the laws of translation in a preface to the English Epistles of Ovid; one of which he translated himself, and another in conjunction with the Earl of Mulgrave.

Absalom and Achitophel is a work so well known, that particular criticism is superfluous. If it be considered as a poem political and controversial, it will be found to comprise all the excellences of which the subject is susceptible; acrimony of censure, elegance of praise, artful delineation of characters, variety and vigour of sentiment, happy turns of language, and pleasing harmony of numbers; and all these raised to such a height as can scarcely be found in any other English composition.

It is not, however, without faults; some lines are inelegant or improper, and too many are irreligiously licentious. The original structure of the poem was defective; allegories drawn to great length will always break; Charles could not run continually parallel with David.

The subject had likewise another inconvenience: it admitted little imagery or description, and a long poem of mere sentiments easily becomes tedious; though all the parts are forcible, and every line kindles new rapture, the reader, if not relieved by the interposition of something that sooths the fancy, grows weary of admiration, and defers the rest.

As an approach to historical truth was necessary, the action and catastrophe were not in the poet's power; there is

therefore an unpleasing disproportion between the beginning
and the end. We are alarmed by a faction formed out of many
sects various in their principles, but agreeing in their purpose of
mischief, formidable for their numbers, and strong by their
supports, while the king's friends are few and weak. The chiefs
on either part are set forth to view; but when expectation is at
the height, the king makes a speech, and

> Henceforth a series of new times began.

Who can forbear to think of an enchanted castle, with a
wide moat and lofty battlements, walls of marble and gates of
brass, which vanishes at once into air, when the destined
knight blows his horn before it?

In the second part, written by *Tate*, there is a long
insertion, which, for poignancy of satire, exceeds any part of
the former. Personal resentment, though no laudable motive
to satire, can add great force to general principles. Self-love is
a busy prompter.

The *Medal*, written upon the same principles with
Absalom and Achitophel, but upon a narrower plan, gives less
pleasure, though it discovers equal abilities in the writer. The
superstructure cannot extend beyond the foundation; a single
character of incident cannot furnish as many ideas, as a series
of events, or multiplicity of agents. This poem therefore, since
time has left it to itself, is not much read, nor perhaps generally
understood, yet it abounds with touches both of humorous and
serious satire. The picture of a man whose propensions to
mischief are such, that his best actions are but inability of
wickedness, is very skillfully delineated and strongly coloured.

> Power was his aim: but, thrown from that pretence,
> The wretch turn'd loyal in his own defence,
> And malice reconcil'd him to his Prince.
> Him, in the anguish of his soul, he serv'd;
> Rewarded faster still than he deserv'd:
> Behold him now exalted into trust;
> His counsels oft convenient, seldom just.
> Ev'n in the most sincere advice he gave,
> He had a grudging still to be a knave.
> The frauds he learnt in his fanatic years,
> Made him uneasy in his lawful gears:
> At least as little honest as he cou'd:
> And, like white witches, mischievously good.
> To this first bias, longingly, he leans;
> And rather would be great by wicked means.

The *Threnodia*, which, by a term I am afraid neither
authorized nor analogical, he calls *Augustalis*, is not among
his happiest productions. Its first and obvious defect is the
irregularity of its metre, to which the ears of that age, however,
were accustomed. What is worse, it has neither tenderness nor
dignity, it is neither magnificent nor pathetick. He seems to
look round him for images which he cannot find, and what he
has he distorts by endeavouring to enlarge them. He is, he says,
petrified with grief; but the marble sometimes relents, and
trickles have in a joke.

> The sons of art all med'cines try'd,
> And every noble remedy apply'd;
>   With emulation each essay'd
>   His utmost skill; *nay more they pray'd:*
> Never was losing game with better conduct play'd.

He had been a little inclined to merriment before upon
the prayers of a nation for their dying sovereign, nor was he
serious enough to keep heathen fables out of his religion.

> With him th' innumerable crowd of armed prayers
> Knock'd at the gates of heaven, and knock'd aloud;
> *The first well-meaning rude petitioners,*

> All for his life assail'd the throne,
> All would have brib'd the skies by offering up their
>   own.
> So great a throng not heaven itself could bar;
> 'Twas almost borne by force *as in the giants' war.*
>   The prayers, at least, for his reprieve were heard;
> His death, like Hezekiah's, was deferr'd.

There is throughout the composition a desire of splendor
without wealth. In the conclusion he seems too much pleased
with the prospect of the new reign to have lamented his old
master with much sincerity.

He did not miscarry in this attempt for want of skill either
in lyrick or elegiack poetry. His poem 'On the death of Mrs.
Killigrew,' is undoubtedly the noblest ode that our language
has ever produced. The first part flows with a torrent of
enthusiasm. *Fervet immensusque ruit.* All the stanzas indeed
are not equal. An imperial crown cannot be one continued
diamond; the gems must be held together by some less valuable
matter.

In his first ode for Cecila's day, which is lost in the
splendor of the second, there are passages which would have
dignified any other poet. The first stanza is vigorous and
elegant, though the word *diapason* is too technical, and the
rhymes are too remote from one another.

> From harmony, from heavenly harmony,
>   This universal frame began:
> When nature underneath a heap of jarring atoms
>   lay,
>   And could not heave her head,
> The tuneful voice was heard from high,
>   Arise ye more than dead.
> Then cold and hot, and moist and dry,
> In order to their stations leap,
>   And musick's power obey.
> From harmony, from heavenly harmony,
>   This universal frame began:
>   From harmony to harmony
> Through all the compass of the notes it ran,
>   The diapason closing full in man.

The conclusion is likewise striking, but it includes an
image so awful in itself, that it can owe little to poetry; and I
could wish the antithesis of *musick untuning* had found some
other place.

> As from the power of sacred lays
>   The spheres began to move,
> And sung the great Creator's praise
>   To all the bless'd above.
> So when the last and dreadful hour
> This crumbling pageant shall devour,
> The trumpet shall be heard on high,
> The dead shall live, the living die,
> And musick shall untune the sky.

Of his skill in Elegy he has given a specimen in his
'Eleonora', of which the following lines discover their author:

> Though all these rare endowments of the mind
> Were in a narrow space of life confin'd,
> The figure was with full perfection crown'd;
> Though not so large an orb, as truly round:
> As when in glory, through the public place,
> The spoils of conquer'd nations were to pass,
> And but one day for triumph was allow'd,
> The consul was constrain'd his pomp to crowd;
> And so the swift procession hurry'd on,
> That all, though not distinctly, might be shown:

So in the straiten'd bounds of life confin'd,
She gave but glimpses of her glorious mind:
And multitudes of virtues pass'd along;
Each pressing foremost in the mighty throng,
Ambitious to be seen, and then make room
For greater multitudes that were to come.
Yet unemploy'd no minute slipp'd away;
Moments were precious in so short a stay.
The haste of heaven to have her was so great,
That some were simple acts, though each compleat;
And every act stood ready to repeat.

This piece, however, is not without its faults; there is so much likeness in the initial comparison, that there is no illustration. As a king would be lamented, Eleonora was lamented.

As when some great and gracious monarch dies,
Soft whispers, first, and mournful murmurs rise
Among the sad attendants; then the sound
Soon gathers voice, and spreads the news around,
Through town and country, till the dreadful blast
Is blown to distant colonies at last;
Who, then, perhaps, were offering vows in vain,
For his long life, and for his happy reign:
So slowly by degrees, unwilling fame
Did matchless Eleonora's fate proclaim,
Till publick as the loss the news became.

This is little better than to say in praise of a shrub, that it is as green as a tree, or of a brook, that it waters a garden, as a river waters a country.

Dryden confesses that he did not know the lady whom he celebrates; the praise being therefore inevitably general, fixes no impression upon the reader, nor excites any tendency to love, nor much desire of imitation. Knowledge of the subject is to the poet what durable materials are to the architect.

The *Religio Laici*, which borrows its title from the *Religio Medici* of Browne, is almost the only work of Dryden which can be considered as a voluntary effusion; in this, therefore, it might be hoped, that the full effulgence of his genius would be found. But unhappily the subject is rather argumentative than poetical: he intended only a specimen of metrical disputation.

And this unpolish'd rugged verse I chose,
As fittest for discourse, and nearest prose.

This, however, is a composition of great excellence in its kind, in which the familiar is very properly diversified with the solemn, and the grave with the humorous; in which metre has neither weakened the force, nor clouded the perspicuity of argument; nor will it be easy to find another example equally happy of this middle kind of writing, which, though prosaick in some parts, rises to high poetry in others, and neither towers to the skies, nor creeps along the ground.

Of the same kind, or not far distant from it, is the *Hind and Panther*, the longest of all Dryden's original poems; an allegory intended to comprise and to decide the controversy between the Romanists and Protestants. The scheme of the work is injudicious and incommodious; for what can be more absurd than that one beast should counsel another to rest her faith upon a pope and council? He seems well enough skilled in the usual topicks of argument, endeavours to shew the necessity of an infallible judge, and reproaches the Reformers with want of unity; but is weak enough to ask, why since we see without knowing how, we may not have an infallible judge without knowing where.

The *Hind* at one time is afraid to drink at the common brook, because she may be worried; but walking home with the *Panther*, talks by the way of the *Nicene Fathers*, and at last declares herself to be the Catholic Church.

This absurdity was very properly ridiculed in the *City Mouse and the Country Mouse* of *Montague* and *Prior*; and in the detection and censure of the incongruity of the fiction, chiefly consists the value of their performance, which, whatever reputation it might obtain by the help of temporary passions, seems to readers almost a century distant, not very forcible or animated.

Pope, whose judgement was perhaps a little bribed by the subject, used to mention this poem as the most correct specimen of Dryden's versification. It was indeed written when he had completely formed his manner, and may be supposed to exhibit, negligence excepted, his deliberate and ultimate scheme of metre.

We may therefore reasonably infer, that he did not approve the perpetual uniformity which confines the sense to couplets, since he has broken his lines in the initial paragraph.

A milk-white Hind, immortal and unchang'd,
Fed on the lawns, and in the forest rang'd;
Without unspotted, innocent within,
She fear'd no danger, for she knew no sin.
Yet had she oft been chac'd with horns and hounds
And Scythian shafts, and many winged wounds
Aim'd at her heart; was often forc'd to fly,
And doom'd to death, though fated not to die.

These lines are lofty, elegant, and musical, notwithstanding the interruption of the pause, of which the effect is rather increase of pleasure by variety, than offence by ruggedness.

To the first part it was his intention, he says, *to give the majestick turn of heroick poesy*; and perhaps he might have executed his design not unsuccessfully, had not an opportunity of satire, which he cannot forbear, fallen sometimes in his way. The character of a Presbyterian, whose emblem is the *Wolf*, is not very heroically majestick.

More haughty than the rest, the wolfish race
Appear with belly gaunt and famish'd face:
Never was so deform'd a beast of grace.
His ragged tail betwixt his legs he wears,
Close clapp'd for shame; but his rough crest he rears,
And pricks up his predestinating ears.

His general character of the other sorts of beasts that never go to church, though spritely and keen, has, however, not much of heroick poesy.

These are the chief; to number o'er the rest,
And stand like Adam naming every beast,
Were weary work; nor will the Muse describe
A slimy-born, and sun-begotten tribe;
Who, far from steeples and their sacred sound,
In fields their sullen conventicles found.
These gross, half-animated, lumps I leave;
Nor can I think what thoughts they can conceive;
But if they think at all, 'tis sure no higher
Than matter, put in motion, may aspire;
Souls that can scarce ferment their mass of clay;
So drossy, so divisible are they,
As would but serve pure bodies for allay:
Such souls as shards produce, such beetle things
As only buz to heaven with evening wings;
Strike in the dark, offending but by chance;
Such are the blindfold blows of ignorance.
They know not beings, and but hate a name;
To them the Hind and Panther are the same.

One more instance, and that taken from the narrative art,

where style was more in his choice, will shew how steadily he
kept his resolution of heroick dignity.

> For when the herd, suffic'd, did late repair
> To ferny heaths, and to their forest lair,
> She made a mannerly excuse to stay,
> Proffering the Hind to wait her half the way:
> That, since the sky was clear, an hour of talk
> Might help her to beguile the tedious walk.
> With much good-will the motion was embrac'd,
> To chat awhile on their adventures past:
> Nor had the grateful Hind so soon forgot
> Her friend and fellow-sufferer in the plot.
> Yet, wondering how of late she grew estrang'd,
> Her forehead cloudy and her count'nance chang'd,
> She thought this hour th' occasion would present
> To learn her secret cause of discontent,
> Which well she hop'd, might be with ease redress'd,
> Considering her a well-bred civil beast,
> And more a gentlewoman than the rest.
> After some common talk what rumours ran,
> The lady of the spotted muff began.

The second and third parts he professes to have reduced to
diction more familiar and more suitable to dispute and
conversation; the difference is not, however, very easily perceived; the first has familiar, and the two others have sonorous,
lines. The original incongruity runs through the whole; the
king is now *Caesar*, and now the *Lyon*; and the name *Pan* is
given to the Supreme Being.

But when this constitutional absurdity is forgiven, the
poem must be confessed to be written with great smoothness of
metre, a wide extent of knowledge, and an abundant multiplicity of images; the controversy is embellished with pointed
sentences, diversified by illustrations, and enlivened by sallies
of invective. Some of the facts to which allusions are made, are
now become obscure, and perhaps there may be many satirical
passages little understood.

As it was by its nature a work of defiance, a composition
which would naturally be examined with the utmost acrimony
of criticism, it was probably laboured with uncommon attention; and there are, indeed, few negligences in the subordinate
parts. The original impropriety, and the subsequent unpopu-
larity of the subject, added to the ridiculousness of its first
elements, has sunk it into neglect; but it may be usefully
studied, as an example of poetical ratiocination, in which the
argument suffers little from the metre.

In the poem on 'The Birth of the Prince of Wales,'
nothing is very remarkable but the exorbitant adulation, and
that insensibility of the precipice on which the king was then
standing, which the laureate apparently shared with the rest of
the courtiers. A few months cured him of controversy, dismissed him from court, and made him again a playwright and
translator.

Of Juvenal there had been a translation by Stapylton, and
another by Holiday; neither of them is very poetical. Stapylton
is more smooth, and Holiday's is more esteemed for the
learning of his notes. A new version was proposed to the poets
of that time, and undertaken by them in conjunction. The
main design was conducted by Dryden, whose reputation was
such that no man was unwilling to serve the Muses under him.

The general character of this translation will be given,
when it is said to preserve the wit, but to want the dignity of the
original. The peculiarity of Juvenal is a mixture of gaiety and
stateliness, of pointed sentences and declamatory grandeur.
His points have not been neglected; but his grandeur none of
the band seemed to consider as necessary to be imitated, except

Creech, who undertook the thirteenth satire. It is therefore
perhaps possible to give a better representation of that great
satirist, even in those parts which Dryden himself has translated, some passages excepted, which will never be excelled.

With Juvenal was published Persius, translated wholly by
Dryden. This work, though like all the other productions of
Dryden it may have shining parts, seems to have been written
merely for wages, in an uniform mediocrity, without any eager
endeavour after excellence, or laborious effort of the mind.

There wanders an opinion among the readers of poetry,
that one of these satires is an exercise of the school. Dryden
says that he once translated it at school; but not that he
preserved or published the juvenile performance.

Not long afterwards he undertook perhaps the most
arduous work of its kind, a translation of Virgil, for which he
had shewn how well he was qualified by his version of the
Pollio, and two episodes, one of Nisus and Euryalus, the other
of Mezentius and Lausus.

In the comparison of Homer and Virgil, the discriminative excellence of Homer is elevation and comprehension of
thought, and that of Virgil is grace and splendor of diction.
The beauties of Homer are therefore difficult to be lost, and
those of Virgil difficult to be retained. The massy trunk of
sentiment is safe by its solidity, but the blossoms of elocution
easily drop away. The author, having the choice of his own
images, selects those which he can best adorn: the translator
must, at all hazards, follow his original, and express thoughts
which perhaps he would not have chosen. When to this
primary difficulty is added the inconvenience of a language so
much inferior in harmony to the Latin, it cannot be expected
that they who read the *Georgick* and the *Eneid* should be much
delighted with any version.

All these obstacles Dryden saw, and all these he determined to encounter. The expectation of his work was undoubtedly great; the nation considered its honour as interested in the
event. One gave him the different editions of his author, and
another helped him in the subordinate parts. The arguments of
the several books were given him by Addison.

The hopes of the publick were not disappointed. He
produced, says Pope, *the most noble and spirited translation
that I know in any language*. It certainly excelled whatever had
appeared in English, and appears to have satisfied his friends,
and, for the most part, to have silenced his enemies. Milbourne, indeed, a clergyman, attacked it; but his outrages seem
to be the ebullitions of a mind agitated by stronger resentment
than bad poetry can excite, and previously resolved not to be
pleased. ⟨. . .⟩

When admiration had subsided, the translation was more
coolly examined, and found like all others, to be sometimes
erroneous, and sometimes licentious. Those who could find
faults, thought they could avoid them; and Dr. Brady attempted in blank verse a translation of the Eneid, which, when
dragged into the world, did not live long enough to cry. I have
never seen it; but that such a version there is, or has been,
perhaps some old catalogue informed me.

With not much better success, Trapp, when his Tragedy
and his Prelections had given him reputation, attempted
another blank version of the Eneid; to which, notwithstanding
the slight regard with which it was treated, he had afterwards
perseverance enough to add the Eclogues and Georgicks. His
book may continue its existence as long as it is the clandestine
refuge of school-boys.

Since the English ear has been accustomed to the
mellifluence of Pope's numbers, and the diction of poetry has
become more splendid, new attempts have been made to

translate Virgil; and all his works have been attempted by men better qualified to contend with Dryden. I will not engage myself in an invidious comparison by opposing one passage to another; a work of which there would be no end, and which might be often offensive without use.

It is not by comparing line with line that the merit of great works is to be estimated, but by their general effects and ultimate result. It is easy to note a weak line, and write one more vigorous in its place; to find a happiness of expression in the original, and transplant it by force into the version: but what is given to the parts, may be subducted from the whole, and the reader may be weary, though the critick may commend. Works of imagination excel by their allurement and delight; by their power of attracting and detaining the attention. That book is good in vain, which the reader throws away. He only is the master, who keeps the mind in pleasing captivity; whose pages are perused with eagerness, and in hope of new pleasure are perused again; and whose conclusion is perceived with an eye of sorrow, such as the traveller casts upon departing day.

By his proportion of this predomination I will consent that Dryden should be tried; of this, which, in opposition to reason, makes Ariosto the darling and the pride of Italy; of this, which, in defiance of criticism, continues Shakespeare the sovereign of the drama.

His last work was his *Fables*, in which he gave us the first example of a mode of writing which the Italians call *refacimento*, a renovation of ancient writers, by modernizing their language. Thus the old poem of *Boiardo* has been new-dressed by *Domenichi* and *Berni*. The works of Chaucer, upon which this kind of rejuvenescence has been bestowed by Dryden, require little criticism. The tale of the Cock seems hardly worth revival; and the story of *Palamon* and *Arcite*, containing an action unsuitable to the times in which it is placed, can hardly be suffered to pass without censure of the hyperbolical commendation which Dryden has given it in the general Preface, and in a poetical Dedication, a piece where his original fondness of remote conceits seems to have revived.

Of the three pieces borrowed from Boccace, *Sigismunda* may be defended by the celebrity of the story. *Theodore* and *Honoria*, though it contains not much moral, yet afforded opportunities of striking description. And *Cymon* was formerly a tale of such reputation, that, at the revival of letters, it was translated into Latin by one of the *Beroalds*.

Whatever subjects employed his pen, he was still improving our measures and embellishing our language.

In this volume are interspersed some short original poems, which, with his prologues, epilogues, and songs, may be comprised in Congreve's remark, that even those, if he had written nothing else, would have entitled him to the praise of excellence in his kind.

One composition must, however, be distinguished. The ode for *St. Cecilia's* Day, perhaps the last effort of his poetry, has been always considered as exhibiting the highest flight of fancy, and the exactest nicety of art. This is allowed to stand without a rival. If indeed there is any excellence beyond it, in some other of Dryden's works that excellence must be found. Compared with the Ode on Killigrew, it may be pronounced perhaps superior in the whole; but without any single part, equal to the first stanza of the other.

It is said to have cost Dryden a fortnight's labour; but it does not want its negligences: some of the lines are without correspondent rhymes; a defect, which I never detected but after an acquaintance of many years, and which the enthusiasm of the writer might hinder him from perceiving.

His last stanza has less emotion than the former; but it is not less elegant in the diction. The conclusion is vicious; the musick of *Timotheus*, which *raised a mortal to the skies*, had only a metaphorical power; that of *Cecilia*, which *drew an angel down*, had a real effect; the crown therefore could not reasonably be divided.

In a general survey of Dryden's labours, he appears to have a mind very comprehensive by nature, and much enriched with acquired knowledge. His compositions are the effects of a vigorous genius operating upon large materials.

The power that predominated in his intellectual operations, was rather strong reason than quick sensibility. Upon all occasions that were presented, he studied rather than felt, and produced sentiments not such as Nature enforces, but meditation supplies. With the simple and elemental passions, as they spring separate in the mind, he seems not much acquainted; and seldom describes them but as they are complicated by the various relations of society, and confused in the tumults and agitations of life.

What he says of love may contribute to the explanation of his character:

> Love various minds does variously inspire;
> It stirs in gentle bosoms gentle tire,
> Like that of incense on the altar laid;
> But raging flames tempestuous souls invade;
> A fire which every windy passion blows,
> With pride it mounts, or with revenge it glows.

Dryden's was not one of the *gentle bosoms*: Love, as it subsists in itself, with no tendency but to the person loved, and wishing only for correspondent kindness; such love as shuts out all other interest; the Love of the Golden Age, was too soft and subtle to put his faculties in motion. He hardly conceived it but in its turbulent effervescence with some other desires; when it was inflamed by rivalry, or obstructed by difficulties: when it invigorated ambition, or exasperated revenge.

He is therefore, with all his variety of excellence, not often pathetick; and had so little sensibility of the power of effusions purely natural, that he did not esteem them in others. Simplicity gave him no pleasure; and for the first part of his life he looked on *Otway* with contempt, though at last, indeed very late, he confessed that in his play *there* was *Nature, which is the chief beauty*.

We do not always know our own motives. I am not certain whether it was not rather the difficulty which he found in exhibiting the genuine operations of the heart, than a servile submission to an injudicious audience, that filled his plays with false magnificence. It was necessary to fix attention; and the mind can be captivated only by recollection, or by curiosity; by reviving natural sentiments, or impressing new appearances of things: sentences were readier at his call than images; he could more easily fill the ear with some splendid novelty, than awaken those ideas that slumber in the heart.

The favourite exercise of his mind was ratiocination; and, that argument might not be too soon at an end, he delighted to talk of liberty and necessity, destiny and contingence; these he discusses in the language of the school with so much profundity, that the terms which he uses are not always understood. It is indeed learning, but learning out of place.

When once he had engaged himself in disputation, thoughts flowed in on either side: he was now no longer at a loss; he had always objections and solutions at command: *verbaque provisam rem*—give him matter for his verse, and he finds without difficulty verse for his matter.

In Comedy, for which he professes himself not naturally

qualified, the mirth which he excites will perhaps not be found so much to arise from any original humour, or peculiarity of character nicely distinguished and diligently pursued, as from incidents and circumstances, artifices and surprises; from jests of action rather than of sentiment. What he had of humorous or passionate, he seems to have had not from nature, but from other poets; if not always as a plagiary, at least as an imitator.

Next to argument, his delight was in wild and daring sallies of sentiment, in the irregular and excentrick violence of wit. He delighted to tread upon the brink of meaning, where light and darkness begin to mingle; to approach the precipice of absurdity, and hover over the abyss of unideal vacancy. This inclination sometimes produced nonsense, which he knew; as,

> Move swiftly, sun, and fly a lover's pace,
> Leave weeks and months behind thee in thy race.
> Amariel flies
> To guard thee from the demons of the air;
> My flaming sword above them to display,
> All keen, and ground upon the edge of day.

And sometimes it issued in absurdities, of which perhaps he was not conscious:

> Then we upon our orb's last verge shall go,
>   And see the ocean leaning on the sky;
> From thence our rolling neighbours we shall know,
>   And on the lunar world securely pry.

These lines have no meaning; but may we not say, in imitation of Cowley on another book,

> 'Tis so like *sense* 'twill serve the turn as well?

This endeavour after the grand and the new, produced many sentiments either great or bulky, and many images either just or splendid:

> I am as free as Nature first made man,
> Ere the base laws of servitude began,
> When wild in woods the noble savage ran.
> —'Tis but because the Living death n'er knew,
> They fear to prove it as a thing that's new:
> Let me th' experiment before you try,
> I'll shew you first how easy 'tis to die.
>
> —There with a forest of their darts he strove,
> And stood like *Capaneus* defying Jove;
> With his broad sword the boldest beating down,
> While Fate grew pale lest he should win the town,
> And turn'd the iron leaves of his dark book
> To make new dooms, or mend what it mistook.
>
> —I beg no pity for this mouldering clay;
> For if you give it burial, there it takes
> Possession of your earth;
> If burnt, and scatter'd in the air, the winds
> That strew my dust diffuse my royalty,
> And spread me o'er your clime; for where one atom
> Of mine shall light, know there Sebastian reigns.

Of these quotations the two first may be allowed to be great, the two latter only tumid.

Of such selection there is no end. I will add only a few more passages; of which the first, though it may perhaps not be quite clear in prose, is not too obscure for poetry, as the meaning that it has is noble:

> No, there is a necessity in Fate,
> Why still the brave bold man is fortunate;
> He keeps his object ever full in sight,
> And that assurance holds him firm and right,
> True, 'tis a narrow way that leads to bliss,
> But right before there is no precipice;

> Fear makes men look aside, and so their footing
>   miss.

Of the images which the two following citations afford, the first is elegant, the second magnificent; whether either be just, let the reader judge:

> What precious drops are these,
> Which silently each other's track pursue,
> Bright as young diamonds in their infant dew?
>
> ——Resign your castle——
> —Enter, brave Sir; for when you speak the word,
> The gates shall open of their own accord;
> The genius of the place its Lord shall meet,
> And bow its towery forehead at your feet.

These bursts of extravagance Dryden calls the *Dalilahs* of the Theatre; and owns that many noisy lines of Maxamin and Almanzor call out for vengeance upon him; but *I knew*, says he, *that they were bad enough to please, even when I wrote them*. There is surely reason to suspect that he pleased himself as well as his audience; and that these, like the harlots of other men, had his love, though not his approbation.

He had sometimes faults of a less generous and splendid kind. He makes, like almost all other poets, very frequent use of mythology, and sometimes connects religion and fable too closely without distinction.

He descends to display his knowledge with pedantick ostentation; as when, in translating Virgil, he says *tack to the larboard*—and *veer starboard*; and talks, in another work, of *virtue spooming before the wind*. His vanity now and then betrays his ignorance:

> They Nature's king through Nature's opticks view'd;
> Revers'd they view'd him lessen'd to their eyes.

He had heard of reversing a telescope, and unluckily reverses the object.

He is sometimes unexpectedly mean. When he describes the Supreme Being as moved by prayer to stop the Fire of London, what is his expression?

> A hollow crystal pyramid he takes,
>   In firmamental waters dipp'd above,
> Of this a broad *extinguisher* he makes,
>   And *hoods* the flames that to their quarry strove.

When he describes the Last Day, and the decisive tribunal, he intermingles this image:

> When rattling bones together fly,
> From the four quarters of the sky.

It was indeed never in his power to resist the temptation of a jest. In his Elegy on Cromwell:

> No sooner was the Frenchman's cause embrac'd,
> Than the *light Monsieur* the *grave Don* outweigh'd;
> His fortune turn'd the scale——

He had a vanity, unworthy of his abilities, to shew, as may be suspected, the rank of the company with whom he lived, by the use of French words, which had then crept into conversation; such as *fraîcheur* for *coolness*, *fougue* for *turbulence*, and a few more, none of which the language has incorporated or retained. They continue only where they stood first, perpetual warnings to future innovators.

These are his faults of affectation; his faults of negligence are beyond recital. Such is the unevenness of his compositions, that ten lines are seldom found together without something of which the reader is ashamed. Dryden was no rigid judge of his own pages; he seldom struggled after supreme excellence, but snatched in haste what was within his reach; and when he could content others, was himself contented. He did not keep present to his mind an idea of pure perfection; nor compare his works, such as they were, with what they might be made. He knew to whom he should be opposed. He had more musick than Waller, more vigour than Denham, and more nature than Cowley; and from his contemporaries he was in no danger. Standing therefore in the highest place, he had no care to rise by contending with himself; but while there was no name above his own, was willing to enjoy fame on the easiest terms.

He was no lover of labour. What he thought sufficient, he did not stop to make better; and allowed himself to leave many parts unfinished, in confidence that the good lines would overbalance the bad. What he had once written, he dismissed from his thoughts; and, I believe, there is no example to be found of any correction or improvement made by him after publication. The hastiness of his productions might be the effect of necessity; but his subsequent neglect could hardly have any other cause than impatience of study.

What can be said of his versification will be little more than a dilatation of the praise given it by Pope.

> Waller was smooth; but Dryden taught to join
> The varying verse, the full-resounding line,
> The long majestick march, and energy divine.

Some improvements had been already made in English numbers; but the full force of our language was not yet felt; the verse that was smooth was commonly feeble. If Cowley had sometimes a finished line, he had it by chance. Dryden knew how to chuse the flowing and the sonorous words; to vary the pauses, and adjust the accents; to diversify the cadence, and yet preserve the smoothness of his metre.

Of Triplets and Alexandrines, though he did not introduce the use, he established it. The triplet has long subsisted among us. Dryden seems not to have traced it higher than to Chapman's Homer; but it is to be found in Phaer's Virgil, written in the reign of Mary, and in Hall's Satires, published five years before the death of Elizabeth.

The Alexandrine was, I believe, first used by Spenser, for the sake of closing his stanza with a fuller sound. We had a longer measure of fourteen syllables, into which the Eneid was translated by Phaer, and other works of the ancients by other writers; of which Chapman's Iliad was, I believe, the last.

The two first lines of *Phaer's* third Eneid will exemplify this measure:

> When Asia's state was overthrown, and Prima's king-
>   dom stout,
> All guiltless, by the power of gods above was rooted
>   out.

As these lines had their break, or *caesura*, always at the eighth syllable, it was thought, in time, commodious to divide them; and quatrains of lines, alternately, consisting of eight and six syllables, make the most soft and pleasing of our lyric measures; as,

> Relentless Time, destroying power,
>   Which stone and brass obey,
> Who giv'st to every flying hour
>   To work some new decay.

In the Alexandrine, when its power was once felt, some poems, as *Drayton's Polyolbion*, were wholly written; and sometimes the measures of twelve and fourteen syllables were interchanged with one another. Cowley was the first that inserted the Alexandrine at pleasure among the heroick lines of ten syllables, and from him Dryden professes to have adopted it.

The Triplet and Alexandrine are not universally approved. *Swift* always censured them, and wrote some lines to ridicule

them. In examining their propriety, it is to be considered that the essence of verse is regularity, and its ornament is variety. To write verse, is to dispose syllables and sounds harmonically by some known and settled rule; a rule, however, lax enough to substitute similitude for identity, to admit change without breach of order, and to relieve the ear without disappointing it. Thus a Latin hexameter is formed from dactyls and spondees differently combined; the English heroick admits of acute or grave syllables variously disposed. The Latin never deviates into seven feet, or exceeds the number of seventeen syllables; but the English Alexandrine breaks the lawful bounds, and surprises the reader with two syllables more than he expected.

The effect of the Triplet is the same: the ear has been accustomed to expect a new rhyme in every couplet; but is on a sudden surprised with three rhymes together, to which the reader could not accommodate his voice, did he not obtain notice of the change from the braces of the margins. Surely there is something unskilful in the necessity of such mechanical direction.

Considering the metrical art simply as a science, and consequently excluding all casualty, we must allow that Triplets and Alexandrines, inserted by caprice, are interruptions of that constancy to which science aspires. And though the variety which they produce may very justly be desired, yet to make our poetry exact, there ought to be some stated mode of admitting them.

But till some such regulation can be formed, I wish them still to be retained in their present state. They are sometimes grateful to the reader, and sometimes convenient to the poet. *Fenton* was of opinion that Dryden was too liberal and Pope too sparing in their use.

The rhymes of Dryden are commonly just, and he valued himself for his readiness in finding them; but he is sometimes open to objection.

It is the common practice of our poets to end the second line with a weak or grave syllable:

> Together o'er the Alps methinks we fly,
>   Fill'd with ideas of fair *Italy*.

Dryden sometimes puts the weak rhyme in the first:

> Laugh all the powers that favour *tyranny*,
>   And all the standing army of the sky.

Sometimes he concludes a period or paragraph with the first line of a couplet, which, though the French seem to do it without irregularity, always displeases in English poetry.

The Alexandrine, though much his favourite, is not always very diligently fabricated by him. It invariably requires a break at the sixth syllable; a rule which the modern French poets never violate, but which Dryden sometimes neglected:

> And with paternal thunder vindicates his throne.

Of Dryden's works it was said by Pope, that *he could select from them better specimens of every mode of poetry than any other English writer could supply*. Perhaps no nation ever produced a writer that enriched his language with such variety of models. To him we owe the improvement, perhaps the completion of our metre, the refinement of our language, and much of the correctness of our sentiments. By him we were taught *sapere et fari*, to think naturally and express forcibly. Though Davis has reasoned in rhyme before him, it may be perhaps maintained that he was the first who joined argument with poetry. He shewed us the true bounds of a translator's liberty. What was said of Rome, adorned by Augustus, may be applied by an easy metaphor to English poetry embellished by Dryden, *lateritiam invenit, marmoream reliquit*, he found it brick, and he left it marble.

THOMAS BABINGTON MACAULAY
From "John Dryden" (1828)
Critical, Historical, and Miscellaneous Essays
1860, Volume 1, pp. 351–75

Everything about Milton is wonderful; but nothing is so wonderful as that, in an age so unfavourable to poetry, he should have produced the greatest of modern epic poems. We are not sure that this is not in some degree to be attributed to his want of sight. The imagination is notoriously most active when the external world is shut out. In sleep its illusions are perfect. They produce all the effect of realities. In darkness its visions are always more distinct than in the light. Every person who amuses himself with what is called building castles in the air must have experienced this. We know artists who, before they attempt to draw a face from memory, close their eyes, that they may recall a more perfect image of the features and the expression. We are therefore inclined to believe that the genius of Milton may have been preserved from the influence of times so unfavourable to it by his infirmity. Be this as it may, his works at first enjoyed a very small share of popularity. To be neglected by his contemporaries was the penalty which he paid for surpassing them. His great poem was not generally studied or admired till writers far inferior to him had, by obsequiously cringing to the public taste, acquired sufficient favour to reform it.

Of these, Dryden was the most eminent. Amidst the crowd of authors who, during the earlier years of Charles the Second, courted notoriety by every species of absurdity and affectation, he speedily became conspicuous. No man exercised so much influence on the age. The reason is obvious. On no man did the age exercise so much influence. He was perhaps the greatest of those whom we have designated as the critical poets; and his literary career exhibited, on a reduced scale, the whole history of the school to which he belonged,—the rudeness and extravagance of its infancy,—the propriety, the grace, the dignified good sense, the temperate splendour of its maturity. His imagination was torpid, till it was awakened by his judgment. He began with quaint parallels and empty mouthing. He gradually acquired the energy of the satirist, the gravity of the moralist, the rapture of the lyric poet. The revolution through which English literature has been passing, from the time of Cowley to that of Scott, may be seen in miniature within the compass of his volumes.

His life divides itself into two parts. There is some debatable ground on the common frontier; but the line may be drawn with tolerable accuracy. The year 1678 is that on which we should be inclined to fix as the date of a great change in his manner. During the preceding period appeared some of his courtly panegyrics,—his *Annus Mirabilis*, and most of his plays; indeed, all his rhyming tragedies. To the subsequent period belong his best dramas,—*All for Love, The Spanish Friar*, and *Sebastian*,—his satires, his translations, his didactic poems, his fables, and his odes.

Of the small pieces which were presented to chancellors and princes it would scarcely be fair to speak. The greatest advantage which the Fine Arts derive from the extension of knowledge is, that the patronage of individuals becomes unnecessary. Some writers still affect to regret the age of patronage. None but bad writers have reason to regret it. It is always an age of general ignorance. Where ten thousand readers are eager for the appearance of a book, a small contribution from each makes up a splendid remuneration for the author. Where literature is a luxury, confined to few, each

of them must pay high. If the Empress Catherine, for example, wanted an epic poem, she must have wholly supported the poet;—just as, in a remote country village, a man who wants a mutton-chop is sometimes forced to take the whole sheep;—a thing which never happens where the demand is large. But men who pay largely for the gratification of their taste will expect to have it united with some gratification to their vanity. Flattery is carried to a shameless extent; and the habit of flattery almost inevitably introduces a false taste into composition. Its language is made up of hyperbolical common-places,—offensive from their triteness,—still more offensive from their extravagance. In no school is the trick of overstepping the modesty of nature so speedily acquired. The writer, accustomed to find exaggeration acceptable and necessary on one subject, uses it on all. It is not strange, therefore, that the early panegyrical verses of Dryden should be made up of meanness and bombast. They abound with the conceits which his immediate predecessors had brought into fashion. But his language and his versification were already far superior to their's.

The *Annus Mirabilis* shows great command of expression, and a fine ear for heroic rhyme. Here its merits end. Not only has it no claim to be called poetry, but it seems to be the work of a man who could never, by any possibility, write poetry. Its affected similes are the best part of it. Gaudy weeds present a more encouraging spectacle than utter barrenness. There is scarcely a single stanza in this long work to which the imagination seems to have contributed anything. It is produced, not by creation, but by construction. It is made up, not of pictures, but of inferences. We will give a single instance, and certainly a favourable instance—a quatrain which Johnson has praised. Dryden is describing the sea-fight with the Dutch.—

> Amidst whole heaps of spices lights a ball;
> And now their odours armed against them fly
> Some preciously by shattered porcelain fall,
> And some by aromatic splinters die.

The poet should place his readers, as nearly as possible, in the situation of the sufferers or the spectators. His narration ought to produce feelings similar to those which would be excited by the event itself. Is this the case here? Who, in a sea-fight, ever thought of the price of the china which beats out the brains of a sailor; or of the odour of the splinter which shatters his leg? It is not by an act of the imagination, at once calling up the scene before the interior eye, but by painful meditation,—by turning the subject round and round,—by tracing out facts into remote consequences,—that these incongruous topics are introduced into the description. Homer, it is true, perpetually uses epithets which are not peculiarly appropriate. Achilles is the swift-footed, when he is sitting still. Ulysses is the much-enduring, when he has nothing to endure. Every spear casts a long shadow, every ox has crooked horns, and every woman a high bosom, though these particulars may be quite beside the purpose. In our old ballads a similar practice prevails. The gold is always red, and the ladies always gay, though nothing whatever may depend on the hue of the gold, or the temper of the ladies. But these adjectives are mere customary additions. They merge in the substantives to which they are attached. If they at all colour the idea, it is with a tinge so slight as in no respect to alter the general effect. In the passage which we have quoted from Dryden the case is very different. *Preciously* and *aromatic* divert our whole attention to themselves, and dissolve the image of the battle in a moment. The whole poem reminds us of Lucan, and of the worst parts of Lucan,—the sea-fight in the Bay of Marseilles, for example. The description of the two fleets during the night is perhaps the only passage which ought to be exempted from this censure. If it was from the *Annus Mirabilis* that Milton formed his opinion, when he pronounced Dryden a good rhymer but no poet, he certainly judged correctly. But Dryden was, as we have said, one of those writers in whom the period of imagination does not precede, but follow, the period of observation and reflection.

His plays, his rhyming plays in particular, are admirable subjects for those who wish to study the morbid anatomy of the drama. He was utterly destitute of the power of exhibiting real human beings. Even in the far inferior talent of composing characters out of those elements into which the imperfect process of our reason can resolve them, he was very deficient. His men are not even good personifications; they are not well-assorted assemblages of qualities. Now and then, indeed, he seizes a very coarse and marked distinction, and gives us, not a likeness, but a strong caricature, in which a single peculiarity is protruded, and everything else neglected; like the Marquis of Granby at an inn-door, whom we know by nothing but his baldness; or Wilkes, who is Wilkes only in his squint. These are the best specimens of his skill. For most of his pictures seem, like Turkey carpets, to have been expressly designed not to resemble anything in the heavens above, in the earth beneath, or in the waters under the earth.

The latter manner he practises most frequently in his tragedies, the former in his comedies. The comic characters are, without mixture, loathsome and despicable. The men of Etherege and Vanbrugh are bad enough. Those of Smollett are perhaps worse. But they do not approach to the Celadons, the Wildbloods, the Woodalls, and the Rhodophils of Dryden. The vices of these last are set off by a certain fierce hard impudence, to which we know nothing comparable. Their love is the appetite of beasts; their friendship the confederacy of knaves. The ladies seem to have been expressly created to form helps meet for such gentlemen. In deceiving and insulting their old fathers they do not perhaps exceed the license which, by immemorial prescription, has been allowed to heroines. But they also cheat at cards, rob strong boxes, put up their favours to auction, betray their friends, abuse their rivals in the style of Billingsgate, and invite their lovers in the language of the Piazza. These, it must be remembered, are not the valets and waiting-women, the Mascarilles and Nerines, but the recognised heroes and heroines, who appear as the representatives of good society, and who, at the end of the fifth act, marry and live very happily ever after. The sensuality, baseness, and malice of their natures is unredeemed by any quality of a different description,—by any touch of kindness,—or even by any honest burst of hearty hatred and revenge. We are in a world where there is no humanity, no veracity, no sense of shame,—a world for which any good-natured man would gladly take in exchange the society of Milton's devils. But, as soon as we enter the regions of Tragedy, we find a great change. There is no lack of fine sentiment there. Metastasio is surpassed in his own department. Scuderi is out-scuderied. We are introduced to people whose proceedings we can trace to no motive,—of whose feelings we can form no more idea than of a sixth sense. We have left a race of creatures, whose love is as delicate and affectionate as the passion which an alderman feels for a turtle. We find ourselves among beings, whose love is a purely disinterested emotion,—a loyalty extending to passive obedience,—a religion, like that of the Quietists, unsupported by any sanction of hope or fear. We see nothing but despotism without power, and sacrifices without compensation.

We will give a few instances. In *Aurengzebe*, Arimant, governor of Agra, falls in love with his prisoner Indamora. She rejects his suit with scorn; but assures him that she shall make great use of her power over him. He threatens to be angry. She answers, very coolly:

> Do not: your anger, like your love, is vain:
> Whene'er I please, you must be pleased again.
> Knowing what power I have your will to bend,
> I'll use it; for I need just such a friend.

This is no idle menace. She soon brings a letter addressed to his rival,—orders him to read it,—asks him whether he thinks it sufficiently tender,—and finally commands him to carry it himself. Such tyranny as this, it may be thought, would justify resistance. Arimant does indeed venture to remonstrate:—

> This fatal paper rather let me tear,
> Than, like Bellerophon, my sentence bear.

The answer of the lady is incomparable:—

> You may; but 'twill not be your best advice;
> 'Twill only give me pains of writing twice.
> You know you must obey me, soon or late.
> Why should you vainly struggle with your fate?

Poor Arimant seems to be of the same opinion. He mutters something about fate and free-will, and walks off with the billet-doux.

In the Indian Emperor, Montezuma presents Almeria with a garland as a token of his love, and offers to make her his queen. She replies:—

> I take this garland, not as given by you;
> But as my merit's and my beauty's due;
> As for the crown which you, my slave, possess,
> To share it with you would but make me less.

In return for such proofs of tenderness as these, her admirer consents to murder his two sons and a benefactor to whom he feels the warmest gratitude. Lyndaraxa, in the Conquest of Granada, assumes the same lofty tone with Abdelmelech. He complains that she smiles upon his rival.

Lynd.: And when did I my power so far resign,
    That you should regulate each look of mine?
Abdel.: Then, when you gave your love, you gave
    that power.
Lynd.: 'Twas during pleasure—'tis revoked this hour.
Abdel.: I'll hate you, and this visit is my last.
Lynd.: Do, if you can: you know I hold you fast.

That these passages violate all historical propriety, that sentiments to which nothing similar was ever even affected except by the cavaliers of Europe, are transferred to Mexico and Agra, is a light accusation. We have no objection to a conventional world, an Illyrian puritan, or a Bohemian sea-port. While the faces are good, we care little about the back-ground. Sir Joshua Reynolds says that the curtains and hangings in a historical painting ought to be, not velvet or cotton, but merely drapery. The same principle should be applied to poetry and romance. The truth of character is the first object; the truth of place and time is to be considered only in the second place. Puff himself could tell the actor to turn out his toes, and remind him that Keeper Hatton was a great dancer. We wish that, in our own time, a writer of a very different order from Puff had not too often forgotten human nature in the niceties of upholstery, millinery, and cookery.

We blame Dryden, not because the persons of his dramas are not Moors or Americans, but because they are not men and women;—not because love, such as he represents it, could not exist in a harem or in a wigwam, but because it could not exist anywhere. As is the love of his heroes, such are all their other emotions. All their qualities, their courage, their generosity, their pride, are on the same colossal scale. Justice and prudence are virtues which can exist only in a moderate degree, and which change their nature and their name if pushed to excess. Of justice and prudence, therefore, Dryden leaves his favourites destitute. He did not care to give them what he could not give without measure. The tyrants and ruffians are merely the heroes altered by a few touches, similar to those which transformed the honest face of Sir Roger de Coverley into the Saracen's head. Through the grin and frown the original features are still perceptible.

It is in the tragi-comedies that these absurdities strike us most. The two races of men, or rather the angels and the baboons, are there presented to us together. We meet in one scene with nothing but gross, selfish, unblushing, lying libertines of both sexes, who, as a punishment, we suppose, for their depravity, are condemned to talk nothing but prose. But, as soon as we meet with people who speak in verse, we know that we are in society which would have enraptured the Cathos and Madelon of Molière, in society for which Oroondates would have too little of the lover, and Clelia too much of the coquette.

As Dryden was unable to render his plays interesting by means of that which is the peculiar and appropriate excellence of the drama, it was necessary that he should find some substitute for it. In his comedies he supplied its place, sometimes by wit, but more frequently by intrigue, by disguises, mistakes of persons, dialogues at cross purposes, hair-breadth escapes, perplexing concealments, and surprising disclosures. He thus succeeded at least in making these pieces very amusing.

In his tragedies he trusted, and not altogether without reason, to his diction and his versification. It was on this account, in all probability, that he so eagerly adopted, and so reluctantly abandoned, the practice of rhyming in his plays. What is unnatural appears less unnatural in that species of verse than in lines which approach more nearly to common conversation; and in the management of the heroic couplet Dryden has never been equalled. It is unnecessary to urge any arguments against a fashion now universally condemned. But it is worthy of observation, that, though Dryden was deficient in that talent which blank verse exhibits to the greatest advantage, and was certainly the best writer of heroic rhyme in our language, yet the plays which have, from the time of their first appearance, been considered as his best, are in blank verse. No experiment can be more decisive.

It must be allowed that the worst even of the rhyming tragedies contains good description and magnificent rhetoric. But, even when we forget that they are plays, and, passing by their dramatic improprieties, consider them with reference to the language, we are perpetually disgusted by passages which it is difficult to conceive how any author could have written, or any audience have tolerated, rants in which the raving violence of the manner forms a strange contrast with the abject tameness of the thought. The author laid the whole fault on the audience, and declared that, when he wrote them, he considered them bad enough to please. This defence is unworthy of a man of genius, and, after all, is no defence. Otway pleased without rant; and so might Dryden have done, if he had possessed the powers of Otway. The fact is, that he had a tendency to bombast, which, though subsequently corrected by time and thought, was never wholly removed, and which showed itself in performances not designed to please the rude mob of the theatre.

Some indulgent critics have represented this failing as an indication of genius, as the profusion of unlimited wealth, the wantonness of exuberant vigour. To us it seems to bear a nearer affinity to the tawdriness of poverty, or the spasms and convulsions of weakness. Dryden surely had not more imagination than Homer, Dante, or Milton, who never fall into this vice. The swelling diction of Æschylus and Isaiah resembles that of Almanzor and Maximin no more than the tumidity of a muscle resembles the tumidity of a boil. The former is symptomatic of health and strength, the latter of debility and disease. If ever Shakspeare rants, it is not when his imagination is hurrying him along, but when he is hurrying his imagination along,—when his mind is for a moment jaded,—when, as was said of Euripides, he resembles a lion, who excites his own fury by lashing himself with his tail. What happened to Shakspeare from the occasional suspension of his powers happened to Dryden from constant impotence. He, like his confederate Lee, had judgment enough to appreciate the great poets of the preceding age, but not judgment enough to shun competition with them. He felt and admired their wild and daring sublimity. That it belonged to another age than that in which he lived and required other talents than those which he possessed, that, in aspiring to emulate it, he was wasting, in a hopeless attempt, powers which might render him pre-eminent in a different career, was a lesson which he did not learn, till late. As those knavish enthusiasts, the French prophets, courted inspiration by mimicking the writhings, swoonings, and gaspings which they considered as its symptoms, he attempted, by affected fits of poetical fury, to bring on a real paroxysm; and, like them, he got nothing but his distortions for his pains.

Horace very happily compares those who, in his time, imitated Pindar to the youth who attempted to fly to heaven on waxen wings, and who experienced so fatal and ignominious a fall. His own admirable good sense preserved him from this error, and taught him to cultivate a style in which excellence was within his reach. Dryden had not the same self-knowledge. He saw that the greatest poets were never so successful as when they rushed beyond the ordinary bounds, and that some inexplicable good fortune preserved them from tripping even when they staggered on the brink of nonsense. He did not perceive that they were guided and sustained by a power denied to himself. They wrote from the dictation of the imagination; and they found a response in the imaginations of others. He, on the contrary, sat down to work himself, by reflection and argument, into a deliberate wildness, a rational frenzy.

In looking over the admirable designs which accompany the Faust, we have always been much struck by one which represents the wizard and the tempter riding at full speed. The demon sits on his furious horse as heedlessly as if he were reposing on a chair. That he should keep his saddle in such a posture, would seem impossible to any who did not know that he was secure in the privileges of a superhuman nature. The attitude of Faust, on the contrary, is the perfection of horsemanship. Poets of the first order might safely write as desperately as Mephistophiles rode. But Dryden, though admitted to communion with higher spirits, though armed with a portion of their power, and intrusted with some of their secrets, was of another race. What they might securely venture to do, it was madness in him to attempt. It was necessary that taste and critical science should supply his deficiencies.

We will give a few examples. Nothing can be finer than the description of Hector at the Grecian wall:—

ὁ δ᾽ ἄρ᾽ ἔσθορε φαίδιμος Ἕκτωρ,
Νυκτὶ θοῇ ἀτάλαντος ὑπώπια· λάμπε δὲ χαλκῷ

Σμερδαλέῳ, τὸν ἔεστο περὶ χροΐ· ὁοιὰ δὲ χερσὶ
Δοῦρ' ἔχεν· οὐκ ἄν τίς μιν ἐρυκάκοι
    ἀντιβολήσας,
Νόσφι θεῶν, ὅτ' ἐσᾶλτο πύλας· πυρὶ δ' ὄσσε
    δεδήει.—
'Αυτίκα δ' ὁι μὲν τεῖχος ὑπέρβασαν, ὁι δέ κατ'
    ἀυτὰς
Ποιητὰς ἐσέχυντο πύλας· Δαναιοὶ δ' ἐφόβηθεν
Νῆας ἀνὰ γλαφυράς· ὅμαδος δ' ἀλίαστος
    ἐτύχθη.

What daring expressions! Yet how significant! How picturesque! Hector seems to rise up in his strength and fury. The gloom of night in his frown,—the fire burning in his eyes,—the javelins and the blazing armour,—the mighty rush through the gates and down the battlements,—the trampling and the infinite roar of the multitude,—everything is with us, everything is real.

Dryden has described a very similar event in Maximin, and has done his best to be sublime, as follows:—

There with a forest of their darts he strove,
And stood like Capaneus defying Jove;
With his broad sword the boldest beating down,
Till Fate grew pale, lest he should win the town,
And turned the iron leaves of its dark book
To make new dooms, or mend what it mistook.

How exquisite is the imagery of the fairy songs in the *Tempest* and in the *Midsummer Night's Dream*; Ariel riding through the twilight on the bat, or sucking in the bells of flowers with the bee; or the little bower-women of Titania, driving the spiders from the couch of the Queen! Dryden truly said, that

Shakspeare's magic could not copied be:
Within that circle none durst walk but he.

It would have been well if he had not himself dared to step within the enchanted line, and drawn on himself a fate similar to that which, according to the old superstition, punished such presumptuous interference. The following lines are parts of the song of his fairies:—

Merry, merry, merry, we sail from the East,
Half-tippled at a rainbow feast.
In the bright moonshine, while winds whistle loud,
Tivy, tivy, tivy, we mount and we fly,
All racking along in a downy white cloud;
And lest our leap from the sky prove too far,
We slide on the back of a new falling star,
And drop from above
In a jelly of love.

These are very favourable instances. Those who wish for a bad one may read the dying speeches of Maximin, and may compare them with the last scenes of *Othello* and *Lear*.

If Dryden had died before the expiration of the first of the periods into which we have divided his literary life, he would have left a reputation, at best, little higher than that of Lee or Davenant. He would have been known only to men of letters; and by them he would have been mentioned as a writer who threw away, on subjects which he was incompetent to treat, powers which, judiciously employed, might have raised him to eminence; whose diction and whose numbers had sometimes very high merit; but all whose works were blemished by a false taste, and by errors of gross negligence. A few of his prologues and epilogues might perhaps still have been remembered and quoted. In these little pieces he early showed all the powers which afterwards rendered him the greatest of modern satirists. But, during the latter part of his life, he gradually abandoned

the drama. His plays appeared at longer intervals. He renounced rhyme in tragedy. His language became less turgid—his characters less exaggerated. He did not indeed produce correct representations of human nature; but he ceased to daub such monstrous chimeras as those which abound in his earlier pieces. Here and there passages occur worthy of the best ages of the British stage. The style which the drama requires changes with every change of character and situation. He who can vary his manner to suit the variation is the great dramatist; but he who excels in one manner only will, when that manner happens to be appropriate, appear to be a great dramatist; as the hands of a watch which does not go point right once in the twelve hours. Sometimes there is a scene of solemn debate. This a mere rhetorician may write as well as the greatest tragedian that ever lived. We confess that to us the speech of Sempronius in Cato seems very nearly as good as Shakspeare could have made it. But when the senate breaks up, and we find that the lovers and their mistresses, the hero, the villain, and the deputy-villain, all continue to harangue in the same style, we perceive the difference between a man who can write a play and a man who can write a speech. In the same manner, wit, a talent for description, or a talent for narration, may, for a time, pass for dramatic genius. Dryden was an incomparable reasoner in verse. He was conscious of his power; he was proud of it; and the authors of the *Rehearsal* justly charged him with abusing it. His warriors and princesses are fond of discussing points of amorous casuistry, such as would have delighted a Parliament of Love. They frequently go still deeper, and speculate on philosophical necessity and the origin of evil.

There were, however, some occasions which absolutely required this peculiar talent. Then Dryden was indeed at home. All his best scenes are of this description. They are all between men; for the heroes of Dryden, like many other gentlemen, can never talk sense when ladies are in company. They are all intended to exhibit the empire of reason over violent passion. We have two interlocutors, the one eager and impassioned, the other high, cool, and judicious. The composed and rational character gradually acquires the ascendency. His fierce companion is first inflamed to rage by his reproaches, then overawed by his equanimity, convinced by his arguments, and soothed by his persuasions. This is the case in the scene between Hector and Troilus, in that between Antony and Ventidius, and in that between Sebastian and Dorax. Nothing of the same kind in Shakspeare is equal to them, except the quarrel between Brutus and Cassius, which is worth them all three.

Some years before his death, Dryden altogether ceased to write for the stage. He had turned his powers in a new direction, with success the most splendid and decisive. His taste had gradually awakened his creative faculties. The first rank in poetry was beyond his reach; but he challenged and secured the most honorable place in the second. His imagination resembled the wings of an ostrich. It enabled him to run, though not to soar. When he attempted the highest flights, he became ridiculous; but, while he remained in a lower region, he outstripped all competitors.

All his natural and all his acquired powers fitted him to found a good critical school of poetry. Indeed he carried his reforms too far for his age. After his death, our literature retrograded: and a century was necessary to bring it back to the point at which he left it. The general soundness and healthfulness of his mental constitution, his information of vast superficies though of small volume, his wit scarcely inferior to that of the most distinguished followers of Donne, his eloquence, grave, deliberate, and commanding, could not save him from disgraceful failure as a rival of Shakspeare, but raised him far above the level of Boileau. His command of language was immense. With him died the secret of the old poetical diction of England,—the art of producing rich effects by familiar words. In the following century, it was as completely lost as the Gothic method of painting glass, and was but poorly supplied by the laborious and tesselated imitations of Mason and Gray. On the other hand, he was the first writer under whose skilful management the scientific vocabulary fell into natural and pleasing verse. In this department, he succeeded as completely as his contemporary Gibbons succeeded in the similar enterprise of carving the most delicate flowers from heart of oak. The toughest and most knotty parts of language became ductile at his touch. His versification in the same manner, while it gave the first model of that neatness and precision which the following generation esteemed so highly, exhibited, at the same time, the last examples of nobleness, freedom, variety of pause, and cadence. His tragedies in rhyme, however worthless in themselves, had at least served the purpose of nonsense-verses; they had taught him all the arts of melody which the heroic couplet admits. For bombast, his prevailing vice, his new subjects gave little opportunity; his better taste gradually discarded it.

He possessed, as we have said, in a pre-eminent degree, the power of reasoning in verse; and this power was now peculiarly useful to him. His logic is by no means uniformly sound. On points of criticism, he always reasons ingeniously; and, when he is disposed to be honest, correctly. But the theological and political questions which he undertook to treat in verse were precisely those which he understood least. His arguments, therefore, are often worthless. But the manner in which they are stated is beyond all praise. The style is transparent. The topics follow each other in the happiest order. The objections are drawn up in such a manner that the whole fire of the reply may be brought to bear on them. The circumlocutions which are substituted for technical phrases are clear, neat, and exact. The illustrations at once adorn and elucidate the reasoning. The sparkling epigrams of Cowley, and the simple garrulity of the burlesque poets of Italy, are alternately employed, in the happiest manner, to give effect to what is obvious, or clearness to what is obscure.

His literary creed was catholic, even to latitudinarianism; not from any want of acuteness, but from a disposition to be easily satisfied. He was quick to discern the smallest glimpse of merit; he was indulgent even to gross improprieties, when accompanied by any redeeming talent. When he said a severe thing, it was to serve a temporary purpose,—to support an argument, or to tease a rival. Never was so able a critic so free from fastidiousness. He loved the old poets, especially Shakspeare. He admired the ingenuity which Donne and Cowley had so wildly abused. He did justice, amidst the general silence, to the memory of Milton. He praised to the skies the school-boy lines of Addison. Always looking on the fair side of every object, he admired extravagance on account of the invention which he supposed it to indicate; he excused affectation in favour of wit; he tolerated even tameness for the sake of the correctness which was its concomitant.

It was probably to this turn of mind, rather than to the more disgraceful causes which Johnson has assigned, that we are to attribute the exaggeration which disfigures the panegyrics of Dryden. No writer, it must be owned, has carried the flattery of dedication to a greater length. But this was not, we suspect, merely interested servility: it was the overflowing of a mind singularly disposed to admiration,—of a mind which diminished vices, and magnified virtues and obligations. The

most adulatory of his addresses is that in which he dedicates the *State of Innocence* to Mary of Modena. Johnson thinks it strange that any man should use such language without self-detestation. But he has not remarked that to the very same work is prefixed an eulogium on Milton, which certainly could not have been acceptable at the court of Charles the Second. Many years later, when Whig principles were in a great measure triumphant, Sprat refused to admit a monument of John Philips into Westminster Abbey—because, in the epitaph, the name of Milton incidently occurred. The walls of his church, he declared, should not be polluted by the name of a republican! Dryden was attached, both by principle and interest, to the Court. But nothing could deaden his sensibility to excellence. We are unwilling to accuse him severely, because the same disposition, which prompted him to pay so generous a tribute to the memory of a poet whom his patrons detested, hurried him into extravagance when he described a princess distinguished by the splendour of her beauty and the graciousness of her manners.

This is an amiable temper; but it is not the temper of great men. Where there is elevation of character, there will be fastidiousness. It is only in novels and on tombstones that we meet with people who are indulgent to the faults of others, and unmerciful to their own; and Dryden, at all events, was not one of these paragons. His charity was extended most liberally to others; but it certainly began at home. In taste he was by no means deficient. His critical works are, beyond all comparison, superior to any which had, till then, appeared in England. They were generally intended as apologies for his own poems, rather than as expositions of general principles; he, therefore, often attempts to deceive the reader by sophistry which could scarcely have deceived himself. His dicta are the dicta, not of a judge, but of an advocate;—often of an advocate in an unsound cause. Yet, in the very act of misrepresenting the laws of composition, he shows how well he understands them. But he was perpetually acting against his better knowledge. His sins were sins against light. He trusted that what was bad would be pardoned for the sake of what was good. What was good, he took no pains to make better. He was not, like most persons who rise to eminence, dissatisfied even with his best productions. He had set up no unattainable standard of perfection, the contemplation of which might at once improve and mortify him. His path was not attended by an unapproachable mirage of excellence, for ever receding, and for ever pursued. He was not disgusted by the negligence of others; and he extended the same toleration to himself. His mind was of a slovenly character,—fond of splendour, but indifferent to neatness. Hence most of his writings exhibit the sluttish magnificence of a Russian noble, all vermin and diamonds, dirty linen and inestimable sables. Those faults which spring from affectation, time and thought in a great measure removed from his poems. But his carelessness he retained to the last. If towards the close of his life he less frequently went wrong from negligence, it was only because long habits of composition rendered it more easy to go right. In his best pieces we find false rhymes,—triplets, in which the third line appears to be a mere intruder, and, while it breaks the music, adds nothing to the meaning,—gigantic Alexandrines of fourteen and sixteen syllables, and truncated verses for which he never troubled himself to find a termination or a partner.

Such are the beauties and the faults which may be found in profusion throughout the later works of Dryden. A more just and complete estimate of his natural and acquired powers,—of the merits of his style and of its blemishes,—may be formed from the *Hind and Panther*, than from any of his other writings. As a didactic poem, it is far superior to the *Religio Laici*. The satirical parts, particularly the character of Burnet, are scarcely inferior to the best passages in *Absalom and Achitophel*. There are, moreover, occasional touches of a tenderness which effects us more, because it is decent, rational, and manly, and reminds us of the best scenes in his tragedies. His versification sinks and swells in happy unison with the subject; and his wealth of language seems to be unlimited. Yet, the carelessness with which he has constructed his plot, and the innumerable inconsistencies into which he is every moment falling, detract much from the pleasure which such various excellence affords.

In *Absalom and Achitophel* he hit upon a new and rich vein, which he worked with signal success. The ancient satirists were the subjects of a despotic government. They were compelled to abstain from political topics, and to confine their attention to the frailties of private life. They might, indeed, sometimes venture to take liberties with public men,

Quorum Flaminia tegitur cinis atque Latina.

Thus Juvenal immortalised the obsequious senators who met to decide the fate of the memorable turbot. His fourth satire frequently reminds us of the great political poem of Dryden; but it was not written till Domitian had fallen: and it wants something of the peculiar flavour which belongs to contemporary invective alone. His anger has stood so long that, though the body is not impaired, the effervescence, the first cream, is gone. Boileau lay under similar restraints; and, if he had been free from all restraint, would have been no match for our countryman.

The advantages which Dryden derived from the nature of his subject he improved to the very utmost. His manner is almost perfect. The style of Horace and Boileau is fit only for light subjects. The Frenchman did indeed attempt to turn the theological reasonings of the *Provincial Letters* into verse, but with very indifferent success. The glitter of Pope is cold. The ardour of Persius is without brilliancy. Magnificent versification and ingenious combinations rarely harmonise with the expression of deep feeling. In Juvenal and Dryden alone we have the sparkle and the heat together. Those great satirists succeeded in communicating the fervour of their feelings to materials the most incombustible, and kindled the whole mass into a blaze, at once dazzling and destructive. We cannot, indeed, think, without regret, of the part which so eminent a writer as Dryden took in the disputes of that period. There was, no doubt, madness and wickedness on both sides. But there was liberty on the one, and despotism on the other. On this point, however, we will not dwell. At Talavera the English and French troops for a moment suspended their conflict, to drink of a stream which flowed between them. The shells were passed across from enemy to enemy without apprehension or molestation. We, in the same manner, would rather assist our political adversaries to drink with us of that fountain of intellectual pleasure, which should be the common refreshment of both parties, than disturb and pollute it with the havock of unseasonable hostilities.

Macflecnoe is inferior to *Absalom and Achitophel*, only in the subject. In the execution it is even superior. But the greatest work of Dryden was the last, the "Ode on Saint Cecilia's day." It is the master-piece of the second class of poetry, and ranks but just below the great models of the first. It reminds us of the Pedasus of Achilles—

ὅς, καὶ θνητὸς ἐὼν, ἔπεθ᾽ ἵπποις, ἀθανάτοισι.

By comparing it with the impotent ravings of the heroic tragedies, we may measure the progress which the mind of Dryden had made. He had learned to avoid a too audacious competition with higher natures, to keep at a distance from the verge of bombast or nonsense, to venture on no expression which did not convey a distinct idea to his own mind. There is none of that "darkness visible" of style which he had formerly affected, and in which the greatest poets only can succeed. Everything is definite, significant, and picturesque. His early writings resembled the gigantic works of those Chinese gardeners who attempt to rival nature herself, to form cataracts of terrific height and sound, to raise precipitous ridges of mountains, and to imitate in artificial plantations the vastness and the gloom of some primeval forest. This manner he abandoned; nor did he ever adopt the Dutch taste which Pope affected, the trim parterres, and the rectangular walks. He rather resembled our Kents and Browns, who, imitating the great features of landscape without emulating them, consulting the genius of the place, assisting nature and carefully disguising their art, produced, not a Chamouni or a Niagara, but a Stowe or a Hagley.

We are, on the whole, inclined to regret that Dryden did not accomplish his purpose of writing an epic poem. It certainly would not have been a work of the highest rank. It would not have rivalled the *Iliad*, the *Odyssey*, or the *Paradise Lost*; but it would have been superior to the productions of Apollonius, Lucan, or Statius, and not inferior to the *Jerusalem Delivered*. It would probably have been a vigorous narrative, animated with something of the spirit of the old romances, enriched with much splendid description, and interspersed with fine declamations and disquisitions. The danger of Dryden would have been from aiming too high; from dwelling too much, for example, on his angels of kingdoms, and attempting a competition with that greater writer who in his own time had so incomparably succeeded in representing to us the sights and sounds of another world. To Milton, and to Milton alone, belonged the secrets of the great deep, the beach of sulphur, the ocean of fire, the palaces of the fallen dominations, glimmering through the everlasting shade, the silent wilderness of verdure and fragrance where armed angels kept watch over the sleep of the first lovers, the portico of diamond, the sea of jasper, the sapphire pavement empurpled with celestial roses, and the infinite ranks of the Cherubim, blazing with adamant and gold. The council, the tournament, the procession, the crowded cathedral, the camp, the guardroom, the chase, were the proper scenes for Dryden.

But we have not space to pass in review all the works which Dryden wrote. We, therefore, will not speculate longer on those which he might possibly have written. He may, on the whole, be pronounced to have been a man possessed of splendid talents, which he often abused, and of a sound judgment, the admonitions of which he often neglected; a man who succeeded only in an inferior department of his art, but who, in that department, succeeded pre-eminently; and who, with a more independent spirit, a more anxious desire of excellence, and more respect for himself, would, in his own walk, have attained to absolute perfection.

JAMES RUSSELL LOWELL
From "Dryden" (1868)
Among My Books
1870, pp. 4–24, 79–80

Dryden has now been in his grave nearly a hundred and seventy years; in the second class of English poets perhaps no one stands, on the whole, so high as he; during his lifetime, in spite of jealousy, detraction, unpopular politics, and a suspicious change of faith, his pre-eminence was conceded; he was the earliest complete type of the purely literary man, in the modern sense; there is a singular unanimity in allowing him a certain claim to *greatness* which would be denied to men as famous and more read,—to Pope or Swift, for example; he is supposed, in some way or other, to have reformed English poetry. It is now about half a century since the only uniform edition of his works was edited by Scott. No library is complete without him, no name is more familiar than his, and yet it may be suspected that few writers are more thoroughly buried in that great cemetery of the "British Poets." If contemporary reputation be often deceitful, posthumous fame may be generally trusted, for it is a verdict made up of the suffrages of the select men in succeeding generations. This verdict has been as good as unanimous in favor of Dryden. It is, perhaps, worth while to take a fresh observation of him, to consider him neither as warning nor example, but to endeavor to make out what it is that has given so lofty and firm a position to one of the most unequal, inconsistent, and faulty writers that ever lived. He is a curious example of what we often remark of the living, but rarely of the dead,—that they get credit for what they might be quite as much as for what they are,—and posterity has applied to him one of his own rules of criticism, judging him by the best rather than the average of his achievement, a thing posterity is seldom wont to do. On the losing side in politics, it is true of his polemical writings as of Burke's,—whom in many respects he resembles, and especially in that supreme quality of a reasoner, that his mind gathers not only heat, but clearness and expansion, by its own motion,— that they have won his battle for him in the judgment of after times.

To us, looking back at him, he gradually becomes a singularly interesting and even picturesque figure. He is, in more senses than one, in language, in turn of thought, in style of mind, in the direction of his activity, the first of the moderns. He is the first literary man who was also a man of the world, as we understand the term. He succeeded Ben Jonson as the acknowledged dictator of wit and criticism, as Dr. Johnson, after nearly the same interval, succeeded him. All ages are, in some sense, ages of transition; but there are times when the transition is more marked, more rapid; and it is, perhaps, an ill fortune for a man of letters to arrive at maturity during such a period, still more to represent in himself the change that is going on, and to be an efficient cause in bringing it about. Unless, like Goethe, he is of a singularly uncontemporaneous nature, capable of being *tutta in se romita*, and of running parallel with his time rather than being sucked into its current, he will be thwarted in that harmonious development of native force which has so much to do with its steady and successful application. Dryden suffered, no doubt, in this way. Though in creed he seems to have drifted backward in an eddy of the general current; yet of the intellectual movement of the time, so far certainly as literature shared in it, he could say, with Æneas, not only that he saw, but that himself was a great part

of it. That movement was, on the whole, a downward one, from faith to scepticism, from enthusiasm to cynicism, from the imagination to the understanding. It was in a direction altogether away from those springs of imagination and faith at which they of the last age had slaked the thirst or renewed the vigor of their souls. Dryden himself recognized that indefinable and gregarious influence which we call nowadays the Spirit of the Age, when he said that "every Age has a kind of universal Genius."[1] He had also a just notion of that in which he lived; for he remarks, incidentally, that "all knowing ages are naturally sceptic and not at all bigoted, which, if I am not much deceived, is the proper character of our own."[2] It may be conceived that he was even painfully half-aware of having fallen upon a time incapable, not merely of a great poet, but perhaps of any poet at all; for nothing is so sensitive to the chill of a sceptical atmosphere as that enthusiasm which, if it be not genius, is at least the beautiful illusion that saves it from the baffling quibbles of self-consciousness. Thrice unhappy he who, born to see things as they might be, is schooled by circumstances to see them as people say they are,—to read God in a prose translation. Such was Dryden's lot, and such, for a good part of his days, it was by his own choice. He who was of a stature to snatch the torch of life that flashes from lifted hand to hand along the generations, over the heads of inferior men, chose rather to be a link-boy to the stews.

As a writer for the stage, he deliberately adopted and repeatedly reaffirmed the maxim that

He who lives to please, must please to live.

Without earnest convictions, no great or sound literature is conceivable. But if Dryden mostly wanted that inspiration which comes of belief in and devotion to something nobler and more abiding than the present moment and its petulant need, he had, at least, the next best thing to that,—a thorough faith in himself. He was, moreover, a man of singularly open soul, and of a temper self-confident enough to be candid even with himself. His mind was growing to the last, his judgment widening and deepening, his artistic sense refining itself more and more. He confessed his errors, and was not ashamed to retrace his steps in search of that better knowledge which the omniscience of superficial study had disparaged. Surely an intellect that is still pliable at seventy is a phenomenon as interesting as it is rare. But at whatever period of his life we look at Dryden, and whatever, for the moment, may have been his poetic creed, there was something in the nature of the man that would not be wholly subdued to what it worked in. There are continual glimpses of something in him greater than he, hints of possibilities finer than anything he has done. You feel that the whole of him was better than any random specimens, though of his best, seem to prove. *Incessu patet*, he has by times the large stride of the elder race, though it sinks too often into the slouch of a man who has seen better days. His grand air may, in part, spring from a habit of easy superiority to his competitors; but must also, in part, be ascribed to an innate dignity of character. That this pre-eminence should have been so generally admitted, during his life, can only be explained by a bottom of good sense, kindliness, and sound judgment, whose solid worth could afford that many a flurry of vanity, petulance, and even error should flit across the surface and be forgotten. Whatever else Dryden may have been, the last and abiding impression of him is, that he was thoroughly manly; and while it may be disputed whether he was a great poet, it may be said of him, as Wordsworth said of Burke, that "he was by far the greatest man of his age, not only abounding in knowledge himself, but feeding, in various directions, his most able contemporaries."[3] ⟨. . .⟩

In his *Aurengzebe* (1675) there is a passage, of which, as it is a good example of Dryden, I shall quote the whole, though my purpose aims mainly at the latter verses:—

When I consider life, 't is all a cheat;
Yet, fooled with Hope, men favor the deceit,
Trust on, and think to-morrow will repay;
To-morrow's falser than the former day,
Lies worse, and, while it says we shall be blest
With some new joys, cuts off what we possess.
Strange cozenage! none would live past years again,
Yet all hope pleasure in what yet remain,
And from the dregs of life think to receive
What the first sprightly running could not give.
I'm tired of waiting for this chymic gold
Which fools us young and beggars us when old.

The "first sprightly running" of Dryden's vintage was, it must be confessed, a little muddy, if not beery; but if his own soil did not produce grapes of the choicest flavor, he knew where they were to be had; and his product, like sound wine, grew better the longer it stood upon the lees. He tells us, evidently thinking of himself, that in a poet, "from fifty to threescore, the balance generally holds even in our colder climates, for he loses not much in fancy, and judgment, which is the effect of observation, still increases. His succeeding years afford him little more than the stubble of his own harvest, yet, if his constitution be healthful, his mind may still retain a decent vigor, and the gleanings of that of Ephraim, in comparison with others, will surpass the vintage of Abiezer."[4] Since Chaucer, none of our poets has had a constitution more healthful, and it was his old age that yielded the best of him. In him the understanding was, perhaps, in overplus for his entire good fortune as a poet, and that is a faculty among the earliest to mature. We have seen him, at only ten years, divining the power of reason in Polybius.[5] The same turn of mind led him later to imitate the French school of tragedy, and to admire in Ben Jonson the most correct of English poets. It was his imagination that needed quickening, and it is very curious to trace through his different prefaces the gradual opening of his eyes to the causes of the solitary pre-eminence of Shakespeare. At first he is sensible of an attraction towards him which he cannot explain, and for which he apologizes, as if it were wrong. But he feels himself drawn more and more strongly, till at last he ceases to resist altogether, and is forced to acknowledge that there is something in this one man that is not and never was anywhere else, something not to be reasoned about, ineffable, divine; if contrary to the rules, so much the worse for *them*. It may be conjectured that Dryden's Puritan associations may have stood in the way of his more properly poetic culture, and that his early knowledge of Shakespeare was slight. He tells us that Davenant, whom he could not have known before he himself was twenty-seven, first taught him to admire the great poet. But even after his imagination had become conscious of its prerogative, and his expression had been ennobled by frequenting this higher society, we find him continually dropping back into that *sermo pedestris* which seems, on the whole, to have been his more natural element. We always feel his epoch in him, that he was the lock which let our language down from its point of highest poetry to its level of easiest and most gently flowing prose. His enthusiasm needs the contagion of other minds to arouse it; but his strong sense, his command of the happy word, his wit, which is distinguished by a certain breadth and, as it were, power of generalization, as Pope's by keenness of edge and point, were his, whether he would or no.

Accordingly, his poetry is often best and his verse more flowing where (as in parts of his version of the twenty-ninth ode of the third book of Horace) he is amplifying the suggestions of another mind.[6] Viewed from one side, he justifies Milton's remark of him, that "he was a good rhymist, but no poet." To look at all sides, and to distrust the verdict of a single mood, is, no doubt, the duty of a critic. But how if a certain side be so often presented as to thrust forward in the memory and disturb it in the effort to recall that total impression (for the office of a critic is not, though often so misunderstood, to say *guilty* or *not guilty* of some particular fact) which is the only safe ground of judgment? It is the weight of the whole man, not of one or the other limb of him, that we want. *Expende Hannibalem.* Very good, but not in a scale capacious only of a single quality at a time, for it is their union, and not their addition, that assures the value of each separately. It was not this or that which gave him his weight in council, his swiftness of decision in battle that outran the forethought of other men,—it was Hannibal. But this prosaic element in Dryden will force itself upon me. As I read him, I cannot help thinking of an ostrich, to be classed with flying things, and capable, what with leap and flap together, of leaving the earth for a longer or shorter space, but loving the open plain, where wing and foot help each other to something that is both flight and run at once. What with his haste and a certain dash, which, according to our mood, we may call florid or splendid, he seems to stand among poets where Rubens does among painters,—greater, perhaps, as a colorist than an artist, yet great here also, if we compare him with any but the first.

⟨. . .⟩ the authentic and unmistakable Dryden first manifests himself in some verses addressed to his friend Dr. Charlton in 1663. We have first his common sense, which has almost the point of wit, yet with a tang of prose:—

The longest tyranny that ever swayed
Was that wherein our ancestors betrayed
Their freeborn reason to the Stagyrite,
And made his torch their universal light.
So truth, while only one supplied the state,
Grew scarce and dear and yet sophisticate.
Still it was bought, like emp'ric wares or charms,
Hard words sealed up with Aristotle's arms.

Then we have his graceful sweetness of fancy, where he speaks of the inhabitants of the New World:—

Guiltless men who danced away their time,
Fresh as their groves and happy as their clime.

And, finally, there is a hint of imagination where "mighty visions of the Danish race" watch round Charles sheltered in Stonehenge after the battle of Worcester. These passages might have been written by the Dryden whom we learn to know fifteen years later. They have the advantage that he wrote them to please himself. His contemporary, Dr. Heylin, said of French cooks, that "their trade was not to feed the belly, but the palate." Dryden was a great while in learning this secret, as available in good writing as in cookery. He strove after it, but his thoroughly English nature, to the last, would too easily content itself with serving up the honest beef of his thought, without regard to daintiness of flavor in the dressing of it.[7] Of the best English poetry, it might be said that it is understanding aërated by imagination. In Dryden the solid part too often refused to mix kindly with the leaven, either remaining lumpish or rising to a hasty puffiness. Grace and lightness were with him much more a laborious achievement than a natural gift, and it is all the more remarkable that he should so often have attained to what seems such an easy perfection in both.

Always a hasty writer,[8] he was long in forming his style, and to the last was apt to snatch the readiest word rather than wait for the fittest. He was not wholly and unconsciously poet, but a thinker who sometimes lost himself on enchanted ground and was transfigured by its touch. This preponderance in him of the reasoning over the intuitive faculties, the one always there, the other flashing in when you least expect it, accounts for that inequality and even incongruousness in his writing which makes one revise his judgment at every tenth page. In his prose you come upon passages that persuade you he is a poet, in spite of his verses so often turning state's evidence against him as to convince you he is none. He is a prose-writer, with a kind of Æolian attachment. For example, take this bit of prose from the dedication of his version of Virgil's *Pastorals*, 1694: "He found the strength of his genius betimes, and was even in his youth preluding to his *Georgicks* and his *Æneis*. He could not forbear to try his wings, though his pinions were not hardened to maintain a long, laborious flight; yet sometimes they bore him to a pitch as lofty as ever he was able to reach afterwards. But when he was admonished by his subject to descend, he came down gently circling in the air and singing to the ground, like a lark melodious in her mounting and continuing her song till she alights, still preparing for a higher flight at her next sally, and tuning her voice to better music." This is charming, and yet even this wants the ethereal tincture that pervades the style of Jeremy Taylor, making it, as Burke said of Sheridan's eloquence, "neither prose nor poetry, but something better than either." Let us compare Taylor's treatment of the same image: "For so have I seen a lark rising from his bed of grass and soaring upwards, singing as he rises, and hopes to get to heaven and climb above the clouds; but the poor bird was beaten back by the loud sighings of an eastern wind, and his motion made irregular and inconstant, descending more at every breath of the tempest than it could recover by the libration and frequent weighing of his wings, till the little creature was forced to sit down and pant, and stay till the storm was over, and then it made a prosperous flight, and did rise and sing as if it had learned music and motion of an angel as he passed sometimes through the air about his ministries here below." Taylor's fault is that his sentences too often smell of the library, but what an open air is here! How unpremeditated it all seems! How carelessly he knots each new thought, as it comes, to the one before it with an *and*, like a girl making lace! And what a slidingly musical use he makes of the sibilants with which our language is unjustly taxed by those who can only make them hiss, not sing! There are twelve of them in the first twenty words, fifteen of which are monosyllables. We notice the structure of Dryden's periods, but this grows up as we read. It gushes, like the song of the bird itself,—

> In profuse strains of unpremeditated art.

Let us now take a specimen of Dryden's bad prose from one of his poems. I open the *Annus Mirabilis* at random, and hit upon this:—

> Our little fleet was now engaged so far,
> That, like the swordfish in the whale, they fought:
> The combat only seemed a civil war,
> Till through their bowels we our passage wrought.

Is this Dryden, or Sternhold, or Shadwell, those Toms who made him say that "dulness was fatal to the name of Tom"? The natural history of Goldsmith in the verse of Pye! His thoughts did not "voluntary move harmonious numbers." He had his choice between prose and verse, and seems to be poetical on second thought. I do not speak without book. He was more than half conscious of it himself. In the same letter

to Mrs. Steward, just cited, he says, "I am still drudging on, always a poet and never a good one"; and this from no mock-modesty, for he is always handsomely frank in telling us whatever of his own doing pleased him. This was written in the last year of his life, and at about the same time he says elsewhere: "What judgment I had increases rather than diminishes, and thoughts, such as they are, come crowding in so fast upon me that my only difficulty is to choose or to reject, to run them into verse or to give them the other harmony of prose; I have so long studied and practised both, that they are grown into a habit and become familiar to me."[9] I think that a man who was primarily a poet would hardly have felt this equanimity of choice. ⟨. . .⟩

Was he, then, a great poet? Hardly, in the narrowest definition. But he was a strong thinker who sometimes carried common sense to a height where it catches the light of a diviner air, and warmed reason till it had wellnigh the illuminating property of intuition. Certainly he is not, like Spenser, the poets' poet, but other men have also their rights. Even the Philistine is a man and a brother, and is entirely right so far as he sees. To demand more of him is to be unreasonable. And he sees, among other things, that a man who undertakes to write should first have a meaning perfectly defined to himself, and then should be able to set it forth clearly in the best words. This is precisely Dryden's praise,[10] and amid the rickety sentiment looming big through misty phrase which marks so much of modern literature, to read him is as bracing as a northwest wind. He blows the mind clear. In ripeness of mind and bluff heartiness of expression, he takes rank with the best. His phrase is always a short-cut to his sense, for his estate was too spacious for him to need that trick of winding the path of his thought about, and planting it out with clumps of epithet, by which the landscape-gardeners of literature give to a paltry half-acre the air of a park. In poetry, to be next-best is, in one sense, to be nothing; and yet to be among the first in any kind of writing, as Dryden certainly was, is to be one of a very small company. He had, beyond most, the gift of the right word. And if he does not, like one or two of the greater masters of song, stir our sympathies by that indefinable aroma so magical in arousing the subtile associations of the soul, he has this in common with the few great writers, that the winged seeds of his thought embed themselves in the memory and germinate there. If I could be guilty of the absurdity of recommending to a young man any author on whom to form his style, I should tell him that, next to having something that will not stay unsaid, he could find no safer guide than Dryden.

Notes

1. *Essay on Dramatick Poesy.*
2. *Life of Lucian.*
3. "The great man must have that intellect which puts in motion the intellect of others."—LANDOR, *Im. Con.*, Diogenes and Plato.
4. Dedication of the *Georgics*.
5. Dryden's penetration is always remarkable. His general judgment of Polybius coincides remarkably with that of Mommsen. (*Röm. Gesch.* II. 448, *seq.*)
6. "I have taken some pains to make it my masterpiece in English." Preface to *Second Miscellany*. Fox said that it "was better than the original." J. C. Scaliger said of Erasmus. "Ex alieno ingenio poeta, ex suo versificator."
7. In one of the last letters he ever wrote, thanking his cousin Mrs. Steward for a gift of marrow-puddings, he says: "A chine of honest bacon would please my appetite more than all the marrow-puddings; for I like them better plain, having a very vulgar stomach." So of Cowley he says: "There was plenty enough, but ill sorted, whole pyramids of sweetmeats for boys and women, but little of solid meat for men." The physical is a truer antitype of the

spiritual man than we are willing to admit, and the brain is often forced to acknowledge the inconvenient country-cousinship of the stomach.

8. In his preface to *All for Love,* he says, evidently alluding to himself: "If he have a friend whose hastiness in writing is his greatest fault, Horace would have taught him to have minced the matter, and to have called it readiness of thought and a flowing fancy." And in the Preface to the *Fables* he says of Homer: "This vehemence of his, I confess, is more suitable to my temper." He makes other allusions to it.

9. Preface to the *Fables.*

10. "Nothing is truly sublime," he himself said, "that is not just and proper."

GEORGE SAINTSBURY
From "Later Dramas and Prose Works"
Dryden
1881, pp. 121–31

The subject of Dryden's prose work is intimately connected with that of his dramatic performances. Had it not been for the interest he felt in matters dramatic, he might never have ventured into anything longer than a preface; and his prefaces would certainly have lacked the remarkable interest in the history of style and in the history of criticism which they now possess. At the time when he first began to write, the accepted prose style of English was in much greater need of reform and reinforcement than the accepted poetical style; or, to speak more properly, there was no accepted prose style at all. Great masters—Bacon, Hooker, Clarendon, Milton, Taylor, Hobbes, Bunyan, and some others—may be quoted from the first two-thirds of the seventeenth century; but their excellences, like the excellences of the writers of French prose somewhat earlier, were almost wholly individual, and provided in no way a model whereby the average writer might form himself for average purposes. Now, prose is above all things the instrument of the average purpose. Poetry is more or less intolerable if it be not intrinsically and peculiarly good; prose is the necessary vehicle of thought. Up to Dryden's time no such generally available vehicle had been attempted or achieved by any one. Clarendon had shown how genius can make the best of the worst style, which from any general point of view his must probably be pronounced to be. In his hands it is alternately delightful or tolerable; in the hands of anybody else it would be simply frightful. His parentheses, his asides, his endless involutions of phrase and thought, save themselves as if by miracle, and certainly could not be trusted so to save themselves in any less favoured hands. Bacon and Hooker, the former in an ornate, the latter in a simple style, reproduce classical constructions and forms in English. Taylor and Milton write poetry in prose. Quaintness and picturesque matter justify, and more than justify, Fuller and Browne. Bunyan puts the vernacular into print with a sublime assurance and success. Hobbes, casting off all ornament and all pretence of ornament, clothes his naked strength in the simplest garment of words competent to cover its nakedness. But none of these had elaborated, or aimed at elaborating, a style suited for every-day use—for the essayist and the pamphleteer, the preacher and the lay orator, the historian and the critic. This was what Dryden did with little assistance from any forerunner, if it were not Tillotson, to whom, as we know from Congreve, he acknowledged his indebtedness. But Tillotson was not a much older man than Dryden himself, and at least when the latter began to write prose, his work was neither bulky nor particularly famous. Nor in reading Tillotson, though it is clear that he and Dryden were in some sort working on the same lines, is it possible to trace much indebtedness on the part of the poet. The sometime archbishop's sermons are excellent in their combination of simplicity with a certain grace, but they are much less remarkable than Dryden's own work for the union of the two. The great fault of the elders had been, first, the inordinate length of their sentences; secondly—and this was rather a cause of the first fault than an additional error— their indulgence in parenthetic quotations, borrowed arguments, and other strengtheners of the position of the man who has to rely on authority; thirdly, the danger to which they were always exposed, of slipping into clumsy classicisms on one side, or inelegant vernacular on the other. Dryden avoided all these faults, though his avoidance was not a matter of a day or a year, nor was it, as far as can be made out, altogether an avoidance of malice prepense. Accident favoured him in exactly the reverse way to that in which it had favoured the reformer of French prose half a century or so before. Balzac had nothing to say, and therefore was extremely careful and exquisite in his manner of saying it. Dryden had a great deal to say, and said it in the plain, straightforward fashion which was of all things most likely to be useful for the formation of a workman-like prose style in English.

The influences of the post-Restoration period which, by their working, produced the splendid variety and efficiency of prose in the eighteenth century—the century, *par excellence,* of prose in English—were naturally numerous; but there were four which had an influence far surpassing that of the rest. These four were the influences of the pulpit, of political discussion, of miscellaneous writing—partly fictitious, partly discursive—and lastly, of literary criticism. In this last Dryden himself was the great authority of the period, and for many years it was in this form that he at once exercised himself and educated his age in the matter of prose writing. Accident and the circumstances of the time helped to give him a considerable audience, and an influence of great width, the critical spirit being extensively diffused at the time. This critical spirit was to a great extent a reflection of that which, beginning with Malherbe, and continuing with the institution and regulation of the Academy, had for some time been remarkable in France. Not long after the Restoration one of the subtlest and most accomplished of all French critics took up his residence in England, and gave further impulse to the fashion which Charles himself and many other cavaliers had already picked up. Saint Evremond lived in England for some forty years, and during the greater part of that time was an oracle of the younger men of wit and pleasure about London. Now Saint Evremond was a remarkable instance of that rare animal, the born critic; even nowadays his critical dicta are worthy of all attention. He had a kind of critical intuition, which is to be paralleled only by the historical and scientific intuition which some of the greatest historians and men of science have had. With national and characteristic indolence he never gave himself the trouble to learn English properly, and it is doubtful whether he could have read a single English play. Yet his critical remarks on some English poets, not borrowed from his friends, but constructed from their remarks, as a clever counsel would construct a pleading out of the information furnished him, are extraordinarily acute and accurate. The relish for literary discussion which Saint Evremond shows was no peculiarity of his, though he had it in super-eminent measure. It was fashionable in France, and he helped to make it fashionable in England.

I have seen this style of criticism dismissed contemptuously as "trifling;" but this is only an instance of the strange power of reaction. Because for many years the plan of criticising by rule and line was almost exclusively pursued, and, as happens in the case of almost all exclusive pursuits, was followed too far, it seems to some people nowadays, that criticism ought to be confined to the expression, in more or less elegant language, of the feelings of admiration or dislike which the subject criticised may excite in the critic's mind. The critic ought to give this impression, but he ought not to leave the other task unattempted, and the result of leaving it unattempted is to be found in the loose and haphazard judgments which now too often compose what is called criticism. The criticism of the Gallic School, which Dryden and Saint Evremond helped so much to naturalize in England, was at least not afraid of giving a reason for the faith that was in it. The critics strove to examine the abstract value of this or that literary form, the propriety of this or that mode of expression, the limits to be imposed on the choice and disposition of this or that subject. No doubt this often resulted in looking merely at the stopwatch, as Sterne's famous phrase has it. But it often resulted in something better, and it at least produced something like reasonable uniformity of judgment.

Dryden's criticisms took, as a rule, the form of prefaces to his plays, and the reading of the play ensured, to some considerable extent, the reading of the preface. Probably the pattern may be found in Corneille's *Examens*. Nor must it be forgotten that the questions attacked in these disquisitions were of real interest at the time to a large number of persons; to a very much larger number relatively, perhaps even to a much larger number absolutely, than would now be the case. The first instance of a considerable piece of prose written by Dryden was not, indeed, a preface, though it was of the nature of one. The *Essay on Dramatic Poesy* was written, according to its own showing, in the summer of 1665, and published two or three years later. It takes the form of a dialogue between interlocutors, who are sufficiently identified with Dorset, Sedley, Sir Robert Howard, and Dryden himself. The argument turns on various questions of comparison between classical French and English dramas, and especially between English dramas of the old and of the newer type, the latter of which Dryden defends. It is noticeable, however, that this very essay contained one of the best worded and best thought-out of the author's many panegyrics upon Shakspeare. Viewed simply from the point of view of style this performance exhibits Dryden as already a considerable master of prose, though, so far as we know, he had had no practice in it beyond a few Prefaces and Dedications, if we except the unacknowledged hackwork which he is sometimes said to have performed for the bookseller Herringman. There is still something of the older, lengthy sentence, and of the tendency to elongate it by joint on joint as fresh thoughts recur to the writer. But these elongations rarely sacrifice clearness, and there is an almost total absence, on the one hand, of the cumbrous classical constructions of the elders; on the other, of the quaint colloquialisms which generally make their appearance when this more ambitious style is discarded. The Essay was quickly followed by a kind of reply from Sir Robert Howard, and Dryden made a somewhat sharp rejoinder to his brother-in-law in the defence of the Essay which he prefixed to his play of *The Indian Emperor*. He was evidently very angry with Sir Robert, who had, indeed, somewhat justified Shadwell's caricature of him as "Sir Positive At-All;" and this anger is not without effects on the style of the defence. Its sentences are sharper, shorter, more briskly and flippantly moulded than those of the Essay. Indeed, about this time—the time of his greatest prosperity—Dryden seems to

have passed, somewhat late in life, through a period of flippancy. He was for a few years decidedly prosperous, and his familiarity with men of rank and position seems a little to have turned his head. It was at this time, and at this time only, that he spoke disrespectfully of his great predecessors, and insinuated, in a manner which, I fear, must be called snobbish, that his own familiarity with such models of taste and deportment as Rochester put him in a very superior position for the drawing of character to such humble and home-keeping folks as the old dramatists. These prefaces and dedications, however, even where their matter is scarcely satisfactory, show an ever-growing command of prose style, and very soon the resipiscence of Dryden's judgment, and the result of his recently renewed study of the older writers. The Preface to *All for Love*, though short, and more familiar in style than the earlier work, is of excellent quality; and the same may be said of those to *Troilus and Cressida* and the *Spanish Friar*, the latter of which is especially characteristic, and contains some striking remarks on the old dramatists. The great poetical works of the period between 1680 and 1687 are also attended by prose introductions, and some of these are exceedingly well done. The *Epistle to the Whigs*, which forms the preface to the *Medal*, is a piece of political writing such as there had been hitherto but very little in English, and it was admirably followed up by the *Vindication of the Duke of Guise*. On the other hand, the preface to *Religio Laici*, though partly also polemical, is a model of what may be called the expository style. Dryden obtained no great credit for his controversy with Stillingfleet, his *Life of St. Francis Xavier*, or his *History of the League*, all of which were directly or indirectly controversial, and concerned with the political events of the time. As his lengthiest prose works, however, they can hardly be passed over without notice.

The Revolution, in throwing Dryden back upon purely literary pursuits, did him no more harm in the way of prose than of poetical composition. Not a few of his Translations have prose prefaces of peculiar excellence prefixed. The sketch of Satire which forms the preface to the *Juvenal* is one of the best of its author's performances. The *Æneid* is introduced by an admirable dedication to Mulgrave; but the essay on the *Georgics*, though it is not, indeed, Dryden's own, is almost more interesting in this connexion than if it were; for this essay came from the pen of no less a person than Addison, then a young man of five-and-twenty, and it enables us to judge of the indebtedness of the Queen Anne men to Dryden, in prose as well as in poetry. It would be a keen critic who, knowing Addison only from the *Spectator*, could detect his hand in this performance. But it does not require much keenness in any one who knows Dryden's prose and Addison's, to trace the link of connexion which this piece affords. It lies much nearer to the former than the latter, and it shows clearly how the writer must have studied those "prefaces of Dryden" which Swift chose to sneer at. As in poetry, however, so in prose, Dryden's best, or almost his best work, was his last. The dedication of the *Fables* to the Duke of Ormond is the last and the most splendid of his many pieces of polished flattery. The preface which follows it is the last and one of the best examples of his literary criticism.

It has been justly observed of Dryden's prose style that it is, for the style of so-distinguished a writer, singularly destitute of mannerism. If we father any particular piece upon him without knowing it to be his, it is not, as in the case of most writers, because of some obvious trick of arrangement or phraseology. The truth is, or at least the probability, that Dryden had no thought of inventing or practising a definite prose style, though he had more than once a very definite intention in his practice of matters poetical. Poetry was with him, as, indeed, it should be, an end in itself; prose, as perhaps it should also be for the most part, only a means to an end. He wanted, from time to time, to express his ideas on certain points that interested him; to answer accusations which he thought unjust; to propitiate powerful patrons; sometimes, perhaps, merely to discharge commissions with which he had been intrusted. He found no good instrument ready to his hand for these purposes, and so, with that union of the practical and literary spirit which distinguished him so strongly, he set to work to make one. But he had no special predilection for the instrument, except in so far as it served its turn, and he had, therefore, no object in preserving any special peculiarities in it except for the same reason. His poetical and dramatic practice, and the studies which that practice implied, provided him with an ample vocabulary, a strong, terse method of expression, and a dislike to archaism, vulgarity, or want of clearness. He therefore let his words arrange themselves pretty much as they would, and probably saw no object in such devises as the balancing of one part of a sentence by another, which attracted so many of his successors. The long sentence, with its involved clauses, was contrary to his habit of thought, and would have interfered with his chief objects—clearness and precision. Therefore he, in the main, discarded it; yet if at any time a long and somewhat complicated sentence seemed to him to be appropriate, he did not hesitate to write one. Slipshod diction and cant vulgarities revolted his notions of correctness and elegance, and therefore he seldom uses them; yet there are not very many writers in whom colloquialisms occasionally occur with happier effect. If a fault is to be found with his style, it probably lies in a certain abuse of figures and of quotation, for both of which his strong tincture of the characteristics of the first half of the century may be responsible, while the former, at least, is natural to a poet. Yet, on the whole, his style, if compared either with Hooker and Clarendon, Bacon and Milton, on the one hand, or with Addison, and still more the later eighteenth century writers, on the other, is a distinctly plain and homely style. It is not so vernacular as Bunyan or Defoe, and not quite so perfect in simplicity as Swift. Yet with the work of these three writers it stands at the head of the plainer English prose styles, possessing at the same time a capacity of magnificence to which the others cannot pretend. As there is no original narrative of any length from Dryden's hand in prose, it is difficult to say whether he could have discharged satisfactorily this part of the prose-writer's functions. The *Life of Xavier* is good, but not of the best. For almost any other function, however, the style seems to be well adapted.

Now this, it must be remembered, was the great want of the day in matter of prose style—a style, namely, that should be generally flexible and capable of adaptation, not merely to the purposes of the erudite and ambitious, but to any purpose for which it might be required, and in which the vernacular and the literary elements should be properly blended and adjusted. It is scarcely too much to say that if, as some critics have inclined to think, the influence of Dryden tended to narrow the sphere and cramp the efforts of English poetry, it tended equally to enlarge the sphere and develope the energies of English prose. It has often been noticed that poets, when they have any faculty for prose writing, are among the best of prose writers, and of no one is this more true than it is of Dryden.

JOHN AMPHLETT EVANS
"Dryden and Ben Jonson"
Temple Bar, May 1892, pp. 101–12

When the writings and the conduct of a man like Dryden have been estimated from the moral point of view, and labelled for praise or blame accordingly, it is obvious that the last word has not yet been said about him. We have not really added much to our knowledge until we have inquired into his literary influence on posterity, and also (which is the subject of the present paper) into the causes which made him what he was.

In this branch of the subject the moral and literary defects of an author may be of equal value with his excellences, as equally pointing back to the causes which led up to them. And if we elect to proceed by way of a comparison with the typical representative of the generation immediately preceding, a position which Ben Jonson may be accepted as holding with regard to Dryden, we may expect beforehand that such a comparison will be extremely instructive.

Among the writers of the seventeenth century these two may be placed in a class by themselves, as having founded, or endeavoured to found, a new critical school of literature, enforcing its principles both by precept and example. The difference between them seems to be that the influence of the older writer died out, while that of the younger continues to this day—in other words, that Dryden succeeded where Jonson failed. If this point be either admitted or demonstrated, and if it be further possible to show that Dryden began by a conscious reference backwards to Jonson, of whose mistakes his own are in almost every case imitations, and that Dryden's work improved in course of time, in proportion as he freed himself from Jonsonian influences, it will be seen that the establishment of such a parallel may be a matter of importance.

Ben Jonson was a man of great natural ability, keen observation, and broad humour. As regards the external circumstances which made him what he was, they may be summed up by saying that he was formed by the Renaissance, and that he was the Poet-Laureate of James I. The term "Renaissance," however, may be very misleading if it causes us to draw too strong a line, for example, between the works of Chaucer and those of Shakespeare. As the English language, viewed in its entirety as an instrument for the expression of thought, is very largely a romance-language, so the English literature, in its birth and growth, is to all intents and purposes a romance-literature. The influences which formed Chaucer were French, Italian, and Provençal. The same influences appear in Shakespeare and Spenser, although by their time the Italian element had become so strong, that it is often the only one of the three that need be considered. Shakespeare and Spenser may thus be viewed as Romance (not to say Italianised) writers, partially modified by the influences of ancient Greece and Rome, which were recalled to strong life by the Renaissance. The comparative elevation and purity of tone which marks the era of the "Maiden Queen" is an attribute which was destined to be subsequently overcast, however strongly it reappears in Milton and some others. The falling off is due to a corresponding variation in the tone of the Court, which in the times of Elizabeth, James I., and Charles II., respectively, wielded a literary influence capable of a ready explanation, though stronger than can be easily realised by us of the present time. Those who live to please must please to live; and if Dryden, as representing the Restoration, has incurred just and severe censure, he was, after all, not so much more blame-worthy than his official predecessor in the Laureateship.

The atmosphere of the Court of James I. was poisonous to Jonson's work as to some other things. Murders, or suspected murders, low and gross language, a tone of mind which nothing disgusts, a depraved liking for literary stiffness and pedantry, a taste for horrors in tragedy, and for unsavoury jests in comedy—something like this made up the literary spirit which Jonson, as the Poet-Laureate, was bound to represent. There is not here much question of private character; as a morally robust and manly individual, Jonson was probably a better man than Dryden; but this does not prevent the existence of blemishes in his work from which the latter would have shrunk. To mention one instance only, the list of characters in *Volpone*, esteemed one of the best of Jonson's comedies, is such as cannot be found in Shakespeare or Dryden either. Macaulay has compared the Restoration dramatists to animals which are protected by their scent. The same remark applies, with at least equal force, to Jonson.

The dramatic work of Ben Jonson had, in its earlier stages, the unique advantage of being carried on under the influence and auspices of Shakespeare, who developed in him the natural gift by which he is most widely and most worthily remembered, that of lyrical poetry. The author of "Drink to me only with thine eyes," and of "Still to be neat, still to be drest," has certainly taken a first class in that branch of literature. The first and perhaps the best of Jonson's comedies (though herein we are at issue with Dryden, who prefers the *Silent Woman*) was *Every Man in his Humour*, which was played in the last years of Elizabeth's reign—Shakespeare himself taking a part in it—and which was thought worthy of revival in our own time by Charles Dickens himself. In its broad and rich humour there is much to remind us of the creator of Falstaff; but indications are not wanting of the faults, presently to be noticed, which have tended to make Jonson, like Dryden, rather a name than a reality to the general reader.

That our two poets both worked under the deliberate consciousness that they were the exponents of certain critical principles is sufficiently proved by their prefaces. The elder writer, in particular, had so much of the schoolmaster in him as to publish an English grammar.

What then were Jonson's weak points, and how did Dryden deal with them? If we can imagine Jonson drawing up a list of practical rules for literary, and especially for dramatic work, they might have included the following:

(1.) One can never have too much of a good thing. In dramatic composition, brevity and terseness need by no means be considered.

(2.) The Greek and Latin writers are classic in the strictest sense of the word. The more we imitate them and copy from them, the better. Long translations from Ovid and Juvenal are perfectly in place in an English comedy; and a London audience will always be gratified by a word or line reproduced in the original language.

(3.) The object of an author is to instruct. We must not, therefore, be afraid of abstruse and learned allusion. For example, every Englishman should be acquainted with the laws of his country, and a string of legal maxims may be effectively used to brighten up a comic scene. The Latin language should in this case be employed.

(4.) The drama should always have a moral tendency. But as regards separate expressions and allusions, our classical models will support us in an unbounded liberty.

(5.) The Italian masque is so noble a branch of the drama, that the more you have of it, and the more lengthy, the better.

(6.) The humour of an individual character consists in a single eccentricity harped upon until a baby would understand it. For example, a gentleman who dislikes noise may be made very funny on the stage. By all means introduce such a one, and work his peculiarity to the last gasp. If it is the only point of the least interest about him, that will not matter.

(7.) It is a mistake to think that puns are out of place in a regular comedy. On the contrary, you can hardly have too many of them. "Peace" and "pease" makes a very good one; so does "poesy" and "posy." "Roger Bacon" pronounced "Rasher Bacon" ought to bring down the house. If one of your characters has to say something like this, "Open the book and read the contents," the proper reply, "This contents me not," will at once suggest itself to you.

(8.) The three unities of time, place, and action are to be maintained as far as possible.

(9.) There is a valuable literary artifice which my name-sake, Samuel Johnson, will one day describe as a mark of the school which he calls "metaphysical," by which I suppose he means "hyper-physical," or unnatural. This consists in hunting over all nature and art for the most far-fetched comparisons, such as no unlearned person could possibly dream of. My follower, Mr. Cowley, will illustrate this by giving a medical turn to his appeal to a cruel mistress, as thus:

> Gently, ah, gently, Madam, touch
> The wounds which you yourself have made:
> That pain must needs be very much
> Which makes me of your hand afraid.
> Cordials of pity give me now,
> For I too weak for purgings grow.

The case may be briefly stated thus. The ideas of literary art that prevailed from 1550 to 1650 were such as would make any work tedious and unreadable. The genius of Shakespeare did not entirely save itself from this danger, while that of Spenser was almost overwhelmed by it. Its effect on Bacon was, that his best writing is in Latin, not English. Liberty where there ought to have been restriction, and restriction where there ought to have been liberty, combined in Jonson's case to destroy the effect which might have been expected from a great genius trained by Shakespeare. Tediousness is, according to Dr. Johnson, the most fatal of all literary defects, and Ben Jonson may too truly be charged with it.

But this was just the fault which the Court of the Restoration, the most lively, witty, and literary ever known in England, was the least likely to endure. We are then to imagine Dryden, early in the year 1662, attempting dramatic work which should please the new generation, and yet maintain a link with the past. He at once laid his finger on several weak points. Lengthiness, wordiness, atrocious puns, were to be things forbidden. From the very first his scenes are much shorter, with a more continual variety, and a pointed dialogue developing into the battledore-and-shuttlecock of repartee. These points reserved, he then looked back, as was probably his wisest course, to the earliest comedy of Jonson, and produced his own *Wild Gallant*, which bears witness to a study of *Every Man in his Humour*, and contains more than one quotation from Shakespeare. It is the only comedy of Dryden in which low-class characters appear, after the manner of Captain Bobadil and his acquaintances. It was brought out a few months before Dryden's marriage with Lady Elizabeth Howard; and its leading character is a "Lady" Constance, the only case in which Dryden employs that title. Possibly this may have been intended as a compliment, though a rather equivocal one, on the whole, to his future wife.

His next play, the *Rival Ladies,* may be described as a shadow of the *Two Gentlemen of Verona,* with a Spanish plot, and a rhymed dialogue in the serious parts.

At this point begins the radical though gradual change which was Dryden's contribution to the development of literature in England. The Latin and Italian models having been permanently discarded, ideas were now adopted from France, and plots from Spain, in about equal measure for tragedy and comedy. For this there was much to be said. The history of Spain must then have seemed more interesting than that of Ferdinand and Charles V., with the conquests of Granada, Mexico, and Peru. Dryden made full use of these subjects in his tragedies, wherein he has been followed by others. He adopted the Spanish comedy of intrigue, often placing his plots in the country from which it came. The rhymed dialogue of his tragedies came from France—his comedies were not uninfluenced by Molière. In this way began the school of "genteel comedy," so called, which maintained itself down to the time of Sheridan inclusive, and which exhibits groups of brilliant and cultivated people engaged in a continual fence of witty repartee—the natural result of a recoil from Jonsonian vulgarity and tediousness; and, "artificial" as it is sometimes called, at all events more agreeably artificial than the school which preceded it. Its weak points are really two: the one, to put it mildly, that the sacredness of marriage is completely ignored by it, by Sheridan as much as by Congreve or Dryden; the other that it represents only one class of society, the valets and waiting-maids who appear in it being merely conventional instruments of the plot. The time had not yet come when a gallery crowded with working men and women were to laugh and cry over the adventures of Sam Gerridge and the Eccles family.

In the year 1672, when this revolution was pretty well completed, Dryden became involved in a controversy arising out of some severe remarks made by him on the Elizabethan writers in general, and on Jonson in particular: not excluding Shakespeare himself from censure. Dryden had claimed a superior refinement for the writers of his own day, and implicitly for himself, produced by a genteel association with the Court. His explanation of this was much more satisfactory than might be expected. His allegations against the older school were, on the whole, such as have been already described; and he had shown quite enough admiration of both Shakespeare and Jonson to be acquitted of any unworthy desire to disparage them. "I know," he says, "I honour Ben Jonson more than my little critics; because, without vanity, I may own I understand him better." He praises Jonson for the strong and well-maintained articulation of his plots and for the broad humour of his characters.

"But," he says, "the poets of this age will be more wary than to imitate the meanness of his persons. Gentlemen will now be entertained with the follies of each other; and the conversation which they would avoid in the street can be no jest to them in the theatre."

So wrote the initiator of the style which produced the *School for Scandal,* and it may well be questioned whether anything so good as that comedy could ever have proceeded from the school of Jonson. The truth is, that a comedy of life which should represent all ranks equally well would require such a fund of experiences in the writer, and such a power of reproducing them, as could hardly be expected to exist in any one man, unless he were a second Shakespeare. But the work left by the late Mr. Robertson may go far towards showing us that such a thing is still possible.

Dryden explains the reference to his own association with the Court in a way which may be accepted, on Sir Walter Scott's authority, as containing much sober truth. He says that the French polish introduced by Charles II. had broken through the English stiffness and reserve, so that "the fire of the English wit, which was before stifled under a constrained, melancholy way of breeding, began first to display its force, by mixing the solidity of our nation with the air and gaiety of our neighbours." He adds that the poets of his time were only following the lead of the whole nation, by reproducing the brilliant conversation of the Court. This lends force to the strong view which may fairly be held as to the amount which our nation has learnt, and has still to learn, from France.

Of Dryden's comedies, then, it may be sufficient to say that, while they missed success themselves for very cogent reasons, they yet paved the way for the success of others. Of the blank-verse tragedies, which are esteemed the best of his dramatic works, we have nothing particular to say. But the rhymed heroic tragedies, whatever else may be said of them, are very remarkable productions, which maintained their popularity for some time. On the one hand, they have been unmercifully and very cleverly parodied, on the other they were written by a theatrical manager well versed in the business of the stage; they were clearly used as libretti for spectacular melodrama; and lastly, they, along with many successful French tragedies, point to the conclusion that rhyme has more dramatic value than may hitherto have been supposed. If there is room for the display of tragic power in an Italian opera, and if music may even assist the dramatic effect, why should either metre or rhyme be such a hindrance to it? As to what may be said against the rhymed dialogue of repartee, the short quotation made by Sir Walter Scott from Butler's lengthy parody, entitled, "Repartees between Cat and Puss," may be partly copied here, as showing the general character of a dialogue in this style between a hero and a heroine, and also the nature of the objections to it (puss, on the tiles, claws his interlocutor, who thus replies):

Cat: Forbear, foul ravisher, this rude address:
    Canst thou at once both injure and caress?
Puss: Thou hast bewitched me with thy powerful charms,
    And I, by drawing blood, would cure my harms.
Cat: He that does love would set his heart a tilt,
    Ere one drop of his lady's should be spilt.
Puss: Your wounds are but without, and mine within,
    You wound my heart, and I but prick your skin;
    And while your eyes pierce deeper than my claws,
    You blame the effect, of which you are the cause.
Cat: How could my guiltless eyes your heart invade,
    Had it not first been by your own betrayed?
    Hence 'tis, my greatest crime has only been
    (Not in mine eyes, but yours) in being seen.

This is a good parody. But one story is good until another is told. What really was the thing parodied? A sample of it may be found in the *Indian Emperor,* more artificial than anything else of the kind in Dryden, inasmuch as it is written, not in couplets, but in the difficult quatrain stanza. Montezuma, Emperor of Mexico, has a stately and beautiful daughter, Cydaria, between whom and Cortez, the Spanish invader, there is of course a love affair. When they are left alone together for the first time, the following dialogue occurs:

Cydaria (aside): My father's gone, and yet I cannot go;
    Sure I have something lost or left behind!

Cortez (aside): Like travellers who wander in the
  snow,
  I on her beauty gaze till I am blind.
Cyd.: Thick breath, quick pulse and heaving of my
  heart,
  All signs of some unwonted change appear;
  I find myself unwilling to depart,
  And yet I know not why I would be here.
  Stranger, you raise such torments in my breast,
  That when I go (if I must go again)
  I'll tell my father you have robbed my rest,
  And to him of your injuries complain.
Cort.: Unknown, I swear, those wrongs were which
  I wrought,
  But my complaints will much more just appear,
  Who from another world my freedom brought,
  And to your conquering eyes have lost it here.
Cyd.: Where is that other world from whence you
  came?
Cort.: Beyond the ocean, far from hence it lies!
Cyd.: Your other world I fear, is then the same,
  That souls must go to when the body dies.
  But what's the cause that keeps you here with
  me?
  That I may know what keeps me here with you?
Cort.: Mine is a love which must perpetual be
  If you can be so just as I am true.

The dialogue is here broken off. There can be no doubt
that Dryden wrote it with a view to its effect on the stage, and
we can imagine that, delivered by competent actors, the effect
might be considerable. The charge of hasty work often made
against Dryden must fail in this case. Nothing was ever more
carefully and deliberately constructed. It is essentially a lyrical
dialogue—in other words it is "spoken opera," only one degree
less artificial than if it were set to music. If it were ever to be so
employed, the composition which had such a libretto should
be of a high order indeed. Those who admire it as it stands will
probably have learnt the value of form in relation to material,
as illustrated by the similar work of Victor Hugo. Like much
else of Dryden's work, it is curious, if not unique.

Dryden's theory of the dramatic unities was not essentially
different from Jonson's. Whether admittedly or not, they
represent practical rules which are not wholly neglected by any
dramatic author of importance. The "metaphysical" heresy
which prevailed in Dryden's youth retained its influence with
him long enough to get him into serious hot water with the
critics. His schoolboy effusion has not been spared, in which,
on the subject of the small-pox which killed a schoolfellow, he
had written:

  Each little pimple had a tear in it
  To wail the fault its rising did commit.
  No comet need foretell his change drew on,
  Whose corpse might seem a con-stell-a-ti-on.

Annus Mirabilis itself has been satirised often enough for
defects of this kind, and the last notable instance of it is just as
bad as any other, where Montezuma, after arguing a theological point with considerable acumen while stretched on the
rack, finds a neat and appropriate simile on which to expend
his last breath:

  Still less and less my boiling spirits flow,
  And I grow stiff, as cooling metals do. (*Dies.*)

And with the last breath of Montezuma evaporates finally the
influence of Jonson.

It might at first sight seem strange enough that even in
such a cursory account of those times as this is, the name of

Milton should have hardly occurred at all. And when it is
further remembered that Dryden revered and admired the great
epic poet of England at a time when very few were found to do
so, it might have been expected that something should be said
of him beyond the mere reference to Dryden's rather dubious
adaptation from the *Paradise Lost,* and to a few scattered
Miltonian expressions of his, which it would of course be
possible to make. The truth is, that in our literary history both
Shakespeare and Milton stand apart by themselves, too inimitable and too spontaneous either to found a critical school or
to carry with them any long train of followers. And as regards
Milton, he may be viewed as a gigantic survival of the
Elizabethan period, more Italianised than Spenser, more of
the Puritan Englishman than was Shakespeare. "His soul was
like a star, and dwelt apart."

If there is one fault more fatal than another to the poet
and dramatist, it is the unseasonable desire to be instructive.
Both Jonson and Dryden were something of culprits in this
way, as may be shown by a short extract from the dialogue
above referred to between the dying Montezuma and a
Christian priest. It must have been written by one who, having
something to say, did not care how he said it, if only it reached
the ears of the public. It is useless to complain of the dramatic
incongruity of a passage which should rather be classed with
Religio Laici and the *Hind and Panther,* as exhibiting a stage in
the growth of Dryden's religious opinions.

Montezuma: Since all religions with each other
  fight,
  While only one can lead us in the right,
  Until that one hath some more certain mark,
  Poor human kind must wander in the dark.
Priest: All, under various names, adore and love
  One Power immense, which ever rules above:
  Vice to abhor, and virtue to pursue,
  Is both believed and taught by us and you;
  But here our worship takes another way—
Mont.: Where both agree, 'tis there most safe to stay.
Priest: If in this middle way you still pretend
  To stay, your journey never will have end.
Mont.: Howe'er, 'tis better in the midst to stay,
  Than wander farther in uncertain way.
Priest: But we by martyrdom our faith avow.
Mont.: You do no more than I for ours do now.
Priest: Since age by erring childhood is misled,
  Refer yourself to our unerring head.
Mont.: Man, and not err! what reason can you give?
Priest: Renounce that carnal reason, and believe.
Mont.: The light of nature should I thus betray,
  'Twere to wink hard, that I might see the day.

That Dryden knew little and cared little about theology
has been asserted by Macaulay and others. How far his beliefs
influenced his conduct is another question; but his writings
continually exhibit that infusion of Biblical and theological
ideas which indicates a strong and spontaneous interest in these
subjects. In this, as in all other points, Dryden was the creation
and the representative of his period.

The exclusive attention that has been given in this paper
to the dramatic works of Dryden is, it need hardly be said, not
produced by any material difference from the general opinion,
which prefers Dryden's adapted tales, and especially his satires.
It is his unique position in these matters which makes them
difficult to handle from our present point of view, which has
sought as far as possible to trace out causes and effects. Who
can say where that great power of satire comes from, which he
certainly learnt from no one else? And what school of satirists

(did the demand for it exist) was such an inimitable worker likely to leave behind him? But his dramatic works are on common ground with those that preceded and followed them, and it is by them, and by his essays written in connection with them, that we are enabled to fix the very important place which he holds in the history of English literature.

Sir Walter Scott and Mr. Saintsbury have provided us with a list of Drydenian localities. Most of them are in Northamptonshire, those in the valley of the Nene including Aldwinkle Vicarage, where the room is known in which he was born; Tichmarsh, where his parents lived; Oundle, which may have been his preparatory school, and others. In the same county is Blakesley, where he owned land, and Castle Ashby, the seat of the Dryden family. To these we have to add the well-known house in Gerrard Street, where he lived many years and died; Charlton, in Wiltshire, a possession of his wife's family, where *Annus Mirabilis* was written; a "Dryden's Walk" at Croxall in Staffordshire, where Dryden is said to have visited Lord Dorset; also Westminster School and Trinity College, Cambridge, the places of his education. *The Hind and Panther* is traditionally said to have been written in the woodland glades of Rushton near Kettering, once the seat of the Tresham family. But we are enabled to meet this by another tradition, so far better established that it has been handed down to the present time through a single family. The place that competes with Rushton for this distinction is Ugbrooke Park. By the courtesy of Lord Clifford, whose words it will be perhaps better to copy, the following facts are now presented to the reader:

> In the rookery about three or four hundred yards from the house is a spot that has always been called Dryden's Seat. It stands at the termination of what were undoubtedly the gardens and pleasure-grounds of the old house, which existed in Dryden's time.

That Dryden was a friend of the first Lord Clifford of Chudleigh and of his son, is evidenced by the fact that his translation of Virgil is dedicated to Hugh, the second lord. In that dedication he says that he "could not possibly have chosen better than the worthy son of an illustrious father. He was the patron of my manhood, when I flourished in the opinion of the world, though with small advantage to my fortune, till he awakened the remembrance of my Royal master. He was that Pollio and that Varus who introduced me to Augustus." That Dryden had visited Lord Clifford at Ugbrooke is therefore most probable, but I do not like to say so much for the tradition that he wrote there 'The Hind and the Panther,' the opening lines of which are supposed to have been suggested by a peculiar species of white deer still existing in the park. It is possible that the idea of the work may have been suggested at Ugbrooke and written elsewhere.

If any visitor to Ugbrooke, led up the nettle-covered hill, past a laurel, gnarled as any ancient yew might be, under lofty elms that must be seen to be believed in, reaches the circular foundation of crumbling stones that marks the place where Dryden sat, and, looking thence over the waving sea of trees, catches sight of a lovely milk-white fawn bounding by the side of her dun-coloured elders, that visitor will surely recognise the true descendant of the "milk-white hind immortal and unchanged;" he will see the very water where the beasts went down to drink; he will feel that if the panther, wolf, and the rest of them were not there at that time, they ought to have been, and he will fearlessly assert the claims of Ugbrooke against Rushton or anywhere else.

And with this undoubted contribution to the ascertained results of historical research, the present series of papers comes to a not undignified conclusion.

DANIEL DEFOE

DANIEL DEFOE

1660–1731

Daniel Defoe, novelist and political pamphleteer, was born in London, probably in the latter half of 1660. His father, who was of Flemish descent, was a tallow-chandler. Defoe's family were Nonconformists, and he attended the Rev. James Fisher's school at Dorking, and later the Rev. Charles Morton's academy for Dissenters at Newington Green. Defoe had intended to enter the ministry, but by 1683 he had become a hosiery merchant instead, after traveling extensively in Britain and on the Continent. Around the same time (1683–84) he married Mary Tuffley.

Defoe began writing political pamphlets in 1683. As a Dissenter he opposed the Catholic James II and took part in the disastrous Monmouth rebellion of 1685; in 1688 he joined the forces of William III. Defoe's first important work was *An Essay upon Projects* (1697), which was followed by a satirical attack on prejudice against kings of foreign birth; this poem, *The True-Born Englishman* (1701), sold more copies than any other yet written in English. In 1702 Defoe issued *The Shortest Way with the Dissenters*, in which, with savage irony, he wrote in the persona of an opponent of Nonconformism; for this offense he was fined, imprisoned in May 1703, and pilloried. While in prison he wrote his mock-Pindaric ode *Hymn to the Pillory* (1703). Defoe was released in November 1703 through the intercession of the Tory politician Robert Harley, who then employed him as a secret agent. Between 1703 and 1714 he traveled around the country monitoring public opinion for Harley, and later for Sidney Godolphin. He also served as a government official for both Tory and Whig ministries, and in 1704 began *The Review*, which became the main government organ; he produced it almost singlehandedly until the fall of the Tories in 1714. Even though the Whigs, when still the opposition party, had briefly imprisoned Defoe in 1713 on account of certain anti-Jacobite pamphlets, the new Whig ministry now employed him to censor various Tory journals. In 1715 he had libel charges brought against him for having implied that Lord Annesley was a Jacobite; he was convicted, but escaped punishment when Townshend, the Whig Secretary of State, intervened.

It was not until 1719 that Defoe produced *Robinson Crusoe*, his first extended piece of fiction. One of the most famous books ever written, it was followed by Crusoe's *Farther Adventures* (1719), and, to complete the trilogy, his *Serious Reflections* (1720). Continuing in this vein, he produced *The Life and Adventures of Duncan Campbell*, *Memoirs of a Cavalier*, and *The Life of Captain Singleton*, all in 1720. *Moll Flanders*, *A Journal of the Plague Year*, and *Colonel Jack* were all published in 1722, followed by *Roxana*, his last major work of fiction, in 1724. Other important works include the *Tour through the Whole Island of Great Britain* (3 vols., 1724–26), *The Complete English Tradesman* (1726), *Augustus Triumphans* (1728), *A Plan of the English Commerce* (1728), and *The Complete English Gentleman* (published 1890).

In all Defoe produced some 560 books, pamphlets, and journals. He has been called both the author of the first novel and the father of modern journalism. Defoe died in London on April 24, 1731.

Personal

And lastly, those weekly libellers, whenever they get a tale by the end relating to Ireland, without ever troubling their thoughts about the truth, always end it with an application against the Sacramental Test, and the absolute necessity there is of repealing it in both kingdoms. I know it may be reckoned a weakness to say anything of such trifles as are below a serious man's notice; much less would I disparage the understanding of any party to think they would choose the vilest and most ignorant among mankind, to employ them for assertors of a cause. I shall only say, that the scandalous liberty those wretches take would hardly be allowed, if it were not mingled with opinions that *some men* would be glad to advance. Besides, how insipid soever those papers are, they seem to be levelled to the understandings of a great number; they are grown a necessary part in coffee-house furniture, and some time or other may happen to be read by customers of all ranks, for curiosity and amusement; because they lie always in the way. One of these authors (the fellow that was pilloried I have forgot his name) is indeed so grave, sententious, dogmatical a rogue, that there is no enduring him.—JONATHAN SWIFT, "Letter from a Member of the House of Commons in Ireland to a Member of the House of Commons in England concerning the Sacramental Test," 1708

Mr. *Daniel De Foe* is a man of good parts, and very clear sense: His conversation is brisk and ingenious enough. The World is well satisfied that he's enterprizing and *bold*; but, alas! had his prudence only weighed a few grains more, he'd certainly have writ his *Shortest Way* a little more at length. There have been some men in all ages, who have taken that of Juvenal for their motto:

> Aude aliquid brevibus Gyaris et carcere dignum
> Si vis esse aliquis

Had he writ no more than his *True-Born Englishman*, and spared some particular Characters that are too vicious for the very Originals, he had certainly deserved applause; but it is hard to leave off when not only the itch and the inclination, but the necessity of writing, lies so heavy upon a man. Should I defend his good-nature and his honesty, and the world would not believe me, 'twould be labour in vain. Mr. Foe writ for me the "Character of Dr. Annesley," and a "Pindarick in honour of the Athenian Society," which was prefixed to the History of it. And he might have asked me the question, before he inserted either of them in the Collection of his Works, in regard he writes so bitterly against the same injustice in others.—JOHN DUNTON, *The Life and Errors of John Dunton*, 1705

I remember an Author in the World some years ago, who was generally upbraided with Ignorance, and called an "Illiterate Fellow," by some of the *Beau-Monde* of the last Age. ⟨. . .⟩ I happened to come into this Person's Study once, and I found him busy translating a Description of the Course of the River Boristhenes, out of *Bleau's* Geography, written in *Spanish*. Another Time I found him translating some Latin Paragraphs out of *Leubinitz Theatri Cometici*, being a learned Discourse upon Comets; and that I might see whether it was genuine, I looked on some part of it that he had finished, and found by it that he understood the Latin very well, and had perfectly taken the sense of that difficult Author. In short, I found he understood the *Latin*, the *Spanish*, the *Italian*, and could read the *Greek*, and I knew before that he spoke *French* fluently— *yet this Man was no Scholar*. As to Science, on another Occasion, I heard him dispute (in such a manner as surprised me) upon the motions of the Heavenly Bodies, the Distance, Magnitude, Revolutions, and especially the Influences of the Planets, the Nature and probable Revolutions of Comets, the excellency of the New Philosophy, and the like; *but this Man was no Scholar.* ⟨. . .⟩ This put me upon wondering, ever so long ago, what this *strange Thing* called a Man of Learning *was*, and what is it that constitutes a *Scholar?* For, *said I*, here's a man speaks five Languages and reads the Sixth, is a master of Astronomy, Geography, History, and abundance of other useful Knowledge (which I do not mention, that you may not guess at the Man, who is too Modest to desire it), and yet, they say *this Man is no Scholar.*—DANIEL DEFOE, *Applebee's Journal*, 1720–26

> While pensive Poets painful vigils keep,
> Sleepless themselves to give their readers sleep.
> Much to the mindful Queen the feast recalls,
> What City-Swans once sung within the walls;
> Much she revolves their arts, their ancient praise,
> And sure succession down from Heywood's days.
> She saw with joy the line immortal run,
> Each sire imprest and glaring in his son;
> So watchful Bruin forms with plastic care
> Each growing lump, and brings it to a Bear.
> She saw old Pryn in restless Daniel shine,
> And Eusden eke out Blackmore's endless line;
> She saw slow Philips creep like Tate's poor page,
> And all the Mighty Mad in Dennis rage.
>   . . .
> Earless on high, stood un-abash'd Defoe,
> And Tutchin flagrant from the scourge, below.
>   —ALEXANDER POPE, *The Dunciad*, 1728, Bk. 1,
>   ll. 91–104, Bk. 2, ll. 139–40

> Few will acknowledge all they owe
> To persecuted, brave Defoe.
> Achilles, in Homeric song,
> May, or he may not, live so long
> As Crusoe; few their strength had tried
> Without so staunch and safe a guide.
> What boy is there who never laid
> Under his pillow, half afraid,
> That precious volume, lest the morrow
> For unlearnt lesson might bring sorrow?

> But nobler lessons he has taught
> Wide-awake scholars who fear'd naught:
> A Rodney and a Nelson may
> Without him not have won the day.
>   —WALTER SAVAGE LANDOR, "Daniel Defoe,"
>   c. 1840

General

Foe, as well as the Lord Treasurer, had been a rank Presbyterian, and their genius was so near akin that Harley could not but take him into his confidence as soon as he got acquainted with him. He was adored and caressed by that mighty statesman, who gave him, as that mercenary said himself, to the value of one thousand pounds in one year. Foe's business was only to puzzle the cause by mercantile cant and bold sophistry.—JOHN OLDMIXON, *History of England*, 1739

The first part of *Robinson Crusoe* is very good.—Defoe wrote a vast many things; and none bad, though none excellent, except this. There is something good in all he has written. —ALEXANDER POPE (1742–43), cited in Joseph Spence, *Anecdotes, Observations and Characters of Books and Men*, ed. S. W. Singer, 1820

I have nothing of Defoe's but two or three Novels, and the *Plague History*. I can give you no information about him. As a slight general character of what I remember of them (for I have not look'd into them latterly) I would say that 'in the appearance of *truth* in all the incidents and conversations that occur in them they exceed any works of fiction I am acquainted with. It is perfect illusion. The *Author* never appears in these self-narratives (for so they ought to be called or rather Autobiographies) but the *narrator* chains us down to an implicit belief in every thing he says. There is all the minute detail of a log-book in it. Dates are painfully pressed upon the memory. Facts are repeated over and over in varying phrases, till you cannot chuse but believe them. It is like reading Evidence given in a Court of Justice. So anxious the story-teller seems, that the truth should be clearly comprehended, that when he has told us a matter of fact, or a motive, in a line or two farther down he *repeats* it with his favorite figure of speech, "I say" so and so,—though he had made it abundantly plain before. This is in imitation of the common people's way of speaking, or rather of the way in which they are addressed by a master or mistress, who wishes to impress something upon their memories; and has a wonderful effect upon matter-of-fact readers. Indeed it is to such principally that he writes. His style is elsewhere beautiful, but plain & *homely. Robinson Crusoe* is delightful to all ranks and classes, but it is easy to see that it is written in phraseology peculiarly adapted to the lower conditions of readers: hence it is an especial favorite with seafaring men, poor boys, servant maids &c. His novels are capital kitchen-reading, while they are worthy from their deep interest to find a shelf in the Libraries of the wealthiest, and the most learned. His passion for *matter of fact narrative* sometimes betrayed him into a long relation of common incidents which might happen to any man, and have no interest but the intense appearance of truth in them, to recommend them. The whole latter half, or two thirds, of *Colonel Jack* is of this description. The beginning of *Colonel Jack* is the most affecting natural picture of a young thief that was ever drawn. His losing the stolen money in the hollow of a tree, and finding it again when he was in despair, and then being in equal distress at not knowing how to dispose of it, and several similar touches in the early history of the Colonel, evince a deep knowledge of human nature; and, putting out of question the superior *romantic* interest of the latter, in my mind very much exceed *Crusoe*. *Roxana* (1st Edition) is the next in Interest, though he left out the best part of it in subsequent Editions from a foolish hypercriticism of his friend, Southerne. But *Moll Flanders*, the account of the Plague &c. &c. are all of one family, and have the same stamp of character.'—CHARLES LAMB, Letter to Walter Wilson (Dec. 16, 1822)

The works of De Foe seemed alternately to delight and disgust. His *Robinson Crusoe* is the most enchanting domestic Romance in the world: but his *Fortunes and Misfortunes of Moll Flanders*, and his *Life of Col. Jaque*, are such low-bred productions, as to induce us to put an instantaneous negative on their admission into our Cabinets.—THOMAS FROGNALL DIBDIN, *The Library Companion*, 1824

We pass on to his Novels, and are sorry that we must hasten over them. We owe them to the ill odour into which he had fallen as a politician. His fate with his party reminds one a little of the reception which the heroine of the *Heart of Mid-Lothian* met with from her sister, because she would not tell a lie for her; yet both were faithful and true to their cause. Being laid aside by the Whigs, as a suspected person, and not choosing to go over to the other side, he retired to Stoke-Newington, where, as already mentioned, he had an attack of apoplexy, which had nearly proved fatal to him. Recovering, however, and his activity of mind not suffering him to be idle, he turned his thoughts into a new channel, and, as if to change the scene entirely, set about writing Romances. The first work that could come under this title was *The Family Instructor;*—a sort of controversial narrative, in which an argument is held through three volumes, and a feverish interest is worked up to the most tragic height, on 'the abomination' (as it was at that time thought by many people, and among others by Defoe) of letting young people go to the play. The implied horror of dramatic exhibitions, in connexion with the dramatic effect of the work itself, leaves a curious impression. Defoe's polemical talents are brought to bear to very good purpose in this performance, which was in the form of Letters; and it is curious to mark the eagerness with which his pen, after having been taken up for so many years with dry debates and doctrinal points, flies for relief to the details and incidents of private life. His mind was equally tenacious of facts and arguments, and fastened on each, in its turn, with the same strong and unremitting grasp. *Robinson Crusoe*, published in 1719, was the first of his performances in the acknowledged shape of a romance; and from this time he brought out one or two every year to the end of his life. As it was the first, it was decidedly the best; it gave full scope to his genius; and the subject mastered his prevailing bias to religious controversy, and the depravity of social life, by confining him to the unsophisticated views of nature and the human heart. His other works of fiction have not been read, (in comparison)—and one reason is, that many of them, at least, are hardly fit to be read, whatever may be said to the contrary. We shall go a little into the theory of this.

We do not think a person brought up and trammelled all his life in the strictest notions of religion and morality, and looking at the world, and all that was ordinarily passing in it, as little better than a contamination, is, *a priori*, the properest person to write novels: it is going out of his way—it is 'meddling with the unclean thing.' Extremes meet, and all extremes are bad. According to our author's overstrained Puritanical notions, there were but two choices, God or the Devil—Sinners and Saints—the Methodist meeting or the Brothel—the school of the press-yard of Newgate, or atten-

dance on the refreshing ministry of some learned and pious dissenting Divine. As the smallest falling off from faith, or grace, or the most trifling peccadillo, was to be reprobated and punished with the utmost severity, no wonder that the worst turn was given to every thing; and that the imagination having once overstepped the formidable line, gave a loose to its habitual nervous dread, by indulging in the blackest and most frightful pictures of the corruptions incident to human nature. It was as well (in the cant phrase) 'to be in for a sheep as a lamb,' as it cost nothing more—the sin might at least be startling and uncommon; and hence we find, in this style of writing, nothing but an alternation of religious horrors and raptures, (though these are generally rare, as being a less tempting bait,) and the grossest scenes of vice and debauchery: we have either saintly, spotless purity, or all is rotten to the core. How else can we account for it, that all Defoe's characters (with one or two exceptions for form's sake) are of the worst and lowest description—the refuse of the prisons and the stews—thieves, prostitutes, vagabonds, and pirates—as if he wanted to make himself amends for the restraint under which he had laboured 'all the fore-end of his time' as a moral and religious character, by acting over every excess of grossness and profligacy by proxy! How else can we comprehend that he should really think there was a salutary moral lesson couched under the history of *Moll Flanders*; or that his romance of *Roxana, or the Fortunate Mistress*, who rolls in wealth and pleasure from one end of the book to the other, and is quit for a little death-bed repentance and a few lip-deep professions of the vanity of worldly joys, showed, in a striking point of view, the advantages of virtue, and the disadvantages of vice? It cannot be said, however, that these works have an *immoral* tendency. The author has contrived to neutralise the question; and (as far as in him lay) made vice and virtue equally contemptible or revolting. In going through his pages, we are inclined to vary Mr. Burke's well-known paradox, that 'vice, by losing all its grossness, loses half its evil,' and say that vice, by losing all its refinement, loses all its attraction. We have in them only the pleasure of sinning, and the dread of punishment here or hereafter;—gross sensuality, and whining repentance. The morality is that of the inmates of a house of correction; the piety, that of malefactors in the condemned hole. There is no sentiment, no atmosphere of imagination, no 'purple light' thrown round virtue or vice;—all is either physical gratification on the one hand, or a selfish calculation of consequences on the other. This is the necessary effect of allowing nothing to the frailty of human nature;—of never strewing the flowers of fancy in the path of pleasure, but always looking that way with a sort of terror as to forbidden ground: nothing is left of the common and mixed enjoyments and pursuits of human life but the coarsest and criminal part; and we have either a sour, cynical, sordid self-denial, or (in the despair of attaining this) a reckless and unqualified abandonment of all decency and character alike:—it is hard to say which is the most repulsive. Defoe runs equally into extremes in his male characters as in his heroines. *Captain Singleton* is a hardened, brutal desperado, without one redeeming trait, or almost human feeling; and, in spite of what Mr. Lamb says of his lonely musings and agonies of a conscience-stricken repentance, we find nothing of this in the text: the captain is always merry and well if there is any mischief going on; and his only qualm is, after he has retired from his trade of plunder and murder on the high seas, and is afraid of being assassinated for his ill-gotten wealth, and does not know how to dispose of it. Defoe (whatever his intentions may be) is led, by the force of truth and circumstances, to give the Devil his due—he puts no gratuitous remorse into his adventurer's mouth, nor spoils the *keeping* by expressing one relenting pang, any more than his hero would have done in reality. This is, indeed, the excellence of Defoe's representations, that they are perfect *fac-similes* of the characters he chooses to pourtray; but then they are too often the worst specimens he can collect out of the dregs and sink of human nature. *Colonel Jack* is another instance, with more pleasantry, and a common vein of humanity; but still the author is flung into the same walk of flagrant vice and immorality;—as if his mind was haunted by the entire opposition between grace and nature—and as if, out of the sphere of spiritual exercise and devout contemplation, the whole actual world was a necessary tissue of what was worthless and detestable.

We have, we hope, furnished a clue to this seeming contradiction between the character of the author and his works; and must proceed to a conclusion. Of these novels we may, nevertheless, add, for the satisfaction of the inquisitive reader, that *Moll Flanders* is utterly vile and detestable: Mrs. Flanders was evidently born in sin. The best parts are the account of her childhood, which is pretty and affecting; the fluctuation of her feelings between remorse and hardened impenitence in Newgate; and the incident of her leading off the horse from the inn-door, though she had no place to put it in after she had stolen it. This was carrying the love of thieving to an *ideal* pitch, and making it perfectly disinterested and mechanical. *Roxana* is better—soaring a higher flight, instead of grovelling always in the mire of poverty and distress; but she has neither refinement nor a heart; we are only dazzled with the outward ostentation of jewels, finery, and wealth. The scene where she dances in her Turkish dress before the king, and obtains the name of Roxana, is of the true romantic cast. The best parts of *Colonel Jack* are the early scenes, where there is a spirit of mirth and good fellowship thrown over the homely features of low and vicious life;—as where the hero and his companion are sitting at the three-halfpenny ordinary, and are delighted, even more than with their savoury fare, to hear the waiter cry, 'Coming, gentlemen, coming,' when they call for a cup of small-beer; and we rejoice when we are told as a notable event, that 'about this time the Colonel took upon him to wear a shirt.' The *Memoirs of a Cavalier* are an agreeable mixture of the style of history and fiction. These Memoirs, as is well known, imposed upon Lord Chatham as a true history. In his *History of Apparitions*, Defoe discovers a strong bias to a belief in the marvellous and preternatural; nor is this extraordinary, for, to say nothing of the general superstition of the times, his own impressions of whatever he chose to conceive are so vivid and literal, as almost to confound the distinction between reality and imagination. He could 'call spirits from the vasty deep,' and they 'would come when he did call for them.' We have not room for an enumeration of even half his works of fiction. We give the bust, and must refer to Mr. Wilson for the whole length. After *Robinson Crusoe*, his *History of the Plague* is the finest of all his works. It has an epic grandeur, as well as heart-breaking familiarity, in its style and matter.—WILLIAM HAZLITT, "Wilson's Life and Times of Daniel Defoe," 1830

It has happened not seldom that one work of some author has so transcendantly surpassed in execution the rest of his compositions, that the world has agreed to pass a sentence of dismissal upon the latter, and to consign them to total neglect and oblivion. It has done wisely in this, not to suffer the contemplation of excellencies of a lower standard to abate, or stand in the way of the pleasure it has agreed to receive from the master-piece.

Again it has happened, that from no inferior merit of execution in the rest, but from superior good fortune in the choice of its subject, some single work shall have been suffered to eclipse, and cast into shade the deserts of its less fortunate brethren. This has been done with more or less injustice in the case of the popular allegory of Bunyan, in which the beautiful and scriptural image of a pilgrim or wayfarer (we are all such upon earth), addressing itself intelligibly and feelingly to the bosoms of all, has silenced, and made almost to be forgotten, the more awful and scarcely less tender beauties of the *Holy War made by Shaddai upon Diabolus*, of the same author; a romance less happy in its subject, but surely well worthy of a secondary immortality. But in no instance has this excluding partiality been exerted with more unfairness than against what may be termed the secondary novels or romances of De Foe.

While all ages and descriptions of people hang delighted over the *Adventures of Robinson Crusoe*, and shall continue to do so we trust while the world lasts, how few comparatively will bear to be told, that there exist other fictitious narratives by the same writer—four of them at least of no inferior interest, except what results from a less felicitous choice of situation. Roxana—Singleton—Moll Flanders—Colonel Jack—are all genuine offspring of the same father. They bear the veritable impress of De Foe. An unpractised midwife that would not swear to the nose, lip, forehead, and eye, of every one of them! They are in their way as full of incident, and some of them every bit as romantic; only they want the uninhabited Island, and the charm that has bewitched the world, of the striking solitary situation.

But are there no solitudes out of the cave and the desert? or cannot the heart in the midst of crowds feel frightfully alone? Singleton, on the world of waters, prowling about with pirates less merciful than the creatures of any howling wilderness; is he not alone, with the faces of men about him, but without a guide that can conduct him through the mists of educational and habitual ignorance; or a fellow-heart that can interpret to him the newborn yearnings and aspirations of unpractised penitence? Or when the boy Colonel Jack, in the loneliness of the heart (the worst solitude), goes to hide his ill-purchased treasure in the hollow tree by night, and miraculously loses, and miraculously finds it again—whom hath he there to sympathise with him? or of what sort are his associates?

The narrative manner of De Foe has a naturalness about it, beyond that of any other novel or romance writer. His fictions have all the air of true stories. It is impossible to believe, while you are reading them, that a real person is not narrating to you every where nothing but what really happened to himself. To this, the extreme *homeliness* of their style mainly contributes. We use the word in its best and heartiest sense—that which comes *home* to the reader. The narrators everywhere are chosen from low life, or have had their origin in it; therefore they tell their own tales, (Mr. Coleridge has anticipated us in this remark,) as persons in their degree are observed to do, with infinite repetition, and an overacted exactness, lest the hearer should not have minded, or have forgotten, some things that had been told before. Hence the emphatic sentences marked in the good old (but deserted) Italic type; and hence, too, the frequent interposition of the reminding old colloquial parenthesis, "I say"—"mind"—and the like, when the story-teller repeats what, to a practised reader, might appear to have been sufficiently insisted upon before: which made an ingenious critic observe, that his works, in this kind, were excellent reading for the kitchen. And, in truth, the heroes and heroines of De Foe, can never again hope to be popular with a much higher class of readers, than that of the servant-maid or the sailor. Crusoe keeps its rank only by tough prescription; Singleton, the pirate—Colonel Jack, the thief—Moll Flanders, both thief and harlot—Roxana, harlot and something worse—would be startling ingredients in the bill of fare of modern literary delicacies. But, then, what pirates, what thieves, and what harlots is *the thief, the harlot,* and *the pirate* of De Foe? We would not hesitate to say, that in no other book of fiction, where the lives of such characters are described, is guilt and delinquency made less seductive, or the suffering made more closely to follow the commission, or the penitence more earnest or more bleeding, or the intervening flashes of religious visitation, upon the rude and uninstructed soul, more meltingly and fearfully painted. They, in this, come near to the tenderness of Bunyan; while the livelier pictures and incidents in them, as in Hogarth or in Fielding, tend to diminish that "fastidiousness to the concerns and pursuits of common life, which an unrestrained passion for the ideal and the sentimental is in danger of producing."—CHARLES LAMB, "Estimate of De Foe's Secondary Novels," 1830

While Defoe would have been fairly entitled to immortality had he never written *Robinson Crusoe,* yet his many other very excellent writings have nearly faded from our attention, in the superior lustre of the Adventures of the Mariner of York. What better possible species of reputation could the author have desired for that book than the species which it has so long enjoyed? It has become a household thing in nearly every family in Christendom! Yet never was admiration of any work—universal admiration—more indiscriminately or more inappropriately bestowed. Not one person in ten—nay, not one person in five hundred, has, during the perusal of *Robinson Crusoe,* the most remote conception that any particle of genius, or even of common talent, has been employed in its creation! Men do not look upon it in the light of a literary performance. Defoe has none of their thoughts—Robinson all. The powers which have wrought the wonder have been thrown into obscurity by the very stupendousness of the wonder they have wrought! We read, and become perfect abstractions in the intensity of our interest—we close the book, and are quite satisfied that we could have written as well ourselves. All this is effected by the potent magic of verisimilitude. Indeed the author of *Crusoe* must have possessed, above all other faculties, what has been termed the faculty of *identification*—that dominion exercised by volition over imagination which enables the mind to lose its own, in a fictitious, individuality. This includes, in a very great degree, the power of abstraction; and with these keys we may partially unlock the mystery of that spell which has so long invested the volume before us. But a complete analysis of our interest in it cannot be thus afforded. Defoe is largely indebted to his subject. The idea of man in a state of perfect isolation, although often entertained, was never before so comprehensively carried out. Indeed the frequency of its occurrence to the thoughts of mankind argued the extent of its influence on their sympathies, while the fact of no attempt having been made to give an embodied form to the conception, went to prove the difficulty of the undertaking. But the true narrative of Selkirk in 1711, with the powerful impression it then made upon the public mind, sufficed to inspire Defoe with both the necessary courage for his work, and entire confidence in its success. How wonderful has been the result!

Besides *Robinson Crusoe,* Defoe wrote no less than *two hundred and eight* works. The chief of these are the *Speculum Crape-Gownorum,* a reply to Roger L'Estrange, and characterized principally by intemperate abuse—a *Treatise against the*

Turks, written for the purpose of showing England "that if it was the interest of Protestantism not to increase the influence of a Catholic power, it was infinitely more so to oppose a Mohammedan one"—an *Essay on Projects,* displaying great ingenuity, and mentioned in terms of high approbation by our own Franklin—the *Poor Man's Plea,* a satire levelled against the extravagances of the upper ranks of British society—the *Trueborn Englishman,* composed with a view of defending the king from the abuse heaped upon him as a foreigner—the *Shortest Way with the Dissenters,* a work which created strong excitement, and for which the author suffered in the pillory—the *Reformation of Manners,* a satirical poem, containing passages of uncommon force, that is to say, uncommon for Defoe, who was no poet—*More Reformation,* a continuation of the above—*Giving Alms no Charity,* an excellent treatise—a *Preface to a translation of Drelincourt on Death,* in which is contained the "true narrative" of Mrs. Veal's apparition—the *History of the Union,* a publication of much celebrity in the days of its author, and even now justly considered as placing him among the "soundest historians of his time"—the *Family Instructor,* "one of the most valuable systems of practical morality in the language"—the *History of Moll Flanders,* including some striking but coarsely executed paintings of low life—the *Life of Colonel Jaque,* in which an account is given of the hero's residence in Virginia—the *Memoirs of a Cavalier,* a book belonging more properly to History than to Fictitious Biography, and which has been often mistaken for a true narrative of the civil wars in England and Germany—the *History of the Plague,* which Dr. Mead considered an authentic record—and *Religious Courtship,* which acquired an extensive popularity, and ran through innumerable editions. In the multiplicity of his other publications, and amid a life of perpetual activity, Defoe found time, likewise, to edit his *Review,* which existed for more than nine years, commencing in February 1704, and ending in May 1713. This periodical is justly entitled to be considered the original of the Tatlers and Spectators, which were afterwards so fashionable. Political intelligence, however, constituted the greater portion of its *materiel.*—EDGAR ALLAN POE, "Daniel Defoe" (1836), *Essays and Reviews,* ed. G. R. Thompson, 1984, pp. 201–3

De Foe is the only author known who has so plausibly circumstantiated his false historical records as to make them pass for genuine, even with literary men and critics. In his *Memoirs of a Cavalier,* one of his poorest forgeries, he assumes the character of a soldier who had fought under Gustavus Adolphus (1628–31), and afterwards (1642–45) in our own Parliamentary War; in fact, he corresponds chronologically to Captain Dalgetty. In other works he personates a sea-captain, a hosier, a runaway apprentice, an officer under Lord Peterborough in his Catalonian expedition. In this last character he imposed upon Dr. Johnson; and, by men better read in History than Dr. Johnson, he has actually been quoted as a regular historical authority. How did he accomplish so difficult an end? Simply by inventing such little circumstantiations of any character or incident as seem, by their apparent inertness of effect, to verify themselves; for, where the reader is told that such a person was the posthumous son of a tanner, that his mother married afterwards a Presbyterian schoolmaster, who gave him a smattering of Latin, but, the schoolmaster dying of the plague, that he was compelled at sixteen to enlist for bread—in all this, as there is nothing at all amusing, we conclude that the author could have no reason to detain us with such particulars but simply because they were true. To invent, when nothing at all is gained by inventing, there seems no imaginable temptation. It never occurs to us that this very construction of the case, this very inference from such neutral details, was precisely the object which De Foe had in view— was the very thing which he counted on, and by which he meant to profit. He thus gains the opportunity of impressing upon his tales a double character: he makes them so amusing that girls read them for novels; and he gives them such an air of verisimilitude that men read them for histories.—THOMAS DE QUINCEY, "Homer and the Homeridae" (1841), *Collected Writings*, ed. David Masson, Vol. 6, pp. 84–85

Of *Robinson Crusoe* it is needless to speak. Was there ever any thing written by mere man but this, asked Doctor Johnson, that was wished longer by its readers? It is a standard Piece in every European language; its popularity has extended to every civilized nation. The traveller Burckhardt found it translated into Arabic, and heard it read aloud among the Arabs in the cool hours of evening. It is devoured by every boy; and, as long as a boy exists, he will clamour for *Robinson Crusoe*. It sinks into the bosom, while the bosom is most capable of pleasurable impressions from the adventurous and the marvellous. It is not, perhaps, too much to say, that neither the *Iliad* nor the *Odyssey*, in the much longer course of ages, has incited so many to enterprise, or to reliance on their own powers and capacities. We need scarcely repeat, what has been said so well by many critics, that the secret of its fascination is its Reality. The same is to be said, in a no less degree, of the *History of the Plague*; which, for the grandeur of the theme, and the profoundly affecting familiarity of its treatment, is one of the noblest prose epics of the language. These are the masterpieces of De Foe. But, while open to objections on another score, the *Moll Flanders*, the *Colonel Jack*, and the *Roxana*, are not less decisive examples of a wonderful genius. In their day, too, they had no unwise or hurtful effect. They had a tendency to produce a more indulgent morality, and larger fair play to all. But we question the wisdom of now reviving them as they were written, we will frankly confess. As models of fictitious narrative, in common with all the writings of De Foe, they are supreme; the art of natural story-telling has had no such astonishing illustrations. High authorities have indeed thought them entitled to still higher dignity. Some one asked Doctor Robertson to advise him as to a good historical style. 'Read De Foe,' replied the great historian. Colonel Jack's life has been commonly reprinted in the genuine accounts of Highwaymen; Lord Chatham thought the Cavalier a real person, and his description of the Civil Wars the best in the language; Doctor Mead quoted the book of the Plague as the narrative of an eyewitness; and Doctor Johnson sat up all night over Captain Carleton's Memoirs, as a new work of English history he wondered not to have seen before. In particular scenes, too, of the three tales we are more immediately considering, (those of the Prison in *Moll Flanders*, of Susannah in *Roxana*, and of the Boyhood in *Colonel Jack*,) the highest masters of prose fiction have never surpassed them. But it will remain the chief distinction of De Foe, in these minor tales of English life, to have been the father of the illustrious family of the English Novel. Swift directly copied from him; Richardson founded his style of minute narrative wholly upon him; Fielding, Smollett, and Goldsmith, Godwin, Scott, and Dickens, have been more or less indebted to him. Shall we scruple to add, then, that while he remains unapproached in his two great masterpieces, he has been surpassed in his minor works by these his successors? His language is as easy and copious, but less elegant and harmonious; his insight into character is as penetrating, but

not so penetrating into the heart; his wit and irony are as playful, but his humour is less genial and expansive; and he wants the delicate fancy, the richness of imagery, the sympathy, the pathos, which will keep the later Masters of our English Novel the delightful companions, the gentle monitors, the welcome instructors, of future generations. So true it is, that every great writer promotes the next great writer one step; and in some cases gets himself superseded by him. —JOHN FORSTER, "Daniel De Foe," *Edinburgh Review*, Oct. 1845, pp. 530–31

He was a very honest man, and very good at conceiving matters of fact; but it is curious to see how impossible he finds it, even in a fiction, to present any thing to his imagination which does not come palpably home to a man's worldly or other-worldly interest and importance; and how fond he is, whether alone or in company, of being all in all; of playing the "monarch of all he surveys," and dictating people's religion and politics to them the moment he catches a listener. He was the prose half of as inventive a genius as ever existed: and his footstep on the sea-shore has left its mark within the borders of the greatest poetry; but it originated, so to speak, in the same intense spirit of self-reference. It was the one isolated Robinson Crusoe reflected by some one other tremendous individual, come to contest with him his safety and his independence. The abstract idea of a multitude followed it; but what would their presence have been in comparison? What would a thousand footsteps have been? The face of things would have been changed at once, and Crusoe's face have no longer matched it. All the savages afterwards never tread out that footmark: nor does Crusoe allow them to remain, and run the chance of it.

It is observable, that De Foe never invented a hero to write about greater than himself; while, at the same time, he willingly recorded such as were inferior. No rogue or vagabond came amiss to him, any more than a mariner or a merchant. And it is curious to consider how heartily such a minute dealer in matter of fact could set about telling a lie;—at least what a deliberate and successful one he told about the "Ghost of Mrs. Veal"; a long-credited fiction which he invented at the request of a bookseller, in order to sell a devout publication. His *History of the Plague* was long considered equally true, and reaped a like success. But the fact is, it is a mistake to suppose De Foe a lover of truth in any other sense than that of a workman's love for his tools, or for any other purpose than that of a masterly use of it, and a consciousness of the mastery. We do not mean to dispute his veracity between man and man: though his peculiar genius may not have been without its recommendation of him to that secret government agency in which he was at one time employed under his hero, William the Third. But the singularly material and mechanical nature of that genius, great as it was, while it hindered him from missing no impressions which could be made personally on himself as a creature of flesh and blood, kept him unembarrassed with any of the more perplexing truths suggested by too much thought and by imaginations poetical; and hence it is, that defect itself conspired to perfect and keep clear his astonishing impress of matter of fact, and render him an object of admiration, great, but not of an exalted kind. De Foe was in one respect as unvulgar a man as can be conceived; nobody but Swift could have surpassed him in such a work as *Robinson Crusoe*; yet we cannot conceal from ourselves, that something vulgar adheres to our idea of the author of *Moll Flanders*, the *Complete English Tradesman*, and even of *Robinson* himself. He has no music, no thorough style, no accomplishments, no love; but he can make wonderful shift without them all; was great in the company of man Friday; and he has rendered his shipwrecked solitary immortal.—LEIGH HUNT, *A Book for a Corner*, 1849

If Swift, in his fictions, is the satirist of his age, Defoe, in most of his, is its chronicler or newspaper-reporter. He had been well beaten about in his life, and had been in many occupations—a hosier, a tile-maker, a dealer in wool; he had travelled abroad and in Scotland; and he was probably as familiar with the middle and lower strata of London society as any man living. He had been in prison and in the pillory, and knew the very face of the mob and ragamuffinism in its haunts. Hence, although he too had been a political pamphleteer, and had written with a blunt, straightforward energy, and even with a sarcastic irony, in the cause of liberty and Whiggism, yet, when he betook himself to concocting stories, the sale of which might bring him in more money than he could earn as a journalist, he was content to make them plain narrations, or little more. In the main, as all know, he drew upon his knowledge of low English life, framing imaginary histories of thieves, courtesans, buccaneers, and the like, of a kind to suit a coarse, popular taste. He was a great reader, and a tolerable scholar, and he may have taken the hint of his method from the Spanish picaresque Novel, as Swift adopted his from Rabelais. On the whole, however, it was his own robust sense of reality that led him to his style. There is none of the sly humour of the foreign picaresque Novel in his representations of English ragamuffin life; there is nothing of allegory, poetry, or even of didactic purpose; all is hard, prosaic, and matter-of-fact, as in newspaper paragraphs, or the pages of the Newgate Calendar. Much of his material, indeed, may have been furnished by his recollections of occurrences, or by actual reports and registers; but it is evident that no man ever possessed a stronger imagination of that kind which, a situation being once conceived, teems with circumstances in exact keeping with it. When the ghost of Mrs. Veal appears to Mrs. Bargrave, at Canterbury, it is in "a scoured silk newly made up;" and when, after chatting with Mrs. Bargrave, and recommending to her Drelincourt's Book on Death, the ghost takes her leave of the worthy woman, who has been quite unconscious all the time of the disembodied nature of her visitor, it is at Mrs. Bargrave's door, "in the street, in the face of the beast-market, on, a Saturday, being market-day at Canterbury, at three-quarters after one in the afternoon." This minuteness of imagined circumstance and filling up, this power of fiction in facsimile of nature, is Defoe's unfailing characteristic. Lord Chatham is said to have taken the *History of a Cavalier* for a true biography; and the *Account of the Plague of London* is still read by many under a similar delusion. There is no doubt that these, as well as the fictions laid more closely in the author's own time, are, for the purposes of historical instruction, as good as real. It is in the true spirit of a realist, also, that Defoe, though he is usually plain and prosaic, yet, when the facts to be reported are striking or horrible, rises easily to their level. His description of London during the Plague leaves an impression of desolation far more death-like and dismal than the similar descriptions in Thucydides, Boccaccio, and Manzoni. It is a happy accident, too, that the subject of one of his fictions, and that the earliest on a great scale, was of a kind in treating which his genius in matter of fact necessarily produced the effect of a poem. The conception of a solitary mariner thrown on an uninhabited island was one as really belonging to the fact of that time as those which formed the subject of Defoe's less-read fictions of coarse English life. Dampier and the Buccaneers were roving the South Seas; and there yet remained parts of the

land-surface of the earth of which man had not taken possession, and on which sailors were occasionally thrown adrift by the brutality of captains. Seizing this text, more especially as offered in the story of Alexander Selkirk, Defoe's matchless power of inventing circumstantial incidents made him more a master even of its poetic capabilities than the rarest poet then living could have been; and now that, all round our globe, there is not an unknown island left, we still reserve in our mental charts one such island, with the sea breaking round it, and we would part any day with ten of the heroes of antiquity rather than with Robinson Crusoe and his man Friday.
—DAVID MASSON, *British Novelists and Their Styles*, 1859, pp. 95–98

However we regard his life, we see only prolonged efforts and persecutions. Joy seems to be wanting; the idea of the beautiful never enter. When he comes to fiction, it is like a Presbyterian and a plebeian, with low subjects and moral aims, to treat of the adventures and reform the conduct of thieves and prostitutes, workmen and sailors. His whole delight was to think that he had a service to perform, and that he was performing it:

> He that opposes his own judgment against the current of the times ought to be backed with unanswerable truth; and he that has truth on his side, is a fool as well as a coward, if he is afraid to own it, because of the multitude of other men's opinions. 'Tis hard for a man to say, all the world is mistaken, but himself. But if it be so, who can help it?

De Foe is like one of those brave, obscure, and useful soldiers who, with empty belly and burdened shoulders, go through their duties with their feet in the mud, pocket blows, receive day by day the fire of the enemy, and sometimes that of their friends into the bargain, and die sergeants, happy if it has been their lot to get hold of the legion of honor.

He had the kind of mind suitable to such a hard service, solid, exact, entirely destitute of refinement, enthusiasm, pleasantness. His imagination was that of a man of business, not of an artist, crammed and, as it were, jammed down with facts. He tells them as they come to him, without arrangement or style, like a conversation, without dreaming of producing an effect or composing a phrase, employing technical terms and vulgar forms, repeating himself at need, using the same thing two or three times, not seeming to suspect that there are methods of amusing, touching, engrossing, or pleasing, with no desire but to pour out on paper the fulness of the information with which he is charged. Even in fiction his information is as precise as in history. He gives dates, year, month, and day; notes the wind, north-east, south-west, north-west; he writes a log book, an invoice, attorneys' and shopkeepers' bills, the number of moidores, interest, specie payments, payments in kind, cost and sale prices, the share of the king, of religious houses, partners, brokers, net totals, statistics, the geography and hydrography of the island, so that the reader is tempted to take an atlas and draw for himself a little map of the place, to enter into all the details of the history as clearly and fully as the author. It seems as though he had performed all Crusoe's labors, so exactly does he describe them, with numbers, quantities, dimensions, like a carpenter, potter, or an old tar. Never was such a sense of the real before or since. Our realists of to-day, painters, anatomists, decidedly men of business, are very far from this naturalness; art and calculation crop out amidst their too minute descriptions. De Foe creates illusion; for it is not the eye which deceives us, but the mind, and that literally: his account of the great plague has more than once passed for true; and Lord Chatham took his

Memoirs of a Cavalier for authentic. This was his aim, In the preface to the old edition of *Robinson Crusoe*, it is said:

> The story is told . . . to the instruction of others by this example, and to justify and honor the wisdom of Providence. The editor believes the thing to be a just history of facts; neither is there any appearance of fiction in it.

All his talents lie in this, and thus even his imperfections aid him; his lack of art becomes a profound art; his negligence, repetitions, prolixity, contribute to the illusion: we cannot imagine that such and such a detail, so minute, so dull, is invented; an inventor would have suppressed it; it is too tedious to have been put in on purpose: art chooses, embellishes, interests; art, therefore, cannot have piled up this heap of dull and vulgar accidents; it is the truth.—HIPPOLYTE TAINE, *History of English Literature*, tr. H. Van Laun, 1871, Bk. 3, Ch. 6

The aims in life of Defoe's thieves and pirates are at bottom very little different from the ambition which he undertakes to direct in the *Complete English Tradesman*, and their maxims of conduct have much in common with this ideal. Self-interest is on the look-out, and Self-reliance at the helm.

> A tradesman behind his counter must have no flesh and blood about him, no passions, no resentment; he must never be angry—no, not so much as seem to be so, if a customer tumbles him five hundred pounds' worth of goods, and scarce bids money for anything; nay, though they really come to his shop with no intent to buy, as many do, only to see what is to be sold, and though he knows they cannot be better pleased than they are at some other shop where they intend to buy, 'tis all one; the tradesman must take it, he must place it to the account of his calling, that 'tis his business to be ill-used, and resent nothing; and so must answer as obligingly to those who give him an hour or two's trouble, and buy nothing, as he does to those who, in half the time, lay out ten or twenty pounds. The case is plain; and if some do give him trouble, and do not buy, others make amends and do buy; and as for the trouble, 'tis the business of the shop.

All Defoe's heroes and heroines are animated by this practical spirit, this thoroughgoing subordination of means to ends. When they have an end in view, the plunder of a house, the capture of a ship, the ensnaring of a dupe, they allow neither passion, nor resentment, nor sentiment in any shape or form to stand in their way. Every other consideration is put on one side when the business of the shop has to be attended to. They are all tradesmen who have strayed into unlawful courses. They have nothing about them of the heroism of sin; their crimes are not the result of ungovernable passion, or even of antipathy to conventional restraints; circumstances and not any law-defying bias of disposition have made them criminals. How is it that the novelist contrives to make them so interesting? Is it because we are a nation of shopkeepers, and enjoy following lines of business which are a little out of our ordinary routine? Or is it simply that he makes us enjoy their courage and cleverness without thinking of the purposes with which these qualities are displayed? Defoe takes such delight in tracing their bold expedients, their dexterous intriguing and manœuvring, that he seldom allows us to think of anything but the success or failure of their enterprises. Our attention is concentrated on the game, and we pay no heed for the moment to the players or the stakes. Charles Lamb says of *The Complete English Tradesman* that "such is the bent of the book

to narrow and to degrade the heart, that if such maxims were as catching and infectious as those of a licentious cast, which happily is not the case, had I been living at that time, I certainly should have recommended to the grand jury of Middlesex, who presented *The Fable of the Bees*, to have presented this book of Defoe's in preference, as of a far more vile and debasing tendency." Yet if Defoe had thrown the substance of this book into the form of a novel, and shown us a tradesman rising by the sedulous practice of its maxims from errand-boy to gigantic capitalist, it would have been hardly less interesting than his lives of successful thieves and tolerably successful harlots, and its interest would have been very much of the same kind, the interest of dexterous adaptation of means to ends.—WILLIAM MINTO, *Daniel Defoe*, 1879, pp. 152–54

Defoe is one of the most voluminous of English writers. During a long life his pen was scarcely ever out of his hand. A complete edition of his works has never yet been, and, the ephemeral interest of many of them considered, is scarcely ever likely to be published; nor probably, for all the industry of Mr. William Lee and others, has a complete list of them yet been made out, so much that he wrote being anonymous. Some years ago some 210 books and pamphlets could be plausibly assigned to his authorship. Such immense practice gave him a wonderful facility of style. Probably from the beginning he wrote with little effort. Certainly—later in life he wrote as readily as he thought. He expressed whatever ideas came into his mind—and his mind was never idle—with the utmost ease and fluency. He formed the habit of thinking aloud, so to speak, of thinking in a printable way; that is, it became as natural to him to write as to think. His thoughts took at once a literary, at least a journalistic shape.

Of matter there was never any lack. He was a man of endless curiosities and interests. He might truly say that for him *nihil humanum*, or even *nihil mundanum*, was *alienum*. He lived in a time of innumerable and pauseless controversies. And there were few of these in which he did not take part. His brain was singularly active and fecund. He had his own views upon all the current questions, and he was eager and resolute to say his say about them. And many questions he himself started, and urged upon his age with characteristic pertinacity and vigour. He was an indefatigable journalist, and struck out new lines in journalism, so that he has left a permanent impression upon our periodical press. The leading article may be said to be one of his creations, or a development of one of them. He was a trenchant pamphleteer, and twice received from the government the painful compliment of imprisonment for his brilliant success in that department. In the fierce clamours of his time one may incessantly—one might almost say always—detect his voice, clear, irrepressible, effective.

Such incessant occupation with burning questions, and such amazing productiveness might well have prepared us to expect little or nothing of permanent literary value from Defoe. The shrewd remark that easy writing makes hard reading at once recurs to us. The man whose tongue is never quiet seldom utters anything worth hearing. The thoughts of him who perpetually thinks aloud are apt to be wanting in finish and in weight. The *calamus* that is always *currens* must surely run away with him who holds it, or tries to hold it. But all such criticisms must be applied with caution to the case of Defoe. He had in an eminent degree the gift of ready writing, and this gift he assiduously cultivated, so that to write, and what is more to write with success, was as easy to him as to speak. He never let his gift of ready writing prove his ruin. For usually men are betrayed and ruined by such facility. They cease to be the masters but become the mere slaves of it. They are confounded and confused by their own abundance. Defoe kept his gift well in hand. He never permitted himself to be merely self-confident and careless. Nor, after all, incessantly as he wrote, did he ever yield idly to the impulse to say something when in fact he had nothing to say.

But he never aimed at being a stylist in the ordinary sense of the term—at writing elaborately and with the idea of producing what was exquisite in form and expression for its own sake or partly for its own sake. He had no æsthetic purpose; but was always eminently earnest and practical and didactic, a man of affairs and of business. His great object was to speak clearly and forcibly, not to turn out sentences of fine rhythm and choice phrasing. What he specially studied was directness and cogency. For the most part, till the last dozen years of his life, he dealt merely with the questions of the day; he addressed an audience that was excited and inflamed, on which any elegancies of style would have been wholly wasted. Thus for any ornamenting of his weapon, to speak metaphorically, he cared little or nothing; his one supreme care was that it should be trenchant—that it should do its work and go home.

And few men have more completely succeeded in their aim than Defoe. He became a potent master of language, and made it do exactly his bidding, such as it was. To play with words—to group them in new and surprising and charming combinations (Horace's *callidæ juncturæ*), to place them in novel situations and bring out unrecognised graces—this was not at all his way, not at all his end. Language was with him a mere instrument of expression, not in itself a thing of beauty with claims of its own for consideration. It was his slave rather than his mistress.

But it would be a great misuse of terms to say that Defoe was no artist. Rather within his limits he was an admirable and a most successful artist. He produced precisely the effects he wished to produce; and used always his material with singular judgment and skill. We may feel his world of thought somewhat narrow, and, as we enter it, may be keenly aware that there are more things in heaven and earth—so many more!—than are dreamt of in his philosophy; but in that world he is supreme. Thus no one has ever equalled Defoe in the art of literary deception, that is, in the art of making his own inventions pass for realities, in the art of "lying like truth": no one has ever so frequently and completely taken in his readers. Again and again his fictions have been cited as genuine and original records: from time to time even now is heard a doubt whether *The Memoirs of a Cavalier*, for instance, is not really a transcript of some seventeenth-century MS. It was once said that Defoe had in fact Alexander Selkirk's papers before him when he wrote *Robinson Crusoe*; but there is not the least shadow of support for that statement. It is undoubtedly baseless. This art of deception he evidently studied with infinite zest and care. *Populus vult decipi*, he might have said to himself, and perhaps did say, *et decipiatur*. In his actual life there was much dissembling and much simulation, however he reconciled his conduct with his conscience. In his novels he carried this art, such as it is, to the highest possible perfection. On internal evidence only it is often not possible to distinguish his fiction from fact. The imposition is absolute. Defoe is the arch deceiver of literature.

In his *Robinson Crusoe* this sovereign lord of illusion has given us one of the most popular books of the world. And here happily we have not only to admire the incomparable realism of the rendering, but to be grateful for a quite inestimable embodiment of a resolute and indomitable spirit, not to be crushed by any adversities, but making good out of bad—making the best out of the worst. Rousseau might well except it from the ban he pronounced on the literature commonly put into the hands of children. This is certainly Defoe's most important claim on our remembrance; it is in it that he still lives and moves and has his being amongst us. The author of such a book must for ever be held in high esteem as a friend of the human race.—JOHN W. HALES, "Defoe," *English Prose*, ed. Henry Craik, 1894, Vol. 3, pp. 356–59

Defoe, ⟨. . .⟩ like Le Sage, was a story-teller above all things; he had this precious faculty in the highest degree, and perhaps he had little else.—BRANDER MATTHEWS, "The Gift of Story-Telling," *Aspects of Fiction*, 1896, pp. 231–32

If Steele be the father of fiction, Defoe is the parent of journalism. Defoe, again, is no paragon. He was a struggling man of restless enterprise, who lived from hand to mouth—a manufacturer, a merchant adventurer, a reformer, and an author. He mastered every practical department except success. William had listened to his schemes of finance. A bankrupt himself, he projected bankruptcy reforms. In the days of the Second George he was still inditing manuals of trade. In Queen Anne's time he conducted the *Review*. It would be difficult to define his politics. He spied for Harley as he had spied for Godolphin. It would be difficult to define his creed. The indignant Dissenter who penned the "Legion" pamphlet was the same who assured Harley, "Nay, even the Dissenters, like Casha (*sic*) to Cæsar, lift up the first dagger at me. I confess it makes me reflect on the whole body of the Dissenters with something of contempt." The informer against Sacheverell to the Whigs was the same who, in the autumn of 1710, "was concerned to see people spread the grossest absurdities, by which they would make their disgusts at the late changes appear rational." But, with all inconsistencies, he was a patriot and a reformer. By perpetual projects of improvement, by a voluminous trick of emphatic expansion which suited his audience, he appealed to the *bourgeoisie* and the artisan. That religion should be real, that law should be simplified, that commerce should walk honest and erect, he wrestled like a giant and roared like a Stentor. His newspaper differed from the lucubrations of the Tory Roper and Leslie or the Whig Ridpath and Tutchin, from the *Postboy* or the *Flying Post*, from the mere News Letters of Boyer, from the *Observator* or the *Rehearsal*, much more than these did from the surviving *Daily Courant* or the obsolete *Mercuries*. It was a broad sheet full of sense and suggestion, over-ambitious rather than unpresuming. A Democrat, he was also an Imperialist; an anti-Churchman, he abhorred fanaticism. A man of the people, he invented a kinship with the De Beauforts of Warwick, and smacks his lips over the ducal glories of Canons. With a vivid speed of graphic presentation he flutters off from scheme to scheme and from criticism to criticism. Himself our first actual, though too often our dreariest novelist, he, in fiction as in journalism, was long-winded, and never knew when to pause. He was inartistic; he was devoid alike of sentiment, tact, or elegance; but he could scent and stimulate the national feeling; he could prick and strengthen the national conscience. His industry is without parallel. Whether roaming at will across England or ferreting for the Government in Scotland, whether dealing in wine or exploiting pottery, or improving manufactures, or inveighing against abuses, or propounding heroic remedies, the pen was always in his hands and the ledger always on his desk. He, like Dickens, travelled for the great "Firm of Human Interest Brothers."—WALTER SICHEL, *Bolingbroke and His Times*, 1901, Vol. 1, pp. 120–21

Works

THE REVIEW

As to our Weekly Papers, the Poor *Review* is quite exhausted, and grown so very Contemptible, that tho' he has provoked all his Brothers of the Quill round, none of them will enter into a Controversy with him. This Fellow, who had excellent Natural Parts, but wanted a small Foundation of Learning, is a lively instance of those Wits, who, as an Ingenious Author says, will endure but one Skimming.—JOHN GAY, "The Present State of Wit," 1711

One of the leading objects of the *Review*, after the discussion of politics, was to correct the vices of the times. Throughout the work, the writer carries on an unsparing warfare against folly and vice, in all their forms and disguises. In forcible terms he inveighs against the fashionable practice of immoderate drinking, the idle propensity to swearing, the little regard that was paid to the marriage vow, and the loose conversation and habits of men in general. In well-pointed satire, he chastises the licentiousness of the stage; and condemns, in strong language, the barbarous practice of duelling. He has also some just remarks upon the rage for gambling speculations, which, in this reign, had risen to a great height. Upon all these subjects, he brings forth his capacious stores of wit and humour to the assistance of grave reasoning, adducing examples occasionally of the flagitious courses he condemns; but with sufficient delicacy to shew that his aim was the reformation, rather than the exposure, of the offender. No man paid a greater regard to those decencies of expression which have so much influence in regulating the intercourses of life; and although few individuals had greater provocation, from the coarse and illiberal writers of the day, yet he rarely suffers his temper to be disturbed, or departs from courtesy of language towards even his bitterest opponents.—WALTER WILSON, *Memoirs of the Life and Times of Daniel De Foe*, 1830, Vol. 2, p. 201

A reason for the rarity of *The Review* becomes obvious to any one who reads or even glances over the complete copy in the British Museum. *The Review* found its way to the uses of waste-paper as worthless in literature. Brilliant passages are to be found in it by one who searches for them, and the conclusion naturally reached during the search is, that Defoe contributed these, and the rest was supplied by some dreary compiler. But it is awkward to hold by this theory in the face of repeated assurances that all is written by Defoe himself. There is another possible theory of the imperfections of the work. Defoe had gained a reputation that secured a wide and rapid sale for anything that bore his name. Apollo's bow is not always bent, and the divine Homer sometimes nods. So it was that Defoe, with something like a suspension of intellectual animation, could write what is colloquially called "twaddle" as fast as his pen could be driven over the paper; and that he so wrote, and sold what he wrote, because he wanted money. —JOHN HILL BURTON, *A History of the Reign of Queen Anne*, 1880, Vol. 3, pp. 95–96

ROBINSON CRUSOE

If ever the Story of any private Man's Adventures in the World were worth making Publick, and were acceptable when Publish'd, the Editor of this Account thinks this will be so.

The Wonders of this Man's Life exceed all that (he thinks) is to be found extant; the Life of one Man being scarce capable of a greater Variety.

The Story is told with Modesty, with Seriousness, and with a religious Application of Events to the Uses to which wise Men always apply them *(viz.)* to the Instruction of others by this Example, and to justify and honour the Wisdom of Providence in all the Variety of our Circumstances, let them happen how they will.

The Editor believes the thing to be a just History of Fact; neither is there any Appearance of Fiction in it: And however thinks, because all such things are dispatch'd, that the Improvement of it, as well to the Diversion, as to the Instruction of the Reader, will be the same; and as such, he thinks, without farther Compliment to the World, he does them a great Service in the Publication.—DANIEL DEFOE, "Preface" to *The Life and Strange Surprizing Adventures of Robinson Crusoe, of York, Mariner*, 1719

We may remember that we have been most of us, when Children, wonderfully pleased with the achievements of *Tom Thumb*, *Jack the Giant-Killer*, *Don Bellianis of Greece*, *The Seven Champions of Christendom*, and such like extraordinary Heroes; and many of us, in our more advanced Age, are little less delighted with such Books as *The Life and Adventures of Robinson Crusoe*; which seems to have had that uncommon Run upon the Town for some Years past, for no other Reason but that it is a *most palpable Lye*, from Beginning to End; and I doubt not that the famous Passage of his *Swimming to Shore* Naked, *with his* Pockets *full of Biscuits*, tho' a most notorious *Blunder* in the Author, has pass'd for a very good Jest, and been received with abundance of Pleasure by many of his Readers.—BENJAMIN HOADLY, *London Journal*, Sept. 4, 1725

Since we must have books, there is one which, to my mind, furnishes the finest of treatises on education according to nature. My Émile shall read this book before any other; it shall for a long time be his entire library, and shall always hold an honorable place. It shall be the text on which all our discussions of natural science shall be only commentaries. It shall be a test for all we meet during our progress toward a ripened judgment, and so long as our taste is unspoiled, we shall enjoy reading it. What wonderful book is this? Aristotle? Pliny? Buffon? No; it is *Robinson Crusoe*.—JEAN JACQUES ROUSSEAU, *Émile*, 1762

Robinson Crusoe must be allowed, by the most rigid moralists, to be one of those novels which one may read, not only with pleasure, but also with profit. It breathes throughout a spirit of piety and benevolence; it sets in a very striking light ⟨. . .⟩ the importance of the mechanic arts, which they, who know not what it is to be without them, are apt to undervalue: it fixes in the mind a lively idea of the horrors of solitude, and, consequently, of the sweets of social life, and of the blessings we derive from conversation and mutual aid; and it shows, how, by labouring with one's own hands, one may secure independence, and open for one's self many sources of health and amusement. I agree, therefore, with Rousseau, that this is one of the best books that can be put in the hands of children. —JAMES BEATTIE, *Dissertations Moral and Critical*, 1783

No fiction, in any language, was ever better supported than the *Adventures of Robinson Crusoe*. While it is carried on with that appearance of truth and simplicity, which takes a strong hold of the imagination of all Readers, it suggests, at the same time, very useful instruction; by showing how much the native powers of man may be exerted for surmounting the difficulties of any external situation.—HUGH BLAIR, *Lectures on Rhetoric and Belles Lettres*, 1783, Lecture 37

"Alas, Madam! (continued ⟨Johnson⟩) how few books are there

of which one ever can possibly arrive at the *last* page! Was there ever yet any thing written by mere man that was wished longer by its readers, excepting *Don Quixote, Robinson Crusoe,* and the *Pilgrim's Progress?*"—HESTER LYNCH PIOZZI, *Anecdotes of the Late Samuel Johnson,* 1786

The charm of De Foe's works, especially of *Robinson Crusoe,* is founded on the same principle. It always interests, never agitates. Crusoe himself is merely a representative of humanity in general; neither his intellectual nor his moral qualities set him above the middle degree of mankind; his only prominent characteristic is the spirit of enterprise and wandering, which is, nevertheless, a very common disposition. You will observe that all that is wonderful in this tale is the result of external circumstances—of things which fortune brings to Crusoe's hand.—SAMUEL TAYLOR COLERIDGE, *A Course of Lectures* (1818), *Literary Remains,* ed. Henry Nelson Coleridge, 1836, Vol. 1, p. 189

The progress of a nation from barbarism to civilisation produces a change similar to that which takes place during the progress of an individual from infancy to mature age. What man does not remember with regret the first time that he read *Robinson Crusoe?* Then, indeed, he was unable to appreciate the powers of the writer; or, rather, he neither knew nor cared whether the book had a writer at all. He probably thought it not half so fine as some rant of Macpherson about dark-browed Foldath, and white-bosomed Strinadona. He now values Fingal and Temora only as showing with how little evidence a story may be believed, and with how little merit a book may be popular. Of the romance of Defoe he entertains the highest opinion. He perceives the hand of a master in ten thousand touches which formerly he passed by without notice. But, though he understands the merits of the narrative better than formerly, he is far less interested by it. Xury and Friday, and pretty Poll, the boat with the shoulder-of-mutton sail, and the canoe which could not be brought down to the water edge, the tent with its hedge and ladders, the preserve of kids, and the den where the old goat died, can never again be to him the realities which they were. The days when his favourite volume set him upon making wheel-barrows and chairs, upon digging caves and fencing huts in the garden, can never return. Such is the law of our nature. Our judgment ripens; our imagination decays. We cannot at once enjoy the flowers of the spring of life and the fruits of its autumn, the pleasures of close investigation and those of agreeable error. We cannot sit at once in the front of the stage and behind the scenes. We cannot be under the illusion of the spectacle, while we are watching the movements of the ropes and pulleys which dispose it.—THOMAS BABINGTON MACAULAY, "John Dryden" (1828), *Critical, Historical, and Miscellaneous Essays,* 1860, Vol. 1, pp. 331–32

One excellence of De Foe, amongst many, is his sacrifice of lesser interest to the greater because more universal. Had he (as without any improbability he might have done) given his Robinson Crusoe any of the turn for natural history, which forms so striking and delightful a feature in the equally uneducated Dampier;—had he made him find out qualities and uses in the before (to him) unknown plants of the island, discover, for instance, a substitute for hops, or describe birds, &c.—many delightful pages and incidents might have enriched the book;—but then Crusoe would have ceased to be the universal representative, the person, for whom every reader could substitute himself. But now nothing is done, thought, suffered, or desired, but what every man can imagine himself doing, thinking, feeling, or wishing for. Even so very easy a problem as that of finding a substitute for ink, is with exquisite judgment made to baffle Crusoe's inventive faculties. And in what he does, he arrives at no excellence; he does not make basket work like Will Atkins; the carpentering, tailoring, pottery, &c. are all just what will answer his purposes, and those are confined to needs that all men have, and comforts that all men desire. Crusoe rises only to the point to which all men may be made to feel that they might, and that they ought to, rise in religion,—to resignation, dependence on, and thankful acknowledgment of, the divine mercy and goodness.—SAMUEL TAYLOR COLERIDGE, "Notes on *Robinson Crusoe*" (1830), *Literary Remains,* ed. Henry Nelson Coleridge, 1836, Vol. 1, pp. 196–97

I now took up the third book. It did not resemble the others, being longer and considerably thicker; the binding was of dingy calf-skin. I opened it, and as I did so another strange thrill of pleasure shot through my frame. The first object on which my eyes rested was a picture; it was exceedingly well executed, at least the scene which it represented made a vivid impression upon me, which would hardly have been the case had the artist not been faithful to nature. A wild scene it was—a heavy sea and rocky shore, with mountains in the background, above which the moon was peering. Not far from the shore, upon the water, was a boat with two figures in it, one of which stood at the bow, pointing with what I knew to be a gun at a dreadful shape in the water; fire was flashing from the muzzle of the gun, and the monster appeared to be transfixed. I almost thought I heard its cry. I remained motionless, gazing upon the picture, scarcely daring to draw my breath, lest the new and wondrous world should vanish of which I had now obtained a glimpse. "Who are those people, and what could have brought them into that strange situation?" I asked of myself; and now the seed of curiosity, which had so long lain dormant, began to expand, and I vowed to myself to become speedily acquainted with the whole history of the people in the boat. After looking on the picture till every mark and line in it were familiar to me, I turned over various leaves till I came to another engraving; a new source of wonder—a low sandy beach on which the furious sea was breaking in mountain-like billows; cloud and rack deformed the firmament, which wore a dull and leaden-like hue; gulls and other aquatic fowls were toppling upon the blast, or skimming over the tops of the maddening waves—"Mercy upon him! he must be drowned!" I exclaimed, as my eyes fell upon a poor wretch who appeared to be striving to reach the shore; he was upon his legs but was evidently half-smothered with the brine; high above his head curled a horrible billow, as if to engulf him for ever. "He must be drowned! he must be drowned!" I almost shrieked, and dropped the book. I soon snatched it up again, and now my eye lighted on a third picture: again a shore, but what a sweet and lovely one, and how I wished to be treading it; there were beautiful shells lying on the smooth white sand, some were empty like those I had occasionally seen on marble mantelpieces, but out of others peered the heads and bodies of wondrous crayfish; a wood of thick green trees skirted the beach and partly shaded it from the rays of the sun, which shone hot above, while blue waves slightly crested with foam were gently curling against it; there was a human figure upon the beach, wild and uncouth, clad in the skins of animals, with a huge cap on his head, a hatchet at his girdle, and in his hand a gun; his feet and legs were bare; he stood in an attitude of horror and surprise; his body was bent far back, and his eyes, which seemed starting out of his head, were fixed upon a mark on the sand—a large distinct mark—a human footprint!

Reader, is it necessary to name the book which now stood open in my hand, and whose very prints, feeble expounders of its wondrous lines, had produced within me emotions strange and novel? Scarcely, for it was a book which has exerted over the minds of Englishmen an influence certainly greater than any other of modern times, which has been in most people's hands, and with the contents of which even those who cannot read are to a certain extent acquainted; a book from which the most luxuriant and fertile of our modern prose writers have drunk inspiration; a book, moreover, to which, from the hardy deeds which it narrates, and the spirit of strange and romantic enterprise which it tends to awaken, England owes many of her astonishing discoveries both by sea and land, and no inconsiderable part of her naval glory.

Hail to thee, spirit of De Foe! What does not my own poor self owe to thee? England has better bards than either Greece or Rome, yet I could spare them easier far than De Foe, "unabashed De Foe," as the hunchbacked rhymer styled him.

The true chord had now been touched. A raging curiosity with respect to the contents of the volume, whose engravings had fascinated my eye, burned within me, and I never rested until I had fully satisfied it. Weeks succeeded weeks, months followed months, and the wondrous volume was my only study and principal source of amusement. For hours together I would sit poring over a page till I had become acquainted with the import of every line. My progress, slow enough at first, became by degrees more rapid, till at last, under "a shoulder of mutton sail," I found myself cantering before a steady breeze over an ocean of enchantment, so well pleased with my voyage that I cared not how long it might be ere it reached its termination.

And it was in this manner that I first took to the paths of knowledge.—GEORGE BORROW, *Lavengro*, 1851, Ch. 3

Since Robinson Crusoe's experiences are a favorite theme with political economists, let us take a look at him on his island. Moderate though he be, yet some few wants he has to satisfy, and must therefore do a little useful work of various sorts, such as making tools and furniture, taming goats, fishing and hunting. Of his prayers and the like we take no account, since they are a source of pleasure to him, and he looks upon them as so much recreation. In spite of the variety of his work, he knows that his labour, whatever its form, is but the activity of one and the same Robinson, and consequently, that it consists of nothing but different modes of human labour. Necessity itself compels him to apportion his time accurately between his different kinds of work. Whether one kind occupies a greater space in his general activity than another, depends on the difficulties, greater or less as the case may be, to be overcome in attaining the useful effect aimed at. This our friend Robinson soon learns by experience, and having rescued a watch, ledger, and pen and ink from the wreck, commences, like a true-born Briton, to keep a set of books. His stock-book contains a list of the objects of utility that belong to him, of the operations necessary for their production; and lastly, of the labour time that definite quantities of those objects have, on an average, cost him. All the relations between Robinson and the objects that form this wealth of his own creation, are here so simple and clear as to be intelligible without exertion, even to Mr. Sedley Taylor. And yet those relations contain all that is essential to the determination of value.

Let us now transport ourselves from Robinson's island bathed in light to the European middle ages shrouded in darkness. Here, instead of the independent man, we find everyone dependent, serfs and lords, vassals and suzerains, laymen and clergy. Personal dependence here characterises the social relations of production just as much as it does the other spheres of life organized on the basis of that production. But for the very reason that personal dependence forms the groundwork of society, there is no necessity for labour and its products to assume a fantastic form different from their reality. They take the shape, in the transactions of society, of services in kind and payments in kind. Here the particular and natural form of labour, and not, as in a society based on production of commodities, its general abstract form is the immediate social form of labour. Compulsory labour is just as properly measured by time, as commodity-producing labour; but every serf knows that what he expends in the service of his lord, is a definite quantity of his own personal labour-power. The tithe to be rendered to the priest is more matter of fact than his blessing. No matter, then, what we may think of the parts played by the different classes of people themselves in this society, the social relations between individuals in the performance of their labour, appear at all events as their own mutual personal relations, and are not disguised under the shape of social relations between the products of labour.

For an example of labour in common or directly associated labour, we have no occasion to go back to that spontaneously developed form which we find on the threshold of the history of all civilized races. We have one close at hand in the patriarchal industries of a peasant family, that produces corn, cattle, yarn, linen, and clothing for home use. These different articles are, as regards the family, so many products of its labour, but as between themselves, they are not commodities. The different kinds of labour, such as tillage, cattle tending, spinning, weaving and making clothes, which result in the various products, are in themselves, and such as they are, direct social functions, because functions of the family, which just as much as a society based on the production of commodities, possesses a spontaneously developed system of division of labour. The distribution of the work within the family, and the regulation of the labour-time of the several members, depend as well upon differences of age and sex as upon natural conditions varying with the seasons. The labour-power of each individual, by its very nature, operates in this case merely as a definite portion of the whole labour-power of the family, and therefore, the measure of the expenditure of individual labour-power by its duration, appears here by its very nature as a social character of their labour.

Let us now picture to ourselves, by way of change, a community of free individuals, carrying on their work with the means of production in common, in which the labour-power of all the different individuals is consciously applied as the combined labour-power of the community. All the characteristics of Robinson's labour are here repeated, but with this difference, that they are social, instead of individual. Everything produced by him was exclusively the result of his own personal labour, and therefore simply an object of use for himself. The total product of our community is a social product. One portion serves as fresh means of production and remains social. But another portion is consumed by the members as means of subsistence. A distribution of this portion amongst them is consequently necessary. The mode of this distribution will vary with the productive organization of the community, and the degree of historical development attained by the producers. We will assume, but merely for the sake of a parallel with the production of commodities, that the share of each individual producer in the means of subsistence is determined by his labour-time. Labour-time would, in that case, play a double part. Its apportionment in accordance with a definite social plan maintains the proper proportion between the different kinds of work to be done and the various wants of the community. On the other hand, it also serves as a measure of the portion of the common labour borne by each individual and of his share in the part of the total product destined for individual consumption. The social relations of the individual producers, with regard both to their labour and to its products, are in this case perfectly simple and intelligible, and that with regard not only to production but also to distribution.—KARL MARX, *Das Kapital*, 1867, Vol. 1, Pt. 1, Ch. 1, Sec. 4

When a boy I loved those books that other boys love, and I love them still. I well remember a little scene which took place when I was a child of eight or nine. *Robinson Crusoe* held me in his golden thrall, and I was expected to go to church. I hid beneath a bed with *Robinson Crusoe*, and was in due course discovered by an elder sister and a governess, who, on my refusing to come out, resorted to force. Then followed a struggle that was quite Homeric. The two ladies tugged as best they might, but I clung to *Crusoe* and the legs of the bed, and kicked till, perfectly exhausted, they took their departure in no very Christian frame of mind, leaving me panting, indeed, but triumphant.—H. RIDER HAGGARD, *Books Which Have Influenced Me*, 1887, p. 66

No theory as to children's books would be worth much attention which found itself obliged to exclude that memorable work. Although it submits in a certain measure to classification, it is almost *sui generis*; no book of its kind, approaching it in merit, has ever been written. In what, then, does its fascination consist? There is certainly nothing hermetic about it; it is the simplest and most studiously matter-of-fact narrative of events, comprehensible without the slightest effort, and having no meaning that is not apparent on the face of it. And yet children, and grown people also, read it again and again, and cannot find it uninteresting. I think the phenomenon may largely be due to the nature of the subject, which is really of primary and universal interest to mankind. It is the story of the struggle of man with wild and hostile nature,—in the larger sense an elementary theme,—his shifts, his failures, his perils, his fears, his hopes, his successes. The character of Robinson is so artfully generalized or universalized, and sympathy for him is so powerfully aroused and maintained, that the reader, especially the child reader, inevitably identifies himself with him, and feels his emotions and struggles as his own. The ingredient of suspense is never absent from the story, and the absence of any plot prevents us from perceiving its artificiality. It is, in fact, a type of the history of the human race, not on the higher plane, but on the physical one; the history of man's contest with and final victory over physical nature. The very simplicity and obviousness of the details give them grandeur and comprehensiveness: no part of man's character which his contact with nature can affect or develop is left untried in Robinson. He manifests in little all historical earthly experiences of the race; such is the scheme of the book; and its permanence in literature is due to the sobriety and veracity with which that scheme is carried out. To speak succinctly, it does for the body what the hermetic and cognate literature does for the soul; and for the healthy man, the body is not less important than the soul in its own place and degree. It is not the work of the Creator, but it is contingent upon creation.—JULIAN HAWTHORNE, "Literature for Children," *Confessions and Criticisms*, 1887, pp. 122–24

Defoe's prominence in my mind is based upon his ability to transmute a fictional narrative into a record of facts; things which might have been became, in his hands, things which actually were. But it is to the story itself that his supremacy as a fictional writer is confined; it does not extend to his personages. It is in the relation of a story, not in the delineation of character, that this great author excels.

Robinson Crusoe himself is not a very interesting personage. We believe in him, but we do not care very much for him. We may not concur in the opinion of the old sea captain and think him a fool, but we must admit that he very often failed to make good use of his exceptional opportunities. He was extremely commonplace in the most extraordinary situation. As to the man Friday, he could have been done as well by Mungo Park. Had the worthy ex-cannibal been less melodramatic, though quite as faithful, he might have possessed a stronger personal interest. The merchants, the pirates, the natives, the English, and the Spaniards of the story could all have held their place in literature, and perhaps a better place, without the aid of Daniel Defoe, but without Defoe there could never have been the immortal story.

To reduce romance to realism without depriving the former of any of its charms was the example set by Defoe to the writers of English fiction. His characters, his situations, his incidents, his material, and his machinery have all been surpassed, but his story telling never.

It was not merely the careful collection and arrangement of details which gave to the work of Defoe its unique effect. Herodotus and Trollope were masters of detail, and neither of them lost an opportunity of training his imagination to act as the exponent of facts, but in both, under the real clothes and accouterments of noted personages we see the figures of wax and wire. There have been artists, other than Meissonier, who could paint well the texture of cloth and the texture of skin, buckles, swords, and feathers; but if the figures on the canvases of these other artists should suddenly be imbued with life, would they possess practical skin and garments, and would their swords come out of their scabbards, and would their feathers wave in the wind? If all the machinery of *Robinson Crusoe*, from the beginning of the story to the end of it, could be set in motion by some magic wand, it would move as smoothly, as steadily, and as accurately as the mechanism of a Jacquard loom. Not a cog would fail to catch, not a pivot be wanting, not a thread be dropped, not a color misplaced.

I do not intend to analyze or endeavor to explain the method by which Defoe gave life to his fictitious work. It would be very easy to dissect this method and to examine all its structural parts, but if we were to do so we should find that all these parts had been used over and over again by writers of many ages and climes, some of these authors, in fact, having used all of them and in almost the same combinations; but the soul of Defoe's method, which gives it its actual life, is his own actual belief in the reality of his work.

While writing his "Surprising Narrative," Defoe must have known, if he thought of the matter at all, that other men had written narratives more surprising, the characters of which were more worthy of attention and literary immortality than those which he put into his own story. He must have known, too, that his story would have been much improved if he had left out of it a good deal that he put into it, but this knowledge had no effect whatever upon him. He knew that he was not writing the adventures of a Scotchman named Alexander Selkirk, who had been left on a desert island, but that he was telling, in the most straightforward manner, what had happened to the son of a certain foreigner of Bremen who acquired a good estate as a merchant at Hull and afterwards settled at

York. The adventures which befell this man were known only to Defoe, and he told them to the rest of the world just as they had occurred; and when a thing happened to Crusoe which had no effect upon the story one way or the other, it was related because it had happened. If days passed without the occurrence of anything which could give an excuse for record, that fact was stated, and the dates of uneventful days set down, and this for the simple reason that there had been such days.

When Crusoe found in the hull of the wrecked vessel a roll of sheet lead too heavy for him to lift, and which he left where it was because he could not lift it; when he took a dose of tobacco tea because he was sick and almost frightened to death, and at that immortal moment when he saw the footprint on the sand, he was always the real man who was doing things and having things happen to him, and Defoe was another man who was making a record of those things just as they were done and just as they had happened.

Cervantes did not believe in *Don Quixote*, and still less did he believe in *Sancho Panza*; but he believed in the purpose of his story, and the characters and events were obliged to accord themselves to that purpose. Defoe had no purpose in writing *Robinson Crusoe* except to relate events which, when he was describing them, he believed had truly happened. But when Defoe wrote what he could not believe, because he knew but little about his subject, and therefore could not compel his imagination to put his material before his eyes as if it had all been real, living, and true, then he failed. The second part of *Robinson Crusoe* was not successful. Defoe did not believe in this work, and he should not have expected other people to be interested in it. In this estimation of the author of *Robinson Crusoe*, I do not consider his other works. Some of them are well worthy of him, but none of them shows that rare power which breathes actual life into inanimate fiction.

I may sum up what I have to say about Defoe in the statement that it is the telling of his story and not the story itself which charms me and holds me to my allegiance. *Robinson Crusoe* is not the best work of English fiction, but it is, in my opinion, the best told story.—FRANK R. STOCKTON, "My Favorite Novelist and His Best Book," *Munsey's Magazine*, June 1897, pp. 352–53

SIR WALTER SCOTT
From "Daniel De Foe" (c. 1821)
Miscellaneous Works

1861, Volume 4, pp. 247–81

We must, in the first place, remark, that the fertility of De Foe was astonishing. He wrote on all occasions, and on all subjects, and seemingly had little time for preparation upon the subject in hand, but treated it from the stores which his memory retained of early reading, and such hints as he had caught up in society, not one of which seems to have been lost upon him. A complete list of De Foe's works, notwithstanding the exertions of the late George Chalmers, has not yet been procured, and a perfect collection even of such books as he is well known to have written, can scarce be procured, even by the most active bibliomaniac.[1] The preceding memoir does not notice one half of his compositions, all, even the meanest of which, have something in them to distinguish them as the works of an extraordinary man. It cannot, therefore, be doubted, that he possessed a powerful memory to furnish him with materials, and a no less copious vein of imagination to weave them up into a web of his own, and supply the rich embroidery which in reality constitutes their chief value. De Foe does not display much acquaintance with classic learning, neither does it appear that his attendance on the Newington seminary had led him deep into the study of ancient languages. His own language is genuine English, often simple even to vulgarity, but always so distinctly impressive, that its very vulgarity had, as we shall presently show, an efficacy in giving an air of truth or probability to the facts and sentiments it conveys. Exclusive of politics, De Foe's studies led chiefly to those popular narratives, which are the amusement of children and of the lower classes; those accounts of travellers who have visited remote countries; of voyagers who have made discoveries of new lands and strange nations; of pirates and bucaniers who have acquired wealth by their desperate adventures on the ocean. His residence at Limehouse, near the Thames, must have made him acquainted with many of those wild mariners, half privateers, half robbers, whom he must often have heard relate their adventures, and with whose manners and sentiments he thus became intimately acquainted. There is reason to believe, from a passage in his *Review*, (we have unfortunately mislaid the reference,) that he was acquainted with Dampier, a mariner, whose scientific skill in his profession and power of literary composition were at that time rarely found in his profession, especially among those rough sons of the ocean who acknowledged no peace beyond the Line, and had as natural an enmity to a South-American Spaniard as a greyhound to a hare, and who, though distinguished by the somewhat milder term of bucanier, were little better than absolute pirates. The English Government, it is well known, were not, however, very active in destroying this class of adventurers while they confined their depredations to the Dutch and Spaniards, and, indeed, seldom disturbed them, if they returned from their roving life, and sat down to enjoy their ill-gotten gains. The courage of these men, the wonderful risks which they incurred, their hair-breadth escapes, and the romantic countries through which they travelled, seem to have had infinite charms for De Foe. He has written several books on this subject, all of which are entertaining, and remarkable for the accuracy with which he personates the character of a bucaniering adventurer. The *New Voyage round the World*, the *Voyages and Piracies of Captain Singleton*, are of this class, and the second part of *Robinson Crusoe* properly belongs to it. De Foe's general acquaintance with nautical affairs has not been doubted, as he is said never to misapply the various sea-phrases, or show an ignorance unbecoming the character under which he wrote. His remarks upon trade, which are naturally mixed with these accounts of foreign parts, might naturally be expected from one whose speculations in every channel of trade had enabled him to write *An Account of Commerce*, and also a work called the *English Tradesman*, from which he appears to have been familiar with foreign countries, their produce, their manners, and government, and whatever rendered it easy or difficult to enter into trade with them. We may therefore conclude that *Purchas's Pilgrim*, *Hackluyt's Voyages*, and the other ancient authorities, had been curiously examined by him, as well as those of his friend Dampier, of Wafer, and others who had been in the South Seas, whether as privateers, or, as it was then called, *Upon the account*.

Shylock observes, there are land thieves and water thieves; and as De Foe was familiar with the latter, so he was not without some knowledge of the practices and devices of the former. We are afraid we must impute to his long and repeated imprisonments, the opportunity of becoming acquainted with the secrets of thieves and mendicants, their acts of plunder, concealment, and escape. But whatever way he acquired his knowledge of low life, De Foe certainly possessed it in the most extensive sense, and applied it in the composition of several works of fiction, in the style termed by the Spaniards *Gusto Picaresco*, of which no man was ever a greater master. This class of the fictitious narrative may be termed the Romance of Roguery, the subjects being the adventures of thieves, rogues, vagabonds, and swindlers, including viragoes and courtezans. The improved taste of the present age has justly rejected this coarse species of amusement, which is, besides, calculated to do an infinite deal of mischief among the lower classes, as it presents in a comic, or even heroic shape, the very crimes and vices to which they are otherwise most likely to be tempted. Nevertheless, the strange and blackguard scenes which De Foe describes, are fit to be compared to the gipsy-boys of the Spanish painter Murillo, which are so justly admired, as being, in truth of conception, and spirit of execution, the very *chef d'œuvres* of art, however low and loathsome the originals from which they are taken. Of this character is the *History of Colonel Jack*, for example, which had an immense popularity among the lower classes; that of *Moll Flanders*, a shoplifter and prostitute; that of *Mrs Christian Davis*, called *Mother Ross*; and that of *Roxana*, as she is termed, a courtezan in higher life. All of these contain strong marks of genius; in the last they are particularly predominant. But from the coarseness of the narrative, and the vice and vulgarity of the actors, the reader feels as a well-principled young man may do, when seduced by some entertaining and dissolute libertine into scenes of debauchery, that, though he may be amused, he must be not a little ashamed of that which furnishes the entertainment. So that, though we could select from these *picaresque* romances a good deal that is not a little amusing, we let them pass by, as we would persons, howsoever otherwise interesting, who may not be in character and manners entirely fit for good society.

A second species of composition, to which the author's active and vigorous genius was peculiarly adapted, was the account of great national convulsions, whether by war, or by the pestilence, or the tempest. These were tales which are sure, when even moderately well told, to arrest the attention, and which, narrated with that impression of reality which De Foe knew so well how to convey, make the hair bristle and the skin creep. In this manner he has written the *Memoirs of a Cavalier*, which have been often read and quoted as a real production of a real personage. Born himself almost immediately after the Restoration, De Foe must have known many of those who had been engaged in the civil turmoils of 1642–6, to which the period of these memoirs refers. He must have lived among them at that age when boys, such as we conceive De Foe must necessarily have been, cling to the knees of those who can tell them of the darings and the dangers of their youth, at a period when their own passions, and views of pressing forward in life, have not begun to operate upon their minds, and while they are still pleased to listen to the adventures which others have encountered on that stage, which they themselves have not yet entered upon. The *Memoirs of a Cavalier* have certainly been enriched with some such anecdotes as were likely to fire De Foe's active and powerful imagination, and hint to him in what colours the subject ought to be treated. ⟨. . .⟩

The *History of the Great Plague in London* is one of that particular class of compositions which hovers between romance and history. Undoubtedly De Foe embodied a number of traditions upon this subject with what he might actually have read,

or of which he might otherwise have received direct evidence. The subject is hideous almost to disgust, yet, even had he not been the author of *Robinson Crusoe*, De Foe would have deserved immortality for the genius which he has displayed in this work, as well as in the *Memoirs of a Cavalier*. This dreadful disease, which, in the language of Scripture, might be described as "the pestilence which walketh in darkness, and the destruction that wasteth at noon-day," was indeed a fit subject for a pencil so veracious as that of De Foe; and, accordingly, he drew pictures almost too horrible to look upon.

It is a wonder how so excellent a subject as the Great Fire of London, should have escaped the notice of De Foe, so eager for subjects of a popular character. Yet we can hardly regret this, since besides the verses of Dryden in the *Annus Mirabilis*, the accounts by two contemporaries, Evelyn and Pepys, have sketched it in all its terrible brilliancy.

The Great Storm, which, on 26th November, 1703, in Addison's phrase, "o'er pale Britannia pass'd," was seized upon by De Foe as a subject for the exercise of his powers of description. But as it consists in a great measure of letters from the country, wretched pastoral poetry, (for De Foe was only a poet in prose,) and similar buckram and binding used by bookmakers, it does not do the genius of the author the same credit as the works before named.

A third species of composition, for which this multifarious author showed a strong predilection, was that upon theurgy, magic, ghost-seeing, witchcraft, and the occult sciences. De Foe dwells on such subjects with so much unction, as to leave us little doubt that he was to a certain point a believer in something resembling an immediate communication between the inhabitants of this world, and of that which we shall in future inhabit. He is particularly strong on the subject of secret forebodings, mysterious impressions, bodements of good or evil, which arise in our own mind, but which yet seem impressed there by some external agent, and not to arise from the course of our natural reflections. Perhaps he even acted upon these supposed inspirations; for the following passage plainly refers to his own history, though, whether he speaks for the nonce, or means to be seriously understood, we cannot pretend to judge, though we incline to the latter opinion.

> I know a man who made it his rule always to obey these silent hints, and he has often declared to me, that when he obeyed them, he never miscarried; and if he neglected them, or went on contrary to them, he never succeeded; and gave me a particular case of his own, among a great many others, wherein he was thus directed. He had a particular case befallen him, wherein he was under the displeasure of the government, and was prosecuted for a misdemeanour, and brought to a trial in the King's Bench Court, where a verdict was brought against him, and he was cast; and times running very hard at that time against the party he belonged to, he was afraid to stand the hazard of a sentence, and absconded, taking care to make due provision for his bail, and to pay them whatever they might suffer. In this circumstance he was in great distress, and no way presented unto him but to fly out of the kingdom, which, being to leave his family, children, and employment, was very bitter to him, and he knew not what to do; all his friends advising him not to put himself into the hands of the law, which, though the offence was not capital, yet, in his circumstances, seemed to threaten his utter ruin. In this extremity, he felt one morning, (just as he had awaked, and the

thoughts of his misfortune began to return upon him,) I say he felt a strong impulse darting into his mind thus, *Write a letter to them*: It spoke so distinctly to him, and as it were forcibly, that, as he has often said since, he can scarce persuade himself not to believe but that he heard it; but he grants that he did not really hear it, too.

However, it repeated the words daily and hourly to him, till at length, walking about in his chamber where he was hidden, very pensive and sad, it jogged him again, and he answered aloud to it, as if it had been a voice, *Whom shall I write to?* It returned immediately, *Write to the judge.* This pursued him again for several days, till at length he took his pen, ink, and paper, and sat down to write, but knew not one word of what he should say; but, *Dabitur in hac hora*, he wanted not words. It was immediately impressed on his mind, and the words flowed upon his pen in a manner that even charmed himself, and filled him with expectations of success.

This letter was so strenuous in argument, so pathetic in its eloquence, and so moving and persuasive, that, as soon as the judge read it, he sent him word he should be easy, for he would endeavour to make that matter light to him, and, in a word, never left till he obtained to stop prosecution, and restore him to his liberty and his family.[2]

Whatever were De Foe's real sentiments on those mystic subjects, there is no doubt that he was fond of allowing his mind to dwell on them; and, either from his own taste, or because he reckoned them peculiarly calculated to attract the notice of a numerous class of readers, many of his popular publications turn upon supernatural visitation. Thus he wrote "An Essay on the history and reality of Apparitions; being an account of what they are, and what they are not; whence they come, and whence they come not; as also how we may distinguish between the apparitions of good and evil spirits, and how we ought to behave to them." This *Essay on Apparitions* was afterwards published under the name of Morton. De Foe, under the name of John Beaumont, Esq., wrote A *Treatise of Spirits, Apparitions, Witchcraft, and other Magical Practices; containing an Account of Genii and Familiar Spirits, &c.* In both of these works De Foe's reasoning, if it can be called such, belongs to the Platonic System of Dr Henry More, but is not very consistent either with that or with itself. On the other hand, the examples, or, in other words, the stories of ghosts and magic, with which we are favoured, are remarkably well told, or, rather, we should say, composed, and that with an air of perfect veracity, which nobody so well knew how to preserve as our author. To this class of his writings must be added the *Life of Duncan Campbell, the Conjurer and Fortune-teller*, a fellow who pretended to be deaf and dumb, and to tell fortunes, and whose reputation was such at the time, that De Foe thought his name would sell more than one book, and also wrote the *Spy on the Conjurer*; for, pressed by his circumstances to seek out such subjects as were popular for the moment, our author was apt to adhere to those which he had already treated with approbation. Thus, he not only wrote a second part to *Robinson Crusoe*, which is greatly inferior to the first part of that inimitable romance, but he drew a third draft on the popularity which it had acquired him, by a work of the mystical kind to which we have just alluded. This last seems the perfection of book-making. It is termed, *Serious Reflections during the Life of Robinson Crusoe, with his Vision of the Angelic World.* The contents are, in general, trite enough reflections upon moral subjects; and though Robinson

Crusoe's solitary state is sometimes referred to, and the book is ornamented with a bird's-eye view of the memorable island, yet it contains few observations that might not have been made by any shopkeeper living at Charing Cross. Thus may the richest source of genius be exhausted, and the most plentiful flow of invention drained off to the very dregs.

Besides those three several species of romantic fiction, in each of which Daniel De Foe was a copious author, his unwearied pen was also turned to moral and philosophical subjects, to those which relate to the economy of life, to history, and to statistics and descriptive subjects. He wrote *Travels in North and South Britain*; he wrote a *History of the Union*; he wrote an incorrect *History of the Church of Scotland, from the Restoration to the Revolution*. None of these historical works are of much value, except, perhaps, the *History of the Union*, which is little more than a dry journal of what passed in the Scottish Parliament upon that remarkable occasion; yet De Foe must have had an interesting tale to tell, if he had chosen it. But, writing under Harley's patronage, he cramped his genius, probably, to avoid the risk of giving offence to the irritable Scottish nation. Among his numerous political tracts, the most interesting perhaps is, *The History of Addresses*, which, written with great power of sarcasm, places in a ludicrous and contemptible light, that mode of communication between the people and the throne. All must recollect the story of Richard Cromwell, who, in removing from Whitehall, no longer his own, begged that particular care might be taken of a large chest, which contained, he said, "all the lives and fortunes of England," pledged, of course, in support of the Second Protector, by those who now saw him, with the utmost indifference, dragged from the seat of government.

It is not, however, of such political subjects that we have undertaken to treat. The multifarious author whose head imagined, and whose pen executed, such variety of works upon them, that it is a labour even to collect their names, must be now treated of solely in his character of a writer of fictitious composition.

And here, before proceeding to attempt a few observations on *Robinson Crusoe* in particular, it may be necessary to consider what is the particular charm which carries the reader through, not that *chef-d'œuvre* alone, but others of De Foe's compositions, and inspires a reluctance to lay down the volume till the tale is finished; and the desire, not generally felt in the perusal of works of fiction, to read every sentence and word upon every leaf, instead of catching up as much of the story as may enable us to understand the conclusion.

It cannot be the beauty of the style which thus commands the reader's attention; for that of De Foe, though often forcible, is rather rendered so by the interest of a particular situation than by the art of the writer. In general the language is loose and inaccurate, often tame and creeping, and almost always that of the lower classes in society. Neither does the charm depend upon the character of the incidents; for although in *Robinson Crusoe*, the incidents are very fine, yet in the *History of the Plague* the events are disgusting, and scarce less in those works where the scene lies in low life. Yet, like Pistol eating his leek, we go on growling and reading to the end of the volume, while we nod over many a more elegant subject, treated by authors who exhibit a far greater command of language. Neither can it be the artful conducting of the story, by which we are so much interested. De Foe seems to have written too rapidly to pay the least attention to this circumstance; the incidents are huddled together like paving-stones discharged from a cart, and have as little connexion between the one and the other. The scenes merely follow, without at all depending on each other. They are not like those of the regular drama, connected together by a regular commencement, continuation, and conclusion, but rather resemble the pictures in a showman's box, which have no relation further than as being enclosed within the same box, and subjected to the action of the same string.

To what, then, are we to ascribe this general charm attached to the romances of De Foe? We presume to answer, that it is chiefly to be ascribed to the unequalled dexterity with which our author has given an appearance of REALITY to the incidents which he narrates. Even De Foe's deficiencies in style, his homeliness of language, his rusticity of thought, expressive of what is called the *Crassa Minerva*, seem to claim credit for him as one who speaks the truth, the rather that we suppose he wants the skill to conceal or disguise it. The principle is almost too simple to need illustration; and yet, as it seems to include something of a paradox, since in fact it teaches that with the more art a story is told, the less likely it is to attract earnest attention, it may be proved by reference to common life. If we meet with a friend in the street, who tells us a story containing something beyond usual interest, and not of everyday occurrence, our feeling with respect to the truth of the story will be much influenced by the character of the narrator. If he is a man of wit or humour, and places the ludicrous part of the tale in the most prominent point of view, the hearer will be apt to recollect that his friend is a wag, and make some grains of allowance accordingly. On the other hand, supposing the person who communicates the narrative to be of a sentimental or enthusiastic character, with romantic ideas and a store of words to express them, you listen to his tale with a sort of suspicion that it is *too well* told to be truly told, and that though it may be at bottom real, yet it has been embroidered over by the flourishes of the narrator. But if the same fact be told by a man of plain sense, and sufficient knowledge of the world, the minuteness with which he tells the story, mixing up with it a number of circumstances, which are not otherwise connected with it, than as existing at the same moment, seems to guarantee the truth of what he says; and the bursts, whether of mirth or of emotion, which accompany the narrative, appear additional warrants of his fidelity, because neither is the usual mood of his mind. You believe, as coming from such a person, that which upon other information you might have thought an imposition, as Benedick credits the report of Beatrice's affection towards him, because "the fellow with the grey beard said it."

In the testimony of such a person upon a subject which is at all interesting, we generally detect some point which ascertains the eyewitness, and some expression which would seem to have only occurred to an individual who had heard and seen the facts to which he speaks. Those who are in the habit of attending courts of justice, during the leading of evidence, frequently hear, not only from men or women of observation, but from "iron-witted fools and unrespective boys," such striking circumstances as the following: A horrible murder had been committed by a man upon a person whom he had invited into his house in friendship; they were alone together when the deed was done, and the murderer, throwing on his coat, hastily left the house before the deed was discovered. A child of twelve or thirteen years old gave evidence that she was playing in the under part of the dwelling, and heard the accused person run hastily down stairs, and stumble at the threshold. She said she was very much frightened at the noise she heard; and being asked whether she had ever before thought of being frightened by a man running

hurriedly down stairs, she replied no; but the noise then made was like no other she had ever heard before. The poet of the most active imagination would hardly have dared to ascribe such impressive effects to the wild and precipitate retreat of guilt in making its escape from justice. This peculiar effect upon the child's imagination we might have doubted if we had read it in fiction, and yet how striking it becomes, heard from the mouth of the child herself!

It is no doubt true, that, in assuming this peculiar style of narrative, the author does so at a certain risk. He debars himself from the graces of language, and the artifice of narrative; he must sometimes seem prolix, sometimes indistinct and obscure, though possessing occasional points of brilliancy; in which respect his story may resemble some old Catholic towns on the Continent, where the streets are left in general darkness, save at those favoured spots where lamps are kept burning before the altars of particular saints; whereas, a regularly composed narrative represents an English country town, so well lighted throughout, that no particular spot, scarce even the dwelling of Mr Mayor, or the window of the apothecary, can exhibit any glow of peculiar lustre. And certainly it is the last style which should be attempted by a writer of inferior genius; for though it be possible to disguise mediocrity by fine writing, it appears in all its native inanity, when it assumes the garb of simplicity. Besides this peculiar style of writing requires that the author possess King Fadlallah's secret of transmigrating from one body to another, and possessing himself of all the qualities which he finds in the assumed character, retaining his own taste and judgment to direct them.

Sometimes this is done, by the author avowedly taking upon himself an imaginary personage, and writing according to his supposed feelings and prejudices. What would be the Vicar of Wakefield's history unless told by the kindest and worthiest pedant that ever wore a cassock, namely the Vicar himself? And what would be the most interesting and affecting, as well as the most comic, passages of *Castle Rackrent*, if narrated by one who had a less regard for "the family" than the immortal Thady, who, while he sees that none of the dynasty which he celebrates were perfectly right, has never been able to puzzle out wherein they were certainly wrong. Mr Galt's country Provost, and still more his reverend Annalist of the Parish should be also distinguished in this class. Wordsworth, himself, has assumed, in one of his affecting poems, the character of a sea-faring person retired to settle in the country.

These are, however, all characters of masquerade: We believe that of De Foe was entirely natural to him. The high-born Cavalier, for instance, speaks nearly the same species of language, and shows scarce a greater knowledge of society than Robinson Crusoe; only he has a cast of the grenadier about him, as the other has the trim of a seaman. It is greatly to be doubted whether De Foe could have changed his colloquial, circuitous, and periphrastic style for any other, whether more coarse or more elegant. We have little doubt it was connected with his nature, and the particular turn of his thoughts and ordinary expressions, and that he did not succeed so much by writing in an assumed manner, as by giving full scope to his own.

The subject is so interesting, that it is worth while examining it a little more closely; with which view we have reprinted, as illustrating our commentary on what may be called the *plausible* style of composition, "The True History of the Apparition of one Mrs Veal the next day after her Death, to one Mrs Bargrave, at Canterbury, the eighth of September, 1705, which Apparition recommends the perusal of Drelincourt's Book of Consolation against the Fears of Death."

We are induced to this, because the account of the origin of the pamphlet is curious, the pamphlet itself short, and, though once highly popular, now little read or known, and particularly because De Foe has put in force, within these few pages, peculiar specimens of his art of recommending the most improbable narrative, by his specious and serious mode of telling it.

An adventurous bookseller had ventured to print a considerable edition of a work by the Reverend Charles Drelincourt, minister of the Calvinist Church in Paris, and translated by M. D'Assigny, under the title of the *Christian's Defence against the Fear of Death, with several directions how to prepare ourselves to die well*. But however certain the prospect of death, it is not so agreeable (unfortunately) as to invite the eager contemplation of the public; and Drelincourt's book, being neglected, lay a dead stock on the hands of the publisher. In this emergency, he applied to De Foe to assist him (by dint of such means as were then, as well as now, pretty well understood in the literary world) in rescuing the unfortunate book from the literary death to which general neglect seemed about to consign it.

De Foe's genius and audacity devised a plan, which, for assurance and ingenuity, defied even the powers of Mr Puff in the *Critic*; for who but himself would have thought of summoning up a ghost from the grave to bear witness in favour of a halting body of divinity? There is a matter-of-fact, businesslike style in the whole account of the transaction, which bespeaks ineffable powers of self-possession. The narrative is drawn up "by a gentleman, a *Justice of Peace* at Maidstone, in Kent, a very intelligent person." And, moreover, "the discourse is attested by a very sober and understanding gentlewoman, who lives in Canterbury, within a few doors of the house in which Mrs Bargrave lives." The Justice believes his kinswoman to be of so discerning a spirit, as not to be put upon by any fallacy—and the kinswoman positively assures the Justice, "that the whole matter, as it is related and laid down, is really true, and what she herself heard, as near as may be, from Mrs Bargrave's own mouth, who, she knows, had no reason to invent or publish such a story, or any design to forge and tell a lie, being a woman of so much honesty and virtue, and her whole life a course, as it were, of piety." Scepticism itself could not resist this triple court of evidence so artfully combined, the Justice attesting for the discerning spirit of the sober and understanding gentlewoman his kinswoman, and his kinswoman becoming bail for the veracity of Mrs Bargrave. And here, gentle reader, admire the simplicity of those days. Had Mrs Veal's visit to her friend happened in our time, the conductors of the daily press would have given the word, and seven gentlemen, unto the said press belonging, would, with an obedient start, have made off for Kingston, for Canterbury, for Dover,—for Kamtschatka if necessary,—to pose the Justice, cross-examine Mrs Bargrave, confront the sober and understanding kinswoman, and dig Mrs Veal up from her grave, rather than not get to the bottom of the story. But in our time we doubt and scrutinize: our ancestors wondered and believed.

Before the story is commenced, the understanding gentlewoman, (not the Justice of Peace,) who is the reporter, takes some pains to repel the objections made against the story by some of the friends of Mrs Veal's brother, who consider the marvel as an aspersion on their family, and do what they can to laugh it out of countenance. Indeed, it is allowed, with admirable impartiality, that Mr Veal is too much of a gentleman to suppose Mrs Bargrave invented the story—scandal itself could scarce have supposed that—although one notorious liar, who is chastised towards the conclusion of the story, ventures to throw out such an insinuation. No reasonable or respectable person, however, could be found to countenance the suspicion, and Mr Veal himself opined that Mrs Bargrave had been driven crazy by a cruel husband, and dreamed the whole story of the apparition. Now all this is sufficiently artful. To have vouched the fact as universally known, and believed by every one, *nem. con.*, would not have been half so satisfactory to a sceptic as to allow fairly that the narrative had been impugned, and hint at the character of one of those sceptics, and the motives of another, as sufficient to account for their want of belief. Now to the fact itself.

Mrs Bargrave and Mrs Veal had been friends in youth, and had protested their attachment should last as long as they lived; but when Mrs Veal's brother obtained an office in the customs at Dover, some cessation of their intimacy ensued, "though without any positive quarrel." Mrs Bargrave had removed to Canterbury, and was residing in a house of her own, when she was suddenly interrupted by a visit from Mrs Veal, as she was sitting in deep contemplation of certain distresses of her own. The visitor was in a riding-habit, and announced herself as prepared for a distant journey, (which seems to intimate that spirits have a considerable distance to go before they arrive at their appointed station, and that the females at least put on a *habit* for the occasion.) The spirit, for such was the seeming Mrs Veal, continued to wave the ceremony of salutation, both in going and coming, which will remind the reader of a ghostly lover's reply to his mistress in the fine old Scottish ballad:

> Why should I come within thy bower?
> I am no earthly man:
> And should I kiss thy rosy lips,
> Thy days would not be lang.

They then began to talk in the homely style of middle-aged ladies, and Mrs Veal proses concerning the conversations they had formerly held, and the books they had read together. Her very recent experience probably led Mrs Veal to talk of death, and the books written on the subject, and she pronounced, *ex cathedrâ*, as a dead person was best entitled to do, that "Drelincourt's book on death was the best book on the subject ever written." She also mentioned Dr. Sherlock, two Dutch books which had been translated, and several others; but Drelincourt, she said, had the clearest notions of death and the future state of any who had handled that subject. She then asked for the work, [we marvel the edition and impress had not been mentioned] and lectured on it with a great eloquence and affection. Dr Kenrick's *Ascetick* was also mentioned with approbation by this critical spectre [the Doctor's work was no doubt a tenant of the shelf in some favourite publisher's shop]; and Mr Norris's *Poem on Friendship*, a work which, I doubt, though honoured with a ghost's approbation, we may now seek for as vainly as Correlli tormented his memory to recover the sonata which the devil played to him in a dream. Presently after, from former habits we may suppose, the guest desires a cup of tea; but, bethinking herself of her new character, escapes from her own proposal by recollecting that Mr Bargrave was in the habit of breaking his wife's china. It would have been indeed strangely out of character if the spirit had lunched, or breakfasted upon tea and toast. Such a consummation would have sounded as ridiculous as if the statue of the Commander in *Don Juan* had not only accepted of the invitation of the libertine to supper, but had also committed a beef-steak to his flinty jaws and stomach of adamant. A little more conversation ensued of a less serious nature, and tending to show that even the passage from life to death leaves the female anxiety about person and dress somewhat alive. The ghost asked Mrs Bargrave whether she did not think her very much altered, and Mrs Bargrave of course complimented her on her good looks. Mrs Bargrave also admired the gown which Mrs Veal wore, and as a mark of her perfectly restored confidence, the spirit let her into the important secret, that it was a *scoured silk*, and lately made up. She informed her also of another secret, namely, that one Mr Bretton had allowed her ten pounds a-year; and, lastly, she requested that Mrs Bargrave would write to her brother, and tell him how to distribute her mourning rings, and mentioned there was a purse of gold in her cabinet. She expressed some wish to see Mrs Bargrave's daughter; but when that good lady went to the next door to seek her, she found on her return the guest leaving the house. She had got without the door, in the street, in the face of the beast market, on a Saturday, which is market day, and stood ready to part. She said she must be going, as she had to call upon her cousin Watson, (this appears to be a *gratis dictum* on the part of the ghost,) and, maintaining the character of mortality to the last, she quietly turned the corner, and walked out of sight.

Then came the news of Mrs Veal's having died the day before at noon. Says Mrs Bargrave, "I am sure she was with me on Saturday almost two hours." And in comes Captain Watson, and says Mrs Veal was certainly dead. And then come all the pieces of evidence, and especially the striped silk gown. Then Mrs Watson cried out, "You have seen her indeed, for none knew but Mrs Veal and I that that gown was scoured;" and she cried that the gown was described exactly, for, said she, "I helped her to make it up." And next we have the silly attempts made to discredit the history. Even Mr Veal, her brother, was obliged to allow that the gold was found, but with a difference, and pretended it was not found in a cabinet, but elsewhere; and, in short, we have all the gossip of *says I*, and *thinks I*, and *says she*, and *thinks she*, which disputed matters usually excite in a country town.

When we have thus turned the tale, the seam without, it may be thought too ridiculous to have attracted notice. But whoever will read it as told by De Foe himself, will agree that, could the thing have happened in reality, so it would have been told. The sobering the whole supernatural visit into the language of middle or low life, gives it an air of probability even in its absurdity. The ghost of an exciseman's housekeeper, and a seamstress, were not to converse like Brutus with his Evil Genius. And the circumstances of scoured silks, broken tea-china, and suchlike, while they are the natural topics of such persons' conversation, would, one might have thought, be the last which an inventor would have introduced into a pretended narrative betwixt the dead and living. In short, the whole is so distinctly circumstantial, that, were it not for the impossibility, or extreme improbability at least, of such an occurrence, the evidence could not but support the story.

The effect was most wonderful. *Drelincourt upon Death*, attested by one who could speak from experience, took an unequalled run. The copies had hung on the bookseller's hands as heavy as a pile of lead bullets. They now traversed the town in every direction, like the same balls discharged from a field-piece. In short, the object of Mrs Veal's apparition was perfectly attained. ⟨. . .⟩

Pathos is not De Foe's general characteristic; he had too little delicacy of mind; when it comes, it comes uncalled, and is created by the circumstances, not sought for by the author. The excess for instance, of the natural longing for human society which Crusoe manifests while on board of the stranded Spanish vessel, by falling into a sort of agony, as he repeated the words, "Oh, that but one man had been saved!—Oh, that there had been but one!" is in the highest degree pathetic. The agonizing reflections of the solitary, when he is in danger of being driven to sea, in his rash attempt to circumnavigate his island, are also affecting.

In like manner we may remark, that De Foe's genius did not approach the grand or terrific. The battles, which he is fond of describing, are told with the indifference of an old bucanier, and probably in the very way in which he may have heard them recited by the actors. His goblins, too, are generally a commonplace sort of spirits, that bring with them very little of supernatural terror; and yet the fine incident of the print of the naked foot on the sand, with Robinson Crusoe's terrors in consequence, never fail to leave a powerful impression upon the reader.

The supposed situation of his hero was peculiarly favourable to the circumstantial style of De Foe. Robinson Crusoe was placed in a condition where it was natural that the slightest event should make an impression on him; and De Foe was not an author who would leave the slightest event untold. When he mentions that two shoes were driven ashore, and adds that they were not neighbours, we feel it an incident of importance to the poor solitary.

The assistance which De Foe derived from Selkirk's history, seems of a very meagre kind. It is not certain that he was obliged to the real hermit of Juan Fernandez even for the original hint; for the putting mutineers or turbulent characters on shore upon solitary places, was a practice so general among the bucaniers, that there was a particular name for the punishment; it was called *marooning* a man. De Foe borrowed, perhaps, from the account in Woodes Rogers, the circumstance of the two huts, the abundance of goats, the clothing made out of their skins; and the turnips of Alexander Selkirk may have perhaps suggested the corn of Robinson Crusoe. Even these incidents, however, are so wrought up and heightened, and so much is added to make them interesting, that the bare circumstances occurring elsewhere, cannot be said to infringe upon the author's claim to originality. On the whole, indeed, Robinson Crusoe is put to so many more trials of ingenuity, his comforts are so much increased, his solitude is so much diversified, and his account of his thoughts and occupations so distinctly traced, that the course of the work embraces a far wider circle of investigation into human nature, than could be derived from that of Selkirk, who, for want of the tools and conveniences supplied to Crusoe by the wreck, relapses into a sort of savage state, which could have afforded little scope for delineation. It may, however, be observed, that De Foe may have known so much of Selkirk's history as to be aware how much his stormy passions were checked and tamed by his long course of solitude, and that, from being a kind of Will Atkins, a brawling dissolute seaman, he became (which was certainly the case) a grave, sober, reflective man. The manner in which Robinson Crusoe's moral sense and religious feeling are awakened and brought into action, are important passages in the work.[3]

Amid these desultory remarks, it may be noticed, that, though all his romances, De Foe has made a great deal of the narrative depend upon lucky hits and accidents, which, as he is usually at some pains to explain, ought rather to be termed providential occurrences. This is coupled with a belief in spiritual communication in the way of strong internal suggestions, to which De Foe, as we have seen, was himself sufficiently willing to yield belief. Odd and surprising accidents do, indeed, frequently occur in human life; and when we hear them narrated, we are interested in them, not only from the natural tendency of the human mind towards the extraordinary and wonderful, but also because we have some disposition to receive as truths circumstances, which, from their improbability, do not seem likely to be invented. It is the kind of good fortune, too, which every one wishes to himself, which comes without exertion, and just at the moment it is wanted; so that it gives a sort of pleasure to be reminded of the possibility of its arrival even in fiction.

The continuation of Robinson Crusoe's history after he obtains the society of his man Friday, is less philosophical than that which turns our thoughts upon the efforts which a solitary individual may make for extending his own comforts in the melancholy situation in which he is placed, and upon the natural reflections suggested by the progress of his own mind. The character of Friday is nevertheless extremely pleasing; and the whole subsequent history of the shipwrecked Spaniards and the pirate vessel is highly interesting. Here certainly the *Memoirs of Robinson Crusoe* ought to have stopped. The Second Part, though containing many passages which display the author's genius, does not rise high in character above the *Memoirs of Captain Singleton*, or the other imaginary voyages of the author.

There scarce exists a work so popular as *Robinson Crusoe*. It is read eagerly by young people; and there is hardly an elf so devoid of imagination as not to have supposed for himself a solitary island in which he could act *Robinson Crusoe*, were it but in the corner of the nursery. To many it has given the decided turn of their lives, by sending them to sea. For the young mind is much less struck with the hardships of the anchorite's situation than with the animating exertions which he makes to overcome them; and *Robinson Crusoe* produces the same impression upon an adventurous spirit which the *Book of Martyrs* would do on a young devotee, or the *Newgate Calendar* upon an acolyte of Bridewell; both of which students are less terrified by the horrible manner in which the tale terminates, than animated by sympathy with the saints or depredators who are the heroes of their volume. Neither does a re-perusal of *Robinson Crusoe*, at a more advanced age, diminish our early impressions. The situation is such as every man may make his own, and, being possible in itself, is, by the exquisite art of the narrator, rendered as probable as it is interesting. It has the merit, too, of that species of accurate painting which can be looked at again and again with new pleasure.

Neither has the admiration of the work been confined to England, though Robinson Crusoe himself, with his rough good sense, his prejudices, and his obstinate determination not to sink under evils which can be surpassed by exertion, forms no bad specimen of the True-Born Englishman. The rage for imitating a work so popular seems to have risen to a degree of frenzy; and, by a mistake not peculiar to this particular class of the *servum pecus*, the imitators did not attempt to apply De Foe's manner of managing the narrative to some situation of a different kind, but seized upon and caricatured the principal incidents of the shipwrecked mariner and the solitary island. It is computed that within forty years from the appearance of the original work, no less than forty-one different *Robinsons* appeared, besides fifteen other imitations, in which other titles were used. Finally, though perhaps it is no great recommendation, the anti-social philosopher Rousseau will allow no other book than *Robinson Crusoe* in the hands of Emilius. Upon the whole, the work is as unlikely to lose its celebrity as it is to be equalled in its peculiar character by any other of similar excellence.

Notes

1. The author has long sought for his poem termed "Caledonia," without being able to obtain a sight of it.
2. *Robinson Crusoe's Vision of the Angelic World*, pp. 48, 49, 50. London, 1720.
3. We should say more on this subject, were it not that Mr Howel, of Edinburgh, a person every way qualified for the task, has collected several particulars concerning the history of Selkirk, the prototype of Robinson Crusoe, which he designs shortly to lay before the public.

SIR LESLIE STEPHEN
"De Foe's Novels" (1868)
Hours in a Library (1874–79)
1904, Volume 1, pp. 1–63

According to the high authority of Charles Lamb, it has sometimes happened "that from no inferior merit in the rest, but from some superior good fortune in the choice of a subject, some single work" (of a particular author) "shall have been suffered to eclipse, and cast into the shade, the deserts of its less fortunate brethren." And after quoting the case of Bunyan's *Holy War*, as compared with the *Pilgrim's Progress*, he adds that, "in no instance has this excluding partiality been exerted with more unfairness than against what may be termed the secondary novels or romances of De Foe." He proceeds to declare that there are at least four other fictitious narratives by the same writer—*Roxana, Singleton, Moll Flanders*, and *Colonel Jack*—which possess an interest not inferior to *Robinson Crusoe*—"except what results from a less felicitous choice of situation." Granting most unreservedly that the same hand is perceptible in the minor novels as in *Robinson Crusoe*, and that they bear at every page the most unequivocal symptoms of De Foe's workmanship, I venture to doubt the "partiality" and the "unfairness" of preferring to them their more popular rival. The instinctive judgment of the world is not really biassed by anything except the intrinsic power exerted by a book over its sympathies; and as in the long run it has honoured *Robinson Crusoe*, in spite of the critics, and has comparatively neglected *Roxana* and the companion stories, there is probably some good cause for the distinction. The apparent injustice to books resembles what we often see in the case of men. A. B. becomes Lord Chancellor, whilst C. D. remains for years a briefless barrister; and yet for the life of us we cannot tell but that C. D. is the abler man of the two. Perhaps he was wanting in some one of the less conspicuous elements that are essential to a successful career; he said "Open, wheat!" instead of "Open, sesame!" and the barriers remained unaffected by his magic. The secret may really be simple enough. The complete success of such a book as *Robinson* implies, it may be, the precise adaptation of the key to every ward of the lock. The felicitous choice of situation to which Lamb refers gave just the required fitness; and it is of little use to plead that *Roxana, Colonel Jack*, and others might have done the same trick if only they had received a little filing, or some slight change in shape: a shoemaker might as well argue that if you had only one toe less his shoes would n't pinch you.

To leave the unsatisfactory ground of metaphor, we may find out, on examination, that De Foe had discovered in *Robinson Crusoe* precisely the field in which his talents could be most effectually applied; and that a very slight alteration in the subject-matter might change the merit of his work to a disproportionate extent. The more special the idiosyncrasy upon which a man's literary success is founded, the greater, of course, the probability that a small change will disconcert him. A man who can only perform upon the drum will have to wait for certain combinations of other instruments before his special talent can be turned to account. Now, the talent in which De Foe surpasses all other writers is just one of those peculiar gifts which must wait for a favourable chance. When a gentleman, in a fairy story, has a power of seeing a hundred miles, or covering seven leagues at a stride, we know that an opportunity will speedily occur for putting his faculties to use. But the gentleman with the seven-leagued boots is useless when the occasion offers itself for telescopic vision, and the eyes are good for nothing without the power of locomotion. To De Foe, if we may imitate the language of the *Arabian Nights*, was given a tongue to which no one could listen without believing every word that he uttered—a qualification, by the way, which would serve its owner far more effectually in this common-place world than swords of sharpness or cloaks of darkness or other fairy paraphernalia. In other words, he had the most marvellous power ever known of giving verisimilitude to his fictions; or, in other words again, he had the most amazing talent on record for telling lies. We have all read how the *History of the Plague*, the *Memoirs of a Cavalier*, and even, it is said, *Robinson Crusoe*, have succeeded in passing themselves off for veritable narratives. The *Memoirs of Captain Carleton* long passed for De Foe's, but the Captain has now gained admission to the biographical dictionary and is credited with his own memoirs. In either case, it is as characteristic that a genuine narrative should be attributed to De Foe, as that De Foe's narrative should be taken as genuine. An odd testimony to De Foe's powers as a liar (a word for which there is, unfortunately, no equivalent that does not imply some blame) has been mentioned. Mr. M'Queen, quoted in Captain Burton's *Nile Basin*, names *Captain Singleton* as a genuine account of travels in Central Africa, and seriously mentions De Foe's imaginary pirate as "a claimant for the honour of the discovery of the sources of the White Nile." Probably, however, this only proves that Mr. M'Queen had never read the book.

Most of the literary artifices to which De Foe owed his power of producing this illusion are sufficiently plain. Of all the fictions which he succeeded in palming off for truths none is more instructive than that admirable ghost, Mrs. Veal. Like the sonnets of some great poets, it contains in a few lines all the essential peculiarities of his art, and an admirable commentary has been appended to it by Sir Walter Scott. The first device which strikes us is his ingenious plan for manufacturing corroborative evidence. The ghost appears to Mrs. Bargrave. The story of the apparition is told by a "very sober and understanding gentlewoman, who lives within a few doors of Mrs. Bargrave;" and the character of this sober gentlewoman is supported by the testimony of a justice of the peace at Maidstone, "a very intelligent person." This elaborate chain of evidence is intended to divert our attention from the obvious circumstance that the whole story rests upon the authority of the anonymous person who tells us of the sober gentlewoman, who supports Mrs. Bargrave, and is confirmed by the intelligent justice. Simple as the artifice appears, it is one which is constantly used in supernatural stories of the present day. One of those improving legends tells how a ghost appeared to two officers in Canada, and how, subsequently, one of the officers met the ghost's twin brother in London, and straightway exclaimed, "You are the person who appeared to me in Canada!" Many people are diverted

from the weak part of the story by this ingenious confirmation, and, in their surprise at the coherence of the narrative, forget that the narrative itself rests upon entirely anonymous evidence. A chain is no stronger than its weakest link; but if you show how admirably the last few are united together, half the world will forget to test the security of the equally essential links which are kept out of sight. De Foe generally repeats a similar trick in the prefaces of his fictions. "'T is certain," he says, in the *Memoirs of a Cavalier*, "no man could have given a description of his retreat from Marston Moor to Rochdale, and thence over the moors to the North, in so apt and proper terms, unless he had really travelled over the ground he describes," which, indeed, is quite true, but by no means proves that the journey was made by a fugitive from that particular battle. He separates himself more ostentatiously from the suppositious author by praising his admirable manner of relating the memoirs, and the "wonderful variety of incidents with which they are beautified;" and, with admirable impudence, assures us that they are written in so soldierly a style, that it "seems impossible any but the very person who was present in every action here related was the relater of them." In the preface to *Roxana*, he acts, with equal spirit, the character of an impartial person, giving us the evidence on which he is himself convinced of the truth of the story, as though he would, of all things, refrain from pushing us unfairly for our belief. The writer, he says, took the story from the lady's own mouth: he was, of course, obliged to disguise names and places; but was himself "particularly acquainted with this lady's first husband, the brewer, and with his father, and also with his bad circumstances, and knows that first part of the story." The rest we must, of course, take upon the lady's own evidence, but less unwillingly, as the first is thus corroborated. We cannot venture to suggest to so calm a witness that he has invented both the lady and the writer of her history; and, in short, that when he says that A. says that B. says something, it is, after all, merely the anonymous "he" who is speaking. In giving us his authority for *Moll Flanders*, he ventures upon the more refined art of throwing a little discredit upon the narrator's veracity. She professes to have abandoned her evil ways, but, as he tells us with a kind of aside, and as it were cautioning us against over-incredulity, "it seems" (a phrase itself suggesting the impartial looker-on) that in her old age "she was not so extraordinary a penitent as she was at first; it seems only" (for, after all, you must n't make *too* much of my insinuations) "that indeed she always spoke with abhorrence of her former life." So we are left in a qualified state of confidence, as if we had been talking about one of his patients with the wary director of a reformatory.

This last touch, which is one of De Foe's favourite expedients, is most fully exemplified in the story of Mrs. Veal. The author affects to take us into his confidence, to make us privy to the pros and cons in regard to the veracity of his own characters, till we are quite disarmed. The sober gentlewoman vouches for Mrs. Bargrave; but Mrs. Bargrave is by no means allowed to have it all her own way. One of the ghost's communications related to the disposal of a certain sum of 10*l.* a year, of which Mrs. Bargrave, according to her own account, could have known nothing, except by this supernatural intervention. Mrs. Veal's friends, however, tried to throw doubt upon the story of her appearance, considering that it was disreputable for a decent woman to go abroad after her death. One of them, therefore, declared that Mrs. Bargrave was a liar, and that she had, in fact, known of the 10*l.* beforehand. On the other hand, the person who thus attacked Mrs. Bargrave had himself the "reputation of a notorious liar." Mr. Veal, the ghost's brother, was too much of a gentleman to make such gross imputations. He confined himself to the more moderate assertion that Mrs. Bargrave had been crazed by a bad husband. He maintained that the story must be a mistake, because, just before her death, his sister had declared that she had nothing to dispose of. This statement, however, may be reconciled with the ghost's remarks about the 10*l.*, because she obviously mentioned such a trifle merely by way of a token of the reality of her appearance. Mr. Veal, indeed, makes rather a better point by stating that a certain purse of gold mentioned by the ghost was found, not in the cabinet where she told Mrs. Bargrave that she had placed it, but in a comb-box. Yet, again, Mr. Veal's statement is here rather suspicious, for it is known that Mrs. Veal was very particular about her cabinet, and would not have let her gold out of it. We are left in some doubts by this conflict of evidence, although the obvious desire of Mr. Veal to throw discredit on the story of his sister's appearance rather inclines us to believe in Mrs. Bargrave's story, who could have had no conceivable motive for inventing such a fiction. The argument is finally clenched by a decisive coincidence. The ghost wears a silk dress. In the course of a long conversation she incidentally mentioned to Mrs. Bargrave that this was a scoured silk, newly made up. When Mrs. Bargrave reported this remarkable circumstance to a certain Mrs. Wilson, "You have certainly seen her," exclaimed that lady, "for none knew but Mrs. Veal and myself that the gown had been scoured." To this crushing piece of evidence it seems that neither Mr. Veal nor the notorious liar could invent any sufficient reply.

One can almost fancy De Foe chuckling as he concocted the refinements of this most marvellous narrative. The whole artifice is, indeed, of a simple kind. Lord Sunderland, according to Macaulay, once ingeniously defended himself against a charge of treachery, by asking whether it was possible that any man should be so base as to do that which he was, in fact, in the constant habit of doing. De Foe asks us in substance, Is it conceivable that any man should tell stories so elaborate, so complex, with so many unnecessary details, with so many inclinations of evidence this way and that, unless the stories were true? We instinctively answer, that it is, in fact, inconceivable; and, even apart from any such refinements as those noticed, the circumstantiality of the stories is quite sufficient to catch an unworthy critic. It is, indeed, perfectly easy to tell a story which shall be mistaken for a *bonâ fide* narrative, if only we are indifferent to such considerations as making it interesting or artistically satisfactory.

The praise which has been lavished upon De Foe for the verisimilitude of his novels seems to be rather extravagant. The trick would be easy enough, if it were worth performing. The storyteller cannot be cross-examined; and if he is content to keep to the ordinary level of commonplace facts, there is not the least difficulty in producing conviction. We recognise the fictitious character of an ordinary novel, because it makes a certain attempt at artistic unity, or because the facts are such as could obviously not be known to, or would not be told by, a real narrator, or possibly because they are inconsistent with other established facts. If a man chooses to avoid such obvious confessions of unreality, he can easily be as lifelike as De Foe. I do not suppose that foreign correspondence of a newspaper is often composed in the Strand; but it is only because I believe that the honesty of writers in the press is far too great to allow them to commit a crime which must be speedily detected by independent evidence. Lying is, after all, the easiest of all things, if the liar be not too ambitious. A little clever circumstantiality will lull any incipient suspicion; and it must

be added that De Foe, in adopting the tone of a *bonâ fide* narrator, not unfrequently overreaches himself. He forgets his dramatic position in his anxiety to be minute. Colonel Jack, at the end of a long career, tells us how one of his boyish companions stole certain articles at a fair, and gives us the list, of which this is a part: "5thly, a silver box, with 7*s.* in small silver; 6, a pocket-handkerchief; 7, *another*; 8, a jointed baby, and little looking-glass." The affectation of extreme precision, especially in the charming item "another," destroys the perspective of the story. We are listening to a contemporary, not to an old man giving us his fading recollections of a disreputable childhood.

The peculiar merit, then, of De Foe must be sought in something more than the circumstantial nature of his lying, or even the ingenious artifices by which he contrives to corroborate his own narrative. These, indeed, show the pleasure which he took in simulating truth; and he may very probably have attached undue importance to this talent in the infancy of novel-writing, as in the infancy of painting it was held for the greatest of triumphs when birds came and pecked at the grapes in a picture. It is curious, indeed, that De Foe and Richardson, the founders of our modern school of fiction, appear to have stumbled upon their discovery by a kind of accident. As De Foe's novels are simply history *minus* the facts, so Richardson's are a series of letters *minus* the correspondents. The art of novel-writing, like the art of cooking pigs in Lamb's most philosophical as well as humorous apologue, first appeared in its most cumbrous shape. As Hoti had to burn his cottage for every dish of pork, Richardson and De Foe had to produce fiction at the expense of a close approach to falsehood. The division between the art of lying and the art of fiction was not distinctly visible to either; and both suffer to some extent from the attempt to produce absolute illusion, where they should have been content with portraiture. And yet the defect is balanced by the vigour naturally connected with an unflinching realism. That this power rested, in De Foe's case, upon something more than a bit of literary trickery, may be inferred from his fate in another department of authorship. He twice got into trouble for a device exactly analogous to that which he afterwards practised in fiction. On both occasions he was punished for assuming a character for purposes of mystification. In the latest instance, it is seen, the pamphlet called *What if the Pretender Comes?* was written in such obvious irony, that the mistake of his intentions must have been wilful. The other and better-known performance, *The Shortest Way with the Dissenters*, seems really to have imposed upon some of his readers. It is difficult in these days of toleration to imagine that any one can have taken the violent suggestions of the *Shortest Way* as put forward seriously. To those who might say that persecuting the Dissenters was cruel, says De Foe:

> I answer, 't is cruelty to kill a snake or a toad in cold blood, but the poison of their nature makes it a charity to our neighbours to destroy those creatures, not for any personal injury received, but for prevention. . . . Serpents, toads, and vipers, &c., are noxious to the body, and poison the sensitive life: these poison the soul, corrupt our posterity, ensnare our children, destroy the vital of our happiness, our future felicity, and contaminate the whole mass.

And he concludes:

> Alas, the Church of England! What with Popery on the one hand, and schismatics on the other, how has she been crucified between two thieves! *Now let us crucify the thieves!* Let her foundations be estab-

lished upon the destruction of her enemies: the doors of mercy being always open to the returning part of the deluded people; let the obstinate be ruled with a rod of iron!

It gives a pleasant impression of the spirit of the times, to remember that this could be taken for a genuine utterance of orthodoxy; that De Foe was imprisoned and pilloried, and had to write a serious protestation that it was only a joke, and that he meant to expose the non-juring party by putting their secret wishes into plain English. "'T is hard," he says, "that this should not be perceived by all the town; that not one man can see it, either Churchman or Dissenter." It certainly was very hard; but a perusal of the whole pamphlet may make it a degree more intelligible. Ironical writing of this kind is in substance a *reductio ad absurdum*. It is a way of saying the logical result of your opinions is such or such a monstrous error. So long as the appearance of logic is preserved, the error cannot be stated too strongly. The attempt to soften the absurdity so as to take in an antagonist is injurious artistically, if it may be practically useful. An ironical intention which is quite concealed might as well not exist. And thus the unscrupulous use of the same weapon by Swift is now far more telling than De Foe's comparatively guarded application of it. The artifice, however, is most skilfully carried out for the end which De Foe had in view. The *Shortest Way* begins with a comparative gravity to throw us off our guard; the author is not afraid of imitating a little of the dulness of his supposed antagonists, and repeats with all imaginable seriousness the very taunts which a High Church bigot would in fact have used. It was not a sound defence of persecution to say that the Dissenters had been cruel when they had the upper hand, and that penalties imposed upon them were merely retaliation for injuries suffered under Cromwell and from Scottish Presbyterians; but it was one of those topics upon which a hot-headed persecutor would naturally dwell, though De Foe gives him rather more forcible language than he would be likely to possess. It is only towards the end that the ironical purpose crops out in what we should have thought an unmistakable manner. Few writers would have preserved their incognito so long. The caricature would have been too palpable, and invited ridicule too ostentatiously. An impatient man soon frets under the mask and betrays his real strangeness in the hostile camp.

De Foe in fact had a peculiarity at first sight less favourable to success in fiction than in controversy. Amongst the political writers of that age he was, on the whole, distinguished for good temper and an absence of violence. Although a party man, he was by no means a man to swallow the whole party platform. He walked on his own legs, and was not afraid to be called a deserter by more thorough-going partisans. The principles which he most ardently supported were those of religious toleration and hatred to every form of arbitrary power. Now, the intellectual groundwork upon which such a character is formed has certain conspicuous merits, along with certain undeniable weaknesses. Amongst the first may be reckoned a strong grasp of facts—which was developed to an almost disproportionate degree in De Foe— and a resolution to see things as they are without the gloss which is contracted from strong party sentiment. He was one of those men of vigorous common-sense, who like to have everything down plainly and distinctly in good unmistakable black and white, and indulge a voracious appetite for facts and figures. He was, therefore, able—within the limits of his vision—to see things from both sides, and to take his adversaries' opinions as calmly as his own, so long, at least, as they dealt with the class of considerations with which he was

accustomed to deal; for, indeed, there are certain regions of discussion to which we cannot be borne on the wings of statistics, or even of common-sense. And this, the weak side of his intellect, is equally unmistakable. The matter-of-fact man may be compared to one who suffers from colour-blindness. Perhaps he may have a power of penetrating, and even microscopic vision; but he sees everything, in his favourite black and white or grey, and loses all the delights of gorgeous, though it may be deceptive, colouring. One man sees everything in the forcible light and shade of Rembrandt: a few heroes stand out conspicuously in a focus of brilliancy from a background of imperfectly defined shadows, clustering round the centre in strange but picturesque confusion. To another, every figure is full of interest, with singular contrasts and sharply-defined features; the whole effect is somewhat spoilt by the want of perspective and the perpetual sparkle and glitter; yet when we fix our attention upon any special part, it attracts us by its undeniable vivacity and vitality. To a third, again, the individual figures become dimmer, but he sees a slow and majestic procession of shapes imperceptibly developing into some harmonious whole. Men profess to reach their philosophical conclusions by some process of logic; but the imagination is the faculty which furnishes the raw material upon which the logic is employed, and, unconsciously to its owners, determines, for the most part, the shape into which their theories will be moulded. Now, De Foe was above the ordinary standard, in so far as he did not, like most of us, see things merely as a blurred and inextricable chaos; but he was below the great imaginative writers in the comparative coldness and dry precision of his mental vision. To him the world was a vast picture, from which all confusion was banished; everything was definite, clear and precise as in a photograph; as in a photograph, too, everything could be accurately measured, and the result stated in figures; by the same parallel, there was a want of perspective, for the most distant objects were as precisely given as the nearest; and yet further, there was the same absence of the colouring which is caused in natural objects by light and heat, and in mental pictures by the fire of imaginative passion. The result is a product which is to Fielding or Scott what a portrait by a first-rate photographer is to one by Vandyke or Reynolds, though, perhaps, the peculiar qualifications which go to make a De Foe are almost as rare as those which form the more elevated artist.

To illustrate this a little more in detail, one curious proof of the want of the passionate element in De Foe's novels is the singular calmness with which he describes his villains. He always looks at the matter in a purely business-like point of view. It is very wrong to steal, or break any of the commandments: partly because the chances are that it won't pay, and partly also because the devil will doubtless get hold of you in time. But a villain in De Foe is extremely like a virtuous person, only that, so to speak, he has unluckily backed the losing side. Thus, for example, Colonel Jack is a thief from his youth up; Moll Flanders is a thief, and worse; Roxana is a highly immoral lady, and is under some suspicion of a most detestable murder; and Captain Singleton is a pirate of the genuine buccaneering school. Yet we should really doubt, but for their own confessions, whether they have villainy enough amongst them to furnish an average pickpocket. Roxana occasionally talks about a hell within, and even has unpleasant dreams concerning "apparitions of devils and monsters, of falling into gulphs, and from off high and steep precipices." She has, moreover, excellent reasons for her discomfort. Still, in spite of a very erroneous course of practice, her moral tone is all that can be desired. She discourses about the importance of keeping to the paths of virtue with the most exemplary punctuality, though she does not find them convenient for her own personal use. Colonel Jack is a young Arab of the streets—as it is fashionable to call them nowadays—sleeping in the ashes of a glass-house by night, and consorting with thieves by day. Still, the exemplary nature of his sentiments would go far to establish Lord Palmerston's rather heterodox theory of the innate goodness of man. He talks like a book from his earliest infancy. He once forgets himself so far as to rob a couple of poor women on the highway instead of picking rich men's pockets; but his conscience pricks him so much that he cannot rest till he has restored the money. Captain Singleton is a still more striking case: he is a pirate by trade, but with a strong resemblance to the ordinary British merchant in his habits of thought. He ultimately retires from a business in which the risks are too great for his taste, marries, and settles down quietly on his savings. There is a certain Quaker who joins his ship, really as a volunteer, but under a show of compulsion, in order to avoid the possible inconveniences of a capture. The Quaker always advises him in his difficulties in such a way as to avoid responsibility. When they are in action with a Portuguese man-of-war, for example, the Quaker sees a chance of boarding, and, coming up to Singleton, says very calmly, "Friend, what dost thou mean? why dost thou not visit thy neighbour in the ship, the door being open for thee?" This ingenious gentleman always preserves as much humanity as is compatible with his peculiar position, and even prevents certain negroes from being tortured into confession, on the unanswerable ground that, as neither party understands a word of the other's language, the confession will not be to much purpose. "It is no compliment to my moderation," says Singleton, "to say I was convinced by these reasons; and yet we had all much ado to keep our second lieutenant from murdering some of them to make them tell."

Now, this humane pirate takes up pretty much the position which De Foe's villains generally occupy in good earnest. They do very objectionable things; but they always speak like steady respectable Englishmen, with an eye to the main chance. It is true that there is nothing more difficult than to make a villain tell his own story naturally; in a way, that is, so as to show at once the badness of the motive and the excuse by which the actor reconciles it to his own mind. De Foe is entirely deficient in this capacity of appreciating a character different from his own. His actors are merely so many repetitions of himself placed under different circumstances and committing crimes in the way of business, as De Foe might himself have carried out a commercial transaction. From the outside they are perfect; they are evidently copied from the life; and Captain Singleton is himself a repetition of the celebrated Captain Kidd, who indeed is mentioned in the novel. But of the state of mind which leads a man to be a pirate, and of the effects which it produces upon his morals, De Foe has either no notion or is, at least, totally incapable of giving us a representation. All that goes by the name of psychological analysis in modern fiction is totally alien to his art. He could, as we have said, show such dramatic power as may be implied in transporting himself to a different position, and looking at matters even from his adversary's point of view; but of the further power of appreciating his adversary's character he shows not the slightest trace. He looks at his actors from the outside, and gives us with wonderful minuteness all the details of their lives; but he never seems to remember that within the mechanism whose working he describes there is a soul very different from that of Daniel De Foe. Rather, he seems to see in mankind nothing but so many million Daniel De Foes; they

are in all sorts of postures, and thrown into every variety of difficulty, but the stuff of which they are composed is identical with that which he buttons into his own coat; there is variety of form, but no colouring, in his pictures of life.

We may ask again, therefore, what is the peculiar source of De Foe's power? He has little or no dramatic power, in the higher sense of the word, which implies sympathy with many characters and varying tones of mind. If he had written *Henry IV.*, Falstaff and Hotspur, and Prince Hal would all have been as like each other as are generally the first and second murderer. Nor is the mere fact that he tells a story with a strange appearance of veracity sufficient; for a story may be truth-like and yet deadly dull. Indeed, no candid critic can deny that this is the case with some of De Foe's narratives; as, for example, the latter part of *Colonel Jack*, where the details of management of a plantation in Virginia are sufficiently uninteresting in spite of the minute financial details. One device, which he occasionally employs with great force, suggests an occasional source of interest. It is generally reckoned as one of his most skilful tricks that in telling a story he cunningly leaves a few stray ends, which are never taken up. Such is the well-known incident of Xury in *Robinson Crusoe*. This contrivance undoubtedly gives an appearance of authenticity, by increasing the resemblance to real narratives; it is like the trick of artificially roughening a stone after it has been fixed into a building, to give it the appearance of being fresh from the quarry. De Foe, however, frequently extracts a more valuable piece of service from these loose ends. The situation which has been most praised in De Foe's novels is that which occurs at the end of *Roxana*. Roxana, after a life of wickedness, is at last married to a substantial merchant. She has saved from the wages of sin the convenient sum of 2,056*l*. a year, secured upon excellent mortgages. Her husband has 17,000*l*. in cash, after deducting a "black article of 8,000 pistoles," due on account of a certain lawsuit in Paris, and 1,320*l*. a year in rent. There is a satisfaction about these definite sums which we seldom receive from the vague assertions of modern novelists. Unluckily, a girl turns up at this moment who shows great curiosity about Roxana's history. It soon becomes evident that she is, in fact, Roxana's daughter by a former and long since deserted husband; but she cannot be acknowledged without a revelation of her mother's subsequently most disreputable conduct. Now, Roxana has a devoted maid, who threatens to get rid, by fair means or foul, of this importunate daughter. Once she fails in her design, but confesses to her mistress that, if necessary, she will commit the murder. Roxana professes to be terribly shocked, but yet has a desire to be relieved at almost any price from her tormentor. The maid thereupon disappears again; soon afterwards the daughter disappears too; and Roxana is left in terrible doubt, tormented by the opposing anxieties that her maid may have murdered her daughter, or that her daughter may have escaped and revealed the mother's true character. Here is a telling situation for a sensation novelist; and the minuteness with which the story is worked out, whilst we are kept in suspense, supplies the place of the ordinary rant; to say nothing of the increased effect due to apparent veracity, in which certainly few sensation novelists can even venture a distant competition. The end of the story differs still more widely from modern art. Roxana has to go abroad with her husband, still in a state of doubt. Her maid after a time joins her, but gives no intimation as to the fate of the daughter; and the story concludes by a simple statement that Roxana afterwards fell into well deserved misery. The mystery is certainly impressive; and Roxana is heartily afraid of the devil and the gallows, to say nothing of the chance of losing her fortune.

Whether, as Lamb maintained, the conclusion in which the mystery is cleared up is a mere forgery, or was added by De Foe to satisfy the ill-judged curiosity of his readers, I do not profess to decide. Certainly it rather spoils the story; but in this, as in some other cases, one is often left in doubt as to the degree in which De Foe was conscious of his own merits.

Another instance on a smaller scale of the effective employment of judicious silence, is an incident in *Captain Singleton*. The Quaker of our acquaintance meets with a Japanese priest who speaks a few words of English, and explains that he has learnt it from thirteen Englishmen, the only remnant of thirty-two who had been wrecked on the coast of Japan. To confirm his story, he produces a bit of paper on which is written, in plain English words, "We came from Greenland and from the North Pole." Here are claimants for the discovery of a North-west Passage, of whom we would gladly hear more. Unluckily, when Captain Singleton comes to the place where his Quaker had met the priest, the ship in which he was sailing had departed; and this put an end to an inquiry, and perhaps "may have disappointed mankind of one of the most noble discoveries that ever was made or will again be made, in the world, for the good of mankind in general; but so much for that."

In these two fragments, which illustrate a very common device of De Foe's, we come across two elements of positive power over our imaginations. Even De Foe's imagination recognised and delighted in a certain margin of mystery to this harsh world of facts and figures. He is generally too anxious to set everything before us in broad daylight; there is too little of the thoughts and emotions which inhabit the twilight of the mind; of those dim half-seen forms which exercise the strongest influence upon the imagination, and are the most tempting subjects for the poet's art. De Foe, in truth, was little enough of a poet. Sometimes by mere force of terse idiomatic language he rises into real poetry, as it was understood in the days when Pope and Dryden were our lawgivers. It is often really vigorous. The well-known verses—

> Wherever God erects a house of prayer
> The devil always builds a chapel there—

which begin the *True-born Englishman*, or the really fine lines which occur in the "Hymn to the Pillory," that "hieroglyphic state machine, contrived to punish fancy in," and ending—

> Tell them that placed him here,
> They 're scandals to the times,
> Are at a loss to find his guilt,
> *And can't commit his crimes*—

may stand for specimens of his best manner. More frequently he degenerates into the merest doggerel, e.g.—

> No man was ever yet so void of sense,
> As to debate the right of self-defence,
> A principle so grafted in the mind,
> With nature born, and does like nature bind;
> Twisted with reason, and with nature too,
> As neither one nor t' other can undo—

which is scarcely a happy specimen of the difficult art of reasoning in verse. His verse is at best vigorous epigrammatic writing, such as would now be converted into leading articles, twisted with more or less violence into rhyme. And yet there is a poetical side to his mind, or at least a susceptibility to poetical impressions of a certain order. And as a novelist is on the border-line between poetry and prose, and novels should be, as it were, prose saturated with poetry, we may expect to come in this direction upon the secret of De Foe's power. Although De Foe for the most part deals with good tangible subjects, which

he can weigh and measure and reduce to moidores and pistoles, the mysterious has a very strong though peculiar attraction for him. It is indeed that vulgar kind of mystery which implies nothing of reverential awe. He was urged by a restless curiosity to get away from this commonplace world, and reduce the unknown regions beyond to scale and measure. The centre of Africa, the wilds of Siberia, and even more distinctly the world of spirits, had wonderful charms for him. Nothing would have given him greater pleasure than to determine the exact number of the fallen angels and the date of their calamity. In the *History of the Devil* he touches, with a singular kind of humorous gravity, upon several of these questions, and seems to apologise for his limited information. "Several things," he says, "have been suggested to set us a-calculating the number of this frightful throng of devils who, with Satan the master-devil, was thus cast out of heaven." He declines the task, though he quotes with a certain pleasure the result obtained by a grave calculator, who found that in the first line of Satan's army there were a thousand times a hundred thousand million devils, and more in the other two. He gives a kind of arithmetical measure of the decline of the devil's power by pointing out that "he who was once equal to the angel who killed eighty thousand men in one night, is not able now, without a new commission, to take away the life of one Job." He is filled with curiosity as to the proceedings of the first parliament (p——t as he delicately puts it) of devils; he regrets that as he was not personally present in that "black divan"—at least, not that he can remember, for who can account for his pre-existent state?—he cannot say what happened; but he adds,

> If I had as much personal acquaintance with the devil as would admit it, and could depend upon the truth of what answer he would give me, the first question would be, what measures they (the devils) resolved on at their first assembly?

and the second how they employed the time between their fall and the creation of the man? Here we see the instinct of the politician; and we may add that De Foe is thoroughly dissatisfied with Milton's statements upon this point, though admiring his genius; and goes so far as to write certain verses intended as a correction of, or interpolation into, *Paradise Lost*.

Mr. Ruskin, in comparing Milton's Satan with Dante's, somewhere remarks that the vagueness of Milton, as compared with the accurate measurements given by Dante, is so far a proof of less activity of the imaginative faculty. It is easier to leave the devil's stature uncertain than to say that he was eighteen feet high. Without disputing the proposition as Mr. Ruskin puts it, we fancy that he would scarcely take De Foe's poetry as an improvement in dignity upon Milton's. We may, perhaps, guess at its merits from this fragment of a speech in prose, addressed to Adam by Eve:

> What ails the sot? [says the new termagant]. What are you afraid of? . . . Take it, you fool, and eat. . . . Take it, I say, or I will go and cut down the tree, and you shall never eat any of it at all; and you shall still be a fool, and be governed by your wife for ever.

This, and much more gross buffoonery of the same kind, is apparently intended to recommend certain sound moral aphorisms to the vulgar; but the cool arithmetical method by which De Foe investigates the history of the devil, his anxiety to pick up gossip about him, and the view which he takes of him as a very acute and unscrupulous politician—though impartially vindicating him for some of Mr. Milton's aspersions—is exquisitely characteristic.

If we may measure the imaginative power of great poets by the relative merits of their conceptions of Satan, we might find a humbler gauge for inferior capacities in the power of summoning awe-inspiring ghosts. The difficulty of the feat is extreme. Your ghost, as Bottom would have said, is a very fearful wild-fowl to bring upon the stage. He must be handled delicately, or he is spoilt. Scott has a good ghost or two; but Lord Lytton, almost the only writer who has recently dealt with the supernatural, draws too freely upon our belief, and creates only melodramatic spiritual beings, with a strong dash of the vulgarising element of modern "spiritualism." They are scarcely more awful beings than the terrible creation of the raw-head-and-bloody-bones school of fiction.

Amongst this school we fear that De Foe must, on the whole, be reckoned. We have already made acquaintance with Mrs. Veal, who, in her ghostly condition, talks for an hour and three-quarters with a gossip over a cup of tea; who, indeed, so far forgets her ghostly condition as to ask for a cup of the said tea, and only evades the consequences of her blunder by one of those rather awkward excuses which we all sometimes practice in society; and who, in short, is the least ethereal spirit that was ever met with outside a table. De Foe's extraordinary love for supernatural stories of the gossiping variety found vent in *A History of Apparitions* and his *System of Magic*. The position which he takes up is a kind of modified rationalism. He believes that there are genuine apparitions which personate our dead friends, and give us excellent pieces of advice on occasion; but he refuses to believe that the spirits can appear themselves, on account "of the many strange inconveniences and ill consequences which would happen if the souls of men and women, unembodied and departed, were at liberty to visit the earth." De Foe is evidently as familiar with the habits of spirits generally as of the devil. In that case, for example, the feuds of families would never die, for the injured person would be always coming back to right himself. He proceeds upon this principle to account for many apparitions, as, for example, one which appeared in the likeness of a certain J. O. of the period, and strongly recommended his widow to reduce her expenses. He won't believe that the Virgin appeared to St. Francis, because all stories of that kind are mere impostures of the priests; but he thinks it very likely that he was haunted by the devil, who may have sometimes taken the Virgin's shape. In the *History of Witchcraft* De Foe tells us how, as he was once riding in the country, he met a man on the way to inquire of a certain wizard. De Foe, according to his account, which may or may not be intended as authentic, waited the whole of the next day at a public-house in a country-town, in order to hear the result of the inquiry; and had long conversations, reported in his usual style, with infinite "says he's" and "says I's," in which he tried to prove that the wizard was an impostor. This lets us into the secret of many of De Foe's apparitions. They are the ghosts that frighten villagers as they cross commons late at night, or that rattle chains and display lights in haunted houses. Sometimes they have vexed knavish attorneys by discovering long-hidden deeds. Sometimes they have enticed highwaymen into dark corners of woods, and there the wretched criminal finds in their bags (for ghosts of this breed have good substantial luggage) nothing but a halter and a bit of silver (value exactly 13½*d*.) to pay the hangman. When he turns to the owner, he has vanished. Occasionally, they are the legends told by some passing traveller from distant lands—probably genuine superstitions in their origin, but amplified by tradition into marvellous exactitude of detail, and garnished with long gossiping conversations.

Such a ghost, which, on the whole, is my favourite, is the mysterious Owke Mouraski. This being, whether devil or good spirit, no man knows, accompanied a traveller for four years through the steppes of Russia, and across Norway, Turkey, and various other countries. On the march he was always seen a mile to the left of the party, keeping parallel with them, in glorious indifference to roads. He crossed rivers without bridges, and the sea without ships. Everywhere, in the wild countries, he was known by name and dreaded; for if he entered a house, some one would die there within a year. Yet he was good to the traveller, going so far, indeed, on one occasion, as to lend him a horse, and frequently treating him to good advice. Towards the end of the journey Owke Mouraski informed his companion that he was "the inhabitant of an invisible region," and afterwards became very familiar with him. The traveller, indeed, would never believe that his friend was a devil, a scepticism of which De Foe doubtfully approves. The story, however, must be true, because, as De Foe says, he saw it in manuscript many years ago; and certainly Owke is of a superior order to most of the pot-house ghosts.

De Foe, doubtless, had an insatiable appetite for legends of this kind, talked about them with infinite zest in innumerable gossips, and probably smoked pipes and consumed ale in abundance during the process. The ghosts are the substantial creations of the popular fancy, which no longer nourished itself upon a genuine faith in a more lofty order of spiritual beings. It is superstition become gross and vulgar before it disappears for ever. Romance and poetry have pretty well departed from these ghosts, as from the witches of the period, who are little better than those who still linger in our country villages and fill corners of newspapers, headed "Superstition in the nineteenth century." In his novels De Foe's instinct for probability generally enables him to employ the marvellous moderately, and, therefore, effectively; he is specially given to dreams; they are generally verified just enough to leave us the choice of credulity or scepticism, and are in excellent keeping with the supposed narrator. Roxana tells us how one morning she suddenly sees her lover's face as though it were a death's head, and his clothes covered with blood. In the evening the lover is murdered. One of Moll Flanders' husbands hears her call him at a distance of many miles—a superstition, by the way, in which Boswell, if not Johnson, fully believed. De Foe shows his usual skill in sometimes making the visions or omens fail of a too close fulfilment, as in the excellent dream where Robinson Crusoe hears Friday's father tell him of the sailors' attempt to murder the Spaniards: no part of the dream, as he says, is specifically true, though it has a general truth; and hence we may, at our choice, suppose it to have been supernatural, or to be merely a natural result of Crusoe's anxiety. This region of the marvellous, however, only affects De Foe's novels in a subordinate degree. The Owke Mouraski suggests another field in which a lover of the mysterious could then find room for his imagination. The world still presented a boundless wilderness of untravelled land. Mapped and explored territory was still a bright spot surrounded by chaotic darkness, instead of the two being in the reverse proportions. Geographers might fill up huge tracts by writing "here is much gold," or putting "elephants instead of towns." De Foe's gossiping acquaintance, when they were tired of ghosts, could tell of strange adventures in wild seas, where merchantmen followed a narrow track, exposed to the assaults of pirates; or of long journeys over endless steppes, in the days when travelling was travelling indeed; when distances were reckoned by months, and men might expect to meet undiscovered tribes and monsters unimagined by natural historians. Doubtless he had listened greedily to the stories of sea-faring men and merchants from the Gold Coast or the East. *Captain Singleton*, to omit *Robinson Crusoe* for the present, shows the form into which these stories moulded themselves in his mind. Singleton, besides his other exploits, anticipated Livingstone in crossing Africa from sea to sea. De Foe's biographers rather unnecessarily, admire the marvellous way in which his imaginary descriptions have been confirmed by later travellers. And it is true that Singleton found two great lakes, which may, if we please, be identified with those of recent discoverers. His other guesses are not surprising. As a specimen of the mode in which he filled up the unknown space we may mention that he covers the desert "with a kind of thick moss of a blackish dead colour," which is not a very impressive phenomenon. It is in the matter of wild beasts, however, that he is strongest. Their camp is in one place surrounded by "innumerable numbers of devilish creatures." These creatures were as "thick as a drove of bullocks coming to a fair," so that they could not fire without hitting some; in fact, a volley brought down three tigers and two wolves, besides one creature "of an ill-gendered kind, between a tiger and a leopard." Before long they met an "ugly, venomous, deformed kind of a snake or serpent," which had "a hellish, ugly, deformed look and voice;" indeed, they would have recognised in it the being who most haunted De Foe's imaginary world—the devil—except that they could not think what business the devil could have where there were no people. The fauna of this country, besides innumerable lions, tigers, leopards, and elephants, comprised "living creatures as big as calves, but not of that kind," and creatures between a buffalo and a deer, which resembled neither; they had no horns, but legs like a cow, with a fine head and neck, like a deer. The "ill-gendered" beast is an admirable specimen of De Foe's workmanship. It shows his moderation under most tempting circumstances. No dog-headed men, no men with eyes in their breasts, or feet that serve as umbrellas, will suit him. He must have something new, and yet probable; and he hits upon a very serviceable animal in this mixture between a tiger and a leopard. Surely no one could refuse to honour such a moderate draft upon his imagination. In short, De Foe, even in the wildest of regions, where his pencil might have full play, sticks closely to the commonplace, and will not venture beyond the regions of the easily conceivable.

The final element in which De Foe's curiosity might find a congenial food consisted of the stories floating about contemporary affairs. He had talked with men who had fought in the Great Rebellion, or even in the old German wars. He had himself been out with Monmouth, and taken part in the fight at Sedgemoor. Doubtless that small experience of actual warfare gave additional vivacity to his descriptions of battles, and was useful to him, as Gibbon declares that his service with the militia was of some assistance in describing armies of a very different kind. There is a period in history which has a peculiar interest for all of us. It is that which lies upon the borderland between the past and present; which has gathered some romance from the lapse of time, and yet is not so far off but that we have seen some of the actors, and can distinctly realise the scenes in which they took part. Such to the present generation is the era of the Revolutionary wars. "Old men still creep among us," who lived through that period of peril and excitement, and yet we are far enough removed from them to fancy that there were giants in those days. When De Foe wrote his novels the battles of the great Civil War and the calamities of the Plague were passing through this phase; and to them we owe two of his most interesting books, the *Memoirs of a Cavalier* and the *History of the Plague*.

When such a man spins us a yarn the conditions of its being interesting are tolerably simple. The first condition obviously is, that the plot must be a good one, and good in the sense that a representation in dumb-show must be sufficiently exciting, without the necessity of any explanation of motives. The novel of sentiment or passion or character would be altogether beyond his scope. He will accumulate any number of facts and details; but they must be such as will speak for themselves without the need of an interpreter. For this reason we do not imagine that *Roxana, Moll Flanders, Colonel Jack*, or *Captain Singleton* can fairly claim any higher interest than that which belongs to the ordinary police report, given with infinite fulness and vivacity of detail. In each of them there are one or two forcible situations. Roxana pursued by her daughter, Moll Flanders in prison, and Colonel Jack as a young boy of the streets, are powerful fragments, and well adapted for his peculiar method. He goes on heaping up little significant facts, till we are able to realise the situation powerfully, and we may then supply the sentiment for ourselves. But he never seems to know his own strength. He gives us at equal length, and with the utmost plain-speaking, the details of a number of other positions, which are neither interesting nor edifying. He is decent or coarse, just as he is dull or amusing, without knowing the difference. The details about the different connections formed by Roxana and Moll Flanders have no atom of sentiment, and are about as wearisome as the journal of a specially heartless lady of the same character would be at the present day. He has been praised for never gilding objectionable objects, or making vice attractive. To all appearance, he would have been totally unable to set about it. He has only one mode of telling a story, and he follows the thread of his narrative into the back-slums of London, or lodging-houses of doubtful character, or respectable places of trade, with the same equanimity, at a good steady jog-trot of narrative. The absence of any passion or sentiment deprives such places of the one possible source of interest; and we must confess that two-thirds of each of these novels are deadly dull; the remainder, though exhibiting specimens of his genuine power, is not far enough from the commonplace to be specially attractive. In short, the merit of De Foe's narrative bears a direct proportion to the intrinsic merit of a plain statement of the facts; and, in the novels already mentioned, as there is nothing very surprising, certainly nothing unique, about the story, his treatment cannot raise it above a very moderate level.

Above these stories comes De Foe's best fragment of fictitious history.[1] The *Memoirs of a Cavalier* is a very amusing book, though it is less fiction than history, interspersed with a few personal anecdotes. In it there are some exquisite little bits of genuine De Foe. The Cavalier tells us, with such admirable frankness, that he once left the army a day or two before a battle, in order to visit some relatives at Bath, and excuses himself so modestly for his apparent neglect of military duty, that we cannot refuse to believe in him. A novelist, we say, would have certainly taken us to the battle, or would, at least, have given his hero a more heroic excuse. The character, too, of the old soldier, who has served under Gustavus Adolphus, who is disgusted with the raw English levies, still more disgusted with the interference of parsons, and who has a respect for his opponents—especially Sir Thomas Fairfax—which is compounded partly of English love of fair play, and partly of the indifference of a professional officer—is better supported than most of De Foe's personages. An excellent Dugald Dalgetty touch is his constant anxiety to impress upon the Royalist commanders the importance of a particular trick which he has learned abroad of mixing foot soldiers with the cavalry. We must leave him, however, to say a few words upon the *History of the Plague*, which seems to come next in merit to *Robinson Crusoe*. Here De Foe has to deal with a story of such intrinsically tragic interest that all his details become affecting. It needs no commentary to interpret the meaning of the terrible anecdotes, many of which are doubtless founded on fact. There is the strange superstitious element brought out by the horror of the sudden visitation. The supposed writer hesitates as to leaving the doomed city. He is decided to stay at last by opening the Bible at random and coming upon the text, "He shall deliver thee from the snare of the fowler, and from the noisome pestilence." He watches the comets: the one which appeared before the Plague was "of a dull, languid colour, and its motion heavy, solemn, and slow;" the other, which preceded the Great Fire, was "bright and sparkling, and its motion swift and furious." Old women, he says, believed in them, especially "the hypochondriac part of the other sex," who might, he thinks, be called old women too. Still he half-believes himself, especially when the second appears. He does not believe that the breath of the plague-stricken upon a glass would leave shapes of "dragons, snakes, and devils, horrible to behold;" but he does believe that if they breathed on a bird they would kill it, or "at least make its eggs rotten." However, he admits that no experiments were tried. Then we have the hideous, and sometimes horribly grotesque, incidents. There is the poor naked creature, who runs up and down, exclaiming continually, "Oh, the great and the dreadful God!" but would say nothing else, and speak to no one. There is the woman who suddenly opens a window and "calls out, 'Death, death, death!' in a most inimitable tone, which struck me with horror and chillness in the very blood." There is the man who, with death in his face, opens the door to a young apprentice sent to ask him for money: "Very well, child," says the living ghost; "go to Cripplegate Church, and bid them ring the bell for me;" and with those words shuts the door, goes upstairs, and dies. Then we have the horrors of the dead-cart, and the unlucky piper who was carried off by mistake. De Foe, with his usual ingenuity, corrects the inaccurate versions of the story, and says that the piper was not blind, but only old and silly; and that he does not believe that, as "the story goes," he set up his pipes while in the cart. After this we cannot refuse to admit that he was really carried off and all but buried. Another device for cheating us into acceptance of his story is the ingenious way in which he imitates the occasional lapses of memory of a genuine narrator, and admits that he does not precisely recollect certain details; and still better is the conscientious eagerness with which he distinguishes between the occurrences of which he was an eye-witness and those which he only knew by hearsay.

This book, more than any of the others, shows a skill in selecting telling incidents. We are sometimes in doubt whether the particular details which occur in other stories are not put in rather by good luck than from a due perception of their value. He thus resembles a savage, who is as much pleased with a glass bead as with a piece of gold; but in the *History of the Plague* every detail goes straight to the mark. At one point he cannot help diverging into the story of three poor men who escape into the fields, and giving us, with his usual relish, all their rambling conversations by the way. For the most part, however, he is less diffusive and more pointed than usual; the greatness of the calamity seems to have given more intensity to his style; and it leaves all the impression of a genuine narrative, told by one who has, as it were, just escaped from the valley of the shadow of death, with the awe still upon him, and every terrible sight and sound fresh in his memory. The amazing

truthfulness of the style is here in its proper place; we wish to be brought as near as may be to the facts; we want good realistic painting more than fine sentiment. The story reminds us of certain ghastly photographs published during the American War, which had been taken on the field of battle. They gave a more forcible impression of the horrors of war than the most thrilling pictures drawn from the fancy. In such cases we only wish the narrator to stand as much as possible on one side, and just draw up a bit of the curtain which conceals his gallery of horrors.

It is time, however, to say enough of *Robinson Crusoe* to justify its traditional superiority to De Foe's other writings. The charm, as some critics say, is difficult to analyse; and I do not profess to demonstrate mathematically that it must necessarily be, what it is, the most fascinating boy's book ever written, and one which older critics may study with delight. The most obvious advantage over the secondary novels lies in the unique situation. Lamb, in the passage from which I have quoted, gracefully evades this point. "Are there no solitudes," he says, "out of the cave and the desert? or cannot the heart, in the midst of crowds, feel frightfully alone?" Singleton, he suggests, is alone with pirates less merciful than the howling monsters, the devilish serpents, and ill-gendered creatures of De Foe's deserts. Colonel Jack is alone amidst the London thieves when he goes to bury his treasures in the hollow tree. This is prettily said; but it suggests rather what another writer might have made of De Foe's heroes, than what De Foe made of them himself. Singleton, it is true, is alone amongst the pirates, but he takes to them as naturally as a fish takes to the water, and, indeed, finds them a good, honest, respectable, stupid sort of people. They stick by him and he by them, and we are never made to feel the real horrors of his position. Colonel Jack might, in other hands, have become an Oliver Twist, less real perhaps than De Foe has made him, but infinitely more pathetic. De Foe tells us of his unpleasant sleeping-places, and his occasional fears of the gallows; but of the supposed mental struggles, of the awful solitude of soul, we hear nothing. How can we sympathise very deeply with a young gentleman whose recollections run chiefly upon the exact numbers of shillings and pence captured by himself and his pocket-picking "pals"? Similarly Robinson Crusoe dwells but little upon the horrors of his position, and when he does is apt to get extremely prosy. We fancy that he could never have been in want of a solid sermon on Sunday, however much he may have missed the church-going bell. But in *Robinson Crusoe*, as in the *History of the Plague*, the story speaks for itself. To explain the horrors of living among thieves, we must have some picture of internal struggles, of a sense of honour opposed to temptation, and a pure mind in danger of contamination. De Foe's extremely straightforward and prosaic view of life prevents him from setting any such sentimental trials before us; the lad avoids the gallows, and in time becomes the honest master of a good plantation; and there's enough. But the horrors of abandonment on a desert island can be appreciated by the simplest sailor or schoolboy. The main thing is to bring out the situation plainly and forcibly, to tell us of the difficulties of making pots and pans, of catching goats and sowing corn, and of avoiding audacious cannibals. This task De Foe performs with unequalled spirit and vivacity. In his first discovery of a new art he shows the freshness so often conspicuous in first novels. The scenery was just that which had peculiar charms for his fancy; it was one of those half-true legends of which he had heard strange stories from seafaring men, and possibly from the acquaintances of his hero himself. He brings out the shrewd vigorous character of the Englishman thrown upon his own resources with evident enjoyment of his task. Indeed, De Foe tells us very emphatically that in Robinson Crusoe he saw a kind of allegory of his own fate. He had suffered from solitude of soul. Confinement in his prison is represented in the book by confinement in an island; and even a particular incident, here and there, such as the fright he receives one night from something in his bed, "was word for word a history of what happened." In other words, this novel too, like many of the best ever written, has in it the autobiographical element which makes a man speak from greater depths of feeling than in a purely imaginary story.

It would indeed be easy to show that the story, though in one sense marvellously like truth, is singularly wanting as a psychological study. Friday is no real savage, but a good English servant without plush. He says "muchee" and "speakee," but he becomes at once a civilised being, and in his first conversation puzzles Crusoe terribly by that awkward theological question, why God did not kill the devil—for characteristically enough Crusoe's first lesson includes a little instruction upon the enemy of mankind. He found, however, that it was "not so easy to imprint right notions in Friday's mind about the devil, as it was about the being of a God." This is comparatively a trifle; but Crusoe himself is all but impossible. Steele, indeed, gives an account of Selkirk, from which he infers that "this plain man's story is a memorable example that he is happiest who confines his wants to natural necessities;" but the facts do not warrant this pet doctrine of an old-fashioned school. Selkirk's state of mind may be inferred from two or three facts. He had almost forgotten to talk; he had learnt to catch goats by hunting them on foot; and he had acquired the exceedingly difficult art of making fire by rubbing two sticks. In other words, his whole mind was absorbed in providing a few physical necessities, and he was rapidly becoming a savage—for a man who can't speak and can make fire is very near the Australian. We may infer, what is probable from other cases, that a man living fifteen years by himself, like Crusoe, would either go mad or sink into the semi-savage state. De Foe really describes a man in prison, not in solitary confinement. We should not be so pedantic as to call for accuracy in such matters; but the difference between the fiction and what we believe would have been the reality is significant. De Foe, even in *Robinson Crusoe*, gives a very inadequate picture of the mental torments to which his hero is exposed. He is frightened by a parrot calling him by name, and by the strangely picturesque incident of the footmark on the sand; but, on the whole, he takes his imprisonment with preternatural stolidity. His stay on the island produces the same state of mind as might be due to a dull Sunday in Scotland. For this reason, the want of power in describing emotion as compared with the amazing power of describing facts, *Robinson Crusoe* is a book for boys rather than men, and, as Lamb says, for the kitchen rather than for higher circles. It falls short of any high intellectual interest. When we leave the striking situation and get to the second part, with the Spaniards and Will Atkins talking natural theology to his wife, it sinks to the level of the secondary stories. But for people who are not too proud to take a rather low order of amusement, *Robinson Crusoe* will always be one of the most charming of books. We have the romantic and adventurous incidents upon which the most unflinching realism can be set to work without danger of vulgarity. Here is precisely the story suited to De Foe's strength and weakness. He is forced to be artistic in spite of himself. He cannot lose the thread of the narrative and break it into disjointed fragments, for the limits of the island confine him as well as his hero. He cannot tire us with details, for all the details of such a story are interesting; it is made up of petty incidents, as much as the life

of a prisoner reduced to taming flies, or making saws out of penknives. The island does as well as the Bastille for making trifles valuable to the sufferer and to us. The demand for romantic power to press them home to us; and the efforts to give an air of authenticity to the story, which sometimes make us smile, and sometimes rather bore us, in other novels are all to the purpose; for there is a real point in putting such a story in the mouth of the sufferer, and in giving us for the time an illusory belief in his reality. It is one of the exceptional cases in which the poetical aspect of a position is brought out best by the most prosaic accuracy of detail; and we imagine that Robinson Crusoe's island, with all his small household torments, will always be more impressive than the more gorgeously coloured island of Enoch Arden. When we add that the whole book shows the freshness of a writer employed on his first novel—though at the mature age of fifty-eight; seeing in it an allegory of his own experience embodied in the scenes which most interested his imagination, we see some reasons why *Robinson Crusoe* should hold a distinct rank by itself amongst his works. As De Foe was a man of very powerful but very limited imagination—able to see certain aspects of things with extraordinary distinctness, but little able to rise above them—even his greatest book shows his weakness, and scarcely satisfies a grown-up man with a taste for high art. In revenge, it ought, according to Rousseau, to be for a time the whole library of a boy, chiefly, it seems, to teach him that the stock of an ironmonger is better than that of a jeweller. We may agree in the conclusion without caring about the reason; and to have pleased all the boys in Europe for near a hundred and fifty years is, after all, a remarkable feat.

One remark must be added, which scarcely seems to have been sufficiently noticed by De Foe's critics. He cannot be understood unless we remember that he was primarily and essentially a journalist, and that even his novels are part of his journalism. He was a pioneer in the art of newspaper writing, and anticipated with singular acuteness many later developments of his occupation. The nearest parallel to him is Cobbett, who wrote still better English, though he could hardly have written a *Robinson Crusoe*. De Foe, like Cobbett, was a sturdy middle-class Englishman, and each was in his time the most effective advocate of the political views of his class. De Foe represented the Whiggism, not of the great "junto" or aristocratic ring, but of the dissenters and tradesmen whose prejudices the junto had to turn to account. He would have stood by Chatham in the time of Wilkes and of the American War; he would have demanded parliamentary reform in the time of Brougham and Bentham, and he would have been a follower of the Manchester school in the time of Bright and Cobden. We all know the type, and have made up our minds as to its merits. When De Foe came to be a subject of biography in this century, he was of course praised for his enlightenment by men of congenial opinions. He was held up as a model politician, not only for his creed but for his independence. The revelations of his last biographer, Mr. Lee, showed unfortunately that considerable deductions must be made from the independence. He was, as we now know, in the pay of Government for many years, while boasting of his perfect purity; he was transferred, like a mere dependent, from the Whigs to the Tories and back again. In the reign of George I. he consented to abandon his character in order to act as a spy upon unlucky Jacobite colleagues. It is to the credit of Harley's acuteness that he was the first English minister to make a systematic use of the press and was the patron both of Swift and De Foe. But to use the press was then to make a mere tool of the author. De Foe was a journalist, living, and supporting a family, by his pen, in the days when a journalist had to choose between the pillory and dependence. He soon had enough of the pillory and preferred to do very dirty services for his employer. Other journalists, I fear, since his day have consented to serve masters whom in their hearts they disapproved. It may, I think, be fairly said on behalf of De Foe that in the main he worked for causes of which he really approved; that he never sacrificed the opinions to which he was most deeply attached; that his morality was, at worst, above that of many contemporary politicians; and that, in short, he had a conscience, though he could not afford to obey it implicitly. He says himself, and I think the statement has its pathetic side, that he made a kind of compromise with that awkward instinct. He praised those acts only of the Government which he really approved, though he could not afford to denounce those from which he differed. Undoubtedly, as many respectable moralists have told us, the man who endeavours to draw such lines will get into difficulties and probably emerge with a character not a little soiled in the process. But after all as things go, it is something to find that a journalist has really a conscience, even though his conscience be a little too open to solid arguments. He was still capable of blushing. Let us be thankful that in these days our journalists are too high-minded to be ever required to blush. Here, however, I have only to speak of the effect of De Foe's position upon his fictions. He had early begun to try other than political modes of journalism. His account of the great storm of 1703 was one of his first attempts as a reporter; and it is characteristic that, as he was in prison at the time, he had already to report things seen only by the eye of faith. He tried at an early period to give variety to his *Review* by some of the "social" articles which afterwards became the staple of the *Tatler* and *Spectator*. When, after the death of Queen Anne, there was a political lull he struck out new paths. It was then that he wrote lives of highwaymen and dissenting divines, and that he patched up any narratives which he could get hold of, and gave them the shape of authentic historical documents. He discovered the great art of interviewing, and one of his performances might still pass for a masterpiece. Jack Sheppard, when already in the cart beneath the gallows, gave a paper to a bystander, of which the life published by De Foe on the following day professed to be a reproduction. Nothing that could be turned into copy for the newspaper or the sixpenny pamphlet of the day came amiss to this forerunner of journalistic enterprise. This is the true explanation of *Robinson Crusoe* and its successors. *Robinson Crusoe*, in fact, is simply an application on a larger scale of the device which he was practising every day. It is purely and simply a masterly bit of journalism. It affects to be a true story, as, of course, every story in a newspaper affects to be true; though De Foe had made not the very remote discovery that it is often easier to invent the facts than to investigate them. He is simply a reporter *minus* the veracity. Like any other reporter, he assumes that the interest of his story depends obviously and entirely upon its verisimilitude. He relates the adventures of the genuine Alexander Selkirk, only elaborated into more detail, just as a modern reporter might give us an account of Mr. Stanley's African expedition if Mr. Stanley had been unable to do so for himself. He is always in the attitude of mind of the newspaper correspondent, who has been interviewing the hero of an interesting story and ventures at most a little safe embroidery. This explains a remark made by Dickens, who complained that the account of Friday's death showed an "utter want of tenderness and sentiment," and says somewhere that *Robinson Crusoe* is the only great novel which never moves either to laughter or to tears. The creator of Oliver Twist and Little Nell was naturally scandalised by De Foe's dry and

matter-of-fact narrative. But De Foe had never approached the conception of his art which afterwards became familiar. He had nothing to do with sentiment or psychology; those elements of interest came in with Richardson and Fielding; he was simply telling a true story and leaving his readers to feel what they pleased. It never even occurred to him, more than it occurs to the ordinary reporter, to analyse character or describe scenery or work up sentiment. He was simply a narrator of plain facts. He left poetry and reflection to Mr. Pope or Mr. Addison, as your straightforward annalist in a newspaper has no thought of rivalling Lord Tennyson or Mr. Froude. His narratives were fictitious only in the sense that the facts did not happen; but that trifling circumstance was to make no difference to the mode of writing them. The poetical element would have been as much out of place as it would have been in a merchant's ledger. He could not, indeed, help introducing a little moralising, for he was a typical English middle-class dissenter. Some of his simple-minded commentators have even given him credit, upon the strength of such passages, for lofty moral purpose. They fancy that his lives of criminals, real or imaginary, were intended to be tracts showing that vice leads to the gallows. No doubt, De Foe had the same kind of solid homespun morality as Hogarth, for example, which was not in its way a bad thing. But one need not be very cynical to believe that his real object in writing such books was to produce something that would sell, and that in the main he was neither more nor less moral than the last newspaper writer who has told us the story of a sensational murder.

De Foe, therefore, may be said to have stumbled almost unconsciously into novel-writing. He was merely aiming at true stories, which happened not to be true. But accidentally, or rather unconsciously, he could not help presenting us with a type of curious interest; for he necessarily described himself and the readers whose tastes he understood and shared so thoroughly. His statement that *Robinson Crusoe* was a kind of allegory was truer than he knew. In *Robinson Crusoe* is De Foe, and more than De Foe, for he is the typical Englishman of his time. He is the broad-shouldered, beef-eating John Bull, who has been shouldering his way through the world ever since. Drop him in a desert island, and he is just as sturdy and self-composed as if he were in Cheapside. Instead of shrieking or writing poetry, becoming a wild hunter or a religious hermit, he calmly sets about building a house and making pottery and laying out a farm. He does not accommodate himself to his surroundings; they have got to accommodate themselves to him. He meets a savage and at once annexes him, and preaches him such a sermon as he had heard from the exemplary Dr. Doddridge. Cannibals come to make a meal of him, and he calmly stamps them out with the means provided by civilisation. Long years of solitude produce no sort of effect upon him morally or mentally. He comes home as he went out, a solid keen tradesman, having, somehow or other, plenty of money in his pocket and ready to undertake similar risks in the hope of making a little more. He has taken his own atmosphere with him to the remotest quarters. Wherever he has set down his solid foot, he has taken permanent possession of the country. The ancient religions of the primæval East or the quaint beliefs of savage tribes make no particular impression upon him, except a passing spasm of disgust at anybody having different superstitions from his own; and, being in the main a good-natured animal in a stolid way of his own, he is able to make use even of popish priests if they will help to found a new market for his commerce. The portrait is not the less effective because the artist was so far from intending it that he could not even conceive of anybody being differently constituted from himself. It shows us all the more vividly what was the manner of man represented by the stalwart Englishman of the day; what were the men who were building up vast systems of commerce and manufacture; shoving their intrusive persons into every quarter of the globe; evolving a great empire out of a few factories in the East; winning the American continent for the dominant English race; sweeping up Australia by the way as a convenient settlement for convicts; stamping firmly and decisively on all toes that got in their way; blundering enormously and preposterously, and yet always coming out steadily planted on their feet; eating roast beef and plum-pudding; drinking rum in the tropics; singing *God Save the King* and intoning Watts's hymns under the nose of ancient dynasties and prehistoric priesthoods; managing always to get their own way, to force a reluctant world to take note of them as a great if rather disagreeable fact, and making it probable that, in long ages to come, the English of *Robinson Crusoe* will be the native language of inhabitants of every region under the sun.

Notes

1. De Foe may have had some materials for this story; but there seems to be little doubt that it is substantially his own.

GEORGE A. AITKEN
"Defoe's 'Apparition of Mrs. Veal'"
Nineteenth Century, January 1895, pp. 95–100

Thanks to Sir Walter Scott, few of Defoe's works are better known than the pamphlet which he called 'A True Relation of the Apparition of one Mrs. Veal, the next day after her death, to one Mrs. Bargrave, at Canterbury, the 8th of September, 1705.' In this piece, which appeared in July 1706, we are told how a maiden lady of about thirty, named, as was then usual, 'Mrs.' Veal, who had kept house at Dover for her only brother, an officer in the Custom House service, called upon an old friend, Mrs. Bargrave, of Canterbury, at noon on the 8th of September, 1705. They had not seen one another for two years and a half, and Mrs. Bargrave was surprised at the visit. Mrs. Veal explained that she was going a journey, and had a great mind to see Mrs. Bargrave first. Mrs. Bargrave had felt hurt at the previous neglect of her old friend, attributing it to Mrs. Veal's prosperity; she herself led an unfortunate life, through 'the unheard of ill-usage of a very wicked husband.' The ladies talked of their early intercourse, and of the comfort they had derived from Drelincourt's book upon Death, from Dr. Sherlock, and others. 'But Drelincourt,' Mrs. Veal said, 'had the clearest notions of death and of the future state of any who had handled that subject.' Much edifying conversation followed, and Mrs. Veal, who had not been well said, 'Mrs. Bargrave, don't you think I am mightily impaired by my fits?' to which Mrs. Bargrave replied that she thought her friend looked as well as ever she knew her.

Mrs. Veal then surprised Mrs. Bargrave by requesting her to write to Mr. Veal about the persons to whom she wished certain rings and a purse of gold to be given. Mrs. Bargrave feared that a fit was approaching, and began to talk about her visitor's gown. Mrs. Veal said it was "a scoured silk, and newly made up.' At last Mrs. Bargrave consented to write to Mrs. Veal's brother, and went out to fetch her daughter. When she returned, Mrs. Veal had come out of the house into the street, 'in the face of the beast-market, on a Saturday (which is market-day).' She said she must be going, but would see Mrs. Bargrave again at her cousin Watson's, in the city. She then

walked away, 'till a turning interrupted the sight of her, which was three-quarters after one in the afternoon.'

On Monday Mrs. Bargrave astonished the Watsons by inquiring if Mrs. Veal was there. Mrs. Watson said there must have been a mistake: if Mrs. Veal had visited Canterbury she would certainly have called upon them. While they were talking, Captain Watson came in, and announced that Mrs. Veal had died on the seventh, at noon, of her fits—that is, twenty-four hours before she appeared to Mrs. Bargrave. When Mrs. Bargrave said that Mrs. Veal had told her that her dress was scoured, Mrs. Watson cried out, 'You have seen her indeed, for none knew but Mrs. Veal and myself that the gown was scoured.' Mrs. Watson owned that the description of the dress, which she had herself helped to make, was correct. When the story got abroad, many gentlemen went to see Mrs. Bargrave, and they were favourably impressed by her manner. One material thing more Mrs. Veal told Mrs. Bargrave—'that old Mr. Breton allowed Mrs. Veal ten pounds a year, which was a secret.'

Mrs. Bargrave never varied in her story. A servant next door heard her talking to some one at the time, and, immediately after Mrs. Veal had gone, Mrs. Bargrave told her neighbour of the ravishing conversation she had had with an old friend. 'Drelincourt's *Book of Death* is, since this happened, bought up strangely.' Mr. Veal tried to throw discredit upon the story, though why he thought it a reflection was not clear. As Mrs. Bargrave said, she had no interest in making people believe the narrative; in fact, she had been put to much trouble by it. One gentleman came thirty miles to hear the tale from her own mouth.

Such, with innumerable details which add to the air of verisimilitude, was the story told by Defoe; but in the preface he said, 'This relation is matter of fact. It was sent by a Justice of the Peace at Maidstone to his friend in London, as here written, and it was attested by a sober gentlewoman, his kinswoman, who lived near Mrs. Bargrave, and had heard the story from Mrs. Bargrave's own mouth. This lady, who was not a person to be easily deceived, testified that Mrs. Bargrave was a pious and honest woman.' The moral, added Defoe, is the reality of a future life, and the need of repentance and right living in the present world.

Scott analysed this story with loving care, and said that, however improbable it seems when described in bald outline, 'whoever will read it as told by Defoe himself will agree that, could the thing have happened in reality, so it would have been told.' In our day, Scott added, journalists would have cross-questioned Mrs. Bargrave and the rest, and would have dug up Mrs. Veal's body rather than not get to the bottom of the matter; but our ancestors wondered and believed. Being himself a romancer, Scott accepted and expanded a circumstantial account of what caused Defoe to write the tale. The publisher of Drelincourt's heavy book (*The Christian's Defence against the Fears of Death*) could not make it sell; he therefore employed Defoe to describe how a ghost, which could speak from experience, recommended Drelincourt as giving the most reliable account of Heaven. Defoe's tale was appended to the unsaleable volume, which then became a most popular manual. Now, Mr. Lee has shown that this account given by Scott is fictitious. Drelincourt was widely read, first in France and then in other countries, long before Defoe wrote his pamphlet, and the English translation had reached a fourth edition in 1701. Moreover, some subsequent editions of Drelincourt did not contain Defoe's story, and the first edition which did contain it sold rather slowly. The pamphlet, too, was published first in separate form by Benjamin Bragg, whereas Drelincourt was published by

J. Robinson and others, who must have made arrangements with Bragg for permission to reprint the tale. But the original pamphlet had at the end an advertisement, stating that many thousand copies of Drelincourt had been sold already, and that the character given it in the 'True Relation' had caused the fourth impression to be nearly sold off.

Later critics have followed Scott in praising 'Mrs. Veal' as an early example of Defoe's power of making fiction appear to be fact. Mr. Leslie Stephen has dwelt upon the skill shown in disarming criticism by giving all the arguments for and against the veracity of the characters. Thus we are told that one person said Mrs. Bargrave had known beforehand of the annuity of 10*l*. a year given to Mrs. Veal by Mr. Breton; but this person, Defoe adds, had the 'reputation of a notorious liar.' 'One can almost fancy Defoe chuckling as he concocted the refinements of this most marvellous narrative.' Professor Raleigh, in his recent book on the English novel, in speaking of the 'True Relation' as the first of Defoe's realistic fictions, remarks that 'the ordinary reader becomes so interested in the opinion that Defoe's characters have of one another's veracity that he forgets to ask whether they exist.' Yet another writer said the other day, 'We would as soon believe in the apparition of Mrs. Veal in her scoured silk dress' as in a certain theory about Defoe.

It has been reserved for Mr. Wright, in his new *Life of Defoe*, to suggest whether 'a lady of Defoe's acquaintance, to whom he gives the name of Mrs. Bargrave, did not tell him, and in good faith, this story.' Before I read this passage I had obtained a clue which now enables me to substitute for Mr. Wright's acute conjecture actual proof that the piece was, as Defoe said, 'a *true* relation' of 'matter of fact.' Whether the apparition really was seen must continue to depend, as Defoe put it, upon the evidence as to Mrs. Bargrave's veracity, and the question may be left to the Psychical Research Society; but, for the rest, I shall be able to show that nearly all the details are true, that the characters are real persons, and that, in fact, Defoe invented nothing, or next to nothing, but simply told, very skilfully, a ghost story which was attracting notice at the time. Perhaps he had done what Scott suggested would now be done—interviewed Mrs. Bargrave; at any rate he had heard the whole tale from some one, as he describes in his preface. Defoe was a born journalist, always ready to glean interesting matter from anybody who had anything to tell which was of general interest.

In collating the text of the 'True Relation'—the modern reprints are very inaccurate—I found in the British Museum a copy of the pamphlet called the 'fourth edition,' which, as appears from a catchword, once formed the introductory sheet to an edition of Drelincourt, printed about 1710. Of no value in itself, I noticed some manuscript notes in a contemporary handwriting, and on examination I found at the beginning a long note in Latin, of which this is a translation: 'On the 21st of May, 1714, I asked Mrs. Bargrave whether the matters contained in this narrative are true, to which she replied that she had neither written the printed narrative nor published it, nor did she know the editor; all things contained in it, however, were true, as regards the event itself, or points of importance; but one or two circumstances relating to the affair were not described with perfect accuracy by the editor. The editor, no doubt, learned all particulars by word of mouth from Mrs. Bargrave, and then published them without her knowledge. Some things added in this copy were changed for the better by Mrs. Bargrave herself.'

Was Mrs. Bargrave, then, a real person? Here we have a contemporary owner of the book placing it on record that he saw her, and that she said that the narrative was, in all essentials, true. She added little; her interviewer corrected with his pen only four passages, and of these one is clearly a mistake. After 'She was with me on Saturday almost two hours' the writer inserts 'from twelve till near two.' Among the devotional works recommended by Mrs. Veal he mentions Scott's *Christian Life*; and after Mrs. Bargrave's offer of tea to her visitor ('and so it passed') we find this addition: 'Something was also mentioned in this conversation of the former times when the Dissenters were persecuted by King Charles the Second. At which, says Mrs. Veal: "People should not persecute one another whilst they all are upon the road to Eternity."' These remarks are just such as Mrs. Veal might make, and her friend recall to memory afterwards. For the rest, the printed narrative was accepted by Mrs. Bargrave.

My next business was to find what was known of the persons mentioned in the pamphlet. In Hasted's *Kent* there are many particulars of the Bargrave and Veal families. A Bargrave was Dean of Canterbury under Charles the First, and from Berry's *Kent Pedigrees* we learn that a Robert Bargrave, of Doctors' Commons, had, by his wife Sarah, an only daughter Elizabeth, who married in 1715. Now, Mrs. Bargrave, in 1705, had a daughter for whom Mrs. Veal inquired. In view, however, of the bad character given of Mrs. Bargrave's husband, it would be unkind to identify him too positively. Perhaps he was the Richard Bargrave of Bridge, maltster, who married Barbara Smith, widow, by licence, on the 11th of January, 1700 (N.S.), at St. Alphage's, Canterbury. From Mr. Cowper's reprints of the registers we know that he was buried at St. Paul's, Canterbury, in July 1726, and that 'the widow Bargrave' followed him in January 1727–8.

We are on more certain ground when we turn to the Veals. There had been De Veals in very early times, but the family seems to have sunk into obscurity. There were Veals at Canterbury in Defoe's day, but those with whom we are concerned belonged to Dover, as he says. Mrs. Veal's brother, with whom she lived, was, as is stated, 'in the Custom House;' for by 1719 he was Comptroller of the Customs at Dover. This William Veal married soon after his sister's death in 1705, for a 'young son' of his was baptised at St. Mary's, Dover, on the 10th of August, 1707. His wife was a widow named Minet, and another Minet, rector of Eythorne, married William Veal's daughter in 1724. Veal died in 1729, and was buried at Capel, where he owned an estate. But the most important fact for us is that the register of St. Mary's, Dover, records the burial, on the 10th of September, 1705, of 'Mrs. Veal,' the central figure of the narrative. She died, it will be remembered, on the 7th of September, according to Defoe, whose account is thus completely substantiated.

But other details can be verified. There were several Watsons in Canterbury at the time, one of whom, no doubt, was Mrs. Veal's cousin, Captain Watson. And, curiously enough, we can identify the 'old Mr. Breton' who had given Mrs. Veal an annuity of 10*l*. He was Robert Breton, of the Elms, near Dover, of whom particulars will be found in Berry's *Pedigrees*. He died in 1708, three years after Mrs. Veal, and was called 'old' Mr. Breton, no doubt, because he had a son Moyle, born in 1692. Thus the whole narrative is literally true, and I have only to thank the Rev. A. L. Palmer, of Dover, the Rev. J. C. W. Valpy, of Alkham, and Mr. S. Wilson and Mr. J. B. Jones, of Dover, for the help they have given me in tracing the various characters. No doubt Mrs. Veal's dress had been scoured, though this is now hardly capable of proof. Who can say, however, that the account for the cleaning of the gown will not some day be found?

May we not draw a moral, after the manner of Defoe, from the result of this inquiry? The fact that there is no record of Defoe's story being contradicted by contemporary writers might have suggested that it was at least based on fact; for enemies were not slow to blame Defoe for saying that *Robinson Crusoe* and other tales were true. It has become the fashion of late to assume that Defoe was romancing when he said his narratives were true histories, and the more he has asserted it the more critics have laughed at his skill or abused him for the immorality of his devices, according to the way the matter struck them. This scepticism has been extended to matters relating to Defoe's own life and character, and the late Professor Minto went so far as to say that he was 'perhaps the greatest liar that ever lived.' The result of this attitude has been a marked change in the common estimate of Defoe, as shown by the chance notices of him in the newspapers. I hope to have an opportunity of speaking at greater length on this question in another place; but does not the story told in this paper show that we should be at least as likely to arrive at the truth by believing what Defoe says, in the absence of proof to the contrary?

G. H. MAYNADIER
From "Introduction"
The Works of Daniel Defoe
1903, Volume 1, pp. xix–xxviii

Defoe is a singular character among our men of letters. There was in him a lack of fine feeling, an intrinsic vulgarity, manifest as well in his political deceits as in his fondness for attracting attention, and in his attempt, by changing his name, to make his family out better than it was. Professing to be a moralist, he always had an eye for the main chance; and at times he had a convenient way of suppressing his opinions—without actually changing them—for the sake of money. Were he alive to-day, we should expect him to be either a very "yellow" journalist or a theatrical or circus manager, unrivalled for sensational, unscrupulous advertising. And yet, so far as we know, Defoe was an upright man in his family relations; he was a man of indomitable courage; and in politics, if not always openly, he was yet consistently, and apparently conscientiously, a Whig, at a time when the Whigs saved English liberty, and when political steadfastness was what few public men could boast of. Either his political services or his journalistic work would entitle him to a place in the *Dictionary of National Biography*, but more than the two combined, his prose fiction puts him there. In the history of our literature, he is important chiefly for his influence on that kind of writing which, within twenty years of his death, was to come, in the works of Fielding, as near perfection as it has ever come.

In *Robinson Crusoe*, his first considerable attempt at fiction to be published, Defoe cannot be said to have invented a new kind of writing. Like most of his narratives, this belongs, broadly speaking, to the division of literature known as the "picaresque novel," a kind of fiction which arose in Spain in the sixteenth century. The *Lazarillo de Tormes*, the first of the kind, was published in 1553. Written in the first person, as if autobiographical, it tells how its hero, whom we see first a poor boy of eight, passed through various adventures, trusting to his wits to extricate him from such difficulties as he got into. The *Lazarillo* met with much favour both at home and abroad; before the century was out, it was translated into German, French, and English. Imitations followed, all, like the origi-

nal, dealing with the fortunes of clever rogues or adventurers. The most important of these in England before the eighteenth century was *The English Rogue*, by Richard Head and Francis Kirkman, which came out in four parts during Defoe's boyhood.[1]

What Defoe did in *Robinson Crusoe* that was new in picaresque novels was to send his hero to a desert island in the tropics, thus setting a fashion for "desert-island" tales that has lasted to our own day. For this novelty he was doubtless indebted to the story of Alexander Selcraig (or Selkirk, as he has been more often called), a Scotchman, who spent four years and four months alone on the island of Juan Fernandez off the coast of Chile. This Selcraig, who was making a voyage round the world with Captain Dampier, as sailing-master of one of his two ships, the *Cinque Ports*, chose to stay on the island rather than continue with the captain of his ship, a certain Stradling, with whom he had quarrelled. From the solitary life which ensued Selcraig was rescued in February, 1709, by Captain Woodes Rogers in command of the *Duke*, a ship fitted out at Bristol for an expedition against the French and Spanish. Rogers published an account of his travels in 1712, in which he tells the story of Selcraig. In *The Englishman* in December, 1713,[2] Steele, who had interviewed the desert-islander, published another account of his adventures. And so it will be seen that Defoe had good opportunity to become acquainted with the story of Selcraig.

As a result of Defoe's acquaintance with this story, we have in the first part of *Robinson Crusoe* what is, with one exception, the most artistic long narrative from his pen. Here is an apparent unity, rare alike in Defoe's other stories and in most picaresque tales of adventure. The reason is that once the hero reaches his desert island, his adventures are of necessity limited; all that happens now bears on one question—how is he going to support himself without human aid? From this all-important question we never get away. Moreover, as a solitary on a desert island would naturally find interest in the most trivial details, Defoe's enumeration of unimportant incidents does not become tedious or exaggerated, as it too often does in his other works. It seems only natural and proper; it adds to the probability of the story.

From the nature of its subject, *Robinson Crusoe* derives something more than a kind of artistic unity. When Crusoe, in his *Farther Adventures*, speaks of "the life I lived in my kingdom, the island, where I suffered no more corn to grow because I did not want it; and bred no more goats, because I had no more use for them; where the money lay in the drawer till it grew mouldy, and had scarce the favour to be looked upon in twenty years"—when Crusoe speaks thus, he touches on a kind of life which, however impossible, has always had some charm for civilisation-wearied man. This charm and the skill of the story-teller together produce that deep interest in the first part of *Robinson Crusoe* which seems likely to last as long as the English tongue. It is, to a large extent, this interest in his island adventures which makes us glad to follow Crusoe in his *Farther Adventures* (published only four months later) through China, Siberia, and Russia. But with all our prepossession in his favour, we find it hard to keep up our interest when we come to his *Serious Reflections*. It matters not that this gives us some information about the author's personal history, as in his declaring—probably untruthfully—that the *Adventures of Robinson Crusoe* was meant for an allegorical history of his own life. *The Serious Reflections . . . of Robinson Crusoe. With his Vision of the Angelic World* is exceedingly hard reading.

Even the charm of the peaceful island life and the unity

of the narrative would not sustain our interest in the first part of *Robinson Crusoe*, were it not for the intense reality of its scenes—a reality characteristic of Defoe's work. Similar reality is apparent in the *Farther Adventures of Robinson Crusoe*, and at least to some extent in every bit of fiction which Defoe ever wrote. The secret of it is that Defoe had an unbounded imagination for fact. It is not enough that Defoe tells us that Crusoe stripped to shirt, drawers, and shoes, the second time he swam out to the wreck. No, he says that Crusoe had "nothing on but a chequered shirt and a pair of linen drawers, and a pair of pumps." And so Defoe almost always goes into minute details, adding one little fact to another, till a reader feels that the man must be telling what he has seen himself. He even goes beyond minutiæ. Whether as a finished artist, or as a hasty writer who allowed himself no time for excision, Defoe is a past master at giving unnecessary detail.

Moreover, Defoe was such a careful student of geography, he was so well read in books of travel, that he has seldom made mistakes in his geographical facts. Now and then he makes a slip, but for the most part, he writes of the Barbary States, North America, South America, Madagascar, the East Indies, the South Seas, China, or Siberia, as if he had visited the regions he describes. His interest in such distant regions, and in the connection of his country with them, marks him as one of the earliest "imperialists" of the English race.

Marvellous reality of scene, a verisimilitude in detached incidents unsurpassed and almost unequalled in English fiction, is not the only product of Defoe's imagination for fact. Because his imagination so seldom goes beyond fact, he has seldom succeeded in imparting reality to a story as a whole. While we read, we accept as real each particular event, but when we come to the end of the book, we do not feel that we have had a bit of real life. The reason is that, to the majority of people, fact is not the whole of life. Most of us are more emotional than Defoe or the creatures of his fiction. Most of us, for example, would have felt more romantic despair than Crusoe at his loneliness; had we been in his place, we should have felt oftener such piercing sorrow as came over him when he found that no one was saved from the wrecked Spanish ship.

Because Crusoe had so little emotion, is one reason that he is not individual. He is, as critics have been pleased to remark again and again, just a typical, common-sense, practical, English colonist, who sets to work with all his ability to make the most he can out of existing conditions. As such, he is true to life so far as the representative of a type can be, but the representative of a type is not an individual human being. Defoe had not the kind of imagination which would give his characters individuality. He tried hard to do so, and in some instances, no doubt, prided himself on his character-drawing. I am inclined to think that he felt he had succeeded in individualising Friday, and William, the Quaker, in *Captain Singleton*, and several others of his personages; but to me they are all wooden. The least so are two of his women, Moll Flanders and Roxana, but even they are far from thoroughly vitalised. Though Defoe could give perfect reality to incidents, he could not impart life to his characters. Not even the best known of them, Robinson Crusoe himself, ever "walks out of the page" (if I may use this overworked expression) as do Fielding's characters and a good many of Smollett's.

It is partly on account of Defoe's inability to make his characters real that some critics have been unwilling to call his stories novels. There is another reason why we should refuse this name to them. As I have tried to point out in the introductions to Fielding's works, by a novel we commonly understand to-day a book that one reads not only for the persuasive reality of its scenes and characters, but also for its plot. Not every novel by any means has real characters, real scenes, and a good plot; but in the best novels, you will find these three elements happily united. The only one of them which we see distinctly in Defoe's works is reality of scene. There is no more plot, there are no more living persons in his stories, than there are in most mediæval romances, in which the storyteller made conventional knights and ladies go through adventures that he terminated summarily or continued indefinitely, as he saw fit. It is chiefly in the fact that their incidents are possible, and that their characters are seen in the garish light of humble realism and not in a knightly mediæval glamour, that the stories of Defoe (and indeed picaresque stories in general) differ from the romances of the Round Table. *Robinson Crusoe* and *Colonel Jacque* are no more organic than the mediæval *Merlin* or *Sir Lancelot du Lake*; nor have they more vivified characters. They are not novels in the sense that *Tom Jones* and *Humphry Clinker* are novels. Professor Minto is right in delcaring that Defoe's narratives are not realistic novels but realistic biographies.[3]

It by no means follows from this that Defoe's narratives are not interesting. From the beginning of literature, men have liked to read about the adventures of other men. We like to read of them as befalling either in the civilised society with which we are familiar, or (even as our mediæval ancestors in the days of Marco Polo) in distant lands which few white people have seen. There is no reason to suppose that this fondness for reading of adventure is not a permanent attribute of the human race. Now in Defoe's stories, adventures follow one another with that quick movement which has always been characteristic of the best narrative. Till human nature changes, therefore, Defoe's narratives, plotless and mostly characterless though they be, are likely to possess interest for readers.

Defoe's stories have yet another permanent claim to interest in being the first good examples in English of the picaresque novel, whose history I have already sketched in this introduction. In the eighteenth century, before Fielding showed that the English novel was a literary form unsurpassed for picturing actual life, there had been two different promises of what the novel might be. On the one hand, there were the sketches of "polite" society which Addison and Steele had made in various numbers of their periodicals, especially in the Sir Roger de Coverley papers—sketches which peopled drawing-rooms, clubs, and country-houses with real personages. Had the incidents which these early essayists related been connected by a plot, we should have had our first English novel a good thirty years before *Joseph Andrews*. The other early eighteenth-century promise for the English novel is found in the picaresque stories of Defoe with their humble, vulgar realism. What the development of the English novel would have been without the picaresque element, it is impossible to say. Perhaps it would have been charged with the forced, hot-house atmosphere which we breathe in Richardson's didactic novels; we should hardly have got the stronger air—sometimes sweet with country freshness, again, heavy with tobacco smoke and the fumes of punch, or reeking with kitchen and stable odours—which Fielding makes us inhale. For Fielding, in his novels, followed the growing tendency of fiction, already apparent in Defoe, to picture even the lowest phases of humanity as truthfully as possible. In doing so he but set the example for all his great successors. Not all, indeed, have a picaresque element in their work, but all have made at least some slight attempt to introduce humble realism. It is because Defoe was the great pioneer in this that he is important in our literary history. And because *Robinson Crusoe* was the first of his long pieces of fiction—because, thanks to the success of this, Defoe was encouraged to give to the world others more in the line of development of the English novel—for these reasons, apart from its intrinsic interest, *Robinson Crusoe* holds an important place in the history of our literature.

Notes

1. 1665, 1668, and two parts in 1671.
2. Both Rogers's account and Steele's are published in the appendix to the third volume of this edition.
3. *Daniel Defoe*, London, 1879, p. 137.

ALEXANDER POPE

ALEXANDER POPE

1688–1744

Alexander Pope, poet and satirist, was born in London on May 21, 1688. His father, a Roman Catholic linen merchant, retired from business in the year of his son's birth, and in 1700 moved to Windsor Forest, where the young Pope largely educated himself. Alexander traveled to London frequently and became acquainted with William Wycherley, William Walsh, and others. His *Essay on Criticism* (1711) introduced him into the circle of Addison and Steele, who published his *Messiah* in *The Spectator* in 1712. Pope's famous mock-heroic poem, *The Rape of the Lock* (1712/ 1714) was followed in 1713 by *Windsor-Forest*, which pleased the Tories by its references to the Peace of Utrecht and made him a friend of Swift's; indeed, Pope soon drifted away from Addison and Steele, and became a member of the Scriblerus Club with Swift, Gay, Arbuthnot, and others. In 1715 he issued the first volume of his translation in heroic couplets of Homer's *Iliad*; this project was completed in 1720, and was followed in 1726 by his translation of the *Odyssey*, written with William Broome and Elijah Fenton. The proceeds from these two translations made him financially independent, and in 1718 he moved to Twickenham, where he spent the rest of his life.

In 1717 the first volume of Pope's *Works* appeared; this included *Eloisa to Abelard* and "Verses to the Memory of an Unfortunate Lady," two poems which, uncharacteristically for Pope, are concerned with romantic love. About this time Pope became friendly with Martha Blount and with Lady Mary Wortley Montagu.

Pope's satires made him numerous enemies, and involved him in endless literary sparring. In 1728 he published the first edition of *The Dunciad*, a satire on "Dulness" in which the central character was Lewis Theobald, who had criticized Pope's edition of Shakespeare (1725); an enlarged version appeared in 1729, and was followed by *The New Dunciad* (1742), inspired, it appears, by a rivalry with Warburton, and by the complete *Dunciad* (four books; 1743), in which Colley Cibber replaces Theobald as the protagonist.

In the 1730s Pope issued a series of moral and philosophical poems, including *An Essay on Man* (1733–34) and *Moral Essays* (1731–35), which in part reflected the influence of the philosophy of his friend Bolingbroke. The *Imitations of Horace*, in which Pope defends his own character, appeared in 1733; the success of this work led to the publication of ten more *Imitations* (1733–38), in which paraphrases of Horatian themes are modernized. Pope's *Epistle to Dr. Arbuthnot* was published in 1735, as a prologue to his *Imitations*; this piece, considered one of his most brilliant, contains a famous portrait of Addison as well as attacks on various minor critics and a certain amount of autobiographical detail. In 1738 two satirical dialogues entitled *One Thousand Seven Hundred and Thirty Eight* were published; these were followed by *The New Dunciad* and the complete *Dunciad*, after which no other completed work appeared. Pope's later years were occupied with the publication of his correspondence, and he also began work on *Brutus*, an epic poem in blank verse, which was left unfinished when he died on May 30, 1744.

Personal

The most eminent Persons of our Assembly are a little Poet, a little Lover, a little Politician, and a little Heroe. The first of these, *Dick Distick* by Name, we have elected President, not only as he is the shortest of us all, but because he has entertain'd so just a Sense of the Stature, as to go generally in Black that he may appear yet Less. Nay, to that Perfection is he arrived, that he *stoops* as he walks. The Figure of the Man is odd enough; he is a lively little Creature, with long Arms and Legs: A Spider is no ill Emblem of him. He has been taken at a Distance for a *small Windmill*. But indeed what principally moved us in his Favour was his Talent in Poetry, for he hath promised to undertake a long Work in *short Verse* to celebrate the Heroes of our Size. He has entertained so great a Respect for *Statius*, on the Score of that Line,

Major in exiguo regnabat corpore virtus,

that he once designed to translate the whole *Thebaid* for the sake of little *Tydeus*.—ALEXANDER POPE, *The Guardian*, No. 92 (June 26, 1713)

With Age decay'd, with Courts and Bus'ness tir'd,
Caring for nothing but what Ease requir'd,
Too serious now a wanton Muse to court,
And from the Criticks safe arriv'd in Port;
I little thought of launching forth agen,
Amidst advent'rous Rovers of the Pen;
And, after some small undeserv'd Success,
Thus hazarding at last to make it less.
   Encomiums suit not this censorious Time,
Itself a Subject for Satirick Rhyme;
Ignorance honour'd, Wit and Worth defam'd,
Folly triumphant, and ev'n HOMER blam'd.
   But to this Genius, join'd with so much Art,
Such various Learning mix'd in ev'ry Part,
Poets are bound a loud Applause to pay;
APOLLO bids it, and they must obey.
   And yet so wond'rous, so sublime a thing,
As the great *Iliad*, scarce should make me sing;
Except I justly could at once commend
A good Companion, and as firm a Friend.
One moral, or a mere well-natur'd Deed,
Can all Desert in Sciences exceed.

'Tis great Delight to laugh at some Mens Ways;
But a much greater to give Merit Praise.
—JOHN SHEFFIELD, DUKE OF BUCKINGHAM, "On
Mr. Pope, and His Poems," 1717

Mr. Pope, the Poët, who is now publishing Homer in English Verse (three Volumes of the *Iliads*, in 4to, being already come out), was born in the Parish of Binfield, near Ockingham in Berks. He is a Papist, as is also his Father, who is a sort of a broken Merchant. The said Mr. Pope was patronized and encouraged by the late Sir William Trumbull. He lived in Binfield Parish 'till of late, when he removed to Chiswick in Surrey. He is most certainly a very ingenious Man. He is deformed.—THOMAS HEARNE, *Reliquiae Hearnianae*, Aug. 7, 1717

"Let Envy," he reply'd, "all ireful rise,
Envy pursues alone the brave and wise;
Maro and Socrates inspire her pain,
And Pope the monarch of the tuneful train!
To whom be Nature's and Britannia's praise!
All their bright honours rush into his lays!
And all that glorious warmth his lays reveal,
Which only poets, kings, and patriots feel!
Tho' gay as Mirth, as curious Thought sedate,
As Elegance polite, as Pow'r elate;
Profound as Reason, and as Justice clear;
Soft as Compassion, yet as Truth severe;
As Bounty copious, as Persuasion sweet,
Like Nature various, and like Art complete;
So fine her morals, so sublime her views,
His life is almost equall'd by his Muse.
"O Pope!—since Envy is decreed by Fate,
Since she pursues alone the wise and great,
In one small emblematic landscape see
How vast a distance 'twixt thy foe and thee!
Truth from an eminence surveys our scene,
(A hill, where all is clear and all serene)
Rude earth-bred sotrms o'er meaner vallies blow,
And wand'ring mists roll, black'ning far below;
Dark and debas'd, like them, is Envy's aim,
And clear and eminent, like Truth, thy fame."
—RICHARD SAVAGE, *The Wanderer*, 1729, Canto
1, ll. 353–78

Mr. Alexander Pope, the Poet's Father, was a poor ignorant man, a tanner at Binfield in Berks. This Mr. Alex. Pope had a little house there, that he had from his Father, but hath now sold it to one Mr. Tanner, an honest man. This Alexander Pope, tho' he be an English Poet, yet he is but an indifferent scholar, mean at Latin and can hardly read Greek. He is a very ill-natured man, and covetous and excessively proud.—THOMAS HEARNE, *Reliquiae Hearnianae*, July 18, 1729

Hail! happy *Pope*, whose gen'rous Mind,
Detesting all the Statesmen kind,
Contemning *Courts*, at *Courts* unseen,
Refus'd the Visits of a Queen;
A Soul with ev'ry Virtue fraught
By *Sages*, *Priests*, or *Poets* taught;
Whose filial Piety excels
Whatever *Grecian* Story tells:
A Genius for all Stations fit,
Whose *meanest Talent* is his *Wit*:
His Heart too Great, though Fortune little,
To lick a *Rascal Statesman's* Spittle.
Appealing to the Nation's Taste,
Above the Reach of Want is plac't:
By *Homer* dead was taught to thrive,
Which *Homer* never cou'd alive.

And, sits aloft on *Pindus* Head,
Despising *Slaves* that *cringe* for Bread.
—JONATHAN SWIFT, "A Libel on D—— D——
and a Certain Great Lord," 1730

O fam'd for judging, as for writing well,
That rarest science, where so few excel;
Whose life, severely scann'd, transcends thy lays,
For wit supreme is but thy second praise:
'Tis thine, O Pope, who choose the better part,
To tell how false, how vain, the scholiast's art,
Which nor to taste, nor genius has pretence,
And, if 'tis learning, is not common sense.
—DAVID MALLET, "Of Verbal Criticism," 1733

Mr. Pope's not being richer may be easily accounted for.—He never had any love for money: and though he was not extravagant in any thing, he always delighted, when he had any sum to spare, to make use of it in giving, lending, building, and gardening; for those were the ways in which he disposed of all the overplus of his income.—If he was extravagant in any thing it was in his grotto, for that, from first to last, cost him above a thousand pounds.—MRS. BLOUNT (1737–39), cited in Joseph Spence, *Anecdotes, Observations and Characters of Books and Men*, ed. S. W. Singer, 1820

Mr. Pope was born on the 21st day of May, 1688.—His first education was extremely loose and disconcerted. He began to learn Latin and Greek together (as is customary in the schools of the Jesuits, and which he seemed to think a good way), under Banister their family priest, whom, he said, was living about two years ago at St. Harry Tichburne's.—He then learned his accidence at Twiford, where he wrote a satire on some faults of his master.—He was then, a little while, at Mr. Deane's seminary at Marylebone; and sometime under the same, after he removed to Hyde-Park Corner.—After this, he taught himself both Greek and Latin.—"I did not follow the grammar; but rather hunted in the authors, for a syntax of my own: and then began translating any parts that pleased me particularly, in the best Greek and Latin poets: and by that means formed my taste; which, I think, verily, about sixteen, was very near as good as it is now."—ALEXANDER POPE (1742–43), cited in Joseph Spence, *Anecdotes, Observations and Characters of Books and Men*, ed. S. W. Singer, 1820

I can say no more for Mr Pope, (for what You keep in Reserve may be worse than all the Rest) it is natural to wish the finest Writer, one of them, we ever had should be an honest Man. it is for the Interest even of that Virtue, whose Friend he profess'd himself, & whose Beauties he sung, that he should not be found a dirty Animal. but however this is Mr Warburton's Business, not mine, who may scribble his Pen to the Stumps & all in vain, if these Facts are so. it is not from what he told me about himself that I thought well of him, but from a Humanity & Goodness of Heart, ay, & Greatness of Mind, that runs thro his private Correspondence, not less apparent than are a thousand little Vanities & Weaknesses mixed with those good Qualities, for no body ever took him for a Philosopher.—THOMAS GRAY, Letter to Horace Walpole (Feb. 3, 1746)

For to have been one of the first poets in the world is but his second praise. He was in a higher class. He was one of the "noblest works of God." He was an "honest man,"—a man who alone possessed more real virtue than, in very corrupt times, needing a satirist like him, will sometimes fall to the share of multitudes. In this history of his life, will be contained a large account of his writings, a critique on the nature, force, and extent of his genius, exemplified from these writings; and a vindication of his moral character, exemplified by his more distinguished virtues,—his filial piety, his disinterested friendships, his reverence for the constitution of his country, his love and admiration of virtue, and (what was the necessary effect) his hatred and contempt of vice, his extensive charity to the indigent, his warm benevolence to mankind, his supreme veneration of the Deity, and above all his sincere belief of Revelation. Nor shall his faults be concealed. It is not for the interests of his virtues that they should. Nor indeed could they be concealed, if we were so disposed, for they shine through his virtues, no man being more a dupe to the specious appearances of virtue in others. In a word, I mean not to be his panegyrist but his historian. And may I, when envy and calumny have taken the same advantage of my absence (for, while I live, I will freely trust it to my life to confute them) may I find a friend as careful of my honest fame as I have been of his! Together with his works, he hath bequeathed me his dunces. So that as the property is transferred, I could wish they would now let his memory alone. The veil which death draws over the good is so sacred, that to tear it, and with sacrilegious hands, to throw dirt upon the shrine, gives scandal even to barbarians. And though Rome permitted her slaves to calumniate her best citizens on the day of triumph, yet the same petulancy at their funeral would have been rewarded with execration and a gibbet. The public may be malicious: but is rarely vindictive or ungenerous. It would abhor all insults, on a writer dead, though it had borne with the ribaldry, or even set the ribalds on work, when he was alive. And in this there is no great harm, for he must have a strange impotency of mind indeed whom such miserable scribblers can disturb or ruffle. Of all that gross Beotian phalanx who have written scurrilously against the editor, he knows not so much as one whom a writer of reputation would not wish to have his enemy, or whom a man of honour would not be ashamed to own for his friend. He is indeed but slightly conversant in their works, and knows little of the particulars of their defamation. To his authorship they are heartily welcome. But if any of them have been so far abandoned by truth as to attack his moral character in any respect whatsoever, to all and every one of these and their abettors, he gives the lie in form, and in the words of honest Father Valerian, *mentiris impudentissime.*—WILLIAM WARBURTON, "Advertisement" to *The Works of Alexander Pope*, 1751

As we walked along to a particular part of the temple (Westminster Abbey), "There," says the gentleman, pointing with his finger, "that is the Poets' Corner; there you see the monuments of Shakespeare, and Milton, and Prior, and Drayton." "Drayton!" I replied, "I never heard of him before; but I have been told of one Pope; is he there?" "It is time enough," replied my guide, "these hundred years; he is not long dead; people have not done hating him yet." "Strange," cried I; "can any be found to hate a man whose life was wholly spent in entertaining and instructing his fellow-creatures?" "Yes," says my guide, "they hate him for that very reason. There is a set of men called answerers of books, who take upon them to watch the republic of letters, and distribute reputation by the sheet; they somewhat resemble the eunuchs in a seraglio, who are incapable of giving pleasure themselves, and hinder those that would. These answerers have no other employment but to cry out Dunce, and Scribbler; to praise the dead, and revile the living; to grant a man of confessed abilities some small share of merit; to applaud twenty blockheads, in order to gain the reputation of candor; and to revile the moral character of the man whose writings they cannot injure. Such wretches are kept in pay by some mercenary bookseller, or

more frequently the bookseller himself takes this dirty work off their hands, as all that is required is to be very abusive and very dull. Every poet of any genius is sure to find such enemies; he feels, though he seems to despise, their malice; they make him miserable here, and, in the pursuit of empty fame, at last he gains solid anxiety."—OLIVER GOLDSMITH, *The Citizen of the World*, 1762, Letter 13

O great misery of length of days, to preserve life only to know its little value! Pope had but one great end in view to render this world supportable to him. That was *Friendship, the peculiar gift of heaven.* This did he nobly deserve and obtain; but for how short a time! Jealousy deprived him of the affection he assiduously sought from Mr. Wycherly, and many others; but Death cruel Death was far more cruel. The dearest ties of his heart all yielded to his stroke. The modest Digby, the gentle virtuous Gay, the worthy Arbuthnot, the exiled Atterbury—but why should I enumerate these excellent men, when their very names deject me? But in nothing does Pope equally charm me as in his conduct to his mother: it is truly noble. He gives up all his time, thought, and attention to her ease and comfort. I dare not begin to mention his long friendship with the admirable Swift, because I shall not know where to stop, for the attachment of such eminent men to one another has something in it that almost awes me, and at the same time inexpressibly delights me. I must tear myself from this.—FANNY BURNEY, *Diary*, Dec. 8, 1771

Sir Joshua Reynolds once saw Pope. It was about the year 1740, at an auction of books or pictures. He remembers that there was a lane formed to let him pass freely through the assemblage, and he proceeded along bowing to those who were on each side. He was, according to Sir Joshua's account, about four feet six high; very humpbacked and deformed; he wore a black coat; and according to the fashion of that time, had on a little sword. Sir Joshua adds that he had a large and very fine eye, and a long handsome nose; his mouth had those peculiar marks which always are found in the mouths of crooked persons; and the muscles which run across the cheek were so strongly marked as to appear like small cords. Roubilliac, the statuary, who made a bust of him from life, observed that his countenance was that of a person who had been much afflicted with headache, and he should have known the fact from the contracted appearance of the skin between his eyebrows, though he had not been otherwise apprised of it.—EDMOND MALONE, "Maloniana" (1783), cited in Sir James Prior, *The Life of Edmond Malone*, 1860, pp. 428–29

I have hung up Pope, and a gem it is, in my town room; I hope for your approval. Though it accompanies the *Essay on Man*, I think that was not the poem he is here meditating. He would have looked up, somehow affectedly, if he were just conceiving 'Awake, my St. John.' Neither is he in the *Rape of the Lock* mood exactly. I think he has just made out the last lines of the 'Epistle to Jervis,' between gay and tender,

> And other beauties envy Worsley's eyes.

I'll be damn'd if that isn't the line. He is brooding over it, with a dreamy phantom of Lady Mary floating before him. He is thinking which is the earliest possible day and hour that she will first see it. What a miniature piece of gentility it is! Why did you give it me? I do not like you enough to give you anything so good.—CHARLES LAMB, Letter to B. W. Procter (April 13, 1823)

His own life was one long series of tricks, as mean and as malicious as that of which he suspected Addison and Tickell. He was all stiletto and mask. To injure, to insult, and to save himself from the consequences of injury and insult by lying and equivocating, was the habit of his life. He published a lampoon on the Duke of Chandos; he was taxed with it; and he lied and equivocated. He published a lampoon on Aaron Hill; he was taxed with it; and he lied and equivocated. He published a still fouler lampoon on Lady Mary Wortley Montague; he was taxed with it; and he lied with more than usual effrontery and vehemence. He puffed himself and abused his enemies under feigned names. He robbed himself of his own letters, and then raised the hue and cry after them. Besides his frauds of malignity, of fear, of interest, and of vanity, there were frauds which he seems to have committed from love of fraud alone. He had a habit of stratagem, a pleasure in outwitting all who came near him. Whatever his object might be, the indirect road to it was that which he preferred. For Bolingbroke, Pope undoubtedly felt as much love and veneration as it was in his nature to feel for any human being. Yet Pope was scarcely dead when it was discovered that, from no motive except the mere love of artifice, he had been guilty of an act of gross perfidy to Bolingbroke.—THOMAS BABINGTON MACAULAY, "The Life and Writings of Addison" (1843), *Critical, Historical, and Miscellaneous Essays*, 1860, Vol. 5, p. 408

General

> When *Pope*'s harmonious Muse with pleasure roves,
> Amidst the Plains, the murm'ring Streams, and Groves,
> Attentive Eccho pleas'd to hear his Songs,
> Thro' the glad Shade each warbling Note prolongs;
> His various Numbers charm our ravish'd Ears,
> His steady Judgment far out-shoots his Years,
> And early in the Youth the God appears.
> —JOHN GAY, "On a Miscellany of Poems," 1711

I am always highly delighted with the Discovery of any rising Genius among my Countrymen. For this Reason I have read over, with great Pleasure, the late Miscellany published by Mr. *Pope*, in which there are many Excellent Compositions of that ingenious Gentleman.—JOSEPH ADDISON, *The Spectator*, No. 523 (Oct. 30, 1712)

> To praise, yet still with due respect to praise,
> A bard triumphant in immortal bays,
> The learn'd to show, the sensible commend,
> Yet still preserve the province of the friend,
> What life, what vigour, must the lines require!
> What music tune them! what affection fire!
>
> O might thy genius in my bosom shine!
> Thou shouldst not fail of numbers worthy thine,
> The brightest ancients might at once agree
> To sing within my lays, and sing of thee.
>
> Horace himself would own thou dost excel
> In candid arts to play the critic well.
>
> Ovid himself might wish to sing the dame
> Whom Windsor forest sees a gliding stream;
> On silver feet, with annual osier crown'd,
> She runs for ever through poetic ground.
>
> How flame the glories of Belinda's hair,
> Made by thy Muse the envy of the fair
> Less shone the tresses Egypt's princess wore,
> Which sweet Callimachus so sung before.
> Here courtly trifles set the world at odds,
> Belles war with beaux, and whims descend for gods.
> The new machines in names of ridicule,
> Mock the grave phrenzy of the chymic fool:

> But know, ye fair, a point conceal'd with art,
> The Sylphs and Gnomes are but a woman's heart:
> The Graces stand in sight; a Satyr train
> Peep o'er their heads, and laugh behind the scene.
>
> In Fame's fair temple, o'er the boldest wits
> Inshrin'd on high the sacred Virgil sits,
> And sits in measures, such as Virgil's Muse
> To place thee near him might be fond to choose.
> How might he tune th' alternate reed with thee,
> Perhaps a Strephon thou, a Daphnis he,
> While some old Damon o'er the vulgar wise,
> Thinks he deserves, and thou deserv'st the prize!
> Rapt with the thought my fancy seeks the plains,
> And turns me shepherd while I hear the strains.
> Indulgent nurse of every tender gale,
> Parent of flowerets, old Arcadia, hail!
> Here in the cool my limbs at ease I spread,
> Here let thy poplars whisper o'er my head;
> Still slide thy waters soft among the trees,
> Thy aspins quiver in a breathing breeze;
> Smile all thy valleys in eternal spring,
> Be hush'd, ye winds! while Pope and Virgil sing.
>
> In English lays, and all sublimely great,
> Thy Homer warms with all his ancient heat;
> He shines in council, thunders in the fight,
> And flames with every sense of great delight.
> Long has that poet reign'd, and long unknown,
> Like monarchs sparkling on a distant throne;
> In all the majesty of Greek retir'd,
> Himself unknown, his mighty name admir'd;
> His language failing, wrapp'd him round with night,
> Thine, rais'd by thee, recalls the work to light.
> So wealthy mines, that ages long before
> Fed the large realms around with golden ore,
> When chok'd by sinking banks, no more appear,
> And shepherds only say, the mines were here!
> Should some rich youth, if nature warm his heart,
> And all his projects stand inform'd with art,
> Here clear the caves, there ope the leading vein;
> The mines detected flame with gold again.
>
> How vast, how copious are thy new designs!
> How every music varies in thy lines!
> Still as I read, I feel my bosom beat,
> And rise in raptures by another's heat.
> Thus in the wood, when summer dress'd the days
> When Windsor lent us tuneful hours of ease,
> Our ears the lark, the thrush, the turtle blest,
> And Philomela, sweetest o'er the rest:
> The shades resound with song—O softly tread!
> While a whole season warbles round my head.
>
> This to my friend—and when a friend inspires,
> My silent harp its master's hand requires,
> Shakes off the dust, and makes these rocks resound,
> For fortune plac'd me in unfertile ground;
> Far from the joys that with my soul agree,
> From wit, from learning,—far, O far from thee!
> Here moss-grown trees expand the smallest leaf,
> Here half an acre's corn is half a sheaf;
> Here hills with naked heads the tempest meet,
> Rocks at their side, and torrents at their feet;
> Or lazy lakes, unconscious of a flood,
> Whose dull brown Naiads ever sleep in mud.
>
> Yet here content can dwell, and learned ease,
> A friend delight me, and an author please;
> Even here I sing, while Pope supplies the theme,
> Show my own love, though not increase his fame.
> —THOMAS PARNELL, "To Mr. Pope," 1717

Vain human Kind! Fantastick Race!
Thy various Follies, who can trace?
Self-love, Ambition, Envy, Pride,
Their Empire in our Hearts divide:
Give others Riches, Power, and Station,
'Tis all on me an Usurpation.
I have not Title to aspire;
Yet, when you sink, I seem the higher.
In POPE, I cannot read a Line,
But with a Sigh, I wish it mine:
When he can in one Couplet fix
More Sense than I can do in Six:
It gives me such a jealous Fit,
I cry, Pox take him, and his Wit.
—JONATHAN SWIFT, *Verses on the Death of
Dr. Swift*, 1731

Pope and Boileau are certainly the best two poets of all the
moderns. They both write extremely well; but I should prefer
Pope to Boileau, because he excels in what is most material in
the character of a poet. Boileau writes more correctly, and better
than Pope; but Pope thinks more nobly, and has much more of
the true spirit of poetry than Boileau.—CHEVALIER RAMSAY
(1732–33), cited in Joseph Spence, *Anecdotes, Observations,
and Characters of Books and Men*, ed. S. W. Singer, 1820

⟨. . .⟩ Pope ⟨. . .⟩ is, I think, the most elegant, the most correct
and, what is much more, the most musical poet England has
ever had. He has reduced the harsh blarings of the English
trumpet to the soft sounds of the flute; he can be translated
because he is extremely clear, and his subjects are usually
general and applicable to all nations.—FRANÇOIS MARIE
AROUET DE VOLTAIRE, *Letters on England* (*Lettres Philosophiques*), tr. Leonard Tancock, 1734

You are very wrong in thinking that Mr. Pope could write
blank verse well: he has got a knack, indeed, of writing the
other, but was he to attempt blank verse, I dare say he would
appear quite contemptible in it.—LADY MARY WORTLEY
MONTAGU (1740–41), cited in Joseph Spence, *Anecdotes,
Observations and Characters of Books and Men*, ed. S. W.
Singer, 1820

Thus I have endeavoured to give a critical account, with
freedom, but it is hoped with impartiality, of each of POPE's
works; by which review it will appear, and the *largest* portion of
them is of the *didactic*, *moral*, and *satyric* kind; and consequently, not of the most *poetic* species *of poetry*; whence it is
manifest, that *good sense* and *judgment* were his characteristical excellencies, rather than *fancy* and *invention*; not that the
author of the *Rape of the Lock*, and *Eloisa*, can be thought to
want *imagination*, but because his *imagination* was not his
predominant talent, because he indulged it not, and because
he gave not so many proofs of *this* talent as of the *other*. This
turn of mind led him to admire French models; he studied
Boileau attentively; formed himself upon *him*, as *Milton*
formed himself upon the Grecian and Italian sons of *Fancy*.
He stuck to describing *modern manners*; but those *manners*,
because they are *familiar, uniform, artificial*, and *polished*,
are, in their very nature, unfit for any lofty effort of the Muse.
He gradually became one of the most correct, even, and exact
poets that ever wrote; polishing his pieces with a care and
assiduity, that no business or avocation ever interrupted: so that
if he does not frequently ravish and transport his reader, yet he
does not disgust him with unexpected inequalities, and absurd
improprieties. Whatever poetical enthusiasm he actually possessed, he withheld and stifled. The perusal of him affects not
our minds with such strong emotions as we feel from *Homer*

and *Milton*; so that no man of a true poetical spirit, *is master
of himself while he reads* them. Hence, he is a writer fit for
universal perusal; adapted to all ages and stations; for the old
and for the young; the man of business and the scholar. He
who would think the *Faery Queen*, *Palamon* and *Arcite*, the
Tempest or *Comus*, childish and romantic, might relish POPE.
Surely it is no narrow and niggardly encomium to say he is the
great Poet of Reason, the *First* of *Ethical* authors in verse. And
this species of writing is, after all, the surest road to an
extensive reputation. It lies more level to the general capacities
of men, than the higher flights of more genuine poetry. We all
remember when even a *Churchill* was more in vogue than a
Gray. He that treats of fashionable follies, and the topics of the
day, that describes present persons and recent events, finds
many readers, whose understandings and whose passion he
gratifies. The name of *Chesterfield* on one hand, and of
Walpole on the other, failed not to make a poem bought up
and talked of. And it cannot be doubted, that the *Odes* of
Horace which celebrated, and the satires which ridiculed,
well-known and real characters at Rome, were more eagerly
read, and more frequently cited, than the *Æneid* and the
Georgic of Virgil.

Where then, according to the question proposed at the
beginning of this Essay, shall we with justice be authorized to
place our admired POPE? Not, assuredly, in the same rank with
Spencer, Shakespeare, and *Milton*; however justly we may applaud the *Eloisa* and *Rape of the Lock*; but, considering the
correctness, elegance, and utility of his works, the weight of
sentiment, and the knowledge of man they contain, we may
venture to assign him a place *next to Milton*, and *just* above
Dryden. Yet, to bring our minds steadily to make this decision,
we must forget, for a moment, the divine *Music Ode* of *Dryden*;
and may perhaps then be compelled to confess, that though
Dryden be the greater genius, yet *Pope* is the better artist.

The preference here given to POPE, above other modern
English poets, it must be remembered, is founded on the
excellencies of his works *in general*, and *taken all together*; for
there are *parts* and *passages* in other modern authors, in *Young*
and in *Thomson*, for instance, equal to any of POPE; and he has
written nothing in a strain so truly sublime, as the *Bard* of
Gray.—JOSEPH WARTON, *An Essay on the Genius and Writings of Pope*, 1756–82, Vol. 2, pp. 408–11

Would not ⟨. . .⟩ Pope have succeeded better in an original
attempt? Talents untried are talents unknown. All that I know
is, that, contrary to these sentiments, he was not only an
avowed professor of imitation, but a zealous recommender of it
also. Nor could he recommend any thing better, except
emulation, to those who write. One of these all writers must
call to their aid; but aids they are of unequal repute. Imitation
is inferiority confessed, emulation is superiority contested or
denied; imitation is servile, emulation generous; that fetters,
this fires; that may give a name, this a name immortal. This
made Athens to succeeding ages the rule of taste, and the
standard of perfection. Her men of genius struck fire against
each other; and kindled, by conflict, into glories, which no
time shall extinguish. We thank Æschylus for Sophocles, and
Parrhasius for Zeuxis, emulation for both. That bids us fly the
general fault of imitators; bids us not to be struck with the loud
report of former fame as with a knell, which damps the spirits,
but as with a trumpet, which inspires ardour to rival the
renowned. Emulation exhorts us, instead of learning our
discipline for ever, like raw troops, under ancient leaders in
composition, to put those laurelled veterans in some hazard of
losing their superior posts in glory.

Such is Emulation's high-spirited advice, such her immortalizing call. Pope would not hear, pre-engaged with Imitation, which blessed him with all her charms. He chose rather, with his namesake of Greece, to triumph in the old world, than to look out for a new. His taste partook the error of his religion,—it denied not worship to saints and angels; that is, to writers who, canonized for ages, have received their apotheosis from established and universal fame. True poesy, like true religion, abhors idolatry; and though it honours the memory of the exemplary, and takes them willingly (yet cautiously) as guides in the way to glory, real (though unexampled) excellence is its only aim; nor looks it for any inspiration less than divine.—EDWARD YOUNG, *Conjectures on Original Composition*, 1759

> In polish'd numbers, and majestic sound,
> Where shall thy rival, POPE, be ever found?
> But whilst each line with equal beauty flows,
> E'en excellence, unvary'd, tedious grows.
> Nature, thro' all her works, in great degree,
> Borrows a blessing from VARIETY.
> Music itself her needful aid requires
> To rouze the soul, and wake our dying fires.
> Still in one key, the Nightingale would teize:
> Still in one key, not BRENT would always please.
> —CHARLES CHURCHILL, *The Apology*, 1761

⟨. . .⟩ if Dryden founds any claim of preference on the originality of his manner, we shall venture to affirm, that Pope may found a similar claim, and with equal justice, on the perfection of his taste; and that, if the critical writings of the first are more voluminous, those of the second are more judicious; if Dryden's inventions are more diversified, those of Pope are more regular, and more important. Pope's style may be thought to have less simplicity, less vivacity, and less of the purity of the mother-tongue; but is at the same time more uniformly elevated, and less debased by vulgarism, than that of his great master:—and the superior variety that animates the numbers of the latter, will perhaps be found to be compensated by the steadier and more majestic modulation of the former. Thus far their merits would appear to be pretty equally balanced.—But if the opinion of those critics be true, who hold that the highest regions of Parnassus are appropriated to pathos and sublimity, Dryden must after all confess, that he has never ascended so far as his illustrious imitator: there being nothing in the writings of the first so pathetic as the *Epistle of Eloisa*, or the "Elegy on the Unfortunate Lady"; nor so uniformly sublime as the *Essay on Man*, or the *Pastoral of the Messiah*. This last is indeed but a selection and imitation of choice passages; but it bespeaks a power of imitation, and a taste in selection, that Dryden does not seem to have possessed. To all which I may not be permitted to add, what I think I could prove, that the pathos of Homer is frequently improved by Pope, and that of Virgil very frequently debased by Dryden?

The writings of Dryden are stamped with originality, but are not always the better for that circumstance. Pope is an imitator professedly, and of choice; but to most of those whom he copies he is at least equal, and to many of them superior: and it is pleasing to observe, how he rises in proportion to his originals. Where he follows Denham, Buckingham, Roscommon, and Rochester, in his *Windsor-forest*, *Essay on Criticism*, and poem on Silence, he is superior indeed, but does not soar very high above them. When he versifies Chaucer, he catches, as by instinct, the ease, simplicity, and spirit of Dryden, whom he there emulates. In the *Rape of the Lock* he outshines Boileau, as much as the sylphs that flutter round Belinda

exceed in sprightliness and luminous beauty those mechanical attendants of the goddess of luxury, who knead up plumpness for the chin of the canon, and pound vermilion for the cheek of the monk. His Eloisa is beyond all comparison more sublime and more interesting than any of Ovid's Heroines. His imitations of Horace equal their archetypes in elegance, and often surpass them in energy and fire. In the lyric style, he was no match for Dryden: but when he copies the manner of Virgil, and borrows the thoughts of Isaiah, Pope is superior not only to himself, but to almost all other poets.—JAMES BEATTIE, *Essays on Poetry and Music* (1776), 1779, pp. 18–19

In the last Review, I mean the last but one, I saw Johnson's Critique upon Prior and Pope. I am bound to acquiesce in his Opinion of the latter, because it has always been my own. I could never agree with those who preferred him to Dryden, nor with others (I have known such and persons of taste and discernment too) who could not allow him to be a Poet at all. He was certainly a mechanical maker of verses, and in every line he wrote we see indubitable marks of the most indefatigable Industry and Labour. Writers who find it necessary to make such strenuous and painfull exertions, are generally as phlegmatic as they are correct; but Pope was in this respect exempted from the common Lot of Authors of that class. With the unwearied application of a plodding Flemish painter who draws a Shrimp with the most minute exactness, he had all the Genius of one of the first Masters. Never, I believe, were such talents and such drudgery united. But I admire Dryden most, who has succeeded by mere dint of Genius, and in spite of a laziness and a carelessness almost peculiar to himself. His faults are numberless, but so are his beauties. His faults are those of a great man, and his beauties are such, at least sometimes, as Pope with all his touching and retouching could never equal.—WILLIAM COWPER, Letter to William Unwin (Jan. 5, 1782)

Mr. Pope's *Ethical Epistles* deserve to be mentioned with signal honour, as a model, next to perfect, of ⟨didactic⟩ Poetry. Here, perhaps, the strength of his genius appeared. In the more sublime parts of Poetry, he is not so distinguished. In the enthusiasm, the fire, the force and copiousness of poetic genius, Dryden, though a much less correct Writer, appears to have been superior to him. One can scarce think that he was capable of Epic or Tragic Poetry; but within a certain limited region, he has been outdone by no Poet. His translation of the *Iliad* will remain a lasting monument to his honour, as the most elegant and highly finished translation, that, perhaps, ever was given to any poetical work. That he was not incapable of tender Poetry, appears from the epistle of Eloisa to Abelard, and from the verses to the memory of an Unfortunate Lady, which are almost his only sentimental productions; and which indeed are excellent in their kind. But the qualities for which he is chiefly distinguished are, judgment and wit, with a concise and happy expression, and a melodious versification. Few Poets ever had more wit, and at the same time more judgment, to direct the proper employment of that wit. This renders his *Rape of the Lock* the greatest master-piece that perhaps was ever composed, in the gay and sprightly Style; and in his serious works, such as his *Essay on Man*, and his *Ethic Epistles*, his wit just discovers itself as much, as to give a proper seasoning to grave reflections. His imitations of Horace are so peculiarly happy, that one is at a loss, whether most to admire the original or the copy; and they are among a few imitations extant, that have all the grace and ease of an original. His paintings of characters are natural and lively in a high degree; and never was any Writer so happy in that concise spirited

Style, which gives animation to Satyres and Epistles.—HUGH BLAIR, *Lectures on Rhetoric and Belles Lettres*, 1783, Lecture 40

> But ever since Pope spoiled the ears of the town
> With his cuckoo-song verses, half up and half down,
> There has been such a doling and sameness, by Jove,
> I'd as soon have gone down to see Kemble in love.
> —LEIGH HUNT, *The Feast of the Poets* (1811), 1814

The arts by which Pope ⟨. . .⟩ contrived to procure to himself a more general and a higher reputation than perhaps any English Poet ever attained during his life-time, are known to the judicious. And as well known is it to them, that the undue exertion of those arts is the cause why Pope has for some time held a rank in literature, to which, if he had not been seduced by an over-love of immediate popularity, and had confided more in his native genius, he never could have descended. He bewitched the nation by his melody, and dazzled it by his polished style, and was himself blinded by his own success. Having wandered from humanity in his Eclogues with boyish inexperience, the praise, which these compositions obtained, tempted him into a belief that Nature was not to be trusted, at least in pastoral Poetry. To prove this by example, he put his friend Gay upon writing those Eclogues which their author intended to be burlesque. The instigator of the work, and his admirers, could perceive in them nothing but what was ridiculous. Nevertheless, though these Poems contain some detestable passages, the effect, as Dr. Johnson well observes, 'of reality and truth became conspicuous even when the intention was to show them grovelling and degraded.' The Pastorals, ludicrous to such as prided themselves upon their refinement, in spite of those disgusting passages, 'became popular, and were read with delight, as just representations of rural manners and occupations.'—WILLIAM WORDSWORTH, "Essay, Supplementary to the Preface" (1815), *Lyrical Ballads* (1798), 1815

I was not blind to the merits of ⟨Pope's⟩ school, yet as from inexperience of the world and consequent want of sympathy with the general subjects of these poems they gave me little pleasure, I doubtless undervalued the *kind*, and with the presumption of youth withheld from its masters the legitimate name of poets. I saw that the excellence of this kind consisted in just and acute observations on men and manners in an artificial state of society as its matter and substance—and in the logic of wit conveyed in smooth and strong epigrammatic couplets as its form. Even when the subject was addressed to the fancy or the intellect, as in the *Rape of the Lock* or the *Essay on Man*; nay, when it was a consecutive narration, as in that astonishing product of matchless talent and ingenuity, Pope's translation of the *Iliad*; still a *point* was looked for at the end of each second line, and the whole was as it were a sorites or, if I may exchange a logical for a grammatical metaphor, a *conjunction disjunctive* of epigrams. Meantime the matter and diction seemed to me characterized not so much by poetic thoughts as by thoughts *translated* into the language of poetry.—SAMUEL TAYLOR COLERIDGE, *Biographia Literaria*, 1817, Ch. 1

The attempt of the poetical populace of the present day to obtain an ostracism against Pope is as easily accounted for as the Athenian's shell against Aristides; they are tired of hearing him always called 'the Just.' They are also fighting for life; for, if he maintains his station, they will reach their own—by falling. They have raised a mosque by the side of a Grecian temple of the purest architecture; and, more barbarous than the barbarians from whose practice I have borrowed the figure, they are not contented with their own grotesque edifice, unless they destroy the prior, and purely beautiful fabric which preceded, and which shames them and theirs for ever and ever. I shall be told that amongst those I *have* been (or it may be still *am*) conspicious—true, and I am ashamed of it. I *have* been amongst the builders of this Babel, attended by a confusion of tongues, but *never* amongst the envious destroyers of the classic temple of our predecessor. I have loved and honoured the fame and name of that illustrious and unrivalled man, far more than my own paltry renown, and the trashy jingle of the crowd of 'Schools' and upstarts, who pretend to rival, or even surpass him. Sooner than a single leaf should be torn from his laurel, it were better that all which these men, and that I, as one of their set, have ever written, should

> Line trunks, clothe spice, or, fluttering in a row,
> Befringe the rails of Bedlam, or Soho!

There are those who will believe this, and those who will not. You, sir, know how far I am sincere, and whether my opinion, not only in the short work intended for publication, and in private letters which can never be published, has or has not been the same. I look upon this as the declining age of English poetry; no regard for others, no selfish feeling, can prevent me from seeing this, and expressing the truth. There can be no worse sign for the taste of the times than the depreciation of Pope. It would be better to receive for proof Mr. Cobbett's rough but strong attack upon Shakespeare and Milton, than to allow this smooth and 'candid' undermining of the reputation of the most *perfect* of our poets, and the purest of our moralists. Of his power in the *passions*, in description, in the mock heroic, I leave others to descant. I take him on his strong ground as an *ethical* poet: in the former, none excel; in the mock heroic and the ethical, none equal him; and, in my mind, the latter is the highest of all poetry, because it does that in *verse*, which the greatest of men have wished to accomplish in prose. If the essence of poetry must be a *lie*, throw it to the dogs, or banish it from your republic, as Plato would have done. He who can reconcile poetry with truth and wisdom, is the only true '*poet*' in its real sense, 'the *maker*,' 'the *creator*,'—why must this mean the 'liar,' the 'feigner,' the 'tale-teller?' A man may make and create better things than these.

I shall not presume to say that Pope is as high a poet as Shakespeare and Milton, though his enemy, Warton, places him immediately under them. I would no more say this than I would assert in the mosque (once Saint Sophia's), that Socrates was a greater man than Mahomet. But if I say that he is very near them, it is no more than has been asserted of Burns, who is supposed

> To rival all but Shakespeare's name below.

I say nothing against this opinion. But what '*order*,' according to the poetical aristocracy, are Burns's poems? There are his *opus magnum*, 'Tam O'Shanter,' a *tale*; the Cotter's Saturday Night, a descriptive sketch; some others in the same style: the rest are songs. So much for the *rank* of his *productions*; the *rank* of Burns is the very first of his art. Of Pope I have expressed my opinion elsewhere, as also of the effect which the present attempts at poetry have had upon our literature. If any great national or natural convulsion could or should overwhelm your country in such sort as to sweep Great Britain from the kingdoms of the earth, and leave only that, after all, the most living of human things, a *dead language*, to be studied and read, and imitated by the wise of future and far generations, upon foreign shores; if your literature should become the learning of mankind, divested of party cabals, temporary fashions, and national pride and prejudice;—an Englishman, anxious that the posterity of strangers should know that there had been such a thing as a British Epic and Tragedy, might wish for the preservation of Shakespeare and Milton; but the surviving World would snatch Pope from the wreck, and let the rest sink with the people. He is the moral poet of all civilisation; and as such, let us hope that he will one day be the national poet of mankind. He is the only poet that never shocks; the only poet whose *faultlessness* has been made his reproach. Cast your eye over his productions; consider their extent, and contemplate their variety:—pastoral, passion, mock heroic, translation, satire, ethics,—all excellent, and often perfect. —GEORGE GORDON, LORD BYRON, "Letter to —— ——, Esqre, on the Rev. W. L. Bowles's Strictures on the Life and Writings of Pope," 1821

We return to the generation of Dryden and to Pope his inheritor—Pope, the perfecter, as we have already taken occasion to call him—who stood in the presence of his father Dryden, before that energetic soul, weary with its long literary work which was not always clean and noble, had uttered its last wisdom or foolishness through the organs of the body. Unfortunately, Pope had his advisers apart from his muses; and their counsel was "be correct." To be correct, therefore, to be great through correctness, was the end of his ambition, an inspiration scarcely more calculated for the production of noble poems than the philosophy of utilitarianism is for that of lofty virtues. Yet correctness seemed a virtue rare in the land; Dr. Johnson having crowned Lord Roscommon over Shakespeare's head, "the only correct writer before Addison." The same critic predicated of Milton, that he could not cut figures upon cherry-stones. Pope glorified correctness, and dedicated himself to cherry-stones from first to last. A cherry-stone was the apple of his eye.

Now we are not about to take up any popular cry against Pope; he has been over-praised and is under-praised; and, in the silence of our poetical experience, ourselves may confess personally to the guiltiness of either extremity. He was not a great poet; he meant to be a correct poet, and he was what he meant to be, according to his construction of the thing meant: there are few amongst us who fulfil so literally their ambitions. Moreover we will admit to our reader in the confessional, that, however convinced in our innermost opinion of the superiority of Dryden's genius, we have more pleasure in reading Pope than we ever could enjoy or imagine under Pope's master. We incline to believe that Dryden being the greatest poet-power, Pope is the best poet-manual; and that whatever Dryden has done—we do not say conceived, we do not say suggested, but *done*—Pope has done that thing better. For translations, we hold up Pope's Homer against Dryden's Virgil and the world. Both translations are utterly and equally contrary to the antique, both bad with the same sort of excellence; but Pope's faults are Dryden's faults, while Dryden's are not Pope's. We say the like of the poems from Chaucer; we say the like of the philosophic and satirical poems; the art of reasoning in verse is admirably attained by either poet, but practised with more grace and point by the later one. To be sure, there is the "Alexander's Feast" ode, called, until people half believed what they said, the greatest ode in the language! But here is, to make the scales even again, the *Eloisa*, with tears on it—faulty but tender—of a sensibility which glorious John was not born with a heart for. To be sure, it was not necessary that John Dryden should keep a Bolingbroke to think for him: but to be

sure again, it is something to be born with a heart, particularly for a poet. We recognise besides, in Pope, a delicate fineness of tact, of which the precise contrary is unpleasantly obvious in his great master: Horace Walpole's description of Selwyn, *une bête inspirée*, with a restriction of *bête* to the animal sense, fitting glorious John like his crown. Now there is nothing of this coarseness of the senses about Pope; the little pale Queen Anne's valetudinarian had a nature fine enough to stand erect upon the point of a needle like a schoolman's angel; and whatever he wrote coarsely, he did not write from inward impulse, but from external conventionality, from a bad social Swift-sympathy. For the rest, he carries out his master's principles into most excellent and delicate perfection: he is rich in his degree. And there is, indeed, something charming even to an enemy's ear in this exquisite balancing of sounds and phrases, these "shining rows" of oppositions and appositions, this glorifying of commonplaces by antithetic processes, this catching, in the rebound, of emphasis upon rhyme and rhyme; all, in short, of this Indian jugglery and Indian carving upon— cherry-stones! "and she herself" (that is, poetry)—

And she herself one fair Antithesis.

When Voltaire threw his *Henriade* into the fire and Hénault rescued it, "Souvenez-vous," said the president to the poet, "that I burnt my lace ruffles for the sake of your epic." It was about as much as the epic was worth. For our own part, we would sacrifice not only our point, but the prosperity of our very fingers, to save from a similar catastrophe these works of Pope; and this, although the most perfect and original of all of them, *The Rape of the Lock*, had its fortune in a fire-safe. They are the works of a master. A great poet? Oh no! A true poet?— perhaps not. Yet a man, be it remembered, of such mixed gracefulness and power, that Lady Mary Wortley deigned to coquet with him, and Dennis shook before him in his shoes. —ELIZABETH BARRETT BROWNING, *The Book of the Poets* (1842), *Life, Letters and Essays of Elizabeth Barrett Browning*, 1863

But the moral character of Pope is of secondary interest: we are concerned with it only as connected with his great intellectual power. There are three errors which seem current upon this subject: *First*, that Pope drew his impulses from French literature; *secondly*, that he was a poet of inferior rank; *thirdly*, that his merit lies in superior "correctness." With respect to the first notion, it has prevailed by turns in every literature. One stage of society, in every nation, brings men of impassioned minds to the contemplation of manners, and of the social affections of man as exhibited in manners. With this propensity co-operates, no doubt, some degree of despondency when looking at the great models of the literature who have usually pre-occupied the grander passions, and displayed their movements in the earlier periods of literature. Now, it happens that the French, from an extraordinary defect in the higher qualities of passion, have attracted the notice of foreign nations chiefly to that field of their literature in which the taste and the unimpassioned understanding preside. But in all nations such literature is a natural growth of the mind, and would arise equally if the French literature had never existed. The wits of Queen Anne's reign, or even of Charles II's, were not French by their taste or their imitation. Butler and Dryden were surely not French; and of Milton we need not speak; as little was Pope French, either by his institution or by his models. Boileau he certainly admired too much; and, for the sake of a poor parallelism with a passage about Greece in Horace, he has falsified history in the most ludicrous manner, without a shadow of countenance from facts, in order to make out that we, like the Romans, received laws of taste from those whom we had conquered. But these are insulated cases and accidents, not to insist on his known and most profound admiration, often expressed, for Chaucer and Shakspere and Milton. Secondly, that Pope is to be classed as an inferior poet has arisen purely from a confusion between the departments of poetry which he cultivated and the merit of his culture. The first place must undoubtedly be given for ever,—it cannot be refused,—to the impassioned movements of the tragic, and to the majestic movements of the epic, muse. We cannot alter the relations of things out of favour to an individual. But in his own department, whether higher or lower, that man is supreme who has not yet been surpassed; and such a man is Pope. As to the final notion, first started by Walsh, and propagated by Warton, it is the most absurd of all the three; it is not from superior correctness that Pope is esteemed more correct, but because the compass and sweep of his performance lie more within the range of ordinary judgments. Many questions that have been raised upon Milton and Shakspere, questions relating to so subtle a subject as the flux and reflux of human passion, lie far above the region of ordinary capacities; and the indeterminateness or even carelessness of the judgment is transferred by a common confusion to its objects. But, waiving this, let us ask what is meant by "correctness"? Correctness in what? In developing the thought? In connecting it, or effecting the transitions? In the use of words? In the grammar? In the metre? Under every one of these limitations of the idea, we maintain that Pope is *not* distinguished by correctness; nay, that, as compared with Shakspere, he is eminently incorrect. Produce us from any drama of Shakspere one of those leading passages that all men have by heart, and show us an eminent defect in the very sinews of the thought. It is impossible; defects there may be, but they will always be found irrelevant to the main central thought, or to its expression. Now, turn to Pope. The first striking passage which offers itself to our memory is the famous character of Addison, ending thus:—

> Who would not laugh, if such a man there be,
> Who but must weep if Atticus were he?

Why must we laugh? Because we find a grotesque assembly of noble and ignoble qualities. Very well; but why, then, must we weep? Because this assemblage is found actually existing in an eminent man of genius. Well, that is a good reason for weeping; we weep for the degradation of human nature. But then revolves the question, Why must we laugh? Because, if the belonging to a man of genius were a sufficient reason for weeping, so much we know from the very first. The very first line says, "Peace to all such. But were there one whose fires *true genius kindles* and fair fame inspires." Thus falls to the ground the whole antithesis of this famous character. We are to change our mood from laughter to tears upon a sudden discovery that the character belonged to a man of genius; and this we had already known from the beginning. Match us this prodigious oversight in Shakspere. Again, take the *Essay on Criticism*: it is a collection of independent maxims, tied together into a fasciculus by the printer, but having no natural order or logical dependency: generally so vague as to mean nothing: like the general rules of justice, &c., in ethics, to which every man assents; but, when the question comes about any practical case, *is* it just? The opinions fly asunder as far as the poles. And, what is remarkable, many of the rules are violated by no man so often as by Pope, and by Pope nowhere so often as in this very poem. As a single instance, he proscribes monosyllabic lines; and in no English poem of any pretensions are there so many lines of that class as in this. We

have counted above a score, and the last line of all is monosyllabic.

Not, therefore, for superior correctness, but for qualities the very same as belong to his most distinguished brethren, is Pope to be considered a great poet: for impassioned thinking, powerful description, pathetic reflection, brilliant narration. His characteristic difference is simply that he carried these powers into a different field, and moved chiefly amongst the social paths of men, and viewed their characters as operating through their manners. And our obligations to him arise chiefly on this ground,—that, having already, in the persons of earlier poets, carried off the palm in all the grander trials of intellectual strength, for the majesty of the epopee and the impassioned vehemence of the tragic drama, to Pope we owe it that we can now claim an equal pre-eminence in the sportive and aërial graces of the mock heroic and satiric muse; that in the *Dunciad* we possess a peculiar form of satire, in which (according to a plan unattempted by any other nation) we see alternately her festive smile and her gloomiest scowl; that the grave good sense of the nation has here found its brightest mirror; and, finally, that through Pope the cycle of our poetry is perfected and made orbicular,—that from that day we might claim the laurel equally, whether for dignity or grace. —THOMAS DE QUINCEY, "Alexander Pope" (c. 1842), *Collected Writings*, ed. David Masson, Vol. 4, pp. 278–81

The tastes and sensibilities of Pope, which led him to cultivate the society of persons of fine manners, or wit, or taste, or beauty, caused him to shrink equally from that shabby and boisterous crew which formed the rank and file of literature in his time: and he was as unjust to these men as they to him. The delicate little creature sickened at habits and company which were quite tolerable to robuster men: and in the famous feud between Pope and the Dunces, and without attributing any peculiar wrong to either, one can quite understand how the two parties should so hate each other. As I fancy, it was a sort of necessity that when Pope's triumph passed, Mr. Addison and his men should look rather contemptuously down on it from their balcony; so it was natural for Dennis and Tibbald, and Webster and Cibber, and the worn and hungry pressmen in the crowd below, to howl at him and assail him. And Pope was more savage to Grub-street, than Grub-street was to Pope. The thong with which he lashed them was dreadful; he fired upon that howling crew such shafts of flame, and poison, he slew and wounded so fiercely, that in reading the *Dunciad* and the prose lampoons of Pope, one feels disposed to side against the ruthless little tyrant, at least to pity those wretched folks upon whom he was so unmerciful. It was Pope, and Swift to aid him, who established among us the Grub-street tradition. He revels in base descriptions of poor men's want; he gloats over poor Dennis's garret, and flannel night-cap, and red stockings; he gives instructions how to find Curll's authors, the historian at the tallow-chandler's under the blind arch in Petty France, the two translators in bed together, the poet in the cock-loft in Budge Row, whose landlady keeps the ladder. It was Pope, I fear, who contributed, more than any man who ever lived, to depreciate the literary calling. It was not an unprosperous one before that time, as we have seen; at least there were great prizes in the profession which had made Addison a minister, and Prior an ambassador, and Steele a commissioner, and Swift all but a bishop. The profession of letters was ruined by that libel of the *Dunciad*. If authors were wretched and poor before, if some of them lived in haylofts, of which their landladies kept the ladders, at least nobody came to disturb them in their straw; if three of them had but one coat between them, the two remained invisible in the garret, the third, at any rate, appeared decently at the coffee-house, and paid his twopence like a gentleman. It was Pope that dragged into light all this poverty and meanness, and held up those wretched shifts and rags to public ridicule. It was Pope that has made generations of the reading world (delighted with the mischief, as who would not be that reads it?) believe that author and wretch, author and rags, author and dirt, author and drink, gin, cowheel, tripe, poverty, duns, bailiffs, squalling children, and clamorous landladies, were always associated together. The condition of authorship began to fall from the days of the *Dunciad:* and I believe in my heart that much of that obloquy which has since pursued our calling was occasioned by Pope's libels and wicked wit. Everybody read those. Everybody was familiarised with the idea of the poor devil author. The manner is so captivating, that young authors practise it, and begin their career with satire. It is so easy to write, and so pleasant to read! to fire a shot that makes a giant wince, perhaps; and fancy one's self his conqueror. It is easy to shoot—but not as Pope did—the shafts of his satire rise sublimely: no poet's verse ever mounted higher than that wonderful flight with which the *Dunciad* concludes:—

> She comes, she comes! the sable throne
>   behold!
> Of night primeval and of Chaos old;
> Before her, Fancy's gilded clouds decay,
> And all its varying rainbows die away;
> Wit shoots in vain its momentary fires,
> The meteor drops, and in a flash expires.
> As, one by one, at dread Medea's strain
> The sick'ning stars fade off the ethereal plain;
> As Argus' eye, by Hermes' wand oppress'd,
> Closed one by one to everlasting rest;—
> Thus, at her fell approach and secret might,
> Art after Art goes out, and all is night.
> See skulking Faith to her old cavern fled,
> Mountains of casuistry heaped o'er her head;
> Philosophy that leaned on Heaven before,
> Shrinks to her second cause and is no more.
> Religion, blushing, veils her sacred fires,
> And unawares Morality expires.
> No public flame, nor private, dares to shine,
> Nor human spark is left, nor glimpse divine.
> Lo! thy dread empire, Chaos, is restored.
> Light dies before thy uncreating word;
> Thy hand, great Anarch, lets the curtain fall,
> And universal darkness buries all.

In these astonishing lines Pope reaches, I think, to the very greatest height which his sublime art has attained, and shows himself the equal of all poets of all times. It is the brightest ardour, the loftiest assertion of truth, the most generous wisdom, illustrated by the noblest poetic figure, and spoken in words the aptest, grandest, and most harmonious. It is heroic courage speaking: a splendid declaration of righteous wrath and war. It is the gage flung down, and the silver trumpet ringing defiance to falsehood and tyranny, deceit, dulness, superstition. It is Truth, the champion, shining and intrepid, and fronting the great world-tyrant with armies of slaves at his back. It is a wonderful and victorious single combat, in that great battle which has always been waging since society began.

In speaking of a work of consummate art one does not try to show what it is, for that were vain; but what it is like, and what are the sensations produced in the mind of him who views it. And in considering Pope's admirable career, I am forced

into similitudes drawn from other courage and greatness, and into comparing him with those who achieved triumphs in actual war. I think the works of young Pope as I do of the actions of young Bonaparte or young Nelson. In their common life you will find frailties and meannesses, as great as the vices and follies of the meanest men. But in the presence of the great occasion, the great soul flashes out, and conquers transcendent. In thinking of the splendour of Pope's young victories, of his merit, unequalled as his renown, I hail and salute the achieving genius, and do homage to the pen of a Hero.—WILLIAM MAKEPEACE THACKERAY, *The English Humourists of the Eighteenth Century*, 1853, pp. 182–86

As a poet, Cowper belongs, though with some differences, to the school of Pope. Great question, as is well known, has been raised whether that very accomplished writer was a poet at all; and a secondary and equally debated question runs side by side, whether, if a poet, he were a great one. With the peculiar genius and personal rank of Pope we have in this article nothing to do. But this much may be safely said, that according to the definition which has been ventured of the poetical art, by the greatest and most accomplished master of the other school, his works are delicately-finished specimens of artistic excellence in one branch of it. 'Poetry,' says Shelley, who was surely a good judge, 'is the expression of the imagination,' by which he meant of course not only the expression of the interior sensations accompanying the faculty's employment, but likewise, and more emphatically, the exercise of it in the delineation of objects which attract it. Now society, viewed as a whole, is clearly one of those objects. There is a vast assemblage of human beings, of all nations, tongues, and languages each with ideas and a personality and a cleaving mark of its own, yet each having somewhat that resembles something of all, much that resembles a part of many—a motley regiment, of various forms, of a million impulses, passions, thoughts, fancies, motives, actions; a 'many-headed monster thing;' a Bashi Bazouk array; a clown to be laughed at; a hydra to be spoken evil of; yet, in fine, our all—the very people of the whole earth. There is nothing in nature more attractive to the fancy than this great spectacle and congregation. Since Herodotus went to and fro to the best of his ability over all the earth, the spectacle of civilisation has ever drawn to itself the quick eyes and quick tongues of seeing and roving men. Not only, says Goethe, is man ever interesting to man, but 'properly there is nothing else interesting.' There is a distinct subject for poetry—at least according to Shelley's definition—in selecting and working out, in idealising, in combining, in purifying, in intensifying the great features and peculiarities which make society, as a whole, interesting, remarkable, fancy-taking. No doubt it is not the object of poetry to versify the works of the eminent narrators, 'to prose,' according to a disrespectful description, 'o'er books of travelled seamen,' to chill you with didactic icebergs, to heat you with torrid sonnets. The difficulty of reading such local narratives is now great—so great that a gentleman in the reviewing department once wished 'one man would go everywhere and say everything,' in order that the limit of his labour at least might be settled and defined. And it would certainly be much worse if palm trees were of course to be in rhyme, and the dinner of the migrator only recountable in blank verse. We do not wish this. We only maintain that there are certain principles, causes, passions, affections, acting on and influencing communities at large, permeating their life, ruling their principles, directing their history, working as a subtle and wandering principle over all their existence. These have a somewhat abstract character, as compared with the soft ideals and passionate incarnations of purely individual character, and seem dull beside the stirring lays of eventful times, in which the earlier and bolder poets delight. Another cause co-operates. The tendency of civilisation is to pare away the oddness and licence of personal character, and to leave a monotonous agreeableness as the sole trait and comfort of mankind. This obviously tends to increase the efficacy of general principles, to bring to view the daily efficacy of constant causes, to suggest the hidden agency of subtle abstractions. Accordingly as civilisation augments and philosophy grows, we commonly find a school of 'common-sense poets,' as they may be called, arise and develop, who proceed to depict what they see around them, to describe its *natura naturans*, to delineate its *natura naturata*, to evolve productive agencies, to teach subtle ramifications. Complete, as the most characteristic specimen of this class of poets, stands Pope. He was, some one we think has said, the sort of person we cannot even conceive existing in a barbarous age. His subject was not life at large, but fashionable life. He described the society in which he was thrown—the people among whom he lived. His mind was a hoard of small maxims, a quintessence of petty observations. When he described character, he described it, not dramatically, nor as it is in itself; but observantly and from without, calling up in the mind not so much a vivid conception of the man, of the real, corporeal, substantial being, as an idea of the idea which a metaphysical bystander might refine and excruciate concerning him. Society in Pope is scarcely a society of people, but of pretty little atoms, coloured and painted with hoops or in coats—a miniature of metaphysics, a puppet-show of sylphs. He elucidates the doctrine, that the tendency of civilised poetry is towards an analytic sketch of the existing civilisation. Nor is the effect diminished by the pervading character of keen judgment and minute intrusive sagacity; for no greater painter of English life can be without a rough sizing of strong sense, or he would fail from want of sympathy with his subject. Pope exemplifies the class and type of 'common-sense' poets who substitute an animated '*catalogue raisonné*' of working thoughts and operative principles—a sketch of the then present society, as a whole and as an object, for the κλέα ἀνδρῶν, the tale of which is one subject of early verse, and the stage effect of living, loving, passionate, impetuous men and women, which is the special topic of another.—WALTER BAGEHOT, "William Cowper" (1855), *Works*, ed. Norman St. John Stevas, Vol. 1, pp. 289–91

I confess that I come to the treatment of Pope with diffidence. I was brought up in the old superstition that he was the greatest poet that ever lived; and when I came to find that I had instincts of my own, and my mind was brought in contact with the apostles of a more esoteric doctrine of poetry, I felt that ardent desire for smashing the idols I had been brought up to worship, without any regard to their artistic beauty, which characterizes youthful zeal. What was it to me that Pope was called a master of style? I felt, as Addison says in his *Freeholder* when answering an argument in favor of the Pretender because he could speak English and George I. could not, "that I did not wish to be tyrannized over in the best English that ever was spoken." The young demand thoughts that find an echo in their real and not their acquired nature, and care very little about the dress they are put in. It is later that we learn to like the conventional, as we do olives. There was a time when I could not read Pope, but disliked him on principle, as old Roger Ascham seems to have felt about Italy when he says, "I was once in Italy myself, but I thank God my abode there was only nine days."

But Pope fills a very important place in the history of English poetry, and must be studied by every one who would come to a clear knowledge of it. I have since read over every line that Pope ever wrote, and every letter written by or to him, and that more than once. If I have not come to the conclusion that he is the greatest of poets, I believe that I am at least in a condition to allow him every merit that is fairly his. I have said that Pope as a literary man represents precision and grace of expression; but as a poet he represents something more,—nothing less, namely, than one of those eternal controversies of taste which will last as long as the imagination and understanding divide men between them. It is not a matter to be settled by any amount of argument or demonstration. There are born Popists or Wordsworthians, Lockists, or Kantists, and there is nothing more to be said of the matter. ⟨. . .⟩

It will hardly be questioned that the man who writes and is still piquant and rememberable, a century and a quarter after his death, was a man of genius. But there are two modes of uttering such things as cleave to the memory of mankind. They may be said or sung. I do not think that Pope's verse anywhere sings, but it should seem that the abiding presence of fancy in his best work forbids his exclusion from the rank of poet. The atmosphere in which he habitually dwelt was an essentially prosaic one, the language habitual to him was that of conversation and society, so that he lacked the help of that fresher dialect which seems like inspiration in the elder poets. His range of associations was of that narrow kind which is always vulgar, whether it be found in the village or the court. Certainly he has not the force and majesty of Dryden in his better moods, but he has a grace, a finesse, an art of being pungent, a sensitiveness to impressions, that would incline us to rank him with Voltaire (whom in many ways he so much resembles), as an author with whom the gift of writing was primary, and that of verse secondary. No other poet that I remember ever wrote prose which is so purely prose as his; and yet, in any impartial criticism, the *Rape of the Lock* sets him even as a poet far above many men more largely endowed with poetic feeling and insight than he.

A great deal must be allowed in Pope for the age in which he lived, and not a little, I think, for the influence of Swift. In his own province he still stands unapproachably alone. If to be the greatest satirist of individual men, rather than of human nature, if to be the highest expression which the life of the court and the ball-room has ever found in verse, if to have added more phrases to our language than any other but Shakespeare, if to have charmed four generations make a man a great poet,—then he is one. He was the chief founder of an artificial style of writing, which in his hands was living and powerful, because he used it to express artificial modes of thinking and an artificial state of society. Measured by any high standard of imagination, he will be found wanting; tried by any test of wit, he is unrivalled.—JAMES RUSSELL LOWELL, "Pope" (1871), *Works*, Riverside ed., Vol. 4, pp. 25–27, 56–57

It seems to me this kind of talent is made for light verses. It is factitious, and so are the manners of society. To make pretty speeches, to prattle with ladies, to speak elegantly of their chocolate or their fan, to jeer at fools, to criticise the last tragedy, to be good at compliments or epigrams,—this, it seems, is the natural employment of a mind such as this, but slightly impassioned, very vain, a perfect master of style, as careful of his verses as a dandy of his coat. Pope wrote the *Rape of the Lock* and the *Dunciad*; his contemporaries went into ecstasies on the charm of his badinage and the exactness of his raillery, and believed that he had surpassed Boileau's *Lutrin* and *Satires*.

That may well be; at all events the praise would be scanty. In Boileau there are, as a rule, two kinds of verse, as was said by a man of wit; most of which seem to be those of a sharp schoolboy in the third class, the rest those of a good schoolboy in the upper division. Boileau wrote the second verse before the first; this is why once out of four times his first verse only serves to stop a gap. Doubtless Pope had a more brilliant and adroit mechanism; but this facility of hand does not suffice to make a poet, even a poet of the boudoir. There, as elsewhere, we need genuine passions, or at least genuine tastes. When we wish to paint the pretty nothings of conversation and the world, we must like them. We can only paint well what we love. Is there no charming grace in the prattle and frivolity of a pretty woman? Painters, like Watteau, have spent their lives in feasting on them. A lock of hair which is lifted up, a pretty arm peeping from underneath a great deal of lace, a stooping figure making the bright folds of a petticoat sparkle, and the arch, half-engaging, half-mocking smile of the pouting mouth,— these are enough to transport an artist. Certainly he will be aware of the influence of the toilet, as much so as the lady herself, and will never scold her for passing three hours at her glass; there is poetry in elegance. He enjoys it as a picture; enjoys the refinements of worldly life, the long quiet lines of the lofty, wainscoted drawing-room, the soft reflection of the high mirrors and glittering porcelain, the careless gayety of the little sculptured Loves, locked in an embrace above the mantelpiece, the silvery sound of these soft voices, buzzing scandal round the tea-table. Pope hardly, if at all, rejoices in them; he is satirical and English amidst this amiable luxury, introduced from France. Although he is the most worldly of English poets, he is not enough so; nor is the society around him. Lady Mary Wortley Montague, who was in her time "the pink of fashion," and who is compared to Madame de Sévigné, has such a serious mind, such a decided style, such a precise judgment, and such a harsh sarcasm, that you would take her for a man. In fine, the English, even Lord Chesterfield and Horace Walpole, never mastered the true tone of the *salon*. Pope is like them; his voice thunders, and then suddenly becomes biting. Every instant a harsh mockery blots out the graceful images, which he began to arouse.—HIPPOLYTE TAINE, *History of English Literature*, tr. H. Van Laun, 1871, Bk. 3, Ch. 7

> From mortal Gratitude, decide, my Pope,
> Have Wits Immortal more to fear or hope?
> Wits toil and travail round the Plant of Fame,
> Their Works its Garden, and its Growth their Aim,
> Then Commentators, in unwieldy Dance,
> Break down the Barriers of the trim Pleasance,
> Pursue the Poet, like Actæon's Hounds,
> Beyond the fences of his Garden Grounds,
> Rend from the singing Robes each borrowed Gem,
> Rend from the laurel'd Brows the Diadem,
> And, if one Rag of Character they spare,
> Comes the Biographer, and strips it bare!
>
> Such, Pope, has been thy Fortune, such thy Doom.
> Swift the Ghouls gathered at the Poet's Tomb,
> With Dust of Notes to clog each lordly Line,
> Warburton, Warton, Croker, Bowles, combine!
> Collecting Cackle, Johnson condescends
> To *interview* the Drudges of your Friends.
> Though still your Courthope holds your merits high,
> And still proclaims your Poems *Poetry*,
> Biographers, un-Boswell-like, have sneered,
> And Dunces edit him whom Dunces feared!

> They say; what say they? Not in vain You ask.
> To tell you what they say, behold my Task!
> "Methinks already I your Tears survey"
> As I repeat "the horrid Things they say."
>
> Comes El—n first: I fancy you'll agree
> Not frenzied Dennis smote so fell as he;
> For El—n's Introduction, crabbed and dry,
> Like Churchill's Cudgel's marked with Lie, and Lie!
>
> "Too dull to know what his own System meant,
> Pope yet was skilled new Treasons to invent;
> A Snake that puffed himself and stung his Friends,
> Few Lied so frequent, for such little Ends;
> His mind, like Flesh inflamed, was raw and sore,
> And still, the more he writhed, he stung the more!
>
> Oft in a Quarrel, never in the Right,
> His Spirit sank when he was called to fight.
> Pope, in the Darkness mining like a Mole,
> Forged on Himself, as from Himself he stole,
> And what for Caryll once he feigned to feel,
> Transferred, in Letters never sent, to Steele!
> Still he denied the Letters he had writ,
> And still mistook Indecency for Wit.
> His very Grammar, so De Quincey cries,
> 'Detains the Reader, and at times defies!'"
>
> Fierce El—n thus: no Line escapes his Rage,
> And furious Foot-notes growl 'neath every Page:
> See St–ph–n next take up the woful Tale,
> Prolong the Preaching, and protract the Wail!
> "Some forage Falsehoods from the North and South,
> But Pope, poor D——l, lied from Hand to Mouth;
> Affected, hypocritical, and vain,
> A Book in Breeches, and a Fop in Grain;
> A Fox that found not the high Clusters sour,
> The Fanfaron of Vice beyond his power,
> Pope yet possessed"—(the Praise will make you start)—
> "Mean, morbid, vain, he yet possessed a Heart!
> And still we marvel at the Man, and still
> Admire his Finish, and applaud his Skill:
> Though, as that fabled Bark, a phantom Form,
> Eternal strains, nor rounds the Cape of Storm,
> Even so Pope strove, nor ever crossed the Line
> That from the Noble separates the Fine!"
>
> The Learned thus, and who can quite reply,
> Reverse the Judgment, and Retort the Lie?
> You reap, in armèd Hates that haunt Your name,
> Reap what you sowed, the Dragon's Teeth of Fame:
> You could not write, and from unenvious Time
> Expect the Wreath that crowns the lofty Rhyme,
> You still must fight, retreat, attack, defend,
> And oft, to snatch a Laurel, lose a Friend!
> The Pity of it! And the changing Taste
> Of changing Time leaves half your Work a Waste!
> My Childhood fled your couplet's clarion tone,
> And sought for Homer in the Prose of Bohn.
> Still through the Dust of that dim Prose appears
> The Flight of Arrows and the Sheen of Spears;
> Still we may trace what Hearts heroic feel,
> And hear the Bronze that hurtles on the Steel!
> But, ah, your Iliad seems a half-pretence,
> Where Wits, not Heroes, prove their Skill in Fence,
> And great Achilles' Eloquence doth show
> As if no Centaur trained him, but Boileau!
> Again, your Verse is orderly,—and more,—
> "The Waves behind impel the Waves before;"
>
> Monotonously musical they glide,

Till Couplet unto Couplet hath replied.
But turn to Homer! How his Verses sweep!
Surge answers Surge and Deep doth call on Deep;
This Line in Foam and Thunder issues forth,
Spurred by the West or smitten by the North,
Sombre in all its sullen Deeps, and all
Clear at the Crest, and foaming to the Fall,
The next with silver Murmur dies away,
Like Tides that falter to Calypso's Bay!

Thus Time, with sordid Alchemy and dread,
Turns half the Glory of your Gold to Lead;
Thus Time—at Ronsard's wreath that vainly bit—
Has marred the Poet to preserve the Wit,
Who almost left on Addison a stain,
Whose knife cut cleanest with a poisoned pain,—
Yet Thou (strange Fate that clings to all of Thine!)
When most a Wit dost most a Poet shine.
In Poetry thy Dunciad expires,
When Wit has shot "her momentary Fires."
'T is Tragedy that watches by the Bed
"Where tawdry Yellow strove with dirty Red,"
And Men, remembering all, can scarce deny
To lay the Laurel where thine Ashes lie!
 —ANDREW LANG, "Epistle to Mr. Alexander
    Pope," *Letters to Dead Authors*, 1886, pp.
    45–49

What is Pope's position as a poet? Time, that great practitioner of the exhaustive process, "sifting alway, sifting ever," even to the point of annihilation, has well-nigh answered the question. No one now, except the literary historian or the student of versification, is ever likely to consult the *Pastorals* or *Windsor Forest*. Men will in all probability continue to quote "Hope springs eternal in the human breast" and "A little learning is a dangerous thing," without the least suspicion that the one comes from the seldom read *Essay on Criticism* and the other from the equally seldom-read *Essay on Man*. Here and there a professor (like the late Professor Conington) will praise the "unhasting unresting flow" of the translations from Homer, but the next generation will read its *Iliad* in the Greek, or in some future successor to Mr. William Morris or Mr. Way. Few will now re-echo the praises which the critics of fifty years ago gave to the "Elegy on an Unfortunate Lady" and *Eloisa to Abelard*, and none but the habitual pilgrims of the by-ways of literature will devote any serious attention to the different versions of the *Dunciad*. But there is no reason why *The Rape of the Lock* should not find as many admirers a hundred years hence as it does to-day, or why—so long as men remember the poems of the friend of Mæcenas—the *Satires and Epistles* should fail of an audience. In these Pope's verse is as perfect as it is anywhere, and his subject is borrowed, not from his commonplace book, but from his own experiences. He wants the careless ease, the variety, the unemphatic grace of Horace, it is true. But he has many of the qualities of his master, and it is probable that only when men weary of hearing how Horace strolled down the Sacred Way and met an intolerable Bore—only then, or perhaps a little earlier, will they cease to hearken how Alexander Pope bade John Searle bar the door at Twickenham against the inroads of Bedlam and Parnassus.
 —AUSTIN DOBSON, "Alexander Pope," *Scribner's Magazine*,
May 1888, p. 547

Pope I will not defend so warmly (as Dryden), and yet Pope also was a great poet. Two of my American critics, bent on refuting me, have severally availed themselves of a somewhat unexpected weapon. Each of them reminds me that Mr. Lang,

in some recent number of a magazine, has said that Pope is not a poet at all. Research might prove that this heresy is not entirely unparalleled, yet I am unconvinced. I yield to no one in respect and affection for Mr. Lang, but in criticising that with which he feels no personal sympathy, he is merely a "young light-hearted master of the oar" of temperament. When Mr. Lang blesses, the object is blest; when he curses, he may bless to-morrow. Some day he will find himself alone in a country-house with a Horace; old chords will be touched, the mystery of Pope will reveal itself to him, and we shall have a panegyric that will make Lady Mary writhe in her grave. Let no transatlantic, or cisatlantic, infidel of letters be profane at the expense of a classic by way of pleasing Mr. Lang; his next emotion is likely to be *"un sentiment obscur d'avoir embrassé la Chimère."*

To justify one's confidence in the great poetic importance of Pope is somewhat difficult. It needs a fuller commentary and a longer series of references than can be given here. But let us recollect that the nature-worship and nature-study of today may grow to seem a complete fallacy, a sheer persistence in affectation, and that then, to readers of new tastes and passions, Wordsworth and Shelley will be as Pope is now, that is to say, supported entirely by their individual merits. At this moment, to the crowd, he is doubtless less attractive than they are; he is on the shady side, they on the sunny side of fashion. But the author of the end of the second book of *The Rape of the Lock*, of the close of *The New Dunciad*, of the Sporus portrait, and of the *Third Moral Essay*, has qualities of imagination, applied to human character, and of distinction, applied to a formal and delicately-elaborated style, which are unsurpassed, even perhaps by Horace himself. Satirist after satirist has chirped like a wren from the head of Pope; where are they now? Where is the great, the terrific, the cloud-compelling Churchill? Meanwhile, in the midst of a generation persistently turned away from all his ideas and all his models, the clear voice of Pope still rings from the arena of Queen Anne.
 —EDMUND GOSSE, "What Is a Great Poet?" (1889), *Questions at Issue*, 1893, pp. 103–5

There was born in eighteenth century England a pale little diseased wretch of a boy. Since it was evident that he would never be fit for any healthy and vigorous trade, and that he must all his life be sickly and burdensome to himself, and since it is the usual way of such unhappy beings to add to their unhappiness by their own perversities of choice, he naturally became a poet. And after living for long in a certain miserable state called glory, reviled and worshipped and laughed at and courted, despised by the women he loved, very ill looked after, amid the fear and malignity of many and the affection of very few, the wizened little suffering monstrosity died, and was buried in Westminster Abbey, by way of encouraging others to follow in his footsteps. And though a large number of others have done so with due and proper misfortune, in all the melancholy line there is, perhaps, no such destined a wretch as Alexander Pope. What fame can do to still the cravings of such a poor prodigal of song, in the beggarly raiment of his tattered body, that it did for him. The husks of renown he had in plenty, and had them all his life, as no other poet has had. But Voltaire testified that the author of that famous piece of philosophy, "Whatever is, is right," was the most miserable man he had ever known.

This king of the eighteenth century is still the king of the eighteenth century by general consent. Dryden was a greater poet, *meo judicio*, but he did not represent the eighteenth century so well as Pope. All that was elegant and airy in the polished artificiality of that age reaches its apotheosis in the *Rape of the Lock*. It is Pope's masterpiece, a Watteau in verse. The poetry of manners could no further go than in this boudoir epic, unmatched in any literature. It is useless, I may here say, to renew the old dispute whether Pope was a poet. Call his verse poetry or what you will, it is work in verse which could not have been done in prose, and, of its kind, never equalled. Then the sylph machinery in *The Rape of the Lock* is undoubted work of fancy: the fairyland of powder and patches, A *Midsummer Night's Dream* seen through chocolate-fumes. The *Essay on Man* is nought to us nowadays, as a whole. It has brilliant artificial passages. It has homely aphorisms such as only Pope and Shakespeare could produce—the quintessence of pointed common sense: many of them have passed into the language, and are put down, by three out of five who quote them, to Shakespeare. But, as a piece of reasoning in verse, the *Essay on Man* is utterly inferior to Dryden's *Hind and Panther*. Even that brilliant achievement could not escape the doom which hangs over the didactic poem pure and simple; and certain, therefore, was the fate of the *Essay on Man*.

The *Dunciad* De Quincey ranked even above the *Rape of the Lock*. At my peril I venture to question a judgment backed by all the ages. The superb satire of parts of the poem I admit; I admit the exceedingly fine close, in which Pope touched a height he never touched before or after; I admit the completeness of the scheme. But from that completeness comes the essential defect of the poem. He adapted the scheme from Dryden's *MacFlecknoe*. But Dryden's satire is at once complete and succinct: Pope has built upon the scheme an edifice greater than it will bear; has extended a witty and ingenious idea to a portentous extent at which it ceases to be amusing. The mock solemnity of Dryden's idea becomes a very real and dull solemnity when it is extended to literal epic proportions. A serious epic is apt to nod, with the force of a Milton behind it; and epic satire fairly goes to sleep. A pleasantry in several books is past a pleasantry. And it is bolstered out with a great deal which is sheer greasy scurrility. The mock-heroic games of the poets are in large part as dully dirty as the waters into which Pope makes them plunge. If the poem had been half as long, it might have been a masterpiece. As it is, unless we are to reckon masterpieces by avoirdupois weight, or to assign undue value to mere symmetry of scheme, I think we must look for Pope's satirical masterpieces elsewhere. Not in the satire on women, where Pope seems hardly to have his heart in his work; but in the imitations from Horace, those generally known as Pope's *Satires*. Here he is at his very best and tersest. They are as brilliant as anything in the *Dunciad*, and they are brilliant right through; the mordant pen never flags. It matters not that they are imitated from Horace. They gain by it: their limits are circumscribed, their lines laid down, and Pope writes the better for having these limits set him, this tissue on which to work. Not a whit does he lose in essential originality: nowhere is he so much himself. It is very different from Horace, say the critics. Surely that is exactly the thing for which to thank poetry and praise Pope. It has not the pleasant urbane good humour of the Horatian spirit. No, it has the spirit of Pope—and satire is the gainer. Horace is the more charming companion; Pope is the greater satirist. In place of an echo of Horace (and no verse translation was ever anything but feeble which attempted merely to echo the original), we have a new spirit in satire; a fine series of English satirical poems, which in their kind are unapproached by the Roman, and in his kind wisely avoid the attempt to approach him. "Satires after Horace" would have been a better title than "Imitations"; for less imitative poems in essence were never written. These and the *Rape of the Lock* are

Pope's finest title to fame. The "Elegy on an Unfortunate Lady," has at least one part which shows a pathos, little to have been surmised from his later work; and so, perhaps (in a much less degree, I think), have fragments of the once famous *Eloisa to Abelard*. But the *Pastorals*, and the *Windsor Forest*, and the "Ode on St. Cecilia's Day," and other things in which Pope tried the serious or natural vein, are only fit to be remembered with Macpherson's Ossian and the classical enormities of the French painter David.

On the whole, it is as a satirist we must think of him, and the second greatest in the language. The gods are in pairs, male and female; and if Dryden was the Mars of English satire, Pope was the Venus—a very eighteenth century Venus, quite as conspicuous for malice as for elegance. If a woman's satire were informed with genius, and cultivated to the utmost perfection of form by lifelong and exclusive literary practice, one imagines it would be much like Pope's. His style seems to me feminine in what it lacks; the absence of any geniality, any softening humour to abate its mortal thrust. It is feminine in what it has, the malice, the cruel dexterity, the delicate needle point which hardly betrays its light and swift entry, yet stings like a bee. Even in his coarseness—as in the *Dunciad*—Pope appears to me female. It is the coarseness of the fine ladies of that material time, the Lady Maries and the rest of them. Dryden is a rough and thick-natured man, cudgelling his adversaries with coarse speech in the heat of brawl and the bluntness of his sensibilities; a country squire, who is apt at times to use the heavy end of his cutting whip; but when Pope is coarse he is coarse with effort, he goes out of his way to be nasty, in the evident endeavour to imitate a man. It is a girl airing the slang of her schoolboy brother. The one thing, perhaps, which differentiates him from a woman, and makes it possible to read his verse with a certain pleasure, without that sense of unrelieved cruelty which repels one in much female satire, is his artist's delight in the exercise of his power. You feel that, if there be malice, intent to wound, even spite, yet none of these count for so much with him as the exercise of his superb dexterity in fence. He is like Ortheris fondly patting his rifle after that long shot which knocked over the deserter, in Mr. Kipling's story. After all, you reflect, it is fair fight; if his hand was against many men, many men's hands were against him. So you give yourself up to admire the shell-like epigram, the rocketing and dazzling antithesis, the exquisitely deft play of point, by which the little invalid kept in terror his encompassing cloud of enemies—many of them adroit and formidable wits themselves. And you think, also, that the man who was loved by Swift, the professional hater, was not a man without a heart; though he wrote the most finished and brilliant satire in the language.—FRANCIS THOMPSON, "Pope," *Academy*, July 3, 1897, pp. 13–14

Works

PASTORALS

He (Wycherley) shall bring with him, if you will, a young Poet, newly inspir'd, in the Neighbourhood of *Coopers-Hill*, whom he and *Walsh* have taken under their Wing; his Name is *Pope*; he is not above Seventeen or Eighteen Years of Age, and promises Miracles: If he goes on as he has begun, in the Pastoral way, as *Virgil* first try'd his Strength, we may hope to see *English* Poetry vie with the *Roman*, and this Swan of *Windsor* sing as sweetly as the *Mantuan*.—GEORGE GRANVILLE, LORD LANSDOWNE, "A Letter with a Character of Mr. Wycherly" (c. 1706), *Genuine Works in Verse and Prose*, 1736, Vol. 2, p. 113

Sir,—I have lately seen a pastoral of yours in mr. Walsh's & mr Congreves hands, which is extreamly ffine & is generally approv'd off by the best Judges in poetry. I Remember I have formerly seen you at my shop & am sorry I did not Improve my Accquaintance with you. If you design your Poem for the Press no person shall be more Carefull in the printing of it, nor no one can give a greater Incouragement to it; than Sir Your Most Obedient Humble Servant.—JACOB TONSON, Letter to Alexander Pope (April 20, 1706)

In these more dull as more censorious Days,
When few dare give, and fewer merit Praise;
A Muse sincere, that never Flatt'ry knew,
Pays what to Friendship and Desert is due.
Young, yet Judicious; in your Verse are found
Art strengthning Nature, Sense improv'd by Sound:
Unlike those Wits, whose Numbers glide along
So smooth, no Thought e'er interrupts the Song;
Laboriously enervate they appear,
And write not to the Head, but to the Ear:
Our Minds unmov'd and unconcern'd, they lull,
And are, at best, most Musically dull.
So purling Streams with even Murmurs creep,
And hush the heavy Hearers into Sleep.
As smoothest Speech is most deceitful found,
The smoothest Numbers oft are empty Sound,
And leave our lab'ring Fancy quite a-ground.
But Wit and Judgment join at once in you,
Sprightly as Youth, as Age consummate too:
Your Strains are Regularly Bold, and please
With unforc'd Care, and unaffected Ease,
With proper Thoughts, and lively *Images*:
Such, as by Nature to the Ancients shown,
Fancy improves, and Judgment makes your own;
For great Men's Fashions to be follow'd are,
Altho' disgraceful 'tis their Clothes to wear.
Some in a polish'd Stile write Pastoral,
Arcadia speaks the Language of the *Mall*,
Like some fair Shepherdess, the *Sylvan* Muse,
Deck't in those Flowr's her native Fields produce,
With modest Charms wou'd in plain Neatness please;
But seems a Dowdy in the Courtly Dress,
Whose aukward Finery allures us less.
But the true Measure of the Shepherd's Wit
Shou'd, like his Garb, be for the Country fit;
Yet must his pure and unaffected Thought
More nicely than the common Swain's be wrought.
So, with becoming Art, the Players dress
In Silks, the Shepherd and the Shepherdess;
Yet still unchang'd the Form and Mode remain,
Shap'd like the homely Russet of the Swain.
Your Rural Muse appears, to Justify
The long-lost Graces of Simplicity;
So Rural Beauties captivate our Sense,
With Virgin Charms, and Nature's Excellence.
Yet long her Modesty those Charms conceal'd,
'Till by Men's Envy to the World reveal'd;
For Wits Industrious to their Trouble seem,
And needs will Envy what they must Esteem.
Live, and enjoy their Spite! nor mourn that Fate
Which wou'd, if *Virgil* liv'd, on *Virgil* wait,
Whose Muse did once, like thine, in Plains delight;
Thine shall, like his, soon take a higher Flight;
So Larks which first from lowly Fields arise,
Mount by degrees, and reach at last the Skies.
—WILLIAM WYCHERLEY, "To my Friend, Mr. Pope, on his Pastorals," 1709

Neither Mr. Pope's, nor Mr. Philips's Pastorals, do any great

honour to the English Poetry. Mr. Pope's were composed in his youth; which may be an apology for other faults, but cannot well excuse the barrenness that appears in them. They are written in remarkably smooth and flowing numbers: and this is their chief merit; for there is scarcely any thought in them which can be called his own; scarcely any description, or any image of nature, which has the marks of being original, or copied from nature herself; but a repetition of the common images that are to be found in Virgil, and in all Poets who write of rural themes.—HUGH BLAIR, *Lectures on Rhetoric and Belles Lettres*, 1783, Lecture 39

The Pastorals have been seriously criticised; but they are, in truth, mere school-boy exercises; they represent nothing more than so many experiments in versification. The pastoral form had doubtless been used in earlier hands to embody true poetic feeling; but in Pope's time it had become hopelessly thread-bare. The fine gentlemen in wigs and laced coats amused themselves by writing about nymphs and "conscious swains," by way of asserting their claims to elegance of taste. Pope, as a boy, took the matter seriously, and always retained a natural fondness for a juvenile performance upon which he expended great labour, and which was the chief proof of his extreme precocity. He invites attention to his own merits, and claims especially the virtue of propriety. He does not, he tells us, like some other people, make his roses and daffodils bloom in the same season, and cause his nightingales to sing in November; and he takes particular credit for having remembered that there were no wolves in England, and having accordingly excised a passage in which Alexis prophesied that those animals would grow milder as they listened to the strains of his favourite nymph. When a man has got so far as to bring to England all the pagan deities, and rival shepherds contending for bowls and lambs in alternate strophes, these niceties seem a little out of place. After swallowing such a camel of an anachronism as is contained in the following lines, it is ridiculous to pride oneself upon straining at a gnat:—
Inspire me, says Strephon,

Inspire me, Phœbus, in my Delia's praise
With Waller's strains or Granville's moving lays.
A milk-white bull shall at your altars stand,
That threats a fight, and spurns the rising sand.

Granville would certainly not have felt more surprised at meeting a wolf than at seeing a milk-white bull sacrificed to Phœbus on the banks of the Thames. It would be a more serious complaint that Pope, who can thus admit anachronisms as daring as any of those which provoked Johnson in Lycidas, shows none of that exquisite feeling for rural scenery which is one of the superlative charms of Milton's early poems. Though country-bred, he talks about country sights and sounds as if he had been brought up at Christ's Hospital, and read of them only in Virgil. But, in truth, it is absurd to dwell upon such points. The sole point worth notice in the Pastorals is the general sweetness of the versification. Many corrections show how carefully Pope had elaborated these early lines, and by what patient toil he was acquiring the peculiar qualities of style in which he was to become pre-eminent. We may agree with Johnson that Pope performing upon a pastoral pipe is rather a ludicrous person, but for mere practice even nonsense verses have been found useful.—SIR LESLIE STEPHEN, *Alexander Pope*, 1880, pp. 23–24

AN ESSAY ON CRITICISM

In our own Country a Man seldom sets up for a Poet, without attacking the Reputation of all his Brothers in the Art. The

Ignorance of the Moderns, the Scriblers of the Age, the Decay of Poetry are the Topicks of Detraction, with which he makes his Entrance into the World ⟨. . .⟩

I am sorry to find that an Author, who is very justly esteemed among the best Judges, has admitted some Stroaks of this Nature into a very fine Poem, I mean *The Art of Criticism*, which was published some months since, and is a Master-piece in its kind. The Observations follow one another like those in *Horace's Art of Poetry*, without that Methodical Regularity which would have been requisite in a Prose Author. They are some of them uncommon, but such as the Reader must assent to, when he sees them explained with that Elegance and Perspicuity in which they are delivered. As for those which are the most known, and the most received, they are placed in so beautiful a Light, and illustrated with such apt Allusions, that they have in them all the Graces of Novelty, and make the Reader, who was before acquainted with them, still more convinced of their Truth and Solidity. And here give me leave to mention what Monsieur *Boileau* has so very well enlarged upon in the Preface to his Works, that Wit and fine Writing doth not consist so much in advancing things that are new, as in giving things that are known an agreeable Turn. It is impossible, for us who live in the later Ages of the World, to make Observations in Criticism, Morality, or in any Art or Science, which have not been touched upon by others. We have little else left us, but to represent the common Sense of Mankind in more strong, more beautiful, or more uncommon Lights. If a Reader examines *Horace's Art of Poetry*, he will find but very few Precepts in it, which he may not meet with in *Aristotle*, and which were not commonly known by all the Poets of the Augustan Age. His way of Expressing and Applying them, not his Invention of them, is what we are chiefly to admire.

For this reason I think there is nothing in the World so tiresom as the Works of those Criticks, who write in a positive Dogmatick Way, without either Language, Genius or Imagination. If the Reader would see how the best of the *Latin* Criticks writ, he may find their manner very beautifully described in the Characters of *Horace*, *Petronius*, *Quintilian* and *Longinus*, as they are drawn in the Essay of which I am now speaking.

Since I have mentioned *Longinus*, who in his Reflections has given us the same kind of Sublime, which he observes in the several Passages that occasioned them; I cannot but take notice, that our *English* Author has after the same manner exemplified several of his Precepts in the very Precepts themselves. I shall produce two or three Instances of this kind. Speaking of the insipid Smoothness which some Readers are so much in love with, he has the following Verses.

> These *Equal Syllables* alone require,
> Tho' oft the Ear the *open* Vowels tire,
> While *Expletives* their feeble Aid *do* join,
> And ten low Words oft creep in one dull Line.

The gaping of the Vowels in the second Line, the Expletive *do* in the third, and the ten Monosyllables in the fourth, give such a Beauty to this Passage, as would have been very much admired in an Ancient Poet.—JOSEPH ADDISON, *The Spectator*, No. 253 (Dec. 20, 1711)

A most notorious Instance of this Depravity of Genius and Tast, is the Essay upon which the following Reflections are writ, and the Approbation which it has met with. I will not deny but that there are two or three Passages in it with which I am not displeas'd; but what are two or three Passages as to the whole?

> Fit Chœrilus ille
> Quem bis terq; bonum cum risu miror.

The approving two or Three Passages amongst a multitude of bad ones, is by no means advantageous to an Author. That little that is good in him does but set off its contrary, and make it appear more extravagant. The Thoughts, Expressions, and Numbers of this Essay are for the most part but very indifferent, and indifferent and execrable in Poetry are all one. But what is worse than all the rest, we find throughout the whole a deplorable want of that very Quality, which ought principally to appear in it, which is Judgment; and I have no Notion that where there is so great a want of Judgment, there can be any Genius.—JOHN DENNIS, *Reflections Critical and Satyrical, upon a Late Rhapsody, Call'd*, An Essay upon Criticism, 1711

I dare not say any Thing of the last *Essay* on *Criticism* in Verse, but that if any more curious Reader has discovered in it something new, which is not in *Dryden's Prefaces, Dedications*, and his *Essay* on *Dramatick Poetry*, not to mention the *French* Criticks, I should be very glad to have the Benefit of the Discovery.—JOHN OLDMIXON, *An Essay on Criticism*, 1728, p. 2

He who reads with discernment and choice, will acquire less learning, but more knowledge: and as this knowledge is collected with design, and cultivated with art and method, it will be at all times of immediate and ready use to himself and others.

> Thus useful arms in magazines we place,
> All rang'd in order; and disposed with grace:
> Nor thus alone the curious eye to please;
> But to be found, when need requires, with ease.

You remember the verses, my lord, in our friend's *Essay on Criticism*, which was the work of his childhood almost; but is such a monument of good sense and poetry as no other, that I know, has raised in his riper years.—HENRY ST. JOHN, VISCOUNT BOLINGBROKE, *Letters on the Study and Use of History*, c. 1735, Letter 4

I admired Mr. Pope's *Essay on Criticism* at first, very much, because I had not then read any of the antient critics, and did not know that it was all stolen.—LADY MARY WORTLEY MONTAGU (1740–41), cited in Joseph Spence, *Anecdotes, Observations and Characters of Books and Men*, ed. S. W. Singer, 1820

It will be observed that the critical sense of the *Essay* is most warmly appreciated by those who are nearest to it in point of time, and is coldly spoken of in proportion as the practical value of its maxims becomes less apparent. It is further seen that those who praise it for its matter do not claim for it much novelty, and those who depreciate it, for its lack of novelty in matter, yet speak highly of the beauty of its form. The question between the two sets of critics, therefore, narrows itself to a very definite issue. Is Mr. Stephen right in making its sole excellence consist in the 'coining of aphorisms out of commonplace,' or Addison, in saying that its observations 'are placed in so beautiful a light, and illustrated with such apt illusions, that they have in them all the graces of novelty, and make the reader who was before acquainted with them, still more convinced of their truth and solidity'? For if what is said in the *Essay* be of the nature of platitude, no amount of skill in the manner of saying it can make it of any value: if, on the other hand, the truths that it conveys are such as, though not doubtful, are not known intuitively, but can only be discovered by experience and reflection; if, indeed, we see them every day openly disregarded by writers of talent and distinction; then these truths are not correctly described as 'commonplace.' It becomes, therefore, of importance to understand fully the poet's design, and the light in which his *Essay* presented itself to the minds of contemporary readers.

And in the first place, there is a great deal of significance in the title—'An *Essay* on Criticism'; an attempt at *Criticism*, not an Art of Poetry like Boileau's. Up to that moment it may be said that the art of Criticism was not in existence in England. Two opposite streams of opinion divided men's minds, the tradition of Mediævalism, and the tradition of the Renaissance; the former seeking to preserve venerable forms from which the vital spirit had departed, the latter to revive old prescriptions which were unsuited to modern circumstances. Mediævalism is perhaps best represented in England by the very ingenious *Art of English Poesie*, written in the reign of Elizabeth, and commonly assigned to George Puttenham; while the chief advocate of Classicalism at the end of the seventeenth century was Thomas Rymer, a great enemy of Shakespeare and Milton, and so much a slave of Aristotle, that he wished to restore the Chorus to the English stage. Of criticism in the modern sense of the word the only examples were, in prose, the scattered Prefaces of Dryden, and, in verse, the commonplace Essays of Mulgrave and Roscommon on Satire and the Art of Translation. Nevertheless, in spite of the absence of any settled code of taste, the coffee-houses were filled with wits and critics who pronounced with a loud confidence on the merits of every work newly submitted to the public. The result was a Babel of ignorance, caprice, and contradiction. Young as he was, Pope perceived the necessity of reducing this chaos to order; his *Essay*, ostensibly merely a collection of maxims for the benefit of critics, is in reality the first attempt to trace for English readers the just boundaries of taste.

Though the *Essay on Criticism* is far from being the systematic treatise that Warburton pretends, it has more method than Addison in the *Spectator* seems disposed to allow it, being indeed a series of loosely connected observations, kept together by the obvious drift of the poet's thought in one direction. Pope observes the prevailing discord of taste:

'Tis with our judgments as our watches, none
Goes just alike, yet each consults his own.

But, in spite of all differences, he perceives that 'each has the seeds of judgment in his mind,' which he therefore holds to be sown there by Nature. Everything in the *Essay* turns on this fundamental idea of Nature, and three main principles underlie Pope's reasoning: (1) That all sound judgment and true 'wit' is founded on the observation of Nature; (2) That false 'wit' arises from a disregard of Nature and an excessive affection for the conceptions of the mind; (3) That the true standard for determining what is 'natural' in poetry is to be found in the best works of the ancients. ⟨. . .⟩

The effect of the *Essay on Criticism*, or at least of the current of thought which it represents, on the taste of the age was profound. Wit, or the practice of finding resemblances in objects apparently dissimilar, as it was cultivated throughout the seventeenth century by poets like Donne, Crashaw, Quarles, and Cowley, disappears altogether from the literary aims of the eighteenth century. With it vanishes the crowd of metaphors, similes, and hyperboles by which these poets sought to recommend their manner of thinking. Wit, as we see from the *Essay on Criticism*, was regarded in the early part of

the century as a proper object in poetry, but as the conceptions of the poet were now based upon Nature itself, its operations gradually restricted themselves to satire or to moral and didactic reflection. Thus, while the range of imagination became more limited, its objects became more clear and definite. An analogous change took place in the form of poetry. In emulation of the classical authors, the followers of the new mode paid great attention to the selection of subject, to the arrangement of the fable or design of their composition, and to the just distribution of all its parts. Instead of ingenuity in the discovery of unheard-of metaphors, which was the ambition of the typical seventeenth-century poet, the poet of the eighteenth century sought to present a general thought in the language best adapted to bring it forcibly before the mind of the reader. In this respect, works so unlike each other as Thomson's *Seasons*, Gray's *Elegy in a Country Churchyard*, the *Deserted Village* of Goldsmith, and *The Village* of Crabbe, may all be said to be the fruits of the *Essay on Criticism*.

I do not for a moment seek to deny that Pope's enthusiasm for classical antiquity frequently betrayed him into narrow and fallacious views. In his rebound from the affectations of an obsolete mediævalism, he closed his eyes to the fact that the works of the great mediæval authors were founded on a perception of Nature fundamentally as true and clear as that of Homer himself. He failed to perceive, also, what scope and extension the materials of romance and theology gave to the imagination of later poets such as Shakespeare and Milton; what delightful associations of idea, and what subtle melodies of language, were at the command of those who, living on the verge of the old and new worlds, were able to invest genuinely classical modes of conception with all the richness and colour of Gothic fancy.

The critical defects of a work so designed lie naturally on the surface. The Essay has many incorrect observations, and, in spite of its own axioms, many bad rhymes, many faulty grammatical constructions. But these cannot weigh against the substantial merit of the performance. They cannot obscure the truth that the poem is, what its title pretends, an *Essay on Criticism*, an attempt made, for the first time in English literature, and in the midst of doubts, perplexities, and distractions, of which we, in our position of the idle heirs of that age, can only have a shadowy conception, to erect a standard of judgment founded in justice and thought and accuracy of expression. Nor will it be denied that, as a poem, the critical and philosophical nature of the subject is enlivened by bold, brilliant, and beautiful imagery. Lastly, when it is remembered that this extraordinary soundness of judgment and maturity of style are exhibited by a young man who was only twenty-three when the poem was published, and may have been under twenty-one when it was composed, the panegyric of Johnson, startling as it seems at first sight, will not be thought after all to be greatly exaggerated.—WILLIAM JOHN COURTHOPE, *The Works of Alexander Pope*, 1889, Vol. 5, pp. 47–49, 68–70

THE RAPE OF THE LOCK

I have accidentally met with your *Rape of the Lock* here, having never seen it before. Stile, Painting, Judgment, Spirit, I had already admired in others of your Writings; but in this I am charm'd with the magic of your *Invention*, with all those images, allusions, and inexplicable beauties, which you raise so surprizingly and at the same time so naturally, out of a trifle. —GEORGE BERKELEY, Letter to Alexander Pope (May 1, 1714)

The stealing of Miss Belle Fermor's hair, was taken too seriously, and caused an estrangement between the two families, though they had lived so long in great friendship before. A common acquaintance and well-wisher to both, desired me to write a poem to make a jest of it, and laugh them together again. It was with this view that I wrote the *Rape of the Lock*; which was well received, and had its effect in the two families.—Nobody but Sir George Brown was angry, and he was a good deal so, and for a long time. He could not bear, that Sir Plume should take nothing but nonsense.—Copies of the poem got about, and it was like to be printed; on which I published the first draught of it (without the machinery), in a *Miscellany* of Tonson's. The machinery was added afterwards, to make it look a little more considerable, and the scheme of adding it was much liked and approved of by several of my friends, and particularly by Dr. Garth: who, as he was one of the best natured men in the world, was very fond of it. —ALEXANDER POPE (1737–39), cited in Joseph Spence, *Anecdotes, Observations and Characters of Books and Men*, ed. S. W. Singer, 1820

I have been assured by a most intimate friend of Mr. Pope's, that the Peer in the *Rape of the Lock* was Lord Petre; the person who desired Mr. Pope to write it, old Mr. Caryl, of Sussex; and that what was said of Sir George Brown in it, was the very picture of the man.—JOSEPH SPENCE (1737–39), cited in Joseph Spence, *Anecdotes, Observations and Characters of Books and Men*, ed. S. W. Singer, 1820

This seems to be Mr. Pope's most finished production, and is, perhaps, the most perfect in our language. It exhibits stronger powers of imagination, more harmony of numbers, and a greater knowledge of the world, than any other of this poet's works: and it is probable, if our country were called upon to shew a specimen of their genius to foreigners, this would be the work here fixed upon.—OLIVER GOLDSMITH, *The Beauties of English Poetry*, 1767

⟨Parnell's⟩ translation of a part of the *Rape of the Lock* into monkish verse, serves to shew what a master Parnell was of the Latin; a copy of verses made in this manner, is one of the most difficult trifles that can possibly be imagined. I am assured that it was written upon the following occasion. Before the *Rape of the Lock* was yet completed, Pope was reading it to his friend Swift, who sat very attentively, while Parnell, who happened to be in the house, went in and out without seeming to take any notice. However he was very diligently employed in listening, and was able, from the strength of his memory, to bring away the whole description of the toilet pretty exactly. This he versified in the manner now published in his works, and the next day when Pope was reading the poem to some friends, Parnell insisted that he had stolen that part of the description from an old monkish manuscript. An old paper with the Latin verses was soon brought forth, and it was not till after some time that Pope was delivered from the confusion which it at first produced.—OLIVER GOLDSMITH, *The Life of Dr. Parnell*, 1770

In my eyes, the *Lutrin*, the *Dispensary* and the *Rape of the Lock*, are standards of grace and elegance, not to be paralleled by antiquity ⟨. . .⟩ the *Rape of the Lock*, besides the originality of great part of the invention, is a standard of graceful writing.—HORACE WALPOLE, Letter to John Pinkerton (June 26, 1785)

THE ILIAD OF HOMER

I am pleas'd beyond measure with your design of translating Homer: The tryals which you have already made and published on some parts of that author have shewn that you

are equal to so great a task: and you may therefore depend upon the utmost services I can do you in promoting this work, or any thing that may be for your service.—GEORGE GRANVILLE, LORD LANSDOWNE, Letter to Alexander Pope (Oct. 21, 1713)

I borrow'd your Homer from the Bishop (mine is not yet landed) and read it out in two evenings. If it pleases others as well as me, you have got your end in profit and reputation: Yet I am angry at some bad Rhymes and Triplets, and pray in your next do not let me have so many unjustifiable Rhymes to *war* and *gods*. I tell you all the faults I know, only in one or two places you are a little obscure; but I expected you to be so in one or two and twenty. I have heard no soul talk of it here, for indeed it is not come over; nor do we very much abound in judges, at least I have not the honour to be acquainted with them. Your Notes are perfectly good, and so are your Preface and Essay.—JONATHAN SWIFT, Letter to Alexander Pope (June 28, 1715)

⟨. . .⟩ I have read with Pleasure the new *Translation* of the first *eight* Books of *Homer*, and if I were to commend the Author, I should do it in these excellent Lines of a Modern to Mr. *Dryden*:

> The Copy casts a fairer Light on all,
> And still out-shines the bright Original.

The Spirit of *Homer* breaths all through this Translation, and I am in doubt whether I should most admire the Justness of the Original, or the Force and Beauty of the Language, or the sounding Variety of the Numbers; but when I find all these meet, it puts me in mind of what the Poet says of one of his Heroes, that he *alone* raised and flung with ease a weighty Stone that Two common Men could not lift from the Ground; just so one single Person has performed in this Translation, what I once despaired to have seen done by the force even of several masterly Hands.—LEWIS THEOBALD, *The Censor*, No. 33 (Jan. 5, 1717)

> Long hast thou, Friend, been absent from thy Soil,
>   Like patient *Ithacus* at Siege of Troy:
> I have been witness of thy Six Years toil,
>   Thy daily labours, and thy night's annoy
> Lost to thy Native Land with great turmoil
>   On the wide Sea, oft threatning to destroy;
> Methinks with thee I've trod Sigaean ground
> And heard the Shores of Hellespont resound.
>
> Did I not See thee, when thou first Sett'st sail
>   To seek adventures fair in *Homer* Land
> Did I not see thy sinking Spirits fail,
>   And wish thy Bark had never left the Strand?
> Ev'n in mid Ocean often did'st thou Quail,
>   And oft lift up thy holy Eye & Hand,
> Praying the Virgin Dear & Saintly Choir
> Back to yᵉ Port to bring thy bark entire.
>
> Chear up, my friend, thy dangers now are o'er
>   Methinks—Nay Sure the rising coasts appear
> Hark how the guns salute from either Shore
>   As thy trim vessell cuts the Thames so fair:
> Shouts answe'ring Shouts from Kent and Essex roar,
>   And bells break loud thro every gust of Air:
> Bonefires do blaze, & Bones & Cleavers ring
> As at the coming of some mighty King.
>
> . . .
>
> How lov'd! how honour'd thou! yet be not vain
>   And sure thou art not for I hear thee Say
> All this my friends I owe to *Homers* strain
>   On whose Strong *Pinions* I exalt my Lay

What from contending Cities did he gain?
  And what rewards his gratefull Country pay?
None none were pay'd—why then all this for me?
These Honours *Homer*, had been just to thee.
            —JOHN GAY, "Mr Popes Welcome from Greece a
              copy of Verses wrote by Mr Gay upon M^r
              Popes having finisht his Translation of Homers
              Ilias," 1720

All the crime that I have committed is saying that he is no
master of Greek; and I am so confident of this, that if he can
translate ten lines of Eustathius I'll own myself unjust and
unworthy.—WILLIAM BROOME, Letter to Elijah Fenton (June
5, 1727)

    Three times I've read your *Iliad* o'er:
      The first time pleas'd me *well*;
    New Beauties unobserv'd before,
      Next pleas'd me *better* still.

    Again I try'd to find a Flaw,
      Examin'd ilka Line;
    The third time pleas'd me *best* of a',
      The Labour seem'd divine.

    Henceforward I'll not tempt my Fate,
      On dazling Rays to stare,
    Lest I should tine dear Self- conceit,
      And read and write nae mair.
            —ALLAN RAMSAY, "To Mr. Pope," *Poems*, 1728

The *Iliad* took me up six years; and during that time, and
particularly the first part of it, I was often under great pain and
apprehension. Though I conquered the thoughts of it in the
day, they would frighten me in the night.—I sometimes, still,
even dream of being engaged in that translation; and got about
half way through it: and being embarrassed and under dread of
never completing it.—ALEXANDER POPE (1742–43), cited in
Joseph Spence, *Anecdotes, Observations and Characters of
Books and Men*, ed. S. W. Singer, 1820

With regard to Homer's Style and manner of Writing, it is easy,
natural, and, in the highest degree, animated. It will be
admired by such only as relish ancient simplicity, and can
make allowance for certain negligencies and repetitions, which
greater refinement in the Art of Writing has taught succeeding,
though far inferior, Poets to avoid. For Homer is the most
simple in his Style of all the great Poets, and resembles most
the Style of the poetical parts of the Old Testament. They can
have no conception of his manner, who are acquainted with
him in Mr. Pope's Translation only. An excellent poetical
performance that Translation is, and faithful in the main to the
Original. In some places, it may be thought to have even
improved Homer. It has certainly softened some of his
rudenesses, and added delicacy and grace to some of his
sentiments. But withal, it is no other than Homer modernised.
In the midst of the elegance and luxuriancy of Mr. Pope's
language, we lose sight of the old Bard's simplicity. I know
indeed no Author, to whom it is more difficult to do justice in
a Translation, than Homer. As the plainness of his diction,
were it literally rendered, would often appear flat in any
modern language; so, in the midst of that plainness, and not a
little heightened by it, there are every where breaking forth
upon us flashes of native fire, of sublimity and beauty, which
hardly any language, except his own, could preserve. His
versification has been universally acknowledged to be uncommonly melodious; and to carry, beyond that of any Poet, a
resemblance in the sound to the sense and meaning.—HUGH
BLAIR, *Lectures on Rhetoric and Belles Lettres*, 1783, Lecture
43

Before I left Kingston school, I was well acquainted with Pope's
Homer, and the Arabian Nights Entertainments, two books
which will always please by the moving picture of human
manners and specious miracles. The verses of Pope accustomed my ear to the sound of poetic harmony: in the death of
Hector and the shipwreck of Ulysses I tasted the new emotions
of terror and pity, and seriously disputed with my aunt on the
vices and virtues of the heroes of the Trojan War.—EDWARD
GIBBON, *Memoirs of My Life*, 1792–93

⟨. . .⟩ the translator of Homer should penetrate himself with a
sense of the plainness and directness of Homer's style; of the
simplicity with which Homer's thought is evolved and expressed. He has Pope's fate before his eyes, to show him what
a divorce may be created even between the most gifted
translator and Homer by an artificial evolution of thought and
a literary cast of style.—MATTHEW ARNOLD, *On Translating
Homer*, 1861

THE DUNCIAD

On the 12th of March, 1729, at St. James's, that poem was
presented to the King and Queen (who had before been pleased
to read it) by the Right Honourable Sir Robert Walpole: and
some days after the whole impression was taken and dispersed
by several noblemen and persons of the first distinction. It is
certainly a true observation, that no people are so impatient of
censure as those who are the greatest slanderers: which was
wonderfully exemplified on this occasion. On the day the book
was first vended, a crowd of authors besieged the shop; entreaties, advices, threats of law, and battery, nay, cries of treason
were all employed, to hinder the coming out of the *Dunciad*;
on the other side, the booksellers and hawkers made as great
efforts to procure it: what could a few poor authors do against
so great a majority as the public? There was no stopping a torrent
with a finger, so out it came. Some false editions of the book
having an owl in their frontispiece, the true one, to distinguish
it, fixed in its stead an ass laden with authors. Then another
surreptitious one being printed with the same ass, the new
edition in octavo returned for distinction to the owl again.
Hence arose a great contest of booksellers against booksellers,
and advertisements against advertisements; some recommended
the "Edition of the Owl," and others the "Edition of the Ass;"
by which names they came to be distinguished, to the great
honour also of the gentlemen of the *Dunciad*.—RICHARD
SAVAGE, *An Account of* The Dunciad, 1732

As you have for several Years past (particularly in your Poetical
Works) mentioned my Name, without my desiring it; give me
leave, at last, to make my due Compliments to *Yours* in Prose,
which I should not choose to do, but that I am really driven to
it (as the Puff in the Play-Bills says) *At the Desire of several
Persons of Quality*.

If I have lain so long stoically silent, or unmindful of your
satyrical Favours, it was not so much for want of a proper
Reply, as that I thought they never needed a Publick one: For
all People of Sense would know, what Truth or Falshood there
was in what you have said of me, without my wisely pointing
it out to them. Nor did I choose to follow your Example of
being so much a Self-Tormentor, as to be concern'd at
whatever Opinion of me any publish'd Invective might infuse
into People unknown to me: Even the Malicious, though they
may like the Libel, don't always believe it. But since the
Publication of your last new *Dunciad* (where you still seem to
enjoy your so often repeated Glory of being bright upon my
Dulness) my Friends now insist, that it will be thought Dulness
indeed, or a plain Confession of my being a Bankrupt in Wit,

if I don't immediately answer those Bills of Discredit you have drawn upon me: For, say they, your dealing with him, like a Gentleman, in your *Apology for your own Life*, &c. you see, has had no sensible Effect upon him, as appears by the wrong-headed Reply his Notes upon the new *Dunciad* have made to it: For though, in that *Apology* you seem to have offer'd him a friendly release of all Damages, yet as it is plain he scorns to accept it, by his still holding you at Defiance with fresh Abuses, you have an indisputable Right to resume that Discharge, and may now, as justly as ever, call him to account for his many bygone Years of Defamation. But pray, Gentlemen, said I, if, as you seem to believe, his Defamation has more of Malice than Truth in it, does he not blacken himself by it? Why then should I give myself the trouble to prove, what you, and the World are already convinc'd of? and since after nearly twenty Years having been libell'd by our Daily-paper Scriblers, I never was so hurt, as to give them one single Answer, why would you have me seem to be more sore now, than at any other time?

As to those dull Fellows, they granted my Silence was right; yet they could not but think Mr. *Pope* was too eminent an Author to justify my equal Contempt of him; and that a Disgrace, from such a Pen, might stick upon me to Posterity: In fine, that though I could not be rouz'd from my Indifference, in regard to myself, yet for the particular Amusement of my Acquaintance, they desired I would enter the Lifts with you; notwithstanding I am under the Disadvantage of having only the blunt and weak weapon of Prose, to oppose you, or defend myself, against the Sharpness of Verse, and that in the Hand of so redoubted an Author as Mr. *Pope*.—COLLEY CIBBER, *A Letter from Mr. Cibber to Mr. Pope*, 1742

> To cast a Shadow o'er the spotless Fame,
> Or dye the Cheek of Innocence with Shame;
> To swell the Breast of Modesty with Care,
> Or force from Beauty's Eye a secret Tear;
> And, not by Decency or Honour sway'd,
> Libel the Living, and asperse the Dead:
> Prone where he ne'er receiv'd to give Offence,
> But most averse to Merit and to Sense;
> Base to his Foe, but baser to his Friend,
> Lying to blame, and sneering to commend:
> Defaming those whom all but he must love,
> And praising those whom none but he approve.
> Then let him boast that honourable Crime,
> Of making those who fear not God, fear him;
> When the great Honour of that Boast is such
> That Hornets and Mad Dogs may boast as much.
> Such is th' Injustice of his daily Theme,
> And such the Lust that breaks his nightly Dream;
> That vestal Fire of undecaying Hate,
> Which Time's cold Tide itself can ne'er abate,
> But like *Domitian*, with a murd'rous Will,
> Rather than nothing, Flies he likes to kill.
> And in his Closet stabs some obscure Name,
> Brought by this Hangman first to Light and Shame.
> —JOHN, LORD HERVEY, *The Difference between Verbal and Practical Virtue*, 1742

My brother does not seem to know what fear is. When some of the people that he had put into his *Dunciad*, were so much enraged against him, and threatened him so highly: he loved to walk out alone, and particularly went often to Mr. Fortescue's at Richmond. Only he would take Bounce with him; and for some time carried pistols in his pocket. He used then to say, when we talked to him about it; that with pistols the least man in England was above a match for the largest.—MRS. RACKET

(1742–43), cited in Joseph Spence, *Anecdotes, Observations and Characters of Books and Men*, ed. S. W. Singer, 1820

This king John ⟨Dryden⟩ had a very long reign, though a very unquiet one; for there were several pretenders to the throne of wit in his time, who formed very considerable parties against him, and gave him great uneasiness, of which his successor hath made mention in the following lines:

> Pride, folly, malice, against Dryden rose,
> In various shapes of parsons, critics, beaus.

Besides which, his finances were in such disorder, that it is affirmed, his treasury was more than once entirely empty.

He died, nevertheless, in a good old age, possessed of the kingdom of wit, and was succeeded by king Alexander, surnamed Pope.

This prince enjoyed the crown many years, and is thought to have stretched the prerogative much farther than his predecessor: he is said to have been extremely jealous of the affections of his subjects, and to have employed various spies, by whom, if he was informed of the least suggestion against his title, he never failed of branding the accused person with the word *dunce* on his forehead in broad letters; after which the unhappy culprit was obliged to lay by his pen for ever; for no bookseller would venture to print a word that he wrote.

He did indeed put a total restraint on the liberty of the press; for no person durst read any thing which was writ without his licence and approbation; and this licence he granted only to four during his reign, namely, to the celebrated Dr. Swift, to the ingenious Dr. Young, to Dr. Arbuthnot, and to one Mr. Gay, four of his principal courtiers and favourites.

But without diving any deeper into his character, we must allow that king Alexander had great merit as a writer, and his title to the kingdom of wit was better founded at least than his enemies have pretended.—HENRY FIELDING, *The Covent-Garden Journal*, No. 23 (March 21, 1752)

The *Dunciad* of Mr. Pope is an everlasting monument of how much the most correct, as well as the most elegant and harmonious of all the English poets, had been hurt by the criticisms of the lowest and most contemptible authors.—ADAM SMITH, *The Theory of Moral Sentiments*, 1759, Pt. 3, Ch. 2

The *Dunciad* is blemished by the offensive images of the games, but the poetry appears to me admirable; and though the fourth book has obscurities, I prefer it to the three others. It has descriptions not surpassed by any poet that ever existed; and which surely a writer merely ingenious will never equal. The lines on Italy, on Venice, on convents, have all the grace for which I contend as distinct from poetry, though united with the most beautiful.—HORACE WALPOLE, Letter to John Pinkerton (June 26, 1785)

AN ESSAY ON MAN

> Was ever work to such perfection wrought?
> How elegant the diction! pure the thought!
> Not sparingly adorn'd with scatter'd rays,
> But one bright beauty, one collected blaze:
> So breaks the day upon the shades of night,
> Enliv'ning all with one unbounded light.
>   To humble man's proud heart thy great design;
> But who can read this wondrous work divine,
> So justly plann'd, and so politely writ,
> And not be proud, and boast of human wit?
>   Yet just to thee, and to thy precepts true,
> Let us know man, and give to God his due;
> His image we, but mix'd with coarse allay,
> Our happiness to love, adore, obey;

To praise him for each gracious boon bestow'd,
For this thy work, for ev'ry lesser good,
With prostrate hearts before his throne to fall,
And own the great Creator all in all.
    The Muse, which should instruct, now entertains,
On trifling subjects, in enervate strains;
Be it thy talk to set the wand'rer right,
Point out her way in her aërial flight;
Her noble mien, her honours lost, restore,
And bid her deeply think, and proudly soar.
Thy theme sublime, and easy verse, will prove
Her high descent, and mission from above.
    Let others now translate; thy abler pen
Shall vindicate the ways of God to men;
In virtue's cause shall gloriously prevail,
When the bench frowns in vain and pulpits fail.
Made wise by thee, whose happy style conveys
The purest morals in the softest lays.
As angels once, so now we mortals bold
Shall climb the ladder Jacob view'd of old;
Thy kind reforming Muse shall lead the way
To the bright regions of eternal day.
      —WILLIAM SOMERVILLE, "To the Author of the
        Essay on Man," c. 1732

It were an easy, but invidious task to expose, in a much greater variety of examples, the fallacious and dangerous reasonings of this infamous Essay. As a moral philosopher, Mr. Pope is justly blameable for excluding from his system, or, at least, throwing, as it might well be supposed, purposely into the shade, that great principle, without which there is no essential or practical difference between Deism and Atheism—the immortality of the soul. At the same time, it would be injustice not to acknowledge that his poem abounds with striking and elevated reflections, admirably calculated to excite a spirit of rational and philosophical devotion; and there is good reason to entertain so favorable an opinion of his general character, as to believe, with a firm assurance, that if he had really conceived this Essay to be injurious to the cause of religion and virtue, he would have disdained to court any increase of poetical fame by its publication: and, as on a former occasion, with a noble indignation, would have exclaimed,

    Oh! teach me, Heaven! to scorn the guilty bays;
    Drive from my breast such wretched lust of praise.
    Unblemish'd let me live, or die unknown;
    Oh! grant an honest fame, or grant me none!
      —W. BELSHAM, "Remarks on Pope's *Essay on
        Man,*" *Essays Philosophical and Moral, His-
        torical and Literary,* 1799, Vol. 1, p. 361

The *Essay on Man* has been supposed to derive all its worth from the doctrines which Bolingbroke has contributed to it. Might it not be much more fairly described as a stately mausoleum in which these doctrines have been saved from putrefaction? They are not more vague and declamatory in their rhymed than in their prose form, but far more distinct and pointed. The folds of affectation and conceit in which they were wrapped have in great measure been stripped off from them. We now see what there was in them which accorded with the temper of the age, what had a suitableness to the poet's own temper and circumstances, what had a permanent worth. A time which despaired of the ocean of Being, and yet clung to the old name of God, and desired to confess Him as exercising some providence over the universe, would welcome the precept, "Presume not God to scan." It would be specially acceptable to a man of letters bred in Romanism, with no special turn for speculation, bewildered by the various opinions

which he heard in a circle consisting of Atterbury, Garth, Swift, Bolingbroke; frequented sometimes by Berkeley, now and then visited by Addison. Most of these would, on the whole, be willing to adopt the maxim. The position that the "proper study of mankind is man" would at once commend itself to a writer who felt how much his own particular tastes or gifts inclined and enabled him to take notice of the passing humours and habits of his fellow-creatures. A general optimism was not unsuitable to one of a sickly constitution, inclined to benevolence, feeling keenly the vexations and falsehoods of the world of letters and of fashion; not much acquainted with the region that lies beyond its flaming walls. But beneath all this was the conviction of an order not created by man, to which it is well that he should yield himself; a conviction for which Pope might be grateful to any man from whom he thought he had derived it; which we may be grateful to him for strengthening in us, even if we have found that it needs the support of other truths which he did not as clearly perceive.—FREDERICK DENISON MAURICE, *Moral and Metaphysical Philosophy,* 1862

The *Essay on Man* is Pope's most ambitious, though not his most successful, work. One great, and indeed insuperable, difficulty which made it unsatisfactory from the first, shows the radical unfitness of the philosophy of the time for poetical, and therefore for religious purposes. The *Essay on Man* aspires to be, like Leibnitz's celebrated work, a *Theodicæa.* The first paragraph ends, like the first paragraph of *Paradise Lost,* with the statement that the poet hopes to 'vindicate the ways of God to man.' Elsewhere, Pope boasts, in a phrase adopted from the first stanza of the *Faerie Queen,* that

    Not in Fancy's maze he wandered long,
    But stoop'd to truth and moralised his song.

The relation between the three poems is, indeed, characteristic. Milton and Spenser could utter their deepest thoughts about man's position in the universe and his moral nature by aid of a symbolism intelligible to themselves and their readers. But where was Pope to turn for concrete symbols sufficiently expressive of his thought? The legends of the Bible claimed too little reverence. Even in the majestic poetry of Milton we are unpleasantly reminded of the fact that the mighty expounder of Puritan thought is consciously devising a conventional imagery. The old romance which had fed Spenser's imagination was too hopelessly dead to serve the purpose. It had left behind a wearisome spawn of so-called romances; it had been turned into mere ribaldry by Butler; and Pope wisely abandoned his cherished project of an epic poem, though feebler hands attempted the task. The *Essay on Man* is substantially a versification of the most genuine creed of the time; of that Deism which took various shapes with Clarke, Tindal, and Shaftesbury, and which Bolingbroke seems to have more or less put into shape to be elaborated into poetry by his friends. But the thought had generated no concrete imagery. It remained of necessity what it was at first—a mere bare skeleton of logic, never clothed upon by imaginative flesh and blood. As in Clarke's sermons, we have diagrams instead of pictures; a system of axioms, deductions, and corollaries instead of a rich mythology; a barren metaphysico-mathematical theory of the universe, which might satisfy the intellect, but remained hopelessly frigid for the emotional nature.

    Pope's poetry is thus forced to become didactic, and not only didactic, but ratiocinative. It consists of a series of arguments, and, what is worse, of incoherent argument hitched into rhyme. The emotion is always checked by the sense that the Deity, whose ways are indicated, is after all but a barren abstraction in no particular relation to our race or its history. He never touches the circle of human interests. We believe in a mathematical proposition without caring whether it was known to Archimedes or to Newton; and the God whose existence is proved like a proposition in Euclid brings us into no sympathy with the saints and heroes of old. Primitive imaginings as to the nature of God had become for Pope a meaningless jargon like the speculations of Ptolemaic astronomers. Theology divorced from history does not take us back to the Garden of Eden, but to some conventional age of which we know, and the poet knows, that it never existed except as a metaphysical hypothesis. We have no visions of heaven and hell, regions which obviously lie beyond the range of philosophy; and though Pope was of course attacked for omitting them, their appearance in his poem would have been æsthetically discordant as well as logically absurd. He deals with demonstration, not with tradition. History is a miscellaneous collection of precedents more or less applicable to modern times, but not the record of earlier stages of processes still at work. The new enlightenment had made men more conscious than their ancestors of the difference between the thoughts of succeeding ages, and made them incapable of the old naïve identification of classical, mediæval, and modern types; it had not yet revealed the identities which produce a new interest in the ancient forms as containing the germs of the new. Thus limited to the sphere of abstract logic, only one practical conclusion emerges in the doctrine to which the essay finally leads us, 'that whatever is is right.' Nothing is less poetical than optimism; for the essence of a poet's function is to harmonise the sadness of the universe.—SIR LESLIE STEPHEN, *History of English Thought in the Eighteenth Century*, 1876

Pope was accustomed to talk with much solemnity of his ethical system, of which the *Essay on Man* is but a fragment, but we need not trouble ourselves about it. Dr. Johnson said about *Clarissa Harlowe* that the man who read it for the story might hang himself; so we may say about the poetry of Pope: the man who reads it for its critical or ethical philosophy may hang himself. We read Pope for pleasure, but a bit of his philosophy may be given—

> Presumptuous man! the reason wouldst thou find,
> Why formed so weak, so little, and so blind?
> First, if thou canst, the harder reason guess
> Why formed no weaker, blinder, and no less?
> Ask of thy mother Earth why oaks are made
> Taller and stronger than the weeds they shade?
> Or ask of yonder argent fields above
> Why Jove's satellites are less than Jove!

To this latter interrogatory presumptuous science, speaking through the mouth of Voltaire, was ready with an answer. If Jupiter were less than his satellites they would n't go round him. Pope can make no claim to be a philosopher, and had he been one, Verse would have been a most improper vehicle to convey his speculations. No one willingly fights in handcuffs or wrestles to music. For a man with novel truths to promulgate, or grave moral laws to expound, to postpone doing so until he had hitched them into rhyme would be to insult his mission. Pope's gifts were his wit, his swift-working mind, added to all the cunning of the craft and mystery of composition. He could say things better than other men, and hence it comes that, be he a great poet or a small one, he is a great writer, an English classic.—AUGUSTINE BIRRELL, "Pope," *Obiter Dicta: Second Series*, 1887

CORRESPONDENCE

I have read the collection of letters you mention and was delighted with nothing more than that air of sincerity, those professions of esteem and respect, and that deference paid to his friend's judgment in poetry which I have sometimes seen expressed to others, and I doubt not with the same cordial affection. If they are read in that light, they will be very entertaining and useful in the present age; but in the next, Cicero, Pliny, and Voiture may regain their reputation.—ELIJAH FENTON, Letter to William Broome (Sept. 1726)

Pope courted with the utmost assiduity all the old men from whom he could hope a Legacy: the Duke of Buckingham, Lord Peterborrough, Sir G. Kneller, Lord Bolingbroke, Mr. Wycherly, Mr. Congreve, Lord Harcourt etc., and I do not doubt projected to sweep the Dean's whole inheritance if he could have persuaded him to throw up his Deanery and come die in his House; and his general preaching against money was meant to induce people to throw it away that he might pick it up. There cannot be a stronger proofe of his being capable of any Action for the sake of Gain than publishing his Literary Correspondance, which lays open such a mixture of Dullness and iniquity that one would imagine it visible even to his most passionate admirers, if Lord O⟨rrery⟩ did not show that smooth lines have as much influence over some people as the Authority of the Church in these Countrys, where it can not only veil but sanctifye any absurdity or Villainy whatever.—LADY MARY WORTLEY MONTAGU, Letter to the Countess of Bute (June 23, 1754)

⟨. . .⟩ in all his letters, as well as those of *Swift*, there runs a strain of pride, as if the world talked of nothing but themselves. *Alass,* says he, in one of them, *the day after I am dead, the sun will shine as bright as the day before, and the world will be as merry as usual!* Very strange, that neither an eclipse nor an earthquake should follow the loss of a Poet!—OLIVER GOLDSMITH, *The Life of Richard Nash*, 1762

It is a mercy to have no character to maintain. Your predecessor Mr Pope laboured his letters as much as the *Essay on Man,* and as they were written to everybody, they do not look as if they had been written to anybody.—HORACE WALPOLE, Letter to William Mason (March 13, 1777)

Your Mother communicated to me the Satisfaction you expressed in my Correspondence, that you thought me Entertaining and Clever and so forth. Now you must know I Love Praise dearly, especially from the Judicious, and those who have so much Delicacy themselves as not to Offend mine in giving it. But then I found this consequence attending, or likely to attend the Eulogium you bestowed. If my Friend thought me Witty before, he shall think me ten times more Witty hereafter, where I Joked Once, I will Joke 5 times, and for One Sensible Remark, I will send him a Dozen. Now this foolish Vanity would have spoiled me quite, and would have made me as disgusting a Letter: Writer as Pope, who seems to have thought that unless a Sentence was well turned, and every Period pointed with some Conceit, it was not worth the Carriage. Accordingly he is to me, except in very few Instances, the most disagreeable Maker of Epistles that ever I met with.—WILLIAM COWPER, Letter to William Unwin (June 8, 1780)

The most distinguished collection of Letters in the English Language, is that of Mr. Pope, Dean Swift, and their friends; partly published in Mr. Pope's Works, and partly in those of Dean Swift. This Collection is, on the whole, an entertaining and agreeable one; and contains much wit and ingenuity. It is not, however, altogether free of the fault which I imputed to Pliny's Epistles, of too much study and refinement. ⟨ . . . ⟩ The censure of writing Letters in too artificial a manner, falls heaviest on Mr. Pope himself. There is visibly more study, and less of nature and the heart in his Letters, than in those of some of his correspondents. He had formed himself on the manner of Voiture, and is too fond of writing like a wit. His Letters to Ladies are full of affectation.—HUGH BLAIR, *Lectures on Rhetoric and Belles Lettres*, 1783, Lecture 37

JOHN DENNIS

A *True Character of Mr. Pope, and His Writings*

1716

I have read over the *Libel*, which I received from you the Day before Yesterday. Yesterday I received the same from another Hand, with this Character of the Secret Author of so much stupid Calumny.

That he is one, whom God and Nature have mark'd for want of Common Honesty, and his own Contemptible Rhimes for want of Common Sense, that those Rhimes have found great Success with the Rabble, which is a Word almost as comprehensive as Mankind; but that the Town, which supports him, will do by him, as the Dolphin did by the Ship-wrack'd *Monkey*, drop him as soon as it finds him out to be a Beast, whom it fondly now mistakes for a Human Creature. 'Tis, *says he*, a very little but very comprehensive Creature, in whom all Contradictions meet, and all Contrarieties are reconcil'd; when at one and the same time, like the Ancient *Centaurs*, he is a Beast and a Man, a Whig and a Tory, a virulent *Papist* and yet forsooth, a Pillar of the Church of *England*, a Writer at one and the same time, of *GUARDIANS* and of *EXAMINERS*, an assertor of Liberty and of the Dispensing Power of Kings; a Rhimester without Judgment or Reason, and a Critick without Common Sense; a Jesuitical Professor of Truth, a base and a foul Pretender to Candour; a Barbarous Wretch, who is perpetually boasting of Humanity and Good Nature, a lurking way-laying Coward, and a Stabber in the Dark; who is always pretending to Magnanimity, and to sum up all Villains in one, a Traytor-Friend, one who has betrayed all Mankind, and seems to have taken his great Rule of Life from the following lines of *Hudibras*.

> For 'tis easier to *Betray*
> Than Ruin any other way,
> As th' Earth is soonest undermin'd,
> By vermin Impotent and Blind.

He is a Professor of the worst Religion, which he laughs at, and yet has most inviolably observ'd the most execrable Maxim in it, *That no Faith is to be kept with Hereticks.* A wretch, whose true Religion is his Interest, and yet so stupidly blind to that Interest, that he often meets her, without knowing her, and very grosly Affronts her. His Villainy is but the natural Effect of his want of Understanding, as the sowerness of Vinegar proceeds from its want of Spirit; and yet, *says My Friend,* notwithstanding that Shape and that Mind of his, some Men of good Understanding, value him for his Rhimes, as they would be fond of an *Asseinego,* that could sing his part in a Catch, or of a *Baboon* that could whistle *Walsingham.* The grosser part of his gentle Readers believe the Beast to be more than Man; as Ancient Rusticks took his Ancestors for those Demy-Gods they call *Fauns* and *Satyrs.*

This was the Character, which my Friend gave to the Author of this miserable Libel, which immediately made me apprehend that it was the very same Person, who endeavour'd to expose you in a *Billinsgate* Libel, at the very time that you were doing him a Favour at his own earnest Desire, who attempted to undermine Mr. *PHILIPS* in one of his *Guardians,* at the same time that the *Crocodile* smil'd on him, embrac'd him, and called him Friend, who wrote a Prologue in praise of *CATO,* and teaz'd *Lintott* to publish Remarks upon it; who at the same time, that he openly extoll'd Sir *Richard Steele* in the highest manner, secretly publish'd the Infamous Libel of Dr. *Andrew Tripe* upon him; who, as he is in Shape a *Monkey,* is so in his every Action; in his senseless Chattering, and his merry Grimaces, in his doing hourly Mischief and hiding himself, in the variety of his Ridiculous Postures, and his continual Shiftings, from Place to Place, from Persons to Persons, from Thing to Thing. But whenever he Scribbles, he is emphatically a *Monkey,* in his awkward servile Imitations. For in all his Productions, he has been an *Imitator,* from his Imitation of *VIRGILS Bucolicks,* to this present Imitation of *HORACE.* ——His *Pastorals* were writ in Imitation of *VIRGIL,*——His *Rape of the Lock* of BOILEAU,——His *Essay on Criticism,* of the present Duke of *Buckingham,* and of my Lord *Roscommon,*——His *Windsor-Forest* of Sir *John Denham,*—— His *Ode upon St. Cæcilia* of Mr. *Dryden,* and——His *Temple of Fame,* of CHAUCER.

Thus for fifteen Years together this Ludicrous Animal has been a constant *Imitator.* Yet he has rather mimick'd these great Genius's, than he has Imitated them. He has given a False and a Ridiculous Turn to all their good and their great Qualities, and has, as far as in him lies, Burlesqu'd them without knowing it. But after having been for fifteen Years as it were an *Imitator,* he has made no Proficiency. His first Imitations, tho' bad, are rather better than the Succeeding, and this last Imitation of *HORACE,* the most execrable of them all.

> For as a Dog that turns the Spitt,
> Bestirs himself and plies his Feet
> To climb the Wheel, but all in vain,
> His own Weight brings him down again,
> And still he's in the self same place,
> Where at his setting out he was,
> So in the Circle of the Arts,
> Does he Advance his natural Parts.
>
> (Hud.)

If you should chance, Sir, to shew this LETTER to any of your Acquaintance who have perus'd his Senseless Calumnies, they may think perhaps that we follow his Example, and retort Slander upon him. I Desire that you would have the Goodness to assure such, that in the Moral part of his Character, and all that relates to matter of Fact, there is no manner of Rhetorick us'd, all is exactly and litterally true, for which we appeal to those Poetical Persons, with whom we have been most Conversant in *Covent-Garden.* We have always been of Opinion that he who invents, or pretends, or falsifies Matter of Fact, in order to slander any one, deserves an Infamous Punishment, and we have always had before our Eyes the following Verses out of *Horace,*

> Absentem qui rodit amicum,
> Qui non defendit alio culpante, solutos
> Qui captat risus Hominum, famamq; dicacis,
> Fingere qui non visa potest, commissa tacere,
> Qui nequit, hic niger est, hunc tu Romane,
> caveto, &c.

As to what relates to the *Person* of this wretched Libeller, if in that there may be some trifling Exaggerations, yet even that is not design'd to Deceive or Impose upon any to whom you may happen to shew it, but is intended to lead them to an exact Knowledge of the Truth by a very little enlarging upon it.

But if any one appears to be concern'd at our Upbraiding him with his Natural Deformity, which did not come by his own Fault, but seems to be the Curse of God upon him; we desire that Person to consider, that this little Monster has upbraided People with their Calamities and their Diseases, and Calamities and Diseases, which are either false or past, or which he himself gave them by administring Poison to them; we desire that Person to consider, that Calamities and Diseases, if they are neither false nor past, are common to all Men; that a Man can no more help his Calamities and his Diseases, than a Monster can his Deformity; that there is no Misfortune, but what the Generality of Mankind are liable too, and that there is no one Disease, but what all the rest of Men are subject too; whereas the Deformity of this Libeller, is Visible, Present, Lasting, Unalterable, and Peculiar to himself. 'Tis the mark of God and Nature upon him, to give us warning that we should hold no Society with him, as a Creature not of our Original, nor of our Species. And they who have refus'd to take this Warning which God and Nature have given them, and have in spight of it, by a Senseless Presumption, ventur'd to be familiar with him, have severely suffer'd for it, by his Perfidiousness. They tell me, he has been lately pleas'd to say, *That 'tis Doubtful if the Race of Men are the Offspring of* Adam *or of the* Devil. But if 'tis doubtful as to the Race of Men, 'tis certain at least, that his Original is not from *Adam*, but from the *Divel*. By his constant and malicious Lying, and by that Angel Face and Form of his, 'tis plain that he wants nothing but Horns and Tayl, to be the exact Resemblance, both in Shape and Mind, of his Infernal Father. Thus, Sir, I return you Truth for Slander, and a just Satire for an Extravagant Libel, which is therefore ridiculously call'd an Imitation of *Horace*. You know very well, Sir, that the Difference between *Horace*, and such an Imitation of him, is almost Infinite; and I leave you to consider what Influence such an Imitation must have upon its Readers of both Kinds, both upon those who are acquainted with that Great Poet, and with those that know him not; how contemptible it must render *Horace* to the latter, and his Imitator to the former, who when they shall behold the Ghost of their old and their valued Friend, raised up before them, by this awkward Conjurer, in a Manner so ridiculously frightful, when they behold him thus miserably mangled, and reflect at once with Contempt and Horrour, upon this Barbarous Usage of him, will not be able to refrain from exclaiming in the most vehement Manner.

Qualis adest, Quantum mutatus ab illo, &c.

They must think that their old and valued Friend had a Prophetick Spirit, and seem'd to foretel the Usage, which he has lately received from this Barbarian and his Brethren, when in the fourth Ode of his Third Book he cryed.

Visam Britannos Hospitibus feros.

But as for the other sorts of Readers, the Readers who have no Knowledge of *Horace*, but from this contemptible Imitation; what must they think, Sir, of those great Men, who extol him, for the second Genius of the *Roman-Empire*. Illustrious for so many great Qualities which are to be found in him alone? Must they not look upon all his Admirers, as so many Learned Idiots, and upon the *Roman-Empire* it self, as a vast Nation of Fools?

You know very well, Sir, that as *Horace* had a firmness of Judgment, and a sureness and truth of Taste; he never once

form'd a wrong Judgment to himself, either of the Actions of Men in general, or of the particular Worth and Merit of Authors; he had an Honour and a Rectitude of Soul, that would have oblig'd him to die a thousand times rather than to Write any thing against his Conscience.

Pejusque letho flagitium timet.

He was capable indeed of being provok'd to expose either a Fool or a Knave, whom otherwise he might have suffer'd to have remain'd in Obscurity; but the most Barbarous Usage of his most Malicious Enemy, could never urge him to Slander that Enemy. From this Force and Clearness of his Understanding, and this Noble Rectitude of his Will, it has proceeded that all his Censures are like so many *Decrees*, that have all been affirm'd by Posterity, the only Supream Court of Judicature, for the Distribution of Fame and Infamy, from which Mankind can have no Appeal. That Supream, Impartial, Incorruptible Judicature, has the same Opinions of Persons and Things, and especially of Authors that he had. The same high Value for *Tibullus*, for *Pollio*, for *Varius*, for *Virgil*; and the same Contempt for *Bavius*, for *Mœvius*, for *Crispinus*, for *Alpinus*, for *Fannius*, and for a thousand more.

The same Justness and Fineness of Discernment, and the same noble Rectitude of Will, appear in the *French Satirist*, which make the most considerable Share of his Merit, and the most Distinguishing part of his Character, if we will believe what he says of himself, in his Admirable Epistle to *Monsieur SEIGNELEY*. You know, Sir, that what *Boileau* says there of himself is exactly true in Fact. The Persons whom he has attack'd in his Writings have been for the most part Authors, and most of those Authors Poets. The Censures which he has pass'd on them have been confirm'd by all *Europe*. But at the same time that judicious Poet, has been as liberal of his Praise to his Contemporaries, who were excellent in their Kinds, as *Corneille*, *Racine*, *Moliere*, and *La Fontaine*. Nay, he was generous enough to defend *Racine*, and to support and strengthen him, when a clamorous crou'd of miserable Authors endeavoured to oppress him, as appears by his Admirable Epistle addrest to that Tragick Poet.

You, and I, both know very well, Sir, that there has been never wanting a Floud of such Authors, neither in *England* nor *France*, who being like this Imitator, in ev'ry Respect, the reverse of *Horace*, in Honour, in Discernment, in Genius; have always combin'd to attack any thing that has appear'd above their own dull Level, while they have hug'd and admir'd each other, Authors who have thought to be too hard for their Adversaries by opposing *Billinsgate* to Reason, and Dogmatical Assertion to Moral Demonstration; and who have been Idiots enough to believe that their Noise and Impudence could alter the Nature of Things, and the Notions of Men of Sense.

Of all these Libellers, the present Imitator is the most Impudent, and the most Incorrigible, who has lately pester'd and plagu'd the World with Five or Six Scandalous Libels, in Prose, that are all of them at once so Stupid, and so Malicious, that Men of Sense are Doubtful, if they should attribute them to the Libellers Native Idiotism, or to Accidental Madness.

In all these Libels, the chief Objects of his Scandal and Malice, have been Persons of distinguish'd Merit, and among these he has fallen upon none so foully as his Friends and Benefactors. Among these latter, he has attack'd no one so often, or with so much ridiculous, impotent Malice, as Sir *Richard Blackmore*; who is Estimable for a thousand good and great Qualities. And what time has he chosen to do this? Why, just after the Gentleman had laid very great Obligations on him; and just after he had oblig'd the World with so many

Editions of his Excellent _Poem_ upon CREATION, which _Poem_ alone is worth all the _Folios_, that this Libeller will ever write, and which will render its Author the Delight and Admiration of Posterity. So that 'tis hard to determine whether this Libeller is more remarkable for his Judgment or his Gratitude.

I dare venture to affirm, that there is not an Author living so little Qualified for a Censurer as himself. I know nothing for which he is so ill Qualified as he is for Judging, unless it be for Translating HOMER. He has neither Taste nor Judgment, but is, if you will pardon a Quibble, the very necessity of _Parnassus_; for he has none of the Poetical Laws; or if he has the Letter of any, He has it without the Spirit. Whenever he pretends to Criticise, I fancy I see _Shamwell_ or _Cheatly_ in the Squire of _Alsatia_, cutting a Sham or Banter to abuse some Bubble. The _Preface_ is full of gross Errours, and he has shewn himself in it, a Dogmatical, Ignorant, Impudent Second-Hand Critick. As for the _Poem_, however he may cry up HOMER for being every where a _Grecian-Trumpeter_ in the Original, I can see no _Trumpeter_ in the _Translator_, but the King of _Spain's_. But since his Friends will alledge 'tis easie to say this, I desire that it may go for nothing, till I have so plainly prov'd it, that the most Foolish, and the most Partial of them shall not be able to deny it.

As for what they call his _Verses_, he has, like Mr. _Bayes_, got a notable knack of Rhimeing and Writing smooth Verse, but without either Genius or Good Sense, or any tolerable Knowledge of _English_, as I believe I shall shew plainly, when I come to the rest of his Imitations. As for his Translation of HOMER, I could never borrow it, till this very Day, and design to read it over to Morrow; so that shortly you may expect to hear more of it. I will only tell you beforehand, that HOMER seems to me to be untranslatable in any Modern Language. That great Poet is just in his Designs, admirable in his Characters, and for the most part exact in his Reasoning, and correct in his Noble Sentiments, but these are Excellencies, which may be already seen in the Prose Translations of Him.

The Qualities which so admirably distinguish HOMER from most other Writers, and which therefore a Translator in Verse is particularly oblig'd to show, because they cannot be shown in Prose, are the Beauty of his Diction, and the various Harmony of his Versification. But 'tis as Ridiculous to pretend to make these Shine out in _English_ Rhimes, as it would be to emulate upon a _Bag-pipe_, the Solemn and Majestick Thorough Basse of an _Organ_.

But you may suddenly expect more of this, if what I have already said, happens to entertain you.

I am
Sir,
Your, &c.

ALEXANDER POPE
"Preface"
The Works of Mr. Alexander Pope
1717

I am inclined to think that both the writers of books, and the readers of them, are generally not a little unreasonable in their expectations. The first seem to fancy that the world must approve whatever they produce, and the latter to imagine that authors are obliged to please them at any rate. Methinks as on the one hand, no single man is born with a right of controuling the opinions of all the rest; so on the other, the world has no title to demand, that the whole care and time of any particular person should be sacrificed to its entertainment. Therefore I cannot but believe that writers and readers are under equal obligations, for as much fame, or pleasure, as each affords the other.

Every one acknowledges, it would be a wild notion to expect perfection in any work of man: and yet one would think the contrary was taken for granted, by the judgment commonly past upon Poems. A Critic supposes he has done his part, if he proves a writer to have fail'd in an expression, or err'd in any particular point: and can it then be wonder'd at, if the Poets in general seem resolv'd not to own themselves in any error? For as long as one side will make no allowances, the other will be brought to no acknowledgements.

I am afraid this extreme zeal on both sides is ill-plac'd; Poetry and Criticism being by no means the universal concern of the world, but only the affair of idle men who write in their closets, and of idle men who read there.

Yet sure upon the whole, a bad Author deserves better usage than a bad Critic: for a Writer's endeavour, for the most part, is to please his Readers, and he fails merely through the misfortune of an ill judgment; but such a Critic's is to put them out of humor; a design he could never go upon without both that and an ill temper.

I think a good deal may be said to extenuate the fault of bad Poets. What we call a Genius, is hard to be distinguish'd by a man himself, from a strong inclination: and if his genius be ever so great, he can not at first discover it any other way, than by giving way to that prevalent propensity which renders him the more liable to be mistaken. The only method he has, is to make the experiment by writing, and appealing to the judgment of others: now if he happens to write ill (which is certainly no sin in itself) he is immediately made an object of ridicule. I wish we had the humanity to reflect that even the worst authors might, in their endeavour to please us, deserve something at our hands. We have no cause to quarrel with them but for their obstinacy in persisting to write; and this too may admit of alleviating circumstances. Their particular friends may be either ignorant, or insincere; and the rest of the world in general is too well bred to shock them with a truth, which generally their Booksellers are the first that inform them of. This happens not till they have spent too much of their time, to apply to any profession which might better fit their talents; and till such talents as they have are so far discredited, as to be but of small service to them. For (what is the hardest case imaginable) the reputation of a man generally depends upon the first steps he makes in the world, and people will establish their opinion of us, from what we do at that season when we have least judgment to direct us.

On the other hand, a good Poet no sooner communicates his works with the same desire of information, but it is imagin'd he is a vain young creature given up to the ambition of fame; when perhaps the poor man is all the while trembling with the fear of being ridiculous. If he is made to hope he may please the world, he falls under very unlucky circumstances; for from the moment he prints, he must expect to hear no more truth, than if he were a Prince, or a Beauty. If he has not very good sense (and indeed there are twenty men of wit, for one man of sense) his living thus in a course of flattery may put him in no small danger of becoming a Coxcomb: If he has, he will consequently have so much diffidence, as not to reap any great satisfaction from his praise; since if it be given to his face, it can scarce be distinguish'd from flattery, and if in his absence, it is hard to be certain of it. Were he sure to be commended by the best and most knowing, he is as sure of being envy'd by the worst and most ignorant, which are the majority; for it is with a fine Genius as with a fine fashion, all those are displeas'd at it who are not able to follow it: And 'tis to be fear'd that esteem will seldom do any man so much good, as ill-will does him harm. Then there is a third class of people who make the largest part of mankind, those of ordinary or indifferent capacities; and these (to a man) will hate, or suspect him: a hundred honest gentlemen will dread him as a wit, and a hundred innocent women as a satyrist. In a word, whatever be his fate in Poetry, it is ten to one but he must give up all the reasonable aims of life for it. There are indeed some advantages accruing from a Genius to Poetry, and they are all I can think of: the agreeable power of self-amusement when a man is idle or alone; the privilege of being admitted into the best company; and the freedom of saying as many careless things as other people, without being so severely remark'd upon.

I believe, if any one, early in his life should contemplate the dangerous fate of authors, he would scarce be of their number on any consideration. The life of a Wit is a warfare upon earth; and the present spirit of the learned world is such, that to attempt to serve it (any way) one must have the constancy of a martyr, and a resolution to suffer for its sake. I could wish people would believe what I am pretty certain they will not, that I have been less concern'd about Fame than I durst declare till this occasion, when methinks I should find more credit than I could heretofore: since my writings have had their fate already, and 'tis too late to think of prepossessing the reader in their favour. I would plead it as some merit in me, that the world has never been prepared for these Trifles by Prefaces, byast by recommendations, dazled with the names of great Patrons, wheedled with fine reasons and pretences, or troubled with excuses. I confess it was want of consideration that made me an author; I writ because it amused me; I corrected because it was as pleasant to me to correct as to write; and I publish'd because I was told I might please such as it was a credit to please. To what degree I have done this, I am really ignorant; I had too much fondness for my productions to judge of them at first, and too much judgment to be pleas'd with them at last. But I have reason to think they can have no reputation which will continue long, or which deserves to do so: for they have always fallen short not only of what I read of others, but even of my own Ideas of Poetry.

If any one should imagine I am not in earnest, I desire him to reflect, that the Ancients (to say the least of them) had as much Genius as we; and that to take more pains, and employ more time, cannot fail to produce more complete pieces. They constantly apply'd themselves not only to that art, but to that single branch of an art, to which their talent was most powerfully bent; and it was the business of their lives to correct and finish their works for posterity. If we can pretend to have used the same industry, let us expect the same immortality: Tho' if we took the same care, we should still lie under a farther misfortune: they writ in languages that became universal and everlasting, while ours are extremely limited both in extent, and in duration. A mighty foundation for our pride! when the utmost we can hope, is but to be read in one Island, and to be thrown aside at the end of one Age.

All that is left us is to recommend our productions by the imitation of the Ancients: and it will be found true, that in every age, the highest character for sense and learning has been obtain'd by those who have been most indebted to them. For to say truth, whatever is very good sense must have been common sense in all times; and what we call Learning, is but the knowledge of the sense of our predecessors. Therefore they

who say our thoughts are not our own because they resemble the Ancients, may as well say our faces are not our own, because they are like our Fathers: And indeed it is very unreasonable, that people should expect us to be Scholars, and yet be angry to find us so.

I fairly confess that I have serv'd my self all I could by reading; that I made use of the judgment of authors dead and living; that I omitted no means in my power to be inform'd of my errors, both by my friends and enemies. But the true reason these pieces are not more correct, is owing to the consideration how short a time they, and I, have to live: One may be ashamed to consume half one's days in bringing sense and rhyme together; and what Critic can be so unreasonable as not to leave a man time enough for any more serious employment, or more agreeable amusement?

The only plea I shall use for the favour of the publick, is, that I have as great a respect for it, as most authors have for themselves; and that I have sacrificed much of my own self-love for its sake, in preventing not only many mean things from seeing the light, but many which I thought tolerable. I would not be like those Authors, who forgive themselves some particular lines for the sake of a whole Poem, and *vice versa* a whole Poem for the sake of some particular lines. I believe no one qualification is so likely to make a good writer, as the power of rejecting his own thoughts; and it must be this (if any thing) that can give me a chance to be one. For what I have publish'd, I can only hope to be pardon'd; but for what I have burn'd, I deserve to be prais'd. On this account the world is under some obligation to me, and owes me the justice in return, to look upon no verses as mine that are not inserted in this collection. And perhaps nothing could make it worth my while to own what are really so, but to avoid the imputation of so many dull and immoral things, as partly by malice, and partly by ignorance, have been ascribed to me. I must farther acquit my self of the presumption of having lent my name to recommend any Miscellanies, or works of other men, a thing I never thought becoming a person who has hardly credit enough to answer for his own.

In this office of collecting my pieces, I am altogether uncertain, whether to look upon my self as a man building a monument, or burying the dead?

If time shall make it the former, may these Poems (as long as they last) remain as a testimony, that their Author never made his talents subservient to the mean and unworthy ends of Party or self-interest; the gratification of publick prejudices, or private passions; the flattery of the undeserving, or the insult of the unfortunate. If I have written well, let it be consider'd that 'tis what no man can do without good sense, a quality that not only renders one capable of being a good writer, but a good man. And if I have made any acquisition in the opinion of any one under the notion of the former, let it be continued to me under no other title than that of the latter.

But if this publication be only a more solemn funeral of my Remains, I desire it may be known that I die in charity, and in my senses; without any murmurs against the justice of this age, or any mad appeals to posterity. I declare I shall think the world in the right, and quietly submit to every truth which time shall discover to the prejudice of these writings; not so much as wishing so irrational a thing, as that every body should be deceiv'd, meerly for my credit. However, I desire it may then be consider'd, that there are very few things in this collection which were not written under the age of five and twenty; so that my youth may be made (as it never fails to be in Executions) a case of compassion. That I was never so concern'd about my works as to vindicate them in print, believing if any thing was good it would defend itself, and what was bad could never be defended. That I used no artifice to raise or continue a reputation, depreciated no dead author I was oblig'd to, brib'd no living one with unjust praise, insulted no adversary with ill language, or when I could not attack a Rival's works, encourag'd reports against his Morals. To conclude, if this volume perish, let it serve as a warning to the Critics, not to take too much pains for the future to destroy such things as will die of themselves; and a *Memento mori* to some of my vain cotemporaries the Poets, to teach them that when real merit is wanting, it avails nothing to have been encourag'd by the great, commended by the eminent, and favour'd by the publick in general.

SAMUEL JOHNSON
From "Pope"
Lives of the English Poets
1779–81

The person of Pope is well known not to have been formed by the nicest model. He has, in his account of the *Little Club*, compared himself to a spider, and by another is described as protuberant behind and before. He is said to have been beautiful in his infancy; but he was of a constitution originally feeble and weak; and as bodies of a tender frame are easily distorted, his deformity was probably in part the effect of his application. His stature was so low, that, to bring him to a level with common tables, it was necessary to raise his seat. But his face was not displeasing, and his eyes were animated and vivid.

By natural deformity, or accidental distortion, his vital functions were so much disordered, that his life was a *long disease*. His most frequent assailant was the headach, which he used to relieve by inhaling the steam of coffee, which he very frequently required.

Most of what can be told concerning his petty peculiarities was communicated by a female domestick of the Earl of Oxford, who knew him perhaps after the middle of life. He was then so weak as to stand in perpetual need of female attendance; extremely sensible of cold, so that he wore a kind of fur doublet, under a shirt of a very coarse warm linen with fine sleeves. When he rose, he was invested in bodice made of stiff canvas, being scarce able to hold himself erect till they were laced, and then he put on a flannel waistcoat. One side was contracted. His legs were so slender, that he enlarged their bulk with three pairs of stockings, which were drawn on and off by the maid; for he was not able to dress or undress himself, and neither went to bed nor rose without help. His weakness made it very difficult for him to be clean.

His hair had fallen almost all away; and he used to dine sometimes with Lord Oxford, privately, in a velvet cap. His dress of ceremony was black with a tye-wig, and a little sword.

The indulgence and accommodation which his sickness required, had taught him all the unpleasing and unsocial qualities of a valetudinary man. He expected that every thing should give way to his ease or humour, as a child, whose parents will not hear her cry, has an unresisted dominion in the nursery.

> C'est que l'enfant toujours est homme,
> C'est que l'homme est toujours enfant.

When he wanted to sleep he *nodded in company*; and once slumbered at his own table while the Prince of Wales was talking of poetry.

The reputation which his friendship gave, procured him many invitations; but he was a very troublesome inmate. He brought no servant, and had so many wants, that a numerous attendance was scarcely able to supply them. Wherever he was, he left no room for another, because he exacted the attention, and employed the activity of the whole family. His errands were so frequent and frivolous, that the footmen in time avoided and neglected him; and the Earl of Oxford discharged some of the servants for their resolute refusal of his messages. The maids, when they had neglected their business, alleged that they had been employed by Mr. Pope. One of his constant demands was of coffee in the night, and to the woman that waited on him in his chamber he was very burthensome; but he was careful to recompense her want of sleep; and Lord Oxford's servant declared, that in a house where her business was to answer his call, she would not ask for wages.

He had another fault, easily incident to those who, suffering much pain, think themselves entitled to whatever pleasures they can snatch. He was too indulgent to his appetite; he loved meat highly seasoned and of strong taste; and, at the intervals of the table, amused himself with biscuits and dry conserves. If he sat down to a variety of dishes, he would oppress his stomach with repletion, and though he seemed angry when a dram was offered him, did not forbear to drink it. His friends, who knew the avenues to his heart, pampered him with presents of luxury, which he did not suffer to stand neglected. The death of great men is not always proportioned to the lustre of their lives. Hannibal, says Juvenal, did not perish by a javelin or a sword; the slaughters of Cannae were revenged by a ring. The death of Pope was imputed by some of his friends to a silver saucepan, in which it was his delight to heat potted lampreys.

That he loved too well to eat, is certain; but that his sensuality shortened his life will not be hastily concluded, when it is remembered that a conformation so irregular lasted six and fifty years, notwithstanding such pertinacious diligence of study and meditation.

In all his intercourse with mankind, he had great delight in artifice, and endeavoured to attain all his purposes by indirect and unsuspected methods. *He hardly drank tea without a stratagem.* If, at the house of his friends, he wanted any accommodation, he was not willing to ask for it in plain terms, but would mention it remotely as something convenient; though, when it was procured, he soon made it appear for whose sake it had been recommended. Thus he teized Lord Orrery till he obtained a screen. He practised his arts on such small occasions, that Lady Bolingbroke used to say, in a French phrase, that *he plaid the politician about cabbages and turnips*. His unjustifiable impression of the *Patriot King*, as it can be imputed to no particular motive, must have proceeded from his general habit of secrecy and cunning; he caught an opportunity of a sly trick, and pleased himself with the thought of outwitting Bolingbroke.

In familiar or convivial conversation, it does not appear that he excelled. He may be said to have resembled Dryden, as being not one that was distinguished by vivacity in company. It is remarkable, that, so near his time, so much should be known of what he has written, and so little of what he has said: traditional memory retains no sallies of raillery, nor sentences of observation; nothing either pointed or solid, either wise or merry. One apophthegm only stands upon record. When an objection raised against his inscription for Shakespeare was defended by the authority of *Patrick*, he replied—*horresco referens*—that *he would allow the publisher of a Dictionary to know the meaning of a single word, but not of two words put together.*

He was fretful, and easily displeased, and allowed himself to be capriciously resentful. He would sometimes leave Lord Oxford silently, no one could tell why, and was to be courted back by more letters and messages than the footmen were willing to carry. The table was indeed infested by Lady Mary Wortley, who was the friend of Lady Oxford, and who, knowing his peevishness, could by no intreaties be restrained from contradicting him, till their disputes were sharpened to such asperity, that one or the other quitted the house.

He sometimes condescended to be jocular with servants or inferiors; but by no merriment, either of others or his own, was he ever seen excited to laughter.

Of his domestick character, frugality was a part eminently remarkable. Having determined not to be dependent, he determined not to be in want, and therefore wisely and magnanimously rejected all temptations to expence unsuitable to his fortune. This general care must be universally approved; but it sometimes appeared in petty artifices of parsimony, such as the practice of writing his composition on the back of letters, as may be seen in the remaining copy of the *Iliad*, by which perhaps in five years five shillings were saved; or in a niggardly reception of his friends, and scantiness of entertainment, as, when he had two guests in his house, he would set at supper a single pint upon the table; and having himself taken two small glasses, would retire, and say, *Gentlemen, I leave you to your wine*. Yet he tells his friends, that *he has a heart for all, a house for all, and, whatever they may think, a fortune for all*.

He sometimes, however, made a splendid dinner, and is said to have wanted no part of the skill or elegance which such performances require. That this magnificence should be often displayed, that obstinate prudence with which he conducted his affairs would not permit; for his revenue, certain and casual, amounted only to about eight hundred pounds a year, of which, however, he declares himself able to assign one hundred to charity.

Of this fortune, which as it arose from publick approbation was very honourably obtained, his imagination seems to have been too full: it would be hard to find a man, so well entitled to notice by his wit, that ever delighted so much in talking of his money. In his Letters, and in his Poems, his garden and his grotto, his quincunx and his vines, or some hints of his opulence, are always to be found. The great topick of his ridicule is poverty; the crimes with which he reproaches his antagonists are their debts, their habitation in the Mint, and their want of a dinner. He seems to be of an opinion not very uncommon in the world, that to want money is to want every thing.

Next to the pleasure of contemplating his possessions, seems to be that of enumerating the men of high rank with whom he was acquainted, and whose notice he loudly proclaims not to have been obtained by any practices of meanness or servility; a boast which was never denied to be true, and to which very few poets have ever aspired. Pope never set genius to sale; he never flattered those whom he did not love, or praised those whom he did not esteem. Savage however remarked, that he began a little to relax his dignity when he wrote a distich for *his Highness's dog*.

His admiration of the Great seems to have increased in the advance of life. He passed over peers and statesmen to inscribe his *Iliad* to Congreve, with a magnanimity of which the praise had been compleat, had his friend's virtue been equal to his wit. Why he was chosen for so great an honour, it is not now possible to know; there is no trace in literary history

of any particular intimacy between them. The name of Congreve appears in the Letters among those of his other friends, but without any observable distinction or consequence.

To his latter works, however, he took care to annex names dignified with titles, but was not very happy in his choice; for, except Lord Bathurst, none of his noble friends were such as that a good man would wish to have his intimacy with them known to posterity: he can derive little honour from the notice of Cobham, Burlington, or Bolingbroke.

Of his social qualities, if an estimate be made from his Letters, an opinion too favourable cannot easily be formed; they exhibit a perpetual and unclouded effulgence of general benevolence, and particular fondness. There is nothing but liberality, gratitude, constancy, and tenderness. It has been so long said as to be commonly believed, that the true characters of men may be found in their Letters, and that he who writes to his friend lays his heart open before him. But the truth is, that such were the simple friendships of the *Golden Age*, and are now the friendships only of children. Very few can boast of hearts which they dare lay open to themselves, and of which, by whatever accident exposed, they do not shun a distinct and continued view; and, certainly, what we hide from ourselves we do not shew to our friends. There is, indeed, no transaction which offers stronger temptations to fallacy and sophistication than epistolary intercourse. In the eagerness of conversation the first emotions of the mind often burst out, before they are considered; in the tumult of business, interest and passion have their genuine effect; but a friendly Letter is a calm and deliberate performance, in the cool of leisure, in the stillness of solitude, and surely no man sits down to depreciate by design his own character.

Friendship has no tendency to secure veracity; for by whom can a man so much wish to be thought better than he is, as by him whose kindness he desires to gain or keep? Even in writing to the world there is less constraint; the author is not confronted with his reader, and takes his chance of approbation among the different dispositions of mankind; but a Letter is addressed to a single mind, of which the prejudices and partialities are known; and must therefore please, if not by favouring them, by forbearing to oppose them.

To charge those favourable representations, which men give of their own minds, with the guilt of hypocritical falsehood, would shew more severity than knowledge. The writer commonly believes himself. Almost every man's thoughts, while they are general, are right; and most hearts are pure, while temptation is away. It is easy to awaken generous sentiments in privacy; to despise death when there is no danger; to glow with benevolence when there is nothing to be given. While such ideas are formed they are felt, and self-love does not suspect the gleam of virtue to be the meteor of fancy.

If the Letters of Pope are considered merely as compositions, they seem to be premeditated and artificial. It is one thing to write because there is something which the mind wishes to discharge, and another, to solicit the imagination because ceremony or vanity requires something to be written. Pope confesses his early Letters to be vitiated with *affectation and ambition*: to know whether he disentangled himself from these perverters of epistolary integrity, his book and his life must be set in comparison.

One of his favourite topicks is contempt of his own poetry. For this, if it had been real, he would deserve no commendation, and in this he was certainly not sincere; for his high value of himself was sufficiently observed, and of what could he be proud but of his poetry? He writes, he says, when *he has just nothing else to do;* yet Swift complains that he was never at leisure for conversation, because he *had always some poetical scheme in his head.* It was punctually required that his writing-box should be set upon his bed before he rose; and Lord Oxford's domestick related, that, in the dreadful winter of Forty, she was called from her bed by him four times in one night, to supply him with paper, lest he should lose a thought.

He pretends insensibility to censure and criticism, though it was observed by all who knew him that every pamphlet disturbed his quiet, and that his extreme irritability laid him open to perpetual vexation; but he wished to despise his criticks, and therefore hoped that he did despise them.

As he happened to live in two reigns when the Court paid little attention to poetry, he nursed in his mind a foolish disesteem of Kings, and proclaims that *he never sees Courts.* Yet a little regard shewn him by the Prince of Wales melted his obduracy; and he had not much to say when he was asked by his Royal Highness, *how he could love a Prince while he disliked Kings?'*

He very frequently professes contempt of the world, and represents himself as looking on mankind, sometimes with gay indifference, as on emmets of a hillock, below his serious attention; and sometimes with gloomy indignation, as on monsters more worthy of hatred than of pity. These were dispositions apparently counterfeited. How could he despise those whom he lived by pleasing, and on whose approbation his esteem of himself was superstructed? Why should he hate those to whose favour he owed his honour and his ease? Of things that terminate in human life, the world is the proper judge; to despise its sentence, if it were possible, is not just; and if it were just, is not possible. Pope was far enough from this unreasonable temper; he was sufficiently *a fool to Fame,* and his fault was that he pretended to neglect it. His levity and his sullenness were only in his Letters; he passed through common life, sometimes vexed, and sometimes pleased, with the natural emotions of common men.

His scorn of the Great is repeated too often to be real; no man thinks much of that which he despises; and as falsehood is always in danger of inconsistency, he makes it his boast at another time that he lives among them.

It is evident that his own importance swells often in his mind. He is afraid of writing, lest the clerks of the Post-office should know his secrets; he has many enemies; he considers himself surrounded by universal jealousy; *after many deaths, and many dispersions, two or three of us,* says he, *may still be brought together, not to plot, but to divert ourselves, and the world too, if it pleases;* and they can live together, and *shew what friends wits may be, in spite of all the fools in the world.* All this while it was likely that the clerks did not know his hand; he certainly had no more enemies than a publick character like his inevitably excites, and with what degree of friendship the wits might live, very few were so much fools as ever to enquire.

Some part of this pretended discontent he learned from Swift, and expresses it, I think, most frequently in his correspondence with him. Swift's resentment was unreasonable, but it was sincere; Pope's was the mere mimickry of his friend, a fictitious part which he began to play before it became him. When he was only twenty-five years old, he related that *a glut of study and retirement had thrown him on the world,* and that there was danger lest *a glut of the world should throw him back upon study and retirement.* To this Swift answered with great propriety, that Pope had not yet either acted or suffered enough in the world to have become weary of it. And, indeed, it must be some very powerful reason that can drive back to solitude him who has once enjoyed the pleasures of society.

In the Letters both of Swift and Pope there appears such narrowness of mind, as makes them insensible of any excellence that has not some affinity with their own, and confines their esteem and approbation to so small a number, that whoever should form his opinion of the age from their representation, would suppose them to have lived amidst ignorance and barbarity, unable to find among their contemporaries either virtue or intelligence, and persecuted by those that could not understand them.

When Pope murmurs at the world, when he professes contempt of fame, when he speaks of riches and poverty, of success and disappointment, with negligent indifference, he certainly does not express his habitual and settled sentiments, but either wilfully disguises his own character, or, what is more likely, invests himself with temporary qualities, and sallies out in the colours of the present moment. His hopes and fears, his joys and sorrows, acted strongly upon his mind; and if he differed from others, it was not by carelessness; he was irritable and resentful; his malignity to Philips, whom he had first made ridiculous, and then hated for being angry, continued too long. Of his vain desire to make Bentley contemptible, I never heard any adequate reason. He was sometimes wanton in his attacks; and, before Chandos, Lady Wortley, and Hill, was mean in his retreat.

The virtues which seem to have had most of his affection were liberality and fidelity of friendship, in which it does not appear that he was other than he describes himself. His fortune did not suffer his charity to be splendid and conspicuous; but he assisted Dodsley with a hundred pounds, that he might open a shop; and of the subscription of forty pounds a year that he raised for Savage, twenty were paid by himself. He was accused of loving money, but his love was eagerness to gain, not solicitude to keep it.

In the duties of friendship he was zealous and constant; his early maturity of mind commonly united him with men older than himself, and therefore, without attaining any considerable length of life, he saw many companions of his youth sink into the grave; but it does not appear that he lost a single friend by coldness or by injury; those who loved him once, continued their kindness. His ungrateful mention of Allen in his will, was the effect of his adherence to one whom he had known much longer, and whom he naturally loved with greater fondness. His violation of the trust reposed in him by Bolingbroke could have no motive inconsistent with the warmest affection; he either thought the action so near to indifferent that he forgot it, or so laudable that he expected his friend to approve it.

It was reported, with such confidence as almost to enforce belief, that in the papers intrusted to his executors was found a defamatory Life of Swift, which he had prepared as an instrument of vengeance to be used, if any provocation should be ever given. About this I enquired of the Earl of Marchmont, who assured me that no such piece was among his remains.

The religion in which he lived and died was that of the Church of Rome, to which in his correspondence with Racine he professes himself a sincere adherent. That he was not scrupulously pious in some part of his life, is known by many idle and indecent applications of sentences taken from the Scriptures; a mode of merriment which a good man dreads for its profaneness, and a witty man disdains for its easiness and vulgarity. But to whatever levities he has been betrayed, it does not appear that his principles were ever corrupted, or that he ever lost his belief of Revelation. The positions which he transmitted from Bolingbroke he seems not to have understood, and was pleased with an interpretation that made them orthodox.

A man of such exalted superiority, and so little moderation, would naturally have all his delinquencies observed and aggravated: those who could not deny that he was excellent, would rejoice to find that he was not perfect.

Perhaps it may be imputed to the unwillingness with which the same man is allowed to possess many advantages, that his learning has been depreciated. He certainly was in his early life a man of great literary curiosity; and when he wrote his *Essay on Criticism* had, for his age, a very wide acquaintance with books. When he entered into the living world, it seems to have happened to him as to many others, that he was less attentive to dead masters; he studied in the academy of Paracelsus, and made the universe his favourite volume. He gathered his notions fresh from reality, not from the copies of authors, but the originals of Nature. Yet there is no reason to believe that literature ever lost his esteem; he always professed to love reading; and Dobson, who spent some time at his house translating his *Essay on Man*, when I asked him what learning he found him to possess, answered, *More than I expected*. His frequent references to history, his allusions to various kinds of knowledge, and his images selected from art and nature, with his observations on the operations of the mind and the modes of life, shew an intelligence perpetually on the wing, excursive, vigorous, and diligent, eager to pursue knowledge, and attentive to retain it.

From this curiosity arose the desire of travelling, to which he alludes in his verses to Jervas, and which, though he never found an opportunity to gratify it, did not leave him till his life declined.

Of his intellectual character, the constituent and fundamental principle was Good Sense, a prompt and intuitive perception of consonance and propriety. He saw immediately, of his own conceptions, what was to be chosen, and what to be rejected; and, in the works of others, what was to be shunned, and what was to be copied.

But good sense alone is a sedate and quiescent quality, which manages its possessions well, but does not increase them; it collects few materials for its own operations, and preserves safety, but never gains supremacy. Pope had likewise genius; a mind active, ambitious, and adventurous, always investigating, always aspiring; in its widest searches still longing to go forward, in its highest flights still wishing to be higher; always imagining something greater than it knows, always endeavouring more than it can do.

To assist these powers, he is said to have had great strength and exactness of memory. That which he had heard or read was not easily lost; and he had before him not only what his own meditation suggested, but what he had found in other writers, that might be accommodated to his present purpose.

These benefits of nature he improved by incessant and unwearied diligence; he had recourse to every source of intelligence, and lost no opportunity of information; he consulted the living as well as the dead; he read his compositions to his friends, and was never content with mediocrity when excellence could be attained. He considered poetry as the business of his life, and however he might seem to lament his occupation, he followed it with constancy; to make verses was his first labour, and to mend them was his last.

From his attention to poetry he was never diverted. If conversation offered anything that could be improved, he committed it to paper; if a thought, or perhaps an expression more happy than was common, rose to his mind, he was careful to write it; an independent distich was preserved for an opportunity of insertion, and some little fragments have been found containing lines, or parts of lines, to be wrought upon at some other time.

He was one of those few whose labour is their pleasure: he was never elevated to negligence, nor wearied by impatience; he never passed a fault unamended by indifference, nor quitted it by despair. He laboured his works first to gain reputation, and afterwards to keep it.

Of composition there are different methods. Some employ at once memory and invention, and, with little intermediate use of the pen, form and polish large masses by continued meditation, and write their productions only when, in their own opinion, they have completed them. It is related of Virgil, that his custom was to pour out a great number of verses in the morning, and pass the day in retrenching exuberances and correcting inaccuracies. The method of Pope, as may be collected from his translation, was to write his first thoughts in his first words, and gradually to amplify, decorate, rectify, and refine them.

With such faculties, and such dispositions, he excelled every other writer in *poetical prudence*; he wrote in such a manner as might expose him to few hazards. He used almost always the same fabrick of verse; and, indeed, by those few essays which he made of any other, he did not enlarge his reputation. Of this uniformity the certain consequence was readiness and dexterity. By perpetual practice, language had in his mind a systematical arrangement; having always the same use for words, he had words so selected and combined as to be ready at his call. This increase of facility he confessed himself to have perceived in the progress of his translation.

But what was yet of more importance, his effusions were always voluntary, and his subjects chosen by himself. His independence secured him from drudging at a task, and labouring upon a barren topick: he never exchanged praise for money, nor opened a shop of condolence or congratulation. His poems, therefore, were scarce ever temporary. He suffered coronations and royal marriages to pass without a song, and derived no opportunities from recent events, nor any popularity from the accidental disposition of his readers. He was never reduced to the necessity of soliciting the sun to shine upon a birthday, of calling the Graces and Virtues to a wedding, or of saying what multitudes have said before him. When he could produce nothing new, he was at liberty to be silent.

His publications were for the same reason never hasty. He is said to have sent nothing to the press till it had lain two years under his inspection: it is at least certain, that he ventured nothing without nice examination. He suffered the tumult of imagination to subside, and the novelties of invention to grow familiar. He knew that the mind is always enamoured of its own productions, and did not trust his first fondness. He consulted his friends, and listened with great willingness to criticism; and, what was of more importance, he consulted himself, and let nothing pass against his own judgement.

He professed to have learned his poetry from Dryden, whom, whenever an opportunity was presented, he praised through his whole life with unvaried liberality; and perhaps his character may receive some illustration, if he be compared with his master.

Integrity of understanding and nicety of discernment were not allotted in a less proportion to Dryden than to Pope. The rectitude of Dryden's mind was sufficiently shewn by the dismission of his poetical prejudices and the rejection of unnatural thoughts and rugged numbers. But Dryden never desired to apply all the judgement that he had. He wrote, and professed to write, merely for the people; and when he pleased others, he contented himself. He spent no time in struggles to rouse latent powers; he never attempted to make that better which was already good, nor often to mend what he must have known to be faulty. He wrote, as he tells us, with very little consideration; when occasion or necessity called upon him, he poured out what the present moment happened to supply, and, when once it had passed the press, ejected it from his mind; for when he had no pecuniary interest, he had no further solicitude.

Pope was not content to satisfy; he desired to excel, and therefore always endeavoured to do his best: he did not court the candour, but dared the judgement of his reader, and, expecting no indulgence from others, he shewed none to himself. He examined lines and words with minute and punctilious observation, and retouched every part with indefatigable diligence, till he had left nothing to be forgiven.

For this reason he kept his pieces very long in his hands, while he considered and reconsidered them. The only poems which can be supposed to have been written with such regard to the times as might hasten their publication, were the two satires of *Thirty-eight*; of which Dodsley told me, that they were brought to him by the author, that they might be fairly copied. 'Almost every line,' he said, 'was then written twice over; I gave him a clean transcript, which he sent some time afterwards to me for the press, with almost every line written twice over a second time.'

His declaration, that his care for his works ceased at their publication, was not strictly true. His parental attention never abandoned them; what he found amiss in the first edition, he silently corrected in those that followed. He appears to have revised the *Iliad*, and freed it from some of its imperfections; and the *Essay on Criticism* received many improvements after its first appearance. It will seldom be found that he altered without adding clearness, elegance, or vigour. Pope had perhaps the judgement of Dryden; but Dryden certainly wanted the diligence of Pope.

In acquired knowledge, the superiority must be allowed to Dryden, whose education was more scholastick, and who before he became an author had been allowed more time for study, with better means of information. His mind has a larger range, and he collects his images and illustrations from a more extensive circumference of science. Dryden knew more of man in his general nature, and Pope in his local manners. The notions of Dryden were formed by comprehensive speculation, and those of Pope by minute attention. There is more dignity in the knowledge of Dryden, and more certainty in that of Pope.

Poetry was not the sole praise of either; for both excelled likewise in prose; but Pope did not borrow his prose from his predecessor. The style of Dryden is capricious and varied, that of Pope is cautious and uniform; Dryden obeys the motions of his own mind, Pope constrains his mind to his own rules of composition. Dryden is sometimes vehement and rapid; Pope is always smooth, uniform, and gentle. Dryden's page is a natural field, rising into inequalities, and diversified by the varied exuberance of abundant vegetation; Pope's is a velvet lawn, shaven by the scythe, and levelled by the roller.

Of genius, that power which constitutes a poet; that quality without judgement is cold and knowledge is inert; that energy which collects, combines, amplifies, and animates; the superiority must, with some hesitation, be allowed to Dryden. It is not to be inferred that of this poetical vigour Pope had only a little, because Dryden had more; for every other writer since Milton must give place to Pope; and even of Dryden it must be said, that if he has brighter paragraphs, he has not better poems. Dryden's performances were always hasty, either

excited by some external occasion, or extorted by domestick necessity; he composed without consideration, and published without correction. What his mind could supply at call, or gather in one excursion, was all that he sought, and all that he gave. The dilatory caution of Pope enabled him to condense his sentiments, to multiply his images, and to accumulate all that study might produce, or chance might supply. If the flights of Dryden therefore are higher, Pope continues longer on the wing. If of Dryden's fire the blaze is brighter, of Pope's the heat is more regular and constant. Dryden often surpasses expectation, and Pope never falls below it. Dryden is read with frequent astonishment, and Pope with perpetual delight.

This parallel will, I hope, when it is well considered, be found just; and if the reader should suspect me, as I suspect myself, of some partial fondness for the memory of Dryden, let him not too hastily condemn me; for meditation and enquiry may, perhaps, shew him the reasonableness of my determination.

The Works of Pope are now to be distinctly examined, not so much with attention to slight faults or petty beauties, as to the general character and effect of each performance.

It seems natural for a young poet to initiate himself by Pastorals, which, not professing to imitate real life, require no experience, and, exhibiting only the simple operation of unmingled passions, admit no subtle reasoning or deep enquiry. Pope's Pastorals are not however composed but with close thought; they have reference to the time of the day, the seasons of the year, and the periods of human life. The last, that which turns the attention upon age and death, was the author's favourite. To tell of disappointment and misery, to thicken the darkness of futurity, and perplex the labyrinth of uncertainty, has been always a delicious employment of the poets. His preference was probably just. I wish, however, that his fondness had not overlooked a line in which the *Zephyrs* are made *to lament in silence*.

To charge these Pastorals with want of invention, is to require what was never intended. The imitations are so ambitiously frequent, that the writer evidently means rather to shew his literature than his wit. It is surely sufficient for an author of sixteen not only to be able to copy the poems of antiquity with judicious selection, but to have obtained sufficient power of language, and skill in metre, to exhibit a series of versification, which had in English poetry no precedent, nor has since had an imitation.

The design of *Windsor Forest* is evidently derived from *Cooper's Hill*, with some attention to Waller's poem on *The Park*; but Pope cannot be denied to excel his masters in variety and elegance, and the art of interchanging description, narrative, and morality. The objection made by Dennis is the want of plan, of a regular subordination of parts terminating in the principal and original design. There is this want in most descriptive poems, because as the scenes, which they must exhibit successively, are all subsisting at the same time, the order in which they are shewn must by necessity be arbitrary, and more is not to be expected from the last part than from the first. The attention, therefore, which cannot be detained by suspense, must be excited by diversity, such as his poem offers to its reader.

But the desire of diversity may be too much indulged; the parts of *Windsor Forest* which deserve the least praise, are those which were added to enliven the stillness of the scene, the appearance of Father Thames, and the transformation of *Lodona*. Addison had in his *Campaign* derided the *Rivers* that *rise from their oozy beds* to tell stories of heroes, and it is therefore strange that Pope should adopt a fiction not only unnatural but lately censured. The story of *Lodona* is told with sweetness; but a new metamorphosis is a ready and puerile expedient; nothing is easier than to tell how a flower was once a blooming virgin, or a rock an obdurate tyrant.

The *Temple of Fame* has, as Steele warmly declared, *a thousand beauties*. Every part is splendid; there is great luxuriance of ornaments; the original version of Chaucer was never denied to be much improved; the allegory is very skillfully continued, the imagery is properly selected, and learnedly displayed: yet, with all this comprehension of excellence, as its scene is laid in remote ages, and its sentiments, if the concluding paragraph be excepted, have little relation to general manners or common life, it never obtained much notice, but is turned silently over, and seldom quoted or mentioned with either praise or blame.

That the *Messiah* excells the *Pollio* is no great praise, if it be considered from what original the improvements are derived.

The 'Verses on the unfortunate Lady' have drawn much attention by the illaudable singularity of treating suicide with respect; and they must be allowed to be written in some parts with vigorous animation, and in others with gentle tenderness; nor has Pope produced any poem in which the sense predominates more over the diction. But the tale is not skilfully told; it is not easy to discover the character of either the Lady or her Guardian. History relates that she was about to disparage herself by a marriage with an inferior; Pope praises her for the dignity of ambition, and yet condemns the unkle to detestation for his pride; the ambitious love of a niece may be opposed by the interest, malice, or envy of an unkle, but never by his pride. On such an occasion a poet may be allowed to be obscure, but inconsistency never can be right.

The 'Ode for St. Cecilia's Day' was undertaken at the desire of Steele: in this the author is generally confessed to have miscarried, yet he has miscarried only as compared with Dryden; for he has far outgone other competitors. Dryden's plan is better chosen; history will always take stronger hold of the attention than fable: the passions excited by Dryden are the pleasures and pains of real life, the scene of Pope is laid in imaginary existence; Pope is read with calm acquiescence, Dryden with turbulent delight; Pope hangs upon the ear, and Dryden finds the passes of the mind.

Both the odes want the essential constituent of metrical compositions, the stated recurrence of settled numbers. It may be alleged, that Pindar is said by Horace to have written *numeris lege solutis*: but as no such lax performances have been transmitted to us, the meaning of that expression cannot be fixed; and perhaps the like return might properly be made to a modern Pindarist, as Mr. Cobb received from Bentley, who, when he found his criticisms upon a Greek exercise, which Cobb had presented, refuted one after another by Pindar's authority, cried out at last, *Pindar was a bold fellow, but thou art an impudent one*.

If Pope's ode be particularly inspected, it will be found that the first stanza consists of sounds well chosen indeed, but only sounds.

The second consists of hyperbolical commonplaces, easily to be found, and perhaps without much difficulty to be as well expressed.

In the third, however, there are numbers, images, harmony, and vigour, not unworthy the antagonist of Dryden. Had all been like this—but every part cannot be the best.

The next stanzas place and detain us in the dark and dismal regions of mythology, where neither hope nor fear, neither joy nor sorrow can be found: the poet however

faithfully attends us; we have all that can be performed by elegance of diction, or sweetness of versification; but what can form avail without better matter?

The last stanza recurs again to commonplaces. The conclusion is too evidently modelled by that of Dryden; and it may be remarked that both end with the same fault, the comparison of each is literal on one side, and metaphorical on the other.

Poets do not always express their own thoughts; Pope, with all this labour in the praise of Musick, was ignorant of its principles, and insensible of its effects.

One of his greatest though of his earliest works is the *Essay on Criticism*, which, if he had written nothing else, would have placed him among the first cricks and the first poets, as it exhibits every mode of excellence that can embellish or dignify didactick composition, selection of matter, novelty of arrangement, justness of precept, splendour of illustration, and propriety of digression. I know not whether it be pleasing to consider that he produced this piece at twenty, and never afterwards excelled it: he that delights himself with observing that such powers may be so soon attained, cannot but grieve to think that life was ever after at a stand.

To mention the particular beauties of the Essay would be unprofitably tedious; but I cannot forbear to observe, that the comparison of a student's progress in the sciences with the journey of a traveller in the Alps, is perhaps the best that English poetry can shew. A simile, to be perfect, must both illustrate and ennoble the subject; must shew it to the understanding in a clearer view, and display it to the fancy with greater dignity; but either of these qualities may be sufficient to recommend it. In didactick poetry, of which the great purpose is instruction, a simile may be praised which illustrates, though it does not ennoble; in heroicks, that may be admitted which ennobles, though it does not illustrate. That it may be complete, it is required to exhibit, independently of its references, a pleasing image; for a simile is said to be a short episode. To this antiquity was so attentive, that circumstances were sometimes added, which, having no parallels, served only to fill the imagination, and produced what Perrault ludicrously called *comparisons with a long tail*. In their similes the greatest writers have sometimes failed; the ship-race, compared with the chariot-race, is neither illustrated nor aggrandised; land and water make all the difference: when Apollo, running after Daphne, is likened to a greyhound chasing a hare, there is nothing gained; the ideas of pursuit and flight are too plain to be made plainer, and a god and the daughter of a god are not represented much to their advantage, by a hare and dog. The simile of the Alps has no useless parts, yet affords a striking picture by itself; it makes the foregoing position better understood, and enables it to take faster hold on the attention; it assists the apprehension, and elevates the fancy.

Let me likewise dwell a little on the celebrated paragraph, in which it is directed that *the sound should seem an echo to the sense*; a precept which Pope is allowed to have observed beyond any other English poet.

This notion of representative metre, and the desire of discovering frequent adaptations of the sound to the sense, have produced, in my opinion, many wild conceits and imaginary beauties. All that can furnish this representation are the sounds of the words considered singly, and the time in which they are pronounced. Every language has some words framed to exhibit the noises which they express, as *thump*, *rattle*, *growl*, *hiss*. These, however, are but few, and the poet cannot make them more, nor can they be of any use but when sound is to be mentioned. The time of pronunciation was in the dactylick measures of the learned languages capable of considerable variety; but that variety could be accommodated only to motion or duration, and different degrees of motion were perhaps expressed by verses rapid or slow, without much attention of the writer, when the image had full possession of his fancy; but our language having little flexibility, our verses can differ very little in their cadence. The fancied resemblances, I fear, arise sometimes merely from the ambiguity of words; there is supposed to be some relation between a *soft* line and *soft* couch, or between *hard* syllables and *hard* fortune.

Motion, however, may be in some sort exemplified; and yet it may be suspected that even in such resemblances the mind often governs the ear, and the sounds are estimated by their meaning. One of the most successful attempts has been to describe the labour of Sisyphus:

> With many a weary step, and many a groan,
> Up the high hill he heaves a huge round stone;
> The huge round stone, resulting with a bound,
> Thunders impetuous down, and smoaks along the
> ground.

Who does not perceive the stone to move slowly upward, and roll violently back? But set the same numbers to another sense;

> While many a merry tale, and many a song,
> Cheer'd the rough road, we wish'd the rough road
> long.
> The rough road then, returning in a round,
> Mock'd our impatient steps, for all was fairy ground.

We have now surely lost much of the delay, and much of the rapidity.

But to shew how little the greatest master of numbers can fix the principles of representative harmony, it will be sufficient to remark that the poet, who tells us, that

> When Ajax strives—the words move slow.
> Not so when swift Camilla scours the plain,
> Flies o'er th' unbending corn, and skims along the
> main;

when he had enjoyed for about thirty years the praise of Camilla's lightness of foot, tried another experiment upon *sound* and *time*, and produced this memorable triplet:

> Waller was smooth; but Dryden taught to join
> The varying verse, the full resounding line,
> The long majestick march, and energy divine.

Here are the swiftness of the rapid race, and the march of slow-paced majesty, exhibited by the same poet in the same sequence of syllables, except that the exact prosodist will find the line of *swiftness* by one time longer than that of *tardiness*.

Beauties of this kind are commonly fancied; and when real, are technical and nugatory, not to be rejected, and not to be solicited.

To the praises which have been accumulated on *The Rape of the Lock* by readers of every class, from the critick to the waiting-maid, it is difficult to make any addition. Of that which is universally allowed to be the most attractive of all ludicrous compositions, let it rather be now enquired from what sources the power of pleasing is derived.

Dr. Warburton, who excelled in critical perspicacity, has remarked that the preternatural agents are very happily adapted to the purposes of the poem. The heathen deities can no longer gain attention: we should have turned away from a contest between Venus and Diana. The employment of allegorical persons always excites conviction of its own absurdity; they may produce effects, but cannot conduct actions; when the phantom is put in motion, it dissolves; thus *Discord* may raise

a mutiny, but *Discord* cannot conduct a march, nor besiege a town. Pope brought into view a new race of Beings, with powers and passions proportionate to their operation. The sylphs and gnomes act at the toilet and the tea-table, what more terrifick and more powerful phantoms perform on the stormy ocean, or the field of battle; they give their proper help, and do their proper mischief.

Pope is said, by an objector, not to have been the inventor of this petty nation; a charge which might with more justice have been brought against the author of the *Iliad*, who doubtless adopted the religious system of his country; for what is there but the names of his agents which Pope has not invented? Has he not assigned them characters and operations never heard of before? Has he not, at least, given them their first poetical existence? If this is not sufficient to denominate his work original, nothing original ever can be written.

In this work are exhibited, in a very high degree, the two most engaging powers of an author. New things are made familiar, and familiar things are made new. A race of aerial people, never heard of before, is presented to us in a manner so clear and easy, that the reader seeks for no further information, but immediately mingles with his new acquaintance, adopts their interests, and attends their pursuits, loves a sylph, and detests a gnome.

That familiar things are made new, every paragraph will prove. The subject of the poem is an event below the common incidents of common life; nothing real is introduced that is not seen so often as to be no longer regarded, yet the whole detail of a female-day is here brought before us invested with so much art of decoration, that, though nothing is disguised, every thing is striking, and we feel all the appetite of curiosity for that from which we have a thousand times turned fastidiously away.

The purpose of the Poet is, as he tells us, to laugh at *the little unguarded follies of the female sex*. It is therefore without justice that Dennis charges the *Rape of the Lock* with the want of a moral, and for that reason sets it below the *Lutrin*, which exposes the pride and discord of the clergy. Perhaps neither Pope nor Boileau has made the world much better than he found it; but if they had both succeeded, it were easy to tell who would have deserved most from publick gratitude. The freaks, and humours, and spleen, and vanity of women, as they embroil families in discord, and fill houses with disquiet, do more to obstruct the happiness of life in a year than the ambition of the clergy in many centuries. It has been well observd, that the misery of man proceeds not from any single crush of overwhelming evil, but from small vexations continually repeated.

It is remarked by Dennis likewise, that the machinery is superfluous; that, by all the bustle of preternatural operation, the main event is neither hastened nor retarded. To this charge an efficacious answer is not easily made. The sylphs cannot be said to help or to oppose, and it must be allowed to imply some want of art, that their power has not been sufficiently intermingled with the action. Other parts may likewise be charged with want of connection; the game at *ombre* might be spared, but if the Lady had lost her hair while she was intent upon her cards, it might have been inferred that those who are too fond of play will be in danger of neglecting more important interests. Those perhaps are faults; but what are such faults to so much excellence!

The Epistle of *Eloise to Abelard* is one of the most happy productions of human wit: the subject is so judiciously chosen, that it would be difficult, in turning over the annals of the world, to find another which so many circumstances concur to recommend. We regularly interest ourselves most in the fortune of those who most deserve our notice. Abelard and

Eloise were conspicuous in their days for eminence of merit. The heart naturally loves truth. The adventures and misfortunes of this illustrious pair are known from undisputed history. Their fate does not leave the mind in hopeless dejection; for they both found quiet and consolation in retirement and piety. So new and so affecting is their story, that it supersedes invention, and imagination ranges at full liberty without straggling into scenes of fable.

The story, thus skilfully adopted, has been diligently improved. Pope has left nothing behind him, which seems more the effect of studious perseverance and laborious revisal. Here is particularly observable the *curiosa felicitas*, a fruitful soil, and careful cultivation. Here is no crudeness of sense, nor asperity of language.

The sources from which sentiments, which have so much vigour and efficacy, have been drawn, are shewn to be the mystick writers by the learned author of the *Essay on the Life and Writings of Pope*; a book which teaches how the brow of Criticism may be smoothed, and how she may be enabled, with all her severity, to attract and to delight.

The train of my disquisition has now conducted me to that poetical wonder, the translation of the *Iliad*; a performance which no age or nation can pretend to equal. To the Greeks translation was almost unknown; it was totally unknown to the inhabitants of Greece. They had no recourse to the Barbarians for poetical beauties, but sought for every thing in Homer, where, indeed, there is but little which they might not find.

The Italians have been very diligent translators; but I can hear of no version, unless perhaps Anguillara's Ovid may be excepted, which is read with eagerness. The *Iliad* of Salvini every reader may discover to be punctiliously exact; but it seems to be the work of a linguist skilfully pedantick, and his countrymen, the proper judges of its power to please, reject it with disgust.

Their predecessors the Romans have left some specimens of translation behind them, and that employment must have had some credit in which Tully and Germanicus engaged; but unless we suppose, what is perhaps true, that the plays of Terence were versions of Menander, nothing translated seems ever to have risen to high reputation. The French, in the meridian hour of their learning, were very laudably industrious to enrich their own language with the wisdom of the ancients; but found themselves reduced, by whatever necessity, to turn the Greek and Roman poetry into prose. Whoever could read an author, could translate him. From such rivals little can be feared.

The chief help of Pope in this arduous undertaking was drawn from the versions of Dryden. Virgil had borrowed much of his imagery from Homer, and part of the debt was now paid by his translator. Pope searched the pages of Dryden for happy combinations of heroick diction; but it will not be denied that he added much to what he found. He cultivated our language with so much diligence and art, that he has left in his *Homer* a treasure of poetical elegances to posterity. His version may be said to have tuned the English tongue; for since its appearance no writer, however deficient in other powers, has wanted melody. Such a series of lines so elaborately corrected, and so sweetly modulated, took possession of the publick ear; the vulgar was enamoured of the poem, and the learned wondered at the translation.

But in the most general applause discordant voices will always be heard. It has been objected by some, who wish to be numbered among the sons of learning, that Pope's version of Homer is not Homerical; that it exhibits no resemblance of the original characteristick manner of the Father of Poetry, as it wants his awful simplicity, his artless grandeur, his unaffected majesty. This cannot be totally denied; but it must be remembered that *necessitas quod cogit defendit*; that may be lawfully done which cannot be forborn. Time and place will always enforce regard. In estimating this translation, consideration must be had of the nature of our language, the form of our metre, and, above all, of the change which two thousand years have made in the modes of life and the habits of thought. Virgil wrote in a language of the same general fabrick with that of Homer, in verses of the same measure, and in an age nearer to Homer's time by eighteen hundred years; yet he found, even then, the state of the world so much altered, and the demand for elegance so much increased, that mere nature would be endured no longer; and perhaps, in the multitude of borrowed passages, very few can be shewn which he has not embellished.

There is a time when nations emerging from barbarity, and falling into regular subordination, gain leisure to grow wise, and feel the shame of ignorance and the craving pain of unsatisfied curiosity. To this hunger of the mind plain sense is grateful; that which fills the void removes uneasiness, and to be free from pain for a while is pleasure; but repletion generates fastidiousness; a saturated intellect soon becomes luxurious, and knowledge finds no willing reception till it is recommended by artificial diction. Thus it will be found, in the progress of learning, that in all nations the first writers are simple, and that every age improves in elegance. One refinement always makes way for another, and what was expedient to Virgil was necessary to Pope.

I suppose many readers of the English *Iliad*, when they have been touched with some unexpected beauty of the lighter kind, have tried to enjoy it in the original, where, alas! it was not to be found. Homer doubtless owes to his translator many *Ovidian* graces not exactly suitable to his character; but to have added can be no great crime, if nothing be taken away. Elegance is surely to be desired, if it be not gained at the expence of dignity. A hero would wish to be loved, as well as to be reverenced.

To a thousand cavils one answer is sufficient; the purpose of a writer is to be read, and the criticism which would destroy the power of pleasing must be blown aside. Pope wrote for his own age and his own nation: he knew that it was necessary to colour the images and point the sentiments of his author; he therefore made him graceful, but lost him some of his sublimity.

The copious notes with which the version is accompanied, and by which it is recommended to many readers, though they were undoubtedly written to swell the volumes, ought not to pass without praise: commentaries which attract the reader by the pleasure of perusal have not often appeared; the notes of others are read to clear difficulties, those of Pope to vary entertainment.

It has however been objected, with sufficient reason, that there is in the commentary too much of unseasonable levity and affected gaiety; that too many appeals are made to the Ladies, and the ease which is so carefully preserved is sometimes the ease of a trifler. Every art has its terms, and every kind of instruction its proper style; the gravity of common criticks may be tedious, but is less despicable than childish merriment.

Of the *Odyssey* nothing remains to be observed: the same general praise may be given to both translations, and a particular examination of either would require a large volume. The notes were written by Broome, who endeavoured not unsuccessfully to imitate his master.

Of the *Dunciad* the hint is confessedly taken from Dryden's *Mac Flecknoe*; but the plan is so enlarged and diversified as justly to claim the praise of an original, and affords perhaps the best specimen that has yet appeared of personal satire ludicrously pompous.

That the design was moral, whatever the author might tell either his readers or himself, I am not convinced. The first motive was the desire of revenging the contempt with which Theobald had treated his *Shakespeare*, and regaining the honour which he had lost, by crushing his opponent. Theobald was not of bulk enough to fill a poem, and therefore it was necessary to find other enemies with other names, at whose expence he might divert the publick.

In this design there was petulance and malignity enough; but I cannot think it very criminal. An author places himself uncalled before the tribunal of criticism, and solicits fame at the hazard of disgrace. Dulness or deformity are not culpable in themselves, but may be very justly reproached when they pretend to the honour of wit or the influence of beauty. If bad writers were to pass without reprehension, what should restrain them? *impune diem consumpserit ingens Telephus*; and upon bad writers only will censure have much effect. The satire which brought Theobald and Moore into contempt, dropped impotent from Bentley, like the javelin of Priam.

All truth is valuable, and satirical criticism may be considered as useful when it rectifies error and improves judgement; he that refines the publick taste is a publick benefactor.

The beauties of this poem are well known; its chief fault is the grossness of its images. Pope and Swift had an unnatural delight in ideas physically impure, such as every other tongue utters with unwillingness, and of which every ear shrinks from the mention.

But even this fault, offensive as it is, may be forgiven for the excellence of other passages; such as the formation and dissolution of Moore, the account of the Traveller, the misfortune of the Florist, and the crowded thoughts and stately numbers which dignify the concluding paragraph.

The alterations which have been made in the *Dunciad*, not always for the better, require that it should be published, as in the last collection, with all its variations.

The *Essay on Man* was a work of great labour and long consideration, but certainly not the happiest of Pope's performances. The subject is perhaps not very proper for poetry, and the poet was not sufficiently master of his subject; metaphysical morality was to him a new study, he was proud of his acquisitions, and, supposing himself master of great secrets, was in haste to teach what he had not learned. Thus he tells us, in the first Epistle, that from the nature of the Supreme Being may be deduced an order of beings such as mankind, because Infinite Excellence can do only what is best. He finds out that these beings must be *somewhere* and that *all the question is whether man be in a wrong place*. Surely if, according to the poet's Leibnitian reasoning, we may infer that man ought to be, only because he is, we may allow that his place is the right place, because he has it. Supreme Wisdom is not less infallible in disposing than in creating. But what is meant by *somewhere* and *place*, and *wrong place*, it had been vain to ask Pope, who probably had never asked himself.

Having exalted himself into the chair of wisdom, he tells us much that every man knows, and much that he does not know himself; that we see but little, and that the order of the universe is beyond our comprehension; an opinion not very uncommon; and that there is a chain of subordinate beings *from infinite to nothing*, of which himself and his readers are equally ignorant. But he gives us one comfort, which, without his help, he supposes unattainable, in the position *that though we are fools, yet God is wise*.

This Essay affords an egregious instance of the predominance of genius, the dazzling splendour of imagery, and the seductive powers of eloquence. Never was penury of knowledge and vulgarity of sentiment so happily disguised. The reader feels his mind full, though he learns nothing; and when he meets it in its new array, no longer knows the talk of his mother and his nurse. When these wonder-working sounds sink into sense, and the doctrine of the Essay, disrobed of its ornaments, is left to the powers of its naked excellence, what shall we discover? That we are, in comparison with our Creator, very weak and ignorant; that we do not uphold the chain of existence, and that we could not make one another with more skill than we are made. We may learn yet more; that the arts of human life were copied from the instinctive operations of other animals; that if the world be made for man, it may be said that man was made for geese. To these profound principles of natural knowledge are added some moral instructions equally new; that self-interest, well understood, will produce social concord; that men are mutual gainers by mutual benefits; that evil is sometimes balanced by good; that human advantages are unstable and fallacious, of uncertain duration, and doubtful effect; that our true honour is, not to have a great part, but to act it well: that virtue only is our own; and that happiness is always in our power.

Surely a man of no very comprehensive search may venture to say that he has heard all this before; but it was never till now recommended by such a blaze of embellishment, or such sweetness of melody. The vigorous contraction of some thoughts, the luxuriant amplification of others, the incidental illustrations, and sometimes the dignity, sometimes the softness of the verses, enchain philosophy, suspend criticism, and oppress judgement by overpowering pleasure.

This is true of many paragraphs; yet if I had undertaken to exemplify Pope's felicity of composition before a rigid critick, I should not select the *Essay on Man*; for it contains more lines unsuccessfully laboured, more harshness of diction, more thoughts imperfectly expressed, more levity without elegance, and more heaviness without strength, than will easily be found in all his other works.

The *Characters of Men and Women* are the product of diligent speculation upon human life; much labour has been bestowed upon them, and Pope very seldom laboured in vain. That his excellence may be properly estimated, I recommend a comparison of his *Characters of Women* with Boileau's *Satire*; it will then be seen with how much more perspicacity female nature is investigated, and female excellence selected; and he surely is no mean writer to whom Boileau shall be found inferior. The *Characters of Men*, however, are written with more, if not with deeper, thought, and exhibit many passages exquisitely beautiful. The 'Gem and the Flower' will not easily be equalled. In the women's part are some defects; the character of *Atossa* is not so neatly finished as that of *Clodio*; and some of the female characters may be found perhaps more frequently among men; what is said of *Philomede* was true of *Prior*.

In the Epistles to Lord Bathurst and Lord Burlington, Dr. Warburton has endeavoured to find a train of thought which was never in the writer's head, and, to support his hypothesis, has printed that first which was published last. In one, the most valuable passage is perhaps the elogy on *Good Sense*; and the other the *End of the Duke of Buckingham*.

The Epistle to Arbuthnot, now arbitrarily called the *Prologue to the Satires*, is a performance consisting, as it seems, of many fragments wrought into one design, which by this union of scattered beauties contains more striking paragraphs than could probably have been brought together into an occasional work. As there is no stronger motive to exertion than self-defence, no part has more elegance, spirit, or dignity, than the poet's vindication of his own character. The meanest passage is the satire upon *Sporus*.

Of the two poems which derived their names from the year, and which are called the *Epilogue to the Satires*, it was very justly remarked by Savage, that the second was in the whole more strongly conceived, and more equally supported, but that it had no single passages equal to the contention in the first for the dignity of Vice, and the celebration of the triumph of Corruption.

The *Imitations of Horace* seem to have been written as relaxations of his genius. This employment became his favourite by its facility; the plan was ready to his hand, and nothing was required but to accommodate as he could the sentiments of an old author to recent facts or familiar images; but what is easy is seldom excellent; such imitations cannot give pleasure to common readers. The man of learning may be sometimes surprised and delighted by an unexpected parallel; but the comparison requires knowledge of the original, which will likewise often detect strained applications. Between Roman images and English manners there will be an irreconcilable dissimilitude, and the work will be generally uncouth and party-coloured; neither original nor translated, neither ancient nor modern.

Pope had, in proportions very nicely adjusted to each other, all the qualities that constitute genius. He had *Invention*, by which new trains of events are formed, and new scenes of imagery displayed, as in the *Rape of the Lock*; and by which extrinsick and adventitious embellishments and illustrations are connected with a known subject, as in the *Essay on Criticism*. He had *Imagination*, which strongly impresses on the writer's mind, and enables him to convey to the reader, the various forms of nature, incidents of life, and energies of passion, as in his *Eloisa*, *Windsor Forest*, and the *Ethick Epistles*. He had *Judgement* which selects from life or nature what the present purpose requires, and, by separating the essence of things from its concomitants, often makes the representation more powerful than the reality: and he had colours of language always before him, ready to decorate his matter with every grace of elegant expression, as when he accommodates his diction to the wonderful multiplicity of Homer's sentiments and descriptions.

Poetical expression includes sound as well as meaning; *Musick*, says Dryden, *is inarticulate poetry*; among the excellences of Pope, therefore, must be mentioned the melody of his metre. By perusing the works of Dryden, he discovered the most perfect fabrick of English verse, and habituated himself to that only which he found the best; in consequence of which restraint, his poetry has been censured as too uniformly musical, and as glutting the ear with unvaried sweetness. I suspect this objection to be the cant of those who judge by principles rather than perception: and who would even themselves have less pleasure in his works, if he had tried to relieve attention by studied discords, or affected to break his lines and vary his pauses.

But though he was thus careful of his versification, he did not oppress his powers with superfluous rigour. He seems to have thought with Boileau, that the practice of writing might be refined till the difficulty should overbalance the advantage. The construction of his language is not always strictly grammatical; with those rhymes which prescription had conjoined

he contented himself, without regard to Swift's remonstrances, though there was no striking consonance; nor was he very careful to vary his terminations, or to refuse admission at a small distance to the same rhymes.

To Swift's edict for the exclusion of alexandrines and triplets he paid little regard; he admitted them, but, in the opinion of Fenton, too rarely; he uses them more liberally in his translation than his poems.

He has a few double rhymes; and always, I think, unsuccessfully, except once in the *Rape of the Lock*.

Expletives he very early ejected from his verses; but he now and then admits an epithet rather commodious than important. Each of the first six lines of the *Iliad* might lose two syllables with very little diminution of the meaning; and sometimes, after all his art and labour, one verse seems to be made for the sake of another. In his latter productions the diction is sometimes vitiated by French idioms, with which Bolingbroke had perhaps infected him.

I have been told that the couplet by which he declared his own ear to be most gratified, was this:

Lo, where Maeotis sleeps, and hardly flows
The freezing Tanais through a waste of snows.

But the reason of this preference I cannot discover.

It is remarked by Watts, that there is scarcely a happy combination of words, or a phrase poetically elegant in the English language, which Pope has not inserted into his version of Homer. How he obtained possession of so many beauties of speech, it were desirable to know. That he gleaned from authors, obscure as well as eminent, what he thought brilliant or useful, and preserved it all in a regular collection, is not unlikely. When, in his last years, Hall's *Satires* were shewn him, he wished that he had seen them sooner.

New sentiments and new images others may produce; but to attempt any further improvement of versification will be dangerous. Art and diligence have now done their best, and what shall be added will be the effort of tedious toil and needless curiosity.

After all this, it is surely superfluous to answer the question that has once been asked, Whether Pope was a poet? otherwise than by asking in return, If Pope be not a poet, where is poetry to be found? To circumscribe poetry by a definition will only shew the narrowness of the definer, though a definition which shall exclude Pope will not easily be made. Let us look round upon the present time, and back upon the past; let us enquire to whom the voice of mankind has decreed the wreath of poetry; let their productions be examined, and their claims stated, and the pretensions of Pope will be no more disputed. Had he given the world only his version, the name of poet must have been allowed him: if the writer of the *Iliad* were to class his successors, he would assign a very high place to his translator, without requiring any other evidence of Genius.

WILLIAM HAZLITT
From *Lectures on the English Poets*
1818

The question, whether Pope was a poet, has hardly yet been settled, and is hardly worth settling; for if he was not a great poet, he must have been a great prose-writer, that is, he was a great writer of some sort. He was a man of exquisite faculties, and of the most refined taste; and as he chose verse (the most obvious distinction of poetry) as the vehicle to express his ideas, he has generally passed for a poet, and a good one. If, indeed, by a great poet, we mean one who gives the utmost grandeur to our conceptions of nature, or the utmost force to the passions of the heart, Pope was not in this sense a great poet; for the bent, the characteristic power of his mind, lay the clean contrary way; namely, in representing things as they appear to the indifferent observer, stripped of prejudice and passion, as in his Critical Essays; or in representing them in the most contemptible and insignificant point of view, as in his Satires; or in clothing the little with mock-dignity, as in his poems of Fancy; or in adorning the trivial incidents and familiar relations of life with the utmost elegance of expression, and all the flattering illusions of friendship or self-love, as in his Epistles. He was not then distinguished as a poet of lofty enthusiasm, of strong imagination, with a passionate sense of the beauties of nature, or a deep insight into the workings of the heart; but he was a wit, and a critic, a man of sense, of observation, and the world, with a keen relish for the elegances of art, or of nature when embellished by art, a quick tact for propriety of thought and manners as established by the forms and customs of society, a refined sympathy with the sentiments and habitudes of human life, as he felt them within the little circle of his family and friends. He was, in a word, the poet, not of nature, but of art; and the distinction between the two, as well as I can make it out, is this—The poet of nature is one who, from the elements of beauty, of power, and of passion in his own breast, sympathises with whatever is beautiful, and grand, and impassioned in nature, in its simple majesty, in its immediate appeal to the senses, to the thoughts and hearts of all men; so that the poet of nature, by the truth, and depth, and harmony of his mind, may be said to hold communion with the very soul of nature; to be identified with and to foreknow and to record the feelings of all men at all times and places, as they are liable to the same impressions; and to exert the same power over the minds of his readers, that nature does. He sees things in their eternal beauty, for he sees them as they are; he feels them in their universal interest, for he feels them as they affect the first principles of his and our common nature. Such was Homer, such was Shakspeare, whose works will last as long as nature, because they are a copy of the indestructible forms and everlasting impulses of nature, welling out from the bosom as from a perennial spring, or stamped upon the senses by the hand of their maker. The power of the imagination in them, is the representative power of all nature. It has its centre in the human soul, and makes the circuit of the universe.

Pope was not assuredly a poet of this class, or in the first rank of it. He saw nature only dressed by art; he judged of beauty by fashion; he sought for truth in the opinions of the world; he judged of the feelings of others by his own. The capacious soul of Shakspeare had an intuitive and mighty sympathy with whatever could enter into the heart of man in all possible circumstances: Pope had an exact knowledge of all that he himself loved or hated, wished or wanted. Milton has winged his daring flight from heaven to earth, through Chaos and old Night. Pope's Muse never wandered with safety, but from his library to his grotto, or from his grotto into his library back again. His mind dwelt with greater pleasure on his own garden, than on the garden of Eden; he could describe the faultless whole-length mirror that reflected his own person, better than the smooth surface of the lake that reflects the face of heaven—a piece of cut glass or a pair of paste buckles with more brilliance and effect, than a thousand dew-drops glittering in the sun. He would be more delighted with a patent lamp, than with 'the pale reflex of Cynthia's brow,' that fills the skies with its soft silent lustre, that trembles through the

cottage window, and cheers the watchful mariner on the lonely wave. In short, he was the poet of personality and of polished life. That which was nearest to him, was the greatest; the fashion of the day bore sway in his mind over the immutable laws of nature. He preferred the artificial to the natural in external objects, because he had a stronger fellow-feeling with the self-love of the maker or proprietor of a gewgaw, than admiration of that which was interesting to all mankind. He preferred the artificial to the natural in passion, because the involuntary and uncalculating impulses of the one hurried him away with a force and vehemence with which he could not grapple; while he could trifle with the conventional and superficial modifications of mere sentiment at will, laugh at or admire, put them on or off like a masquerade-dress, make much or little of them, indulge them for a longer or a shorter time, as he pleased; and because while they amused his fancy and exercised his ingenuity, they never once disturbed his vanity, his levity, or indifference. His mind was the antithesis of strength and grandeur; its power was the power of indifference. He had none of the enthusiasm of poetry; he was in poetry what the sceptic is in religion.

It cannot be denied, that his chief excellence lay more in diminishing, than in aggrandizing objects; in checking, not in encouraging our enthusiasm; in sneering at the extravagances of fancy or passion, instead of giving a loose to them; in describing a row of pins and needles, rather than the embattled spears of Greeks and Trojans; in penning a lampoon or a compliment, and in praising Martha Blount.

Shakspeare says,

> In Fortune's ray and brightness
> The herd hath more annoyance by the brize
> Than by the tyger: but when the splitting wind
> Makes flexible the knees of knotted oaks,
> And flies fled under shade, why then
> The thing of courage,
> As roused with rage, with rage doth sympathise;
> And with an accent tuned in the self-same key,
> Replies to chiding Fortune.

There is none of this rough work in Pope. His Muse was on a peace-establishment, and grew somewhat effeminate by long ease and indulgence. He lived in the smiles of fortune, and basked in the favour of the great. In his smooth and polished verse we meet with no prodigies of nature, but with miracles of wit; the thunders of his pen are whispered flatteries; its forked lightnings pointed sarcasms; for 'the gnarled oak,' he gives us 'the soft myrtle': for rocks, and seas, and mountains, artificial grass-plats, gravel-walks, and tinkling rills; for earthquakes and tempests, the breaking of a flower-pot, or the fall of a china jar; for the tug and war of the elements, or the deadly strife of the passions, we have

> Calm contemplation and poetic ease.

Yet within this retired and narrow circle how much, and that how exquisite, was contained! What discrimination, what wit, what delicacy, what fancy, what lurking spleen, what elegance of thought, what pampered refinement of sentiment! It is like looking at the world through a microscope, where every thing assumes a new character and a new consequence, where things are seen in their minutest circumstances and slightest shades of difference; where the little becomes gigantic, the deformed beautiful, and the beautiful deformed. The wrong end of the magnifier is, to be sure, held to every thing, but still the exhibition is highly curious, and we know not whether to be most pleased or surprised. Such, at least, is the best account I am able to give of this extraordinary man, without doing injustice to him or others. It is time to refer to particular instances in his works.—The *Rape of the Lock* is the best or most ingenious of these. It is the most exquisite specimen of *fillagree* work ever invented. It is admirable in proportion as it is made of nothing.

> More subtle web Arachne cannot spin,
> Nor the fine nets, which oft we woven see
> Of scorched dew, do not in th' air more lightly flee.

It is made of gauze and silver spangles. The most glittering appearance is given to every thing, to paste, pomatum, billet-doux, and patches. Airs, languid airs, breathe around;—the atmosphere is perfumed with affectation. A toilette is described with the solemnity of an altar raised to the Goddess of vanity, and the history of a silver bodkin is given with all the pomp of heraldry. No pains are spared, no profusion of ornament, no splendour of poetic diction, to set off the meanest things. The balance between the concealed irony and the assumed gravity, is as nicely trimmed as the balance of power in Europe. The little is made great, and the great little. You hardly know whether to laugh or weep. It is the triumph of insignificance, the apotheosis of foppery and folly. It is the perfection of the mock-heroic! ⟨. . .⟩

The *Rape of the Lock* is a double-refined essence of wit and fancy, as the *Essay on Criticism* is of wit and sense. The quantity of thought and observation in this work, for so young a man as Pope was when he wrote it, is wonderful: unless we adopt the supposition, that most men of genius spend the rest of their lives in teaching others what they themselves have learned under twenty. The conciseness and felicity of the expression are equally remarkable. Thus in reasoning on the variety of men's opinion, he says—

> 'Tis with our judgments, as our watches; none
> Go just alike, yet each believes his own.

Nothing can be more original and happy than the general remarks and illustrations in the *Essay*: the critical rules laid down are too much those of a school, and of a confined one. There is one passage in the *Essay on Criticism* in which the author speaks with that eloquent enthusiasm of the fame of ancient writers, which those will always feel who have themselves any hope or chance of immortality. I have quoted the passage elsewhere, but I will repeat it here.

> Still green with bays each ancient altar stands,
> Above the reach of sacrilegious hands;
> Secure from flames, from envy's fiercer rage,
> Destructive war, and all-involving age.
> Hail, bards triumphant, born in happier days,
> Immortal heirs of universal praise!
> Whose honours with increase of ages grow,
> As streams roll down, enlarging as they flow.

These lines come with double force and beauty on the reader, as they were dictated by the writer's despair of ever attaining that lasting glory which he celebrates with such disinterested enthusiasm in others, from the lateness of the age in which he lived, and from his writing in a tongue, not understood by other nations, and that grows obsolete and unintelligible to ourselves at the end of every second century. But he needed not have thus antedated his own poetical doom—the loss and entire oblivion of that which can never die. If he had known, he might have boasted that 'his little bark' wafted down the stream of time,

> With *theirs* should sail,
> Pursue the triumph and partake the gale—

if those who know how to set a due value on the blessing, were

not the last to decide confidently on their own pretensions to it.

There is a cant in the present day about genius, as every thing in poetry: there was a cant in the time of Pope about sense, as performing all sorts of wonders. It was a kind of watchword, the shibboleth of a critical party of the day. As a proof of the exclusive attention which it occupied in their minds, it is remarkable that in the Essay on Criticism (not a very long poem) there are no less than half a score successive couplets rhyming to the word *sense*. This appears almost incredible without giving the instances, and no less so when they are given. ⟨. . .⟩

I have mentioned this the more for the sake of those critics who are bigotted idolisers of our author, chiefly on the score of his correctness. These persons seem to be of opinion that 'there is but one perfect writer, even Pope.' This is, however, a mistake: his excellence is by no means faultlessness. If he had no great faults, he is full of little errors. His grammatical construction is often lame and imperfect. In the *Abelard and Eloise*, he says—

> There died the best of passions, Love and Fame.

This is not a legitimate ellipsis. Fame is not a passion, though love is: but his ear was evidently confused by the meeting of the sounds 'love and fame,' as if they of themselves immediately implied 'love, and love of fame.' Pope's rhymes are constantly defective, being rhymes to the eye instead of the ear; and this to a greater degree, not only than in later, but than in preceding writers. The praise of his versification must be confined to its uniform smoothness and harmony. In the translation of the *Iliad*, which has been considered as his masterpiece in style and execution, he continually changes the tenses in the same sentence for the purposes of the rhyme, which shews either a want of technical resources, or great inattention to punctilious exactness. But to have done with this.

The epistle of *Eloise to Abelard* is the only exception I can think of, to the general spirit of the foregoing remarks; and I should be disingenuous not to acknowledge that it is an exception. The foundation is in the letters themselves of Abelard and Eloise, which are quite as impressive, but still in a different way. It is fine as a poem: it is finer as a piece of high-wrought eloquence. No woman could be supposed to write a better love-letter in verse. Besides the richness of the historical materials, the high *gusto* of the original sentiments which Pope had to work upon, there were perhaps circumstances in his own situation which made him enter into the subject with even more than a poet's feeling. The tears shed are drops gushing from the heart: the words are burning sighs breathed from the soul of love. Perhaps the poem to which it bears the greatest similarity in our language, is Dryden's *Tancred and Sigismunda*, taken from Boccaccio. Pope's Eloise will bear this comparison; and after such a test, with Boccaccio for the original author, and Dryden for the translator, it need shrink from no other. There is something exceedingly tender and beautiful in the sound of the concluding lines:

> If ever chance two wandering lovers brings
> To Paraclete's white walls and silver springs, &c.

The *Essay on Man* is not Pope's best work. It is a theory which Bolingbroke is supposed to have given him, and which he expanded into verse. But 'he spins the thread of his verbosity finer than the staple of his argument.' All that he says, 'the very words, and to the self-same tune,' would prove just as well that whatever is, is *wrong*, as that whatever is, is *right*. The *Dunciad* has splendid passages, but in general it is dull, heavy, and mechanical. The sarcasm already quoted on Settle, the Lord Mayor's poet, (for at that time there was a city as well as a court poet)

> Now night descending, the proud scene is o'er,
> But lives in Settle's numbers one day more—

is the finest inversion of immortality conceivable. It is even better than his serious apostrophe to the great heirs of glory, the triumphant bards of antiquity! ⟨. . .⟩

His Satires are not in general so good as his Epistles. His enmity is effeminate and petulant from a sense of weakness, as his friendship was tender from a sense of gratitude. I do not like, for instance, his character of Chartres, or his characters of women. His delicacy often borders upon sickliness; his fastidiousness makes others fastidious. But his compliments are divine; they are equal in value to a house or an estate. Take the following. In addressing Lord Mansfield, he speaks of the grave as a scene,

> Where Murray, long enough his country's pride,
> Shall be no more than Tully, or than Hyde.

To Bolingbroke he says—

> Why rail they then if but one wreath of mine,
> Oh all-accomplish'd St. John, deck thy shrine?

Again, he has bequeathed this praise to Lord Cornbury—

> Despise low thoughts, low gains:
> Disdain whatever Cornbury disdains;
> Be virtuous and be happy for your pains.

One would think (though there is no knowing) that a descendant of this nobleman, if there be such a person living, could hardly be guilty of a mean or paltry action.

The finest piece of personal satire in Pope (perhaps in the world) is his character of Addison; and this, it may be observed, is of a mixed kind, made up of his respect for the man, and a cutting sense of his failings. The other finest one is that of Buckingham, and the best part of that is the pleasurable.

> Alas! how changed from him,
> That life of pleasure and that soul of whim:
> Gallant and gay, in Cliveden's proud alcove,
> The bower of wanton Shrewsbury and love!

⟨. . .⟩ Pope's letters and prose writings neither take away from, nor add to his poetical reputation. There is, occasionally, a littleness of manner, and an unnecessary degree of caution. He appears anxious to say a good thing in every word, as well as every sentence. They, however, give a very favourable idea of his moral character in all respects; and his letters to Atterbury, in his disgrace and exile, do equal honour to both. If I had to choose, there are one or two persons, and but one or two, that I should like to have been better than Pope!

SIR LESLIE STEPHEN
"Pope as a Moralist" (1873)
Hours in a Library (1874–79)
1904, Volume 1, pp. 128–85

The vitality of Pope's writings, or at least of certain fragments of them, is remarkable. Few reputations have been exposed to such perils at the hands of open enemies or of imprudent friends. In his lifetime "the wasp of Twickenham" could sting through a sevenfold covering of pride or stupidity. Lady Mary and Lord Hervey writhed and retaliated with little more success than the poor denizens of Grub Street. But it is more remarkable that Pope seems to be stinging well into the

second century after his death. His writings resemble those fireworks which, after they have fallen to the ground and been apparently quenched, suddenly break out again into spluttering explosions. The waters of a literary revolution have passed over him without putting him out. Though much of his poetry has ceased to interest us, so many of his brilliant couplets still survive that probably no dead writer, with the solitary exception of Shakespeare, is more frequently quoted at the present day. It is in vain that he is abused, ridiculed, and often declared to be no poet at all. The school of Wordsworth regarded him as the embodiment of the corrupting influence in English poetry; and it is only of late that we are beginning to aim at a more catholic spirit in literary criticism. It is not our business simply to revile or to extol the ideals of our ancestors, but to try to understand them. The passionate partisanship of militant schools is pardonable in the apostles of a new creed, but when the struggle is over we must aim at saner judgments. Byron was impelled by motives other than the purely judicial when he declared Pope to be the "great moral poet of all times, of all climes, of all feelings, and of all stages of existence;" and it is not less characteristic that Byron was at the same time helping to dethrone the idol before which he prostrated himself. A critic whose judgments, however wayward, are always keen and original, has more recently spoken of Pope in terms which recall Byron's enthusiasm. "Pope," says Mr. Ruskin, in one of his Oxford lectures, "is the most perfect representative we have since Chaucer of the true English mind;" and he adds that his hearers will find, as they study Pope, that he has expressed for them,

> in the strictest language, and within the briefest limits, every law of art, of criticism, of economy, of policy, and finally of a benevolence, humble, rational, and resigned, contented with its allotted share of life, and trusting the problem of its salvation to Him in whose hand lies that of the universe.

These remarks are added by way of illustrating the relation of art to morals, and enforcing the great principle that a noble style can only proceed from a sincere heart. "You can only learn to speak as these men spake by learning what these men were." When we ask impartially what Pope was, we may possibly be inclined to doubt the complete soundness of the eulogy upon his teaching. Meanwhile, however, Byron and Mr. Ruskin agree in holding up Pope as an instance, almost as the typical instance, of that kind of poetry which is directly intended to enforce a lofty morality. Though we can never take either Byron or Mr. Ruskin as the representative of sweet reasonableness, their admiration is some proof that Pope possessed great merits as a poetical interpreter of morals. Without venturing into the wider ocean of poetical criticism, I will endeavour to consider what was the specific element in Pope's poetry which explains, if it does not justify, this enthusiastic praise.

I shall venture to assume, indeed, that Pope was a genuine poet. Perhaps, as M. Taine thinks, it is a proof of our British grossness that we still admire the *Rape of the Lock*, yet I must agree with most critics that it is admirable after its kind. Pope's sylphs, as Mr. Elwin says, are legitimate descendants from Shakespeare's fairies. True, they have entered into rather humiliating bondage. Shakespeare's Ariel has to fetch the midnight dew from the still-vexed Bermoothes; he delights to fly—

> To swim, to dive into the fire, to ride
> On the curl'd clouds—

whereas the "humbler province" of Pope's Ariel is "to tend the fair"—

To steal from rainbows, ere they drop in showers,
A brighter wash; to curl their waving hairs,
Assist their blushes, and inspire their airs,
Nay, oft in dreams invention we bestow
To change a flounce or add a furbelow.

Prospero, threatening Ariel for murmuring, says "I will

rend an oak
And peg thee in his knotty entrails, until
Thou has howled away twelve winters.

The fate threatened to a disobedient sprite in the later poem is that he shall

Be stuff'd in vials, or transfixed with pins,
Or plunged in lakes of bitter washes lie,
Or wedged whole ages in a bodkin's eye.

Pope's muse—one may use the old-fashioned word in such a connection—had left the free forest for Will's Coffee-house, and haunted ladies' boudoirs instead of the brakes of the enchanted island. Her wings were clogged with "gums and pomatums," and her "thin essence" had shrunk "like a rivel'd flower." But a delicate fancy is a delicate fancy still, even when employed about the paraphernalia of modern life; a truth which Byron maintained, though not in an unimpeachable form, in his controversy with Bowles. We sometimes talk as if our ancestors were nothing but hoops and wigs; and forget that they had a fair allowance of human passions. And consequently we are very apt to make a false estimate of the precise nature of that change which fairly entitles us to call Pope's age prosaic. In showering down our epithets of artificial, sceptical, and utilitarian, we not seldom forget what kind of figure we are ourselves likely to make in the eyes of our own descendants.

Whatever be the position rightly to be assigned to Pope in the British Walhalla, his own theory has been unmistakably expressed. He boasts

That not in fancy's maze he wandered long,
But stooped to truth and moralised his song.

His theory is compressed into one of the innumerable aphorisms which have to some degree lost their original sharpness of definition, because they have passed, as current coinage, through so many hands.

The proper study of mankind is man.

The saying is in form nearly identical with Goethe's remark that man is properly the only object which interests man. The two poets, indeed, understood the doctrine in a very different way. Pope's interpretation strikes the present generation as narrow and mechanical. He would place such limitations upon the sphere of human interest as to exclude, perhaps, the greatest part of what we generally mean by poetry. How much, for example, would have to be suppressed if we sympathised with Pope's condemnation of the works in which

Pure description holds the place of sense.

Nearly all the works of such poets as Thomson and Cowper would disappears, Wordsworth's pages would show fearful gaps, and Keats would be in risk of summary suppression. We may doubt whether much would be left of Spenser, from whom both Keats and Pope, like so many other of our poets, drew inspiration in their youth. Fairy-land would be deserted, and the poet condemned to working upon ordinary commonplaces in broad daylight. The principle which Pope proclaimed is susceptible of the inverse application. Poetry, as it proves, may rightly concern itself with inanimate nature, with pure description, or with the presentation of lovely symbols not definitely identified with any cut-and-dried saws of moral wisdom; because there is no part of the visible

universe to which we have not some relation, and the most ethereal dreams that ever visited a youthful poet "on summer eve by haunted stream" are in some sense reflections of the passions and interests that surround our daily life. Pope, however, as the man more fitted than any other fully to interpret the mind of his own age, inevitably gives a different construction to a very sound maxim. He rightly assumes that man is his proper study; but then by man he means not the genus, but a narrow species of the human being. "Man" means Bolingbroke, and Walpole, and Swift, and Curll, and Theobald; it does not mean man as the product of a long series of generations and part of the great universe of inextricably involved forces. He cannot understand the man of distant ages; Homer is to him not the spontaneous voice of the heroic age, but a clever artist whose gods and heroes are consciously-constructed parts of an artificial "machinery." Nature has, for him, ceased to be inhabited by sylphs and fairies, except to amuse the fancies of fine ladies and gentlemen, and has not yet received a new interest from the fairy tales of science. The old idea of chivalry merely suggests the sneers of Cervantes, or even the buffoonery of Butler's wit, and has not undergone restoration at the hands of modern romanticists. Politics are not associated in his mind with any great social upheaval, but with a series of petty squabbles for places and pensions, in which bribery is the great moving force. What he means by religion is generally not so much the existence of a divine element in the world as a series of bare metaphysical demonstrations too frigid to produce enthusiasm or to stimulate the imagination. And, therefore, he inevitably interests himself chiefly in what is certainly a perennial source of interest—the passions and thoughts of the men and women immediately related to himself; and it may be remarked, in passing, that if this narrows the range of Pope's poetry, the error is not so vital as a modern delusion of the opposite kind. Because poetry should not be brought into too close a contact with the prose of daily life, we sometimes seem to think that it must have no relation to daily life at all, and consequently convert it into a mere luxurious dreaming, where the beautiful very speedily degenerates into the pretty or the picturesque. Because poetry need not be always a point-blank fire of moral platitudes, we occasionally declare that there is no connection at all between poetry and morality, and that all art is good which is for the moment agreeable. Such theories must end in reducing all poetry and art to be at best more or less elegant trifling for the amusement of the indolent; and to those who uphold them Pope's example may be of some use. If he went too far in the direction of identifying poetry with preaching, he was not wrong in assuming that poetry should involve preaching, though by an indirect method. Morality and art are not independent, though not identical. Both, as Mr. Ruskin urges in the passage just quoted, are only admirable when the expression of healthful and noble natures. But, without discussing that thorny problem and certainly without committing myself to an approval of Mr. Ruskin's solution, I am content to look at it for the time from Pope's standpoint.

Taking Pope's view of his poetical office, there remain considerable difficulties in estimating the value of the lesson which he taught with so much energy. The difficulties result both from that element which was common to his contemporaries and from that which was supplied by Pope's own idiosyncrasies. The commonplaces in which Pope takes such infinite delight have become very stale for us. Assuming their perfect sincerity, we cannot understand how anybody should have thought of enforcing them with such amazing emphasis. We constantly feel a shock like that which surprises the reader of Young's *Night Thoughts* when he finds it asserted, in all the pomp of blank verse that

> Procrastination is the thief of time.

The maxim has rightly been consigned to copybooks. And a great deal of Pope's moralising is of the same order. We do not want denunciations of misers. Nobody at the present day keeps gold in an old stocking. When we read the observation,

> 'Tis strange the miser should his cares employ
> To gain the riches he can ne'er enjoy,

we can only reply that we have heard something like it before. In fact, we cannot place ourselves in the position of men at the time when modern society was first definitely emerging from the feudal state, and everybody was sufficiently employed in gossiping about his neighbours. We are perplexed by the extreme interest with which they dwell upon the little series of obvious remarks which have been worked to death by later writers. Pope, for example, is still wondering over the first appearance of one of the most familiar of modern inventions. He exclaims,

> Blest paper credit! last and best supply!
> That lends corruption lighter wings to fly!

He points out, with an odd superfluity of illustration, that bank-notes enable a man to be bribed much more easily than of old. There is no danger, he says, that a patriot will be exposed by a guinea dropping out of his pocket at the end of an interview with the minister; and he shows how awkward it would be if a statesman had to take his bribes in kind, and his servants should proclaim,

> Sir, Spain has sent a thousand jars of oil;
> Huge bales of British cloth blockade the door;
> A hundred oxen at your levees roar.

This, however, was natural enough when the South Sea scheme was for the first time illustrating the powers and the dangers of extended credit. To us, who are beginning to fit our experience of commercial panics into a scientific theory, the wonder expressed by Pope sounds like the exclamations of a savage over a Tower musket. And in the sphere of morals it is pretty much the same. All those reflections about the little obvious vanities and frivolities of social life which supplied two generations of British essayists, from the *Tatler* to the *Lounger*, with an inexhaustible fund of mild satire, have lost their freshness. Our own modes of life have become so complex by comparison, that we pass over these mere elements to plunge at once into more refined speculations. A modern essayist starts where Addison or Johnson left off. He assumes that his readers know that procrastination is an evil, and tries to gain a little piquancy by paradoxically pointing out the objections to punctuality. Character, of course, becomes more complex, and requires more delicate modes of analysis. Compare, for example, the most delicate of Pope's delineations with one of Mr. Browning's elaborate psychological studies. Remember how many pages of acute observations are required to set forth Bishop Blougram's peculiar phase of worldliness, and then turn to Pope's descriptions of Addison, or Wharton, or Buckingham. Each of those descriptions is, indeed, a masterpiece in its way; the language is inimitably clear and pointed; but the leading thought is obvious, and leads to no intricate problems. Addison—assuming Pope's Addison to be the real Addison—might be cold-blooded and jealous; but he had not worked out that elaborate machinery for imposing upon himself and others which is required in a more critical age. He wore a mask, but a mask of simple construction; not one of those complex contrivances of modern invention which are so like the real skin that it requires the acuteness and patience of a scientific

observer to detect the difference and point out the nature of the deception. The moral difference between such an Addison and a Blougram is as great as the difference between an old stagecoach and a steam-engine, or between the bulls and bears which first received the name in Law's time and their descendants on the New York Stock Exchange.

If, therefore, Pope gains something in clearness and brilliancy by the comparative simplicity of his art, he loses by the extreme obviousness of its results. We cannot give him credit for being really moved by such platitudes. We have the same feeling as when a modern preacher employs twenty minutes in proving that it is wrong to worship idols of wood and stone. But, unfortunately, there is a reason more peculiar to Pope which damps our sympathy still more decidedly. Recent investigations have strengthened those suspicions of his honesty which were common even amongst his contemporaries. Mr. Elwin was (very excusably) disgusted by the revelations of his hero's baseness, till his indignation became a painful burden to himself and his readers. Speaking bluntly, indeed, we admit that lying is a vice, and that Pope was in a small way one of the most consummate liars that ever lived. He speaks himself of "equivocating pretty genteelly" in regard to one of his peccadilloes. Pope's equivocation is to the equivocation of ordinary men what a tropical fern is to the stunted representatives of the same species in England. It grows until the fowls of the air can rest on its branches. His mendacity in short amounts to a monomania. That a man with intensely irritable nerves, and so fragile in constitution that his life might, without exaggeration, be called a "long disease," should defend himself by the natural weapons of the weak, equivocation and subterfuge, when exposed to the brutal horse-play common in that day, is indeed not surprising. But Pope's delight in artifice was something unparalleled. He could hardly drink tea without "a stratagem," or, as Lady Bolingbroke put it, was a politician about cabbages and turnips; and certainly he did not despise the arts known to politicians on a larger stage. Never, surely, did all the arts of the most skilful diplomacy give rise to a series of intrigues more complex than those which attended the publication of the *P. T. Letters*. An ordinary man says that he is obliged to publish by request of friends, and we regard the transparent device as, at most, a venial offence. But in Pope's hands this simple trick becomes a complex apparatus of plots within plots, which have only been unravelled by the persevering labours of most industrious literary detectives. The whole story was given for the first time at full length in Mr. Elwin's edition of Pope, and the revelation borders upon the incredible. How Pope became for a time two men; how in one character he worked upon the wretched Curll through mysterious emissaries until the piratical bookseller undertook to publish the letters already privately printed by Pope himself; how Pope in his other character protested vehemently against the publication and disavowed all complicity in the preparations; how he set the House of Lords in motion to suppress the edition; and how, meanwhile, he took ingenious precautions to frustrate the interference which he provoked; how in the course of these manœuvres his genteel equivocation swelled into lying on the most stupendous scale—all this story, with its various ins and outs, may be now read by those who have the patience. The problem may be suggested to casuists how far the iniquity of a lie should be measured by its immediate purpose, or how far it is aggravated by the enormous mass of superincumbent falsehoods which it inevitably brings in its train. We cannot condemn very seriously the affected coyness which tries to conceal a desire for publication under an apparent yielding to extortion; but we must certainly admit that the stomach of any other human being of whom a record has been preserved would have revolted at the thought of wading through such a waste of falsification to secure so paltry an end. Moreover, this is only one instance, and by no means the worst instance, of Pope's regular practice in such matters. Almost every publication of his life was attended with some sort of mystification passing into downright falsehood, and, at times, injurious to the character of his dearest friends. We have to add to this all the cases in which Pope attacked his enemies under feigned names and then disavowed his attacks; the malicious misstatements which he tried to propagate in regard to Addison; and we feel it a positive relief when we are able to acquit him, partially at least, of the worst charge of extorting 1,000*l.* from the Duchess of Marlborough for the suppression of a satirical passage.

Whatever minor pleas may be put forward in extenuation, it certainly cannot be denied that Pope's practical morality was defective. Genteel equivocation is not one of the Christian graces; and a gentleman convicted at the present day of practices comparable to those in which Pope indulged so freely might find it expedient to take his name off the books of any respectable club. Now, if we take literally Mr. Ruskin's doctrine that a noble morality must proceed from a noble nature, the inference from Pope's life to his writings is not satisfactory.

We may, indeed, take it for demonstrated that Pope was not one of those men who can be seen from all points of view. There are corners of his nature which will not bear examination. We cannot compare him with such men as Milton, or Cowper, or Wordsworth, whose lives are the noblest commentary on their works. Rather he is one of the numerous class in whom the excessive sensibility of genius has generated very serious disease. In more modern days we may fancy that his views would have taken a different turn, and that Pope would have belonged to the Satanic school of writers, and instead of lying enormously, have found relief for his irritated nerves in reviling all that is praised by ordinary mankind. But we must hesitate before passing from his acknowledged vices to a summary condemnation of the whole man. Human nature (the remark is not strictly original) is often inconsistent; and, side by side with degrading tendencies, there sometimes lie not only keen powers of intellect, but a genuine love for goodness, benevolence, and even for honesty. Pope is one of those strangely mixed characters which can only be fully delineated by a masterly hand, and Mr. Courthope in the life which concludes the definitive edition of the works has at last performed the task with admirable skill and without too much shrouding his hero's weaknesses. Meanwhile our pleasure in reading him is much counterbalanced by the suspicion that those pointed aphorisms which he turns out in so admirably polished a form may come only from the lips outwards. Pope, it must be remembered, is essentially a parasitical writer. He was a systematic appropriator—I do not say plagiarist, for the practice seems to be generally commendable—of other men's thoughts. His brilliant gems have often been found in some obscure writer, and have become valuable by the patient care with which he has polished and mounted them. We doubt their perfect sincerity because, when he is speaking in his own person, we can often prove him to be at best under a curious delusion. Take, for example, the *Epistle to Dr. Arbuthnot*, which is his most perfect work. Some of the boasts in it are apparently quite justified by the facts. But what are we to say to such a passage as this?—

I was not born for courts or great affairs;
I pay my debts, believe, and say my prayers;

Can sleep without a poem in my head,
Nor know if Dennis be alive or dead.

Admitting his independence, and not inquiring too closely into his prayers, can we forget that the gentleman who could sleep without a poem in his head called up a servant four times in one night of "the dreadful winter of Forty" to supply him with paper, lest he should lose a thought? Or what is the value of a professed indifference to Dennis from the man distinguished beyond all other writers for the bitterness of his resentment against all small critics; who disfigured his best poems by his petty vengeance for old attacks; and who could not refrain from sneering at poor Dennis, even in the Prologue which he condescended to write for the benefit of his dying antagonist? Or, again, one can hardly help smiling at his praises of his own hospitality. The dinner which he promises to his friend is to conclude with—

Cheerful healths (your mistress shall have place),
And, what's more rare, a poet shall say grace.

The provision made for the "cheerful healths," as Johnson lets us know, consisted of the remnant of a pint of wine, from which Pope had taken a couple of glasses, divided amongst two guests. There was evidently no danger of excessive conviviality. And then a grace in which Bolingbroke joined could not have been a very impressive ceremony.

Thus, we are always pursued, in reading Pope, by disagreeable misgivings. We don't know what comes from the heart, and what from the lips: when the real man is speaking, and when we are only listening to old commonplaces skilfully vamped. There is always, if we please, a bad interpretation to be placed upon his finest sentiments. His indignation against the vicious is confused with his hatred of personal enemies; he protests most loudly that he is honest when he is "equivocating most genteelly;" his independence may be called selfishness or avarice; his toleration simply indifference; and even his affection for his friends a decorous fiction, which will never lead him to the slightest sacrifice of his own vanity or comfort. A critic of the highest order is provided with an Ithuriel spear, which discriminates the sham sentiments from the true. As a banker's clerk can tell a bad coin by its ring on the counter, without need of a testing apparatus, the true critic can instinctively estimate the amount of bullion in Pope's epigrammatic tinsel. But criticism of this kind, as Pope truly says, is as rare as poetical genius. Humbler writers must be content to take their weights and measures, or, in other words, to test their first impressions, by such external evidence as is available. They must proceed cautiously in these delicate matters, and instead of leaping to the truth by a rapid intuition, patiently enquire what light is thrown upon Pope's sincerity by the recorded events of his life, and a careful cross-examination of the various witnesses to his character. They must, indeed, keep in mind Mr. Ruskin's excellent canon—that good fruit, even in moralising, can only be borne by a good tree. Where Pope has succeeded in casting into enduring form some valuable moral sentiment, we may therefore give him credit for having at least felt it sincerely. If he did not always act upon it, the weakness is not peculiar to Pope. Time, indeed, has partly done the work for us. In Pope, more than in almost any other writer, the grain has sifted itself from the chaff. The jewels have remained after the flimsy embroidery in which they were fixed has fallen into decay. Such a result was natural from his mode of composition. He caught at some inspiration of the moment; he cast it roughly into form; brooded over it; retouched it again and again; and when he had brought it to the very highest polish of which his art was capable, placed it in a pigeon-hole to be fitted, when the opportunity offered, into an appropriate corner of his mosaic work. We can see him at work, for example, in the passage about Addison and the celebrated concluding couplet. The epigrams in which his poetry abounds have obviously been composed in the same fashion, for that "masterpiece of man," as South is made to call it in the *Dunciad*, is only produced in perfection when the labour which would have made an ode has been concentrated upon a couple of lines. There is a celebrated recipe for dressing a lark, if we remember rightly, in which the lark is placed inside a snipe, and the snipe in a woodcock, and so on till you come to a turkey, or if procurable, to an ostrich; then, the mass having been properly stewed, the superincumbent envelopes are all thrown away, and the essences of the whole are supposed to be embodied in the original nucleus. So the perfect epigram, at which Pope is constantly aiming, should be the quintessence of a whole volume of reflection. Such literary cookery, however, implies not only labour, but an unwearied vividness of thought and feeling. The poet must put his soul into the work as well as his artistic power. Thus, if we may take Pope's most vigorous expressions as an indication of his strongest convictions, and check their conclusions by his personal history and by the general tendency of his writings, we might succeed in putting together something like a satisfactory statement of the moral system which he expressed forcibly because he believed in it sincerely.

Without following the proofs in detail, let us endeavour to give some statement of the result. What, in fact, did Pope learn by his study of man, such as it was? What does he tell us about the character of human beings and their position in the universe which is either original or marked by the freshness of independent thought? Perhaps the most characteristic vein of reflection is that which is embodied in the *Dunciad*. There, at least, we have Pope speaking energetically and sincerely. He really detests, abjures, and abominates as impious and heretical, without a trace of mental reservation, the worship of the great goddess Dulness. The *Dunciad* does not show the quality in which Pope most excels, that which makes his best satires resemble the quintessence of the most brilliant thought of his most brilliant contemporaries. But it has more energy and continuity than most of his other poetry. The *Dunciad* often flows in a continuous stream of eloquence, instead of dribbling out in little jets of epigram. If there are fewer points, there are more frequent gushes of sustained rhetoric. Even when Pope condescends—and he condescends much too often—to pelt his antagonist with mere filth, he does it with a touch of boisterous vigour. He laughs out. He catches something from his patron Swift when he

Laughs and shakes in Rabelais's easy chair.

His lungs seem to be fuller and his voice to lose for the time its tricks of mincing affectation. Here, indeed, there can be no question of insincerity. Pope's scorn of folly is to be condemned only so far as it was connected with too bitter a hatred of fools. He has suffered, as Swift foretold, by the insignificance of the enemies against whom he rages with superfluous vehemence. But for Pope, no one in this generation would have heard of Arnall, and Moore, and Breval, and Bezaleel Morris, and fifty more ephemeral denizens of Grub Street. The fault is, indeed, inherent in the plan. It is in some degree creditable to Pope that his satire was on the whole justified, so far as it could be justified, by the correctness of his judgment. The only great man whom he has seriously assaulted is Bentley; and to Pope, Bentley was of necessity not the greatest of classical critics, but the tasteless mutilator of Milton, and, as we must perhaps add, the object

of the hatred of Pope's particular friends, Atterbury and Warburton. The misfortune is that the more just his satire, the more perishable is its interest; and if we regard the *Dunciad* simply as an assault upon the vermin who then infested literature, we must consider him as a man who should use a steamhammer to crack a flea. Unluckily for ourselves, however, it cannot be admitted so easily that Curll and Dennis and the rest had a merely temporary interest. Regarded as types of literary nuisances—and Pope does not condescend in his poetry, though the want is partly supplied in the notes, to indulge in much personal detail—they may be said by cynics to have a more enduring vitality. Of course there is at the present day no such bookseller as Curll, living by piratical invasions of established rights, and pandering to the worst passions of ignorant readers; no writer who could be fitly called, like Concanen

A cold, long-winded native of the deep,

and fitly sentenced to dive where Fleet Ditch

Rolls the large tribute of dead dogs to Thames;

and most certainly we must deny the present applicability of the note upon "Magazines" compiled by Pope, or rather by Warburton, for the episcopal bludgeon is perceptible in the prose description. They are not at present

the eruption of every miserable scribbler, the scum of every dirty newspaper, or fragments of fragments picked up from every dirty dunghill . . . equally the disgrace of human wit, morality, decency, and common sense.

But if the translator of the *Dunciad* into modern phraseology would have some difficulty in finding a head for every cap, there are perhaps some satirical stings which have not quite lost their point. The legitimate drama, so theatrical critics tell us, has not quite shaken off the rivalry of sensational scenery and idiotic burlesque, though possibly we do not produce absurdities equal to that which, as Pope tells us, was actually introduced by Theobald, in which

Nile rises, Heaven descends, and dance on earth
Gods, imps, and monsters, music, rage, and mirth,
A fire, a jig, a battle and a ball,
Till one wide conflagration swallows all.

There is still facetiousness which reminds us too forcibly that

Gentle Dulness ever loves a joke,

and even sermons, for which we may apologise on the ground that

Dulness is sacred in a sound divine.

Here and there, too, if we may trust certain stern reviewers, there are writers who have learnt the principle that

Index learning turns no student pale,
Yet holds the eel of Science by the tail.

And the first four lines, at least, of the great prophecy at the conclusion of the third book is thought by the enemies of muscular Christianity to be possibly approaching its fulfilment:

Proceed, great days! till learning fly the shore,
Till birch shall blush with noble blood no more,
Till Thames see Eton's sons for ever play,
Till Westminster's whole year be holiday,
Till Isis' elders reel, their pupils sport,
And Alma Mater lies dissolved in Port!

No! So far as we can see, it is still true that

Born a goddess, Dulness never dies.

Men, we know it on high authority, are still mostly fools. If Pope be in error, it is not so much that his adversary is beneath him, as that she is unassailable by wit or poetry. Weapons of the most ethereal temper spend their keenness in vain against the "anarch old" whose power lies in utter insensibility. It is fighting with a mist, and firing cannon-balls into a mudheap. As well rave against the force of gravitation, or complain that our gross bodies must be nourished by solid food. If, however, we should be rather grateful than otherwise to a man who is sanguine enough to believe that satire can be successful against stupidity, and that Grub Street, if it cannot be exterminated, can at least be lashed into humility, we might perhaps complain that Pope has taken rather too limited a view of the subject. Dulness has other avatars besides the literary. In the last and finest book, Pope attempts to complete his plan by exhibiting the influence of dulness upon theology and science. The huge torpedo benumbs every faculty of the human mind, and paralyses all the Muses, except "mad Mathesis," which, indeed, does not carry on so internecine a war with the general enemy. The design is commendable, and executed, so far as Pope was on a level with his task, with infinite spirit. But, however excellent the poetry, the logic is defective, and the description of the evil inadequate. Pope has but a vague conception of the mode in which dulness might become the leading force in politics, lower religion till it became a mere cloak for selfishness, and make learning nothing but laborious and pedantic trifling. Had his powers been equal to his goodwill, we might have had a satire far more elevated than anything which he has attempted; for a man must be indeed a dull student of history who does not recognise the vast influence of dulness-worship in the whole period which has intervened between Pope and ourselves. Nay, it may be feared that it will yet be some time before education bills and societies for university extension will have begun to dissipate the evil. A modern satirist, were satire still alive, would find an ample occupation for his talents in a worthy filling out of Pope's incomplete sketch. But though I feel, I must endeavour to resist the temptation of indicating some of the probable objects of his antipathy.

Pope's gallant assault on the common enemy indicates, meanwhile, his characteristic attitude. Pope is the incarnation of the literary spirit. He is the most complete representative in our language of the intellectual instincts which find their natural expression in pure literature, as distinguished from literature applied to immediate practical ends, or enlisted in the service of philosophy or science. The complete antithesis to that spirit is the evil principle which Pope attacks as dulness. This false goddess is the literary Ahriman; and Pope's natural antipathies, exaggerated by his personal passions and weaknesses to extravagant proportions, express themselves fully in his great mock-epic. His theory may be expressed in a parody of Nelson's immortal advice to his midshipmen: "Be an honest man and hate dulness as you do the devil." Dulness generates the asphyxiating atmosphere in which no true literature can thrive. It oppresses the lungs and irritates the nerves of men whose keen, brilliant intellects mark them as the natural servants of literature. Seen from this point of view, there is an honourable completeness in Pope's career. Possibly a modern subject of literature may, without paradox, express a certain gratitude to Pope for a virtue which he would certainly be glad to imitate. Pope was the first man who made an independence by literature. First and last, he seems to have received over 8,000*l.* for his translation of Homer, a sum then amply sufficient to enable him to live in comfort. No sum at all comparable to this was ever received by a poet or novelist until the era of Scott and Byron. Now, without challenging admiration for Pope on the simple ground that he made his fortune,

it is difficult to exaggerate the importance of this feat at the time. A contemporary who, whatever his faults, was a still more brilliant example than Pope of the purely literary qualities, suggests a curious parallel. Voltaire, as he tells us, was so weary of the humiliations that dishonour letters, that to stay his disgust he resolved to make "what scoundrels call a great fortune." Some of Voltaire's means of reaching this end appear to have been more questionable than Pope's. But both of these men of genius early secured their independence by raising themselves permanently above the need of writing for money. It may be added in passing that there is a curious similarity in intellect and character between Pope and Voltaire which would on occasion be worth fuller exposition. The use, too, which Pope made of his fortune was thoroughly honourable. We scarcely give due credit, as a rule, to the man who has the rare merit of distinctly recognising his true vocation in life, and adhering to it with unflinching pertinacity. Probably the fact that such virtue generally brings a sufficient personal reward in this world seems to dispense with the necessity of additional praise. But call it a virtuous or merely a useful quality, we must at least admit that it is the necessary groundwork of a thoroughly satisfactory career. Pope, who, from his infancy, had

Lisped in numbers, for the numbers came,

gained by his later numbers a secure position, and used his position to go on rhyming to the end of his life. He never failed to do his very best. He regarded the wealth which he had earned as a retaining fee, not as a discharge from his duties. Comparing him with his contemporaries, we see how vast was the advantage. Elevated above Grub Street, he had no temptation to manufacture rubbish or descend to actual meanness like De Foe. Independent of patronage, he was not forced to become a "tame cat" in the hands of a duchess, like his friend Gay. Standing apart from politics, he was free from those disappointed pangs which contributed to the embitterment of the later years of Swift, dying "like a poisoned rat in a hole;" he had not, like Bolingbroke, to affect a philosophical contempt for the game in which he could no longer take a part; nor was he even, like Addison and Steele, induced to "give up to party what was meant for mankind." He was not a better man than some of these, and certainly not better than Goldsmith and Johnson in the succeeding generation. Yet, when we think of the amount of good intellect that ran to waste in the purlieus of Grub Street, or in hunting for pensions in ministerial ante-chambers, we feel a certain gratitude to the one literary magnate of the century, whose devotion, it is true, had a very tangible reward, but whose devotion was yet continuous, and free from any distractions but those of a constitutional irritability. Nay, if we compare Pope to some of the later writers who have wrung still princelier rewards from fortune, the result is not unfavourable. If Scott had been as true to his calling, his life, so far superior to Pope's in most other respects, would not have presented the melancholy contrast of genius running to waste in desperate attempts to win money at the cost of worthier fame.

Pope, as a Roman Catholic, and as the adherent of a defeated party, had put himself out of the race for pecuniary reward. His loyal adherence to his friends, though, like all his virtues, subject to some deduction, is really a touching feature in his character. His Catholicism was of the most nominal kind. He adhered in name to a depressed Church chiefly because he could not bear to give pain to the parents whom he loved with an exquisite tenderness. Granting that he would not have had much chance of winning tangible rewards by the baseness of a desertion, he at least recognised his true position; and instead of being soured by his exclusion from the general competition, or wasting his life in frivolous regrets, he preserved a spirit of tolerance and independence, and had a full right to the boasts in which he certainly indulged a little too freely:

> Not Fortune's worshipper, nor Fashion's fool,
> Not Lucre's madman, nor Ambition's's tool;
> Not proud, nor servile—be one poet's praise
> That, if he pleased, he pleased by manly ways;
> That flattery, even to kings, he held a shame,
> And thought a lie in prose or verse the same.

Admitting that the last line suggests a slight qualm, the portrait suggested in the rest is about as faithful as one can expect a man to paint from himself.

And hence we come to the question, what was the morality which Pope dispensed from this exalted position? Admitting his independence, can we listen to him patiently when he proclaims himself to be

> Of virtue only, and her friends, the friend;

or when he boasts in verses noble if quite sincere—

> Yes, I am proud; I must be proud to see
> Men not afraid of God, afraid of me;
> Safe from the Bar, the Pulpit, and the Throne,
> Yet touched and shamed by ridicule alone.

Is this guardian of virtue quite immaculate, and the morality which he preaches quite of the most elevated kind? We must admit, of course, that he does not sound the depths, or soar to the heights, in which men of loftier genius are at home. He is not a mystic, but a man of the world. He never, as we have already said, quits the sphere of ordinary and rather obvious maxims about the daily life of society, or quits it at his peril. His independence is not like Milton's, that of an ancient prophet, consoling himself by celestial visions for a world given over to baseness and frivolity; nor like Shelley's, that of a vehement revolutionist, who has declared open war against the existing order; it is the independence of a modern gentleman, with a competent fortune, enjoying a time of political and religious calm. And therefore his morality is in the main the expression of the conclusions reached by supreme good sense, or, as he puts it,

> Good sense, which only is the gift of heaven,
> And though no science, fairly worth the seven.

Good sense is one of the excellent qualities to which we are scarcely inclined to do justice at the present day; it is the guide of a time of equilibrium, stirred by no vehement gales of passion, and we lose sight of it just when it might give us some useful advice. A man in a passion is never more irritated than when advised to be sensible; and at the present day we are permanently in a passion, and therefore apt to assert that, not only for a moment, but as a general rule, men do well to be angry. Our art critics, for example, are never satisfied with their frame of mind till they have lashed themselves into a fit of rhetoric. Nothing more is wanted to explain why we are apt to be dissatisfied with Pope, both as a critic and a moralist. In both capacities, however, Pope is really admirable. Nobody, for example, has ridiculed more happily the absurdities of which we sometimes take him to be a representative. The recipe for making an epic poem is a perfect burlesque upon the pseudo-classicism of his time. He sees the absurdity of the contemporary statues, whose grotesque medley of ancient and modern costume is recalled in the lines—

> That livelong wig, which Gorgon's self might own,
> Eternal buckle takes in Parian stone.

The painters and musicians come in for their share of ridicule, as in the description of Timon's Chapel, where

> Light quirks of music, broken and uneven,
> Make the soul dance upon a jig to heaven;
> On painted ceilings you devoutly stare,
> Where sprawl the saints of Verrio and Laguerre.

Pope, again, was one of the first, by practice and precept, to break through the old formal school of gardening, in which

> No pleasing intracacies intervene,
> No artful wildness to perplex the scene;
> Grove nods at grove, each alley has a brother,
> And half the platform just reflects the other.
> The suffering eye inverted Nature sees,
> Trees cut to statues, statues thick as trees,
> With here a fountain never to be played,
> And there a summer-house that knows no shade;
> Here Amphitrite sails through myrtle bowers,
> There gladiators fight or die in flowers;
> Unwatered see the drooping sea-horse mourn,
> And swallows roost in Nilus' dusty urn.

It would be impossible to hit off more happily the queer formality which annoys us, unless its quaintness makes us smile, in the days of good Queen Anne, when Cato still appeared with a

> Long wig, flowered gown, and lacquered chair.

Pope's literary criticism, too, though verging too often on the commonplace, is generally sound as far as it goes. If, as was inevitable, he was blind to the merits of earlier schools of poetry, he was yet amongst the first writers who helped to establish the rightful supremacy of Shakespeare.

But in what way does Pope apply his good sense to morality? His favourite doctrine about human nature is expressed in the theory of the "ruling passion" which is to be found in all men, and which, once known, enables us to unravel the secret of every character. As he says in the *Essay on Man*—

> On life's vast ocean diversely we sail,
> Reason the card, but passion is the gale.

Right reason, therefore, is the power which directs passions to the worthiest end; and its highest lesson is to enforce

> The truth (enough for man to know)
> Virtue alone is happiness below.

The truth, though admirable, may be suspected of commonplace; and Pope does not lay down any propositions unfamiliar to other moralists, nor, it is to be feared, enforce them by preaching of more than usual effectiveness. His denunciations of avarice, of corruption, and of sensuality were probably of little more practical use than his denunciation of dulness. The "men not afraid of God" were hardly likely to be deterred from selling their votes to Walpole by fear of Pope's satire. He might

> Goad the Prelate slumbering in his stall

sufficiently to produce the episcopal equivalent for bad language; but he would hardly interrupt the bishop's slumbers for many moments; and, on the whole, he might congratulate himself, rather too cheaply, on being animated by

> The strong antipathy of good to bad.

Without exaggerating its importance, however, we may seek to define the precise point on which Pope's morality differed from that of many other writers who have expressed their general approval of the ten commandments. A healthy strain of moral feeling is useful, though we cannot point to the individuals whom it has restrained from picking pockets.

The defective side of the morality of good sense is, that it tends to degenerate into cynicism, either of the indolent variety which commended itself to Chesterfield, or of the more vehement sort, of which Swift's writings are the most powerful embodiment. A shrewd man of the world, of placid temperament, accepts placidly the conclusion that as he can see through a good many people, virtue generally is a humbug. If he has grace enough left to be soured by such a conclusion, he raves at the universal corruption of mankind. Now Pope, notwithstanding his petty spite, and his sympathy with the bitterness of his friends, always shows a certain tenderness of nature which preserves him from sweeping cynicism. He really believes in nature, and values life for the power of what Johnson calls reciprocation of benevolence. The beauty of his affection for his father and mother, and for his old nurse, breaks pleasantly through the artificial language of his letters, like a sweet spring in barren ground. When he touches upon the subject in his poetry, one seems to see tears in his eyes, and to hear his voice tremble. There is no more beautiful passage in his writings than the one in which he expresses the hope that he may be spared

> To rock the cradle of reposing age,
> With lenient arts extend a mother's breath,
> Make languor smile, and smooth the bed of death;
> Explore the thought, explain the asking eye,
> And keep awhile one parent from the sky.

Here at least he is sincere beyond suspicion; and we know from unimpeachable testimony that the sentiment so perfectly expressed was equally exemplified in his life. It sounds easy, but unfortunately the ease is not always proved in practice, for a man of genius to be throughout their lives an unmixed comfort to his parents. It is unpleasant to remember that a man so accessible to tender emotions should jar upon us by his language about women generally. Byron countersigns the opinion of Bolingbroke that he knew the sex well; but testimony of that kind hardly prepossesses us in his favour. In fact, the school of Bolingbroke and Swift, to say nothing of Wycherley, was hardly calculated to generate a chivalrous tone of feeling. His experience of Lady Mary gave additional bitterness to his sentiments. Pope, in short, did not love good women—

> Matter too soft a lasting mark to bear,
> And best distinguished as black, brown, or fair,

as he impudently tells a lady—as a man of genius ought; and women have generally returned the dislike. Meanwhile the vein of benevolence shows itself unmistakably in Pope's language about his friends. Thackeray seizes upon this point of his character in his lectures on the English Humourists, and his powerful, if rather too favourable, description brings out forcibly the essential tenderness of the man who, during the lucid intervals of his last illness, was "always saying something kindly of his present or absent friends." Nobody, as has often been remarked, has paid so many exquisitely turned compliments. There is something which rises to the dog-like in his affectionate admiration for Swift and for Bolingbroke, his rather questionable "guide, philosopher, and friend." Whenever he speaks of a friend, he is sure to be felicitous. There is Garth, for example:

> The best good Christian he,
> Although he knows it not.

There are beautiful lines upon Arbuthnot, addressed as—

> Friend to my life, which did not you prolong,
> The world had wanted many an idle song.

Or we may quote, though one verse has been spoilt by familiarity, the lines in which Bolingbroke is coupled with Peterborough:

> There St. John mingles with my friendly bowl
> The feast of reason and the flow of soul;
> And he whose lightning pierced the Iberian lines
> Now farms my quincunx, and now ranks my vines,
> And tames the genius of the stubborn plain
> Almost as quickly as he conquered Spain.

Or again, there are the verses in which he anticipates the dying words attributed to Pitt:

> And you, brave Cobham, to the latest breath,
> Shall feel the ruling passion strong in death;
> Such in those moments, as in all the past,
> "Oh, save my country, Heaven!" shall be your last.

Cobham's name, again, suggests the spirited lines—

> Spirit of Arnall! aid me while I lie,
> Cobham's a coward, Polwarth is a slave,
> And Lyttelton a dark, designing knave;
> St. John has ever been a wealthy fool—
> But let me add Sir Robert's mighty dull,
> Has never made a friend in private life,
> And was, besides, a tyrant to his wife.

Perhaps the last compliment is ambiguous, but Walpole's name again reminds us that Pope could on occasion be grateful even to an opponent. "Go see Sir Robert," suggests his friend in the epilogue to the Satires; and Pope replies:

> See him I have; but in his happier hour
> Of social pleasure, ill exchanged for power;
> Seen him uncumbered with the venal tribe
> Smile without art, and win without a bribe;
> Would he oblige me? Let me only find
> He does not think me what he thinks mankind;
> Come, come; at all I laugh, he laughs no doubt;
> The only difference is, I dare laugh out.

But there is no end to the delicate flattery which may be set off against Pope's ferocious onslaughts upon his enemies. If one could have a wish for the asking, one could scarcely ask for a more agreeable sensation than that of being titillated by a man of equal ingenuity in caressing one's pet vanities. The art of administering such consolation is possessed only by men who unite such tenderness to an exquisitely delicate intellect. This vein of genuine feeling sufficiently redeems Pope's writings from the charge of a commonplace worldliness. Certainly he is not one of the "genial" school, whose indiscriminate benevolence exudes over all that they touch. There is nothing mawkish in his philanthropy. Pope was, if anything, too good a hater; "the portentous cub never forgives," said Bentley; but kindliness is all the more impressive when not too widely diffused. Add to this his hearty contempt for pomposities, humbugs, and stupidities of all kinds, and above all the fine spirit of independence, in which we have again the real man, and which expresses itself in such lines as these:

> Oh, let me live my own, and die so too!
> (To live and die is all I have to do);
> Maintain a poet's dignity and ease,
> And see what friends and read what books I please.

And we may admit that Pope, in spite of his wig and his stays, his vanities and his affectations, was in his way as fair an embodiment as we would expect of that "plain living and high thinking" of which Wordsworth regretted the disappearance. The little cripple, diseased in mind and body, spiteful and occasionally brutal, had in him the spirit of a man. The monarch of the literary world was far from immaculate; but he was not without a dignity of his own.

We come, however, to the question, what had Pope to say upon the deepest subjects with which human beings can concern themselves? The most explicit answer must be taken from the *Essay on Man*, and the essay must be acknowledged to have more conspicuous faults than any of Pope's writings. The art of reasoning in verse is so difficult that we may doubt whether it is in any case legitimate, and must acknowledge that it has been never successfully practised by any English writer. Dryden's *Religio Laici* may be better reasoning, but it is worse poetry than Pope's Essay. It is true, again, that Pope's reasoning is intrinsically feeble. He was no metaphysician, and confined himself to putting together incoherent scraps of different systems. Some of his arguments strike us as simply childish, as, for example, the quibble derived from the Stoics, that

> The blest to-day is as completely so
> As who began a thousand years ago.

Nobody, we may safely say, was ever much comforted by that reflection. Nor, though the celebrated argument about the scale of beings, which Pope but half understood, was then sanctioned by the most eminent contemporary names, do we derive any deep consolation from the remark that

> in the scale of reasoning life, 't is plain,
> There must be somewhere such a rank as man.

To say no more of these frigid conceits, as they now appear to us, Pope does not maintain the serious temper which befits a man pondering upon the deep mysteries of the universe. Religious meditation does not harmonise with epigrammatical satire. Admitting the value of the reflection that other beings besides man are fitting objects of the Divine benevolence, we are jarred by such a discord as this:

> While man exclaims, See all things for my use!
> See man for mine! replies a pampered goose.

The goose is appropriate enough in Charron or Montaigne, but should be kept out of poetry. Such a shock, too, follows when Pope talks about the superior beings who

> Showed a Newton as we show an ape.

Did anybody, again, ever complain that he wanted "the strength of bulls, the fur of bears?"[1] Or could it be worth while to meet his complaints in a serious poem? Pope, in short, is not merely a bad reasoner, but he wants that deep moral earnestness which gives a profound interest to Johnson's satires—the best productions of his school—and the deeply pathetic religious feeling of Cowper.

Admitting all this, however, and more, the *Essay on Man* still contains many passages which not only testify to the unequalled skill of this great artist in words, but show a certain moral dignity. In the Essay, more than in any of his other writings, we have the difficulty of separating the solid bullion from the dross. Pope is here pre-eminently parasitical, and it is possible to trace to other writers, such as Montaigne, Pascal, Leibniz, Shaftesbury, Locke, and Wollaston, as well as to the inspiration of Bolingbroke, nearly every argument which he employs. He unfortunately worked up the rubbish as well as the gems. When Mr. Ruskin says that his "theology was two centuries in advance of his time," the phrase is curiously inaccurate. He was not really in advance of the best men of his own time; but they, it is to be feared, were considerably in advance of the average opinion of our own. What may be said with more plausibility is, that whilst Pope frequently wastes his

skill in gilding refuse, he is really most sensitive to the noblest sentiments of his contemporaries, and that, when he has good materials to work upon, his verse glows with unusual fervour, often to sink with unpleasant rapidity into mere quibbling or epigrammatic pungency. The real truth is that Pope precisely expresses the position of the best thinkers of his day. He did not understand the reasoning, but he fully shared the sentiments of the philosophers among whom Locke and Leibniz were the great lights. Pope is to the deists and semi-deists of his time what Milton was to the Puritans or Dante to the Schoolmen. At times he writes like a Pantheist, and then becomes orthodox, without a consciousness of the transition; he is a believer in universal predestination, and saves himself by inconsistent language about "leaving free the human will;" his views about the origin of society are an inextricable mass of inconsistency; and he may be quoted in behalf of doctrines which he, with the help of Warburton, vainly endeavoured to disavow. But, leaving sound divines to settle the question of his orthodoxy, and metaphysicians to crush his arguments, if they think it worth while, we are rather concerned with the general temper in which he regards the universe, and the moral which he draws for his own edification. The main doctrine which he enforces is, of course, one of usual commonplaces. The statement that "whatever is, is right," may be verbally admitted, and strained to different purposes by half a dozen differing schools. It may be alleged by the cynic, who regards virtue as an empty name; by the mystic, who is lapped in heavenly contemplation from the cares of this troublesome world; by the sceptic, whose whole wisdom is concentrated in the duty of submitting to the inevitable; or by the man who, abandoning the attempt of solving inscrutable enigmas, is content to recognise in everything the hand of a Divine ordainer of all things. Pope, judging him by his most forcible passages, prefers to insist upon the inevitable ignorance of man in presence of the Infinite:

> 'Tis but a part we see, and not the whole;

and any effort to pierce the impenetrable gloom can only end in disappointment and discontent:

> In pride, in reasoning pride, our error lies.

We think that we can judge the ways of the Almighty, and correct the errors of His work. We are as incapable of accounting for human wickedness as for plague, tempest, and earthquake. In each case our highest wisdom is an humble confession of ignorance; or, as he puts it,

> In both, to reason right is to submit.

This vein of thought might, perhaps, have conducted him to the scepticism of his master, Bolingbroke. He unluckily fills up the gaps of his logical edifice with the untempered mortar of obsolete metaphysics, long since become utterly uninteresting to all men. Admitting that he cannot explain, he tries to manufacture sham explanations out of the "scale of beings," and other scholastic rubbish. But, in a sense, too, the most reverent minds will agree most fully with Pope's avowal of the limitation of human knowledge. He does not apply his scepticism or his humility to stimulate to vain repining against the fetters with which our minds are bound, or an angry denunciation, like that of Bolingbroke, of the solutions in which other souls have found a sufficient refuge. The perplexity in which he finds himself generates a spirit of resignation and tolerance.

> Hope humbly, then; with trembling pinions soar;
> Wait the great teacher, Death, and God adore.

That is the pith of his teaching. All optimism is apt to be a little irritating to men whose sympathies with human suffering are unusually strong; and the optimism of a man like Pope, vivacious rather than profound in his thoughts and his sympathies, annoys us at times by his calm complacency. We cannot thrust aside so easily the thought of the heavy evils under which all creation groans. But we should wrong him by a failure to recognise the real benevolence of his sentiment. Pope indeed becomes too pantheistic for some tastes in the celebrated fragment—the whole poem is a conglomerate of slightly connected fragments—beginning,

> All are but parts of one stupendous whole,
> Whose body Nature is, and God the soul.

But his real fault is that he is not consistently pantheistic. Pope was attacked both for his pantheism and fatalism and for having borrowed from Bolingbroke. It is curious enough that it was precisely these doctrines which he did not borrow. Bolingbroke, like most feeble reasoners, believed firmly in Free Will; and though a theist after a fashion, his religion had not emotional depth or logical coherence enough to be pantheistic. Pope, doubtless, did not here quit his master's guidance from any superiority in logical perception. But he did occasionally feel the poetical value of pantheistic conception of the universe. Pantheism, in fact, is the only poetical form of the metaphysical theology current in Pope's day. The old historical theology of Dante, or even of Milton, was too faded for poetical purposes; and the "personal Deity," whose existence and attributes were proved by the elaborate reasonings of the apologists of that day, was unfitted for poetical celebration by the very fact that his existence required proof. Poetry deals with intuitions, not with remote inferences, and therefore in his better moments Pope spoke not of the intelligent moral Governor discovered by philosophical investigation, but of the Divine Essence immanent in all nature, whose "living raiment" is the world. The finest passages in the *Essay on Man*, like the finest passages in Wordsworth, are an attempt to expound that view, though Pope falls back too quickly into epigram, as Wordsworth into prose. It was reserved for Goethe to show what a poet might learn from the philosophy of Spinoza. Meanwhile Pope, uncertain as is his grasp of any philosophical conceptions, shows, not merely in set phrases, but in the general colouring of his poem, something of that width of sympathy which should result from the pantheistic view. The tenderness, for example, with which he always speaks of the brute creation is pleasant in a writer so little distinguished as a rule by an interest in what we popularly call nature. The "scale of being" argument may be illogical, but we pardon it when it is applied to strengthen our sympathies with our unfortunate dependants on the lower steps of the ladder. The lamb who

> Licks the hand just raised to shed his blood

is a second-hand lamb, and has, like so much of Pope's writing, acquired a certain tinge of banality, which must limit quotation; and the same must be said of the poor Indian, who

> thinks, admitted to that equal sky,
> His faithful dog will bear him company.

But the sentiment is as right as the language (in spite of its familiarity we can still recognise the fact) is exquisite. Tolerance of all forms of faith, from that of the poor Indian upwards, is so characteristic of Pope as to have offended some modern critics who might have known better. We may pick holes in the celebrated antithesis:

> For forms of government let fools contest:
> Whate'er is best administered is best;
> For forms of faith let graceless zealots fight,
> He can't be wrong whose life is in the right.

Certainly, they are not mathematically accurate formulæ; but they are generous, if imperfect, statements of great truths, and not unbecoming in the mouth of the man who, as the member of an unpopular sect, learnt to be cosmopolitan rather than bitter, and expressed his convictions in the well-known words addressed to Swift: "I am of the religion of Erasmus, a Catholic; so I live, so I shall die; and hope one day to meet you, Bishop Atterbury, the younger Craggs, Dr. Garth, Dean Berkeley, and Mr. Hutchinson in heaven." Who would wish to shorten the list? And the scheme of morality which Pope deduced for practical guidance in life is in harmony with the spirit which breathes in those words just quoted. A recent dispute in a court of justice shows that even our most cultivated men have forgotten Pope so far as to be ignorant of the source of the familiar words—

> What can ennoble sots, or slaves, or cowards?
> Alas! not all the blood of all the Howards.

It is therefore necessary to say explicitly that the poem where they occur, the fourth epistle of the *Essay on Man*, not only contains half a dozen other phrases equally familiar—*e.g.*, "An honest man's the noblest work of God;"[2] "Looks through nature up to nature's God;" "From grave to gay, from lively to severe"—but breathes throughout sentiments which it would be credulous to believe that any man could express so vigorously without feeling profoundly. Mr. Ruskin has quoted one couplet as giving "the most complete, the most concise, and the most lofty expression of moral temper existing in English words"—

> Never elated, while one man's oppressed;
> Never dejected, whilst another's blessed.

The passage in which they occur is worthy of this (let us admit, just a little over-praised) sentiment; and leads not unfitly to the conclusion and summary of the whole, that he who can recognise the beauty of virtue knows that

> Where Faith, Law, Morals, all began,
> All end—in love of God and love of man.

I know but too well all that may be said against this view of Pope's morality. He is, as Sainte-Beuve says, the easiest of all men to caricature; and it is equally easy to throw cold water upon his morality. We may count up his affectations, ridicule his platitudes, make heavy deductions for his insincerity, denounce his too frequent indulgence in a certain love of dirt, which he shares with, and in which indeed he is distanced by, Swift; and decline to believe in the virtue, or even in the love of virtue, of a man stained by so many vices and weaknesses. Yet I must decline to believe that men can gather grapes off thorns, or figs off thistles, or noble expressions of moral truth from a corrupt heart thinly varnished by a coating of affectation. Turn it how we may, the thing is impossible. Pope was more than a mere literary artist, though he was an artist of unparalleled excellence in his own department. He was a man in whom there was the seed of many good thoughts, though choked in their development by the growth of innumerable weeds. And I will venture, in conclusion, to adduce one more proof of the justice of a lenient verdict. I have had already to quote many phrases familiar to every one who is tinctured in the slightest degree with a knowledge of English literature; and yet have been haunted by a dim suspicion that some of my readers may have been surprised to recognise their author. Pope, we have seen, is recognised even by judges of the land only through the medium of Byron; and therefore the "Universal Prayer" may possibly be unfamiliar to some readers. If so, it will do them no harm to read over again a few of its verses. Perhaps, after that experience, they will admit that the little cripple of Twickenham, distorted as were his instincts after he had been stretched on the rack of this rough world, and grievous as were his offences against the laws of decency and morality, had yet in him a noble strain of eloquence significant of deep religious sentiment. A phrase in the first stanza may shock us as bordering too closely on the epigrammatic; but the whole poem from which I take these stanzas must, I think, be recognised as the utterance of a tolerant, reverent, and kindly heart:

> Father of all! in every age,
>   In every clime adored,
> By saint, by savage, and by sage—
>   Jehovah, Jove, or Lord!
>
> Thou great First Cause, least understood,
>   Who all my sense confined
> To know but this, that thou art good,
>   And that myself am blind.
>
>   . . .
>
> What conscience dictates to be done,
>   Or warns me not to do,
> This, teach me more than hell to shun;
>   That, more than heaven pursue.
>
> What blessings thy free bounty gives
>   Let me not cast away;
> For God is paid when man receives—
>   To enjoy is to obey.
>
> Yet not to earth's contracted span
>   Thy goodness let me bound,
> Or think thee Lord alone of man,
>   When thousand worlds are round.
>
> Let not this weak, unknowing hand
>   Presume thy bolts to throw,
> Or deal damnation round the land
>   On each I judge thy foe.
>
> If I am right, they grace impart
>   Still in the right to stay:
> If I am wrong, oh, teach my heart
>   To find that better way.

These stanzas, I am well aware, do not quite conform to the modern taste in hymns, nor are they likely to find favour with admirers of the *Christian Year*. Another school would object to them on a very different ground. The deism of Pope's day was not a stable form of belief; but in the form in which it was held by the pure deists of the Toland and Tindal school, or by the disguised deists who followed Locke or Clarke, it was the highest creed then attainable; and Pope's prayer is an adequate impression of its best sentiment.

Notes

1. The remark was perhaps taken from Sir Thomas Browne: "Thus have we no just quarrel with nature for leaving us naked; or to envy the horns, hoofs, skins, and furs of other creatures; being provided with reason that can supply them all."—*Religio Medici*, Part I, sec. 18.
2. This sentiment, by the way, was attacked by Darnley, in his edition of Beaumont and Fletcher, as "false and degrading to man, derogatory to God." As I have lately seen the remark quoted with approbation, it is worth noticing the argument by which Darnley supports it. He says that an honest able man is nobler than an honest man, and Aristides with the genius of Homer nobler than Aristides with the dulness of a clown. Undoubtedly! But surely a man might say that English poetry is the noblest in the world, and yet admit that Shakespeare was a nobler poet than Tom Moore. Because honesty is nobler than any other quality, it does not follow that all honest men are on a par. This bit of cavilling reminds one of De Quincey's elaborate argument against the lines:

    > Who would not laugh, if such a man there be?
    > Who would not weep, if Atticus were he?

De Quincey says that precisely the same phenomenon is supposed to make you laugh in one line and weep in the other; and that therefore the thought is inaccurate. As if it would not be a fit cause for tears to discover that one of our national idols was a fitting subject for laughter!

H. D. TRAILL
From "Pope"

National Review, December 1889, pp. 493–503

Every age has its own definition of poetry, and the present age, it appears, has chosen so to define it as to exclude Pope from the rank of poet, or, at any rate, of great poet, by very force of the defining terms. It might almost seem as if we had constructed our theory of the poetic function with a direct eye to that part of the poet's work which Pope, in the judgment even of his warmest admirers in this age, was least capable of performing to the satisfaction of the modern mind and heart. We have altered the rules of the game, as it were, and now point to the fact that the players of that day, and he, the master of all of them, would be no match for the accomplished "performers" among ourselves as if that were a proof of our own natural superiority to those disqualified ones. The mistake, in my opinion, on the part of the nineteenth-century Popian—I do not charge Mr. Courthope with committing it, though he seems to me, I own, to come parlously near it sometimes—is to meet this charge against Pope by a denial of it, instead of by what the old pleaders used to call a plea "in confession and avoidance." It really does not bear a moment's disputing that Nature, and all that we in these days mean by Nature, had scarcely a touch of that significance for Pope which it has for the man of average sensibility at the present day. To deny this, or to endeavour to make out that if Pope does not express for us this attitude of man towards Nature, he gives us something else that will do equally well, is futile. What the author of *Windsor Forest* and the imitator of *Pollio* gives us will not do equally well; it will not do at all. It would be as absurd to pretend that it does, as idle to feign belief in its adequacy, as it would be for a physician of the present day to attempt to square his diagnoses with the doctrines of the "humoral pathology," or for a lecturer in physiology to make believe that he could instruct his class satisfactorily without any positive rejection of the theory that the arteries contain not blood but "animal spirits." Nothing is gained by disguising the fact that the mental and emotional relation of civilized man to the external world has undergone as distinct and irrevocable a change, since Pope wrote, as has passed over his scientific conception of the structure and functions of his body since Harvey ascertained the most fundamental of all its physiological truths. It is true, of course, that the former change, unlike the latter, was not determined by any one specific *revelation*—though, to be sure, the work of Wordsworth is sometimes spoken of, erroneously and exaggeratively, as if it had effected this very thing; it was gradual, and its phases are to be traced not only through Cowper, but through a yet earlier poet, Gray. No one can, I think, deny that when the *Elegy on a Country Churchyard* was written, only five years after the death of Pope, the "modern feeling" for Nature was already born into the world. That the poet of *The Task* is instinct with it—nay, that it inspires him in a form of, so to speak, a more equable purity, if of nothing like the potency with which it was afterwards to inspire the poet of the *Excursion*, appears to me, at least, to be just as undeniable. But, however opinions may differ as to the point or phase in the movement which individual poets represent, there can be no difference of opinion as to the distance traversed by it between the first half of the eighteenth century and the present day. It amounts to this: that when Pope speaks to us of the external world, when he tells us what Nature looks like to him, in her fields and flowers, her woods and waters, her dawns and sunsets, he speaks to us in a language which, rich, varied, picturesque, as it often is, and masterly as almost always is the skill with which he uses it, no more responds to the emotional needs of the modern mind than if it were so much geometrical demonstration.

No doubt the *advocatus diaboli* might go a good deal farther than this in his opposition to Pope's canonization. He might urge that, though the attitude of the great Elizabethans, the attitude of Milton, the attitude, say, of Andrew Marvell or George Herbert—to take two widely differing types of the seventeenth-century mind—towards Nature was as far as or farther removed than that of Pope from our own, they nevertheless bring themselves, in many and many a passage of descriptive poetry, into very close sympathy with the modern feeling. He might add that even such a poet of the artificial period of which Pope is the consummate expression as James Thomson has it in him to touch and move us as Pope never can; and that Pope's poetry must, therefore, have been chilled by some essential frigidity of imagination for which the man himself was responsible, and not his age. And if this charge were to be pressed against him, I for one should not care to combat it. But neither am I concerned to adopt it and rely upon it. It is enough for me that the poetry of Pope is manifestly obnoxious to the earlier objection alleged against it—namely, that it absolutely fails to fulfil that function to which the criticism of our day assigns the supreme place in the poet's work; absolutely fails, that is to say, to satisfy the emotional needs which are awakened in the modern mind by the contemplation of external nature.

But then the question arises, How far are we justified in elevating the function in question to that supreme place in poetry which, as I have said, it at present occupies? Or, assuming that the claim of this function to supremacy may with propriety be admitted let us ask whether the ever-growing tendency to treat it as though it were not the highest merely, but the sole office of the poet to interpret to man the message of external nature is itself legitimate. In the essay prefixed to the new edition of *The Human Tragedy*, Mr. Alfred Austin deprecates the disfavour into which narrative poetry has fallen. This decline will, of course, be deplored the most deeply by those who accept Mr. Austin's graduation of the various orders of poetic production—who agree with him, that is to say, in assigning to epic and dramatic, the two forms of narrative poetry, that place of primacy which Aristotle claimed for them, and who hold with him that from the descriptive to the lyrical, from the lyrical to the reflective, and from the reflective to the epic and dramatic orders of poetry, "there is an ascending scale of growth and dignity." But if anyone chose to challenge the accuracy of this "Table of Precedence," it would not be necessary to my present purpose to defend it. My point is that whether descriptive and lyrical poetry be or be not inferior in degree to reflective and narrative poetry, the two former kinds have most assuredly no right to monopolize the name which is common to them all. Yet what else can be said of nine-tenths of contemporary poetic production, and a full half of contemporary criticism, than that the one embodies, and the other implies, the assumption that descriptive and lyrical poetry constitute the beginning and end of the poetic art; that they *are*

poetry and that there is no other? Year after year the stream of rhymed and metrical matter issuing from the press increases not, I fear, in depth, but undoubtedly in volume. It would be mere prejudice to deny the very considerable exaltation of its standard which has taken place during the last quarter of a century. Without exactly embracing the creed that true poetic genius has become so common now-a-days as to flourish unnoticed by the wayside, one must admit that a vast amount of genuine poetic feeling, an amount far in excess of what is to be traced in the comparatively obscure and fugitive literature of an earlier day, finds voice every year in verse to which the quality of genuine poetic expression cannot be denied. The experience of every competent critic who has watched the yearly "output" of the press with any attention may safely be appealed to for confirmation of this; and indeed the fact, I think, may be almost claimed as one of general acknowledgment. Yet what is the prevailing, I might almost say the invariable characteristic, of all the flood of verse? It is almost wholly descriptive-lyrical. One cannot call it by either name alone, for its *manner* is nothing if not descriptive, and its *motive* nothing if not lyrical. In it we find the plainest evidence of these three things: first, that the poet's personal emotions, sometimes his momentary mood, form the habitual inspiration of his verse; secondly, that he instinctively turns to the contemplation of external nature to give expression to it; and thirdly, that his passion, whatever it may be, appears to find relief in the elaborate and often successful attempt to portray Nature (as an object of perception, not of thought) with truth and subtlety of observation, and with vigour and delicacy of touch. Nor, I think, can anyone who has noticed this have failed to notice also the further fact that for nine-tenths of those who endeavour, with greater or less success, after the realisation of this kind of poetic thought in this form of poetic expression, it evidently constitutes the be-all and end-all of the poetic art. They have manifestly no conception of poetry which is not this, and probably, if they met with anything not being this, and yet claiming to be poetry, they would contemptuously reject the claim.

An age which insists on limiting the definition of poetry after this fashion is obviously the most unfit of judges to pronounce on the question whether Pope (who admittedly fails to satisfy the requirements of the age in the matter of poetry as so defined) is or is not a poet. It is getting almost unfit to pronounce on the question whether Byron is a poet or not; it has already disqualified itself, as it seems to me, to assign Byron his true rank among poets, for the reason that it dwells exclusively on the lyrical and egotistically subjective side of Byron's genius, and has no feeling whatever for that magnificent epic and dramatic energy about it, which in everything except metrical quality (a terrible exception, it shall be freely granted to Mr. Swinburne), gives to even an imperfect piece of work like *Sardanapalus* or *Marino Faliero*, a life, a glow, a movement which are absolutely wanting to such a far more finished work of art as the *Cenci*. Wherever, therefore, the verse of Pope is avowedly dealing with subjects of a different order of poetry from the descriptive or the lyrical; wherever he may have tried to strike dramatically the note of passion; wherever he may have responded or endeavoured to respond to the inspiration of some great impersonal thought—then it follows that contemporary taste, so far at least as the dominant poetical canons of the day represent it, has no right to sit in judgment. It is like a juror who must be challenged as having already in general terms delivered a verdict which covers and must form his decision on the particular case before him. What, for instance, is the good of a critic's declaring that *Eloisa* to *Abelard* is "not poetry," when he consciously or unconsciously excludes the dramatic imagination and all its works from his conception of what poetry is. In the *Eloisa to Abelard* there is undoubtedly much that no longer rings true to the modern ear; there are passages here and there which it is difficult to think of as having ever rung true to the ear of any man, even to that of the poet himself; there are lines in it, though but a few, which are of a taste that never could be otherwise than false and unsound in any poet of any age; it contains at least one line of which we can agree with Mr. Swinburne in thinking that "no woman could read it without a blush, nor any man without a laugh." Yet he who can read its last hundred lines, with the struggle between Love and Devotion thrilling and throbbing through them, and not hear in them the true note, the unmistakable cry of human passion, uttered as only poetry can give it utterance, may rest assured that his natural sympathies and sentiments have been dwarfed and sophisticated by theory, and that from dogmatizing overmuch about what poetry ought to be he has blunted some of the sensibilities which should tell him what poetry *is*. Or if he be himself a verse-maker instead of or as well as a critic, he has probably so enslaved himself to the subjective, that he can realise no Abelard who does not correspond with some complacent projection of his own personality, nor any Eloisa who does not reproduce some passionately yearning, but desperately bloodless young woman of his own dreams.

Moreover, though it would be dangerous indeed to press an identity of names too far, it should not be forgotten that the "classic manner" is essentially a manner of reserve, and that in so far as Pope succeeded in approaching those antique models which he so greatly admired, emotion as adequately expresses itself through the severe correctness of his verse as it does through the statuesque calm of a Sophocles, or the stately movement of a Virgil among the Shades. Instances in plenty will suggest themselves; but it may suffice to take that famous epitaph alone, "the most valuable," as Johnson called it, of all Pope's epitaphs, and almost the only one, I may add, which has escaped his usually too captious censures—the inscription on the tomb of Mrs. Corbet. The often-quoted couplets with which it closes appear to me to furnish one of the most admirable examples of that pathos, the more eloquent for repression, which results from the classically perfect utterance not, primarily, of any emotion whatever, but simply of a thought.

> So unaffected, so composed a mind,
> So firm yet soft, so strong yet so refined.
> Heaven, as its purest gold, by tortures tried;
> The Saint sustained it, but the Woman died.

So far is this from being formally emotional that it is actually, in form, an epigram. Every word in it, taken singly, is as cold and colourless as the marble on which it is graven. Yet by sheer force of style, so to speak, by pure virtue of literary completeness, the thought conveyed in it comes charged with a fuller measure of emotional significance than would serve to freight a whole score of impassioned elegiacs. I should, indeed, have little hesitation in proposing this epitaph as the test of a reader's capacity for appreciating the power of any other poetry than that which wears its heart habitually on its sleeve. Nor do I think that, save in an age which has too unreservedly surrendered itself to the worship of poetry of the heart-on-the-sleeve order, could the true poetic value of such a passage fail of recognition.

I do not say, for I do not think, that Pope is always or everywhere as successful in adapting the chosen form of his poetry to the expression of the stronger human feelings; but I do with confidence maintain that the too common complaint of its uniform inadequacy for this purpose is due, in a great measure, to our effeminate desire in these days that every poet should "unpack his heart with words." And, what is more, I vehemently suspect that in spite of the lip service which we still render to the models of classical antiquity, a goodly proportion of those among us who now-a-days find Pope unvaryingly "cold" would confess, if they are candid, that they are equally chilled by the unimpassioned manner of those ancient poets whom they profess to admire. Do they, I would ask, feel quite satisfied with the ten lines of Catullus's stern lament over the tomb of his brother? Might not Virgil have told us more about the *infantum animæ flentes in limine primo* than the two following lines contain? Could not the piteous yearnings of those who *stabant orantes primi transmittere cursum, Tendebantque manus ripæ ulterioris amore,* have been described with advantage in greater detail? And does not the bald, brief intimation that the hound Argus died, "having seen his master in the twentieth year," appear to them a somewhat jejune and unsatisfying statement of the case? Or, to take the greatest of modern studies from the classical antique, are they sure that Meleager's dying farewell to his mother in *Atalanta in Calydon,* does not strike them, for all its grave and noble tenderness, as a trifle "cold"? I would not of course be understood to suggest that the manner of Catullus, or Virgil, or Homer, or of Mr. Swinburne in the passage referred to, resembles the manner of Pope in any other respect than that of dealing in an unemotional fashion with situations of a profoundly emotional kind. But to say that they all resemble each other in this respect alone is equivalent to saying that they all alike leave something to the imagination of the reader, and that therefore the coldness which he may think he finds in any one of them may belong not to the poet's method but to the reader's imagination. If Pope is not as "passionate" or "intense" as the modern poetic taste would like him to be, it should be remembered that there is no such thing as an "intense" substantive or a "passionate" adjective in the whole Greek and Latin vocabularies; and that those who feel the undercurrent of passion and intensity in the Greek and Latin poetry can only feel it in virtue of precisely that imaginative sympathy and literary sensibility which they seem unable or unwilling to bring to the study of Pope. It now only remains to consider that portion, by far the most considerable, of the poet's work to which Mr. Courtney refers in the following passage:

> To say that one species of poetry is more *poetic* than another is like saying that one species of horse, the race-horse, is more equine than the carriage-horse or the hunter. It may be fairly said that a great epic or dramatic poem, as being more imaginative, more pathetic, more sublime, is therefore much more admirable as a work of poetry than a fine satire; but to deny (as Warton in effect does) to good moral or satiric verse the title of poetry is to maintain a paradox in the face of common sense and general language. Juvenal and Boileau have written nothing considerable except satiric or ethical verse; instinct and usage nevertheless allow them the name of poets in their own class, though not for one moment ranking such poets in the same class with Homer, Virgil, and Milton.

Such is the plea, stated with refreshing plainness and decision, which Mr. Courtney urges for the admittance of Pope to the company of poets on the strength of the work which he has done, imperishable so long as the language endures, in the *Essay on Man*, the *Essay on Criticism*, and the *Moral Essays*. There is, however, no denying, I fear, that modern ideas are very much in accord with Warton, and that many people professing to speak with authority on the subject would withhold the title of poetry from all "moral and satiric" verse whatsoever. Probably they would defend themselves by contending that it is impossible even for the best verse in this form to display those peculiar qualities of "inspiration," of "magic," and so forth, which distinguish the "sacred thing" in its other forms from even the most masterly counterfeits. In a certain sense this is true, but whether it contains enough truth for the purpose of their argument depends mainly on the relative values to be attached respectively to conception and expression as formative elements in poetry. And it must be pointed out that the argument, as employed in this connection, starts from the assumption that *technique* itself can have no inspiration or magic of its own, and that the workmanship of Pope, say in the second of the *Moral Essays*, differs only in degree and not in kind of excellence from that of Garth's *Dispensary*; an assumption only possible to those whose feeling for style, whatever their case may be as regards any other part of the critic's equipment, is exceedingly imperfect. Those in whom this feeling is at all adequately developed will, I am confident, agree in recognizing that the art of Pope, when his moral and satiric verse is at its best, is just as different from and just as unapproachable by the work of any other artist in the same order as, for instance, the enchanted music of the opening lines of *Lycidas* is different from and unapproachable by the more or less melodious wailings of other elegists before or since.

Anyone who is disposed to under-estimate Pope's extraordinary, his unprecedented and never-repeated pre-eminence in pure artistic mastery over all other writers of poetry or, if we please, of "verse," should consider what sort of subject matter it is to which this consummate workmanship has imparted such immortal literary life. The *Moral Essays* and the *Epistle to Dr. Arbuthnot* are almost the only pieces, perhaps, which we could conceive our reading with any pleasure for the sake of the ideas conveyed in them, if treated by an inferior hand. But the reputation—nay, even the vitality of these works is not so great as belongs to the *Dunciad* and the *Essay on Man*. And what, in the name of fitness, are these? The one an entomologist's case of mouldy moths, and the other a writing master's collection of edifying moralities. Who but Pope could have enabled any reader of the *Dunciad* to watch with patience, at this distance of time, the descent of such a storm of insults, insolences, and scurrilities on such a crowd of obscure and forgotten heads? As for the *Essay on Man*, even Mr. Courthope, who does ample justice to its extraordinary artistic merits, admits to the full the poverty of its matter; and Johnson, who was too often an unfair and captious critic of Pope, did no injustice to its philosophic pretensions in the trenchant criticsm in which he disposes of them. It is true of the poet here, that "having exalted himself into the chair of wisdom, he tells us much that every man knows, and much that he does not know himself; as, for instance, that we see but little, and that the order of the universe is beyond our comprehension; an opinion not very uncommon; and that there is a chain of subordinate beings from infinite to nothing, of which himself and his readers are ignorant." Nor is it possible to impeach the substantial accuracy of the following admirably put *resumé* of the work.

> Never were penury of knowledge and vulgarity
> of sentiment so happily disguised. The reader feels

his mind full, though he learns nothing; and when he meets it in its new array, no longer knows the talk of his mother and his nurse. When these wonder-working sounds sink into sense, and the doctrine of the Essay is divested of its ornaments, is left to the power of its naked excellence, what shall we discover? That we are, in comparison with our Creator, very weak and ignorant; that we do not uphold the chain of existence; and that we could not make one another with more skill than we are made. . . . To these profound principles of natural knowledge are added some moral instructions equally new; that self-interest, well understood, will produce social concord; that men are mutual gainers by mutual benefits; that evil is sometimes balanced by good; that human advantages are unstable and fallacious, of uncertain duration and doubtful effect; that our true honour is not to have a great part, but to act it well; that virtue only is our own, and that happiness is always in our power.

Yet Johnson's remark that "surely a man of no very comprehensive search may venture to say that he has heard all this before," is not more just than the qualifying observation that "it was never till now recommended by such a blaze of embellishments, or such sweetness of melody."

And not only the poet's own countrymen, but all civilized humanity, as Mr. Courthope points out, has agreed to regard this glittering rosary of commonplaces as an offering dedicated to the whole world of letters. Seven times has it been translated into French verse; once into French prose, and four times into German; the last time as recently as 1874. Five Italian translations of it are in existence, two Portuguese, and one Polish. It was imitated by Voltaire and Wieland, and Kant was in the frequent habit of quoting from it in his lectures. Stronger testimony to Pope's unequalled power of expression there could not be; nor is it credible that such power could have been exerted with results so triumphant upon any subject in which the writer's emotions were not in some measure engaged. It is easy enough to cite evidence—such, for instance, as the famous insertion of the negative in the line which, as it originally stood, declared the world to be a planless maze—in support of the theory that the sentiment of natural religion in the poem is only rhetorically felt; but these arguments, after all, do but go to show that Pope's attitude towards his creed was not—what his nature forbade it to be—the attitude of an impassioned devotee. They fail to show that he did not feel it with all the intensity of which that nature was capable; nor does it seem to me possible to conceive otherwise of the production of the poem. Let us grant that Bolingbroke's "ready-made system of philosophy" was not one pre-eminently calculated to arouse enthusiasm even in a mind predisposed to such an affection, and that Pope's religious sensibilities were not such as to be readily raised to any high temperature even by a far more enkindling subject. Still there is every reason to suppose that all the sparks which such a steel could strike from such a flint were in fact generated, and that it was under a genuine inspiration, so far as it went, that Pope called upon "his St. John" to "awake and leave all meaner things," and himself took up his pen to formulate his queer doctrine of fatalistic Deism, in a confession which for lucidity of statement, brilliancy of wit, and splendidly unflagging animation of movement stands alone in the history alike of creeds and letters.

But one ought not now-a-days to need to say so much in defence of a poem whose workmanship so far surpasses its subject. For if the frigid respect, which is all that Pope can be said to receive from the taste of the present day, be explicable enough when we consider the subject matter of much of his poetry, it is far less easy to explain how it is that he commands no warmer sentiment in respect of his manner. No competent critic has ever disputed, none such critic now disputes, his achievement of a nearly absolute perfection of form. And seeing that we live in times when, to put it broadly, poetic workmanship is regarded by multitudes of people as everything and design and material as nothing, or almost nothing, we should certainly have expected that Pope, considered merely as a literary artist, would be studied with reverential enthusiasm. In an age so much of whose poetry hardly professes to be any more than the "exquisite carving of cherrystones," it might have been thought that that transcendent and glorified piece of cherrystone carving the *Rape of the Lock* would have been recommended by every latter-day poet to his fellows with a *Nocturnâ versate manu versate diurnâ*. It will hardly do to connect the neglect of it with the mere disuse of the heroic metre—for Pope's artistic perfection is not alone, or perhaps even chiefly, metrical. His lines, indeed, have been objected to, even from the metrist's point of view, as pushing smoothness to monotony; the complaint of the "perpetual see-saw" of his couplet is not an unfounded one. Assuredly, it might be possible for some of our modern masters of poetic "vocalization" occasionally to vary Pope's cadences to the relief of the reader's ear. The impossibility would be to relieve the ear by this means without displeasing the mind. The impossibility would be to modify the cæsura of the line, or to diversify the pauses of the couplet, without marring the matchless accommodation of word to thought. This is an excellence of Pope's poetry which has nothing to do with his metre, and which it is possible to strive after, though it may be hopeless to attain it, in any metre whatsoever. How comes it, then, one wonders, that a poetic literature, characterized like ours by an almost painful straining after perfection of poetic expression, should be almost disdainfully indifferent to so supreme a model? The explanation, one must suppose, is to be found in the phenomenon which has been dwelt upon at some length in the foregoing remarks. It is in the perfect and final presentment, not of *impressions*, not of *emotions*, but of *thoughts* that Pope's consummate artistry is principally displayed. His verse may fail to reproduce the perceptions of the senses with the force and truth which many lesser artists of our own day can command; it may often—nay, it does very often—give but inadequate utterance to the experiences of the soul; but over the operations of the mind it is the complete and unerring master. It may present the impression dimly, the emotion coldly, but the thought never fails to emerge from it a flawless jewel. And that I suggest as the reason why a poetry which is given over like ours of to-day to the impression and the emotion, and sets so little store by the thought—which is satisfied with making people see with its own half-sensuous, half-melancholy eyes, and sympathize, if so it may be, with its vague and dreamy moods—can find neither inspiration in the masterly artistic method of Pope nor pattern in his unsurpassable art.

G. K. CHESTERTON
"Pope and the Art of Satire" (1902)
Varied Types
1908, pp. 43–55

The general critical theory common in this and the last century is that it was very easy for the imitators of Pope to write English poetry. The classical couplet was a thing that anyone could do. So far as that goes, one may justifiably answer by asking anyone to try. It may be easier really to have wit, than really, in the boldest and most enduring sense, to have imagination. But it is immeasurably easier to pretend to have imagination than to pretend to have wit. A man may indulge in a sham rhapsody, because it may be the triumph of a rhapsody to be unintelligible. But a man cannot indulge in a sham joke, because it is the ruin of a joke to be unintelligible. A man may pretend to be a poet: he can no more pretend to be a wit than he can pretend to bring rabbits out of a hat without having learnt to be a conjuror. Therefore, it may be submitted, there was a certain discipline in the old antithetical couplet of Pope and his followers. If it did not permit of the great liberty of wisdom used by the minority of great geniuses, neither did it permit of the great liberty of folly which is used by the majority of small writers. A prophet could not be a poet in those days, perhaps, but at least a fool could not be a poet. If we take, for the sake of example, such a line as Pope's:

Damn with faint praise, assent with civil leer,

the test is comparatively simple. A great poet would not have written such a line, perhaps. But a minor poet could not.

Supposing that a lyric poet of the new school really had to deal with such an idea as that expressed in Pope's line about man:

A being darkly wise and rudely great,

Is it really so certain that he would go deeper into the matter than that old antithetical jingle goes? I venture to doubt whether he would really be any wiser or weirder or more imaginative or more profound. The one thing that he would really be, would be longer. Instead of writing,

A being darkly wise and rudely great,

the contemporary poet, in his elaborately ornamented book of verses, would produce something like the following:

A creature
Of feature
More dark, more dark, more dark than skies,
Yea, darkly wise, yea, darkly wise:
Darkly wise as a formless fate.
And if he be great,
If he be great, then rudely great,
Rudely great as a plough that plies,
And darkly wise, and darkly wise.

Have we really learnt to think more broadly? Or have we only learnt to spread our thoughts thinner? I have a dark suspicion that a modern poet might manufacture an admirable lyric out of almost every line of Pope.

There is, of course, an idea in our time that the very antithesis of the typical line of Pope is a mark of artificiality. I shall have occasion more than once to point out that nothing in the world has ever been artificial. But certainly antithesis is not artificial. An element of paradox runs through the whole of existence itself. It begins in the realm of ultimate physics and metaphysics, in the two facts that we cannot imagine a space that is infinite, and that we cannot image a space that is finite.

It runs through the inmost complications of divinity, in that we cannot conceive that Christ in the wilderness was truly pure, unless we also conceive that he desired to sin. It runs, in the same manner, through all the minor matters of morals, so that we cannot imagine courage existing except in conjunction with fear, or magnanimity existing except in conjunction with some temptation to meanness. If Pope and his followers caught this echo of natural irrationality, they were not any the more artificial. Their antitheses were fully in harmony with existence, which is itself a contradiction in terms.

Pope was really a great poet; he was the last great poet of civilisation. Immediately after the fall of him and his school come Burns and Byron, and the reaction towards the savage and the elemental. But to Pope civilisation was still an exciting experiment. Its perruques and ruffles were to him what feathers and bangles are to a South Sea Islander—the real romance of civilisation. And in all the forms of art which peculiarly belong to civilisation, he was supreme. In one especially he was supreme—the great and civilised art of satire. And in this we have fallen away utterly.

We have had a great revival in our time of the cult of violence and hostility. Mr. Henley and his young men have an infinite number of furious epithets with which to overwhelm anyone who differs from them. It is not a placid or untroubled position to be Mr. Henley's enemy, though we know that it is certainly safer than to be his friend. And yet, despite all this, these people produce no satire. Political and social satire is a lost art, like pottery and stained glass. It may be worth while to make some attempt to point out a reason for this.

It may seem a singular observation to say that we are not generous enough to write great satire. This, however, is approximately a very accurate way of describing the case. To write great satire, to attack a man so that he feels the attack and half acknowledges its justice, it is necessary to have a certain intellectual magnanimity which realises the merits of the opponent as well as his defects. This is, indeed, only another way of putting the simple truth that in order to attack an army we must know not only its weak points, but also its strong points. England in the present season and spirit fails in satire for the same simple reason that it fails in war: it despises the enemy. In matters of battle and conquest we have got firmly rooted in our minds the idea (an idea fit for the philosophers of Bedlam) that we can best trample on a people by ignoring all the particular merits which give them a chance of trampling upon us. It has become a breach of etiquette to praise the enemy; whereas, when the enemy is strong, every honest scout ought to praise the enemy. It is impossible to vanquish an army without having a full account of its strength. It is impossible to satirise a man without having a full account of his virtues. It is too much the custom in politics to describe a political opponent as utterly inhuman, as utterly careless of his country, as utterly cynical, which no man ever was since the beginning of the world. This kind of invective may often have a great superficial success: it may hit the mood of the moment; it may raise excitement and applause; it may impress millions. But there is one man among all those millions whom it does not impress, whom it hardly ever touches; that is the man against whom it is directed. The one person for whom the whole satire has been written in vain is the man whom it is the whole object of the institution of satire to reach. He knows that such a description of him is not true. He knows that he is not utterly unpatriotic, or utterly self-seeking, or utterly barbarous and revengeful. He knows that he is an ordinary man, and that he can count as many kindly memories, as many humane instincts, as many hours of decent work and responsibility as any other ordinary man. But behind all this he has his real weaknesses, the real ironies of his soul: behind all these ordinary merits lie the mean compromises, the craven silences, the sullen vanities, the secret brutalities, the unmanly visions of revenge. It is to these that satire should reach if it is to touch the man at whom it is aimed. And to reach these it must pass and salute a whole army of virtues.

If we turn to the great English satirists of the seventeenth and eighteenth centuries, for example, we find that they had this rough, but firm, grasp of the size and strength, the value and the best points of their adversary. Dryden, before hewing Ahitophel in pieces, gives a splendid and spirited account of the insane valour and inspired cunning of the

> daring pilot in extremity,

who was more untrustworthy in calm than in storm, and

> Steered too near the rocks to boast his wit.

The whole is, so far as it goes, a sound and picturesque version of the great Shaftesbury. It would, in many ways, serve as a very sound and picturesque account of Lord Randolph Churchill. But here comes in very pointedly the difference between our modern attempts at satire and the ancient achievement of it. The opponents of Lord Randolph Churchill, both Liberal and Conservative, did not satirise him nobly and honestly, as one of those great wits to madness near allied. They represented him as a mere puppy, a silly and irreverent upstart whose impudence supplied the lack of policy and character. Churchill had grave and even gross faults, a certain coarseness, a certain hard boyish assertiveness, a certain lack of magnanimity, a certain peculiar patrician vulgarity. But he was a much larger man than satire depicted him, and therefore the satire could not and did not overwhelm him. And here we have the cause of the failure of contemporary satire, that it has no magnanimity, that is to say, no patience. It cannot endure to be told that its opponent has his strong points, just as Mr. Chamberlain could not endure to be told that the Boers had a regular army. It can be content with nothing except persuading itself that its opponent is utterly bad or utterly stupid—that is, that he is what he is not and what nobody else is. If we take any prominent politician of the day—such, for example, as Sir William Harcourt—we shall find that this is the point in which all party invective fails. The Tory satire at the expense of Sir William Harcourt is always desperately endeavouring to represent that he is inept, that he makes a fool of himself, that he is disagreeable and disgraceful and untrustworthy. The defect of all that is that we all know that it is untrue. Everyone knows that Sir William Harcourt is not inept, but is almost the ablest Parliamentarian now alive. Everyone knows that he is not disagreeable or disgraceful, but a gentleman of the old school who is on excellent social terms with his antagonists. Everyone knows that he is not untrustworthy, but a man of unimpeachable honour who is much trusted. Above all, he knows it himself, and is therefore affected by the satire exactly as any one of us would be if we were accused of being black or of keeping a shop for the receiving of stolen goods. We might be angry at the libel, but not at the satire: for a man is angry at a libel because it is false, but at a satire because it is true.

Mr. Henley and his young men are very fond of invective and satire; if they wish to know the reason of their failure in these things, they need only turn to the opening of Pope's superb attack upon Addison. The Henleyite's idea of satirising a man is to express a violent contempt for him, and by the heat of this to persuade others and himself that the man is contemptible. I remember reading a satiric attack on Mr. Gladstone by one of the young anarchic Tories, which began by asserting that Mr. Gladstone was a bad public speaker. If these people would, as I have said, go quietly and read Pope's "Atticus," they would see how a great satirist approaches a great enemy:

> Peace to all such! But were there one whose fires
> True genius kindles, and fair fame inspires,
> Blest with each talent, and each art to please,
> And born to write, converse, and live with ease.
> Should such a man—

And then follows the torrent of that terrible criticism. Pope was not such a fool as to try to make out that Addison was a fool. He knew that Addison was not a fool, and he knew that Addison knew it. But hatred, in Pope's case, had become so great and, I was almost going to say, so pure, that it illuminated all things, as love illuminates all things. He said what was really wrong with Addison; and in calm and clear and everlasting colours he painted the picture of the evil of the literary temperament:

> Bear, like the Turk, no brother near the throne,
> View him with scornful, yet with jealous eyes,
> And hate for arts that caused himself to rise.
>
> . . .
>
> Like Cato give his little Senate laws,
> And sit attentive to his own applause.
> While wits and templars every sentence raise,
> And wonder with a foolish face of praise.

This is the kind of thing which really goes to the mark at which it aims. It is penetrated with sorrow and a kind of reverence, and it is addressed directly to a man. This is no mock-tournament to gain the applause of a crowd. It is a deadly duel by the lonely seashore.

In current political materialism there is everywhere the assumption that, without understanding anything of his case or his merits, we can benefit a man practically. Without understanding his case and his merits, we cannot even hurt him.

JONATHAN SWIFT

JONATHAN SWIFT

1667–1745

Jonathan Swift was born in Dublin on November 30, 1667, seven months after his father's death. He was the son of Jonathan Swift and Abigail Erick (or Herrick); since both parents were from England, Swift, though born and educated in Ireland, did not think of himself as Irish. He attended Kilkenny Grammar School and Trinity College, Dublin, where, because of disciplinary problems, he obtained his B.A. degree only by "special grace" (*speciale gratia*).

In 1689 Swift left for England, becoming secretary to Sir William Temple, through whom he apparently hoped to achieve some advancement in political affairs. Nothing came of this association, however, and, having received his M.A. degree in 1692 from Hart Hall, Oxford, Swift took orders as a priest of the Anglican Church of Ireland early in 1695, more to achieve independence than out of any particular religious fervor.

After spending an unhappy year as prebendary of Kilroot, Swift returned to England and remained with Temple at Moor Park until 1699. It was during this period that he began his literary career, writing Pindarics and, in 1697, *The Battle of the Books*, which was inspired by Temple's involvement in the "Phalaris" controversy.

Temple died in 1699, leaving Swift without a patron. He returned to Ireland, settling this time in Dublin as the chaplain to Lord Berkeley, the new Lord Justice of Ireland. In 1704 Swift published *A Tale of a Tub* (along with *The Battle of the Books*), which was primarily an attack on various religious abuses. Swift's outspokenness, manifested also in a number of pamphlets on religious questions, such as *An Argument against Abolishing Christianity* (1708), made it harder for Swift to gain the preferment that would have enabled him to leave Ireland. He was, however, a frequent visitor to England, where he gained a literary reputation, became acquainted with Addison, Steele, Pope, and Congreve, and was briefly, in 1714, a member of the Scriblerus Club with Pope, Gay, Arbuthnot, and others. In 1710 he switched his political allegiance to the Tories, and was active as a political journalist, writing poems and tracts in support of the Tory ministry and editing *The Examiner* for four years. Events in Swift's personal life are reflected in the *Journal to Stella* (1710–13) and in the poem *Cadenus and Vanessa* (1713).

In 1713 Swift became Dean of St. Patrick's Cathedral in Dublin, the highest position he was ever to achieve. The death of Queen Anne in 1714 put an end to his political career and ensured that he would remain in Ireland for most of the rest of his life. He wrote several pamphlets in defense of Irish rights, most notably the *Drapier's Letters* (1724), which frustrated an attempt to circulate debased currency in Ireland.

Swift published *Gulliver's Travels* in 1726; it satirized contemporary politics and the conventions of both philosophical and "factual" tales of exploration. *The Grand Question Debated* and *A Modest Proposal* were published in 1729, and *Verses on the Death of Dr. Swift* in 1731. Having suffered since his twenty-third year from a condition now called Ménière's disease, which causes nausea and loss of equilibrium, Swift developed a brain tumor late in life; in 1742 he lapsed into dementia and died on October 19, 1745.

Personal

Hee has latine and greek, some french, writes a very good and current hand, is very honest and diligent.—SIR WILLIAM TEMPLE, Letter to Sir Robert Southwell (May 29, 1690)

Swift came into the coffee-house, and had a bow from everybody but me. When I came to the antechamber to wait before prayers Dr. Swift was the principal man of talk and business, and acted as Minister of Requests. He was soliciting the Earl of Arran to speak to his brother, the Duke of Ormond, to get a chaplain's place established in the garrison of Hull for Mr. Fiddes, a clergyman in that neighborhood, who had lately been in jail, and published sermons to pay fees. He was promising Mr. Thorold to undertake with my Lord Treasurer that according to his petition he should obtain a salary of 200*l* per annum, as minister of the English Church at Rotterdam. He stopped F. Gwynne, Esq., going in with the red bag to the Queen, and told him aloud he had something to say to him from my Lord Treasurer. He talked with the son of Dr. Davenant to be sent abroad, and took out his pocket-book and wrote down several things as *memoranda* to do for him. He turned to the fire, and took out his gold watch, and telling him the time of day, complained it was very late. A gentleman said, "it was too fast." "How can I help it," says the Doctor, "if the courtiers give me a watch that won't go right?" Then he instructed a young nobleman that the best poet in England was Mr. Pope (a Papist), who had begun a translation of Homer into English verse for which, he said, he must have them all subscribe. "For," says he, "the author *shall not* begin to print till I *have* a thousand guineas for him." Lord Treasurer, after leaving the Queen, came through the room, beckoning Dr. Swift to follow him; both went off just before prayers.—WHITE KENNETT, *Diary*, 1713

J.S. D.D., and D of St P—— was the onely son of Jonathan Swift, who was the seventh or eighth son of Mr Thomas Swift above mentioned, so eminent for his Loyalty and his sufferings.

His Father dyed young, about two years after his marriage. He had some employments, and agencyes. his death was much lamented on account of his reputation for integrity with a tolerable good understanding.

He married Mrs Abigail Erich of Leicester-shire, descended from the most antient family of Ericks, who derive their Lineage from Erick the Forester, a great Commander, who raised an army to oppose the Invasion of William the Conqueror, by whom he was vanquished, but afterwards employed to command that Prince's forces, and in his old age retired to his house in Leicester-shire where his family hath continued ever since, but declining every age, and are now in the condition of very private Gentlemen.

This marriage was on both sides very indiscreet, for his wife brought her husband little or no fortune, and his death happening so suddenly before he could make a sufficient establishment for his family: And his son (not then born) hath often been heard to say that he felt the consequences of that marriage not onely through the whole course of his education, but during the greatest part of his life.

He was born in Dublin on St Andrews day, and when he was a year old, an event happened to him that seems very unusuall; for his Nurse who was a woman of Whitehaven, being under an absolute necessity of seeing one of her relations, who was then extremely sick, and from whom she expected a Legacy; and being at the same time extremely fond of the infant, she stole him on shipboard unknown to his Mother and Uncle, and carryed him with her to Whitehaven, where he continued for almost three years. For when the matter was discovered, His Mother sent orders by all means not to hazard a second voyage, till he could be better able to bear it. The nurse was so carefull of him that before he returnd he had learnt to spell, and by the time that he was three years old he could read any chapter in the Bible.

After his return to Ireld, he was sent at six years old to the School of Kilkenny, from whence at fourteen he was admitted into the University at Dublin, where by the ill Treatment of his nearest Relations, he was so discouraged and sunk in his Spirits, that he too much neglected his Academical Studyes, for which he had no great relish by Nature, and turned himself to reading History and Poetry. So that when the time came for taking his degree of Batchlor, although he had lived with great Regularity and due Observance of the Statutes, he was stopped of his Degree, for Dullness and Insufficiency, and at last hardly admitted in a manner little to his Credit, which is called in that College *Speciali gratia*, and this discreditable mark as I am told, stands upon record in their College Registry.

The Troubles then breaking out, he went to his Mother, who lived in Leicester, and after continuing there some Months, he was received by Sr Wm Temple, whose Father had been a great Friend to the Family, and who was now retired to his House called Moorpark near Farnham in Surrey, where he continued for about two years. For he happened before twenty years old, by a Surfeit of fruit to contract a giddyness and coldness of Stomach, that almost brought him to his Grave, and this disorder pursued him with Intermissions of two or three years to the end of his Life. Upon this Occasion he returned to Ireld by advice of Physicians, who weakly imagined that his native air might be of some use to recover his Health. But growing worse, he soon went back to Sr Wm Temple; with whom growing into some confidence, he was often trusted with matters of great Importance. King William had a high esteem for Sr Wm Temple by a long acquaintance, while that Gentlmn was Ambassador and Mediator of a Generall peace at Nimeguen. The King soon after his Expedition to England, visited his old Friend often at Sheen, and took his advice in affairs of greatest consequence. But Sr W. T. weary of living so

near London, and resolving to retire to a more private Scene, bought an Estate near Farnham in Surrey of about 100 ll a year, where Mr Swift accompanied him.

About that time a Bill was brought in to the H. of Commons for Triennial Parlmts, against which the King who was a stranger to our Constitution, was very averse, by the Advice of some weak People, who persuaded the Earl of Portland that K.Ch. 1st lost his Crown and Life by consenting to pass such a bill. The Earl who was a weak man, came down to Moorpark by His Majesty's orders to have Sr Wm Temple's advice, who said much to show him the Mistake. But he continued still to advise the King against passing the Bill. Whereupon Mr Swift was sent to Kensington with the whole Account of that matter, in writing, to convince the King and the Earl how ill they were informed. He told the Earl to whom he was referred by His Majesty, (and gave it in writing) that the Ruin of K. Charles the 1st was not owing to his passing the Triennial bill, which did not hinder him from dissolving any Parlmt, but to the passing another bill, which put it out of his power to dissolve the Parliamt then in being, without the consent of the House. Mr Swift who was well versed in English History although he were then under twenty one years old, gave the King a short account of the Matter, but a more large one to the Earl of Portland; but all in vain: For the King by ill advisers was prevayled upon to refuse passing the Bill. This was the first time that Mr Swift had ever any converse with Courts, and he told his friends it was the first incident that helped to cure him of vanity. The Consequence of this wrong Step in His Majesty was very unhappy; For it put that Prince under a necessity of introducing those People called Whigs into power and Employments, in order to pacify them. For, although it be held a part of the Kings Prerogative to refuse passing Bills, Yet the Learned in the Law, think otherwise, from that Expression used at the Coronation wherein the Prince obligeth himself to consent to all Laws *quas vulgus elegerit*.

Mr Swift lived with him some time, but resolving to settle himself in some way of living, was inclined to take orders. However, although his fortune was very small, he had a scruple of entring into the Church meerly for support, and Sr Wm Temple then being Master of the Rolls in Ireland offered him an Employ of about 120 ll a year in that office, whereupon Mr Swift told him, that since he had now an opportunity of living without being driven into the Church for a maintenance, he was resolved to go to Ireld and take holy Orders. He was recommended to the Lord Capel, then Ld Deputy, who gave him a Prebend in the North, worth about 100 ll a year, of which growing weary in a few months, he returned to England; resigned his Living in favor of a Friend, and continued in Sr W Temple's house till the Death of that great Man, who besides a Legacy left him the care and trust and Advantage of publishing his posthumous Writings.

Upon this Event Mr Swift removed to London, and applyed by Petition to King William, upon the Claym of a Promise his Majesty had made to Sr W T that he would give Mr Swift a Prebend of Canterbury or Westminster. The Earl of Rumney who professed much friendship for him, promised to second his Petition, but, as he was an old vitious illiterate Rake without any sense of Truth or Honor, said not a word to the King: And Mr Swift after long attendance in vain; thought it better to comply with an Invitation given him by the E. of Berkeley to attend him to Ireland as his Chaplain and private Secretary; His Lordship having been appointed one of the Lords Justices of that Kingdom. He attended his Lordship; who landed near Waterford, and Mr. Swift acted as Secretary the whole Journy to Dublin. But another Person had so far insinuated himself into the Earls favor, by telling him, that the Post of Secretary was not proper for a Clergyman, nor would be of any advantage to one who aimed onely at Church-preferments, that his Lordship after a poor Apology gave that Office to the other.

In some Months, the Deanry of Derry fell vacant; and it was the Earl of Berkeley's turn to dispose of it. Yet things were so ordered that the Secretary having received a Bribe, the Deanry was disposed of to another, and Mr Swift was put off with some other Church-livings not worth above a third part of that rich Deanry, and at this present time, not a sixth. The Excuse pretended was his being too young, although he were then 30 years old.—JONATHAN SWIFT, "Family of Swift," c. 1727

Dr. Swift has an odd blunt way, that is mistaken, by strangers, for ill-nature.—'Tis so odd that there's no describing it but by facts.—I'll tell you one that just comes into my head. One evening Gay and I went to see him: you know how intimately we were all acquainted. On our coming in; "Hey-day, gentlemen," says the Doctor, "what's the meaning of this visit? How come you to leave all the great lords, that you are so fond of, to come hither to see a poor Dean?"—Because we would rather see you than any of them.—"Ay, any one that did not know you so well as I do, might believe you. But, since you are come, I must get some supper for you, I suppose?"—No, Doctor, we have supped already.—"Supped already! that's impossible: why, 'tis not eight o'clock yet."—Indeed we have.—"That's very strange: but if you had not supped, I must have got something for you.—Let me see, what should I have had? a couple of lobsters? ay, that would have done very well;—two shillings: tarts; a shilling. But you will drink a glass of wine with me, though you supped so much before your usual time, only to spare my pocket?"—No, we had rather talk with you, than drink with you.—"But if you had supped with me, as in all reason you ought to have done, you must have drank with me.—A bottle of wine; two shillings.—Two and two, is four; and one is five: just two and sixpence a piece. There, Pope, there's half-a-crown for you; and there's another for you, sir: for I won't save any thing by you I am determined." This was all said and done with his usual seriousness on such occasions; and in spite of every thing we could say to the contrary, he actually obliged us to take the money.—ALEXANDER POPE (1728–30), cited in Joseph Spence, *Anecdotes, Observations and Characters of Books and Men*, ed. S. W. Singer, 1820

Rollin has written a letter very full of compliments to Dr. Swift.—"Has not he affronted him by it?"—No:—the doctor does not hate praise, he only dislikes it when 'tis extravagant or coarse.—When B—— told him he loved him more than all his friends and relations; the dean made him no manner of answer; but said afterwards: "the man's a fool!"—I once said to him, "There's a lady, doctor, that longs to see you, and admires you above all things."—"Then I despise her heartily!" said he.—ALEXANDER POPE (1742–43), cited in Joseph Spence, *Anecdotes, Observations and Characters of Books and Men*, ed. S. W. Singer, 1820

He was in the decline of life when I knew him. His friendship was an honour to me, and to say the truth, I have even drawn advantage from his errors. I have beheld him in all humours and dispositions, and I have formed various speculations from the several weaknesses, to which I observed him liable. His capacity and strength of mind were undoubtedly equal to any task whatever. His pride, his spirit, or his ambition, call it by what name you please, was boundless: but, his views were

checked in his younger years, and the anxiety of that disappointment had a visible effect upon all his actions. He was sour and severe, but not absolutely ill-natured. He was sociable only to particular friends, and to them only at particular hours. He knew politeness more than he practised it. He was a mixture of avarice, and generosity: the former, was frequently prevalent, the latter, seldom appeared, unless excited by compassion. He was open to adulation, and could not, or would not distinguish between low flattery, and just applause. His abilities rendered him superiour to envy. He was undisguised and perfectly sincere. I am induced to think, that he entered into orders, more from some private and fixed resolution, than from absolute choice: be that as it may, he performed the duties of the church with great punctuality, and a decent degree of devotion. He read prayers rather in a strong nervous voice, than in a graceful manner: and altho' he has often been accused of irreligion, nothing of that kind appeared in his conversation or behaviour. His cast of mind induced him to think, and speak more of politics than of religion. His perpetual views were directed towards power: and his chief aim was to be removed into *England*: but when he found himself entirely disappointed, he turned his thoughts to opposition, and became the patron of *Ireland*, in which country he was born.—JOHN BOYLE, EARL OF ORRERY, *Remarks on the Life and Writings of Dr. Jonathan Swift*, 1752, pp. 4–6

I really think my Lord Orrery, in his *Life of Swift*, has intended to be laudably impartial. I have no notion of that friendship which makes a man think himself obliged to gloss over the faults of a man whom he wishes not to have great ones. Is it not a strong proof of the sacred authority of the Scriptures, that the histories of David, Solomon, and its other heros, are handed down to us with their mixture of vices and virtues? Lord Orrery says very high and very great things of Swift. The bad ones we knew, in part, before. Had he attempted to whiten them over, would it not have weakened the credibility of what he says in his favour? I am told, that my Lord is mistaken in some of his facts: for instance, in that, wherein he asserts that Swift's learning was a late acquirement. I am very well warranted by the son of an eminent divine, a prelate, who was for three years what is called his *chum*, in the following account of that fact: Dr. Swift made as great a progress in his learning, at the University of Dublin, in his youth, as any of his cotemporaries; but was so very ill-natured and troublesome, that he was made *Terrae-filius*, (Sir Roger will explain what that means, if your Ladyship is unacquainted with the University term) on purpose to have a pretence to expel him. He raked up all the scandal against the Heads of that University that a severe inquirer, and a still severer temper, could get together into his harangue. He was expelled in consequence of his abuse, and, having his *decessit*, afterwards got admitted, at Oxford, to his degrees.

I cannot find that my Lord was very intimate with him. As from a man of quality, and the son of a nobleman who had been obnoxious to ministers, no doubt but the Dean might countenance those professions of friendship which the young Lord might be forward to make to a man who was looked upon as the genius of Ireland and the fashion. But he could be only acquainted with him in the decline of the Dean's genius.

My Lord, I think, has partly drawn censure upon himself, by a little piece of affectation. *My friends* will, he says, by way of preface to some of the things that the friends of Swift think the severest. I was a little disgusted, as I read it, at these ill-placed assumptions of friendship in words. I thought these affectations below Lord Orrery, as it seemed, by them, as if he was proud of being thought of, as a friend, by the man, who, whatever his head was, had not, I am afraid, near so good a heart as his own.

Mr. Temple, nephew to Sir William Temple, and brother to Lord Palmerston, who lately died at Bath, declared, to a friend of mine, that Sir William hired Swift, at his first entrance into the world, to read to him, and sometimes to be his amanuensis, at the rate of 20£ a year and his board, which was then high preferment to him; but that Sir William never favoured him with his conversation, because of his ill qualities, nor allowed him to sit down at table with him. Swift, your Ladyship will easily see by his writings, had bitterness, satire, moroseness, that must make him insufferable both to equals and inferiors, and unsafe for his superiors to countenance. Sir William Temple was a wise and discerning man. He could easily see through a young fellow taken into a low office, and inclined to forget himself. Probably, too, the Dean was always unpolite, and never could be a man of breeding. Sir William Temple was one of the politest men of his time.

Whoever the lady be, who is so severe upon Lord Orrery, I cannot but think that she is too severe. The story of Swift's marriage, and behaviour to a worthy, very worthy wife, I have been told long before Lord Orrery's history of him came out. It was not, as the angry lady charges, a chimera, but a certain truth. And this I was informed of by a lady of goodness, and no enemy, but to what was bad in Swift. Surely this lady, who calls my Lord to account for his unchristian-like usage of a dead friend, should have shewn a little more of the Christian in her invectives. Near twenty years ago I heard from a gentleman now living, with whom Vanessa lived, or lodged, in England, an account of the Dean's behaviour to the unhappy woman, much less to his reputation than the account my Lord gives of that affair. According to this gentleman's account, she was not the creature that she became when she was in Ireland, whither she followed him, and, in hopes to make herself an interest with his vanity, threw herself into glare and expense; and, at last, by disappointment, into a habit of drinking, till grief and the effects of that vice destroyed her. You may gather from that really pretty piece of his, *Cadenus and Vanessa*, how much he flattered her, and that he took great pains to gloss over that affair. I remember once to have seen a little collection of letters and poetical scraps of Swift's, which passed between him and Mrs. Van Homrigh, this same Vanessa, which the bookseller then told me were sent him to be published, from the originals, by this lady, in resentment of his perfidy. . . .—SAMUEL RICHARDSON, Letter to Lady Bradshaigh (April 22, 1752)

To sum up all—he lived long an honour to the powers of the human mind: and died (as he had lived for some few later years) a sad monument of the infirmities incident to it in this house of clay: and a melancholly mortifying memento to the vanity of the pride of parts. His little power and fortune, whilst he enjoyed them, were in miniature, a resemblance of that great tree which shadowed out the grandeur, might, magnificence and munificence of NEBUCHADNEZZAR: it protected, as far as it could, all those that resorted to it for shade and shelter: and supported those that fled to it, for relief and sustenance; and this was cut down as that was, when God *had purposed to stain the pride of all glory.*

My Lord, when you consider SWIFT's singular, peculiar, and most variegated vein of wit, always rightly intended (although not always so rightly directed) delightful in many instances, and salutary, even where it is most offensive; when you consider his strict truth, his fortitude in resisting oppression, and arbitrary power; his fidelity in friendship; his sincere love and zeal for religion; his uprightness in making right resolutions, and his steadiness in adhering to them: his care of his church, its choir, its œconomy, and its income: his attention to all those that preached in his cathedral, in order to their amendment in pronunciation and style; as also his remarkable attention to the interest of his successors, preferably to his own present emoluments; his invincible patriotism, even to a country which he did not love; his very various, well devised, well judged, and extensive charities, throughout his life; and his whole fortune (to say nothing of his wife's) conveyed to the same christian purposes at his death: charities from which he could enjoy no honour, advantage, or satisfaction of any kind, in this world.

When you consider his ironical and humorous, as well as his serious schemes for the promotion of true religion and virtue; his success in solliciting for the first fruits and twentieths, to the unspeakable benefit of the established church of *Ireland*; and his felicity (to rate it no higher) in giving occasion to the building of fifty new churches in *London*.

All this considered, the character of his life will appear like that of his writings; they will both bear to be re-considered and re-examined with the utmost attention; and will always discover new beauties and excellencies, upon every examination.

They will bear to be considered as the sun, in which the brightness will hide the blemishes; and whenever petulant ignorance, pride, malice, malignity, or envy interposes, to cloud, or sully his fame, I will take upon me to pronounce, that the eclipse will not last long.

To conclude,—no man ever deserved better of any country than SWIFT did of his. A steady, persevering, inflexible friend; a wife, a watchful, and a faithful counsellor under many severe trials, and bitter persecutions, to the manifest hazard, both of his liberty and fortune!

He lived a blessing, he died a benefactor, and his name will ever live an honour to *Ireland.*—PATRICK DELANY, *Observations upon Lord Orrery's* Remarks on the Life and Writings of Dr. Jonathan Swift, 1754, pp. 288–91

I knew him well, tho I never was within side of his house, because I could not flatter, cringe, or meanly humour the extravagances of any man. I am sure I knew him better than any of those friends he entertained twice a-week at the Deanery; *Stella* excepted. I had him often to myself in his rides, and walks, and have studied his soul when he little thought what I was about. As I lodged for a year within a few doors of him, I knew his times of going out to a minute, and generally nicked the opportunity. He was fond of company upon these occasions, and glad to have any rational to talk to: for, whatever was the meaning of it, he rarely had any of his friends attending him at his exercises. One servant only, and no companion, he had with him, as often as I have met him, or came up with him. What gave me the easier access to him, was my being tolerably well acquainted with our politics and history, and knowing many places, things, people, and parties, civil and religious, of his beloved England. Upon this account he was glad I joined him. We talked generally of factions and religion, states, revolutions, leaders, and pieties. Sometimes we had other subjects. Who I was he never knew: nor did I seem to know he was the Dean for a long time; not till one Sunday evening that his Verger put me into his seat at St. Patrick's prayers; without my knowing the Doctor sat there. Then I was obliged to recognize the great man, and seemed in a very great surprize. This pretended ignorance of mine as to the person of the Dean, had given me an opportunity of discoursing more freely with, and of receiving more information from the Doctor, than otherwise I could have enjoyed. The Dean was proud beyond all other mortals that I have seen, and quite another man when he was known.—THOMAS AMORY, "The History of These Memoirs," *Memoirs of Several Ladies of Great Britain*, 1755, pp. xxviii–xxix

SWIFT in his private character was a man of fine address, and perfectly well bred: He knew to a point all the modes and variations of complaisance and politeness. And yet his manners were not framed like the manners of any other mortal: But, corrected by general observation, and adapted to his own peculiar observation, turn of genius, they shone forth, always enlivened more or less with some spirit of dominion, in a blaze of politeness, so inimitably, and so determinately his own, that in effect they seemed to be the result of pure nature, uncopied from any the brightest, or the fairest original.

SWIFT talked a great deal in all companies, without engrossing the conversation to himself. His rule of politeness in this case was, that every man had a right to speak for a minute; and when that minute was out, if nobody else took up the discourse, after a short pause of two or three moments, the same person had an equal right with any of the rest of the company, to speak again, and again, and again, and so on during the whole evening. His chief delight, however, was to entertain, and be entertained, in small circles; which he liked the better, if two or three women of good understanding happened to be of the party; the delicacy of their sentiments, like the delicacy of their frame, being in all likelihood providentially designed, to embellish and refine our conversation, as well as to smooth and polish the roughness of our nature: Which indeed is remarked by SWIFT himself, in his letter to my lord Treasurer OXFORD. "Since the women (saith he) have been left out of all meetings, except parties of play, or where worse designs are carried on, our conversation hath very much degenerated." But, in the character of a *tête à tête* companion, according to the best judgment that I can form of his great abilities, if I may be allowed the expression, he rather excelled himself. Few that are equal to him in that respect, perhaps none that are his superiors, can be found upon earth. He was by no means in the class with those, who pour down their eloquence like a torrent, driving all before it. Far from my desires of that sort, he equally loved to speak, and loved to hearken: Like FALSTAFF, he not only had wit himself, but frequently was the cause of wit in others. However indeed, that universal reverence which was paid to his great abilities, frequently struck a damp on the spirits of those who were not perfectly well acquainted with him; an effect of modesty, which however did not always happen to be construed to their advantage, unless it were in the case of very young people. For, when such persons were gone, if none but his intimates were present, he would express himself with some degree of emotion; and cry, Such a one, I have heard, is a very great man; or such a one, they say, has abundance of learning; or, such a one, I have been told, has an excellent understanding; but GOD deliver me from such companions!—DEANE SWIFT, *An Essay upon the Life, Writings, and Character, of Dr. Jonathan Swift*, 1755, pp. 365–67

Swift was a wild beast, who baited and worried all mankind almost, because his intolerable arrogance, vanity, pride, and ambition were disappointed—he abused Lady Suffolk who tried and wished to raise him, only because she had not power to do so; and one is sure that a man who could deify that silly woman Queen Anne, would have been more profuse of incense to Queen Caroline, who had sense, if the court he paid to her had been crowned with success.—HORACE WALPOLE, Letter to Sir Horace Mann (Jan. 13, 1780)

It is a wonder that, in these days of scientific criticism, the melancholy ocean (ocean, the very reverse of melancholy, breather of health, bringer of food) has not been summoned to account for the dark and tempestuous temper of Swift. The stage-manager of the world's tragi-comedy doubtless needed his pessimism and despair as a foil to the amiable ethics of Addison and the smooth optimism of Pope. What gives his rage against life its peculiar character is that Swift's genius was not speculative, nor in a high sense imaginative, but was eminently practical and positive. He is not confounded by the thought of man's mingled greatness and misery—"how noble in reason! how infinite in faculty!" and yet "the quintessence of dust." "Le silence éternel de ces espaces infinis m'effraie," exclaimed Pascal; but if the eternal silence drives us in from the outposts of creation upon our central self it also invites us to escape from self, and be at rest. Swift never reached out to the eternal silence; the din of this world clattered upon his ears perpetually. He did not expect infinite things from life—infinite love, boundless knowledge, absolute beauty. But he thought men and women might at least be clean, healthy, industrious, quiet, comfortable, honest, friendly, temperate, rational. Was it a too ambitious programme? And he found, or thought he found, them nasty, slothful, diseased, malicious, vain—creatures by so much more hateful than the Yahoo as corrupted reason is worse than brutality itself. Yet his last word in *Gulliver* is one of reconciliation, not of revolt. The sometime pupil of the noble Houyhnhyms will try to apply their lessons of virtue; he will try to enjoy his own speculations in his little garden at Redriff; he will instruct the Yahoos of his own family so far as they are docible animals; he will behold his figure often in a glass, and thus, if possible, habituate himself by time to tolerate the sight of a human creature. Only the pride of a Yahoo drives him mad.

And yet what contradictions! What Titanic pride to strive to see things as a god; to dwarf man's glory or aggrandise his vices with planetary magnifying or diminishing glasses; to distort his features in the concave mirror of the heavens! The Houyhnhyms—Swift's ideals of moral excellence—are calm, rational, benevolent creatures, devoid of passions: and he himself is devoured by scorn and hate. They have not learnt to say the thing that is not: and Swift does not scruple to print monstrous falsehoods for a party purpose. They are modest and cleanly: and Swift flings ordure in the faces of women and of little children. They have tranquil deaths, towards which they move with resignation: and he makes his exit in a rage. —EDWARD DOWDEN, *Academy*, Sept. 30, 1882, p. 233

General

Urg'd by the warmth of Friendship's sacred flame,
But more by all the glories of thy fame;
By all those offsprings of thy learned mind,
In judgment solid, as in wit refin'd,
Resolv'd I sing. Though labouring up the way
To reach my theme, O Swift, accept my lay.
Rapt by the force of thought, and rais'd above,
Through Contemplation's airy fields I rove;
Where powerful Fancy purifies my eye,
And lights the beauties of a brighter sky;
Fresh paints the meadows, bids green shades ascend,
Clear rivers wind, and opening plains extend;
Then fills its landscape through the varied parts
With Virtues, Graces, Sciences, and Arts:

Superior forms, of more than mortal air,
More large than mortals, more serenely fair.
Of these two chiefs, the guardians of thy name,
Conspire to raise thee to the point of fame.
Ye future times, I heard the silver sound!
I saw the Graces form a circle round!
Each, where she fix'd, attentive seem'd to root,
And all, but Eloquence herself, was mute.

High o'er the rest I see the goddess rise,
Loose to the breeze her upper garment flies:
By turns, within her eyes the passions burn,
And softer passions languish in their turn;
Upon her tongue persuasion or command,
And decent action dwells upon her hand.

From out her breast ('twas there the treasure lay)
She drew thy labours to the blaze of day;
Then gaz'd, and read the charms she could inspire,
And taught the listening audience to admire,
How strong thy flight, how large thy grasp of
    thought,
How just thy schemes, how regularly wrought;
How sure you wound when ironies deride,
Which must be seen, and feign to turn aside.
'Twas thus exploring she rejoic'd to see
Her brightest features drawn so near by thee;
"Then here," she cries, "let future ages dwell,
And learn to copy, where they can't excel."

She spake. Applause attended on the close.
Then Poesy, her sister-art, arose;
Her fairer sister, born in deeper ease,
Not made so much for business, more to please.
Upon her cheek sits Beauty ever young;
The soul of Music warbles on her tongue;
Bright in her eyes a pleasing ardour glows,
And from her heart the sweetest temper flows:
A laurel wreath adorns her curls of hair,
And binds their order to the dancing air:
She shakes the colours of her radiant wing,
And, from the spheres, she takes a pitch to sing.
"Thrice happy genius his, whose works have hit
The lucky point of business and of wit.
They seem like showers, which April months prepare
To call their flowery glories up to air:
The drops, descending, take the painted bow,
And dress with sunshine, while for good they flow.
To me retiring oft, he finds relief
In slowly-wasting care, and biting grief:
From me retreating oft, he gives to view
What eases care and grief in others too.
Ye fondly grave, be wise enough to know,
'Life ne'er unbent, were but a life of woe.'
Some, full in stretch for greatness, some for gain,
On his own rack each puts himself to pain.
I'll gently steal you from your toils away,
When balmy winds with scents ambrosial play;
Where, on the banks as crystal rivers flow,
They teach immortal amaranths to grow;
Then, from the mild indulgence of the scene,
Restore your tempers strong for toils again."

She ceas'd. Soft music trembled in the wind,
And sweet delight diffus'd through every mind;
The little Smiles, which still the goddess grace,
Sportive arose, and ran from face to face.
But chief (and in that place the Virtues bless)
A gentle band their eager joy express:
Here, Friendship asks, and Love of Merit longs

To hear the goddesses renew their songs;
Here great Benevolence to Man is pleas'd;
These own their Swift, and grateful hear him prais'd.
You gentle band, you well may bear your part,
You reign superior graces in his heart.

O Swift! if fame be life (as well we know
That bards and heroes have esteem'd it so),
Thou canst not wholly die. Thy works will shine
To future times, and life in fame be thine.
      —THOMAS PARNELL, "To Dr. Swift, On his
        Birthday, November 30th, 1713," 1713

⟨. . .⟩ the books of the ingenious Dr Swift, called the English Rabelais, will never be properly understood in France. He has the honour of being a priest, like Rabelais, and of mocking everything, like Rabelais, but it does him a great disservice, in my humble opinion, to call him by that name. Rabelais, in his extravagant and incomprehensible book, manifested extreme gaiety and even greater impertinence; he was lavish with erudition, obscenities and boredom—a good story in two pages at the expense of volumes of rubbish. Only a few people of peculiar taste fancy themselves able to understand and appreciate the whole of this work; the rest of the nation laughs at Rabelais' jokes and despises the book. He is looked upon as the first of the clowns, and people are sorry that a man with so much intelligence put it to such miserable use. He is a drunken philosopher who only wrote when he was drunk.

Swift is a sensible Rabelais living in civilized society. He lacks, it is true, the gaiety of the earlier writer, but he has all the finesse, reason, discrimination and good taste lacking in our Curé of Meudon. His poems have a strange and almost inimitable flavour, he is full of good fun in verse and prose alike, but to understand him you must travel a bit in his country.—FRANÇOIS MARIE AROUET DE VOLTAIRE, "Letter 22: On Mr Pope and Some Other Famous Poets," *Letters on England (Lettres Philosophiques)*, tr. Leonard Tancock, 1734

When Swift and I were once in the country for some time together, I happened one day to be saying, "that if a man was to take notice of the reflections that came into his mind on a sudden as he was walking in the fields, or sauntering in his study, there might be several of them perhaps as good as his most deliberate thoughts."—On this hint, we both agreed to write down all the volunteer reflections that should thus come into our heads, all the time we staid there. We did so: and this was what afterwards furnished out the maxims published in our miscellanies. Those at the end of one volume are mine; and those in the other Dr. Swift's.—ALEXANDER POPE (1734–36), cited in Joseph Spence, *Anecdotes, Observations and Characters of Books and Men*, ed. S. W. Singer, 1820

Swift has stolen all his humour from Cervantes and Rabelais.—LADY MARY WORTLEY MONTAGU (1740–41), cited in Joseph Spence, *Anecdotes, Observations and Characters of Books and Men*, ed. S. W. Singer, 1820

   "Now mark, SERENA!" (the mild Guide began)
"The proudest Phantom of the gloomy clan,
Appointed, by this surly Monarch's grace,
High-priest of all his Misanthropic race!
See o'er the crowd a throne of vapours lift
That strange and motley form, the shade of SWIFT!
Now shalt thou view" (the guardian Sprite pursues)
"His horrid pennance, that each day renews:
Perchance its terrors may o'erwhelm thy sense,
But trust my care to bear thee safely hence!"
As thus she spoke, above the gazing throng,
High in a sailing cloud the Spectre swept along.

Vain of his power, of elocution proud,
In mystic language he harangu'd the crowd;
The bounds he mark'd, with measure so precise,
Of Equine virtue, and of Human vice,
That, cursing Nature's gifts, without remorse,
Each sullen hearer wish'd himself a Horse.
Pleas'd with the pure effect his sermon wrought,
Th' ambitious Priest a rich Tiara caught,
Which, hovering o'er his high-aspiring head,
Sarcastic Humour dangled by a thread.
The rich Tiara, for his temples fit,
Blaz'd with each polish'd gem of brilliant wit;
And sharp-fac'd Irony, his darling Sprite,
Who rais'd her patron to this giddy height,
Fast on his brow the dangerous honour bound,
But, in the moment that her Priest was crown'd,
His airy throne dissolv'd, and thunder rent the
    ground.
Forth from the yawning earth, with lightning's
    speed,
Sprung the fierce phantom of a fiery Steed,
Spurring his sides, whence bloody poison flow'd,
The ghastly-grinning Fiend, Derision, rode.
In her right-hand a horrid whip she shakes,
Whose sounding lash was form'd of knotted snakes:
An uncouth bugle her left-hand display'd,
From a grey monkey's skull by Malice made;
As her distorted lips this whistle blew,
Forth rush'd the Spectre of a wild Yahoo.
See the poor Wit in hasty terror spring,
And fly for succour to his grisly King!
In vain his piercing cries that succour court:
The grisly King enjoys the cruel sport.
Behold the fierce Yahoo, her victim caught,
Drive her sharp talons thro' the seat of thought!
That copious fountain, which too well supplied
Perverted Ridicule's malignant tide.
Quick from her steed the grinning Fiend descends,
From the pierc'd skull the spleenful brain she rends,
To black Misanthropy, her ghastly King,
See the keen Hag this horrid present bring!
Her daily gift! for, as each day arrives,
Her destin'd victim for new death revives.
The Huntress now, this direst pageant past,
On her wild bugle blew so dread a blast,
The sharp sound pierc'd thro' all the depths of Hell;
The Fiends all answer'd in one hideous yell,
And in a fearful trance the soft SERENA fell.
Hence from the lovely Nymph her senses fled,
Till, thro' the parted curtains of her bed,
The amorous Sun, who now began to rise,
Kist, with a sportive beam, her opening eyes.
—WILLIAM HAYLEY, *The Triumphs of Temper*,
    1781, Canto 3, ll. 587–648

Nature imparting her satyric gift,
Her serious mirth, to Arbuthnot and Swift,
With droll sobriety they rais'd a smile
At folly's cost, themselves unmov'd the while.
That constellation set, the world in vain
Must hope to look upon their like again.
    WILLIAM COWPER, *Table Talk*, 1782, ll.
    656–61

⟨. . .⟩ Dean Swift ⟨. . .⟩ may be placed at the head of those that have employed the plain style. Few writers have discovered more capacity. He treats every subject which he handles, whether serious or ludicrous, in a masterly manner. He knew, almost beyond any man, the purity, the extent, the precision of the English language; and therefore, to such as wish to attain a pure and correct style, he is one of the most useful models. But we must not look for much ornament and grace in his language. His haughty and morose genius made him despise any embellishment of this kind as beneath his dignity. He delivers his sentiments in a plain downright positive manner, like one who is sure he is in the right; and is very indifferent whether you be pleased or not. His sentences are commonly negligently arranged; distinctly enough as to the sense; but without any regard to smoothness of sound; often without much regard to compactness or elegance. If a metaphor, or any other figure, chanced to render his satire more poignant, he would, perhaps, vouchsafe to adopt it, when it came in his way; but if it tended only to embellish and illustrate, he would rather throw it aside. Hence, in his serious pieces, his style often borders upon the dry and unpleasing; in his humorous ones, the plainness of his manner sets off his wit to the highest advantage. There is no froth, nor affectation in it; it seems native and unstudied; and while he hardly appears to smile himself, he makes his reader laugh heartily. To a writer of such a genius as Dean Swift, the plain style was most admirably fitted.—HUGH BLAIR, *Lectures on Rhetoric and Belles Lettres*, 1783, Lecture 17

Swift having been mentioned, Johnson, as usual, treated him with little respect as an authour. Some of us endeavoured to support the Dean of St. Patrick's by various arguments. One in particular praised his *Conduct of the Allies*. JOHNSON. 'Sir, his *Conduct of the Allies* is a performance of very little ability.' 'Surely, Sir, (said Dr. Douglas,) you must allow it has strong facts.' JOHNSON. 'Why yes, Sir; but what is that to the merit of the composition? In the Sessions-paper of the Old Bailey there are strong facts. Housebreaking is a strong fact; robbery is a strong fact; and murder is a *mighty* strong fact; but is great praise due to the historian of those strong facts? No, Sir. Swift has told what he had to tell distinctly enough, but that is all. He had to count ten, and he has counted it right.'—JAMES BOSWELL, *Life of Johnson*, 1791

A vulgar scribbler, certes, stands disgraced
In this nice age, when all aspire to taste;
The dirty language, and the noisome jest,
Which pleased in Swift of yore, we now detest;
Proscribed not only in the world polite,
But even too nasty for a city knight!
    Peace to Swift's faults! his wit hath made them
        pass,
Unmatch'd by all, save matchless Hudibras!
Whose author is perhaps the first we meet,
Who from our couplet lopp'd two final feet;
Nor less in merit than the longer line,
This measure moves a favourite of the Nine.
    —GEORGE GORDON, LORD BYRON, *Hints from
        Horace*, 1811

In Swift's writings there is a false misanthropy grounded upon an exclusive contemplation of the vices and follies of mankind, and this misanthropic tone is also disfigured or brutalized by his obtrusion of physical dirt and coarseness. I think *Gulliver's Travels* the great work of Swift. In the voyages to Lilliput and Brobdingnag he displays the littleness and moral contemptibility of human nature; in that to the Houyhnhnms he represents the disgusting spectacle of man with the understanding only, without the reason or the moral feeling, and in his horse he gives the misanthropic ideal of man—that is, a being virtuous from rule and duty, but untouched by the principle of love.—SAMUEL TAYLOR

COLERIDGE, A *Course of Lectures* (1818), *Literary Remains*, ed. Henry Nelson Coleridge, 1836, Vol. 1, p. 140

Swift's reputation as a poet has been in a manner obscured by the greater splendour, by the natural force and inventive genius of his prose writings; but if he had never written either the *Tale of a Tub* or *Gulliver's Travels*, his name merely as a poet would have come down to us, and have gone down to posterity with well-earned honours. His *Imitations of Horace*, and still more his *Verses on his own Death*, place him in the first rank of agreeable moralists in verse. There is not only a dry humour, an exquisite tone of irony, in these productions of his pen; but there is a touching, unpretending pathos, mixed up with the most whimsical and eccentric strokes of pleasantry and satire. His "Description of the Morning in London," and of a "City Shower," which were first published in the *Tatler*, are among the most delightful of the contents of that very delightful work. Swift shone as one of the most sensible of the poets; he is also distinguished as one of the most nonsensical of them. No man has written so many lack-a-daisical, slip-shod, tedious, trifling, foolish, fantastical verses as he, which are so little an imputation on the wisdom of the writer; and which, in fact, only shew his readiness to oblige others, and to forget himself. He has gone so far as to invent a new stanza of fourteen and sixteen syllable lines for Mary the cookmaid to vent her budget of nothings, and for Mrs. Harris to gossip with the deaf old housekeeper. Oh, when shall we have such another Rector of Laracor!—The *Tale of a Tub* is one of the most masterly compositions in the language, whether for thought, wit, or style. It is so capital and undeniable a proof of the author's talents, that Dr. Johnson, who did not like Swift, would not allow that he wrote it. It is hard that the same performance should stand in the way of a man's promotion to a bishopric, as wanting gravity, and at the same time be denied to be his, as having too much wit. It is a pity the Doctor did not find out some graver author, for whom he felt a critical kindness, on whom to father this splendid but unacknowledged production. Dr. Johnson could not deny that *Gulliver's Travels* were his; he therefore disputed their merits, and said that after the first idea of them was conceived, they were easy to execute; all the rest followed mechanically. I do not know how that may be; but the mechanism employed is something very different from any that the author of *Rasselas* was in the habit of bringing to bear on such occasions. There is nothing more futile, as well as invidious, than this mode of criticising a work of original genius. Its greatest merit is supposed to be in the invention; and you say, very wisely, that it is not *in the execution*. You might as well take away the merit of the invention of the telescope, by saying that, after its uses were explained and understood, any ordinary eyesight could look through it. Whether the excellence of *Gulliver's Travels* is in the conception or the execution, is of little consequence; the power is somewhere, and it is a power that has moved the world. The power is not that of big words and vaunting common places. Swift left these to those who wanted them; and has done what his acuteness and intensity of mind alone could enable any one to conceive or to perform. His object was to strip empty pride and grandeur of the imposing air which external circumstances throw around them; and for this purpose he has cheated the imagination of the illusions which the prejudices of sense and of the world put upon it, by reducing every thing to the abstract predicament of size. He enlarges or diminishes the scale, as he wishes to shew the insignificance or the grossness of our overweening self-love. That he has done this with mathematical precision, with complete presence of mind and perfect keeping, in a manner that comes equally home to the understanding of the man and of the child, does not take away from the merit of the work or the genius of the author. He has taken a new view of human nature, such as a being of a higher sphere might take of it; he has torn the scales from off his moral vision; he has tried an experiment upon human life, and gifted its pretensions from the alloy of circumstances; he has measured it with a rule, has weighed it in a balance, and found it, for the most part, wanting and worthless—in substance and in shew. Nothing solid, nothing valuable is left in his system but virtue and wisdom. What a libel is this upon mankind! What a convincing proof of misanthropy! What presumption and what *malice prepense*, to shew men what they are, and to teach them what they ought to be! What a mortifying stroke aimed at national glory, is that unlucky incident of Gulliver's wading across the channel and carrying off the whole fleet of Blefuscu! After that, we have only to consider which of the contending parties was in the right. What a shock to personal vanity is given in the account of Gulliver's nurse Glumdalclitch! Still, notwithstanding the disparagement to her personal charms, her good-nature remains the same amiable quality as before. I cannot see the harm, the misanthropy, the immoral and degrading tendency of this. The moral lesson is as fine as the intellectual exhibition is amusing. It is an attempt to tear off the mask of imposture from the world; and nothing but imposture has a right to complain of it. It is, indeed, the way with our quacks in morality to preach up the dignity of human nature, to pamper pride and hypocrisy with the idle mockeries of the virtues they pretend to, and which they have not: but it was not Swift's way to cant morality, or any thing else; nor did his genius prompt him to write unmeaning panegyrics on mankind!

I do not, therefore, agree with the estimate of Swift's moral or intellectual character, given by an eminent critic, who does not seem to have forgotten the party politics of Swift. I do not carry my political resentments so far back: I can at this time of day forgive Swift for having been a Tory. I feel little disturbance (whatever I might think of them) at his political sentiments, which died with him, considering how much else he has left behind him of a more solid and imperishable nature! If he had, indeed, (like some others) merely left behind him the lasting infamy of a destroyer of his country, or the shining example of an apostate from liberty, I might have thought the case altered.

The determination with which Swift persisted in a preconcerted theory, savoured of the morbid affection of which he died. There is nothing more likely to drive a man mad, than the being unable to get rid of the idea of the distinction between right and wrong, and an obstinate, constitutional preference of the true to the agreeable. Swift was not a Frenchman. In this respect he differed from Rabelais and Voltaire. They have been accounted the three greatest wits in modern times; but their wit was of a peculiar kind in each. They are little beholden to each other; there is some resemblance between Lord Peter in the *Tale of a Tub*, and Rabelais' Friar John; but in general they are all three authors of a substantive character in themselves. Swift's wit (particularly in his chief prose works) was serious, saturnine, and practical; Rabelais' was fantastical and joyous; Voltaire's was light, sportive, and verbal. Swift's wit was the wit of sense; Rabelais', the wit of nonsense; Voltaire's, of indifference to both. The ludicrous in Swift arises out of his keen sense of impropriety, his soreness and impatience of the least absurdity. He separates, with a severe and caustic air, truth from falsehood, folly from wisdom, 'shews vice her own image, scorn her own feature'; and it is the force, the precision, and the honest abruptness with which the separation is made, that excites our surprise, our admiration, and laughter. He sets a mark of reprobation on that which offends good sense and good manners, which cannot be mistaken, and which holds it up to our ridicule and contempt ever after. His occasional disposition to trifling (already noticed) was a relaxation from the excessive earnestness of his mind. *Indignatio facit versus*. His better genius was his spleen. It was the biting acrimony of his temper that sharpened his other faculties. The truth of his perceptions produced the pointed coruscations of his wit; his playful irony was the result of inward bitterness of thought; his imagination was the product of the literal, dry, incorrigible tenaciousness of his understanding. He endeavoured to escape from the persecution of realities into the regions of fancy, and invented his Lilliputians and Brobdingnagians, Yahoos, and Houynhyms, as a diversion to the more painful knowledge of the world around him: *they* only made him laugh, while men and women made him angry. His feverish impatience made him view the infirmities of that great baby the world, with the same scrutinizing glance and jealous irritability that a parent regards the failings of its offspring; but, as Rousseau has well observed, parents have not on this account been supposed to have more affection for other people's children than their own. In other respects, and except from the sparkling effervescence of his gall, Swift's brain was as 'dry as the remainder biscuit after a voyage.'—WILLIAM HAZLITT, *Lectures on the English Poets*, 1818

Swift was *anima Rabelaisii habitans in sicco*,—the soul of Rabelais dwelling in a dry place.—SAMUEL TAYLOR COLERIDGE, *Table Talk*, June 15, 1830

By far the greatest man of that time, I think, was Jonathan Swift: Dean Swift, a man entirely deprived of his natural nourishment, but of great robustness; of genuine Saxon mind, not without a feeling of reverence, though, from circumstances, it did not awaken in him, for he got unhappily, at the outset, into the Church, not having any vocation for it. It is curious to see him arranging, as it were, a little religion to himself. Some man found him one day giving prayers to his servants in a kind of secret manner, which he did, it seems, every morning, for he was determined, at any rate, to get out of cant; but he was a kind of cultivated heathen, no Christianity in him. He saw himself in a world of confusion and falsehood. No eyes were clearer to see into it than his. He was great from being of acrid temperament: painfully sharp nerves in body as well as soul, for he was constantly ailing, and his mind, at the same time, was soured with indignation at what he saw around him. He took up therefore, what was fittest for him, namely, sarcasm, and he carried it quite to an epic pitch. There is something great and fearful in his irony, for it is not always used for effect, or designedly to depreciate. There seems often to be a sympathy in it with the thing he satirises; occasionally it was even impossible for him so to laugh at any object without a sympathy with it, a sort of love for it; the same love as Cervantes universally shows for his own objects of merit. In his conduct, there is much that is sad and tragic, highly blameable; but I cannot credit all that is said of his cruel unfeeling dissipation. There are many circumstances to show that by nature he was one of the truest of men, of great pity for his fellow-men. For example, we read that he set up banks for the poor Irish in his neighborhood, and required nothing of them but that they should keep their word with him, when they came to borrow. 'Take your own time,' he said, 'but don't come back if you fail to keep the time you tell me.' And if they

had failed, he would tell them, 'Come no more to me, if you have not so much method as to keep your time; if you cannot keep your word, what are you fit for?' All this proves him to have been a man of much affection, but too impatient of others' infirmities. But none of us can have any idea of the bitter misery which lay in him; given up to ambition, confusion, and discontent. He fell into fatalism at last, and madness, that was the end of it. The death of Swift was one of the awfullest; he knew his madness to be coming. A little before his death he saw a tree withered at the top, and he said that, 'like that tree, he, too, was dying at the top.' He was well called by Johnson a driveller and a show, a stern lesson to ambitious people.—THOMAS CARLYLE, *Lectures on the History of Literature*, 1838

We think ⟨. . .⟩ that the obligations which the mind of Swift owed to that of Temple were not inconsiderable. Every judicious reader must be struck by the peculiarities which distinguish Swift's political tracts from all similar works produced by mere men of letters. Let any person compare, for example, the *Conduct of the Allies*, or the *Letter to the October Club*, with Johnson's *False Alarm*, or *Taxation no Tyranny*, and he will be at once struck by the difference of which we speak. He may possibly think Johnson a greater man than Swift. He may possibly prefer Johnson's style to Swift's. But he will at once acknowledge that Johnson writes like a man who has never been out of his study. Swift writes like a man who has passed his whole life in the midst of public business, and to whom the most important affairs of state are as familiar as his weekly bills.

> Turn him to any cause of policy,
> The Gordian knot of it he will unloose,
> Familiar as his garter.

The difference, in short, between a political pamphlet by Johnson, and a political pamphlet by Swift, is as great as the difference between an account of a battle by Mr. Southey and the account of the same battle by Colonel Napier. It is impossible to doubt that the superiority of Swift is to be, in a great measure, attributed to his long and close connection with Temple.—THOMAS BABINGTON MACAULAY, "Sir William Temple" (1838), *Critical, Historical, and Miscellaneous Essays*, 1860, Vol. 4, pp. 102–3

He moves laughter, but never joins in it. He appears in his works such as he appeared in society. All the company are convulsed with merriment, while the Dean, the author of all the mirth, preserves an invincible gravity, and even sourness of aspect, and gives utterance to the most eccentric and ludicrous fancies, with the air of a man reading the commination service.—THOMAS BABINGTON MACAULAY, "The Life and Writings of Addison" (1843), *Critical, Historical, and Miscellaneous Essays*, 1860, Vol. 5, pp. 376–77

Now ⟨. . .⟩ you, commonplace reader, that (as an old tradition) believe Swift's style to be a model of excellence, hereafter I shall say a word to you, drawn from deeper principles. At present I content myself with these three propositions; which overthrow if you can:—

1. That the merit which justly you ascribe to Swift is *vernacularity*, and nothing better or finer: he never forgets his mother-tongue in exotic forms, unless we may call Irish exotic; for some Hibernicisms he certainly has. This merit, however, is exhibited—not, as *you* fancy, in a graceful artlessness, but in a coarse inartificiality. To be artless, and to be inartificial, are very different things,—as different as being natural and being gross, as different as being simple and being homely.

2. That, whatever, meantime, be the particular sort of excellence, or the value of the excellence, in the style of Swift, he had it in common with multitudes besides of that age. Defoe wrote a style for all the world the same as to kind and degree of excellence, only pure from Hibernicisms. So did every honest skipper (Dampier was something more) who had occasion to record his voyages in this world of storms. So did many a hundred of religious writers. And what wonder should there be in this, when the main qualification for such a style was plain good sense, natural feeling, unpretendingness, some little scholarly practice in putting together the clockwork of sentences so as to avoid mechanical awkwardness of construction, but above all the advantage of a *subject* such in its nature as instinctively to reject ornament, lest it should draw off attention from itself? Such subjects are common; but grand impassioned subjects insist upon a different treatment; and *there* it is that the true difficulties of style commence, and there it is that your worshipful Master Jonathan would have broke down irrecoverably.

3. (Which partly is suggested by the last remark.) That nearly all the blockheads with whom I have at any time had the pleasure of conversing upon the subject of style (and pardon me for saying that men of the most sense are apt, upon two subjects—viz. poetry and style—to talk *most* like blockheads) have invariably regarded Swift's style not as if *relatively* good (*i.e. given* a proper subject), but as if *absolutely* good—good unconditionally, no matter what the subject. Now, my friend, suppose the case that the Dean had been required to write a pendant for Sir Walter Raleigh's immortal apostrophe to Death, or to many passages that I could select in Sir Thomas Browne's *Religio Medici* and his *Urn-Burial*, or to Jeremy Taylor's inaugural sections of his *Holy Living and Dying*, do you know what would have happened? Are you aware what sort of ridiculous figure your poor bald Jonathan would have cut? About the same that would be cut by a forlorn scullion from a greasy eating-house at Rotterdam, if suddenly called away in vision to act as seneschal to the festival of Belshazzar the king before a thousand of his lords.—THOMAS DE QUINCEY, "Schlosser's Literary History of the Eighteenth Century" (1847), *Collected Writings*, ed. David Masson, Vol. 11, pp. 17–18

As for the famous Dr. Swift, I can say of him, "Vidi tantum." He was in London all these years up to the death of the Queen; and in a hundred public places where I saw him, but no more; he never missed Court of a Sunday, where once or twice he was pointed out to your grandfather. He would have sought me out eagerly enough had I been a great man with a title to my name, or a star on my coat. At Court the Doctor had no eyes but for the very greatest. Lord Treasurer and St. John used to call him Jonathan; and they paid him with this cheap coin for the service they took of him. He writ their lampoons, fought their enemies, flogged and bullied in their service, and it must be owned with a consummate skill and fierceness. 'Tis said he hath lost his intellect now, and forgotten his wrongs and his rage against mankind. I have always thought of him and of Marlborough as the two greatest men of that age. I have read his books (who doth not know them?) here in our calm woods, and imagine a giant to myself as I think of him, a lonely fallen Prometheus, groaning as the vulture tears him. Prometheus I saw, but when first I ever had any words with him, the giant stepped out of a sedan chair in the Poultry, whither he had come with a tipsy Irish servant parading before him, who announced him, bawling out his Reverence's name, whilst his master below was as yet haggling with the chairman. I disliked

this Mr. Swift, and heard many a story about him, of his conduct to men, and his words to women. He could flatter the great as much as he could bully the weak; and Mr. Esmond, being younger and hotter in that day than now, was determined, should he ever meet this dragon, not to run away from his teeth and his fire.—WILLIAM MAKEPEACE THACKERAY, *The History of Henry Esmond, Esq.*, 1852, Bk. 3, Ch. 5

How realistic or materialistic in treatment of his subject is Swift. He describes his fictitious persons as if for the police. —RALPH WALDO EMERSON, "Literature," *English Traits*, 1856

Indubitably one of the most robust minds of his age, Swift, in the first place, went wholly along with his age, nay, tore it along with him faster than it could decorously go, in its renunciation of romance and all "the sublimities." He, a surpliced priest (as Rabelais had also been), a commissioned expositor of things not seen, *was* an expositor of things not seen; but it was of those that are unseen because they have to be dug for down in the concealing earth, and not of those that fill the upward azure, and tremble by their very nature beyond the sphere of vision. The age for him was still too full of the cant of older beliefs, preserved in the guise of "respectabilities;" and, to help to clear it of this, he would fix its gaze on its own roots, and on the physical roots of human nature in general, down in the disgusting and the reputedly bestial. I say this not in the way of judgment, but of fact. It is what we all know of Swift—they who see good in his merciless method, as well as they who abhor it. But, with all this excess of his age in its own spirit, even to what was considered profanity and blasphemy, Swift, in many respects, adjusted himself to it. He flung himself, none more energetically, into its leading controversy of Whiggism and Toryism. He was at first, somewhat anomalously, a Whig in civil politics and ecclesiastically a High Churchman, consenting to changes in the secular system of the State, but zealous for the preservation and extension of that apparatus of bishoprics, churches, and endowments, which the past had consolidated—though for what end, save that Swifts, as well as Cranmers and Lauds, could work it, he hardly permits us to infer. Later, he was a Tory in state-politics as well. In both stages of his political career, he took an active interest in current social questions. He was as laborious as a prime minister in his partisanship, as vehement and minute in his animosities. He had some peculiar tenets which he perseveringly inculcated—among which was that now called "The Emancipation of Women."

And yet, though he concerned himself in this manner with the controversies and social facts of his time, how, underneath such concern, we see a raging tumult of thought about humanity as a whole, over which all these facts and controversies of his time must have really floated as things ludicrous and contemptible! It is one of the peculiarities of Swift that, though belonging to an age in which Whiggism and Toryism had come in lieu of older distinctions and beliefs, and though himself sharing in the renunciation of these as effete fanaticism, yet in him, more than in any other man of his time, we see a mind bursting the bounds of Whiggism and Toryism, not dwelling in them, seeing round and round them, and familiar in its own recesses with more general and more awful contemplations. True, Swift's philosophy of human nature, in which his partisanship was engulphed, was not the same as that of the elder men—the Shakespeares and the Miltons, whose souls had also tended to the boundless and the general. It was a philosophy of misanthropy rather than of benevolence, of universal despair rather than of hope, of the blackness under the earth, and the demons tugging there at their connexions with man, rather than of the light and evangelism of the countervailing Heaven. But herein at least was a source of strength which made him terrible among his contemporaries. He came among them by day as one whose nights were passed in horror; and hence in all that he said and did there was a vein of ferocious irony.

While all Swift's fictions reveal his characteristic satirical humour, they reveal it in different degrees and on different themes and occasions. In some of his smaller squibs of a fictitious kind we see him as the direct satirist of a political faction. In the *Battle of the Books* we have a satire directed partly against individuals, partly against a prevailing tone of opinion and criticism. In the *Tale of a Tub* he appears as the satirist of the existing Christian Churches, the Papal, the Anglican, and the Presbyterian—treating each with the irreverence of an absolute sceptic in all that Churches rest upon, but arguing in behalf of the second. In the four parts of *Gulliver* he widens the ground. In the Voyage to Laputa, &c., we have a satire on various classes of men and their occupations; and in the Voyages to Lilliput and Brobdingnag, and still more in the story of the Houynhmns and Yahoos, we have satires on human nature and human society, down to their very foundations. With what power, what genius in ludicrous invention, these stories are written, no one needs to be reminded. Schoolboys, who read for the story only, and know nothing of the satire, read *Gulliver* with delight; and our literary critics, even while watching the allegory and commenting on the philosophy, break down in laughter from the sheer grotesqueness of some of the fancies, or are awed into pain and discomfort by the ghastly significance of others. Of Swift we may surely say, that, let our literature last for ages, he will be remembered in it, and chiefly for his fictions, as one of the greatest and most original of our writers—the likest author we have to Rabelais, and yet with British differences. In what cases one would recommend Swift is a question of large connexions. To all strong men he is and will be congenial, for they can bear to look round and round reality on all sides, even on that which connects us with the Yahoos. Universality is best. In our literature, however, there are varieties of spirits—

> Black spirits and white,
> Green spirits and grey;

And so,

> Mingle, mingle, mingle,
> Ye that mingle may.

—DAVID MASSON, *British Novelists and Their Styles*, 1859, pp. 90–94

In truth, the nature of Swift was one of those which neither seek nor obtain the sympathy of ordinary men. Through his whole life his mind was positively diseased, and circumstances singularly galling to a great genius and a sensitive nature combined to aggravate his malady. Educated in poverty and neglect, passing then under the yoke of an uncongenial patron and of an unsuitable profession, condemned during his best years to offices that were little more than menial, consigned after a brief period of triumph to life-long exile in a torpid country, separated from all his friends and baffled in all his projects, he learned to realise the bitterness of great powers with no adequate sphere for their display—of a great genius passed in every walk of worldly ambition by inferior men. His character was softened and improved by prosperity, but it became acrid and virulent in adversity. Hating hypocrisy, he often threw himself into the opposite extreme, and concealed his virtues as other men their vices. Possessing powers of satire perhaps as terrible as have ever been granted to a human being,

he employed them sometimes in lashing impostors like Partridge, or arrogant lawyers like Bettesworth, but very often in unworthy personal or political quarrels. He flung himself unreservedly into party warfare, and was often exceedingly unscrupulous about the means he employed; and there is at least one deep stain on his private character; but he was capable of a very genuine patriotism, of an intense hatred of injustice, of splendid acts of generosity, of a most ardent and constant friendship, and it may be truly said that it was those who knew him best who admired him most. He was also absolutely free from those literary jealousies which were so common among his contemporaries, and from the levity and shallowness of thought and character that were so characteristic of his time.

Of the intellectual grandeur of his career it is needless to speak. The chief sustainer of an English Ministry, the most powerful advocate of the Peace of Utrecht, the creator of public opinion in Ireland, he has graven his name indelibly in English history, and his writings, of their own kind, are unique in English literature. It has been the misfortune of Pope to produce a number of imitators, who made his versification so hackneyed that they produced a reaction against his poetry in which it is often most unduly underrated. Addison, though always read with pleasure, has lost much of his old supremacy. A deeper criticism, a more nervous and stimulating school of political writers have made much that he wrote appear feeble and superficial, and even in his own style it would be possible to produce passages in the writings of Goldsmith and Lamb that might be compared without disadvantage with the best papers of the *Spectator*. But the position of Swift is unaltered. *Gulliver* and the *Tale of a Tub* remain isolated productions, unrivalled, unimitated, and inimitable.—W. E. H. LECKY, "Jonathan Swift," *The Leaders of Public Opinion in Ireland*, 1861

We cannot properly understand Swift's cynicism and bring it into any relation of consistency with our belief in his natural amiability without taking his whole life into account. Few give themselves the trouble to study his beginnings, and few, therefore, give weight enough to the fact that he made a false start. He, the ground of whose nature was an acrid commonsense, whose eye magnified the canker till it effaced the rose, began as what would now be called a romantic poet. With no mastery of verse, for even the English heroic (a balancing-pole which has enabled so many feebler men to walk the ticklish rope of momentary success) was uneasy to him, he essayed the Cowleian Pindarique, as the adjective was then rightly spelled with a hint of Parisian rather than Theban origin. If the master was but a fresh example of the disasters that wait upon every new trial of the flying-machine, what could be expected of the disciple who had not even the secret of the mechanic wings, and who stuck solidly to the earth while with perfect good faith he went through all the motions of soaring? Swift was soon aware of the ludicrousness of his experiment, though he never forgave Cousin Dryden for being aware of it also, and the recoil in a nature so intense as his was sudden and violent. He who could not be a poet if he would, angrily resolved that he would not if he could. Full-sail verse was beyond his skill, but he could manage the simpler fore-and-aft rig of Butler's octosyllabics. As Cowleyism was a trick of seeing everything as it was not, and calling everything something else than it was, he would see things as they were—or as, in his sullen disgust, they seemed to be—and call them all by their right names with a resentful emphasis. He achieved the naked sincerity of a Hottentot—nay, he even went beyond it in rejecting the feeble compromise of the breech-clout. Not only would he be naked and not ashamed, but everybody else should be so with a blush of conscious exposure, and human nature should be stripped of the hypocritical fig-leaves that betrayed by attempting to hide its identity with the brutes that perish. His sincerity was not unconscious, but self-willed and aggressive. But it would be unjust to overlook that he began with himself. He despised mankind because he found something despicable in Jonathan Swift, as he makes Gulliver hate the Yahoos in proportion to their likeness with himself. He had more or less consciously sacrificed self-respect for that false consideration which is paid to a man's accidents; he had preferred the vain pomp of being served on plate, as no other "man of his level" in Ireland was, to being happy with the woman who had sacrificed herself to his selfishness, and the independence he had won turned out to be only a morose solitude after all. "Money," he was fond of saying, "is freedom," but he never learned that self-denial is freedom with the addition of self-respect. With a hearty contempt for the ordinary objects of human ambition, he could yet bring himself for the sake of them to be the obsequious courtier of three royal strumpets. How should he be happy who had defined happiness to be "the perpetual possession of being well deceived," and who could never be deceived himself? It may well be doubted whether what he himself calls "that pretended philosophy which enters into the depth of things and then comes gravely back with informations and discoveries that in the inside they are good for nothing," be of so penetrative an insight as it is apt to suppose, and whether the truth be not rather that to the empty all things are empty. Swift's diseased eye had the miscroscopic quality of Gulliver's in Brobdignag, and it was the loathsome obscenity which this revealed in the skin of things that tainted his imagination when it ventured on what was beneath. But with all Swift's scornful humor, he never made the pitiful mistake of his shallow friend Gay that life was a jest. To his nobler temper it was always profoundly tragic, and the salt of his sarcasm was more often, we suspect, than with most humorists distilled out of tears. The lesson is worth remembering that *his* apples of Sodom, like those of lesser men, were plucked from boughs of his own grafting.—JAMES RUSSELL LOWELL, "Forster's Life of Swift," *Nation*, April 20, 1876, p. 265

Too strong and terrible for Thackeray and Macaulay, Swift is much more so for the average middle-class John Bull, who, while among the bravest of the brave in many respects, is one of the most timorous of mortals face to face with disagreeable truths, truths that perturb his eupeptic comfort, truths hostile to his easy old-fashioned way of thinking without thought, especially if these truths affront his fat inertia in religious, moral, or social questions. This middle-class John Bull, well-fed, well-clothed, well-housed, with a snug balance at his banker's, is the most self-satisfied of optimists, and is simply disgusted and alarmed by a fellow, who as a Dean ought surely to have been contented and sleekly jolly, who never omitted when his birthday came round to read the words of Job: "Let the day perish wherein I was born, and the night in which it was said, There is a man child conceived;" who asked a friend, "Do not the corruptions and villanies of men eat your flesh and exhaust your spirits?" and who wrote of himself in his epitaph: "*Ubi sæva indignatio ulterius cor lacerare nequit.*" —JAMES THOMSON, "A Note on Forster's Life of Swift" (1876), *Essays and Phantasies*, 1881, pp. 287–88

A word must here be said of the most unpleasant part of Swift's character. A morbid interest in the physically disgusting is shown in several of his writings. Some minor pieces, which ought to have been burnt, simply make the gorge rise. Mrs.

Pilkington tells us, and we can for once believe her, that one "poem" actually made her mother sick. It is idle to excuse this on the ground of contemporary freedom of speech. His contemporaries were heartily disgusted. Indeed, though it is true that they revealed certain propensities more openly, I see no reason to think that such propensities were really stronger in them than in their descendants. The objection to Swift is not that he spoke plainly, but that he brooded over filth unnecessarily. No parallel can be found for his tendency even in writers, for example, like Smollett and Fielding, who can be coarse enough when they please, but whose freedom of speech reveals none of Swift's morbid tendency. His indulgence in revolting images is to some extent an indication of a diseased condition of his mind, perhaps of actual mental decay. Delany says that it grew upon him in his later years, and, very gratuitously, attributes it to Pope's influence. The peculiarity is the more remarkable, because Swift was a man of the most scrupulous personal cleanliness. He was always enforcing this virtue with special emphasis. He was rigorously observant of decency in ordinary conversation. Delany once saw him "fall into a furious resentment" with Stella for "a very small failure of delicacy." So far from being habitually coarse, he pushed fastidiousness to the verge of prudery. It is one of the superficial paradoxes of Swift's character that this very shrinking from filth became perverted into an apparently opposite tendency. In truth, his intense repugnance to certain images led him to use them as the only adequate expression of his savage contempt. Instances might be given in some early satires, and in the attack upon dissenters in the *Tale of a Tub*. His intensity of loathing leads him to besmear his antagonists with filth. He becomes disgusting in the effort to express his disgust. As his misanthropy deepened, he applied the same method to mankind at large. He tears aside the veil of decency to show the bestial elements of human nature; and his characteristic irony makes him preserve an apparent calmness during the revolting exhibition. His state of mind is strictly analogous to that of some religious ascetics, who stimulate their contempt for the flesh by fixing their gaze upon decaying bodies. They seek to check the love of beauty by showing us beauty in the grave. The cynic in Mr. Tennyson's poem tells us that every face, however full—

> Padded round with flesh and blood,
> Is but moulded on a skull.

Swift—a practised self-tormentor, though not in the ordinary ascetic sense—mortifies any disposition to admire his fellows by dwelling upon the physical necessities which seem to lower and degrade human pride. Beauty is but skin deep; beneath it is a vile carcase. He always sees the "flayed woman" of the *Tale of a Tub*. The thought is hideous, hateful, horrible, and therefore it fascinates him. He loves to dwell upon the hateful, because it justifies his hate. He nurses his misanthropy, as he might tear his flesh to keep his mortality before his eyes.—SIR LESLIE STEPHEN, *Swift*, 1882, pp. 179–81

Judged with reference to their object, ⟨the⟩ pamphlets of Swift are among the best things in our literature. They have lost much of their interest now that the occasions which prompted them are forgotten. Their constant bitterness, and now and then their nastiness, make them distasteful to sensitive readers. Their simplicity of style seems poverty-stricken to those who think that good writing means fine writing. But those who know what style means will own these pamphlets models of literary art. To be perfectly familiar yet by no means vulgar, to be precise without being pedantic, to argue without becoming tedious, to tell impossible things in a way which makes them seem quite natural, to prejudice your reader whilst yourself seemingly un-prejudiced, to stir him to madness whilst yourself seemingly unmoved, to employ every artifice of the most dexterous advocate whilst never dropping the disguise of the modest parish priest or homely tradesman; all this Swift has done so often and with so much address, that after reading him it seems quite easy to do, and one forgets for a moment that in our literature it has been done by Swift alone. He has done the feat best in the *Drapier's Letters.* I know of nothing else like them, and I know of nothing else which may wait longer for a rival. The reader feels that they could not have been written by a tradesman; yet he cannot well believe that they were written by the Dean. The language has all the literary qualities, yet is that of an illiterate man. The arguments are often unsound enough to find general acceptance, yet the author conceals admirably his knowledge of their unsoundness. The result of the blending of the real author and his imagined trader is as piquant to us as it was exciting to his countrymen.

About the efficacy of Swift's polemical writings there can be no question; but there has been much question as to the nature of Swift's personal opinions. Nor is this surprising when we consider Swift's peculiar position. He put forth all his powers on behalf of the Tories; but he had reached middle-life before he quitted the Whigs. He fought the battles of the Church; but he certainly had no clerical vocation. He pleaded the cause of Ireland, but the country he disliked and the bulk of the people he despised. It is therefore natural that many, especially those who disagreed with him, should have regarded this puissant champion as a mere soldier of fortune, careless for whom he fought, and chagrined only because he failed to secure his booty. What seems to confirm their suspicion is the impartial and unqualified scorn which Swift, in his freer moods, pours out upon all factions, civil or ecclesiastical. What he thought of our venerable Constitution he has betrayed in Gulliver's conversation with the King of Brobdingnag. What he thought of politicians he has told us in the last of the *Drapier's Letters.* "Few politicians, with all their schemes, are half so useful members of a commonwealth as an honest farmer; who, by skilfully draining, fencing, manuring and planting, hath increased the intrinsic value of a piece of land, and thereby done a perpetual service to his country, which it is a great controversy whether any of the former ever did since the creation of the world; but no controversy that ninety-nine in a hundred have done abundant mischief." What Swift thought of ecclesiastical disputes he has pretty plainly told in his *Tale of a Tub,* and still more plainly in those famous lines on the Last Judgment, which, although disputed, seem too pungent to have come from any other author. Such a man might have been expected to set less store by the contentions of Whig and Tory, and to tolerate Nonconformists in a petty allowance of power and preferment. Yet as a Tory and Churchman Swift may have been sincere. If little prone to glorify an established order, he was apt enough to cry down the capacity of mankind. Vicious and foolish as they are, he seems to say, it is odd that they should have been able to set up any civil or ecclesiastical polity. What they have set up may be a poor contrivance; but it is as good as could be expected from them. Why trouble yourself to alter mere mechanical arrangements of state when the men upon whom all depends and for whom all exists are naturally base and necessarily miserable? Why vex your soul with the interminable wrangle of theologians when the very little which we know, or need to know, about religion is plain to every man possessed of common sense, if not puffed up with vanity and presumption? Rather let everything be and possess your soul in patience; for wisdom and endurance lessen the evils which they cannot cure. Let knaves and enthusiasts bawl for reformation; they know not what they want, or if they do, they know that they want their own advantage, not the public good.

Such, we may conjecture, was the real unaffected temper of Swift's mind. Expecting little from change, he was naturally conservative. Knowing how trivial are many of the subjects of political and ecclesiastical debate, he thought the disputants fools, and their noise a nuisance to be suppressed as speedily as possible. Sensitive to everything grotesque or frantic, he preferred a decent routine to the vagaries of enthusiasm. Constitutionally imperious and despotic, he followed his bent on taking the side of authority. Having chosen the clerical profession, he was confirmed in all those innate propensities. He took orders at a time when the Church was making her last effort to retain exclusive domination. He felt as a personal wrong the dissidence of the crowd, the unbelief of the fine gentlemen, and the mean estimation in which his calling was held. Upon considering all these things, we shall be surprised rather at his so long remaining a Whig than at his finally becoming a Tory. Once engaged in a party conflict, he was carried by his fierce, overbearing disposition into every excess which his keen, sceptical intellect might have been expected to condemn. The inconsistency may point his own satire upon man, it should surprise only those who have been able to regulate their lives by strict syllogism.—F. C. MONTAGUE, "Political Pamphlets by Men of Genius," *Murray's Magazine,* Nov. 1891, pp. 751–54

"Proper words, in proper places, make the true definition of a style." This is Swift's own maxim in his *Letter to a Young Clergyman,* dated 1719. It has the common defect of such apophthegms, that we are left to interpret it each in his own way. But Swift has developed his views upon style with some fulness in several passages; and from these we can gather what his ideal was, although it is only natural that a genius such as his refused in practice to be bound very strictly by his own theories. In the *Tatler* for 28th September 1710 he commented severely upon the defects of contemporary prose—the mutilation of words and syllables, the introduction of what we should now call slang, and the sacrifice of dignity, taste, and orderly arrangement to caprice, affectation, and ever-changing fashion. He elaborated this more fully in his *Letter to the Lord Treasurer* (Lord Oxford) of the following year, in which he urged the minister to use his influence to check the vulgarising of our language, by founding an academy which should be empowered to regulate and fix the language, and preserve it against the changing whims of fashion. The project was a strange one, and it may be doubted whether there is not something of irony in Swift's advocacy of it; but his hatred of the absurd straining after originality, which succeeded only in attaining to an affected oddity and eccentricity, was not only serious and earnest, but was of a piece with the whole body of Swift's thought and taste. In both these pieces he points to the prose of the Elizabethan age as the most perfect type. Its distinctive mark he asserts to have been its simplicity—"The best and truest ornament of most things in human life," or, as he repeats in the *Letter to a Young Clergyman,* "That simplicity without which no human performance can arrive to any great perfection." As instances of this perfection he adduces Parsons the Jesuit and Hooker, and he contrasts them with the over-elaboration which was distinctive of the following age. Repeatedly he urges this as the first and most essential quality in good prose, and he found the excellence of the prose writers of the reign of Charles I. to be due to their having recovered for a few years some of the simplicity which marked the Elizabethan age. Clarendon was warmly admired by Swift, and was in great measure his model in his chief historical work, the *Memoirs of the Last Four Years of the Queen*, and he tells with approval of Lord Falkland's practice of testing the intelligibility of a word by consulting a servant, and being guided "by her judgment whether to receive or reject it." There is another passage—this time from Mrs. Pilkington's *Memoirs*—which helps us to understand Swift's conception of good prose. "I would have every man write his own English," said the Dean to Mrs. Pilkington; and when she assented, he followed up his dictum by asking her to explain it. "Not to confine one's self to a set of phrases, as some of our ancient English historians, Camden in particular, seems to have done, but to make use of such words as naturally occur on the subject." It was thus that Mrs. Pilkington represents herself to have replied. Swift seems to have approved the interpretation, and we may reasonably guess that he had given Mrs. Pilkington some help towards it.

These indications of the Dean's opinions are not without interest; but he was the last man to be bound by rules, even of his own making. He inveighs against grammatical errors and looseness of construction, but there is scarcely a page of his own writings in which some trifling infringement of grammatical accuracy is not to be found. Of all prose styles his is perhaps the least subject to parody or to imitation, because it is so admirably adapted to each variety in subject, in tone, in treatment. He wields it with the elastic power of the consummate master, so that, once expressed, each thought seems to be fitted with its natural dress, and no variation in the expression is conceivable without the obscuring and even the destruction of the thought. To the genuine lover of Swift the *Tale of a Tub* will probably always be the chief treasure in his works; and it is there that his style is seen at its perfection. The mere story in the book is of the flimsiest description, and the fact that the story is an allegory rather weakens than increases its interest. Its genius lies in the range of thought, in the light play of fancy, in the absolute ease with which he passes, in one undeviating mood of contemptuous sarcasm, through every varying phase of human interest—metaphysical and social, literary and historical, ecclesiastical and political, with no sign of effort, and yet without relaxing for one moment the restrained irony which dominates the reader with a sense of reserved power.

This is the quality of Swift's prose in which his genius shows its mastery. That genius had, of course, other elements; but merely as a writer of prose, Swift's highest excellence is his consummate ease, his absolute concealment of the art and the artist, and the perfect subordination of his instruments to his subject. It is a necessary consequence of this that his style should have variety; but although it is easy to trace the deliberate effort to assume a certain dialect with a view to dramatic effect, yet Swift never allows his reader to be impressed with the fact that the dialect is purposely assumed. Thus in the *Drapier Letters* there is a distinct homeliness of tone, but he is always careful to avoid any exaggeration; and he never openly imitates a jargon or reproduces peculiarities throughout a prose piece as he frequently does in his verse. Master of prose as he was, he yet denied himself any but what he deemed legitimate methods, and even in *Gulliver's Travels*, his imitations of nautical jargon are never carried on for more than a few lines, and even then they are introduced not so much for the purpose of caricature as to heighten the effect of reality in the narrative.

Of all English prose Swift's has the most of flexibility, the most of nervous and of sinewy force; it is the most perfect as an instrument, and the most deadly in its unerring accuracy of aim. It often disdains grammatical correctness, and violates not infrequently the rules of construction and arrangement. But it is significant that Swift attained the perfection of his art, not by deliberately setting aside the proprieties of diction, but by setting before himself consistently the first and highest ideal of simplicity, by disdaining eccentricity and paradox and the caprice of fashion, and that although he wrote "his own English," as no other did before or since, he was inspired from first to last by a deep reverence for the language, and an ardent desire to maintain its dignity and its purity unchanged and unimpaired.—HENRY CRAIK, "Jonathan Swift," *English Prose*, ed. Henry Craik, 1894, Vol. 3, pp. 387–90

We have hitherto said nothing of Jonathan Swift, yet he flows right across the present field of our vision, from William III. to George II. His course is that of a fiery comet that dashes through the constellation of the wits of Anne, and falls in melancholy ashes long after the occultation of the last of them. The friend and companion of them for a season, he pursues his flaming course with little real relation to their milder orbits, and is one of the most singular and most original figures that our history has produced. Swift was a bundle of paradoxes—a great churchman who has left not a trace on our ecclesiastical system, an ardent politician who was never more than a fly on the wheel. He is immortal on the one side on which he believed his genius ephemeral; he survives solely, but splendidly, as a man of letters. His career was a failure: he began life as a gentleman's dependent, he quitted it "like a poisoned rat in a hole"; with matchless energy and ambition, he won neither place nor power; and in the brief heyday of his influence with the Ministry, he who helped others was impotent to endow himself. Swift is the typical instance of the powerlessness of pure intellect to secure any but intellectual triumphs. But even the victories of his brain were tainted; his genius left a taste of brass on his own palate. That Swift was ever happy, that his self-torturing nature was capable of contentment, is not certain; that for a long period of years he was wretched beyond the lot of man is evident, and those have not sounded the depths of human misery who have not followed in their mysterious obscurity the movements of the character of Swift.

His will was too despotic to yield to his misfortunes; his pride sustained him, and in middle life a fund of restless animal spirits. We know but little of his early years, yet enough to see that the *splendida bilis*, the *sæva indignatio*, which ill-health exacerbated, were his companions from the first. We cannot begin to comprehend his literary work without recognising this. His weapon was ink, and he loved to remember that gall and copperas went to the making of it. It was in that deadest period, at the very close of the seventeenth century, that his prodigious talent first made itself apparent. With no apprenticeship in style, no relation of discipleship to any previous French or English writer, but steeped in the Latin classics, he produced, at the age of thirty, two of the most extraordinary masterpieces of humour and satire which were ever written, the *Tale of a Tub* and the *Battle of the Books*. It was not until five or six years later (1704) that he gave them together, anonymously, to the press. In the *Tale of a Tub* every characteristic of Swift's style is revealed—the mordant wit, the vehement graceful ease, the stringent simplicity. To the end of his days he never wrote better things than the description of the goddess of Criticism drawn by geese in a chariot, the dedication to Prince Posterity with its splendid hilarity and irony, the doubly distilled allegorical apologue of the Spider and the Bee. In his poisonous attacks on the deists, in his gleams of sulky misanthropy, in the strange filthiness of his fancy, in the stranger exhilaration which seizes him whenever the idea of madness is introduced—in all these things Swift reveals his essential character in this his first and perhaps greatest book. Although every one admired it, the *Tale of a Tub* was doubtless fatal to his ambition, thus wrecked at the outset on the reef of his ungovernable satire. The book, to be plain, is a long gibe at theology, and it is not surprising that no bishopric could ever be given to the inventor of the Brown Loaf and the Universal Pickle. He might explain away his mockery, declare it to have been employed in the Anglican cause, emphasise the denial that his aim was irreligious; the damning evidence remained that when he had had the sacred garments in his hands he had torn away, like an infuriated ape, as much of the gold fringe as he could. The fact was that, without any design of impiety, he knew not how to be devout. He always, by instinct, saw the hollowness and the seamy side. His enthusiasms were negative, and his burning imagination, even when he applied it to religion, revealed not heaven but hell to him.

The power and vitality of such a nature could not be concealed; they drew every sincere intellect towards him. Already, in 1705, Addison was hailing Swift as "the most agreeable companion, the truest friend, and the greatest genius of the age." We take him up again in 1711, when the slender volume of *Miscellanies* reminds us of what he had been as a writer from the age of thirty-five to forty-five. The contents of this strange book name for us the three caustic religious treatises, the first of Swift's powerful political tracts (the *Sacramental Test*), various other waifs and rags from his culminating year, 1708, gibes and flouts of many kinds revealing the spirit of "a very positive young man," trifles in verse and prose to amuse his friends the Whig Ministers or the ladies of Lord Berkeley's family. Nothing could be more occasional than all this; nothing, at first sight, less imbued with intensity or serious feeling. Swift's very compliments are impertinent, his arguments in favour of Christianity subversive. But under all this there is the passion of an isolated intellect, and he was giving it play in the frivolities of a compromising humour.

The published writings of Swift during the first forty-four years of his life were comprised in two volumes of very moderate dimensions. But if the purely literary outcome of all this period had been exiguous, it was now to grow scantier still. At the very moment when the group of Anne wits, led by Pope and Addison, were entering with animation upon their best work, Swift, almost ostentatiously, withdrew to the sphere of affairs, and for ten years refrained entirely from all but political authorship. His unexampled *Journal to Stella*, it is true, belongs to this time of obscuration, but it is hardly literature, though of the most intense and pathetic interest. Swift now stood "ten times better" with the new Tories than ever he did with the old Whigs, and his pungent pen poured forth lampoons and satirical projects. The influence of Swift's work of this period upon the style of successive English publicists is extremely curious; he began a new order of political warfare, demanding lighter arms and swifter manœuvres than the seventeenth century had dreamed of. Even Halifax seems cold and slow beside the lightning changes of mood, the inexorable high spirits of Swift. That such a tract as the *Sentiments of a Church of England Man*, with its gusts of irony, its white heat of preposterous moderation, led on towards Junius is obvious; but Swift is really the creator of the whole school of eighteenth-century rhetorical diatribe on its better side, wherever it is not leaden and conventional. It may be said that he invented a vital polemical system, which was used through the remainder of the century by every one who dealt in that kind of literature,

and who was at the same time strong enough to wield such thunderbolts.—EDMUND GOSSE, *A Short History of Modern English Literature*, 1897, pp. 220–24

Works

A TALE OF A TUB

⟨June 15, 1704⟩ I beg your Lordship (if the book is come down to Exon) to read the *Tale of a Tub*. For, bating the profaneness of it in some places, it is a book to be valued, being an original in it's kind, full of wit, humour, good sense and learning. It comes from Christ Church; and a good part of it is written in defence of Mr. Boyle against Wotton and Bentley. The town is wonderfully pleased with it.

⟨July 1, 1704⟩ The author of A *Tale of a Tub* will not as yet be known; and if it be the man I guess, he hath reason to conceal himself, because of the prophane strokes in that piece, which would do his reputation and interest in the world more harm than the wit can do him good. I think your Lordship hath found out a very proper employment for his pen, which he would execute very happily. Nothing can please more than that book doth here at London.—FRANCIS ATTERBURY, Letters to Bishop Trelawney (1704)

I am of your mind as to the *Tale of a Tub*. I am not alone in the opinion, as you are there; but I am pretty near it, having but very few on my side; but those few are worth a million. However, I have never spoke my sentiments, not caring to contradict a multitude. Bottom admires it, and cannot bear my saying, I confess I was diverted with several passages when I read it, but I should not care to read it again. That he thinks not commendation enough.—WILLIAM CONGREVE, Letter to Joseph Keally (Oct. 28, 1704)

Another pernicious Abuse of Wit is that which appears in the Writings of some ingenious Men, who are so hardy as to expose from the Press the most venerable Subjects, and treat Vertue and Sobriety of Manners with Raillery and Ridicule. Several, in their Books, have many sarcastical and spiteful Strokes at Religion in general, while others make themselves pleasant with the Principles of the Christian. Of the last kind this Age has seen a most audacious Example in the Book intitul'd, A *Tale of a Tub*. Had this Writing been publish'd in a Pagan or Popish Nation, who are justly impatient of all Indignity offer'd to the Establish'd Religion of their Country, no doubt but the Author would have receiv'd the Punishment he deserv'd. But the Fate of this impious Buffoon is very different; for in a Protestant Kingdom, zealous of their Civil and Religious Immunities, he has not only escap'd Affronts and the Effects of publick Resentment, but has been caress'd and patroniz'd by Persons of great Figure and of all Denominations. Violent Party Men, who differ'd in all Things besides, agreed, in their Turn, to shew particular Respect and Friendship to this insolent Derider of the Worship of his Country, till at last the reputed Writer is not only gone off with Impunity, but triumphs in his Dignity and Preferment. I do not know, that any Inquiry or Search was ever made after this Writing, or that any Reward was ever offer'd for the Discovery of the Author, or that the infamous Book was ever condemn'd to be burnt in Publick: Whether this proceeds from the excessive Esteem and Love that Men in Power, during the late Reign, had for Wit, or their defect of Zeal and Concern for the Christian Religion, will be determin'd best by those, who are best acquainted with their Character.—SIR RICHARD BLACKMORE, "An Essay upon Wit," *Essays upon Several Subjects*, 1716, pp. 217–18

The *Tale of a Tub* is a work, of perhaps greater felicity of wit, and more ludicrous combinations of ideas, than any other book in the world. It is however, written in so strange a style of "banter," to make use of one of the author's words, or rather in so low and anomalous a slang, which perhaps Swift considered as the necessary concomitant of wit; that it is by no means proper to be cited as an example of just composition.—WILLIAM GODWIN, "Of English Style," *The Enquirer*, 1797, p. 444

It would not, perhaps, be unfair to bring within the pale of the seventeenth century an effusion of genius, sufficient to redeem our name in its annals of fiction. The *Tale of a Tub*, though not published till 1704, was chiefly written, as the author declares, eight years before; and the *Battle of the Books* subjoined to it has every appearance of recent animosity against the opponents of Temple and Boyle, in the question of Phalaris. The *Tale of a Tub* is, in my apprehension, the masterpiece of Swift; certainly Rabelais has nothing superior, even in invention, nor any thing so condensed, so pointed, so full of real meaning, of biting satire, of felicitous analogy.—HENRY HALLAM, *Introduction to the Literature of Europe*, 1837–39, Pt. 4, Ch. 7, Par. 61

The very extraordinary treatise called *A Tale of a Tub* is allowed to rank among the first of its author's productions. It displays his finest qualities of imagination and irony when they were in their freshest and most ebullient condition. Swift himself is said to have remarked, at the close of his life, "Good God, what a genius I had when I wrote that book." It is not long, and it is divided into so many varied sections that it seems shorter than it is. The reader is carried along so gaily on this buoyant tide of wit, that he puts the book down with regret to find it ended, when it seemed but just begun. In this, *A Tale of a Tub* forms a surprising contrast to almost all the prose which had preceded it for half a century, the writers of the Restoration, even where they are most correct and graceful, being devoid of this particular sparkle and crispness of phrase. The book is an allegorical romance, but surrounded by so many digressions, one outside the other, like the parts of an ivory puzzle-ball, that scarcely half of it is even nominally narrative. The name is given from the supposed custom of sailors to throw a tub to a whale to prevent him from rolling against their ship; the treatise being a tub for the leviathans of scepticism to sport with, instead of disturbing the orthodox commonwealth. ⟨. . .⟩

In *A Tale of a Tub* the intellectual interest never halts for a moment. There is infinite variety, and the reader is tantalised by the prodigality of wit, never fatigued for a moment by its expression. In pure style Swift never excelled this his first important essay. The polemical and humorous parts are direct and terse beyond anything that had preceded them in English, and when the author permits himself for a moment to be serious, he speaks with the tongue of angels. In the midst of the profane section on the Æolists, there is a page which reaches as far as our language can reach in the direction of dignity and music; and at all times it may be noted that Swift in this work and in *The Battle of the Books* is more picturesque than anywhere else.—EDMUND GOSSE, *A History of Eighteenth Century Literature*, 1888, pp. 144–47

That Swift was able, when he chose, to fulfil the conditions of the allegory is abundantly proved by *The Tale of a Tub*. This work, written before he had reached his thirtieth year, is full of spirit, wit, and power. The reader of such vigorous and effective English, employed with so much directness and point, cannot but sympathize with the feeling which prompted him to say in his old age, when his mind was gradually failing, "Good God, what a genius I had when I wrote that book!" Not

only is the book his masterpiece, but it is also his best allegory; indeed one would hazard little in making the assertion that it is the best sustained allegory that ever was written.

Three brothers, born at a birth, named Peter, Martin, and Jack, represent the Roman Catholics, the Church of England, and the Dissenters. To these brothers their fathers had bequeathed a coat with strict injunctions never to make any alteration in it; this coat is evidently the Christian religion. In his will, that is, the Bible, were careful instructions as to how the coat should be worn. After seven years, that is, centuries, of faithful obedience, the brothers fell in with three ladies in great reputation at that time, the Duchess d'Argent, Madame de Grand Titres, and the Countess d'Orgueil. A short digression gives us the germ of the "clothes-philosophy," afterwards developed by Carlyle, whereby fine feathers make fine birds. This philosophy being in vogue at that time, as since, the three brothers found their coats decidedly out of fashion and themselves out of favor. Though the will said not a word about shoulder-knots, which were then "the only wear," yet one of the brothers, "more book-learned than the other two," found that the various letters of the word could be picked out separately, with the exception of K; and it was soon discovered that C was the equivalent of K. The interpretation is obvious. In the same skillful manner are allegorized tampering with manuscripts, oral tradition, the use of images, withholding the Bible from the common people, the temporal sovereignty of the Pope, the doctrine of purgatory, penance, confession, absolution, indulgences, holy water, the celibacy of the clergy, transubstantiation, withholding the cup from the laity. Starting with the three brothers, the coat, and the will, as the basis of his allegory, he follows with amazing ingenuity the history of the Church through the centuries of corruption to the Reformation, and thence onward far enough to show the divisions that arose after the Reformation and the growth of sects. Such close and logical correspondence between the sign and the thing signified, it would be difficult to parallel elsewhere in an allegory that possesses a vital interest.

Macaulay's statement that *The Tale of a Tub* swarms with errors in the conduct of its allegory, is not borne out by examination. Some parts, indeed, are expressed more directly than others; such are the celibacy of the clergy and the temporal power of the Pope, which it is scarcely possible to express otherwise than directly. In the entire narrative there are no personifications save those named above of wealth, ambition and pride. The allegory is necessarily historical, and that this is not the highest kind of allegory I shall have occasion later to show. In such an allegory and with the kind of figures that Swift habitually employed, there was little opportunity for true and ennobling symbolism. Setting aside all that should be deducted for the absence of two so important aids to the highest degree of success, and bearing in mind what Swift undertook to do, his allegory is well nigh perfect. The main lines of his narrative were already marked out for him; troublesome details he could omit, if he chose, but in the more important points he had no power of choice. His task was to contrive a close correspondence to the actual history of the church; and this he did in a masterly manner.—HERBERT EVELETH GREENE, "The Allegory as Employed by Spenser, Bunyan, and Swift," *PMLA*, 1889, pp. 168–70

THE DRAPIER'S LETTERS

Let Ireland tell, how Wit upheld her cause,
Her Trade supported, and supply'd her Laws;
And leave on SWIFT this grateful verse ingrav'd,
The Rights a Court attack'd, a Poet sav'd.

Behold the hand that wrought a Nation's cure,
Stretch'd to relieve the Idiot and the Poor,
Proud Vice to brand, or injur'd Worth adorn,
And stretch the Ray to Ages yet unborn.
—ALEXANDER POPE, *Imitations of Horace*, 1737,
Ep. II.i.221–28

On this gloom, one luminary rose; and Ireland worshipped it with almost Persian idolatry: personal resentment was, perhaps, the first motive of the patriotism of SWIFT, but it assumed in its progress a higher port, and directed itself by nobler considerations. The jealousy of the partisan soon expanded into the generous devotion of a patriot, and the power of his mind and the firmness of his character raised him to an ascendancy which no other individual ever attained or deserved; above suspicion, he was trusted; above envy, he was beloved; above rivalry, he was obeyed. His wisdom was at once practical and prophetic; remedial for the present, warning for the future: he first taught Ireland that she might become a nation, and England that she might cease to be a despot. But he was a churchman. His gown impeded his course, and entangled his efforts; guiding a senate, or heading an army, he had perhaps been equal to Cromwell, and Ireland not less than England: as it was, he saved her by his courage, improved her by his authority, adorned her by his talents, and exalted her by his fame. His mission was but of ten years; and for ten years only did his personal power mitigate the government: but when no longer feared by the great, he was yet not forgotten by the wise; his influence, like his writings, has survived a century; and the foundations of whatever prosperity we have since erected, are laid in the disinterested and magnanimous patriotism of Swift.—JOHN WILSON CROKER, *A Sketch of the State of Ireland, Past and Present*, 1808

The Drapier's Letters are the best known of Swift's efforts for Ireland, but were perhaps no more useful than the tracts published subsequently, which are, says Scott, "a bright record of the unceasing zeal with which he continued, through successive years and until the total decay of his mental faculties, to watch over the interests of Ireland,—to warn his countrymen of their errors, to laugh them out of their follies, to vindicate their rights against the oppressions of their powerful neighbors, and to be, in the expressive language of Scripture, the man set for their watchman to blow the trumpet and warn the people." He inveighed, not always in the politest terms, against the luxury and extravagance of women, the folly of improvident marriages, the absenteeism of landlords, the extortions of their agents, the expenditure in England of money wrung from Irish tenants. He described the condition of the unhappy kingdom;—spacious harbors without shipping; fertile soil, capable of producing needed corn and potatoes, but grazed on by sheep whose wool was useless, since its exportation was forbidden; undrained morasses; unrepaired fences; wretched hovels; wretched roads; able-bodied laborers without work; beggars swarming everywhere: and, over all, the English governors, civil, military, clerical, whose sole anxiety was to squeeze as much as possible out of their subjects. Swift's was the single voice crying in that wilderness loudly enough to be heard across the Channel. With bursts of indignation against the oppressor who would not hear, and against the oppressed who, hearing, did not understand, he pleaded for his country, appealing to every motive that could influence the master or the slave. In one pamphlet he suggested, as the only remaining means of relief, that the people should sell their children to the rich, as a new delicacy for the table, and with the proceeds keep the wolf from their doors a little longer. The wonderful irony with which the advantages of

the scheme are set forth, the scientific coolness with which the problem is worked out like a sum in arithmetic, so shocked the sensibilities of Thackeray, that he calls Swift an "ogre" in the nursery. But the meaning of the writer is apparent in every line. In numerous passages in previous tracts he had shown how inapplicable to Ireland was the generally received maxim that "People are the riches of a nation." If Swift played the ogre, it was not for the purpose of frightening children, but to warn parents, their landlords and rulers. England was the ogre whose part he assumed, in order the more forcibly to impress the fearful consequences of persistency in the policy which was ruining Ireland. Having assumed the part, he played it to the life, thinking less perhaps of the feelings of Thackeray and the ladies than of the serious work in hand. Bully Bottom had not been his instructor.—ADAMS SHERMAN HILL, "The Character of Jonathan Swift," *North American Review*, Jan. 1868, pp. 85–86

The Drapier's Letters are epoch-making in that they first taught Ireland the policy and the power of union, of dogged inert resistance, and of strategically organized and directed agitation. Their effect was, in fact, commensurate with their power, and their power of its kind was supreme. It is the power of a deft, vigorous, intent and unerring-eyed wielder of a hammer, who hits each nail on the head and home without one single feint, or flourish, or one single short, or wide, or weak, or wasted stroke. Swift's consummate mastery of the art which conceals art was never shown to such perfection as in these Letters, whose naked simplicity is so like naked truth as to be confounded with it. Yet there was about as much naked truth in them as in *Gulliver's Travels!*—RICHARD ASHE KING, *Swift in Ireland*, 1895, pp. 108–9

GULLIVER'S TRAVELS

Here is a book come out, that all our people of taste run mad about. 'Tis no less than the united Work of a dignify'd clergyman, an Eminent Physician, and the first poet of the Age, and very wonderfull it is, God knows. Great Eloquence have they employ'd to prove themselves Beasts, and show such a veneration for Horses that since the Essex Quaker no body has appear'd so passionately devoted to that species; and to say truth, they talk of a stable with so much warmth and Affection I can't help suspecting some very powerfull Motive at the bottom of it.—LADY MARY WORTLEY MONTAGU, Letter to the Countess of Mar (Nov. 1726)

Your books shall be sent as directed: they have been printed above a month, but I cannot get my subscribers' names. I will make over all my profits to you for the property of *Gulliver's Travels*, which, I believe, will have as great a run as John Bunyan. Gulliver is a happy man that at his age can write such a merry work.
⟨. . .⟩ Lord Scarborough, who is no inventor of stories, told me, that he fell in company with a master of a ship, who told him, that he was very well acquainted with Gulliver, but that the printer had mistaken, that he lived in Wapping, and not in Rotherhithe. I lent the book to an old gentleman, who went immediately to his map to search for Lilliput.—JOHN ARBUTHNOT, Letter to Jonathan Swift (Nov. 8, 1726)

About ten days ago a book was published here of the travels of one Gulliver, which has been the conversation of the whole town ever since: the whole impression sold in a week, and nothing is more diverting than to hear the different opinions people give of it, though all agree in liking it extremely. It is generally said that you are the author; but I am told, the bookseller declares, he knows not from what hand it came. From the highest to the lowest it is universally read, from the cabinet-council to the nursery. The politicians to a man agree, that it is free from particular reflections, but that the satire on general societies of men is too severe. Not but we now and then meet with people of greater perspicuity, who are in search for particular applications in every leaf; and it is highly probable we shall have keys published to give light into Gulliver's design. Lord ⟨Bolingbroke⟩ is the person who least approves it, blaming it as a design of evil consequence to depreciate human nature, at which it cannot be wondered that he takes most offence, being himself the most accomplished of his species, and so losing more than any other of that praise which is due both to the dignity and virtue of a man. Your friend, my Lord Harcourt, commends it very much, though he thinks in some places the matter too far carried. The Duchess Dowager of Marlborough is in raptures at it; she says she can dream of nothing else since she read it; she declares that she has now found out, that her whole life has been lost in caressing the worst part of mankind, and treating the best as her foes; and that if she knew Gulliver, though he had been the worst enemy she ever had, she should give up her present acquaintance for his friendship.

You may see by this, that you are not much injured by being supposed the author of this piece. If you are, you have disobliged us, and two or three of your best friends, in not giving us the least hint of it while you were with us; and in particular Dr. Arbuthnot, who says it is ten thousand pities he had not known it, he could have added such abundance of things upon every subject. Among lady critics, some have found out that Mr. Gulliver had a particular malice to maids of honour. Those of them who frequent the Church, say, his design is impious, and that it is an insult on Providence depreciating the works of the Creator. Notwithstanding, I am told the Princess has read it with great pleasure. As to other critics, they think the flying island is the least entertaining; and so great an opinion the town have of the impossibility of Gulliver's writing at all below himself, it is agreed that part was not writ by the same hand, though this has its defenders too. It has passed Lords and Commons, *nemine contradicente*; and the whole town, men, women, and children are quite full of it. Perhaps I may all this time be talking to you of a book you have never seen, and which has not yet reached Ireland. If it has not, I believe what we have said will be sufficient to recommend it to your reading, and that you will order me to send it to you. But it will be much better to come over yourself, and read it here, where you will have the pleasure of variety of commentators, to explain the difficult passages to you.—JOHN GAY, ALEXANDER POPE, Letter to Jonathan Swift (Nov. 17, 1726)

⟨. . .⟩ O Gulliver, dost thou not shudder at thy brother Lucian's vultures hovering over thee? Shudder on! They cannot shock thee more than decency has been shocked by thee. How have thy Houynhunms thrown thy judgment from its seat, and laid thy imagination in the mire! In what ordure hast thou dipped thy pencil! What a monster hast thou made of the "human face divine!" This writer has so satirised human nature, as to give a demonstration in himself, that it deserves to be satirised. "But," say his wholesale admirers, "few *could* so have written." True, and fewer *would*. If it required great abilities to commit the fault, greater still would have saved him from it. But whence arise such warm advocates for such a performance? From hence, namely, Before a character is established, merit makes fame; afterwards fame makes merit. Swift is not com-

mended for this piece, but this piece for Swift. He has given us some beauties which deserve all our praise; and our comfort is, that his faults will not become common; for none can be guilty of them but who have wit as well as reputation to spare. His wit had been less wild, if his temper had not jostled his judgment. If his favourite Houynhunms could write, and Swift had been one of them, every horse with him would have been an ass, and he would have written a panegyric on mankind, saddling with much reproach the present heroes of his pen: on the contrary, being born amongst men, and, of consequence, piqued by many, and peevish at more, he has blasphemed a nature little lower than that of angels, and assumed by far higher than they. But surely the contempt of the world is not a greater virtue, than the contempt of mankind a vice. Therefore I wonder that, though forborne by others, the laughter-loving Swift was not reproved by the venerable dean, who could sometimes be very grave.—EDWARD YOUNG, *Conjectures on Original Composition*, 1759

The two nations of the giants and the fairies had long been mortal enemies, and most cruel wars had happened between them. At last in the year 2000096 Oberon the 413th had an only daughter who was called Illipip, which signified the corking-pin, from her prodigious stature, she being full eighteen inches high, which the fairies said was an inch taller than Eve the first fairy. Gob, the Emperor of the giants, had an only son, who was as great a miracle for his diminutiveness, for at fifteen he was but seven and thirty feet high, and though he was fed with the milk of sixteen elephants every day, and took three hogsheads of jelly of lions between every meal, he was the most puny child that ever was seen, and nobody expected that he would ever be reared to man's estate. However as it was indispensably necessary to marry him, that the imperial family might not be extinct, and as an opportunity offered of terminating the long wars between the two nations by an union of the hostile houses, ambassadors were sent to demand the Princess of the Fairies, for the Prince of the Giants, who I forgot to say was called the Delicate Mountain. The Queen of the Fairies, who was a woman of violent passions, was extremely offended at the proposal, and vowed that so hopeful a girl as Corking-Pin should not be thrown away upon a dwarf—however as Oberon was a very sage monarch and loved his people, he overruled his wife's impetuosity and granted his daughter. Still the Queen had been so indiscreet as to drop hints of her dissatisfaction before the Princess, and Corking-Pin set out with a sovereign contempt for her husband, whom she said she supposed she should be forced to keep in her toothpick-case for fear of losing him. This witticism was so applauded by all the Court of Fairy that it reached the ears of Emperor Gob and had like to have broken off the match.

On the frontiers of the two kingdoms the Princess was met by the Emperor's carriages. A litter of crimson velvet, embroidered with seed pearls as big as ostriches' eggs, and a little larger than a cathedral was destined for the Princess, and was drawn by twelve dromedaries. At the first stage she found the bridegroom, who for fear of catching cold, had come in a close sedan, which was but six and forty feet high. He had six under-waistcoats of bear-skin, and a white handkerchief about his neck twenty yards long. He had the misfortune of having weak eyes, and when the Princess descended from her litter to meet him he could not distinguish her. She was wonderfully shocked at his not saluting her, but when his governor whispered to him which was she, he spit upon his finger, and stretched out his hand to bring her nearer to his eye, but unluckily fixed upon the great Mistress of the Queen's Household and lifted her up in the air in a very unseemly attitude, to the great diversion of the young fairy lords. The lady squalled dreadfully, thinking the Prince was going to devour her. As misfortune would have it, notwithstanding all the Empress's precautions, the Prince had taken cold, and happening at that very instant to sneeze, he blew the old lady ten leagues off, into a millpond, where it was forty to one but she had been drowned. The whole cavalcade of the fairies was put into great disorder likewise by this untoward accident, and the cabinet councillors deliberated whether they should not carry back the Princess immediately to her father—but Corking-Pin it seems had not found the Prince quite so disagreeable as she had expected, and declared that she would not submit to the disgrace of returning without a husband. Nay, she said, that to prevent any more mistakes, she would have the marriage solemnized that night. The nuptial ceremony was accordingly performed by the Archbishop of Saint Promontory, but the governor declaring that he had the Empress's express injunctions not to let them live together for two years in consideration of the Prince's youth and tender constitution, the Princess was in such a rage, that she swore and stamped like a madwoman, and spit in the Archbishop's face. Nothing could equal the confusion occasioned by this outrage. By the laws of Giantland it was death to spit in a priest's face. The Princess was immediately made close prisoner, and couriers were dispatched to the two courts to inform them of what had happened. By good fortune the chief of the law, who did not love the Archbishop, recollected an old law which said that no woman could be put to death for any crime committed on her wedding day. This discovery split the whole nation of giants into two parties, and occasioned a civil war which lasted till the whole nation of giants was exterminated; and as the fairies from a factious spirit took part with the one side or other, they were all trampled to death, and not a giant or fairy remained to carry on either race.—HORACE WALPOLE, "The Sequel to *Gulliver's Travels*" (Letter to the Countess of Upper Ossery, Dec. 14, 1771)

Critical ingenuity has laboured to discover the sources of the peculiar form taken by this celebrated romance. The author presented the world with one obvious suggestion by stating, in a mock prefatory epistle, that he was the cousin of William Dampier, the famous navigator of the preceding generation. But *Gulliver's Travels* owes most of its external shape to the *Vera Historia* of Lucian, itself a travesty of lost works on geography. The French poet Cyrano de Bergerac (1620–1655) had written a *Voyage à la lune* and a *Histoire comique des états empires du Soleil*, from which Fontenelle had borrowed some hints. Several slight points which Swift used he is said to have taken from a tract by Francis Goodwin, Bishop of Llandaff. There can be no doubt, moreover, that the particular narrative manner of Defoe, whose *Robinson Crusoe* had appeared in 1719, produced an effect upon Swift. All these critical speculations, however, are rather curious than essential. Swift, always among the most original of writers, is nowhere more thoroughly himself than in his enchanting romance of Lemuel Gulliver. Whether we read it, as children do, for the story, or as historians, for the political allusions, or as men of the world, for the satire and philosophy, we have to acknowledge that it is one of the wonderful and unique books of the world's literature.

From internal evidence, it is highly probable that the composition of *Gulliver's Travels* was distributed over a good many years. In the voyages to Lilliput and Brobdingnag there is but little to justify the charges of brutality and cruel violence which are brought against Swift's later satires. They belong to the period of his mental health. The third section of *Gulliver's Travels* is really a miscellany: it has never interested the public so much as the rest of the book; it deals with speculations with which, it is supposed, Swift could not deal without help from Arbuthnot; and it holds no very distinct place among the leading works of the writer. The floating island, though described with unusual picturesqueness of phrase, baffles the most willing faith. When he comes to Lagado, Swift flies too modestly beneath the wing of Rabelais. In Glubbdubdrib the reader soon grows like the narrator, and finds that the domestic spectres "give him no emotion at all." Indeed, this portion of *Gulliver's Travels* would hardly live, were it not for the pathetic imagination of the Struldbrugs, a people whose peculiarities appeal to the most secret instincts of mankind. But in all these miscellaneous excursions there is little or nothing which displays to us the darker side of Swift's genius. That side is, however, exemplified to excess in the final part, the Voyage to the Country of the Houyhnhnms. It is difficult not to believe that this was written during the last illness of Stella, when Swift was aware that his best companion was certainly leaving him, and when that remorse which he could not but feel for his conduct to the woman who had so long loved him was turning what milk remained in his nature to gall. In the summer of 1726 the loss of Stella's conversation made him, he tells us, weary of life, and he fled from Ireland in a horror lest he should be a witness of her end. Delany tells us that from the time of her death, and probably from a few months earlier, Swift's character and temper underwent a change. His vertigo became chronic, and so did his misanthropy, and it seems probable that the first literary expression of his rage and despair was the awful satire of the Yahoos. It was with the horrible satisfaction of disease that Swift formed a story which would enable him to describe men as being, though "with some appearance of cunning, and the strongest disposition to mischief, yet the most unteachable of all brutes," and there is something which suggests a brain not wholly under control in the very machinery of this part of the romance. In Lilliput and in Brobdingnag we are struck by the ingenious harmony of the whole design, there being no detail which is not readily credible if we admit the possibility of the scheme; but among the Houyhnhnms probability is ruthlessly sacrificed to the wild pleasure the author takes in trampling human pride in the mire of his sarcasm. Of the horrible foulness of this satire on the Yahoos enough will have been said when it is admitted that it banishes from decent households a fourth part of one of the most brilliant and delightful of English books.—EDMUND GOSSE, *A History of Eighteenth Century Literature*, 1888, pp. 160–62

⟨. . .⟩ *Gulliver's Travels* is the one work of Swift's which is known to the universal reading public, I suppose, in all European countries. It is in every way his greatest and most characteristic work. Swift's purely intellectual gifts are there in perfection; his vigour, clearness, and ease of style; invention of the first order; wit and humour of the most exquisite. We read it in an abridged form as children; for its marvels, and for the verisimilitude which makes them seem possible, if not wholly credible, and for the Defoe-like handling of detail, which makes it so like what a man would have written had he had such adventures as Gulliver. We are not surprised at the Irish bishop who pronounced it most interesting, but added there were things in it which he could hardly believe. Then, as we grow older, our eyes are opened to the pungent satire scattered through the narrative, upon the trivial or foolish quarrels of men or nations, on the pomps and vanities which men will live and die for; the wars of the "Big-endians" and the "Little-endians," of which, with amazing gravity (and this gravity is a special feature of Swift's irony), the author relates that "it is computed that eleven thousand persons have at several times suffered death rather than submit to break their eggs at the smaller end." We become aware what is meant by the strips of blue and red ribbon for which prominent men at court would contend by jumping over sticks; and it is not till last of all, the sublime audacity of the whole purpose flashes upon the reader. For, besides the incidental satire upon particular blemishes and weaknesses in any one particular state of society, such as that among which Swift dwelt, Swift, by the machinery of his allegory, was able to inflict a deeper, wider wound upon the credit of human nature. He wielded a two-edged sword—a two-handed engine. For the Lilliputians and Brobdingnagians were *men*, though on vaster or more diminutive scale than ordinary; and Swift thereby contrives, without showing that he had any such intention, to show human nature as contemptible when exhibited in the manikins of Lilliput, and gross, horrible, and revolting when magnified into the size of the Brobdingnagian. Samuel Gulliver, from this point of view, is the author himself, looking from a height of calm contemplation, alternately on the pettiness and on the grossness of human vanities or pursuits. And this is what, of course, makes *Gulliver* Swift's most characteristic, most representative work, and places it in a different category from that earlier satire, the *Tale of a Tub*. Taking up that book once in the years of his decay, he was heard to exclaim, "What a genius I had when I wrote that book!" But, brilliant as it is, it is not Swift's masterpiece. There was underlying it—for those who had eyes to see—the scorn for his kind, the grudge and the impeachment of human nature. It was then in the germ, as we have seen, but though the book was profane enough, Swift had not conceived the more profane, the more awful idea, of cursing the very image of his Maker, and hooting and yelling at the flesh and blood which he, the author, was himself compelled to wear. And *Gulliver* belongs, as we see, to Swift's matured powers, if not matured judgment, and the years which should have brought the philosophic mind, but which had brought him only a deadlier hate and scorn. *Gulliver* is the key to Swift's life and works. Swift, writing about human nature, is always either in Lilliput or in Brobdingnag—either pitying and scorning its littleness, or enlarging and dilating on its horror. Yet no one who has watched, in friend and neighbour, or in himself, the manifold inconsistencies which make up the individual life will be surprised that the man who thus looked upon his kind was at the same time capable of affection and admiration for individuals. Swift could love Arbuthnot and Gay and Addison, while he affected to loathe the clay out of which they were formed. Yes, and worse than this, he could be drawn to, and dearly love, the converse and the sympathy of women like Stella and Vanessa, and be aware at the same time that, in accordance with this creed, he was bound to loathe and despise them; yes, and to loathe and despise himself for not being superior to the vulgar affections and needs of mankind. And here may well have been a clue to some portion of his conduct, and to certain elements of his misery. His heart and his creed were in deadly conflict. His heart pleaded with him to be human; his creed said, "to be human is to be despicable or brutal." When he looked on Stella, his heart may have often said, "take her, and be happy"; his creed said, "no, wedded love is also a delusion and a snare." Samuel Taylor Coleridge, in familiar lines, has told us that "to be wrath with one we love, doth work like madness in the brain." But what is even

that struggle between love and anger to compare with this conflict of love and scorn, this self-imposed obligation of disgust and revolt. "I have just beheld," said the Archbishop of Dublin to a friend, after an interview with Swift, "the most miserable man in the world"; and one thinks he must have deserved this description, as truly as any man that ever lived.

Of *Gulliver* the world at large knows chiefly the portions referring to Lilliput and Brobdingnag. It is these only, and then only with careful editings, that one cares to leave about in the schoolroom. The other portions are most surely not "meat for babes"; not because of immorality, or even of coarseness, as ordinarily understood, but because of the horror of the continuous presentation of human nature in every light that can lower it and make it hateful. To compare it unfavourably with the lower animals—such as that indeed noble animal "the horse"—to exaggerate the *animal* aspect of the man, and minimise the spiritual, by ignoring, not only the soul, but *any* sense of dignity and self-respect in the creature—this is the ignoble work Swift set himself to do. And the disastrous character of his method lies in its very skill and adroitness. Here is no Thersites, scattering abuse and ribaldry right and left, but a man, standing a head and shoulders, in cleverness and plausibility, above his contemporaries; employing this ability to sow broadcast the seeds of misanthropy; for though the satire is ostensibly directed against Swift's own country, by making the criticisms of it proceed from a kind of "Utopia," the censure passed is not on this or that country at all, but on the human subject.—ALFRED AINGER, "Swift—His Life and Genius" (1894), *Lectures and Essays*, 1905, Vol. 1, pp. 252–56

The close simulation of the truth employed by Defoe to gain credence for the story of *Robinson Crusoe* was imitated by Swift to lend plausibility to the *Travels into Several remote Nations of the World by Lemuel Gulliver* (1726–1727). Imaginary voyages and travels cannot, for the most part, be regarded as pure romances; they have generally some ulterior purpose in view, political or satirical. Thus Sir Thomas More's *Utopia* (1516) pictures an ideal polity; Francis Godwin's *The Man in the Moon*, written before 1603, borrows its inspiration from Lucian; Bacon's fragment called *The New Atlantis* (1635) sets forth a scheme for the advancement of science; the Duchess of Newcastle's *Description of New World, called the Blazing World* (1666), tells mechanical wonders of a fairy people living at the North Pole; the anonymous *Memoirs of Gaudentio di Lucca* (1737), by Simon Berington, describe an imaginary State conducted on philanthropic principles under a patriarchal government; and Swift's great work, after storming the outposts of human policy and human learning, breaks at last in a torrent of contempt and hatred on the last stronghold of humanity itself. The strength of Swift's work as a contribution to the art of fiction lies in the portentous gravity and absolute mathematical consistency wherewith he developes the consequences of his modest assumptions. In the quality of their realism the voyages to Lilliput and Brobdingnag are much superior to the two later and more violent satires: he was better fitted to ridicule the politics of his time than to attack the "men of Gresham," of whose true aims and methods he knew little or nothing; and the imagination stumbles at many of the details of the last book. But the wealth of illustration whereby he maintains the interest of his original conception of pigmies and giants is eternally surprising and delightful. Defoe could have made of Captain Lemuel Gulliver a living man; he, too, could have recorded with the minutest circumstance of date and place the misadventures and actions of his hero: it may well be doubted whether he could have carried into an unreal world that literalism, accuracy of proportion, and imaginative vividness of detail wherewith Swift endows it. The cat in Brobdingnag makes a noise in purring like "a dozen Stocking-weavers at work;" Gulliver is clad in clothes of the thinnest silk, "not much thicker than an English blanket, very cumbersome, till I was accustomed to them;" the sailing-boat wherein he shows his skill in navigation is taken, when he has done, and hung upon a nail to dry. These are the sources of the pleasure that children take in the book; the astonishing strokes of savage satire that are its chief attraction for their elders derive most of their force from the imperturbable innocence and quietude of manner that disarms suspicion. Like Iago, Gulliver is a fellow "of exceeding honesty," and he goes about his deadly work the better for his bluntness and scrupulous pretence of veracity. But the design of the book forbids its classification among works of pure fiction; it is enough to remark that in *Gulliver* realism achieved one of the greatest of its triumphs before its ultimate conquest of the novel.—WALTER RALEIGH, *The English Novel*, 1894, pp. 136–38

POETRY

I heard my father say, that Mr. Elijah Fenton, who was his intimate friend, and had been his master, informed him that Dryden, upon seeing some of Swift's earliest verses, said to him "Young man, you will never be a poet!"—JOSEPH WARTON, *An Essay on the Genius and Writings of Pope*, 1756–82

Of his Poetry, we do not think there is much to be said;—for we cannot persuade ourselves that Swift was in any respect a poet. It would be proof enough, we think, just to observe, that, though a popular and most miscellaneous writer, he does not mention the name of Shakespeare above two or three times in any part of his works, and has nowhere said a word in his praise. His partial editor admits that he has produced nothing which can be called either sublime or pathetic; and we are of the same opinion as to the beautiful. The merit of correct rhymes and easy diction, we shall not deny him; but the diction is almost invariably that of the most ordinary prose, and the matter of his pieces no otherwise poetical, than that the Muses and some other persons of the Heathen mythology are occasionally mentioned. He has written lampoons and epigrams, and satirical ballads and abusive songs in great abundance, and with infinite success. But these things are not poetry;—and are better in verse than in prose, for no other reason than that the sting is more easily remembered, and the ridicule occasionally enhanced, by the hint of a ludicrous parody, or the drollery of an extraordinary rhyme. His witty verses, where they are not made up of mere filth and venom, seem mostly framed on the model of *Hudibras*; and are chiefly remarkable, like those of his original, for the easy and apt application of homely and familiar phrases, to illustrate ingenious sophistry or unexpected allusions. One or two of his imitations of Horace, are executed with spirit and elegance, and are the best, we think, of his familiar pieces; unless we except the verses on his own death, in which, however, the great charm arises, as we have just stated, from the singular ease and exactness with which he has imitated the style of ordinary society, and the neatness with which he has brought together and reduced to metre such a number of natural, characteristic and commonplace expressions. The *Cadenus and Vanessa* is, of itself, complete proof that he had in him none of the elements of poetry. It was written when his faculties were in their perfection, and his heart animated with all the tenderness of which it was ever capable—and yet it is as cold and as flat as the ice of Thule. Though describing a real passion, and a real perplexity, there is not a spark of fire, nor a throb of emotion in it from one end to the other. All the return he makes to the warm-hearted creature who had put her destiny into his hands, consists in a frigid mythological fiction, in which he sets forth, that Venus and the Graces lavished their gifts on her in her infancy, and moreover got Minerva, by a trick, to inspire her with wit and wisdom. The style is mere prose—or rather a string of familiar and vulgar phrases tacked together in rhyme, like the general tissue of his poetry.—FRANCIS, LORD JEFFREY, "Scott's Edition of Swift," *Edinburgh Review*, Sept. 1816, pp. 49–50

Will poetry calm such a mind? Here, as elsewhere, he is most unfortunate. He is excluded from great transports of imagination, as well as from the lively digressions of conversation. He can attain neither the sublime nor the agreeable; he has neither the artist's rapture, nor the entertainment of the man of the world. Two similar sounds at the end of two equal lines have always consoled the greatest troubles; the old muse, after three thousand years, is a young and divine nurse; and her song lulls the sickly natures whom she still visits, like the young, flourishing races amongst whom she has appeared. The involuntary music, in which thought wraps itself, hides ugliness and unveils nature. Feverish man, after the labors of the evening and the anguish of the night; sees at morning the beaming whiteness of the opening heaven; he gets rid of himself and the joy of nature from all sides enters with oblivion into his heart. If misery pursues him, the poetic afflatus, unable to wipe it out, transforms it; it becomes ennobled, he loves it, and thenceforth he bears it; for the only thing to which he cannot resign himself is littleness. Neither Faust nor Manfred have exhausted human grief; they drank from the cruel cup a generous wine, they did not reach the dregs. They enjoyed themselves and nature; they tasted the greatness which was in them, and the beauty of creation; they pressed with their bruised hands all the thorns with which necessity has made our way thorny, but they saw them blossom with roses, fostered by the purest of their noble blood. There is nothing of the sort in Swift: what is wanting most in his verses is poetry. The positive mind can neither love nor understand it; it sees therein only a machine or a fashion, and employs it only for vanity and conventionality. When in his youth he attempted Pindaric odes, he failed lamentably. I cannot remember a line of his which indicates a genuine sentiment of nature: he saw in the forests only logs of wood, and in the fields only sacks of corn. He employed mythology, as we put on a wig, ill-timed, wearily and scornfully. ⟨. . .⟩

But in prosaic subjects, what truth and force! How this masculine nakedness crushes the artificial poetry of Addison and Pope! There are no epithets; he leaves his thought as he conceived it, valuing it for and by itself, needing neither ornaments, nor preparation, nor extension; above the tricks of the profession, scholastic conventionalisms, the vanity of the rhymester, the difficulties of the art; master of his subject and of himself. This simplicity and naturalness astonish us in verse. Here, as elsewhere, his originality is entire, and his genius creative; he surpasses his classical and timid age; he tyrannizes over form, breaks it, dare utter anything, spares himself no strong word. Acknowledge the greatness of this invention and audacity; he alone is a superior, who finds everything and copies nothing.

⟨. . .⟩ All poetry exalts the mind, but this depresses it; instead of concealing reality, it unveils it; instead of creating illusions, it removes them. When he wishes to give a *description of morning*, he shows us the street-sweepers, the "watchful bailiffs," and imitates the different street cries. When he wishes to paint the rain, he describes "filth of all hues and odors," the "swelling kennels," the "dead cats," "turnip-tops," "stinking sprats," which "come tumbling down the flood." His long verses whirl all this filth in their eddies. We smile to see poetry degraded to this use; we seem to be at a masquerade; it is a queen travestied into a rough country girl. We stop, we look on, with the sort of pleasure we feel in drinking a bitter draught. Truth is always good to know, and in the splendid piece which artists show us, we need a manager to tell us the number of the hired applauders and of the supernumeraries.—HIPPOLYTE TAINE, *History of English Literature*, tr. H. Van Laun, 1871, Bk. 3, Ch. 5

Dryden, then the veteran of our literature, sitting in the dictator's chair left vacant by Ben Jonson and waiting for Samuel Johnson, having perused an ode on the Athenian Society dating from Moor Park, February 14, 1691, hazarded the prediction, 'Cousin Swift, you will never be a poet.' The unforgiven criticism has received from the judgment of posterity an assent qualified by respect for the strongest satirist of England and for an ability which cannot help making itself here and there manifest even in his verse.

Swift's satire is of two kinds: the party polemic of his earlier years, which culminated in 1724 in the *Drapier's Letters*, and the expression of a misanthropy as genuine as that of Shakespeare's Timon, of a rage directed not against Dissent or Church or Whig or Tory, but mankind, finding mature vent in the most terrible libel that has ever been imagined—a libel on the whole of his race—the hideous immortal mockery of the closing voyage of Gulliver. Such a work could only have been written by one born a cynic, doubly soured by some mysterious affliction, and by having had

To fawn, to crouch, to wait, to ride, to run,
To spend, to give, to want, to be undone,

till he had lost any original capacity he may have had for becoming a poet. His genius, moreover, was from the first as far removed from that peculiar to poetry as it is possible for any genius of the first rank to be. The power of Swift's prose was the terror of his own, and remains the wonder of after times. With the exception of a few clumsy paragraphs thrown off in haste, he says what he means in the homeliest native English that can be conceived. Disdaining even those refinements or shades of expression to which most writers touching on delicate or dangerous subjects feel compelled to resort, he owes almost nothing to foreign influence. 'I am,' he wrote, 'for every man's working on his own materials, and producing only what he can find within himself': he consistently carved everything he had to set before his readers out of the plain facts with which he professed to deal. In his masterpieces there is scarce a hint from any known source, rarely a quotation: his sentences are self-sufficient, and fit the occasion as a glove the hand. In the *Tale of a Tub* he anticipates Teufelsdröckh in his contempt for trappings of speech as of person; he regarded fine language as leather and prunella. Though Swift's Allegories are abundant, he disdained ordinary metaphor, in the spirit in which Bentham defined poetry as misrepresentation. But towards the close of the seventeenth and during the end of the eighteenth centuries, almost every English writer—apart from those purely scientific—had to pay toll to what he called the Muses. Bunyan seems to have written his bad lines to italicise the distinction between the most highly imaginative prose and poetry. In the next age no one who addressed the general public could escape the trial; and Swift's verses are at least as worthy of preservation as Addison's. In following a fashion he also gratified a talent,—nor Pope nor Byron had a greater,—for random rhyme. Generally careless, often harsh, his versification is seldom laboured: his pen may run till it wearies the reader; but we see no reason in fall of energy why Swift's Hudibrastic jingle should cease, any more than why the waves of Spenser's stanza should not roll for ever. The other merits of our author's verse are those of his prose—condensation, pith, always the effect, generally the reality, of sincere purpose, and, with few exceptions, simplicity and directness. The exceptions are in his unhappy Pindaric odes, and some of his later contributions to the pedantry of the age. The former could scarcely be worse, for they have almost the contortions of Cowley, without his occasional flow and elevation. Take the following lines from the 'Athenian Ode':

Just so the mighty Nile has suffered in its fame
Because 'tis said (and perhaps only said)
We've found a little inconsiderable head
That feeds the huge, unequal stream.

And again:

And then how much and nothing is mankind,
Whose reason is weighed down by popular air,
Who by that vainly talks of baffling death:
And hopes to lengthen life by a transfusion of breath,
Which yet whoe'er examines right will find
To be an art as vain as bottling up of wind.

As in Congreve's 'Address to Silence' the force of cacophony can no further go. It may be said that these lines were the products of 'green, unknowing youth,' but during the same years the same writer was maturing the *Tale of a Tub*. Swift had no ear save for the discords of the world, and in such cases a stiff regular measure, which is a sort of rhythmic policeman, is the only safe guard. Pindaric flights, unless under the guidance of the genius that makes music as it runs, invariably result in confusion worse confounded. Not least among our debts to Dryden may be ranked his fencing the ode from his cousin Swift. Of the pseudo-classic efforts of the latter, *Cadenus and Vanessa*, published in 1723, probably written about ten years earlier, may be taken as a type. No selection from his verses would be esteemed satisfactory that did not exhibit a sample of this once celebrated production: but, apart from the tragic interest of the personal warning it conveys, it is, as M. Taine says, 'a threadbare allegory in which the author's prosaic freaks tear his Greek frippery.' The same critic justly remarks that Swift 'wore his mythology like a wig: that his pleading before Venus is like a legal procedure,' and that he habitually 'turns his classic wine to vinegar.' The other writers of the time had turned it into milk and water, but Prior and the rest had a grace to which Swift was a stranger. Their laughter is genuine though light; his was funereal and sardonic. His pleasantry is rarely pleasant, and he is never at heart more gloomy than when he affects to be gay. Most of his occasional verses, written at intervals from 1690 till 1733, are either frigid compliments or thinly veiled invectives, many of which, like the epigrams that disfigure the otherwise exquisite pages of Herrick, have all the coarseness with only half the wit of Martial. His addresses to women are, as might be expected, singularly unfortunate. He says truly of himself that he

could praise, esteem, approve,
But understood not what it was to love.

He can never get out of his satiric pulpit, and while saluting his mistresses as nymphs, he lectures them as school-girls. His verses to Stella, whom he came as near to loving as was for him possible, and whose death certainly hastened his mental ruin, are as unimpassioned as those to Vanessa, with whose affec-

tions he merely trifled. Swift's tendency to dwell on the
meaner, and even the revolting facts of life, pardonable in his
prose, is unpardonable in those tributes to Venus Cloacina, in
which he intrudes on a lady's boudoir with the eye of a surgeon
fresh from a dissecting-room or an hospital. His society verses
are like those of a man writing with his feet, for he delights to
trample on what others caress. Often he seems, among singing
birds, a vulture screeching over carrion.

Of Swift's graver satiric pieces, the *Rhapsody on Poetry*
has the fatal drawback of suggesting a comparison with *The
Dunciad*. In *The Beast's Confession*, vivid and trenchant
though it be, the author appears occasionally to intrude on the
gardens of Prior and Gay. Had he been an artist in verse, he
might have written something in English more like the sixth
satire of Juvenal than Churchill ever succeeded in doing. But
Swift despised art: he rode rough-shod, on his ambling cynic
steed, through bad double rhyme and halting rhythm, to his
end. War with the cold steel of prose was his business: his
poems are the mere side-lights and pastimes of a man too grim
to join heartily in any game. Only here and there among
them, as in the strange medley of pathos and humour on his
own death, there is a flash from the eyes which Pope—good
hater and good friend—said were azure as the heavens, a
touch of the hand that was never weary of giving gifts to the
poor and blows to the powerful, a reflection of the universal
condottiere, misanthrope and sceptic, who has a claim to our
forbearance in that he detested, as Johnson and as Byron
detested, cowardice and cant.—J. NICHOL, "Jonathan Swift,"
The English Poets, ed. Thomas Humphry Ward, 1880, Vol. 3,
pp. 35–38

JONATHAN SWIFT
From *Verses on the Death of Dr. Swift*

1731

The Time is not remote, when I
Must by the Course of Nature dye:
When I foresee my special Friends,
Will try to find their private Ends:
'Tho' it is hardly understood,
Which way my Death can do them good;
Yet, thus methinks, I hear 'em speak;
See, how the Dean begins to break:
Poor Gentleman, he droops apace,
You plainly find it in his Face:
That old Vertigo in his Head,
Will never leave him, till he's dead:
Besides, his Memory decays,
He recollects not what he says;
He cannot call his Friends to Mind;
Forgets the Place where last he din'd:
Plyes you with Stories o'er and o'er,
He told them fifty Times before.
How does he fancy we can sit,
To hear his out-of-fashion'd Wit?
But he takes up with younger Fokes,
Who for his Wine will bear his Jokes:
Faith, he must make his Stories shorter,
Or change his Comrades once a Quarter:
In half the Time, he talks them round;
There must another Sett be found.

For Poetry, he's past his Prime,
He takes an Hour to find a Rhime:
His Fire is out, his Wit decay'd,
His Fancy sunk, his Muse a Jade.
I'd have him throw away his Pen;

But there's no talking to some Men.

AND, then their Tenderness appears,
By adding largely to my Years:
"He's older than he would be reckon'd,
And well remembers *Charles* the Second.
"He hardly drinks a Pint of Wine;
And that, I doubt, is no good Sign.
His Stomach too begins to fail:
Last Year we thought him strong and hale;
But now, he's quite another Thing;
I wish he may hold out till Spring.

"THEN hug themselves, and reason thus;
It is not yet so bad with us."

IN such a Case they talk in Tropes,
And, by their Fears express their Hopes:
Some great Misfortune to portend,
No Enemy can match a Friend;
With all the Kindness they profess,
The Merit of a lucky Guess,
(When daily Howd'y's come of Course,
And Servants answer; *Worse and Worse*)
Wou'd please 'em better than to tell,
That, GOD be prais'd, the Dean is well.
Then he who prophecy'd the best,
Approves his Foresight to the rest:
"You know, I always fear'd the worst,
And often told you so at first:"
He'd rather chuse that I should dye,
Than his Prediction prove a Lye.
Not one foretels I shall recover;
But, all agree, to give me over.

YET shou'd some Neighbour feel a Pain,
Just in the Parts, where I complain;
How many a Message would he send?
What hearty Prayers that I should mend?
Enquire what Regimen I kept;
What gave me Ease, and how I slept?
And more lament, when I was dead,
Than all the Sniv'llers round my Bed.

MY good Companions, never fear,
For though you may mistake a Year;
Though your Prognosticks run too fast,
They must be verify'd at last.

"BEHOLD the fatal Day arrive!
How is the Dean? He's just alive.
Now the departing Prayer is read:
He hardly breathes. The Dean is dead.
Before the Passing-Bell begun,
The News thro' half the Town has run.
O, may we all for Death prepare!
What has he left? And who's his Heir?
I know no more than what the News is,
'Tis all bequeath'd to publick Uses.
To publick Use! A perfect Whim!
What had the Publick done for him!
Meer Envy, Avarice, and Pride!
He gave it all:—But first he dy'd.
And had the Dean, in all the Nation,
No worthy Friend, no poor Relation?
So ready to do Strangers good,
Forgetting his own Flesh and Blood?"

Now Grub-Street Wits are all employ'd;
With Elegies, the Town is cloy'd:
Some Paragraph in ev'ry Paper,
To *curse* the *Dean*, or *bless* the *Drapier*. [1]

THE Doctors tender of their Fame,

Wisely on me lay all the Blame:
"We must confess his Case was nice;
But he would never take Advice:
Had he been rul'd, for ought appears,
He might have liv'd these Twenty Years:
For when we open'd him we found,
That all his vital Parts were sound."

FROM *Dublin* soon to *London* spread,
'Tis told at Court, the Dean is dead.[2]

KIND Lady *Suffolk* in the Spleen,[3]
Runs laughing up to tell the Queen.
The Queen, so Gracious, Mild, and Good,
Cries, "Is he gone? 'Tis time he shou'd.
He's dead you say; why let him rot;
I'm glad the Medals were forgot.[4]
I promis'd them, I own; but when?
I only was the Princess then;
But now as Consort of the King,
You know 'tis quite a different Thing."

Now, *Chartres*[5] at Sir *Robert*'s Levee,
Tells, with a Sneer, the Tidings heavy:
"Why, is he dead without his Shoes?"
(Cries *Bob*)[6] "I'm Sorry for the News;
Oh, were the Wretch but living still,
And in his Place my good Friend *Will*;[7]
Or, had a Mitre on his Head
Provided *Bolingbroke*[8] were dead."

Now *Curl*[9] his Shop from Rubbish drains;
Three genuine Tomes of *Swift*'s Remains.
And then to make them pass the glibber,
Revis'd by *Tibbalds, Moore, and Cibber*.[10]
He'll treat me as he does my Betters.
Publish my Will, my Life, my Letters.[11]
Revive the Libels born to dye;
Which POPE must bear, as well as I.

HERE shift the Scene, to represent
How those I love, my Death lament.
Poor POPE will grieve a Month; and GAY
A Week; and ARBUTHNOTT a Day.

ST. JOHN himself will scarce forbear,
To bite his Pen, and drop a Tear.
The rest will give a Shrug and cry,
I'm sorry; but we all must dye.
Indifference clad in Wisdom's Guise,
All Fortitude of Mind supplies:
For how can stony Bowels melt,
In those who never Pity felt;
When *We* are lash'd, *They* kiss the Rod;
Resigning to the Will of God.

THE Fools, my Juniors by a Year,
Are tortur'd with Suspence and Fear.
Who wisely thought my Age a Screen,
When Death approach'd, to stand between:
The Screen remov'd, their Hearts are trembling,
They mourn for me without dissembling.

MY female Friends, whose tender Hearts
Have better learn'd to act their Parts.
Receive the News in *doleful Dumps*,
"The Dean is dead, (*and what is Trumps?*)
Then Lord have Mercy on his Soul.
(Ladies I'll venture for the *Vole*.)
Six Deans they say must bear the Pall.
(I wish I knew what *King* to call.)
Madam, your Husband will attend
The Funeral of so good a Friend.

No Madam, 'tis a shocking Sight,
And he's engag'd To-morrow Night!
My Lady *Club* wou'd take it ill,
If he shou'd fail her at *Quadrill*.
He lov'd the Dean. (*I lead a Heart*.)
But dearest Friends, they say, must part.
His Time was come, he ran his Race;
We hope he's in a better Place."

WHY do we grieve that Friends should dye?
No Loss more easy to supply.
One Year is past; a different Scene;
No further mention of the Dean;
Who now, alas, no more is mist,
Than if he never did exist.
Where's now this Fav'rite of *Apollo*?
Departed; *and his Works must follow*:
Must undergo the common Fate;
His Kind of Wit is out of Date.
Some Country Squire to *Lintot*[12] goes,
Enquires for SWIFT in Verse and Prose:
Says *Lintot*, "I have heard the Name:
He dy'd a Year ago." The same.
He searcheth all his Shop in vain;
"Sir you may find them in *Duck-lane*:[13]
I sent them with a Load of Books,
Last *Monday* to the Pastry-cooks.
To fancy they cou'd live a Year!
I find you're but a Stranger here.
The Dean was famous in his Time;
And had a Kind of Knack at Rhyme:
His way of Writing now is past;
The Town hath got a better Taste:
I keep no antiquated Stuff;
But, spick and span I have enough.
Pray, do but give me leave to shew 'em;
Here's *Colley Cibber*'s Birth-day Poem.
This Ode you never yet have seen,
By *Stephen Duck*, upon the Queen.
Then, here's a Letter finely penn'd
Against the *Craftsman* and his Friend;
It clearly shews that all Reflection
On Ministers, is disaffection.
Next, here's Sir *Robert*'s Vindication,[14]
And Mr. *Henly*'s[15] last Oration:
The Hawkers have not got 'em yet,
Your Honour please to buy a Set?

"HERE'S *Wolston*'s[16] Tracts, the twelfth
    Edition;
'Tis read by ev'ry Politician:
The Country Members, when in Town,
To all their Boroughs send them down:
You never met a Thing so smart;
The Courtiers have them all by Heart:
Those Maids of Honour (who can read)
Are taught to use them for their Creed.
The Rev'rend Author's good Intention,
Hath been rewarded with a Pension:
He doth an Honour to his Gown,
By bravely running *Priest-craft* down:
He shews, as sure as GOD's in *Gloc'ster*,
That *Jesus* was a Grand Impostor:
That all his Miracles were Cheats,
Perform'd as Juglers do their Feats:
The Church had never such a Writer:
A Shame, he hath not got a Mitre!"

SUPPOSE me dead; and then suppose
A Club assembled at the *Rose*;

Where from Discourse of this and that,
I grow the Subject of their Chat:
And, while they toss my Name about,
With Favour some, and some without;
One quite indiff'rent in the Cause,
My Character impartial draws:

"THE Dean, if we believe Report,
Was never ill receiv'd at Court:
As for his Works in Verse and Prose,
I own my self no Judge of those:
Nor, can I tell what Criticks thought 'em;
But, this I know, all People bought 'em;
As with a moral View design'd
To cure the Vices of Mankind:
His Vein, ironically grave,
Expos'd the Fool, and lash'd the Knave:
To steal a Hint was never known,
But what he writ was all his own.

"HE never thought an Honour done him,
Because a Duke was proud to own him:
Would rather slip aside, and chuse
To talk with Wits in dirty Shoes:
Despis'd the Fools with Stars and Garters,
So often seen caressing *Chartres*: [17]
He never courted Men in Station,
Nor Persons had in Admiration;
Of no Man's Greatness was afraid,
Because he sought for no Man's Aid.
Though trusted long in great Affairs,
He gave himself no haughty Airs:
Without regarding private Ends,
Spent all his Credit for his Friends:
And only chose the Wise and Good;
No Flatt'rers; no Allies in Blood;
But succour'd Virtue in Distress,
And seldom fail'd of good Success;
As Numbers in their Hearts must own,
Who, but for him, had been unknown.

"WITH Princes kept a due Decorum,
But never stood in Awe before 'em:
He follow'd *David*'s Lesson just,
In Princes never put thy Trust.
And, would you make him truly sower;
Provoke him with *a slave in Power:*
The *Irish* Senate, if you nam'd,
With what Impatience he declaim'd!
Fair LIBERTY was all his Cry;
For her he stood prepar'd to die;
For her he boldly stood alone;
For her he oft expos'd his own.
Two Kingdoms, just as Faction led, [18]
Had set a Price upon his Head;
But, not a Traytor cou'd be found,
To sell him for Six Hundred Pound.

"HAD he but spar'd his Tongue and Pen,
He might have rose like other Men:
But, Power was never in his Thought;
And, Wealth he valu'd not a Groat:
Ingratitude he often found,
And pity'd those who meant the Wound:
But, kept the Tenor of his Mind,
To merit well of human Kind:
Nor made a Sacrifice of those
Who still were true, to please his Foes.
He labour'd many a fruitless Hour [19]
To reconcile his Friends in Power;
Saw Mischief by a Faction brewing,

While they pursu'd each others Ruin.
But, finding vain was all his Care,
He left the Court in meer Despair.

"AND, oh! how short are human Schemes!
Here ended all our golden Dreams.
What ST. JOHN's Skill in State Affairs,
What ORMOND's *Valour*, OXFORD's Cares,
To save their sinking Country lent,
Was all destroy'd by one Event.
Too soon that precious Life was ended, [20]
On which alone, our Weal depended.
When up a dangerous Faction starts, [21]
With Wrath and Vengeance in their Hearts:
By solemn League and Cov'nant bound,
To ruin, slaughter, and confound;
To turn Religion to a Fable,
And make the Government a *Babel:*
Pervert the Law, disgrace the Gown,
Corrupt the Senate, rob the Crown;
To sacrifice old *England*'s Glory,
And make her infamous in Story.
When such a Tempest shook the Land,
How could unguarded Virtue stand?

"WITH Horror, Grief, Despair the Dean
Beheld the dire destructive Scene:
His Friends in Exile, or the Tower,
Himself within the Frown of Power; [22]
Pursu'd by base envenom'd Pens,
Far to the Land of Slaves and Fens; [23]
A servile Race in Folly nurs'd,
Who truckle most, when treated worst.

"BY Innocence and Resolution,
He bore continual Persecution;
While Numbers to Preferment rose;
Whose Merits were, to be his Foes.
When, *ev'n his own familiar Friends*
Intent upon their private Ends;
Like Renegadoes now he feels,
Against him lifting up their Heels.

"THE Dean did by his Pen defeat
An infamous destructive Cheat. [24]
Taught Fools their Int'rest how to know;
And gave them Arms to ward the Blow.
Envy hath own'd it was his doing,
To save that helpless Land from Ruin,
While they who at the Steerage stood,
And reapt the Profit, sought his Blood.

"To save them from their evil Fate,
In him was held a Crime of State.
A wicked Monster on the Bench, [25]
Whose Fury Blood could never quench;
As vile and profligate a Villain,
As modern *Scroggs*, or old *Tressilian;* [26]
Who long all Justice had discarded,
Nor fear'd he GOD, nor Man regarded;
Vow'd on the Dean his Rage to vent,
And make him of his Zeal repent;
But Heav'n his Innocence defends,
The grateful People stand his Friends:
Not Strains of Law, nor Judges Frown,
Nor Topicks brought to please the Crown,
Nor Witness hir'd, nor Jury pick'd,
Prevail to bring him in convict.

"IN Exile [27] with a steady Heart,
He spent his Life's declining Part;
Where, Folly, Pride, and Faction sway,

Remote from St. John, [28] Pope, and Gay.

"His Friendship there to few confin'd, [29]
Were always of the midling Kind:
No Fools of Rank, a mungril Breed,
Who fain would pass for Lords indeed:
Where Titles give no Right or Power, [30]
And Peerage is a wither'd Flower,
He would have held it a Disgrace,
If such a Wretch had known his Face.
On Rural Squires, that Kingdom's Bane,
He vented oft his Wrath in vain:
Biennial Squires, to Market brought; [31]
Who sell their Souls and Votes for Naught;
The Nations stript go joyful back,
To rob the Church, their Tenants rack,
Go Snacks with Thieves and Rapparees, [32]
And, keep the Peace, to pick up Fees:
In every Jobb to have a Share,
A Jayl or Barrack [33] to repair;
And turn the Tax for publick Roads
Commodious to their own Abodes.

"Perhaps I may allow, the Dean
Had too much Satyr in his Vein;
And seem'd determin'd not to starve it,
Because no Age could more deserve it.
Yet, Malice never was his Aim;
He lash'd the Vice but spar'd the Name.
No Individual could resent,
Where Thousands equally were meant.
His Satyr points at no Defect,
But what all Mortals may correct;
For he abhorr'd that senseless Tribe,
Who call it Humour when they jibe:
He spar'd a Hump or crooked Nose,
Whose Owners set not up for Beaux.
True genuine Dulness mov'd his Pity,
Unless it offer'd to be witty.
Those, who their Ignorance confess'd,
He ne'er offended with a Jest;
But laugh'd to hear an Idiot quote,
A Verse from *Horace*, learn'd by Rote.

"He knew an hundred pleasant Stories,
With all the Turns of *Whigs* and *Tories*:
Was chearful to his dying Day,
And Friends would let him have his Way.

"He gave the little Wealth he had,
To build a House for Fools and Mad:
And shew'd by one satyric Touch,
No Nation wanted it so much:
That Kingdom [34] he hath left his Debtor,
I wish it soon may have a Better.

Notes

1. The Author imagines, that the Scriblers of the prevailing Party, which he always opposed, will libel him after his Death; but that others will remember him with Gratitude, who consider the Service he had done to *Ireland*, under the Name of *M. B.* Drapier, by utterly defeating the destructive Project of *Wood's* Half-pence, in five Letters to the People of *Ireland*, at that Time read universally, and convincing every Reader.
2. The Dean supposeth himself to dye in *Ireland*.
3. Mrs. *Howard*, afterwards Countess of *Suffolk*, then of the Bedchamber to the Queen, professed much Friendship for the dean. The Queen then Princess, sent a dozen times to the Dean (then in *London*) with her Command to attend her; which at last he did, by advice of all his Friends. She often sent for him afterwards, and always treated him very Graciously. He taxed her with a Present

worth Ten Pounds, which she promised before he should return to *Ireland*, but on his taking Leave, the Medals were not ready.
4. The Medals were to be sent to the Dean in four Months, but she forgot them, or thought them too dear. The Dean, being in *Ireland*, sent Mrs. *Howard* a Piece of *Indian* Plad made in that Kingdom: which the Queen seeing took from her, and wore it herself, and sent to the Dean for as much as would cloath herself and Children, desiring he would send the Charge of it. He did the former. It cost thirty-five Pounds, but he said he would have nothing except the Medals. He was the Summer following in *England*, was treated as usual, and she being then queen, the Dean was promised a Settlement in *England*, but returned as he went, and, instead of Favour or Medals, hath been ever since under her Majesty's Displeasure.
5. *Chartres* is a most infamous, vile Scoundrel, grown from a Foot-Boy, or worse, to a prodigious Fortune both in *England* and *Scotland*: He had a Way of insinuating himself into all Ministers under every Change, either as Pimp, Flatterer, or Informer. He was Tryed at Seventy for a Rape, and came off by sacrificing a great Part of his Fortune (he is since dead, but this Poem still preserves the Scene and Time as was writ in.)
6. Sir *Robert Walpole*, Chief Minister of State, treated the *Dean* in 1726, with great Distinction, invited him to Dinner at *Chelsea*, with the *Dean's* Friends chosen on Purpose; appointed an Hour to talk with him of *Ireland*, to which *Kingdom* and *People* the *Dean* found him no great Friend; for he defended *Wood's* Project of Half-pence, &c. The *Dean* would see him no more, and upon his next Year's return to *England*, Sir *Robert* on an accidental Meeting, only made a civil Compliment, and never invited him again.
7. Mr. *William Pultney*, from being Mr. *Walpole's* intimate Friend, detesting his Administration, opposed his Measures, and joined with my *Lord Bolingbroke*, to represent his Conduct in an excellent Paper, called the *Craftsman*, which is still continued.
8. Henry *St. John*, Lord Viscount *Bolingbroke*, Secretary of State to Queen *Anne* of blessed Memory. He is reckoned the most Universal Genius in *Europe*; *Walpole* dreading his Abilities, treated him most injuriously, working with King *George*, who forgot his promise of restoring the said Lord, upon the restless Importunity of *Walpole*.
9. *Curl* hath been the most infamous Bookseller of any Age or Country: His Character in Part may be found in Mr. Pope's *Dunciad*. He published three Volumes all charged on the Dean, who never writ three Pages of them: He hath used many of the Dean's Friends in almost as vile a Manner.
10. Three stupid Verse Writers in *London*, the last to the Shame of the Court, and the highest Disgrace to Wit and Learning, was made Laureat. *Moore*, commonly called *Jemmy Moore*, Son of *Arthur Moore*, and *Tibbalds*, *Theobald* in the *Dunciad*.
11. *Curl* is notoriously infamous for publishing the Lives, Letters, and last Wills and Testaments of the Nobility and Ministers of State, as well as of all the Rogues, who are hanged at *Tyburn*. He hath been in Custody of the House of Lords for publishing or forging the Letters of many Peers; which made the Lords enter a Resolution in their Journal Book, that no Life or Writings of any Lord should be published without the Consent of the next Heir at Law, or Licence from their House.
12. *Bernard Lintot*, a Bookseller in *London*. Vide Mr. Pope's *Dunciad*.
13. A Place in *London* where old Books are sold.
14. *Walpole* hires a Set of Party Scriblers, who do nothing else but write in his Defence.
15. *Henly* is a Clergyman who wanting both Merit and Luck to get Preferment, or even to keep his Curacy in the Established Church, formed a new Conventicle, which he calls an Oratory. There, at set Times, he delivereth strange Speeches compiled by himself and his Associates, who share the Profit with him. Every Hearer pays a Shilling each Day for Admittance. He is an absolute Dunce, but generally reputed crazy.
16. *Wolston* was a Clergyman, but for want of Bread, hath in several Treatises, in the most blasphemous Manner, attempted to turn *Our Saviour* and his Miracles into Ridicule. He is much caressed

by many great Courtiers, and by all the Infidels, and his Books read generally by the Court Ladies.

17. See the Notes before on *Chartres*.

18. In the Year 1713, the late Queen was prevailed with by an Address of the House of Lords in *England*, to publish a Proclamation, promising Three Hundred Pounds to whatever Person would discover the Author of a Pamphlet called, *The Publick Spirit of the Whiggs*; and in *Ireland*, in the Year 1724, my Lord *Carteret* at his first coming into the Government, was prevailed on to issue a Proclamation for promising the like Reward of Three Hundred Pounds, to any Person who could discover the Author of a Pamphlet called, *The Drapier's Fourth Letter*, &c. writ against that destructive Project of coining Half-pence for *Ireland*; but in neither Kingdoms was the Dean discovered.

19. Queen ANNE's Ministry fell to Variance from the first Year after their Ministry began: *Harcourt* the Chancellor, and Lord *Bolingbroke* the Secretary, were discontented with the Treasurer *Oxford*, for his too much Mildness to the Whig Party; this Quarrel grew higher every Day till the Queen's death: The Dean, who was the only Person that endeavoured to reconcile them, found it impossible; and thereupon retired to the Country about ten Weeks before that fatal Event: Upon which he returned to his Deanry in *Dublin*, where for many Years he was worryed by the new People in Power, and had Hundreds of Libels writ against him in *England*.

20. In the Height of the Quarrel between the Ministers, the Queen died.

21. Upon Queen ANNE's death the Whig Faction was restored to Power, which they exercised with the utmost Rage and Revenge; impeached and banished the Chief Leaders of the Church Party, and stripped all their Adherents of what Employments they had, after which *England* was never known to make so mean a Figure in *Europe*. The greatest Preferments in the Church in both Kingdoms were given to the most ignorant Men, Fanaticks were publickly caressed, *Ireland* utterly ruined and enslaved, only great Ministers heaping up Millions, and so Affairs continue until this present third Day of May, 1732, and are likely to go on in the same Manner.

22. Upon the Queen's Death, the Dean returned to live in *Dublin*, at his Deanry-House: Numberless Libels were writ against him in *England*, as a Jacobite; he was insulted in the Street, and at Nights was forced to be attended by his Servants armed.

23. The Land of Slaves and Fens, is *Ireland*.

24. One *Wood*, a Hardware-man from *England*, has a Patent for coining Copper Half-pence in *Ireland*, to the Sum of 108.000 l. which in the Consequence, must leave that Kingdom without Gold or Silver (see *Drapier's* Letters).

25. One *Whitshed* was then Chief Justice: He had some Years before prosecuted a Printer for a Pamphlet writ by the Dean, to persuade the People of *Ireland* to wear their own Manufactures. *Whitshed* sent the Jury down eleven Times, and kept them nine Hours, until they were forced to bring in a special Verdict. He sat as Judge afterwards on the Tryal of the Printer of the *Drapier's* Fourth Letter; but the Jury, against all he could say or swear, threw out the Bill: All the Kingdom took the *Drapier's* Part, except the Courtiers, or those who expected Places. The *Drapier* was celebrated in many Poems and Pamphlets: His Sign was set up in most Streets of *Dublin* (where many of them still continue) and in several Country Towns.

26. *Scroggs* was Chief Justice under King *Charles* the Second: His Judgment always varied in State Tryals, according to Directions from Court. *Tressilian* was a wicked Judge, hanged above three hundred Years ago.

27. In *Ireland*, which he had Reason to call a Place of Exile; to which Country nothing could have driven him, but the Queen's Death, who had determined to fix him in *England*, in Spight of the Dutchess of *Somerset*, &c.

28. *Henry St. John*, Lord Viscount *Bolingbroke*, mentioned before.

29. In *Ireland* the Dean was not acquainted with one single Lord Spiritual or Temporal. He only conversed with private Gentlemen of the Clergy or Laity, and but a small Number of either.

30. The Peers of *Ireland* lost a great Part of their Jurisdiction by one single Act, and tamely submitted to this infamous Mark of Slavery without the least Resentment, or Remonstrance.

31. The Parliament (as they call it) in *Ireland* meet but once in two Years; and, after giving five Times more than they can afford, return Home to reimburse themselves by all Country Jobs and Oppressions, of which some few only are here mentioned.

32. The Highway-Men in *Ireland* are, since the late Wars there, usually called Rapparees, which was a name given to those *Irish* soldiers who in small Parties used, at that time, to plunder the Protestants.

33. The Army in *Ireland* is lodged in Barracks, the building and repairing whereof, and other Charges, have cost a prodigious Sum to that unhappy Kingdom.

34. Meaning *Ireland*, where he now lives, and probably may dye.

SAMUEL JOHNSON
From "Swift"
Lives of the English Poets
1779–81

When Swift is considered as an author, it is just to estimate his powers by their effects. In the reign of Queen Anne he turned the stream of popularity against the Whigs, and must be confessed to have dictated for a time the political opinions of the English nation. In the succeeding reign he delivered Ireland from plunder and oppression; and shewed that wit, confederated with truth, had such force as authority was unable to resist. He said truly of himself, that Ireland *was his debtor*. It was from the time when he first began to patronize the Irish, that they may date their riches and prosperity. He taught them first to know their own interest, their weight, and their strength, and gave them spirit to assert that equality with their fellow-subjects to which they have ever since been making vigorous advances, and to claim those rights which they have at last established. Nor can they be charged with ingratitude to their benefactor; for they reverenced him as a guardian, and obeyed him as a dictator.

In his works, he has given very different specimens both of sentiment and expression. His *Tale of a Tub* has little resemblance to his other pieces. It exhibits a vehemence and rapidity of mind, a copiousness of images, and vivacity of diction, such as he afterwards never possessed, or never exerted. It is of a mode so distinct and peculiar, that it must be considered by itself; what is true of that, is not true of any thing else which he has written.

In his other works is found an equable tenour of easy language, which rather trickles than flows. His delight was in simplicity. That he has in his works no metaphor, as has been said, is not true; but his few metaphors seem to be received rather by necessity than choice. He studied purity; and though perhaps all his strictures are not exact, yet it is not often that solecisms can be found; and whoever depends on his authority may generally conclude himself safe. His sentences are never too much dilated or contracted; and it will not be easy to find any embarrassment in the complication of his clauses, and inconsequence in his connections, or abruptness in his transitions.

His style was well suited to his thoughts, which are never subtilised by nice disquisitions, decorated by sparkling conceits, elevated by ambitious sentences, or variegated by far-sought learning. He pays no court to the passions; he excites neither surprise nor admiration; he always understands himself: and his reader always understands him: the peruser of Swift wants little previous knowledge: it will be sufficient that he is acquainted with common words and common things; he is neither required to mount elevations, nor to explore profundities; his passage is always on a level, along solid ground, without asperities, without obstruction.

This easy and safe conveyance of meaning it was Swift's desire to attain, and for having attained he deserves praise, though perhaps not the highest praise. For purposes merely didactick, when something is to be told that was not known before, it is the best mode, but against that inattention by which known truths are suffered to lie neglected, it makes no provision; it instructs, but does not persuade.

By his political education he was associated with the Whigs; but he deserted them when they deserted their principles, yet without running into the contrary extreme; he continued throughout his life to retain the disposition which he assigns to the *Church-of-England Man*, of thinking commonly with the Whigs of the State, and with the Tories of the Church.

He was a churchman rationally zealous; he desired the prosperity, and maintained the honour of the Clergy; of the Dissenters he did not wish to infringe the toleration, but he opposed their encroachments.

To his duty as Dean he was very attentive. He managed the revenues of his church with exact oeconomy; and it is said by Delany, that more money was, under his direction, laid out in repairs than had ever been in the same time since its first erection. Of his choir he was eminently careful; and, though he neither loved nor understood musick, took care that all the singers were well qualified, admitting none without the testimony of skilful judges.

In his church he restored the practice of weekly communion, and distributed the sacramental elements in the most solemn and devout manner with his own hand. He came to church every morning, preached commonly in his turn, and attended the evening anthem, that it might not be negligently performed.

He read the service *rather with a strong nervous voice than in a graceful manner; his voice was sharp and high-toned, rather than harmonious.*

He entered upon the clerical state with hope to excel in preaching; but complained, that, from the time of his political controversies, *he could only preach pamphlets.* This censure of himself, if judgement be made from those sermons which have been published, was unreasonably severe.

The suspicions of his irreligion proceeded in a great measure from his dread of hypocrisy; instead of wishing to seem better, he delighted in seeming worse than he was. He went in London to early prayers, lest he should be seen at church; he read prayers to his servants every morning with such dexterous secrecy, that Dr. Delany was six months in his house before he knew it. He was not only careful to hide the good which he did, but willingly incurred the suspicion of evil which he did not. He forgot what himself had formerly asserted, that hypocrisy is less mischievous than open impiety. Dr. Delany, with all his zeal for his honour, has justly condemned this part of his character.

The person of Swift had not many recommendations. He had a kind of muddy complexion, which, though he washed himself with oriental scrupulosity, did not look clear. He had a countenance sour and severe, which he seldom softened by any appearance of gaiety. He stubbornly resisted any tendency to laughter.

To his domesticks he was naturally rough; and a man of a rigorous temper, with that vigilance of minute attention which his works discover, must have been a master that few could

bear. That he was disposed to do his servants good, on important occasions, is no great mitigation; benefaction can be but rare, and tyrannick peevishness is perpetual. He did not spare the servants of others. Once, when he dined alone with the Earl of Orrery, he said of one that waited in the room, *That man has, since we sat to the table, committed fifteen faults.* What the faults were, Lord Orrery, from whom I heard the story, had not been attentive enough to discover. My number may perhaps not be exact.

In his oeconomy he practised a peculiar and offensive parsimony, without disguise or apology. The practice of saving being once necessary became habitual, and grew first ridiculous, and at last detestable. But his avarice, though it might exclude pleasure, was never suffered to encroach upon his virtue. He was frugal by inclination, but liberal by principle; and if the purpose to which he destined his little accumulations be remembered, with his distribution of occasional charity, it will perhaps appear that he only liked one mode of expence better than another, and saved merely that he might have something to give. He did not grow rich by injuring his successors, but left both Laracor and the Deanery more valuable than he found them.—With all this talk of his covetousness and generosity, it should be remembered that he was never rich. The revenue of his Deanery was not much more than seven hundred a year.

His beneficence was not graced with tenderness or civility; he relieved without pity, and assisted without kindness, so that those who were fed by him could hardly love him.

He made a rule to himself to give but one piece at a time, and therefore always stored his pocket with coins of different value.

Whatever he did, he seemed willing to do in a manner peculiar to himself, without sufficiently considering that singularity, as it implies a contempt of the general practice, is a kind of defiance which justly provokes the hostility of ridicule; he therefore who indulges peculiar habits is worse than others, if he be not better. ⟨. . .⟩

In the intercourse of familiar life, he indulged his disposition to petulance and sarcasm, and thought himself injured if the licentiousness of his raillery, the freedom of his censures, or the petulance of his frolicks, was resented or repressed. He predominated over his companions with very high ascendency, and probably would bear none over whom he could not predominate. To give him advice was, in the style of his friend Delany, *to venture to speak to him.* This customary superiority soon grew too delicate for truth; and Swift, with all his penetration, allowed himself to be delighted with low flattery.

On all common occasions, he habitually affects a style of arrogance, and dictates rather than persuades. This authoritative and magisterial language he expected to be received as his peculiar mode of jocularity; but he apparently flattered his own arrogance by an assumed imperiousness, in which he was ironical only to the resentful, and to the submissive sufficiently serious.

He told stories with great felicity, and delighted in doing what he knew himself to do well. He was therefore captivated by the respective silence of a steady listener, and told the same tales too often.

He did not, however, claim the right of talking alone; for it was his rule, when he had spoken a minute, to give room by a pause for any other speaker. Of time, on all occasions, he was an exact computer, and knew the minutes required to every common operation.

It may be justly supposed that there was in his conversation, what appears so frequently in his Letters, an affectation of familiarity with the Great, an ambition of momentary equality sought and enjoyed by the neglect of those ceremonies which custom has established as the barriers between one order of society and another. This transgression of regularity was by himself and his admirers termed greatness of soul. But a great mind disdains to hold any thing by courtesy, and therefore never usurps what a lawful claimant may take away. He that encroaches on another's dignity, puts himself in his power; he is either repelled with helpless indignity, or endured by clemency and condescension.

Of Swift's general habits of thinking, if his Letters can be supposed to afford any evidence, he was not a man to be either loved or envied. He seems to have wasted life in discontent, by the rage of neglected pride, and the languishment of unsatisfied desire. He is querulous and fastidious, arrogant and malignant; he scarcely speaks of himself but with indignant lamentations, or of others but with insolent superiority when he is gay, and with angry contempt when he is gloomy. From the Letters that pass between him and Pope it might be inferred that they, with Arbuthnot and Gay, had engrossed all the understanding and virtue of mankind, that their merits filled the world; or that there was no hope of more. They shew the age involved in darkness, and shade the picture with sullen emulation.

When the Queen's death drove him into Ireland, he might be allowed to regret for a time the interception of his views, the extinction of his hopes, and his ejection from gay scenes, important employment, and splendid friendships; but when time had enabled reason to prevail over vexation, the complaints, which at first were natural, became ridiculous because they were useless. But querulousness was now grown habitual, and he cried out when he probably had ceased to feel. His reiterated wailings persuaded Bolingbroke that he was really willing to quit his deanery for an English parish; and Bolingbroke procured an exchange, which was rejected, and Swift still retained the pleasure of complaining.

The greatest difficulty that occurs, in analysing his character, is to discover by what depravity of intellect he took delight in revolving ideas, from which almost every other mind shrinks with disgust. The ideas of pleasure, even when criminal, may solicit the imagination; but what has disease, deformity, and filth, upon which the thoughts can be allured to dwell? Delany is willing to think that Swift's mind was not much tainted with this gross corruption before his long visit to Pope. He does not consider how he degrades his hero, by making him at fifty-nine the pupil of turpitude, and liable to the malignant influence of an ascendant mind. But the truth is, that Gulliver had described his *Yahoos* before the visit, and he that had formed those images had nothing filthy to learn.

I have here given the character of Swift as he exhibits himself to my perception; but now let another be heard, who knew him better; Dr. Delany, after long acquaintance, describes him to Lord Orrery in these terms:

'My Lord, when you consider Swift's singular, peculiar, and most variegated vein of wit, always rightly intended (although not always so rightly directed), delightful in many instances, and salutary, even where it is most offensive; when you consider his strict truth, his fortitude in resisting oppression and arbitrary power; his fidelity in friendship, his sincere love and zeal for religion, his uprightness in making right resolutions, and his steadiness in adhering to them; his care of his church, its choir, its oeconomy, and its income; his attention to all those that preached in his cathedral, in order to their amendment in pronunciation and style; as also his remarkable attention to the interest of his successors, preferably

to his own present emoluments; invincible patriotism, even to a country which he did not love; his very various, well-devised, well-judged, and extensive charities, throughout his life, and his whole fortune (to say nothing of his wife's) conveyed to the same Christian purposes at his death; charities from which he could enjoy no honour, advantage or satisfaction of any kind in this world. When you consider his ironical and humorous, as well as his serious schemes, for the promotion of true religion and virtue; his success in soliciting for the First Fruits and Twentieths, to the unspeakable benefit of the Established Church of Ireland; and his felicity (to rate it no higher) in giving occasion to the building of fifty new churches in London.

'All this considered, the character of his life will appear like that of his writings; they will both bear to be re-considered and re-examined with the utmost attention, and always discover new beauties and excellences upon every examination.

'They will bear to be considered as the sun, in which the brightness will hide the blemishes; and whenever petulant ignorance, pride, malice, malignity, or envy, interposes to cloud or sully his fame, I will take upon me to pronounce that the eclipse will not last long.

'To conclude—No man ever deserved better of any country than Swift did of his. A steady, persevering, inflexible friend; a wise, a watchful, and a faithful counsellor, under many severe trials and bitter persecutions, to the manifest hazard both of his liberty and fortune.

'He lived a blessing, he died a benefactor, and his name will ever live an honour to Ireland.'

In the Poetical Works of Dr. Swift there is not much upon which the critick can exercise his powers. They are often humorous, almost always light, and have the qualities which recommend such compositions, easiness and gaiety. They are, for the most part, what their author intended. The diction is correct, the numbers are smooth, and the rhymes exact. There seldom occurs a hard-laboured expression, or a redundant epithet; all his verses exemplify his own definition of a good style, they consist of *proper words in proper places*.

To divide this Collection into classes, and shew how some pieces are gross, and some are trifling, would be to tell the reader what he knows already, and to find faults of which the author could not be ignorant, who certainly wrote not often to his judgement, but his humour.

It was said, in a Preface to one of the Irish editions, that Swift had never been known to take a single thought from any writer, ancient or modern. This is not literally true; but perhaps no writer can easily be found that has borrowed so little, or that in all his excellences and all his defects has so well maintained his claim to be considered as original.

DAVID MASSON
From "Dean Swift"
Essays Biographical and Critical
1856, pp. 169–77

Have we said too much in declaring that of all the men who illustrated that period of our literary history which lies between the Revolution of 1688 and the beginning or middle of the reign of George II., Swift alone (excepting Pope, and excepting him only on certain definite and peculiar grounds) fulfils to any tolerable extent those conditions which would entitle him to the epithet of "great," already refused by us to his age as a whole? We do not think so. Swift *was* a great genius; nay, if by *greatness* we understand general mass and energy rather than any preconceived peculiarity of quality, he was the greatest genius of his age. Neither Addison, nor Steele, nor Pope, nor Defoe, possessed, in anything like the same degree, that which Goethe and Niebuhr, seeking a name for a certain attribute found always present, as they thought, in the higher and more forcible order of historic characters, agreed to call the *demoniac* element. Indeed very few men in our literature, from first to last, have had so much of this element in them—the sign and source of all real greatness—as Swift. In him it was so obvious as to attract notice at once. "There is something in your looks," wrote Vanessa to him, "so awful that it strikes me dumb;" and again, "Sometimes you strike me with that prodigious awe, I tremble with fear;" and again, "What marks are there of a deity that you are not known by?" True, these are the words of a woman infatuated with love; but there is evidence that wherever Swift went, and in whatever society he was, there was this magnetic power in his presence. Pope felt it; Addison felt it; they all felt it. We question if, among all our literary celebrities, from first to last, there has been one more distinguished for being personally formidable to all who came near him.

And yet in calling Swift a great genius we clearly do not mean to rank him in the same order of greatness with such men among his predecessors as Spenser, or Shakespeare, or Milton, or such men among his successors, as Scott, Coleridge and Wordsworth. We even retain instinctively the right of not according to him a certain kind of admiration which we bestow on such men of his own generation as Pope, Steele, and Addison. How is this? What is the drawback about Swift's genius which prevents us from referring him to that highest order of literary greatness to which we do refer others, who in respect of hard general capacity were apparently not superior to him, and on the borders of which we also place some who in that respect were certainly his inferiors? To make the question more special, why do we call Milton great in quite a different sense from that in which we consent to confer the same epithet on Swift?

Altogether, it will be said, Milton was a greater man than Swift; his intellect was higher, richer, deeper, grander; his views of things are more profound, grave, stately, and exalted. This is a true enough statement of the case; and we like that comprehensive use of the word intellect which it implies, wrapping up, as it were, all that is in and about a man in this one word, so as to dispense with the distinctions between imaginative and non-imaginative, spiritual and unspiritual natures, and make every possible question about a man a mere question in the end as to the size or degree of his intellect. But such a mode of speaking is too violent and recondite for common purposes. According to the common use of the word intellect, it might be maintained (we do not say it would) that Swift's intellect, meaning his strength of mental grasp, was equal to Milton's; and yet that, by reason of the fact that his intellectual style was deficient, that he did not grasp things precisely in the Miltonic way, a distinction might be drawn unfavourable, on the whole, to his genius as compared with that of Milton. According to such a view, we must seek for that in Swift's genius, upon which it depends that while we accord to it all the admiration we bestow on strength, our sympathies with height or sublimity are left unmoved. Nor have we far to seek. When Goethe and Niebuhr generalized in the phrase, "the demoniac element," that mystic something which they seemed to detect in all men of unusual potency among their fellows, they used the word "demoniac," not in its English

sense, as signifying what appertains specially to the demons or powers of darkness, but in its Greek sense, as equally implying the unseen agencies of light and good. The demoniac element in a man, therefore, may in one case be the demoniac of the etherial and celestial, in another the demoniac of the Tartarean and infernal. There is a demoniac of the supernatural—angels, and seraphs, and white-winged airy messengers swaying men's phantasies from above; and there is a demoniac of the infra-natural—fiends and shapes of horror tugging at men's thoughts from beneath. The demoniac in Swift was of the latter kind. It is false, it would be an entire mistake as to his genius, to say that he regarded, or was inspired by, only the worldly and the secular; that men, women, and their relations in the little world of visible life, were all that his intellect cared to recognise. He also, like our Miltons and our Shakespeares, and all our men who have been anything more than prudential and pleasant writers, had his being anchored in things and imaginations beyond the visible verge. But while it was given to them to hold rather by things and imaginations belonging to the region of the celestial, to hear angelic music and the rustling of seraphic wings; it was his unhappier lot to be related rather to the darker and subterranean mysteries. One might say of Swift that he had far less of belief in a God than of belief in a devil. He is like a man walking on the earth and among the busy haunts of his fellow-mortals, observing them and their ways, and taking his part in the bustle; all the while, however, conscious of the tuggings downward of secret chains reaching into the world of the demons. Hence his ferocity, his misan-thropy, his *sæva indignatio*, all of them true forms of energy, imparting unusual potency to a life; but forms of energy bred of communion with what outlies nature on the lower or infernal side.

Swift, doubtless, had this melancholic tendency in him constitutionally from the beginning. From the first we see him an unruly, rebellious, gloomy, revengeful, unforgiving spirit, loyal to no authority, and gnashing under every restraint. With nothing small or weak in his nature, too proud to be dishonest, bold and fearless in his opinions, capable of strong attachments and of hatred as strong, it was to be predicted that if the swarthy Irish youth, whom Sir William Temple received into his house, when his college had all but expelled him for contu-macy, should ever be eminent in the world, it would be for fierce and controversial, and not for beautiful or harmonious, activity. It is clear, however, on a survey of Swift's career, that the gloom and melancholy which characterised it, was not altogether congenital, but in part, at least grew out of some special circumstance or set of circumstances, having a precise date and locality among the facts of his life. In other words, there was some secret in Swift's life, some root of bitterness or remorse, diffusing a black poison throughout his whole exist-ence. That communion with the invisible almost exclusively on the infernal side—that consciousness of chains wound round his own moving frame at the one end, and at the other tugged at by demons in the depths of their populous pit, while no cords of love were felt sustaining him from the countervail-ing heaven—had its origin, in part at least, in some one recollection or cause of dread. It was some one demon down in that pit that tugged the chains; the others but assisted him. Thackeray's perception seems to us exact when he says of Swift that "he goes through life, tearing, like a man possessed with a devil;" or again, changing the form of the figure, that, "like Abudah, in the Arabian story, he is always looking out for the Fury, and knows that the night will come, and the inevitable hag with it." What was this Fury, this hag that duly came in the night, making the mornings horrible by the terrors of recollection, the evenings horrible by those of anticipation, and leaving but a calm hour at full mid-day? There was a secret in Swift's life; what was it? His biographers as yet have failed to agree on this dark topic. Thackeray's hypothesis, that the cause of Swift's despair was chiefly his consciousness of disbelief in the creed to which he had sworn his professional faith, does not seem to us sufficient. In Swift's days, and even with his frank nature, we think that difficulty could have been got over. There was nothing, at least, so unique in the case as to justify the supposition that this was what Archbishop King referred to in that memorable saying to Dr. Delany, "You have just met the most miserable man on earth; but on the subject of his wretchedness you must never ask a question." Had Swift made a confession of scepticism to the Archbishop, we do not think the prelate would have been taken so very much by surprise. Nor can we think, with some, that Swift's vertigo (now pronounced to have been increasing congestion of the brain) and his life-long certainty that it would end in idiotcy or madness, are the true explanation of this interview and of the mystery which it shrouds. There was cause enough for melancholy here, but not exactly the cause that meets the case. Another hypothesis there is of a physical kind, which Scott and others hint at, and which finds great acceptance with the medical philosophers. Swift, it is said, was of "a cold temperament," &c. &c. But why a confession on the part of Swift that he was not a marrying man, even had he added that he desired, above all things in the world, to be a person of this sort, should have so moved the heart of an Archbishop, we cannot conceive. Besides, although this hypothesis might explain much of the Stella and Vanessa imbroglio, it would not explain all; nor do we see on what foundation it could rest. Scott's assertion that all through Swift's writings there is no evidence of his having felt the tender passion, is simply untrue. On the whole, the hypothesis which has been started of a too near consanguinity between Swift and Stella, either known from the first to one or both, or discovered too late, would most nearly suit the conditions of the case. And yet, so far as we have seen, this hypothesis also rests on air, with no one fact to support it. Could we suppose that Swift, like another Eugene Aram, went through the world with a murder on his mind, it might be taken as a solution of the mystery; but as we cannot do this, we must be content with supposing that either some one of the foregoing hypotheses, or some combination of them, is to be accepted, or that the matter is altogether inscrutable.

Such by constitution as we have described him—with an intellect strong as iron, much acquired knowledge, an ambition all but insatiable, and a decided desire to be wealthy—Swift, almost as a matter of course, flung himself impetuously into the Whig and Tory controversy, which was the question paramount in his time. In that he laboured as only a man of his powers could, bringing to the side of the controversy on which he chanced to be—and we believe when he was on a side it was honestly because he found a certain preponderance of right in it—a hard and ruthless vigour which served it immensely. But from the first, and, at all events, after the disappointments of a political career had been experienced by him, his nature would not work alone in the narrow warfare of Whiggism and Toryism, but overflowed in general bitterness of reflection on all the customs and ways of humanity. The following passage in *Gulliver's Voyage to Brobdingnag*, describing how the politics of Europe appeared to the King of Brobdingnag, shows us Swift himself in his larger mood of thought.

This prince took a pleasure in conversing with me, inquiring into the manners, religion, laws, government, and learning of Europe; wherein I gave him the best account I was able. His apprehension was so clear, and his judgment so exact, that he made very wise reflections and observations upon all I said. But I confess that after I had been a little too copious in talking of my own beloved country, of our trade, and wars by sea and land, of our schisms in religion, and parties in the state, the prejudices of his education prevailed so far that he could not forbear taking me up in his right hand, and stroking me gently with the other, after an hearty fit of laughing, asking me, whether I was a Whig or Tory. Then turning to his first minister, who waited behind him with a white staff nearly as tall as the mainmast of the 'Royal Sovereign,' he observed how contemptible a thing was human grandeur, which could be mimicked by such diminutive insects as I; 'And yet,' says he, 'I dare engage these creatures have their titles and distinctions of honour; they contrive little nests and burrows, that they call houses and cities; they make a figure in dress and equipage; they love, they fight, they dispute, they cheat, they betray.' And thus he continued on, while my colour came and went several times with indignation to hear our noble country, the mistress of arts and arms, the scourge of France, the arbitress of Europe, the seat of virtue, piety, honour, truth, the pride and envy of the world, so contemptuously treated.

Swift's writings, accordingly, divide themselves, in the main, into two classes,—pamphlets, tracts, lampoons, and the like, bearing directly on persons and topics of the day, and written with the ordinary purpose of a partisan; and satires of a more general aim, directed, in the spirit of a cynic philosopher, against humanity on the whole, or against particular human classes, arrangements, and modes of thinking. In some of his writings the politician and the general satirist are seen together. The *Drapier's Letters* and most of the poetical lampoons, exhibit Swift in his direct mood as a party-writer; in the *Tale of a Tub* we have the ostensible purpose of a partisan masking a reserve of general scepticism; in the *Battle of the Books* we have a satire partly personal to individuals, partly with a reference to a prevailing tone of opinion; in the *Voyage to Laputa* we have a satire on a great class of men; and in the *Voyages to Lilliput* and *Brobdingnag*, and still more in the story of the *Houynhnms* and *Yahoos*, we have human nature itself analysed and laid bare.

Swift took no care of his writings, never acknowledged some of them, never collected them, and suffered them to find their way about the world as chance, demand, and the piracy of publishers directed. As all know, it is in his character as a humorist, an inventor of the preposterous as a medium for the reflective, and above all as a master of irony, that he takes his place as one of the chiefs of English literature. There can be no doubt that, as regards the literary form which he affected most, he took hints from Rabelais, as the greatest original in the realm of the absurd. Sometimes, as in his description of the Strulbrugs in the *Voyage to Laputa*, he approaches the ghastly power of that writer; on the whole, however, there is more of stern English realism in him, and less of sheer riot and wildness. Sometimes, however, Swift throws off the guise of the humorist, and speaks seriously and in his own name. On such occasions we find ourselves simply in the presence of a man of strong, sagacious, and thoroughly English mind, content, as is the habit of Englishmen, with vigorous proximate sense, expressed in plain and rather coarse idiom. For the speculative he shows in these cases neither liking nor aptitude;

he takes obvious reasons and arguments as they come to hand, and uses them in a robust, downright Saxon manner. In one respect he stands out conspicuously even among plain Saxon writers—his total freedom from cant. Johnson's advice to Boswell, "above all things to clear his mind of cant," was perhaps never better illustrated than in the case of Dean Swift. Indeed, it might be given as a summary definition of Swift's character that he had cleared his mind of cant, without having succeeded in filling the void with song. It was Swift's intense hatred of cant—cant in religion, cant in morality, cant in literature—that occasioned many of those peculiarities which shock people in his writings. His principle being to view things as they are, irrespective of all the accumulated cant of orators and poets, he naturally prosecuted his investigations into those classes of circumstances which orators and poets have omitted as unsuitable for their purposes. If they had viewed men as angels, he would view them as Yahoos. If they had placed the springs of action among the fine phrases and the sublimities, he would trace them down into their secret connexions with the bestial and the obscene. Hence—as much as for any of those physiological reasons which some of his biographers assign for it—his undisguised delight in filth. And hence, also, probably—seeing that among the forms of cant he included the traditional manner of speaking of women in their relations to men—his studious contempt, whether in writing for men or women, of all the accustomed decencies. It was not only the more obvious forms of cant, however, that Swift had in aversion. Even to that minor form of cant which consists in the "trite" he gave no quarter. Whatever was habitually said by the majority of people, seemed to him, for that very reason, not worthy of being said at all, much less put into print. A considerable portion of his writings, as, for example, his *Tritical Essay on the Faculties of the Mind*, and his *Art of Polite Conversation*—in the one of which he strings together a series of the most threadbare maxims and quotations to be found in books, offering the compilation as an original disquisition of his own; and, in the other, imitates the insipidity of ordinary table-talk in society—may be regarded as showing a systematic determination on his part to turn the trite into ridicule. Hence, in his own writings, though he abstains from the profound, he never falls into the commonplace. Apart from all Swift's other merits, there are to be found scattered through his writings not a few distinct propositions of an innovative and original character respecting our social arrangements. We have seen his doctrine as to the education of women; and we may mention, as an instance of the same kind, his denunciation of the institution of standing armies as incompatible with freedom. Curiously enough, also, it was Swift's belief that, Yahoos as we are, the world is always in the right.

CHARLES COWDEN CLARKE
From "On the Comic Writers of England: VI. Swift"

Gentleman's Magazine, September 1871, pp. 436–56

Had Swift written no other verses than those on his own death, he would have deserved honourable mention among our national poets; had he written no other history than the *Tale of a Tub* he must have ranked among our greatest wits; had he produced no other work of imagination than *Gulliver's Travels*, he would have been great among the greatest satirists;

had he put forth no other tracts than the *Drapier Letters*, he would have deserved a votive offering from the nation whose interests he had undertaken to protect; and had he projected no other scheme than the plan of an Academy for the correcting and enlarging, polishing and fixing of his native language, he might have claimed the gratitude and reverence of the whole British people. Even one of these productions would furnish an ample capital to establish and support a good literary reputation; and a single one of them (the *Gulliver*) has perhaps commanded a more extended share of popularity than any prose work in the language (*Robinson Crusoe* excepted); and it will continue to be a stable satire so long as court servility, national vanity and conceit, with the mania for scheme-projection, shall continue to form a feature in the human character, and to maintain an influence over human action. Swift's other great satire, the *Tale of a Tub*, will retain every particle of its freshness and verdure so long as the three master-dogmas of the Christian religion (those of the Roman, the Lutheran, and the Calvinistic Churches) shall preserve their sway in the Christian world. The subjects of his two great satires being quite as familiar with our every-day habits, feelings, and associations, as they were with society at the period of their production; to all appearance they will continue so after very many generations shall have passed away; and this circumstance has given Swift an advantage over his brother satirists, who, in attacking the epidemic weaknesses, follies, or vices of their contemporaries, which were the mania of their age, and not of universal humanity, have passed into matter of curious investigation with the literary antiquary, and are not familiar with or cognisable by the million. Who, for example, would be bold enough to name the period when it shall become a question of legendary history, and not, as it now is, a matter of every day notoriety, that the leaders in the different sects of Christianity have interpreted the doctrinal portions of Scripture in conformity with their own articles of faith, warping the texts by the heat of argument; or, where they happen to be stubbornly plain, denying their authenticity altogether? and this, in the *Tale of a Tub*, Swift has, with a caustic satire, represented under the form of the three brothers interpreting their father's will. When will the allegory of Brother Peter's loaf, which comprised the essence of beef, partridge, apple-pie, and custard, require a black-letter annotator to expound its interpretation? The *Tale of a Tub* was written when Swift was but nineteen years old. This circumstance renders the performance of the work the more surprising; not on account of the invention and learning displayed in it, neither of which was miraculous in a naturally strong mind, and in one educated for the clerical profession: but the staidness with which the history is conducted, and the consistency preserved throughout, have all the air of matured practice in authorship. The style, too, is so easy, and so purely idiomatical, that none of his later works exhibits material improvement upon it in this respect. There is a remarkable determination of purpose in the style of Swift, with perfect transparency; and these are but the reflexes of the natural man, for these were the prominent features of his character. It will be observed that in his writings we rarely meet with a superfluous word, and never with a superfluous epithet. Now this is one of the besetting sins of modern writing. Swift is the most English, the most thoroughly national in his diction of all our classic writers. On no occasion does he employ an exotic term, if one indigenous to the language be at hand. He is also sparing of connecting particles and introductory phrases and flourishes; using also the simplest forms of construction; and, moreover, he is master of the idiomatic peculiarities, and lurking, unapparent resources of the language to a degree of perfection that leaves him almost without a competitor. The cultivation of a plain, unornamented style demands considerably more care and research than that of the florid and redundant style; and for this obvious reason, that, in the one instance, it is a task of no ordinary severity to restrain, retrench, and condense, remaining all the while clear and perspicuous; whereas, in the inflated, verbose style, the very redundancy of words pressed into the service is commonly the result of indolence, indifference, and carelessness. The former, on account of its simplicity in appearance, is thought to be easily imitable, while the latter has the effect of laborious and scientific construction,— than which a greater mistake does not exist. For the one man who by bestowing thought and care shall be able to write with the nervous plainness and perspicuity of Swift, fifty could with little exertion imitate the artificial manner of Dr. Johnson; and hence the number of followers and admirers of the latter. "Fit words in fit places" is the best and indeed the only axiom to form the best style in writing: for in expressing our thoughts there may be several native words, which differ only in shades of meaning, that are all available for carrying out the idea; nevertheless, each word or term must express the thought with varied force and propriety; but out of all these there is only one we really want, and that is *the* one which punctually accords with the idea we design to convey. The usages of society have apportioned to each word employed in common conversation its conventional associations and graduated tints of meaning; and the stubbornness of custom has assigned to each its nicety of distinction. The having all these ready for use, with the judgment to decide upon the one best fitted for the occasion, constitutes the clearest conversational prose style; and that is the finest diction which most nearly approaches a familiar and refined discourse. In the florid and artificial style of writing the same tax of selection, and the same niceness of propriety, are not severely demanded. It is sufficient that, in construction, the members of sentences be involved, that qualifying terms and epithets be multiplied, and the employment of learned words from the classical and dead languages be not spared. One cannot be supposed familiar with the minute varieties and shades of signification in a language that has no longer a "local habitation." The attainment of this last finish in writing is sufficiently perplexing even in the living dialects; the broadly accepted meaning, therefore, of dead foreign words is sufficient for the cultivator of the artificial and florid style; and they offer this advantage to the writer, that they all impose upon the general reader, because they are out of the every-day familiar path of language; and the more *un*familiar and occult the words, the more learned and grand, of course, will be thought the style. The location of words, rather than the novelty of ideas, soonest attracts the reading million. A verbose commonplace will gain the day over simple originality—at least where the election goes by "universal suffrage." Swift's own designation of the three styles of writing cannot be too often repeated. "There is one style (he says) that cannot be understood; and there is another that can be understood: but there is a third style, that cannot be *mis*understood, and that is the best;" and it is eminently characteristic of his own, for it may be safely affirmed that throughout the whole of his voluminous writings not a single sentence occurs the meaning of which any intellect above a baboon's need stumble at. The most remarkable style of our own day for simplicity, with clearness and brevity, was, perhaps, that of the late Duke of Wellington. I know of nothing in writing more suited to their subject-matter than those official despatches. They are to be studied for their economy and yet sufficiency of language. They are models for young men who may be employed in business correspondence. A principal clerk in one of our public offices told me that at one period, when they were not much engaged, he was in the habit of receiving official communications from the Duke, and that he used to amuse himself by endeavouring to express the same ideas in fewer words, but that he remembered in no instance to have succeeded. And now to return to our *Tale of a Tub*.

One curious feature in the work is the several introductory papers that the author has appended before the reader is ushered into the "real presence;" like passing a suite of rooms in progress to a Prince at his levee. There is first an "Apology," or defence of the character and principles of the tale; wherein, defending the freedom with which he has assailed the superstition and folly of the religious sectaries, he concludes with the question, "Why any clergyman of our Church should be angry to see the follies of fanaticism and superstition exposed, though in the most ridiculous manner; since that is the most probable way to cure them, or at least to hinder them from farther proceeding?" and he frankly adds, that he "will forfeit his life if any one opinion can be fairly deduced from the book, which is contrary to religion or morality." The "Apology" comprises sixteen pages of small type, closely printed, and ably written with temper and judgment. This is followed by a "Postscript," which is succeeded by a noble and worthy "Dedication" to the great Lord Chancellor Somers, one of the most shining lights of his age. The language of this dedication is of itself calculated to exalt Swift in our esteem; for in addressing this nobleman, he has shown how (like all magnanimous spirits) he could sink the mere party-politician in the intellectual cosmopolite. Swift was a Tory, and Somers was the Whig Chancellor; nevertheless, the tribute to the public virtues of the first patron of the *Paradise Lost* is urged with as much neatness and elegance of wit as manliness of spirit. ⟨. . .⟩

The weight and force of Swift's argumentative power, with perspicuity of thought and transparency of diction, are seen to great advantage in that admirable series of political essays known under the title of *The Drapier Letters*, a collection of papers drawn up in so masterly a manner, and directed to their object of attack with such vehemence and effect, that his single energy and exertion withstood the unconstitutional attempt of the whole Ministerial phalanx to debase the Irish coin; and, finally, he succeeded in frustrating their iniquitous purpose. The event, which forms a prominent feature in Swift's career, was briefly this: In the year 1724 an obscure tradesman, and a bankrupt, of the name of Wood, alleging the great want of copper money in Ireland, obtained a patent for issuing one hundred and eight thousand pounds in that metal, to pass there as current money; the metal for which, however, was so debased that six parts out of seven were composed of brass. Swift at this period had almost wholly withdrawn from political writing; but, seeing at a glance the fatal consequences that would ensue to the whole kingdom if the measure were allowed to succeed, and believing it to be a vile job from the beginning to the end, and that the chief procurers of the patent were to be sharers in the profits which would arise from the ruin of a kingdom, he rushed from his retirement to the rescue, and in the first instance drew up a remonstrance to both Houses of Parliament, in which, after a number of masterly arguments, he makes the following nervous appeal:—"Is it, was it, can it, or will it ever be a question, not whether such a kingdom, or William Wood, should be a gainer; but whether such a kingdom should be wholly undone, destroyed, sunk, depopulated, made a scene of misery and desolation, for the sake of William Wood? God of His infinite mercy avert this dreadful judgment; and it is our universal wish that God would put it into your hearts to be His instrument for so good a work." And he concludes with the following determination in case the Parliament should persist in urging on the measure:—"For my own part, who am but one man, of obscure condition, I do solemnly declare, in the presence of Almighty God, that I will suffer the most ignominious and torturing death, rather than submit to receive this accursed coin, or any other that shall be liable to the same objections, until they shall be forced upon me by a *law of my own country*" [the Irish, it will be remembered, had then a Parliament of their own]; "and if that shall ever happen, I will transport myself into some foreign land, and eat the bread of poverty among a free people." Well may it be said: "When shall the Irish have such another rector of Laracor?"

The Ministry, however, persisted in their injustice; and then Swift began his famous attack in the series of letters (there are seven of them) under the signature "M. B. Drapier" (a supposed tradesman), which are dictated in so plain a language that the most barren capacity could understand them. His arguments are so naturally adduced, and his principles are so clear and homely, that perusal and conviction are simultaneous. So perfectly did he sustain the character of the writer he had assumed, that the letters have all the appearance of being the common-sense outpourings of an honest, homespun shop-keeper, who had issued from his obscurity, and had perforce turned author, through indignation at the insolence of power exerted over himself and fellow-citizens. And yet, plain and simple as these compositions appear at first sight, and such as any ordinary writer might imagine he himself could produce, as he would a letter of ceremony; yet inspect them critically, and they will be found to have been constructed with consummate art and skill. Moreover, Swift has displayed a thoroughly comprehensive view of his subject, and shown himself to have been a political economist (especially as regards the monetary question) of no ordinary standard. Had this iniquitous job (for "job" it certainly was—there is no courtlier term for it) been forced upon the Irish people, their trading interest must have been swamped. His attacks, therefore, are terrific, from their force and certainty of aim. They are rifle-cannon shot. His fourth letter brought out a proclamation from the Lord Lieutenant (Carteret) offering £300 reward for the discovery of the author of it. The printer was imprisoned; a bill was sent to the grand jury. Swift addressed a letter to every member of the pannel—so convincing in its argument, that, to a man, they threw out the bill; and so furious was the then tide of party, that the time-serving Lord Chief Justice, Whitshed, in his rage, unconstitutionally discharged the whole of the grand jury; and when the Parliament refused to impeach the judge for his breach of the law of the land, Swift darted upon him like a bull-dog, tore, and worried him out of all his patience by squibs, epigrams, and bitter attacks in all directions, till he made him ridiculous, as well as odious, to the whole country—in short, he succeeded in making the universal trading community of Ireland determine to refuse the coin in payment for their goods. ⟨. . .⟩

What service Demosthenes rendered to the Athenians by his renowned orations, the author of these remarkable, yet unostentatious, letters effected for his countrymen by his silent pen. This is the true and the most effective "agitation;" steam-force arguments, with a righteous cause to back them; and indeed Swift undertook a greater labour, and produced a greater effect, than any single man, before or since, has been able to accomplish. "Every person, of every rank, party, and denomination, was convinced," says Lord Orrery; "the Papist, the fanatic, the Tory, the Whig, all listed themselves volun-

teers under the banner of M. B. Drapier, and were all equally zealous to serve the common cause. Much heat, and many fiery speeches against the Administration, were the consequences of this union." All the threats and proclamations of the Government produced not the slightest effect till the coin was totally suppressed and Wood had withdrawn his patent. As a proof of the intrinsic merit of these letters, as compositions, they are so interesting that the reader must indeed be inert who can quit them; or who, as he reads on, does not so identify himself with the object they are intended to serve as to revive their local political interest after a lapse of more than a hundred and forty years. Swift was a thorough master of "political agitation." It is curious, and as amusing, to note the various measures in which he harps upon that odious coin, constantly using the word "brass." When he was not writing essays, addresses, petitions, and letters, he let off squibs and epigrams, and all addressed to the level of the common intellect. The circumstance of Lord Carteret succeeding the unprincipled Duke of Grafton in the government of Ireland, supplied him with an epigram:

> Cart'ret was welcom'd to the shore,
> First with the *brazen* cannons' roar;
> To meet him next the soldier comes,
> With *brazen* trumps and *brazen* drums;
> Approaching near the town, he hears
> The *brazen* bells salute his ears;
> But when Wood's *brass* began to sound,
> Guns, trumpets, drums, and bells were drown'd.

It was not at all Swift's vein to cant about the "dignity and morality of virtue," or to pat his brethren on the back and to assure them that, after all, men are not so bad as they are represented; he left that course to the dealers in hypocrisy and mouth honour; but he has, by implication, constantly shown his reverence for *true* honour, social worth, and unpalavering integrity; and "he that runneth may read" this moral throughout his most popular prose satire, meaning the *Gulliver's Travels*. We have the meanness, the littleness, the low cunning, the national conceit and chicanery, in the small people of Lilliput. Just so long as blue ribands and red ribands, and silver sticks and gold sticks, and other trumpery are retained and revered as the insignia of services performed, just so long will the leaps and the vaultings and the summersaults of my lord Flimnap and his noble competitors at the Court of Lilliput be appreciated by and amuse the reflecting reader. And as long as men will prostrate their souls in the mire of servility and dishonour, in order that they may bask in the sunshine of favour, so long will the service in the Court of Lilliput rebound from every worthy breast, that the chief merit of every courtier there is made to consist in the neatness with which he licks up the dust while crawling upon his hands and knees to the foot of the throne. All these acts are the characteristics of miniature-minded and low people. On the other hand, to the gigantic Brobdignagians he has dispensed a bland nature and a large benevolence, the baser properties being the result of diminutive intellectual conformation. Swift, therefore, as it appears, designs to portray that true grandeur of character and magnanimity consist in gentleness, sympathy, and an expansive benevolence. His prototype, Rabelais, has anticipated him in this moral of his allegory; for Gargantua and his father, Grangousier, are the most forbearing and beneficent of giants. How agreeable is the description of Gulliver's nurse, Glumdalclitch; and how fine and racy the satire put into the mouth of the good-tempered King. How triumphant his reception of the little traveller's account of the wars and disputes in his own country—religious and political—after a hearty laugh asking him whether he was a Whig or a Tory. What a capital rebuke to the fussiness of party! And how stinging the concluding remark of his Brobdignagian majesty:—

> Then turning to his First Minister, who waited behind him with a white staff near as tall as the mainmast of the *Royal Sovereign*, he observed how contemptible a thing was human grandeur, which could be mimicked by such contemptible creatures as I; and yet, says he, I dare engage, these creatures have their titles and distinctions of honour; they contrive little nests and burrows, that they call houses and cities; they make a figure in dress and equipage; they love, they fight, they dispute, they cheat, they betray.

The only malicious creature among the whole race is the Dwarf.

Throughout this masterly work, Swift has taken such a view of human nature as might be supposed to emanate from a being of a higher sphere and in a superior state of existence. Who more contemptuously than he has exposed the worthlessness, if not the wickedness, of party feud? two races in a nation tearing each other to pieces in order that the question may be decided whether they shall break their eggs at the big or the little end: as Voltaire, in his biting way, records of the Spaniards in America, "They roasted thirty thousand people at slow fires, in order to *convert* them."

Dr. Johnson, who seems to have had a personal antipathy to Swift, has endeavoured to depreciate his literary reputation by denying—or, at all events, questioning—that, in the one case, he was the author of the *Tale of a Tub*; and, in the other, by asserting that there was no merit in *Gulliver* beyond the mechanical execution of the story; because the first idea of it was taken from the *Gargantua* of Rabelais.

That Swift was answerable for all the merits and demerits in the allegory of the Brothers Peter, Martin, and Jack, its internal evidence of style and manner were alone all but sufficient. Johnson should have said who was the author, if Swift was not. His biographer and friend, Dr. Sheridan, however, speaks of the work as though its authenticity could not for one moment be questioned; besides, an anecdote is somewhere upon record that in his advanced age, and when his faculties were upon the waver, he was heard to mutter to himself, while reading the book, "What a fine genius I had when I wrote this!" Moreover, so little doubt existed with the Ministers of the day, and at Court, of his being the author, that the fact obstructed his promotion to a vacant bishopric. It savours, therefore, of the bitterness of antipathy to take that from a man's literary fame which stood in the way of his worldly success. And as to the want of originality in the first thought of the *Gulliver*—that of making the agents of disproportioned size, to suit the purpose of his satire—there can be no serious ground taken for detraction on that score; for we must remember that this employment of the gigantic agency did not come from the corner-stone of Rabelais's satire, whereas it constitutes both the groundwork and the entire elevation of that of Swift; he has availed himself of a similar material, but he has made a totally different disposal of it. Is every one who writes an epic poem in twenty-four books, in the heroic stanza, with episode and simile interspersed, a copyist of Homer? And, lastly, and to dispose of the question of the "execution" of the *Gulliver's Travels*, which Dr. Johnson pronounced to be so easy and mechanical—after he had wrenched the original invention from the author—it can only be said that we may look in vain for equal ease and propriety of

action in the mechanism of the *Rasselas*, or in the "Voyage of Life," in the *Idler*; and with no greater hope of success for any originality in the allegory, the design, or the satire of either. It was as unwise as it was invidious in Dr. Johnson (himself so exposed to detraction) to adopt such a course for lessening a great man's fame. The fact is, that the mere machinery of the *Gulliver* (easy of achievement as it was in Dr. Johnson's estimation) is so correct through all its proportions that this alone constitutes no small share of the merit of the work, and (united with the invention) it has become one of those effective levers that have pushed on the social world.

The poetry of Swift has been wholly—at all events, in a great degree—eclipsed by the predominant excellence of his prose inventions and dissertations. The same strong sense, however, the same natural, indigenous diction, and the same caustic humour characterise his poetical effusions as his satires and essays. There is an austere drollery and a most pure vein of irony in some of the poems of Swift that are extremely amusing: and now and then we come upon a golden thread of pathos (unpremeditated and unaffected) which appeals at once to the tribunal of sentiment and good feeling. Swift was the poet of sterling, downright sense, and not of speculative fancy, or of excursive imagination. So little congeniality, indeed, has he with that higher region of poetry, that it must have been interesting to have heard what his mathematical, utilitarian mind would have to say about the *Faërie Queene*, or the *Midsummer Night's Dream*. He would not have talked the amazing nonsense that Dr. Johnson did; but, with the same hard cynical faculty, he would have bound them to the Procrustes' bed of the French school of criticism, and by that code he might, perhaps (while he showed that they "*proved* nothing"), have missed the subtleties in that *mens divinior* which can "take the imprisoned soul and lap it in elysium." Even in his wit, Swift is serious and saturnine—not sportive and wanton. He did not *laugh* at the follies and vices of mankind—he was never seen to laugh; but he was impatient with them, and they made him angry. I know that there is an opinion prevailing with regard to the satires of Swift—most especially his prose ones—that they have an injurious tendency, inasmuch as they induce a degrading, and even desponding, sense of human nature. For my own part I do not feel this to be the case; and this feeling may arise from self-conceit, but more, I believe, from the sense I entertain of the dignity of the human creation. One exception I must allow, and that is, in the story of the Houynhyms and Yahoos; and that bitter satire, I suppose, was penned when the redeeming milk of hope and forbearance with regard to his species had all but dried up in his nature. ⟨. . .⟩

If Swift wrote much that deserved to survive, and which will survive, to the latest posterity (for he is a British classic), he has also left a prodigious quantity that no mortal would care to look at twice. Few men perhaps, with equal grasp of mind, have written so much trumpery, and few so many ineffective, uninteresting, and nonsensical verses, as he. Fortunate for his executors and editors that he could not retrace his steps after quitting this world; since they would assuredly have felt the weight of his indignation due to their intemperate zeal in pouring out upon the public all the waifs and strays, scraps, odds and ends, tag-rag and bob-tail, scattered among his books and papers. If they had found a receipt for pickling cabbage, I verily believe that it would have been installed among his "works." Nevertheless, it is neither a fruitless nor a worthless employment to contemplate a mind like that of Swift during its carnival of negligence and frivolity. It is pleasant, in the first place, to notice the stern, unbending patriot, the haughty politician, who kept the Prime Minister, Oxford, at arm's length, and sent him to Coventry till he had apologised for an affront that that lord had passed upon him; for at the Queen's levee he no more noticed that principal officer of the Government than if he had been Silver or Gold Stick; and when alluding to the circumstance in his journal to Stella, he adds, in the spirit of an intellectual autocrat: "If we let these Ministers pretend too much, there will be no *governing* them." The man who bearded the Viceroy at his own levee in Dublin Castle, and made the roof ring with his indignant remonstrance at the unconstitutional acts of the English Parliament; who, by his own robust sense, unflinching and uncompromising firmness of purpose, and integrity of principle reconciled a bickering and unstable Ministry, and, for months, forcibly, and by his own unaided genius, kept them at the political helm—the eminent Bolingbroke being one of them—it is pleasant, I say, to see such a sturdy spirit bending to the relaxations of a drawing-room dilettante; writing Lilliputian odes, in lines of three syllables; Latin doggrels, puns and charades to Dr. Sheridan, and slip-shod verses from Mary the cook to the deaf old housekeeper. What pleasant humour in the poem, whether "Hamilton's bawn shall be converted into a barrack or a malt-house." What a spirited sketch of a militia captain, and how genuine (for that age) the soldiers' oaths, and rough handling of the canonical cloth. What excellent travesty upon rural poetry, in what he styles a "Town Eclogue; or, London in a Shower." ⟨. . .⟩

So little concern did this remarkable man evince for his literary fame that, of all his works, not one was subscribed with his name, except the letter upon the English language, and that he addressed to the Earl of Oxford, the Prime Minister. Not one of his most intimate friends was aware of his being the author of the *Gulliver's Travels*. Gay wrote over to him in Ireland, describing the sensation the book was producing in all circles, telling him that even the publisher was ignorant of its author, and adding, "If you are the man, as we suspect, your friends have reason to feel disobliged at your giving them no hint of the matter." Swift had none of the coquetry or pettiness of authorship; he could afford to wait till the world found him out; and he was even less regardful of the author's pecuniary emolument; for in one of his letters he declared that he never got a farthing for anything he had written, except once, and then he was indebted to the vigilance of Pope; and even this sum he abandoned to his friend. It is plausible to infer that the history of authorship does not furnish a parallel to the extent of this sacrifice. He never asked a favour (for himself) of king or statesman; still less would he condescend to dandle palms with the critics. Swift was the most stubbornly proud man of his age; and this bearing he supported in his tone of thought as well as action; for, in directing his genius, he followed no man as a model. In short, he was not only the most original, but, take him in all his phases of authorship, he was the most powerful and perhaps the most various writer of the century in which he flourished.

To sum up his character in few words, he was, as Sir Walter Scott says in his Life of him, a compound of anomaly and paradox. He was a strenuous believer, and yet was refused a diocese through the instrumentality of the Archbishop of York, who told Queen Anne that she ought to be certain that the man she was going to create a bishop was a Christian. This opposition arose from his irrepressible spirit of satirical levity, both in speaking and writing. The wonder is, that the Archbishop did not pronounce him a subtle Atheist.

In his politics he adhered to the Tory party—he was a sublime Tory. And yet no man has said or done stronger things in behalf of democratic freedom. Had he adhered to his first party and principles, he would have been as sublime a Whig. He entertained a rugged antipathy to his countrymen; and yet he seized the first opportunity to vindicate their rights and liberties, and to rescue them from unjust oppression. And this he did after the most disgraceful outrages on their part offered to his own person. When he first went over to Dublin to occupy his living, the Whig party pursued him there; and such was the coarse political spirit of the age that he was not unfrequently pelted with mud as he walked the streets.

He lay all his life under the stigma of being penurious (this charge arose from his being orderly and *strict* in the employment of his revenue), and yet he was greatly and secretly bountiful.

He was avowedly the most classical writer of his day, and yet he could not take his degree at college.

He was the sole prop and stay of the Tory Administration; he had obtained promotion for numbers in the Church, and yet could not compass for himself the only place he desired.

He was actuated by strong impulses of kindness and affection—upon one occasion hurrying into a closet to weep when he saw the pictures taken down at his friend Sheridan's, who was removing from him; yet this friend he arrested for debt, and broke the hearts of two amiable women, whom there is little doubt he sincerely respected, if not loved; for all those poems to Stella, and that constant journal, proclaim him to have been—for the time, at all events, and for a long time, too—a sincere man; or, indeed, he was an astounding and gratuitous hypocrite, a charge that no one will be hardy enough to file against him. But, in fact, no man was more wilful, and less patient of dictation; and this, it may be, was the dormant seed in his nature, which in latter life, fungus-like, overgrew and smothered his reason. We may feel for him in his secret thoughts—which at times must have been awful, since he evidently anticipated for years his own mental decay. He told Dr. Young—pointing to the blasted summit of a tree—that that was the way in which he himself should decline. With all his wilfulness and impatience, however, he would frequently, as an author, yield upon the tenderest points—that of deferring to the opinion of others. He struck out forty verses, and added the same number to one of his poems, in compliance with a suggestion of Addison's. Upon another occasion he altered two paragraphs in a pamphlet in opposition to his own judgment; and when, after the publication, his adviser became sensible that the changes were to its detriment, and expressed his regret and surprise that they had been adopted, Swift, with all the indifference of conscious power, answered, "I made them without hesitation, lest, had I stood up for their defence, you might have imputed it to the vanity of an author unwilling to hear of his errors, and by this ready compliance I hoped you would at all times hereafter be the more free in your remarks."

He constantly manifests in his works—more especially in the latter ones—a bitter misanthropy; and yet in his "heart of heart" he was an enduring friend, a firm and devoted patriot, a foot-to-foot partisan, a bountiful patron. The fund he appropriated in small loans to assist needy traders and even the poor basket-women in the streets, which consisted of the first £500 he himself had saved, is a proof that his misanthropy was little more than a skin-deep irritation; and as sympathy begets sympathy, no man, perhaps (not even excepting the famous "Agitator" of our own day—need I say Daniel O'Connell?), possessed so absolute a dominion over the affections of the commonalty. When the Archbishop of Dublin publicly charged Swift with inflaming the people against him—"I inflame them!" retorted the triumphant dictator; "had I but lifted my finger they would have torn you to pieces." Oh! truly, and indeed, we may parody Marc Antony's eulogy of the great Brutus, and say of Swift—"This was the noblest 'Tory' of them all"—

> All the "party-mongers," save only he,
> Did what they did in envy of "Whiggery;"
> He only, in a general honest thought,
> And common good to all, made one of them.

I cannot pursue my parody, and say: "His life was *gentle*" (for it was anything but that); we may add, however:—

> The elements
> So mixed in him, that nature might stand up
> And say to all the World: *This was a man.*

Truly may we exclaim with Hazlitt, "When shall we have another Rector of Laracor?"

JOHN CHURTON COLLINS
From "Characteristics"
Jonathan Swift: A Biographical and Critical Study
1893, pp. 241–68

I

The chief peculiarity of Swift's temper lay in the coexistence not merely of opposite qualities but of opposite natures. The union of a hard, cold, logical intellect with a heart of almost feminine tenderness is no uncommon anomaly. But the anomaly which Swift presents is not an anomaly of this kind. In acute susceptibility to sensuous and emotional impression he resembled Rousseau and Shelley. His nervous organisation was quite as exquisite, his sensibility as keen, his perceptions as nice. He was as dependent on human sympathy and on human affection; he was as passionately moved by what men less finely tempered regard with composure. The sight of a fellow-creature in distress or pain, the spectacle of an unjust or cruel action, a fancied slight conveyed in a word or look, an offensive or disagreeable object, were to him, as to them, little less than torture. Thus on the sensuous and emotional side he had the temperament of the poet and the enthusiast. But Nature had not completed what she had begun. She had bestowed on him the *cor cordium*; she had endowed him with 'the love of love' and 'the hate of hate'; she had been lavish of the gifts which are the poet's most painful inheritance; but from all else, from all that constitutes the poet's solaces, the poet's charm, the poet's power, she had excluded him. Utterly devoid of a sense of the beautiful, of the beautiful in nature, in the human form, in morals, in art, in philosophy, he neither sought it nor recognised it when seen. Its representation in concrete form is always perverted by him into the grotesque and ugly. As a critic and philosopher he has only one criterion—plain good sense in the one case, practical utility in the other. Of any perception of the ideal, of any sympathy with effort or tendency to aspire to it, he was as destitute as Sancho Panza and Falstaff. On no class of people have the shafts of his contemptuous raillery fallen thicker than on those who would seek for finer bread than is made of flour, and on the originators of Utopian schemes. His own ideal of life began and ended, as he himself frankly admitted, with the attainment of worldly success. [1] Of transcendental imagination, nay, of the transcendental instinct, he had nothing. He never appears to have had even a glimpse of those truths which lie outside the scope of the senses and the reason, and which find their

expression in poetry and in sentimental religion. He never refers to them as embodied in the first without ridicule and contempt, nor as embodied in the second without coldly resolving them into compulsory dogmas. 'Violent zeal for Truth,' he observes, 'has a hundred to one odds to be either petulancy, ambition, or pride.' [2] If he does not deny the divine element in man and in the world, it is only because it forms an article of the creed which for other reasons he thought it expedient to uphold. But what he did not deny he either ignored or obscured. A conception of human nature and of human life more inconsistent than his with any theory of divinity either within man or without it would be impossible to find, even in the writings of professed atheists. 'Miserable mortals!' he exclaims in his *Thoughts on Religion*, 'can we contribute to the honour and glory of God? I could wish that expression were struck out of our prayer-books.' His whole conception of religion appears to have been almost purely political. What Fielding puts into the mouth of Thwackum is literally descriptive of Swift's attitude: 'When I mention religion I mean the Christian religion; and not only the Christian religion, but the Protestant; and not only the Protestant, but the Church of England.' He makes no distinction between Deists and Nonconformists, between Roman Catholics and Infidels. They are all equally denounced, and regarded as equally excluded from the pale of what constitutes 'religion.' And what constitutes religion has been prescribed by the State. To that every man should be compelled to adhere. In relation to its essence and apart from its accidents he never contemplates it. 'Religion,' he insists, 'supposes Heaven and Hell, the Word of God, and Sacraments.' [3] He complains bitterly that men should be allowed a freedom in religious matters which they are not allowed in political; that a citizen who prefers a commonwealth to monarchy, and who should endeavour to establish one, would be punished with the utmost rigour of the law, but that a citizen who prefers Nonconformity to Episcopalianism is at perfect liberty to choose the one instead of the other. [4] So completely are the spiritual and essential elements of religion subordinated to its political and temporal utility, that he contends boldly that the truth or falsehood of the fundamental opinions on which the creed of the Christian rests are of comparatively little moment compared with the mischief involved in questioning them; that it is not requisite for a man to believe what he professes; and that it matters little what doubts and scruples he may have, provided he keeps them to himself. [5] A man may be allowed, he observes elsewhere in reference to this subject, to keep poisons in his closet, but not to vend them about for cordials. [6] If, as has been sometimes supposed, he depicts his ideal man in the King of Brobdingnag, and his ideal of human excellence in the Houyhnhnms, it is remarkable that religion has no place in the education and life of either. The virtues of the former are those of pure stoicism; the virtues of the latter are summed up in friendship, benevolence, temperance, industry, and cleanliness.

It is, of course, impossible to say, but it is very doubtful whether Swift's own opinions inclined certainly towards belief in the promises of Christianity, or even in a future state. The balance of probability is decidedly adverse to the first supposition, and wavers very uncertainly in favour of the second. His attitude towards the metaphysics of Christianity is always the same; he never dwells on them, and whenever it is possible he avoids them. In his sermon on the Trinity he speaks of his theme as 'a subject which probably I should not have chosen if I had not been invited to it.' Rigidly orthodox, he repeats over and over again that what the Church teaches is no matter for argument and question, but must be accepted implicitly and in its integrity. Episcopal Protestant Christianity supplies as a co-ercive moral agency what no system of morality apart from it is able to supply; it must, therefore, be retained, and if it is not retained with all its dogmas it ceases to be Christianity.[7] This is his note throughout in apology as in exegesis. Without unc-tion, without fervour, without sentiment, he leaves us with the impression that he neither sought nor found in the Gospel which he accepted and delivered so faithfully anything that illuminated or anything that cheered. Of its power as a source of consolation in sorrow he was well aware. 'Take courage from Christianity,' he writes to Mrs. Whiteway, 'which will assist you when humanity fails.' But he took from it, or seems to have taken from it, little courage himself. It is mournfully apparent that no ray from the creed of faith and hope pierced the gloom of that long night which descended on the winter of his life.

Assuming, as a churchman, the truth of Christianity, he was bound also, as a churchman, to assume the existence of a future state. But the evidence for supposing that it formed any article of his personal belief is very slight. In his *Thoughts on Religion* he makes no reference to it, but observes of death that a thing so natural, so necessary, and so universal could not have been designed by Providence as an evil to mankind. In his sermons he never dwells on it. In his letters of consolation in bereavement he wrote, of course, as propriety dictated that a clergyman should write. And yet even here his expressions are frequently very guarded and sometimes ambiguous. 'Religion regards life,' he writes to Mrs. Moore on the death of her daughter, 'only as a preparation for a better, which you are taught to be certain that so innocent a person is now in possession of.'[8] He would, he said to Pope, exchange youth for advanced old age, if he could be as secure of a better life as Mrs. Pope deemed herself.[9] 'If,' he remarked when his mother died, 'the way to Heaven be through piety, truth, justice and charity, she is there.' In his reflections on the death of Esther Johnson he makes no reference to immortality. In the prayers which he offered for her in her last illness he expresses a hope that she 'may be received into everlasting habitations,' but there is nothing to indicate that he felt the smallest confidence in the realisation of such hopes. His own epitaph is without a trace of Christian sentiment—that he had found in the grave a haven *ubi sæva indignatio ulterius cor lacerare nequit*—that he had left in his life an example which all who loved liberty would do well to imitate—this was the only assurance, this the only admonition, which he desired to proclaim from the tomb. It is possible, of course, that his reticence and reserve on religious subjects had its origin in the same cause which led him to conceal so studiously from guests in his house the fact that he daily read prayers to his servants—that it arose from his detestation of pretence and especially of pretentious piety. And this is by no means improbable, for there can be little doubt that, had he been as convinced of the truth of the Christian dogmas as St. Paul himself, he would have avoided ostenta-tious or enthusiastic profession.[10] But a distinction must be made between the avoidance of ostentatious or enthusiastic profession and such an attitude as Swift's. We must take into consideration the whole tenor of his character and writings, and the impression conveyed by them is that of a man who was endeavouring honestly to support a part. He was convinced of the absolute necessity of maintaining, in the interests of society as well as of particular individuals, the Christian religion with all its dogmas; he felt that the balance of what he could accept as sound and true in its teaching was more and much more than a counterpoise to what might be unsound and untrue; and he probably felt that what he could not accept he could not absolutely pronounce to be false. Applying the test of the

politician, the magistrate, and the philanthropist, he was content to dispense with the test of the transcendental philos-opher.[11] Hence his habit of avoiding all discussion of such subjects as the immortality of the soul and a future state, his guarded phrases, his plain unwillingness to commit himself to expressions of his personal opinions, his appeals to reason rather than to faith, the ethical as distinguished from the theological character of his teaching, the absence, in the stress of affliction, of any indication of faith and hope.

His deficiency on the side of what we commonly call sentiment is not less remarkable. Sentiment is never likely to be found in any great degree where the transcendental instinct is lacking. But the total atrophy, or rather non-existence, of both in a man of strong affections and of acute susceptibility to emotional impression is an anomaly rare indeed in the temper of men. Of sentiment Swift was so wholly devoid that it was unintelligible to him. Its expression in language he regarded as cant, its expression in action as affectation and folly. For him life had no illusions, man no mystery, nature no charm. He looked on woman's beauty with the eye of an anatomist, on earth's beauties with the eye of a chemist. In the passion which not unfrequently transforms even the grossest and most com-monplace of human beings into poets he saw only brutal appetite, masquerading in fantastic frippery. And his delight was to strip it bare. All that fancy, all that imagination, all that sentiment had woven round it torn contemptuously away, he gloated with horrid glee over the naked shame of nature. For religious enthusiasm he could discern only physical causes; sometimes he refers it to hysterics or to sexual excitement taking a wrong turn, sometimes to a diseased and disordered brain. More generally he regards it as mere affectation assumed for the purpose of making money or of gratifying vanity by acquiring notoriety. His sole criterion as a critic and judge was unsublimated reason. In his estimate of men he made no allowance for impulse and passion except as indicating deprav-ity or weakness. In his estimate of life and the world generally he saw everything in the clear cold light of the pure intellect. From no mind of which we have expression in record had the Spectres of the Tribe, the Den, the Forum, and the Theatre been so completely exorcised. But, as the eyes of the body may be blinded by excess of light, so the eyes of the mind may by excess of reason be blinded—by the very power which should give them sight. Of the truth by which men live, mere reason indeed obscures almost as much as she reveals. If life took its colour and its pattern from the philosophy of Swift as that philosophy finds embodiment in his ideal king and in his ideal creatures, how insipid would it become, how torpid, how inglorious! Swift's philosophy is indeed in essence precisely the philosophy of Falstaff in his soliloquy on honour:—

> What need I be so forward with him that calls not on me? Well, 'tis no matter; honour pricks me on. Yea, but how if honour prick me off when I come on? how then? Can honour set to a leg? no: or an arm? no: or take away the grief of a wound? no. Honour hath no skill in surgery, then? no. What is honour? a word. What is in that word honour? what is that honour? air. A trim reckoning! Who hath it? he that died o' Wednesday. Doth he feel it? no. Doth he hear it? no. 'Tis insensible, then. Yea, to the dead. But will it not live with the living? no. Why? detraction will not suffer it. Therefore I'll none of it. Honour is a mere scutcheon: and so ends my catechism.

Now, apart from transcendental considerations, apart from sentiment, apart, in fine, from all that Swift ignores, how unanswerable is logic like this, how irrefutable the reasoning! But it is reasoning against which all that constitutes the true dignity and beauty of human life rises in revolt. It would paralyse the wings of the soul, dwarf and blight the heroic virtues, and degrade the whole level of action and aspiration. As Shakespeare's generous enthusiast so well says:—

> Manhood and honour
> Should have hare hearts, would they but fat their
>   thoughts
> With this cramm'd reason: reason and respect
> Make livers pale, and lustihood deject.

Swift said himself that his favourite author was La Rochefoucauld, 'because I find my whole character in him.'[12] The remark is significant, and the resemblance in some respects between them unquestionable. But his true prototype was Hobbes. Hobbes had none of Swift's acute sensibility, none of his tense and vehement seriousness, nothing of his Titanism, nothing of his humour. But for the rest the analogy between them was complete. The intelligence of both moved only in the sphere of the senses and the pure reason. Pessimists and cynics by both temper and conviction, they were deficient in all those instincts and sympathies on which every true estimate and every true philosophy of humanity must be based. Both resolved mankind into mere animals, and the Yahoos of Swift are the 'natural men' of Hobbes. Both reduced all that ennobles, all that beautifies, all that consecrates life, to a *caput mortuum*. Both denied practically, and even ridiculed as metaphysical thinkers, what they asserted and maintained as ethical political legislators. Both, in effect, eliminated the element of supernaturalism, and defended religion on civil grounds. Hobbes based its sanction and authority on the will of the State, Swift practically on the will of the State Church. When Hobbes wrote 'It is with the mysteries of our religion as with wholesome pills for the sick, which, swallowed whole, have the virtue to cure, but chewed are for the most part cast up again without effect,'[13] he condensed what is in essence the argument of Swift. Both, by nature pure despots, regarded the mass of their fellow-men as fools and knaves, to be ruled with justice indeed, and, if possible, with clemency, but to be ruled with a rod of iron.

But it must not be forgotten that, if this anti-ideality and cynicism found its intensest and most powerful expression in Swift, it was essentially characteristic of the age into which he was born and in which he died. That age may be compared to a deep valley between two eminences. On the one side are the heights to which the enthusiasm of the Renaissance and the enthusiasm of Puritanism had elevated the national spirit; on the other side is the ascent sloping upwards to the equally lofty tablelands of the idealists of the New World. Between the year of Swift's birth and the first administration of Pitt, it may be safely said that in all that ennobles and in all that beautifies human life and human nature England had reached her lowest level. The morals and temper of the London of the Restoration would have disgusted the Romans of St. Paul, while much of its literature would hardly have been tolerated by the friends of Trimalchion. After the accession of Anne, it is generally supposed that the evil spirit of the preceding era was exorcised, and that a new and good spirit entered in. And this is to some extent true. The example set by the Queen herself, the decency and decorum observed at her Court, and the writings of Addison and his circle, undoubtedly exercised a salutary influence on society. But all that was touched was the surface. The change was more apparent than real. The filth, the cynicism, the inhumanity, the unbelief of the former age underlay—a foul substratum—the specious exterior. The accession of George I.

rendered concealment no longer necessary, and with some slight modification all became as all had been before.[14] Wherever we turn we find variously diluted and variously coloured what we find condensed in Swift. What is Prior but the poet of disillusion? His most elaborate poem was written to show the nothingness of man and of the world, his *Alma* to ridicule metaphysics, his most successful tales to laugh romance to scorn; his best lyrics are but cynical trifles. What is Gay but an elegant fribble, who ordered a flippant jest to be inscribed as his epitaph?[15] Even the fine genius of Pope is without wings, and many of the passages which exhibit his powers in their highest perfection are directed to the ignoble purpose of degrading his species. Mandeville's *Fable of the Bees* is as shameless a libel on humanity as the *Voyage to the Houyhnhnms*, and his *Virgin Unmasked* would have disgraced Wycherley. In the *Richardsoniana* we have the very alcohol of cynicism. The greatest painter of the age devoted his talents to bringing into prominence all that is most humiliating and odious in man, and the pens of De Foe and Smollett vied with the pencil of Hogarth in depicting and heightening moral and physical ugliness and depravity. Nor is this spirit less apparent when it finds urbaner and more refined expression. The correspondence of Pope, of Bolingbroke, of Lady Mary Wortley Montagu, the conversations recorded by Spence, the *Memoirs* of Lord Hervey, and, indeed, the greater part of the polite literature and all the *ana* of the age, are the records of a society which, with *Que sçais-je?* for its motto, and *Nil admirari* for its creed, prided itself on its superiority to enthusiasm, to sentiment, to the ideal. If we turn to theology and philosophy, we find ourselves on the same low level. When Reid wrote, 'Philosophy has no other root but the principles of common sense; it grows out of them; it draws its nourishment from them; severed from this root its honours wither, its sap is dried up, it dies and rots;[16] and when Pope wrote

> Good sense, which only is the gift of Heaven,
> And, though no science, fairly worth the seven,

they merely expressed what has expression everywhere in the writings of their immediate predecessors and contemporaries. It was the age of the Deistic Controversy, of the sermons of Wake, Gibson, Sherlock, and Hare. The test of religious truth was social utility—its sanction, reason. 'I send my servants to church,' said Anthony Collins, 'that they may neither rob nor murder me'; and if he spoke as a freethinker he adduced what was practically the chief argument of the most orthodox theologians of that day in favour of supernaturalism. As the apostle of ideal truth not simply in the technical but in the comprehensive sense of the term, Berkeley stood absolutely alone. To eliminate as far as possible the transcendental element from religion, and to show how life may be sustained upon a minimum of moral and spiritual assumption, appears to have been the main object of the divines and moralists of those times.

But to return. Thackeray, in speaking of Swift's last days, has finely said: 'So great a man he seems to me, that thinking of him is like thinking of an empire falling.' The expression is not exaggerated. Swift is the one figure of colossal proportions in the age to which he belonged. Nay, we may go further. Among men whose fame depends mainly on their writings, there is, if we except Aristotle, Shakespeare, and perhaps Bacon, probably no man on record who impresses us with a sense of such enormous intellectual power. He has always the air of a giant sporting among pigmies, crushing or scrutinising, helping or thwarting them, as the mood takes him. Immense strength, immense energy, now frittering themselves away on trifles, now roused for a moment to concentrated action by passion, interest, or benevolence, but never assuming their true proportions, never developing into full activity—this is what we discern in Swift. We feel how miserably incommensurate was the part he played with the part which Nature had fitted him to play, how contracted was the stage, how mighty the capacities of the actor. In his pamphlets, in his two great satires, in his poems, in his correspondence, is the impression of a character which there is no mistaking. And it is not among philosophers, poets, and men of letters that we are to look for its prototype or its analogy, but among those who have made and unmade nations—among men like Cæsar and men like Napoleon.

A comparison between Napoleon at St. Helena and Swift in Ireland has more than once been drawn. With two great distinctions between them, namely, that Napoleon was, morally speaking, an essentially bad man, and Swift an essentially good man, and that the one was without heart and the other with the heart of a woman, it would be possible to institute a parallel not simply between their relative position as exiles but between their temper and characteristics. Both scorned the homage which they punctiliously exacted, and the prizes for which they fought. Devouring ambition, finding in itself not merely the motive but the centre of action, and originating, if partly from the lust of dominion, partly also from the restless importunity of superabundant, nay almost preternatural energy, was the ruling passion of both.[17] Egotists, despots, and cynics, each owned no equal, each had no real confidant. The one towered over his kind on the sublime heights of power, the other in the proud solitude of his own consciousness. What was potential in the one found full and unimpeded expression; what was potential in the other perished undeveloped in embryo. But the genius which could indemnify itself for the lack of the material and conventional symbols of supremacy by writing *Gulliver's Travels* was in essence of the same superhuman type as the genius which half realised universal empire.

What Swift suffered in failing to attain the prizes which his haughty spirit coveted is only too plain from his diaries and correspondence. His pride amounted to disease. He was always on the watch for fancied slights. If a great man left a letter unanswered for a few days, or a friend let fall an ambiguous word, he was miserable. A man passing him in the streets without touching his hat or a woman failing to drop a curtsey seriously discomposed him.[18] To whatever degree of mere intimacy he admitted a person who could amuse or entertain him, he guarded his dignity with the most jealous care. 'He could not,' says Deane Swift, 'endure to be treated with any sort of familiarity, or that any man living, his three or four old acquaintances with whom he corresponded to the last only excepted, should rank himself in the number of his friends.'[19] His superiority to envy, of which he had not, we are told, the smallest tincture, his indifference to literary fame, and his scrupulous truthfulness in all that related to himself, had their origin in the same lofty consciousness of supereminence.

Such were the characteristics and temper of Swift. And it would seem as if Fortune, perceiving what opportunities Nature had given her for malicious sport, had in some spiteful mood resolved to make his life her cruel plaything. Everything that could depress, annoy, and irritate was his lot in youth. His early manhood, initiated by the fatal blunder he made in taking orders, miserable in itself, involved him in deeper miseries still. An

abandon'd wretch, by hope forsook,
Forsook by hopes, ill fortune's last relief,
Assign'd for life to unremitting grief;

For, let Heaven's wrath enlarge these weary days,
If Hope e'er dawns the smallest of its rays[20]
—it was thus that he could write of himself at a time when most men are bounding blithely from the starting-post of life. Whenever a ray seemed to pierce the gloom it was always illusory. Hope after hope glimmered only to be extinguished. Even the paltry prizes he despised were beyond his reach, and his forty-third year found him eating out his heart in an obscure Irish vicarage. Then came power and eminence, without the glory and without the guerdon. A dictator and an underling, a despot and a tool, for nearly four years of his life, all that could pamper and flatter, and all that could gall and irritate his arrogant and sensitive spirit were his mingled portion. With exile as the reward of services great beyond any expression of gratitude, in that exile were accumulated tenfold all causes of irritation, till irritation became torture, till torture goaded passion into fury. And brooding over the life of this unhappy man, wretched alike in what he owed to Nature and in the spite of Fortune, hung a phantom horror. As there can be no doubt that Swift was never insane, and that the maladies from which he suffered had no connection with insanity, so there can equally be no doubt that he was himself convinced of the contrary—was convinced that he carried within him the gradually developing germs of madness, and that his terrible doom was inevitable.[21]

It has been sometimes supposed that Swift's rage for obscenity, so inconsistent with the austere purity of his morals and with his aversion to anything approaching indecency in conversation, had its origin in physical disease—that it was, as it so often is, a phase of insanity. But it is perfectly explicable without resorting to any such hypothesis. An observation of his own furnishes us with the true key—a nice man is a man of nasty ideas;[22] and he was one of the nicest and most fastidious of men. But its expression in its most offensive forms is to be attributed partly to misanthropy, intensifying this depraved sensibility, and partly to a desire to furnish dissuasives from vice. Of such poems as the 'Lady's Dressing Room' Delany observes, and probably with perfect justice, that they were 'the prescriptions of an able physician, who had the health of his patients at heart, but laboured to attain that end not only by strong emetics, but also by all the most offensive drugs and potions that could be administered.' He was, in truth, doing nothing more than the Saints and Fathers of the Church have habitually done, and with the same object. There are passages, for example, in St. Chrysostom and in St. Gregory, which are as nauseous and disgusting as anything that can be found in Swift. But this plea cannot be always, or indeed generally, urged in his defence; and how, in allowing himself such licence, he could see nothing incompatible with his position and behaviour as a clergyman, must remain a mystery.[23] Something is no doubt to be attributed to the age in which he lived, something to his constitution, and more to his rage against his kind. What is certain is that, as his misanthropy intensified, his imagination grew fouler and his filth became more noisome.

II

The writings of Swift are the exact reflection of his character, variously expressing itself on its various sides. Affectation and pretentiousness were his abhorrence; for literary fame he cared nothing, and he had therefore no inducement to aspire beyond the natural level of his powers. He wrote out of the fulness of his mind, as impulse or passion directed, practically, for the attainment of some immediate object, or idly, to amuse himself. To books he owed comparatively little.

Butler was his model in verse. If he had any models in prose, they were the tracts of Father Parsons, and one of the most powerful political pieces extant in our language, Silas Titus' *Killing No Murder*. As a political pamphleteer, Swift is without a rival. Fénelon observed of Cicero, that when the Romans heard him they exclaimed, 'It is the voice of a God;' and of Demosthenes, that when the Athenians heard him they cried, 'Let us march against Philip.' The remark indicates the distinction between Swift's political pieces and the political pieces of such writers as Bolingbroke, Junius, and Burke. Compared with him, they appear to be but splendid sophists, maintaining with all the resources of rhetoric, and all the experience and skill of practised advocates, a case for the prosecution or a case for the defence. If the truth is of little moment to us, we concede to admiration what we ought to concede only to conviction. But the impression produced by Swift is the impression produced by a powerful and logical mind, with no object but the investigation of truth, amply furnished with the means of ascertaining it, and convinced itself before attempting to convince others. His profound knowledge of human nature and his experience of affairs enabled him to bring every point home, and to assume naturally, and with propriety, an air of authority such as in any mere man of letters would be affectation.

Swift is a poet only by courtesy. Good sense, humour, and wit are as a rule the distinguishing characteristics of his poetry, though, as Scott well observes, the intensity of his satire sometimes gives to his verses an emphatic violence which borders on grandeur, as in the *Rhapsody* and in the poem on the Last Day. But, if Apollo disowned him, he was not altogether deserted by the Graces, as *Cadenus and Vanessa* shows; and of the attributes of the poet a touch of fancy may certainly be claimed for him. It would, however, be doing him great injustice to deny his claim to a high place among masters of the *sermo pedestris*. As descriptive pieces his 'City Shower' and his 'Early Morning in London' are pictures worthy of Hogarth; his adaptations from Horace and Ovid are eminently felicitous and pleasing, while the verses on his own death and the 'Grand Question Debated' are among the best things of their kind. Some of his other trifles, particularly his Epistles, will always find delighted readers. His verse, though too mechanically monotonous, is unlaboured and flowing, his diction terse and yet easy and natural. In the art of rhyming, an accomplishment on which he especially prided himself, he has few superiors, and his rhymes are as exact and correct as they are ingenious and novel. Even the author of *Don Juan* spoke of himself as contemplating Swift's mastery over rhyme with admiring despair.

It is, of course, as a humorist and satirist that Swift is and will continue to be a power in literature. Models as his political pieces are—in their style nervous, simple, trenchant—in their method lucid, logical—in their tone masculine, vehement— few perhaps but historical students will turn to them, for to none but historical students will their ephemeral matter be intelligible. Two-thirds of his other writings have long ceased to be of interest to the many, but the *Battle of the Books*, the *Tale of a Tub*, the *Arguments against Abolishing Christianity*, the *Modest Proposal*, a dozen or two of his poems, and *Gulliver*, will keep his fame fresh in every generation. Here, then, are to be found the qualities upon which his claim to a place among classics must rest. They are easily distinguished. The first attribute of genius is originality, and Swift was essentially original. It is true that he was indebted to others for the hint of his three chief satires, but, as he has himself observed, if a man lights his candle at his neighbour's fire it does not affect his property in the candle which he lights. [24] Probably no other writer with the exception of Dickens has borrowed so little. His images and ideas are almost always his own; his humour is his own; his style is his own. In a well-known passage he claims to have been the first to introduce and teach the use of irony:—

> Arbuthnot is no more my friend,
> Who does to irony pretend,
> Which I was born to introduce,
> Refin'd it first, and taught its use.

This was not strictly true, as he had been anticipated by De Foe, whose *Shortest Way with the Dissenters* appeared nearly two years before the earliest of Swift's writings had been published. But a title to a place among classics depends not merely on originality—it depends also on quality, on the intrinsic value and interest of what is produced. Swift's serious reflections and remarks are the perfection of homely good sense—shrewd, trenchant, pointed, enriching life with new and useful truths. But his good sense is without refinement, without imagination, and without subtlety. The sphere in which his intelligence worked and within which his sympathy and insight were bounded was, comparatively speaking, a narrow one. He had the eye of a lynx for all that moves on the surface of life and for all that may be found on the beaten highway of commonplace experience, but the depths he neither explored nor perhaps even suspected. In his innumerable aphorisms, generalisations, and precepts it would be impossible to find one which either indicates delicate discrimination or reveals a glimpse of ideal truth.

His style has in itself little distinction and no charm, but for his purposes it is the more effective from the absence of distinction. A pure medium of expression, it owes nothing to art, for he disdained ornament and he disdained elaboration. To eloquence he makes no pretension. Proper words in proper places was his own ideal of a good style, and he was satisfied with attaining it.

As a master of irony he has few if any equals. It was his favourite weapon, tempered as finely as that with which the Platonic Socrates disarmed Protagoras and Hippias, and as that with which the author of the *Provincial Letters* lacerated the disciples of Le Moine and Father Annat. But the fineness of its temper constituted its chief resemblance to the irony of Plato and Pascal. It is without urbanity, without lightness, and without grace. Austere and saturnine, bitter and intense, it would seem strangely out of place as the ally of pleasantry; and yet seldom has pleasantry been so happily mated. Other humorists may move us to merriment and convulse us with laughter, but the irony of Swift is a source of more delicious enjoyment, of more exquisite pleasure. In its lighter forms it springs from a nice and subtle perception of the unbecoming and the ridiculous in their lighter and more trivial aspects, tempered with scorn and contempt; in its severer, from a similar perception of the same improprieties in their most impressive and most serious aspects, tempered not with scorn merely but with loathing, not with contempt merely but with horror and rage. The extremes are marked by the Dissertations in the *Tale of a Tub* and by the *Directions to Servants* on the one side, by the *Modest Proposal* and the *Voyage to the Houyhnhnms* on the other. And the mean is in the *Voyage to Brobdingnag*. It is in irony that Swift's humour most generally finds expression, and always finds its most characteristic expression. And naturally. Wherever intelligence of clairvoyant insight, however narrow its area, together with a calm or contemptuous consciousness of superiority, is united with acute sensibility and with the keenest perception of the difference between things as they seem and things as they are, irony will always be the note.

The attitude of Swift towards life and man is precisely that of Juvenal's deity—*ridet et odit*—he laughs and loathes. And his humour is the laughter. It is never good-natured. It is always sardonic, presenting a complete contrast to that of Cervantes and to that of Shakespeare. When we turn to the line which Shakespeare put into the mouth of Puck, 'Lord, what fools these mortals be!' and to the *Tempest*, and then to the *Voyage to the Houyhnhnms*, and to the poem in which the Deity dismisses his cowering creatures from the judgment bar, as too despicable to be damned—

> I to such blockheads set my wit!
> I damn such fools! Go go—*you're bit*—

we measure the difference between the humour 'which sees life steadily and sees it whole' and the humour of the mere Titan.

Swift forms one of an immortal trio. In the writings of Addison will be mirrored for all time the image of a beautiful human soul. Humour genial and kindly as it is exquisite, wit refined and polished as it is rich and abundant, and a style approaching as nearly to perfection as it is perhaps possible for style to do, will unite with the charm of his character in keeping his memory green. If the poetry of Pope has not the vogue it once had, the fame of the most brilliant of poets is secure. He may not have the homage of the multitude, but he will have in every generation, as long as our language lasts, the homage of all who can discern. He stands indeed with Horace, Juvenal, and Dryden at the head of a great department of poetry—the poetry of ethics and satire. But the third of the trio will as a name and as a power overshadow the other two. Before his vast proportions they seem indeed to dwindle into insignificance. And what figure in that eighteenth century of time is not dwarfed beside this Momus-Prometheus? Among men, but not of them, at war with himself, with the world, and with destiny, he set at naught the warning which Greek wisdom was never weary of repeating—

Born into life we are, and life must be our mould.

He was in temper all that Pindar symbolises in Typhon, and all that revolts Plato in the inharmonious and unmusical soul. And so, while his writings bear the impress of powers such as have rarely been conceded to man, they reflect and return with repulsive fidelity the ugliness and discord of the Titanism which inspired them. Without reverence and without reticence, he gloried in the licence which to the Greeks constituted the last offence against good taste and good sense, and out of the indulgence in which they have coined a synonym for shamelessness—the indiscriminate expression of what ought and what ought not to be said. A cynic and a misanthrope in principle, his philosophy of life is ignoble, base, and false, and his impious mockery extends even to the Deity. A large portion of his works exhibit, and in intense activity, all the worst attributes of our nature—revenge, spite, malignity, uncleanness. His life, indeed, afforded a noble example of duty conscientiously fulfilled, of great services done to his kind, and of an active benevolence which knew no bounds. But it is not by these virtues that he will be remembered. He will live as one of the most commanding and fascinating figures which has ever appeared on the stage of life, and as the protagonist of a drama which can never cease to interest the student of human life and of human nature. In every generation his works will be read, but they will be read not so much for themselves as for their association. The fame of the man will preserve and

support the fame of the author. For there is probably no writer of equal power and eminence in whose judgments and conclusions, in whose precepts and teaching, the instincts and experience of progressive humanity will find so little to corroborate.

Notes

1. 'All my endeavours, from a boy, to distinguish myself were only for the want of a great title and fortune, that I might be used like a lord by those who have an opinion of my parts, whether right or wrong it is no great matter; and so the reputation of wit and great learning does the office of a blue ribbon or of a coach and six horses.' (Letter to Bolingbroke, April 5, 1729.)
2. *Thoughts on Religion* (*Works*, Bohn ed. viii. 173).
3. *Advice to a Young Poet* (*Works*, ix. 392).
4. *Thoughts on Religion* (*Id.* viii. 176).
5. *Thoughts on Religion* (*Works*, viii. 174).
6. *Gulliver's Travels*—*Voyage to Brobdingnag*.
7. See Sermons, *passim*, but particularly that on the Testimony of Conscience.
8. See his beautiful letter (*Works*, xvii. 197).
9. Letter to Pope, Id. p. 224.
10. 'There was no vice,' says Delany, 'he so much abhorred as hypocrisy, and of consequence nothing he dreaded so much as to be suspected of it, and this made him often conceal his piety with more care than others take to conceal their vices.'—*Observations*, pp. 43–44.
11. Swift's opinions on religion probably differed little from those expressed so admirably by Polybius, vi. ch. 56, 57; by Strabo, i. ch. 2, 8; and by Cicero, *De Legibus*, ii. ch. 7.
12. Letter to Pope, Nov. 26, 1725.
13. *Leviathan*, ch. xxxii.
14. For the temper and tone of the England of Swift see particularly Hartley's *Observations on Man*, ii. 441, not published till 1749, but written many years before; Butler's *Preface to the Analogy*; Warburton's *Dedication to the Divine Legation*; Whiston's *Memoirs*, Part III. pp. 142–213; Voltaire, *Lettres sur les Anglais*; Montesquieu, *Notes on England*, where he says, 'Point de religion en Angleterre; si quelqu'un parle de religion, tout le monde se met à rire'; Hervey's *Memoirs*; the *Suffolk Papers*; Atterbury's *Representation*.
15.
> Life is a jest: and all things show it.
> I thought so once, and now I know it.
16. *Inquiry into the Human Mind*. Introduction, p. 4.
17. To this constitutional restlessness, to this morbid activity of mind, which was so striking a trait of Napoleon, Swift frequently refers. Thus in a letter to Kendall, dated February, 1691/2, he says, 'A person of great honour in Ireland used to tell me that my mind was like a conjured spirit that would do mischief if I did not give it employment. It is this humour which makes me so busy.' Again, in a letter recently printed by the Historical Manuscripts Commissioners, 'I myself was never very miserable while my thoughts were in a ferment, for I imagine a dead calm is the troublesomest of our voyage through the world.'
18. To confine illustrations to the diary at Holyhead—'The master of the pacquet boat hath not treated me with the least civility, altho' Watt gave him my name . . . yet my hat is worn to pieces by answering the civilities of the poor inhabitants as they pass by. . . . I am as insignificant here as Parson Brooke is in Dublin. By my conscience, I believe Cæsar would be the same without his army at his back. . . . Not a soul is yet come to Holyhead except a young fellow who smiles when he meets me and would fain be my companion, but it is not come to that yet . . . if I stay here much longer I am afraid all my pride and grandeur will truckle to comply with him.'
19. *Essay on Swift*, p. 361.
20. 'Verses on Sir W. Temple's Illness and Recovery,' written at Moor Park in 1693.
21. This is placed beyond doubt by the well-known incident recorded by Young in his *Conjectures on Original Composition*. The

incident almost certainly occurred in or about 1717. See Scott, i. 443–44.
22. *Thoughts on Various Subjects*.
23. What is still more surprising is that, although these productions appeared anonymously, it was no secret that they were from the pen of the Dean of St. Patrick's; and how Swift, who in private life and in conversation never forgot and never allowed others to forget the respect due to his cloth, could expose himself to the derogatory retorts which his licence in this respect provoked is inexplicable. Yet so it was. See a ribald poem called 'The Dean's Provocation', which professes to account for the reason of his writing the 'Lady's Dressing Room'.
24. *Advice to a Young Poet*.

HERBERT PAUL
"The Prince of Journalists"

Nineteenth Century, January 1900, pp. 73–87

Journalists have acquired a habit of talking about each other. Twenty years, or even ten years, ago, they were as little inclined to blow the trumpet of their profession—occupation they would have called it then—as the permanent members of the Civil Service, who, as the late Lord Farrer so admirably said, prefer power to fame. Even their consciousness of one another's infirmities, always perhaps acute, was confined to private conversation. Journalism might have withstood all attacks upon its shrinking modesty but for the establishment of that excellent society, the Institute of Journalists. One form of self-assertion leads to another, and a presumptuous person ventured last summer to deliver at Oxford, in academic disguise, a lecture on Modern Journalism. In the course of it he expressed the opinion that the greatest journalist who ever lived was Jonathan Swift. As I think he was right on that point, however mistaken he may have been on others, I should like to support and develop the paradox. I use the word paradox in its proper sense of what is contrary to accepted belief, but is nevertheless true. If a paradox be not true, it is mere nonsense.

No one, or scarcely any one, thinks of Swift as connected with the press. As a satirist, as a poet, above all as a humourist, he is of course an English classic. Politicians, if they have read him, know that, in spite of his cloth, he was pre-eminently a statesman. But few of those who admire him the least have gone so far as to suggest that he was a journalist. Yet he wrote regularly, he wrote anonymously, he wrote on politics, and, if any further proof be needed, he wrote on both sides. He did not indeed write against time. His were days of leisure, not of morning and evening papers. Nor did he write ostensibly for money. But the Deanery of St. Patrick's was a reward for his political services, and may, I suppose, be reckoned as deferred pay. I doubt whether any great writer has put his name to so few productions as Swift. To the day of his death he never would acknowledge the work which prevented him from becoming a Bishop, the *Tale of a Tub*. The most famous of his controversial tracts were ascribed by a transparent fiction to a draper of Dublin. The one essay which appeared with Swift's name upon the title-page was the plea for setting up an English Academy of Letters, which, if it did not lower his reputation, has certainly not raised it. The robust common sense of Dr. Johnson, who knew the virtues and the foibles of Englishmen with a perfect knowledge, supplied in a single sentence the epitaph of that proposal. If such an academy were created, he said, most men would be willing, and many men would be proud, to disobey its decrees. With that solitary and perfunctory exception, Swift left his arguments and his illustrations,

his invective and his sarcasm, to make their own mark upon the world. That that mark would be deep and ineffaceable, he must have known long before his mind sank into prematurely senile decay. No man was more fully conscious of his own tremendous powers. His genius burst, almost without an effort, the bonds of poverty and obscurity, of an uncontrollable temper and a sullen pride. He trampled on the insufferable patronage of the conventionally great with an arrogance more excessive than their own. He propitiated no one, he conciliated no one, and when he was doing the work of a Tory Ministry, he insisted upon a deference from Tory Ministers which in that ceremonious age must have seemed even stranger than it would now. After the death of Sir William Temple, upon whom he was dependent, and to whom in his way he was grateful, he called no man master. Indeed he called hardly any man equal. The force which he wielded without fear or pity, without mercy or scruple, was the force of sheer intellectual supremacy. Of his literary friends the only one who could be compared with him was Pope, and Swift came far nearer to Pope in verse than Pope came to Swift in prose. Among the public men with whom he associated there was none except Lord Oxford and Lord Carteret upon whom he did not look down. 'Send us back our boobies,' he exclaimed when Carteret came as Viceroy to Dublin. 'What do we want with men like you?' A characteristic compliment, characteristically worded.

Mr. Lecky has very properly included Swift among the leaders of Irish opinion. Yet there were few things which annoyed him so much as to be called an Irishman. That he was born in Ireland he could not deny. But he was ready with an answer. A man, he said, is not a horse because he was born in a stable. Much of his life, as everybody knows, was spent in Ireland, and the whole Cathedral of St. Patrick's, not otherwise interesting, is overshadowed by the awful inscription engraved by his own desire upon his tomb. The boast which he there somewhat inappropriately makes is a true one.[1] He did fight manfully and consistently for what he believed to be the liberties of Ireland. But by Ireland he meant Protestant Ireland, and her liberties were bound up for him in a Parliament where no Catholic could sit or be represented. Even upon the Irish House of Commons, when it presumed to touch the rights of the Protestant Church, he turned with a concentrated fury which makes the *Legion Club* almost terrifying to read after the lapse of more than a century and a half. Swift did not regard the Irish Catholics as citizens. He considered them, in Mr. Gladstone's picturesque phrase, to have nothing human about them except the form. In one respect only he was their friend. Despite his parsimonious habits, the indelible result of early indigence, he was generous to the poor. But his political sympathies and his political support were confined to the Protestants and to the Pale. Swift's politics are not, I think, difficult to understand. He was educated by Sir William Temple in loyalty to the Revolution of 1688, and he received some personal kindness from the King. He never became a Jacobite, or a thorough-going supporter of hereditary right. The Whigs did nothing for him after Temple's death, and he had a special grievance against Lord Somers. But his removal from one party to the other was not the mere consequence of personal disappointment. He had to choose between being a High Churchman and being a Whig. He chose not to be a Whig.

The position of a Whig clergyman has always been difficult. His politics are apt to make him ashamed of his profession. His profession is apt to make him afraid of his politics. The keen intellect and wholesome character of Sydney Smith raised him above shame or fear. He held that the Whig party and the Church of England were co-ordinate and providential instruments for the promotion of human happiness. Swift's intellect was as subtle as it was capacious, as clear as it was profound. But his character was warped and morbid, perverted by some insidious disease which has puzzled all his biographers, and will puzzle them till the end of time. While his logical powers were singularly acute and penetrating, his passions, and especially the passion of hatred, were altogether beyond the control of his will. If he hated the Whigs for not advancing him in the Church, he hated them also for making light of the holy orders which he had chosen to take. He used to say himself that while the Whigs detested the Church, they were mighty civil to parsons, whereas the Tory high-fliers, who exalted the Church above measure, treated the heirs of the apostolic succession as a kind of upper servants. If Swift had been a layman he would probably have remained a Whig. Why he took orders, except that there was no other visible opening for him, it is difficult to say. But having once put on the gown, he remained throughout his life as staunch to the Church of England and of Ireland as ever was soldier to his regiment or politician to his party. If he had been a student of Shakespeare, which he certainly was not, he might have said with Sir Oliver Martext, 'Not a fantastical fool of them all shall flout me out of my calling.' Sir Walter Scott, in his fascinating *Life of Swift* which can never be superseded until another man of genius undertakes the task, describes Swift as deeply and sincerely religious. It is presumptuous either to disagree with Sir Walter, or to probe the recesses of the human soul. We cannot follow Swift into his private chapel, or his secret devotions. We can only judge him by his works. There may be religion in the *Tale of a Tub*, though for my part I think that Queen Anne and Voltaire were right when from their different points of view they regarded it as casting ridicule upon all forms of the Christian faith. It certainly did for Swift what *Tristram Shandy* did for Sterne. It cost him his chance of a bishopric. And much as one may be disposed to take the side of brilliant eccentricity against orthodox dulness, it is impossible to say that in these instances the royal objections were unfounded.

The man who can find religion in Swift's sermons must have a microscopic eye. Tried even by the standard of the eighteenth century, they are singularly secular. But perhaps the surest indication of his real creed is given in the striking verses on the Day of Judgment, which were not published till long after his death. They were privately sent by Chesterfield in a letter to Voltaire, but everybody now knows the vigorous lines:

> Ye who in diverse sects were shammed,
> And came to see each other damned;
> (For so folks told you, but they knew
> No more of Jove's designs than you).
> The world's mad business now is o'er,
> And Jove resents such pranks no more.
> I to such blockheads set my wit!
> I damn such fools! Go, go, you're bit.

The ingenious critic is at liberty to observe that Jove is an abbreviation of Jupiter, and that Jupiter was a heathen divinity not entitled to the respect of Christians. Such criticism would prove Montaigne to have believed in miracles.

It is of course true that in theological or ecclesiastical controversy Swift always took the orthodox side. He writes as one equally averse from the doctrines of Rome and the doctrines of Geneva. He was as 'sound on the goose' as Parson Thwackum himself. When he said religion he meant the Christian religion; when he said the Christian religion, he meant the Protestant religion; and by the Protestant religion he meant the religion of the Church of England. For the Deists of his time, such as

Toland, Asgill, Collins, and Coward, he had a profound and a just contempt. He refers to 'that quality of their voluminous writings which the poverty of the English language compels me to call their style.' In his famous argument upon the inconveniences which would result from the immediate abolition of Christianity by law, he drenches them with vitriolic scorn. But it is all purely intellectual. 'As if Christianity wasn't good enough, and far too good, for such as you,' is the sentiment which underlies the invective. Professor Huxley was not an orthodox Christian. Yet he said that if Bishop Butler were alive, he would put to silence the shallow infidelity of the day. Swift showed no indignation against Bolingbroke, who was a notorious sceptic, nor against Pope, who was certainly not a Protestant, and was a Catholic only in name. It was the material property, not the spiritual influence of the Church, for which he was most eager to fight. His clear strong mind was fretted by the pretentious cleverness of men who acquired a spurious reputation for wit and learning by their attacks upon established beliefs. If that is religion, then Swift was religious. But so far as religion is contained in the Sermon on the Mount, or the thirteenth chapter of the first epistle to the Corinthians, Swift had no more of it than Bolingbroke and a good deal less than Voltaire. He had the honesty to keep every vestige of it out of his own epitaph on himself.

Swift was by far the greatest writer who ever devoted himself to the service of the Tory party. Johnson's political pamphlets are worthless compared with Swift's, and when Burke thundered against the French Revolution he spoke for a large number of Whigs. Although I should not myself rate *The Conduct of the Allies* so high as *The Anatomy of an Equivalent*, or *Thoughts on the Causes of the Present Discontents*, I know of no other English pamphleteer who could be put on a level with Halifax, Swift and Burke. But whereas Halifax was for years what we should call a Cabinet Minister, and Burke the greatest orator in the House of Commons, Swift was disqualified from even entering Parliament. Nor was he really trusted by the Ministers whom he served. As Mr. Morley says, he was the dupe of his great friends. They called him Jonathan; they treated him with every external mark of confidence and attention. If they had not, he would have turned upon them with the utmost ferocity. But they did not tell him that they were Jacobites at heart, and in communication with the King over the water. It was not special knowledge that gave Swift the mastery, but the fact that he had a statesman's mind. Macaulay has written in the margin of the letter to the October Club that a man must have been behind the scenes in politics to understand the excellence of this pamphlet. It might, he says, have been written in defence of the Whig Government from 1835 to 1841. It might, I add, have been an apology for the Liberal Government from 1892 to 1895. It is the old dilatory plea against expecting everything at once, wanting the millennium, as Mr. Anthony Hope says, in a Pickford van, but expressed with a plausible and persuasive subtlety that takes in almost everyone, except the author. Yet even then when his object was to conciliate the country and allay dissatisfaction with Lord Oxford, Swift cannot refrain from irony. Eminent statesmen, he remarked, had sometimes told him that politics were only common sense. It was the one thing they told him that was true, and the one thing they wished him not to believe. More delicate, and not less deadly, is the account of the Minister who, because he can judge better than the public when he knows more than they, thinks that he must be wiser than the rest of the world when their information is the same as his own. In practical sagacity Swift may be compared with the favourite object of his aversion, Sir Robert Walpole. He had one of those intellects which no sophistry can delude, and which are incapable of deviating from the path of reason. When the nation was mad over the South Sea Bubble, Swift, in a few simple stanzas, exposed the whole fabric of deception in a manner intelligible to a child.

What they do in heaven, said Swift, we know not; what they do not we know. They neither marry, nor are given in marriage. *Chatter about Harriet* was the late Professor Freeman's epigrammatic summary of recent literature on Shelley. There is nothing new to be said about the relations between Swift and Stella. Sir Henry Craik, in his exhaustive biography, has collected the evidence in favour of the marriage. Mr. Churton Collins, one of the few people who write too little, has argued with great ability the negative case. Every detail of Swift's career is interesting. But as the alleged marriage was a nominal, and not a real one, it is possible to exaggerate the importance of this particular incident. Upon the general subject of Swift's conduct to women Sir Walter Scott has said the last, or the last profitable, word. With exquisite delicacy, and with true insight, he has shown that Swift's passions were of another kind, and that he was incapable of falling in love. Unfortunately he could inspire feelings which he could not return. But that is a subject which Thackeray has made his own for ever. It is, of course, to Swift's friendship for Stella, whatever its precise nature may have been, that we owe the celebrated *Journal*, with its 'baby language,' its unflinching revelation of character, and its great historical value. I cannot see the tenderness which some have found or thought they found in it. It was written at the happiest, or least unhappy, period of his life, and yet it is full of gloomy pride, of obstinate isolation, of implacable revenge. For acute observation of men and manners, for lurid insight into hidden motives, for a haughtiness of temper which no despot could have surpassed, it is singular in the documents of autobiography. It was Swift's curse that nothing mean or vile or low or nasty ever escaped the pitiless keenness of his penetrating eye. He employed his unrivalled powers of ridicule and invective on the side of religion and virtue, but of decency he did not know the meaning. Even the 'troughs of Zolaism' contain nothing fouler than some of Swift's so-called poems. These are only fit to be burned by the common hangman, and it is wonderful that they should have been preserved. Some of his best and gravest work contains expressions from which most laymen would have shrunk, and of which any clergyman should have been ashamed. But Swift was ashamed of nothing. He was exempt from moral and apparently even from physical nausea. No idea was too disgusting for his imagination, no image too loathsome for his pen. The *Journal to Stella* owes, I cannot help thinking, some of its charm to its freedom from this disfiguring grossness. For this must be said of Swift, whether it be against him or in his favour, he neither conceals what is repulsive nor varnishes what is foul. Filthy he often is, prurient never. He cannot have made vice attractive to man or woman.

He was, in sober truth and earnest, a real cynic and misanthrope. Born with a temper which was a greater misfortune than any corporal defect, he nursed and cherished the *sæva indignatio* of which he boasts on his tomb until it subdued his will, overpowered his reason, and left him to expire a driveller and a show. He is the only great writer who did actually hate his fellow-men. The ordinary characteristics of human nature were to him odious in themselves. And when they appeared most fair, his terrible fancy transformed them. He could not see a beautiful woman without fancying how coarse her skin would look under a microscope. *Gulliver's Travels* has been called a political satire. It is a satire and a libel

on humanity. More and more savage does the author grow with the progress of his work, until in the last part he is like the demoniac raging among the tombs. Critics have praised the verisimilitude of *Gulliver*, and told the story of the Irish Bishop who said he did not believe a word of it. There is a humorous exactness of detail in the wildest extravagances of the fiction, no doubt. But Swift had not the peculiar gift of Defoe. He does not inspire belief in everything he says, like that most imaginative and unscrupulous of romancers. To do so a man must have his prejudices and passions under control. Swift could govern himself well enough when he was writing on politics or upon any abstract question. It is in dealing with mankind that his fury carries him away.

Only such an intellect could have been proof so long against such a temper. Only such a temper could in the end have ruined such an intellect. It was said of a former Speaker that he always flew into a passion in Parliamentary English. Swift's irritability, to use a mild word, did no injury to his style. Of Swift's prose it seems to me almost impossible to speak too highly. It has not the splendour of Milton's, or Dryden's, or Burke's. But as a method of conveying thought it is perfect. Nothing once said by Swift could ever be said again without being spoiled in the saying. Absolute and utter simplicity is the distinguishing mark of his style. No doubt this simplicity is a highly artificial product. It is the result of pruning, of trimming, of cutting down. The result and the object of these processes is to leave the reader face to face with the precise idea which the writer wished to convey. There is no veil, however thin, between the mind of the author and the mind of the public. Clearness and force could not be more harmoniously combined. Swift's reasoning faculty, when he used it at all, worked with consummate accuracy and without the slightest friction. There were very few things he could not understand, and whatever he could understand he could explain to the humblest capacity. His mind supplied him with an endless succession of ludicrous images, but he used them only when they assisted the point he wished to drive home. Tricks and mannerisms he discarded and abhorred. After the lapse of nearly two hundred years his best work shows little or no trace of obsolete phrases and idioms. It was the choicest English then, it is the choicest English now. The *Drapier's Letters* deal with the coinage of Wood's halfpence. Nobody except an historical student cares any longer for Wood, and the copper coins he introduced into Ireland under contract with the Government. But the *Drapier's Letters* can be read with delight by all who enjoy masculine reasoning, simple eloquence, and racy humour.

Swift's prose masterpiece is now, I think, commonly admitted to be the *Argument against the Abolition of Christianity*. The *Mechanical Operation of the Spirit* is almost equal to it. The *Drapier's Letters* are as much superior to Junius as Junius is superior to Wilkes. The Dean's own judgment upon the *Tale of a Tub* is well known. 'What a genius I had when I wrote that book!' he said in his clouded and declining years. The *Tale of a Tub* has passed beyond criticism and become a standard of satirical excellence. It is from no affectation of singularity that I prefer the later produce of that 'savage and unholy genius' to this early effort. There is genius in the *Tale*, of course. Swift was right in that. It is an exuberant genius, bursting all bounds of taste and congruity, with all Voltaire's license and none of Voltaire's tact. As one grows older one comes back to Horace:

Est modus in rebus, sunt certi denique fines.

With all Swift's admiration for the *Tale of a Tub*, he did not repeat the experiment. He had, in a literary sense, sown his wild oats. He began to curb not his irony, but his fancy, and the soberer he grew the more deadly he became. Under the frown or smile of that irony everything pretentious shrivelled up and disappeared. The Dean detested hypocrisy so bitterly that he railed even against ordinary devotion. The tears of a widow weeping for her husband were to him a cloak for her wish to find another. He could not believe in purity of motive or unselfishness of aim. Yet he was not without virtues of his own. He gave away money to the needy, though no professional miser loved money more. He risked the loss of his own liberty in order to fight, if not for the liberties of Irishmen, at least for the liberties of Ireland. His patriotism was genuine and incorruptible. If he sometimes trampled on the weak, he never stooped to flatter the strong. Although his early opinions were liberal, there is no reason to doubt the sincerity of his later Toryism. The truth is that as Burke bowed down and worshipped the British Constitution, so Swift bent the knee to the Established Church. Both may have been wrong, but one was as honest as the other.

Swift taught by example, and not by precept. It may be doubted whether he had any theories of style. He was a sound classical scholar, though, like most men of his time, especially Pope and Addison, he studied Latin rather than Greek. Ignorance of the Greek language accounts for Sir William Temple's belief that the *Letters of Phalaris* were genuine, and Bentley's monumental treatise was out of Swift's depth altogether. But he knew Horace and Virgil a good deal better than he knew Shakespeare or Milton. He had the classical standard of taste, with a rooted dislike of anything tawdry, showy, or 'flash.' His criticisms on Bishop Burnet exhibit an equal abhorrence of the Bishop's politics, which were Whiggery of the purest water, and the Bishop's English, which was anything but pure. He was the master, not the servant, of language, and he could always make it do exactly what he wanted. For slovenly writing, as for slovenly knowledge, he had an irrepressible contempt.

> The most accomplished way [he says in the *Tale of the Tub*], the most accomplished way of using books at present is two-fold: either, first, as some men do Lords, learn their titles exactly, and then brag of their acquaintance. Or secondly, which is indeed the choicer, the profounder and polite method, to get a thorough insight into the index, by which the whole book is governed and turned, like fishes by the tail. For to enter the palace of learning by the great gate requires an expense of time and forms. Therefore men of much taste and little ceremony are content to get in by the back door.

One is reminded of the well-known couplet:

> For index-learning turns no student pale,
> Yet holds the eel of science by the tail.

'As some men do Lords' cannot, I suppose, be grammatically defended. Like other masters of English, such as Newman and Froude in our own day, Swift is occasionally careless of minute accuracy, and his dullest editors have an obvious satisfaction in pointing out these trivial defects. A mistake showing real ignorance is not to be found in Swift.

It was from the *Battle of the Books*, not one of Swift's happiest efforts, that Matthew Arnold took one of his most successful and popular phrases. The *Battle of the Books* is, we may be thankful to reflect, all that remains of the foolish controversy over the rival merits of ancient and modern literature. The disputants might as profitably have employed themselves in comparing the relative excellence of Virgil and Dryden, or of Homer and Pope. Swift, in gratitude to Temple, who oddly took the side of authors he could not read, came forward as their champion.

> As for us, the ancients [he wrote], we are content with the bee to pretend to nothing of our own beyond our wings and our voice; that is to say, our flights and our language. For the rest, whatever we have got, has been by infinite labour and search, and ranging through every corner of nature. The difference is that instead of dirt and poison we have rather chose to fill our hives with honey and wax, thus furnishing mankind with the two noblest things, which are sweetness and light.

There is an imaginative beauty in this passage to which Swift seldom attains. His habitual vein was irony, which came as surely and as naturally to him as the rhymed couplet came to Pope. There is scarcely a better specimen of this, his favourite weapon, to be found in all his works than the final sentences of the strange and sinister *Argument*, to which I have so often referred. He had already asked what young men of wit and fashion would have for the object of their raillery if the Christian religion were abolished; how Freethinkers could gain a reputation for learning; and what could hinder Popery from being put in the place of religion. Then comes the climax:—

> To conclude, whatever some may think of the great advantage to trade by this favourite scheme, I do very much apprehend that in six months time after the Act is passed for the extirpation of the Gospel the Bank and East India Stock may fall at least 1 per cent. And since that is fifty times more than ever the wisdom of our age thought fit to venture for the preservation of Christianity, there is no reason why we should be at so great a loss merely for the sake of destroying it.

That seems to me finer than anything in Voltaire. Voltaire always seems to be conscious of his own cleverness, to be showing what he can do. Very wonderful his performances are. But in Swift's best work, this *Argument* for example, the strokes descend upon the victims with the grim, relentless force of circumstance or fate. It is not so much Swift as the naked truth of things, stripped of all subterfuge and disguise, speaking through Swift's mouth, while upon Swift's face there is never the flicker of a smile.

In his *Thoughts on Various Subjects* Swift displays a lighter and, if such a word may be used of such a man, a more genial mood. The sarcasm is there, as indeed it is everywhere. But it is of a less cruel and more human sort. 'The reason why so few marriages are happy is because young ladies spend their time in making nets, not in making cages.' For exquisite felicity of diction that little apophthegm is unapproached and unapproachable. Like all the best verbal wit, it is not merely verbal. It is worth, to my mind, half a dozen essays from the *Spectator*. Somewhat grimmer is the following:—

> Venus, a beautiful, good-natured lady, was the goddess of love; Juno, a terrible shrew, the goddess of marriage; and they were always mortal enemies.

But, after all, this was the last subject on which Swift could pose as an authority. Here is a judgment more in his line:—

> As universal a practice as lying is, and as easy a one as it seems, I do not remember to have heard three good lies in all my conversation, even from those who were most celebrated in that faculty.

From the friend of Pope this is much. But we could wish that the Dean had given us the two.

> True genuine dulness moved his pity,
> Unless it offered to be witty.

So wrote Swift with truth and sincerity, in the most celebrated of all his poems. The Dean's most shining merit was his hatred of cant. Carlyle attacked the cant of philanthropy, forgetting that there was a cant of misanthropy as well, and that malevolence may be quite as sentimental as its opposite. But Swift detested shams in general, not merely the shams obnoxious to himself in particular. His loathing of his own kind was not affectation. It was an awful reality. In more wholesome ways, and from more manly motives, he despised from the bottom of his soul all who pretended to gifts or virtues which they did not possess. Intellectual contempt was at the root of his animosity against superficial deism and against the false wit which would amuse no one if it were not profane. His *Letter to a Young Clergyman* shows that he applied the same principle with strict impartiality to those of his own cloth. Swift indeed felt for the clergy as Johnson felt for Garrick. He would not suffer any one else to criticise them without rushing to their defence, and yet no one criticised them more severely than himself. His advice to this young man might have been read and pondered with advantage by the contemporary school of divines, whose sermons Archbishop Tait once described as like essays from the *Spectator* without the Addisonian eloquence.

> I cannot forbear warning you in the most earnest manner against endeavouring at wit in your sermons, because by the strictest computation it is very near a million to one that you have none; and because too many of your calling have made themselves everlastingly ridiculous by attempting it. I remember several young men in the town who could never leave the pulpit under half a dozen conceits; and the faculty adhered to those gentlemen a longer or shorter time, exactly in proportion to their several degrees of dulness. Accordingly I am told that some of them retain it to this day. I heartily wish the brood was at an end.

About Swift's own sermons there is some uncertainty. There are not many of them extant, and it is doubtful whether they were preached. The religious or spiritual element is as conspicuously absent from most of them as it is from Sterne's. With all his staunch Protestantism, and his not less resolute High Churchmanship, in which may be traced a curious resemblance between him and Archbishop Laud, Swift could be coarser than Rabelais, and profaner than Voltaire. Men have been convicted and imprisoned in this country for treating sacred subjects less offensively than Swift treats the Holy Communion in the *Tale of a Tub*. The only distinction which could have been drawn by the most ingenious counsel for the defence is that the ostensible object of Swift's satire was not the Christian religion, but the Church of Rome, and the essence of blasphemy is not so much its objects as the methods by which those objects are attempted or achieved. The following passage from Swift's sermon on the fate of Eutychus, though it may be unsuitable to the pulpit, is not unfit for publication, and is certainly neither 'conceited' nor dull:—

> The accident which happened to this young man in the text hath not been sufficient to discourage his successors; but because the preachers now in the world, however they may exceed St. Paul in the art of setting men to sleep, do extremely fall short of him in the working of miracles, therefore men are become so cautious as to choose more safe and conve-

nient stations and postures for taking their repose without hazard of their persons; and upon the whole matter choose rather to entrust their destruction to a miracle than their safety.

That has all the best qualities of Swift's humour without any of the faults which sometimes disfigure it. The ideas are intensely ludicrous, and the images by which they are conveyed excessively comical. And yet there is all the appearance of grave reasoning, of flawless logic, and of an obvious reflection which almost apologises for being a platitude. The little phrase 'upon the whole matter' is inserted with admirable artifice. It suggests the imperturbable demeanour of a dignified judge, calmly weighing the reasons on both sides, and concluding that it was better to sit in church upon a bench from which there was no possibility of falling.

Swift was not only a statesman and a satirist. He was also the father of what is now called Society Verse. It is curious that before he hit upon the form which best suited him, and in which the inimitable stanzas on his own death were composed, he should have perpetrated some of those crazy Pindarics which were fashionable when he was young. The 'Odes' to Archbishop Sancroft and to Sir William Temple, particularly the latter, are not to be matched for badness among the worst imitations of Cowley. It was a strange theory that because Pindar wrote Greek poetry of the highest excellence in a rather difficult and complicated metre, therefore English poetry could be written in no metre at all. Fortunately the error came to a speedy and ignominious death at the hands of Swift himself. Well might Dryden, who died in 1700, say, 'Cousin Swift, you will never be a poet.' Swift never forgave the insult, and he says, in the *Tale of a Tub*, with a malignity which for once was stupid, that Dryden would never have been taken for a great poet if he had not in his own Prefaces so often made the assertion. But he profited by the condemnation, and wrote no more Pindarics. In 1698 he produced the first of the poems, if poems they are to be termed, which will be read with pleasure and copied with freedom so long as English verse remains a vehicle of thought. I mean of course the famous lines, 'Written in a Lady's Ivory Table-Book.'

> Here you may read, 'Dear charming saint;'
> Beneath, 'A new receipt for paint;'
> Here, in beau spelling, 'Tru tel deth,'
> There, in her own, 'For an el breth;'
> Here, 'Lovely nymph pronounce my doom!'
> There, 'A safe way to use perfume;'
> Here, a page filled with billet-doux;
> On t'other side, 'Laid out for shoes;'
> 'Madam, I die without your grace,'
> 'Item, for half a yard of lace.'

Two years afterwards, when chaplain to Lord Berkeley in Ireland, Swift wrote 'Mrs. Harris's Petition,' which as a bit of low comedy is unsurpassed in literature. Has Dryden's prophecy been fulfilled? That depends upon the definition of poetry, which has never yet, and perhaps never will be, authoritatively defined. But those who deny the title of poet to Swift must deny it also to Pope. They stand and fall together. Pope was Swift's avowed model. He never, he said, could read a line of Pope's without wishing it were his own. Is there such a thing as the poetry of common sense? Horace thought there was, and by his judgment I am content to abide. Swift, like Pope, creeps on the ground. He does not strike the stars. He has no height of imagination, no depth of passion, and, even in his verses to Stella, no store of tenderness. Few lines of his are more characteristic than his playful exposure of the South Sea Bubble:—

A shilling in the bath you fling;
    The silver takes a nobler hue
By magic virtue in the spring,
    And seems a guinea to your view.
But as a guinea will not pass
    At market for a farthing more,
Shown through a multiplying glass
    Than what it always did before.
So cast it in the Southern Seas,
    And view it through a Jobber's Bill,
Put on what spectacles you please,
    Your guinea's but a guinea still.

This is quite conclusive and entirely prosaic. Swift became with practice a perfect master of form in verse, and the lines on his own death are flawless from beginning to end. In this respect he far excelled his contemporary Prior, and has not been outdone by his successor Praed. Cowper was his admiring student, and Johnson's birthday odes to Mrs. Thrale were modelled on Swift's to Mrs. Johnson. The consummate mastery which Swift gradually obtained over his instrument, and the perfect ease with which he wielded it, are perhaps the secret of its permanent charm. The satiric humour, which in his prose is apt to be savage, and in the *Legion Club* is ferocious, is mellowed and chastened with social playfulness in *Cadenus and Vanessa*, or *Baucis and Philemon*.

As Rochefoucauld from nature drew
His maxims, I believe them true;
They argue no corrupted mind
In him, the fault is in mankind.

Swift's estimate of the illustrious Frenchman is sound and just. The cynicism of La Rochefoucauld was the cynicism of an outraged sentimentalist. He expected too much of men and women. Because they were not angels, because their lives did not square with their theories, he believed the mass of them to be utterly base. But he always recognised that there was a noble remnant. He stopped far short of Swift's universal misanthropy. *Il y a peu d'honnêtes femmes*, he says, in the bitterest of all his maxims, *qui ne soient lasses de leur métier*. There were a few, and to La Rochefoucauld it was the minority that made the world fit for human habitation. It was not a high standard of morals, nor a small capacity for belief, that drove Swift into cursing and railing. It was constitutional distemper and despair. If Archbishop King knew the secret of his misery, he kept it like a gentleman and carried it to the grave. The death of Stella, as Thackeray says, extinguished his last ray of hope, and almost his last gleam of reason. 'After that darkness and utter night fell upon him.' If one cannot truly say 'What a noble mind was here o'erthrown,' one may at least feel that a gigantic intellect sank suddenly into the abyss. There was no warning. Until Swift became a lunatic, his mind cut like a diamond through the hardest substances in its way. No sophistry ever deceived him. No difficulty ever puzzled him. There was nothing he thought which he could not express. The pellucid simplicity of his style, both in prose and in verse,

came of clear thinking and sound reasoning, assisted by the habit of daily explanation to unlettered women. It is easy to understand him, because he understood so easily himself. A great deal of time is wasted by the 'general reader' in guessing at the meaning of authors who did not mean anything in particular. Uncertainty is the fruitful parent of obscurity, and many people write obscurely in the hope that they will be thought profound. Like the subaltern who would not form his letters distinctly lest his correspondents should find out how he spelt, there is a class of writers who will not be plain lest the poverty of their thoughts should be exposed. Swift, it must in fairness be admitted, did not treat of questions which transcend the powers of human language. His prose is never metaphorical, and his poetry could always be translated into prose. He had what the French call an *esprit positif*. Philosophical speculation did not attract him, and if he inwardly cultivated any religious mysticism, he kept it entirely to himself. Eloquent he was not. He seldom rises and seldom falls. What made him the prince of journalists was his mental tact. He had the public ear. He knew precisely when the anvil was hot, and when he ought to strike it. To say that he never took a bad point would be to exaggerate, though there are not many controversialists who took so few. When he turned Bishop Burnet's fears of a Jacobite restoration into ridicule, he merely showed that the worthy Bishop knew the danger, and that he did not. That any one should ever have thought Harley a greater minister than Walpole seems incomprehensible to us, and though it may have been true friendship, it was false judgment. But Swift's particular errors are quite unimportant now. His value to posterity lies in his matchless humour, his statesmanlike wisdom, his hatred of pretence and sham, his intellectual integrity, and above all the sustained perfection of his English style.

Notes
1.

> Hic depositum est corpus
> Jonathan Swift, S.T.P.,
> Hujus Ecclesiæ Cathedralis
> Decani:
> Ubi sæva indignatio
> Ulterius cor lacerare nequit.
> Abi Viator,
> Et imitare, si poteris,
> Strenuum pro virili libertatis vindicem.
> Obiit anno (1745)
> Mensis Octobris die (19)
> Ætatis anno (78).

(Here lies the body of Jonathan Swift, Doctor of Divinity, Dean of this Cathedral Church, where fierce rage can tear the heart no more. Go, traveller, and imitate, if you can, an earnest, manly champion of freedom. He died on the 19th of October, 1745, in the 78th year of his age.)

The dates were of course left blank by Swift. No alteration was made in the epitaph, except to fill them in.

HENRY FIELDING

HENRY FIELDING

1707–1754

Henry Fielding, novelist and playwright, was born, probably at Sharpham Park in Somerset, on April 22, 1707. The son of a lieutenant, he was educated at Eton where he was friendly with Lord Lyttelton and the elder Pitt. After leaving Eton in 1725 he moved to London to become a dramatist, and in 1728 had his play *Love in Several Masques* produced. In that same year he began to study classics at the University of Leiden where he remained for eighteen months. In 1729 he returned to London and wrote some twenty-five dramas between 1729 and 1737, including *The Author's Fame*; *Rape upon Rape* (performed 1730), a bitter, satirical commentary on the contemporary practices of the law; and *Tom Thumb* (1730; extended edition published as *The Tragedy of Tragedies; or The Life of Tom Thumb the Great*, 1731), a burlesque of a fashionable type of tragedy. In 1734 *Don Quixote in England*, which is part satire, part tribute to Cervantes, was performed, and in the same year he married Charlotte Cradock, after whom Sophia in *Tom Jones* and the heroine of *Amelia* were modeled.

In 1736 Fielding became manager of the New Theatre, for which he wrote the highly successful satirical comedy *Pasquin* (1736), which attacked various religious and political abuses; another even fiercer political satire was *The Historical Register for 1736* (1737), which greatly antagonized Walpole's government. Shortly after the production of this latter play Fielding's career as a playwright was brought to an abrupt end by the Licencing Act of 1737, which required that all plays be licensed by the Lord Chamberlain before they could legally be performed.

Fielding entered the Middle Temple in 1737 and began to read for the bar, to which he was called in 1740. From 1739 to 1741 he was also editor of the anti-Jacobite journal *The Champion*. His first novel appeared pseudonymously in 1741; this satirical work, *An Apology for the Life of Mrs. Shamela Andrews*, was prompted by Fielding's dislike for Samuel Richardson's epistolary novel *Pamela*. Meanwhile, increasing ill-health made it impossible for Fielding to continue his legal career with any consistency, and he turned instead to the production of his novel *The Adventures of Joseph Andrews, and of His Friend, Mr. Abraham Adams* (1742). In 1743 he published his *Miscellanies*, which most notably includes two prose satires, *A Journey from This World to the Next*, and *The Life of Mr. Jonathan Wild the Great*. In 1744 Fielding's wife died, to his great sorrow; three years later he married her maid, Mary Daniel, which caused some scandal. His novel *The History of Tom Jones, A Foundling* appeared in 1749. Shortly before its publication Fielding had been appointed Justice of the Peace (1748), and by 1749 his jurisdiction extended over the whole county of Middlesex. He wrote various influential legal pamphlets, and in 1751 published *Amelia*, in his own time the best selling of all his novels. After *Amelia* his main publications were the reform-minded *Covent-Garden Journal* (1752), and *The Journal of a Voyage to Lisbon* (published posthumously, 1755), which describes a voyage taken to improve his health. He died in Lisbon on October 8, 1754.

Fielding has been widely credited with developing the first novel in English. In creating a new form, which he described as "comic epics in prose," he can be seen as the direct predecessor of Dickens and Thackeray.

Personal

This enterprising Person, I say (whom I do not chuse to name, unless it could be to his Advantage, or that it were of Importance) had Sense enough to know that the best Plays with bad Actors would turn but to a very poor Account; and therefore found it necessary to give the Publick some Pieces of an extraordinary Kind, the Poetry of which he conceiv'd ought to be so strong that the greatest Dunce of an Actor could not spoil it: He knew, too, that as he was in haste to get Money, it would take up less time to be intrepidly abusive than decently entertaining; that to draw the Mob after him he must rake the Channel and pelt their Superiors; that, to shew himself somebody, he must come up to *Juvenal's* Advice and stand the Consequence:

> Aude aliquid brevibus Gyaris, & carcere dignum
> Si vis esse aliquis—
>
> (Juv. *Sat.* I.)

Such, then, was the mettlesome Modesty he set out with; upon this Principle he produc'd several frank and free Farces that seem'd to knock all Distinctions of Mankind on the Head: Religion, Laws, Government, Priests, Judges, and Ministers, were all laid flat at the Feet of this *Herculean* Satyrist! This *Drawcansir* in Wit, that spared neither Friend nor Foe! who to make his Poetical Fame immortal, like another *Erostratus*, set Fire to his Stage by writing up to an Act of Parliament to demolish it. I shall not give the particular Strokes of his Ingenuity a Chance to be remembered by reciting them; it may be enough to say, in general Terms, they were so openly flagrant, that the Wisdom of the Legislature thought it high time to take a proper Notice of them.—COLLEY CIBBER, *An Apology for the Life of Mr. Colley Cibber*, 1739

I wish you had been with me last week, when I spent two evenings with Fielding and his sister, who wrote *David Simple*, and you may guess I was very well entertained. The lady indeed retir'd pretty soon, but Russell and I sat up with the Poet till one or two in the morning, and were inexpressibly diverted. I find he values, as he justly may, his *Joseph Andrews* above all his writings: he was extremely civil to me, I fancy, on my Father's account.—JOSEPH WARTON, Letter to Thomas Warton (Oct. 29, 1746)

I could not help laughing in myself t'other day as I went through Holborn in a very hot day, at the dignity of human nature; all those foul old-clothes women panting without handkerchiefs, and mopping themselves all the way down within their loose jumps. Rigby gave me as strong a picture of nature; he and Peter Bathurst t'other night carried a servant of the latter's who had attempted to shoot him, before Fielding, who to all his other vocations has, by the grace of Mr Lyttelton, added that of Middlesex justice. He sent them word he was at supper, that they must come next morning. They did not understand that freedom and ran up, where they found him banqueting with a blind man, three Irishmen, and a whore, on some cold mutton and a bone of ham, both in one dish, and the cursedest dirty cloth! He never stirred nor asked them to sit. Rigby, who had seen him so often come to beg a guinea of Sir Charles Williams, and Bathurst at whose father's he had lived for victuals, understood that dignity as little, and pulled themselves chairs, on which he civilized.—HORACE WALPOLE, Letter to George Montagu (May 18, 1749)

I advise Mr. Spondy to give him the refusal of this same pastoral; who knows but he may have the good fortune of being listed in the number of his beef-eaters, in which case he may, in process of time, be provided for in the Customs or the Church; *when he is inclined to marry his own cook-wench his gracious patron may condescend to give the bride away; and may finally settle him, in his old age, as a trading Westminster Justice.*—TOBIAS SMOLLETT, *The Adventures of Peregrine Pickle*, 1751

I am sorry for Henry Fielding's Death, not only as I shall read no more of his writings, but I beleive he lost more than others, as no Man enjoy'd life more than he did, thô few had less reason to do so, the highest of his preferment being raking in the lowest sinks of vice and misery. I should think it a nobler and less nauseous employment to be one of the staff officers that conduct the Nocturnal Weddings. His happy Constitution (even when he had, with great pains, halfe demolish'd it) made him forget every thing when he was before a venison Pasty or over a Flask of champaign, and I am perswaded he has known more happy moments than any Prince upon Earth. His natural Spirits gave him Rapture with his Cookmaid, and chearfullness when he was Fluxing in a Garret. There was a great similitude between his character and that of Sir Richard Steele. He had the advantage both in Learning and, in my Opinion, Genius. They both agreed in wanting money in spite of all their Freinds, and would have wanted it if their Hereditary Lands had been as extensive as their Imagination, yet each of them so form'd for Happiness, it is pity they were not Immortal.—LADY MARY WORTLEY MONTAGU, Letter to the Countess of Bute (Sept. 22, 1755)

⟨. . . Lady Mary Wortley Montagu was⟩ well informed of every particular that concerned her relation Henry Fielding; nor was she a stranger to that beloved first wife whose picture he drew in his *Amelia*, where, as she said, even the glowing language he knew how to employ did not do more than justice to the amiable qualities of the original, or to her beauty, although this had suffered a little from the accident related in the novel—a frightful overturn, which destroyed the gristle of her nose. He loved her passionately, and she returned his affection; yet led no happy life, for they were almost always miserably poor, and seldom in a state of quiet and safety. All the world knows what was his imprudence; if ever he possessed a score of

pounds, nothing could keep him from lavishing it idly, or make him think of to-morrow. Sometimes they were living in decent lodgings with tolerable comfort; sometimes in a wretched garret without necessaries; not to speak of the spunging-houses and hiding-places where he was occasionally to be found. His elastic gaiety of spirit carried him through it all; but, meanwhile, care and anxiety were preying upon her more delicate mind, and undermining her constitution. She gradually declined, caught a fever, and died in his arms.

His biographers seem to have been shy of disclosing that after the death of this charming woman he married her maid. And yet the act was not so discreditable to his character as it may sound. The maid had few personal charms, but was an excellent creature, devotedly attached to her mistress, and almost broken-hearted for her loss. In the first agonies of his own grief, which approached to frenzy, he found no relief but from weeping along with her; nor solace, when a degree calmer, but in talking to her of the angel they mutually regretted. This made her his habitual confidential associate, and in process of time he began to think he could not give his children a tenderer mother, or secure for himself a more faithful housekeeper and nurse. At least this was what he told his friends; and it is certain that her conduct as his wife confirmed it, and fully justified his good opinion.

Lady Mary Wortley had a great regard for Fielding; she pitied his misfortunes, excused his failings, and warmly admired his best writings; above all *Tom Jones*, in her own copy of which she wrote *Ne plus ultra*. Nevertheless, she frankly said she was sorry he did not himself perceive that he had made Tom Jones a scoundrel; alluding to the adventure with Lady Bellaston.—LADY LOUISA STUART, "Introductory Anecdotes," *The Letters and Works of Lady Mary Wortley Montagu*, ed. Lord Wharncliffe, 1837, Vol. 1

But though a man may think wisely, and admonish with sagacity, he yet may not be always capable of acting prudently. And such, certainly, was the case with Fielding in the early period of his career. But this arose from the enthusiastic ardour of his social affections, which urged him to share in the cordial pleasures of society, where the shining qualities of his admirable wit and humour could not fail to make him a conspicuous ornament. His carelessness, too, in regard to money, and his kindly and liberal tendencies, were calculated to render the promptings of frugality nugatory, even supposing such salutary warnings to have arisen; and thus was he compelled to crave the aid of men in power, who lay under obligations to him for his political writings.

And what was his reward, after wasting disappointments? The then not very reputable post of Middlesex magistrate at Bow Street. But, to his credit be it told, the corrupt practices which disgraced that important though subordinate seat of criminal justice were swept away by his judicious and indefatigable management, and from being a nest rather for the nursing care of some delinquents than for their utter extermination, it became in his hands the dread of incorrigible evil-doers; while the weary and heavy-laden met with compassionate consideration. Of these facts there is no one but must feel assured who has read what may be called his dying words, which are so impressively told in his *Voyage to Lisbon*—his last resting-place.—JAMES P. BROWNE, "Preface" to *The Works of Henry Fielding, Esq.*, 1872, Vol. 11, pp. 17–18

I do not believe that Henry Fielding was ever in love. —ROBERT LOUIS STEVENSON, *Virginibus Puerisque*, 1881

    He looked on naked Nature unashamed,
    And saw the Sphinx, now bestial, now divine,

In change and rechange; he nor praised nor blamed,
But drew her as he saw with fearless line.
Did he good service? God must judge, not we;
Manly he was, and generous and sincere;
English in all, of genius blithely free:
Who loves a Man may see his image here.
—JAMES RUSSELL LOWELL, "Inscription for a
Memorial Bust of Fielding," 1883

Not from the ranks of those we call
Philosopher or Admiral,—
Neither as LOCKE was, nor as BLAKE,
Is that Great Genius for whose sake
We keep this Autumn festival.

And yet in one sense, too, was he
A soldier—of humanity;
And, surely, philosophic mind
Belonged to him whose brain designed
That teeming COMIC EPOS where,
As in CERVANTES and MOLIÈRE
Jostles the medley of Mankind.

Our ENGLISH NOVEL's pioneer!
His was the eye that first saw clear
How, not in natures half-effaced
By cant of Fashion and of Taste,—
Not in the circles of the Great,
Faint-blooded and exanimate,—
Lay the true field of Jest and Whim,
Which we to-day reap after him.
No:—he stepped lower down and took
The piebald PEOPLE for his Book!

Ah, what a wealth of Life there is
In that large-laughing page of his!
What store and stock of Common-Sense,
Wit, Wisdom, Books, Experience!
How his keen Satire flashes through,
And cuts a sophistry in two!
How his ironic lightning plays
Around a rogue and all his ways!
Ah, how he knots his lash to see
That ancient cloak, Hypocrisy!

Whose are the characters that give
Such round reality?—that live
With such full pulse? Fair SOPHY yet
Sings *Bobbing Joan* at the spinet;
We see AMELIA cooking still
That supper for the recreant WILL;
We hear Squire WESTERN's headlong tones
Bawling 'Wut ha?—wut ha?' to JONES.
Are they not present now to us,—
The Parson with his *Aeschylus?*
SLIPSLOP the frail, and NORTHERTON,
PARTRIDGE, and BATH, and HARRISON?—
Are they not breathing, moving,—all
The motley, merry carnival
That FIELDING kept, in days agone?
He was the first that dared to draw
Mankind the mixture that he saw;
Not wholly good nor ill, but both,
With fine intricacies of growth.
He pulled the wraps of flesh apart,
And showed the working human heart;
He scorned to drape the truthful nude
With smooth, decorous platitude!

He was too frank, may be; and dared
Too boldly. Those whose faults be bared,
Writhed in the ruthless grasp that brought

Into the light their secret thought.
Therefore the TARTUFFE-throng who say
'*Couvrez ce sein,*' and look that way,—
Therefore the Priests of Sentiment
Rose on him with their garments rent.
Therefore the gadfly swarm whose sting
Plies ever round some generous thing,
Buzzed of old bills and tavern-scores,
Old 'might-have-beens' and 'heretofores';—
Then, from that garbled record-list,
Made him his own Apologist.

And was he? Nay,—let who has known
Nor Youth nor Error, cast the stone!
If to have sense of Joy and Pain
Too keen,—to rise, to fall again,
To live too much,—be sin, why then,
This was no pattern among men.
But those who turn that later page,
The Journal of his middle-age,
Watch him serene in either fate,—
Philanthropist and Magistrate;
Watch him as Husband, Father, Friend,
Faithful, and patient to the end;

Grieving, as e'en the brave may grieve,
But for the loved ones he must leave:
These will admit—if any can—
That 'neath the green Estrella trees,
No artist merely, but a MAN,
Wrought on our noblest island-plan,
Sleeps with the alien Portuguese.
—AUSTIN DOBSON, "Henry Fielding (To James
Russell Lowell)," 1883

It is sufficiently appropriate that a recognition in this way of the Somersetshire novelist should be made in his native county. But the real monument which Fielding's memory most needs is one that does not ask for the chisel of any sculptor or the voice of any orator. It is, moreover, a memorial which it would neither be difficult to raise nor pecuniarily unprofitable. That memorial is a complete edition of his writings. Though one hundred and thirty years have gone by since his death, this act of justice to his reputation has never yet been performed. Apparently, it has never once been contemplated. A portion of his work—and, in a certain way, of work especially characteristic—is practically inaccessible to the immense majority of English-speaking men. We are the losers by this neglect more than he. The mystery that envelops much of Fielding's career can never be cleared away, the estimate of his character and conduct can never be satisfactorily fixed, until everything he wrote has been put into the hands of independent investigators pursuing separate lines of study. Equally essential is such a collection to our knowledge of the literary, the social, and even the political history of his time.—T. R. LOUNSBURY, "Letter on Fielding's Bust," *Century*, Feb. 1884, p. 635

General

I have myself, upon your recommendation, been reading *Joseph Andrews*. The incidents are ill laid and without invention; but the characters have a great deal of nature, which always pleases even in her lowest shapes. Parson Adams is perfectly well; so is Mrs. Slipslop, and the story of Wilson; and throughout he shews himself well read in Stage-Coaches, Country Squires, Inns, and Inns of Court. His reflections upon high people and low people, and misses and masters, are very good.—THOMAS GRAY, Letter to Richard West (April 8, 1742)

I have been very well entertained lately with the two first volumes of *The Foundling*, which is written by Mr. Fielding, but not to be published till the 22nd of January; and if the same spirit runs through the whole work, I think it will be much preferable to *Joseph Andrews*.—FRANCES THYNNE HERTFORD, DUCHESS OF SOMERSET, Letter to Lady Luxborough (Nov. 20, 1748)

You guess that I have not read *Amelia*. Indeed I have read but the first volume. I had intended to go through with it; but I found the characters and situations so wretchedly low and dirty, that I imagined I could not be interested for any one of them; and to read and not to care what became of the hero and heroine, is a task that I thought I would leave to those who had more leisure than I am blessed with.

Parson Young sat for Fielding's Parson Adams, a man he knew, and only made a little more absurd than he is known to be. The best story in the piece, is of himself and his first wife. In his *Tom Jones*, his hero is made a natural child, because his own first wife was such. Tom Jones is Fielding himself, hardened in some places, softened in others. His Lady Bellaston is an infamous woman of his former acquaintance. His Sophia is again his first wife. Booth, in his last piece, again himself; Amelia, even to her noselessness, is again his first wife. His brawls, his jarrs, his gaols, his spunging-houses, are all drawn from what he has seen and known. As I said (witness also his hamper plot) he has little or no invention: and admirably do you observe, that by several strokes in his Amelia he designed to be good, but knew not how, and lost his genius, low humour, in the attempt.—SAMUEL RICHARDSON, Letter to Anne Donnellan (Feb. 22, 1752)

Through all Mr. Fielding's inimitable comic romances, we perceive no such thing as personal malice, no private character dragged into light; but every stroke is copied from the volume which nature has unfolded to him; every scene of life is by him represented in its natural colours, and every species of folly or humour is ridiculed with the most exquisite touches. A genius like this is perhaps more useful to mankind, than any class of writers; he serves to dispel all gloom from our minds, to work off our ill-humours by the gay sensations excited by a well directed pleasantry, and in a vein of mirth he leads his readers into the knowledge of human nature.—CHRISTOPHER SMART, Prefatory Letter to *The Hilliad*, 1752

Of the Comic Epopee we have two exquisite models in English, I mean the *Amelia* and *Tom Jones* of Fielding. The introductory part of the latter follows indeed the historical arrangement, in a way somewhat resembling the practice of Euripides in his Prologues, or at least as excuseable: but, with this exception, we may venture to say, that both fables would bear to be examined by Aristotle himself, and, if compared with those of Homer, would not greatly suffer in the comparison. This author, to an amazing variety of probable occurrences, and of characters well drawn, well supported, and finely contrasted, has given the most perfect unity, by making them all co-operate to one and the same final purpose. It yields a very pleasing surprise to observe, in the unravelling of his plots, particularly that of *Tom Jones*, how many incidents, to which, because of their apparent minuteness, we had scarce attended as they occurred in the narrative, are found to have been essential to the plot. And what heightens our idea of the poet's art is, that all this is effected by natural means, and human abilities, without any machinery:——while his great master Cervantes is obliged to work a miracle for the cure of Don Quixote.——Can any reason be assigned, why the inimitable Fielding, who was so perfect in Epic fable, should have succeeded so indifferently in Dramatic? Was it owing to the peculiarity of his genius, or of his circumstances? to any thing in the nature of Dramatic writing in general, or of that particular taste in Dramatic Comedy which Congreve and Vanburgh had introduced, and which he was obliged to comply with?—JAMES BEATTIE, *An Essay on Poetry and Music*, 1762, Pt. 1, Ch. 5, Note

The cultivated genius of Fielding entitles him to a high rank among the classics. His works exhibit a series of pictures drawn with all the descriptive fidelity of a Hogarth. They are highly entertaining, and will always be read with pleasure; but they likewise disclose scenes, which may corrupt a mind unseasoned by experience.—VICESIMUS KNOX, *Essays, Moral and Literary* (1777), 1782, Essay 14

I never saw Johnson really angry with me but once; and his displeasure did him so much honour that I loved him the better for it. I alluded rather flippantly, I fear, to some witty passage in *Tom Jones*: he replied, "I am shocked to hear you quote from so vicious a book. I am sorry to hear you have read it; a confession which no modest lady should ever make. I scarcely know a more corrupt work." I thanked him for his correction; assured him I thought full as ill of it now as he did, and had only read it at an age when I was more subject to be caught by the wit, than able to discern the mischief. Of *Joseph Andrews* I declared my decided abhorrence. He went so far as to refuse to Fielding the great talents which were ascribed to him, and broke out into a noble panegyric on his competitor Richardson; who, he said, was as superior to him in talents as in virtue, and whom he pronounced to be the greatest genius that had shed its lustre on this path of literature.—HANNAH MORE (1780), *Memoirs of the Life and Correspondence of Mrs. Hannah More*, ed. William Roberts, 1835, Vol. 1

Mr. Fielding's Novels are highly distinguished for their humour; a humour which, if not of the most refined and delicate kind, is original, and peculiar to himself. The characters which he draws are lively and natural, and marked with the strokes of a bold pencil. The general scope of his stories is favourable to humanity and goodness of heart; and in *Tom Jones*, his greatest work, the artful conduct of the fable, and the subserviency of all the incidents to the winding up of the whole, deserve much praise.—HUGH BLAIR, *Lectures on Rhetoric and Belles Lettres*, 1783, Lecture 37

It always appeared to me that he estimated the compositions of Richardson too highly, and that he had an unreasonable prejudice against Fielding. In comparing those two writers, he used this expression: 'that there was as great a difference between them as between a man who knew how a watch was made, and a man who could tell the hour by looking on the dial-plate.' This was a short and figurative state of his distinction between drawing characters of nature and characters only of manners. But I cannot help being of opinion, that the neat watches of Fielding are as well constructed as the large clocks of Richardson, and that his dial-plates are brighter. Fielding's characters, though they do not expand themselves so widely in dissertation, are as just pictures of human nature, and I will venture to say, have more striking features, and nicer touches of the pencil; and though Johnson used to quote with approbation a saying of Richardson's, 'that the virtues of Fielding's heroes were the vices of a truly good man,' I will venture to add, that the moral tendency of Fielding's writings, though it does not encourage a strained and rarely possible virtue, is ever favourable to honour and honesty, and cherishes the benevolent and generous affections. He who is as good as Fielding would make him, is an amiable member of society, and may be led on by more regulated instructors, to a higher state of ethical perfection.—JAMES BOSWELL, *Life of Johnson*, 1791

On Monday, April 6 ⟨1772⟩, I dined with him ⟨Johnson⟩ at Sir Alexander Macdonald's, where was a young officer in the regimentals of the Scots Royal, who talked with a vivacity, fluency, and precision so uncommon, that he attracted particular attention. He proved to be the Honourable Thomas Erskine, youngest brother to the Earl of Buchan, who has since risen into such brilliant reputation at the bar in Westminster-hall.

Fielding being mentioned, Johnson exclaimed, 'he was a blockhead;' and upon my expressing my astonishment at so strange an assertion, he said, 'What I mean by his being a blockhead is that he was a barren rascal.' BOSWELL. 'Will you not allow, Sir, that he draws very natural pictures of human life?' JOHNSON. 'Why, Sir, it is of very low life. Richardson used to say, that had he not known who Fielding was, he should have believed he was an ostler. Sir, there is more knowledge of the heart in one letter of Richardson's, than in all *Tom Jones*. I, indeed, never read *Joseph Andrews*.' ERSKINE. 'Surely, Sir, Richardson is very tedious.' JOHNSON. 'Why, Sir, if you were to read Richardson for the story, your impatience would be so much fretted that you would hang yourself. But you must read him for the sentiment, and consider the story as only giving occasion to the sentiment.'—I have already given my opinion of Fielding; but I cannot refrain from repeating here my wonder at Johnson's excessive and unaccountable depreciation of one of the best writers that England has produced. *Tom Jones* has stood the test of publick opinion with such success, as to have established its great merit, both for the story, the sentiments, and the manners, and also the varieties of diction, so as to leave no doubt of its having an animated truth of execution throughout.—JAMES BOSWELL, *Life of Johnson*, 1791

Fielding had all the ease which Richardson wanted, a genuine flow of humour, and a rich variety of comic character; nor was he wanting in strokes of an amiable sensibility, but he could not describe a consistently virtuous character, and in deep pathos he was far excelled by his rival. When we see Fielding parodying *Pamela*, and Richardson asserting, as he does in his letters, that the run of *Tom Jones* is over, and that it would soon be completely forgotten; we cannot but smile on seeing the two authors placed on the same shelf, and going quietly down to posterity together.—ANNA LAETITIA BARBAULD, "Introduction" to *The Correspondence of Samuel Richardson*, 1804, Vol. 1, p. 79

Fielding will for ever remain the delight of his country, and will always retain his place in the library of Europe, notwithstanding that unfortunate grossness which is the mark of an uncultivated taste, and which, if not yet entirely excluded from conversation, has been for some time banished from our writings, where, during the best age of national genius, it prevailed more than in those of any other polished nation. —SIR JAMES MACKINTOSH, "Godwin's Lives of Edward and John Philips, Nephews of Milton," *Edinburgh Review*, Oct. 1815, p 485

If I could not discover the place of Camöens's interment, I at least found out the grave and tombstone of the author of *Tom Jones*. Fielding, who terminated his life, as is well known, at Lisbon, in 1754, of a complication of disorders, at little more than forty seven years of age, lies buried in the Cemetery appropriated to the English Factory. I visited his grave, which was already nearly concealed by weeds and nettles. Though he

did not suffer the extremity of distress under which Camöens and Cervantes terminated their lives; yet his extravagance, a quality so commonly characteristic of men distinguished by talents, embittered the evening of his days. Fielding, Richardson, and Le Sage, seem to have attained the highest eminence in that seductive species of composition, unknown to antiquity, which we denominate *Novels*. Crebillon, Marivaux, and Smollett, only occupy the second place. Voltaire and Rousseau are rather satirical or philosophical moralists, than Novelists. *Don Quixote* is a work *sui generis*, and not amenable to ordinary rules. *Gil Blas* seems to stand alone, and will probably be read with avidity in every age, and every country. Though the scene lies in Spain, and the characters are Spaniards, the manners are universal; and true to nature equally in Madrid, in Paris, or in London. Richardson and Fielding are more national, and cannot be read with the same delight on the banks of the Seyne, or the Tyber, as on those of the Thames; though the former writer transports us to Bologna, in his *Sir Charles Grandison*. Fielding never attempts to carry us out of England, and his actors are all Aborigines. Foreigners neither can taste his works, nor will he ever attain to the fame of Richardson, beyond the limits of his own country. *Clementina* and *Clarissa* will penetrate, where *Sophia Western* and *Parson Adams* never can be known. *Joseph Andrews* and *Amelia* are, in point of composition, to Fielding, what *Pamela* is to Richardson.—SIR NATHANIEL WILLIAM WRAXALL, *Historical Memoirs of My Time*, 1815

⟨. . .⟩ the *prose* Homer of human nature.—GEORGE GORDON, LORD BYRON, *Journal*, Jan. 4, 1821

Have you read Fielding's novels? they are genuine things; though if you were not a decent fellow, I should pause before recommending them, their morality is so loose.—THOMAS CARLYLE, Letter to John A. Carlyle (Nov. 11, 1823)

Many people find fault with Fielding's Tom Jones as gross and immoral. For my part, I have doubts of his being so very handsome from the author's always talking about his beauty, and I suspect he was a clown, from being constantly assured he was so very genteel. Otherwise, I think Jones acquits himself very well both in his actions and speeches, as a lover and as a *trencher-man* whenever he is called upon. Some persons, from their antipathy to that headlong impulse, of which Jones was the slave, and to that morality of good-nature which in him is made a foil to principle, have gone so far as to prefer Blifil as the *prettier fellow* of the two. I certainly cannot subscribe to this opinion, which perhaps was never meant to have followers, and has nothing but its singularity to recommend it. Joseph Andrews is a hero of the shoulder-knot: it would be hard to canvass his pretensions too severely, especially considering what a patron he has in Parson Adams. That one character would cut up into a hundred fine gentlemen and novel-heroes! Booth is another of the good-natured tribe, a fine man, a very fine man! But there is a want of spirit to animate the well-meaning mass. He hardly deserved to have the hashed mutton kept waiting for him. The author has redeemed himself in Amelia; but a heroine with a *broken nose* and who was a married woman besides, must be rendered truly interesting and amiable to make up for superficial objections. The character of the Noble Peer in this novel is *not* insipid. If Fielding could have made virtue as admirable as he could make vice detestable, he would have been a greater master even than he was. I do not understand what those critics mean who say he got all his characters out of ale-houses. It is true he did some of them.—WILLIAM HAZLITT, "Why the Heroes of Romances Are Insipid," 1827

Try what you can remember about Fielding for me. The *Voyage to Lisbon* is the most remarkable example I ever met with of native cheerfulness triumphant over bodily suffering and surrounding circumstances of misery and discomfort. —ROBERT SOUTHEY, Letter to Caroline Bowles (Feb. 15, 1830)

Jonathan Wild is assuredly the best of all the fictions in which a villain is throughout the prominent character. But how impossible it is by any force of genius to create a sustained attractive interest for such a groundwork, and how the mind wearies of, and shrinks from, the more than painful interest, the μισητὸν, of utter depravity,—Fielding himself felt and endeavoured to mitigate and remedy by the (on all other principles) far too large a proportion, and too quick recurrence, of the interposed chapters of moral reflection, like the chorus in the Greek tragedy,—admirable specimens as these chapters are of profound irony and philosophic satire.—SAMUEL TAYLOR COLERIDGE, "Notes on *Jonathan Wild*" (1832), *Literary Remains*, ed. Henry Nelson Coleridge, 1836, Vol. 2

What a master of composition Fielding was! Upon my word, I think the *Œdipus Tyrannus*, the *Alchymist*, and *Tom Jones* the three most perfect plots ever planned. And how charming, how wholesome, Fielding always is! To take him up after Richardson is like emerging from a sick-room heated by stoves into an open lawn on a breezy day in May.—SAMUEL TAYLOR COLERIDGE, *Table Talk*, July 5, 1834

Yet when we read Fielding's novels after those of Richardson, we feel as if a stupendous pressure were removed from our souls. We seem suddenly to have left a palace of enchantment, where we have past through long galleries filled with the most gorgeous images, and illumined by a light not quite human nor yet quite divine, into the fresh air, and the common ways of this "bright and breathing world." We travel on the high road of humanity, yet meet in it pleasanter companions, and catch more delicious snatches of refreshment, than ever we can hope elsewhere to enjoy. The mock heroic of Fielding, when he condescends to that ambiguous style, is scarcely less pleasing than its stately prototype. It is a sort of spirited defiance to fiction, on the behalf of reality, by one who knew full well all the strongholds of that nature which he was defending. There is not in Fielding much of that which can properly be called ideal—if we except the character of Parson Adams; but his works represent life as more delightful than it seems to common experience, by disclosing those of its dear immunities, which we little think of, even when we enjoy them. How delicious are all his refreshments at all his inns! How vivid are the transient joys of his heroes, in their checkered course— how full and overflowing are their final raptures! His *Tom Jones* is quite unrivalled in plot, and is to be rivalled only in his own works for felicitous delineation of character. The little which we have told us of Allworthy, especially that which relates to his feelings respecting his deceased wife, makes us feel for him, as for one of the best and most revered friends of our childhood. Was ever the "soul of goodness in things evil" better disclosed, than in the scruples and the dishonesty of Black George, that tenderest of gamekeepers, and truest of thieves? Did ever health, good-humour, frankheartedness, and animal spirits hold out so freshly against vice and fortune as in the hero? Was ever so plausible a hypocrite as Blifil, who buys a Bible of Tom Jones so delightfully, and who, by his admirable imitation of virtue, leaves it almost in doubt,

whether, by a counterfeit so dexterous, he did not merit some share of her rewards? Who shall gainsay the cherry lips of Sophia Western? The story of Lady Bellaston we confess to be a blemish. But if there be any vice left in the work, the fresh atmosphere diffused over all its scenes, will render it innoxious. *Joseph Andrews* has far less merit as a story—but it depicts Parson Adams, whom it does the heart good to think on. He who drew this character, if he had done nothing else, would not have lived in vain. We fancy we can see him with his torn cassock, (in honour of his high profession,) his volumes of sermons, which we really wish had been printed, and his Æschylus, the best of all the editions of that sublime tragedian! Whether he longs after his own sermons against vanity—or is absorbed in the romantic tale of the fair Leonora—or uses his ox-like fists in defence of the fairer Fanny, he equally imbodies in his person, "the homely beauty of the good old cause," of high thoughts, pure imaginations, and manners unspotted by the world.—T. NOON TALFOURD, "On the British Novels and Romances," *Critical and Miscellaneous Writings*, 1842

Is the forthcoming critique on Mr. Thackeray's writings in the *Edinburgh Review* written by Mr. Lewes? I hope it is. Mr. Lewes, with his penetrating sagacity and fine acumen, ought to be able to do the author of *Vanity Fair* justice. Only he must not bring him down to the level of Fielding—he is far, far above Fielding. It appears to me that Fielding's style is arid, and his views of life and human nature coarse, compared with Thackeray's.—CHARLOTTE BRONTË, Letter to W. S. Williams (Dec. 23, 1847)

Resemblances have been found, and may be admitted to exist, between the Reverend Charles Primrose and the Reverend Abraham Adams. They arose from kindred genius; and from the manly habit which Fielding and Goldsmith shared, of discerning what was good and beautiful in the homeliest aspects of humanity. In the parson's saddle-bag of sermons would hardly have been found this prison sermon of the vicar; and there was in Mr. Adams not only a capacity for beef and pudding, but for beating and being beaten, which would ill have consisted with the simple dignity of Doctor Primrose. But unquestionable learning, unsuspecting simplicity, amusing traits of credulity and pedantry, and a most Christian purity and benevolence of heart, are common to both these master-pieces of English fiction; and are in each with such exquisite touch discriminated, as to leave no possible doubt of the originality of either. Anything like the charge of imitation is preposterous. Fielding's friend, Young, sat for the parson, as in Goldsmith's father, Charles, we have seen the original of the vicar; and as long as nature pleases to imitate herself, will such simple-hearted spirits reveal kindred with each other. At the same time, and with peculiar mastery, art vindicates also in such cases her power and skill; and the general truth of resemblance is, after all, perceived to be much less striking than the local accidents of difference. Does it not well-nigh seem incredible, indeed, comparing the tone of language and incident in the two stories, that a space of twenty years should have comprised *Joseph Andrews* and the *Vicar of Wakefield?* —JOHN FORSTER, *The Life and Times of Oliver Goldsmith*, 1848, Bk. 3, Ch. 13

Independently of their value as the creations of genius, the novels of Fielding are inestimable as genuine pictures of English manners in the middle of the last century. 'Oh!' exclaimed Dr. Arnold, 'if we had but a *Tom Jones* of the times of Augustus!' As an instance, I may mention that from this novel we learn that it was so much the custom at that time for ladies to travel on horseback, that side-saddles were kept at all the inns throughout the country. I do not recollect to have met with any allusion to this custom in any other work, novel, play, or poem of that time. Sir Walter Scott also observes that Fielding's novels are so thoroughly English that no one can perfectly understand them who has not been born, or at least lived some time, in England. Of the truth of this remark I can myself bear witness; for I thought I understood them thoroughly till I went to live for some time in one of the southern counties, when I discovered many traits of manners in them, of the existence of which I had previously been unconscious.

Without possessing the grace and elegance of Addison and Goldsmith, the lightness and vivacity of Lesage, or the dignity and rotundity of Cervantes, Fielding was master of a vigorous, manly, and truly English style, though occasionally incorrect. His most remarkable peculiarity is the constant employment, no matter who is the speaker, of *hath* and *doth* for *has* and *does*. This occurs, I believe, in no other writer of the eighteenth century.

Fielding is to be classified among those writers who are invidiously styled *egotists* because they speak freely of themselves, their feelings, opinions, affairs, and works. This *formula* contains many great names—such as Horace, Montaigne, Milton, Boileau, Pope, and others (and most, if not all of these were eminent for good taste and knowledge of the world); besides the whole band of autobiographers. If I may judge by my own feelings, writers of this class are the most delightful. I never, in fact, could read the *Exegi monumentum* of Horace, or the *Address to Fame* of Fielding, without a secret elation of mind and rejoicing at seeing their anticipations so fully verified. The proper place for this *egotism* is the preface, which I regard as the author's manor, for a well-constructed work requires no preface; and if he adheres rigidly to truth, and endeavours to form a just estimate of himself and his powers, though the envious, and little-minded may carp and sneer, he may be sure that he will command the sympathy of all whose minds have been cast in the mould of taste, good feeling, and generosity.—THOMAS KEIGHTLEY, "On the Life and Writings of Henry Fielding," *Fraser's Magazine*, Feb. 1858, p. 217

The least objectionable, according to modern notions, of Fielding's novels, is *Amelia*. There is much less coarseness, and also *less* licentiousness. His object is to portray the conduct of a virtuous wife, who adores her husband and children; and she is really a charming character. Scenes of course are introduced in which the old, old story of illicit love goes on; but they are wholly unknown to her, and they serve only to enhance, by the force of contrast, the innocence and purity of her mind.—WILLIAM FORSYTH, *The Novels and Novelists of the Eighteenth Century*, 1871, p. 274

But, although Fielding was dramatic, in so far as conversation and incident led the story on from point to point with a certain degree of system, combined with spontaneity, he did not carry the dramatic movement far enough. When all was over, his tale would remain but a rambling, aimless concatenation, terminating in nothing but an end of the adventures. His great power lay in the observation of manners and natures; but he was content to offer the results of this observation in a crude, digressive form, somewhat lacking—if it may be said—in principle. He was fond of whipping in and out among his characters, in person, and did so with a sufficiently cheery and pleasant defiance of all criticism; but the practice injured his art, nevertheless. In a word, he seems to have written as much for his own amusement as for that of his reader; and although he sedulously endeavored to identify these two interests, he did

not hesitate, when he felt like discharging a little dissertation on love, or classical learning, or what not, to do this at any cost, either of artistic propriety or the reader's patience. And, worst of all, he frequently dissected his *dramatis personœ* in full view of the audience, giving an epitome of their characters off-hand, or chatting garrulously about them, when the mood took him. These shortcomings withheld from him the possibility of grouping his keen observations firmly about some centre of steady and assimilative thought. With Fielding, nothing crystallized, but all was put together in a somewhat hastily gathered bundle; and the parts have a semi-detached relation. He hardly dreamed of that suggestive and deeply significant order of novel which our own day has seen almost perfected in the hands of George Eliot. And yet, what a brilliant retinue has Fielding had! Scott, Dickens, Thackeray —George Eliot herself—and many more besides, have followed in the path which he opened. He had an alert and energetic mind, and heartily and impartially enjoyed life, wherever and whatever it might be found; and this capacity for a healthy participation in the business of the people who surround him remains now, as it then was, an indispensable qualification in the novelist. But the best allegiance to Fielding must move men to further explorations in that province which he, in his day, so despotically governed. His greatest successors in empire have done this; but in what degrees, it will be interesting to consider. If, too, we find their efforts crowned by a constant though gradual progress, we shall perhaps think the conclusion justified, that new avenues to new goals of art remain yet to be adventured on.—G. P. LATHROP, "The Growth of the Novel," *Atlantic*, June 1874, pp. 686–87

Fielding is often censured by moralists for the coarseness of his novels. But had he not been coarse he would not have been true. He described life as it was in the eighteenth century, as he had seen it in the ups and downs of a checkered career. His characters were taken from the higher ranks and the lower. He placed the house, the amusements, the habits of a country-gentleman before the reader with the faithfulness of a man who had hunted, feasted, and got drunk with country-gentlemen. He described the miserable prisons of his time as he only could who had mingled with their degraded inmates, and had exerted his power as a police magistrate to break up the gangs of ruffians who infested the streets. Thus Fielding's novels have a high historical, as well as a literary value.—BAYARD TUCKERMAN, *A History of English Prose Fiction*, 1882, p. 204

In *Joseph Andrews*, Fielding's work had been mainly experimental. He had set out with an intention which had unexpectedly developed into something else. That something else, he had explained, was the comic epic in prose. He had discovered its scope and possibilities only when it was too late to re-cast his original design; and though *Joseph Andrews* has all the freshness and energy of a first attempt in a new direction, it has also the manifest disadvantages of a mixed conception and an uncertain plan. No one had perceived these defects more plainly than the author; and in *Tom Jones* he set himself diligently to perfect his new-found method. He believed that he foresaw a "new Province of Writing," of which he regarded himself with justice as the founder and lawgiver; and in the "prolegomenous, or introductory Chapters" to each book— those delightful resting-spaces where, as George Eliot says, "he seems to bring his arm-chair to the proscenium and chat with us in all the lusty ease of his fine English"—he takes us, as it were, into his confidence, and discourses frankly of his aims and his way of work. He looked upon these little "initial

Essays" indeed, as an indispensable part of his scheme. They have given him, says he more than once, "the greatest Pains in composing" of any part of his book, and he hopes that, like the Greek and Latin mottoes in the *Spectator*, they may serve to secure him against imitation by inferior authors. Naturally a great deal they contain is by this time commonplace, although it was unhackneyed enough when Fielding wrote. The absolute necessity in work of this kind for genius, learning, and knowledge of the world, the constant obligation to preserve character and probability—to regard variety and the law of contrast:—these are things with which the modern tiro (however much he may fail to possess or observe them) is now supposed to be at least theoretically acquainted. But there are other chapters in which Fielding may also be said to reveal his personal point of view, and these can scarcely be disregarded. His "Fare," he says, following the language of the table, is "HUMAN NATURE," which he shall first present "in that more plain and simple Manner in which it is found in the Country," and afterwards "hash and ragoo it with all the high *French* and *Italian* seasoning of Affectation and Vice which Courts and Cities afford." His inclination, he admits, is rather to the middle and lower classes than to "the highest Life," which he considers to present "very little Humour or Entertainment." His characters (as before) are based upon actual experience; or, as he terms it, "Conversation." He does not propose to present his reader with "Models of Perfection;" he has never happened to meet with those "faultless Monsters." He holds that mankind is constitutionally defective, and that a single bad act does not, of necessity, imply a bad nature. He has also observed, without surprise, that virtue in this world is not always "the certain Road to Happiness," nor "Vice to Misery." In short, having been admitted "behind the Scenes of this Great Theatre of Nature," he paints humanity as he has found it, extenuating nothing, nor setting down aught in malice, but reserving the full force of his satire and irony for affectation and hypocrisy.—AUSTIN DOBSON, *Fielding* (1883), 1889, pp. 121–23

Let it suffice here to state generally the reasons for which we set a high value on this man whose bust we unveil to-day. Since we are come together, not to judge, but only to commemorate, perhaps it would be enough to say, in justification of to-day's ceremony, that Fielding was a man of genius; for it is hardly once in a century, if so often, that a whole country catches so rare and shy a specimen of the native fauna, and proportionably more seldom that a county is so lucky. But Fielding was something more even than this. It is not extravagant to say that he marks an epoch, and that we date from him the beginning of a consciously new form of literature. It was not without reason that Byron, expanding a hint given somewhere by Fielding himself, called him "the prose Homer of human nature." He had more than that superficial knowledge of literature which no gentleman's head should be without. He knew it as a craftsman knows the niceties and traditions of his craft. He saw that since the epic in verse ceased to be recited in the market-places, it had become an anachronism; that nothing but the charm of narrative had saved Ariosto, as Tasso had been saved by his diction, and Milton by his style; but that since Milton every epic had been born as dead as the Pharaohs—more dead, if possible, than the *Columbiad* of Joel Barlow and the *Charlemagne* of Lucien Bonaparte are to us. He saw that the novel of actual life was to replace it, and he set himself deliberately (after having convinced himself experimentally in Parson Adams that he could create character) to produce an epic on the lower and more neighborly level of prose. However opinions may differ as to the other merits of

Tom Jones, they are unanimous as to its harmony of design and masterliness of structure.

Fielding, then, was not merely, in my judgment at least, an original writer, but an originator. He has the merit, whatever it may be, of inventing the realistic novel, as it is called.—JAMES RUSSELL LOWELL, "Address on Unveiling the Bust of Fielding (1883)," *Works*, Riverside ed., Vol. 6, pp. 63–64

Finally, in the last week of 1751 appeared his latest novel *Amelia*, in four volumes. It might be separated from *Tom Jones* by twenty years, instead of two, so obvious is the sense of failing health, so ripe and melancholy the fulness of experience. When we speak of the proofs of failing health, we refer to no decline in force or genius, but to lessened animal spirits, to a quieter and sadder ideal of life. There is far more shadow and less sunshine in *Amelia* than in *Tom Jones*, while in some respects it is certainly much more humane and tender. Those who have preferred *Amelia* to its predecessors must, we think, have been over-enchanted by the character of its patient and saintly heroine, without whom the book would fall in pieces. Her husband, Captain Booth, on whom it can scarcely be doubted that the world has unjustly built its conception of Fielding himself, is very natural and human, but unstable to the last degree, and noticeably stupid. Many of the incidents are crudely introduced, being no doubt actual history which the novelist did not take the trouble to work into his picture. *Amelia* was not popular in its own day, but rose into favour at the beginning of the present century; and Thackeray, who did not wholly appreciate the morals of *Tom Jones* or *Joseph Andrews*, found those of Fielding's latest novel entirely to his taste. On the other hand, it is, surely, what they certainly are not, a little dull.—EDMUND GOSSE, *A History of Eighteenth Century Literature*, 1888, pp. 256–57

Take the pair, they seem like types: Fielding, with all his faults, was undeniably a gentleman; Richardson, with all his genius and his virtues, as undeniably was not. And now turn to their works. In *Tom Jones*, a novel of which the respectable profess that they could stand the dulness if it were not so blackguardly, and the more honest admit they could forgive the blackguardism if it were not so dull—in *Tom Jones*, with its voluminous bulk and troops of characters, there is no shadow of a gentleman, for Allworthy is only ink and paper. In *Joseph Andrews*, I fear I have always confined my reading to the parson; and Mr. Adams, delightful as he is, has no pretension "to the genteel." In *Amelia*, things get better; all things get better; it is one of the curiosities of literature that Fielding, who wrote one book that was engaging, truthful, kind, and clean, and another book that was dirty, dull, and false, should be spoken of, the world over, as the author of the second and not the first, as the author of *Tom Jones*, not of *Amelia*. And in *Amelia*, sure enough, we find some gentlefolk; Booth and Dr. Harrison will pass in a crowd, I dare not say they will do more.—ROBERT LOUIS STEVENSON, "Some Gentlemen in Fiction," *Scribner's Magazine*, June 1888, p. 766

But Fielding cannot be kept in prison long. His noble English, his sonorous voice must be heard. There is somewhat inexpressibly heartening, to me, in the style of Fielding. One seems to be carried along, like a swimmer in a strong, clear stream, trusting one's self to every whirl and eddy, with a feeling of safety, of comfort, or delightful ease in the motion of the elastic water. He is a scholar, nay more, as Adams had his innocent vanity, Fielding has his innocent pedantry. He likes to quote Greek (fancy quoting Greek in a novel of to-day!) and to make the rogues of printers set it up correctly. He likes to air his ideas on Homer, to bring in a piece of Aristotle—not hackneyed—to show you that if he is writing about 'characters and situations so wretchedly low and dirty,' he is yet a student and critic. —ANDREW LANG, *Letters on Literature*, 1889, pp. 38–39

Perhaps Fielding's characters are not altogether real. That self-righteous prig, Adam Bede, is more real, if not more agreeable, than the sanctimonious Blifil. Fielding's portrait-painting is rough at the best. But his error is overstatement and not the fatal error of suppression, and at any rate he gives a true social picture of his time.—WALTER LEWIN, "The Abuse of Fiction," *Forum*, Aug. 1889, pp. 667–68

Fielding is one of the most striking figures in our literary history, and he is one of the most popular as well. But it is questionable if many people know very much about him after all, or if the Fielding of legend—the potwalloper of genius at whom we have smiled so often—has many things in common with the Fielding of fact, the indefatigable student, the vigorous magistrate, the great and serious artist. You hear but little of him from himself; for with that mixture of intellectual egoism and moral unselfishness which is a characteristic of his large and liberal nature he was as careless of Henry Fielding's sayings and doings and as indifferent to the fact of Henry Fielding's life and personality as he was garrulous in respect of the good qualities of Henry Fielding's friends and truculently talkative about the vices of Henry Fielding's enemies. And what is exactly known people have somehow or other contrived to misapprehend and misapply. They have preferred the evidence of Horace Walpole to that of their own senses. They have suffered the brilliant antitheses of Lady Mary to obscure and blur the man as they might have found him in his work. Booth and Jones have been taken for definite and complete reflections of the author of their being: the parts for the whole, that is—a light-minded captain of foot and a hot-headed and soft-hearted young man about town for adequate presentments of the artist of a new departure and the writer of three or four books of singular solidity and finish. Whichever way you turn, you are confronted with appearances each more distorted and more dubious than the other. Some have chosen to believe the foolish fancies of Murphy, and have pictured themselves a Fielding begrimed with snuff, heady with champagne, and smoking so ferociously that out of the wrappings of his tobacco he could keep himself in paper for the manuscripts of his plays. For others the rancour of Smollett calls up a Fielding who divides his time and energy between blowing a trumpet on a Smithfield show and playing Captain Bilkum to a flesh-and-blood Stormandra at the establishment of a living, breathing, working Mother Punchbowl. With Dr. Rimbault and Professor Henry Morley others yet evolve from their inner consciousness a Fielding with a booth in Smithfield, buffooning for the coppers of a Bartlemy Fair audience. The accomplished lawyer has had as little place in men's thoughts as the tender father, the admirable artist as little as the devoted husband and the steadfast friend. Fielding has been so often painted a hard drinker that few have thought of him as a hard reader; he has been suspected of conjugal infidelity, so it has seemed impossible that he should be other than a violent Bohemian. In certain chapters of *Jonathan Wild the Great* there is enough of sustained intellectual effort to furnish forth a hundred modern novels; but you only think of Fielding reeling home from the Rose, and refuse to consider him except as sitting down with his head in a wet towel to scribble immodest and ruffianly trash for the players! A consequence of all these exercises in sentiment and imagination has been that, while many have

been ready to deal with Fielding as the text for a sermon or the subject of an essay, as the point of a moral or the adornment of a tale, few have cared to think of him as worthy to dispute the palm with Cervantes and Sir Walter as the heroic man of letters.

He is before all things else a writer to be studied. He wrote for the world at large and to the end that he might be read eternally. His matter, his manner, the terms of his philosophy, the quality of his ideals, the nature of his achievement, proclaim him universal. Like Scott, like Cervantes, like Shakespeare, he claims not merely our acquaintance but an intimate and abiding familiarity. He has no special public, and to be only on nodding terms with him is to be practically dead to his attraction and unworthy his society. He worked not for the boys and girls of an age but for the men and women of all time; and both as artist and as thinker he commands unending attention and lifelong friendship. He is a great inventor, an unrivalled craftsman, a perfect master of his material. His achievement is the result of a lifetime of varied experience, of searching and sustained observation, of unwearying intellectual endeavour. The sound and lusty types he created have an intellectual flavour peculiar to themselves. His novels teem with ripe wisdom and generous conclusions and beneficent examples.—W. E. HENLEY, "Fielding," *Views and Reviews*, 1890, pp. 229–32

Fielding's strong, healthy, unconventional nature revolted from the moral priggishness of *Virtue Rewarded*. It angered him that crowds of ladies sighed and wept over Richardson's ponderous, long-drawn, and fictitious tales, with their wearisome platitudes, their attenuated moral maxims, their morbid tone, and their impossible situations. Fielding resolved to write a contrast and corrective, purporting to be the adventures of Pamela's brother, *Joseph Andrews*; but, in quizzing Richardson, he opened up an original vein of his own. His *Jonathan Wild* is a masterpiece of irony. *Tom Jones* is a marvel of invention, character, and wit, of which readers never weary; with its amusing scenes and adventures, its sparkling sketches of high and low life, its genial satire, and its scorn of meanness and hypocrisy. He has stronger claims to be a writer of history than the authors of many elaborate fictions known under that name. Before he discovered the true bent of his genius, he wasted his powers in writing third-rate plays until he was thirty-five. He died twelve years later in Lisbon.—W. H. S. AUBREY, *The Rise and Growth of the English Nation*, 1895, Vol. 3, p. 121

As a master of style, Fielding has a claim on our admiration, apart from all the other attributes of his genius. It seems strange in regard to Fielding to set aside all the wealth of human sympathy, all the range of humour, all the vividness of character-drawing, and to restrict ourselves solely to the one aspect that interests us here, his place as a writer of prose. His style reflects much that is distinctive of his genius, its massive carelessness, its strong simplicity, its clearness of outline, and its consummate ease. But above all things he repeats two leading characteristics of his age, its irony and its scholarship. Fielding was from first to last a man of letters, as the character was conceived in his time—without pedantry, without strain, without the constraint of subtlety, but always imbued with the instinct of the scholar, never forgetting that, in the full rush of his exuberant fancy and his audacious humour, he must give to his style that indescribable quality that makes it permanent, that forces us to place it in the first rank of literary effort, that, even when irregular, pleads for no allowance on the score of neglect of art. He challenges comparison on merely literary grounds with the best models of literary art, and he is no loser by the comparison.—HENRY CRAIK, "Introduction" to *English Prose*, ed. Henry Craik, 1895, Vol. 4, pp. 10–11

Yet Fielding had, and had eminently, the style which belongs to his own kind of work. The picked and outlandish epithets, the elaborately set conceits, of some writers would have been not more or less inappropriate to his downright and massive grasp of human nature, than the flourish and ornament of others, would have been awkwardly suited with his direct and piercing irony, his simple and sincere humour. It was not his object, and it would not have fitted his nature, to give his readers "blessed words" to chew and puzzle over, conundrums to guess, dainty tissues of writing to admire independently of the subject and the meaning. He might, if his education and early practice had been different, have written with more formal correctness and yet none the worse; he could hardly, if the paradox may be pardoned, have written otherwise than he did and yet have written much the better. Of no one is the much-quoted and much-misquoted maxim of Buffon more justified than of him. His style is exactly suited to his character and his production—which latter, be it remembered, considering the pleasures of his youth and the business of his age, was very considerable. No fault of his style can ever, either in the general reader or in the really qualified critic, have hindered the enjoyment of the best part of his work: and like the work itself the style in which it is clothed is eminently English. It is English no less in its petty shortcomings of correctness, precision, and grace, than in its mighty merits of power and range. Of the letter Fielding may be here and there a little neglectful; in the spirit he always holds fast to the one indispensable excellence, the adjustment of truth and life to art.—GEORGE SAINTSBURY, "Fielding," *English Prose*, ed. Henry Craik, 1895, Vol. 4, pp. 114–15

Very different in kind, though of equal value to literature, is the gift to his generation of Henry Fielding, whose *Joseph Andrews* in 1742 succeeds so oddly to the *Pamela* of 1740–41. He also set out to copy human nature faithfully and minutely, but his view of life was more eclectic than that of Richardson. A much greater writer, in his own virile way one of the most skilful of all manipulators of English, he is saved by his wider learning and experience from the banality of Richardson. As Mr. Leslie Stephen has well said, Fielding, more than any other writer, gives the very form and pressure of the eighteenth century. He is without the sensibility of Richardson, which he disdained; his observation of the movements of the heart is more superficial; he cannot probe so deeply into the fluctuating thoughts of woman. He has the defects of too great physical health; he is impatient of the half-lights of character, of nervous impressionability. He can spare few tears over Clarissa, and none at all over Clementina; he laughs in the sunshine with Ariosto. He also is a moralist, but of quite another class than Richardson; he is pitiful of the frailties of instinct, sorry for those who fall from excess of strength. Hence, while Richardson starts the cloistered novel of psychology, of febrile analysis, Fielding takes a manlier note, and deals with conduct from its more adventurous side.

The various qualities of Fielding are seen to successive advantage in *Joseph Andrews* (1742) with its profuse humour, in *Jonathan Wild* (1743) with its cynical irony, in *Amelia* (1751) with its tenderness and sentiment; but it is in *Tom Jones* (1749) that the full force of the novelist is revealed. This was the first attempt made by any writer to depict in its fulness the life of a normal man, without help from extraordinary conditions or events, without any other appeal to the reader

than that made simply to his interest in a mirror of his own affections, frailties, hopes, and passions. Fielding, in each of his works, but in *Tom Jones* pre-eminently, is above all things candid and good-humoured. He is a lover of morals, but he likes them to be sincere; he has no palliation for their rancid varieties. He has his eye always on conduct; he is keen to observe not what a man pretends or protests, but what he does, and this he records to us, sometimes with scant respect for our susceptibilities. But it has been a magnificent advantage for English fiction to have near the head of it a writer so vigorous, so virile, so devoid of every species of affectation and hypocrisy. In all the best of our later novelists there has been visible a strain of sincere manliness which comes down to them in direct descent from Fielding, and which it would be a thousand pities for English fiction to relinquish.—EDMUND GOSSE, A *Short History of Modern English Literature*, 1897, pp. 243–44

Works

DRAMAS

F——g, who *yesterday* appear'd so rough,
Clad in *coarse Frize*, and plaister'd down with *Snuff*,
See how his *Instant* gaudy Trappings shine;
What *Play-house* Bard was ever seen so fine!
But this, not from his *Humour* flows, you'll say,
But mere *Necessity*;—for last Night lay
In *Pawn*, the *Velvet* which he wears to-Day.
          —JAMES BRAMSTON, *Seasonable Reproof*, 1736

'Twas from a sense of this concluding Jumble, this unnatural huddling of Events, that a witty Friend of mine, who was himself a Dramatic Writer ⟨Fielding⟩, used pleasantly, tho' perhaps rather freely, *to damn the man, who invented Fifth Acts*.—JAMES HARRIS, *Philological Inquiries*, c. 1750, Pt. 2, Ch. 7

Fielding was a comic writer, as well as a novelist; but his comedies are very inferior to his novels: they are particularly deficient both in plot and character. The only excellence which they have is that of the style, which is the only thing in which his novels are deficient. The only dramatic pieces of Fielding that retain possession of the stage are, the *Mock Doctor* (a tolerable translation from Molière's Medecin Malgrè Lui), and his *Tom Thumb*, a very admirable piece of burlesque.—WILLIAM HAZLITT, *Lectures on the English Comic Writers*, 1818

It has been well remarked, indeed, of Fielding's dramatic character, that though the plan of his pieces is not always regular, yet he is often happy in his style and diction, and in every group that he has exhibited there are to be seen particular delineations that will amply recompense the attention bestowed upon them. Though no man in the opinion of that ingenious and discriminating biographer, Dr. Aikin, had a stronger perception of the ludicrous in characters, and though he painted the detached scenes with humour, yet a want of true delicacy to distinguish between the comic, or the grotesque and extravagant, and defect of care and judgment in the business of the drama, prevented him from obtaining excellence in this species of composition.

It is most probable, however, that his inferiority as a dramatist is partly to be attributed to the rapid manner in which he composed his plays, and to the unfavourable situation in which he was placed, as well as to the disadvantage of his having commenced so difficult a species of composition at too early a period of life. Perhaps, also, he possessed greater talent for painting in detail, than for placing a variety of characters before the spectator, by a few bold decided strokes of the pencil; for it is thought, that two different classes of mind are required for these distinct species of production, and the same writer, it has been remarked, rarely succeeds in both. It would appear equally true of a sister art, for the ingenious Retsch, who is considered so incomparable in his dramatic outlines, is very inferior to himself, in respect to finished composition. From the haste, moreover, in which Fielding wrote to supply his continually recurring necessities, without even revising or correcting many of his pieces, he may be said to have furnished rather the materials than the wrought productions of art, calculated for brilliant scenic effect. He was known frequently to enter into an engagement over night with some manager, to bring him a play at a certain hour, and then to go to his lodgings after spending the evening at a tavern (the club assembly of the day), and write a scene on the papers in which he had wrapped his tobacco; and to be ready with his composition for the players next morning to rehearse it. We must remember, at the same time, with regard to these extempore efforts, that not a few of Fielding's pieces are little more than free translation, or adaptations from the French, and among these, perhaps, that of *L'Avare* of Molière, presented under the title of *The Miser*, was one of the most successful. In some of his satirical passages, the author touched (too freely for a corrupt court and ministry) upon political topics, and he was one of the writers who, by indulging their bold and caustic vein, particularly in the cutting satire of his *Pasquin*, contributed to the act for limiting the number of theatres, and submitting dramatic performances to the cruel process of the pruning knife, in the hands of the Lord Chamberlain. The satire of Fielding's comedy is exceedingly keen and severe on the characters of "the great," as he ironically calls them, and on the habits of fashionable life; and for this reason, perhaps, they would have been eminently adapted, with greater care and revision, to appear with advantage before the public. "If the comedy of *Pasquin*," says Mr. Murphy, "were restored to the stage, it would be a more favourite entertainment with our audiences than the much admired *Rehearsal*." A more rational one it certainly would be, as it must undoubtedly be better understood. Though its success was considerable, it never shone forth with a lustre equal to its merit; and yet it is a composition that might have done honour to the Athenian stage, when the middle comedy, under the authority of the laws, made use of fictitious names, to satirise vice and folly, however disguised by honours and employments. But the middle comedy did not flourish long at Athens; the archness of its aim, and the poignancy of its satire, soon became offensive to the officers of state; a law was made to prohibit those oblique strokes of wit; and the comic muse was restrained from all indulgences of personal satire, however humorously drawn under the appearance of imaginary characters. The same fate attended the use of the middle comedy in England; and it is said, that the wit and humour of our modern Aristophanes, whose quarry in some of his pieces, particularly the 'Historical Register,' was higher game than in prudence he should have chosen, were principal instruments in provoking that law under which the British theatre has groaned ever since. It has been also observed by Warburton, the author of the *Divine Legation*, that comic satire is like a two-edged sword, and is susceptible of great abuse; which he illustrates by an anecdote of the court of Charles II. "This weapon in the dissolute times of Charles II. completed the ruin of the best minister of that age. The historians tell us that chancellor Hyde was brought into his majesty's contempt by this odd court

argument; they mimicked his walk and gesture, with a fire-shovel and bellows for the mace and purse. Thus, it being the representation, and not the object represented, which strikes the fancy, vice and virtue must fall indifferently before it."

The objects, however, of Fielding's satire were always of a legitimate kind; and in no part of his works do we find anything like a sneer, either against religion or virtue. His farces partook all of the same character; they were admirable burlesque representations, and they were almost invariably successful. The production only of two or three mornings, and struck off in the heat of the moment, they nevertheless pleased the public, and still continue to enliven our winters on the stage, by the exquisite manner in which they hit the object at which they are aimed. "The representations," says Bishop Hurd, "of common nature may either be taken accurately, so as to reflect a faithful and exact image of their original, which alone is that I should call comedy; or they may be forced or overcharged above the simple and just proportions of nature, as when the excesses of a few are given for standing characters; when not the man in general, but the passion is described, or when, in the draught of the man, the leading feature is extended beyond measure; and in these cases, the representation holds of the province of farce." This is a just and accurate definition, and the farces of Fielding comprehend all that is required: the mock tragedy 'Tom Thumb' is considered replete with as fine a parody as perhaps has ever been written; the *Lottery*, *The Intriguing Chambermaid*, and the *Virgin Unmasked*, besides the real entertainment they afford, had also, on their first appearance, the merit of bringing out the comic genius of some of our best actresses. Of Mrs. Clive in particular, the author observes in one of his prefaces—"I cannot help reflecting that the town has one obligation to me, who made the first discovery of your just capacity, and brought you earlier forward on the theatre than the ignorance of some, and the envy of others, would otherwise have permitted. I shall not here dwell on anything so well known as your theatrical merit; which one of the finest judges, and the greatest man of his age, hath acknowledged to exceed, in humour, that of any of your predecessors in his time."

Notwithstanding the indisputable merit of some of his comic productions, Fielding's finances continued still in a dilapidated condition; for the remuneration he obtained was decidedly inadequate to his expenses. When we consider that by his own account he gained by the *Wedding Day*, which was performed six nights with unremitted applause, only fifty pounds, we are not surprised that he should have required the occasional assistance of his friends. And fortunately he now extended his acquaintance, with a few persons of merit as well as distinction; and the refinement of modern clubs being unknown, the grand resort of literary wit and fashion, and too often of dissipation, were the favourite taverns of the day.—THOMAS ROSCOE, "Life and Works of Henry Fielding," *The Works of Henry Fielding*, 1840

We have seen that, during the ten years that Fielding was a dramatist, he averaged about two plays a year. The composition of these occupied but a comparatively small portion of his time. He would sometimes contract to write a farce or comedy in the evening, pass a good portion of the night convivially, and bring in a whole scene the next morning, written on the paper in which his darling tobacco was wrapped. His plays never met with any brilliant success, and failed to provide for his wants. He said himself, that he left off writing for the stage at the period when he should have begun. There are some indications of his genius scattered over his comedies, though but little evidence is given of dramatic art. As a playwright, he never reached the success which was afterwards obtained by such men as Holcroft, Morton, and Reynolds.—EDWIN P. WHIPPLE, "The Life and Works of Henry Fielding," *North American Review*, Jan. 1849, p. 51

TOM JONES

From the name of my patron, indeed, I hope my reader will be convinced, at his very entrance on this work, that he will find in the whole course of it nothing prejudicial to the cause of religion and virtue, nothing inconsistent with the strictest rules of decency, nor which can offend even the chastest eye in the perusal. On the contrary, I declare, that to recommend goodness and innocence hath been my sincere endeavour in this history. This honest purpose you have been pleased to think I have attained: and to say the truth, it is likeliest to be attained in books of this kind; for an example is a kind of picture, in which virtue becomes, as it were, an object of sight, and strikes us with an idea of that loveliness, which Plato asserts there is in her naked charms.

Besides displaying that beauty of virtue which may attract the admiration of mankind, I have attempted to engage a stronger motive to human action in her favour, by convincing men that their true interest directs them to a pursuit of her. For this purpose I have shown that no acquisitions of guilt can compensate the loss of that solid inward comfort of mind, which is the sure companion of innocence and virtue; nor can in the least balance the evil of that horror and anxiety which, in their room, guilt introduces into our bosoms. And again, that as these acquisitions are in themselves generally worthless, so are the means to attain them not only base and infamous, but at best incertain, and always full of danger. Lastly, I have endeavoured strongly to inculcate that virtue and innocence can scarce ever be injured but by indiscretion; and that it is this alone which often betrays them into the snares that deceit and villainy spread for them. A moral which I have the more industriously laboured, as the teaching it is, of all others, the likeliest to be attended with success; since, I believe, it is much easier to make good men wise, than to make bad men good.

For these purposes I have employed all the wit and humour of which I am master in the following history; wherein I have endeavoured to laugh mankind out of their favourite follies and vices. How far I have succeeded in this good attempt, I shall submit to the candid reader, with only two requests: First, that he will not expect to find perfection in this work; and Secondly, that he will excuse some parts of it, if they fall short of that little merit which I hope may appear in others.—HENRY FIELDING, Dedication to George, Lord Lyttelton, *Tom Jones*, 1749

Mean while, it is an honest pleasure, which we take in adding, that (exclusive of one wild, detach'd, and independent Story of a *Man of the Hill*, that neither brings on Anything, nor rose from Anything that went before it) All the changefull windings of the Author's Fancy carry on a course of regular Design; and end in an extremely moving Close, where Lives that seem'd to wander and run different ways, meet, All, in an instructive Center.

The whole Piece consists of an inventive Race of Disappointments and Recoveries. It excites Curiosity, and holds it watchful. It has just and pointed Satire; but it is a partial Satire, and confin'd, too narrowly: It sacrifices to Authority, and Interest. Its *Events* reward Sincerity, and punish and expose Hypocrisy; shew Pity and Benevolence in amiable Lights, and Avarice and Brutality in very despicable ones. In every Part It

has Humanity for its Intention: In too many, it *seems* wantoner than It was meant to be: It has bold shocking Pictures; and (I fear) not unresembling ones, in high Life, and in low. And (to conclude this too adventurous Guess-work, from a Pair of forward Baggages) woud, every where, (we think,) *deserve* to please,—if stript of what the Author thought himself most sure to *please by*.

And thus, Sir, we have told you our sincere opinion of *Tom Jones*.—ASTRAEA AND MINERVA HILL, Letter to Samuel Richardson (July 27, 1749)

I must confess, that I have been prejudiced by the Opinion of Several judicious Friends against the truly coarse-titled *Tom Jones*; and so have been discouraged from reading it.—I was told, that it was a rambling Collection of Waking Dreams, in which Probability was not observed: And that it had a very bad Tendency. And I had Reason to think that the Author intended for his Second View (His *first*, to fill his Pocket, by accommodating it to the reigning Taste) in writing it, to whiten a vicious Character, and to make Morality bend to his Practices. What Reason has he to make his Tom illegitimate, in an Age where Keeping is become a Fashion? Why did he make him a common—What shall I call it?—And a Kept Fellow, the Lowest of all Fellows, yet in Love with a Young Creature who was trapsing after him, a Fugitive from her Father's House?— Why did he draw his Heroine so fond, so foolish, and so insipid?—Indeed he has one Excuse—He knows now how to draw a delicate Woman—He has not been accustomed to such Company—And is too prescribing, too impetuous, too immoral, I will venture to say, to take any other Byass than that a perverse and crooked Nature has given him; or Evil Habits, at least, have confirm'd in him. Do Men expect Grapes of Thorns, or Figs of Thistles? But, perhaps, I think the worse of the Piece because I know the Writer, and dislike his Principles, both Public and Private, tho' I wish well to the *Man*, and Love Four worthy Sisters of his, with whom I am well acquainted. And indeed should admire him, did he make the Use of his Talents which I wish him to make; For the Vein of Humour, and Ridicule, which he is Master of, might, if properly turned, do great Service to ye Cause of Virtue.

But no more of this Gentleman's Work, after I have said, That the favourable Things, you say of the Piece, will tempt me, if I can find Leisure, to give it a Perusal.—SAMUEL RICHARDSON, Letter to Astraea and Minerva Hill (Aug. 4, 1749)

Unfortunate *Tom Jones!* how sadly has he mortify'd Two sawcy Correspondents of your making! They are with me now: and bid me tell you, You have spoil'd 'em Both, for Criticks.— Shall I add, a Secret which they did not bid me tell you?— They, Both, fairly *cry'd*, that You shou'd think it possible they cou'd approve of Any thing, in Any work, that had an *Evil Tendency*, in any Part or Purpose of it. They maintain their Point so far, however, as to be convinc'd they say, that *you* will disapprove this over-rigid Judgment of those Friends, who cou'd not find a Thread of Moral Meaning in Tom Jones, quite independent of the Levities they justly censure.—And, as soon as you have Time to read him, for yourself, tis there, pert Sluts, they will be bold enough to rest the Matter.—Mean while, they love and honour you and your opinions.—AARON HILL, Letter to Samuel Richardson (Aug. 11, 1749)

> Long, thro' the mimic scenes of motly life,
> Neglected *Nature* lost th' unequal strife;
> Studious to show, in mad, fantastic shape,
> Each grinning gesture of his kindred ape,
> Man lost the name: while each, in artful dress,

Appear'd still something more or something less:
Virtue and vice, unmix'd, in fancy stood,
And all were vilely bad, or greatly good;
Eternal distance ever made to keep,
Exciting horrour, or promoting sleep:
   Sick of her fools, great *Nature* broke the jest,
And *Truth* held out each character to test,
When *Genius* spoke: Let *Fielding* take the pen!
Life dropt her mask, and all mankind were men.
     —THOMAS CAWTHORN, "To Henry Fielding,
     Esq.; On Reading His Inimitable *History of
     Tom Jones*," *Gentleman's Magazine*, Sept.
     1749, p. 371

There is lately sprung up among us a species of narrative poem, representing likewise the characters of common life. It has the same relation to comedy that the epic has to tragedy, and differs from the epic in the same respect that comedy differs from tragedy; that is, in the actions and characters, both which are much nobler in the epic than in it. It is therefore, I think, a legitimate kind of poem; and, accordingly, we are told, Homer wrote one of that kind, called *Margites*, of which some lines are preserved. The reason why I mention it is, that we have, in English, a *poem* of that kind, (for so I will call it) which has more of character in it than any work, antient or modern, that I know. The work I mean is, the *History of Tom Jones*, by Henry Fielding, which, as it has more personages brought into the story than any thing of the poetic kind I have ever seen; so all those personages have characters peculiar to them, in so much, that there is not even an host or an hostess upon the road, hardly a servant, who is not distinguished in that way; in short I never saw any thing that was so much animated, and, as I may say, *all alive* with characters and manners, as the *History of Tom Jones*.—JAMES BURNETT, LORD MONBODDO, *Of the Origin and Progress of Language*, 1773–92, Pt. 2, Bk. 4, Ch. 8

He was the author of a romance, entitled *The History of Joseph Andrews*, and of another, *The Foundling, or the History of Tom Jones*, a book seemingly intended to sap the foundation of that morality which it is the duty of parents and all public instructors to inculcate in the minds of young people, by teaching that virtue upon principle is imposture, that generous qualities alone constitute true worth, and that a young man may love and be loved, and at the same time associate with the loosest women. His morality, in respect that it resolves virtue into good affections, in contradiction to moral obligation and a sense of duty, is that of Lord Shaftesbury vulgarized, and is a system of excellent use in palliating the vices most injurious to society. He was the inventor of that cant phrase, goodness of heart, which is every day used as a substitute for probity, and means little more than the virtue of a horse or dog; in short, he has done more towards corrupting the rising generation than any writer we know of.—SIR JOHN HAWKINS, *The Life of Samuel Johnson, LL.D.*, 1787

Our immortal Fielding was of a younger branch of the Earls of Denbigh who draw their origin from the Counts of Habsburg, the lineal descendants of Eltrico, in the seventh century Duke of Alsace. Far different have been the fortunes of the English and German divisions of the family of Habsburg. The former, the knights and sheriffs of Leicestershire, have slowly risen to the dignity of a peerage: the latter, the Emperors of Germany, and Kings of Spain, have threatened the liberty of the old and invaded the treasures of the new world. The successors of Charles the Fifth may disdain their brethren in England: but the romance of *Tom Jones*, that exquisite picture of human

manners, will outlive the palace of the Escurial and the imperial eagle of the house of Austria.—EDWARD GIBBON, *Memoirs of My Life*, 1792–93

Tom Jones cannot be considered simply a novel; the abundance of philosophical ideas, the hypocrisy of society, and the contrast of natural qualities, are brought into action with an infinity of art; and love, as I have observed before, it is only a vehicle to introduce these.—MADAME DE STAËL, *The Influence of Literature upon Society*, 1800, Ch. 15

As a story, *Tom Jones* seems to have only one defect, which might have been so easily remedied, that it is to be regretted that it should have been neglected by the author. Jones, after all, proves illegitimate, when there would have been no difficulty for the author to have supposed that his mother had been privately married to the young clergyman. This would not only have removed the stain from the birth of the hero, but, in the idea of the reader, would have given him better security for the property of his uncle Allworthy. In fact, in a miserable continuation which has been written of the history of *Tom Jones*, the wrongheaded author (of whom Blifil was the favourite,) has made his hero bring an action against Tom after the death of Mr. Allworthy, and oust him from his uncle's property.—JOHN DUNLOP, *The History of Fiction* (1814), 1842, Ch. 14

Shall I say which was the first book that most strongly excited my curiosity, and interested my sensibility? It was *Tom Jones*. My female Mentor tantalized me without mercy. She would let me have but one volume at a time; and not only would not afford me any clue to the concluding catastrophe, but rather put me upon a wrong scent. Sometimes too when my impatience of expectation was at the very highest point possible, the succeeding volume was mislaid, was lent, was not impossibly lost. However, after a long and most severe trial, after hating Blifil with no common hatred, forming a most friendly intimacy with Partridge, loving Sophia with rapturous extravagance, I complacently accompanied dear wicked Tom to the nuptial altar. I endeavoured of course to procure the other productions of this popular author, but I well remember that I did not peruse any of them, no not within a hundred degrees of the satisfaction, which the Foundling communicated.—WILLIAM BELOE, *The Sexagenarian*, 1817, Vol. 1, p. 13

Manners change from generation to generation, and with manners morals appear to change,—actually change with some, but appear to change with all but the abandoned. A young man of the present day who should act as Tom Jones is supposed to act at Upton, with Lady Bellaston, &c. would not be a Tom Jones; and a Tom Jones of the present day, without perhaps being in the ground a better man, would have perished rather than submit to be kept by a harridan of fortune. Therefore this novel is, and indeed, pretends to be, no exemplar of conduct. But, notwithstanding all this, I do loathe the cant which can recommend *Pamela* and *Clarissa Harlowe* as strictly moral, though they poison the imagination of the young with continued doses of *tinct. lyttæ*, while *Tom Jones* is prohibited as loose. I do not speak of young women;—but a young man whose heart or feelings can be injured, or even his passions excited, by aught in this novel, is already thoroughly corrupt. There is a cheerful, sun-shiny, breezy spirit that prevails everywhere, strongly contrasted with the close, hot, day-dreamy continuity of Richardson. Every indiscretion, every immoral act, of Tom Jones, (and it must be remembered that he is in every one taken by surprise—his inward principles remaining firm—) is so instantly punished by embarrassment and unanticipated evil consequences of his folly, that the reader's mind is not left for a moment to dwell or run riot on the criminal indulgence itself. In short, let the requisite allowance be made for the increased refinement of our manners,—and then I dare believe that no young man who consulted his heart and conscience only, without adverting to what the world would say—could rise from the perusal of Fielding's *Tom Jones, Joseph Andrews,* or *Amelia,* without feeling himself a better man;—at least, without an intense conviction that he could not be guilty of a base act.—SAMUEL TAYLOR COLERIDGE, "Notes on *Tom Jones,*" *Literary Remains,* ed. Henry Nelson Coleridge, 1836, Vol. 2, pp. 374–75

While on this visit I saw for the first time an odd volume of *Tom Jones;* but I have not the slightest intention of describing the wonder and the feeling with which I read it. No pen could do justice to that. It was the second volume; of course the story was incomplete, and, as a natural consequence, I felt something amounting to agony at the disappointment—not knowing what the *dénouement* was.—WILLIAM CARLETON (c. 1869), *The Life of William Carleton: Being His Autobiography and Letters,* ed. David J. O'Donoghue, 1896, Vol. 1, p. 74

Our great eighteenth century novelists have won a place in the abiding literature of the world—a place beside the poets more specially so called. Their knowledge of human nature, their humour, their dramatic skill, their pathos, make them peers of those who have used the forms of verse, and it is in the form and not in substance that they may rank below the masters of the creative art in verse. First among them all is the generous soul of Fielding, to whom so much is forgiven for the nobleness of his great heart. On him and on the others there rests the curse of their age, and no incantation can reverse the sentence pronounced upon those who deliberately stoop to the unclean. It is a grave defect in the splendid tale of *Tom Jones*— of all prose romances the most rich in life and the most artistic in construction—that a Bowdlerised version of it would be hardly intelligible as a tale. Grossness, alas! has entered into the marrow of its bones. Happily, vice has not; and amidst much that is repulsive, we feel the good man's reverence for goodness, and the humane spirit's honour of every humane quality, whilst the pure figure of the womanly Sophia (most womanly of all women in fiction) walks in maiden meditation across the darkest scenes, as the figure of the glorified Gretchen passes across the revel in the Walpurgis-Nacht.—FREDERIC HARRISON, "The Choice of Books" (1879), *The Choice of Books and Other Literary Pieces,* 1886, p. 63

Novelists who have undertaken to write the life of a hero or heroine have generally considered their work completed at the interesting period of marriage, and have contented themselves with the advance in taste and manners which are common to all boys and girls as they become men and women. Fielding, no doubt, did more than this in *Tom Jones,* which is one of the greatest novels in the English language, for there he has shown how a noble and sanguine nature may fall away under temptation and be again strengthened and made to stand upright. —ANTHONY TROLLOPE, *An Autobiography,* 1883, Ch. 17

Tom Jones was published in 1749. It stands for the fulness of Fielding's art and manhood. Into it Fielding has compressed his richest observations on life and his ripest thought; and expended in its composition 'some thousands of hours.' *Tom Jones* is the consummation of his earlier plan of transforming comedy into the comic epic. Fielding still writes with his eye upon Aristotle and the Greek drama. He keeps from the reader the secret of Jones's parentage, which he manages with greater

artistic effect than the similar secret in *Joseph Andrews.* It becomes a directing force on the course of events, and an element of interest to the reader. The discovery, when it comes, is not a fantastic surprise operated by the machinery of gypsies and the exchange of children in the cradle; the reader has been looking forward to it, for he has been prepared for it. The scenes are still constructed as in comedy. As we read on, it is as if we were assisting at the representation of a score of comedies, parallel and successive; some pathetic, some burlesque, others possessing the gay wit of Vanbrugh and Congreve—all of which, after a skilfully manipulated revolution of circumstances, are united in a brilliant conclusion. Instead of being burdened, as were the earlier epic romancers, with a number of narratives to be gathered up in the last chapters, Fielding in the main becomes his own story-teller throughout. Character is unfolded, and momentum is given to his plot by direct, not reported, conversations. All devices to account for his subject-matter, such as bundles of letters, fragmentary or rat-eaten manuscripts, found by chance, or given to the writer in keeping, are brushed aside as cheap and silly. Fielding throws off the mask of anonymity, steps out boldly, and asks us to accept his omniscience and omnipresence.—WILBUR L. CROSS, *The Development of the English Novel,* 1899, pp. 45–46

The two hundredth anniversary of Henry Fielding is very justly celebrated, even if, as far as can be discovered, it is only celebrated by the newspapers. It would be too much to expect that any such merely chronological incident should induce the people who write about Fielding to read him; this kind of neglect is only another name for glory.⟨. . .⟩

There seems to be an extraordinary idea abroad that Fielding was in some way an immoral or offensive writer. I have been astounded by the number of the leading articles, literary articles, and other articles written about him just now in which there is a curious tone of apologising for the man. One critic says that after all he couldn't help it, because he lived in the eighteenth century; another says that we must allow for the change of manners and ideas; another says that he was not altogether without generous and humane feelings; another suggests that he clung feebly, after all, to a few of the less important virtues. What on earth does all this mean? Fielding described Tom Jones as going on in a certain way, in which, most unfortunately, a very large number of young men do go on. It is unnecessary to say that Henry Fielding knew that it was an unfortunate way of going on. Even Tom Jones knew that. He said in so many words that it was a very unfortunate way of going on; he said, one may almost say, that it had ruined his life; the passage is there for the benefit of any one who may take the trouble to read the book. There is ample evidence (though even this is of a mystical and indirect kind), there is ample evidence that Fielding probably thought that it was better to be Tom Jones than to be an utter coward and sneak. There is simply not one rag or thread or speck of evidence to show that Fielding thought that it was better to be Tom Jones than to be a good man. All that he is concerned with is the description of a definite and very real type of young man; the young man whose passions and whose selfish necessities sometimes seemed to be stronger than anything else in him.

The practical morality of Tom Jones is bad, though not so bad, *spiritually* speaking, as the practical morality of Arthur Pendennis or the practical morality of Pip, and certainly nothing like so bad as the profound practical immorality of Daniel Deronda. The practical morality of Tom Jones is bad;

but I cannot see any proof that his theoretical morality was particularly bad. There is no need to tell the majority of modern young men even to live up to the theoretical ethics of Henry Fielding. They would suddenly spring into the stature of archangels if they lived up to the theoretic ethics of poor Tom Jones. Tom Jones is still alive, with all his good and all his evil; he is walking about the streets; we meet him every day. We meet with him, we drink with him, we smoke with him, we talk with him, we talk about him. The only difference is that we have no longer the intellectual courage to write about him. We split up the supreme and central human being, Tom Jones, into a number of separate aspects. We let Mr. J. M. Barrie write about him in his good moments, and make him out better than he is. We let Zola write about him in his bad moments, and make him out much worse than he is. We let Maeterlinck celebrate those moments of spiritual panic which he knows to be cowardly; we let Mr. Rudyard Kipling celebrate those moments of brutality which he knows to be far more cowardly. We let obscene writers write about the obscenities of this ordinary man. We let puritan writers write about the purities of this ordinary man. We look through one peephole that makes men out as devils, and we call it the new art. We look through another peephole that makes men out as angels, and we call it the New Theology. But if we pull down some dusty old books from the bookshelf, if we turn over some old mildewed leaves, and if in that obscurity and decay we find some faint traces of a tale about a complete man, such a man as is walking on the pavement outside, we suddenly pull a long face, and we call it the coarse morals of a bygone age.

The truth is that all these things mark a certain change in the general view of morals; not, I think, a change for the better. We have grown to associate morality in a book with a kind of optimism and prettiness; according to us, a moral book is a book about moral people. But the old idea was almost exactly the opposite; a moral book was a book about immoral people. A moral book was full of pictures like Hogarth's "Gin Lane" or "Stages of Cruelty," or it recorded, like the popular broadsheet, "God's dreadful judgment" against some blasphemer or murderer. There is a philosophical reason for this change. The homeless scepticism of our time has reached a sub-conscious feeling that morality is somehow merely a matter of human taste—an accident of psychology. And if goodness only exists in certain human minds, a man wishing to praise goodness will naturally exaggerate the amount of it that there is in human minds or the number of human minds in which it is supreme. Every confession that man is vicious is a confession that virtue is visionary. Every book which admits that evil is real is felt in some vague way to be admitting that good is unreal. The modern instinct is that if the heart of man is evil, there is nothing that remains good. But the older feeling was that if the heart of man was ever so evil, there was something that remained good—goodness remained good. An actual avenging virtue existed outside the human race; to that men rose, or from that men fell away. Therefore, of course, this law itself was as much demonstrated in the breach as in the observance. If Tom Jones violated morality, so much the worse for Tom Jones. Fielding did not feel, as a melancholy modern would have done, that every sin of Tom Jones was in some way breaking the spell, or we may even say destroying the fiction of morality. Men spoke of the sinner breaking the law; but it was rather the law that broke him. And what modern people call the foulness and freedom of Fielding is generally the severity and moral stringency of Fielding. He would not have thought that he was serving morality at all if he had written a book all about nice people. Fielding would have considered Mr Ian

Maclaren extremely immoral; and there is something to be said for that view. Telling the truth about the terrible struggle of the human soul is surely a very elementary part of the ethics of honesty. If the characters are not wicked, the book is.

This older and firmer conception of right as existing outside human weakness and without reference to human error can be felt in the very lightest and loosest of the works of old English literature. It is commonly unmeaning enough to call Shakspere a great moralist; but in this particular way Shakspere is a very typical moralist. Whenever he alludes to right and wrong it is always with this old implication. Right is right, even if nobody does it. Wrong is wrong, even if everybody is wrong about it.—G. K. CHESTERTON, "Tom Jones and Morality," *All Things Considered*, 1907, pp. 193–99

ARTHUR MURPHY
From "An Essay on the Life and
Genius of Henry Fielding, Esq."
Collected Works of Henry Fielding, Esq.

1762

And now we are arrived at the second grand epoch of Mr. Fielding's genius, when all his faculties were in perfect unison, and conspired to produce a complete work. If we consider *Tom Jones* in the same light in which the ablest critics have examined the *Iliad*, the *Æneid*, and the *Paradise Lost*, namely, with a view to the fable, the manners, the sentiments, and the stile, we shall find it standing the test of the severest criticism, and indeed bearing away the envied praise of a complete performance. In the first place, the action has that unity, which is the boast of the great models of composition; it turns upon a single event, attended with many circumstances, and many subordinate incidents, which seem, in the progress of the work, to perplex, to entangle, and to involve the whole in difficulties, and lead on the reader's imagination, with an eagerness of curiosity, through scenes of prodigious variety, till at length the different intricacies and complications of the fable are explained after the same gradual manner in which they had been worked up to a crisis: incident arises out of incident; the seeds of every thing that shoots up, are laid with a judicious hand, and, whatever occurs in the latter part of the story, seems naturally to grow out of those passages which preceded; so that, upon the whole, the business with great propriety and probability works itself up into various embarrassments, and then afterwards, by a regular series of events, clears itself from all impediments, and brings itself inevitably to a conclusion; like a river, which, in its progress, foams amongst fragments of rocks, and for a while seems pent up by unsurmountable oppositions; then angrily dashes for a while, then plunges under ground into caverns, and runs a subterraneous course, till at length it breaks out again, meanders round the country, and with a clear placid stream flows gently into the ocean. By this artful management, our author has given us the perfection of fable; which, as the writers upon the subject have justly observed, consists in such obstacles to retard the final issue of the whole, as shall at least, in their consequences, accelerate the catastrophe, and bring it evidently and necessarily to that period only, which, in the nature of things, could arise from it; so that the action could not remain in suspense any longer, but must naturally close and determine itself. It may be proper to add, that no fable whatever affords, in its solution, such artful states of suspence, such beautiful turns of surprise, such unexpected incidents, and such sudden discoveries, sometimes apparently embarrassing, but always promising the catastrophe, and eventually promoting the completion of the whole. *Vida*, the celebrated critic of Italy, has transmitted down to us, in his Art of Poetry, a very beautiful idea of a well-concerted fable, when he represents the reader of it in the situation of a traveller to a distant town, who, when he perceives but a faint shadowy glimmering of its walls, its spires, and its edifices, pursues his journey with more alacrity than when he cannot see any appearances to notify the place to which he is tending, but is obliged to pursue a melancholy and forlorn road through a depth of vallies, without any object to flatter or to raise his expectation.

> Haud aliter, longinqua petit qui fortè viator
> Mœnia, si positas altis in collibus arces
> Nunc etiam dubias oculis videt, incipit ultrò
> Lætior ire viam, placidumque urgere laborem,
> Quam cum nusquam ullæ cernuntur quas adit
>   arces,
> Obscurum sed iter tedit convallibus imis.

In the execution of this plan, thus regular and uniform, what a variety of humorous scenes of life, of descriptions, and characters has our author found means to incorporate with the principal action; and this too, without distracting the reader's attention with objects foreign to his subject, or weakening the general interest by a multiplicity of episodical events? Still observing the grand essential rule of unity in the design, I believe, no author has introduced a greater diversity of characters, or displayed them more fully, or in more various attitudes. *Allworthy* is the most amiable picture in the world of a man who does honour to his species: in his own heart he finds constant propensities to the most benevolent and generous actions, and his understanding conducts him with discretion in the performance of whatever his goodness suggests to him. And though it is apparent that the author laboured this portrait *con amore*, and meant to offer it to mankind as a just object of imitation, he has soberly restrained himself within the bounds of probability, nay, it may be said, of strict truth; as in the general opinion, he is supposed to have copied here the features of a worthy character still in being. Nothing can be more entertaining than WESTERN; his rustic manners, his natural undisciplined honesty, his half-enlightened understanding, with the self-pleasing shrewdness which accompanies it, and the biass of his mind to mistaken politicks, are all delineated with precision and fine humour. The sisters of those two gentlemen are aptly introduced, and give rise to many agreeable scenes. *Tom Jones* will at all times be a fine lesson to young men of good tendencies to virtue, who yet suffer the impetuosity of their passions to hurry them away. *Thackwum* and *Square* are excellently opposed to each other; the former is a well drawn picture of a *divine*, who is neglectful of the moral part of his character, and ostentatiously talks of religion and grace; the latter is a strong ridicule of those, who have high ideas of the dignity of our nature, and of the native beauty of virtue, without owning any obligations of conduct from religion. But grace, without practical goodness, and the moral fitness of things, are shewn, with a fine vein of ridicule, to be but weak principles of action. In short, all the characters down to Partridge, and even to a maid or an hostler at an inn, are drawn with truth and humour: and indeed they abound so much, and are so often brought forward in a dramatic manner, that every thing may be said to be here in action; every thing has MANNERS; and the very manners which belong to it in human life. They look, they act, they speak to our imaginations just as they appear to us in the world. The SENTIMENTS

which they utter, are peculiarly annexed to their habits, passions, and ideas; which is what poetical propriety requires; and, to the honour of the author, it must be said, that, whenever he addresses us in person, he is always in the interests of virtue and religion, and inspires, in a strain of moral reflection, a true love of goodness, and honour, with a just detestation of imposture, hypocrisy, and all specious pretences to uprightness.

There is, perhaps, no province of the comic muse that requires so great a variety of stile as this kind of description of men and manners, in which Mr. Fielding so much delighted. The laws of the mock-epic, in which this species of writing is properly included demand, that, when trivial things are to be represented with a burlesque air, the language should be raised into a sort of tumor of dignity, that by the contrast between the ideas and the pomp in which they are exhibited, they may appear the more ridiculous to our imaginations. Of our author's talent in this way, there are instances in almost every chapter; and were we to align a particular example, we should refer to the relation of a battle in the *Homerican Stile*. On the other hand, when matters, in appearance, of higher moment, but, in reality, attended with incongruous circumstances, are to be set forth in the garb of ridicule, which they deserve, it is necessary that the language should be proportionably lowered, and that the metaphors and epithets made use of be transferred from things of a meaner nature, that so the false importance of the object described may fall into a gay contempt. The first specimen of this manner that occurs to me is in the *Jonathan Wild*: "For my own part," says he, "I confess I look on this death of hanging to be as proper for a hero as any other; and I solemnly declare, that had Alexander the Great been hanged, it would not in the least have diminished my respect to his memory." A better example of what is here intended might, no doubt, be chosen, as things of this nature may be found almost every where in *Tom Jones*, or *Joseph Andrews*; but the quotation here made will serve to illustrate and that is sufficient. The mock-epic has likewise frequent occasion for the gravest irony, for florid description, for the true sublime, for the pathetic, for clear and perspicuous narrative, for poignant satire, and generous panegyrick. For all these different modes of eloquence, Mr. Fielding's genius was most happily versatile, and his power in all of them is so conspicuous, that he may justly be said to have had the rare skill, required by Horace, of giving to each part of his work its true and proper colouring.

> —Servare vices, operumquè colores.

In this consists the specific quality of fine writing: and thus our author being confessedly eminent in all the great essentials of composition, in fable, character, sentiment, and elocution; and as these could not all be united in so high an assemblage, without a rich invention, a fine imagination, an enlightened judgment, and a lively wit, we may fairly here decide his character, and pronounce him the ENGLISH CERVANTES. ⟨. . .⟩

HENRY FIELDING was in stature rather rising above six feet; his frame of body large, and remarkably robust, till the gout had broke the vigour of his constitution. Considering the esteem he was in with all the artists, it is somewhat extraordinary that no portrait of him had ever been made. He had often promised to sit to his friend Hogarth, for whose good qualities and excellent genius he always entertained so high an esteem, that he has left us in his writings many beautiful memorials of his affection: unluckily, however, it so fell out that no picture of him was ever drawn; but yet, as if it was intended that some traces of his countenance should be perpetuated, and that too by the very artist whom our author preferred to all others, after

Mr. Hogarth had long laboured to try if he could bring out any likeness of him from images existing in his own fancy; and just as he was despairing of success, for want of some rule to go by in the dimensions and outlines of the face, fortune threw the grand *desideratum* in the way. A lady, with a pair of scissars, had cut a profile, which gave the distances and proportions of his face sufficiently to restore his lost ideas of him. Glad of an opportunity of paying his last tribute to the memory of an author whom he admired, Mr. Hogarth caught at this outline with pleasure, and worked with all the attachment of friendship till he finished that excellent drawing, which stands at the head of this work, and recalls to all, who have seen the original, a corresponding image of the man.

Had the writer of this Essay the happy power of delineation which distinguishes the artist just mentioned, he would here attempt a portrait of Mr. Fielding's mind: of the principal features, such as they appear to him, he will at least endeavour to give a sketch, however imperfect. His passions, as the poet expresses it, were tremblingly alive all o'er: whatever he desired, he desired ardently; he was alike impatient of disappointment, or ill-usage, and the same quickness of sensibility rendered him elate in prosperity, and overflowing with gratitude at every instance of friendship or generosity: steady in his private attachments, his affection was warm, sincere, and vehement; in his refinements he was manly, but temperate, seldom breaking out in his writings into gratifications of ill-humour, or personal satire. It is to the honour of those whom he loved, that he had too much penetration to be deceived in their characters; and it is to the advantage of his enemies, that he was above passionate attacks upon them. Open, unbounded, and social in his temper, he knew no love of money; but inclining to excess even in his very virtues, he pushed his contempt of avarice into the opposite extreme of imprudence and prodigality. When young in life he had a moderate estate, he soon suffered hospitality to devour it; and when in the latter end of his days he had an income of four or five hundred a-year, he knew no use of money, but to keep his table open to those who had been his friends when young, and had impaired their own fortunes. Though disposed to gallantry by his strong animal spirits, and the vivacity of his passions, he was remarkable for tenderness and constancy to his wife, and the strongest affection for his children. Of sickness and poverty he was singularly patient, and under the pressure of those evils, he could quietly read *Cicero de Consolatione*; but if either of them threatened his wife, he was impetuous for her relief: and thus often from his virtues arose his imperfections. A sense of honour he had as lively and delicate as most men, but sometimes his passions were too turbulent for it, or rather his necessities were too pressing; in all cases where delicacy was departed from, his friends know how his own feelings reprimanded him. The interests of virtue and religion he never betrayed; the former is amiably enforced in his works; and, for the defence of the latter, he had projected a laborious answer to the posthumous philosophy of Bolingbrook; and the preparation he had made for it of long extracts and arguments from the fathers and the most eminent writers of controversy, is still extant in the hands of his brother, Sir John Fielding. In short, our author was unhappy, but not vicious in his nature; in his understanding lively, yet solid; rich in invention, yet a lover of real science; an observer of mankind, yet a scholar of enlarged reading; a spirited enemy, yet an indefatigable friend; a satirist of vice and evil manners, yet a lover of mankind; an useful citizen, a polished and instructive wit; and a magistrate zealous for the order and welfare of the community which he served.

Such was the man, and such the author, whose works we now offer to the public. Of this undertaking we shall only say, that the proprietor was above taking advantage of the author's established reputation to enhance the price, but studied principally to send it into the world at as cheap a purchase as possible; and the editor, from the prodigious number of materials before him, was careful, after communicating with the ablest and best of the author's friends, to reprint every thing worthy of a place in this edition of his Works; which is intended, and, no doubt, will prove, A LASTING MONUMENT OF THE GENIUS OF HENRY FIELDING.

WILLIAM HAZLITT
From *Lectures on the English Comic Writers*
1818

There is very little to warrant the common idea that Fielding was an imitator of Cervantes, except his own declaration of such an intention in the title-page of *Joseph Andrews*, the romantic turn of the character of Parson Adams (the only romantic character in his works), and the proverbial humour of Partridge, which is kept up only for a few pages. Fielding's novels are, in general, thoroughly his own; and they are thoroughly English. What they are most remarkable for, is neither sentiment, nor imagination, nor wit, nor even humour, though there is an immense deal of this last quality; but profound knowledge of human nature, at least of English nature; and masterly pictures of the characters of men as he saw them existing. This quality distinguishes all his works, and is shown almost equally in all of them. As a painter of real life, he was equal to Hogarth; as a mere observer of human nature, he was little inferior to Shakspeare, though without any of the genius and poetical qualities of his mind. His humour is less rich and laughable than Smollett's; his wit as often misses as hits; he has none of the fine pathos of Richardson or Sterne; but he has brought together a greater variety of characters in common life, marked with more distinct peculiarities, and without an atom of caricature, than any other novel writer whatever. The extreme subtlety of observation on the springs of human conduct in ordinary characters, is only equalled by the ingenuity of contrivance in bringing those springs into play, in such a manner as to lay open their smallest irregularity. The detection is always complete, and made with the certainty and skill of a philosophical experiment, and the obviousness and familiarity of a casual observation. The truth of the imitation is indeed so great, that it has been argued that Fielding must have had his materials ready-made to his hands, and was merely a transcriber of local manners and individual habits. For this conjecture, however, there seems to be no foundation. His representations, it is true, are local and individual; but they are not the less profound and conclusive. The feeling of the general principles of human nature operating in particular circumstances, is always intense, and uppermost in his mind; and he makes use of incident and situation only to bring out character.

It is scarcely necessary to give any illustrations. *Tom Jones* is full of them. There is the account, for example, of the gratitude of the elder Blifil to his brother, for assisting him to obtain the fortune of Miss Bridget Alworthy by marriage; and of the gratitude of the poor in his neighborhood to Alworthy himself, who had done so much good in the country that he had made every one in it his enemy. There is the account of the Latin dialogues between Partridge and his maid, of the assault made on him during one of these by Mrs. Partridge, and the severe bruises he patiently received on that occasion, after which the parish of Little Baddington rung with the story, that the school-master had killed his wife. There is the exquisite keeping in the character of Blifil, and the want of it in that of Jones. There is the gradation in the lovers of Molly Seagrim; the philosopher Square succeeding to Tom Jones, who again finds that he himself had succeeded to the accomplished Will. Barnes, who had the first possession of her person, and had still possession of her heart, Jones being only the instrument of her vanity, as Square was of her interest. Then there is the discreet honesty of Black George, the learning of Thwackum and Square, and the profundity of Squire Western, who considered it as a physical impossibility that his daughter should fall in love with Tom Jones. We have also that gentleman's disputes with his sister, and the inimitable appeal of that lady to her niece.—'I was never so handsome as you, Sophy: yet I had something of you formerly. I was called the cruel Parthenissa. Kingdoms and states, as Tully Cicero says, undergo alteration, and so must the human form!' The adventure of the same lady with the highwayman, who robbed her of her jewels, while he complimented her beauty, ought not to be passed over, nor that of Sophia and her muff, nor the reserved coquetry of her cousin Fitzpatrick, nor the description of Lady Bellaston, nor the modest overtures of the pretty widow Hunt, nor the indiscreet babblings of Mrs. Honour. The moral of this book has been objected to, without much reason; but a more serious objection has been made to the want of refinement and elegance in two principal characters. We never feel this objection, indeed, while we are reading the book: but at other times, we have something like a lurking suspicion that Jones was but an awkward fellow, and Sophia a pretty simpleton. I do not know how to account for this effect, unless it is that Fielding's constantly assuring us of the beauty of his hero, and the good sense of his heroine, at last produces a distrust of both. The story of Tom Jones is allowed to be unrivalled: and it is this circumstance, together with the vast variety of characters, that has given the history of a Foundling so decided a preference over Fielding's other novels. The characters themselves, both in *Amelia* and *Joseph Andrews*, are quite equal to any of those in *Tom Jones*. The account of Miss Matthews and Ensign Hibbert, in the former of these; the way in which that lady reconciles herself to the death of her father; the inflexible Colonel Bath; the insipid Mrs. James, the complaisant Colonel Trent, the demure, sly, intriguing, equivocal Mrs. Bennet, the lord who is her seducer, and who attempts afterwards to seduce Amelia by the same mechanical process of a concert-ticket, a book, and the disguise of a great coat; his little, fat, short-nosed, red-faced, good-humoured accomplice, the keeper of the lodging-house, who, having no pretensions to gallantry herself, has a disinterested delight in forwarding the intrigues and pleasures of others, (to say nothing of honest Atkinson, the story of the miniature-picture of Amelia, and the hashed mutton, which are in a different style,) are masterpieces of description. The whole scene at the lodging-house, the masquerade, &c. in *Amelia*, are equal in interest to the parallel scenes in *Tom Jones*, and even more refined in the knowledge of character. For instance, Mrs. Bennet is superior to Mrs. Fitzpatrick in her own way. The uncertainty, in which the event of her interview with her former seducer is left, is admirable. Fielding was a master of what may be called the *double entendre* of character, and surprises you no less by what he leaves in the dark, (hardly known to the persons themselves) than by the unexpected discoveries he makes of the real traits and circumstances in a character with which, till then, you find you were un-

acquainted. There is nothing at all heroic, however, in the usual style of his delineations. He does not draw lofty characters or strong passions; all his persons are of the ordinary stature as to intellect; and possess little elevation of fancy, or energy of purpose. Perhaps, after all, Parson Adams is his finest character. It is equally true to nature, and more ideal than any of the others. Its unsuspecting simplicity makes it not only more amiable, but doubly amusing, by gratifying the sense of superior sagacity in the reader. Our laughing at him does not once lessen our respect for him. His declaring that he would willingly walk ten miles to fetch his sermon on vanity, merely to convince Wilson of his thorough contempt of this vice, and his consoling himself for the loss of his Æschylus, by suddenly recollecting that he could not read it if he had it, because it is dark, are among the finest touches of *naïveté*. The night-adventures at Lady Booby's with Beau Didapper, and the amiable Slipslop, are the most ludicrous; and that with the huntsman, who draws off the hounds from the poor Parson, because they would be spoiled by following *vermin*, the most profound. Fielding did not often repeat himself; but Dr. Harrison, in *Amelia*, may be considered as a variation of the character of Adams: so also is Goldsmith's *Vicar of Wakefield*; and the latter part of that work, which sets out so delightfully, an almost entire plagiarism from Wilson's account of himself, and Adams's domestic history.

SIR WALTER SCOTT
From "Fielding" (1820)
Lives of the Novelists
1825

Of all the works of imagination to which English genius has given origin, the novels of the celebrated Henry Fielding are, perhaps, most decidedly and exclusively her own. They are not only altogether beyond the reach of translation, in the proper sense and spirit of the word, but we even question whether they can be fully understood, or relished to the highest extent, by such natives of Scotland and Ireland, as are not habitually acquainted with the character and manners of Old England. Parson Adams, Towwouse, Partridge, above all, Squire Western, are personages as peculiar to England as they are unknown to other countries. Nay, the actors whose character is of a more general cast, as Allworthy, Mrs. Miller, Tom Jones himself, and almost all the subordinate agents in the narrative, have the same cast of nationality, which adds not a little to the versimilitude of the tale. The persons of the story live in England, travel in England, quarrel and fight in England; and scarce an incident occurs without its being marked by something which could not well have happened in any other country. This nationality may be ascribed to the author's own habits of life, which rendered him conversant, at different periods, with all the various classes of English society, specimens of which he has selected, with inimitable spirit of choice and description, for the amusement of his readers. Like many other men of talent, Fielding was unfortunate: his life was a life of imprudence and uncertainty. But it was, while passing from the high society to which he was born, to that of the lowest and most miscellaneous kind, that he acquired the extended familiarity with the English character, in every rank and aspect, which has made his name immortal as a painter of national manners. ⟨. . .⟩

The novel of *Pamela*, published in 1740, had carried the

fame of Richardson to the highest pitch; and Fielding, whether he was tired of hearing it over praised (for a book, several passages of which would now be thought highly indelicate, was in those days even recommended from the pulpit), or whether, as a writer for daily subsistence, he caught at whatever interested the public for the time; or whether, in fine, he was seduced by that wicked spirit of wit, which cannot forbear turning into ridicule the idol of the day, resolved to caricature the style, principles, and personages of this favourite performance. As Gay's desire to satirize Philips gave rise to the *Shepherd's Week*, so Fielding's purpose to ridicule *Pamela* produced the *History of Joseph Andrews*; and, in both cases, but especially in the latter, a work was executed infinitely better than could have been expected to arise out of such a motive, and the reader received a degree of pleasure far superior to what the author himself appears to have proposed. There is, indeed, a fine vein of irony in Fielding's novel, as will appear from comparing it with the pages of *Pamela*. But *Pamela*, to which that irony was applied, is now in a manner forgotten, and *Joseph Andrews* continues to be read, for the admirable pictures of manners which it presents; and, above all, for the inimitable character of Mr. Abraham Adams, which alone is sufficient to stamp the superiority of Fielding over all writers of his class. His learning, his simplicity, his evangelical purity of mind, and benevolence of disposition, are so admirably mingled with pedantry, absence of mind, and with the habit of athletic and gymnastic exercise, then acquired at the universities by students of all descriptions, that he may be safely termed one of the richest productions of the Muse of fiction. Like Don Quixote, Parson Adams is beaten a little too much, and too often; but the cudgel lights upon his shoulders, as on those of the honoured Knight of La Mancha, without the slightest stain to his reputation, and he is bastinadoed without being degraded. The style of this piece is said, in the preface, to have been an imitation of Cervantes; but both in *Joseph Andrews* and *Tom Jones*, the author appears also to have had in view the *Roman Comique* of the once celebrated Scaron. From this authority he has copied the mock-heroic style, which tells ludicrous events in the language of the classical epic; a vein of pleasantry which is soon wrought out, and which Fielding has employed so often as to expose him to the charge of pedantry.

Joseph Andrews was eminently successful; and the aggrieved Richardson, who was fond of praise even to adulation, was proportionally offended, while his group of admirers, male and female, took care to echo back his sentiments, and to heap Fielding with reproach. Their animosity survived his life, and we find the most ungenerous reproaches thrown upon his memory, in the course of Richardson's correspondence. Richardson was well acquainted with Fielding's sisters, and complained to them—not of Fielding's usage of himself, that he was too wise, or too proud to mention, but—of his unfortuate predilection to what was mean and low in character and description. The following expressions are remarkable, as well for the extreme modesty of the writer, who thus rears himself into the paramount judge of Fielding's qualities, and for the delicacy which could intrude such observations on the ear of his rival's sister: "Poor Fielding, I could not help telling his sister, that I was equally surprised at, and concerned for, his continued lowness. Had your brother, said I, been born in a stable, or been a runner at a spunging-house, one should have thought him a genius, and wished he had had the advantage of a liberal education, and of being admitted into good company!" After this we are not surprised at its being alleged that Fielding was destitute of invention and talents; that the run of

his best works was nearly over; and that he would soon be forgotten as an author. Fielding does not appear to have retorted any of this ill will, so that, if he gave the first offence, and that an unprovoked one, he was also the first to retreat from the contest, and to allow to Richardson those claims which his genius really demanded from the liberality of his contemporaries. In the fifth number of the Jacobite Journal, Fielding highly commends *Clarissa*, which is by far the best and most powerful of Richardson's novels; and, with those scenes in *Sir Charles Grandison* which refer to the history of Clementina, contains the passages of deep pathos on which his claim to immortality must finally rest. Perhaps this is one of the cases in which one would rather have sympathized with the thoughtless offender, than with the illiberal and ungenerous mind which so long retained its resentment.

After the publication of *Joseph Andrews*, Fielding had again recourse to the stage, and brought out *The Wedding-Day*, which, though on the whole unsuccessful, produced him some small profit. This was the last of his theatrical efforts which appeared during his life. The manuscript comedy of *The Fathers* was lost by Sir Charles Hanbury Williams, and, when recovered, was acted, after the author's death, for the benefit of his family. An anecdote respecting the carelessness with which Fielding regarded his theatrical fame, is thus given by former biographers:—

"On one of the days of its rehearsal (i.e. the rehearsal of the *Wedding-Day*) Garrick, who performed a principal part, and who was even then a favourite with the public, told Fielding he was apprehensive that the audience would make free with him in a particular passage; and remarked that, as a repulse might disconcert him during the remainder of the night, the passage should be omitted:——'No, d——n 'em,' replied he, 'if the scene is not a good one, let them find *that* out.' Accordingly the play was brought out without alteration, and, as had been foreseen, marks of disapprobation appeared. Garrick, alarmed at the hisses he had met with, retired into the green-room, where the author was solacing himself with a bottle of champagne. He had by this time drank pretty freely—and glancing his eye at the actor, while clouds of tobacco issued from his mouth, cried out, 'What's the matter, Garrick? what are they hissing now?' 'Why the scene that I begged you to retrench,' replied the actor; 'I knew it would not do; and they have so frightened me, that I shall not be able to collect myself again the whole night.' 'Oh! d——n 'em,' rejoined he, with great coolness, 'they *have* found it out, have they?'"

Besides various fugitive pieces, Fielding published, in or about 1743, a volume of Miscellanies, including *The Journey from this World to the Next*, a tract containing a good deal of Fielding's peculiar humour, but of which it is difficult to conceive the plan or purport. *The History of Jonathan Wild the Great* next followed. It is not easy to see what Fielding proposed to himself by a picture of complete vice, unrelieved by any thing of human feeling, and never, by any accident, even deviating into virtue; and the ascribing a train of fictitious adventures to a real character has in it something clumsy and inartificial on the one hand, and, on the other, subjects the author to a suspicion that he only used the title of Jonathan Wild in order to connect his book with the popular renown of that infamous depredator. But there are few passages in Fielding's more celebrated works more marked by his peculiar genius than the scene betwixt his hero and the ordinary when in Newgate.

Besides these more permanent proofs of his industrious application to literature, the pen of Fielding was busily employed in the political and literary controversies of the times. He conducted one paper called *The Jacobite Journal*, the object of which was to eradicate those feelings and sentiments which had been already so effectually crushed upon the Field of Culloden. *The True Patriot* and *The Champion* were works of the same kind, which he entirely composed, or in which, at least, he had a principal share. In these various papers he steadily advocated what was then called the whig cause, being attached to the principles of the revolution, and the royal family of Brunswick, or, in other words, a person well affected to church and state. His zeal was long unnoticed, while far inferior writers were enriched out of the secret service money with unexampled prodigality. At length, in 1749, he received a small pension, together with the then disreputable office of a justice of peace for Westminster and Middlesex, of which he was at liberty to make the best he could by the worst means he chose. This office, such as it was, he owed to the interference of Mr. afterwards Lord Lyttleton. ⟨. . .⟩

The *History of a Foundling* was composed under all the disadvantages incident to an author, alternately pressed by the disagreeable task of his magisterial duties, and by the necessity of hurrying out some ephemeral essay or pamphlet to meet the demands of the passing day. It is inscribed to the Honourable Mr. Lyttleton, afterward Lord Lyttleton, with a dedication, in which he intimates, that, without his assistance and that of the Duke of Bedford, the work had never been completed, as the author had been indebted to them for the means of subsistence while engaged in composing it. Ralph Allen, the friend of Pope, is also alluded to as one of his benefactors, but unnamed, by his own desire: thus confirming the truth of Pope's beautiful couplet:—

> Let humble Allen, with an awkward shame,
> Do good by stealth and blush to find it fame.

It is said that this munificent and modest patron made Fielding a present of 200*l.* at one time, and that even before he was personally acquainted with him.

Under such precarious circumstances, the first English novel was given to the public, which had not yet seen any works of fiction founded upon the plan of painting from nature. Even Richardson's novels are but a step from the old romance, approaching, indeed, more nearly to the ordinary course of events, but still dealing in improbable incidents, and in characters swelled out beyond the ordinary limits of humanity. The *History of a Foundling* is truth and human nature itself, and there lies the inestimable advantage which it possesses over all previous fictions of this particular kind. It was received with unanimous acclamation by the public, and proved so productive to Millar, the publisher, that he handsomely added 100*l.* to 600*l.*, for which he had purchased the work from the author.

The general merits of this popular and delightful work have been so often dwelt upon, and its imperfections so frequently censured, that we can do little more than hastily run over ground which has been so repeatedly occupied. The felicitous contrivance and happy extrication of the story, where every incident tells upon and advances the catastrophe, while, at the same time, it illustrates the characters of those interested in its approach, cannot too often be mentioned with the highest approbation. The attention of the reader is never diverted or puzzled by unnecessary digressions, or recalled to the main story by abrupt and startling recurrences; he glides down the narrative like a boat on the surface of some broad navigable stream, which only winds enough to gratify the voyager with the varied beauty of its banks. One exception to this praise, otherwise so well merited, occurs in the story of the Old Man of the Hill; an episode, which, in compliance with a custom introduced by Cervantes, and followed by Le Sage, Fielding has thrust into the midst of his narrative, as he had formerly introduced the History of Leonora, equally unnecessarily and inartificially, into that of *Joseph Andrews*. It has also been wondered why Fielding should have chosen to leave the stain of illegitimacy on the birth of his hero; and it has been surmised that he did so in allusion to his own first wife, who was also a natural child.

A better reason may be discovered in the story itself; for, had Miss Bridget been privately married to the father of Tom Jones, there could have been no adequate motive assigned for keeping his birth secret from a man so reasonable and compassionate as Allworthy.

But even the high praise due to the construction and arrangement of the story is inferior to that claimed by the truth, force, and spirit of the characters, from Tom Jones himself, down to Black George the game-keeper, and his family. Amongst these, Squire Western stands alone; imitated from no prototype, and in himself an inimitable picture of ignorance, prejudice, irascibility, and rusticity, united with natural shrewdness, constitutional good-humour, and an instinctive affection for his daughter—all which qualities, good and bad, are grounded upon that basis of thorough selfishness natural to one bred up from infancy where no one dared to contradict his arguments, or to control his conduct. In one incident alone, we think Fielding has departed from this admirable sketch. As an English squire, Western ought not to have taken a beating so unresistingly from the friend of Lord Fellamar. We half suspect that the passage is an interpolation. It is inconsistent with the squire's readiness to engage in rustic affrays. We grant a pistol or sword might have appalled him, but Squire Western should have yielded to no one in the use of the English horsewhip—and as, with all his brutalities, we have a sneaking interest in the honest, jolly country gentleman, we would willingly hope there is some mistake in this matter.

The character of Jones, otherwise a model of generosity, openness, manly spirit mingled with thoughtless dissipation, is in like manner unnecessarily degraded by the nature of his intercourse with Lady Bellaston; and this is one of the circumstances which incline us to believe that Fielding's ideas of what was gentleman-like and honourable, had sustained some depreciation, in consequence of the unhappy circumstances of his life, and of the society to which they condemned him.

A more sweeping and general objection was made against the *History of a Foundling* by the admirers of Richardson, and has been often repeated since. It is alleged that the ultimate moral of *Tom Jones*, which conducts to happiness, and holds up to our sympathy and esteem, a youth who gives way to licentious habits, is detrimental to society, and tends to encourage the youthful reader in the practice of those follies, to which his natural passions and the usual course of the world but too much direct him. French delicacy, which, on so many occasions, has strained at a gnat and swallowed a camel, saw this fatal tendency in the work, and, by an *arret*, discharged the circulation of a bungled abridgment by De la Place, entitled a translation. To this charge Fielding himself might probably have replied, that the vices into which Jones suffers himself to fall are made the direct cause of placing him in the distressful situation which he occupies during the greater part of the narrative: while his generosity, his charity, and his amiable qualities, become the means of saving him from the consequences of his folly. But we suspect, with Doctor Johnson, that there is something of cant both in the objection and in the answer to it. "Men," says that moralist, "will not become highwaymen because Macheath is acquitted on the stage;" and, we add, they will not become swindlers and thieves because they sympathize with the fortunes of the witty picaroon Gil Blas, or licentious debauchees, because they read *Tom Jones*. The professed moral of a piece is usually what the reader is least interested in; it is like the mendicant who cripples after some gay and splendid procession, and in vain solicits the attention of those who have been gazing upon it. Excluding from consideration those infamous works which address themselves directly to awakening the grosser passions of our nature, we are inclined to think the worst evil to be apprehended from the perusal of novels is, that the habit is apt to generate an indisposition to real history and useful literature; and that the best which can be hoped is, that they may sometimes instruct the youthful mind by real pictures of life, and sometimes awaken their better feelings and sympathies by strains of generous sentiments, and tales of fictitious wo. Beyond this point thay are a mere elegance, a luxury contrived for the amusement of polished life, and the gratification of that half love of literature which pervades all ranks in an advanced stage of society, and are read much more for amusement than with the least hope of deriving instruction from them. The vices and follies of Tom Jones are those which the world soon teaches to all who enter on the career of life, and to which society is unhappily but too indulgent; nor do we believe that, in any one instance, the perusal of Fielding's novel has added one libertine to the large list who would not have been such, had it never crossed the press. And it is with concern that we add our sincere belief, that the fine picture of frankness and generosity exhibited in that fictitious character has had as few imitators as the career of his follies. Let it not be supposed that we are indifferent to morality, because we treat with scorn that affectation which, while in common life it connives at the open practice of libertinism, pretends to detest the memory of an author who painted life as it was, with all its shades, and more than all the lights which it occasionally exhibits to relieve them. For particular passages of the work, the author can only be defended under the custom of his age, which permitted, in certain cases, much stronger language than ours. He has himself said that there is nothing which can offend the chastest eye in the perusal, and he spoke probably according to the ideas of his time. But, in modern estimation, there are several passages at which delicacy may justly take offence; and, we can only say, that they may be termed rather jocularly coarse than seductive, and that they are atoned for by the admirable mixture of wit and argument, by which, in others, the cause of true religion and virtue is supported and advanced.

Fielding considered his works as an experiment in British literature; and, therefore, he chose to prefix a preliminary chapter to each book, explanatory of his own views, and of the rules attached to this mode of composition. Those critical introductions, which rather interrupt the course of the story, and the flow of the interest at the first perusal, are found, on a second or third, the most entertaining chapters of the whole work.

The publication of *Tom Jones* carried Fielding's fame to its height; but seems to have been attended with no consequences to his fortune, beyond the temporary relief which the copy money afforded him. It was after this period that he published his proposal for making an effectual provision for the poor, formerly noticed, and a pamphlet relating to the mysterious case of the celebrated Elizabeth Canning, in which he adopted the cause of common sense against popular prejudice, and failed, in consequence, in the object of his publication.

Amelia was the author's last work of importance. It may be termed a continuation of Tom Jones, but we have not the same sympathy for the ungrateful and dissolute conduct of Booth, which we yield to the youthful follies of Jones. The character of Amelia is said to have been drawn for Fielding's second wife. If he put her patience, as has been alleged, to tests of the same kind, he has, in some degree, repaid her, by the picture he has drawn of her feminine delicacy and pure tenderness. Fielding's novels show few instances of pathos; it was, perhaps, inconsistent with the life which he was compelled to lead; for those who see most of human misery, become necessarily, in some degree, hardened to its effects. But few scenes of fictitious distress are more affecting than that in which Amelia is described as having made her little preparations for the evening, and sitting in anxious expectation of the return of her unworthy husband, whose folly is, in the mean time, preparing for her new scenes of misery. But our sympathy for the wife is disturbed by our dislike of her unthankful husband; and the tale is, on the whole, unpleasing, even though relieved by the humours of the doughty Colonel Bath, and the learned Dr. Harrison, characters drawn with such force and precision as Fielding alone knew how to employ.

Millar published *Amelia* in 1751. He had paid a thousand pounds for the copyright; and when he began to suspect that the work would be judged inferior to its predecessor, he employed the following stratagem to push it upon the trade. At a sale made to the booksellers, previous to the publication, Millar offered his friends his other publications on the usual terms of discount; but when he came to *Amelia*, he laid it aside, as a work in such demand, that he could not afford to deliver it to the trade in the usual manner. The *ruse* succeeded, the impression was anxiously bought up, and the bookseller relieved from every apprehension of a slow sale.

Notwithstanding former failures, Fielding, in 1752, commenced a new attempt at a literary newspaper and review, which he entitled the *Covent Garden Journal*, to be published twice a week, and conducted by Sir Alexander Drawcansir. It was the author's failing that he could not continue any plan of this nature, for which otherwise his ready pen, sharp wit, and classical knowledge, so highly fitted him, without involving himself in some of the party squabbles, or petty literary broils of the day. On the present occasion, he was not long ere he involved himself in a quarrel with Dr. Hill, and other periodical writers. Among the latter, we are sorry to particularize Smollett, although possessed of the most kindred genius to Fielding's, which has yet appeared in British literature. The warfare was of short duration, and neither party would obtain honour by an inquiry into the cause or conduct of its hostilities.

Meanwhile, Fielding's life was fast decaying; a complication of diseases had terminated in a dropsical habit, which totally undermined his strong constitution. The Duke of Newcastle, then prime minister, was desirous of receiving assistance from him in the formation of a plan for the remedy and prevention of secret robberies, and improving the police of the metropolis. For the small consideration of 600*l.*, paid by the government, Fielding engaged to extirpate several gangs of daring ruffians, which at this time infested London and its vicinity; and though his health was reduced to the last extremity, he continued himself to superintend the conduct of his agents, to take evidence, and make commitments, until this great object was attained.

These last exertions seem to have been fatal to his exhausted frame, which suffered at once under dropsy, and jaundice, and asthma. The Bath waters were tried in vain, and various modes of cure or alleviation were resorted to, of which tapping only appears to have succeeded to a certain extent. The medical attendants gave their last sad advice in recommending a milder climate. Of his departure for Lisbon, in conformity with their advice, he has himself left the following melancholy record, painting the man and his situation a thousand times better than any other pen could achieve.

"On this day, Wednesday, June 26th, 1754,"[1] he says, "the most melancholy sun I had ever beheld arose, and found me awake at my house at Fordhook. By the light of this sun I was, in my own opinion, last to behold and take leave of some of those creatures on whom I doated with a mother-like fondness, guided by nature and passion, and uncured and unhardened by all the doctrine of that philosophical school, where I had learned to bear pains, and to despise death. In this situation, as I could not conquer nature, I submitted entirely to her, and she made as great a fool of me, as she had ever done of any woman whatsoever; under pretence of giving me leave to enjoy, she drew me in to suffer the company of my little ones, during eight hours; and I doubt not whether, in that time, I did not undergo more than in all my distemper. At twelve precisely my coach was at the door, which was no sooner told me, than I kissed my children round, and went into it with some little resolution. My wife, who behaved more like a heroine and philosopher, though at the same time the tenderest mother in the world, and my eldest daughter, followed me. Some friends went with us, and others took their leave; and I heard my behaviour applauded, with many murmurs and praises, to which I well knew I had no title."

This affecting passage makes a part of his *Journey to Lisbon*, a work which he commenced during the voyage, with a hand trembling in almost its latest hour. It remains a singular example of Fielding's natural strength of mind, that, while struggling hard at once with the depression, and with the irritability of disease, he could still exhibit a few flashes of that bright wit, which could once set the "world" in a roar. His perception of character, and power of describing it, had not forsaken him in those sad moments; for the master of the ship in which he sailed, the scolding landlady of the Isle of Wight, the military coxcomb, who visits their vessel, are all portraits, marked with the master-hand which traced Parson Adams and Squire Western.

The *Journey to Lisbon* was abridged by fate. Fielding reached that city, indeed, alive, and remained there two months; but he was unable to continue his proposed literary labours. The hand of death was upon him, and seized upon his prey in the beginning of October, 1754. He died in the 48th year of his life, leaving behind him a widow, and four children, one of whom died soon afterwards. His brother Sir John Fielding, well known as a magistrate, aided by the bounty of Mr. Allen, made suitable provision for the survivors; but of their fate we are ignorant.

Thus lived and thus died, at a period of life when the world might have expected continued delight from his matured powers, the celebrated Henry Fielding, father of the English novel; and in his powers of strong and national humour, and forcible yet natural exhibition of character, unapproached, as yet, even by his successful followers.

Notes
1. *Voyage to Lisbon*, p. 1.

WILLIAM MAKEPEACE THACKERAY
From "Hogarth, Smollett, and Fielding"
The English Humourists of the Eighteenth Century

1853

I cannot offer or hope to make a hero of Harry Fielding. Why hide his faults? Why conceal his weaknesses in a cloud of periphrases? Why not show him, like him as he is, not robed in a marble toga, and draped and polished in an heroic attitude, but with inked ruffles, and claret-stains on his tarnished laced coat, and on his manly face the marks of good-fellowship, of illness, of kindness, of care, and wine. Stained as you see him, and worn by care and dissipation, that man retains some of the most precious and splendid human qualities and endowments. He has an admirable natural love of truth, the keenest instinctive antipathy to hypocrisy, the happiest satirical gift of laughing it to scorn. His wit is wonderfully wise and detective; it flashes upon a rogue and lightens up a rascal like a policeman's lantern. He is one of the manliest and kindliest of human beings: in the midst of all his imperfections, he respects female innocence and infantine tenderness, as you would suppose such a great-hearted, courageous soul would respect and care for them. He could not be so brave, generous, truth-telling as he is, were he not infinitely merciful, pitiful, and tender. He will give any man his purse— he can't help kindness and profusion. He may have low tastes, but not a mean mind; he admires with all his heart good and virtuous men, stoops to no flattery, bears no rancour, disdains all disloyal arts, does his public duty uprightly, is fondly loved by his family, and dies at his work.[1]

If that theory be—and I have no doubt it is—the right and safe one, that human nature is always pleased with the spectacle of innocence rescued by fidelity, purity, and courage; I suppose that of the heroes of Fielding's three novels, we should like honest Joseph Andrews the best, and Captain Booth the second, and Tom Jones the third.[2]

Joseph Andrews, though he wears Lady Booby's cast-off livery, is, I think, to the full as polite as Tom Jones in his fustian-suit, or Captain Booth in regimentals. He has, like those heroes, large calves, broad shoulders, a high courage, and a handsome face. The accounts of Joseph's bravery and good qualities; his voice, too musical to halloo to the dogs; his bravery in riding races for the gentlemen of the county, and his constancy in refusing bribes and temptation, have something affecting in their *naïveté* and freshness, and prepossess one in favour of that handsome young hero. The rustic bloom of Fanny, and the delightful simplicity of Parson Adams, are described with a friendliness which wins the reader of their story; we part from them with more regret than from Booth and Jones.

Fielding, no doubt, began to write this novel in ridicule of *Pamela*, for which work one can understand the hearty contempt and antipathy which such an athletic and boisterous genius as Fielding's must have entertained. He couldn't do otherwise than laugh at the puny cockney bookseller, pouring out endless volumes of sentimental twaddle, and hold him up to scorn as a mollcoddle and a milksop. *His* genius had been nursed on sack-posset, and not on dishes of tea. *His* muse had sung the loudest in tavern choruses, had seen the daylight streaming in over thousands of emptied bowls, and reeled home to chambers on the shoulders of the watchman. Richardson's goddess was attended by old maids and dowagers, and fed on muffins and bohea. "Milksop!" roars Harry

Fielding, clattering at the timid shop-shutters. "Wretch! Monster! Mohock!" shrieks the sentimental author of "Pamela;"[3] and all the ladies of his court cackle out an affrighted chorus. Fielding proposes to write a book in ridicule of the author, whom he disliked and utterly scorned and laughted at; but he is himself so generous, jovial, and kindly a turn that he begins to like the characters which he invents, can't help making them manly and pleasant as well as ridiculous, and before he has done with them all, loves them heartily every one.

Richardson's sickening antipathy for Harry Fielding is quite as natural as the other's laughter and contempt at the sentimentalist. I have not learned that these likings and dislikings have ceased in the present day: and every author must lay his account not only to misrepresentation, but to honest enmity among critics, and to being hated and abused for good as well as for bad reasons. Richardson disliked Fielding's works quite honestly: Walpole quite honestly spoke of them as vulgar and stupid. Their squeamish stomachs sickened at the rough fare and the rough guests assembled at Fielding's jolly revel. Indeed the cloth might have been cleaner: and the dinner and the company were scarce such as suited a dandy. The kind and wise old Johnson would not sit down with him.[4] But a greater scholar than Johnson could afford to admire that astonishing genius of Harry Fielding: and we all know the lofty panegyric which Gibbon wrote of him, and which remains a towering monument to the great novelist's memory. "Our immortal Fielding," Gibbon writes, "was of the younger branch of the Earls of Denbigh, who drew their origin from the Counts of Hapsburgh. The successors of Charles V. may disdain their brethren of England: but the romance of *Tom Jones*, that exquisite picture of humour and manners, will outlive the palace of the Escurial and the Imperial Eagle of Austria."

There can be no gainsaying the sentence of this great judge. To have your name mentioned by Gibbon, is like having it written on the dome of St. Peter's. Pilgrims from all the world admire and behold it.

As a picture of manners, the novel of *Tom Jones* is indeed exquisite: as a work of construction quite a wonder: the by-play of wisdom; the power of observation, the multiple felicitous turns and thoughts; the varied character of the great Comic Epic: keep the reader in a perpetual admiration and curiosity. But against Mr. Thomas Jones himself we have a right to put in a protest, and quarrel with the esteem the author evidently has for that character. Charles Lamb says finely of Jones, that a single hearty laugh from him "clears the air"—but then it is in a certain state of the atmosphere. It might clear the air when such personages as Blifil or Lady Bellaston poison it. But I fear very much that (except until the very last scene of the story), when Mr. Jones enters Sophia's drawing-room, the pure air there is rather tainted with the young gentleman's tobacco-pipe and punch. I can't say that I think Mr. Jones a virtuous character; I can't say but that I think Fielding's evident liking and admiration for Mr. Jones shows that the great humourist's moral sense was blunted by his life, and that here, in Art and Ethics, there is a great error. If it is right to have a hero whom we may admire, let us at least take care that he is admirable: if, as is the plan of some authors (a plan decidedly against their interests, be it said), it is propounded that there exists in life no such being, and therefore that in novels, the picture of life, there should appear no such character; then Mr. Thomas Jones becomes an admissible person, and we examine his defects and good qualities, as we do those of Parson Thwackum, or Miss Seagrim. But a hero with a flawed reputation; a hero spunging for a guinea; a hero who can't pay his landlady, and is obliged

to let his honour out to hire, is absurd, and his claim to heroic rank untenable. I protest against Mr. Thomas Jones holding such rank at all. I protest even against his being considered a more than ordinary young fellow, ruddy-cheeked, broad-shouldered, and fond of wine and pleasure. He would not rob a church, but that is all; and a pretty long argument may be debated, as to which of these old types, the spendthrift, the hypocrite, Jones and Blifil, Charles and Joseph Surface,—is the worst member of society and the most deserving of censure. The prodigal Captain Booth is a better man than his predecessor Mr. Jones, in so far as he thinks much more humbly of himself than Jones did: goes down on his knees, and owns his weaknesses, and cries out, "Not for my sake, but for the sake of my pure and sweet and beautiful wife Amelia, I pray you, O critical reader, to forgive me." That stern moralist regards him from the bench (the judge's practice out of court is not here the question), and says, "Captain Booth, it is perfectly true that your life has been disreputable, and that on many occasions you have shown yourself to be no better than a scamp—you have been tippling at the tavern, when the kindest and sweetest lady in the world has cooked your little supper of boiled mutton and awaited you all the night; you have spoilt the little dish of boiled mutton thereby, and caused pangs and pains to Amelia's tender heart.[5] You have got into debt without the means of paying it. You have gambled the money with which you ought to have paid your rent. You have spent in drink or in worse amusements the sums which your poor wife has raised upon her little home treasures, her own ornaments, and the toys of her children. But, you rascal! you own humbly that you are no better than you should be; you never for one moment pretend that you are anything but a miserable weak-minded rogue. You do in your heart adore that angelic woman, your wife, and for her sake, sirrah, you shall have your discharge. Lucky for you and for others like you, that in spite of your failings and imperfections, pure hearts pity and love you. For your wife's sake you are permitted to go hence without a remand; and I beg you, by the way, to carry to that angelical lady the expression of the cordial respect and admiration of this court." Amelia pleads for her husband, Will Booth: Amelia pleads for her reckless kindly old father, Harry Fielding. To have invented that character, is not only a triumph of art, but it is a good action. They say it was in his own home that Fielding knew her and loved her: and from his own wife that he drew the most charming character in English fiction. Fiction! why fiction? why not history? I know Amelia just as well as Lady Mary Wortley Montagu. I believe in Colonel Bath almost as much as in Colonel Gardiner or the Duke of Cumberland. I admire the author of "Amelia," and thank the kind master who introduced me to that sweet and delightful companion and friend. *Amelia* perhaps is not a better story than *Tom Jones*, but it has the better ethics; the prodigal repents at least, before forgiveness,—whereas the odious broad-backed Mr. Jones carries off his beauty with scarce an interval of remorse for his manifold errors and shortcomings; and is not half punished enough before the great prize of fortune and love falls to his share. I am angry with Jones. Too much of the plum-cake and rewards of life fall to that boisterous, swaggering young scapegrace. Sophia actually surrenders without a proper sense of decorum; the fond, foolish, palpitating little creature!—"Indeed, Mr. Jones," she says,—"it rests with you to appoint the day." I suppose Sophia is drawn from life as well as Amelia; and many a young fellow, no better than Mr. Thomas Jones, has carried by a *coup de main* the heart of many a kind girl who was a great deal too good for him.

What a wonderful art! What an admirable gift of nature

was it by which the author of these tales was endowed, and which enabled him to fix our interest, to waken our sympathy, to seize upon our credulity, so that we believe in his people—speculate gravely upon their faults or their excellences, prefer this one or that, deplore Jones's fondness for drink and play, Booth's fondness for play and drink, and the unfortunate position of the wives of both gentlemen—love and admire those ladies with all our hearts, and talk about them as faithfully as if we had breakfasted with them this morning in their actual drawing-rooms, or should meet them this afternoon in the Park! What a genius! what a vigour! what a bright-eyed intelligence and observation! what a wholesome hatred for meanness and knavery! what a vast sympathy! what a cheerfulness! what a manly relish of life! what a love of human kind! what a poet is here!—watching, meditating, brooding, creating! What multitudes of truths has that man left behind him! What generations he has taught to laugh wisely and fairly! What scholars he has formed and accustomed to the exercise of thoughtful humour and the manly play of wit! What a courage he had! What a dauntless and constant cheerfulness of intellect, that burned bright and steady through all the storms of his life, and never deserted its last wreck! It is wonderful to think of the pains and misery which the man suffered; the pressure of want, illness, remorse which he endured; and that the writer was neither malignant nor melancholy, his view of truth never warped, and his generous human kindness never surrendered.

In the quarrel mentioned before, which happened on Fielding's last voyage to Lisbon, and when the stout captain of the ship fell down on his knees and asked the sick man's pardon—"I did not suffer," Fielding says, in his hearty, manly way, his eyes lighting up as it were with their old fire—"I did not suffer a brave man and an old man to remain a moment in that posture, but immediately forgave him." Indeed, I think, with his noble spirit and unconquerable generosity, Fielding reminds one of those brave men of whom one reads in stories of English shipwrecks and disasters—of the officer on the African shore, when disease has destroyed the crew, and he himself is seized by fever, who throws the lead with a death-stricken hand, takes the soundings, carries the ship out of the river or off the dangerous coast, and dies in the manly endeavour—of the wounded captain, when the vessel founders, who never loses his heart, who eyes the danger steadily, and has a cheery word for all, until the inevitable fate overwhelms him, and the gallant ship goes down. Such a brave and gentle heart, such an intrepid and courageous spirit, I love to recognize in the manly, the English Harry Fielding.

Notes

1. He sailed for Lisbon, from Gravesend, on Sunday morning, June 30th, 1754; and began *The Journal of a Voyage* during the passage. He died at Lisbon, in the beginning of October of the same year. He lies buried there, in the English Protestant churchyard, near the Estrella Church, with this inscription over him:—
HENRICUS FIELDING.
LUGET BRITANNIA GREMIO NON DATUM
FOVERE NATUM
2. Fielding himself is said by Dr. Warton to have preferred *Joseph Andrews* to his other writings.
3. "Richardson," says a worthy Mrs. Barbauld, in her Memoir of him, prefixed to his Correspondence, "was exceedingly hurt at this (*Joseph Andrews*), the more so as they had been on good terms, and he was very intimate with Fielding's two sisters. He never appears cordially to have forgiven it (perhaps it was not in human nature he should), and he always speaks in his letters with a great deal of asperity of *Tom Jones*, more indeed than was quite graceful in a rival author. No doubt he himself thought his indignation was solely

excited by the loose morality of the work and of its author, but he could tolerate Cibber."
4. It must always be borne in mind, that besides that the Doctor couldn't be expected to like Fielding's wild life (to say nothing of the fact that they were of opposite sides in politics), Richardson was one of his earliest and kindest friends. Yet Johnson too (as Boswell tells us) read *Amelia* through without stopping.
5. Fielding's first wife was Miss Craddock, a young lady from Salisbury, with a fortune of 1,500*l.*, whom he married in 1736. About the same time he succeeded, himself, to an estate of 200*l.* per annum, and on the joint amount he lived for some time as a splendid country gentleman in Dorsetshire. Three years brought him to the end of his fortune; when he returned to London, and became a student of law.

HIPPOLYTE TAINE
From "Fielding"
History of English Literature
tr. H. Van Laun
1871, Book 3, Chapter 6

Fielding protests on behalf of nature; and certainly, to see his actions and his persons, we might think him made expressly for that; a robust, strongly-built man, above six feet high, sanguine, with an excess of good humor and animal spirits, loyal, generous, affectionate, and brave, but imprudent, extravagant, a drinker, a royster, ruined as it were by heirloom, having seen the ups and downs of life, bespattered, but always jolly. Lady Wortley Montague says of him: "His happy constitution made him forget everything when he was before a venison pasty, or over a flask of champagne."[1] Nature sways him; he is somewhat coarse but generous. He does not restrain himself, he indulges, he follows nature's bent, not too choice in his course, not confining himself to banks, muddy, but abundantly and in a broad channel. From the outset an abundance of health and physical impetuosity plunges him into gross jovial excess, and the immoderate sap of youth bubbles up in him until he marries and becomes ripe in years. He is gay, and seeks gayety; he is careless, and has not even literary vanity. One day Garrick begged him to cut down an awkward scene, and told him "that a repulse would flurry him so much, he should not be able to do justice to the part." "If the scene is not a good one, let them find that out." Just as was foreseen, the house made a violent uproar, and the performer tried to quell it by retiring to the green-room, where the author was supporting his spirits with a bottle of champagne. "What is the matter, Garrick? are they hissing me now?" "Yes, just the same passage that I wanted you to retrench." "Oh," replied the author, "I did not give them credit for it; they have found it out, have they?"[2] In this easy manner he took all mischance. He went ahead without feeling the bruises much, like a confident man, whose heart expands and whose skin is thick. When he inherited some money, he feasted, gave dinners to his neighbors, kept a pack of hounds and a lot of magnificent lackeys in yellow livery. In three years he had spent it all; but courage remained, he finished his law studies, wrote two folios on the rights of the crown, became a magistrate, destroyed bands of robbers, and earned in the most insipid of labors "the dirtiest money upon earth." Disgust, weariness did not affect him; he was too solidly made to have the nerves of a woman. Force, activity, invention, tenderness, all overflowed in him. He had a mother's fondness for his children, adored his wife, became almost mad when he lost her, found no other consolation than to weep with his maid-servant, and ended by marrying that good and honest girl, that he might give a mother to his children; the last trait in the portrait of this valiant plebeian heart, quick in telling all, possessing no dislikes, but all the best parts of man, except delicacy. We read his books as we drink a pure, wholesome, and rough wine, which cheers and fortifies us, and which wants nothing but bouquet.

Such a man was sure to dislike Richardson. He who loves expansive and liberal nature, drives from him like foes the solemnity, sadness, and pruderies of the Puritans. To begin with, he caricatures Richardson. His first hero, Joseph, is the brother of Pamela, and resists the proposals of his mistress, as Pamela does those of her master. The temptation, touching in the case of a girl, becomes comical in that of a young man, and the tragic turns into the grotesque. Fielding laughs heartily, like Rabelais, like Scarron. He imitates the emphatic style; ruffles the petticoats and bobs the wigs; upsets with his rude jests all the seriousness of conventionality. If you are refined, or simply well dressed, don't go along with him. He will take you to prisons, inns, dunghills, the mud of the roadside; he will make you flounder among rollicking, scandalous, vulgar adventures, and crude pictures. He has plenty of words at command, and his sense of smell is not delicate. Mr. Joseph Andrews, after leaving Lady Booby, is felled to the ground, left naked in a ditch, for dead; a stagecoach came by; a lady objects to receive a naked man inside; and the gentleman, "though there were several greatcoats about the coach," could not spare them; the coachman, who had two greatcoats spread under him, refused to lend either, lest they should be made bloody.[3] This is but the outset, judge of the rest. Joseph and his friend, the good Parson Adams, give and receive a vast number of cuffs; blows resound; cans of pigs' blood are thrown at their heads; dogs tear their clothes to pieces; they lose their horse. Joseph is so good-looking, that he is assailed by the maid-servant, "obliged to take her in his arms and to shut her out of the room;"[4] they have never any money; they are threatened with being sent to prison. Yet they go on in a merry fashion, as their brothers in Fielding's other novels, Captain Booth and Tom Jones. These hailstorms of blows, these tavern brawls, this noise of broken warming-pans and basins flung at heads, this medley of incidents and downpouring of mishaps, combine to make the most joyous music. All these honest folk fight well, walk well, eat well, drink still better. It is a pleasure to observe these potent stomachs; roast-beef goes down into them as to its natural place. Do not say that these good arms practice too much on their neighbors' skins: the neighbors' hides are healthy, and always heal quickly. Decidedly life is a good thing, and we will go along with Fielding, smiling by the way, with a broken head and a bellyful.

Shall we merely laugh? There are many things to be seen on our journey: the sentiment of nature is a talent, like the understanding of certain rules; and Fielding, turning his back on Richardson, opens up a domain as wide as that of his rival. What we call nature is this brood of secret passions, often malicious, generally vulgar, always blind, which tremble and fret within us, ill-covered by the cloak of decency and reason under which we try to disguise them; we think we lead them, and they lead us; we think our actions our own, they are theirs. They are so many, so strong, so interwoven, so ready to rise, break forth, be carried away, that their movements elude all our reasoning and our grasp. This is Fielding's domain; his art and pleasure, like Molière's, are in lifting a corner of the cloak; his characters parade with a rational air, and suddenly, through a vista, the reader perceives the inner turmoil of vanities, follies, lusts, and secret rancors which make them move.

Thus, when Tom Jones' arm is broken, philosopher Square comes to console him by an application of stoical maxims; but to prove to him that pain is an indifferent matter, he bites his tongue, and lets slip an oath or two; whereupon Parson Thwackum, his opponent and rival, assures him that his mishap is a warning of Providence, and both are nearly coming to blows.[5] Another time, the prison chaplain having aired his eloquence, and entreated the condemned man to repent, accepts from him a bowl of punch, because Scripture says nothing against this liquor; and after drinking, repeats his last sermon against the pagan philosophers. Thus unveiled, natural impulse has a grotesque appearance; the people advance gravely, cane in hand, but in our eyes they are all naked. Understand, they are every whit naked; and some of their attitudes are very lively. Ladies will do well not to enter here. This powerful genius, frank and joyous, loves boisterous fairs like Rubens; the red faces, beaming with good humor, sensuality, and energy, move about his pages, flutter hither and thither, and jostle each other, and their overflowing instincts break forth in violent actions. Out of such he creates his chief characters. He has none more lifelike than these, more broadly sketched in bold and dashing outline, with a more wholesome color. If sober people like Allworthy remain in a corner of his vast canvas, characters full of natural impulse, like Western, stand out with a relief and brightness, never seen since Falstaff. Western is a country squire, a good fellow in the main, but a drunkard, always in the saddle, full of oaths, ready with coarse language, blows, a sort of dull carter, hardened and excited by the brutality of the race, the wildness of a country life, by violent exercises, by abuse of coarse food and strong drink, full of English and rustic pride and prejudice, having never been disciplined by the constraint of the world, because he lives in the country; nor by that of education, since he can hardly read; nor of reflection, since he cannot put two ideas together; nor of authority, because he is rich and a justice of the peace, and given up like a noisy and creaking weathercock, to every gust of passion. When contradicted, he grows red, foams at the mouth, wishes to thrash some one. "Doff thy clothes." They are even obliged to stop him by main force. He hastens to go to Allworthy to complain of Tom Jones, who has dared to fall in love with his daughter:

> It's well for un I could not get at un: I'd a licked un: I'd a spoiled his caterwauling; I'd a taught the son of a whore to meddle with meat for his master. He shan't ever have a morsel of meat of mine, or a varden to buy it. If she will ha un, one smock shall be her portion. I'd sooner give my estate to the sinking fund, that it may be sent to Hanover, to corrupt our nation with.[6]

Allworthy says he is very sorry for it:

> Pox o' your sorrow. It will do me abundance of good, when I have lost my only child, my poor Sophy, that was the joy of my heart, and all the hope and comfort of my age. But I am resolved I will turn her out o' doors; she shall beg, and starve, and rot in the streets. Not one hapenny, not a hapenny shall she ever hae o' mine. The son of a bitch was always good at finding a hare sitting and be rotted to'n; I little thought what puss he was looking after. But it shall be the worst he ever vound in his life. She shall be no better than carrion; the skin o'er it all he shall ha, and zu you may tell un.[7]

His daughter tries to reason with him; he storms. Then she speaks of tenderness and obedience; he leaps about the room for joy, and tears come to his eyes. Then she recommences her prayers; he grinds his teeth, clinches his fists, stamps his feet:

> I am determined upon this match, and ha him you shall, damn me, if shat unt. Damn me, if shat unt, though dost hang thyself the next morning. [8]

He can find no reason; he can only tell her to be a good girl. He contradicts himself, defeats his own plans; is like a blind bull, which butts to right and left, doubles on his path, touches no one, and paws the ground. At the least sound he rushes head foremost, offensively, knowing not why. His ideas are only starts or transports of flesh and blood. Never has the animal so completely covered and absorbed the man. It makes him grotesque; he is so natural and so brute-like: he allows himself to be led, and speaks like a child. He says:

> I don't know how 'tis, but, Allworthy, you make me do always just as you please; and yet I have as good an estate as you, and am in the commission of the peace just as yourself. [9]

Nothing holds or lasts with him; he is impulsive in everything; he lives but for the moment. Rancor, interest, no passions of long continuance affect him. He embraces people whom he just before wanted to knock down. Everything with him disappears in the fire of the passion of the hour, which comes over his brain, as it were, in sudden waves, which drown the rest. Now that he is reconciled to Tom, he cannot rest until Tom marries his daughter:

> To her, boy, to her, go to her. That's it, little honeys, O that's it. Well, what, is it all over? Hath she appointed the day, boy? What, shall it be to-morrow or next day? I shan't be put off a minute longer than next day, I am resolved. . . . I tell thee it is all flimflam. Zoodikers! she'd have the wedding to-night with all her heart. Would'st not, Sophy? . . . Where the devil is Allworthy? . . . Harkee, Allworthy, I bet thee five pounds to a crown, we have a boy to-morrow nine months. But prithee, tell me what wut ha? Wut ha Burgundy, Champagne, or what? For please Jupiter, we'll make a night on't. [10]

And when he becomes a grandfather, he spends his time in the nursery, "where he declares the tattling of his little granddaughter, who is above a year and a half old, is sweeter music than the finest cry of dogs in England."[11] This is pure nature, and no one has displayed it more free, more impetuous, ignoring all rule, more abandoned to physical passions, than Fielding.

It is not because he loves it like the great impartial artists, Shakspeare and Goethe; on the contrary, he is eminently a moralist; and it is one of the great marks of the age, that reformatory designs are as decided with him as with others. He gives his fictions a practical aim, and commends them by saying that the serious and tragic tone sours, whilst the comic style disposes men to be "more full of good humour and benevolence."[12] Moreover, he satirizes vice; he looks upon the passions not as simple forces, but as objects of approbation or blame. At every step he suggests moral conclusions; he wants us to take sides; he discusses, excuses, or condemns. He writes an entire novel in an ironical style,[13] to attack and destroy rascality and treason. He is more than a painter, he is a judge, and the two parts agree in him. For a psychology produces a morality: where there is an idea of man, there is an ideal of man; and Fielding, who has seen in man nature as opposed to law, praises in man nature as opposed to law; so that, according to him, virtue is but an instinct. Generosity in his eyes is, like all sources of action, a primitive inclination; like all sources of

action, it flows on, receiving no good from catechisms and phrases; like all sources of action, it flows at times too copious and quick. Take it as it is, and do not try to oppress it under a discipline, or to replace it by an argument. Mr. Richardson, your heroes, so correct, constrained, so carefully made up with their impedimenta of maxims, are cathedral vergers, of use but to drone in a procession. Square or Thwackum, your tirades on philosophical or Christian virtue are mere words, only fit to be heard after dinner. Virtue is in the mood and the blood; a gossipy education and cloistral severity do not assist it. Give me a man, not a show-mannikin or a mere machine, to spout phrases. My hero is the man who is born generous, as a dog is born affectionate, and a horse brave. I want a living heart, full of warmth and force, not a dry pedant, bent on squaring all his actions. This ardent character will perhaps carry the hero too far; I pardon his escapades. He will get drunk unawares; he will pick up a girl on his way; he will hit out with a zest; he will not refuse a duel; he will suffer a fine lady to appreciate him, and will accept her purse; he will be imprudent, will injure his reputation, like Tom Jones; he will be a bad manager, and will get into debt, like Booth. Pardon him for having muscles, nerves, senses, and that overflow of anger or ardor which urges forward animals of a noble breed. But he will let himself be beaten till he bleeds, before he betrays a poor gamekeeper. He will pardon his mortal enemy readily, from sheer kindness, and will send him money secretly. He will be loyal to his mistress, and will be faithful to her, spite of all offers, in the worst destitution, and without the least hope of winning her. He will be liberal with his purse, his trouble, his sufferings, his blood; he will not boast of it; he will have neither pride, vanity, affectation, nor dissimulation; bravery and kindness will abound in his heart, as good water in a good spring. He may be stupid, like Captain Booth, a gambler, even extravagant, unable to manage his affairs, liable one day through temptation to be unfaithful to his wife; but he will be so sincere in his repentance, his error will be so involuntary, he will be so carefully, genuinely tender, that she will love him exceedingly,[14] and in good truth he will deserve it. He will be a nurse to her when she is ill, behave as a mother to her; he will himself see to her lying-in; he will feel towards her the adoration of a lover, always, before all the world, even before Miss Matthews, who seduced him. He says: "If I had the world, I was ready to lay it at my Amelia's feet; and so, Heaven knows, I would ten thousand worlds."[15] He weeps like a child on thinking of her; he listens to her like a little child. "I believe I am able to recollect much the greatest part (of what she uttered); for the impression is never to be effaced from my memory."[16] "He dressed himself, with all the expedition imaginable, singing, whistling, hurrying, attempting by every method to banish thought,"[17] and galloped away because he cannot endure her tears. In this soldier's body, under this brawler's thick breastplate, there is a true woman's heart, which melts, which a trifle disturbs, when she whom he loves is in question; timid in its tenderness, inexhaustible in devotion, in trust, in self-denial, in the communication of its feelings. When a man possesses this, overlook the rest; with all his excesses and his follies, he is better than your well-dressed devotees.

To this we reply: You do well to defend nature, but let it be on condition that you suppress nothing. One thing is wanted in your strongly-built folks—refinement; the delicate dreams, enthusiastic elevation, and trembling delicacy, exist in nature equally with coarse vigor, noisy hilarity, and frank kindness. Poetry is true, like prose; and if there are eaters and boxers, there are also knights and artists. Cervantes, whom you imitate, and Shakespeare, whom you recall, had this refinement, and they have painted it; in this abundant harvest, with which you fill your arms, you have forgotten the flowers. We tire at last of your fisticuffs and tavern bills. You flounder too readily in cowhouses, among the ecclesiastical pigs of Parson Trulliber. We would fain see you have more regard for the modesty of your heroines; wayside accidents raise their tuckers too often; and Fanny, Sophia, Mrs. Heartfree, may continue pure, yet we cannot help remembering the assaults which have lifted their petticoats. You are so rude yourself, that you are insensible to what is atrocious. You persuade Tom Jones falsely, yet for an instant, that Mrs. Waters, whom he has made his mistress, is his mother, and you leave the reader long buried in the shame of this supposition. And then you are obliged to become unnatural in order to depict love; you can give but constrained letters; the transports of your Tom Jones are only the author's phrases. For want of ideas he declaims odes. You are only aware of the impetuosity of the senses, the upwelling of the blood, the effusion of tenderness, but not of the nervous exaltation and poetic rapture. Man, such as you conceive him, is a good buffalo; and perhaps he is the hero required by a people which is itself called John Bull.

Notes

1. *Lady Montague's Letters*, ed. Lord Wharncliffe, 2d ed. 3 vols. 1837; Letter to the Countess of Bute, iii. 120.
2. Roscoe's *Life of Fielding*, p. xxv.
3. *The Adventures of Joseph Andrews*, bk. i. ch. xii.
4. Ibid. i. ch. xviii.
5. *History of a Foundling*, bk. v. ch. ii.
6. *History of a Foundling*, bk. vi. ch. x.
7. Ibid.
8. Ibid. xvi. ch. ii.
9. *History of a Foundling*, xviii. ch. ix.
10. Ibid. xviii. ch. xii.
11. Last chapter of the *History of a Foundling*.
12. Preface to *Joseph Andrews*.
13. *Jonathan Wilde*.
14. Amelia is the perfect English wife, an excellent cook, so devoted as to pardon her husband his accidental infidelities, always looking forward to the accoucheur. She says even (bk. iv. ch. vi.) "Dear Billy, though my understanding be much inferior to yours," etc. She is excessively modest, always blushing and tender. Bagillard having written her some love-letters, she throws them away, and says (bk. iii. ch. ix.): "I would not have such a letter in my possession for the universe; I thought my eyes contaminated with reading it."
15. *Amelia*, bk. ii. ch. viii.
16. Ibid. bk. iii. ch. i.
17. Ibid. bk. iii. ch. ii.

CHARLES COWDEN CLARKE
From "On the Comic Writers of England: XIV. Fielding, Smollett and Sterne"

Gentleman's Magazine, May 1872, pp. 556–65

The anecdote is upon record, that when Reynolds first met with Johnson's *Life of Savage*, he commenced reading it with one elbow resting on the mantel-piece, and that he never moved from that position till he had finished the biography, when he found his arm so benumbed as to be scarcely able to move it. It were difficult to conceive of even few circumstances more gratifying to the honest self-love of an author than the record of such a fact, coming, too, from a man possessing the graceful perception and cultivated understanding of the

first President of our Academy of Painting. As a pendant to the above anecdote, I was acquainted with an old gentleman who told me that when he received the "New Novel" of *Tom Jones* from his bookseller, he never left his seat till he closed the last volume at the last page: and no wonder, for it is a story of a life that grapples the attention of the reader—particularly the English reader—"with hooks of steel;" for no novelist before him, and but few of eminence after him, have been so thoroughly indigenous in scene, in character, in feeling, and in manners, as Fielding; and not only are all his novels thoroughly English, but they are as thoroughly *his own*. In reading them, we feel as if they were the social and domestic history of the early part of the last century; and there can be little doubt that such is the case, for Fielding drew all his characters from the life, his plots from his own invention; and these are almost equal in merit to the other, for I suppose that no one, from his own to the present day, when reading the book, ever anticipated the origin of Tom Jones. He must, indeed, have been a "wise child" could he, or any one else, have guessed the Foundling's father *or* mother; and yet the ease and natural development of the story are such, there is so little of the artifice, the machinery of plot in it, that it has all the effect of certainly a romantic, but yet of a true biography. In reading the novels of Fielding, and tracing his characters, we never catch ourselves exclaiming, "Oh, that is very improbable, that character is much overdrawn!" Even his Parson Adams (perhaps the most fanciful in all his gallery of portraits) is nevertheless a *vera effigies*; and I, in my contracted worldly experience, could have closely paralleled that original for an almost incredible homeliness and simplicity of mind, and he also a Christian minister. It is hazardous to pronounce what character is improbable, what combination monstrous. The "yarn of our life is so mingled," we have all so many antagonistic and contradictory qualities, that that artist draws the most natural character who is not over anxious about its uniformity in good or evil.

Not only, however, is Fielding distinguished by the fidelity of his characters, but with an almost prophetic inspiration he reveals to us the penetralia of the human heart, its secret and profound movements, with the causes and consequences of volition and action. Moreover, with that expanded knowledge and experience, he constantly exhibits a strong sympathy with his species, and which, with his great master (Shakespeare) he ratifies by insisting upon the redeeming presence of "good in things evil." The most enlarged and the soundest in knowledge are ever tolerant of the defects and infirmities of others. So accurate, so natural, in short, are Fielding's charts of characters, that it has been urged by some that he must have had his materials ready-made to his hands, as Defoe is said to have had with many of his extraordinary histories and biographies. Indeed there is little doubt that he had, and amply did he avail himself of his resources, and so has every one who has an eye in his head, and a head to concoct and record all that he perceives transacting around him. The great book of Nature is open to us all to copy from, and all the human characters that we see emblazoned in works of fiction are only just so many copies of what the writers have witnessed in real life, as the same writers describe the scenery appropriate to the circumstances associate and congenial with the time and action of their characters. Every writer of fiction selects for the purpose of his story persons whom he has seen and noted in real life. The merit consists in causing the persons to talk like themselves. That is the only "invention" in a novelist (after his plot), and very great *is* that invention—the greater, of course, the more nearly the ideas and the order of language harmonise with the order of character. As there is "nothing new under the sun" in human character; all is but an endless system of permutation; so, when we say of any newly-introduced individual in a novel, "That is an original character," it is but one more in the long train of beings that has hitherto escaped the graphic eye of the historian. It will readily be believed that there is no intention to depreciate the merits of a man like Fielding; for, after all, the seeing and the recording of that which we have seen constitute the talent of the artist; the more faithfully, the more meritorious the transmission.

Fielding, in his public capacity of magistrate, as well as in the public career he pursued, had an infinite variety of characters come under his notice; and his order of mind and natural tendency being that of studying the evolutions of human action, the whole animus of his genius was directed to that order of delineation. Hence is to be noticed in his novels how very meagre are his descriptions of scenery, particularly of rural scenery. Compare them with Walter Scott's, whose order of mind was absolutely panoramic. Scott was a true poet. Fielding had very little *external* imagination, and even less fancy; he never went out of the scenes in which he had been accustomed to move. He busied himself solely with human nature; and rarely has any one turned his studies to more ample account than he. Its principles, and general, intimate, and remote feelings, acting under particular circumstances and impressions, moved him to an intense degree. They were ever present with him; and, as Hazlitt has well observed, "he makes use of incident and situation only to bring out character." Instances of these might be enumerated to a remarkable extent. In *Tom Jones* alone they recur constantly. In all the collisions between Squire Western and Sophia, his utter incapacity in the first instance to conceive that his daughter should or could fall in love with Tom Jones; his fury against him for daring so bold a flight as the aspiring to her heart; his coarse and insane denunciations of her for daring to make her own election; his scouring the country after her when she has eloped, with that clever touch of the wild animal instinct in him; leaving the pursuit of her (whom he most loves upon earth—after himself) when he hears the cry of the hounds, in order that he may join in the fox-chase; his swine-like obstinacy and tyranny being perfectly consistent with his love of his daughter; but even that subservient to his passion for hunting. And at the close of the history, when matters have been cleared to the hero's advantage, and he has received the consent of the Squire to claim his daughter's hand, the transport of his rage upon finding that now that daughter has an objection of her own against the man for whom she formerly had asserted her right of preference in contradiction to his will, he having no idea of any will being superior to his own on this side of Omnipotence; and he has, indeed, but a limited idea of any thing beyond the circle of his own fireside and his dog-kennel, in both spheres wherein he reigns autocrat.

Again, the elegant squabbles we are entertained with between him and his sister: his constantly taunting her with her defection from the good old Jacobite principles; all disorder, all misrule, civil or domestic, all inconvenience, all disagreeables, being the result of our importation of the "Hanover rats." That prodigy of a so-called argument between them regarding Sophia's elopement; Miss Western's assertion of her sex's prerogative, with her reference, as an authority, to Milton; and the Squire's answer, winding up the controversy, by damning Milton.

There is little doubt that the portrait of Western is a faithful one of a Somersetshire Squire of that age, and Fielding having resided among the gentry of that district for some time, he had notable subjects to sketch from at full leisure.

Then the extraordinary force of delineation in the characters of the Blifils; the contempt of Mrs. B. for her husband, the captain, and the intensely cordial hatred, the unmitigated, the saturated disgust of the captain for his wife; his loathing of her merging into a religion; the exquisitely refined satire in describing her behaviour upon receiving the news of his sudden death, ending in the immortal epitaph inscribed on his tombstone, a stereotype of the conventional decency to be observed in those matrimonial alliances which have existed in loathing and ended in joy to the survivor. "Here lies, in expectation of a joyful rising, the body of Captain John Blifil. London had the honour of his birth; Oxford of his education. His parts were an honour to his profession and to his country; his life to his religion and human nature. He was a dutiful son, a tender husband, an affectionate father, a most kind brother, a sincere friend, a devout Christian, and a good man. His inconsolable widow hath erected this stone, the monument of his virtues and her affection." The triumph—the climax of this polished satire—is, that every word of the composition comprises a falsehood.

Again, as instances of his using "incident and situation *only* to bring out *character*," may be noticed the scenes with Molly Seagrim, and the graduated preferences she shows for her several lovers. For Jones, through vanity; for Philosopher Square, through mere pecuniary interest; and for Will Barnes, through instinct, as being the only one on a level with herself. The scenes again with Lady Bellaston; the one with Sophia's muff; but *the* one in which, to my own feeling, the fine nature of Fielding comes forth, and his contempt is displayed for the odious insincerity of a large class in society who pass for very virtuous and very proper people, occurs in that scene in *Joseph Andrews*, where the hero is robbed, beaten, and stripped by highwaymen, and left for dead by the roadside; and when discovered by the stage-coach party that were passing the same way, the postillion having first heard his groans and insisted on dismounting to see what was the matter; the consternation of the gentlemen upon finding that he had been robbed, and their proposing to hasten on immediately lest they should be robbed also. The wish of the young lawyer that "they had *happened* to have passed by *without taking any notice*, but that now they might be proved to have been last in his company, and that if he should die they might be called to some account for the murder." The horror of the lady passenger at the idea of a naked and bleeding man being taken into the carriage, and her ordering the coachman to drive on, and, as a winding up of the event, the means by which he was relieved from his misery. The author says: "Though there were several great-coats about the coach the two gentlemen complained they were cold and could not spare a rag, the man of wit saying, with a laugh, that 'Charity began at home,' and the coachman, who had two great-coats spread under him, refused to lend either lest they should be made bloody. The lady's footman desired to be excused for the same reason, which the lady herself, notwithstanding her abhorrence of a naked man, approved; and it is more than probable that poor Joseph, who obstinately adhered to his modest resolution of not appearing among the party in that state, must have perished unless the postillion (a lad who has since been transported for robbing a hen-roost) had voluntarily stripped off a great-coat, his only garment, at the same time swearing a great oath (for which he was rebuked by the passengers), 'that he would rather ride in his shirt all his life, than suffer a fellow creature to die in so miserable a condition.'"

Upon numbers of such occasions as this the humane philosophy of this great writer is displayed, and always with so finely polished a vein of satire, that he is to be studied for the sake of his language alone, his sentences being constructed with the most perfect appropriateness, without betraying the slightest appearance of effort or elaboration.

The moral tendency of *Tom Jones* has been objected to, but I must honestly confess that I think with undue rigidity. That lad must have had from his birth but questionable *home* examples who shall become enamoured of the Foundling's vagabond career, and even in his disreputable alliances I do not find him to be envied in his successes, and on few occasions is his general character to be respected. Certainly Tom Jones is not mean, or treacherous, but open, liberal, and humane; still, withal, he is essentially a most commonplace fellow.

The character, too, of Sophia, the heroine, was doubtless formed upon the author's *own* ideas of female perfection. She is, of course, beautiful, generous, amiable in temper, dotingly fond, and constant to her lover. But it is to be remarked that Fielding had not the true lofty sense of the female character. Upon this point he as much depressed the higher qualities in his women as Richardson labours to elevate them. Fielding seems to think that the *ne plus ultra* of perfection in woman consists in implicit yielding. Alworthy tells Sophia that the great charm he had observed in her conduct was the deference she always manifested for the opinions and judgment of men; and, with the exception of Alworthy himself, only think of the "men" by whom Sophia was surrounded! So glaring is this prejudice in Fielding, that he almost always associates anything of a learned accomplishment in women with some disgusting quality or propensity. Jenny, the reputed mother of Tom Jones, has a spice of learning; the same accomplishment is bestowed upon the odious Mrs. Bennett, in his novel of *Amelia*. Squire Western's sister, too, would, in his day, pass for a learned woman. Fielding having been a gay man of the world, a reckless expensive one, and somewhat licentious in his habits, and consequently selfish, it would almost naturally follow that he was not intimate with the finest specimens of the female sex, and that he would eulogise those characters among them who would be the most subservient to his humours, caprices, and sensual indulgences. The most perfect character, therefore (selfishly speaking), that he has drawn, is the wife of Booth, in his novel of *Amelia*. Dotingly fond, constant, forbearing, patient, uncomplaining, sacrificing all, even to her jewels and other personal property, pawning her clothes and furniture to pay his *gambling debts*, and this conduct on her part (which it were scarcely a harsh term to call imbecile) is exalted by the author into a moral canonization. While, on the part of Booth himself (in whose character Fielding is said to have portrayed his own), we are introduced to a man described as being passionately in love with his wife, not so much so however as to preclude his occasionally lapsing into infidelities. He is good-natured, it is true, but recklessly extravagant, and so regardless of her sufferings that I recollect no instance of a sacrifice that he makes for her comfort, while he graciously receives (as a duty to a higher nature) all the lavishings that she pours out upon him. Now, all this appears to me no more than selfishness on the one side, and amiable profusion on the other; and really, so to speak, Amelia, upon more than one occasion, is weakness itself. Of the same complexion with Amelia is the character of Mrs. Heartfree in the "Jonathan Wild." Personally attractive, perfectly doting, and obedient, even against her reason, and these qualities appear to comprise the whole category of a woman's perfections in Fielding's estimation. Such are evidently the favourites

with him; yet the facility and even the weakness of Mrs. Heartfree's judgment upon more than one occasion during her career exhibits her as little better than a born fool.

But the force of Fielding's genius lay (as already observed) in an acute perception of the niceties—particularly the imperfections—of character, with a richly gifted vein of satire. This talent always appears in great force whenever he has the two professions of law and medicine under his lash. The consultation of the doctors upon the cause of Blifil's death, and their coming to the unanimous opinion that it is not necessary to administer medicine to him because he is already dead, is worthy of Molière himself; and Voltaire could not with a finer pungency have described a justice of the peace than Fielding has done in the opening of his novel of *Amelia*. The satire is keen enough, because it is true in the aged experience of some of us. This is the passage alluded to: "Mr. Thrasher, however, the justice before whom the prisoners were now brought, had some few imperfections in his magistratical capacity. I own I have been sometimes inclined to think that this office of a justice of peace requires some knowledge of the law, for this simple reason, because in every case which comes before him he is to judge and act according to law. Again, as these laws are contained in a great variety of books (the statutes which relate to the office of a justice of peace making themselves two large volumes in folio, and that part of his jurisdiction which is founded on the common law being disposed in a hundred volumes), I cannot conceive how this knowledge should be acquired without reading, and yet, certain it is, Mr. Thrasher never read one syllable of the matter.

"This, perhaps, was a defect, but this was not all, for where mere ignorance is to decide a point between two litigants, it will always be an even chance whether it decide right or wrong. But sorry am I to say right was often in a much worse situation than this, and wrong has often had five hundred to one on his side before that magistrate, who, if he was ignorant of the laws of England, was yet well versed in the laws of nature. He perfectly well understood that fundamental principle laid down in the Institutes of the learned Rochefoucault, by which the duty of self-love is so strongly enforced, and every man is taught to consider himself as the centre of gravity, and to attract all things thither. To speak the truth plainly, the justice was never indifferent in a cause but when he could get nothing on either side."

In this same scene it is that the watchmen have always in stock, and at hand, a battered lantern, which they produce in every assault case as evidence against the prisoners. Upon occasions like this Fielding's wit and humour appear to advantage; in the latter quality (of humour) he was as far behind, as in the former and higher quality (of wit) he surpassed Smollett. Fielding's coarser scenes of low humour, and his coarse description of them (those at inns for instance), are, to my own feeling, absolutely disagreeable, and they are frequently repeated.

The peculiar vein of Fielding's genius, that of satire, appears in its greatest force and lustre in his *History of Jonathan Wild the Great*. For a finely and consistently-sustained vein of irony throughout the whole of the pretended biography of that illustrious thief and blood-money dealer, I think its rival will scarcely be found in the language.

Having stated the thesis of his argument, that "greatness consists in bringing all manner of mischief on mankind, and goodness in removing it from them," in contradistinction to what he amusingly terms the "obsolete doctrines of a set of simple fellows called, in derision, sages or philosophers, who have confounded the ideas of greatness and goodness, no two things being more distinct from each other," he cites two eminent historical examples of what the world have deemed great in action in the characters of Alexander and Julius Cæsar; and from these two he deduces the inference that his own hero, Mr. Jonathan Wild, advanced equal claims to the cognomen of great. "For instance," he says, "in the histories of Alexander and Cæsar we are frequently reminded of their benevolence and generosity. When the former had with fire and sword overrun a whole empire, and destroyed the lives of millions of innocent people, we are told, as an example of his benevolence, that he did not cut the throat of an old woman, and carry her daughters into captivity. And when the mighty Cæsar had with wonderful 'greatness' of mind destroyed the liberties of his country, and gotten all the power into his own hands, we receive, as an instance of his generosity, his largesses to his followers and tools, by whose means he had accomplished his purpose, and by whose assistance he was to establish it." And so, upon this principle of pure selfishness, he conducts his history of Mr. Jonathan Wild, the thief and blood-money dealer. The steady and sedate manner in which he narrates an act of perfidy, treachery, or cruelty in his hero (and always with the epithet of "great" attached to it), becomes positively humorous by the force of contrast. Upon the principle, too, of Shakespeare's aphorism: "Base things, sire, base; Nature hath meal and bran, contempt and grace," Fielding, in his genealogy of the Wild family, traces the great qualities in his hero to the renowned Wolfstan Wild, who came over with Hengist, and eminently distinguished himself at that famous festival where the Britons were so treacherously murdered by the Saxons. "For," he says, "when the word was given, 'Nemet eour saxes' ('Take out your swords'), this gentleman, being a little hard of hearing, mistook the sound for 'Nemet her sacs' ('Take out their purses'); instead, therefore, of applying to the throat, he immediately applied to the pocket of his guest, and contented himself with taking all that he had without attempting his life."

Again, in his account of Master Jonathan's infant life, Fielding gives us one of those biting sarcasms for which he is so celebrated. In recording the early indications of the little gentleman's sweetness of temper, he says:—"Though he was by no means to be terrified into compliance, yet might he by a sugar-plum be brought to your purpose. Indeed, to say the truth, he was to be bribed to any thing, which made many say he was certainly born to be a great man." But the book teems with shrewd and caustic axioms. Mr. Wild has no objection to "borrow" of his friend, Mr. Bagshot, for it is as good a way of "taking" as any, and it is the "genteelest kind of sneaking-budge."

The "force of habit," as exemplified in the actions of his hero, and of his friend, Count la Ruse, the blackleg, is another example of Fielding's perception of human nature and character. He says: "The two friends sat down to cards, a circumstance I should not have mentioned but for the sake of observing the prodigious force of habit; for, though the Count knew, if he won ever so much from Mr. Wild, he should not receive a shilling, yet could he not refrain from packing the cards; nor could Wild keep his hands out of his friend's pockets, although he knew there was nothing in them." The scene again between Wild and Bagshot upon the division of a booty that Bagshot has been induced to risk his neck in plundering, with Wild's argument why he, who had not shared in the toil and danger, should nevertheless receive three-fourths of the amount for his own share, is a masterly satire upon the unequal division of labour and reward in the great world.

Again, Mr. Wild's dissertation upon "honour"—a string of pungent sarcasms. His argument, also, that one feature of

greatness, in worldly estimation, consists in the employment or non-employment of others' hands; that, had a "prig" as many tools as an Alexander, or a Prime Minister, he would be as "great" a man.

Yet again, his scorn of good-natured people, who, he says, "are sent into the world by nature, with the same design as men put little fish into a pike-pond in order to be devoured by that voracious water-hero." What fine sarcasm! what fine morality, too, in Mr. Marybone the highwayman's contempt of the baser and meaner species of robbery called "cheating," and which he calls "robbery within the law."

And (to crown all) in summing up the character of his hero, like an orthodox biographer, after that hero has consummated his last act of "greatness," and in the way, as our historian says, all should do, whom the world styles "great"— by quitting this world for the next at Tyburn, he winds up with a choice selection of his axioms upon worldly conduct and wisdom, found in his study after his decease, and which are so many concentrated drops of the keenest irony. In short, the whole work is, I should think, one of the acutest and most stinging satires ever penned.

Those readers who are unacquainted with Fielding's *Miscellanies* will find their time agreeably spent in reading that very original Record, his *Journey from this World to the Next*, his *Essay on Nothing*, his satirical papers upon the *Chrysippus, or Golden Guinea, proposed to be read before the Royal Society*, and especially in the last of his productions, the diary he kept during his voyage to Lisbon, where he died.

The best of all—as I believe it was the precursor of all our dramatic burlesques, *Tom Thumb the Great*,—was written by Fielding. The original edition, accompanied by copious illustrative notes in burlesque, is extremely amusing.

SIR LESLIE STEPHEN
"Fielding's Novels" (1877)
Hours in a Library (1874–79)
1904, Volume 3, pp. 1–43

A double parallel has often been pointed out between the two pairs of novelists who were most popular in the middle of our own and of the preceding century. The intellectual affinity which made Smollett the favourite author of Dickens is scarcely so close as that which commended Fielding to Thackeray. The resemblance between *Pickwick* and *Humphrey Clinker*, or between *David Copperfield* and *Roderick Random*, consists chiefly in the exuberance of animal spirits, the keen eye for external oddity, the consequent tendency to substitute caricature for portrait, and the vivid transformation of autobiography into ostensible fiction, which are characteristic of both authors. Between Fielding and Thackeray the resemblance is closer. The peculiar irony of *Jonathan Wild* has its closest English parallel in *Barry Lyndon*. The burlesque in *Tom Thumb* of the Lee and Dryden school of tragedy may remind us of Thackeray's burlesques of Scott and Dumas. The characters of the two authors belong to the same family. *Vanity Fair* has grown more decent since the days of Lady Bellaston, but the costume of the actors has changed more than their nature. Rawdon Crawley would not have been surprised to meet Captain Booth in a sponging-house; Shandon and his friends preserved the old traditions of Fielding's Grub Street; Lord Steyne and Major Pendennis were survivals from the more congenial period of Lord Fellamar and Colonel James; and the two

Amelias represent cognate ideals of female excellence. Or, to take an instance of similarity in detail, might not this anecdote from *The Covent Garden Journal* have rounded off a paragraph in the *Snob Papers*? A friend of Fielding saw a dirty fellow in a mud-cart lash another with his whip, saying, with an oath, "I will teach you manners to your betters." Fielding's friends wondered what could be the condition of this social inferior of a mud-cart driver, till he found him to be the owner of a dust-cart driven by asses. The great butt of Fielding's satire is, as he tells us, affectation; the affectation which he specially hates is that of strait-laced morality; Thackeray's satire is more generally directed against the particular affectation called snobbishness; but the evil principle attacked by either writer is merely one avatar of the demon assailed by the other.

The resemblance, which extends in some degree to style, might perhaps be shown to imply a very close intellectual affinity. I am content, however, to notice the literary genealogy as illustrative of the fact that Fielding was the ancestor of one great race of novelists. "I am," he says expressly in *Tom Jones*, "the founder of a new province of writing." Richardson's *Clarissa*[1] and Smollett's *Roderick Random* were indeed published before *Tom Jones*; but the provinces over which Richardson and Smollett reigned were distinct from the contiguous province of which Fielding claimed to be the first legislator. Smollett (who comes nearest) professed to imitate *Gil Blas* as Fielding professed to imitate Cervantes. Smollett's story inherits from its ancestry a reckless looseness of construction. It is a series of anecdotes strung together by the accident that they all happen to the same person. *Tom Jones*, on the contrary, has a carefully constructed plot, if not, as Coleridge asserts, one of the three best plots in existence (its rivals being *Œdipus Tyrannus* and *The Alchemist*). Its excellence depends upon the skill with which it is made subservient to the development of character and the thoroughness with which the working motives of the persons involved have been thought out. Fielding claims—even ostentatiously—that he is writing a history, not a romance; a history not the less true because all the facts are imaginary, for the fictitious incidents serve to exhibit the most general truths of human character. It is by this seriousness of purpose that his work is distinguished from the old type of novel, developed by Smollett, which is but a collection of amusing anecdotes; or from such work as De Foe's, in which the external facts are given with almost provoking indifference to display of character and passion. Fielding's great novels have a true organic unity as well as a consecutive story, and are intended in our modern jargon as genuine studies in psychological analysis.[2]

Johnson, no mean authority when in his own sphere and free from personal bias, expressly traversed this claim; he declared that there was more knowledge of the human heart in a letter of *Clarissa* than in the whole of *Tom Jones*; and said more picturesquely, that Fielding could tell the hour by looking at the dial-plate, whilst Richardson knew how the clock was made.[3] It is tempting to set this down as a Johnsonian prejudice, and to deny or retort the comparison. Fielding, we might say, paints flesh and blood; whereas Richardson consciously constructs his puppets out of frigid abstractions. Lovelace is a bit of mechanism; Tom Jones a human being. In fact, however, such comparisons are misleading. Nothing is easier than to find an appropriate ticket for the objects of our criticism, and summarily pigeon-hole Richardson as an idealist and Fielding as a realist; Richardson as subjective and morbid, Fielding as objective and full of coarse health; or to attribute to either of them the deepest knowledge of the human heart. These are the mere banalities

of criticism; and I can never hear them without a suspicion that a professor of æsthetics is trying to hoodwink me by a bit of technical platitude. The cant phrases which have been used so often by panegyrists too lazy to define their terms, have become almost as meaningless as the complimentary formulæ of society.

Knowledge of the human heart in particular is a phrase which covers very different states of mind. It may mean that power by which the novelist or dramatist identifies himself with his characters; sees through their eyes and feels with their senses; it is the product of rich nature, a vivid imagination, and great powers of sympathy, and draws a comparatively small part of its resources from external experience. The novelist knows how his characters would feel under given conditions, because he feels it himself; he sees from within, not from without; and is almost undergoing an actual experience instead of condensing his observations on life. This is the power in which Shakespeare is supreme; which Richardson proved himself, in his most powerful passages, to possess in no small degree; and which in Balzac seems to have generated fits of absolute hallucination.

Fielding's novels are not without proof of this power, as no great imaginative work can be possible without it; but the knowledge for which he is specially conspicuous differs almost in kind. This knowledge is drawn from observation rather than intuitive sympathy. It consists in great part of those weighty maxims which a man of keen powers of observation stores up in his passage through a varied experience. It is the knowledge of Ulysses, who has known

Cities of men
And manners, climates, councils, governments;

the knowledge of a Macchiavelli, who has looked behind the screen of political hypocrisies; the knowledge of which the essence is distilled in Bacon's *Essays*; or the knowledge of which Polonius seems to have retained many shrewd scraps even when he had fallen into his dotage. In reading *Clarissa* or *Eugenie Grandet* we are aware that the soul of Richardson or Balzac has transmigrated into another shape; that the author is projected into his character, and is really giving us one phase of his own sentiments. In reading Fielding we are listening to remarks made by a spectator instead of an actor; we are receiving the pithy recollections of the man about town; the prodigal who has been with scamps in gambling-houses, and drunk beer in pothouses and punch with country squires; the keen observer who has judged all characters, from Sir Robert Walpole down to Betsy Canning;[4] who has fought the hard battle of life with unflagging spirit, though with many falls; and who, in spite of serious stains, has preserved the goodness of his heart and the soundness of his head. The experience is generally given in the shape of typical anecdotes rather than in explicit maxims; but it is not the less distinctly the concentrated essence of observation, rather than the spontaneous play of a vivid imagination. Like Balzac, Fielding has portrayed the "Comédie Humaine;" but his imagination has never overpowered the coolness of his judgment. He shows a superiority to his successor in fidelity almost as marked as his inferiority in vividness. And, therefore, it may be said in passing, it is refreshing to read Fielding at a time when this element of masculine observation is the one thing most clearly wanting in modern literature. Our novels give us the emotions of young ladies, which, in their way, are very good things; they reflect the sentimental view of life, and the sensational view, and the commonplace view, and the high philosophical view. One thing they do not tell us. What does the world look like to a shrewd police-magistrate, with a keen eye in his head and a sound heart in his bosom? It might be worth knowing. Perhaps (who can tell?) it would still look rather like Fielding's world.

The peculiarity is indicated by Fielding's method. Scott, who, like Fielding, generally describes from the outside, is content to keep himself in the background. "Here," he says to his readers, "are the facts; make what you can of them." Fielding will not efface himself; he is always present as chorus; he tells us what moral we ought to draw; he overflows with shrewd remarks, given in their most downright shape, instead of obliquely suggested through the medium of anecdotes; he likes to stop us as we pass through his portrait gallery; to take us by the button-hole and expound his views of life and his criticisms on things in general. His remarks are often so admirable that we prefer the interpolations to the main current of narrative. Whether this plan is the best must depend upon the idiosyncrasy of the author; but it goes some way to explain one problem, over which Scott puzzles himself—namely, why Fielding's plays are so inferior to his novels. There are other reasons, external and internal; but it is at least clear that a man who can never retire behind his puppets is not in the dramatic frame of mind. He is always lecturing where a dramatist must be content to pull the wires. Shakespeare is really as much present in his plays as Fielding in his novels; but he does not let us know it; whereas the excellent Fielding seems to be quite incapable of hiding his broad shoulders and lofty stature behind his little puppet-show.

There are, of course, actors in Fielding's world who can be trusted to speak for themselves. Tom Jones, at any rate, who is Fielding in his youth, or Captain Booth, who is the Fielding of later years, are drawn from within. Their creator's sympathy is so close and spontaneous that he has no need of his formulæ and precedents. But elsewhere he betrays his methods by his desire to produce his authority. You will find the explanation of a certain line of conduct, he says, in "human nature, page almost the last." He is a little too fond of taking down that volume with a flourish; of exhibiting his familiarity with its pages, and referring to the passages which justify his assertions. Fielding has an odd touch of the pedant. He is fond of airing his classical knowledge; and he is equally fond of quoting this imaginary code which he has had to study so thoroughly and painfully. The effect, however, is to give an air of artificiality to some of his minor characters. They show the traces of deliberate composition too distinctly, though the blemish may be forgiven in consideration of the genuine force and freshness of his thinking. If manufactured articles, they are not second-hand manufactures. His knowledge, unlike that of the good Parson Adams, comes from life, not books.

The worldly wisdom for which Fielding is so conspicuous had indeed been gathered in doubtful places, and shows traces of its origin. He had been forced, as he said, to choose between the positions of a hackney coachman and of a hackney writer. "His genius," said Lady M. W. Montagu, who records the saying, "deserves a better fate." Whether it would have been equally fertile, if favoured by more propitious surroundings, is one of those fruitless questions which belong to the boundless history of the might-have-beens. But one fact requires to be emphasised. Fielding's critics and biographers have dwelt far too exclusively upon the uglier side of his Bohemian life. They have presented him as yielding to all the temptations which can mislead keen powers of enjoyment, when the purse is one day at the lowest ebb and the next overflowing with the profits of some lucky hit at the theatre. Those unfortunate yellow liveries which contributed to dissipate his little fortune have scandalised posterity as they scandalised his country neigh-

bours. [5] But it is essential to remember that the history of the Fielding of later years, of the Fielding to whom we owe the novels, is the record of a manful and persistent struggle to escape from the mire of Grub Street. During that period he was studying the law with the energy of a young student; redeeming the office of magistrate from the discredit into which it had fallen in the hands of fee-hunting predecessors; considering seriously, and making practical proposals to remedy, the evils which then made the lowest social strata a hell upon earth; sacrificing his last chances of health and life to put down with a strong hand the robbers who infested the streets of London; and clinging with affection to his wife and children. He never got fairly clear of that lamentable slough of despond into which his follies had plunged him. His moral tone lost what delicacy it had once possessed; he had not the strength which enabled Johnson to gain elevation even from the temptations which then beset the unlucky "author by profession." Some literary hacks of the day escaped only by selling themselves, body and soul; others sank into misery and vice, like poor Boyce, a fragment of whose poem has been preserved by Fielding, and who appears in literary history scribbling for pay in a sack arranged to represent a shirt. Fielding never let go his hold of the firm land, though he must have felt through life like one whose feet are always plunging into a hopeless quagmire. To describe him as a mere reckless Bohemian, is to overlook the main facts of his story. He was manly to the last, not in the sense in which man means animal; but with the manliness of one who struggles bravely to redeem early errors, and who knows the value of independence, purity, and domestic affection. The scanty anecdotes which do duty for his biography reveal little of his true life. We know indeed, from a spiteful and obviously exaggerated story of Horace Walpole's, that he once had a very poor supper in doubtful company; and from another anecdote, of slightly apocryphal flavour, that he once gave to "friendship" the money which ought to have been given to the collector of rates. But really to know the man, we must go to his books.

What did Fielding learn of the world which had treated him so roughly? That the world must be composed of fools because it did not bow before his genius, or of knaves because it did not reward his honesty? Men of equal ability have drawn both those and the contradictory conclusions from experience. Human nature, as philosophers assure us, varies little from age to age; but the pictures drawn by the best observers vary so strangely as to convince us that a portrait depends as much upon the artist as upon the sitter. One can see nothing but the baser, and another nothing but the nobler, passions. To one the world is like a masque representing the triumph of vice; and another placidly assures us that virtue is always rewarded by peace of mind, and that even the temporary prosperity of the wicked is an illusion. On one canvas we see a few great heroes stand out from a multitude of pygmies; on its rival, giants and dwarfs appear to have pretty much the same stature. The world is a scene of unrestrained passions impelling their puppets into collision or alliance without intelligible design; or a scene of domestic order, where an occasional catastrophe interferes as little with ordinary lives as a comet with the solar system. Blind fate governs one world of the imagination, and beneficent Providence another. The theories embodied in poetry vary as widely as the philosophies on which they are founded; and to philosophise is to declare the fundamental assumptions of half the wise men of the world to be transparent fallacies.

We need not here attempt to reconcile these apparent contradictions. As little need we attempt to settle Fielding's philosophy, for it resembles the snakes in Iceland. It seems to have been his opinion that philosophy is, as a rule, a fine word for humbug. That was a common conviction of his day; but his acceptance of it doubtless indicates the limits of his power. In his pages we have the shrewdest observation of man in his domestic relations; but we scarcely come into contact with man as he appears in presence of the infinite, and therefore with the deepest thoughts and loftiest imaginings of the great poets and philosophers. Fielding remains inflexibly in the regions of common-sense and everyday experience. But he has given an emphatic opinion of that part of the world which was visible to him, and it is one worth knowing. In a remarkable conversation, reported in Boswell, Burke and Johnson, two of the greatest of Fielding's contemporaries, seem to have agreed that they had found men less just and more generous than they could have imagined. People begin by judging the world from themselves, and it is therefore natural that two men of great intellectual power should have expected from their fellows a more than average adherence to settled principles. Thus Johnson and Burke discovered that reason, upon which justice depends, has less influence than a young reasoner is apt to fancy. On the other hand, they discovered that the blind instincts by which the mass are necessarily guided are not so bad as they are represented by the cynics. The Rochefoucauld or Mandeville who passes off his smart sayings upon the public as serious, knows better than anybody that a man must be a fool to take them literally. The wisdom which he affects is very easily learnt, and is more often the product of the premature sagacity dear to youth than of a ripened judgment. Good-hearted men, at least, like Johnson and Burke, shake off cynicism whilst others are acquiring it.

Fielding's verdict seems to differ at first sight. He undoubtedly lays great stress upon the selfishness of mankind. He seldom admits of an apparently generous action without showing its alloy of selfish motive, and sometimes showing that it is a mere cloak for selfish motives. In a characteristic passage of his *Voyage to Lisbon* he applies his theory to his own case. When the captain falls on his knees, he will not suffer a brave man and an old man to remain for a moment in that posture, but forgives him at once. He hastens, however, utterly to disclaim all praise, on the ground that his true motive was simply the convenience of forgiveness. "If men were wiser," he adds, "they would be oftener influenced by that motive." This kind of inverted hypocrisy, which may be graceful in a man's own case (for nobody will doubt that Fielding was less guided by calculation than he asserts) is not so graceful when applied to his neighbours. And perhaps some readers may hold that Fielding pitches the average strain of human motive too low. I should rather surmise that he substantially agrees with Johnson and Burke. The fact that most men attend a good deal to their own interests is one of the primary data of life. It is a thing at which we have no more right to be astonished than at the fact that even saints and martyrs have to eat and drink like other persons, or that a sound digestion is the foundation of much moral excellence. It is one of those facts which people of a romantic turn of mind may choose to overlook, but which no honest observer of life can seriously deny. Our conduct is determined through some thirty points of the compass by our own interest; and, happily, through at least nine-and-twenty of those points is rightfully so determined. Each man is forced, by an unavoidable necessity, to look after his own and his children's bread and butter, and to spend most of his efforts on that innocent end. So long as he does not pursue his interests wrongfully, nor remain dead to other calls when they happen, there is little cause for complaint, and certainly there is none for surprise.

Fielding recognises, but never exaggerates, this homely truth. He has a hearty and generous belief in the reality of good impulses, and the existence of thoroughly unselfish men. The main actors in this world are not, as in Balzac's, mere hideous incarnations of selfishness. The superior sanity of his mind keeps him from nightmares, if its calmness is unfavourable to lofty visions. With Balzac, women like Lady Bellaston become the rule instead of the exception, and their evil passions are the dominant forces in society. Fielding, though he recognises their existence, tells us plainly that they are exceptional. Society, he says, is as moral as it ever was, and given more to frivolity than to vice[6]—a statement judiciously overlooked by some of the critics who want to make graphic history out of his novels. Fielding's mind had gathered coarseness, but it had not been poisoned. He sees how many ugly things are covered by the superficial gloss of fashion, but he does not condescend to travesty the facts in order to gratify a morbid taste for the horrible. When he wants a good man or woman he knows where to find them, and paints from Allen or his own wife with obvious sincerity and hearty sympathy. He is less anxious to exhibit human selfishness than to show us that an alloy of generosity is to be found even amidst base motives. Some of his happiest touches are illustrations of this doctrine. His villains (with a significant exception) are never monsters. They have some touch of human emotion. No desert, according to him, is so bare but that some sweet spring blends with its brackish waters. His grasping landladies have genuine movements of sympathy; and even the scoundrelly Black George, the gamekeeper, is anxious to do Tom Jones a good turn, without risk, of course, to his own comfort, by way of compensation for previous injuries. It is this impartial insight into the ordinary texture of human motive that gives a certain solidity and veracity to Fielding's work. We are always made to feel that the actions spring fairly and naturally from the character of his persons, not from the exigencies of his story or the desire to be effective. The one great difficulty in *Tom Jones* is the assumption that the excellent Allworthy should have been deceived for years by the hypocrite Blifil, and blind to the substantial kindliness of his ward. Here we may fancy that Fielding has been forced to be unnatural by his plot. Yet he suggests a satisfactory solution with admirable skill. Allworthy is prejudiced in favour of Blifil by the apparently unjust prejudice of Blifil's mother in favour of the jovial Tom. A generous man may easily become blind to the faults of a supposed victim of maternal injustice; and even here Fielding fairly escapes from the blame due to ordinary novelists, who invent impossible misunderstandings in order to bring about intricate perplexities.

Blifil is perhaps the one case (for *Jonathan Wild* is a satire, not a history, or as M. Taine fancies, a tract) in which Fielding seems to lose his unvarying coolness of judgment; and the explanation is obvious. The one fault to which he is, so to speak, unjust, is hypocrisy. Hypocrisy, indeed, cannot well be painted too black, but it should not be made impossible. When Fielding has to deal with such a character, he for once loses his self-command, and, like inferior writers, begins to be angry with his creatures. Instead of analysing and explaining, he simply reviles and leaves us in the presence of a moral anomaly. Blifil is not more wicked than Iago, but we seem to understand the psychical chemistry by which an Iago is compounded; whereas Blifil can only be regarded as a devil (if the word be not too dignified) who does not really belong to this world at all. The error, though characteristic of a man whose great intellectual merit is his firm grasp of realities, and whose favourite virtue is his downright sincerity, is not the less a blemish. Hatred of pedantry too easily leads to hatred of culture, and hatred of hypocrisy to distrust of the more exalted virtues. Fielding cannot be just to motives lying rather outside his ordinary sphere of thought. He can mock heartily and pleasantly enough at the affectation of philosophy, as in the case where Parson Adams, urging poor Joseph Andrews, by considerations drawn from the Bible and from Seneca, to be ready to resign his Fanny "peaceably, quietly, and content-edly," suddenly hears of the supposed loss of his own little child, and is called upon to act instead of to preach. But this satire upon all characters and creeds which embody the more exalted strains of feeling is apt to be indiscriminate. A High Churchman, according to him, is a Pharisee who prefers orthodoxy to virtue; a Methodist a mere mountebank, who counterfeits spiritual raptures to impose upon dupes; a Free-thinker is a man who weaves a mask of fine phrases, under which to cover his aversion to the restraints of religion. Fielding's religion consists chiefly of a solid homespun moral-ity, and he is more suspicious of an excessive than of a defective zeal. Similarly he is a hearty Whig, but no revolu-tionist. He has as hearty a contempt for the cant about liberty[7] as Dr. Johnson himself, and has very stringent remedies to propose for regulating the mob. The bailiff in *Amelia*, who, whilst he brutally maltreats the unlucky prisoners for debt, swaggers about the British Constitution, and swears that he is "all for liberty," recalls the boatman who ridiculed French slavery to Voltaire, and was carried off next day by a pressgang. Fielding, indeed, is no fanatical adherent of our blessed Constitution, which, as he says, has been pronounced by some of our wisest men to be too perfect to be altered in any particular, and which a number of the said wisest men have been mending ever since. He hates cant on all sides impar-tially, though, as a sound Whig, he specially hates Papists and Jacobites as the most offensive of all Pharisees, marked for detestation by their taste for frogs and French wine in prefer-ence to punch and roast beef. He is a patriotic Briton, whose patriotism takes the genuine shape of a hearty growl at English abuses, with a tacit assumption that things are worse elsewhere.

The reflection of this quality of solid good sense, abso-lutely scorning any ailment except that of solid facts, is the so-called realism of Fielding's novels. He is, indeed, as hearty a realist as Hogarth, whose congenial art he is never tired of praising with all the cordiality of his nature, and to whom he refers his readers for portraits of several characters in *Tom Jones*. His scenery is as realistic as a photograph. Tavern kitchens, sponging-house parlours, the back-slums of London streets, are drawn from the realities with unflinching vigour. We see the stains of beer-pots and smell the fumes of stale tobacco as distinctly as in Hogarth's engravings. He shrinks neither from the coarse nor the absolutely disgusting. It is enough to recall the female boxing or scratching matches which are so frequent in his pages. On one such occasion his language seems to imply that he had watched such battles in the spirit of a connoisseur in our own day watching less inexpressibly disgusting prize-fights. Certainly we could wish that, if such scenes were to be depicted, there might have been a clearer proof that the artist had a nose and eyes capable of feeling offence.

But the nickname "realist" slides easily into another sense. The realist is sometimes supposed to be more shallow as well as more prosaic than the idealist; to be content with the outside where the idealist pierces to the heart. He gives the bare fact, where his rival gives the idea symbolised by the fact, and therefore rendering it attractive to the higher intellect. Fielding's view of his own art is instructive in this as in other matters. Poetic invention, he says, is generally taken to be a

creative faculty; and if so, it is the peculiar property of the romance-writers, who frankly take leave of the actual and possible. Fielding disavows all claim to this faculty; he writes histories, not romances. But, in his sense, poetic invention means, not creation, but "discovery;" that is, "a quick, sagacious penetration into the true essence of all objects of our contemplation." Perhaps we may say that it is chiefly a question of method whether a writer should portray men or angels—the beings, that is, of everyday life—or beings placed under a totally different set of circumstances. The more vital question is whether, by one method or the other, he shows us a man's heart or only his clothes; whether he appeals to our intellects or imaginations, or amuses us by images which do not sink below the eye. In scientific writings a man may give us the true law of a phenomenon, whether he exemplifies it in extreme or average cases, in the orbit of a comet or the fall of an apple. The romance writer should show us what real men would be in dreamland, the writer of "histories" what they are on the knifeboard of an omnibus. True insight may be shown in either case, or may be absent in either, according as the artist deals with the deepest organic laws or the more external accidents. *The Ancient Mariner* is an embodiment of certain simple emotional phases and moral laws amidst the phantasmagoric incidents of a dream, and De Foe does not interpret them better because he confines himself to the most prosaic incidents. When romance becomes really arbitrary, and is parted from all basis of observation, it loses its true interest and deserves Fielding's condemnation. Fielding conscientiously aims at discharging the highest function. He describes, as he says in *Joseph Andrews*, "not men, but manners; not an individual, but a species." His lawyer, he tells us, has been alive for the last four thousand years, and will probably survive four thousand more. Mrs. Towwouse lives wherever turbulent temper, avarice, and insensibility are united; and her sneaking husband wherever a good inclination has glimmered forth, eclipsed by poverty of spirit and understanding. But the type which shows best the force and the limits of Fielding's genius is Parson Adams. He belongs to a distinguished family, whose members have been portrayed by the greatest historians. He is a collateral descendant of Don Quixote, for whose creation Fielding felt a reverence exceeded only by his reverence for Shakespeare.[8] The resemblance is, of course, distant, and consists chiefly in this, that the parson, like the knight, lives in an ideal world, and is constantly shocked by harsh collision with facts. He believes in his sermons instead of his sword, and his imagination is tenanted by virtuous squires and model parsons instead of Arcadian shepherds, or knight-errants and fair ladies. His imagination is not exalted beyond the limits of sanity, but only colours the prosaic realities in accordance with the impulses of a tranquil benevolence. If the theme be fundamentally similar, it is treated with a far less daring hand.

Adams is much more closely related to Sir Roger de Coverley, the Vicar of Wakefield, or Uncle Toby. Each of these lovable beings invites us at once to sympathise with and to smile at the unaffected simplicity which, seeing no evil, becomes half ludicrous, and half pathetic in this corrupt world. Adams stands out from his brethren by this intense reality. If he smells too distinctly of beer and tobacco, we believe in him more firmly than in the less full-blooded creations of Sterne and Goldsmith. Parson Adams, indeed, has a startling vigour of organisation. Not merely the hero of a modern ritualist novel, but Amyas Leigh or Guy Livingstone himself, might have been amazed at his athletic prowess. He stalks ahead of the stage-coach (favoured doubtless by the bad roads of the period) as though he had accepted the modern principle about fearing God and walking a thousand miles in a thousand hours. His mutton fist and the crab-tree cudgel which swings so freely round his clerical head would have daunted the contemporary gladiators, Slack and Broughton. He shows his Christian humility not merely by familiarity with his poorest parishioners, but in sitting up whole nights in tavern kitchens, drinking unlimited beer, smoking inextinguishable pipes, and revelling in a ceaseless flow of gossip. We smile at the good man's intense delight in a love-story, at the simplicity which makes him see a good Samaritan in Parson Trulliber, at the absence of mind which makes him pitch his Æschylus into the fire, or walk a dozen miles in profound oblivion of the animal which should have been between his knees; but his contemporaries were provoked to horse-laugh, and when we remark the tremendous practical jokes which his innocence suggests to them, we admit that he requires his whole athletic vigour to bring so tender a heart safely through so rough a world.

If the ideal hero is always to live in fancy-land and talk in blank verse, Adams has clearly no right to the title; nor, indeed, has Don Quixote. But the masculine portraiture of the coarse realities is not only indicative of intellectual vigour, but artistically appropriate. The contrast between the world and its simple-minded inhabitant is the more forcible in proportion to the firmness and solidity of Fielding's touch. Uncle Toby proves that Sterne had preserved enough tenderness to make an exquisite plaything of his emotions. The Vicar of Wakefield proves that Goldsmith had preserved a childlike innocence of imagination, and could retire from duns and publishers to an idyllic world of his own. Joseph Andrews proves that Fielding was neither a child nor a sentimentalist, but that he had learnt to face facts as they are, and set a true value on the best elements of human life. In the midst of vanity and vexation of spirit, he could find some comfort in pure and strong domestic affection. He can indulge his feelings without introducing the false note of sentimentalism, or condescending to tone his pictures with rose-colour. He wants no illusions. The exemplary Dr. Harrison in *Amelia* held no action unworthy of him which could protect an innocent person or "bring a rogue to the gallows." Good Parson Adams could lay his cudgel on the back of a villain with hearty goodwill. He believes too easily in human goodness, but there is not a maudlin fibre in his whole body. He would not be the man to cry over a dead donkey whilst chidren are in want of bread. He would be slower than the excellent Dr. Primrose to believe in the reformation of a villain by fine phrases, and if he fell into such a weakness, his biographer would not, like Goldsmith, be inclined to sanction the error. A villain is induced to reform, indeed, by the sight of Amelia's excellence, but Fielding is careful to tell us that the change was illusory, and that the villain ended on a gallows. We are made sensible that if Adams had his fancies they were foibles, and therefore sources of misfortune. We are to admire the child-like character, but not to share its illusions. The world is not made of moonshine. Hypocrisy, cruelty, avarice, and lust have to be stamped out by hard blows, not cured by delicate infusion of graceful sentimentalisms.

So far Fielding's portrait of an ideal character is all the better for his masculine grasp of fact. It must, however, be admitted that he fails a little on the other side of the contrast. He believes in a good heart, but scarcely in very lofty motive. He tells us in *Tom Jones*[9] that he has painted no perfect character, because he never happened to meet one. His stories, like *Vanity Fair*, may be described as novels without a hero. It is not merely that his characters are imperfect, but that they are deficient in the finer ingredients which go to make up the

nearest approximations of our imperfect natures to heroism. Colonel Newcome was not perhaps so good a man as Parson Adams, but he had a certain delicacy of sentiment which led him, as we may remember, to be rather hard upon Tom Jones, and which Fielding (as may be gathered from Bath in *Amelia*) would have been inclined to ridicule. Parson Adams is simple enough to become a laughing-stock to the brutal, but he never consciously rebels against the dictates of the plainest common-sense. His theology comes from Tillotson and Hoadly; he has no eye for the romantic side of his creed, and would be apt to condemn a mystic as simply a fool. His loftiest aspiration is not to reform the world or any part of it, but to get a modest bit of preferment (he actually receives it, we are happy to think, in *Amelia*), enough to pay for his tobacco and his children's schooling. Fielding's dislike to the romantic makes him rather blind to the elevated. He will not only start from the actual, but does not conceive the possibility of an infusion of loftier principles. The existing standard of sound sense prescribes an impassable limit to his imagination. Parson Adams is an admirable incarnation of certain excellent and honest impulses. He sets forth the wisdom of the heart and the beauty of the simple instincts of an affectionate nature. But we are forced to admit that he is not the highest type conceivable, and might, for example, learn something from his less robust colleague, Dr. Primrose.

This remark suggests the common criticism, expounded with his usual brilliancy by M. Taine. Fielding, he tells us, loves nature, but he does not love it "like the great impartial artists, Shakespeare and Goethe." He moralises incessantly—which is wrong. Moreover, his morality appears to be very questionable. It consists in preferring instinct to reason. The hero is the man who is born generous as a dog is born affectionate. And this, says M. Taine, might be all very well were it not for a great omission. Fielding has painted nature, but nature without refinement, poetry, and chivalry. He can only describe the impetuosity of the senses, not the nervous exaltation and the poetic rapture. Man is with him "a good buffalo; and perhaps he is a hero required by a people which is itself called John Bull." In all which there is an undoubted vein of truth. Fielding's want of refinement, for example, is one of those undeniable facts which must be taken for granted. But, without seeking to set right some other statements implied in M. Taine's judgment, it is worth while to consider a little more fully the moral aspect of Fielding's work. Much has been said upon this point by some who, with M. Taine, take Fielding for a mere "buffalo," and by others who, like Coleridge,—a safer and more sympathetic critic—hold *Tom Jones* to be, on the whole, a sound exposition of healthy morality.

Fielding, on the "buffalo" view, is supposed to be simply taking one side in one of those perpetual controversies which has occupied many generations and never approaches a settlement. He prefers nature to law, instinct to reasoned action; he is on the side of Charles as against Joseph Surface; he admires the publican, and condemns the Pharisee without reserve; he loves the man who is nobody's enemy but his own, and despises the prudent person whose charity ends at his own door-step. Such a doctrine—so absolutely stated—is rather a negation of all morality than a lax morality. If it implies a love of generous instincts, it denies that a man should have any regard for moral rules, which are needed precisely in order to control our spontaneous instincts. Virtue is amiable, but ceases to be meritorious. Nothing would be easier than to quote passages in which Fielding expressly repudiates such a theory; but, of course, a writer's morality must be judged by the conceptions embodied in his work, not by the maxims scattered through it. Nor, for the same reason, can we pay much attention to Fielding's express assertion that he is writing in the interests of virtue; for Smollett, and less scrupulous writers than Smollett, have found their account in similar protestations. Yet anybody, I think, who will compare *Joseph Andrews* with that intentionally most moral work, *Pamela*, will admit that Fielding's morality goes deeper than this. Fielding at least makes us love virtue, and is incapable of the solecism which Richardson commits in substantially preaching that virtue means standing out for a higher price. That Fielding's reckless heroes have a genuine sensibility to the claims of virtue, appears still more unmistakably when we compare them with the heartless fine gentlemen of the Congreve school and of his own early plays, or put the faulty Captain Booth beside such an unredeemed scamp as Peregrine Pickle.

It is clear, in short, that the aim of Fielding (whether he succeeds or not) is the very reverse of that attributed to him by M. Taine. *Tom Jones* and *Amelia* have, ostensibly at least, a most emphatic moral attached to them; and not only attached to them, but borne in mind and even too elaborately preached throughout. That moral is the one which Fielding had learnt in the school of his own experience. It is the moral that dissipation bears fruit in misery. The remorse, it is true, which was generated in Fielding and in his heroes was not the remorse which drives a man to a cloister, or which even seriously poisons his happiness. The offences against morality are condoned too easily, and the line between vice and virtue drawn in accordance with certain distinctions which even Parson Adams could scarcely have proved. Vice, he seems to say, is altogether objectionable only when complicated by cruelty or hypocrisy. But if Fielding's moral sense in not very delicate, it is vigorous. He hates most heartily what he sees to be wrong, though his sight might easily be improved in delicacy of discrimination. The truth is simply that Fielding accepted that moral code which the better men of the world in his time really acknowledged, as distinguished from that by which they affected to be bound. That so wide a distinction should generally exist between these codes is a matter for deep regret. That Fielding in his hatred for humbug should have condemned purity as puritanical is clearly lamentable. The confusion, however, was part of the man, and, as already noticed, shows itself in one shape or other through his work. But it would be unjust to condemn him upon that ground as antagonistic or indifferent to reasonable morality. His morality is at the superior antipodes from the cynicism of a Wycherley; and far superior to the prurient sentimentalism of Sterne or the hot-pressed priggishness of Richardson, or even the reckless Bohemianism of Smollett.

There is a deeper question, however, beneath this discussion. The morality of those "great impartial artists" of whom M. Taine speaks differs from Fielding's in a more serious sense. The highest morality of a great work of art depends upon the power with which the essential beauty and ugliness of virtue and vice are exhibited by an impartial observer. The morality, for example, of Goethe and Shakespeare appears in the presentation of such characters as Iago and Mephistopheles. The insight of true genius shows us by such examples what is the true physiology of vice; what is the nature of the man who has lost all faith in virtue and all sympathy with purity and nobility of character. The artist of inferior rank tries to make us hate vice by showing that it comes to a bad end precisely because he has an adequate perception of its true nature. He can see that a drunkard generally gets into debt or incurs an attack of *delirium tremens*, but he does not exhibit the moral disintegration which is the underlying cause of the misfortune,

and which may be equally fatal, even if it happens to evade the penalty. The distinction depends upon the power of the artist to fulfil Fielding's requirement of penetrating to the essence of the objects of his contemplation. It corresponds to the distinction in philosophy between a merely prudential system of ethics—the system of the gallows and the gaol—and the system which recognises the deeper issues perceptible to a fine moral sense.

Now, in certain matters, Fielding's morality is of the merely prudential kind. It resembles Hogarth's simple doctrine that the good apprentice will be Lord Mayor and the bad apprentice get into Newgate. So shrewd an observer was indeed well aware, and could say very forcibly, [10] that virtue in this world might sometimes lead to poverty, contempt, and imprisonment. He does not, like some novelists, assume the character of a temporal Providence, and knock his evil-doers on the head at the end of the story. He shows very forcibly that the difficulties which beset poor Jones and Booth are not to be fairly called accidents, but are the difficulties to which bad conduct generally leads a man, and which are all the harder when not counterbalanced by a clear conscience. He can even describe with sympathy such a character as poor Atkinson in *Amelia*, whose unselfish love brings him more blows than favours of fortune. But it is true that he is a good deal more sensible to what are called the prudential sanctions of virtue, at least of a certain category of virtues, than to its essential beauty. So far the want of refinement of which M. Taine speaks does, in fact, lower, and lower very materially, his moral perception. A man of true delicacy could never have dragged Tom Jones into his lowest degradation without showing more forcibly his abhorrence of his loose conduct. This is, as Colonel Newcome properly points out, the great and obvious blot upon the story, which no critics have missed, and we cannot even follow the leniency of Coleridge, who thinks that a single passage introduced to express Fielding's real judgment would have remedied the mischief. It is too obvious to be denied without sophistry that Tom, though he has many good feelings, and can preach very edifying sermons to his less scrupulous friend Nightingale, requires to be cast in a different mould. His whole character should have been strung to a higher pitch to make us feel that such degradation would not merely have required punishment to restore his self-complacency, but have left a craving for some thorough moral ablution.

Granting unreservedly all that may be urged upon this point, we may still agree with the judgment pronounced by the most congenial critics. Fielding's pages reek too strongly of tobacco; they are apt to turn delicate stomachs; but the atmosphere is, on the whole, healthy and bracing. No man can read them without prejudice and fail to recognise the fact that he has been in contact with something much higher than a "good buffalo." He has learnt to know a man, not merely full of animal vigour, not merely stored with various experience of men and manners, but also in the main sound and unpoisoned by the mephitic vapours which poisoned the atmosphere of his police office. If the scorn of hypocrisy is too fully emphasised, and the sensitiveness to ugly and revolting objects too much deadened by a rough life, yet nobody could be more heartily convinced of the beauty and value of those solid domestic instincts on which human happiness must chiefly depend. Put Fielding beside the modern would-be satirists who make society—especially French society[11]—a mere sink of nastiness, or beside the more virtuous persons whose favourite affectation is simplicity, and who labour most spasmodically to be masculine, and his native vigour, his massive common-sense, his wholesome views of men and manners, stand out in solid relief. Certainly he was limited in perception, and not so elevated in tone as might be desired; but he is a fitting representative of the stalwart vigour and the intellectual shrewdness evident in the best men of his time. The English domestic life of the period was certainly far from blameless, and anything but refined; but if we have gained in some ways, we are hardly entitled to look with unqualified disdain upon the rough vigour of our beer-drinking, beef-eating ancestors.

We have felt, indeed, the limitations of Fielding's art more clearly since English fiction found a new starting point in Scott. Scott made us sensible of many sources of interest to which Fielding was naturally blind. He showed us especially that a human being belonged to a society going through a long course of historical development, and renewed the bonds with the past which had been rudely snapped in Fielding's period. Fielding only deals, it may be roughly said, with men as members of a little family circle, whereas Scott shows them as members of a nation rich in old historical traditions, related to the past and the future, and to the external nature in which it has been developed. A wider set of forces is introduced into our conception of humanity, and the romantic element, which Fielding ignored, comes again to life. Scott, too, was a greater man than Fielding, of wider sympathy, loftier character, and, not the least, with an incomparably keener ear for the voices of the mountains, the sea, and the sky. The more Scott is studied, the higher, I believe, the opinion that we shall form of some of his powers. But in one respect Fielding is his superior. It is a kind of misnomer which classifies all Scott's books as novels. They are embodied legends and traditions, descriptions of men, and races, and epochs of history; but many of them are novels, as it were, by accident, and modern readers are often disappointed because the name suggests misleading associations. They expect to sympathise with Scott's heroes, whereas the heroes are generally dropped in from without, just to give ostensible continuity to the narrative. The apparent accessories are really the main substance. The Jacobites and not Waverley, the Borderers, not Mr. Van Beest Brown, the Covenanters, not Morton or Lord Evandale, are the real subjects of Scott's best romances. Now Fielding is really a novelist in the more natural sense. We are interested, that is, by the main characters, though they are not always the most attractive in themselves. We are really absorbed by the play of their passions and the conflict of their motives, and not merely taking advantage of the company to see the surrounding scenery or phases of social life. In this sense Fielding's art is admirable, and surpassed that of all of his English predecessors as of most of his successors. If the light is concentrated in a narrow focus, it is still healthy daylight. So long as we do not wish to leave his circle of ideas, we see little fault in the vigour with which he fulfils his intention. And therefore, whatever Fielding's other faults, he is beyond comparison the most faithful and profound mouthpiece of the passions and failings of a society which seems at once strangely remote and yet strangely near to us. When seeking to solve that curious problem which is discussed in one of Hazlitt's best essays—what characters one would most like to have met?—and running over the various claims of a meeting at the Mermaid with Shakespeare and Jonson, a "neat repast of Attic taste" with Milton, a gossip at Button's with Addison and Steele, a club-dinner with Johnson and Burke, a supper with Lamb, or (certainly the least attractive) an evening at Holland House, I sometimes fancy that, after all, few things would be pleasanter than a pipe and a bowl of punch with Fielding and Hogarth. It is true that for such a purpose I provide myself in imagination with a new set of sturdy nerves, and with a digestion such as that which was once equal to the horrors of

an undergraduates' "wine party." But having made that trifling assumption, I fancy that there would be few places where one would hear more good mother wit, shrewder judgments of men and things, or a sounder appreciation of those homely elements of which human life is in fact chiefly composed. Common-sense in the highest degree—whether we choose to identify it or contrast it with genius—is at least one of the most enduring and valuable of qualities in literature as everywhere else; and Fielding is one of its best representatives. But perhaps one is unduly biassed by the charm of a complete escape in imagination from the thousand and one affectations which have grown up since Fielding died and we have all become so much wiser and more learned than all previous generations.

Notes

1. Richardson wrote the first part of *Pamela* between November 10, 1739, and January 10, 1740. *Joseph Andrews* appeared in 1742. The first four volumes of *Clarissa Harlowe* and *Roderick Random* appeared in the beginning of 1748; *Tom Jones* in 1749.
2. See some appreciative remarks upon this in Scott's preface to *The Monastery*.
3. It is rather curious that Richardson uses the same comparison to Miss Fielding. He assures her that her brother only knew the outside of a clock, whilst she knew all the finer springs and movements of its inside.
4. Fielding blundered rather strangely in the celebrated Betsy Canning case, as Balzac did in the *Affaire Peytel*; but the story is too long for repetition in this place. The trials of Miss Canning and her supposed kidnappers are amongst the most amusing in the great collection of *State Trials*. Fielding's defence of his own conduct in the matter is reprinted in his *Miscellanies and Poems*, being the supplementary volume of the last collected edition of his works.
5. They were really the property not of Fielding but of the once famous "beau Fielding." See *Dictionary of National Biography*.
6. See *Tom Jones*, book xiv., chap. 1.
7. See *Voyage to Lisbon* (July 21) for some very good remarks upon this word, which, as he says, no two men understand in the same sense.
8. In his interesting Life of Godwin, Mr. Paul claims for his hero (I dare say rightly) that he was the first English writer to give a "lengthy and appreciative notice" of *Don Quixote*. But when he infers that Godwin was also the first English writer who recognised in Cervantes a great humourist, satirist, moralist, and artist, he seems to me to overlook Fielding and others. So Warton in his essay on *Pope* calls *Don Quixote* the "most original and unrivalled work of modern times." The book must have been popular in England from its publication, as we know from the preface to Beaumont and Fletcher's *Knight of the Burning Castle*; and numerous translations and imitations show that Cervantes was always enjoyed, if not criticised. Fielding's frequent references to *Don Quixote* (to say nothing of his play, *Don Quixote in England*) imply an admiration fully as warm as that of Godwin. *Don Quixote*, says Fielding, is more worthy the name of history than Mariana, and he always speaks of Cervantes in the tone of an affectionate disciple. Fielding, I will add, seems to me to have admired Shakespeare more heartily and intelligently than ninety-nine out of a hundred modern supporters of Shakespeare societies; though these gentlemen are never happier than when depreciating English eighteenth-century critics to exalt vapid German philosophising. Fielding's favourite play seems from his quotations to have been *Othello*.
9. Book x., chap. i.
10. *Tom Jones*, Book xv., chap. i.
11. For Fielding's view of the French novels of his day, see *Tom Jones*, Book xiii., chap. ix.

CLARA THOMSON
"A Note on Fielding's *Amelia*"
Westminster Review, November 1899, pp. 579–88

Owing, perhaps, to his supreme success in the delineation of one woman, and to the patience and delicacy with which this character is conducted through the painful intricacies of her story, and sacrificed at last to the tragic necessity of her fate, Richardson has been credited with having achieved the greatest triumph of the eighteenth century as an interpreter of feminine character. Yet, in spite of the profound effect that Clarissa Harlowe must have on every persevering reader, in spite of the tribute that every unprejudiced critic must pay to the genius of her creator, it must be confessed that she moves in a narrow sphere and exhibits in a very partial manner the characteristics of that infinitely complex nature of which she is so often taken as a type. Richardson did one thing excellently, and the poverty of his attainment in other directions induced his admirers to accumulate all their praise on his single achievement. He has been considered as *par excellence* the delineator and exponent of feminine character.

His position being thus secured, it has become a matter of tradition, and historians of literature (a class especially prone to generalisations) have established the convention that, while Richardson was supremely successful in his studies of women, Fielding excelled in masculine portraiture, and that the heroines of the latter are wanting in vigour and character. According to this convention, even Sophia Western, one of the most charming and spirited women that any English novelist has created, is depreciated, and it has been taken for granted that since Fielding drew men to the life he could not be equally happy in his treatment of their female relations.

And all this in the face of the fact that one of Fielding's three great novels is purely and simply a study of feminine character! The figure of Amelia dominates the story that bears her name as powerfully as that of Clarissa Harlowe absorbs all the interest in Richardson's novel; but the impression made by the latter is more forcible, partly because her fate is more tragic, and partly because the subsidiary characters in this book are less numerous and less lifelike.

Clarissa Harlowe is a woman placed in extraordinary and, it may be added, improbable circumstances, and the art of the novelist consists in knowing and revealing how such a woman so circumstanced would behave. Amelia, no less heroic in her own way, moves in ordinary and commonplace, almost sordid, surroundings. One knows that she is too sensible and discreet for the perils she encounters to have a tragic ending, and in her last resort she has the muscular, if not always intelligently guided, arm of her husband to defend her. But as she comes more within the range of the reader's own experience and of probable situations, no great effort of imagination is required to follow her adventures, and while one feels that if she had been put to the same test she would have behaved every whit as nobly as Clarissa, our sympathy accompanies her with less strain because her emotions are more intelligible to us.

Nor is *Amelia* the only novel in which Fielding vindicates his right to be considered a skilful delineator of women. Even in *Tom Jones*, besides Sophia, there are at least three or four women who are masterpieces of characterisation. Sophia's aunt, for instance, and Mrs. Waters, and Miss Biddy, and Mrs. Fitzpatrick. All these persons are utterly unlike one another, and yet perfectly lifelike. But in *Amelia* (and this is the one point in which the novel is superior to *Tom Jones*) the women

are even better. Just as Richardson, after having delineated an ideal feminine character in Clarissa Harlowe, attempted her masculine counterpart in Sir Charles Grandison, so Fielding, after the creation of Tom Jones, turned to that of Amelia. But it may be observed of both these writers that they are more successful in the idealistic treatment of women than in that of men. Richardson failed ludicrously when he tried to depict a perfect hero, and Tom Jones shows scarcely any idealisation at all. Critics have cavilled at the portrait of Captain Booth, and have said that "he only exists to be forgiven." But the fact is that Booth is simply a good fellow, without any particular mental or moral strength, drawn to the life, while Amelia is a good woman, very much idealised, yet with sufficient leaven of human nature to make her quite probable and extremely interesting.

But, though many readers have shared the admiration of Dr. Johnson and Thackeray for the heroine, her story has not always elicited equally cordial praise, and it has even been reluctantly hinted that the book is somewhat dull. One critic accounts for this by the fact that the novel begins when the romance of courtship is over. It is a story of married life, and married life, apparently, cannot be made interesting unless it is associated with unlawful passion. Surely this is a mistake, for the secret histories of even happy and successful marriages are not without their painful episodes, verging on tragedy, where, indeed, tragedy is only averted by patience and good sense and loyal forbearance. And such episodes, if they do not provide the unhealthy excitement of a certain class of French novels, may form the material of many a tender and diverting page. As, indeed, Fielding would show us in this very book, but that our taste is spoiled by more highly seasoned provender, and we are not always in the mood to appreciate less stimulating fare.

The mistake seems to lie here. Our estimate of Fielding and of what to expect from Fielding is generally formed from *Tom Jones*. Now, *Tom Jones* has all the good qualities of *Amelia*, and, in addition, a most elaborate and carefully constructed plot; the excitement and interest of the reader are sustained by the vigorous description of adventures which follow one another in such quick succession that there is no time for the attention to flag. These adventures, moreover, are all encountered by the hero, who himself has a very interesting and attractive personality. But in *Amelia*, though skilful construction is by no means absent, the subject of the adventures described is not the subject of the book. When Booth is arrested for debt our sympathy is evoked, not primarily for him, but for Amelia, who suffers through him. A woman whose qualities are essentially domestic cannot well be made the heroine of a picturesque novel; yet one side of Fielding's genius impelled him in this direction, while his profound knowledge of human nature, and the wide experience of mankind obtained in his office as a London magistrate, inclined him to character study and what is now called the psychological novel. In *Tom Jones* the two sides of his genius are equally balanced, but in *Amelia* the latter is predominant. This gives the book a more sombre and reflective tone. Mr. Austin Dobson has remarked that the difference in tone between the two novels would lead one to suppose that a long interval of time had elapsed between the dates of their production. This was not the case, yet *Amelia* is a far sadder, perhaps a wiser, certainly a less witty book than its predecessor. It is a monument to a dead woman, and in raising it to her memory her husband has laboured with a graver touch, a less exuberant, if not less vigorous energy.

And so, to appreciate *Amelia* one must put aside the memory of *Tom Jones*, and view it from a different standpoint.

Johnson once said that, "If you were to read Richardson for the story, your impatience would be so much fretted that you would hang yourself. But you must read him for the sentiment, and consider the story as only giving occasion to the sentiment." The same criticism applies in a less degree to *Amelia*. The subject is, briefly, the story of the misfortunes and difficulties of a young married couple who are defrauded of their inherited fortune. Dismissed on half pay, the husband, who has done good service in the army, takes to farming, but is unsuccessful, and is arrested for debt. He and his family are therefore obliged to live within the verge of court, but even this limited freedom cannot keep the too impulsive captain out of mischief. He is again arrested for a gaming debt, and is only rescued by the kind intervention of an old clergyman called Dr. Harrison, who acts the part of *deus ex machina* throughout the book. Finally the fortune is restored, and prosperity once more smiles on the sufferers. The story is varied by the account of the advances made to Booth by an adventuress named Miss Matthews, and by corresponding difficulties innocently incurred by Amelia; but, as the affections of neither husband nor wife are concerned in these adventures, little anxiety is felt by the reader as to their ultimate issue.

It will be seen, therefore, that the plot of *Amelia* is far less complicated than that of *Tom Jones*. We have, in fact, a study rather than a story, a study of married life and a study of feminine character. And this study of feminine character is so powerful that it has thrown into the shade the other personages of the story, who have received less than their due from the majority of critics.

This especially applies to Booth, who is often represented as merely an amiable blockhead. Professor Saintsbury is extremely severe on him, and on Amelia for her devotion to him.

> One could have better pardoned her forgiveness of her husband if she had, in the first place, been a little more conscious of what there was to forgive; and in the second, a little more romantic in her attachment to him. As it is, he was *son homme*, he was handsome, he had broad shoulders, he had a sweet temper, he was the father of her children, and that was enough. At least we are allowed to see in Mr. Booth no qualities other than these, and in her no imagination even of any other qualities.[1]

But as regards the first part of this criticism one must take into consideration contemporary matters, which allowed a greater moral license than our own time permits. Fielding lived in an age of low morality, and our wonder is not that he allowed his heroes to indulge in sins of the flesh, but that he never failed to punish them for so doing. Compare his treatment of such questions with that of Smollett, and the difference in moral tone is striking. And not only in Fielding's and Smollett's novels, but in those of their contemporaries, even women whose lives have been scarcely respectable are admitted to decent society, and mingle with good and noble women who know all about their antecedents. So that if Amelia judged her husband more leniently than, according to our notions, he deserved, it was because she was a woman of the eighteenth century and conformed with established contemporary custom, not because she personally was less virtuous or pure-minded than her modern sister. The lapse of fidelity wounded her as such lapses will wound loving and devoted wives in all time, and no passage in the book is more pathetic and convincing than that in which she is described as thinking that Booth has returned to his disloyalty. But once reassured concerning this, and convinced of his restored faith, she takes

the contemporary view of the heinousness of his sin. And let those who can affirm that their own standard of morality is altogether disassociated from the custom and conventions of their time first cast a stone.

But, further, allowing that Amelia's leniency was justifiable, would not our opinion of her good sense and intelligence be lessened if Fielding had represented her husband as so absolutely inane as Professor Saintsbury would have us think? Only compare Captain Booth with Sir Charles Grandison. The one is faulty, impulsive, weak, credulous, stupid, if you will, but instinct with life, and at least a man; the other, immaculate, deliberate, the pillar and prop of his acquaintance, the quintessence of honour and wisdom, but how dull, how mechanical, how tiresome! Booth is not merely handsome and broad-shouldered, not merely sweet-tempered and domesticated. He belongs to a type common enough among the English upper classes. Without great intellectual power (for his pedantic debate with the author in Bondum's house is not in keeping with the rest of his character, and is, as Mr. Austin Dobson has told us, a reminiscence of one of Fielding's early plays), but possessing plenty of common sense, generous and unsuspicious, a loyal friend and a brave soldier, he is in the main a thoroughly good fellow. His very weaknesses, his physical susceptibility to women (for no genuine passion for Miss Matthews is hinted), his want of reflection and his financial imprudence, are all characteristic of the class he illustrates, a class familiar to us all, and as common among us as among our great-grandfathers. Without wishing to palliate Booth's failings or to pardon him for the one grave infidelity of which he is made guilty, we are at liberty to appreciate his good qualities and to respect him for the indignation with which he views the advances of the "noble lord" to Amelia, though his necessities have obliged him to supplicate favours for himself. The dialogue of husband and wife on the subject of the children's visit to their patron is admirable, and the justice of the argument is all on Booth's side. Amelia has been telling him of the peer's generosity.

> Booth, instead of making a direct answer to what Amelia had said, cried coldly, "But do you think, my dear, it was right to accept all those expensive toys which the children brought home? And I ask you again, what return we are to make for these obligations?"
>
> "Indeed, my dear," cries Amelia, "you see this matter in too serious a light. Though I am the last person in the world who would lessen his lordship's goodness (indeed I shall always think we are both infinitely obliged to him), yet sure you must allow the expense to be a mere trifle to such a vast fortune. As for return, his own benevolence in the satisfaction it receives more than repays itself, and I am convinced he expects no other."
>
> "Very well, my dear," cries Booth, "you shall have your own way. I must confess I never yet found any reason to blame your discernment, and perhaps I have been in the wrong to give myself so much uneasiness on this account."
>
> "Uneasiness, child," said Amelia eagerly. "Good heavens! hath this made you uneasy?"
>
> "I do own it hath," answered Booth, "and it hath been the only cause of breaking my repose."
>
> "Why, then, I wish," cries Amelia, "all the things had been at the devil before ever the children had seen them; and whatever I may think myself, I promise you they shall never more receive the value of a farthing: if upon this occasion I have been the

cause of your uneasiness, you will do me the justice to believe that I was totally innocent."

At these words Booth caught her in his arms, and with the tenderest embrace emphatically repeating the word "innocent," cried, "Heaven forbid I should think otherwise. Oh, thou art the best of creatures that ever blessed a man."

"Well, but," said she, smiling, "do confess, my dear, the truth. I promise you I won't blame you nor disesteem you for it; but is not pride really at the bottom of this fear of obligation?"

"Perhaps it may be," answered he, "or if you wish you may call it fear. I own I am afraid of obligation as the worst kind of debts, for I have generally observed those who confer them expect to be repaid a thousand-fold."[2]

Nothing could exhibit the two in a better light—Booth, tormented by the hint that his friend James had given him as to their patron's character, yet unable to explain to his wife the real grounds for his fear; Amelia, blinded by maternal vanity as to the real significance of the peer's attention; ready, as ever, to follow her husband's desires as regards her course of action, yet with sufficient independence of judgment to keep her own opinion about the matter.

Nor is this the only occasion on which this devoted couple are represented as disagreeing with one another. Take, again, the discussion over the masquerade ticket. Booth objects, in the presence of Mrs. Ellison, to Amelia accepting it from their noble friend. Amelia, to preserve her husband's dignity, upholds his authority before a third person, but demands an explanation when the two are alone. He fears to tell her frankly, and begs her to be content with knowing his wish on the matter.

"I will appeal to yourself," answered she, "whether this be not using me too much like a child, and whether I can possibly help being a little offended at it?"

"Not in the least," replied he; "I use you only with the tenderness of a friend. I would only endeavour to conceal that from you which I think would give you uneasiness if you knew. These are called the pious frauds of friendship."

"I detest all fraud," says she, "and pious is too good an epithet to be joined to so odious a word. . . . If, after all this, you still insist on keeping the secret, I will convince you I am not ignorant of the duty of a wife by my obedience; but I cannot help telling you at the same time you will make me one of the most miserable of women."

"That is," cries he, "in other words, my dear Emily, to say I will be contented without the secret, but I am resolved to know it nevertheless."

"Nay, if you say so," cries she, "I am convinced you will tell me. Positively, dear Billy, I must and will know."

"Why then, positively," says Booth, "I will tell you. And I think I shall then show you that however well you may know the duty of a wife, I am not always able to behave like a husband. In a word, then, my dear, the secret is no more than this: I am unwilling you should receive any more presents from my lord."[3]

So Booth is forced by his affection, against his better judgment, to reveal the causes of his alarm; with the result that he had feared. Amelia is keenly wounded and passionately indignant at such a suggestion. She is hurt both in her affections and in her mind by the hint. She considers that the mere idea is an affront both to her virtue and to her intelligence, for how, she says, could such designs be unperceived by the person principally concerned, unless that person were an utter fool? She does not see that she is disarmed by her own innocence, and that her very want of suspicion may lead her into danger. But when the outburst of indignation has subsided, husband and wife are reconciled with mutual regrets, though Amelia, with characteristic tenacity, still thinks herself in the right. Fielding has learned the secret of happiness in marriage—the lesson of compromise.

"It is my opinion," he says in another place, "that we can have but little love for the person whom we will never indulge in an unreasonable demand."[4]

On the whole one likes Booth. If he sins he is heavily punished, and his conscience never becomes hardened. He is irresponsible, but he is not a fool. Fielding was a true artist when he put this born soldier into circumstances that needed the attainments of a man of business, and showed thereby that the qualities which were winning for us our colonial empire would not ensure financial success to their possessor. There is no subject on which our author waxes more indignant than the ingratitude shown by the Government to officers of distinguished merit who were so unfortunate as to lack interest in high places. But Booth's military training is apparent throughout the book. As far as his own sufferings are concerned he has plenty of pluck; it is the misery of those dear to him that disturbs his fortitude. When Amelia tries to deter him from foreign service for her sake, his tender heart is torn for his wife, while his honour as a soldier bids him go. And honour wins the day in spite of Amelia's entreaties. This man, after all, has some spirit, and is not simply a foolish prodigal, alternately uxorious and licentious.

For such a man Amelia's devotion is not altogether incompresible. His weakness and dependence are marked enough to bring into play that maternal element in her affection which is hardly ever absent from the love of good women. But, at the same time, he is not a despicable mate, and his wife's devotion to him need not in any degree detract from our opinion of her good sense.

And this is the quality for which Amelia is particularly remarkable. She is true to the ideal of her century in this, and if she is not very learned nor very "cultured," she has far more practical wisdom and capacity than the average nineteenth-century woman who clamours for independence and is in perpetual revolt against the conditions imposed by her sex. On occasion, as will be seen from the above extracts, she can employ forcible language, but she is wonderfully self-controlled, and not at all subject to what her contemporaries called the "vapours." From this steady self-control much of her dignity and serenity is derived, and when her husband, writhing under the double sting of fresh debt and suspicion of a friend, accuses her of having had secrets from him, she answers him with an affectionate reproof that at once recalls him to himself. "When you are calm," said she, "I will speak, but not before." It is this reserve of power that gives her so much influence over others. The foolish, repentant Mrs. Atkinson, who has not learned wisdom through her sorrows, and who, with twice the knowledge of the world that Amelia possesses, has not half her prudence, comes to her at once for sympathy, although she has quarreled with her immediately before. The relations of Amelia with her, and with Mrs. James, are especially interesting, as they show that our heroine was one of those rare women who can keep up a friendship after marriage. She has not narrowed all her interests to the home, not become so absorbed in wifely and maternal cares as to have no thought for those outside her domestic circle.

Yet how charming are these little pictures of home life, like firelit interiors revealing to the outsider fascinating glimpses of quiet happiness or pathetic devotion. Amelia putting her children to bed, walking with them in the park, gently reproving them and weeping over the misfortunes which she feels far more on their account than her own—all these beautiful and tender scenes add enormously to the convincing effect of the book. Fielding's references to children are always sympathetic, which is the more surprising since he wrote in an age that was far from idealising childhood as our own does. One remembers the scene with Parson Adams and his little boy (which foreshadows a similar one in the *Vicar of Wakefield*), the picture of Squire Western in Sophia's nursery listening to the tattling of his little daughter, and declaring it to be "sweeter than the finest cry of any dogs of England," and that most touching passage in the *Voyage to Lisbon* which relates the author's farewell to his own children before his departure on that journey from which he never returned.

But, after all, it is in her relations with her husband that the heroic side of Amelia's character is developed. The instinct of maternal love compels unselfishness with regard to children even in naturally selfish and egotistic women. But if there is one grievance that such women are inclined to magnify and resent above all others, it is the grievance, real or supposed, of the slightest approach to neglect on the part of their husbands. It is here that Amelia's generosity and magnanimity become truly sublime. Her large charity and sympathy, and her swift intuition, help her in some degree to regard things from the masculine standpoint, and to realise that a sudden gust of passion may drive a well-meaning man from the straight path for a time; but that if he be a good man he will return to it. No doubt she attributed Booth's lapse to the wiles and schemes of Miss Matthews; what woman would not? No doubt she gave the temptress all the blame and framed tender excuses for the beloved sinner; but her forgiveness is none the less great and grand for all that. How touching is the scene in which she hears her husband's confession of his guilt—a confession the humiliation of which she feels as much as he, so entirely has she made his honour her own.

> When he had ended his narration, Amelia, after a short silence, answered, "Indeed, I firmly believe every word you have said, but I cannot now forgive you the fault you have confessed; and my reason is—because I have forgiven it long ago. Here, my dear," said she, "is an instance that I am likewise capable of keeping a secret."
>
> She then delivered her husband a letter which she had some time ago received from Miss Matthews, and which was the same which that lady had mentioned, and supposed, as Booth had never heard of it, that it had miscarried, for she sent it by the penny post. In this letter, which was signed by a feigned name, she had acquainted Amelia with the infidelity of her husband, and had besides very greatly abused him, taxing him with many falsehoods, and, among the rest, with having spoken very slightingly and disrespectfully of his wife.

Amelia never shined forth to Booth in so amiable and great a light, nor did his own unworthiness ever appear to him so mean and contemptible, as at this instant. However, when he had read the letter, he uttered many violent protestations to her that all which related to herself was absolutely false.

> "I am convinced it is," said she. "I would not have a suspicion to the contrary for the world. I assure you I had, till last night revived it in my memory, almost forgot the letter; for, as I well knew from whom it came, by her mentioning obligations which she had conferred on you, and which you had more than once spoken to me of, I made large allowances for the situation you were then in; and I was the more satisfied, as the letter itself, as well as many other circumstances, convinced me the affair was at an end." [5]

And there, indeed, the matter is concluded. One cannot imagine that Amelia, in those other less serious differences that must have arisen between them even after prosperity had returned, ever reproached her husband with what had passed, or reminded him of former offences. What she loved and believed in in Booth was his higher nature, the nature that ached with remorse at the memory of sin. And so, by believing him incapable of the worst offences, she made him incapable of them; partaking the serene atmosphere that lay around her, he would himself be purified and raised to her level.

It has been said that the low moral tone of the eighteenth century is indicated by the want of respect with which women are treated in literature. By Swift and Pope, even by the genial Addison, they are regarded as inferiors in every respect, as toys and amusing companions for hours of relaxation, as fit subjects for more or less good-natured banter, but never as equals either in character or intellect.

Was it a sign of better things that just as the first half of the century approached its close *Clarissa Harlowe* appeared above the horizon, followed at no long distance by *Amelia*? From them it is an easy transition to Wordsworth's ideal, the "perfect woman, nobly planned"; though our heroine's character is perhaps better summed up in the less hackneyed lines of Tennyson:

> The mellow'd reflex of a winter moon;
> A clear stream flowing with a muddy one,
> Till in its onward current it absorbs
> With swifter movement and in purer light
> The vexed eddies of its wayward brother;
> A leaning and upbearing parasite,
> Clothing the stem, which else had fallen quite,
> With cluster'd flower-bells, and ambrosial orbs
> Of rich fruit bunches leaning on each other,
> Shadow forth thee: the world hath not another
> (Tho' all her fairest forms are types of thee,
> And thou of God in thy great charity)
> Of such a finish'd, chasten'd purity.

Notes

1. *Amelia*. Published by J.M. Dent & Co., 1893. "Introduction", p. 16.
2. *Amelia*. Vol. II, pp. 62–3.
3. *Amelia*. Vol. II, pp. 82 3.
4. *Amelia*. Vol. I, p. 137.
5. *Amelia*. Vol. III, pp. 186–7.

LAURENCE STERNE

LAURENCE STERNE

1713–1768

Laurence Sterne, novelist, was born at Clonmel, Ireland, on November 24, 1713. The son of a soldier, he spent his early years moving about as he and his mother followed his father's regiment. Around 1723 he was sent to a grammar school near Halifax; he never again returned to Ireland. In 1733 he entered Jesus College, Cambridge, where he studied classics and divinity and received a B.A. At Cambridge he discovered the philosophy of Locke, which was to have a great influence on his novels, and also became friendly with John Hall (later Hall-Stevenson).

Around 1737 Sterne was ordained into the Church of England as a deacon. In the following year he became a priest and was granted the living of Sutton-on-the-Forest, Yorkshire; the neighboring living of Stillington was added in 1744. In 1741 he married Elizabeth Lumley, who gave birth to seven children, of whom only his daughter Lydia (b. 1749) survived.

In 1743 Sterne submitted to the *Gentleman's Magazine* a poem entitled "The Unknown World: Verses Occasion'd by Hearing a Pass-Bell," but with the exception of two sermons, *The Case of Elijah* (1747) and *The Abuses of Conscience* (1750), he published nothing else before 1759. In 1758 Sterne became involved in an ecclesiastical controversy, and as a way of mocking the opposition he composed his *Political Romance* (1759), later renamed *The History of a Good Warm Watchcoat* (1769). Although this pamphlet was almost immediately suppressed, the writing of it gave Sterne the confidence to progress to more ambitious projects; very shortly he began to work on the novel *Tristram Shandy*, eventually published in nine volumes between 1759 and 1767. The first two volumes, released in 1759, were an immediate success, and a second edition, with an engraving by William Hogarth, appeared soon after. In 1760 Sterne published two volumes of sermons as *The Sermons of Mr. Yorick*, using the name under which he had portrayed himself in *Tristram Shandy*.

Sterne, who had contracted tuberculosis while at Cambridge, was by 1762 seriously ill, and in an attempt to regain his health he traveled to France with his wife and daughter. When he returned to England in 1764 his wife remained behind, as they were by then estranged. Sterne made a second trip to the Continent in 1765, and for eight months traveled in France and Italy. In 1767, after returning to England, he met Eliza Draper, the twenty-three-year-old wife of an official of the East India Company, and during the three months before she returned to her husband Sterne fell deeply in love with her. Throughout the summer of 1767, after she had left for India, he kept a diary now known as the *Journal to Eliza*. The last work by Sterne to appear was his *Sentimental Journey through France and Italy* (1768), a fictionalized account of his two trips to the Continent. Sterne died of tuberculosis on March 18, 1768.

Personal

Lord Ossory told Us that the famous Dr. Sterne dyed that Morning; he seem'd to lament him very much. Lord Eglington said (but not in a ludicrous manner) that he had taken his "Sentimental journey."—LADY MARY COKE, *Journal*, March 14, 1768

> Shall pride a heap of sculptur'd marble raise,
> Some worthless, unmourn'd titled fool to praise;
> And shall we not by one poor grave-stone learn
> Where genius, wit, and humour sleep with *Sterne?*
> —DAVID GARRICK, "Epitaph on Laurence Sterne," c. 1768

The celebrated writer Sterne, after being long the idol of this town, died in a mean lodging without a single friend who felt interest in his fate except Becket, his bookseller, who was the only person that attended his interment. He was buried in a graveyard near Tyburn, belonging to the parish of Marylebone, and the corpse being marked by some of the *resurrection men* (as they are called), was taken up soon afterward and carried to an anatomy professor of Cambridge. A gentleman who was present at the dissection told me, he recognized Sterne's face the moment he saw the body.—EDMOND MALONE, "Maloniana" (1787), cited in Sir James Prior, *Life of Edmond Malone*, 1860, pp. 373–74

It having been observed that there was little hospitality in London;—JOHNSON. 'Nay, Sir, any man who has a name, or who has the power of pleasing, will be very generally invited in London. The man, Sterne, I have been told, has had engagements for three months.' GOLDSMITH. 'And a very dull fellow.' JOHNSON. 'Why no, Sir.'—JAMES BOSWELL, *Life of Johnson*, 1791

Ah, I am as bad as that dog Sterne, who preferred whining over "a dead ass to relieving a living mother"—villain—hypocrite—slave—sycophant! but *I* am no better.—GEORGE GORDON, LORD BYRON, *Journal*, Dec. 1, 1813

In him also there was a great quantity of good struggling through the superficial evil. He terribly failed in the discharge of his duties, still, we must admire in him that sportive kind of geniality and affection, still a son of our common mother, not cased up in buckram formulas as the other writers were, clinging to forms, and not touching realities. And, much as has been said against him, we cannot help feeling his immense love for things around him; so that we may say of him, as of Magdalen, 'much is forgiven him, because he loved much.' A good simple being after all.—THOMAS CARLYLE, *Lectures on the History of Literature*, 1838

Though the mind of Sterne was deeply imbued with a sense of the ludicrous, yet his versatile nature was so alive to the charms of what is beautiful in all things—whether of a material or spiritual nature—that it tinged his predominant jollity with that fine spirit of whim for which he was so remarkably distinguished. Few men were possessed of a finer perception of form, whether it be displayed in painting or in sculpture; and, had he given his mind to either, there is reason to think that he would have been successful as an artist. In this faculty he differed much from his contemporary, Smollett, who saw but little beauty, if any, in the Venus de Medici, for which want of taste he was laughed at by Sterne, who nicknamed him Smellfungus.

Sterne had much musical taste, and played well upon the viol. Love of the drama was also a marked feature of his mind; and from these sources he chose, for his faculty of comparison, materials which render his similes animated and pleasing. He was fonder of fame than of power. His ardour in pursuit of pleasure amounted to unrestrained selfishness; but his selfishness was not the result of self-love, engendered by self-esteem. It arose rather from the excessive fervour of his feelings, by which he allowed himself to be carried beyond the bounds of propriety, owing to want of firmness and due consideration for his own dignity. He was hurried on in these courses, so fatal to his good name, not so much by gross and vicious tendencies, as by a rare buoyancy of spirit proceeding from unflagging hope and unbounded mirthfulness; accompanied with a keen perception of graceful form, which enabled him to appreciate female beauty, and caused him to yield to those allurements which so often attend its presence, and which his instincts were too prone to sympathise with and admire.

To a man of such a turn of mind the unprecedented honours he met with in London, on the publication of the two first volumes of *Tristram Shandy*, must have been hurtful; and that this was the case we have the authority of his warmly-attached friend, Garrick, who said, sorrowfully, "He degenerated in London, like an ill-transplanted shrub. The incense of the great spoiled his head, and their ragouts his stomach."
—JAMES P. BROWNE, "Preface" to *The Works of Laurence Sterne*, 1873, Vol. 1, pp. 26–27

General

Tristram Shandy is still a greater object of admiration, the Man as well as the Book. one is invited to dinner, where he dines, a fortnight beforehand. his portrait is done by Reynolds, & now engraving. Dodsley gives 700£ for a second edition, & two new volumes not yet written; & tomorrow will come out two Volumes of Sermons by him. your Friend Mr. Hall has printed two Lyric Epistles, one to my Cousin Shandy on his coming to Town, the other to the grown Gentlewomen, the Misses of York: they seem to me to be absolute madness.—THOMAS GRAY, Letter to Thomas Wharton (April 22, 1760)

> Could I, whilst Humour held the quill,
> Could I digress with half that skill;
> Could I with half that skill return,
> Which we so much admire in Sterne,
> Where each digression, seeming vain,
> And only fit to entertain,
> Is found, on better recollection,
> To have a just and nice connexion,
> To help the whole with wondrous art,
> Whence it seems idly to depart;
> Then should our readers ne'er accuse
> These wild excursions of the Muse.
> —CHARLES CHURCHILL, *The Ghost*, 1762, Bk. 3, ll. 967–78

And now, Sir, our day of combat is come.—You deny Sterne originality—and say that no classic ear can endure his style. These assertions more than surprise—they astonish me. What!—that imagination, which I have always thought of such exquisite, such original colouring!—that penetration which seems to have an hundred eyes with which to look into the human heart!—that happy, thrice happy, mixture of the humorous and the pathetic, in which he stands alone amongst all other writers out of the dramatic scale; resembling none, and whom not one, amongst his numerous imitators, have attempted to copy, without proving, by their total failure, the difficulty of acquiring a manner so singularly, so curiously original. Like ether, its spirit is too subtile and volatile to become the vehicle of any other person's ideas. And then that frolic fancy!—that all-atoning wit!—that style which my ear finds so natural, easy, animated, and eloquent!—how could you thus scorn them?

My dear Sir, *who* are they from whom he has borrowed? Some slight, very slight, resemblance perhaps exists between the best sallies of Swift's humour and Sterne's: but Swift has not any of Sterne's pathos, and Sterne has none of the filthiness of Swift,—though too apt to sport licentiously with comic double-meanings. His fault, in that respect, however justly censurable, has no tendency to injure the minds of his readers by inflaming their passions. Swift and Rabelais, whom he is also accused of copying, never interest the affections, while Sterne guides, turns, and precipitates them into any channel he pleases.

I can believe that he took the hint of character for his sub-acid philosopher from the Martinus Scriblerius of Pope, Swift, and Arbuthnot; but there is an immense superiority in the vividness with which he has coloured his Shandy; in the dramatic spirit he has infused into the character; in the variety of situations in which he has placed the hypothesis-monger,—all natural, probable, and exquisitely humorous. We see and hear the little domestic group at Shandy-hall; nor can we help an involuntary conviction, not only that they all existed, but that they had been of our acquaintance; and where may be found even the most shadowy prototype in books, of uncle Toby and his Trim, of Mrs Shandy and Dr Slop?

At last this note of your's in your great work against Sterne—this note,

> At which my very locks have stood on end,
> Like quills upon the fretful porcupine,

Confirms anew an observation of mine, long since made;—that I never knew a man or woman of letters, however ingenious, ingenuous, and judicious, as to their general taste, but there was some one fine writer, at least, to which their "Lynx's beam became the mole's dim curtain." Mason, Hayley, and Boothby, are moles to Ossian. Gray was a mole to Rousseau.—Darwin is a mole to Milton, and that you will say is indeed a *molism*. Envy made Johnson a mole to all our best poets, except Dryden and Pope. You are a mole to Sterne;—and I—for why should not my portly self run in amongst you intellectually greater folk?—ANNA SEWARD, Letter to George Gregory (Dec. 5, 1787)

Of Sterne and Rousseau it is difficult to speak without being misunderstood; yet it is impossible to deny the praise of wit and originality to Yorick, or of captivating eloquence to the philosopher of vanity. Their imitators are below notice.
—THOMAS JAMES MATHIAS, *The Pursuits of Literature* (1794), 1798, p. 59, Note

About fifty years ago a very singular work appeared, somewhat in the guise of a novel, which gave a new impulse to writings of this stamp; namely, *The Life and Opinions of Tristram Shandy*, followed by *The Sentimental Journey*, by the rev. Mr. Sterne, a clergyman of York. They exhibit much originality, wit, and beautiful strokes of pathos, but a total want of plan or adventure, being made up of conversations and detached incidents. It is the peculiar characteristic of this writer, that he affects the heart, not by long drawn tales of distress, but by light electric touches which thrill the nerves of the reader who possesses a correspondent sensibility of frame. His characters, in like manner, are struck out by a few masterly touches. He resembles those painters who can give expression to a figure by two or three strokes of bold outline, leaving the imagination to fill up the sketch; the feelings are awakened as really by the story of *Le Fevre*, as by the narrative of *Clarissa*. The indelicacies of these volumes are very reprehensible, and indeed in a clergyman scandalous, particularly in the first publication, which however has the richest vein of humour. The two *Shandys*, *Trim*, *Dr. Slop*, are all drawn with a masterly hand. It is one of the merits of Sterne that he has awakened the attention of his readers to the wrongs of the poor negroes, and certainly a great spirit of tenderness and humanity breathes throughout the work. It is rather mortifying to reflect how little the power of expressing these feelings is connected with moral worth; for Sterne was a man by no means attentive to the happiness of those connected with him; and we are forced to confess that an author may conceive the idea of "brushing away flies without killing them," and yet behave ill in every relation of life.

It has lately been said that Sterne has been indebted for much of his wit to *Burton's Anatomy of Melancholy*. He certainly exhibits a good deal of reading in that and many other books out of the common way, but the wit is in the application, and that is his own. This work gave rise to the vapid effusions of a crowd of sentimentalists, many of whom thought they had seized the spirit of Sterne, because they could copy him in his breaks and asterisks. The taste spread, and for a while, from the pulpit to the playhouse, the reign of sentiment was established. Among the more respectable imitators of Sterne may be reckoned Mr. Mackenzie in his *Man of Feeling* and his *Julia de Roubigné*, and Mr. Pratt in his *Emma Corbett*.—ANNA LAETITIA BARBAULD, "On the Origin and Progress of Novel-Writing," *The British Novelists*, 1810, Vol. 1, pp. 40–42

I have very few heresies in English literature. I do not remember any serious one, but my moderate opinion of Sterne.—SIR JAMES MACKINTOSH (May 31, 1811), cited in Robert James Mackintosh, *Memoirs of the Life of Sir James Mackintosh*, 1853, Vol. 2, p. 102

It remains to speak of Sterne; and I shall do it in few words. There is more of *mannerism* and affectation in him, and a more immediate reference to preceding authors; but his excellences, where he is excellent, are of the first order. His characters are intellectual and inventive, like Richardson's; but totally opposite in the execution. The one are made out by continuity, and patient repetition of touches: the others, by glancing transitions and graceful apposition. His style is equally different from Richardson's: it is at times the most rapid, the most happy, the most idiomatic of any that is to be found. It is the pure essence of English conversational style. His works consist only of *morceaux*—of brilliant passages. I wonder that Goldsmith, who ought to have known better, should call him 'a dull fellow.' His wit is poignant, though artificial; and his characters (though the groundwork of some of them had been laid before) have yet invaluable original

differences; and the spirit of the execution, the master-strokes constantly thrown into them, are not to be surpassed. It is sufficient to name them;—Yorick, Dr. Slop, Mr. Shandy, My Uncle Toby, Trim, Susanna, and the Widow Wadman. In these he has contrived to oppose, with equal felicity and originality, two characters, one of pure intellect, and the other of pure good nature, in My Father and My Uncle Toby. There appears to have been in Sterne a vein of dry, sarcastic humour, and of extreme tenderness of feeling; the latter sometimes carried to affectation, as in the tale of Maria, and the apostrophe to the recording angel: but at other times pure, and without blemish. The story of Le Fevre is perhaps the finest in the English language. My Father's restlessness, both of body and mind, is inimitable. It is the model from which all those despicable performances against modern philosophy ought to have been copied, if their authors had known any thing of the subject they were writing about. My Uncle Toby is one of the finest compliments ever paid to human nature. He is the most unoffending of God's creatures; or, as the French express it, *un tel petit bon homme!* Of his bowling-green, his sieges, and his amours, who would say or think any thing amiss!—WILLIAM HAZLITT, *Lectures on the English Comic Writers*, 1818

Sterne says that the liveliest of our pleasures ends with a shudder which is almost painful. Unbearable observer! He should have kept it to himself; many people wouldn't have noticed it.—ALEXANDER PUSHKIN, "Fragments from Letters, Thoughts, and Notes" (1827), *The Critical Prose of Alexander Pushkin*, ed. and tr. Carl R. Proffer, 1969, p. 49

I think highly of Sterne; that is, of the first part of *Tristram Shandy*: for as to the latter part, about the widow Wadman, it is stupid and disgusting; and the *Sentimental Journey* is poor sickly stuff. There is a great deal of affectation in Sterne, to be sure; but still the characters of Trim and the two Shandies are most individual and delightful. Sterne's morals are bad, but I don't think they can do much harm to any one whom they would not find bad enough before. Besides, the oddity and erudite grimaces under which much of his dirt is hidden, take away the effect for the most part; although, to be sure, the book is scarcely readable by women.—SAMUEL TAYLOR COLERIDGE, *Table Talk*, Aug. 18, 1833

We think that, on the whole, Mackenzie is the first master of this delicious style. Sterne, doubtless, has deeper touches of humanity in some of his works. But there is no sustained feeling—no continuity of emotion—no extended range of thought, over which the mind can brood in his ingenious and fantastical writings. His spirit is far too mercurial and airy to suffer him tenderly to linger over those images of sweet humanity which he discloses. His cleverness breaks the charm which his feeling spreads, as by magic, around us. His exquisite sensibility is ever counteracted by his perceptions of the ludicrous, and his ambition after the strange. No harmonious feeling breathes from any of his pieces. He sweeps "that curious instrument, the human heart," with hurried fingers, calling forth in rapid succession its deepest and its liveliest tones, and making only marvellous discord. His pathos is, indeed, most genuine while it lasts; but the soul is not suffered to cherish the feeling which it awakens.—T. NOON TALFOURD, "Mackenzie," *Critical and Miscellaneous Writings*, 1842, p. 7

⟨. . .⟩ he used to blubber perpetually in his study, and finding his tears infectious, and that they brought him a great popularity, he exercised the lucrative gift of weeping: he utilized it, and cried on every occasion. I own that I don't value or respect much the cheap dribble of those fountains. He fatigues me with his perpetual disquiet and his uneasy appeals to my risible or sentimental faculties. He is always looking in my face, watching his effect, uncertain whether I think him an imposter or not; posture-making, coaxing, and imploring me. "See what sensibility I have—own now that I'm very clever—do cry now, you can't resist this." The humour of Swift and Rabelais, whom he pretended to succeed, poured from them as naturally as song does from a bird; they lose no manly dignity with it, but laugh their hearty great laugh out of their broad chests as nature bade them. But this man—who can make you laugh, who can make you cry too—never lets his reader alone, or will permit his audience repose: when you are quiet, he fancies he must rouse you, and turns over head and heels, or sidles up and whispers a nasty story. The man is a great jester, not a great humourist. He goes to work systematically and of cold blood; paints his face, puts on his ruff and motley clothes, and lays down his carpet and tumbles on it.—WILLIAM MAKEPEACE THACKERAY, *The English Humourists of the Eighteenth Century*, 1853

Never did Hogg utter (to use his own favourite phrase) a truer "apophthegm." Sterne is one of the men, with world-famous reputation, of whom his native Ireland has small cause to be proud. He was five-and-forty before he commenced *Tristram Shandy*—the wit and pathos of which took the town by storm. Bishop Warburton (author of the Divine Legation of Moses,) publicly declaring that it was the English Rabelais, while he privately warned the author that its "violations of decency and good manners" were numerous and blamable. Soon after, Warburton pronounced him to be "an irrecoverable scoundrel." Sterne expected even a mitre, but the accession of George III, a moral man, deprived him of all hope of rising in the church, where he already had several benefices. Continuing *Tristram Shandy*, making it more and more indecent—reading chapter after chapter, as composed, to his wife,—making his only child, a girl of fourteen, copy it for the press, he produced further volumes, the success of which naturally encouraged him to write more; to put the jester's cap and bells upon the head of the divine. So infamous was his private character, that when he entered the pulpit to preach in York Minster, of which he was a prebend, many of the congregation rose from their seats and left the cathedral. His conduct and temper so much provoked his wife, a loving and patient woman, that she was compelled to live away from him. With health so broken that his continued existence appeared almost miraculous, he entered into an intrigue with a married woman, and, at the age of 54, openly speculating on the prospect of marrying her, when his own wife as well as the lady's husband should die! The only redeeming feeling in his life, was his devoted love for his daughter, for whom, however, he made not the slightest provision. He died, in lodgings in London, and his attendants robbed him of his gold shirt-buttons as he lay helpless in bed. His letters, which fully expose his profligacy, were published, seven years after his death, by his daughter—so reduced to poverty by his extravagance that she was compelled to barter his reputation for bread. It is almost inexplicable how such a man as Sterne could have lived so loosely and produced such a pure-minded original as My Uncle Toby, and such a faithful serving man as Corporal Trim, maternal grandfather to Sam Weller, in all probability.—R. SHELTON MACKENZIE, Note to John Wilson, *Noctes Ambrosianae*, 1854, Vol. 4, p. 214

The humour of Sterne is not only very different from that of Fielding and Smollett, but is something unique in our literature. He also was a professed admirer of Cervantes; to as large an extent as Swift he adopted the whimsical and perpetually digressive manner of Rabelais; and there is proof that he was well acquainted with the works of preceding humorists less familiarly known in England. But he was himself a humorist by nature—a British or Irish Yorick, with differences from any of those who might have borne that name before him after their imaginary Danish prototype; and, perpetually as he reminds us of Rabelais, his Shandean vein of wit and fancy is not for a moment to be regarded as a mere variety of Pantagruelism. There is scarcely anything more intellectually exquisite than the humour of Sterne. To very fastidious readers much of the humour of Fielding or of Smollett might come at last to seem but buffoonery; but Shakespeare himself, as one fancies, would have read Sterne with admiration and pleasure.

Tristram Shandy and the *Sentimental Journey* were certainly novelties in English prose writing. The first peculiarity that strikes us in them, considered as novels, is the thin style of the fiction in comparison either with that of Fielding or with that of Smollett. There is little or no continuous story. That special constituent of epic interest which arises from the fable or the action is altogether discarded, and is even turned into jest; and all is made to depend on what the critics called the characters, the sentiments, and the diction. As to the characters, who knows not that group of originals, Shandy the elder, Uncle Toby, Corporal Trim, Dr. Slop, the Widow Wadman, &c.? These were "characters of nature," and not "characters of manners,"—creations of a fine fancy working in an ideal element, and not mere copies or caricatures of individualities actually observed. And how *good* they all are, what heart as well as oddity there is in them! One feels that one could have lived cheerfully and freely in the vicinity of Shandy Hall, whereas it is only now and then among the characters of Fielding and Smollett that this attraction is felt by the reader. Coleridge, who has noted as one of Sterne's great merits this faith in moral good as exhibited in his favourite characters, noted also his physiognomic skill and his art in bringing forward and giving significance to the most evanescent minutiæ in thought, feeling, look, and gesture. In the dissertations, digressions, and interspersed whimsicalities of Sterne we see the same art of minute observation displayed; while we are perpetually entertained and surprised by reminiscences from out-of-the-way authors (many of them plagiarisms from Burton), by remarks full of wit and sense, by subtleties of a metaphysical intellect, and by quaint flights of a gay and delicate, but bold imagination. The "tenderness" of Sterne, his power of "pathetic" writing, all his readers have confessed; nor even can the artificiality of much of his pathos take away the effect on our sympathies. Sensibility—a capacity for being easily moved—was the quality he gave himself out as possessing personally in a high degree, and as most desirous of representing and diffusing by his writings, and he certainly succeeded. So far as sensibility can be taught by fiction, his works teach it, and perhaps it was one of his uses at the time when he lived that he had chosen to be the apostle of a quality which was otherwise greatly at a discount in contemporary literature. Add to all the exquisite accuracy and finish of Sterne's diction. Even now the grace, the insinuating delicacy, the light lucidity, the diamond-like sparkle of Sterne's style make reading him a peculiar literary pleasure. One could cull from his pages, and especially from his *Tristram Shandy*, a far greater number of passages for a book of elegant extracts than from the works of Fielding or Smollett. Several such passages are universal favourites already.—DAVID MASSON, *British Novelists and Their Styles*, 1859, pp. 145–48

Even Jean Paul, the greatest of German humorous authors, and never surpassed in comic conception or in the pathetic quality of humor, is not to be named with his master, Sterne, as a creative humorist. What are Siebenkäs, Fixlein, Schmelzle, and Fibel, (a single lay-figure to be draped at will with whimsical sentiment and reflection, and put in various attitudes,) compared with the living reality of Walter Shandy and his brother Toby, characters which we do not see merely as puppets in the author's mind, but poetically projected from it in an independent being of their own?—JAMES RUSSELL LOWELL, "Lessing" (1866), *Works*, Riverside ed., Vol. 2, p. 170

It must be confessed that Sterne has not paid quite attention enough to this law of the style. He is tedious, lengthy, wearisome, obscure, repellent, to such an extent that his books, *Tristram Shandy* especially, are little read nowadays. And yet *Tristram* is a masterpiece: the characters of my Uncle Toby and of Corporal Trim are real creations. There is nothing more original, nothing more thoroughly worked out, in any literature; but nothing less than these admirable portraits and some charming passages could have succeeded in saving Sterne's books. The mere style which he created, and to which his name remains in some sort attached, the style of humorous fantasy, would not have sufficed to do it.

⟨. . .⟩ Unluckily Sterne is never natural for long; if he possesses a style of his own, a substratum of real originality, he possesses also affectations, a method, and a great deal of both. He is a mannerist. He tries to be odd, which is the worst way of attaining oddity. He lays himself out to astonish us, which is the worst way of succeeding in doing so. He begins his story by the first end he can catch hold of, and then goes on anyhow, dropping the clue every moment, piling up interruptions, digressions, discussions; affecting not to know what he is going to write next sentence; building his theatre before us, and insisting that we shall see its tricks and dodges; appearing in person on the scene with fool's cap on head, and warning us that he is going to do so; jingling his bells, pirouetting, shouting words of double meaning at us, playing tricks on the audience. These devices are by no means invariably amusing—very far from it. How is one to be amused by chapters in reverse order, blank pages, blacked pages, haphazard diagrams? Can Sterne possibly have thought all this quaint and witty? Can the exquisite author of the story of Le Fevre have mistaken, as so often happens, the strength and the weakness of his genius, holding as its true originality what was only slag and dross? What is certain is that Sterne keeps afloat to-day on the current of literature with some difficulty, and that it is the fault of the very eccentricities on which he plumed himself. For he does plume himself on them, and this is what sets us against him; his drolleries are sought for, his caprices deliberate. There is affectation in his letting himself go; he is the most learned of buffoons, the most sophisticated of simpletons, so much so that you are sure of nothing in him, neither of his tears nor of his laughter.—EDMOND SCHERER, "Laurence Sterne, or The Humorist" (1870), *Essays on English Literature*, tr. George Saintsbury, 1891, pp. 161, 172–73

After devoting a chapter to the charges of plagiarism contained in Dr. Ferriar's *Illustrations* (which is as much as they deserve), Mr. Traill proceeds to the consideration of Sterne's style, of his general characteristics, of his humour and sentiment. He thinks that to talk of the "style" of Sterne is as though one should say "the form of Proteus," so uniformly eccentric and regularly irregular he considers him. He thinks Sterne's mode of expression is destitute of precision, and in many cases

a perfect marvel of literary slipshod. This is no doubt just criticism; and in all essential features Sterne's writing resembled his talk, which has been described as always animated, often brilliant, rarely correct, and never clerical. His "style" was no doubt consciously founded upon that of Rabelais; and certainly, in discursiveness, in deliberate buffoonery, in extravagant eccentricity, and in solemn and ingenious pretence of a measureless profundity of meaning where no meaning whatever existed or was intended—in a word, in a brilliant sense, and yet more brilliant nonsense, the style of Sterne does gravitate towards that of the master of wits. It is hardly necessary to say that the parallel goes no farther. Between the occult truths, political and philosophical, which Rabelais was often compelled to hide behind a masquerade of pure buffoonery, and the transparent absurdities which Sterne, as a mode of attracting attention, concealed behind a veil of mysterious significance, there is indeed a whole world of purpose which forbids that we should unite the names of these writers. The real excellence of Sterne's writing, however, is obvious enough, his sputterings, dashes, blank pages, and countless affectations notwithstanding. He excels, perhaps, as Walter Bagehot said, all other writers in simple and direct description of common human action; and therein his genius was continually developing, the *Sentimental Journey* being superior to *Tristram Shandy* in that form of realistic force. Mr. Traill is justly severe on Sterne's claims as a man of sentiment; he thinks nearly all the pet bits of pathos on which the writer prided himself, and for which he has been extolled are complete failures as serious appeals to the heart, and failures traceable to Sterne's artistic error of obtruding his own personality, and begging the reader to "turn from the picture to the artist, to cease gazing for a moment on his touching creation, and to admire the fine feeling, the exquisitely sympathetic nature, of the man who created it." No doubt there is truth in this, but it is not the whole truth. It is not a fact that the primary condition of success in realistic pathos is that the writer should erase himself from the reader's consciousness altogether. It will be found that the most profoundly moving passages in fiction are concerned not only with the sad or tragic events they record, but also, in a secondary degree, with the emotions of the spectator or narrator who, from first to last, floods his dramatic narrative with subjective passion. This interposition of an outside intelligence seems always necessary to interpret our feelings to ourselves, and to make us realise that the pathos of the recorded scene comes from someone, instead of living merely in an atmosphere of cold drama. In Sterne the "artistic error" lies deeper than Mr. Traill indicates in his just strictures on Sterne's confusion of artistic methods. Sterne is as self-conscious a humorist as the melancholy Jacques; but he is as deliberate a jester as Touchstone. He loves to suck melancholy out of any passing event "as a weasel sucks eggs;" but he also delights to thrust constantly before our eyes the cap and bells; not that he intends the smile to compete with the tear, but that he prides himself on his personal freedom from the torturing sensibilities over which he claims to have absolute command. Immediately after one of his famous sentimental outbursts, he tells us how good the inn is at Moulines. This is an outrage of a kind he delighted to perpetrate. It seems to say: "Behold! what a master I am! How I can harrow up your feelings! and now I'm off to eat a muttonchop." It is the grimace of a bad actor before the tragic business is over, before he quits the stage, and while his face is still turned towards his audience. Of Sterne's humour Mr. Traill does not seem to say much that is new. He speaks of it as Cervantic; and, in estimating the net sum of Sterne's creative power, he says the writer will live by virtue of his one individual creation—Capt. Tobias Shandy. He cannot mean that the humour of Uncle Toby's character is the Cervantic element in Sterne, for that is obviously centred in the elder Shandy. Walter Shandy is the only Don Quixote of English fiction, and, therefore, the only character in Sterne that is essentially Cervantic, the humour of Uncle Toby and of Sterne's own character being distinctly Shaksperean.

That Thackeray should have denied to Sterne the character of a great humorist, and attributed to him only the qualities of a great wit, proves how astoundingly untrustworthy the criticism must be that is founded on, and begins with, an illiberal estimate of personal character. Sterne was vain; he was licentious; he was insincere. Be it so. On the other hand, he was courageous under bodily suffering; he was totally free from literary envy; and he never pretended (his accidental clerical functions out of the count) to be a better man than he was. He stole unblushingly from earlier writers, but never from lack of originality; and his plagiarisms are only more obvious than other people's because more undisguised. In short, neither in the bad qualities nor in the good qualities he had can he be considered much more reprehensible than writers before him and after, whose ill-luck it never was to be held up to the ridicule of popular audiences by the brilliant satirist who loathed and despised Sterne, and read his more sentimental utterances with a mock solemnity of tone that made his hearers laugh until the tears rolled down their cheeks.—HALL CAINE, *Academy*, Nov. 4, 1882, pp. 321–22

So it is that although *Tristram Shandy* continues one of the most popular classics in the language, nobody dares to confess his debt to Sterne except in discreet terms of apology.

But the fellow wrote the book. You can't deny *that*, though Thackeray may tempt you to forget it. (What proportion does My Uncle Toby hold in that amiable Lecture?) The truth is that the elemental simplicity of Captain Shandy and Corporal Trim did not appeal to the author of *The Book of Snobs* in the same degree as the pettiness of the man Sterne appealed to him: and his business in Willis's Rooms was to talk, not of Captain Shandy, but of the man Sterne, to whom his hearers were to feel themselves superior as members of society. I submit that this was not a worthy task for a man of letters who was also a man of genius. I submit that it was an inversion of the true critical method to wreck Sterne's *Sentimental Journey* at the outset by picking Sterne's life to pieces, holding up the shreds, and warning the reader that any nobility apparent in his book will be nothing better than a sham. Sterne is scarcely arrived at Calais and in conversation with the Monk before you are cautioned how you listen to the imposter. "Watch now," says the critic; "he'll be at his tricks in a moment. Hey, *paillasse!* There!—didn't I tell you?" And yet I am as sure that the opening pages of the *Sentimental Journey* are full of genuine feeling as I am that if Jonathan Swift had entered the room while the Lecture upon him was going forward, he would have eaten William Makepeace Goliath, white waistcoat and all.

Frenchmen, who are either less awed than we by lecturers in white waistcoats, or understand the methods of criticism somewhat better, cherish the *Sentimental Journey* (in spite of its indifferent French) and believe in the genius that created it. But the Briton reads it with shyness, and the British critic speaks of Sterne with bated breath, since Thackeray told it in Gath that Sterne was a bad man, and the daughters of Philistia triumphed.—SIR ARTHUR QUILLER-COUCH, "Laurence Sterne" (1891), *Adventures in Criticism*, 1896, pp. 43–44

Sterne, far more than Thackeray, hated "the artificialities of civilization," and although his characters have nothing of "the violent blackguard" about them, his philosophy of human conduct is substantially the philosophy of Rousseau. The two writers were contemporary, Rousseau having been born in 1712, Sterne in 1713. There is no reason to believe that Sterne ever read a line of Rousseau, but it may be that the same reactionary feeling, spoken of by Maine, affected the English novelist as well as the French philosopher. At all events, we find in Sterne's fiction the very embodiment and concrete working out of Rousseau's theory of human conduct.—HENRY CHILDS MERWIN, "The Philosophy of Sterne," *Atlantic*, Oct. 1894, p.523

Laurence Sterne was a born humorist, but his humor was the humor of whimsicality, and at times his oddity grows wearisome. He is too artful to be sympathetic, and his artifice is too obvious. Besides, he is over-fond of innuendo; slyly playing back and forth, he now pretends an innocence more impertinent than diverting, and now suggests that his reader is deeper in the mire than he is; always exhibiting a genius in the art with which he stimulates the latent wickedness whose presence in weak human nature this worldly Ecclesiastes understands all too well. It hardly need be said that it is not for his sermons in six volumes that we remember Laurence Sterne. His two works, *Tristram Shandy* and *The Sentimental Journey*, are the memorials which keep his memory green. The latter of these two productions is merely a sketchy account of a supposititious journey over the usual continental route of that day, interlarded with bits of sentimental pathos and apparent sensibility, which Thackeray, in his *English Humorists*, rightly characterizes as artificial and insincere. It is in no sense a novel, although intended as an essay in delineation of character.

The Life and Opinions of Tristram Shandy, Gentleman (1759–1767), a cleverly constructed series of eight volumes (originally nine), details with great accuracy and minute circumstance the incidents attending the nativity of the gentleman whose autobiographical idiosyncrasies we are supposed to be enjoying. The affectation of ingenuity, and the very pertness of the narrative at last become wearisome; while the humor, which is genuine enough, is vitiated by the vulgarity and the indecency of its allusions. The use of *double-entendre*, of coarse word-play, of pure obscenity, in fact, becomes so frequent and so elaborate that its lack of spontaneity makes intolerable what, in works of that period, is sometimes condoned because of its naturalness and robust vivacity. The hero of the novel, if novel it may be called, presumably the "Gentleman" whose name adorns the titlepage, does not appear in his own proper person throughout the length and breadth of the entire nine volumes. There is, however, some capital character painting in the work. Mr. Shandy, father of the hero, is exceeding real; Dr. Slop, although bordering upon the verge of caricature, possesses an individuality of his own; while the character of Uncle Toby stands out immeasurably above and beyond all the rest, not merely for the consistency and clearness of the portraiture, but for the very lovableness of the conception, which goes far to atone its author's faults and to stamp him the genius that he undoubtedly was. Uncle Toby and his body-servant, Corporal Trim, who is as much a part of Uncle Toby as is the latter's wig or stick, belong to the great character portraits in our gallery of English fiction.—WILLIAM EDWARD SIMONDS, *An Introduction to the Study of English Fiction*, 1894, pp. 51–52

Upon us, who read him to-day, he no longer produces, to the same extent, the effect of novelty. But we can understand that his method must have seemed new in his time. Sterne writes without a plan, without arrangement, one might almost say without an object: he lets his soul wander where it lists. His whole work is, in reality, nothing more than a long account of journeyings—always sentimental—through the world. —JOSEPH TEXTE, *Jean-Jacques Rousseau and the Cosmopolitan Spirit in Literature* (1895), tr. J. W. Matthews, 1899, p. 288

By Laurence Sterne the course of fiction was reversed a little way towards Addison and Steele in the two incomparable books which are his legacy to English literature. We call *Tristram Shandy* (1760–67) and *A Sentimental Journey* (1768) novels, because we know not what else to call them; nor is it easy to define their fugitive and rare originality. Sterne was not a moralist in the mode of Richardson or of Fielding; it is to be feared that he was a complete ethical heretic; but he brought to his country as gifts the strained laughter that breaks into tears, and the melancholy wit that saves itself by an outburst of buffoonery. He introduced into the coarse and heavy life of the eighteenth century elements of daintiness, of persiflage, of moral versatility; he prided himself on the reader's powerlessness to conjecture what was coming next. A French critic compared Sterne, most felicitously, to one of the little bronze satyrs of antiquity in whose hollow bodies exquisite odours were stored. He was carried away by the tumult of his nerves, and it became a paradoxical habit with him to show himself exactly the opposite of what he was expected to be. You had to unscrew him for the aroma to escape. His unseemly, passionate, pathetic life burned itself away at the age of fifty-four, only the last eight of which had been concerned with literature. Sterne's influence on succeeding fiction has been durable but interrupted. Ever and anon his peculiar caprices, his selected elements, attract the imitation of some more or less analogous spirit. The extreme beauty of his writing has affected almost all who desire to use English prose as though it were an instrument not less delicate than English verse. Nor does the fact that a surprising number of his "best passages" were stolen by Sterne from older writers militate against his fame, because he always makes some little adaptation, some concession to harmony, which stamps him a master, although unquestionably a deliberate plagiarist. This fantastic sentimentalist and disingenuous idealist comes close, however, to Richardson in one faculty, the value which he extracts from the juxtaposition of a variety of trifling details artfully selected so as to awaken the sensibility of ordinary minds.—EDMUND GOSSE, *A Short History of Modern English Literature*, 1897, pp. 244–45

Works

TRISTRAM SHANDY

But to be serious if I can—I will use all reasonable caution— Only with this caution along with it, not to spoil My Book;— that is the air and originality of it, which must resemble the Author—& I fear 'tis a Number of these slighter touches which Mark this resemblance & Identify it from all Others of the [same] Stamp—Which this understrapping Virtue of Prudence woud Oblige Me to strike out. A Very Able Critick & Onc of My Colour too—who has Read Over tristram—Made Answer Upon My saying I Would consider the colour of My Coat, as I corrected it—That that very Idea in My head would render My Book not worth a groat—still I promise to be Cautious— but I deny I have gone as farr as Swift—He keeps a due distance from Rabelais—& I keep a due distance from him— Swift has said a hundred things I durst Not Say—Unless I was

Dean of St. Patricks—LAURENCE STERNE, Letter (Summer 1759)

Never poor Wight of a Dedicator had less hopes from his Dedication, than I have from this of mine; for it is written in a bye corner of the kindgom, and in a retir'd thatch'd house, where I live in a constant endeavour to fence against the infirmities of ill health, and other evils of life, by mirth; being firmly persuaded that every time a man smiles,——but much more so, when he laughs, it adds something to this Fragment of Life.

I humbly beg, Sir, that you will honour this book, by taking it——(not under your Protection,——it must protect itself, but)——into the country with you; where, if I am ever told, it has made you smile; or can conceive it has beguiled you of one moment's pain——I shall think myself as happy as a minister of state;——perhaps much happier than any one (one only excepted) that I have read or heard of.

> I am, GREAT SIR,
> (and what is more to your Honour)
> I am, GOOD SIR,
> Your Well-wisher, and
> most humble Fellow-subject.
> —LAURENCE STERNE, "Dedication to Mr. Pitt,"
> *The Life and Opinions of Tristram Shandy,
> Gent.*, 1760

At present nothing is talked of, nothing admired, but what I cannot help calling a very insipid and tedious performance: it is a kind of novel called, *The Life and Opinions of Tristram Shandy*; the great humour of which consists in the whole narration always going backwards. I can conceive a man saying that it would be droll to write a book in that manner, but have no notion of his persevering in executing it. It makes one smile two or three times in the beginning, but in recompense makes one yawn for two hours. The characters are tolerably kept up; but the humour is forever attempted and missed. The best thing in it is a sermon—oddly coupled with a good deal of bawdy, and both the composition of a clergyman. The man's head indeed was a little turned before, now topsyturvy with his success and fame. Dodsley has given him £650 for the second edition and two more volumes (which I suppose will reach backwards to his great-grandfather); Lord Falconberg a donative of £160 a year; and Bishop Warburton gave him a purse of gold and this compliment (which happened to be a contradiction) *that it was quite an original composition, and in the true Cervantic vein*—the only copy that ever was an original except in painting, where they all pretend to be so. Warburton, however, not content with this, recommended the book to the bench of bishops and told them Mr Sterne, the author, was the English Rabelais—they had never heard of such a writer. —HORACE WALPOLE, Letter to David Dalrymple (April 4, 1760)

However, I pride myself in having warmly recommended *Tristram Shandy* to all the best company in town, except that at Arthur's. I was charged in a very grave assembly, as Dr. Newton can tell him, for a particular patronizer of the work; and how I acquitted myself of the imputation, the said Doctor can tell him. I say all this to show how ready I was to *do justice* to a stranger. This is all I expect from a stranger. From my friends, indeed, I expect, because I stand in need of, much *indulgence*. To them, (being without reserve,) I show my weaknesses. To strangers I have the discretion not to show them; at least, those *writing* strangers, I mentioned before, have not yet had the wit to find them out.

If Mr. Sterne will take me with all my infirmities, I shall be glad of the honour of being better known to him; and he has the additional recommendation of being your friend.—WILLIAM WARBURTON, Letter to David Garrick (May 13, 1760)

If I did not mention *Tristram* to you, it was because I thought I had done so before. there is much good fun in it, & humour sometimes hit & sometimes mist. I agree with your opinion of it, & shall see the two future volumes with pleasure. have you read his Sermons (with his own comic figure at the head of them)? they are in the style I think most proper for the Pulpit, & shew a very strong imagination & a sensible heart: but you see him often tottering on the verge of laughter, & ready to throw his perriwig in the face of his audience.—THOMAS GRAY, Letter to Thomas Wharton (c. June 20, 1760)

Sterne has published his fifth and sixth Volumes of *Tristram*. They are wrote pretty much like the first and second; but whether they will restore his reputation as a writer with the public, is another question.—The fellow himself is an irrecoverable scoundrel.—WILLIAM WARBURTON, Letter to Richard Hurd (Dec. 27, 1761)

There are several very dull fellows, who, by a few mechanical helps, sometimes learn to become extremely brilliant and pleasing; with a little dexterity in the management of the eyebrows, fingers, and nose. By imitating a cat, a sow and pigs; by a loud laugh, and a slap on the shoulder; the most ignorant are furnished out for conversation. But the writer finds it impossible to throw his winks, his shrugs, or his attitudes upon paper; he may borrow some assistance, indeed, by printing his face at the title-page; but, without wit, to pass for a man of ingenuity, no other mechanical help but downright obscenity will suffice. By speaking to some peculiar sensations, we are always sure of exciting laughter, for the jest does not lie in the writer, but in the subject.—OLIVER GOLDSMITH, *The Citizen of the World*, 1762, Letter 53

The best Book, that has been writ by any Englishman these thirty Years (for Dr Franklyn is an American) is *Tristram Shandy*, bad as it is. A Remark which may astonish you; but which you will find true on Reflection.—DAVID HUME, Letter to William Strahan (Jan. 30, 1773)

⟨Johnson:⟩ 'Nothing odd will do long. *Tristram Shandy* did not last.'—JAMES BOSWELL, *Life of Johnson*, 1791

To these three—Richardson, Fielding and Smollett—I have now only to add the name of Laurence Sterne, whose *Tristram Shandy* appeared in 1759, in order to complete a group of novel writers whose moral outcome is much the same and who are still reputed in all current manuals as the classic founders of English fiction. I need give no characterization of Sterne's book, which is probably the best known of all. Every one recalls the Chinese puzzle of humor in *Tristram Shandy*, which pops something grotesque or indecent at us in every crook. As to its morality, I know good people who love the book; but to me, when you sum it all up, its teaching is that a man may spend his life in low, brutish, inane pursuits and may have a good many little private sins on his conscience,—but will nevertheless be perfectly sure of heaven if he can have retained the ability to weep a maudlin tear over a tale of distress; or, in short, that a somewhat irritable state of the lachrymal glands will be cheerfully accepted by the Deity as a substitute for saving grace or a life of self-sacrifice. As I have said, these four writers still maintain their position as the classic novelists and their moral influence is still copiously extolled; but I cannot help believing that much of this praise is simply well-meaning ignorance. I protest that I can read none of these books without feeling as if my soul had been in the rain, draggled, muddy, miserable. In other words, they play upon life as upon a violin without a bridge, in the deliberate endeavor to get the most depressing tones possible from the instrument. This is done under the pretext of showing us vice.—SIDNEY LANIER, *The English Novel*, 1883, pp. 186–87

Mr. Traill concludes his pleasant *Life of Sterne* in a gloomy vein, which I cannot for the life of me understand. He says: 'The fate of Richardson might seem to be close behind him' (Sterne). Even the fate of *Clarissa* is no hard one. She still numbers good intellects, and bears her century lightly. Diderot, as Mr. Traill reminds us, praised her outrageously—but Mr. Ruskin is not far behind; and from Diderot to Ruskin is a good 'drive.' But *Tristram* is a very different thing from *Clarissa*. I should have said, without hesitation, that it was one of the most popular books in the language. Go where you will amongst men—old and young, undergraduates at the Universities, readers in our great cities, old fellows in the country, judges, doctors, barristers—if they have any tincture of literature about them, they all know their 'Shandy' at least as well as their 'Pickwick.' What more can be expected? 'True Shandeism,' its author declares, 'think what you will against it, opens the heart and lungs.' I will be bound to say that Sterne made more people laugh in 1893 than in any previous year; and, what is more, he will go on doing it—'"that is, if it please God," said my Uncle Toby.'—AUGUSTINE BIRRELL, *Essays about Men, Women, and Books*, 1894, pp. 36–37

There is a singular blend of two qualities in Sterne's writing, as in his character. Humour and pathos are never in their nature far apart; in Sterne they are almost inextricably combined. His laughter and his tears are both so facile, and their springs lie so near together, that the one almost infallibly provokes the other; he will laugh at sorrow and find matter of sentiment in a comical mishap. It is his keenest pleasure to juggle with these two effects; a solemn occasion is to him an irresistible provocative to burlesque, and his pathetic sensibility responds to a touch so light that to a less highly strung nature his tears will seem affected. Yet herein lies the delicacy of his writing, and of those exquisite effects, the despair of many a more robust artist, which are as hard to describe as an odour is to remember. His reader must be incessantly on the alert for surprises; it is only prudent, at a funeral where Parson Sterne officiates, for the guest to attend with a harlequin's suit beneath his decent garb of black, prepared for either event.

The same perpetual faculty of surprise is seen in his whimsical digressive style; the same sensitive delicacy makes itself felt in his subtle analytic treatment of gesture, expression, intonation, all the evanescent details that together make up character. "The circumstances with which everything in this world is begirt, give everything in this world its size and shape:" none knew it better than Sterne, and he makes it an excuse for expatiating at length upon the circumstances, and omitting the thing itself. The humorous description of gesture that he learned from Rabelais is applied by him to the minute delineation of character, in and for itself. The story he has to tell, if it can be supposed to exist, is nothing but a starting-point for digressions, an occasion for defining all that is not his story, but—to use the favourite figure of Mr. Walter Shandy—might, could, would, or should have some possible, probable, or conceivable bearing on what would be, or ought to be, his story. Tristram Shandy himself, whose life and opinions the author promises to record, just succeeds in being born, and little more. ⟨. . .⟩

In the much agitated question concerning the debts of Sterne to previous writers, sufficient stress has always been laid on his obligation to Cervantes, whose main conception, borrowed and altered, is the soul of his work. On the other hand, perhaps too little has been made of the similarity of his central character to Cornelius, the father of the hero in Arbuthnot's posthumous *Memoirs of Martinus Scriblerus* (1741). The harangues which Cornelius delivers to his wife before their child is born, wherein he insists that the child shall not be swaddled lest the flexibility of his ears be lost, and that he shall be a great traveller, are met precisely as Mrs. Shandy would have met them—"My dear . . . we have but one child, and cannot afford to throw him away upon experiments." Arbuthnot, no doubt, borrowed much from Rabelais, but what he borrowed he handed on to Sterne enriched by his own additions, which reappear in *Tristram Shandy.*—WALTER RALEIGH, *The English Novel,* 1894, pp. 195–98

For to call *Tristram Shandy* the best of novels would be a very revolutionary proceeding, since it could be justified only by throwing aside and disregarding utterly all the rules, canons, standards, and marks by which it is customary to try and test novels at the high bar of criticism. (And, after all, most of them only aimed at being amusing, poor things!)

It is indeed a strange book, certainly not everybody's book. To start with, it is often tedious, sometimes silly, not seldom downright nasty. It does not begin at the end, because it has no end to begin at; but it does begin very nearly as far on as it ever gets, and goes back great distances in between. If anything at all happens—and it is possible to disentangle two or three events—it happens quite out of its right order; if the vehicle moves at all, it is with the cart before the horse; it is purposely so mixed up that a page of uninterrupted narrative is hardly to be found in it. It is a mass of tricks and affectations, some amusing, some very wearisome. To say that it has no plot is nothing; it takes the utmost pains to persuade you that it has not a plan. It is sometimes obviously and laboriously imitative. Its pathos, sometimes superb, is sometimes horribly maudlin. We must not ask for good taste, and can by no means rely on decency; there is even a perverse spirit of impropriety which seizes occasions and topics apparently quite innocent. This is not a complete catalogue of its sins; these are only a few points which occur to an old friend, a few characteristics which it is well to mention, lest those who do not know the book should suffer too severe a shock on making its acquaintance. For the difficulty with it is in the beginning; to read it the first time is almost hard; every reading after that goes more easily. Nevertheless, although there are, I believe, fanatic admirers who read all of it every time, I am not of those. I think I have earned the right to skip, and I exercise it freely, without qualms of conscience. What's the use of being on intimate terms with a book if you cannot have that liberty?

So many much better qualified people have set out to describe the attraction of *Tristram Shandy* that I hesitate to try my hand; but after what I have said against it I must give one or two of my own impressions about it, jotted down with a want of system appropriate to the subject. To me, infinitely the greatest charm lies in the talk. In this there is a peculiar flavor, so far as I know proper to Sterne, and to him only. It has all the discursiveness of actual conversation; the interruptions are as vital as the theme. It is developed through the mouths of characters admirably contrasted. Three occur at once to the mind, *Mr. Shandy,* his wife, and *Uncle Toby.* These might perhaps be roughly described as representing the speculative, the traditional, and the quietest types of humanity. Nothing

ever presents itself to one of them in the same light in which it appears to another. They are thinking either about different things, or about the same thing in utterly different ways. The comment of the audience is never in the least what the speaker expects it to be. Sterne suddenly presents, in a sentence, with marvelous terseness, the point of view most opposed to that which he has been developing; a gulf of difference, intellectual or moral, is shown in a word, almost as it seems in a look. This diverse spirit of the interlocutors imparts to the dialogue an extraordinary piquancy, a quality of unexpectedness. The reader never knows what is coming next, and Sterne, quite alive to the value of keeping him in this state of suspense, constantly interrupts the sentence in the middle by a description of the air or the gestures which accompanied the remark.

This last habit may perhaps be called a mere trick, but it has immense value, first in the way to which I have referred, secondly as serving the purpose of most admirably apt and pointed stage directions. You seem to see and hear the man speaking. You wait while he fills his pipe, and, impatient as you grow, you watch how he fills it; for that throws out a hint of what he is going to say. And yet, surprising as the comment is, viewed in relation to the topic, it is always perfectly true to the character of the person uttering it. In this respect Sterne's dialogue is unrivaled within the range of my reading; there is an absolute sinking of the writer in the character.

But there is more in the matter than this. Sterne fits himself with a cast of characters so chosen and so handled that, in the course of a whimsical and fantastic record of trivial, and meaner than trivial, occurrences (and very few of those), he seems to travel over so large an extent of human nature, and to embrace so many varieties of human character, that it is impossible to read his book without recognizing the hand and the insight of a master. In a way, it is a most personal book; that is, it is redolent of the author's individuality, and he himself is obtruded at every turn. None the less—and no paradoxes seem really paradoxical in this connection—it exhibits a power of equal sympathy with, and understanding of, the most widely different types of man and modes of thought; and these are exhibited with the richest sense of the humorous conflict and contrast between one and another of them—exhibited with no apparent elaboration, very rarely with any apparent seriousness. Indeed, they are made to show themselves accidentally, as it were, in the course of talk, in the pursuit of absurd hobbies and pottering occupations. This is, of course, very fine art, although it seems nothing of the kind as you read with an easy languor and a luxurious smile.—ANTHONY HOPE, "My Favorite Novelist and His Best Book," *Munsey's Magazine,* Dec. 1897, pp. 351–53

A SENTIMENTAL JOURNEY

Sterne has published two little volumes, called, *Sentimental Travels.* They are very pleasing, though too much dilated, and infinitely preferable to his tiresome *Tristram Shandy,* of which I never could get through three volumes. In these there is great good nature and strokes of delicacy.—HORACE WALPOLE, Letter to Sir George Montagu (March 12, 1768)

I am now going to *charm* myself for the third time with poor Sterne's *Sentimental Journey.*—FANNY BURNEY, *Diary,* Spring 1769

We neither know nor care whether Laurence Sterne really went to France, whether he was there accosted by the Franciscan, at first rebuked him unkindly, and then gave him a peace offering: or whether the whole be not fiction. In either case we equally are sorrowful at the rebuke, and secretly resolve *we* will never do so: we are pleased with the subsequent atonement, and view with emulation a soul candidly acknowleging it's fault and making a just reparation. Considering history as a moral exercise, her lessons would be too infrequent if confined to real life.—THOMAS JEFFERSON, Letter to Robert Skipwith (Aug. 3, 1771)

I casually took a volume of what is called *A Sentimental Journey through France and Italy. Sentimental!* what is that? It is not English; he might as well say *Continental*. It is not sense. It conveys no determinate idea; yet one fool makes many. And this nonsensical word (who would believe it?) is become a fashionable one! However, the book agrees full well with the title, for one is as queer as the other. For oddity, uncouthness, and unlikeness to all the world beside, I suppose, the writer is without a rival.—JOHN WESLEY, *Journal,* Feb. 11, 1772

Much of Sterne's journey is certainly founded on fiction; but it has nevertheless afforded a model to those, who have pretended to relate nothing but the truth. His sentimental and excessive sensibility was found so engaging, that most of the subsequent authors of travels have been induced to interweave into the body of their work an amorous episode.—VICESIMUS KNOX, "On the Manner of Writing Voyages and Travels," *Essays, Moral and Literary* (1777), 1782, No. 24

GEORGE WHITFIELD (OR WHITEFIELD)
*A Letter from the Rev. George Whitfield, B.A.
to the Rev. Laurence Sterne, M.A.*

1760

Perhaps you may expect from me, notwithstanding my sacred function an idle tale tending to excite laughter, but if you do you are disappointed; I address you in a letter, but my letter shall contain a sermon; this is a truly apostolical practice. St. Paul, and many other saints, wrote epistles, but I never yet heard of a saint's writing a bawdy novel; 'tis true that many pastors of your church have done it as well as yourself, but the pastors of your church have long since erred and strayed like lost sheep, and therefore it is no wonder the flock should forsake the truth, and seek after ungodly and sinful fancies. 'Tis an old proverb but a very true one, that "one scabby sheep spoils a "whole flock;" but alas! how dreadful must the condition of the flock be, when the shepherd himself is scabby.

Oh *Sterne!* thou art scabby, and such is the leprosy of thy mind that it is not to be cured like the leprosy of the body, by dipping nine times in the river Jordan. Thy prophane history of *Tristram Shandy* is as it were an anti-gospel, and seems to have been penned by the hand of Antichrist himself; it tends to excite laughter, but you should remember that the wisest man that ever was, that the great king Solomon himself said of laughter "it is mad," and of mirth "what doth it?" *Sterne!* (for brother I can no longer call thee, though I look upon the clergy of the Church of England as my brethren, when they discharge conscientiously the duties of their function) *Sterne,* apostate *Sterne!* if Solomon was now alive, he would not put the question, "What doth mirth." Thy book would fully shew him, that mirth is nearly akin to wickedness, and that the tickling of laughter is occasioned by the obscene Devil.

Had John Bunyan been now alive to behold thy abominable work, he would have cried out, "Antichrist is come, Antichrist has published his antichristian gospel; and lo there shall arise other Antichrists, his disciples, who shall write books

filled with obscenity, and these obscene books shall be read in a degenerate age, when the sacred oracles are neglected. The ministers of the gospel shall cease to point out the way that leads to the New Jerusalem, and, deserting the paths of grace, shall give themselves up to the evil spirit Mammon, and lead their flocks to Babylon. But the time shall come, when the cup of wrath shall be poured down their throats, and when that time is come, it will be more tolerable for the inhabitants of Sodom and Gomorrah than for them."

In words like these the pious John Bunyan might have addressed thee, if he was alive, but since he is not, I must supply his place, and reprove thee with meekness of spirit. Faith might have made thee whole, but thy worldly practices have render'd thee unsound; thy mind is cankered, and the vanities of the world have so taken hold of thy sense, that all true believers must despair of thy regeneration. We have no hopes that thou wilt ever put off the old man; by the old man I mean *Yorick,* a name that Shakespear or the Devil must have put into thy head, and which thou hast prophanely prefixed to two volumes of sermons.

The nobility and gentry have likewise been led astray by the same evil spirit; they have encouraged thee, and thus thou art become a deceitful teacher of mankind; but though thy light shineth, 'twere much better for thy soul's health that thou hadst hid it under a bushel; for the hour will come, and perhaps it is not far off, when the light of thy wit and humour shall be extinguished, and *Tristram Shandy* shall know his place no more. It shall come like a thief in the night, and deprive thee of life, it shall pick thy vital pockets, as thou hast pickt the pockets of all the nobility and gentry. Then wilt thou mourn thy past follies, when thou shalt no longer meet with a harlot at St. James's Park, or lasciviously yield to the temptations of the flesh at Ranelagh, but become a feast; a feast where thou shalt not but be eaten; a certain convocation of politic worms shall feed upon thy body, and there shall remain to thy soul only a fearful looking for of judgment.

Therefore, think of it in this thy day, though regeneration is not the work of a day, repentance is often the work of a few moments, and repentance may at last, by the assistance of the spirit, lead you up the high road of contrition, and conduct you, though a reprobate, to grace. If you once get thither, it will give me the highest satisfaction, and, in order to prepare your way, I must heartily exhort you to frequent the *Tabernacle,* where you will not want spiritual assistance, and J—s—s Ch—st may perhaps redeem you from the world, the flesh, and the Devil.

Thou hast studied prophane plays more than the word of God, and thy text is generally taken from the writings of Shakespear, an author who never had any idea of the new birth, and yet without the new birth it will be in vain for you to hope for salvation; unless you enter again into your mother's womb, you never can be saved. Come, I'll tell you a story upon the new birth, and God send it may turn your heart to grace, *Amen* and *Amen.*

A wicked prophane author that had wrote as much like a libertine as yourself, was once taken ill, but not thinking his disorder dangerous, he made a jest of it, and in a gamesome mood, sent for a minister of the gospel; when the minister was come, he desired him to read a chapter in the Bible to him, "For, says he, I very much want sleep, and I am sure that will very soon make me sleep." A few days after his disorder increased, and when he saw himself upon the point of death, he sent again to the man of God, and intreated him to read one of his sermons to him, in order to awaken him to a true sense of his deplorable condition, and conduct him to the narrow path that leads to life. Upon this says the man of God, "The path that leads to life is very narrow, and so sometimes is the path that leads to death; those that are hanged at Tyburn always find it so, for they stand upon a board not two inches broad; but now you are in the broad way, and you have so often resisted the motions of the spirit, that your journey must be all down hill."

Thus you see that vengeance overtakes the unrighteous, repent therefore, for the day of judgment was never nearer than it is now; in that dreadful day you will cry out to the booksellers shops, "Fall upon me," and to the counters "Conceal and cover me." But the spirit, if resisted thro' life, will with-hold its influence, and as thy days were graceless, thou wilt be given up to a reprobate sense. The lamb that bled did not bleed for thee, if thou dost turn aside from thy faith, and, though a clergyman, give thyself up to secular whimsies and wanton back-sliding. He that was wounded was not wounded for thee, since by thy prophane writings thou hast crucified him anew in the flesh.

Thou art the man of sin, and in thee the Scripture is fulfilled, and the measure of thine iniquity shall soon be full; thou hast mocked at religion, virtue, and honour, but know that there is one that will mock when your fear cometh.

Fly, therefore, in time from the wrath to come; for if adulterers and fornicators enter into the lake, surely he that writes to please whoremasters and adulterers must be plunged into the lake likewise.

You have forsaken the ministry, you have deserted the faith, you have had recourse to vile expedients to procure bread; but you seem to have totally forgotten him who with a loaf and five fishes gave a repast to a multitude, who rose up cramm'd, as if from a clergy or a city feast.

Learn to chew the cud of piety, make a hearty meal upon faith, and you'll find it very different from Dr. *Slop*'s wafer; not that I would be understood to reflect upon the Papists, Christians may enter to the throne of salvation through many doors. For example, there are four doors at the *Tabernacle*, where I preach sometimes; some enter at the East, some at the West, some at the North, and some at the South; but that does not hinder us from being all comfortably assembled together, and when two or three are gathered together, the holy spirit is always in the midst of them.

But now I talk of two or three, come to the *Tabernacle*, where you shall see seven or eight thousand pious souls assembled together, and there I'll preach a sermon for your conversion; for all I desire is to bring over as many souls as possible to J—s—s Ch—st, the only door through which you, or I, or any body else, can enter to salvation.

Come, though your sins are as red as scarlet, I'll wash them as white as snow, and though you have drank deep of the whore of Babylon's cup, become one of my followers and you shall drink the juice of the grape; not the grape that is pressed by peasants in Burgundy, but the grape from which celestial wine is extracted in Paradise.

Oh *Sterne!* forsake the paths that lead unto Ranelagh, take no more walks in St. James's Park, but come to me and I'll make you take a spiritual walk; a walk even up to the top of mount Tabor.

'Tis that holy mount you should endeavour to ascend; but you have followed the evil spirit who hath led you to the highest pinnacle of the temple and from thence shewn you all the vanities of this wicked world, with which thou hast been so bewitched, that thou hast fallen upon thy knees and worship'd him. Thou hast received the mark of the beast, and thy return to grace is, at present, almost totally despaired of.

But turn again to the way of truth and I will be your guide,

I'll lead you from the path that leads to perdition to the turnpike of grace; and, when thou entrest thereat, thou wilt find that her ways are ways of pleasantness, and all her paths are peace.

Though thou art a sinner, I wish for thy regeneration; but expect not the new birth, till thou turnest thy heart to J—s—s Ch—st; become entirely a Methodist, I say entirely, for, wicked and prophane as thou art, I can discover some principles of Methodism in thy writings; nay, I can easily prove that you and your brethren of the Church of England are all rank Methodists, do you not know it?

There I'll warrant you'll cry out, "Sir, you're beginning to deal in mystery, I suppose you'll prophesy by and by." But stay a while, Mr. *Sterne*, or Mr. *Tristram Shandy*, or Mr. *Yorick*, and I'll prove what I advanced.

You'll ask me, without doubt, how I can prove it? Why, I'll prove it by a dilemma; either you of the church of England sleep in your churches, or you don't understand what you hear there, or else you are all downright Methodists.

You have undoubtedly often heard and often yourself pronounced these words of the liturgy of the church of England: "The peace of God which passes all understanding, keep your hearts and minds, in the knowledge and love of God, and the blessing of God Almighty the Father, the Son, and the Holy Ghost, be amongst you and remain with you always."

"The peace of God,"——That smells rankly of Methodism, but indeed, *Lawrence* I am sorry to say, that peace does not dwell with thee. But come to me, or some other man of God, and thou mayst still partake of the fellowship of the Holy Ghost. "The fellowship of Holy Ghost!"——This smells still stronger of Methodism.

Come, perhaps I may make a convert of you yet; I have converted many sinners as hardened as yourself, for the new birth comes in a manner not to be explained. Regeneration is a greater mystery than any mystery of our holy religion, but thou seemest more inclined to rely upon a mystery of iniquity than upon the mystery of regeneration; yet even thy prophane *Yorick*, and thy prophane Shakespear, might have given thee a glimmering of the new birth,

> Get thee to my lady's chamber, and tell her, let
> her lay it on an inch thick to this favour.

Why, what is this, but an exhortation to put off the old man? Depend upon it, the poet, prophane as he was, had regeneration in view. But how is this great work of regeneration to be brought about? Who can deliver you from the womb of sin, and happily restore you to the new birth, and make you a child of God?

'Tis not Dr. *Slop* the man-midwife, 'tis not a papist quack that can by obstetric art, make you again enter your mother's womb, or come out of it again; Dr. *Slop* can never make you a child of election. There is but one man-midwife that can procure you a new birth, and that man-midwife is no other than the man J—s—s Ch—st.

Midwives upon earth have various ways of bringing a child into the world; sometimes they take it by the head, sometimes by the heels, but the great man-midwife of souls will at once take you by the head and shoulders, and, by the comfort of the spirit, throw you into the lap of regeneration.

You say that *Tristram Shandy*'s misfortunes began nine months before he was born, and I really believe that your perverseness and prophane turn began nine months before you were born.

Pray then for the new birth; there will be no occasion for

winding up a clock, regeneration does not depend upon wheels and springs; it depends only upon the spirit, it depends upon grace, and not upon mechanism.

Sterne, you have a hobby-horse and that hobby-horse may lead you to destruction, except you listen to some man of God. But I'll warrant if you were to see a man of God at the other end of the street, you'd run into some alehouse or tavern, and if he was to follow you thither, you'd say to him "Hast thou found me, O my enemy."

When men are given over to a reprobate sense, they look upon the men of God as intruders; nay, what is still worse, they look upon J—s—s Ch—st as an intruder. But the Lord is not mocked; though thou hast laugh'd every thing serious to scorn, thou wilt cry another time, a time will come when thou wilt say in the bitterness of thy heart, "Lord be merciful to me a sinner."

Listen therefore to the advice I give you, and don't despise it, because it is given by a poor Methodist preacher. I know you are a scholar, but should you be puffed up with the pride of human learning, and criticise the words I utter, should you look upon the words of sobriety as folly and enthusiasm, God forgive you.

Come, I'll tell you a story, but it shan't be a story in the *Shandy* taste, it shall be a story of righteousness.

Once upon a time a graceless author took it into his head to write several tracts against Christianity, but being soon taken desperately ill, he sent for a clergyman, and expressed himself as follows. Alas! I fear my works "have perverted half mankind; I have done my utmost to propagate infidelity, and though I have acquired a great reputation, it avails me nothing, since I run a risque of losing my own soul." Hereupon the man of God desired him not to be uneasy on that account; "For, says he, your books are all so weakly written, that no man of common sense can give them a reading, without, at the same time, discovering their futility."

Such was his answer, and really I think your writings might be answered much in the same manner; for, though the town has been taken in by them, the criticks, I mean the judicious criticks, will always look upon them as the productions of a crazy head and a depraved heart.

I speak to you with freedom, but the spirit will re-eccho my voice, and when thou art upon thy death-bed, thou wilt in vain hope for the beatific vision; for beatific vision is not to be obtained by such wretches as thee; thou hast forsaken the paths of grace, and vanity, like an *ignis fatuus*, will lead thee to unavoidable destruction.

The pit of destruction gapes, and will soon open to receive thee, if thou dost not, in this thy day turn thy heart to righteousness; by righteousness, I here mean faith.

Good works will be insufficient to rescue thy soul from the power of sin; for, to use the words of the liturgy of the church of England, "In the sight of God shall no man living be justified."

When the blessed martyr Stephen was stoned, it did not appear that he was full of self-righteousness, or good works; the testimony that the spirit gave of him, is, that he was full of faith, and of the Holy Ghost.

Sterne, Sterne! if thou hadst been full of the Holy Ghost, thou would'st never have written that prophane book, *The Life and Opinions of Tristram Shandy*, to judge of which, by the hand that wrote it, one would think the author had a cloven foot.

Thou art puffed up with spiritual pride, and the vanity of human learning has led thee aside into the paths of prophaneness.

Thou hast even been so far elated as to give the likeness of thyself before thy sermons, but, though it is the likeness of something upon earth, I shrewdly doubt that it will never be the likeness of any thing in heaven.

Return therefore to grace, before it is too late; throw aside Shakespear, and take up the word of God.

Read, mark, learn, and inwardly digest it, and you may, perhaps, by patience and comfort of the holy name of J—s—s Ch—st, be again led into the way of truth, from which you have deviated.

To facilitate your regeneration, I heartily pray, that the great *Philanthropist* of souls, that J—s—s Ch—st himself may be your man-midwife; he only can bring you to the new birth.

So, to his care I recommend you, and heartily pray for, and wish your regeneration.

May J—s—s Ch—st assist at your delivery from sin, and regeneration render you a new man.

May your mind forsake wit, and have recourse to faith; for by faith alone thou canst be made whole.

Oh, what a happiness it is to be a poor contrite sinner, and to be convinced that salvation is to be obtained by J—s—s Ch—st alone! to whose mercy and mediation I earnestly exhort you to have recourse.

To promote thy conversion, I shall subjoin a hymn upon regeneration.

> What is there on earth,
> For Christian souls, but the new birth?
> Oh, perverse degenerate nation,
> Hope not to escape damnation,
> Without true faith and regeneration.
> J—s—s on the cross was pierced,
> Because wicked man transgressed,
> Crucify him not anew,
> Since he bled for sinful you;
> For the new birth sincerely strive,
> And you shall save your soul alive.

SIR WALTER SCOTT
From "Sterne" (1821)
Lives of the Novelists
1825

If we consider Sterne's reputation as chiefly founded upon *Tristram Shandy*, he must be considered as liable to two severe charges;—those, namely, of indecency, and of affectation. Upon the first accusation Sterne himself was peculiarly sore, and used to justify the licentiousness of his humour by representing it as a mere breach of decorum, which had no perilous consequence to morals. The following anecdote we have from a sure source. Soon after *Tristram* had appeared, Sterne asked a Yorkshire lady of fortune and condition whether she had read his book. "I have not, Mr. Sterne," was the answer; "and to be plain with you, I am informed it is not proper for female perusal."—"My dear good lady," replied the author, "do not be gulled by such stories; the book is like your young heir there, (pointing to a child of three years old, who was rolling on the carpet in his white tunics) he shows at times a good deal that is usually concealed, but it is all in perfect innocence!" This witty excuse may be so far admitted; for it cannot be said that the licentious humour of *Tristram Shandy* is of the kind which applies itself to the passions, or is calculated to corrupt society. But it is a sin against taste, if allowed to be harmless as to morals. A handful of mud is neither a fire brand nor a stone; but to fling it about in sport, argues a coarseness of taste, and want of common manners.

Sterne, however, began and ended by braving the censure of the world in this particular. A remarkable passage in one of his letters shows how lightly he was disposed to esteem the charge; and what is singular enough, his plan for turning it into ridicule seems to have been serious. "Crebillon (*le fils*) has made a convention with me, which, if he is not too lazy, will be no bad *persiflage*. As soon as I get to Toulouse, he has agreed to write me an expostulatory letter on the indecencies of *Tristram Shandy*—which is to be answered by recrimination upon the liberties in his own works. These are to be printed together—Crebillon against Sterne—Sterne against Crebillon—the copy to be sold, and the money equally divided: this is good Swiss policy."

In like manner, the greatest admirers of Sterne must own, that his style is affected, eminently, and in a degree which even his wit and pathos are inadequate to support. The style of Rabelais, which he assumed for his model, is to the highest excess rambling, excursive, and intermingled with the greatest absurdities. But Rabelais was in some degree compelled to adopt this harlequin's habit, in order that, like licensed jesters, he might, under the cover of his folly, have permission to vent his satire against church and state. Sterne assumed the manner of his master, only as a mode of attracting attention, and of making the public stare; and, therefore, his extravagances, like those of a feigned madman, are cold and forced, even in the midst of his most irregular flights. A man may, in the present day, be, with perfect impunity, as wise or as witty as he can, without assuming the cap and bells of the ancient jester as an apology; and, that Sterne chose voluntarily to appear under such a disguise, must be set down as mere affectation, and ranked with the tricks of black or marbled pages, as used merely *ad captandum vulgus*. All popularity thus founded, carries in it the seeds of decay; for eccentricity in composition, like fantastic modes of dress, however attractive when first introduced, is sure to be caricatured by stupid imitators, to become soon unfashionable, and of course to be neglected.

If we proceed to look more closely into the manner of composition which Sterne thought proper to adopt, we find a sure guide in the ingenious Dr. Ferriar, of Manchester, who, with most singular patience, has traced our author through the hidden sources whence he borrowed most of his learning, and many of his most striking and peculiar expressions. Rabelais (much less read than spoken of) the lively but licentious miscellany called *Moyen de parvenir*, and D'Aubigné's *Baron de Fæneste*, with many other forgotten authors of the sixteenth century, were successively laid under contribution. Burton's celebrated work on Melancholy, (which Dr. Ferriar's Essay instantly raised to double price in the book-market) afforded Sterne an endless mass of quotations, with which he unscrupulously garnished his pages, as if they had been collected in the course of his own extensive reading. The style of the same author, together with that of Bishop Hall, furnished the author of *Tristram* with many of those whimsical expressions, similes, and illustrations, which were long believed the genuine productions of his own eccentric wit. For proofs of this sweeping charge, we must refer the readers to Dr. Ferriar's well-known Essay and Illustrations, as he delicately terms them, of Sterne's Writing's, in which it is clearly shown, that he, whose manner and style were so long thought original, was, in fact, the most unhesitating plagiarist who ever cribbed from his predecessors in order to garnish his own pages. It must be owned, at the same time, that Sterne selects the materials of his mosaic work with so much art, places them so well, and

polishes them so highly, that in most cases we are disposed to pardon the want of originality, in consideration of the exquisite talent with which the borrowed materials are wrought up into the new form.

One of Sterne's most singular thefts, considering the tenor of the passage stolen, is his declamation against literary depredators of his own class: "Shall we," says Sterne, "for ever make new books, as apothecaries make new medicines, by pouring only out of one vessel into another? Are we for ever to be twisting and untwisting the same rope—for ever in the same track—for ever at the same pace?" The words of Burton are, "As apothecaries, we make new mixtures, every day pour out of one vessel into another; and as the Romans robbed all the cities in the world to set out their bad-sited Rome, we skim the cream of other men's wits, pick the choice flowers of their tilled gardens, to set out our own sterile plots. We weave the same web, still twist the same rope again and again." We cannot help wondering at the coolness with which Sterne could transfer to his own work so eloquent a tirade against the very arts which he was practising.

Much has been said about the right of an author to avail himself of his predecessors' labours; and, certainly, in a general sense, he that revives the wit and learning of a former age, and puts it in a form likely to captivate his own, confers a benefit on his contemporaries. But to plume himself with the very language and phrases of former writers, and to pass their wit and learning for his own, was the more unworthy in Sterne, as he had enough of original talent, had he chosen to exert it, to have dispensed with all such acts of literary petty larceny.

Tristram Shandy is no narrative, but a collection of scenes, dialogues and portraits, humorous or affecting, intermixed with much wit and with much learning, original or borrowed. It resembles the irregularities of a gothic room, built by some fanciful collector, to contain the miscellaneous remnants of antiquity which his pains have accumulated, and bearing as little proportion in its parts, as the pieces of rusty armour with which it is decorated. Viewing it in this light, the principal figure is Mr. Shandy the elder, whose character is formed, in many respects, upon that of Martinus Scriblerus. The history of Martin was designed by the celebrated club of wits, by whom it was commenced, as a satire upon the ordinary pursuits of learning and science. Sterne, on the contrary, had no particular object of ridicule; his business was only to create a person, to whom he could attach the great quantity of extraordinary reading, and antiquated learning which he had collected. He, therefore, supposed in Mr. Shandy a man of an active and metaphysical, but at the same time, a whimsical cast of mind, whom too much and too miscellaneous learning had brought within a step or two of madness, and who acts, in the ordinary affairs of life, upon the absurd theories adopted by the pedants of past ages. He is most admirably contrasted with his wife, well described as a good lady of the true *poco-curante* school, who neither obstructed the progress of her husband's hobby-horse, to use a phrase which Sterne has rendered classical, nor could be prevailed upon to spare him the least admiration for the grace and dexterity with which he managed it.

Yorick, the lively, witty, sensitive, and heedless parson, is the well-known personification of Sterne himself, and undoubtedly, like every portrait of himself, drawn by a master of the art, bore a strong resemblance to the original. Still, however, there are shades of simplicity thrown into the character of Yorick, which did not exist in that of Sterne. We cannot believe that the jests of the latter were so void of malice prepense, or that his satire entirely flowed out of honesty of mind and mere jocundity of humour. It must be owned, moreover, that Sterne was more likely to have stolen a passage out of Stevinus, if he could have found one to his purpose, than to have left one of his manuscripts in the volume, with the careless indifference of Yorick. Still, however, we gladly recognise the general likeness between the author and the child of his fancy, and willingly pardon the pencil which in the delicate task of self delineation, has softened some traits, and improved others.

Uncle Toby, with his faithful squire, the most delightful characters in the work, or perhaps in any other, are drawn with such a pleasing force and discrimination that they more than entitle the author to a free pardon for his literary speculations, his indecorum, and his affectation; nay, authorize him to leave the court of criticism, not forgiven only, but applauded and rewarded, as one who has exalted and honoured humanity, and impressed upon his readers such a lively picture of kindness and benevolence, blended with courage, gallantry, and simplicity, that their hearts must be warmed by it when ever it is recalled to memory. Sterne, indeed, might boldly plead in his own behalf that the passages which he borrowed from others were of little value, in comparison to those which are exclusively original; and that the former might have been written by many persons, while in his own proper line he stands alone and inimitable. Something of extravagance may, perhaps, attach to Uncle Toby's favourite amusements. Yet in England, where men think and act with little regard to the ridicule or censure of their neighbours, there is no impossibility, perhaps no great improbability, in supposing, that a humourist might employ such a mechanical aid as my Uncle's bowling-green, in order to encourage and assist his imagination, in the pleasing but delusive task of castle building. Men have been called children of a larger growth, and among the antic toys and devices with which they are amused, the device of my Uncle, with whose pleasures we are so much disposed to sympathize, does not seem so unnatural upon reflection, as it may appear at first sight.

It is well known (through Dr. Ferriar's labours) that Dr. Slop, with all his obstetrical engines, may be identified with Dr. Burton, of York who published a treatise of Midwifery in 1751. This person, as we have elsewhere noticed, was on bad terms with Sterne's uncle; and though there had come strife and unkindness between the uncle and the nephew, yet the latter seems to have retained aversion against the enemy of the former. But Sterne, being no politician, had forgiven the Jacobite, and only persecutes the Doctor with his raillery, as a quack and a catholic.

It is needless to dwell longer on a work so generally known. The style employed by Sterne is fancifully ornamented, but at the same time vigorous and masculine, and full of that animation and force which can only be derived by an intimate acquaintance with the early English prose-writers. In the power of approaching and touching the finer feelings of the heart, he has never been excelled, if indeed, he has ever been equalled; and may be at once recorded as one of the most affected, and one of the most simple writers—as one of the greatest plagiarists, and one of the most original geniuses whom England has produced. Dr. Ferriar, who seemed born to trace and detect the various mazes through which Sterne carried on his depredations upon ancient and dusty authors, apologizes for the rigour of his inquest, by doing justice to those merits which were peculiarly our author's own. We cannot better close this article than with the sonnet in which his ingenious inquisitor makes the *amende honorable* to the shade of Yorick.

Sterne, for whose sake I plod through miry ways,
Of antique wit and quibbling mazes drear,
Let not thy shade malignant censure fear,
Though ought of borrowed mirth my search betrays.
Long slept that mirth in dust of ancient days;
(Erewhile to guise or wanton Valois dear)
Till waked by thee, in Skelton's joyous pile,
She flung on Tristram her capricious rays;
But the quick tear that checks our wondering smile,
In sudden pause, or unexpected story,
Owns thy true mastery—and Lefever's woes,
Maria's wanderings, and the prisoner's throes,
Fix thee conspicuous on the throne of glory.

WHITWELL ELWIN
From "Sterne"
Quarterly Review, March 1854, pp. 334–40

The leading idea of Sterne was to represent his characters enthusiastic in pursuits which, either from their eccentric nature, or the disproportionate attention they engaged, appear ridiculous to ordinary people. In the phrase which he himself has engrafted into the English language, his principal personages had each their 'hobbyhorse.' Of all the creations of this description, Don Quixote is, perhaps, the first in time, and, beyond question, is the first in excellence. Sterne, while avowing that he took Cervantes for his model, did not attempt a feeble copy of an inimitable original. He borrowed the conception of a man mastered by a fantastic passion, and gave it an application thoroughly novel. Uncle Toby is the happiest delineation in the group, and in accounting for his propensities Sterne has even outdone Cervantes. The madness of Don Quixote is beyond the limits of nature. That he should have heated his imagination with reading books of chivalry is sufficiently probable; that he should have resolved to imitate the heroes he worshipped is no incredible consequence: but that he should mistake windmills for giants, and flocks of sheep for armies; that he should act steadily upon such suppositions and never deviate from his delusion, exceeds, we believe, all the flights of insanity which are yet upon record. But grant Cervantes his premises, and nothing can be more truthful than his mode of applying them. Though Don Quixote is only crazed upon a single point, it is a point which affects the whole system of his life. In the complication of the poor knight's acts and speeches, Cervantes draws the line between sense and lunacy with admirable skill; and the extravagances which the Don commits, and the rational sentiments which he utters, are never out of keeping. There is a consistency in his behaviour, relatively to the conditions which are stated at starting, most difficult to contrive and most unerringly preserved. Modern campaigns are to Uncle Toby what knight-errantry was to Don Quixote. Captain Shandy, however, is sane. His imagination has not got the better of his senses, and if his military enthusiasm almost rivals the chivalrous frenzy of Don Quixote, it is due to disease of the body instead of the mind. The genius of our author, often wild and wayward, has here displayed an exquisite tact, which becomes strikingly apparent when we disentangle the character from the rhapsodies and digressions in which Sterne has involved it.

Uncle Toby was wounded at the siege of Namur in his groin by a piece of stone splintered off from the fortifications. He returned to England, and a succession of exfoliations from the injured bones confined him to his room. His brother, with whom he was housed, conducted every visitor to his apartment that they might assist to beguile the anguish of the wound and the tedium of the confinement. The conversation naturally turned upon the accident, and the mode in which he met with it. From thence Uncle Toby proceeded to speak of the siege, and having no ideas which were not professional, he soon grew copious upon this single topic. The more he was minute the less lucid he became. He got so entangled in the technicalities of the fortifications, and in the dykes and streams of the surrounding country, that he lost himself and bewildered his hearers. The thought struck him to procure a military map for the illustration of his lecture, and the map again suggested an expansion of the scheme. He had before descanted chiefly upon that portion of the siege of which he was the eye-witness and the hero; he now purchased books to enable him to develope the entire history. Every taste of the spring increased the longing for a deeper draught. He bought plans of other towns, and more books to teach the art of attacking and defending them. Disabled for ever, without a possibility of turning his acquisitions to account, he was yet so entranced in his studies that he grudged to shave or change his shirt, and constantly forgot his dinner, his wound, and the world. The next stage to which he rode his hobby-horse brought him to the point which completed his happiness and gave piquancy to his character.

The maps, books, and instruments of Uncle Toby had outgrown his table. He ordered Corporal Trim to bespeak another twice the size, and the Corporal replied by expressing a hope that his honour would soon be well enough to leave London for his little estate in the country. There, upon a rood and a half of ground, Trim could execute a model of the fortifications, while Uncle Toby sat in the sun and directed the works. The capabilities of the scheme developed themselves on the instant in the good enthusiast's brain. 'Trim,' said he, with a face crimson with joy, 'thou hast said enough.' But Trim enlarged on the hint. 'Say no more,' exclaimed the enraptured Captain, and the proud Corporal continued his discourse on the pleasures and advantages of the plan. 'Say no more,' reiterated Uncle Toby; and as often as he repeated the phrase, no cheers that ever greeted orator could have afforded equal encouragement to Trim to proceed in his harangue. Unable to contain himself, the Captain leaped upon his sound leg, thrust a guinea into Trim's hand, and bid him bring up supper directly. Supper came, but Uncle Toby could not eat. 'Get me,' he said, 'to bed;' but Uncle Toby could not sleep. A delicious waking dream had filled his imagination, and absorbed all his faculties, mental and corporeal.

Hitherto Uncle Toby had borne his wound and imprisonment without a murmur. From the time he was fairly mounted on his hobby he had grown quite indifferent to his groin, except that he disliked the interruption of having it dressed; but on the morning which succeeded his supperless and sleepless night, he remonstrated with the surgeon on the protraction of the cure. With much pathos, and at great length, he expatiated upon the misery of four years of captivity, and declared, that unless for his brother's tenderness he must have sunk beneath the load. Uncle Toby was without guile; he understood no artifice, and would have disdained to practise it. He was the dupe of his own exaggeration when he applied to the whole of his sickness the feelings of impatience which were barely twelve hours old. His brother wept; the surgeon was petrified. For a man who never once had breathed a complaint, who seldom inquired after the wound, or concerned himself about the answer, suddenly to sum into one grand total all the items of a four years' account was embarassing in the

extreme. When the surgeon was sufficiently collected to speak, he promised the Captain a speedy recovery, and named five or six weeks. To the feverish longing of the patient weeks and ages were the same. He determined inwardly to take the field without delay, and his mode of executing the resolve is an example of Sterne's delicate discrimination of character.

Uncle Toby was without a misgiving upon the importance of his pursuit, but he was sensible that the world was not upon his side. To relinquish a sick chamber at the risk of exasperating an ugly wound, and take a tedious journey into the country for the purpose of digging mimic fortifications in his garden, was what he could justify to no understanding besides the Corporal's and his own. He therefore decided to elope. A chariot and four was ordered for twelve o'clock when his brother was at the Exchange, and with his books, maps, instruments, and dressings, a pioneer's spade, a shovel and a pickaxe, he set off full speed to Shandy Hall. The whole vigour of his mind being directed to the toy in the bowling-green, his inventive faculties were continually suggesting some extension of the works. Now he bethought himself of providing batteries of miniature cannon, now of throwing a drawbridge over the ditch he called a moat, now of procuring a number of doll-houses, constructed according to the system of architecture prevalent abroad, and which he arranged in the form of whatever city was besieged by the allies. The war was carried on at Shandy in rigorous imitation of the war on the continent. When Marlborough dug a trench, Uncle Toby furrowed his bowling-green; when Marlborough opened his batteries, Uncle Toby's cannon kept up a ceaseless pop; and when Marlborough effected a breach, Uncle Toby's works met with a similar catastrophe. Between pulling everything to pieces in taking one town, and putting them together again preparatory to besieging another, the Captain was in a perpetual heat of excitement and delight; and having arrived at that pitch of fervour in which no suspicion of the futility of his proceedings ever troubled his pleasure, he had all the animation and pride of conquest without its dangers and fatigues.

The character of Uncle Toby is thus evolved naturally out of the circumstances in which he is placed, and has the merits so hard to unite of being as original as any monstrosity of the imagination, and as truthful as any transcript from commonplace life. He may be purely a creation of fancy, and may never have had an original, but he acts according to verified laws of the mind, and is like the countenance in an historical picture, which may resemble no one that ever lived, and yet be a perfect type of humanity.

The eccentricity, which is only laughable, raises no respect. One of the triumphs of the novelist's art is to dignify the ludicrous element by noble traits without breaking in upon the consistency of the character. Cervantes, who must certainly have been a delighted devourer of the books he satirized, and who employed his reason to make a jest of his tastes, has displayed much of this blending skill. In reducing the rhodomontade of fiction to a rule of conduct, the knight of La Mancha outchivalries chivalry. His romantic daring which no disasters can abate, his fortitude under suffering, his lofty principles, his generous zeal in the cause of the oppressed, qualify our laughter with a compassionate respect. Sterne has redeemed his hero from farcical contempt—nay, has rendered him far more loveable than ridiculous, by combining with his professional whims an exquisitely winning benignity of disposition. A warmer and gentler heart than that which inspired the martial courage and enthusiasm of Uncle Toby never beat in a bosom, nor could any one have surpassed the author of *Tristram Shandy* in the taste and judgment with which he has portrayed the union of meek and manly qualities. There is nothing sickly, affected, or ostentatious. Uncle Toby's benevolence sits as natural upon him as his bravery. 'There never,' says Corporal Trim, 'was a better officer in the king's army, or a better man in God's world.'

The attendants of Don Quixote and Uncle Toby differ even more than their respective leaders. Two persons could not be represented as both insane upon the point of knight-errantry, nor could the Don's delusion have been so humorously exposed with a sympathising as with a dissimilar associate. Cervantes has, therefore, availed himself of the power of contrast;—selfishness and disinterestedness, cowardice and courage, gross sense and wild fancy, are brought out with augmented force from their unceasing collision. It is solely the credulity of ignorance which keeps Sancho Panza in the train of Don Quixote. He is sufficiently aware of many of the knight's misconceptions to be always laughing at him in his sleeve; but he is imposed upon by the higher flights of his master's extravagance; and, when he listens to his rhapsodical discourses, and witnesses his deeds of frantic daring, he is constrained to credit his pretensions. Trim, instead of being the opposite, is, in his notions, the duplicate of Uncle Toby. Every fresh access of the captain's military fever infected the corporal in a like degree; and, indeed, they keep up a mutual excitement, which renders both more eager in the pursuit than either would have been without the other. Yet, with an identity of disposition, the character of the common soldier is nicely discriminated from that of the officer. His whole carriage bears traces of the drill-yard, which are wanting in his superior. Under the name of a servant he is in reality a companion, and he is a delightful mixture of familiarity in the essence, and the most deferential respect in forms. Of his simplicity and humanity it is enough to say that he was worthy to walk behind his master.

The crude conception of the character of Uncle Toby's brother is clearly borrowed from that of the elder Scriblerus, but it is worked out with a dramatic skill to which the original has no pretension. Mr. Shandy had been formerly a Turkey merchant, and, from reading antiquated books in the intervals of business, had got his mind imbued with obsolete fancies and theories. To lose himself in these idle and intricate speculations, to urge them upon others, to apply them to the actual affairs of life, has become the single thought of his existence. A considerable amount of shrewdness and humour mingle with his absurdity. A leading article of his creed is, that the characters of mankind are influenced by their Christian names. 'Your son,' he would say to those that maintained that names were a matter of indifference, 'your dear son, from whose sweet and open temper you have so much to expect,—your Billy, Sir,—would you for the world have called him JUDAS?' 'I never,' adds Sterne, 'knew a man able to answer this argument.' Though by native disposition a benevolent person, the kindliness of Mr. Shandy never stands in the way of his systems. He has no more feeling on such occasions than the withered mummies of the ages from which he has fetched not a few of his notions; for his fantastical ideas are paramount above all things, and a good heart has been entirely vanquished by a maggoty head. He has a notion, supported by plausible reasoning, that the Cæsarean operation was favourable to the genius of the child. 'He mentioned the thing one afternoon to my mother, merely as a matter of fact; but seeing her turn as pale as ashes at the very mention of it, as much as the operation flattered his hopes, he thought it as well to say no more of it, contenting himself with admiring what he thought was to no purpose to propose.' Mrs. Shandy, in the question,

is nothing more to him than a *corpus vile*. Sterne explains that his design in the character was to laugh learned dunces out of countenance. In this respect the satire is a failure. The speculations of Mr. Shandy are too remote from ordinary pedantry for the cap to fit. He must be considered as *sui generis*, an exceptional eccentricity; and, thus viewed, the portrait is conceived with infinite humour and tact.

The brothers have retired to their ancestral village, where they pass their lives together, and the action of one upon the other is managed with wonderful address. They both ride their hobby-horses incessantly, but it is in parallel lines, which never meet at a single point, or rather, they proceed in opposite directions and are constantly coming into collision. The elder Mr. Shandy can never get above a step or two in a demonstration before the use of a word, which is common to civil and military affairs, carries Uncle Toby off into a professional digression; and Uncle Toby's martial harangues are, in like manner, cut short by Mr. Shandy's scholastic commentaries. In general the captain looks upon his brother's abstruse speculations as beyond his comprehension, and contents himself with occasionally whistling Lilibulero when something is advanced which shocks his common sense. Mr. Shandy, on the other hand, holds Uncle Toby's military mania in complete contempt, laughs at it when he is in good humour, and inveighs against it when he is in bad. The blending quality which binds these unsympathising enthusiasts into social and fraternal harmony is a benevolence of soul, in which again the dispositions of the brothers are nicely distinguished, for, while the heart of the captain overflows with affection, the modified return which Mr. Shandy makes to it is not so much spontaneous as generated by the excess of the quality in Uncle Toby. The strokes with which the portraits are drawn are altogether so deep and yet so delicate, so truthful and yet so novel, so simple in the outline, and yet so varied in the details, so laughable and yet so winning, that we question if, out of Shakspeare, there is a single character in English fiction depicted with greater or even equal power.

HENRY T. TUCKERMAN
From "The Sentimentalist: Laurence Sterne"
Essays, Biographical and Critical
1857, pp. 327–41

It detracts nothing from Sterne's originality, that the prototypes of his characters have been, in many instances, identified. It is the coloring, rather than the invention, of his writings, in which consists their peculiar charm. As in the plots of Shakspeare, and the travels of Byron, what of mere incident occurs is chiefly important as a nucleus for his idiosyncrasies. It is the treatment, and not the theme, that wins our sympathies. To use a chemical figure of speech, the scenes and personages to which he introduces us serve mainly to precipitate the humor and sentiment of the author. The papers on Sterne by Dr. Ferriar, preserved in the *Transactions of the Manchester Society*, are but curious literary researches, and throw comparatively no light on the real genius of Yorick. However largely he was indebted to old Burton and Rabelais, the individuality of his conceptions remains. Take away the plot, the scholarship, and the anecdotical episodes, and we have still a fund of quaint generalization, a special vein of pathetic and humorous sentiment, which constitutes the real claim of Sterne as an author. The delight which Dr. Ferriar derived from him was quite independent of his borrowed plumes; it came from the cleverness of his satire, and the power of inducing a mood of quiet emotion and gentle mirth; and especially from a suggestive faculty, in which no English author excels him.

He opened to the mass of English readers that attractive domain in literature, which Rousseau in France, and Richter in Germany, made popular; though in him, unfortunately, it was not linked with aspirations for social amelioration, as in Jean Jacques, nor with deep-hearted sympathies, as in Jean Paul. Sterne was organized to feel and to evolve, but not to hallow and realize, those beautiful emotions of the soul in which so essentially consist its glory and its bane. In his hands the work degenerated too often into "the art of talking amusing nonsense;" it was debased by indecency, and made contemptible by caprice. Burns declared that he put himself on the regimen of admiring a fine woman, in order to secure inspiration. Sterne said that he had been in love with some Dulcinea, all his life, because it "sweetened his temper." He was an amorous jester, a sentimental epicure, and his theory was to make the most of life by adroitly skimming its surface. The tender passion was a means of casual luxury, not a serious experience. He protested against gravity, and, as Goldoni fought off the spleen by habitually standing on his guard like a wary fencer, Sterne adopted mirth as a panacea, clutching at the straws on the tide of sorrow with the childish impulse of desperation. "I am fabricating them" (the last volume of *Tristram Shandy*), he says, "for the laughing part of the world; for the melancholy part of it, I have nothing but my prayers."

There was a decided taste in Sterne's day for those colloquial treatises, lay sermons, and minor speculations, which, under the name of the British Essayists, form a department of literature peculiar to England; and this taste was united in the uneducated with a love of narrative and fiction, to which De Foe, and other *raconteurs*, ministered. The two were admirably combined in Sterne; his writings are made up, in about equal proportions, of speculation and description— now a portrait, and now a reverie; on one page ingenious argument, on the next, humorous anecdote. Thus something seems provided for every literary palate; and his desultory plan, or want of plan, became a chief source of his popularity. That he was conscious of an original vein, notwithstanding the abundant material of which he availed himself, may be inferred from his self-complacent query, "Shall we forever make new books, as the apothecaries make new mixtures, by pouring only out of one vessel into another?"

Perhaps the absence of constructive art increased the popularity of Sterne. To many readers there is a charm in the boldness which sets rules at defiance; and the author of *Tristram Shandy* not only braved that sense of propriety which is an instinct of better natures, but seemed to take a wanton delight in writing a book without any regard to established precedents, either in its arrangement or the development of its subject. He was the reverse of careless, however, in his habits of composition, and, running through all his apparent indifference of mood, there is obvious a trick of art. It is in the use of his materials, rather than in style, that he violates the order of a finished narration. Gathering from the storehouse of a tenacious memory what he had heard of fortifications, camp life, obstetrics, and foreign countries, and linking them together with curious gleanings of erudition, he gave vitality and interest to the whole by the introduction of several original and well-sustained characters, and occasional passages of skilful dialogue and pathetic story. The result was a *mélange*, whose fragmentary shape and indecent allusions were counterbalanced, though by

no means atoned for, by felicitous creations, and the graphic limning of still-life. He has candidly given us his own theory of authorship. "Digressions," he says, "are the sunshine; they are the life and soul of reading." Instead of apologizing for an episode, he calls it "a master stroke of digressive skill." "To write a book," he elsewhere observes, "is for all the world like humming a song; be but in tune with yourself, 'tis no matter how high or how low you take it." ⟨. . .⟩

The most interesting problem involved in his career as an author is the rank he holds as an expositor of sentiment. Critics have viewed him, in this regard, at the two extremes of hypocrisy and sincerity, of artifice and truth. In order justly to estimate Sterne with reference to this, his most obvious claim and purpose, we must consider the true relation between human feeling and its written expression.

Sentiment, as an element of literature, is the intellectual embodiment of feeling; it is thought imbued with a coloring and an atmosphere derived from emotion. Its reality, duration, and tone, depend in books, as in character, upon alliance with other qualities; and there is no fallacy more common than that which tests its sincerity in the author by the permanent traits of the man. It may be quite subordinate as a motive of action, and altogether secondary as a normal condition, and yet it is none the less real while it lasts. In each artist and author, sentiment exists in relation to other qualities, which essentially modify it while they do not invalidate its claim. To say that a man who writes an elegy which moves us to tears, and at the same time displays the most heartless conduct in his social life, is therefore a hypocrite, is to reason without discrimination. The adhesiveness, the conscience, and the temperament, of each individual, directly influence his sentiment; in one case giving it to the intensity of passion, in another the sustained dignity of principle, now causing it to appear as an incidental mood, and again as a permanent characteristic. United to strength of will or to earnestness of spirit, it is worthy of the highest confidence; in combination with a feeble and impressible mind, or a lightsome and capricious fancy, or a selfish disposition, it is quite unreliable. In either case, however, the quality itself is genuine; its type and degree only are to be questioned. Thus regarded, the apparent incongruity between its expression and its actual condition vanishes.

Sentiment in Burns was essentially modified by tenderness, in Byron by passion, in Shelley by imagination; meditation fostered it in Petrarch, extreme susceptibility in Kirke White. In the French Quietists it took the form of religious ecstasy. In the Old English drama it is robust, in the Spanish ballads chivalric, in Hamlet abstract and intellectual, in *As You Like It* full of airy fancifulness. Miss Edgeworth and Jane Austen exhibited it as governed by prudence and common sense; Mrs. Radcliffe, as rendered mysterious by superstition. Scott delighted to interpret it through local and legendary accessories, under the influence of a sensuous temperament. In the Dantesque picture of Francesca da Rimini it is full of tragic sweetness, and in Paul and Virginia perverted by artificial taste. In Charles Lamb it is quaint, in Hood deeply human, in Cowper alternately natural and morbid, in Mackenzie soft and pale as moonlight, and in Boccaccio warm as the glow of a Tuscan vintage. Chastened by will, it is as firm and cold as sculpture in Alfieri, and melted by indulgence, it is as insinuating as the most delicious music in Metastasio. Pure and gentle in Raphael, it is half savage in Salvator and Michael Angelo; severely true in Vandyke, it is luscious and coarse in Rubens. And yet, to a certain extent and under specific modifications, every one of these authors and artists possessed sentiment; but, held in solution by character, in some it governed, in others it served genius; in some it was a predominant source of enjoyment and suffering, and in others but an occasional stimulus or agency. Who doubts, over a page of the Nouvelle Heloise, that sentiment in all its tearful bliss was known to Rousseau? The abandonment of his offspring to public charity does not disprove its existence, but only shows that in his nature it was a mere selfish instinct. The history of philanthropic enterprise indicates the same contradiction. Base cruelty has at times deformed the knight, gross appetites the crusader, hypocrisy the missionary, and the men whose names figure in the so-called charitable movements of our day are often the last to whom we should appeal for personal kindness and sympathy. The same inconsistency is evident in that large class of women in whose characters the romantic predominates over the domestic instincts. "Confessions" form a popular department of French literature, and are usually based on sentiment. Yet their authors are frequently thorough men of the world and intense egotists. It is this want of harmony between expression and life, between the eloquent avowal and the practical influence of sentiment, patriotic, religious, and humane, which gave rise to the invective of Carlyle, and the other stern advocates of fact, of action, and of reality. Meanwhile the beauty, the high capacity, the exalted grace of sentiment itself, is uninvaded. We must learn to distinguish its manifestations, to honor its genuine power, to distrust its rhetorical exaggeration.

The truth is, that Sterne's heart was more sensitive than robust. It was like "wax to receive," but not like "marble to retain," impressions. Their evanescence, therefore, does not impugn their reality. Perhaps we owe the superiority of their artistic expression to this want of stability. Profound and continuous emotion finds but seldom its adequate record. Men thus swayed recoil from self-contemplation; their peace of mind is better consulted by turning from than by dwelling upon their states of feeling; whereas more frivolous natures may dally with and make capital of their sentiment without the least danger of insanity. We have but to study the portrait of Sterne in order to feel that a highly nervous organization made him singularly alive to the immediate, while it unfitted him for endurance and persistency. That thin, pallid countenance, that long, attenuated figure, the latent mirth of the expression, the predominance of the organs of wit and ideality, betoken a man to "set the table in a roar,"—one who passes easily from smiles to tears, from whose delicately strung yet unheroic mould the winds of life draw plaintive and gay, but transient music;—a being more artistic than noble, more susceptible than generous, capable of a shadowy grace and a fitful brilliancy, but without the power to dignify and elevate sensibility. His fits of depression, his recourse to amusement, his favorite watchword, *"Vive la bagatelle,"* his caprice and trifling, his French view of life, his alternate gayety and blue devils, attest one of those ill-balanced characters, amusing in society, ingenious in literature, but unsatisfactory in more intimate relations and higher spheres.

WALTER BAGEHOT

From "Sterne and Thackeray" (1864)
Collected Works, ed. Norman St. John-Stevas
1965, Volume 2, pp. 288–98

The real excellence of Sterne is single and simple; the defects are numberless and complicated. He excels, perhaps, all other writers in mere simple description of common sensitive human action. He places before you in their simplest form the elemental facts of human life; he does not view them through the intellect, he scarcely views them through the imagination; he does but reflect the unimpaired impression which the facts of life, which does not change from age to age, make on the deep basis of human feeling, which changes as little though years go on. The example we quoted just now is as good as any other, though not better than any other. Our readers should go back to it again, or our praise may seem overcharged. It is the portrait-painting of the heart. It is as pure a reflection of mere natural feeling as literature has ever given, or will ever give. The delineation is nearly perfect. Sterne's feeling in his higher moments so much overpowered his intellect, and so directed his imagination, that no intrusive thought blemishes, no distorting fancy mars, the perfection of the representation. The disenchanting facts which deface, the low circumstances which debase, the simpler feelings oftener than any other feelings, his art excludes. The feeling which would probably be coarse in the reality is refined in the picture. The unconscious tact of the nice artist heightens and chastens reality, but yet it is reality still. His mind was like a pure lake of delicate water: it reflects the ordinary landscape, the rugged hills, the loose pebbles, the knotted and the distorted firs perfectly and as they are, yet with a charm and fascination that they have not in themselves. This is the highest attainment of art: to be at the same time nature and something more than nature.

But here the great excellence of Sterne ends as well as begins. In *Tristram Shandy* especially there are several defects which, while we are reading it, tease and disgust so much that we are scarcely willing even to admire as we ought to admire the nice pictures of human emotion. The first of these, and perhaps the worst, is the fantastic disorder of the form. It is an imperative law of the writing art that a book should go straight on. A great writer should be able to tell a great meaning as coherently as a small writer tells a small meaning. The magnitude of the thought to be conveyed, the delicacy of the emotion to be painted, render the introductory touches of consummate art not of less importance, but of more importance. A great writer should train the mind of the reader for his greatest things; that is, by first strokes and fitting preliminaries he should form and prepare his mind for the due appreciation and the perfect enjoyment of high creations. He should not blunder upon a beauty, nor, after a great imaginative creation, should he at once fall back to bare prose. The high-wrought feeling which a poet excites should not be turned out at once and without warning into the discomposing world. It is one of the greatest merits of the greatest living writer of fiction—of the authoress of *Adam Bede*—that she never brings you to anything without preparing you for it; she has no loose lumps of beauty; she puts in nothing at random; after her greatest scenes, too, a natural sequence of subordinate realities again tones down the mind to this sublunary world. Her logical style—the most logical, probably, which a woman ever wrote—aids in this matter her natural sense of due proportion. There is not a space of incoherency—not a gap. It is not natural to begin with the point of a story, and she does not begin with it. When some great marvel has been told, we all wish to know what came of it, and she tells us. Her natural way, as it seems to those who do not know its rarity, of telling what happened produces the consummate effect of gradual enchantment and as gradual disenchantment. But Sterne's style is *un*natural. He never begins at the beginning and goes straight through to the end. He shies in a beauty suddenly; and just when you are affected he turns round and grins at it. 'Ah,' he says, 'is it not fine?' And then he makes jokes which at that place and that time are out of place, or passes away in scholastic or other irrelevant matter, which simply disgusts and disheartens those whom he has just delighted. People excuse all this iregularity of form by saying that it was imitated from Rabelais. But this is nonsense. Rabelais, perhaps, could not in his day venture to tell his meaning straight out; at any rate, he did not tell it. Sterne should not have chosen a model so monstrous. Incoherency is not less a defect because an imperfect foreign writer once made use of it. 'You may have, sir, a reason,' said Dr. Johnson, 'for saying that two and two make five, but they will still make four.' Just so, a writer may have a reason for selecting the defect of incoherency, but it is a defect still. Sterne's best things read best out of his books—in Enfield's *Speaker* and other places—and you can say no worse of any one as a continuous artist.

Another most palpable defect—especially palpable nowa-days—in *Tristram Shandy* is its indecency. It is quite true that the customary conventions of writing are much altered during the last century, and much which would formerly have been deemed blameless would now be censured and disliked. The audience has changed; and decency is of course in part dependent on who is within hearing. A divorce case may be talked over across a club-table with a plainness of speech and development of expression which would be indecent in a mixed party, and scandalous before young ladies. Now, a large part of old novels may very fairly be called club-books; they speak out plainly and simply the notorious facts of the world, as men speak of them to men. Much excellent and proper masculine conversation is wholly unfit for repetition to young girls; and just in the same way books written—as was almost all old literature,—for men only, or nearly only, seem coarse enough when contrasted with novels written by young ladies upon the subjects and in the tone of the drawing-room. The change is inevitable; as soon as works of fiction are addressed to boys and girls, they must be fit for boys and girls; they must deal with a life which is real so far as it goes, but which is yet most limited; which deals with the most passionate part of life, and yet omits the errors of the passions; which aims at describing men in their relations to women, and yet omits an all but universal influence which more or less distorts and modifies all these relations.

As we have said, the change cannot be helped. A young ladies' literature must be a limited and truncated literature. The indiscriminate study of human life is not desirable for them, either in fiction or in reality. But the habitual formation of a scheme of thought and a code of morality upon incom-plete materials is a very serious evil. The readers for whose sake the omissions are made cannot fancy what is left out. Many a girl of the present day reads novels, and nothing but novels; she forms her mind by them, as far as she forms it by reading at all; even if she reads a few dull books, she soon forgets all about them, and remembers the novels only; she is more influenced by them than by sermons. They form her idea of the world, they define her taste, and modify her morality; not so much in explicit thought and direct act as unconsciously and in her floating fancy. How is it possible to convince such a girl, especially if she is clever, that on most points she is all wrong? She has been reading most excellent descriptions of mere society; she comprehends those descriptions perfectly, for her own experience elucidates and confirms them. She has a vivid picture of a *patch* of life. Even if she admits in words that there is something beyond, something of which she has no idea, she will not admit it really and in practice. What she has mastered and realised will incurably and inevitably overpower the unknown something of which she knows nothing, can imagine nothing, and can make nothing. 'I am not sure,' said an old

lady, 'but I think it's the novels that make my girls so *heady*.' It is the novels. A very intelligent acquaintance with limited life makes them think that the world is far simpler than it is, that men are easy to understand, 'that mamma is *so* foolish.'

The novels of the last age have certainly not this fault. They do not err on the side of reticence. A girl may learn from them more than it is desirable for her to know. But, as we have explained, they were meant for men and not for girls; and if *Tristram Shandy* had simply given a plain exposition of necessary facts—necessary, that is, to the development of the writer's view of the world, and to the telling of the story in hand—we should not have complained; we should have regarded it as the natural product of a now extinct society. But there are most unmistakable traces of 'Crazy Castle' in *Tristram Shandy*. There is indecency for indecency's sake. It is made a sort of recurring and even permeating joke to mention things which are not generally mentioned. Sterne himself made a sort of defence, or rather denial, of this. He once asked a lady if she had read *Tristram*. 'I have not, Mr. Sterne,' was the answer; 'and, to be plain with you, I am informed it is not proper for female perusal.' 'My dear good lady,' said Sterne, 'do not be gulled by such stories; the book is like your young heir there' (pointing to a child of three years old who was rolling on the carpet in white tunics): 'he shows at times a good deal that is usually concealed, but it is all in perfect innocence.' But a perusal of *Tristram* would not make good the plea. The unusual publicity of what is ordinarily imperceptible is not the thoughtless accident of amusing play; it is deliberately sought after as a nice joke; it is treated as a good in itself.

The indecency of *Tristram Shandy*—at least of the early part, which was written before Sterne had been to France—is especially an offence against taste, because of its ugliness. *Moral* indecency is always disgusting. There certainly is a sort of writing which cannot be called decent, and which describes a society to the core immoral, which nevertheless is no offence against art; it violates a higher code than that of taste, but it does not violate the code of taste. The *Mémoires de Gram-mont*—hundreds of French memoirs about France—are of this kind, more or less. They describe the refined, witty, elegant immorality of an idle aristocracy. They describe a life 'unsuitable to such a being as man in such a world as the present one,' in which there are no high aims, no severe duties, where some precepts of morals seem not so much to be sometimes broken as to be generally suspended and forgotten; such a life, in short, as God has never suffered men to lead on this earth long, which He has always crushed out by calamity and revolution. This life, though an offence in morals, was not an offence in taste. It was an elegant, a *pretty* thing while it lasted. Especially in enhancing description, where the alloy of life may be omitted, where nothing vulgar need be noticed, where everything elegant may be neatly painted,—such a world is elegant enough. Morals and policy must decide how far such delineations are permissible or expedient; but the art of beauty—art criticism,—has no objection to them. They are pretty paintings of pretty objects, and that is all it has to say. They may very easily do harm; if generally read among the young of the middle class, they would be sure to do harm: they would teach not a few to aim at a sort of refinement denied them by circumstances, and to neglect the duties allotted them; it would make shopmen 'bad imitations of polished ungodli-ness,' and also bad shopmen. But still, though it would in such places be noxious literature, in itself it would be pretty literature. The critic must praise it, though the moralist must condemn it, and perhaps the politician forbid it.

But *Tristram's* indecency is the very opposite to this

refined sort. It consists in allusions to certain inseparable accompaniments of actual life which are not beautiful, which can never be made interesting, which would, *if* they were decent, be dull and uninteresting. There is, it appears, a certain excitement in putting such matters into a book: there is a minor exhilaration even in petty crime. At first such things look so odd in print that you go on reading them to see what they look like; but you soon give up. What is disenchanting or even disgusting in reality does not become enchanting or endurable in delineation. You are more angry at it in literature than in life; there is much which is barbarous and animal in reality that we could wish away; we endure it because we cannot help it, because we did not make it and cannot alter it, because it is an inseparable part of this inexplicable world. But why we should put this coarse alloy, this dross of life, into the *optional* world of literature, which we can make as we please, it is impossible to say. The needless introduction of accessory ugliness is always a sin in art, and is not at all less so when such ugliness is disgusting and improper. *Tristram Shandy* is incurably tainted with a pervading vice; it dwells at length on, it seeks after, it returns to, it gloats over, the most unattractive part of the world.

There is another defect in *Tristram Shandy* which would of itself remove it from the list of first-rate books, even if those which we have mentioned did not do so. It contains eccentric characters only. Some part of this defect may be perhaps explained by one peculiarity of its origin. Sterne was so sensitive to the picturesque parts of life, that he wished to paint the picturesque parts of the people he hated. Country-towns in those days abounded in odd character. They were out of the way of the great opinion of the world, and shaped themselves to little opinions of their own. They regarded the customs which the place had inherited as the customs which were proper for it, and which it would be foolish, if not wicked, to try to change. This gave English country-life a motley picturesqueness then, which it wants now, when London ideas shoot out every morning, and carry on the wings of the railway a uniform creed to each cranny of the kingdom, north and south, east and west. These little public opinions of little places wanted, too, the crushing power of the great public opinion of our day; at the worst, a man could escape from them into some different place which had customs and doctrines that suited him better. We now may fly into another 'city,' but it is all the same Roman empire; the same uniform justice, the one code of heavy laws, press us down and make us—the sensible part of us at least—as like other people as we can make ourselves. The public opinion of county-towns yielded soon to individual exceptions; it had not the confidence in itself which the opinion of each place now receives from the accordant and simultaneous echo of a hundred places. If a man chose to be queer, he was bullied for a year or two, then it was settled that he was 'queer;' that was the fact about him, and must be accepted. In a year or so he became an 'institution' of the place, and the local pride would have been grieved if he had amended the oddity which suggested their legends and added a flavour to their life. Of course, if a man was rich and influential, he might soon disregard the mere opinion of the petty locality. Every place has wonderful traditions of old rich men who did exactly as they pleased, because they could set at naught the opinions of the neighbours, by whom they were feared; and who did not, as now, dread the unanimous conscience which does not fear even a squire of £2000 a year, or a banker of £800, because it is backed by the wealth of London and the magnitude of all the country. There is little oddity in county-towns now; they are detached scraps of great

places; but in Sterne's time there was much, and he used it unsparingly.

Much of the delineation is of the highest merit. Sterne knew how to describe eccentricity, for he showed its relation to our common human nature: he showed how we were related to it, how in some sort and in some circumstances we might ourselves become it. He reduced the abnormal formation to the normal rules. Except upon this condition, eccentricity is no fit subject for literary art. Every one must have known characters which, if they were put down in books, barely and as he sees them, would seem monstrous and disproportioned, which would disgust all readers, which every critic would term unnatural. While characters are monstrous, they should be kept out of books; they are ugly unintelligibilities, foreign to the realm of true art. But as soon as they can be explained to us, as soon as they are shown in their union with, in their outgrowth from, common human nature, they are the best subjects for great art—for they are new subjects. They teach us, not the old lesson which our fathers knew, but a new lesson which will please us and make us better than them. Hamlet is an eccentric character, one of the most eccentric in literature; but because, by the art of the poet, we are made to understand that he is a possible, a *vividly* possible man, he enlarges our conceptions of human nature; he takes us out of the bounds of commonplace. He 'instructs us by means of delight.' Sterne does this too. Mr. Shandy, Uncle Toby, Corporal Trim, Mrs. Shandy,—for in strictness she too is eccentric from her abnormal commonplaceness,—are beings of which the possibility is brought home to us, which we feel we could under circumstances and by influences become, which, though contorted and twisted, are yet spun out of the same elementary nature, the same thread, as we are. Considering how odd these characters are, the success of Sterne is marvellous, and his art in this respect consummate. But yet on a point most nearly allied it is very faulty. Though each individual character is shaded off into human nature, the whole is not shaded off into the world. This society of originals and oddities is left to stand by itself, as if it were a natural and ordinary society,—a society easily conceivable and needing no explanation. Such is not the manner of the great masters; in their best works a constant atmosphere of half commonplace personages surrounds and shades off, illustrates and explains, every central group of singular persons.

On the whole, therefore, the judgment of criticism on *Tristram Shandy* is concise and easy. It is immortal because of certain scenes suggested by Sterne's curious experience, detected by his singular sensibility, and heightened by his delineative and discriminative imagination. It is defective because its style is fantastic, its method illogical and provoking; because its indecency is of the worst sort, as far as in such matters an artistic judgment can speak of worst and best; because its world of characters forms an incongruous group of singular persons utterly dissimilar to, and irreconcilable with, the world in which we live. It is a great work of art, but of barbarous art. Its mirth is boisterous. It is *provincial*. It is redolent of an inferior society; for those who think crude animal spirits in themselves delightful, who do not know that, without wit to point them or humour to convey them, they are disagreeable to others; who like disturbing transitions, blank pages, and tricks of style; who do not know that a simple and logical form of expression is the most effective, if not the easiest,—the least laborious to readers, if not always the most easily attained by writers.

The oddity of *Tristram Shandy* was, however, a great aid to its immediate popularity. If an author were to stand on his head now and then in Cheapside, his eccentricity would bring him into contact with the police, but it would advertise his writings; they would sell better: people would like to see what was said by a great author who was so odd as to stand so. Sterne put his eccentricity into his writings, and therefore came into collision with the critics; but he attained the same end. His book sold capitally. As with all popular authors, he went to London; he was *fêted*. 'The *man* Sterne,' growled Dr. Johnson, 'has dinner engagements for three months.' The upper world,—ever desirous of novelty, ever tired of itself, ever anxious to be amused,—was in hopes of a new wit. It naturally hoped that the author of *Tristram* would talk well, and it sent for him to talk.

He did talk well, it appears, though not always very correctly, and never very clerically. His appearance was curious, but yet refined. Eager eyes, a wild look, a long lean frame, and what he called a cadaverous bale of goods for a body, made up an odd exterior, which attracted notice, and did not repel liking. He looked like a scarecrow with bright eyes. With a random manner, but not without a nice calculation, he discharged witticisms at London parties. His keen nerves told him which were fit witticisms; *they* took, and *he* was applauded.

He published some sermons too. That tolerant age liked, it is instructive as well as amusing to think, sermons by the author of *Tristram Shandy*. People wonder at the rise of Methodism; but ought they to wonder? If a clergyman publishes his sermons *because* he has written an indecent novel— a novel which is purely pagan—which is outside the ideas of Christianity, whose author can scarcely have been inside of them,—if a man so made and so circumstanced is *as such* to publish Christian sermons, surely Christianity is a joke and a dream. Wesley was right in this at least; if Christianity be true, the upper life of the last century was based on rotten falsehood. A world which is really secular—which professes to be Christian, is the worst of worlds.

The only point in which Sterne resembles a clergyman of our own time is that he lost his voice. That peculiar affection of the chest and throat, which is hardly known among barristers, but which inflicts such suffering upon parsons, attacked him also. Sterne too, as might be expected, went abroad for it. He 'spluttered French,' he tells us, with success in Paris; the accuracy of the grammar some phrases in his letters would lead us to doubt; but few, very few Yorkshire parsons could then talk French at all, and there was doubtless a fine tact and sensibility in what he said. A literary phenomenon wishing to enjoy society, and able to amuse society, has ever been welcome in the Parisian world. After Paris, Sterne went to the south of France, and on to Italy, lounging easily in pretty places, and living comfortably, as far as one can see, upon the profits of *Tristram Shandy*. Literary success has seldom changed more suddenly and completely the course of a man's life. For years Sterne resided in a country parsonage, and the sources of his highest excitement were a country-town full of provincial oddities, and a 'Crazy Castle' full of the license and the whims of a country squire. On a sudden London, Paris, and Italy were opened to him. From a few familiar things he was suddenly transferred to many unfamiliar things. He was equal to them, though the change came so suddenly in middle life; though the change from a secluded English district to the great and interesting scenes was far greater, far fuller of unexpected sights and unforeseen phenomena, than it can be now, when travelling is common, when the newspaper is 'abroad,' when every one has in his head some feeble image of Europe and the world. Sterne showed the delicate docility which belongs to a sensitive and experiencing nature. He understood and enjoyed very much of this new and strange life, if not the whole.

The proof of this remains written in the *Sentimental Journey*. There is no better painting of first and easy impressions than that book. After all which has been written on the *ancien régime*, an Englishman at least will feel a fresh instruction on reading these simple observations. They are instructive *because* of their simplicity. The old world at heart was not like that; there were depths and realities, latent forces and concealed results, which were hidden from Sterne's eye, which it would have been quite out of his way to think of or observe. But the old world *seemed* like that. This was the spectacle of it as it was seen by an observing stranger; and we take it up, not to know what was the truth, but to know what we should have thought to be the truth if we had lived in those times. People say *Eöthen* is not like the real East; very likely it is not, but it is like what an imaginative young Englishman would *think* the East. Just so the *Sentimental Journey* is not the true France of the old monarchy, but it is exactly what an observant quick-eyed Englishman might fancy that France to be. This has given it popularity; this still makes it a valuable relic of the past. It is not true to the outward nature of real life, but it is true to the reflected image of that life in an imaginative and sensitive man.

HIPPOLYTE TAINE
From *History of English Literature*
tr. H. Van Laun
1871, Book 2, Chapter 6

Figure to yourself a man who goes on a journey, wearing on his eyes a pair of marvellously magnifying spectacles. A hair on his hand, a speck on a tablecloth, a fold of a moving garment, will interest him: at this rate he will not go very far; he will go six steps in a day, and will not quit his room. So Sterne writes four volumes to record the birth of his hero. He perceives the infinitely little, and describes the imperceptible. A man parts his hair on one side: this, according to Sterne, depends on his whole character, which is of a piece with that of his father, his mother, his uncle, and his whole ancestry; it depends on the structure of his brain, which depends on the circumstances of his conception and his birth, and these on the fancies of his parents, the humor of the moment, the talk of the preceding hour, the contrarieties of the last curate, a cut thumb, twenty knots made on a bag; I know not how many things besides. The six or eight volumes of *Tristram Shandy* are employed in summing them up; for the smallest and dullest incident, a sneeze, a badly-shaved beard, drags after it an inextricable network of inter-involved causes which from above, below, right and left, by invisible prolongations and ramifications, are buried in the depths of a character and in the remote vistas of events. Instead of extracting, like the novel-writers, the principal root, Sterne, with marvellous devices and success, devotes himself to drawing out the tangled skein of numberless threads, which are sinuously immersed and dispersed, so as to suck in from all sides the sap and the life. Slender, intertwined, buried as they are, he finds them; he extricates them without breaking, brings them to the light; and there, where we fancied was but a stalk, we see with wonder the underground mass and vegetation of the multiplied fibres and fibrils, by which the visible plant grows and is supported.

This is truly a strange talent, made up of blindness and insight, which resembles those diseases of the retina in which the over-excited nerve becomes at once dull and penetrating, incapable of seeing what the most ordinary eyes perceive, capable of observing what the most piercing sight misses. In fact, Sterne is a sickly and eccentric humorist, an ecclesiastic and a libertine, a fiddler and a philosopher, "who whimpered over a dead donkey, but left his mother to starve," selfish in act, selfish in word, who in everything is the reverse of himself and of others. His book is like a great storehouse of articles of *virtù*, where the curiosities of all ages, kinds, and countries lie jumbled in a heap; texts of excommunication, medical consultations, passages of unknown or imaginary authors, scraps of scholastic erudition, strings of absurd histories, dissertations, addresses to the reader. His pen leads him; he has neither sequence nor plan; nay, when he lights upon anything orderly, he purposely contorts it; with a kick he sends the pile of folios next to him over the history he has commenced, and dances on the top of them. He delights in disappointing us, in sending us astray by interruptions and outrages. Gravity displeases him, he treats it as a hypocrite; to his liking folly is better, and he paints himself in Yorick. In a well-constituted mind ideas march one after another, with uniform motion or acceleration; in this uncouth brain they jump about like a rout of masks at a carnival, in troops, each dragging his neighbor by the feet, head, coat, amidst the most promiscuous and unforeseen hubbub. All his little lopped phrases are somersaults; we pant as we read. the tone is never for two minutes the same; laughter comes, then the beginning of emotion, then scandal, then wonder, then tenderness, then laughter again. The mischievous joker pulls and entangles the threads of all our feelings, and makes us go hither, thither, irregularly, like puppets. Amongst these various threads there are two which he pulls more willingly than the rest. Like all men who have nerves, he is subject to tenderness; not that he is really kindly and tender; on the contrary, his life is that of an egotist; but on certain days he must needs weep, and he makes us weep with him. He is moved on behalf of a captive bird, of a poor ass, which, accustomed to blows, "looked up pensive," and seemed to say, "Don't thrash me with it (the halter); but if you will, you may."[1] He will write a couple of pages on the attitude of this donkey, and Priam at the feet of Achilles was not more touching. Thus in a silence, in an oath, in the most trifling domestic action, he hits upon exquisite refinements and little heroisms, a sort of charming flowers, invisible to everybody else, which grow in the dust of the dryest road. One day Uncle Toby, the poor sick captain, catches, after "infinite attempts, a big buzzing fly, who has cruelly tormented him all dinnertime; he gets up, crosses the room on his suffering leg, and opening the window, cries: "Go, poor devil, get thee gone; why should I hurt thee? This world surely is wide enough to hold both thee and me."[2] This womanish sensibility is too fine to be described; we should have to give a whole story—that of Lefevre, for instance—that the perfume might be inhaled; this perfume evaporates as soon as we touch it, and is like the weak fleeting odor of the plants, brought for one moment into a sick-chamber. What still more increases this sad sweetness, is the contrast of the free and easy waggeries which, like a hedge of nettles, encircles them on all sides. Sterne, like all men whose mechanism is over-excited, has irregular appetites. He loves the nude, not from a feeling of the beautiful, and in the manner of painters, not from sensuality and frankness like Fielding, not from a search after pleasure, like Dorat, Boufflers, and all those refined pleasure-seekers, who at the same time were rhyming and enjoying themselves in France. If he

goes into dirty places, it is because they are forbidden and not frequented. What he seeks there is singularity and scandal. The allurement of this forbidden fruit is not the fruit, but the prohibition; for he bites by preference where the fruit is withered or worm-eaten. That an epicurean delights in detailing the pretty sins of a pretty woman is nothing wonderful; but that a novelist takes pleasure in watching the bedroom of a musty, fusty old couple, in observing the consequences of the fall of a burning chestnut in a pair of breeches,[3] in detailing the questions of Mrs. Wadman on the consequences of wounds in the groin,[4] can only be explained by the aberration of a perverted fancy, which finds its amusement in repugnant ideas, as spoiled palates are pleased by the pungent flavor of mouldy cheese.[5] Thus, to read Sterne we should wait for days when we are in a peculiar kind of humour, days of spleen, rain, or when through nervous irritation we are disgusted with rationality. In fact, his characters are as unreasonable as himself. He sees in man nothing but fancy, and what he calls the hobby-horse— Uncle Toby's taste for fortifications, Mr. Shandy's fancy for oratorical tirades and philosophical systems. This hobby-horse, according to him, is like a wart, so small at first that we hardly perceive it, and only when it is in a strong light; but it gradually increases, becomes covered with hairs, grows red, and buds out all around: its possessor, who is pleased with and admires it, nourishes it, until at last it is changed into a vast wen, and the whole face disappears under the invasion of the parasite excrescence. No one has equalled Sterne in the history of these human hypertrophies; he puts down the seed, feeds it gradually, makes the propagating threads creep round about, shows the little veins and microscopic arteries which inosculate within, counts the palpitations of the blood which passes through them, explains their changes of color and increase of bulk. The psychological observer attains here one of his extreme developments. A far advanced art is necessary to describe, beyond the confines of regularity and health, the exception or the degeneration; and the English novel is completed here by adding to the representation of form the picture of deformations.

Notes

1. Sterne's Works, 7 vols., 1783, 3; *The Life and Opinions of Tristram Shandy*, vii. ch. xxxii.
2. Ibid. ii. ch. xii.
3. Ibid. iv. ch. xxvii.
4. Ibid. ix. ch. xx.
5. Sterne, Goldsmith, Burke, Sheridan, Moore, having a tone of their own, which comes from their blood, or from their proximate or distant parentage—the Irish tone. So Hume, Robertson, Smollett, W. Scott, Burns, Beattie, Reid, D. Stewart, etc., have the Scotch tone. In the Irish or Celtic tone we find an excess of chivalry, sensuality, expansion; in short, a mind less equally balanced, more sympathetic and less practical. The Scotchman on the other hand, is an Englishman, either slightly refined or narrowed, because he has suffered more and fasted more.

CHARLES COWDEN CLARKE
From "On the Comic Writers of England: XIV. Fielding, Smollett and Sterne"
Gentleman's Magazine, May 1872, pp. 575–80

There is more originality of manner, and more mannerism in his originality; more sudden and unaffected strokes of nature, and more palpable affectation; more genuinely idiomatical power, and conversational ease in his style, and more constrained and far-fetched attempts to be unconstrained and easy, than in any eminent classical writer of our language that I am acquainted with. When I speak of Sterne's "originality," I would merge it rather in an oddness of manner, a bold and self-satisfied eccentricity (for no writer was ever on better terms with himself than Sterne), than any new range of thought or invention, for much of his manner, much of his thought, and much of his oddity are referable to wits and writers that had gone before him. Rabelais' *History of Gargantua*, and Burton's *Anatomy of Melancholy* must have been his literary household gods. His imitations (I will not say plagiarisms) of Rabelais are most palpable.

His strokes of nature and pathos frequently reach the very seat of feeling and true sentiment, but he did not always know when to leave well alone. He sometimes spoils all by an artificial dilation, an anticlimax. He will run a description of a pathetic scene into trifling, as if he himself had thrust his tongue into his cheek (as Garrick, when he had uttered the curse in *Lear*), and was laughing at the effect he had produced; or, on the other hand, if he have achieved a piece of fine sentiment, he will strive to make it more fine by a miserable artifice. For one example in evidence of the former, the reader may be referred to Trim's account of Master Bobby Shandy's death, which ends in burlesque; and for the latter, to the passage about the "accusing" and the "recording angel" in the story of Le Fevre—a story which, for exquisite and simple pathos, I should think is without a rival in the language. Any writer might be allowed to think with complacency of his own talent who had so told that tender tale. As another example of his artifice (by which I mean that he himself did not consistently accompany in feeling what he was putting down), I would refer to the story of "Maria," in *The Sentimental Journey*, and which, in modern language, would be called "twaddle;" to the account also of the "Dead Ass," and to that of the ass with his panniers in the *Tristram Shandy*, the chief portion of which is excellent, both in sense and diction. The amusing gravity of his reason why he would rather hold conversation with an ass than with any other animal is a complete specimen of that mixture of nature and art, truth and artifice, that we constantly encounter in Sterne. "In truth," he says, "it is the only creature of all the classes of beings below me with whom I can do this; for parrots, jackdaws, &c., I can never exchange a word with them, nor with apes, &c., for pretty near the same reason; they act by rote, as the others speak by it, and equally make me silent; nay, my dog and my cat, though I value them both (and for my dog, he would speak if he could), yet, somehow or other, they neither of them possess the talents for conversation; I can make nothing of a discourse with them beyond the proposition, the reply, and the rejoinder, but with an ass I can commune for ever."

The conversational ease of Sterne's style is at times perfect; it is brisk, felicitous, brief, and idiomatic. Nothing can be finer than the dialogues between Mr. Shandy and Dr. Slop, with those inimitably humourous parenthetical objections now and then thrown in, like hand-grenades, by Uncle Toby, so effectually checking and disconcerting the self-satisfied garrulity of the others; the "excommunication" scene; and when the Doctor begins to read the Pope's curse, Uncle Toby throwing back his head, and giving a monstrous, long, loud "Wh—e—w!" with that magnificent comment at the close of it—"'I declare,' quoth my Uncle Toby, 'my heart would not let me curse the devil himself with so much bitterness.' 'He is the father of curses,' replied Dr. Slop. 'So am not I,' replied my uncle. 'But he is cursed and damned already to all eternity,' replied Dr. Slop. 'I am sorry for it,' quoth my uncle Toby."

The eccentricities of manner in Sterne are, no doubt, frequently amusing; but, as eccentricities, they almost as frequently bring their annoyances with them. The wayward ramblings in the story of *Tristram Shandy*; the unlooked for jerks, dislocations, and digressions; the never knowing when and where to have him, convey much more the air of preparation and artifice, not to say of affectation, than a naturally inconsequent and unconstrained manner. Moreover, it will be difficult to discern anything beyond mere eccentricity (with the affectation of it) in those sudden chapters of one and two lines only, and even chapters about nothing at all. Such gyrations of the fancy are, at all events, easy of invention, and as futile as easy.

But the most objectionable feature in this author is the unpleasant way in which he selects subjects connected with the infirmities of our nature to joke upon, and even to ridicule with ungenial hardness. I allude especially to the early accounts of Mrs. Shandy. One can tolerate and laugh at his impudent inuendos, and sly, roguish insinuations—the more of such the merrier, for we have not too much of these carnivals of the fancy in the present day; but there are feelings connected with our nature in its weakness, and in its painful prostrations, that are much too sacred to be made the subjects of ribald jests, chapter after chapter; for it is not a passing joke and away; but there are numbers of pages of it. This it is that induces the suspicion (with the other reasons adduced) that in Sterne's mental composition, sentiment, real sentiment, sentiment of the heart (not professional sentiment), was, after all, but a skin-deep affair with him. Nay, indeed, to speak sincerely, it is difficult to avoid the impression that there was a prodigious deal of talky-talk, with no parsimonious infusion of what the French call "blague," and his natives, "blarney," in his sentimentality.

His wit, however, if it be artificial, as some critics have pronounced it, is nevertheless most poignant; and his vein of humour dry, sarcastic, and quite his own. His principal characters, too, are said to be traceable in their ground work elsewhere. Possibly; but I protest that I am ignorant of the quarry whence they were extracted; and sure I am, that in the remodelling, and the grouping, he has all but made them his own. And surely no one will deny that Corporal Trim is an original; if so, where is his prototype? Who has ever produced anything comparable or at all like his report of his visit to the dying Le Fevre? Here is Trim's practical illustration of the Fifth Commandment:—

> "Pr'ythee, Trim," quoth my father, "what dost *thou* mean by 'honouring thy father and thy mother?'" "Allowing them, an' please your honour, three halfpence a day out of my pay when they grow old." "And didst thou do that, Trim?" said Yorick. "He did indeed," replied my uncle Toby. "Then, Trim," said Yorick, springing out of his chair, and taking the corporal by the hand, "thou art the best commentator upon that part of the Decalogue; and I honour thee more for it, Corporal Trim, than if thou hadst had a hand in the Talmud itself."

Uncle Toby, however, is the favourite of all the characters, and naturally so; for he is one of Nature's own gentlemen—gentle in every thought and action. His apostrophe to the fly—a piece of truth in the abstract, but in the reality another example of the author's artifice; for, in his vocation, Uncle Toby would have hewn up a fellow creature, and sent him shrieking out of life; and yet could be very considerate towards the feelings of a blue-bottle—not to say that this is unnatural; we all are inconsistent creatures, and surrounded with artifice and conventionalities. But Uncle Toby's character is finely sustained throughout. With his simple, plain-sailing sense, and with those interjectional comments of his during their conversations, uttered between the whiffs of his pipe, he keeps up a running satire upon, and upsets the pedantic book-learning of his formal-minded and prosing brother. It will be recollected that he makes but one speech through the whole book, and that is his famous apology for wishing a continuance of the war. And in his love-campaign with the Widow Wadman he is the same unsophisticated, unsuspicious, natural being. The pretty widow's generalship, together with her long-range artillery, proved too heavy metal for the redoubt of the captain's heart to withstand; and who, indeed, ought to have held out against so fair a daughter of Eve? This portion of the book is one of the most humorous—quietly humorous, and well-sustained scenes that ever was penned. Of his bowling-green and his fortifications, his sieges and his mortars, his field-pieces, and his jack-boots stuffed with tobacco, to puff away at the enemy; they are amusing enough, and part and parcel of his simplicity of nature; but, indeed, both he and Trim, in this scene of their career, come rather under the denomination of childish than child-like in their evolutions.

Dear Uncle Toby! thou art a most divine-hearted and unoffending creature; and one towards whom it were quite as easy to commit a violence—either in word or deed—as against the loveliest emanation of Universal Benevolence. We will give thy author all the merit due, and our gratitude into the bargain, for having imagined and produced so sweet a character; but when we are informed (as we have been) that Shakespeare never originated so perfect a character as Uncle Toby, we naturally pause, and call up in review before "the mind's eye" Mr. Justice Shallow and Master Slender; Sir Andrew Aguecheek and Malvolio; and if these were all sunk in the sea of oblivion, we would take our stand upon immortal Sir John Falstaff alone. One would avoid committing oneself with a real opinion upon reading these small pickthankings of the greatest imaginative intellect that the world has yet produced.

Uncle Toby is *the* character always recurred to when thinking or talking of this admirable work; but I am not quite sure that Mr. Shandy is not the most original and consistent, as well as artistical invention of the whole company. He is a perfect specimen of an old married bachelor: formal in body, formal in mind, and restless in both; a mere compilation upon the thoughts and actions of his predecessors. Mr. Shandy is a personification of rule and precedent. He would as soon reverse the common law of all nature, as he would an opinion of the most obsolete classic. His notions of marriage are comprehended in the one idea of having a son to continue the Shandy generation; and he has no other idea of Mrs. Shandy than that she is to fulfil her destiny in giving him a son. As for Mrs. Shandy herself, she has not a single opinion in opposition to her husband,—except the good old orthodox one, of being paramount when women are in that blessed state those "wish to be who love their lords." But we are never let into the secret that Mrs. Shandy does "love her lord." She is his wife by ecclesiastical and civil law, and no more. She never contradicts him—even upon the momentous question of Master Tristram being breeched; and while dialogue (by the way) is eminently characteristic of that unique couple. Most methodical and one-sided is the conduct of the debate; Mr. Shandy suggesting the most fit materials and fashions, and Mrs. Shandy coinciding implicitly in every one of them.

If we consider the *Tristram Shandy* as an integral production; or even if we balance its defects against its merits, we must come to the conclusion that it is a work of uncommon

versatility, and as uncommon vigour of talent in that versatility. The wit does not fail before the humour; nor the pathos before the homely narrative; while the characteristic development in the whole *dramatis personæ* soars over all in triumphant perfection. But Sterne, I suspect, will always be more remembered for his vagaries and eccentricities, than for the more staid, and the deeper effusions of his genius; and this is unfortunate, since it proves that those are so prominent in the mind of the reader, as to bring them, at all events, to an equipoise. In short, there is so much of idiosyncrasy in his style and manner, that they cannot be reproduced. They are like the hybrid vagaries in nature, that come forth and remain in anomalous singularity. Imitations of them have been attempted, and with the success they deserved, not having the wit of the original to sustain them.

One circumstance must always be regretted as regards Sterne's position in society, and which no doubt his own spirit constantly fretted and chafed at; that is, that he ever became a clergyman.

SIR LESLIE STEPHEN
"Sterne" (1880)
Hours in a Library (1874–79)
1904, Volume 4, pp. 57–101

It is impossible for any one with the remotest taste for literary excellence to read *Tristram Shandy* or the *Sentimental Journey* without a sense of wondering admiration. One can hardly read the familiar passages without admitting that Sterne was perhaps the greatest artist in the language. No one at least shows more inimitable felicity in producing a pungent effect by a few touches of exquisite precision. He gives the impression that the thing has been done once for all; he has hit the bull's eye round which inspiring marksmen go on blundering indefinitely without any satisfying success. Two or three of the scenes in which Uncle Toby expresses his sentiments are as perfect in their way as the half-dozen lines in which Mrs. Quickly describes the end of Falstaff, and convince us that three strokes from a man of genius may be worth more than the life's labour of the cleverest skilled literary workmen. And it may further be said that Uncle Toby, like his kinsmen in the world of humour, is an incarnation of most lovable qualities. In going over the list—a short list in any case—of the immortal characters in fiction, there is hardly any one in our literature who would be entitled to take precedence of him. To find a distinctly superior type, we must go back to Cervantes, whom Sterne idolised and professed to take for his model. But to speak of a character as in some sort comparable to Don Quixote, though without any thought of placing him on the same level, is to admit that he is a triumph of art. Indeed, if we take the other creator of types, of whom it is only permitted to speak with bated breath, we must agree that it would be difficult to find a figure even in the Shakesperean gallery more admirable in its way. Of course, the creation of a Hamlet, an Iago, or a Falstaff implies an intellectual intensity and reach of imaginative sympathy altogether different from anything which his warmest admirers would attribute to Sterne. I only say that there is no single character in Shakespeare whom we see more vividly and love more heartily than Mr. Shandy's uncle.

It should follow, according to the doctrine just set forth, that we ought to love Uncle Toby's creator. But here I fancy that everybody will be sensible of a considerable difficulty. The judgment pronounced upon Sterne by Thackeray seems to me to be substantially unimpeachable. The more I know of the man, for my part, the less I like him. It is impossible to write his biography (from the admiring point of view) without making it a continuous apology. His faults may be extenuated by the customary devices; but there is a terrible lack of any positive merits to set against them. He seems to have been fond of his daughter and tolerant of his wife. The nearest approach to a good action recorded of him is that when they preferred remaining in France to following him to England, he took care that they should have the income which he had promised. The liberality was nothing very wonderful. He knew that his wife was severely economical, as she had good reason to be; inasmuch as his own health was most precarious, and he was spending his income with a generous freedom which left her in destitution at his death. Still we are glad to give him all credit for not being a grudging paymaster. Some better men have been less good-natured. The rest of his panegyric consists of excuses for his shortcomings. We know the regular formulæ. He had bad companions, it is said, in his youth. Men who show a want of principle in later life have a knack of picking up bad companions at their outset. We are reminded as usual that the morals of the time were corrupt. It is a very difficult question how far this is true. We can only make a rough guess as to the morals of our own time; some people can see steady improvement, where others see nothing but signs of growing corruption; but when we come to speak of the morals of an age more or less removed, there are so many causes of illusion that our estimates have very small title to respect. It is no doubt true that the clergy of the Church of England in Sterne's day took a less exalted view than they now do of their own position and duties; that they were frequently pluralists and absentees; that patrons had small sense of responsibility; and that, as a general rule, the spiritual teachers of the country took life easily, and left an ample field for the activity of Wesley and his followers. But, making every allowance for this, it would be grossly unfair to deny, what is plainly visible in all the memoirs of the time, that there were plenty of honest squires and persons in every part of the country leading wholesome domestic lives.

But, in any case, such apologies rather explain how a man came to be bad, than prove that he was not bad. They would show at most that we were making an erroneous inference if we inferred badness of heart from conduct which was not condemned by the standard of his own day. This argument, however, is really inapplicable. Sterne's faults were of a kind for which if anything there was less excuse then than now. The faults of his best-known contemporaries, of men like Fielding, Smollett, or Churchill, were the faults of robust temperament with an excess of animal passions. Their coarseness has left a stain upon their pages as it injured their lives. But, however much we may lament or condemn, we do not feel that such men were corrupt at heart. And that, unfortunately, is just what we are tempted to feel about Sterne. When the huge, brawny parson, Churchill, felt his unfitness for clerical life, he pitched his cassock to the dogs and blossomed out in purple and gold. He set the respectabilities at defiance, took up with Wilkes and the reprobates, and roared out full-mouthed abuse against bishops and ministers. He could still be faithful to his friends, observe his own code of honour, and do his best to make some atonement to the victims of his misconduct. Sterne, one feels, differs from Churchill not really as being more virtuous, but in not having the courage to be so openly vicious. Unlike Churchill, he could be a consummate sneak. He was quite as ready to flatter Wilkes or to be on intimate terms with atheists and libertines, with Holbach and Crébillon, when his bishop and his parishioners could not see him. His most intimate friend from early days was John Hall Stevenson—the country squire whose pride it was to ape in the provinces the orgies of the monks of Medmenham Abbey, and once notorious as the author of a grossly indecent book. The dog-Latin letter in which Sterne informs this chosen companion that he is weary of his life contains other remarks sufficiently significant of the nature of their intimacy. The age was not very nice; but it was quite acute enough to see the objections to a close alliance between a married ecclesiastic of forty-five[1] and the rustic Don Juan of the district. But his cynicism becomes doubly disgusting when we remember that Sterne was all the time as eager as any patronage hunter to ingratiate himself into the good graces of bishops. Churchill, we remember, lampooned Warburton with savage ferocity. Sterne tried his best to conciliate the most conspicuous prelate of the day. He never put together a more elaborately skilful bit of writing than the letter which he wrote to Garrick, with the obvious intention that it should be shown to Warburton. He humbly says that he has no claim to an introduction, except "what arises from the honour and respect which, in the progress of my work, will be shown the world I owe so great a man." The statement was probably meant to encounter a suspicion which Warburton entertained that he was to be introduced in a ridiculous character in *Tristram Shandy*. The bishop was sufficiently soothed to administer not only good advice but a certain purse of gold, which had an unpleasant resemblance to hush-money. It became evident, however, that the author of *Tristram Shandy* was not a possible object of episcopal patronage; and, indeed, he was presently described by the bishop as an "irrevocable scoundrel." Sterne's "honour and respect" never found expression in his writings; but he ingeniously managed to couple the *Divine Legation*—the work which had justified Warburton's elevation to the bench—with the *Tale of a Tub*, the audacious satire upon orthodox opinions which had been an insuperable bar to Swift's preferment. The insinuation had its sting, for there were plenty of critics in those days who maintained that Warburton's apology was really more damaging to the cause of orthodoxy than Swift's burlesque. We cannot resist the conviction that if Warburton had been more judicious in his distribution of patronage, he would have received a very different notice in return. The blow from Churchill's bludgeon was, on any right, given by an open enemy. This little stab came from one who had been a servile flatterer.

No doubt Sterne is to be pitied for his uncongenial position. The relations who kindly took him off the hands of his impecunious father could provide for him most easily in the Church; and he is not the only man who has been injured by being forced by such considerations into a career for which he was unfitted. In the same way we may pity him for having become tired of his wife whom he seems to have married under a generous impulse—she was no doubt a very tiresome woman—and try to forgive him for some of his flirtations. But it is not so easy to forgive the spirit in which he conducted them. One story, as related by an admiring biographer, will be an amply sufficient specimen. He fell in love with a Miss Fourmantelle, who was living at York when he was finishing the first volumes of *Tristram Shandy* at the ripe age of forty-six. He introduced her into that work as "dear, dear Jenny." He writes to her in his usual style of love-making. He swears that he loves her "to distraction," and will love her "to eternity." He declares that there is "only one obstacle to their happiness"—obviously Mrs. Sterne—and solemnly prays to God that she may so live and love him as one day to share in his great good fortune. Precisely similar aspirations we note in passing, were to be soon afterwards addressed to Mrs. Draper, on the hypothesis that two obstacles to their happiness might be removed namely, Mr. Draper and Mrs. Sterne. Few readers are likely to be edified by the sacred language used by a clergyman on such an occasion; though biographical zeal has been equal even to this emergency. But the sequel to the Fourmantelle story is the really significant part. Mr. Sterne goes to London to reap the social fruits of his amazing success with *Tristram Shandy*. The whole London world falls at his feet; he is overwhelmed with invitations, and deafened with flattery; and poor literary drudges like Goldsmith are scandalised by so overpowering a triumph. Nobody had thought it worth while to make a fuss about the author of the *Vicar of Wakefield*. Sterne writes the accounts of his unprecedented success to Miss Fourmantelle: he snatches moments in the midst of his crowded levees to tell her that he is hers for ever and ever, that he would "give a guinea for a squeeze of her hand;" and promises to use his influence in some affair in which she is interested. Hereupon Miss Fourmantelle follows him to London. She finds him so deeply engaged that he cannot see her from Sunday till Friday; though he is still good enough to say that he would wish to be with her always, were it not for "fate." And, hereupon, Miss Fourmantelle vanishes out of history, and Mr. Sterne ceases to trouble his head about her. It needs only to be added that this is but one episode in Sterne's career out of several of which the records have been accidentally preserved. Mrs. Draper seems to have been the most famous case; but, according to his own statement, he had regularly on hand some affair of the sort, and is proud of the sensibility which they indicate.

Upon such an occurrence only one comment is possible from the moralist's point of view, namely, that a brother of Miss Fourmantelle, had she possessed a brother would have been justified in administering a horse-whipping. I do not, however, wish to preach a sermon upon Sterne's iniquities, or to draw any edifying conclusions upon the present occasion. We have only to deal with the failings of the man so far as they are reflected in the author. Time enables us to abstract and distinguish. A man's hateful qualities may not be of the essence of his character, or they may be only hateful in certain specific relations which do not now affect us. Moreover, there is some kind of immorality—spite and uncharitableness, for example—which is not without its charm. Pope was in many ways a far worse man than Sterne; he was an incomparably more elaborate liar, and the amount of gall with which his constitution was saturated would have been enough to furnish a whole generation of Sternes. But we can admire the brilliance of Pope's epigrams without bothering ourselves with the reflection that he told a whole series of falsehoods as to the date of their composition. We can enjoy the pungency of his indignant satire without asking whether it was directed against deserving objects. Atticus was perhaps a very cruel caricature of Addison; but the lines upon Atticus remain as an incomparably keen dissection of a type which need not have been embodied in this particular representative. Some people, indeed, may be too virtuous or tender-hearted to enjoy any exposure of human weakness. I make no pretensions to such amiability, and I can admire the keenness of the wasp's sting when it is no longer capable of touching me and my friends. Indeed, almost any genuine ebullition of human passion is interesting in its way, and it would be pedantic to be scandalised whenever it is rather more vehement than a moralist would approve, or happens to break out on the wrong occasion. The reader can apply the

correction for himself; he can read satire in his moments of virtuous indignation, and twist it in his own mind against some of those people—they are generally to be found—who really deserve it. But the case is different when the sentiment itself is offensive, and offensive by reason of insincerity. When the very thing by which we are supposed to be attracted is the goodness of a man's heart, a suspicion that he was a mere Tartufe cannot enter our minds without injuring our enjoyment. We may continue to admire the writer's technical skill, but he cannot fascinate us unless he persuades us of his sincerity. One might, to take a parallel case, admire Reynolds for his skill of hand, and fine perception of form and colour, if he had used them only to represent objects as repulsive as the most hideous scenes in Hogarth. One loves him, because of the exquisite tenderness of nature implied in the representations of infantile beauty. And if it were possible to feel that this tenderness was a mere sham, that his work was that of a dexterous artist skilfully flattering the fondness of parents, the charm would vanish. The children would breathe affectation instead of simplicity, and provoke only the sardonic sneer which is suggested by most of the infantile portraits collected in modern exhibitions.

It is with something of this feeling that we read Sterne. Of the literary skill there cannot be a moment's question; but if we for a moment yield to the enchantment, we feel ashamed, at the next moment, of our weakness. We have been moved on false pretences; and we seem to see the sham Yorick with that unpleasant leer upon his too expressive face, chuckling quietly at his successful imposition. It is no wonder if many of his readers have revolted, and even been provoked to an excessive reaction of feeling. The criticism was too obvious to be missed. Horace Walpole indulged in a characteristic sneer at the genius who neglected a mother and snivelled over a dead donkey. (The neglect of a mother, we may note in passing, is certainly not proven.) Walpole was too much of a cynic, it may be said, to distinguish between sentimentalism and genuine sentiment, or rather so much of a cynic that one is surprised at his not liking the sentimentalism more. But Goldsmith at least was a man of real feeling, and as an artist in some respects superior even to Sterne. He was moved to his bitterest outburst of satire by *Tristram Shandy*. He despised the charlatan who eked out his defects of humour by the paltry mechanical devices of blank pages, disordered chapters, and a profuse indulgence in dashes. He pointed out with undeniable truth the many grievous stains by which Sterne's pages are defaced. He spoke with disgust of the ladies who worshipped the author of a book which they should have been ashamed to read, and found the whole secret of Sterne's success in his pertness and indecency. Goldsmith may have been yielding unconsciously to a not unnatural jealousy, and his criticism certainly omits to take into account Sterne's legitimate claims to admiration. It is happily needless to insist at the present day upon the palpable errors by which the delicate and pure-minded Goldsmith was offended. It is enough to indulge in a passing word of regret that a man of Sterne's genius should have descended so often to mere buffoonery or to the most degrading methods of meeting his reader's interest. *The Sentimental Journey* is a book of simply marvellous cleverness, to which one can find no nearer parallel than Heine's *Reisebilder*. But one often closes it with a mixture of disgust and regret. The disgust needs no explanation; the regret is caused by our feeling that something has been missed which ought to have been in the writer's power. He has so keen an eye for picturesque effects; he is so sensitive to a thousand little incidents which your ordinary traveller passes with eyes riveted to his guidebook, or which

"Smelfungus" Smollett disregarded in his surly British pomposity; he is so quick at appreciating some delicate courtesy in humble life or some pathetic touch of commonplace suffering, that one grows angry when he spoils a graceful scene by some prurient double meaning, and wastes whole pages in telling a story fit only for John Hall Stevenson. One feels that one has been rambling with a discreditable parson, who is so glad to be free from the restraints of his parish or of Mrs. Sterne's company that he is always peeping into forbidden corners, and anxious to prove to you that he is as knowing in the ways of a wicked world as a raffish undergraduate enjoying a stolen visit to London. Goldsmith's idyllic pictures of country life may be a little too rose-coloured, but at least they are harmonious. Sterne's sudden excursions into the nauseous are like the brutal practical jokes of a dirty boy who should put filth into a scent bottle. We feel that if he had entered the rustic paradise, of which Dr. and Mrs. Primrose were the Adam and Eve, half his sympathies would have been with the wicked Squire Thornhill; he would have been quite as able to suit that gentleman's tastes as to wheedle the excellent Vicar; and his homage to Miss Olivia would have partaken of the nature of an insult. A man of Sterne's admirable delicacy of genius, writing always with an eye to the canons of taste approved in Crazy Castle, must necessarily produce painful discords, and throw away admirable workmanship upon contemptible ribaldry. But the very feeling proves that there was really a finer element in him. Had he been thoroughly steeped in the noxious element, there would have been no discord. We might simply have set him down as a very clever reprobate. But, with some exceptions, we can generally recognise something so amiable and attractive as to excite our regret for the waste of genius even in his more questionable passages.

Coleridge points out, with his usual critical acuteness, that much of *Tristram Shandy* would produce simple disgust were it not for the presence of that wonderful group of characters who are antagonistic to the spurious wit based upon simple shocks to a sense of decency. That group redeems the book, and we may say that it is the book. We must therefore admit that the creator of Uncle Toby and his family must not be unreservedly condemned. To admit that one thoroughly dislikes Sterne is not to assert that he was a thorough hypocrite of the downright Tartufe variety. His good feelings must be something more than a mere sham or empty formula; they are not a flimsy veil thrown over degrading selfishness or sensuality. When he is attacked upon this ground, his apologists may have an easy triumph. The true statement is rather that Sterne was a man who understood to perfection the art of enjoying his own good feelings as a luxury without humbling himself to translate them into practice. This is the definition of sentimentalism when the word is used in a bad sense. Many admirable teachers of mankind have held the doctrine that all artistic indulgence is universally immoral, because it is all more or less obnoxious to this objection. So far as a man saves up his good feelings merely to use them as the raw material of poems, he is wasting a force which ought to be applied to the improvement of the world. What have we to do with singing and painting when there are so many of our fellow-creatures whose sufferings might be relieved and whose characters might be purified if we turned our songs into sermons, and, instead of staining canvas, tried to purify the dwellings of the poor? There is a good deal to be said for the thesis that all fiction is really a kind of lying, and that art in general is a luxurious indulgence, to which we have no right whilst crime and disease are rampant in the outer world.

I think, indeed, that I could detect some flaws in the logic by which this conclusion is supported, but I confess that it often seems to possess a considerable plausibility. The peculiar sentimentalism of which Sterne was one of the first mouthpieces would supply many effective illustrations of the argument; for it is a continuous manifestation of extraordinary skill in providing "sweet poison for the age's tooth." He was exactly the man for his time, though, indeed, so clever a man would probably have been equally able to flatter the prevailing impulse of any time in which his lot had been cast. M. Taine has lately described with great skill the sort of fashion of philanthropy which became popular among the upper classes in France in the pre-revolutionary generation. The fine ladies and gentlemen who were so soon to be crushed as tyrannical oppressors of the people had really a strong impression that benevolence was a branch of social elegance which ought to be assiduously cultivated by persons of taste and refinement. A similar tendency, though less strongly marked, is observable amongst the corresponding class in English society. From causes which may be analysed by historians, the upper social stratum was becoming penetrated with a vague discontent with the existing order and a desire to find new outlets for emotional activity. Between the reign of comfortable common-sense, represented by Pope and his school, and the fierce outbreak of passion which accompanied the crash of the revolution, there was an interregnum marked by a semi-conscious fore-feeling of some approaching catastrophe; a longing for fresh excitement, and tentative excursions into various regions of thought, which have since been explored in a more systematic fashion. Sentimentalism was the word which represented one phase of this inarticulate longing, and which expresses pretty accurately the need of having some keen sensations without very well knowing in what particular channels they were to be directed. The growth of the feminine influence in literature had no doubt some share in this development. Women were no longer content to be simply the pretty fools of the *Spectator*, unworthy to learn the Latin grammar or to be admitted to the circle of wits; though they seldom presumed to be independent authors, they were of sufficient importance to have a literature composed for their benefit.

The phrase "sentimentalism" became common towards the middle of the century, as I have remarked in speaking of Richardson. Some time earlier Sterne was writing a love letter to his future wife, lamenting the "quiet and sentimental repasts" which they had had together, and weeping "like a child" (so he writes) at the sight of his single knife and fork and plate. We have known the same spirit in many incarnations in later days. Sterne, who made the word popular in literature, represents what may be considered as sentimentalism in its purest form; that which corresponds most closely to its definition as sentiment running to waste; for in Sterne there is no thought of any moral, or political, or philosophical application. He is as entirely free as a man can be from any suspicion of "purpose." He tells us as frankly as possible that he is simply putting on the cap and bells for our amusement. He must weep and laugh just as the fancy takes him; his pen, he declares, is the master of him, not he the master of his pen. This, being interpreted, means, of course, something rather different from its obvious sense. Nobody, it is abundantly clear, could be a more careful and deliberate artist, though he aims at giving a whimsical and arbitrary appearance to his most skilfully devised effects. The author Sterne has a thorough command of his pen; he only means that the parson Sterne is not allowed to interfere in the management. He has no doctrine which he is in the least ambitious of expounding. He does not even wish to tell us, like some of his successors, that the world is out of joint;

that happiness is a delusion, and misery the only reality; nor, what often comes to just the same thing, is he anxious to be optimistic, and to declare, in the vein of some later humourists, that the world should be regarded through a rose-coloured mask, and that a little effusion of benevolence will summarily remove all its rough places. Undoubtedly it would be easy to argue—were it worth the trouble—that Sterne's peculiarities of temperament would have rendered certain political and religious teachings more congenial to him than others. But he did not live in stirring times, when every man is forced to translate his temperament by a definite creed. He could be as thoroughgoing and consistent an Epicurean as he pleased. Nothing matters very much (that seems to be his main doctrine), so long as you possess a good temper, a soft heart, and have a flirtation or two with pretty women. Though both men may be called sentimentalists, Sterne must have regarded Rousseau's vehement social enthusiasm as so much insanity. The poor man took life in desperate earnest, and instead of keeping his sensibility to warm his own hearth, wanted to set the world on fire. When rambling through France, Sterne had an eye for every pretty vignette by the roadside, for peasants' dances, for begging monks, or smart Parisian grisettes; he received and repaid the flattery of the drawing-rooms, and was, one may suppose, as absolutely indifferent to omens of coming difficulties as any of the free-thinking or free-living abbés who were his most congenial company. Horace Walpole was no philosopher, but he shook his head in amazement over the audacious scepticism of French society. Sterne, so far as one can judge from his letters, saw and heard nothing in this direction; and one would as soon expect to find a reflection upon such matters in the *Sentimental Journey* as to come upon a serious discussion of theological controversy in *Tristram Shandy*. Now and then some such question just shows itself for an instant in the background. A negro wanted him to write against slavery; and the letter came just as Trim was telling a pathetic story to Uncle Toby, and suggesting doubtfully that a black might have a soul. "I am not much versed, Corporal," quoth my Uncle Toby, "in things of that kind; but I suppose God would not have made him without one any more than thee or me." Sterne was quite ready to aid the cause of emancipation by adding as many picturesque touches as he could devise to Uncle Toby, or sentimentalising over jackdaws and prisoners in the *Sentimental Journey*; but more direct agitation would have been as little in his line as travelling through France in the spirit of Arthur Young to collect statistics about rent and wages. Sterne's sermons, to which one might possibly turn with a view to discovering some serious opinions, are not without an interest of their own. They show touches of the Shandy style and efforts to escape from the dead level. But Sterne could not be really at home in the pulpit, and all that can be called original is an occasional infusion of a more pungent criticism of life into the moral commonplaces of which sermons were then chiefly composed. The sermon in *Tristram Shandy* supplies a happy background to Uncle Toby's comments; but even Sterne could not manage to interweave them into the text.

The very essence of the Shandy character implies this absolute disengagement from all actual contact with sublunary affairs. Neither Fielding nor Goldsmith can be accused of preaching in the objectionable sense; they do not attempt to supply us with pamphlets in the shape of novels, but in so far as they draw from real life they inevitably suggest some practical conclusions. Reformers, for example, might point to the prison experiences of Dr. Primrose or of Captain Booth, as well as to the actual facts which they represent; and Smollett's account of

the British navy is a more valuable historical document than any quantity of official reports. But in Uncle Toby's bowling-green we have fairly shut the door upon the real world. We are in a region as far removed from the prosaic fact as in Aladdin's wondrous subterranean garden. We mount the magical hobby-horse, and straightway are in an enchanted land, "as though of hemlock we had drunk," and if the region is not altogether so full of delicious perfume as that haunted by Keats's nightingale, and even admits occasional puffs of rather unsavoury odours, it has a singular and characteristic influence of its own. Uncle Toby, so far as his intellect is concerned, is a full-grown child; he plays with his toys, and rejoices over the manufacture of cannon from a pair of jack-boots, precisely as if he were still in petticoats; he lives in a continuous daydream framed from the materials of adult experience, but as unsubstantial as any childish fancies; and when he speaks of realities it is with the voice of one half-awake, and in whose mind the melting vision still blends with the tangible realities. Mr. Shandy has a more direct and conscious antipathy to reality. The actual world is commonplace; the events there have a trick of happening in obedience to the laws of nature; and people not unfrequently feel what one might have expected beforehand that they would feel. One can express them in cut-and-dried formulæ. Mr. Shandy detests this monotony. He differs from the ordinary pedant in so far as he values theories not in proportion to their dusty antiquity, but in proportion to their unreality, the pure whimsicality and irrationality of the heads which contained them. He is a sort of inverted philosopher, who loves the antithesis of the reasonable as passionately as your commonplace philosopher professes to love the reasonable. He is ready to welcome a *reductio ad absurdum* for a demonstration; yet he values the society of men of the ordinary turn of mind precisely because his love of oddities make him relish a contradiction. He is enabled to enjoy the full flavour of his preposterous notions by the reaction of other men's astonished common-sense. The sensation of standing upon his head is intensified by the presence of others in the normal position. He delights in the society of the pragmatic and contradictious Dr. Slop, because Slop is like a fish always ready to rise at the bait of a palpable paradox, and quite unable to see with the prosaic humourist that paradoxes are the salt of philosophy. Poor Mrs. Shandy drives him to distraction by the detestable acquiescence with which she receives his most extravagant theories, and the consequent impossibility of ever (in the vulgar phrase) getting a rise out of her.

A man would be priggish indeed who could not enjoy this queer region where all the sober proprieties of ordinary logic are as much inverted as in Alice's Wonderland; where the only serious occupation of a good man's life is in playing an infantile game; where the passion of love is only introduced as a passing distraction when the hobby-horse has accidentally fallen out of gear; where the death of a son merely supplies an affectionate father with a favourable opportunity for airing his queer scraps of outworn moralities, and the misnaming of an infant casts him into a fit of profound melancholy; where everything, in short, is topsy-turvy, and we are invited to sit down, consuming a perpetual pipe in an old-fashioned arbour, dreamily amusing ourselves with the grotesque shapes that seem to be projected, in obedience to no perceptible law, upon the shifting wreaths of smoke. It would be as absurd to lecture the excellent brothers upon the absurdity of their mode of life as to preach morality to the manager of a Punch show, or to demand sentiment in the writer of a mathematical treatise.

I believe in my soul [says Sterne, rather audaciously] that the hand of the supreme Maker and Designer of all things never made or put a family together, where the characters of it were cast and contrasted with so dramatic a felicity as ours was, for this end; or in which the capacities of affording such exquisite scenes, and the powers of shifting them perpetually from morning to night, were lodged and entrusted with so unlimited a confidence as in the Shandy family.

The grammar of the sentence is rather queer, but we can hardly find fault with the substance. The remark is made *à propos* of Mr. Shandy's attempt to indoctrinate his brother with the true theory of noses, which is prefaced by the profoundly humorous sentence which expresses the leading article of Mr. Shandy's creed: "Learned men, brother Toby, don't write dialogues upon long noses for nothing." And, in fact, one sees how admirably the simplicity of each brother plays into the eccentricity of the other. The elder Shandy could not have found in the universe a listener more admirably calculated to act as whetstone for his strangely constructed wit, to dissent in precisely the right tone, not with a brutal intrusion of common-sense, but with the gentle horror of innocent astonishment at the paradoxes, mixed with veneration for the portentous learning of his senior. By looking at each brother alternately through the eyes of his relative, we are insensibly infected with the intense relish which each feels for the cognate excellence of the other. When the characters are once familiar to us, each new episode in the book is a delightful experiment upon the fresh contrasts which can be struck out by skilfully shifting their positions and exchanging the parts of clown and chief actor. The light is made to flash from a new point, as the gem is turned round by skilled hands. Sterne's wonderful dexterity appears in the admirable setting which is thus obtained for his most telling remarks. Many of the most famous sayings, such as Uncle Toby's remark about the fly, or the recording angel, are more or less adapted from other authors, but they come out so brilliantly that we feel that he has shown a full right to property which he can turn to such excellent account. Sayings quite as witty, or still wittier, may be found elsewhere. Some of Voltaire's incomparable epigrams, for example, are keener than Sterne's, but they owe nothing to the Zadig or Candide who supplies the occasion for the remark. They are thrown out in passing, and shine by their intrinsic brilliancy. But when Sterne has a telling remark, he carefully prepares the dramatic situation in which it will have the whole force due to the concentrated effect of all the attendant circumstances. "Our armies swore terribly in Flanders," cried my Uncle Toby, "but nothing to this." Voltaire could not have made a happier hit at the excess of the *odium theologicum*, but the saying comes to us armed with the authority of the whole Shandy conclave. We have a vision of the whole party sitting round, each charged with his own peculiar humour. There is Mr. Shandy, whose fancy has been amazingly tickled by the portentous oath of Ernulfus, as regards antiquarian curiosity, and has at once framed a quaint theory of the advantages of profane swearing in order to justify his delight in the tremendous formula. He regards his last odd discovery with the satisfaction of a connoisseur; "I defy a man to swear out of it!" It includes all oaths from that of William the Conqueror to that of the humblest scavenger, and is a perfect institute of swearing collected from all the most learned authorities. And there is the unlucky Dr. Slop, cleverly enticed into the pitfall by Mr. Shandy's simple cunning, and induced to exhibit himself as a monster of ecclesiastical ferocity by thundering

forth the sounding anathema at the ludicrously disproportioned case of Obadiah's clumsy knot-tying; and to bring out the full flavour of the grotesque scene, we see it as represented to the childlike intelligence of Uncle Toby, taking it all in sublime seriousness, whistling lilliburlero to soothe his nerves under this amazing performance, in sheer wonder at the sudden revelation of the potentialities of human malediction, and compressing his whole character in that admirable cry of wonder, so phrased as to exhibit his innocent conviction that the habits of the armies in Flanders supplied a sort of standard by which the results of all human experience might be appropriately measured, and to even justify it in some degree by the queer felicity of the particular application. A formal lecturer upon the evils of intolerance might argue in a set of treatises upon the light in which such an employment of sacred language would strike the unsophisticated common-sense of a benevolent mind. The imaginative humourist sets before us a delicious picture of two or three concrete human beings, and is then able at one stroke to deliver a blow more telling than the keenest flashes of the dry light of logical understanding. The more one looks into the scene and tries to analyse the numerous elements of dramatic effect to which his total impression is owing, the more one admires the astonishing skill which has put so much significance into a few simple words. The colouring is so brilliant and the touch so firm that one is afraid to put any other work beside it. Nobody before or since has had so clear an insight into the meaning which can be got out of a simple scene by a judicious selection and skilful arrangement of the appropriate surroundings. Sterne's comment upon the mode in which Trim dropped his hat at the peroration of his speech upon Master Bobby's death, affecting even the "fat, foolish scullion," is significant.

> Had he flung it, or thrown it, or skimmed it, or squirted it, or let it slip or fall in any possible direction under Heaven—or in the best direction that could have been given to it—had he dropped it like a goose, like a puppy, like an ass, or in doing it, or even after he had done it, had he looked like a fool, like a ninny, like a nincompoop, it had failed, and the effect upon the heart had been lost.

Those who would play upon human passions and, those who are played upon, or, in Sterne's phrase those who drive, and those who are driven, like turkeys to market, with a stick and a red clout, are invited to meditate upon Trim's hat; and so may all who may wish to understand the secret of Sterne's art.

It is true, unfortunately, that this singular skill—the felicity with which Trim's cap, or his Montero cap, or Uncle Toby's pipe—is made to radiate eloquence, sometimes lead to a decided bathos. The climax so elaborately prepared too often turns out to be a faded bit of sentimentalism. We rather resent the art which is thrown away to prepare us for the assertion that "When a few weeks will rescue misery out of her distress, I hate the man who can be a churl of them." So we hate the man who can lift his hand upon a woman save in the way of kindness, but we do not want a great writer to adorn that unimpeachable sentiment with all the jewels of rhetoric. It is just in these very critical passages that Sterne's taste is defective, because his feeling is not sound. We are never sure that we can distinguish between the true gems and the counterfeit. When the moment comes at which he suddenly drops the tear of sensibility, he is almost as likely to provoke sneers as sympathy. There is, for example, the famous donkey, and it is curious to compare the donkey fed with macaroons in the *Tristram Shandy* with the dead donkey of the *Sentimental Journey*, whose weeping master lays a crust of bread on the now vacant bit of his bridle. It is obviously the same donkey, and Sterne has reflected that he can squeeze a little more pathos out of the animal by actually killing him, and providing a sentimental master. It seems to me that, in trying to heighten the effect, he has just crossed the dangerous limit which divides sympathetic from derisive laughter; and whereas the macaroon-fed animal is a possible, straight-forward beast, he becomes (as higher beings have done) a humbug in his palpably hypocritical epitaph. Sterne tries his hand in the same way at improving Maria, who is certainly an effective embodiment of the mad young woman who has tried to move us in many forms since the days of Ophelia. In her second appearance, she comes in to utter the famous sentiment about the wind and the shorn lamb. It has become proverbial, and been even credited in the popular mind with a scriptural origin; and considering such a success, one has hardly the right to say that it has gathered a certain sort of banality. Yet it is surely on the extreme verge at which the pathetic melts into the ludicrous. The reflection, however, occurs more irresistibly in regard to that other famous passage about the recording angel. Sterne's admirers held it to be sublime at the time, and he obviously shared the opinion. And it is undeniable that the story of Le Fevre, in which it is the most conspicuous gem, is a masterpiece in its way. No one can read it, or better still, hear it from the lips of a skilful reader, without admitting the marvellous felicity with which the whole scene is presented. Uncle Toby's oath is a triumph fully worthy of Shakespeare. But the recording angel, though he certainly comes in effectively, is a little suspicious to me. It would have been a sacrifice to which few writers could have been equal, to suppress or soften that brilliant climax; and, yet, if the angel had been omitted, the passage would, I fancy, have been really stronger. We might have been left to make the implied comment for ourselves. For the angel seems to introduce an unpleasant air as of eighteenth-century politeness; we fancy that he would have welcomed a Lord Chesterfield to the celestial mansions with a faultless bow and a dexterous compliment; and somehow he appears, to my imagination at least, apparelled in theatrical gauze and spangles rather than in the genuine angelic costume. Some change passes over every famous passage; the bloom of its first freshness is rubbed off as it is handed from one quoter to another; but where the sentiment has no false ring at the beginning, the colours may grow faint without losing their harmony. In this angel, and some other of Sterne's best-known touches, we seem to feel that the baser metal is beginning to show itself through the superficial enamel.

And this suggests the criticism which must still be made in regard even to the admirable Uncle Toby. Sterne has been called the English Rabelais, and was apparently more ambitious himself of being considered as an English Cervantes. To a modern English reader he is certainly far more amusing than Rabelais, and he can be appreciated with less effort than Cervantes. But it is impossible to mention these great names without seeing the direction in which Sterne falls short of the highest excellence. We know that, on clearing away the vast masses of buffoonery and ribaldry under which Rabelais was forced, or chose, to hide himself we come to the profound thinker and powerful satirist. Sterne represents a comparatively shallow vein of thought. He is the mouthpiece of a sentiment which had certainly its importance in so far as it was significant of a vague discontent with things in general, and a desire for more exciting intellectual food. He was so far ready to fool the age to the top of its bent; and in the course of his ramblings he strikes some hard blows at various types of hide-bound pedantry. But he is too systematic a trifler to be reckoned with any

plausibility amongst the spiritual leaders of any intellectual movement. In that sense, *Tristram Shandy* is a curious symptom of the existing currents of emotion, but cannot, like the *Emile* or the *Nouvelle Héloïse*, be reckoned as one of the efficient causes. This complete and characteristic want of purpose may indeed be reckoned as a literary merit, so far as it prevented *Tristram Shandy* from degenerating into a mere tract. But the want of intellectual seriousness has another aspect, which comes out when we compare Tristram Shandy, for example, with Don Quixote. The resemblance, which has been often pointed out (as indeed Sterne is fond of hinting at it himself) consists in this, that in both cases we see lovable characters through a veil of the ludicrous. As Don Quixote is a true hero, though he is under a constant hallucination, so Uncle Toby is full of the milk of human kindness, though his simplicity makes him ridiculous to the piercing eyes of common-sense. In both cases, it is inferred, the humourist is discharging this true function of showing the lovable qualities which may be associated with a ludicrous outside.

The Don and the Captain both have their hobbies, which they ride with equal zeal, and there is a close analogy between them. Uncle Toby makes his own apology in the famous oration upon war.

> What is war [he asks] but the getting together of quiet and harmless people with swords in their hands, to keep the turbulent and ambitious within bounds? And heaven is my witness, brother Shandy, that the pleasure I have taken in these things, and that infinite delight in particular which has attended my sieges in the bowling-green, has arisen within me, and I hope in the Corporal too, from the consciousness that in carrying them on we were answering the great ends of our creation.

Uncle Toby's military ardour undoubtedly makes a most piquant addition to his simple-minded benevolence. The fusion of the gentle Christian with the chivalrous devotee of honour is perfect; and the kindliest of human beings, who would not hurt a hair of the fly's head, most delicately blended with the gallant soldier who, as Trim avers, would march up to the mouth of a cannon though he saw the match at the very touchhole. Should any one doubt the merits of the performance, he might reassure himself by comparing the scene in which Uncle Toby makes the speech, just quoted, with a parallel passage in *The Caxtons*, and realise the difference between extreme imitative dexterity and the force of real genius.

It is only when we compare this exquisite picture with the highest art that we are sensible of its comparative deficiency. The imaginative force of Cervantes is proved by the fact that Don Quixote and his followers have become the accepted symbols of the most profoundly tragic element in human life—of the contrast between the lofty idealism of the mere enthusiast and the sturdy common-sense of ordinary human beings—between the utilitarian and the romantic types of character; and as neither aspect of the truth can be said to be exhaustive, we are rightly left with our sympathies equally balanced. The book may be a sad one to those who prefer to be blind; but in proportion as we can appreciate a penetrative insight into the genuine facts of life, we are impressed by this most powerful presentation of the never-ending problem. It is impossible to find in *Tristram Shandy* any central conception of this breadth and depth. If Trim had been as shrewd as Sancho, Uncle Toby would appear like a mere simpleton. Like a child, he requires a thoroughly sympathetic audience who will not bring his playthings to the brutal test of actual facts.

The high and earnest enthusiasm of the Don can stand the contrast of common-sense, though at the price of passing into insanity. But Trim is forced to be Uncle Toby's accomplice, or his Commander would never be able to play at soldiers. If Don Quixote had simply amused himself at a mock tournament, and had never been in danger of mistaking a puppet-show for a reality, he would certainly have been more credible, but in the same proportion he would have been commonplace. The whole tragic element which makes the humour impressive would have disappeared. Sterne seldom ventures to the limit of the tragic. The bowling-green of Mr. Shandy's parlance is too exclusively a sleepy hollow. The air is never cleared by a strain of lofty sentiment. When Yorick and Eugenius form part of the company, we feel that they are rather too much at home with offensive suggestions. When Uncle Toby's innocence fails to perceive their coarse insinuations, we are credited with clearer perception, and expected to sympathise with the spurious wit which derives its chief zest from the presence of the pure-minded victim. And so Uncle Toby comes to represent that stingless virtue, which never gets beyond the ken or hurts the feelings of the easy-going epicurean. His perceptions are too slow and his temper too mild to resent an indecency as his relative, Colonel Newcome, would have done. He would have been too complacent, even to the outrageous Costigan. He is admirably kind when a comrade falls ill at his door; but his benevolence can exhale itself sufficiently in the intervals of hobby-riding, and his chivalrous temper in fighting over old battles with the Corporal. We feel that he must be growing fat; that his pulse is flabby and his vegetative functions predominant. When he falls in love with the repulsive (for she is repulsive) widow Wadman, we pity him as we pity a poor soft zoophyte in the clutches of a rapacious crab; but we have no sense of a wasted life. Even his military ardour seems to present itself to our minds as due to the simple affection which makes his regiment part of his family rather than to any capacity for heroic sentiment. His brain might turn soft; it would never spontaneously generate the noble madness of a Quixote, though he might have followed that hero with a more canine fidelity than Sancho.

Mr. Matthew Arnold says of Heine, as we all remember, that—

> The spirit of the world,
> Beholding the absurdity of men—
> Their vanities, their feats—let a sardonic smile
> For one short moment wander o'er his lips—
>   That smile was Heine.

There is a considerable analogy, as one may note in passing, between the two men; and if Sterne was not a poet, his prose could perhaps be even more vivid and picturesque than Heine's. But his humour is generally wanting in the quality suggested by Mr. Arnold's phrase. We cannot represent it by a sardonic smile, or indeed by any other expression which we can very well associate with the world-spirit. The imaginative humourist must in all cases be keenly alive to the "absurdity of man;" he must have a sense of the irony of fate, of the strange interlacing of good and evil in the world, and of the baser and nobler elements in human nature. He will be affected differently according to his temperament and his intellectual grasp. He may be most impressed by the affinity between madness and heroism; by the waste of noble qualities on trifling purposes; and, if he be more amiable, by the goodness which may lurk under ugly forms. He may be bitter and melancholy, or simply serious in contemplating the fantastic tricks played by mortals before high heaven. But, in any case, some real

undercurrent of deeper feeling is essential to the humourist who impresses us powerfully, and who is equally far from mere buffoonery and sentimental foppery. His smile must be at least edged with melancholy, and his pathos too deep for mere "snivelling."

Sterne is often close to this loftier region of the humorous; sometimes he fairly crosses it; but his step is uncertain as of one not feeling at home. The absurdity of man does not make him "sardonic." He takes things too easily. He shows us the farce of life, and feels that there is a tragical background to it all; but somehow he is not usually much disposed to cry over it, and he is obviously proud of the tears which he manages to produce. The thought of human folly and suffering does not usually torment and perplex him. The highest humourist should be the laughing and weeping philosopher in one; and in Sterne the weeping philosopher is always a bit of a humbug. The pedantry of the elder Shandy is a simple whim, not a misguided aspiration; and Sterne is so amused with his oddities that he even allows him to be obtrusively heartless. Uncle Toby undoubtedly comes much nearer to complete success; but he wants just that touch of genuine pathos which he would have received from the hands of the greatest writers. But the performance is so admirable in the best passages, where Sterne can drop his buffoonery and his indecency, that even a criticism which sets him below the highest place seems almost unfair.

And this may bring us back for a moment to the man himself. Sterne avowedly drew his own portrait in Yorick. That clerical jester, he says, was a mere child, full of whim and gaiety, but without an ounce of ballast. He had no more knowledge of the world at 26 than a "romping unsuspicious girl of 13." His high spirits and frankness were always getting him into trouble. When he heard of a spiteful or ungenerous action he would blurt out that the man was a dirty fellow. He would not stoop to set himself right, but let people think of him what they would. Thus his faults were all due to his extreme candour and impulsiveness. It wants little experience of the world to recognise the familiar portrait of an impulsive and generous fellow. It represents the judicious device by which a man reconciles himself to some very ugly actions. It provides by anticipation a complete excuse for thoughtlessness and meanness. If he is accused of being inconstant, he points out the extreme goodness of his impulses; and if the impulses were bad, he argues that at least they did not last very long. He prides himself on his disregard to consequences, even when the consequences may be injurious to his friends. His feelings are so genuine for the moment that his conscience is satisfied without his will translating them into action. He is perfectly candid in expressing the passing phrase of sentiment, and therefore does not trouble himself to ask whether what is true to-day will be true to-morrow. He can call an adversary a dirty fellow, and is very proud of his generous indiscretion. But he is also capable of gratifying the dirty fellow's vanity by high-flown compliments if he happens to be in the enthusiastic vein; and somehow the providence which watches over the thoughtless is very apt to make his impulses fall in with the dictates of calculated selfishness. He cannot be an accomplished courtier, because he is apt to be found out; but he can crawl and creep for the nonce with any one. In real life such a man is often as delightful for a short time as he becomes contemptible on a longer acquaintance. When we think of Sterne as a man, and try to frame a coherent picture of his character, we must give a due weight to the baser elements of his composition. We cannot forget his shallowness of feeling and the utter want of self-respect which prompted him to condescend to be a mere mountebank, and to dabble in filth for the amusement of graceless patrons. Nor is it really possible entirely to throw aside this judgment even in reading his works; for even after abstracting our attention from the rubbish and the indecency, we are haunted in the really admirable parts by our misgivings as to their sincerity. But the problem is one to tax critical acumen. It is one aspect of a difficulty which meets us sometimes in real life. Every man flatters himself that he can detect the mere hypocrite. We seem to have a sufficient instinct to warn us against the downright pitfalls where an absolute void is covered by an artificial stratum of mere verbiage. Perhaps even this is not so easy as we sometimes fancy; but there is a more refined sort of hypocrisy which requires keener dissection. How are men to draw the narrow and yet all-important line which separates—not the genuine from the feigned emotion—but the emotion which is due to some real cause, and that which is a cause in itself? Some people we know fall in love with a woman, and others are really in love with the passion. Grief may be the sign of lacerated affection, or it may be a mere luxury indulged in for its own sake. The sentimentalism which Sterne represented corresponded in the main to this last variety. People had discovered the art of extracting direct enjoyment from their own "sensibility," and Sterne expressly gives thanks for his own as the great consolation of his life. He has the heartiest possible relish for his tears and lamentations, and it is precisely his skill in marking this vein of interest which gives him his extraordinary popularity. So soon as we discover that a man is enjoying his sorrow our sympathy is killed within us, and for that reason Sterne is apt to be repulsive to humourists whose sense of the human tragi-comedy is deeper than his own. They agree with him that the vanity of human dreams may suggest a mingling of tears and laughter; but they grieve because they must, not because they find it a pleasant amusement. Yet it is perhaps unwise to poison our pleasure by reflections of this kind. They come with critical reflection, and may at least be temporarily suppressed when we are reading for enjoyment. We need not sin ourselves by looking a gift horse in the mouth. The sentiment is genuine at the time. Do not inquire how far it has been deliberately concocted and stimulated. The man is not only a wonderful artist, but he is right in asserting that his impulses are clear and genuine. Why should not that satisfy us? Are we to set up for so rigid a nature that we are never to consent to sit down with Uncle Toby and take him as he is made? We may wish, if we please, that Sterne had always been in his best, and that his tears flowed from a deeper source. But so long as he really speaks from his heart—and he does so in all the finer parts of the Toby drama—why should we remember that the heart was rather flighty, and regarded with too much conscious complacency by its proprietor? The Shandyism upon which he prided himself was not a very exalted form of mind, nor one which offered a very deep or lasting satisfaction. Happily we can dismiss an author when we please; give him a cold shoulder in our more virtuous moods, and have a quiet chat with him when we are graciously pleased to relax. In those times we may admit Sterne as the best of jesters, though it may remain an open question whether the jester is on the whole an estimable institution.

Notes

1. Sterne says in the letter that Hall was over forty; and he was five years older than Hall.

H. D. TRAILL
"Laurence Sterne"
English Prose, ed. Henry Craik
1895, Volume 4, pp. 207–10

To talk of "the style" of Sterne is almost to play one of those tricks with language of which he himself was so fond. For there is hardly any definition of the word which can make it possible to describe him as having any style at all. It is not only that he manifestly recognised no external canons whereto to conform the expression of his thoughts, but he had apparently no inclination to invent and observe, except indeed in the most negative of senses, any style of his own. The "style of Sterne," in short, is as though one should say "the form of Proteus."

He was determined to be uniformly eccentric, regularly irregular, and that was all. His digressions, his "asides," and his fooleries, in general, would of course have in any case necessitated a certain jerkiness of manner; but this need hardly have extended itself habitually to the structure of his individual sentences, and as a matter of fact he can at times write, as he does for the most part in his sermons, in a style which is not the less vigorous for being fairly correct. But as a rule his mode of expressing himself is destitute of any pretensions to precision; and in many instances it is a perfect marvel of literary slipshod. Nor is there any ground for believing that the slovenliness was invariably intentional. Sterne's truly hideous French—French at which even the average English tourist would stand aghast—is in itself sufficient evidence of a natural insensibility to grammatical accuracy. Here there can be no suspicion of designed defiance of rules; and more than one solecism of rather a serious kind in his use of English words and phrases affords confirmatory testimony to the same point. His punctuation is fearful and wonderful, even for an age in which the *rationale* of punctuation was more imperfectly understood than it is at present; and this, though an apparently slight matter, is not without value as an indication of ways of thought. But if we can hardly describe Sterne's style as being in the literary sense a style at all, it has a very distinct colloquial character of its own, and as such it is nearly as much deserving of praise as from the literary point of view it is open to exception. Chaotic as it is in the syntactical sense, it is a perfectly clear vehicle for the conveyance of thought. We are as rarely at a loss for the meaning of one of Sterne's sentences, as we are, for very different reasons, for the meaning of one of Macaulay's. And his language is so full of life and colour, his tone so animated and vivacious, that we forget we are reading and not listening, and we are as little disposed to be exacting in respect to form as though we were listeners in actual fact. Sterne's manner, in short, may be that of a bad and careless writer, but it is the manner of a first-rate talker; and this of course enhances rather than detracts from the unwearying charm of his wit and humour.

It is by the latter of these qualities—though he had the former in almost equal abundance—that he lives. No doubt he valued himself no less, perhaps even more highly, on his sentiment, and was prouder of his acute sensibility to the sorrows of mankind, than of his keen eye for their absurdities, and his genially satiric appreciation of their foibles. But posterity has not confirmed Sterne's judgment of himself. His passages of pathos, sometimes genuine and deeply moving, too often on the other hand only impress the modern reader with their artificial and overstrained sentimentalism. The affecting too often degenerates into the affected. To trace the causes of this degeneration would be a work involving too complex a process of analysis to be undertaken in this place. But the sum of the whole matter seems to be that the "sentiment" on which Sterne so prided himself—the acute sensibilities which he regarded with such extraordinary complacency—were in reality the weakness and not the strength of his pathetic style. When Sterne the artist is uppermost, when he is surveying the characters with that penetrating eye of his, and above all when he is allowing his subtle and tender humour to play around them unrestrained, he can touch the cords of compassionate emotion in us with a potent and unerring hand. But when Sterne the man is uppermost, when he is looking inward and not outward, contemplating his own feelings and not those of his personages, his cunning fails him altogether. In other words he is at his best in pathos when he is most the humourist; or rather, we may almost say, his pathos is never true unless when it is closely interwoven with his humour.

Still it is comparatively seldom that this foible of Sterne obtrudes itself upon the strictly narrative and dramatic part of his work. It is, generally speaking, in the episodical passages, such, for instance, as the story of the distraught Maria of Moulines, or that incident of the dead donkey of Nampont which Thackeray so mercilessly, though not unfairly, ridiculed, that Sterne most "lays himself out" to be pathetic; it is in these digressions, as they may almost be called, that he becomes lugubrious "of malice aforethought," so to say; and it is therefore only in such exceptional cases that the expectation is disappointed, and the critical judgment offended, by the failures of the kind above described. On the main road of his story—if it can be said to have a main road—he is usually saved from such lapses of artistic taste by his strong dramatic instinct. Perpetual as are his affectations, and tiresome as his eternal self-consciousness, when he is speaking in his own person, often becomes, yet when once this dramatic instinct fairly lays hold of him there is no writer who can make us more completely forget him in the presence of his characters, none who can bring them and their surroundings, their looks and words before us with such convincing force of reality.

But if he makes us see them thus clearly, and thus plainly hear them, it is of course because of the matchless vigour and truth of touch with which their figures are first made to stand forth upon his canvass. And it is in fact the union with Sterne's other rare intellectual and artistic qualities of this rarest gift of all which has won for him his unique place in our literature. Neither wit, nor humour, nor creative power, nor skill of dramatic handling, would have done that for him if it had stood alone. They might, any of them, have made him famous in his time; but, except in conjunction, they could not have raised him to the rank he holds among the classics of English prose fiction. The extravagant Rabelaisian drollery that revels through the pages of *Tristram Shandy*, the marvellous keenness of eye, the inimitable delicacy of touch to which we owe the exquisite vignettes of the *Sentimental Journey*, would hardly of themselves have secured the place for Sterne. But it is for ever assured to him in right of that combination of subjective and personal with objective and dramatic humour in which he has never been excelled by any one save the creator of Falstaff. In Mr. Shandy and his wife, in Corporal Trim, in Yorick, and above all in that masterpiece of mirthful, subtle, tenderly humorous portraiture, "My Uncle Toby," Sterne has created imperishable types of character and made them remarkably his own.

HERBERT PAUL
From "Sterne"
Nineteenth Century, December 1896, pp. 997–1000

A great French critic, the late M. Taine, in his spirited and ingenious history of English literature dismisses Sterne with a few contemptuous pages. He could see nothing in him but the eccentric and grotesque. But that is to miss the whole reason of Sterne's popularity and the whole source of his power. Dr. Johnson was right in his general principle, though wrong in his particular instance. Nothing merely odd does last. *Tristram Shandy* is not merely odd. Its oddity is on the surface. The author has ways and tricks which perplex some readers, and annoy others. But they are not of the essence of his work. They are superficial. What lies below is a profound knowledge of men and women, a subtle sympathy with human weakness, a consummate art of putting the great commonplaces of life in a form which makes them seem original. 'Difficile est proprie communia dicere.' It is difficult, but it is worth doing, for the prize is literary immortality. M. Taine, who so thoroughly appreciated and so nobly expressed the genius of Swift, could see in Sterne only a writer who ended where he ought to have begun, who prosed upon the conjugal endearments of an elderly merchant and his wife, who had strange theories of trivial things, who dragged in legal pedantry and theological disputes and the jargon of the schools without reason or excuse. No such book could have lived a hundred and thirty-six years, or thirty-six without the hundred. It may be that, as Mr. Fitzgerald says, *Tristram Shandy* is more talked about than read. All the masterpieces of literature are. If every copy of *Tristram Shandy* were destroyed to-morrow its influence upon style and thought would remain. Sterne had one great quality besides humour in common with Swift. He wrote his own English. I sometimes doubt whether justice has ever been done to the simplicity and beauty of it. The *Sentimental Journey* and the fragment of autobiography are almost perfect. The familiar description of the accusing spirit and the recording angel have been made ridiculous, and the intrusion or even the misplacement of a word would have spoiled it. As it stands it is the admiration of every one who reads and the despair of every one who writes. The brief sketch of Uncle Toby's funeral, characteristically introduced in the middle of a book which leaves him perfectly well at the end of it, is a flawless and exquisite vignette in words. Sterne, like Swift, eschewed the mannerisms of his own age. There is hardly a phrase in *Tristram Shandy* or in *Gulliver's Travels* which would fix the date of either. They wrote for posterity, and, unlike the too famous ode, they have reached their address.

It is, perhaps, less strange that M. Taine should underrate Sterne than that Sterne should have become the rage in the Paris of Louis Quinze. Whatever may be said of the *Sentimental Journey* there is no more thoroughly English book than *Tristram Shandy*. But the Anglomania of 1760 was equal to anything, and the fine French ladies who thought Hume handsome found that Shandyism was just the thing to suit them. Sterne's own French seems to have been as bad as Lord Brougham's. But *Tristram Shandy* was translated as it came out, and the Parisians bought it, if they did not read it. Long afterwards Madame de Beaumont, whose humour was not her strong point, carried *Tristram Shandy* about with her among her favourite volumes in the strange company of Voltaire's *Letters* and the Platonic Dialogue which describes the death of Socrates. It was not all Anglomania or affectation. It was also a conclusive tribute to the universality of the book. We know the sources from which Sterne's characters were drawn. Uncle Toby was a compound of his own father, concerning whom he says in the autobiography that 'you might have cheated him ten times a day if nine had not been sufficient for your purpose,' and Captain Hinde, of Preston Castle, in Hertfordshire. Yorick is, of course, himself, or one side of himself, for there is a great deal of Sterne in Mr. Shandy. Mrs. Shandy is said, alas! to have been his wife. Eugenius was John Hall Stevenson, owner of Crazy Castle, which was unfortunately destroyed, and author of *Crazy Tales*, which have been unfortunately preserved. Ernulphus is Bishop Warburton, Dr. Slop is Dr. Burton, and so forth. These facts are not without their interest, and it is still disputed, I believe, whether Dr. Burton was really a Roman Catholic and whether he was actually upset in the mud. The industrious inquirer who set himself to discover whether the husband of the nurse in *Romeo and Juliet* was really a merry man, or whether she was deceived into thinking him so by affectionate partiality for his memory, belonged to a class more numerous than less energetic people might suppose. 'The best in this kind are but shadows, and the worst are no worse, if imagination amend them.' But the shadows outlast the substance. They are too immaterial to feel the hand of death. They are like the songs of the old Greek, αἰσιν ὁ πάντων ἀρπακτὴρ ᾿Αΐδης οὐκ ἐπὶ χειρα βαλει. There is not much superficial resemblance between Laurence Sterne and Jane Austen; but both drew their characters from their own immediate and not remarkable surroundings. Both drew them in such a fashion that all classes of readers can equally enjoy them. The early editions of *Tristram Shandy* bore on the title page a motto from Aristotle which gives the key to the whole work. Men are troubled, said the philosopher, not by facts, but by opinions about facts. Charles Lamb used to call himself a matter of fiction man. Walter Shandy is the type and presentment of the speculative mind. Nothing strikes him as it strikes other people. He judges everything by reference to a theory, and his theories have no necessary connection the one with the other. Yet his unfailing humour shines through his pedantry and, except when he lies on the bed, saves him from appearing ridiculous.

Sterne laughed at his critics, and their successors have not forgiven him. Bishop Warburton, after extolling him, oddly enough, as the English Rabelais, excommunicated him with bell, book, and candle, as Bishop Monk long afterwards did to Sydney Smith. The result in both cases was a deplorably easy triumph for the inferior clergy. Warburton lives as Ernulphus, and the *Divine Legation* is dead. Monk's *Euripides* reposes in the libraries of the curious. But everybody remembers him in connection with those 'cephalic animalculæ' protesting against the use of small-tooth combs. It is a dangerous thing to run across a man of genius before he is dead. When Boswell depreciated the *Dunciad* Johnson told him that he had missed his chance of immortality by coming too late into the world. Thackeray, who devoted half a lecture to abuse of Sterne, and many volumes to the sincerest form of flattering him, took him, if one may say so with all respect, by the wrong side. The laughter of fools, said the wise man in one of his wisest sayings, is like the crackling of thorns under a pot. To Mr. Thackeray, with his sensitive and beautiful reverence for the serious side of life, Sterne's laughter was hollow and his mockery hideous. Sterne's sentiment, which is no more exclusively Sterne's than it is Shakespeare's or Nature's, may be found in *Esmond* and *The Newcomes* as much as in the *Sentimental Journey* itself. The fascinating spirit of the eighteenth century, as perilous and attractive as the Hill of Venus in mediæval romance, is summed up in Sterne as in no other man. It was the century of Wesley as well as of Voltaire, and of Johnson as well as of Rousseau. Sterne and Wesley hardly seem to belong to the same species. We are not all made to understand each other. Voltaire, with his noble hatred of persecution and love of intellectual freedom, did undoubtedly sometimes direct the terrible engine of his ridicule against 'the last restraint of the powerful and the last hope of the wretched.' Sterne did not. 'There never,' said Trim of his master, 'was a better officer in the king's army, or a better man in God's world,' and the character of Uncle Toby is a faithful portrait lovingly drawn.

WILBUR L. CROSS
From "Laurence Sterne"
The Development of the English Novel
1899, pp. 70–76

Sterne, like all writers, had his antecedents; and some of them were very remote from his time. He has furnished the reader of *Tristram Shandy* with a very full list of them, in which are his 'dear Rabelais and dearer Cervantes.' He found in old English and French humorists a body of stories, jests, and witticisms,—learned, heavy, quaint, and salacious,—and he helped himself. He might, like honest Burton, 'have given every man his own,' but it was his whim not to do so. The contribution of the *Anatomy* to *Shandy*, in respect to suggestion and actual material, is immense. The influence of Cervantes on Sterne was all pervading; when a friend criticised him for describing too minutely Slop's fall in *Shandy*, Sterne appealed, not to nature, not to the laws of the imagination, but to Cervantes. Rabelais led him to seek wit in questionable sources. He also drew freely upon a group of Queen Anne wits, of which Swift was the centre. For the general plan of *Tristram Shandy*, he was surely indebted to the *Memoirs of Martinus Scriblerus*, written mostly by Dr. John Arbuthnot, and first published with Pope's prose works, in 1741. *Martinus Scriblerus* is a satire in the Cervantic manner on 'the abuses of human learning.' It's out-of-the-way medical knowledge, its account of the birth of Scriblerus, its disquisitions on playthings and education—all have their more Quixotic counterpart in the first volumes of *Shandy*. The purpose of Sterne, however, is not satire, except perhaps in the delineation of Dr. Slop; he is trying to see how much sport he can get out of good-natured men who have lost their wits by their learning.

The formlessness of Smollett becomes with Sterne an affectation. The title, *The Life and Opinions of Tristram Shandy, Gent.*, is a misnomer. Tristram is not born until near the end of the third volume, and he is not put into breeches until the sixth. Sterne deserts his characters in the most ridiculous situations,—Mrs. Shandy with ear placed against the keyhole, Walter and Toby conversing on the stairway,—and runs off into digression after digression, which are called 'the sunshine, the life, and the soul of reading.' He tampers with his pagination, and abounds in dashes, asterisks, indexhands, and 'and-so-forths'; he leaves entire chapters for the imagination of the reader to construct, and then unexpectedly returns to these blanks, filling them in himself; he writes a sentence and calls it a chapter; or begins a chapter, breaks off suddenly, and starts in anew; and of one of his volumes he plots the curve, showing twistings, retrogressions, and plungings. Nothing was left for Sterne's imitators but to write their words upside down. Undoubtedly there is method in this madness.

Sterne was not a careless or hasty writer; he selected and presented his material with infinite pains. 'I have burnt,' he writes ambiguously in one of his letters, 'more wit than I have published.' But it was a sad day for English fiction when a writer of genius came to look upon the novel as the repository for the crotchets of a lifetime. This is the more to be lamented when we reflect that Sterne, unlike Smollett, could tell a story in a straightforward manner when he chose to do so. Had the time he wasted in dazzling his friends with literary fireworks been devoted to a logical presentation of the wealth of his experiences, fancies, and feelings, he might have written one of the most perfect pieces of compositions in the English language. As it is, the novel in his hands, considered from the standpoint of structure, reverted to what it was when left by the wits of the Renaissance.

There is, however, in Sterne a great though not a full compensation for his eccentricities of form. In passages now immortal, as that one in which the recording angel drops a tear upon an oath of Uncle Toby's, he strove to write prose that should possess the precision, the melody, and the sensuousness of the highest poetic expression. The proverb, 'God tempers the wind to the shorn lamb,' belongs in its present form to Sterne; clergymen have taken it for a text to their sermons, and then searched the Scriptures for it in vain. In indicating delicate shades of feeling, he refined upon Marivaux and Fielding. And in the course of his work he created great and extraordinary characters.

Fielding, Smollett, and Sterne, all had the reputation in their time of taking their leading characters from actual experience. Fielding selected, and, except in *Amelia*, made men and women conform to a theory of the ludicrous. Smollett drenched his rogues and seamen in a bath of indignation, brutality, and revenge. Sterne was more an idealist than either. Characters which had a real basis in his boyhood observations in English and Irish barracks, in his association with droll and not over-fastidious Yorkshire wits, and in his French travels, he lifted into 'the clear climate of fantasy.' Hypocrisy, vanity, affectation, and ruling passions—the material which Fielding and Smollett worked—he subtilized into the strangest whims; as, for example, the hobby that our whole success in life depends upon the name with which we happen to be christened. These faint shadows of real life, though they do speak, converse with us quite as much through attitude, gesture, and movement. Trim is discoursing upon life and death. 'Are we not here now, continued the Corporal (striking the end of his stick perpendicularly upon the floor, so as to give an idea of health and stability)—and are we not—(dropping his hat upon the ground) gone! in a moment!—'Twas infinitely striking! Susannah burst into a flood of tears.' Passages might be selected to show that Sterne was capable of descending to the antics of a jester or to the pantomime of a Parisian music hall; but at his best, he displayed in the study of gesture a fine and high art. He enlarged for the novelist the sphere of character-building, by bringing over into fiction the pose and the attitude of the sculptor and the painter, combined with a graceful and harmonious movement, which he justly likened to the transitions of music.

Sterne's characters belong to that Shakesperean brother hood of fools which Macaulay must have had in mind when he sketched Boswell. Mrs. Shandy on the famous 'bed of justice,' echoing her husband's observations on Tristram's need of breeches, is that delightfully stupid Justice Shallow who, standing by Westminster Abbey, gave his assent to the absurd remarks of Falstaff and Pistol, with 'It doth' and ''Tis so

indeed.' Dr. Slop is of the dull and blundering class. Trim is the pragmatic fool, haunted at times by a deep philosophy. Walter Shandy is the learned fool, whose poor brain, involved in a labyrinth of *a priori* reasoning, is now and then visited by gleams of intelligence. Listen to him on his favorite hypothesis: 'How many CÆSARS and POMPEYS, he would say, by mere inspiration of the names, have been rendered worthy of them? And how many, he would add, are there, who might have done exceeding well in the world had not their characters and spirits been totally depressed and NICODEMUSED into nothing!' Uncle Toby is the innocent gentleman who knows nothing of the real world; who sits in his sentry-box, pipe in hand, looking into Widow Wadman's left eye for 'moat or chaff or speck,' wholly unaware that it is 'one lambent, delicious fire,' shooting into his own. And in their kindness of heart, all Sterne's characters are cousins to that Yorick whose lips Hamlet 'kissed how oft.' Walter Shandy, though sometimes assuming a subacid humor, never does so without a prick of conscience. Uncle Toby's heart goes out in sympathy for all in misfortune and distress. Aged and infirm as he is, he would walk through darkness and storm to console a dying soldier. Sterne writes:

> My Uncle Toby had scarce a heart to retaliate upon a fly.—Go—says he, one day at dinner, to an over-grown one which had buzzed about his nose, and tormented him cruelly all dinner-time,—and which, after infinite attempts, he had caught at last, as it flew by him. I'll not hurt thee, says my Uncle Toby, rising from his chair, and going across the room with the fly in his hand,—I'll not hurt a hair of thy head:—Go,—says he, lifting up the sash, and opening his hand as he spoke to let it escape;—go, poor devil, get thee gone, why should I hurt thee?—This world surely is wide enough to hold both thee and me.

Before Sterne, there was in our literature no incident like this. To characterize the soft state of the feelings and the imagination that could originate it, Sterne himself was apparently the first to use the epithet sentimental; and by a curious coincidence he so employed it in the very year Richardson published *Pamela*. Viewed largely, Richardson is a sentimentalist by virtue of the fact that he dwells upon the sin and shame of a world given over to the debauchee. Rousseau, when he sits down by Lake Geneva, and watches his tears as they drip into the water, is asking the spectator to sympathize with the wrongs—real or imaginary—which he has endured. Sterne never takes a lyrical view of life. He listens to the tale of human misery only because it gives him 'sweet and pleasurable nerve vibrations.' In his sentiment is always involved the ludicrous. He moves into ripple our feelings by the starling which ought to be set free, by the fly, the hair of whose head ought not to be injured, and by the donkey which ought to be chewing a macaroon instead of an artichoke. When he seeks to awaken pleasure in a real distress, then he seems ignoble, until we reflect that author and work are an immense hoax. The absurdity lurking in special scenes of the *Sentimental Journey* is elusive; but it is there. It is a kind of humor that evokes only the gentlest emotions of pity, to be followed by the smile. It enfranchises the heart, purging it of melancholy, and giving zest to the mere bagatelles of existence. When Sterne's influence began to be felt throughout Europe, in translations and imitations—zigzag journeys here and there—it did more than all else to free literature from the depression of the serious sentimentalism of Richardson, Rousseau, and their school.

THOMAS GRAY

THOMAS GRAY

1716–1771

Thomas Gray was born in London on December 26, 1716. He was the son of a scrivener and was educated at Eton, where he became friendly with Horace Walpole, and then at Peterhouse, Cambridge, which he left in 1738 without taking a degree. Between 1739 and 1741 Gray and Walpole toured France and Italy, but had a falling out and returned home separately.

After living briefly with his mother at Stoke Poges in Buckinghamshire, Gray moved to Cambridge in 1742. He lived as a guest of the university for the rest of his life, first at Peterhouse and then at Pembroke. In 1741–42 Gray began to compose his first odes, having previously only written brief verses in Latin. His friend Richard West died in June 1742, just after Gray had sent him his "Ode on the Spring" (1748), and in tribute Gray composed his "Sonnet on the Death of West." He also wrote the "Ode on a Distant Prospect of Eton College" and "The Hymn to Adversity" (both 1747) and continued the philosophical poem in Latin, *De Principiis Cogitandi*, that he had begun earlier in Florence.

In 1745 Gray was reconciled with his old friend Walpole; in 1747, after the death of Walpole's pet, he sent him his "Ode on the Death of a Favourite Cat" (1748). In 1751 Gray published the *Elegy Written in a Country Church-Yard*, completed in 1750 but probably begun as early as 1742. This poem quickly achieved an immense popularity, but Gray's reaction was somewhat ambivalent: his next major work, a Pindaric ode entitled *The Progress of Poesie* (1754), was intentionally more obscure. This was followed in 1757 by another somewhat esoteric poem, *The Bard*, set in ancient Wales; later in 1757 these two poems, printed together, became the initial publication of Walpole's Strawberry Hill Press. Despite the mixed reception accorded these two works, Gray was by this time an extremely popular poet; upon the death of Cibber in 1757 he was offered the poet laureateship but declined it.

Thereafter Gray wrote no major poetical works but devoted himself mainly to a range of botanical and antiquarian interests, including preparing translations from the Welsh and the Icelandic. He was much taken by *The Poems of Ossian*, spurious Gaelic verses supposedly discovered by James Macpherson, and he produced various imitations of Old Norse and Welsh poems including "The Fatal Sisters" and "The Descent of Odin" (both written in 1761 and published in 1768). He traveled in Scotland and the Lake District, and kept a *Journal* (1775) of one of his visits to the Lakes. Gray died at Pembroke on July 30, 1771. His correspondence, edited by P. Toynbee and L. Whibley, was published in three volumes in 1935.

Personal

I agree with you most absolutely in your opinion about Gray; he is the worst company in the world—from a melancholy turn, from living reclusely, and from a little too much dignity, he never converses easily—all his words are measured, and chosen, and formed into sentences; his writings are admirable; he himself is not agreeable.—HORACE WALPOLE, Letter to George Montague (Sept. 3, 1748)

Mr. Gray, our elegant poet, and delicate Fellow-Commoner of Peter House, has just removed to Pembroke Hall, in resentment of some usage he met with at the former place. The case is much talked of, and is this:—He is much afraid of fire, and was a great sufferer in Cornhill; he has ever since kept a ladder of ropes by him, soft as the silky cords by which Romeo ascended to his Juliet, and has had an iron machine fixed to his bedroom window. The other morning Lord Percival and some Petreuchians, going a hunting, were determined to have a little sport before they set out, and thought it would be no bad diversion to make Gray bolt, as they called it, so ordered their man, Joe Draper, to roar out "fire." A delicate white night-cap is said to have appeared at the window; but finding the mistake, retired again to the couch. The young fellows, had he descended, were determined, they said, to have whipped the Butterfly up again.—JOHN SHARP, Letter (March 12, 1756)

I am sorry you did not see Mr. Gray on his return; you would have been much pleased with him. Setting aside his merit as a poet which, however, is greater in my opinion than any of his contemporaries can boast, in this or any other nation, I found him possessed of the most exact taste, the soundest judgment, and the most extensive learning. He is happy in a singular facility of expression. His composition abounds with original observations, delivered in no appearance of sententious formality, and seeming to arise spontaneously without study or premeditation. I passed two days with him at Glammis, and found him as easy in his manners, and as communicative and frank as I could have wished.—JAMES BEATTIE, Letter to Sir William Forbes (1765)

Perhaps he was the most learned man in Europe. He was equally acquainted with the elegant and profound parts of science, and that not superficially, but thoroughly. He knew every branch of history, both natural and civil; had read all the original histories of England, France, and Italy; and was a great antiquarian. Criticism, metaphysics, morals, politics, made a principal part of his study; voyages and travels of all sorts were his favourite amusements; and he had a fine taste in paintings, prints, architecture, and gardening. With such a fund of knowledge, his conversation must have been equally instructing and entertaining; but he was also a good man, a man of virtue and humanity. There is no character without some speck, some imperfection; and I think the greatest defect in his was an affectation in delicacy, or rather effeminacy, and a visible fastidiousness, or contempt and disdain of his inferiors in science.—WILLIAM TEMPLE, Letter to James Boswell (1772)

Gray on Himself—he has left a few lines thus entitled—is worth quoting.

> Too pure for a bribe, and too proud to importune,
> He had not the method of making a fortune;
> Could love and could hate, so 'twas thought some-
>   thing odd;
> No very great wit, he believed in a God.
> A post or a pension he did not desire,
> But left church and state to Charles Townshend and
>   Squire.

Under a jocular form, these lines seem to present a very fair picture of the author, so far as they go. He was essentially a man of virtue and humanity; not eager for money or *éclat*; helpful to the poor; amiable, temperate, and unpresuming. Though he "could love and could hate," his affections were perhaps cool rather than otherwise, his disposition sedate. He had a healthy indifference to criticism, but it was to some extent a weakness that he wished (like Congreve) to be looked upon as a private independent gentleman who read for his amusement, rather than as a professional man of letters. His greatest defect, says the masculine Johnson, was "an affectation of delicacy, or rather effeminacy, and a visible fastidiousness, or contempt and disdain of his inferiors in science." This effeminacy was indeed mostly put on in the company of people whom Gray did not wish to please; it seems however that he was careful of himself to the extent of timorousness, and we are told that, when he was in the Lake-country, this backwardness made him miss the finest views. He had also the indolence natural to a placid and unenterprising scholar. Let us enjoy here—on more accounts than one—his description of the only occasion (or he affects to speak of it as solitary) on which he saw the sun rise: he had been making a trip on the south-west coast in 1769. "I must not close my letter without giving you one principal event of my history; which was that, in the course of my late tour, I set out one morning before five o'clock, the moon shining through a dark and misty autumnal air, and got to the sea-coast time enough to be at the sun's levee. I saw the clouds and dark vapours open gradually to right and left, rolling over one another in great smoky wreaths, and the tide, as it flowed gently in upon the sands, first whitening, then slightly tinged with gold and blue, and all at once a little line of insufferable brightness that (before I can write these five words) was grown to half an orb, and now to a whole one too glorious to be distinctly seen. It is very odd it makes no figure on paper: yet I shall remember it as long as the sun, or at least as I endure. I wonder whether anybody ever saw it before: I hardly believe it."—In conversation with intimate friends Gray was learned and witty; but his talk was mostly scanty, and somewhat stilted as well. If Walpole (or his informant Lady Ailesbury) is to be believed, the poet, on passing a day in the society of her ladyship and others, "never opened his lips but once, and then only said, 'Yes, my lady, I believe so.'" His religious opinions are not very definitely known. His own expression that "he believed in a God" may suggest to some readers that he believed in not much more: one may peruse many of his letters, and find that, though religious considerations are sometimes raised, the christian faith forms no element in them. None the less he appears, with the true temper of an academic scholar, conservatively indifferent and unaggressive, to have been hostile to any general dissemination of sceptical or subversive opinions. In a letter to Beattie, dated in 1770, *à propos* of the *Essay on Truth*, written in opposition to Hume and the sceptical system, he says: "I have always thought David

Hume a pernicious writer, and believe he has done as much mischief here as he has in his own country. A professed sceptic can be guided by nothing but his present passions (if he has any) and interests."—WILLIAM MICHAEL ROSSETTI, "Thomas Gray," *Lives of Famous Poets*, 1878, pp. 154–56

General

> What Muse like Gray's shall pleasing pensive flow
> Attemper'd sweetly to the rustic woe?
> Or who like him shall sweep the Theban lyre,
> And, as his master, pour forth thoughts of fire?
> —ROBERT LLOYD, *An Epistle to C. Churchill,
> Author of* The Rosciad, 1762

I have been reading Grey's Works, and think him the only Poet since Shakespear entitled to the Character of Sublime. Perhaps you will remember that I once had a different Opinion of him: I was prejudiced; he did not belong to our Thursday Society & was an Eaton man, which lower'd him prodigiously in our Esteem. I once thought Swift's Letters the best that could be written, but I like Grey's better; his Humour or his Wit, or whatever it is to be called is never illnatur'd or offensive, & yet I think equally poignant with the Dean's.—WILLIAM COWPER, Letter to Joseph Hill (April 20, 1777)

> Not that her blooms are mark'd with beauty's hue,
> My rustic Muse her votive chaplet brings;
> Unseen, unheard, O GRAY, to thee she sings!—
> While slowly-pacing thro' the churchyard dew,
> At curfeu-time, beneath the dark-green yew,
> Thy pensive genius strikes the moral strings;
> Or borne sublime on Inspiration's wings,
> Hears Cambria's bards devote the dreadful clue
> Of Edward's race, with murthers foul defil'd;
> Can aught my pipe to reach thine ear essay?
> No, bard divine! For many a care beguil'd
> By the sweet magic of thy soothing lay,
> For many a raptur'd thought, and vision wild,
> To thee this strain of gratitude I pay.
> —THOMAS WARTON, "To Mr. Gray," 1777

⟨Johnson:⟩ 'Sir, I do not think Gray a first-rate poet. He has not a bold imagination, nor much command of words. The obscurity in which he has involved himself will not persuade us that he is sublime. His *Elegy in a Church-yard* has a happy selection of images, but I don't like what are called his great things. His Ode which begins

> Ruin seize thee, ruthless King,
> Confusion on thy banners wait!

has been celebrated for its abruptness, and plunging into the subject all at once. But such arts as these have no merit, unless when they are original. We admire them only once; and this abruptness has nothing new in it. We have had it often before. Nay, we have it in the old song of Johnny Armstrong:

> Is there ever a man in all Scotland
> From the highest estate to the lowest degree, &c.

And then, Sir,

> Yes, there is a man in Westmoreland,
> And Johnny Armstrong they do him call.

There, now, you plunge at once into the subject. You have no previous narration to lead you to it. The two next lines in that Ode are, I think, very good:

> Though fanned by conquest's crimson wing,
> They mock the air with idle state.'

Here let it be observed, that although his opinion of Gray's poetry was widely different from mine, and I believe from that of most men of taste, by whom it is with justice highly admired, there is certainly much absurdity in the clamour which has been raised, as if he had been culpably injurious to the merit of that bard, and had been actuated by envy. Alas! ye little short-sighted criticks, could JOHNSON be envious of the talents of any of his contemporaries? That his opinion on this subject was what in private and in publick he uniformly expressed, regardless of what others might think, we may wonder, and perhaps regret; but it is shallow and unjust to charge him with expressing what he did not think. ⟨. . .⟩

Next day ⟨March 28, 1775⟩ I dined with Johnson at Mr. Thrale's. He attacked Gray, calling him a 'dull fellow.' BOSWELL. 'I understand he was reserved, and might appear dull in company; but surely he was not dull in poetry.' JOHNSON. 'Sir, he was dull in company, dull in his closet, dull every where. He was dull in a new way, and that made many people think him GREAT. He was a mechanical poet.' He then repeated some ludicrous lines, which have escaped my memory, and said, 'Is not that GREAT, like his Odes?' Mrs. Thrale maintained that his Odes were melodious; upon which he exclaimed,

Weave the warp, and weave the woof;—

I added, in a solemn tone,

The winding-sheet of Edward's race.

'There is a good line.' 'Ay, (said he,) and the next line is a good one,' (pronouncing it contemptuously;)

Give ample verge and room enough.—

'No, Sir, there are but two good stanzas in Gray's poetry, which are in his *Elegy in a Country Church-yard*.' He then repeated the stanza,

For who to dumb forgetfulness a prey, &c.

mistaking one word; for instead of *precincts* he said *confines*. He added, 'The other stanza I forget.'—JAMES BOSWELL, *Life of Johnson*, 1791

If in a Poem there should be found a series of lines, or even a single line, in which the language, though naturally arranged and according to the strict laws of metre, does not differ from that of prose, there is a numerous class of critics who, when they stumble upon these prosaisms as they call them, imagine that they have made a notable discovery, and exult over the Poet as over a man ignorant of his own profession. Now these men would establish a canon of criticism which the Reader will conclude he must utterly reject if he wishes to be pleased with these volumes. And it would be a most easy task to prove to him that not only the language of a large portion of every good poem, even of the most elevated character, must necessarily, except with reference to the metre, in no respect differ from that of good prose, but likewise that some of the most interesting parts of the best poems will be found to be strictly the language of prose when prose is well written. The truth of this assertion might be demonstrated by innumerable passages from almost all the poetical writings, even of Milton himself. I have not space for much quotation; but, to illustrate the subject in a general manner, I will here adduce a short composition of Gray, who was at the head of those who by their reasonings have attempted to widen the space of separation betwixt Prose and Metrical composition, and was more than any other man curiously elaborate in the structure of his own poetic diction.

In vain to me the smiling mornings shine,
And reddening Phœbus lifts his golden fire:
The birds in vain their amorous descant join,
Or chearful fields resume their green attire:
These ears alas! for other notes repine;

A different object do these eyes require;
My lonely anguish melts no heart but mine;
And in my breast the imperfect joys expire;
Yet Morning smiles the busy race to cheer,
And new-born pleasure brings to happier men;
The fields to all their wonted tribute bear;
To warm their little loves the birds complain.
I fruitless mourn to him that cannot hear
And weep the more because I weep in vain.

It will easily be perceived that the only part of this Sonnet which is of any value is the lines printed in Italics: it is equally obvious that except in the rhyme, and in the use of the single word "fruitless" for fruitlessly, which is so far a defect, the language of these lines does in no respect differ from that of prose.—WILLIAM WORDSWORTH, "Preface" (1800) to *Lyrical Ballads* (1798), 1800

Gray failed as a Poet, not because he took too much pains, and so extinguished his animation; but because he had little of that fiery quality to begin with; and his pains were of the wrong sort. He wrote English Verses, as he and other Eton school-Boys wrote Latin: filching a phrase now from one author, and now from another. I do not profess to be a person of very various reading; nevertheless if I were to pluck out of Grays tail all the feathers which, I know, belong to other Birds he would be left very bare indeed. Do not let any Body persuade you that any quantity of good verses can ever be produced by mere felicity; or that an immortal *style* can be the growth of mere Genius— Multa *tulit* fecitque, must be the motto of all those who are to last.—WILLIAM WORDSWORTH, Letter to R. P. Gillics (April 15, 1816)

I should conceive that Collins had a much greater poetical genius than Gray: he had more of that fine madness which is inseparable from it, of its turbid effervescence, of all that pushes it to the verge of agony or rapture. Gray's *Pindaric Odes* are, I believe, generally given up at present: they are stately and pedantic, a kind of methodical borrowed phrenzy. But I cannot so easily give up, nor will the world be in any haste to part with his *Elegy in a Country Church-yard*: it is one of the most classical productions that ever was penned by a refined and thoughtful mind, moralising on human life. Mr. Coleridge (in his *Literary Life*) says, that his friend Mr. Wordsworth had undertaken to shew that the language of the *Elegy* is unintelligible: it has, however, been understood! The 'Ode on a Distant Prospect of Eton College' is more mechanical and common-place; but it touches on certain strings about the heart, that vibrate in unison with it to our latest breath. No one ever passes by Windsor's 'stately heights,' or sees the distant spires of Eton College below, without thinking of Gray. He deserves that we should think of him; for he thought of others, and turned a trembling, ever-watchful ear to 'the still sad music of humanity.'—His Letters are inimitably fine. If his poems are sometimes finical and pedantic, his prose is quite free from affectation. He pours his thoughts out upon paper as they arise in his mind; and they arise in his mind without pretence, or constraint, from the pure impulse of learned leisure and contemplative indolence. He is not here on stilts or in buckram; but smiles in his easy chair, as he moralises through the loopholes of retreat, on the bustle and raree-show of the world, or on 'those reverend bedlams, colleges and schools!' He had nothing to do but to read and to think, and to tell his friends what he read and thought. His life was a luxurious, thoughtful dream. 'Be mine,' he says in one of his Letters, 'to read eternal new romances of Marivaux and Crebillon.' And in another, to shew his contempt for action and the turmoils of ambition, he says to some one, 'Don't you remember Lords —— and ——, who are now great statesmen, little dirty boys playing at cricket? For my part, I do not feel a bit wiser, or bigger, or older than I did then.' What an equivalent for not being wise or great, to be always young! What a happiness never to lose or gain any thing in the game of human life, by being never any thing more than a looker-on!—WILLIAM HAZLITT, *Lectures on the English Poets*, 1818

The obscurity so often objected to in him is certainly a defect not to be justified by the authority of Pindar, more than anything else that is intrinsically objectionable. But it has been exaggerated. He is nowhere so obscure as not to be intelligible by recurring to the passages. And it may be further observed, that Gray's lyrical obscurity never arises, as in some writers, from undefined ideas or paradoxical sentiments. On the contrary, his moral spirit is as explicit as it is majestic; and deeply read as he was in Plato, he is never metaphysically perplexed. The fault of his meaning is to be latent, not indefinite or confused. When we give his beauties re-perusal and attention, they kindle and multiply to the view. The thread of association that conducts to his remote allusions, or that connects his abrupt transitions, ceases then to be invisible. His lyrical pieces are like paintings on glass, which must be placed in a strong light to give out the perfect radiance of their colouring.—THOMAS CAMPBELL, *Specimens of the British Poets*, 1819

No wonder he should describe so well what he saw, for he seems to have been present at life rather as a spectator than an actor.

When he wrote, it was more to exercise his mind, or entertain his fancy, than from any ambition to please or be admired by others.

England had not sent abroad so elegant a scholar since the days of Milton; but he did not, like Milton, seek for distinction in the company of the learned. Whatever was going forward, he was anxious to observe, but cared not how little he was himself seen.

The few incidents in his life are to be collected from his letters, which were written with no view to publication, and on that account show to more advantage the excellence of his character, his duty and affection as a son, his cordiality and sincerity as a friend, his diligence, accuracy and elegance as a scholar, and the high sense of probity and honour that actuated his whole conduct.—HENRY FRANCIS CARY, "Notices of Miscellaneous English Poets" (1823), cited in Henry Cary, *Memoirs of the Rev. Henry Francis Cary*, 1847, Vol. 2, p. 293

⟨. . .⟩ the poetry of Gray ⟨is . . .⟩ a laborious mosaic, through the hard stiff lineaments of which little life or true grace could be expected to look: real feeling, and all freedom of expressing it, are sacrificed to pomp, to cold splendour; for vigour we have a certain mouthing vehemence, too elegant indeed to be tumid, yet essentially foreign to the heart, and seen to extend no deeper than the mere voice and gestures. Were it not for his *Letters*, which are full of warm exuberant power, we might almost doubt whether Gray was a man of genius; nay, was a living man at all, and not rather some thousand-times more cunningly devised poetical turning-loom, than that of Swift's Philosophers in Laputa.—THOMAS CARLYLE, "Goethe" (1828), *Critical and Miscellaneous Essays*, 1839–69

I think there is something very majestic in Gray's Installation Ode; but as to the *Bard* and the rest of his lyrics, I must say I think them frigid and artificial. There is more real lyric feeling in Cotton's "Ode on Winter."—SAMUEL TAYLOR COLERIDGE, *Table Talk*, Oct. 23, 1833

And GRAY, while Windsor's antique towers shall stand,
Or spring revisit Britain's favour'd land;
While those old bards whose praise he sung so well
Shall keep their place in memory's haunted cell;
While the green churchyard and the hallow'd tower
Attract your steps at eve's soft, solemn hour;
As long as men can read, and boys recite,
As long as critics sneer, and bards endite,
And lavish lords shall print their jingling stuff,
Mid ample margin, leaving verge enough;
So long shall GRAY, and all he said and sung,
Tang the shrill accents of the school-girl's tongue;
So long his Ode, his Elegy, and Bard,
By lisping prodigies be drawl'd and marr'd.
　　　—HARTLEY COLERIDGE, "Young and His Contemporaries," *Sketches of English Poets*, 1849

The poetry of Gray which treats of familiar subjects belongs to the first period of his English compositions. In them he drew from the spontaneous emotions of his heart, and the native melancholy, plaintive but not morbid, with which he coloured everything, is one of the causes of the hold which his pieces take on the mind. He there displays the real bent of his genius, which was rather tender than sublime. What Johnson said of his Pindaric Odes—that they were forced plants raised in a hot-bed, and again that Gray was tall by walking on tiptoe—is not devoid of justice. This is now a more common opinion than it used to be formerly. "They are, I believe," says Hazlitt, "generally given up at present: they are stately and pedantic, a kind of methodical borrowed frenzy." Sir Walter Scott thought them stiff and artificial, and Lord Byron considered that Gray's reputation would have been higher if he had written nothing except his Elegy. To us it appears that his Odes, and especially *The Bard*, which is much the finest, contain delicious strains, but that taken as a whole they are not first-rate. The words and verse of the *Progress of Poetry* are glowing enough, but many of the ideas are frigid and far-fetched. The *Bard* is a grand conception, and has more vigour of sentiment than the companion Ode, but the dramatic energy, so conspicuous in the opening burst, is not well sustained. Whatever bears the marks of painful elaboration must be to some extent formal; fervour is the impulse of the moment; and in passages intended to be passionate, the smell of the lamp destroys the nature and mars the effect.

The language of his other pieces is rich, but not luxuriant; in his Pindarics it is ornate to excess, and the metaphors and personifications, a few of which are superb, are sometimes pushed to the boundaries of extravagance, and even cross the confines. The praise of Shakspeare, which was a favourite passage with the author because he thought it had the merit of being original where novelty was hardly possible, is an instance of the defect. The picture of Nature presenting the pencil and keys to the child, and of his smiling at her awful face, is grotesque in proportion to the vividness with which it is realised, and is not redeemed by any ingenuity in the conception. The representation, too, of the mighty mother as wearing a terrible countenance, is peculiarly inapplicable to the universal genius of Shakspeare, whose comic powers are not inferior to his tragic. In the lines which follow on Milton, the ascribing his blindness to his contemplation of the dazzling glories of heaven, which he only viewed in imagination, is certainly a conceit, but there is a grandeur in the passage, which even this blemish, serious as it is, could not destroy.

If Gray had been more sparing of his metaphors they would have gained in effect, and we should have had less of that obscurity, which it is idle to defend, and which, in the *The Progress of Poetry*, is entirely produced by the resolution to tell everything in the high figurative style. He frequently fails to preserve consistency in his images. Dr. Akenside remarked that the keys in the panegyric on Shakspeare, which are employed at first to unlock a gate, are made at the end 'to ope a *source.*' Dr. Johnson has exposed some similar slips, and throughout Gray's poems there is often a want of coherence between the parts of a sentence, either of grammar or of sense. The fault arose from his mode of composition. Instead of putting down his thoughts as they sprung up in his mind, he polished every line as he proceeded, and in the repeated changes of expression, a later verse, which was correct in the first conception, came to harmonize imperfectly with what went before.

In the management of his metre Gray has no superior. His ear was exquisite, and the few harsh lines, and very harsh they are, which are to be found in his poetry, were evidently left because he preferred to sacrifice the melody to the expression. The greatness of his reputation, contrasted with the small extent of the compositions upon which it is built, is the strongest proof of their singular excellence. Whether the slow and mosaic workmanship of Gray was an indication of genius, has often been questioned, but none except the few, who were jealous of his popularity, have ever hesitated to admit that his happiest poetry must be classed among the most perfect in the world.—WHITWELL ELWIN, "Life and Works of Gray," *Quarterly Review*, Jan. 1854, pp. 25–26

Gray, if we may believe the commentators, has not an idea, scarcely an epithet, that he can call his own; and yet he is, in the best sense, one of the classics of English literature. He had exquisite felicity of choice; his dictionary had no vulgar word in it, no harsh one, but all culled from the luckiest moods of poets, and with a faint but delicious aroma of association; he had a perfect sense of sound, and one idea without which all the poetic outfit (*si absit prudentia*) is of little avail,—that of combination and arrangement, in short, of art. The poets from whom he helped himself have no more claim to any one of his poems as wholes, than the various beauties of Greece (if the old story were true) to the Venus of the artist.—JAMES RUSSELL LOWELL, "Carlyle" (1866), *Works*, Riverside ed., Vol. 2, pp. 80–81

Neither in respect of the quantity nor the quality of his verse could Gray's manner of composition be described as spontaneous. Compared with Wordsworth's numerous volumes of poetry, the slender volume that contains the poetry of Gray looks meagre indeed; yet almost every poem in this small collection is a considered work of art. To begin with *The Bard*. Few readers, we suppose, would rise from this ode without a sense of its poetical 'effect.' The details may be thought to require too much attention; the allusions, from the nature of the subject, are, no doubt, difficult; but a feeling of loftiness, of harmony, of proportion, remains in the mind at the close of the poem, which is not likely to pass away. How, then, was this effect produced? First of all we see that Gray had selected a good subject; his raw materials, so to speak, were poetical. The imagination, unembarrassed by common associations, breathes freely in its own region, and is instinctively elevated as it moves among the great events of the past, dwelling on the misfortunes of monarchs, the rise of dynasties, and the splendours of literature. But in the second place, when he has chosen his subject, it is the part of the poet to impress the great ideas derived from it on the feelings and the memory by the distinctness of the form

under which he presents it; and here poetical invention first begins to work. By the imaginative fiction of *The Bard*, Gray is enabled to cast the whole course of English history into the form of a prophecy, and to excite the patriotic feelings of the reader, as Virgil roused the pride of his own countrymen, by Anchises' forecast of the grandeur of Rome. Finally, when the main design of the poem is thus conceived, observe with what art all the different parts are made to emphasise the beauty of the general conception; with what dramatic propriety the calamities of the conquering Plantagenet are prophesied by his vanquished foe; while on the other hand, the literary glories of the Tudor Elizabeth awaken the triumph of the patriot and the poet; how martial and spirited is the opening of the poem! how lofty and enthusiastic its close! Perhaps there is no English lyric which, animated by equal fervour, displays so much architectural genius as *The Bard*.

Take, again, the 'Ode on the Prospect of Eton College.' A subject better adapted for the indulgence of personal feeling, or for those sentimental confidences between the reader and the poet, in which the modern muse so much delights, could not be imagined. But what do we find? The theme is treated in the most general manner. Though emphasising the irony of his reflection by the beautiful touch of memory in the second stanza, the poet speaks throughout as a moralist or spectator; from first to last he seems to lose all thought of himself in contemplating the tragedies he foresees for others; the subject is in fact handled with the most skilful rhetoric, and every stanza is made to strengthen and elaborate the leading thought. In the *Progress of Poesy*, though the general constructive effect is perhaps inferior to *The Bard*, we see the same evidence of careful preconsideration, while the course of the poem is particularly distinguished by the beauty of the transitions. Of the form of the *Elegy* it is superfluous to speak; a poem so dignified and yet so tender, appeals immediately, and will continue to appeal, to the heart of every Englishman, so long as the care of public liberty and love of the soil maintain their hold in this country. In this poem, as indeed in all that Gray ever wrote, we find it his first principle *to prefer his subject to himself;* he never forgot that while he was a man he was also an artist, and he knew that the function of art was not merely to indulge nature, but to dignify and refine it.

Yet, in spite of his love of form, there is nothing frigid or statuesque in the genius of Gray. A vein of deep melancholy, evidently constitutional, runs through his poetry, and, considering how little he produced, the number of personal allusions in his verses is undoubtedly large. But he is entirely free from that egotism which we have had frequent occasion to blame as the prevailing vice of modern poetry. For whereas the modern poet thrusts his private feelings into prominence, and finds a luxury in the confession of his sorrows, Gray's references to himself are introduced on public grounds, or, in other words, with a view to poetical effect.—W. J. COURTHOPE, "Wordsworth and Gray," *Quarterly Review*, Jan. 1876, pp. 58–59

In Collins we have seen Nature described with a perfect grace of language and a penetrating of the forms and colors of things with human sentiment, that far outwent the minute and faithful descriptions of Thomson. This same movement was maintained, I cannot say advanced, by Gray. That he had a fine feeling for Nature is apparent in his letters, which show more minute observation and greater descriptive power than his poetry. In these the beautiful scenery around the Westmoreland Lakes finds the earliest notice.

In dealing with scenery, as with other things, Nature without Art, and Art without Nature, are alike inadequate. To hit the balance is no easy task. To let in Nature fully upon the heart, by means of an art which is colorless and unperceived—this English poetry was struggling toward, and Gray helped it forward, though he himself only attained partial success. Often the art is too apparent; a false classicism is sometimes thrust in between the reader and the fresh outer world. Wordsworth has laid hold of a sonnet of Gray's as a text to preach against false poetic diction. And yet Gray, notwithstanding his often too elaborate diction, deserves better of lovers of English poetry than to have his single sonnet thus gibbeted, merely because, instead of saying the sun rises, it makes

Reddening Phœbus lift his golden fire.

In the ode on Spring, it is "the rosy-bosomed hours, fair Venus' train," which bring spring in. Venus is thrust between you and the advent of spring, much as Adversity is made "the daughter of Jove." For the nightingale we have "the Attic warbler," as in another ode, for the yellow corn-fields we have "Ceres' golden reign." It is needless to say how abhorrent this sort of stuff is to the modern feeling about Nature. And yet, notwithstanding these blemishes, Gray did help forward the movement to a more perfect and adequate style, in which Nature should come direct to the heart, through a perfectly transparent medium of art. When he is at his best, as in the Elegy, Nature and human feeling so perfectly combine that the mind finds in all the images satisfaction and relief. There is in the Elegy no image from Greece or Rome, no intrusive heathen deity, to jar upon the feeling. From the common English landscape alone is drawn all that is needed to minister to the quiet but deep pathos of the whole.—J. C. SHAIRP, *On Poetic Interpretation of Nature*, 1877, pp. 209–10

As to Gray—Ah, to think of that little Elegy inscribed among the Stars, while Browning, Swinburne & Co., are blazing away with their Fireworks here below. I always think there is more Genius in most of the three volume Novels than in Gray: but by the most exquisite Taste, and indefatigable lucubration, he made of his own few thoughts, and many of other men's, a something which we all love to keep ever about us. I do not think his scarcity of work was from Design: he had but a little to say, I believe, and took his time to say it.—EDWARD FITZGERALD, Letter to James Russell Lowell (June 13, 1879)

"Knowledge, penetration, seriousness, sentiment, humour"—so Mr. Matthew Arnold counts over the five talents committed to Gray. Five talents; yet it is not easy to think of him as ever to be a ruler of five cities. With his gathered learning, his insight and his power of organising knowledge, his judgment at once delicate and solid, his feeling for beauty in nature and in art, his amiable irony and his brightness of style, why was Gray a failure, and why does the story of his life hang weights upon our courage and our hope? One can imagine his biographer protesting in lively tones against the word "failure." Gray created a style in English poetry; he was perhaps the most cultured Englishman of his generation; he interpreted Icelandic literature; he heralded the romantic revival; he felt the beauty of Gothic architecture; he revealed the wonders of lake and crag in Cumberland and Westmoreland; he sustained classical learning in his university; he made true friends and kept them. And, doubtless, compared with many lives, that of Gray may almost deserve to be called a success. Yet, on the other hand, there have been gallant defeats which, compared with such success as his, look like victories. After all contentions to the contrary, the settled conviction returns and maintains its hold upon our minds that Gray failed to work out the possibilities of his nature; that, but for some enervating

cause within, some retarding cause without, his powers must have carried him much farther than they actually did.

"Spirits failing and health not sound" is part of Mr. Arnold's proposed explanation; and it is certain that thunder-clouds of melancholy passion are less depressing to genius than the long, low-lying cloud of habitual *ennui*. But one great thought, one sudden ardour, has proved itself able at times to pierce and break up such a cloud of barren sadness. With Gray it was not so; the cloud hung lower and grew denser towards the close. "Gray, a born poet, fell upon an age of prose," adds Mr. Arnold; and this it was, in his opinion, which gave power to Gray's reclusion and ill-health to induce his sterility. "He fell upon an age whose task was such as to call forth in general men's powers of understanding, wit, and cleverness rather than their deepest powers of mind and soul." True; yet the age which gave birth to *Clarissa* and *Tom Jones* was not without its imaginative creations, its tragedy, its comedy, and was not wholly unfavourable to seriousness, sentiment, humour. Gray's Odes, novel in style, were called obscure, and he addressed them συνετοῖσι; but his *Elegy* received a prompt and universal welcome. He was acknowledged to be the chief living poet of England; yet in the decade of his highest fame he made "less and less effort," says Mr. Gosse, "to concentrate his powers." To quote the text of Mr. Arnold's discourse, "he never spoke out."

Gray was an elegiac and a lyric poet; a poet of sentiment and reflection in the *Elegy* and in the minor Odes; a poet of imaginative enthusiasm of a sustained and deliberate kind in the greater Odes. Never, perhaps, did a distinguished lyrical poet possess so little of native passion. The poet, we all know, is born,

With golden stars above,
Dower'd with the hate of hate, the scorn of scorn,
The love of love.

Whether Gray felt the influence of golden stars in Cornhill, or at Stoke Pogis, or in Cambridge, where the wild beasts of the deserts dwelt and the great owl made his nest, may be doubted. He was a languid hater; his scorn was the delicate satire of an onlooker at the follies of life, amused more than indignant, and sometimes wearied more than amused. His love—alas, his pallid passion which died before it was born, Delia's gentlest philanderings, his "amatory lines"! And yet ideal topics through his imagination could excite in Gray an ideal passion. No pressure of personal feeling compelled him to song; but the "Lyric Muse," as Gray knew her, was willing, "like other fine ladies, to be courted," and the poet's imaginative passion rose with the occasion. "I *was* the Bard," he said, when asked how he felt when writing that Ode. And Nicholls speaks of his awe at the lightning of Gray's eye, "at that *folgorante sguardo*, as the Tuscans term it." But a lyric poet who does not sing as the bird sings, but must court the Muse, requires a faith in himself, a strength of will, a power of strenuous self-sacrifice—sacrifice of inferior appetites and faculties of the mind for the sake of the higher faculty—and to these Gray did not attain. "If I do not write much," he said, "it is because I cannot." And this is true; but sterility was inevitable for one who lacked energy of soul to live in his highest faculties, who would not place his noblest power at the head of the rest to lead them all on to victory, who would not tax the inferior powers in the service of the superior, who chose rather the luxury of endless intellectual acquisition, the ease of one who is increased in goods, the narcotic of erudition. Yet the still small voice of poetry was never quite silenced within him, and his was the grief of those who know that the purpose of their lives is frustrate through the sin

1590

Of the unlit lamp and the ungirt loin.

This is a severe judgment; but if Gray's life tells us anything it tells us that an ascetic principle is needed in the intellectual and spiritual life.

As a poet "of sentiment and reflection," Gray's view of the world is in large part that of his age. In the *saeculum rationalisticum* a temper of moderation was predominant. There were no transcendental views as to the individual man; no one had announced that each of us is a part of "the vesture of the Unnamed;" nor was there yet any extravagant hope of a sudden Millennium for society, any widespread faith in a remote yet glorious triumph of humanity to which each of us may contribute a little. To Gray the general aspect of society was saddening; life upon the whole seemed a poor affair.

> How vain the ardour of the crowd,
> How low, how little are the proud,
> How indigent the great.

What are mortal men but a tribe of insects? What their strivings but an aimless fluttering? And what am I, poor moralist, adds Gray, but a fly like them, and, unlike them, a sad and solitary fly? To escape from the folly of life, to conquer its pain—this is what we need. Even the escape through ignorance and youth and animal spirits has in it something which assuages while we contemplate it; therefore, let the Eton school-boy chase the hoop and urge the ball—"Thought would destroy his paradise." Some of Gray's delight in his mercurial friend, Bonstetten, doubtless arose from the pathetic interest of the contrast between himself, the frustrate man who knew everything, and this immortal boy who promised to be all that Gray was not, and who seemed never to feel the weight of years or custom. Happier, however, than the average Eton lad, by-and-by to degrade into a member of the House of Lords, is the peasant "whose sober wishes never learned to stray," and who will rest so well at last in his village churchyard. Gray felt deeply the worth of simple goodness even while doing honour to genius, and the peasant and the poet of his *Elegy* are two of those who have escaped from the vain turmoil of human life. Even in a stern retreat from the world dwells truer happiness than in its tumult; such happiness is that of the monk of the Grande Chartreuse, whose silent abode and quietude were envied by Gray. Unhappily, Pembroke was no Carthusian monastery; but the harpischord, and the mignonette, and the china jars, and an eye which took an amused interest in the foibles and follies of those around him, made amends. It is a pity that some poetical medium was not discovered by Gray in which his humour, his sentiment, his knowledge, his wisdom of life, could all have coalesced—some medium which might have been to Gray what the blank verse of *The Task* was to Cowper. Perhaps Gray thought of this, and then took a dose of his favourite anodyne, *fastidium.*—EDWARD DOWDEN, *Academy*, July 22, 1882, pp. 58–59

It may ⟨. . .⟩ be accepted that in ⟨Gosse's⟩ edition we have the whole outcome of Gray's literary life. The quantity must be conceded to be extraordinarily small for a modern author. It is inevitable, therefore, that in any consideration of his achievement the question should invariably come up why it was that he wrote so little. A favorite theory, perhaps the present favorite theory, is that this paucity of production was due to the character of the age and not to that of the man. The eighteenth century is steadily patronized by the nineteenth in a way which suggests to the doubting heart unpleasant possibilities as to the attitude which the twentieth century may take toward the nineteenth. In no one thing, however, does it hold its predecessor more responsible than for the character and extent

of Gray's poetical achievement. He was, it is said, a poet in an age of prose. He was a sort of literary Robinson Crusoe, wrecked in the unimaginative, unspiritual, watery waste of the eighteenth century. This view has been lately enforced with his usual clearness and acuteness by Matthew Arnold; and to that author Mr. Gosse dedicates this edition of Gray in terms which seem to indicate that he too accepts this opinion. Still, the authority of any names, however great, can hardly convince us that this theory is true. It is by the nature of the man and not of the century that Gray's barrenness of production is to be explained. The causes that limited it do not seem hard to find. He never felt through life the pressure of necessity. He was not rich, but he had enough. He lived a life of lettered ease; and a life of lettered ease is not favorable to literary fertility, unless the love of fame acts as an unusually powerful stimulant. This in Gray's case could hardly be said to act as a stimulant at all. Moreover, while he had the genius of the poet, he had the tastes and inclinations of the scholar, or perhaps it would be truer to say, of the student. These, when strongly developed, are unfavorable in a high degree to original composition; for by those possessing them the luxury of the acquisition of knowledge will always be preferred to the toil involved in the creation of literature. Milton's case is in many respects analogous. He was everlastingly occupying his leisure with the compilation of histories, of systems of divinity, of Latin dictionaries; and had he not been prevented by blindness from indulging these tastes, it is surely among the possibilities that he would never have found the time to complete his early-planned but long-deferred great work. It is certain that, had he died at the age at which Gray died, his published poetical production would have rivalled the latter's in scantiness. In a similar way Gray was writing notes on classical authors, compiling chronological tables, and planning works never to be completed, involving study rather than genius; and no slight share of his literary labor was given up to the composition of Latin verse—an occupation which makes the pursuits of the schoolmen respectable.

In addition to all this, Gray was a consummate literary artist, and had all the fastidiousness and the self-dissatisfaction which go with the artistic nature. The same sort of feeling that led him to throw out one beautiful stanza which was included in the *Elegy* when first printed, acted, we may be sure, in a thousand cases of which we have no knowledge. Each of these reasons is sufficient to explain his silence without seeking for its cause in something outside of himself. The eighteenth century has sins enough of literary commission to answer for without making it responsible for sins of literary omission on the part of its individual members.

The further question arises here, if this paucity of production has not been on the whole a benefit to Gray's fame—at any rate to the universality of it. The bulk exhibited by his poetry may not seem imposing to the critic, but it does not frighten the reader. It is natural for us to wish that a writer of Gray's order of genius should have produced some one large work; not because size is essential to greatness, but because it is necessary to the display of invention on a grand scale, and to the development of passions and activities working through mighty agencies. Yet it is extremely doubtful if his fame would have been enhanced in the slightest measure if he had accomplished what it is so natural for us to desire. He probably knew the limits of his own powers better than his friends or critics. The unpublished fragments which he left do not, on the whole, make us regret very deeply that he never completed long and ambitious works. They would certainly have contained many fine lines, and might have contained many fine passages; but the spread of his reputation would most probably have been hindered rather than helped by the weight it had to carry. In nothing was the wisdom of the ancients more clearly expressed than in the story of the Sibylline books. The value remained the same after two-thirds of them had been destroyed; and the surviving three would doubtless have been more frequently consulted than the original nine had they possessed the same existence in fact as in fable. Of the majority of even writers of genius, it can truly be said that they would be read a great deal more had they written a great deal less. Gray is one of the very few poets whose productions are mastered in their entirety; and the actual familiarity with them, so general among educated men, is due in no slight degree to their fewness. His fame might possibly have been more imposing, but it certainly would not have been broader than it is now, if he had been selected as the official mouthpiece of the muse of long-windedness.—THOMAS R. LOUNSBURY, "Gray's Works," *Nation*, March 5, 1885, pp. 205–6

In spite of unjust depreciation and misapplied criticism, he holds his own and bids fair to last as long as the language which he knew how to write so well and of which he is one of the glories. Wordsworth is justified in saying that he helped himself from everybody and everywhere—and yet he made such admirable use of what he stole (if theft there was) that we should as soon think of finding fault with a man for pillaging the dictionary. He mixed himself with whatever he took—an incalculable increment. In the editions of his poems, the thin line of text stands at the top of the page like cream, and below it is the skim-milk drawn from many milky mothers of the herd out of which it has risen. But the thing to be considered is that, no matter where the material came from, the result is Gray's own. Whether original or not, he knew how to make a poem, a very rare knowledge among men. The thought in Gray is neither uncommon nor profound, and you may call it beatified commonplace if you choose. I shall not contradict you. I have lived long enough to know that there is a vast deal of commonplace in the world of no particular use to anybody, and am thankful to the man who has the divine gift to idealize it for me. Nor am I offended with this odor of the library that hangs about Gray, for it recalls none but delightful associations. It was in the very best literature that Gray was steeped and I am glad that both he and we should profit by it. If he appropriated a fine phrase wherever he found it, it was by right of eminent domain, for surely he was one of the masters of language. His praise is that what he touched was idealized, and kindled with some virtue that was not there before, but came from him.—JAMES RUSSELL LOWELL, "Gray," *New Princeton Review*, March 1886, pp. 175–76

Gray and Collins, distinct enough in character to the careful critical inspector, have to the outward eye a curious similarity. They were contemporaries; they wrote very little, and that mostly in the form of odes; they both affected personation and allegorical address to a very unusual extent; both studied effects which were Greek in their precision and delicacy; both were learned and exact students of periods of literature now reinstated in critical authority, but in their day neglected. Yet, while Gray was the greater intellectual figure of the two, the more significant as a man and a writer, Collins possessed something more thrilling, more spontaneous, as a purely lyrical poet. When they are closely examined, their supposed similarity fades away; and, without depreciating either, we discover that each was typical of a class—that Collins was the type of the poet who sings, as the birds do, because he must; and Gray of the artist in verse, who has learned everything which the most consummate attention to workmanship can

teach him, when added to the native faculty of a singularly delicate ear. Each has his separate charm, but we must not stultify our own enjoyment of either by pushing too far a parallelism which, though strongly marked, turns out to be mainly superficial. ⟨. . .⟩

Against the right of Gray to be considered one of the leading English men of letters no more stringent argument has been produced than is founded upon the paucity of his published work. It has fairly been said that the springs of originality in the brain of a great inventive genius are bound to bubble up more continuously and in fuller volume than could be confined within the narrow bounds of the poetry of Gray. But the sterility of the age, the east wind of discouragement steadily blowing across the poet's path, had much to do with this apparent want of fecundity, and it would be an error to insist too strongly on a general feature of the century in this individual case. When we turn to what Gray actually wrote, although the bulk of it is small, we are amazed at the originality and variety, the freshness and vigour of the mind that worked thus tardily and in miniature. As a poet Gray closes the period we have been discussing in the present chapter, and then passes beyond it. His metrical work steadily advances: we have the somewhat cold and timid odes of his youth; we proceed to the superb *Elegy*, in which the Thomsonian school reaches its apex, and expires; we cross over to the elaborate Pindaric odes, in which Gray throws off the last shackles of Augustan versification, and prepares the way for Shelley; and lastly, we have the purely romantic fragments of the close of his life, those lyrics inspired by the Edda and by Ossian, in which we step out of the eighteenth century altogether, and find ourselves in the full stream of romanticism.

In no sketch of the genius of Gray, however slight, can we afford to ignore the range and singular fulness of his intellectual acquirements. He was described by one well qualified to judge as being in his time "perhaps the most learned man in Europe." His knowledge of Greek literature, and especially Greek poetry, was as deep as it was subtle; he was equally keen in his study of all that suited his own peculiar habits of mind in the authors of modern Europe, and when he was already advanced in life he mastered Icelandic, at that time a language almost unknown even in continental Scandinavia. His tendency of mind was to be habitually dejected; he was solitary, and a hypochondriac. Against this constitutional melancholy, intellectual activity was his great resource, and his favourite saying was, "to be employed is to be happy." We are fortunately able to follow the development of this exquisite and sequestered mind in the copious series of his letters to his private friends, first imperfectly collected in 1775; in this remarkable correspondence, which yields to none in the language in brightness and elegance, we observe the movements of the fastidious brain and melancholy conscience, illuminated and gilded by the light of such spontaneous humour as the sprightlier poems of the writer ought to have prepared us for.

Among the writings of Gray it is unquestionable that the *Churchyard Elegy* stands first. In other poems he has during brief passages displayed higher qualities than are illustrated here, but in no second work is the noble tone of tenderness and distinction preserved at such a uniform level of perfection. By credit of this single piece Gray stands easily at the head of all the English elegiac poets, and, as Mr. Swinburne puts it, "holds for all ages to come his unassailable and sovereign station." Encrusted as it is with layers upon layers of eulogy, bibliography, and criticism, we have but to scrape these away to find the immortal poem beneath as fresh, as melodious, as inspiring as ever. With regard to the two great Pindaric odes, criticism has by no means spoken with the same unanimity. The contemporaries of Gray found these elaborate pieces difficult to the verge of unintelligibility. Later critics, who have not pretended to find them unmeaning, have yet objected to their overblown magnificence, their excess of allegorical apparatus, and their too manifest metrical artifice. That they do not belong to the school of simplicity may be freely admitted, but there are certain themes, suggestively described by De Quincey, in the treatment of which simplicity is out of place. The *Progress of Poesy* and the prophetic raptures of a dying bard may be recognised as belonging to the same class of subjects as Belshazzar's Feast. The qualities rather to be regarded in these elaborate pieces of poetic art are their originality of structure, the varied music of their balanced strophes, as of majestic antiphonal choruses answering one another in some antique temple, and the extraordinary skill with which the evolution of the theme is observed and restrained. It is in this latter characteristic that Gray shows himself, as an artist, to be far superior to Collins. The student will not fail, in some of Gray's minor writings, in the sonorous "Stanzas to Mr. Bentley," in the thrilling flute-like tones and nature-sketches of the fragmentary "Ode on Vicissitude," in the Gothic picturesqueness of "The Descent of Odin," to detect notes and phrases of a more delicate originality than are to be found even in his more famous writings, and will dwell with peculiar pleasure on those passages in which Gray freed himself of the trammels of an artificial and conventional taste, and prophesied of the new romantic age that was coming. The faults of Gray's poetry are obvious, especially in his earlier writing; they are the results of an exaggerated taste for rhetoric and for allegory. But the main features of his work are such that we may frankly acknowledge him to have succeeded when he tells us that "the style I have aimed at is extreme conciseness of expression, yet pure, perspicuous, and musical."—EDMUND GOSSE, *A History of Eighteenth Century Literature*, 1888, pp. 235–41

It is scarcely a paradox to say that he has left much that is incomplete, but nothing that is unfinished. His handwriting represents his mind; I have seen and transcribed many and many a page of it, but I do not recollect to have noticed a single carelessly written word, or even letter. The mere sight of it suggests refinement, order, and infinite pains. A mind searching in so many directions, sensitive to so many influences, yet seeking in the first place its own satisfaction in a manner uniformly careful and artistic, is almost foredoomed to give very little to the world; it must be content, as the excellent Matthias says, to be 'its own exceeding great reward.' But what is given is a little gold instead of much silver; a legal tender at any time, though it has never been soiled in the market. He claims our honour as one of those few who in any age have lived in the pursuit of the absolute best, and who help us to mistrust the glib facility with which we are apt to characterize epochs. In all that he has left, there is independence, sincerity, thoroughness; the highest exemplar of the critical spirit; a type of how good work of any kind should be done. He studied Greek when few studied it, and when much that is now familiar to schoolboys was unknown to scholars, yet he read with all the exactness he could command as well as in the large fashion of a man of letters. He wrote with accents, generally, I believe, rightly placed; though in this respect his editors have declined to copy him. His notes, designed for his own use, have been frequently quoted by the late Master of Trinity; they prove very extensive reading and comparison of authorities; we may infer that in the absence of adequate aids he was often

guided to the meaning more by the context than by verbal scholarship. To history he brought the modern spirit of research, which, like the curiosity of Herodotus and Froissart, is a kind of guarantee of impartiality, and virtually leaves to the secure judgment of the world the task of pronouncing sentence. His critical opinions are safe, because they are not controversial nor addressed to a public, but the outcome of impressions gathered at leisure by a mind at once comprehensive and exact. We are no losers by the circumstance that they were communicated only to his friends, for next in sincerity to the good criticism which may be found in some poetry, is that which we can extract from private letters. And though Gray lived so much in the past, he is receptive in the present, cognizant of new tendencies and apt to resign himself to them, and to forego his penetration when these are concerned; he would willingly believe in Macpherson's Ossian; he is perhaps the only Englishman of note whom it affects, as it affected the Continentals; this is because his sensitive genius has a little shudder of presentiment, at this first breath of the reviving spirit of Romance. It is these characteristics which make him, as I have said, still modern for us in the best sense and justify the curious and minute interest which some feel in him now; it is at any rate the best account I am able to give of a sort of homage which seems to belong to much greater names, and yet which inclines one who has given much time to Gray, whilst perhaps half-smiling at his own enthusiasm, to repeat to his fascinating shade the invocation

> Vagliami 'l lungo studio e 'l grande amore
> Che m' han fatto cercar lo tuo volume.
> —DUNCAN C. TOVEY, "Introductory Essay" to
> *Gray and His Friends: Letters and Relics*,
> 1890, pp. 32–33

"In Gray's Commonplace Books at Pembroke College there is much interesting matter," says Dr. Bradshaw (*Aldine Edition* of Gray's Poetical Works, ed. 1891), "and many notes and essays that have never been printed," though Mr. Gosse has drawn from them in his *Works of Gray in Prose and Verse*. But the prose writings by which Gray is best known, and deserves to be best known, the contents of his MSS. being for the most part of the nature of notes and fragments, are certainly his Letters.

Letter-writing was an art carefully and assiduously cultivated in the last century, as never before, and never comparably since. In many instances beyond doubt a correspondent fully entertained the idea of future publication. He wrote consciously for the press, and not only for the private perusal of his friend. In any case he would be assured that generally what he wrote would be read, not only by his friend, but by his friend's circle. Hence special pains were taken with this kind of composition, and it became a branch of literature. Thus a habit of epistolary care and finish was formed; and a certain ease and charm marks even the most ordinary communications. Now, if such attention to style was common, as it was, we may be sure it is to be found in a high degree in Gray's correspondence. A man so critical and fastidious as Gray could indeed do nothing carelessly and like a sloven. The idea of perfection was ever before his eyes. Even his handwriting was significant in this respect. "I have seen and transcribed many and many a page of it," says Mr. Tovey, in his interesting volume entitled *Gray and His Friends*; "but I do not recollect to have noticed a single carelessly written word, or even a letter. The mere sight of it suggests refinement, order, and infinite pains." Lady Jane Grey, in a well-known anecdote of her given by Ascham, complains that whatever she had to do before her father or mother—whether to "speak or keep silence, sit, stand, or go, eat, drink, be merry or sad, be sewing, playing, dancing, or doing anything else"—she was expected to do it "as it were, in such weight, measure, and number, even so perfectly, as God made the world," or else she had a very bad time, being "sharply taunted" and "cruelly threatened" and pinched and nipped and otherwise tortured. Gray was scarcely less exacting and stern towards himself than those austere parents in the old house in Bradgate Park towards their child. He was one of the severest of self-critics. Was ever any other poet so remorseless with himself? Those stanzas omitted from the *Elegy written in a Country Church-yard* we believe Gray's taste was sound and true in excising; still they are in themselves such as perhaps no other author would have had the heart to excise. And yet both in his poetry and, what now more closely concerns us, in his prose, he exhibits the art of concealing his art. We feel ourselves in the presence of a most finished artist, but we do not see him mixing his colours, or fingering his brushes. We enjoy the effect without having thrust upon our notice the process or processes by which it has been produced. In his Letters the habit of a refined and polished manner has become second nature. He writes like a scholar, but without stiffness or effort. He is classical, but never pedantic.

In addition to all the culture that so eminently distinguished Gray, he possessed natural gifts without which all his culture would have done little to endear him to the general reader. He had a genuine vein of humour, which not only prevents his being dull, but makes him at times highly entertaining. He had a keen sense of the beauty of landscape, and one of his greatest pleasures was to gaze upon it and to describe it. He was Wordsworthian before Wordsworth was born. Lastly, though reserved and seemingly dry and cynical, he was a man of the tenderest affections. He does not wear his heart upon his sleeve; but it would be a gross mistake to conclude because he does not so wear it, that he had none to wear. "*Sunt lacrimæ rerum et mentem mortalia tangunt*" was a saying he felt deeply. His intimate friend West died in 1742; but we are told that all the rest of his life he never heard his name mentioned without a change of countenance—without a thrill of pain. In the *Elegy*, begun when the sorrow of that bereavement was still fresh, he writes of himself—

He gained from Heaven—'twas all he wished—a friend;

and this gain of "all he wished" was in one sense never lost; it was a blessed experience that was never forgotten, but to the end saved him from the dangers of self-absorption and misanthropy.

And so he happily remained capable of forming fresh friendships. Not only, to use his own exquisite words, is it "the parting soul" that "on some fond breast relies," but the soul throughout its period of embodiment. And Gray must needs have his confidants, to whom he could unbosom himself in prose at least, and speak of the high enjoyments he derived both from nature and art. His mother and father, West, Horace Walpole, Ashton, Wharton, Mason, Norton, Nicholls—all these and others, in a greater or less degree of frankness and fulness, this Cambridge recluse admits to a share of his thoughts and observations.

And of thoughts and observations there was not any lack, however quiet and retired his life, however "far from the madding crowd." At Cambridge his books were his world, and a world he keenly explored. In the summer he surrendered himself to the beauties of natural scenery. He was the earliest

annual tourist, in this respect as in many others anticipating the taste of a coming age. These wanderings in the more picturesque parts of the country, often companionless, became a passion with him; and it was a real relief to detail them to an appreciative friend with a faithful and loving pen that was also exquisitely skilful and graphic.—JOHN W. HALES, "Thomas Gray," *English Prose*, ed. Henry Craik, 1895, Vol. 4, pp. 221–24

Works

ELEGY

As you have brought me into a little Sort of Distress, you must assist me, I believe, to get out of it, as well as I can. yesterday I had the Misfortune of receiving a Letter from certain Gentlemen (as their Bookseller expresses it) who have taken the *Magazine of Magazines* into their Hands. they tell me, that an *ingenious* Poem, call'd, *Reflections* in a Country-Churchyard, has been communicated to them, wch they are printing forthwith: that they are inform'd, that the *excellent* Author of it is I by name, & that they beg not only his *Indulgence*, but the *Honor of his Correspondence*, &c: as I am not at all disposed to be either so indulgent, or so correspondent, as they desire; I have but one bad Way left to escape the Honour they would inflict upon me. & therefore am obliged to desire you would make Dodsley print it immediately (wch may be done in less than a Week's time) from your Copy, but without my Name, in what Form is most convenient for him, but in his best Paper & Character. he must correct the Press himself, & print it without any Interval between the Stanza's, because the Sense is in some Places continued beyond them; & the Title must be, *Elegy, wrote in a Country Church-yard*. if he would add a Line or two to say it came into his Hands by Accident, I should like it better.—THOMAS GRAY, Letter to Horace Walpole (Feb. 11, 1751)

The following *Poem* came into my hands by Accident, if the general Approbation with which this little Piece has been spread, may be call'd by so slight a term as Accident. It is this Approbation which makes it unnecessary for me to make any Apology but to the Author: As he cannot but feel some Satisfaction in having pleas'd so many Readers already, I flatter myself he will forgive my communicating that Pleasure to many more. The Editor.—HORACE WALPOLE, "Advertisement" to *Elegy Written in a Country Church-Yard*, 1751

This is a very fine poem, but overloaded with epithet. The heroic measure, with alternate rhyme, is very properly adapted to the solemnity of the subject, as it is the slowest movement that our language admits of. The latter part of the poem is pathetic and interesting.—OLIVER GOLDSMITH, *The Beauties of English Poetry*, 1767

Had Gray written nothing but his *Elegy*, high as he stands, I am not sure that he would not stand higher; it is the corner-stone of his glory: without it, his odes would be insufficient for his fame.—GEORGE GORDON, LORD BYRON, "Letter to —— ——, Esqre, on the Rev. W. L. Bowles's Strictures on the Life and Writings of Pope," 1821

Gray's *Elegy* will be read as long as any work of Shakespeare, despite of its moping owl and the tin-kettle of an epitaph tied to its tail. It is the first poem that ever touched my heart, and it strikes it now just in the same place. Homer, Shakespeare, Milton, Dante, the four giants who lived before our last Deluge of poetry, have left the ivy growing on the churchyard wall.—WALTER SAVAGE LANDOR, "The *Elegy in a Country*

Churchyard" (1843), cited in John Forster, *Walter Savage Landor: A Biography*, 1869, p. 570

Gray's *Elegy* describes a mood which Gray felt more than other men, but which most others, perhaps all others, feel too. It is more popular, perhaps, than any English poem, because that sort of feeling is the most diffused of high feelings, and because Gray added to a singular nicety of fancy an habitual proneness to a *contemplative*—a discerning but unbiassed—meditation on death and on life. Other poets cannot hope for such success: a subject so popular, so grave, so wise, and yet so suitable to the writer's nature is hardly to be found. ⟨. . .⟩

What sort of literatesque types are fit to be described in the sort of literature called poetry, is a matter on which much might be written. Mr. Arnold, some years since, put forth a theory that the art of poetry could only delineate *great actions*. But though, rightly interpreted and understood—using the word action so as to include high and sound activity in contemplation—this definition may suit the highest poetry, it certainly cannot be stretched to include many inferior sorts and even many good sorts. Nobody in their senses would describe Gray's *Elegy* as the delineation of a 'great action;' some kinds of mental contemplation may be energetic enough to deserve this name, but Gray would have been frightened at the very word. He loved scholarlike calm and quiet inaction; his very greatness depended on his *not* acting, on his 'wise passiveness,' on his indulging the grave idleness which so well appreciates so much of human life.—WALTER BAGEHOT, "Wordsworth, Tennyson, and Browning; or, Pure, Ornate, and Grotesque Art in English Poetry," 1864

ODES

I do not know why you should thank me for what you had a right and title to; but attribute it to the excess of your politeness, and the more so because almost no one else has made me the same compliment. As your acquaintance in the University (you say) do me the honour to admire, it would be ungenerous in me not to give them notice that they are doing a very unfashionable thing, for all people of condition are agreed not to admire, nor even to understand: one very great man, writing to an acquaintance of his and mine, says that he had read them seven or eight times, and that now, when he next sees him, he shall not have above thirty questions to ask. Another, a peer, believes that the last stanza of the Second Ode relates to King Charles the First and Oliver Cromwell. Even my friends tell me they do not succeed, and write me moving topics of consolation on that head; in short, I have heard of nobody but a player ⟨Garrick⟩ and a doctor of divinity ⟨John Brown⟩ that profess their esteem for them.—THOMAS GRAY, Letter to Richard Hurd (Aug. 25, 1757)

As this publication seems designed for those who have formed their taste by the models of antiquity, the generality of Readers cannot be supposed adequate Judges of its merit; nor will the Poet, it is presumed, be greatly disappointed if he finds them backward in commending a performance not entirely suited to their apprehensions. We cannot, however, without some regret behold those talents so capable of giving pleasure to all, exerted in efforts that, at best, can amuse only the few; we cannot behold this rising Poet seeking fame among the learned, without hinting to him the same advice that Isocrates used to give his Scholars, *Study the People*. This study it is that has conducted the great Masters of antiquity up to immortality. Pindar himself, of whom our modern Lyrist is an imitator, appears entirely guided by it. He adapted his works exactly to the dispositions of his countrymen. Irregular, enthusiastic, and

quick in transition,—he wrote for a people inconstant, of warm imaginations, and exquisite sensibility. He chose the most popular subjects, and all his allusions are to customs well known, in his days, to the meanest person.

His English Imitator wants those advantages. He speaks to a people not easily impressed with new ideas; extremely tenacious of the old; with difficulty warmed; and as slowly cooling again.—How unsuited then to our national character is that species of poetry which rises upon us with unexpected flights! Where we must hastily catch the thought, or it flies from us; and, in short, where the Reader must largely partake of the Poet's enthusiasm, in order to taste his beauties. To carry the parallel a little farther; the Greek Poet wrote in a language the most proper that can be imagined for this species of composition; lofty, harmonious, and never needing rhyme to heighten the numbers. But, for us, several unsuccessful experiments seem to prove that the English cannot have Odes in blank Verse; while, on the other hand, a natural imperfection attends those which are composed in irregular rhymes:—the similar sound often recurring where it is not expected, and not being found where it is, creates no small confusion to the Reader,—who, as we have not seldom observed, beginning in all the solemnity of poetic elocution, is by frequent disappointments of the rhyme, at last obliged to drawl out the uncomplying numbers into disagreeable prose.

It is, by no means, our design to detract from the merit of our Author's present attempt: we would only intimate, that an English Poet,—one whom the Muse has *mark'd for her own*, could produce a more luxuriant bloom of flowers, by cultivating such as are natives of the soil, than by endeavouring to force the exotics of another climate: or, to speak without a metaphor, such a genius as Mr. Gray might give greater pleasure, and acquire a larger portion of fame, if, instead of being an imitator, he did justice to his talents, and ventured to be more an original. These two Odes, it must be confessed, breath much of the spirit of Pindar, but then they have caught the seeming obscurity, the sudden transition, and hazardous epithet, of his mighty master; all which, though evidently intended for beauties, will, probably, be regarded as blemishes, by the generality of his Readers. In short, they are in some measure, a representation of what Pindar now appears to be, though perhaps, not what he appeared to the States of Greece, when they rivalled each other in his applause, and when Pan himself was seen dancing to his melody.

In conformity to the antients, these Odes consist of the *Strophe*, *Antistrophe*, and *Epode*, which, in each Ode, are thrice repeated. The Strophes have a correspondent resemblance in their structure and numbers: and the Antistrophe and Epode also bear the same similitude. The Poet seems, in the first Ode particularly, to design the Epode as a complete air to the Strophe and Antistrophe, which have more the appearance of Recitative. There was a necessity for these divisions among the antients, for they served as directions to the dancer and musician; but we see no reason why they should be continued among the moderns; for, instead of assisting, they will but perplex the Musician, as our music requires a more frequent transition from the Air to the Recitative than could agree with the simplicity of the antients.—OLIVER GOLDSMITH, "*Odes*, by Mr. Gray," *Monthly Review*, Sept. 1757

Gray (who joins to the sublimity of Milton the elegance and harmony of Pope, and to whom nothing is wanting to render him, perhaps, the first poet in the English language, but to have written a little more) is said to have been so much hurt by a foolish and impertinent parody of two of his finest odes, that he never afterwards attempted any considerable work.—ADAM SMITH, *The Theory of Moral Sentiments* (1759), 1790, Sec. 3, Ch. 2

Talking of Gray's *Odes*, he said, 'They are forced plants raised in a hot-bed; and they are poor plants; they are but cucumbers after all.' A gentleman present, who had been running down Ode-writing in general, as a bad species of poetry, unluckily said, 'Had they been literally cucumbers, they had been better things than Odes.'—'Yes, Sir, (said Johnson,) for a *hog*.' —BENNET LANGTON (1780), cited in James Boswell, *Life of Johnson*, 1791

I yet reflect with pain upon the cool reception which those noble odes, *The Progress of Poetry* and *The Bard*, met with at their first publication; it appeared that there were not twenty people in England who liked them.—THOMAS WHARTON, Letter to William Mason (May 29, 1781)

I have this evening been reading a few pages in Gray's Odes. I am very much pleased with them. The *Progress of Poesy* and the ode "To Eton College" are admirable. And many passages in *The Bard*, tho' I confess, quite obscure to me, seem to partake in a great degree of the sublime. Obscurity is the great objection which many urge against Gray. They do not consider that it contributes in the highest degree to sublimity. And he certainly aim'd at sublimity in these Lyrical Odes. If he did not, so much the more honour to him, for he has certainly attained it, whether sought or unsought. Tho' not in themselves entirely original, they were quite so to me—and, of course very amusing. Every one admires his Elegy and if they do not his odes, they must attribute it to their own *want of taste*—en Français *Gout*.—HENRY WADSWORTH LONGFELLOW, Letter to Zilpah Longfellow (April 1823)

CORRESPONDENCE

Gray's *style* in prose, as exhibited in his correspondence, is confessedly delightful. Though somewhat quaint, it is an easy quaintness. He was infinitely more natural in prose than verse. Horace Walpole lets us into the secret of this. "Gray," says that piercing reader of such characters as came within the scope of his actual observation, *"never wrote anything easily but things of humour;"*—and humour, his natural gift, is the characteristic of his correspondence. If not the best letter-writer in the language, he is the best letter-writer of all the professed *scholars*. Addison himself does not more happily combine humour with elegance; nor can even Walpole throw a more intellectual grace over familiar trifles.—EDWARD BULWER-LYTTON, "Gray's Works" (1837), *Miscellaneous Works*, 1868, Vol. 1, p. 153

Gray appears to us to be the best letter-writer in the language. Others equal him in particular qualities, and surpass him in amount of entertainment; but none are so nearly faultless. Chesterfield wants heart, and even his boasted "delicacy;" Bolingbroke and Pope want simplicity; Cowper is more lively than strong; Shenstone reminds you of too many rainy days, Swift of too many things which he affected to despise, Gibbon too much of the formalist and the *littérateur*. The most amusing of all our letter-writers are Walpole and Lady Mary Wortley Montagu; but though they had abundance of wit, sense, and animal spirits, you are not always sure of their veracity. Now, "the first quality in a companion," as Sir William Temple observes, "is truth;" and Gray's truth is as manifest as his other good qualities. He has sincerity, modesty, manliness (in spite of a somewhat effeminate body), learning, good-nature, playfulness, a perfect style; and if an air of

pensiveness breathes over all, it is only of that resigned and contemplative sort which completes our sympathy with the writer.

Mark what he says in these letters about his sitting in the forest; about Southern; about lords and their school-days; about Shaftesbury; about having a "garding" of one's own; about Akenside compared with himself; about the Southampton Abbot, the Grand Duchess of Tuscany, &c. &c.; and about sunrise—wondering "whether anybody ever saw it before," he is so astonished at their not having said more on the subject.

Gray is the "melancholy Jaques" of English literature, without the sullenness or causticity. His melancholy is of the diviner sort of Milton and Beaumont and is always ready to assume a kindly cheerfulness.—LEIGH HUNT, *A Book for a Corner*, 1849

Every one knows the letters of Gray, and remembers the lucid simplicity and directness, mingled with the fastidious sentiment of a scholar, of his description of such scenes as the Chartreuse. That is a well-known description, but those in his journal of a *Tour in the North* have been neglected, and they are especially interesting since they go over much of the country in which Wordsworth dwelt, and of which he wrote. They are also the first conscious effort—and in this he is a worthy forerunner of Wordsworth—to describe natural scenery with the writer's eye upon the scene described, and to describe it in simple and direct phrase, in distinction to the fine writing that was then practised. And Gray did this intentionally in the light prose journal he kept, and threw by for a time the refined carefulness and the insistence on human emotion which he thought necessary in poetic description of Nature. In his prose, then, though not in his poetry, we have Nature loved for her own sake.—STOPFORD A. BROOKE, *Theology in the English Poets*, 1874

However people may differ in their estimate of Gray as a poet, as a man he is secure of our affection, so soon as we get to know him, and any one may know him who will read his letters. Here, surely, there is no want of speaking out. Indeed, there are few literary men of so attractive a nature as Gray. Perhaps he is the most lovable of all except Charles Lamb, and with Lamb, despite many obvious differences, he has many points in common. They were both solitary creatures, living a recluse life in the world, but not of it, their best friends among the dead; they were both exquisite critics and no mean writers of poetry; they were both a prey to melancholy or rather, as Gray says, to "leucocholy"; they had both a delicate and delightful humour; they were both the very soul of gentle goodness. And so it comes about that their letters, in which they live to us, are among the few external good things which are necessary to happiness.

The charm of a letter of Gray's lies partly in this interest of his character, and partly in the perfect felicity with which everything is said. There is nothing slovenly or far-fetched or makeshift; even in the shortest and apparently most hasty note his touch is perfectly sure and his taste faultless.—H. C. BEECHING, *Academy*, Jan. 24, 1885, p. 53

———

SAMUEL JOHNSON
From "Gray"
Lives of the English Poets
1779–81

Gray's Poetry is now to be considered; and I hope not to be looked on as an enemy to his name, if I confess that I contemplate it with less pleasure than his life.

His 'Ode on Spring' has something poetical, both in the language and the thought; but the language is too luxuriant, and the thoughts have nothing new. There has of late arisen a practice of giving to adjectives, derived from substantives, the termination of participles; such as the *cultured* plain, the *daisied* bank; but I was sorry to see, in the lines of a scholar like Gray, the *honied* Spring. The morality is natural, but too stale; the conclusion is pretty.

The poem on the 'Cat' was doubtless by its author considered as a trifle, but it is not a happy trifle. In the first stanza *the azure flowers* that *blow*, shew resolutely a rhyme is sometimes made when it cannot easily be found. *Selima*, the Cat, is called a nymph, with some violence both to language and sense; but there is good use made of it when it is done; for of the two lines,

> What female heart can gold despise?
> What cat's averse to fish?

the first relates merely to the nymph, and the second only to the cat. The sixth stanza contains a melancholy truth, that *a favourite has no friend*; but the last ends in a pointed sentence of no relation to the purpose; if *what glistered* had been *gold*, the cat would not have gone into the water; and, if she had, would not less have been drowned.

The 'Prospect of Eton College' suggests nothing to Gray, which every beholder does not equally think and feel. His supplication to father *Thames*, to tell him who drives the hoop or tosses the ball, is useless and puerile. Father *Thames* has no better means of knowing than himself. His epithet *buxom health* is not elegant; he seems not to understand the word. Gray thought his language more poetical as it was more remote from common use: finding in Dryden *honey redolent of Spring*, an expression that reaches the utmost limits of our language, Gray drove it a little more beyond apprehension, by making *gales* to be *redolent of joy and youth*.

Of the 'Ode on Adversity,' the hint was at first taken from *O Diva, gratum quae regis Antium*; but Gray has excelled his original by the variety of his sentiments, and by their moral application. Of this piece, at once poetical and rational, I will not by slight objections violate the dignity.

My process has now brought me to the *Wonderful Wonder of Wonders*, the two Sister Odes; by which, though either vulgar ignorance or common sense at first universally rejected them, many have been since persuaded to think themselves delighted. I am one of those that are willing to be pleased, and therefore would gladly find the meaning of the first stanza of *The Progress of Poetry*.

Gray seems in his rapture to confound the images of *spreading sound* and *running water*. A *stream of musick* may be allowed; but where does *Musick*, however *smooth and strong*, after having visited the *verdant vales, rowl down the steep amain*, so as that *rocks and nodding groves rebellow to the roar?* If this be said of *Musick*, it is nonsense; if it be said of *Water*, it is nothing to the purpose.

The second stanza, exhibiting Mars's car and Jove's eagle, is unworthy of further notice. Criticism disdains to chase a schoolboy to his common-places.

To the third it may likewise be objected, that it is drawn from Mythology, though such as may be more easily assimilated to real life. Idalia's *velvet-green* has something of cant. An epithet or metaphor drawn from Nature ennobles Art; an epithet or metaphor drawn from Art degrades Nature. Gray is too fond of words arbitrarily compounded. *Many-twinkling* was formerly censured as not analogical; we may say *many-spotted*, but scarcely *many-spotting*. This stanza, however, has something pleasing.

Of the second ternary of stanzas, the first endeavours to tell something, and would have told it, had it not been crossed by Hyperion: the second describes well enough the universal prevalence of Poetry; but I am afraid that the conclusion will not rise from the premises. The caverns of the North and the plains of Chili are not the residences of *Glory and generous Shame*. But that Poetry and Virtue go always together is an opinion so pleasing, that I can forgive him who resolves to think it true.

The third stanza sounds big with *Delphi*, and *Egean*, and *Ilissus*, and *Meander*, and *hallowed fountain* and *solemn sound*; but in all Gray's odes there is a kind of cumbrous splendour which we wish away. His position is at last false: in the time of Dante and Petrarch, from whom he derives our first school of Poetry, Italy was overrun by *tyrant power* and *coward vice*; nor was our state much better when we first borrowed the Italian arts.

Of the third ternary, the first gives a mythological birth of Shakespeare. What is said of that mighty genius is true; but it is not said happily: the real effects of this poetical power are put out of sight by the pomp of machinery. Where truth is sufficient to fill the mind, fiction is worse than useless; the counterfeit debases the genuine.

His account of Milton's blindness, if we suppose it caused by study in the formation of his poem, a supposition surely allowable, is poetically true, and happily imagined. But the *car* of Dryden, with his *two coursers*, has nothing in it peculiar; it is a car in which any other rider may be placed.

The Bard appears, at the first view, to be, as Algarotti and others have remarked, an imitation of the prophecy of Nereus. Algarotti thinks it superior to its original; and, if preference depends only on the imagery and animation of the two poems, his judgement is right. There is in *The Bard* more force, more thought, and more variety. But to copy is less than to invent, and the copy has been unhappily produced at a wrong time. The fiction of Horace was to the Romans credible; but its revival disgusts us with apparent and unconquerable falsehood. *Incredulus odi*.

To select a singular event, and swell it to a giant's bulk by fabulous appendages of spectres and predictions, has little difficulty, for he that forsakes the probable may always find the marvellous. And it has little use; we are affected only as we believe; we are improved only as we find something to be imitated or declined. I do not see that *The Bard* promotes any truth, moral or political.

His stanzas are too long, especially his epodes; the ode is finished before the ear has learned its measures, and consequently before it can receive pleasure from their consonance and recurrence.

Of the first stanza the abrupt beginning has been celebrated; but technical beauties can give praise only to the inventor. It is in the power of any man to rush abruptly upon his subject, that has read the ballad of 'Johnny Armstrong',

Is there ever a man in all Scotland—

The initial resemblances, or alliterations, *ruin, ruthless, helm or hauberk*, are below the grandeur of a poem that endeavours at sublimity.

In the second stanza *The Bard* is well described; but in the third we have the puerilities of obsolete mythology. When we are told that *Cadwallo hush'd the stormy main*, and that *Modred* made *huge Plinlimmon bow his cloud-top'd head*, attention recoils from the repetition of a tale that, even when it was first heard, was heard with scorn.

The *weaving* of the *winding sheet* he borrowed, as he owns, from the northern Bards; but their texture, however, was very properly the work of female powers, as the art of spinning the thread of life in another mythology. Theft is always dangerous; Gray has made weavers of slaughtered bards, by a fiction outrageous and incongruous. They are then called upon to *Weave the warp, and weave the woof*, perhaps with no great propriety; for it is by crossing the *woof* with the *warp* that men *weave* the *web* or piece; and the first line was dearly bought by the admission of its wretched correspondent, *Give ample room and verge enough*. He has, however, no other line as bad.

The third stanza of the second ternary is commended, I think, beyond its merit. The personification is indistinct. *Thirst* and *Hunger* are not alike; and their features, to make the imagery perfect, should have been discriminated. We are told, in the same stanza, how *towers* are *fed*. But I will no longer look for particular faults; yet let it be observed that the ode might have been concluded with an action of better example; but suicide is always to be had, without expence of thought.

These odes are marked by glittering accumulations of ungraceful ornaments; they strike, rather than please; the images are magnified by affectation; the language is laboured into harshness. The mind of the writer seems to work with unnatural violence. *Double, double, toil and trouble*. He has a kind of strutting dignity, and is tall by walking on tiptoe. His art and his struggle are too visible, and there is too little appearance of ease and nature.

To say that he has no beauties, would be unjust: a man like him, of great learning and great industry, could not but produce something valuable. When he pleases least, it can only be said that a good design was ill directed.

His translations of Northern and Welsh poetry deserve praise; the imagery is preserved, perhaps often improved; but the language is unlike the language of other poets.

In the character of his *Elegy* I rejoice to concur with the common reader; for by the common sense of readers uncorrupted with literary prejudices, after all the refinements of subtilty and the dogmatism of learning, must be finally decided all claim to poetical honours. The *Churchyard* abounds with images which find a mirrour in every mind, and with sentiments to which every bosom returns an echo. The four stanzas beginning *Yet even these bones*, are to me original: I have never seen the notions in any other place; yet he that reads them here, persuades himself that he has always felt them. Had Gray written often thus, it had been vain to blame, and useless to praise him.

SIR LESLIE STEPHEN
From "Gray and His School" (1879)
Hours in a Library (1874–79)
1904, Volume 4, pp. 13–33

Gray, beyond all doubt, was the one man of genius of the school after the early death of Collins, for it would be strained to give a higher name than talent even to Horace Walpole's remarkable intellectual vivacity. Tom Warton's biographer (it is impossible to speak of Thomas) has drawn an elaborate parallel, in the proper historical fashion, between his hero and Gray. They were both dons, professors, students of antiquities, lovers of nature and of the romantic, composers of odes, and so forth. The parallel contains a good deal of truth, but it is consistent with an amusing contrast. Tom Warton was the thoroughly jovial, undignified don of the period. His poetry—even if his "Triumph of Isis" the superior to Mason's "Isis," and his sonnets deserve some praise in a century barren of sonnets—is not generally refreshing; the poor man had to construct some of those fanciful pieces of verse which laureates in those days were bound to manufacture for the sovereign's birthday, and one cannot glance at them (nobody can read them) without profound sympathy. But his humorous verses have still a pleasant ring about them. There is a contagion in the enthusiasm with which he celebrates the virtues of Oxford ale. When he imagines himself discommuned for his indulgence, and unable even to get longer "tick" at the pothouse, he daringly compares himself to Adam exiled from Paradise. In another poem we have the characteristic triumph of the steady don, who has stuck to a bachelor life, over the misguided victim to matrimony and a college living. Thus will the poor fellow lament as butchers' bills and school fees become heavier year by year:—

> Why did I sell my college life
> (He cries) for benefice and wife?
> Return, ye days when endless pleasure
> I found in reading or in leisure,
> When calm around the common room
> I puffed my daily pipe's perfume,
> Rode for a stomach, and inspected
> At annual bottlings corks selected,
> And din'd untaxed, untroubled, under
> The portrait of our pious founder!

These of course are youthful productions; but, if all tales be true, the tastes described did not die out. Once, it is said, Warton's presence was required on some grand public function. The professor was not to be found till an ingenious person suggested that a drum and fife should be sent through the streets performing a jovial and Jacobite tune; and before long the sweet notes enticed Warton from a public-house, pipe in mouth and with rumpled bands, to be miserably deceived in his hopes of fun. More creditable, and apparently more authentic, anecdotes relate how he took part in the boyish pranks of his brother's pupils at Winchester, and once at least composed a copy of Latin verses for a youthful companion, and insisted upon taking the half-crown which had been offered as a reward for their excellence before the mild imposture was detected.

Most men grow tired of pipes and ale and the jolly bachelor life of common rooms soon after they have put on their master's hood. In the old days, before commissions and reform, when the Universities were more frequently regarded as a permanent retreat for men who could find a pipe a sufficient substitute for a wife, such jolly fellows as Warton formed a larger part of the college society. Most of them, however, were duller dogs than Tom Warton, who, with all his enjoyment of such heavy festivities, managed to write some laborious books. A proud, fastidious, and exquisitely sensitive man like Gray looked upon the whole scene with infinite contempt and scorn. It does not appear to be very clearly made out why he should have resided permanently at Cambridge, except for the sake of the libraries. Apparently he had resented some of Walpole's supercilious conduct, and possibly conduct which deserves a harsher name; for it is said that Walpole opened a letter addressed to Gray in the expectation of finding some disrespectful notice of himself. Anyhow, Gray erased Walpole from his list of friends, though he consented to resume acquaintanceship. He might previously have condescended to accept some of the appointments which Walpole could have easily procured during his father's ministry. But the father was turned out of office whilst the son was a discarded friend, and Gray, unwilling to enter the struggle of professional life, settled down at the University, though he always regarded it and its inhabitants with unqualified contempt. Gray—as his letters prove—had a very keen sense of humour, and when he chose could put a very sharp edge to his tongue. He let his fellow-residents know that he thought them fools—an opinion which they were perverse enough to resent. The poem with which he greeted Cambridge on first returning from his travels, headed a "Hymn to Ignorance," is a curious contrast to Warton's enthusiastic "Triumph of Isis."

> Hail, horrors, hail! ye ever gloomy bowers,
> Ye Gothic fanes and antiquated towers,
> Where rushy Camus' slowly winding flood
> Perpetual draws his humid train of mud—

is the opening of his uncomplimentary address to his *alma mater.*

> At the very time [says Parr, in that style of delicious pomposity which smells of his immortal wig], in which Mr. Gray spoke so contemptuously of Cambridge, that very University abounded in men of erudition and science, with whom the first scholars would not have disdained to converse; and who shall convict me of exaggeration when I bring forward the names

of the immortal so-and-so? The names include, it is true, some which have still a claim upon our respect—Bentley, Waterland, and Conyers Middleton, for example—but the most eminent were just dead or dying when Gray came into residence, and dignified heads of houses, like Bentley and Waterland, were in a seventh heaven of dignity, quite inaccessible to the youthful poet. It does not now appear that it can ever have been a great privilege to live in the same town with "Provost Snape," "Tunstall the public orator," or "Asheton of Jesus." Gray knew something of Middleton (who died in 1750, when Gray was 34), and speaks of his house as the only one in Cambridge where it was easy to converse; and he takes care to add that even Middleton was only an "old acquaintance," which is but an indifferent likeness of a friend. He made a few intimacies—chiefly with younger men, like Mason, who soon ceased to be residents—but the bulk of the University was in his eyes contemptible; and, on the whole, contemporary evidence would lead to the conclusion that his opinion was not far wrong. Cambridge had possessed very eminent men in the days of Bentley, Newton, Waterland, Sherlock, and Middleton, and it has had very eminent men at a later period, but Gray was himself almost the only man in the middle of the

eighteenth century whom anybody need care to remember now. At any rate, there was a large proportion of that ale-drinking, tobacco-smoking element amongst the jolly fellows of the combination room, whose society Warton might relish, but whom Gray regarded with supreme contempt. The fellow-commoners appear by his account to have exceeded in audacity the young gentlemen who lately exhibited their sense of playful humour by defacing certain statues at Oxford. The wits of an earlier day put poor Gray in fear of his life. He ordered a rope ladder, to be able to escape from his rooms in case they set the college on fire; and, if I remember the tradition rightly, they set a "booby trap" for the poet, and, raising an alarm, induced him to descend his rope ladder into a water-butt. Anyhow, poor Gray was driven from Peterhouse to Pembroke, and there abstracted his mind from the academical noises by a course of study which, according to his admirers (but who shall answer for the admirers?), made him profoundly familiar with every branch of learning except mathematics. Meanwhile his appearance and manners were calculated to intensify the mutual dislike between himself and his rougher surroundings. His rooms were scrupulously neat, with mignonette in the windows and flowers elegantly planted in china vases; he spoke little in general society, and compiled biting epigrams or classical puns with a derisory application to his special associates. In short, in outward appearance he belonged to the class fop or *petit-maître,* mincing, precise, affected, and as little in harmony with the rowdy fellow-commoners as Hotspur's courtier with the rough soldiers on the battlefield.

The want of harmony between Gray and his surroundings goes far to explain his singular want of fertility. In fact, we may say—without any want of respect for a venerable institution—that Gray could hardly have found a more uncongenial residence. Cambridge boasts of its poets; and a University may well be proud which has had, amongst many others, such inmates as Spenser, Milton, Dryden, Gray, Coleridge, Wordsworth, Byron, and Tennyson. If a sceptic chooses to ask what share the University can claim in stimulating the genius of those illustrious men, the answer might be difficult. But, in any case, no poet except Gray loved his University well enough to become a resident. If it were not for Gray, I should be inclined to guess that a poet don was a contradiction in terms. The reason is very obvious to any one who has enjoyed the latter title. It is simply that no atmosphere can be conceived more calculated to stimulate that excessive fastidiousness which all but extinguished Gray's productive faculties. He might wrap himself in simple contempt for the ale-drinking vanity of the don. He could, in the old college slang, "sport his oak" and despise their railings, and even the shouts of "Fire!" of the worthy fellow-commoners. But a poet requires some sympathy, and, if possible, some worshippers. The inner circle of Gray's intimates was naturally composed of men fastidious like himself, and all of them more or less critics by profession. The reflection would be forced upon his mind, whenever he thought of publishing, What will be thought of my poems by Provost Snape, and Mr. Public-Orator Tunstall, and Asheton of Jesus, and those other luminaries whom Dr. Parr commemorates? And undoubtedly their first thought would be to show their claim to literary excellence by picking holes in their friend's compositions. They would rejoice greatly when they could show that faculties sharpened by the detection of false quantities and slips of grammar in their pupils' Latin verses were equal to the discovery of solecisms and defective rhymes in the work of a living poet. Gray's extreme sensitiveness to all such quillets of criticism is marked in every poem he wrote.

Had he been forced to fight his way in literature he would have learnt to swallow his scruples and take the chance in a free give-and-take struggle for fame. In a country living he might have forgotten his tormentors and have married a wife to secure at least one thoroughly appreciative and intelligent admirer. But to be shut up in a small scholastic clique, however little he might respect their individual merits, to have the chat of combination rooms ever in his ears, to be worried by bands of professional critics at every turn, was as though a singing bird should build over a wasp's nest. The *Elegy* and the *Odes* just struggled into existence, though much of them was written before he settled down as a resident; but Gray, like many another don of great abilities, finished but a minute fragment of the work of which he more or less contemplated the execution. The books contemplated but never carried out by men in his position would make a melancholy and extensive catalogue. The effect of these influences upon his work is palpable to every reader of Gray. No English poet has ever given more decisive proof that he shared that secret of clothing even an obvious thought in majestic and resounding language, which we naturally call Miltonic. Though he modestly asserts that he inherits

> Nor the pride nor ample pinion
> That the Theban eagle bear,
> Sailing with supreme dominion
> Through the azure deep of air,

yet we feel that none of his contemporaries—perhaps none of his successors—could have equalled, in dignity and richness of style, the noble passage in which that phrase occurs. And yet we must also feel that if his "car," as he says of Dryden's, is borne by "coursers of ethereal race," they are constantly checked before they can get into full career. He takes flight as if the azure deep were the natural home in which he could sail suspended like the eagle without perceptible effort. But the wings droop before they are well unfurled, and the magnificent strain ceases without giving the promised satisfaction. Even the *Elegy* flags a little towards the end; the "hoary-headed swain" becomes rather flat in his remarks, and the concluding epitaph has just a little too much twang of epigrammatic smartness. I sometimes agree, indeed, with Wolfe that it was a far greater achievement to write the *Elegy* than to storm the heights of Abram, and then hold (though I also incline to a different opinion) that only a soldier, or author, or civilian of ultra-military enthusiasm could suppose that such a comparison involved condescension on the side of the general. Gray and his personal admirers seem to have been annoyed at the preference given to this above his other writings. It proved, so he argued, that the stupid public cared for the subject instead of the art; that they liked the *Elegy* as they liked Blair's *Grave*, and would have liked it as well if the same thoughts had been expressed in prose. Undoubtedly the public will always refuse to make that distinction between form and matter which seems so important to the critical mind. It is not, however, that they are unaffected by the artistic skill, but that they are affected unconsciously. The meditations of Blair, of Young, and of Hervey, equally popular in their day, have fallen into disrepute for want of the exquisite felicity of language which has preserved the *Elegy*. It is a commonplace thing to say that the power of giving freshness to commonplace is amongst the highest proofs of poetical genius. One reason is, apparently, that it is so difficult to extract the pure and ennobling element from the coarser materials in which any obvious truth comes to be imbedded. The difficulty of feeling rightly is as great as the difficulty of finding a worthy utterance of the feeling. Every-

body may judge of the difficulty of Gray's task who will attend to what passes at a funeral. On such an occasion one is inclined to fancy, *a priori*, mourners will drop all affectation and speak poetically because they will speak from their hearts; but, as a matter of fact, there is no occasion on which there is generally such a lavish expenditure of painful and jarring sentiment, of vulgarity, affectation, and insincerity; and thus Gray's meditations stand out from other treatments of a similar theme not merely by the technical merits of the language, but by the admirable truth and purity of the underlying sentiment. The temptation to be too obtrusively moral and improving, to indulge in inappropriate epigram, in sham feeling, in idle sophistry, in strained and exaggerated gloominess, or even on occasion to heighten the effect by inappropriate humour, is so strong with most people that Gray's kindness and delicacy of feeling, qualities which were perceptible to the despised public, must be regarded as contributing quite as much to the success of the *Elegy* as the technical merits of form, which, moreover, can hardly be separated from the merits of substance.

Indeed, when we come to the other odes which have similar qualities of mere style, we are at no loss to explain the difference of reception. The beautiful "Ode upon Eton," for example, comes into conflict with one's common-sense. We know too well that an Eton boy is not always the happy and immaculate creature of Gray's fancy; and one feels that the reflections upon his probable degradation imply a fit of temporary ill-humour in the poet, supervening, no doubt, upon a deeper vein of melancholy. The sentiment is too splenetic to be pleasing. The *Bard*, which has, I suppose, been recited by schoolboys as frequently as the *Elegy*, is a more curious indication of the peculiarities of Gray's method of composition. Mason gives an account of the remarkable transformation which it underwent. Gray's first intention, it appears, was that the bard should declare prophetically that poets should never be wanting "to celebrate true virtue and valour in immortal strains, to expose vice and infamous pleasure, and boldly censure tyranny and oppression." Undoubtedly this gives a meaning to the ode worthy of the beginning. The victim could not make a more effective retort. But, unluckily, when the bard had got into full swing, it struck him that the facts were not what his theory required. Shakespeare, says Mason, liked Falstaff in spite of his vices; Milton censured tyranny in prose; Dryden was a court parasite; Pope, a Tory; and Addison, "though a Whig," was a poor poet. The poor bard was therefore in the miserable position—one of the most wretched known to humanity—of a man who has begun a fine speech and does not see his way out of it. If Gray had taken a wider view of the poet's true function, he might still have found some embodiment for his thoughts; for English poetry, though it may not have been Whiggish, may certainly be regarded as the fullest expression of the more liberal and humanising conceptions of the world which have to struggle against the pedantry and narrowness of prosaic professional theorisers. But the bard required sound Whig precedent to point his moral, and it was not forthcoming. Consequently he has to take refuge in the very scanty consolation afforded by the bare reflection that Spenser, Shakespeare, and Milton would begin to write some time after the descendants of a Welshman had ascended the throne. One would not grudge any satisfaction to an unfortunate gentleman just about to commit suicide; but one must admit that he was easily pleased.

This want of any central idea converts the ode into a set of splendid fragments of verse, which scarcely hold together. Contemporary critics complained grievously of its "obscurity"—a phrase which seems ill placed to us who know by experience what obscurity may really mean. An obscurity removable by a slight knowledge of English history and a recollection of the fact that Richard II. is said to have been starved instead of stabbed, as in Shakespeare, by Exton, is not of a very grievous kind; but the absence of any intelligible motive in the bard's final rupture is more serious. A poet surely might have acted upon the *tant pis pour les faits* theory, and proceeded to make his general assertion without waiting for confirmatory evidence. A writer who, like Gray, secretes his poetry line by line and spreads the process over years, seems to fall into the same faults which are more frequently due to haste. He pores over his conceptions so long that he becomes blind to defects obvious to a fresh observer, and rather misses his point, as he introduces minute alterations without noticing their effect on the context. One wonders how a man of Gray's exquisite perception could have introduced the lines—

> And gorgeous dames, and statesmen old
> In bearded majesty appear—

without seeing that we are only saved by a comma, and a comma easily neglected, from assuming that a Julia Pastrana would have been a usual phenomenon at the court of Elizabeth. Correction continued after the freshness of the impression has died away is apt to lead to such oversight.

The learned and fastidious don shows through the inspired "bard" by many equally unmistakable indications. His editor, Mitford, collected a number of parallel passages which curiously indicate the degree in which his mind was saturated with recollections of poetical literature. It seems to be now considered as unjustifiable plagiarism for a poet to assimilate the phrases of his predecessors. We may, indeed, find abundant proofs of familiarity with Shakespeare in Shelley, and in more recent writers; but they are generally of the unconscious kind, and would otherwise be avoided as sins against originality. The poets of the last century, such as Goldsmith, and especially Pope, had no scruples in the matter. Their work did not profess to be a sudden and spontaneous inspiration. It was a slow elaboration, with which it was perfectly allowable to interweave any quantity of previously manufactured material so long as the juncture was not palpable. Gray's adaptations seem sometimes to make the whole tissue of his poetry. He owns to an unconscious appropriation from Green (author of the *Spleen*) of the main thought of his "Ode to the Spring," the comparison of men to ephemeral insects. But everywhere he is giving out phrases which he has previously assimilated. So in the very spirited translation from the Norse, "Uprose the king of men with speed," we have a verse from the "Allegro"—"Right against the Eastern Gate"—cropping up naturally in quite a fresh connection. A single phrase seems to combine several semi-conscious recollections. The words in the *Bard*, "dear as the ruddy drops that warm my heart" come from Shakespeare, and the preceding "dear as the light that visits those sad eyes" are perhaps from Otway. But it is useless to accumulate instances of so palpable a process.

It is only in character, again, that Gray should have clung to a peculiar dictum, as he would have insisted upon wearing his proper academical costume in a performance in the senate-house. He would no more have dropped into Wordsworth's vernacular than he would have smoked a pipe in one of Warton's pot-houses. Wordsworth considered this dignity to be unnatural pomposity; and undoubtedly the language is frequently conventional and "unnatural," and a stumbling-block of offence to the generation which gave up wigs. Equally annoying was Gray's immense delight in semi-allegorical figures. We have whole catalogues of abstract qualities scarcely personified. Ambition, bitter Scorn, grinning Infamy, Falsehood, hard Unkindness, keen Remorse, and moody Madness are all collected in one stanza not exceptional in style—beings which to us are almost as offensive as the muse whom he has pretty well ceased to invoke, though he still appeals to his lyre. This fashion reached its culminating point in the celebrated invocation somewhere recorded by Coleridge, "Inoculation, heavenly maid!" The personified qualities are a kind of fading "survival"—ghosts of the old allegorical persons who put on a rather more solid clothing of flesh and blood with Spenser, and with Gray scarcely putting in a stronger claim to vitality than is implied in the use of capital letters. The "muses" were nearly extinct, and in Pope's time the gods and goddesses had come to be regarded as so much "machinery" invented by Homer to work his epic poetry. They were, in fact, passions and qualities in masquerade; and they therefore found it very easy, in the next generation, to drop even this thin disguise, and fit themselves for poetic usage, not by taking the name of a pagan deity, but by a simple typographical device.

What would Gray have done under more congenial circumstances if he produced such inimitable fragments under such adverse conditions—when his learning threatened to choke his fire, when his exquisite taste was pampered with excessive fastidiousness, and his temper and position alienated him from the most vigorous intellectual movement of the day? Perhaps—for the region of the might-have-been is boundless—he would have produced a masterpiece of the "grand style," worthy of a place by Milton's finest work; or, as possibly, he would have done nothing. It is an amusing exercise of the imagination to place our favourite authors in different countries and centuries, and to trace their hypothetical development a century earlier. I fancy that Gray would have buried himself still more profoundly from the political convulsions which attracted Milton's sterner and more active spirit; he would have studied Plotinus and Maimonides, and found sympathetic companionship amongst the Cambridge Platonists; he would have written some fragment of semi-mystical reverie, showing stupendous learning and philosophic breadth of thought, and possibly have composed some divine poems for the admiration of Henry More or John Norris. Warton, doubtless, would at any period have enjoyed Oxford ale, and joined in the jolly song, "Back and side go bare, go bare;" he would have sometimes accompanied Burton on the rambles where he was thrown into fits of laughter by listening to the ribaldry of the bargees at the bridge end; he would still have been an antiquarian, and his note-book might have contributed quaint scraps of learning to the *Anatomy of Melancholy*. Mason, anxious not to sink the man of the world in the country parson, would have racked his unfortunate brains for conceits worthy to be placed beside the most fashionable compositions of Donne or Cowley. Horace Walpole would, of course, have been at any time the prince of gossips; he would have kept most judiciously on the safe side in the most dangerous revolutions, and have come just near enough to collect the most interesting scandals in the courts of the Stuarts; but probably his lively intellect would have led him to drop in occasionally at the meetings of the infant Royal Society, and to have been one of the early cultivators of a taste for ancient marbles or a judicious patron of Vandyke. It is, perhaps, harder to assign the precise place in our own days, when the separate niches are not so distinctly marked off, and even the universities scarcely afford a satisfactory refuge for the would-be recluse; but at least one may assume that each of them would have been æsthetic to his fingers' ends, and have been thoroughly on a level with the last new developments of taste, whether for mediæval architecture or the art of the Renaissance, or that style which is called after Queen Anne. The snapdragon which Cardinal Newman saw from his windows of Trinity, and took for the emblem of his perpetual residence in the University, was probably flourishing when Warton's residence in the same college ceased; and Warton, in spite of that love of ale which is perhaps more prominent than it should be in our impressions of his character, would beyond all doubt have been a member of that school of which his successor was the greatest ornament, and which has given a new meaning to the old phrase "High Church." It was amongst the Wartons and their friends that the word "Gothic," used by earlier writers as a simple term of abuse, came to have a more appreciative meaning; they were the originators of the so-called romanticism made popular by Scott, and which counts for so much in the Anglo-Catholic development.

MATTHEW ARNOLD
From "Thomas Gray"
The English Poets, ed. Thomas Humphry Ward
1880, Volume 3, pp. 303–16

James Brown, Master of Pembroke Hall at Cambridge, Gray's friend and executor, in a letter written a fortnight after Gray's death to another of his friends, Dr. Wharton of Old Park, Durham, has the following passage:—

'Everything is now dark and melancholy in Mr. Gray's room, not a trace of him remains there; it looks as if it had been for some time uninhabited, and the room bespoke for another inhabitant. The thoughts I have of him will last, and will be useful to me the few years I can expect to live. He never spoke out, but I believe from some little expressions I now remember to have dropped from him, that for some time past he thought himself nearer his end than those about him apprehended.'

He never spoke out. In these four words is contained the whole history of Gray, both as a man and as a poet. The words fell naturally, and as it were by chance, from their writer's pen; but let us dwell upon them, and press into their meaning, for in following it we shall come to understand Gray.

He was in his fifty-fifth year when he died, and he lived in ease and leisure, yet a few pages hold all his poetry; *he never spoke out* in poetry. Still, the reputation which he has achieved by his few pages is extremely high. True, Johnson speaks of him with coldness and disparagement. Gray disliked Johnson, and refused to make his acquaintance; one might fancy that Johnson wrote with some irritation from this cause. But Johnson was not by nature fitted to do justice to Gray and to his poetry; this by itself is a sufficient explanation of the deficiencies of his criticism of Gray. We may add a further explanation of them which is supplied by Mr. Cole's papers. 'When Johnson was publishing his Life of Gray,' says Mr. Cole, 'I gave him several anecdotes, *but he was very anxious as soon as possible to get to the end of his labours.*' Johnson was not naturally in sympathy with Gray, whose life he had to write, and when he wrote it he was in a hurry besides. He did Gray injustice, but even Johnson's authority failed to make injustice, in this case, prevail. Lord Macaulay calls the Life of Gray the worst of Johnson's Lives, and it had found many censurers before Macaulay. Gray's poetical reputation grew and flourished in spite of it. The poet Mason, his first biographer, in his epitaph equalled him with Pindar. Britain has known, says Mason,

a Homer's fire in Milton's strains,
A Pindar's rapture in the lyre of Gray.

The immense vogue of Pope and of his style of versification had at first prevented the frank reception of Gray by the readers of poetry. The *Elegy* pleased; it could not but please: but Gray's poetry, on the whole, astonished his contemporaries at first more than it pleased them; it was so unfamiliar, so unlike the sort of poetry in vogue. It made its way, however, after his death, with the public as well as with the few; and Gray's second biographer, Mitford, remarks that 'the works which were either neglected or ridiculed by their contemporaries have now raised Gray and Collins to the rank of our two greatest lyric poets.' Their reputation was established, at any rate, and stood extremely high, even if they were not popularly read. Johnson's disparagement of Gray was called 'petulant,' and severely blamed. Beattie, at the end of the eighteenth century, writing to Sir William Forbes, says: 'Of all the English poets of this age Mr. Gray is most admired, and I think with justice.' Cowper writes: 'I have been reading Gray's works, and think him the only poet since Shakespeare entitled to the character of sublime. Perhaps you will remember that I once had a different opinion of him. I was prejudiced.' Adam Smith says: 'Gray joins to the sublimity of Milton the elegance and harmony of Pope; and nothing is wanting to render him, perhaps, the first poet in the English language, but to have written a little more.' And, to come nearer to our own times, Sir James Mackintosh speaks of Gray thus: 'Of all English poets he was the most finished artist. He attained the highest degree of splendour of which poetical style seemed to be capable.'

In a poet of such magnitude, how shall we explain his scantiness of production? Shall we explain it by saying that to make of Gray a poet of this magnitude is absurd; that his genius and resources were small and that his production, therefore, was small also, but that the popularity of a single piece, the *Elegy*,—a popularity due in great measure to the subject,—created for Gray a reputation to which he has really no right? He himself was not deceived by the favour shown to the *Elegy*. 'Gray told me with a good deal of acrimony,' writes Dr. Gregory, 'that the *Elegy* owed its popularity entirely to the subject, and that the public would have received it as well if it had been written in prose.' This is too much to say; the *Elegy* is a beautiful poem, and in admiring it the public showed a true feeling for poetry. But it is true that the *Elegy* owed much of its success to its subject, and that it has received a too unmeasured and unbounded praise.

Gray himself, however, maintained that the *Elegy* was not his best work in poetry, and he was right. High as is the praise due to the *Elegy*, it is yet true that in other productions of Gray he exhibits poetical qualities even higher than those exhibited in the *Elegy*. He deserves, therefore, his extremely high reputation as a poet, although his critics and the public may not always have praised him with perfect judgment. ⟨. . .⟩

Bonstetten, that mercurial Swiss who died in 1832 at the age of eighty-seven, having been younger and livelier from his sixtieth year to his eightieth than at any other time in his life, paid a visit in his early days to Cambridge, and saw much of Gray, to whom he attached himself with devotion. Gray, on his part, was charmed with his young friend; 'I never saw such a boy,' he writes; 'our breed is not made on this model.' Long afterwards, Bonstetten published his reminiscences of Gray. 'I used to tell Gray,' he says, 'about my life and my native country, but *his* life was a sealed book to me; he never would talk of himself, never would allow me to speak to him of his poetry. If I quoted lines of his to him, he kept silence like an obstinate child. I said to him sometimes: "Will you have the goodness to give me an answer?" But not a word issued from his lips.' *He never spoke out.* Bonstetten thinks that Gray's life was poisoned by an unsatisfied sensibility, was withered by his having never loved; by his days being passed in the dismal cloisters of Cambridge, in the company of a set of monastic bookworms, 'whose existence no honest woman ever came to cheer.' Sainte-Beuve, who was much attracted and interested by Gray, doubts whether Bonstetten's explanation of him is admissible; the secret of Gray's melancholy he finds rather in the sterility of his poetic talent, 'so distinguished, so rare, but so stinted;' in the poet's despair at his own unproductiveness.

But to explain Gray, we must do more than allege his sterility, as we must look further than to his reclusion at Cambridge. What caused his sterility? Was it his ill-health, his hereditary gout? Certainly we will pay all respect to the powers of hereditary gout for afflicting us poor mortals. But Goethe, after pointing out that Schiller, who was so productive, was 'almost constantly ill,' adds the true remark that it is incredible how much the spirit can do, in these cases, to keep up the body. Pope's animation and activity through all the course of what he pathetically calls 'that long disease, my life,' is an example presenting itself signally, in Gray's own country and time, to confirm what Goethe here says. What gave the power to Gray's reclusion and ill-health to induce his sterility?

The reason, the indubitable reason as I cannot but think it, I have already given elsewhere. Gray, a born poet, fell upon an age of prose. He fell upon an age whose task was such as to call forth in general men's powers of understanding, wit and cleverness, rather than their deepest powers of mind and soul. As regards literary production, the task of the eighteenth century in England was not the poetic interpretation of the world, its task was to create a plain, clear, straightforward, efficient prose. Poetry obeyed the bent of mind requisite for the due fulfilment of this task of the century. It was intellectual, argumentative, ingenious; not seeing things in their truth and beauty, not interpretative. Gray, with the qualities of mind and soul of a genuine poet, was isolated in his century. Maintaining and fortifying them by lofty studies, he yet could not fully educe and enjoy them; the want of a genial atmosphere, the failure of sympathy in his contemporaries, were too great. Born in the same year with Milton, Gray would have been another man; born in the same year with Burns, he would have been another man. A man born in 1608 could profit by the larger and more poetic scope of the English spirit in the Elizabethan age; a man born in 1759 could profit by that European renewing of men's minds of which the great historical manifestation is the French Revolution. Gray's alert and brilliant young friend, Bonstetten, who would explain the void in the life of Gray by his having never loved, Bonstetten himself loved, married, and had children. Yet at the age of fifty he was bidding fair to grow old, dismal and torpid like the rest of us, when he was roused and made young again for some thirty years, says M. Sainte-Beuve, by the events of 1789. If Gray, like Burns, had been just thirty years old when the French Revolution broke out, he would have shown, probably, productiveness and animation in plenty. Coming when he did and endowed as he was, he was a man born out of date, a man whose full spiritual flowering was impossible. The same thing is to be said of his great contemporary, Butler, the author of the *Analogy*. In the sphere of religion, which touches that of poetry, Butler was impelled by the endowment of his nature to strive for a profound and adequate conception of religious things, which was not pursued by his contemporaries, and which at that time, and in that atmosphere of mind, was not

fully attainable. Hence, in Butler too, a dissatisfaction, a weariness, as in Gray; 'great labour and weariness, great disappointment, pain and even vexation of mind.' A sort of spiritual east wind was at that time blowing; neither Butler nor Gray could flower. They *never spoke out.*

Gray's poetry was not only stinted in quantity by reason of the age wherein he lived, it suffered somewhat in quality also. We have seen under what obligation to Dryden Gray professed himself to be; 'if there was any excellence in his numbers, he had learned it wholly from that great poet.' It was not for nothing that he came when Dryden had lately 'embellished,' as Johnson says, English poetry; had 'found it brick and left it marble.' It was not for nothing that he came just when 'the English ear,' to quote Johnson again, 'had been accustomed to the mellifluence of Pope's numbers, and the diction of poetry had grown more splendid.' Of the intellectualities, ingenuities, personifications, of the movement and diction of Dryden and Pope, Gray caught something, caught too much. We have little of Gray's poetry, and that little is not free from the faults of his age. Therefore it was important to go for aid, as we did, to Gray's life and letters, to see his mind and soul there, and to corroborate from thence that high estimate of his quality which his poetry, indeed, calls forth, but does not establish so amply and irresistibly as one could desire.

For a just criticism it does, however, clearly establish it. The difference between genuine poetry and the poetry of Dryden, Pope, and all their school, is briefly this; their poetry is conceived and composed in their wits, genuine poetry is conceived and composed in the soul. The difference between the two kinds of poetry is immense. They differ profoundly in their modes of language, they differ profoundly in their modes of evolution. The poetic language of our eighteenth century in general is the language of men composing *without their eye on the object*, as Wordsworth excellently said of Dryden; language merely recalling the object, as the common language of prose does, and then dressing it out with a certain smartness and brilliancy for the fancy and understanding. This is called 'splendid diction.' The evolution of the poetry of our eighteenth century is likewise intellectual; it proceeds by ratiocination, antithesis, ingenious turns and conceits. This poetry is often eloquent, and always, in the hands of such masters as Dryden and Pope, clever; but it does not take us much below the surface of things, it does not give us the emotion of seeing things in their truth and beauty. The language of genuine poetry, on the other hand, is the language of one composing with his eye on the object; its evolution is that of a thing which has been plunged in the poet's soul until it comes forth naturally and necessarily. This sort of evolution is infinitely simpler than the other, and infinitely more satisfying; the same thing is true of the genuine poetic language likewise. But they are both of them, also, infinitely harder of attainment; they come only from those who, as Emerson says, 'live from a great depth of being.'

Goldsmith disparaged Gray who had praised his *Traveller*, and indeed in the poem on the 'Alliance of Education and Government' had given him hints which he used for it. In retaliation let us take from Goldsmith himself a specimen of the poetic language of the eighteenth century.

No cheerful murmurs fluctuate in the gale—

there is exactly the poetic diction of our prose century! rhetorical, ornate,—and, poetically, quite false. Place beside it a line of genuine poetry, such as the

In cradle of the rude, imperious surge

of Shakespeare; and all its falseness instantly becomes apparent.

Dryden's poem on the death of Mrs. Killigrew is, says Johnson, 'undoubtedly the noblest ode that our language ever has produced.' In this vigorous performance Dryden has to say, what is interesting enough, that not only in poetry did Mrs. Killigrew excel, but she excelled in painting also. And thus he says it:—

> To the next realm she stretch'd her sway,
> For Painture near adjoining lay—
> A plenteous province and alluring prey.
> A Chamber of Dependencies was framed
> (As conquerors will never want pretence
> When arm'd, to justify the offence).
> And the whole fief, in right of Poetry, she claim'd.

The intellectual, ingenious, superficial evolution of poetry of this school could not be better illustrated. Place beside it Pindar's

αἰὼν ἀσφαλὴς
οὐκ ἔγεντ' οὔτ' Αἰακίδα παρὰ Πηλει,
οὔτε παρ' ἀντιθέῳ Κάδμῳ . . .

> A secure time fell to the lot neither of Peleus the son of Æacus nor of the godlike Cadmus; howbeit these are said to have had, of all mortals, the supreme of happiness, who heard the golden snooded Muses sing,—on the mountain the one heard them, the other in seven-gated Thebes.

There is the evolution of genuine poetry, and such poetry kills Dryden's the moment it is put near it.

Gray's production was scanty, and scanty, as we have seen, it could not but be. Even what he produced is not always pure in diction, true in evolution. Still, with whatever drawbacks, he is alone or almost alone (for Collins has something of the like merit) in his age. Gray said himself that 'the style he aimed at was extreme conciseness of expression, yet pure, perspicuous, and musical.' Compared, not with the work of the great masters of the golden ages of poetry, but with the poetry of his own contemporaries in general, Gray's may be said to have reached, in his style, the excellence at which he aimed; while the evolution, also, of such a piece as his *Progress of Poesy*, must be accounted not less noble and sound than its style.

A. C. BENSON

"Thomas Gray" (1888)

Essays (1896)

1907, pp. 119–46

Every boy who leaves Eton creditably is presented with a copy of the works of Gray, for which everything has been done that the art of printers, bookbinders and photographers can devise. This is one of the most curious instances of the triumphs of genius, for there is hardly a single figure in the gallery of Etonians who is so little characteristic of Eton as Gray. His only poetical utterance about his school is one which is hopelessly alien to the spirit of the place, though the feelings expressed in it are an exquisite summary of those sensations of pathetic interest which any rational man feels at the sight of a great school. And yet, though the attitude of the teacher of youth is professedly and rightly rather that of encouragement than of warning, though he points to the brighter hopes of life rather than brandishes the horrors that

infest it, yet the last word that Eton says to her sons is spoken in the language of one to whom elegy was a habitual and deliberate tone.

Gray's was in many ways a melancholy life. His vitality was low, and such happiness as he enjoyed was of a languid kind. Physically and emotionally he was unfit to cope with realities, and this though he never felt the touch of some of the most crushing evils that humanity sustains. He was never poor, he was never despised, he had many devoted friends; but on the other hand he had a wretched and diseased constitution, he suffered from all sorts of prostrating complaints, from imaginary insolences, violent antipathies, and want of sympathy. Fame such as is rarely accorded to men came to him: he was accepted as without doubt the first of living English poets; but he took no kind of pleasure in it. He was horrified to find himself a celebrity; he declined to be Poet Laureate; he refused honorary degrees; when at Cambridge the young scholars are said to have left their dinners to see him as he passed in the street, it was a sincere pain to him. Cowper counterbalanced his fits of unutterable melancholy by his hours of tranquil serenity over teacups and muffins and warm coal-fires, with the curtains drawn close. Johnson enlivened his boding depression by tyrannizing over an adoring circle. But Gray's only compensations were his friends. Any one who knows Gray's letters to and about his young friend Bonstetten, knows how close and warm it is possible for friendship to be.

No biography is more simple than Gray's. From Eton he passed to Cambridge, which was practically his home for the rest of his life. He went as a young man on a long foreign tour of nearly three years with Horace Walpole, quarrelled, and came back alone, both afterwards claiming to have been in the wrong; he travelled in England and Scotland a little; he lived a little in London and a good deal at Stoke Poges, where he kept a perfect menagerie of aged aunts, and he died somewhat prematurely at the age of fifty. He spent in all more than twenty years at Cambridge—the only event that interrupted his life there being his move from Peterhouse to Pembroke, across the road, in consequence of an offensive practical joke played on him by some undergraduates, who, working on his morbid dread of fire, induced him by their cries to leave the window of his room by means of a rope-ladder, and descend into a tub of water placed ready for this purpose. The authorities at Peterhouse seem to have made no sort of attempt to punish this wanton outrage, nor to have been anxious to keep him at their college.

So he lived on at Cambridge, hating the "silly dirty place," as he calls it. The atmosphere, physical and mental, weighed on his spirits with leaden dulness. In one of his early letters he speaks of it as the land indicated by the prophet, where the ruined houses were full of owls and doleful creatures. He often could not bring himself to go there, and once there, his spirits sank so low that he could not prevail on himself to move. Almost the only part he took in the public life of the place was to write and circulate squibs and lampoons on people and local politics, most of which have fortunately perished; those that remain are coarse and vindictive. Nevertheless he had some true friends there: Mason, his worshipper and biographer, Dr. Brown, the Master of Pembroke, in whose arms he died, and several others. He held no office there and did no work for the place, till late in his life the Professorship of Modern History, a mere sinecure, for which he had unsuccessfully applied six years previously, came to him unsolicited. It was his aim throughout to be considered a gentleman who read for his own amusement, and with that curious fastidiousness which was so characteristic of him, he considered it beneath him to receive money for his writings, the copyrights of which he bestowed upon his publisher. Forty pounds for a late edition of his poems is said to be the only money of this kind that he ever handled. But he was, as has been said, well off, at least in his later years. He had a country-house at Wanstead which he let, a house in Cornhill, property at Stoke, and, though he sank some money in a large annuity, he died worth several thousand pounds.

It might be thought that such a life, meagre and solitary as it was, would furnish few details to a biographer, and this is to a certain extent true; but about Gray there is a peculiar atmosphere of attractiveness. He went his own way, thought his own thoughts, and did not concern himself in the least with the ordinary life of people round about him, except to despise them. This disdainful attitude is always an attractive one. The recluse stimulates curiosity; and when we pass behind the scenes and see the high purity of the life, the wide and deep ideals always floating before such a man, the wonder grows. He lived unconsciously at so high a level that he could not conceive how low and animal lives were possible to men; he owned to no physical impulses; he held that there was no knowledge unworthy of the philosopher, except theology; and over the whole of his existence hung that shadow of doom which lends a pathetic interest to the lives of the meanest of mankind.

When such a man is the author of the most famous poem of pure sentiment in the English language, as well as of smaller pieces by which some readers are fascinated, most impressed, and each of which has enriched the world with one or more eternal phrases, our interest is indefinitely increased, because isolation only ceases to be interesting when it is self-absorbed and self-centred. Gray, on the other hand, suppressed himself so effectually in his writings that he even caused them for some readers to forfeit that personal interest that is so attractive to most. "We are all condemned," he says, "to lonely grief,"— "the tender for another's pain, the unfeeling for his own;" one of the latter could never have written these words.

The deeper that we enter into such a life, the more fascinating it becomes. All Gray's tastes were natural and yet high; whatever he sets his hand to ceases to be dull; he had a transfiguring touch, he was moreover a strangely unconscious precursor of modern tastes and fancies, in such things as his self-created taste for architecture and antiquities, by communicating which to Horace Walpole (for Gray's influence can be surely traced in Horace's artistic development) he succeeded in making fashionable; his dignified preferences in art, his rapturous devotion to music, especially to Pergolesi and the contemporary Roman school, whose airs he would sit crooning to himself, playing his own accompaniment on the harpsichord in the high unvisited rooms at Pembroke; his penchant for heraldry, his educational theories, his minute and accurate investigations of Nature, as close and loving as Gilbert White's, recording as he does the break of dry clear weather into warm wet winds, the first flight of ladybirds, the first push of crocuses, the first time he heard the redstart's note in the bushes and the thrush fluting about the butts of the old college gardens, "scattering," as he said in a lovely impromptu line that he made in a walk near Cambridge, "her loose notes in the waste of air." In 1740 he wrote from Florence to a friend:

"To me there hardly appears any medium between a public life and a private one; he who prefers the first must feel himself in a way of being serviceable to the rest of mankind, if he has a mind to be of any consequence among them. Nay, he must not refuse being in a certain degree dependent upon some men who are so already; if he has the good fortune to light on

such as will make no ill use of his humility, there is no shame in this. If not, his ambition ought to give place to a reasonable pride, and he should apply to the cultivation of his own mind those abilities which he has not been permitted to use for others' service; such a private happiness (supposing a small competence of fortune) is almost in every one's power, and is the proper enjoyment of age, as the other is the proper employment of youth."

And this was the programme to which Gray settled down. In what vast schemes of study he indulged we do not know; but we do know that he gave five years to a comprehensive survey of Greek literature, taking prose and verse alternately, like bread and cheese; he contemplated and wrote notes for an edition of Strabo; he translated many Greek epigrams into Latin verse, curiously weighing his words for weeks together; he read history exhaustively, with such tenacious accuracy that he could correct in the margin with the everlasting pencil dates and names in a Chinese dynasty—"a dismal waste of energy and power," sigh his biographers. No, it was no waste, for this was Gray. He wrote no more poetry, except a few "autumnal verses" still unidentified. He could not write any. Mr. Matthew Arnold, in his delicate essay, blames the age for this; he puts Gray's reticence down to a want of literary sympathy and intellectual stimulus. Had Gray been born with Milton or with Burns, he says he would have been a different man. We may thankfully doubt it. Gray's nature, Gray's powers of production, would have been far more liable to be crushed into extinction by the consciousness of the existence of a superior artist, fluent and sublime. He would have read and wondered, and thrown aside his pen. The fact that he could strike out better verse and nobler thoughts than his contemporaries, though it did not urge him to prolific production, made him at least not ashamed of work that gained by comparison with the work of all living artists; but a genius on the scene would have elbowed Gray out altogether. To take the very first instance that comes to hand of his fastidious discontent, consider the two exquisite stanzas which he struck out of the *Elegy* for no more adequate reason than that "they made too long a parenthesis."

There scattered oft, the earliest of the year,
  By hands unseen, are showers of violets found;
The redbreast loves to build and warble there,
  And little footsteps lightly print the ground.

Him have we seen the greenwood side along,
  While o'er the heath we hied, our labours done,
Oft as the woodlark piped her farewell song,
  With wistful eyes pursue the setting sun.

Akenside or Mason, Dyer or Armstrong, if they had lit upon any one of these delightful lines, would have made a whole poem in which to set it, and have been well content.

Perhaps his own words best describe the intrinsic characteristics of his writings: "Thoughts that breathe and words that burn." Gray's thoughts, the elegiac poet's thoughts, are common property, after all; every one has felt them, or something like them; the poet has got, so to speak, to make a formula which shall cover all the vague, blind variations of which every one is conscious. When he has thus made thought live, expression comes next, and here Gray surpasses almost every English poet. The words literally eat their way into memory and imagination; the epithets seize upon the nouns and crown them. Take such a stanza as the one to which Dr. Johnson gave a grudging admiration:

For who to dumb forgetfulness a prey,
  This pleasing anxious being e'er resigned,

Left the warm precincts of the cheerful day,
   Nor cast one longing lingering look behind?

Try the effect of substitution or suppression on a stanza like that! Nothing can be spared; the gap if created could not be filled. A good instance of this is in a little posthumous poem of Gray's, written on a sheet of paper from which the lower right-hand corner has been unfortunately torn, thus depriving the last three lines of the last stanza of their last words. Both Mason and Mitford tried their hands at restoring the text. Mason's is the best, but they are both hopelessly far away. The lines run thus, Mitford's emendations being given above Mason's.

Enough to me if to some feeling breast
             convey,
My lines a secret sympathy impart,
              is exprest
And as the pleasing influence flows confest
           dies away.
A sigh of soft reflection heaves the heart.

The only thing of which we feel certain is that neither is near the truth.

It is not only in Gray's poetry that this sure touch is visible. I do not know any more simple or yet more worthy epitaph than the one that he wrote for his mother. "In the same pious confidence, beside her friend and sister, sleep the remains of Dorothy Gray, widow, the careful tender mother of many children, one of whom alone had the misfortune to survive her." Given the circumstances and, so to speak, the sense, how many people could have produced such an ideal of tender dignity?

It is not within the scope of these essays to make large quotations, but page after page of Gray's letters illustrate this felicitous and apposite handling. In Horace Walpole's quaint diction: "His letters are the best I ever saw, and had more novelty and wit." But besides the perfection of style they have a charming meditative tone, combined with a certain subtle humour running through them. Moreover, Gray exercised to the full the privilege of allusion. Out of his teeming mind, echoes and memories, images and unsuspected likenesses streamed, encircling all that he thought or wrote. The perfection of classical culture, the departure of which we cannot help deploring, even though it may have been succeeded by a wider and freer sentiment, is seen in him; not only are his quotations exquisite, but there is a forgotten music which haunts his sentences and words, even in the very nicknames with which it was his delight to dub his friends.

I venture to quote the exquisite description of Burnham Beeches, which cannot be too well-known.

"I have, at the distance of half a mile through a green lane, a forest (the vulgar call it a common) all my own, at least as good as so, for I spy no human thing in it but myself. It is a little chaos of mountains and precipices, mountains, it is true, that do not ascend much above the clouds, nor are the declivities quite so amazing as Dover Cliff, but just such hills as people who love their necks as well as I do may venture to climb, and crags that give the eye as much pleasure as if they were more dangerous. Both vale and hill are covered with most venerable beeches and other very reverend vegetables, that like most other ancient people are always *dreaming out their old stories to the winds.* At the foot of one of these squats ME (Il Penseroso), and there I grow to the trunk for a whole morning. The timorous hare and sportive squirrel gambol around me like Adam in Paradise before he had an Eve, but I think he did not use to read Virgil as I commonly do."

In this letter emerges that fact which at least no one disputes, that Gray discovered and introduced the taste for natural scenery. He was nearly the first to love the hills and woods for themselves. He found out Wordsworth's favourite prospects in the lakes when Wordsworth was a dumb baby; he gazed upon Scotland and the Alps with a reverent awe. It was a time when writers about Nature's loveliness were accustomed to describe her with their back to the study-window, and the only Nature that such men as Shenstone and Akenside revelled in was Nature as they had themselves adapted her. Gray was the first to take her as he found her.

To any one who is familiar with it, the quiet Buckinghamshire country where Gray lived comes to have a peculiar charm. Lower down, nearer the Thames, the land is oppressively flat, but Burnham and Stoke are on higher ground, broken into innumerable little undulations, with copses in the hollows, and little lanes, meandering about for no apparent purpose except their own pleasure. It is a gravel soil, and immemorial excavations which indent the surfaces of all the hills and fields give a pleasant character to the whole. The wayfarer is for ever looking down into pits full nearly to the brim of ferns and brambles, elder plants and young ash-suckers; the great bare sweeps of the fields, with the rounded gravel lying thick among the thin vegetation, are broken by little hollows full of ragwort and the brisk hardy bugloss and a dozen other light-soil plants. Of Burnham Beeches itself it is unnecessary to speak. The old wreathed trunks full of gaping mouths and eyes, standing in the green twilight knee-deep in ferns, have a character that no other trees wear, and the breaks of moorland scenery, heathery sweeps dotted with tall fir spinnies, out of which the owls call on summer nights—all this is true forest, and needs no praise; but the roads and lanes themselves, with the venerable hump-backed Buckinghamshire cottages, with houseleek and stonecrop on the roof, the moated farms, the parks set with noble cedars, the high-shouldered barns, all these are full of delight. The pedestrian may climb the long slope to Burnham and gaze up its straggling red-brick street; the quaint cupola of the church, familiar to Gray, has lately, alas! fallen before a whirlwind of restoration, and given place to a neat spire; he may pass on to Britwell, a house, half-grange, half-mansion, with a modern tower, where Gray used to live with his gouty uncle, a Nimrod *emeritus,* who, too broken to ride out, used to regale himself upon the "comfortable sound and stink" of his hounds. The elm-girt paddocks and the tall plane-trees must be much as they were then. By Nut Hall, with its close of ancient walnuts, he may pass through East Burnham village, and finally descend upon Stoke itself by West-end House, still nestling in trees, where Gray was petted and coddled by his old aunts till he was too lazy even to go down to Eton, which lay full in view from the brow that spread half a mile below him. The tall chimneys of the manor, the hideous white dome of the park, the church ivy-girt and irregular, the churchyard surrounded by old brick walls on three sides, over which tower the foliage of yews and cedars—all these he may see. The only memorial of Gray, save a tablet, is the one thing which he himself would have loathed. On a rising ground stands a huge cube of stone with marble panels, crowned with a sarcophagus of the kind that suggests a hopeless prisoner for ever trying to force up the lid. This was the best that they could do for Gray!

It is only quite lately that the aid of Mr. Thornycroft, a sculptor of a genius akin to Gray's, has been invoked to decorate her hall with a worthy monument of the poet.

Shelley's letters are said by some to be the best ever written, but I cannot think that they come near to Gray's. With that independence so characteristic of him, Gray and Horace Walpole are perhaps the only writers of the time who entirely escape the Johnsonian contagion. Johnson's style, as written by Johnson himself, has indeed most of the elements of magnificence; unfortunately it is also very useful for concealing the absence of ideas. Gray's English, on the other hand, is pure and stately, and never diffuse; he said what he had to say and was done with it; he never appears to be endeavouring to "get in diction," as so many of the imitators of the Doctor undeniably did. In this respect it resembles Johnson's conversation, and for the art of statement it is hardly possible to say more.

Some slight affectation is traceable in the earliest letters. They are mostly written to his young and brilliant friend, West, by whose premature death literature, we may believe, was a loser. "Take my word and experience upon it," he writes for example, "doing nothing is a most amusing business, and yet neither something nor nothing give me any pleasure. For this little while past I have been playing at Statius. We yesterday had a game of quoits together. You will easily forgive me for having broke his head, as you have a little pique with him." He means to say that he has been translating him. West replies in the same strain. "I agree with you that you have broke Statius' head, but it is in like manner as Apollo broke Hyacinth's—you have foiled him infinitely at his own weapons."

This is sad posturing, and only excusable in very young and clever men. These letters are, however, fortunately relieved by a short note, in which he is very humanly rude to his tutor.

As a specimen of the early style at its best, I may quote the following, written from Rome in imitation of a classical epistle:

"I am to-day just returned from Alba, a good deal fatigued, for you know the Appian is somewhat tiresome. We dined at Pompey's; he indeed was gone for a few days to his Tusculan, but by the care of his villicus we made an admirable meal. We had the dugs of a pregnant sow, a peacock, a dish of thrushes, a noble scarus just fresh from the Tyrrhene, and some conchylia of the lake with garum sauce. For my part I never eat better at Lucullus' table. We drank half a dozen cyathi apiece of ancient Alban to Pholoe's health, and after bathing and playing an hour at ball, we mounted our essedum again, and proceeded up the mount to the temple. The priests there entertained us with an account of a wonderful shower of birds' eggs that had fallen two days before, which had no sooner touched the ground but they were converted into gudgeons; as also that the night past a dreadful voice had been heard out of the Adytum, which spoke Greek during a full half hour, but nobody understood it."

That is nothing short of admirable; it catches the subtle classical flavour, and intermingles it with the later humour of which the Roman mind seemed so singularly destitute.

Among these earlier letters, however, there are charming passages in his natural manner. What could be better than this humorous description of Peterhouse and his life there?

"My motions at present (which you are pleased to ask after) are much like those of a pendulum or oscillatory. I swing from Chapel or Hall home, and from home to Chapel or Hall. All the strange incidents that happen in my journeys and returns I shall be sure to acquaint you with. The most wonderful is that it now rains exceedingly; this has refreshed the prospect, as the way for the most part lies between green fields on either hand terminated with buildings at some distance—castles I presume, and of great antiquity. The roads are very good, being as I presume the work of Julius Cæsar's army, for they still preserve in many places the appearance of a pavement in pretty good repair, and if they were not so near home, might perhaps be as much admired as the Via Appia. There are at present several rivulets to be crossed, and which serve to enliven the view all around; the country is exceeding fruitful in ravens and such black cattle; but not to trouble you with my travels I abruptly conclude."

But perhaps the most striking characteristic throughout the whole series are the extraordinarily felicitous criticisms, and the soundness of the taste which he brought to bear on an author. It is true he made mistakes; he spoke of Collins as a writer that deserved to live, but that would not; and he, like many other clever men, was carried off his feet by the rage for Ossian. Like other critics he was misled by the accounts of interviews with Macpherson, who appeared to be a dull, unintelligent person, incapable of originating or of putting together even such a composition as *Fingal*; besides, the difficulty of getting solid testimony on the subject seems to have been extreme. Gray's last word on the subject is: "For me, I admire nothing but *Fingal*, yet I remain still in doubt about the authenticity of these poems, though inclining to believe them genuine in spite of the world. Whether they are the inventions of antiquity, or of a modern Scotchman, either case is to me alike unaccountable. *Je m'y perds.*" We, nowadays, with all the barbarous treasures of Indian and Scandinavian literatures about us, find it hard to understand how fascinating the opening of such a mine must have been, even when the ore extracted was such thin stuff as Ossian; the old rude primitive world, as simple as Homer, fighting and singing in desolate Northern forests, seems to have been altogether too much even for the discrimination of Gray; his imagination was taken captive; he dreamed of little else; we have several disappointing attempts of his own to imitate the ancient Icelandic staves, and of Ossian, or rather Macpherson, he writes: "This man in short is the very Dæmon of poetry, or he has lighted on a treasure hid for ages." We may forgive him for having floundered here. Dr. Johnson, whose imagination was not so strong as his common-sense, was the only man not misled.

But Gray on Aristotle, Gray on Froissart is admirable; his pungent criticism on Shaftesbury, too long to quote, is a perfect masterpiece; even his verbal criticisms on the poor stuff with which Mason inundated him, are wonderfully patient and acute. It may be worth while to hear Gray on other people's elegies. He writes to Mason: "All I can say is, that your elegy must not end with the worst line in it; it is flat, it is prose, whereas that above all ought to sparkle, or at least to shine. If the sentiment must stand, twist it a little into an apophthegm, stick a flower into it, gild it with a costly expression, let it strike the fancy, the ear or the heart, and I am satisfied." Again he writes, on the nature of elegiac writing: "Nature and sorrow and tenderness are the true genius of such things; poetical ornaments are foreign to the purpose—for they only show that a man is not sorry—and devotion worse, for that teaches him that he ought not to be sorry, which is all the pleasure of the thing."

Yet he could condescend to a little good-natured puffing of his friend's writings. He sends Mason's tragedy, *Caractacus*, a tiresome work, to a friend. "You will receive to-morrow *Caractacus*, piping hot, I hope before any one else has it. Observe it is I that send it, for Mason makes no presents to any one whatever; and moreover you are desired to lend it to nobody, that we may sell the more of them,—for money, not fame, is the declared purpose of all we do. He has had infinite fits of affectation as the hour approached, and is now gone into the country for a week, like a new-married couple."

He mistrusts his powers as a critic: "You know I do not

love, much less pique myself on criticism, and think even a bad verse as good a thing or better than the best observation that was ever made upon it." Indeed his diffidence with regard to his own work was profound. This is the first announcement of the completion of the *Elegy*: "I have been here at Stoke a few days, and having put an end to a thing, whose beginning you have seen long ago, I immediately send it to you. You will, I hope, look upon it in the light of a thing with an end to it, a merit that most of my writings have wanted and are like to want."

The following contains a pathetic touch; the diffident man's silent hankering after recognition: "I cannot brag of my spirits, my situation, my employments, or my fertility; the days and the nights pass, and I am never the nearer to anything but that one to which we are all tending. Yet I love people that leave some traces of their journey behind them, and have strength enough to advise you to do so while you can; winter is the season of harvest to an author."

This is his own account of his powers of composition: "I by no means pretend to inspiration, but yet I affirm that the faculty in question [of composition] is by no means voluntary. It is the result (I suppose) of a certain disposition of mind, which does not depend on one's self, and which I have not felt this long time. You that are a witness how seldom this spirit has moved me in my life, may easily give credit to what I say." The great Doctor, whose favourite maxim it was that any one can write at any time who sets himself "doggedly" to it, was profoundly irritated by this. He speaks of Gray's "fantastic" notion that he could not write except at happy moments; a "foppery," he adds, "to which my kindness for a man of learning makes me wish that he had been superior."

Gray was a master of the art of delicate moralising. I cannot help wondering that more literary apophthegms have not been extracted from his writings. Here is one for example: "I am persuaded that the whole matter is to have always something going forward." And again: "You mistake me, I was always a friend to employment and no foe to money; but they are no friends to each other. Promise me to be always busy, and I will allow you to be rich." Or more solemnly still:

"A life spent out of the world has its hours of despondence, its inconveniences, its sufferings as numerous and real (though not quite of the same sort) as a life spent in the midst of it. The power we have, when we will exert it, over our own minds, joined to a little strength and consolation, nay, a little pride we catch from those that seem to love us, is our only support in either of these conditions. I am sensible I cannot return to you so much of this assistance as I have received from you. I can only tell you that one who has far more reason than you I hope will ever have, to look on life with something worse than indifference, is yet no enemy to it, and can look back on many bitter moments, partly with satisfaction, and partly with patience, and forward too, on a scene not very promising, with some hope and some expectations of a better day."

The last extract is particularly characteristic, and strikes a note which sounds again and again throughout the letters. Gray was deeply serious. Seriousness unrelieved by humour is tiresome; but Gray, however melancholy he felt, could always retire a few paces and view himself as a spectator, with a smile. It is the truth that we do not really love a man unless we are sure that he is serious; he may amuse us and fascinate us, but he does nothing more. And Gray was never cynical; below his humour and contempt lay a deep regard for the holiness of life, for friendship and loyalty and old-fashioned virtues. Shelley attracts us, but we do not feel sure of him: our respect for Gray grows with every page we turn.

Of his humour it is difficult to give specimens. Isolated from the connection in which they occur they lose half their charm; there is a habitual tone, a point of view, of which extracts can give no idea. But it may perhaps be worth while to give a sentence or two to illustrate his habit of viewing himself. On settling in London he writes: "I am just settled in my new habitation in Southampton Row; and though a solitary and dispirited creature, not ungenial nor wholly unpleasant to myself. I live in the Museum and write volumes of antiquity." That was the sort of life that suited him. Nothing tires him, he declares, more than being entertained. "I am come to my resting-place, and find it very necessary, after living for a month in a house with three women, that laughed from morning to night, and would allow nothing to the sulkiness of my disposition. Company and cards at home, parties by land and water abroad, and (what they call) *doing something*, that is, racketing about from morning to night, are occupations I find that wear out my spirits, especially in a situation where one might sit still and be alone with pleasure; for the place was a hill like Clifden, opening to a very extensive and diversified landscape, with the Thames, which is navigable, running at its foot."

He does not indulge much in anecdote, nor indeed in witticisms of a direct kind, but when he met with a story that pleased him, he sent it on. The following seems to have taken his fancy, as it occurs more than once; and it may be noted in passing that Gray was never averse to reproducing a letter almost verbally for the benefit of two or three friends: there are several instances of these duplicate letters. "An old Alderman I knew, who after living forty years on the fat of the land (not milk and honey, but arrack-punch and venison) and losing his great toe with a mortification, said to the last that he owed it to two grapes which he ate one day after dinner. He felt them lie cold at his stomach the minute they were down." Again, when he was told that a certain Dr. Plumptre, a plethoric pluralist, had had his picture painted by Wilson with his family motto below, *Non magna loquimur sed vivimus*—Gray humorously suggests a rendering: "We don't say much, but we hold good livings."

Apart from actual letters, his diaries are delightfully suggestive reading; and there is a peculiar freshness about them, because the taste for natural scenery was not then universal. It was impossible that there should be any cant about it then; any one who delighted in it was peculiar in his tastes; and Gray, who practically visited all the English districts where Nature shows herself on a more striking scale, met with little sympathy from his friends who were writing about her with their back to the window. It is impossible to illustrate this by quotation; but I may perhaps be excused for giving a well-known sentence, into which is concentrated a wealth of sympathetic observation; it suggests lonely evenings, when the winds were blustering round the little college-court or moaning in the tall chimneys of Stoke; for after all it is an indoors-criticism. "Did you never observe (while rocking winds are piping loud) that pause, as the gust is re-collecting itself, and rising upon the ear in a shrill and plaintive note, like the swell of an Æolian harp? I do assure you there is nothing in the world so like the voice of a spirit."

It was not, of course, likely that Gray's letters would ever attain a very wide popularity; to appreciate them, they require a rather minute study of a very peculiar character, and a certain familiarity with the leisurely movements of a very uneventful life. And they are moreover touched throughout with a stately refinement, a certain delicacy and remoteness which need almost an initiation to comprehend. In days when vulgar romances run in a few weeks into a circulation of thousands, it is only to be wondered at that such things as these letters get readers at all; for they are high literature, not spiced for a jaded taste, but somewhat austere and solemn—the intimate thoughts of a high-minded man.

Much has been said that is wide of the mark about Gray's religious belief. The fact was that he was a pagan of the grand type. He was not really a Christian, but he had no wish to tilt against orthodoxies and accepted dogmas. The most that can be traced in his writings is a solemn Theism. He recognised the huge inscrutable fate that lay behind the inexplicable fabric of human life and human history, but of the God with men, of the Divine hope, the consecration of life, the self-abnegation of the Christian, he had no real cognizance. This, I think, cannot be doubted. His contemptuous hatred of theology and of creeds is marked; he had no patience with them; of worship he knew nothing. It has been said that he would have found a medicine for his unhappiness in wedded love; he would have found more than a medicine in religion.

The stately pathos of such a life is indisputable. The pale little poet, with greatness written so largely on all his works, with keen, deep eyes, the long aquiline nose, the heavy chin, the thin compressed lips, the halting affected gait, is a figure to be contemplated with serious and loving interest, spoiled for life, as he said, by retirement. How he panted for strength and serenity! How far he was from reaching either! Yet the bitter dignity of his thought, the diffident and fastidious will, are of a finer type than we often meet with. We cannot spare the men of action, it is true; yet the contemplative soul, with the body so pitifully unequal to sustain its agonizing struggle, is an earnest of higher things. In the valley of shadows he walked, and entered the gate without repining. All are equal there; and the memory that he left, and the characters that he graved on the rock, while they move our pity, stir our wonder too.

TOBIAS SMOLLETT

TOBIAS SMOLLETT

1721–1771

Tobias George Smollett, novelist and man of letters, was born in March 1721 near Cardross in Dunbarton, Scotland. The son of a Scottish laird, he probably attended Glasgow University and in 1736 was apprenticed to two Glasgow surgeons. Smollett moved to London in 1739 after being released from his apprenticeship in 1738 upon developing a cough; with him he brought the completed manuscript of *The Regicide*, a tragedy which he tried unsuccessfully to produce. In 1740 he became a naval surgeon, and is believed to have been present during the abortive attack in 1741 on the Spanish in Cartagena, about which he later wrote in *Roderick Random* and (if the work is his) *A Compendium of Authentic and Entertaining Voyages* (1756). Between 1742 and 1744 Smollett lived in Jamaica; while there he married Anne Lassells, heiress to a Jamaican plantation owner, who outlived him by twenty years. Returning to London in 1744, Smollett set himself up as a surgeon, first in Downing Street and then in 1746 in Chapel Street in Mayfair, although he never enjoyed much success in his medical career.

Smollett's first publication, the poem *A New Song*, which later occurs in revised form in *Roderick Random*, appeared in either 1744 or 1745, with music by James Oswald. This was followed by another poem set to music by Oswald, *The Tears of Scotland* (1746), about atrocities committed by the Duke of Cumberland's troops at Culloden during the Jacobite Rebellion. Later that year appeared *Advice*, a verse satire on London life, followed by a sequel, *Reproof* (1747). Also in 1747, or perhaps early in 1748, Smollett's only child was born, a daughter named Elizabeth (d. 1763).

Smollett's first novel, *The Adventures of Roderick Random*, was published in 1748 and became a lasting success. In the summer of 1749 Smollett paid the first of several visits to the Continent. In 1750 he received a medical degree from Marischal College, Aberdeen; he then moved to Old Chelsea, where he remained until 1763. Smollett's second novel, *The Adventures of Peregrine Pickle* (1751), partly reflected his experiences in Paris; this long and often extremely libelous book, which Smollett later revised, was only a moderate success. Smollett may have been the author of *The Faithful Narrative of Habbakkuk Hilding* (1752), an attack upon Fielding.

In his remaining twenty years Smollett wrote a great deal, much of it hack work. His nonfiction writings included *A Complete History of England* (4 vols., 1757–58), *The Continuation of the Complete History of England* (5 vols., 1760–65), *Travels through France and Italy* (1766), and *The Present State of All Nations* (8 vols., 1768–69). He was extremely active as a journalist and was the founder and editor of the *Critical Review* (1756–63), the *British Magazine* (founded with Oliver Goldsmith in 1760 and co-edited by Smollett until 1767), and the Tory journal *The Briton* (1762–63). In addition, he published many volumes of translations of works by Le Sage, Cervantes, Voltaire, and others.

Smollett published his third novel, *The Adventures of Ferdinand Count Fathom*, in 1753; this was followed by a play, *The Reprisal*, first produced in 1757; a fourth novel, *The Adventures of Sir Launcelot Greaves* (serialized 1760–61; published in book form 1762); and a political satire almost certainly by Smollett, *The History and Adventures of an Atom* (1769).

The epistolary novel *The Expedition of Humphry Clinker*, generally considered Smollett's masterpiece, was published in London in 1771, several months before his death from an acute intestinal infection on September 17, 1771. Smollett died at his home near Leghorn, Italy, where he had settled in 1769 in an attempt to regain his health. His reputation as a novelist suffered a decline in the nineteenth and early twentieth centuries, but he is now once again rated very highly.

Personal

Is there a man, in vice and folly bred,
To sense of honour as to virtue dead;
Whom ties nor human, nor divine, can bind;
Alien to GOD, and foe to all mankind;
Who spares no character; whose ev'ry word,
Bitter as gall, and sharper than the sword,
Cuts to the quick; whose thoughts with rancour swell:
Whose tongue, on earth, performs the work of Hell?
If there be such a monster, the REVIEWS
Shall find him holding forth against Abuse.
'Attack Profession!—'tis a deadly breach!
'The Christian laws another lesson teach:—
'Unto the end should charity endure,
'And Candour hide those faults it cannot cure.'
Thus Candour's maxims flow from Rancour's throat,
As devils, to serve their purpose, Scripture quote.
—CHARLES CHURCHILL, *The Apology*, 1761, ll. 298–313

Next Smollett came. What author dare resist
Historian, critic, bard, and novelist?
"To reach thy temple, honour'd Fame," he cried,
"Where, where's an avenue I have not tried?
But since the glorious present of to-day
Is meant to grace alone the poet's lay,
My claim I waive to ev'ry art beside,
And rest my plea upon the Regicide.
But if, to crown the labours of my muse,

Thou, inauspicious, shouldst the wreath refuse,
Whoe'er attempts it in this scribbling age,
Shall feel the Scottish pow'rs of critic rage:
Thus spurn'd, thus disappointed of my aim,
I'll stand a bugbear in the road to Fame;
Each future minion's infant hopes undo,
And blast the budding honours of his brow."
　　　—CUTHBERT SHAW, *The Race*, 1766

⟨. . .⟩ a most worthless and dangerous fellow, and capable of any mischief.—HORACE WALPOLE, Letter to Sir Horace Mann (March 15, 1770)

Smollets disposition was roving and unsettled; nor had he judgment to investigate a matter with sagacity: however, he had some humour, but then it was of a kind ludicrously cruel, and if once prejudiced he would propogate with his utmost dexterity of insinuation, a report hurtful to the innocent, would first condemn anonymous productions, and then ascribe them possitively to people who did not know what size they were of: However it is a kind of honour to his tomb, that it was taken notice of by Doctor Samuel Johnson, the man who could represent an island as an entire square, which in many places is actually indented with Bays.—ANDREW HENDERSON, *A Second Letter to Dr. Samuel Johnson*, 1775

Smollet was a Man of very agreable Conversation, and of much Genuine Humour, and tho' not a profound Scholar, Possess'd a Philosophical Mind, and was capable of making the Soundest Observations on Human Life, and of Discerning the Excellence, or Seeing the Ridicule of Every Character he met with. Fielding only excell'd him in Giving a Dramatick Story to his Novels, but in my Opinion was Inferior to him in the true Comick Vein. He was one of the many very pleasant men with whom it was my Good Fortune to be Intimatly Acquainted.—ALEXANDER CARLYLE, *Anecdotes and Characters of the Times*, 1800–05

There is a vein in Smollett—a Scotch vein—which is always disgusting to people of delicacy; but it is enough to say of him in this work, that he is an invalid with whom even invalids cannot sympathise—one has no patience with his want of patience. (Is not this a touch of *natural* criticism?)—LEIGH HUNT, "Memorandum" (March 17, 1813), *The Correspondence of Leigh Hunt*, 1853, Vol. 1, p. 80

It has been remarked that during his life he was more generally read, owing to the rich entertainment he afforded, than he was applauded or approved; for his powers were unequal and variable, and blended with his unrivalled qualities were defects and blemishes, occasional breaches of propriety and good taste, which offended the judgment, though they could not detract from the admirable portraiture of life and manners, from the wit and humour which held the reader captive. Fertility of imagination, striking imagery, rich fancy, and a flowing style, throw a ceaseless charm over his narrative. Quick and penetrating, with strong sense and a retentive memory, his writings all exhibit proofs of versatility as well as vigour of talent. Though neither erudite nor profound, he displays a competent knowledge both of Greek and Roman literature, and he was sufficiently skilled in the various branches of modern learning. Though a fair historian, he was but a feeble controversialist, and a weak politician; his inventive powers were not adapted to the close reasoning, the condensed argument, and overwhelming weight of bitter invective deduced from them, which crushes with its wit and sarcasm what it cannot confute—a power, happily for its opponents, rare—and of which we find in the writings of

Junius a celebrated and striking exemplification. No wonder that Smollett, with all his finer weapons of fancy, wit, and humour, fell before the close heavy hammer of the Thor of his desperate day, clothed in his arms of proof. Neither his learning, nor his familiarity with the history and politics of Europe, with the constitution and government of his country, availed him in a conflict like this. His peculiar power of observation; his insight into the foibles of character, and the eccentricities of manner, profession, life, and human nature itself, were here unavailing; and his nicer distinctions of natural and of moral beauty and deformity were rather an incumbrance in an arbitrary and conventional battle of naked gladiatorial weapons, in which he possessed neither the skill nor strength of his adversary.

The intellect of Smollett, acute and penetrating, enabled him to dive a certain way, but not as with the genius of a Fielding, into the very recesses of the human mind. His humour, lively and versatile as it was, lay rather in broad and strong painting, approaching caricature, than in situation and incident, which require no comment, which possess the soul and naked power of wit, without the ornament of language. Yet he could paint vividly and accurately the weaknesses and absurdities which presented themselves in ludicrous points of view. He had a clear conception, and he conveyed it in a perspicuous and forcible style. He combines simplicity with correctness, and elegance and ease with grace. His wit, bold and sudden, never fails to strike and it is keen as it is strong and manly. His humour, though exquisite at times, and always lively, cannot compete with the innate power of Fielding, nor with that of Swift and Congreve. Nor as a general writer does he possess the delicate taste or chastened moral, with the poignant satire and pleasing variety of Addison, but his great forte lay in displaying the various incongruities of conduct and manners, as well as the sources of human actions, in all which he proved himself no unworthy rival of Theophrastus, of Bruyere, and Molière.

Of Smollett's social qualities and style of living, we are happily presented with a lively and interesting sketch from his own pen, in the *Expedition of Humphry Clinker*, in the account of young Melford, when accompanied by Dick Ivy, he proceeds to dine with the author at his house in Chelsea. "He carried me to dine with S——, whom you and I have long known by his writings. He lives in the skirts of the town, and every Sunday his house is open to all unfortunate brothers of the quill. I was civilly received in a plain, yet decent habitation, which opened backwards into a very pleasant garden, kept in excellent order; and indeed I saw none of the outward signs of authorship, either in the house, or the landlord, who is one of the few writers of the age that stand upon their own foundation, without patronage, and above dependence. If there was nothing characteristic in the entertainer, the company made ample amends for his want of singularity. After dinner we adjourned into the garden, when I observed S—— gave a separate audience to every individual, in a small remote filbert walk, from whence most of them dropped off; but they were replaced by fresh recruits of the same clan, who came to make an afternoon's visit. After coffee, I took my leave of S——, with proper acknowledgments of his civility, and was extremely well pleased with the entertainment of the day, though not yet satisfied with respect to the nature of the connexion betwixt a man of character in the literary world, and a parcel of authorlings, who, in all probability, would never be able to acquire any degree of reputation by their labours. On this head, I interrogated my conductor, who answered me to this effect:—Those people, whom he knows to be bad men, as well as bad writers, are cunning enough to make him their property. There is not one of them who does not owe him particular obligations. Those who are in distress he supplies with money, when he has it, and with his credit when he is out of cash. When they want business, he either finds employment for them in his own service, or recommends them to booksellers to execute some project he has formed for their subsistence. They are always welcome to his table, which, though plain, is plentiful, and to his good offices as far as they will go; and, when they see occasion, they make use of his name with the most petulant familiarity; nay, they do not scruple to arrogate to themselves the merit of some of his performances, and have been known to sell their own lucubrations as the produce of his brain. I still expressed a desire to know his real motives for continuing his friendship to a set of rascals equally ungrateful and insignificant. He said, he did not pretend to assign any reasonable motive; that, if the truth must be told, the man was, in point of conduct, a most incorrigible fool; that, though he pretended to have a knack at hitting off characters, he blundered strangely in the distribution of his favours, which were generally bestowed on the most undeserving of those who had recourse to his assistance. By all accounts, S—— is not without weakness and caprice; yet he is certainly good humoured and civilized; nor do I find that there is any thing overbearing, cruel, or implacable in his disposition." —THOMAS ROSCOE, "Life and Works of Tobias Smollett" (1840), *Miscellaneous Works of Tobias Smollett*, 1856, Vol. 1, pp. 32–33

Most obscure among the other items in that Armada of Sir Chaloner's, just taking leave of England; most obscure of the items then, but now most noticeable, or almost alone noticeable, is a young Surgeon's-Mate,—one Tobias Smollett; looking over the waters there and the fading coasts, not without thoughts. A proud, soft-hearted, though somewhat stern-visaged, caustic and indignant young gentleman. Apt to be caustic in speech, having sorrows of his own under lock and key, on this and subsequent occasions. Excellent Tobias; he has, little as he hopes it, something considerable by way of mission in this Expedition, and in this Universe generally. Mission to take Portraiture of English Seamanhood, with the due grimness, due fidelity; and convey the same to remote generations, before it vanish. Courage, my brave young Tobias; through endless sorrows, contradictions, toils and confusions, you will do your errand in some measure; and that will be something!—THOMAS CARLYLE, *History of Friedrich II. of Prussia*, 1858–65, Bk. 12, Ch. 12

He was not intemperate, nor yet was he extravagant, but by nature hospitable and of a cheerful temperament; his housekeeping was never niggardly, so long as he could employ his pen. Thus his genius was too often degraded to the hackney-tasks of booksellers; while a small portion of those pensions which were so lavishly bestowed upon ministerial dependants and placemen would have enabled him to turn his mind to its congenial pursuits, and probably to still further elevate the literary civilization of his country. But if there be satisfaction in the thought that a neglect similar to that which befell so bright a genius as his could no longer occur in England, there is food likewise for reflection in the change that has come over the position in which men of letters lived in those days towards the public, and even towards each other.—W. SARGENT, "Some Inedited Memorials of Smollett," *Atlantic*, June 1859, p. 702

General

Smollet inherited from nature a strong sense of ridicule, a great fund of original humour, and a happy versatility of talent, by which he could accommodate his style to almost every species of writing. He could adopt alternately the solemn, the lively, the sarcastic, the burlesque, and the vulgar. To these qualifications he joined an inventive genius, and a vigorous imagination. As he possessed talents equal to the composition of original works of the same species with the romance of Cervantes; so it is not perhaps possible to conceive a writer more completely qualified to give a perfect translation of that romance.—ALEXANDER FRASER TYTLER, LORD WOODHOUSELEE, *Essay on the Principles of Translation*, 1791

Smollett had much penetration, though he is frequently too vulgar to please; but his knowledge of men and manners is unquestionable.—THOMAS JAMES MATHIAS, *The Pursuits of Literature* (1794), 1798, p. 59, Note

He has published more volumes, upon more subjects, than perhaps any other author of modern date; and, in all, he has left marks of his genius. The greater part of his novels are peculiarly excellent. He is nevertheless a hasty writer; when he affects us most, we are aware that he might have done more. In all his works of invention, we find the stamp of a mighty mind. In his lightest sketches, there is nothing frivolous, trifling and effeminate. In his most glowing portraits, we acknowledge a mind at ease, rather essaying its powers, than tasking them. We applauded his works; but it is with profounder sentiment that we meditate his capacity. The style of Smollett has never been greatly admired, and it is brought forward here merely to show in what manner men of the highest talents, and of great eminence in the *belles lettres*, could write forty or fifty years ago.—WILLIAM GODWIN, "Of English Style," *The Enquirer*, 1797, p. 467

Smollett, though not equal to Fielding, is yet possessed of a most excellent vein of humour. His characters are in general not quite so natural as those of Fielding; but we must except his sea personages, who are unrivalled. Perhaps he is not quite equal to his great original, at least as far as respects *Tom Jones*, in the skill and address of conducting a plot, and winding it up in a dramatic manner; yet his novels never fail of exciting the most lively interest in his reader. *Roderic Random* is very superior to his *Peregrine Pickle*, independently of the gross deficiency in moral, which is a censure that justly attaches to the latter work. Indeed *Tom Jones* is in some measure culpable in this respect; for actual vice is treated too much as venial levity, and exhibited in too amiable and alluring a light not to be injurious to young readers. *Humphrey Clinker*, though it has little of plot or story, keeps attention alive by the constant display of odd characters well caricatured, and by an uninterrupted flow of genuine humour. No man can read these performances without regretting that the time and genius of Smollett, instead of pursuing a track for which he was so admirably adapted by nature, should have been wasted on the compilation of a dull, and in all respects very indifferent history.—GEORGE GREGORY, *Letters on Literature, Taste, and Composition*, 1808, Vol. 2, pp. 72–73

Something like this censure, or perhaps something more severe, may be passed upon the *Roderick Random* and *Peregrine Pickle* of Smollet; whose humour is inferior to that of Fielding, and his objectionable scenes wrought up with still less regard to decency. In fact, the female who has read these novels has nothing bad to learn.

Nearly all the splendid qualities of *Roderick Random* and *Peregrine Pickle* are subservient to licentious purposes. Their characters, and those of the minor agents in each piece, may be, and I dare say sometimes are, drawn with a strict attention to nature: but I trust I shall never know whether many of them are so or not.

The author is not satisfied with expatiating on the revelry of the stews, and the vile debaucheries of the bully and the harlot; but thinks it incumbent on him to subjoin nastiness to obscenity; and brings into full view the infirmities by which man is degraded; the ravages of loathsome distemper, and the stench and the vermin of the hospital.—EDWARD MANGIN, *An Essay on Light Reading*, 1808, pp. 50–51

As an author, Dr. Smollett is universally allowed the praise of original genius displayed with an ease and variety which are rarely found. Yet this character belongs chiefly to his novels. In correct delineation of life and manners, and in drawing characters of the humorous class, he has few equals. But when this praise is bestowed, every critic who values what is more important than genius itself, the interest of morals and decency, must surely stop. It can be of no use to analyze each individual scene, incident, or character in works which, after all, must be pronounced unfit to be read.

But if the morals of the reader were in no danger, his taste can hardly escape being insulted or perverted. Smollett's humour is of so low a cast, and his practical jokes so frequently end in what is vulgar, mean, and filthy, that it would be impossible to acquire a relish for them, without injury done to the chaster feelings, and to the just respect due to genuine wit. No novel writer seems to take more delight in assembling images and incidents that are gross and disgusting: nor has he scrupled to introduce, with more than slight notice, those vices which are not fit even to be named. If this be a just representation of his most favourite novels, it is in vain to oppose it by pointing out passages which do credit to his genius, and more vain to attempt to prove that virtue and taste are not directly injured by such productions.

As a historian, Smollett's reputation has certainly not been preserved. When he published his *History*, something of the kind was wanted, and it was executed in a manner not unworthy of his talents. But the writings of Hume, Robertson, and Gibbon have introduced a taste for a higher species of historical composition: and, if I am not mistaken, there has been no complete edition of Smollett's *History*, but that which he published. Had he been allowed the proper time for revision and reflection, it cannot be doubted that he might have produced a work deserving of more lasting fame. His *History*, even as we have it, when we advert to the short time he took for its completion, is a very extraordinary effort, and instead of blaming him for occasionally following his authorities too servilely, the wonder ought to be that he found lesiure to depart from them so frequently, and to assign reasons, which are not those of a superficial thinker. It is impossible, however, to quit this subject without adverting to the mode of publication which dispersed the work among a class of persons, the purchasers of sixpenny numbers, whom Smollett too easily took for the learned and discerning part of the public. This fallacious encouragement afforded fuel to his irritable temper, by inciting him, not only to the arts of puffing, by which the literary character is degraded, but to those vulgar and splenetic recriminations of which a specimen has been given, and which must have lowered him yet more in the opinion of the eminent characters of his day.

Smollett was not successful in his dramatic attempts.

Those who judged from the ease and vivacity of his pictures of life and manners in his novels, no doubt thought themselves justified in encouraging him in this species of composition. But all experience shows that the talents necessary for the prose epic, and those for the regular drama, are essentially different, and have rarely met in one man. Fielding, a novelist greatly superior, and who after the trials of more than half a century, may be pronounced inimitable, was yet foiled in his dramatic attempts, although he returned to the charge with fresh courage and skill.

As a poet, in which character only Smollett is here introduced, although his pieces are few, they must be allowed to confer a very high rank. It is, indeed, greatly to be lamented that he did not cultivate his poetical talents more frequently and more extensively. "The Tears of Scotland" and the "Ode to Independence," particularly the latter, are equal to the highest efforts in the pathetic and sublime. In the "Ode to Independence" there is evidently the inspiration of real genius, free from all artificial aid, or meretricious ornament. It may be questioned whether there are many compositions in our language which more forcibly charm by all the enchantments of taste, expression, and sentiment. Some observations on this ode, and usually printed with it, are the production of professor Richardson. It may be necessary to add that this ode was left in manuscript by Smollett, and published at Glasgow and London in 1773.—ALEXANDER CHALMERS, "The Life of Tobias Smollett, M.D.," *The Works of the English Poets*, 1810, Vol. 15, pp. 551–53

Of the writings of Smollett, by far the most original is *Humphry Clinker*. In this novel the author most successfully executes, what had scarcely ever been before attempted—a representation of the different effects which the same scenes, and persons, and transactions, have on different dispositions and tempers. He exhibits through the whole work a most lively and humorous delineation, confirming strongly the great moral truth, that happiness and all our feelings are the result, less of external circumstances, than the constitution of the mind. In his other writings, the sailors of Smollett are most admirably delineated—their mixture of rudeness and tenderness—their narrow prejudices—thoughtless extravagance—dauntless valour—and warm generosity. In his *Peregrine Pickle*, Smollett's sea characters are a little caricatured, but the character of Tom Bowling, in *Roderick Random*, has something even sublime, and will be regarded in all ages as a happy exhibition of those naval heroes, to whom Britain is indebted for so much of her happiness and glory.—JOHN DUNLOP, *The History of Fiction* (1814), 1842, Vol. 2, p. 408

Smollett's first novel, *Roderick Random*, which is also his best, appeared about the same time as Fielding's *Tom Jones*; and yet it has a much more modern air with it: but this may be accounted for, from the circumstance that Smollett was quite a young man at the time, whereas Fielding's manner must have been formed long before. The style of *Roderick Random* is more easy and flowing than that of *Tom Jones*; the incidents follow one another more rapidly (though, it must be confessed, they never come in such a throng, or are brought out with the same dramatic effect); the humour is broader, and as effectual; and there is very nearly, if not quite, an equal interest excited by the story. What then is it that gives the superiority to Fielding? It is the superior insight into the springs of human character, and the constant developement of that character through every change of circumstance. Smollett's humour often arises from the situation of the persons, or the peculiarity of their external appearance; as, from Roderick Random's carrotty locks, which hung down over his shoulders like a pound of candles, or Strap's ignorance of London, and the blunders that follow from it. There is a tone of vulgarity about all his productions. The incidents frequently resemble detached anecdotes taken from a newspaper or magazine; and, like those in *Gil Blas*, might happen to a hundred other characters. He exhibits the ridiculous accidents and reverses to which human life is liable, not 'the stuff' of which it is composed. He seldom probes to the quick, or penetrates beyond the surface; and, therefore, he leaves no stings in the minds of his readers, and in this respect is far less interesting than Fielding. His novels always enliven, and never tire us: we take them up with pleasure, and lay them down without any strong feeling of regret. We look on and laugh, as spectators of a highly amusing scene, without closing in with the combatants, or being made parties in the event. We read *Roderick Random* as an entertaining story; for the particular accidents and modes of life which it describes have ceased to exist: but we regard *Tom Jones* as a real history; because the author never stops short of those essential principles which lie at the bottom of all our actions, and in which we feel an immediate interest—*intus et in cute*. Smollett excels most as the lively caricaturist: Fielding as the exact painter and profound metaphysician. I am far from maintaining that this account applies uniformly to the productions of these two writers; but I think that, as far as they essentially differ, what I have stated is the general distinction between them. *Roderick Random* is the purest of Smollett's novels: I mean in point of style and description. Most of the incidents and characters are supposed to have been taken from the events of his own life; and are, therefore, truer to nature. There is a rude conception of generosity in some of his characters, of which Fielding seems to have been incapable, his amiable persons being merely good-natured. It is owing to this that Strap is superior to Partridge; as there is a heartiness and warmth of feeling in some of the scenes between Lieutenant Bowling and his nephew, which is beyond Fielding's power of impassioned writing. The whole of the scene on ship-board is a most admirable and striking picture, and, I imagine, very little if at all exaggerated, though the interest it excites is of a very unpleasant kind, because the irritation and resistance to petty oppression can be of no avail. The picture of the little profligate French friar, who was Roderick's travelling companion, and of whom he always kept to the windward, is one of Smollett's most masterly sketches.—*Peregrine Pickle* is no great favourite of mine, and *Launcelot Greaves* was not worthy of the genius of the author.

Humphry Clinker and *Count Fathom* are both equally admirable in their way. Perhaps the former is the most pleasant gossiping novel that ever was written; that which gives the most pleasure with the least effort to the reader. It is quite as amusing as going the journey could have been; and we have just as good an idea of what happened on the road, as if we had been of the party. Humphry Clinker himself is exquisite; and his sweetheart, Winifred Jenkins, not much behind him. Matthew Bramble, though not altogether original, is excellently supported, and seems to have been the prototype of Sir Anthony Absolute in the *Rivals*. But Lismahago is the flower of the flock. His tenaciousness in argument is not so delightful as the relaxation of his logical severity, when he finds his fortune mellowing in the wintry smiles of Mrs. Tabitha Bramble. This is the best preserved, and most severe of all Smollett's characters. The resemblance to *Don Quixote* is only just enough to make it interesting to the critical reader, without giving offence to any body else. The indecency and filth in this novel, are what must be allowed to all Smollett's writings.—

The subject and characters in *Count Fathom* are, in general, exceedingly disgusting: the story is also spun out to a degree of tediousness in the serious and sentimental parts; but there is more power of writing occasionally shewn in it than in any of his works. I need only to refer to the fine and bitter irony of the Count's address to the country of his ancestors on his landing in England; to the robber scene in the forest, which has never been surpassed; to the Parisian swindler who personates a raw English country squire (Western is tame in the comparison); and to the story of the seduction in the west of England. It would be difficult to point out, in any author, passages written with more force and mastery than these.—WILLIAM HAZLITT, *Lectures on the English Comic Writers*, 1818

You ask me what degrees there are between Scotts Novels and those of Smollet—They appear to me to be quite distinct in every particular—more especially in their Aim—Scott endeavours to throw so interesting and ramantic a colouring into common and low Characters as to give them a touch of the Sublime—Smollet on the contrary pulls down and levels what with other Men would continue Romance. The Grand parts of Scott are within the reach of more Minds that the finest humours in *Humphrey Climker*—I forget whether that fine thing of the Sargeant is Fielding's or Smollets but it gives me more pleasure that the whole Novel of the Antiquary—you must remember what I mean. Some one says to the Sargeant "thats a non sequiter," "if you come to that" replies the Sargeant "you're another."—JOHN KEATS, Letter to George and Thomas Keats (Jan. 5, 1818)

Fielding and Smollett, however clever in their delineations and sometimes caricatures of life, offend by, we had almost said, the studied coarseness of even their best scenes and descriptions; and if, as we have assumed, the most popular fiction may be taken as a measure of the taste and morals of the age which admired them, we must place those of our ancestors very low.—GEORGE ELIOT, "The Progress of Fiction as an Art," *Westminster Review*, Oct. 1853, p. 355

We have before us, and painted by his own hand, Tobias Smollett, the manly, kindly, honest and irascible; worn and battered, but still brave and full of heart, after a long struggle against a hard fortune. His brain had been busied with a hundred different schemes; he had been reviewer and historian, critic, medical writer, poet, pamphleteer. He had fought endless literary battles; and braved and wielded for years the cudgels of controversy. It was a hard and savage fight in those days, and a niggard pay. He was oppressed by illness, age, narrow fortune; but his spirit was still resolute, and his courage steady; the battle over, he could do justice to the enemy with whom he had been so fiercely engaged, and give a not unfriendly grasp to the hand that had mauled him. He is like one of those Scotch cadets, of whom history gives us so many examples, and whom, with a national fidelity, the great Scotch novelist has painted so charmingly. Of gentle birth and narrow means, going out from his northern home to win his fortune in the world, and to fight his way, armed with courage, hunger, and keen wits. His crest is a shattered oak tree, with green leaves yet springing from it. On his ancient coat-of-arms there is a lion and a horn; this shield of his was battered and dinted in a hundred fights and brawls, through which the stout Scotchman bore it courageously. You see somehow that he is a gentleman, through all his battling and struggling, his poverty, his hard-fought successes, and his defeats. His novels are recollections of his own adventures; his characters drawn, as I should think, from personages with whom he became acquainted in his own career of life. Strange companions he must have had; queer acquaintances he made in the Glasgow College—in the country apothecary's shop; in the gun-room of the man-of-war where he served as surgeon, and in the hard life on shore, where the sturdy adventurer struggled for fortune. He did not invent much, as I fancy, but had the keenest perceptive faculty, and described what he saw with wonderful relish and delightful broad humour. I think Uncle Bowling, in *Roderick Random*, is as good a character as Squire Western himself; and Mr. Morgan, the wild apothecary, is as pleasant as Dr. Caius. What man who has made his inestimable acquaintance—what novel reader who loves Don Quixote and Major Dalgetty—will refuse his most cordial acknowledgments to the admirable Lieutenant Lismahago. The novel of *Humphrey Clinker* is, I do think, the most laughable story that has ever been written since the goodly art of novel-writing began. Winifred Jenkins and Tabitha Bramble must keep Englishmen on the grin for ages yet to come; and in their letters and the story of their loves there is a perpetual fount of sparkling laughter, as inexhaustible as Bladud's well.—WILLIAM MAKEPEACE THACKERAY, *The English Humourists of the Eighteenth Century*, 1853

Smollett succeeds—a rough, roaring, ill-natured, and yet originally kind-hearted Scotchman of the last century, with three powers in extraordinary development: self-will, humor, and a certain strong poetical gift, which could only be, and was only now and then, *stung* into action. To see his self-will, in its last soured and savage state, let us consult his *Travels*. He was the "Smelfungus" of Sterne, who traveled from Dan to Beersheba, and found all barren. We are among the very few who have read the book. It is a succession of asthmatic gasps and groans, with not a particle of the humor of *Humphrey Clinker*. Among his novels, *Roderick Random* is the most popular, *Peregrine Pickle* the filthiest, *Sir Launcelot Greaves* the silliest, *Clinker* the most delightful, and *Ferdinand Fathom*, in parts, the most original and profound. There is a robber scene in a forest, in this last novel, surpassed by nothing in Scott, or anywhere else. His "Ode to Independence" should have been written by Burns. How that poet's lips must have watered as he repeated the lines,

> Lord of the lion heart and eagle eye,

and remembered he was not their author! He said he would have given ten pounds to have written "Donocht-head;" he would have given ten times ten, if he had had them, poor fellow! to have written the "Ode to Independence." Thackeray, who is in chase of Fielding, finds nothing very new to say of Smollett, and ignores his most peculiar and powerful works. His best sentence about him is, that he went to London, "armed with courage, hunger, and keen wits."—GEORGE GILFILLAN, "Thackeray," A *Third Gallery of Portraits*, 1854, p. 230

P.S.—*Humphry Clinker* is certainly Smollett's best. I am rather divided between *Peregrine Pickle* and *Roderick Random*, both extraordinarily good in their way, which is a way without tenderness; but you will have to read them both, and I send the first volume of *Peregrine* as the richer of the two.—CHARLES DICKENS, Letter to Frank Stone (May 30, 1854)

He was by no means the idle half-reprobate he represents in his Roderick Random. He was often wrong and always irascible, continually fancying himself aggrieved, and always with a quarrel on his hands; but he was as proud, warm-hearted, and mettlesome a Scot as had then crossed the Tweed—of a spirit so independent, we are told, that he never asked a favour for

himself from any great man in his life; paying his way honestly, and helping liberally those about him who were in distress; and altogether, so far from being a mere pleasure-seeker, that there was probably no man then in or near London, who stayed more at home, or worked more incessantly and laboriously to prevent the world from being a shilling the worse for him. He ruined his health by over-work. ⟨. . .⟩

On a comparison of Fielding with Smollett it is easy to point out subordinate differences between them. Critics have done this abundantly and accurately enough. Smollett, they tell us, is even more historical in his method, deals more in actual observation and reminiscence, and less in invention and combination of reminiscence, than Fielding. His notion of a story, still more than Fielding's, is that of a traveller, moving over a certain extent of ground, and through a succession of places, each full of things to be seen and of odd physiognomies to be quizzed. Fielding's construction is the more careful and well considered, his evolution of his story the more perfect and harmonious, his art altogether the more classic and exquisite. His humour too, is the finer and more subtle, like that of a well-wrought comedy; while Smollett's is the coarser and more outrageous like that of a broad farce. Both are satirists; but Fielding's satire is that of a man of joyous and self-possessed temperament, who has come to definite conclusions as to what is to be expected in the world, while Smollett writes with pain and under irritation. Fielding has little scruple in hanging his villains, as if he had made up his mind that the proper treatment of villains was their physical annihilation; Smollett, with all his fiercer indignation, punishes his villains too, but generally deals with them in the end as if they might be curable. If Fielding's, on the whole, as Mr. Thackeray and most critics argue, is "the greater hand," there are peculiarities in Smollett in virtue of which Scott and others have hesitated to admit his absolute inferiority so easily as might be expected, and have ranked him, all in all, as Fielding's rival. Some of Smollett's characters are as powerful creations as any in Fielding; and he has given us a range of sea characters in Tom Bowling, Trunnion, Hatchway, &c., to which there is nothing similar in the works of the other. In sheerly ludicrous episode, also—in the accumulation of absurd and grotesque detail till the power of laughter can endure no more—Smollett has perhaps surpassed Fielding. There is also a rhetorical strength of language in Smollett which Fielding rarely exhibits; a power of melodramatic effect to which Fielding does not pretend; and a greater constitutional tendency to the sombre and the terrible. There was potentially more of the poet in Smollett than in Fielding; and there are passages in his writings approaching nearer, both in feeling and in rhythm, to lyric beauty. Lastly, Smollett possesses one interesting peculiarity for readers north of the Tweed, in his Scotticism. Had he remained in Scotland, becoming an Edinburgh lawyer like his cousins, or settling in medical practice in Glasgow, the probability is that he would still have pursued authorship, and have left writings in his own peculiar vein, more Scottish in their substance than those that now bear his name, and so perhaps linking the infancy of North-British literature in Allan Ramsay, with its maturity in Burns and Sir Walter. But though his fortunes carried him out of Scotland, the Scot was always strong in him. In his first novel, it is as a young Scot that he starts on the voyage of life; throughout his whole career he looks back with affection to the land of his birth, and even fights her political battles against what he considers to be English misconception and prejudice; and his last novel of all, written when he was a lingering invalid on the Italian coast, is the dying Scotchman's farewell to Scotland. Curiously enough, this last novel, though the most literally historical of all that he wrote, is, in its spirit and matter, the finest and mellowest, the most truly classical and poetical. Though *Roderick Random* and *Peregrine Pickle* should cease to be read, Scotchmen would still have an interest in preserving *Humphry Clinker.*—DAVID MASSON, *British Novelists and Their Styles*, 1859, pp. 133–45

I have read over *Roderick Random*, too—an odd contrast—but did not learn anything new from it. I found I knew Smollett well enough before. However, I shall get *Peregrine Pickle* for the sake of Trunnion and Pipes, who are grown very dim to me. Fielding's coarseness belongs to his time, Smollett's is of all time.—JAMES RUSSELL LOWELL, Letter to Charles Eliot Norton (July 8, 1867)

The jolly, riotous kind of life which I have spoken of as characteristic of one class of novels of the last century is fully displayed in the pages of Smollett. He reflects, in many respects, the character of the age more fully than any other writer,—its material pleasures—its coarse amusements—its hard drinking, loud swearing, and practical jokes. His heroes are generally libertines, full of mirth and animal spirits, who make small account of woman's chastity; and whose adventures are intrigues, and their merriment broad farce. Such are the chief features of *Roderick Random* and *Peregrine Pickle*— neither of which, however, is so offensive as the *Adventures of Ferdinand, Count Fathom*, the hero of which is a blackguard and a scoundrel, without a redeeming virtue.—WILLIAM FORSYTH, *The Novels and Novelists of the Eighteenth Century*, 1871, p. 278

We must now hastily pass to the third so-called classic writer in English fiction, Tobias Smollett, who, after being educated as a surgeon, and having experiences of life as surgeon's mate on a ship of the line in the expedition to Carthagena, spent some time in the West Indies, returned to London, wrote some satires, an opera, &c., and presently when he was still only twenty-seven years old captivated England with his first novel, *Roderick Random*, which appeared in 1748, the same year with *Clarissa Harlowe*. In 1751 came Smollett's *Peregrine Pickle*, famous for its bright fun and the caricature it contains of Akenside—*Pleasures of Imagination* Akenside—who is represented as the host in a very absurd entertainment after the ancient fashion. In 1752 Smollett's *Adventures of Ferdinand Count Fathom* gave the world a new and very complete study in human depravity. In 1769, appeared his *Adventures of an Atom*: a theme which one might suppose it difficult to make indecorous and which was really a political satire; but the unfortunate liberty of locating his atom as an organic particle in various parts of various successive human bodies gave Smollett a field for indecency which he cultivated to its utmost yield. A few months before his death in 1771 appeared his *Expedition of Humphrey Clinker*, certainly his best novel. It is worth while noticing that in *Humphrey Clinker* the veritable British poorly-educated and poor-spelling woman begins to express herself in the actual dialect of the species, and in the letters of Mrs. Winifred Jenkins to her fellow maid-servant Mrs. Mary Jones at Brambleton Hall, during a journey made by the family to the North, we have some very worthy and strongly-marked originals not only of Mrs. Malaprop and Mrs. Partington, but of the immortal Sairey Gamp and of scores of other descendants in Thackeray and Dickens, here and there.—SIDNEY LANIER, *The English Novel*, 1883, p. 185

Our age has to blame Sir Robert Walpole and the Duke of Newcastle for the works their neglect compelled Smollett to

undertake even more than for the possible *Peregrine Pickles* and *Roderick Randoms* it has lost us. The versatility of genius was never more fully proved than when Smollett turned historian. Put to the trade of book-making he became the ideal book-maker. The language cannot show a more complete example of the dismal art than the history compiled by a prince of the domain of fiction, a master of fancy as fertile, and of a pen as vivid as English literature has ever produced. To Smollett's *Continuation of Hume*, and the book trade which tyrannically forced it upon several much-enduring generations of readers, must be imputed not a little of the extraordinary superstition that the eighteenth century is the most tedious portion of English history.—WILLIAM STEBBING, *Some Verdicts of History Reviewed*, 1887, pp. 6–7

While Smollett occasionally rises above Fielding, he does not maintain the same high level, and though free of digression, to which Fielding was prone, he is of coarser tastes. He is remarkable for a variety of incidents and characters almost bewildering in their abundance, and expressed in an easy, flowing style which is never obscure or tedious. If Fielding anticipated Thackeray, Smollett was the forerunner of Dickens. His love of fun leads him often to the verge of caricature. He painted a whole gallery of original characters, among which are the life-like portraits of Squire Bramble and Lieutenant Lesmahago, Commodore Trunnion and Jack Hatchway, Morgan and Tom Bowling, besides Strap, and Pipes, and Winifred Jenkins.—J. LOGIE ROBERTSON, A *History of English Literature*, 1894, pp. 234–35

As a novelist he stands among the British classics, probably unsurpassed in his own region—an amusing delineation of the stronger humours and absurdities of character.—GEORGE EYRE-TODD, *Scottish Poetry of the Eighteenth Century*, 1896, Vol. 1, p. 151

If in Sterne the qualities of imagination were heightened, and the susceptibilities permitted to become as feverish and neurotic as possible, the action of Tobias Smollett was absolutely the reverse. This rough and strong writer was troubled with no superfluous refinements of instinct. He delighted in creating types of eccentric profligates and ruffians, and to do this was to withdraw from the novel as Richardson, Fielding, and Sterne conceived it, back into a form of the picaresque romance. He did not realise what his greatest compeers were doing, and when he wrote *Roderick Random* (1748) he avowedly modelled it on *Gil Blas*, coming, as critics have observed, even closer to the Spanish *picaros* spirit than did Le Sage himself. If Smollett had gone no further than this, and had merely woven out of his head one more romance of the picaresque class, we should never have heard of him. But his own life, unlike those of his three chief rivals, had been adventurous on land and under sail, and he described what he had seen and suffered. Three years later he published *Peregrine Pickle* (1751), and just before he died, in 1771, *Humphrey Clinker*. The abundant remainder of his work is negligible, these three books alone being worthy of note in a sketch of literature so summary as this.

⟨. . .⟩ But Smollett was not great enough to continue this admirable innovation; he went back to the older, easier, method of gibbeting a peculiarity and exaggerating an exception. He was also much inferior to his rivals in the power of constructing a story, and in his rude zeal to "subject folly to ridicule, and vice to indignation," he raced from one rough episode to another, bestowing very little attention upon that evolution of character which should be the essence of successful fiction. The proper way to regard Smollett is, doubtless, as a man of experience and energy, who was encouraged by the success of the realistic novel to revive the old romance of adventure, and to give it certain new features. The violence of Smollett is remarkable; it was founded on a peculiarity of his own temper, but it gives his characters a sort of contortion of superhuman rage and set grimaces that seem mechanically horrible. When young Roderick Random's cousin wishes to tease him, he has no way of doing it short of hunting him with beagles, and when it is desired that Mrs. Pickle should be represented as ill tempered, a female like one of the Furies is evoked. But while it is easy to find fault with Smollett's barbarous books, it is not so easy to explain why we continue to read them with enjoyment, nor why their vigorous horse-play has left its mark on novelists so unlike their author as Lever, Dickens, and Charles Reade. Smollett's best book, moreover, is his latest, and its genial and brisk comicality has done much to redeem the memory of earlier errors of taste.—EDMUND GOSSE, *A Short History of Modern English Literature*, 1897, pp. 245–47

⟨. . .⟩ his novels, excellent in themselves, are of the highest historical importance. It has been said that he fell back on the adventure-scheme. Plot he hardly attempted; and even, as regards incident, he probably, as Thackeray says, "did not invent much," his own varied experiences and his sharp eye for humorous character giving him abundant material. In *Roderick Random* he uses his naval experiences, and perhaps others, to furnish forth the picture of a young Scotchman, arrogant, unscrupulous, and not too amiable, but bold and ready enough; in *Peregrine Pickle* he gives that of a spendthrift scapegrace, heir to wealth; in *Fathom* he draws a professional *chevalier d'industrie*. The strange fancy which made him attempt a sort of "New Quixote" in *Sir Lancelot Greaves* has seldom been regarded as happy, either in inception or in result; but in *Humphrey Clinker* we have the very best of all his works. It is written in the letter form, the scenes and humours of many places in England and Scotland are rendered with admirable picturesqueness, while the book has seldom been excelled for humorous character of the broad and farcical kind. Matthew Bramble, the testy hypochondriac squire who is at heart one of the best of men, and in head not one of the foolishest; his sour-visaged and greedy sister Tabitha; her maid Winifred Jenkins, who has learnt the art of grotesque misspelling from Swift's Mrs. Harris, and has improved upon the teaching; the Scotch soldier of fortune, Lismahago,—these are among the capital figures of English fiction, as in the earlier books are the Welsh surgeon's mate Morgan, Commodore Trunnion, and others.

Besides this conception of humorous if somewhat rough character, and a remarkable faculty of drawing interiors which accompanies it, and in which he perhaps even excels Fielding, Smollett made two very important contributions to the English novel. The first was the delineation of national types in which he, almost for the first time, reduced and improved the stock exaggerations of the stage to a human and artistic temper. The second, not less important, was the introduction, under proper limitations, of the professional interest. He had, though less of universality than Fielding, yet enough of it to be successful with types in which he had only observation, not experiment, to guide him, but he was naturally most fortunate with what he knew from experience, sailors and "medical gentlemen." Until his time the sailor had been drawn almost entirely from the outside in English literature. Smollett first gives him to us in his habit as he lived, and long continued to live. To these great merits must be added one or two drawbacks—a hardness and

roughness of tone approaching ferocity, and not more distinguished from the somewhat epicene temper of Richardson than from the manly but kindly spirit of Fielding, and an extreme coarseness of imagery and language—a coarseness which can hardly be called immoral, but which is sometimes positively revolting.—GEORGE SAINTSBURY, *A Short History of English Literature*, 1898, pp. 606–7

Smollett's chief fault is a certain hard and shameless indelicacy of imagination and perception, which makes it impossible for him to enter deeply or sympathetically into some essentials of human character, and to say anything worth heeding of the niceties of human intercourse. There is no greater ruffian in literature than Roderick Random, unless it be Peregrine Pickle; yet he started with the notice that in Roderick he would incarnate "modest merit"; and in the end he is perfectly satisfied with his results. And Roderick, between the first and last chapters of his history, scarce ever appears excepting as a sharking rascal, who has few other virtues than the very doubtful one of being as free with his own money as he is with other people's, and whose selfishness is of so lusty a type that he is content to reward his faithful Strap with, as Scott said, a cast mistress and a Highland farm. Of this hero's original relations with Miss Williams I forbear to speak: the curious may look into them for themselves. Here I shall but note that there is in them a peculiarity of squalor, an intimate and ineradicable unpleasantness, which make the lady's subsequent connexion with Narcissa one of the unpardonable things in fiction. Nobody minds, however, in the book; and as Narcissa herself is moved to distinguish "modest merit" in a footman's habit, one may infer that Narcissa, did she know, would mind as little as Miss Williams does, or Roderick, or the common author of their being. And this same indelicacy is of the very stuff of Smollett's mind. You would say that, thanks to his Scots breeding, or his professional training, or both, he had neither sense of privacy nor olfactory nerves. More: he is indecent naturally, yet deliberately: indecent because he must be, but also because he will. People talk and write about the "cynicism" of Thackeray. If they want the real thing—(but they don't)—let them look for it in the Smollett of *Random* and *Pickle*. They will find more in a single character of the earlier artist's—his Crabtree, say—than there is in all the sentimental carpings of the Middle-Victorian moralist; and they will think better of their Thackeray than they ever thought before.

I have said what I believe to be the worst that can be said of Smollett. Now for the other side. He has—and I take it to be his master-quality—a peculiar power of realizing a character, not by description and analysis but, out of the character's own mouth. He sees his people mostly as personages in a farce; but he knows all he wants you to know about them from the beginning, and with three strokes of his pen he makes you also know it. His Morgan, for instance: is it possible to forget that first appearance in the surgeon's berth of H.M.S. *Thunder?* It is all over in no time (so to say); yet, once and forever, there is Morgan. It is the same, in a greater or less degree, with Weazle and Miss Ramper, with Narcissa's aunt and Pipes and Hatchway, with Jack Rattlin and Oakum and Mrs. Trunnion-Hatchway, with Potion and Crab and Lavement, with Winifred Jenkins and Tabitha Bramble and Jackson: in fact, with almost any one of the many whom their author deigns to individualize. And when he goes deeper—when he is interested enough to be intimate—then you get creations like Bowling and Trunnion, like Lismahago and Matthew Bramble, like Pipes and Strap; and with these you are well into literature. And his narrative is of the same instant, peremptory type. He writes good, nervous forth-right English; knows exactly what he wants to say; and says it exactly as he means it to be said: as, to take three very different examples, the story of Random and Strap in London, the "Night in the Forest" episode in *Fathom*, and that unparalleled digression concerning Pipes and the beggar maid, which does so much to reconcile one with the ostentatious blackguardism of *Pickle*—as these, I say, exist to show. Comes in the last instance, Smollett the humourist—hard and immodest but copious and authentic, if in the main inalterably farcical; and, as I think, the secret of the perennial popularity of some (at least) of him lies open, even to him that runs and reads.

Says Mr Raleigh, finally:—"His zest in life is real and infectious, and his purely external treatment gives a certain refreshing quality to his pages; over his books at least it is possible to 'unbend the mind.'" That, if our standard be that of great literature, is good enough for Smollett; and I know not if there be more to say about him. But literature is not all great; and outside the pleasaunce, where Fielding ironizes with Cervantes, and Shakespeare discusses an intonation with Dickens, while Scott and Thackeray pause in their talk to hear what's said, and Sterne reads Trim and Toby and "My Father" into them all—outside, I say, the scene of these august familiarities there is honourable room for Smollett. For, take it how you will, he anglicized Le Sage, and so was one ancestor of *Pickwick*; he created Pipes and Trunnion and Bowling, and in this wise cleared the way for Chucks, and Mesty, and O'Brien—to name but these; in *Ferdinand Count Fathom* he struck a note and suggested a set of possibilities with which romance yet thrills; he was the first (so far as I can find) to write a novel for publication in serial form, and herein he has had some forty thousand imitators; finally, he was beloved of the boy Dickens, who remembered and imitated him, and so he takes hands with one of the greatest in English Letters. One may like him or not; but one has to admit that he builded better than, with all his full-sailed vanity, he knew, and, at the worst, was full of most excellent differences: that, in so many words, English literature would have been appreciably the poorer, if "Dr Toby" had not lived and worked.—W. E. HENLEY, "Introduction" to *The Works of Tobias Smollett*, 1899, Vol. 1, pp. 44–48

In comparing a novelist like Smollett with the best in English fiction to-day, the final thought, nevertheless, is likely to be—with all recognition of his talent and sturdy force—that the gains in both art and ethics have been substantial. The careless rough-and-tumble display of venality, profligacy, and brutality in these eighteenth century pages is all unconsciously a revelation of how far we have since advanced in decency, in refinement, in spiritual ideals. And quite as truly, the progress in the technique of novel-making since Smollett's time is a matter for satisfaction. No novelist of our day has more genius for fiction than had Henry Fielding; but all novelists of the first rank now will avoid Fielding's defects and those of his contemporaries: the carelessness of construction in the bringing in of loose, rambling episodic material; the failure to respect truth rather than theatric effect of scene and character; the lapses from the clean, the frank catering to gutter tastes; the clumsiness in attempting to make dialectic or other variations from normal English speech. Yet, since life is more than art, those earlier novelists often have an effect of power, of reality, of the atmosphere that makes for illusion, that has not since been surpassed. And Smollett, in his obvious faults and equally obvious virtues, stands at Fielding's shoulder, a doughty

lieutenant of that incomparable captain.—RICHARD BURTON, "The Vigorous Dr. Smollett," *Dial*, Feb. 1, 1902, p. 83

Works

RODERICK RANDOM

Smollet seems to have had more touch of romance than Fielding, but not so profound and intuitive a knowledge of humanity's hidden treasures. There is nothing in his works comparable to Parson Adams; but then, on the other hand, Fielding has not any thing of the kind equal to Strap. Partridge is dry, and hard, compared with this poor barber-boy, with his generous overflowings of affection. *Roderick Random*, indeed, with its varied delineation of life, is almost a romance. Its hero is worthy of his name. He is the sport of fortune rolled about through the "many ways of wretchedness" almost without resistance, but ever catching those tastes of joy which are every where to be relished by those who are willing to receive them. We seem to roll on with him, and get delectably giddy in his company.—T. NOON TALFOURD, "On British Novels and Romances," *Critical and Miscellaneous Writings*, 1842, pp. 14–15

Smollett's first, and, beyond all comparison, his best novel, is *Roderick Random*; whether it be received in point of force and completeness of character, apart from extravagance and incongruity, or of coherence and propriety of design in its plot, or, lastly, of vividness and vigour in the scenic descriptions. The story itself exhibits the career of a friendless orphan, with no very exalted principle, exposed to the snares and pit-falls of the knavish world. Roderick is not a gentleman born, he has no pretensions to be styled a gentleman either in his habits or deportment, and consequently the author has, with perfect consistency, supported his character throughout. But Roderick is not a gentleman at *heart*, and this appears to me a crying defect in the book. It was not called for that the hero of the story, who is described as a raw-boned, uncouth lad, that had never derived the early benefit of one hour's social polish or example, should suddenly, upon entering the world, conduct himself in such a manner as to be a pattern to his species for chivalrous and elegant deportment; but, as the hero of a story, he should scarcely be distinguished for meanness, and still less for ingratitude and unkindness. Roderick's treatment of Strap (who has infinitely the finer nature of the two) is rarely what it should be, and often what it should not be, for he is under constant obligations to Strap, yet he always assumes to be the higher being, and at times he behaves towards him with positive brutality. His deportment towards his mistress, Narcissa, is that of a man acquainted with women only under the most degrading of positions, while his proposal to marry an old woman, solely for money, sinks him at once to the level of a mere scoundrel, and, what is worse, a sordid scoundrel. Such a character, it is true, is often heard of in real life; but such a character is scarcely fit to be the hero of a story, the more especially as we constantly encounter beggings of the question in his favour, and that, upon the whole, we are called upon to receive and to congratulate him upon his final triumph, and the respectable position he has attained in society.

It is of no use to mince the matter; nothing could make Roderick Random respectable with such qualifications to form the groundwork of his moral nature. If Smollett designed to represent a purely commonplace character, with a considerable portion of very base alloy in it, and without reference to the moral canons in romance composition, he has eminently succeeded in his construction of that of Roderick Random, but, to repeat, such a one is not a subject for heroic life.

But Smollett's talent lay in vigorous descriptions of broad humour, whether in person, character, action, or scenery, and in these it may be said he has been surpassed by few. The scenes he had witnessed in life he described in the broadest sunlight of vividness. He had been a surgeon on board of a man-of-war, and every portion of his novels that have any reference to the seaman or a seafaring life may be given in upon evidence and sworn to. The whole scene on board the man-of-war is as minute and true as a Dutch painting. Smollett's language, moreover, is admirably adapted for humorous description, being natural, easy, concise, and home-striking to the point. He likewise possesses amazing power in narrations of terrific adventure, as, witness the forest scene with the robbers in *Count Fathom*. And for his humour, all the night adventures in inns may be quoted. What can surpass in drollery of thought his making one of the land-ladies rush forth upon an occasion of alarm, installed in that never-described article of her husband's wardrobe, with the wrong side before? The humour of the circumstance may surely plead for this allusion to it. All the scenes with Captain Weasel, and in the waggon, together with multitudes of others that might be recalled, proclaim him a farcist of the highest order.

Of sentiment, delicacy, and refinement; above all, refinement of the heart, if Smollett possessed and exhibited any in his personal associations in the world, he cared little to exemplify them in his writings; for in these qualifications his heroes are positively naught; his heroines are distilled mawkishness, and his subordinate women (when unpleasant) are awful. His common, inferior characters, when good, have a fine rough and sturdy perfection about them. Roderick's uncle, Lieutenant Bowling, is a man to take to one's heart. For correctness, as well as consistency, that character may stand "unbonneted" before any one that has been described in ancient or modern fiction. It is nature herself; and nature in rough, unhewn simplicity and goodness. The character, too, of Strap is, I believe, quite as accurately as it is humourously drawn. If a romantic attachment such as he manifests for Roderick be questioned in the great working-day world of real life, I can only say that I could formerly have quoted a parallel to the friendly devotion of that simple-hearted barber. The remonstrance that he makes to his friend, when he offers to pawn everything he has in the world—even his razors—to assist him in his necessities, is at once touching and humourous, and (as it should be) more touching even than humourous.—CHARLES COWDEN CLARKE, "On the Comic Writers of England: XIV. Fielding, Smollett and Sterne," *Gentleman's Magazine*, May 1872, pp. 565–67

A work of fiction may easily be more valuable than a history. Smollett's *Roderick Random* is better worth preserving than the same author's continuation of Hume.—MARK PATTISON, "Pope and His Editors" (1872), *Essays*, ed. Henry Nettleship, 1889, Vol. 2, p. 356

The most interesting naval character in *Roderick Random* is the hero's maternal uncle, Lieutenant Bowling. In him Smollett seized at once, and fixed for ever, the old type of seaman—rough as a polar bear, brave, simple, kindly—and out of his element everywhere except afloat. Bowling has left his mark in many a sea novel, the key to his eccentricities being that he, and such as he, did really live more afloat than ashore; and in days when the shore life had not a fiftieth part of the close influence on the sea life which it has now. Hence, of course, his very language has little in common with that of other people—a peculiarity now seen nowhere except in stage sailors, of whom the world (as we have hinted already) has shown itself to be fairly tired—except, of course, in such exceptional cases as "Black-Eyed Susan," written by a man of genius, who had himself been at sea. Bowling certainly carries the habit of professional speech as far as the limits of art will allow. At the death-bed of the mean old curmudgeon, Roderick Random's grandfather, the lieutenant observes, "Yes, yes, he's a-going; the land-crabs will have him, I see that; his anchor's a-peak, i' faith." And he startles the greedy relatives, after the old man's death, with "Odd's fish! now my dream is out, for all the world. I thought I stood upon the forecastle, and saw a parcel of carrion crows foul of a dead shark that floated alongside, and the Devil perching upon our sprit-sail yard in the likeness of a blue bear, who, d'ye see, jumped overboard upon the carcase, and carried it to the bottom in his claws." Yet the lieutenant is a good fellow, and of more tenderness than most men. Only his own sort of qualities are precisely the opposite of those of worldlings, and hypocrites; while sea life and war, and the hardening habits of the service, have made him indifferent to the social softening down of things, which, without amending hearts, refines manners. Bowling blurts out what his contemporary, Lord Chesterfield, might have equally said, but in a whisper and in an epigram. The frankness, which is still a marked characteristic of our naval officers, is only the freedom of the Bowling school strained, as it were, through three generations of increasing culture and amenity. The oak has got polished, and that is all; and there is a mighty difference between kinds of refinement, between polished oak and veneered deal.

Commodore Trunnion is, perhaps, more amusing than Bowling. He is not such a likeable man; and we are even left to doubt whether his wounds were all gained in action. But how irresistibly comic he is! His beating to windward in the lanes, his involuntary part in the fox-hunt—what capital specimens these are of that hearty natural comedy which is good not merely for the spirits and temper of the reader, but for his very lungs and digestion. Without disparaging the charm of subtle analysis of character, delicate tracing of sentiment, rare, choice ease of wit and irony—is it not good for us all, every now and then, to go back to those masters who honestly devote themselves to giving us downright fun? We laugh, inwardly, with the poetic and philosophical humourists: we laugh, outwardly, with Smollett, and those who resemble Smollett. There was no gentle tickling about his satire. It was all hard hitting, whether the subject be the brutal bullies, Dr. Mackshane and Captain Oakhum, or the loathsome fop, Captain Whiffle, radiant in silk, lace, and diamond buckles, who, when Random comes to bleed him, exclaims, "Hast thou ever blooded anybody but brutes?—But I need not ask thee, for thou wilt tell me a most damnable lie." The reader to whom such subjects are new is surprised to find in Smollett a dandy glittering with gems, drenched with essences, and talking like the latest fashion of fool of quality, alongside the tarry veterans in check shirts, odorous only of pitch, tobacco, and rum. But the truth is, that this juxtaposition of opposite types was of very ancient date in the history of the Navy, and has only lately disappeared. There were good officers who were gentlemen, and there were good officers who were "tarpaulings." But the fools of each type supplied the comic material—such as the Whiffle we have just seen, of the one sort, or the Oakhum, to whose command he succeeds, of the other. Both were usually tyrants; but the best seaman of the two was rather the tyrant who smelt of tar than the tyrant who smelt of lavender water.

In painting these queer portraits, and showing their action

upon the life of ships and squadrons, the naval novelist becomes a contributor to his country's naval history. What can the ordinary reader, indeed, make of naval history, generally, with its diagrams and technicalities—even of such excellent books as those of James, Captain Brenton, or Admiral Ekins? He must make preparatory studies if he really means to read them. But in a good sea novel, a sea fight is made living and intelligible, and the kind of men that the fighters were is brought home to him with a reality beyond the historian's reach. Hence, when Mr. Carlyle, in his great work on Frederick, has to touch on the Carthagena expedition, he quotes *Roderick Random* as the best authority on the subject. —JAMES HANNAY, "Sea Novels—Captain Marryat," *Cornhill Magazine*, Feb. 1873, pp. 173–75

It must be apparent now why, in spite of its faults, *Roderick Random* is one of the great English novels. Though the book is inorganic, its style is easy and polished, and it is enlivened by delicious humour and keen satire. Of Smollett, as of Defoe, it has been justly said that much of his work is clever reporting, but reporting which preserves the life about him for all time. In one respect, however, Smollett's *Roderick Random* is far ahead of anything of his famous predecessor. Most of its characters are thoroughly alive—sometimes, to be sure, eccentric to the point of unnaturalness, but even so, vivified and amusing. And as they pass back and forth, and smile and scold, and vex and comfort one another, they seem above all things a marvellously human set of individuals—the more marvellously so, if one stops to reflect that Smollett was only twenty-six when he created them. They may not be people with whom it is well for every youthful reader to come in contact; we might like them better if they exchanged some of their rationalism for idealism; but even taking them just as they are, we find in their life, with all its roughness, a stimulating robustness which is in wholesome contrast to the rather morbid and effeminate spirituality of some later fiction.—G. H. MAYNADIER, "Introduction" to *The Adventures of Roderick Random*, 1902, Vol. 1, pp. 26–27

PEREGRINE PICKLE

The author of the adventures of *Peregrine Pickle*, had before given, in those of *Roderick Random*, a specimen of his talents for this species of writing, which had been so well received by the public, as to encourage his entering on the present work.

The first volume is chiefly taken up with introductory accounts of the family of *Peregrine Pickle*, who is the hero of the piece, of incidents which preceded his birth—His boyish pranks—His mother's capricious aversion to him, which, after a fruitless appeal to his own father, who is too much wife-ridden to do his son natural justice, throws him into an intire dependence on his uncle—His falling in love with *Emilia*, the consequences of this passion, and several juvenile sallies, and adventures, till he arrives at a competent age for setting out on his travels to *France*.

In this volume, the author seems to have aimed more at proportioning his style to his subject, in imitation of *Lazarillo de Tormes, Guzman d' Alfarache, Gil Blas de Santillane*, and *Scarron's Comic Romance*, than he has respected the delicacy of those readers, who call every thing *Low* that is not taken from high-life, which is, however, rarely susceptible of that humour and drollery which occur in the more familiar walks of common life. But, to pronounce with an air of decision, that he has every where preserved propriety and nature, would sound more towards interested commendation than genuine criticism.—JOHN CLELAND, *Monthly Review*, March 1751, pp. 357–58

At candlelight D. D., and I read by turns, and what do *you think* has been part of our study?—why truly *Peregrine Pickle!* We never undertook it before, but *it is wretched stuff*; only Lady V's. history is a curiosity.—MARY DELANY, Letter to Mrs. Dewes (1752)

> Or with poor Smollett, fain for gold to tickle,
> Wrought up with liquorish gust, the feats of Pickle;
> Or, sinning deeper, like repentant Punk,
> Call'd gloating females to abhor the Monk;
> —LADY ANNE HAMILTON, *The Epics of the Ton*, 1807

> The characters in *Peregrinus Pickle*
> All teach us wisdom, while our sides they tickle;
> They argue not from what their acts ensue,
> But tell us what they are from what they do.
> —ROBERT DWER JOYCE, "Reflections," *Scribner's Monthly Magazine*, Aug. 1877, p. 446

FERDINAND COUNT FATHOM

The novel in question is *The Adventures of Ferdinand Count Fathom*, published in two volumes 12mo, in 1753; and a portion of the apologetic dedication prefixed to it is:—"Know then, I can despise your pride while I honour your integrity; and applaud your taste, while I am shocked at your ostentation. I have known you trifling, superficial, and obstinate in dispute; meanly jealous, and awkwardly reserved; rash and haughty in your resentments; and coarse and lowly in your connexions. I have blushed at the weakness of your conversation, and trembled at the errors of your conduct. Yet, as I own you possess certain good qualities which overbalance these defects, and distinguish you on this occasion as a person for whom I have the most perfect attachment and esteem, you have no cause to complain of the indelicacy with which your faults are reprehended; and as they are chiefly the excesses of a sanguine disposition and looseness of thought, impatient of caution or control; you may, thus stimulated, watch over your own intemperance and infirmity with redoubled vigilance and consideration, and for the future profit by the severity of my reproof."

Talk like this in a dedication to a new book by a genius all in flame, still struggling at thirty-two years of age, eager to excel all at once, and painfully sensible of the inconvenience of talk in another strain, is dogged with a sense of blended apology and advertisement, and with a suspicion that it squirts from a source about as profound as the tongue and the tips of two fingers and a thumb. The talk, let us hope, will by and bye proceed in an opposite direction. When a man begins to say such things to himself, all alone and in the strictest confidence, he is in a hopeful way; and in some score of years or so, more or less, according to the bulk of certain elements of an earthy sort, and according to the action of certain incidents of a torturing kind, the spirit of the talk will perhaps have inspired the temper, and become a law of life to it. As an account of the inner man, Smollett, it has, no doubt, a good deal of truth in it. Many years later he drew only a line, and laid down two points, of the outer man in the face. Tabitha Bramble's tongue is the black-lead used. She says, when comparing Humphry Clinker's features to the family portrait, "I do think he has got the trick of the eye, and the tip of the nose of my uncle Lloyd of Flluydwelltyn; and, as for the long chin, it is the very moral of the governor's."

Ferdinand Count Fathom never became a classical novel. All the biographers have found a reason for this ready to hand in the author's unwise words in his dedication to the individual already identified. The words are: "Let me not be condemned for having chosen my principal character from the purlieus of treachery and fraud, when I declare my purpose is to set him up as a beacon for the benefit of the unexperienced and unwary." Here was ready to hand a necessary and sufficient explanation of a difficulty. The author had begun to work another vein for a metal seen to be different from what he had previously sent to the market; but who was to explain the difference? He had not, wise workman as he was, cleaned out the one from which he had previously taken two tremendous hauls. But variety would please himself and amuse his customers. He would introduce mystery. This would be something new. Everything had been naked and open hitherto. But now a chapter headed, "The mystery unfolded. Another recognition which, it is hoped, the reader could not foresee," would at least give the author a thrill of fresh sensation in the preparation of it. And then description of scenery had not been his forte thus far. He had ventured on a short description of a storm at sea. Now he would try a land-storm in the Black Forest, and a robber's hut, and the bloody doings of cut-throats and a beldame. These accordingly were conceived and brought forth by that healthy generation of intellect of which only genius is capable. But all this, being new, was strange and difficult to an intelligent public. Random and Pickle had shown a faint outline of the genteelest comedy, crammed with the broadest and coarsest farce. But here was melo-drama looking as like tragedy as a black cloak and a scowl look like deeds of terror and death. Random was a roisterer, Pickle was a trickster, but both were full of fun; Fathom was a cheat, and incapable of a thoughtless joke. Above all, Random and Pickle had both been brought out of their scrapes. Their end was social success. Fathom was a social failure. As to moral failure or success, there was not much to choose among the three. But socially there was all the difference. All these things, the last especially, puzzled the public. An explanation was wanted, the critics were looked to, and the author supplied the key. He, like Sir Walter Scott, when he gossiped so unwarily about his poetry, threw up his own brief. All the biographers have informed us of the fact; and the badness of Fathom's character has gratified the sense of goodness in people whose goodness has not extended to their judgment. There is a toughness in the novel-reading faculty which can stand, and has frequently stood, far worse than Fathom, when Random and Pickle have not gone before. *Ferdinand Count Fathom* coming first from an author, or following novels in its own line, would not have been a drag on his reputation. But coming from Smollett, after he had balanced himself on the very apex of the comical cone, was more than his public could stand or understand.

In one respect this novel is like the other two: Le Sage is still the master, and *Gil Blas* the model.—DAVID HERBERT, "Life of Tobias George Smollett," *The Works of Tobias Smollett,* 1870

HISTORY OF ENGLAND

With respect to the History now before us, the Compiler does not pretend to have discovered any hidden records, or authentic materials, that have escaped the notice of former Writers; or to have thrown such lights upon contested events, or disputed characters, as may serve to rectify any mistaken opinions mankind may have entertained, with respect to either. His care is rather to disburthen former Histories of those tedious vouchers, and proofs of authenticity, which, in his opinion, only serve to swell the page, and exercise the Reader's patience. He seldom quotes authorities in support of his representations; and if he now and then condescends to cite the testimony of former Writers, he never points to the page, but leaves the sceptical Reader to supply any defect of this kind, by an exertion of that industry which the Author disdains: and thus, on the veracity of the Relator are we to rest our conviction, and accept his own word for it, that he has no intention to deceive or mislead us.

That this Author, however, has no such design, may be fairly presumed from his declining all attempts to bias us by any remarks of his own. Determined to avoid all *useless disquisitions,* as his plan professes, he steers wide indeed of that danger, and avoids all *disquisition* as *useless.* A brief recital of facts is chiefly what the public is to expect from this performance. But, with submission, we think the ingenious Author might have afforded us something more. He has undoubted ability; and he well knows, that a moderate interspersion of manly and sensible observations, must have greatly enlivened his work, and would hardly have been deemed superfluous by such Readers as have any turn for reflection.

With respect to the stile of this Historian, it is, in general clear, nervous, and flowing; and we think it impossible for a Reader of taste not to be pleased with the perspicuity, and elegance of his manner. But what he seems principally to value himself upon, and what his Patronizers chiefly mention in praise of his performance, are the characters he has summed up, at the close of every reign.—OLIVER GOLDSMITH, "Smollet's *History of England,*" *Monthly Review,* June 1757, pp. 531–32

⟨. . .⟩ Smollot, who I am sorry disgraces his Talent by writeing those Stupid Romances commonly call'd History.—LADY MARY WORTLEY MONTAGU, Letter to the Countess of Bute (Oct. 3, 1758)

Robertson's History is, I think, extremely well written.—It was well observed, that nobody in the Augustan age could conceive that so soon after, a Horse should be made Consul: and yet matters were so well prepared by the time of Caligula, that nobody was surprised at the matter. So when Clarendon and Temple wrote History, they little thought the time was so near when a vagabond Scot should write nonsense ten thousand strong.—WILLIAM WARBURTON, Letter to Richard Hurd (Jan. 30, 1759), *Letters from a Late Eminent Prelate,* 1808

I am reading again, the *History of England,* that of Smollet. ⟨. . .⟩ I have read to the reign of George the Second, and, in spight of the dislike I have to Smollet's language and style of writing, I am much entertained, for scarce a name is now mentioned that is not familiar to my ear, and I delight in thus *tracing* the *rise* and *progress* of the great characters of the age. —FANNY BURNEY, *Diary,* April 1770

Smollett's work is a rapid performance, but not worthy of its author. Smollett was a man, not only possessed of a strong vein of coarse humor, but one of laborious activity and of a powerful mind, fitted therefore to succeed in a literary enterprise. On this occasion, however, it is understood that he was only desirous, and only employed, to draw up a narrative on the Tory side of the question. It was his fate, as it has been but too often the unhappy fate of men of genius, to be obliged to convert literature into a means of subsistence.—WILLIAM SMYTH, *Lectures on Modern History,* 1840, Lecture 26

TRAVELS THROUGH FRANCE AND ITALY

I was best pleased with my old and excellent friend Smollett, testy and discontented as he is, he writes with perspicuity; his observations are generally sensible, and even his oddities are entertaining.—FRANCIS GARDEN, LORD GARDENSTONE, *Travelling Memoranda,* 1792–95

His journal is, for the most part, an unattractive record of annoyances and discomforts, marked by considerable energy of expression, but wearisome from its sameness. With innkeepers, ostlers, and postilions, especially, he seems to have been in a state of perpetual war; and he fell into so many quarrels with them that the wonder is, considering the revengeful and vindictive character of the lower class of Italians, that he ever got out of the country alive. He is every where devoured by vermin, poisoned with bad food, and pillaged by extortionate landlords. Indeed, making all allowances for his diseased state of mind and body, travelling in Italy at that period must have been a very uncomfortable experience, requiring patience, animal spirits, and a well-stocked purse to make it at all endurable. ⟨. . .⟩

That Smollett, in recording the incidents of such a journey, should have put a good deal of gall into his ink, is not a matter of surprise; but it is rather remarkable that his journal should be so devoid of literary merit. The author of *Humphrey Clinker* seems to have packed his genius away at the bottom of his trunk, and not taken it out during his whole tour. His spirit is all put forth in vituperation; but otherwise he is tame and commonplace.—GEORGE STILLMAN HILLARD, *Six Months in Italy*, 1853, Vol. 2, pp. 375–77

Few books have ever been more heartily abused than Smollett's *Travels*, and of late years few have been less read. The faults of the book lie very plainly on the surface. It is written in a bad temper, to begin with, and with a decided wilfulness that rather enjoys giving offence. On all matters appertaining to art, it is invariably provoking and usually wrong. The coarseness of the novels is in it, with comparatively little of that boisterous humour which in the novels redeems the coarseness. To use the slang of the day—for slang is by no means confined to the vulgar—it is essentially the work of a Philistine—ay, and of a man who decidedly glories in his Philistinism. All this may readily be granted. Squeamish people will find the book unsavoury, connoisseurs will declare it heretical, and the lovers of "the picturesque" had much better give it a wide berth. To sum up its defects, it was written by a man whose life had been comparatively a failure, who had just been beaten down by a heavy domestic sorrow, and whose health had failed him—a man who had all the prejudices of his contemporaries and many of his own; who was irritable, violent, and coarse. Sentimentally journeying, Sterne could have fallen in with no volume more offensive. When one walks through life in a genteel way, with an embroidered handkerchief at one's eyes, it is positively distressing to run against such a "rough" as Smollett—such a lump of mere raw manhood, and choleric bravery, and cynical kindness, and—worst of all—"bad taste." Hence, the mellifluous wanderer starts aside, distinctly declines to journey with such an objectionable fellow-traveller, and, leaving Dr. Smollett to complain of being badly fed by an avaricious innkeeper, turns politely away to have a good cry over the famous dead donkey. Smollett shall figure, henceforward, as "Smellfungus;" all the complaints which he tells to the world "he had better have told to his physician!" ⟨. . .⟩

The faults of the book admitted, it is quite time to assert—which I do with considerable confidence—that it has merits equally conspicuous. The absolute frankness and sincerity with which Smollett speaks his mind may lead him into many outrages upon good breeding, but assuredly must be considered well worth having, even at that heavy price. There is not a more truthful book in the language. I make no attempt to

defend its criticisms on art; but I may perhaps venture to hint that some of the notions which were considered almost blasphemous by the dilettante of the last century would pass for very pardonable heresies in 1869. Out and away, however, from the debateable land of art, Smollett's admirable keenness and precision of observation impress themselves more and more forcibly upon you the more you read him. He may not know how to look at a statue or a picture; he may be culpably indifferent to the Correggioscity of Correggio; but for the actual incidents of life and aspects of nature he has as keen an eye as any traveller of his day.—W. J. PROWSE, "Smollett at Nice," *Macmillan's Magazine*, April 1870, pp. 529–30

HUMPHRY CLINKER

Little less offence was taken at a party novel, written by the profligate hireling Smollett, to vindicate the Scots and cry down juries.—HORACE WALPOLE, *Memoirs of the Reign of King George the Third*, 1771

The very ingenious scheme of describing the various effects produced upon different members of the same family by the same objects, was not original, though it has been supposed to be so. Anstey, the facetious author of the *New Bath Guide*, had employed it six or seven years before *Humphrey Clinker* appeared. But Anstey's diverting satire was but a light sketch compared to the finished and elaborate manner in which Smollett has, in the first place, identified his characters, and then fitted them with language, sentiments, and powers of observation, in exact correspondence with their talents, temper, condition, and disposition. The portrait of Matthew Bramble, in which Smollett described his own peculiarities, using towards himself the same rigid anatomy which he exercised upon others, is unequalled in the line of fictitious composition. It is peculiarly striking to observe, how often, in admiring the shrewd and sound sense, active benevolence, and honourable sentiments combined in Matthew, we lose sight of the humorous peculiarities of his character, and with what effect they are suddenly recalled to our remembrance, just at the time and in the manner when we least expect them. All shrewish old maids, and simple waitingwomen, which shall hereafter be drawn, must be contented with the praise of approaching in merit to Mrs. Tabitha Bramble and Winifred Jenkins. The peculiarities of the hotheaded young Cantab, and the girlish romance of his sister, are admirably contrasted with the sense and pettish half-playful misanthropy of their uncle; and Humphrey Clinker (who by the way resembles Strap, supposing that excellent person to have a turn towards methodism) is, as far as he goes, equally delightful. Captain Lismahago was probably no violent caricature, allowing for the manners of the time. We can remember a good and gallant officer who was said to have been his prototype, but believe the opinion was only entertained from the striking resemblance which he bore in externals to the doughty captain.

When *Humphrey Clinker* appeared in London, the popular odium against the Scotch nation, which Wilkes and Churchill had excited, was not yet appeased, and Smollett had enemies amongst the periodical critics, who failed not to charge him with undue partiality to his own country. They observed, maliciously, but not untruly, that the cynicism of Matthew Bramble becomes gradually softened as he journeys northward, and that he who equally detested Bath and London, becomes wonderfully reconciled to walled cities and the hum of men, when he finds himself an inhabitant of the northern metropolis. It is not worth defending so excellent a work against so weak an objection. The author was a dying man, and his thoughts were turned towards the scenes of youthful gaiety and the abode of early friends, with a fond partiality, which had they been even less deserving of his attachment, would have been not only pardonable, but praiseworthy.

> Moritur, et moriens dulces reminiscitur Argos.

Smollett failed not, as he usually did, to introduce himself, with the various causes which he had to complain of the world, into the pages of this delightful romance. He appears as Mr. Serle, and more boldly under his own name, and in describing his own mode of living, he satirizes without mercy the book-makers of the day, who had experienced his kindness without repaying him by gratitude. It does not, however, seem perfectly fair to make them atone for their ungracious return to his hospitality, by serving up their characters as a banquet to the public; and, in fact, it too much resembles the design of which Pallet accuses the Physician, of converting his guests into patients, in order to make him amends for the expense of the entertainment.—SIR WALTER SCOTT, "Tobias Smollett" (1821), *Lives of the Novelists*, 1825

Smollett had long broken away from Le Sage; there is not a nail-head of the framework of *Gil Blas* in *Humphry Clinker.* Sir Walter Scott in *Redgauntlet* and *Guy Mannering* has made effective use of its plan of carrying on the story in letters; and others, such as Miss Muloch, have followed Sir Walter Scott. It is to be noted, however, as peculiar to Smollett, that the story is carried on by letters not replied to. In the letters of Tabitha Bramble and Winifred Jenkins we have early and the very best specimens of wit, which wings itself out upon bad spelling. This work is the *Logos* of Tobias George Smollett purified and obedient. It is the man himself again after many evil spirits which took early possession of him were cast out. He is now neither a Random Scotchman nor an English Pickle, but a humble Welsh Bramble of Brambleton Hall.—DAVID HERBERT, "Life of Tobias George Smollett," *The Works of Tobias Smollett*, 1870

At Pisa he was visited by Sir Horace Mann, who did what he could for him; and among other work he wrote his charming novel of *Humphrey Clinker*, in which he has evidently figured himself under the character of Matthew Bramble, whom Hannay calls "the most credible specimen of the *bourru bienfaisant* in literature." The charm of the book lies in its sweetness, which is the ripe product of Southern influence combined with ill health.—EUGENE SCHUYLER, "Smollett in Search of Health" (1889), *Italian Influences*, 1901, p. 242

'No one will contend,' says Henry Fielding in the Preface to one of his sister's books, 'that the epistolary Style is in general the most proper to a Novelist, or that [and here he was plainly thinking of a certain work called *Pamela*] it hath been used by the best Writers of this Kind.' The former part of the proposition is undeniable; but however true the latter may have been when Fielding wrote in 1747, it is scarcely as true now. Even if we omit for the moment all consideration of modern examples, *Clarissa* and *Sir Charles Grandison*—both of them novels told by letters, and in one of which Richardson emphatically vindicated his claim to rank among the 'best Writers'—followed *Pamela* before Fielding's death. Half-a-dozen years after that event, another and a greater than Richardson adopted the same medium for a masterpiece; and the sub-title of Rousseau's *Nouvelle Héloïse* is, *Lettres de deux amants, habitants d'une petite ville au pied des Alpes.* Still later—in 1771—the 'epistolary Style' was chosen, for his final fiction, by one of Fielding's own countrymen; and in the success of the enterprise, the fact that it was achieved in what Mrs. Barbauld correctly defines as 'the most natural and the least probable way of telling a story,' has fallen out of sight. To think of *Grandison* or *Clarissa* is to remember that the prolixity of those prolix performances is increased by the form; but in Smollett's *Expedition of Humphry Clinker* the form is scarcely felt as an objection, assuredly not as an obstruction. It is true, also, that between Smollett's last and best book and the books of the authors mentioned there are some other not unimportant differences. One of these lies in the circumstance that his communications are never replied to—a detail which, however irritating in a practical correspondence, obviates in a novel much of the wearisome repetition usually charged against epistolary narrative; another difference is, that there is no serious approach to anything like a connected story in the detached recollections of travel recorded by the characters in *Humphry Clinker.* Entertaining in themselves, those characters in their progress encounter other characters who are equally entertaining, and an apology for a conclusion is obtained by the conventional cluster of marriages at the end; but as far as the intrigue itself is concerned, the book would have been just as amusing if Tabitha Bramble had never become Mrs. Lismahago, or if Winifred Jenkins, in her 'plain pea-green tabby sack, Runnela cap, ruff toupee and side curls,' had declined to bestow herself upon the fortunate foundling who gives his name to the volumes, although—to quote a contemporary critic—he 'makes almost as inconsiderable a figure in the work as the dog does in the history of Tobit.'

But it is not our present intention to hunt old trails with a new 'appreciation' of the misnamed *Expedition of Humphry Clinker.* Matthew Bramble and Obadiah Lismahago, the squire's sister and her Methodist maid, have passed permanently into literature, and their places are as secure as those of Partridge and Parson Adams, of Corporal Trim and 'my Uncle Toby.' Not even the Malapropoism of Sheridan or Dickens is quite as riotously diverting, as rich in its unexpected turns, as that of Tabitha Bramble and Winifred Jenkins, especially Winifred, who remains delightful even when deduction is made of the poor and very mechanical fun extracted from the parody of her pietistic phraseology. That it could ever have been considered witty to spell 'grace' 'grease,' and 'Bible' 'byebill,' can only be explained by the indiscriminate hostility of the earlier assailants of Enthusiasm. Upon this, as well as upon a particularly evil-smelling taint of coarseness which, to the honour of the author's contemporaries, was fully recognized in his own day as offensive, it is needless now to dwell. But there is an aspect of *Humphry Clinker* which has been somewhat neglected—namely, its topographical side; and from the fact that Smollett, in the initial pages, describes it as *Letters upon Travels*, it is clear that he himself admitted this characteristic of his work. When he wrote it at Leghorn in 1770, he was using his gamut of personages mainly to revive, from different points of view, the impressions he had received in his last visits to Bath, to London, and to certain towns in his native North. We are told by Chambers that his pictures of life at these places were all accepted by his relatives as personal records; and though some of the first reviews condemned him for wasting time on descriptions of what every one then knew by heart, we are not likely to insist upon that criticism now, when nearly a century and a quarter of change has lent to those descriptions all the charm—the fatal charm—of the remote and the half-forgotten.—AUSTIN DOBSON, "The Topography of *Humphry Clinker*," *Eighteenth Century Vignettes: Second Series*, 1894

POETRY

This ode ⟨"The Tears of Scotland"⟩, by Dr. Smollet, does rather more honour to the author's feelings than his taste. The mechanical part, with regard to numbers and language, is not so perfect as so short a work as this requires; but the pathetic it contains, particularly in the last stanza but one, is exquisitely fine.—OLIVER GOLDSMITH, *The Beauties of English Poetry*, 1767

The few poems which he has left have a portion of delicacy which is not to be found in his novels; but they have not, like those prose fictions, the strength of a master's hand. Were he to live over again, we might wish him to write more poetry, in the belief that his poetical talent would improve by exercise; but we should be glad to have more of his novels just as they are.—THOMAS CAMPBELL, *Specimens of the British Poets*, 1819

So long as his odes to "Leven Water" and to "Independence" exist Smollett can never fail to be admired as a poet, nor can a feeling of regret be avoided that he did not devote more of his genius to poetic compositions. We cannot take leave of this distinguished Scotchman—distinguished as a historian, as a novelist, and as the author of lines which possess the masculine strength of Dryden—without alluding to a passage in his novel of *Peregrine Pickle*, that passage so inexpressibly touching where the Jacobite exiles stand every morning on the coast of France to contemplate the blue hills of their native land, to which they are never to return!—JAMES GRANT WILSON, *The Poets and Poetry of Scotland*, 1876, Vol. 1, p. 203

ROBERT ANDERSON
From "The Life of Tobias Smollett, M.D."
The History of England by Tobias Smollett

1805, Volume 1, pp. 107–13, 123–25

The character of Smollett, at the present period, when prejudice and partiality have, in a great measure, subsided, will be better understood by this account of his life, than by any laboured comment; yet, as he has had the lot to be more read than applauded, and less applauded than he deserves, it may not be superfluous here to attempt to collect, into one point of view, his most prominent excellencies and defects, and to endeavour, by stating his literary pretensions, and estimating his worth, to ascertain the rank to which he is entitled among the writers of our nation.

In his person and manners, Smollett was fashioned to prepossess all men in his favour. His figure was manly, graceful and handsome, and in his air and manner there was a dignity that commanded respect, joined with a benignity that inspired affection. With the most polished manners, and the finest address, he possessed a loftiness and elevation of sentiment and character, without vanity or affectation. His general behaviour bore the genuine stamp of true politeness, the result of an overflowing humanity and goodness of heart. He was a man of upright principles, and of great and extensive benevolence. The friend of sense and of virtue, he not only embraced, but sought occasions of doing good. He was the reliever of the distressed, the protector of the helpless, and the encourager of merit. His conversation was sprightly, instructive, and agreeable; like his writings, pregnant with wit and intelligence, and animated with sallies of humour and pleasantry. In his opinions of mankind, except where his personal and political prejudices were concerned, he was candid and liberal. To those who were above him he allowed the due superiority, but

he did not willingly associate with his superiors, and always with a consciousness of his personal dignity, and with evident indications of pride and reserve. To his equals and inferiors he behaved with ease and affability, without the insolence of familiarity, or the parade of condescension. With his amiable qualities and agreeable manners, he united courage and independence. In the declaration of his opinions he was open; in his actions he was intrepid, and often imprudent; a gentleman in principle, independent in spirit, and fearless of enemies, however powerful from their malignity, or formidable from their rank, no danger could prevent him from saying or doing those things which he conceived in themselves to be right, and in their consequences to be useful to his friends or his country. He had been bred a whig, and generally adhered to the principles of that party, which suited the independent turn of his mind; but impressed with a regard for public order and national tranquillity, he maintained a great reserve on the principles of resistance and opposition, amidst acknowledgments of their just foundation, and a sense of the benefits which arise to mankind from their seasonable operation. Regarding liberty as one great basis of national prosperity, he was jealous alike of encroachments on political freedom, and of the abuse of it. He was so far a tory, as to love and revere the monarchy; he was so far a whig, as to laugh at the notions of indefeasible right and non-resistance. He had a sincere love for his country, and a diffusive benevolence for the whole human race. His experience in the world inflamed his indignation against oppression, and his detestation of vice and corruption, in proportion to his love of virtue and zeal for the public good; and he thought it no violation of charity to stigmatize fraud, profligacy, and hypocrisy. But in his support of persons and measures, he sometimes considered only the persons and measures, without taking other objects and relations into the account. He was more frequently influenced by personal attachment, and hurried on by present impulse, than guided by comparative views of real advantage, examined by impartial reason. His opposition to men in power, often, in its warmth, exceeded the importance of the subject. He was occasionally misled, by a heated imagination, strong resentment, and the mortification of disappointed hope, into bitterness and party violence, long kept alive by the indecent and irritating provocations of triumphant adversaries. Under these impressions, his descriptions as an *historian* were often distorted, and his decisions as a *critic*, on the literary productions of some of his contemporaries, were sometimes warped by personal prejudice, and expressed in the harsh terms of contempt. He was jealous of his own fame, almost the sole reward of his labours, but he was not envious of that of others; he was easily provoked, and vindictive when provoked; but the vengeance he took was public, not circulated in whispers. Whatever end he pursued, he followed with an eagerness that was not necessary to compass it. The defects in his temperament, natural or habitual, made him unprosperous and unhappy. His sensibility was too ardent; his passions were too easily moved, and too violent and impetuous. His disposition was irritable, imprudent, and capricious; his candour frequently became credulity; his liberality often subjected him to deception; his favours were generally bestowed on the most undeserving of those who had recourse to his assistance; not so much from want of discernment, as want of resolution; for he had not fortitude to resist the importunity of even the most worthless and insignificant. He neglected sometimes to make use himself of the acute remarks he has made on the characters and conduct of others. In the domestic relations, his conduct was tender, affectionate, and exemplary. In friendship, he was ardent and steady; and the cordial esteem of his friends and acquaintance, is an honourable testimony to his moral and social character; but in the latter part of his life, he sometimes, very feelingly, bewailed the neglect and ingratitude he had experienced, in consequence of the mistaken connections he had formed, and to which every man of warm attachments will be exposed. He was known, however, to no man by whom his loss was not sincerely regretted. In the practice of physic, for want of suppleness, application and perseverance, he never was eminent. As an author, he was less successful than his happy genius and acknowledged merit certainly deserved. His connections were extensive, and his friends numerous and respectable; he was intimately acquainted with the most eminent of his literary and poetical contemporaries; he was respected by the world as a man of superior talents, wit, and learning, and had rendered himself serviceable to men in power; but he never acquired a patron among the great, who, by his favour or beneficence, relieved him from the necessity of writing for a subsistence. Booksellers may be said to have been his only patrons; and without doubt he made a great deal of money by his connections with them: and had he been a rigid economist, and endowed with the gift of retention, he might have lived and died very independent. He was not of that turn of mind which disposes men to become rich, and probably could not have made a fortune in any situation of life. But his difficulties, whatever they were, proceeded not from ostentation or extravagance. He was hospitable, but not ostentatiously so; his table was plentiful, but not extravagant. An irritable and impatient temper, and a proud, improvident disposition, were his greatest failings. In alleviation of his defects, let it be remembered, that a composed and happy temper, a heart at ease, and an independent situation, the most favourable circumstances perhaps in an author's fortune, were not the lot of Smollett. With a necessary indulgence for his frailties and errors, and making due allowance for a spirit cramped by a narrow fortune, wounded by ingratitude, and irritated by the malignant shafts of envy, dulness, and profligacy, it would be difficult to name a man so respectable for the extraordinary powers of his genius, and the generous qualities of his heart.

The predominant excellencies of his mind were fertility of invention, vigorous sense, brilliant fancy, and versatile humour. His understanding was quick and penetrating, his imagination lively, his memory retentive, and his humour original. In the course of his literary career, he has written variously, and much. His writings must be allowed as proofs of a versatility, as well as a fecundity of talents, not to be disputed, and perhaps seldom or ever exceeded by any writer in the same period of years. In extent and variety of science and erudition he has been surpassed by many, but he shows in his compositions that he was intimately acquainted with Greek and Roman literature, and had studied with success the various branches of modern learning. He had an extensive knowledge not only in physic, and the arts and sciences in general, but in moral and political philosophy, in ancient and modern history, in the laws and institutions of Europe, and in the constitution and government of his country. But the principal subject of his deliberate inquiry was the human character; and, in his literary progress, the representation of life and manners his principal object. Man he surveyed with the most accurate observation. His understanding, acute and vigorous, was well fitted for diving into the human mind. He had a strong sense of impropriety, and a nice discernment, both of natural and moral beauty and deformity. His humour, lively and versatile, could paint justly and agreeably what he saw in absurd or ludicrous aspects. He possessed a rapid and

clear conception, with an animated, unaffected, and graceful style. With much simplicity, he has much purity, and is, at the same time, both forcible and copious. His observations on life and manners are commonly just, strong, and comprehensive, and his reasoning generally sound and conclusive. His perceptions of beauty and deformity are vivid and distinct, his feelings ardent, his taste correct. His wit is prompt and natural, yet keen and manly. His humour, though lively and pungent, is not perhaps equal in strength and elegance to that of Congreve and Swift. In chastity and delicacy, it is inferior to that of Addison, but equal in purity and moral tendency to that of his contemporary, Fielding; it is poignant, sprightly, variegated, and founded on truth; it exposes successfully hypocrisy, impropriety, and such vices as are objects of ridicule. To trace the latent sources of human actions, and to develope the various incongruities of conduct arising from them, was the favourite bent of his mind; and in describing objects of this kind, whether in the way of fabulous narration, or dramatic composition, he is so peculiarly happy, that as a natural and humorous painter of life and manners, he has reflected the highest honour on the place of his nativity, and must ever be considered by his country among the first of her sons in literary reputation. ⟨. . .⟩

As a writer of that species of modern romance which has been denominated a *novel*, he is entitled to the praise of being one of the greatest that our nation has produced. He ranks with Cervantes, Le Sage, Marivaux, Rousseau, Richardson and Fielding, the great masters of prosaic fiction; and though we cannot say he has surpassed them, he has entered into a noble competition. He proves himself to have possessed, in an eminent degree, the powers which are required to excel in this species of composition; an extensive acquaintance with human nature, an acute discernment, and exact discrimination of characters, a correct judgment of probability in situations, an active imagination in devising and combining incidents, with command of language for describing them. His novels exhibit the features that give most dignity to this species of fiction, the artful conduct of an interesting plot, the dramatic delineation of characters drawn from actual observation, the accurate and captivating representation of real domestic life, without offending the modesty of nature, which are found in great perfection in the novels of Le Sage, professedly adopted by him as models of imitation. The vivacity of his characters, the interesting nature of his incidents, the epigrammatic turn of his dialogues, and the sly elliptical vein of satire by which he inculcates his moral, and endeavours to reform the follies of various orders in society, have perhaps been equalled, but certainly have not been surpassed, by Smollett. In representing the characters of men as they are, not as they ought to be, which seems to have been the object of Le Sage in his various works, Smollett displays much the spirit and humour of his model, and copies from nature with the pleasantry and descriptive fidelity of a Hogarth. In the knowledge of human nature, masculine humour, just observations on life, great variety of original characters, and the powers of his invention, he is equal to Richardson and Fielding; but he is inferior to them in pathos, sublimity, contrast of character, and regularity of fable. By perusing the pages of *Clarissa*, and *Tom Jones*, the passions are affected, the understanding is instructed, mirth is excited, and all the purposes of moral improvement are attained. The romances of Smollett are equally distinguished by a fertility of interesting incidents, and a strong, lively, and picturesque description of characters. They exhibit a series of natural pictures of life and manners, which rival the masterly productions of the moral, the sublime, the pathetic, but the tiresome

Richardson, with all his profound and accurate knowledge of the various movements of the passions; and the ingenious, the humourous, the diffuse Fielding, with all his wit, learning, and knowledge of mankind. Though Fielding displays an intimate acquaintance with human nature, and deserves the highest praise for his humour, the very skilful management of his fable, and the variety and contrast of his characters, and innumerable passages may be pointed out in Richardson, which do infinite credit to the goodness of his heart and the depth of his understanding, superior to the best efforts of Smollett; yet, after perusing the wire-drawn history of *Clarissa*, and the diffuse narrative of *Tom Jones*, we never quit them with so much reluctance as we feel in closing the pages of Smollett, who, with less regularity of fable, and without introducing so many observations of a moral tendency, or so much of what may be called fine writing, possesses, in an eminent degree, the art of rousing the feelings and fixing the attention of his readers. The style is characterised by a just selection of appropriate terms and descriptive expressions, by turns, easy, elegant, and pathetic. With so much merit, he is not without his faults. His style is sometimes course, his characters are sometimes overcharged, his humour is often indelicate, and he has exhibited some scenes which may corrupt a mind unseasoned by experience. His system of youthful profligacy, as exemplified in some of his libertines, is without excuse: Of genteel life, he has few portraits, and these are not executed in the most successful manner; his fine ladies and gentlemen are not favourites with his readers in general. Profligates, misanthropes, gamblers, and duellists, are among his favourite characters. His novels, however, are of a moral tendency; they have spirit, humour and morality, and display the beauties of that genius which allures and rewards the attention of the discreet reader. Unguarded as they are in many of their representations, they are highly entertaining, and will be always read with pleasure.

SIR WALTER SCOTT
From "Tobias Smollett" (1821)
Lives of the Novelists
1825

The person of Smollett was eminently handsome, his features prepossessing, and, by the joint testimony of all his surviving friends, his conversation in the highest degree instructive and amusing. Of his disposition, those who have read his works (and who has not done so?) may form a very accurate estimate; for in each of them he has presented, and sometimes under various points of view, the leading features of his own character, without disguising the most unfavourable of them. Nay, there is room to believe, that he rather exaggerated than softened that cynical turn of temper, which was the principal fault of his disposition, and which engaged him in so many quarrels. It is remarkable, that all his heroes, from Roderick Random downward, possess a haughty, fierce irritability of disposition, until the same features appear softened, and rendered venerable by age and philosophy, in Matthew Bramble. The sports in which they most delight are those which are attended with disgrace, mental pain, and bodily mischief to others; and their humanity is never represented as interrupting the course of their frolics. We know not that Smollett had any other marked failing, save that which he himself has so often and so liberally acknowledged. When

unseduced by his satirical propensities, he was kind, generous, and humane to others; bold, upright, and independent in his own character; stooped to no patron, sued for no favour, but honestly and honourably maintained himself on his literary labours; when, if he was occasionally employed in work which was beneath his talents, the disgrace must remain with those who saved not such a genius from the degrading drudgery of compiling and translating. He was a doating father and an affectionate husband; and the warm zeal with which his memory was cherished by his surviving friends, showed clearly the reliance which they placed upon his regard. Even his resentments, though often hastily adopted, and incautiously expressed, were neither ungenerous nor enduring. He was open to conviction, and ready to make both acknowledgment and allowance when he had done injustice to others, willing also to forgive and to be reconciled when he had received it at their hand.

Churchill, and other satirists, falsely ascribe to Smollett the mean passion of literary envy, to which his nature was totally a stranger. The manner in which he mentions Fielding and Richardson in the account of the literature of the century, shows how much he understood, and how liberally he praised, the merit of those, who, in the view of the world, must have been regarded as his immediate rivals. "The genius of Cervantes," in his generous expression, "was transfused into the novels of Fielding, who painted the characters, and ridiculed the follies of life, with equal strength, humour, and propriety;"—a passage which we record with pleasure, as a proof that the disagreement which existed betwixt Smollett and Fielding did not prevent his estimating with justice, and recording in suitable terms the merits of the Father of the English Novel. His historian, with equal candour, proceeds to tell his reader, that "the laudable aim of enlisting the passions on the side of virtue was successfully pursued by Richardson in his *Pamela*, *Clarissa*, and *Grandison*, a species of writing equally new and extraordinary, where, mingled with much superfluity and impertinence, we find a sublime system of ethics, an amazing knowledge and command of human nature."

In leaving Smollett's personal for his literary character, it is impossible not to consider the latter as contrasted with that of his eminent contemporary, Fielding. It is true, that such comparisons, though recommended by the example of Plutarch, are not in general the best mode of estimating individual merit. But in the present case, the contemporary existence, the private history, accomplishments, talents, pursuits, and, unfortunately, the fates of these two great authors, are so closely allied, that it is scarce possible to name the one without exciting recollections of the other. Fielding and Smollett were both born in the highest rank of society, both educated to learned professions, yet both obliged to follow miscellaneous literature as a means of subsistence. Both were confined, during their lives, by the narrowness of their circumstances,—both united a humorous cynicism with generosity and good-nature,—both died of the diseases incident to a sedentary life, and to literary labour,—and both drew their last breath in a foreign land, to which they retreated under the adverse circumstances of a decayed constitution, and an exhausted fortune.

Their studies were no less similar than their lives. They both wrote for the stage, and neither of them successfully. They both meddled in politics, and never obtained effectual patronage; they both wrote travels, in which they showed that their good humour was wasted under the sufferings of their disease; and, to conclude, they were both so eminently successful as novelists, that no other English author of that class has a right to be mentioned in the same breath with Fielding and Smollett.

If we compare the works of these two great masters yet more closely, we may assign to Fielding, with little hesitation, the praise of a higher and a purer taste than was shown by his rival; more elegance of composition and expression; a nearer approach to the grave irony of Swift and Cervantes; a great deal more address or felicity in the conduct of his story; and, finally, a power of describing amiable and virtuous characters, and of placing before us heroes, and especially heroines, of a much higher as well as more pleasing character than Smollett was able to present.

Thus the art and felicity with which the story of *Tom Jones* evolves itself, is nowhere found in Smollett's novels, where the heroes pass from one situation in life, and from one stage of society, to another totally unconnected, except that, as in ordinary life, the adventures recorded, though not bearing upon each other, or on the catastrophe, befall the same personage. Characters are introduced and dropped without scruple, and, at the end of the work, the hero is found surrounded by a very different set of associates from those with whom his fortune seemed at first indissolubly connected. Neither are the characters which Smollett designed should be interesting, half so amiable as his readers could desire. The low-minded Roderick Random, who borrows Strap's money, wears his clothes, and, rescued from starving by the attachment of that simple and kind-hearted adherent, rewards him by squandering his substance, receiving his attendance as a servant, and beating him when the dice ran against him, is not to be named in one day with the open-hearted, good-humoured, and noble-minded Tom Jones, whose libertinism (one particular omitted) is perhaps rendered but too amiable by his good qualities. We believe there are few readers who are not disgusted with the miserable reward assigned to Strap in the closing chapter of the novel. Five hundred pounds (scarce the value of the goods he had presented to his master), and the hand of a reclaimed street-walker, even when added to a Highland farm, seem but a poor recompense for his faithful and disinterested attachment. The Englishman is a hundred times more grateful to Partridge (whose morality is very questionable, and who follows Jones's fortunes with the self-seeking fidelity of a cur, who, while he loves his master, has his eye upon the flesh-pots), than Roderick Random shows himself towards the disinterested and generous attachment of poor Strap. There may be one way of explaining this difference of taste betwixt these great authors, by recollecting, that in Scotland, at that period, the absolute devotion of a follower to his master was something which entered into, and made part of the character of the lower ranks in general; and therefore domestic fidelity was regarded as a thing more of course than in England, and received less gratitude than it deserved, in consideration of its more frequent occurrence.

But to recur to our parallel betwixt the characters of Fielding and those of Smollett, we should do Jones great injustice by weighing him in the balance with the wild and ferocious Pickle, who,—besides his gross and base brutality towards Emilia, besides his ingratitude to his uncle, and the savage propensity which he shows, in the pleasure he takes to torment others by practical jokes resembling those of a fiend in glee,—exhibits a low and ungentleman-like tone of thinking, only one degree higher than that of Roderick Random. The blackguard frolic of introducing a prostitute, in a false character, to his sister, is a sufficient instance of that want of taste and feeling which Smollett's admirers are compelled to acknowledge, may be

detected in his writings. It is yet more impossible to compare Sophia or Amelia to the females of Smollett, who (excepting Aurelia Darnel) are drawn as the objects rather of appetite than of affection, and excite no higher or more noble interest than might be created by the houris of the Mahomedan paradise.

It follows from this superiority on the side of Fielding, that his novels exhibit, more frequently than those of Smollett, scenes of distress, which excite the sympathy and pity of the reader. No one can refuse his compassion to Jones, when, by a train of practices upon his generous and open character, he is expelled from his benefactor's house under the foulest and most heart-rending accusations; but we certainly sympathize very little in the distress of Pickle, brought on by his own profligate profusion, and enhanced by his insolent misanthropy. We are only surprised that his predominating arrogance does not weary out the benevolence of Hatchway and Pipes, and scarce think the ruined spendthrift deserves their persevering and faithful attachment.

But the deep and fertile genius of Smollett afforded resources sufficient to make up for these deficiencies; and when the full weight has been allowed to Fielding's superiority of taste and expression, his northern contemporary will still be found fit to balance the scale with his great rival. If Fielding had superior taste, the palm of more brillancy of genius, more inexhaustible richness of invention, must in justice be awarded to Smollett. In comparison with his sphere, that in which Fielding walked was limited and compared with the wealthy profusion of varied character and incident which Smollett has scattered through his works, there is a poverty of composition about his rival. Fielding's fame rests on a single *chef d'œuvre*; and the art and industry which produced *Tom Jones*, was unable to rise to equal excellence in *Amelia*. Though, therefore, we must prefer *Tom Jones* as the most masterly example of an artful and well-told novel, to any individual work of Smollett; yet *Roderick Random, Peregrine Pickle*, and *Humphrey Clinker*, do each of them far excel *Joseph Andrews* or *Amelia*; and, to descend still lower, *Jonathan Wild*, or *The Journey to the next World*, cannot be put into momentary comparison with *Sir Lancelot Greaves*, or *Ferdinand Count Fathom*.

Every successful novelist must be more or less a poet, even although he may never have written a line of verse. The quality of imagination is absolutely indispensable to him; his accurate power of examining and embodying human character and human passion, as well as the external face of nature, is not less essential; and the talent of describing well what he feels with acuteness, added to the above requisites, goes far to complete the poetic character. Smollett was, even in the ordinary sense, which limits the name to those who write verses, a poet of distinction; and in this particular, superior to Fielding, who seldom aims at more than a slight translation from the classics. Accordingly, if he is surpassed by Fielding in moving pity, the northern novelist soars far above him in his powers of exciting terror. Fielding has no passages which approach in sublimity to the robber-scene in *Count Fathom*; or to the terrible description of a sea-engagement, in which Roderick Random sits chained and exposed upon the poop, without the power of motion or exertion, during the carnage of a tremendous engagement. Upon many other occasions, Smollett's descriptions ascend to the sublime; and, in general, there is an air of romance in his writings, which raises his narratives above the level and easy course of ordinary life. He was, like a pre-eminent poet of our own day, a searcher of dark bosoms, and loved to paint characters under the strong agitation of fierce and stormy passions. Hence misanthropes, gamblers, and duellists, are as common in his works, as robbers in those of Salvator Rosa, and are drawn, in most cases, with the same terrible truth and effect. To compare *Ferdinand Count Fathom* to the *Jonathan Wild* of Fielding, would be perhaps unfair to the latter author; yet, the works being composed on the same plan (a very bad one, as we think), we cannot help placing them by the side of each other; when it becomes at once obvious that the detestable Fathom is a living and existing miscreant, at whom we shrink as if from the presence of an incarnate fiend, while the villain of Fielding seems rather a cold personification of the abstract principle of evil, so far from being terrible, that notwithstanding the knowledge of the world argued in many passages of his adventures, we are compelled to acknowledge him absolutely tiresome.

It is, however, chiefly in his profusion, which amounts almost to prodigality, that we recognise the superior richness of Smollett's fancy. He never shows the least desire to make the most either of a character, a situation, or an adventure, but throws them together with a carelessness which argues unlimited confidence in his own powers. Fielding pauses to explain the principles of his art, and to congratulate himself and his readers on the felicity with which he constructs his narrative, or makes his characters evolve themselves in its progress. These appeals to the reader's judgment, admirable as they are, have sometimes the fault of being diffuse, and always the great disadvantage that they remind us we are perusing a work of fiction; and that the beings with whom we have been conversant during the perusal, are but a set of evanescent phantoms, conjured up by a magician for our amusement. Smollett seldom holds communication with his readers in his own person. He manages his delightful puppet-show without thrusting his head beyond the curtain, like Gines de Passamont, to explain what he is doing; and hence, besides that our attention to the story remains unbroken, we are sure that the author, fully confident in the abundance of his materials, has no occasion to eke them out with extrinsic matter.

Smollett's sea-characters have been deservedly considered as inimitable; and the power with which he has diversified them, in so many instances, distinguishing the individual features of each honest tar, while each possesses a full proportion of professional manners and habits of thinking, is a most absolute proof of the richness of fancy with which the author was gifted, and which we have noticed as his chief advantage over Fielding. Bowling, Trunnion, Hatchway, Pipes, and Crowe, are all men of the same class, habits, and tone of thinking, yet so completely differenced by their separate and individual characters, that we at once acknowledge them as distinct persons, while we see and allow that every one of them belongs to the old English navy. These striking portraits have now the merit which is cherished by antiquaries—they preserve the memory of the school of Benbow and Boscawen, whose manners are now banished from the quarter-deck to the forecastle. The naval officers of the present day, the splendour of whose actions has thrown into shadow the exploits of a thousand years, do not now affect the manners of foremast-men, and have shown how admirably well their duty can be discharged without any particular attachment to tobacco or flip, or the decided preference of a check shirt over a linen one. But these, when memory carries them back thirty or forty years, must remember many a weather-beaten veteran, whose appearance, language, and sentiments free Smollett from the charge of extravagance in his characteristic sketches of British seamen of the last century.

In the comic part of their writings, we have already said,

Fielding is pre-eminent in grave irony, a Cervantic species of pleasantry, in which Smollett is not equally successful. On the other hand, the Scotchman, notwithstanding the general opinion denies that quality to his countrymen, excels in broad and ludicrous humour. His fancy seems to run riot in accumulating ridiculous circumstances one upon another, to the utter destruction of all power of gravity; and perhaps no books ever written have excited such peals of inextinguishable laughter as those of Smollett. The descriptions which affect us thus powerfully, border sometimes upon what is called farce or caricature; but if it be the highest praise of pathetic composition that it draws forth tears, why should it not be esteemed the greatest excellence of the ludicrous that it compels laughter? The one tribute is at least as genuine an expression of natural feeling as the other; and he who can read the calamitous career of Trunnion and Hatchway, when run away with by their mettled steeds, or the inimitable absurdities of the Feast of the Ancients, without a good hearty burst of honest laughter, must be well qualified to look sad and gentleman-like with Lord Chesterfield and Master Stephen.

Upon the whole, the genius of Smollett may be said to resemble that of Rubens. His pictures are often deficient in grace; sometimes coarse, and even vulgar in conception; deficient in keeping, and in the due subordination of parts to each other; and intimating too much carelessness on the part of the artist. But these faults are redeemed by such richness and brilliancy of colours; such a profusion of imagination—now bodying forth the grand and terribly—now the natural, the easy, and the ludicrous; there is so much of life, action, and bustle, in every group he has painted; so much force and individuality of character,—that we readily grant to Smollett an equal rank with his great rival Fielding, while we place both far above any of their successors in the same line of fictitious composition.

HIPPOLYTE TAINE
From *History of English Literature*
tr. H. Van Laun
1871, Book 3, Chapter 6

Now open a more literal copyist of life; they are doubtless all such, and declare—Fielding amongst them—that if they imagine a feature, it is because they have seen it; but Smollett has this advantage, that, being mediocre, he chalks out the figures insipidly, prosaically, without transforming them by the illumination of genius: the joviality of Fielding and the rigor of Richardson are not there to light up or ennoble the pictures. Observe carefully Smollett's manners; listen to the confessions of this imitator of Le Sage, who reproaches that author with being gay, and jesting with the mishaps of his hero. He says:

> The disgraces of Gil Blas are, for the most part, such as rather excite mirth than compassion; he himself laughs at them, and his transitions from distress to happiness, or at least ease, are so sudden that neither the reader has time to pity him, nor himself to be acquainted with affliction. This conduct . . . prevents struggling with every difficulty to which a friendless orphan is exposed from his own want of experience as well as from the selfishness, envy, malice, and base indifference of mankind. [1]

It is no longer merely showers of blows, but also of knife and sword thrusts, as well as pistol shots. In such a world, when a girl goes out she runs the risk of coming back a woman; and when a man goes out, he runs the risk of not coming back at all. The women bury their nails in the faces of the men; the well-bred gentlemen, like Peregrine Pickle, whip gentlemen soundly. Having deceived a husband, who refuses to demand satisfaction, Peregrine calls his two servants, "and ordered them to duck him in the canal."[2] Misrepresented by a curate, whom he has horsewhipped, he gets an innkeeper "to rain a shower of blows upon his (the priest's) carcass," who also "laid hold of one of his ears with his teeth, and bit it unmercifully."[3] I could quote from memory a score more of outrages begun or completed. Savage insults, broken jaws, men on the ground beaten with sticks, the churlish sourness of conversations, the coarse brutality of jests, give an idea of a pack of bull-dogs eager to fight each other, who, when they begin to get lively, still amuse themselves by tearing away pieces of flesh. A Frenchman can hardly endure the story of *Roderick Random*, or rather that of Smollett, when he is in a man-of-war. He is pressed, that is to say, carried off by force, knocked down, attacked with "cudgels and drawn cutlasses," "pinioned like a malefactor," and rolled on board, covered with blood, before the sailors, who laugh at his wounds; and one of them, "seeing my hair clotted together with blood, as it were, into distinct cords, took notice that my bows were manned with the red ropes, instead of my side."[4] "He desired one of his fellow-captives, who was unfettered, to take a handkerchief out of his pocket, and tie it round his head to stop the bleeding; he pulled out his handkerchief, 'tis true, but sold it before my face to a bum-boat woman for a quart of gin." Captain Oakum declares he will have no more sick in his ship, ordered them to be brought on the quarter-deck, commanded that some should receive a round dozen; some spitting blood, others fainting from weakness, whilst not a few became delirious; many died, and of the sixty-one sick, only a dozen remained alive.[5] To get into this dark, suffocating hospital, swarming with vermin, it is necessary to creep under the close hammocks, and forcibly separate them with the shoulders, before you can reach the patients. Read the story of Miss Williams, a wealthy young girl, of good family, reduced to the trade of a prostitute, robbed, hungry, sick, shivering, strolling about the streets in the long winter nights, amongst "a number of naked wretches reduced to rags and filth, huddled together like swine, in the corner of a dark alley," who depend "upon the addresses of the lowest class, and are fain to allay the rage of hunger and cold with gin; degenerate into a brutal insensibility, rot and die upon a dunghill."[6] She was thrown into Bridewell, where, she says, "in the midst of a hellish crew I was subjected to the tyranny of a barbarian, who imposed upon me tasks that I could not possibly perform, and then punished my incapacity with the utmost rigor and inhumanity. I was often whipped into a swoon, and lashed out of it, during which miserable intervals I was robbed by my fellow-prisoners of everything about me, even to my cap, shoes, and stockings: I was not only destitute of necessaries, but even of food, so that my wretchedness was extreme." One night she tried to hang herself. Two of her fellow-prisoners, who watched her, prevented her. "In the morning my attempt was published among the prisoners, and punished with thirty stripes, the pain of which, co-operating with my disappointment and disgrace, bereft me of my senses, and threw me into an ecstasy of madness, during which I tore the flesh from my bones with my teeth, and dashed my head · against the pavement."[7] In vain you turn your eyes on the hero of the novel, Roderick Random, to repose a little after such a spectacle. He is sensual and coarse, like Fielding's heroes, but not good and jovial as these. The generous wine of Fielding, in Smollett's hands, becomes brandy of the dram-shop. His heroes are selfish; they revenge themselves barbarously. Roderick oppresses the faithful Strap, and ends by marrying him to a prostitute. Peregrine Pickle attacks by a most brutal and cowardly plot the honor of a young girl, whom he wants to marry, and who is the sister of his best friend. We get to hate his rancorous, concentrated, obstinate character, which is at once that of an absolute king accustomed to please himself at the expense of others' happiness, and that of a boor with only the varnish of education. We should be uneasy at living near him; he is good for nothing but to shock or tyrannize over others. We avoid him as we would a dangerous beast; the sudden rush of animal passion and the force of his firm will are so overpowering in him, that when he fails he becomes outrageous. He draws his sword against an innkeeper; he must bleed him, grows mad. Everything, even to his generosities, is spoiled by pride; all, even to his gayeties, is clouded by harshness. Peregrine's amusements are barbarous, and those of Smollett are after the same style. He exaggerates caricature; he thinks to amuse us by showing us mouths gaping to the ears, and noses half-a-foot long; he magnifies a national prejudice or a professional trick until it absorbs the whole character; he jumbles together the most repulsive oddities,—a Lieutenant Lismahago half roasted by Red Indians; old jack-tars who pass their life in shouting and travestying all sorts of ideas into their nautical jargon; old maids as ugly as monkeys, as withered as skeletons, and as sour as vinegar; maniacs steeped in pedantry, hypochondria, misanthropy, and silence. Far from sketching them slightly, as Le Sage does in *Gil Blas*, he brings into prominent relief each disagreeable feature, overloads it with details, without considering whether they are too numerous, without reflecting that they are excessive, without feeling that they are odious, without perceiving that they are disgusting. The public whom he addresses is on a level with his energy and his coarseness; and in order to move such nerves, a writer cannot strike too hard.

But, at the same time, to civilize this barbarity and to control this violence, a faculty appears, common to all, authors and public: serious reflection attached to the observation of character. Their eyes are turned toward the inner man. They note exactly the individual peculiarities, and mark them with such a precise imprint that their personage becomes a type, which cannot be forgotten. They are psychologists. The title of a comedy of old Ben Johnson's, *Every Man in his Humor*, indicates how this taste is ancient and national amongst them. Smollett writes a whole novel, *Humphrey Clinker*, on this idea. No action; the book is a collection of letters written during a tour in Scotland and England. Each of the travellers, after his bent of mind, judges variously of the same objects. A generous, grumbling old gentleman, who amuses himself by thinking himself ill, a crabbed old maid in search of a husband; a lady's maid, ingenuous and vain, who bravely mutilates her spelling; a series of originals, who one after another bring their oddities on the scene,—such are the characters: the pleasure of the reader consists in recognizing their humor in their style, in foreseeing their follies, in perceiving the thread which pulls each of their motions, in verifying the agreement of their ideas and their actions. Push this study of human peculiarities to excess, and you will come upon the origin of Sterne's talent.

Notes
1. "Preface" to *Roderick Random*.
2. *Peregrine Pickle*, ch. lx.
3. Ibid. ch. xxix.
4. Ibid. ch. xxiv.
5. Ibid. ch. xxvii.
6. Ibid. ch. xxiii.
7. Ibid. ch. xxiii.

GEORGE BARNETT SMITH
"Tobias Smollett"

Gentleman's Magazine, June 1875, pp. 729–37

Dickens in early childhood sat at the feet of Tobias Smollett. From the author of *Roderick Random* came to the author of *David Copperfield* the first inspiration of the story-teller. Each of these two men was the most popular fiction writer of his time, and there cannot be a doubt that the artist whose loss from among us we have not yet ceased to mourn gathered something both in style and substance from the novelist whose fictions so delighted his own childhood. It is not then quite wise in us, whose moral and intellectual lives have been largely influenced by Dickens, to pass by wholly unheeded the old master whom the child Dickens studied so intently and to such great purpose.

But for the brilliant genius of Henry Fielding, Smollett must have stood the most important figure among British novelists till the appearance of Sir Walter Scott. In depicting certain aspects of human nature, the author of *Roderick Random* is the chief of humourists; but when we weigh his talent generally against that of his rival, the gold is not quite so pure and genuine. There was an admixture of simulation in him which was absent from Fielding, and is indeed absent from all really lofty and creative minds. To Smollett it was necessary that he should have a predecessor; Fielding, on the contrary, was spontaneous and original, and the founder of a race. He made successors, but was himself no man's successor. The third novelist of the same illustrious age, Samuel Richardson, had little in common with either, nor did he reach to their height. He was less able than they to assimilate the lessons of humanity, or to reproduce individual character.

Smollett, however much we may dislike his method, is remarkably truthful in his delineations. His pictures of rollicking sailors are as realistic as the works of Hogarth, with whose genius his own had some affinity. Unless expurgated, he is scarcely a fit subject for illustrative readings in the drawing-room, but then the same may be said to a large extent of almost every other prominent literary man of his own or any preceding era. We condone his offences against purity because of his great gifts. Smollett's most important work is indubitably *Roderick Random*. It exhibits in the strongest degree all the qualities which rendered him famous. Here we meet with, in all their fullness, the uproarious mirthfulness and the broad farce which are never wholly absent from any of his conceptions in fiction. His characters are not overdrawn, as some are in the habit of thinking. Le Sage was the writer most frequently in his thoughts, and the touches of realism to be met with throughout the work are almost unique.

Smollett has not made the friendless orphan the paragon of virtue which he would inevitably have been in the hands of most novelists. He presents him to us "with all his imperfections on his head," a faithful picture of what life would be under the disadvantageous circumstances of Roderick's history.

The evolution of the story affords the author that opportunity for reproving the baseness and the hollowness of men for which he was so well fitted, and the various situations of life are painted with admirable vigour and local colouring. The name of Bowling alone has passed into a synonym for all that is honest and manly in the sailor, and the character of the Lieutenant remains still unmatched by any similar creation. To the essentially comic characters of the novel almost the same high praise must be awarded. While doubtless written with a view to the promotion of good morals, it is not to be supposed that Smollett intends to hold up Roderick Random as an individual character worthy of imitation. Like Fielding, this other master of fiction did not assume at any time to draw perfect characters. The simpering perfections of the ordinary heroes of fiction would have been abhorrent to him, utterly devoid of resemblance to the people of real life. As he conceives the novelist's duty, it stands upon higher ground than the mere cutting out of faultless, pasteboard men, in which neither art nor truth is required.

Besides its excellence in striking and bold portraiture, *Roderick Random* is distinguished for the simplicity and ease of its narrative. Although the writing is not so exquisite as that to be found in the pages of Fielding, it yet varies on occasion from the intensely humorous to the genuinely pathetic. I do not attempt to conceal the disappointment which we must all feel that Smollett has made his heroes generally of so coarse a texture. They have in them—or at least many of them strike us in this manner—a good deal of grossness which cannot be excused, and are frequently overbearing, swaggering, and offensive in their manners. Roderick Random, for instance, deserved the severest physical castigation, at certain stages of his career, and so did Peregrine Pickle.

The author's genius has been not inaptly compared to that of Rubens. In both we get richness of colouring, though the two artists are frequently vulgar in idea, and exhibit an overcharged animalism in their pictures. I must protest, nevertheless, against the judgment that Smollett, "being mediocre, chalks out the figures tamely, prosaically, without transforming them by the illumination of genius." This exhibits a very deficient grasp of the novelist's talent. His manners may be vulgar, but his genius is undeniable.

Can any one who has studied *Peregrine Pickle* affirm for a moment that the figures which are prominent in that novel are sketched prosaically? Surely if there is one feeling uppermost after reading this work, it is that it is lightened and illumined by the power of real genius! Sir Walter Scott said of it:— "*Peregrine Pickle* is more finished, more sedulously laboured into excellence, exhibits scenes of more accumulated interest, and presents a richer variety of character and adventure than *Roderick Random.*" And with this verdict the bulk of mankind will agree. The interest in the novel never flags between the two covers; and it was a totally new attempt in fiction. The idea of these Adventures has been considerably worked upon in our own day. Smollett worked out this fiction with much more than his usual elaboration. *Roderick Random* has a greater air of spontaneity, but *Peregrine Pickle* is more polished, even while it is as uproariously mirthful. It is doubtful whether the sale of the latter during its author's lifetime would have borne comparison with that of the former novel but for one adventitious circumstance. Embedded in the story are certain "Memoirs of a Lady of Quality," which have no connection whatever with the novel itself. These memoirs were founded on fact, and contain the history of Lady Vane, a contemporary of Smollett's, who was celebrated for her beauty and her intrigues. So far from blushing at the revelation of her own life, or feeling herself degraded by the scandal attaching thereto, it is affirmed that she rewarded the novelist handsomely for incorporating the disclosures in his work. Exhibiting an astounding taste for celebrity, she even furnished the materials herself for the story. The town speedily rang with the history of Lady Vane, and the consequence was a great popular demand for the novel.

There is genuine comedy in this fiction from beginning to end. It teems with humorous situations; and although Trunnion and Hatchway may be considered by many to be stamped with exaggeration, the interest we take in their fortunes is intense and real. We get, too, in *Peregrine Pickle* Smollett's best attempt at a heroine, in the person of Emilia. His previous story was utterly unsatisfactory in this respect, women being apparently dragged in because the *dramatis personae* would not be complete without them. Emilia is not perfect, and entangles herself on one occasion in a manner which should have been avoided; but she is still pure, and displays admirable heroism and endurance. In Smollett's time people used plain language on particular subjects, and women were familiarised with vice in a way that has now gone out of date. When all this is remembered we must do Smollett the justice of admitting that in his novel he really appears to be striving after what is good and noble. If he reproduces the follies and the vices of his time he nowhere hints that he desires to be the laureate of these things. Side by side with the powerful indignation against hypocrisy, pride, and cruelty, is also apparent a reverence for a high morality and a desire to lead men into the ways of virtue. Of Pipes, one of the leading characters, it is worth recording that Edmund Burke was wondrously delighted with him, and thought him the most humorous and highly finished character that ever was invented. The whole narrative hangs well together, the various incidents are excellently told, and the reconciliation between the two lovers is well led up to.

Cumberland the dramatist very happily touched off the literary character of Smollett in his allegorical representation of him, together with Fielding and Richardson. He observed that "there was a third, somewhat posterior in time, not in talent, who was indeed a rough driver, and rather too severe to his cattle; but in faith he carried us at a merry pace over land or sea: nothing came amiss to him, for he was up to both elements, and a match for nature in every shape, character, and degree. He was not very courteous, it must be owned, for he had a capacity for higher things, and was above his business; he wanted only a little more suavity and discretion to have figured with the best."

Count Fathom is an extraordinary revelation of villainy, as remarkable indeed for its portraiture of vice in the upper classes as *Jonathan Wild* is in the lower. Smollett himself apprehended that he might be attacked for this singular work, and makes a long prefatory explanation in consequence. He declares his purpose to be to set up the Count "as a beacon for the benefit of the inexperienced and unwary, who, from the perusal of these memoirs, may learn to avoid the manifold snares with which they are continually surrounded in the paths of life, while those who hesitate on the brink of iniquity may be terrified from plunging into that irremediable gulf by surveying the deplorable fate of Ferdinand, Count Fathom." Certainly, if anything is to be gained of a deterrent nature from the contemplation of vice, it ought to be gathered here; for I do not bear in memory a single narrative so surcharged with it. The virtuous character raised up in opposition to the Count, to give a certain relief to the story (as the novelist informs us), is a mere puppet without life as compared with the human fiend who furnishes the title of the novel, and though at the close the

author makes virtue triumphant, the strongest and most indelible realism is thrown round the character of the villain. This, of course, only proves the power of the narrator's art. Altogether the work is not a pleasant one, but it is not without its uses, and offers a very distinctive moral.

Perhaps Smollett's best work for natural movement was his *Expedition of Humphrey Clinker*. The probabilities are not outraged in this narrative, which deals with the ordinary events of every-day life in a simple and forcible manner. The situations are never unduly forced, nor are the characters lifted out of the common run. It was an attempt in quite a new direction, and it has since been extensively imitated, notably by a popular author of fiction now living, who has written one story closely upon its lines. Humour and observation are as rich and striking as in any of his novels, and he writes with all his old freshness and freedom, even after he has suffered misfortune, and his life has been embittered with affliction. Matthew Bramble is an original character who divides our esteem and our humorous condolence; whilst Tabitha is even a more singular character still for her forcible delineation. Humphrey Clinker himself is not so remarkable a creation as many others in the Adventures, but he serves admirably as a centre round which the other characters revolve. The letters are capital reading, and afford many truthful pictures of scenery and observations upon manners. Manifestly it was not the author's intention to depend upon plot for the success of his work. Of story there is little or none; but of portraiture of real life there is abundance. Dr. Moore, the best of the novelist's biographers, says of *Humphrey Clinker*, with much justice:—"From the assemblies of high life Dr. Smollett thought that humour was banished by ceremony, affectation, and cards; that nature being castigated almost to still life, mirth never appeared but in an insipid grin. His extreme fondness for humour, therefore, led him to seek it where it was to be found, namely, in the inferior societies of life, which in spite of the acuteness with which he seized and described it, has exposed him to the censure of the fastidious. Dr. Smollett seems, when he wrote *Humphrey Clinker*, to have been conscious of the discontent and fretfulness that appear in his letters from France and Italy; and to have had a just notion of his own character. Neither Le Sage nor Fielding, had they been intimately acquainted with him, could have drawn it more truly nor with more humour than it appears in the letters of Matthew Bramble."

There are passages in the book which a man of more refined mind would have omitted. Smollett, with his splendid capacity for humour, seems never to have been content unless he reproduced with the wit or the sarcasm the coarse jest and the objectionable gesture with which the characters themselves would have embellished their deeds and speech in actual life. It is here, I think, that he has a little overstepped the boundary even of license, and committed the unpardonable sin. He behaves in a more unseemly manner than the other humorous novelists of the age; and however much we may be disposed to forgive him for the sake of his wonderful genius, it is impossible to help feeling a little angry at his too literal a rendering of the grossness of character. That *Humphrey Clinker* displays some amount of peevishness is a charge which should cause us but little surprise. A disappointed man is in the habit of occasionally venting his spleen upon the world through the best medium that is open to him; and Smollett would have been more than human if, with his power of pen, he had always neglected the opportunity of castigating his species.

Sir Launcelot Greaves is a book to please the few, but not likely to retain much hold upon people generally. Yet, it presents us with several most natural scenes, and the character of the chivalrous young knight is, notwithstanding the author's disclaimer, suggested, I think, by the writings of the immortal Cervantes. This style of composition has gone completely out of vogue now, and I am not aware that in inferior cases—that is, the cases of authors who are not conspicuous for original talent—it would ever be a style that could be justified. The profit to be derived from works of this stamp would be very small; and even in the hands of a master we can only tolerate the burlesque for the excellence of the wit. Extravagance of conception is not a very difficult thing to accomplish; the real power of genius consists in investing the ordinary with the highest amount of interest possible.

The happiest excursion of Smollett into the realms of mock history is to be found in his *Adventures of an Atom*. It is full of extravagance, wit, and learning. The singular groundwork of the romance is the endowment of an atom, by supposed transmigration, with reason and speech. This speaks through one Mr. Nathaniel Peacock, and causes him to write down exactly what it dictates respecting past history. There are numerous satirical touches upon prominent Whig politicians, and very strange digressions upon all kinds of topics, in which the author casually shows the depth of his erudition. Many of the allusions are beyond the apprehension of the reader simply from lapse of time; but the romance is worth perusal as showing the fruitfulness and versatility of the author's mind. The work is a curiosity.

Concerning Smollett's Letters from Abroad much need not be said. They are far from being without glimpses of the man in his best style, and they light up objects and places to the untravelled man with many vivid touches and references; but they occupy small ground towards forming an estimate of the value of the novelist's intellectual labours.

Critics have greatly differed as to Smollett's merits as a poet. Some perceive in him only the ordinary versifier, while others see in what he has done the germ of a talent which might have been developed to an extraordinary degree. The truth lies between the two extremes, and is a good way removed from either. Smollett certainly did not write doggrel; his faculty for apprehending the ludicrous aspect of things would have led him to eschew the muse altogether rather than do that; but then, on the other hand, he was not sufficiently musical or imaginative ever to become the lofty and impassioned poet. His power in tragedy was inferior to any other literary faculty he possessed, but in his odes there is some really fine and spirited work. One commentator remarks on this head:—"His 'Ode to Independence' is the greatest effort of his genius, and rivals in spirit and sublimity, in strength of conception and beauty of colouring, the sublime odes of Dryden, Collins, and Gray, the great masters of the British lyre." It is just this kind of wholesale eulogy which succeeds in placing an author in a false position. To say deliberately that Smollett equals Dryden in the writing of odes is to show a total want of discrimination and critical capacity. A man may be a very fine poet without attaining to that height; and Smollett has unquestionably written many noble strains. Take the opening, for instance, of the "Ode to Independence" just cited—

> Thy spirit, Independence, let me share,
>   Lord of the lion-heart and eagle-eye;
> Thy steps I follow with my bosom bare,
>   Nor heed the storm that howls along the sky.
> Deep in the frozen regions of the north
> A goddess violated brought thee forth,
> In mortal liberty, whose look sublime

> Hath bleach'd the tyrant's cheek in every varying
>   clime,
>   What time the iron-hearted Gaul,
> With frantic Superstition for his Guide,
>   Arm'd with the dagger and the pall,
> The sons of Woden to the field defied;
>   The ruthless hag, by Weser's flood,
> In heaven's name urg'd th' infernal blow;
> And red the stream began to flow—
>   The vanquish'd were baptis'd with blood!

The Ode retains its excellence and force to the end, and is in every respect successful. It appears to be just one of those happy efforts which come to men but once in their lives, when they are almost astonished with themselves at the results they achieve. To "The Tears of Scotland," which is full of pathos, it is impossible to do justice by the mere quotation of a stanza, but in considering Smollett as a poet, here is one song which proves his command over another style of verse. It has elements of grace and delicacy:—

> To fix her—'twere a task as vain
> To combat April drops of rain,
> To sow in Afric's barren soil,
> Or tempests hold within a toil.
>
> I know it, friend, she's light as air,
> False as the fowler's artful snare;
> Inconstant as the passing wind,
> As winter's dreary frost unkind.
>
> She's such a miser, too, in love;
> Its joys she'll neither share nor prove,
> Though hundreds of gallants await
> From her victorious eyes their fate.
>
> Blushing at such inglorious reign,
> I sometimes strive to break her chain;
> My reason summon to my aid,
> Resolv'd no more to be betray'd.
>
> Ah! friend, 'tis but a short-liv'd trance,
> Dispell'd by one enchanting glance;
> She need but look, and I confess
> Those looks completely curse or bless.
>
> So soft, so elegant, so fair,
> Sure something more than human's there;
> I must submit, for strife is vain,
> 'Twas destiny that forg'd the chain.

The miseries and misfortunes of literary men have formed a frequent topic of reflection in the world's history, and Smollett adds one more name to the long roll of the unfortunate. Never reduced to the terrible depths of deprivation which marked the career of a Savage or a Chatterton, yet he had his own peculiar trials and difficulties to encounter. Isaac Disraeli, in his *Calamities of Authors*, says: "Of most authors by profession, Who has displayed a more fruitful genius, and exercised more intense industry, with a loftier sense of his independenece, than Smollett? But look into his life, and enter into his feelings, and we shall be shocked at the disparity of his situation with the genius of the man. His life was a succession of struggles, vexations, and disappointments—yet of success in his writings. Smollett, who is a great poet though he has written little in verse, and whose rich genius had composed the most original pictures of human life, was compelled by his wants to debase his name by selling his *Voyages and Travels*, which he could never have read. When he had worn himself down in the service of the public, or the booksellers, there remained not of all his slender remunerations, in the last stage of life, sufficient to convey him to a cheap country and a restorative air on the

Continent." This is the old story of humanity from the blind and sublime vagrant Homer downwards. Earthly rewards are extended with a niggard's hand to the illustrious in literature. But Smollett, one of the few creators of types, and brother to the select band of the highest humourists, need not be ashamed of the company which he keeps. Nor was it without salutary effect, probably, upon his own nature that he passed through troubled depths. The purest song, and song which has risen to its grandest height, has alas! with much of the living prose of this mighty language, been too often the outcome of suffering, deprivation, or persecution. England herein is a sister of other nations. Yet, what matters it now that Camoens died of want and that even Cervantes suffered hunger? Their reward is assured. Kings and peoples usually reserve their acclamations and laurels for the warrior; but posterity crowns the author. The distribution remains not unequal for ever. The man who has generated thought, and who has scaled the lofty heights of genius, looks down through the ages and beholds his fame increasing with the passing of the years—for the fiat has gone forth that the offspring of the mind is immortal, and that he who has touched the intellect and the soul into activity at any stage of the world's history is the real prince and leader among men.

EDMUND GOSSE
From "The Novelists"
A History of Eighteenth Century Literature
1888, pp. 258–64

Richardson was an elderly man, Fielding in the ripeness of manhood, and Smollett quite young, when each flourished as a novelist; and hence, though more than thirty years separated the birth of the first from that of the third, they are to be considered as contemporaries—*Roderick Random*, indeed, being exactly contemporaneous with *Clarissa*, and a little older than *Tom Jones*. Tobias George Smollett was brought up in a beautiful valley of Dumbartonshire by his grandfather, Sir James Smollett of Bonhill, whose death in 1740 left the youth with no other provision than an excellent education. He was already something of a poet, and had come up to London in 1739 with a very bad tragedy, *The Regicide*, which Garrick refused. Smollett was obliged to become surgeon's mate on board a man-of-war, and served in the affair of Carthagena. He left the fleet and settled in the West Indies, somewhat longer than Roderick Random did. In Jamaica he married one who at least had seemed to be an heiress, Miss Nancy Lascelles. After a world of adventures he found himself in London again in 1744, trying to combine the professions of medicine and literature, and scourging the follies of the age from a garret. In January 1748 Smollett published, in two volumes, his first novel, *The Adventures of Roderick Random*. This book is a good instance of his method, and exemplifies the merits as well as the defects of his style. It takes the form of an autobiography; the hero is a Scotchman who is singularly like Smollett himself in the nature of his adventures. He is even shipped off to the West Indies as a surgeon, and there can be no doubt that the author was mainly repeating, but also, one hopes, exaggerating, what he himself had seen and experienced. *Roderick Random* is intentionally modelled on the plan of Lesage, and here, as elsewhere, Smollett shows himself less original than either Richardson or Fielding. He can hardly be said to invent or to construct; he simply reports. He does this with infinite spirit and variety. Comedy and tragedy, piety and farce, follow one another in bewildering alternation. But although he dazzles and entertains us, he does not charm. The book is ferocious to a strange degree, and so foul as to be fit only for a very well-seasoned reader. The hero, in whom Smollett complacently could see nothing but a picture of "modest merit struggling with every difficulty," is a selfish bully, whose faults it is exasperating to find condoned. The book, of course, is full of good things. The hero is three separate times hurried off to sea, and the scenes of rough sailor-life, though often disgusting, are wonderfully graphic. Tom Bowling, Jack Rattlin, and the proud Mr. Morgan are not merely immortal among salt-sea worthies, but practically the first of a long line of sailors of fiction. There is, moreover, the meek and gentle Strap, so ungenerously treated by the hero, that we almost throw the book from us in anger, when at last Random is permitted, on the last page, to crown his own ill-gotten gains with the fortune of the lovely Narcissa.

The same inconsistent qualities, mingled, however, with considerably greater breadth and freedom, go to make up the four volumes of *The Adventures of Peregrine Pickle* (1751), which is not a better novel than its predecessors, but possesses finer passages. This is, indeed, a very difficult book to criticise, so great is the inequality of its execution. The first volume is in Smollett's best style, displaying his faults of coarseness and satiric ferocity to the full, but concise, brisk, and exquisitely humorous. The second, which is mainly occupied with the French and Flemish passages, is vivacious, but to a much less degree, and by fits and starts. Two-thirds of the third volume are taken up by the nauseous and impertinent "Memoirs of a Lady of Quality," a fungoid growth of episode. The fourth is weighted through its first half by Smollett's passion for elaborate social satire, but wakes up again into pure and lively fiction towards the close. Here, as in *Roderick Random*, the personal unloveliness of the hero's character is annoying. Peregrine is a handsome, swaggering swashbuckler, ungenerous and untrustworthy to the highest degree, with hardly any virtue but that of brute courage. Smollett, nevertheless, smiles at him all through, and seems to be assuring us that he is only sowing his wild oats. The extraordinary violence of the characters, which is more marked here than in any other book of the author's, becomes fatiguing at length. The internecine animosities of Mrs. Trunnion and Mrs. Pickle, the bitter inhumanity of almost everybody in the book, leave us at first exasperated and then incredulous. It is difficult to say why a novel so very disagreeable and so full of faults does, nevertheless, impress the reader as a work of genius. The humours of Commodore Trunnion and Lieutenant Jack Hatchway are still unsurpassed in their kind, though they have inspired so many later hands. The long and stately comedy of the Roman dinner is still a masterpiece of elaborate, learned fooling. Nor are the treasures of the author's studied and artificial humour anywhere scattered with more careless profusion than over the earlier pages of this unequal book.

Smollett was not happily inspired in his next novel. *The Adventures of Ferdinand, Count Fathom* (1753), is more serious than its predecessors; the author's intentions seem to have been romantic. But the hero, once more, and more than ever, is a repulsive scoundrel, and the forest-scenes, which have been praised for their poetical force, appear to us to be simply brutal when they are not bombastic. The public, at all events, rejected *Count Fathom*, and Smollett turned to other branches of literature. He translated *Don Quixote* (1755); he started the *Critical Review*, a newspaper, mainly consisting of short notices of books, which Smollett edited, and partly wrote, with the help of a staff of six or seven hacks. He had an old grudge against one of the Carthagena admirals, and he used the *Critical Review* as a vehicle for censuring this man anonymously in terms which went beyond all possible endurance. Smollett acknowledged the authorship of the article, and was imprisoned as well as fined for the libel. While he was in gaol, he amused himself by imitating Cervantes in a novel in two volumes, *The Adventures of Sir Lancelot Greaves*, printed in 1761, an absurd and exaggerated satire which added nothing to his fame.

Emulous of the success which was attending his countrymen, the Scotch historians, Smollett undertook to write a *Complete History of England*, from Julius Cæsar down to the year 1748; this he afterwards continued to the year 1765. The first edition of the perfunctory work appeared in 1758; Smollett was no born historian, but he wrote with verve and confidence, and when he approached the events of his own age, he prepared himself to treat them with the vivacity of a novelist. If he did not lift his style to a level with that of Hume or Robertson, he easily surpassed the Guthries and Campbells of his day; and from this period we have to think of him as famous. Unfortunately, with success in authorship came the utter ruin of his health, and the loss of his only child, a charming daughter. Smollett was ordered to Italy by his doctors, and he spent two years on the continent of Europe in desultory travel, out of sympathy with what he saw, and ignorantly prejudiced against all customs that clashed in any degree with British habit. He was the original of Smelfungus, who "set out with the spleen and jaundice, and every object he passed by was discoloured and distorted." Sterne, who did not err from want of sympathy, wittily says of Smollett's opinions of the works of art in Italy, that they should have been reserved for his physician. The *Travels in France and Italy*, which he published in 1766, throw more light upon the author than upon the countries he traversed.

Smollett, indeed, was now a wreck; he enjoyed a slight respite in the village of his birth by his native lake, which suited him far better than Bolsena or Garda. His praises of Leven Water, in *Humphrey Clinker*, both in prose, and in his graceful ode, are among the best specimens we possess of his descriptive powers, and show that he could be deeply moved by landscape, when its associations assisted the impression. Any return to cheerfulness or ease, however, was but temporary. The angry and tortured spirit produced in 1769 a fantastic story in two volumes, *The Adventures of an Atom*, one of the foulest and most distressing works ever published, in which the firebrands of indiscriminate satire are hurled hither and thither without aim or purpose. The only part of this Japanese monstrosity which is worth remembering is the attack on Yak-strot, the Earl of Bute. Smollett certainly possessed, with his own Jan-ki-dtzin, "the art of making balls of filth, which were famous for sticking and stinking." This dreadful book was the last that he wrote in England. Utterly shattered and exhausted, he went abroad again, and settled in a villa near Leghorn, under the care of the amiable poet-physician Armstrong. And now a miracle took place, almost unparalleled in literature. For ten years the imaginative powers of Smollett had shown signs of steady decline, and had in his last novel sunk below toleration. What he wrote had long been dull and vindictive, the outcome of a dying mind that sought in filth and peevishness a counterirritant to its exhaustion. But at Leghorn, during the last year of his life, all the wasted powers of the brain appeared to flicker up in a last flame, and it was almost on his deathbed that Smollett wrote the best of all his books, that masterpiece of wit and frolic, the inimitable *Expedition of Humphrey Clinker*, published in three volumes, in 1771, a few weeks before he died.

It may, perhaps, be questioned whether certain isolated passages of *Peregrine Pickle* do not surpass, in graphic power, any one page of *Humphrey Clinker;* but no critic can well question that the latter is the best sustained, the most complete, and the least disagreeable of Smollett's novels. It is written in the form of letters; it should more properly be called the Expedition of Matthew Bramble, for Humphrey is merely a Methodist postilion picked up by the family of that gentleman near the end of the first volume, and no very prominent character anywhere. The adventures of Mr. Bramble, who sallies forth in search of health at Bath, in London, at Harrogate, at Scarborough, in the Scottish Highlands, at Buxton, and at Gloucester, are no doubt mainly those of Smollett himself, and the only disagreeable parts of the book are the pages in which the old gentleman dwells with the gusto of an invalid on the symptoms of himself or of his fellow-patients. Mr. Bramble is accompanied, however, by his sister Tabitha, a treasure, and by his excellent niece and nephew; it is the letters of all these persons, with those of their servants, that make up the tale. There is a pretty love-intrigue going on all the time between the niece Lydia and a mysterious stranger; but as a rule the novel is distinctly comic in tone, yet with none of the ferocity, the tendency to scourge society, which is so marked elsewhere in Smollett. There is noticeable, moreover, for the first time, in *Humphrey Clinker*, a power of creating characters which are not caricatures, and a sympathy for average human nature. In short, this swan-song of the novelist is in the highest degree tantalising as showing us what he could have done throughout his life if he had cared to cultivate the best part of his genius. If we had more examples of the gaiety that presided at the birth of Winifred Jenkins and Tabitha Bramble we should not doubt, as we now do, whether we are justified in naming Smollett in the same breath with Richardson and Fielding. Looking at his work, however, from the broadest point of view, and acknowledging all its imperfections as well as its imitative quality, we have also to acknowledge that it bears upon it the stamp of a vigorous individuality, and that it has extended no little fascination to later masters of English fiction. Without Smollett Dickens would no more be what he is than Thackeray would be without Fielding.

WALTER RALEIGH
From "The Novels of the Eighteenth Century"
The English Novel
1894, pp. 185–90

Smollett avows frankly in his preface that his book is written in imitation of the *Gil Blas* of Lesage. In the first chapter of a later work, *Ferdinand, Count Fathom*, he gives a fuller list of his originals, enumerating *Guzman d'Alfarache*, *Don Quixote*, Scarron's *Roman Comique*, and *Gil Blas* as works which delight those very readers who profess disgust at scenes of low life described in the English tongue. The existence of these works certainly gave Smollett some advantage over Nash, who had written his *Jacke Wilton* when only *Lazarillo de Tormes* was available as a model in this kind. Even Defoe had died before the completion of *Gil Blas* in 1735, but Defoe had shown small inclination to borrow from any of them. He knew, as Smollett also knew, that for the realistic novel of humour and adventure, which in the country of its invention has been called picaresque, the purely literary inspiration is hopelessly inadequate. And Smollett fails where he most trusts to it. His later direct imitation of *Don Quixote, The Adventures of Sir Launcelot Greaves* (1762) is poor indeed compared with the full-blooded vitality and jollity of his earliest novel.

"A novel," says Smollett in one of his dedications, "is a large diffused picture, comprehending the characters of life, disposed in different groups and exhibited in various attitudes, for the purposes of an uniform plan." And he gives what is at least a characteristic of his own novels when he adds that "this plan cannot be executed with propriety, probability, or success, without a principal personage to attract the attention, unite the incidents, unwind the clue of the labyrinth, and at last close the scene, by virtue of his own importance." Such unity of design as his novels may claim is entirely due to this device of the "principal personage." But his constructive power is small, and the merits of *Roderick Random* are more apparent in the parts than in the whole. It is a very lively panorama, the incidents and characters of which he borrowed directly from his life and experience, leaving it to his invention to give them a certain comic distortion. The known facts of Smollett's life correspond exactly with what he relates of his hero. The same birth, the same education, the same naval adventures lead up to the close of the book in a marriage very like that which, in 1747, had closed the first chapter of Smollett's life. So close is the correspondence that his biographers have felt warranted in eking out the facts of his life with inferences drawn from this novel.

The success of *Roderick Random* turned Smollett finally to literature as a profession, and for the next twenty years the irascible strenuous Scot was a well-known character in London. Hardly a well-known figure, for his hot temper and ostentatious independence made him a difficult friend; "far more disposed to cultivate the acquaintance of those he could serve, than of those who could serve him." He came only into casual contact with Johnson's circle, and was very far indeed from relishing Johnson's favourite joke. But he was never a misanthrope like his friend and fellow-countryman Dr. John Armstrong, of whom Beattie said that he seemed "to have conceived a rooted aversion against the whole human race, except a few friends, which it seems are dead."

Some light is thrown on his methods as a novelist, by the fact that he travelled to Paris in the company of his friend and disciple, Dr. John Moore, with no ostensible purpose save the acquisition of new literary capital. This was duly employed in the *Adventures of Peregrine Pickle* (1751), a longer and more disjointed work than his first. The autobiographic method did not prove pleasing to Akenside and others, whose characters were burlesqued in this novel; and Smollett could hardly employ the excuse of Dr. John Shebbeare, who says that novelists are like army-tailors, they make suits for all mankind, to be taken and fitted on to their persons by Tom, Dick, and Harry. For Smollett fitted his descriptions to the individual, and took care that they should suit no one else. His method is minute and his satire savage and personal.

One more novel, this time on the model of *Jonathan Wild*, was produced by Smollett before journalism, translation, and history absorbed his time and turned his attention from fiction. *The Adventures of Ferdinand, Count Fathom* (1753), is as inferior to its prototype in conception and execution as Smollett is inferior in mind and art to Fielding. Count Fathom is a feeble knave compared with the great Jonathan, and the ironic conception that is the basis of Fielding's book is here missing. Smollett boasts in his preface that he has attempted

"to subject folly to ridicule and vice to indignation," and has at least "adorned virtue with honour and applause." These are really the weaknesses of the book. Indignation is out of place, and the applause bestowed on virtue only helps to confuse and disaffect the reader, who is kept throughout in the company of vice. It is a coarse morality at best that is taught by repulsion from vice, and the plea is often hypocritical. All the more, therefore, is the absence felt of some such intellectual standpoint as Fielding's, to give unity and meaning to the book. Wild, led by his author in triumph to "a death as glorious as his life," and exhibited under the gallows picking the officiating parson's pocket of a "bottle-screw," is a more instructive and a more impressive figure than Fathom, who slinks out of the story to be reformed elsewhere.

Of *Sir Launcelot Greaves*, originally contributed as a serial to *The British Review*, the scheme, as one of the characters remarks, "is somewhat too stale and extravagant." The plot is the merest excuse for variety of scene, and the characters do not live. What he borrowed from Cervantes is as little put to its proper use by Smollett as what he borrowed from Fielding. His work loses its chief merit when he attempts to exchange his own method of reminiscence for a wider imaginative scheme.

His visit to Scotland in the summer of 1766 furnished him with material for his last and best novel, *The Expedition of Humphrey Clinker*, which was completed at Leghorn and published in 1771, the year of his death. The opportunity of treating Scottish scenes and characters, the pleasure of escaping from politics, and perhaps also the influence of a new writer, Sterne, combined to make of this the gentlest and most humorous of his novels.

Smollett was not a great man; he has none of Johnson's massive dignity, or Goldsmith's charm, or Fielding's generous strength. His combative intensity made it impossible for him to take the detached view of life that is characteristic of a great humourist. His expedients for raising a laugh are seldom intellectual. His stories, as has been observed by a writer in the *Quarterly Review* (No. 205), display "such a bustle of coarse life, such swearing and rioting and squalor, and, above all, such incessant thumping and fighting and breaking each others' heads and kicking each others' shins as could never have taken place in any conceivable community, or under any system of police, unless the human skeleton had been of much harder construction than it is at present." Only those whose bodily vigour is at its height can derive unfailing pleasure from seeing one buffoon knock another down. Smollett's own pleasure in the adventures he relates is obviously akin to the physical; the accidents that crowd his pages have none of that intellectual appeal which glorifies the muddiest misadventures of Parson Adams in Parson Trulliber's pigsty. But his zest in life is real and infectious, and his purely external treatment gives a certain refreshing quality to his pages; over his books at least it is possible "to unbend the mind."

Of his chief opportunity for the display of character he does not make full use. The nominal heroes of his novels are not the most interesting of his characters. His seafaring men, Tom Bowling, Commodore Trunnion, Lieutenant Hatchway, and the rest, have generally been considered his chief contribution to character in fiction. They are happy and early creations of that burlesque humour which applies to the whole of life the technical terms drawn from a single art, profession, or trade. And the death of the Commodore in *Peregrine Pickle* deserves the praise that has been given it. But even the extraordinary wealth of Smollett's nautical vocabulary does not prevent the infliction of a certain fatigue by these gentlemen, who will wrap up the Lord's Prayer or a request for grog with equal ease in a superfluity of far-fetched and monotonous metaphor.

Yet Smollett cannot be robbed of what, after all, is his chief praise; he knew the very spirit of adventure, and gave a long lease of life in England to his revival of the picaresque romance. For his method, less original than Fielding's or Richardson's, was more easily imitated, and the public was long regaled with every conceivable variety of adventures.

GEORGE SAINTSBURY
"Tobias Smollett"
English Prose, ed. Henry Craik
1895, Volume 4, pp. 257–60

It is probable that in that vague reflection of critical opinion in general judgment which rarely goes very far wrong, Smollett takes on the whole the lowest place among the four great novelists of the mid-eighteenth century in England. Scott indeed tried to make him out Fielding's equal; but this was the almost solitary example of national prejudice warping that sane and shrewd intellect. Smollett is undoubtedly far more amusing to the general reader than Richardson; and it may be contended that his altogether astonishing foulness (which exceeds as a pervading trait if it does not equal in individual instances the much discussed failing of Swift) is not to a nice morality more offensive than the sniggering indelicacy of Sterne. With very young readers who are not critical from the literary side, Smollett is probably the most popular of the four.

But the reader who begins to "pull him to pieces," to ask what is his idiosyncrasy, what his special contribution to letters, cannot very long remain in doubt as to the fact and the reason of his inferiority. Thackeray, with the native shrewdness of a critic and the acquired tact of a brother of the mystery, hit one side of this inferiority in the remark, "He did not invent much, I fancy." In truth, observation, and observation of the outside rather than of the inside, is Smollett's characteristic. He had seen much; he had felt much; he had desired, and enjoyed, and failed in, and been indignant at much. And he related these experiences, or something like them, with a fresh and vigorous touch, giving them for the most part true life and nature, but not infusing any great individuality into them either from the artistic or the ethical side. He was a good writer but not one of distinction. He never takes the very slightest trouble about construction: his books are mere lengths cut off from a conceivably infinite bead-roll of adventures. Vivid as are his sketches they all run (except perhaps in his last and best book) to types. His humour though exuberant is for the most part what has been called "the humour of the stick." He has no commanding or profound knowledge of human nature below the surface. And this brings us to the one idiosyncrasy or characteristic which Smollett did very unfortunately succeed in impressing on his books, and not least on those of them which have survived—the novels. He seems himself to have had many good personal qualities, to have been a fervent lover, a staunch friend, a steadfast politician, a generous acquaintance and patron, a man of dauntless courage and (except in the ugly passage of his taking money to foist in the "Memoirs of a Lady of Quality" into *Peregrine Pickle*) of incorruptible integrity. But these good things were "dashed and brewed" not merely with the above-mentioned coarseness but with a savage ferocity of temper, which not only vented itself on the unlucky

authors whom he criticised and the unlucky patrons who did not patronise him enough, but took form in his two first heroes, Roderick and Peregrine—two of the most unmitigated young ruffians who ever escaped condign punishment. The good-natured and often quite valid plea of "dramatic presentment" will not avail here; for Roderick and Peregrine are not merely presented without the slightest effort on the part of their introducer to apologise for them, but the keynote of both characters corresponds only too exactly to that of the character of the *Critical* journalist, the traveller in France and Italy, and the chronicler of the *Atom*. When to this drawback is added the others above referred to, especially the almost total absence of construction, and of what may be called projection of character, in the earlier novels, it becomes tolerably easy to understand why Smollett has not on the whole been a favourite with critics, and why he pleases far more at a first, especially an early and unfastidious reading, than at nicer reperusal in later years.

Yet no estimate which refused him a very high place among those who do not attain the highest would be either critical or generous. The profusion of scene and incident which led Scott into the undoubted blunder of ascribing to Smollett "more brilliancy of genius and more inexhaustible fertility of invention" than to Fielding, as well as into the particular oddity of preferring *Ferdinand, Count Fathom*, to *Jonathan Wild*, is real and wonderful, while the naval personages in both *Roderick Random* and *Peregrine Pickle*, the scenes on shipboard in the former novel, the "Roman dinner" in the latter, the forest adventures of Fathom, and even not a few passages in that rather unjustly depreciated book *Sir Launcelot Greaves*, remain as masterpieces of their kind. If Smollett adds nothing to the pillar-to-post manner of the Spaniards and of Le Sage he is a thorough adept in it, and succeeds in holding the reader's interest perhaps better than any of them. And if he never communicates to any character, much less to any story, the subtle truth and nature of which Fielding was a master, it can hardly be said that any of his characters are distinctly untrue or lacking in life. Nor did his plans and schemes lack a general verisimilitude save only in the singular crotchet which made him attribute to his Sir Launcelot the actual costume and procedure as well as the crazes and virtues of Don Quixote.

There can, however, be very little doubt that if he had left nothing but *Humphry Clinker*, though the body and variety of delight which he would have given to readers would have been much less, his literary standing would have been higher. In this charming book his defects appear softened and his merits heightened in a way difficult to parallel elsewhere in any single work of a voluminous and strongly-gifted author. Hardly any novel better carries off the too frequently troublesome and teasing scheme of epistolary narrative; the false spelling of Winifred Jenkins if it is only farce, and rather facile farce, is excellently funny, and has never been so well done by any one except by Thackeray who copied it; the stream of loosely connected adventure never flags or becomes monotonous; while here, and perhaps here only, Smollett has really created characters as well as "humours." Bramble and Lismahago by common consent need not fear to hold their head up (a process to which both were well inclined) in any fictitious company; and the others are not far behind them. Such an increase of mellowness and art with such a maintenance of vigour and resource are indeed rare in the work of a hack of letters who has been writing at full speed and on almost every subject for nearly five and twenty years.

It has not seemed necessary in the brief space available

here to draw on anything except the novels. The *History*, still venal at every stall and obvious on many shelves, is but hack-work, and not eminent hack-work of its kind, though it is very fairly written. Indeed Smollett is, as regards the mechanical minutenesses of composition, a very careful and correct craftsman. The criticism has the same drawback, not to mention that Smollett was one of those who mistake criticism for fault-finding, and who confuse the scholarly with the vulgar meaning of "censure." The *Travels* though not contemptible are too ill-tempered, too ambitious, and too much stuffed with guide-book detail; and I am sure that no one who has twice read the ferocious nastiness of the *Adventures of an Atom* would feel tempted to cull from them. Nature had made Smollett a novelist; only necessity, assisted by ill-health and ill-temper, made him a miscellaneous writer. So let us take the advice of a creation of his greatest follower and "make the best of him, not the worst."

OLIPHANT SMEATON
From *Tobias Smollett*
1897, pp. 122–46
Smollett as a Novelist

Smollett, although gaining distinction in other branches of literature, was primarily and essentially a novelist. He wrote history, and wrote it well; drama, and wrote it only passably; travels but little better, and poetry decidedly mechanically, save in the 'Ode to Independence.' In the novel alone did he by prescriptive right take his place in the front rank of British writers of fiction. Wherein then lay his strength, and in what respects did he differ from Richardson and Fielding? To institute any comparative estimate between the three is foolish in the last degree. The grounds for such a comparison do not exist, save in the initial fact that all three wrote novels!

Smollett was, like Scott, an unequalled observer. Nothing missed his 'inevitable eye,' either in a situation, an incident, or a landscape. If he had not Fielding's keen power of vision into the mental and moral characteristics of his fellow-men, he had twice his aptness of objective photography. The ludicrous aspects of a circumstance or of a saying impressed him deeply. He never seemed to forget the humorous bearings of any experience through which he had passed, or of which he had learned. The *affaire de cœur* with Melinda in *Roderick Random*, the challenge and arrest through the affection of Strap, also the inimitable 'banquet after the manner of the ancients' in *Peregrine Pickle*, were described from incidents occurring in Smollett's own history. To few writers has the faculty been given in measure so rich of projecting objectively the scenes he was describing upon some outward, yet imaginary canvas, whence he transferred them to his pages. The naturalness of setting in the case of all the incidents is so marked, and stands out in such glaring contrast to those recorded in the *Memoirs of a Lady of Quality* (published in *Peregrine Pickle*), that one scarcely knows which to admire most—the originality of the genius or the wonderful fidelity and impressiveness of the painter's reproduction.

Smollett's strength lay in his great power of self-restraint. He knew what he could do, and with rare wisdom he kept himself within the limits of his imaginative ability. He could very easily have made either Roderick Random or Peregrine Pickle a sentimental amorist, sighing after his mistress, and suffering all the delicious hopes and fears and ups and downs of the knights-errant of love. But therein he would have trenched upon Richardson's province, and placed himself in a decidedly unfavourable comparison with the author of *Pamela* and *Clarissa Harlowe*. He might have developed a splendid character-study out of the colossal Borgia-like wickedness of Ferdinand Count Fathom, who can alone claim kindred, in the pitiless thirst for crime which possesses him, with that repulsively brutal creation of Shakespeare's early days, Aaron in *Titus Andronicus*, who, when dying, curses the world with the words—

> If one good deed in all my life I did,
> I do repent it from my very soul.

But had he done so, he would have entered into direct competition with Fielding; a competition he knew he was unfitted to support. But in his own department he was supreme. In fertility of invention and apt adaptation of means to end he had no rival. His novels present one bewildering succession of accidents, entanglements, escapes, imprisonments, love-makings, and what not, until the mind positively becomes cloyed with the banquet of incident provided for it. A less profound genius than Smollett would in all probability have worn itself out in a vain attempt to rival his great contemporaries, on the principle 'never venture, never win.' Smollett was a surer critic, on this point at least, than many of his friends, who were continually urging him to attempt something in the mode of Fielding. 'There is but one husbandman can reap that field,' he replied. He knew what he *could* do and what he *could not* do, and therein, as has been said, lay his strength.

Viewing his novels as a whole,—*Roderick Random*, *Peregrine Pickle*, *Ferdinand Count Fathom*, *Launcelot Greaves*, *The Adventures of an Atom*, and *Humphrey Clinker*,—the first quality which strikes a critical reader is the family likeness existing between all the leading characters. Dissimilar though Roderick Random and Ferdinand Count Fathom may be in their impulses toward evil, distinct though Peregrine Pickle is from Launcelot Greaves, Matthew Bramble, and Lismahago in what may be termed his nobler qualities, there is nevertheless in all that happy-go-lucky carelessness, that supreme indifference to consequences, that courage that never flinches from the penalties of its own misdeeds, but accepts them without a murmur—in a word, a *bonhomie* diversified by egotism, that appears in equal measure in no other novelist of his time. Richardson displays that sentimental, melodramatic, watery 'gush' which the taste of last century denominated pathos—the sort of thing Dickens long after described in the phrase 'drawing tears from his eyes and a handkerchief from his pocket'; but of that quality there is not the faintest trace in Smollett. If anything, his characters are too callous, too fond of the rough-and-tumble Tom-and-Jerry life in which their creator so perceptibly revelled. Fielding, on the other hand, patiently elaborates his characters, adding here a line and there a curve, heightening the light in one place, deepening the shading in another, never picturing an incident or a trait without some definite end to be served in perfecting the final portrait. Smollett never takes time for such microscopic character studies. He is a veritable pen-and-ink draughtsman. With bold, rapid, vigorous strokes, he sketches, through the agency of incident, the outlines of his characters, filling in these outlines with but few subsidiary details regarding the feelings and moral impulses of his creations. For such he has neither the time nor the space. Let any reader lift the conceptions of Roderick Random, or Peregrine Pickle, or Matthew Bramble out of the setting of the story and study them apart, paying no heed to anything affecting the other personages, and he will see at once how completely Smollett relied on incident to do the work of explaining and analysing the feelings of his heroes. Fielding was the greater artist, Smollett the better story-teller; Fielding was the greater moral teacher, Smollett the more vigorous painter of contemporary manners. Further, let the reader carefully study Lovelace in Richardson's *Clarissa Harlowe*, Blifil in Fielding's novel of *Tom Jones*, and Smollett's Ferdinand Count Fathom, and he will perceive in even a stronger degree the diverse method of the three great novelists. Richardson builds up what might be called the 'architectonic' of the creation by a series of great scenes wherein dialogue plays the greatest part. Lovelace has all the light-hearted villainy of a man to whom virtue is a myth, who has no conscience, and whose standard of right is his gross animal devilishness. Richardson does everything by square and rule. He expends at the outset a wealth of ingenuity in portraying the most insignificant qualities of Lovelace's nature. And so fully does he make us acquainted with his nature, that at the end of the novel we know in reality very little more of him than we did at the outset. Fielding, on the other hand, winds his way into the very heart of a character, 'like a serpent round its prey,' as Goldsmith said of Burke's treatment of a subject in conversation. Every chapter gives us some addition to the creation, even to the very close of the novel. But when that is reached, the great synthesis is complete. Not a trait is lacking, and Master Blifil stands pilloried to all time as the type of everything that is contemptible and deceitful. Not so Smollett. In the case of Ferdinand Count Fathom the initial description of the character is reduced to a minimum. Everything is left to the effect produced by incident. All Fathom's pitilessness, his absolute love of vice for its own sake, his colossal selfishness, are in reality merely suggested to the reader's own mind, by the thread of rapidly succeeding incident, not formally labelled as such. In the case of both Richardson and Fielding the author is constantly present in his creation. So with Smollett, he is ever in evidence. None of them attain that superb art of Walter Scott, who simply effaces himself in his creations, or, as Hazlitt says: 'He sits like a magician in his cell and conjures up all shapes and sights to the view; but in the midst of all this phantasmagoria the author himself never appears to take part with his characters. It is the perfection of art to conceal art, and this is here done so completely, that, while it adds to our pleasure in the work, it seems to take away from the merit of the author. As he does not thrust himself into the foreground, he loses the credit of the performance.'

By the critical student closely attentive to the development of Smollett's genius, the fact will assuredly be noted that in the gallery of his characters, chronologically considered, there is a definitely progressive growth or increase in the power wherewith he limned character. Bearing in mind our initial position, that in Smollett's art incident was the prime element, and the delineation of character subordinate to the artistic arrangement of the links in the chain of circumstance, I would invite attention to the following analysis, as being, in my opinion, the conclusion to be deduced from a patient, faithful, and impartial study of the personages named. My contention is that in the character sequence we have a series of ascending psychologic gradations, each one presenting features of greater complexity and philosophic force, as the author realised more clearly the value of a system in that concatenation of event which influenced so intimately his personages.

Roderick Random is little else than the *Gil Blas* of Le Sage Anglified, with some hints borrowed from the excellent *Lazarillo de Tormes* of Hurtado de Mendoza. In his Preface to the novel Smollett acknowledges his indebtedness to French and Spanish fiction, and announces his conviction of the superiority of the novel of circumstance over all others. *Roderick Random*, therefore, as a novel consists of a succession of incidents, some startling, some improbable, some foolish, and some highly effective, but all loosely strung together without much artistic arrangement or relative affinity to each other. The book is a record of the 'adventures' of the hero from his cradle to his marriage. As in the case of all such books, the peg whereon the incidents are hung is very slender. All is loose and disjointed, happy-go-lucky in narration, rapid, swift, and evanescent in the mental pictures produced. Roderick is only a big schoolboy, full of animal spirits and animal passions, far, very far from being a saint, yet as far from being an irreclaimable sinner. He is the plaything of his passions, carried like a straw on the stream of circumstance. He takes everything as it comes, be it weal be it woe, be it good fortune or evil, with supreme nonchalance. He shows little regard or gratitude to his uncle, Lieutenant Bowling. He treats his poor friend Strap, whose only fault was his fidelity, worse than indifferently. He is not by any means faithful, and certainly not very respectful, to his lady-love, Narcissa; nay, he even takes the discovery of his long-lost father—a circumstance materially altering his social station—quite as a matter of course. Roderick Random was the spirit incarnate of the cold-blooded, coarse-fibred, religionless eighteenth century—a century wherein virtue was perpetually on the lips, and vice as perpetually in the hearts of its men, a century wherein its women were colourless puppets, without true individuality or definite aims, but oscillating aimlessly between Deism and Methodism to escape from the ennui that resulted from the lack of true culture. Roderick Random as a creation was a purely adventitious one, resulting from the fortuitous concourse of incidents. How the character was to shape itself, morally or mentally, seemed to trouble the creator little, provided the events were sufficiently lively and brisk, and the interest in the story was maintained unflaggingly. Incidents were piled up, whether tending to heighten the effect of the *dramatis personæ* or not. There was no conservation of material, no wise economy, no evidence of careful selection. Prodigality and profusion were everywhere present, with the signs of youth and inexperience writ large over all. In fact, the character of Roderick Random, critically estimated as a work of art, is little better than Lobeyra's Amadis de Gaul, a portrait limned wholly out of incident, flung on the canvas without premeditation, and frequently presenting inconsistencies and conflicting traits. There is no gradual development of character contemporaneously with the evolution of event. The character has gathered no wisdom during its course. It is represented to us in quite as immature a state at the end of the story as at the beginning. There is a heartlessness, a moral callousness about Roderick which all his experiences never seemed to remove. Excessively repulsive is this phase of the hero's character; nay, the novel is only saved from being as darkly shaded and as morally repellent as Count Fathom, by the pathetic doglike fidelity of poor Strap, who exhibits more true nobility of nature in a chapter, than Roderick Random in the whole book.

From the criticisms on *Roderick Random*, Smollett learned many lessons. He noted that, though his free and easy method of letting character shape itself through the medium of incident had its advantages, these were liable to be counterbalanced unless the chain of incident was so forged that each link would be related to the leading characters of the novel, so as to promote their development and tend to fill in the bare black and white outlines by some distinguishing trait, mannerism, or eccentricity. In *Peregrine Pickle*, therefore, the characters are seen to be more vertebrate. They are no longer the stalking lay figures of the first novel. Albeit Peregrine is only Roderick under another name, and endowed with a year or two more of experience and sense,—the subtle differentiation of personages visible in *Humphrey Clinker* having yet to be learned,—there is a marked improvement in the *technique* of the novel. The chain of incident is every whit as varied, the events as events are more stirring and startling than in the first novel, but there is now the attempt—though as yet but an attempt—to subject the unflagging flow of incident to an artistic adaptation towards definite ends. Incident is no longer piled on incident regardless of the fact whether it tend to advance the development of the characters or not. Then Smollett has learned the value of contrast in character-painting. Peregrine is contrasted with such humorous creations as Godfrey Gauntlet, Commodore Hawser Trunnion, Lieutenant Hatchway, and Bo'sun Tom Pipes. The virtue of relative proportion among his characters according to their ratio of importance in influencing the story, though still faulty, has been carefully studied. Peregrine therefore is supreme as hero. There is no Strap to dispute the honours with him, and as a portrait he is more consistent than in the case of Roderick. Though the same callous indifference to morality is manifest, though the likeness to Lazarillo de Tormes is even more patent in this latter creation than in the former, though the same polite villainy passes current under the name of gallantry, the same cheap appreciation of female honour,—witness that degrading scene so reprobated by Sir Walter Scott, where Peregrine assails Emilia Gauntlet's chastity,—the hero is not so glaring a moral imbecile as Roderick. He has gleams of better things. But, as in the former novel so in the latter, the noblest character of the book is the foil or contrast to Peregrine—Godfrey Gauntlet, on whom Smollett seems to lavish all his powers.

Then comes *Ferdinand Count Fathom*, indicating a still further advance in the *technique* of novel-writing. In this work the stage is not so crowded as in *Roderick Random* and *Peregrine Pickle*. The whole interest centres in the career of crime of this archfiend, this pitiless Nero, Iago, and Cæsar Borgia in one. A more terrible picture of human depravity has never been drawn unless in *Othello* and *Titus Andronicus*. But Smollett had now learned the lesson of the conservation of imaginative power. There are no needless incidents in this novel. Everyone reveals the character of the hero in a new light. Relative proportion, differentiation, and contrast have all been carefully studied. Notwithstanding our loathing of crimes so unspeakable, notwithstanding our hatred of animalism so unbridled as would sacrifice the trustful Monimia to his base passions, a sort of sneaking sympathy with Fathom begins to find entrance into the breast. As in *Paradise Lost* one feels a sorrow for Satan's position after his magnificent resistance to the Almighty, so here the same sentiment finds place. One hopes Fathom may have time given him wherein to repent. But Smollett was now too consummate an artist for that concession to sentimentalism. In *Roderick Random* he might have committed such an artistic mistake. Not now. Fathom receives retributive justice, and only repents when he has expiated to the uttermost his sins and wrongdoings.

Passing by *Sir Launcelot Greaves* and *The History of an Atom* as outside the pale of our criticism, inasmuch as they were written when he was worried and distracted with other matters, besides being in wretched health, so that they are unworthy of his genius, we come to the consideration of Matthew Bramble and Lieutenant Lismahago in *Humphrey Clinker*. They are undoubtedly the two greatest characters in the Smollett gallery

of imaginative portraits. They must be viewed together. To separate them is to lose the reflected lustre they cast by contrast on each other. Likenesses many and important they have. Both are sufferers from the world's fickle changes. Both are weary and irritated with society's meannesses and petty falsehoods. Both are testy, tetchy, and prickly-tempered. But how truly men! Smollett had now reached the meridian of his powers. He realised now that in a great novel incident and the delineation of character must occupy co-ordinate positions. To assign excessive predominance to either, is to mar the ultimate effect. Therefore in *Humphrey Clinker*, while still revelling in inexhaustible variety of incident, Smollett assigns to the synthesis of character its proper place. In place of portraying the characters himself, he adopted the course, so favoured by his great rival Richardson, and long years after to be employed with such rare effect by Walter Scott and William Makepeace Thackeray, of achieving the evolution of character through the medium of letters, a mutual analysis as well as a distinctive synthesis. Risky though the expedient was, for it demanded a man of the highest genius to make the letters popular, in Smollett's hands it proved eminently successful. We accordingly have Matthew Bramble alternately described by himself and Jerry Melford, each giving varying phases of the same kindly, dogmatic, generously obstinate, and wholly noble-hearted fellow. Lismahago's character, besides being drawn by the two above-named fellow-travellers in that expedition to Scotland wherein Humphrey Clinker was the footman and hero, has the blanks in the portrait filled in by Miss Tabitha Bramble, the bitter-sweet spinster whom he afterwards married, and the inimitably delightful lady's-maid, Winnifred Jenkins. More highly finished pictures could scarcely be desired. Side by side with Scott's Dugald Dalgetty and Thackeray's Esmond, Lismahago may assuredly be placed, while Matthew Bramble falls little short, in completeness of details, of Jonathan Oldbuck in the *Antiquary*. Yet Bramble is still Roderick Random and Peregrine Pickle purged of their faults and follies, and with the experience of years upon them. We realise that Bramble possesses all their shortcomings, albeit held in check by his strong good sense, while they potentially had all his virtues, though the fever of youth i' the blood obscured them for the nonce. A noble gallery do these five characters compose. If Fathom be the Cain or the Esau of the company, he has many of the family features to show to what race he belongs.

In one imaginative type Smollett has never been approached as a creator, to wit, in his delineation of British seamen. Captain Marryat exhibits a greater knowledge of nautical affairs than Smollett, but nothing in the younger novelist quite touches the racy humour of Commodore Hawser Trunnion, Lieutenant Bowling, Hatchway, and Pipes. David Hannay, in his introduction to *Japhet in Search of a Father*, says: 'Captain Savage of the *Diomede*, Captain M—— of the *King's Own*, Captain Hector Maclean in *Jacob Faithful*, Terence O'Brien, the mate Martin, the midshipman Gascoigne, Thomas Saunders the boatswain's mate, and Swinburne the quartermaster, are beyond all question not less lifelike portraits of the officers and men of the navy than Trunnion and Bowling, Pipes and Hatchway. In one respect Marryat had an inevitable advantage over his predecessor. Smollett never shows us the seaman at his work. He could not, because he did not know it sufficiently well to understand it himself.' That is perfectly true. But, on the other hand, Marryat's intimate knowledge was often a hindrance to his art. It led him to inflict the minutiæ of the service on his readers more than was needful. Hence the reason why some parts of Marryat's books are decidedly tiresome. Smollett's are never so. His sense of artistic proportion was finer than Marryat's, and he avoided the pitfall whereinto the other fell. As a delineator of the nautical character, Mr. Clark Russell is the greatest we have had since Smollett, and in him the latter finds his most dangerous rival. Yet, if Mr. Russell has equalled his master in many other respects, it is doubtful if he has quite reached the high-water mark of Commodore Trunnion and Lismahago.

Finally, Smollett's women are deserving of a word. Sainte Beuve said he judged a novelist's powers by the manner in which he drew his female characters. If so, Smollett would not have excited much sympathy in the mind of the brilliant author of the *Causeries du Lundi*. His women are of varying excellence. Narcissa in *Roderick Random* and Emilia in *Peregrine Pickle* are only sweet dolls. Until his closing years he could not differentiate between puling sentimentality and piquancy. Into the charming perversity, the delightful contradictoriness, that often make up for us one-half the attractiveness of the female character, he could not enter. To rise to the height of spiritual insight that was requisite to conceive and execute a Di Vernon, an Ethel Newcome, or a Rose Vincy, was for him impossible, simply because he could not realise in his earlier years of authorship that women are the equals, not the inferiors of man. The hapless Miss Williams in *Roderick Random* exhibits this feeling on the part of Smollett. She was nobility itself in character, yet she was made over to Strap. One of the finest of his creations is the hapless Monimia in *Count Fathom*. Tenderness, purity, grace, and beauty are all united in her. She falls, it is true, but her fall left her virtue unimpugned, seeing that her betrayer resorted to means as cruel as they were irresistible to accomplish his diabolic purpose. Monimia occupies a pedestal apart, but, she excepted, the two most delightful creations in all his works are those in *Humphrey Clinker*, Tabitha Bramble and Winnifred Jenkins. Lydia Melford is too milk-and-waterish, but the two first-named are drawn with masterly precision and force. Tabitha Bramble is a capital portrait of the soured, disappointed old maid, whose lover had died long before, but to whose memory she had been ever faithful—a woman whose nature is only encrusted with prejudice, not interpenetrated by it, so that we may justly hope that, under the loving care of Lieutenant Lismahago, her frigidity may thaw, and that in matrimony she may discover the world not to be so very bad after all. Winnifred Jenkins is the prototype of Mrs. Malaprop in Sheridan's *Rivals*, and is infinitely more amusing. All the vanity, self-assertiveness, and jealousy of a small mind, conjointly with the love of appearing to move in a higher circle of society than she really does, are admirably sketched, while her misappropriate use of the language of that circle is most felicitously rendered. The portrait is Smollett's best, and no touch is finer than Winnifred's conduct in the menagerie. Let her speak for herself. 'Last week I went with mistress to the Tower to see the crowns and wild beastis. There was a monstracious lion with teeth half a quarter long, and a gentleman bid me not go near him if I wasn't a maid, being as how he would roar, and tear, and play the dickens. Now I had no mind to go near him, for I cannot abide such dangerous honeymils, not I—but mistress would go, and the beast kept such a roaring and bouncing that I tho't he would have broke his cage and devoured us all; and the gentleman tittered forsooth; but I'll go death upon it, I will, that my lady is as good a firgkin as the child unborn; and therefore either the gentleman told a phib, or the lion ought to be set in the stocks for bearing false witness against his neighbour.' Tabitha Bramble and Win Jenkins are those two in Smollett's gallery of fiction which the world will not willingly let die.

Such, then, is Smollett as a novelist—the great master of incident and humorous narration, the painter of the faults, foibles, and eccentricities of his fellow-men. In his own sphere he was unrivalled, and he in nothing showed more saliently his good sense than by refusing to attempt works for which he knew he was both by temperament and training unfitted. I cannot quite agree with Professor Saintsbury's view in his charming and sympathetic "Life of Smollett," prefixed to what bids fair to be the standard edition of his works. [1] 'The only one of the deeper and higher passions which seems to have stirred Smollett was patriotism, in which a Scot rarely fails, unless he is an utter gaby or an utter scoundrel.' Does not the worthy Professor, following the popular definition, fail to differentiate between an *emotion* and a *passion*. In depicting the passions, Smollett, I grant, was singularly deficient; in such emotions as patriotism, sympathy with the oppressed, and a pure devotion to the cause of truth, he showed himself a man whose heart was permeated with the warmest and deepest enthusiasm.

Smollett as Historian and Critic

A hundred and thirty years ago, if one had been asked to name the six great historians then alive, Smollett with marked unanimity would have been mentioned amongst the first. In fact, Hume, Robertson, and he were then reckoned as the illustrious triumvirate of Scots whose genius, in default of others native born, had been consecrated to the task of lauding for bread and fame the annals of the land whose glories were supposed to be to them so distasteful. The Union of the countries was not yet sufficiently remote to have borne as its fruit that harvest of commercial, political, and agricultural benefits that have accrued to both lands as its result. The jealousy wherewith Scotsmen were regarded in England was a legacy from the days when the subjugation of the territory north of Tweed was a standing item in English foreign policy, from the reign of that greatly misjudged monarch, Edward I. (Longshanks), to the days of the fourth of his name, who recognised the younger brother of James III., the exiled Duke of Albany, as King of Scots under the title of Alexander IV., on condition that he acknowledged Edward as lord paramount and feudal superior.

The school of historians represented by Rapin, Oldmixon, Tindal, Carte, and Hooke, honest, hard-working investigators, but without any sense of method or proportion in classifying or arranging materials, and vigorous anti-Scots, was alarmed by the success attending the publication of Hume's *History of England* in 1754–61, Principal Robertson's *History of Scotland* in 1758–59, and Smollett's *History of England* in 1758. When the Continuation by the last-named appeared in 1762, it was exposed, as we have seen, to a perfect broadside of misrepresentation and unjust reflections, prompted by the historians above-named and their booksellers, whose literary property seemed to them to be endangered. That some of the criticisms were just, and founded upon the discovery of genuine errors and blemishes in the history, cannot be denied. But, on the other hand, three-fourths of the allegations were baseless, because proceeding from spleen, and not from genuine enthusiasm in the cause of historic truth.

For example, the objections urged by the friends and supporters of Rapin's History were that Smollett was too hurried in his survey, that he took too many facts on trust, that he was unfair in his critical estimates of eminent personages, and finally, that his style was one better adapted for the novel than for historical compositions. To these allegations the friends of Oldmixon added that he permitted party prejudice to colour all his judgments. In replying to such charges we virtually analyse Smollett's merits as a historian. A double duty is therefore discharged by so doing.

Smollett as a historian might say with Horace, and assuredly with truth, '*Nullius addictus jurare in verba magistri*—a slavish disciple of the tenets of no master am I.' Though unstinted in his praise of Hume's calm, lucid survey, of his careful generalisations and eminently comprehensive method, though likewise a generous admirer of Robertson's brilliant word-pictures and glowingly eloquent narrative, wherein the long dead seemed to live again, he had his own ideal of the writing of history, and it savoured rather of Tacitus than of Thucydides. His method consisted in presenting a series of great outstanding events covering the entire period under notice, and round these to group the subordinate occurrences either resulting from or happening contemporaneously with them. He was a firm believer in the doctrine that political freedom and commercial honesty are the two great bulwarks of any State. Though a Tory in name, he was in reality more of a philosophical Whig, rather a champion of the rights of the people than a lover and defender of aristocracies, oligarchies, and monopolies. 'That country only is truly prosperous that is in the highest sense free, and that country alone is free where a hierarchy of knowledge governs, uninfluenced by faction and undisturbed by prejudice,' he wrote in the *Critical Review*. The sentiments are somewhat vague and indefinite, but they show that he was striving to emancipate himself from the leading-strings of party prejudice.

Although the fact is beyond doubt that Smollett's historical works were written exceedingly rapidly, on the other hand, we must remember that the rapidity of production merely applied to the mechanical work of transcribing what had been already carefully thought out. Like Dr. Johnson, Smollett was possessed of a most retentive memory. He rarely committed any of his works to paper until he had thoroughly thought them out in his mind, and had tested them over and over again in that searching alembic. In neither case, therefore, was the *composition* hurried. All that was done was to expedite its transcription. Smollett's historical judgments, in place of being hastily formed, were the result of patient study and thought. On this point we have the evidence of Wilkes, who, in one of his epigrams, more forcible than delicate, remarked that Smollett travailed over the birth of his historical judgments so much that he (Wilkes) had often to play the part of the critical midwife.

The next charge, that Smollett was too prone to take his information at second hand, cannot be altogether controverted, though it was not yet the custom of historians to betake themselves to the MS. repositories of the country for their materials. More mutual reliance was placed by historians on each other's *bonâ fides* and faculty of critical selection than seems to be the case now. But we have it on his own assurance that he consulted over three hundred authorities for his facts. That number may be small compared with those eight hundred names which Buckle prints at the commencement of his noble and imperishable *History of Civilisation in England*, but in Smollett's day the number of his references was considered phenomenal. He greatly surpassed Hume in the range and appropriateness of his references, and rather prided himself on the collateral evidences of facts which he was able to adduce from his miscellaneous reading. That Smollett was consciously unfair in his judgment of any character in his historical works cannot be credited. He was too warm a friend of truth to be seduced into wilfully distorting the plain and straightforward deductions from ascertained facts. That he may have been misled I do not deny, that his political predilections may have led him insensibly to colour his judgments at times with the jaundice of partisanship, is quite possible, yet that such was done deliberately, no student of Smollett's character for a moment will credit. Many of his political opponents were castigated, it is true, so were many of his political friends; but, on the other hand, the fact is to be taken into account that many of his bitterest enemies obtained a just and impartial criticism from Smollett when such was denied to them by many of the writers numbered among their own friends. Finally, that his style was more adapted to the treatment of imaginative themes than of sober historical narrative, was a charge that might have some weight in the middle decades of last century. It can have none now. No special style is distinctively to be employed in historical composition. It affords scope for all. True it is that Echard and his school, in the early decades of the eighteenth century, contended that history should be written in a style of sober commonplace altogether divested of ornament, as thereby the judgment was not likely to be led astray. But such nonsensical reservations have long since been relegated to the limbo of exploded theories, and in historical composition the brilliancy of a Macaulay and of an Alison finds a place as well as the sober sense of a Hallam or a Stubbs; the picturesqueness of a Froude, as well as the earnest vigour and tireless industry of a Freeman. Smollett's style, so nervous, pointed, and epigrammatic, so full of strength and beauty as well as of scintillating sparkle, was somewhat of a surprise in his day. Hume's easy, flowing, pithy Saxon, and Robertson's stately splendour, had both carried the honours in historical composition to the grey metropolis of the North. The fact that another Scot, albeit resident in London, should repeat the success, and in some respects excel both, was the most crushing blow the elder school of history had received. Thenceforward we hear nothing of them. Rapin and Oldmixon slumbered with the spiders on the remotest shelves of the great libraries. Their day was past. A new school of British historians had arisen.

Smollett's historical works, his *History of England*, his *Continuation of the History of England*, his *Histories of France, Italy, and Germany*, are characterised by the following sterling qualities:—a felicity of method whereby the narrative flows on easily and consecutively from beginning to end, and whereby, through its division into chapters, representing definite epochs, one is able to discover with ease any specific point that may be desired; an exhibition of the principles whereon just and equitable government should proceed, namely, that of a limited monarchy; a judicious subordination of the less to the more important events in the narrative; short, pithy, but eminently fair and appreciative criticisms of all the more outstanding personages in the country under treatment, and a convincing testimony borne to the axiom that only by national virtue and the conservation of national honour can any nation either reach greatness or retain it. If Smollett did not possess Hume's power of reaching back to first principles in tracing the evolution of a country's greatness, or Robertson's stimulating eloquence that fired the heart with noble sentiments, he had the virtue, scarcely less valuable, of keeping more closely to his theme than either of them, and of producing works that read like a romance. If Hume were the superior in what may be styled the philosophy of history, if Robertson in picturesqueness and eloquence, Smollett was the better narrator of the circumstances and facts as they actually occurred. In many respects he resembles Diderot, and the analogy is not lessened when we compare the private lives of the two men. To Smollett history was only of value insomuch as we are able to read the present by the key of the past, and to influence the future by avoiding the mistakes of the past and present. Smollett was a patriot in the broad catholic signification of the word. He had no sympathy with the patriotism that is synonymous with national or racial selfishness. More crimes have stained the annals of humanity under the guise of patriotism than can be atoned for by cycles of penitence. To Smollett the soul of patriotism was summed up in sinking the name of Scot in the generic one of Briton, and in endeavouring to stamp out that pitiful provincialism that considered one's love of country to be best manifested in perpetuating quarrels whereon the mildew of centuries had settled. Smollett in his historical works showed himself a truer patriot than that. Though a leal-hearted Scot, he was likewise a magnanimous-spirited Briton, ready to judge as he would wish to be judged. Writing of the Union of 1707, he remarks in his *Continuation*: 'The majority of both nations believed that the treaty would produce violent convulsions, or, at best, prove ineffectual. But we now see it has been attended with none of the calamities that were prognosticated, that it quietly took effect, and answered all the purposes for which it was intended. Hence we may learn that many great difficulties are surmounted because they are not seen by those who direct the execution of any great project; and that many great schemes which theory deems impracticable will yet succeed in the experiment.'

Some critics have urged that Smollett might have taken a broader view of the sources and progress of national expansion and development. Minto rather off-handedly designates his style as 'fluent and loose, possessing a careless vigour where the subject is naturally exciting,' and concluding with the words, 'the history *is said* to be full of errors and inconsistencies.'[2] Now, this last clause is taken word for word from Chambers's *Cyclopædia of English Literature*, who took it from Angus's *English Literature*, who borrowed it from Macaulay, who annexed it from the *Edinburgh Review*, which journal had originally adopted it with alterations from Smollett's own prefatory remarks in the first edition of the book. How many of these authors had read the history for themselves, to see if it really contained such errors and inconsistencies? Criticism conducted on that mutual-trust principle is very convenient for the critic; is it quite fair to the author? Now, anyone who faithfully reads Smollett's *History of England* and its *Continuation* will not discover a larger percentage of either errors or inconsistencies than appear in the works of his contemporary historians, Tytler, Hume, and Robertson. Smollett is as distinguishingly fair and impartial as it was possible for one to be, influenced so profoundly by his environment as were all the historians of the eighteenth century. The mind of literary Europe was already tinged by that spiritual unrest and moral callousness that was to induce the new birth of the French Revolution.

As a literary critic, during his tenure of the editorial chair of the *Critical Review*, Smollett's judgments were frequently called in question, especially in the case of Dr. Grainger, the translator of *Tibullus* and of the Greek dramatists, and author of the *Ode to Solitude*; Shebbeare, a well-known political writer of the period, whose seditious utterances had been chastised; Home, the author of *Douglas*, and Wilkie of the *Epigoniad*. Now, in nearly all the cases wherein exception was taken to the articles, these were not written by Smollett. But even as regards those of his own composition that have been complained of, careful perusal alike of the volume criticised and of the critique evince Smollett to have been as just and fair in the circumstances as he could well be. For example, the opinion he formed of Churchill's Poems was that in which the British public within thirty years was to acquiesce,—nay, is that

which to-day is the prevailing literary verdict upon these once popular works. Smollett unfortunately left his contributors a perfectly free hand. Many of them were men of no principle, who permitted private grudges to colour their critical estimate of literary works produced by those with whom they had some quarrel or disagreement. Smollett was to blame for not exercising his editorial scissors more freely on the verdicts of his *collaborateurs*. His own opinions of current literature were expressed with a fairness leaving little to be desired. Though not a Sainte Beuve in critical appreciation of the work of others, though his verdicts never possessed the keen spiritual and emotional insight of the famous *Causeries du Lundi* in the Paris *Constitutional*, still they are the fair, honest, outspoken opinions of a man who, as Morton said of Knox, 'never feared the face of man,' and therefore would not be biassed by favour or fear. Dr. Johnson was at the same time criticising literature in his new *Literary Magazine*. Interesting it is to compare the two opinions on the books they dealt with. Smollett's style is well-nigh as distinguishable as Johnson's among his fellow-contributors. If the decrees of 'the Great Cham of Literature'[3] are more authoritative, they are but little more incisive and searching than those of the author of *Roderick Random*. The former had a more extensive vocabulary, the latter was the more consummate literary critic. Wit, humour, pathos, and epigram were all at the service of Smollett, and though, in depth of thought and soaring sublimity of reasoning powers, the author of the *Rambler* excelled his contemporary, in the lighter graces of style Smollett was the better of the two. Though he had not Johnson's Jove-like power of driving home a truth, he frequently persuaded, by his calm and lucid logic, where the thunder of the Great Cham only repelled. If blame be his, then, with regard to the exercise of his critical authority, it was due more to sins of omission than of commission, more to believing that others were actuated by the same high ideals in criticism as himself. In reading some of the numbers of the *Critical Review* for the purposes of this biography, nothing struck me more in those papers that were plainly from the pen of Smollett, than the power he possessed of placing himself at the point of view assumed by the writer of the work under criticism, so that he might be thoroughly *en rapport* with the author's sympathies. How few critics have either the inclination or the ability to do likewise!

Notes

1. *Works of T. G. Smollett*, edited by George Saintsbury. London: Gibbings & Co.
2. *Manual of English Prose Literature*.
3. The title Smollett gave to Johnson when requesting the aid of Wilkes to free Francis Barber, Johnson's black servant, from service on board the *Stag*. It is the older form of *Khan*.

WILBUR L. CROSS
"Tobias Smollett"
The Development of the English Novel
1899, pp. 63–69

The first novels of Tobias Smollett appeared when Richardson and Fielding were doing their maturest work. *Roderick Random* (1748) immediately follows *Clarissa Harlowe*, and immediately precedes *Tom Jones*. *Peregrine Pickle* (1751) falls between *Tom Jones* and *Amelia*. *The Adventures of Ferdinand, Count Fathom* was published in 1753. Smollett's other novels belong to a later period. *The Adventures of Sir*

Launcelot Greaves—a too patent imitation of *Don Quixote*—was published in 1762, and *Humphry Clinker* in 1771.

Smollett and Fielding professed the same source of inspiration—Spain. The Spanish picaresque stories of Aleman, Cervantes, Quevedo, and others, and the French offshoots of them by Sorel, Scarron, and Furetière had all found their way into English. Beginning with *The Fraternity of Vagabonds* (1561) by John Awdeley, there was a long line of English picaresque sketches and stories extending down to Defoe. Fielding evidently read considerably in this fiction, and Smollett evidently read all at his command, whether Spanish, French, or English. More particularly, both Smollett and Fielding informed the reader that their models were Cervantes and Lesage. As a result, Fielding and Smollett have much in common; a novel, as they conceived of it, is a union of intrigue and adventure. But in the disposition of their material they were far apart. Fielding when at his best grouped and arranged incidents for dramatic effect, with his final chapter in view. Smollett, too, brought his stories to a close in the manner of *Tom Jones*, with a marriage and a description of the charms of the bride; yet there was no logic in this; it was merely a mechanical device for stopping somewhere. Smollett's novels are strings of adventure and personal histories, and it is not quite clear to the reader why they might not be shuffled into any other succession than the one they have assumed. A literary form cannot exist without its art. If a fable may drift along at the pleasure of an author, with the episode thrust in at will, then anybody can write a novel. This inference was drawn by the contemporaries of Smollett. Between 1750 and 1770 the press was burdened with slipshod adventures, the writers of which did not possess Smollett's picturesqueness and immense strength of style. The novel thus put into the hands of the mob ceased to be a serious literary product; and, in consequence, its decline was rapid from what it was as left by Richardson and Fielding.

Fielding based his art as humorist and realist on the commonplace observation that we are not what we seem. His province as novelist was to remove the mask of affectation, that we may be seen as we really are. Except where his motive is purely literary, as in *Jonathan Wild*, his principal characters are never 'sordid and vicious'; his Trulliber and Blifil come only by the way. Smollett, in his first novels, puts first 'the selfishness, envy, malice, and base indifference of mankind'; he does not strip his rogues, for they are stripped when introduced; he at once exposes to view 'those parts of life where the humors and passions are undisguised by affectation, ceremony, or education.' The least varnished scenes in our fiction are in *Roderick Random*: the flogging of Dr. Syntax, the impressment of Roderick, Dr. Macshane's review of the sick on the quarter-deck of the *Thunder*, and the duel between Roderick and Midshipman Crampley. It was the boast of Smollett that in drawing them 'nature is appealed to in every particular.' In *Peregrine Pickle* and *Count Fathom*, he is equally outspoken, but there his realism is somewhat artificial; he is writing to order for a public who find humor in the practical joke, or who would like to see refurbished those scenes in Richardson between Lord B—— and Pamela. In his ruffianism, and his savage analysis of motive, Smollett intensifies, enforces, and completes the reaction against Richardson.

Yet Smollett's realism is marked by the spot of decay. All his first novels have one characteristic of the fictions of Mrs. Manley and Mrs. Haywood, Tom Brown, and numerous other early eighteenth-century writers: he crowds his pages with well-known characters of his own time, usually for the purpose of fierce satire. He is a Swift without Swift's clear and wide vision. He ridicules Fielding for marrying his 'cook-maid'; Akenside—

a respectable poet and scholar—is a mere 'index-hunter who holds the eel of science by the tail'; Garrick is 'a parasite and buffoon, whose hypocrisy is only equalled by his avarice'; Lyttelton is 'a dunce'; he insults Newcastle, Bute, and Pitt, and sneers at his king, and the 'sweet princes of the royal blood.' In making his characters at will the mouthpiece of his venom, he takes no pains to preserve their consistency; and frequently, under the excitement of his ferocious hate, he forgets they are there, and speaks out in his own name. This kind of work, though done brilliantly and under the inspiration of robust indignation, does not form a novel. The logical outcome was his own *History of an Atom* and Charles Johnstone's *History of a Guinea*—pamphlets and libels *in extenso*.

In the *débris* of the novel thus wrecked by Smollett, there are new scenes and characters. *Roderick Random* is our first novel of the sea. Defoe and the romancers and the picaresque writers before him transferred imaginary adventure to an imaginary sea. It remained for Smollett to bring into the novel the real sea, a real ship, a real voyage, and the real English tars. As an example of Smollett's realism, Lieutenant Bowling may be contrasted with Crusoe: 'He was a strong built man, somewhat bandy-legged, with a neck like that of a bull, and a face which (you might easily perceive) had withstood the most obstinate assaults of the weather.' He has forgotten the language of landsmen and speaks only the 'seamen's phrase'; had the occasion occurred, he would have fought and died at his post with the cheerfulness of a Grenville. The English sailor lingers on in *Peregrine Pickle* and *Humphry Clinker*. In the former appears Commodore Trunnion, Smollett's most amusing seaman, who, retiring into the country with Lieutenant Hatchway and Tom Pipes, turns his house into a garrison; and, after nursing his whims and superstitions for a period of years, dies in a hiccough and a groan. Smollett's land characters are as novel as his seamen; his Scotchmen, his Irishmen, his Welshmen, and his Jews,—drawn at full length, as Lieutenant Lishmahago, or characterized by a happy phrase, as the Scotch schoolmaster who advertises to teach Englishmen the correct pronunciation of the English language. They are caricature types, at once professional and national. As national types they are the first in English fiction.

The author of *Humphry Clinker* is also the exponent of a new kind of humor. Written while Smollett was dying at Leghorn, the novel is milder in tone than the rest; fierce satire has disappeared. Though thrown together like his other novels, it is most brilliant in conception. Matthew Bramble, a bachelor well on in years, the master of Brambleton Hall in Monmouthshire, is a sufferer from the gout and many imaginary diseases. At the advice of his physician, Dr. Lewis, he takes a circular tour through England and Scotland for his health, visiting Bath, London, Scarborough, Edinburgh, Glasgow, and the Western Highlands. He is accompanied by his shrewish sister Tabitha Bramble, her dog Chowder, her maid Winifred Jenkins, and his niece and nephew, Miss Lydia Melford and Mr. Jeremiah Melford. Smollett's object is to excite continuous laughter by farcical situations. The novel thus announces the broad comedy of Dickens, so different from the pure comedy of Fielding, and best characterized by *funny*, a word then just coming into use.

Smollett, however, is never merely funny. In this one instance he tells his story by means of letters from the various characters to their various friends, in which the same scenes are described as viewed by a hypochondriac, a man of the world, a sentimental young woman, an aged spinster seeking a husband, and a waiting-maid who has never before crossed the Severn. Lydia thus writes of Ranelagh to her friend Laetitia:—

Ranelagh looks like the enchanted palace of a genie, adorned with the most exquisite performances of painting, carving, and gilding, enlightened with a thousand golden lamps that emulate the noonday sun; crowded with the great, the rich, the gay, the happy, and the fair; glittering with cloth of gold and silver, lace, embroidery, and precious stones. While these exulting sons and daughters of felicity tread this round of pleasure, or regale in different parties and separate lodges, with fine imperial tea and other delicious refreshments, their ears are entertained with the most ravishing delights of music, both instrumental and vocal.

Then Matthew Bramble gives his impression of Ranelagh in a letter to Dr. Lewis:—

What are the amusements at Ranelagh? One half of the company are following one another in an eternal circle; like so many blind asses in an olive-mill, where they can neither discourse, distinguish, nor be distinguished; while the other half are drinking hot water, under the denomination of tea, till nine or ten o'clock at night, to keep them awake for the rest of the evening. As for the orchestra, the vocal music especially, it is well for the performers that they cannot be heard distinctly.

This is comedy become philosophic; it is comedy which arises (to use a popular current phrase) from profound insight into the relativity of knowledge.

Finally, Smollett's novels look toward the new romance which was soon to displace the novel of sentiment and ridicule. Smollett's imagination delighted in terror. A tragic gloom colors many a scene on board the *Thunder*, especially that one where Roderick, chained to the deck on a dark night, lies exposed to the furious broadside of a French man-of-war. It pervades *Count Fathom*, his most romantic novel; and perhaps above all his scenes of horror, rises the midnight the count passes in the robbers' cave. Here are the shadows, the poniard, the bleeding corpse, the cold sweat, and the trance machinery which usher in Gothic romance.

OLIVER GOLDSMITH

OLIVER GOLDSMITH

c. 1730–1774

Oliver Goldsmith, novelist, poet, and comic dramatist, was born on November 10, 1730 or 1731, probably at Pallas, County Longford, Ireland. He spent much of his childhood at Lissoy and attended schools at Elphin, Athlone, and Edgeworthstown. In 1745 he entered Trinity College, Dublin, as a sizar. Goldsmith was involved in a college riot in 1747 and left school temporarily, but he returned and in 1749 received his B.A. He then decided to follow in his father's footsteps and prepared for holy orders, but upon presenting himself for ordination he was rejected by the Bishop of Elphin.

In 1752 Goldsmith left Ireland permanently. He briefly studied medicine in Edinburgh (1753) and Leyden (1754), although he did not receive a degree. Between 1755 and 1756 he traveled on foot throughout northern Italy, Switzerland, France, and perhaps Germany. Returning to England in February 1756, he worked at various odd jobs and then in 1757 began his literary career as a reviewer for the *Monthly Review*. Early in 1758 he published a translation of Jean Marteille's *Memoirs of a Protestant, Condemned to the Galleys of France*, and later that year attempted but failed to qualify as a hospital-mate on board a ship bound for India.

Goldsmith's first important work, *An Enquiry into the Present State of Polite Learning in Europe*, was published in 1759. By this time he was contributing to several periodicals and was employed by Smollett for his *British Magazine* and by John Newbery for his *Public Ledger*. Between October 6 and November 24 Goldsmith published eight issues of his own periodical, *The Bee*. In 1760 his *Chinese Letters* appeared in installments in the *Public Ledger*; these letters, modeled on Montesquieu's *Persian Letters*, are written from the viewpoint of a Chinaman in London, and were reprinted in 1762 as *The Citizen of the World*. Goldsmith became editor of the *Lady's Magazine* in 1761; in that year he met Samuel Johnson, who invited him to become one of the first members of Johnson's Club. By that time Goldsmith had also become friendly with Thomas Percy, Sir Joshua Reynolds, David Garrick, Edmund Burke, and James Boswell. Despite having risen from an obscure hack writer to an associate of such famous men, he was still frequently on the brink of financial ruin, mostly because of his extravagance. In 1762 Johnson saved him from being arrested for debt by arranging for the sale of the first third of Goldsmith's novel, *The Vicar of Wakefield*, and Goldsmith himself quickly turned out various biographies, compilations, translations, and abridgements in order to support himself. Works of this nature include, out of more than forty volumes, the *Memoirs of M. de Voltaire* (1761), *The Life of Richard Nash, Esq.* (1762), an abridgement of Plutarch's *Lives* (5 vols., 1762), *An History of England in a Series of Letters of a Nobleman to His Son* (2 vols., 1764), a *Roman History* (2 vols., 1769), a *Grecian History* (2 vols., 1774), a *Life of Bolingbroke* (1770), and a *Life of Parnell* (1770).

In 1764 Goldsmith established his reputation as a poet with the publication of *The Traveller*, a work much admired by Samuel Johnson, Charles James Fox, and others. *The Vicar of Wakefield*, for which he is now best remembered, was also published in that year but did not attract much attention. Goldsmith then tried his hand at theatrical comedy, and wrote two plays, *The Good Natur'd Man*, produced in 1768, and *She Stoops to Conquer*, produced with much greater success in 1773. In the meantime he had published his most famous poem, *The Deserted Village* (1770), and in the following years wrote other lighter verses, such as *Retaliation* (1774) and *The Haunch of Venison* (1776). His fantastical *History of the Earth and Animated Nature* was published posthumously in 1774, shortly after Goldsmith's death on March 25 of that year.

Personal

Here Hermes, says Jove who with nectar was mellow,
Go fetch me some clay—I will make an odd fellow:
Right and wrong shall be jumbled—much gold and some dross;
Without cause be he pleas'd, without cause be he cross;
Be sure as I work to throw in contradictions,
A great love of truth; yet a mind turn'd to fictions;
Now mix these ingredients, which warm'd in the baking,
Turn to learning, and gaming, religion and raking.
With the love of a wench, let his writings be chaste;
Tip his tongue with strange matter, his pen with fine taste;
That the rake and the poet o'er all may prevail,
Set fire to the head, and set fire to the tail:
For the joy of each sex, on the world I'll bestow it:

This Scholar, Rake, Christian, Dupe, Gamester and Poet,
Thro' a mixture so odd, he shall merit great fame,
And among brother mortals—be GOLDSMITH his name!
When on earth this strange meteor no more shall appear,
You, Hermes, shall fetch him—to make us sport here!
—DAVID GARRICK, "Jupiter and Mercury: A Fable," n.d.

Of all solemn coxcombs, Goldsmith is the first; yet sensible—but affects to use Johnson's hard words in conversation.
—THOMAS WARTON, Letter to Joseph Warton (Jan. 22, 1765)

From our Goldsmith's anomalous character, who
Can withhold his contempt, and his reverence too?
From a poet so polished, so paltry a fellow!
From critic, historian, or vile Punchinello!

From a heart in which meanness had made her abode,
From a foot that each path of vulgarity trod;
From a head to invent, and a hand to adorn,
Unskilled in the schools, a philosopher born.
By disguise undefended, by jealousy smit,
This *lusus naturæ*, nondescript in wit,
May best be compared to those Anamorphòses,
Which for lectures to ladies th' optician proposes;
All deformity seeming, in some points of view,
In others quite accurate, regular, true:
Till the student no more sees the figure that shock'd her,
But all in his likeness—our odd little doctor.
> —HESTER LYNCH PIOZZI, "The Streatham Por-
> traits" (1773), *Autobiography, Letters and Lit-
> erary Remains*, ed. A. Hayward, 1861, Vol. 2,
> pp. 12–13

With the greatest pretensions to polished manners he was rude, and, when he most meant the contrary, absurd. He affected Johnson's style and manner of conversation, and, when he had uttered, as he often would, a laboured sentence, so tumid as to be scarce intelligible, would ask, if that was not truly Johnsonian; yet he loved not Johnson, but rather envied him for his parts; and once entreated a friend to desist from praising him, 'for in doing so,' said he, 'you harrow up my very soul.'

He had some wit, but no humour, and never told a story but he spoiled it.—SIR JOHN HAWKINS, *The Life of Samuel Johnson, LL.D.*, 1787

As Dr. Oliver Goldsmith will frequently appear in this narrative, I shall endeavour to make my readers in some degree acquainted with his singular character. He was a native of Ireland, and a contemporary with Mr. Burke at Trinity College, Dublin, but did not then give much promise of future celebrity. He, however, observed to Mr. Malone, that 'though he made no great figure in mathematicks, which was a study in much repute there, he could turn an Ode of Horace into English better than any of them.' He afterwards studied physick at Edinburgh, and upon the Continent; and I have been informed, was enabled to pursue his travels on foot, partly by demanding at Universities to enter the list as a disputant, by which, according to the custom of many of them, he was entitled to the premium of a crown, when luckily for him his challenge was not accepted; so that, as I once observed to Dr. Johnson, he *disputed* his passage through Europe. He then came to England, and was employed successively in the capacities of an usher to an academy, a corrector of the press, a reviewer, and a writer for a news-paper. He had sagacity enough to cultivate assiduously the acquaintance of Johnson, and his faculties were gradually enlarged by the contemplation of such a model. To me and many others it appeared that he studiously copied the manner of Johnson, though, indeed, upon a smaller scale.

At this time I think he had published nothing with his name, though it was pretty generally known that *one Dr. Goldsmith* was the authour of *An Enquiry into the present State of polite Learning in Europe*, and of *The Citizen of the World*, a series of letters supposed to be written from London by a Chinese. No man had the art of displaying with more advantage as a writer, whatever literary acquisitions he made. '*Nihil quod tetigit non ornavit.*' His mind resembled a fertile, but thin soil. There was a quick, but not a strong vegetation, of whatever chanced to be thrown upon it. No deep root could be struck. The oak of the forest did not grow there; but the elegant shrubbery and the fragrant parterre appeared in gay succession. It has been generally circulated and believed that

he was a mere fool in conversation; but, in truth, this has been greatly exaggerated. He had, no doubt, a more than common share of that hurry of ideas which we often find in his countrymen, and which sometimes produces a laughable confusion in expressing them. He was very much what the French call *un étourdi*, and from vanity and an eager desire of being conspicuous wherever he was, he frequently talked carelessly without knowledge of the subject, or even without thought. His person was short, his countenance coarse and vulgar, his deportment that of a scholar aukwardly affecting the easy gentleman. Those who were in any way distinguished, excited envy in him to so ridiculous an excess, that the instances of it are hardly credible. When accompanying two beautiful young ladies with their mother on a tour in France, he was seriously angry that more attention was paid to them than to him; and once at the exhibition of the *Fantoccini* in London, when those who sat next him observed with what dexterity a puppet was made to toss a pike, he could not bear that it should have such praise, and exclaimed with some warmth, 'Pshaw! I can do it better myself.'

He, I am afraid, had no settled system of any sort, so that his conduct must not be strictly scrutinised; but his affections were social and generous, and when he had money he gave it away very liberally. His desire of imaginary consequence predominated over his attention to truth. When he began to rise into notice, he said he had a brother who was Dean of Durham, a fiction so easily detected, that it is wonderful how he should have been so inconsiderate as to hazard it. He boasted to me at this time of the power of his pen in commanding money, which I believe was true in a certain degree, though in the instance he gave he was by no means correct. He told me that he had sold a novel for four hundred pounds. This was his *Vicar of Wakefield*. But Johnson informed me, that he had made the bargain for Goldsmith, and the price was sixty pounds. 'And, Sir, (said he,) a sufficient price too, when it was sold; for then the fame of Goldsmith had not been elevated, as it afterwards was, by his *Traveller*; and the bookseller had such faint hopes of profit by his bargain, that he kept the manuscript by him a long time, and did not publish it till after *The Traveller* had appeared. Then, to be sure, it was accidentally worth more money.'
—JAMES BOSWELL, *Life of Johnson*, 1791

He was subject to severe fits of the stranguary, owing probably to the intemperate manner in which he confined himself to the desk, when he was employed in his compilations, often indeed for several weeks successively without taking exercise. On such occasions he usually hired lodgings in some farm house a few miles from London, and wrote without cessation till he had finished his task. He then carried his copy to the bookseller, received his compensation, and gave himself up perhaps for months without interruption, to the gaieties, amusements, and societies of London.

And here it may be observed, once for all, that his elegant and enchanting style in prose flowed from him with such facility, that in whole quires of his histories, *Animated Nature*, &c. he had seldom occasion to correct or alter a single word; but in his verses, especially his two great ethic poems, nothing could exceed the patient and incessant revisal, which he bestowed upon them. To save himself the trouble of transcription, he wrote the lines in his first copy very wide, and would so fill up the intermediate space with reiterated corrections, that scarcely a word of his first effusions was left unaltered.—THOMAS PERCY, "Life of Dr. Oliver Goldsmith," *The Miscellaneous Works of Oliver Goldsmith*, 1801

A lady, who was a great friend of Dr. Goldsmith, earnestly desired to have a lock of his hair to keep as a memorial of him; and his coffin was opened again, after it had been closed up, to procure this lock of hair from his head; this relick is still in the possession of the family, and is the only one of the kind which has been preserved of the Doctor.

An observation of Dr. Beattie, respecting the deceased poet, in a letter to Mrs. Montague, must not be passed over. "I am sorry for poor Goldsmith. There were some things in his temper which I did not like; but I liked many things in his genius; and I was sorry to find, last summer, that he looked upon me as a person who seemed to stand between him and his interest. However, when *next* we meet, all this will be forgotten, and the jealousy of authors, which, Dr. Gregory used to say, was next to that of physicians, will be no more."

Soon after Goldsmith's death, some people dining with Sir Joshua were commenting rather freely on some part of his works, which, in their opinion, neither discovered talent nor originality. To this, Dr. Johnson listened, in his usual growling manner, for some time; when, at length, his patience being exhausted, he rose, with great dignity, looked them full in the face, and exclaimed, "If nobody was suffered to abuse poor Goldy, but those who could write as well, he would have few censors."

Yet, on another occasion, soon after the death of Goldsmith, a lady of his acquaintance was condoling with Dr. Johnson on their loss, saying, "Poor Goldsmith! I am exceedingly sorry for him; he was every man's friend!"

"No, Madam," answered Johnson, "he was no man's friend!"

In this seemingly harsh sentence, however, he merely alluded to the careless and imprudent conduct of Goldsmith, as being no friend even to himself, and when that is the case, a man is rendered incapable of being of any essential service to any one else.

It has been generally circulated, and believed by many, that Goldsmith was a mere fool in conversation; but, in truth, this has been greatly exaggerated by such as were really fools. In allusion to this notion Mr. Horace Walpole, who admired his writings, said he was "an inspired idiot," and Garrick described him as one,

> for shortness call'd Noll,
> Who wrote like an angel, but talk'd like poor Poll.

Sir Joshua Reynolds mentioned to Boswell that he frequently had heard Goldsmith talk warmly of the pleasure of being liked, and observe how hard it would be if literary excellence should preclude a man from that satisfaction, which he perceived it often did, from the envy which attended it; and therefore Sir Joshua was convinced, that he was intentionally more absurd, in order to lessen himself in social intercourse, trusting that his character would be sufficiently supported by his works. If it was his intention to appear absurd in company, he was often very successful. This, in my own opinion, was really the case; and I also think Sir Joshua was so sensible of the advantage of it, that he, yet in a much less degree, followed the same idea, as he never had a wish to impress his company with any awe of the great abilities with which he was endowed, especially when in the society of those high in rank.

I have heard Sir Joshua say, that he has frequently seen the whole company struck with an awful silence at the entrance of Goldsmith, but that Goldsmith has quickly dispelled the charm, by his boyish and social manners, and he then has soon become the plaything and favorite of the company.—JAMES

NORTHCOTE, *Memoirs of Sir Joshua Reynolds, Knt.*, 1813, pp. 210–12

Dr. Goldsmith and I never quarrelled; for he was convinced that I had a real regard for him; but a kind of civil sparring continually took place between us. "You are so attached," says he, "to Hurd, Gray, and Mason, that you think nothing good can proceed, but out of that formal school;—now, I'll mend Gray's *Elegy,* by leaving out an idle word in every line!"—"And, for me, Doctor, completely spoil it."

> The curfew tolls the knell of day,
>   The lowing herd winds o'er the Lea;
> The plowman homeward plods his way,
>   And——

"Enough, enough, I have no ear for more."

"Cradock (after a pause), I am determined to come down into the country, and make some stay with you, and I will build you an ice-house."—"Indeed, my dear Doctor," I replied, "you will not; you have got the strangest notion in the world of making amends to your friends, where-ever you go; I hope, if you favour me with a visit, that you will consider that your own company is the best recompence." "Well," says Goldsmith, "that is civilly enough expressed; but I should like to build you an ice-house; I have built two already; they are perfect, and this should be a pattern to all your county."

"I dined yesterday," says he, laying down his papers, "in company with three of your friends, and I talked at every thing."—"And they would spare you in nothing."—"I cared not for that, I persisted; but I declare solemnly to you, that though I angled the whole evening I never once obtained a bite."

"You are all of you," continued he, "absolutely afraid of Johnson,—now I attack him boldly, and without the least reserve."—"You do, Doctor, and sometimes catch a Tartar." "If it were not for me, he would be insufferable; if you remember, the last time we ever supped together, he sat sulky and growling, but I resolved to fetch him out;"—"you did, and at last he told you that he would have no more of your fooleries."

It was always thought fair by some persons to make what stories they pleased of Dr. Goldsmith, and the following was freely circulated in ridicule of him, "That he attended the Fantoccini in Penton-street, and that from envy he wished to excel the dexterity of one of the puppets." I was of the party, and remember no more, than that the Doctor, the Rev. Mr. Ludlam of St. John's College, and some others, went together to see the puppetshew; that we were all greatly entertained, and many idle remarks might possibly be made by all of us during the evening. Mr. Ludlam afterwards laughingly declared, that he believed he must shut up all his experiments at Cambridge and Leicester in future, and take lectures only during the winter, from Fantoccinis, and the expert mechanists of both the Royal Theatres."

The greatest real fault of Dr. Goldsmith was, that if he had thirty pounds in his pocket, he would go into certain companies in the country, and in hopes of doubling the sum, would generally return to town without any part of it.—JOSEPH CRADOCK, *Literary and Miscellaneous Memoirs,* 1828, Vol. 1, pp. 230–32

Oliver Goldsmith, several years before my luckless presentation to Johnson, proved how *"Doctors differ."*—I was only five years old when Goldsmith took me on his knee, while he was drinking coffee, one evening, with my father, and began to play with me,—which amiable act I return'd with the ingratitude of a peevish brat, by giving him a very smart slap in the face;—it must have been a tingler;—for it left the marks of my little spiteful paw upon his cheek. This infantile outrage was follow'd by summary justice; and I was lock'd up by my indignant father, in an adjoining room, to undergo solitary imprisonment, in the dark. Here I began to howl and scream, most abominably; which was no bad step towards liberation, since those who were not inclined to pity me might be likely to set me free, for the purpose of abating a nuisance.

At length a generous friend appear'd to extricate me from jeopardy; and that generous friend was no other than the man I had so wantonly molested; by assault and battery;—it was the tender-hearted Doctor himself, with a lighted candle in his hand, and a smile upon his countenance, which was still partially red, from the effects of my petulance.—I sulk'd and sobb'd, and he fondled and sooth'd;—till I began to brighten. Goldsmith, who, in regard to children, was like the Village Preacher he has so beautifully described,—for

Their welfare pleased him, and their cares distress'd,

seized the propitious moment of returning good-humour;—so he put down the candle, and began to conjure. He placed three hats, which happen'd to be in the room, upon the carpet, and a shilling under each:—the shillings, he told me, were England, France, and Spain. "Hey, presto, cockolorum!" cried the Doctor,—and, lo! on uncovering the shillings which had been dispersed, each beneath a separate hat, they were all found congregated under one.—I was no Politician at five years old,—and, therefore, might not have wonder'd at the sudden revolution which brought England, France, and Spain, all under one Crown; but, as I was also no Conjuror, it amazed me beyond measure. Astonishment might have amounted to awe for one who appear'd to me gifted with the power of performing miracles, if the good-nature of the man had not obviated my dread of the magician;—but, from that time, whenever the Doctor came to visit my father,

I pluck'd his gown, to share the good man's smile;

a game at romps constantly ensued, and we were always cordial friends, and merry play-fellows. Our unequal companionship varied somewhat, in point of sports, as I grew older, but it did not last long;—my senior playmate died, alas! in his forty-fifth year, some months after I had attain'd my eleventh. His death, it has been thought, was hasten'd by "mental inquietude;"—if this supposition be true, never did the turmoils of life subdue a mind more warm with sympathy for the misfortune of our fellow-creatures;—but his character is familiar to every one who reads:—in all the numerous accounts of his virtues and his foibles,—his genius and absurdities, his knowledge of nature, and his ignorance of the world,—his "compassion for another's woe" was always predominant; and my trivial story, of his humouring a froward child, weighs but as a feather in the recorded scale of his benevolence.—GEORGE COLMAN THE YOUNGER, *Random Records*, 1830, Vol. 1, pp. 110–12

From the general tone of Goldsmith's biography, it is evident that his faults, at the worst, were but negative, while his merits were great and decided. He was no one's enemy but his own; his errors, in the main, inflicted evil on none but himself, and were so blended with humorous, and even affecting circumstances, as to disarm anger and conciliate kindness. Where eminent talent is united to spotless virtue, we are awed and dazzled into admiration, but our admiration is apt to be cold and reverential; while there is something in the harmless infirmities of a good and great, but erring individual, that pleads touchingly to our nature; and we turn more kindly towards the object of our idolatry, when we find that, like ourselves, he is mortal and is frail. The epithet so often heard, and in such kindly tones, of "poor Goldsmith," speaks volumes. Few, who consider the real compound of admirable and whimsical qualities which form his character, would wish to prune away its eccentricities, trim its grotesque luxuriance, and clip it down to the decent formalities of rigid virtue. "Let not his frailties be remembered," said Johnson; "he was a very great man." But, for our part, we rather say "Let them be remembered," since their tendency is to endear; and we question whether he himself would not feel gratified in hearing his reader, after dwelling with admiration on the proofs of his greatness, close the volume with the kind hearted phrase, so fondly and familiarly ejaculated, of "POOR GOLDSMITH."—WASHINGTON IRVING, *Oliver Goldsmith: A Biography*, 1849

Forgettest thou thy bard, who hurried home
From distant lands and, bent by poverty,
Reposed among the quiet scenes he loved
In native Auburn, nor disdain'd to join
The village dancers on the sanded floor?
No poet since hath Nature drawn so close
To her pure bosom as her Oliver.
—WALTER SAVAGE LANDOR, "Erin," *Heroic Idyls*, 1863

General

⟨. . .⟩ we do not mean to insinuate, that his lucubrations ⟨in *The Bee*⟩ are so void of merit, as not to deserve the public attention. On the contrary, we must confess ourselves to have found no inconsiderable entertainment in their perusal. His stile is not the worst, and his manner is agreeable enough, in our opinion, however it may have failed of exciting universal admiration. The truth is, most of his subjects are already sufficiently worn out, and his observations frequently trite and common. A Writer must, therefore, possess very extraordinary talents, of spirit, humour, and variety of expression, to please, under such disadvantages.—WILLIAM KENRICK, *Monthly Review*, June 1760, p. 39

The trading Wits endeavor to attain,
Like Booksellers, the Worlds first Idol Gain:
For this they puff the heavy Goldsmiths Line.
And hail his Sentiment tho' trite, divine.
—THOMAS CHATTERTON, "The Art of Puffing by a Bookseller's Journeyman," 1770

Goldsmith being mentioned; JOHNSON. 'It is amazing how little Goldsmith knows. He seldom comes where he is not more ignorant than any one else.' SIR JOSHUA REYNOLDS. 'Yet there is no man whose company is more liked.' JOHNSON. 'To be sure, Sir. When people find a man of the most distinguished abilities as a writer, their inferiour while he is with them, it must be highly gratifying to them. What Goldsmith comically says of himself is very true,—he always gets the better when he argues alone; meaning, that he is master of a subject in his study, and can write well upon it; but when he comes into company, grows confused, and unable to talk. Take him as a poet, his *Traveller* is a very fine performance; ay, and so is his *Deserted Village*, were it not sometimes too much the echo of his *Traveller*. Whether, indeed, we take him as a poet,—as a comick writer,—or as an historian, he stands in the first class.' BOSWELL. 'An historian! My dear Sir, you surely will not rank his compilation of the Roman History with the works of other historians of this age?" JOHNSON. 'Why, who are before him?' BOSWELL. 'Hume,—Robertson,—Lord Lyttleton.' JOHNSON (his antipathy to the Scotch beginning to rise). 'I have not read Hume; but, doubtless, Goldsmith's *History* is better than the *verbiage* of Robertson, or the foppery of Dalrymple.'—JAMES BOSWELL, *Life of Johnson*, 1791

There is something in Goldsmith's prose, that to my ear is uncommonly sweet and harmonious; it is clear, simple, easy to be understood; we never want to read his period twice over, except for the pleasure it bestows; obscurity never calls us back to a repetition of it. That he was a poet there is no doubt, but the paucity of his verses does not allow us to rank him in that high station, where his genius might have carried him. There must be bulk, variety and grandeur of design to constitute a first-rate poet. The *Deserted Village*, *Traveller* and *Hermit* are all specimens beautiful as such, but they are only birds eggs on a string, and eggs of small birds too. One great magnificent *whole* must be accomplished before we can pronounce upon the *maker* to be the ὁ ποιήτης. Pope himself never earned this title by a work of any magnitude but his Homer, and that being a translation only constitutes him an accomplished versifier. Distress drove Goldsmith upon undertakings, neither congenial with his studies, nor worthy of his talents. I remember him, when in his chamber in the Temple, he shewed me the beginning of his *Animated Nature*; it was with a sigh, such as genius draws, when hard necessity diverts it from its bent to drudge for bread, and talk of birds and beasts and creeping things, which Pidcock's show-man would have done as well. Poor fellow, he hardly knew an ass from a mule, nor a turkey from a goose, but when he saw it on the table. But publishers hate poetry, and Paternoster-Row is not Parnassus. Even the mighty Doctor Hill, who was not a very delicate feeder, could not make a dinner out of the press till by a happy transformation into Hannah Glass he turned himself into a cook, and sold receipts for made-dishes to all the savoury readers in the kingdom. Then indeed the press acknowledged him second in fame only to John Bunyan; his feasts kept pace in sale with Nelson's fasts, and when his own name was fairly written out of credit, he wrote himself into immortality under an alias. Now though necessity, or I should rather say the desire of finding money for a masquerade, drove Oliver Goldsmith upon abridging histories and turning Buffon into English, yet I much doubt if without that spur he would ever have put his Pegasus into action; no, if he had been rich, the world would have been poorer than it is by the loss of all the treasures of his genius and the contributions of his pen. —RICHARD CUMBERLAND, *Memoirs of Richard Cumberland*, 1807, Vol. 1, pp. 351–53

⟨. . .⟩ it is in the narrowness of his range, and in the close identity of his characters with his own heart and experience, that we are to find the main cause of Goldsmith's universal and unfading popularity. He had in himself an original to draw from, with precisely those qualities which win general affection. Loveable himself, in spite of all his grave faults, he makes loveable the various copies that he takes from the master portrait. His secret is this—the emotions he commands are pleasureable. He is precisely what Johnson calls him, the '*affectuum lenis* '*dominator*'—*potens* because *lenis*. He is never above the height of the humblest understanding; and, by touching the human heart, he raises himself to a level with the loftiest. He has to perfection what the Germans call *Anmuth*. His Muse wears the zone of the Graces.

There is another peculiarity in Goldsmith. Precisely because his ideas are not numerous, he has the most complete command over them. They have all the versatility of a practised company. He can make them do duty alike in a poem, a comedy, a novel, an essay. Like Bobadil, he selects 'but nineteen more to himself—gentlemen of good spirit, strong and able constitutions, teaches them the special rules—your punto, your reverso,' and may then boast, with more truth than Bobadil, that he can make them a match for 'forty thousand strong.' Various, in the larger sense of the word, as we apply it to Goethe or Shakspeare, he was not; but he was wonderfully versatile. He always addresses the same feelings, presents the same phrases of life, the same family of thought—but then it is in all ways, which are rarely indeed at the command of the same man. Whether you read *The Deserted Village*, *The Vicar of Wakefield*, *The Goodnatured Man*, or *The Citizen of the World*, you find at the close that much the same emotions have been created—the heart has been touched much in the same place. But with what pliant aptitude the form and mode are changed and disguised! Poem, novel, essay, drama, how exquisite of its kind! The humour that draws tears, and the pathos that provokes smiles, will be popular to the end of the world. That these merits imply an extraordinary charm of style, is self-evident. 'The style is the man,' says a French authority;—at all events, the style is the writer. But where in this irregular course of study—where in his college associations or his village festivities—did this man, with his rustic manners and Irish brogue, pick up a style so pure, so delicate? How comes it that in all the miry paths of life that he had trod, no speck ever sullied the robe of his modest and graceful muse? How, amidst all that love for inferior company, which never to the last forsook him, did he keep his genius so free from every touch of vulgarity? What style in the English language is more thoroughly elegant and high bred—more impressed with the stamp of gentleman—its ease so polished, its dignity so sweet? Johnson says that 'Goldsmith was a plant that flowered late.' This is not strictly true. In the earlier letters of Goldsmith, those, for instance, written from Edinburgh, we see (as has been before implied) the same peculiar graces of diction, the same happy humour, with its undercurrent of tenderness, which make the works of his maturity so delightful. On examining narrowly the character of Goldsmith, we find, even in what are regarded its defects, and what served to render him ridiculous in the circles of London, some clue to the enigma of the contrast between the habits of the man and the style of the writer. Goldsmith never, from the period at which he lounged at the college gates as a sizar to the time when his peach-blossom coat attracted the mirth of Garrick, divested himself of the notion that he was a gentleman. This conviction was almost the strongest he possessed; the more it was invaded the more he clung to it. He surrounded it with all the keenest susceptibilities of his sensitive nature. Nothing so galled and offended him as a hint to the contrary. To be liked as a jester, not companion—to be despised for his poverty—to be underrated as a sizar—to be taunted by a schoolboy with a question of his gentility—were cruelties beyond all others that fate could inflict. This conviction, and its concomitant yearning for respect, could not influence conventional manners, formed under auspices the least propitious. It could not invest with dignity the stunted and awkward figure; it could not check the lively impulses of a quick blundering Irish temper; but in that best and most sacred part of him—his genius—it moulded his taste to instinctive refinement. Here he was always true to his ideal. There is something to us expressibly touching in the jealous religion with which this man, exposed to the rough trials and coarse temptations of life, preserved the sanctity of his muse. The troops of Comus in vain 'knit hands and beat the ground' by the stream in which that pure Sabrina 'commends her fair innocence to the flood:'—

Summer drouth or singed air
Never scorch those tresses fair,
Nor wet October's torrent flood
The molten chrystal fills with mud.

To judge by Goldsmith's early letters, we are inclined to believe that Le Sage was one of his first models in diction. When we read them, with their naïve accounts of his own credulity—the amusing adventures they recite—their mingled simplicity and shrewdness—we seem to be opening a new chapter in the youthful history of Gil Blas. Goldsmith, indeed, was in himself a kind of young Irish Gil Blas, terminating in a Fabricio instead of a minister's secretary and retired statesman. But if Le Sage did really influence his earlier mode of description and his easy views of life, he added in his maturer years the grace of a sentiment and the softness of a pathos all his own. He never attained to that wonderful knowledge of the world, that careless comprehension of external character in its widest varieties, which render *Gil Blas* the wisest novel that man ever wrote; but with much of Le Sage's polished facility of narrative he combined a command over emotions Le Sage never aspired to reach. He added poetry to the Frenchman's prose,—for Goldsmith was a poet, Le Sage was not.—EDWARD BULWER-LYTTON, "Goldsmith," *Edinburgh Review*, July 1848, pp. 206–8

But gentler GOLDSMITH, whom no man could hate,
Beloved by Heaven, pursued by wayward fate,
Whose verse shall live in every British mind,
Though sweet, yet strong; though nervous, yet refined;—
A motley part he play'd in life's gay scene,
The dupe of vanity and wayward spleen;
Aping the world, a strange fantastic elf;
Great, generous, noble, when he was himself.
　　　　—HARTLEY COLERIDGE, "Young and His Con-
　　　　temporaries," *Sketches of English Poets*, 1849

Who, of the millions whom he has amused, does not love him? To be the most beloved of English writers, what a title that is for a man! A wild youth, wayward but full of tenderness and affection, quits the country village where his boyhood has been passed in happy musing, in idle shelter, in fond longing to see the great world out of doors, and achieve name and fortune—and after years of dire struggle, and neglect and poverty, his heart turning back as fondly to his native place, as it had longed eagerly for change when sheltered there, he writes a book and a poem, full of the recollections and feelings of home—he paints the friends and scenes of his youth, and peoples Auburn and Wakefield with remembrances of Lissoy. Wander he must, but he carries away a home-radio with him, and dies with it on his breast. His nature is truant; in repose it longs for change: as on the journey it looks back for friends and quiet. He passes to-day in building an air castle for to-morrow, or in writing yesterday's elegy; and he would fly away this hour; but that a cage necessity keeps him. What is the charm of his verse, of his style, and humour? His sweet regrets, his delicate compassion, his soft smile, his tremulous sympathy, the weakness which he owns? Your love for him is half pity. You come hot and tired from the day's battle, and this sweet minstrel sings to you. Who could harm the kind vagrant harper? Whom did he ever hurt? He carries no weapon—save the harp on which he plays to you; and with which he delights great and humble, young and old, the Captains in the tents, or the soldiers round the fire, or the women and children in the villages, at whose porches he stops and sings his simple songs of love and beauty. With that sweet story of the *Vicar of Wakefield*, he has found entry into every castle and every hamlet in Europe. Not one of us, however busy or hard, but once or twice in our lives, has passed an evening with him, and undergone the charm of his delightful music.—WILLIAM MAKEPEACE THACKERAY, *The English Humourists of the Eighteenth Century*, 1853

His name has been used to glorify a sham Bohemianism—a Bohemianism that finds it easy to live in taverns, but does not find it easy, so far as one sees, to write poems like the *Deserted Village*. His experiences as an author have been brought forward to swell the cry about neglected genius—that is, by writers who assume their genius in order to prove the neglect. The misery that occasionally befell him during his wayward career has been made the basis of an accusation against society, the English constitution, Christianity—Heaven knows what. It is time to have done with all this nonsense. Goldsmith resorted to the hackwork of literature when every thing else had failed him; and he was fairly paid for it. When he did better work, when he "struck for honest fame," the nation gave him all the honor that he could have desired. With an assured reputation, and with ample means of subsistence, he obtained entrance into the most distinguished society then in England—he was made the friend of England's greatest in the arts and literature—and could have confined himself to that society exclusively if he had chosen. His temperament, no doubt, exposed him to suffering; and the exquisite sensitiveness of a man of genius may demand our sympathy; but in far greater measure is our sympathy demanded for the thousands upon thousands of people who, from illness or nervous excitability, suffer from quite as keen a sensitiveness without the consolation of the fame that genius brings.

In plain truth, Goldsmith himself would have been the last to put forward pleas humiliating alike to himself and to his calling. Instead of beseeching the State to look after authors; instead of imploring society to grant them "recognition;" instead of saying of himself "he wrote, and paid the penalty;" he would frankly have admitted that he chose to live his life his own way, and therefore paid the penalty. This is not written with any desire of upbraiding Goldsmith. He did choose to live his own life his own way, and we now have the splendid and beautiful results of his work; and the world—looking at these with a constant admiration, and with a great and lenient love for their author—is not anxious to know what he did with his guineas, or whether the milkman was ever paid. "He had raised money and squandered it, by every artifice of acquisition and folly of expense. BUT LET NOT HIS FRAILTIES BE REMEMBERED: HE WAS A VERY GREAT MAN ." This is Johnson's wise summing up; and with it we may here take leave of gentle Goldsmith.—WILLIAM BLACK, *Goldsmith*, 1878, pp. 150–52

The most thoughtful, the most gentle, the most truly humorous of all the writers of his age or of any age, he is, on the whole, the most attractive figure in our literary history. He has touched every kind of composition, history, poetry, drama, fiction, and criticism, and he has touched them all with a master's hand. The greater part of his writings were miscellaneous "hack work" for different booksellers, for his engagements with these gentlemen usually terminated abruptly. Goldsmith is an Addison with a rich vein of true poetry and true compassion added. The pleasure derived from the style of his writings is akin to that derived from reading the *Spectator*: the later writer is equally polished and more metaphorical, or rather his metaphors are derived more from actual life than

Addison's. We feel that to him writing could have been no effort whatever, whereas Addison must have sat down to compose his *Spectators* much as he would to compose his beautiful Latin verses. Each is the man

Qui mores hominum multorum vidit et urbes.

The difference between them lies in the spirit with which they have looked upon these things. Goldsmith's humour and pathos are both beyond all praise. Who has not been moved almost to tears by the affecting comicality of Beau Tibbs? Who would be ashamed to confess that he has been upset by one or two passages in that perfect little human epic, the *Vicar of Wakefield?* The description of London misery in the *Letters of the Citizen of the World* proves conclusively that the art of pathetic touches lies in their rarity. Goldsmith's mind was of such a happy equable temperament that he avoided every trace of the sickly sentimentality which, it is to be feared, took the place of active benevolence among some writers of the day. He is at the head of the novelists of the century; his pen was pure without the pruderies which are apparent in the earlier leaders of the reaction against Smollett and Fielding. In style, as in matter, Goldsmith's armour is proof against all the arrows of criticism, yet no writer was ever more careless of the estimation in which his works would be held by posterity.—C. R. L. FLETCHER, *The Development of English Prose Style*, 1881, pp. 22–23

By the side of Johnson, like an antelope accompanying an elephant, we observe the beautiful figure of Oliver Goldsmith. In spite of Johnson's ascendency, and in spite of a friendship that was touching in its nearness, scarcely a trace of the elder companion is to be discovered in the work of the younger. Johnson's style is massive, sonorous, ponderous; enamoured of the pomp of language, he employs its heaviest artillery for trifles, and points his cannon at the partridge on the mountains. The word which Johnson uses is always the correct one so far as meaning goes, but it is often more weighty than the occasion demands, and more Latin. Hence it was, no doubt, that his spoken word, being more racy and more Saxon, was often more forcible than his printed word. There is no ponderosity about Goldsmith, whose limpid and elegant simplicity of style defies analysis. In that mechanical and dusty age he did not set up to be an innovator. We search in vain, in Goldsmith's verse or prose, for any indication of a consciousness of the coming change. He was perfectly contented with the classical traditions, but his inborn grace and delicacy of temper made him select the sweeter and the more elegant among the elements of his time. As a writer, purely, he is far more enjoyable than Johnson; he was a poet of great flexibility and sensitiveness; his single novel is much fuller of humour and nature than the stiff *Rasselas*; as a dramatist he succeeded brilliantly in an age of failures; he is one of the most perfect of essayists. Nevertheless, with all his perennial charm, Goldsmith, in his innocent simplicity, does not attract the historic eye as the good giant Johnson does, seated for forty years in the undisputed throne of letters.—EDMUND GOSSE, *A Short History of Modern English Literature*, 1897, pp. 253-54

Works

THE VICAR OF WAKEFIELD

There are an hundred faults in this Thing, and an hundred things might be said to prove them beauties. But it is needless. A book may be assuming with numerous errors, or it may be very dull without a single absurdity. The hero of this piece unites in himself the three greatest characters upon earth; he is

a priest, an husbandman, and the father of a family. He is drawn as ready to teach, and ready to obey, as simple in affluence, and majestic in adversity. In this age of opulence and refinement whom can such a character please? Such as are fond of high life, will turn with disdain from the simplicity of his country fireside. Such as mistake ribaldry for humour, will find no wit in his harmless conversation; and such as have been taught to deride religion, will laugh at one whose chief stores of comfort are drawn from futurity.—OLIVER GOLDSMITH, "Advertisement" to *The Vicar of Wakefield*, 1766

I have this very moment finish'd reading a novel call'd the *Vicar of Wakefield*. It was wrote by Dr. Coldsmith, author of the comedy of the *Good-Natured Man*, and several essays. His style is rational and sensible and I knew it again immediately. This book is of a very singular kind—I own I began it with distaste and disrelish, having just read the elegant *Letters of Henry*,—the beginning of it, even disgusted me—he mentions his wife with such indifference—such contempt—the contrast of Henry's treatment of Frances struck me—the more so, as it is real—while this tale is fictitious—and then the style of the latter is so elegantly natural, so tenderly manly, so unassumingly rational!—I own I was tempted to thro' the book aside—but there was something in the situation of his family, which if it did not interest me, at least drew me on—and as I proceeded, I was better pleased.—The description of his rural felicity, his simple, unaffected contentment—and family domestic happiness, gave me much pleasure—but still, I was not satisfied, a *something* was wanting to make the book satisfy me—to make me *feel* for the Vicar in every line he writes, nevertheless, before I was half thro' the first volume, I was, as I may truly express myself, *surprised into tears*—and in the second volume, I really sobb'd. It appears to me, to be impossible any person could read this book thro' with a dry eye at the same time the best part of it is that which turns one's grief out of doors, to open them to laughter. He advances many very bold and singular opinions—for example, he avers that murder is the sole crime for which death ought to be the punishment, he goes even farther, and ventures to affirm that our laws in regard to penalties and punishments are *all* too severe. This doctrine might be contradicted from the very essence of our religion—Scripture for . . . in the Bible—in Exodus particularly, death is commanded by God himself, for many crimes besides murder. But this author shews in all his works a love of peculiarity and of making originality of character in others; and therefore I am not surprised he possesses it himself. This Vicar is a very venerable old man—his distresses *must* move you. There is but very little story, the plot is thin, the incidents very rare, the sentiments uncommon, the vicar is contented, humble, pious, virtuous, [quite a darling character,] but upon the whole how far more was I pleased with the genuine productions of Mr. Griffith's pen—for that is the real name of Henry,—I hear that more volumes are lately published. I wish I could get them, I have read but two—the elegance and delicacy of the manner—expressions—style or that book are so superiour!—How much I should like to be acquainted with the writers of it!—Those Letters are doubly pleasing, charming to me, for being genuine—they have encreased my relish for *minute, heartfelt* writing, and encouraged me in my attempt to give an opinion of the books I read.—FANNY BURNEY, *Diary*, 1768

In the meantime I will hope the best, and endeavour to pursue Oliver Cromwell, through all his crooked paths. I have gone but a short way, my attention having been completely engrossed by a book that has bewitched me for the time; it is the *Vicar of Wakefield*, which you must certainly read. Goldsmith puts one in mind of Shakespeare; his narrative is improbable and absurd in many instances, yet all his characters do and say so exactly what might be supposed of them, if so circumstanced, that you willingly resign your mind to the sway of this pleasing enchanter; laugh heartily at improbable incidents, and weep bitterly for impossible distresses. But his personages have all so much nature about them! Keep your gravity if you can, when Moses is going to market with the colt, in his waistcoat of gosling-green; when the Vicar's family make the notable procession on Blackberry and his companion; or, when the fine ladies dazzle the Flamboroughs with taste, Shakspeare, and the musical glasses; not to mention the polemical triumphs of that redoubted monogamist the Vicar. 'Tis a thousand pities Goldsmith had not patience, or art, to conclude suitably a story so happily conducted; but the closing events which rush on so precipitately, are managed with so little skill, and wound up in such a hurried and really bungling manner, that you seem hastily awaked from an affecting dream.—ANNE GRANT, *Letters from the Mountains*, June 20, 1773

Mrs. Piozzi and Sir John Hawkins have strangely mis-stated the history of Goldsmith's situation and Johnson's friendly interference, when this novel was sold. I shall give it authentically from Johnson's own exact narration:—'I received one morning a message from poor Goldsmith that he was in great distress, and, as it was not in his power to come to me, begging that I would come to him as soon as possible. I sent him a guinea, and promised to come to him directly. I accordingly went as soon as I was drest, and found that his landlady had arrested him for his rent, at which he was in a violent passion. I perceived that he had already changed my guinea, and had got a bottle of Madeira and a glass before him. I put the cork into the bottle, desired he would be calm, and began to talk to him of the means by which he might be extricated. He then told me that he had a novel ready for the press, which he produced to me. I looked into it, and saw its merit; told the landlady I should soon return, and having gone to a bookseller, sold it for sixty pounds. I brought Goldsmith the money, and he discharged his rent, not without rating his landlady in a high tone for having used him so ill.'—JAMES BOSWELL, *Life of Johnson*, 1791

It would not be easy to find, within the compass of light literature, any thing more perfect in its kind than the scene unfolded in the opening chapters of the *Vicar of Wakefield*: it abounds in strokes of humour and tenderness; and fixes the attention by a most affecting picture of a happy *home*, enjoyed by persons in the middle rank of life, citizens of a free country, and possessing competent means and innocent minds. The group of characters, their circumstances, and local situation, are truly *English*, and could only belong to the enviable land within those confines the scene is laid.

In England alone, amongst the nations of the earth, could such an individual as the vicar be supposed. Idolatry, Mahometanism, and superstition have indeed their priests; and the minister of religion exists alike under the fervour of Indian skies, and in the twilights of Lapland; in the cloisters of Madrid, and the conventicles of Philadelphia: but England only can exhibit the original from which the inimitable portrait of Dr. Primrose is taken.

He is drawn as pious, learned, charitable, hospitable; fearless in the cause of sanctity and rectitude; in affliction, at once magnanimous and resigned; in prosperity, grateful and humble; a kind and sympathizing neighbour; a most affection-

ate parent; and, as a pastor, almost worshipped for his virtues by the flock under his care.

As a shade, to counteract the dazzling effect of so much excellence, his learning is represented as not quite unmixed with inoffensive pedantry; and the awe inspired by his good natural understanding, is admirably tempered with a very endearing cast of simplicity; and the solemnity of his deportment relieved, by a well-managed introduction of comic traits.

If any thing can equal this portrait of the vicar, it is the delicacy with which his story is related; and the art shown by the author in conducting the personages of his fable through various vicissitudes, without the least appearance of exaggeration or force. The reader sheds tears at their sorrows, and exults in their restoration to felicity: but the depression of spirits created by the perusal has in it nothing shocking, nothing disgusting; it is rather the *"luxury of grief:"* and the most unsullied chastity may, without self-reproach, smile at all the pleasantries of Goldsmith.

This dexterity in the author of a novel cannot be too highly praised; particularly if we consider the period when Goldsmith wrote, the opportunities his own hard lot in life had afforded him of becoming acquainted with every phrase of vulgar humour, and how strongly (had he pleased to do so) he might have pourtrayed many of the incidents in his narrative.

His powers of description and command of language were nearly unlimited, and many of the events in the *Vicar of Wakefield* are such as would have tempted a writer of meaner talents and less true sensibility, to exceed those boundaries which he scorned to overleap; confident that the object in view might be otherwise attained, and that success would be purchased at too great a price by an outrage against the morals of his country.—EDWARD MANGIN, *An Essay on Light Reading*, 1808, pp. 123–28

How far I must have been behind in modern literature one may conclude from the kind of life which I led at Frankfort, from the studies to which I had devoted myself; nor could my residence in Strasburg advance me in this respect. Now came Herder, and together with his great knowledge brought many other aids and the newer publications as well. Among these he announced to us *The Vicar of Wakefield* as an excellent work, with the German translation of which he wished to make us acquainted by reading it aloud to us himself. ⟨. . .⟩

A Protestant country clergyman is, perhaps, the most beautiful subject of a modern idyl; he appears, like Melchizedek, a priest and a king in one person. To the most innocent situation which can be imagined on earth, to that of husbandman, he is for the most part united by similarity of occupation, as well as by family relationships; he is a father, master of a family, an agriculturist, and thus fully a member of the community. On this pure, beautiful, earthly foundation rests his higher calling; to him is it given to guide men into life, to take care of their spiritual education, to bless them at all the leading epochs of their existence, to instruct, to strengthen, to console them, and, if consolation for the present is not sufficient, to call up and guarantee the hope of a happier future. Imagine such a man with pure human sentiments, strong enough not to deviate from them under any circumstances, and by this already elevated above the multitude, of whom one cannot expect purity and firmness; grant him the learning necessary to his office, as well as cheerful, equable activity, which is even passionate, as it neglects no moment to do good, and you will have him well endowed. But at the same time one must add the necessary limitation, that he must not only remain in a small circle, but may also pass over to a smaller; grant him good nature, placability, steadfastness, and everything else praiseworthy which springs from a decided character, and over all this a cheerful and smiling toleration of his own and others' failings, so you will have pretty well put together the picture of our excellent Wakefield.

The delineation of this character in his course of life through joys and sorrows, the ever-increasing interest of the story by the combination of the entirely natural with the strange and singular, makes this novel one of the best which has ever been written; besides this, it has the great advantage that it is quite moral, nay, in a pure sense, Christian: represents the reward of a good will and perseverance in the right, strengthens an unconditional confidence in God, and attests the final triumph of good over evil—and all this without a trace of cant or pedantry. From both of these the author was preserved by an elevation of mind which shows itself throughout in the form of irony, by which this little work must appear to us as wise as it is pleasing. The author, Dr Goldsmith, without question, has great insight into the moral world, into its strength and its weakness, but at the same time he can thankfully acknowledge that he is an Englishman, and reckon highly the advantages which his country and his nation afford him. The family, with the description of which he is occupied, stands upon one of the lowest steps of citizen comfort, and yet comes in contact with the highest; its narrow circle, which becomes still more contracted through the natural and civil course of things, touches upon the great world; this little craft floats upon the rich, agitated waves of English life, and in weal or woe it has to expect injury or help from the vast fleet which sails around it.

I may suppose that my readers know this work and have it in memory; he who hears it named for the first time here, as well as he who is stirred to read it again, will both thank me. For the former, I remark only in passing that the wife of the Vicar is of that good, active sort, who allows herself and her own to want for nothing, but who is also somewhat vain of herself and her family. Two daughters—Olivia, handsome and more devoted to the outside of things; Sophia, charming and more given to what is inward: I will not omit to mention an industrious son, Moses, who is somewhat blunt, and emulous of his father.—JOHANN WOLFGANG VON GOETHE, *Autobiography*, 1811, tr. R. O. Moon

As a novelist, his *Vicar of Wakefield* has charmed all Europe. What reader is there in the civilised world, who is not the better for the story of the washes which the worthy Dr. Primrose demolished so deliberately with the poker—for the knowledge of the guinea which the Miss Primroses kept unchanged in their pockets—the adventure of the picture of the Vicar's family, which could not be got into the house—and that of the Flamborough family, all painted with oranges in their hands—or for the story of the case of shagreen spectacles and the cosmogony?

As a comic writer, his Tony Lumpkin draws forth new powers from Mr. Liston's face. That alone is praise enough for it. Poor Goldsmith! how happy he has made others! how unhappy he was in himself! He never had the pleasure of reading his own works! He had only the satisfaction of good-naturedly relieving the necessities of others, and the consolation of being harassed to death with his own! He is the most amusing and interesting person, in one of the most amusing and interesting books in the world, Boswell's *Life of Johnson*. His peach-coloured coat shall always bloom in Boswell's writings, and his fame survive in his own!—His genius was a mixture of originality and imitation: he could do nothing without some model before him, and he could copy nothing that he did not adorn with the graces of his own mind. Almost all the latter part of the *Vicar of Wakefield*, and a great deal of the former, is taken from *Joseph Andrews*; but the circumstances I have mentioned above are not.—WILLIAM HAZLITT, *Lectures on the English Poets*, 1818

Expecting some short Tales, Goldsmith gave to the department of the novelist only one work—the inimitable *Vicar of Wakefield*. We have seen that it was suppressed for nearly two years, until the publication of the *Traveller* had fixed the author's fame. Goldsmith had, therefore, time for revisal, but he did not employ it. He had been paid for his labour, as he observed, and could have profited nothing by rendering the work ever so perfect. This, however, was false reasoning, though not unnatural in the mouth of the author who must earn daily bread by daily labour. The narrative, which in itself is as simple as possible, might have been cleared of certain improbabilities, or rather impossibilities, which it now exhibits. We cannot, for instance, conceive how Sir William Thornhill should contrive to masquerade under the name of Burchell among his own tenantry, and upon his own estate; and it is absolutely impossible to see how his nephew, the son, doubtless, of a younger brother, (since Sir William inherited both title and property,) should be nearly as old as the Baronet himself. It may be added, that the character of Burchell, or Sir William Thornhill, is in itself extravagantly unnatural. A man of his benevolence would never have so long left his nephew in the possession of wealth which he employed to the worst of purposes. Far less would he have permitted his scheme upon Olivia in a great measure to succeed, and that upon Sophia also to approach consummation; for, in the first instance, he does not interfere at all, and in the second, his intervention is accidental. These, and some other little circumstances in the progress of the narrative, might easily have been removed upon revisal.

But whatever defects occur in the tenor of the story, the admirable ease and grace of the narrative, as well as the pleasing truth with which the principal characters are designed, make the *Vicar of Wakefield* one of the most delicious morsels of fictitious composition on which the human mind was ever employed. The principal character, that of the simple Pastor himself, with all the worth and excellency which ought to distinguish the ambassador of God to man, and yet with just so much of pedantry and literary vanity as serves to show that he is made of mortal mould, and subject to human failings, is one of the best and most pleasing pictures ever designed. It is perhaps impossible to place frail humanity before us in an attitude of more simple dignity than the Vicar, in his character of pastor, of parent, and of husband. His excellent helpmate, with all her motherly cunning, and housewifely prudence, loving and respecting her husband, but counterplotting his wisest schemes, at the dictates of maternal vanity, forms an excellent counterpart. Both, with their children around them, their quiet labour and domestic happiness, compose a fireside picture of such a perfect kind, as perhaps is nowhere else equalled. It is sketched indeed from common life, and is a strong contrast to the exaggerated and extraordinary characters and incidents which are the resource of those authors, who, like Bayes, make it their business to elevate and surprise; but the very simplicity of this charming book renders the pleasure it affords more permanent. We read the *Vicar of Wakefield* in youth and in age— We return to it again and again, and bless the memory of an author who contrives so well to reconcile us to human nature. Whether we choose the pathetic and distressing incidents of the fire, the scenes at the jail, or the lighter and humorous parts of the story, we find the best and truest sentiments enforced in the most beautiful language; and perhaps there are few characters of purer dignity have been described than that of the excellent pastor, rising above sorrow and oppression, and labouring for the conversion of those felons, into whose company he had been thrust by his villanous creditor. In too many works of this class, the critics must apologize for or censure particular passages in the narrative, as unfit to be perused by youth and innocence. But the wreath of Goldsmith is unsullied; he wrote to exalt virtue and expose vice; and he accomplished his task in a manner which raises him to the highest rank among British authors. We close his volume, with a sigh that such an author should have written so little from the stores of his own genius, and that he should have been so prematurely removed from the sphere of literature, which he so highly adorned.—SIR WALTER SCOTT, "Oliver Goldsmith" (1823), *Lives of the Novelists*, 1825

It is a dissertation in the English style, made up of close reasoning, seeking only to establish that, from the nature of pleasure and pain, the wretched must be repaid the balance of their sufferings in the life hereafter. We see the sources of this virtue, born of Christianity and natural kindness, but long nourished by inner reflection. Meditation, which usually produces only phrases, results with Dr. Primrose in actions. Verily reason has here taken the helm, and it has taken it without oppressing other feelings; a rare and excellent spectacle, which, uniting and harmonizing in one character the best features of the manners and morals of the time and country, creates an admiration and love for pious and orderly, domestic and disciplined, laborious and rural life. Protestant and English virtue has not a more approved and amiable exemplar. Religious, affectionate, rational, the Vicar unites dispositions which seemed irreconcilable; a clergyman, a farmer, a head of a family, he enhances those characters which appeared fit only for comic or homely parts.—HIPPOLYTE TAINE, *History of English Literature*, tr. H. Van Laun, 1871, Bk. 3, Ch. 6

POETRY

What true and pretty Pastoral images has Goldsmith in his *Deserted Village*—that beat all Pope and Philips and Spenser too in my opinion, that is in the Pastoral—for I go no further— Our own manners afford food enough for Poetry if we knew how to dress it.—EDMUND BURKE, Letter to Richard Shackleton (May 6, 1780)

Goldsmith being mentioned, Johnson observed, that it was long before his merit came to be acknowledged. That he once complained to him, in ludicrous terms of distress, 'Whenever I write any thing, the publick *make a point* to know nothing about it:' but that his *Traveller* brought him into high reputation. LANGTON. 'There is not one bad line in that poem; not one of Dryden's careless verses.' SIR JOSHUA. 'I was glad to hear Charles Fox say, it was one of the finest poems in the English language.' LANGTON, 'Why was you glad? You surely had no doubt of this before.' JOHNSON. 'No; the merit of *The Traveller* is so well established, that Mr. Fox's praise cannot augment it, nor censure diminish it.' SIR JOSHUA. 'But his friends may suspect they had too great a partiality for him.' JOHNSON. 'Nay, Sir, the partiality of his friends was all against him. It was with difficulty we could give him a hearing. Goldsmith had no settled notions upon any subject; so he talked always at random. It seemed to be his intention to blurt out whatever was in his mind, and see what would become of it. He was angry too, when catched in an absurdity; but it did not prevent him from falling into another the next minute. I remember Chamier, after talking with him for some time, said, "Well, I do believe he wrote this poem himself: and, let me tell you, that is believing a great deal." Chamier once asked him, what he meant by *slow*, the last word in the first line of *The Traveller*,

Remote, unfriended, melancholy, slow.

Did he mean tardiness of locomotion? Goldsmith, who would say something without consideration, answered, "Yes." I was sitting by, and said, "No Sir; you do not mean tardiness of locomotion; you mean, that sluggishness of mind which comes upon a man in solitude." Chamier believed then that I had written the line as much as if he had seen me write it. Goldsmith, however, was a man, who, whatever he wrote, did it better than any other man could do. He deserved a place in Westminster-Abbey, and every year he lived, would have deserved it better. He had, indeed, been at no pains to fill his mind with knowledge. He transplanted it from one place to another; and it did not settle in his mind; so he could not tell what was in his own books.'—JAMES BOSWELL, *Life of Johnson*, 1791

He *could* not be affected or uninteresting upon any subject. A profound, powerful, or subtle thinker he was not, and his culture, of course, was exceedingly desultory and imperfect. But there lay in him a vein as exquisitely natural and true, within its limits, as any writer ever possessed. When we analyze his genius, we find it to be composed of the following elements:—a keen perception and enjoyment of the surface beauties of nature; an intuitive knowledge of the human heart; a power of instinct or common sense which supplies the lack of logic and learning, and is all the more powerfully displayed in his writings, that none of it was diverted to the regulation of his conduct or life; a fine healthy tone of moral feeling; an exquisite taste; a mild but sincere enthusiasm; a humour at once rich and delicate; and a style yielding in felicity, transparency, and grace, to Addison's alone. Imagination of the highest order—of that order which constructs great epics, swelters out deep tragedies, or soars up into lofty odes— Goldsmith did not possess, and, with all his vanity, never dreamed that he did. But he had a fine fancy, which sometimes, as in *The Traveller*, and portions of *The Deserted Village*, verges on the imaginative, and produces short-lived bursts of grandeur. He has pathos, too, of a very tender and touching kind. He opens up at times, as in portions of *The Citizen of the World*, a vein of quiet, serious reflection, which, if never profound, is very pleasing and poetical. Best of all is a childlike simplicity, which, wherever it is found in an author, servers to cover a multitude of sins, but which, in Goldsmith, co-exists with manly sense, acute appreciation of character, and refined native genius. His literary faults are, as we have hinted, very few. He is sometimes too severe in his judgments of other writers. His ease of style occasionally degenerates into carelessness; and he often exhibits a dogmatism which his resources are not able to support—a fault incident, we suspect, to all half-taught writers.

His *Traveller* is a poem in the style of Pope—less thoroughly finished than *his* masterpieces, but warmed by a finer poetic enthusiasm, and abounding in those slight, successful touches which best exhibit the artist's hand. He takes you with him in every step of his tour; you

Run the great circle, and are still at home.

And the moral he draws from the whole, if not strictly correct, is ideally beautiful—none the less so that the words expressing it are lines which Johnson contributed to the poem—

> How small, of all that human hearts endure,
> That part which laws or kings can cause or cure!
> Still to ourselves in every place consign'd,
> Our own felicity we make or find.

In his *Deserted Village* he chooses a less ambitious, but a more interesting field. Like the chased hare, he flies back to his form—his dear native village; and the poem is just a daguerre-otype of Lishoy and its inhabitants—only so far coloured as memory colours all the past with its own poetic hues. The same power of delicate, minute, and rapid painting he has applied, in *Retaliation,* to living men; and Plutarch, as a character-painter, is a dauber to Oliver Goldsmith; nor has Reynolds himself, in those portraits of his in which, according to Burke, he has combined the "invention of history and the amenity of landscape," excelled these little sketches, where the artist not only draws the literal features, but gives at once the inner soul and the future history of his subjects. The characters of Garrick and Burke have never been surpassed, and have been approached only by Lowell, in his "Fable for Critics"—a poem formed upon the model (and the motive, too!) of *Retaliation.*
—GEORGE GILFILLAN, "The Life of Oliver Goldsmith," *The Poetical Works of Goldsmith, Collins, and T. Warton,* 1854, pp. xxiv–xxvi

In mere diction and versification this celebrated poem ⟨*The Deserted Village*⟩ is fully equal, perhaps superior, to the *Traveller;* and it is generally preferred to the *Traveller* by that large class of readers who think, with Bayes in the *Rehearsal,* that the only use of a plan is to bring in fine things. More discerning judges, however, while they admire the beauty of the details, are shocked by one unpardonable fault which pervades the whole. The fault we mean is not that theory about wealth and luxury which has so often been censured by political economists. The theory is indeed false: but the poem, considered merely as a poem, is not necessarily the worse on that account. The finest poem in the Latin language, indeed the finest didactic poem in any language, was written in defence of the silliest and meanest of all systems of natural and moral philosophy. A poet may easily be pardoned for reasoning ill; but he cannot be pardoned for describing ill, for observing the world in which he lives so carelessly that his portraits bear no resemblance to the originals, for exhibiting as copies from real life monstrous combinations of things which never were and never could be found together. What would be thought of a painter who should mix August and January in one land-scape, who should introduce a frozen river into a harvest scene? Would it be a sufficient defence of such a picture to say that every part was exquisitely coloured, that the green hedges, the apple-trees loaded with fruit, the waggons reeling under the yellow sheaves, and the sun-burned reapers wiping their foreheads, were very fine, and that the ice and the boys sliding were also very fine? To such a picture the *Deserted Village* bears a great resemblance. It is made up of incongruous parts. The village in its happy days is a true English village. The village in its decay is an Irish village. The felicity and the misery which Goldsmith has brought close together belong to two different countries, and to two different stages in the progress of society. He had assuredly never seen in his native island such a rural paradise, such a seat of plenty, content, and tranquility, as his "Auburn." He had assuredly never seen in England all the inhabitants of such a paradise turned out of

their homes in one day and forced to emigrate in a body to America. The hamlet he had probably seen in Kent; the ejectment he had probably seen in Munster: but, by joining the two, he has produced something which never was and never will be seen in any part of the world.—THOMAS BABINGTON MACAULAY, "Oliver Goldsmith" (1856), *Critical, Historical, and Miscellaneous Essays,* 1860, Vol. 6, pp. 162–63

The amiable and versatile Goldsmith looks at Nature, as he passes along, with a less moralizing eye than the sombre-minded Gray. In his earliest long poem, *The Traveller,* published in 1765, though he surveys many lands, his eye dwells on man and society rather than on the outward world. In remarkable contrast to more recent English poets, though he passes beneath the shadow of the Alps, he looks up to them with shuddering horror rather than with any kindling of soul. The mountain glory had not yet burst on the souls of men. The one thought that strikes him is the hard lot of the mountain-eers. Such conventional lines as these are all that he has for the mountains themselves:—

> No vernal blooms their torpid rocks array,
> But winter lingers in the lap of May;
> No zephyr fondly sues the mountain's breast,
> But meteors glare, and stormy glooms invest.

It is only when he thinks of the Switzer's love for them that they become interesting:—

> Dear is the shed to which his soul conforms,
> And dear that hill which lifts him to the storms;
> And as a child, when scaring sounds molest,
> Clings close and closer to his mother's breast,
> So the loud torrent, and the whirlwind's roar,
> But bind him to his native mountains more.

This poem, however, is remarkable as the first expression in English verse of that personal interest in foreign scenes and people which has kindled so many a splendid strain of our more recent poetry. But it is in *The Deserted Village,* his best known poem, that he has most fully shown the grace and truthfulness with which he could touch natural scenes. Lissoy, an Irish village where the poet's brother had a living, is said to have been the original from which he drew. In the poem, the church which crowns the neighboring hill, the mill, the brook, the hawthorn-tree, are all taken straight from the outer world. The features of Nature and the works of man, the parsonage, the school-house, the ale-house, all harmonize in one picture, and though the feeling of desolation must needs be a melancholy one, yet it is wonderfully varied and relieved by the uncolored faithfulness of the pictures from Nature and the kindly humor of those of man. It is needless to quote from a poem which every one knows so well. The verse of Pope is not the best vehicle for rural description, but it never was employed with greater grace and transparency than in *The Deserted Village.* In that poem there is fine feeling for Nature, in her homely forms, and truthful description of these, but beyond this Goldsmith does not venture. The pathos of the outward world in its connection with man is there, but no reference to the meaning of Nature in itself, much less any question of its relation to the Divine Being and a supersensible world.—J. C. SHAIRP, *On Poetic Interpretation of Nature,* 1877, pp. 211–13

Of all the classes of writing which Goldsmith thus embellished, the only one which I need here deal with is the poetic; and we find amid the small bulk of his poetry that the only two compositions of any considerable importance are *The Traveller* and *The Deserted Village,*—most of the residue have a playful turn.

Goldsmith is remarkable among our poets for having little which can be expressly fixed upon as poetry—although there is undoubtedly an abundance of felicitous diction, and glowing appositeness of thought. Good feeling, right sense, genuine observation, descriptive and expressive language, flowing, harmonious, and accomplished verse—all these are present, and avail to make the work soundly poetical, if not poetry in its ultimate essence. The genial and tender nature of the man forms the great, the paramount charm of the verse. Goldsmith did not care for elaborate art, or rules of art. In the dedication of *The Traveller*, addressed to his brother Henry, he says that Poetry suffers 'from the mistaken efforts of the learned to improve it. What criticisms have we not heard of late in favour of blank verse and Pindaric odes, choruses, anapæsts, and iambics, alliterative care and happy negligence! Every absurdity has now a champion to defend it; and, as he is generally much in the wrong, so he has always much to say, for Error is ever talkative." Goldsmith's poems are in fact matter fit for either poetry or prose, and manner which would be almost as fit for prose as for poetry, were it not for the simple consideration that they are written in excellent verse, with such elevation and refinement of method, and such turns of phrase, as verse naturally and properly entails.—WILLIAM MICHAEL ROSSETTI, "Oliver Goldsmith," *Lives of Famous Poets*, 1878, pp. 174–75

DRAMA

Dr. Goldsmith has written a comedy ⟨*She Stoops to Conquer*⟩—no, it is the lowest of all farces, it is not the subject I condemn, though very vulgar, but the execution. The drift tends to no moral, no edification of any kind—the situations however are well imagined, and make one laugh in spite of the grossness of the dialogue, the forced witticisms, and total improbability of the whole plan and conduct. But what disgusts me most, is that though the characters are very low, and aim at low humour, not one of them says a sentence that is natural or marks any character at all. It is set up in opposition to sentimental comedy, and is as bad as the worst of them. Garrick would not act it, but bought himself off by a poor prologue.—HORACE WALPOLE, Letter to William Mason (May 27, 1773)

She Stoops to Conquer, notwithstanding many improbabilities in the economy of the plot, several farcical situations, and some characters which are rather exaggerated, is a lively and faithful representation of nature; genius presides over every scene of this play; the characters are either new, or varied improvements from other plays.

Marlow has a slight resemblance of Charles in *The Fop's Fortune*, and something more of Lord Hardy in Steele's *Funeral*; and yet, with a few shades of these parts, he is discriminated from both. Tony Lumpkin is a vigorous improvement of Humphry Gubbins, and a more diverting picture of ignorance, rusticity, and obstinacy; Hardcastle, his wife, and daughter, I think, are absolutely new; the language is easy and characteristical; the manners of the times are slightly, but faithfully, represented; the satire is not ostentatiously displayed, but incidentally involved in the business of the play; and the suspense of the audience is artfully kept up to the last. This comedy was very well acted; Lewis played Marlow with the ease of a gentleman; Hardcastle and Tony Lumpkin were supported in a masterly style by Shuter and Quick; so was Miss Hardcastle by Mrs. Bulkeley. Mrs. Green, in Mrs. Hardcastle, maintained her just title to one of the best comic actresses of the age.—THOMAS DAVIES, *Memoirs of the Life of David Garrick*, 1780

Goldsmith, who has done honour to English literature; who was the best meaning, strange, good, whimsical creature in the world; whose intentions, though always right, by doing nothing like any body else he executed always wrong; whose writings, which are a mixture of merit and singularity, scarcely had a part that did not contain some trait of himself; who has left two beautiful poems, a sweet ballad, and a charming novel, wrote successfully for the stage, but not up to the standard of his other productions.

The Good Natured Man was brought out at Covent-Garden, exactly at the moment when the public began to be under the influence of the sentimental mania. There is nothing, however, better than Croker, and the incident of the incendiary letter; but Bailiffs were introduced on the stage, which had been done an hundred times before, and has been an hundred times since, and it was enough that the audience did not like such vulgar acquaintance. There have been times when, if they had been real bailiffs, the managers would have sympathized with the audience. To see however that the public are a very short time deluded when they adopt false taste without consideration, they were glad of the next opportunity Goldsmith gave them of laughing away the gloom that had been thrown over their minds by the introduction of an infatuation so totally contrary to the English character.

She Stoops to Conquer Goldsmith considered as a desperate remedy for a desperate disease. It operated effectually; indeed like electricity. The audiences seemed as if they had been at some place the reverse of the Cave of Trophonius, for they went in sad and came out merry. This piece was a good deal abused, and no wonder, for it went to the ruin of dull authors. Its efficacy, however, was confirmed; and, whatever absurdities the public taste may have assumed at times, it has not since then trenched upon the pulpit. Goldsmith also altered for QUICK's benefit, the *Grumbler*, from SEDLEY. —CHARLES DIBDIN, *A Complete History of the Stage*, 1795, Vol. 5, pp. 282–84

Goldsmith was, perhaps, in relation to Sheridan, what Vanburgh was to Congreve. His comedies turn on an extravagance of intrigue and disguise, and so far belong to the Spanish school. But the ease of his humorous dialogue, and the droll, yet true conception of the characters, made sufficient amends for an occasional stretch in point of probability. If all who draw on the spectators for indulgence, were equally prepared to compensate by a corresponding degree of pleasure, they would have little occasion to complain.—SIR WALTER SCOTT, "An Essay on the Drama," 1819

It is when we pass from some of the things now playing, to Goldsmith's *She Stoops to Conquer*, at the St James's Theatre, that we may well despair of the English drama. Light and darkness, brilliancy and stupidity, nature and affectation, life and death, are not more opposed. But it seems a wonder how this immortal comedy 'got into this galley;' it is as strange among its fellows, as was Rip Van Winkle after his return. It is, alas! a little strange also to the audience, who, though amused, seem but half satisfied, as though this was not the sort of thing they liked. The truth is, their stomachs are so accustomed to rich loaded sauces and greasy stews, they cannot as yet relish prime well-dressed meats. Audiences have to be educated as well as actors, who are now unequal to such a task, and really find it far above their strength. Their tongues are itching for the easy and rollicking familiarities of the every-day farce, or their limbs yearning for the easy 'breakdown.' And, indeed, this play, like others of the same importance, was written for very great players, and was meant to be a stock piece at that one house. It was not intended to be carried over the kingdom and played by every journeyman corps that could get permission to do so. It belonged to the original actors. So long as they survived, and young Marlow was to be convertible with Lee Lewes, and Miss Hardcastle with Mrs Bulkeley, it made no itinerant course.

That delightful comedy, *She Stoops to Conquer*, would indeed deserve a volume, and is the best specimen of what an English comedy should be. It illustrates excellently what has been said as to the necessity of the plot depending on the characters, rather than the characters depending on the plot, as the fashion is at present. How would our modern playwright have gone to work, should he have lighted on this good subject for a piece—that of a gentleman's house being taken for an inn, and the mistakes it might give rise to? He would have an irascible old proprietor, who would be thrown into contortions of fury by the insults he was receiving; visitors free and easy, pulling the furniture about, ransacking the wardrobes, with other farcical pranks, such as would betray that they were *not* gentlemen, or such as guests at an inn would never dream of doing. But farce would be got out of it somehow. We might also swear that the real 'fun' of the whole would be fetched out of the servants, the part of a drawling flunkey being specially 'written up' for Mr ——, or Mr ——. The visitor's 'hown' valet, a fine London domestic, would have a great deal of 'business,' and his love-makings and freedoms with the 'land-lady' would have a great share in the piece.

Very different were the principles of Goldsmith. He had this slight shred of a plot to start with; but it was conceived *at the same moment with the character of Marlow*—the delicacy and art of which conception is beyond description. It was the character of all others to bring out the farce and humour of the situation, viz. a character with its two sides—one that was forward and impudent with persons of the class he believed his hosts to belong to, but liable at any crisis, on the discovery of the mistake, to be reduced to an almost pitiable state of shyness and confusion. it is the consciousness that this change is *in petto* at any moment, that the cool town man may be hoisted in a second on this petard, that makes all so piquant for the spectator.—PERCY FITZGERALD, *Principles of Comedy and Dramatic Effect*, 1870, pp. 91–93

JOHN AIKIN
"On the Poetry of Dr. Goldsmith"
The Poetical Works of Oliver Goldsmith
1796

Among those false opinions which, having once obtained currency, have been adopted without examination, may be reckoned the prevalent notion, that, notwithstanding the improvement of this country in many species of literary composition, its poetical character has been on the decline ever since the supposed Augustan age of the beginning of this century. No one poet, it is true, has fully succeeded to the laurel of Dryden or Pope; but if without prejudice we compare the minor poets of the present age (*minor*, I mean, with respect to the *quantity* not the *quality* of their productions), with those of any former period, we shall, I am convinced, find them greatly superior not only in taste and correctness, but in every other point of poetical excellence. The works of many late and present writers might be confidently appealed to in proof of this assertion; but it will suffice to instance the author who is the subject of the present Essay; and I cannot for a moment hesitate

to place the name of GOLDSMITH as a poet, above that of Addison, Parnell, Tickell, Congreve, Lansdown, or any of those who fill the greater part of the voluminous collection of the *English Poets*. Of these, the main body has obtained a prescriptive right to the honor of classical writers; while their works ranged on the shelves as necessary appendages to a modern library, are rarely taken down, and contribute very little to the stock of literary amusement. Whereas the pieces of GOLDSMITH are familiar companions; and supply passages for recollection, when our minds are either composed to moral reflection or warmed by strong emotions and elevated conceptions. There is, I acknowledge, much of habit and accident in the attachments we form to particular writers; yet I have little doubt, that if the lovers of English poetry were confined to a small selection of authors, GOLDSMITH would find a place in the favorite list of a great majority. And it is, I think, with much justice that a great modern critic has ever regarded this concurrence of public favor as one of the least equivocal tests of uncommon merit. Some kinds of excellence, it is true, will more readily be recognized than others; and this will not always be in proportion to the degree of mental power employed in the respective productions: but he who obtains general and lasting applause in any work of art, must have happily executed a design judiciously formed. This remark is of fundamental consequence in estimating the poetry of GOLDSMITH; because it will enable us to hold the balance steady, when it might be disposed to incline to the superior claims of a style of loftier pretension, and more brilliant reputation.

Compared with many poets of deserved eminence, GOLDSMITH will appear characterized by his *simplicity*. In his language will be found few of those figures which are supposed *of themselves* to constitute poetry;—no violent transpositions; no uncommon meanings and constructions; no epithets drawn from abstract and remote ideas; no coinage of new words by the ready mode of turning nouns into verbs; no bold prosopopœia, or audacious metaphor:—it scarcely contains an expression which might not be used in eloquent and descriptive prose. It is replete with imagery; but that imagery is drawn from obvious sources, and rather enforces the simple idea, than dazzles by new and unexpected ones. It rejects not common words and phrases; and, like the language of Dryden and Otway, is thereby rendered the more forcible and pathetic. It is eminently nervous and concise; and hence affords numerous passages which dwell on the memory. With respect to his matter, it is taken from human life, and the objects of nature. It does not body forth things unknown, and create new beings. Its humbler purpose is to represent manners and characters as they really exist; to impress strongly on the heart moral and political sentiments; and to fill the imagination with a variety of pleasing or affecting objects selected from the stores of nature. If this be not the highest department of poetry, it has the advantage of being the most universally agreeable. To receive delight from the sublime fictions of Milton, the allegories of Spenser, the learning of Gray, and the fancy of Collins, the mind must have been prepared by a course of particular study; and perhaps, at a certain period of life, when the judgment exercises a severer scrutiny over the sallies of the imagination, the relish for artificial beauties will always abate, if not entirely desert us. But at every age, and with every degree of culture, correct and well-chosen representations of nature must please. We admire them when young; we recur to them when old; and they charm us till nothing longer can charm. Farther, in forming a scale of excellence for artists, we are not only to consider who works upon the noblest design, but who fills his design best. It is, in reality, but a poor excuse for a slovenly performer to '*magnis tamen excidit ausis;*' and the addition of one masterpiece of any kind to the stock of art is a greater benefit than that of a thousand abortive and mis-shapen wonders.

If GOLDSMITH then be referred to the class of *descriptive poets*, including the description of moral as well as of physical nature, it will next be important to inquire by what means he has attained the rank of a master in his class. Let us then observe how he has selected, combined, and contrasted his objects, with what truth and strength of coloring he has expressed them, and to what end and purpose.

As poetry and eloquence do not describe by an exact enumeration of every circumstance, it is necessary to *select* certain particulars which may excite a sufficiently distinct image of the thing to be presented. In this *selection*, the great art is to give *characteristic marks*, whereby the object may at once be recognized, without being obscured in a mass of common properties, which belong equally to many others. Hence the great superiority of *particular* images to *general* ones in description: the former identify, while the latter disguise. Thus, all the hackneyed representations of the country in the works of ordinary versifiers, in which groves, and rills, and flowery meads are introduced just as the rhyme and measure require, present nothing to the fancy but an indistinct daub of coloring, in which all the diversity of nature is lost and confounded. To catch the discriminating features, and present them bold and prominent, by few but decisive strokes, is the talent of a master; and it will not be easy to produce a superior to GOLDSMITH in this respect. The mind is never in doubt as to the meaning of his figures, nor does it languish over the survey of trivial and unappropriated circumstances. All is alive—all is filled—yet all is clear.

The proper *combination* of objects refers to the impression they are calculated to make on the mind; and requires that they should harmonize, and reciprocally enforce and sustain each other's effect. They should unite in giving one leading tone to the imagination: and without a sameness of form, they should blend in an uniformity of hue. This, too, has very successfully been attended to by GOLDSMITH, who has not only sketched his single figures with truth and spirit, but has combined them into the most harmonious and impressive groups. Nor has any descriptive poet better understood the great force of *contrast*, in setting off his scenes, and preventing any approach to weari-someness by repetition of kindred objects. And, with great skill, he has contrived that both parts of his contrast should conspire in producing one intended moral effect. Of all these excel-lences, examples will be pointed out as we take a cursory view of the particular pieces.

In addition to the circumstances already noted, the *force* and *clearness* of representation depend also on the diction. It has already been observed, that GOLDSMITH's language is remarkable for its general simplicity, and the direct and proper use of words. It has ornaments, but these are not far-fetched. The epithets employed are usually qualities strictly belonging to the subject, and the true coloring of the simple figure. They are frequently contrived to express a necessary circumstance in the description, and thus avoid the usual imputation of being expletive. Of this kind are 'the *rattling* terrors of the *vengeful* snake;' '*indurated* heart;' 'shed *intolerable* day;' '*matted* woods;' '*ventrous* ploughshare;' '*equinoctial* fervors.' The examples are not few of that indisputable mark of true poetic language, where a single word conveys an image; as in these instances: 'resignation gentle *slopes* the way;' '*scoops out* an empire;' 'the vessel, idly waiting, *flaps* with every gale;' 'to *winnow* fra-grance;' 'murmurs *fluctuate* in the gale.' All metaphor, in-deed, does this in some degree; but where the accessory idea is either indistinct or incongruous, as frequently happens when it is introduced as an artifice to force language up to poetry, the effect is only a gaudy obscurity.

The *end* and *purpose* to which description is directed is what distinguishes a well-planned piece from a loose effusion; for though a vivid representation of striking objects will ever afford some pleasure, yet if aim and design be wanting, to give it a basis, and stamp it with the dignity of meaning, it will in a long performance prove flat and tiresome. But this is a want which cannot be charged on GOLDSMITH; for both the *Traveller* and the *Deserted Village* have a great moral in view, to which the whole of the description is made to tend. I do not now inquire into the legitimacy of the conclusions he has drawn from his premises; it is enough to justify his plans, that such a purpose is included in them.

The *versification* of GOLDSMITH is formed on the general model that has been adopted since the refinement of English poetry, and especially since the time of Pope. To manage rhyme couplets so as to produce a pleasing effect on the ear has since that period been so common an attainment, that it merits no particular admiration. GOLDSMITH may, I think, be said to have come up to the usual standard of proficiency in this respect, without having much surpassed it. A musical ear, and a familiarity with the best examples, have enabled him, without much apparent study, almost always to avoid defect, and very often to produce excellence. It is no censure of this poet to say that his versification presses less on the attention than his matter. In fact he has none of those peculiarities of verifying, whether improvements or not, that some who aim at distinction in this point have adopted. He generally suspends or closes the sense at the end of the line or of the couplet; and therefore does not often give examples of that greater compass and variety of melody which is obtained by longer clauses, or by breaking the coincidences of the cadence of sound and meaning. He also studiously rejects triplets and alexandrines. But allowing for the want of these sources of variety, he has sufficiently avoided monotony; and in the usual flow of his measure, he has gratified the ear with as much change, as judiciously shifting the line-pause can produce.

Having made these general observations on the nature of GOLDSMITH's poetry, I proceed to a survey of his principal pieces.

The *Traveller, or Prospect of Society*, was first sketched out by the author during a tour in Europe, great part of which he performed on foot, and in circumstances which afforded him the fullest means of becoming acquainted with the most numerous class in society, peculiarly termed *the people*. The date of the first edition is 1765. It begins in the gloomy mood natural to genius in distress, when wandering alone,

> Remote, unfriended, melancholy, slow.

After an affectionate and regretful glance to the peaceful seat of fraternal kindness, and some expressions of self-pity, the Poet sits down amid Alpine solitudes to spend a pensive hour in meditating on the state of mankind. He finds that the natives of every land regard their own with preference: whence he is led to this proposition,—that if we impartially compare the advantages belonging to different countries, we shall conclude that an equal portion of good is dealt to all the human race. He farther supposes, that every nation, having in view one peculiar species of happiness models life to that alone; whence this favorite kind, pushed to an extreme, becomes a source of peculiar evils. To exemplify this by instances, is the business of the subsequent descriptive part of the piece.

Italy is the first country that comes under review. Its general landscape is painted by a few characteristic strokes, and the felicity of its climate is displayed in appropriate imagery. The revival of arts and commerce in Italy, and their subsequent decline, are next touched upon; and hence is derived the present disposition of the people—easily pleased with splendid trifles, the wrecks of their former grandeur; and sunk into an enfeebled moral and intellectual character, reducing them to the level of children.

From these he turns with a sort of disdain, to view a nobler race, hardened by a rigorous climate, and by the necessity of unabating toil. These are the *Swiss*, who find, in the equality of their condition, and their ignorance of other modes of life, a source of content which remedies the natural evils of their lot. There cannot be a more delightful picture than the poet has drawn of the Swiss peasant, going forth to his morning's labor, and returning at night to the bosom of domestic happiness. It sufficiently accounts for that *patriot passion* for which they have ever been so celebrated, and which is here described in lines that reach the heart, and is illustrated by a beautiful simile. But this state of life has also its disadvantages. The sources of enjoyment being few, a vacant listlessness is apt to creep upon the breast; and if nature urges to throw this off by occasional bursts of pleasure, no stimulus can reach the purpose but gross sensual debauch. Their morals, too, like their enjoyments, are of a coarse texture. Some sterner virtues hold high dominion in their breast, but all the gentler and more refined qualities of the heart which soften and sweeten life, are exiled to milder climates.

To the more genial climate of *France* the traveller next repairs, and in a very pleasing rural picture he introduces himself in the capacity of musician to a village party of dancers beside the murmuring Loire. The leading feature of this nation he represents as being the love of praise; which passion, while it inspires sentiments of honor, and a desire of pleasing, also affords a free course to folly, and nourishes vanity and ostentation. The soul, accustomed to depend for its happiness on foreign applause, shifts its principles with the change of fashion, and is a stranger to the value of self-approbation.

The strong contrast to this national character is sought in *Holland*; a most graphical description of the scenery presented by that singular country introduces the moral portrait of the people. From the necessity of unceasing labor, induced by their peculiar circumstances, a habit of industry has been formed, of which the natural consequence is a love of gain. The possession of exuberant wealth has given rise to the arts and conveniences of life; but at the same time has introduced a crafty, cold, and mercenary temper, which sets everything, even liberty itself, at a price. How different, exclaims the poet, from their Belgian ancestors! how different from the present race of Britain!

To Britain, then, he turns, and begins with a slight sketch of the country, in which, he says, the mildest charms of creation are combined.

Extremes are only in the master's mind.

He then draws a very striking picture of a stern, thoughtful, independent freeman, a creature of reason, unfashioned by the common forms of life, and loose from all its ties;—and this he gives as the representative of the English character. A society formed by such unyielding, self-dependent beings, will naturally be a scene of violent political contests, and ever in a ferment with party. And a still worse fate awaits it; for the ties of nature, duty, and love, failing, the fictitious bonds of wealth and law must be employed to hold together such a reluctant

association; whence the time may come, that valor, learning, and patriotism, may all lie levelled in one sink of avarice. These are the ills of freedom; but the Poet, who would only repress to secure, goes on to deliver his ideas of the cause of such mischiefs, which he seems to place in the usurpations of aristocratical upon regal authority; and with great energy he expresses his indignation at the oppressions the poor suffer from their petty tyrants. This leads him to a kind of anticipation of the subject of his *Deserted Village*, where, laying aside the politician, and resuming the poet, he describes, by a few highly pathetic touches, the depopulated fields, the ruined village, and the poor, forlorn inhabitants driven from their beloved home, and exposed to all the perils of the transatlantic wilderness. It is by no means my intention to enter into a discussion of GOLDSMITH's political opinions, which bear evident marks of confused notions and a heated imagination. I shall confine myself to a remark upon the English national character, which will apply to him in common with various other writers, native and foreign.

This country has long been in the possession of more unrestrained freedom of thinking and acting than any other perhaps that ever existed; a consequence of which has been that all these peculiarities of character, which in other nations remain concealed in the general mass, have here stood forth prominent and conspicuous; and these being from their nature calculated to draw attention, have by superficial observers been mistaken for the general character of the people. This has been particularly the case with political distinction. From the publicity of all proceedings in the legislative part of our constitution and the independence with which many act, all party differences are strongly marked, and public men take their side with openness and confidence. Public topics, too, are discussed by all ranks; and whatever seeds there are in any part of the society of spirit and activity, have full opportunity of germinating. But to imagine that these busy and high-spirited characters compose a majority of the community, or perhaps a much greater proportion than in other countries, is a delusion. This nation, as a body, is, like all others, characterized by circumstances of its situation; and a rich commercial people, long trained to society, inhabiting a climate where many things are necessary to the comfort of life, and under a government abounding with splendid distinctions cannot possibly be a knot of philosophers and patriots.

To return from this digression. Though it is probable that few of GOLDSMITH's readers will be convinced, even from the instances he has himself produced, that the happiness of mankind is everywhere equal, yet all will feel the force of the truly philosophical sentiment which concludes the piece,— that man's chief bliss is ever seated in his mind; and that but a small part of real felicity consists in what human governments can either bestow or withhold.

The *Deserted Village*, first printed in 1769, is the companion piece of the *Traveller*, formed, like it, upon a plan which unites description with sentiment, and employs both in inculcating a political moral. It is a view of the prosperous and ruined state of a country village, with reflections on the causes of both. Such it may be defined in prose; but the disposition, management and coloring of the piece are all calculated for poetical effect. It begins with a delightful picture of *Auburn*, when inhabited by a happy people. The view of the village itself, and the rural occupations and pastimes of its simple natives, is in the best style of painting, by a selection of characteristic circumstances. It is immediately contrasted by a similar bold sketch of its ruined and desolated condition. Then succeeds an imaginary state of England, in a kind of golden age of equality; with its contrast likewise. The apostrophe that follows, the personal complaint of the poet, and the portrait of a sage in retirement, are sweetly sentimental touches that break the continuity of description.

He returns to *Auburn*, and having premised another masterly sketch of its two states, in which the images are chiefly drawn from sounds, he proceeds to what may be called the interior history of the village. In his first figure he has tried his strength with Dryden. The *parish priest* of that great poet, improved from Chaucer, is a portrait full of beauty, but drawn in a loose, unequal manner, with the flowing vein of digressive thought and imagery that stamps his style. The subject of the draught, too, is considerably different from that of GOLDSMITH, having more of the ascetic and mortified cast in conformity to the saintly model of the Roman Catholic priesthood. The pastor of *Auburn* is more *human*, but is not on that account a less venerable and interesting figure; though I know not whether all will be pleased with his familiarity with vicious characters, which goes beyond the purpose of mere reformation. The description of him in his professional character is truly admirable; and the similes of the bird instructing its young to fly, and the tall cliff rising above the storm have been universally applauded. The first, I believe, is original;—the second is not so, though it has probably never been so well drawn and applied. The subsequent sketches of the village schoolmaster and alehouse are close imitations of nature in low life, like the pictures of Teniers and Hogarth. Yet even these humorous scenes slide imperceptibly into sentiment and pathos; and the comparison of the simple pleasures of the poor, with the splendid festivities of the opulent, rises to the highest style of moral poetry. Who has not felt the force of that reflection,

The heart distrusting asks, if this be joy?

The writer then falls into a strain of reasoning against luxury and superfluous wealth, in which the sober inquirer will find much serious truth, though mixed with poetical exaggeration. The description of the contrasted scenes of magnificence and misery in a great metropolis, closed by the pathetic figure of the forlorn, ruined female, is not to be surpassed.

Were not the subjects of GOLDSMITH's description so skilfully varied, the uniformity of manner, consisting in an enumeration of single circumstances, generally depicted in single lines, might tire; but where is the reader who can avoid being hurried along by the swift current of imagery, when to such a passage as the last succeeds a landscape fraught with all the sublime terrors of the torrid zone;—and then an exquisitely tender history-piece of the departure of the villagers concluded with a group (slightly touched indeed) or allegorical personages? A noble address to the Genius of Poetry, in which is compressed the moral of the whole, gives a dignified finishing to the work.

If we conjure these two principal poems of GOLDSMITH, we may say that the *Traveller* is formed on a more regular plan, has a higher purpose in view, more abounds in thought, and in the expression of moral and philosophical ideas; the *Deserted Village* has more imagery, more variety, more pathos, more of the peculiar character of poetry. In the first, the moral and natural descriptions are more general and elevated, in the second, they are more particular and interesting. Both are truly original productions; but the *Deserted Village* has less peculiarity, and indeed has given rise to imitations which may stand in some parallel with it; while the *Traveller* remains an *unique*.

With regard to GOLDSMITH's other poems, a few remarks will suffice. The *Hermit*, printed in the same year with the *Traveller*, has been a very popular piece, as might be expected of a tender tale prettily told. It is called a 'Ballad,' but I think with no correct application of that term, which properly means a story related in language either naturally or affectedly rude and simple. It has been a sort of a fashion to admire these productions; yet in the really ancient ballads, for one stroke of beauty, there are pages of insipidity and vulgarity; and the imitations have been pleasing in proportion as they approached more finished compositions. In GOLDSMITH's *Hermit* the language is always polished, and often ornamented. The best things in it are some neat turns of moral and pathetic sentiment, given with a simple conciseness that fits them for being retained in the memory. As to the story, it has little fancy or contrivance to recommend it.

We have already seen that GOLDSMITH possessed humor; and, exclusively of his comedies, pieces professedly humorous form a part of his poetical remains. His imitations of Swift are happy, but they *are* imitations. His tale of the 'Double Transformation' may vie with those of Prior. His own natural vein of easy humor flows freely in his 'Haunch of Venison' and *Retaliation*; the first, an admirable specimen of a very ludicrous story made out of a common incident by the help of conversation and character; the other, an original thought, in which his talent at drawing portraits, with a mixture of the serious and the comic, is most happily displayed.

E. T. CHANNING
From "Prior's Life of Goldsmith"
North American Review, July 1837, pp. 106–16

It is not our object, in what follows, to give a history or analysis of his writings, but to speak of a few of his most obvious and pleasing peculiarities; and though much of what is said may apply to his political histories, and his *History of the Earth* and *Animated Nature*, yet we have particularly in view his *Miscellaneous Works*. In the course of time, one after another of even his lighter pieces has passed gently out of sight, or they are of interest to none but literary men; while two or three of his works are more popularly known than any writings of the last century, and probably are not surpassed by any books in the language for their power of interesting a great variety of readers. To be sure, new editions of his collected miscellanies are not rare, and Mr. Prior announces still another with recently discovered pieces; but what is or will be the consumption of these, compared with that of the few favorites that are published separately? A great author may be pardoned for promising himself inmortality; but he should not venture to say which of his numerous works he shall be remembered for. That which cost him least pains, and to whose fate he was indifferent, may be the one that strikes the never-dying note in human hearts, and gives a kind of perpetuity to all the rest. There is an artificial or conventional fame which is created, and for its day sustained, by the efforts of a small set of admirers or applauders. Sometimes the mere force of custom will keep a book in the rank of a classic, while to all important purposes it is dead in literature. And there is a natural fame, which is nothing more than the response of the general mind. It is liable to suffer obscuration, with the revolutions in every thing human; but we never doubt that it will from time to time recover its brightness, with the return of a natural state of feeling in men.

It may be thought that a work of genius cannot be strictly

popular; that is, it cannot be generally understood and felt; and that if the people praise it, they do so with exceedingly vague impressions, and more from deference to high names than any distinct perception and hearty delight. This is to say, that if a book is really popular, it cannot be of the highest order. But without entering into the question, or stating reasons for thinking that it is a much narrower one than it may at first appear, we would inquire who are the most fervent admirers of books that everybody allows to be truly popular; such as *The Vicar of Wakefield, Robinson Crusoe, Pilgrim's Progress*, and parts, at least, of *Gulliver's Travels*. Are they children, and the less cultivated? Does a moderate development of the faculties, or the freshness and liberty of youth prepare one for the truest estimate of the simple tale, which seems to have been composed purposely to suit the comprehension and taste of the humblest reader? There are secret beauties in this general favorite, principles of art, results of high inventive genius, on which its very popularity depends, and which he alone will perceive and value who is capable of estimating what are called the grandest compositions. Whether the amount of his pleasure be greater on the whole than that of a less accomplished reader, is another question. And whether all products of genius are of equal compass and dignity, is no question at all. It is enough if we have raised a doubt in the minds of any, who would exclude a book from the ranks of genius, because it is simple and familiar, and recommends itself to the general apprehension and favor.

The most popular of Goldsmith's *Miscellaneous Works*, are his two larger poems and the ballad, his Novel, *The Citizen of the World*, the little collection of Essays, published in 1765, and his still acted play of *She Stoops to Conquer*. Of these, *The Vicar of Wakefield* and *The Deserted Village* are known to everybody, and of as familiar reference as any thing in the language. What a variety of literature is here offered in three or four small volumes! Dramas, essays, poetry, and prose fiction; some of them the elaborate productions of his happier days, and others struck off in haste to supply his urgent wants; but all marked alike with his genius and memorable style.

Nothing seems more easy at first, than to point out what it chiefly is that constitutes the attraction of these writings. But the critic, after carefully distinguishing this and that property, and applying all the discriminating terms of his art, will sometime own that he knows little more of the secret than the simple-hearted admirer. There is a charm, an effect, and *that* we all feel; and we might almost as well try to produce as to express it. Still there is nothing in the thoughts, the plots, the characters, or the verse, that is difficult to understand. Nobody makes discoveries in Goldsmith. If another points out a beauty to us which we had never stated as such to ourselves, he only revives or defines an old idea or feeling. The impression received in his own time was just the same that he makes now, and just the same in boy and man. Different minds may speculate about him in a different manner, and prefer different things, but there will be found among them all a remarkable general agreement, and but one kind of feeling. At the same time that every thing is so obvious, that the mind scarcely seems to be exercised beyond what is necessary for receiving; yet, when we come to think over the matter, and find scenes, reflections, feelings, whole passages, and simple saying, not merely remembered, but so wrought into the mind that they are a part of itself, rather than its furniture, and that our tempers have been softened by them, our characters and sentiments moulded, and our happiness increased, we own that some power, deep as any philosophy, has been operating without our knowledge to produce effects like these, and that,

while reading, we little thought of the mild, tender, yet clear light, which made the images at once distinct and lovely.

Goldsmith's popularity is as natural as our instinctive attachments. It springs not from our studying his beauties and admiring his skill, and stopping to observe the perpetual evidence of his resources; and it depends in no degree upon our finding that others have read him, and talking with them about his excellences. We are pleased off hand and by himself, and for a reason of our own. We should like him in precisely the same degree, if we had happened upon him accidentally, and without ever having heard of him.

Every reader calls him entertaining; and he is eminently, it might also be said, constantly so. And more is meant by this, than his power of agreeable narrative, description, and dialogue; more than that we have been amused by his humor, or thoughtlessly carried along by a light, graceful, desultory manner, which never wearies, because it never detains. We mean, that he gives a charm to every thing, that he recommends it. We receive agreeably the gravest thoughts, such as we should not for a moment call diverting, and we can never think of them as separated from the pleasure. Our happy emotion belongs to the sentiment itself, and seems in no respect to be produced by any accidental beauty with which he had clothed it, as if to make a disagreeable or indifferent thing welcome. Our minds are exercised, but without the least effort; we get at the full meaning without seeking for it. If his reflections rarely lead us directly to further thoughts, still they put the mind in a good state, and dispose it to work for itself. Instead of fearing that we have been indulging ourselves with a debilitating luxury, or at best a mere relaxation, as is the effect of too many things that we find entertaining, we know that a great mind has been in familiar communication with ours, and we are exhilarated and strengthened much in the same way as when we contemplate material beauty or breathe a wholesome atmosphere.

Next to his humor, we believe his style of narrative has been most admired. What we particularly observe in this is, that while things are related in a simple, straight-forward manner, so that the merely literary beauty may escape notice and no contrivance of art may be seen, yet it is impossible that any writer with any manner should give us a livelier and more agreeable succession of scenes and actions, and this too with very few occurrences to fill out a story. He seems to bring both the dramatic art and that of painting to his aid, to make his little collection of facts consistent and animated. Thus in his *Letters on English History*, whatever omissions there may be, he certainly carries us into the very heart of the times, and makes us acquainted with people. So in his Novel; up to the time of Olivia's flight, we feel as if we have been living some years with a great number and variety of persons, and gradually becoming accustomed to their tempers, eccentricities, and ways of life, and acquiring no small amount of common experience; and yet every distinct fact could be soon enumerated, and all this part of the story is comprised in a few short chapters. Richardson produced his great effects in a very different manner.

The Vicar of Wakefield is a plain tale of English rural life. We are set down in a country which we have never thought very picturesque, though the Vicar's thatched house of one story is beautifully situated. There are scattered cottages, near enough however to make a neighbourhood; and next to him is Mr. Flamborough, whom we see smoking his pipe at his door, as the Vicar approaches after his great bargain at the fair. The farms are generally small, but sufficiently productive to supply the comforts of life. The population is evidently of old standing. There are no new comers, save the Vicar himself and his family, and none rich or ambitious enough to run to the city for sights and to bring back the fashions. We are all acquainted with the localities; the short foot-way to the church, and the five-mile route on which the ladies were "thrown from their horses,"—the bank overshadowed with hawthorn and honeysuckle, where in fine weather the family "usually sat together to enjoy an extensive landscape in the calm of the evening," and the grass plot before the door where Mr. Thornhill gave the ball by moonlight to the young ladies.

Upon the sudden loss of an ample fortune the Vicar retires to this scene of antique simplicity, where he had been offered a small cure of fifteen pounds a year, and probably regretting most of all that he can no longer appropriate the profits of his living in the poor. This reverse in his circumstances is important, for his character is to be seen and felt the best among strong contrasts both of fortune and people. Nothing can be more steady than his Christian philosophy under the experience of what is commonly thought to be the good and ill of human life. If he can bring up a virtuous family, discharge his sacred office faithfully, and enjoy his principles of strict monogamy without molestation, the temptations of riches and want are as nothing.

He has his weak side,—great tenacity upon some harmless point, great self-complacency in his sole perception of its importance, great confidence in his own judgment, and upon those matters especially where experience, which he had not, was alone wanted; and all the disappointments and mortifications in the world will not cure him. But vanity and self-sufficiency together are generally too much to permit perfect self-satisfaction; and we are not surprised to see his courage fail him, when, after some of his misadventures, he has to meet his own family. For though they held him in the highest reverence, yet they had so many points of their own to carry against his better judgment, that their eyes would not be shut; and the advantage was too tempting not to be taken, the next time he should overwhelm them with commonplace warnings and oracular doubts. He had failed where he had been confident, and was downright ashamed for the moment; but each case of the kind soon comes to be looked at as an exception, and his frailty, though wounded, is soon as active as ever.

And to all appearance it does him no harm; for look at him in any point where high, true feeling is involved; where honor, generosity, integrity, or parental love is touched; and what is all the wisdom of this world by the side of his clear sense of wrong, and the utter surrender of self at the thought of the only real sufferer,—the offender? His heart is wise; and in a real conflict, his courage is that of a hero or martyr. After a long life of speculation, conceit, credulity, and domestic happiness, his time of action and adventure begins with his journey in pursuit of his daughter. Observe, through the whole of his wanderings, the absence of all sentimentality and exhibition of grief. It is just what we should expect. He knows the full extent of his calamity, and is prepared for the worst. His object is nothing less than to reclaim a lost child, and without losing sight of it, he retains his interest in common affairs; he is ready to enter into conversation with travellers on the road or at the inns, and is as positive and communicative as ever. This immutable simplicity is the truth of nature. The beauty and pathos with which he describes his return to his own door make the scene imperishable.

The hired horse that we rose was to be put up that night at an inn by the way, within about five miles from my house; and as I was willing to prepare my family for my daughter's reception, I determined to leave her that night at the inn, and to return for her, accompanied by my daughter Sophia, early the next morning. It was night before we reached our appointed stage; however, after seeing her provided with a decent apartment, and having ordered the hostess to prepare proper refreshments, I kissed her, and proceeded towards home. And now my heart caught new sensations of pleasure the nearer I approached that peaceful mansion. As a bird that had been frighted from its nest, my affections outwent my haste, and hovered round my little fireside with all the rapture of expectation. I called up the many fond things I had to say, and anticipated the welcome I was to receive. I already felt my wife's tender embrace, and smiled at the joy of my little ones. As I walked but slowly, the night waned apace. The laborers of the day were all retired to rest; the lights were out in every cottage; no sounds were heard but of the shrilling cock and the deep-mouthed watchdog at hollow distance. I approached my little abode of pleasure and before I was within a furlong of the place, our honest mastiff came running to welcome me.

It was now near midnight that I came to knock at my door;—all was still and silent;—my heart dilated with unutterable happiness, when, to my amazement, I saw the house bursting out in a blaze of fire, and every aperture red with conflagration. I gave a loud, convulsive outcry, and fell upon the pavement insensible.—Chap. 22.

The elements of the Vicar's character are certainly very common. We recognise an old acquaintance, and no study or ingenuity can make him any thing else than what he appears to plain men at the first reading. It is needless to add, that in spite of this, or in consequence of it, it is known all over the world as a master-work of genius. At the close, the Vicar, like the Patriarch, has his blessings doubled upon him; and we feel as if all his good fortune were wrought out by his virtues, though, to look at the case truly, every event of his life appears to be brought about by others, and his own will and wisdom to be powerless.

Many of the qualities of this novel will be found in some of the other prose works which we have named; the same unobserved, indefinable fitness of composition, which is satisfied with accomplishing its purpose, and asks no notice the same unobtrusive, ever-varying humor, seen equally in deeds, words, characters, and situations, calling for no sagacity in us to catch it, and producing no surprise. We have felt inclined to qualify this last remark, with respect to many passages in the plays. Still these might succeed perfectly in acting; and it would require more than a hint to show the difference between a drama and a story, between the position and circumstances of a reader and spectator, and that possibly the whole theatrical apparatus helps to give effect to humor in a play, as the narrative certainly does to conversation in a novel. As the *Vicar* is formed upon English habits and manners of the time in a certain sphere, so in the *Essays* and *Citizen of the World* we have life and character, as they appeared in parts at least of London. Though there are fancy sketches, and a variety of subjects, yet we remember nothing so distinctly, as that we are in the company of a wise, pleasant, acute observer of common life, who has delightful narratives in store, to set out the simple truths that he lets fall;—as when he puts to shame the complaints of the great by the story of the poor soldier with a wooden leg, whom he met begging at one of the outlets of the town; and shows the irksomeness of the company of fools in his sketches of that matchless compound of superficiality, pretension, tawdriness, and self-content, the little second-rate beau, Mr. Tibbs. And so, if allowable, we might go on with instances of situations, occurrences, and characters, which are either fraught with instruction, or give the mind health by surrounding it with truth,—no matter how familiar, if it be so offered that it is *felt* to be truth. But we are talking of old and well-known things; and though we might expect the reader's sympathy whenever we were fortunate enough to revive early recollections and feeling, yet we should consider that there are few who have not as good memories and as distinct impressions as ourselves.

And for the same reason, we need say little of his Poetry. We observe in his two larger poems (and to these our remarks will be limited), that, except in the descriptions of the village school and inn, there is a want of his customary humor, even of the most delicate kind; and this is not wholly explained by their serious subject and aim, for humor is always natural to him, and can seldom harm any thing. One explanation might be suggested by his complaint in the *Inquiry*, that the "critics have almost got the victory over humor," and that "the most trifling performance now assumes all the didactic stiffness of wisdom." But he, at the same time, derides this false solemnity, and begs people to write naturally, and visits the critics with the most hearty contempt. Another explanation may be sought in the fact, that these poems were deeply studied and slowly finished. Goldsmith deliberately proposed to establish his name upon them, and hence his mind may have been under restraint, and a gay variety of thoughts obstructed. The purpose of carrying out an idea to as great perfection as possible, may defeat those free touches which sometimes accomplish more than the most diligent, intentional adherence to propriety. But the ease and fluent sweetness of the thoughts and verse, forbid the idea that he was under alarm or constraint. Though, undoubtedly, the topics show one steady direction of his mind, and the tone of the composition never varies, unless it be, that there is more tenderness in the *Deserted Village*, and more ardor of denunciation in *The Traveller*, yet there is no indication that he ever suppresses what he feels, or inserts what he does not.

The reader sees that Goldsmith is writing of what he had witnessed and felt in early life. He turns to this period as to a dream, whose very sorrows he would recover, and whose delights are the dearer, that they are dimmed and saddened. The seasons of inward solitude which often visit the opening and joyous spirit of youth, seasons, when the heart reports not its wants, and knows not on what it shall fasten, to supply them, are the best remembered in after life, and give a color to every recollection that we value. While important events, as they then appeared, have faded, many a trifling occasion or object is invested with strange beauty, and breathes softness and peace over our hearts. We know not what gives them this importance. The association was early made, but not perceived fully till years afterwards. It is in the midst of such recollections that Goldsmith writes. Though professing to have public evils in view, he is thinking of private losses, domestic changes, those humble, well-remembered revolutions, that pass between boyhood and matured years. Some of his most affecting descriptions are little more than a series of such recollections, arranged with slight regard to order, and apparently not moulded in the least by the imagination; perhaps stated as they casually rose to his mind, in a time of grief and depression. In this respect they resemble elegiac poetry, and many passages have the true spirit of a pastoral lament.

How often have I paused on every charm,
The sheltered cot, the cultivated farm,
The never-failing brook, the busy mill,
The decent church that topped the neighbouring hill,
The hawthorn bush, with seats beneath the shade,
For talking age and whispering lovers made.
How often have I blest the coming day
When toil remitting lent its turn to play!
Sweet was the sound, when oft, at evening's close,
Up yonder hill the village murmur rose.
There, as I passed with careless steps and slow,
The mingling notes came softened from below;
The swain responsive as the milk-maid sung,
The sober herd that lowed to meet their young;
The noisy geese that gabbled o'er the pool,
The playful children just let loose from school;
The watch-dog's voice that bayed the whispering wind,
And the loud laugh that spoke the vacant mind.

He laments the decay of simplicity in manners and tastes, and the depopulation of the country, in consequence of the gradual amassing of wealth in single hands, and the abandonment of agriculture for trade. In his comparative view of states he does not overlook the blessing which justify patriotism in each; but he misses something which he deems essential to happiness, and falls into a natural exaggeration of what is lost, and sees not that changes may have been for the better. But none of us probably ever think of weighing his political opinions, or his claims to the title of a great philosophical poet. His fame and influence depend on neither. We are not grateful to him because he possesses extraordinary poetical power. There is so much of genuine feeling, just thought, true description, and sound moral distinction in these poems, the language is so clear, the strain so liquid, the general style, not quite magnificent, but yet of such an easy, natural elevation and dignity, that they glide into our affections and memory in youth, and we are never displaced, we apprehend, by the more exciting pleasures, the more subtile and complicated conceptions, which we owe in later years to poetry of a far higher and infinitely more varied character.

We do ourselves wrong to compare him injuriously with others. We are losers by it. We cannot and ought not to be satisfied with his poetry, and seek nothing higher and different; yet if we forget it, or even think less of it, the change will not be owing to our worship of greater genius, but to a feverish love of idols. Indeed, the relish of such poetry is some evidence of an uncorrupted taste. It owes nothing to affectation, and is in nothing more original than its serenity or tempered feeling. While the glory of greater artists is in subduing their inspiration to their conception of perfect workmanship, his distinction is that he is willing not to stimulate his powers to false efforts. He effects one purpose of all real poetry, by refining the perception and multiplying the sources of truth. Excitement and exhilaration, tears and laughter, all feelings and signs of feeling may be produced both by ordinary and by powerful writers, in a wholly false way. The right instrument has been touched by both, and abused; both have trusted to our weakness or ignorance, and succeeded; little thinking that there were principles in our nature, which would not long endure this tampering, if the note of a true minstrel, though the humblest, was yet to be heard.

LEIGH HUNT
From *Wit and Humour*
1846

GOLDSMITH excelled all his contemporaries in variety of genius but VOLTAIRE. If he was less of the profound thinker than JOHNSON, who scarcely ever thought otherwise than profoundly, he was a greater humourist, and what is more, a greater poet. The author, whose pen can move from novel writing to history, from history to poetry, and from poetry to natural philosophy, always with elegance, if not always with felicity, will boast a greater number of readers and consequently of admirers than him, who is greatest of the great in only one species of writing.

Though the chief excellence of GOLDSMITH is in prose, yet his poetry is so happily adapted to general understandings, that it is more universally admired. It is not however of the highest class: it always pleases with delicacy, and sometimes elevates with grandeur, but it never astonishes with enthusiastic daring. Of his first composition, the *Traveller*, Dr. JOHNSON said that 'there had not been so fine a poem since the days of POPE:' but this word *fine* is of so vague a meaning, that it is difficult to comprehend what the critic intended by his panegyric, when THOMSON had published the *Seasons*, and COLLINS had produced an ode that rivalled DRYDEN: if he designed to say, that there had not been so fine a poem in POPE's style, the praise may be allowed; it has all the flow of thought and clear exposition of that exact poet; its style is generally vigorous and melodious, and its metaphorical allusion easy and appropriate; in the *application* of epithets, which are the touchstones of true poetry, it would be difficult to find a more skilful master: but these beauties are difficult of *creation*: the '*bleak Swiss*' is surely a very violent illustration; to apply the elementary effect of winds and storms to the inhabitants of a stormy region is little better than to call the African the *electrifying negro*, because it perpetually lightens in Africa, GOLDSMITH's figures of speech however seldom start into this violence, though they are powerful upon powerful occasions: there are few metaphors so happy as that picture of a factious state, when

——overwrought, the gen'ral system feels
Its motion stop, or frenzy fire the wheels.

But no heroic versifier since the days of POPE has been unchangeably vigorous in a long rhyming poem; SOUTHEY and COWPER, the most original poets of our time, are often unpardonably feeble in this respect, the one through an affectation of simplicity, and the other, singularly enough, of, dignity. Metrical weakness is owing in most cases to paucity of emphasis; but GOLDSMITH in his *Traveller* is feeble in misplaced emphasis; for his words are of sufficient length and sound to be pompous in a better situation: he slides now and then into a kind of hurried halt, which is as lame as the feebleness of monosyllables. ⟨. . .⟩ These debilities of verse could not have been the effect of negligence; for GOLDSMITH, though he was rapid in prose composition, polished his verses with the slowest attention: they must be reckoned among those infelicities of composition, which sometimes escape the self-love of an author fond of his first ideas. No poet however should hesitate to blot such lines; for what he may gain in vigour of thought, he loses in feebleness of language.

There is something peculiarly beautiful in what may be called the plot of the poem: the *Traveller* seats himself on Alpine solitudes to moralize on the world beneath him; he takes a mental survey of the character as well as landscape of different nations, and in such a situation is naturally inspired with serious and pathetic reflections on human nature; but he has caught the general melancholy of moralists, and his conclusions, like those of all systematic complainers, are not invariably just: he laments every thing, advantageous or unprofitable, happy or unhappy; if a nation is poor, it has the vices of poverty; if it is rich, it has the vices of riches: first the Swiss is lucky in his want of refinement, then he is unlucky; the Hollander is industrious, but then industry makes him avaricious; the Englishman is free, but then liberty makes him factious: thus in the first part of its character every nation is wise or happy, but in the next paragraph you find it both foolish and miserable. These descriptions of universal evil are always exaggerated; the generality of mankind will never think of their condition as irritable poets and gloomy philosophers chuse to think for them: at the very moment the author is endeavouring to prove that every man makes his own happiness, he judges of the happiness of others by his own idea of felicity, and pronounces them unhappy because he could not be easy in their condition. The fact is, that GOLDSMITH thought he was reasoning finely, when he was writing fine poetry only. It is the fault of poetical argument that the reasoner is apt to forget his logic in his fancy; he catches at a brilliant line, or a brilliant idea; his imagination fires; and his reason, that serves merely to overshadow its brightness, rolls from it like smoke. It is well for the generality of readers, that melancholy disquisitions in poetry have not the doleful effect of such disquisitions in prose. Poetry scatters so many flowers on the most rugged arguments, that the weariness of the road is insensibly beguiled. If the *Traveller* had been written in prose, or were stripped of its poetical ornament, it would allure no readers at all; and I am much afraid, that with the same alteration many an argument in DRYDEN and POPE would share the same fate. The nearer logic is allied to poetry, the faster it loses its strength to the greater power. How poetical, how wild is PLATO! How unpoetical, how rational is LOCKE!

But GOLDSMITH was attached to fictitious sorrows, and he could not help fancying a new subject of complaint for his *Deserted Village*. In this poem he describes a village depopulated by the grasping luxury of the neighbouring gentry, a circumstance which was much disputed in the poet's time, and notwithstanding the frequent oppression of enclosures, has never since been proved. Poetically considered, the *Deserted Village* is a more beautiful production than the *Traveller*. It is more original, more vigorous, more characteristic in its description. The strength of the poetry is not suddenly lost in those feeble lines that give his *Traveller* the air of an interpolated copy: it is full of the natural domestic images which endear the author to us as a man, while they recommend him as an observer of life. The village landscape, its sports, its domestic sounds, and its snug alehouse shining in all the comforts of clean sand and furniture, with the exception perhaps of the rural dances, which are rather French than British, must be familiar to every body who has been ten miles from London; the mock-heroic dignity of the schoolmaster, whose jokes are studiously laughed at by the boys, is superior to that of SHENSTONE's *Schoolmistress*, whose humour consists chiefly in externals. But the amiable cares of the parish curate compose the finest part of the poem. Though they occasionally rise into a grander spirit of poetry, they possess that simple pathos, which brings an unconscious smile upon the lips, while it reaches the heart. That affecting couplet,

E'en children followed with endearing wile,
And pluck'd his gown to share the good man's smile,

seems to me perfectly original; so does the noble simile that compares the holy preacher to a bird *tempting its new-fledg'd offspring to the skies*. But a critic should be cautious in bestowing the praise of poetical invention on GOLDSMITH. He has imitated all our best poets; and though he was indignant enough, when his ideas were copied without acknowledgment by others, he does not seem to have been eager in confessing his own imitations. The general idea of the parish priest is borrowed from DRYDEN, who improved it from CHAUCER; and the sublime comparison of the religious man to the mountain circled with clouds and topped with sunshine, is copied almost literally from CLAUDIAN. What he borrows however he never degrades; it is always excellently adapted to the nature of the production. He has beauties of his own too that might have been imitated by the best poets; the aged widow who picks water-cresses, and is the only inhabitant left in the desolated village,

> The sad historian of the pensive plain,

is a novel and picturesque image; and the six lines beginning 'Ill fares the land,' and those in praise of retirement, are as vigorous as the best moral verses of POPE. No poem is at the same time more decidedly marked with the manner of its author. GOLDSMITH throughout his works was very fond of repeating what he thought his happiest ideas. He so often uses some peculiar turns of language in which he delighted, that the reader who has discovered the trick sometimes fancies he has discovered an old idea, when it is nothing but an old peculiarity of manner. But he was also fond, even to an unpardonable vanity, of repeating his sentiments almost word for word. Dr. JOHNSON objected to the *Deserted Village*, that it was too often an echo of the *Traveller*; but the fact is, that all his productions are in some degree echoes of each other. Of three comparisons in the *Essay on the State of Polite Learning* he appears to have been particularly fond, and has introduced them with a trifling variation of phrase into three of his other works. GOLDSMITH should have been superior to this vain repetition, which is as little allowable to wit as it is to dullness. It is like one of those conversation humourists, who if they cannot labour a new pun or a new allusion to set your faculties at work, nail down your escape by some such recollection as 'By the bye, let me remind you of a deuced good thing I said upon a former occasion.'

Of his lesser poems the general character is tenderness and vivacity. The *Hermit* is admired by readers of every age and intellect; it is one of the very few modern ballads which possess simplicity without affectation. Compositions of this kind are generally either elevated into a dignity incompatible with the ballad, or incongruously sprinkled with old English phrases and expletives, with *dids* and with *doths*, that have the feebleness without the respectability of age, and are helps to nobody's understanding but the author's. The *Hermit*, TICKELL's *Colin and Lucy*, and SHENSTONE's *Jemmy Dawson*, are the three best ballads in the language. ⟨. . .⟩

The Stanzas on Woman are exquisitely pathetic. Our language has no morsel that exhibits so true a simplicity of taste, while its effect is heightened with such poetical artifice. The question and answer so equally divided, so apparently artless, and the beautiful climax in the second stanza, are managed with felicity that turns criticism into mere praise. These stanzas seem to have attained perfection; they are short, but they leave us nothing to desire. Pathos as well as wit is always more effectual, in proportion as it is more concise.

It appears surprising that GOLDSMITH, whose prose works abound with humour, should in his poetry have been so sparing of his first talent. He seems to have laboured at a

prologue or an epilogue, and to have lost his more elegant vivacity, in adapting himself to the manner of its speaker. The epilogue however, spoken by Mr. LEE LEWES in the character of Harlequin, is vigorous, and well adapted to the occasion. Of all our prologue writers DRYDEN seems to have been the most witty, FOOTE the most humourous, and GARRICK, whose profession taught him every artifice of theatrical effect, the most generally pleasing. But tasks like these require very little genius; the writer has nothing to do but to make an audience good-humoured, and wit on such occasions is lost on three parts of the theatre.

Our author's pieces in professed imitation of SWIFT, possess neither the wit nor the ease of his model, whose social familiarity is more attained by the 'Haunch of Venison,' which does not profess to imitate. But *Retaliation* would have been owned with pleasure by SWIFT himself; the style is perfectly easy, and the characters, especially that of GARRICK, exhibit much knowledge of human nature. The character of CUMBERLAND however, who is compared with TERENCE, and yet is said not to draw from nature, is dramatically inconsistent: GOLDSMITH disliked sentimental comedy, and therefore found it difficult to praise. The poem is also unfortunately divided into two characteristic descriptions, the one metaphorical, and the other personal; first his friends are dishes, then they are men. And lastly, it is still more unfortunate, that his company must be intoxicated before their epitaphs are written: the wise REYNOLDS, the good Dean, and CUMBERLAND, the mender of hearts, make very awkward figures *sunk under the table*. But the general manner of the poem is certainly original; and the imitations it has provoked sufficiently prove its claim to reputation.

I do not know why I should criticise the comedies of GOLDSMITH among his poetical works, nor how those familiar dramas, which are poetry neither to the eye nor the imagination, can be called poetical. The ancient comedians, and those of the English who wrote metrically, may claim the title of poets; but if they who write mere prosaic dialogues for the stage are to be honoured with the appellation, you must call LE SAGE, RICHARDSON, and MISS EDGEWORTH poets, for some of their works are dialogues: upon this reasoning the *Devil upon Two Sticks* becomes a poem, for it is almost an entire drama, of which the Devil and the Student are the two persons. The only difference between such novels and most of our comedies is, that the former are never acted. If a work is not written in verse the only quality that can give it the name of a poem is imagination or poetical invention. Thus *Ossian* and *Telemachus* are called poems, because they want nothing but rhythm, which is the mere body, as imagination is the soul of poetry.

But the comedies of GOLDSMITH have nothing poetical about them: he seems to have avoided every studied ornament, in his dislike to sentimental comedy, from which he was anxious to divert the taste of the day. This taste however was so prevalent, that in his first comedy, the *Good-natured Man*, he restrained his acknowledged fondness for caricature and became more natural than I believe he was willing to be. There is much easy dialogue in this play, and most of the characters are to be found in nature; but the servant, Jarvis, like all dramatic servants, has too much sense and importance about him: from TERENCE down to the huge farce-writers of the present day, a footman is a very different being in real life and on the stage. The character of Croaker, who is always anticipating misfortunes, is an imitation of Suspirius in the *Rambler*: both the imitation and the original are caricatures, but the dramatic one is certainly the least unnatural; for he does utter a sentence now and then without misery in it. No character in nature ever confined his speech like Suspirius to one passion or one subject: there must be a time, when the common interests of life will compel him to accommodate his speech to his society. In the picture of the *Good-natured Man*, which is drawn with correctness and vivacity, there may be distinguished the usual fondness of GOLDSMITH for introducing himself into his works; he had gathered much experience during the wandering life he originally led, and was very skilful in applying it in a literary, if not in a practical way. I have no doubt that the *Good-natured Man* was a personification of his own accommodating careless temper: in his principal poems he is always an actor as well as a speaker; the adventures of the *Vicar of Wakefield*'s son George are supposed to comprehend some of his own; and a ludicrous mistake which he made in one of his Irish journies formed the plot of his next comedy, *She Stoops to Conquer*, in which two gentlemen mistake an old country house for an inn, and are indulged in their error by the master of it, who is a humourist. Such a plot does not promise much nature either in the incidents or the characters, and in reality the production is merely a large farce with the name of comedy. Tony Lumpkin is certainly a most original personage; his subjection at home and his domination abroad, his uncouth bashfulness at the gallantries of his female cousin, and his love of mischievous fun, present an inimitable picture of broad rusticity: the natural contempt which he shews for his mother, who has indulged him till he is too old to play the child, enforces an excellent moral in the midst of the most laughable caricature. But the characters are exaggerated throughout, and most of the incidents are inconsistent and improbable. It is from this play and the grinning comedies of O'KEEFE, have arisen those monstrous farces of the present stage, which may, for ought I know, attain the end of comedy, for they are certainly satires on human nature.

It is from his prose works that GOLDSMITH will obtain his best reputation with the critic. In these his judgment becomes more correct, and he adapts his fancy to his subject rather than his subject to his fancy. If his sentiments in verse are little better than vehicles for poetical ornament, they become their own ornament in prose; they want no glare of dress to conceal poverty; their manner is chearful, their language unaffected and elegant. The style of almost every celebrated writer preceding GOLDSMITH is remarkable for some prominent quality, which is more immediately his own: thus SWIFT is plain, JOHNSON dignified, BOLINGBROKE ardent; and critics have said that a manner is as indicative of great authors as it is of great painters. But each of these writers wants the quality of the other, and certainly it were better to be distinguished by united than by individual excellence. ADDISON gained pre-eminence over all the writers of his age by an union of the qualities of style: he is deservedly celebrated for his simplicity; yet even ADDISON wants strength. It is most probable that his occasional weakness proceeded from affectation; for though his natural taste produced a style almost always unaffected, yet as he knew his talent, he might sometimes consider it too much, and the very wish to be artless would lead him into artifice: but a writer's artifice is always detected; if he escapes the criticism, he will be detected by the feelings of his reader. An author after all merely talks to his reader by signs instead of speech; and therefore the most perfect style seems to be that which avoids the negligence while it preserves the spirit of conversation. If no exclusive peculiarity of style would be proper in social intercourse,—if the majesty of JOHNSON would only awe his hearers, and the short decision of SWIFT intimidate them, an union of the elegant and the vigorous, of the attractive and the unaffected, is necessary to the beauty and the end of writing.

This end seems to have been attained more nearly by GOLDSMITH than by any single writer before or after him; and JOHNSON pronounced his own condemnation, when he characterised him as an author, 'who had the art of being minute without tediousness, and general without confusion; whose language was copious without exuberance, exact without constraint, and easy without weakness.' This is not mere eulogy; it is a criticism worthy its author and its subject. GOLDSMITH had united the chief beauties of his predecessors and contemporaries in a style the most adapted to miscellaneous writing: he had preserved all the ease of ADDISON, while he rejected his feebleness and indecision; he had shone in all the perspicuity of SWIFT, and added to perspicuity the ornament of elegance; and though his period were sonorous and often grand, his friendship with JOHNSON had never led him to assume that studied loftiness which had become even fashionable. It was reserved for a future age however to conquer every minute feebleness of writing, to get rid of the *namelys* and *therebys*, of sentences ending with prepositions, and of relative pronouns that have no substantive relation. I have never met with a single author, who was invariably right in placing the adverb *only*: BLAIR, who detects its dislocation in ADDISON, uses it most unmercifully himself.

The earliest production of GOLDSMITH, an *Enquiry into the State of Polite Learning* in 1759, introduced him to the public in all his beauties of style and original turns of thought. Perhaps there never was an author who united such liveliness of manner with so melancholy a system of opinion. His writings abound with complaints on the unsuccessful toils of genius, and on the general misery of human life; and he began a literary career, which was to confer new laurels on the age, by writing an essay on the universal decline of letters. Much of this decline seems to have been imaginary: perhaps the despondent fancy was natural to a writer, who with all the consciousness of merit was struggling in obscurity to procure his daily subsistence. GOLDSMITH, like most writers vain of their genius, and impatient of the idea of censure, indulged in a contemptuous dislike of critics, whom he represented as 'the natural destroyers of polite learning:' but when he tells us that 'critics are always more numerous as learning is more diffused,' and that 'an increase of criticism has always portended a decay' of literature, he becomes feeble and inconsistent. Would it not follow, that when learning is not diffused, criticism would not be diffused; and therefore that when the 'natural destroyer of learning' no longer existed, the latter would revive in all its bloom?

England is perhaps of all countries the best adapted to vigorous knowledge. An Englishman not only thinks but speaks what he pleases; and therefore he excels in those arts which require a liberty of thought and speech, in political writing, in oratory, and particularly in logic: VOLTAIRE pronounced us the only nation in Europe who think profoundly. Such a nation wants nothing but the patronage of the great to excel in every department of literature; and GOLDSMITH might have allowed criticism a little respite from his rage, and attributed the decay of English genius to this simple deficiency. Some few of our latter writers indeed have received pensions from the state; but instead of receiving them as incentives to further exertion during the vigour of their health and powers, the money had dropped upon them when they have learnt to bear poverty and have almost lost both.

When literature wants patronage, men of taste become indolent and fall into imitation: from this cause has arisen that universal but elegant mediocrity of genius which characterises the present age. Every author imitates somebody's opinions or somebody's style; or if one more independent than the rest attempts to become original, he runs into the opposite extreme, and in his determination to remind us of no author good or bad, wanders into a vicious singularity. ⟨. . .⟩ COWPER of all the poets of our age is the most correctly original; his thoughts were entirely his own, and therefore naturally produced a new style: he excels in domestic pathos; and in natural strength of reasoning may rank next to DRYDEN and POPE. But in his contempt of imitation he has fallen into the error of SOUTHEY: that air of candid familiarity, which his heart led him to indulge, feeling itself sufficiently at ease out of the fetters of rhyme, relaxes too often into the prosaic; and he has furnished another hopeless instance of the inefficacy of blank-verse in artless composition. The productions of this poet however have not developed his powers in all their strength: the distempered severity of his religious doctrines, nourished by the bigotry of mistaken friends, was perpetually at variance with his philanthropic mildness of spirit, and the struggle injured his genius while it was fatal to his repose; if he had felt less acutely for the follies of mankind, he would have become a great satirist. SHERIDAN is the best dramatist since the days of CONGREVE; his comedy of the *Rivals* is perhaps the only instance of broad humour uninjuring and uninjured by nature. With the exception of this writer and MURPHY, whose farce of the *Citizen* is the best in the language, our stage is wretchedly degenerate; but this degeneracy exhibits itself in a manner the very reverse of that which GOLDSMITH lamented in his time. Instead of the everlasting revival of old plays and the total disregard of living authors which he so feelingly laments, we are presented with the hasty comedies, or rather with nothing but the bloated farces of mercenary writers, who are in fact stipendiaries of the theatre, some of them being absolutely engaged by a permanent salary. Thus a modern dramatist, who has nothing in view but the service of his employers and his own payment, is in the situation of a journeyman mechanic, with this simple difference, that the manufacturer of clocks or of cupboards is of public utility, while the manufacturer of plays is the depraver of public taste, and consequently of public morals. ⟨. . .⟩

As to the criticism of our reviews and magazines, which GOLDSMITH considers so alarming, the public do not rest so implicit a confidence in their authority as they used to do; a bad critic is as little regarded as a bad poet; we begin to judge by our feelings rather than our learning; and it is by appealing to taste and not to ARISTOTLE that the merits of a work are determined. At the same time, if the majority of our reviews are not worth attention, there have been lately some spirited attempts to rescue criticism from the charge of ignorance and corruption; it has lost much of that assertive and dogmatical tone which disdains to give a reason for its decision, and has become more philosophical and enlarged in its views. Criticism like this promotes literature instead of retarding it; a hundred reviews, thus combined to praise genius and to ridicule folly, would be nothing but a hundred incentives to merit; for though applause be compared to air, yet it is the air necessary to an author's existence. ⟨. . .⟩

I have been thus diffuse in criticising the *Essay on the State of Polite Learning*, because it was in some measure prophetically addressed to our own times. It possesses many individual beauties both of language and thought; its figures of speech are generally strong and well chosen; and that dry humour, which has so peculiar an effect in its own apparent unconsciousness, and which was afterwards proved to be GOLDSMITH's best originality, always catches at the proper objects of ridicule, and sparkles with ready illustration. The

chapter on universities is full of judicious observation; it is almost a string of aphorisms, the more valuable as they were formed by experience, which is the logic of fact. It will be seen however that the prophetic warnings of the Essay have not generally become true, and that the effects which the author deplores are not always deduced from their real causes. His temper too often betrays itself, and leads him into conclusions without conclusion; he is too apt to confound false criticism with true, and decides too strongly from conjecture. In fact it is a very difficult, not to say an impossible task to settle the literary merits of contemporary nations, whose writers are often unknown beyond their native country; and the consciousness of this difficulty led the author into that unlucky assertion, which measured a country's *reputation* by writers who confer *fame on others without receiving any portion of it themselves*. GOLDSMITH by his own unconscious acknowledgement could no more pronounce on the contemporary literature of Italy or Germany than LOPE DE VEGA could have prounced on the literature of the contemporary English poets, of whom he knew nothing. ⟨. . .⟩

GOLDSMITH does not appear to have possessed an attention sufficiently persevering to pursue one individual subject through a long maze of reasoning. Hence he was fond of detached essays, into which he could throw the result of his meditations and his experience without tiring himself or his readers. Though he had such a host of predecessors in this species of writing, he seems to have imitated nothing either of their sentiment or style: in style he excelled them all; in sentiment he was sprightly yet sententious; and perhaps he is the only successor of ADDISON who indulges his readers in broad laughter while he gives them sound reason. The *Citizen of the World*, or as it was originally entitled, *Letters from a Chinese Philosopher in London to his Friends in the East*, afford the best specimen of GOLDSMITH's genius, both as an observer and a man of wit. The letters are upon the manners of the English; and in fact are merely a set of essays slightly connected by the supposition of an epistolary correspondence. Some of them possess nothing of the Chinese writer, and little of the epistolary form but the *address* at the beginning, and the *farewell* at the end; consequently the author, who was fond of seeing himself reflected in all his publications, printed many of them at various times, under the title of *Essays*. ⟨. . .⟩

As a Novelist GOLDSMITH has less faults perhaps than in any other species of writing. He seems to have introduced among us a new species of novel, the simple domestic: in no novel indeed is there an assemblage of characters so equally natural as in the *Vicar of Wakefield*: if there is a degree of romance about the pretended Mr. Burchell, it is well repaid by little touches of natural amiableness which endear this character almost as much to his readers as to the Vicar's little children. The contented liveliness, credulity, and good-natured disputes of the venerable pair, the Vicar's patient philanthropy and the wife's holiday vanity, the credulous importance of his logical son Moses, and the manly frankness equally credulous of George, with the beautiful contrast of the two sisters, and one overpowering with gaiety, the other winning with modest sensibility, compose a family picture unequalled in lively nature. The two first pages of the book present one of the best specimens of the author's dry simplicity of style, and the latter chapters abound with a domestic pathos, the more powerful as the writer seems unconscious of his powers, and we are reminded by no artifice of language or sentiment to keep our tears for a less designing pathos. The morality is unexceptionable: I know not a single novel, which could give young readers a better insight into the habits and follies of human life with less danger in the disclosure.

If GOLDSMITH were characterised in a few words, I would describe him as a writer generally original yet imitative of the best models; from these he gathered all the chief qualities of style, and became elegant and animated in his language while from experience rather than from books he obtained his knowledge, and became natural and original in his thoughts. His poetry has added little to English literature, because nothing that is not perfectly and powerfully original can be said to add to the poetical stock of a nation; but his prose exhibits this quality in the highest degree: if he was more of the humourist than the wit, it was not for want of invention; humour was the familiar delight, wit the occasional exercise of his genius. In short he is one of those happy geniuses who are welcome to a reader in every frame of mind, for his seriousness and his gaiety are equally unaffected and equally instructive.

HENRY GILES
From "Oliver Goldsmith"
Lectures and Essays
1850, Volume 1, pp. 235–57

As a historian, Goldsmith accomplishes all at which he aims. He does not promise much, but he does more than he promises. He takes, it is true, facts which had been already collected, but he shapes them with an art that is all his own. He has the rare faculty of being brief without being dry; of being at once perspicuous and compressed, and of giving to the merest abridgment the interest of dramatic illusion. Doctor Johnson set a high value on Goldsmith, if not as a historian, at least as a narrator; and Dr. Johnson was a man, whose critical austerity even friendship rarely softened. Dr. Johnson went so far, as to place Goldsmith above Robertson. When we have taken into consideration Johnson's prejudices against Robertson for being a Scotchman and a Presbyterian, a worth will still remain in the opinion, which we must allow to Goldsmith. Robertson, Johnson represents as crushed under his own weight; or as like a man that packs gold in wool, the wool taking more room than the gold. Goldsmith, he says, puts into his book as much as his book will hold. No man, he asserts, will read Robertson's cumbrous detail a second time; but Goldsmith's plain narrative will please again and again. Johnson remarked of Goldsmith in one of his conversations,—"He is now writing a Natural History, and he will make it as entertaining as a Persian Tale." With these histories of Goldsmith we cannot dispense; a beautiful mixture of the agreeable and the useful, they are dear to us with all their imperfections; they are lessons for our childhood, and relaxation for our maturity. They have a permanent existence in our literature, and they deserve it. They deserve it, not alone for their charms of expression, but for qualities of higher worth; for purity of sentiment, for honesty of purpose, for benevolence of heart, for the wisdom of a liberal spirit, and the moderation of a humane temper.

As an essayist, Goldsmith ranks with the highest in our language. With a keen observation of life and manners, he unites delightful ease; and he softens caustic sarcasm with a pleasant humor. Amidst a varied experience, he preserved a simple heart; and he drew human nature as he found it, with the freedom of a satirist, but never with the coldness of a cynic. The essays of Goldsmith are wise as well as amusing, and display as much sagacity as variety. They abound in impressive

moral teachings, in apt examples, and in beautiful illustrations. Serious, when soberness is wisdom, and gay when laughter is not folly; they can prompt the smile, they can also start the tear; inspiration comes with the occasion, in unexpected eloquence, and in unbidden pathos.

To speak of Goldsmith as an essayist, is to suggest a comparison of his merits with writers whose excellence in didactic and humorous composition forms an elevated and a severe standard. But Goldsmith will bear the comparison. He has not, indeed, the indefinable grace of Addison; nor the solemn wisdom of Johnson. But neither has Addison his freshness, his hearty and broad ridicule, the cheerful comicry which will not be satisfied with an elegant simper, but must have the loud and open laugh. Johnson on the solemn themes of humanity maintains a melancholy grandeur; he sits in despondency and solitude; his general reflections on life and destiny are the deep sighings of a heart that seeks for hope, but has not found it; the pantings of a troubled soul alarmed by superstition, but wanting faith; they are lofty, but cheerless; they are eloquent, but monotonous; they have music, but it is the music of lamentation; they are the modulations of a dirge. Johnson knew well the dark abstractions which belong to our nature; but he did not understand the details of common existence as Goldsmith did. He could moralize, but he could not paint; he has splendid passages, but no pictures; he could philosophize, but he could not create. He has, therefore, left us no special individualities, to which our fancies can give local habitations; he has made no addition to that world of beings, whose population and whose history belong to imagination; he has given it no new inhabitant, none to walk beside the "Vicar of Wakefield," or "Sir Roger de Coverly." As for "Rasselas," he is a declamatory shadow; and cloud-formed as he is, the vapor does not long preserve a shape; for the outlines soon melt into the illimitable expanse of gloomy meditation.

After reading a paper in the *Rambler*, or a chapter in *Rasselas*, I take up Goldsmith's *Citizen of the World* with a new relish; and when I have perused some pages, I feel resuscitated from depression by its satire, its shrewdness, its pleasantry, and good sense. What a pungent impersonation of poverty and folly is Beau Tibbs, such an admirable combination of the dandy and the loafer. Johnson could have no more conceived of Beau Tibbs, than he could have invented a dialect for little fishes. Goldsmith at one time told the critic, that if he gave little fishes language, that he would make little fishes speak like whales. So he would make Beau Tibbs speak like "The Last Man." But Goldsmith understood what little fishes should say, if they had the gift of speech; it is no wonder, that he knew the proper phraseology of Beau Tibbs, who had that gift with a most miraculous fluency.

Beau Tibbs is a perfect character of the Jeremy Diddler school. Dressed in the finery of rag-fair, he talks of the balls and assemblies he attends. He has invitations to noblemen's feasts for a month to come; yet he jumps at an offer to share a mug of porter; he bets a thousand guineas, and in the same breath, it is "Dear Drybone, lend me half-a-crown for a minute or two." Once in company with his Chinese friend, the Citizen of the World, they are asked twenty pounds for a seat to see the coronation. The Chinese sage inquires, whether a coronation will clothe, or feed, or fatten him. "Sir," replied the man, "you seem to be under a mistake; all you can bring away is the pleasure of having it to say, that you saw the coronation." "Blast me," cries Tibbs, "if that be all, there is no need of paying for that, since I am resolved to have that pleasure, whether I am there or not."

Beau Tibbs, then, is a character, and so is the "Man in

Black." Where will you find more originality? A most delightful compound is the "Man in Black;" a rarity not to be met with often; a true oddity, with the tongue of Timon, and the heart of Uncle Toby. He proclaims war against pauperism, yet he cannot say "no" to a beggar. He ridicules generosity, yet would he share with the poor whatever he possessed. He glories in having become a niggard, as he wishes to be thought, and thus describes his conversion. Having told how he quitted the folly of liberality, "I now," said he, "pursued a course of uninterrupted frugality, seldom wanted a dinner, and was consequently invited to twenty. I soon began to get the character of a saving hunks, that had money, and insensibly I grew into esteem. Neighbors have asked my advice in the disposal of their daughters, and I have always taken care not to give any. I have contracted a friendship with an alderman only by observing, that if we take a farthing from a thousand pounds, it will be a thousand pounds no longer. I have been invited to a pawnbroker's table by pretending to hate gravy, and am now actually on a treaty of marriage with a rich widow, for only having observed that bread was rising. If ever I am asked a question, whether I know it or not, instead of answering it, I only smile, and look wise. If a charity is proposed, I go about with the hat, but put nothing in myself. If a wretch solicits my pity, I observe that the world is filled with impostors, and take a certain method of not being deceived by never relieving."

As a dramatist, Goldsmith is amusing; and if to excite laughter be, as Johnson asserts it is, the chief end of comedy, Goldsmith attains it. His plots, however, are extravagant, and his personages are oddities rather than characters. Goldsmith's plays want the contrivance which belongs to highest art; but they have all those ingenious accidents which are suitable for stage effect. They are, in fact, deficient in that insight, which pertains only to great dramatic genius. *The Good-natured Man* is an agreeable satire on the follies of benevolence, and *She Stoops to Conquer*, a laughable burlesque on a very improbable mistake. Croaker, in the one, is an effective caricature on men of groaning and long faces; and Tony Lumpkin, in the other, is a broad, grinning stereotype of a foolish mother's fool. These two comedies comprise all Goldsmith's theatrical writings. Both of them abound in drollery and strong touches of nature; but they do not give the author an exalted position among dramatists, and they do not promise that he could have reached it.

In referring to Goldsmith as a poet, I have no intention to commit the impertinence of formal criticism. I have an easy and a pleasant work. I have nothing to defend, and nothing to refute. I have only to call up simple recollections, which are endeared to us all by the unanimous experience of a common pleasure. Who has not read *The Traveller*, and *The Deserted Village*, and *The Hermit*, and *Retaliation?* And who that has read them will forget, or not recall them, as among the sweetest melodies which his thoughts preserve? *The Traveller* has the most ambitious aim of Goldsmith's poetical compositions. The author, placed on a height of the Alps, muses and moralizes on the countries around him. His object, it appears, is to show the equality of happiness, which consists with diversities of circumstances and situations. The poem is, therefore, mainly didactic. Description and reflection are subservient to an ethical purpose, and this purpose is never left out of sight. The descriptive passages are all vivid, but some of them are imperfect. Italy, for instance, in its prominent aspects, is boldly sketched. We are transported to the midst of its mountains, woods, and temples; we are under its sunny skies, we are embosomed in its fruits and flowers, we breathe its fragrant air, and we are charmed by its matchless landscapes; but we miss the influence of its arts, and the solemn impression of its

former grandeur. We are made to survey a nation in degeneracy and decay; but we are not relieved by the glow of Raffael, or excited by the might of the Colliseum. ⟨. . .⟩

Goldsmith is one of those whom we cannot help liking, and whom we cannot criticise; yet he is one that should be praised with caution, if in our age there was much danger of his being imitated. We are too busy for meditative vagrancy; we are too practical for the delusions of scholarship; even with the felicitous genius of Goldsmith, the literary profession would now be an insecure basis for subsistence, and none at all for prodigality. Extent of competition, the rigor of criticism, the difficulty of acting on an immensely multiplied reading public, repress the efforts of vanity; yet, except in few instances, they do not compensate the efforts of power; the vain are driven to obscurity, but the powerful have little more than their fame. And though we possessed the abilities of Goldsmith, and were tempted to his follies, his life is before us for a memento, and his experience is sufficient for a warning. Yet is it agreeable to lay aside our prudence for a little, and enjoy with him, in fancy at least, the advantage of the hour; to participate in his thoughtless good nature, and to enter into his careless gaiety; to sit with him in some lonely Swiss glen; or to listen to his flute among the peasantry of France; or to hear him debate logical puzzles in monastic Latin; to share the pride of his new purple coat, which Johnson would not praise, and which Boswell could not admire. More grateful still, is the relief which we derive from the perusal of his works; for in these we have the beauty of his mind, and no shade upon its wisdom; the sweetness of humanity, and its dignity also.

We need the mental refreshment, which writers like Goldsmith afford. Our active and our thoughtful powers are all on the stretch; and such, unless it has appropriate relaxations, is not a state of nature or a state of health. From the troubles of business, which absorb the attention or exhaust it; from the acclivities of society, which exemplify, in the same degrees, the force of mechanism and the force of will; from the clamor of politics, from the asperity of religious discussions, we turn to philosophy and literature for less fatiguing or less disquieting interests. But our philosophy, when not dealing with matter, is one which, in seeking the limits of reason, carries it ever into the infinite and obscure; our literature is one which, in its genuine forms, has equal intensity of passion and intensity of expression; which, in its spurious forms, mistakes extravagance for the one, and bombast for the other. Our genuine literature is the production of natural causes, and has its peculiar excellence. But from the excitement of our present literature, whether genuine or spurious, it is a pleasant change to take up the tranquil pages of Goldsmith; to feel the sunny glow of his thoughts upon our hearts, and on our fancies the gentle music of his words. In laying down his writings, we are tempted to exclaim, "O that the author of *The Deserted Village* had written more poetry! O that the author of *The Vicar of Wakefield* had written more novels!"

EDWARD DOWDEN

"Oliver Goldsmith"

The English Poets, ed. Thomas Humphry Ward

1880, Volume 3, pp. 368–72

The poems of Goldsmith make but a small fragment of his work; they are, however, more finely wrought and of a costlier material than the rest. 'I cannot afford to court the draggle-tail Muses,' he said, 'they would let me starve.' And so he turned to the booksellers' task-work, bestowing on that task-work a grace which was all his own; and, the drudgery ended, he took his wages and was light of heart. But poetry belonged to his higher self, to his affections, to his imagination. Goldsmith could not have written *The Deserted Village* to the order of Griffiths or Newbery; and it is told—nor is the story incredible—that he went back with the note for one hundred pounds in his pocket, and insisted that his publisher should not ruin himself by paying 'five shillings a couplet.' The rustic maid Poetry whom he loved was not quite penniless; still Goldsmith felt that the attachment was imprudent, and she was none the less dear to his foolish heart on that account:

> Dear charming nymph, neglected and decried,
> My shame in crowds, my solitary pride.
> Thou source of all my bliss and all my woe,
> That found'st me poor at first, and keep'st me so.

His poems won for Goldsmith friendships and fame, yet he felt truly that his was not a poetic age. The keenest intellects and the most powerful imaginations of the time found their proper utterance in prose. The high tragedy of that period is *Clarissa*; the broadest and brightest study of the *comédie humaine* is *Tom Jones*. Johnson in his essays had dignified the minor morals of Addison, and breathed into them the spirit of a courageous melancholy. Burke by breadth of vision and largeness of character was transforming the political pamphlet from a thing of party to a thing for mankind. Hume had shown how the facts of history may be artfully disposed, and their ragged edges smoothed away, until a graceful narrative emerges from the confusion. Gibbon was already projecting the lines of his Roman road through the centuries. It was the age of prose. The poets themselves had turned critics, making but timid experiments in verse; the more exquisite their culture, the less was their poetic courage. One or two indeed might appear more robust, but by a well-instructed eye their force was seen to be but turbulence. As for the rest they handed their verses around in manuscript; then perhaps contributed them to a poetical miscellany; finally, collected them in a tiny volume, or a quarto pamphlet of ample margin.

Goldsmith, whose genius slumbered late, was in no hurry to be a poet, and he looked carefully to make sure of himself and of his way. With a happy instinct he discerned his own gift, and it was his virtue, amid all his wanderings, and with all his seeming recklessness, to be faithful to that gift. Should he apply his humour to base uses and follow in the steps of Churchill? Goldsmith affected no airs of dignity in what he wrote, and did not fear that word of reproach in his day, *low*; but his gentle heart, his kindly wisdom, made it impossible for him to follow Churchill. He did not covet the reputation of a literary bully; his was no loud contentious voice; if he hated anything, he hated the rage of party spirit. But might he not accept Gray as a master? Goldsmith has left on record his estimate of Gray, and the words express a qualified enthusiasm, a certain official admiration as critic. But in truth, to please him poetry should address the heart, and he felt cold towards the fastidious flights of *The Bard* and *The Progress of Poetry*. He ventured to hint to Gray the advice that Isocrates used to give his scholars, *study the people*. Pindar had been popular—Pan himself was once dancing to his melody. The seeming obscurity, the sudden transitions, the hazardous epithet of that mighty master had been caught by Gray; the directness, the life, the native energy of classical poetry he had not discovered. And Gray's imitators, what did they produce but 'tawdry things . . . in writing which the poet sits down without any plan, and heaps up splendid images without any selection'? Last, there

was the didactic essay or epistle in verse. Should Goldsmith become the successor of Akenside? Goldsmith highly esteemed the didactic poem; he looked on it as characteristic of England. But, at least, let it be written in our old rhymed couplet, not in pedantic blank-verse; and as for the pompous epithet, the licentious transposition, the unnatural construction, let these be reformed altogether. Why too should dulness be an essential of didactic poetry? Goldsmith could not endure its 'disgusting solemnity of manner'; he loved innocent gaiety, and found much wisdom in that agreeable trifling which often 'deceives us into instruction.'

With such views, and at a time of life when all his powers were ripe and mellow, Goldsmith published his *Traveller*. Some fragments, perhaps a first sketch of the poem, had been sent from Switzerland to his brother Henry in 1755. *The Traveller*, as we know it, is an attempt to unite the didactic with the descriptive poem. But Goldsmith does not begin with theory, and proceed to illustrate his theory by a series of pictures. He begins with a sigh for kindred and for home. The poem is personal; the reflections, except perhaps the closing ones, which came from Johnson, are such as naturally arose in his mind in the days of his wandering. It would have been easy to have thrown *The Traveller* into the form of an Essay on the Happiness of Nations, or *The Deserted Village* into that of an Epistle on the Dangers of Luxury, and then the wanderer sounding his flute beside the Loire might have risen to the stature of a philosophic spectator with a classical name; sweet Auburn might have appeared as minor term of a syllogism concerned with the abuse of wealth. Goldsmith chose a simpler method, more wholesome and sweet. He had actually smiled at sight of the old dames of the province in their quaint French caps leading out the little boys and girls to foot it while he piped; he had turned away disappointed from the Carinthian peasant's inhospitable door; he had breasted the keen air with the Alpine herdsman; he had lazily stared from the towing-path at the Dutchman squat on his brown canal-boat. Seeking neither wealth, nor advancement, nor toilful learning, unencumbered by possessions of his own, he had looked on all with a sympathetic eye, an open heart, an innocent delight in human gladness, a kindly smile at human frailty, a sigh and a tear for human woe; and from all he had gathered a store of gentle wisdom, of dear remembrance. He needed only to select from his recollections whatever was most full of charm, what was gayest, tenderest, most pleasantly coloured, and with these to mingle some natural thoughts, some natural feelings. Surely an easy thing; and yet none except Goldsmith had the secret how to do this, to unite such various elements into a delightful whole,—description, reflection, mirth, sadness, memory and love. No one like Goldsmith could pass so tranquilly from grave to gay, still preserving the delicate harmony of tone. No one like Goldsmith knew how to be at once natural and exquisite, innocent and wise, a man and still a child.

The naturalness and ease of his poetry are those of an accomplished craftsman. His verse, which flows towards the close of the period with such a gentle yet steady advance, is not less elaborated than that of Pope, and Goldsmith conceived his verse more in paragraphs than in couplets. His subdued brilliancy was perhaps harder to attain than the point and polish of *The Rape of the Lock*. His artless words were, each one, delicately chosen; his simple constructions were studiously sought. Cooke, Goldsmith's neighbour in the Temple, speaks of the Doctor's slowness in writing poetry 'not from tardiness of fancy, but from the time he took in pointing the sentiment, and polishing the versification.' In writing *The Deserted Village* the Doctor, as Cooke again tells us, 'first sketched a part of his design in prose, in which he threw out his ideas as they occurred to him; he then sat down carefully to versify them, correct them, and add such other ideas as he thought better fitted to the subject; and if sometimes he would exceed his prose design by writing several verses impromptu, these he would take singular pains afterwards to revise, lest they should be found unconnected with his main design.' When Cooke entered the Doctor's chamber one morning Goldsmith with some elation read aloud to him the ten lines beginning

> Dear lovely bowers of innocence and ease,
> Seats of my youth, when every sport could please.

'Come, let me tell you this is no bad morning's work,' he said; 'and now, my dear boy, if you are not better engaged, I should be glad to enjoy a Shoemaker's Holiday with you.'

Whether *The Traveller* or *The Deserted Village* be the more admirable poem, whether Auburn be an English village or the Irish Lissoy, or both in one, whether Goldsmith's political economy be solid or sentimental, it is perhaps not necessary once more to discuss. Perhaps Auburn bordered on Shakespeare's Forest of Arden, and the doctrines concerning agricultural and commercial prosperity were suited to that neighbourhood. It would be pleasant to hear Jaques and Touchstone discuss them, taking opposite sides. Certainly Auburn is English, but certainly too Paddy Byrne kept school there, and Uncle Contarine or Henry Goldsmith occupied the rectory. In whatever shire or county situated, we know Auburn better than any other village; its sweet confusion of rural sounds is in our ears; we have seen its children hanging on the venerable preacher's gown; we have played truant from the stern schoolmaster, and trembled in his presence; we know the clicking of the ale-house clock, and have felt the old, plain pathos of the woodman's ballad! And we grieve that Auburn is departed. It may be a weak retreat into the age of sentiment and simplicity and Rousseau; perhaps we ought rather exult in the triumphs of modern civilisation and the progress of modern science. Still the flowers of an old garden-croft smell sweet, and the hawthorn bush is white under which lovers whisper.

The ballad of 'Edwin and Angelina', 'The Haunch of Venison', and *Retaliation* mark the extremes of Goldsmith's somewhat limited range in verse. Any reader of the ballad who pleases may make a wry face, along with Kenrick of Grub Street, at the insipidity of Dr. Goldsmith's negus, and may seek elsewhere some livelier liquor. We feel differently, for we have heard this ballad in the open air from Mr. Burchell's manly throat, while Sophia in her new ribbons languished in the hay. To us, the love-lorn stranger is an eighteenth-century cousin—and so perhaps a little modish—of Rosalind and Viola. Those earlier disguisers bore themselves no doubt more gallantly, with more of saucy archness; but none was more sweetly discovered than Goldsmith's pretty pilgrim by her mantling blush, and bashful glance, and rising breast. In 'The Haunch of Venison' we have a miniature farce, and Goldsmith good-naturedly includes himself among the persons to be laughed at. *Retaliation* is the most mischievous, and the most playful, the friendliest and the faithfulest of satires. How much better we know Garrick because Goldsmith has shown him to us in his acting off the stage! And do we as often think of Reynolds in any attitude as in that of smiling non-listener to the critical coxcombs

> When they talked of their Raphaels, Correggios and
>   stuff,
> He shifted his trumpet and only took snuff.

Would that portraits of Johnson and Boswell had been added!

AUSTIN DOBSON
"The Citizen of the World"
Eighteenth Century Vignettes: First Series
1892

W hat was it that suggested to Goldsmith *The Citizen of the World?* Biographers and commentators have pointed to more than one plausible model,—the *Lettres Persanes* of Montesquieu, the *Lettres d'une Péruvienne* of Madame de Graffigny, the *Lettres Chinoises* of the Marquis d'Argens, the 'Asiatic' of Voltaire's *Lettres Philosophiques*. But it is sometimes wise, especially in such hand-to-mouth work as journalism, which was all Goldsmith at first intended, to seek for origins in the immediate neighbourhood rather than in remoter places. In 1757 Horace Walpole published anonymously, in pamphlet form, a clever little squib upon Admiral Byng's trial in particular and English inconstancy in general, which he entitled A *Letter from Xo Ho, a Chinese Philosopher at London, to his friend Lien Chi, at Peking*. This was briefly noticed in the May issue of the *Monthly Review*, where Goldsmith was then acting as scribbler-general to Griffiths, the proprietor of the magazine (his reviews of Home's *Douglas* and of Burke's *Sublime and Beautiful* appeared in the same number), and it was described as in Montesquieu's manner. A year later Goldsmith is writing mysteriously to his friend Bob Bryanton, of Ballymulvey, in Ireland, about a 'Chinese whom he shall soon make talk like an Englishman;' and when at last his *Chinese Letters*, as they were called at first, begin to appear in Newbery's *Public Ledger*, he takes for the name of his Oriental, Lien Chi Altangi, one of Walpole's imaginary correspondents having been Lien Chi. This chain of association, if slight, is strong enough to justify some connection. The fundamental idea, no doubt, was far older than either Walpole or Goldsmith; but it is not too much to suppose that Walpole's *jeu d'esprit* supplied just that opportune suggestion which produced the remarkable and now too-much-neglected series of letters afterwards reprinted under the general title of *The Citizen of the World*.

'The metaphors and allusions,' says Goldsmith in one of those admirable prefaces of which he possessed the secret, 'are all drawn from the East;' and in another place he tells us that a certain apostrophe is wholly translated from Ambulaaohamed, a real (or fictitious) Arabian poet. To these ingenuities he no doubt attached the exaggerated importance habitually assigned to work which has cost its writer pains. But it is not the adroitness of his adaptations from Le Comte and Du Halde that most detains us now. The purely Oriental part of the work—although it includes the amusing story (an 'Ephesian Matron' *à la Chinoise*) of the widow who, in her haste to marry again, fans her late husband's grave to dry it quicker, and the apologue of Prince Bonbennin and the White Mouse—is practically dead wood. It is Goldsmith under the transparent disguise of Lien Chi—Goldsmith commenting, after the manner of Addison and Steele, upon Georgian England, that attracts and interests the modern reader. His Chinese Philosopher might well have wondered at the lazy puddle moving muddily along the ill kept London streets, at the large feet and white teeth of the women, at the unwieldy signs with their nondescript devices, at the unaccountable fashion of lying-in-state; but it is Goldsmith, and Goldsmith only, who could have imagined the admirable humour of the dialogue on liberty between a prisoner (through his grating), a porter pausing from his burden to denounce slavery and the French, and a soldier who, with a tremendous oath, advocates, above all, the importance of religion. It is Goldsmith again—the Goldsmith of Green-Arbour Court and Griffiths' back-parlour—who draws from a harder experience than could have been possible to Lien Chi, the satiric picture of the so-called republic of letters which forms his twentieth epistle. 'Each looks upon his fellow as a rival, not an assistant in the same pursuit. They calumniate, they injure, they despise, they ridicule each other: if one man writes a book that pleases, others shall write books to show that he might have given still greater pleasure, or should not have pleased. If one happens to hit on something new, there are numbers ready to assure the public that all this was no novelty to them or the learned; that Cardanus or Brunus, or some other author too dull to be generally read, had anticipated the discovery. Thus, instead of uniting like the members of a commonwealth, they are divided into almost as many factions as there are men; and their jarring constitution, instead of being styled a republic of letters, should be entitled, an anarchy of literature.' One rubs one's eyes as one reads; one asks oneself under one's breath if it is of our day that the satirist is speaking. No; it is of the reign of the second of the Georges, before Grub Street was turned into Milton Street.

Literature, in its different aspects, plays not a small part in the lucubrations of Lien Chi. Two of the best letters are devoted to a whimsical description of the vagaries of some of its humbler professors, who hold a Saturday Club at the 'Broom' at Islington; others treat of the decay of poetry; of novels, and *Tristram Shandy* in particular; of the necessity of intrigue or riches as a means to success. Nor are Art and the Drama neglected. The virtuoso, who afforded such a fund of amusement to Fielding and Smollett, receives his full share of attention; and in the papers upon acting and actors, Goldsmith once more displays that critical common-sense which he had shown so conspicuously in *The Bee*. Travellers and their trivialities are freely ridiculed; there are papers on Newmarket, on the Marriage Act, on the coronation, on the courts of justice; on quacks, gaming, paint, mourning, and mad dogs. There is a letter on the irreverent behaviour of the congregation in St. Paul's; there is another on the iniquity of making shows of public monuments. Now and then a more serious note is touched, as when the author is stirred to unwonted gravity by the savage penal code of his day, which, 'cementing the laws with blood,' closed every avenue with a gibbet, and against which Johnson too lifted his sonorous voice.

> Scarce can our fields, such crowds at Tyburn die,
> With hemp the gallows and the fleet supply,—

he sang in *London*, anticipating his later utterances in *The Rambler*. Goldsmith, on the other hand, crystallized in his verse the raw material of which he made his Chinese philosopher the mouthpiece. Several of the best known passages of his two longest poems have their first form in the prose of Lien Chi. Indeed, one actual line of *The Traveller*, 'A land of tyrants, and a den of slaves,' is simply a textual quotation from *The Citizen of the World*.

But what in the Chinese letters is even more remarkable than their clever raillery of social incongruities and abuses, is their occasional indication of the author's innate but hitherto undisclosed gift for the delineation of humorous character. Up to this time he had exhibited no particular tendency in this direction. The little sketches of Jack Spindle and 'my cousin Hannah,' in *The Bee*, go no farther than the corresponding personifications of particular qualities in the *Spectator* and *Tatler*; and they are not of the kind which, to employ a French figure, 'enter the skin' of the personality presented. But in the case of the eccentric philanthropist of *The Citizen of the World*,

whom he christens the 'Man in Black,' he comes nearer to such a definite embodiment as Addison's 'Will Wimble.' The 'Man in Black' is evidently a combination of some of those Goldsmith family traits which were afterwards so successfully recalled in Dr. Primrose, Mr. Hardcastle, and the clergyman of *The Deserted Village*. The contrast between his credulous charity and his expressed distrust of human nature, between his simulated harshness and his real amiability, constitutes a type which has since been often used successfully in English literature; it is clear, too, that in the account of his life he borrows both from his author and his author's father. When he speaks of his unwillingness to take orders, of his dislike to wear a long wig when he preferred a short one, or a black coat when he dressed in brown, he is only giving expression to that imcompatibility of temper which led to Goldsmith's rejection for ordination by the Bishop of Elphin; while in his picture of his father's house, with its simple, kindly prodigality, its little group of grateful parasites who laugh, like Mr. Hardcastle's servants, at the host's old jokes, and the careless paternal benevolence which makes the children 'mere machines of pity,' 'instructed in the art of giving away thousands before they were taught the more necessary qualifications of getting a farthing,' one recognizes the environment of that emphatically Irish household on the road from Ballymahon to Athlone, in which Goldsmith's own boyhood had been spent.

Excellent as he is, however, the 'Man in Black,' with his grudging generosity and his 'reluctant goodness,' is surpassed in completeness of characterization by the more finished portrait of Beau Tibbs. The poor little pinched pretender to fashion, with his tarnished finery and his reed-voiced, simpering helpmate,—with his coffee-house cackle of my Lord Mudler and the Duchess of Piccadilly, and his magnificent promises of turbot and ortolan, which issue pitifully in postponed ox-check and bitter beer,—approaches the dimensions of a masterpiece. Charles Lamb, one would think, must have rejoiced over the reckless assurance which expatiates on the charming view of the Thames from the garret of a back-street in the suburbs, which glorifies the 'paltry, unframed pictures' on its walls into essays in the manner of the celebrated Grisoni, and transforms a surly Scotch bag-of-all-work into an old and privileged family-servant,—the gift 'of a friend of mine, a Parliament man from the Highlands.' Nor are there many pages in Dickens more perennially humorous than the scene in which the 'Man in Black,' his *inamorata* the pawnbroker's widow, and Mr. and Mrs. Tibbs, all make a party to the picturesque old Vauxhall Gardens of Jonathan Tyers. The inimitable sparring which ensues between the second-hand gentility of the beau's lady and the moneyed vulgarity of the tradesman's relict, their different and wholly irreconcilable views of the entertainment, and the tragic termination of the whole, by which the widow is balked of 'the waterworks' because good manners constrain her to sit out the wire-drawn *roulades* and quavers or Mrs. Tibbs—these are things which age cannot wither nor custom stale. If Goldsmith had written nothing but this miniature trilogy or Beau Tibbs,—if Dr. Primrose were uninvented and Tony Lumpkin non-existent,—he would still have earned a perpetual place among English humourists.

Something of this, undoubtedly, he owed to the fortunate instinct which dictated his choice of his material. The forerunner of Dickens,—the disciple, although he knew it not, of Fielding,—he makes his capital by his disregard of the reigning models of his time. Declining to select his characters from the fashionable abstractions of Sentimental Comedy and the mechanical puppets of conventional High Life, he turns aside to the moving, various, many-coloured middle-classes, from whose ranks originality has not yet been banished, or nature cast out. Of these he had knowledge and experience; of those he had seen but little. Upon the other walk, his labours might have been as forgotten as the 'Henry' of Richard Cumberland or the 'Henrietta' of Mrs. Charlotte Lenox. But he took his own line; and in consequence, Beau Tibbs and the pawnbroker's widow (with her rings and her green damask) are as much alive to-day as Partridge or Mrs. Nickleby.

HENRY JAMES
"Introduction"
The Vicar of Wakefield
1900

It is a sign of the wonderful fortune of *The Vicar of Wakefield* that the properest occasions for speaking of it continue to present themselves. Everything has been said about it, and said again and again, but the book has long since diffused an indulgence that extends even to commentators. In the degree of its fortune, indeed, it seems almost single of its kind. Stretch the indulgence as we may, Goldsmith's story still fails, somehow, on its face, to account for its great position and its remarkable career. Read as one of the masterpieces by a person not acquainted with our literature, it might easily give an impression that this literature is not immense. It has been reproduced, at all events, in a thousand editions, and the end is not yet. All the arts of book-making and of editing, all the graces of typography and of illustration, have been lavished upon its text. Painters, playwrights, and musicians have again and again drawn upon it, and there is not a happy turn in it, not a facetious figure nor a vivid image, that has not become familiar and famous. We point our phrases with its good things, and the fact that everybody knows them seems only to make them better.

If, therefore, I speak of something disproportionate in the case, between effect and cause, between so many honors and the object they are heaped upon, it is to couple the matter with an instant confession. If I have just re-read the book, I have re-read it after years, and the length of the interval has perhaps something to do with the force of the conviction brought freshly home to me—the idea that a literary production may have its luck as well as its merit, and an author his star as well as his genius. We are tempted to say of *The Vicar of Wakefield* that it has been happy in the manner in which a happy man is happy—a man, say, who has married an angel or been appointed to a sinecure. These various fates of books are to some extent a mystery and a riddle; but what is most striking in the fortune of Goldsmith's story is that, though we fail to explain it completely, we grudge it perhaps less than in any other case. The thing has succeeded by its incomparable amenity. That is a quality by itself, and *The Vicar* gives us the best chance we shall meet to catch this particular influence in the very fact. It has operated here as almost never—for it has operated almost singly—to produce a classic; and we say much in recognizing that under its charm we really resist the irritation of having to define that character. It makes us wonder once more what a classic consists of, and offers us abundant occasion for the study of the question, which it presents in conditions singularly simple and undisturbed.

What we most seem to gather, in the light of this truth, is that if a book have amenity it may, at a stretch, have scarcely anything else. It would not be difficult, on some such ground,

I think, to go into the question of how little else, really, *The Vicar* has. I have felt its natural note, on this renewal, as much as ever, but, one by one and page after page, I have missed other matters. Nothing, perhaps, could be, critically, more interesting than to see them successively go and still leave the soft residuum that keeps the work green. It brings us back, of course, to the old, old miracle of style, and puts us in danger of relapsing again into the new, new heresy that style is everything; only to wake up, however, with the shock of the sense that that way madness lies, that *a priori* such a doctrine is fatal. And yet, as our masterpiece stands, we feel that, on other counts, it is really the infancy of art. A mature reader may well be stupefied at some of the claims that have been made for it in respect of skill of portraiture and liveliness of presentation. The first hundred pages—the first half of the first volume of the original edition—contain nearly all the happiest strokes. These, therefore, are comprised in but a quarter of the whole, and I suspect, moreover, that if we shoud reckon them up—I mean the felicities that have become familiar and famous—they would be found to consist of no great number: of the blue bed and the brown, of Moses and his spectacles, of the Flamboroughs and their oranges, of the family piece by the 'limner,'—the prettiest page of all,—of Shakspere and the musical glasses, of Jernigan and the garters, of Mr. Burchell and his 'Fudge.'

Add to the above the few comparatively sharp little lights in the image of Mrs. Primrose, and what we are left to fall back upon is mere lovability. As a story, as we say nowadays, I am so unconscious of anything vivid in the several figures that I can only be astonished at the claim for difference and contrast in Olivia and Sophia. Such results are easily produced, surely, if the claim is just. The young rake, the base seducer, has so little dramatic substance that we almost resent, on behalf of the lovely Olivia, and indeed on behalf of the whole amiable family, that so much ravage should be represented as wrought by so immaterial a presence. The young man never sounds, never looks at us; and his kinsman, the virtuous Burchell, keeps him nebulous company. The thing goes to pieces—so far as it has been held together at all—from the moment little Dick comes in with the cry that his sister has gone. We are made, in a manner, to see the scene before the child's entrance—it gives us the climax of what is vivid in the first volume; but what immediately ensues illustrates the faintness of the author's touch in any business of emotion or action. His pathos and his tragedy fall, throughout, much below his humor, and the second half of the tale, dropping altogether, becomes almost infantine in its awkwardness, its funny coincidences, and big stitches of white thread.

No one would say as much as this, I hasten to add, and mean it as a reproach. Criticism, I think, does not get near the thing at all, for it only goes so far as to suggest that if it *were* to criticize—In fact, it never pretends to that, for it feels that we are never really troubled, and that to do so would spoil one of the most delicate of all artistic oddities. *The Vicar* throws itself upon our sensibility with a slenderness of means that suggests—for this very slimness—some angular, archaic nudity. I spoke above of some passages as 'faint,' and the privilege of the whole thing is just to be delightfully so. This faintness, like the faded tone of an old sampler, an old spinet, the ink of an old letter, is of the positive essence of the charm and spell, so that here and there the least little lights gleam in it with effect: we just catch the white stocking of Moses and the brown of the hair that his sisters have tied with ribbon; we catch, in the pleasant paleness, the deep hue of the Flamborough oranges. In short, we make to our own mind, all the while, a plea for the peculiar grace, and feel that, in the particulars, it loses nothing through the want of art. One admits the particulars with the sense that, as regards the place the thing has taken, it remains, by a strange little law of its own, quite undamaged—simply stands there smiling with impunity.

It is the spoiled child of our literature. We cling to it as to our most precious example that we, too, in prose, have achieved the last amiability. Thus it is that the book converts everything it contains into a happy case of exemption and fascination—a case of imperturbable and inscrutable classicism. It is a question of tone. The tone is exquisite, and that's the end of it. It takes us through all the little gaps and slips, through all the artless looseness of the Vicar's disasters and rescues, through his confused and unconvincing captivity and his wonderful accidents and recognitions. It makes these things amusing, makes them most human even when—for there is no other way of putting it—they are most absurd. I will not say it makes them live, for I think it scarce does that at all, but leaves them to linger on as spiced, dead rose-leaves in a bowl, inanimate, fragrant, intensely present. There is not a small drollery at the end that does not work into the very texture that takes us: the punishment of the wicked seducer by being cut down to a single footman; the retinue of so many of these who attest, at the final hour, the real philanthropy of Sir William; the perpetual food that makes its appearance as the climax of everything; the supper of two well-dressed dishes that dissipates the gloom of the prison; the delightful forty pounds distributed among the captives, and the still more delightful 'coarser provisions' scattered among the populace.

If the tone is the great thing, this comes, doubtless, to saying that the Vicar himself is, and that the book has flourished through having so much of him. It is he who is the success of his story; he is always kept true, is what we call to-day 'sustained,' without becoming pompous or hollow. The especial beauty of this is surely that it contains something of the very soul of Goldsmith. It is the most natural imagination of the unspotted that any production, perhaps, offers, and

the exhibition of the man himself—by which I mean of the author—combines with his instinctive taste to make the classicism for which we praise him. These two things, the frankness of his sweetness and the beautiful ease of his speech, melt together—with no other aid, as I have hinted, worth mentioning—to form his style. I am afraid I cannot go further than this in the way of speculation as to how a classic is grown. In the open air is perhaps the most we can say. Goldsmith's style is the flower of what I have called his amenity, and his amenity the making of that independence of almost everything by which *The Vicar* has triumphed. The books that live, apparently, are very personal, though there are many defunct, of course, even with that qualification.

The author of this one never, at any rate, lets go our hand; and we, on our side, keep hold with a kind of sense, which is one of the most touching things our literature gives us, of all that, by doing so, we make up to him for. It helps us to look with a certain steadiness on his battered and miserable life. It helps us even to evoke with a certain joy the free, incurable Irish play of fancy and of character that, in the most English of all English ages and circles, drew down on him so much ridicule. There was scarce a difficulty, a disappointment, an humiliation, or a bitterness of which he had not intimate and repeated knowledge; and yet the heavy heart that went through all this overflows in the little book as optimism of the purest water—as good humor, as good taste, and as a drollery that, after all, has oftener its point than its innocence. For these reasons, it would seem, fortune has singled him out, distinguished him with extraordinary favor, decreed that he should be forever known to us in an exceptionally human way. Never was such a revenge against the superior and the patronizing. The spirit still speaks to us of all that was taken to produce it, all the privation and pain and abasement, all the ugliness of circumstance and air; so we piously pluck it and keep it, press it between the leaves of the English prose that we show and boast of, treat it as a rare, fine flower that has sprouted in a rough, hard soil.

DAVID HUME

DAVID HUME

1711–1776

David Hume was born at Edinburgh on May 7, 1711. After attending Edinburgh University and working for several months at a merchant's office in Bristol, Hume in 1734 left for France, where he remained until 1737. While in France he composed his *Treatise of Human Nature*; to Hume's disappointment, it was largely ignored after its publication in 1738–40. This first book, like all the philosophical works to follow, was a systematic attempt to develop the empiricism of Locke and Berkeley to its furthest logical conclusion.

Hume's second book, his *Essays, Moral and Political*, appeared in 1741–42. Encouraged by rather more favorable reaction, Hume applied in 1744 for a chair in philosophy at Edinburgh University, but was rejected. Between 1746 and 1749 he was a secretary to General St. Clair on a military expedition to Brittany and a diplomatic mission to Vienna and Turin. Meanwhile, in 1748, his revision of the first part of the *Treatise* appeared under the title *Philosophical Essays concerning Human Understanding*; in 1751 a second edition was published as *An Enquiry concerning Human Understanding*. *An Enquiry concerning the Principles of Morals*, essentially a re-working of the third part of the *Treatise*, also appeared in 1751.

In 1752 Hume at last established a considerable reputation with the publication of his *Political Discourses*. He wrote no further important philosophical works aside from the *Four Dissertations* (1757) and the *Dialogues concerning Natural Religion*, published posthumously in 1759 and probably written in the 1750s. From 1752 to 1757 Hume was librarian for the Faculty of Advocates in Edinburgh, where access to a large book collection encouraged him to begin work on his last major project, a *History of Great Britain*, which appeared in four volumes between 1754 and 1762.

In 1763 Hume returned to France as private secretary to Lord Hertford, British ambassador to Paris. In Paris, where he was for a time *chargé d'affaires*, Hume came to know the French *philosophes* associated with the *Encyclopedia*, and on returning to England in 1766 he brought back with him Jean Jacques Rousseau, who soon, however, began unjustly to suspect Hume of plotting against him. Between 1767 and 1768 Hume briefly served as an Under-secretary of State; in 1769 he retired permanently and returned to Edinburgh, where he died on August 25, 1776.

Personal

Ever since I was acquainted with your works, your talents as a writer have, notwithstanding some differences in abstract principles, extorted from me the highest veneration. But I could scarce have thought that, in spite of differences of a more interesting nature, even such as regard morals and religion, you could ever force me to love and honour you as a man. —DR. CAMPBELL, Letter to David Hume (June 25, 1762)

With respect to myself, I am sorry I cannot have the pleasure of taking leave of you in person, before I go into perpetual exile. I sincerely wish you all health and happiness. In whatever part of the earth it may be my fate to reside, I shall always remember with pleasure, and recapitulate with pride, the friendly intercourse I have maintained with one of the best men, and undoubtedly the best writer of the age.—TOBIAS SMOLLETT, Letter to David Hume (Aug. 31, 1768)

Yesterday about 4 o'clock afternoon Mr Hume expired. The immediate approach of his Death became evident in the night between Thursday and Friday when the looseness became very excessive and was attended with vomiting now and then. This continued the greater part of the time that remained and soon weakened him so much that he could no longer rise out of his bed. He continued to the last perfectly sensible and free from much pain or feelings of distress. He never dropped the smallest expression of impatience but when he had occasion to speak to the people about him always did it with affection and tenderness. I thought it improper to write to bring you over, especially as I heard that he had dictated a letter to you on Thursday or wednesday desiring you not to come. When he became very weak it cost him an effort to speak and he died in such a happy composure of mind that nothing could have made it better.—JOSEPH BLACK, Letter to Adam Smith (Aug. 26, 1776)

Thus died out most excellent, and never to be forgotten friend; concerning whose philosophical opinions men will, no doubt, judge variously, every one approving or condemning them, according as they happen to coincide or disagree with his own; but concerning whose character and conduct there can scarce be a difference of opinion. His temper, indeed, seemed to be more happily balanced, if I may be allowed such an expression, than that perhaps of any other man I have ever known. Even in the lowest state of his fortune, his great and necessary frugality never hindered him from exercising, upon proper occasions, acts both of charity and generosity. It was a frugality founded, not upon avarice, but upon the love of independency. The extreme gentleness of his nature never weakened either the firmness of his mind, or the steadiness of his resolutions. His constant pleasantry was the genuine effusion of good-nature and good-humour, tempered with delicacy and modesty, and without even the slightest tincture of malignity, so frequently the disagreeable source of what is called wit in other men. It never was the meaning of his raillery to mortify; and therefore, far from offending, it seldom failed to please and delight, even those who were the objects of it. To his friends, who were frequently the objects of it, there was not perhaps any one of all his great and amiable qualities, which contributed more to endear his conversation. And that gaiety of temper, so agreeable in society, but which is so often accompanied with frivolous and superficial qualities, was in him certainly attended with the most severe application, the most extensive learning, the greatest depth of thought, and a capacity in every respect the most comprehensive. Upon the whole, I have always considered him, both in his lifetime and since his death, as approaching as nearly to the idea of a perfectly wise and virtuous man, as perhaps the nature of human frailty will permit.—ADAM SMITH, Letter to William Strahan (Nov. 9, 1776)

⟨Johnson:⟩ "And as to Hume—a man who has so much conceit as to tell all mankind that they have been bubbled for ages and he is the wise man who sees better than they, a man who has so little scrupulosity as to venture to oppose those principles which have been thought necessary to human happiness—is he to be surprised if another man comes and laughs at him? If he is the great man he thinks himself, all this cannot hurt him; it is like throwing peas against a rock." He added *"something much too rough,"* both as to Mr. Hume's head and heart, which I suppress. Violence is, in my opinion, not suitable to the Christian cause. Besides, I always lived on good terms with Mr. Hume, though I have frankly told him I was not clear that it was right in me to keep company with him. "But," said I, "how much better are you than your books!" He was cheerful, obliging, and instructive; he was charitable to the poor; and many an agreeable hour have I passed with him. I have preserved some entertaining and interesting memoirs of him, particularly when he knew himself to be dying, which I may some time or other communicate to the world. I shall not, however, extol him so very highly as Dr. Adam Smith does, who says in a letter to Mr. Strahan the printer (not a confidential letter to his friend, but a letter which is published with all formality), "Upon the whole, I have always considered him, both in his lifetime and since his death, as approaching as nearly to the idea of a perfectly wise and virtuous man as perhaps the nature of human frailty will permit." Let Dr. Smith consider: was not Mr. Hume blessed with good health, good spirits, good friends, a competent and increasing fortune? And had he not also a perpetual feast of fame? But, as a learned friend has observed to me, "What trials did he undergo to prove the perfection of his virtue? Did he ever experience any great instance of adversity?" When I read this sentence, delivered by my old Professor of Moral Philosophy, I could not help exclaiming with the Psalmist, "Surely I have now more understanding than my teachers!"—JAMES BOSWELL, *Journal of a Tour to the Hebrides,* 1785

Mr. Burke told me he was well acquainted with David Hume, and that he was a very easy, pleasant, unaffected man, till he went to Paris as secretary to Lord Hertford. There the attention paid him by the French *belles savants* had the effect of making him somewhat of a literary coxcomb.—EDMOND MALONE, "Maloniana" (1787), cited in Sir James Prior, *Life of Edmond Malone,* 1860, p. 368

At this Time ⟨1753⟩ David Hume was Living in Edin!. and composing his *History of Great Brittain.* He was a Man of Great Knowledge and of a Social and Benevolent Temper, and truly the Best Natur'd Man in the World. He was Branded with the Title of Atheist, on account of the many attacks on Reveald Religion, that is to be found in his Philosophical Works, and in many Places of his History. The Last of which are still more objectionable than the First, which a friendly Critick might Call only Sceptical. Apropos of this, when M.ʳ Rob!. Adam the celebrated architect and his Brother Liv'd in Ed!. with their Mother, an aunt of D.ʳ Robertson, and a very respectable woman, she said to her Son, I shall be glad to see any of your

Companions to Dinner, But I hope you will never bring the Atheist here to Disturb my Peace. But Robert soon fell on a Method to reconcile her to him, for he introduc'd him under another Name, or Conceal'd it carefully from her. When the Company parted she said to her Son, I must confess that you bring very agreeable Companions about you, But the Large Jolly Man who sate next me is the most agreable of them all. This was the very Atheist (said he) Mother that you was so much affraid of. Well says she, you may bring him here as much as you please, for he's the most agreable Facetious Man I ever met with. This was truly the case with him, for tho' he had much Learning and a Fine Taste, and was professedly a Sceptick, tho' by no means an Atheist, he had the Greatest Simplicity of Mind and Manners with the utmost Facility and Benevolence of Temper of any Man I ever knew. His Conversation was truly Irresistable, For while it was enlighten'd it was naive almost to puerility. At this period when he first Liv'd in Edin!. and was writing his *History of England,* his circumstances were narrow, and he accepted the office of Librarian to the Faculty of Advocates, worth £40—p.ʳ ann. But it was not for the Sallary, that he accepted this Employment; but that he might have Easy access to the Books in that Celebrated Library, for to my Certain Knowledge he gave every farthing of it to Family's in Distress. Of a piece with this temper was his Curiosity and Credulity, which were without Bounds. A Specimen of which shall be afterwards Given, when I come down to Militia and the Poker. His Oeconymy was strict, as he lov'd independency, and yet he was able at that time to Give Suppers to his Friends in his small lodging in the Cannongate. He took much to the Company of the younger Clergy, not from a wish to bring them over to his Opinions, for he never attempted to overturn any Mans principles, but they best understood his Notions, and could furnish him with Literary Conversation. Robertson, and John Home and Bannatyne and I liv'd all in the Country, and came only periodically to the Town; Blair and Jardine both liv'd in it—and Supper being the only Fashionable meal at that time, we Din'd where we best could, and by Cadies assembled our Friends to meet us in a Tavern by nine aclock—and a Fine time it was when we could Collect David Hume and Adam Smith, and Adam Ferguson, and L.ᵈ Elibank and D.ʳ Blair and Jardine on an Hours warning. I Remember one Night, that Dav. Hume who having din'd abroad came Rather late to us, and Directly pull'd a large Key from his Pocket which he Laid on the Table—This he said was Given him by his maid Peggy, (much more Like a Man than a Woman) That she might not sit up for him, for she said, When the Honest Fellows came in from the Country, he never Return'd home till after one aclock. This Intimacy of the Young Clergy with David Hume Enrag'd the Zealots on the Opposite Side, who little knew how Impossible it was for him, had he been willing, to Shake their Principles.

As M.ʳ Hume's Circumstances Improv'd, he Enlarg'd his Mode of Living and instead of the Roosted Hen, and Minc'd Collops, and a Bottle of Punch, he Gave both Elegant Dinners and Suppers, and the Best Claret. And which was best of all, he furnish'd the Entertainment, with the most Instructive and pleasing Conversation, for he assembled whomsoever were most knowing and agreable, among either the Laity or Clergy. This he always Did, but still more unsparingly, when he became what he Call'd Rich. For Innocent Mirth and Agreable Raillery, I never knew his Match—Jardine who sometimes bore Hard upon him, for he had much Drollery and Wit tho' but little Learning, never could overturn his Temper. L.ᵈ Elibank Resembled David in his Talent for Collecting agreable Companies together, and had a House in Town for Several Winters, Chiefly for that Purpose. —ALEXANDER CARLYLE, *Anecdotes and Characters of the Times*, 1800–05

General

Let David Hume, from the remotest north,
In see-saw sceptic scruples hint his worth;
David, who there supinely deigns to lye
The fattest hog of Epicurus' sty;
Tho' drunk with Gallic wine, and Gallic praise,
David shall bless Old England's halcyon days.
—WILLIAM MASON, "An Heroic Epistle to Sir
William Chambers, Knight," 1773

The conversation now turned upon Mr. David Hume's style. JOHNSON. 'Why, Sir, his style is not English; the structure of his sentences is French. Now the French structure and the English structure may, in the nature of things, be equally good. But if you allow that the English language is established, he is wrong. My name might originally have been Nicholson, as well as Johnson; but were you to call me Nicholson now, you would call me very absurdly.'—JAMES BOSWELL, *Life of Johnson*, 1791

Next comes the Scotch Goliath, David Hume; but where is the accomplished stripling who can cut off his most metaphysical head? Who is he that can stand up before him & prove the existence of the Universe, & of its Founder? He hath an adroiter wit than all his forefathers in philosophy if he will confound this Uncircumcised. The long & dull procession of Reasoners that have followed since, have challenged the awful shade to duel, & struck the air with their puissant arguments. But as each new comer blazons 'Mr Hume's objections' on his pages, it is plain they are not satisfied the victory is gained. Now though every one is daily referred to his own feelings as a triumphant confutation of the glozed lies of this Deciever, yet, it assuredly would make us feel safer & prouder, to have our victorious answer set down in impregnable propositions. —RALPH WALDO EMERSON, Letter to Mary Moody Emerson (Oct. 16, 1823)

Samuel Johnson and David Hume, as was observed, were children nearly of the same year: through life they were spectators of the same Life-movement; often inhabitants of the same city. Greater contrast, in all things, between two great men, could not be. Hume, well-born, competently provided for, whole in body and mind, of his own determination forces a way into Literature: Johnson, poor, moonstruck, diseased, forlorn, is forced into it 'with the bayonet of necessity at his back.' And what a part did they severally play there! As Johnson became the father of all succeeding Tories; so was Hume the father of all succeeding Whigs, for his own Jacobitism was but an accident, as worthy to be named Prejudice as any of Johnson's. Again, if Johnson's culture was exclusively English; Hume's, in Scotland, became European;—for which reason too we find his influence spread deeply over all quarters of Europe, traceable deeply in all speculation, French, German, as well as domestic; while Johnson's name, out of England, is hardly anywhere to be met with. In spiritual stature they are almost equal; both great, among the greatest: yet how unlike in likeness! Hume has the widest, methodising, comprehensive eye; Johnson the keenest for perspicacity and minute detail: so had, perhaps chiefly, their education ordered it. Neither of the two rose into Poetry; yet both to some approximation thereof: Hume to something of an Epic clearness and method, as in his delineation of the Commonwealth Wars; Johnson to many a deep Lyric tone of plaintiveness and impetuous graceful power, scattered over his fugitive compositions. Both, rather to the general surprise, had a certain rugged Humour shining through their earnestness: the

indication, indeed, that they *were* earnest men, and had *subdued* their wild world into a kind of temporary home and safe dwelling. Both were, by principle and habit, Stoics: yet Johnson with the greater merit, for he alone had very much to triumph over; farther, he alone ennobled his Stoicism into Devotion. To Johnson Life was as a Prison, to be endured with heroic faith: to Hume it was little more than a foolish Bartholomew-Fair Show-booth, with the foolish crowdings and elbowings of which it was not worth while to quarrel; the whole would break up, and be at liberty, so *soon*. Both realised the highest task of Manhood, that of living like men; each died not unfitly, in his way: Hume as one, with factitious, half-false gaiety, taking leave of what was itself wholly but a Lie: Johnson as one, with awe-struck, yet resolute and piously expectant heart, taking leave of a Reality, to enter a Reality still higher. Johnson had the harder problem of it, from first to last: whether, with some hesitation, we can admit that he was intrinsically the better-gifted, may remain undecided.—THOMAS CARLYLE, "Boswell's Life of Johnson" (1832), *Critical and Miscellaneous Essays*, 1839–69

Hume is always idiomatic, but his idioms are constantly wrong; many of his best passages are, on that account, curiously grating and puzzling; you feel that they are very like what an Englishman would say, but yet that, after all, somehow or other, they are what he never would say;—there is a minute seasoning of imperceptible difference which distracts your attention, and which you are for ever stopping to analyse. —WALTER BAGEHOT, "Adam Smith as a Person," 1864

Hume's place in literature is not, at the present moment, adequate to what we know of his powers of intellect or to his originality as a thinker. He is acknowledged to be a great man, but he is very little read. His *History*, in fragments, and his "Essay on Miracles," which still enjoys a kind of success of scandal, are all that the general reader knows of Hume. If we deplore this fact, it must be admitted that his cool and unimpassioned criticism of belief, his perpetual return to the destructive standpoint, yet without vivacity, as one who undermines rather than attacks an opposing body, his colourless grace, the monotony of his balanced and faultless sentences, offer to us qualities which demand respect but scarcely awaken zeal, and, in short, that Hume although a real is a somewhat uninspiring classic. His great merit as a writer is his lucidity, his perfectly straightforward and competent expression of the particular thing he has it on his mind to say. To demand from him the fire of Berkeley or the splendour of Gibbon would be to expect from an essentially frigid writer an effect which he does not even desire to produce. It is only right to add that several distinguished critics of the present century have expressed for the style of Hume an admiration which we cannot help believing to be a little in excess of its merits.—EDMUND GOSSE, *A History of Eighteenth Century Literature*, 1888, pp. 299–300

Hume's pre-eminence in the field of speculation has somewhat thrown into the shade his merits as a man of letters; and, in truth, he has been surpassed by none of his countrymen in the acuteness, the penetration, and the intrepidity with which he treated the problems of philosophy. While his opponents must concede that he possessed the courage of his opinions in no ordinary degree, and that he never shrank from following whither the argument seemed to lead, but, on the contrary, applied his canons with a consistency as admirable as it was singular, his supporters would find it hard to point to any subsequent writer who has presented the case for the philosophy of Experience with greater—or even with equal—thoroughness and cogency. The discoveries of modern science have supplied the empirical philosopher with no weapon which may not be found in Hume's well-stocked armoury; while, as a political enquirer, he attained a position second only to that of his close friend, Adam Smith.

A studied and artful—sometimes a strained—simplicity is the chief characteristic of his style. He never attempts the majestic periods of Johnson or Gibbon; while a certain air of stiffness and precision effectually prevents his being spirited on the one hand, or colloquial on the other. His prose flows on with a steady and even motion, which no obstacle ever retards, nor any passion ever agitates. In the whole of his writings there is scarce one of those outbursts of emotion which at times animate the pages even of the coolest metaphysicians. Scorn there is in abundance; but it is the amused and pitying contempt of a superior being who watches from afar the frailties and vices from which himself is consciously exempt. Enthusiasm, or righteous indignation, was a total stranger to Hume's cast of mind. But his sneer and his sarcasm, though by far less elaborate and less diligently sustained, are hardly less effective and pointed than Gibbon's. As a historian, he makes little pretence to absolute impartiality, but his opinions are insinuated with the utmost delicacy and address; and at least he never wilfully falsifies his facts. He appeals little to the modern taste in the capacity either of the pedant or the journalist; yet his judgment of character is at once cautious and discriminating, and he interjects many shrewd and dry remarks. Such, for example, is the observation that to inspire the Puritans with a better humour was, both for their own sake and that of the public, a laudable intention of the Court; "but whether pillories, fines, and prisons were proper expedients for that purpose may admit of some question"; or the description of the Solemn League and Covenant as "composed of many invectives, fitted to inflame the minds of men against their fellow-creatures, whom Heaven has enjoined them to cherish and to love."

Hume's vocabulary is copious and well chosen, but never picturesque. He compiled for his own guidance a list of Scotticisms; and it argues a nice literary sense and an attentive study of the best models that, having in him a strong dash of the provincial, he should have not only sought but contrived to avoid these not unnatural solecisms. Many men have written English prose with greater ease, fluency, and freedom, and many with greater dignity and effect; but few with more accuracy, purity, and elegance of diction than David Hume.—J. H. MILLAR, "David Hume," *English Prose*, ed. Henry Craik, 1895, Vol. 4, pp. 187–88

His philosophical importance has lasted better than his historical, because his history, though full of ability, was written without access to many documents since laid open, and with a somewhat insufficient attention to careful use of those that were accessible; while his philosophy, needing nothing but the furniture of his own mind, and employing that in the best way on one side of perennially interesting and insoluble questions, remains a *point de repère* for ever. It is indeed admitted to have practically restarted all philosophical inquiry, being as much the origin of German and other theory as of the Scottish school and of later English negative materialism. Luckily, too, the value of literary work as such is far more enduring than that of either philosophy or history by themselves. For they may be superseded, but it never can. And Hume's expression was for his special purposes supreme—perfectly clear, ironical, but not to the point of suspicious frivolity, and as polished as the somewhat dead and flat colour of the style of the time would

admit.—GEORGE SAINTSBURY, *A Short History of English Literature*, 1898, pp. 623–24

Works

ESSAYS

I am strongly tempted too to have a stroke at Hume in parting. He is the author of a little book called *Philosophical Essays*, in one part of which he argues against the being of a God, and in another, (very needlessly you will say,) against the possibility of miracles. He has crowned the liberty of the press. And yet he has a considerable post under the Government. I have a great mind to do justice on his arguments against miracles, which I think might be done in few words. But does he deserve notice? Is he known amongst you? Pray answer me these questions. For if his own weight keeps him down, I should be sorry to contribute to his advancement to any place but the pillory.—WILLIAM WARBURTON, Letter to Richard Hurd (Sept. 28, 1749), *Letters from a Late Eminent Prelate*, 1808

I have not yet read the last *Review*, but dipping into it, accidentally fell upon their account of Hume's essays on suicide. I am glad that they have liberality enough to condemn the licentiousness of an Author whom they so much admire. I say liberality—for there is as much Bigotry in the world to that man's errors, as there is in the hearts of some Sectaries to their peculiar modest Tenets. He is the Pope of thousands as blind and as presumptuous as himself. God certainly infatuates those who will not see. It were otherwise impossible that a man naturally shrewd and sensible, and whose understanding had all the advantages of constant exercise and cultivation, could have satisfied himself, or have hoped to satisfy others with such palpable sophistry as has not even the grace of fallacy to recommend it. His silly assertion that because it would be no Sin to divert the course of the Danube, therefore it is none to let out a few ounces of blood from an artery, would justify not Suicide only but Homicide too. For the lives of ten thousand men are of less consequence to their country, than the course of that river to the regions through which it flows. Population would soon make Society amends for the loss of her ten thousand members, but the loss of the Danube would be felt by all the millions that dwell upon its banks to all generations. But the life of a man and the water of a River can never come into competition with each other in point of value, unless in the estimation of an unprincipled philosopher.—WILLIAM COWPER, Letter to William Unwin (July 12, 1784)

I am highly indebted to you for Hume. I like his essays better than any thing I have read these many days. He has prejudices, he does maintain errors—but he defends his positions, with so much ingenuity, that one would be almost sorry to see him dislodged. His Essays on 'Superstition & Enthusiasm,' on 'the Dignity & meanness of Human Nature' and several others, are in my opinion admirable both in matter & manner:—particularly the first where his conclusions might be verified by instances, with which we are all acquainted. The manner, indeed, of all is excellent:—the highest & most difficult effect of art—the appearance of its absence—appears throughout. But many of his opinions are not to be adopted—How odd does it look for instance to refer *all* the modifications of 'National character,' to the influence of moral causes. Might it not be asserted with some plausibility, that even those which he denominates moral causes, originate from physical circumstances? Whence but from the perpetual contemplation of his dreary glaciers & rugged glens—from his dismal broodings in his long & almost solitary nights, has the Scandinavian conceived his ferocious Odin, & his horrid 'spectres of the deep'? Compare this with the copper-castles and celestial gardens of the Arabian—and we must admit that physical causes *have* an influence on man. I read 'the Epicurean,' 'the Stoic,' 'the Platonist' & 'the Sceptic' under some disadvantage. They are perhaps rather clumsily executed ⟨. . .⟩ As a whole however I am delighted with the book, and if you can want it, I shall moreover give it a second perusal.—THOMAS CARLYLE, Letter to Thomas Mitchell (May 24, 1815)

HISTORY OF ENGLAND

Hume has out-done himself in this new *History*, in shewing his contempt of Religion. This is one of those proof charges which Arbuthnot speaks of in his treatise of *political lying*, to try how much the public will bear. If his history be well received, I shall conclude that there is even an end of all pretence to Religion. But I should think it will not: because I fancy the good reception of Robertson's proceeded from the *decency* of it.—Hume carries on his system here, to prove we had *no Constitution* till the struggles with James and Charles procured us one. And he has contrived an effectual way to support his system, by beginning the History of England with Henry VII. and *shutting out* all that preceded, by assuring his reader that the earlier history is worth no one's while to inquire after—Should you not take notice of this address? I take it for granted you will read his *History*—say nothing of it till it be published, for I engaged my word to Millar to be silent about it till that time.—WILLIAM WARBURTON, Letter to Richard Hurd (March 3, 1759), *Letters from a Late Eminent Prelate*, 1808

He acknowledged to Mr. Boswell that he did not take much pains in examining the old historians while writing the early part of his history. He dipped only into them so as to make out a pleasing narrative. It is manifest to me on reading Bacon's *Life of Henry VII.*, that *that* was the model on which Hume founded his plan. Bacon particularly recommends to the historian a review at the end of every reign of the laws enacted; of the progress of manners, arts, &c., which Hume has so successfully followed.

It is surprising, on examining any particular point, how superficial Hume is, and how many particulars are omitted that would have made his book much more entertaining; but perhaps we have no right to expect this in a general history. For my own part, I am much more entertained with memoirs and letters written at the time, in which everything is alive, and passes in motion before the eye.—EDMOND MALONE, "Maloniana" (1787), cited in Sir James Prior, *Life of Edmond Malone*, 1860, pp. 369–70

For a judicious choice of materials, and a happy disposition of them, together with perspicuity of style in recording them, this writer was hardly ever exceeded; especially in the latter part of his work, which is by far the most elaborate. The earlier part of his history is too superficial. He has endeavoured to trace the progress of our constitution, and has descended more into the internal state of the nation, in exhibiting a view of the manners and sentiments of each age, the state of property and personal security, with the improvements in the conveniences of life, than most other writers; but he has represented the ancient government as much more arbitrary than it really was, as will appear by the much more accurate accounts of Dr. Sullivan, and especially Mr. Millar, whose work on the English constitution I cannot too strongly recommend. Some great faults in Mr. Hume's history were well pointed out by Dr. Towers. Mr. Hume is also thought by many to have given too favourable an idea of the characters of our princes of the Stewart family, by omitting to mention those particulars in their conduct which have been most objected to; and it was probably with a view to exculpate them, that he has taken so much pains to give the colour that he has done to the preceding periods of our history. A good antidote to what is unfavourable to liberty in Mr. Hume will be found in the very masterly history of Mrs. Macaulay. Though the style of Mr. Hume is, upon the whole, excellent, yet he has departed more than any other writer of the present age from the true English idiom, and leaned more to that of the French.—JOSEPH PRIESTLEY, *Lectures on History and General Policy*, 1788, Lecture 27

The old reproach, that no British altars had been raised to the Muse of history, was recently disproved by the first performances of Robertson and Hume, the histories of Scotland and of the Stuarts. I will assume the presumption to say that I was not unworthy to read them; nor will I disguise my different feelings in the repeated perusals. The perfect composition, the nervous language, the well-turned periods of Dr Robertson inflamed me to the ambitious hope that I might one day tread in his footsteps; the calm philosophy, the careless inimitable beauties of his friend and rival often forced me to close the volume, with a mixed sensation of delight and despair.—EDWARD GIBBON, *Memoirs of My Life*, 1792–93

The great standards of historical composition which England produced during the eighteenth century are among the most important features of belles lettres. In this species of literature they have surpassed all other nations, if only in leading the way, and as historical models for foreign imitation. Unless I am mistaken, Hume ranks with the foremost in this department. But however great a safeguard scepticism may be in the process of historic investigation of facts, in which it can hardly be carried to excess, yet if the effects of doubting be to attack, to shake, nay, utterly to demolish the great bulwark of moral and religious principles, it little becomes the historian of a powerful nation, who aims at exercising permanent and extensive influence.

Narrow principles, views not perfectly correct are, in this case, much better and more productive than a deadening want of sentiment, feeling, and love. A tendency to opposition to prevalent opinions, a leaning to paradox, are all that remain to invest history, when framed after this manner, with any degree of interest. Now such a tendency to opposition is unmistakeable in Hume. In his time, the republican spirit of the Whigs biassed English literature almost as completely as it now does, and with equally doubtful influence on the country's welfare. How salutary soever, then, it may have seemed to him to abandon the prevalent Anglican severity of party and, attaching himself to the Opposition, to tinge a most important part of the national annals with evident predilection for the unfortunate house of Stuart and sympathy with Tory principles, he can only be regarded as an eminent party-historian, the first in his peculiar method and view, not the truly great author of a performance at once national in spirit and in genius. His description of earlier times is very unsatisfactory: having no affection for them, he could not sufficiently realize them.—FRIEDRICH SCHLEGEL, *Lectures on the History of Literature*, 1815

Hume is an accomplished advocate. Without positively asserting much more than he can prove, he gives prominence to all the circumstances which support his case, he glides lightly over those which are unfavourable to it; his own witnesses are applauded and encouraged; the statements which seem to throw discredit on them are controverted; the contradictions into which they fall are explained away; a clear and connected abstract of their evidence is given. Everything that is offered on the other side is scrutinised with the utmost severity; every suspicious circumstance is a ground for comment and invective; what cannot be denied is extenuated, or passed by without notice; concessions even are sometimes made; but this insidious candour only increases the effect of the vast mass of sophistry.—THOMAS BABINGTON MACAULAY, "History" (1828), *Critical, Historical, and Miscellaneous Essays*, 1860, Vol. 1, p. 420

A man of his exceedingly inquiring and unrestrained mind, living in the midst of the eighteenth century, might have been expected to have espoused what is called the popular side in the great questions of English history, the side, in later language, of the movement. Yet we know that Hume's leaning is the other way. Accidental causes may perhaps have contributed to this; the prejudice of an ingenious mind against the opinions which he found most prevalent around him; the resistance of a restless mind to the powers that be, as natural as implicit acquiescence in them is to an indolent mind. But the main cause apparently is to be sought in his abhorrence of puritanism, alike repugnant to him in its good and its evil. His subtle and active mind could not bear its narrowness and bigotry, his careless and epicurean temper had no sympathy with its earnestness and devotion. The popular cause in our great civil contests was in his eyes the cause of fanaticism; and where he saw fanaticism he saw that from which his whole nature recoiled, as the greatest of all conceivable evils.—THOMAS ARNOLD, *Introductory Lectures on Modern History*, 1842, Lecture 5

Hume had little of the more recently developed conscientiousness about the use of materials. If he found a statement quoted, he would indolently adopt it without troubling to refer to the original document. He was willing to make lavish use of the collections of Thomas Carte, a laborious and unfortunate predecessor of his, whose Jacobite prejudices had concealed his considerable pretensions as an historical compiler. Carte died just when Hume's first volume appeared, and this fact perhaps saved Hume from some unpleasant animadversions. Modern critics have shown that Hume's pages swarm with inaccuracies, and that, what is a worse fault, his predilections for Tory ideas lead him to do wilful injustice to the opponents of arbitrary power. All this, however, is little to the point; Hume is no longer appealed to as an authority. He is read for his lucid and beautiful English, for the skill with which he marshals vast trains of events before the mental eye, for his almost theatrical force in describing the evolution of a crisis. If we compare his work from this point of view with all that had preceded it in English literature, we shall see how eminent is the innovation we owe to Hume. He first made history readable.—EDMUND GOSSE, *A Short History of Modern English Literature*, 1897, pp. 256–57

PHILOSOPHY

The whole of his reasoning depends upon this maxim, that when once we have traced an effect up to its cause, we can never ascribe any thing to the cause but what is precisely proportioned to the effect, and what we ourselves discern to be so: nor can we infer any thing farther concerning the cause, than what the effect, or the present appearance of it, necessarily leads to. He had to the same purpose observed in a former essay; that "it is allowed by all philosophers, that the effect is the measure of the power." But this is far from being universally true. For we in many instances clearly perceive, that a cause can produce an effect which it doth not actually produce, or a greater effect than it hath actually produced. This gentleman's whole reasoning proceeds upon confounding necessary and free causes; and indeed he seems not willing to allow any distinction between them, or that there are any other but necessary and material causes. A necessary cause acts up to the utmost of its power, and therefore the effect must be exactly proportioned to it. But the case is manifestly different as to free and voluntary causes. They may have a power of producing effects, which they do not actually produce. And as they act from discernment and choice, we may, in many cases, reasonably ascribe to them farther views than what we discern or discover in their present course of action. This author himself owns, that this may be reasonably done with respect to man whom we know by experience, and whose nature and conduct we are acquainted with; but denies that the same way of arguing will hold with respect to the Deity. But surely when once we come from the consideration of his works to the knowlege of a self-existent and absolutely perfect Being, we may from the nature of that self-existent and absolutely perfect cause reasonably conclude, that He is able to produce certain effects beyond what actually come under our present notice and observation, and indeed that He can do whatsoever doth not imply a contradiction. This Universe is a vast, a glorious, and amazing system, comprehending an infinite variety of parts. And it is but a small part of it that comes under our own more immediate notice. But we know enough to be convinced, that it demonstrateth a wisdom as well as power beyond all imagination great and wonderful. And we may justly conclude the same concerning those parts of the Universe that we are not acquainted with. And for any man to say, that we cannot reasonably ascribe any degree of wisdom or power to God but what is exactly proportioned to that part of the universal frame which comes under our own particular observation, is a very strange way of arguing. The proofs of the wisdom and power of God, as appearing in our part of the system, are so striking, that it is hard to conceive, how any man that is not under the influence of the most obstinate prejudice, can refuse to submit to their force. And yet there are many phænomena, the reasons and ends of which we are not at present able to assign. The proper conduct in such a case, is to believe there are most wise reasons for these things, though we do not now discern those reasons, and to argue from the uncontested characters of wisdom in things that we do know, that this most wise and powerful agent, the author of nature, hath also acted with admirable wisdom in those things, the designs and ends of which we do not know. It would be wrong therefore to confine the measures of his wisdom precisely to what appeareth to our narrow apprehensions in that part of his works, which falleth under our immediate inspection. This was the great fault of the *Epicureans*, and other atheistical philosophers, who judging by their own narrow views, urged several things as proofs of the want of wisdom and contrivance, which upon a fuller knowlege of the works of nature, furnish farther convincing proofs of the wisdom of the great Former of all things.

In like manner with respect to his goodness, there are numberless things in this present constitution, which lead us to regard him as a most benign and benevolent Being. And therefore it is highly reasonable, that when we meet with any phænomena, which we cannot reconcile with our ideas of the divine goodness, we should conclude, that it is only for want of having the whole of things before us, and considering them in their connexion and harmony, that they appear to us with a disorderly aspect. And it is very just in such a case to make use of any reasonable hypothesis, which tendeth to set the goodness of God in a fair and consistent light.

The same way of reasoning holds with regard to the justice and righteousness of God as the great Governor of the world. We may reasonably conclude from the intimate sense we have of the excellency of such a character, and the great evil and deformity of injustice and unrighteousness, which sense is implanted in us by the author of our beings, and from the natural rewards of virtue, and punishment of vice even in the present constitution of things; that he is a lover of righteousness and virtue, and an enemy to vice and wickedness. Our author himself makes his *Epicurean* friend acknowlege, that in the present order of things, virtue is attended with more peace of mind, and with many other advantages above vice. And yet it cannot be denied, that there are many instances obvious to common observation, in which vice seemeth to flourish and prosper, and virtue to be exposed to great evils and calamities. What is to be concluded from this? Is it that because the justice of God here sheweth itself only *in part*, and not *in its full extent* (to use our author's expression), therefore righteousness as in God is imperfect in its degree, and that he doth not possess it in the full extent of that perfection, nor will ever exert it any farther than we see him exert it in this present state? This were an unreasonable conclusion, concerning a being of such admirable perfection, whose righteousness as well as wisdom must be supposed to be infinitely superior to ours. It is natural therefore to think that this present life is only a part of the divine scheme, which shall be compleated in a future state. —JOHN LELAND, A *View of the Principal Deistical Writers*, 1754–56

I shall always avow myself your disciple in metaphysics. I have learned more from your writings in this kind, than from all others put together. Your system appears to me not only coherent in all its parts, but likewise justly deduced from principles commonly received among philosophers; principles which I never thought of calling in question, until the conclusions you draw from them in the *Treatise of Human Nature* made me suspect them. If these principles are solid, your system must stand; and whether they are or not, can better be judged after you have brought to light the whole system that grows out of them, than when the greater part of it was wrapped up in clouds and darkness. I agree with you, therefore, that if this system shall ever be demolished, you have a just claim to a great share of the praise, both because you have made it a distinct and determinate mark to be aimed at, and have furnished proper artillery for the purpose.—THOMAS REID, Letter to David Hume (March 18, 1763)

When we were alone, I introduced the subject of death, and endeavoured to maintain that the fear of it might be got over. I told him that David Hume said to me, he was no more uneasy to think he should *not be* after this life, than that he *had not been* before he began to exist. JOHNSON. 'Sir, if he really thinks so, his perceptions are disturbed; he is mad: if he does not think so, he lies. He may tell you, he holds his finger in the flame of a candle, without feeling pain; would you believe him? When he dies, he at least gives up all he has.'—JAMES BOSWELL, *Life of Johnson*, 1791

The system which founds morality on utility, an utility, let it be *always* remembered, confined to the purposes of the present world, issued with ill omen from the school of infidelity. It was first broached, I believe, certainly first brought into general notice, by Mr. Hume, in his *Treatise on Morals*, which he himself pronounced *incomparably the best* he ever wrote. It

was incomparably the best for his purpose; nor is it easy to imagine a mind so acute as his did not see the effect it would have in setting morality and religion afloat, and substituting for the stability of principle the looseness of speculation and opinion. It has since been rendered popular by a succession of eminent writers; by one especially (I doubt not with intentions very foreign from those of Mr. Hume), whose great services to religion in other respects, together with my high reverence for his talents, prevent me from naming him. This venerable author, it is probable, little suspected to what lengths the principle would be carried, or to what purposes it would be applied in other hands. Had he foreseen this, I cannot but imagine he would have spared this part of his acute speculations.—ROBERT HALL, "The Sentiments Proper to the Present Crisis" (1803), *Miscellaneous Works and Remains*, 1846, pp. 357–58

The man who gave the whole philosophy of Europe a new impulse and direction, and to whom, mediately or immediately, must be referred every subsequent advance in philosophical speculation, was our countryman,—David Hume. In speaking of this illustrious thinker, I feel anxious to be distinctly understood. I would, therefore, earnestly request of you to bear in mind, that religious disbelief and philosophical scepticism are not merely not the same, but have no natural connection; and that while the one must ever be a matter of reprobation and regret, the other is in itself deserving of applause. Both were united in Hume; and this union has unfortunately contributed to associate them together in popular opinion, and to involve them equally in one vague condemnation. They must, therefore, I repeat, be accurately distinguished; and thus, though decidedly opposed to one and all of Hume's theological conclusions, I have no hesitation in asserting of his philosophical scepticism, that this was not only beneficial in its results, but, in the circumstances of the period, even a necessary step in the progress of Philosophy towards truth. In the first place, it was requisite in order to arouse thought from its lethargy. Men had fallen asleep over their dogmatic systems. In Germany, the Rationalism of Leibnitz and Wolf; in England, the Sensualism of Locke, with all its melancholy results, had subsided almost into established faiths. The Scepticism of Hume, like an electric spark, sent life through the paralysed opinions; philosophy awoke to renovated vigour, and its problems were again to be considered in other aspects, and subjected to a more searching analysis.

In the second place, it was necessary in order to manifest the inadequacy of the prevailing system. In this respect, scepticism is always highly advantageous; for scepticism is only the carrying out of erroneous philosophy to the absurdity which it always virtually involved. The sceptic, *qua* sceptic, cannot himself lay down his premises; he can only accept them from the dogmatist; if true, they can afford no foundation for the sceptical inference; if false, the sooner they are exposed in their real character the better. Accepting his principles from the dominant philosophies of Locke and Leibnitz, and deducing with irresistible evidence these principles to their legitimate results, Hume showed, by the extreme absurdity of these results themselves, either that Philosophy altogether was a delusion, or that the individual systems which afforded the premises, were erroneous or incomplete. He thus constrained philosophers to the alternative,—either of surrendering philosophy as null, or of ascending to higher principles, in order to re-establish it against the sceptical reduction. The dilemma of Hume constitutes, perhaps, the most memorable crisis in the history of philosophy; for out of it the whole subsequent

Metaphysic of Europe has taken its rise.—WILLIAM HAMILTON, "Fragments on the Scottish Philosophy" (1836), *Lectures on Metaphysics and Logic*, 1859

Hume, the prince of *dilletanti*, from whose writings one will hardly learn that there is such a thing as truth, far less that it is attainable; but only that the *pro* and *con* of everything may be argued with infinite ingenuity, and furnishes a fine intellectual exercise. This absolute scepticism in speculation very naturally brought him round to Toryism in practice; for if no faith can be had in the operations of human intellect, and one side of every question is about as likely as another to be true, a man will commonly be inclined to prefer that order of things which, being no more wrong than every other, he has hitherto found compatible with his private comforts. Accordingly Hume's scepticism agreed very well with the comfortable classes, until it began to reach the uncomfortable: when the discovery was made that, although men could be content to be rich without a faith, men would not be content to be poor without it, and religion and morality came into fashion again as the cheap defence of rent and tithes.—JOHN STUART MILL, "Bentham" (1838), *Dissertations and Discussions*, 1859, Vol. 1

Hume's abstractions are not deep or wise. He owes his fame to one keen observation, that no copula had been detected between any cause and effect, either in physics or in thought; that the term cause and effect was loosely or gratuitously applied to what we know only as consecutive, not at all as causal.—RALPH WALDO EMERSON, "Literature," *English Traits*, 1856

Hume lived in a dark age—dark, we mean, as regards religion. The eighteenth century had so many men remarkable for their virtues, their great human gifts, and their practical common sense, that we often wish it were possible to vindicate it from the usual charge of irreligion. But all the evidence is against us. Hume says that the clergy had lost their credit; their pretensions and doctrines were ridiculed; and even religion could scarcely support itself in the world. We have the same testimony from Bishop Butler, Archbishop Secker, and others. Hume was penetrated with the spirit of the age. There is no great man of whom we know anything who had by nature so little of the sentiment of religion. His mind was essentially pagan, without one Shemetic element. The whole spirit of the Bible was alien to him. He does not seem to have had even a taste for its literature or its lessons of human wisdom. In every great English writer, passages, similes, or illustrations from Scripture are plentiful in almost every page, interweaving themselves in the happiest sentences of our most brilliant orators and our most finished essayists; but in all Hume's philosophical writings we have marked only two references to the Scriptures. One of them is about the treasures of Hezekiah. It is introduced in a political essay, and with the indifferent words, *if I remember right*. In the whole history of his life there is but one occasion where he ever manifests the least sense for religious feeling. When in London he learned of the death of his mother. His sorrow was overwhelming. His friend Mr. Boyle said to him, "You owe this uncommon grief to having thrown off the principles of religion, for if you had not, you would have been consoled with the firm belief that the good lady, who was not only the best of mothers, but the most pious of Christians, was completely happy in the realms of the just." To which Hume answered, "Though I throw out my speculations to entertain the learned and metaphysical world, yet in other things I do not think so differently from the rest of the world as you imagine." This is a solitary instance, and, if really

genuine, is altogether exceptional. When he drew near his own end, with all his faculties entire, he amused himself and his friends with jests about crossing the Styx, and how he would banter old Charon, and how he could detain him as long as he could on this side the river before he entered the ferry-boat.—JOHN HUNT, "David Hume," *Contemporary Review*, May 1869, pp. 99–100

In his principal philosophical work, the *Enquiry concerning Human Understanding*, after announcing as his purpose, not a mere exhortation to virtue, but a thoroughgoing examination of the powers of man and of the limits of our knowledge—hence, not a merely popular, but a scientific philosophic investigation, in which, nevertheless, he proposes, as far as possible, to combine exactness with clearness—Hume proceeds first to inquire into the origin of ideas. He distinguishes between impressions and ideas or thoughts; under the former he understands the lively sensations which we have when we hear, see, feel, or love, hate, desire, will, and under the latter, the less lively ideas of memory or imagination, of which we become conscious when we reflect on any impression. The creative power of thought extends no further than to the faculty of combining, transposing, augmenting, or diminishing the material furnished by the senses and by experience. All the materials of thought are given us through external or internal experience; only their combination is the work of the understanding or the will. All our ideas are copies of perceptions. The idea of God furnishes no exception to this rule; the mind obtains that idea by magnifying the human attributes of wisdom and goodness beyond all limits. The joining of different ideas with each other depends on the three principles of association: similarity, union in space and time, and cause and effect.

All subjects of human reason or inquiry can be divided into two classes: relations of ideas, and facts. To the first class belong the propositions of geometry, arithmetic, and algebra, and, in general, all judgments the evidence of which is founded on intuition of demonstration. All propositions of this kind are discovered by the sole agency of the faculty of thought; they are altogether independent of reality. Even though no circle or triangle existed in nature, the statements of geometry would still be true. But propositions which relate to matters of objective fact have neither the same degree nor the same kind of evidence. The truth or falsity of such propositions is not demonstrable by ideas alone; for if it were so the supposition of the contrary must involve a contradiction, which is not the case. All reasoning about facts appears to be founded on the relation of cause and effect. It is presupposed that there is a causal connection between the present fact and that which is inferred from it, so that the one is the cause of the other, or both are co-ordinate effects of the same cause. If, therefore, we would obtain a satisfactory insight into the nature of the certainty of inferred facts, we must inquire in what manner we obtain the knowledge of cause and effect.

We acquire, says Hume, the knowledge of the causal nexus in no case by *à priori* inferences, but solely through experience, which shows us certain objects connected according to a constant rule. The effect is entirely different from the cause, and can, consequently, not be discovered in the idea of the latter, nor learned inferentially by the understanding without the aid of experience. A stone or piece of metal left in the air without support falls at once to the ground. This, experience teaches us. But can we possibly discover by *à priori* reasonings the least ground for supposing that the stone or metal might not as well move upwards as towards the centre of the earth? Still less, than the nature of the effect, can the understanding know *á priori* the necessary invariable connection between cause and effect. It follows, hence, that the highest end of human knowledge consists in summing up the empirically discovered causes of natural phenomena, and arranging the multitude of particular effects under a few general causes. But our pains are lost if we attempt to ascertain the causes of these general causes. The ultimate grounds of things are utterly inaccessible to the curiosity and investigation of man. Elasticity, gravity, the cohesion of parts, and the communication of motion by impulsion, are probably the most general causes to which we can trace back the phenomena of nature; but even thus our ignorance of nature is only removed a few degrees further backwards. The like is true in reference to moral philosophy and the science of knowledge. Geometry, great as is her well-deserved renown in respect of the conclusiveness and rigor of her demonstrations, can yet not help us to the knowledge of the ultimate causes in nature; for her only use is in the discovery and application of natural laws; but these laws themselves must be known through experience.

When we perceive similar sensible qualities, we expect from them effects similar to those we have already experienced as arising from them. But it may further be asked, on what this expectation is founded. Were it, by any means, supposable that the course of nature might change, and that the past would furnish no rule for the future, then all experience would be useless, and no more inferences could be drawn from it. The principle which determines all our expectations of similar effects is not any knowledge of the hidden force, through which the one thing brings another into being—for no such force can we observe, whether without or within us; but this principle is habit; the mind is led by habit, on the repetition of similar instances, to expect, with the appearance of the one event, the ordinary accompanying event, and to believe that it will really take place. This connection of events, which we feel in the mind, this habitual transition from one object to its customary accompaniment, is the sensation or impression from which we form the conception of a force or necessary connection. When successive phenomena are continually perceived to be connected, we *feel* the accustomed connection of ideas, which feeling we transfer to the subjects of the perceived phenomena, just as, in general, we are wont to ascribe to external objects the sensations which are occasioned in us by them.

Hume's philosophical significance is connected principally with his speculations concerning causality. His skepticism is founded on the assertion, that the causal idea, owing to its origin in habit, admits of use only within the field of experience: to reason from data given empirically to that which is transcendent (or lies beyond the whole range of experience), like God and immortality, appears to Hume unlawful. To this is to be added that Hume, particularly in his earliest treatise, expresses an equally negative judgment concerning the idea of substance; the I, he argues, is a complex of ideas, for which we have no right to posit a single substratum or underlying substance. Hume's ethical principle is the feeling of the happiness and misery of man. The moral judgment is based on the satisfaction or disapprobation which an action excites in him who witnesses it. Owing to the natural sympathy of man for his fellows, an action performed in the interest of the common welfare calls forth approbation, and one of an opposite nature, disapprobation.—FRIEDRICH ÜBERWEG, *History of Philosophy*, tr. George S. Morris, 1871

His theory of causation undermines the argument for the divine existence. He carefully abstains from dwelling on this in his great philosophic work, but he expounds it at great length, and with all his intellectual power, in his *Dialogues on Natural Religion*. We know nothing of cause, except that it has been observed to be the antecedent of its effect; when we have noticed an occurrence usually preceded by another occurrence, we may on discovering the one look for the other. But when we have never seen the events together, we have really nothing to guide us in arguing from the one to the other. We can argue that a watch implies a watchmaker, for we have observed them together; but never having had any experience of the making of a world, we cannot argue that the existence of a world implies the existence of a world maker. There is no effective way of answering this objection, but by maintaining that an effect necessarily implies a cause. It was on this ground that he was met by Reid, who argues that traces of design in God's works argue an intelligent cause. Kant deprived himself of the right to argue in this way, by making the mind itself impose the relation of causation on events, so that we cannot argue that there is a corresponding law in the things themselves. Hume urges with great force and ingenuity, as Kant did after him, that if we are compelled to seek for a cause of every object, we must also seek for a cause of the Divine Being. This is to be met by showing that our intuitive conviction simply requires us to seek for a cause of a new occurrence. He argues, as Kant also did after him, that the existence of order in the universe could at best prove merely a finite and not an infinite cause. The reply is, that we must seek for the evidence of the infinity of God in the peculiar conviction of the mind in regard to the infinite and the perfect.

This may be the most expedient place for stating and examining his famous argument against miracles, as advanced in his essay on the subject. It is clear that he could not argue, as some have done, that a miracle is an impossibility, or that it is contrary to the nature of things. He assails not the possibility of the occurrence of a miraculous event, but the proof of it. Experience being with him the only criterion of truth, it is to experience he appeals. He maintains that there has been an invariable experience in favor of the uniformity of nature, and that a miracle being a violation of a law of nature, can never be established by as strong proof as what can be urged against it. He then exerts his ingenuity in disparaging the evidence usually urged in behalf of miraculous occurrences, by showing how apt mankind are to be swayed on these subjects by such principles as fear, wonder, and fancy. We are not sure whether Hume has always been opposed in a wise or judicious manner by his opponents on this subject. It is of little use showing that there is some sort of original instinct leading us to believe in testimony; for this instinct, if it exists, often leads us astray, and we must still go to experience to indicate what we are to trust in and what we are to discard. But the opponents of Hume were perfectly right when they showed, that in maintaining that nature always acted according to certain mundane laws, he was assuming the point in dispute. Let us admit that the whole question is to be decided by experiential evidence. Let us concede that in the present advanced state of science there is ample evidence that there is a uniformity in nature; but then let us place alongside of this a counterpart fact, that there is a sufficient body of evidence in favor of there being a supernatural system. For this purpose let the cumulative proofs in behalf of Christianity, external and internal, be adduced; those derived from testimony and from prophecy, and those drawn from the unity of design in the revelation of doctrine and morality, and from the character of Jesus; and we shall find that in their consistency and congruity they are not unlike those which can be advanced in behalf of the existence of a natural system.—JAMES McCOSH, *The Scottish Philosophy*, 1874, pp. 145–47

Hume has not discussed the theological theory of the obligations of morality, but it is obviously in accordance with his view of the nature of those obligations. Under its theological aspect, morality is obedience to the will of God; and the ground for such obedience is twofold; either we ought to obey God because He will punish us if we disobey Him, which is an argument based on the utility of obedience; or our obedience ought to flow from our love towards God, which is an argument based on pure feeling and for which no reason can be given. For, if any man should say that he takes no pleasure in the contemplation of the ideal of perfect holiness, or, in other words, that he does not love God, the attempt to argue him into acquiring that pleasure would be as hopeless as the endeavour to persuade Peter Bell of the "witchery of the soft blue sky."

In whichever way we look at the matter, morality is based on feeling, not on reason; though reason alone is competent to trace out the effects of our actions and thereby dictate conduct. Justice is founded on the love of one's neighbour; and goodness is a kind of beauty. The moral law, like the laws of physical nature, rests in the long run upon instinctive intuitions, and is neither more nor less "innate" and "necessary" than they are. Some people cannot by any means be got to understand the first book of Euclid; but the truths of mathematics are no less necessary and binding on the great mass of mankind. Some there are who cannot feel the difference between the *Sonata Appassionata* and *Cherry Ripe*; or between a gravestone-cutter's cherub and the Apollo Belvidere; but the canons of art are none the less acknowledged. While some there may be, who, devoid of sympathy are incapable of a sense of duty; but neither does their existence affect the foundations of morality. Such pathological deviations from true manhood are merely the halt, the lame, and the blind of the world of consciousness; and the anatomist of the mind leaves them aside, as the anatomist of the body would ignore abnormal specimens.

And as there are Pascals and Mozarts, Newtons and Raffaelles, in whom the innate faculty for science or art seems to need but a touch to spring into full vigour, and through whom the human race obtains new possibilities of knowledge and new conceptions of beauty: so there have been men of moral genius, to whom we owe ideals of duty and visions of moral perfection, which ordinary mankind could never have attained; though, happily for them, they can feel the beauty of a vision, which lay beyond the reach of their dull imaginations, and count life well spent in shaping some faint image of it in the actual world.—THOMAS HENRY HUXLEY, *Hume*, 1879, pp. 207–8

By none of his contemporaries was he fully understood. A few saw the results of his teaching, but they could not comprehend its deeper significance, nor its relation to the past. They did not see that, in its initial stages, it was merely a development of the method of Socrates, and of the Cartesian doubt; and that, in its completed form, it was the "honest doubt" in which—if there did not "live more faith" than "in half the creeds" it overthrew—there was at least neither an iota of scorn, nor that "vaunting of itself," which has been the bane of many a positive philosophy. Even to this day it is difficult for some persons to see that the sceptic's function is a necessary one in every age; and that it must always assert itself, after a period of uncritical faith, or dogmatic affirmation. Adequately to recognise this may be the best antidote to the evil which a

one-sided scepticism breeds. It is, moreover, a very obvious corollary of one of the simplest of truths—viz. this, that no intellectual conclusion, come to by the speculative reason, however clearly realised, can possibly continue to satisfy it; nay, that every time it is grasped by the mind, after its first recognition, it of necessity assumes a different aspect. It comes back altered in the very act of reapprehension; partly because it is seen each time from a different point of view, under an altered light, and partly because it returns associated with other truths, or views of the universe. Every intellectual system is thus of necessity transient; but if, in virtue of this almost elementary fact, one were to maintain that all truth was fluid, and that no standard of the true or the good was obtainable, a dogma would underlie the doubt, and even contradict it. Already, in the very statement of the sceptic's position, a dogma lies in germ, and that dogma, dragged out into daylight, becomes, as much as the most elaborate system, open to the attack which scepticism initiates.

Occasionally dogmatic Hume could not fail to be; dogmatic, that is to say, in his avowal that an ultimate dogma, whether as to nature of substance or of cause, was unattainable. But dogmatism was not the prevailing tone of his mind. It was rather that of suspense, or uncertainty, as to all ultimate things; and when he had once "made up his mind" in reference to any minor question, within the range of phenomenal fact or law, he did not care to reopen it. As he grew older, he became increasingly averse to speculative inquiry as such. As he said to Blair, in reference to Dr Campbell's discourses on miracles, "I have long since done with all inquiries into such subjects." That was the form which the conservative instinct of advancing age assumed in Hume; but it was simply because he believed the problem to be an insoluble one, and because he therefore bowed to the inevitable. There was not a spark of irreverence in Hume; and his bitterest opponents never charged him with intolerance, or with antagonism to religion. On the contrary, he was recognised as a reasonable conformist to religious practice, even while he was intellectually unconvinced as to the data on which that practice rested. All his contemporaries—excepting those who were, let us say, constitutionally biassed against him—join in honouring him for his honesty, his sincerity, his generosity, his unbounded good-humour, his cheerful spirit, and the calm tranquillity of his outlook. His cheerfulness never forsook him, while the malady that killed him advanced with rapid step. But, on the other hand, there was a certain rigidity of mind, and even a ponderousness, in the way in which he dealt with the problems which he finally set aside. To be prosaic rather than poetic he would himself have regarded as a title to honour amongst philosophers; but in consequence of this, and from the very want of the "inward eye," he never saw the ideal side of things. To Hume the ideal was equivalent to the fantastic; and his want of idealism—his habit of prosaic literalness—cut him off from appreciating one half of the philosophy, the art, the literature, and the life of the world.—WILLIAM KNIGHT, *Hume*, 1886, pp. 231–33

Hume was first and chiefly a speculative thinker; intensely interested in the difficulties besetting all research, he consecrated the best efforts of his life to penetrate into the conditions of certainty in knowledge. He prosecuted his task without misgiving, and was willing to bear all the consequences, however trying to reputation and ambition. Amongst these the loss of an Academic chair was by far the bitterest experience. He had shown in many ways his conviction that philosophic research can be successfully conducted only in silent retreat, with attention concentrated undisturbed on all complexities of thought. He even refused to discuss philosophic themes in general company, and hardly relaxed this rule in the select gatherings of thinkers fully competent for the discussion required. As a thinker, he really lived apart, feeling that his speculations could be known only through the printed page, read deliberately and silently as it had been written. When, however, he closed his studies for the time, he abandoned all concern with them; he returned into society with the alacrity of one who seeks relaxation, and with the overflowing humour of one ready for amusement under any conditions. In the same spirit his familiar correspondence was conducted, allowing himself often freedom for the utmost playfulness—not infrequently for unrestrained exaggeration, liable to misunderstanding by those who were not familiar with the licence he allowed himself in the familiarity of friendship.—HENRY CALDERWOOD, *David Hume*, 1888, p. 32

David Hume was without question the man of greatest mental grasp whom Scotland produced in the eighteenth century. His central ambition was literary fame, the absorbing pleasure of his life literary interest, and he contemplated the controversies of his day with a serene and imperturbable ease and indifference to which his contemporaries were strangers. It cost him no trouble to grasp the fact that the so-called philosophy of his day was a mass of disordered fragments, and that the nonchalant materialism of Locke was destructive of any creed based on a sure foundation. He carried that system only a step further in showing that on its basis all knowledge was accidental, and that the theories that were propounded with so much confidence were conjectures only. It was not his to reconstruct a system of metaphysics: that was left for a later age and for another country. But the work he did he did for all time; and it was to show that a system of knowledge based only on experience could attain no higher authority than that which experience could give. In practice and in character he was a philosopher in a sense that none of the others were: serene in temper, unmoved by attack, calm in the face of an almost sublime abnegation of all that gave life its deepest meaning to most men, and looking down with an indifference, which only genius could prevent from degenerating into arrogance, on all the wrangling of the day. No man could carry a creed of despair with more imperturbable good-humour, or could maintain a standard of morality with more perfect consistency upon the somewhat meagre motives of innate pride and dignity. The reason was that Hume's literary genius made him express something that is more or less a truth of every man's experience; and that his literary sympathy enabled him to understand and appreciate, if he did not share, the religious motives that stand as sentinels to human conduct. It has often been the habit to represent Hume's formal deference to the dictates of revealed religion as only a species of elaborate sarcasm. It is hard to say on what proof such a forced interpretation rests. The symptoms of religious feeling which showed themselves in his temperament—symptoms supported by too many authorities to be easily ignored—have been studiously minimised: but to do this is only to misunderstand the nature of the man, and to be blind to that wide range of literary sympathy which made all human feelings find some echo in his heart.—HENRY CRAIK, *A Century of Scottish History*, 1901, pp. 440–41

DAVID HUME
"My Own Life" (1776)
The Life of David Hume, Esq.
1777

It is difficult for a man to speak long of himself without vanity; therefore, I shall be short. It may be thought an instance of vanity that I pretend at all to write my life; but this Narrative shall contain little more than the History of my Writings; as, indeed, almost all my life has been spent in literary pursuits and occupations. The first success of most of my writings was not such as to be an object of vanity.

I was born the 26th of April 1711, old style, at Edinburgh. I was of a good family, both by father and mother: my father's family is a branch of the Earl of Home's, or Hume's; and my ancestors had been proprietors of the estate, which my brother possesses, for several generations. My mother was daughter of Sir David Falconer, President of the College of Justice: the title of Lord Halkerton came by succession to her brother.

My family, however, was not rich, and being myself a younger brother, my patrimony, according to the mode of my country, was of course very slender. My father, who passed for a man of parts, died when I was an infant, leaving me, with an elder brother and a sister, under the care of our mother, a woman of singular merit, who, though young and handsome, devoted herself entirely to the rearing and educating of her children. I passed through the ordinary course of education with success, and was seized very early with a passion for literature, which has been the ruling passion of my life, and the great source of my enjoyments. My studious disposition, my sobriety, and my industry, gave my family a notion that the law was a proper profession for me; but I found an unsurmountable aversion to every thing but the pursuits of philosophy and general learning; and while they fancied I was poring upon Voet and Vinnius, Cicero and Virgil were the authors which I was secretly devouring.

My very slender fortune, however, being unsuitable to this plan of life, and my health being a little broken by my ardent application, I was tempted, or rather forced, to make a very feeble trial for entering into a more active scene of life. In 1734, I went to Bristol, with some recommendations to eminent merchants, but in a few months found that scene totally unsuitable to me. I went over to France, with a view of prosecuting my studies in a country retreat; and I there laid that plan of life, which I have steadily and successfully pursued. I resolved to make a very rigid frugality supply my deficiency of fortune, to maintain unimpaired my independency, and to regard every object as contemptible, except the improvement of my talents in literature.

During my retreat in France, first at Reims, but chiefly at La Fleche, in Anjou, I composed my *Treatise of Human Nature*. After passing three years very agreeably in that country, I came over to London in 1737. In the end of 1738, I published my Treatise, and immediately went down to my mother and my brother, who lived at his country-house, and was employing himself very judiciously and successfully in the improvement of his fortune.

Never literary attempt was more unfortunate than my *Treatise of Human Nature*. It fell *dead-born from the press*, without reaching such distinction, as even to excite a murmur among the zealots. But being naturally of a cheerful and sanguine temper, I very soon recovered the blow, and prosecuted with great ardour my studies in the country. In 1742, I printed at Edinburgh the first part of my Essays: the work was favourably received, and soon made me entirely forget my former disappointment. I continued with my mother and brother in the country, and in that time recovered the knowledge of the Greek language, which I had too much neglected in my early youth.

In 1745, I received a letter from the Marquis of Annandale, inviting me to come and live with him in England; I found also, that the friends and family of that young nobleman were desirous of putting him under my care and direction, for the state of his mind and health required it. I lived with him a twelvemonth. My appointments during that time made a considerable accession to my small fortune. I then received an invitation from General St. Clair to attend him as a secretary to his expedition, which was at first meant against Canada, but ended in an incursion on the coast of France. Next year, to wit, 1747, I received an invitation from the General to attend him in the same station in his military embassy to the courts of Vienna and Turin. I then wore the uniform of an officer, and was introduced at these courts as aid-de-camp to the general, along with Sir Harry Erskine and Captain Grant, now General Grant. These two years were almost the only interruptions which my studies have received during the course of my life: I passed them agreeably, and in good company; and my appointments, with my frugality, had made me reach a fortune, which I called independent, though most of my friends were inclined to smile when I said so; in short, I was now master of near a thousand pounds.

I had always entertained a notion, that my want of success in publishing the *Treatise of Human Nature*, had proceeded more from the manner than the matter, and that I had been guilty of a very usual indiscretion, in going to the press too early. I, therefore, cast the first part of that work anew in the *Enquiry concerning Human Understanding*, which was published while I was at Turin. But this piece was at first little more successful than the *Treatise of Human Nature*. On my return from Italy, I had the mortification to find all England in a ferment, on account of Dr. Middleton's *Free Enquiry*, while my performance was entirely overlooked and neglected. A new edition, which had been published at London of my Essays, moral and political, met not with a much better reception.

Such is the force of natural temper, that these disappointments made little or no impression on me. I went down in 1749, and lived two years with my brother at his country-house, for my mother was now dead. I there composed the second part of my Essays, which I called *Political Discourses*, and also my *Enquiry concerning the Principles of Morals*, which is another part of my treatise that I cast anew. Meanwhile, my bookseller, A. Millar, informed me, that my former publications (all but the unfortunate *Treatise*) were beginning to be the subject of conversation; that the sale of them was gradually increasing, and that new editions were demanded. Answers by Reverends, and Right Reverends, came out two or three in a year; and I found, by Dr. Warburton's railing, that the books were beginning to be esteemed in good company. However, I had fixed a resolution, which I inflexibly maintained, never to reply to any body; and not being very irascible in my temper, I have easily kept myself clear of all literary squabbles. These symptoms of a rising reputation gave me encouragement, as I was ever more disposed to see the favourable than unfavourable side of things; a turn of mind which it is more happy to possess, than to be born to an estate of ten thousand a year.

In 1751, I removed from the country to the town, the true scene for a man of letters. In 1752, were published at Edinburgh, where I then lived, my *Political Discourses*, the only work of mine that was successful on the first publication. It was well received abroad and at home. In the same year was published at London, my *Enquiry concerning the Principles of Morals*; which, in my own opinion (who ought not to judge on that subject), is of all my writings, historical, philosophical, or literary, incomparably the best. It came unnoticed and unobserved into the world.

In 1752, the Faculty of Advocates chose me their Librarian, an office from which I received little or no emolument, but which gave me the command of a large library. I then formed the plan of writing the *History of England*; but being frightened with the notion of continuing a narrative through a period of 1700 years, I commenced with the accession of the House of Stuart, an epoch when, I thought, the misrepresentations of faction began chiefly to take place. I was, I own, sanguine in my expectations of the success of this work. I thought that I was the only historian, that had at once neglected present power, interest, and authority, and the cry of popular prejudices; and as the subject was suited to every capacity, I expected proportional applause. But miserable was my disappointment: I was assailed by one cry of reproach, disapprobation, and even detestation; English, Scotch, and Irish, Whig and Tory, churchman and sectary, freethinker and religionist, patriot and courtier, united in their rage against the man, who had presumed to shed a generous tear for the fate of Charles I. and the Earl of Strafford; and after the first ebullitions of their fury were over, what was still more mortifying, the book seemed to sink into oblivion. Mr. Millar told me, that in a twelvemonth he sold only forty-five copies of it. I scarcely, indeed, heard of one man in the three kingdoms, considerable for rank or letters, that could endure the book. I must only except the primate of England, Dr. Herring, and the primate of Ireland, Dr. Stone, which seem two odd exceptions. These dignified prelates separately sent me messages not to be discouraged.

I was, however, I confess, discouraged; and had not the war been at that time breaking out between France and England, I had certainly retired to some provincial town of the former kingdom, have changed my name, and never more have returned to my native country. But as this scheme was not now practicable, and the subsequent volume was considerably advanced, I resolved to pick up courage and to persevere.

In this interval, I published at London my *Natural History of Religion*, along with some other small pieces: its public entry was rather obscure, except only that Dr. Hurd wrote a pamphlet against it, with all the illiberal petulance, arrogance, and scurrility which distinguish the Warburtonian school. This pamphlet gave me some consolation for the otherwise indifferent reception of my performance.

In 1756, two years after the fall of the first volume, was published the second volume of my History, containing the period from the death of Charles I. till the Revolution. This performance happened to give less displeasure to the Whigs, and was better received. It not only rose itself, but helped to buoy up its unfortunate brother.

But though I had been taught by experience, that the Whig party were in possession of bestowing all places, both in the state and in literature, I was so little inclined to yield to their senseless clamour, that in above a hundred alterations, which farther study, reading, or reflection engaged me to make in the reigns of the first two Stuarts, I have made all of them invariably to the Tory side. It is ridiculous to consider the English constitution before that period as a regular plan of liberty.

In 1759, I published my *History of the House of Tudor*. The clamour against this performance was almost equal to that against the History of the two first Stuarts. The reign of Elizabeth was particularly obnoxious. But I was now callous against the impressions of public folly, and continued very peaceably and contentedly in my retreat at Edinburgh, to finish, in two volumes, the more early part of the *English History*, which I gave to the public in 1761, with tolerable, and but tolerable success.

But notwithstanding this variety of winds and seasons, to which my writings had been exposed, they had still been making such advances, that the copy-money given me by the booksellers, much exceeded any thing formerly known in England; I was become not only independent, but opulent. I retired to my native country of Scotland, determined never more to set my foot out of it; and retaining the satisfaction of never having preferred a request to one great man, or even making advances of friendship to any of them. As I was now turned of fifty, I thought of passing all the rest of my life in this philosophical manner, when I received, in 1763, an invitation from the Earl of Hertford, with whom I was not in the least acquainted, to attend him on his embassy to Paris, with a near prospect of being appointed secretary to the embassy; and, in the meanwhile, of performing the functions of that office. This offer, however inviting, I at first declined, both because I was reluctant to begin connexions with the great, and because I was afraid that the civilities and gay company of Paris, would prove disagreeable to a person of my age and humour: but on his lordship's repeating the invitation, I accepted of it. I have every reason, both of pleasure and interest, to think myself happy in my connexions with that nobleman, as well as afterwards with his brother, General Conway.

Those who have not seen the strange effects of modes, will never imagine the reception I met with at Paris, from men and women of all ranks and stations. The more I resiled from their excessive civilities, the more I was loaded with them. There is, however, a real satisfaction in living at Paris, from the great number of sensible, knowing, and polite company with which that city abounds above all places in the universe. I thought once of settling there for life.

I was appointed secretary to the embassy; and in summer 1765, Lord Hertford left me, being appointed Lord Lieutenant of Ireland. I was *chargé d'affaires* till the arrival of the Duke of Richmond, towards the end of the year. In the beginning of 1766, I left Paris, and next summer went to Edinburgh, with the same view as formerly, of burying myself in a philosophical retreat. I returned to that place, not richer, but with much more money, and a much larger income, by means of Lord Hertford's friendship, than I left it; and I was desirous of trying what superfluity could produce, as I had formerly made an experiment of a competency. But, in 1767, I received from Mr. Conway an invitation to be Under-secretary; and this invitation, both the character of the person, and my connexions with Lord Hertford, prevented me from declining. I returned to Edinburgh in 1769, very opulent (for I possessed a revenue of 1000 £. a year), healthy, and though somewhat stricken in years, with the prospect of enjoying long my ease, and of seeing the increase of my reputation.

In spring 1775, I was struck with a disorder in my bowels, which at first gave me no alarm, but has since, as I apprehend it, become mortal and incurable. I now reckon upon a speedy dissolution. I have suffered very little pain from my disorder; and what is more strange, have, notwithstanding the great decline of my person, never suffered a moment's abatement of my spirits; insomuch, that were I to name the period of my life, which I should most choose to pass over again, I might be tempted to point to this later period. I possess the same ardour as ever in study, and the same gaiety in company. I consider, besides, that a man of sixty-five, by dying, cuts off only a few years of infirmities; and though I see many symptoms of my literary reputation's breaking out at last with additional lustre, I knew that I could have but few years to enjoy it. It is difficult to be more detached from life than I am at present.

To conclude historically with my own character. I am, or rather was (for that is the style I must now use in speaking of myself, which emboldens me the more to speak my sentiments); I was, I say, a man of mild dispositions, of command of temper, of an open, social, and cheerful humour, capable of attachment, but little susceptible of enmity, and of great moderation in all my passions. Even my love of literary fame, my ruling passion, never soured my temper, notwithstanding my frequent disappointments My company was not unacceptable to the young and careless, as well as to the studious and literary; and as I took a particular pleasure in the company of modest women, I had no reason to be displeased with the reception I met with from them. In a word, though most men anywise eminent, have found reason to complain of calumny, I never was touched, or even attacked by her baleful tooth: and though I wantonly exposed myself to the rage of both civil and religious factions, they seemed to be disarmed in my behalf of their wonted fury. My friends never had occasion to vindicate any one circumstance of my character and conduct: not but that the zealots, we may well suppose, would have been glad to invent and propagate any story to my disadvantage, but they could never find any which they thought would wear the face of probability. I cannot say there is no vanity in making this funeral oration of myself, but I hope it is not a misplaced one; and this is a matter of fact which is easily cleared and ascertained.

WALTER SAVAGE LANDOR
"David Hume and John Home"
Imaginary Conversations: Second Series
1824

Hume: We Scotchmen, sir, are somewhat proud of our families and relationships: this is however a nationality which perhaps I should not have detected in myself, if I had not been favoured with the flattering present of your tragedy. Our names, as often happens, are spelled differently; but I yielded with no reluctance to the persuasion, that we are, and not very distantly, of the same stock.

Home: I hope, sir, our mountains will detain you among them some time, and I presume to promise you that you will find in Edinburgh a society as polished and literate as in Paris.

Hume: As literate I can easily believe, my cousin, and perhaps as polished, if you reason upon the ingredients of polish: but there is certainly much more amenity and urbanity at Paris than anywhere else in the world, and people there are less likely to give and take offence. All topics may be discussed without arrogance and super-ciliousness: an atheist would see you worship a stool or light a candle at noon without a sneer at you; and a bishop, if you were well-dressed and perfumed, would argue with you calmly and serenely, though you doubted the whole Athanasian creed.

Home: So much the worse: God forbid we should ever experience this lukewarmness in Scotland.

Hume: God, it appears, has forbidden it: for which reason, to show my obedience and submission, I live as much as possible in France, where at present God has forbidden no such thing.

Home: Religion, my dear sir, can alone make men happy and keep them so.

Hume: Nothing is better calculated to make men happy than religion, if you will allow them to manage it according to their minds; in which case the strong men hunt down others, until they can fold them, entrap them, or noose them. Here however let the discussion terminate. Both of us have been in a cherry orchard, and have observed the advantages of the jacket, hat, and rattle.

Home: Our reformed religion does not authorise any line of conduct diverging from right reason: we are commanded by it to speak the truth to all men.

Hume: Are you likewise commanded to hear it from all men?

Home: Yes, let it only be proved to be truth.

Hume: I doubt the observance: you will not even let the fact be proved: you resist the attempt: you blockade the preliminaries. Religion, as you practise it in Scotland, in some cases is opposite to reason and subversive of happiness.

Home: In what instance?

Hume: If you had a brother whose wife was unfaithful to him without his suspicion; if he lived with her happily; if he had children by her; if others of which he was fond could be proved by you, and you only, not to be his; what would you do?

Home: O the harlot! we have none such here, excepting the wife indeed (as we hear she is) of a little lame blear-eyed lieutenant, brought with him from Sicily, and bearing an Etna of her own about her, and truly no quiescent or intermittent one, which Mungo Murray (the apprentice of Hector Abercrombie) tells me he has engulfed half the dissolutes in the parish. Of the married men who visited her, there was never one whose boot did not pinch him soon after, or the weather was no weather for corns and rheumatisms, or he must e'en go to Glasgow to look after a bad debt, the times being too ticklish to bear losses. I run into this discourse, not fearing that another philosopher will, like Empedocles, precipitate himself into the crater, but merely to warn you against the husband, whose intrepidity on entering the houses of strangers has caught many acute and wary folks. After the first compliments, he will lament to you that elegant and solid literature is more neglected in our days than it ever was. He will entreat you to recommend him to your bookseller; his own having been too much enriched by him had grown insolent. It is desirable that it should be one who could advance three or four guineas: not that he cares about the money, but that it is always best to have a check upon these people. You smile: he has probably joined you in the street already, and found his way into your study, and requested of you *by the bye* a trifling loan, as being the only person in the world with whom he could take such a liberty.

Hume: You seem to forget that I am but just arrived, and never knew him.

Home: That is no impediment: on the contrary, it is a reason the more. A new face is as inviting to him as to the mosquitoes in America. If you lend him a guinea to be rid of him, he will declare the next day that he borrowed it at your own request, and that he returned it the same evening.

Hume: Such men perhaps may have their reasons for being here; but the woman must be, as people say, like a fish out of water. Again to the question. Come now, if you had a brother, I was supposing whose wife—

Home: Out upon her! should my brother cohabit with her? should my nephews be defrauded of their patrimony by bastards?

Hume: You would then destroy his happiness, and his children's: for, supposing that you preserved to them a scanty portion more of fortune (which you could not do), still the shame they would feel from their mother's infamy would much outweigh it.

Home: I do not see clearly that this is a question of religion.

Hume: All the momentous actions of religious men are referable to their religion, more or less nearly; all the social duties, and surely these are implicated here, are connected with it. Suppose again that you knew a brother and sister, who, born in different countries, met at last, ignorant of their affinity, and married.

Home: Poor blind sinful creatures! God be merciful to them!

Hume: I join you heartily in the prayer, and would only add to it, man be merciful to them also! Imagine them to have lived together ten years, to have a numerous and happy family, to come and reside in your parish, and the attestation of their prior relationship to be made indubitable to you by some document which alone could establish and record it: what would you do?

Home: I would snap asunder the chain that the devil had ensnared them in, even if he stood before me; I would implore God to pardon them, and to survey with an eye of mercy their unoffending bairns.

Hume: And would not you be disposed to behold them with an eye of the same materials?

Home: Could I leave them in mortal sin? a prey to the ensnarer of souls! No; I would rush between them as with a flaming sword; I would rescue them by God's help from perdition.

Hume: What misery and consternation would this rescue bring with it!

Home: They would call upon the hills to cover them, to crush and extinguish their shame.

Hume: Those who had lived together in love and innocence and felicity? A word spoken to them by their pastor brings them into irremediable guilt and anguish. And you would do this?

Home: The laws of God are above all other laws: his ways are inscrutable: thick darkness covers his throne.

Hume: My cousin, you who have written so elegant and pathetic a tragedy, cannot but have read the best-contrived one in existence, the Œdipus of Sophocles.

Home: It has wrung my heart; it has deluged my eyes with weeping.

Hume: Which would you rather do; cause and excite those sufferings, or assuage and quell them?

Home: Am I a Scotchman or an islander of the Red Sea, that a question like this should be asked me?

Hume: You would not then have given to Œdipus that information which drove him and Jocasta to despair?

Home: As a Christian and a minister of the gospel, I am commanded to defy the devil, and to burst asunder the bonds of sin.

Hume: I am certain you would be greatly pained in doing it.

Home: I should never overcome the grief and anxiety so severe a duty would cause me.

Hume: You have now proved, better than I could have done in twenty *Essays*, that, if morality is not religion, neither is religion morality. Either of them, to be good (and the one must be and the other should be so), will produce good effects from the beginning to the end, and be followed by no remorse or repentance.

It would be presumptuous in me to quote the Bible to you, who are so much more conversant in it: yet I cannot refrain from repeating, for my own satisfaction, the beautiful sentence on Holiness; that "all her ways are pleasantness, and all her paths are peace." It says, not one or two paths, but *all*: for vice hath one or two passably pleasant in the season, if we could forget that, when we would return, the road is difficult to find, and must be picked out in the dark. Imagine anything in the semblance of a duty attended by regret and sorrow, and be assured that Holiness has no concern in it. Admonition, it is true, is sometimes of such a nature, from that of the irregularity it would correct, as to occasion a sigh or a blush to him who gives it; in this case, the sensation so manifested adds weight to the reproof and indemnifies the reprover. He is happy to have done, what from generosity and tenderness of heart he was sorry and slow to do; and the person in whose behalf he acted must be degraded beneath the dignity of manhood, if he feels less for himself than another has felt for him. The regret is not at the performance of his duty, but at the failure of its effect.

To produce as much happiness as we can, and to prevent as much misery, is the proper aim and end of true morality and true religion. Only give things their right direction; do but place and train them well, and there is room to move easily and pleasantly in the midst of them.

Home: What! in the midst of vice and wickedness? and must we place and train those?

Hume: There was a time when what is wine was not wine, when what is vinegar was not vinegar, when what is corruption was not corruption. That which would turn into vice, may not only not turn into it, but may, by discreet and attentive management, become the groundwork of virtue. A little watchfulness over ourselves will save us a great deal of watchfulness over others, and will permit the kindliest of religions to drop her inconvenient and unseemly talk, of enmity and strife, cuirasses and breastplates, battles and exterminations.

Home: These carnal terms are frequent in the books of the Old Testament.

Hume: Because the books of the Old Testament were written when the world was much more barbarous and ferocious than it is at present; and legislators must accommodate their language to the customs and manners of the country.

Home: Apparently you would rather abolish the forcible expressions of our pious reformers than the abominations at which their souls revolted. I am afraid you would hesitate as little to demolish kirks as convents, to drive out ministers as monks.

Hume: I would let ministers and their kirks alone. I would abolish monasteries; but gradually and humanely; and not until I had discovered how and where the studious and pious could spend their time better. I hold religion in the light of a medal which has contracted rust from ages. This rust seems to have been its preserver for many centuries, but after some few more will certainly be its consumer, and leave no vestige of effigy or superscription behind: it should be detached carefully and patiently, not ignorantly and rudely scoured off. Happiness may be taken away from many with the design of communicating it to more: but that which is a grateful and refreshing odor in a limited space, would be none whatever in a larger; that which is comfortable warmth to the domestic circle, would not awaken the chirping of a cricket, or stimulate the

flight of a butterfly, in the forest; that which satisfies a hundred poor monks, would, if thrown open to society at large, contribute not an atom to its benefit and emolument. Placid tempers, regulated habitudes, consolatory visitations, are suppressed and destroyed, and nothing rises from their ruins. Better let the cell be standing, than level it only for the thorn and nettle.

Home: What good do these idlers, with their cords and wallets, or, if you please, with their regularities?

Hume: These have their value, at least to the possessor and the few about him. Ask rather, what is the worth of his abode to the prince or to the public? who is the wiser for his cowl, the warmer for his frock, the more contented for his cloister, when they are taken from him? Monks, it is true, are only as stars that shine upon the desert: but tell me, I beseech you, who caused such a desert in the moral world? And who rendered so faint a light, in some of its periods, a blessing? Ignorant rulers, must be the answer, and inhuman laws. They should cease to exist some time before their antidotes, however ill-compounded, are cast away.

If we had lived seven or eight centuries ago, John Home would probably have been saying mass at the altar, and David Hume, fatter and lazier, would have been pursuing his theological studies in the convent. We are so much the creatures of times and seasons, so modified and fashioned by them, that the very plants upon the wall, if they were as sensible as some suppose them to be, would laugh at us.

Home: Fantastic forms and ceremonies are rather what the philosopher will reprehend. Strip away these, reduce things to their primitive state of purity and holiness, and nothing can alter or shake us, clinging, as we should, to the anchor of Faith.

Hume: People clung to it long ago; but many lost their grasp, benumbed by holding too tightly. The church of Scotland brings close together the objects of veneration and abhorrence. The evil principle, or devil, was, in my opinion, hardly worth the expense of his voyage from Persia; but, since you have him, you seem resolved to treat him nobly, hating him, defying him, and fearing him nevertheless. I would not however place him so very near the Creator, let his pretensions, from custom and precedent, be what they may.

Home: He is always marring the fair works of our heavenly Father: in this labour is his only proximity.

Hume: You represent him as spurring men on to wickedness, from no other motive than the pleasure he experiences in rendering them miserable.

Home: He has no other, excepting his inveterate spite and malice against God; from which indeed, to speak more properly, this desire originates.

Hume: Has he lost his wits, as well as his station, that he fancies he can render God unhappy by being spiteful and malicious? You wrong him greatly; but you wrong God more. For in all Satan's attempts to seduce men into wickedness, he leaves everyone his free will either to resist or yield; but the heavenly Father, as you would represent him, predestines the greater part of mankind to everlasting pains and torments, antecedently to corruption or temptation. There is no impiety in asking you which is the worst: for impiety most certainly does not consist in setting men right on what is demonstrable in their religion, nor in proving to them that God is greater and better than, with all their zeal for him, they have ever thought him.

Home: This is to confound religion with philosophy, the source of nearly every evil in conduct and of every error in ethics.

Hume: Religion is the eldest sister of Philosophy: on whatever subjects they may differ, it is unbecoming in either to quarrel, and most so about their inheritance.

Home: And have you nothing, sir, to say against the pomps and vanities of other worships, that you should assail the institutions of your native country? To fear God, I must suppose then, is less meritorious than to build steeples, and embroider surplices, and compose chants, and blow the bellows of organs.

Hume: My dear sir, it is not because God is delighted with hymns and instruments of music, or prefers base to tenor or tenor to base, or Handel to Giles Halloway, that nations throng to celebrate in their churches his power and his beneficence: it is not that Inigo Jones or Christopher Wren could erect to him a habitation more worthy of his presence than the humblest cottage on the loneliest moor: it is that the best feelings, the highest faculties, the greatest wealth, should be displayed and exercised in the patrimonial palace of every family united. For such are churches both to the rich and poor.

Home: Your hand, David! Pardon me, sir; the sentiment carried me beyond custom; for it recalled to me the moments of blissful enthusiasm when I was writing my tragedy, and charmed me the more as coming from you.

Hume: I explain the causes of things, and leave them.

Home: Go on, sir, pray go on; for here we can walk together. Suppose that God never heard us, never cared for us: do those care for you or hear you whose exploits you celebrate at public dinners, our Wallaces and Bruces? yet are not we thence the braver, the more generous, the more grateful?

Hume: I do not see clearly how the more grateful: but I would not analyse by reducing to a cinder a lofty sentiment.

Home: Surely we are grateful for the benefits our illustrious patriots have conferred on us: and every act of gratitude is rewarded by reproduction. Justice is often pale and melancholy; but Gratitude, her daughter, is constantly in the flow of spirits and the bloom of loveliness. You call out to her when you fancy she is passing; you want her for your dependents, your domestics, your friends, your children. The ancients, as you know, habitually asked their Gods and Goddesses by which of their names it was most agreeable to them to be invoked: now let Gratitude be, what for the play of our fancy we have just imagined her, a sentient living power; I can not think of any name more likely to be pleasing to her, than Religion. The simplest breast often holds more reason in it than it knows of, and more than Philosophy looks for or suspects. We almost as frequently despise what is not despicable as we admire and reverence what is. No nation in the world was ever so enlightened, and in all parts and qualities so civilised, as the Scotch. Why would you shake or unsettle or disturb those principles which have rendered us peaceable and contented?

Hume: I would not by any means.

Home: Many of your writings have evidently such a tendency.

Hume: Those of my writings to which you refer will be read by no nation: a few speculative men will take them; but none will be rendered more gloomy, more dissatisfied, or more unsocial by them. Rarely will you find one who, five minutes together, can fix his mind even on the surface: some new tune, some idle project, some light thought, some impracticable wish, will generally run, like the dazzling haze of summer on the dry heath, betwixt them and the reader. A bagpipe will swallow them up, a strathspey will dissipate them, or Romance with the death-rattle in her throat will drive them away into dark staircases and charnel-houses.

You and I, in the course of our conversation, have been at variance, as much as discreet and honest men ought to be: each knows that the other thinks differently from him, yet each esteems the other. I can not but smile when I reflect that a few paces, a glass of wine, a cup of tea, conciliate those whom Wisdom would keep asunder.

Home: No wonder you scoff emphatically, as you pronounce the word *wisdom*.

Hume: If men would permit their minds, like their children, to associate freely together, if they would agree to meet one another with smiles and frankness, instead of suspicion and defiance, the common stock of intelligence and of happiness would be centupled. Probably those two men who hate each other most, and whose best husbandry is to sow burs and thistles in each other's path, would, if they had ever met and conversed familiarly, have been ardent and inseparable friends. The minister who may order my book to be burnt to-morrow by the hangman, if I, by any accident, had been seated yesterday by his side at dinner, might perhaps in another fortnight recommend me to his master, for a man of such gravity and understanding as to be worthy of being a privy councillor, and might conduct me to the treasury-bench.

EUGENE LAWRENCE
From "David Hume"
The Lives of the British Historians
1855, Volume 2, pp. 194–215

The chief element of Hume's mental power was its skepticism. From this sprang his novelty, strength and profuse fertility. He was born to doubt. At sixteen, if not long before, we have evidence that he had cast aside many of the prevailing modes of belief. The principle grew stronger as his intellect matured. His skepticism in metaphysics, commencing in early youth, gave rise to those novel inquiries into the mental constitution, which gave to the science of the mind a new fertility. From the doubts of Hume sprang up new schools of philosophy. He found, indeed, few followers, but he gained what pleased him almost as well—many opponents. Reid and the Scottish thinkers, driven by his subtle reasoning from the old basis of the science, called in a new ally, which they called common sense. By a single doubt, Hume created the Scottish metaphysical school. In Germany, his opponents fled to the opposite pole. Kant, after long labors, produced a theory laden with mystic technicalities, by which he believed he could refute the ingenious skeptic. He declared the mind to be self-creative, producing its own cognitions, and while thus isolating the intellect in order to defend it from materialism, gave rise to that transcendental philosophy, which has gradually faded into the dreams of Fichte and Hegel. France, meanwhile, excited by the impulse from Germany and Scotland, sought to build up an eclectic philosophy of her own, more satisfactory to her modern thinkers than the analytical school of Des Cartes.

Such has been the power of Hume's skepticism in a single science. In politics, it has been no less destructive of ancient creeds. His essays and political discourses, so new and surprising in their day, gave a strong impulse to the study of political economy. They excited men to think upon topics which had been hitherto neglected. They aroused in England a class of reasoners who soon discovered the falseness of many of the prevailing views in trade and commercial legislation. Adam Smith developed Hume's doubts in his able treatise on the wealth of nations, and each succeeding writer upon political topics has owed much to Hume's novel inquiries. Bentham, Malthus, Brougham, and Ricardo have discussed and studied the questions which he proposed. In France, the effect of his writings was still more wonderful; they made political economy a popular study, and directed the attention of the best minds of that country to the subject of political reform. No little share of that free spirit, which led to the first Revolution, was due to the influence of Hume.

In literature, however, Hume's skepticism was strangely silent. Here he bowed superstitiously before the oracles of ancient criticism and the borrowed taste of Paris. He could approve nothing in tragedy that was not modelled after Sophocles, or in poetry that was not a reflection of Virgil. Shakspeare was to him a wild and savage genius, and Milton barbarously sublime. Even Homer had not that charm for him which he professes. He enjoyed the smooth and easy flow of Tasso and Virgil, better than the majestic ballads that have been woven into the *Iliad* and *Odyssey*. In this spirit of deference to antiquity he always wrote. His style has nothing of that boldness with which Milton asserted his mastery over his native tongue, or with which Johnson, diving deep into the wells of English lore, drew forth the pearls of his powerful diction. Hume never doubted that the classical models were to be implicitly followed, both in style and manner. His history he formed upon the model of the Greeks, neglecting all the suggestions which the enlarged inquiries of modern times demanded. He recommended Robertson to write biographies after the manner of Plutarch, and would himself have sunk into a mere imitator of Thucydides, had not his earnest doubts in religion, politics and character lent an interest to the history, which animates its classic style with vital fire, and gives it a novelty which no classic has attained.

From this singular exception to his general skepticism, Hume's criticisms are valueless. His literary history is without a novel thought. You anticipate his judgment before it is uttered. You see whom he will condemn and where will be the fatal fault. He mows down the fairest flowers in the gardens of English poetry with a hand more relentless than that of time. He aims vain blows at the greatest English dramatist, and the lord of English poets. Bacon, he ranks below Galileo, and Spenser, imaginative and harmonious, for him had written in vain. On the whole, he had little respect for English literature, and looked rather to Scotland, with its Wilkie and Home, to redeem the nation from the reproach of deficiency in taste and genius.

In another field of thought his skepticism was unusually active, and was again the ruling principle of his intellect. Religion to him had no existence; and his doubt of religion has stirred the mind of the world. "God, immortality, and liberty," the ideas which Kant makes the necessary offspring of mentality, Hume argued against as non-existent. His doubt, inconclusive as it was, proved the source of much that is peculiar and powerful in his writings. From the publication of the *Treatise*, his whole series of productions owe their interest to the artful ingenuity, with which his want of faith is developed and defended. History, essay, and metaphysical inquiry, all echo with the startling cry, "There is no God!" and the chief aim of his powerful intellect is to enforce this dreadful proposition—"Let us eat and drink, for to-morrow we die." These infidelities were not new in themselves, but by the manner in which Hume discovered and defended them. He drew them out of the deeps of metaphysical inquiry, and so arranged and adorned them in his novel speculations, that they were made singularly startling to the age in which he lived.

A skeptic by necessity, Hume fortunately possessed other mental traits which kept him from the sluggishness of doubt: he was untiringly inquisitive. In all subjects for which he was fitted by nature, he labored for knowledge. It is told of him that in company he would sit leaning on his hand, and lifting his eyes only to ask a question. This trait pursued him in his studies. In morals, metaphysics, and politics he was constantly an inquirer. Yet he seldom ventured a conclusion. His power lay in asking suggestively. Whenever he dogmatizes, as in literary criticism, he is usually wanting in novelty and truth.

Skepticism implies a want of the imaginative power. The skeptic may invent ingenious systems of argument, and delight in intellectual exercises; but he can know nothing of that fertility of form and imagery which springs from the influence of faith. Poets and painters are never skeptical. And Hume, believing as little as possible, destroyed whatever fancy had lingered to him from his youth. In his essays he emulates the gay and fanciful manner of Addison in vain, and Addison must have smiled at his uncourtly imitator. In history he carefully avoids all scenic display. His characters are well known intellectually; but never in their common dress and every-day pursuits. We almost forget that Queen Elizabeth wore a ruff; or that Mary's court shone with beautiful women, and glittered with Parisian fashions. He paints no stately pageants, nor lingers over the manners and amusements of the times. No opening diorama unfolds to us the men who sat in the Long Parliament, nor do we see the countenance and bearing of the daring Oliver, or the brave Montrose. To Hume, victim or victor were only portions of an interesting political discussion. He would have them animated arguments: he paints with clearness the outlines of their mental character, and leads Charles I. to the scaffold in a manner that touches every heart. But in all this, imagination has little share. He wanted wholly the creative power, and his characters live in the thoughts of the reader not as individuals, but as parts of an ingenious argument.

Yet Hume was not insensible to the finer feelings. The most captivating trait in his historical style is the readiness with which he seizes upon the tender and affecting elements of his narrative. While pursuing the cold and common details of political life, he constantly surprises us by an appeal to the softer sentiments of our nature, and is always successful in calling forth the emotion which he wishes to excite. His account of the last days of Elizabeth, of the execution of King Charles, of the death of the beautiful Mary, and the virtuous Russell, is singularly moving; and excels anything that can be found in his classic models.

Knowing his own powers, Hume aimed at nothing which he could not reach. In early youth he perhaps believed that he might write a poem after the manner of Virgil, cold, polished, and imitative; but as no trace of his early poetry remains, he must have prudently destroyed all his early attempts; and soon ceased to think himself a poet. His later efforts in verse, if those attributed to him are his, were mere literary recreations. He was vain of his poor attempts at humor; but these were only the trifles of the moment. He soon discovered that he was to be a philosopher and a prose writer, and with this design, gave himself up to reflection, looking in upon the movements of his own mind.

In style, he knew but one standard of excellence, and that he constantly strove to attain. We have seen the eagerness with which he strove to banish Scotticisms; he labored all his life to improve his style, and he made it more perfect than that of any other historian. It is faultless. Gibbon, Robertson, and their successors, have each some peculiar fault, which, amid their many excellences, leaves dissatisfaction upon the mind. But no man can rise from the study of Hume's writings, without feeling that language was never more delicately moulded or thought more artlessly expressed.

His style has an endless rhythm like the verse of Shakspeare, and never fails in harmony. Melody, the offspring of true genius, is unattainable by common minds. It was the charm of the Greek historians and has descended to a few modern writers. Hume's rhythm is peculiar to himself. It differs from that of Robertson or Gibbon, and the latter declared that he listened to it in despair. It has no resemblance to the sounding periods of Jeremy Taylor, or the simpler flow of Addison. Hume's ear for harmony was perfect, and his great thoughts shaped themselves into delicate modulations of language as naturally as those of Homer compressed themselves in verse.

To preserve this harmony he uses an easy flow of words. He never condenses; his thought are all broadly presented to the reader. There is no trace of the study of the elder English writers in his prose, and to him they were, probably, all barbarians. He had read little of Taylor, Barrow, or Burton. His thoughts never rise into artificial periods like those of Johnson, or contract into concise novelty like those of Bacon. He sought rather to utter his peculiar views in a language almost conversational, and distinguished from conversation only by its pleasing modulations. He uses the plainest Saxon; but he does this not from any acquaintance with Anglo-Saxon literature, but because he found that language the best to express his meaning. He has plainly studied the French writers diligently, but he has carefully shunned the measured and stilted tone assumed by the writers under Louis XIV. He has none of the declamation, the repetitions, the contrasts and antithesis that mark the eloquence of Massillon and Bossuet; he has even less of Voltaire's flippancy and satire; and his style is simply that of a wise and thoughtful mind addressing minds as thoughtful and as earnest as itself.

To attain this purity of style he was forced to labor incessantly. His handwriting was clear, yet even his familiar letters were made obscure by his efforts to remove all defects. It will be remembered, that he wrote a long letter to Dr. Clephane, asking him if the word "enow" was in use in good company in London. In reviewing Dr. Reid's manuscript, the only defect that he notices is the misuse of a single word. One of his last letters to Dr. Robertson contains a half-serious remonstrance against the "old-fashioned, dangling word '*wherewith*,' and the tribe of whereupon, whereto, and wherein." And as he went over his *History*, in preparing new editions, we find him constantly exercising this delicate verbal criticism. His various editions show the progress and growing nicety of his taste. In the first edition he writes "Scotch," in the new one "Scottish." Betwixt becomes "between," "under pretext" is "on pretence," "confined in the Tower"—"confined to the Tower," "effectuate a marriage"—"effect a marriage." "Had sat" the hardly more pleasing "had sitten," "reduced to shifts" becomes the less vulgar "reduced to extremities," and in the sentence "his dignity was exempted from pride," the Latin Scotticism is made "his dignity was free from pride."

Such careful word-study was enforced upon Hume and his literary circle by their Scottish origin. Speaking the broad dialect of their country, it is the more wonderful that Smith and Robertson and Hume should have so fully succeeded in attaining an almost perfect English. For this purpose, Robertson gave his days and nights to the study of Swift, and Hume, perhaps, to Addison. Yet they still labored under the disadvantage of writing, as it were, in a foreign language, and wanting the freedom and perfect mastery which only early habit can give, were forced to become classics in order to write with any ease.

Hume was not an eminently learned man. He was never fond of gathering the thoughts of other men in his commonplace book, or of fixing them in his memory. His mind, unlike the intellects of Warburton or Gibbon, those vast storehouses of knowledge, was occupied chiefly with looking in upon itself. He read few books, but those carefully and often. He always said that there were but few books worth reading. But upon small materials of research and study, he delighted to weave the vast fabrics of his own speculations. His mind, producing abundantly from its native strength, seemed to require little renewal to enable it to maintain its fertility.

Among his Scottish contemporaries, however, Hume passed for learned. By the side of Robertson or Kames, Smith and Reid, he was no doubt widely read. His friends, even more than himself, depended chiefly upon the native fertility of their minds. And in fact, of the two national intellects, the Scottish seems best fitted for speculation, the English for collecting knowledge. By the side of Johnson, Gibbon, or Gray, Hume's learning was dwarfed and feeble. His acquaintance with the languages was very imperfect. Even in Latin he was plainly deficient; and for its prosody he had no ear. His quotations of the Latin poets from memory, are usually deficient in grammar and always in verse. He may have read Latin easily, but he made errors in writing it that would have disgraced a schoolboy. Greek he professes to have "recovered," after he was thirty, but he makes such miserable mistakes in quoting it that it is not likely he could ever have read it with ease. French he spoke tolerably, was afraid to write, and perhaps had read extensively. It could hardly have happened that he should have spent three years of his youth in France without at least being able to understand the niceties of the language. Machiavelli and Tasso he professes to have read in their native tongue; certainly he had nothing else. He evidently had no readiness in acquiring languages, and must have been indebted chiefly to translations for his knowledge of the Greek masters who were his models in poetry, and the historians whom he imitated in prose.

With science, art, and mechanics he was wholly unfamiliar. No traces of geographical knowledge is to be found in his history. But the most striking instance of his ignorance is to be found in the two unfortunate first volumes of that work. Hume has written of the days of Alfred and Edward the Confessor, of the manners and genius of the Anglo-Saxon race, without any attempt to understand the true spirit of that remarkable people. To their poetical and prose compositions, their men of wonderful learning, and their intelligent and noble hearted monarchs he was wholly a stranger. Of the formation of the English language he knew nothing. He believed it to consist for the most part of French derivatives, an error that the analyzation of a few sentences must have instantly revealed. "From this," he writes, "proceeded that mixture of French which is at present to be found in the English tongue, and which composes the greatest and best part of our language," a statement altogether unfounded. The English language far from being chiefly Norman French, is chiefly pure Saxon, and derives its excellence from that circumstance. In its composition the Celtic and Danish have as large a share, the Latin a far more important one, than the language of its conquerors. The attempt of the victorious Normans to introduce the French into the schools and the literature of England, was unsuccessful, and the language of the conquered people gradually became that of the victors.

Of the Anglo-Saxons themselves he is no better informed. He classes them together as a people "rude and uncultivated, ignorant of letters, ungovernable and addicted to riot and disorder." As compared with the Normans they were barbarians, and from the Normans they received the first impulse towards knowledge and civilization. And this is told of a people who had already made great progress in learning and letters, who had produced learned historians, pleasing poets, and princes distinguished by a love of literature, a wisdom, and a political liberality such as no Norman duke had ever been known to display. A people whose monasteries produced scholars educated under Bede, and Egbert and Alfred, and whose famous Alcuin was the founder of the University of Paris, and had imparted the first elements of civilization to the subjects of Charlemagne.

But ignorance might have been pardoned if Hume had not added a graver fault. The ideal of a perfect historian is one who shall labor for truthfulness; a philosophical historian, one would suppose, of all others must display this peculiar trait. He should be the most careful and accurate of writers. But far different is it with Hume. He evidently commenced his *History* as an agreeable mental exercise. He selected an interesting hero. It was Charles I. Whether from the mere love of paradox or from a lingering taint of Jacobitism which was in his family, he resolved to lend all the influence of his subtile reasoning, and pathetic narrative, to the side of the tyrannical monarch. Charles was to rise from his grave arrayed in white robes of a martyr. To clothe in this garb of purity a monarch who had attempted to rule his people without a parliament, and to take their money from them at pleasure; who had frequently violated his pledged word and had acted upon the maxim that kings should keep no faith with their subjects, was not easy. Yet Hume essayed and accomplished it. But he did this by violating the truth of history. He invented indeed, no new facts, but he accomplished his design by omitting much that was important. He passed lightly over the faults of Charles to dwell upon his virtues. He blinds himself and his readers to the great qualities of those heroes of the middle classes who asserted the liberties of Englishmen, Hampden and Pym, Waller and Cromwell. The Parliament he represents as factious and designing, the king as grave, beneficent and ill-used. That vast body of Englishmen who had risen in arms against oppression, he depicts as little better than a factious mob. That austere army, which gave to war a higher aspect and robbed it of half its brutality, to Hume was composed of canting hypocrites, and that mighty genius who, on the death of Charles, ruled England with more than the energy of Elizabeth, was only a whining brewer who could not speak two words consecutively with clearness, and whose life and example of rigid virtue was all hypocrisy and guile.

This false representation was met by a public reprobation. Yet Hume clung to his theory. All the remaining volume of his work bear upon the character of his hero, Charles. He wrote the history of the Tudors to prove that Charles was justifiable in tyranny, and he pursues the theme back to the Conquest. Wherever he can extend the prerogative, he has done so; wherever he could set out of view the rights of the people, he has seized the opportunity. For the Parliament he has everywhere a sneer, for the prince a word of applause: a course the more inexcusable, since in his political essays he had unfolded a liberality of political sentiment that would have graced a Hampden or a Milton.

Hume's *History*, therefore, is scarcely better than a fiction. It is hardly more reliable than the works of Carte or Oldmixon; and far less excusable, since it pretends to philo-

sophic impartiality. A witness on the stand, who should give such an account of facts with which he was familiar, omitting those that made against his purpose, and dwelling on those that favored it, would be guilty of a suppression of the truth, and would violate his oath. An historian, pretending to impartiality, who thus distorts the truth, is guilty of the greatest offence. He is telling to posterity a tale that he knows to be false.

The only excuse for Hume is that he took a low view of the morals of history. He seems to have thought that the first duty of an historian was to relate an interesting story. If he carefully labored his style, and collected amusing details from various sources, if he could produce an authority for every circumstance, and could tell Charles Townsend, who doubted his accuracy, that he would find every incident in the records: he believed his duty was fulfilled. He had written a work interesting, full of ingenious theories and happy speculations, teeming with the evidences of taste and genius; and what more could posterity ask?

Is it possible that this false pleader, this avowed traducer, this narrator of a garbled story, can be the first of British historians? That a writer so unreliable can have won the attention and the applause of the best minds of his own and all succeeding ages? That Mackintosh and Brougham and Romilly can have united to place him where he now stands, first among his rivals; while the honest intellect of the Anglo-Saxons of every land cherishes as a priceless treasure this work, in which there is so much that is false and so much that is unworthy?

There can only be applied to this singular problem in literature the simplest solution. What we admire in Hume's *History* is the display of intellectual power. We read it, not so much for information, as for an agreeable intellectual exercise. In this view it was written, in this it is read. We admire its subtile disputations, its artful array of facts, the genius which shines in its false narrative, and illuminates its unsound disputations. The consciousness that its narrative is unsound heightens the interest of the tale. We yield to the skillful partisan as the spectator yields to the gifted tragedian. Its scenes of pathos fascinate us, although we feel that our pity is wrongly bestowed. Its nice balance of opposing arguments, with a bias ever to one side, satisfies our judgment as a specimen of peculiar mental power. It is the skillful by-play of the barrister defending an almost defenceless cause solely by his own ingenuity; and we rank Hume the first of historians, not because he has written a truthful narrative, but because he has shown what an admirable book he would have made, had he taken up a better cause.

One trait which modern historians claim as their peculiar excellence was first adopted by Hume. He was inquisitive with regard to all matters of political economy. In his essays he had been accustomed to examine into curious statistics, and now he was the first of the English historians who added to his history an account of the manners of the times of which he wrote. The appendix which he attached to each important period was not only a new feature, but must have been attended with considerable labor and research. He here descends from the dignity of history to give minute details of common life; to tell how much a capon sold for under Henry VIII., how much corn brought in the reign of Elizabeth; what was the price of land, the wages of labor, the cost of transportation, the gross amount of commerce and trade. He also notices slightly the amusements and tastes of the people, the employments of the court and city, and tells something of the condition of the masses in regard to food and living. Invariably he closes his account of manners with those criticisms upon literature so well meant, but so ill done, and which, valueless in themselves, betray the strength of his national prejudices and the narrow range of his taste.

For scenery and nature he had little love. In all his writings there is not a single description of a scene from nature. His journal down the Rhine and the Danube may seem an exception to this; but the faint praise and general account which he gives of the finest landscapes in Europe, shows how slight was the impression with which they affected him. He simply remarks that the banks of this river are wild, of that are well cultivated; but he never pauses to select some particular view, and to produce it to the fancy of the reader. Drachenfels and Ehrenbreitstein are to him only common castles: he is more struck by the deformities of the peasants of Styria than delighted with the wild and lovely landscape through which he travelled. It is always the curious traits of every scene rather than the beautiful, upon which he delights to dwell. For strange and novel facts he is ever on the watch: but for mere beauty he has no leisure.

This want of perception of physical beauty is felt in his history. Writing of a country of great natural charms, he might well have paused in his details of politics, to rescue some single landscape from neglect, to paint a battlefield or to describe the physical advance of his country. He might have defined the landscape amid which Mary passed her long imprisonment, and upon which her sad eyes so often rested in hope of deliverance; or he might have drawn, with his master hand, the fine scenery amid which Falkland fell. But of nature he gives us not a glimpse. Even in his appendix he aims to give no general view of the condition of the country, whether it was covered with cottages, or studded only with gloomy castles; where cornfields smiled, or where the ravages of war or the barrenness of the soil enforced a perpetual sterility. Such descriptions he did not think worthy of a place in history, nor is it probable that had he attempted it, he could have given a much better account of a fine landscape, than he could of a fine poem or a fine play.

Great intellects are of necessity refined. There is a common standard to which they all aspire. Hume was right, therefore, in endeavoring by ceaseless labor to cast off his faults of education, to refine and chasten his genius, and to approach as near as possible to his highest standard—the ancients. To become a classic was his constant aim; and if that term mean an union of the greatest mental power with the highest limit of refinement, he succeeded. Fortunately for his fame, he did not lose his originality in his effort to approach his great models. Each one of his writings is marked by a novelty which separates it from all other productions, and gives it a striking individuality. The *Treatise*, polished and pruned by his youthful taste, still possesses more rude strength than any of his works. But the *History* never grows tame or feeble, however much he labors to remove its superfluities, and to conform it to a classical design. His style, delicately wrought and purified, was entirely his own. His method and arrangement, clear, simple and philosophical, no other writer has since been able to rival. And it is the highest proof of the originality of his genius that, although always studying and imitating high models, in all his writings he shows no trace of imitation.

As an historian Hume takes the chief place in the literature of his country. There he has been placed not only by the ablest critics but by the common agreement of all reading men. And it is doubtful whether, since the age of Tacitus, there has arisen in all modern literature an historical writer who has combined so many remarkable traits. Niebuhr, if he be more than an historical critic, is far more learned. Guicciardini more patriotic, and Voltaire more acute; but Hume is more thor-

oughly than either the great historian. He seems to have had a fitness for this vocation more than any other man. And all his faculties, conspiring happily together, blend in his great work the highest excellences of historical composition.

In essay writing he was less happy. His shorter pieces are wonderful for method and order. If argumentative, they conduct the mind to their conclusion without a shade of obscurity or a needless pause. If more fanciful, they are always clear and refined. But they are not essays in the true sense of that word; they are not the genuine descendants of the *Spectator* and the *Tatler*; they want the lively play of fancy, the wide range of illustration, and the happy flow of style that mark the true offspring of the great British essayists. For illustration Hume was wholly at a loss. He knew nothing of nature and of the thousand images and pleasant conceptions, which she offers to the imaginative mind. From poetry he could borrow no beauties, since he was altogether incapable of perceiving what was its crowning charm; association and romantic legends and curious lore, he had not taste for; pleasant fancies and inventions he had no power to summon to his aid. His style was bare and unenriched from the abundant stores which lie at the call of the genial essayist, like Lamb or Macaulay, but which were to him all sealed and unknown. His language had no richness of expression, no powerful and impetuous flow. His essays, therefore, are simply disquisitions; as arguments they are admirable, as examples of subtle reasoning they have a singular charm. But it is impossible to call Hume an essayist, as Addison was an essayist, or to rank him among that delightful band of writers, peculiar to England, who have done more than any other class for the improvement and embellishment of their native literature.

As a metaphysical author he stands again, in novelty of conception and in greatness of influence, at the summit of renown. Locke and Berkeley have both sunk into provincials before his world-wide fame. Reid and Stewart are by reaction his disciples. Yet Hume fails wholly in method in treating of metaphysics. His first work, the *Treatise*, was an incongruous medley. Professing to treat of the human understanding, its second part ran into moral disquisitions, and its third was of "virtue and vice." He seems to have flung to the press a mass of discursive thoughts under a title altogether inappropriate. From this fault he never recovered and never ceased to lament it. His style, however, made amends for his want of method. He conveys the most difficult conceptions in the plainest language. Later writers have been driven to the formation of technical phrases to convey their metaphysical meaning. Kant has formed a vocabulary of the science, the meaning of which his disciples labor in vain to unfold; and his method has been adopted by most modern metaphysicians with, perhaps, some benefit. But Hume never felt this necessity. Novel as were his theories, he could unfold them with perfect clearness in the common dialect. He never veils himself in a wise obscurity, or uses sounding words to which none but himself can attach a meaning. His own conceptions were singularly clear and well defined, and his style was so pure that it revealed the depths of his intellect to the common observer, as the clear water of an inland lake its pebbly bottom.

SIR LESLIE STEPHEN
From *History of English Thought
in the Eighteenth Century*
1876

Hume, unlike Berkeley or Locke, was absolutely free from theological prepossessions. He, and he alone, amongst contemporary thinkers, followed logic wherever it led him. Hume, indeed, may be accused of some divergence from the straight path under the influence of literary vanity. To that cause we must partly attribute his singular attempt to extinguish his early and most complete work, the *Treatise on Human Nature*. During his youth, however, he was a reasoner pure and simple, and the subsequent change in his literary activity probably implied some real dissatisfaction with part of the earlier treatise, whilst we shall see that, in another sense, it was a legitimate consequence of the principles to which he still undoubtedly adhered. Hume's scepticism completes the critical movement of Locke. It marks one of the great turning-points in the history of thought. From his writings we may date the definite abandonment of the philosophical conceptions of the preceding century, leading in some cases to an abandonment of the great questions as insoluble, and, in others, to an attempt to solve them by a new method. Hume did not destroy ontology or theology, but he destroyed the old ontology; and all later thinkers who have not been content with the mere dead bones of extinct philosophy, have built up their systems upon entirely new lines.

Hume starts from the positions occupied by Locke and Berkeley. He regards innate ideas as exploded; he accepts Berkeley's view of abstraction (as he understands it) and of the distinction between primary and secondary qualities; he applies and carries out more systematically the arguments by which Berkeley had assailed the hypothetical substratum of material qualities. But with Hume the three substances disappear together. The soul is dissolved by the analysis which has been fatal to its antithesis. All grounds for an *a priori* theology are cut away, though his conclusion is, for obvious reasons, not so unequivocally displayed in the treatise. All our knowledge is framed out of 'impressions' and 'ideas,' ideas being simply decaying impressions. The attempt to find a reality underlying these impressions is futile, and even self-contradictory. We are conscious only of an unceasing stream of more or less vivid feelings, generally cohering in certain groups. The belief that anything exists outside our mind, when not actually perceived, is a 'fiction.' The belief in a continuous subject which perceives the feelings is another fiction. The only foundation of the belief that former coherences will again cohere is custom. Belief is a 'lively idea related to or associated with a present impression.' Reason is 'nothing but a wonderful and unintelligible instinct in our souls, which carries us along a certain train of ideas, and endows them with particular qualities according to their particular situations and relations.' Association is in the mental what gravitation is in the natural world. The name signifies the inexplicable tendency of previously connected ideas and impressions to connect themselves again. We can only explain mental processes of any kind by resolving them into such cases of association. Thus reality is to be found only in the ever-varying stream of feelings, bound together by custom, regarded by a 'fiction' or set of fictions as implying some permanent set of external or internal relations, and becoming beliefs only as they acquire liveliness. Chance, instead of order, must, it would seem, be the ultimate objective fact, as custom, instead of reason, is the ultimate subjective

fact. We have reached, it is plain, the fullest expression of scepticism, and are not surprised when Hume admits that his doubts disappear when he leaves his study. The old bonds which held things together have been completely dissolved. Hume can see no way to replace them, and Hume, therefore, is a systematic sceptic.

I must attempt, however, to define rather more closely the nature of this destructive conclusion. Hume assails the old theory of perception and the old theory of causation. What are the elements of which the universe is composed, and how are they woven into a continuous whole? 'I see the sun.' How does that statement differ from the statement, 'I have certain sensations of light and heat'? 'I believe that the sun will rise to-morrow.' What do I mean by belief, and what is my warrant for this particular belief? Hume's analysis of this last question involves the theory of causation, which is his most celebrated contribution to philosophy. It became the prominent thesis of the *Essays*, which gave Hume's later version of his philosophy; it suggested Kant's inquiry into the foundations of philosophy, and it was accepted with little alteration by the school which followed Hume's lead in England. It is, however, closely connected with his other theories. The question, Why do I conceive of the world as something different from a series of sensations? is bound up with the further inquiry, Why do I regard the world thus constituted as regulated by certain invariable relations? Whether reasonably or otherwise, we do in fact interpret the stream of feelings of which consciousness is composed as implying an organised system of real existences or potentialities of experience, underlying each other in infinite complexity. As a fact, we believe in a set of permanent relations independent of our individual consciousness. How, and in what sense, is this to be 'explained'?

Let us begin with the theory of perception. Every perception must depend upon the perceiving subject. My sight depends upon my eyes. If they were differently constituted, I should see differently. Therefore, it was argued by Locke, colour is a secondary quality. It depends upon the perceiver as well as upon the thing perceived. Therefore it cannot have that reality which is to be found in the transcendental world alone, where it is assumed we might see things unaffected by the character of our eyes. Hume, following Berkeley, has only to apply this method to the primary qualities. They, as much as the secondary qualities, are perceived through the senses, and are equally unreal, if the presence of a subjective factor implies unreality. The ideas of colour, sounds, tastes, and smells, are inseparably connected with the ideas of extension or solidity. Each implies the other, and to remove one set of ideas is to remove the other. If we take an object to pieces in our imagination, we find that, when we have removed all the qualities known to us by our senses, we have removed everything. The supposed 'abstract idea,' which remains behind, is, as Berkeley has shown, a mere empty word. A thing is the sum of its qualities; and what we call the abstract idea of a triangle is but the idea of a particular triangle regarded as representative of an indefinite multitude of other triangles. Thus, whenever an idea is suggested as corresponding to some independent reality, Hume challenges it to give an account of itself. Can we trace its derivation to some previous impression? If we cannot, it is an empty word. If we can, it must share the unreality of the impression which it represents.

How then do we come by the distinction between external and internal? If every object of thought is either a sensation or the representative of a sensation, an actual or a decaying impression, how can we even think of things as existing outside of us? 'It is impossible for us,' says Hume, 'so much as to conceive or form an idea of anything specifically different from ideas and impressions. Let us fix our attention out of ourselves as much as possible. Let us chase our imaginations to the heavens, or to the utmost limits of the universe; we never can really advance a step beyond ourselves, nor can conceive any kind of existence but those perceptions which have appeared in that narrow compass. This is the universe of the Imagination, nor have we any idea but what is there produced.' So great is our weakness that Hume notices as anomalous the case in which we form an idea of a particular shade of blue, when we have only perceived contiguous shades. The mind is supposed to have no faculty except that of reviewing past impressions, modified only by their gradual decay.

Yet it is a plain fact of consciousness that we think of a table or a house as somehow existing independently of our perception of it. The mind is conscious of a series of sensations of colour, form, and so forth. Some of these recur frequently in the same relative positions, though interrupted by other terms of the series. Why does the mind, which can only, as Hume says, reproduce its impressions and ideas, and reproduce them in their old form, identify the recurrent terms, and then suppose them to exist behind the interrupting terms? Why are not the group of sensations which we call table supposed to vanish when they are not felt like the group of sensations which we call toothache? 'As far as the senses are judges,' he says, 'all perceptions are the same in the manner of their existence.' The so-called qualities of bodies are sensations; the pain caused by a blow, the colours of the striking body, its extension and solidity, are equally feelings in the mind. We have, it would seem, in each case, the same ground, or absence of ground, for inferring a corresponding external existence in one case as in the other. Both inferences are alike reasonable or unreasonable. As reason does not infer the external existence in the case of a pain, it should not do so in the case of colour; and we must therefore refer to the imagination as the source of our belief in external existence. Hume traces, in a very ingenious chapter, the mode in which the coherence and consistency of certain groups of feelings make it easy for the imagination to regard the series of similar but intermittent sensations as continuous and identical. As the attempt to satisfy the imagination, which thus suggests an independent existence of our perceptions, and the reason which refuses to recognise an unperceived perception as possible, philosophers have hit upon the expedient of attributing interruption to our perceptions and independent continuity to 'objects.' But as an object can only be a perception—for we can imagine nothing but our feelings—the contradiction is really concealed, not evaded. Here, says Hume, is the sceptical doubt which can never be 'radically cured.' The subjective element implies unreality. All perceptions have a subjective element. Therefore, the supposed reality must be a 'fiction.'

The doubt, in fact, has not been even yet radically cured. The struggle between realists and idealists continues, and every philosopher has his own solution. All that can be here attempted is to indicate the direction impressed upon later speculations by the doubt thus formally articulated. We may, perhaps, admit that Hume's account of the process by which a belief in an external world is actually suggested is fairly accurate, or that it coincides, as far as the contemporary state of psychology would allow, with the explanations given by later thinkers of his school.[1] Further, the process described is not strictly reason. A simple inspection of a sensation will not reveal an external object to which it corresponds. Nor can we say that the object, in the sense of a continuous something as it exists out of relation to the mind, 'resembles' the sensation, for that would be to attempt the contradictory feat of contemplating an unrelated relation. Still further, we may admit that the philosophy attacked by Hume, and the popular conceptions upon which it was based, did involve an element of 'fiction.' The whole history of philosophical thought is but a history of attempts to separate the object and the subject, and each new attempt implies that the previous line of separation was erroneously drawn or partly 'fictitious.' Such a familiar fact again as the belief that an object felt in the dark is coloured as we see it in the light, illustrates the popular tendency described by Hume to attribute an objective existence to our own sensations—in others words, to believe in a 'fiction.'

In what direction, then, are we to escape? Granting that Hume has exposed certain contradictions involved in contemporary philosophy and in all popular conceptions, are we to regard those contradictions as insoluble? The first remark will probably be that Hume's 'fiction' implies the existence of a condition which he tends to ignore. If we are unable accurately to draw the line between the objective and subjective, and even forced to admit that the attempt to separate the two elements in perceptions common to the race implies a contradictory attempt to get outside of our own minds, we must still admit that the primitive elements of consciousness imply the necessity of recognising the distinction. They have, that is, an objective and subjective aspect, and the power of thus organising impressions implies the existence of an organised mind. Hume's analysis seems to recognise no difference between the mind of a man and a polyp, between the intellectual and the merely sensitive animal. The mind is a bare faculty for repeating impressions. The power of grouping and arranging them is regarded as somehow negligeable. Agreeing that all materials of thought are derived from experience, we yet have to account for the form impressed upon them. The destruction of innate ideas seemed to him, as to the philosophers whom he assailed, almost to imply the annihilation even of mental faculties. He could not allow that the function depended upon the organ without seeming to admit that the organ either created materials for itself, or was supplied with them from some source independent of experience. And, in the next place, the doctrine that belief in the external world is a 'fiction' is apparently self-destructive. If all reason is fiction, fiction is reason. It is indeed true that the process by which the belief is generated is not what we call reason. It does not imply a reference to general rules; but that is because it generates the rules. Feeling precedes reason, and is the material out of which reason is evolved. We become reasonable as we become conscious of the law by which our feelings have been unconsciously determined. Slowly and tentatively we arrive at a true conception of the division between the external and internal world by a series of approximate assumptions, each involving a slowly diminishing amount of error, and our belief is justified in proportion as the assumption thus blindly felt out gives coherent and accurate results. Hume follows the ontologists in trying to find a reason for reason, and to get the why of the wherefore. When he comes upon a process which underlies reason, instead of being deduced from it, he pronounces it to be fictitious as they call it transcendental. Thus we should say that, whilst Hume was right in limiting the mind to experience, and in declaring the existing distinction of object and subject to involve an error, he was wrong in not observing that the very possibility of making the distinction implied an operative mind, and in not seeing that the process by which the distinction works itself into correspondence with facts is legitimate, though not, in his sense, reasoning. He cannot account for the existence of the organising power, and he does not understand the process by which the facts are finally organised.

Hume's attack on the theory of causation follows the same lines. We have nothing to deal with but a series of impressions and ideas. The hypothetical objects to which the ideas were taken to correspond have vanished, and the powers inherent in them must vanish equally. The idea of 'power' cannot be traced to any impression, and is therefore, by Hume's ordinary test, no idea at all, but an empty word. We say, for example, that fire burns. That, on the old interpretation, was explained to mean that fire had a latent power, which started into activity under certain conditions. But what is this power? We have an 'idea' of fire, because we once had an 'impression' of fire. The mental picture is a copy of a previous sensation. Similarly we have an idea of 'burning'—of a piece of paper, for example, turning black and crumpling up when exposed to fire. But of the power as an independent entity, existing independently of the two phenomena, we have no idea at all, for we can never have had an impression. Or contemplate the same facts from the subjective side. One thing, it had been held, was the cause of another when the existence of the second followed from the definition of the first. If we could define fire adequately—that is, if the definition expressed its essence—we could deduce the proposition 'fire burns,' as we deduce from the definition of a circle the proposition expressive of its various properties. Now, in this sense, as Hume argues, we can never know a cause. The various combinations of colour, form, and so on, might, for anything that we can tell, be replaced by any other combinations. We can separate in imagination any two ideas which have been combined; for what is distinguishable is separable. We can think of fire without thinking of it as burning, of a planet without regarding it as gravitating; and similarly in all other cases. But, if the existence of one thing logically implied the existence of another thing, such a separation would imply a contradiction. Erroneous logic may always be forced to yield such a contradiction by accurate analysis. In other words, the relation of cause and effect can never correspond to an *a priori* logical nexus; for it can never imply a contradiction in terms to suppose one body annihilated whilst others remain unaltered. But if logic implied any necessary connections between ideas, a contradiction must emerge in such cases. Hence the objective and the subjective links disappear together, and we are forced to admit that 'the uniting principle amongst our internal perceptions is as unintelligible as that among external objects, and it is not known to us in any other way than by experience.'

The nature of this celebrated argument, and its affiliation to previous theories, may perhaps be more closely exhibited by an illustration given by Reid. A magnet attracts iron. In the earlier stage of thought this phenomenon, if observed, might have been explained by the assumption that the magnet had an appetite for iron like that of a human being for food. As the points of unlikeness became evident, this appetite would gradually fade away into an occult power inherent in the magnet, and called forth on the approach of iron. The magnet, regarded as the active factor, was the cause; the movement produced in the iron would be the effect. Philosophers supposed that, from a complete definition of the magnet, this iron-attracting power might be deduced as a necessary consequence of the definition. Hume then argues that we can form no idea whatever of this supposed power, regarded as an independent entity. He observes, moreover, that our knowledge of its existence is nothing else than a knowledge that, as a matter of fact, magnets have been observed in previous cases to attract iron. Further, it is impossible to show by an *a priori* process that magnets must

attract iron; were that possible, it would be impossible to conceive of a magnet as not attracting iron; whereas nothing is easier than to imagine the magnet and the iron co-existing without attraction. All that is left, therefore, is, on the one hand, the fact that magnets have attracted iron, and, on the other, the 'custom' set up in the mind of expecting a similar combination in future. Experience is all, and experience can never give rise to any logical inference beyond itself. All such inferences then are illogical or customary.

If now we examine the case more closely, we may see that Hume has made an omission similar to the omission already noticed in his theory of perception. He is perfectly right in asserting that our knowledge of this property of magnets depends upon experience alone. He is right, again, in a certain sense, in saying that we may conceive of a magnet not attracting iron. We have, that is, no *a priori* ground for the assertion that all the other qualities discovered in the magnet its weight, colour, chemical composition, and so forth—may not be hereafter discovered in a body which does not attract iron. But he implicitly makes another assertion, easily confounded with this last, and yet involving a fundamental error— the assertion, namely, that we might expect to find a magnet identical in all respects with the first magnet which yet would not attract iron. This statement implies the existence of chance as something more than a name for our ignorance, and must therefore be denied by all who (on whatever grounds) believe in the validity of reason, or the correlative doctrine of the regularity of the external world. Suppose, in fact, that we found that a so-called magnet did not attract iron, we should be entitled to conclude peremptorily that it was wanting in some quality, discoverable or not, which exists in true magnets. Its molecular composition, or the state of its molecules, must be in some way altered. We cannot hold that the magnet loses one quality whilst all the others are unchanged, though it may be that all the discovered, or even all the discoverable, qualities remain unchanged. In the last case, there is an element of chance in the sense, that is, that undiscoverable conditions are present; but there cannot be in the sense that the same conditions exist and produce different results. Metaphysicians may still dispute what is our warrant for this assumption, but its validity is implied in all reasonings about the external world; for otherwise the world is not a system of permanent relations. Hume has here again come upon an ultimate process implied in all reason, and not being able to find a further justification for it, pronounces it to be a mere 'custom.'

The point may be stated in a slightly different form. Every phenomenon is known as the sum of a set of relations. The total phenomenon—the attraction of the iron by the magnet— is the effect. The separate factors, the presence of the iron and the magnet, each of which is decomposable into various groups of relations to the perceiving subject, and to each other, are the causes. The same phenomenon can always be resolved into the same causes. If the phenomenon differs, some one or more of the components must differ. In this sense the assertion of the uniformity of causation is resolvable into something like an identical truth, or at least a statement of the postulate implied in all reason, and which constitutes the very reasoning process, that we can make identical propositions in identical cases. We thus come upon the fundamental illusion which underlies Hume's scepticism, and which was inherited by him from preceding thinkers. We fancy that we can separate the two terms of a relation without altering them. We take the magnet which is not magnetic, the fire which does not burn, the planet which does not gravitate, and suppose that the idea remains unaltered even in the act of altering it. Hence we come to the contradictory conceptions of unperceivable perceptions and inactive activities. The magnet has no power of attracting independently of the iron. The two are equally essential factors in the phenomenon; and when we separate them, and then try to mend the conception by the fiction of an occult power, we are led to scepticism by discarding one factor whilst continuing to regard the other of the connected objects as still entitled to the name of cause. The true answer to Hume's scepticism is, therefore, that we cannot conceive of a non-magnetic magnet; for that is to conceive of a magnet deprived of the quality which makes it a magnet. But it remains true, as Hume says, that this quality is revealed to us by experience alone, and that we have no right in any given case to appeal to an *a priori* reason. What remains after Hume's scepticism has been allowed full play is the objective fact of the regularity of the external world, and the subjective faculty which corresponds to it, in virtue of which we assert, not that this or that truth, revealed by experience, is universally true, but that every experience implicitly contains a universal truth. When two experiences differ, we are entitled, that is, to assume that there is some difference in the conditions which may or may not be evident to our senses. To make this assumption is to reason. Hume's scepticism is justified in so far as it denies the existence in the mind of a certain list of self-evidencing truths independent of all experience. It is erroneous in confounding this denial with the suicidal denial that the mind possesses, or rather is constituted by a certain faculty involved in the recombination of experience. Having emptied the mind of its supposed innate ideas and *a priori* truths, he fancies that the mind itself is dissolved, and that reason is shown to be 'custom.' The organism remains, though the laws of its operation are only revealed to us by the experience upon which it operates.

The critical movement, then, of which Hume gave the last word amounted to the final destruction of the old assumptions by which philosophers, developing and modifying the earliest modes of conception, had reconciled the doctrines of the regularity of the universe and the validity of reason with the observation that all phenomena are incessantly changing, and that knowledge of the visible universe can only be derived from the impressions made by these changing phenomena on the senses. The assumptions, themselves the phantoms of earlier assumptions, are shown to involve irreconcilable contradictions. The sceptic pulls the constructions of the dogmatist to pieces, and assumes that no dogmas can be discovered. From the dogmatist he adopts the introspective method, or, in other words, assumes that the ultimate truths, if such truths exist, may be found by simply inspecting our own minds. Now, such inspection cannot reveal the observing faculty itself, but only the varying set of experiences which it has observed. Hence, truth can only be discovered if the mind is stocked with certain ideas miraculously inserted prior to all experience. But the sceptic proves against the dogmatist that no such idea is discoverable. Every idea that can be assigned is traceable to certain observations, which must be affected by the mind of the observer, or have a 'subjective' element. But the sceptic assumes, again, with the dogmatist, that the subjective element implies unreality. Hence there is no truth discoverable. This mode of analysis applied to the three great ideas shows them to be unreal. The bond which holds the external universe together is non-existent or essentially undiscoverable. The bond which holds together the corresponding mental construction must be equally undiscoverable, for the innate ideas and principles upon which it must be founded have failed to stand the accepted test. Briefly, the method by which alone, as

dogmatists and sceptics agreed, truth could be discoverable, led to the hopeless attempt of getting out of ourselves and seeing things as we do not see them. Scepticism, therefore, was inevitable, unless a different method could be suggested. It had shown beyond all dispute that the old conceptions involved an element of fiction, and, in fact, they were thenceforward exorcised from living philosophy. Ontology revived, but it revived by striking out a new path. The conceptions of God, the soul, and matter were not destroyed, but they were transformed.

A line of escape from these difficulties was indicated by Kant's theory of time and space. The mind is conceived as a mould which imposes its own form upon the experience which it received. In every act of perception there are two factors, the objective and subjective, neither of which can be conceived apart from the other. Reality does not imply the absence of a subjective organ, but only that the organ is operating according to universal laws. It is not necessary for the discovery of truth to know things as they cannot be known, or to discover propositions existing independently of a relation between the perceiving and the perceived. The two terms of relation, which had been arbitrarily separated, are again brought together, and the hopeless attempt to get outside ourselves is abandoned. It is fortunately needless, however, to touch upon the many problems suggested by this conception, even in the briefest terms. Kant's philosophy did not react upon English thought till a period later than that with which I am dealing. If Kant had never lived, or had lived in Pekin, English thinkers in the eighteenth century would not have been less conscious of his position. It is enough to mention the difficulty which would have made his view unacceptable to such a mind as Hume's, even if it had been presented to him. The theory of a mind imposing its own forms upon experience seems to introduce an *a priori* element. If that element can in any way be separated in thought from its correlative, there still seems to be a road to the otherwise hopeless attempt of constructing a philosophy independent of experience; and the experiment was made by some of Kant's German successors. To admit the existence of an *a priori* factor in thought might be as dangerous as to admit the existence of *a priori* truths in the soul. Locke's attempt to expel the unknowable, and the scholasticism founded upon it, might be evaded by a more refined procedure. Modern thinkers of Hume's school meet the difficulty by distinguishing between the *a priori* element in the individual mind and in the mind of the race. Each man brings with him certain inherited faculties, if not inherited knowledge; but the faculties have been themselves built up out of the experience of the race. Such a conception, however, was beyond Hume's sphere of thought, and obviously could not be attained so long as it was held to be possible to account for knowledge by simple introspection or the examination of the individual mind. Experience must be understood in a far wider sense than that in which Hume could possibly understand it, before it could explain the elementary phenomena of thought. Thus we may say that his scepticism expresses the natural result of trying to explain thought exclusively by individual experience, and declaring the unexplained residuum to be mere 'fiction' or custom, as the dogmatic theory is the result of the same attempt when the unexplained residuum is assumed to imply innate ideas. It is in this sense a crude attempt to apply a sound criterion, but a criterion which is only sound when applied with a sufficient appreciation of its meaning.

Here, then, we have the last word of the English criticism. What would be the natural working of Hume's scepticism, so far as it was accepted by his contemporaries? Absolute scepticism, it may be said, is an unthinkable state of mind. So far as Hume's reasoning tended to show that all reasoning was absurd, it was self-contradictory and inoperative. He admits the fact himself in the concluding section of the fourth part of his treatise, where he says that his doubts vanish as soon as he leaves his study for the streets. The most unflinching sceptic, of course, believes in the objections to knocking his head against a post as implicitly as the most audacious dogmatist. To say that belief as belief is absurd is not only practically, but theoretically, puerile. Belief is only a custom, therefore it is unreasonable to believe. But if reason is only customary, this can only mean that it is not customary to believe. Lower the intensity of all belief, and you do nothing; for custom being everything, the custom which preponderates in one direction will be just as effective as the reason which you have abolished. And, in fact, though Hume affects to attack equally all reasoning which has to do with the external world, his scepticism is really directed against the superfluous hypothesis of an absolute substratum distinct from the world. The custom which induces us to act upon evidence is still left for guidance in practical affairs; the supposed entities which lie behind the phenomena are shown, so far as his logic is valid, to be superfluous or meaningless.

Thus the moral which Hume naturally drew from his philosophy was the necessity of turning entirely to experience. Experience, and experience alone, could decide questions of morality or politics; and Hume put his theory in practice when he abandoned speculation to turn himself to history. Whether because they shared Hume's doubts, or because, without much speculation, they recognised the failure of previous philosophers to reach any fruitful conclusions, and saw no more promising road to success, Hume's ablest contemporaries followed his example. The last half of the eighteenth century, as we shall hereafter see more fully, is specially characterised by its tendency to historical enquiry. But it must further be remarked that historical enquiry thus divorced from philosophy leads in the first instance only to crude results. The histories of Hume, Robertson, and Gibbon, the great triumvirate of the day, have a common weakness, though Gibbon's profound knowledge has enabled his great work to survive the more flimsy productions of his colleagues. The fault, briefly stated, seems to be an incapacity to recognise the great forces by which history is moulded, and the continuity which gives to it a real unity. We have but a superficial view; a superficiality, in the cases of Hume and Robertson, implying inadequate research; and both in their case and Gibbon's implying a complete acquiescence in the external aspects of events, and the accidental links of connection, without any attempt to penetrate to the underlying and ultimately determining conditions. The defect was inevitable from the point of view of Hume's philosophy, or in the absence of all philosophy. The formula that 'anything may be the cause of anything else' must obviously lead to a perfunctory discharge of the duties of a philosophical historian. Any superficial combination may be expected to produce results entirely incommensurate with its apparent importance. The slightest accident may change, not only a dynasty or a form of government, but the whole social constitution or the beliefs of the human race. The first crude interrogation of experience reveals to us only varieties of external conformation, without exhibiting the governing forces which mould the internal constitution. Hume's philosophy, in fact, when applied to the examination of history, falls in with a crude empiricism instead of an experiential philosophy. The world is a chaos, not an organised whole; and we are content with detecting random resemblances and contrasts here and there without resolving them into more simple and general uniformities. A form of government, for example, is characteristically regarded as possessing an independent virtue, without regard to the conditions of the time or the race. We look at the outward conformation of the mass without asking what are the molecular forces which bind it together. To apply the inductive method effectually, it is necessary that the data given by experience should be properly sorted and arranged. Our mere collection of curiosities must be formed into an organised museum. Hume's cruder method tempted the historian to overlook this necessary process. It must, indeed, be added that the general desire to appeal to experience was an essential step towards something better. This kind of historical empiricism was gradually to lead to a genuine historical method. We may see the germs of a more fruitful investigation of some important problems in such books as Horne Tooke's *Diversions of Purley*, which is a premature attempt to apply philological enquiries to the history of thought; or, in Sir W. Jones's studies of Oriental literature, which helped to found the science of comparative mythology, and in various attempts, some of which will hereafter be noticed, to apply a truly historical method to various theological and political problems. Still, the narrowness and comparative fruitlessness of the English movement, when set beside contemporary German thought, is generally and perhaps rightly brought to show that even an unsatisfactory philosophy may be better than no philosophy at all. In the last half of the century, that which is permanently valuable may be regarded as a feeling after the historical method; and really great results were obtained in one direction by Adam Smith, and in another by the admirable genius of Burke.

Notes

1. Compare, for example, Hume's *Treatise*, part iv. § 2, with Mr. Herbert Spencer's *Principles of Psychology*, part vii. ch. xvi. xvii. xviii. Mr. Spencer, of course, differs from Hume's conclusions, and enlarges greatly his account of the constructive process; but the germs of his doctrine are to be found in Hume.

JOSIAH ROYCE
From *The Spirit of Modern Philosophy*
1892, pp. 93–98

Hume is, I think, next to Hobbes, the greatest of British speculative thinkers, Berkeley occupying the third place in order of rank. I cannot undertake to describe to you in this place the real historical significance of Hume, his subtlety, his fearlessness, his fine analysis of certain of the deepest problems, his place as the inspirer of Kant's thought, his whole value as metaphysical teacher of his time. What you will see in him is merely the merciless skeptic, and, in this superficial sketch of the rediscovery of the inner consciousness, I don't ask you to see more. Hume accepted Locke's belief that reason is merely the recorder of experience. He carries out this view to its remotest consequences. Our minds consist, as he says, of impressions and ideas. By impressions he means the experiences of sense; by ideas he means the remembered copies of these experiences. You see, feel, smell, taste; and you remember having seen, felt, tasted or smelt. That is all. You have no other knowledge. Upon some of your ideas, namely those of quantity and number, you can reason, and can even discover novel and necessary truth about them. This is owing to the peculiarity of these ideas and of the impressions on which they are founded. For these ideas, also, even all the subtleties of mathematical science, are faded and blurred impressions of sense. And, as it chances, on just these faded impressions you can reason. But Berkeley was wrong in thinking that you can by searching find out God, or anything else supersensual. Science concerns matters of fact, as the senses give them, and ends with these.

With this general view in mind, let us examine, in Hume's fashion, certain of the most familiar conceptions of human reason. Hume is afraid of nothing, not even of the presumptions at the basis of physical science. Matters of fact he respects, but not universal principles. "There are," says Hume, "no ideas . . . more obscure than those of power, force, or necessary connection." Let us look a little more closely at these ideas. Let us clear them up if we can. How useful they seem. How much we hear in exact science about something called the law of causation, which says that there is a necessary connection between causes and effects, that given natural conditions have a "power" to bring to pass certain results, that the forces of nature *must* work as they do. Well, apply to such sublime and far-reaching ideas,—just such ideas, you will remember, as seemed to Spinoza so significant,—apply to them Hume's simple criterion. Ideas, in order to have a good basis, must, Hume declares, stand for matters of fact, given to us in the senses. "It is impossible for us to *think* of anything which we have not antecedently *felt*, either by our external or internal senses." "By what invention, then," says Hume, "can we throw light" upon ideas that, being simple, still pretend to be authoritative, "and render them altogether precise and determinate to our intellectual view?" Answer: "Produce the impressions or original sentiments from which the ideas are copied." These impressions will "admit of no ambiguity." So, then, let us produce the original impression from which the idea of causation, of necessary connection, or of power is derived. You say that in nature there is and must be *necessity*. Very well, let us ask ourselves afresh the questions that we asked of Locke. Did you ever see necessity? Did you ever hear or touch causation? Did you ever taste or smell necessary connection? Name us the original impression whence comes your idea. "When," says Hume, "we look about us towards external objects, and consider the operation of causes, we are never able, in any single instance, to discover any power or necessary connection, any quality which binds the effect to the cause, and renders the one an infallible consequence of the other. We only find that the one does actually in fact follow the other. The impulse of one billiard ball is attended with motion in the second. That is the whole that appears to the outward senses." "In reality, there is no part of matter that does ever by its sensible qualities discover any power or energy, or give us ground to imagine that it could produce anything," until we have found out by experience what happens in consequence of its presence. Thus outer sense gives us facts, but no necessary laws, no true causation, no real connection of events.

We must, then, get our idea of power, of necessary connection, from within. And so, in fact, many have thought that we do. If in outer nature I am only impressed by matters of fact about billiard balls and other such things, and if there I never learn of causation, do I not, perchance, directly feel my own true power, my own causal efficacy, my own will, making acts result in a necessary way from my purposes? No, answers Hume. If I examine carefully I find that my own deeds also are merely matters of fact, with nothing causally efficacious about my own conscious nature to make them obviously necessary. After all, "is there any principle in nature more mysterious than the union of soul with body?" "Were we empowered," adds Hume, "to remove mountains, or control the planets in their orbit, this extensive authority would not be more extraordinary, or more beyond our comprehension," than is the bare matter of fact that we now can control our bodies by our will. In inner experience, then, just as in outer, we get no direct impression of *how* causes produce effects. We only see *that* things *do* often happen in regular ways. In experience, then, "all events seem entirely loose and separate. One event follows another; but we can never observe any tie between them. They seem *conjoined*, but never *connected*. But as we can have no idea of anything which never appeared to our outward sense or inward sentiment, the necessary conclusion *seems* to be, that we have no idea of connection or power at all, and that these words are absolutely without any meaning." From this seeming conclusion, Hume makes, indeed, an escape, but one that is, in fact, not less skeptical than his result as first reached. The true original of our idea of power, and so of causation, he says, is simply this, that "after a repetition of similar instances, the mind is carried, by habit, upon the appearance of one event, to expect its usual attendant, and to believe that it will exist." "The first time a man saw the communication of motion by impulse, as by the shock of the two billiard balls, he could not pronounce that the one event was *connected*, but only that it was *conjoined*, with the other. After he has observed several instances of this nature, he then pronounces them to be *connected*. What alteration has happened to give rise to this new idea of *connection*? Nothing but that now he *feels* these two events to be *connected* in his imagination." Custom, then, mere habit of mind, is the origin of the idea of causation. We see no necessity in the world. We only *feel* it there, because that is our habit of mind, our fashion of mentally regarding an often-repeated experience of similar successions.

The importance of all this skepticism lies, as you of course see, in its removal from our fact-world of just the principles that the seventeenth century had found so inspiring. "It is of the nature of reason," Spinoza had said, "to regard things as necessary." Upon that rock he had built his faith. His wisdom had reposed secure in God, in whom were all things, just because God's nature was the highest form of necessity, the law of laws. And now comes Hume, and calls this "nature of reason" a mere feeling, founded on habit, a product of our imagination, no matter of fact at all. What becomes, then, of Spinoza's divine order? Has philosophy fallen by its own hands? Is the eternal in which we had trusted really, after all, but the mass of the flying and disconnected impressions of sense? All crumbles at the touch of this criticism of Hume's. All becomes but the aggregate of the disconnected sense-impressions. Nay, if we find the Holy Grail itself, it, too, will fade and crumble into dust. Hume is aware of some such result. He skillfully and playfully veils the extreme consequences at times by the arts of his beautiful dialectic. But he none the less rejoices in it, with all the fine joy of the merciless foe of delusions:—*matters of fact, relations of ideas*,—these are all that his doctrine leaves us. "When," he once says, "we run through libraries, persuaded of these principles, what havoc must we make? If we take in our hand any volume of divinity or school metaphysics, for instance, let us ask, *Does it contain any abstract reasoning concerning quantity or number*? No. *Does it contain any experimental reasoning concerning matter of fact and existence*? No. Commit it then to the flames, for it can contain nothing but sophistry and illusion."

SAMUEL JOHNSON

SAMUEL JOHNSON

1709–1784

Samuel Johnson was born at Lichfield, Staffordshire, on September 18, 1709. The son of a bookseller, he was educated at Lichfield Grammar School (1716–26) and in 1728 entered Pembroke College, Oxford, which he left a year later when he could no longer afford the tuition. He worked briefly as an undermaster at the Market Bosworth Grammar School in 1732, then moved to Birmingham, where he contributed essays (none of which survive) to the *Birmingham Journal*. In 1733 he prepared a translation from the French of Father Lobo's *Voyage to Abyssinia*, published anonymously in 1735. In that same year he married Elizabeth Porter, a forty-six-year-old widow, and started a private school at Edial, near Lichfield. Johnson had difficulty attracting students, and after two years was forced to shut the school down.

In 1737 he went to London with his former pupil David Garrick, and in 1738 began to write for the *Gentleman's Magazine*, founded by Edward Cave. Also in that year he published his satirical poem *London*, written in imitation of Juvenal's Third Satire. This was well received, by Pope among others, but Johnson was still obliged to do a great deal of literary hackwork in order to survive.

In 1744 Johnson published *The Life of Richard Savage*, later included in *Lives of the English Poets* and written to commemorate the death of his friend in 1743. In 1746 he contracted with Robert Dodsley and others to compile a dictionary, and eventually set up an office in Fleet Street with a staff of six assistants. His *Plan of a Dictionary* (1747) was dedicated to the Earl of Chesterfield, who was not, however, responsive, much to Johnson's annoyance. Johnson's poem *The Vanity of Human Wishes*, an imitation of the Tenth Satire of Juvenal, was published in 1749, and in that year *Irene*, a tragedy written in 1736, was produced by David Garrick at the Drury Lane Theatre. In March 1750 Johnson started the *Rambler*, a twice-weekly periodical for which he wrote most of the essays. This was quite successful and ran until March 1752, the year in which Johnson suffered the loss of his much-loved wife. Between March 1753 and March 1754 Johnson contributed regularly to John Hawkesworth's *Adventurer*, and in 1755 his *Dictionary of the English Language* appeared in print after nine laborious years. Upon its publication Chesterfield wrote two papers in the *World* praising it highly; Johnson responded to this belated attention with his celebrated letter to Chesterfield. Between 1758 and 1760 Johnson contributed the *Idler* essays to the *Universal Chronicle*, and in 1759 he wrote the didactic romance *Rasselas, Prince of Abyssinia* in one week to pay for his mother's funeral. George III granted Johnson a pension of £300 a year in 1762, and Johnson was at last freed from the necessity of doing tedious hackwork.

In 1763 Johnson met James Boswell, then aged twenty-two, who became his biographer. From that time onward his life is described by Boswell in great detail. Johnson's club (later known as the Literary Club) was formed in 1764, and Boswell's biography also contains portraits of its members, including Reynolds, Burke, Goldsmith, Garrick, and Gibbon. In 1765 Johnson's edition of Shakespeare appeared, followed in 1775 by *A Journey to the Western Islands of Scotland*, recording his travels with Boswell in Scotland and the Hebrides during 1773. In 1777 Johnson was commissioned to write a series of biographical prefaces for an edition of the works of various English poets from the time of Milton onward, and when these prefaces were completed they were published separately in 1779–81 as *Lives of the English Poets*. Two years later Johnson became seriously ill, and on December 13, 1784, he died at his house in Bolt Court. Boswell's *Life of Johnson* appeared in 1791. Other biographies include *Anecdotes of the Late Samuel Johnson* (1786) by Hester Lynch Piozzi (Mrs. Thrale) and a *Life* by Sir John Hawkins (1787).

Personal

I am again your Petitioner in behalf of that great Cham of Literature, Samuel Johnson. His Black Servant, whose name is Francis Barber, has been pressed on board the Stag Frigate, Capt. Angel, and our Lexicographer is in great Distress. He says the Boy is a sickly Lad of a delicate frame, and particularly subject to a malady in his Throat which renders him very unfit for his majesty's Service. You know what matter of animosity the said Johnson has against you, and I dare say you desire no other opportunity of resenting it than that of laying him under an obligation. He was humble enough to desire my assistance on this occasion, though he and I were never cater-cousins, and I gave him to understand that I would make application to my Friend Mr. Wilkes who perhaps by his Interest with Dr. Hay and Mr. Elliot might be able to procure the Discharge of his Lacquey. It would be superfluous to say more on the subject which I leave to your Consideration, but I cannot let slip this opportunity of declaring that I am with the most inviolable Esteem and Attachment, Dear Sir, your affectionate, obliged humble Servt.—TOBIAS SMOLLETT, Letter to John Wilkes (March 16, 1759)

The day after I wrote my last letter to you I was introduced to Mr. Johnson by a friend: we passed through three very dirty rooms to a little one that looked like an old counting-house, where this great man was sat at his breakfast. The furniture of this room was a very large deal writing-desk, an old walnut-tree table, and five ragged chairs of four different sets. I was very much struck with Mr. Johnson's appearance, and could hardly help thinking him a madman for some time, as he sat waving over his breakfast like a lunatic.

He is a very large man, and was dressed in a dirty brown coat and waistcoat, with breeches that were brown also (though they had been crimson), and an old black wig: his shirt collar and sleeves were unbuttoned; his stockings were down about his feet, which had on them, by way of slippers, an old pair of shoes. He had not been up long when we called on him, which was near one o'clock: he seldom goes to bed till near two in the morning; and Mr. Reynolds tells me he generally drinks tea about an hour after he has supped. We had been some time with him before he began to talk, but at length he began, and, faith, to some purpose! every thing he says is as *correct* as a *second edition:* 't is almost impossible to argue with him, he is so sententious and so knowing. ⟨. . .⟩

When Mr. Johnson understood that I had lived some time in Bath, he asked me many questions that led, indeed, to a general description of it. He seemed very well pleased; but remarked that men and women bathing together as they do at Bath is an instance of barbarity that he believed could not be paralleled in any part of the world. He entertained us about an hour and a half in this manner; then we took our leave. I must not omit to add, that I am informed he denies himself many conveniences, though he cannot well afford any, that he may have more in his power to give in charities.—OZIAS HUMPHREY, Letter to William Humphrey (Sept. 19, 1764)

> Here Johnson comes—unblest with outward grace,
> His rigid morals stamp'd upon his face,
> While strong conceptions struggle in his brain
> (For even wit is brought to bed with pain).
> To view him, porters with their loads would rest,
> And babes cling frighted to the nurse's breast.
> With looks convuls'd he roars in pompous strain,
> And, like an angry lion, shakes his mane.
> The *Nine,* with terror struck, who ne'er had seen
> Aught human with so horrible a mien,
> Debating, whether they should stay or run—
> Virtue steps forth, and claims him for her son.
> With gentle speech she warns him not to yield,
> Nor strain his glories in the doubtful field.
> But, wrapt in conscious worth, content sit down,
> Since Fame resolv'd his various pleas to crown,
> Though forc'd his present claim to disavow,
> Had long reserv'd a chaplet for his brow.
> He bows; obeys—for Time shall first expire,
> Ere Johnson stay, when virtue bids retire.
> —CUTHBERT SHAW, *The Race,* 1766

With a lumber of learning and some strong parts, Johnson was an odious and mean character. By principle a Jacobite, arrogant, self-sufficient, and over-bearing by nature, ungrateful through pride, and of *feminine bigotry,* he had prostituted his pen to party even in a dictionary, and had afterwards, for a pension, contradicted his own definitions. His manners were sordid, supercilious and brutal, his style ridiculously bombastic and vicious; and, in one word, with all the pedantry he had all the gigantic littleness of a country schoolmaster.—HORACE WALPOLE, *Memoirs of the Reign of King George the Third,* 1771

The time is again at which, since the death of my poor dear Tetty, on whom God have mercy, I have annually commemorated the mystery of Redemption, and annually purposed to amend my life. My reigning sin, to which perhaps many others are appendent, is waste of time, and general sluggishness, to which I was always inclined and in part of my life have been almost compelled by morbid melancholy and disturbance of mind. Melancholy has had in me its paroxisms and remissions, but I have not improved the intervals, nor sufficiently resisted my natural inclination, or sickly habits. I will resolve henceforth to rise at eight in the morning, so far as resolution is proper, and will pray that God will strengthen me. I have begun this morning.—SAMUEL JOHNSON, *Diaries, Prayers, and Annals,* April 7, 1776

He is, indeed, very ill-favoured; is tall and stout; but stoops terribly; he is almost bent double. His mouth is almost constantly opening and shutting, as if he was chewing. He has a strange method of frequently twirling his fingers, and twisting his hands. His body is in continual agitation, *see-sawing* up and down; his feet are never a moment quiet; and, in short, his whole person is in *perpetual motion.* His dress, too, considering the times, and that he had meant to put on his *best becomes,* being engaged to dine in a large company, was as much out of the common road as his figure; he had a large wig, snuff-colour coat, and gold buttons, but no ruffles to his shirt, doughty fists, and black worsted stockings. He is shockingly near-sighted, and did not, till she held out her hand to him, even know Mrs. Thrale. He *poked his nose* over the keys of the harpsichord, till the duet was finished, and then my father introduced Hetty to him as an old acquaintance, and he cordially kissed her! When she was a little girl, he had made her a present of *The Idler.*—FANNY BURNEY, Letter to Samuel Crisp (March 28, 1777)

Poor Johnson is in a bad state of health; I fear his constitution is broken up: I am quite grieved at it, he will not leave an abler defender of religion and virtue behind him, and the following little touch of tenderness which I heard of him last night from one of the Turk's Head Club, endears him to me exceedingly. There are always a great many candidates ready, when any vacancy happens in that club, and it requires no small interest and reputation to get elected; but upon Garrick's death, when numberless applications were made to succeed him, Johnson was deaf to them all; he said, No, there never could be found any successor worthy of such a man; and he insisted upon it there should be a year's widowhood in the club, before they thought of a new election. In Dr. Johnson some contrarieties very harmoniously meet; if he has too little charity for the opinions of others, and too little patience with their faults, he has the greatest tenderness for their persons. He told me the other day, he hated to hear people whine about metaphysical distresses, when there was so much want and hunger in the world. I told him I supposed then he never wept at any tragedy but Jane Shore, who had died for want of a loaf. He called me a saucy girl, but did not deny the inference.—HANNAH MORE (c. April 1782), *Memoirs of the Life and Correspondence of Mrs. Hannah More,* ed. William Roberts, 1835, Vol. 1, p. 249

I have lately been in the almost daily habit of contemplating a very melancholy spectacle. The great Johnson is here, labouring under the paroxysms of a disease, which must speedily be fatal. He shrinks from the consciousness with the extremest horror. It is by his repeatedly expressed desire that I visit him often: yet I am sure he neither does, nor ever did feel much regard for me; but he would fain escape, for a time, in any society, from the terrible idea of his approaching dissolution. I never would be awed by his sarcasms, or his frowns, into acquiescence with his general injustice to the merits of *other* writers; with his national, or party aversions; but I feel the truest compassion for his present sufferings, and fervently wish

I had power to relieve them.—ANNA SEWARD, Letter to Miss Weston (Oct. 29, 1784)

Went to Dr. Johnson's about two o'clock, met Mrs. Hoole coming from thence as he was asleep, took her back with me—found Sir John Hawkins with him;—the Doctor's conversation tolerably cheerful: Sir John reminded him that he had express'd a desire to leave some small memorials to his friends particularly a Polyglot Bible to Mr. Langton, and asked if they should add the Codicil then—the Doctor reply'd 'he had forty things to add but could not do it at that time.' Sir John then took his leave, Mr. Sastres came next into the Diningroom where I was with Mrs. Hoole. I then went again to the Doctor and told him that Mrs. Hoole sent her kindest remembrance—on hearing she was in the next room, he bade me bring her to him: he received her with great affection, took her by the hand and said nearly these words, 'My dear God-daughter I feel great tenderness for you: think of the situation in which you see me, profit by it, and God Almighty keep you for Jesus Christ's sake, Amen!' He then asked if we would both stay and dine with him; Mrs. Hoole said she could not but I agreed to stay. We then left the chamber in great trouble, and on our return to Mr. Sastres were all inconceivably afflicted for the situation of our friend. Upon my saying to the Doctor that Dr. Heberden would visit him that morning his answer was: 'God has called me and Dr. Heberden comes too late.' Soon after Dr. Heberden came: we soon overheard them in earnest discourse and found that they were talking over the affair of the King and Chancellor: we overheard Dr. Heberden say 'All you did was extremely proper.' After Dr. Heberden was gone Mr. Sastres and I returned into the chamber. Dr. Johnson complained this day that Sleep had powerful dominion over him, that he waked with great struggle and difficulty and that probably he should go off in one of these paroxysms. Afterwards he said that he hoped his sleep was the effect of opium which he had taken some days before, and which might not be worked off. We dined together, the Doctor, Mr. Sastres, a Mrs. Davies and myself: he eat a pretty good dinner with seeming appetite, but being rather impatient at being asked unnecessary and frivolous questions, he said he often thought of Macbeth, 'Question enrages him.' He retired immediately after dinner, and we soon went at his desire; Mr. Sastres and I and sate with him till tea. He said little but dozed at times. At six he ordered Tea for us, and we went out to drink it with Mrs. Davies; the Doctor drank none. The Rev. Dr. Taylor of Ashbourne came soon after and Dr. Johnson sent a message desiring our attendance at prayers. We all went into the chamber and Dr. Taylor read prayers. Not seeing me in the room with the rest, he asked with some warmth, 'Where is Mr. Hoole?' Mr. Ryland came and sate some time with him; he thought him much better. Mr. Sastres and I continued with him the remainder of the evening, and he exhorted Mr. Sastres in nearly these words. 'There is no one who has shewn me more attention than you have done, and it is now right you should claim some attention from me. You are a young man and are to struggle through life: you are in a profession that I dare say you will exercise with great fidelity and innocence, but let me exhort you always to think of my situation which must one day be yours. always remember that Life is short, and that Eternity never ends! I say nothing of your Religion, for if you conscientiously keep to it I have little doubt but you may be saved: if you read the controversy I think we have the right on our side, but if you do not read it, be not persuaded from any worldly consideration to alter the religion in which you were educated; change not but from conviction of reason: when any temptation offers, reflect

that this leads to Hell!—consider every pain that you feel here and what that must be forever! Remember all this and God bless You! Write down what I have said. I think you are the third person I have bid do this.' At ten o'clock he dismissed us thanking us for a visit which he said could not have been very pleasant to us.—JOHN HOOLE, *Journal Narrative Relative to Doctor Johnson's Last Illness Three Weeks before His Death*, Nov. 28, 1784

45 Minutes past 10 P.M.—While I was writing the adjoining articles I received the fatal account, so long dreaded, that Dr. Johnson was no more!

    May those prayers which he incessantly poured from a heart fraught with the deepest devotion, find that acceptance with Him to whom they were addressed, which piety, so humble and so fervent, may seem to promise! ⟨. . .⟩

    On dissection of the body, vesicles of wind were found on the lungs (which Dr. Heberden said he had never seen, and of which Cruikshank professed to have seen only two instances), one of the kidneys quite gone, a gall stone in the bladder, I think; no water in the chest, and little in the abdomen, no more than might have found its way thither after death. —WILLIAM WINDHAM, *Diary*, Dec. 13, 1784

Yesterday, my dear Sir, I followed our ever to be lamented friend, Dr. Johnson, to his last mansion—non omnis moriar—multaque pars mei vitabit Libitinam—should be engraven on his stone. He died with the same piety with which he lived; and bestowed much pains during his last illness in endeavouring to convince some of his friends, who were in doubt, about the truth of the Christian religion. He has left behind him a collection of small Latin compositions in verse. They are principally translations of Collects and Greek epigrams. He was followed to the Abbey by a large troop of friends. Ten mourning coaches were ordered by the executors for those invited. Besides these, eight of his friends or admirers clubbed for two more carriages, in one of which I had a seat. But the executor, Sir John Hawkins, did not manage things well, for there was no anthem, or choir service performed—no lesson—but merely what is read over every old woman that is buried by the parish. Surely, surely, my dear Sir, this was wrong, very wrong. Dr. Taylor read the service—but so-so. He lies nearly under Shakespeare's monument, with Garrick at his right hand, just opposite to the monument erected not long ago for Goldsmith by him and some of his friends.—CHARLES BURNEY, Letter to Samuel Parr (Dec. 21, 1784), cited in *The Works of Samuel Parr*, ed. John Johnstone, 1828, Vol. 1, p. 535

He gave himself very much to companionable friends for the last years of his life (for he was delivered from the daily labour of the pen, and he wanted relaxation), and they were eager for the advantage and reputation of his conversation. Therefore he frequently left his own home (for his household gods were not numerous or splendid enough for the reception of his great acquaintance), and visited them both in town and country. This was particularly the case with Mr. and Mrs. Thrale (*ex uno disce omnes*), who were the most obliging and obliged of all within his intimacy, and to whom he was introduced by his friend Murphy. He lived with them a great part of every year. He formed at Streatham a room for a library, and increased by his recommendation the number of books. Here he was to be found (himself a library) when a friend called upon him; and by him the friend was sure to be introduced to the dinner-table, which Mrs. Thrale knew how to spread with the utmost plenty and elegance; and which was often adorned with such guests, that to dine there was, *epulis accumbere divum*. Of Mrs. Thrale, if mentioned at all, less cannot be said, than that in one of the latest opinions of Johnson, 'if she was not the wisest woman in the world, she was undoubtedly one of the wittiest.' She took or caused such care to be taken of him, during an illness of continuance, that Goldsmith told her, 'he owed his recovery to her attention.' She taught him to lay up something of his income every year. Besides a natural vivacity in conversation, she had reading enough, and the gods had made her poetical. *The Three Warnings* (the subject she owned not to be original) are highly interesting and serious, and literally come home to every body's breast and bosom. The writer of this would not be sorry if this mention could follow the lady to Venice. At Streatham, where our Philologer was also guide, philosopher, and friend, he passed much time. His inclinations here were consulted, and his will was a law. With this family he made excursions into Wales and to Brighthelmstone. Change of air and of place were grateful to him, for he loved vicissitude. But he could not long endure the illiteracy and rusticity of the country, for woods and groves, and hill and dale, were not his scenes:

> Tower'd cities please us then,
> And the busy hum of men.
> —THOMAS TYERS, "A Biographical Sketch of Dr. Samuel Johnson," *Gentleman's Magazine*, Dec. 1784

Dr. Samuel Johnson's character—religious, moral, political, and literary—nay, his figure and manner, are, I believe, more generally known than those of almost any man, yet it may not be superfluous here to attempt a sketch of him. Let my readers then remember that he was a sincere and zealous Christian, of high-Church-of-England and monarchical principles, which he would not tamely suffer to be questioned; steady and inflexible in maintaining the obligations of piety and virtue, both from a regard to the order of society and from a veneration for the Great Source of all order; correct, nay stern, in his taste; hard to please and easily offended, impetuous and irritable in his temper, but of a most humane and benevolent heart; having a mind stored with a vast and various collection of learning and knowledge, which he communicated with peculiar perspicuity and force, in rich and choice expression. He united a most logical head with a most fertile imagination, which gave him an extraordinary advantage in arguing, for he could reason close or wide as he saw best for the moment. He could, when he chose it, be the greatest sophist that ever wielded a weapon in the schools of declamation, but he indulged this only in conversation, for he owned that he sometimes talked for victory; he was too conscientious to make error permanent and pernicious by deliberately writing it. He was conscious of his superiority. He loved praise when it was brought to him, but was too proud to seek for it. He was somewhat susceptible of flattery. His mind was so full of imagery that he might have been perpetually a poet. It has been often remarked that in his poetical pieces (which it is to be regretted are so few, because so excellent) his style is easier than in his prose. There is deception in this: it is not easier but better suited to the dignity of verse; as one may dance with grace whose motions in ordinary walking—in the common step—are awkward. He had a constitutional melancholy the clouds of which darkened the brightness of his fancy and gave a gloomy cast to his whole course of thinking; yet, though grave and awful in his deportment when he thought it necessary or proper, he frequently indulged himself in pleasantry and sportive sallies. He was prone to superstition but not to

credulity. Though his imagination might incline him to a belief of the marvellous and the mysterious, his vigorous reason examined the evidence with jealousy. He had a loud voice and a slow deliberate utterance which no doubt gave some additional weight to the sterling metal of his conversation. Lord Pembroke said once to me at Wilton, with a happy pleasantry and some truth, that "Dr. Johnson's sayings would not appear so extraordinary were it not for his *bow-wow-way*," but I admit the truth of this only on some occasions. The *Messiah* played upon the Canterbury organ is more sublime than when played upon an inferior instrument, but very slight music will seem grand when conveyed to the ear through that majestic medium. *While therefore Doctor Johnson's sayings are read, let his manner be taken along with them.* Let it, however, be observed that the sayings themselves are generally great; that, though he might be an ordinary composer at times, he was for the most part a Handel.—His person was large, robust, I may say approaching to the gigantic, and grown unwieldly from corpulency. His countenance was naturally of the cast of an ancient statue, but somewhat disfigured by the scars of that *evil* which it was formerly imagined the *royal touch* could cure. He was now in his sixty-fourth year, and was become a little dull of hearing. His sight had always been somewhat weak, yet so much does mind govern and even supply the deficiency of organs that his perceptions were uncommonly quick and accurate. His head and sometimes also his body shook with a kind of motion like the effect of a palsy; he appeared to be frequently disturbed by cramps or convulsive contractions, of the nature of that distemper called St. Vitus's dance. He wore a full suit of plain brown clothes with twisted-hair buttons of the same colour, a large bushy greyish wig, a plain shirt, black worsted stockings, and silver buckles. Upon this tour (to the Hebrides), when journeying, he wore boots and a very wide brown cloth greatcoat with pockets which might have almost held the two volumes of his folio dictionary, and he carried in his hand a large English oak stick. Let me not be censured for mentioning such minute particulars. Everything relative to so great a man is worth observing. I remember Dr. Adam Smith, in his rhetorical lectures at Glasgow, told us he was glad to know that Milton wore latchets in his shoes instead of buckles. When I mention the oak stick, it is but letting Hercules have his club; and by and by my readers will find this stick will bud and produce a good joke.—JAMES BOSWELL, *Journal of a Tour to the Hebrides with Samuel Johnson, LL.D.*, 1785

Dr. Johnson delighted in the company of women. 'There are few things,' he would say, 'that we so unwillingly give up, even in an advanced age, as the supposition that we have still the power of ingratiating ourselves with the Fair Sex.' Among his singularities, his love of conversing with the prostitutes whom he met with in the streets was not the least. He has been known to carry some of these unfortunate creatures into a tavern, for the sake of striving to awaken in them a proper sense of their condition. His younger friends now and then affected to tax him with less chastised intentions. But he would answer—'No Sir; we never proceeded to the *Opus Magnum*. On the contrary, I have rather been disconcerted and shocked by the replies of these giddy wenches, than flattered or diverted by their tricks. I remember asking one of them for what purpose she supposed her Maker had bestowed on her so much beauty? Her answer was—"To please the gentlemen, to be sure; for what other use could it be given me?"'—GEORGE STEEVENS, "Johnsoniana," *Gentleman's Magazine*, Jan. 1785

The piety of Dr. Johnson was exemplary and edifying: he was punctiliously exact to perform every public duty enjoined by the church, and his spirit of devotion had an energy that affected all who ever saw him pray in private. The coldest and most languid hearers of the word must have felt themselves animated by his manner of reading the holy scriptures; and to pray by his sick bed, required strength of body as well as of mind, so vehement were his manners, and his tones of voice so pathetic. I have many times made it my request to heaven that I might be spared the sight of his death; and I was spared it!

Mr. Johnson, though in general a gross feeder, kept fast in Lent, particularly the holy week, with a rigour very dangerous to his general health; but though he had left off wine (for religious motives as I always believed, though he did not own it), yet he did not hold the commutation of offences by voluntary penance, or encourage others to practise severity upon themselves. He even once said, 'that he thought it an error to endeavour at pleasing God by taking the rod of reproof out of his hands.' And when we talked of convents, and the hardships suffered in them—'Remember always (said he) that a convent is an idle place, and where there is nothing to be *done* something must be *endured*: mustard has a bad taste *per se* you may observe, but very insipid food cannot be eaten without it.'

His respect however for places of religious retirement was carried to the greatest degree of earthly veneration: the Benedictine convent at Paris paid him all possible honours in return, and the Prior and he parted with tears of tenderness. Two of that college sent to England on the mission some years after, spent much of their time with him at Bolt Court I know, and he was ever earnest to retain their friendship; but though beloved by all his Roman Catholic acquaintance, particularly Dr. Nugent, for whose esteem he had a singular value, yet was Mr. Johnson a most unshaken church of England man; and I think, or at least I once *did* think, that a letter written by him to Mr. Barnard the King's librarian, when he was in Italy collecting books, contained some very particular advice to his friend to be on his guard against the seductions of the church of Rome.

The settled aversion Dr. Johnson felt towards an infidel he expressed to all ranks, and at all times, without the smallest reserve; for though on common occasions he paid great deference to birth or title, yet his regard for truth and virtue never gave way to meaner considerations. We talked of a dead wit one evening, and somebody praised him—'Let us never praise talents so ill employed, Sir; we foul our mouths by commending such infidels' (said he). Allow him the *lumières* at least, intreated one of the company—'I do allow him, Sir (replied Johnson) just enough to light him to hell.'—Of a Jamaica gentleman, then lately dead—'He will not, whither he is now gone (said Johnson), find much difference, I believe, either in the climate or the company.'—The Abbé Reynal probably remembers that, being at the house of a common friend in London, the master of it approached Johnson with that gentleman so much celebrated in his hand, and this speech in his mouth: Will you permit me, Sir, to present to you the Abbé Reynal? 'No, Sir,' (replied the Doctor very loud) and suddenly turned away from them both.—HESTER LYNCH PIOZZI, *Anecdotes of the Late Samuel Johnson, LL.D.*, 1786

Here lies Sam Johnson:—Reader, have a care,
Tread lightly, lest you wake a sleeping bear:
Religious, moral, generous, and humane
He was; but self-sufficient, proud, and vain,
Fond of, and overbearing in dispute,
A Christian, and a scholar—but a brute.
  —SOAME JENYNS, "Epitaph on Dr. Samuel Johnson," c. 1787

His discourse, which through life was of the didactic kind, was replete with original sentiments expressed in the strongest and most correct terms, and in such language, that whoever could have heard and not seen him would have thought him reading. For the pleasure he communicated to his hearers he expected not the tribute of silence: on the contrary he encouraged others, particularly young men, to speak, and paid a due attention to what they said; but his prejudices were so strong and deeply rooted, more especially against Scotchmen and Whigs, that whoever thwarted him ran the risque of a severe rebuke, or at best became entangled in an unpleasant altercation. He was scarce settled in town before this dogmatical behaviour, and his impatience of contradiction, became a part of his character, and deterred many persons of learning, who wished to enjoy the delight of his conversation, from seeking his acquaintance. There were not wanting those among his friends who would sometimes hint to him, that the conditions of free conversation imply an equality among those engaged in it, which are violated whenever superiority is assumed: their reproofs he took kindly, and would in excuse for what they called the pride of learning, say, that it was of the defensive kind. The repetition of these had, however, a great effect on him; they abated his prejudices, and produced a change in his temper and manners that rendered him at length a desirable companion in the most polite circles.

In the lesser duties of morality he was remiss: he slept when he should have studied, and watched when he should have been at rest: his habits were slovenly, and the neglect of his person and garb so great as to render his appearance disgusting. He was an ill husband of his time, and so regardless of the hours of refection, that at two he might be found at breakfast, and at dinner at eight. In his studies, and I may add, in his devotional exercises, he was both intense and remiss, and in the prosecution of his literary employments, dilatory and hasty, unwilling, as himself confessed, to work, and working with vigour and haste.

His indolence, or rather the delight he took in reading and reflection, rendered him averse to bodily exertions. He was ill made for riding, and took so little pleasure in it, that, as he once told me, he has fallen asleep on his horse. Walking he seldom practised, perhaps for no better reason, than that it required the previous labour of dressing. In a word, mental occupation was his sole pleasure, and the knowledge he acquired in the pursuit of it he was ever ready to communicate: in which faculty he was not only excellent but expert; for, as it is related of lord Bacon by one who knew him, that 'in all companies he appeared a good proficient, if not a master, in those arts entertained for the subject of every one's discourse,' and that 'his most casual talk deserved to be written,' so it may be said of Johnson, that his conversation was ever suited to the profession, condition, and capacity of those with whom he talked.—SIR JOHN HAWKINS, *The Life of Samuel Johnson, LL.D.*, 1787

Methinks I view his full plain suit of brown,
The large grey bushy wig that graced his crown,
Black worsted stockings, little silver buckles,
And shirt that had no ruffles for his knuckles.
I mark the brown great-coat of cloth he wore,
That two huge Patagonian pockets bore,
Which Patagonians (wondrous to unfold!)
Would fairly both his Dictionaries hold.
I see the Rambler on a large bay Mare,
Just like a Centaur, every danger dare;
On a full gallop dash the yielding wind,
The Colt and Bozzy scampering close behind.
  —JOHN WOLCOT (as "Peter Pindar"), *A Poetical*

and Congratulatory Epistle to James Boswell, Esq., on His Journal of a Tour to the Hebrides with the Celebrated Doctor Johnson, 1787

When a friend told Johnson that he was much blamed for having unveiled the weakness of Pope, "Sir," said he, "if one man, undertake to write the life of another, he undertakes to exhibit his true and real character: but this can be done only by a faithful and accurate delineation of the particulars which discriminate that character."

The biographers of this great man seem conscientiously to have followed the rule thus laid down by him, and have very fairly communicated all they knew, whether to his advantage or otherwise. Much concern, disquietude, and offence, have been occasioned by this their conduct in the minds of many who apprehend, that the cause in which he stood forth will suffer by the infirmities of the advocate being thus exposed to the prying and malignant eye of the world.

But did these persons then ever suppose, or did they imagine that the world ever supposed, Dr. Johnson to have been a perfect character? Alas! no; we all know how that matter stands, if we ever look into our own hearts, and duly watch the current of our own thoughts, words, and actions. Johnson was honest, and kept a faithful diary of these, which is before the public. Let any man do the same for a fortnight, and publish it: and if, after that, he should find himself so disposed, let him "cast a stone." At that hour when the failings of all shall be made manifest, the attention of each individual will be confined to his own.

It is not merely the name of Johnson that is to do service to any cause. It is his genius, his learning, his good sense, the strength of his reasonings, and the happiness of his illustrations. These all are precisely what they were: once good, and always good. His arguments in favour of self-denial do not lose their force, because he fasted; nor those in favour of devotion, because he said his prayers. Grant his failings were, if possible, still greater than these: will a man refuse to be guided by the sound opinion of a counsel, or resist the salutary prescription of a physician, because they who give them are not without their faults? A man may do so; but he will never be accounted a wise man for doing it.

Johnson, it is said, was superstitious. But who shall exactly ascertain to us what superstition is? The Romanist is charged with it by the church-of-England man; the churchman by the presbyterian; the presbyterian by the independent; all by the deist; and the deist by the atheist. With some it is superstition to pray, with others to receive the sacrament, with others to believe in revelation, with others to believe in God. In some minds it springs from the most amiable disposition in the world—a pious awe, and fear to have offended; a wish rather to do too much than too little. Such a disposition one loves and wishes always to find in a friend; and it cannot be disagreeable in the sight of him who made us; it argues a sensibility of heart, a tenderness of conscience, and the fear of God. Let him, who finds it not in himself, beware lest, in flying from superstition, he fall into irreligion and profaneness.

That persons of eminent talents and attainments in literature have been often complained of as—dogmatical, boisterous, and inattentive to the rules of good breeding, is well known. But let us not expect every thing from every man. There was no occasion that Johnson should teach us to dance, to make bows, or turn compliments. He could teach us better things. To reject wisdom, because the person of him who communicates it is uncouth, and his manners are inelegant—

what is it, but to throw away a pine-apple, and assign for a reason the roughness of its coat? Who quarrels with a botanist for not being an astronomer, or with a moralist for not being a mathematician? As it is said in concerns of a much higher nature, "every man hath his gift, one after this manner and another after that;" it is our business to profit by all, and to learn of each that in which each is best qualified to instruct us.

That Johnson was generous and charitable, none can deny. But he was not always judicious in the selection of his objects; distress was a sufficient recommendation, and he did not scrutinize into the failings of the distressed. May it be always my lot to have such a benefactor! Some are so nice in a scrutiny of this kind, that they can never find any proper objects of their benevolence, and are necessitated to save their money. It should doubtless be distributed in the best manner we are able to distribute it; but what would become of us all, if he, on whose bounty all depend, should be "extreme to mark that which is done amiss"?

It is hard to judge any man, without a due consideration of all circumstances. Here were stupendous abilities, and suitable attainments; but then here were hereditary disorders of body and mind reciprocally aggravating each other; a scrofulous frame, and a melancholy temper; here was a life, the greater part of which passed in making provision for the day, under the pressure of poverty and sickness, sorrow and anguish. So far to gain the ascendant over these, as to do what Johnson did, required very great strength of mind indeed. Who can say, that, in a like situation, he should long have possessed, or been able to exert it?

From the mixture of power and weakness in the composition of this wonderful man, the scholar should learn humility. It was designed to correct that pride which great parts and great learning are apt to produce in their possessor. In him it had the desired effect. For though consciousness of superiority might sometimes induce him to carry it high with man (and even this was much abated in the latter part of life), his devotions have shewn to the whole world, how humbly he walked at all times with his God.

His example may likewise encourage those of timid and gloomy dispositions not to despond, when they reflect, that the vigour of such an intellect could not preserve its possessor from the depredations of melancholy. They will cease to be surprised and alarmed at the degree of their own sufferings: they will resolve to bear, with patience and resignation, the malady to which they find a Johnson subject, as well as themselves: and if they want words, in which to ask relief from him who alone can give it, the God of mercy, and Father of all comfort, language affords no finer than those in which his prayers are conceived. Child of sorrow, whoever thou art, use them; and be thankful, that the man existed, by whose means thou hast them to use.

His eminence and his fame must of course have excited envy and malice: but let envy and malice look at his infirmities and his charities, and they will quickly melt into pity and love.

That he should not be conscious of the abilities with which Providence had blessed him, was impossible. He felt his own powers; he felt what he was capable of having performed; and he saw how little, comparatively speaking, he had performed. Hence his apprehensions on the near prospect of the account to be made, viewed through the medium of constitutional and morbid melancholy, which often excluded from his sight the bright beams of divine mercy. May those beams ever shine upon us! But let them not cause us to forget, that talents have been bestowed, of which an account must be rendered; and that the fate of the "unprofitable servant" may justly beget apprehensions in the stoutest mind. The indolent man, who is without such apprehensions, has never yet considered the subject as he ought. For one person who fears death too much, there are a thousand who do not fear it enough, nor have thought in earnest about it. Let us only put in practice the duty of self-examination; let us inquire into the success we have experienced in our war against the passions, or even against undue indulgence of the common appetites, eating, drinking, and sleeping; we shall soon perceive how much more easy it is to form resolutions, than to execute them; and shall no longer find occasion, perhaps to wonder at the weakness of Johnson.—GEORGE HORNE, *The Olla Podrida*, No. 13 (June 9, 1787)

From passion, from the prevalence of his disposition for the minute, he was constantly acting contrary to his own reason, to his principles. It was a frequent subject of animadversion with him, how much authors lost of the pleasure and comfort of life by their carrying always about them their own consequence and celebrity. Yet no man in mixed company,—not to his intimates, certainly, for that would be an insupportable slavery,—ever acted with more circumspection to his character than himself. The most light and airy dispute was with him a dispute on the arena. He fought on every occasion as if his whole reputation depended upon the victory of the minute, and he fought with all the weapons. If he was foiled in argument he had recourse to abuse and rudeness. That he was not thus strenuous for victory with his intimates in tête-à-tête conversations when there were no witnesses, may be easily believed. Indeed, had his conduct been to them the same as he exhibited to the public, his friends could never have entertained that love and affection for him which they all feel and profess for his memory.

But what appears extraordinary is that a man who so well saw, himself, the folly of this ambition of shining, of speaking, or of acting always according to the character ⟨he⟩ imagined ⟨he⟩ possessed in the world, should produce himself the greatest example of a contrary conduct.

Were I to write the Life of Dr. Johnson I would labour this point, to separate his conduct that proceeded from his passions, and what proceeded from his reason, from his natural disposition seen in his quiet hours.—SIR JOSHUA REYNOLDS (c. 1792), cited in C. R. Leslie, Tom Taylor, *Life and Times of Sir Joshua Reynolds*, 1865

It is now some three quarters of a century that Johnson has been the Prophet of the English; the man by whose light the English people, in public and in private, more than by any other man's, have guided their existence. Higher light than that immediately *practical* one; higher virtue than an honest PRUDENCE, he could not then communicate; nor perhaps could they have received: such light, such virtue, however, he did communicate. How to thread this labyrinthic Time, the fallen and falling Ruin of Times; to silence vain Scruples, hold firm to the last the fragments of old Belief, and with earnest eye still discern some glimpses of a true path, and go forward thereon, 'in a world where there is much to be done, and little to be known:' this is what Samuel Johnson, by act and word, taught his Nation; what his Nation received and learned of him, more than of any other. We can view him as the preserver and transmitter of whatsoever was genuine in the spirit of Toryism; which genuine spirit, it is now becoming manifest, must again embody itself in all new forms of Society, be what they may, that are to exist, and have continuance—elsewhere than on Paper. The *last* in many things, Johnson was the last genuine Tory; the last of Englishmen who, with strong voice

and wholly-believing heart, preached the Doctrine of Standing still; who, without selfishness or slavishness, reverenced the existing Powers, and could assert the privileges of rank, though himself poor, neglected and plebeian; who had heart-devoutness with heart-hatred of cant, was orthodox-religious with his eyes open; and in all things and everywhere spoke out in plain English, from a soul wherein jesuitism could find no harbour, and with the front and tone not of a diplomatist, but of a man.—THOMAS CARLYLE, "Boswell's *Life of Johnson*" (1832), *Critical and Miscellaneous Essays*, 1839–69

Dr. Johnson's fame now rests principally upon Boswell. It is impossible not to be amused with such a book. But his *bow-wow* manner must have had a good deal to do with the effect produced; for no one, I suppose, will set Johnson before Burke, and Burke was a great and universal talker; yet now we hear nothing of this, except by some chance remarks in Boswell. The fact is, Burke, like all men of genius who love to talk at all, was very discursive and continuous; hence he is not reported; he seldom said the sharp short things that Johnson almost always did, which produce a more decided effect at the moment, and which are so much more easy to carry off. Besides, as to Burke's testimony to Johnson's powers, you must remember that Burke was a great courtier; and after all, Burke said and wrote more than once that he thought Johnson greater in talking than in writing, and greater in Boswell than in real life.—SAMUEL TAYLOR COLERIDGE, *Table Talk*, July 4, 1833

Lichfield signifies "The Field of the Dead Bodies"—an epithet, however, which the town did not assume in remembrance of a battle, but which probably sprung up by a natural process, like a sprig of rue or other funereal weed, out of the graves of two princely brothers, sons of a pagan King of Mercia, who were converted by Saint Chad, and afterwards martyred for their Christian faith. Nevertheless, I was but little interested in the legends of the remote antiquity of Lichfield, being drawn thither partly to see its beautiful Cathedral, and still more, I believe, because it was the birthplace of Dr. Johnson, with whose sturdy English character I became acquainted, at a very early period of my life, through the good offices of Mr. Boswell. In truth, he seems as familiar to my recollection, and almost as vivid in his personal aspect to my mind's eye, as the kindly figure of my own grandfather. It is only a solitary child—left much to such wild modes of culture as he chooses for himself while yet ignorant what culture means, standing on tiptoe to pull down books from no very lofty shelf, and then shutting himself up, as it were, between the leaves, going astray through the volume at his own pleasure, and comprehending it rather by his sensibilities and affections than his intellect—that child is the only student that ever gets the sort of intimacy which I am now thinking of, with a literary personage. I do not remember, indeed, ever caring much about any of the stalwart Doctor's grandiloquent productions, except his two stern and masculine poems, *London*, and *The Vanity of Human Wishes*; it was as a man, a talker, and a humorist, that I knew and loved him, appreciating many of his qualities perhaps more thoroughly than I do now, though never seeking to put my instinctive perception of his character into language.

Beyond all question, I might have had a wiser friend than he. The atmosphere in which alone he breathed was dense; his awful dread of death showed how much muddy imperfection was to be cleansed out of him, before he could be capable of spiritual existence; he meddled only with the surface of life, and never cared to penetrate farther than to plough-share depth; his very sense and sagacity were but a one-eyed clear-sightedness. I laughed at him, sometimes, standing beside his knee. And yet, considering that my native propensities were towards Fairy Land, and also how much yeast is generally mixed up with the mental sustenance of a New Englander, it may not have been altogether amiss, in those childish and boyish days, to keep pace with this heavy-footed traveller and feed on the gross diet that he carried in his knapsack. It is wholesome food even now. And, then, how English! Many of the latent sympathies that enabled me to enjoy the Old Country so well, and that so readily amalgamated themselves with the American ideas that seemed most adverse to them, may have been derived from, or fostered and kept alive by, the great English Moralist. Never was a descriptive epithet more nicely appropriate than that! Dr. Johnson's morality was as English an article as a beef-steak.—NATHANIEL HAWTHORNE, "Lichfield and Uttoxeter," *Our Old Home*, 1863

Dr. Johnson was a man of no profound mind,—full of English limitations, English politics, English Church, Oxford philosophy; yet, having a large heart, mother-wit and good sense which impatiently overleaped his customary bounds, his conversation as reported by Boswell has a lasting charm. Conversation is the vent of character as well as of thought; and Dr. Johnson impresses his company, not only by the point of the remark, but also, when the point fails, because *he* makes it. His obvious religion or superstition, his deep wish that they should think so or so, weighs with them,—so rare is depth of feeling, or a constitutional value for a thought or opinion, among the light-minded men and women who make up society; and though they know that there is in the speaker a degree of shortcoming, of insincerity and of talking for victory, yet the existence of character, and habitual reverence for principles over talent or learning, is felt by the frivolous.—RALPH WALDO EMERSON, "Clubs," *Society and Solitude*, 1870

General

Dr. Johnson's works have obtained so much reputation, and the execution of them, from partiality to his abilities, has been rated so far above their merit, that, without detracting from his capacity or his learning, it may be useful to caution young authors against admiration of his *style* and *manner*; both of which are uncommonly vicious, and unworthy of imitation by any man who aims at excellence in writing his own language.

A marked *manner*, when it runs through all the compositions of any master, is a defect in itself, and indicates a deviation from nature. The writer betrays his having been struck by some particular tint, and his having overlooked nature's variety. It is true that the greatest masters of composition are so far imperfect, as that they always leave some marks by which we may discover their *hand*. He approaches the nearest to universality, whose works make it difficult for our quickness or sagacity to observe certain characteristic touches which ascertain the specific author.

Dr. Johnson's works are as easily distinguished as those of the most affected writer; for exuberance is a fault as much as quaintness. There is meaning in almost every thing Johnson says; he is often profound, and a just reasoner—I mean, when prejudice, bigotry, and arrogance do not cloud or debase his logic. He is benevolent in the application of his morality; dogmatically uncharitable in the dispensation of his censures; and equally so, when he differs with his antagonist on general truths or partial doctrines.

The first criterion that stamps Johnson's works for his, is the loaded style. I will not call it verbose, because verbosity generally implies unmeaning verbiage; a censure he does not deserve. I have allowed and do allow, that most of his words

have an adequate, and frequently an illustrating purport, the true use of epithets; but then his words are indiscriminately select, and too forceful for ordinary occasions. They form a hardness of diction and a muscular toughness that resist all ease and graceful movement. Every sentence is as high-coloured as any: no paragraph improves; the position is as robust as the demonstration; and the weakest part of the sentence (I mean, in the effect, not in the solution) is generally the conclusion: he illustrates till he fatigues, and continues to prove, after he has convinced. This fault is so usual with him, he is so apt to charge with three different set of phrases of the same calibre, that, if I did not condemn his laboured coinage of new words, I would call his threefold inundation of synonymous expressions, *triptology*.

He prefers learned words to the simple and common. He is never simple, elegant or light. He destroys more enemies with the weight of his shield than with the point of his spear, and had rather make three mortal wounds in the same part than one. This monotony, the grievous effect of pedantry and self-conceit, prevents him from being eloquent. He excites no passions but indignation: his writings send the reader away more satiated than pleased. If he attempts humour, he makes your reason smile, without making you gay; because the study that his learned mirth requires, destroys cheerfulness. It is the clumsy gambol of a lettered elephant. We wonder that so grave an animal should have strayed into the province of the ape; yet admire that practice should have given the bulky quadruped so much agility.

Upon the whole, Johnson's style appears to me so encumbered, so void of ear and harmony, that I know no modern writer whose works can be redde aloud with so little satisfaction. I question whether one should not read a page of equal length in any modern author, in a minute's time less than one of Johnson's, all proper pauses and accents being duly attended to in both.

His works are the antipodes of taste, and he a schoolmaster of truth, but never its parent; for his doctrines have no novelty, and are never inculcated with indulgence either to the froward child or to the dull one. He has set nothing in a new light, yet is as diffuse as if we had every thing to learn. Modern writers have improved on the ancients only by conciseness. Dr. Johnson, like the chymists of Laputa, endeavours to carry back what has been digested, to its pristine and crude principles. He is a standing proof that the Muses leave works unfinished, if they are not embellished by the Graces.—HORACE WALPOLE, "General Criticism on Dr. Johnson's Writings" (c. 1779), *Works*, 1798, Vol. 4, pp. 361–62

Here Johnson lies—a sage, by all allow'd,
Whom to have bred may well make England proud;
Whose prose was eloquence by wisdom taught,
The graceful vehicle of virtuous thought;
Whose verse may claim—grave, masculine, and strong,
Superior praise to the mere poet's song;
Who many a noble gift from heav'n possess'd,
And faith at last—alone worth all the rest.
Oh man immortal by a double prize!
By Fame on earth—by Glory in the skies!
    —WILLIAM COWPER, "Epitaph on Dr. Johnson," 1785

Though Johnson's merits thus I freely scan,
And paint the foibles of this wond'rous man;
Yet can I coolly read, and not admire,
When Learning, Wit and Poetry conspire
To shed a radiance o'er his moral page,
And spread truth's sacred light to many an age:

For all his works with innate lustre shine,
Strength all his own, and energy divine:
While through life's maze he darts his piercing view,
His mind expansive to the object grew.
    In judgment keen he acts the critick's part,
By reason proves the feelings of the heart;
In thought profound, in nature's study wise,
Shews from what source our fine sensations rise;
With truth, precision, fancy's claims defines,
And throws new splendour o'er the poet's lines.
    When specious sophists with presumption scan
The source of evil, hidden still from man;
Revive Arabian tales, and vainly hope
To rival St. John, and his scholar, Pope;
Though metaphysics spread the gloom of night,
By reason's star he guides our aching sight;
The bounds of knowledge marks; and points the way
To pathless wastes, where wilder'd sages stray;
Where, like a farthing linkboy, J⟨enyn⟩s stands,
And the dim torch drops from his feeble hands.
    Impressive truth, in splendid fiction drest,
Checks the vain wish, and calms the troubled breast;
O'er the dark mind a light celestial throws,
And sooths the angry passions to repose:
As oil effus'd illumes and smooths the deep,
When round the bark the swelling surges sweep.—
With various stores of erudition fraught,
The lively image, the deep-searching thought,
Slept in repose;—but when the moment press'd,
The bright ideas stood at once confess'd;
Instant his genius sped its vigorous rays,
And o'er the letter'd world diffus'd a blaze:
As womb'd with fire the cloud electrick flies,
And calmly o'er the horizon seems to rise;
Touch'd by the pointed steel, the lightning flows,
And all the expanse with rich effulgence glows.
      —JOHN COURTENAY, *A Poetical Review of the Literary and Moral Character of the Late Samuel Johnson LL.D.*, 1786

Johnson, I think, was far from a great character; he was continually sinning against his conscience, and then afraid of going to hell for it. A Christian and a man of the town, a philosopher and a bigot, acknowledging life to be miserable, and making it more miserable through fear of death; professing great distaste to the country, and neglecting the urbanity of towns; a Jacobite, and pensioned; acknowledged to be a giant in literature, and yet we do not trace him, as we do Locke, or Rousseau, or Voltaire, in his influence on the opinions of the times. We cannot say Johnson first opened this vein of thought, led the way to this discovery or this turn of thinking. In his style he is original, and there we can track his imitators. In short, he seems to me to be one of those who have shone in the *belles lettres*, rather than, what he is held out by many to be, an original and deep genius in investigation.—ANNA LAETITIA BARBAULD, Letter to John Aikin (May 1791), *Works*, 1825, Vol. 2, p. 158

    Here, peaceable at last
    are deposited the remains
    of Dr. Samuel Johnson,
    the Poet
    the Critic
    the Periodical Essayist
    the Novellist
    the Politico-polemic,
    the Lexicographer,
    Topographer,

Biographer.
The Public taste
Patron of every novelty,
Cherished his writings for a while,
as most extraordinary specimens
of pedantic verbosity;
even the matchless insipidity of *Rasselas*
was tolerated.
His political and poetical talents
differed widely from each other.
A bigoted education
had taught him to maintain
long-exploded absurdities
in maxims of government.
His own failures in poetry
made him a perfect leveler
throughout the region of the Muses.
Incompetent critic from hebetude,
Credulous retailer of calumnies;
illiberal in his censures;
Cynical in his expressions;
he acquired the literary title of
Snarler General.
To the manes of poets
whom Johnson slandered in their graves,
be this an expiatory offering.
    —GEORGE MASON, *Gentleman's Magazine*, 1796, pp. 758–59

Style is, of course, nothing else but the art of conveying the meaning appropriately and with perspicuity, whatever that meaning may be, and one criterion of style is that it shall not be translateable without injury to the meaning. Johnson's style has pleased many from the very fault of being perpetually translateable; he creates an impression of cleverness by never saying any thing in a common way.—SAMUEL TAYLOR COLERIDGE, *A Course of Lectures* (1818), *Literary Remains*, ed. Henry Nelson Coleridge, 1836, Vol. 1, p. 239

The dramatic and conversational tone which forms the distinguishing feature and greatest charm of the *Spectator* and *Tatler*, is quite lost in the *Rambler* by Dr. Johnson. There is no reflected light thrown on human life from an assumed character, nor any direct one from a display of the author's own. The *Tatler* and *Spectator* are, as it were, made up of notes and memorandums of the events and incidents of the day, with finished studies after nature, and characters fresh from the life, which the writer moralises upon, and turns to account as they come before him: the *Rambler* is a collection of moral Essays, or scholastic theses, written on set subjects, and of which the individual characters and incidents are merely artificial illustrations, brought in to give a pretended relief to the dryness of didactic discussion. The *Rambler* is a splendid and imposing common-place-book of general topics, and rhetorical declamation on the conduct and business of human life. In this sense, there is hardly a reflection that had been suggested on such subjects which is not to be found in this celebrated work, and there is, perhaps, hardly a reflection to be found in it which had not been already suggested and developed by some other author, or in the common course of conversation. The mass of intellectual wealth here heaped together is immense, but it is rather the result of gradual accumulation, the produce of the general intellect, labouring in the mine of knowledge and reflection, than dug out of the quarry, and dragged into the light by the industry and sagacity of a single mind. I am not here saying that Dr. Johnson was a man without originality, compared with the ordinary run of men's minds, but he was not a man of original thought or genius, in the sense in which Montaigne or Lord Bacon was. He opened no new vein of precious ore, nor did he light upon any single pebbles of uncommon size and unrivalled lustre. We seldom meet with any thing to 'give us pause;' he does not set us thinking for the first time. His reflections present themselves like reminiscences; do not disturb the ordinary march of our thoughts; arrest our attention by the stateliness of their appearance, and the costliness of their garb, but pass one and mingle with the throng of our impressions. After closing the volumes of the *Rambler*, there is nothing that we remember as a new truth gained to the mind, nothing indelibly stamped upon the memory; nor is there any passage that we wish to turn to as embodying any known principle or observation, with such force and beauty that justice can only be done to the idea in the author's own words. Such, for instance, are many of the passages to be found in Burke, which shine by their own light, belong to no class, have neither equal nor counterpart, and of which we say that no one but the author could have written them! There is neither the same boldness of design, nor mastery of execution in Johnson. In the one, the spark of genius seems to have met with its congenial matter: the shaft is sped; the forked lightning dresses up the face of nature in ghastly smiles, and the loud thunder rolls far away from the ruin that is made. Dr. Johnson's style, on the contrary, resembles rather the rumbling of mimic thunder at one of our theatres; and the light he throws upon a subject is like the dazzling effect of phosphorus, or an *ignis fatuus* of words. There is a wide difference, however, between perfect originality and perfect common-place: neither ideas nor expressions are trite or vulgar because they are not quite new. They are valuable, and ought to be repeated, if they have not become quite common; and Johnson's style both of reasoning and imagery holds the middle rank between startling novelty and vapid commonplace. Johnson has as much originality of thinking as Addison; but then he wants his familiarity of illustration, knowledge of character, and delightful humour.—What most distinguishes Dr. Johnson from other writers is the pomp and uniformity of his style. All his periods are cast in the same mould, are of the same size and shape, and consequently have little fitness to the variety of things he professes to treat of. His subjects are familiar, but the author is always upon stilts. He has neither ease nor simplicity, and his efforts at playfulness, in part, remind one of the lines in Milton:—

The elephant
To make them sport wreath'd his proboscis lithe.

His Letters from Correspondents, in particular, are more pompous and unwieldy than what he writes in his own person. This want of relaxation and variety of manner has, I think, after the first effects of novelty and surprise were over, been prejudicial to the matter. It takes from the general power, not only to please, but to instruct. The monotony of style produces an apparent monotony of ideas. What is really striking and valuable, is lost in the vain ostentation and circumlocution of the expression; for when we find the same pains and pomp of diction bestowed upon the most trifling as upon the most important parts of a sentence or discourse, we grow tired of distinguishing between pretension and reality, and are disposed to confound the tinsel and bombast of the phraseology with want of weight in the thoughts. Thus, from the imposing and oracular nature of the style, people are tempted at first to imagine that our author's speculations are all wisdom and profundity: till having found out their mistake in some instances, they suppose that there is nothing but common-place

in them, concealed under verbiage and pedantry; and in both they are wrong. The fault of Dr. Johnson's style is, that it reduces all things to the same artificial and unmeaning level. It destroys all shades of difference, the association between words and things. It is a perpetual paradox and innovation. He condescends to the familiar till we are ashamed of our interest in it: he expands the little till it looks big. 'If he were to write a fable of little fishes,' as Goldsmith said of him, 'he would make them speak like great whales.' We can no more distinguish the most familiar objects in his descriptions of them, than we can a well-known face under a huge painted mask. The structure of his sentences, which was his own invention, and which has been generally imitated since his time, is a species of rhyming in prose, where one clause answers to another in measure and quantity, like the tagging of syllables at the end of a verse; the close of the period follows as mechanically as the oscillation of a pendulum, the sense is balanced with the sound; each sentence, revolving round its centre of gravity, is contained with itself like a couplet, and each paragraph forms itself into a stanza. Dr. Johnson is also a complete balance-master in the topics of morality. He never encourages hope, but he counteracts it by fear; he never elicits a truth, but he suggests some objection in answer to it. He seizes and alternately quits the clue of reason, lest it should involve him in the labyrinths of endless error: he wants confidence in himself and his fellows. He dares not trust himself with the immediate impressions of things, for fear of compromising his dignity; or follow them into their consequences, for fear of committing his prejudices. His timidity is the result, not of ignorance, but of morbid apprehension. 'He runs the great circle, and is still at home.' No advance is made by his writings in any sentiment, or mode of reasoning. Out of the pale of established authority and received dogmas, all is sceptical, loose, and desultory: he seems in imagination to strengthen the dominion of prejudice, as he weakens and dissipates that of reason; and round the rock of faith and power, on the edge of which he slumbers blindfold and uneasy, the waves and billows of uncertain and dangerous opinion roar and heave for evermore. His *Rasselas* is the most melancholy and debilitating moral speculation that ever was put forth. Doubtful of the faculties of his mind, as of his organs of vision, Johnson trusted only to his feelings and his fears. He cultivated a belief in witches as an out-guard to the evidences of religion; and abused Milton, and patronised Lauder, in spite of his aversion to his countrymen, as a step to secure the existing establishment in church and state. This was neither right feeling nor sound logic.—WILLIAM HAZLITT, *Lectures on the English Comic Writers*, 1818

Rough Johnson, the great moralist, profess'd,
Right honestly, 'he liked an honest hater!'—
The only truth that yet has been confest
Within these latest thousand years or later.
—GEORGE GORDON, LORD BYRON, *Don Juan*,
1823, Canto 13, Stanza 7

With respect to the mind of Johnson, it was undoubtedly one of the very first order. ⟨. . .⟩ His conversation, which is perhaps the best test of real ability, is unrivalled for its point, brilliancy, and power; and if in some respects he appears to take narrow views of important subjects, it was evidently a voluntary bondage, and from his own choice if he moved in chains. In fact, we cannot tell whether we have his real opinions; he considered conversation an exhibition of skill; and he delighted to put his shoulder under a fallen theory or forsaken cause, to show what his ingenuity and power could do. Many suggestions, which were hastily thrown out by him in this way and forgotten, have been regarded as his deliberate convictions; the superstition, for example, which is supposed to have been his weakness; and various other frailties of mind, which have now become, by a not unmerited retribution, inseparably attached to his memory, in consequence of the intellectual duels in which he was constantly engaged. Many have professed to wonder, that he should have been permitted to exercise such a despotism in society; but his society consisted not of the fashionable nor the great, but of intellectual men, who admired his talent, and were content to keep silence or humor his caprice, for the sake of enjoying his inspirations. With his ready wit, shrewdness, and overpowering ability, he could not fail to predominate in any circle where he might be thrown. It is true, there were great men about him; but Fox was easy and unambitious, except in the House of Commons. In these conversations, he seems to have been too indolent or careless to take any leading part. Burke was distinguished every where; in vigor of mind he was equal to Johnson, and in comprehension, probably superior; but the careless prodigality with which he threw out his resources, sometimes made his hearers insensible of their value. In conversation he was less impressive than Johnson, from this very overflow of thought; as the roar of the cataract is less startling than the sudden thunder of the gun. To us it seems plain, that were Johnson now living, such a master of the social power would hold the same ascendency over an intellectual society, as was conceded to him in his own day.

It has been commonly said of him, that he was not remarkable for learning; but we apprehend that this only means, that his works were rather of the literary than of the learned kind. He drew his illustrations less from classical sources, than from the inexhaustible fountains of his own invention; but it would be difficult to point out the place where he showed any deficiency in those various and important attainments, which a profound scholar might be expected to possess. Doubtless there were those, who went beyond him in every single department of learning; but we strongly doubt whether England has ever produced a scholar, whose treasures of the kind were more useful to his purpose, or one who had a greater power of recalling his acquisitions just where they happened to be wanted, or of suiting them to the demands of the occasion. That he was deficient, is matter of inference altogether; and how cautious one should be in drawing such conclusions, was well suggested by Jacob Bryant in a conversation with Gifford, to whom he gave a lesson of modesty, which, it is a pity to reflect, was entirely thrown away. Gifford became acquainted with Bryant at Lord Grosvenor's. The conversation one day turned on a Greek criticism by Dr. Johnson, in some volume on the table, which Gifford thought incorrect, and pointed out as such to the veteran Grecian. Bryant hesitated to acquiesce, and in order to overcome his scruples, Gifford remarked, that Johnson himself admitted that he was not a good Greek scholar. 'Sir,' said Bryant, with a very expressive manner, 'it is not for us to say, what such a man as Johnson would call a good Greek scholar.' We are glad that Gifford had the grace to record this story; and we hope that our readers will remember it when any thing is said in dispraise of men with whom young pretenders are disgusted, because the world has so long delighted to honor them. Much has been said also, in derision of the style of Johnson. Many writers speak of style, as if it were formed and changed at pleasure; but it seems to us as absurd to give rules for the formation of style, after the mysteries of grammar are understood, as to determine what expression the countenance shall wear. The first object is

to think clearly, and then to express the thought in the most direct and natural manner. This was the course taken by Johnson; the movements of his mind were heavy and powerful, like those of some mighty enginery, and his style assumed the same form, not by any effort or ambition, but simply by following the dictate of his nature. In his later years, when the labor of thought grew easier, and he felt more secure of fame, his style underwent a corresponding change; but from first to last, it was solemn, imposing, and majestic, and was in every respect an exact expression of the habits and character of his mind. We wish this truth were more generally understood, that the style indicates the habits of thought, though it does not always indicate the measure of strength which belongs to the mind; for we have observed in some able writers an attempt to write in an obscure and shadowy style, thinking, perhaps, that as objects are lifted and magnified by a mist, their conceptions, dimly expressed, will swell into gigantic proportions. The author of the Pelham novels is an example of this affectation, and the writer of an article on Burns in a late *Edinburgh Review*, a man of much higher order, brought his talent into suspicion by a similar style. Johnson's was what a style should be,—a natural expression of his mind; and those who attempted to ridicule it by travesty, overlooked the fact, that little men might appear very absurdly dressed in Johnson's clothes: and the garments might, nevertheless, sit very well on him.

There has been an impression, that Johnson's writings have had their day; and the *Rambler* is cited as a work which has been much admired, and is now but little read. This may be true; but the change of taste proves nothing against its excellence. New works, suited to the varying feelings of the times, have come forward, and though the *Rambler* is still admired, others stand more directly before the public eye. We should be sorry to estimate the merit of the *Paradise Lost* by the number of its readers. It is partly owing to Johnson himself, that his morality is neglected; for his original and striking maxims impressed the public mind so forcibly shortly after they appeared, that they became incorporated with the common sense of mankind, and thus by lifting man to the height where he himself stood, he rendered his own observations unnecessary. They became as 'a lamp despised in the thought of him that is at ease;' and thus the decay into which his morality has fallen, proves at once its power, and the good which it has done. It must be remarked, too, that moral writings, not being particularly sprightly, have but little attraction for men at large, when they are no longer new. Nicol Jarvie was not singular, when he spent the Sabbath evening in reading good books and gaping. The reason is, that in order to gain popular favor, all works in which abstract truth is taught, must be made palatable by some kind of attraction; and Johnson's style, which in his own age was a recommendation, has lost its interest by the lapse of time.

If Johnson's circumstances had been favorable to the cultivation of his poetical talent, he would have been very much distinguished for the brilliancy of his imagination. Poetry, in the richest forms of image and sentiment, flashes out in almost all his writings. His poetical writings, as we now have them, abound in faults, but they are all such as practice would have cured. In his imitations of Juvenal, his thought is condensed and energetic, in order to resemble the original; but as often as he forgets his copy and breathes out his own mind and spirit, the tones of the organ are not so deep and full as his poetry in its grand and melancholy flow. It does not appear that he could ever have excelled in tragedy, even if he had not been shackled by a system, which agreed neither with public taste nor with English nature; he was far too stately and unbending, to follow the play and change of the passions. Lyrical poetry would have suited him no better; but in the moral and didactic department, to which his genius was eminently adapted, we believe that the prophetic suggestion which Pope made of his future greatness, would have been more than realized, and that he would have been the most impressive and inspiring poetical moralist the world ever saw.

We have no reason, however, to complain, since in the latter part of his life he accidentally took the employment of a critic on poetry, a field in which his splendid powers appeared to the best advantage. The *Lives of the Poets* has been by far the most popular of his works, and is doubtless the one for which he will be most reverenced in future times. It afforded room for the display of every kind of talent; of his critical sagacity, his burning imagination, his learned research, and that memory by which he retained many curious anecdotes and traits of character, which would otherwise have been lost. No doubt a prejudiced air is given to the work by his political prepossessions, and he has done injustice to some distinguished names; but he wrote what he thought, and treated his subjects as he believed they deserved. It is now clear that he was wrong in some respects; but he did not err in malice, and how was it reasonable to expect, that he should follow the prejudices of others in preference to his own? The portion of this work which he esteemed the best, was the essay on the metaphysical poets, an affected race, to whom Byron's word 'metaquizzical' would much better apply. It was, however, wasting too much ingenuity on their *Euphuistical* conceits; and the happiest parts of the book, in our opinion, are those in which he was best pleased with his subject, and gave it his manly praise. The world is deeply indebted to him for this great work; and if there are instances in which injustice has been done by it, it has come to pass as he expected, that there have been enough to correct his errors, and to redeem from reproach every deserving fame.

It is but a part of his works to which we have alluded. His dictionary, a vast undertaking, from which his feelings and habits revolted, which was wrought out without aid or patronage, and in seasons of poverty and sorrow, has supplied a broad and deep foundation, on which all future improvements in the language can be built. His *Preface to Shakespeare*, in which he fearlessly assaulted a feeling second in strength only to religious reverence,—his dedications, many of which are eminently beautiful and happy, show how every subject was illuminated, when he held it in the concentrated light of his mind. All who are able to estimate talent, will be found among the admirers of Johnson. They will acknowledge, that there were those among the sons of light, who towered in a higher sphere, and took wider and more inspiring views of the ways of God and the duty and destiny of man; but they will not suffer him to be degraded beneath the place, which the sentence of the world has assigned him. They will forgive his imperfections and reverence his virtues; they will defend his character when it is attacked by thoughtless folly, though, to adopt his own sentiment, a reputation established like his, has little to fear from censure, and nothing to hope from praise.—W. B. O. PEABODY, "Croker's Boswell," *North American Review*, Jan. 1832, pp. 100–104

"Dr. Johnson," Goldsmith said one day to him, "if you were to make little fishes talk, they would talk like whales." In fact, his phraseology rolls always in solemn and majestic periods, in which every substantive marches ceremoniously, accompanied by its epithet; great, pompous words peal like an organ; every proposition is set forth balanced by a proposition of equal length; thought is developed with the compassed regularity and official splendor of a procession. Classical prose attains its perfection in him, as classical poetry in Pope. Art cannot be more consummate, or nature more forced. No one has confined ideas in more strait compartments; none has given stronger relief to dissertation and proof; none has imposed more despotically on story and dialogue the forms of argumentation and violent declamation; none has more generally mutilated the flowing liberty of conversation and life by antitheses and technical words. It is the completion and the excess, the triumph and the tyranny, of oratorical style. We understand now that an oratorical age would recognize him as a master, and attribute to him in eloquence the primacy which is attributed to Pope in verse.

We wish to know what ideas have made him popular. Here the astonishment of a Frenchman redoubles. We vainly turn over the pages of his *Dictionary*, his eight volumes of essays, his ten volumes of biographies, his numberless articles, his conversation so carefully collected; we yawn. His truths are too true; we already know his precepts by heart. We learn from him that life is short, and we ought to improve the few moments accorded to us; that a mother ought not to bring up her son as a dandy; that a man ought to repent of his crimes, and yet avoid superstition; that in everything we ought to be active, and not hurried. We thank him for these sage counsels, but we mutter to ourselves that we could have done very well without them. We should like to know who could have been the lovers of *ennui* who have bought up thirteen thousand copies. We then remember that sermons are liked in England, and that these *Essays* are sermons. We discover that men of reflection do not need bold or striking ideas, but palpable and profitable truths. They demand to be furnished with a useful provision of authentic documents on man and his existence, and demand nothing more. No matter if the idea is vulgar; meat and bread are vulgar, too, and are no less good. They wish to be taught the kinds and degrees of happiness and unhappiness, the varieties and results of characters and conditions, the advantages and inconveniences of town and country, knowledge and ignorance, wealth and poverty, because they are moralists and utilitarians; because they look in a book for the knowledge to turn them from folly, and motives to confirm them in uprightness; because they cultivate in themselves sense, that is to say, practical reason. A little fiction, a few portraits, the least amount of amusement, will suffice to adorn it. This substantial food only needs a very simple seasoning. It is not the novelty of the dishes, nor dainty cookery, but solidity and wholesomeness, which they seek. For this reason the *Essays* are a national food. It is because they are insipid and dull for us that they suit the taste of an Englishman. We understand now why they take for a favorite the respectable, the unbearable Samuel Johnson.—HIPPOLYTE TAINE, *History of English Literature*, tr. H. Van Laun, 1871, Bk. 3, Ch. 6

Johnson escaped from the hell of Swift's passion by virtue of that pathetic tenderness of nature which lay beneath his rugged outside. If Swift excites a strange mixture of repulsion and pity, no one can know Johnson without loving him. And what was Johnson's special message to the world? He has given it most completely in *Rasselas*; and the curious coincidence between *Rasselas* and *Candide* has been frequently noticed. Voltaire, the arch-iconoclast, Johnson, last of the Tories, agree in making the protest against optimism the topic of their most significant works. Besides the vast difference in style between the greatest master of literary expression and the powerful writer whose pen seems to be paralysed by his constitutional depression, there is another striking difference. The moral of *Candide* is, in one sense, speculative. The result, it is true, is purely negative. Optimism, that is Voltaire's thesis, will not fit the facts of the world. Johnson, on the other hand, is exclusively moral. A disciple of Voltaire would learn to 'cultivate his garden' and abandon speculation; but then, with speculation, he would abandon all theology. A disciple of Johnson learns the futility of enquiring into the ultimate purposes of the Creator; but he would acquiesce in the accepted creed. It is as good as any other, considered as a philosophy, and much better considered as supplying motives for the conduct of life. Johnson's fame amongst his contemporaries was that of a great moralist; and the name represents what was most significant in his teaching.

He was as good a moralist as a man can be who regards the ultimate foundations of morality as placed beyond the reach of speculation. 'We know we are free, and there's an end on't,' is his answer to the great metaphysical difficulty. He 'refutes' Berkeley by kicking a stone. He thinks that Hume is a mere trifler, who has taken to 'milking the bull' by way of variety. He laughs effectually at Soame Jenyns's explanation of the origin of evil; but leaves the question as practically insoluble, without troubling himself as to why it is insoluble, or what consequences may follow from its insolubility. Speculation, in short, though he passed for a philosopher, was simply abhorrent to him. He passes by on the other side, and leaves such puzzles for triflers. He has made up his mind once for all that religion is wanted, and that the best plan is to accept the established creed. And thus we have the apparent paradox that, whilst no man sets a higher value upon truthfulness in all the ordinary affairs of life than Johnson, no man could care less for the foundations of speculative truth. His gaze was not directed to that side. Judging in all cases rather by intuition than by logical processes, he takes for granted the religious theories which fall in sufficiently with his moral convictions. To all speculation which may tend to loosen the fixity of the social order he is deaf or contemptuously averse. The old insidious Deism seems to him to be mere trash; and he would cure the openly aggressive Deism of Rousseau by sending its author to the plantations. Indifference to speculation generates a hearty contempt for all theories. He has too firm a grasp of facts to care for the dreams of fanciful Utopians; his emotions are too massive and rigid to be easily excited by enthusiasts. He ridicules the prevailing cry against corruption. The world is bad enough, in all conscience, but it will do no good to exaggerate or to whine. He has no sympathy with believers in the speedy advent of a millennium. The evils under which creation groans have their causes in a region far beyond the powers of constitution-mongers and political agitators.

How small of all that human hearts endure
That part which laws or kings can cause or cure!

These words sum up his political theory. Subordination is the first necessity of man, whether in politics or religion. To what particular form of creed or constitution men are to submit is a matter of secondary importance. No mere shifting of the superficial arrangements of society will seriously affect the condition of mankind. Starvation, poverty, and disease are evils beyond the reach of a Wilkes or a Rousseau. Stick to the facts, and laugh at fine phrases. Clear your mind of cant. Work and don't whine. Hold fast by established order, and resist anarchy as you would resist the devil. That is the pith of Johnson's answer to the vague declamations symptomatic of the growing unrest of European society. All such querulous complaints were classed by him with the fancies of a fine lady

who has broken her china, or a fop who has spoilt his fine clothes by a slip in the kennel. He under-estimated the significance of the symptoms, because he never appreciated the true meaning of Hume or Voltaire. But the stubborn adherence of Johnson, and such men as Johnson, to solid fact, and their unreasonable contempt for philosophy, goes far to explain how it came to pass that England avoided the catastrophe of a revolution. The morality is not the highest, because it implies an almost wilful blindness to the significance of the contemporary thought, but appropriate to the time, for it expresses the resolute determination of the dogged English mind not to loosen its grasp on solid fact in pursuit of dreams; and thoroughly masculine, for it expresses the determination to see the world as it is, and to reject with equal decision the optimism of shallow speculation, and the morbid pessimism of such misanthropists as Swift.—Sir Leslie Stephen, *History of English Thought in the Eighteenth Century*, 1876

Johnson gained his reputation by his unrivalled power of concentrating his own forces, of defending himself against the aggression of outer influences,—and striking a light in the process. Of course Johnson was a man of very strong general understanding. Had he not been so, he could not have commanded the respect he did, for those who do not in a considerable degree understand others, will never be themselves understood. Still, admitting freely that it both takes a man of some character as well as insight, to understand distinctly what is beyond his own sphere, and a man of some insight as well as character, to teach others to understand distinctly what is within himself, it is clear that Johnson's genius lay in the latter, not in the former direction,—in maintaining himself against the encroachments of the world, and in interpreting himself to that world, not in enlarging materially the world's sympathies and horizons, except so far as he taught them to include himself. The best things he did of any kind were all expressions of himself. His poems,—*London* and *The Vanity of Human Wishes*,—many parts even of his biographies, like his *Life of Savage*,—almost all his moral essays of any value, and above everything, his brilliant conversation, were all shadows or reflections of that large and dictatorial, but in the main, benign character which he has stamped for us on all he did. Of his companions and contemporaries, all but himself won their fame by entering into something different from themselves,—Burke by his political sagacity, Garrick by imitating men and manners, Goldsmith by reflecting them, Reynolds by painting them, Boswell by devoting his whole soul to the faithful portraiture of Johnson. But Johnson became great by concentrating his power in himself, though in no selfish fashion, for he concentrated it even more vigorously in his unselfish tastes,—for example, in the home which he so generously and eccentrically made for so many unattractive dependents,—than in the mere self-assertion of his impressions and his convictions. What made Johnson loom so large in the world was this moral concentrativeness, this incapacity for ceasing to be himself, and becoming something different in deference to either authority or influence. His character was one the surface of which was safe against rust, or any other moral encroachment by things without. And it is his capacity for not only making this visible, but for making it visible by a sort of electric shock which announces his genius for repelling any threatening influence, that constitutes the essence of his humour. Some of his finest sayings are concessions *in form* to his opponent, while in reality they reassert with far greater strength his original position. They are, in fact, fortifications of his personal paradox, instead of modifications of it,—the fortification being all the more telling because it took the form of an apparent concession. Thus when he said of the poet Gray, "He was dull in company, dull in his closet, dull everywhere,—he was dull in a new way, and that made people think him great," his concession of novelty to Gray was, in fact, an aggravation of his attack upon him. And still more effective was his attack on Gray's friend, Mason. When Boswell said that there were good passages in Mason's *Elfrida*, Johnson replied that "there were now and then some good imitations of Milton's bad manner." Or take his saying of Sheridan, "Why, Sir, Sherry is dull, naturally dull; but it must have taken him a great deal of pains to become what we now see him. Such an excess of stupidity, Sir, is not in nature." Of course you are not prepared to find that Sheridan's improvements on "nature" were all in the direction of the dulness of which Johnson had been accusing him. Johnson's humour, indeed, generally consists in using the forms of speech appropriate to giving way, just as he puts the crown on his self-assertion, as in the celebrated case of his attack on Scotch scenery, in answer to the Scotchman's praise of the "noble, wild prospects" to be found in Scotland:— "I believe, Sir, you have a great many. Norway, too, has noble, wild prospects, and Lapland is remarkable for prodigious noble, wild prospects. But, Sir, let me tell you, the noblest prospect which a Scotchman ever sees, is the high-road that leads him to England."

But this curious power of Johnson's of strengthening himself in his position the moment it was threatened, was the secret of a great deal that was morally grand in him, as well as of a great deal of his humour. His great saying to Boswell, on which Carlyle lays so much stress, that he should clear his mind of cant, and not affect a depression about public affairs which he did not really feel, was, in fact, a protest against the demands which conventionalism makes on men's sincerity. Distinctly aware, as he was, that the state of public affairs seldom or never made him really unhappy, he resented the habit of speaking as if it did, as an act of treachery to his own self-respect. So nothing irritated him like a sentimental eulogy on "a state of nature," because it demanded from him an admission that one of the strongest and soundest of his own instincts was utterly untrustworthy. When somebody had told him with admiration of the soliloquy of an officer who lived in the wilds of America,—"Here am I free and unrestrained, amidst the rude magnificence of nature, with the Indian woman by my side, and this gun, with which I can procure food when I want it! What more can be desired for human happiness?"—Johnson, well aware that what he, and indeed what every sane man, valued most was partly the product of intellectual labour and civilisation, retorted, "Do not allow yourself, Sir, to be imposed upon by such gross absurdity. It is sad stuff. It is brutish. If a bull could speak, he might as well exclaim, 'Here am I, with this cow and this grass; what being can enjoy greater felicity?'" Nor would Johnson ever allow himself to be betrayed into pretending to approve what he hated, simply because such approval would have fitted in with other prejudices and tastes that were very deep in him. High Tory as he was, when any one defended slavery he would burst out into vehement attacks. On one occasion, says Mr. Stephen, he gave as a toast to some "very grave men" at Oxford, "Here's to the next insurrection of negroes in the West Indies"; and he was accustomed to ask, "How is it that we always have the loudest yelps for liberty amongst the drivers of negroes?" Indeed, the hearty old man would have been a most valuable ally during the American Civil War of seventeen years back, when English society got quite sentimental about slave-drivers who were yelping their loudest for liberty to drive slaves.

But no matter what the subject was, nor what was to be the logical or analogical consequence of his confession of his own belief,—whether he were to be called cold-hearted for confessing (perhaps mistakenly) that he should not eat one bit of plum pudding the less if an acquaintance of his were found guilty of a crime and condemned to die,—or were to be branded as grossly inconsistent for admiring such a "bottomless Whig" as Burke,—or were to be taxed with ridiculing Garrick one day as a mere trick-playing monkey, and defending him vigorously the next when attacked by some one else,—Johnson was always determined to be himself, and always was himself. He was himself in collecting round him so strange a household of companions, who would have been miserable but for his generosity, and were to some extent miserable, and the causes of misery, in spite of his generosity, and in remaining true to them in spite of their taunts and complaints against him. He was himself, in spurning the patronage of Chesterfield when he found out its utter insincerity; himself, in his strange acts of occasional penance; in his loudly and even scornfully avowed value for his dinner,—and for a good dinner; himself, in his strange and tender acts of humanity to the lower animals; himself, in his knock-down blows to his conversational companions; himself, in his curious superstitions, and in his not less curious scepticisms. For a long time he disbelieved, as Mr. Stephen notes, the earthquake which destroyed Lisbon, though he believed in the Cock Lane Ghost. But whatever he did or declined to do, whatever he believed or rejected, he was always the first to avow it, and to assert himself as not only not ashamed, but eager to avow it, even though it were an act which he thought a blot on his own past life. It was this indomitable self-respect and dignity, in the highest sense, which gave not only much of the freshness and force to his conversation but the grandeur to his life. His devotion to his wife and to his wife's memory,—she was said by those who knew her to have been an affected woman, who painted herself, and took on her all the airs and graces of an elderly beauty, though she was fifteen years older than he was,—his courage in carrying home a half-dying woman of bad character whom he found in the streets, and did his best to cure and to reform,—his incessant, though rough benevolence to his poor dependents, and indeed almost all the traits of his remarkable character, bespeak a man who was never ashamed of himself when he thought himself right, and was never ashamed to be publicly ashamed of himself, when he thought himself wrong. It was this quality, almost as much as his great wit and strength of conversation, which made him the literary dictator of his time,—and it is in this quality that our own day needs his example most. A day in which men are almost ashamed to be odd, and quite ashamed to be inconsistent, in which a singular life, even if the result of intelligent and intelligible purpose, is almost regarded as a sign of insanity, and in which society imposes its conventional assumptions and insincerities on almost every one of us, is certainly a day when it will do more than usual good to revive the memory of that dangerous and yet tender literary bear who stood out amongst the men even of his day as one who, whatever else he was, was always true to himself, and that too almost at the most trying time of all, even when he had not been faithful to himself,—a man who was more afraid of his conscience than of all the world's opinion—and who towers above our own generation, just because he had the courage to be what so few of us are,—proudly independent of the opinion in the midst of which he lived.—Richard Holt Hutton, "Mr. Leslie Stephen on Johnson" (1878), *Criticisms of Contemporary Thought and Thinkers*, 1894, Vol. 1, pp. 164–70

The most able criticism of the 18th century was Johnson's; he may be called in fact the first really systematic critic of English literature; for, although his remarks on other authors are scattered all about his own miscellaneous writings, it may be confidently stated that he made criticism his profession, and earned his living by it. He is an important link in the chain of English prose writers, for he is the first author whose whole thoughts were turned to the works of his predecessors.—C. R. L. Fletcher, *The Development of English Prose Style*, 1881, p. 19

I never for an instant compared Johnson to Scott, Pope, Byron, or any of the really great writers whom I loved. But I at once and forever recognized in him a man entirely sincere, and infallibly wise in the view and estimate he gave of the common questions, business, and ways of the world. I valued his sentences not primarily because they were symmetrical, but because they were just, and clear; it is a method of judgment rarely used by the average public, who ask from an author always, in the first place, arguments in favour of their own opinions, in elegant terms; and are just as ready with their applause for a sentence of Macaulay's, which may have no more sense in it than a blot pinched between doubled paper, as to reject one of Johnson's, telling against their own prejudice,—though its symmetry be as of thunder answering from two horizons. I hold it more than happy that, during those continental journeys, in which the vivid excitement of the greater part of the day left me glad to give spare half-hours to the study of a thoughtful book, Johnson was the one author accessible to me. No other writer could have secured me, as he did, against all chance of being misled by my own sanguine and metaphysical temperament. He taught me carefully to measure life, and distrust fortune; and he secured me, by his adamantine common-sense, for ever, from being caught in the cobwebs of German metaphysics, or sloughed in the English drainage of them.—John Ruskin, *Praeterita*, 1885, Vol. 1, p. 416

Johnson stands out pre-eminently as the one man for whom biography has done more than she has done for any other. By her help he is no mere name in literary history, but a personal friend and acquaintance, whose strength and whose weakness we know by heart; whose picture is impressed upon us down to the smallest details with a vivid force. The powerful personality of the man, and the perfection of the portrait, have obscured the fame that properly belongs to him as an author; and the popular notion of his work is based upon little more than a superficial tradition, which is rarely corrected by any real familiarity with his writings. Johnson is conceived as a man of pedantic turn of mind, cumbrous in his ideas and inflated in his diction; the slave of convention, the enemy of humour, dictatorial in argument, without tolerance for the graces of simplicity, and lacking all keenness of critical insight. It would be hard to conceive any picture more unlike the truth. Johnson rightly despised the easy triumph of paradox and eccentricity. He saw—just as the best of the previous generation had seen—that excellence in literature must be based on form, and that its advances, to be sure, must be secured by rigid adherence to rule. The masters of English prose in the Augustan age had all of them protested against anarchy in literature, and with all their variety, they had been careful to claim for themselves no right to set convention at

defiance. Dryden, Swift, and Addison had never permitted themselves to forget that English prose had to obey a certain law that was fixing on it more and more of order and regularity. They had, it is true, by their genius, breathed into that order and regularity their own force, and directness, and easy familiarity. But these last were the supreme effect of their own individual genius: neither the impetuous flow of Dryden's prose, nor the easy lissomeness of Swift's, nor the delicate conversational tone of Addison's, could repeat or perpetuate themselves in English prose, and establish a common model for all time. What was necessary in the generation when Johnson wrote, was some commanding authority that might set a standard of prose style, that might establish its laws beyond all gainsaying, and that by the force of its own virility might compel obedience. This was just what Johnson did. It was hardly possible that this work could be done without occasional austerity. Prose that aimed at a certain formal sequence, that preserved an equable balance of clause against clause, that imposed a certain uniformity in the use of pronouns, and that sought to impress by clear and forcible antithesis, could not avoid formality. The mannerisms are apt to assume undue prominence, and lend themselves to imitation and to parody. The popular impression ends there. It fancies that it has caught the trick of Johnson's style when it has adopted a certain arrangement of pronouns, when it has marshalled the sentences in well-drilled parallels of antithetical clauses, when it has sprinkled the whole with sesquipedalian words, and given an air of pedantic solemnity to the treatment of the subject. This is to miss all that is really characteristic in Johnson's style. Our debt to him is twofold. In the first place, he preserved us against the inevitable triviality and feebleness that would have come from the imitation of Addison's prose by the ordinary writer, who had not the secret of Addison's genius. Had not such a dictator as Johnson arisen, English prose would inevitably have dwindled into decay, pleasing itself all the while with the fancy that it was repeating the subtle and inimitable achievements of the preceding generation. In the next place, he set a model which could be safely followed, and which was secure for a generation at least, against the intrusion of slipshod banality. For more than a generation after his death, the impression of his sovereignty remained; and it is not too much to say that no competent writer of prose since Johnson's day, has not, in spite of all diversities of genius, and in spite even of earnest resistance to his sway, owed much of such rhythm, and balance, and lucidity as he has attained, to the example and the model set by Johnson. In some of the authors who might least of all be supposed to accept his dictatorship, it will be interesting to trace examples of this unconscious influence, in the later pages of this selection.

When we turn to an examination of Johnson's own style, we shall find that its characteristics are very different from those of the parody which lives in the popular estimation. No man could better discard long words, and use more pithy English when he chose, than could Johnson. "Wit is that which he who hath never found it wonders how he missed;" such a sentence shows that Johnson could express himself tersely when it suited him to do so. Often the long words and the formal expression are adopted of a set purpose, which is humorous much more than pedantic. No man could assume a manner of greater ease and directness, and no one could achieve with more perfect art that most difficult of literary manoeuvres, the introduction of a convenient but entirely irrelevant digression. We have only to turn over a few pages of the *Lives of the Poets* to see how a stinging sarcasm no less than a touch of playful humour, is enhanced by the formal dignity of manner, and would have lost half its raciness if the ceremonial stateliness of phraseology were absent.

One of the secrets of Johnson's style is that it was hammered out upon the anvil of conversational combat. It was wrought into shape by no persevering and continuous labour. His work was done, all his life through, in those sudden starts by which he shook off the lethargy that burdened him, and toiled with fierce and untiring energy, with all the muscles of his mind strained to tensity. So it was with his conversation and with the style that grew out of that conversational habit. All his thoughts turned upon questions of direct human interest, upon the science of character, and the casuistry of ethics. These were just the questions that rejected all technical terms, and Johnson is singularly free from technicalities: they were also the questions that admitted most variety of treatment, in regard to which Johnson might most readily alter his position with the ease of the intellectual athlete; which admitted of endless disputation, and in regard to which skilful argument, clear exposition, and ready epigram could best win a conversational triumph. Addison's style was conversational in its ease and its familiarity: Johnson's style has not the ease, but it has the force, the epigram, and the dialectical readiness of successful conversation. We have his own account of it to Sir Joshua Reynolds: "He told him that he had early laid it down as a rule to do his best on every occasion and in every company; to impart whatever he knew in the most forceful language he could put it in; and that, by constant practice, and never suffering any careless expression to escape him, or attempting to deliver his thoughts without arranging them in the clearest manner, it became habitual to him" (BOSWELL).

Another characteristic of Johnson's work which largely affects his style, is its occasional calm and condescending frankness. It is not the frankness of a familiar friend. When he confesses to his dislike of tedious investigation and elaborate research, it is with the frankness which despises concealment, not with that which deprecates criticism or craves indulgence. When he draws aside the curtain and speaks of the loneliness and ill health and poverty under which he toiled, he gives the confidence with the air of one who defies sympathy, not with the humility of one who begs for pity. But in both cases, the effect on his style is the same, to increase the force of its dignified formality, which can on occasion be frank and even confidential, but which indicates clearly enough that he will neither welcome nor permit the slightest intrusion beyond the limits he has set to that confidence.

The first specimens of Johnson's original prose were the parliamentary debates (composed almost entirely according to his own notion of probabilities) which he contributed to the *Gentleman's Magazine*. The *Rambler* was written in the midst of his most severe and prolonged toil, and under conditions of grinding poverty, and in point of style it has more than his usual stateliness, and less than his usual variety and humour. The *Idler* was written when he had escaped from the long burden of the *Dictionary* and was already a literary dictator, and its style is more varied by light and shade, more quickened by humour; but the weight of poverty still pressed him, and its sadness still hangs heavily over *Rasselas*, which was written in order to pay for his mother's funeral. It represents perhaps the best specimen of Johnson's more formal style. From first to last it has a strain of melancholy, relieved by few lighter touches; but its literary skill is seen in the perfect symmetry, and completeness of its construction, all the more remarkable because it wants beginning, and end, and story.

But Johnson's style is not seen in its richness and perfection, nor in its consummate ease, until we come to his last and greatest work—the *Lives of the Poets*. That was not begun until he was nearly seventy years of age. His time for careful and methodic labour was now past. His opinions were fixed, and he was not likely to examine or modify them. He was undisputed literary dictator, and indisposed to bend to others' views. But all these circumstances contributed to the consummate literary qualities of the book. This is not the place either to impugn or defend the justice of his literary criticisms. But for vigour and ease and variety of style, for elasticity of confidence, for keenness of sarcasm, for brightness of humour, the *Lives* hold the first place, absolutely free from competition, amongst all works of English criticism of similar range. We may carp at Johnson's judgments, and rail against the prejudice and injustice of his decrees. We may be disposed to accord to more modern critics, all the advantages of balanced judgment and sympathetic insight which they may claim; but they must yield to Johnson the palm for boldness, for wit, for extent of range, and for brilliancy of style.

To those at least, who, like the present writer, look upon Johnson as a man and as a genius with the most profound admiration, it may be permitted to point to passages, to be found even amongst the scanty selections that follow, which may fitly take rank amongst the most consummate and perfect specimens of English prose, clothing thoughts of highest wisdom in language which is a model of dignity and grace.
—HENRY CRAIK, "Samuel Johnson," *English Prose*, ed. Henry Craik, 1895, Vol. 4, pp. 135–40

During the later part of his lifetime Johnson was undoubtedly regarded as a sort of unofficial head of English literature, and also as a great philosopher and sage; while the reaction and oblivion which so often follow in such cases were prevented by the singular charms of Boswell's *Life* ⟨. . .⟩ But the Romantic school bitterly disliked Johnson's literary principles and practice, though not his political and religious theories, while these latter have become unpopular since. It has thus been usual during the greater part of the nineteenth century to extol Johnson's moral character, and feel or affect delight in his biography, while assigning him no high place as a writer. It is true that with the not quite certain exception of the *Lives of the Poets*, Johnson can claim no single work uniting bulk with value of matter and originality of form. His work in verse is very small, and though all of it is scholarly and some elegant, it is universally composed in obedience to a very narrow and jejune theory of English versification and English poetics generally. Nothing perhaps but the beautiful epitaph on his friend Levett, and the magnificent statement of his religious pessimism in *The Vanity of Human Wishes*, distinctly transcends mediocrity. His tragedy of *Irene* is a not very good example of an entirely artificial and lifeless kind. Although his essays have been oftener under- than over-valued of late, they are far from original in conception, and those at least of the *Rambler* are too often injured by the excessively stiff and cumbrous style which has been rather unjustly identified with Johnson's manner of writing generally. His *Dictionary*, though a wonderful monument of enterprise and labour, and though containing many acute and some witty definitions, is, as he well knew himself, but "drudgery," and his political pamphlets, though forcible and sensible, and his *Journey to the Hebrides*, though interesting, suffer also from "Johnsonese." His often beautiful prayers and meditations, his occasional work in inscriptions and the like, are, as well as the *Dictionary*, not easily classifiable literature, though, like that, they testify to the literary saturation of his mind and thought. *Rasselas*, an admirable though a mannered composition, and perhaps the chief document for Johnson's practical though melancholy wisdom, must always underlie the objection that it holds itself out as a story, but has really no story to tell, nor even (save in Imlac, who is partly Johnson) any character to bring out.

It is extremely fortunate that very late, and as it were accidentally, he was induced to leave an adequate and permanent monument of his powers in the *Lives of the Poets*. In these literary biographies, of which long before he had given an example in the *Life of Savage*, he practically struck into a new development of the essay—one to which Dryden had sometimes come near, and which he would have carried out with surpassing excellence had the time been ripe, but which had not been actually anticipated by any. It is no matter that Johnson's standards and view-points are extravagantly and exclusively of his time, so that occasionally—the cases of Milton and Gray are the chief—he falls into critical errors almost incomprehensible except from the historic side. Even these extravagances fix the critical creed of the day for us in an inestimable fashion, while in the great bulk of the Lives this criticism does no harm, being duly adjusted to the subjects. Johnson's estimate of Chaucer doubtless would have been, as his *Rambler* remarks on Spenser actually are, worthless, except as a curiosity. But of Dryden, of Pope, and of the numerous minor poets of their time and his, he could speak with a competently adjusted theory, with admirable literary knowledge and shrewdness, and with a huge store of literary tradition which his long and conversation-loving life had accumulated, and which would have been lost for us had he not written.

But it would be unjust to limit Johnson's literary value to this book, or even to this *plus The Vanity of Human Wishes*, *Rasselas*, and the best of his essays. It was far more extensive, and the above-referred-to Johnsonese, the "great-whale" style which Goldsmith so wittily reprehended, was only an exaggeration of its good influence. Of the alternate fashions of prose which we have already surveyed in some instances, and shall survey in more, the dangers are also alternate. The ornate and fanciful style tends to the florid and the extravagant, and needs to be restrained and tamed; the plain style tends to the slipshod and jejune, and needs to be raised and inspired. We have seen how, during the earlier prevalence of this latter, Addison and Swift came to its rescue from the mere colloquialism which distinguishes writers like L'Estrange. So Johnson in its later came (as in different ways did Gibbon and Burke) to its rescue from the jejuneness and lack of colour which distinguish writers like Middleton.

His means may not have been perfect. His Latinising (not improbably helped by some early work of his on Sir Thomas Browne), his somewhat ponderous swing of balanced phrase, his too mechanical antithesis, lie open to much easy ridicule and to some just censure. But even his more pompous and rhetorical style has nobility and dignity, while the vigorous conversational directness which he always maintained in speech, and by no means neglected wholly in writing, served to preserve it from mere stilted bombast. And as this characteristic pervades all his prose work, all his prose work possesses, and to the true historic judgment will always retain, interest and value accordingly. As a poet he can only rely on a few trifles, playful or pathetic, and on the gorgeous declamation, rising to the level of true verse-eloquence, of *The Vanity of Human Wishes*.—GEORGE SAINTSBURY, *A Short History of English Literature*, 1898, pp. 615–17

Works

POETRY

⟨. . .⟩ *London* is to me one of those few imitations, that have all the ease and all the spirit of an original.—THOMAS GRAY, Letter to Horace Walpole (c. Jan. 1748)

This poem of Mr. Johnson's ⟨*London*⟩ is the best imitation of the original that has appeared in our language, being possessed of all the force and satirical resentment of Juvenal. Imitation gives us a much truer idea of the ancients than ever translation could do.—OLIVER GOLDSMITH, *The Beauties of English Poetry*, 1767

His *Vanity of Human Wishes* has less of common life, but more of a philosophick dignity than his *London*. More readers, therefore, will be delighted with the pointed spirit of *London*, than with the profound reflection of *The Vanity of Human Wishes*. Garrick, for instance, observed in his sprightly manner, with more vivacity than regard to just discrimination, as is usual with wits, 'When Johnson lived much with the Herveys, and saw a good deal of what was passing in life, he wrote his *London*, which is lively and easy. When he became more retired, he gave us his *Vanity of Human Wishes*, which is as hard as Greek. Had he gone on to imitate another satire, it would have been as hard as Hebrew.'

But *The Vanity of Human Wishes* is, in the opinion of the best judges, as high an effort of ethick poetry as any language can shew. The instances of variety of disappointment are chosen so judiciously and painted so strongly, that, the moment they are read, they bring conviction to every thinking mind. That of the scholar must have depressed the too sanguine expectations of many an ambitious student. That of the warrior, Charles of Sweden, is, I think, as highly finished a picture as can possibly be conceived.—JAMES BOSWELL, *Life of Johnson*, 1791

Dined. Read Johnson's *Vanity of Human Wishes*,—all the examples and mode of giving them sublime, as well as the latter part, with the exception of an occasional couplet. I do not so much admire the opening. I remember an observation of Sharpe's (the *Conversationist*, as he was called in London, and a very clever man) that the first line of this poem was superfluous, and that Pope (the best of poets, *I* think,) would have begun at once, only changing the punctuation—

Survey mankind from China to Peru!

The former line, "Let observation" &c., is certainly heavy and useless. But 'tis a grand poem—and *so true!*—true as the 10th of Juvenal himself. The lapse of ages *changes* all things—time—language—the earth—the bounds of the sea—the stars of the sky, and every thing "about, around, and underneath" man, *except man himself*, who has always been, and always will be, an unlucky rascal. The infinite variety of lives conduct but to death, and the infinity of wishes lead but to disappointment. All the discoveries which have yet been made have multiplied little but existence. An extirpated disease is succeeded by some new pestilence; and a discovered world has brought little to the old one, except the pox   first and freedom afterwards—the *latter* a fine thing, particularly as they gave it to Europe in exchange for slavery. But it is doubtful whether "the Sovereigns" would not think the *first* the best present of the two to their subjects.—GEORGE GORDON, LORD BYRON, *Journals*, Jan. 9, 1821

Johnson may be said to occupy the central place in that highly characteristic school of didactic poetry which was originated by

Pope and completed by Goldsmith. The essence of Pope's didactic compositions is personal satire. It is true that he specially prides himself on being the champion of virtue and the great promoter of moral truth. But the virtue which he had invariably before his imagination was his own, and throughout his *Imitations of Horace* morality is always exalted in the person of the poet, and always seems to be endangered by the wicked virulence of his private enemies. In consequence of their intense personality, Pope's didactic poems fail in point of poetical design. In the *Essay on Man* the subject-matter is Bolingbroke's rather than Pope's, and the conduct of the argument is extraordinarily confused; while in the *Moral Essays* and *Satires*, what really pleases is the beauty of detail, the terse epigrams, the brilliant images, and above all the matchless portraiture of particular characters. The great beauty of Goldsmith's poems, on the other hand, lies in the justness of their design, the relation of the means to the end, and of the parts to the whole. He relies hardly at all on personal interest for his effects; but he is perhaps the most persuasive of all didactic poets, from the extraordinary art which he possesses of enlisting simple and universal feelings in behalf of the moral principle which he seeks to establish.

Johnson unites in his own style many of the opposite excellences exhibited by his predecessor and his friend. It was impossible that the bias of his strong character should be altogether concealed in his verse, and *London* in particular appears to have been largely inspired by personal motives like those which suggested to Pope his *Imitations of Horace*. But the different genius of the two poets is seen in the selection of their respective originals. Pope was struck by the many superficial points of resemblance between himself and the lively egotistical Horace, and seized eagerly on the opportunity of presenting his own virtues, friendships, and enmities to the public under a transparent veil of imitation. Johnson, on the contrary, who, as an unknown writer, could not hope to interest the public in his personal concerns, chose a general theme, and imitated the satirist whose denunciations of Roman vice offered, in many respects, an apt parallel to the manners of his own age. *London* is marked by genuine public spirit; at the same time we see quite as much of the man as of the moralist in the poet's characteristic allusions to the penalties of poverty, his antipathy to the Whigs, and his dislike of foreigners. The story that 'Thales' was meant for Savage, and that the occasion of the poem was the departure of the latter from London after his trial, is confuted by dates, but we may be sure that the poem gives us a real representation of Johnson's feelings as a struggling author and a political partisan.

The Vanity of Human Wishes marks a calmer and more prosperous epoch in the poet's life, and its philosophical generalising spirit is an anticipation of Goldsmith's *Traveller*. Johnson was now relieved from the immediate pressure of want; and in his second *Imitation* he takes a wider survey of mankind; he suppresses all personal satire, and fetches the illustrations of his argument from distant times. The style of this poem is also completely different from that of *London*: in the latter he is ardent, animated, and colloquial, while in the *Vanity of Human Wishes* he speaks with the gravity of a moralist, making his periods swelling and sonorous, balancing his verses against each other, and equalling Pope himself in the condensation of his language. Nevertheless, the whole spirit of the composition, though professedly an imitation, is highly characteristic of the man: we see in it the melancholy gloom that darkened all his view of human existence, while at the same time the noble lines of the conclusion recall the language

of those touching fragments of prayer which Boswell discovered among his papers and has preserved in his *Life*.

His Prologues are of the highest excellence; indeed it may be confidently affirmed that he is the best writer of prologues in the language. No man was ever so well qualified to strike that just mean between respectfulness and authority which such addresses to the public require. His sound critical power and elevated feeling are well exemplified in the 'Prologue spoken at the opening of Drury Lane Theatre'; and there is true greatness of spirit in his Prologue to *Comus*, in which he claims the liberality of the audience for Milton's granddaughter as a tardy redress for the injustice shown by the nation to the genius of the poet himself. His admirable independence of character is perhaps even better seen in the Prologue to *A Word to the Wise*, a play which at its first exhibition was damned in consequence of political prejudices against the author, but was revived after his death. Nothing can be better than the dignity with which Johnson, in this address, while recognising the judicial authority of the audience, indirectly reproves them for their previous disregard of the laws of humanity by which all their verdicts ought to be determined.—W. J. COURTHOPE, "Samuel Johnson," *The English Poets*, ed. Thomas Humphry Ward, 1880, Vol. 3, pp. 245–47

THE RAMBLER

Though I have constantly been a purchaser of the *Ramblers* from the first five that you were so kind as to present me with, yet I have not had time to read any farther than those first five, till within these two or three days past. But I can go no further than the thirteenth, now before me, till I have acquainted you, that I am inexpressibly pleased with them. I remember not any thing in the *Spectators*, in those *Spectators* that I read, for I never found time—(Alas! my life has been a trifling busy one) to read them all, that half so much struck me; and yet I think of them highly.

I hope the world tastes them; for its own sake, I hope the world tastes them! The author I can only guess at. There is but one man, I think, that could write them; I desire not to know his name; but I should rejoice to hear that they succeed; for I would not, for any consideration, that they should be laid down through discouragement.

I have, from the first five, spoke of them with honour. I have the vanity to think that I have procured them admirers; that is to say, *readers*. And I am vexed that I have not taken larger draughts of them before, that my zeal for their merit might have been as glowing as now I find it.—SAMUEL RICHARDSON, Letter to Edward Cave (Aug. 9, 1750)

The *Rambler* is certainly a strong misnommer. He allwaies plods in the beaten road of his Predecessors, following the *Spectator* (with the same pace a Pack horse would do a Hunter) in the style that is proper to lengthen a paper. These writers may perhaps be of Service to the Public (which is saying a great deal in their Favor). There are numbers of both Sexes who never read any thing but such productions, and cannot spare time from doing nothing to go through a sixpenny Pamphlet. Such gentle Readers may be improv'd by a moral hint which, thô repeated over and over from Generation to Generation, they never heard in their Lives. I should be glad to know the name of this Laborious Author.—LADY MARY WORTLEY MONTAGU, Letter to the Countess of Bute (July 23, 1754)

I have lately been reading one or two volumes of *The Rambler*; who, excepting against some few hardnesses in his manner, and the want of more examples to enliven, is one of the most *nervous*, most *perspicuous*, most concise, and most harmonious prose-writers I know. A learned diction improves by time.—WILLIAM SHENSTONE, Letter to Richard Graves (Feb. 9, 1760)

Dr. Johnson seems to have been really more powerful in discoursing *viva voce* in conversation than with his pen in hand. It seems as if the excitement of company called something like reality and consecutiveness into his reasonings, which in his writings I can not see. His antitheses are almost always verbal only; and sentence after sentence in the *Rambler* may be pointed out to which you can not attach any definite meaning whatever. In his political pamphlets there is more truth of expression than in his other works, for the same reason that his conversation is better than his writings in general.
—SAMUEL TAYLOR COLERIDGE, *Table Talk*, Nov. 1, 1833

There is no denying that some of Johnson's works, from the meagreness of the material and the regularity of the monotous style, are exceedingly little adapted to reading. They are flimsy, and they are dull; they are pompous, and though full of undeniable, indeed self-evident truths, they are somewhat empty; they are, moreover, wrapt up in a style so disproportioned in its importance, that the perusal becomes very tiresome, and is soon given up. This character belongs more especially to the *Rambler*, the object of such unmeasured praises among his followers, and from which he derived the title of the Great Moralist. It would not be easy to name a book more tiresome, indeed more difficult to read, or one which gives moral lessons in a more frigid tone, with less that is lively or novel in the matter, in a language more heavy and monotonous. The measured pace, the constant balance of the style, becomes quite intolerable; for there is no interesting truth there to be inculcated remote from common observation, nor is there any attack carried on against difficult positions, nor is there any satirical warfare maintained either with opinions or with persons. There is wanting, therefore, all that makes us overlook the formality and even lumbering heaviness of Johnson's style in his other works; and in this the style forms a very large proportion of the whole, as the workmanship does of filagree or lace, the lightness of which, however, is a charm that Johnson's work wholly wants. It is singular to observe how vain are all his attempts in these papers to escape from his own manner, even when it was most unsuited to the occasion. Like Addison and Steele, he must needs give many letters from correspondents by way of variety; but these all write in the same language, how unlike soever their characters. So that anything less successful in varying the uniformity of the book, or anything less resembling the lightness, the graces, the eloquent and witty simplicity of the great masters, can hardly be imagined. Thus we not only find maiden ladies, like Tranquilla, describing themselves as "having danced the round of gaiety amidst the murmurs of envy and the gratulations of applause; attended from pleasure to pleasure by the great, the sprightly, and the vain; their regard solicited by the obsequiousness of gallantry, the gaiety of wit, and the timidity of love;" and spoilt beauties, like Victoria, "whose bosom was rubbed with a pomade, of virtue to discuss pimples and clear discolorations;" but we have Bellaria, at fifteen, and hating books, who "distinguishes the glitter of vanity from the solid merit of understanding," and describes her guardians as telling her, but telling her in vain, "that reading would fill up the vacuities of life, without the help of silly or dangerous amusements, and preserve from the snares of idleness and the inroads of temptation;" and Myrtella, at sixteen, who had "learnt all the commun rules of decent behaviour and standing maxims of domestic prudence," till Flavia came down to the

village, "at once easy and officious, attentive and unembarrassed," when a struggle commenced with the old aunt, who found "girls grown too wise and too stubborn to be commanded, but was resolved to try who should govern, and would thwart her mere humour till she broke her spirit."

Ponderous as such levities are after the *Spectator* and the *Tatler*, and heavy indeed as the whole of the *Rambler* proves to every reader, it is impossible to deny that it contains a great profusion of sensible reflection, or to refuse it the praise of having been produced with a facility altogether astonishing, considering it to bear so manifestly the mark of great labour. The papers were always written in the utmost haste; a part of each being sent to the press, and the rest written while it was printing. Nor did the author almost ever read over what he had written until he saw it in print. ⟨. . .⟩ Indeed, Johnson appears to have composed so easily, that he could write as fast as he could copy.—HENRY, LORD BROUGHAM, "Johnson," *Lives of Men of Letters and Science Who Flourished in the Time of George III*, 1846, Vol. 2, pp. 32–34

DICTIONARY

I heard the other day with great pleasure from my worthy friend Mr. Dodsley, that Mr. Johnson's *English Dictionary*, with a grammar and history of our language prefixed, will be published this winter in two large volumes in folio.

I had long lamented that we had no lawful standard of our language set up, for those to repair to, who might choose to speak and write it grammatically and correctly: and I have as long wished that either some one person of distinguished abilities would undertake the work singly, or that a certain number of gentlemen would form themselves, or be formed by the government, into a society for that purpose. The late ingenious Doctor Swift proposed a plan of this nature to his friend (as he thought him) the lord treasurer Oxford, but without success; precision and perspicuity not being in general the favourite objects of ministers, and perhaps still less so of that minister, than of any other.

Many people have imagined that so extensive a work would have been best performed by a number of persons who should have taken their several departments, of examining, sifting, winnowing (I borrow this image from the Italian *Crusca*), purifying, and finally fixing, our language, by incorporating their respective funds into one joint stock. But whether this opinion be true or false, I think the public in general, and the republic of letters in particular, greatly obliged to Mr. Johnson, for having undertaken and executed so great and desirable a work. Perfection is not to be expected from man; but if we are to judge by the various works of Mr. Johnson already published, we have good reason to believe that he will bring this as near to perfection as any one man could do. The plan of it, which he published some years ago, seems to me to be a proof of it. Nothing can be more rationally imagined, or more accurately and elegantly expressed. I therefore recommend the previous perusal of it to all those who intend to buy the dictionary, and who, I suppose, are all those who can afford it. ⟨. . .⟩

P.S. I hope that none of my courteous readers will upon this occasion be so uncourteous, as to suspect me of being a hired and interested puff of this work; for I most solemnly protest that neither Mr. Johnson, nor any person employed by him, nor any bookseller or booksellers concerned in the success of it, have ever offered me the usual compliment of a pair of gloves or a bottle of wine; nor has even Mr. Dodsley, though my publisher, and, as I am informed, deeply interested in the sale of this dictionary, so much as invited me to take a bit of mutton with him.—PHILIP DORMER STANHOPE, EARL OF CHESTERFIELD, *The World*, No. 100 (Nov. 28, 1754)

Talk of war with a Briton, he'll boldly advance,
That one English soldier will beat ten of France;
Would we alter the boast from the sword to the pen,
Our odds are still greater, still greater our men:
In the deep mines of science tho' Frenchmen may toil,
Can their strength be compar'd to Locke, Newton, and Boyle?
Let them rally their heroes, send forth all their pow'rs,
Their verse-men, and prose-men; then match them with ours!
First Shakespeare and Milton, like gods in the fight,
Have put their whole drama and epic to flight;
In satires, epistles, and odes would they cope,
Their numbers retreat before Dryden and Pope;
And Johnson, well arm'd, like a hero of yore,
Has beat forty French, and will beat forty more.
      —DAVID GARRICK, "On Johnson's Dictionary,"
      1755

The present undertaking is very extensive. A dictionary of the English language, however useful, or rather necessary, has never been hitherto attempted with the least degree of success. To explain hard words and terms of art seems to have been the chief purpose of all the former compositions which have borne the title of English dictionaries. Mr. Johnson has extended his views much farther, and has made a very full collection of all the different meanings of each English word, justified by examples from authors of good reputation. When we compare this book with other dictionaries, the merit of its author appears very extraordinary. Those which in modern languages have gained the most esteem, are that of the French academy, and that of the academy Della Crusca. Both these were composed by a numerous society of learned men, and took up a longer time in the composition, than the life of a single person could well have afforded. The dictionary of the English language is the work of a single person, and composed in a period of time very inconsiderable, when compared with the extent of the work. The collection of words appears to be very accurate, and must be allowed to be very ample. Most words, we believe, are to be found in the dictionary that ever were almost suspected to be English; but we cannot help wishing, that the author had trusted less to the judgment of those who may consult him, and had oftener passed his own censure upon those words which are not of approved use, tho' sometimes to be met with in authors of no mean name. Where a work is admitted to be highly useful, and the execution of it intitled to praise; the adding, that it might have been more useful, can scarcely, we hope, be deemed a censure of it. The merit of Mr. Johnson's dictionary is so great, that it cannot detract from it to take notice of some defects, the supplying which, would, in our judgment, add a considerable share of merit to that which it already possesses. Those defects consist chiefly in the plan, which appears to us not to be sufficiently grammatical. The different significations of a word are indeed collected; but they are seldom digested into general classes, or ranged under the meaning which the word principally expresses. And sufficient care has not been taken to distinguish the words apparently synonomous.

⟨. . .⟩ Any man who was about to compose a dictionary or rather a grammar of the English language, must acknowledge himself indebted to Mr. Johnson for abridging at least one half of his labour. All those who are under any difficulty with respect to a particular word or phrase, are in the same situation. The dictionary presents them a full collection of examples; from whence indeed they are left to determine, but

by which the determination is rendered easy. In this country, the usefulness of it will be soon felt, as there is no standard of correct language in conversation; if our recommendation could in any degree incite to the perusal of it, we would earnestly recommend it to all those who are desirous to improve and correct their language, frequently to consult the dictionary. Its merit must be determined by the frequent resort that is had to it. This is the most unerring test of its value; criticisms may be false, private judgments ill-founded; but if a work of this nature be much in use, it has received the sanction of the public approbation.—ADAM SMITH, *Edinburgh Review*, May 1755

Much indeed has been done of late to ascertain and fix the English tongue. Johnson's *Dictionary* is a most important, and, considered as the work of one man, a most wonderful performance. It does honour to England, and to human genius; and proves, that there is still left among us a force of mind equal to that which formerly distinguished a Stephanus or a Varro. Its influence in diffusing the knowledge of the language, and retarding its decline; is already observable:

    Si Pergama dextra
Defendi possent, etiam hac defensa fuissent.

And yet, within the last twenty years, and since this great work was published, a multitude of new words have found their way into the English tongue, and, though both unauthorised and unnecessary, seem likely to remain in it.—JAMES BEATTIE, "Remarks on the Usefulness of Classical Learning" (1769), *Essays on Poetry and Music* (1776), 1779, pp. 511–12

How should puny scribblers be abashed and disappointed, when they find him displaying a perfect theory of lexicographical excellence, yet at the same time candidly and modestly allowing that he 'had not satisfied his own expectations.' Here was a fair occasion for the exercise of Johnson's modesty, when he was called upon to compare his own arduous performance, not with those of other individuals, (in which case his inflexible regard to truth would have been violated, had he affected diffidence,) but with speculative perfection; as he, who can outstrip all his competitors in the race, may yet be sensible of his deficiency when he runs against time. Well might he say, that 'the *English Dictionary* was written with little assistance of the learned,' for he told me, that the only aid which he received was a paper containing twenty etymologies, sent to him by a person then unknown, who he was afterwards informed was Dr. Pearce, Bishop of Rochester. The etymologies, though they exhibit learning and judgement, are not, I think, entitled to the first praise amongst the various parts of this immense work. The definitions have always appeared to me such astonishing proofs of acuteness of intellect and precision of language, as indicate a genius of the highest rank. This it is which marks the superiour excellence of Johnson's *Dictionary* over others equally or even more voluminous, and must have made it a work of much greater mental labour than mere Lexicons, or *Word-books*, as the Dutch call them. They, who will make the experiment of trying how they can define a few words of whatever nature, will soon be satisfied of an unquestionable justice of this observation, which I can assure my readers is founded upon much study, and upon communication with more minds than my own.

A few of his definitions must be admitted to be erroneous. Thus, *Windward* and *Leeward*, though directly of opposite meaning, are defined identically the same way; as to which inconsiderable specks it is enough to observe, that his Preface announces that he was aware there might be many such in so immense a work; nor was he at all disconcerted when an instance was pointed out to him. A lady once asked him how he came to define *Pastern* the *knee* of a horse: instead of making an elaborate defence, as she expected, he at once answered, 'Ignorance, Madam, pure ignorance.' His definition of *Network* has been often quoted with sportive malignity, as obscuring a thing in itself very plain. But to these frivolous censures no other answer is necessary than that with which we are furnished by his own Preface.

'To explain, requires the use of terms less abstruse than that which is to be explained, and such terms cannot always be found. For as nothing can be proved but by supposing something intuitively known, and evident without proof, so nothing can be defined but by the use of words too plain to admit of definition. Sometimes easier words are changed into harder; as, *burial*, into *sepulture* or *interment*; *dry*, into *desiccative*; *dryness*, into *siccity or aridity*; *fit*, into *paroxysm*; for the *easiest* word, whatever it be, can never be translated into one more easy.'

His introducing his own opinions, and even prejudices, under general definitions of words, while at the same time the original meaning of the words is not explained, as his *Tory*, *Whig*, *Pension*, *Oats*, *Excise*, and a few more, cannot be fully defended, and must be placed to the account of capricious and humourous indulgence. Talking to me upon this subject when we were at Ashbourne in 1777, he mentioned a still stronger instance of the predominance of his private feelings in the composition of this work, than any now to be found in it. 'You know, Sir, Lord Gower forsook the old Jacobite interest. When I came to the word *Renegado*, after telling that it meant "one who deserts to the enemy, a revolter," I added, *Sometimes we say a* GOWER. Thus it went to the press; but the printer had more wit than I, and struck it out.'

Let it, however, be remembered, that this indulgence does not display itself only in sarcasm towards others, but sometimes in playful allusion to the notions commonly entertained of his own laborious task. Thus: '*Grub-street*, the name of a street in London, much inhabited by writers of small histories, *dictionaries*, and temporary poems; whence any mean production is called *Grub-street*.'—'*Lexicographer*, a writer of dictionaries, a *harmless drudge*.'—JAMES BOSWELL, *Life of Johnson*, 1791

Extravagant praise of any human production, like indiscriminate censure, is seldom well founded; and both are evidence of want of candor or want of discernment. On a careful examination of the merits of Johnson's *Dictionary*, it will unquestionably appear that the blind admiration which would impose it upon the world as a very accurate and indisputable authority errs as much upon one extreme as the pointed condemnation of the whole work does upon the other. But it is the fate of man to vibrate from one extreme to another. The great intellectual powers of Dr. Johnson, displayed in many of his works but especially in his *Rambler* and his *Rasselas*, have raised his reputation to high distinction and impressed upon all his opinions a stamp of *authority*, which gives them currency among men, without an examination into their intrinsic value. The character of correctness must depend chiefly on observation and on reading that requires little labor; while his *Dictionary*, the accuracy of which must depend on minute distinctions or laborious researches into unentertaining books, may be left extremely imperfect and full of error.

These circumstances, however, are seldom considered; and Johnson's writings had in philology the effect, which Newton's discoveries had in mathematics, to interrupt for a

time the progress of this branch of learning; for when any man has pushed his researches so far beyond his contemporaries that all men despair of proceeding beyond him, they will naturally consider his principles and decisions as the limit of perfection on that particular subject, and repose their opinions upon his authority without examining into their validity.

⟨. . .⟩ What are the excellencies in the work to which it owes its reputation? To this inquiry the answer is obvious: Dr. Johnson has given many definitions of words which his predecessors had omitted, and added illustrations which in many instances are very valuable. These real improvements could not fail to be duly appreciated, while the display of erudition in numerous extracts from English writers, concurring with the reputation which the author derived from his other writings, have led the public to repose an undue confidence in his opinions. This is probably the sense in which we are to understand Mr. Horne Tooke ⟨. . .⟩, in which he declares that the portion of merit which the *Dictionary* possesses renders it the more dangerous. Indeed, in any branch of literature nothing is so dangerous as the errors of a great man.

But the great advances in philology which have been made in Europe within the last twenty years enable us to disabuse ourselves of these prepossessions. And I am firmly persuaded that, whatever prejudices my fellow citizens now entertain, they will be satisfied at a period not very remote that this subject is far better understood now than it was in the age of Dr. Johnson.—NOAH WEBSTER, Letter to David Ramsay (Oct. 1807)

The celebrated Dr. Samuel Johnson—an ignorant philologist, following in the track of still more ignorant predecessors—maintained, in his famous *Dictionary*, that the original inhabitants of England, who spoke Keltic, one of the oldest languages in the world, though spared by the Romans during five hundred years of occupation, were *exterminated* at a later period by their Saxon conquerors, and that, being exterminated, their language was necessarily exterminated with them; that the few miserable fugitives who escaped the incredible massacre took refuge in Wales and the Highlands of Scotland; and that the remnants of their language which they carried along with them to their all but inaccessible mountain fastnesses were mere gibberish, unworthy of the attention of philologists and students of language.

He based his *Dictionary* on this unfounded assertion, and persuaded himself, his contemporaries, and successors in the industry of compiling Dictionaries, that the English language was almost wholly a variety of the Teutonic, enriched and extended by the Latin, and the Norman French, and that it was in no degree indebted to the British of the early inhabitants. —CHARLES MACKAY, *Through the Long Day*, 1887, Vol. 2, pp. 395–96

RASSELAS

I have lately read the *Prince of Abissinia*—I am almost equally charm'd and shocked at it—the style, the sentiments are inimitable—but the subject is dreadful—and handled as it is by Dr. Johnson, might make *any* young, perhaps old, person tremble. O, how dreadful, how terrible is it to be told by a man of his genius and knowledge, in so affectingly probable a manner, that true, real, happiness is ever unattainable in this world!—Thro' all the scenes, publick or private, domestick or solitary, that Nekaya or Rasselas pass, real felicity eludes their pursuit and mocks their solicitude. In high life, superiority, envy and haughtiness baffle the power of preferment, favour and greatness—and, with or without them, all is animosity, suspicion, apprehension, and misery!—in private families, disagreement, jealousy and partiality, destroy all domestick felicities and all social cheerfulness, and all is peevishness, contradiction, ill-will, and wretchedness! And in solitude, imagination paints the world in a new light, every bliss which was wanting when in it, appears easily attained when away from it, but the loneliness of retirement seems unsocial, dreary, savouring of misanthropy and melancholy—and all is anxiety, doubt, fear and anguish! In this manner does Mr. Johnson proceed in his melancholy conviction of the impossibility of all human enjoyments and the impossibility of all earthly happiness. One thing during the course of the successless enquiry struck me, which gave me much comfort, which is, that those who wander in the world avowedly and purposely in search of happiness, who view every scene of present joy with an eye to what may succeed, certainly are more liable to disappointment, misfortune and unhappiness, than those who give up their fate to chance and take the goods and evils of fortune as they come, without making happiness their study or misery their foresight.—FANNY BURNEY, *Diary*, July 17, 1768

Considering the large sums which have been received for compilations, and works requiring not much more genius than compilations, we cannot but wonder at the very low price which he was content to receive for this admirable performance; which, though he had written nothing else, would have rendered his name immortal in the world of literature. None of his writings has been so extensively diffused over Europe; for it has been translated into most, if not all, of the modern languages. This Tale, with all the charms of oriental imagery, and all the force and beauty of which the English language is capable, leads us through the most important scenes of human life, and shews us that this stage of our being is full of 'vanity and vexation of spirit.' To those who look no further than the present life, or who maintain that human nature has not fallen from the state in which it was created, the instruction of this sublime story will be of no avail. But they who think justly, and feel with stronger sensibility, will listen with eagerness and admiration to its truth and wisdom. Voltaire's *Candide*, written to refute the system of Optimism, which it has accomplished with brilliant success, is wonderfully similar in its plan and conduct to Johnson's *Rasselas*; insomuch, that I have heard Johnson say, that if they had not been published so closely one after the other that there was not time for imitation, it would have been in vain to deny that the scheme of that which came latest was taken from the other. Though the proposition illustrated by both these works was the same, namely, that in our present state there is more evil than good, the intention of the writers was very different. Voltaire, I am afraid, meant only by wanton profaneness to obtain a sportive victory over religion, and to discredit the belief of a superintending Providence: Johnson meant, by shewing the unsatisfactory nature of things temporal, to direct the hopes of man to things eternal. *Rasselas*, as was observed to me by a very accomplished lady, may be considered as a more enlarged and more deeply philosophical discourse in prose, upon the interesting truth, which in his *Vanity of Human Wishes* he had so successfully enforced in verse.—JAMES BOSWELL, *Life of Johnson*, 1791

Of *Rasselas*, translated into so many languages, and so widely circulated through the literary world, the merits have been long justly appreciated. It was composed in solitude and sorrow; and the melancholy cast of feeling which it exhibits, sufficiently evinces the temper of the author's mind. The

resemblance, in some respects, betwixt the tenor of the moral and that of *Candide*, is striking, and Johnson himself admitted, that if the authors could possibly have seen each other's manuscript, they could not have escaped the charge of plagiarism. But they resemble each other like a wholesome and a poisonous fruit. The object of the witty Frenchman is to induce a distrust of the wisdom of the great Governor of the Universe, by presuming to arraign him of incapacity before the creatures of his will. Johnson uses arguments drawn from the same premises, with the benevolent view of encouraging men to look to another and a better world, for the satisfaction of wishes, which in this seem only to be awakened in order to be disappointed. The one is a fiend—a merry devil, we grant—who scoffs at and derides human miseries; the other, a friendly though grave philosopher, who shows us the nothingness of earthly hopes, to teach us that our affections ought to be placed higher.

The work can scarce be termed a narrative, being in a great measure void of incident; it is rather a set of moral dialogues on the various vicissitudes of human life, its follies, its fears, its hopes, its wishes, and the disappointment in which all terminate. The style is in Johnson's best manner; enriched and rendered sonorous by the triads and quaternions which he so much loved, and balanced with an art which perhaps he derived from the learned Sir Thomas Brown. The reader may sometimes complain, with Boswell, that the unalleviated picture of human helplessness and misery, leaves sadness upon the mind after perusal. But the moral is to be found in the conclusion of the *Vanity of Human Wishes*, a poem which treats of the same melancholy subject, and closes with this sublime strain of morality:—

Pour forth thy fervours for a healthful mind,
Obedient passions, and a will resign'd;
For Love, which scarce collective man can fill;
For Patience, sovereign o'er transmuted ill;
For Faith, that, panting for a happier seat,
Counts death kind nature's signal of retreat:
These goods for man the laws of Heaven ordain;
These goods He grants, who grants the power to gain
With these celestial Wisdom calms the mind,
And makes the happiness she cannot find.
                —SIR WALTER SCOTT, "Samuel Johnson"
                (1821), *Lives of the Novelists*, 1825

I forgot old Sam—a jewel rough set, yet shining like a star; and though sand-blind by nature, and bigoted by education, one of the truly great men of England, and "her men are of men the chief," alike in the dominions of the understanding, the reason, the passions, and the imagination. No prig shall ever persuade me that *Rasselas* is not a noble performance,—in design and in execution. Never were the expenses of a mother's funeral more gloriously defrayed by son, than the funeral of Samuel Johnson's mother by the price of *Rasselas*, written for the pious purpose of laying her head decently and honourably in the dust.—JOHN WILSON (as "Christopher North"), *Noctes Ambrosianae* (April 1829), 1854

About the plan of *Rasselas* little was said by the critics; and yet the faults of the plan might seem to invite severe criticism. Johnson has frequently blamed Shakspeare for neglecting the proprieties of time and place, and for ascribing to one age or nation the manners and opinions of another. Yet Shakspeare has not sinned in this way more grievously than Johnson. Rasselas and Imlac, Nekayah and Pekuah, are evidently meant to be Abyssinians of the eighteenth century: for the Europe which Imlac describes is the Europe of the eighteenth century;

and the inmates of the Happy Valley talk familiarly of that law of gravitation which Newton discovered, and which was not fully received even at Cambridge till the eighteenth century. What a real company of Abyssinians would have been may be learned from Bruce's *Travels*. But Johnson, not content with turning filthy savages, ignorant of their letters, and gorged with raw steaks cut from living cows, into philosophers as eloquent and enlightened as himself or his friend Burke, and into ladies as highly accomplished as Mrs. Lennox or Mrs. Sheridan, transferred the whole domestic system of England to Egypt. Into a land of harems, a land of polygamy, a land where women are married without ever being seen, he introduced the flirtations and jealousies of our ball-rooms. In a land where there is boundless liberty of divorce, wedlock is described as the indissoluble compact. "A youth and maiden meeting by chance, or brought together by artifice, exchange glances, reciprocate civilities, go home, and dream of each other. Such," says Rasselas, "is the common process of marriage." Such it may have been, and may still be, in London, but assuredly not at Cairo. A writer who was guilty of such improprieties had little right to blame the poet who made Hector quote Aristotle, and represented Julio Romano as flourishing in the days of the oracle of Delphi.—THOMAS BABINGTON MACAULAY, "Samuel Johnson" (1856), *Critical, Historical, and Miscellaneous Essays*, 1860, Vol. 6, pp. 197–98

It has been doubted whether *Rasselas* may justly be considered as a novel at all. The conversations held between the characters, it has been pointed out, are to be criticized, not in relation to circumstance and verisimilitude, but after the manner of an essay, in relation to truth. And certainly the strong moral and didactic purpose cannot be gainsaid. But the youth of the modern novel was a season of experiment, no rules of form had been determined, and a moral directly inculcated had never been disallowed. Far later in the century a noted literary critic, out of compliment to Richardson, refused to his works the title of novels, preferring to class them as excursions in "imaginative ethics." The sermon has played its part, as well as the drama, the epic, and the narrative poem, in shaping the form of the novel.

Sermon or novel, *Rasselas* was written at a time when Johnson had first attained his full command of literary expression. In the essays of *The Rambler*, begun some nine years earlier, his inversions, abstractions, monotonous sentences, and long words seem almost to exhibit, if the thought be not heresy, an imperfectly educated person struggling to acquire a polite diction. They certainly make his style as unsuitable for narrative as for the light ridicule of social foibles. *The Rambler* is not easy to read; or rather, to speak as the case demands, the otiose prolongation of the periods and the superabundance of polysyllabic vocables render the task of the intrepid adventurer who shall endeavour to peruse the earlier performances of this writer an undertaking of no inconsiderable magnitude. On the other hand, the later highly finished and effective style of the *Lives of the Poets* has an epigrammatic quality, a studied balance of phrase and a dogmatic ring, like the stroke of a hammer, that would infallibly interrupt the flow of imaginative narrative. In *Rasselas* the merits of both manners are combined to produce that ease of narration and those memorable and weighty turns of phrase which give it its principal distinction.

The main theme is never forgotten. The prince, educated in the happy valley, and taken with his sister into the world, is acquainted with human aims and human enjoyments, only

that their futility and insufficiency may be demonstrated, and the verdict again and again recorded with merciless severity. The "choice of life" is indeed difficult. The pastoral life is marred by ignorance, discontent, and stupid malevolence. Prosperity means disquiet and danger. Is happiness to be found in solitude? "The life of a solitary man will be certainly miserable, but not certainly devout." Is marriage to be preferred? "I know not whether marriage be more than one of the innumerable modes of human misery." Will varied pleasures serve to wile away the time? "Pleasures never can be so multiplied and continued as not to leave much of life unemployed." May the true solution be found in the pursuit of virtue? "All that virtue can afford is quietness of conscience, a steady prospect of a happier state; this may enable us to endure calamity with patience; but remember that patience must suppose pain."

All the sterner traits of Johnson's character, his uncompromising rectitude, his steadiness of outlook on unrelieved gloom, his hatred of sentimental and unthinking optimism, have left their mark on *Rasselas*. What was perhaps less to be expected, the structure of the plot is masterly, the events are arranged in a skilful climax, culminating in the story of the mad astronomer, whose delusions supply the picture with a shade darker than death itself. "Few can attain this man's knowledge," says Imlac, "and few practise his virtues, but all may suffer his calamities. Of the uncertainties of our present state the most dreadful and alarming is the uncertain continuance of reason." And a note of personal sadness is struck towards the close in the declaration of the virtuous sage, who confesses that praise has become to him an empty sound. "I have neither mother to be delighted with the reputation of her son, nor wife to partake the honours of her husband." The words recall a similar phrase in the famous letter to Lord Chesterfield, but the defiant strain that they there introduce is exchanged for a subdued and deepened melancholy. Taken as a whole, *Rasselas* is one of the most powerful of moral fables to be found in any literature, and the lighter and wittier passages, such as those on the functions of a poet and on the definition of a life "according to nature," relieve its inspissated tenebrosity with something like an air of comedy.—WALTER RALEIGH, *The English Novel*, 1894, pp. 203–6

LIVES OF THE ENGLISH POETS

I am glad we agree in our opinion of King Critic, and the writers on whom he has bestowed his animadversions. It is a matter of indifference to me whether I think with the world at large or not, but I wish my friends to be of my mind. The same work will wear a different appearance in the eyes of the same man according to the different views with which he reads it; if merely for his amusement, his candour being in less danger of a twist from interest or prejudice, he is pleased with what is really pleasing, and is not over curious to discover a blemish, because the exercise of a minute exactness is not consistent with his purpose. But if he once becomes a critic by trade, the case is altered. He must then at any rate establish, if he can, an opinion in every mind, of his uncommon discernment, and his exquisite taste. This great end he can never accomplish by thinking in the track that has been beaten under the hoof of public judgement. He must endeavour to convince the world, that their favourite authors have more faults than they are aware of, and such as they have never suspected. Having marked out a writer universally esteemed, whom he finds it for that very reason convenient to depreciate and traduce, he will overlook some of his beauties, he will faintly praise others, and

in such a manner as to make thousands, more modest, though quite as judicious as himself, question whether they are beauties at all. Can there be a stronger illustration of all that I have said, than the severity of Johnson's remarks upon Prior, I might have said the injustice? His reputation as an author who, with much labour indeed, but with admirable success, has embellished all his poems with the most charming ease, stood unshaken till Johnson thrust his head against it. And how does he attack him in this his principal fort? I cannot recollect his very words, but I am much mistaken indeed if my memory fails me with respect to the purport of them. 'His words,' he says, 'appear to be forced into their proper places; there indeed we find them, but find likewise that their arrangement has been the effect of constraint, and that without violence they would certainly have stood in a different order.' By your leave, most learned Doctor, this is the most disingenuous remark I ever met with, and would have come with a better grace from Curl or Dennis. Every man conversant with verse-writing knows, and knows by painful experience, that the familiar style is of all styles the most difficult to succeed in. To make verse speak the language of prose, without being prosaic,—to marshal the words of it in such an order as they might naturally take in falling from the lips of an extempory speaker, yet without meanness, harmoniously, elegantly, and without seeming to displace a syllable for the sake of the rhyme, is one of the most arduous tasks a poet can undertake. He that could accomplish this task was Prior; many have imitated his excellence in this particular, but the best copies have fallen far short of the original. And now to tell us, after we and our fathers have admired him for it so long, that he is an easy writer indeed, but that his ease has an air of stiffness in it, in short, that his ease is not ease, but only something like it, what is it but a self-contradiction, an observation that grants what it is just going to deny, and denies what it has just granted, in the same sentence, and in the same breath? But I have filled the greatest part of my sheet with a very uninteresting subject. I will only say, that as a nation we are not much indebted, in point of poetical credit, to this too sagacious and unmerciful judge; and that for myself in particular, I have reason to rejoice that he entered upon and exhausted the labours of his office before my poor volume could possibly become an object of them.
—WILLIAM COWPER, Letter to William Unwin (Jan. 17, 1782)

Towards the end of his life, when intercourse with the world had considerably softened his style, he published his *Lives of the English Poets*, a work of which the subject ensures popularity, and on which his fame probably now depends. He seems to have poured into it the miscellaneous information which he had collected, and the literary opinions which he had formed, during his long reign over the literature of London. The critical part has produced the warmest agitations of literary faction. The time may perhaps now be arrived for an impartial estimate of its merits. Whenever understanding alone is sufficient for poetical criticism, the decisions of Johnson are generally right. But the beauties of poetry must be felt before their causes are investigated. There is a poetical sensibility which in the progress of the mind becomes as distinct a power as a musical ear or a picturesque eye. Without a considerable degree of this sensibility it is as vain for a man of the greatest understanding to speak of the higher beauties of poetry, as it is for a blind man to speak of colours. To adopt the warmest sentiments of poetry, to realise its boldest imagery, to yield to every impulse of enthusiasm, to submit to the illusions of fancy, to retire with the poet into his ideal worlds, were

dispositions wholly foreign from the worldly sagacity and stern shrewdness of Johnson. As in his judgment of life and character, so in his criticism on poetry, he was a sort of Freethinker. He suspected the refined of affectation, he rejected the enthusiastic as absurd, and he took it for granted that the mysterious was unintelligible. He came into the world when the school of Dryden and Pope gave the law to English poetry. In that school he had himself learned to be a lofty and vigorous declaimer in harmonious verse; beyond that school his unforced admiration perhaps scarcely soared; and his highest effort of criticism was accordingly the noble panegyric on Dryden. His criticism owed its popularity as much to its defects as to its excellencies. It was on a level with the majority of readers—persons of good sense and information, but of no exquisite sensibility, and to their minds it derived a false appearance of solidity from that very narrowness which excluded those grander efforts of imagination to which Aristotle and Bacon confined the name of poetry. If this unpoetical character be considered, if the force of prejudice be estimated, if we bear in mind that in this work of his old age we must expect to find him enamoured of every observation which he had thrown into a striking form, and of every paradox which he had supported with brilliant success, and that an old man seldom warmly admires those works which have appeared since his sensibility has become sluggish and his literary system formed, we shall be able to account for most of the unjust judgments of Johnson, without recourse to any suppositions inconsistent with honesty and magnanimity. Among the victories gained by Milton, one of the most signal is that which he obtained over all the prejudices of Johnson, who was compelled to make a most vigorous, though evidently reluctant, effort to do justice to the fame and genius of the greatest of English poets. The alacrity with which he seeks every occasion to escape from this painful duty in observation upon Milton's Life and Minor Poems sufficiently attest the irresistible power of *Paradise Lost*. As he had no feeling of the lively and graceful, we must not wonder at his injustice to Prior. Some accidental impression, concurring with a long habit of indulging and venting every singularity, seems necessary to account for his having forgotten that Swift was a wit. As the *Seasons* appeared during the susceptible part of Johnson's life, his admiration of Thomson prevailed over the ludicrous prejudice which he professed against Scotland, perhaps because it was a Presbyterian country. His insensibility to the higher poetry, his dislike of a Whig university, and his scorn of a fantastic character, combined to produce that monstrous example of critical injustice which he entitles the "Life of Gray."—SIR JAMES MACKINTOSH (Dec. 1811), cited in Robert James Mackintosh, *Memoirs of the Life of Sir James Mackintosh*, 1835, Vol. 2, pp. 170–71

⟨. . .⟩ in writing *The Lives of the Poets*, one of the Doctor's latest works, he had learned caution. Malice, he found, was not always safe; and it might sometimes be costly. Still, there was plenty of game to be had without too much risk. And the Doctor, prompted by the fiend, resolved to "take a shy," before parting, at the most consecrated of Milton's creations. It really vexes me to notice this second case at all in a situation where I have left myself so little room for unmasking its hollowness. But a whisper is enough if it reaches a watchful ear. What, then, is the supreme jewel which Milton has bequeathed to us? Nobody can doubt that it is *Paradise Lost*.

Into this great *chef-d'œuvre* of Milton it was no doubt Johnson's secret determination to send a telling shot at parting. He would lodge a little *gage d'amitié*, a farewell pledge of hatred, a trifling token (trifling, but such things are not estimated in money) of his eternal malice. Milton's admirers might divide it among themselves; and, if it should happen to fester and rankle in their hearts, so much the better; they were heartily welcome to the poison: not a jot would he deduct for himself if a thousand times greater. O Sam! kill us not with munificence. But now, as I must close within a minute or so, what *is* that pretty souvenir of gracious detestation with which our friend took his leave? The *Paradise Lost*, said he, in effect, is a wonderful work; wonderful; grand beyond all estimate; sublime to a fault. But—well, go on; we are all listening. But—I grieve to say it, wearisome. It creates a world of admiration (*one* world, take notice); but—oh, that I, senior offshoot from the house of Malagrowthers, should live to say it!—ten worlds of *ennui*: one world of astonishment; ten worlds of *tædium vitæ*. Half and half might be tolerated—it is often tolerated by the bibulous and others; but one against ten? No, no!

This, then, was the farewell blessing which Dr. Johnson bestowed upon the *Paradise Lost!* What is my reply? The poem, it seems, is wearisome; Edmund Waller called it *dull*. A man, it is alleged by Dr. Johnson, opens the volume; reads a page or two with feelings allied to awe: next he finds himself rather jaded; then sleepy; naturally shuts up the book; and forgets ever to take it down again. Now, when any work of human art is impeached as wearisome, the first reply is— wearisome to *whom?* For it so happens that nothing exists, absolutely nothing, which is not at some time, and to some person, wearisome or even potentially disgusting. There is no exception for the works of God. "Man delights not me, nor woman either," is the sigh which breathes from the morbid misanthropy of the gloomy but philosophic Hamlet. Weariness, moreover, and even sleepiness, is the natural reaction of awe or of feelings too highly strung; and this reaction in some degree proves the sincerity of the previous awe. In cases of that class, where the impressions of sympathetic veneration have been really unaffected, but carried too far, the mistake is—to have read too much at a time. But these are exceptional cases: to the great majority of readers the poem is wearisome through mere vulgarity and helpless imbecility of mind; not from overstrained excitement, but from pure defect in the *capacity* for excitement. And a moment's reflection at this point lays bare to us the malignity of Dr. Johnson. The logic of that malignity is simply this: that he applies to Milton, as if separately and specially true of *him*, a rule abstracted from human experience spread over the total field of civilisation. All nations are here on a level. Not a hundredth part of their populations is capable of any unaffected sympathy with what is truly great in sculpture, in painting, in music, and by a transcendent necessity in the supreme of Fine Arts—Poetry. To be popular in any but a meagre comparative sense as an artist of whatsoever class is to be *confessedly* a condescender to human infirmities. And, as to the test which Dr. Johnson, by implication, proposes as trying the merits of Milton in his greatest work, viz. the degree in which it was read, the Doctor knew pretty well,—and when by accident he did *not* was inexcusable for neglecting to inquire,—that by the same test all the great classical works of past ages, Pagan or Christian, might be branded with the mark of suspicion as works that had failed of their paramount purpose, viz. a deep control over the modes of thinking and feeling in each successive generation. Were it not for the continued succession of academic students having a contingent *mercenary* interest in many of the great authors surviving from the wrecks of time, scarcely one edition of fresh copies would be called for in each period of fifty years. And, as

to the arts of sculpture and painting, were the great monuments in the former art, those, I mean, inherited from Greece, such as the groups, &c., scattered through Italian mansions,— the Venus, the Apollo, the Hercules, the Faun, the Gladiator, and the marbles in the British Museum, purchased by the Government from the late Lord Elgin,—stripped of their metropolitan advantages, and left to their own unaided attraction in some provincial town, they would not avail to keep the requisite officers of any establishment for housing them in salt and tobacco. We may judge of this by the records left behind by Benjamin Haydon of the difficulty which *he* found in simply upholding their value as wrecks of the Phidian æra. The same law asserts itself everywhere. What is *ideally* grand lies beyond the region of ordinary human sympathies; which must, by a mere instinct of good sense, seek out objects more congenial and upon their own level. One answer to Johnson's killing shot, as he kindly meant it, is that our brother is not dead but sleeping. Regularly as the coming generations unfold their vast processions, regularly as these processions move forward upon the impulse and summons of a nobler music, regularly as the dormant powers and sensibilities of the intellect in the working man are more and more developed, the *Paradise Lost* will be called for more and more: less and less continually will there be any reason to complain that the immortal book, being once restored to its place, is left to slumber for a generation. So far as regards the Time which is coming; but Dr. Johnson's insulting farewell was an arrow feathered to meet the Past and Present. We may be glad at any rate that the supposed neglect is not a wrong which Milton does, but which Milton suffers. Yet that Dr. Johnson should have pretended to think the case in any special way affecting the reputation or latent powers of Milton,—Dr. Johnson, that knew the fates of Books, and had seen by moonlight, in the Bodleian, the ghostly array of innumerable books long since departed as regards all human interest or knowledge—a review like that in Béranger's Dream of the First Napoleon at St. Helena, reviewing the buried forms from Austerlitz or Borodino, horses and men, trumpets and eagles, all phantom delusions, vanishing as the eternal dawn returned,—might have seemed incredible except to one who knew the immortality of malice,—that for a moment Dr. Johnson supposed himself seated on the tribunal in the character of judge, and that Milton was in fancy placed before him at the bar,—

> Quem si non aliquâ nocuisset, mortuus esset.
> —THOMAS DE QUINCEY, "Postscript Respecting Johnson's Life of Milton" (1859), *Collected Writings*, ed. David Masson, Vol. 4, pp. 113–17

The only writing in which we see a distinct reflection of Johnson's talk is the *Lives of the Poets*. The excellence of that book is of the same kind as the excellence of his conversation. Johnson wrote it under pressure, and it has suffered from his characteristic indolence. Modern authors would fill as many pages as Johnson has filled lines, with the biographies of some of his heroes. By industriously sweeping together all the rubbish which is in any way connected with the great man, by elaborately discussing the possible significance of infinitesimal bits of evidence, and by disquisition upon general principles or the whole mass of contemporary literature, it is easy to swell volumes to any desired extent. The result is sometimes highly interesting and valuable, as it is sometimes a new contribution to the dust-heaps; but in any case the design is something quite different from Johnson's. He has left much to be supplied and corrected by later scholars. His aim is simply to give a vigorous summary of the main facts of his heroes' lives, a pithy analysis of their character, and a short criticism of their productions. The strong sense which is everywhere displayed, the massive style, which is yet easier and less cumbrous than in his earlier work, and the uprightness and independence of the judgments, make the book agreeable even where we are most inclined to dissent from its conclusions.

The criticism is that of a school which has died out under the great revolution of modern taste. The booksellers decided that English poetry began for their purposes with Cowley, and Johnson has, therefore, nothing to say about some of the greatest names in our literature. The loss is little to be regretted, since the biographical part of earlier memoirs must have been scanty, and the criticism inappreciative. Johnson, it may be said, like most of his contemporaries, considered poetry almost exclusively from the didactic and logical point of view. He always inquires what is the moral of a work of art. If he does not precisely ask "what it proves," he pays excessive attention to the logical solidity and coherence of its sentiments. He condemns not only insincerity and affectation of feeling, but all such poetic imagery as does not correspond to the actual prosaic belief of the writer. For the purely musical effects of poetry he has little or no feeling, and allows little deviation from the alternate long and short syllables neatly bound in Pope's couplets.

To many readers this would imply that Johnson omits precisely the poetic element in poetry. I must be here content to say that in my opinion it implies rather a limitation than a fundamental error. Johnson errs in supposing that his logical tests are at all adequate; but it is, I think, a still greater error to assume that poetry has no connexion, because it has not this kind of connexion, with philosophy. His criticism has always a meaning, and in the case of works belonging to his own school a very sound meaning. When he is speaking of other poetry, we can only reply that his remarks may be true, but that they are not to the purpose.—SIR LESLIE STEPHEN, *Samuel Johnson*, 1878, pp. 186–87

No one needs an excuse for re-opening the *Lives of the Poets*; the book is too delightful. It is not, of course, as delightful as Boswell; but who re-opens Boswell? Boswell is in another category; because, as every one knows, when he has once been opened he can never be shut. But, on its different level, the *Lives* will always hold a firm and comfortable place in our affections. After Boswell, it is the book which brings us nearer than any other to the mind of Dr. Johnson. That is its primary import. We do not go to it for information or for instruction, or that our tastes may be improved, or that our sympathies may be widened; we go to it to see what Dr. Johnson thought. Doubtless, during the process, we are informed and instructed and improved in various ways; but these benefits are incidental, like the invigoration which comes from a mountain walk. It is not for the sake of the exercise that we set out; but for the sake of the view. The view from the mountain which is Samuel Johnson is so familiar, and has been so constantly analysed and admired, that further description would be superfluous. It is sufficient for us to recognise that he is a mountain, and to pay all the reverence that is due. In one of Emerson's poems a mountain and a squirrel begin to discuss each other's merits; and the squirrel comes to the triumphant conclusion that he is very much the better of the two, since he can crack a nut, while the mountain can do no such thing. The parallel is close enough between this impudence and the attitude—implied, if not expressed—of too much modern criticism towards the sort of qualities—the

easy, indolent power, the searching sense of actuality, the combined command of sanity and paradox, the immovable independence of thought—which went to the making of the *Lives of the Poets*. There is only, perhaps, one flaw in the analogy: that, in this particular instance, the mountain was able to crack nuts a great deal better than any squirrel that ever lived.

That the *Lives* continue to be read, admired, and edited, is in itself a high proof of the eminence of Johnson's intellect; because, as serious criticism, they can hardly appear to the modern reader to be very far removed from the futile. Johnson's æsthetic judgments are almost invariably subtle, or solid, or bold; they have always some good quality to recommend them—except one: they are never right. That is an unfortunate deficiency; but no one can doubt that Johnson has made up for it, and that his wit has saved all. He has managed to be wrong so cleverly, that nobody minds. When Gray, for instance, points the moral to his poem on Walpole's cat with a reminder to the fair that all that glisters is not gold, Johnson remarks that this is 'of no relation to the purpose; if *what glistered* had been *gold*, the cat would not have gone into the water; and, if she had, would not less have been drowned.' Could anything be more ingenious, or more neatly put, or more obviously true? But then, to use Johnson's own phrase, could anything be of less 'relation to the purpose'? It is his wit—and we are speaking, of course, of wit in its widest sense—that has sanctified Johnson's perversities and errors, that has embalmed them for ever, and that has put his book, with all its mass of antiquated doctrine, beyond the reach of time.

For it is not only in particular details that Johnson's criticism fails to convince us; his entire point of view is patently out of date. Our judgments differ from his, not only because our tastes are different, but because our whole method of judging has changed. Thus, to the historian of letters, the *Lives* have a special interest, for they afford a standing example of a great dead tradition—a tradition whose characteristics throw more than one curious light upon the literary feelings and ways which have become habitual to ourselves. Perhaps the most striking difference between the critical methods of the eighteenth century and those of the present day, is the difference in sympathy. The most cursory glance at Johnson's book is enough to show that he judged authors as if they were criminals in the dock, answerable for every infraction of the rules and regulations laid down by the laws of art, which it was his business to administer without fear or favour. Johnson never inquired what poets were trying to do; he merely aimed at discovering whether what they had done complied with the canons of poetry. Such a system of criticism was clearly unexceptionable, upon one condition—that the critic was quite certain what the canons of poetry were; but the moment that it became obvious that the only way of arriving at a conclusion upon the subject was by consulting the poets themselves, the whole situation completely changed. The judge had to bow to the prisoner's ruling. In other words, the critic discovered that his first duty was, not to criticise, but to understand the object of his criticism. That is the essential distinction between the school of Johnson and the school of Sainte-Beuve. No one can doubt the greater width and profundity of the modern method; but it is not without its drawbacks. An excessive sympathy with one's author brings its own set of errors: the critic is so happy to explain everything, to show how this was the product of the age, how that was the product of environment, and how the other was the inevitable result of inborn qualities and tastes—that he sometimes forgets to mention whether the work in question has any value. It is then that one cannot help regretting the Johnsonian black cap.

But other defects, besides lack of sympathy, mar the *Lives of the Poets*. One cannot help feeling that no matter how anxious Johnson might have been to enter into the spirit of some of the greatest of the masters with whom he was concerned, he never could have succeeded. Whatever critical method he might have adopted, he still would have been unable to appreciate certain literary qualities, which, to our minds at any rate, appear to be the most important of all. His opinion of 'Lycidas' is well known: he found that poem 'easy, vulgar, and therefore disgusting.' Of the songs in *Comus* he remarks: 'they are harsh in their diction, and not very musical in their numbers.' He could see nothing in the splendour and elevation of Gray, but 'glittering accumulations of ungraceful ornaments.' The passionate intensity of Donne escaped him altogether; he could only wonder how so ingenious a writer could be so absurd. Such preposterous judgments can only be accounted for by inherent deficiencies of taste; Johnson had no ear, and he had no imagination.—LYTTON STRACHEY, "The Lives of the Poets" (1906), *Literary Essays*, 1949, pp. 94–97

THOMAS BABINGTON MACAULAY
From "Samuel Johnson" (1831)
Critical, Historical, and Miscellaneous Essays
1860, Volume 2, pp. 398–426

Johnson came up to London precisely at the time when the condition of a man of letters was most miserable and degraded. It was a dark night between two sunny days. The age of patronage had passed away. The age of general curiosity and intelligence had not arrived. The number of readers is at present so great that a popular author may subsist in comfort and opulence on the profits of his works. In the reigns of William the Third, of Anne, and of George the First, even such men as Congreve and Addison would scarcely have been able to live like gentlemen by the mere sale of their writings. But the deficiency of the natural demand for literature was, at the close of the seventeenth and at the beginning of the eighteenth century, more than made up by artificial encouragement, by a vast system of bounties and premiums. There was, perhaps, never a time at which the rewards of literary merit were so splendid, at which men who could write well found such easy admittance into the most distinguished society, and to the highest honours of the state. The chiefs of both the great parties into which the kingdom was divided patronised literature with emulous munificence. Congreve, when he had scarcely attained his majority, was rewarded for his first comedy with places which made him independent for life. Smith, though his *Hippolytus* and *Phædra* failed, would have been consoled with three hundred a year but for his own folly. Rowe was not only Poet Laureate, but also land-surveyor of the customs in the port of London, clerk of the council to the Prince of Wales, and secretary of the Presentations to the Lord Chancellor. Hughes was secretary to the Commissions of the Peace. Ambrose Philips was judge of the Prerogative Court in Ireland. Locke was Commissioner of Appeals and of the Board of Trade. Newton was Master of the Mint. Stepney and Prior were employed in embassies of high dignity and importance. Gay, who commenced life as apprentice to a silk mercer, became a secretary of legation at five-and-twenty. It was to a poem on the Death of Charles the Second, and to the City and Country Mouse, that Montague owed his introduc-

tion into public life, his earldom, his garter, and his Auditorship of the Exchequer. Swift, but for the unconquerable prejudice of the queen, would have been a bishop. Oxford, with his white staff in his hand, passed through the crowd of his suitors to welcome Parnell, when that ingenious writer deserted the Whigs. Steele was a commissioner of stamps and a member of Parliament. Arthur Mainwaring was a commissioner of the customs, and auditor of the imprest. Tickell was secretary to the Lords Justices of Ireland. Addison was secretary of state.

This liberal patronage was brought into fashion, as it seems, by the magnificent Dorset, almost the only noble versifier in the court of Charles the Second who possessed talents for composition which were independent of the aid of a coronet. Montague owed his elevation to the favour of Dorset, and imitated through the whole course of his life the liberality to which he was himself so greatly indebted. The Tory leaders, Harley and Bolingbroke in particular, vied with the chiefs of the Whig party in zeal for the encouragement of letters. But soon after the accession of the house of Hanover a change took place. The supreme power passed to a man who cared little for poetry or eloquence. The importance of the House of Commons was constantly on the increase. The government was under the necessity of bartering for Parliamentary support much of that patronage which had been employed in fostering literary merit; and Walpole was by no means inclined to divert any part of the fund of corruption to purposes which he considered as idle. He had eminent talents for government and for debate. But he had paid little attention to books, and felt little respect for authors. One of the coarse jokes of his friend, Sir Charles Hanbury Williams, was far more pleasing to him than Thomson's *Seasons* or Richardson's *Pamela*. He had observed that some of the distinguished writers whom the favour of Halifax had turned into statesmen had been mere encumbrances to their party, dawdlers in office, and mutes in Parliament. During the whole course of his administration, therefore, he scarcely befriended a single man of genius. The best writers of the age gave all their support to the opposition, and contributed to excite that discontent which, after plunging the nation into a foolish and unjust war, overthrew the minister to make room for men less able and equally immoral. The opposition could reward its eulogists with little more than promises and caresses. St. James's would give nothing: Leicester house had nothing to give.

Thus, at the time when Johnson commenced his literary career, a writer had little to hope from the patronage of powerful individuals. The patronage of the public did not yet furnish the means of comfortable subsistence. The prices paid by booksellers to authors were so low that a man of considerable talents and unremitting industry could do little more than provide for the day which was passing over him. The lean kine had eaten up the fat kine. The thin and withered ears had devoured the good ears. The season of rich harvests was over, and the period of famine had begun. All that is squalid and miserable might now be summed up in the word Poet. That word denoted a creature dressed like a scarecrow, familiar with compters and spunging-houses, and perfectly qualified to decide on the comparative merits of the Common Side in the King's Bench prison and of Mount Scoundrel in the Fleet. Even the poorest pitied him; and they well might pity him. For if their condition was equally abject, their aspirings were not equally high, nor their sense of insult equally acute. To lodge in a garret up four pair of stairs, to dine in a cellar among footmen out of place, to translate ten hours a day for the wages of a ditcher, to be hunted by bailiffs from one haunt of beggary and pestilence to another, from Grub Street to St. George's Fields, and from St. George's Fields to the alleys behind St. Martin's church, to sleep on a bulk in June and amidst the ashes of a glass-house in December, to die in an hospital and to be buried in a parish vault, was the fate of more than one writer who, if he had lived thirty years earlier, would have been admitted to the sittings of the Kitcat or the Scriblerus club, would have sat in Parliament, and would have been entrusted with embassies to the High Allies; who, if he had lived in our time, would have found encouragement scarcely less munificent in Albemarle Street or in Paternoster Row.

As every climate has its peculiar diseases, so every walk of life has its peculiar temptations. The literary character, assuredly, has always had its share of faults, vanity, jealousy, morbid sensibility. To these faults were now superadded the faults which are commonly found in men whose livelihood is precarious, and whose principles are exposed to the trial of severe distress. All the vices of the gambler and of the beggar were blended with those of the author. The prizes in the wretched lottery of book-making were scarcely less ruinous than the blanks. If good fortune came, it came in such a manner that it was almost certain to be abused. After months of starvation and despair, a full third night or a well-received dedication filled the pocket of the lean, ragged, unwashed poet with guineas. He hastened to enjoy those luxuries with the images of which his mind had been haunted while he was sleeping amidst the cinders and eating potatoes at the Irish ordinary in Shoe Lane. A week of taverns soon qualified him for another year of night-cellars. Such was the life of Savage, of Boyse, and of a crowd of others. Sometimes blazing in gold-laced hats and waistcoats; sometimes lying in bed because their coats had gone to pieces, or wearing paper cravats because their linen was in pawn; sometimes drinking Champagne and Tokay with Betty Careless; sometimes standing at the window of an eating-house in Porridge island, to snuff up the scent of what they could not afford to taste; they knew luxury; they knew beggary; but they never knew comfort. These men were irreclaimable. They looked on a regular and frugal life with the same aversion which an old gipsy or a Mohawk hunter feels for a stationary abode, and for the restraints and securities of civilised communities. They were as untameable, as much wedded to their desolate freedom, as the wild ass. They could no more be broken into the offices of social man than the unicorn could be trained to serve and abide by the crib. It was well if they did not, like beasts of a still fiercer race, tear the hands which ministered to their necessities. To assist them was impossible; and the most benevolent of mankind at length became weary of giving relief which was dissipated with the wildest profusion as soon as it had been received. If a sum was bestowed on the wretched adventurer, such as, properly husbanded, might have supplied him for six months, it was instantly spent in strange freaks of sensuality, and, before forty-eight hours had elapsed, the poet was again pestering all his acquaintance for twopence to get a plate of shin of beef at a subterraneous cook-shop. If his friends gave him an asylum in their houses, those houses were forthwith turned into bagnios and taverns. All order was destroyed; all business was suspended. The most good-natured host began to repent of his eagerness to serve a man of genius in distress when he heard his guest roaring for fresh punch at five o'clock in the morning.

A few eminent writers were more fortunate. Pope had been raised above poverty by the active patronage which, in his youth, both the great political parties had extended to his Homer. Young had received the only pension ever bestowed,

to the best of our recollection, by Sir Robert Walpole, as the reward of mere literary merit. One or two of the many poets who attached themselves to the opposition, Thomson in particular and Mallet, obtained, after much severe suffering, the means of subsistence from their political friends. Richardson, like a man of sense, kept his shop; and his shop kept him, which his novels, admirable as they are, would scarcely have done. But nothing could be more deplorable than the state even of the ablest men, who at that time depended for subsistence on their writings. Johnson, Collins, Fielding, and Thomson, were certainly four of the most distinguished persons that England produced during the eighteenth century. It is well known that they were all four arrested for debt.

Into calamities and difficulties such as these Johnson plunged in his twenty-eighth year. From that time till he was three or four and fifty, we have little information respecting him; little, we mean, compared with the full and accurate information which we possess respecting his proceedings and habits towards the close of his life. He emerged at length from cock-lofts and sixpenny ordinaries into the society of the polished and the opulent. His fame was established. A pension sufficient for his wants had been conferred on him; and he came forth to astonish a generation with which he had almost as little in common as with Frenchmen or Spaniards.

In his early years he had occasionally seen the great; but he had seen them as a beggar. He now came among them as a companion. The demand for amusement and instruction had, during the course of twenty years, been gradually increasing. The price of literary labour had risen; and those rising men of letters with whom Johnson was henceforth to associate were for the most part persons widely different from those who had walked about with him all night in the streets for want of a lodging. Burke, Robertson, the Wartons, Gray, Mason, Gibbon, Adam Smith, Beattie, Sir William Jones, Goldsmith, and Churchill, were the most distinguished writers of what may be called the second generation of the Johnsonian age. Of these men Churchill was the only one in whom we can trace the stronger lineaments of that character which, when Johnson first came up to London, was common among authors. Of the rest, scarcely any had felt the pressure of severe poverty. Almost all had been early admitted into the most respectable society on an equal footing. They were men of quite a different species from the dependents of Curll and Osborne.

Johnson came among them the solitary specimen of a past age, the last survivor of the genuine race of Grub Street hacks; the last of that generation of authors whose abject misery and whose dissolute manners had furnished inexhaustible matter to the satirical genius of Pope. From nature, he had received an uncouth figure, a diseased constitution, and an irritable temper. The manner in which the earlier years of his manhood had been passed had given to his demeanour, and even to his moral character, some peculiarities appalling to the civilised beings who were the companions of his old age. The perverse irregularity of his hours, the slovenliness of his person, his fits of strenuous exertion, interrupted by long intervals of sluggishness, his strange abstinence, and his equally strange voracity, his active benevolence, contrasted with the constant rudeness and the occasional ferocity of his manners in society, made him, in the opinion of those with whom he lived during the last twenty years of his life, a complete original. An original he was, undoubtedly, in some respects. But if we possessed full information concerning those who shared his early hardships, we should probably find that what we call his singularities of manner were, for the most part, failings which he had in common with the class to which he belonged. He ate at Streatham Park as he had been used to eat behind the screen at St. John's Gate, when he was ashamed to show his ragged clothes. He ate as it was natural that a man should eat, who, during a great part of his life, had passed the morning in doubt whether he should have food for the afternoon. The habits of his early life had accustomed him to bear privation with fortitude, but not to taste pleasure with moderation. He could fast; but, when he did not fast, he tore his dinner like a famished wolf, with the veins swelling on his forehead, and the perspiration running down his cheeks. He scarcely ever took wine. But when he drank it, he drank it greedily and in large tumblers. These were, in fact, mitigated symptoms of that same moral disease which raged with such deadly malignity in his friends Savage and Boyse. The roughness and violence which he showed in society were to be expected from a man whose temper, not naturally gentle, had been long tried by the bitterest calamities, by the want of meat, of fire, and of clothes, by the importunity of creditors, by the insolence of booksellers, by the derision of fools, by the insincerity of patrons, by that bread which is the bitterest of all food, by those stairs which are the most toilsome of all paths, by that deferred hope which makes the heart sick. Through all these things the ill-dressed, coarse, ungainly pedant had struggled manfully up to eminence and command. It was natural that, in the exercise of his power, he should be "eo immitior, quia toleraverat," that, though his heart was undoubtedly generous and humane, his demeanour in society should be harsh and despotic. For severe distress he had sympathy, and not only sympathy, but munificent relief. But for the suffering which a harsh world inflicts upon a delicate mind he had no pity; for it was a kind of suffering which he could scarcely conceive. He would carry home on his shoulders a sick and starving girl from the streets. He turned his house into a place of refuge for a crowd of wretched old creatures who could find no other asylum; nor could all their peevishness and ingratitude weary out his benevolence. But the pangs of wounded vanity seemed to him ridiculous; and he scarcely felt sufficient compassion even for the pangs of wounded affection. He had seen and felt so much of sharp misery, that he was not affected by paltry vexations; and he seemed to think that every body ought to be as much hardened to those vexations as himself. He was angry with Boswell for complaining of a headache, with Mrs. Thrale for grumbling about the dust on the road, or the smell of the kitchen. These were, in his phrase, "foppish lamentations," which people ought to be ashamed to utter in a world so full of sin and sorrow. Goldsmith crying because the *Good-natured Man* had failed, inspired him with no pity. Though his own health was not good, he detested and despised valetudinarians. Pecuniary losses, unless they reduced the loser absolutely to beggary, moved him very little. People whose hearts had been softened by prosperity might weep, he said, for such events; but all that could be expected of a plain man was not to laugh. He was not much moved even by the spectacle of Lady Tavistock dying of a broken heart for the loss of her lord. Such grief he considered as a luxury reserved for the idle and the wealthy. A washerwoman, left a widow with nine small children, would not have sobbed herself to death.

A person who troubled himself so little about small or sentimental grievances was not likely to be very attentive to the feelings of others in the ordinary intercourse of society. He could not understand how a sarcasm or a reprimand could make any man really unhappy. "My dear doctor," said he to Goldsmith, "what harm does it do to a man to call him Holofernes?" "Pooh, ma'am," he exclaimed to Mrs. Carter,

"who is the worse for being talked of uncharitably?" Politeness has been well defined as benevolence in small things. Johnson was impolite, not because he wanted benevolence, but because small things appeared smaller to him than to people who had never known what it was to live for fourpence halfpenny a day.

The characteristic peculiarity of his intellect was the union of great powers with low prejudices. If we judged of him by the best parts of his mind, we should place him almost as high as he was placed by the idolatry of Boswell; if by the worst parts of his mind, we should place him even below Boswell himself. Where he was not under the influence of some strange scruple, or some domineering passion, which prevented him from boldly and fairly investigating a subject, he was a wary and acute reasoner, a little too much inclined to scepticism, and a little too fond of paradox. No man was less likely to be imposed upon by fallacies in argument or by exaggerated statements of fact. But if, while he was beating down sophisms and exposing false testimony, some childish prejudices, such as would excite laughter in a well managed nursery, came across him, he was smitten as if by enchantment. His mind dwindled away under the spell from gigantic elevation to dwarfish littleness. Those who had lately been admiring its amplitude and its force were now as much astonished at its strange narrowness and feebleness as the fisherman in the Arabian tale, when he saw the Genie, whose stature had overshadowed the whole seacoast, and whose might seemed equal to a contest with armies, contract himself to the dimensions of his small prison, and lie there the helpless slave of the charm of Solomon.

Johnson was in the habit of sifting with extreme severity the evidence for all stories which were merely odd. But when they were not only odd but miraculous, his severity relaxed. He began to be credulous precisely at the point where the most credulous people begin to be sceptical. It is curious to observe, both in his writings and in his conversation, the contrast between the disdainful manner in which he rejects unauthenticated anecdotes, even when they are consistent with the general laws of nature, and the respectful manner in which he mentions the wildest stories relating to the invisible world. A man who told him of a water-spout or a meteoric stone generally had the lie direct given him for his pains. A man who told him of a prediction or a dream wonderfully accomplished was sure of a courteous hearing. "Johnson," observed Hogarth, "like King David, says in his haste that all men are liars." "His incredulity," says Mrs. Thrale, "amounted almost to disease." She tells us how he browbeat a gentleman, who gave him an account of a hurricane in the West Indies, and a poor quaker who related some strange circumstance about the red-hot balls fired at the siege of Gibraltar. "It is not so. It cannot be true. Don't tell that story again. You cannot think how poor a figure you make in telling it." He once said, half jestingly we suppose, that for six months he refused to credit the fact of the earthquake at Lisbon, and that he still believed the extent of the calamity to be greatly exaggerated. Yet he related with a grave face how old Mr. Cave of St. John's Gate saw a ghost, and how this ghost was something of a shadowy being. He went himself on a ghost-hunt to Cock Lane, and was angry with John Wesley for not following up another scent of the same kind with proper spirit and perseverance. He rejects the Celtic genealogies and poems without the least hesitation; yet he declares himself willing to believe the stories of the second sight. If he had examined the claims of the Highland seers with half the severity with which he sifted the evidence for the genuineness of Fingal, he would, we suspect, have come away from Scotland with a mind fully made up. In his *Lives of the*

Poets, we find that he is unwilling to give credit to the accounts of Lord Roscommon's early proficiency in his studies; but he tells with great solemnity an absurd romance about some intelligence preternaturally impressed on the mind of that nobleman. He avows himself to be in a great doubt about the truth of the story, and ends by warning his readers not wholly to slight such impressions.

Many of his sentiments on religious subjects are worthy of a liberal and enlarged mind. He could discern clearly enough the folly and meanness of all bigotry except his own. When he spoke of the scruples of the Puritans, he spoke like a person who had really obtained an insight into the divine philosophy of the New Testament, and who considered Christianity as a noble scheme of government, tending to promote the happiness and to elevate the moral nature of man. The horror which the sectaries felt for cards, Christmas ale, plum-porridge, mince-pies, and dancing bears, excited his contempt. To the arguments urged by some very worthy people against showy dress he replied with admirable sense and spirit, "Let us not be found, when our Master calls us, stripping the lace off our waistcoats, but the spirit of contention from our souls and tongues. Alas! sir, a man who cannot get to heaven in a green coat will not find his way thither the sooner in a grey one." Yet he was himself under the tyranny of scruples as unreasonable as those of Hudibras or Ralpho, and carried his zeal for ceremonies and for ecclesiastical dignities to lengths altogether inconsistent with reason or with Christian charity. He has gravely noted down in his diary that he once committed the sin of drinking coffee on Good Friday. In Scotland, he thought it his duty to pass several months without joining in public worship, solely because the ministers of the kirk had not been ordained by bishops. His mode of estimating the piety of his neighbours was somewhat singular. "Campbell," said he, "is a good man, a pious man. I am afraid he has not been in the inside of a church for many years; but he never passes a church without pulling off his hat: this shows he has good principles." Spain and Sicily must surely contain many pious robbers and well-principled assassins. Johnson could easily see that a Roundhead who named all his children after Solomon's singers, and talked in the House of Commons about seeking the Lord, might be an unprincipled villain whose religious mummeries only aggravated his guilt. But a man who took off his hat when he passed a church episcopally consecrated must be a good man, a pious man, a man of good principles. Johnson could easily see that those persons who looked on a dance or a laced waistcoat as sinful, deemed most ignobly of the attributes of God and of the ends of revelation. But with what a storm of invective he would have overwhelmed any man who had blamed him for celebrating the redemption of mankind with sugarless tea and butterless buns.

Nobody spoke more contemptuously of the cant of patriotism. Nobody saw more clearly the error of those who regarded liberty, not as a means, but as an end, and who proposed to themselves, as the object of their pursuit, the prosperity of the state as distinct from the prosperity of the individuals who compose the state. His calm and settled opinion seems to have been that forms of government have little or no influence on the happiness of society. This opinion, erroneous as it is, ought at least to have preserved him from all intemperance on political questions. It did not, however, preserve him from the lowest, fiercest, and most absurd extravagances of party-spirit, from rants which, in every thing but the diction, resembled those of Squire Western. He was, as a politician, half ice and half fire. On the side of his intellect he was a mere Pococurante, far too apathetic about

public affairs, far too sceptical as to the good or evil tendency of any form of polity. His passions, on the contrary, were violent even to slaying against all who leaned to Whiggish principles. The well-known lines which he inserted in Goldsmith's *Traveller* express what seems to have been his deliberate judgment:

> How small, of all that human hearts endure,
> That part which kings or laws can cause or cure!

He had previously put expressions very similar into the mouth of Rasselas. It is amusing to contrast these passages with the torrents of raving abuse which he poured forth against the Long Parliament and the American Congress. In one of the conversations reported by Boswell this inconsistency displays itself in the most ludicrous manner.

"Sir Adam Ferguson," says Boswell, "suggested that luxury corrupts a people, and destroys the spirit of liberty. JOHNSON: 'Sir, that is all visionary. I would not give half a guinea to live under one form of government rather than another. It is of no moment to the happiness of an individual. Sir, the danger of the abuse of power is nothing to a private man. What Frenchman is prevented passing his life as he pleases?' SIR ADAM: 'But, sir, in the British constitution it is surely of importance to keep up a spirit in the people, so as to preserve a balance against the crown.' JOHNSON: 'Sir, I perceive you are a vile Whig. Why all this childish jealousy of the power of the crown? The crown has not power enough.'"

One of the old philosophers, Lord Bacon tells us, used to say that life and death were just the same to him. "Why then," said an objector, "do you not kill yourself?" The philosopher answered, "Because it is just the same." If the difference between two forms of government be not worth half a guinea, it is not easy to see how Whiggism can be viler than Toryism, or how the crown can have too little power. If the happiness of individuals is not affected by political abuses, zeal for liberty is doubtless ridiculous. But zeal for monarchy must be equally so. No person would have been more quick-sighted than Johnson to such a contradiction as this in the logic of an antagonist.

The judgments which Johnson passed on books were, in his own time, regarded with superstitious veneration, and, in our time, are generally treated with indiscriminate contempt. They are the judgments of a strong but enslaved understanding. The mind of the critic was hedged round by an uninterrupted fence of prejudices and superstitions. Within his narrow limits, he displayed a vigour and an activity which ought to have enabled him to clear the barrier that confined him.

How it chanced that a man who reasoned on his premises so ably, should assume his premises so foolishly, is one of the great mysteries of human nature. The same inconsistency may be observed in the schoolmen of the middle ages. Those writers show so much acuteness and force of mind in arguing on their wretched data, that a modern reader is perpetually at a loss to comprehend how such minds came by such data. Not a flaw in the superstructure of the theory which they are rearing escapes their vigilance. Yet they are blind to the obvious unsoundness of the foundation. It is the same with some eminent lawyers. Their legal arguments are intellectual prodigies, abounding with the happiest analogies and the most refined distinctions. The principles of their arbitrary science being once admitted, the statute-book and the reports being once assumed as the foundations of reasoning, these men must be allowed to be perfect masters of logic. But if a question arises as to the postulates on which their whole system rests, if they are called upon to vindicate the fundamental maxims of that system which they have passed their lives in studying, these very men often talk the language of savages or of children. Those who have listened to a man of this class in his own court, and who have witnessed the skill with which he analyses and digests a vast mass of evidence, or reconciles a crowd of precedents which at first sight seem contradictory, scarcely know him again when, a few hours later, they hear him speaking on the other side of Westminster Hall in his capacity of legislator. They can scarcely believe that the paltry quirks which are faintly heard through a storm of coughing, and which do not impose on the plainest country gentleman, can proceed from the same sharp and vigorous intellect which had excited their admiration under the same roof, and on the same day.

Johnson decided literary questions like a lawyer, not like a legislator. He never examined foundations where a point was already ruled. His whole code of criticism rested on pure assumption, for which he sometimes quoted a precedent or an authority, but rarely troubled himself to give a reason drawn from the nature of things. He took it for granted that the kind of poetry which flourished in his own time, which he had been accustomed to hear praised from his childhood, and which he had himself written with success, was the best kind of poetry. In his biographical work he has repeatedly laid it down as an undeniable proposition that during the latter part of the seventeenth century, and the earlier part of the eighteenth, English poetry had been in a constant progress of improvement. Waller, Denham, Dryden, and Pope, had been, according to him, the great reformers. He judged of all works of the imagination by the standard established among his own contemporaries. Though he allowed Homer to have been a greater man than Virgil, he seems to have thought the *Æneid* a greater poem than the *Iliad*. Indeed he well might have thought so; for he preferred Pope's *Iliad* to Homer's. He pronounced that, after Hoole's translation of Tasso, Fairfax's would hardly be reprinted. He could see no merit in our fine old English ballads, and always spoke with the most provoking contempt of Percy's fondness for them. Of the great original works of imagination which appeared during his time, Richardson's novels alone excited his admiration. He could see little or no merit in *Tom Jones*, in *Gulliver's Travels*, or in *Tristram Shandy*. To Thomson's *Castle of Indolence*, he vouchsafed only a line of cold commendation, of commendation much colder than what he has bestowed on the *Creation* of that portentous bore, Sir Richard Blackmore. Gray was, in his dialect, a barren rascal. Churchill was a blockhead. The contempt which he felt for the trash of Macpherson was indeed just; but it was, we suspect, just by chance. He despised the *Fingal* for the very reason which led many men of genius to admire it. He despised it, not because it was essentially common-place, but because it had a superficial air of originality.

He was undoubtedly an excellent judge of compositions fashioned on his own principles. But when a deeper philosophy was required, when he undertook to pronounce judgment on the works of those great minds which "yield homage only to eternal laws," his failure was ignominious. He criticized Pope's *Epitaphs* excellently. But his observations on Shakspeare's plays and Milton's poems seem to us for the most part as wretched as if they had been written by Rymer himself, whom we take to have been the worst critic that ever lived.

Some of Johnson's whims on literary subjects can be compared only to that strange nervous feeling which made him uneasy if he had not touched every post between the Mitre tavern and his own lodgings. His preference of Latin epitaphs to English epitaphs is an instance. An English epitaph, he said,

would disgrace Smollett. He declared that he would not pollute the walls of Westminster Abbey with an English epitaph on Goldsmith. What reason there can be for celebrating a British writer in Latin, which there was not for covering the Roman arches of triumph with Greek inscriptions, or for commemorating the deeds of the heroes of Thermopylæ in Egyptian hieroglyphics, we are utterly unable to imagine.

On men and manners, at least on the men and manners of a particular place and a particular age, Johnson had certainly looked with a most observant and discriminating eye. His remarks on the education of children, on marriage, on the economy of families, on the rules of society, are always striking, and generally sound. In his writings, indeed, the knowledge of life which he possessed in an eminent degree is very imperfectly exhibited. Like those unfortunate chiefs of the middle ages who were suffocated by their own chain-mail and cloth of gold, his maxims perish under that load of words which was designed for their defence and their ornament. But it is clear from the remains of his conversation, that he had more of that homely wisdom which nothing but experience and observation can give than any writer since the time of Swift. If he had been content to write as he talked, he might have left books on the practical art of living superior to the *Directions to Servants*.

Yet even his remarks on society, like his remarks on literature, indicate a mind at least as remarkable for narrowness as for strength. He was no master of the great science of human nature. He had studied, not the genus man, but the species Londoner. Nobody was ever so thoroughly conversant with all the forms of life and all the shades of moral and intellectual character which were to be seen from Islington to the Thames, and from Hyde-Park corner to Mile-end green. But his philosophy stopped at the first turnpike-gate. Of the rural life of England he knew nothing; and he took it for granted that every body who lived in the country was either stupid or miserable. "Country gentlemen," said he, "must be unhappy; for they have not enough to keep their lives in motion;" as if all those peculiar habits and associations which made Fleet Street and Charing Cross the finest views in the world to himself had been essential parts of human nature. Of remote countries and past times he talked with wild and ignorant presumption. "The Athenians of the age of Demosthenes," he said to Mrs. Thrale, "were a people of brutes, a barbarous people." In conversation with Sir Adam Ferguson he used similar language. "The boasted Athenians," he said, "were barbarians. The mass of every people must be barbarous where there is no printing." The fact was this: he saw that a Londoner who could not read was a very stupid and brutal fellow: he saw that great refinement of taste and activity of intellect were rarely found in a Londoner who had not read much; and, because it was by means of books that people acquired almost all their knowledge in the society with which he was acquainted, he concluded, in defiance of the strongest and clearest evidence, that the human mind can be cultivated by means of books alone. An Athenian citizen might possess very few volumes; and the largest library to which he had access might be much less valuable than Johnson's bookcase in Bolt Court. But the Athenian might pass every morning in conversation with Socrates, and might hear Pericles speak four or five times every month. He saw the plays of Sophocles and Aristophanes: he walked amidst the friezes of Phidias and the paintings of Zeuxis: he knew by heart the choruses of Æschylus: he heard the rhapsodist at the corner of the street reciting the shield of Achilles or the Death of Argus: he was a legislator, conversant with high questions of alliance, revenue, and war: he was a soldier, trained under a liberal and generous discipline: he was a judge, compelled every day to weigh the effect of opposite arguments. These things were in themselves an education, an education eminently fitted, not, indeed, to form exact or profound thinkers, but to give quickness to the perceptions, delicacy to the taste, fluency to the expression, and politeness to the manners. All this was overlooked. An Athenian who did not improve his mind by reading was, in Johnson's opinion, much such a person as a Cockney who made his mark, much such a person as black Frank before he went to school, and far inferior to a parish clerk or a printer's devil.

Johnson's friends have allowed that he carried to a ridiculous extreme his unjust contempt for foreigners. He pronounced the French to be a very silly people, much behind us, stupid, ignorant creatures. And this judgment he formed after having been at Paris about a month, during which he would not talk French, for fear of giving the natives an advantage over him in conversation. He pronounced them, also, to be an indelicate people, because a French footman touched the sugar with his fingers. That ingenious and amusing traveller, M. Simond, has defended his countrymen very successfully against Johnson's accusation, and has pointed out some English practices which, to an impartial spectator, would seem at least as inconsistent with physical cleanliness and social decorum as those which Johnson so bitterly reprehended. To the sage, as Boswell loves to call him, it never occurred to doubt that there must be something eternally and immutably good in the usages to which he had been accustomed. In fact, Johnson's remarks on society beyond the bills of mortality, are generally of much the same kind with those of honest Tom Dawson, the English footman in Dr. Moore's *Zeluco*. "Suppose the king of France has no sons, but only a daughter, then, when the king dies, this here daughter, according to that there law, cannot be made queen, but the next near relative, provided he is a man, is made king, and not the last king's daughter, which, to be sure, is very unjust. The French footguards are dressed in blue, and all the marching regiments in white, which has a very foolish appearance for soldiers; and as for blue regimentals, it is only fit for the blue horse or the artillery."

Johnson's visit to the Hebrides introduced him to a state of society completely new to him; and a salutary suspicion of his own deficiencies seems on that occasion to have crossed his mind for the first time. He confessed, in the last paragraph of his *Journey*, that his thoughts on national manners were the thoughts of one who had seen but little, of one who had passed his time almost wholly in cities. This feeling, however, soon passed away. It is remarkable that to the last he entertained a fixed contempt for all those modes of life and those studies which tend to emancipate the mind from the prejudices of a particular age or a particular nation. Of foreign travel and of history he spoke with the fierce and boisterous contempt of ignorance. "What does a man learn by travelling? Is Beauclerk the better for travelling? What did Lord Charlemont learn in his travels, except that there was a snake in one of the pyramids of Egypt?" History was, in his opinion, to use the fine expression of Lord Plunkett, an old almanack: historians could, as he conceived, claim no higher dignity than that of almanack-makers; and his favourite historians were those who, like Lord Hailes, aspired to no higher dignity. He always spoke with contempt of Robertson. Hume he would not even read. He affronted one of his friends for talking to him about Catiline's conspiracy, and declared that he never desired to hear of the Punic war again as long as he lived.

Assuredly one fact which does not directly affect our own interests, considered in itself, is no better worth knowing than another fact. The fact that there is a snake in a pyramid, or the fact that Hannibal crossed the Alps, are in themselves as unprofitable to us as the fact that there is a green blind in a particular house in Threadneedle Street, or the fact that a Mr. Smith comes into the city every morning on the top of one of the Blackwall stages. But it is certain that those who will not crack the shell of history will never get at the kernel. Johnson, with hasty arrogance, pronounced the kernel worthless, because he saw no value in the shell. The real use of travelling to distant countries and of studying the annals of past times is to preserve men from the contraction of mind which those can hardly escape whose whole communion is with one generation and one neighbourhood, who arrive at conclusions by means of an induction not sufficiently copious, and who therefore constantly confound exceptions with rules, and accidents with essential properties. In short, the real use of travelling and of studying history is to keep men from being what Tom Dawson was in fiction, and Samuel Johnson in reality.

Johnson, as Mr. Burke most justly observed, appears far greater in Boswell's books than in his own. His conversation appears to have been quite equal to his writings in matter, and far superior to them in manner. When he talked, he clothed his wit and his sense in forcible and natural expressions. As soon as he took his pen in his hand to write for the public, his style became systematically vicious. All his books are written in a learned language, in a language which nobody hears from his mother or his nurse, in a language in which nobody ever quarrels, or drives bargains, or makes love, in a language in which nobody ever thinks. It is clear that Johnson himself did not think in the dialect in which he wrote. The expressions which came first to his tongue were simple, energetic, and picturesque. When he wrote for publication, he did his sentences out of English into Johnsonese. His letters from the Hebrides to Mrs. Thrale are the original of that work of which the *Journey to the Hebrides* is the translation; and it is amusing to compare the two versions. "When we were taken up stairs," says he in one of his letters, "a dirty fellow bounced out of the bed on which one of us was to lie." This incident is recorded in the *Journey* as follows: "Out of one of the beds on which we were to repose started up, at our entrance, a man black as a Cyclops from the forge." Sometimes Johnson translated aloud. *"The Rehearsal,"* he said, very unjustly, "has not wit enough to keep it sweet;" then, after a pause, "it has not vitality enough to preserve it from putrefaction."

Mannerism is pardonable, and is sometimes even agreeable, when the manner, though vicious, is natural. Few readers, for example, would be willing to part with the mannerism of Milton or of Burke. But a mannerism which does not sit easy on the mannerist, which has been adopted on principle, and which can be sustained only by constant effort, is always offensive. And such is the mannerism of Johnson.

The characteristic faults of his style are so familiar to all our readers, and have been so often burlesqued, that it is almost superfluous to point them out. It is well known that he made less use than any other eminent writer of those strong plain words, Anglo-Saxon or Norman-French, of which the roots lie in the inmost depths of our language; and that he felt a vicious partiality for terms which, long after our own speech had been fixed, were borrowed from the Greek and Latin, and which, therefore, even when lawfully naturalised, must be considered as born aliens, not entitled to rank with the king's English. His constant practice of padding out a sentence with useless epithets, till it became as stiff as the bust of an exquisite, his antithetical forms of expression, constantly employed even where there is no opposition in the ideas expressed, his big words wasted on little things, his harsh inversions, so widely different from those graceful and easy inversions which give variety, spirit, and sweetness to the expression of our great old writers, all these peculiarities have been imitated by his admirers and parodied by his assailants, till the public has become sick of the subject.

Goldsmith said to him, very wittily and very justly, "If you were to write a fable about little fishes, doctor, you would make the little fishes talk like whales." No man surely ever had so little talent for personation as Johnson. Whether he wrote in the character of a disappointed legacy-hunter or an empty town fop, of a crazy virtuoso or a flippant coquette, he wrote in the same pompous and unbending style. His speech, like Sir Piercy Shafton's Euphuistic eloquence, bewrayed him under every disguise. Euphelia and Rhodoclea talk as finely as Imlac the poet, or Seged, Emperor of Ethiopia. The gay Cornelia describes her reception at the country-house of her relations, in such terms as these: "I was surprised, after the civilities of my first reception, to find, instead of the leisure and tranquillity which a rural life always promises, and, if well conducted, might always afford, a confused wildness of care, and a tumultuous hurry of diligence, by which every face was clouded, and every motion agitated." The gentle Tranquilla informs us, that she "had not passed the earlier part of life without the flattery of courtship, and the joys of triumph; but had danced the round of gaiety amidst the murmurs of envy and the gratulations of applause, had been attended from pleasure to pleasure by the great, the sprightly, and the vain, and had seen her regard solicited by the obsequiousness of gallantry, the gaiety of wit, and the timidity of love." Surely Sir John Falstaff himself did not wear his petticoats with a worse grace. The reader may well cry out, with honest Sir Hugh Evans, "I like not when a 'oman has a great peard: I spy a great peard under her muffler."[1]

We had something more to say. But our article is already too long; and we must close it. We would fain part in good humour from the hero, from the biographer, and even from the editor, who, ill as he has performed his task, has at least this claim to our gratitude, that he has induced us to read Boswell's book again. As we close it, the club-room is before us, and the table on which stands the omelet for Nugent, and the lemons for Johnson. There are assembled those heads which live for ever on the canvass of Reynolds. There are the spectacles of Burke and the tall thin form of Langton, the courtly sneer of Beauclerk and the beaming smile of Garrick, Gibbon tapping his snuff-box and Sir Joshua with his trumpet in his ear. In the foreground is that strange figure which is as familiar to us as the figures of those among whom we have been brought up, the gigantic body, the huge massy face, seamed with the scars of disease, the brown coat, the black worsted stockings, the grey wig with the scorched foretop, the dirty hands, the nails bitten and pared to the quick. We see the eyes and mouth moving with convulsive twitches; we see the heavy form rolling; we hear it puffing; and then comes the "Why, sir!" and the "What then, sir?" and the "No, sir!" and the "You don't see your way through the question, sir!"

What a singular destiny has been that of this remarkable man! To be regarded in his own age as a classic, and in ours as a companion. To receive from his contemporaries that full homage which men of genius have in general received only from posterity! To be more intimately known to posterity than other men are known to their contemporaries! That kind of fame which is commonly the most transient is, in his case, the most durable. The reputation of those writings, which he probably expected to be immortal, is every day fading; while those peculiarities of manner and that careless table-talk the memory of which, he probably thought, would die with him, are likely to be remembered as long as the English language is spoken in any quarter of the globe.

Notes

1. It is proper to observe that this passage bears a very close resemblance to a passage in the *Rambler* (No. 20). The resemblance may possibly be the effect of unconscious plagiarism.

THOMAS CARLYLE
From "The Hero as Man of Letters"
On Heroes, Hero-Worship and the Heroic in History
1841

As for Johnson, I have always considered him to be, by nature, one of our great English souls. A strong and noble man; so much left undeveloped in him to the last: in a kindlier element what might he not have been,—Poet, Priest, sovereign Ruler! On the whole, a man must not complain of his 'element,' of his 'time,' or the like; it is thriftless work doing so. His time is bad: well then, he is there to make it better!— Johnson's youth was poor, isolated, hopeless, very miserable. Indeed, it does not seem possible that, in any the favourablest outward circumstances, Johnson's life could have been other than a painful one. The world might have had more of profitable *work* out of him, or less; but his *effort* against the world's work could never have been a light one. Nature, in return for his nobleness, had said to him, Live in an element of diseased sorrow. Nay, perhaps the sorrow and the nobleness were intimately and even inseparably connected with each other. At all events, poor Johnson had to go about girt with continual hypochondria, physical and spiritual pain. Like a Hercules with the burning Nessus'-shirt on him, which shoots-in on him dull incurable misery: the Nessus'-shirt not to be stript-off, which is his own natural skin! In this manner *he* had to live. Figure him there, with his scrofulous diseases, with his great greedy heart, and unspeakable chaos of thoughts; stalking mournful as a stranger in this Earth; eagerly devouring what spiritual thing he could come at: school-languages and other merely grammatical stuff, if there were nothing better! The largest soul that was in all England; and provision made for it of 'fourpence-halfpenny a day.' Yet a giant invincible soul; a true man's. One remembers always that story of the shoes at Oxford: the rough, seamy-faced, rawboned College Servitor stalking about, in winter-season, with his shoes worn-out; how the charitable Gentleman Commoner secretly places a new pair at his door; and the rawboned Servitor, lifting them, looking at them near, with his dim eyes, with what thoughts,— pitches them out of window! Wet feet, mud, frost, hunger or what you will; but not beggary: we cannot stand beggary! Rude stubborn self-help here; a whole world of squalor, rudeness, confused misery and want, yet of nobleness and manfulness withal. It is a type of the man's life, this pitching-away of the shoes. An original man; not a secondhand, borrowing or begging man. Let us stand on our own basis, at any rate! On such shoes as we ourselves can get. On frost and mud, if you will, but honestly on that;—on the reality and substance which Nature gives *us*, not on the semblance, on the thing she has given another than us!—

And yet with all this rugged pride of manhood and self-help, was there ever soul more tenderly affectionate, loyally submissive to what was really higher than he? Great souls are always loyally submissive, reverent to what is over them; only small mean souls are otherwise. I could not find a better proof of what I said the other day, That the sincere man was by nature the obedient man; that only in a World of Heroes was there loyal Obedience to the Heroic. The essence of *originality* is not that it be *new:* Johnson believed altogether in the old; he found the old opinions credible for him, fit for him; and in a right heroic manner lived under them. He is well worth study in regard to that. For we are to say that Johnson was far other than a mere man of words and formulas; he was a man of truths and facts. He stood by the old formulas; the happier was it for him that he could so stand: but in all formulas that *he* could stand by, there needed to be a most genuine substance. Very curious how, in that poor Paper-age, so barren, artificial, thick-quilted with Pedantries, Hearsays, the great Fact of this Universe glared in, for ever wonderful, indubitable, unspeakable, divine-infernal, upon this man too! How he harmonised his Formulas with it, how he managed at all under such circumstances: that is a thing worth seeing. A thing 'to be looked at with reverence, with pity, with awe.' That Church of St. Clement Danes, where Johnson still *worshipped* in the era of Voltaire, is to me a venerable place.

It was in virtue of his *sincerity*, of his speaking still in some sort from the heart of Nature, though in the current artificial dialect, that Johnson was a Prophet. Are not all dialects 'artificial'? Artificial things are not all false;—nay every true Product of Nature will infallibly *shape* itself; we may say all artificial things are, at the starting of them, *true*. What we call 'Formulas' are not in their origin bad; they are indispensably good. Formula is *method*, habitude; found wherever man is found. Formulas fashion themselves as Paths do, as beaten Highways, leading towards some sacred or high object, whither many men are bent. Consider it. One man, full of heartfelt earnest impulse, finds-out a way of doing somewhat,—were it of uttering his soul's reverence for the Highest, were it but of fitly saluting his fellow-man. An inventor was needed to do that, a *poet*; he has articulated the dim-struggling thought that dwelt in his own and many hearts. This is his way of doing that; these are his footsteps, the beginning of a 'Path.' And now see: the second man travels naturally in the footsteps of his foregoer; it is the *easiest* method. In the footsteps of his foregoer; yet with improvements, with changes where such seem good; at all events with enlargements, the Path ever *widening* itself as more travel it;—till at last there is a broad Highway whereon the whole world may travel and drive. While there remains a City or Shrine, or any Reality to drive to, at the farther end, the Highway shall be right welcome! When the City is gone, we will forsake the Highway. In this manner all Institutions, Practices, Regulated Things in the world have come into existence, and gone out of existence. Formulas all begin by being *full* of substance; you may call them the *skin*, the articulation into shape, into limbs and skin, of a substance that is already there: *they* had not been there otherwise. Idols, as we said, are not idolatrous till they become doubtful, empty for the worshipper's heart. Much as we talk against Formulas, I hope no one of us is ignorant withal of the high significance of *true* Formulas; that they were, and will ever be, the indispensablest furniture of our habitation in this world.—

Mark, too, how little Johnson boasts of his 'sincerity.' He has no suspicion of his being particularly sincere,—of his being particularly anything! A hard-struggling, weary-hearted man, or 'scholar' as he calls himself, trying hard to get some honest livelihood in the world, not to starve, but to live—

without stealing! A noble unconsciousness is in him. He does not 'engrave *Truth* on his watch-seal'; no, but he stands by truth, speaks by it, works and lives by it. Thus it ever is. Think of it once more. The man whom Nature has appointed to do great things is, first of all, furnished with that openness to Nature which renders him incapable of being *in*sincere! To his large, open, deep-feeling heart Nature is a Fact: all hearsay is hearsay; the unspeakable greatness of this Mystery of Life, let him acknowledge it or not, nay even though he seem to forget it or deny it, is ever present to *him*,—fearful and wonderful, on this hand and on that. He has a basis of sincerity; unrecognised, because never questioned or capable of question. Mirabeau, Mahomet, Cromwell, Napoleon: all the Great Men I ever heard-of have this as the primary material of them. Innumerable commonplace men are debating, are talking everywhere their commonplace doctrines, which they have learned by logic, by rote, at secondhand: to that kind of man all this is still nothing. He must have truth; truth which *he* feels to be true. How shall he stand otherwise? His whole soul, at all moments, in all ways, tells him that there is no standing. He is under the noble necessity of being true. Johnson's way of thinking about this world is not mine, any more than Mahomet's was: but I recognise the everlasting element of heart-*sincerity* in both; and see with pleasure how neither of them remains ineffectual. Neither of them is as *chaff* sown; in both of them is something which the seed-field will *grow*.

Johnson was a Prophet to his people; preached a Gospel to them,—as all like him always do. The highest Gospel he preached we may describe as a kind of Moral Prudence: 'in a world where much is to be done, and little is to be known,' see how you will *do* it! A thing well worth preaching. 'A world where much is to be done, and little is to be known': do not sink yourselves in boundless bottomless abysses of Doubt, of wretched god-forgetting Unbelief;—you were miserable then, powerless, mad: how could you *do* or work at all? Such Gospel Johnson preached and taught;—coupled, theoretically and practically, with this other great Gospel, 'Clear your mind of Cant!' Have no trade with Cant: stand on the cold mud in the frosty weather, but let it be in your own *real* torn shoes: 'that will be better for you,' as Mahomet says! I call this, I call these two things *joined together*, a great Gospel, the greatest perhaps that was possible at that time.

Johnson's Writings, which once had such currency and celebrity, are now, as it were, disowned by the young generation. It is not wonderful; Johnson's opinions are fast becoming obsolete: but his style of thinking and of living, we may hope, will never become obsolete. I find in Johnson's Books the indisputablest traces of a great intellect and great heart;—ever welcome, under what obstructions and perversions soever. They are *sincere* words, those of his; he means things by them. A wondrous buckram style,—the best he could get to then; a measured grandiloquence, stepping or rather stalking along in a very solemn way, grown obsolete now; sometimes a tumid *size* of phraseology not in proportion to the contents of it: all this you will put-up with. For the phraseology, tumid or not, has always *something within it*. So many beautiful styles and books, with *nothing* in them;—a man is a *male*factor to the world who writes such! *They* are the avoidable kind!—Had Johnson left nothing but his *Dictionary*, one might have traced there a great intellect, a genuine man. Looking to its clearness of definition, its general solidity, honesty, insight and successful method, it may be called the best of all Dictionaries. There is in it a kind of architectural nobleness; it stands there like a great solid square-built edifice, finished, symmetrically complete: you judge that a true Builder did it.

One word, in spite of our haste, must be granted to poor Bozzy. He passes for a mean, inflated, gluttonous creature; and was so in many senses. Yet the fact of his reverence for Johnson will ever remain noteworthy. The foolish conceited Scotch Laird, the most conceited man of his time, approaching in such awestruck attitude the great dusty irascible Pedagogue in his mean garret there: it is a genuine reverence for Excellence; a *worship* for Heroes, at a time when neither Heroes nor worship were surmised to exist. Heroes, it would seem, exist always, and a certain worship of them! We will also take the liberty to deny altogether that of the witty Frenchman, that no man is a Hero to his valet-de-chambre. Or if so, it is not the Hero's blame, but the Valet's: that his soul, namely, is a mean *valet*-soul! He expects his Hero to advance in royal stage-trappings, with measured step, trains borne behind him, trumpets sounding before him. It should stand rather, No man can be a *Grand-Monarque* to his valet-de-chambre. Strip your Louis Quatorze of his king-gear, and there *is* left nothing but a poor forked radish with a head fantastically carved;—admirable to no valet. The Valet does not know a Hero when he sees him! Alas, no: it requires a kind of *Hero* to do that;—and one of the world's wants, in *this* as in other senses, is for most part want of such.

On the whole, shall we not say, that Boswell's admiration was well bestowed; that he could have found no soul in all England so worthy of bending down before? Shall we not say, of this great mournful Johnson too, that he guided his difficult confused existence wisely; led it *well*, like a right-valiant man? That waste chaos of Authorship by trade; that waste chaos of Scepticism in religion and politics, in life-theory and life-practice; in his poverty, in his dust and dimness, with the sick body and the rusty coat: he made it do for him, like a brave man. Not wholly without a loadstar in the Eternal; he had still a loadstar, as the brave all need to have: with his eye set on that, he would change his course for nothing in these confused vortices of the lower sea of Time. 'To the Spirit of Lies, bearing death and hunger, he would in no wise strike his flag.' Brave old Samuel: *ultimus Romanorum!*

SIR LESLIE STEPHEN
"Dr. Johnson's Writings"
Hours in a Library (1874–79)
1904, Volume 2, pp. 146–88

A book appeared not long ago of which it was the professed object to give to the modern generation of lazy readers the pith of Boswell's immortal biography. I shall, for sufficient reasons, refrain from discussing the merits of the performance. One remark, indeed, may be made in passing. The circle of readers to whom such a book is welcome must, of necessity, be limited. To the true lovers of Boswell it is, to say the least, superfluous; the gentlest omissions will always mangle some people's favourite passages, and additions, whatever skill they may display, necessarily injure that dramatic vivacity which is one of the great charms of the original. The most discreet of cicerones is an intruder when we open our old favourite, and, without further magic, retire into that delicious nook of eighteenth-century society. Upon those, again, who cannot appreciate the infinite humour of the original, the mere excision of the less lively pages will be thrown away. There remains only that narrow margin of readers whose appetites, languid but not extinct, can be titillated by the promise that

they shall not have the trouble of making their own selection. Let us wish them good digestions, and, in spite of modern changes of fashion, more robust taste for the future. I would still hope that to many readers Boswell has been what he has certainly been to some, the first writer who gave them a love of English literature, and the most charming of all companions long after the bloom of novelty has departed. I subscribe most cheerfully to Mr. Lewes's statement that he estimates his acquaintances according to their estimate of Boswell. A man, indeed, may be a good Christian and an excellent father of a family, without loving Johnson or Boswell, for a sense of humour is not one of the primary virtues. But Boswell's is one of the very few books which, after many years of familiarity, will still provoke a hearty laugh even in the solitude of a study; and the laughter is of that kind which does one good.

I do not wish, however, to pronounce one more eulogy upon an old friend, but to say a few words on a question which he sometimes suggests. Macaulay's well-known but provoking essay is more than usually lavish in overstrained paradoxes. He has explicitly declared that Boswell wrote one of the most charming of books because he was one of the greatest of fools. And his remarks suggest, if they do not implictly assert, that Johnson wrote some of the most unreadable of books, although, if not because, he possessed one of the most vigorous intellects of the time. Carlyle has given a sufficient explanation of the first paradox; but the second may justify a little further inquiry. As a general rule, the talk of a great man is the reflection of his books. Nothing is so false as the common saying that the presence of a distinguished writer is generally disappointing. It exemplifies a very common delusion. People are so impressed by the disparity which sometimes occurs, that they take the exception for the rule. It is, of course, true that a man's verbal utterances may differ materially from his written utterances. He may, like Addison, be shy in company; he may, like many retired students, be slow in collecting his thoughts; or he may, like Goldsmith, be over-anxious to shine at all hazards. But a patient observer will even then detect the essential identity under superficial differences; and in the majority of cases, as in that of Macaulay himself, the talking and the writing are palpably and almost absurdly similar. The whole art of criticism consists in learning to know the human being who is partially revealed to us in his spoken or his written words. Whatever the means of communication, the problem is the same. The two methods of inquiry may supplement each other; but their substantial agreement is the test of their accuracy. If Johnson, as a writer, appears to us to be a mere windbag and manufacturer of sesquipedalian verbiage, whilst, as a talker, he appears to be one of the most genuine and deeply feeling of men, we may be sure that our analysis has been somewhere defective. The discrepancy is, of course, partly explained by the faults of Johnson's style; but the explanation only removes the difficulty a degree further. "The style is the man" is a very excellent aphorism, though some eminent writers have lately pointed out that Buffon's original remark was *le style c'est de l'homme*. That only proves that, like many other good sayings, it has been polished and brought to perfection by the process of attrition in numerous minds, instead of being struck out at a blow by a solitary thinker. From a purely logical point of view, Buffon may be correct; but the very essence of an aphorism is that slight exaggeration which makes it more biting whilst less rigidly accurate. According to Buffon, the style might belong to a man as an acquisition rather than to natural growth. There are parasitical writers who, in the old phrase, have "formed their style" by the imitation of accepted models, and who have, therefore, possessed it only by right of appropriation. Boswell has a discussion as to the writers who may have served Johnson in this capacity. But, in fact, Johnson, like all other men of strong idiosyncrasy, formed his style as he formed his legs. The peculiarities of his limbs were in some degree the result of conscious efforts in walking, swimming, and "buffeting with his books." This development was doubtless more fully determined by the constitution which he brought into the world, and the circumstances under which he was brought up. And even that queer Johnsonese, which Macaulay supposes him to have adopted in accordance with a more definite literary theory, will probably appear to be the natural expression of certain innate tendencies, and of the mental atmosphere which he breathed from youth. To appreciate fairly the strangely cumbrous form of his written speech, we must penetrate more deeply than may at first sight seem necessary beneath the outer rind of this literary Behemoth. The difficulty of such spiritual dissection is, indeed, very great; but some little light may be thrown upon the subject by following out such indications as we possess.

The talking Johnson is sufficiently familiar to us. So far as Boswell needs an interpreter, Carlyle has done all that can be done. He has concentrated and explained what is diffused, and often unconsciously indicated in Boswell's pages. When reading Boswell, we are half ashamed of his power over our sympathies. It is like turning over a portfolio of sketches, caricatured, inadequate, and each giving only some imperfect aspect of the original. Macaulay's smart paradoxes only increase our perplexity by throwing the superficial contrasts into stronger relief. Carlyle, with true imaginative insight, gives us at once the essence of Johnson; he brings before our eyes the luminous body of which we had previously been conscious only by a series of imperfect images refracted through a number of distorting media. To render such a service effectually is the highest triumph of criticism; and it would be impertinent to say again in feebler language what Carlyle has expressed so forcibly. We may, however, recall certain general conclusions by way of preface to the problem which he has not expressly considered, how far Johnson succeeded in expressing himself through his writings.

The world, as Carlyle sees it, is composed, we all know, of two classes: there are "the dull millions, who, as a dull flock, roll hither and thither, whithersoever they are led," and there are a few superior natures who can see and can will. There are, in other words, the heroes, and those whose highest wisdom is to be hero-worshippers. Johnson's glory is that he belonged to the sacred band, though he could not claim within it the highest, or even a very high, rank. In the current dialect, therefore, he was "nowise a clothes-horse or patent digester, but a genuine man." Whatever the accuracy of the general doctrine, or of certain corollaries which are drawn from it, the application to Johnson explains one main condition of his power. Persons of colourless imagination may hold—nor will we dispute their verdict—that Carlyle overcharges his lights and shades, and brings his heroes into too startling a contrast with the vulgar herd. Yet it is undeniable that the great bulk of mankind are transmitters rather than originators of spiritual force. Most of us are necessarily condemned to express our thoughts in formulas which we have learnt from others and can but slightly tinge with our feeble personality. Nor, as a rule, are we even consistent disciples of any one school of thought. What we call our opinions are mere bundles of incoherent formulæ, arbitrarily stitched together because our reasoning faculties are too dull to make inconsistency painful. Of the vast piles of books which load our libraries, ninety-nine hundredths

and more are but printed echoes: and it is the rarest of pleasures to say, Here is a distinct record of impressions at first hand. We commonplace beings are hurried along in the crowd, living from hand to mouth on such slices of material and spiritual food as happen to drift in our direction, with little more power of taking an independent course, or of forming any general theory, than the polyps which are carried along by an oceanic current. Ask any man what he thinks of the world in which he is placed: whether, for example, it is on the whole a scene of happiness or misery, and he will either answer by some cut-and-dried fragments of what was once wisdom, or he will confine himself to a few incoherent details. He had a good dinner today and a bad toothache yesterday, and a family affliction or blessing the day before. But he is as incapable of summing up his impressions as an infant of performing an operation in the differential calculus. It is as rare as it is refreshing to find a man who can stand on his own legs and be conscious of his own feelings, who is sturdy enough to react as well as to transmit action, and lofty enough to raise himself above the hurrying crowd and have some distinct belief as to whence it is coming and whither it is going. Now Johnson, as one of the sturdiest of mankind, had the power due to a very distinct sentiment, if not to a very clear theory, about the world in which he lived. It had buffeted him severely enough, and he had formed a decisive estimate of its value. He was no man to be put off with mere phrases in place of opinions, or to accept doctrines which were not capable of expressing genuine emotion. To this it must be added that his emotions were as deep and tender as they were genuine. How sacred was his love for his old and ugly wife; how warm his sympathy wherever it could be effective; how manly the self-respect with which he guarded his dignity through all the temptations of Grub Street, need not be once more pointed out. Perhaps, however, it is worth while to notice the extreme rarity of such qualities. Many people, we think, love their fathers. Fortunately, that is true; but in how many people is filial affection strong enough to overpower the dread of eccentricity? How many men would have been capable of doing penance in Uttoxeter market years after their father's death for a long-passed act of disobedience? Most of us, again, would have a temporary emotion of pity for an outcast lying helplessly in the street. We should call the police, or send her in a cab to the workhouse, or, at least, write to the *Times* to denounce the defective arrangements of public charity. But it is perhaps better not to ask how many good Samaritans would take her on their shoulders to their own homes, care for her wants, and put her into a better way of life.

In the lives of most eminent men we find much good feeling and honourable conduct; but it is an exception, even in the case of good men, when we find that a life has been shaped by other than the ordinary conventions, or that emotions have dared to overflow the well-worn channels of respectability. The love which we feel for Johnson is due to the fact that the pivots upon which his life turned are invariably noble motives, and not mere obedience to custom. More than one modern writer has expressed a fraternal affection for Addison, and it is justified by the kindly humour which breathes through his *Essays*. But what anecdote of that most decorous and successful person touches our hearts or has the heroic ring of Johnson's wrestlings with adverse fortune? Addison showed how a Christian could die—when his life has run smoothly through pleasant places, secretaryships of state, and marriages with countesses, and when nothing—except a few overdoses of port wine—has shaken his nerves or ruffled his temper. A far deeper emotion rises at the deathbed of the rugged old pilgrim, who has fought his way to peace in spite of troubles within and without, who has been jeered in Vanity Fair and has descended into the Valley of the Shadow of Death, and escaped with pain and difficulty from the clutches of Giant Despair. When the last feelings of such a man are tender, solemn, and simple, we feel ourselves in a higher presence than that of an amiable gentleman who simply died, as he lived, with consummate decorum.

On turning, however, from Johnson's life to his writings, from Boswell to the *Rambler*, it must be admitted that the shock is trying to our nerves. The *Rambler* has, indeed, high merits. The impression which it made upon his own generation proves the fact; for the reputation, however temporary, was not won by a concession to the fashions of the day, but to the influence of a strong judgment uttering itself through uncouth forms. The melancholy which colours its pages is the melancholy of a noble nature. The tone of thought reminds us of Bishop Butler, whose writings, defaced by a style even more tiresome, though less pompous than Johnson's, have owed their enduring reputation to a philosophical acuteness in which Johnson was certainly very deficient. Both of these great men, however, impress us by their deep sense of the evils under which humanity suffers, and their rejection of the superficial optimism of the day. Butler's sadness, undoubtedly, is that of a recluse, and Johnson's that of a man of the world; but the sentiment is fundamentally the same. It may be added, too, that here, as elsewhere, Johnson speaks with the sincerity of a man drawing upon his own experience. He announces himself as a scholar thrust out upon the world rather by necessity than choice; and a large proportion of the papers dwell upon the various sufferings of the literary class. Nobody could speak more feelingly of those sufferings, as no one had a closer personal acquaintance with them. But allowing to Johnson whatever credit is due to the man who performs one more variation on the old theme, *Vanitas vanitatum*, we must in candour admit that the *Rambler* has the one unpardonable fault: it is unreadable.

What an amazing turn it shows for commonplaces! That life is short, that marriages from mercenary motives produce unhappiness, that different men are virtuous in different degrees, that advice is generally ineffectual, that adversity has its uses, that fame is liable to suffer from detraction;—these and a host of other such maxims are of the kind upon which no genius and no depth of feeling can confer a momentary interest. Here and there, indeed, the pompous utterance invests them with an unlucky air of absurdity. "Let no man from this time," is the comment in one of his stories, "suffer his felicity to depend on the death of his aunt." Every actor, of course, uses the same dialect. A gay young gentleman tells us that he used to amuse his companions by giving them notice of his friends' oddities. "Every man," he says, "has some habitual contortion of body, or established mode of expression, which never fails to excite mirth if it be pointed out to notice. By premonition of these particularities, I secured our pleasantry." The feminine characters, Flirtillas, and Cleoras, and Euphelias, and Penthesileas, are, if possible, still more grotesque. Macaulay remarks that he wears the petticoat with as ill a grace as Falstaff himself. The reader, he thinks, will cry out with Sir Hugh, "I like not when a 'oman has a great peard! I spy a great peard under her muffler." Oddly enough Johnson gives the very same quotation; and goes on to warn his supposed correspondents that Phyllis must send no more letters from the Horse Guards; and that Belinda must "resign her pretensions to female elegance till she has lived three weeks without hearing the politics of Button's Coffee House." The Doctor was probably sensible enough of his own defects. And yet there is a

still more wearisome set of articles. In emulation of the precedent set by Addison, Johnson indulges in the dreariest of allegories. Criticism, we are told, was the eldest daughter of Labour and Truth, but at last resigned in favour of Time, and left Prejudice and False Taste to reign in company with Fraud and Mischief. Then we have the genealogy of Wit and Learning, and of Satire, the Son of Wit and Malice, and an account of their various quarrels, and the decision of Jupiter. Neither are the histories of such semi-allegorical personages as Almamoulin, the son of Nouradin, or of Anningait and Ayut, the Greenland lovers, much more refreshing to modern readers. That Johnson possessed humour of no mean order, we know from Boswell; but no critic could have divined his power from the clumsy gambols in which he occasionally recreates himself. Perhaps his happiest effort is a dissertation upon the advantage of living in garrets; but the humour struggles and gasps dreadfully under the weight of words.

> There are [he says] some who would continue blockheads [the Alpine Club was not yet founded], even on the summit of the Andes or the Peak of Teneriffe. But let not any man be considered as unimprovable till this potent remedy has been tried; for perhaps he was found to be great only in a garret, as the joiner of Aretæus was rational in no other place but his own shop.

How could a man of real power write such unendurable stuff? Or how, indeed, could any man come to embody his thoughts in the style of which one other sentence will be a sufficient example? As it is afterwards nearly repeated, it may be supposed to have struck his fancy. The remarks of the philosophers who denounce temerity are, he says,

> too just to be disputed and too salutary to be rejected; but there is likewise some danger lest timorous prudence should be inculcated till courage and enterprise are wholly repressed and the mind congested in perpetual inactivity by the fatal influence of frigorifick wisdom.

Is there not some danger, we ask, that the mind will be benumbed into perpetual torpidity by the influence of this soporific sapience? It is still true, however, that this Johnsonese, so often burlesqued and ridiculed, was, as far as we can judge, a genuine product. Macaulay says that it is more offensive than the mannerism of Milton or Burke, because it is a mannerism adopted on principle and sustained by constant effort. Facts do not confirm the theory. Milton's prose style seems to be the result of a conscious effort to run English into classical moulds. Burke's mannerism does not appear in his early writings, and we can trace its development from the imitation of Bolingbroke to the last declamation against the Revolution. But Johnson seems to have written Johnsonese from his cradle. In his first original composition, the preface to Father Lobo's *Abyssinia*, the style is as distinctive as in the *Rambler*. The Parliamentary reports in the *Gentleman's Magazine* make Pitt and Fox express sentiments which are probably their own in language, which is as unmistakably Johnson's. It is clear that his style, good or bad, was the same from his earliest efforts. It is only in his last book, the *Lives of the Poets*, that the mannerism, though equally marked, is so far subdued as to be tolerable. What he himself called his habit of using "too big words and too many of them" was no affectation, but as much the result of his special idiosyncrasy as his queer gruntings and twitchings. Sir Joshua Reynolds indeed maintained, and we may believe so attentive an observer, that his strange physical contortions were the result of bad habit, not of actual disease.

Johnson, he said, could sit as still as other people when his attention was called to it. And possibly, if he had tried, he might have avoided the fault of making "little fishes talk like whales." But how did the bad habits arise? According to Boswell, Johnson professed to have "formed his style" partly upon Sir W. Temple, and on *Chambers's Proposal for his Dictionary*. The statement was obviously misinterpreted: but there is a glimmering of truth in the theory that the "style was formed"—so far as those words have any meaning—on the "giants of the seventeenth century," and especially upon Sir Thomas Browne. Johnson's taste, in fact, had led him to the study of writers in many ways congenial to him. His favourite book, as we know, was Burton's *Anatomy of Melancholy*. The pedantry of the older school did not repel him; the weighty thought rightly attracted him; and the more complex structure of sentence was perhaps a pleasant contrast to an ear saturated with the Gallicised neatness of Addison and Pope. Unluckily, the secret of the old majestic cadence was hopelessly lost. Johnson though spiritually akin to the giants, was the firmest ally and subject of the dwarfish dynasty which supplanted them. The very faculty of hearing seems to change in obedience to some mysterious law at different stages of intellectual development; and that which to one generation is delicious music is to another a mere droning of bagpipes or the grinding of monotonous barrel-organs.

Assuming that a man can find perfect satisfaction in the versification of the *Essay on Man*, we can understand his saying of "Lycidas," that "the diction is harsh, the rhymes uncertain, and the numbers unpleasing." In one of the *Ramblers* we are informed that the accent in blank verse ought properly to rest upon every second syllable throughout the whole line. A little variety must, he admits, be allowed to avoid satiety; but all lines which do not go in the steady jog-trot of alternate beats as regularly as the piston of a steam engine, are more or less defective. This simple-minded system naturally makes wild work with the poetry of the "mighty-mouthed inventor of harmonies." Milton's harsh cadences are indeed excused on the odd ground that he who was "vindicating the ways of God to man" might have been condemned for "lavishing much of his attention upon syllables and sounds." Moreover, the poor man did his best by introducing sounding proper names, even when they "added little music to his poem:" an example of this feeble though well-meant expedient being the passage about the moon, which—

> The Tuscan artist views
> At evening, from the top of Fiesole
> Or in Valdarno, to descry new lands, etc.

This profanity passed at the time for orthodoxy. But the misfortune was, that Johnson, unhesitatingly subscribing to the rules of Queen Anne's critics, is always instinctively feeling after the grander effects of the old school. Nature prompts him to the stateliness of Milton, whilst art orders him to deal out long and short syllables alternately, and to make them up in parcels of ten, and then tie the parcels together in pairs by the help of a rhyme. The natural utterance of a man of strong perceptions, but of unwieldy intellect, of a melancholy temperament, and capable of very deep, but not vivacious emotions, would be in stately and elaborate phrases. His style was not more distinctly a work of art than the style of Browne or Milton, but, unluckily, it was a work of bad art. He had the misfortune, not so rare as it may sound, to be born in the wrong century; and is, therefore, a giant in fetters; the amplitude of stride is still there, but it is checked into mechanical regularity. A similar phenomenon is observable in other writers of the time. The blank verse of Young, for example, is generally set to Pope's tune with the omission of the rhymes, whilst Thomson, revolting more or less consciously against the canons of his time, too often falls into mere pompous mouthing. Shaftesbury, in the previous generation, trying to write poetical prose, becomes as pedantic as Johnson, though in a different style; and Gibbon's mannerism is a familiar example of a similar escape from a monotonous simplicity into awkward complexity. Such writers are like men who have been chilled by what Johnson would call the "frigorifick" influence of the classicism of their fathers, and whose numbed limbs move stiffly and awkwardly in a first attempt to regain the old liberty. The form, too, of the *Rambler* is unfortunate. Johnson has always Addison before his eyes; to whom it was formerly the fashion to compare him for the same excellent reason which has recently suggested comparisons between Dickens and Thackeray—namely, that their works were published in the same external shape. Unluckily Johnson gave too much excuse for the comparison by really imitating Addison. He has to make allegories and to give lively sketches of feminine peculiarities and to ridicule social foibles of which he was, at most, a distant observer. The inevitable consequence is, that though here and there we catch a glimpse of the genuine man, we are, generally, too much provoked by the awkwardness of his costume to be capable of enjoying, or even reading him.

In many of his writings, however, Johnson manages, almost entirely, to throw off these impediments. In his deep capacity for sympathy and reverence, we recognise some of the elements that go to the making of a poet. He is always a man of intuitions rather than of discursive intellect; often keen of vision, though wanting in analytical power. For poetry, indeed, as it is often understood now, or even as it was understood by Pope, he had little enough qualification. He had not the intellectual vivacity implied in the marvellously neat workmanship of Pope, and still less the delight in all natural and artistic beauty which we generally take to be essential to poetic excellence. His contempt for *Lycidas* is sufficently significant upon that head. Still more characteristic is the incapacity to understand Spenser, which comes out incidentally in his remarks upon some of those imitations, which even in the middle of the eighteenth century showed that sensibility to the purest form of poetry was not by any means extinct amongst us. But there is a poetry, though we sometimes seem to forget it, which is the natural expression of deep moral sentiment; and of this Johnson has written enough to reveal very genuine power. The touching verses upon the death of Levett are almost as pathetic as Cowper; and fragments of the two imitations of Juvenal have struck deep enough to be not quite forgotten. We still quote the lines about pointing a moral and adorning a tale, which conclude a really noble passage. We are too often reminded of his melancholy musings over the

> Fears of the brave and follies of the wise,

and a few of the concluding lines of the *Vanity of Human Wishes*, in which he answers the question whether man must of necessity

> Roll darkling down the torrent of his fate,

in helplessness and ignorance, may have something of a familiar ring. We are to give thanks, he says,

> For love, which scarce collective man can fill;
> For patience, sovereign o'er transmuted ill;
> For faith, that, panting for a happier seat,
> Counts death kind nature's signal for retreat;

These goods for man, the laws of heaven ordain,
These goods He grants, who grants the power to gain,
With these celestial wisdom calms the mind,
And makes the happiness she does not find.

These lines, and many others which might be quoted, are noble in expression, as well as lofty and tender in feeling. Johnson, like Wordsworth, or even more deeply than Wordsworth, had felt all the "heavy and the weary weight of all this unintelligible world;" and, though he stumbles a little in the narrow limits of his versification, he bears himself nobly, and manages to put his heart into his poetry. Coleridge's paraphrase of the well-known lines, "Let observation with extensive observation, observe mankind from China to Peru," would prevent us from saying that he had thrown off his verbiage. He has not the felicity of Goldsmith's *Traveller*, though he wrote one of the best couplets in that admirable poem; but his ponderous lines show genuine vigour, and can be excluded from poetry only by the help of an arbitrary classification.

The fullest expression, however of Johnson's feeling is undoubtedly to be found in *Rasselas*. The inevitable comparison with Voltaire's *Candide*, which, by an odd coincidence, appeared almost simultaneously, suggests some curious reflections. The resemblance between the moral of the two books is so strong that, as Johnson remarked, it would have been difficult not to suppose that one had given a hint to the other but for the chronological difficulty. The contrast, indeed, is as marked as the likeness. *Candide* is not adapted for family reading, whereas *Rasselas* might be a textbook for young ladies studying English in a convent. *Candide* is a marvel of clearness and vivacity; whereas to read *Rasselas* is about as exhilarating as to wade knee-deep through a sandy desert. Voltaire and Johnson, however, the great sceptic and the last of the true old Tories, coincide pretty well in their view of the world, and in the remedy which they suggest. The world is, they agree, full of misery, and the optimism which would deny the reality of the misery is childish. *Il faut cultiver notre jardin* is the last word of *Candide*, and Johnson's teaching, both here and elsewhere, may be summed up in the words "Work, and don't whine." It need not be considered here, nor, perhaps, is it quite plain, what speculative conclusions Voltaire meant to be drawn from his teaching. The peculiarity of Johnson is, that he is apparently indifferent to any such conclusion. A dogmatic assertion, that the world is on the whole a scene of misery, may be pressed into the service of different philosophies. Johnson asserted the opinion resolutely, both in writing and in conversation, but apparently never troubled himself with any inferences but such as have a directly practical tendency. He was no "speculatist"—a word which now strikes us as having an American twang, but which was familiar to the lexicographer. His only excursion to the borders of such regions was in the very forcible review of Soane Jenyns, who had made a jaunty attempt to explain the origin of evil by the help of a few of Pope's epigrams. Johnson's sledge-hammer smashes his flimsy platitudes to pieces with an energy too good for such a foe. For speculation, properly so called, there was no need. The review, like *Rasselas*, is simply a vigorous protest against the popular attempt to make things pleasant by a feeble dilution of the most watery kind of popular teaching. He has no trouble in remarking that the evils of poverty are not alleviated by calling it "want of riches," and that there is a poverty which involves want of necessaries. The offered consolation, indeed, came rather awkwardly from the elegant country gentleman to the poor scholar who had just known by experience what it was to live upon fourpence-halfpenny a day. Johnson resolutely looks facts in the face, and calls ugly things by their right names. Men, he tells us over and over again, are wretched, and there is no use in denying it. This doctrine appears in his familiar talk, and even in the papers which he meant to be light reading. He begins the prologue to a comedy with the words—

Pressed with the load of life, the weary mind
Surveys the general toil of human kind.

In the *Life of Savage* he makes the common remark that the lives of many of the greatest teachers of mankind have been miserable. The explanation to which he inclines is that they have not been more miserable than their neighbours, but that their misery has been more conspicuous. His melancholy view of life may have been caused simply by his unfortunate constitution; for everybody sees in the disease of his own liver a disorder of the universe; but it was also intensified by the natural reaction of a powerful nature against the fluent optimism of the time, which expressed itself in Pope's aphorism, "Whatever is, is right." The strongest men of the time revolted against that attempt to cure a deep-seated disease by a few fine speeches. The form taken by Johnson's revolt is characteristic. His nature was too tender and too manly to incline to Swift's misanthropy. Men might be wretched, but he would not therefore revile them as filthy Yahoos. He was too reverent and cared too little for abstract thought to share the scepticism of Voltaire. In this miserable world the one worthy object of ambition is to do one's duty, and the one consolation deserving the name is to be found in religion. That Johnson's religious opinions sometimes took the form of rather grotesque superstition may be true; and it is easy enough to ridicule some of its manifestations. He took the creed of his day without much examination of the evidence upon which its dogmas rested; but a writer must be thoughtless indeed who should be more inclined to laugh at his superficial oddities, than to admire the reverent spirit and the brave self-respect with which he struggled through a painful life. The protest of *Rasselas* against optimism is therefore widely different from the protest of Voltaire. The deep and genuine feeling of the Frenchman is concealed under smart assaults upon the dogmas of popular theology; the Englishman desires to impress upon us the futility of all human enjoyments, with a view to deepen the solemnity of our habitual tone of thought. It is true, indeed, that the evil is dwelt upon more forcibly than the remedy. The book is all the more impressive. We are almost appalled by the gloomy strength which sees so forcibly the misery of the world and rejects so unequivocally all the palliatives of sentiment and philosophy. The melancholy is intensified by the ponderous style, which suggests a man weary of a heavy burden. The air seems to be filled with what Johnson once called "inspissated gloom." *Rasselas*, one may say, has a narrow escape of being a great book, though it is ill calculated for the hasty readers of to-day. Indeed, the defects are serious enough. The class of writing to which it belongs demands a certain dramatic picturesqueness to point the moral effectively. Not only the long-winded sentences, but the slow evolution of thought and the deliberation with which he works out his pictures of misery, makes the general effect dull beside such books as *Candide* or *Gulliver's Travels*. A touch of epigrammatic exaggeration is very much needed; and yet anybody who has the courage to read it through will admit that Johnson is not an unworthy guide into those gloomy regions of imagination which we all visit sometimes, and which it is as well to visit in good company.

After his fashion, Johnson is a fair representative of Greatheart. His melancholy is distinguished from that of feebler men by the strength of the conviction that "it will do no good to whine." We know his view of the great prophet of the Revolutionary school.

> Rousseau [he said, to Boswell's astonishment] is a very bad man. I would sooner sign a sentence for his transportation than that of any felon who has gone from the Old Bailey these many years. Yes, I should like to have him work in the plantations.

That is a fine specimen of the good Johnsonese prejudices of which we hear so much; and, of course, it is easy to infer that Johnson was an ignorant bigot, who had not in any degree taken the measure of the great moving forces of his time. Nothing, indeed, can be truer than that Johnson cared very little for the new gospel of the rights of man. His truly British contempt for all such fancies ("for anything I see," he once said, "foreigners are fools") is one of his strongest characteristics. Now, Rousseau and his like took a view of the world as it was quite as melancholy as Johnson's. They inferred that it ought to be turned upside down, assured that the millennium would begin as soon as a few revolutionary dogmas were accepted. All their remedies appeared to the excellent Doctor as so much of that cant of which it was a man's first duty to clear his mind. The evils of life were far too deeply seated to be caused or cured by kings or demagogues. One of the most popular commonplaces of the day was the mischief of luxury. That we were all on the high road to ruin on account of our wealth, our corruption, and the growth of the national debt, was the text of any number of political agitators. The whole of this talk was, to his mind, so much whining and cant. Luxury did no harm, and the mass of the people, as indeed was in one sense obvious enough, had only too little of it. The pet "state of nature" of theorists was a silly figment. The genuine savage was little better than an animal; and a savage woman, whose contempt for civilised life had prompted her to escape to the forest, was simply a "speaking cat." The natural equality of mankind was mere moonshine. So far is it from being true, he says, that no two people can be together for half an hour without one acquiring an evident superiority over the other. Subordination is an essential element of human happiness. A Whig stinks in his nostrils because to his eye modern Whiggism is "a negation of all principles." As he said of Priestley's writings, it unsettles everything and settles nothing. "He is a cursed Whig, a *bottomless* Whig as they all are now," was his description apparently of Burke. Order, in fact, is a vital necessity; what particular form it may take matters comparatively little; and therefore all revolutionary dogmas were chimerical as an attack upon the inevitable conditions of life, and mischievous so far as productive of useless discontent. We need not ask what mixture of truth and falsehood there may be in these principles. Of course, a Radical, or even a respectable Whig, like Macaulay, who believed in the magical efficacy of the British Constitution, might shriek or laugh at such doctrine. Johnson's political pamphlets, besides the defects natural to a writer who was only a politician by accident, advocate the most retrograde doctrines. Nobody at the present day thinks that the Stamp Act was an admirable or justifiable measure; or would approve of telling the Americans that they ought to have been grateful for their long exemption instead of indignant at the imposition. "We do not put a calf into the plough; we wait till he is an ox"—was not a judicious taunt. He was utterly wrong; and, if everybody who is utterly wrong in a political controversy deserves unmixed contempt, there is no more to be said for him. We might indeed argue that Johnson was in some ways entitled to the sympathy of

enlightened people. His hatred of the Americans was complicated by his hatred of slave-owners. He anticipated Lincoln in proposing the emancipation of the negroes as a military measure. His uniform hatred for the slave trade scandalised poor Boswell, who held that its abolition would be equivalent to "shutting the gates of mercy on mankind." His language about the blundering tyranny of the English rule in Ireland would satisfy Mr. Froude, though he would hardly have loved a Home Ruler. He denounces the frequency of capital punishment and the harshness of imprisonment for debt, and he invokes a compassionate treatment of the outcasts of our streets as warmly as the more sentimental Goldsmith. His conservatism may be at times obtuse, but it is never of the cynical variety. He hates cruelty and injustice as righteously as he hates anarchy. Indeed, Johnson's contempt for mouthing agitators of the Wilkes and Junius variety is one which may be shared by most thinkers who would not accept his principles. There is a vigorous passage in the *False Alarm* which is scarcely unjust to the patriots of the day. He describes the mode in which petitions are generally got up. They are sent from town to town, and the people flock to see what is to be sent to the king.

> One man signs because he hates the Papists; another because he has vowed destruction to the turnpikes; one because it will vex the parson; another because he owes his landlord nothing; one because he is rich; another because he is poor; one to show that he is not afraid, and another to show that he can write.

The people, he thinks, are as well off as they are likely to be under any form of government; and grievances about general warrants or the rights of juries in libel cases are not really felt so long as they have enough to eat and drink and wear. The error, we may probably say, was less in the contempt for a very shallow agitation than in the want of perception that deeper causes of discontent were accumulating in the background. Wilkes in himself was a worthless demagogue; but Wilkes was the straw carried by the rising tide of revolutionary sentiment, to which Johnson was entirely blind. Yet whatever we may think of his political philosophy, the value of these solid sturdy prejudices is undeniable. To the fact that Johnson was the typical representative of a large class of Englishmen, we owe it that the Society of Rights did not develop into a Jacobin Club. The fine phrases on which Frenchmen became intoxicated never turned the heads of men impervious to abstract theories and incapable of dropping substances for shadows. There are evils in each temperament; but it is as well that some men should carry into politics that rooted contempt for whining which lay so deep in Johnson's nature. He scorned the sickliness of the Rousseau school as, in spite of his constitutional melancholy, he scorned valetudinarianism whether of the bodily or the spiritual order. He saw evil enough in the world to be heartily, at times too roughly, impatient of all fine ladies who made a luxury of grief or of demagogues who shrieked about theoretical grievances which did not sensibly affect the happiness of one man in a thousand. The lady would not have time to nurse her sorrows if she had been a washer-woman; the grievances with which the demagogues yelled themselves hoarse could hardly be distinguished amidst the sorrows of the vast majority condemned to keep starvation at bay by unceasing labour. His incapacity for speculation makes his pamphlets worthless beside Burke's philosophical discourses; but the treatment, if wrong and defective on the theoretical side, is never contemptible. Here, as elsewhere, he judges by his intuitive aversions. He rejects too hastily whatever seems insipid or ill-flavoured to his spiritual appetite. Like all the shrewd and sensible part of mankind he condemns as mere moonshine what may be really the first faint dawn of a new daylight. But then his intuitions are noble, and his fundamental belief is the vital importance of order, of religion, and of morality, coupled with a profound conviction, surely not erroneous, that the chief sources of human suffering lie far deeper than any of the remedies proposed by constitution-mongers and fluent theorists. The literary version of these prejudices or principles is given most explicitly in the *Lives of the Poets*—the book which is now the most readable of Johnson's performances, and which most frequently recalls his conversational style. Indeed, it is a thoroughly admirable book, and but for one or two defects might enjoy a much more decided popularity. It is full of shrewd sense and righteous as well as keen estimates of men and things. The *Life of Savage*, written in earlier times, is the best existing portrait of that large class of authors who, in Johnson's phrase, "hung loose upon society," in the days of the Georges. The Lives of Pope, Dryden, and others have scarcely been superseded, though much fuller information has since come to light; and they are all well worth reading. But the criticism, like the politics, is woefully out of date. Johnson's division between the shams and the realities deserves all respect in both cases, but in both cases he puts many things on the wrong side of the dividing line. His hearty contempt for sham pastorals and sham love-poetry will be probably shared by modern readers.

> Who will hear of sheep and goats and myrtle bowers and purling rivulets through five acts? Such scenes please barbarians in the dawn of literature, and children in the dawn of life, but will be for the most part thrown away as men grow wise and nations grow learned.

But elsewhere he blunders into terrible misapprehensions. Where he errs by simply repeating the accepted rules of the Pope school, he for once talks mere second-hand nonsense. But his independent judgments are interesting even when erroneous. His unlucky assault upon "Lycidas," already noticed, is generally dismissed with a pitying shrug of the shoulders.

> Among the flocks and copses and flowers appear the heathen deities; Jove and Phœbus, Neptune and Æolus, with a long train of mythological imagery, such as a college easily supplies. Nothing can less display knowledge, or less exercise invention, than to tell how a shepherd has lost his companions, and must now feed his flocks alone; how one god asks another god what has become of Lycidas, and how neither god can tell. He who thus grieves can excite no sympathy; he who thus praises will confer no honour.

Of course every tyro in criticism has his answer ready; he can discourse about the æsthetic tendencies of the *Renaissance* period, and explain the necessity of placing one's self at a writer's point of view and entering into the spirit of the time. He will add, perhaps, that "Lycidas" is a test of poetical feeling, and that he who does not appreciate its exquisite melody has no music in his soul. The same writer who will tell us all this, and doubtless with perfect truth, would probably have adopted Pope or Johnson's theory with equal confidence if he had lived in the last century. "Lycidas" repelled Johnson by incongruities, which, from his point of view, were certainly offensive. Most modern readers, I will venture to suggest, feel the same annoyances, though they have not the courage to avow them freely. If poetry is to be judged exclusively by the simplicity

and force with which it expresses sincere emotion, "Lycidas" would hardly convince us of Milton's profound sorrow for the death of King, and must be condemned accordingly. To the purely pictorial or musical effects of a poem Johnson was nearly blind; but that need not suggest a doubt as to the sincerity of his love for the poetry which came within the range of his own sympathies. Every critic is in effect criticising himself as well as his author; and I confess that to my mind an obviously sincere record of impressions however one-sided they may be, is infinitely refreshing, as revealing at least the honesty of the writer. The ordinary run of criticism generally implies nothing but the extreme desire of the author to show that he is open to the very last new literary fashion. I should welcome a good assault upon Shakespeare which was not prompted by a love of singularity; and there are half a dozen popular idols—I have not the courage to name them—a genuine attack upon whom I could witness with entire equanimity not to say some complacency. If Johnson's blunder in this case implied sheer stupidity, one can only say that honest stupidity is a much better thing than clever insincerity or fluent repetition of second-hand dogmas. But, in fact, this dislike of "Lycidas," and a good many instances of critical incapacity might be added, is merely a misapplication of a very sound principle. The hatred of cant and humbug and affectation of all vanity is a most salutary ingredient even in poetical criticism. Johnson, with his natural ignorance of that historical method, the exaltation of which threatens to become a part of our contemporary cant, made the pardonable blunder of supposing that what would have been gross affectation in Gray must have been affectation in Milton. His ear had been too much corrupted by the contemporary school to enable him to recognise beauties which would even have shone through some conscious affectation. He had the rare courage—for, even then, Milton was one of the tabooed poets—to say what he thought as forcibly as he could say it; and he has suffered the natural punishment of plain speaking. It must, of course, be admitted that a book embodying such principles is doomed to become more or less obsolete, like his political pamphlets. And yet, as significant of the writer's own character, as containing many passages of sound judgment, expressed in forcible language, it is still, if not a great book, really impressive within the limits of its capacity.

After this imperfect survey of Johnson's writings, it only remains to be noticed that all the most prominent peculiarities are the very same which give interest to his spoken utterances. The doctrine is the same, though the preacher's manner has changed. His melancholy is not so heavy-eyed and depressing in his talk, for we catch him at moments of excitement; but it is there, and sometimes breaks out emphatically and unexpectedly. The prospect of death often clouds his mind, and he bursts into tears when he thinks of his past sufferings. His hearty love of truth, and uncompromising hatred of cant in all its innumerable transmutations, prompt half his most characteristic sayings. His queer prejudices take a humorous form, and give a delightful zest to his conversation. His contempt for abstract speculation comes out when he vanquishes Berkeley, not with a grin, but by "striking his foot with mighty force against a large stone." His arguments, indeed, never seem to have owed much to such logic as implies systematic and continuous thought. He scarcely waits till his pistol misses fire to knock you down with the butt-end. The merit of his best sayings is not that they compress an argument into a phrase, but that they are vivid expressions of an intuitive judgment. In other words, they are always humorous rather than witty. He holds his own belief with so vigorous a grasp that all argumentative devices for loosening it seem to be thrown away. As Boswell says, he is through your body in an instant without any preliminary parade; he gives a deadly lunge, but cares little for skill of fence. "We know we are free and there's an end of it," is his characteristic summary of a perplexed bit of metaphysics; and he would evidently have no patience to wander through the labyrinths in which men like Jonathan Edwards delighted to perplex themselves. We should have been glad to see a fuller report of one of those conversations in which Burke "wound into a subject like a serpent" and contrast his method with Johnson's downright hitting. Boswell had not the power, even if he had the will, to give an adequate account of such a "wit combat."

That such a mind should express itself most forcibly in speech is intelligible enough. Conversation was to him not merely a contest, but a means of escape from himself. "I may be cracking my joke," he said to Boswell, "and cursing the sun: Sun, how I hate thy beams!" The phrase sounds exaggerated, but it was apparently his settled conviction that the only remedy for melancholy, except indeed the religious remedy, was in hard work or in the rapture of conversational strife. His little circle of friends called forth his humour as the House of Commons excited Chatham's eloquence; and both of them were inclined to mouth too much when deprived of the necessary stimulus. Chatham's set speeches were as pompous as Johnson's deliberate writing. Johnson and Chatham resemble the chemical bodies which acquire entirely new properties when raised beyond a certain degree of temperature. Indeed, we frequently meet touches of the conversational Johnson in his controversial writing. *Taxation no Tyranny* is at moments almost as pithy as Swift, though the style is never so simple. The celebrated Letter to Chesterfield, and the letter in which he tells MacPherson that he will not be "deterred from detecting what he thinks a cheat by the menaces of a ruffian," are as good specimens of the smashing repartee as anything in Boswell's reports. Nor, indeed, does his pomposity sink to mere verbiage so often as might be supposed. It is by no means easy to translate his ponderous phrases into simple words without losing some of their meaning. The structure of the sentences is compact, though they are too elaborately balanced and stuffed with superfluous antitheses. The language might be simpler, but it is not a mere sham aggregation of words. His written style, however faulty in other respects, is neither slipshod nor ambiguous, and passes into his conversational style by imperceptible degrees. The radical identity is intelligible, though the superficial contrast is certainly curious. We may perhaps say that his century, unfavourable to him as a writer, gave just what he required for talking. If, as is sometimes said, the art of conversation is disappearing, it is because society has become too large and diffuse. The good talker, as indeed the good artist of every kind, depends upon the tacit co-operation of the social medium. The chorus, as Johnson has himself shown very well in one of the *Ramblers*, is quite as essential as the main performer. Nobody talks well in London, because everybody has constantly to meet a fresh set of interlocutors, and is as much put out as a musician who has to be always learning a new instrument. A literary dictator has ceased to be a possibility, so far as direct personal influence is concerned. In the club, Johnson knew how every blow would tell, and in the rapid thrust and parry dropped the heavy style which muffled his utterances in print. He had to deal with concrete illustrations, instead of expanding into platitudinous generalities. The obsolete theories which impair the value of his criticism and his politics, become amusing in the form of pithy sayings, though they weary us when asserted in

formal expositions. His greatest literary effort, the *Dictionary*, has of necessity become antiquated in use, and, in spite of the intellectual vigour indicated, can hardly be commended for popular reading. And thus but for the inimitable Boswell, it must be admitted that Johnson would probably have sunk very deeply into oblivion. A few good sayings would have been preserved by Mrs. Thrale and others, or have been handed down by tradition, and doubtless assigned in process of time to Sydney Smith and other conversational celebrities. A few couplets from the *Vanity of Human Wishes* would not yet have been submerged, and curious readers would have recognised the power of *Rasselas* and been delighted with some shrewd touches in the *Lives of the Poets*. But with all desire to magnify critical insight, it must be admitted that that man would have shown singular penetration, and been regarded as an eccentric commentator, who had divined the humour and the fervour of mind which lay hid in the remains of the huge lexicographer. And yet when we have once recognised his power, we can see it everywhere indicated in his writings, though by an unfortunate fatality the style or the substance was always so deeply affected by the faults of the time, that the product is never thoroughly sound. His tenacious conservatism caused him to cling to decaying materials for the want of anything better, and he has suffered the natural penalty. He was a great force half wasted, so far as literature was concerned, because the fashionable costume of the day hampered the free exercises of his powers, and because the only creeds to which he could attach himself were in the phase of decline and inanition. A century earlier or later he might have succeeded in expressing himself through books as well as through his talk; but it is not given to us to choose the time of our birth, and some very awkward consequences follow.

MATTHEW ARNOLD
From "Johnson's Lives"
Macmillan's Magazine, June 1878, pp. 153–60

Da mihi, Domine, scire quod sciendum est—"Grant that the knowledge I get may be the knowledge which is worth having!"—the spirit of that prayer ought to rule our education. How little it does rule it, every discerning man will acknowledge. Life is short, and our faculties of attention and of recollection are limited; in education we proceed as if our life were endless, and our powers of attention and recollection inexhaustible. We have not time or strength to deal with half of the matters which are thrown upon our minds, and they prove a useless load to us. When some one talked to Themistocles of an art of memory, he answered: "Teach me rather to forget!" The sarcasm well criticises the fatal want of proportion between what we put into our minds and their real needs and powers.

From the time when first I was led to think about education, this want of proportion is what has most struck me. It is the great obstacle to progress, yet it is by no means remarked and contended against as it should be. It hardly begins to present itself until we pass beyond the strict elements of education—beyond the acquisition, I mean, of reading, of writing, and of calculating so far as the operations of common life require. But the moment we pass beyond these, it begins to appear. Languages, grammar, literature, history, geography, mathematics, the knowledge of nature—what of these is to be taught, how much, and how? There is no clear, well-grounded consent. The same with religion. Religion is surely to be taught, but what of it is to be taught, and how? A clear, well-grounded consent is again wanting. And taught in such fashion as things are now, how often must a candid and sensible man, if he could be offered an art of memory to secure all that he has learned of them, as to a very great deal of it be inclined to say with Themistocles: "Teach me rather to forget!"

In England the common notion seems to be that education is advanced in two ways principally: by for ever adding fresh matters of instruction, and by preventing uniformity. I should be inclined to prescribe just the opposite course; to prescribe a severe limitation of the number of matters taught, a severe uniformity in the line of study followed. Wide ranging, and the multiplication of matters to be investigated, belong to private study, to the development of special aptitudes in the individual learner, and to the demands which they raise in him. But separate from all this should be kept the broad plain lines of study for almost universal use. I say *almost* universal, because they must of necessity vary a little with the varying conditions of men. Whatever the pupil finds set out for him upon these lines, he should learn; therefore it ought not to be too much in quantity. The essential thing is that it should be well chosen. If once we can get it well chosen, the more uniformly it can be kept to, the better. The teacher will be more at home; and besides, when we have got what is good and suitable, there is small hope of gain, and great certainty of risk, in departing from it.

No such lines are laid out, and perhaps no one could be trusted to lay them out authoritatively. But to amuse oneself with laying them out in fancy is a good exercise for one's thoughts. One may lay them out for this or that description of pupil, in this or that branch of study. The wider the interest of the branch of study taken, and the more extensive the class of pupils concerned, the better for our purpose. Suppose we take the department of letters. It is interesting to lay out in one's mind the ideal line of study to be followed by all who have to learn Latin and Greek. But it is still more interesting to lay out the ideal line of study to be followed by all who are concerned with that body of literature which exists in English, because this class is so much more numerous amongst us. The thing would be, one imagines, to begin with a very brief introductory sketch of our subject; then to fix a certain series of works to serve as what the French, taking an expression from the builder's business, call *points de repère*—points which stand as so many natural centres, and by returning to which we can always find our way again, if we are embarrassed; finally, to mark out a number of illustrative and representative works, connecting themselves with each of these *points de repère*. In the introductory sketch we are amongst generalities, in the group of illustrative works we are amongst details; generalities and details have, both of them, their perils for the learner. It is evident that, for purposes of education, the most important parts by far in our scheme are what we call the *points de repère*. To get these rightly chosen and thoroughly known is the great matter. For my part, in thinking of this or that line of study which human minds follow, I feel always prompted to seek, first and foremost, the leading *points de repère* in it.

In editing for the use of the young the group of chapters which are now commonly distinguished as those of the Babylonian Isaiah, I drew attention to their remarkable fitness for serving as a point of this kind to the student of universal history. But a work which by many is regarded as simply and solely a document of religion, there is difficulty, perhaps, in employing for historical and literary purposes. With works of a secular character one is on safer ground. And for years past, whenever I have had occasion to use Johnson's *Lives of the*

Poets, the thought has struck me how admirable a *point de repère*, or fixed centre of the sort described above, these lives might be made to furnish for the student of English literature. If we could but take, I have said to myself, the most important of the lives in Johnson's volumes, and leave out all the rest, what a text-book we should have! The volumes at present are a work to stand in a library, "a work which no gentleman's library should be without." But we want to get from them a text-book, to be in the hands of every one who desires even so much as a general acquaintance with English literature;—and so much acquaintance as this who does not desire? The work as Johnson published it is not fitted to serve as such a text-book; it is too extensive, and contains the lives of many poets quite insignificant. Johnson supplied lives of all whom the booksellers proposed to include in their collection of British Poets; he did not choose the poets himself, although he added two or three to those chosen by the booksellers. Whatever Johnson did in the department of literary biography and criticism possesses interest and deserves our attention. But in his *Lives of the Poets* there are six of pre-eminent interest; the lives of six men who, while the rest in the collection are of inferior rank, stand out as names of the first class in English literature—Milton, Dryden, Swift, Addison, Pope, Gray. These six writers differ among themselves, of course, in power and importance, and every one can see, that, if we were following certain modes of literary classification, Milton would have to be placed on a solitary eminence far above any of them. But if, without seeking a close view of individual differences, we form a large and liberal first class among English writers, all these six personages—Milton, Dryden, Swift, Addison, Pope, Gray—must, I think, be placed in it. Their lives cover a space of more than a century and a half, from 1608, the year of Milton's birth, down to 1771, the date of the death of Gray. Through this space of more than a century and a half the six lives conduct us. We follow the course of what Warburton well calls "the most agreeable subject in the world, which is literary history," and follow it in the lives of men of letters of the first class. And the writer of their lives is himself, too, a man of letters of the first class. Malone calls Johnson "the brightest ornament of the eighteenth century." He is justly to be called, at any rate, a man of letters of the first class, and the greatest power in English letters during the eighteenth century. And in these characteristic lives, not finished until 1781, and "which I wrote," as he himself tells us, "in my usual way, dilatorily and hastily, unwilling to work and working with vigour and haste," we have Johnson mellowed by years, Johnson in his ripeness and plentitude, treating the subject which he loved best and knew best. Much of it he could treat with the knowledge and sure tact of a contemporary; even from Milton and Dryden he was scarcely further separated than our generation is from Burns and Scott. Having all these recommendations, his *Lives of the Poets* do indeed truly stand for what Boswell calls them, "the work which of all Dr. Johnson's writings will perhaps be read most generally and with most pleasure." And in the lives of the six chief personages of the work, the lives of Milton, Dryden, Swift, Addison, Pope, and Gray, we have its very kernel and quintessence; we have the work relieved of whatever is less significant, retaining nothing which is not highly significant, brought within easy and convenient compass, and admirably fitted to serve as a *point de repère*, a fixed and thoroughly known centre of departure and return, to the student of English literature.

I know of no such first-rate piece of literature, for supplying in this way the wants of the literary student, existing at all in any other language; or existing in our own language, for any period except the period which Johnson's six lives cover. A student cannot read them without gaining from them, consciously or unconsciously, an insight into the history of English literature and life. He would find great benefit, let me add, from reading in connection with each biography something of the author with whom it deals; the first two books, say, of *Paradise Lost*, in connection with the life of Milton; *Absalom and Achitophel*, and the Dedication of the *Æneis*, in connection with the life of Dryden; in connection with Swift's life, the *Battle of the Books*; with Addison's, the *Coverley Papers*; with Pope's, the imitations of the *Satires* and *Epistles* of Horace. The *Elegy in a Country Churchyard* everybody knows, and will have it present to his mind when he reads the life of Gray. But of the other works which I have mentioned how little can this be said; to how many of us are Pope and Addison and Dryden and Swift, and even Milton himself, mere names, about whose date and history and supposed characteristics of style we may have learnt by rote something from a handbook, but of the real men and of the power of their works we know nothing! From Johnson's biographies the student will get a sense of what the real men were, and with this sense fresh in his mind he will find the occasion propitious for acquiring also, in the way pointed out, a sense of the power of their works.

This will seem to most people a very unambitious discipline. But the fault of most of the disciplines proposed in education is that they are by far too ambitious. Our improvers of education are almost always for proceeding by way of augmentation and complication; reduction and simplification, I say, is what is rather required. We give the learner too much to do, and we are over-zealous to tell him what he ought to think. Johnson himself has admirably marked the real line of our education through letters. He says in his life of Pope:— "Judgment is forced upon us by experience. He that reads many books must compare one opinion or one style with another; and when he compares, must necessarily distinguish, reject, and prefer." The aim and end of education through letters is to get this experience. Our being told by another what its results will properly be found to be, is not, even if we are told aright, at all the same thing as getting the experience for ourselves. The discipline, therefore, which puts us in the way of getting it, cannot be called an inconsiderable or ineffacacious one. We should take care not to imperil its acquisition by refusing to trust to it in its simplicity, by being eager to add, set right, and annotate. It is much to secure the reading, by young English people, of the lives of the six chief poets of our nation between the years 1650 and 1750, related by our foremost man of letters of the eighteenth century. It is much to secure their reading, under the stimulus of Johnson's interesting recital and forcible judgments, famous specimens of the authors whose lives are before them. Do not let us insist on also reviewing in detail and supplementing Johnson's work for them, on telling them what they ought really and definitively to think about the six authors and about the exact place of each in English literature. Perhaps our pupils are not ripe for it; perhaps, too, we have not Johnson's interest and Johnson's force; we are not the power in letters for our century which he was for his. We may be pedantic, obscure, dull, everything that bores, rather than everything that attracts; and so Johnson and his lives will repel, and will not be received, because we insist on being received along with them. Again, as we bar a learner's approach to Homer and Virgil by our *chevaux de frise* of elaborate grammar, so we are apt to stop his way to a piece of English literature by imbedding it in a mass of notes and additional matter. Mr. Croker's edition of Boswell's *Life of*

Johnson is a good example of the labour and ingenuity which may be spent upon a masterpiece, with the result, after all, really of rather encumbering than illustrating it. All knowledge may be in itself good, but this kind of editing seems to proceed upon the notion that we have only one book to read in the course of our life, or else that we have eternity to read in. What can it matter to our generation whether it was Molly Aston or Miss Boothby whose preference for Lord Lyttelton made Johnson jealous, and produced in his "Life of Lyttelton" a certain tone of disparagement? With the young reader, at all events, our great endeavour should be to bring him face to face with masterpieces, and to hold him there, not distracting or rebutting him with needless excursions or trifling details.

I should like, therefore, to reprint Johnson's six chief lives, simply as they are given in the edition in four volumes octavo,—the edition which passes for being the first to have a correct and complete text,—and to leave the lives, in that natural form, to have their effect upon the reader. I should like to think that a number of young people might thus be brought to know an important period of our literary and intellectual history, by means of the lives of six of its leading and representative authors, told by a great man. I should like to think that they would go on, under the stimulus of the lives, to acquaint themselves with some leading and representative work of each author. In the six lives they would at least have secured, I think, a most valuable *point de repère* in the history of our English life and literature, a point from which afterwards to find their way; whether they might desire to ascend upwards to our anterior literature, or to come downwards to the literature of yesterday and of the present.

The six lives cover a period of literary and intellectual movement in which we are all profoundly interested. It is the passage of our nation to prose and reason; the passage to a type of thought and expression, modern, European, and which on the whole is ours at the present day, from a type antiquated, peculiar, and which is ours no longer. The period begins with a prose like this of Milton: "They who to states and governors of the commonwealth direct their speech, high court of parliament! or wanting such access in a private condition, write that which they foresee may advance the public good; I suppose them, if at the beginning of no mean endeavour, not a little altered and moved inwardly in their minds." It ends with a prose like this of Smollett: "My spirit began to accommodate itself to my beggarly fate, and I became so mean as to go down towards Wapping, with an intention to inquire for an old schoolfellow, who, I understood, had got the command of a small coasting vessel then in the river, and implore his assistance." These are extreme instances; but they give us no unfaithful notion of the change in our prose between the reigns of Charles I. and George III. Johnson has recorded his own impression of the extent of the change and of its salutariness. Boswell gave him a book to read, written in 1702 by the English chaplain of a regiment stationed in Scotland. "It is sad stuff, sir," said Johnson, after reading it; "miserably written, as books in general then were. There is now an elegance of style universally diffused. No man now writes so ill as Martins' *Account of the Hebrides* is written. A man could not write so ill if he should try. Set a merchant's clerk now to write, and he'll do better." ⟨. . .⟩

Do not let us ⟨. . .⟩ hastily despise Johnson and his century for their defective poetry and criticism of poetry. True, Johnson is capable of saying: "Surely no man could have fancied that he read 'Lycidas' with pleasure had he not known the author!" True, he is capable of maintaining "that the description of the temple in Congreve's *Mourning Bride* was the finest poetical passage he had ever read—he recollected none in Shakespeare equal to it." But we are to conceive of Johnson and of his century as having a special task committed to them, the establishment of English prose; and as capable of being warped and narrowed in their judgments of poetry by this exclusive task. Such is the common course and law of progress; one thing is done at a time, and other things are sacrificed to it. We must be thankful for the thing done, if it is valuable, and we must put up with the temporary sacrifice of other things to this one. The other things will have their turn sooner or later. Above all, a nation with profound poetical instincts, like the English nation, may be trusted to work itself right again in poetry after periods of mistaken poetical practice. Even in the midst of an age of such practice, and with his style frequently showing the bad influence of it, Gray was saved, we may say, and remains a poet whose work has high and pure worth, simply by knowing the Greeks thoroughly, more thoroughly than any English poet had known them since Milton. Milton was a survivor from the great age of poetry; Dryden, Addison, Pope, and Swift were mighty workers for the age of prose. Gray, a poet in the midst of the age of prose, a poet, moreover, of by no means the highest force and of scanty productiveness, nevertheless claims a place among the six chief personages of Johnson's lives, because it was impossible for an English poet, even in that age, who knew the great Greek masters intimately, not to respond to their good influence, and to be rescued from the false poetical practice of his contemporaries. Of such avail to a nation are deep poetical instincts even in an age of prose. How much more may they be trusted to assert themselves after the age of prose has ended, and to remedy any poetical mischief done by it! And meanwhile the work of the hour, the necessary and appointed work, has been done, and we have got our prose.

Let us always bear in mind, therefore, that the century so well represented by Dryden, Addison, Pope, and Swift, and of which the literary history is so powerfully written by Johnson in his lives, is a century of prose—a century of which the great work in literature was the formation of English prose. Johnson was himself a labourer in this great and needful work, and was ruled by its influences. His blame of genuine poets like Milton and Gray, his over-praise of artificial poets like Pope, are to be taken as the utterances of a man who worked for an age of prose, who was ruled by its influences, and could not but be ruled by them. Of poetry he speaks as a man whose sense for that with which he is dealing is in some degree imperfect.

Yet even on poetry Johnson's utterances are valuable, because they are the utterances of a great and original man. That indeed he was; and to be conducted by such a man through an important century cannot but do us good, even though our guide may in some places be less competent than in others. Johnson was the man of an age of prose. Furthermore, he was a strong force of conservation and concentration, in an epoch which by its natural tendencies seemed moving towards expansion and freedom. But he was a great man, and great men are always instructive. The more we study him, the higher will be our esteem for the power of his mind, the width of his interests, the largeness of his knowledge, the freshness, fearlessness, and strength of his judgments. The higher, too, will be our esteem for his character. His well-known lines on Levett's death, beautiful and touching lines, are still more beautiful and touching because they recall a whole history of Johnson's goodness, tenderness, and charity. Human dignity, on the other hand, he maintained, we all know how well, through the whole long and arduous struggle of his life, from his servitor days at Oxford, down to the *Jam*

moriturus of his closing hour. His faults and strangenesses are on the surface, and catch every eye. But on the whole we have in him a good and admirable type, worthy to be kept in our view for ever, of "the ancient and inbred integrity, piety, good nature and good humour of the English people."

A volume giving us Johnson's Lives of Milton, Dryden, Swift, Addison, Pope, Gray, would give us, therefore, the compendious story of a whole important age in English literature, told by a great man, and in a performance which is itself a piece of English literature of the first class. If such a volume could but be prefaced by Lord Macaulay's *Life of Johnson*, it would be perfect.

AUGUSTINE BIRRELL
From "Dr. Johnson" (1885)
Obiter Dicta: Second Series
1887, pp. 126–48

Johnson the author is not always fairly treated. Phrases are convenient things to hand about, and it is as little the custom to inquire into the truth as it is to read the letterpress on banknotes. We are content to count banknotes, and to repeat phrases. One of these phrases is, that whilst everybody reads Boswell, nobody reads Johnson. The facts are otherwise. Everybody does not read Boswell, and a great many people do read Johnson. If it be asked, What do the general public know of Johnson's nine volumes octavo? I reply, Beshrew the general public! What in the name of the Bodleian has the general public got to do with literature? The general public subscribes to Mudie, and has its intellectual, like its lacteal sustenance, sent round to it in carts. On Saturdays these carts, laden with 'recent works in circulation,' traverse the Uxbridge Road; on Wednesdays they toil up Highgate Hill, and if we may believe the reports of travellers, are occasionally seen rushing through the wilds of Camberwell and bumping over Blackheath. It is not a question of the general public, but of the lover of letters. Do Mr. Browning, Mr. Arnold, Mr. Lowell, Mr. Trevelyan, Mr. Stephen, Mr. Morley, know their Johnson? 'To doubt would be disloyalty.' And what these big men know in their big way hundreds of little men know in their little way. We have no writer with a more genuine literary flavour about him than the great Cham of literature. No man of letters loved letters better than he. He knew literature in all its branches—he had read books, he had written books, he had sold books, he had bought books, and he had borrowed them. Sluggish and inert in all other directions, he pranced through libraries. He loved a catalogue; he delighted in an index. He was, to employ a happy phrase of Dr. Holmes, at home amongst books, as a stable-boy is amongst horses. He cared intensely about the future of literature and the fate of literary men. 'I respect Millar,' he once exclaimed; 'he has raised the price of literature.' Now Millar was a Scotchman. Even Horne Tooke was not to stand in the pillory: 'No, no, the dog has too much literature for that.' The only time the author of *Rasselas* met the author of the *Wealth of Nations* witnessed a painful scene. The English moralist gave the Scotch one the lie direct, and the Scotch moralist applied to the English one a phrase which would have done discredit to the lips of a costermonger; but this notwithstanding, when Boswell reported that Adam Smith preferred rhyme to blank verse, Johnson hailed the news as enthusiastically as did Cedric the Saxon the English origin of the bravest knights in the retinue of the Norman king. 'Did

Adam say that?' he shouted: 'I love him for it. I could hug him!' Johnson no doubt honestly believed he held George III. in reverence, but really he did not care a pin's fee for all the crowned heads of Europe. All his reverence was reserved for 'poor scholars.' When a small boy in a wherry, on whom had devolved the arduous task of rowing Johnson and his biographer across the Thames, said he would give all he had to know about the Argonauts, the Doctor was much pleased, and gave him, or got Boswell to give him, a double fare. He was ever an advocate of the spread of knowledge amongst all classes and both sexes. His devotion to letters has received its fitting reward, the love and respect of all 'lettered hearts.'

Considering him a little more in detail, we find it plain that he was a poet of no mean order. His resonant lines, informed as they often are with the force of their author's character—his strong sense, his fortitude, his gloom—take possession of the memory, and suffuse themselves through one's entire system of thought. A poet spouting his own verses is usually a figure to be avoided; but one could be content to be a hundred and thirty next birthday to have heard Johnson recite, in his full sonorous voice, and with his stately elocution, *The Vanity of Human Wishes*. When he came to the following lines, he usually broke down, and who can wonder?—

> Proceed, illustrious youth,
> And virtue guard thee to the throne of truth!
> Yet should thy soul indulge the gen'rous heat
> Till captive science yields her last retreat;
> Should reason guide thee with her brightest ray,
> And pour on misty doubt resistless day;
> Should no false kindness lure to loose delight,
> Nor praise relax, nor difficulty fright;
> Should tempting novelty thy cell refrain,
> And sloth effuse her opiate fumes in vain;
> Should beauty blunt on fops her fatal dart,
> Nor claim the triumph of a lettered heart;
> Should no disease thy torpid veins invade,
> Nor melancholy's phantoms haunt thy shade;
> Yet hope not life from grief or danger free,
> Nor think the doom of man revers'd for thee.
> Deign on the passing world to turn thine eyes,
> And pause a while from letters to be wise;
> There mark what ills the scholar's life assail,
> Toil, envy, want, the patron and the gaol
> See nations, slowly wise and meanly just,
> To buried merit raise the tardy bust.
> If dreams yet flatter, once again attend,
> Hear Lydiat's life, and Galileo's end.

If this be not poetry, may the name perish! ⟨. . .⟩

Johnson's prologues, and his lines on the death of Robert Levet, are well known. Indeed, it is only fair to say that our respected friend, the General Public, frequently has Johnsonian tags on its tongue:—

> Slow rises worth by poverty depressed.
> The unconquered lord of pleasure and of pain.
> He left the name at which the world grew pale
> To point a moral or adorn a tale.
> Death, kind nature's signal of retreat.
> Panting time toiled after him in vain.

All these are Johnson's, who, though he is not, like Gray, whom he hated so, all quotations, is yet oftener in men's mouths than they perhaps wot of.

Johnson's tragedy, *Irene*, need not detain us. It is unreadable; and to quote his own sensible words, 'It is useless to criticise what nobody reads.' It was indeed the expressed opinion of a contemporary, called Pot, that *Irene* was the finest tragedy of modern times; but on this judgment of Pot's being made known to Johnson, he was only heard to mutter, 'If Pot says so, Pot lies,' as no doubt he did.

Johnson's Latin Verses have not escaped the condemnation of scholars. Whose have? The true mode of critical approach to copies of Latin verse is by the question—How bad are they? Croker took the opinion of the Marquess Wellesley as to the degree of badness of Johnson's Latin Exercises. Lord Wellesley, as became so distinguished an Etonian, felt the solemnity of the occasion, and, after bargaining for secrecy, gave it as his opinion that they were all very bad, but that some perhaps were worse than others. To this judgment I have nothing to add.

As a writer of English prose, Johnson has always enjoyed a great, albeit a somewhat awful reputation. In childish memories he is constrained to be associated with dust and dictionaries, and those provoking obstacles to a boy's reading—'long words.' It would be easy to select from Johnson's writings numerous passages written in that essentially vicious style to which the name Johnsonese has been cruelly given; but the searcher could not fail to find many passages guiltless of this charge. The characteristics of Johnson's prose style are colossal good sense, though with a strong sceptical bias, good humour, vigorous language, and movement from point to point, which can only be compared to the measured tread of a well-drilled company of soldiers. Here is a passage from the Preface to Shakspeare:—'Notes are often necessary, but they are necessary evils. Let him that is yet unacquainted with the powers of Shakspeare, and who desires to feel the highest pleasure that the drama can give, read every play from the first scene to the last, with utter negligence of all his commentators. When his fancy is once on the wing, let it not stoop at correction or explanation. When his attention is strongly engaged, let it disdain alike to turn aside to the name of Theobald and of Pope. Let him read on, through brightness and obscurity, through integrity and corruption; let him preserve his comprehension of the dialogue and his interest in the fable. And when the pleasures of novelty have ceased, let him attempt exactness and read the commentators.'

Where are we to find better sense, or much better English?

In the pleasant art of chaffing an author Johnson has hardly an equal. De Quincey too often overdoes it. Macaulay seldom fails to excite sympathy with his victim. In playfulness Mr. Arnold perhaps surpasses the Doctor, but then the latter's playfulness is always leonine, whilst Mr. Arnold's is surely, sometimes, just a trifle kittenish. An example, no doubt a very good one, of Johnson's humour must be allowed me. Soame Jenyns, in his book on the *Origin of Evil*, had imagined that, as we have not only animals for food, but choose some for our diversion, the same privilege may be allowed to beings above us, 'who may deceive, torment, or destroy us for the ends only of their own pleasure.'

On this hint writes our merry Doctor as follows:—

'I cannot resist the temptation of comtemplating this analogy, which I think he might have carried farther, very much to the advantage of his argument. He might have shown that these "hunters, whose game is man," have many sports, analogous to our own. As we drown whelps or kittens they amuse themselves now and then with sinking a ship, and stand round the fields of Blenheim, or the walls of Prague, as we encircle a cockpit. As we shoot a bird flying, they take a man in the midst of his business or pleasure, and knock him down with an apoplexy. Some of them perhaps are virtuosi, and delight in the operations of an asthma, as a human philosopher in the effects of the air-pump. Many a merry bout have these frolick beings at the vicissitudes of an ague, and good sport it is to see a man tumble with an epilepsy, and revive, and tumble again, and all this he knows not why. The paroxysms of the gout and stone must undoubtedly make high mirth, especially if the play be a little diversified with the blunders and puzzles of the blind and deaf. . . . One sport the merry malice of these beings has found means of enjoying, to which we have nothing equal or similar. They now and then catch a mortal, proud of his parts, and flattered either by the submission of those who court his kindness, or the notice of those who suffer him to court theirs. A head thus prepared for the reception of false opinions, and the projection of vain designs, they easily fill with idle notions, till, in time, they make their plaything an author; their first diversion commonly begins with an ode or an epistle, then rises perhaps to a political irony, and is at last brought to its height by a treatise of philosophy. Then begins the poor animal to entangle himself in sophisms and to flounder in absurdity.'

The author of the philosophical treatise *A Free Inquiry into the Nature and Origin of Evil* did not at all enjoy this 'merry bout' of the 'frolick' Johnson.

The concluding paragraphs of Johnson's Preface to his *Dictionary* are historical prose; and if we are anxious to find passages fit to compare with them in the melancholy roll of their cadences and in their grave sincerity and manly emotion, we must, I think, take a flying jump from Dr. Johnson to Dr. Newman.

For sensible men the world offers no better reading than the *Lives of the Poets*. They afford an admirable example of the manner of man Johnson was. The subject was suggested to him by the booksellers, whom as a body he never abused. Himself the son of a bookseller, he respected their calling. If they treated him with civility, he responded suitably. If they were rude to him, he knocked them down. These worthies chose their own poets. Johnson remained indifferent. He knew everybody's poetry, and was always ready to write anybody's Life. If he knew the facts of a poet's life—and his knowledge was enormous on such subjects—he found room for them; if he did not, he supplied their place with his own shrewd reflections and sombre philosophy of life. It thus comes about that Johnson is every bit as interesting when he is writing about Sprat, or Smith, or Fenton, as he is when he has got Milton or Gray in hand. He is also much less provoking. My own favourite Life is that of Sir Richard Blackmore.

The poorer the poet the kindlier is the treatment he receives. Johnson kept all his rough words for Shakspeare, Milton, and Gray.

In this trait, surely an amiable one, he was much resembled by that eminent man the late Sir George Jessel, whose civility to a barrister was always in inverse ratio to the barrister's practice; and whose friendly zeal in helping young and nervous practitioners over the stiles of legal difficulty was only equalled by the fiery enthusiasm with which he thrust back the Attorney and Solicitor-General and people of that sort.

As a political thinker Johnson has not had justice. He has been lightly dismissed as the last of the old-world Tories. He was nothing of the sort. His cast of political thought is shared by thousands to this day. He represents that vast army of electors whom neither canvasser nor caucus has ever yet cajoled or bullied into a polling-booth. Newspapers may scold, platforms may shake; whatever circulars can do may be done,

all that placards can tell may be told; but the fact remains that one-third of every constituency in the realm shares Dr. Johnson's 'narcotic indifference,' and stays away.

It is, of course, impossible to reconcile all Johnson's recorded utterances with any one view of anything. When crossed in conversation or goaded by folly he was, like the prophet Habakkuk (according to Voltaire), *capable du tout*. But his dominant tone about politics was something of this sort. Provided a man lived in a state which guaranteed him private liberty and secured him public order, he was very much of a knave or altogether a fool if he troubled himself further. To go to bed when you wish, to get up when you like, to eat and drink and read what you choose, to say across your port or your tea whatever occurs to you at the moment, and to earn your living as best you may—this is what Dr. Johnson meant by private liberty. Fleet Street open day and night—this is what he meant by public order. Give a sensible man these, and take all the rest the world goes round. Tyranny was a bugbear. Either the tyranny was bearable, or it was not. If it was bearable, it did not matter; and as soon as it became unbearable the mob cut off the tyrant's head, and wise men went home to their dinner. To views of this sort he gave emphatic utterance on the well-known occasion when he gave Sir Adam Ferguson a bit of his mind. Sir Adam had innocently enough observed that the Crown had too much power. Thereupon Johnson:—

'Sir, I perceive you are a vile Whig. Why all this childish jealousy of the power of the Crown? The Crown has not power enough. When I say that all governments are alike, I consider that in no government power can be abused long; mankind will not bear it. If a sovereign oppresses his people, they will rise and cut off his head. There is a remedy in human nature against tyranny that will keep us safe under every form of government.'

This is not and never was the language of Toryism. It is a much more intellectual 'ism.' It is indifferentism. So, too, in his able pamphlet, *The False Alarm*, which had reference to Wilkes and the Middlesex election, though he no doubt attempts to deal with the constitutional aspect of the question, the real strength of his case is to be found in passages like the following:—

'The grievance which has produced all this tempest of outrage, the oppression in which all other oppressions are included, the invasion which has left us no property, the alarm that suffers no patriot to sleep in quiet, is comprised in a vote of the House of Commons, by which the freeholders of Middlesex are deprived of a Briton's birthright—representation in Parliament. They have, indeed, received the usual writ of election; but that writ, alas! was malicious mockery; they were insulted with the form, but denied the reality, for there was one man excepted from their choice. The character of the man, thus fatally excepted, I have no purpose to delineate. Lampoon itself would disdain to speak ill of him of whom no man speaks well. Every lover of liberty stands doubtful of the fate of posterity, because the chief county in England cannot take its representative from a gaol.'

Temperament was of course at the bottom of this indifference. Johnson was of melancholy humour and profoundly sceptical. Cynical he was not—he loved his fellow-men; his days were full of

> Little, nameless, unremembered acts
> Of kindness and of love.

But he was as difficult to rouse to enthusiasm about humanity as is Mr. Justice Stephen. He pitied the poor devils, but he did not believe in them. They were neither happy nor wise, and he saw no reason to believe they would ever become either. 'Leave me alone,' he cried to the sultry mob, bawling 'Wilkes and Liberty.' 'I at least am not ashamed to own that I care for neither the one nor the other.'

No man, however, resented more fiercely than Johnson any unnecessary interference with men who were simply going their own way. The Highlanders only knew Gaelic, yet political wiseacres were to be found objecting to their having the Bible in their own tongue. Johnson flew to arms: he wrote one of his monumental letters; the opposition was quelled, and the Gael got his Bible. So too the wicked interference with Irish enterprise, so much in vogue during the last century, infuriated him. 'Sir,' he said to Sir Thomas Robinson, 'you talk the language of a savage. What, sir! would you prevent any people from feeding themselves, if by any honest means they can do so?'

Were Johnson to come to life again, total abstainer as he often was, he would, I expect, denounce the principle involved in 'Local Option.' I am not at all sure he would not borrow a guinea from a bystander and become a subscriber to the 'Property Defence League;' and though it is notorious that he never read any book all through, and never could be got to believe that anybody else ever did, he would, I think, read a larger fraction of Mr. Spencer's pamphlet, '*Man* versus *the State*,' than of any other 'recent work in circulation.' The state of the Strand, when two vestries are at work upon it, would, I am sure, drive him into open rebellion.

As a letter-writer Johnson has great merits. Let no man despise the epistolary art. It is said to be extinct. I doubt it. Good letters were always scarce. It does not follow that, because our grandmothers wrote long letters, they all wrote good ones, or that nobody nowadays writes good letters because most people write bad ones. Johnson wrote letters in two styles. One was monumental—more suggestive of the chisel than the pen. In the other there are traces of the same style, but, like the old Gothic architecture, it has grown domesticated, and become the fit vehicle of plain tidings of joy and sorrow—of affection, wit, and fancy. The letter to Lord Chesterfield is the most celebrated example of the monumental style. From the letters to Mrs. Thrale many good examples of the domesticated style might be selected. ⟨. . .⟩

Johnson's literary fame is, in our judgment, as secure as his character. Like the stone which he placed over his father's grave at Lichfield, and which, it is shameful to think, has been removed, it is 'too massy and strong' to be ever much affected by the wind and weather of our literary atmosphere. 'Never,' so he wrote to Mrs. Thrale, 'let critcisms operate upon your face or your mind; it is very rarely that an author is hurt by his critics. The blaze of reputation cannot be blown out; but it often dies in the socket. From the author of *Fitzosborne's Letters* I cannot think myself in much danger. I met him only once, about thirty years ago, and in some small dispute soon reduced him to whistle.' Dr. Johnson is in no danger from anybody. None but Gargantua could blow him out, and he still burns brightly in his socket.

How long this may continue who can say? It is a far cry to 1985. Science may by that time have squeezed out literature, and the author of the *Lives of the Poets* may be dimly remembered as an odd fellow who lived in the Dark Ages, and had a very creditable fancy for making chemical experiments. On the other hand, the Spiritualists may be in possession, in which case the Cock Lane Ghost will occupy more of public attention than Boswell's hero, who will, perhaps, be reprobated as the profane utterer of these idle words: 'Suppose I

know a man to be so lame that he is absolutely incapable to move himself, and I find him in a different room from that in which I left him, shall I puzzle myself with idle conjectures, that perhaps his nerves have by some unknown change all at once become effective? No, sir, it is clear how he got into a different room—he was *carried*.'

We here part company with Johnson, bidding him a most affectionate farewell, and leaving him in undisturbed possession of both place and power. His character will bear investigation and some of his books perusal. The latter, indeed, may be submitted to his own test, and there is no truer one. A book, he wrote, should help us either to enjoy life or to endure it. His frequently do both.

GEORGE BIRKBECK HILL
"Dr. Johnson as a Radical"
Contemporary Review, June 1889, pp. 888–99

I happened to mention to a politician the other day my intention to write something on the Radical side of Dr. Johnson's character. "The Radical side!" he exclaimed; "you would require a microscope to discover it." As my friend belongs to that numerous class of men who talk confidently of Johnson without having first given themselves the trouble to read Boswell, I was not much moved by his opinion. I knew very well that from Johnson's writings and sayings it would be easy for me to gather more passages that have the true Radical ring than most people would find patience to read. I must admit that the very founder of modern Radicalism, Jeremy Bentham, failed to recognize in him a forerunner, though the two men, as I have but lately discovered, belonged to the same club—that City Club which met at the Queen's Arms in St. Paul's Churchyard. "Johnson," Boswell records, "told Mr. Hoole that he wished to have a City Club, and asked him to collect one; but said he, 'Don't let them be patriots.'" *Patriot*, it will be remembered, he defined in a late edition of his Dictionary, as "a factious disturber of the Government." Among the non-patriots who were thus gathered together was the founder of the Utilitarian philosophy, at that time about three-and-thirty years old, and still in politics a Tory. In his boyhood he had been so fortunate as to be present at the coronation of George III., and had described him as "a most beautiful person." Nay even, at an earlier time, by standing on tip-toe he had once to his ineffable delight caught sight of the top of the wig of his gracious Majesty George II. It is some satisfaction to me to reflect that as one of my uncles, who died but a few years ago, knew Bentham, I am separated but by two steps from that august vision. All the Radical philosopher's loyal feelings had long passed away when in his old age he came to describe the City Club. The poet who collected it he spoke of as "Tasso Hoole, one of Dr. Johnson's lickspittles." Johnson himself he called "the miserable and misery-propagating ascetic and instrument of despotism," "the pompous preacher of melancholy moralities." Yet the conversation might easily have taken such a turn as would have called forth a sentence, uttered "in the loud voice and with a slow, deliberate utterance" that would have scared the City Tories, and roused strange feelings in the future Radical leader. The talk might have fallen on slavery; a toast might have been called for, and Johnson might have startled "the very grave men" of London, as he had once startled "the very grave men" of Oxford, by drinking "to the next insurrection of the negroes in the West Indies." The talk might have fallen on Ireland, and

Johnson might have exclaimed—"Let the authority of the English government perish rather than be maintained by iniquity." The talk might have fallen on the miserable state of the crofters in the Hebrides, and Johnson might have lamented that "the chiefs were gradually degenerating from patriarchal rulers to rapacious landlords;" and he might have gone on to repeat his suggestion that "the general good requires that the landlords be for a time restrained in their demands, and kept quiet by pensions proportionate to their loss." Had emigration been suggested as a measure of relief, he might have remarked that "to hinder insurrection by driving away the people, and to govern peaceably by having no subjects, is an expedient that argues no great profundity of politics. . . . It affords a legislator little self-applause to consider that where there was formerly an insurrection there is now a wilderness." The talk might have turned on the savage cruelty of the criminal law, in the reform of which Bentham was to gain one of his noblest triumphs, and Johnson might have lifted up his voice once more, as he had lifted it up thirty years earlier, against "the legal massacre" which takes place "on the days when the prisons of this city are emptied into the grave." He might once more have pointed out "that all but murderers have at their last hour the common sensations of mankind pleading in their favour. . . . They who would rejoice at the correction of a thief are yet shocked at the thought of destroying him. His crime shrinks to nothing compared with his misery, and severity defeats itself by exciting pity." Bentham might have heard him take the part of the unhappy inmates of the debtors' prisons, and have felt the fire kindle within him as the old man said: "Let those whose writings form the opinions and the practices of their contemporaries endeavour to transfer the reproach of imprisonment from the debtor to the creditor, till universal infamy shall pursue the wretch whose wantonness of power, or revenge of disappointment, condemns another to torture and ruin; till he shall be hunted through the world as an enemy to man, and find in riches no shelter from contempt." Bentham might have been still further roused as he heard him maintain that "no scheme of policy has in any country yet brought the rich and poor on equal terms into courts of judicature."

In truth, there is no knowing what startling sentiments "the sensible, well-behaved company" which Boswell met at the Queen's Arms, under the shadow of the great Cathedral, might have heard fall from Johnson's lips, had fortune only proved favourable. It was well observed of him by one who had known him long: "In general you may tell what the man to whom you are speaking will say next. This you can never do of Johnson." How astonished, for instance, must the foolish Yorkshire baronet have looked—Long Sir Thomas Robinson—when, on his observing that certain laws, which were for the benefit of Ireland, might be prejudicial to the corn-trade of England, Johnson cried out—"Sir Thomas, you talk the language of a savage: what, sir, would you prevent any people from feeding themselves, if by any honest means they can do it?" It was this unexpectedness in his talk which gave it no small part of its interest. It was due not only to the great variety of ways in which he could regard and handle almost all questions, but also to the striking dissimilarities in his own character. Tory though he was, he was a man sprung from the people—not for one moment ashamed of his origin—to whom the people were ever dear; who made their happiness, and not the happiness of any one class, his sole standard of good government. "Where a great proportion of the people," he said, "are suffered to languish in helpless misery, that country must be ill-policed and wretchedly governed: a decent provision for the poor is the true test of civilization." "The true state

of every nation," he maintained at another time, "is the state of common life. . . . As the great mass of the people approach to delicacy a nation is refined; as their conveniences are multiplied, a nation, at least a commercial nation, must be denominated wealthy." "An English king," he wrote, "has no great right to quiet when his people are in misery."

He admitted the lawfulness of rebellion. "In no Government," he maintained, "can power be abused long. Mankind will not bear it. If a Sovereign oppresses his people to a great degree, they will rise up and cut off his head. There is a remedy in human nature against tyranny that will keep us safe under every form of Government." "If the abuse be enormous," he said on another occasion, "Nature will rise up, and claiming her original rights, overturn a corrupt political system." When he uttered these words he was not so very far removed from "the sacred right of insurrection" of the French Republicans; nor did he need Boswell's father to teach him that the good which Cromwell did was that "he gart kings ken that they had a lith in their neck." To the danger of irresponsible power he was fully alive. "There are few minds," he wrote, "to which tyranny is not delightful; power is nothing but as it is felt, and the delight of superiority is proportionate to the resistance overcome." He judged much more indulgently of peoples than of rulers. "Governors," he said, "being accustomed to hear of more crimes than they can punish, and more wrongs than they can redress, set themselves at ease by indiscriminate negligence, and presently forget the request when they lose sight of the petitioner." So patient are the common people, that "the general story of mankind will evince that lawful and settled authority is very seldom resisted when it is well employed. . . . Though men are drawn by their passions into forgetfulness of invisible rewards and punishments, yet they are easily kept obedient to those who have temporal dominion in their hands, till their veneration is dissipated by such wickedness and folly as can neither be defended nor concealed." He attacked the system under which the governors of our colonies were appointed, and compared it with that of the French. "To be a bankrupt at home, or to be so infamously vicious that he cannot be decently protected in his own country, seldom recommends any man to the government of a French colony."

For kings he often shows no great respect. He laughs at "the attendant on a Court, whose business is to watch the looks of a being weak and foolish as himself, and whose vanity is to recount the names of men who might drop into nothing and leave no vacuity." "Princes," he wrote, "are commonly the last by whom merit is distinguished." Speaking of Queen Mary, the wife of William III., he said: "Her character has hitherto had this great advantage that it has only been compared with that of kings." He defends monarchs against the reproach which had been cast on them that they show little care for posterity. "Are not pretenders, mock patriots, masquerades, operas, birthnights, treaties, conventions, reviews, drawing-rooms, the births of heirs and the deaths of queens, sufficient to overwhelm any capacity but that of a king?" "The acquisitions of kings," he says, "are always magnified." He accounts Frederick the Great fortunate in "the difficulties of his youth. . . . Kings, without this help from temporary infelicity, see the world in a mist, which magnifies everything near them, and bounds their view to a narrow compass, which few are able to extend by the mere force of curiosity."

When Voltaire "censured Shakespeare's kings as not completely royal—thinking, perhaps, that decency was violated when the Danish usurper is represented as a drunkard," Johnson replied that "Shakespeare knew that kings love wine like other men, and that wine exerts its natural power upon kings." In a note on *The Winter's Tale*, on a speech of Leontes, king of Sicilia, in which he suggests that instead of "fact" we should read "pack," he says: "Pack is a low, coarse word, well suited to the rest of this royal invective." When Theobald, in a note on another passage in the same play, says that "it is certainly too gross and blunt in Paulina to call the king downright a fool," Johnson writes: "Poor Mr. Theobald's courtly remark cannot be thought to deserve much notice." When some one spoke to him of George the Third's neglect of Reynolds, he said he thought it a matter of little consequence. "His Majesty's neglect could never do Sir Joshua any prejudice; but it would reflect eternal disgrace on the king not to have employed Sir Joshua Reynolds."

Some of his political definitions might have excited the envy even of Cobbett or of O'Connell—"*Pension*. In England it is generally understood to mean pay given to a State hireling for treason to his country." "*Excise*. A hateful tax levied upon commodities, and adjudged not by the common judges of property, but wretches hired by those to whom excise is paid." "*Favourite*. A mean wretch whose whole business is by any means to please."

He scoffs at "the little tyrants of the fields" as much as at the great tyrants of nations. He describes how "the pride which under the check of public observation would have been only vented among servants and domestics becomes in a country baronet the torment of a province, and instead of terminating in the destruction of chinaware and glasses, ruins tenants, dispossesses cottagers, and harasses villages with actions of trespass and bills of indictment." He has a hope, though but a faint hope, that he may excite men of rank "to prefer books and manuscripts to equipage and luxury, and to forsake noise and diversion for the conversation of the learned and the satisfaction of extensive knowledge." Very curious is the account which Mme. D'Arblay gives of his treatment of Fulk Greville, the "superb Greville," a man "who was," she says, "generally looked up to as the finest gentleman about town." This glorious being had wished to meet Johnson; and Dr. Burney accordingly had invited the two men to his house. Greville, to use Mme. D'Arblay's words—

> took the field with the aristocratic armour of pedigree and distinction. Aloof, therefore, he kept from all; and assuming his most supercilious air of distant superiority, planted himself immovable as a noble statue upon the hearth, as if a stranger to the whole set. . . . Johnson remained silent, composedly at first and afterwards abstractedly . . . completely absorbed in silent rumination; sustaining nevertheless a grave and composed demeanour, with an air by no means wanting in dignity any more than in urbanity. Very unexpectedly, however, ere the evening closed, he showed himself alive to what surrounded him by one of those singular starts of vision that made him seem at times—though purblind to things in common, and to things inanimate—gifted with an eye of instinct for espying any action or position that he thought merited reprehension; for all at once, looking fixedly on Mr. Greville, who, without much self-denial, the night being very cold, pertinaciously kept his station before the chimney-piece, he exclaimed: "If it were not for depriving the ladies of the fire, I should like to stand upon the hearth myself!" A smile gleamed upon every face at this pointed speech. Mr. Greville tried to smile himself, though faintly and scoffingly. He tried also to hold to his post . . . for two or three minutes he disdained to

move, but the awkwardness of a general pause impelled him ere long to glide back to his chair; but he rang the bell with force as he passed it, to order his carriage. It is probable that Dr. Johnson had observed the high air and mien of Mr. Greville, and had purposely brought forth that remark to disenchant him from his self-consequence.

Wars and conquests Johnson hated with a hatred worthy of John Bright. "I would wish," he writes, "Cæsar and Catiline, Xerxes and Alexander, Charles and Peter, huddled together in obscurity or detestation." Clive he described as a man who, "loaded" as he was "with wealth and honours, had acquired his fortune by such crimes, that his consciousness of them impelled him to cut his own throat." Lord Macaulay places Clive's name "in the list of those who have done and suffered much for the happiness of mankind." Mr. Bright, speaking in 1862 of our government in India, said: "I have always described it as a piratical joint-stock company, beginning with Lord Clive and ending, as I now hope it has ended, with Lord Dalhousie." How much nearer to Johnson is the Radical orator than the Whig historian? How the grand old Quaker would have applauded him when he maintained "that the martial character cannot prevail in a whole people but by the diminution of all other virtues." No less would he have praised his assertion that "among the calamities of war may be justly numbered the diminution of the love of truth by the falsehoods which interest dictates and credulity encourages. A peace will equally leave the warrior and relater of wars destitute of employment; and I know not whether more is to be dreaded from streets filled with soldiers accustomed to plunder, or from garrets filled with scribblers accustomed to lie." Johnson describes in a fable a mother vulture telling her little one, who had been watching a battle, that "man is the only beast who kills that which he does not devour, and this quality makes him so much a benefactor to our species." He scoffs at "the feudal gabble" of the great Earl of Chatham, who wished to plunge the nation into war for the possession of Falkland's Island—"a bleak and gloomy solitude, an island thrown aside from human use; stormy in winter and barren in summer; an island which not the southern savages have dignified with habitation. . . . This is the country," he continues, "of which we have now possession, and of which a numerous party pretends to wish that we had murdered thousands for the titular sovereignty"—"murdered," that is to say, in a war with Spain.

Had I space, I would quote the splendid passage in his "Falkland's Islands," in which he attacks "the coolness and indifference with which the greater part of mankind see war commenced," and teaches us that "the life of a modern soldier is ill-represented by heroic fiction." What a contrast to his hatred of war do we find in the pages of an early number of the great Whig Review—the Review of Jeffrey and Brougham, of Sidney Smith, and Francis Horner.

> The evils of increasing capital [writes the reviewer], like the evils of increasing population, are felt long before the case has become extreme, and a nation, it may be observed, is much more likely (at least in the present state of commercial policy) to suffer from increasing wealth than from increasing numbers of people. Are there no checks provided by the constitution of human nature and the construction of civil society for the one as well as for the other of these evils? Mr. Malthus has pointed out the manner in which the principle of population is counteracted, and we apprehend that causes nearly analogous will be found to check the progressive

increase of capital. Luxurious living and other kinds of unnecessary expenditure—above all, political expenses, and chiefly the expenses of war—appear to us to furnish those necessary checks to the indefinite augmentation of wealth, which there was reason *a priori* to suppose would be somewhere provided by the wise regulations of Nature.

This passage was written at a time when from bad harvests, war taxes, and corn laws, the people were on the brink of starvation. Johnson would have upbraided it as even more the language of a savage than the talk of Long Sir Thomas Robinson.

Should prolonged wars and extravagance have piled up the national debt, he was not troubled by Hume's fears that "inevitable ruin" must follow. "It was," he said, "an idle dream to suppose that the country could sink under the debt. Let the public creditors be ever so clamorous, the interest of millions must ever prevail over that of thousands." In other words, if the debt threatened to overwhelm the State, repudiation, partial or complete, must follow.

Writing about the approaching coronation of George III., he expresses the hope "that the number of foot-soldiers will be diminished, since it cannot but offend every Englishman to see troops of soldiers placed between him and his Sovereign, as if they were the most honourable of the people, or the king required guards to secure his person from his subjects. As their station makes them think themselves important, their insolence is always such as may be expected from servile authority; and the impatience of the people under such immediate oppression always produces quarrels, tumults, and mischief." In one of his *Idlers* he introduces "the second son of a gentleman whose estate was barely sufficient to support himself and his heir in the dignity of killing game;" the young man had, therefore, gone into the army. "I passed," he writes, "some years in the most contemptible of all human stations—that of a soldier in time of peace."

Cobden, in his pamphlets on our wars with Burmah, has not spoken more strongly against the annexation of that part of the Eastern peninsula than Johnson always spoke against conquest in every part of the globe. "I do not much wish well to discoveries," he said; "for I am always afraid they will end in conquest and robbery. To find a new country and to invade it has always been the same." Of Christopher Columbus he said that "no part of the world has yet had reason to rejoice that he found at last reception [at the Court of Spain] and employment. In the same year, in a year hitherto disastrous to mankind, by the Portuguese was discovered the passage of the Indies, and by the Spaniards the coast of America." It "was with great emotion," Boswell tells us, that he exclaimed, "I love the University of Salamanca; for when the Spaniards were in doubt as to the lawfulness of their conquering America, the University of Salamanca gave it as their opinion that it was not lawful." The war between the English and the French in America he looked upon as a contest in which "no honest man can heartily wish success to either party. . . . It is only the quarrel of two robbers for the spoils of a passenger." He introduces in a tale an Indian chief bidding his countrymen "remember that the death of every European delivers the country from a tyrant and a robber," and this he published when the story of Wolfe's conquest of Quebec was but a fortnight old, and the church-bells, to use Horace Walpole's striking words, "were worn threadbare with ringing for victories." Of the colonies, such as Pennsylvania, that were established "on the fairest terms," he says that "they have no other merit than that of a scrivener who ruins in silence over a plunderer that seizes by force." Of the cessions that were said

to have been made by the princes of the North American nations he writes: "There is no great malignity in suspecting that those who have robbed have also lied." How far he would have been from reproaching any one of his fellow-subjects, even "a black man," for his colour, he shows by his assertion that "it is ridiculous to imagine that the friendship of nations, whether civil or barbarous, can be gained and kept but by kind treatment; and surely they who intrude uncalled upon the country of a distant people ought to consider the natives as worthy of common kindness, and content themselves to rob without insulting them."

He was hopeful of better times to come. "There is reason to expect that, as the world is more enlightened, policy and morality will at last be reconciled, and that nations will learn not to do what they would not suffer." He seems almost to anticipate "The parliament of man, the federation of the world," of the poet; for in his writings we come across such expressions as "the universal league of social beings," "the great republic of human nature," "the great republic of humanity," against which "it is not easy to commit more atrocious treason than by falsifying its records, and misguiding its decrees." Against wreckers, on whatever coast they may be found, he proposes "a general insurrection of all social beings."

For Ireland he always had a strong feeling of pity. "The Irish," he said, "are in a most unnatural state, for we see there the minority prevailing over the majority." He praises Swift in that "he delivered Ireland from plunder and oppression, and showed that wit confederated with truth, had such force as authority was unable to resist. . . . Swift," he continues, "taught the Irish first to know their own interest, their weight, and their strength, and gave them spirit to assert that equality with their fellow-subjects to which they have ever since been making vigorous advances, and to claim those rights which they have at last established." When the Irish patriot, Dr. Lucas, had to flee from his country to escape the imprisonment with which he was threatened, "in the common hall of the prisons among the felons," Johnson wrote: "Let the man thus driven into exile for having been the friend of his country be received in every other place as a confessor of liberty, and let the tools of power be taught in time that they may rob but cannot impoverish." He points out that "no oppression is so heavy or lasting as that which is inflicted by the perversion and exorbitance of legal authority. . . . When plunder bears the name of impost, and murder is perpetrated by a judicial sentence, fortitude is intimidated, and wisdom confounded: resistance shrinks from an alliance with rebellion, and the villain remains secure in the robes of the magistrate." The sight of the wretched hovels in the Hebrides—"a heap of loose stones and turf in a cavity between rocks, where a being, born with all those powers which education expands, and all those sensations which culture refines, is condemned to shelter itself from the wind and rain"—the sight of such abodes of squalor moved Johnson to write—

> That gloomy tranquillity, which some may call fortitude and others wisdom, was, I believe, for a long time to be very frequently found in these dens of poverty; every man was content to live like his neighbours, and never wandering from home saw no mode of life preferable to his own, except at the house of the laird, or the laird's nearest relations, whom he considered as a superior order of beings, to whose luxuries or honours he had no pretensions. But the end of this reverence and submission seems now approaching; the Highlanders have learned that there are countries less bleak and barren than their

own, where, instead of working for the laird, every man may till his own ground, and eat the produce of his own labour.

Slavery at all times roused his deepest indignation—"the most calamitous estate in human life," he called it—"a state which has always been found so destructive to virtue that in many languages a slave and a thief are expressed by the same word." In our war with our American colonies he proposed that "the slaves should be set free and furnished with firearms for defence,. . . . settled in some simple form of government within the country, they may be more grateful and honest than their masters." This scheme shocked the caution of Edmund Burke. "Slaves," Burke said, "are often much attached to their masters. A general wild offer of liberty would not always be accepted. History furnishes few instances of it. It is sometimes as hard to persuade slaves to be free as it is to compel freemen to be slaves; and in this auspicious scheme we should have both these pleasing tasks on our hands at once." Of fugitive negroes Johnson wrote that "they asserted their natural right to liberty and independence." Jamaica he described as "a place of great wealth and dreadful wickedness, a den of tyrants and a dungeon of slaves."

No man was more eager for general education. "He that voluntarily continues ignorance is guilty," he asserts, "of all the crimes which ignorance produces. . . . The efficacy of ignorance," he continues, "has been long tried, and has not produced the consequence expected. Let knowledge, therefore, take its turn." He shows why it is that education is dreaded by a ruling race. "It is found that ignorance is most easily kept in subjection, and that by enlightening the mind with truth fraud and usurpation would be made less practicable and less secure." There were men who maintained "that those who are born to poverty and drudgery should not be deprived by an improper education of the opiate of ignorance." But he replied, even if this be granted, we have first to determine "who are those that are born to poverty. To entail irreversible poverty upon generation after generation only because the ancestor happened to be poor is in itself cruel, if not unjust."

To him might justly be applied the words which he used of Savage: "He has asserted the natural equality of mankind, and endeavoured to suppress that pride which inclines men to imagine that right is the consequence of power." One who knew him well described him as a man who "supported his philosophical character with dignity, was extremely jealous of his personal liberty and independence, and could not brook the smallest appearance of neglect or insult even from the highest personages."

Few men held more strongly to the faith that,

The rank is but the guinea stamp,
The man's the gowd for a' that.

Few men more steadily maintained that, however high the dignities may be, nevertheless

The pith o' sense and pride o' worth
Are higher ranks than a' that.

From him may be learnt the danger which the Radical runs when he mixes with the great. He warns his readers against "that cowardice which always encroaches fast upon such as spend their lives in the company of persons higher than themselves." "Such," he says, "is the state of the world, that the most obsequious of the slaves of pride, the most rapturous of the gazers upon wealth, the most officious of the whisperers of greatness, are collected from seminaries appropriated to the study of wisdom and of virtue, where it was intended that appetite should learn to be content with little, and that hope

should aspire only to honours which no human power can give or take away." "Such," writes Boswell, "was his inflexible dignity of character, that he could not stoop to court the great." "No man," he adds, "had a higher notion of the dignity of literature, or was more determined in maintaining the respect which he justly considered as due to it." This Boswell exemplifies by the following anecdote: "Goldsmith, in his diverting simplicity, complained one day, in a mixed company, of Lord Camden. 'I met him,' said he, 'at Lord Clare's house in the country, and he took no more notice of me than if I had been an ordinary man.' The company having laughed heartily, Johnson stood forth in defence of his friend. 'Nay, gentlemen,' said he, 'Dr. Goldsmith is in the right. A nobleman ought to have made up to such a man as Goldsmith; and I think it is much against Lord Camden that he neglected him.'" His letter to Lord Chesterfield—to Chesterfield, the great nobleman, the statesman, "the most distinguished orator in the Upper House, and the undisputed sovereign of wit and fashion"—has surely the true Radical ring. He carried his Radicalism to the family hearth. "A father," he maintained, "had no right to control the inclinations of his daughters in marriage." Writing of those who were despotic in their disposal of the hands of their daughters, he says: "It may be urged, in extenuation of this crime, which parents, not in any other respect to be numbered with robbers and assassins, frequently commit, that in their estimation riches and happiness are equivalent terms."

It may be objected that in applying the term *Radicalism* to the age of Johnson, I am as much the father of an anachronism as ever Mr. Caxton was when his son was christened Peisistratus. I am supported, however, by the reflection that Johnson himself, in contempt of all recognized systems of chronology, applied the term *Whig* to a very early period indeed in the world's history. "The first Whig," he said, "was the devil." Whiggism, therefore, is of far greater antiquity than its name, and so is Radicalism. At all events, for want of a better word, I must use it to describe that strongly marked vein which, as the passages that I have thus brought together show, under-ran "his high Church of England and monarchical principles." It is shown, moreover, in the whole conduct of his life; in his steady and bold assertion of the high merits and claim to respect of the awkward son of the bankrupt country bookseller, even in the midst of his greatest poverty and surrounded by the highest society. It is shown in the indignation with which in his college days he threw away the pair of new shoes which some unknown friend had set at his door. It is shown in his letter to Lord Chesterfield; in the pride with which he brought out his great Dictionary—"I deliver it to the world," he said in his Preface, "with the spirit of a man that has endeavoured well;" in his assertion that "the chief glory of every nation arises," not from its kings, its nobles, its statesmen, its warriors, but from the class to which he himself belonged—"its authors." It is shown from the beginning to the end of his interview with the king, in his never failing for one moment even before Majesty in the respect which he owed to himself. It is shown in that "blunt dignity which there was about him on every occasion;" in that fact which was found so remarkable by one who had seen no small variety of men, that however meagre might be his surroundings in his home, "no external circumstances ever prompted him to make any apology, or to seem even sensible of their existence." It is shown in the timid care with which his society was shunned by "great lords and great ladies"—a class which does not "love to have their mouths stopped." It is shown in the proud way in which he always acted up to his own noble words: "He that lives well cannot be despised."

WALTER RALEIGH
From "Samuel Johnson" (1907)
Six Essays on Johnson
1910, pp. 9–31

The accident which gave Boswell to Johnson and Johnson to Boswell is one of the most extraordinary pieces of good fortune in literary history. Boswell was a man of genius; the idle paradox which presents him in the likeness of a lucky dunce was never tenable by serious criticism, and has long since been rejected by all who bring thought to bear on the problems of literature. If I had to find a paradox in Boswell I should find it in this, that he was a Scot. His character was destitute of all the vices, and all the virtues, which are popularly, and in the main rightly, attributed to the Scottish people. The young Scot is commonly shy, reserved, and self-conscious; independent in temper, sensitive to affront, slow to make friends, and wary in society. Boswell was the opposite of all these things. He made himself at home in all societies, and charmed others into a like ease and confidence. Under the spell of his effervescent good-humour the melancholy Highlanders were willing to tell stories of the supernatural. 'Mr. Boswell's frankness and gayety,' says Johnson, 'made everybody communicative.' It was no small part of Boswell's secret that he talked with engaging freedom, and often, as it seemed, with childish vanity, of himself. He had the art of interesting others without incurring their respect. He had no ulterior motives. He desired no power, only information, so that his companions recognized his harmlessness, and despised him, and talked to him without a shadow of restraint. He felt a sincere and unbounded admiration for greatness or originality of intellect. 'I have the happiness,' he wrote to Lord Chatham, 'of being capable to contemplate with supreme delight those distinguished spirits by which God is sometimes pleased to honour humanity.' But indeed he did not confine his interest to the great. He was an amateur of human life; his zest in its smallest incidents and his endless curiosity were infectious and irresistible. No scientific investigator has ever been prompted by a livelier zeal for knowledge; and his veracity was scrupulous and absolute. 'A Scotchman must be a very sturdy moralist,' said Johnson, 'who does not love Scotland better than truth.' Boswell was very far indeed from being a sturdy moralist, but he loved truth better than Scotland, better even than himself. Most of the stories told against him, and almost all the witticisms reported at his expense, were first narrated by himself. He had simplicity, candour, fervour, a warmly affectionate nature, a quick intelligence, and a passion for telling all that he knew. These are qualities which make for good literature. They enabled Boswell to portray Johnson with an intimacy and truth that has no parallel in any language.

We owe such an enormous debt of gratitude to Boswell that it seems ungrateful to suggest what is nevertheless obviously true, that the Johnson we know best is Boswell's Johnson. The *Life* would be a lesser work than it is if it had not the unity that was imposed upon it by the mind of its writer. The portrait is so broad and masterly, so nobly conceived and so faithful in detail, that the world has been content to look at Johnson from this point of view and no other. Yet it cannot be denied, and Boswell himself would have been the first to admit it, that there are aspects and periods of Johnson's career which are not and could not be fully treated in the *Life*. When Johnson first saw Boswell in Tom Davies's back shop, he was fifty-four years old and Boswell was twenty-two. The year before the meeting Johnson had been rescued, by the grant of an honourable pension, from the prolonged struggle with poverty which makes up so great a part of the story of his life. He had conquered his world; his circumstances were now comparatively easy and his primacy was universally acknowledged. All these facts have left their mark on Boswell's book. We have some trivial and slight memorials of Shakespeare by men who treated him on equal terms of friendship or rivalry. But Johnson, in our conception of him, is always on a pedestal. He is Doctor Johnson; although he was sixty-six years of age when his own University gave him its honorary degree. The fact is that we cannot escape from Boswell any more than his hero could; and we do not wish to escape, and we do not try. There are many admirers and friends of Johnson who are familiar with every notable utterance recorded by Boswell, who yet would be hard put to it if they were asked to quote a single sentence from *The Rambler*. That splendid repository of wisdom and truth has ceased to attract readers: it has failed and has been forgotten in the unequal contest with Boswell. 'It is not sufficiently considered,' said Johnson, in an early number of *The Rambler*, 'that men more frequently require to be reminded than informed.' I desire to remind you of the work of Johnson, the writer of prose; and I am happy in my subject, for the unique popularity of Boswell has given to the study of Johnson's own works a certain flavour of novelty and research.

It will be wise to face at once the charge so often brought against these writings, that they are dull. M. Taine, who somehow got hold of the mistaken idea that Johnson's periodical essays are the favourite reading of the English people, has lent his support to this charge. Wishing to know what ideas had made Johnson popular, he turned over the pages of his *Dictionary*, his eight volumes of essays, his biographies, his numberless articles, his conversation so carefully collected, and he yawned. 'His truths,' says this critic, 'are too true, we already know his precepts by heart. We learn from him that life is short, and we ought to improve the few moments granted us; that a mother ought not to bring up her son as a fop; that a man ought to repent of his faults and yet avoid superstition; that in everything we ought to be active and not hurried. We thank him for these sage counsels, but we mutter to ourselves that we could have done very well without them.' I will not continue the quotation. It is clear that M. Taine's study of Johnson was limited to a table of contents. What he says amounts to this— that Johnson's writings are a treasury of commonplaces; and in this opinion he certainly has the concurrence of a good many of Johnson's fellow countrymen, who have either refused to read the works or have failed after a gallant attempt.

A commonplace, I take it, is an oft-repeated truth which means nothing to the hearer of it. But for the most perfect kind of commonplace we must enlarge this definition by adding that it means nothing also to the speaker of it. Now it cannot be denied that Johnson's essays are full of commonplace in the first and narrower sense. When he came before the public as a periodical writer, he presented the world with the odd spectacle of a journalist who cared passionately for truth and nothing at all for novelty. The circulation of *The Rambler* was about five hundred copies, and the only number of it which had a great sale was a paper by Richardson, teaching unmarried ladies the advantages of a domestic reputation and a devout bearing at church as effective lures for husbands. Johnson's papers often handle well-worn moral themes in general and dogmatic language, without any effort to commend them to the reader by particular experiences. He did not conceal from himself the difficulty of making any impression on the wider public—'a multitude fluctuating in pleasures or immersed in business, without time for intellectual amusements.' In many passages of his works he shows a keen appreciation of the obstacles to be surmounted before an author can capture the attention and wield the sympathies of his readers. The chief of these obstacles is the deep and sincere interest which every author feels in his own work and which he imagines will be communicated automatically to the reader. 'We are seldom tiresome to ourselves.' Every book that can be called a book has had one interested and excited reader. It is surely a strange testimony to the imperfection of human sympathy and the isolation of the single mind that some books have had only one.

An author's favourite method of attack in the attempt to cross the barrier that separates him from his reader is the method of surprise. The writer who can startle his public by an immediate appeal to the livelier passions and sentiments is sure of a hearing, and can thereafter gain attention even for the commonplace. This method was never practised by Johnson. He despised it, for he knew that what he had to say was no commonplace, so far as he himself was concerned. Among all his discourses on human life he utters hardly a single precept which had not been brought home to him by living experience. The pages of *The Rambler*, if we can read them, are aglow with the earnestness of dear-bought conviction, and rich in conclusions gathered not from books but from life and suffering. It is here that the biography of the writer helps us. If he will not come to meet us, we can go to meet him. Any reader who acquaints himself intimately with the records of Johnson's life, and then reads *The Rambler*, must be very insensible if he does not find it one of the most moving of books. It was so to Boswell, who says that he could never read the following sentence without feeling his frame thrill: 'I think there is some reason for questioning whether the body and mind are not so proportioned that the one can bear all which can be inflicted on the other; whether virtue cannot stand its ground as long as life, and whether a soul well principled will not be separated sooner than subdued.'

Almost every number of *The Rambler* contains reflections and thoughts which cease to be commonplace when the experiences that suggested them are remembered. For more than thirty years of his mature life Johnson was poor, often miserably poor. There are three degrees of poverty, he said—want of riches, want of competence, and want of necessaries. He had known them all. He spoke little of this in his later years; there is no pleasure, he said, in narrating the annals of beggary. But his knowledge of poverty has expressed itself more than once in the quiet commonplaces of *The Rambler*. Again, he was tortured by what he called indolence, but what was more probably natural fatigue consequent upon the excessive nervous expenditure of his bouts of hard work. And this too finds expression in *The Rambler*. 'Indolence,' he says, 'is one of the vices from which those whom it infects are seldom reformed. Every other species of luxury operates upon some appetite that is quickly satiated, and requires some concurrence of art or accident which every place will not supply; but the desire of ease acts equally at all hours, and the longer it is indulged is the more increased. To do nothing is in every man's power; we can never want an opportunity of omitting duties.' The topics of *The Rambler* are many, but the great majority of them are drawn from the graver aspects of life, and it is when he treats of fundamental duties and inevitable sorrows, bereavement, and disease, and death, that Johnson rises to his full stature. When he ventures to emulate the tea-table morality of the *Spectator* he has not a light or happy touch. Yet his knowledge of the human mind is not only much more profound than Addison's, it is also more curious and subtle. In an essay on bashfulness he first investigates its causes, and finds the chief of them in too

high an opinion of our own importance. Then he applies the remedy:

'The most useful medicines are often unpleasing to the taste. Those who are oppressed by their own reputation will, perhaps, not be comforted by hearing that their cares are unnecessary. But the truth is that no man is much regarded by the rest of the world. He that considers how little he dwells upon the condition of others, will learn how little the attention of others is attracted by himself. While we see multitudes passing before us, of whom, perhaps, not one appears to deserve our notice, or excite our sympathy, we should remember that we likewise are lost in the same throng; that the eye which happens to glance upon us is turned in a moment on him that follows us, and that the utmost which we can reasonably hope or fear is, to fill vacant hour with prattle, and be forgotten.'

This is prose that will not suffer much by comparison with the best in the language. It is strange to remember, as we read some of the noblest of Johnson's sentences, that they were written in a periodical paper for the entertainment of chance readers. His essay on Revenge concludes with an appeal not often to be found in the pages of a society journal: 'Of him that hopes to be forgiven, it is indispensably required that he forgive. It is therefore superfluous to urge any other motive. On this great duty eternity is suspended; and to him that refuses to practice it, the throne of mercy is inaccessible, and the Saviour of the world has been born in vain.'

The passages that I have quoted from *The Rambler* are perhaps enough to illustrate what Johnson means when he speaks, in the last number, of his services to the English language. 'Something, perhaps, I have added to the elegance of its construction, and something to the harmony of its cadence.' Later criticism has been inclined to say rather that he subdued the syntax of his native tongue to a dull mechanism, and taught it a drowsy tune. But this is unjust. It is true that he loved balance and order, and that the elaborate rhetorical structure of his sentences is very ill-adapted to describe the trivial matters to which he sometimes applies it, such as the arrival of a lady at a country house. 'When a tiresome and vexatious journey of four days had brought me to the house, where invitation, regularly sent for seven years together, had at last induced me to pass the summer, I was surprised, after the civilities of my first reception, to find, instead of the leisure and tranquillity which a rural life always promises, and, if well conducted, might always afford, a confused wildness of care, and a tumultuous hurry of diligence, by which every face was clouded and every motion agitated.' In a sentence like this, the ear, which has been trained to love completeness and symmetry, shows itself exorbitant in its demands, and compels even the accidents of domestic life to happen in contrasted pairs. The idle antithetical members of the sentence have been compared to those false knobs and handles which are used, for the sake of symmetry, in a debased style of furniture. But this occasional fault of the formal Johnsonian syntax is of a piece with its merits. The sentence is very complex, and when no member of it is idle, when every antithesis makes room for some new consideration, it can be packed full of meaning, so that it exhibits a subject in all its bearings, and in a few lines does the work of a chapter. When Johnson is verbose and languid, it is often because his subject is slight, and does not yield him matter enough to fill his capacious style. The syntax is still a stately organ, fitted to discourse great music, but the bellows are poor and weak. When his mind gets to work on a subject that calls forth all his powers, his vigour and versatility, displayed within a narrow compass, are amazing. There is nothing new to add to his brief conclusion in the question of the second sight, which he investigated with some care during his Highland journey. 'To collect sufficient testimonies,' he says, 'for the satisfaction of the public, or of ourselves, would have required more time than we could bestow. There is, against it, the seeming analogy of things confusedly seen and little understood; and, for it, the indistinct cry of national persuasion, which may be perhaps resolved at last into prejudice and tradition. I never could advance my curiosity to conviction; but came away at last only willing to believe.'

In *The Lives of the Poets* his style reaches its maturity of vigour and ease. The author of these *Lives* is Boswell's Johnson, the brilliant talker, the king of literary society,

> Who ruled, as he thought fit,
> The universal monarchy of wit.

Yet for the light that they throw on Johnson's own character I doubt whether any of the *Lives* can compare with *The Life of Richard Savage*, which was published almost twenty years before the meeting with Boswell. The character of Savage was marked, as Boswell truly observes, by profligacy, insolence, and ingratitude. But Johnson had wandered the streets with him for whole nights together, when they could not pay for a lodging, and had taken delight in his rich and curious stores of information concerning high and low society. The *Life of Savage* is a tribute of extraordinary delicacy and beauty, paid by Johnson to his friend. Only a man of the broadest and sanest sympathies could have performed this task, which Johnson does not seem to find difficult. Towards Savage he is all tenderness and generosity, yet he does not for an instant relax his allegiance to the virtues which formed no part of his friend's character. He tells the whole truth; yet his affection for Savage remains what he felt it to be, the most important truth of all. His morality is so entirely free from pedantry, his sense of the difficulty of virtue and the tragic force of circumstance is so keen, and his love of singularity of character is so great, that even while he points the moral of a wasted life he never comes near to the vanity of condemnation. It is abundantly clear from the facts, which he records with all the impartiality of a naturalist, that Savage, besides being hopelessly self-indulgent and dissolute, was violently egotistic, overbearing, and treacherous to his friends. Johnson's verdict on these faults is given in the closing sentences of the *Life*: 'The insolence and resentment of which he is accused were not easily to be avoided by a great mind, irritated by perpetual hardships, and constrained hourly to return the spurns of contempt and repress the insolence of prosperity; and vanity surely may be readily pardoned in him, to whom life afforded no other comforts than barren praises and the consciousness of deserving them. Those are no proper judges of his conduct, who have slumbered away their time on the down of plenty; nor will any wise man easily presume to say, "Had I been in Savage's condition, I should have lived or written better than Savage."'

If we try to picture Johnson in his most characteristic attitude we usually see him sitting on that throne of human felicity, a chair in a tavern, and roaring down opposition. It was thus that Boswell knew him best, and though the same record exhibits him in many other aspects, yet the predominant impression persists. So Johnson has come to be regarded as a kind of Chairman to humanity, whose business it is to cry 'Order, Order,' an embodiment of corporate tradition and the settled wisdom of the ages.

Yet we may think of him, if we like, in a less public fashion, as a man full of impulse and whim, quaint in humour, passionate in feeling, warm in imagination, and,

above all, original. You can never predict what Johnson will say when his opinion is challenged. Doubtless he loved paradox and argument, but he was no dialectician, and behind the play of talk his fancies and tastes were intensely individual. He disliked all talk that dealt with historical facts, especially the facts of Roman history. He never, while he lived, desired to hear of the Punic War. Others besides Johnson have been distressed and fatigued by talk that is merely an exercise of memory. But his method of escape was all his own. When Mrs. Thrale asked his opinion of the conversational powers of Charles James Fox, 'He talked to me at club one day,' said Johnson, 'concerning Catiline's conspiracy—so I withdrew my attention, and thought about Tom Thumb.'

Johnson is famous for his good sense and sound judgement, but his good sense abounds in surprises. There is a delightful touch of surprise in his comparison of a ship to a jail. 'No man will be a sailor who has contrivance enough to get himself into a jail; for being in a ship is being in a jail, with the chance of being drowned.' And again, 'A man in jail has more room, better food, and commonly better company.' The same dislike of the sea expresses itself in a paper of *The Rambler* which discusses the possibility of varying the monotony of pastoral poetry by introducing marine subjects. But unfortunately the sea has less variety than the land. 'To all the inland inhabitants of every region, the sea is only known as an immense diffusion of waters, over which men pass from one country to another, and in which life is frequently lost.'

Wherever you open the pages of Johnson's works you will find general truths sincerely and vigorously expressed, but behind the brave array of dogma you will find everywhere the strongest marks of an individual mind, and the charm and colour of personal predilections. The Romantic writers must not be allowed the credit of inventing the personal note in literature. What they invented was not themselves, but a certain sentimental way of regarding themselves. Johnson despised all such sentiment. 'When a butcher tells you,' he said, 'that his heart bleeds for his country; he has in fact no uneasy feeling.' Rousseau is not more individual in his cultivation of sentiment than Johnson in his dislike of it. He carried this dislike to strange extremes, so that all gesticulation and expression of the emotions became suspect to him. Of the preaching of Dr. Isaac Watts he says, "He did not endeavour to assist his eloquence by any gesticulations; for, as no corporeal actions have any correspondence with theological truth, he did not see how they could enforce it.' Perhaps the best example of this fixed distaste for demonstrative emotion may be found in his contempt for the actor's profession. It is dangerous to quarrel with Boswell, but it seems to me impossible to accept his suggestion that Johnson's opinions concerning stage-players had their origin in jealousy of the success of Garrick. Such jealousy is utterly unlike all that we know of Johnson. On the other hand, a hatred of show and a fierce resentment at the response of his own feelings to cunningly simulated passion are exactly what we should expect in him. The passages in which he has expressed himself on this matter are too many and too various to be attributed to a gust of personal ill-feeling. One of the most delightful of them occurs in his notes on the character of Bottom in *A Midsummer Night's Dream*. 'Bottom,' he says, 'seems to have been bred in a tiring-room. He is for engrossing every part, and would exclude his inferiors from all possibility of distinction.' Again, 'Bottom discovers a true genius for the stage by his solicitude for propriety of dress, and his deliberation which beard to choose among many beards, all unnatural.'

The sonorous and ponderous rotundity of Johnson's style,

and the unfailing respect that he pays to law and decorum, have partly concealed from view the wilfulness of his native temper. Obedience to law imposed from without can never be the soul of a man or of a writer. It is the converted rebels who give power to the arm of government. If there has ever been a writer of a sober, slow and conforming temper, who has left memorable work behind him, it will be found, I think, that for the greater part of his life he acted as a poor mechanical drudge in the service of his own youthful enthusiasm, and painfully filled out the schemes which were conceived in a happier time. All enduring literary work is the offspring of intense excitement. Johnson did most of his reading piecemeal, in a fever of agitation. If any man praised a book in his presence, he was sure to ask, 'Did you read it through?' If the answer was in the affirmative, he did not seem willing to believe it. He very seldom read a book from beginning to end; his writing, moreover, was done at high speed, and often at a great heat of imagination. Some writers use general statements as a mask to conceal ignorance and emptiness: Johnson prefers them because they lend smoothness and decency to passion. He states only his conclusions; but the premises, although they are not given, are vividly present to his mind. When it becomes necessary, as a guarantee of sincerity and knowledge, to exhibit in full all that is implied in a general statement, he reverses his favourite method, and permits his imagination to expatiate on his material with all the visionary activity of poetry.

⟨. . .⟩ 'Life,' he says, 'must be seen before it can be known.' Because he had seen much of life, his last and greatest work, *The Lives of the Most Eminent English Poets*, is more than a collection of facts: it is a book of wisdom and experience, a treatise on the conduct of life, a commentary on human destiny.

Those *Lives* will never lose their authoritative value as a record. The biographer must often consult them for their facts. The student of Johnson will consult them quite as often for the light that they throw on their author, who moves among the English poets easily and freely, enjoying the society of his peers, praising them without timidity, judging them without superstition, yet ready at all times with those human allowances which are more likely to be kept in mind by a man's intimates than by an indifferent posterity. When Johnson undertook the *Lives* he was almost seventy years of age; he had long been familiar with his subject, and he wrote from a full mind, rapidly and confidently. He spent little time on research. When Boswell tried to introduce him to Lord Marchmont, who had a store of anecdotes concerning Pope, he at first refused the trouble of hearing them. 'I suppose, Sir,' said Mrs. Thrale, with something of the severity of a governess, 'Mr. Boswell thought, that as you are to write Pope's *Life*, you would wish to know about him.' Johnson accepted the reproof, though he might very well have replied that he knew more than was necessary for his purpose. An even better instance of his indifference may be found in his criticism of Congreve. Congreve's dramatic works are not bulky, and were doubtless to be found in any well-appointed drawingroom. But Johnson would not rise from his desk. 'Of Congreve's plays,' he says, 'I cannot speak distinctly; for since I inspected them many years have passed; but what remains upon my memory is, that his characters are commonly fictitious and artificial, with very little of nature and not much of life.' Then follows an admirable critical summary of Congreve's peculiar merits in comedy.

This magnanimous carelessness with regard to detail helped rather than hindered the breadth and justice of Johnson's scheme. There are many modern biographies and histories, full of carefully authenticated fact, which afflict the reader with a weight of indigestion. The author has no right to

his facts, no ownership in them. They have flitted through his mind on a calm five minutes' passage from the notebook to the immortality of the printed page. But no man can hope to make much impression on a reader with facts which he has not thought it worth his own while to remember. Every considerable book, in literature or science, is an engine whereby mind operates on mind. It is an ignorant worship of Science which treats it as residing in books, and reduces the mind to a mechanism of transfer. The measure of an author's power would be best found in the book which he should sit down to write the day after his library was burnt to the ground.

The *Lives of the Poets* has not a few of the qualities of such a book. It is broadly conceived and written, it has a firm grasp of essentials, the portraits are lifelike, and the judgements, on the whole, wonderfully fair. There has been much extravagant talk among Romantic critics of Johnson's prejudices, and even of his incapacity as a judge of poetry. Time will avenge him on these critics; and Time has begun to do its work. The minor poets of our own day may well be glad that Johnson is not alive among them.

His occasional errors cannot be concealed; they are known to every schoolboy. Sometimes he allows his own matured and carefully considered views on certain general literary questions to interfere with the impartial examination of a particular poem. He disliked irregular metres and fortuitous schemes of rhyme. He held the pastoral convention in poetry to be artificial, frigid, and over-worn. These opinions and tastes led him into his notorious verdict on 'Lycidas.' And yet, when the noise of the shouting shall have died away, it may be questioned whether most of the points attacked by Johnson would ever be chosen by admirers of the poem for special commendation. Is there nothing artificial and far-fetched about the satyrs and the fauns with cloven heel? Is the ceremonial procession of Triton, Camus, and St. Peter an example of Milton's imagination as its best? In short, does the beauty and wonder of the poem derive from the allegorical scheme to which Johnson objected? But I am almost frightened at my own temerity, and must be content to leave the question unanswered.

There were certain of the English poets whom Johnson, it is plain, disliked, even while he admired their work. His account of them is inevitably tinged by this dislike; yet his native generosity and justice never shine out more brightly than in the praises that he gives them. He disliked Milton; and no one has ever written a more whole-hearted eulogy of *Paradise Lost*. Unless I am deceived, he disliked many things in the character of Addison, yet any one who would praise Addison nobly and truly will find himself compelled to echo Johnson's praises. A more profound difference of feeling separated him from Swift. He excuses himself from writing a fuller account of Swift's life, on the ground that the task had already been performed by Dr. Hawkesworth. But Hawkesworth's *Life* is a mere piece of book-making, and it seems likely that Johnson was glad to be saved from a duty that had no attractions for him. The contrast between himself and Swift may be best expressed in their own words: 'I heartily hate and detest that animal called man,' said Swift, 'although I heartily love John, Peter, Thomas, and so forth.' Johnson's attitude was the reverse of this. He used to say that the world was well constructed, but that the particular people disgraced the elegance and beauty of the general fabric. Yet it was he, not the hearty lover of 'John, Peter, Thomas, and so forth', who had the deeper sense of the tie that binds man to man. That men should dare to hate each other in a world where they suffer the like trials and await the same doom was hardly conceivable to Johnson. That a man should dare to stand aloof from his kind and condemn them was a higher pitch of arrogance, destined to end in that tempest of madness and hate which is the Fourth Book of *Gulliver's Travels*.

Lastly, it cannot be denied that Johnson did scant justice to Gray; although here, again, his praise of the *Elegy* could hardly be bettered. The causes of this imperfect sympathy are easy to understand. Gray was a recluse poet, shy, sensitive, dainty, who brooded on his own feelings and guarded his own genius from contact with the rough world. 'He had a notion,' says Johnson, 'not very peculiar, that he could not write but at certain times, or at happy moments; a fantastic foppery, to which my kindness for a man of learning and virtue wishes him to have been superior.' Surely this impatience will seem only natural to those who remember the story of Johnson's life. He had lived for thirty years, and had supported others, solely by the labours of his pen. The pay he received was often wretchedly small. Fifteen guineas was the price of the copyright of the *Life of Savage*. He was driven from task to task, compelled to supply the booksellers with what they demanded, prefaces, translations, or sermons at a guinea a piece. In spite of sickness and lassitude and intense disinclination, the day's work had to be done, and when work did not come to hand, it had to be sought and solicited. It is not easy for us to imagine the conditions of literature in London when Johnson first came there, and for many years after,—the crowds of miserable authors, poor, servile, jealous, and venal. Immersed in this society he laboured for years. The laws that he imposed on his drudgery were never broken. He make no personal attacks on others, and answered none on himself. He never complied with temporary curiosity, nor enabled his readers to discuss the topic of the day. He never degraded virtue by the meanness of dedication. There was nothing in his writings to disclaim and nothing to regret, for he always thought it the duty of an anonymous author to write as if he expected to be hereafter known. When at last he was known, there was still no escape from hack-work and the necessities of the day. The books which he has added to the English Classics were written for bread—the *Dictionary*, the periodical papers, *Rasselas*, the Preface and Notes to Shakespeare (which will some day be recognized for what they are, the best and most luminous of eighteenth century commentaries on Shakespeare's drama), and the *Lives of the Poets*.

This is the greatness of Johnson, that he is greater than his works. He thought of himself as a man, not as an author; and of literature as a means, not as an end in itself. Duties and friendships and charities were more to him than fame and honour. The breadth and humanity of temper which sometimes caused him to depreciate the importance of literature, have left their mark on his books. There are some authors who exhaust themselves in the effort to endow posterity, and distil all their virtue in a book. Yet their masterpieces have something inhuman about them, like those jewelled idols, the work of men's hands, which are worshipped by the sacrifice of man's flesh and blood. There is more of comfort and dignity in the view of literature to which Johnson has given large utterance: 'Books without the knowledge of life are useless; for what should books teach but the art of living?'

Edward Gibbon

Edward Gibbon

1737–1794

Edward Gibbon was born at Putney on May 8, 1737. As a child he suffered from frequent illnesses, and his education was irregular. He attended the Westminster School and in 1752 enrolled at Magdalen College, Oxford; his conversion to Roman Catholicism in 1753 led to his exclusion from the college. In a successful attempt to have him reconverted, Gibbon's father sent him to Lausanne, Switzerland, where Gibbon spent the next five years and became engaged to Suzanne Curchod. His father persuaded him to break off this engagement, and in 1758 Gibbon returned to England.

In 1759 he became a captain in the South Hampshire militia, where he remained until 1763. Gibbon published his *Essai sur l'étude de la littérature* in 1761, and in 1763 made a second trip to the Continent. While sightseeing in Rome in 1764 he first conceived of the idea of writing *The Decline and Fall of the Roman Empire*; he did not, however, begin the work until 1773. Gibbon returned to England in 1765, and in 1774 entered Parliament representing Liskeard; in 1779 he was appointed Commissioner of Trade and Plantations.

The first volume of Gibbon's *Decline and Fall* appeared in 1776 and immediately sparked a theological controversy concerning the two celebrated chapters (15 and 16) in which he maintained that the Christian church sapped the will of the Roman people and was the primary cause of the decline of the Roman Empire. Gibbon responded to the many attacks upon him with A *Vindication of Some Passages in the XVth and XVIth Chapters* (1779). The second and third volumes of the *Decline and Fall* were published in 1781, and in that year Gibbon was elected M.P. for Lynnington. Two years later he retired and returned to Lausanne, where in 1787 he completed the *Decline and Fall*; the final three volumes were published in 1788, after his return to England.

Gibbon spent most of the last years of his life at the home of his friend Lord Sheffield, who, after Gibbon's death on January 16, 1794, prepared an edition of his *Miscellaneous Works* (1796), including Gibbon's *Memoirs*. The *Memoirs* (sometimes called the *Autobiography*) exist in several states and were definitively edited by George A. Bonnard in 1966.

They have had great doings here at the christening of Mr. Gibbon's son. I called there last night to ask how they did, and ⟨they⟩ asked me to take a bed there, but I excused myself because of Mr. Thyer. Our landlady says that his lady had no fortune, but was a young lady of good family and reputation, and that old Mr. Gibbon led her to church and back again. —JOHN BYROM, Letter to Mrs. Byrom (May 15, 1737), *The Private Journal and Literary Remains of John Byrom*, ed. Richard Parkinson, 1856, Vol. 2, Pt. 1, p. 158

He is an ugly, affected, disgusting fellow and poisons our literary club to me.—JAMES BOSWELL, Letter to William Temple (May 3, 1779)

Fat and ill-constructed, Mr. Gibbon has cheeks of such prodigious chubbiness, that they envelope his nose so completely, as to render it, in profile, absolutely invisible. His look and manner are placidly mild, but rather effeminate; his voice,—for he was speaking to Sir Joshua at a little distance,— is gentle, but of studied precision of accent. Yet, with these Brobdignatious cheeks, his neat little feet are of a miniature description; and with these, as soon as I turned around, he hastily described a quaint sort of circle, with small quick steps, and a dapper gait, as if to mark the alacrity of his approach, and then, stopping short when full face to me, he made so singularly profound a bow, that—though hardly able to keep my gravity—I felt myself blush deeply at its undue, but palpably intended obsequiousness.—FANNY BURNEY, Letter to Samuel Crisp (1782)

Mr. Gibbon, the historian, is so exceedingly indolent that he never even pares his nails. His servant, while Gibbon is reading, takes up one of his hands, and when he has performed the operation lays it down, and then manages the other—the patient in the meanwhile scarcely knowing what is going on, and quietly pursuing his studies.

The picture of him painted by Sir J. Reynolds, and the prints made from it, are as like the original as it is possible to be. When he was introduced to a blind French lady, the servant happening to stretch out her mistress's hand to lay hold of the historian's cheek, she thought, upon feeling its rounded contour, that some trick was being played upon her with the *sitting* part of a child, and exclaimed, "Fidonc!"

Mr. Gibbon is very replete with anecdotes, and tells them with great happiness and fluency.—EDMOND MALONE, "Maloniana" (1787), cited in Sir James Prior, *Life of Edmond Malone*, 1860, p. 382

I hesitate from the apprehension of ridicule, when I approach the delicate subject of my early love. By this word I do not mean the polite attention, the gallantry without hope or design, which has originated from the spirit of chivalry, and is interwoven with the texture of French manners. I do not confine myself to the grosser appetite which our pride may affect to disdain, because it has been implanted by Nature in the whole animal creation. *Amor omnibus idem.* The discovery of a sixth sense, the first consciousness of manhood, is a very interesting moment of our lives: but it less properly belongs to the memoirs of an individual, than to the natural history of the species. I understand by this passion the union of desire, friendship and tenderness, which is inflamed by a single female, which prefers her to the rest of her sex, and which seeks her possession as the supreme or the sole happiness of our being. I need not blush at recollecting the object of my choice, and though my love was disappointed of success, I am rather proud that I was once capable of feeling such a pure and exalted sentiment. The personal attractions of Mademoiselle Suzanne Curchod were embellished by the virtues and talents of the mind. Her fortune was humble but her family was respectable: her mother, a native of France, had preferred her religion to her country; the profession of her father did not extinguish the moderation and philosophy of his temper, and he lived content with a small salary and laborious duty in the obscure lot of minister of Crassy, in the mountains that separate the Pays de Vaud from the County of Burgundy. In the solitude of a sequestered village he bestowed a liberal and even learned education on his only daughter; she surpassed his hopes by her proficiency in the sciences and languages; and in her short visits to some relations in Lausanne, the wit and beauty and erudition of Mademoiselle Curchod were the theme of universal applause. The report of such a prodigy awakened my curiosity; I saw and loved. I found her learned without pedantry, lively in conversation, pure in sentiment, and elegant in manners; and the first sudden emotion was fortified by the habits and knowledge of a more familiar acquaintance. She permitted me to make her two or three visits at her father's house: I passed some happy days in the mountains of Burgundy; and her parents honourably encouraged a connection which might raise their daughter above want and dependence. In a calm retirement the gay vanity of youth no longer fluttered in her bosom: she listened to the voice of truth and passion; and I might presume to hope that I had made some impression on a virtuous heart.—EDWARD GIBBON, *Memoirs of My Life*, 1792–93

Went to the library of Mr. Gibbon; it still remains here ⟨in Lausanne⟩, though bought seven years ago by Mr. Beckford, of Fonthill, for 950*l.* It consists of nearly 10,000 volumes, and, as far as I could judge by a cursory and (from its present situation) a very inconvenient examination of it, it is, of all the libraries I ever saw, that of which I should most covet the possession— that which seems exactly everything that any gentleman or gentlewoman fond of letters could wish. Although it is in no particular walk of literature a perfect collection, in the classical part perhaps less than any other, and in the Greek less than in the Latin classics, still there are good editions of all the best authors in both languages. The books, though neither magnificent in their editions nor in their bindings, are all in good condition, all clean, all such as one wishes to read, and could have no scruple in using. They are under the care of Mr. Scott, a physician of this place, who made the bargain for Mr. Beckford with Gibbon's heirs in England, and are placed in two small and inconvenient rooms hired for the purpose, and filled with rows of shelves so near as scarcely to admit of looking at the books on the back side of them. Mr. Beckford, when last here in 179-, packed up about 2,500 vols. of what he considered as the choicest of them, in two cases, which he then proposed sending to England directly, but which still remain in their cases with the others.—MARY BERRY, *Journal*, July 6, 1803

I am thus far (kept by stress of weather) on my way back to Diodati (near Geneva) from a voyage in my boat round the lake—& I enclose you a sprig of *Gibbon's Acacia* & some rose leaves from his garden—which with part of his house I have just seen—you will find honourable mention in his life made of this "Acacia" when he walked out on the night of concluding his history.—The garden—& *summer house* where he composed are neglected—& the last utterly decayed—but they still show it as his "Cabinet" & seem perfectly aware of his memory.—GEORGE GORDON, LORD BYRON, Letter to John Murray (June 27, 1816)

One of the first resolutions passed by our committee of six was that each of us should, in rotation, entertain at dinner our two military commanders and the field officers of the regiment. When my turn arrived I invited the four military gentlemen, our committee, and six other persons the best qualified I could meet with, among whom were my father, Lord Carmarthen, and Mr. Gibbon, the historian, who was then at the zenith of his fame, and who certainly was not at all backward in availing himself of the deference universally shown to him, by taking both the lead, and a very ample share of the conversation, in whatever company he might honour with his presence. His conversation was not, indeed, what Dr. Johnson would have called *talk*. There was no interchange of ideas, for no one had a chance of replying, so fugitive, so variable, was his mode of discoursing, which consisted of points, anecdotes, and epigrammatic thrusts, all more or less to the purpose, and all pleasantly said with a French air and manner which gave them great piquancy, but which were withal so desultory and unconnected that, though each separately was extremely amusing, the attention of his auditors sometimes flagged before his own resources were exhausted. At my repast, however, there appeared to be no reason to apprehend such an untoward issue, for one of the principal guests was his *fidus Achates*, Colonel Holroyd, now Lord Sheffield, his admiring friend and future biographer; and the rest of us were young untried men, except my father, who, having never previously been in the company of this celebrated person, was more inclined to listen than to talk.

In these favourable circumstances, Mr. Gibbon, nothing loath, took the conversation into his own hands, and very brilliant and pleasant he was during the dinner and for some time afterwards. He had just concluded, however, one of his best foreign anecdotes, in which he had introduced some of the fashionable levities of political doctrine then prevalent, and, with his customary tap on the lid of his snuff-box, was looking round to receive our tribute of applause, when a deep-toned but clear voice was heard from the bottom of the table, very calmly and civilly impugning the correctness of the narrative, and the propriety of the doctrines of which it had been made the vehicle. The historian, turning a disdainful glance towards the quarter whence the voice proceeded, saw, for the first time, a tall, thin, and rather ungainly-looking young man, who now sat quietly and silently eating some fruit. There was nothing very prepossessing or very formidable in his exterior, but, as the few words he had uttered appeared to have made a considerable impression on the company, Mr. Gibbon, I suppose, thought himself bound to maintain his honour by suppressing such an attempt to dispute his supremacy. He accordingly undertook the defence of the propositions in question, and a very animated debate took place between him and his youthful antagonist, Mr. Pitt, and for some time was conducted with great talent and brilliancy on both sides. At length the genius of the young man prevailed over that of his senior, who, finding himself driven into a corner from which there was no escape, made some excuse for rising from the table and walked out of the room. I followed him and, finding that he was looking for his hat, I tried to persuade him to return to his seat. "By no means," said he. "That young gentleman is, I have no doubt, extremely ingenious and agreeable, but I must acknowledge that his style of conversation is not exactly what I am accustomed to, so you must positively excuse me." And away he went in high dudgeon, notwithstanding that his friend had come to my assistance. When we returned into the dining-room we found Mr. Pitt proceeding very tranquilly with the illustration of the subject from which his opponent had fled, and which he discussed with such ability, strength of argument, and eloquence, that his hearers were filled with profound admiration.—SIR JAMES BLAND BURGES (1818), cited in *Selections from the Letters and Correspondence of Sir James Bland Burges*, ed. James Hutton, 1885, pp. 59–61

The learned Gibbon was a curious counterbalance to the learned, (may I not say *less* learned?) Johnson. Their manners and taste, both in writing and conversation, were as different as their habiliments. On the day I first sat down with Johnson, in his rusty brown, and his black worsteads, Gibbon was placed opposite to me in a suit of flower'd velvet, with a bag and sword. Each had his measured phraseology; and Johnson's famous parallel, between Dryden and Pope, might be loosely parodied, in reference to himself and Gibbon.—Johnson's style was grand, and Gibbon's elegant; the stateliness of the former was sometimes pedantick, and the polish of the latter was occasionally finical. Johnson march'd to kettle-drums and trumpets; Gibbon moved to flutes and haut-boys;—Johnson hew'd passages through the Alps, while Gibbon levell'd walks through parks and gardens.—Maul'd as I had been by Johnson, Gibbon pour'd balm upon my bruises, by condescending, once or twice, in the course of the evening, to talk with me;—the great historian was light and playful, suiting his matter to the capacity of the boy;—but it was done *more suâ*;—still his mannerism prevail'd;—still he tapp'd his snuff-box,—still he smirk'd, and smiled; and rounded his periods with the same air of good-breeding, as if he were conversing with men.—His mouth, mellifluous as Plato's, was a round hole, nearly in the centre of his visage.—GEORGE COLMAN THE YOUNGER, *Random Records*, 1830, Vol. 1, pp. 121–22

Southey, like Gibbon, was a miscellaneous scholar; he, like Gibbon, of vast historical research; he, like Gibbon, signally industrious, and patient, and elaborate in collecting the materials for his historical works. Like Gibbon, he had dedicated a life of competent ease, in a pecuniary sense, to literature; like Gibbon, he had gathered to the shores of a beautiful lake, remote from great capitals, a large, or at least, sufficient library (in each case, I believe, the library ranged, as to the numerical amount, between seven and ten thousand); and, like Gibbon, he was the most accomplished *littérateur* amongst the erudite scholars of his time, and the most of an erudite scholar amongst the accomplished *littérateurs*. After all these points of agreement known, it remains as a pure advantage on the side of Southey—a mere *lucro ponatur*—that he was a poet; and, by all men's confession, a respectable poet, brilliant in his descriptive powers, and fascinating in his narration, however much he might want of

The vision and the faculty divine.

It is remarkable amongst the series of parallelisms that have been or might be pursued between two men, that both had the honour of retreating from a parliamentary life; Gibbon, after some silent and inert experience of that warfare; Southey, with a prudent foresight of the ruin to his health and literary usefulness, won from the experience of his nearest friends. —THOMAS DE QUINCEY, "The Lake Poets: Southey, Wordsworth, and Coleridge," *Literary and Lake Reminiscences*, 1839

It is well known that Fox visited Gibbon at Lausanne; and he was much gratified by the visit. Gibbon, he said, talked a great

deal, walking up and down the room, and generally ending his sentences with a genitive case; every now and then, too, casting a look of complacency on his own portrait by Sir Joshua Reynolds, which hung over the chimney-piece,—that wonderful portrait, in which, while the oddness and vulgarity of the features are refined away, the likeness is perfectly preserved.—Fox used to say that Gibbon's *History* was immortal, because nobody could do without it,—nobody without vast expense of time and labour, could get elsewhere the information which it contains.—I think, and so Lord Grenville thought, that the introductory chapters are the finest part of that history: it was certainly more difficult to write *them* than the rest of the work.—SAMUEL ROGERS, *Table Talk*, c. 1855

General

You wonder, (and I dare say unfeignedly because you do not think yourself entitled to such praise) that I prefer your stile as an Historian to that of the two most renowned and admired Writers of History the present day has seen. That you may not suspect me of having said more than my real opinion will warrant, I will tell you why. In your stile I see no affectation. In every line of theirs, I see nothing else. They disgust me always—Robertson with his pomp and his Strut, and Gibbons with his finical and French manner.—WILLIAM COWPER, Letter to John Newton (July 27, 1783)

Heard of the death of Mr. Gibbon the historian, the calumniator of the despised Nazarene, the derider of Christianity. Awful dispensation! He too was my acquaintance. Lord, I bless thee, considering how much infidel acquaintance I have had, that my soul never came into their secret! How many souls have his writings polluted! Lord, preserve others from their contagion!—HANNAH MORE, *Diary* (Jan. 19, 1784), *Memoirs of the Life and Correspondence of Mrs. Hannah More*, ed. William Roberts, 1835, Vol. 2, p. 413

Gibbon! if sterner patriots than thyself
With firmer foot have stampt our English soil;
If Poesy stood high above thy reach,
She stood with only one on either hand
Upon the cliffs of Albion tall and strong:
Meanwhile gregarious songsters tramp around
On plashy meadow-land, mid noisome flowers
Sprung from the rankness of flush city-drains.
In other regions graver History
Meets her own Muse; nor walk they far below.
   The rivulets and mountain-rills of Greece
Will have dried up while Avon stil runs on;
And those four rivers freshening Paradise
Gush yet, tho' Paradise had long been lost
Had not one man restored it; he was ours.
Not song alone detain'd him, tho' the song
Came from the lips of Angels upon his,
But strenuous action when his country call'd
Drew him from those old groves and that repose
In which the enchantress Italy lulls all.
No Delphic laurel's trembling glimmery leaves
Checkered thy gravel-walk; 'twas evener ground,
Altho' mid shafts and cornices o'ergrown
With nettles, and palatial caverns choakt
With rubbish from obliterated names.
   There are who blame thee for too stately step
And words resounding from inflated cheek.
Words have their proper places, just like men.
I listen to, nor venture to reprove,
Large language swelling under gilded domes,
Byzantine, Syrian, Persepolitan,

Or where the world's drunk master lay in dust.
Fabricius heard and spake another tongue,
And such the calm Cornelia taught her boys,
Such Scipio, Cæsar, Tullius, marshaling,
Cimber and wilder Scot were humanized,
And, far as flew the Eagles, all was Rome.
    Thou lookedst down complacently where brawl'd
The vulgar factions that infest our streets,
And turnedst the black vizor into glass
Thro which men saw the murderer and the cheat
In diadem and cowl. Erectly stood,
After like work with fiercer hand perform'd,
Milton, as Adam pure, as Michael strong,
When brave Britannia struck her bravest blow,
When monstrous forms, half-reptile and half-man,
Snatcht up the hissing snakes from off Hell's floor
And flung them with blind fury at her crest.
Two valiant men sprang up, of equal force,
Protector and *Defender* each alike.
Milton amid the bitter sleet drove on,
Shieldbearer to the statelier one who struck
That deadly blow which saved our prostrate sires
And gave them (short the space!) to breathe once more.
    History hath beheld no pile ascend
So lofty, large, symmetrical, as thine,
Since proud Patavium gave Rome's earlier chiefs
To shine again in virtues and in arms.
Another rises from the couch of pain,
Wounded, and worne with service and with years,
To share fraternal glory, and ward off
(Alas, to mortal hand what vain essay!)
The shafts of Envy.
            May Thucydides,
Recall'd to life among us, close his page
Ere come the Pestilence, ere come the shame
Of impotent and Syracusan war!
Lately (how strange the vision!) o'er my sleep
War stole, in bandages untinged with wounds,
Wheezing and limping on fat nurse's arm
To take a draught of air before the tent,
And for each step too fast or wide rebuked.
Peace stood with folded arms nor ventured near,
But Scorn ran closer, and a shout went up
From north and south above the Euxine wave.
    —WALTER SAVAGE LANDOR, "Gibbon," 1854

For history there is great choice of ways to bring the student through early Rome. If he can read Livy, he has a good book; but one of the short English compends, some Goldsmith or Ferguson, should be used, that will place in the cycle the bright stars of Plutarch. The poet Horace is the eye of the Augustan age; Tacitus, the wisest of historians; and Martial will give him Roman manners,—and some very bad ones,—in the early days of the Empire: but Martial must be read, if read at all, in his own tongue. These will bring him to Gibbon, who will take him in charge and convey him with abundant entertainment down—with notice of all remarkable objects on the way—through fourteen hundred years of time. He cannot spare Gibbon, with his vast reading, with such wit and continuity of mind, that, though never profound, his book is one of the conveniences of civilization, like the new railroad from ocean to ocean,—and, I think, will be sure to send the reader to his *Memoirs of Himself*, and the *Extracts from my Journal*, and *Abstracts of my Readings*, which will spur the laziest scholar to emulation of his prodigious performance.
—RALPH WALDO EMERSON, "Books," *Society and Solitude*, 1870

Although upon the whole Gibbon is one of the rare examples of a writer whose reputation, great and deserved at once, has deservedly increased as time went on, it cannot be said that he has at any time escaped unjust or at least irrelevant detraction. At the time of its appearance, though it could not fail to make its mark, the *Decline and Fall of the Roman Empire* was exposed to misconception from two causes. In respect of one of these the author was justly to be blamed; while in respect of the other he was guiltless. There can be no doubt that Gibbon's attitude towards Christianity and religion generally, was even from the lowest point of view a mistake. It prejudiced one large section of his readers against him; it introduced a disturbing and deluding influence into his own manner of view; and what is more it was already something of an anachronism. Gibbon took it up when it was already losing its hold upon the brighter and more original spirits in all countries, when it was a fashion and not even a very new fashion. Again, the generation for whose benefit the book was written was in the habit of considering the ages with which all the best and most characteristic part of it deals as "dark," sordid, uninteresting, and unworthy the attention of any but pedants and monks. Gibbon's genius indeed compelled them to read; but they cannot but have felt a certain grudge against him for the compulsion. Nor did things improve when a new generation and a new century came into being. The offence to orthodoxy remained, and if the distaste for the subject slowly yielded to the pressure of Romantic feelings, it was replaced by an even stronger distaste for the style, and a sort of double-edged political odium. Tories disliked Gibbon because of his subversive religious opinions; Whigs made as little of him as they could because he was a Tory in politics. Accordingly a collection of curious uncritical omissions or aggressions might be made from the greater critics of the first quarter of this century about him. The remarks of Coleridge, the most scholarly and philosophical, and of Leigh Hunt, the most impulsive and popular, of the Romantic critics on his style are almost equally unfavourable; Sydney Smith, in a context which makes oversight almost impossible, excludes him from the list of "our greatest historians"; Jeffrey, so far as I remember, leaves him severely alone. The massive splendour of his manner had ceased to please a time which was seeking after more fantastic literary ornament; and the incomparable richness and art of his matter did not yet fully appeal to a time which was only beginning the history of the document.

Yet even against these drawbacks Gibbon's wonderful merits made their way; and of late his fame on the side of the matter has risen higher than ever, and on that of form has recovered much and will I think recover more appreciation. The estimate now held by all the best historians of his historical merits is something unique in literary history. For the greater part of the century since his death, and for the whole of its latter half, one unceasing process of unearthing original authorities, and of correcting (not always too critically or generously) the treatment of their subjects by previous writers has been going on. Historian after historian whose name was great with our forefathers, has been justly or unjustly relegated from the shelf of history to that of *belles lettres* if his literary merits happen to have been considerable, and to the garret or the cellar if they were not. Yet every critic who, himself competent to speak even on parts of the subject, has examined these parts with fairness, has confessed with astonishment the adequacy of Gibbon's treatment; while those who are competent to judge the work as a whole have spoken with even greater astonishment of his coordination of the several parts into that whole. In the union of accuracy and grasp indeed Gibbon has absolutely no rival in literature ancient and modern. It constantly happens that a most learned, industrious, and accurate scholar will show himself hopelessly incompetent for the task of arranging his knowledge of something much less than the history of the whole of the western and part of the eastern world for fifteen hundred years. It happens—not much less often—that a man of real historical range and grasp is unequal to the toil, or unprovided with the faculty of ascertaining and stating details with accuracy. But Gibbon is equally great at both these things. It may be that he was not a little indebted to a gift which may be called the gift of sagaciously letting alone; but he certainly did not abuse this gift, and one of his most remarkable characteristics is his faculty of making slight references, which on fuller knowledge of the subject are found to be perfectly exact as far as they go. Every careful critic of his own and other men's work knows that there is no more dangerous point than this one of slight reference or allusion to subjects imperfectly known, nor any in which sciolism or imposture is more certain to be found out. Yet it is scarcely too much to say that Gibbon has never been thus found out. There were some things—not many—which he did not and could not know; but almost everything that there was for him to know he knew.

The merits of his manner must of necessity be far more matters of taste, of opinion, and of variations in both. The simile of the "Hampshire militiaman," which has sometimes been supposed to be justified by his own very innocent remark that his training in drill and tactics had been of use to him on the military side of history is smart enough of course. All that can be said is that it is a very high compliment to the Hampshire militia. To those who insist upon extreme ornamentation, or extreme simplicity of style, Gibbon's, of course, must be distasteful. But to those who judge a thing by its possession of its own excellences, and not by its lack of the excellences of others, it must always be the subject of an immense admiration. In the first place it is perfectly clear, and for all its stateliness so little fatiguing to the reader that true Gibbonians read it, by snatches or in long draughts, as others read a newspaper or a novel for mere pastime. Although full of irony and epigram it is never uneasily charged with either; and the narrative is never broken, the composition never interrupted for the sake of a flourish or a "point." It may be thought by some to abuse antithesis of sense and balance of cadence; but I should say myself that there is fully sufficient variety in the sentences and in the paragraph arrangement to prevent this. Here, no doubt, the *ultima ratio* of individual taste comes in. What is not disputable is that in the style of the balanced sentence, in which antithesis was the chief figure used, and in which the writer depends upon an ironic or declamatory flavouring, as the case might be, to save his manner from stiffness, Gibbon has achieved the "farthest possible." That this was so, may be seen, better perhaps than in any other way by comparing the practice of Macaulay, who may be called a popular nineteenth-century Gibbon. That most ingenious and widely read historian in reality did little more than shorten the Gibbonian antithesis, substitute a sharp quick movement for the former stately roll, exchange irony for a certain kind of wit, and the declamation of oratory for the declamation of debate.

These remarks of necessity apply most to the *Decline and Fall*, but the manner of Gibbon is one and indivisible, and the *Autobiography*, the *Miscellaneous Works*, and even the letters, exhibit no very different characteristics. It would indeed have been surprising if they had. For Gibbon was one of those fortunate and rare men of letters, who early conceiving a great and definite scheme of literary attempt have had the leisure and the means to perfect their literary undertakings. He spent about twenty years on the completion of the work which he was born to do; and everything that as by-work and addition he felt himself inclined to grapple with, had in its preparation and execution an equally unhurried maturity. There may be, and no doubt there were, other instances of faculty which had equal opportunities of developing itself, and failed. In his case the faculty was there, the scheme was there, and the opportunities were there, with the result of a perfect accomplishment. It rests with those who hold that the faculty and the scheme being present but the opportunities absent, the same or any approximately equal result is attainable, to produce an instance justifying their theory.—GEORGE SAINTSBURY, "Edward Gibbon," *English Prose*, ed. Henry Craik, 1895, Vol. 4, pp. 455–59

Works

THE HISTORY OF THE DECLINE AND FALL OF THE ROMAN EMPIRE

It is not my intention to detain the reader by expatiating on the variety or the importance of the subject, which I have undertaken to treat; since the merit of the choice would serve to render the weakness of the execution still more apparent, and still less excusable. But, as I have presumed to lay before the Public a *first* volume only of the History of the Decline and Fall of the Roman Empire, it will perhaps be expected that I should explain, in a few words, the nature and limits of my general plan.

The memorable series of revolutions, which, in the course of about thirteen centuries, gradually undermined, and at length destroyed, the solid fabric of human greatness, may, with some propriety, be divided into the three following periods:

I. The first of these periods may be traced from the age of Trajan and the Antonines, when the Roman monarchy, having attained its full strength and maturity, began to verge towards its decline; and will extend to the subversion of the Western Empire, by the barbarians of Germany and Scythia, the rude ancestors of the most polished nations of modern Europe. This extraordinary revolution, which subjected Rome to the power of a Gothic conqueror, was completed about the beginning of the sixth century.

II. The second period of the Decline and Fall of Rome may be supposed to commence with the reign of Justinian, who by his laws, as well as by his victories, restored a transient splendour to the Eastern Empire. It will comprehend the invasion of Italy by the Lombards; the conquest of the Asiatic and African provinces by the Arabs, who embraced the religion of Mahomet; the revolt of the Roman people against the feeble princes of Constantinople; and the elevation of Charlemagne, who, in the year 800, established the second or German Empire of the West.

III. The last and longest of these periods includes about six centuries and a half; from the revival of the Western Empire till the taking of Constantinople by the Turks and the extinction of a degenerate race of princes, who continued to assume the titles of Cæsar and Augustus, after their dominions were contracted to the limits of a single city; in which the language, as well as manners, of the ancient Romans had been long since forgotten. The writer who should undertake to relate the events of this period would find himself obliged to enter into the general history of the Crusades, as far as they contributed to the ruin of the Greek Empire; and he would scarcely be able to restrain his curiosity from making some enquiry into the state of the city of Rome during the darkness and confusion of the middle ages.

As I have ventured, perhaps too hastily, to commit to the press a work, which, in every sense of the word, deserves the epithet of imperfect, I consider myself as contracting an engagement to finish, most probably in a second volume, the first of these memorable periods; and to deliver to the Public the complete History of the Decline and Fall of Rome, from the age of the Antonines to the subversion of the Western Empire. With regard to the subsequent periods, though I may entertain some hopes, I dare not presume to give any assurances. The execution of the extensive plan which I have described would connect the ancient and modern history of the World; but it would require many years of health, of leisure, and of perseverance.—EDWARD GIBBON, "Preface" to the First Edition of *The History of the Decline and Fall of the Roman Empire*, 1776

After the singular pleasure of reading you, Sir, the next satisfaction is to declare my admiration. I have read great part of your volume, and cannot decide to which of its various merits I give the preference, though I have no doubt of assigning my partiality to one virtue in the author, which, seldom as I meet with it, always strikes me superiorly. Its quality will naturally prevent your guessing which I mean. It is your amiable modesty. How can you know so much, judge so well, possess your subject and your knowledge and your power of judicious reflection so thoroughly, and yet command yourself and betray no dictatorial arrogance of decision? How unlike very ancient and very modern authors! You have unexpectedly given the world a classic history. The fame it must acquire will tend every day to acquit this panegyric of flattery. The impressions it has made on me are very numerous. The strongest is the thirst of being better acquainted with you—but I reflect that I have been a trifling author, and am in no light profound enough to deserve your intimacy, except by confessing your superiority so frankly, that I assure you honestly I already feel no envy, though I did for a moment. The best proof I can give you of my sincerity, is to exhort you warmly and earnestly to go on with your noble work—the strongest, though a presumptuous, mark of my friendship, is to warn you never to let your charming modesty be corrupted by the acclamations your talents will receive. The native qualities of the man should never be sacrificed to those of the author, however shining. I take this liberty as an older man, which reminds me how little I dare promise myself that I shall see your work completed! But I love posterity enough to contribute, if I can, to give them pleasure through you.

I am too weak to say more, though I could talk for hours on your *History*. But one feeling I cannot suppress, though it is a sensation of vanity. I think, nay I am sure I perceive, that your sentiments on government agree with my own. It is the only point on which I suspect myself of any partiality in my admiration. It is a reflection of a far inferior vanity that pleases me in your speaking with so much distinction of that alas! wonderful period in which the world saw five good monarchs succeed each other. I have often thought of treating that Elysian era. Happily it has fallen into better hands!—HORACE WALPOLE, Letter to Edward Gibbon (Feb. 14, 1776)

As I ran through your Volume of History with a great deal of Avidity and Impatience, I cannot forbear discovering somewhat of the same Impatience in returning you thanks for your agreeable Present, and expressing the Satisfaction which the Performance has given me. Whether I consider the Dignity of your Style, the Depth of your Matter, or the Extensiveness of your Learning, I must regard the Work as equally the Object of Esteem; and I own, that if I had not previously had the Happiness of your personal Acquaintance, such a Performance, from an Englishman in our Age, would have given me some Surprize. You may smile at this Sentiment; but as it seems to me that your Countrymen, for almost a whole Generation, have given themselves up to barbarous and absurd Faction, and have totally neglected all polite Letters, I no longer expected any valuable Production ever to come from them. I know it will give you Pleasure (as it did me), to find that all the Men of Letters in this Place concur in their Admiration of your Work, and in their anxious Desire of your continuing it.

When I heard of your Undertaking (which was some time ago), I own I was a little curious to see how you woud extricate yourself from the Subject of your two last Chapters. I think you have observ'd a very prudent Temperament; but it was impossible to treat the Subject so as not to give Grounds of Suspicion against you, and you may expect that a Clamour will arise. This, if anything, will retard your Success with the Public; for in every other respect your Work is calculated to be popular. But, among many other marks of Decline, the Prevalence of Superstition in England, prognosticates the Fall of Philosophy and Decay of Taste; and though no body be more capable than you to revive them, you will probably find a Struggle in your first Advances. ⟨. . .⟩

I must inform you, that we are all very anxious to hear that you have fully collected the Materials for your second Volume, and that you are even considerably advanc'd in the Composition of it. I speak this more in the Name of my Friends than in my own; as I cannot expect to live so long as to see the Publication of it. Your ensuing Volume will be more delicate than the preceding, but I trust in your Prudence for extricating you from the Difficulties; and, in all Events, you have Courage to despise the Clamour of Bigots. I am with great Regard Dear Sir Your most obedient and most humble Servant.—DAVID HUME, Letter to Edward Gibbon (March 18, 1776)

I am ashamed of having deferred so long to thank you for the agreeable presents of your two new volumes, but just as I had finished the first reading of them I was taken ill, and continued, for two or three weeks, nervous, deaf, and languid. I have now recovered as much spirit as to tell you with what perfect satisfaction I have not only perused but studied this part of your work. I knew enough of your talents and industry to expect a great deal, but you have gone far beyond my expectations. I can recollect no historical work from which I ever received so much instruction; and when I consider in what a barren field you had to glean and pick up materials, I am truly astonished at the connected and interesting story you have formed. I like the style of these volumes better than that of the first; there is the same beauty, richness, and perspicuity of language, with less of that quaintness into which your admiration of Tacitus sometimes seduced you. I am highly pleased with the reign of Julian. I was a little afraid that you might lean with some partiality towards him; but even bigots, I should think, must allow that you have delineated his most singular character with a more masterly hand than ever touched it before. You set me a-reading his works, with which I was very slenderly acquainted; and I am much struck with the felicity wherewith you have described that odd infusion of heathen fanaticism and philosophical coxcombry which mingled with the great qualities of a hero and a genius. Your chapter concerning the pastoral nations is admirable; and though I hold myself to be a tolerably good general historian, a great part of it was new to me. As soon as I have leisure I purpose to trace you to your sources of information, and I have no doubt of finding you as exact there as I have found you in other passages where I have made a scrutiny. It was always my idea that a historian should feel himself a witness giving evidence upon oath. I am glad to perceive by your minute scrupulosity that your notions are the same. The last chapter of your work is the only one with which I am not entirely satisfied. I imagine you rather anticipate in describing the jurisprudence and institutions of the Franks, and should think that the account of private war, ordeals, chivalry, &c., would have come in more in its place about the age of Charlemagne or later; but with respect to this and some other petty criticisms I will have an opportunity of talking fully to you soon, as I propose setting out for London on Monday. I have, indeed, many things to say to you; and as my stay in London is to be very short, I shall hope to find your door, at which I will be very often, always open to me. I cannot conclude without approving of the caution with which the new volumes are written; I hope it will exempt you from the illiberal abuse the first volume drew upon you.—WILLIAM ROBERTSON, Letter to Edward Gibbon (May 12, 1781)

You will be diverted to hear that Mr Gibbon has quarrelled with me. He lent me his second volume in the middle of November. I returned it with a most civil panegyric. He came for more incense, I gave it, but alas! with too much sincerity, I added, 'Mr Gibbon, I am sorry *you* should have pitched on so disgusting a subject as the Constantinopolitan history. There is so much of the Arians and Eunomians, and semi-Pelagians; and there is such a strange contrast between Roman and Gothic manners, and so little harmony between a Consul Sabinus and a Ricimer, Duke of the palace, that though you have written the story as well as it could be written, I fear few will have patience to read it.' He coloured; all his round features squeezed themselves into sharp angles; he screwed up his button-mouth and rapping his snuff-box, said, 'It had never been put together before'—*so well* he meant to add—but gulped it. He meant *so well* certainly, for Tillemont, whom he quotes in every page, has done the very thing. Well from that hour to this I have never seen him, though he used to call once or twice a week; nor has sent me the third volume, as he promised. I well knew his vanity, even about his ridiculous face and person, but thought he had too much sense to avow it so palpably. The history is admirably written, especially in the characters of Julian and Athanasius, in both which he has piqued himself on impartiality—but the style is far less sedulously enamelled than the first volume.—HORACE WALPOLE, Letter to William Mason (Jan. 27, 1781)

I now discharge my promise, and complete my design, of writing the History of the Decline and Fall of the Roman Empire, both in the West and the East. The whole period extends from the age of Trajan and the Antonines to the taking of Constantinople by Mohamet the Second; and includes a review of the Crusades and the state of Rome during the middle ages. Since the publication of the first volume, twelve years have elapsed; twelve years, according to my wish, "of health, of leisure and of perseverance". I may now congratulate my deliverance from a long and laborious service, and my satisfaction will be pure and perfect, if the public favour should be extended to the conclusion of my work.

It was my first intention to have collected under one view the numerous authors, of every age and language, from whom I have derived the materials of this history; and I am still convinced that the apparent ostentation would be more than compensated by real use. If I have renounced this idea, if I have declined an undertaking which had obtained the approbation of a master-artist, my excuse may be found in the extreme difficulty of assigning a proper measure to such a catalogue. A naked list of names and editions would not be satisfactory either to myself or my readers: the characters of the principal Authors of the Roman and Byzantine History have been occasionally connected with the events which they describe; a more copious and critical enquiry might indeed deserve, but it would demand, an elaborate volume, which might swell by degrees into a general library of historical writers. For the present I shall content myself with renewing my serious protestation, that I have always endeavoured to draw from the fountain-head; that my curiosity, as well as a sense of duty, has always urged me to study the originals; and that, if they have sometimes eluded my search, I have carefully marked the secondary evidence, on whose faith a passage or a fact were reduced to depend.

I shall soon visit the banks of the lake of Lausanne, a country which I have known and loved from my early youth. Under a mild government, amidst a beauteous landskip, in a life of leisure and independence, and among a people of easy and elegant manners, I have enjoyed, and may again hope to enjoy, the varied pleasures of retirement and society. But I shall ever glory in the name and character of an Englishman: I am proud of my birth in a free and enlightened country; and the approbation of that country is the best and most honourable reward for my labours. Were I ambitious of any other Patron than the Public, I would inscribe this work to a Statesman, who, in a long, a stormy, and at length an unfortunate administration, had many political opponents, almost without a personal enemy: who has retained, in his fall from power, many faithful and disinterested friends; and who, under the pressure of severe infirmity, enjoys the lively vigour of his mind, and the felicity of his incomparable temper. LORD NORTH will permit me to express the feelings of friendship in the language of truth: but even truth and friendship should be silent, if he still dispensed the favours of the crown.

In a remote solitude, vanity may still whisper in my ear that my readers, perhaps, may enquire whether, in the conclusion of the present work, I am now taking an everlasting farewell. They shall hear all that I know myself, all that I could reveal to the most intimate friend. The motives of action or silence are now equally balanced; nor can I pronounce, in my most secret thoughts, on which side the scale will preponderate. I cannot dissemble that twelve ample octavos must have tried, and may have exhausted, the indulgence of the Public; that, in the repetition of similar attempts, a successful Author has much more to lose, than he can hope to gain; that I am now descending into the vale of years; and that the most respectable of my countrymen, the men whom I aspire to imitate, have resigned the pen of history about the same period of their lives. Yet I consider that the annals of ancient and modern times may afford many rich and interesting subjects; that I am still possessed of health and leisure; that by the practice of writing some skill and facility must be acquired; and that in the ardent pursuit of truth and knowledge I am not conscious of decay. To an active mind, indolence is more painful than labour; and the first months of my liberty will be occupied and amused in the excursions of curiosity and taste. By such temptations I have been sometimes seduced from the rigid duty even of a pleasing and voluntary task: but my time will now be my own; and in the use or abuse of independence I shall no longer fear my own reproaches or those of my friends. I am fairly entitled to a year of jubilee: next summer and the following winter will rapidly pass away; and experience only can determine whether I shall still prefer the freedom and variety of study to the design and composition of a regular work, which animates, while it confines, the daily application of the Author. Caprice and accident may influence my choice; but the dexterity of self-love will contrive to applaud either active industry or philosophic repose.—EDWARD GIBBON, "Preface" to the Fourth Volume of the Quarto Edition of *The History of the Decline and Fall of the Roman Empire*, 1788

I finished Mr Gibbon a full fortnight ago, and was extremely pleased. It is a most wonderful mass of information, not only on history, but almost on all the ingredients of history, as war, government, commerce, coin, and what not. If it has a fault, it is in embracing too much, and consequently in not detailing enough, and in striding backwards and forwards from one set of princes to another, and from one subject to another; so that, without much historic knowledge, and without much memory, and much method in one's memory, it is almost impossible not to be sometimes bewildered: nay, his own impatience to tell what he knows, makes the author, though commonly so explicit, not perfectly clear in his expressions. The last chapter of the fourth volume, I own, made me recoil, and I could scarcely push through it. So far from being Catholic or heretic, I wished Mr Gibbon had never heard of Monophysites, Nestorians, or any such fools!—But the sixth volume made ample amends; Mohamet and the popes were gentlemen and good company.—I abominate fractions of theology and reformation.—HORACE WALPOLE, Letter to Thomas Barret (June 5, 1788)

You desire to know my opinion of Mr. Gibbon. I can say very little about him; for such is the affectation of his style, that I could never get through the half of one of his volumes. If any body would translate him into good classical English (such, I mean, as Addison, Swift, Lord Lyttleton, &c. wrote), I should read him with eagerness; for I know there must be much curious matter in his work. His cavils against religion have, I think, been all confuted; he does not seem to understand that part of his subject: indeed I have never yet met with a man, or with an author, who both understood Christianity, and disbelieved it. It is, I am told, the fashion to admire Gibbon's style; my opinion of it however, is supported by great authorities, of whom I need only mention Lord Mansfield, the present Bishop of London, Mrs. Montagu, and Major Mercer. In the Bishop's last letter to me there is the following passage: 'We have been much amused this summer with Keate's Account of the Pelew Islands: and it is almost the only summer book we have had. For Gibbon's three bulky quartos are fit only for the gloom and horror of wintry storms. His style is more obscure and affected than ever; and his insults on Christianity not less offensive.'—JAMES BEATTIE, Letter to the Duchess of Gordon (Nov. 20, 1788), cited in Sir William Forbes, *An Account of the Life and Writings of James Beattie, LL.D.* (1806), 1824, Vol. 2, pp. 225–26

I have ten thousand appologies to make for not having long ago returned you my best thanks for the very agreable present you made me of the three last Volumes of your History. I cannot express to you the pleasure it gives me to find, that by the universal assent of every man of taste and learning, whom I either know or correspond with, it sets you at the very head of the whole literary tribe at present existing in Europe.—ADAM SMITH, Letter to Edward Gibbon (Dec. 10, 1788)

An impartial judge, I think, must allow, that Mr. Gibbon's History is one of the ablest performances of its kind that has ever appeared. His industry is indefatigable; his accuracy scrupulous; his reading, which indeed is sometimes ostentatiously displayed, immense; his attention always awake; his memory retentive; his style emphatic and expressive; his periods harmonious. His reflections are often just and profound; he pleads eloquently for the rights of mankind, and the duty of toleration; nor does his humanity ever slumber, unless when women are ravished, or the Christians persecuted.

Mr. Gibbon shews, it is true, so strong a dislike to Christianity, as visibly disqualifies him for that society, of which he has created Ammianus Marcellinus president. I confess that I see nothing wrong in Mr. Gibbon's attack on Christianity. It proceeded, I doubt not, from the purest and most virtuous motive. We can only blame him for carrying on the attack in an insidious manner, and with improper weapons. He often makes, when he cannot readily find, an occasion to insult our religion; which he hates so cordially, that he might seem to revenge some personal injury. Such is his eagerness in the cause, that he stoops to the most despicable pun, or to the most aukward perversion of language, for the pleasure of turning the Scripture into ribaldry, or of calling Jesus an impostor.

Though his style is in general correct and elegant, he sometimes *draws out the thread of his verbosity finer than the staple of his argument*. In endeavouring to avoid vulgar terms, he too frequently dignifies trifles, and clothes common thoughts in a splendid dress, that would be rich enough for the noblest ideas. In short, we are too often reminded of *that great man*, Mr. Prig, *the auctioneer, whose manner was so inimitably fine, that he had as much to say upon a ribbon as a Raphael.*

Sometimes in his anxiety to vary his phrase, he becomes obscure; and, instead of calling his personages by their names, defines them by their birth, alliance, office, or other circumstances of their history. Thus an honest gentleman is often described by a circumlocution, lest the same word should be twice repeated in the same page. Sometimes epithets are added, which the tenour of the sentence renders unnecessary. Sometimes in his attempts at elegance, he loses sight of English, and sometimes of sense.

A less pardonable fault is that rage for indecency which pervades the whole work, but especially the last volumes. And, to the honour of his consistency, this is the same man who is so prudish that he dares not call Belisarius a cuckold, because it is too bad a word for a *decent* historian to use. If the history were anonymous, I should guess that these disgraceful obscenities were written by some debauchee, who having from age, or accident, or excess, survived the practice of lust, still indulged himself in the luxury of speculation; *and exposed the impotent imbecillity, after he had lost the vigour of the passions.*

But these few faults make no considerable abatement in my general esteem. Notwithstanding all its particular defects, I greatly admire the whole; as I should admire a beautiful face in the author, though it were tarnished with a few freckles; or as I should admire an elegant person and address, though they were blemished with a little affectation.—RICHARD PORSON, "Preface" to *Letters to Mr. Archdeacon Travis*, 1790, pp. xxviii–xxxi

I often mix together in the most confused manner the reading of books of quite opposite quality. As for instance, I lately read at the same time, Gibbon's *Decline and Fall*, and Baxter's *Account of his own Life and Times*. The work of Gibbon excites my utmost admiration; not so much by the immense learning and industry which it displays, as by the commanding intellect, the keen sagacity, apparent in almost every page. The admiration of his ability extends even to his manner of showing his hatred to Christianity, which is exquisitely subtle and acute, and adapted to do very great mischief, even where there is not the smallest avowal of hostility. It is to be deplored that a great part of the early history of the Christian Church was exactly such as a man like him could have wished. There is no doubt that in his hands, Fathers, Councils, and the ancient contests and mutual persecutions of Christian parties, take their worst form; but after every allowance for this historian's malignity, it is impossible not to contemplate with disgust and reprobation a great part of what the Christian world has been accustomed to revere.—JOHN FOSTER, Letter to John Fawcett (May 23, 1805), *The Life and Correspondence of John Foster*, ed. J. E. Ryland, 1846, Vol. 1, p. 262

Gibbon is copious in reflections: his style is, in detail, particularly excellent, but he is too uniformly rich in ornament. His page is replete with Latin and French idiomatic turns: owing to the mixed character of the English language which has no definite fixed boundary of speech. Gibbon's artificial half-Latin manner was more especially introduced by Johnson: in principle, at least, the English have partially given it up, as doing violence to the genius of their language. As regards internal merit, whilst copious and attractive, he is, nevertheless, unsatisfactory: owing to the absence of right feeling, and the presence of Voltaire's spirit of mockery at religion, at all times unworthy of a historian, and not even easy or natural in Gibbon, since it militates against his laboured elegance of expression, and seems an awkward attempt at witticism.—FRIEDRICH SCHLEGEL, *Lectures on the History of Literature*, 1815

Next I read Gibbon's decline and fall of the Roman empire— a work of immense research and splendid execution. Embracing almost all the civilised world, and extending from the time of Trajan to the taking of Constantinople by Mohamet II in 1453, it connects the events of ancient with those of modern history. Alternately delighted and offended by the gorgeous coulouring with which his fancy invests the rude and scanty materials of his narrative; sometimes fatigued by the learning of his notes, occasionally amused by their liveliness frequently disgusted with their obscenity, and admiring or deploring the bitterness of his skilful irony—I toiled through his massy tomes with exemplary patience. His style is exuberant, sonorous and epigrammatic to a degree that is often displeasing. He yields to Hume in elegance and distinctness—to Robertson in talents for general disquisition—but he excels them both in a species of brief & shrewd remark for which he seems to have taken Tacitus as a model, more than any other that I know of. —THOMAS CARLYLE, Letter to Robert Mitchell (Feb. 16, 1818)

Arrived at Bury before tea. My brother and sister were going to hear an astronomical lecture. I stayed alone and read a chapter in Gibbon on the early history of the Germans. Having previously read the two first lectures of Schlegel, I had the pleasure of comparison, and I found much in Gibbon that I had thought original in Schlegel. Their views differ slightly; for the most part in the higher character given by Schlegel to the Germans, the correctness of which I had doubted. It seems absurd to ascribe great effects to the enthusiastic love of nature by a people otherwise so low in civilization. But probably he is justified in the opinion that the Goths were to no great degree the bringers of barbarism. He considers them the great agents in the renovation of society.—HENRY CRABB ROBINSON, *Diary*, April 7, 1820

Less vigorous, less profound, less elevated than Montesquieu, Gibbon appropriated to himself the subject, of which his predecessor had pointed out the extent and rich stores. He carefully traced and untwisted slowly the whole progressive chain of those occurrences, some of which Montesquieu had used, rather as pegs whereon to hang his own ideas, than as guide-posts to show his reader the course and mutual influence of events. The English historian was eminently gifted with the penetration which ascends to causes, and the sagacity which discerns such as are true amid those which are only apparently so; he was born in an age when enlightened curiosity studied the gear of the social machine, and strove to understand the connection of its parts, their working, their use, their effects, and their importance; the pursuits and the stretch of his mind placed him on a level with the lights of his age; the materials— that is, the facts of history he examined and criticised with a judicious erudition; its moral aspect—that is, the relation of events between themselves and with the actors, he regarded with a skilful philosophy. He was aware that a dry detail of facts excites no other interest than the idle curiosity which desires to know the actions of other men; and that history, to be truly useful and serious, must look at the society which it depicts, in all the different points of view in which it is seen by the statesman, the warrior, the magistrate, the financier, the philosopher, and all whose position or knowledge may lay open to them the springs of action. Equally just and noble, this idea, as it appears to me, inspired the author, while composing his *History of the Decline and Fall of the Roman Empire*. It is not a simple recital of the events which agitated the Roman world, from the elevation of Augustus to the taking of Constantinople by the Turks. With this picture we find constantly associated the state of the finances, of opinions, of manners, of the military system, and of all those internal and concealed causes either of prosperity or misery, by which the existence and welfare of society are silently established or secretly undermined. Faithful to that recognized, but neglected law, which prescribes fact as the guide of general reflections, and a step-by-step adherence to its slow but necessary course, Gibbon has produced a work remarkable for the extent of its views, although seldom dignified by exalted ideas; and abounding in positive and interesting results, in spite of its author's scepticism.

The merits of the work are incontestably proved by its success, in an age which had produced Montesquieu; and which, at the time of the publication, still possessed Hume, Robertson, and Voltaire: they are confirmed by the subsequently undisturbed permanence of that success. In the most enlightened countries of Europe, in England, France, and Germany, Gibbon is always quoted as an authority. Even those who have detected his inaccuracies, or do not assent to some of his opinions, never point out his mistakes nor contest his views, but with the respect due to superior merit. My labours have required that I should consult the writings of philosophers who have discussed the financial resources of the Roman empire, of learned men who have studied its chronology, of theologians who have sounded the depths of ecclesiastical history, of lawyers who have carefully investigated the Roman jurisprudence, of oriental scholars well versed in Arab customs and the Koran, and of modern historians who have largely inquired respecting the Crusades and their influence— each of these writers has remarked and indicated in the *History of the Decline and Fall of the Roman Empire*, some instances of negligence, some false, or at least imperfect views, and sometimes even omissions, which it is difficult to consider as not designed; they have set right some facts and advantageously contradicted some assertions; but for the most part, they made the ideas and researches of Gibbon their starting-point, or used them as proofs of whatever new opinions they themselves advanced.—F. P. G. GUIZOT, "Preface" to *The History of the Decline and Fall of the Roman Empire*, 1828

Gibbon's style is detestable; but his style is not the worst thing about him. His history has proved an effectual bar to all real familiarity with the temper and habits of imperial Rome. Few persons read the original authorities, even those which are classical; and certainly no distinct knowledge of the actual state of the empire can be obtained from Gibbon's rhetorical sketches. He takes notice of nothing but what may produce an effect; he skips from eminence to eminence, without ever taking you through the valleys between: in fact, his work is little else but a disguised collection of all the splendid anecdotes which he could find in any book concerning any persons or nations, from the Antonines to the capture of Constantinople. When I read a chapter in Gibbon, I seem to be looking through a luminous haze or fog:—the figures come and go, I know not how or why, all larger than life, or distorted or discolored; nothing is real, vivid, true; all is scenical, and, as it were, exhibited by candle-light. And then to call it a History of the Decline and Fall of the Roman Empire! Was there ever a greater misnomer? I protest I do not remember a single philosophical attempt made throughout the work to fathom the ultimate cause of the decline or fall of that empire. How miserably deficient is the narrative of the important reign of Justinian! And that poor skepticism, which Gibbon mistook for Socratic philosophy, has led him to misstate and mistake the character and influence of Christianity in a way which even an avowed infidel or atheist would not and could not have done. Gibbon was a man of immense reading; but he had no philosophy; and he never fully understood the principle upon which the best of the old historians wrote. He attempted to imitate their artificial construction of the whole work—their dramatic ordonnance of the parts—without seeing that their histories were intended more as documents illustrative of the truths of political philosophy than as mere chronicles of events.—SAMUEL TAYLOR COLERIDGE, *Table Talk*, Aug. 15, 1833

Another very celebrated historian, we mean Gibbon—not a man of mere science and analysis, like Hume, but with some (though not the truest or profoundest) artistic feeling of the picturesque, and from whom, therefore, rather more might have been expected—has with much pains succeeded in producing a tolerably graphic picture of here and there a battle, a tumult, or an insurrection: his book is full of movement and costume, and would make a series of very pretty ballets at the Opera-house, and the ballets would give us fully as distinct an idea of the Roman empire, and how it declined and fell, as the book does. If we want that, we must look for it anywhere but in Gibbon. One touch of M. Guizot removes a portion of the veil which hid from us the recesses of private life under the Roman empire, lets in a ray of light which penetrates as far even as the domestic hearth of a subject of Rome, and shews us the government at work making that desolate; but no similar gleam of light from Gibbon's mind ever reaches the subject; *human life*, in the times he wrote about, is not what he concerned himself with.—JOHN STUART MILL, "Carlyle's French Revolution," 1837

I read a good deal of Gibbon. He is grossly partial to the pagan persecutors; quite offensively so. His opinion of the Christian fathers is very little removed from mine; but his excuses for the

tyranny of their oppressors give to his book the character which Porson describes. He writes like a man who had received some personal injury from Christianity, and wished to be revenged on it and all its professors.—THOMAS BABINGTON MACAULAY, *Diary* (Dec. 22, 1838), cited in G. Otto Trevelyan, *The Life and Letters of Lord Macaulay*, 1876, Vol. 2, p. 40

He had three hobbies which he rode to the death (stuffed puppets as they were), and which he kept in condition by the continual sacrifice of all that is valuable in language. These hobbies were *Dignity—Modulation—Laconism*.

Dignity is all very well; and history demands it for its general tone; but the being everlastingly on stilts is not only troublesome and awkward, but dangerous. He who falls *en homme ordinaire*—from the mere slipping of his feet—is usually an object of sympathy; but all men tumble now and then, and this tumbling from high sticks is sure to provoke laughter.

His modulation, however, is *always* ridiculous; for it is so uniform, so continuous, and so jauntily kept up, that we almost fancy the writer waltzing to his words.

With him, to speak lucidly was a far less merit than to speak smoothly and curtly. There is a way in which, through the nature of the language itself, we may often save a few words by talking backwards; and this is, therefore, a favorite practice with Gibbon. Observe the sentence commencing—"The nature of the soil." The thought expressed could scarcely be more condensed in expression; but, for the sake of this condensation, he renders the idea difficult of comprehension, by subverting the natural order of a simple proposition, and placing a deduction before that from which it is deduced. An ordinary man would have thus written: "As these formidable concussions arise from subterranean fires kindled by the union and fermentation of iron and sulphur, we may judge of the degree in which any region is exposed to earthquake by the presence or absence of these minerals." My sentence has forty words—that of Gibbon thirty-six; but the first cannot fail of being instantly comprehended, while the latter it may be necessary to re-read.

The mere *terseness* of this historian is, however, grossly over-rated. In general, he conveys an idea (although darkly) in fewer words than others of his time; but a habit of straight thinking that rejects non-essentials, will enable any one to say, for example, what was intended above, *both* more briefly and more distinctly. He must abandon, of course, "formidable concussions" and things of that kind.

E. g.—"The sulphur and iron of any region express its liability to earthquake; their fermentation being its cause."

Here are seventeen words in place of the thirty-six; and these seventeen convey the full force of all that it was necessary to say. Such concision is, nevertheless, an error, and, so far as respects the true object of concision, is a *bull*. The most truly concise style is that which most rapidly transmits the sense. What, then, should be said of the concision of Carlyle?—that those are mad who admire a brevity which squanders our time for the purpose of economizing our printing-ink and paper.

Observe, now, the passage above quoted, commencing—"Each year is marked." What is it the historian wishes to say? Not, certainly, that every year was marked by earthquakes that shook Constantinople forty days, and extended to all regions of the earth!—yet this only is the legitimate interpretation. The earthquakes are said to be of *such* duration that Constantinople, &c., and these earthquakes (of *such* duration) were experienced every year. But this is a pure Gibbonism—an original one; no man ever so rhodomontaded before. He means to say merely that the earthquakes were of unusual duration and extent—the duration of one being so long that Constantinople shook for forty days, and the extent of another being so wide as to include the whole empire of Rome—"by which," he adds *sotto voce*—"by which insulated facts the reader may estimate that *average* duration and extent of which I speak"—a thing the reader will find it difficult to do.

A few years hence—and should any one compose a mock heroic in the manner of the *Decline and Fall*, the poem will be torn to pieces by the critics, *instanter*, as an unwarrantable exaggeration of the principles of the burlesque.—EDGAR ALLAN POE, *Marginalia* (1844), *Essays and Reviews*, ed. G. R. Thompson, 1984, pp. 1320–21

In this first volume the historian displayed and developed in the greatest detail the position and constitution of the empire under the Antonines. He carried his explanations back to the policy of Augustus, he depicted in general outlines the reigns and the minds of the five Emperors to whom mankind owed its last great century, the finest and perhaps the most happy of all those which history has recorded; then starting from Commodus he entered upon the unbroken course of his story. The first volume alone contained much matter of different kinds, reflexions remarkable for their arrangement and extent; rapid narratives: the cruelties and strange atrocities of Commodus, Caracalla, Heliogabalus; the useless virtues of Pertinax, Alexander Severus, Probus; the first great effort of the barbarians against the Empire, with a digression upon their manners; Diocletian's able and courageous defence, his new policy which, always keeping an eye on the frontiers, gradually detaches itself from Rome, and which, with a forecast of the act solemnly performed by Constantine, looks to transporting the seat of empire elsewhere; and finally the two chapters relating to the establishment of Christianity and its condition during those first centuries. There was thus an extreme variety of subjects which the author had brought together into one clever tissue, and rendered in a careful and studied style, the elegance of which sometimes reached the point of foppery. In the succeeding volumes the historian relaxed a little and developed more and more; he did not reject any branch of events and of facts which lay in his way over his immense field. His main line is as far as possible Roman, afterwards Byzantine, but there comes a point when by dint of prolonging it he loses it. Think merely that this History which is in contact with Augustus, and actually begins with Trajan, does not end till the fourteenth century, with Rienzi's tribunitian parody and classical revival. Yet Gibbon treats successively and in detail of Goths, Lombards, Franks, Turks, Bulgarians, Croatians, Hungarians, Normans, and twenty races besides; it is the most comprehensive history ever seen. In proportion as the river grows smaller and goes on to lose itself in the sand, it keeps receiving some new and disastrous torrent which completes the destruction of its bank, but at the same time maintains it and feeds it a little longer. The calm and tranquil historian notes all this, accepts and measures it. In these accessory parts he will, as a matter of course, be some day surpassed by those who will make a special study of those devastating races, and will go back to their roots and sources in Asia. Where he remains original is in his setting out of the last great Roman or Byzantine reigns; when he speaks of Diocletian, Constantine, Theodosius; of heroic souls born after their time like Majorian, of Justinian and of Belisarius. Considered from this point of view, his history is like a fine long-continued retreat before swarms of enemies; there is no impetuosity, no fire, but there are tactics and order. He encamps, halts and deploys wherever he can.

I confine myself to rendering the impression which a continuous perusal makes on me, and extracting from it the essential quality of the author's talent and wit. I will say then also that in many cases Gibbon does not produce a perfect light; he stops short of the summit where perhaps it shines. He is excellent at analyzing and bringing out the complicated parts of his subject, but he never brings them together under one swift glance or in one outflow of genius; it is all rather intelligent than elevated. Faithful to his humour, even in the processes of his intellect, he levels everything too much. May I make a joke which is suggested to me by himself? When he has the gout, it never takes him in fits, but treats him very much as it did Fontenelle: it follows a slow and regular course. Similarly, his History goes on uniformly with an even step, without fitfulness, without violence. If a great revolution takes place anywhere in the human soul he will not feel it, he will not call attention to it by lighting a beacon on his tower or sounding a stroke of his silver bell. That is the historical complaint which people have to make against him in regard to his explanation of Christianity. He does not understand that at that moment a wholly new moral view, a new virtue, was coming to birth. That regular, customary, indolent slavery which was the law of the old world and which Gibbon palliates as much as he can, appeared all of a sudden horrible to certain people, and little by little they inoculated nearly all with this horror. The easy tolerance which the ancients had for different opinions and religious beliefs, a tolerance which Gibbon makes so strong a point of displaying, was more than compensated by the slight regard in which people then so usually held human life. Something incomplete comes in even among the just notions which Gibbon enunciates on that subject.

In a word, if he has very well displayed and explained to us the nature of Cicero's, of Trajan's, of Pliny's tolerance—a disposition doubtless humane, but still born of or accompanied by a profound indifference and a secret contempt for the objects of a worship which among the ancients was a matter of custom and exterior form, not of opinion or belief—he has not in the same degree comprehended the new feeling which faced and fought that tolerance, and was in the end to wear it out. Christianity has in fact, and there lies its innovation in morals, implanted in men a livelier and more absolute feeling for truth; it is a religion which takes possession of the whole being. One must, in order to be tolerant, invest oneself with something more, and then one is so in virtue of a principle quite different from that of the ancients, in virtue of charity. Why did not Gibbon, who did justice to the soul of the ancients, do as much for that of the Christians? Why, when he was wholly occupied with defending and justifying the ancient police administration of the Emperors and the methods of the Roman magistrate, did he overlook the introduction into the world and the establishment in men's hearts of a new heroism? He took warning by the effect of his fifteenth and sixteenth chapters, and was in other respects very much more moderate and restrained in the remainder of his History. Robertson, who awaited with some dread his treatment of Julian's reign, congratulates him on having so well touched and characterized in this famous example that grotesque mixture of pagan fanaticism and philosophical fatuity, associated with the merits of a hero and a superior mind. In the portraits of Christians, even of the greatest during these ages, Gibbon is content to be never quite clear. He does not present them on their greater sides, and, as a learned ecclesiastic of our days has remarked, 'his work swarms with equivocal portraits.' Gibbon dwelt with a surely malicious complacency on the wretched theological subtleties, on the infinite division of the sects which divided men's minds during the lower Empire, but he does not approach them in the fashion of Voltaire. Voltaire has a sarcastic laugh and outbreaks of his grin, Gibbon's laugh is composed and silent. He slips it in at the bottom of a note, as for instance that which ends what he says of St. Augustine; like Bayle, he delights, but always in a note, to quote certain passages of erudite and cold indecency, and he comments upon them with an elaborate elegance.

Irony, caustic reserve, comprehensive penetration, easy and natural explanation of many facts which, extraordinary as they seemed, he reduces to an appearance of simplicity, such are his qualities, and many of them go near to be faults. He more than once invokes Montesquieu. He says that at a certain period of his life he read the *Provinciales* every year, but he does not give the same stimulus as Montesquieu and Pascal; he never gives his reader's mind the unexpected impulse which awakens it, transports it, and excites it to discovery. He writes in his armchair and leaves you in yours while you read him; or if he gets up it is only to take two or three turns about his room, while he is arranging his phrase and settling his expression.

⟨. . .⟩ It would not be fair, before quitting the History, if we were not to call attention to some places of a thoroughly literary character and of a happy wealth of matter, in which the author is quite free to apply his natural qualities, and to employ his talent. For example, a carefully written passage on the schools of Greek philosophy at the moment when the edict of Justinian suppressed them, and again, quite at the end of the work, to considerations on the Renaissance in Italy, on the arrival of the scholars from Constantinople, at the regret with which Petrarch received a Homer which he could not read in the original, and on the good luck of Boccaccio, more learned in this respect, and more favoured by fortune. These are fine chapters treated with a sort of predilection, and giving evidence to the very end of copious fertility. Far from ending abruptly, he well enjoys prolonging it. He finishes his long course almost as if it were a walk, and at the moment of putting down his pen, he halts to consider the final surroundings of his subject, and takes his rest in it. He has nothing like Montesquieu's panting cry on reaching the shore, but no more had he his dash, his discoveries of ideas in every direction, or his genius.—C. A. SAINTE-BEUVE, "Gibbon," 1853

I was present on the second day of Hastings's trial in Westminster Hall; when Sheridan was listened to with such attention that you might have heard a pin drop.—During one of those days Sheridan, having observed Gibbon among the audience, took occasion to mention "the luminous author of *The Decline and Fall.*" After he had finished, one of his friends reproached him with flattering Gibbon. "Why, what did I say of him?" asked Sheridan.—"You called him the luminous author," &c.—"Luminous! oh, I meant—*voluminous.*"—SAMUEL ROGERS, *Table Talk*, c. 1855

Gibbon's Decline and Fall has now been jealously scrutinized by two generations of eager and unscrupulous opponents; and I am only expressing the general opinion of competent judges when I say that by each successive scrutiny it has gained fresh reputation. Against his celebrated fifteenth and sixteenth chapters, all the devices of controversy have been exhausted; but the only result has been, that while the fame of the historian is untarnished, the attacks of his enemies are falling into complete oblivion. The work of Gibbon remains; but who is there who feels any interest in what was written against him?—HENRY THOMAS BUCKLE, *History of Civilization in England*, 1857–62

The student must have perceived at once that this unbeliever, however he might adopt the cant of the philosophers, was no mere philosophical historian in the Hume and Voltaire sense of the word; that he had devoted intense labour to his task; that he had succeeded in presenting a picture of the past ages such as had not been presented before. He might detect many sophisms in the arguments of his fifteenth and sixteenth chapters. But what are all these arguments to the actual vision of the evils of human society under the Christian dispensation? It is these that give the special pleas for secondary causes their weight. It is these that tempt to the notion that those secondary causes were many of them not divine, but devilish. If that conviction is truly followed out, Gibbon himself will be the best of preachers. He will be the brilliant and eloquent witness for a divine power which has been at work in all ages to counteract the devilish power; which has been stronger to support a righteous kingdom on earth than all evil influences, proceeding from those who call themselves divine ministers, have been to destroy it. But if his reasoning and facts are merely brought face to face with arguments, to prove that at a certain moment there was launched into the world, with miraculous sanctions, a religion the outward displays of which, through subsequent ages, have been so mixed,—which has apparently prompted so many evil deeds—the result must be, in a multitude of cases, a negative indifferent scepticism, in not a few, a positive infidelity.—FREDERICK DENISON MAURICE, *Moral and Metaphysical Philosophy*, 1862

If you want to know where the world was, and how it fared with it during the first ten centuries of our era, read Gibbon. No other writer can do for you just what he does. No one else has had the courage to attempt his task over again. The laborious student of history may go to the many and obscure sources from which Gibbon drew the materials for his great work, and correct or supplement him here and there, as Milman has done; but the general reader wants the completed structure, and not the mountain quarries from which the blocks came; and the complete structure you get in Gibbon. To omit him is to leave a gap in your knowledge of the history of the world which nothing else can fill. As Carlyle said to Emerson, he 'is the splendid bridge which connects the old world with the new;' very artificial, but very real for all that, and very helpful to any who have business that way.

The case may be even more strongly stated than that. To read Gibbon is to be present at the creation of the world—the modern world. We see the chaos out of which it came; we see the breaking up of the old races, institutions, conditions, and the slow formation of the new. The period which his work covers was the great thaw and dissolution of history—the springtime which preceded the summer of modern civilizations. What anarchy, what confusion, what a giving away of foundations, what a tottering and tumbling of the superb Roman masonry; and yet what budding of new life, what inundations of new fresh humanity, from the North and from the East! A new light was in the world—the light of Christianity; new races also, and the game of life and of nationality was to be played under new conditions and in new fields. What a picture is that which we get in Gibbon of those swarms upon swarms of barbarians, from northern Europe, and central Asia, and finally from southern Arabia, breaking in and overrunning the old Empire! One comes to think of the Roman dominion as a circle more or less filled with light; around it on all sides is darkness, and out of this darkness come fiercely riding these savage hordes, as soon as they cross the line made visible to us. Out of this seething lava of humanity, the modern races and states have arisen. The main push always came from the plains of central Asia; here seems to have been the well-head of mankind. What we see in Roman history is doubtless but a continuation of a process which had been going on for long ages. The westward movement of our Aryan ancestors was an earlier chapter in the same great series of events.

Ruskin objects to Gibbon's style as the 'worst English ever written by an educated Englishman.' It was the style of his age and country brought to perfection, the stately curvilinear or orbicular style; every sentence makes a complete circle; but it is always a real thought, a real distinction that sweeps through the circle. Modern style is more linear, more direct and picturesque; and in the case of such a writer as Ruskin, much more loose, discursive and audacious. The highly artificial buckram style of the age of Gibbon has doubtless had its day, but it gave us some noble literature, and is no more to be treated with contempt than the age which produced it is to be treated with contempt.—JOHN BURROUGHS, "Ruskin's Judgment of Gibbon and Darwin," *Critic*, May 1, 1886, p. 213

Gibbon has a good deal to answer for. You can find nearly every fact in him, but he began by making the subject ridiculous, by trotting out some absurd, and, if possible, indecent anecdote, as if it were a summary of the whole reign. It is that chapter which gives the impression, and those which follow never take it away. I believe that Pippin was made patrician by authority of Constantine Kopronymos, but that Pope Stephen bamboozled them all round.—EDWARD A. FREEMAN, Letter to Goldwin Smith (April 25, 1888), cited in W. R. W. Stephens, *The Life and Letters of Edward A. Freeman*, 1895, Vol. 2, p. 380

If we continue Gibbon in his fame, it will be for love of his art, not for worship of his scholarship. We some of us, nowadays, know the period of which he wrote better even than he did; but which one of us shall build so admirable a monument to ourselves, as artists, out of what we know? The scholar finds his immortality in the form he gives to his work. It is a hard saying, but the truth of it is inexorable: be an artist, or prepare for oblivion.—WOODROW WILSON, "Mere Literature," *Mere Literature and Other Essays*, 1896, p. 22

To Edward Gibbon, who timidly deprecated comparison with Robertson and Hume, criticism is steadily awarding a place higher and higher above them. He is, indeed, one of the great writers of the century, one of those who exemplify in the finest way the signal merits of the age in which he flourished. The book by which he mainly survives, the vast *Decline and Fall of the Roman Empire*, began to appear in 1776, and was not completed until 1788. It was at once discovered by all who were competent to judge, that here was a new thing introduced into the literature of the world. Mézeray and Voltaire had written in French, Hume and Robertson in English, historical works which had charming qualities of the rhetorical order, but which did not pass beyond the rudimentary stage of history, in which the hasty compilation of documents, without close investigation of their value, took the place of genuine and independent research. At length in Gibbon, after a life of forty years mostly spent in study and reflection, a writer was found who united "all the broad spirit of comprehensive survey with the thorough and minute patience of a Benedictine." After long debate, Gibbon fixed upon the greatest historical subject which the chronicle of the world supplied; undaunted by its extreme obscurity and remoteness, he determined to persevere in investigating it, and to sacrifice all other interests and ambitions to its complete elucidation. The mysterious and elaborate story of the transition from the Pagan to the Christian world might well have daunted any mind, but Gibbon kept his thoughts detached from all other ideas, concentrating his splendid intellect on this vast and solitary theme, until his patience and his force moved the mountain, and "the encyclopædic history," as Freeman calls it, "the grandest of all historical designs," took form and shape in six magnificent volumes.

Some modern critics have found the attitude of Gibbon unsympathetic, his manner cold and superficial, his scepticism impervious to the passion of religious conviction. We may admit that these charges are well founded, and set them down to the credit of the age in which he lived, so averse to enthusiasm and ebullition. But to dwell too long on these defects is to miss a recognition of Gibbon's unique importance. His style possesses an extraordinary pomp and richness; ill adapted, perhaps, for the lighter parts of speech, it is unrivalled in the exercise of lofty and sustained heroic narrative. The language of Gibbon never flags; he walks for ever as to the clash of arms, under an imperial banner; a military music animates his magnificent descriptions of battles, of sieges, of panoramic scenes of antique civilisation. He understood, as few historical writers have done, how much the reader's enjoyment of a sustained narrative depends on the appeal to his visual sense. Perhaps he leaned on this strength of his style too much, and sacrificed the abstract to the concrete. But the book is so deeply grounded on personal accurate research, is the result of reflection at once so bold and so broad, with so extraordinary an intuition selects the correct aspect where several points of view were possible, that less than any other history of the eighteenth century does the *Decline and Fall* tend to become obsolete, and of it is still said, what the most scientific of historians said only a generation ago, "Whatever else is read, Gibbon must be read too."—EDMUND GOSSE, *A Short History of Modern English Literature*, 1897, pp. 258–60

Gibbon certainly obeyed the maxim which, if we may believe Juvenal, descended (in the Greek language) from Heaven. He knew himself. It was a fashionable branch of knowledge in the eighteenth century, and Carlyle has not failed to denounce it with his accustomed vigour. But it was even then an accomplishment more often claimed than possessed, and there must have been few men in any age who ordered their own lives with the calm sagacity of Gibbon. 'I have always'—so he wrote to Mrs. Gibbon on the 27th of December, 1783—'I have always valued far above the external gifts of rank and fortune, two qualities for which I stand indebted to the indulgence of Nature, a strong and constant passion for letters, and a propensity to view and to enjoy every object in the most favourable light.' Could the art of happiness be condensed into fewer words? Mr. Gibbon did really resemble the Epicurean philosophers whom he so much admired. There may have been some affectation in his manners. There was none in his opinions. He was, in every sense of the words, *totus teres atque rotundus*. He was never tired of intellectual work. When he had finished the *Decline and Fall*, the tenth part of which would have filled the life of almost any other man, he projected a series of historical biographies which death alone prevented him from accomplishing. Yet he died in his fifty-seventh year, and Macaulay, whose *History of England* is a small fraction of what he contemplated that it should be, lived to be fifty-nine. Macaulay, however, was a practical statesman. He was a Cabinet Minister, a Parliamentary orator, and the author of the Indian Penal Code. He sank the politician in the historian too late for the interests of posterity, though not for his own fame. In one respect he resembled Gibbon. He told Charles Greville that he neglected contemporary literature, and that his mind was in the past. There are few allusions in Gibbon's Correspondence to Johnson or to Goldsmith, to Richardson or to Sterne. Strange as it may seem to the learned men of this age, he was wholly ignorant of German. He preferred the French poets to the English, and among the English poets he reckoned Hayley. He sympathised with Voltaire's estimate of Shakespeare, whom he anticipated Leech's schoolboy and the admirers of Ibsen in considering an overrated individual. With the rhetorical school of poetry, the school of Dryden and Pope, he was familiar, and he did homage to the genius of Milton. The most illustrious man of science that the nineteenth century has produced confessed that absorption in his pursuits gradually diminished, and ultimately destroyed, his enjoyment of literary excellence. Gibbon, though not himself scientific, attended in pursuit of knowledge the lectures of John Hunter, being apparently interested in everyone's anatomy except his own. But, perhaps, like Mr. Darwin he was restricted in the range of his appreciation by the enormous scope and magnitude of his own particular studies. His love of classical literature, however, was unbounded, and it is not the least striking proof of his marvellous powers that he shoud have acquired for himself a mastery of the dead languages which the 'grand old fortifying classical curriculum' seldom imparts. Compared with the aids to learning provided for the modern student his facilities were slight indeed. Such an edition as Professor Jebb's *Sophocles*, or Professor Munro's *Lucretius*, or Professor Robinson Ellis's *Catullus* was as much beyond the imagination of the eighteenth century as a telegraph or a railway. A modern first-class man could hardly decipher the Greek type which was read by Gibbon. For Latin he had Forcellini. But as for Greek, the sight of a Liddell and Scott would have almost induced him to believe that the age of miracles had returned. Even Porson, one of the greatest masters of English who ever lived, wrote his commentaries in Latin. Bentley has been called the first of philologists, and to the results of his researches Gibbon had access. But Bentley unfortunately persuaded himself that the best thing to do with the classics was to rewrite them, and wasted in speculative emendation the time which might have been employed in illustrative comment. If any one will try to read Lucretius as edited before Lachmann had revised the text, he will realise what it was to be a scholar in the days of Gibbon.—HERBERT PAUL, "Gibbon's Life and Letters," *Nineteenth Century*, Feb. 1897, pp. 306–7

MEMOIRS AND MISCELLANEOUS WORKS

Papa has read us several parts of Mr. Gibbon's Memoirs, written so exactly in the style of his conversation that, while we felt delighted at the beauty of the thoughts and elegance of the language, we could not help feeling a severe pang at the idea we should never hear his instructive and amusing conversation any more.—MARIA JOSEPHA HOLROYD, Letter (1793), cited in *The Girlhood of Maria Josepha Holroyd*, ed. J. H. Adeane, 1896, p. 273

The melancholy duty of examining the Papers of my deceased friend devolved upon me at a time when I was depressed by severe afflictions.

In that state of mind, I hesitated to undertake the task of selecting and preparing his Manuscripts for the press. The warmth of my early and long attachment to Mr. Gibbon made me conscious of a partiality, which it was not proper to indulge, especially in revising many of his juvenile and unfinished compositions. I had to guard, not only against a sentiment like my own, which I found extensively diffused, but also against the eagerness occasioned by a very general curiosity to see in print every literary relick, however imperfect, of so distinguished a writer.

Being aware how disgracefully Authors of Eminence have been often treated, by an indiscreet posthumous publication of fragments and careless effusions; when I had selected those Papers which to myself appeared the fittest for the public eye, I consulted some of our common friends, whom I knew to be equally anxious with myself for Mr. Gibbon's fame, and fully competent, from their judgment, to protect it.

Under such a sanction it is, that, no longer suspecting myself to view through too favourable a medium the compositions of my Friend, I now venture to publish them: and it may here be proper to give some information to the Reader, respecting the Contents of these Volumes.

The most important part consists of Memoirs of Mr. Gibbon's Life and Writings, a work which he seems to have projected with peculiar solicitude and attention, and of which he left Six different sketches, all in his own hand-writing. One of these sketches, the most diffuse and circumstantial, so far as it proceeds, ends at the time when he quitted Oxford. Another at the year 1764, when he travelled to Italy. A third, at his father's death, in 1770. A fourth, which he continued to a short time after his return to Lausanne in 1788, appears in the form of Annals, much less detailed than the others. The two remaining sketches are still more imperfect. It is difficult to discover the order in which these several Pieces were written, but there is reason to believe that the most copious was the last. From all these the following Memoirs have been carefully selected, and put together.

My hesitation in giving these Memoirs to the world arose, principally, from the circumstance of Mr. Gibbon's appearing, in some respect, not to have been satisfied with them, as he had so frequently varied their form: yet, notwithstanding this diffidence, the compositions, though unfinished, are so excellent, that they may justly entitle my Friend to appear as his own biographer, rather than to have that task undertaken by any other person less qualified for it.

This opinion has rendered me anxious to publish the present Memoirs, without any unnecessary delay; for I am persuaded, that the Author of them cannot be made to appear in a truer light than he does in the following pages. In them, and in his different Letters, which I have added, will be found a complete picture of his talents, his disposition, his studies, and his attainments.

Those slight variations of character, which naturally arose in the progress of his Life, will be unfolded in a series of Letters, selected from a Correspondence between him and myself, which continued full thirty years, and ended with his death.

It is to be lamented, that all the sketches of the Memoirs, except that composed in the form of Annals, and which seems rather designed as heads for a future Work, cease about twenty years before Mr. Gibbon's death; and consequently, that we have the least detailed account of the most interesting part of his Life. His Correspondence during that period will, in great measure, supply the deficiency. It will be separated from the Memoirs and placed in an Appendix, that those who are not disposed to be pleased with the repetitions, familiarities, and trivial circumstances of epistolary writing, may not be embarrassed by it. By many, the Letters will be found a very interesting part of the present Publication. They will prove, how pleasant, friendly, and amiable Mr. Gibbon was in private life; and if, in publishing Letters so flattering to myself, I incur the imputation of vanity, I shall meet the charge with a frank confession, that I am indeed highly vain of having enjoyed, for so many years, the esteem, the confidence, and the affection of a man, whose social qualities endeared him to the most accomplished society, and whose talents, great as they were, must be acknowledged to have been fully equalled by the sincerity of his friendship.

Whatever censure may be pointed against the Editor, the Public will set a due value on the Letters for their intrinsic merit. I must, indeed, be blinded, either by vanity or affection, if they do not display the heart and mind of their Author, in such a manner as justly to increase the number of his admirers.

I have not been solicitous to garble or expunge passages which, to some, may appear trifling. Such passages will often, in the opinion of the observing Reader, mark the character of the Writer, and the omission of them would materially take from the ease and familiarity of authentic letters.

Few men, I believe, have ever so fully unveiled their own character, by a minute narrative of their sentiments and pursuits, as Mr. Gibbon will here be found to have done; not with study and labour—not with an affected frankness—but with a genuine confession of his little foibles and peculiarities, and a good-humoured and natural display of his own conduct and opinions.—JOHN, LORD SHEFFIELD, "Preface" to *Miscellaneous Works of Edward Gibbon, Esquire*, 1796, Vol. 1, pp. iii–vii

Mr. Burke had not read Lord Sheffield's *Memoirs of Gibbon*. On my observing that Mr. Gibbon declares himself of the same opinion with him on the French Revolution, he said that Gibbon was an old friend of his, and he knew well that before he (Mr. G.) died, that he heartily repented of the anti-religious part of his work for contributing to free mankind from all restraint on their vices and profligacy, and thereby aiding so much the spirit which produced the horrors that blackened the most detestable of all revolutions.—ARTHUR YOUNG, *Autobiography* (entry for May 1, 1796), ed. M. Bentham-Edwards, 1898, pp. 258–59

As is well known, it was my grandfather, the first Earl, who made the historian almost his adopted brother, gave him a home both in town and in country, was his devisee and literary executor, and edited and published the famous *Autobiography*, the letters, and remains. All of these passed under Edward Gibbon's will to Lord Sheffield; and, together with books, relics, portraits, and various mementos, they have been for a century preserved by my father and myself with religious care and veneration in Sheffield Park. The original autograph manuscripts of the *Memoirs*, the *Diaries, Letters, Note-books*, etc., have now become the property of the British Museum, subject to the copyright of all the unpublished parts which was previously assigned to Mr. Murray. And it is with no little pleasure and pride that I have acceded to the request of the publishers that I would introduce these unpublished remains to the world, and thus complete the task of editing the historian, to which my grandfather devoted so great a portion of his time, not only as a testamentary duty, but as a labour of love.

The connection of the historian with my grandfather, his early friend, John Holroyd, and the members of the Holroyd family, forms one of the pleasantest and also most interesting passages in literary history. It was in no way interrupted by Lord Sheffield's public and official duties; it was continued without a cloud to obscure their intimacy, until it was sundered by death; and the Earl, who survived his friend so long, continued to edit and to publish the manuscripts left in his hands for some twenty years after the death of the historian.

By a clause in the will of Edward Gibbon, dated July 14, 1788, his papers were entrusted to Lord Sheffield and Mr. John Batt, his executors, in the following terms:—

"I will that all my Manuscript papers found at the time of my decease be delivered to my executors, and that if any shall appear sufficiently finished for the public eye, they do treat for the purchase of the same with a Bookseller, giving the preference to Mr. Andrew Strahan and Mr. Thomas Cadell, whose liberal spirit I have experienced in similar transactions. And whatsoever monies may accrue from such sale and publication, I give to my much-valued friend William Hayley, Esq., of Eastham, in the County of Sussex. But in case he shall dye before me, I give the aforesaid monies to the Royal Society of London and the Royal Academy of Inscriptions of Paris, share and share alike, in trust to be by them employed in such a manner as they shall deem most beneficial to the cause of Learning."

In pursuance of the directions contained in the will and of many verbal communications, Lord Sheffield, in 1799, published the *Miscellaneous Works of Edward Gibbon, with Memoirs of his Life and Writings*, in 2 vols., 4to. A third volume was added in 1815, and a new edition of the whole, with additions, appeared during the same year in 5 vols., 8vo. In 1837 another edition, in one large 8vo volume, was published.

By a clause in his own will, Lord Sheffield directed that no further publication of the historian's manuscripts should be made.

"And I request of my said trustees and my heirs that none of the said manuscripts, papers, or books of the said Edward Gibbon be published unless my approbation of the publication be directed by some memorandum indorsed and written or signed by me. And I also request the person entitled for the time being to the possession thereof not to suffer the same to be out of his possession or to be improperly exposed."

This direction has been strictly followed by my father, the second Earl, and by myself; and it is believed that no person has ever had access to any of the manuscripts for any literary purpose, excepting the late Dean Milman, who, when editing his well-known edition of the *Decline and Fall*, in 1842, was permitted to inspect the original manuscripts of the Autobiography, on condition of not publishing any new matter.

The commemoration of 1894, however, again raised the question whether such an embargo on giving to the world writings of national importance was ever meant to be, or even ought to be, regarded as perpetual. Whilst persons named in these papers or their children were living, whilst the bitter controversies of the last century were still unforgotten, whilst the fame of Edward Gibbon had hardly yet become one of our national glories, it was a matter of good feeling and sound judgment in Lord Sheffield to exercise an editor's discretion in publishing his friend's confession and private thoughts. Now that more than a hundred years have passed since his death, no such considerations have weight or meaning. And the opinion of those whom I have consulted, both professionally and as private friends, amply corroborates my own conclusion, that it is a duty which I owe to my own ancestor and to the public to give to the world all the remains of the historian which for more than a century have been preserved in the strong room at Sheffield Park.

The unlocking of the cases in which these manuscripts were secured was quite a revelation of literary workmanship, and has led to a most interesting problem in literary history. The manuscripts of the historian are all holographs—the text of the famous *Memoirs* being written with extraordinary beauty of calligraphy, and studied with the utmost care. But, singularly enough, none of the texts are prepared for immediate, or even direct, publication. The historian wrote, at various intervals between 1788 and 1793, no less than *six* different sketches. They are not quite continuous; they partly recount the same incidents in different form; they are written in different tones: and yet no one of them is complete; none of them plainly designed to supersede the rest. There is even a small seventh sketch, from which one of the noblest and most famous passages that Gibbon ever wrote has been excised, and inserted in the published Autobiography.

Lord Sheffield executed his editorial task with extreme judgment, singular ingenuity, but remarkable freedom. He was assisted in preparing the manuscripts for publication by his wife and by Lady Maria Holroyd, his eldest daughter, who became by marriage the first Lady Stanley of Alderley. This very able and remarkable woman, of whose abilities the historian expressed in letters his great admiration, evidently marked the manuscripts in pencil handwriting (now recognized as hers) for the printer's copyist. These pencil deletions, transpositions, and even additions, correspond with the Autobiography as published by Lord Sheffield. Quite a third of the whole manuscript is omitted, and many of the most piquant passages that Gibbon ever wrote were suppressed by the caution or the delicacy of his editor and his family.

The result is a problem of singular literary interest. A piece, most elaborately composed by one of the greatest writers who ever used our language, an autobiography often pronounced to be the best we possess, is now proved to be in no sense the simple work of that illustrious pen, but to have been dexterously pieced together out of seven fragmentary sketches and adapted into a single and coherent narrative. The manner and the extent of this extraordinary piece of editing has been so fully explained in the address of November 15, published by the Centenary Committee, that it is not necessary for me to enlarge upon it further.

No sooner had the discovery of the process by which Gibbon's *Autobiography* had been concocted been made public, than a general desire was expressed to have the originals published in the form in which the historian left them. It was no case of incomplete or illegible manuscripts, nor of rough drafts designed only as notes for subsequent composition. The whole of the seven manuscripts are written with perfect precision; the style is in Gibbon's most elaborate manner; and each piece is perfectly ready for the printer—so far as it goes. It was impossible to do again the task of consolidation so admirably performed by Lord Sheffield. Nothing remained but to print the whole of the pieces *verbatim*, as the historian wrote them, not necessarily in the order of time of their apparent composition, but so as to form a consecutive narrative of the author's life.

The reader may now rest assured that, *for the first time*, he has before him the Autobiographic Sketches of Edward Gibbon in the exact form in which he left them at his death. The portions enclosed in dark brackets are the passages which were omitted by Lord Sheffield, and in the notes are inserted the passages or sentences, few and simple in themselves, which Lord Sheffield added to the original manuscript. For various reasons it was found impracticable to print the six sketches in parallel columns; but the admirers of the historian and all students of English literature will find abundant opportunity for collating the original texts with each other, and with the text as published by the editor, and now for a century current as one of the masterpieces of English literature.—EARL OF SHEFFIELD, "Introduction" to *The Autobiographies of Edward Gibbon*, ed. John Murray, 1896, pp. v–ix

Gibbon's reflections on his own childish reminiscences, in the light of his interest in scientific biology, have a real philosophic interest. He thinks he remembers, at the age of three, shouting out the names of his father's opponents at an election in revenge for a whipping he got: but perhaps "he may only repeat the hearsay of a riper season." It is now clear from the newly published *Letters* that the weakness and extravagances of the elder Gibbon imposed on the younger a life-long burden of anxiety and embarrassment; and we may now more justly estimate the extreme tenderness with which the son alluded to the failings of the parent—failings which the Sheffields sought to cover by the simple process of suppression. There is a clear-cut picture of the Rev. Philip Francis, father of "Junius," and translator of Horace; but all this Lord Sheffield dropped—perhaps in dread of another Philippic from the son. Why should he also have dropped the bitter invective against the sufferings of a delicate schoolboy— a piece to be set beside Cowper's *Tirocinium*—"they labour like the soldiers of Persia under the scourge, and their education is nearly finished before they can apprehend the sense or utility of the harsh lessons which they are forced to repeat"? Gibbon's view on schools and colleges are full of interest and suggestion: but we ought from the first to have had his words in their completeness.

His judgment on Universities has been more curtailed than that which he passes on Schools. It is amusing to note that we now have the names of the authorities of Gibbon's own College, Magdalen, which the delicacy of Lord Sheffield suppressed—as he did the prophetic sentence that "the inveterate evils which are derived from their birth and character must still cleave to our Ecclesiastical corporations." Gibbon's experience in 1752 of the fellows of Magdalen College was that "their conversation stagnated in a round of College business, Tory politics, personal stories, and private scandals." But so slow is the advance of the College "in the progressive movement of the age," or so persistent is its spirit of ill-humour, that it declines to accept from the Commemoration Committee a tablet to the memory of one of the greatest scholars who ever entered its mediæval cloister.—FREDERIC HARRISON, "The New Memoirs of Edward Gibbon," *Forum*, Feb. 1897, pp. 754–55

H. H. MILMAN
From "Guizot's Edition of Gibbon"
Quarterly Review, January 1834, pp. 286–307

The vastness, yet the harmony of his design, is unquestionably that which distinguishes the work of Gibbon from all other great historical compositions. He has first bridged the abyss between ancient and modern times, and connected together the two worlds of history. The great advantage which the classical historians possess over those of modern times is in unity of design, of course greatly facilitated by the narrower sphere to which their researches were confined. Herodotus takes, it is remarkable, the widest and the boldest range. Though the centre towards which his remotest inquiries radiate is the Persian invasion of Greece, yet he combines, as it were, the whole known, almost the whole habitable world within his range; he ascends to the highest accessible period of every national history, of Egypt, of Persia, of Scythia, and though in a manner remarkably inartificial, brings the whole at length to bear upon the declared object of his work. The other great historians of Greece—we exclude the more modern compilers, like Diodorus Siculus—limited themselves to a single period, or at least to the contracted sphere of Grecian affairs. As far as the *Barbarians* trespassed within the Grecian boundary, or were necessarily mingled up with Grecian politics, they were admitted into the pale of Grecian history; but to Thucydides and to Xenophon, excepting in the Persian inroad of the latter, Greece was the world—a natural unity confined their narrative almost to chronological order, the episodes were of rare occurence and extremely brief. To the Roman historians the course was equally clear and defined—Rome was their centre of unity; and the uniformity with which the circle of the Roman dominion spread around, the regularity with which their civil polity expanded, forced, as it were, upon the Roman historian that plan which Polybius announces as the subject of his history, the means and the manner by which the whole world became subject to the Roman sway. How different the complicated politics of the European kingdoms! Every national history, to be complete, must, in a certain sense, be the history of Europe; there is no knowing to how remote a quarter it may be necessary to trace our most domestic events; from a country, how apparently disconnected, may originate the impulse which gives its direction to the whole course of affairs.

In imitation of his classical models, Gibbons places *Rome* as the cardinal point from which his inquiries diverge, and to which they bear constant reference: yet how immeasurable the space over which his inquiries range! how complicated, how confused, how apparently inextricable the causes which tend to the decline of the Roman empire! how countless the nations which swarm forth, in mingling and indistinct hordes, constantly changing the geographical limits—incessantly confounding the natural boundaries! At first sight, the whole period, the whole state of the world seems to offer no more secure footing to an historical adventurer than the chaos of Milton—to be in a state of irreclaimable disorder, best described in the language of the poet:—

> A dark
> Illimitable ocean, without bound,
> Without dimension, where length, breadth, and
>   height,
> And time, and place, are lost. where eldest Night
> And Chaos, ancestors of Nature, hold
> Eternal anarchy, amidst the noise
> Of endless wars, and by confusion stand.

We feel that the unity, the harmony of narrative, which shall comprehend this period of social disorganization, must be ascribed entirely to the skill and luminous disposition of the historian. It is in this sublime Gothic architecture of his work, in which the boundless range, the infinite variety, the, at first sight, incongruous gorgeousness of the separate parts, nevertheless are all subordinate to one main and predominant idea, that Gibbon is unrivalled. The manner in which he masses his materials, and arranges his facts in successive groups, not according to chronological order, but to their moral or political connexion; the distinctness with which he marks his periods of gradually advancing decay; the skill with which, though advancing on separate parallels of history, he shows the common tendency of the slower or more rapid religious or civil innovations: however these principles of composition may demand more than ordinary attention on the part of the reader, they can alone impress upon the memory the real course and the relative importance of the events. Whoever would justly appreciate the superiority of Gibbon's lucid arrangement, should attempt to make his way through the regular but wearisome annals of Tillemont, or even the less ponderous volumes of Le Beau. Both these writers adhere

almost entirely to chronological order; the consequence is, that we are twenty times called upon to break off and resume the thread of six or eight wars in different parts of the empire—to suspend the operations of a military expedition for a court intrigue; to hurry away from a siege to a council; and the same page places us in the middle of a campaign against the barbarians, and in the depths of the Monophysite controversy. In Gibbon it is not always easy to trace the exact dates, [1] but the course of events is ever clear and distinct; like a skilful general, though his troops advance from the most remote and opposite quarters, they are constantly bearing down and concentrating themselves on one point, that which is still occupied by the name and by the waning power of Rome. Whether he traces the progress of hostile religions—or leads from the shores of the Baltic, or the verge of the Chinese empire, the successive hosts of barbarians—though one wave has hardly burst and discharged itself, before another swells up and approaches all is made to flow in the same direction, and the impression which each makes upon the tottering fabric of the Roman greatness, connects their distant movements, and measures the relative importance assigned to them in the panoramic history. The more peaceful and didactic episodes on the development of the Roman law, or even on the details of ecclesiastical history, interpose themselves as resting-places or divisions between the periods of barbaric invasion. In short, though distracted first by the two capitals, and afterwards by the formal partition of the empire, the extraordinary felicity of arrangement maintains an order and a regular progression. As our horizon expands to reveal to us the gathering tempests which are forming far beyond the boundaries of the civilized world—as we follow their successive approach to the trembling frontier—the compressed and receding line is still distinctly visible; though gradually dismembered, and its broken fragments assuming the form of regular states and kingdoms, the real relation of those kingdoms to the empire is maintained and defined; and although the Roman dominion has shrunk into little more than the province of Thrace—though the name of Rome is confined in Italy to the walls of the city—yet it is still the memory, the shade of the Roman greatness, which extends over the wide sphere into which the historian expands his later narrative; the whole blends into the unity, and is manifestly essential to the double catastrophe of his tragic drama. ⟨. . .⟩

We have ourselves followed the track of Gibbon through many parts of his work; we have read his authorities with constant reference to his pages, and we must pronounce our deliberate judgment, in terms of the highest admiration, of his general accuracy. [2] Many of his seeming errors are almost inevitable, from the close condensation of his matter. From the immense range of his history, it was sometimes necessary to compress into a single sentence, a whole vague and diffuse page of a Byzantine chronicler. Perhaps something of importance may thus escape, and his expressions may not quite contain the whole substance of the quotation. His limits, at times, compel him to sketch; where that is the case, it is not fair to expect the full details of the finished picture. At times he can only deal with important results; and in his account of a war, it sometimes requires great attention to discover that the events, which seem to be comprehended in a single campaign, occupy several years. But this admirable skill in selecting and giving prominence to the points which are of real weight and importance—this distribution of light and shade—though perhaps it may occasionally betray him into vague and imperfect statements, is one of the highest excellences of Gibbon's historic manner. It is the more striking, when we pass from the works of his chief authorities, where, after labouring through long, minute and wearisome descriptions of the accessary and subordinate circumstances, a single unmarked and undistinguished sentence, which we may overlook from the inattention of fatigue, contains the great moral and political result.

Gibbon's method of arrangement, though on the whole most favourable to the clear comprehension of the events, leads likewise to apparent inaccuracy. That which we expect to find in one part is reserved for another. The estimate which we are to form, depends on the accurate balance of statements in remote parts of the work; and we have sometimes to correct and modify opinions, formed from one chapter, by those of another.[3] Yet, on the other hand, it is astonishing how rarely we detect apparent contradiction; the mind of the author has already harmonized the whole result to truth and probability; the general impression is almost invariably the same. The quotations of Gibbon have likewise been called in question— we have in general been more inclined to admire their exactitude, than to complain of their indistinctness, or incompleteness. Where they are imperfect, it is oftener from the study of brevity, and from the desire of compressing the substance of his notes into pointed and emphatic sentences, than from dishonesty, or uncandid suppression of truth.

These observations apply more particularly to the accuracy and fidelity of the historian as to his facts; his inferences, of course, are more liable to exception. It is almost impossible to trace the line between unfairness and unfaithfulness; between intentional misrepresentation, and undesigned false colouring. The relative magnitude and importance of events must, in some respect, depend upon the mind before which they are presented; the estimate of character, on the habits and feelings of the reader. Christians, like M. Guizot and ourselves, will see some things and some persons in a different light from the historian of the Decline and Fall. We may deplore the bias of his mind; we may, ourselves, be on our guard against the danger of being misled, and be anxious to warn less wary readers against the same perils; but we must not confound this secret and unconscious departure from truth, with the deliberate violation of that, which is the only title of an historian to our confidence. Gibbon, we will fearlessly assert, is rarely, if ever, chargeable even with the suppression of any material fact, which bears upon individual character; he may, with apparently invidious hostility, enhance the errors and crimes, and disparage the virtues of certain persons; yet he in general leaves us the materials for forming a fairer judgment; and if he is not exempt from his own prejudices, perhaps we might write passions, it must be candidly acknowledged, that his philosophical bigotry is not more unjust than the theological partialities of those ecclesiastical writers who were before in undisputed possession of this province of history.

We are thus naturally led to that great misrepresentation which pervades his history—his false estimate of the nature and influence of Christianity. But before we enter on this point, we would fully acknowledge the justice of certain other charges, which admit of no extenuation. It may be difficult to give a just and properly repulsive picture of a depraved and licentious period, without offending the scrupulous delicacy of modern manners; but it cannot be denied that especially the latter volumes of Gibbon are loaded with much unnecessary indecency. Our readers will permit us to drop the veil on this subject, but we cannot help alluding to a kindred deficiency in moral sensibility, which is almost equally offensive to the pure and generous mind—the perpetual vulgar and sarcastic depreciation of female purity. This is as repugnant to taste as to moral feeling. It was learned in the school of Voltaire, and at best was only a heavy and ungraceful imitation of his manner,

altogether beneath the real dignity of history. That which might extort a smile in the light tale, in 'Candide,' or the 'Ingenu,' was as incongruous as repulsive in the stately periods of the Decline and Fall.

The effect of Gibbon's hostility towards Christianity upon the character of his history has been first fairly and justly appreciated by his French critics. What their complaints dwell upon is not so much his insidious description of the means by which it was propagated, as a general false estimate of its influence upon the social and even political state of mankind. Here the matter has chiefly been considered in a polemical spirit;—abroad in a more enlarged, a more philosophical, and, therefore, in a more wisely Christian point of view—

> Via prima salutis,
> Quod minimè reris, Graiâ pandetur ab urbe.

It is remarkable that in the midst of the indignation of the better part of our community, at the publication of the first volumes of the Decline and Fall, the more distinguished theological writers of the country stood aloof, while the first ranks were filled by rash and feeble volunteers. Gibbon, with a single discharge from his ponderous artillery of learning and sarcasm, laid prostrate the whole disorderly squadron. The Davises, the Chelsums, and the Travises shrunk back into their former insignificance. Their plan of attack was as misjudging as their conduct of it was imbecile. With a very slender stock of learning, hurried together for the occasion, they ventured to impeach the accuracy, and to condemn the false quotations, of a scholar, whose mind was thoroughly saturated with every kind of knowledge which could bear upon his subject; and they could only make up in spleen and intemperance for their lamentable deficiency in all the true qualifications for defenders of Christianity. Watson alone had the good taste to maintain towards his antagonist the dignified courtesy which belonged to his literary character; and the judgment to confine his 'Apology' to one specific point—the inadequacy of Gibbon's arguments to account, from mere human causes, for the propagation of Christianity. But we are not sure that Watson himself has not unconsciously been betrayed, by the consummate skill of his antagonist, to advance beyond that which is the really impregnable position, and to carry on the contest on a far less advantageous ground. The art of Gibbon, or at least the unfair impression produced by these two memorable chapters, consists in confounding together, in one indistinguishable mass, the *origin* and *apostolic* propagation of the new religion, with its *later* progress. No argument for the divine authority of Christianity has been urged with greater force, or developed with higher eloquence, than that deduced from its primary development, explicable on no other hypothesis than a heavenly origin, and from its rapid extension through great part of the Roman empire. But this argument—one, when confined within reasonable limits, of unanswerable force— becomes more feeble and disputable in proportion as it recedes from the birth-place, as it were, of the religion. The further Christianity advanced, the more causes purely human were enlisted in its favour; nor can it be doubted that those expounded with such artful exclusiveness by Gibbon did concur most essentially to its establishment. It is in the Christian dispensation, as in the material world. In both, it is as the great first Cause that the Deity is most undeniably manifest. When once launched in regular motion upon the bosom of space, and endowed with all their properties and relations of weight and mutual attraction, the heavenly bodies appear to pursue their courses according to secondary laws, which account for all their sublime regularity; so Christianity proclaims its Divine Author chiefly in its first origin and development; when it had once received its impulse from above—when it had once been infused into the minds of its first teachers—when it had gained full possession of the reason and affections of the favoured few, it *might be*—and to the Protestant, the rational Christian, it is impossible to define *when* it really *was*—left to make its way by its native force, under the ordinary secret agencies of all-ruling Providence. The main question, the divine origin of the religion, was dexterously eluded, or speciously conceded by Gibbon; his plan enabled him to commence his account, in most parts, *below the apostolic times*; and it was only by the strength of the dark colouring with which he brought out the failings and the follies of the succeeding ages, that a shadow of doubt and suspicion was thrown back upon the primitive period of Christianity.

'The theologian,' says Gibbon, 'may indulge the pleasing task of describing religion as she descended from heaven, arrayed in her native purity; a more melancholy duty is imposed upon the historian:—he must discover the inevitable mixture of error and corruption, which she contracted in a long residence upon earth among a weak and degenerate race of beings.'

Divest this passage of the latent sarcasm betrayed by the subsequent tone of the whole disquisition, and it might commence a Christian history written in the most Christian spirit of candour. But as the historian, by seeming to respect, yet dexterously confounding the limits of the sacred land, contrived to insinuate that it was an Utopia, which had no existence but in the imagination of the theologian—as he *suggested* rather than affirmed that the days of Christian purity were a kind of poetic golden age;—so the theologian, by venturing too far into the domain of the historian, was obliged to contest points on which he had little chance of victory,—to deny facts established on unshaken evidence—and thence, to retire, if not with the shame of defeat, yet with but doubtful and imperfect success.

With the solitary, and partial exception of the Bishop of Llandaff, the more able writers of the English church, it has been said, stood aloof in this contest;—they may have been conscious that ecclesiastical history was not their strong ground:—that branch of study had been comparatively neglected, since the heat of controversy between the rival churches had subsided:—the learning of Horsley himself was, we suspect, rather hastily drawn together for his contest with Priestley; and though it ensured him a superiority over so superficial and ill-grounded an antagonist, was not the profound and mature result of researches previously directed to the subject. But these divines estimated the real nature of the controversy, as much more wisely, as, if they had meddled in it, they would have conducted their battle more ably than the actual champions. Paley, with his intuitive sagacity, saw through the whole case—his emphatic sentence, 'who can refute a sneer,' contains as much truth as point. Gibbon, in fact, is unanswerable by the ordinary arts of controversy. It is not by minute nibbling at a mutilated quotation, by contesting an incorrect statement, or even disputing an unfair inference, that his learning can be impeached, his authority shaken, or the general impression of his work weakened or neutralized. Nothing less is wanting than a Christian account of the whole period, written in an attractive style, and in a vein of true philosophy, fairly tracing and constantly estimating the real effects of the Christian religion on the mind, manners, and destinies of mankind. It must be a history attempted on a totally different plan from any yet published in this country; or indeed, with complete success, elsewhere. It must be very unlike the dry polemic manner of Mosheim, and the more animated but uncritical and sectarian work of Milner. It must obtain its triumph, not by writing down those parts of history on which Gibbon has lavished all the power and splendour of his style, but by writing up Christianity to its proper place in the annals of human civilization. For *here* is the radical defect in the *Decline and Fall*. Christianity alone receives no embellishment from the magic of Gibbon's language; his imagination is dead to its moral dignity; it is kept down by a general tone of jealous disparagement, or neutralized by a painfully elaborate exposition of its darker and degenerate periods. There are occasions, indeed, when its pure and exalted humanity, when its manifestly beneficial influence, can compel even him, as it were, to fairness, and kindle his unguarded eloquence to its usual fervour, but in general he soon relapses into a frigid and passionless apathy: *affects* an ostentatiously severe impartiality; notes all the faults of Christians in every age with bitter and almost malignant sarcasm; reluctantly, and with exception and reservation, admits their claim to admiration. This inextricable bias appears even to influence his manner of composition. While all the other assailants of the Roman empire, whether warlike or religious, the Goth, the Hun, the Arab, the Tartar, Alaric and Attila, Mahomet, and Zengis, and Tamerlane, are each introduced upon the scene almost with dramatic animation—their progress related in a full, complete, and unbroken narrative—the triumph of Christianity alone takes the form of a cold and critical disquisition. The successes of barbarous energy and brute force call forth all the consummate skill of composition;—while the moral triumphs of Christian benevolence—the tranquil heroism of endurance, the blameless purity, the contempt of guilty fame and of honours destructive to the human race, which, had they assumed the proud name of philosophy, would have been blazoned in his brightest words, but because they own religion as their principle, sink into narrow asceticism—the *glories* of Christianity, in short, touch no chord in the heart of the writer; his imagination remains unkindled; his words, though they maintain their stately and measured march, have become cool, argumentative, and inanimate. We would not obscure one hue of that gorgeous colouring in which Gibbon has invested the dying forms of Paganism; nor darken one paragraph in his splendid view of the rise and progress of Mahometanism; we would only have wished that the same equal justice had been done to Christianity; that its real character and deeply penetrating influence had been traced with the same philosophical sagacity, and represented with more sober, as would become its quiet course, and perhaps less picturesque, but still with lively and attractive descriptiveness. He might have thrown aside with the same scorn the mass of ecclesiastical fiction which envelopes the early history of the church, stripped off the legendary romance, and brought out the facts in their primitive nakedness and simplicity—if he had but allowed those facts the benefit of the glowing eloquence which he denied to them alone. He might have annihilated the whole fabric of post-apostolic miracles, if he had left uninjured by sarcastic insinuation those of the New Testament; he might have cashiered, with Dodwell, the whole host of martyrs, which owe their existence to the prodigal invention of later days, had he but bestowed fair room, and dwelt with his ordinary energy, on the sufferings of the genuine witnesses to the truth of Christianity, the Polycarps or the martyrs of Vienne. ⟨. . .⟩

It is a singular but inevitable consequence of the establishment of a very masterly work, as the acknowledged, the authorised history of any particular time or country, that, if it does not arrest the free progress of inquiry, it prevents the general dissemination of any subsequent discoveries in the same province. It has become, as it were, the historic creed of the nation; and all attempts to correct and amend its imperfect representation of the times, are not perhaps met with an open and obstinate appeal to its indefeasible authority, but are either disregarded or obtain no general hearing. Where one man of letters, or one more inquiring lover of truth, reads the less attractive but more accurate statement, hundreds content themselves with the agreeable or eloquent original; and thus errors, which have been exploded for years from the historic belief of the better-informed few, remain inveterately moulded up with the popular instruction. The physical sciences are in a constant state of marked and acknowledged progression. In a certain sense, the last book must always be the best, as containing all the recent discoveries admitted by men of science: no one would think of reading Newton in the present day as a complete treatise on optics. Yet, though even the stanchest Tory must admit the deficiencies of Hume, and acknowledge, that from the public documents alone that have come to light since he wrote, it is impossible that his work should be a perfect or an accurate history of our country, yet, to how many is Hume the *ne plus ultra* of authority! We may remonstrate in learned indignation; we may deplore the indolent and unenquiring spirit of the age; we may lament the superior influence of manner over matter, of the graceful and easy style over solid and accurate information; but after all, the agreeable book will be the popular one; we may recommend one author for depth of research, another for philosophic views, but unless he possess some inherent attractiveness, unless he commend himself to the public taste, he will never supersede the more amusing, or more exciting narrative, which is already in possession of the ground. Thus is error perpetuated and canonized by genius; and the work which reflects the highest credit on a national literature, and during its first days is a source of unmingled good, by promulgating and impressing valuable knowledge upon the public mind in the most effective and lasting manner, becomes incidentally the cause of some mischief, and retards the free promulgation of truth. For though not progressive in the same defined and incontestable manner with science, there can be no doubt that historic knowledge must be constantly on the advance. Each age will have its own characteristic way of looking on the past; each will have its own philosophy of history; each be misled in the appreciation of characters, or in ascertaining the magnitude of events, by the haze of its own passions and prejudices; but we must encourage the hope, that though not altogether clear, our moral sight will become more keen and just; that our judgments on the past will not only be formed on the more complete evidence of more extensive information, but on sounder, wiser, and more truly Christian principles. But it is not so much in the philosophy of history, as in the critical sagacity which is perpetually sifting the materials with more jealous and scrupulous care, and the patient industry, or fortunate discovery, which is constantly accumulating new treasures, that historical knowledge enlarges its sphere. In the case of Gibbon, few discoveries may have been made in ancient literature, which will throw light on the subjects of his inquiries, though even in this province there have been some valuable accessions to our knowledge; but other parts of his history, particularly all that relates to the East, may admit of much improvement from the recently explored treasures of oriental literature. The whole of his narrative of Armenian

affairs, so intimately blended with the political relations of the Byzantine empire, and of the later Persian kingdom, requires to be modified according to the discoveries of M. St Martin among the historians of that country. On another most important point, the origin and affiliation of the barbarous nations which invaded the West, the opinions of the learned have undergone considerable change since the age of Gibbon. The study of languages—since that time pursued with so much wider information, and so much more philosophically, by the Adelungs, Klaproths, Grimms, Remusats, &c.,—has greatly modified many of the views adopted by our historian.

All this may undoubtedly be found in 'a great number of writers,' some of great and deserved popularity, but it is because it is to be found in 'a great number of writers,' that it is little likely to be sought, or at all events applied at the right time. Where one person extends his inquiries so far as to bring a mass of historical reading to bear upon the correction of a standard work, a thousand will acquiesce with unenquiring submission in the statements of an accredited author. But if accuracy of historical knowledge be of importance even in minute points—if it be desirable that erroneous views should not be thus incorporated and perpetuated in our whole system of instruction—any palliative to this growing evil would be a valuable service to our national literature. The only remedy appears to be the republication of such works as are unlikely to be superseded in public estimation and authority, with a body of notes, which may at once correct their errors, and incorporate the more valuable discoveries of modern enquiry. It is time that variorum editions of our standard works should issue from the press. In this the French[4] are setting a good example; and we trust that we shall not long remain behind our enlightened neighbours. The combined motives of admiration for the classical works of our literature—which, in proportion to their merit, we should rejoice in beholding in a more perfect form— and of zeal for the sound and accurate instruction of the people, will we trust, before long, be enlisted in this important cause; and the attempt at least be made to extend and enlarge the general knowledge, not by hasty and temporary compilations, and such shreds and tatters of information as are scattered abroad in the countless cheap publications of the day, but by the continual improvement and completion of the great imperishable works of English literature.

Notes

1. An industrious editor's marginal references, by the way, might remedy this.
2. Perhaps his view of the Crusades is the most inaccurate portion of his history. If we remember right, Mr Hallam has made a similar observation.
3. As an instance of this, we may select M. Guizot's note on his character of Alexander Severus, in which, from inattention to this peculiarity in Gibbon's system of composition, the critic has reproached him with the omission of certain facts, which appear in another part of his work, and in stronger terms than M. Guizot's. 'Alexander received into his chapel all the religions (cultes) which prevailed in the empire. He admitted Jesus Christ, Abraham, Orpheus, Apollonius of Tyana, &c. It is almost certain that his mother Mammæa had instructed him in the morality of Christianity. . . . *Gibbon has not noticed this circumstance,*' &c, &c. Such is M. Guizot's note to chapter vi, of the history. In the memorable sixteenth chapter, after discussing the Christianity of Mammæa, which he gives some valid reason for disbelieving, and after describing her interview with Origen, and the favourable hearing which she gave to his *eloquent exhortations,* Gibbon thus proceeds:—'The sentiments of Mammæa were adopted by her son Alexander, and the philosophic devotion of that emperor was marked by a singular but injudicious regard for the Christian

religion. In his domestic chapel he placed the statues of Abraham, of Orpheus, of Apollonius, and of Christ, as an honour justly due to those respectable sages, who had instructed mankind in various modes of addressing their homage to the Supreme and Universal Deity. *A purer faith as well as worship was openly professed and practised among his household.* Bishops, perhaps for the first time, were seen at court,' &c.

4. Even Rollin—a writer whom it will require much labour and very considerable additions to bring up to the present state of opinion as to ancient history—has been undertaken by a scholar of the high reputation of M. Letronne. The *Histoire du bas empire*, of Le Beau, a work, as an historical composition, immeasurably inferior to Gibbon, is in course of publication. It was commenced and carried nearly through the thirteenth volume by the celebrated Armenian scholar, M. St Martin, who, however, has not confined his annotations to oriental affairs, but has subjoined useful corrections and explanations to every part of the history. Since the death of M. St Martin, the continuation of the work has been confided to M. Brosset.

WALTER BAGEHOT
From "Edward Gibbon" (1856)
Collected Works, ed. Norman St. John-Stevas
1965, Volume 1, pp. 378-91

You should do everything, said Lord Chesterfield, in minuet time. It was in that time that Gibbon wrote his history, and such was the manner of the age. You fancy him in a suit of flowered velvet, with a bag and sword, wisely smiling, composedly rounding his periods. You seem to see the grave bows, the formal politeness, the finished deference. You perceive the minuetic action accompanying the words: 'Give,' it would say, 'Augustus a chair: Zenobia, the humblest of your slaves: Odoacer, permit me to correct the defect in your attire.' As the slap-dash sentences of a rushing critic express the hasty impatience of modern manners, so the deliberate emphasis, the slow acumen, the steady argument, the impressive narration bring before us what is now a tradition, the picture of the correct eighteenth-century gentleman, who never failed in a measured politeness, partly because it was due in propriety towards others, and partly because from his own dignity it was due most obviously to himself.

And not only is this true of style, but may be extended to other things also. There is no one of the many literary works produced in the eighteenth century more thoroughly characteristic of it than Gibbon's history. The special characteristic of that age is its clinging to the definite and palpable; it had a taste beyond everything for what is called solid information. In literature the period may be defined as that in which authors had ceased to write for students, and had not begun to write for women. In the present day no one can take up any book intended for general circulation, without clearly seeing that the writer supposes most of his readers will be ladies or young men; and that in proportion to his judgment, he is attending to their taste. Two or three hundred years ago books were written for professed and systematic students,—the class the fellows of colleges were designed to be,—who used to go on studying them all their lives. Between these there was a time in which the more marked class of literary consumers were strong-headed, practical men. Education had not become so general, or so feminine, as to make the present style—what is called the 'brilliant style'—at all necessary; but there was enough culture to make the demand of common diffused persons more effectual than that of special and secluded scholars. A book-

buying public had arisen of sensible men, who would not endure the awful folio style in which the schoolmen wrote. From peculiar causes, too, the business of that age was perhaps more free from the hurry and distraction which disable so many of our practical men now from reading. You accordingly see in the books of the last century what is called a masculine tone; a firm, strong, perspicuous narration of matter of fact, a plain argument, a contempt for everything which distinct definite people cannot entirely and thoroughly comprehend. There is no more solid book in the world than Gibbon's history. Only consider the chronology. It begins before the year ONE and goes down to the year 1453, and is a schedule or series of schedules of important events during that time. Scarcely any fact deeply affecting European civilisation is wholly passed over, and the great majority are elaborately recounted. Laws, dynasties, churches, barbarians, appear and disappear. Everything changes; the old world—the classical civilisation of form and definition—passes away, a new world of free spirit and inward growth emerges; between the two lies a mixed weltering interval of trouble and confusion, when everybody hates everybody, and the historical student leads a life of skirmishes, is oppressed with broils and feuds. All through this long period Gibbon's history goes with steady consistent pace; like a Roman legion through a troubled country—*hæret pede pes*; up hill and down hill, through marsh and thicket, through Goth or Parthian—the firm defined array passes forward—a type of order, and an emblem of civilisation. Whatever may be the defects of Gibbon's history, none can deny him a proud precision and a style in marching order.

Another characteristic of the eighteenth century is its taste for dignified pageantry. What an existence was that of Versailles! How gravely admirable to see the *grand monarque* shaved, and dressed, and powdered; to look on and watch a great man carefully amusing himself with dreary trifles. Or do we not even now possess an invention of that age—the great eighteenth-century footman, still in the costume of his era, with dignity and powder, vast calves and noble mien? What a world it must have been when all men looked like that! Go and gaze with rapture at the footboard of a carriage, and say, Who would not obey a premier with such an air? Grave, tranquil, decorous pageantry is a part, as it were, of the essence of the last age. There is nothing more characteristic of Gibbon. A kind of pomp pervades him. He is never out of livery. He ever selects for narration those themes which look most like a levee; grave chamberlains seem to stand throughout; life is a vast ceremony, the historian at once the dignitary and the scribe.

The very language of Gibbon shows these qualities. Its majestic march has been the admiration—its rather pompous cadence the sport of all perusers. It has the greatest merit of an historical style; it is always going on; you feel no doubt of its continuing in motion. Many narrators of the reflective class, Sir Archibald Alison for example, fail in this; your constant feeling is, 'Ah! he is pulled up; he is going to be profound; he never will go on again.' Gibbon's reflections connect the events; they are not sermons between them. But, notwithstanding, the manner of the *Decline and Fall* is the last which should be recommended for strict imitation. It is not a style in which you can tell the truth. A monotonous writer is suited only to monotonous matter. Truth is of various kinds—grave, solemn, dignified, petty, low, ordinary; and a historian who has to tell the truth must be able to tell what is vulgar as well as what is great, what is little as well as what is amazing. Gibbon is at fault here. He *cannot* mention Asia *Minor*. The petty order of sublunary matters; the common gross existence of ordinary people; the necessary littlenesses of necessary life, are little suited to his sublime narrative. Men on the *Times* feel this acutely; it is most difficult at first to say many things in the huge imperial manner. And after all you cannot tell everything. 'How, sir,' asked a reviewer of Sydney Smith's life, 'do you say a "good fellow" in print?' 'Mr. ——,' replied the editor, 'you should not say it at all.' Gibbon was aware of this rule: he omits what does not suit him; and the consequence is, that though he has selected the most various of historical topics, he scarcely gives you an idea of variety. The ages change, but the varnish of the narration is the same.

It is not unconnected with this fault that Gibbon gives us but an indifferent description of individual character. People seem a good deal alike. The cautious skepticism of his cold intellect, which disinclined him to every extreme, depreciates great virtues and extenuates great vices; and we are left with a tame neutral character, capable of nothing extraordinary,—hateful, as the saying is, 'both to God and to the enemies of God.'

A great point in favour of Gibbon is the existence of his history. Some great historians seem likely to fail here. A good judge was asked which he preferred, Macaulay's *History of England* or Lord Mahon's. 'Why,' he replied, 'you observe Lord Mahon has written his history; and by what I see Macaulay's will be written not only for but *among* posterity.' Practical people have little idea of the practical ability required to write a large book, and especially a large history. Long before you get to the pen, there is an immensity of pure business; heaps of material are strewn everywhere; but they lie in disorder, unread, uncatalogued, unknown. It seems a dreary waste of life to be analysing, indexing, extracting works and passages, in which one per cent of the contents are interesting, and not half of that percentage will after all appear in the flowing narrative. As an accountant takes up a bankrupt's books filled with confused statements of ephemeral events, the disorderly record of unprofitable speculations, and charges this to that head, and that to this,—estimates earnings, specifies expenses, demonstrates failures; so the great narrator, going over the scattered annalists of extinct ages, groups and divides, notes and combines, until from a crude mass of darkened fragments there emerges a clear narrative, a concise account of the result and upshot of the whole. In this art Gibbon was a master. The laborious research of German scholarship, the keen eye of theological zeal, a steady criticism of eighty years, have found few faults of detail. The account has been worked right, the proper authorities consulted, an accurate judgment formed, the most telling incidents selected. Perhaps experience shows that there is something English in his talent. The Germans are more elaborate in single monographs; but they seem to want the business-ability to work out a complicated narrative, to combine a long whole. The French are neat enough, and the style is very quick; but then it is difficult to believe the facts; the account on its face seems too plain and no true Parisian ever was an antiquary. The great classical histories published in this country in our own time show that the talent is by no means extinct; and they likewise show, what is also evident, that this kind of composition is easier with respect to ancient than with respect to modern times. The barbarians burned the books; and though all the historians abuse them for it, it is quite evident that in their hearts they are greatly rejoiced. If the books had existed, they would have had to read them. Mr. Macaulay has to peruse every book printed with long s's; and it is no use after all; somebody will find some stupid MS., an old account-book of an 'ingenious gentleman,' and with five entries therein destroy a whole hypothesis. But Gibbon was exempt from this; he could count the books the efficient Goths bequeathed; and when he had mastered them he might pause. Still it was no light matter, as any one who looks at the books—awful folios in the grave Bodleian—will most certainly credit and believe. And he did it all himself; he never showed his book to any friend, or asked any one to help him in the accumulating work, not even in the correction of the press. 'Not a sheet,' he says, 'has been seen by any human eyes, excepting those of the author and the printer; the faults and the merits are exclusively my own.' And he wrote most of it with one pen, which must certainly have grown erudite towards the end.

The nature of his authorities clearly shows what the nature of Gibbon's work is. History may be roughly divided into universal and particular; the first being the narrative of events affecting the whole human race, at least the main historical nations, the narrative of whose fortunes is the story of civilisation; and the latter being the relation of events relating to one or a few particular nations only. Universal history, it is evident, comprises great areas of space and long periods of time; you cannot have a series of events visibly operating on all great nations without time for their gradual operation, and without tracking them in succession through the various regions of their power. There is no instantaneous transmission in historical causation; a long interval is required for universal effects. It follows, that universal history necessarily partakes of the character of a summary. You cannot recount the cumbrous annals of long epochs without condensation, selection, and omission; the narrative, when shortened within the needful limits, becomes concise and general. What it gains in time, according to the mechanical phrase, it loses in power. The particular history, confined within narrow limits, can show us the whole contents of these limits, explain its features of human interest, recount in graphic detail all its interesting transactions, touch the human heart with the power of passion, instruct the mind with patient instances of accurate wisdom. The universal is confined to a dry enumeration of superficial transactions; no action can have all its details; the canvas is so crowded that no figure has room to display itself effectively. From the nature of the subject, Gibbon's history is of the latter class; the sweep of the narrative is so wide; the decline and fall of the Roman empire being in some sense the most universal event which has ever happened,—being, that is, the historical incident which has most affected all civilised men, and the very existence and form of civilisation itself,—it is evident that we must look rather for a comprehensive generality than a telling minuteness of delineation. The history of a thousand years does not admit the pictorial detail which a Scott or a Macaulay can accumulate on the history of a hundred. Gibbon has done his best to avoid the dryness natural to such an attempt. He inserts as much detail as his limits will permit; selects for more full description striking people and striking transactions; brings together at a single view all that relates to single topics; above all, by a regular advance of narration, never ceases to imply the regular progress of events and the steady course of time. None can deny the magnitude of such an effort. After all, however, these are merits of what is technically termed composition, and are analogous to those excellencies in painting and sculpture that are more respected by artists than appreciated by the public at large. The fame of Gibbon is highest among writers; those especially who have studied for years particular periods included in his theme (and how many those are; for in the East and West he has set his mark on all that is great for ten centuries!) acutely feel and admiringly observe how difficult it would be to say so much, and leave so little untouched; to compress so many telling points; to present in so few words so apt and embracing a narrative of the whole. But the mere unsophisticated reader scarcely appreciates this; he is rather awed than delighted; or rather, perhaps, he appreciates it for a little while, then is tired by the roll and glare; next on any chance—the creaking of an organ or the stirring of a mouse—in time of temptation he falls away. It has been said, the way to answer all objections to Milton is to take down the book and read him; the way to reverence Gibbon is not to read him at all, but look at him, from outside, in the bookcase, and think how much there is within; what a course of events, what a muster-roll of names, what a steady solemn sound! You will not like to take the book down; but you will think how much you could be delighted if you would.

It may be well, though it can be only in the most cursory manner, to examine the respective treatment of the various elements in this vast whole. The history of the *Decline and Fall* may be roughly and imperfectly divided into the picture of the Roman empire—the narrative of barbarian incursions—the story of Constantinople: and some few words may be hastily said on each.

The picture,—for so, from its apparent stability when contrasted with the fluctuating character of the later period, we may call it,—which Gibbon has drawn of the united empire has immense merit. The organisation of the imperial system is admirably dwelt on; the manner in which the old republican institutions were apparently retained, but really altered, is compendiously explained; the mode in which the imperial will was transmitted to and carried out in remote provinces is distinctly displayed. But though the mechanism is admirably delineated, the dynamical principle, the original impulse, is not made clear. You never feel you are reading about the Romans. Yet no one denies their character to be most marked. Poets and orators have striven for the expression of it.

Mr. Macaulay has been similarly criticised; it has been said, that notwithstanding his great dynamic power, and wonderful felicity in the selection of events on which to exert it, he yet never makes us feel that we are reading about Englishmen. The coarse clay of our English nature *cannot* be represented in so fine a style. In the same way, and to a much greater extent (for this is perhaps an unthankful criticism, if we compare Macaulay's description of anybody with that of any other historian), Gibbon is chargeable with neither expressing nor feeling the essence of the people concerning whom he is writing. There was, in truth, in the Roman people a warlike fanaticism, a puritanical essence, an interior, latent, re-strained, enthusiastic religion, which was utterly alien to the cold skepticism of the narrator. Of course he was conscious of it. He indistinctly felt that at least there was something he did not like; but he could not realise or sympathise with it without a change of heart and nature. The old Pagan has a sympathy with the religion of enthusiasm far above the reach of the modern Epicurean.

It may indeed be said, on behalf of Gibbon, that the old Roman character was in its decay, and that only such slight traces of it were remaining in the age of Augustus and the Antonines that it is no particular defect in him to leave it unnoticed. Yet though the intensity of its nobler peculiarities was on the wane, many a vestige would perhaps have been apparent to so learned an eye, if his temperament and disposition had been prone to seize upon and search for them. Nor is there any adequate appreciation of the compensating element, of the force which really held society together, of the fresh air of the Illyrian hills, of that army which, evermore recruited from northern and rugged populations, doubtless

brought into the very centre of a degraded society the healthy simplicity of a vital if barbarous religion.

It is no wonder that such a mind should have looked with displeasure on primitive Christianity. The whole of his treatment of that topic has been discussed by many pens, and three generations of ecclesiastical scholars have illustrated it with their emendations. Yet if we turn over this, the latest and most elaborate edition, containing all the important criticisms of Milman and of Guizot, we shall be surprised to find how few instances of definite exact error such a scrutiny has been able to find out. As Paley, with his strong sagacity, at once remarked, the subtle error rather lies hid in the sinuous folds than is directly apparent on the surface of the polished style. Who, said the shrewd archdeacon, can refute a sneer? And yet even this is scarcely the exact truth. The objection of Gibbon is, in fact, an objection rather to religion than to Christianity; as has been said, he did not appreciate, and could not describe, the most inward form of pagan piety; he objected to Christianity because it was the intensest of religions. We do not mean by this to charge Gibbon with any denial of, any overt distinct disbelief in the existence of a supernatural Being. This would be very unjust; his cold composed mind had nothing in common with the Jacobinical outbreak of the next generation. He was no doubt a theist after the fashion of natural theology; nor was he devoid of more than scientific feeling. All consti-tuted authorities struck him with emotion, all ancient ones with awe. If the Roman empire had descended to his time, how much he would have reverenced it! He had doubtless a great respect for the 'First Cause;' it had many titles to approbation; 'it was not conspicuous,' he would have said, 'but it was potent.' A sensitive decorum revolted from the jar of atheistic disputation. We have already described him more than enough. A sensible middle-aged man in political life; a bachelor, not himself gay, but living with gay men; equable and secular; cautious in his habits, tolerant in his creed, as Porson said, 'never failing in natural feeling except when women were to be ravished and Christians to be martyred.' His writings are in character. The essence of the far-famed fifteenth and sixteenth chapters is, in truth, but a description of unworldly events in the tone of this world, of awful facts in unmoved voice, of truths of the heart in the language of the eyes. The wary sceptic has not even committed himself to definite doubts. These celebrated chapters were in the first manuscript much longer, and were gradually reduced to their present size by excision and compression. Who can doubt that in their first form they were a clear, or comparatively clear expression of exact opinions on the Christian history, and that it was by a subsequent and elaborate process that they were reduced to their present and insidious obscurity? The toil has been effectual. 'Divest,' says Dean Milman of the introduction to the fifteenth chapter, 'this whole passage of the latent sarcasm betrayed by the subsequent tone of the whole disqui-sition, and it might commence a Christian history, written in the most Christian spirit of candour.'

It is not for us here to go into any disquisition as to the comparative influence of the five earthly causes to whose secondary operation the specious historian ascribes the progress of Christianity. Weariness and disinclination forbid. There can be no question that the polity of the church, and the zeal of the converts, and other such things, did most materially conduce to the progress of the Gospel. But few will now attribute to these much of the effect. The real cause is the heaving of the mind after the truth. Troubled with the perplexities of time, weary with the vexation of ages, the spiritual faculty of man turns to the truth as the child turns to its mother. The thirst of the soul was to be satisfied, the deep torture of the spirit to have rest. There was an appeal to those

> High instincts, before which our mortal Nature
> Did tremble like a guilty Thing surprised.

The mind of man has an appetite for the truth.

> Hence, in a season of calm weather
>   Though inland far we be,
> Our Souls have sight of that immortal sea
>   Which brought us hither,
>   Can in a moment travel thither,
> And see the Children sport upon the shore,
> And hear the mighty waters rolling evermore.

All this was not exactly in Gibbon's way, and he does not seem to have been able to conceive that it was in any one else's. Why his chapters had given offence he could hardly make out. It actually seems that he hardly thought that other people believed more than he did. 'We may be well assured,' says he, of a sceptic of antiquity, 'that a writer conversant with the world would never have ventured to expose the gods of his country to public ridicule, had they not been already the objects of secret contempt among the polished and enlightened orders of society.' 'Had I,' he says of himself, 'believed that the majority of English readers were so fondly attached even to the name and shadow of Christianity, had I foreseen that the pious, the timid, and the prudent would feel, or would affect to feel, with such exquisite sensibility,—I might perhaps have softened the two invidious chapters, which would create many enemies and conciliate few friends.' The state of belief at that time is a very large subject; but it is probable that in the cultivated cosmopolitan classes the continental scepticism was very rife; that among the hard-headed classes the rough spirit of English Deism had made progress. Though the mass of the people doubtless believed much as they now believe, yet the entire upper class was lazy and corrupt, and there is truth in the picture of the modern divine: 'The thermometer of the Church of England sank to its lowest point in the first thirty years of the reign of George III. . . . In their preaching, nineteen clergymen out of twenty carefully abstained from dwelling upon Christian doctrines. Such topics exposed the preacher to the charge of fanaticism. Even the calm and sober Crabbe, who certainly never erred from excess of zeal, was stigmatised in those days by his brethren as a methodist, because he introduced into his sermons the motives of future reward and punishment. An orthodox clergyman (they said) should be content to show his people the worldly advantage of good conduct, and to leave heaven and hell to the ranters. Nor can we wonder that such should have been the notions of country parsons, when, even by those who passed for the supreme arbiters of orthodoxy and taste, the vapid rhetoric of Blair was thought the highest standard of Christian exhortation.' It is among the excuses for Gibbon that he lived in such a world.

There are slight palliations also in the notions then prevalent of the primitive church. There was the Anglican theory, that it was a *via media*, the most correct of periods, that its belief is to be the standard, its institutions the model, its practice the test of subsequent ages. There was the notion, not formally drawn out, but diffused through and implied in a hundred books of evidences,—a notion in opposition to every probability, and utterly at variance with the New Testament,—that the first converts were sober, hard-headed, cultivated inquirers,—Watsons, Paleys, Priestleys, on a small scale; weighing evidence, analysing facts, suggesting doubts, dwelling on distinctions, cold in their dispositions, moderate in their morals,—cautious in their creed. We now know that these were not they of whom the world was not worthy. It is ascertained that the times of the first church were times of excitement; that great ideas falling on a mingled world were distorted by an untrained intellect, even in the moment in which they were received by a yearning heart; that strange confused beliefs, Millennarianism, Gnosticism, Ebionitism, were accepted, not merely by outlying obscure heretics, but in a measure, half-and-half, one notion more by one man, another more by his neighbour, confusedly and mixedly by the mass of Christians; that the appeal was not to the questioning thinking understanding, but to unheeding all-venturing emotion; to that lower class 'from whom faiths ascend,' and not to the cultivated and exquisite class by whom they are criticised; that fervid men never embraced a more exclusive creed. You can say nothing favourable of the first Christians, except that they *were* Christians. We find no 'form nor comeliness' in them; no intellectual accomplishments, no caution in action, no discretion in understanding. There is no admirable quality except that, with whatever distortion, or confusion, or singularity, they at once accepted the great clear outline of belief in which to this day we live, move, and have our being. The offence of Gibbon is his disinclination to this simple essence; his excuse, the historical errors then prevalent as to the primitive Christians, the real defects so natural in their position, the false merits ascribed to them by writers who from one reason or another desired to treat them as 'an authority.'

On the whole, therefore, it may be said of the first, and in some sense the most important part of Gibbon's work, that though he has given an elaborate outline of the framework of society, and described its detail with pomp and accuracy, yet that he has not comprehended or delineated its nobler essence, Pagan or Christian. Nor perhaps was it to be expected that he should, for he inadequately comprehended the dangers of the time; he thought it the happiest period the world has ever known; he would not have comprehended the remark, 'To see the old world in its worst estate we turn to the age of the satirists and of Tacitus, when all the different streams of evil coming from east, west, north, south, the vices of barbarism and the vices of civilization, remnants of ancient cults and the latest refinements of luxury and impurity, met and mingled on the banks of the Tiber. What could have been the state of society when Tiberius, Caligula, Nero, Domitian, Heliogabalus, were the rulers of the world? To a good man we should imagine that death itself would be more tolerable than the sight of such things coming upon the earth.' So deep an ethical sensibility was not to be expected in the first century; nor is it strange when, after seventeen hundred years, we do not find it in their historian.

Space has failed us, and we must be unmeaningly brief. The second head of Gibbon's history—the narrative of the barbarian invasions—has been recently criticised, on the ground that he scarcely enough explains the gradual but unceasing and inevitable manner in which the outer barbarians were affected by and assimilated to the civilisation of Rome. Mr. Congreve has well observed, that the impression which Gibbon's narrative is insensibly calculated to convey is, that there was little or no change in the state of the Germanic tribes between the time of Tacitus and the final invasion of the empire—a conclusion which is obviously incredible. To the general reader there will perhaps seem some indistinctness in this part of the work, nor is a free confused barbarism a congenial subject for an imposing and orderly pencil. He succeeds better in the delineation of the riding monarchies, if we may so term them,—of the equestrian courts of Attila or

Timour, in which the great scale, the concentrated power, the very enormity of the barbarism, give, so to speak a shape to unshapeliness; impart, that is, a horrid dignity to horse-flesh and mare's milk, an imposing oneness to the vast materials of a crude barbarity. It is needless to say that no one would search Gibbon for an explanation of the reasons or feelings by which the northern tribes were induced to accept Christianity.

It is on the story of Constantinople that the popularity of Gibbon rests. The vast extent of the topic; the many splendid episodes it contains; its epic unity from the moment of the far-seeing selection of the city by Constantine to its last fall; its position as a link between Europe and Asia; its continuous history; the knowledge that through all that time it was, as now, a diadem by the water-side, a lure to be snatched by the wistful barbarian, a marvel to the West, a prize for the North and for the East;—these, and such as these ideas, are congenial topics to a style of pomp and grandeur. The East seems to require to be treated with a magnificence unsuitable to a colder soil. The nature of the events, too, is suitable to Gibbon's cursory imposing manner. It is the history of a form of civilisation, but without the power thereof; a show of splendour and vigour, but without bold life or interior reality. What an opportunity for an historian who loved the imposing pageantry and disliked the purer essence of existence! There were here neither bluff barbarians nor simple saints; there was nothing admitting of particular accumulated detail: we do not wish to know the interior of the stage; the imposing movements are all which should be seized. Some of the features, too, are curious in relation to those of the historian's life; the clear accounts of the theological controversies, followed out with an appreciative minuteness so rare in a sceptic, are not disconnected with his early conversion to the scholastic church: the brilliancy of the narrative reminds us of his enthusiasm for Arabic and the East; the minute description of a licentious epoch evinces the habit of a mind which, not being bold enough for the practice of license, took a pleasure in following its theory. There is no subject which combines so much of unity with so much of variety.

It is evident, therefore, where Gibbon's rank as an historian must finally stand. He cannot be numbered among the great painters of human nature, for he has no sympathy with the heart and passions of our race; he has no place among the felicitous describers of detailed life, for his subject was too vast for minute painting, and his style too uniform for a shifting scene. But he is entitled to a high—perhaps to a first place—among the orderly narrators of great events; the composed expositors of universal history; the tranquil artists who have endeavoured to diffuse a cold polish over the warm passions and desultory fortunes of mankind.

SIR LESLIE STEPHEN
From "Gibbon's Autobiography"
Studies of a Biographer
1898, Volume 1, pp. 172–87

He is less sagacious than Horace Walpole, whose extraordinary cleverness was wasted by frivolity. As an outside observer, he might have recognised the importance of the great issues, and shown himself at least on a level with the higher judges of his own time. He was apparently conscious of the gross blunders of George III. and Lord North, but was content to support Ministers, with a lazy indifference to the result. His letters, when they contain any reference to the American War,

treat the matter almost as a jest, and plainly betray that his real interest was much more with Alaric than with Washington. He lived through the most exciting period of the century; he even took an actual, though a very subordinate, part in the operations which involved the foundation of the British Empire in the East and the expulsion of our rivals from the West. He supported the political course which led to the separation of our greatest colonies a few years later; and both at these periods and on the outbreak of the French Revolution afterwards, he seems to have regarded the greatest events of the time chiefly as they affected the comfort of a fat historian in his library. What defence can be made? None truly, if we are measuring Gibbon by a lofty moral standard; but if we are asking the question now under consideration, how a great historian was to be turned out, we shall have to make a very different judgment.

The obvious reproach is summed up by the statement that Gibbon was a cynic. The name suggests the selfish indifference to human welfare which permits a man to treat politics simply as a game played for the stakes of place and pension. It is generally added, though I hardly know whether it is regarded by way of apology, or as a proof of the offence, that all our great-grandfathers were corrupt borough-mongers, forming cliques for the distribution of plunder, and caring nothing for the welfare of the people. We ought, we are often told, to judge a man by the standard of his period. Whatever the period, it can always be plausibly added that it was the most immoral period ever known in history. The argument is familiar, and I cannot attempt to consider its precise application here. But I may try briefly to indicate how it would have struck Gibbon. What would he have said if he could have foreseen the judgment of the coming generation? You call me a cynic, he might have replied, but at least you must admit that I was an honest cynic; I never professed to believe in humbug, though I had to accept it. If you are less cynical, you have made up for it by being more hypocritical. Our party politics meant adherence to some little aristocratic ring. Yours mean servility to a caucus. You cover a real cynicism as deep as mine by shouting with the largest mob. We at least dared to despise a demagogue; you dare not openly deny his inspiration. You manage to use fine phrases so as to cover the desertion of all your principles: you use old war-cries in favour of the very doctrines which you used to condemn, and declare all the time that you are impelled by 'enthusiasm' and sensibility to the voice of the people. Is it not rather subservience to their narrowest prejudices? In my day, he would add, we had examples of the genuine demagogue revealing himself without a blush. When in the militia, in 1762, I saw Colonel Wilkes, the best of companions, at a drunken dinner, full of blasphemy and indecency, glorying in his profligacy, and openly declaring that he had resolved to make his fortune. You have found out that because he made it by flattering the winning side he must have been a saint in disguise. You sneer at my want of 'enthusiasm.' You shudder when you make the remark that enthusiasm was once actually a term of reproach. When we denounced 'enthusiasts,' we denounced a very bad thing. We thought that the false claimants of supernatural powers must be knaves or fools, and we ventured to say so openly. You think that even a charlatan deserves respect if his stock-in-trade is a comfortable superstition. I, too, could claim enthusiasm in your sense. It was in a moment of 'enthusiasm' that I joined the Church of Rome; and though I always scorned to affect what I did not feel, it was with true 'enthusiasm' that I entered Rome, heard the bare-footed friars singing vespers in the Temple of Jupiter, and conceived the first crude idea of my great work. Enthusiasm, in my version, lifted me to the regions of philosophy, and separated me from the vulgar herd. It did not mean the discovery of the *vox dei* in every platform intended to catch the votes of the majority. We did not think ignorance and poverty a sufficient guarantee for political or religious infallibility. But we were not, therefore, as you infer, indifferent to the happiness of mankind. We thought that their happiness was best secured in the ages when a benevolent despotism maintained peace and order throughout the world; when philosophers could rule and the lower orders be confined to the work for which they were really competent. We held in religion pretty much what you hold, only that you try to cover your real meaning under a cloud of words. We accepted my great maxim: To the philosopher all religions are equally false; and to the magistrate equally useful. You try to spin theories which will combine the two opinions—which will allow you to use the most edifying language, while explaining that it means nothing; and to base arguments for 'faith' on the admission that nobody can possibly know anything. We were content to say that it was too much honour to the vulgar to argue as to the truth of their beliefs. We were content to belong to the upper circle of enlightenment in which it was understood that the creeds were meaningless, but without attempting the hopeless task of enlightening the uncultivated mind. Some such retort might be made to the nineteenth century by the eighteenth; and Gibbon is a typical example of the qualities which were denounced in the next generation when they called their immediate predecessors cold, heartless, and materialistic, and looked upon the whole preceding century as a sort of mysterious intercalation, an eclipse of all that was heroic and romantic, and a sudden paralysis of the progressive forces of humanity. Nothing, as I believe, can be more unjust; but rightly or wrongly, there are times when one regrets the reign of cool common sense and of freedom from fads and fussiness. At such moments there is an incidental charm about the intellectual position of our grandfathers. Philosophical problems can hardly be discussed now without suggesting some immediate practical application. Dogmas have become explosive, and suggest at once a reconstruction of society, a revolutionary or a reactionary movement; they are caught up by popular leaders on one side or the other, and abstract speculations are made at once into party watchwords. It must have been pleasant to philosophise in the days when your audience was select, when you could feel that your opinions would be discussed only by a few enlightened people, or would at most spread gradually and slowly force away old prejudices without provoking internecine struggles. You could boast of being a philosopher, and yet be content to allow error to die out among the vulgar without trying to force new ideas upon minds totally incapable of appreciating them. To speak freely and openly is no doubt the best rule in the long-run; but there is, it must be admitted, a real difficulty in proclaiming truth with the knowledge that it will be perverted by the vulgar interpreters. To Gibbon, in his earlier days, that difficulty scarcely presented itself. He fancied that even his chapters upon Christianity would be accepted by all cultivated people, while there should be a faint understanding that the old language should still be kept up 'for the use of the poor.'

Gibbon, indeed, had in time to confess that this view involved an important practical mistake. Philosophy, political and religious, could not permanently remain the esoteric doctrine of a narrow circle; and when hot-headed Rousseaus and the like spread its tenets among the vulgar, it produced an explosion which took the calm philosophers by surprise. Gibbon began to see a good side even in the superstition, the vitality of which had astonished him so much on the publication of his first volume.

This suggests the obvious weakness of his position; nor do I mean to adopt the sentiments which I have ventured to attribute to him. What I desire to indicate is the necessity of this position to the discharge of his function as a historian. We can no doubt conceive of a more excellent way; of a great thinker, who should at once be capable of philosophical detachment, of looking at passing events in their relations to the vast drama of human history on the largest scale without losing his interest in the history actually passing under his eyes. He might take not less but more interest in processes which he saw to be the continuation of the great evolution of thought and society. But the phrase indicates the conception which was necessarily obscure to Gibbon. To have reached that view would in his time have required almost superhuman attributes. Gibbon's merits were at the time inconsistent with the virtues of which we regret the absence. He had to choose, one may say, between two alternatives. If he were to take an active part in the politics of the day, he would have had to be a Wilkes on condition of not being a Wilkeite, or at least, with Burke, to give up to party what was meant for mankind. To save him from such a fate, which would have been a hopeless waste of power, he required to be endowed with an excess of indifference, and a deficiency of close and spontaneous sympathy with men outside of his little inner circle. Of this, I fear, he cannot be acquitted. Indeed, his qualification in this respect went a little too far, for he appears to have been on the very point of accepting a post which would have cut short the *History* half-way. Even his best friends, strangely as it seems to us, pressed him to commit this semi-suicide. Here, therefore, his good genius had once more to interfere by external circumstances. The task was not difficult. A happy dulness to his claims was infused into the minds of the dispensers of patronage; and Gibbon was compelled to retire philosophically to the house at Lausanne, where in due time he was to take the famous stroll in the covered walk of acacias which on 27th June 1787 succeeded the completion of the 'last lines of the last page' of his unique achievement.

We see how strangely Gibbon had been fitted for his task; how fate had turned him out of the quiet grooves down which he might have spun to obscurity, and then applied the goad judiciously whenever he tried to bolt from the predestined course. The task itself was obviously demanded by the conditions of the time, and its importance recognised by other, and in some respects acuter or more powerful, intellects. History was to emerge from the stage of mere personal memoirs and antiquarian annals: A survey from a higher point of view was wanted: a general map or panoramic view of the great field of human progress must be laid down as preparatory to further progress. Such men as Hume and Voltaire, for instance, had clearly seen the need, and had endeavoured in their way to supply it. Gibbon's superiority was, of course, due in the first place to the high standard of accuracy and research which has enabled his work to stand all the tests applied by later critics. His instinctive perception of this necessity, combined with the intellectual courage implied in his choice of so grand a subject, enabled him to combine width of view and fulness of detail with unsurpassed felicity. All this is unanimously granted. But other qualities were equally required, though from a later point of view they account rather for the limitations than the successes of his work. There must be a division of labour between generations as well as between individuals. Kepler had to describe the actual movements of the planets before Newton could determine the nature of the forces implied by the movements. In Gibbon's generation it was necessary to describe the evolutions of the puppets which move across the stage of history. His successors could then, and not till then, attempt to show what were the hidden strings that moved them. Gibbon, it has been said, 'adheres to the obvious surface of events, with little attempt to place them beneath the deeper sky of social evolution.' He appreciates, it is suggested, neither the great spiritual forces nor the economic conditions which lie beneath the surface. He calmly surveys the great stream of history, its mingling currents and deluges and regurgitations, the struggles of priests and warriors and legislators, without suggesting any adequate conceptions of what is called the social dynamics implied. To him history appears to be simply a 'register of the crimes, follies, and misfortunes of mankind.' The criticism, taking its truth for granted, amounts to saying that Gibbon had only gone as far as was in his time possible. He must be philosopher enough to sympathise with the great intellectual movement of his time. Otherwise he could not have risen above the atmosphere of Oxford common-rooms, and could only have written annals or narratives on one side or the other of some forgotten apologetic thesis. But had the philosophic taste predominated, had his passions and his sympathies been more fervid, he must have fallen into the fallacies of his time. The enthusiastic or militant philosopher was, as I certainly think, doing an inestimable service in attacking superstition and bigotry. But he was thereby disqualified as a writer not only of philosophical history, but even of such a record of facts as would serve for later historians. Such a man as d'Alembert was inclined to wish that history in general could be wiped out of human memory. From the point of view characteristic of the eighteenth-century philosophers, history could be nothing but a record of the tyranny of kings and the imposture of priests. Voltaire's *Essai sur les mœurs* is delightful reading, but a caricature of history. Gibbon might sympathise with this sentiment so far as to look with calm impartiality upon all forms of faith and government, but not so far as to pervert his *History* into a series of party pamphlets. To him the American War, or the early democratic movements in England, were simply incidents in his great panorama: like the rise of the Christian Church, or the barbarian Moslems or the Crusades, they were eddies in the great confused gulf-stream of humanity. He could not believe in a sudden revelation of Reason, or the advent of a new millennium any more than in the second coming anticipated by the early Christians. To condemn his coldness may be right; but it is to condemn him for taking the only point of view from which his task could be achieved. He was philosopher enough to be impartial, not enough to be subject to the illusions, useful illusions possibly, of a sudden regeneration of mankind by philosophy. His political position was the necessary complement of his historical position. A later philosophy may have taught us how to see a process of evolution, a gradual working-out of great problems, even in the blind, instinctive aspirations and crude faiths of earlier ages. At Gibbon's time, he had to choose between rejecting them in the mass as mere encumbrances or renouncing them altogether. That is to admit that the one point of view which makes a reasonable estimate possible was practically excluded. On the other hand, his historical instinct forced him at last to set forth the material facts both impartially and so grouped and related as to bring out the great issues. It is easy now both for positivists and believers to show, for example, that his account of the origins of Christianity was entirely insufficient. He explains, as has been remarked, the success of the Church by the zeal of the early disciples, and forgets to explain how they came to be zealous. Undoubtedly that is an omission of importance. What, however, Gibbon did was not the less effectively to bring out the real conditions of any satisfactory solution of the greatest of historical problems. Newman observed how, in a later period, 'Athanasius stands out more grandly in Gibbon

than in the pages of the orthodox ecclesiastical historians.' That is because he places all events in their true historical setting. In the writings of the apologists of the time, the spread of Christianity was treated as though converts had been made by producing satisfactory evidence of miracles in a court of justice. Gibbon's famous chapters, however inadequate, showed at least that the development of the new creed required for its expansion a calm consideration of all the multitudinous forces that go to building up a great ecclesiastical hierarchy, and a testing by careful examination of all the entries about saints and martyrs which flowed so easily from the pens of enthusiastic historians. That his judgment should be final or even coherent was impossible; but it was an essential step towards any such judgment as could pass muster with a historian equipped with the results of later thought and inquiry.

Upon this, however, it would be idle to say more. I have only tried to point an obvious moral; to show what a rare combination of circumstances with character and intellect is required to produce a really monumental work; to show how easy it generally is even for the competent man of genius to mistake his path at starting or to be distracted from it by tempting accidents; how necessary may be not only the intervention of fortunate accidents, but even the presence of qualities which, in other relations, must be regarded as defects. Happily for us, the man came when he was wanted, and just such as he was wanted; but after studying his career, we understand better than ever why great works are so rare. We may probably have known of men—many instances might easily be suggested—who might be compared to Gibbon in natural endowments, and who have left nothing but fragments, or been confined to obscure tasks, the value of which will never be sufficiently recognised. It is only when the right player comes, and the right cards are judiciously dealt to him by fortune, that the great successes can be accomplished.

J. B. BURY
"Introduction" (1896)
The History of the Decline and Fall
of the Roman Empire
1909, pp. vii–xxii

Gibbon is one of those few writers who hold as high a place in the history of literature as in the roll of great historians. He concerns us here as an historian; our business is to consider how far the view which he has presented of the decline and fall of the Roman Empire can be accepted as faithful to the facts, and in what respects it needs correction in the light of discoveries which have been made since he wrote. But the fact that his work, composed more than a hundred years ago, is still successful with the general circle of educated people, and has not gone the way of Hume and Robertson, whom we laud as "classics" and leave on the cold shelves, is due to the singularly happy union of the historian and the man of letters. Gibbon thus ranks with Thucydides and Tacitus, and is perhaps the clearest example that brilliance of style and accuracy of statement are perfectly compatible in an historian.

But Gibbon has his place in literature not only as the stylist, who never lays aside his toga when he takes up his pen, but as the expounder of a large and striking idea in a sphere of intense interest to mankind, and as a powerful representative of certain tendencies of his age. The guiding idea or "moral" of his history is briefly stated in his epigram: "I have described the triumph of barbarism and religion". In other words, the historical development of human societies, since the second century after Christ, was a retrogression (according to ordinary views of "progress"), for which Christianity was mainly to blame.

We are thus taken into a region of speculation where every traveller must make his own chart. But to attempt to deny a general truth in Gibbon's point of view is vain; and it is feeble to deprecate his sneer. We may spare more sympathy than he for the warriors and the churchmen; but all that has since been added to his knowledge of facts has neither reversed nor blunted the point of the *Decline and Fall*. For an inquirer not blinded by religious prepossessions, or misled by comfortable sophistries, Gibbon really expounded one of the chief data with which the philosophy of history has to reckon. How are we to define progress? how recognize retrogression? Is there an end in relation to which such words have their meaning, and is there a law which will explain "the triumph of barbarism and religion" as a necessary moment in a reasonable process towards that end, whatever it may be? Some answers have been given since Gibbon's day, for which he would have the same smile as for Leo's Dogmatic Epistle.

Not the least important aspect of the *Decline and Fall* is its lesson in the continuity of history, the favourite theme of Mr. Freeman. The title displays the cardinal fact that the Empire founded by Augustus fell in 1461; that all the changes which transformed the Europe of Marcus Aurelius into the Europe of Erasmus had not abolished the name and memory of the Empire. And whatever names of contempt—in harmony with his thesis—Gibbon might apply to the institution in the period of its later decline, such as the "Lower Empire," or "Greek Empire," his title rectified any false impressions that such language might cause. On the continuity of the Roman Empire depended the unity of his work. By the emphasis laid on this fact he did the same kind of service to the study of history in England, that Mr. Bryce has done in his *Holy Roman Empire* by tracing the thread which connects the Europe of Francis the Second with the Europe of Charles the Great.

It has sometimes been remarked that those histories are most readable which are written to prove a thesis. The indictment of the Empire by Tacitus, the defence of Cæsarianism by Mommsen, Grote's vindication of democracy, Droysen's advocacy of monarchy, might be cited as examples. All these writers intended to present the facts as they took place, but all wrote with prepossessions and opinions, in the light of which they interpreted the events of history. Arnold deliberately advocated such partiality on the ground that "the past is reflected to us by the present and the partyman feels the present most". Another Oxford Regius Professor remarked that "without some infusion of spite it seems as if history could not be written". On the other side stands the formula of Ranke as to the true task of the historian: "Ich will bloss sagen wie es eigentlich gewesen ist". It cannot be said that Gibbon sat down to write with any ulterior purpose, but fortunately he allowed his temperament to colour his history, and used it to prove a congenial thesis. But, while he put things in the light demanded by this thesis, he related his facts accurately. If we take into account the vast range of his work, his accuracy is amazing. He laboured under some disadvantages, which are set forth in his own *Memoirs*. He had not enjoyed that school and university training in the languages and literatures of Greece and Rome which is probably the best preparation for historical research. His knowledge of Greek was imperfect; he was very far from having the "scrupulous ear of the well-

flogged critic". He has committed errors of translation, and was capable of writing "Gregory of Nazianzen". But such slips are singularly few.

Gibbon's diligent accuracy in the use of his materials cannot be over-praised, and it will not be diminished by giving the due credit to his French predecessor Tillemont. The *Histoire des Empereurs* and the *Mémoires ecclésiastiques*, laborious and exhaustive collections of material, were addressed to the special student and not to the general reader, but scholars may still consult them with profit. It is interesting to find Mommsen in his later years retracting one of his earlier judgments and reverting to a conclusion of Tillemont. In his recent edition [1] of the *Laterculus* of Polemius Silvius, he writes thus:—

L'auteur de la Notice—peritissimi Tillemontii verba sunt (*Hist*. 5, 699)—vivoit en Occident et ne savoit pas trop l'état où estoit l'Oreint; *ei iuvenis contradixi hodie subscribo*.

It is one of Gibbon's merits that he made full use of Tillemont, "whose inimitable accuracy almost assumes the character of genius," as far as Tillemont guided him, up to the reign of Anastasius I.; and it is only just to the work of the Frenchman to impute to him a large share in the accuracy which the Englishman achieved. From the historical, though not from the literary, point of view, Gibbon, deserted by Tillemont, distinctly declines, though he is well sustained through the wars of Justinian by the clear narrative of Procopius. Recognizing that he was accurate, we do not acknowledge by implication that he was always right; for accuracy is relative to opportunities. The discovery of new materials, the researches of numerous scholars, in the course of a hundred years, have not only added to our knowledge of facts, but have modified and upset conclusions which Gibbon with his materials was justified in drawing.

Gibbon's historical sense kept him constantly right in dealing with his sources, but he can hardly be said to have treated them methodically. The growth of German erudition was one of the leading features of the intellectual history of the nineteenth century; and one of its most important contributions to historical method lies in the investigation of sources. Some German scholars have indeed pressed this "Quellenkritik" further than it can safely be pressed. A philologist, writing his doctoral dissertation, will bring plausible reasons to prove where exactly Diodorus ceased to "write out" Ephorus, whose work we do not possess, and began to write out somebody else, whose work is also lost to us. But, though the method lends itself to the multiplication of vain subtleties, it is absolutely indispensable for scientific historiography. It is in fact part of the science of evidence. The distinction of primary and derivative authorities might be used as a test. The untrained historian fails to recognize that nothing is added to the value of a statement of Widukind by its repetition by Thietmar or Ekkehard, and that a record in the Continuation of Theophanes gains no further credibility from the fact that it likewise occurs in Cedrenus, Zonaras, or Glycas. On the other hand, it is irrelevant to condemn a statement of Zonaras as made by a "modern Greek". The question is, where did he get it? [2]

The difficult questions connected with the authorship and compilation of the Historia Augusta have produced a chestful of German pamphlets, but they did not trouble Gibbon. The relationships of the later Greek chronicles and histories are more difficult and intricate even than the questions raised by the Historia Augusta, but he did not even formulate a prudent interrogation. Ferdinand Hirsch, thirty years ago, cleared new roads through this forest, in which George the Monk and the Logothete who continued him, Leo Grammaticus and Simeon Magister, John Scylitzes, George Cedrenus, and Zonaras lived in promiscuous obscurity.

Criticism, too, has rejected some sources from which Gibbon drew without suspicion. In the interest of literature we may perhaps be glad that like Ockley he used with confidence the now discredited Al Wakidi. Before such maintained perfection of manner, to choose is hard; but the chapters on the origin of Mahometanism and its first triumphs against the Empire would alone be enough to win perpetual literary fame. Without Al Wakidi's romance they would not have been written.

In the study of sources, then, our advance has been great, while the labours of an historian have become more arduous. It leads us to another advance of the highest importance. To use historical documents with confidence, an assurance that the words of the writer have been correctly transmitted is manifestly indispensable. It generally happens that our texts have come down in several MSS., of different ages, and there are often various discrepancies. We have then to determine the relation of the MSS. to each other and their comparative values. To the pure philologist this is part of the alphabet of his profession; but the pure historian takes time to realise it, and it was not realised in the age of Gibbon as it is to-day. Nothing forces upon the historian the necessity of having a sound text so impressively as the process of comparing different documents in order to determine whether one was dependent on another,—the process of investigating sources. In this respect we have now to be thankful for many blessings denied to Gibbon and—so recent is our progress—denied to Milman and Finlay. We have Mommsen's editions of Jordanes and the *Variae* of Cassiodorus, his Chronica Minora, including, for instance, Idatius, Prosper, Count Marcellinus, Isidore; we have Peter's *Historia Augusta*, Gardthausen's Ammianus, Birt's Claudian, Leutjohann's Sidonius Apollinaris; Duchesne's *Liber Pontificalis*; and a large number of critical texts of ecclesiastical writers might be mentioned. The Greek historians are also being re-edited. The Bonn edition of the "Byzantine Writers," issued under the auspices of Niebuhr and Bekker in the early part of the nineteenth century, was the most lamentably feeble production ever given to the world by German scholars of great reputation. It marked no advance on the older folio edition, except that it was cheaper, and that one or two new documents were included. But there is now a reasonable prospect that we shall by degrees have a complete series of trustworthy texts. De Boor showed the way by his splendid edition of Theophanes and his smaller texts of Theophylactus Simocatta and the Patriarch Nicephorus, to which his indefatigable industry has since added an edition of George the Monk. Then we have Mendelssohn's Zosimus, Büttner-Wobst's edition of the latter part of Zonaras, Bidez and Parmentier's Evagrius, Reiffersheid's Anna Comnena, Heisenberg's George Acropolites, Förster's Libanius and Haury's Procopius (neither yet completed), to mention only some of the most important.

Besides improved methods of dealing with the old material, much new material of various kinds has been discovered, since the work of Gibbon. To take one department, our coins have increased in number. It seems a pity that he who worked at his Spanheim with such diligence was not able to make use of Eckhel's great work on Imperial coinage which began to appear in 1792 and was completed in 1798. Since then we have had Cohen, and the special works of Saulcy and Sabatier. M. Schlumberger's study of Byzantine sigillography may be mentioned in the same connexion.

The constitution and institutions of the Principate, and the provincial government of the early Emperors, have been placed on an entirely new basis by Mommsen and his school. The Römisches Staatsrecht is a fabric for whose rearing was needed not only improved scholarship but an extensive collection of epigraphic material. The Corpus of Latin Inscriptions is the keystone of the work.

Hence Gibbon's first chapters are somewhat "out of date". But on the other hand his admirable description of the change from the Principate to absolute Monarchy, and of the system of Diocletian and Constantine, is still most valuable. Here inscriptions are less illustrative, and he disposed of much the same material as we, especially the Codex Theodosianus. New light is wanted, and has not been to any extent forthcoming, on the respective contributions of Diocletian and Constantine to the organization of the new monarchy. As to the arrangement of the provinces we have indeed a precious document in the Verona List (published by Mommsen), which, dating from 297 A.D., shows Diocletian's reorganization. The modifications which were made between this year and the beginning of the fifth century when the *Notitia Dignitatum* was drawn up, can largely be determined not only by lists in Rufus and Ammianus, but, as far as the eastern provinces are concerned, by the *Laterculus* of Polemius Silvius. Thus, partly by critical method applied to Polemius, partly by the discovery of a new document, we are enabled to rectify the list of Gibbon, who adopted the simple plan of ascribing to Diocletian and Constantine the detailed organization of the Notitia. Otherwise our knowledge of the changes of Diocletian has not been greatly augmented; but our clearer conception of the Principate and its steady development towards pure monarchy has reflected light on Diocletian's system; and the tendencies of the third century, though still obscure at many points, have been made more distinct. The constitutional and administrative history of the Empire from Diocletian forward has still to be written systematically.

Gibbon's forty-fourth chapter is still not only famous, but admired by jurists as a brief and brilliant exposition of the principles of Roman law. To say that it is worthy of the subject is the best tribute that can be paid to it. A series of foreign scholars of acute legal ability has elaborated the study of the science in the present century. The manuscript of Gaius is the new discovery to be recorded; and we can imagine with what interest Gibbon, were he restored to earth, would compare in Gneist's parallel columns the Institutions with the elder treatise.

But whoever takes up Gibbon's theme now will not be content with an exposition of the Justinianean Law. He must go on to its later development in the subsequent centuries, in the company of Zachariä von Lingenthal and Heimbach. Such a study has been made possible and comparatively easy by the works of Zachariä; among whose achievements I may single out his restoration of the Ecloga, which used to be ascribed to Leo VI., to its true author Leo III.; a discovery which illuminated in a most welcome manner the Isaurian reformation.

Not a few entirely new texts, of considerable importance as historical sources, have been printed during the nineteenth century. Among these may be mentioned the treatise *De Magistratibus* of John Lydus, the History of Psellus, the Memoir of Cecaumenus, the history of the Ottoman conquest by Critobulus.[3] Fresh light has also been thrown on many periods by Syriac, Arabic, Armenian, and Ethiopic sources, drawn from the obscurity of their MSS., such as Zacharias of Mytilene, John of Ephesus, Sebaeos, John of Nikiu, Tabari. I may specially refer to the Book of the Conquest of the Morea, first published by Buchon, and recently edited critically by Schmitt. It is a mixture of fiction and fact, but invaluable for realising the fascinating though complicated history of the "Latin" settlements in Greece. That history was set aside by Gibbon, with the phrase, "I shall not pursue the obscure and various dynasties that rose and fell on the continent or in the isles," though he deigns to give a page or two to Athens. [4] But it is a subject with unusual possibilities for picturesque treatment, and out of which, Gibbon, if he had apprehended the opportunity, and had possessed the materials, would have made a brilliant chapter. Since Finlay, who entered into this episode of Greek history with great fulness, the material has been largely increased by the researches of Hopf.

Having illustrated by examples the advantages open to an historian of the present day, which were not open to Gibbon, for dealing with Gibbon's theme,—improved and refined methods, a closer union of philology with history, and ampler material—we may go on to consider a general defect in his treatment of the Later Empire, and here too exhibit, by a few instances, progress made in particular departments.

Gibbon ended the first half of his work with the so-called fall of the Western Empire in 476 A.D.—a date which has been fixed out of regard for Italy and Rome, and should strictly be 480 A.D. in consideration of Julius Nepos. Thus the same space is devoted to the first three hundred years which is allowed to the remaining nine hundred and eighty. Nor does the inequality end here. More than a quarter of the second half of the work deals with the first two of these ten centuries. The mere statement of the fact shows that the history of the Empire from Heraclius to the last Grand Comnenus of Trebizond is merely a sketch with certain episodes more fully treated. The personal history and domestic policy of all the Emperors, from the son of Heraclius to Isaac Angelus, are compressed into one chapter. This mode of dealing with the subject is in harmony with the author's contemptuous attitude to the "Byzantine" or "Lower" Empire.

But Gibbon's account of the internal history of the Empire after Heraclius is not only superficial; it gives an entirely false impression of the facts. If the materials had been then as well sifted and studied as they are even to-day, he could not have failed to see that beneath the intrigues and crimes of the Palace there were deeper causes at work, and beyond the revolutions of the Capital City wider issues implied. Nor had he any conception of the great ability of most of the Emperors from Leo the Isaurian to Basil II., or, we might say, to Constantine the conqueror of Armenia. The designation of the story of the later Empire as a "uniform tale of weakness and misery" [5] is one of the most untrue, and most effective, judgments ever uttered by a thoughful historian. Before the outrage of 1204, the Empire was the bulwark of the West.

Against Gibbon's point of view there has been a gradual reaction which may be said to have culminated during the last twenty years of the nineteenth century. It was begun by Finlay, whose unprosperous speculations in Greece after the Revolution prompted him to seek for the causes of the insecurity of investments in land, and, leading him back to the year 146 B.C., involved him in a history of the "Byzantine Empire" which embedded a history of Greece. [6] The great value of Finlay's work lies not only in its impartiality and in his trained discernment of the commercial and financial facts underlying the superficial history of the chronicles, but in its full and trustworthy narration of the events. By the time that Mr. Tozer's edition of Finlay appeared in 1876, it was being recognized that Gibbon's word on the later Empire was not the last. Meanwhile Hertzberg was going over the ground in

Germany, and Gfrörer, whose ecclesiastical studies had taken him into those regions, had written a good deal of various value. Hirsch's *Byzantinische Studien* had just appeared, and Rambaud's admirable monograph *l'Empire grec au xme siècle*. M. Sathas was bringing out his Bibliotheca Græca medii aevi—including two volumes of Psellus—and was beginning his Documents inédits. Professor Lambros was working at his Athens in the Twelfth Century and preparing his editio princeps of the great Archbishop Akominatos. Hopf had collected a mass of new materials from the archives of southern cities. In England, Freeman was pointing out the true position of New Rome and her Emperors in the history of Europe.

These tendencies have since increased in volume and velocity. It may be said that the subject entered on a new stage through the publication of Professor Krumbacher's *History of Byzantine Literature*. [7] The importance of this work, of vast scope and extraordinary accuracy, can only be fully understood by the specialist. It has already promoted and facilitated the progress of the study in an incalculable measure; and it was soon followed by the inauguration of a journal, entirely devoted to works on "Byzantine" subjects, by the same scholar. The *Byzantinische Zeitschrift* would have been impossible thirty-five years ago and nothing showed more surely the turn of the tide. Professor Krumbacher's work seems likely to form as important an epoch as that of Ducange. It may be added that designs have been framed for a Corpus of Greek Inscriptions of the Christian period, and for a collection of Greek Acts and Charters of the Middle Ages. [8]

Meanwhile in a part of Europe which deems itself to have received the torch from the Emperors as it has received their torch from the Patriarchs, and which has always had a special regard for the city of Constantine, some excellent work was being done. In Russia, Muralt edited the chronicle of George the Monk and his Continuers, and compiled Byzantine Fasti. The Journal of the Ministry of Public Instruction is the storehouse of a long series of most valuable articles dealing, from various sides, with the history of the later Empire, by those indefatigable workers Vasilievski and Uspenski. In 1894, Krumbacher's lead was followed, and the *Vizantiiski Vremennik*, a Russian counterpart of the *Byzantinische Zeitschrift*, was started under the joint editorship of Vasilievski and Regel. Much good work has also been done by the Russian Archæological Institute of Constantinople.

The study of works of architecture in ancient cities, like Athens, Rome, or Constantinople, naturally entails a study of the topography of the town; and in the case of Constantinople this study is equally important for the historian. Little progress of a satisfactory kind can be made until either Constantinople passes under a European government, or a complete change comes over the spirit of Turkish administration. The region of the Imperial Palace and the ground between the Hippodrome and St. Sophia must be excavated before certainty on the main points can be attained. Labarte's *a priori* reconstruction of the plan of the palace, on the basis of the Ceremonies of Constantine Porphyrogennetos and scattered notices in other Greek writers, was wonderfully ingenious and a certain part of it is manifestly right, though there is much which is not borne out by a more careful examination of the sources. The next step was taken by a Russian scholar Bieliaev who has recently published a most valuable study on the Ceremonies, [9] in which he has tested the reconstruction of Labarte and shown us exactly where we are,—what we know, and what with our present materials we cannot possibly know. Between Labarte and Bieliaev the whole problem was obscured by the diligent unscholarly work of Paspatês, an enthusiastic Greek antiquarian; whose chief merit was that he kept the subject before the world. The general topography of the city has been illuminated by Mordtmann's valuable *Esquisse topographique* (1902), and the special topography of the walls, gates, and adjacent quarters by the admirable work of Professor van Millingen.

On the Slavonic side of the history of the Empire Gibbon is most conspicuously inadequate. Since he wrote, various causes have combined to increase our knowledge of Slavonic antiquity. The Slavs themselves have engaged in methodical investigation of their own past; and, since the entire or partial emancipations of the southern Slavs from Asiatic rule, a general interest in Slavonic civilisation has grown up throughout Europe. Gibbon dismissed the history of the First Bulgarian Kingdom, from its foundation in the reign of Constantine Pogonatus to its overthrow by the second Basil, in two pages. To-day the author of a history of the Empire on the same scale would find two hundred a strict limit. Gibbon tells us nothing of the Slavonic missionaries, Cyril and Methodius, round whose names an extensive literature has been formed. It is only in comparatively recent years that the geography of the Illyrian peninsula has become an accessible subject of study.

The investigation of the history of the northern peoples who came under the influence of the Empire has been stimulated by controversy, and controversy has been animated and even embittered by national pride. The question of Slavonic settlements in Greece has been thoroughly ventilated, because Fallmerayer excited the scholarship of Hellenes and Philhellenes to refute what they regarded as an insulting paradox.[10] So, too, the pride of the Roumanians was irritated by Roesler, who denied that they were descended from the inhabitants of Trajan's Dacia and described them as later immigrants of the thirteenth century. Hungary too has its own question. Are the Magyars to be ethnically associated with the Finns or given over to the family of the Turks, whom as champions of Christendom they had opposed at Mohácz and Varna? It was a matter of pride for the Hungarian to detach himself from the Turk; and the evidence is certainly on his side. Hunfalvy's conclusions have successfully defied the assaults of Vámbéry.[11] Again in Russia there has been a long and vigorous contest, the so-called Norman or Varangian question. No doubt is felt now by the impartial judge as to the Scandinavian origin of the princes of Kiev, and that the making of Russia was due to Northmen or Varangians. Kunik and Pogodin were reinforced by Thomsen of Denmark; and the pure Slavism of Ilovaiski[12] and Gedeonov, though its champions were certainly able, is a lost cause.

From such collisions sparks have flown and illuminated dark corners. For the Slavs the road was first cleared by Šafarik. The development of the comparative philology of the Indo-Germanic tongues has had its effect; the Slavonic languages have been brought into line, chiefly by the lifework of Miklosich; and a special journal for Slavonic studies, edited by Jagič, has existed for many years. The several countries of the Balkan lands have their archæologists and archæological journals; and the difficulty which now meets the historian is not the absence but the plenitude of philological and historical literature.

The foregoing instances will serve to give a general idea of the respects in which Gibbon's history might be described as behind date. To follow out all the highways and byways of progress would mean the usurpation of at least a volume by the editor. What more has to be said, must be said briefly in notes and appendices. That Gibbon is behind date in many details, and in some departments of importance, simply signifies that we and our fathers have not lived in an absolutely incompetent world. But in the main things he is still our master, above and beyond "date". It is needless to dwell on the obvious qualities which secure to him immunity from the common lot of historical writers,—such as the bold and certain measure of his progress through the ages; his accurate vision, and his tact in managing perspective; his discreet reserves of judgment and timely scepticism; the immortal affectation of his unique manner. By virtue of these superiorities he can defy the danger with which the activity of successors must always threaten the worthies of the past. But there is another point which was touched on in an earlier page and to which here, in a different connexion, we may briefly revert. It is well to realise that the greatest history of modern times was written by one in whom a distrust of enthusiasm was deeply rooted.[13] This cynicism was not inconsistent with partiality, with definite prepossessions, with a certain spite. In fact it supplied the antipathy which the artist infused when he mixed his most effective colours. The conviction that enthusiasm is inconsistent with intellectual balance was engrained in his mental constitution, and confirmed by study and experience. It might be reasonably maintained that zeal for men or causes is an historian's marring, and that "reserve sympathy" is the first lesson he has to learn. But without venturing on any generalisation we must consider Gibbon's zealous distrust of zeal as an essential and most suggestive characteristic of the *Decline and Fall.*

Notes

1. In the *Chronica Minora* (M. G. H.), vol. i. 512 sqq.
2. Gibbon had a notion of this, but did not apply it methodically. See in this vol., p. 448, note 60: "but those modern Greeks had the opportunity of consulting many writers which have since been lost". And see, in general, his Preface to the fourth volume of the quarto ed.
3. Some of the new texts which have been published are important for the help they give in determining the relations of our sources, though they supply no new information; e.g., the chronicle of Theodosius of Melitene published by Tafel.
4. The history of mediæval Athens has been recorded at length in an attractive work by Gregorovius, the counterpart of his great history of mediæval Rome.
5. Chap. xlviii. ad init., where a full statement of his view of the later Empire will be found.
6. Since then a Greek scholar, K. Paparrigopulos, has covered the whole history of Greece from the earliest times to the present century, in his Ἱστορία τοῦ Ἑλληνικοῦ ἔθνους.
7. *Geschichte der byzantinischen Litteratur* (565–1453), 1891; second greatly enlarged edition (with co-operation of Ehrhard and Gelzer), 1897.
8. At present we have the valuable but inadequate *Acta et Diplomata* of Miklosich and Müller.
9. *Byzantina, Ocherki, materialy, i zamietki po Vizantiiskim drevnostiam,* 1891–3.
10. Fallmerayer's thesis that there is *no* pure Hellenic blood in Greece was triumphantly refuted. But his antagonists, on their side, have gone much too far. It cannot be denied that there was a large Slavonic element in the country parts, especially of the Peloponnesus.
11. In a paper entitled, "The Coming of the Hungarians," in the *Scottish Review* of July, 1892, I have discussed the questions connected with early Magyar history, and criticized Hunfalvy's *Magyarország Ethnographiája* (1876) and Vámbéry's *A magyarok eredete* (1882). One of the best works dealing with the subject has been written by a Slav (C. Grot).
12. Ilovaiski's work *Istoriia Rossii,* vol. i, (Kiev period), is, though his main thesis as to the origins is a mistake, most instructive.
13. And who regarded history as "little more than the register of the crimes, follies and misfortunes of mankind."

Robert Burns

ROBERT BURNS

1759–1796

Robert Burns was born at Alloway, Scotland, on January 25, 1759. The son of a farmer, he was educated at John Murdoch's school in Alloway Miln and at Hugh Roger's school in Kirkoswald. Much of the young Burns's spare time was spent working on his father's land, and after his father's death in 1784 he and his brother continued to farm at Mossgiel, in the parish of Mauchline. During this period Burns composed several of his most famous poems, including "The Cotter's Saturday Night," "To a Mouse," "To a Mountain Daisy," "Holy Willie's Prayer," and "The Holy Fair." In 1786 Burns began a romance with Jean Armour, who gave birth to twins later that year.

In 1786 Burns sent a collection of his verses to a publisher in Kilmarnock, and they appeared later that year as *Poems, Chiefly in the Scottish Dialect*. The volume was an immediate success, and in 1787 a second edition, with twenty two additional poems, was published at Edinburgh. Burns then traveled in the Highlands and Stirlingshire. On his return he was approached by James Johnson, who asked Burns to help him collect material for his series *The Scots Musical Museum* (1787–1803). Burns eagerly consented, and between 1787 and 1792 collected, edited, and wrote some two hundred poems, all set to music, including some of his best-known lyrics, such as "Auld Lang Syne," "O My Luve's like a red, red rose," "Ye Banks and Braes," and "Scots wha hae."

Late in 1787 Burns became romantically involved with Agnes Maclehose, a married woman, and began a correspondence in which he addressed her as "Clarinda" and signed himself "Sylvander." In the following year he returned to Mauchline, where he married Jean Armour. He purchased a farm in Ellisland in the summer of 1788, and in 1789 became an excise officer. In 1791 Burns published his last major poem, "Tam O'Shanter," in Grose's *Antiquities of Scotland*. Later that year he gave up his farm at Ellisland and moved to Dumfries, where in 1792 he was promoted in his job as exciseman to the Dumfries Port Division. Toward the end of his life he started compiling material for George Thomson's *Select Scottish Airs*, the first volume of which was published in 1793. Burns continued to contribute songs for the next volume, but in 1795 he contracted rheumatic fever and died on July 21, 1796. The standard edition of Burns's *Poems and Songs* was edited by J. Kinsley and published in three volumes in 1968.

Personal

I have written you so often without rec.g any answer, that I would not trouble you again but for the circumstances in which I am.—An illness which has long hung about me in all probability will speedily send me beyond that bourne whence no traveller returns.—Your friendship with which for many years you honored me was a friendship dearest to my soul.— Your conversation & especially your correspondence were at once highly entertaining & instructive.—With what pleasure did I use to break up the seal! The remembrance yet adds one pulse more to my poor palpitating heart! Farewell!!!—ROBERT BURNS, Letter to Frances Dunlop (July 10, 1796)

After all my boasted independance, curst necessity compels me to implore you for five pounds.—A cruel scoundrel of a Haberdasher to whom I owe an account, taking it into his head that I am dying, has commenced a process, & will infallibly put me into jail.—Do, for God's sake, send me that sum, & that by return of post.—Forgive me this earnestness, but the horrors of a jail have made me half distracted.—I do not ask all this gratuitously; for upon returning health, I hereby promise & engage to furnish you with five pounds' worth of the neatest song-genius you have seen.—I tryed my hand on Rothiemurche this morning.—The measure is so difficult, that it is impossible to infuse much genius into the lines—they are on the other side. Forgive me!—ROBERT BURNS, Letter to George Thomson (July 12, 1796)

It will actually be an injustice done to Burns's character, not only by future generations and foreign countries, but even by his native Scotland, and perhaps a number of his cotempo-raries, that he is generally talked of, and considered, with reference to his poetical talents *only*: for the fact is, even allowing his great and original genius its due tribute of admiration, that poetry (I appeal to all who have had the advantage of being personally acquainted with him) was actually not his *forte*. Many others, perhaps, may have ascended to prouder heights in the region of Parnassus, but none certainly ever outshone Burns in the charms—the sorcery, I would almost call it, of fascinating conversation, the spontaneous eloquence of social argument, or the unstudied poignancy of brilliant repartee; nor was any man, I believe, ever gifted with a larger portion of the "*vivida vis animi.*" His personal endowments were perfectly correspondent to the qualifications of his mind: his form was manly; his action, energy itself; devoid in great measure perhaps of those graces, of that polish, acquired only in the refinement of societies where in early life he could have no opportunities of mixing; but where, such was the irresistible power of attraction that encircled him, though his appearance and manners were always peculiar, he never failed to delight, and to excel. His figure seemed to bear testimony to his earlier destination and employments. It seemed rather moulded by nature for the rough exercises of Agriculture, than the gentler cultivation of the Belles Lettres. His features were stamped with the hardy character of independence, and the firmness of conscious, though not arrogant, pre-eminence; the animated expressions of countenance were almost peculiar to himself; the rapid lightnings of his eye were always the harbingers of some flash of genius, whether they darted the fiery glances of insulted and indignant superiority, or beamed with the impassioned sentiment of fervent and impetuous affections. His voice alone could improve upon the magic of his eye: sonorous, replete with the finest modulations, it alternately captivated the ear with the melody of poetic numbers, the perspicuity of nervous reasoning, or the ardent sallies of enthusiastic patriotism. The keenness of satire was, I am almost at a loss whether to say, his forte or his foible; for though nature had endowed him with a portion of the most pointed excellence in that dangerous talent, he suffered it too often to be the vehicle of personal, and sometimes unfounded, animosities. It was not always that sportiveness of humour, that "unwary pleasantry," which *Sterne* has depictured with touches so conciliatory, but the darts of ridicule were frequently directed as the caprice of the instant suggested, or as the altercations of parties and of persons happened to kindle the restlessness of his spirit into interest or aversion. This, however, was not invariably the case; his wit (which is no unusual matter indeed,) had always the start of his judgment, and would lead him to the indulgence of raillery uniformly acute, but often unaccompanied with the least desire to wound. The suppression of an arch and full-pointed bon-mot, from a dread of offending its object, the sage of Zurich very properly classes as a virtue *only to be sought for in the Calendar of Saints*; if so, Burns must not be too severely dealt with for being rather deficient in it. He paid for this mischievous wit as dearly as any one could do. " 'Twas no extravagant arithmetic," to say of him, as was said of Yorick, "that for every ten jokes he got an hundred enemies;" but much allowance will be made by a candid mind for the splenetic warmth of a spirit whom "distress had spited with the world," and which, unbounded in its intellectual sallies and pursuits, continually experienced the curbs imposed by the waywardness of his fortune. The vivacity of his wishes and temper was indeed checked by almost habitual disappointments, which sat heavy on a heart that acknowledged the ruling passion of independence, without having ever been placed beyond the grasp of penury. His soul was never languid or inactive, and his genius was extinguished only with the last sparks of retreating life. His passions rendered him, according as they disclosed themselves in affection or antipathy, an object of enthusiastic attachment, or of decided enmity; for *he* possessed none of that negative insipidity of character, whose love might be regarded with indifference, or whose resentment could be considered with contempt. In this, it should seem, the temper of his associates took the tincture from his own; for *he* acknowledged in the universe but two classes of objects, those of adoration the most fervent, or of aversion the most uncontroulable; and it has been frequently a reproach to him, that, unsusceptible of indifference, often hating, where he ought only to have despised, he alternately opened his heart and poured forth the treasures of his understanding to such as were incapable of appreciating the homage; and elevated to the privileges of an adversary, some who were unqualified in all respects for the honour of a contest so distinguished.—MARIA RIDDELL, Letter to *Dumfries Journal* (Aug. 7, 1796), cited in James Currie, *The Life of Robert Burns*, 1800

His manners were then, as they continued ever afterwards, simple, manly, and independent; strongly expressive of conscious genius and worth; but without any thing that indicated forwardness, arrogance, or vanity. He took his share in conversation, but not more than belonged to him; and listened with apparent attention and deference, on subjects where his want of education deprived him of the means of information. If there had been a little more of gentleness and accommodation in his temper, he would, I think, have been still more interesting; but he had been accustomed to give law in the

circle of his ordinary acquaintance; and his dread of any thing approaching to meanness or servility, rendered his manner somewhat decided and hard. Nothing, perhaps, was more remarkable among his various attainments, than the fluency, and precision, and originality of language, when he spoke in company; more particularly as he aimed at purity in his turn of expression, and avoided more successfully than most Scotchmen, the peculiarities of Scottish phraseology. ⟨. . .⟩

The attentions he received during his stay in town from all ranks and descriptions of persons, were such as would have turned any head but his own. I cannot say that I could perceive any unfavourable effect which they left on his mind. He retained the same simplicity of manners and appearance which had struck me so forcibly when I first saw him in the country; nor did he seem to feel any additional self-importance from the number and rank of his new acquaintance. His dress was perfectly suited to his station, plain and unpretending, with a sufficient attention to neatness. If I recollect right he always wore boots; and, when on more than usual ceremony, buckskin breeches.

Among the subjects on which he was accustomed to dwell, the characters of the individuals with whom he happened to meet, was plainly a favourite one. The remarks he made on them were always shrewd and pointed, though frequently inclining too much to sarcasm. His praise of those he loved was sometimes indiscriminate and extravagant; but this, I suspect, proceeded rather from the caprice and humour of the moment, than from the effects of attachment in blinding his judgment. His wit was ready, and always impressed with the marks of a vigorous understanding; but, to my taste, not often pleasing or happy. His attempts at epigram, in his printed works, are the only performances, perhaps, that he has produced, totally unworthy of his genius.—DUGALD STEWART, Letter to James Currie (c. 1800), cited James Currie, *The Life of Robert Burns*, 1800

Went to the churchyard where Burns is buried, a bookseller accompanied us. He showed us the outside of Burns's house, where he had lived the last three years of his life, and where he died. It has a mean appearance, and is in a bye situation, whitewashed—dirty about the doors, as almost all Scotch houses are—flowering plants in the windows.

⟨. . .⟩ We spoke to the servant-maid at the door, who invited us forward, and we sate down in the parlour. The walls were coloured with a blue wash; on one side of the fire was a mahogany desk, opposite to the window a clock, and over the desk a print from the "Cotter's Saturday Night," which Burns mentions in one of his letters having received as a present. The house was cleanly and neat in the inside, the stairs of stone, scoured white, the kitchen on the right side of the passage, the parlour on the left. In the room above the parlour the poet died, and his son after him in the same room.—DOROTHY WORDSWORTH, *Journal*, Aug. 18, 1803

I shiver, Spirit fierce and bold,
At thought of what I now behold:
As vapours breathed from dungeons cold
　　Strike pleasure dead,
So sadness comes from out the mould
　　Where Burns is laid.

And have I then thy bones so near,
And thou forbidden to appear?
As if it were thyself that's here
　　I shrink with pain;
And both my wishes and my fear
　　Alike are vain.

Off weight—nor press on weight!—away
Dark thoughts!—they came, but not to stay;
With chastened feelings would I pay
    The tribute due
To him, and aught that hides his clay
    From mortal view.

Fresh as the flower, whose modest worth
He sang, his genius 'glinted' forth,
Rose like a star that touching earth,
    For so it seems,
Doth glorify its humble birth
    With matchless beams.

The piercing eye, the thoughtful brow,
The struggling heart, where be they now?—
Full soon the Aspirant of the plough,
    The prompt, the brave,
Slept, with the obscurest, in the low
    And silent grave.

I mourned with thousands, but as one
More deeply grieved, for He was gone
Whose light I hailed when first it shone,
    And showed my youth
How Verse may build a princely throne
    On humble truth.

Alas! where'er the current tends,
Regret pursues and with it blends,—
Huge Criffel's hoary top ascends
    By Skiddaw seen,—
Neighbours we were, and loving friends
    We might have been;

True friends though diversely inclined;
But heart with heart and mind with mind,
Where the main fibres are entwined,
    Through Nature's skill,
May even by contraries be joined
    More closely still.

The tear will start, and let it flow;
Thou 'poor Inhabitant below,'
At this dread moment—even so—
    Might we together
Have sate and talked where gowans blow,
    Or on wild heather.

What treasures would have then been placed
Within my reach; of knowledge graced
By fancy what a rich repast!
    But why go on?—
Oh! spare to sweep, thou mournful blast,
    His grave grass-grown.

There, too, a Son, his joy and pride,
(Not three weeks past the Stripling died,)
Lies gathered to his Father's side,
    Soul-moving sight!
Yet one to which is not denied
    Some sad delight.

For *he* is safe, a quiet bed
Hath early found among the dead,
Harboured where none can be misled,
    Wronged, or distrest;
And surely here it may be said
    That such are blest.

And oh for Thee, by pitying grace
Checked oft-times in a devious race,
May He, who halloweth the place
    Where Man is laid,
Receive thy Spirit in the embrace
    For which it prayed!

Sighing I turned away; but ere
Night fell I heard, or seemed to hear,
Music that sorrow comes not near,
    A ritual hymn,
Chanted in love that casts out fear
    By Seraphim.
      —WILLIAM WORDSWORTH, "At the Grave of
      Burns," 1803

The town, the churchyard, and the setting sun,
  The clouds, the trees, the rounded hills all seem,
  Though beautiful, cold—strange—as in a dream
I dreamèd long ago. Now new begun
The short-lived, paly summer is but won
  From winter's ague, for one hour's gleam;
  Through sapphire-warm, their stars do never
    beam—
All is cold Beauty; pain is never done
For who has mind to relish, Minos wise,
  The real of Beauty, free from that dead hue
    Fickly imagination and sick pride
Cast wan upon it! Burns! with honour due
  I have oft honoured thee. Great shadow, hide
Thy face! I sin against thy native skies.
      —JOHN KEATS, "On Visiting the Tomb of Burns,"
      1818

As for Burns, I may truly say, *Virgilium vidi tantum*. I was a lad of fifteen in 1786–7, when he came first to Edinburgh, but had sense and feeling enough to be much interested in his poetry, and would have given the world to know him; but I had very little acquaintance with any literary people, and still less with the gentry of the west country, the two sets that he most frequented. Mr. Thomas Grierson was at that time a clerk of my father's. He knew Burns, and promised to ask him to his lodgings to dinner, but had no opportunity to keep his word, otherwise I might have seen more of this distinguished man. As it was, I saw him one day at the late venerable Professor Fergusson's, where there were several gentlemen of literary reputation, among whom I remember the celebrated Mr. Dugald Stewart. Of course we youngsters sate silent, looked and listened. The only thing I remember which was remarkable in Burns' manner, was the effect produced upon him by a print of Bunbury's, representing a soldier lying dead on the snow, his dog sitting in misery on the one side, on the other his widow, with a child in her arms. These lines were written beneath,—

  Cold on Canadian hills, or Minden's plain,
  Perhaps that parent wept her soldier slain;
  Bent o'er her babe, her eye dissolved in dew,
  The big drops, mingling with the milk he drew,
  Gave the sad presage of his future years,
  The child of misery baptized in tears.

Burns seemed much affected by the print, or rather the ideas which it suggested to his mind. He actually shed tears. He asked whose the lines were, and it chanced that nobody but myself remembered that they occur in a half-forgotten poem of Langhorne's, called by the unpromising title of "The Justice of the Peace." I whispered my information to a friend present, who mentioned it to Burns, who rewarded me with a look and a word, which, though of mere civility, I then received, and still recollect, with very great pleasure.

His person was strong and robust: his manners rustic, not clownish; a sort of dignified plainness and simplicity, which received part of its effect perhaps from one's knowledge of his extraordinary talents. His features are represented in Mr. Nasmyth's picture, but to me it conveys the idea that they are diminished as if seen in perspective. I think his countenance was more massive than it looks in any of the portraits. I would have taken the poet, had I not known what he was, for a very sagacious country farmer of the old Scotch school—*i.e.* none of your modern agriculturists, who keep labourers for their drudgery, but the *douce gudeman* who held his own plough. There was a strong expression of sense and shrewdness in all his lineaments; the eye alone, I think, indicated the poetical character and temperament. It was large, and of a dark cast, and glowed (I say literally *glowed*) when he spoke with feeling or interest. I never saw such another eye in a human head, though I have seen the most distinguished men in my time. His conversation expressed perfect self-confidence, without the slightest presumption. Among the men who were the most learned of their time and country, he expressed himself with perfect firmness, but without the least intrusive forwardness; and when he differed in opinion, he did not hesitate to express it firmly, yet at the same time with modesty. I do not remember any part of his conversation distinctly enough to be quoted, nor did I ever see him again, except in the street, where he did not recognise me, as I could not expect he should. He was much caressed in Edinburgh, but (considering what literary emoluments have been since his day) the efforts made for his relief were extremely trifling.

I remember on this occasion I mention, I thought Burns' acquaintance with English poetry was rather limited, and also, that having twenty times the abilities of Allan Ramsay and of Ferguson, he talked of them with too much humility as his models; there was doubtless national predilection in his estimate.—SIR WALTER SCOTT, Letter to John Gibson Lockhart (1827), cited in John Gibson Lockhart, *Memoirs of the Life of Sir Walter Scott*, 1837–38,

I, in this year, 1801, when in the company of Dr. Currie, did not forget, and, with some pride I say that I stood alone in remembering, the very remarkable position of Burns: not merely that, with his genius, and with the intellectual pretensions generally of his family, he should have been called to a life of early labour, and of labour unhappily not prosperous, but also that he, by accident about the proudest of human spirits, should have been by accident summoned, beyond all others, to eternal recognitions of some mysterious gratitude which he owed to some mysterious patrons little and great, whilst yet, of all men, perhaps, he reaped the least obvious or known benefit from any patronage that has ever been put on record.—THOMAS DE QUINCEY, "A Liverpool Literary Coterie" (1837), *Collected Writings*, ed. David Masson, Vol. 2, p. 134

If these remarks seem to cast no new light on Burns' character and history, it is partly because on such an inconsistent and anomalous character little satisfactory light *can* be cast; its contradictions were never reconciled, its controversies raged on till the very hour of death, and despair over the unresolved and unresolvable problem of his history, will always mingle with, and shade, the delight with which we peruse the miracles of his genius. Much of this inconsistency may, indeed, be traced to his irregular education, and to his poverty-stricken circumstances, as well as to his want of sound, solid Christian principle. But whatever the cause, the effect is certain. He had no leading principle or guiding star:—not conscience, for that was often asleep; not benevolence, for his humane feelings, though sincere, were fluctuating and uncertain; not religion, for although not an infidel, neither was he a firm believer; not a high ideal of art, for to this he had never risen; not even his boasted independence, for no man, at times, descended,

although it was with reluctance, to more servile flatteries. Impulse was his idol, and this acting on a nature in which the passions were greater than even the powers, made wild work, strengthened what in him was low and animal, weakened what in him was high and noble—infuriated his passions and degraded his genius. Indeed, why have critics and moralists wasted so much time in discussing the moral character of Burns? *He* saw it, at an early period, with his own inevitable eye, and in his "Bard's Epitaph," has, in living colours, at once painted his character, and predicted his fate. In it we see the prophet as well as the poet.—GEORGE GILFILLAN, "Life of Robert Burns," *The Poetical Works of Robert Burns*, 1856, Vol. 1, pp. 29–30

The whole house was pervaded with a frowzy smell, and also a dunghill-odor; and it is not easy to understand how the atmosphere of such a dwelling can be any more agreeable or salubrious morally than it appeared to be physically. No virgin, surely, could keep a holy awe about her while stowed higgledy-piggledy with coarse-natured rustics into this narrowness and filth. Such a habitation is calculated to make beasts of men and women; and it indicates a degree of barbarism which I did not imagine to exist in Scotland, that a tiller of broad fields, like the farmer of Mauchline, should have his abode in a pig-sty. It is sad to think of anybody—not to say a poet, but any human being—sleeping, eating, thinking, praying, and spending all his home-life in this miserable hovel; but, methinks, I never in the least knew how to estimate the miracle of Burns's genius, nor his heroic merit for being no worse man, until I thus learned the squalid hindrances amid which he developed himself. Space, a free atmosphere, and cleanliness have a vast deal to do with the possibilities of human virtue.—NATHANIEL HAWTHORNE, "Some of the Haunts of Burns" (1860), *Old Our Home*, 1863

Another happy man, after all, seems to be Allingham, for all his want of 'success'. Nothing but the most absolute calm and enjoyment of outside nature could account for so much gadding hither and thither on the soles of his two feet. Fancy carrying about grasses for hours and days from the field where Burns ploughed up a daisy. Good God! if I found the daisy itself there, I would sooner swallow it than be troubled to carry it twenty yards.—DANTE GABRIEL ROSSETTI, Letter to William Bell Scott (Aug. 25, 1871)

Poor Burns! One of the most pathetic features in his pathetic life is this constant struggle between pride and the dislike of poverty. We say *the dislike of poverty*, not *poverty* simply, for poverty is a far less terrible thing to some men than to others. Burns' tastes were simple. He would not have known what to do with a large fortune. But he chafed at the lack of consequence which accompanies the lack of this world's goods. Nor had he the typical Scotchman's delight in making sixpence do the work of half-a-crown. The details of economy harassed him; the dread of debt was a nightmare to him; anxiety for his children's future destroyed all present happiness. Some men can deal with sordid cares without loss of mental dignity and calm. Burns could not. He was bitterly conscious that his nature was dragged down by them—that his soul, in the words of Carlyle, wasted itself away in a hopeless struggle with base entanglements. There was in his nature a strain of weakness, a lack of moral fibre, which not infrequently accompanies poetic sensibility, and which may co-exist with strong mental powers and great intellectual vitality. He speaks much of "stubborn independence," much, too, of what has well been called "the barren and unfruitful principle of pride." But, in fact, when evil days came he was glad to avail himself of the help of his fellow-creatures, while his pride chiefly served to make that help a new source of irritation. A robuster character would have refrained from speaking much of his pecuniary difficulties to a woman of well-known wealth and generosity. But Burns' complaints to Mrs. Dunlop of the persistent presence of his "old attendant, poverty," are so frequent and so bitter as to lay him open to the imputation of covert begging.—L. M. ROBERTS, "The Burns and Dunlop Correspondence," *Fortnightly Review*, Nov. 1895, p. 669

General

I know not if I shall be accused of such enthusiasm and partiality, when I introduce to the notice of my readers a poet of our own country, with whose writings I have lately become acquainted; but if I am not greatly deceived, I think I may safely pronounce him a genius of no ordinary rank. The person to whom I allude is ROBERT BURNS, an *Ayrshire* ploughman, whose poems were some time ago published in a country-town in the west of Scotland, with no other ambition, it would seem, than to circulate among the inhabitants of the county where he was born, to obtain a little fame from those who had heard of his talents. I hope I shall not be thought to assume too much, if I endeavour to place him in a higher point of view, to call for a verdict of his country on the merit of his works, and to claim for him those honours which their excellence appears to deserve.

In mentioning the circumstance of his humble station, I mean not to rest his pretensions solely on that title, or to urge the merits of his poetry when considered in relation to the lowness of his birth, and the little opportunity of improvement which his education could afford. These particulars, indeed, might excite our wonder at his productions; but his poetry, considered abstractedly, and without the apologies arising from his situation, seems to me fully intitled to command our feelings, and to obtain our applause. One bar, indeed, his birth and education have opposed to his fame, the language in which most of his poems are written. Even in Scotland, the provincial dialect which Ramsay and he have used is now read with a difficulty which greatly damps the pleasure of the reader: in England it cannot be read at all, without such a constant reference to a glossary, as nearly to destroy that pleasure. ⟨. . .⟩

The power of genius is not less admirable in tracing the manners, than in painting the passions, or in drawing the scenery of Nature. That intuitive glance with which a writer like *Shakespeare* discerns the characters of men, with which he catches the many-changing hues of life, forms a sort of problem in the science of mind, of which it is easier to see the truth than to assign the cause. Though I am very far from meaning to compare our rustic bard to Shakespeare, yet whoever will read his lighter and more humorous poems, his "Dialogue of the Dogs," his "Dedication to G——, H——. Esq."; his "Epistles to a young Friend," and "to W. S——n," will perceive with what uncommon penetration and sagacity this Heaven-taught ploughman, from his humble and unlettered station, has looked upon men and manners.

Against some passages of those last-mentioned poems it has been objected, that they breathe a spirit of libertinism and irreligion. But if we consider the ignorance and fanaticism of the lower class of people in the country where these poems were written, a fanaticism of that pernicious sort which sets *faith* in opposition to *good works*, the falacy and danger of which, a mind so enlightened as our Poet's could not but perceive; we shall not look upon his lighter Muse as the enemy of religion, (of which

in several places he expresses the justest sentiments), tho' she has sometimes been a little unguarded in her ridicule of hypocrisy.

In this, as in other respects, it must be allowed that there are exceptionable parts of the volume he has given to the public, which caution would have suppressed, or correction struck out; but Poet's are seldom cautious, and our Poet had, alas! no friends or companions from whom correction could be obtained. When we reflect on his rank in life, the habits to which he must have been subject, and the society in which he must have mixed, we regret perhaps more than wonder, that delicacy should be so often offended in perusing a volume in which there is so much to interest and to please us.

Burns possesses the spirit as well as the fancy of a poet. That honest pride and independence of soul which are sometimes the Muse's only dower, break forth on every occasion in his works. It may be, then, I shall wrong his feelings, while I indulge my own, in calling the attention of the public to his situation and circumstances. That condition, humble as it was, in which he found content, and wooed the Muse, might not have been deemed uncomfortable; but grief and misfortunes have reached him there; and one or two of his poems hint, what I have learnt from some of his countrymen, that he has been obliged to form the resolution of leaving his native land, to seek under a West-Indian clime that shelter and support which Scotland has denied him. But I trust means may be found to prevent this resolution from taking place; and that I do my country no more than justice, when I suppose her ready to stretch out her hand to cherish and retain this native poet, whose "wood notes wild" possess so much excellence, To repair the wrongs of suffering or neglected merit; to call forth genius from the obscurity in which it had pined indignant, and place it where it may profit or delight the world; these are exertions which give to wealth an enviable superiority, to greatness and to patronage a laudable pride.—HENRY MACKENZIE, *The Lounger*, No. 97 (Dec. 9, 1786)

I have therefore read Burns's Poems, and have read them twice. And though they be written in a language that is new to me, and many of them on subjects much inferior to the author's ability, I think them on the whole a very extraordinary production. He is, I believe, the only Poet these kingdoms have produced in the lower rank of life, since Shakespeare, I should rather say since Prior, who need not be indebted for any part of his praise, to a charitable consideration of his origin, and the disadvantages under which he has laboured. It will be pity if he should not hereafter divest himself of barbarism, and content himself with writing pure English, in which he appears perfectly qualified to excel. He who can command admiration, dishonours himself if he aims no higher than to raise a laugh.—WILLIAM COWPER, Letter to Samuel Rose (July 24, 1787)

Poor Burns loses much of his deserved praise in this country, through our ignorance of his language. I despair of meeting with any Englishman who will take the pains that I have taken to understand him. His candle is bright but shut up in a dark lantern. I lent him to a very sensible neighbour of mine, but his uncouth dialect spoiled all and before he had half read him through, he was quite *ramfeezled*.—WILLIAM COWPER, Letter to Samuel Rose (Aug. 27, 1787)

Robert Burns, a natural poet of the first eminence, does not, perhaps, appear to his usual advantage in song: *non omnia possumus*. The political "fragment," as he calls it, inserted in the second volume of the present collection, has, however, much merit in some of the satirical stanzas, and could it have been concluded with the spirit with which it is commenced, would indisputably have been intitled to great praise; but the character of his favourite minister seems to have operated like the touch of a torpedo; and after vainly attempting something like a panegyric, he seems under the necessity of relinquishing the task. Possibly the bard will one day see occasion to complete his performance as a uniform satire.—JOSEPH RITSON, "A Historical Essay on Scotish Song," *Scotish Song*, 1794, Vol. 1, pp. 74–75

To determine the comparative merit of Burns would be no easy task. Many persons, afterwards distinguished in literature, have been born in as humble a situation of life; but it would be difficult to find any other who, while earning his subsistence by daily labour, has written verses which have attracted and retained universal attention, and which are likely to give the author a permanent and distinguished place among the followers of the muses. If he is deficient in grace, he is distinguished for ease as well as energy; and these are indications of the higher order of genius. The father of Epic poetry exhibits one of his heroes as excelling in strength, another in swiftness—to form his perfect warrior, these attributes are combined. Every species of intellectual superiority admits, perhaps, of a similar arrangement. One writer excels in force—another in ease; he is superior to them both, in whom both these qualities are united. Of Homer himself it may be said, that, like his own Achilles, he surpasses his competitors in mobility as well as strength.

The force of Burns lay in the powers of his understanding, and in the sensibility of his heart; and these will be found to infuse the living principle into all the works of genius which seem destined to immortality. His sensibility had an uncommon range. He was alive to every species of emotion. He is one of the few poets that can be mentioned, who have at once excelled in humour, in tenderness, and in sublimity; a praise unknown to the ancients, and which in modern times is only due to Ariosto, to Shakespeare, and perhaps to Voltaire. To compare the writings of the Scottish peasant with the works of these giants in literature, might appear presumptuous; yet it may be asserted that he has displayed the *foot of Hercules*. How near he might have approached them by proper culture, with lengthened years, and under happier auspices, it is not for us to calculate. But while we run over the melancholy story of his life, it is impossible not to heave a sigh at the asperity of his fortune; and as we survey the records of his mind, it is easy to see, that out of such materials have been reared the fairest and the most durable of the monuments of genius.—JAMES CURRIE, *The Life of Robert Burns*, 1800

Burns was possest of a versatility and strength of genius which might have conducted him to eminence in any department of science or literature. His senses were acute; his affections warm and generous: his imagination was vivid and excursive; his judgment prompt and penetrating. His poetry is the effusion of a vigorous and susceptible mind powerfully affected by the objects of its contemplation. The external beauties of nature, the pleasures and disappointments of love, the characteristics of the peasant's fate, the ridiculous features of hypocrisy and superstition, furnish the principal subjects on which he has exercised his bold and original talents. Most of the occasions which awakened his poetical powers were not fictitious but real; and his sentiments and language are generally those of a man who obeys the strong impulses of unsophisticated feeling. Although he laboured under the disadvantages of a very imperfect education, yet some circumstances of his early life were not altogether unfavourable to the nurture of a poetical

genius. The peculiarity of his fate tended to impress every sentiment more deeply on his mind, and to familiarize him with the habits of profound meditation. The lessons which his father taught him, were those of piety, virtue, and independence; lessons which are scarcely of less importance to the poet than to the man. His early years were indeed consumed in depressing toil: but even while the young peasant was following the plough, his intellectual eye was fixed on immortality. Many of his poems were composed during the hours when he was actually engaged in manual labour: his native energy was unsubdued by illiberal toil, by perpetual mortification, and by his total seclusion from that intercourse which is most calculated to fan the sparks of generous emulation. "This kind of life," says Burns, "the cheerless gloom of a hermit, with the unceasing moil of a galley-slave, brought me to my sixteenth year; a little before which period I first committed the sin of rhyme." Love, he informs us, was the original source of his poetry: "I never had the least thought or inclination of turning poet till I got once heartily in love; and then rhyme and song were in a manner the spontaneous language of my heart."

His principal models of composition were Ramsay and Fergusson. In his letter to Dr Moore, he remarks that he had nearly abandoned poetry, when in his twenty-third year having become acquainted with the works of Fergusson, he "strung a-new his wildly-sounding lyre with emulating vigour." Of classical learning he was totally destitute; and it is not apparent that he was much indebted to his knowledge of the French language. With the best English writers he was however sufficiently conversant: he redd them with avidity, and for the most part with wonderful discernment. Nor was he altogether unacquainted with science: he had at least studied Euclid, Locke, and Smith; he redd and understood Mr Alison's *Essays on the Principles of Taste*.

The most beautiful of his poems are professedly written in the Scotish dialect: but in general they are not deeply tinctured with provincial idioms; many of the stanzas are almost purely English. His verses, though not very polished or melodious, are commonly distinguished by an air of originality which atones for every deficiency. His rhymes are often imperfect, and his expressions indelicate; he passes from ease to negligence, and from simplicity to coarseness. But these peculiarities we may ascribe to his early habits of association.

The poems of Burns, though most remarkable for the quality of humour, exhibit various instances of the true sublime: the vigour of his imagination, and the soundness of his understanding, enabled him to attain a variety of excellence which can only be traced in the productions of original genius. Some of his subjects are sufficiently mean; but he never fails to illumine them with brilliant flashes of intellect. His flights however are sudden and irregular: the strong impulses of his mind were not sufficiently chastened and directed by the wholesome discipline of the schools. His compositions, however beautiful in detached parts, are very often defective in their general plan.

The most exquisite of his serious poems is "The Cotter's Saturday Night." The characters and incidents which the poet here describes in so interesting a manner, are such as his father's cottage presented to his observation; they are such as may every where be found among the virtuous and intelligent peasantry of Scotland.—DAVID IRVING, "The Life of Robert Burns," *The Lives of the Scottish Poets*, 1804, Vol. 2, pp. 487–90

The occasion of this present infliction, my dear friend, proceeds from my desire to vent on some *sympathetic soul*, some *kindred spirit*, three feelings with which I am at present brim-full—admiration, anger, and perplexity. In the first I am sure you will sympathize most cordially, for it is excited by Burns—by Burns, the sweetest, the sublimest, the most tricksy poet who has blest this nether world since the days of Shakespeare! I am just fresh from reading Dr. Currie's four volumes and Cromek's one, which comprise, I believe, all that he ever wrote; and I cannot imagine how I can have wasted my admiration on the little living, and disregarded the mighty dead in the way that I have hitherto done. To make it worse, I had read Dr. Currie's *Life of Burns* before, when I was about twelve or thirteen, and yet I had almost forgotten him. If I forget him again "may my right hand forget its cunning"! Have you lately read that delightful work? If you have not, pray do, and tell me if you do not admire him—not with the flimsy, lackadaisical praise with which certain gentle damsels bedaub his "Mountain Daisy" and his "Woodlark," and talk and sing of the rustic bard as the compeer of Bloomfield, and Stephen Duck, and Mrs. Leapor; but with the strong and manly feeling which his fine and indignant letters, his exquisite and original humour, his inimitable pathos, must awaken in such a mind as yours. Oh, what have they to answer for who let such a man perish! I think there is no poet whose works I have ever read, who interests one so strongly by the display of personal character contained in almost everything he wrote (even in his songs) as Burns. Those songs are for the greater part nearly his best productions; the very best is undoubtedly "Tam o' Shanter." The humour, the grandeur, and the fancy of that poem will never be equalled. What a pity it is that Burns did not follow the advice of my late excellent correspondent and adviser, Lord Woodhouselee, and give the world some more tales on that model! His versatility and his exhaustless imagination would have made it easy to him.—MARY RUSSELL MITFORD, Letter to Sir William Elford (Nov. 10, 1813)

Allen (Lord Holland's Allen—the best informed and one of the ablest men I know—a perfect Magliabecchi—a devourer, a Helluo of books, and an observer of men,) has lent me a quantity of Burns's unpublished, and never-to-be-published, Letters. They are full of oaths and obscene songs. What an antithetical mind!—tenderness, roughness—delicacy, coarseness—sentiment, sensuality—soaring and grovelling, dirt and deity—all mixed up in that one compound of inspired clay!—GEORGE GORDON, LORD BYRON, *Journal*, Dec. 13, 1813

No person can regret more than I do the tendency of *some* of my Brother's writings to represent irregularity of conduct as a consequence of genius, and sobriety the effect of dulness; but surely more has been said on that subject than the fact warrants: and it ought to be remembered that the greatest part of his writings, having that tendency, *were not published by himself, nor intended for publication.* But it may likewise be observed, and every attentive reader of Burns's Works, must have observed, that he frequently presents a caricature of his feelings, and even of his failings—a kind of mock-heroic account of himself and his opinions, which he never supposed could be taken literally. I dare say it never entered into his head, for instance, that when he was speaking in that manner of Milton's Satan, any one should gravely suppose that was the model on which he wished to form his own character. Yet on such rants, which the author evidently intends should be considered a mere play of imagination, joined to some abstract reasoning of the critic, many of the heavy accusations brought against the Poet for bad taste and worse morals, rest.—GILBERT BURNS, Letter to Alexander Peterkin (Sept. 29, 1814), cited in Alexander Peterkin, *Life and Works of Robert Burns*, 1814

But you will perhaps accuse me of refining too much; and it is, I own, comparatively of little importance, while we are engaged in reading the *Iliad*, the *Eneid*, the tragedies of *Othello* and *King Lear*, whether the authors of these poems were good or bad men; whether they lived happily or miserably. Should a thought of the kind cross our minds, there would be no doubt, if irresistible external evidence did not decide the question unfavourably, that men of such transcendent genius were both good and happy: and if, unfortunately, it had been on record that they were otherwise, sympathy with the fate of their fictitious personages would banish the unwelcome truth whenever it obtruded itself, so that it would but slightly disturb our pleasure. Far otherwise is it with that class of poets, the principal charm of whose writings depends upon the familiar knowledge which they convey of the personal feelings of their authors. This is eminently the case with the effusions of Burns,—in the small quantity of narrative that he has given, he himself bears no inconsiderable part, and he has produced no drama. Neither the subjects of his poems, nor his manner of handling them, allow us long to forget their author. On the basis of his human character he has reared a poetic one, which with more or less distinctness presents itself to view in almost every part of his earlier, and, in my estimation, his most valuable verses. This poetic fabric, dug out of the quarry of genuine humanity, is airy and spiritual:—and though the materials, in some parts, are coarse, and the disposition is often fantastic and irregular, yet the whole is agreeable and strikingly attractive. Plague, then, upon your remorseless hunters after matter of fact (who, after all, rank among the blindest of human beings) when they would convince you that the foundations of this admirable edifice are hollow; and that its frame is unsound! Granting that all which has been raked up to the prejudice of Burns were literally true; and that it added, which it does not, to our better understanding of human nature and human life (for that genius is not incompatible with vice, and that vice leads to misery—the more acute from the sensibilities which are the elements of genius—we needed not those communications to inform us) how poor would have been the compensation for the deduction made, by this extrinsic knowledge, from the intrinsic efficacy of his poetry—to please, and to instruct!

In illustration of this sentiment, permit me to remind you that it is the privilege of poetic genius to catch, under certain restrictions of which perhaps at the time of its being exerted it is but dimly conscious, a spirit of pleasure wherever it can be found,—in the walks of nature, and in the business of men.—The poet, trusting to primary instincts, luxuriates among the felicities of love and wine, and is enraptured while he describes the fairer aspects of war: nor does he shrink from the company of the passion of love through immoderate—from convivial pleasure though intemperate—nor from the presence of war though savage, and recognized as the hand-maid of desolation. Frequently and admirably has Burns given way to these impulses of nature; both with reference to himself and in describing the condition of others. Who, but some impenetrable dunce or narrow-minded puritan in works of art, ever read without delight the picture which he has drawn of the convivial exaltation of the rustic adventurer, Tam o' Shanter? The poet fears not to tell the reader in the outset that his hero was a desperate and sottish drunkard, whose excesses were frequent as his opportunities. This reprobate sits down to his cups, while the storm is roaring, and heaven and earth are in confusion;—the night is driven on by song and tumultuous noise—laughter and jest thicken as the beverage improves upon the palate—conjugal fidelity archly bends to the service of general benevolence—selfishness is not absent, but wearing the mask of social cordiality—and, while these various elements of humanity are blended into one proud and happy composition of elated spirits, the anger of the tempest without doors only heightens and sets off the enjoyment within.—I pity him who cannot perceive that, in all this, though there was no moral purpose, there is a moral effect.—WILLIAM WORDSWORTH, *Letter to a Friend of Robert Burns*, 1816

To proceed to the more immediate subject of the present Lecture, the character and writings of Burns.—Shakspeare says of some one, that 'he was like a man made after supper of a cheese-paring.' Burns, the poet, was not such a man. He had a strong mind, and a strong body, the fellow to it. He had a real heart of flesh and blood beating in his bosom—you can almost hear it throb. Some one said, that if you had shaken hands with him, his hand would have burnt yours. The Gods, indeed, 'made him poetical'; but nature had a hand in him first. His heart was in the right place. He did not 'create a soul under the ribs of death,' by tinkling siren sounds, or by piling up centos of poetic diction; but for the artificial flowers of poetry, he plucked the mountain-daisy under his feet; and a field-mouse, hurrying from its ruined dwelling, could inspire him with the sentiments of terror and pity. He held the plough or the pen with the same firm, manly grasp; nor did he cut out poetry as we cut out watch-papers, with finical dexterity, nor from the same flimsy materials. Burns was not like Shakspeare in the range of his genius; but there is something of the same magnanimity, directness, and unaffected character about him. He was not a sickly sentimentalist, a namby-pamby poet, a mincing metre ballad-monger, any more than Shakspeare. He would as soon hear 'a brazen candlestick tuned, or a dry wheel grate on the axletree.' He was as much of a man—not a twentieth part as much of a poet as Shakspeare. With but little of his imagination or inventive power, he had the same life of mind: within the narrow circle of personal feeling or domestic incidents, the pulse of his poetry flows as healthily and vigorously. He had an eye to see; a heart to feel:—no more. His pictures of good fellowship, of social glee, of quaint humour, are equal to any thing; they come up to nature, and they cannot go beyond it. The sly jest collected in his laughing eye at the sight of the grotesque and ludicrous in manners—the large tear rolled down his manly cheek at the sight of another's distress. He has made us as well acquainted with himself as it is possible to be; has let out the honest impulses of his native disposition, the unequal conflict of the passions in his breast, with the same frankness and truth of description. His strength is not greater than his weakness: his virtues were greater than his vices. His virtues belonged to his genius: his vices to his situation, which did not correspond to his genius.—WILLIAM HAZLITT, *Lectures on the English Poets*, 1818

One song of Burns's is of more worth to you than all I could think for a whole year in his native country—His Misery is a dead weight upon the nimbleness of one's quill—I tried to forget it—to drink Toddy without any Care—to write a merry Sonnet—it wont do—he talked with Bitches—he drank with Blackguards, he was miserable—We can see horribly clear in the works of such a man his whole life, as if we were God's spies.—JOHN KEATS, Letter to J. H. Reynolds (July 13, 1818)

Burns has given an elixir of life to his native dialect. The Scottish "Tam o' Shanter" will be read as long as any English production of the same century. The impression of his genius is deep and universal; and, viewing him merely as a poet, there is scarcely any other regret connected with his name, than that

his productions, with all their merit, fall short of the talents which he possessed. That he never attempted any great work of fiction or invention, may be partly traced to the cast of his genius, and partly to his circumstances and defective education. His poetical temperament was that of fitful transports, rather than steady inspiration. Whatever he might have written, was likely to have been fraught with passion. There is always enough of *interest* in life to cherish the feelings of a man of genius; but it requires knowledge to enlarge and enrich his *imagination*. Of that knowledge which unrolls the diversities of human manners, adventures, and characters to a poet's study, he could have no great share; although he stamped the little treasure which he possessed in the mintage of sovereign genius. It has been asserted, that he received all the education which is requisite for a poet: he had learned reading, writing, and arithmetic; and he had dipped into French and geometry. To a poet, it must be owned, the three last of those acquisitions were quite superfluous. His education, it is also affirmed, was equal to Shakespeare's; but, without intending to make any comparison between the genius of the two bards, it should be recollected that Shakspeare lived in an age within the verge of chivalry, an age overflowing with chivalrous and romantic reading; that he was led by his vocation to have daily recourse to that kind of reading; that he dwelt on the spot which gave him constant access to it, and was in habitual intercourse with men of genius. Burns, after growing up to manhood under toils which exhausted his physical frame, acquired a scanty knowledge of modern books, of books tending for the most part to regulate the judgment more than to exercise the fancy. In the whole tract of his reading, there seems to be little that could cherish his inventive faculties. One material of poetry he certainly possessed, independent of books, in the legendary superstitions of his native country. But with all that he tells us of his early love of those superstitions, they seem to have come home to his mind with so many ludicrous associations of vulgar tradition, that it may be doubted if he could have turned them to account in an elevated work of fiction. Strongly and admirably as he paints the supernatural in "Tam o' Shanter," yet there, as every where else, he makes it subservient to comic effect. The fortuitous wildness and sweetness of his strains may, after all, set aside every regret that he did not attempt more superb and regular structures of fancy. He describes, as he says, the sentiments which he saw and felt in himself and his rustic compeers around him. His page is a lively image of the contemporary life and country from which he sprung. He brings back old Scotland to us with all her homefelt endearments, her simple customs, her festivities, her sturdy prejudices, and orthodox zeal, with a power that excites, alternately, the most tender and mirthful sensations. After the full account of his pieces which Dr. Currie has given, the English reader can have nothing new to learn respecting them. On one powerfully comic piece Dr. Currie has not disserted, namely, "The Holy Fair." It is enough, however, to mention the humour of this production, without recommending its subject. Burns, indeed, only laughs at the abuses of a sacred institution; but the theme was of unsafe approach, and he ought to have avoided it.

He meets us, in his compositions, undisguisedly as a peasant. At the same time, his observations go extensively into life, like those of a man who felt the proper dignity of human nature in the character of a peasant. The writer of some of the severest strictures that ever have been passed upon his poetry conceives, that his beauties are considerably defaced by a portion of false taste and vulgar sentiment, which adhere to him from his low education. That Burns's education, or rather the want of it, excluded him from much knowledge, which might have fostered his inventive ingenuity, seems to be clear; but his circumstances cannot be admitted to have communicated vulgarity to the tone of his sentiments. They have not the sordid taste of low condition. It is objected to him, that he boasts too much of his own independence; but, in reality, this boast is neither frequent nor obtrusive; and it is in itself the expression of a manly and laudable feeling. So far from calling up disagreeable recollections of rusticity, his sentiments triumph, by their natural energy, over those false and fastidious distinctions which the mind is but too apt to form in allotting its sympathies to the sensibilities of the rich and poor. He carries us into the humble scenes of life, not to make us dole out our tribute of charitable compassion to paupers and cottagers, but to make us feel with them on equal terms, to make us enter into their passions and interests, and share our hearts with them as with brothers and sisters of the human species.

He is taxed, in the same place, with perpetually affecting to deride the virtues of prudence, regularity, and decency; and with being imbued with the sentimentality of German novels. Any thing more remote from German sentiment than Burns's poetry could not easily be mentioned. But is he depraved and licentious in a comprehensive view of the moral character of his pieces? The overgenial freedom of a few assuredly ought not to fix this character upon the whole of them. It is a charge which we should hardly expect to see preferred against the author of "The Cotter's Saturday Night." He is the enemy, indeed, of that selfish and niggardly spirit which shelters itself under the name of prudence; but that pharisaical disposition has seldom been a favourite with poets. Nor should his maxims, which inculcate charity and candour in judging of human frailties, be interpreted as a serious defence of them, as when he says,

> Then gently scan your brother man,
>   Still gentlier sister woman,
> Though they may gang a kennan wrang;
>   To step aside is human.
> Who made the heart, 'tis he alone
>   Decidedly can try us;
> He knows each chord, its various tone,
>   Each spring its various bias.

It is still more surprising, that a critic, capable of so eloquently developing the traits of Burns's genius, should have found fault with his amatory strains for want of polish, and "of that chivalrous tone of gallantry, which uniformly abases itself in the presence of the object of its devotion." Every reader must recal abundance of thoughts in his love songs, to which any attempt to superadd a tone of gallantry would not be

> To gild refined gold, to paint the rose,
>   Or add fresh perfume to the violet,

but to debase the metal, and to take the odour and colour from the flower. It is exactly this superiority to "abasement" and polish which is the charm that distinguishes Burns from the herd of erotic songsters, from the days of the troubadours to the present time. He wrote from impulses more sincere than the spirit of chivalry; and even Lord Surrey and Sir Philip Sidney are cold and uninteresting lovers in comparison with the rustic Burns.—Thomas Campbell, *Specimens of the British Poets*, 1819

A genius like Burns certainly may do, and doubtless has done, much to diffuse a knowledge and a relish for his native idiom. His character as a poet has been too often canvassed by writers and biographers to require our panegyric. We define it,

perhaps, as concisely as may be, by saying that it consisted of an acute sensibility regulated by uncommon intellectual vigor. Hence his frequent visions of rustic love and courtship never sink into mawkish sentimentality, his quiet pictures of domestic life are without insipidity, and his mirth is not the unmeaning ebullition of animal spirits, but is pointed with the reflection of a keen observer of human nature. This latter talent, less applauded in him than some others, is in our opinion his most eminent. Without the grace of La Fontaine, or the broad buffoonery of Berni, he displays the same facility of illuminating the meanest topics, seasons his humor with as shrewd a moral, and surpasses both in a generous sensibility which gives an air of truth and cordiality to all his sentiments. Lyrical poetry admits of less variety than any other species; and Burns, from this circumstance, as well as from the flexibility of his talents, may be considered as the representative of his whole nation. Indeed, his universal genius seems to have concentrated within itself the rays which were scattered among his predecessors,—the simple tenderness of Crawford, the fidelity of Ramsay, and careless humor of Ferguson. The Doric dialect of his country was an instrument peculiarly fitted for the expression of his manly and unsophisticated sentiments. But no one is more indebted to the national music than Burns: embalmed in the sacred melody, his songs are familiar to us from childhood, and, as we read them, the silver sounds with which they have been united seem to linger in our memory, heightening and prolonging the emotions which the sentiments have excited.—William H. Prescott, "Scottish Song" (1826), *Biographical and Critical Miscellanies*, 1845, pp. 547–48

Porson. What an admirable Spanish scholar must Mr. Wordsworth be! How completely has he transfused into his own compositions all the spirit of those verses! Nevertheless, it is much to be regretted that, in resolving on simplicity, he did not place himself under the tuition of Burns; which quality Burns could have taught him in perfection: but others he never could have imparted to such an auditor. He would have sung in vain to him

> Scots wha hae wi' Wallace bled,—

a song more animating than ever Tyrtæus sang to the fife before the Spartans. But simplicity in Burns is never stale and unprofitable. In Burns there is no waste of words out of an ill-shouldered sack; no troublesome running backward and forward of little, idle, ragged ideas; no ostentation of sentiment in the surtout of selfishness.—Walter Savage Landor, "Southey and Porson: Second Conversation," *Imaginary Conversations: Third Series*, 1828

On one point there can be no controversy; the poetry of Burns has had most powerful influence in reviving and strengthening the national feelings of his countrymen. Amidst penury and labour, his youth fed on the old minstrelsy and traditional glories of his nation, and his genius divined, that what he felt so deeply must belong to a spirit that might lie smothered around him, but could not be extinguished. The political circumstances of Scotland were, and had been, such as to starve the flame of patriotism; the popular literature had striven, and not in vain, to make itself English; and, above all, a new and a cold system of speculative philosophy had begun to spread widely among us. A peasant appeared, and set himself to check the creeping pestilence of this indifference. Whatever genius has since then been devoted to the illustration of the national manners, and sustaining thereby of the national feelings of the people, there can be no doubt that Burns will ever be remembered as the founder, and, alas! in his own person as the martyr, of this reformation.—JOHN GIBSON LOCKHART, *Life of Robert Burns*, 1828, pp. 225–26

Burns is our chief national Poet; he owes nothing of the structure of his verse or of the materials of his poetry to other lands—he is the offspring of the soil; he is as natural to Scotland as the heath is to her hills, and all his brightness, like our nocturnal aurora, is of the north. Nor has he taken up fleeting themes; his song is not of the external manners and changeable affectations of man—it is of the human heart—of the mind's hopes and fears, and of the soul's aspirations. Others give us the outward form and pressure of society—the court-costume of human nature—the laced lapelle and the epauletted shoulder. He gives us flesh and blood; all he has he holds in common with mankind, yet all is national and Scottish. We can see to whom other bards have looked up for inspiration—like fruit of the finest sort, they smack of the stock on which they were grafted. Burns read Young, Thomson, Shenstone, and Shakspeare; yet there is nothing of Young, Thomson, Shenstone, or Shakspeare about him; nor is there much of the old ballad. His light is of nature, like sunshine, and not reflected.—ALLAN CUNNINGHAM, *The Life of Robert Burns*, *The Works of Robert Burns*, 1834, Vol. 1, pp. 365–66

> And Burns, with pungent passionings
> Set in his eyes: deep lyric springs
> Are of the fire-mount's issuings.
> —ELIZABETH BARRETT BROWNING, *A Vision of Poets*, 1844, ll. 403–5

> On, exulting in his magic,
> Swept the gifted peasant on—
> Though his feet were on the greensward,
> Light from Heaven around him shone;
> At his conjuration, demons
> Issued from their darkness drear;
> Hovering round on silver pinions,
> Angels stoop'd his songs to hear;
> Bow'd the Passions to his bidding,
> Terror gaunt, and Pity calm;
> Like the organ pour'd his thunder,
> Like the lute his fairy psalm.
>
> Lo! when clover-swathes lay round him,
> Or his feet the furrow press'd,
> He could mourn the sever'd daisy,
> Or the mouse's ruin'd nest;
> Woven of gloom and glory, visions
> Haunting throng'd his twilight hour;
> Birds enthrall'd him with sweet music,
> Tempests with their tones of power;
> Eagle-wing'd, his mounting spirit
> Custom's rusty fetters spurn'd;
> Tasso-like, for Jean he melted,
> Wallace-like, for Scotland burn'd!
> —DAVID MACBETH MOIR, "Stanzas for the Burns Festival," 1844

> In him there burned that passionate glow,
> All Nature's soul and savor,
> Which gives its hue to every flower,
> To every fruit its flavor:
> Nor less the kindred power he felt;
> That love of all things human
> Whereof the fiery centre is
> The love man bears to woman.
>
> He sang the dignity of man,
> Sang woman's grace and goodness;
> Passed by the world's half-truths, her lies
> Pierced through with lance-like shrewdness.

> Upon life's broad highways he stood,
> And aped nor Greek nor Roman;
> But snatched from heaven Promethean fire
> To glorify things common.
>
> He sang of youth, he sang of age,
> Their joys, their griefs, their labors;
> Felt with, not for, the people, hailed
> All Scotland's sons his neighbors:
> And therefore all repeat his verse—
> Hot youth, or graybeard steady,
> The boatman on Loch Etive's wave,
> The shepherd on Ben Ledi.
>
> He sang from love of song; his name
> Dunedin's cliff resounded:—
> He left her, faithful to a fame
> On truth and nature founded.
> He sought true fame, not loud acclaim;
> Himself and Time he trusted:
> For laurels crackling in the flame
> His fine ear never lusted!
>
> He loved, and reason had to love,
> The illustrious land that bore him:
> Where'er he went like heaven's broad tent
> A star-bright Past hung o'er him.
> Each isle had fenced a saint recluse,
> Each tower a hero dying;
> Down every mountain-gorge had rolled
> The flood of foemen flying.
>
> From age to age that land has paid
> No alien throne submission;
> For feudal faith had been her Law,
> And Freedom her Tradition.
> Where frowned the rocks had Freedom smiled,
> Sung, 'mid the shrill wind's whistle—
> So England prized her garden Rose,
> But Scotland loved her Thistle.
> —AUBREY DE VERE, "To Burns's Highland Mary," 1847

We must listen, too, while in homely Scots vernacular we are told by an Ayrshire ploughman authentic tidings of living instincts, of spontaneous belief, which not all the philosophy in the brain of the intellectual can banish from the breast of the human being.—ARTHUR HUGH CLOUGH, "Lecture on the Development of English Literature" (1852), *Prose Remains*, 1888, p. 350

> No more these simple flowers belong
> To Scottish maid and lover;
> Sown in the common soil of song,
> They bloom the wide world over.
>
> In smiles and tears, in sun and showers,
> The minstrel and the heather,
> The deathless singer and the flowers
> He sang of live together.
>
> Wild heather-bells and Robert Burns!
> The moorland flower and peasant!
> How, at their mention, memory turns
> Her pages old and pleasant!
>
> The gray sky wears again its gold
> And purple of adorning,
> And manhood's noonday shadows hold
> The dews of boyhood's morning.
>
> The dews that washed the dust and soil
> From off the wings of pleasure,
> The sky, that flecked the ground of toil
> With golden threads of leisure.

I call to mind the summer day,
　The early harvest mowing,
The sky with sun and clouds at play,
　And flowers with breezes blowing.

I hear the blackbird in the corn,
　The locust in the haying;
And, like the fabled hunter's horn,
　Old tunes my heart is playing.

How oft that day, with fond delay,
　I sought the maple's shadow,
And sang with Burns the hours away,
　Forgetful of the meadow!

Bees hummed, birds twittered, overhead
　I heard the squirrels leaping,
The good dog listened while I read,
　And wagged his tail in keeping.

I watched him while in sportive mood
　I read "The Twa Dogs'" story,
And half believed he understood
　The poet's allegory.

Sweet day, sweet songs! The golden hours
　Grew brighter for that singing,
From brook and bird and meadow flowers
　A dearer welcome bringing.

New light on home-seen Nature beamed,
　New glory over Woman;
And daily life and duty seemed
　No longer poor and common.

I woke to find the simple truth
　Of fact and feeling better
Than all the dreams that held my youth
　A still repining debtor:

That Nature gives her handmaid, Art,
　The themes of sweet discoursing;
The tender idyls of the heart
　In every tongue rehearsing.

Why dream of lands of gold and pearl,
　Of loving knight and lady,
When farmer boy and barefoot girl
　Were wandering there already?

I saw through all familiar things
　The romance underlying;
The joys and griefs that plume the wings
　Of Fancy skyward flying.

I saw the same blithe day return,
　The same sweet fall of even,
That rose on wooded Craigie-burn,
　And sank on crystal Devon.

I matched with Scotland's heathery hills
　The sweetbrier and the clover;
With Ayr and Doon, my native rills,
　Their wood-hymns chanting over.

O'er rank and pomp, as he had seen,
　I saw the Man uprising;
No longer common or unclean,
　The child of God's baptizing!

With clearer eyes I saw the worth
　Of life among the lowly;
The Bible at his Cotter's hearth
　Had made my own more holy.

And if at times an evil strain,
　To lawless love appealing,
Broke in upon the sweet refrain
　Of pure and healthful feeling,

It died upon the eye and ear,
　No inward answer gaining;
No heart had I to see or hear
　The discord and the staining.

Let those who never erred forget
　His worth, in vain bewailings;
Sweet Soul of Song! I own my debt
　Uncancelled by his failings!

Lament who will the ribald line
　Which tells his lapse from duty,
How kissed the maddening lips of wine
　Or wanton ones of beauty;

But think, while falls that shade between
　The erring one and Heaven,
That he who loved like Magdalen,
　Like her may be forgiven.

Not his the song whose thunderous chime
　Eternal echos render;
The mournful Tuscan's haunted rhyme,
　And Milton's starry splendor!

But who his human heart has laid
　To Nature's bosom nearer?
Who sweetened toil like him, or paid
　To love a tribute dearer?

Through all his tuneful art, how strong
　The human feeling gushes!
The very moonlight of his song
　Is warm with smiles and blushes!

Give lettered pomp to teeth of Time,
　So "Bonnie Doon" but tarry;
Blot out the Epic's stately rhyme,
　But spare his Highland Mary!
　　　—JOHN GREENLEAF WHITTIER, "Burns: On Re-
　　　ceiving a Sprig of Heather in Blossom," 1854

At the first announcement, from I know not whence, that the 25th of January was the hundredth anniversary of the birth of Robert Burns, a sudden consent warmed the great English race, in all its kingdoms, colonies and states, all over the world, to keep the festival. We are here to hold our parliament with love and poesy, as men were wont to do in the Middle Ages. Those famous parliaments might or might not have had more stateliness and better singers than we,—though that is yet to be known,—but they could not have better reason. I can only explain this singular unanimity in a race which rarely acts together, but rather after their watchword, Each for himself,—by the fact that Robert Burns, the poet of the middle class, represents in the mind of men to-day that great uprising of the middle class against the armed and privileged minorities, that uprising which worked politically in the American and French Revolutions, and which, not in governments so much as in education and social order, has changed the face of the world.

In order for this destiny, his birth, breeding and fortunes were low. His organic sentiment was absolute independence, and resting as it should on a life of labor. No man existed who could look down on him. They that looked into his eyes saw that they might look down the sky as easily. His muse and teaching was common sense, joyful, aggressive, irresistible. Not Latimer, nor Luther struck more telling blows against false theology than did this brave singer. The Confession of Augsburg, the Declaration of Independence, the French Rights of Man, and the Marseillaise, are not more weighty documents in the history of freedom than the songs of Burns. His satire has lost none of its edge. His musical arrows yet sing through the air. He is so substantially a reformer that I find his grand plain sense in close chain with the greatest masters,—

Rabelais, Shakspeare in comedy, Cervantes, Butler, and Burns. If I should add another name, I find it only in a living countryman of Burns.

He is an exceptional genius. The people who care nothing for literature and poetry care for Burns. It was indifferent—they thought who saw him—whether he wrote verse or not: he could have done anything else as well. Yet how true a poet is he! And the poet, too, of poor men, of gray hodden and the guernsey coat and the blouse. He has given voice to all the experiences of common life; he has endeared the farmhouse and cottage, patches and poverty, beans and barley; ale, the poor man's wine; hardship; the fear of debt; the dear society of weans and wife, of brothers and sisters, proud of each other, knowing so few and finding amends for want and obscurity in books and thoughts. What a love of Nature, and, shall I say it? of middle-class Nature. Not like Goethe, in the stars, or like Byron, in the ocean, or Moore, in the luxurious East, but in the homely landscape which the poor see around them,—bleak leagues of pasture and stubble, ice and sleet and rain and snow-choked brooks; birds, hares, field-mice, thistles and heather, which he daily knew. How many "Bonny Doons" and "John Anderson my jo's" and "Auld lang synes" all around the earth have his verses been applied to! And his love-songs still woo and melt the youths and maids; the farm-work, the country holiday, the fishing-cobble are still his debtors to-day.

And as he was thus the poet of the poor, anxious, cheerful, working humanity, so had he the language of low life. He grew up in a rural district, speaking a *patois* unintelligible to all but natives, and he has made the Lowland Scotch a Doric dialect of fame. It is the only example in history of a language made classic by the genius of a single man. But more than this. He had that secret of genius to draw from the bottom of society the strength of its speech, and astonish the ears of the polite with these artless words, better than art, and filtered of all offence through his beauty. It seemed odious to Luther that the devil should have all the best tunes; he would bring them into the churches; and Burns knew how to take from fairs and gypsies, blacksmiths and drovers, the speech of the market and street, and clothe it with melody. But I am detaining you too long. The memory of Burns,—I am afraid heaven and earth have taken too good care of it to leave us anything to say. The west winds are murmuring it. Open the windows behind you, and hearken for the incoming tide, what the waves say of it. The doves perching always on the eaves of the Stone Chapel opposite, may know something about it. Every name in broad Scotland keeps his fame bright. The memory of Burns,—every man's, every boy's and girl's head carries snatches of his songs, and they say them by heart, and, what is strangest of all, never learned them from a book, but from mouth to mouth. The wind whispers them, the birds whistle them, the corn, barley, and bulrushes hoarsely rustle them, nay, the music-boxes at Geneva are framed and toothed to play them; the hand-organs of the Savoyards in all cities repeat them, and the chimes of bells ring them in the spires. They are the property and the solace of mankind.—RALPH WALDO EMERSON, "Robert Burns" (1859), *Works*, 1904, Vol. 11, pp. 439–43

His birthday.—Nay, we need not speak
    The name each heart is beating,—
Each glistening eye and flushing cheek
    In light and flame repeating!

We come in one tumultuous tide,—
    One surge of wild emotion,—
As crowding through the Frith of Clyde
    Rolls in the Western Ocean;

As when yon cloudless, quartered moon
    Hangs o'er each storied river,
The swelling breasts of Ayr and Doon
    With sea-green wavelets quiver.

The century shrivels like a scroll,—
    The past becomes the present,—
And face to face, and soul to soul,
    We greet the monarch-peasant.

While Shenstone strained in feeble flights
    With Corydon and Phillis,—
While Wolfe was climbing Abraham's heights
    To snatch the Bourbon lilies,—

Who heard the wailing infant's cry,
    The babe beneath the sheeling,
Whose song to-night in every sky
    Will shake earth's starry ceiling,—

Whose passion-breathing voice ascends
    And floats like incense o'er us,
Whose ringing lay of friendship blends
    With labor's anvil chorus?

We love him, not for sweetest song,
    Though never tone so tender;
We love him, even in his wrong,—
    His wasteful self-surrender.

We praise him, not for gifts divine,—
    His Muse was born of woman,—
His manhood breathes in every line,—
    Was ever heart more human?

We love him, praise him, just for this:
    In every form and feature,
Through wealth and want, through woe and bliss,
    He saw his fellow-creature!

No soul could sink beneath his love,—
    Not even angel blasted;
No mortal power could soar above
    The pride that all outlasted!

Ay! Heaven had set one living man
    Beyond the pedant's tether,—
His virtues, frailties, HE may scan,
    Who weighs them all together!

I fling my pebble on the cairn
    Of him, though dead, undying;
Sweet Nature's nursling, bonniest bairn
    Beneath her daisies lying.

The waning suns, the wasting globe,
    Shall spare the minstrel's story,—
The centuries weave his purple robe,
    The mountain-mist of glory!
        —OLIVER WENDELL HOLMES, "For the Burns Centennial Celebration," 1859

Dear Bard and Brother! let who may
    Against thy faults be railing,
(Though far, I pray, from us be they
    That never had a failing!)
One toast I'll give, and that not long,
    Which thou wouldst pledge if present,—
To him whose song, in nature strong,
    Makes man of prince and peasant!
        —JAMES RUSSELL LOWELL, "At the Burns Centennial," 1859

One circumstance alone is enough to stamp Burns as a man of the highest order of genius. He took a local dialect and made it classical, gave it a character of great universality. I am not ignorant of what the poets who had lived before Burns did for the dialect of Scotland, nor what has been done since by

Walter Scott, whose works are read by everybody, and will be read for ages to come. But the poets of the Scottish dialect before Burns never attained that general and popular perusal which his works have acquired, and it was the good fortune of Scott that he wrote after Burns had made that dialect familiar to all classes of English readers.

It was Burns who taught us all to love the Scottish dialect—its graceful diminutives, its rich store of comic expressions, its homely but intensely significant phrases of pathos and tenderness, which go to the heart. Within his lifetime—and his life was not a long one—his poems were read wherever the English language is spoken: on the banks of the Hudson, of the Ashley and the Santee, of the Mississippi, of the St. Lawrence, of the Ganges, as well as on the banks of the Tweed and the Thames. It is owing to Burns that the natives of Scotland have it in their power to say that to him who has not some knowledge of the Scottish dialect and some relish for its significance there is one chamber of the common treasury of our literature—a chamber filled with gems and jewels—to which he has not the key.—WILLIAM CULLEN BRYANT, "An Address on Burns" (1871), *Prose Writings*, ed. Parke Godwin, 1884, Vol. 2, p. 320

> O Burns! where bid? where bide you now?
> Where are you in this night's full noon,
> Great master of the pen and plough?
> Might you not on yon slanting beam
> Of moonlight, kneeling to the Doon,
> Descend once to this hallow'd stream?
> Sure yon stars yield enough of light
> For heaven to spare your face one night.
>
> O Burns! another name for song,
> Another name for passion—pride;
> For love and poesy allied;
> For strangely blended right and wrong.
>
> I picture you as one who kneel'd
> A stranger at his own hearthstone;
> One knowing all, yet all unknown,
> One seeing all, yet all conceal'd;
> The fitful years you linger'd here,
> A lease of peril and of pain;
> And I am thankful yet again
> The gods did love you, ploughman! peer!
>
> In all your own and other lands,
> I hear your touching songs of cheer;
> The peasant and the lordly peer
> Above your honor'd dust strike hands.
> —JOAQUIN MILLER, "Burns and Byron" (1870),
> *Songs of the Sierras*, 1871, pp. 259–60

He made love the great end of existence, to such a degree that at the club which he founded with the young men of Tarbolton, every member was obliged "to be the declared lover of one or more fair ones." From the age of fifteen this was his main business. He had for companion in his harvest toil a sweet and lovable girl, a year younger than himself:

> In short, she, altogether unwittingly to herself, initiated me in that delicious passion, which, in spite of acid disappointment, gin-horse prudence, and book-worm philosophy, I hold to be the first of human joys, our dearest blessing here below.

He sat beside her, with a joy which he did not understand, to "pick out from her little hand the cruel nettlestings and thistles." He had many other less innocent fancies; it seems to me that he was at bottom in love with all women: as soon as he saw a pretty one, he grew gay; his commonplace book and his songs show that he set off in pursuit after every butterfly, golden or not, which seemed about to settle. Observe that he did not confine himself to Platonic reveries; he was as free of action as of words; obscene jokes come freely in his verses. He calls himself an unregenerate heathen, and he is right. He has even written ribald verses; and Lord Byron refers to a packet of his letters, unedited of course, than which worse could not be imagined: it was the excess of the sap which overflowed in him, and soiled the bark. Doubtless he did not boast about these excesses, he rather repented of them; but as to the uprising and blooming of the free poetic life towards the open air, he found no fault with it. He thought that love, with the charming dreams it brings, poetry, pleasure, and the rest, are beautiful things, appropriate to human instincts, and therefore to the designs of God. In short, in contrast with morose Puritanism, he approved joy and spoke well of happiness. —HIPPOLYTE TAINE, *History of English Literature*, tr. H. Van Laun, 1871, Bk. 4, Ch. 1

Burns imparted to poetry an impulse at once like that given by Cowper and diverse from it. Both were in a high degree natural, spontaneous, sincere; but the sincerity of the one was that of a melancholy and devout temper, and that of the other of a joyous and passionate one. Few characters so elicit sympathy and regard, passing into regret and sadness, as that of Burns. With large and generous impulses and an eager relish for pleasure, he sought it impetuously, and missed it early and almost utterly. His warm, emotional nature made him as ready to impart as to receive enjoyment, yet his fatal haste and disobedience brought the same bitterness to others as to himself. His love was as deadly as the hate of another man. The flowers he planted lost their fragrance, and the blossoms he plucked distilled blood upon his fingers. We share something of his resentment and impatience at the stern, cold, cruel features of the social life and religious faith of his country, yet we are forced to remember, that out of his own more tender sentiments, as expressed in the "Cotter's Saturday-Night," there came no strength, no power to plant, to harvest, or to enjoy the good he coveted. His own failure was early and complete.

As a lyric poet Burns deserves the name of great. In the most essential qualities of this form of verse; in fire, tenderness and naturalness, none have surpassed him. The earnest devotion of Cowper united him in meditative sympathy to nature; the warm passions of Burns set him aglow with human interests, and made him the poet of tender, heroic, mirthful, wilful impulses. He keenly felt, and uttered melodiously what he felt; and by this force of a strong, impetuous nature became a fresh, creative poet, working vigorously for the new era. With lively and sympathetic feelings he entered into the homely experiences of life about him, both frolicsome and serious, gay and sombre; rendered them with his own appreciation, and colored them with his own transfiguring fancy. The human sympathies of Burns wrought like the spiritual sympathies of Cowper, and put him, at times, as in the "Mountain Daisy," in living concord with nature.

The class to which Burns belonged, the dialect in which he wrote, his limited education, all lightened the weight of conventional influences, and left him chiefly to the push of his own nature as he produced his lyrics, first for himself, and later for the world. Though Burns stands at the entrance of the new period, none of the great poets that followed surpassed him in individuality of faculties, a freedom which yet left him in full mastery of a varied and most melodious verse. Here again in the life of Burns we have a large, constitutional, original element, which shaped itself into the development of his times without being governed by it. Pope had been made the subject of admiring study by Burns, yet cast no reflection of himself in the dancing, sparkling, rollicksome stream of his verse.—JOHN BASCOM, *Philosophy of English Literature*, 1874, pp. 220–22

The name of Robert Burns is a well-understood signal for an overflow of all sorts of commonplaces from the right-minded critic. These commonplaces run mainly in three channels:— ecstatic astonishment at finding that a ploughman was also a poet; wringing of hands over the admission that the ploughman and poet was likewise a drunkard, and a somewhat miscel- laneous lover; and caustic severity upon the lionizers and "admirers of native genius" who could find no employment more appropriate than that of excise-officer for the brightest and finest mind of their country and generation. All these commonplaces must stand confessed as warranted by the facts; they are truths, but they are also truisms. We have heard them very often, and have always sat in meek acquiescence and unfeigned concurrence. But the time comes when they have been repeated frequently enough to make the enlarging upon them a weariness, and the profuse and argumentative re- enforcement of them a superfluity.—WILLIAM MICHAEL ROS- SETTI, "Robert Burns," *Lives of Famous Poets*, 1878, p. 189

The spiritual power of poetry, indeed, like that of natural beauty, is immeasurable, and it is not easy to define and describe Burns's service to the world. But, without critical and careful detail of observation, it is plain, first of all, that he interpreted Scotland as no other country has been revealed by a kindred genius. Were Scotland suddenly submerged and her people swept away, the tale of her politics and kings and great events would survive in histories. But essential Scotland, the customs, legends, superstitions, language; the grotesque hu- mor, the keen sagacity, the simple, serious faith, the charac- teristic spirit of the national life, caught up and preserved in the sympathy of poetic genius, would live forever in the poet's verse. The sun of Scotland sparkles in it; the birds of Scotland sing; its breezes rustle, its waters murmur. Each "timorous wee beastie," the "ourie cattle," and the "silly sheep," are softly penned and gathered in this all-embracing fold of song. Over the dauntless battle-hymn of "Scots wha hae wi' Wallace bled" rises the solemn music of the "Cotter's Saturday Night." Through the weird witch romance of "Tam O'Shanter" breathes the scent of the wild rose of Alloway, and the daring and astounding babel of the "Jolly Beggars" is penetrated by the heart-breaking sigh to Jessie:

> Although thou maun never be mine,
>   Although even hope is denied,
> 'Tis sweeter for thee despairing
>   Than aught in the world beside.

The poet touches every scene and sound, every thought and feeling—but the refrain of all is Scotland. To what other man was it ever given so to transfigure the country of his birth and love? Every bird and flower, every hill and dale and river, whispers and repeats his name, and the word Scotland is sweeter because of Robert Burns.

But in thus casting a poetic spell upon everything distinc- tively Scotch, Burns fostered a patriotism which has become proverbial. The latest historian of England says that at the time of Burns's birth England was mad with hatred of the Scots. But when Burns died there was not a Scotchman who was not proud of being a Scotchman. A Scotch ploughman, singing of his fellow-peasants and their lives and loves in their own language, had given them in their own eyes a dignity they had never known:

> A man's a man for a' that

And America is but the sublime endeavor to make the ploughman's words true. Great poets, before and after Burns, have been honored by their countries and by the world; but is there any great poet of any time or country who has so taken the heart of what our Abraham Lincoln, himself one of them, called the plain people, that, as was lately seen in Edinburgh, when he had been dead nearly a hundred years, workmen going home from work begged to look upon this statue for the love and honor they bore to Robbie Burns? They love him for their land's sake, and they are better Scotchmen because of him. England does not love Shakespeare, nor Italy Dante, nor Germany Goethe, with the passionate ardor with which Scotland loves Burns. It is no wonder, for here is Auld Scotia's thistle bloomed out into a flower so fair that its beauty and perfume fill the world with joy.—GEORGE WILLIAM CURTIS, "Robert Burns" (1880), *Orations and Addresses*, ed. Charles Eliot Norton, 1894, Vol. 3, pp. 317–19

> I see amid the fields of Ayr
> A ploughman, who, in foul or fair,
>   Sings at his task,
> So clear we know not if it is
> The laverock's song we hear or his,
>   Nor care to ask.
>
> For him the ploughing of those fields
> A more ethereal harvest yields
>   Than sheaves of grain:
> Songs flush with purple bloom the rye;
> The plover's call, the curlew's cry,
>   Sing in his brain.
>
> Touched by his hand, the way-side weed
> Becomes a flower; the lowliest reed
>   Beside the stream
> Is clothed with beauty; gorse and grass
> And heather, where his footsteps pass,
>   The brighter seem.
>
> He sings of love, whose flame illumes
> The darkness of lone cottage rooms;
>   He feels the force,
> The treacherous under-tow and stress,
> Of wayward passions, and no less
>   The keen remorse.
>
> At moments, wrestling with his fate,
> His voice is harsh, but not with hate;
>   The brush-wood hung
> Above the tavern door lets fall
> Its bitter leaf, its drop of gall,
>   Upon his tongue.
>
> But still the burden of his song
> Is love of right, disdain of wrong;
>   Its master-chords
> Are Manhood, Freedom, Brotherhood;
> Its discords but an interlude
>   Between the words.
>
> And then to die so young, and leave
> Unfinished what he might achieve!
>   Yet better sure
> Is this than wandering up and down,
> An old man, in a country town,
>   Infirm and poor.
>
> For now he haunts his native land
> As an immortal youth; his hand
>   Guides every plough;

He sits beside each ingle-nook;
His voice is in each rushing brook,
    Each rustling bough.
His presence haunts this room to-night,
A form of mingled mist and light,
    From that far coast.
Welcome beneath this room of mine!
Welcome! this vacant chair is thine,
    Dear guest and ghost!
      —HENRY WADSWORTH LONGFELLOW, "Robert
      Burns," *Harper's New Monthly Magazine*, Au-
      gust 1880, pp. 321–23

Very few have given more poetic expression to the everyday incidents and feelings of their lives—the quiet life of home, the common labours by which he won his daily bread, the every-day friends he knew, the social circle he met, the plain but parti-coloured life of the countryside in which he lived, the simplest country tale, the commonest country tradition, the flow of common events, and the thousand little things that make up the daily life of our common humanity. Few also have surpassed him in uttering the varied emotions, "the moods of the mind," the sunshine and the shower, the dreams and aspirations of his deeper heart,—experiences common in their kind to all men, which it only requires the soul and tongue of genius to interpret and to utter.

    It is here that our poet has done vital and lasting service to the race, in expressing the idealism that underlies the commonest of things, the most common-place of lives, the most ordinary of incidents. It is here that Burns has shed the highest glory on Scotland, and the Scotch people, and on mankind. Go where we may, look where we will, in any place in which he has sojourned during his short but pregnant life, we are constantly reminded of the man, his life, his wonderful words, and their ever-widening influence. It is here that his genius most conspicuously appears, in utterances that will speed the time when the world will act on the conviction that the elements of happiness and poetry are more within our reach, here and now, than we have yet dreamt of, and not in some far-off Utopia, in the skies, in dreamland, or in the future, where we have foolishly too much located them; and that

    A man's best things are nearest him;
    Lie close about his feet.

It is here that Burns takes a permanent and paramount place amongst the true poets of nature and humanity, who have increased our power of

    Clothing the palpable and familiar
    With golden exhalations of the dawn.
      —WILLIAM JOLLY, *Robert Burns at Mossgiel*,
      1881, pp. 125–27

'Twas his to feel the anguish keen
Of noblest powers to mortals given,
While tyrant passions chained to earth
    The soul that might have soared to heaven.

'Twas his to feel in one poor heart
    Such war of fierce conflicting feeling
As makes this life of ours too sad
    A mystery for our unsealing;—
The longing for the nobler course,
    The doing of the thing abhorred,—
Because the lower impulse rose
    Resistless as a mountain torrent,—

Resistless to a human will,
    But not to strength that had been given,

Had he but grasped the anchor true
    Of "correspondence fixed wi' heaven."
Ah well! he failed. Yet let us look
    Through tears upon our sinning brother,
As thankful that we are not called
    To hold the balance for each other!
And never lips than his have pled
    More tenderly and pitifully
To leave the erring heart with Him
    Who made it, and will judge it truly.
Nay, more, it is no idle dream
    That we have heard a voice from heaven:
"Behold, *this heart hath loved much,*
    And much to it shall be forgiven!"
      —AGNES MAULE MACHAR, "An Evening with
      Burns," *Century Magazine*, Jan. 1884, p. 479

Sir,—Among men of Genius, and especially among Poets, there are some to whom we turn with a peculiar and unfeigned affection; there are others whom we admire rather than love. By some we are won with our will, by others conquered against our desire. It has been your peculiar fortune to capture the hearts of a whole people—a people not usually prone to praise, but devoted with a personal and patriotic loyalty to you and to your reputation. In you every Scot who *is* a Scot sees, admires, and compliments Himself, his ideal self—independent, fond of whiskey, fonder of the lassies; you are the true representative of him and of his nation. Next year will be the hundredth since the press of Kilmarnock brought to light its solitary master-piece, your Poems; and next year, therefore, methinks, the revenue will receive a welcome accession from the abundance of whiskey drunk in your honor. It is a cruel thing for any of your countrymen to feel that, where all the rest love, he can only admire; where all the rest are idolaters, he may not bend the knee; but stands apart and beats upon his breast, observing, not adoring—a critic. Yet to some of us—petty souls, perhaps, and envious—that loud indiscriminating praise of "Robbie Burns" (for so they style you in their Changehouse familiarity) has long been ungrateful; and, among the treasures of your songs, we venture to select and even to reject. So it must be! We cannot all love Haggis, nor "painch, tripe, and thairm," and all those rural dainties which you celebrate as "warm-reekin, rich!" "Rather too rich," as the Young Lady said on an occasion recorded by Sam Weller.

    Auld Scotland wants nae skinking ware
      That jaups in luggies;
    But, if ye wish her gratefu' prayer,
      Gie her a Haggis!

You *have* given her a Haggis, with a vengeance, and her "gratefu' prayer" is yours forever. But if even an eternity of partridge may pall on the epicure, so of Haggis, too, as of all earthly delights, cometh satiety at last. And yet what a glorious Haggis it is—the more emphatically rustic and even Fescennine part of your verse! We have had many a rural bard since Theocritus "watched the visionary flocks," but you are the only one of them all who has spoken the sincere Doric. Yours is the talk of the byre and the plough-tail; yours is that large utterance of the early hinds. Even Theocritus minces matters, save where Lacon and Comatas quite outdo the swains of Ayrshire. "But thee, Theocritus, wha matches?" you ask, and yourself out-match him in this wide rude region, trodden only by the rural Muse. "*Thy* rural loves are nature's sel';" and the wooer of Jean Armour speaks more like a true shepherd than the elegant Daphnis of the "Oaristys."

    Indeed it is with this that moral critics of your life

reproach you, forgetting, perhaps, that in your amours you were but as other Scotch ploughmen and shepherds of the past and present. Ettrick may still, with Afghanistan, offer matter for idyls, as Mr. Carlyle (your antithesis, and the complement of the Scotch character) supposed; but the morals of Ettrick are those of rural Sicily in old days, or of Mossgiel in your days. Over these matters the Kirk, with all her power, and the Free Kirk too, have had absolutely no influence whatever. To leave so delicate a topic, you were but as other swains, or as "that birkie ca'd a lord," Lord Byron; only you combined (in certain of your letters) a libertine theory with your practice; you poured out in song your audacious raptures, your half-hearted repentance, your shame, and your scorn. You spoke the truth about rural lives and loves. We may like it, or dislike it; but we cannot deny the verity.—ANDREW LANG, "To Robert Burns," *Letters to Dead Authors*, 1886

If the poetry of Cowper belongs to our national school, that of Burns is yet more racy of the soil. He was more fortunately circumstanced for poetry, though he had more to contend with. The period at which he lived furnished materials sufficiently poetical, when presented to his keen insight and vivid sensibilities; and Burns was luckily without that smattering of learning which often leads men from what surrounds them, without enabling them truly to appreciate the spirit of another age. He felt deeply; and he affected nothing foreign to his genius. Song and ballad, and light tale and humorous dialogue, the forms of composition with which the neighbourhood was familiar,—with these, while he "unlocked his heart" he also interpreted that of his country. Most of those qualities which were distributed among his countrymen met in his larger being, or were embraced by his sympathies. It is not chiefly the romantic side of the Scotch character which was represented in Burns,—its imagination, its patriotism, its zealous affectionateness, its love of the legendary, the marvellous and the ancient,—that part, in fact, which belongs most to the highlands: he was more amply furnished with the stronger lowland qualities,—sense, independence, courageous perseverance, shrewdness, and humour, a retentive heart, and a mind truthful alike when fully expressed or when partially reserved. These qualities were united in his abundant nature; and his poetic temperament freed them from the limitations which belong to every character formed upon a local type. The consequence is that his songs are sung at the hearth and on the mountain-side; his pathos is felt and his humour applauded by the village circle; his sharp descriptions and shrewd questions on grave matters are treated as indulgently by ministers of the "National Assembly," the "Free Kirk," and "orthodox dissenters," as Boccaccio's stories once were by the Italian clergy; and for the lonely traveller from the South the one small volume which contains his works is the best of guidebooks,—not indeed to noted spots, legendary or famed for beauty,—but to the manners, the moral soul, and the heart of the Scotch people. Burns is emphatically the most national of poets. —AUBREY DE VERE, "The Two Chief Schools of English Poetry," *Essays Chiefly on Poetry*, 1887, Vol. 2, pp. 120–22

It has always been a mystery to me why Walter Scott stands so low in the estimation of the present race of Scotsmen all over the world, and why Robert Burns, a greatly inferior genius, stands so high. Is it because the majority of the Scotch people are so ultra-democratic that they cannot forgive Scott for being an aristocrat; and that they almost worship Burns because he was born and nurtured and died in poverty, because he was an ultra-plebeian, earning his scanty and precarious bread by the sweat of his brow? Or do the multitude, in all countries, love

their heroes all the more because of their conspicuous human frailties, and have nothing but cold respect for the great men who are only virtuous and respectable?—CHARLES MACKAY, *Through the Long Day*, 1887, Vol. 1, pp. 147–48

In respect of genius, I think it is now universally admitted that our Ayrshire bard has gained for himself, by the number, the variety, and the brilliancy of his productions, a place in the first rank of the great singers of the intellectual world,—Pindar, Chaucer, Horace, Hafiz, Goethe, Béranger, Moore, and if there be any others who enjoy an equally wide recognition. Whatever qualities are necessary to make a lyric poet,—and in the term lyrical we include not only songs in the proper sense composed to be sung, but, for want of a better word, idylls, sketches of character, and, it may be, satirical sideshots, and other short poems meant to be read,—these qualities Burns possessed with a complete equipment; and in addition to these, he was distinguished by certain great human qualities, not always present in great singers, which add the stamp of a vigorous and manly intellect to the charm of a nice emotional sensibility. The fire and fervour without which lyrical poetry is scarce worthy of the name, Burns possessed in a high degree; but it was not merely fire from within, consuming itself in the glow of some special pet enthusiasm, but it was a fire that went out contagiously and seized on whatever fuel it might find in the motley fair of the largest human life. If ever there was a song-writer who could say with the most catholic comprehensiveness in the words of the old comedian, "*I am a man, and all things human are kin to me,*" it was Robert Burns. In this respect he is the Shakespeare of lyric poetry. Some have thought, indeed, that in respect of the fine objective eye, and power of self-transmutation, shown in "The Jolly Beggars," and not a few others of his poems, had he lived his genius might have risen to the dignity of the regular drama. Possibly; but I am inclined to think that, however quick his eye for dramatic peculiarities of character, and however far he was from being the votary of a purely subjective sensibility, the action of his mind was deficient in that continuity of persistent effort which enables a man to build up into a firm structure the complex materials of a drama. In connection with his power of seizing the striking features of character, must be mentioned his tremendous force as a satirist,—for a satirist of the most pungent order unquestionably he was,—too much, in fact, for his own peaceable march through life, and too much sometimes, as we have seen, for his own pleasant reflections on his deathbed, but not too much for public correction and reproof when, as in the case of "Holy Willie" and "The Holy Fair," the lash was wisely and effectively wielded. His admiring friend Mr Ramsay of Ochtertyre, anxious that his genius might reap sweet fruit with as little of the bitter element as possible, wrote to him with an earnest admonition, "to keep clear of the thorny walk of satire, which makes a man a hundred enemies for one friend;" and this was, no doubt, good advice. Only in the passionate love of the beautiful, and the reverential admiration of the sublime, can true poetry find its life-breath; but a satirical fling occasionally at dominant follies, seasoned with kindliness, is perfectly within the province of the poet in a secondary way, when touching on matters that cannot be avoided, and that deserve no better treatment. A song-writer, as we have said, must always be a warm-hearted man,—a cold song is inconceivable; but he is not always a strong man,—he may be weak, with all his warmth. Not so Burns. He was emphatically a strong man; there was, as Carlyle says, "a certain rugged sterling worth about him," which makes his songs as good as sermons sometimes, and sometimes as good as battles. And it was this notable amount of backbone, and force of arm, sensibly felt in his utterances, which gave to his pathos and his tenderness such healthy grace, and such rare freedom from anything that savoured of sentimentality. In Burns the most delicate sensibility to beauty was harmoniously combined with the firmest grip and the most manly stoutheartedness. This sensibility, of course, showed itself most largely in the electric power constantly exercised over him by the presence of God's great masterpiece of creative skill, a lovely woman; but the heather-bell, and the field daisy, and every grassy slope and wooded fringe and wimpling brook of bonnie Ayrshire, were ever as dear to his heart as they were near to his footstep. Nor was it the Platonic admiration of the beautiful only that moved him to sing. The Christian element of pity also had a deep fount in his rich human heart, and a tear of common-blooded affinity was ever ready to be dropt, not only over the sorrows of an injured woman, but over the pangs of a hunted hare or the terror of a startled fieldmouse. Add to all this, extraordinary quickness of apprehension, great vividness of imagination, and great powers of rhythmical utterance, and you have in the Ayrshire ploughman every element that goes to equip a master-spirit in the noble craft of song-writing. But there were also in the composition of Burns certain grand general human qualities which, though not necessary to the highest excellence of the lyrical Muse, are of a nature to adorn and to commend what they cannot create, and to extort admiration from persons the furthest removed from anything that savours of poetical inspiration. First, of course, there came the commendation that he was a man of good personal aspect and manly presentment. He had none of the pale cast of countenance that men of action expect to find in the poet and the philosopher; he was healthy and robust, and could handle the plough or the flail as vigorously as the pen. Then, again, his general vigour of mind was as notable as his vigour of body; he was as strong in thought as intense in emotion. If inferior to Coleridge in ideal speculation, to Wordsworth in harmonious contemplation, and to Southey in book-learning, in all that concerns living men and human life and human society he was extremely sharp-sighted, and not only wise in penetrating to the inmost springs of human thought and sentiment, but in the judgment of conduct eminently shrewd and sagacious; gifted, in the highest degree, with that fundamental virtue of all sound Scotsmen, common-sense, without which great genius in full career is apt to lead a man astray from his surroundings, and make him most a stranger to that with which in common life he ought to be most familiar. One notable feature in his genius—a feature which has not seldom been wanting even in the greatest of minds—is humour, a certain sportive fence of the soul delighting in the significant conjunction of contraries, a quality peculiarly Scotch, and which in Scotsmen seems a counterpoise graciously provided by Nature to that overcharge of thoughtfulness and seriousness which so strikingly contrasts them with their Hibernian cousins across the channel. Burns also was strong in wit, a domain in which Scotsmen generally are weak,—kindred qualities, no doubt, in their root, but in their expression diverse, wit acting by points and by flashes, humour by a general breadth of playful light in the moral atmosphere of the man. Another quality Burns possessed in an eminent degree, a quality which tended to make him the idol of his countrymen, and that was patriotism, a virtue which, as Carlyle remarks, was in the days of Hume and Robertson and Blair anything but common in the literary atmosphere of Scotland. The great Scottish writers of those days, he remarks, had no Scottish culture, scarcely even English; it was almost exclusively French. Finally, let us note what in other walks of literature might have operated as a serious disadvantage, viz., his peasant breeding and rustic habitude; for in the domain of popular song, the familiar intercourse with nature and the natural forms of human life, has a saving virtue to keep a man free from that crop of splendid affectations and dainty conceits, which the hot pressure of literary competition in an age of highly stimulated culture seldom fails to produce.—JOHN STUART BLACKIE, *Life of Robert Burns*, 1888, pp. 157–61

Sweet Singer that I loe the maist
O' ony, sin' wi' eager haste
I smacket bairn-lips ower the taste
    O' hinnied sang,
I hail thee, though a blessed ghaist
    In Heaven lang!

For, weel I ken, nae cantie phrase,
Nor courtly airs, nor lairdly ways,
Could gar me freer blame, or praise,
    Or proffer hand,
Where "Rantin' Robbie" and his lays
    Thegither stand.

And sae these hamely lines I send,
Wi' jinglin' words at ilka end,
In echo o' the sangs that wend
    Frae thee to me
Like simmer-brooks, wi' mony a bend
    O' wimplin' glee.

In fancy, as, wi' dewy een,
I part the clouds aboon the scene
Where thou wast born, and peer atween,
    I see nae spot
In a' the Hielands half sae green
    And unforgot!

I see nae storied castle-hall,
Wi' banners flauntin' ower the wall
And serf and page in ready call,
    Sae grand to me
As ane puir cotter's hut, wi' all
    Its poverty.

There where the simple daisy grew
Sae bonnie sweet, and modest, too,
Thy liltin' filled its wee head fu'
    O' sic a grace,
It aye is weepin' tears o' dew
    Wi' droopit face.

Frae where the heather bluebells fling
Their sangs o' fragrance to the Spring,
To where the lavrock soars to sing,
    Still lives thy strain,
For a' the birds are twittering
    Sangs like thine ain.

And aye, by light o' sun or moon,
By banks o' Ayr, or Bonnie Doon,
The waters lilt nae tender tune
    But sweeter seems
Because they poured their limpid rune
    Through a' thy dreams.

Wi' brimmin' lip, and laughin' ee,
Thou shookest even Grief wi' glee,
Yet had nae niggart sympathy
    Where Sorrow bowed,
But gavest a' thy tears as free
    As a' thy gowd.

And sae it is we loe thy name
To see bleeze up wi' sic a flame,
That a' pretentious stars o' fame

Maun blink asklent,
To see how simple worth may shame
Their brightest glent.
—JAMES WHITCOMB RILEY, "To Robert Burns,"
1888

Adequate length of days is indispensable to the production of any monumental work. Milton spent nearly as much time as was granted for the whole mortal career of Burns in what he regarded as a mere apprenticeship to the art of poetry. It is indispensable too that opportunity should be granted as well as time. Those Greek philosophers, whose superb wisdom, discredited for a while by the youthful self-assurance of modern science, is again enforcing recognition, insist upon nothing so much as the need of σχολή to the noble mind. In this respect Burns was still more unfortunate than in the matter of time. His thirty-seven years of life were shorter for effective purposes of art than the nine-and-twenty of Shelley, hardly longer than the five-and-twenty of Keats.

The crushing weight of circumstance becomes evident when we contemplate his career from his first introduction to the world till his death. A period of ten years passed between the publication of the Kilmarnock edition and the closing of the grave. For the purposes of poetry they ought to have been far more valuable than all the time that went before. They did not prove so. The cause must lie either in the man or his environment. The man was not blameless; but it was not he who was chiefly to blame. Few probably who study Burns will arrive at the conclusion that his was one of those minds which bloom early and fade early. A shrewd observer remarked of his great countryman and successor, Scott, that his sense was even more extraordinary than his genius. Strange as it may seem to many, the same assertion may be made with only a little less truth of Burns. He possessed a clear, penetrating, logical intellect, a sound and vigorous judgment. Once and again in his poems he delights the idealist with his flashes of inspiration; but just as frequently he captivates the man of common sense, who finds his own sober views of life expressed by the poet with infinitely more of force and point than he could give them. But sagacity of judgment and strength of reason are qualities which do not soon decay, which, on the contrary, seldom, in a rich mind, reach their full maturity till an age later than Burns ever saw. And the poems, when closely examined, give no countenance to the notion that Burns's mind was unprogressive. It is rather the limited quantity of the work and the fugitive character of the pieces that occasion disappointment. There is no sustained flight, there are rarely even pieces as long as he had written in his earlier days. On occasion, it is true, as in "Tam o' Shanter," he proves that he can equal anything he had done before; but as a rule he contents himself with the lyric cry, the expression of the moment's emotion in song. It was unfortunately all that increasing responsibilities and cankering disquiet left possible for him. Even in his early manhood Burns had little enough of peace of mind; but he had more than he ever afterwards enjoyed. He had given fewer "hostages to fortune"; he had youthful buoyancy to lift him above his troubles; and the result is seen in the fact that, notwithstanding his youth, his work then is wider in its range than it ever was in his more mature years.

The literary work of Burns is divisible into two periods. The first ends with the publication of the Kilmarnock volume; the second covers the rest of his life. The division is justified by the marked difference in the character of the work produced in the two periods. In the earlier, satires, pictures of rural life, and familiar epistles predominate; in the later, and

in an always increasing degree as time passed, songs take the first place. In each period there is of course an intermixture of the work characteristic of the other; but the dominant note in either case is unmistakeable.

There has always been diversity of opinion as to the relative merits of the two classes of poems, or what comes to much the same thing, the two periods. Perhaps, on the whole, the loss of the songs would be the more irreparable; but it may be questioned whether the miscellaneous poems do not contain more conclusive evidence of the greatness of the poet. The poems composed previous to the first visit to Edinburgh display nearly all Burns's highest powers—his humour, his satire, his pathos, the force and truth of his style, his insight into nature. In so young a man nothing is more remarkable than their wide range. The scathing satire of "Holy Willie's Prayer," the humour tinged with pathos of the "Address to the Deil," the poetic feeling mingling with the ludicrous in "Death and Dr. Hornbook," the elevation of "The Vision," the beautiful descriptions of simple rural peace and piety in "The Cotter's Saturday Night," the sympathy and exquisite purity of style in the verses to the mouse and the daisy, the shrewdness and sober-minded wisdom of the "Epistle to a Young Friend," the astonishing self-knowledge of "The Bard's Epitaph"—these display a range and variety of power which few poets have equalled.—HUGH WALKER, *Three Centuries of Scottish Literature*, 1893, Vol. 2, pp. 147–50

Burns died in 1796, and in the years that correspond to these, a century ago, he was dragging out his hard life to a bitter close. We are near, then, to the centenary of his death; and his fame stands, beyond question, higher than ever; and a fame, let us remember, not of the coteries, but, so to speak, of the equator. That fire was in him, indeed, which though it consumes, casts its reflection far into time. Trying everything in its flame, he suffered and was soon spent; he tried life, and its passions, and its care and delight, and sang them in immortal rhymes full of tears and laughter, and died ere he was forty.

Before we take to moralising him, and nothing is so easy, let us remember that the same passions which led him astray, sped and fired his rhymes. It has been the common responsibility of his biographers to point out how differently he might have lived, how much more wisely he might have ordered his days. More wisely, perhaps, but not so well. There is a diviner economy in these things than we have come to allow. Burns, like Shelley, like Heine, was what he was because he followed his genius. If for these and others like them; lovers of beauty and delight, spoilt children of a fickle mother—the Muse, poets and prodigals, the cup in the end is bitter: they must still drain it. Without it they would not fulfil their destiny, and die that they might live. Better men they might have been, but worse poets,—less moving, less passionate, less instinct with the pity and the delight of life.

Without Burns' fatal love for Mary Campbell, we should not have had the song "Highland Mary," and the lines to Mary in Heaven. Without the incredible episode of his appearance on the Cutty Stool, we should not have had the Epistle to Rankine and other of the poems which followed, inspired first of all by the smart under a crude church discipline. Without those terrible orgies in low taverns, when on occasion Burns locked the door that no roysterer might escape, we should not have had "Tam o' Shanter" and "The Jolly Beggars."

How much better to understand a poet like Burns, whose heart was great, too great indeed for its narrow environment;— to understand him, than take to condemning him for what, his

condition and opportunities being what they were, he could no
more help, than the fire can refrain from kindling. And to
understand him, it is enough to read his life sympathetically,
with a keen eye to his daily cares and circumstance.—ERNEST
RHYS, "Introduction" to *The Lyric Poems of Robert Burns*,
1895, pp. 9–10

A fire of fierce and laughing light
That clove the shuddering heart of night
Leapt earthward, and the thunder's might
    That pants and yearns
Made fitful music round its flight:
    And earth saw Burns.

The joyous lightning found its voice
And bade the heart of wrath rejoice
And scorn uplift a song to voice
    The imperial hate
That smote the god of base men's choice
    At God's own gate.

Before the shrine of dawn, wherethrough
The lark rang rapture as she flew,
It flashed and fired the darkling dew:
    And all that heard
With love or loathing hailed anew
    A new day's word.

The servants of the lord of hell,
As though their lord had blessed them, fell
Foaming at mouth for fear, so well
    They knew the lie
Wherewith they sought to scan and spell
    The unsounded sky.

The god they made them in despite
Of man and woman, love and light,
Strong sundawn and the starry night,
    The lie supreme,
Shot through with song, stood forth to sight
    A devil's dream.

And he that bent the lyric bow
And laid the lord of darkness low
And bade the fire of laughter glow
    Across his grave,
And bade the tides above it flow,
    Wave hurtling wave,

Shall he not win from latter days
More than his own could yield of praise?
Ay, could the sovereign singer's bays
    Forsake his brow,
The warrior's, won on stormier ways,
    Still clasp it now.

He loved, and sang of love: he laughed,
And bade the cup whereout he quaffed
Shine as a planet, fore and aft,
    And left and right,
And keen as shoots the sun's first shaft
    Against the night.

But love and wine were moon and sun
For many a fame long since undone,
And sorrow and joy have lost and won
    By stormy turns
As many a singer's soul, if none
    More bright than Burns.

And sweeter far in grief or mirth
Have songs as glad and sad of birth
Found voice to speak of wealth or dearth
    In joy of life:
But never song took fire from earth

More strong for strife.
The daisy by his ploughshare cleft,
The lips of women loved and left,
The griefs and joys that weave the weft
    Of human time,
With craftsman's cunning, keen and deft,
    He carved in rhyme.

But Chaucer's daisy shines a star
Above his ploughshare's reach to mar,
And mightier vision gave Dunbar
    More strenuous wing
To hear around all sins that are
    Hell dance and sing.

And when such pride and power of trust
In song's high gift to arouse from dust
Death, and transfigure love or lust
    Through smiles or tears
In golden speech that takes no rust
    From cankering years,

As never spake but once in one
Strong star-crossed child of earth and sun,
Villon, made music such as none
    May praise or blame,
A crown of starrier flower was won
    Than Burns may claim.

But never, since bright earth was born
In rapture of the enkindling morn,
Might godlike wrath and sunlike scorn
    That was and is
And shall be while false weeds are worn
    Find word like his.

Above the rude and radiant earth
That heaves and glows from firth to firth
In vale and mountain, bright in dearth
    And warm in wealth,
Which gave his fiery glory birth
    By chance and stealth,

Above the storms of praise and blame
That blur with mist his lustrous name,
His thunderous laughter went and came,
    And lives and flies;
The roar that follows on the flame
    When lightning dies.

Earth, and the snow-dimmed heights of air,
And water winding soft and fair
Through still sweet places, bright and bare,
    By bent and byre,
Taught him what hearts within them were:
    But his was fire.
    —ALGERNON CHARLES SWINBURNE, "Robert
    Burns," *Nineteenth Century*, Feb. 1896, pp.
    181–84

By virtue of his ardent and undisciplined temperament, by his
peasant origin and his experience of the sufferings of the poor,
by that pride of manhood and of genius which made him feel
himself an equal of prince or peer, by the zeal of his
humanitarian sympathies, by his sentimental Jacobitism and
his imaginative enthusiasm for the traditions of Scottish
independence, by the fact that he belonged to the democratic
Presbyterian Church and sympathized with the party of spiritual revolt, Burns was fitted to be a spokesman of the passions
of the time. The passions of the time, for doctrine and theory
took little hold on the mind of Burns until they were caught
into the kindling heat of passion.—EDWARD DOWDEN, *The
French Revolution and English Literature*, 1897, p. 146

It is of importance that we recognize the fact that in Burns the two literary estates, English and Scottish, were united. Until his time there was a sharp distinction between Scottish and English literature; but after him the literature of the two countries became one, both in nature and in name. This was but natural, when we consider that something of the original impulse which moved Burns's genius was English.

When the riches of this noble Scottish house, and of that sister house of Chaucer, Spenser, Shakespeare, and Milton, awaited union in a royal heir, there came a peasant lad from the "auld clay biggin'" in Ayrshire, who, with the simple and graceful dignity of one of nature's noblemen, claimed his own, and there was added a new hereditary peer to the House of Fame.—ANDREW J. GEORGE, *Carlyle's Essay on Burns*, 1897, pp. 114–15

⟨. . .⟩ and in all departments of life among the general the Kirk of Scotland was a paramount influence, and, despite the intrusion of some generous intelligences, was largely occupied with the work of narrowing the minds, perverting the instincts, and constraining the spiritual and social liberties of its subjects. In 1759, however, there was secreted the certainty of a revulsion against its ascendency; for that year saw the birth of the most popular poet, and the most anti-clerical withal, that Scotland ever bred. He came of the people on both sides; he had a high courage, a proud heart, a daring mind, a matchless gift of speech, an abundance of humour and wit and fire; he was a poet in whom were quintessentialized the elements of the Vernacular Genius, in whose work the effects and the traditions of the Vernacular School, which had struggled back into being in the Kirk's despite, were repeated with surpassing brilliancy; and in the matter of the Kirk he did for the people a piece of service equal and similar to that which was done on other lines and in other spheres by Hutcheson and Hume and Adam Smith. He was apostle and avenger as well as maker. He did more than give Scotland songs to sing and rhymes to read: he showed that laughter and the joy of life need be no crimes, and that freedom of thought and sentiment and action is within the reach of him that will stretch forth his hand to take it. He pushed his demonstration to extremes; often his teaching has been grossly misread and misapprehended; no doubt, too, he died of his effort—and himself. But most men do as they must—not as they will. It was Burns's destiny, as it was Byron's in his turn, to be "the passionate and dauntless soldier of a forlorn hope;" and if he fell in midassault, he found, despite the circumstances of his passing, the best death man can find. He had faults and failings not a few. But he was ever a leader among men; and if the manner of his leading were not seldom reckless, and he did some mischief, and gave the Fool a great deal of what passes for good Scripture for his folly, it will be found in the long-run that he led for truth—the truth which "maketh free;" so that the Scotland he loved so well and took such pride in honouring could scarce have been the Scotland she is, had he not been.—W. E. HENLEY, "Robert Burns: Life, Genius, Achievement," *The Complete Poetical Works of Robert Burns*, 1897, Vol. 1, pp. 13–14

A stranger freak of burgess criticism is every-day fare in the odd world peopled by the biographers of Robert Burns. The nature of Burns, one would think, was simplicity itself; it could hardly puzzle a ploughman, and two sailors out of three would call him brother. But he lit up the whole of that nature by his marvellous genius for expression, and grave personages have been occupied ever since in discussing the dualism of his character, and professing to find some dark mystery in the existence of this, that, or the other trait—a love of pleasure, a

hatred of shams, a deep sense of religion. It is common human nature, after all, that is the mystery, but they seem never to have met with it, and treat it as if it were the poet's eccentricity. They are all agog to worship him, and when they have made an image of him in their own likeness, and given it a tin-pot head that exactly hits their taste, they break into noisy lamentation over the discovery that the original was human, and had feet of clay. They deem "Mary in Heaven" so admirable that they could find it in their hearts to regret that she was ever on earth. This sort of admirers constantly refuses to bear a part in any human relationship; they ask to be fawned on, or trodden on, by the poet while he is in life; when he is dead they make of him a candidate for godship, and heckle him. It is a misfortune not wholly without its compensations that most great poets are dead before they are popular. —WALTER RALEIGH, *Style*, 1897, pp. 76–77

Burns, like Homer, is not merely a poet, but a literature. He has succeeded in fulfilling the old savage ideal—he has eaten up all his predecessors, and become possessed of their united powers. It is useless to haggle overmuch about what he borrowed: one can only envy the gigantic luck of his chance. —FRANCIS THOMPSON, "Mr. Henley's *Burns*," *Academy*, March 6, 1897, p. 274

When Burns's poems, therefore, came out, they gave a startling revelation of the power of expression which lay in the despised "vulgar dialect"—its picturesqueness of word and epithet, its capacity to give language to pathos, satire, and humour, its power to utter any mood and feeling with verve and vividness when wielded by one who was at once a master of his native speech and a poet. Very soon it was felt that what had fast been becoming a provincial patois had again become a great written language.—HENRY GREY GRAHAM, "Robert Burns," *Scottish Men of Letters in the Eighteenth Century*, 1901, pp. 382–83

Works

The following trifles are not the production of the Poet, who, with all the advantages of learned art, and perhaps amid the elegancies and idlenesses of upper life, looks down for a rural theme, with an eye to Theocrites or Virgil. To the Author of this, these and other celebrated names (their countrymen) are, in their original languages, 'a fountain shut up, and a book sealed.' Unacquainted with the necessary requisites for commencing Poet by rule, he sings the sentiments and manners he felt and saw in himself and his rustic compeers around him, in his and their native language. Though a Rhymer from his earliest years, at least from the earliest impulses of the softer passions, it was not till very lately that the applause, perhaps the partiality, of Friendship, wakened his vanity so far as to make him think anything of his was worth showing; and none of the following works were ever composed with a view to the press. To amuse himself with the little creations of his own fancy, amid the toil and fatigues of a laborious life; to transcribe the various feelings, the loves, the griefs, the hopes, the fears, in his own breast; to find some kind of counterpoise to the struggles of a world, always an alien scene, a task uncouth to the poetical mind; these were his motives for courting the Muses, and in these he found Poetry to be its own reward.

Now that he appears in the public character of an Author, he does it with fear and trembling. So dear is fame to the rhyming tribe, that even he, an obscure, nameless Bard, shrinks aghast at the thought of being branded as 'An impertinent blockhead, obtruding his nonsense on the world; and because he can make a shift to jingle a few doggerel Scotch rhymes together, looks upon himself as a Poet of no small consequence forsooth.'

It is an observation of that celebrated Poet—whose divine Elegies do honour to our language, our nation, and our species—that 'Humility has depressed many a genius to a hermit, but never raised one to fame.' If any Critic catches at the word *genius*, the Author tells him, once for all, that he certainly looks upon himself as possest of some poetic abilities, otherwise his publishing in the manner he has done, would be a manœuvre below the worst character which, he hopes, his worst enemy will ever give him: but to the genius of a Ramsay, or the glorious dawnings of the poor, unfortunate Ferguson, he, with equal unaffected sincerity, declares that, even in his highest pulse of vanity, he has not the most distant pretensions. These two justly admired Scotch Poets he has often had in his eye in the following pieces; but rather with a view to kindle at their flame, than for servile imitation.

To his Subscribers the Author returns his most sincere thanks. Not the mercenary bow over a counter, but the heart-throbbing gratitude of the Bard, conscious how much he is indebted to Benevolence and Friendship for gratifying him, if he deserves it, in that dearest wish of every poetic bosom— to be distinguished. He begs his readers, particularly the Learned and the Polite, who may honour him with a perusal, that they will make every allowance for Education and Circumstances of Life: but if, after a fair, candid, and impartial criticism, he shall stand convicted of Dulness and Nonsense, let him be done by, as he would in that case do by others—let him be condemned without mercy, to contempt and oblivion.—Robert Burns, "Preface" to *Poems Chiefly in the Scottish Dialect*, 1786

I have been much pleased with the poems of the Scottish ploughman, of which you have had specimens in the *Review*. His "Cotter's Saturday Night" has much of the same kind of merit as the *School-mistress*; and the "Daisy," and the "Mouse," which I believe you have had in the papers, I think are charming. The endearing diminutives, and the Doric rusticity of the dialect, suit such subjects extremely.—Anna Laetitia Barbauld, Letter to Dr. Aikin (Jan. 31, 1787), *The Works of Anna Laetitia Barbauld*, 1825, Vol. 2, p. 151

Some of the poems you have added in this last edition are very beautiful, particularly the "Winter Night," the "Address to Edinburgh," "Green Grow the Rashes," and the two songs immediately following, the latter of which is exquisite. By the way, I imagine you have a peculiar talent for such compositions, which you ought to indulge. No kind of poetry demands more delicacy or higher polishing. Horace is more admired on account of his Odes than all his other writings. But nothing now added is equal to your "Vision" and "Cotter's Saturday Night." In these are united fine imagery, natural and pathetic description, with sublimity of language and thought. It is evident that you already possess a great variety of expression and command of the English language; you ought, therefore, to deal more sparingly for the future in the provincial dialect; why should you, by using that, limit the number of your admirers to those who understand the Scottish, when you can extend it to all persons of taste who understand the English language? In my opinion, you should plan some larger work than any you have as yet attempted. I mean, reflect upon some proper subject, and arrange the plan in your mind, without beginning to execute any part of it till you have studied most of

the best English poets, and read a little more of history.—John Moore, Letter to Robert Burns (May 23, 1787)

I intended writing you last night, but happening to lift the "Cotter's Saturday Night," it was impossible for me to close the book without reading it, tho' for the five hundred time. Do, I beg you, try if you can make anything now like it. I'm sure no one else I have ever seen can; but I'll say no more of it, or I could speak of nothing else.—Frances Dunlop, Letter to Robert Burns (Sept. 23, 1789)

Among the serious poems of Burns, "The Cotter's Saturday Night" is perhaps entitled to the first rank. "The Farmer's Ingle" of Fergusson evidently suggested the plan of this poem, as has been already mentioned; but after the plan was formed, Burns trusted entirely to his own powers for the execution. Fergusson's poem is certainly very beautiful. It has all the charms which depend on rural characters and manners happily portrayed, and exhibited under circumstances highly grateful to the imagination. "The Farmer's Ingle" begins with describing the return of evening. The toils of the day are over, and the farmer retires to his comfortable fire-side. The reception which he and his men-servants receive from the careful housewife, is pleasingly described. After their supper is over, they begin to talk on the rural events of the day.

> 'Bout kirk and market eke their tales gae on,
>   How *Jock* woo'd *Jenny* here to be his bride;
> And there how *Marion* for a bastart son,
>   Upo' the cutty-stool was forced to ride,
> The waefu' scauld o' our *Mess John* to bide.

The "Guidame" is next introduced as forming a circle round the fire, in the midst of her grand-children, and while she spins from the rock, and the spindle plays on her "russet lap," she is relating to the young ones tales of witches and ghosts. The poet exclaims,

> O mock na this my friends! but rather mourn,
>   Ye in life's brawest spring wi' reason clear,
> Wi' eild our idle fancies a' return,
>   And dim our dolefu' days wi' bairnly fear;
> The mind's aye *cradled* when the *grave* is near.

In the mean time the farmer, wearied with the fatigues of the day, stretches himself at length on the *settle*, a sort of rustic couch, which extends on one side of the fire, and the cat and house-dog leap upon it to receive his caresses. Here, resting at his ease, he gives his directions to his men-servants for the succeeding day. The house-wife follows his example, and gives her orders to the maidens. By degrees the oil in the cruise begins to fail; the fire runs low; sleep steals on this rustic group; and they move off to enjoy their peaceful slumbers. The poet concludes by bestowing his blessing on the "husbandman and all his tribe."

This is an original and truly interesting pastoral. It possesses every thing required in this species of composition. We might have perhaps said, every thing that it admits, had not Burns written his "Cotter's Saturday Night."

The cottager returning from his labours, has no servants to accompany him, to partake of his fare, or to receive his instructions. The circle which he joins, is composed of his wife and children only; and if it admits of less variety, it affords an opportunity for representing scenes that more strongly interest the affections. The younger children running to meet him, and clambering round his knee; the elder, returning from their weekly labours with the neighbouring farmers, dutifully depositing their little gains with their parents, and receiving their father's blessing and instructions; the incidents of the courtship of Jenny, their eldest daughter, "woman grown;" are circumstances of the most interesting kind, which are most happily delineated: and after their frugal supper, the representation of these humble cottagers forming a wider circle round their hearth, and uniting in the worship of God, is a picture the most deeply affecting of any which the rural muse has ever presented to the view. Burns was admirably adapted to this delineation. Like all men of genius he was of the temperament of devotion, and the powers of memory co-operated in this instance with the sensibility of his heart, and the fervour of his imagination. "The Cotter's Saturday Night" is tender and moral, it is solemn and devotional, and rises at length into a strain of grandeur and sublimity, which modern poetry has not surpassed. The noble sentiments of patriotism with which it concludes, correspond with the rest of the poem. In no age or country have the pastoral muses breathed such elevated accents, if the *Messiah* of Pope be excepted, which is indeed a pastoral in form only. It is to be regretted that Burns did not employ his genius on other subjects of the same nature, which the manners and customs of the Scottish peasantry would have amply supplied. Such poetry is not to be estimated by the degree of pleasure which it bestows; it sinks deeply into the heart, and is calculated, far beyond any other human means, for giving permanence to the scenes and the characters it so exquisitely describes.—JAMES CURRIE, *The Life of Robert Burns*, 1800

Burns' songs are better than Bulwer's Epics.— CHARLOTTE BRONTË, Letter to W. S. Williams (April 2, 1849)

The rural descriptions and the reflections on the outer world contained in the poetry of Cowper, mark the highest limit which the feeling for Nature had reached in England at the close of last century. But the stream of natural poetry in England, which up to that time had been fed from purely native sources, and which had flowed on through all last century with ever increasing volume, received toward the close of the century affluents from other regions, which tinged the color and modified the direction of its future current. Of these affluents the first and most powerful was the poetry of Burns. It is strange to think that Cowper and he were singing their songs at the same time, each in his own way describing the scenery that surrounded him, and yet that they hardly knew of each other's existence.

Burns not only lived in a world of nature, of society, and of feeling, wholly alien to that of Cowper, but he took for his models far different poets. These models were the Scottish rhymers, Allan Ramsay, Ferguson, and the unknown singers of the native ballads, and especially of the popular songs, of his country. Proud and self-reliant as Burns was, he everywhere speaks of Ramsay and Ferguson as his models and superiors. From these he took the forms of his poems, though into these forms he poured a new and stronger inspiration. Burns's "Halloween" is framed on a model of Ferguson's poem called "Leith Races," and "The Cottar's Saturday Night" is evidently suggested by Ferguson's "Farmer's Ingle;" but poor Ferguson's very mundane view of happiness is, at least in the "Cottar's Saturday Night," by Burns, transfigured by a purer and nobler sentiment. Besides these Burns knew the English poets, such as Pope and Shenstone, but well for the world that he did not come too early under their influence, else we had probably lost much of what is most native and original in him. Somewhere in his later years he marvels at his own audacity in having ventured to use his native Scotch as the vehicle for poetry, and speaks as if, had he earlier known more English literature, he would not have dared to do so. Yet when he does essay to write pure English his poetry becomes only of third or fourth-rate

excellence, just as nothing can be more mawkish and vapid than Ferguson, when he makes Damon and Alexis discourse in his purely English pastorals. Only in one poem, written in pure English, does Burns attain high excellence, and that one is the "Lines to Mary in Heaven." Perhaps in nothing, except it may be in humorous or pathetic feeling, is the Scottish dialect more in place than in describing the native scenery. For, in truth, the features of every county, if possible of each district, ought to be rendered in the very words by which they are known to the natives. When instead of this they are transferred into the literary language, they have lost I know not how much of their life and individuality. If in Scottish scenery, for instance, you speak of a brook and a grove, instead of a burn or a shaw or wood, you have really robbed the locality described of all that belongs to it. The same thing holds still more of mountain scenery, in which, unless you adopt the words which the country people apply to their own hills, you had better leave them undescribed. This feeling has at last forced both poets, and all who attempt to render Highland scenery, to use the Celtic words by which the mountain lineaments are described. We must, if we would name these features at all, speak of the "corrie," the "lochan," the "balloch," and the "screetan" or "sclidder," for the book-English has no words for these things. Hence it is that Scottish Lowland scenery is never so truly and vividly described, as when Burns uses his own vernacular. And yet Burns was no merely descriptive poet. It would be difficult to name one of his poems in which description of Nature is the main object. Everywhere with him, man, his feelings and his fate, stand out in the front of his pictures, and Nature comes in as the delightful background—yet Nature loved with a love, beheld with a rapture, all the more genuine, because his pulses throbbed in such intense sympathy with man.

Three things may be noted as to the influence of Burns on men's feeling for Nature.

First, he was a more entirely open-air poet than any first-rate singer who had yet lived, and as such he dealt with Nature in a more free, close, intimate way than any English poet since the old ballad-singers. He did more to bring the hearts of men close to the outer world, and the outer world to the heart, than any former poet. His keen eye looked directly, with no intervening medium, on the face alike of Nature and of man, and embraced all creation in one large sympathy. With familiar tenderness he dwelt on the lower creatures, felt for their sufferings, as if they had been his own, and opened men's hearts to feel how much the groans of creation are needlessly increased by the indifference or cruelty of man. In Burns, as in Cowper, and in him perhaps more than in Cowper, there was a large going forth of tenderness to the lower creatures, and in their poetry this first found utterance, and in no poet since their time, so fully as in these two.

Secondly, his feeling in Nature's presence was not, as in the English poets of his time, a quiet contemplative pleasure. It was nothing short of rapture. Other more modern poets may have been thrilled with the same delight, he alone of all in the last century expressed the thrill. In this, as in other things, he is the truest herald of that strain of rejoicing in Nature, even to ecstasy, which has formed one of the finest tones in the poetry of this century.

Thirdly, he does not philosophize on Nature or her relation to man; he feels it, alike in his joyful moods and in his sorrowful. It is to him part of what he calls "the universal plan," but he nowhere reasons about the life of Nature as he often does so trenchantly about that of man.—J. C. SHAIRP, *On Poetic Interpretation of Nature*, 1877, pp. 224–30

Burns's most considerable poems, as distinct from his songs, were almost all written before he went to Edinburgh. There is, however, one memorable exception. "Tam o' Shanter," as we have seen, belongs to Ellisland days. Most of his earlier poems were entirely realistic, a transcript of the men and women and scenes he had seen and known, only lifted a very little off the earth, only very slightly idealized. But in "Tam o' Shanter" he had let loose his powers upon the materials of past experiences, and out of them he shaped a tale which was a pure imaginative creation. In no other instance, except perhaps in "The Jolly Beggars," had he done this; and in that cantata, if the genius is equal, the materials are so coarse, and the sentiment so gross, as to make it, for all its dramatic power, decidedly offensive. It is strange what very opposite judgments have been formed of the intrinsic merit of "Tam o' Shanter." Mr. Carlyle thinks that it might have been written "all but quite as well by a man, who, in place of genius, had only possessed talent; that it is not so much a poem, as a piece of sparkling rhetoric; the heart of the story still lies hard and dead," On the other hand, Sir Walter Scott has recorded this verdict: "In the inimitable tale of 'Tam o' Shanter,' Burns has left us sufficient evidence of his abilities to combine the ludicrous with the awful and even the horrible. No poet, with the exception of Shakespeare, ever possessed the power of exciting the most varied and discordant emotions with such rapid transitions. His humorous description of death in the poem on Dr. Hornbrook, borders on the terrific; and the witches' dance in the Kirk of Alloway is at once ludicrous and horrible." Sir Walter, I believe, is right, and the world has sided with him in his judgment about "Tam o' Shanter." Nowhere in British literature, out of Shakespeare, is there to be found so much of the power of which Scott speaks—that of combining in rapid transition almost contradictory emotions—if we except perhaps one of Scott's own highest creations, the tale of Wandering Willie, in *Redgauntlet*.

On the songs of Burns a volume might be written, but a few sentences must here suffice. It is in his songs that his soul comes out fullest, freest, brightest; it is as a song-writer that his fame has spread widest, and will longest last. Mr. Carlyle, not in his essay, which does full justice to Burns's songs, but in some more recent work, has said something like this, "Our Scottish son of thunder had, for want of a better, to pour his lightning through the narrow cranny of Scottish song—the narrowest cranny ever vouchsafed to any son of thunder."— The narrowest, it may be, but the most effective, if a man desires to come close to his fellow-men, soul to soul. Of all forms of literature the genuine song is the most penetrating, and the most to be remembered; and in this kind Burns is the supreme master. To make him this, two things combined. First, there was the great background of national melody and antique verse, coming down to him from remote ages, and sounding through his heart from childhood. He was cradled in a very atmosphere of melody, else he never could have sung so well. No one knew better than he did, or would have owned more feelingly, how much he owed to the old forgotten song-writers of his country, dead for ages before he lived, and lying in their unknown graves all Scotland over. From his boyhood he had studied eagerly the old tunes, and the old words where there were such, that had come down to him from the past, treasured every scrap of antique air and verse, conned and crooned them over till he had them by heart. This was the one form of literature that he had entirely mastered. And from the first he had laid it down as a rule, that the one way to catch the inspiration, and rise to the true fervour of song, was, as he phrased it, "to *sowth* the tune over and over," till the words

came spontaneously. The words of his own songs were inspired by pre-existing tunes, not composed first, and set to music afterwards. But all this love and study of the ancient songs and outward melody would have gone for nothing, but for the second element, that is the inward melody born in the poet's deepest heart, which received into itself the whole body of national song; and then when it had passed through his soul, sent it forth ennobled and glorified by his own genius.

That which fitted him to do this was the peculiar intensity of his nature, the fervid heart, the trembling sensibility, the headlong passion, all thrilling through an intellect strong and keen beyond that of other men. How mysterious to reflect that the same qualities on their emotional side made him the great songster of the world, and on their practical side drove him to ruin! The first word which Burns composed was a song in praise of his partner on the harvest-rig; the last utterance he breathed in verse was also a song—a faint remembrance of some former affection. Between these two he composed from two to three hundred. It might be wished perhaps that he had written fewer, especially fewer love songs; never composed under pressure, and only when his heart was so full he could not help singing. This is the condition on which alone the highest order of songs is born. Probably from thirty to forty songs of Burns could be named which come up to this highest standard. No other Scottish song-writer could show above four or five of the same quality. Of his songs one main characteristic is that their subjects, the substance they lay hold of, belongs to what is most permanent in humanity, those primary affections, those permanent relations of life which cannot change while man's nature is what it is. In this they are wholly unlike those songs which seize on the changing aspects of society. As the phases of social life change, these are forgotten. But no time can superannuate the subjects which Burns has sung; they are rooted in the primary strata, which are steadfast. Then as the subjects are primary, so the feeling with which Burns regards them is primary too—that is, he gives us the first spontaneous gush—the first throb of his heart, and that a most strong, simple, manly heart. The feeling is not turned over in the reflective faculty, and there artistically shaped,—not subtilized and refined away till it has lost its power and freshness; but given at first hand, as it comes warm from within. When he is at his best you seem to hear the whole song warbling through his spirit, naturally as a bird's. The whole subject is wrapped in an element of music, till it is penetrated and transfigured by it. No one else has so much of the native lilt in him. When his mind was at the white heat, it is wonderful how quickly he struck off some of his most perfect songs. And yet he could, when it was required, go back upon them, and retouch them line by line, as we saw him doing in "Ye Banks and Braes." In the best of them the outward form is as perfect as the inward music is all-pervading, and the two are in complete harmony.—J. C. SHAIRP, *Robert Burns*, 1879, pp. 201–5

The love poetry of Burns affords an abundant exemplification of nearly all the known devices peculiar to the theme. Consisting of short effusions, mainly songs, it almost entirely excludes plot-interest, occasionally there is a slight use of narrative, as in 'The Soldier's Return' and 'There was a lass and she was fair'.

In regard to description of the object of love, Burns usually depends on a few unsystematic touches, expressive of the emotion excited. Sometimes, however, he does enter on a regular enumeration of the qualities that charm; but his method even then is rather to elevate the object by comparisons, both figurative and literal, than to give any distinct impression of the personal appearance.⟨. . .⟩

Among charms to be celebrated, Burns does not overlook the mental, especially reciprocated affection. The refrain of one song is, 'She says she lo'es me best of a',' and of another, 'Kind love is in her ee'.

But the largest constituents of Burns's love songs are the expression of the lover's own feelings and the use of harmonizing circumstances. The methods employed under these heads are sufficiently varied.

The pleasure of the loved one's presence, the pain of absence, the memory of past happiness, the hope of meeting again, and the pain of unrequited love are all employed for the purpose; and these are expressed with the hyperbolical intensity appropriate to love.—ALEXANDER BAIN, *English Composition and Rhetoric*, 1888, Pt. 2, pp. 157–58

"The Cotter's Saturday Night" is included in the list of poems mentioned by Burns in his letter to Richmond, 17th February 1786; it was therefore composed between the beginning of November 1785 and that date. Gilbert Burns relates that Robert first repeated it to him in the course of a walk one Sunday afternoon. He also states that the 'hint of the plan, and the title of the poem,' were taken from Fergusson's "Farmer's Ingle."

This is true, but the piece as a whole is formed on English models. It is the most artificial and the most imitative of Burns's works. Not only is the influence of Gray's *Elegy* conspicuous, but also there are echoes of Pope, Thomson, Goldsmith, and even Milton; while the stanza, which was taken, not from Spenser, whom Burns had not then read, but from Beattie and Shenstone, is so purely English as to lie outside the range of Burns's experience and accomplishment.—W. E. HENLEY, THOMAS F. HENDERSON, *The Poetry of Robert Burns*, 1896, Vol. 1, pp. 361–62, Note

In his relation to Nature there was this great difference between Burns and his literary contemporaries and immediate predecessors, that whereas even the best of them wrote rather as pleased spectators of the country, with all its infinite variety of form and colour, of life and sound, of calm and storm, he sang as one into whose very inmost heart the power of these things had entered. For the first time in English literature the burning ardour of a passionate soul went out in tumultuous joy towards Nature. The hills and woods, the streams and dells were to Burns not merely enjoyable scenes to be visited and described. They became part of his very being. In their changeful aspects he found the counterpart of his own variable moods; they ministered to his joys, they soothed his sorrows. They yielded him a companionship that never palled, a sympathy that never failed. They kindled his poetic ardour, and became themselves the subjects of his song. He loved them with all the overpowering intensity of his affectionate nature, and his feelings found vent in an exuberance of appreciation which had never before been heard in verse.

Among the natural objects which exerted this potent sway over the poetry of Burns, the streams of Ayrshire and Nithsdale ever held a foremost place. Their banks were his favourite haunt for reverie. They were familiar to him under every change of sky and season, from firth to fell. Each feature in their seaward course was noted by his quick eye, and treasured in his loving memory. Their union of ruggedness and verdure, of sombre woods and open haughs, of dark cliff and bright meadow, of brawling current and stealthy flow, furnished that variety which captivated his fancy, and found such fitting transposition to his verse. His descriptions and allusions,

however, are never laboured and prominent; they are dashed off with the careless ease of a master-artist, whose main theme is the portrayal of human feeling. Even when the banks and braes have been the immediate source of his inspiration, Burns quickly passes from them into the world of emotion to which he makes them subservient. ⟨. . .⟩

When Burns moved from Ayrshire to Nithsdale, he found at his new home another valley and another river that could minister to his inspiration. The Nith took the place of the Ayr. But it could not wholly fill that place, for its landscape is less ample, the hills come closer down upon the valley, while the river, in its lower course, curves from side to side in a wide alluvial plain, without the variety that marks the lower part of the Ayr. We seem to recognize the influence of these differences in the allusions in the songs.

The landscapes of Burns are marked by some curious limitations. Though he was born within sight of the picturesque mountain group of Arran, it does not come within his poetic outlook. Though the 'craggy ocean pyramid' of the Clyde rose so stupendously from the firth in front of him, he makes no use of it further than to tell how 'Meg was deaf as Ailsa Craig.' Its distant grandeur does not seem to have struck his imagination. Indeed, if we examine his treatment of scenery, we may observe that it is the nearer detail that appeals to him. His pictures are exquisite foregrounds with seldom any distinct distance. But perhaps more remarkable still is the small place which the sea takes in the poetry of Burns. We must bear in mind that he was born and spent his boyhood within sight and hearing of the open Firth of Clyde. The dash of the breakers along the sandy beach behind his father's 'clay biggin' must have been one of the most familiar sounds to his young ears. Yet the allusions to the sea in his poems betray little trace of this association. They are in large measure introduced to mark the wide distance between separated friends.—SIR ARCHIBALD GEIKIE, *Types of Scenery and Their Influence on Literature*, 1898, pp. 26–31

In the preface to his first edition he takes, with other poets, a lowly view of his performance. He confesses that he has not "the advantages of learned art," and that he "does not look down for a rural theme with an eye to Theocritus or Virgil"; his purpose, says he, is "to amuse himself with the little creations of his own fancy"; but these confessions need not be taken too seriously. The oaten reed and the scrannel pipe are the professed heritage of all; and Burns's preface meant no more than the admissions of Herrick, of Milton, or of Pope. In his heart he knew himself a great artist, nor to his friends does he conceal his exultation. But he is a great artist who, happily or unhappily, has become popular, and in the devotion of the crowd his excellencies have been slurred, while his ostensible vices have appeared virtues to the over-sympathetic.

Yet the unbiassed critic has no difficulty in separating the wheat from the chaff. "The Jolly Beggars," long held unworthy the author of "The Cotter's Saturday Night," is an immortal masterpiece of melody and observation. The squalor of the piece is glorified by a style so little rustic that every word and every rhythm is fitted to its purpose. It is the literature of the street, maybe, but the literature of the street made classic for all time; and on either side of it may stand that miracle of quiet irony, "The Twa Dogs," and the grim fantasy from fairyland which is known as "Tam o' Shanter." These are works of invention which might establish a poet's claim to immortality, yet they are but a corner of Burns's achievement. In "Holy Willie's Prayer," and the other poisoned shafts launched at the Kirk, he proves himself a master of satire,—of satire that could wound and render its victim's recovery hopeless. The rarest gift remains untold,—the gift of song which, rather than the composition of epics or the building of plays, justifies the ancient proverb *poeta nascitur*. It is a gift that can neither be fostered nor controlled, and a lyrical voice is as seldom heard as a nightingale in Cheapside. Some years since the French Academy, which has never lacked courage, undertook to award a triennial prize to the worthiest song of the moment. But with all their courage they have never had a chance to make the award, and in sheer despair they are renouncing the responsibility. Yet the voice, once heard, is unmistakeable, and Burns is one of the few singers the world has known. That he regarded this one gift with seriousness is certain. So lofty was his lyric pride that he declined to accept money for his masterpieces, not, as Mr. Stevenson suggests because "his steps led downwards," but because he believed, with a touch of sentiment, that the writing of songs was above price. As we have said, he laid his hand upon whatever material he found suitable, but he himself was the first to declare his indebtedness, and the genius which transformed the hasty sketch into a marvel of music was all his own.—CHARLES WHIBLEY, "Burns," *Macmillan's Magazine*, Jan. 1898, pp. 182–83.

ROBERT BURNS
From a Letter to Dr. John Moore
August 2, 1787

We lived very poorly; I was a dextrous Ploughman for my years; and the next eldest to me was a brother, who could drive the plough very well and help me to thrash.—A Novel-Writer might perhaps have viewed these scenes with some satisfaction, but so did not I: my indignation yet boils at the recollection of the scoundrel tyrant's insolent, threatening epistles, which used to set us all in tears.—

This kind of life, the chearless gloom of a hermit with the unceasing moil of a galley-slave, brought me to my sixteenth year; a little before which period I first committed the sin of RHYME.—You know our country custom of coupling a man and woman together as Partners in the labors of Harvest.—In my fifteenth autumn, my Partner was a bewitching creature who just counted an autumn less.—My scarcity of English denies me the power of doing her justice in that language; but you know the Scotch idiom, She was a bonie, sweet, sonsie lass.—In short, she altogether unwittingly to herself, initiated me in a certain delicious Passion, which in spite of acid Disappointment, gin-horse Prudence and bookworm Philosophy, I hold to be the first of human joys, our dearest pleasure here below.—How she caught the contagion I can't say; you medical folks talk much of infection by breathing the same air, the touch, &c. but I never expressly told her that I loved her.— Indeed I did not well know myself, why I liked so much to loiter behind with her, when returning in the evening from our labors; why the tones of her voice made my heartstrings thrill like an Eolian harp; and particularly, why my pulse beat such a furious ratann when I looked and fingered over her hand, to pick out the nettle-stings and thistles.—Among her other love-inspiring qualifications, she sung sweetly; and 'twas her favorite reel to which I attempted giving an embodied vehicle in rhyme.—I was not so presumtive as to imagine that I could make verses like printed ones, composed by men who had Greek and Latin; but my girl sung a song which was said to be composed by a small country laird's son, on one of his father's maids, with whom he was in love; and I saw no reason why I

might not rhyme as well as he, for excepting smearing sheep and casting peats, his father living in the moors, he had no more Scholarcraft than I had.—

Thus with me began Love and Poesy; which at times have been my only, and till within this last twelvemonth have been my highest enjoyment.—My father struggled on till he reached the freedom in his lease, when he entered on a larger farm about ten miles farther in the country.—The nature of the bargain was such as to throw a little ready money in his hand at the commencement, otherwise the affair would have been impractible.—For four years we lived comfortably here; but a lawsuit between him and his Landlord commencing, after three years tossing and whirling in the vortex of Litigation, my father was just saved from absorption in a jail by phthisical consumption, which after two years promises, kindly stept in and snatch'd him away—"To where the wicked cease from troubling, and where the weary be at rest."

It is during this climacterick that my little story is most eventful.—I was, at the beginning of this period, perhaps the most ungainly, aukward being in the parish.—No Solitaire was less acquainted with the ways of the world.—My knowledge of ancient story was gathered from Salmon's and Guthrie's geographical grammars; my knowledge of modern manners, and of literature and criticism, I got from the *Spectator*.— These, with Pope's works, some plays of Shakespear, Tull and Dickson on Agriculture, The Pantheon, Locke's *Essay on the human understanding*, Stackhouse's *history of the bible*, Justice's British Gardiner's directory, Boyle's lectures, Allan Ramsay's works, Taylor's scripture doctrine of original sin, a select Collection of English songs, and Hervey's meditations had been the extent of my reading.—The Collection of Songs was my vade mecum. I pored over them, driving my cart or walking to labor, song by song, verse by verse; carefully noting the true tender or sublime from affectation and fustian.—I am convinced I owe much to this for my critic-craft such as it is.—

In my seventeenth year, to give my manners a brush, I went to a country dancing school—My father had an unaccountable antipathy against these meetings; and my going was, what to this hour I repent, in absolute defiance of his commands. My father, as I said before, was the sport of strong passions: from that instance of rebellion he took a kind of dislike to me, which, I believe was one cause of that dissipation which marked my future years.—I only say, Dissipation, comparative with the strictness and sobriety of Presbyterean country life; for though the will-o'-wisp meteors of thoughtless Whim were almost the sole lights of my path, yet early ingrained Piety and Virtue never failed to point me out the line of Innocence.—The great misfortune of my life was, never to have AN AIM.—I had felt early some stirrings of Ambition, but they were the blind gropins of Homer's Cyclops round the walls of his cave: I saw my father's situation entailed on me perpetual labor.—The only two doors by which I could enter the fields of fortune were, the most niggardly economy, or the little chicaning art of bargain-making: the first is so contracted an aperture, I never could squeeze myself into it; the last, I always hated the contamination of the threshold.— Thus, abandoned of aim or view in life; with a strong appetite for sociability, as well from native hilarity as from a pride of observation and remark; a constitutional hypochondriac taint which made me fly solitude; add to all these incentives to social life, my reputation for bookish knowledge, a certain wild, logical talent, and a strength of thought something like the rudiments of good sense, made me generally a welcome guest; so 'tis no great wonder that always "where two or three were met together, there was I in the midst of them."—But far beyond all the other impulses of my heart was, un penchant á l'adorable moitiée du genre humain.—My heart was compleatly tinder, and was eternally lighted up by some Goddess or other: and like every warfare in this world, I was sometimes crowned with success, and sometimes mortified with defeat.—At the plough, scythe or reap-hook I feared no competitor, and set Want at defiance; and as I never cared farther for my labors than while I was in actual exercise, I spent the evening in the way after my own heart.—A country lad rarely carries on an amour without an assisting confident.—I possessed a curiosity, zeal and intrepid dexterity in these matters which recommended me a proper Second in duels of that kind; and I dare say, I felt as much pleasure at being in the secret of half the amours in the parish, as ever did Premier at knowing the intrigues of half the courts of Europe.—

The very goosefeather in my hand seems instinctively to know the well-worn path of my imagination, the favorite theme of my song; and is with difficulty restrained from giving you a couple of paragraphs on the amours of my Compeers, the humble Inmates of the farm-house and cottage; but the grave sons of Science, Ambition or Avarice baptize these things by the name of Follies.—To the sons and daughters of labor and poverty they are matters of the most serious nature: to them, the ardent hope, the stolen interview, the tender farewell, are the greatest and most delicious part of their enjoyments.—

Another circumstance in my life which made very considerable alterations in my mind and manners was, I spent my seventeenth summer on a smuggling coast a good distance from home at a noted school, to learn Mensuration, Surveying, Dialling, &c. in which I made a pretty good progress.—But I made greater progress in the knowledge of mankind.—The contraband trade was at that time very successful; scenes of swaggering riot and roaring dissipation were as yet new to me; and I was no enemy to social life.—Here, though I learned to look unconcernedly on a large tavern-bill, and mix without fear in a drunken squabble, yet I went on with a high hand in my Geometry; till the sun entered Virgo, a month which is always a carnival in my bosom, a charming Fillette who lived next door to the school overset my Trigonomertry, and set me off in a tangent from the sphere of my studies.—I struggled on with my Sines and Co-sines for a few days more; but stepping out to the garden one charming noon, to take the sun's altitude, I met with my Angel,

> Like Proserpine gathering flowers,
> Herself a fairer flower

It was vain to think of doing any more good at school.—The remaining week I staid, I did nothing but craze the faculties of my soul about her, or steal out to meet with her; and the two last nights of my stay in the country, had sleep been a mortal sin, I was innocent.—

I returned home very considerably improved.—My reading was enlarged with the very important addition of Thomson's and Shenstone's works; I had seen mankind in a new phasis; and I engaged several of my schoolfellows to keep up a literary correspondence with me.—This last helped me much on in composition.—I had met with a collection of letters by the Wits of Queen Ann's reign, and I pored over them most devoutly.—I kept copies of any of my own letters that pleased me, and a comparison between them and the composition of most of my correspondents flattered my vanity.—I carried this whim so far that though I had not three farthings worth of business in the world, yet every post brought

me as many letters as if I had been a broad, plodding son of Day-book & Ledger.—

My life flowed on much in the same tenor till my twenty third year.—Vive l'amour et vive la bagatelle, were my sole principles of action.—The addition of two more Authors to my library gave me great pleasure; Sterne and Mᶜkenzie.—*Tristram Shandy* and the *Man of Feeling* were my bosom favorites.—Poesy was still a darling walk for my mind, but 'twas only the humour of the hour.—I had usually half a dozen or more pieces on hand; I took up one or other as it suited the momentary tone of the mind, and dismissed it as it bordered on fatigue.—My Passions when once they were lighted up, raged like so many devils, till they got vent in rhyme; and then conning over my verses, like a spell, soothed all into quiet.—None of the rhymes of those days are in print, except, Winter, a dirge, the eldest of my printed pieces; The death of Poor Mailie, John Barleycorn, And songs first, second and third: song second was the ebullition of that passion which ended the forementioned school-business.—

My twenty third year was to me an important era.—Partly thro' whim, and partly that I wished to set about doing something in life, I joined with a flax-dresser in a neighbouring town, to learn his trade and carry on the business of manufacturing and retailing flax.—This turned out a sadly unlucky affair.—My Partner was a scoundrel of the first water who made money by the mystery of thieving; and to finish the whole, while we were giving a welcoming carousal to the New year, our shop, by the drunken carelessness of my Partner's wife, took fire and was burnt to ashes; and left me like a true Poet, not worth sixpence.—I was oblidged to give up business; the clouds of misfortune were gathering thick round my father's head, the darkest of which was, he was visibly far gone in a consumption; and to crown all, a belle-fille whom I adored and who had pledged her soul to meet me in the field of matrimony, jilted me with peculiar circumstances of mortification.—The finishing evil that brought up the rear of this infernal file was my hypochondriac complaint being irritated to such a degree, that for three months I was in a diseased state of body and mind, scarcely to be envied by the hopeless wretches who have just got their mittimus, "Depart from me, ye Cursed."

From this adventure I learned something of a town-life.—But the principal thing which gave my mind a turn was, I formed a bosom-friendship with a young fellow, the first created being I had ever seen, but a hapless son of misfortune.—He was the son of a plain mechanic; but a great Man in the neighbourhood taking him under his patronage gave him a genteel education with a view to bettering his situation in life.—The Patron dieing just as he was ready to launch forth into the world, the poor fellow in despair went to sea; where after a variety of good and bad fortune, a little before I was acquainted with him, he had been set ashore by an American Privateer on the wild coast of Connaught, stript of every thing.—I cannot quit this poor fellow's story without adding that he is at this moment Captain of a large westindiaman belonging to the Thames.—

This gentleman's mind was fraught with courage, independance, Magnanimity, and every noble, manly virtue.—I loved him, I admired him, to a degree of enthusiasm; and I strove to imitate him.—In some measure I succeeded: I had the pride before, but he taught it to flow in proper channels.—His knowledge of the world was vastly superiour to mine, and I was all attention to learn.—He was the only man I ever saw who was a greater fool than myself when WOMAN was the presiding star; but he spoke of a certain fashionable failing with levity, which hitherto I had regarded with horror.—Here his friendship did me a mischief; and the consequence was, that soon after I resumed the plough, I wrote the WELCOME inclosed.—My reading was only encreased by two stray volumes of *Pamela*, and one of *Ferdinand Count Fathom*, which gave me some idea of Novels.—Rhyme, except some religious pieces which are in print, I had given up; but meeting with Fergusson's Scotch Poems, I strung anew my wildly-sounding, rustic lyre with emulating vigour.—When my father died, his all went among the rapacious hell-hounds that growl in the kennel of justice; but we made a shift to scrape a little money in the family amongst us, with which, to keep us together, my brother and I took a neighbouring farm.—My brother wanted my harebrained imagination as well as my social and amorous madness, but in good sense and every sober qualification he was far my superiour.—

I entered on this farm with a full resolution, "Come, go to, I will be wise!"—I read farming books; I calculated crops; I attended markets; and in short, in spite of "The devil, the world and the flesh," I believe I would have been a wise man; but the first year from unfortunately buying in bad seed, the second from a late harvest, we lost half of both our crops: this overset all my wisdom, and I returned "Like the dog to his vomit, and the sow that was washed to her wallowing in the mire.—"

I now began to be known in the neighbourhood as a maker of rhymes.—The first of my poetic offspring that saw the light was a burlesque lamentation on a quarrel between two rev^d Calvinists, both of them dramatis personae in my "Holy Fair."—I had an idea myself that the piece had some merit; but to prevent the worst, I gave a copy of it to a friend who was very fond of these things, and told him I could not guess who was the Author of it, but that I thought it pretty clever.—With a certain side of both clergy and laity it met with a roar of applause.—"Holy Willie's Prayer" next made its appearance, and alarmed the kirk-Session so much that they held three several meetings to look over their holy artillery, if any of it was pointed against profane Rhymers. Unluckily for me, my idle wanderings led me, on another side, point-blank within the reach of their heaviest metal.—This is the unfortunate story alluded to in my printed poem, The Lament.—'Twas a shocking affair, which I cannot yet bear to recollect; and had very nearly given me one or two of the principal qualifications for a place among those who have lost the chart and mistake the reckoning of Rationality.—I gave up my part of the farm to my brother, as in truth it was only nominally mine; and made what little preparation was in my power for Jamaica.—Before leaving my native country for ever, I resolved to publish my Poems.—I weighed my productions as impartially as in my power; I thought they had merit; and 'twas a delicious idea that I would be called a clever fellow, even though it should never reach my ears a poor Negro-driver, or perhaps a victim to that inhospitable clime gone to the world of Spirits.—I can truly say that pauvre Inconnu as I then was, I had pretty nearly as high an idea of myself and my works as I have at this moment.—It is ever my opinion that the great, unhappy mistakes and blunders, both in a rational and religious point of view, of which we see thousands daily guilty, are owing to their ignorance, or mistaken notions of themselves.—To know myself had been all along my constant study.—I weighed myself alone; I balanced myself with others; I watched every means of information how much ground I occupied both as a Man and as a Poet: I studied assiduously Nature's DESIGN where she seem'd to have intended the various LIGHTS and SHADES in my character.—I was pretty sure my Poems would meet with

some applause; but at the worst, the roar of the Atlantic would deafen the voice of Censure, and the novelty of west-Indian scenes make me forget Neglect.—

I threw off six hundred copies, of which I had got subscriptions for about three hundred and fifty.—My vanity was highly gratified by the reception I met with from the Publick; besides pocketing, all expences deducted, near twenty pounds.—This last came very seasonable, as I was about to indent myself for want of money to pay my freight.—So soon as I was master of nine guineas, the price of wafting me to the torrid zone, I bespoke a passage in the very first ship that was to sail, for

Hungry wind ruin had me in the wind

I had for some time been sculking from covert to covert under all the terrors of a Jail; as some ill-advised, ungrateful people had uncoupled the merciless legal Pack at my heels.—I had taken the last farewel of my few friends, my chest was on the road to Greenock; I had composed my last song I should ever measure in Caledonia, "The gloomy night is gathering fast," when a letter from Dr Blacklock to a friend of mine overthrew all my schemes by rousing my poetic ambition.—The Doctor belonged to a set of Critics for whose applause I had not even dared to hope.—His idea that I would meet with every encouragement for a second edition fired me so much that away I posted to Edinburgh without a single acquaintance in town, or a single letter of introduction in my pocket.—The baneful Star that had so long shed its blasting influence in my Zenith, for once made a revolution to the Nadir; and the providential care of a good God placed me under the patronage of one of his noblest creatures, the Earl of Glencairn: "Oublie moi, Grand Dieu, si jamais je l'oublie!"—

I need relate no farther.—At Edin^r I was in a new world: I mingled among many classes of men, but all of them new to me; and I was all attention "to catch the manners living as they rise."—

You can now, Sir, form a pretty near guess what sort of a Wight he is whom for some time you have honored with your correspondence.—That Fancy & Whim, keen Sensibility and riotous Passions may still make him zig-zag in his future path of life, is far from being improbable; but come what will, I shall answer for him the most determinate integrity and honor; and though his evil star should again blaze in his meridian with tenfold more direful influence, he may reluctantly tax Friendship with Pity but no more.—

THOMAS CARLYLE
From "Burns" (1828)
Critical and Miscellaneous Essays
1839–69

Burns first came upon the world as a prodigy; and was, in that character, entertained by it, in the usual fashion, with loud, vague, tumultuous wonder, speedily subsiding into censure and neglect; till his early and most mournful death again awakened an enthusiasm for him, which, especially as there was now nothing to be done, and much to be spoken, has prolonged itself even to our own time. It is true, the 'nine days' have long since elapsed; and the very continuance of this clamour proves that Burns was no vulgar wonder. Accordingly, even in sober judgments, where, as years passed by, he has come to rest more and more exclusively on his own intrinsic merits, and may now be well-nigh shorn of that casual radiance, he appears not only as a true British poet, but as one of the most considerable British men of the eighteenth century. Let it not be objected that he did little. He did much, if we consider where and how. If the work performed was small, we must remember that he had his very materials to discover; for the metal he worked in lay hid under the desert moor, where no eye but his had guessed its existence; and we may almost say, that with his own hand he had to construct the tools for fashioning it. For he found himself in deepest obscurity, without help, without instruction, without model; or with models only of the meanest sort. An educated man stands, as it were, in the midst of a boundless arsenal and magazine, filled with all the weapons and engines which man's skill has been able to devise from the earliest time; and he works, accordingly, with a strength borrowed from all past ages. How different is *his* state who stands on the outside of that storehouse, and feels that its gates must be stormed, or remain forever shut against him! His means are the commonest and rudest; the mere work done is no measure of his strength. A dwarf behind his steam-engine may remove mountains; but no dwarf will hew them down with a pickaxe; and he must be a Titan that hurls them abroad with his arms.

It is in this last shape that Burns presents himself. Born in an age the most prosaic Britain had yet seen, and in a condition the most disadvantageous, where his mind, if it accomplished aught, must accomplish it under the pressure of continual bodily toil, nay, of penury and desponding apprehension of the worst evils, and with no furtherance but such knowledge as dwells in a poor man's hut, and the rhymes of a Ferguson or Ramsay for his standard of beauty, he sinks not under all these impediments: through the fogs and darkness of that obscure region, his lynx eye discerns the true relations of the world and human life; he grows into intellectual strength, and trains himself into intellectual expertness. Impelled by the expansive movement of his own irrepressible soul, he struggles forward into the general view; and with haughty modesty lays down before us, as the fruit of his labour, a gift, which Time has now pronounced imperishable. Add to all this, that his darksome drudging childhood and youth was by far the kindliest era of his whole life; and that he died in his thirty-seventh year: and then ask, If it be strange that his poems are imperfect, and of small extent, or that his genius attained no mastery in its art? Alas, his Sun shone as through a tropical tornado; and the pale Shadow of Death eclipsed it at noon! Shrouded in such baleful vapours, the genius of Burns was never seen in clear azure splendour, enlightening the world: but some beams from it did, by fits, pierce through; and it tinted those clouds with rainbow and orient colours, into a glory and stern grandeur, which men silently gazed on with wonder and tears!

We are anxious not to exaggerate; for it is exposition rather than admiration that our readers require of us here; and yet to avoid some tendency to that side is no easy matter. We love Burns, and we pity him; and love and pity are prone to magnify. Criticism, it is sometimes thought, should be a cold business; we are not so sure of this; but, at all events, our concern with Burns is not exclusively that of critics. True and genial as his poetry must appear, it is not chiefly as a poet, but as a man, that he interests and affects us. He was often advised to write a tragedy: time and means were not lent him for this; but through life he enacted a tragedy, and one of the deepest. We question whether the world has since witnessed so utterly sad a scene; whether Napoleon himself, left to brawl with Sir Hudson Lowe, and perish on his rock 'amid the melancholy main,' presented to the reflecting mind such a 'spectacle of pity and fear' as did this intrinsically nobler, gentler and

perhaps greater soul, wasting itself away in a hopeless struggle with base entanglements, which coiled closer and closer round him, till only death opened him an outlet. Conquerors are a class of men with whom, for most part, the world could well dispense; nor can the hard intellect, the unsympathising loftiness and high but selfish enthusiasm of such persons inspire us in general with any affection; at best it may excite amazement; and their fall, like that of a pyramid, will be beheld with a certain sadness and awe. But a true Poet, a man in whose heart resides some effluence of Wisdom, some tone of the 'Eternal Melodies,' is the most precious gift that can be bestowed on a generation: we see in him a freer, purer development of whatever is noblest in ourselves; his life is a rich lesson to us; and we mourn his death as that of a benefactor who loved and taught us.

Such a gift had Nature, in her bounty, bestowed on us in Robert Burns; but with queenlike indifference she cast it from her hand, like a thing of no moment; and it was defaced and torn asunder, as an idle bauble, before we recognised it. To the ill-starred Burns was given the power of making man's life more venerable, but that of wisely guiding his own life was not given. Destiny,—for so in our ignorance we must speak,—his faults, the faults of others, proved too hard for him; and that spirit, which might have soared could it but have walked, soon sank to the dust, its glorious faculties trodden under foot in the blossom; and died, we may almost say, without ever having lived. And so kind and warm a soul; so full of inborn riches, of love to all living and lifeless things! How his heart flows out in sympathy over universal Nature; and in her bleakest provinces discerns a beauty and a meaning! The 'Daisy' falls not unheeded under his ploughshare; nor the ruined nest of that 'wee, cowering, timorous beastie,' cast forth, after all its provident pains, to 'thole the sleety dribble and cranreuch cauld.' The 'hoar visage' of Winter delights him; he dwells with a sad and oft-returning fondness in these scenes of solemn desolation; but the voice of the tempest becomes an anthem to his ears; he loves to walk in the sounding woods, for 'it raises his thoughts to *Him that walketh on the wings of the wind.*' A true Poet-soul, for it needs but to be struck, and the sound it yields will be music! But observe him chiefly as he mingles with his brother men. What warm, all-comprehending fellow-feeling; what trustful, boundless love; what generous exaggeration of the object loved! His rustic friend, his nut-brown maiden, are no longer mean and homely, but a hero and a queen, whom he prizes as the paragons of Earth. The rough scenes of Scottish life, not seen by him in any Arcadian illusion, but in the rude contradiction, in the smoke and soil of a too harsh reality, are still lovely to him: Poverty is indeed his companion, but Love also, and Courage; the simple feelings, the worth, the nobleness, that dwell under the straw roof, are dear and venerable to his heart: and thus over the lowest provinces of man's existence he pours the glory of his own soul; and they rise, in shadow and sunshine, softened and brightened into a beauty which other eyes discern not in the highest. He has a just self-consciousness, which too often degenerates into pride; yet it is a noble pride, for defence, not for offence; no cold suspicious feeling, but a frank and social one. The Peasant Poet bears himself, we might say, like a King in exile: he is cast among the low, and feels himself equal to the highest; yet he claims no rank, that none may be disputed to him. The forward he can repel, the supercilious he can subdue; pretensions of wealth or ancestry are of no avail with him; there is a fire in that dark eye, under which the 'insolence of condescension' cannot thrive. In his abasement, in his extreme need, he forgets not for a moment the majesty of

Poetry and Manhood. And yet, far as he feels himself above common men, he wanders not apart from them, but mixes warmly in their interests; nay, throws himself into their arms, and, as it were, entreats them to love him. It is moving to see how, in his darkest despondency, this proud being still seeks relief from friendship; unbosoms himself, often to the unworthy; and, amid tears, strains to his glowing heart a heart that knows only the name of friendship. And yet he was 'quick to learn'; a man of keen vision, before whom common disguises afforded no concealment. His understanding saw through the hollowness even of accomplished deceivers; but there was a generous credulity in his heart. And so did our Peasant show himself among us; 'a soul like an Æolian harp, in whose strings the vulgar wind, as it passed through them, changed itself into articulate melody.' And this was he for whom the world found no fitter business than quarrelling with smugglers and vintners, computing excise-dues upon tallow, and gauging alebarrels! In such toils was that mighty Spirit sorrowfully wasted: and a hundred years may pass on, before another such is given us to waste.

All that remains of Burns, the Writings he has left, seem to us, as we hinted above, no more than a poor mutilated fraction of what was in him; brief, broken glimpses of a genius that could never show itself complete; that wanted all things for completeness: culture, leisure, true effort, nay, even length of life. His poems are, with scarcely any exception, mere occasional effusions; poured forth with little premeditation; expressing, by such means as offered, the passion, opinion, or humour of the hour. Never in one instance was it permitted him to grapple with any subject with the full collection of his strength, to fuse and mould it in the concentrated fire of his genius. To try by the strict rules of Art such imperfect fragments, would be at once unprofitable and unfair. Nevertheless, there is something in these poems, marred and defective as they are, which forbids the most fastidious student of poetry to pass them by. Some sort of enduring quality they must have: for after fifty years of the wildest vicissitudes in poetic taste, they still continue to be read; nay, are read more and more eagerly, more and more extensively; and this not only by literary virtuosos, and that class upon whom transitory causes operate most strongly, but by all classes, down to the most hard, unlettered and truly natural class, who read little, and especially no poetry, except because they find pleasure in it. The grounds of so singular and wide a popularity, which extends, in a literal sense, from the palace to the hut, and over all regions where the English tongue is spoken, are well worth inquiring into. After every just deduction, it seems to imply some rare excellence in these works. What is that excellence?

To answer this question will not lead us far. The excellence of Burns is, indeed, among the rarest, whether in poetry or prose; but, at the same time, it is plain and easily recognised: his *Sincerity*, his indisputable air of Truth. Here are no fabulous woes or joys; no hollow fantastic sentimentalities; no wiredrawn refinings, either in thought or feeling: the passion that is traced before us has glowed in a living heart; the opinion he utters has risen in his own understanding, and been a light to his own steps. He does not write from hearsay, but from sight and experience; it is the scenes that he has lived and laboured amidst, that he describes: those scenes, rude and humble as they are, have kindled beautiful emotions in his soul, noble thoughts, and definite resolves; and he speaks forth what is in him, not from any outward call of vanity or interest, but because his heart is too full to be silent. He speaks it with such melody and modulation as he can; 'in homely rustic jingle'; but it is his own, and genuine. This is the grand secret for

finding readers and retaining them: let him who would move and convince others, be first moved and convinced himself. Horace's rule, *Si vis me flere*, is applicable in a wider sense than the literal one. To every poet, to every writer, we might say: Be true, if you would be believed. Let a man but speak forth with genuine earnestness the thought, the emotion, the actual condition of his own heart; and other men, so strangely are we all knit together by the tie of sympathy, must and will give heed to him. In culture, in extent of view, we may stand above the speaker, or below him; but in either case, his words, if they are earnest and sincere, will find some response within us; for in spite of all casual varieties in outward rank or inward, as face answers to face, so does the heart of man to man.

This may appear a very simple principle, and one which Burns had little merit in discovering. True, the discovery is easy enough: but the practical appliance is not easy; is indeed the fundamental difficulty which all poets have to strive with, and which scarcely one in the hundred ever fairly surmounts. A head too dull to discriminate the true from the false; a heart too dull to love the one at all risks, and to hate the other in spite of all temptations, are alike fatal to a writer. With either, or as more commonly happens, with both of these deficiencies combine a love of distinction, a wish to be original, which is seldom wanting, and we have Affectation, the bane of literature, as Cant, its elder brother, is of morals. How often does the one and the other front us, in poetry, as in life! Great poets themselves are not always free of this vice; nay, it is precisely on a certain sort and degree of greatness that it is most commonly ingrafted. A strong effort after excellence will sometimes solace itself with a mere shadow of success; he who has much to unfold, will sometimes unfold it imperfectly. Byron, for instance, was no common man: yet if we examine his poetry with this view, we shall find it far enough from faultless. Generally speaking, we should say that it is not true. He refreshes us, not with the divine fountain, but too often with vulgar strong waters, stimulating indeed to the taste, but soon ending in dislike, or even nausea. Are his Harolds and Giaours, we would ask, real men; we mean, poetically consistent and conceivable men? Do not these characters, does not the character of their author, which more or less shines through them all, rather appear a thing put on for the occasion; no natural or possible mode of being, but something intended to look much grander than nature? Surely, all these stormful agonies, this volcanic heroism, superhuman contempt and moody desperation, with so much scowling, and teeth-gnashing, and other sulphurous humour, is more like the brawling of a player in some paltry tragedy, which is to last three hours, than the bearing of a man in the business of life, which is to last threescore and ten years. To our minds there is a taint of this sort, something which we should call theatrical, false, affected, in every one of these otherwise so powerful pieces. Perhaps *Don Juan*, especially the latter parts of it, is the only thing approaching to a *sincere* work, he ever wrote; the only work where he showed himself, in any measure, as he was; and seemed so intent on his subject as, for moments, to forget himself. Yet Byron hated this vice; we believe, heartily detested it: nay, he had declared formal war against it in words. So difficult is it even for the strongest to make this primary attainment, which might seem the simplest of all: to *read its own consciousness without mistakes*, without errors involuntary or wilful! We recollect no poet of Burns's susceptibility who comes before us from the first, and abides with us to the last, with such a total want of affectation. He is an honest man, and an honest writer. In his successes and his failures, in his greatness and his littleness, he is ever clear, simple, true, and glitters with no lustre but his own. We reckon this to be a great virtue; to be, in fact, the root of most other virtues, literary as well as moral.

Here, however, let us say, it is to the Poetry of Burns that we now allude; to those writings which he had time to meditate, and where no special reason existed to warp his critical feeling, or obstruct his endeavour to fulfil it. Certain of his Letters, and other fractions of prose composition, by no means deserve this praise. Here, doubtless, there is not the same natural truth of style; but on the contrary, something not only stiff, but strained and twisted; a certain high-flown inflated tone; the stilting emphasis of which contrasts ill with the firmness and rugged simplicity of even his poorest verses. Thus no man, it would appear, is altogether unaffected. Does not Shakspeare himself sometimes premeditate the sheerest bombast! But even with regard to these Letters of Burns, it is but fair to state that he had two excuses. The first was his comparative deficiency in language. Burns, though for most part he writes with singular force and even gracefulness, is not master of English prose, as he is of Scottish verse; not master of it, we mean, in proportion to the depth and vehemence of his matter. These Letters strike us as the effort of a man to express something which he has no organ fit for expressing. But a second and weightier excuse is to be found in the peculiarity of Burns's social rank. His correspondents are often men whose relation to him he has never accurately ascertained; whom therefore he is either forearming himself against; or else unconsciously flattering, by adopting the style he thinks will please them. At all events, we should remember that these faults, even in his Letters, are not the rule, but the exception. Whenever he writes, as one would ever wish to do, to trusted friends and on real interests, his style becomes simple, vigorous, expressive, sometimes even beautiful. His letters to Mrs. Dunlop are uniformly excellent.

But we return to his Poetry. In addition to its Sincerity, it has another peculiar merit, which indeed is but a mode, or perhaps a means, of the foregoing: this displays itself in his choice of subjects; or rather in his indifference as to subjects, and the power he has of making all subjects interesting. The ordinary poet, like the ordinary man, is forever seeking in external circumstances the help which can be found only in himself. In what is familiar and near at hand, he discerns no form or comeliness: home is not poetical but prosaic; it is in some past, distant, conventional heroic world, that poetry resides; were he there and not here, were he thus and not so, it would be well with him. Hence our innumerable host of rose-coloured Novels and iron-mailed Epics, with their locality not on the Earth, but somewhere nearer to the Moon. Hence our Virgins of the Sun, and our Knights of the Cross, malicious Saracens in turbans, and copper-coloured Chiefs in wampum, and so many other truculent figures from the heroic times or the heroic climates, who on all hands swarm in our poetry. Peace be with them! But yet, as a great moralist proposed preaching to the men of this century, so would we fain preach to the poets, 'a sermon on the duty of staying at home.' Let them be sure that heroic ages and heroic climates can do little for them. That form of life has attraction for us, less because it is better or nobler than our own, than simply because it is different; and even this attraction must be of the most transient sort. For will not our own age, one day, be an ancient one; and have as quaint a costume as the rest; not contrasted with the rest, therefore, but ranked along with them, in respect of quaintness? Does Homer interest us now, because he wrote of what passed beyond his native Greece, and two centuries before he was born; or because he wrote what passed in God's world, and in the heart of man, which is the same after thirty centuries? Let our poets look to this: is their feeling really finer, truer, and their vision deeper than that of other men,—they have nothing to fear, even from the humblest subject; is it not so,—they have nothing to hope, but an ephemeral favour, even from the highest.

The poet, we imagine, can never have far to seek for a subject: the elements of his art are in him, and around him on every hand; for him the Ideal world is not remote from the Actual, but under it and within it: nay, he is a poet, precisely because he can discern it there. Wherever there is a sky above him, and a world around him, the poet is in his place; for here too is man's existence, with its infinite longings and small acquirings; its ever-thwarted, ever-renewed endeavours; its unspeakable aspirations, its fears and hopes that wander through Eternity; and all the mystery of brightness and of gloom that it was ever made of, in any age or climate, since man first began to live. Is there not the fifth act of a Tragedy in every death-bed, though it were a peasant's, and a bed of heath? And are wooings and weddings obsolete, that there can be Comedy no longer? Or are men suddenly grown wise, that Laughter must no longer shake his sides, but be cheated of his Farce? Man's life and nature is, as it was, and as it will ever be. But the poet must have an eye to read these things, and a heart to understand them; or they come and pass away before him in vain. He is a *vates*, a seer; a gift of vision has been given him. Has life no meanings for him, which another cannot equally decipher; then he is no poet, and Delphi itself will not make him one.

In this respect, Burns, though not perhaps absolutely a great poet, better manifests his capability, better proves the truth of his genius, than if he had by his own strength kept the whole Minerva Press going, to the end of his literary course. He shows himself at least a poet of Nature's own making; and Nature, after all, is still the grand agent in making poets. We often hear of this and the other external condition being requisite for the existence of a poet. Sometimes it is a certain sort of training; he must have studied certain things, studied for instance 'the elder dramatists,' and so learned a poetic language; as if poetry lay in the tongue, not in the heart. At other times we are told he must be bred in a certain rank, and must be on a confidential footing with the higher classes; because, above all things, he must see the world. As to seeing the world, we apprehend this will cause him little difficulty, if he have but eyesight to see it with. Without eyesight, indeed, the task might be hard. The blind or the purblind man 'travels from Dan to Beersheba, and finds it all barren.' But happily every poet is born *in* the world; and sees it, with or against his will, every day and every hour he lives. The mysterious workmanship of man's heart, the true light and the inscrutable darkness of man's destiny, reveal themselves not only in capital cities and crowded saloons, but in every hut and hamlet where men have their abode. Nay, do not the elements of all human virtues and all human vices; the passions at once of a Borgia and of a Luther, lie written, in stronger or fainter lines, in the consciousness of every individual bosom, that has practised honest self-examination? Truly, this same world may be seen in Mossgiel and Tarbolton, if we look well, as clearly as it ever came to light in Crockford's, or the Tuileries itself.

But sometimes still harder requisitions are laid on the poor aspirant to poetry; for it is hinted that he should have *been born* two centuries ago; inasmuch as poetry, about that date, vanished from the earth, and became no longer attainable by men! Such cobweb speculations have, now and then, overhung the field of literature; but they obstruct not the growth of any plant there: the Shakspeare or the Burns, unconsciously and merely as he walks onward, silently brushes them away. Is not every genius an impossibility till he appear? Why do we call him new and original, if *we* saw where his marble was lying, and what fabric he could rear from it? It is not the material but the workman that is wanting. It is not the dark *place* that hinders, but the dim *eye*. A Scottish peasant's life was the meanest and rudest of all lives, till Burns became a poet in it, and a poet of it; found it a *man's* life, and therefore significant to men. A thousand battle-fields remain unsung; but the "Wounded Hare" has not perished without its memorial; a balm of mercy yet breathes on us from its dumb agonies, because a poet was there. Our "Halloween" had passed and repassed, in rude awe and laughter, since the era of the Druids; but no Theocritus, till Burns, discerned in it the materials of a Scottish Idyl: neither was the "Holy Fair" any "Council of Trent" or Roman "Jubilee"; but nevertheless, "Superstition" and "Hypocrisy" and "Fun" having been propitious to him, in this man's hand it became a poem, instinct with satire and genuine comic life. Let but the true poet be given us, we repeat it, place him where and how you will, and true poetry will not be wanting.

Independently of the essential gift of poetic feeling, as we have now attempted to describe it, a certain rugged sterling worth pervades whatever Burns has written; a virtue, as of green fields and mountain breezes, dwells in his poetry; it is redolent of natural life and hardy natural men. There is a decisive strength in him, and yet a sweet native gracefulness: he is tender, he is vehement, yet without constraint or too visible effort; he melts the heart, or inflames it, with a power which seems habitual and familiar to him. We see that in this man there was the gentleness, the trembling pity of a woman, with the deep earnestness, the force and passionate ardour of a hero. Tears lie in him, and consuming fire; as lightning lurks in the drops of the summer cloud. He has a resonance in his bosom for every note of human feeling; the high and the low, the sad, the ludicrous, the joyful, are welcome in their turns to his 'lightly-moved and all-conceiving spirit.' And observe with what a fierce prompt force he grasps his subject, be it what it may! How he fixes, as it were, the full image of the matter in his eye; full and clear in every lineament; and catches the real type and essence of it, amid a thousand accidents and superficial circumstances, no one of which misleads him! Is it of reason, some truth to be discovered? No sophistry, no vain surface-logic detains him; quick, resolute, unerring, he pierces through into the marrow of the question; and speaks his verdict with an emphasis that cannot be forgotten. Is it of description; some visual object to be represented? No poet of any age or nation is more graphic than Burns: the characteristic features disclose themselves to him at a glance; three lines from his hand, and we have a likeness. And, in that rough dialect, in that rude, often awkward metre, so clear and definite a likeness! It seems a draughtsman working with a burnt stick; and yet the burin of a Retzsch is not more expressive or exact.

MATTHEW ARNOLD
From "Introduction"
The English Poets, ed. Thomas Humphry Ward
1880, Volume 1, pp. xli–xlvi

The real Burns is of course in his Scotch poems. Let us boldly say that much of this poetry, a poetry dealing perpetually with Scotch drink, Scotch religion, and Scotch manners, a Scotchman's estimate is apt to be personal. A Scotchman is used to this world of Scotch drink, Scotch religion, and Scotch manners; he has a tenderness for it; he meets its poet half way. In this tender mood he reads pieces like the 'Holy Fair' or 'Halloween.' But this world of Scotch drink, Scotch religion, and Scotch manners is against a poet, not for him, when it is not a partial countryman who reads him; for in itself it is not a beautiful world, and no one can deny that it is of advantage to a poet to deal with a beautiful world. Burns's world of Scotch drink, Scotch religion, and Scotch manners, is often a harsh, a sordid, a repulsive world; even the world of his 'Cotter's Saturday Night' is not a beautiful world. No doubt a poet's criticism of life may have such truth and power that it triumphs over its world and delights us. Burns may triumph over his world, often he does triumph over his world, but let us observe how and where. Burns is the first case we have had where the bias of the personal estimate tends to mislead; let us look at him closely, he can bear it.

Many of his admirers will tell us that we have Burns, convivial, genuine, delightful, here:—

> Leeze me on drink! it gies us mair
>   Then either school or college;
> It kindles wit, it waukens lair,
>   It pangs us fou o' knowledge.
> Be 't whisky gill or penny wheep
>   Or ony stronger potion,
> It never fails, on drinking deep,
>   To kittle up our notion
>   By night or day.

There is a great deal of that sort of thing in Burns, and it is unsatisfactory, not because it is bacchanalian poetry, but because it has not that accent of sincerity which bacchanalian poetry, to do it justice, very often has. There is something in it of bravado, something which makes us feel that we have not the man speaking to us with his real voice; something, therefore, poetically unsound.

With still more confidence will his admirers tell us that we have the genuine Burns, the great poet, when his strain asserts the independence, equality, dignity, of men, as in the famous song 'For a' that and a' that':—

> A prince can mak' a belted knight,
>   A marquis, duke, and a' that;
> But an honest man's aboon his might,
>   Guid faith he mauna fa' that!
>   For a' that, and a' that!
>   Their dignities, and a' that,
>   The pith o' sense, and pride o' worth,
>   Are higher rank than a' that.

Here they find his grand, genuine touches; and still more, when this puissant genius, who so often set morality at defiance, falls moralising:—

> The sacred lowe o' weel-placed love
>   Luxuriantly indulge it;
> But never tempt th' illicit rove,
>   Tho' naething should divulge it.
> I waive the quantum o' the sin,
>   The hazard o' concealing,
> But och! it hardens a' within,
>   And petrifies the feeling.

Or in a higher strain:—

> Who made the heart, 'tis He alone
>   Decidedly can try us;
> He knows each chord, its various tone;
>   Each spring, its various bias.

Then at the balance let's be mute,
    We never can adjust it;
What's *done* we partly may compute,
    But know not what's resisted.

Or in a better strain yet, a strain, his admirers will say, unsurpassable:—

To make a happy fire-side clime
    To weans and wife,
That's the true pathos and sublime
    Of human life.

There is criticism of life for you, the admirers of Burns will say to us; there is the application of ideas to life! There is, undoubtedly. The doctrine of the last-quoted lines coincides almost exactly with what was the aim and end, Xenophon tells us, of all the teaching of Socrates. And the application is a powerful one; made by a man of vigorous understanding, and (need I say?) a master of language.

But for supreme poetical success more is required than the powerful application of ideas to life; it must be an application under the conditions fixed by the laws of poetic truth and poetic beauty. Those laws fix as an essential condition, in the poet's treatment of such matters as are here in question, high seriousness;—the high seriousness which comes from absolute sincerity. The accent of high seriousness, born of absolute sincerity, is what gives to such verse as

In la sua volontade è nostra pace . . .

to such criticism of life as Dante's, its power. Is this accent felt in the passages which I have been quoting from Burns? Surely not; surely, if our sense is quick, we must perceive that we have not in those passages a voice from the very inmost soul of the genuine Burns; he is not speaking to us from these depths, he is more or less preaching. And the compensation for admiring such passages less, from missing the perfect poetic accent in them, will be that we shall admire more the poetry where that accent is found.

No; Burns, like Chaucer, comes short of the high seriousness of the great classics, and the virtue of matter and manner which goes with that high seriousness is wanting to his work. At moments he touches it in a profound and passionate melancholy, as in those four immortal lines taken by Byron as a motto for *The Giaour,* but which have in them a depth of poetic quality such as resides in no verse of Byron's own:—

Had we never loved sae kindly,
Had we never loved sae blindly,
Never met, or never parted,
We had ne'er been broken-hearted.

But a whole poem of that quality Burns cannot make; the rest, in the "Farewell to Nancy," is verbiage.

We arrive best at the real estimate of Burns, I think, by conceiving his work as having truth of matter and truth of manner, but not the accent or the poetic virtue of the highest masters. His genuine criticism of life, when the sheer poet in him speaks, is ironic; it is not:

Thou Power Supreme, whose mighty scheme
    Those woes of mine fulfil,
Here firm I rest, they must be best
    Because they are Thy will!

It is far rather: "Whistle owre the lave o't!" Yet we may say of him as of Chaucer, that of life and the world, as they come before him, his view is large, free, shrewd, benignant,—truly poetic, therefore; and his manner of rendering what he sees is to match. But we must note, at the same time, his great difference from Chaucer. The freedom of Chaucer is heightened, in Burns, by a fiery, reckless energy; the benignity of

Chaucer deepens, in Burns, into an overwhelming sense of the pathos of things;—of the pathos of human nature, the pathos, also, of non-human nature. Instead of the fluidity of Chaucer's manner, the manner of Burns has spring, bounding swiftness. Burns is by far the greater force, though he has perhaps less charm. The world of Chaucer is fairer, richer, more significant than that of Burns; but when the largeness and freedom of Burns get full sweep, as in 'Tam o' Shanter,' or still more in that puissant and splendid production, 'The Jolly Beggars,' his world may be what it will, his poetic genius triumphs over it. In the world of the 'Jolly Beggars' there is more than hideousness and squalor, there is bestiality; yet the piece is a superb poetic success. It has a breadth, truth, and power which make the famous scene in Auerbach's Cellar, of Goethe's *Faust,* seem artificial and tame beside it, and which are only matched by Shakespeare and Aristophanes.

Here, where his largeness and freedom serve him so admirably, and also in those poems and songs, where to shrewdness he adds infinite archness and wit, and to benignity infinite pathos, where his manner is flawless, and a perfect poetic whole is the result,—in things like the address to the Mouse whose home he had ruined, in things like 'Duncan Gray,' 'Tam Glen,' 'Whistle and I'll come to you, my lad,' 'Auld lang syne' (the list might be made much longer),—here we have the genuine Burns, of whom the real estimate must be high indeed. Not a classic, nor with the excellent σπουδαιότης of the great classics, nor with a verse rising to a criticism of life and a virtue like theirs; but a poet with thorough truth of substance and an answering truth of style, giving us a poetry sound to the core. We all of us have a leaning towards the pathetic, and may be inclined perhaps to prize Burns most for his touches of piercing, sometimes almost intolerable, pathos; for verse like:

We twa hae paidl't i' the burn
    From mornin' sun till dine;
But seas between us braid hae roar'd
    Sin auld lang syne . . .

where he is as lovely as he is sound. But perhaps it is by the perfection of soundness of his lighter and archer master-pieces that he is poetically most wholesome for us. For the votary misled by a personal estimate of Shelley, as so many of us have been, are, and will be,—of that beautiful spirit building his many-coloured haze of words and images

Pinnacled dim in the intense inane—

no contact can be wholesomer than the contact with Burns at his archest and soundest. Side by side with the

On the brink of the night and the morning
    My coursers are wont to respire,
But the Earth has just whispered a warning
    That their flight must be swifter than fire . . .

of *Prometheus Unbound,* how salutary, how very salutary, to place this from 'Tam Glen':—

My minnie does constantly deave me
    And bids me beware o' young men;
They flatter, she says, to deceive me;
    But wha can think sae o' Tam Glen?

JOHN SERVICE
From "Robert Burns"
The English Poets, ed. Thomas Humphry Ward
1880, Volume 3, pp. 515–23

His poetry is instinct with the life and movement of one age,—one which was an era of resurrection from the dead and of revolt against all that had lived too long. Any explanation of Burns, however, which is thus to be found where we find an explanation of Europe itself in the spirit of a particular age, is of course partial. Its merit is that it points to what is more essential and more comprehensive than itself. Burns' poetry shares with all poetry of the first order of excellence the life and movement not of one age but of all ages, that which belongs to what Wordsworth calls 'the essential passions' of human nature. It is the voice of nature which we hear in his poetry, and it is of that nature one touch of which makes the whole world kin. It is doubtful whether any poet, ancient or modern, has evoked as much personal attachment of a fervid and perfervid quality as Burns has been able to draw to himself. It is an attachment the amount and the quality of which are not to be explained by anything in the history of the man, anything apart from the exercise of his genius as a poet. His misfortunes, though they were great, do not account for it—these are cancelled by his faults, from which his misfortunes are not easily separated. What renders it at all intelligible is that human nature, in its most ordinary shapes, is more poetical than it looks, and that exactly at those moments of its consciousness in which it is most truly because most vividly and powerfully and poetically itself, Burns has a voice to give to it. He is not the poet's poet, which Shelley no doubt meant to be, or the philosopher's poet, which Wordsworth, in spite of himself, is. He is the poet of homely human nature, not half so homely or prosaic as it seems. His genius, in a manner all its own, associates itself with the fortunes, experiences, memorable moments, of human beings whose humanity is their sole patrimony; to whom 'liberty,' and whatever, like liberty, has the power

To raise a man aboon the brute,
And mak him ken himsel,

is their portion in life; for whom the great epochs and never-to-be-forgotten phases of existence are those which are occasioned by emotions inseparable from the consciousness of existence. For the great majority of his readers, and therefore for the mass of human beings, the sympathy which exists between him and them is sympathy relative to their strongest and deepest feelings, and this is sympathy out of which personal affection naturally springs, and in the strength of which it cannot but grow strong. In this light Burns clubs and Burns celebrations, excursions and pilgrimages to the land of Burns, manifestations of personal affection without parallel for range or depth in the history of literature, instead of misleading the critical judgment as to his poetry, are an infallible index to the truth respecting it—namely, that the passions which live in it and by which it lives are the essential passions of human nature.

Of these plain 'good masters' his princely intellectual gifts are the humble and faithful servants. His imagination, humour, pathos, the qualities in respect of which his genius is most powerful and opulent, are without reserve placed at their disposal and submitted to their dictation. His genius might possibly have elected to move sometimes in a different sphere, but this is the sphere in which its creative force is habitually spent. Words and phrases which derive their significance from what belongs to it are those that recur oftenest in his best and in his worst lines, and linger in our ears with the airs to which his songs are sung. As part and parcel of its contents, and as they are assorted in its compass, 'freedom and whisky gang thegither' in his rhymes; so do mirth and care, despair and rapture, pride of birth and pride of worth, love and sorrow and death, auld acquaintance not to be forgotten, social inequalities not to be forgiven, hypocrisy at its prayers, and commiseration for the wretched which extends to the brute creation and cannot be withheld from the devil. That the worst of it as well as the best of it has power over him is the most that can be said in the way of censure or in the way of excuse in regard to that capital fault of his, a relish for grossness and even obscenity in the choice and treatment of his themes, which gives occasion to turgid moralists to talk of him as at once the glory and the shame of literature, and which, as disfiguring some of his best pieces no one has more reason to regret than he who has to do justice to the genius of the poet by making a selection from his works.

Genius can explain everything except itself. In this limitation of his genius to one sphere of activity we have, however, not only some explanation of the place which Burns occupies in European literature and European history, but also a revelation of the inner structure and quality of his genius. Genius which in every case eludes and defies definition is by this restriction of its operations shown to be in his case, more than most, synonymous with force of mind, that force which cleaves its way through the shows of things to the reality behind them and beyond them:

The heart ay's the part ay
That makes us right or wrang.

To say that this is his poetical creed is to say that poetical genius in his case is akin to or identical with 'majestic common sense,' an intellect of singular power to penetrate appearance and become conversant with reality and truth—that reality and truth which are to be found, if anywhere, in the sphere of the passions and emotions of which he is the laureate. He is closer to this reality than other poets because his mental force is greater than theirs and carries him farther and straighter from the surface of things towards the centre. His poetry makes a gift again to folly of that definition of poetry which was presented by folly to stupidity—that is the best poetry which is the most feigning. It feigns not at all when it is at its best, and hardly any when it is at its worst. So much reality is there in it to the experience of common mortals, that it is commonly mistaken among them for useful information for the people. Where it is not understood as comprehending the choicest products of imagination, humour, pathos, it is admired and valued as a repertory of oracular wisdom. When it is denied the welcome to which it is entitled as song, the gift of the gods, it is sure of applause as the 'pith of sense,' of which every man as he believes has his own share. Genius in the case of Burns is thus shown to be compact of sense, sagacity, intelligence of a powerful and piercing order, general force of mind to which nature and life cannot but yield up their deepest secrets. It is in the sphere of the essential passions of human nature that reality lies. That Burns, in a manner all his own, is rigid, not consciously always, but instinctively, in adhering to this sphere, is evidence that what takes in him the form and fashion of genius is common sense.

A melancholy or rather a mournful interest attaches to several of his poems—'A Bard's Epitaph' for example, and the 'Epistle to a Young Friend'—as showing that intellect and passion were as far from being perfectly adjusted in his life as they have been in the lives of many other sons of genius. That they were not on better terms with each other than they actually were, it may be, is a matter which calls rather for regret than for amazement. Considering what nature made him and what his destiny was, considering how rudely in his case the sensibilities of a gifted soul clashed with the exigencies of a sordid lot, it is possibly not a matter for as much astonishment as has been sometimes expressed, that the last chapter of his history should be one which cannot be read without a pang of sorrow for the degradation of genius. Had he been a struggling tradesman in Paris instead of a struggling farmer in Ayrshire and a measurer of ale-firkins at Dumfries, Burns would no doubt have lived and died with a reputation for sobriety as unimpeachable as that of Beranger. But for that insanity, compounded of headache and melancholy, from which he suffered all his life, as the result of being made to do a man's work when he was a boy; but for his being 'half fed, half sarkit,' too literally and too long not to be rendered 'half mad' as well, it is open to a candid judgment to suppose that the 'thoughtless follies' which 'laid him low,' would not have been committed, at any rate would not have cut half as formidable a figure as they do in the count and reckoning of some of the honorary sheriffs and respectable aldermen of literature. But however it may have been that the relations of intellect and passion were imperfectly or ill adjusted in his life, their perfect harmony is the marvel and the glory of his song. Passages indeed from various pieces of his, perhaps whole pieces, could be cited which fall below the level of poetry in the strictest sense of the word, for which no higher character can be claimed than that of rhymed prose, because sense and sagacity or wit and humour predominate in them in too marked a degree over feeling and imagination. It is as if the balance, 'rarely right adjusted,' in his life, swung heavily sometimes in his verse to the other side. But it is only where it is chargeable with this excess of sense, or where it is written in that English tongue of which he never attained any mastery in verse, that his poetry falls short of excellence as regards the union of intellect and passion, the union of which is the first condition of poetical vitality. His passions, according to a well-known account of them from the best authority, 'raged like so many devils' till they found vent in rhyme. They could not have raged more or raged less any day without perhaps marring the perfection of a stanza or a song which has almost the perfection of the work of Shakespeare or of nature. His one poetical failing, besides being one which leans to virtue's side, is exhibited for the most part only where it is harmless—in his epistles, satires, and especially his epigrams. His songs, on which after all his fame must mainly rest, are free from it, though even in them passion is governed and moderated in such a manner that in the whole collection of them there is abundant evidence of sense and sanity which it would have been fatal to obtrude in any one of them. His claim to be considered the first of song-writers is hardly disputed. It is a claim which rests upon scores of lyrics, each of which might be cited as an instance of lyrical passion at its best and highest. Lyrical passion in his case drew its strength from various and opposite sources, from the clashing experiences, habits and emotions of a nature which needed nothing so much as regulation and harmony. But it is itself harmony as perfect as the song of the linnet and the thrush piping to a summer evening of peace on earth and glory in the western sky. Whatever the poet's eye has seen of beauty, or his heart has felt of mirth or sadness or madness, melts into it and becomes a tone, a chord of music of which, but for one singer, the world should hardly have known the power to thrill the universal

heart. He could not begin to write a song till he had crooned over and got into his head some old air to which words might be adapted. Only when his songs are sung are they legitimately said, is the melody of them vocalised. Their affinity with music by origin and by use is only symbolic of the harmony to which lyrical passion in them has set the incongruous facts and experiences of human life and destiny. The best of them are serious and pathetic, like 'Mary Morison,' 'My Nanie O,' 'Of a' the airts the wind can blaw'; but serious and pathetic like these, or arch and airy and humorous like 'Tam Glen' and 'Duncan Gray,' they draw upon sources of melody of which Tibullus and Petrarch and Beranger had almost as little knowledge as of the sources of the Lugar or of the banks of Bonie Doon.

Like Shakespeare, Burns is almost as great in the matter of borrowing as in that of originality. His measures are without exception those with which he was familiar in his favourites and predecessors, Ramsay and Fergusson, or in the ballads and songs which the stream of time might be said to have brought down to his poetical mill. His 'Cotter's Saturday Night' is modelled upon Fergusson's 'Farmer's Ingle'; his 'Holy Fair' upon the same poet's 'Leith Races.' His epistles are Ramsay's and Fergusson's in form and spirit, only instinct with a kind of genius to which neither Ramsay nor Fergusson had any pretensions. One stanza in which he wrote a great deal, for which among poetical measures he had as much partiality as he had for winter among the seasons, or the mavis among birds, or humanity among the virtues, and which his readers, even Scotch readers, find it sometimes hard to endure, was no doubt made classical to him and informed with music by its having been made use of by predecessors of his, of whose genius he had formed a most generous and uncritical estimate.

His best work is distributed over three periods, into which his poetical life can be most easily divided—the first marked by the publication of his poems at Kilmarnock, 1786, when he was at the age of twenty-seven; the second comprehending the extraordinary fertility of his later residence in Ayrshire (at Mossgiel), and terminating in 1788, and the third being the melancholy last years at Ellisland and Dumfries, in which his recreation was to give to his country and the world a store of songs, original and amended, such as no other country possesses. 'The Jolly Beggars,' that incomparable opéra in which critical genius of the highest order has discovered the highest flight of his poetical genius, belongs to the first period, though not published till after his death, 'The Cotter's Saturday Night' belongs to the same period. 'My Nanie O' is one of its songs. As regards humour and imagination it could be represented either by 'Death and Doctor Hornbook,' or the 'Address to the Deil,' or 'The Holy Fair.' With reference to the work which was done by him before the close of this period, considering its quality and variety, considering how much of it is destined to hold a permanent place in literature, Burns is perhaps to be regarded as the most remarkable instance on record of the precocity of genius, at any rate poetical genius. It would be difficult to point to a single rival for poetical fame who before the age of twenty-six or twenty-seven had contributed as much to the stock of literature, exempt for ever from oblivion. He was in this sense something of the prodigy which, in respect of his being born a peasant, Jeffrey would not allow him to be considered.

In each of these three periods of his poetical life he was at his best in one or other of the departments of song in which his greatness is least open to question. To Ellisland and Dumfries, the last of the three, besides 'Tam o' Shanter' and 'Captain Grose,' belongs the glory of that marvellous series of songs, new and old, original and improved, which it was the unhappy exciseman-poet's one pure delight to contribute to the Miscellanies in which they appeared. Whether his genius was exhausted by the activity of these ten or a dozen years, or whether, if his life had been prolonged, he might not have undertaken and accomplished some even greater task than any he had attempted, is a question to which no very certain answer can be given. He might have done something to diminish the interval between him and the poets of the first order—those whose poetry includes character and action as well as passion. He was ambitious of doing something of the kind. At one time the scheme of an epic, at another the plans for a tragedy were revolved in his mind. But if we may judge from a fragment of his intended drama, from the quality of his English verses, or from the leading features of his character, it seems unlikely that he would under any circumstances have made a nearer approach than he has done, or than that other passionate pilgrim of the realm of song, Byron, has done, to Milton or Shakespeare. His nearest approach to Shakespeare and Milton must be held to be that he wrote for the same theatre as they—not for an age, but for all time.

If only because the essential passions of human nature are so peculiarly and exclusively the sphere in which his genius moves, the question whether on the whole the influence of his poetry is wholesome, is a question touching the perpetuity of his fame. It is the native sphere of morality and religion in which his genius disports itself, and hence, though it cannot be required of poetry that it should directly inculcate virtue and piety, yet poetry like his has only the choice of recognising at their proper value the highest instincts and feelings of human nature, or ensuring its own consignment to neglect and oblivion by clashing with them. For, as critics have at length discovered, poetry is not meant for critics but for mankind. If it is of use to mankind it has a chance of life; if not it must die. On these terms, like other poets, Burns is a competitor for immortality, and on these terms, though his claim has been variously judged, it is now generally admitted to be strong. It is true, as has been already acknowledged, that touches of grossness and obscenity disfigure some of his best pieces, and are the execrable characteristics of some of his worst. It is true also that religious people have had much fault to find with 'The Holy Fair' and 'Holy Willie,' and other satires of his in which religious, or rather ecclesiastical things and personages, have been held up to ridicule and scorn. But the one fault he shares with many of his brother poets whose immortality is not doubtful; the other to most persons is rendered venial by a doubt as to whether it is not rather a capital merit than an unpardonable sin. His morality is not always perfect; sometimes it sanctions or applauds what cannot be defended. But he never ridicules religion except when the religion in question is in the nature of things ridiculous, and only not so by an accident of time or place. On the other hand, it is a world from which virtue and piety are not absent into which he habitually escapes from scenes in the actual world in which, with most of his generation, he was tempted to linger too long and too agreeably. Sordid and even revolting as some of these scenes are, they are yet to the reader of all that he has written only grotesque openings into a world beyond and above them in which everything fair and good has its own place—love and truth, joy in all that is pure and high, sorrow over all that is weak and low and sad, in the life of man. Hypocrisy, superstition, fanaticism owe him a heavy grudge. But in Scotland at least, and where 'The Holy Fair' is remembered and 'Holy Willie' is not unknown, spiritual religion owes him little but thanks.

On this subject only a word more need be said. Burns lives above all, and is destined to live, in his songs. In them, at any rate, he lives for an infinitely larger public than knows much of him as the author of 'Halloween' or 'The Jolly Beggars.' By his songs, though they too furnish his more austere censors with complaint, the service which he rendered to morality and religion is one the value of which can hardly be over-estimated. It is a remarkable fact that a country, the history of which is so much, as that of Scotland is, a history of religious or at any rate ecclesiastical events, especially battles, a country too which has not been unprolific in poetical talent, should have given birth to almost no religious poetry worth the name. Yet hardly is religious poetry a more prolific crop in the country of Dunbar and Burns and Scott than figs or peaches or bananas. It may be after all that other passions than those spiritual ones which find expression for themselves in psalms and hymns and spiritual songs, have been chiefly concerned in those religious movements of which Scottish history is a tedious record. But be that as it may, Burns inherited from his poetical ancestry a wealth not of hymns but of songs and ballads, chiefly of course amatory. They inspired him with harmonies compared with which they are themselves harsh and out of tune—the inimitable airs to which they were sung were reverberated from his mind in words in which there is the very soul of melody. In this process of transmitting what he received from the past to the future to which he looked forward as a better day for all mankind, he changed, as regards morality, silver into gold, dirt into the fragrance of lilies and violets, foul dirt into the breath of meadows and of shady paths through woods and by the banks of murmuring streams. As a reformer of one branch of literature, when centuries that are centuries still have dwindled into years, he may perhaps be named along with John Knox and Walter Scott in the history of the Scottish Reformation. Anyhow, judged by his songs, Burns' fame has little to fear from any question being raised as to whether the tree of knowledge of good and evil in the instance of his poetry is really what it seems—a tree that is good for food and pleasant to the eyes, and a tree to be desired to make one wise.

ROBERT LOUIS STEVENSON
From "Some Aspects of Robert Burns"
Familiar Studies of Men and Books
1882, pp. 95–103

The somewhat cruel necessity which has lain upon me throughout this paper only to touch upon those points in the life of Burns where correction or amplification seemed desirable, leaves me little opportunity to speak of the works which have made his name so famous. Yet, even here, a few observations seem necessary.

At the time when the poet made his appearance and great first success, his work was remarkable in two ways. For, first, in an age when poetry had become abstract and conventional, instead of continuing to deal with shepherds, thunderstorms, and personifications, he dealt with the actual circumstances of his life, however matter-of-fact and sordid these might be. And, second, in a time when English versification was particularly stiff, lame, and feeble, and words were used with ultra-academical timidity, he wrote verses that were easy, racy, graphic, and forcible, and used language with absolute tact and courage as it seemed most fit to give a clear impression. If you take even those English authors whom we know Burns to have most admired and studied, you will see at once that he owed them nothing but a warning. Take Shenstone, for instance, and watch that elegant author as he tries to grapple with the facts of life. He has a description, I remember, of a gentleman engaged in sliding or walking on thin ice, which is a little miracle of incompetence. You see my memory fails me, and I positively cannot recollect whether his hero was sliding or walking; as though a writer should describe a skirmish, and the reader, at the end, be still uncertain whether it were a charge of cavalry or a slow and stubborn advance of foot. There could be no such ambiguity in Burns; his work is at the opposite pole from such indefinite and stammering performances; and a whole lifetime passed in the study of Shenstone would only lead a man farther and farther from writing the "Address to a Louse." Yet Burns, like most great artists, proceeded from a school and continued a tradition; only the school and tradition were Scotch, and not English. While the English language was becoming daily more pedantic and inflexible, and English letters more colorless and slack, there was another dialect in the sister country, and a different school of poetry tracing its descent, through King James I., from Chaucer. The dialect alone accounts for much; for it was then written colloquially, which kept it fresh and supple; and, although not shaped for heroic flights, it was a direct and vivid medium for all that had to do with social life. Hence, whenever Scotch poets left their laborious imitations of bad English verses, and fell back on their own dialect, their style would kindle, and they would write of their convivial and somewhat gross existences with pith and point. In Ramsay, and far more in the poor lad Fergusson, there was mettle, humor, literary courage, and a power of saying what they wished to say definitely and brightly, which in the latter case should have justified great anticipations. Had Burns died at the same age as Fergusson, he would have left us literally nothing worth remark. To Ramsay and to Fergusson, then, he was indebted in a very uncommon degree, not only following their tradition and using their measures, but directly and avowedly imitating their pieces. The same tendency to borrow a hint, to work on some one else's foundation, is notable in Burns from first to last, in the period of song-writing as well as in that of the early poems; and strikes one oddly in a man of such deep originality, who left so strong a print on all he touched, and whose work is so greatly distinguished by that character of "inevitability" which Wordsworth denied to Goethe.

When we remember Burns's obligations to his predecessors, we must never forget his immense advances on them. They had already "discovered" nature; but Burns discovered poetry—a higher and more intense way of thinking of the things that go to make up nature, a higher and more ideal key of words in which to speak of them. Ramsay and Fergusson excelled at making a popular—or shall we say vulgar?—sort of society verses, comical and prosaic, written, you would say, in taverns while a supper party waited for its laureate's word; but on the appearance of Burns, this coarse and laughing literature was touched to finer issues, and learned gravity of thought and natural pathos.

What he had gained from his predecessors was a direct, speaking style, and to walk on his own feet instead of on academical stilts. There was never a man of letters with more absolute command of his means; and we may say of him, without excess, that his style was his slave. Hence that energy of epithet, so concise and telling, that a foreigner is tempted to explain it by some special richness or aptitude in the dialect he wrote. Hence that Homeric justice and completeness of description which gives us the very physiognomy of nature, in body and detail, as nature is. Hence, too, the unbroken literary quality of his best pieces, which keeps him from any slip into the weariful trade of word-painting, and presents everything, as everything should be presented by the art of words, in a clear, continuous medium of thought. Principal Shairp, for instance, gives us a paraphrase of one tough verse of the original; and for those who know the Greek poets only by paraphrase, this has the very quality they are accustomed to look for and admire in Greek. The contemporaries of Burns were surprised that he should visit so many celebrated mountains and waterfalls, and not seize the opportunity to make a poem. Indeed, it is not for those who have a true command of the art of words, but for peddling, professional amateurs, that these pointed occasions are most useful and inspiring. As those who speak French imperfectly are glad to dwell on any topic they may have talked upon or heard others talk upon before, because they know appropriate words for it in French, so the dabbler in verse rejoices to behold a waterfall, because he has learned the sentiment and knows appropriate words for it in poetry. But the dialect of Burns was fitted to deal with any subject; and whether it was a stormy night, a shepherd's collie, a sheep struggling in the snow, the conduct of cowardly soldiers in the field, the gait and cogitations of a drunken man, or only a village cockcrow in the morning, he could find language to give it freshness, body, and relief. He was always ready to borrow the hint of a design, as though he had a difficulty in commencing—a difficulty, let us say, in choosing a subject out of a world which seemed all equally living and significant to him; but once he had the subject chosen, he could cope with nature single-handed, and make every stroke a triumph. Again, his absolute mastery in his art enabled him to express each and all of his different humors, and to pass smoothly and congruously from one to another. Many men invent a dialect for only one side of their nature—perhaps their pathos or their humor, or the delicacy of their senses—and, for lack of a medium, leave all the others unexpressed. You meet such an one, and find him in conversation full of thought, feeling, and experience, which he has lacked the art to employ in his writings. But Burns was not thus hampered in the practice of the literary art; he could throw the whole weight of his nature into his work, and impregnate it from end to end. If Doctor Johnson, that stilted and accomplished stylist, had lacked the sacred Boswell, what should we have known of him? and how should we have delighted in his acquaintance as we do? Those who spoke with Burns tell us how much we have lost who did not. But I think they exaggerate their privilege: I think we have the whole Burns in our possession set forth in his consummate verses.

It was by his style, and not by his matter, that he affected Wordsworth and the world. There is, indeed, only one merit worth considering in a man of letters—that he should write well; and only one damning fault—that he should write ill. We are little the better for the reflections of the sailor's parrot in the story. And so, if Burns helped to change the course of literary history, it was by his frank, direct, and masterly utterance, and not by his homely choice of subjects. That was imposed upon him, not chosen upon a principle. He wrote from his own experience, because it was his nature so to do, and the tradition of the school from which he proceeded was fortunately not opposed to homely subjects. But to these homely subjects he communicated the rich commentary of his nature; they were all steeped in Burns; and they interest us not in themselves, but because they have been passed through the spirit of so genuine and vigorous a man. Such is the stamp of living literature; and there was never any more alive than that of Burns.

What a gust of sympathy there is in him sometimes flowing out in byways hitherto unused, upon mice, and flowers, and the devil himself; sometimes speaking plainly between human hearts; sometimes ringing out in exultation like a peal of bells! When we compare the "Farmer's Salutation to his Auld Mare Maggie," with the clever and inhumane production of half a century earlier, "The Auld Man's Mare's dead," we see in a nutshell the spirit of the change introduced by Burns. And as to its manner, who that has read it can forget how the collie, Luath, in the "Twa Dogs," describes and enters into the merry-making in the cottage?

> The luntin' pipe an' sneeshin' mill,
> Are handed round wi' richt guid will;
> The canty auld folks crackin' crouse,
> The young anes rantin' through the house—
> My heart has been sae fain to see them
> That I for joy hae barkit wi' them

It was this ardent power of sympathy that was fatal to so many women, and, through Jean Armour, to himself at last. His humor comes from him in a stream so deep and easy that I will venture to call him the best of humorous poets. He turns about in the midst to utter a noble sentiment or a trenchant remark on human life, and the style changes and rises to the occasion. I think it is Principal Shairp who says, happily, that Burns would have been no Scotchman if he had not loved to moralize; neither, may we add, would he have been his father's son; but (what is worthy of note) his moralizings are to a large extent the moral of his own career. He was among the least impersonal of artists. Except in the "Jolly Beggars," he shows no gleam of dramatic instinct. Mr. Carlyle has complained that "Tam o' Shanter" is, from the absence of this quality, only a picturesque and external piece of work; and I may add that in the "Twa Dogs" it is precisely in the infringement of dramatic propriety that a great deal of the humor of the speeches depends for its existence and effect. Indeed, Burns was so full of his identity that it breaks forth on every page; and there is scarce an appropriate remark either in praise or blame of his own conduct, but he has put it himself into verse. Alas! for the tenor of these remarks! They are, indeed, his own pitiful apology for such a marred existence and talents so misused and stunted; and they seem to prove forever how small a part is played by reason in the conduct of man's affairs. Here was one, at least, who with unfailing judgment predicted his own fate; yet his knowledge could not avail him, and with open eyes he must fulfil his tragic destiny. Ten years before the end he had written his epitaph; and neither subsequent events, nor the critical eyes of posterity, have shown us a word in it to alter. And, lastly, has he not put in for himself the last unanswerable plea?—

> Then gently scan your brother man,
>   Still gentler sister woman;
> Though they may gang a kennin wrang,
>   To step aside is human:
> One point must still be greatly dark—

One? Alas! I fear every man and woman of us is "greatly dark" to all their neighbors, from the day of birth until death removes them, in their greatest virtues as well as in their saddest faults; and we, who have been trying to read the character of Burns, may take home the lesson and be gentle in our thoughts.

WALT WHITMAN
From "Robert Burns as Poet and Person" (1882/1886)
Prose Works, ed. Floyd Stovall
1964, Volume 2, pp. 558–68

What the future will decide about Robert Burns and his works—what place will be assign'd them on that great roster of geniuses and genius which can only be finish'd by the slow but sure balancing of the centuries with their ample average—I of course cannot tell. But as we know him, from his recorded utterances, and after nearly one century, and its diligence of collections, songs, letters, anecdotes, presenting the figure of the canny Scotchman in a fullness and detail wonderfully complete, and the lines mainly by his own hand, he forms to-day, in some respects, the most interesting personality among singers. Then there are many things in Burns's poems and character that specially endear him to America. He was essentially a Republican—would have been at home in the Western United States, and probably become eminent there. He was an average sample of the good-natured, warm-blooded, proud-spirited, amative, alimentive, convivial, young and early-middle-aged man of the decent-born middle classes everywhere and any how. Without the race of which he is a distinct specimen, (and perhaps his poems) America and her powerful Democracy could not exist to-day—could not project with unparallel'd historic sway into the future.

Perhaps the peculiar coloring of the era of Burns needs always first to be consider'd. It included the times of the '76–'83 Revolution in America, of the French Revolution, and an unparallel'd chaos development in Europe and elsewhere. In every department, shining and strange names, like stars, some rising, some in meridian, some declining—Voltaire, Franklin, Washington, Kant, Goethe, Fulton, Napoleon, mark the era. And while so much, and of grandest moment, fit for the trumpet of the world's fame, was being transacted—that little tragi-comedy of R. B.'s life and death was going on in a country by-place in Scotland! ⟨. . .⟩

I would say a large part of the fascination of Burns's homely, simple dialect-melodies is due, for all current and future readers, to the poet's personal "errors," the general bleakness of his lot, his ingrain'd pensiveness, his brief dash into dazzling, tantalizing, evanescent sunshine—finally culminating in those last years of his life, his being taboo'd and in debt, sick and sore, yaw'd as by contending gales, deeply dissatisfied with everything, most of all with himself—high-spirited too—(no man ever really higher-spirited than Robert Burns.) I think it a perfectly legitimate part too. At any rate it has come to be an impalpable aroma through which only both the songs and their singer must henceforth be read and absorb'd. Through that view-medium of misfortune—of a noble spirit in low environments, and of a squalid and premature death—we view the undoubted facts, (giving, as we read them now, a sad kind of pungency,) that Burns's were, before all else, the lyrics of illicit loves and carousing intoxication. Perhaps even it is this strange, impalpable *post-mortem* comment and influence referr'd to, that gives them their contrast, attraction, making the zest of their author's after fame. If he had lived steady, fat, moral, comfortable, well-to-do years, on his own grade, (let alone what of course was out of the question, the ease and velvet and rosewood and copious royalties of Tennyson or Victor Hugo or Longfellow,) and died well-ripen'd and respectable, where could have come in that burst of passionate sobbing and remorse which well'd forth instantly and generally in Scotland, and soon follow'd everywhere among English-speaking races, on the announcement of his death? and which, with no sign of stopping, only regulated and vein'd with fitting appreciation, flows deeply, widely yet?

Dear Rob! manly, witty, fond, friendly, full of weak spots as well as strong ones—essential type of so many thousands—perhaps the average, as just said, of the decent-born young men and the early mid-aged, not only of the British Isles, but America, too, North and South, just the same. I think, indeed, one best part of Burns is the unquestionable proof he presents of the perennial existence among the laboring classes, especially farmers, of the finest latent poetic elements in their blood. (How clear it is to me that the common soil has always been, and is now, thickly strewn with just such gems.) He is well-called the *Ploughman*. "Holding the plough," said his brother Gilbert, "was the favorite situation with Robert for poetic compositions; and some of his best verses were produced while he was at that exercise." "I must return to my humble station, and woo my rustic muse in my wonted way, at the plough-tail." 1787, to the Earl of Buchan. He has no high ideal of the poet or the poet's office; indeed quite a low and contracted notion of both:

> Fortune! if thou'll but gie me still
> Hale breeks, a scone, and whiskey gill,
> An' rowth o' rhyme to rave at will,
>   Tak' a' the rest.

See also his rhym'd letters to Robert Graham invoking patronage; "one stronghold," Lord Glencairn, being dead, now these appeals to "Fintra, my other stay," (with in one letter a copious shower of vituperation generally.) In his collected poems there is no particular unity, nothing that can be called a leading theory, no unmistakable spine or skeleton. Perhaps, indeed, their very desultoriness is the charm of his songs: "I take up one or another," he says in a letter to Thompson, "just as the bee of the moment buzzes in my bonnet-lug."

Consonantly with the customs of the time—yet markedly inconsistent in spirit with Burns's own case, (and not a little painful as it remains on record, as depicting some features of the bard himself,) the relation called *patronage* existed between the nobility and gentry on one side, and literary people on the other, and gives one of the strongest side-lights to the general coloring of poems and poets. It crops out a good deal in Burns's Letters, and even necessitated a certain flunkeyism on occasions, through life. It probably, with its requirements, (while it help'd in money and countenance) did as much as any one cause in making that life a chafed and unhappy one, ended by a premature and miserable death.

Yes, there is something about Burns peculiarly acceptable to the concrete, human points of view. He poetizes work-a-day agricultural labor and life, (whose spirit and sympathies, as well as practicalities, are much the same everywhere,) and treats fresh, often coarse, natural occurrences, loves, persons, not like many new and some old poets in a genteel style of gilt and china, or at second or third removes, but in their own born atmosphere, laughter, sweat, unction. Perhaps no one ever sang "lads and lasses"—that universal race, mainly the same, too, all ages, all lands—down on their own plane, as he has. He exhibits no philosophy worth mentioning; his morality is hardly more than parrot-talk—not bad or deficient, but cheap, shopworn, the platitudes of old aunts and uncles to the youngsters (be good boys and keep your noses clean.) Only when he gets at Poosie Nansie's, celebrating the "barley bree," or among tramps, or democratic bouts and drinking generally,

(Freedom and whiskey gang thegither,)

we have, in his own unmistakable color and warmth, those interiors of rake-helly life and tavern fun—the cantabile of jolly beggars in highest jinks—lights and groupings of rank glee and brawny amorousness, outvying the best painted pictures of the Dutch school, or any school.

By America and her democracy such a poet, I cannot too often repeat, must be kept in loving remembrance; but it is best that discriminations be made. His admirers (as at those anniversary suppers, over the "hot Scotch") will not accept for their favorite anything less than the highest rank, alongside of Homer, Shakspere, etc. Such, in candor, are not the true friends of the Ayrshire bard, who really needs a different place quite by himself. The Iliad and the Odyssey express courage, craft, full-grown heroism in situations of danger, the sense of command and leadership, emulation, the last and fullest evolution of self-poise as in kings, and godlike even while animal appetites. The Shaksperean compositions, on vertebers and framework of the primary passions, portray (essentially the same as Homer's,) the spirit and letter of the feudal world, the Norman lord, ambitious and arrogant, taller and nobler than common men—with much underplay and gusts of heat and cold, volcanoes and stormy seas. Burns (and some will say to his credit) attempts none of these themes. He poetizes the humor, riotous blood, sulks, amorous torments, fondness for the tavern and for cheap objective nature, with disgust at the grim and narrow ecclesiasticism of his time and land, of a young farmer on a bleak and hired farm in Scotland, through the years and under the circumstances of the British politics of that time, and of his short personal career as author, from 1783 to 1796. He is intuitive and affectionate, and just emerged or emerging from the shackles of the kirk, from poverty, ignorance, and from his own rank appetites—(out of which latter, however, he never extricated himself.) It is to be said that amid not a little smoke and gas in his poems, there is in almost every piece a spark of fire, and now and then the real afflatus. He has been applauded as democratic, and with some warrant; while Shakspere, and with the greatest warrant, has been called monarchical or aristocratic (which he certainly is.) But the splendid personalizations of Shakspere, formulated on the largest, freest, most heroic, most artistic mould, are to me far dearer as lessons, and more precious even as models for Democracy, than the humdrum samples Burns presents. The motives of some of his effusions are certainly discreditable personally—one or two of them markedly so. He has, moreover, little or no spirituality. This last is his mortal flaw and defect, tried by highest standards. The ideal he never reach'd (and yet I think he leads the way to it.) He gives melodies, and now and then the simplest and sweetest ones; but harmonies, complications, oratorios in words, never. (I do not speak this in any deprecatory sense. Blessed be the memory of the warm-hearted Scotchman for what he has left us, just as it is!) He likewise did not know himself, in more ways than one. Though so really free and independent, he prided himself in his songs on being a reactionist and a Jacobite—on persistent sentimental adherency to the cause of the Stuarts—the weakest, thinnest, most faithless, brainless dynasty that ever held a throne.

Thus, while Burns is not at all great for New World study, in the sense that Isaiah and Eschylus and the book of Job are unquestionably great—is not to be mention'd with Shakspere—hardly even with current Tennyson or our Emerson—he has a nestling niche of his own, all fragrant, fond, and quaint and homely—a lodge built near but outside the mighty temple of the gods of song and art—those universal strivers, through their works of harmony and melody and power, to ever show or intimate man's crowning, last, victorious fusion in himself of Real and Ideal. Precious, too—fit and precious beyond all singers, high or low—will Burns ever be to the native Scotch, especially to the working-classes of North Britain; so intensely one of them, and so racy of the soil, sights, and local customs. He often apostrophizes Scotland, and is, or would be, enthusiastically patriotic. His country has lately commemorated him in a statue. His aim is declaredly to be 'a Rustic Bard.' His poems were all written in youth or young manhood, (he was little more than a young man when he died.) His collected works in giving everything, are nearly one half first drafts. His brightest hit is his use of the Scotch patois, so full of terms flavor'd like wild fruits or berries. Then I should make an allowance to Burns which cannot be made for any other poet. Curiously even the frequent crudeness, haste, deficiencies, (flatness and puerilities by no means absent) prove upon the whole not out of keeping in any comprehensive collection of his works, heroically printed, 'following copy,' every piece, every line according to originals. Other poets might tremble for such boldness, such rawness. In 'this odd-kind chiel' such points hardly mar the rest. Not only are they in consonance with the underlying spirit of the pieces, but complete the full abandon and veracity of the farm-fields and the home-brew'd flavor of the Scotch vernacular. (Is there not often something in the very neglect, unfinish, careless nudity, slovenly hiatus, coming from intrinsic genius, and not 'put on,' that secretly pleases the soul more than the wrought and re-wrought polish of the most perfect verse?) Mark the native spice and untranslatable twang in the very names of his songs—"O for ane and twenty, Tam," "John Barleycorn," "Last May a braw Wooer," "Rattlin roarin Willie," "O wert thou in the cauld, cauld blast," "Gude e'en to you, Kimmer," "Merry hae I been teething a Heckle," "O lay thy loof in mine, lass," and others.

The longer and more elaborated poems of Burns are just such as would please a natural but homely taste, and cute but average intellect, and are inimitable in their way. The "Twa Dogs," (one of the best) with the conversation between Cesar and Luath, the "Brigs of Ayr," "the Cotter's Saturday Night," "Tam O'Shanter"—all will be long read and re-read and admired, and ever deserve to be. With nothing profound in any of them, what there is of moral and plot has an inimitably fresh and racy flavor. If it came to question, Literature could well afford to send adrift many a pretensive poem, and even book of poems, before it could spare these compositions.

Never indeed was there truer utterance in a certain range of idiosyncracy than by this poet. Hardly a piece of his, large or small, but has "snap" and raciness. He puts in cantering rhyme (often doggerel) much cutting irony and idiomatic ear-cuffing of the kirk-deacons—drily good-natured addresses to his cronies, (he certainly would not stop us if he were here this moment, from classing that "to the De'il" among them)—"to Mailie and her Lambs," "to auld Mare Maggie," "to a Mouse,"

Wee, sleekit, cowrin, tim'rous beastie:

"to a Mountain Daisy," "to a Haggis," "to a Louse," "to the Toothache," etc.—and occasionally to his brother bards and lady or gentleman patrons, often with strokes of tenderest sensibility, idiopathic humor, and genuine poetic imagination—still oftener with shrewd, original, sheeny, steel-flashes of wit, home-spun sense, or lance-blade puncturing. Then, strangely, the basis of Burns's character, with all its fun and manliness, was hypochondria, the blues, palpable enough in "Despondency," "Man was made to Mourn," "Address to Ruin," a "Bard's Epitaph," &c. From such deep-down elements sprout up, in very contrast and paradox, those riant

utterances of which a superficial reading will not detect the hidden foundation. Yet nothing is clearer to me than the black and desperate background behind those pieces—as I shall now specify them. I find his most characteristic, Nature's masterly touch and luxuriant life-blood, color and heat, not in "Tam O'Shanter," "the Cotter's Saturday Night," "Scots wha hae," "Highland Mary," "the Twa Dogs," and the like, but in "the Jolly Beggars," "Rigs of Barley," "Scotch Drink," "the Epistle to John Rankine," "Holy Willie's Prayer," and in "Halloween," (to say nothing of a certain cluster, known still to a small inner circle in Scotland, but, for good reasons, not published anywhere.) In these compositions, especially the first, there is much indelicacy (some editions flatly leave it out,) but the composer reigns alone, with handling free and broad and true, and is an artist. You may see and feel the man indirectly in his other verses, all of them, with more or less life-likeness—but these I have named last call out pronouncedly in his own voice,

I, Rob, am here.

Finally, in any summing-up of Burns, though so much is to be said in the way of fault-finding, drawing black marks, and doubtless severe literary criticism—(in the present outpouring I have 'kept myself in,' rather than allow'd any free flow)—after full retrospect of his works and life, the aforesaid 'odd-kind chiel' remains to my heart and brain as almost the tenderest, manliest, and (even if contradictory) dearest flesh-and-blood figure in all the streams and clusters of by-gone poets.

GABRIEL SETOUN
"Summary and Estimate"
Robert Burns
1896, pp. 148–60

In Mrs. Riddell's sketch of Burns, which appeared shortly after his death, she starts with the somewhat startling statement that poetry was not actually his *forte*. She did not question the excellence of his songs, or seek to depreciate his powers as a poet, but she spoke of the man as she had known him, and was one of the first to assert that Burns was very much more than an uneducated peasant with a happy knack of versification. Even in the present day we hear too much of the inspired ploughman bursting into song as one that could not help himself, and warbling of life and love in a kind of lyrical frenzy. The fact is that Burns was a great intellectual power, and would have been a force in any sphere of life or letters. All who met him and heard him talk have insisted on the greatness of the man, apart from his achievements in poetry. It was not his fame as a poet that made him the lion of a season in Edinburgh, but the force and brilliancy of his conversation; and it needs more than the reputation of a minstrel to explain the hold he has on the affection and intelligence of the world to-day.

On the other hand, it would be a mistake to accept his intellectual greatness as a mere tradition of those who knew him, and to regret that he has not left us some long and ponderous work worthy of the power he possessed. It is an absurd idea to imagine that every great poet ought to write an epic or a play. Burns's powers were concentrative, and he could put into a song what a dramatist might elaborate into a five-act tragedy; but that is not to say that the dramatist is the greater poet. After all, the song is the more likely to live, and the more likely, therefore, to keep the mission of the poet an enduring and living influence in the lives of men.

Still Burns might have been a great song-writer without becoming the name and power he is in the world to-day. The lyrical gift implies a quick emotional sense, which in some cases may be little more than a beautiful defect in a weak nature. But Burns was essentially a strong man. His very vices are the vices of a robust and healthy humanity. Besides being possessed of all the qualities of a great singer, he was at the same time vigorously human and throbbing with the love and joy of life. It is this sterling quality of manhood that has made Burns the poet and the power he is. He looked out on the world with the eyes of a man, and saw things in their true colours and in their natural relations. He regarded the world into which he had been born, and saw it not as some other poet or an artist or a painter might have beheld it,—for the purposes of art,— but in all its uncompromising realism; and what his eye saw clearly, his lips as clearly uttered. His first and greatest gift, therefore, as a poet was his manifest sincerity. His men and women are living human beings; his flowers are real flowers; his dogs, real dogs, and nothing more. All his pictures are presented in the simplest and fewest possible words. There is no suspicion of trickery; no attempt to force words to carry a weight of meaning they are incapable of expressing. He knew nothing of the deification of style, and on absolute truthfulness and unidealised reality rested his poetical structure. Words-worth speaks of him—

> Whose light I hailed when first it shone,
> And showed my youth
> How verse may build a princely throne
> On humble truth.

It is this quality that made Burns the interpreter of the lives of his fellow-men, not only to an outside world that knew them not, but to themselves. And he has glorified those lives in the interpretation, not by the introduction of false elements or the elimination of unlovely features, but simply by his insis-tence, in spite of the sordidness of poverty, on the naked dignity of man.

Everything he touched became interesting because it was interesting to him, and he spoke forth what he felt. For Burns did not go outside of his own life, either in time or place, for subject. There are poetry and romance, tragedy and comedy ever waiting for the man who has eyes to see them; and Burns's stage was the parish of Tarbolton, and he found his poetry in (or rendered poetical) the ordinary humdrum life round about him. For that reason it is, perhaps, that he has been called the satirist and singer of a parish. Had he lived nowadays, he would have been relegated to the kailyard, there to cultivate his hardy annuals and indigenous daisies. For Burns did not affect exotics, and it requires a specialist in manure to produce blue dandelions or sexless ferns. In the narrow sense of the word he was not parochial. Whilst true to class and country, he reached out a hand to universal man. A Scotsman of Scotsmen, he endeared himself to the hearts of a people; but he was from first to last a man, and so has found entrance to the hearts of all men. Although local in subject, he was artistic in treatment; he might address the men and women of Mauchline, but he spoke with the voice of humanity, and his message was for mankind.

Besides interpreting the lives of the Scottish peasantry, he revived for them their nationality. For he was but the last of the great bards that sang the Iliad of Scotland; and in him, when patriotism was all but dead, and a hybrid culture was making men ashamed of their land and their language, the voices of nameless ballad-makers and forgotten singers blended again

into one great voice that sang of the love of country, till men remembered their fathers, and gloried in the name of Scots-men. His patriotism, however, was not parochial. It was no mere prejudice which bound him hand and foot to Scottish theme and Scottish song. He knew that there were lands beyond the Cheviots, and that men of other countries and other tongues joyed and sorrowed, toiled and sweated and struggled and hoped even as he did. He was attached to the people of his own rank in life, the farmers and ploughmen amongst whom he had been born and bred; but his sympathies went out to all men, prince or peasant, beggar or king, if they were worthy of the name of men he recognised them as brothers. It is this sympathy which gives him his intimate knowledge of mankind. He sees into the souls of his fellows; the thoughts of their hearts are visible to his piercing eye. He who had mixed only with hard-working men, and scarcely ever been beyond the boundary of his parish, wrote of court and parliament as if he had known princes and politicians from his boyhood. The goodwife of Wauchope House would hardly credit that he had come straight from the plough-stilts—

> And then sae slee ye crack your jokes
> O' Willie Pitt and Charlie Fox;
> Our great men a' sae weel descrive,
> And how to gar the nation thrive,
> Ane maist would swear ye dwalt amang them,
> And as ye saw them sae ye sang them.

But his intuitive knowledge of men is apparent in almost all he wrote. Every character he has drawn stands out a living and breathing personality. This is greatly due to the fact that he studied those he met, as *men*, dismissing the circumstance of birth and rank, of costly apparel, or beggarly rags. For rank and station after all are mere accidents, and count for nothing in an estimate of character. Indeed, Burns was too often inclined from his hard experience of life to go further than this, and to count them disqualifying circumstances. This aggressive inde-pendence was, however, always as far removed from insolence as it was from servility. He saw clearly that the 'pith o' sense and pride o' worth' are beyond all the dignities a king can bestow; and he looked to the time when class distinctions would cease, and the glory of manhood be the highest earthly dignity.

> Then let us pray that come it may—
> As come it will for a' that—
> That sense and worth, o'er a' the earth,
> May bear the gree and a' that!
> For a' that, and a' that,
> It's comin' yet, for a' that,
> That man to man, the warld o'er,
> Shall brothers be for a ' that!

Besides this abiding love of his fellow-man, or because of it, Burns had also a childlike love of nature and all created things. He sings of the mountain daisy turned up by his plough; his heart goes out to the mouse rendered homeless after all its provident care. Listening at home while the storm made the doors and windows rattle, he bethought him on the cattle and sheep and birds outside—

> I thought me on the ourie cattle
> Or silly sheep, wha bide this brattle
> O' wintry war,
> And thro' the drift, deep-lairing, sprattle
> Beneath a scaur.

Nor is there in his love of nature any transcendental strain; no mawkish sentimentality, and consequently in its expression no bathos. Everywhere in his poetry nature comes in, at times in artistically selected detail, at times again with a deft suggestive touch that is telling and effective, yet always in harmony with the feeling of the poem, and always subordinate to it. His descriptions of scenery are never dragged in. They are incidental and complementary; human life and human feeling are the first consideration; to this his scenery is but the setting and background. He is never carried away by the force or beauty of his drawing as a smaller artist might have been. The picture is given with simple conciseness, and he leaves it; nor does he ever attempt to elaborate a detail into a separate poem. The description of the burn in "Hallowe'en" is most beautiful in itself, yet it is but a detail in a great picture—

> Whyles owre a linn the burnie plays,
> As thro' the glen it wimpl't;
> Whyles round a rocky scaur it strays;
> Whyles in a wiel it dimpl't;
> Whyles glitter'd to the nightly rays,
> Wi' bickerin', dancin' dazzle;
> Whyles cookit underneath the braes,
> Below the spreading hazel,
> Unseen that night.

That surely is the perfection of description; whilst the wimple of the burn is echoed in the music of the verse!

Allied to the clearness of vision and truthfulness of presentment of Burns, growing out of them it may be, is that graphic power in which he stands unexcelled. He is a great artist, and word-painting is not the least of his many gifts. He combines terseness and lucidity, which is a rare combination in letters; his phrasing is as beautiful and fine as it is forcible, which is a distinction rarer still. Hundreds of examples of his pregnant phrasing might be cited, but it is best to see them in the poems. Many have become everyday expressions, and have passed into the proverbs of the country.

Another of Burns's gifts was the saving grace of humour. This, of course, is not altogether a quality distinct in itself, but rather a particular mode in which love or tenderness or pity may manifest itself. This humour is ever glinting forth from his writings. Some of his poems—"The Farmer's Address to his Auld Mare," for example—are simply bathed in it, and we see the subject glowing in its light, soft and tremulous, as of an autumn sunset. In others, again, it flashes and sparkles, more sportive than tender. But, however it manifest itself, we recognise at once that it has a character of its own, which marks it off from the humour of any other writer; it is a peculiar possession of Burns.

Perhaps the poem in which all Burns's poetic qualities are seen at their best is "The Jolly Beggars." The subject may be low and the materials coarse, but that only makes the finished poem a more glorious achievement. For the poem is a unity. We see those vagabonds for a moment's space holding high revel in Poosie Nansie's; but in that brief glance we see them from their birth to their death. They are flung into the world, and go zigzagging through it, chaffering and cheating, swaggering and swearing; kicked and cuffed from parish to parish; their only joy of existence an occasional night like this, a carnival of drink and all sensuality; snapping their fingers in the face of the world, and as they have lived so going down defiantly to death, a laugh on their lips and a curse in their heart. Every character in it is individual and distinct from his neighbour; the language from first to last simple, sensuous, musical. Of his poem Matthew Arnold says: 'It has a breadth, truth, and power which make the famous scene in Auerbach's cellar of Goethe's *Faust* seem artificial and tame beside it, and which are only matched by Shakspeare and Aristophanes.'

"The Cotter's Saturday Night" has usually, in Scotland, been the most lauded of his poems. Many writers give it as his best. It is a pious opinion, but is not sound criticism. Burns handicapped himself, not only by the stanza he selected for this poem, but also by the attitude he took towards his subject. He is never quite himself in it. We admire its many beauties; we see the life of the poor made noble and dignified; we see, in the end, the soul emerging from the tyranny of time and circumstance; but with all that we feel that there is something awanting. The priest-like father is drawn from life, and the picture is beautiful; not less deftly drawn is the mother's portrait, though it be not so frequently quoted:

> The mother, wi' a woman's wiles, can spy
> What makes the youth so bashfu' and so grave;
> Weel pleased to think her bairn's respected like the lave.

The last line gives one of the most natural and most subtle touches in the whole poem. The closing verses are, I think, unhappy. The poet has not known when to stop, keeps writing after he has finished, and so becomes stilted and artificial.

It is in his songs, however, more than in his poems, that we find Burns most regularly at his best. And excellence in song-writing is a rare gift. The snatches scattered here and there throughout the plays of Shakspeare are perhaps the only collection of lyrics that can at all stand comparison with the wealth of minstrelsy Burns has left behind him. This was his undying legacy to the world. Song-writing was a labour of love, almost his only comfort and consolation in the dark days of his later years. He set himself to this as to a congenial task, and he knew that he was writing himself into the hearts of unborn generations. His songs live; they are immortal, because every one is a bit of his soul. These are no feverish, hysterical jingles of clinking verse, dead save for the animating breath of music. They sing themselves, because the spirit of song is in them. Quite as marvellous as his excellence in this department of poetry is his variety of subject. He has a song for every age; a musical interpretation of every mood. But this is a subject for a book to itself. His songs are sung all over the world. The love he sings appeals to all, for it is elemental, and is the love of all. Heart speaks to heart in the songs of Robert Burns; there is a free-masonry in them that binds Scotsmen to Scotsmen across the seas in the firmest bonds of brotherhood.

What place Burns occupies as a poet has been determined not so much by the voice of criticism, as by the enthusiastic way in which his fellow-mortals have taken him to their heart. The summing-up of a judge counts for little when the jury has already made up its mind. What matters it whether a critic argues Burns into a first or second or third rate poet? His countrymen, and more than his countrymen, his brothers all the world over, who read in his writings the joys and sorrows, the temptations and trials, the sins and shortcomings of a great-hearted man, have accepted him as a prophet, and set him in the front rank of immortals. They admire many poets; they love Robert Burns. They have been told their love is unreasoning and unreasonable. It may be so. Love goes by instinct more than by reason; and who shall say it is wrong? Yet Burns is not loved because of his faults and failings, but in spite of them. His sins are not hidden. He himself confessed them again and again, and repented in sackcloth and ashes. If he did not always abjure his weaknesses, he denounced them, and with no uncertain voice; nor do we know how hardly he strove to do more.

What estimate is to be taken of Burns as a man will have many and various answers. Those who still denounce him as the chief of sinners, and without mercy condemn him out of his own mouth, are those whom Burns has pilloried to all posterity. There are dull, phlegmatic beings with blood no warmer than ditch-water, who are virtuous and sober citizens because they have never felt the force of temptation. What power could tempt them? The tree may be parched and blistered in the heat of noonday, but the parasitical fungus draining its sap reamins cool—and poisonous. So in the glow of sociability the Pharisee remains cold and clammy; the fever of love leaves his blood at zero. How can such anomalies understand a man of Burns's wild and passionate nature, or, indeed, human nature at all? The broad fact remains, however much we may deplore his sins and shortcomings, they are the sins and shortcomings of a large-hearted, healthy, human being. Had he loved less his fellow men and women, he might have been accounted a better man. After all, too, it must be remembered that his failings have been consistently exaggerated. Coleridge, in his habit of drawing nice distinctions, admits that Burns was not a man of degraded genius, but a degraded man of genius. Burns was neither the one nor the other. In spite of the occasional excesses of his later years, he did not degenerate into drunkenness, nor was the sense of his responsibilities as a husband, a father, and a man less clear and acute in the last months of his life than it had ever been. Had he lived a few years longer, we should have seen the man mellowed by sorrow and suffering, braving life, not as he had done all along with the passionate vehemence of undisciplined youth, but with the fortitude and dignity of one who had learned that contentment and peace are gifts the world cannot give, and, if he haply find them in his own heart, which it cannot take away. That is the lesson we read in the closing months of Burns's chequered career.

But it was not to be. His work was done. The message God had sent him into the world to deliver he had delivered, imperfectly and with faltering lips it may be, but a divine message all the same. And because it is divine men still hear it gladly and believe.

Let all his failings and defects be acknowledged, his sins as a man and his limitations as a poet, the want of continuity and purpose in his work and life; but at the same time let his nobler qualities be weighed against these, and the scale 'where the pure gold is, easily turns the balance.' In the words of Angellier: 'Admiration grows in proportion as we examine his

qualities. When we think of his sincertiy, of his rectitude, of his kindness towards man and beast; of his scorn of all that is base, his hatred of all knavery which in itself would be an honour; of his disinterestedness, of the fine impulses of his heart, and the high aspirations of his spirit; of the intensity and idealism necessary to maintain his soul above its circumstances; when we reflect that he has expressed all these generous sentiments to the extent of their constituting his intellectual life; that they have fallen from him as jewels . . . as if his soul had been a furnace for the purification of precious metals, we are tempted to regard him as belonging to the elect spirits of humanity, to those gifted with exceptional goodness. When we recall what he suffered, what he surmounted, and what he has effected; against what privations his genius struggled into birth and lived; the perseverance of his apprenticeship; his intellectual exploits; and, after all, his glory, we are inclined to maintain that what he failed to accomplish or undertake is as nothing in comparison with his achievements. . . . There is nothing left but to confess that the clay of which he was made was thick with diamonds, and that his life was one of the most valiant and the most noble a poet ever has lived.'

With Burns's own words we may fitly conclude. They are words not merely to be read and admired, but to be remembered in our hearts and practised in our lives—

> Then gently scan your brother Man,
>   Still gentler sister Woman;
> Tho' they may gang a kennin wrang,
>   To step aside is human:
> One point must still be greatly dark,
>   The moving *Why* they do it;
> And just as lamely can ye mark,
>   How far perhaps they rue it.
>
> Who made the heart, 'tis He alone
>   Decidedly can try us,
> He knows each chord—its various tone,
>   Each spring—its various bias:
> Then at the balance let's be mute,
>   We never can adjust it;
> What's *done* we partly may compute,
>   But know not what's *resisted*.

Richard Brinsley Sheridan

RICHARD BRINSLEY SHERIDAN

1751–1816

Richard Brinsley Sheridan was born in Dublin in September or October 1751. He was exposed to the theatre at an early age by his father Thomas Sheridan, an actor-manager, and by his mother Frances Sheridan, who was both a novelist and a playwright. When Richard Sheridan was quite young his family moved to England, where he was educated at Harrow and also tutored privately by his father. In 1770 he moved from Soho to Bath to help run his father's new Academy of Oratory, and while in Bath wrote *Ixion*, a burlesque burletta, in collaboration with his friend Nathaniel Halhed, who was then at Oxford. In 1771 he published two satiric poems, "The Ridotto of Bath," and "Clio's Protest," and translated and published (with Halhed) *The Love Epistles of Aristaenetus*.

Sheridan had by this time become infatuated with Elizabeth Linley, whom he married despite parental opposition in April 1773. Two years later his son Thomas was born. After his marriage Sheridan turned to the theatre for a livelihood, and soon arranged to have several of his plays performed at Covent Garden. These were *The Rivals*, *St. Patrick's Day*, and *The Duenna*, all premiered with great success in 1775. In 1776, in partnership with James Ford and Linley, Sheridan took over David Garrick's shares in the Drury Lane Theatre, and in September of that year became the theatre's manager. Sheridan's play *A Trip to Scarborough*, based on Vanbrugh's *The Relapse* (1696), was produced at Drury Lane in 1777, as was *The School for Scandal*, which Garrick helped to make a tremendous success. Another play that was very well received was his adaptation of Buckingham's *The Rehearsal* (1671), produced in 1779 as *The Critic*.

Although he had become one of the most important theatrical figures of his time, Sheridan had not yet realized his greatest ambition—to enter the world of politics. Upon gaining the friendship and support of Charles James Fox he was elected M.P. for Stafford in 1780; thereafter he handed over the direction of his theatre to a succession of managers. While he continued to adapt plays and to supervise spectacular productions, Sheridan wrote only one more full-length piece, *Pizarro* (1799), based on August von Kotzebue's *Die Spanier in Peru* (1796). After only two years as an M.P. he became the Undersecretary for Foreign Affairs in 1782, and in 1783 was appointed Secretary to the Treasury. In the House of Commons he established a reputation as a brilliant orator, and by 1787 he had become an intimate friend of the Prince Regent and other royal figures.

Sheridan's luck began to turn in 1792. In that year his wife and infant daughter died, and the Drury Lane Theatre was declared unsafe and had to be demolished. Although Sheridan was able to raise the money for a new theatre, by doing so he put himself deeply into debt. At the same time his friendship with Fox was fading, and when Grenville formed the "Ministry of all the talents" in 1806 Sheridan was offered only the relatively unimportant post of Treasurer of the Navy. After Fox's death in 1806 Sheridan took over his seat, but he did not win the leadership of the Whig opposition he had hoped for, and one year later was voted out of the seat. In 1809 the Drury Lane Theatre was destroyed by fire, and the company was then re-established at the Lyceum, under the management of Samuel Whitbread. In 1812 Sheridan stood for Stafford again, but was defeated. Having lost his income from the theatre as well as parliamentary seat, Sheridan fell prey to his creditors, and in 1813 he was briefly imprisoned for debt. By this time both he and his second wife were ill, and three years later, on July 7, 1816, Sheridan died in London. Byron's "Monody on the Death of Sheridan" appeared shortly afterwards, and was followed by the biographies of Thomas Moore (1825) and William Smyth (1840).

Personal

Mr. Sheridan has a very fine figure, and a good though I don't think a handsome face. He is tall, and very upright, and his appearance and address are at once manly and fashionable, without the smallest tincture of foppery or modish graces. In short, I like him vastly, and think him every way worthy his beautiful companion.—FANNY BURNEY, *Diary*, 1779

It was some Spirit, SHERIDAN! that breath'd
   O'er thy young mind such wildly-various power!
   My soul hath mark'd thee in her shaping hour,
Thy temples with Hymettian flow'rets wreath'd:
And sweet thy voice, as when o'er LAURA's bier
   Sad Music trembled thro' Vauclusa's glade

Sweet, as at dawn the love-lorn Serenade
That wafts soft dreams to SLUMBER's listening ear.
Now patriot Rage and Indignation high
   Swell the full tones! And now thine eye-beams dance
   Meanings of Scorn and Wit's quaint revelry!
Writhes inly from the bosom-probing glance
The Apostate by the brainless rout ador'd,
As erst that elder Fiend beneath great Michael's sword.
   —SAMUEL TAYLOR COLERIDGE, "To Richard Brinsley Sheridan, Esq.," 1795

Sheridan is very little consulted at present; and it is said, will not have a seat in the cabinet. This is a distressing necessity. His habits of daily intoxication are probably considered as unfitting him for trust. The little that has been confided to him he has been running about to tell; and since Monday, he has been visiting Sidmouth. At a dinner at Lord Cowper's on Sunday last, where the Prince was, he got drunk as usual, and began to speak slightingly of Fox. From what grudge this behaviour proceeds I have not learned. The whole fact is one to investigate with candour, and with a full remembrance of Sheridan's great services, in the worst times, to the principles of liberty.—FRANCIS HORNER, *Journal* (Jan. 29, 1806), *Memoirs and Correspondence of Francis Horner*, ed. Leonard Horner, 1843, Vol. 1, p. 357

I find things settled so that £150 will remove all difficulties. I am absolutely undone and broken-hearted. I shall negotiate for the Plays successfully in the course of a week, when all shall be returned. I have desired Fairbrother to get back the Guarantee for thirty.

They are going to put the carpets out of the window, and break into Mrs. S.'s room and *take me*—for God's sake let me see you.—RICHARD BRINSLEY SHERIDAN, Letter to Samuel Rogers (May 15, 1816)

And here, oh! here, where yet all young and warm,
The gay creations of his spirit charm,
The matchless dialogue, the deathless wit,
Which knew not what it was to intermit;
The glowing portraits, fresh from life, that bring
Home to our hearts the truth from which they spring;
These wondrous beings of his fancy, wrought
To fulness by the fiat of his thought,
Here in their first abode you still may meet,
Bright with the hues of his Promethean heat;
A halo of the light of other days,
Which still the splendour of its orb betrays.

But should there be to whom the fatal blight
Of failing Wisdom yields a base delight,
Men who exult when minds of heavenly tone
Jar in the music which was born their own,
Still let them pause—ah! little do they know
That what to them seem'd Vice might be but Woe.
Hard is his fate on whom the public gaze
Is fix'd for ever to detract or praise;
Repose denies her requiem to his name,
And Folly loves the martyrdom of Fame.
The secret ememy whose sleepless eye
Stands sentinel, accuser, judge, and spy,
The foe, the fool, the jealous, and the vain,
The envious who but breathe in others' pain,
Behold the host! delighting to deprave,
Who track the steps of Glory to the grave,
Watch every fault that daring Genius owes
Half to the ardour which its birth bestows,
Distort the truth, accumulate the lie,
And pile the pyramid of Calumny!
These are his portion—but if join'd to these
Gaunt Poverty should league with deep Disease,
If the high Spirit must forget to soar,
And stoop to strive with Misery at the door,
To soothe Indignity—and face to face
Meet sordid Rage, and wrestle with Disgrace,
To find in Hope but the renew'd caress,
The serpent-fold of further Faithlessness:—
If such may be the ills which men assail,
What marvel if at last the mightiest fail?
Breasts to whom all the strength of feeling given
Bear hearts electric—charged with fire from Heaven,
Black with the rude collision, inly torn,
By clouds surrounded, and on whirlwinds borne,

Driven o'er the lowering atmosphere that nurst
Thoughts which have turn'd to thunder—scorch, and burst.

But far from us and from our mimic scene
Such things should be—if such have ever been;
Ours be the gentler wish, the kinder task,
To give the tribute Glory need not ask,
To mourn the vanish'd beam, and add our mite
Of praise in payment of a long delight.
Ye Orators! whom yet our councils yield,
Mourn for the veteran Hero of your field!
The worthy rival of the wondrous *Three!*
Whose words were sparks of Immortality!
Ye Bards! to whom the Drama's muse is dear,
He was your Master—emulate him *here!*
Ye men of wit and social eloquence!
He was your brother—bear his ashes hence!
While Powers of mind almost of boundless range,
Complete in kind, as various in their change,
While Eloquence, Wit, Poesy, and Mirth,
That humbler Harmonist of care on Earth,
Survive within our souls—while lives our sense
Of pride in Merit's proud pre-eminence,
Long shall we seek his likeness, long in vain,
And turn to all of him which may remain,
Sighing that nature form'd but one such man,
And broke the die—in moulding Sheridan!
　　　　—GEORGE GORDON, LORD BYRON, "Monody on
　　　　　　the Death of the Right Hon. R. B. Sheridan,"
　　　　　　1816, ll. 47–118

Yes, grief will have way—but the fast-falling tear
　Shall be mingled with deep execrations on those
Who could bask in that spirit's meridian career,
　And yet leave it thus lonely and dark at its close:—
Whose vanity flew round him only while fed
　By the odour his fame in its summer-time gave;
Whose vanity now, with quick scent for the dead,
　Like the ghole of the East, comes to feed at his grave

Oh! it sickens the heart to see bosoms so hollow
　And spirits so mean in the great and high-born;
To think what a long line of titles may follow
　The relics of him who died—friendless and lorn!

How proud they can press to the funeral array
　Of one whom they shunned in his sickness and sorrow!
How bailiffs may seize his last blanket to-day,
　Whose pall shall be held up by nobles to-morrow!

And thou, too, whose life, a sick epicure's dream,
　Incoherent and gross, even grosser had passed,
Were it not for that cordial and soul-giving beam
　Which his friendship and wit o'er thy nothingness cast:

No, not for the wealth of the land that supplies thee
　With millions to heap upon foppery's shrine;—
No, not for the riches of all who despise thee,
　Though this would make Europe's whole opulence mine;—

Would I suffer what—even in the heart that thou hast,
　All mean as it is—must have consciously burned,
When the pittance, which shame had wrung from thee at last,
　And which found all his wants at an end, was returned!

'Was *this*, then, the fate'—future ages will say,
　When *some* names shall live but in history's curse;
When Truth will be heard, and these lords of a day
　Be forgotten as fools, or remembered as worse—

'Was this, then, the fate of that high-gifted man,
　The pride of the palace, the bower, and the hall,
The orator—dramatist—minstrel,—who ran
　Through each mode of the lyre, and was master of all!

'Whose mind was an essence, compounded with art
  From the finest and best of all other men's powers—
Who ruled, like a wizard, the world of the heart,
  And could call up its sunshine, or bring down its showers
'Whose humour, as gay as the fire-fly's light,
  Played round every subject, and shone as it played
Whom wit, in the combat, as gentle as bright,
  Ne'er carried a heart-stain away on its blade;
'Whose eloquence—brightening whatever it tried,
  Whether reason or fancy, the gay or the grave—
Was as rapid, as deep, and as brilliant a tide
  As ever bore Freedom aloft on its wave!'
Yes—such was the man, and so wretched his fate;—
  And thus, sooner or later, shall all have to grieve,
Who waste their morn's dew in the beams of the Great,
  And expect 'twill return to refresh them at eve!
In the woods of the North there are insects that prey
  On the brain of the elk till his very last sigh;
Oh, Genius! thy patrons, more cruel than they,
  First feed on thy brains, and then leave thee to die:
       —THOMAS MOORE, "Lines on the Death of
        Sheridan," 1816

Unless Richard Brinsley Sheridan had been immeasurably superior to the majority of the men amongst whom he lived, he *could* not have so overleapt the barriers of poverty, want of connexion, and class jealousies, as to attain the celebrity and position he did attain. He *was* immeasurably superior. And, while nominally acquiescing in the sneers levelled at his origin, I beg to say that those sneers merely prove the ignorance of the writers who so assail him. If he was the son of an actor, he was the grandson of a bishop; and a bishop so conscientiously rigid in his religious opinions that all the worldly prospects of his family were blighted by the self-sacrificing fidelity with which those opinions were maintained.—CAROLINE NORTON, "Books of Gossip: Sheridan and His Biographers," *Macmillan's Magazine*, Jan. 1861, p. 177

Perhaps Sheridan was never a wise man, he can hardly be called a good one, yet he was free from the worst vices of his condition and craft. He never exhibited envy of his favoured rivals; his temper was never soured by misfortune. People said he had stolen his wit and borrowed his plots, that his fertile soil was capable of one crop and no more. But he was too well versed in the infirmities of human nature to look for generosity where he was more likely to meet with malice, and too sensible or too indolent to be angry when his experience justified his insight. Sheridan's own infirmities were inconvenient certainly, but not noxious. ⟨. . .⟩ The man who not only did not answer his letters, but neglected to read them; who not only neglected his appointments, but forgot them; who not only forgot his debts in irregular pursuits and dissipated society, but tacitly defied them, and was known to return home late at night—the muddled reveller—and wedge up his bed-room window, which rattled, with bank-notes out of his impoverished pocket, was not a man likely to prove a stay and a comfort to the people around him. Sheridan had just that minimum of selfishness which perforce adheres to the profligate; he had few or none of the higher virtues which belong to the chivalrous spirit; but force of character he certainly possessed. It is a grave error to say that either the middle or the end of life found him deficient in strength. We cannot talk of him as we have allowed ourselves to talk of Goldsmith. If he had died at thirty-seven years of age, when he stood on that apex of applause and honour which came of having written the three brightest comedies of the time and delivered the finest speech within

living memory, no career would have seemed so brilliant as his, and no character so full of force. Then, indeed, society would have counted as nothing what he sacrificed to its pleasures. But Sheridan lived to be old, to be "a poor, broken-down, dissipated old man;" and hence it is, it seems, open to some of us to talk of him as a man devoid of character, or at least of character meriting respect. The truth is that more of us than would care to own to it rejoice in friend Dogberry's genius for calculating a man's character out of his circumstances. We find, for instance, that poor Steele enjoyed a great reputation for benevolence, but that when he was upon the point of his departure for Wales, and his friends came to lay their heads together, each man was his creditor. So we conclude that this humbugging Dick was a quack. We find that poor Savage spent alternate nights under the piazzas of Covent Garden and among the ribbands of St. James's, and closed his career in a prison at Bristol, so we find it easy to conclude that this second Dick was not only a Bohemian, but a blackguard. If the life of either had been extended or abridged by five poor years our estimate might have been other than it is. And because Sheridan was checkmated at last by Whitbread, because he lost his seat in Parliament and was left by Prince and party to sink or swim, and sank but too rapidly into unknown depths of "debts and duns and drink," most of all because health failed him, and because in the shameful end he was hustled into his coffin and stolen away to the shelter of a friend's house lest he should be arrested dead—because of all this we conclude that our third Dick was a characterless prodigal of genius.

But Sheridan, like Fielding and his two afore-mentioned brothers-by-affinity, was a true son of that most un-English period and place, the eighteenth century in London. Unlike Steele, he did not spend his life in sinning and repenting, in inventing codes of morality and breaking them. Unlike Savage and Fielding, he did not run riot in more than a single sensual excess. But he was at one with all of them in regarding life, as Mrs. Oliphant says, as

> a vulgar sort of drama, a problem without any
> depths—to be solved by plenty of money and wine
> and pleasure, by youth and high spirits, and an easy
> lavishness which was called liberality or even gener-
> osity as occasion served.

And with this view of life they had each of them character enough to carry it through—Steele, like Charles Surface, with a bailiff behind the chair of every guest; Savage with the funds of Tyrconnel; Fielding with those, perhaps, of Allen; and Sheridan with his "mysterious genius for finance." This was all that there was in life for any of them, and they had nothing further to do with it, or to find out about it, at least not until the end, when Steele in Wales and Savage in Bristol, and Fielding in Lisbon and Sheridan in London—all broken in heart and shattered in body—turned pale with awe at the nearness of the death which had rarely before occupied their thoughts. But for each of them it is true, as Mrs. Oliphant eloquently says of Sheridan, that

> the finest thing of all was that death, which in
> England makes all glory possible, and which restores
> to the troublesome bankrupt, the unfortunate prod-
> igal, and all stray sons of fame, at one stroke, their
> friends and their reputation.

    —HALL CAINE, *Academy*, Sept. 15, 1883, pp. 171–72

No man has ever lived in more worlds than Sheridan, or has ever shone with such brilliancy in all. In the world of fashion, in the company of wits, among authors, painters and poets, in the House of Commons, at the Court of the Prince Regent,—whatever society he frequented,—he moved a star. His charming manners, his handsome person, his gaiety, and, above all, his good nature, which was one of his principal characteristics, rendered him universally popular. But these engaging qualities were sometimes marred by the foibles and peculiarities which are most apt to attract attention and to serve as weapons in the hands of a man's enemies. In early manhood he became one of the chiefs of a political party when party strife ran high, and when virulent calumny and abuse, in an age more coarse than ours, were considered legitimate means of offence, and his memory has suffered accordingly. Moreover, from his youth, two impediments clogged and embarrassed his every step,—his poverty and his Irish origin.—MARQUESS OF DUFFERIN AND AVA, "Introduction" to *Sheridan: A Biography* by W. Fraser Rae, 1896, Vol. 1, pp. viii–ix

Sheridan was no ordinary man. He appears to have entered the world to demonstrate by his example and conduct the utter and contemptible absurdity of proclaiming that all men can remain equal, or ought to rest satisfied with their lot. It is unhappily true that a dead level in humanity does exist; but it can only be found within the walls of an asylum for idiots. Sheridan's confidence in himself could not be repressed by penury, nor deadened by the predominance of those who were elevated above him by the accident of high birth or inherited wealth. When a boy he had resolved to rise to the top; he neither flinched nor failed in his upward course, and he lived to look down with serenity from the pinnacle of fame upon the applauding multitude below. It is inspiring to follow his steps; it is instructive to contemplate how he always despised the aid of unworthy means, and disdained employing any of the despicable tricks to which such men as his own Joseph Surface frequently resort for the attainment of their miserable ends. He was always dissatisfied and he was often imprudent; but there is an imprudence which is sublime as well as a discontent which is noble, and their manifestation in his person constitutes one of his titles to esteem. Another is the fact that, in the protracted and keen struggle with competitors, he never lost his self-control and his good humour, or ceased to bear himself with the dignity and grace of a true gentleman. Had the goal of his ambition been reached in 1779, that year would have been the concluding one in his biography. But it merely marks the close of a chapter, instead of being the final date in the diversified story of his adventurous and dazzling career.—W. FRASER RAE, *Sheridan: A Biography*, 1896, Vol. 1, pp. 346–47

Not only was Sheridan lacking in the prerogative of birth, which defect a century ago was no small affair, but he had also the twin misfortune of being a painstaking and highly successful dramatist, and the almost lifelong manager of Drury Lane Theatre. It is difficult to conceive two more absorbing occupations than those of an active parliamentary leader in stirring times, and of the master of a great theatre, respectively. The combination of the two during thirty-one years of parliamentary life, and a still longer period of theatrical possession, is among the most remarkable *tours de force*, so far as my knowledge goes, of which any man has ever made himself the victim. It was also a grave drawback, if not a misfortune, for Sheridan at his date to be an Irishman.—WILLIAM EWART GLADSTONE, "Sheridan," *Nineteenth Century*, June 1896, p. 1037

General

Sheridan, before he was first elected member for Stafford in 1780, had indeed attained the heights of dramatic celebrity; and already, in the opinion of many, rivalled Congreve. I never have, I own, so thought; nor do I consider him as entitled to dispute precedence with the author of *The Way of the World*, and of *Love for Love*. Sheridan's *Duenna*, and still more, his *School for Scandal*, are both unquestionably charming productions; nor does *The Critic* excite less admiration: but they, nevertheless, fall below the comedies of Congreve in brilliancy of wit and strength of composition, though they may possess more stage effect. The plays of Sheridan are likewise free from the licentiousness of Congreve: that defect was, however, the fault of the age, not of the author. Prior, and even Pope, are liable to the same imputation, and so are Vanbrugh and Centlivre: but the facts only prove that our manners under George the Third are much more refined and correct than they were during the reigns of Anne and George the First.

After Sheridan's entrance on the field of politics and parliament, he abandoned the comic muse; a circumstance greatly to be regretted. Perhaps, if Shakspeare or Milton had been so unfortunate as to attain a seat in the legislature, we might never have witnessed *Hamlet* and *Othello*; nor should we have boasted of an epic poem that justly ranks with the *Iliad* and the *Æneid*. Lord Byron, beyond all comparison the first poet of the present age, has purchased his "Parnassian laurels" by the sacrifice or dereliction of his legislative and parliamentary duties. Sheridan combined in himself the talents of Terence and of Cicero, the powers of Demosthenes and of Menander. In the capital of Great Britain, on one and the same day, he has spoken for several hours in Westminster Hall, during the course of Hasting's trial, to a most brilliant and highly-informed audience of both sexes, in a manner so impressive, no less than eloquent, as to extort admiration even from his greatest enemies. Then repairing to the house of commons, he has exhibited specimens of oratory before that assembly, equalling those which he had displayed in the morning, when addressing the peers, as one of Hastings's accusers: while, on the same evening, *The Duenna* has been performed at one theatre, and *The School for Scandal* at the other, to crowded audiences, who received them with unbounded applause. This is a species of double triumph, of the tongue and of the pen, to which antiquity, Athenian or Roman, can lay no claim, and which has not any parallel in our own history.—SIR NATHANIEL WRAXALL (1784), *Posthumous Memoirs of His Own Time*, 1836, Vol. 1, pp. 39–41

Sheridan was abandoned to his own guidance, and left to the resources of his talents at the most dangerous period of youth. At the same age with Congreve, he composed comedies of similar, and one of almost equal, merit: like his great master, he neglected incident and character, and sought only brilliancy of dialogue; what he sought, he attained, even to excess; and his wit was fertile enough to betray him into the splendid fault of rendering his dialogue more dazzling and poignant than suited his own personages, or, indeed, any human conversation. Like Congreve, too, his wit seldom appeared to be struck out at the moment; it was elaborately polished, and equally finished; it demanded somewhat of the same effort of attention with serious eloquence, and disposed the reader or hearer rather to admire than to smile. He wrote some verses of great beauty, though the general structure betrays too obvious marks of art and imitation.

⟨. . .⟩ His education was so early interrupted, and his subsequent life so irregular, that he had little knowledge from books; but his knowledge of men was admirable, and his insight into character keen. No man formed a more just estimate of the result of public measure; he dissuaded his party from all the measures which proved unfortunate to them. In private and in public life, he had generally the good sense to judge aright concerning conduct, though very seldom the prudence to act according to his right judgment. He was a new example of the natural union between good sense and wit, which seems nothing else than the connection between a quick perception of the ridiculous, and a strong disposition to avoid it. Neither the long adversity of his party, nor the slights which he sometimes experienced from them, nor the temptations of poverty, ever shook his adherence to his public principles and attachments. But the union of a fine genius with delightful talents, an excellent understanding, a generous temper, and an incorruptible public character, was insufficient to support him against the depressing power of dissipation, too long continued, and irregularity of every kind almost reduced to system.—SIR JAMES MACKINTOSH, *Journal* (Feb. 7, 1812), cited in Robert James Mackintosh, *Memoirs of the Life of Sir James Mackintosh*, 1853, Vol. 2, pp. 203–4

Lord Holland told me a curious piece of sentimentality in Sheridan. The other night we were all delivering our respective and various opinions on him and other *hommes marquans*, and mine was this. "Whatever Sheridan has done or chosen to do has been, *par excellence*, always the *best* of its kind. He has written the *best* comedy *(School for Scandal)* the *best* drama (in my mind, far before that St. Giles's lampoon, the *Beggar's Opera*), the best farce (the *Critic*—it is only too good for a farce), and the best Address (Monologue on Garrick), and, to crown all, delivered the very best Oration (the famous Begum Speech) ever conceived or heard in this country." Somebody told S. this the next day, and on hearing it he burst into tears!

Poor Brinsley! if they were tears of pleasure, I would rather have said these few, but most sincere, words than have written the *Iliad* or made his own celebrated Philippic. Nay, his own comedy never gratified me more than to hear that he had derived a moment's gratification from any praise of mine, humble as it must appear to "my elders and my betters." —GEORGE GORDON, LORD BYRON, *Journal*, Dec. 17–18, 1813

Mr. Sheridan has been justly called 'a dramatic star of the first magnitude:' and, indeed, among the comic writers of the last century, he 'shines like Hesperus among the lesser lights.' He has left four several dramas behind him, all different or of different kinds, and all excellent in their way;—the *School for Scandal*, the *Rivals*, the *Duenna*, and the *Critic*. The attraction of this last piece is, however, less in the mock-tragedy rehearsed, than in the dialogue of the comic scenes, and in the character of Sir Fretful Plagiary, which is supposed to have been intended for Cumberland. If some of the characters in the *School for Scandal* were contained in Murphy's comedy of *Know Your Own Mind* (and certainly some of Dashwood's detached speeches and satirical sketches are written with quite as firm and masterly a hand as any of those given to the members of the scandalous club, Mrs. Candour or Lady Sneerwell), yet they were buried in it for want of grouping and relief, like the colours of a well-drawn picture sunk in the canvass. Sheridan brought them out, and exhibited them in all their glory. If that gem, the character of Joseph Surface, was Murphy's, the splendid and more valuable setting was Sheridan's. He took Murphy's Malvil from his lurking-place in the closet, and 'dragged the struggling monster into day' upon the stage. That is, he gave interest, life, and action or, in other words, its dramatic being, to the mere conception and written specimens of a character. This is the merit of Sheridan's comedies, that every thing in them *tells*; there is no labour in vain. His Comic Muse does not go about prying into

obscure corners, or collecting idle curiosities, but shews her laughing face, and points to her rich treasure—the follies of mankind. She is garlanded and crowned with roses and vine-leaves. Her eyes sparkle with delight, and her heart runs over with good-natured malice. Her step is firm and light, and her ornaments consummate! The *School for Scandal* is, if not the most original, perhaps the most finished and faultless comedy which we have. When it is acted, you hear people all around you exclaiming, 'Surely it is impossible for any thing to be cleverer.' The scene in which Charles sells all the old family pictures but his uncle's, who is the purchaser in disguise, and that of the discovery of Lady Teazle when the screen falls, are among the happiest and most highly wrought that comedy, in its wide and brilliant range, can boast. Besides the wit and ingenuity of this play, there is a genial spirit of frankness and generosity about it, that relieves the heart as well as clears the lungs. It professes a faith in the natural goodness, as well as habitual depravity of human nature. While it strips off the mask of hypocrisy, it inspires a confidence between man and man. As often as it is acted, it must serve to clear the air of that low, creeping, pestilent fog of cant and mysticism, which threatens to confound every native impulse, or honest conviction, in the nauseous belief of a perpetual lie, and the laudable profession of systematic hypocrisy.—The character of Lady Teazle is not well made out by the author; nor has it been well represented on the stage since the time of Miss Farren.— The *Rivals* is a play of even more action and incident, but of less wit and satire than the *School for Scandal*. It is as good as a novel in the reading, and has the broadest and most palpable effect on the stage. If Joseph Surface and Charles have a smack of Tom Jones and Blifil in their moral constitution, Sir Anthony Absolute and Mrs. Malaprop remind us of honest Matthew Bramble and his sister Tabitha, in their tempers and dialect. Acres is a distant descendant of Sir Andrew Ague-cheek. It must be confessed of this author, as Falstaff says of some one, that 'he had damnable iteration in him!' The *Duenna* is a perfect work of art. It has the utmost sweetness and point. The plot, the characters, the dialogue, are all complete in themselves, and they are all his own; and the songs are the best that ever were written, except those in the *Beggar's Opera*. They have a joyous spirit of intoxication in them, and a strain of the most melting tenderness. Compare the softness of that beginning,

> Had I heart for falsehood framed,

with the spirited defiance to Fortune in the lines,

> Half thy malice youth could bear,
> And the rest a bumper drown.

It would have been too much for the author of these elegant and classic productions not to have had some drawbacks on his felicity and fame. But even the applause of nations and the favour of princes cannot always be enjoyed with impunity.—Sheridan was not only an excellent dramatic writer, but a first-rate parliamentary speaker. His characteristics as an orator were manly, unperverted good sense, and keen irony. Wit, which has been thought a two-edged weapon, was by him always employed on the same side of the question—I think, on the right one. His set and more laboured speeches, as that on the Begum's affairs, were proportionably abortive and unimpressive: but no one was equal to him in replying, on the spur of the moment, to pompous absurdity, and unravelling the web of flimsy sophistry. He was the last accomplished debater of the House of Commons.—His character will, however, soon be drawn by one who has all the ability, and every inclination to do him justice; who knows how to bestow praise and to deserve it; by one who is himself an ornament of private and of public life; a satirist, beloved by his friends; a wit and a patriot to-boot; a poet, and an honest man.—WILLIAM HAZLITT, *Lectures on the English Comic Writers*, 1818

The comedy of the fourth period is chiefly remarkable for exhibiting *The Rivals* and *The School for Scandal*. Critics prefer the latter; while the general audience reap, perhaps, more pleasure from the former; the pleasantry being of a more general cast, the incidents more complicated and varied, and the whole plot more interesting. In both these plays, the gentlemanlike ease of Farquhar is united with the wit of Congreve. Indeed, the wit of Sheridan, though equally brilliant with that of his celebrated predecessor, flows so easily, and is so happily elicited by the tone of the dialogue, that in admiring its sparkles, we never once observe the stroke of the flint which produces them. Wit and pleasantry seemed to be the natural atmosphere of this extraordinary man, whose history was at once so brilliant and so melancholy.—SIR WALTER SCOTT, "An Essay on the Drama," 1819

I must differ from ⟨Thomas⟩ Moore in his view of Sheridan's heart. Notwithstanding his passion for Miss Linley and his grief for his father's death, who used him ill, I question his having a *really good heart*. His making love to Pamela, Madame de Genlis's daughter, so soon after his lovely wife's death, and his marriage, in two years, with a young girl as a *compliment* to her remembrance, renders one very suspicious of the real depth of his passion. No man of wit to the full extent of the word can have a good heart, because he has by nature less regard for the feelings of others than for the brilliancy of his own sayings. There must be more mischief than love in the hearts of all radiant wits.

⟨. . .⟩ Half his dirty tricks were from an intense relish for fun. He forgot the apparent want of principle in the strength of the propensity. God knows everybody has his faults, I more than others; but some of Sheridan's cruelties to others were really unpardonable, and Moore ought not to have concealed them; Storachi's widow, for example, where Sheridan took all the "benefit" money out of the drawer, and walked off with it as his own.

His not relishing Shakespeare, as well as Byron, was *cant*. It was from hopeless envy of rivalling him. Moore, I suspect on this point. All dramatic authors, and many others I have talked with, peck and spit at Shakespeare's overwhelming and gigantic genius. Prince Hoare toddles out his namby-pamby mumblings; Leigh Hunt bows, but "seldom reads" him; Byron dreaded him; Sheridan doubted him—at least they all pretended this. It is extraordinary I never heard any poet quote him but Keats, and one day in a party of literary men I was appealed to about a passage which not one of these worthies remembered: either the play it was in, or the words. Is this not a shame?

Which would you rather be, the author of the *School for Scandal*, or, of the *Merchant of Venice*? The *School for Scandal*, or any of Shakespeare's comedies? It appears to me that all the characters in the *School for Scandal* are too *distinct* to have mingled together. They are set apart as it were to say certain things. Shakespeare's characters, on the contrary, have a natural union. Each becomes the other sometimes, each say things occasionally which any people might say, however distinct their characters. Now, in the *School for Scandal*, every one seems to say: "I am to be a scandalmonger, don't let me forget it. *I* am to be to Charles; *I* am to be Joseph; *I* am to be Sir Peter." At least this is my impression, an unlettered painter.—BENJAMIN ROBERT HAYDON, Letter to Mary Russell Mitford (Dec. 10, 1825)

The dramas of Sheridan have their existence apart from him, and from all the circumstances of his life. They have placed him at the head of the genteel comedy of England; and while truth of character and manners, chastised brilliancy of wit, humour devoid of the least stain of coarseness, exquisite knowledge of stage-effect, and consummate ease and elegance of idiomatic language are appreciated, there can be no doubt that the name of Sheridan will maintain its place.—JOHN WILSON CROKER, "Memoirs of Sheridan by Dr. Watkins and Mr. Moore," *Quarterly Review*, March 1826, pp. 592–93

It would be something of the latest to engage now in a critique on the *Rivals* or the *School for Scandal*; and it would be useless. The public and general judgment is right; both in the very high rank it has assigned to these pieces, and in the exceptions with which it has qualified its praise. They are all over sparkling with wit, and alive with character; and nothing, so much better in its substance than the real conversation of polite society, ever came so near it, in manner. But there is too much merely ornamental dialogue, and, with some very fine theatrical situations, too much intermission in the action and business of the play; and, above all, there is too little real warmth of feeling, and too few indications of noble or serious passion thoroughly to satisfy the wants of English readers and spectators—even in a comedy. Their wit is the best of them;— and we do not mean to deny that it is both genuine and abundant. But it is fashioned rather too much after one pattern; and resolved too often into studied comparisons, and ludicrous and ingenious similes. There is a degree of monotony in this; and its very condensation gives it something of a quaint, elaborate, and ostentatious air. The good things are all detached, and finished, and independent, each in itself; and, accordingly, they do not inform the style with a diffusive splendour, such as the sun sheds on a fine landscape, but sparkle in their separate spheres, more in the manner of nightly illuminations in a luxurious city. It is but a forked and jagged lightning, compared to the broad flashes of Shakespeare, that kindle the whole horizon with their wide and continuous blaze! It is not fair, perhaps, to name that mighty name, in estimating the merits of any other writer. But, since it is done, it may serve still farther to illustrate what we mean, if we add, that, where Sheridan resembles him at all in his wit and humour, it is rather in the ostentatious and determined pleasantries of such personages as Mercutio or Benedict, than in the rich and redundant inventions of Falstaff, the light-hearted gayety of Rosalind, the jollity of Sir Toby, or the inexhaustible humours and fancies of his clowns, fairies, fools, constables, serving-men and justices. What a variety! what force, what facility,—and how little depending on point, epigram, or terseness of expression!—FRANCIS, LORD JEFFREY, "Moore's Life of Sheridan," *Edinburgh Review*, Dec. 1826, pp. 7–8

No writers have injured the Comedy of England so deeply as Congreve and Sheridan. Both were men of splendid wit and polished taste. Unhappily, they made all their characters in their own likeness. Their works bear the same relation to the legitimate drama, which a transparency bears to a painting. There are no delicate touches, no hues imperceptibly fading into each other: the whole is lighted up with an universal glare. Outlines and tints are forgotten in the common blaze which illuminates all. The flowers and fruits of the intellect abound; but it is the abundance of a jungle, not of a garden, unwholesome, bewildering, unprofitable from its very plenty, rank from its very fragrance. Every fop, every boor, every valet, is a man of wit. The very butts and dupes, Tattle, Witwould, Puff,

Acres, outshine the whole Hotel of Rambouillet. To prove the whole system of this school erroneous, it is only necessary to apply the test which dissolved the enchanted Florimel, to place the true by the false Thalia, to contrast the most celebrated characters which have been drawn by the writers of whom we speak with the Bastard in King John, or the Nurse in Romeo and Juliet.—THOMAS BABINGTON MACAULAY, "Machiavelli" (1827), *Critical, Historical, and Miscellaneous Essays*, 1860, Vol. 1, p. 295

Compared even with Congreve himself, he stands high as a dialoguist, for though his wit is not quite so keen or so nimble, or his style quite so polished, his epigrams and jests seem to grow more naturally and unforcedly out of the circumstances of the play; his geniality, too, is much greater, and is contagious. After a play of Sheridan's we feel on better terms with human nature. His plots are admirable—not solutions of any of the problems of social life as, according to some critics, comedies should be, but easy, pleasant, and fluent, and full, as such ease and pleasantness implies, of much concealed art. The spirit of Sheridan's plays is so thoroughly modern, they are salted with so good and true a wit, have so much of honest stage-craft in them, and are so full of a humour which is wholly that of the present period, that a play of his adequately put upon the stage will hold its own to this day triumphantly against the most successful of modern pieces.—OSWALD CRAWFURD, *English Comic Dramatists*, 1883, p. 262

His first appearance was with *The Rivals* (1775), an amazing feat in comedy for a young man of twenty-two, not much resembling life indeed, but full of whim and wit and theatrical activity. In the same year Sheridan not merely brought out a farce, but took the town by storm with the laughable opera of *The Duenna*. In this he owed something to Wycherley, and he borrowed more from Vanbrugh in his comedy of *A Trip to Scarborough* (1777); but in May of the same year he suddenly achieved a very great and entirely original success with what is perhaps the best existing English comedy of intrigue, *The School for Scandal*. This play was produced by Sheridan in his capacity of proprietor of Drury Lane Theatre. For years the popularity of *The School for Scandal* "damped the new pieces," and it is still one of the safest favourites of the public. Two years later the brilliant extravaganza of *The Critic* closed the list of Sheridan's dramatic successes. These dramas are among the most familiar of all products of English genius.—EDMUND GOSSE, *A History of Eighteenth Century Literature*, 1888, pp. 337–38

In that brilliant city ⟨Bath⟩ and in that opulent, insincere, tattling, backbiting society—intermittently, but most of the time—he lived during the perilous years of his youth, from 1770 to 1776; there he loved and won for a wife the beautiful Eliza Linley—eloping with her to France, and fighting duels in her defence when he came back; there he wrote *The Rivals* and *The Duenna*, and there he planned and partly executed the *School for Scandal*. Into *The Rivals* he wrought much of his personal experience, duly and artistically modified and veiled. Into the *School for Scandal* he wrought the results of his observation—working in a manner essentially natural to his order of mind, yet one that was to some extent guided and impelled by the study of Etherege, Wycherley, Farquhar, Vanbrugh, and Congreve, who are his intellectual ancestors. There is more freedom, more freshness of impulse, more kindness, more joy, more nature in *The Rivals* than there is in the *School for Scandal*; but both are artificial; both reflect, in a mirror of artistic exaggeration, the hollow, feverish,

ceremonious, bespangled, glittering, heart-breaking fashionable world, in which their author's mind was developed and in which they were created. The *School for Scandal*, indeed, is completely saturated with artificiality, and the fact that it was intended to satirise and rebuke the faults of an insincere, scandal-mongering society does not—and was not meant to—modify that pervasive and predominant element of its character.

Satire, in order to be effective, must portray the thing that it excoriates. The *School for Scandal* rebukes a vice by depicting it, and makes the rebuke pungent by depicting it in a brilliant and entertaining way; yet there is no considerable comedy in our language, not even one by Etherege or by Congreve—authors whose influence was naturally and cogently operative upon the kindred mind of Sheridan—that stands further off from the simplicity of nature, moves in a more garish light, or requires for its intelligble and effective interpretation a more studied, manufactured, fantastic manner. It contains no person upon whom the imagination can dwell with delight, or to whom the heart can become devoted; no person who either fires the mind by example, or arouses the imagination by romantic nobility, or especially wins esteem whether for worth of character or excellence of conduct. Once or twice indeed—as in Charles's impulsive expression of grateful sentiment toward the bounteous uncle whom he supposes to be absent from the scene of the auction, and in Sir Peter Teazle's disclosure to Joseph of his considerate intentions toward his volatile wife, in the scene of the screen—it imparts a transient thrill of feeling. But it never strikes—and, indeed, it never aims to strike—the note of pathos, in its portraiture of human life; so that, in the main, it contains scarcely a single trait of simple humanity. And yet its fascination is universal, indomitable, irresistible, final—the fascination of buoyant, intellectual character, invincible mirth, pungent satire, and a gorgeous affluence of polished wit. It succeeded when it was first produced, and now, after the lapse of a hundred years and more, it still continues to please, equally when it is acted and when it is read. There is a moral in this which ought to carry comfort to those votaries of art who believe in symbol rather than in fact, the ideal rather than the literal; who know that a dramatic picture of life, in order that it may be made universal in its applicability and incessant in its influence, must be made to present aggregate and comprehensive personifications and not local and particular portraits, and must be painted in colours that are not simply true but delicately exaggerated. This is the great art—the art which has made Shakespeare to survive when Ben Jonson is dead. The absence of genial emotion—of the glow of expansive humanity and of pathos— in the *School for Scandal* is, perhaps, to be regretted; but in this case a deficiency of the melting heart is counterbalanced by a prodigality of the opulent mind. The piece transcends locality and epoch. The resident not only of Bath and of London, but of New York and San Francisco, the denizen not only of great capitals but of provincial villages, the inhabitant of yesterday, to-day, and to-morrow, can perceive the meaning, feel the power, and rejoice in the sparkling gayety of the *School for Scandal*.—WILLIAM WINTER, "Sheridan and *The School for Scandal*," *Old Shrines and Ivy*, 1892, pp. 225–30

Can any one see such plays acted, for instance, as Sheridan's without being forcibly struck by the total absence of spontaneity and the absolute submission to social routine of the average society man and woman of those days. Sheridan's comedies are undoubtedly as true to their times on the one hand as they are to human nature on the other, but the humanity of them is thrown into vivid and strong relief by the artificiality of the elements in the midst of which the chief actors have their being.—F. MARION CRAWFORD, *The Novel: What It Is*, 1893, p. 100

Sheridan brought the comedy of manners to the highest perfection, and *The School for Scandal* remains to this day the most popular comedy in the English language. Some of the characters both in this play and in *The Rivals* have become so closely associated with our current speech that we may fairly regard them as imperishable. No farce of our time has so excellent a chance of immortality as *The Critic*. A playwright of whom these things are commonplaces must have had brilliant qualities for his craft; but the secret in this case, I think, lies in the pervading humanity of Sheridan's work. That is the only preservative against decay.—SIR HENRY IRVING, cited in W. Fraser Rae, *Sheridan: A Biography*, 1896, Vol. 2, p. 322

An extravagant hyperbole of Byron's as to the relative excellence of Sheridan's plays has perhaps done him some harm, but his three best pieces are of extraordinary merit. They were all produced between 1775 and 1779; each is a masterpiece in its kind, and the kinds are not identical. *The Rivals* is artificial comedy, inclining on one side to farce, and, in the parts of Falkland and Julia, to the sentimental. But it is, on its own rather artificial plan, constructed with remarkable skill and tightness; and the characters of Sir Anthony Absolute, Mrs. Malaprop, Sir Lucius O'Trigger, and Bob Acres, with almost all the rest, combine fun with at least theatrical verisimilitude in a very rare way. Indeed, Sir Anthony and Mrs. Malaprop, though heightened from life, can hardly be said to be false to it, and though in the other pair the license of dramatic exaggeration is pushed to its farthest, it is not exceeded. The effect could not have been produced without the sparkling dialogue, but this alone could not have given it.

The School for Scandal flies higher, but not quite so steadily. Pedants of construction fall more foul of it, and even those who do not accept their standards must admit that the characters are less uniformly alive. But they, like the play generally, aim higher; it is no longer artificial comedy with stock personages, but a great comic castigation of manners that is attempted. In *The Rivals* Sheridan has vied with Vanbrugh and had beaten him; in *The School for Scandal* he challenges Molière, and is hardly beaten except in a certain universality. As for his third masterpiece, *The Critic*, it is simply a farce *in excelsis*, designedly extravagant and chaotic, but all the more successful. The mock-play is admittedly almost, if not quite, the best thing of the kind, and the by-play of Sneer, Puff, Dangle, and the immortal Sir Fretful Plagiary requires none of the illegitimate attraction of identification with real personages to give it zest. *The Critic* forms with *The Rehearsal* and *The Rovers* a triad of which English literature may well be proud. It is difficult, allowing for the scale of each, to choose between the three, but in variety and reach *The Critic* may be allowed frankly to carry it.—GEORGE SAINTSBURY, *A Short History of English Literature*, 1898, p. 641

Works

THE RIVALS

The outlines of this play will be found to correspond with the history of Mr. Sheridan's marriage; and the characters are for the most part the same with those that had before been dramatized in a ludicrous manner by Foote in his *Maid of Bath*. One of the personages in the comedy, however, is a palpable copy from an original in the novel of *Joseph Andrews*. But the delineation of a conceited waiting-woman, who affects superiority of mental endowments, by using hard words in a misapplied sense, while it gives inimitable humour to the story of Fielding, becomes extravagantly absurd in the comedy of Sheridan. Slipslop in the novel is just such an affected character as might be found in her situation of life, at any period; but it is ridiculous to suppose that a lady of family and fortune, residing at Bath in the eighteenth century, could be so grossly ignorant as Mrs. Malaprop is described in every sentence that she utters. For instance, she is introduced as giving her opinion upon female education, and saying, that "Greek and Hebrew, Algebra, and *Simony*, are *inflammatory* branches of learning, with which a young woman ought by no means to be acquainted, while it is proper that she should have a *supercilious* knowledge in accounts; and as she grows up be instructed in *geometry*, that she may know something of the *contagious* countries; but above all she should be mistress of *orthodoxy*, that she may not misspell, or mispronounce words so shamefully as girls usually do; and likewise that she may *reprehend* the true meaning of what she is saying."

That the author might have had some particular person in view at the time when he sketched this outrageous caricature is extremely probable, but he has violated all probability in representing such a contemptible compound of ignorance and vanity as a woman of family and fortune. The character of Sir Lucius O'Trigger, an Irish adventurer, who is ready to fight any body, with or without a reason, is happily conceived, and forcibly drawn.—JOHN WATKINS, *Memoirs of Richard Brinsley Sheridan*, 1817, Vol. 1, pp. 145–46

I prefer Sheridan's *Rivals* to his *School for Scandal*; exquisite humour pleases me more than the finest wit.—SAMUEL ROGERS, *Table Talk*, c. 1855

His wit was all his capital, and the first great use he put it to was to compose the comedy of *The Rivals*, produced at Covent Garden on January 19th, 1775. It failed on the first night, partly on account of Lee's bad acting in Sir Lucius, which was violently hissed, partly on account of its great length, and partly through private malice. But a change in the cast and a judicious use of the pruning-knife quickly reversed the verdict, and made it, as it deserved, a complete success. It brought the author some £1,200, which, however, must have been a mere drop against his ocean of difficulties. After the lapse of a hundred years, *The Rivals* still remains, next to its author's greater work, the most popular comedy of the last century. The characters were doubtless drawn from his old Bath experience. Mrs. Malaprop was the portrait of an original, well known at Bath for "the nice derangement of her epitaphs," and he must very frequently have met such irascible old gentlemen as Sir Anthony, such romance-reading sentimentalists as Lydia Languish, such Irish adventurers as Sir Lucius, such country squires as Acres, such footmen as Fag; for the Captain's cool impudence he might have sat himself. Indeed, the audience believed they discovered many allusions to his own love story in the piece. The great blot of the work, according to our present ideas, lies in the forced and pedantic scenes between Julia and Falkland, now almost expunged in acting. Take, for instance, such a passage as the following: "Then on the bosom of your wedded Julia you may lull your keen regrets to slumbering, while virtuous love, with a cherub's hand, shall smooth the brow of upbraiding thought and pluck the thorn from compunction." But this was esteemed the proper language of sentiment by the good people of a hundred years ago.—H. BARTON BAKER, "Richard Brinsley Sheridan," *Gentleman's Magazine*, Sept. 1878, pp. 307–8

The Rivals, from the date of its first night's failure, has neither merited nor enjoyed a like measure of success as, throughout the world, has followed the *School for Scandal*; while I venture to think the incidents of the comedy are too fragile and farcical to bear such elaborate scenic treatment as we endeavoured to depict of last-century life, when Beau Nash reigned in the pump-room at Bath.—SIR SQUIRE BANCROFT, cited in W. Fraser Rae, *Sheridan: A Biography*, 1896, Vol. 2, p. 321

THE DUENNA

At the opening of the ensuing season the *Duenna* was brought out on the same stage, with rapturous applause, which increased at every repetition during seventy-five nights, being ten more than the number of nights on which the celebrated opera of Gay was exhibited in the first run of the performance.

This comic opera, by Sheridan, is a very lively and bustling piece, but the general outline of the plot is not new, being an exact copy of the *Country Wife*, by Wycherly. The principal incidents in the *Duenna* are in direct violation of all probability; for it is utterly incredible that a Spanish nobleman, of ancient pedigree, and considerable estate, should dispose of his daughter to a commercial Jew, recently baptized, and who has nothing but his wealth to recommend him. Yet the scene of this inconsistency is laid in Seville, the seat of the Inquisition, and in a family of the first consequence. Had the author transferred his adventure to Amsterdam, and described the father of the young lady as a penurious burgomaster, there would have been less objection to the story: but as it stands, the warmest admirers of the opera must allow that it is completely at variance with the pride and superstition of the Spanish character. The imposition practised upon the sordid lover is whimsical, and constitutes the principle feature of the piece; yet this also is liable to the same charge of being in every respect unnatural. That a man hackneyed in the ways of the world should mistake an old woman, who, by his own observation, reminded him of his mother, for the daughter of his friend, and accede to her proposal of elopement, is one of those extravagancies which may perhaps find a parallel in the modern drama, but which never could have been realized in any society. The dialogue is easy, and conducted with that quickness of reciprocity which is characteristic of true conversation; but it is somewhat remarkable that there is little wit interspersed even where such sallies might have been most expected. The spectator is excited to laughter more by the equivocal situations of the parties, and their respective blunders, than by the singularity of their conduct, or the humour of their language. The picture of a monastic refectory is amusing, but it is excessively overcharged, and abruptly introduced without any necessary connexion with the plot; and certainly it is not calculated to recommend religion or morality. Whatever may be our ideas of cloistered superstition, and of the abuses which have crept into institutions set apart for the purposes of study and devotion, it should be remembered that the conventual seclusion has been the means of preserving learning and of encouraging hospitality. The balance of good produced by these venerable foundations so far outweighs their temporary and local evils, that the liberal observer of men and manners will be inclined to resent any public ridicule thrown upon them as an ungrateful return for the benefits which we still derive from these memorials of ancient piety. This episode of the priory seems to have been thrust in by the author merely to create some diversion for the support of the piece; but the object is obtained at the risk of endangering the principles of virtue, by making the profession of religion a cloak for intemperance, and shewing that ebriety is practised most where the obligation of abstinence is the strongest. The merriment excited by viewing this scene is congenial with that displayed by Father Paul and his companions on the stage, whose licentiousness is not censured, though their hypocrisy is made conspicuous.—JOHN WATKINS, *Memoirs of Richard Brinsley Sheridan*, 1817, Vol. 1, pp. 147–48

The songs in his opera of the *Duenna* are as superior to the productions of the century before, as they are inferior to those of the Elizabethan age. They have the sharpness and the grace of a fine intaglio: Ovid might have been proud of them: they have as much tenderness as the best portions of his *Amores*, and the *tour de malice* of his epigrammatic couplets. If Sheridan had turned his attention to the writing of lyrical dramas, Gay would have had a formidable rival for his *Beggar's Opera*.—WILLIAM BODHAM DONNE, "Songs from the Dramatists" (1854), *Essays on the Drama*, 1858, p. 117

The characters of *The Duenna* have far less strength, as well as far less originality, than their brothers and sisters in *The Rivals*, in *The School for Scandal*, and in *The Critic*. There is no Sir Anthony Absolute or Mrs. Malaprop, no Sir Peter or Lady Teazle, no Mr. Puff or Sir Fretful Plagiary; there are for the most part nothing but half a dozen of the usual types—the young lover, the romantic girl, the jealous rival, the lively coquette, the arbitrary father, the intriguing old woman. Among all these, the character of the little Portuguese Jew, Isaac Mendoza, stands out in bold relief as the only figure in the play really worthy of its illustrious authorship. He is knavish, and always overreaches himself; like Dickens's Joey Bagstock, who was "sly, devilish sly, sir," he is "a cunning dog, ain't I? A sly little villain, eh?. . . Roguish, you'll say, but keen, hey?—devilish keen?" Did Dickens, I wonder, remember this passage?

Not only in the drawing of character, but also in dialogue, is *The Duenna* inferior to Sheridan's better-known plays. In spite of all its brightness and lightness, it is impossible not to acknowledge that it does not contain his best work. It has few specimens of the recondite wit and quaint fancy which make *The School for Scandal* so brilliant and unequalled a comedy. If Sheridan's wit, like quicksilver, is always glistening, perhaps at times, like mercury, it seems a little heavy. Now and again the dialogue vies in sparkle and point with the talk of its author's other plays, but not as often as might be wished. ⟨. . .⟩

But, as a whole, the dialogue of *The Duenna* is far inferior to that in Sheridan's other plays. It seems hastier work, at once less happy and less polished. One thing to be remarked about all of Sheridan's plays is that the dialogue is easy to speak. The son of an elocutionist and lecturer, and himself an orator, Sheridan worked his words until they fell trippingly from the tongue. And the songs in *The Duenna* have a quality not as common as might be thought: they are all singable. The words of many songs, and especially of many modern songs, are so loaded with harsh consonants and combinations of consonants, and with sounds which shut instead of opening the mouth, that they are very difficult to sing. ⟨. . .⟩

It is a proof of Sheridan's remarkable cleverness that he never failed in anything he attempted, and that while he wrote only six plays, five of them are the best we have, each in its kind—*The Rivals*, in broad comedy; *The School for Scandal*, in the comedy of wit; *The Critic*, in satirical farce; *Pizarro*, in high-flown melodrama; and *The Duenna*, in ballad-opera.

—BRANDER MATTHEWS, "Pinafore's Predecessor," *Harper's New Monthly Magazine*, March 1880, pp. 504–8

THE SCHOOL FOR SCANDAL

Mr Garrick's best Wishes & Comp^ts to Mr Sheridan—how is the Saint to day? a Gentleman who is as mad as myself about y^e *School* remark'd that the Characters upon the Stage at ye falling of ye Screen Stand too long before they speak—I thought so too ye first Night—he said it was ye Same on ye 2^d & was remark'd by others—tho they should be astonish'd & a little petrify'd, yet it may be carry'd to too great a length—all praised at Lord Lucan's last Night.—DAVID GARRICK, Letter to Richard Brinsley Sheridan (May 12, 1777)

I have seen Sheridan's new comedy, and liked it much better than any I have seen since *The Provoked Husband*. There is a great deal of wit and good situations; but it is too long, has two or three bad scenes that might easily be omitted, and seemed to me to want nature and truth of character; but I have not read it, and sat too high to hear it well. It is admirably acted. —HORACE WALPOLE, Letter to William Mason (May 16, 1777)

Amidst the mortifying circumstances attendant upon growing old, it is something to have seen the *School for Scandal* in its glory. This comedy grew out of Congreve and Wycherley, but gathered some allays of the sentimental comedy which followed theirs. It is impossible that it should be now *acted*, though it continues, at long intervals, to be announced in the bills. Its hero, when Palmer played it at least, was Joseph Surface. When I remember the gay boldness, the graceful solemn plausibility, the measured step, the insinuating voice—to express it in a word—the downright *acted* villany of the part, so different from the pressure of conscious actual wickedness,—the hypocritical assumption of hypocrisy,—which made Jack so deservedly a favourite in that character, I must needs conclude the present generation of play-goers more virtuous than myself, or more dense. I freely confess that he divided the palm with me with his better brother; that, in fact, I like him quite as well. Not but there are passages,—like that, for instance, where Joseph is made to refuse a pittance to a poor relation,—incongruities which Sheridan was forced upon by the attempt to join the artificial with the sentimental comedy, either of which must destroy the other—but over these obstructions Jack's manner floated him so lightly, that a refusal from him no more shocked you, than the easy compliance of Charles gave you in reality any pleasure; you got over the paltry question as quickly as you could, to get back into the regions of pure comedy, where no cold moral reigns. The highly artificial manner of Palmer in this character counteracted every disagreeable impression which you might have received from the contrast, supposing them real, between the two brothers. You did not believe in Joseph with the same faith with which you believed in Charles. The latter was a pleasant reality, the former a no less pleasant poetical foil to it. The comedy, I have said, is incongruous; a mixture of Congreve with sentimental incompatibilities: the gaiety upon the whole is buoyant; but it required the consummate art of Palmer to reconcile the discordant elements.—CHARLES LAMB, "On the Artificial Comedy of the Last Century" (1822), *Essays of Elia*, 1823

In the *School for Scandal* the construction, the ordering of the scenes, the development of the elaborate plot is much better than in the comedies of any of Sheridan's contemporaries. A play in those days need not reveal a complete and self-contained plot. Great laxity of episode was not only permitted, but almost praised; and that Sheridan, with a subject which lent itself so readily to digression, should have limited himself as he did, shows his exact appreciation of the source of dramatic effect. But it must be confessed that the construction of the *School of Scandal*, when measured by our modern standards, seems a little loose, a little diffuse, perhaps. It shows the welding of the two distinct plots. There can hardly be seen in it the ruling of a dominant idea, subordinating all the parts to the effect of the whole. But, although the two original motives have been united mechanically, although they have not flowed and fused together in the hot spurt of homogeneous inspiration, the joining has been so carefully concealed, and the whole structure has been overlaid with so much wit, that few people after seeing the play would care to complain. The wit is ceaseless; and wit like Sheridan's would cover sins of construction far greater than those of the *School for Scandal*. It is "steeped in the very brine of conceit, and sparkles like salt in the fire."

In his conception of character Sheridan was a wit rather than a humorist. He created character by a distinctly intellectual process; he did not bring it forth out of the depths, as it were, of his own being. His humor—fine and dry as it was—was the humor of the wit. He had little or none of the rich and juicy, nay, almost oily humor of Falstaff, for instance. His wit was the wit of common-sense, like Jerrold's or Sydney Smith's; it was not wit informed with imagination, like Shakespeare's wit. But this is only to say again that Sheridan was not one of the few world-wide and all-embracing geniuses. He was one of those almost equally few who in their own line, limited though it may be, are unsurpassed. It has been said that poets—among whom dramatists are entitled to stand—may be divided into three classes; those who can say one thing in one way—these are the great majority; those who can say one thing in many ways—even these are not so many as they would be reckoned generally; and those who can say many things in many ways—these are the chosen few, the scant half-dozen who hold the highest peak of Parnassus. In the front rank of the second class stood Sheridan. The one thing he had was wit—and of this in all its forms he was master. His wit in general had a metallic smartness and a crystalline coldness; it rarely lifts us from the real to the ideal; and yet the whole comedy is in one sense, at least, idealized; it bears, in fact, the resemblance to real life that a well-cut diamond has to a drop of water.

Yet, the play is not wholly cold. Sheridan's wit could be genial as well as icy—of which there could be no better proof than the success with which he has enlisted our sympathies for the characters of his comedy. *Sir Peter Teazle* is an old fool, who has married a young wife; but we are all glad when we see a prospect of his future happiness. *Lady Teazle* is flighty and foolish; and yet we cannot help but like her. *Charles* we all wish well; and as for *Joseph*, we feel from the first so sure of his ultimate discomfiture, that we are ready to let him off with the light punishment of exposure. There are, it is true, here and there blemishes to be detected on the general surface, an occasional hardness of feeling, an apparent lack, at times, of taste and delicacy—for instance, the bloodthirsty way in which the scandal-mongers pounce upon their prey, the almost brutal expression by *Lady Teazle* of her willingness to be a widow, the ironical speech of *Charles* after the fall of the screen; but these are perhaps more the fault of the age than of the author. That Sheridan's wit ran away here with him is greatly to be regretted. That in the course of his constant polishing of the play he should not have seen these blots, is only another instance of the blindness with which an author is at times afflicted when he has dwelt long on one work.

The great defect of the *School for Scandal*—the one thing which shows the difference between a comic writer of the type of Sheridan and a great dramatist like Shakespeare—is the unvarying wit of the characters. And not only are the characters all witty, but they all talk alike. Their wit is Sheridan's wit, which is very good wit indeed; but it is Sheridan's own, and not *Sir Peter Teazle's*, or *Backbite's*, or *Careless's*, or *Lady Sneerwell's*. It is one man in his time playing many parts. It is the one voice always; though the hands be the hands of Esau, the voice is the voice of Jacob. And this quick wit and ready repartee is not confined to the ladies and gentlemen; the master is no better off than the man, and *Careless* airs the same wit as *Charles*. As Sheridan said in the *Critic*, he was "not for making slavish distinctions in a free country, and giving all the fine language to the upper sort of people." Now, no doubt the characters do all talk too well; the comedy would be far less entertaining if they did not. The stage is not life, and it is not meant to be; it has certain conventions on the acceptance of which hangs its existence; a mere transcript of ordinary talk would be insufferable. We meet bores enough in the world—let the theatre, at least, be free from them; and therefore condensation is necessary, and selection and a heightening and brightening of talk. No doubt Sheridan pushed this license to its utmost limit,—at times even beyond it; but in consequence his comedy, if a little less artistic in the reading, is far more lively in the acting. It has been said that in Shakespeare we find not the language we would use in the situations, but the language we should wish to use—that we should talk so if we could. We cannot all of us be as witty as the characters of the *School for Scandal*, but who of us would not if he could?—BRANDER MATTHEWS, "Introduction to *The School for Scandal*," *Sheridan's Comedies*, 1891, pp. 196–99

SPEECHES

If you could bring over Mr. Sheridan, you would do something—he talked for five hours and half on Wednesday, and turned everybody's head—one heard everybody in the streets raving on the wonders of that speech—for my part I cannot believe it was so supernatural, as they say—do you believe it was, Madam? I will go to my oracle, who told me of the marvels of the pamphlet, which assures us that Mr Hastings is a prodigy of virtue and abilities—and as you think so too, how should such a fellow as Sheridan, who has no diamonds to bestow, fascinate all the world?—yet witchcraft no doubt there had been, for when did simple eloquence ever convince a majority?—HORACE WALPOLE, Letter to the Countess of Upper Ossory (Feb. 9, 1787)

If you were to form a judgment of Sheridan's speech on Tuesday from this unfavourable introduction, you would certainly be misled, and think much too low of it. It was a very great exertion of talent, understanding, and skill in composition, and was the work of a man of very extraordinary genius. There was not one sentence in which you did not perceive the exercise of a most ingenious, acute, penetrating, and lively mind; and it was strewed very thick with more brilliant periods of eloquence and poetical imagination, and more lively sallies of wit, than could be produced probably by more than one other man in the world, with whom, however, they spring up and shoot out with all the luxuriance and grace of spontaneous nature. This certainly cannot be said of Sheridan's flowers, which are produced by great pains, skill, and preparation, and are delivered in perfect order, ready tied up in regular though *beautiful bouquets*, and very unlike Burke's wild and natural nosegays.

I think in this respect that Sheridan's *excellence* becomes *perversely* a sort of defect; for the finer periods and passages are so *salient* from the rest, are so finished, and bear so strongly the evidence of regular and laborious composition produced by premeditation and delivered by memory, as to give the whole performance a character of design and artificial execution which keeps the author rather than his work, the orator rather than his speech, before you, which draws the attention entirely away from the *purpose* to the *performance*, and which can at most exercise the wonder and admiration of his audience, leaving both their passions and their judgment unaffected. —GILBERT ELLIOT, FIRST EARL OF MINTO, Letter to Lady Elliot (June 5, 1788), cited in the Countess of Minto, *Life and Letters of Sir Gilbert Elliot*, 1874, Vol. 1, pp. 208–9

Mr Sheridan, I hear, did not quite satisfy the passionate expectation that had been raised—But it was impossible he could, when people had worked themselves up into an enthusiasm of offering fifty—aye, *fifty* guineas for a ticket to hear him. Well! we are sunk and deplorable in many points—yet not absolutely gone, when history and eloquence throw out such shoots! I thought I had outlived my country; I am glad not to leave it desperate!—HORACE WALPOLE, Letter to Thomas Barret (June 5, 1788)

Yesterday the august scene was closed for this year. Sheridan surpassed himself, and though I am far from considering him as a perfect Orator, there were many beautiful passages in his speech on Justice, filial love &c, one of the closest chains of argument I ever heard to prove that Hastings was responsible for the acts of Middleton, and a compliment much admired to a certain historian of your acquaintance. Sheridan in the close of his speech, sunk into Burke's arms: but I called this morning, he is perfectly well. A good actor!—EDWARD GIBBON, Letter to Lord Sheffield (June 14, 1788)

The charge touching the spoliation of the Begums was brought forward by Sheridan, in a speech which was so imperfectly reported that it may be said to be wholly lost, but which was, without doubt, the most elaborately brilliant of all the productions of his ingenious mind. The impression which it produced was such as has never been equalled. He sat down, not merely amidst cheering, but amidst the loud clapping of hands, in which the Lords below the bar and the strangers in the gallery joined. The excitement of the House was such that no other speaker could obtain a hearing; and the debate was adjourned. The ferment spread fast through the town. Within four and twenty hours, Sheridan was offered a thousand pounds for the copyright of the speech, if he would himself correct it for the press. The impression made by this remarkable display of eloquence on severe and experienced critics, whose discernment may be supposed to have been quickened by emulation, was deep and permanent. Mr. Windham, twenty years later, said that the speech deserved all its fame, and was, in spite of some faults of taste, such as were seldom wanting either in the literary or the parliamentary performances of Sheridan, the finest that had been delivered within the memory of man. Mr. Fox, about the same time, being asked by the late Lord Holland what was the best speech ever made in the House of Commons, assigned the first place, without hestitation, to the great oration of Sheridan on the Oude charge.—THOMAS BABINGTON MACAULAY, "Warren Hastings" (1841), *Critical, Historical, and Miscellaneous Essays*, 1860, Vol. 5, pp. 121–22

Sheridan, like Whitefield, was a great rhetorician, not a great orator.—A. V. DICEY, "Sheridan," *Nation*, Aug. 14, 1884, p. 137

He cannot be called a classic orator. His oriental exuberance of imagination is Asiatic rather than Greek. With a Celtic intellect that was always in extremes, joined to a native sense of humor he could not be reckoned with the grand orators of the Demosthenean type. Impetuous and heedless he plunged into the very errors he was quick to detect and expose. But for conjuring up a storm of eloquence that should bear his hearers away from their sober sense, stirring their emotions and moving their will his magnetic and impulsive oratory was surpassed by none and equaled by few.—LORENZO SEARS, *The History of Oratory*, 1895, pp. 295–96

THOMAS MOORE
From *Memoirs of the Life of Richard Brinsley Sheridan*
1825, Volume 1, pp. 245–56

The beauties of this Comedy ⟨*The School for Scandal*⟩ are so universally known and felt, that criticism may be spared the trouble of dwelling upon them very minutely. With but little interest in the plot, with no very profound or ingenious development of character, and with a group of personages, not one of whom has any legitimate claims upon either our affection or esteem, it yet, by the admirable skill with which its materials are managed,—the happy contrivance of the situations, at once both natural and striking,—the fine feeling of the ridiculous that smiles throughout, and that perpetual play of wit which never tires, but seems, like running water, to be kept fresh by its own flow,—by all this general animation and effect, combined with a finish of the details almost faultless, it unites the suffrages, at once, of the refined and the simple, and is not less successful in ministering to the natural enjoyment of the latter, than in satisfying and delighting the most fastidious tastes among the former. And this is the true triumph of genius in all the arts;—whether in painting, sculpture, music, or literature, those works which have pleased the greatest number of people of all classes, for the longest space of time, may, without hesitation be pronounced the best; and, however mediocrity may enshrine itself in the admiration of the select few, the palm of excellence can only be awarded by the many.

The defects of *The School for Scandal*, if they can be allowed to amount to defects, are, in a great measure, traceable to that amalgamation of two distinct plots, out of which, as I have already shown, the piece was formed. From this cause,—like an accumulation of wealth from the union of two rich families,—has devolved that excessive opulence of wit, with which, as some critics think, the dialogue is overloaded; and which, Mr. Sheridan himself used often to mention, as a fault of which he was conscious in his work. That he had no such scruple, however, in writing it, appears evident from the pains which he took to string upon his new plot every bright thought and fancy which he had brought together for the two others; and it is not a little curious, in turning over his manuscript, to see how the out-standing jokes are kept in recollection upon the margin, till he can find some opportunity of funding them to advantage in the text. The consequence of all this is, that the dialogue, from beginning to end, is a continued sparkling of polish and point: and the whole of the Dramatis Personæ might be comprised under one common designation of Wits. Even Trip, the servant, is as pointed and shining as the rest, and has his master's wit, as he has his birth-day clothes, "with the gloss on." [1] The only personage among them that shows any "temperance in jesting," is Old Rowley; and he, too, in the

original, had his share in the general largess of *bon-mots*,—one of the liveliest in the piece [2] being at first given to him, though afterwards transferred, with somewhat more fitness, to Sir Oliver. In short, the entire Comedy is a sort of El-Dorado of wit, where the precious metal is thrown about by all classes, as carelessly as if they had not the least idea of its value.

Another blemish that hypercriticism has noticed, and which may likewise be traced to the original conformation of the play, is the uselessness of some of the characters to the action or business of it—almost the whole of the "Scandalous College" being but, as it were, excrescences, through which none of the life-blood of the plot circulates. The cause of this is evident:—Sir Benjamin Backbite, in the first plot to which he belonged, was a principal personage; but, being transplanted from thence into one with which he has no connection, not only he, but his uncle Crabtree, and Mrs. Candour, though contributing abundantly to the animation of the dialogue, have hardly any thing to do with the advancement of the story; and, like the accessories in a Greek drama, are but as a sort of Chorus of Scandal throughout. That this defect, or rather peculiarity, should have been observed at first, when criticism was freshly on the watch for food, is easily conceivable; and I have been told by a friend, who was in the pit on the first night of performance, that a person who sat near him, said impatiently, during the famous scene at Lady Sneerwell's, in the Second Act,—"I wish these people would have done talking, and let the play begin."

It has often been remarked as singular, that the lovers, Charles and Maria, should never be brought in presence of each other till the last scene; and Mr. Sheridan used to say, that he was aware, in writing the Comedy, of the apparent want of dramatic management which such an omission would betray; but that neither of the actors, for whom he had destined those characters, was such as he could safely trust with a love scene. There might, perhaps, too, have been, in addition to this motive, a little consciousness, on his own part, of not being exactly in his element in that tender style of writing, which such a scene, to make it worthy of the rest, would have required; and of which the specimens left us in the serious parts of *The Rivals* are certainly not among his most felicitous efforts.

By some critics the incident of the screen has been censured, as a contrivance unworthy of the dignity of comedy. But in real life, of which comedy must condescend to be the copy, events of far greater importance are brought about by accidents as trivial; and in a world like ours, where the falling of an apple has led to the discovery of the laws of gravitation, it is surely too fastidious to deny to the dramatist the discovery of an intrigue by the falling of a screen. There is another objection as to the manner of employing this machine, which, though less grave, is perhaps less easily answered. Joseph, at the commencement of the scene, desires his servant to draw the screen before the window, because "his opposite neighbour is a maiden lady of so anxious a temper;" yet, afterwards, by placing Lady Teazle between the screen and the window, he enables this inquisitive lady to indulge her curiosity at leisure. It might be said, indeed, that Joseph, with the alternative of exposure to either the husband or neighbour, chooses the lesser evil;—but the oversight hardly requires a defence.

From the trifling nature of these objections to the dramatic merits of *The School for Scandal*, it will be seen that, like the criticism of Momus on the creaking of Venus's shoes, they only show how perfect must be the work in which no greater faults can be found. But a more serious charge has been brought against it on the score of morality; and the gay charm thrown around the irregularities of Charles is pronounced to be dangerous to the interests of honesty and virtue. There is no doubt that, in this character, only the fairer side of libertinism is presented,—that the merits of being in debt are rather too fondly insisted upon, and with a grace and spirit that might seduce even creditors into admiration. It was, indeed, playfully said, that no tradesman who applauded Charles could possibly have the face to dun the author afterwards. In looking, however, to the race of rakes that had previously held possession of the stage, we cannot help considering our release from the contagion of so much coarseness and selfishness to be worth even the increased risk of seduction that may have succeeded to it; and the remark of Burke, however questionable in strict ethics, is, at least, true on the stage,—that "vice loses half its evil by losing all its grossness."

It should be recollected, too, that, in other respects, the author applies the lash of moral satire very successfully. The group of slanderers who, like the Chorus of the Eumenides, go searching about for their prey with "eyes that drop poison," represent a class of persons in society who richly deserve such ridicule, and who—like their prototypes in Æschylus trembling before the shafts of Apollo—are here made to feel the full force of the archery of wit. It is a proof of the effect and use of such satire, that the name of "Mrs. Candour" has become one of those formidable by-words, which have more power in putting folly and ill-nature out of countenance, than whole volumes of the wisest remonstrance and reasoning.

The poetical justice exercised upon the Tartuffe of sentiment, Joseph, is another service to the cause of morals, which should more than atone for any dangerous embellishment of wrong, that the portraiture of the younger brother may exhibit. Indeed, though both these characters are such as the moralist must visit with his censure, there can be little doubt to which we should, in real life, give the preference;—the levities and errors of the one, arising from warmth of heart and of youth, may be merely like those mists that exhale from summer streams, obscuring them awhile to the eye, without affecting the native purity of their waters; while the hypocrisy of the other is like the *mirage* of the desert, shining with promise on the surface, but all false and barren beneath.

In a late work, professing to be the Memoirs of Mr. Sheridan, there are some wise doubts expressed as to his being really the author of *The School for Scandal*, to which, except for the purpose of exposing absurdity, I should not have thought it worth while to allude. It is an old trick of Detraction,—and one, of which it never tires,—to father the works of eminent writers upon others; or, at least, while it kindly leaves an author the credit of his worst performances, to find some one in the back-ground to ease him of the fame of his best. When this sort of charge is brought against a cotemporary, the motive is intelligible; but, such an abstract pleasure have some persons in merely unsettling the crowns of Fame, that a worthy German has written an elaborate book to prove, that *The Iliad* was written, not by that particular Homer the world supposes, but by some *other* Homer! In truth, if mankind were to be influenced by those *Qui tam* critics, who have, from time to time, in the course of the history of literature, exhibited informations of plagiarism against great authors, the property of fame would pass from its present holders into the hands of persons with whom the world is but little acquainted. Aristotle must refund to one Ocellus Lucanus—Virgil must make a *cessio bonorum* in favour of Pisander—the *Metamorphoses* of Ovid must be credited to the account of Parthenius of Nicæa, and (to come to a modern instance) Mr. Sheridan must, according to his biographer, Dr. Watkins, surrender the glory

of having written *The School for Scandal* to a certain anonymous young lady, who died of a consumption in Thames Street!

To pass, however, to less hardy assailants of the originality of this comedy,—it is said that the characters of Joseph and Charles were suggested by those of Bliful and Tom Jones; that the incident of the arrival of Sir Oliver from India is copied from that of the return of Warner in *Sidney Biddulph*; and that the hint of the famous scandal scene at Lady Sneerwell's is borrowed from a comedy of Moliere.

Mr. Sheridan, it is true, like all men of genius, had, in addition to the resources of his own wit, a quick apprehension of what suited his purpose in the wit of others, and a power of enriching whatever he adopted from them with such new grace, as gave him a sort of claim of paternity over it, and made it all his own. "C'est mon bien," said Moliere, when accused of borrowing, "et je le reprens partout où je le trouve;" and next to creation, the re-production, in a new and more perfect form, of materials already existing, or the full developement of thoughts that had but half blown in the hands of others, are the noblest miracles for which we look to the hand of genius. It is not my intention, therefore, to defend Mr. Sheridan from this kind of plagiarism, of which he was guilty in common with the rest of his fellow-descendants from Prometheus, who all steal the spark wherever they can find it. But the instances, just alleged, of his obligations to others, are too questionable and trivial to be taken into any serious account. Contrasts of character, such as Charles and Joseph exhibit, are as common as the lights and shadows of a landscape, and belong neither to Fielding or Sheridan, but to nature. It is in the manner of transferring them to the canvass that the whole difference between the master and the copyist lies; and Charles and Joseph would, no doubt, have been what they are, if Tom Jones had never existed. With respect to the hint supposed to be taken from the novel of his mother, he at least had a right to consider any aid from that quarter as "son bien"—talent being the only partrimony to which he had succeeded. But the use made of the return of a relation in the play is wholly different from that to which the same incident is applied in the novel. Besides, in those golden times of Indian delinquency, the arrival of a wealthy relative from the East was no very unobvious ingredient in a story.

The imitation of Moliere, (if, as I take for granted, *The Misanthrope* be the play, in which the origin of the famous scandal scene is said to be found) is equally faint and remote, and, except in the common point of scandal, untraceable. Nothing, indeed, can be more unlike than the manner in which the two scenes are managed. Célimene, in Moliere, bears the whole *frais* of the conversation; and this female in La Bruyere's tedious and solitary dissections of character would be as little borne on the English stage, as the quick and dazzling movement of so many lancets of wit as operate in *The School for Scandal* would be tolerated on that of the French.

Notes

1. This is one of the phrases that seem to have perplexed the taste of Sheridan,—and upon so minute a point, as, whether it should be "with the gloss on," or, "with the gloss on them." After various trials of it in both ways, he decided, as might be expected from his love of idiom, for the former.
2. The answer to the remark, that "charity begins at home,"—"and his, I presume, is of that domestic sort which never stirs abroad at all."

WILLIAM CULLEN BRYANT
From "The Character of Sheridan" (1826)
Prose Writings, ed. Parke Godwin
1884, Volume 2, pp. 366–69

It was the misfortune of Sheridan that his animal nature, if we may so speak, had so much the mastery over his intellectual. He not only loved pleasure with a more impetuous fondness, but suffered less from the excessive pursuit of it than most men. The strength of his constitution, the possession of high health, the excitability of his feelings, and his fine flow of animal spirits, all either seconded the temptations of the siren, or secured him from the immediate penalties which so often follow her gifts. In proportion to his love of pleasure was his hatred of labor. No man loves labor for its own sake— at least not until long habit has made it necessary—but some seem originally to dread and hate it more vehemently than others. It is almost impossible to imagine anybody more unwilling to look this severe step-mother of greatness and virtue in the face than was Sheridan. This disposition showed itself while he was yet a school-boy, and seems to have lost no strength in his maturer years. He never had, he never would have, any regular pursuit, for neither his connection with the theatre nor his parliamentary career deserve this name. He avoided all periodical industry; it was a principle of his conduct to delay everything to the last possible moment; and his whole life seems to have been a series of experiments to escape, or at least to put off to another day, that greatest of evils—labor. Yet he was capable, in a high degree, of intellectual exertion; and the instances in which he submitted himself to it are so many successful experiments of the force of his genius. His political career was marked by the same unpersevering character as his private life. He was ambitious, but his was not that deep-seated ambition which broods long over its plans, and follows and watches them, year after year, with unexhausted patience. If a single blow could prostrate the party he opposed, Sheridan was the man to strike it—and with great force; but it was not for him to assail it with attacks, continually repeated, till it was overthrown. After a powerful effort, he would turn again to his pleasures and dissipations until they palled upon him, or until the entreaties of friendship, or some sudden excitement of feeling, recalled him to the warfare. That such a man should, notwithstanding, have exerted himself so far as to produce those celebrated comedies and speeches which were the admiration of his age, may be easily accounted for on these views of his character. His indolence was not of that dreamy kind which delights in visions of its own creation; no man was less imaginative than Sheridan. It is true that there are some attempts at fancy in his writings, but they do not seem to be the natural effusions of his mind. They were evidently written for display, and consist of broken images laboriously brought together. Indeed, it would probably have been fortunate for him had he delighted more in reveries of the imagination, for it is the tendency of these to make us look with a kind of dissatisfaction on the world about us; but it was the error and the danger of Sheridan that he loved that world, and its splendors and its pleasures, quite too well. He was not disposed to search for imaginary enjoyments, but to possess himself greedily and immoderately of those within his reach. He was the creature of society; its light and changing excitements were the food of his mind; and to dazzle and astonish it was a pleasure which he enjoyed with the highest zest. This is the secret of those irregular and brief, but for the time vigorous,

sallies of industry. Everything with him was planned for effect; his comedies, his operas, his speeches, are all brilliant, showy, and taking. His more elaborate efforts, however, were stimulated by the additional motive of necessity. *The Rivals* and *The Duenna* were written when he was forced to think of doing something for a livelihood, and the *School for Scandal* at the same period. All his exertions respected some immediate advantage. He loved to shine, but thought not of laying up fame for future ages; just as he loved the enjoyments of wealth, but chose not to perplex himself for its accumulation and preservation. It was characteristic of Sheridan that he was too economical of labor even to labor in vain. All the quips and jests and smart things which came into his head he treasured up for the convivial meeting or the floor of Parliament. He came fresh from his stolen studies, on subjects of which he was before ignorant, to make a splendid speech about them before the vividness of his new impressions had faded from his mind. Among the few papers left behind him, it would seem, from the extracts given us by Mr. Moore, that there was nothing on which much study had been expended, nor which was in itself capable of being made valuable.

Sheridan was a man of quick but not deep feelings; of sudden but not lasting excitements. He was not one of those who suffer a single passion to influence the whole course of their lives. Even the desire to dazzle by his wit, great as was its power over him, was not always awake, for we are told that he would sometimes remain silent for hours in company, too lazy to invent a smart saying for the occasion, but idly waiting for the opportunity to apply some brilliant witticism already in his memory. His writings themselves show that he never dwelt long enough on any particular feeling to analyze it; the few attempts at sentimentalism they contain are excessively false and affected; their excellence lies wholly in a different way. His romantic love for the beautiful, amiable, and accomplished woman who became his wife, though his biographer would have us believe that it continued unabated to the end of her life, seems to have operated on his mind only at intervals, for it is hinted in this very book that it was not steady enough to secure his fidelity. Her death and that of her little daughter, who soon followed her, deeply as they affected him at the time, threw no cloud over his after-life. His griefs might have been violent, but they were certainly brief, and he quickly forgot them when he came to look again at the sunny side of things. Even his political disappointments do not seem in the least to have soured his temper, or abated his readiness to adopt new hopes and new expedients. Indeed, it seems not improbable, from some appearances of pliancy in his political character, that, had not his daily habits enfeebled the vigor of his mind and shortened a life which great robustness of constitution seemed to have marked out for a late old age, he might have long continued a favorite with the present sovereign of England.

Some of the excellences of Sheridan's character were such as could not easily suffer by this disposition to indolence and pleasure. That a man possessing an abundant flow of agreeable animal sensations, determined to make a matter of enjoyment of everything, and to avoid everything in the shape of care, should have possessed likewise an engaging good nature, is by no means extraordinary. That he who had no solitary pleasures, but whose happiness was in some way connected with that of those about him, should be obliging, generous, and humane, is almost a natural consequence. The man who lives only among and by his friends is naturally led to study the art of making friendships. Nor is the frankness and openness of Sheridan's disposition any less in harmony with the rest of his character. It is not among men of his temperament that we are to look for the habit of dissimulation, for concealed designs, and the weaving and carrying on of frauds and artifices. The labor and perplexity of falsehood were with him sufficient objection, had no other existed, to the practice of it. The anxious and persevering necessity to provide against detection he left to those who were more steadily diligent than himself. Had the practice of deceit been as easy as that of integrity, we are not sure that Sheridan would not have fallen into it, induced by the prospect of immediate and present advantages which it always holds out—for it seems that he had not sufficient firmness of principle to resist the temptations of many other vices.

LEIGH HUNT
From "Biographical and Critical Sketch of Richard Brinsley Sheridan"
The Dramatic Works of Richard Brinsley Sheridan
1841

The approaches of want of money, or more likely the pressure of it, appears to have hastened the composition of our author's first drama, *The Rivals*, which was brought out at Covent Garden in January 1775. The admirers of this highly diverting and popular comedy are astonished to hear that it failed on its first night. But the circumstance was attributable, chiefly, to the bad acting of one of the performers; and, on the substitution of another, and the alteration of such passages as a first night's experience generally requires to be corrected, the comedy became the favourite which it remains. The character of Falkland is thought to have been suggested to the author by some tempers of his own during courtship. The wit and trickery of Captain Absolute probably lost nothing from similar self-references: nor may Sir Anthony be supposed to have been the worse for recollections of the paternal will and pleasure of Mr. Sheridan, senior, who was as arbitrary a father as rhetorician. Mrs. Malaprop is a caricature, but a very amusing one, of Mrs. Slipslop. Even her "allegory on the banks of the Nile," however, must yield to the other's anger in behalf of the "frail sect." Sheridan's wit is more sparkling, but does not go so deep as Fielding's. Neither is it so good-natured. There is little intimation of tenderness in it, or of the habitual consideration of anything but some jest at somebody's expense. The kindness of Sir Peter Teazle towards his wife is but a sort of dotage, and mixed up with the selfishness of unequal years. It was not in Sheridan's nature to invent a Parson Adams, or Sir Roger de Coverley; much less to venture upon an heroical character in the shape of a footman.

The gaiety of success, and, some say, gratitude to the good actor who was substituted for the bad one in Sir Lucius O'Trigger, produced in the ensuing spring the farce of *St. Patrick's Day, or the Scheming Lieutenant*, which turns upon an amusing trick *à la Molière*, and met with the like prosperity; and the author's animal spirits thus gaining triumph upon triumph, he devoted the summer to an opera (*The Duenna*), which, assisted by the sprightly and characteristic melodies of his father-in-law, Mr. Linley, came out in the autumn and succeeded to admiration. The incidents are not new, but are very cleverly put together; the dialogue is smart and unsuperfluous, like all his comic writing; the more humorous characters are not very agreeable, and there is too much jesting upon personal defects, but they are very amusing; and if the

poetry has little claim to that most abused term, it is very good town poetry,—full of pretty turns and epigrammatic points, and even as like earnestness of feeling, as such art well can be. It is clear that the heart is generally subordinate to the will, and the passion little but a restless, though elegant, sensuality. His table songs are always admirable. When he was drinking wine, he was thoroughly in earnest.

A passage in one of his letters at this period, shows a strange instance of that subjection of the greater to the less, of the universal to the conventional, which, as it is the very essence of the factitious importance of the leaders of artificial life, becomes the ruin of poetry in their worshippers. But here even wit was dismayed! "Ormsby," says he, "has sent me a silver branch (candlestick) on the score of the *Duenna*. This will cost me, what of all things I am least free of, a letter; and it should have been a poetical one too, if the present had been any piece of plate but a candlestick! I believe I must melt it into a bowl, to make verse on it; for there is no possibility of bringing candle, candlestick, or snuffers, into metre. However, as the gift was owing to the muse, and the manner of it very friendly, I believe I shall try to jingle a little on the occasion; at least, a few such stanzas as might gain a cup of tea from the urn at Bath Easton." Poor victim of the prose of a "candlestick!" Light itself, and the fire of Apollo, could do nothing for him! nor the wax of the bee, nor love, nor lucubration, nor even the Greek Anthology! We wonder what he thought of that pretty feminine speech of the lady in *The Merchant of Venice*, when she is going home, and sees a light in her window:

How far that little *candle* throws its beams!
So shines a good deed in a naughty world.

Or that other in *Romeo and Juliet*, where Shakspeare, applying the word to the very stars, seems to identify them with the artificial lights of our earthly night-time, in order to dismiss them with the better grace before the freshness and hilarity of day-light:

Night's *candles* are burn'd out, and jocund day
Stands tip-toe on the misty mountain tops.

How wit itself seems to vanish, like a squalid reveller, before the coming of that happy god! But Sheridan, if we are not mistaken, was no great believer in Shakspeare.

Our author now became one of the proprietors of Drury Lane Theatre; how, nobody can tell—for nobody knew where the money came from; probably, as in the case of his friend Richardson afterwards, from some wealthy nobleman. This cunning and reserve, mixed with pride, does not sit well upon a jovial man of the town; nor did it do him good afterwards, out of whatever immediate necessities it helped him. It only seemed to tempt him into more; for, strangely enough, where such a quality was present, it was the only provident part of his character. Luxury and delay beset all the rest of it; so that his very wit ended in doing him no good, even as the proprietor of a theatre, but by affording him unwieldy, uneasy, and, finally, insufficient means of warding off debts, and encouraging the ruin it delayed.

Sheridan's animal spirits, however, which were also among the causes of his ruin—perhaps the chief cause, in a worldly sense,—had the good luck, or misfortune, whichever the reader pleases to call it, of making trouble and difficulty less painful to him than to most men. He doubtless extracted a great deal of pleasure from most of the days of his brilliant career, as long as it remained brilliant, and health and strength were not wanting. And we have now come to the moment when he was at the height of it, that of the production of *The School for Scandal*, in the year 1777. It was preceded by the re-fashionment, not worth more than alluding to, of Vanbrugh's *Relapse*, under the title of A *Trip to Scarborough*. He was at this period six-and-twenty, an age at which many prose comic writers have produced their best, though Shakspeare himself could hardly have given us *Lear* and *Hamlet*. But this apparent precocity has excited more admiration than it deserves; for the truth is, that the "great world" of artificial society is a very little world to become intimate with, compared with Shakspeare's. Passions there, like modes, run very much in patterns, and lie on the surface; and folly, which is the object of satire, is by its nature a thing defective, and therefore sooner read through than the wisdom of the wise, or the universality of nature. A man, like Sheridan or Congreve, may very well know all that is to be known in the circles of conventional grace or absurdity, by the time he has spent more than half his life. Feeling he needs but little, imagination not at all. The stars might be put out, the ocean drunk up, almost everything which makes the universe what it is might vanish, including the heart of man in its largest and deepest sense, and if a single ball-room survived, like some foolish fairy corner, he might still be what he is. A little fancy and a good deal of scorn, a terseness, a polish, and a sense of the incongruous, are all the requisites of his nature,—admirable in the result, compared with what is inferior to them,—nothing (so to speak) by the side of the mighty waters, and interminable shores, and everlasting truth and graces, of the masters of the dramatic art *poetical*.

The *School for Scandal*, with the exception of too great a length of dialogue without action in its earlier scenes, is a very concentration and crystallization of all that is sparkling, clear, and compact, in the materials of prose comedy; as elegantly elaborate, but not so redundant or apparently elaborate, as the wittiest scenes of Congreve, and containing the most complete and exquisitely wrought-up bit of effect in the whole circle of comedy—the screen scene. Yet none of the characters, hardly even Sir Peter, can be said to be agreeable; certainly not Charles Surface, unless performed with a flow of spirits perhaps beyond what the author intended. He is almost as selfish as his brother Joseph, and makes pretensions to generosity hardly less provoking. His inclusion of Lady Teazle among the objects of his mockery in the screen-scene, is particularly unhandsome and ungallant. But the author thought it necessary to the perfection of the joke, and therefore nobody was to be spared. Of Sir Peter we have said more in a former passage. It is painful to witness the depth of reverential silence with which the audience see him give his wife a bank-bill for two hundred pounds. The whole commercial heart of England seems to be suddenly on the spot, awed by seeing all that virtue going out of it.

The year 1779 produced *The Critic*; and, after a long political interval, his contributions to the stage concluded in the years 1798 and 1799 with adaptations of other people's versions of *The Stranger* and *Pizarro*. *The Critic*, though in some of its most admired passages little better than an exquisite cento of the wit of satirists before him, is a worthy successor to *The Rehearsal* of the Duke of Buckingham, and even to Beaumont and Fletcher's *Knight of the Burning Pestle*; though the last has the far superior merit to both, of being at once their original, and the work of poetry as well as wit. Sheridan must have felt himself emphatically at home in a production of this kind; for there was every call in it upon the powers he abounded in,—wit, banter, and style,—and none upon his good-nature. It is observable, however, and not a little edifying to observe, that when those who excel in a spirit of satire above everything else, come to attempt serious specimens of the poetry and romance whose exaggerations they ridicule, they make ridiculous mistakes of their own, and of the very same kind: so allied is habitual want of faith with want of all higher power. The style of *The Stranger* is poor and pick-thank enough; but *Pizarro*, in its highest flights, is downright booth at a fair—a tall spouting gentleman in tinsel.

GEORGE GABRIEL SIGMOND
From "The Life of the Right Honourable
Richard Brinsley Sheridan"
The Dramatic Works of Richard Brinsley Sheridan
1848

It would be a task of no small difficulty at this time of day to criticise the *Rivals*, to hold up to admiration the scenes which are most deserving praise, or to point out the delicate touches which distinguish each character. We cannot, however refrain from making an observation in reply to those who have studied the beautiful imaginings of Sheridan, and have found several of those defects, which certainly may exist in the most carefully digested works. They have pointed out that every individual who appears on the scene is a wit of his kind, and that the humblest personage, be he a coachman, a usurer, a valet, or an humble friend, is a humourist in his way, and occasionally much too clever for his situation. To a certain extent this may be correct; but we shall never find a single smart saying, a jest, or a sneer, put into the mouth not adapted for it. Not one single phrase is misplaced; if it came from any one person but the one for whom it was written, it would appear like a daub upon a picture. Not one of his personages but is perfectly distinct in his conversation from his neighbour; a clever thing becomes doubly so, if appropriate to the situation of him who speaks it, and this is precisely the case with these dramas. Nobody else could utter the things which the Coachman or Fag says in the first scene; neither Acres nor Sir Lucius O'Trigger could be borne with, if they had not each their own sly hits and extravagant observations, adapted with admirable judgment to their respective positions, and the characteristics by which they are distinguished. Mrs. Malaprop has been censured by critics as an outrageous caricature; but there are those in Bath to whom it has been handed down that there was an original from whom a tolerably well drawn portrait was taken, and that a lady who distinguished herself as a minuet dancer, was as remarkable for the singular "choice of epitaphs," as the She Dragon whom Sheridan has given to the world. We must confess we find it much more difficult to discover the history of his marriage, and the duel in which he was involved, in the drama. It is true that he has laid the scene in Bath, with which he was familiar; and where such persons as an Irish fortune hunter, a booby squire, a female matrimonial adventurer with a marriageable niece, an irritable country gentleman, and a love sick youth, were likely to rendezvous, but why on this account it should be found to correspond with his own romantic adventures, we cannot imagine. The clever touches at the state of society in that fashionable town, its lounges, its early hours, its circulating libraries, its abbey thickly peopled with the dead, are the natural results of the observation which even a superficial stranger might make, without it being attributed to him that a love of scandal and of satire, was predominant in him. The least interesting of his delineations, Falkland and Julia, partake of the same talent; and although they have been objected to as unnecessary to the general action of the comedy, yet they exhibit an intimate acquaintance with the springs that guide the lover's heart, and the peculiar form of jealousy which is held up to reprobation is one that required castigation. The language which the lovers express themselves in has been considered to exhibit false finery, by one who has himself given to the world much more elaborate ornament, and much more of false taste, than any other author of our age.

The youth of Sheridan must be borne in mind when we pass any critical remarks upon the *Rivals*, and we then shall be disposed to view it as the production of natural genius. At the age of twenty-three, a comedy remarkable for its wit, its ingenuity, and its knowledge of the world, must be the result of innate powers. There had been no time for deep observation, reflection, and the study of human nature. There must have been a quick perception of character, a power of adaptation, and a rapid insight into the effects produced upon an audience by dramatic skill. We find individuals brought before us whom we recognise as the fair objects of legitimate comedy, their peculiarities, their foibles presented to us so as to excite our laughter, without any of that harshness or asperity which demands severe chastisement. In the midst of all their extravagances they have some redeeming good qualities which make us pleased that they sufficiently suffer by the exposure of their follies, and the same holds good with his more matured comedy, *The School for Scandal*. If the *Rivals* does not abound with the same sparkle, if there be less polish in the dialogue, if the turn of satirical wit be less epigrammatic, there is much more of the character of common life about it, there is more ingenuity in the several contrivances, the peculiarities of each individual lead to more decided ends, and are more skilfully combined to produce an effect. It is more like the usual comedies of the stage, and there are more of those conventional personages to whom time has reconciled us, and given to them its acknowledged sanction. We have had most of them placed before us by other comic writers, but they have not been so dexterously managed, nor have they appeared in so vivid a light, or been so cleverly brought together. The materials are of a very slight texture, yet the whole is woven into a solid fabric well suited to the ordinary taste. We are told that Sir Anthony Absolute and Mrs. Malaprop remind us of honest Matthew Bramble and his sister Tabitha, and that Acres is a distinct descendant of Sir Andrew Aguecheek. Granted that it is so; the greater the praise due to Sheridan in having placed in so ingenious a form before us our old favourites; and as much right have we to complain of the want of variety in the lovely flowers that are created by the hand of nature, because the petals of some of them are distinguishable in shape only by very slight apparent variations, and yet when we examine them we find they possess colouring totally distinct, and qualities quite at variance. The Irish fortune hunter, the romantic loving girl, the poltroon, and the dictatorial father, are subjects with whom we daily meet in novels and in plays; but it cannot detract from the originality of Sheridan that he has ingeniously introduced them into a drama, made them act and react upon each other, until they produce a most agreeable impression upon the mind, and give us rational amusement by the display of the singularities which it is the peculiar province of the dramatist to depict.

EDWIN P. WHIPPLE
From "Richard Brinsley Sheridan" (1848)
Essays and Reviews
1850, Volume 2, pp. 262–74

The design of Sheridan in *The Rivals* was not dramatic excellence, but stage effect. In seeing it performed, we overlook, in the glitter and point of the dialogue, the absence of the higher requisites of comedy. The plot is without progress and development. The characters are overcharged into caricatures, and can hardly be said to be conceived, much less sustained. Each has some oddity stuck upon him, which hardly rises to a peculiarity of character, and the keeping of this oddity is carelessly sacrificed at every temptation from a lucky witticism. The comic personages seem engaged in an emulous struggle to outshine each other. What they are is lost sight of in what they say. Sparkling sentences are bountifully lavished upon all. Fag and David are nearly as pungent as their masters. The scene in the fourth act, where Acres communicates to David his challenge to Beverley, is little more than a brilliant string of epigrams and repartees, in which the country clown plays the dazzling fence of his wit with all the skill of Sheridan himself. When Acres says that no gentleman will lose his honor, David is ready with the brisk retort, that it then "would be but civil in honor never to risk the loss of a gentleman." Acres swears "odd crowns and laurels," that he will not disgrace his ancestors by refusing to fight. David assures him, in an acute *non sequitur*, that the surest way of not disgracing his ancestors is to keep as long as he can out of their company. "Look'ee now, master, to go to them in such haste—with an ounce of lead in your brains—I should think might as well be let alone. Our ancestors are a very good sort of folks, but they are the last people we should choose to have a visiting acquaintance with." No dramatist whose conception of character was strong would fall into such shining inconsistencies.

The truth is, in this, as in Sheridan's other comedies, we tacitly overlook the keeping of character in the blaze of the wit. Everybody laughs at Mrs. Malaprop's mistakes in the use of words, as he would laugh at similar mistakes in an acquaintance who was exercising his ingenuity instead of exposing his ignorance. They are too felicitously infelicitous to be natural. Her remark to Lydia, that she is "as headstrong as an allegory on the banks of the Nile,"—her scorn of "algebra, simony, fluxions, paradoxes, and such inflammatory branches of learning,"—her quotation from Hamlet, in which the royal Dane is gifted with the "front of Job himself,"—her fear of going into "hydrostatic fits,"—her pride in the use of "her oracular tongue and a nice derangement of epitaphs,"—are characteristics, not of a mind flippantly stupid, but curiously acute. In the scene where Lydia Languish tells her maid to conceal her novels at the approach of company, the sentimentalist is lost in the witty rake; *Lord Ainsworth* being ordered to be thrust under the sofa, and *The Innocent Adultery* to be put into *The Whole Duty of Man*.

Sir Anthony Absolute is the best character of the piece, and is made up of the elder Sheridan and Smollet's Matthew Bramble. Doubtless Sheridan had many a conversation with his father, of which the first scene between Sir Anthony and Captain Absolute is but a ludicrously heightened description. The scenes, also where the doctrine and discipline of duelling are discussed, and in which Acres and Sir Lucius shine with so much splendor, the author may have obtained in the course of his difficulties with Captain Mathews. Falkland is a satire on a state of mind which Sheridan himself experienced during his courtship of Miss Linley. The fine talk of Falkland and Julia is as unintentionally ludicrous as any comic portion of the play. We can easily imagine how the author himself might have made Puff ridicule it. Indeed, Sheridan's attempts at serious imagery rarely reached beyond capitalizing the names of abstract qualities, or running out commonplace similes into flimsy and feeble allegories. His sentiment, also, is never fresh, generous, and natural, but almost always as tasteless in expression as hollow in meaning. The merit of *The Rivals* is in its fun and farce; and the serious portions, lugged in to make it appear more like a regular comedy, are worse than the attempts of Holcroft, Morton and Reynolds, in the same style.

The farce of *St. Patrick's Day*, which Sheridan brought out a few months after *The Rivals*, though written in evident haste, bears, in a few passages, marks of that elaborate and fanciful wit in which the chief strength of his mind consisted. In the second scene of the first act, the dialogue between Lauretta and her mother, on the relative merits of militia and regular officers, is keen and sparkling. "Give me," says Lauretta, "the bold, upright youth, who makes love to-day, and has his head shot off to-morrow. Dear! to think how the sweet fellows sleep on the ground and fight in silk stockings and lace ruffles." To this animated burst of girlish admiration, Mrs. Bridget contemptuously replies:—"To want a husband that may wed you to-day and be sent the Lord knows where before night; then in a twelvemonth, perhaps, to come home like a Colossus, with one leg at New York and the other at Chelsea Hospital!" This is one of the most startlingly ludicrous fancies in Sheridan's works.

The success of *The Rivals* seems to have inspired Sheridan with industry as well as ambition, for during the summer of this year he wrote the delightful opera of *The Duenna*. It was produced at Covent Garden, in November, 1775, and had the unprecedented run of seventy-five nights, exceeding even the success of *The Beggar's Opera* by twelve nights.

The diction of *The Duenna*, and the management of its character and incident, evince a marked improvement upon *The Rivals*. The wit, though not so intellectual as that of *The School for Scandal*, is so happily combined with heedless animal spirits, as often to produce the effect of humor. It glitters and plays like heat-lightning through the whole dialogue. Epigram, repartee, and jest, sparkle on the lips of every character. The power of permeating everything with wit and glee,—love, rage, cunning, avarice, religion,—is displayed to perfection. It touches lightly, but keenly, on that point in every subject which admits of ludicrous treatment, and overlooks or blinks the rest. The best of the songs are but epigrams of sentiment. There is a spirit of joyous mischievousness and intrigue pervading the piece, which gives a delicious excitement to the brain. Little Isaac, the cunning, overreaching, and overreached Jew, is the very embodiment of gleeful craft,— "roguish, perhaps, but keen, devilish keen." The scene in which he woos the Duenna, and that which succeeds with Don Jerome, are among the most exquisite in the play. The sentiment of the piece is all subordinated to its fun and mischief. The scene in the Priory with the jolly monks is the very theology of mirth. Father Augustine tells his brothers of some sinner who has left them a hundred ducats to be remembered in their masses. Father Paul orders the money to be paid to the wine-merchant, and adds, "'We will remember him in our cups, which will do just as well." When asked if they had finished their devotions, their reply is, "Not by a bottle each."

The wit of *The Duenna* is so diffused through the dialogue as not readily to admit of quotation. It sparkles over the piece like sunshine on the ripples of running water. There are, however, a few sentences which stand apart in isolated brilliancy, displaying that curious interpenetration of fancy and wit, in which Sheridan afterwards excelled. Such is Isaac's description of the proud beauty,—"the very rustling of her silk has a disdainful sound;" and his answer to Don Ferdinand's furious demand to know whither the absconding lovers have gone:—"I will! I will! but people's memories differ; some have a treacherous memory: now, mine is a cowardly memory,—it takes to its heels at the sight of a drawn sword, it does i' faith; and I could as soon fight as recollect." In the same vein is Don Jerome's observation on the face of the Duenna:—"I thought that dragon's front of thine would cry aloof to the sons of gallantry; steel-traps and spring-guns seemed writ in every wrinkle of it." The description of the same old lady's face, as "parchment on which Time and Deformity have engrossed their titles," was omitted in the published copy; though brilliant, he could afford to lose it. The Duenna's delineation of little Isaac, after that deluded Jew has called her as "old as his mother and as ugly as the devil," reaches the topmost height of contemptuous hyperbole. "Dare such a thing as you," she exclaims, "pretend to talk of beauty?—A walking rondeau!—a body that seems to owe all its consequence to the dropsy!—a pair of eyes like two dead beetles in a wad of brown dough!—a beard like an artichoke, with dry, shrivelled jaws which would disgrace the mummy of a monkey!" But perhaps the most purely intellectual stroke of pleasantry is the allusion to Isaac,—who has forsworn the Jewish faith, and "has not had time to get a new one,"—as standing "like a dead wall between church and synagogue, or like the blank leaves between the Old and New Testament." ⟨. . .⟩

Thus, at the age of twenty-eight, Sheridan, the "impenetrable dunce" of his first schoolmaster, had contrived to enrich English letters with a series of plays which are to English prose what Pope's satires are to English verse. We may now pause to consider the nature and extent of his comic powers, and his claim to be ranked among the masters of comic genius.

Sheridan's defects as a dramatist answer to the defects of his mind and character. Acute in observing external appearances, and well informed in what rakes and men of fashion call life, he was essentially superficial in mind and heart. A man of great wit and fancy, he was singularly deficient in the deeper powers of humor and imagination. All his plays lack organic life. In plot, character, and incident, they are framed by mechanical, not conceived by vital, processes. They evince no genial enjoyment of mirth, no insight into the deeper springs of the ludicrous. The laughter they provoke is the laughter of antipathy, not of sympathy. It is wit detecting external inconsistencies and oddities, not humor representing them in connection with the inward constitution whence they spring. The great triumphs of comic genius have been in comic creations, conceived through the processes of imagination and sympathy, and instinct with the vital life of mirth. Such are the comic characters of Shakspeare, of the elder dramatists generally, of Addison, Goldsmith, Fielding, Sterne, Scott, and Dickens. A writer who grasps character in the concrete gives his creation a living heart and brain. His hold upon the general conception is too firm to allow his fancy to seduce him into inconsistencies for the sake of fine separate thoughts. Everything that the character says is an expression of what the character is. Such a creation impresses the mind as a whole. Its unity is never lost in the variety of its manifestation. This is evident enough in the case of Falstaff, for the living idea of the man impressed on our imaginations gives more mirthful delight than his numberless witticisms. The witticisms indeed, owe much of their effect to their intimate relation with the character. But the principle is no less true, though less evident, of Mercutio, Beatrice, and the airier creations of mirth generally. We conceive of them all as living beings, whose wit and humor do not begin with their entrance, or cease with their exit from the scene, but overflow in fun, whether we are by to hear or not. Such creations represent the poetry of mirth, and spring from profound and creative minds.

Now, Sheridan's comic personages display none of this life and genial fun. They seem sent upon the stage simply to utter brilliant things, and their wit goes out with their exit. Everything they say is as good as the original conception of their individuality, and character is therefore lost in the glare of its representation. In truth, Sheridan conceived a character as he conceived a jest. It first flashed upon his mind in an epigrammatic form. In his *Memoranda*, published by Moore, we find the hints of various dramatic personages embodied in smart sayings. Thus, one is indicated in this significant sentence:—"I shall order my valet to shoot me, the first thing he does in the morning." Another is sketched as "an old woman endeavoring to put herself back into a girl;" another, as a man "who changes sides in all arguments, the moment you agree with him;" and another, as a "pretty woman studying looks, and endeavoring to recollect an ogle, like Lady ——, who has learned to play her eyelids like Venetian blinds." In all these we perceive wit laughing at external peculiarities, and subjecting them to the malicious exaggeration of fancy, but not the dramatist searching for internal qualities, and moulding them into new forms of mirthful being. The character is but one of the many pleasantries it is made to speak. In those instances where Sheridan most nearly produces the effects of humor, it is done by the coöperation of brisk animal spirits with fancy, or by adopting and refining upon the delineations of others.

We would not, in these remarks, be considered as underrating Sheridan's real powers. He is undoubtedly to be placed among the wittiest of writers and speakers. His plays, speeches, and the records of his conversation, sparkle with wit of almost all kinds, from the most familiar to the most recondite. Though seldom genial, it is never malignant; and if it rarely reaches far beneath the surfaces of things, it plays over them with wonderful brilliancy. No English comic writer, who was not also a great poet, ever approached him in fineness and remoteness of ludicrous analogy. In delicacy of allusion, in exquisite lightness and certainty of touch, in concise felicity and airiness of expression, his wit is almost unmatched. It has been asserted that he had not a fertile fancy, and that he gained much of his reputation by the care with which he husbanded his stores. He was doubtless often complimented for his readiness when he least deserved it, and was cunning in the concealment of preparation. But we think he was so entirely a wit as to be choice to daintiness in what he employed, and to aim at perfection in its verbal expression. He would not always trust to a mere flow of animal spirits to fashion the light idea of the minute; for his object was not mere hilarity, but the keen, subtile, piercing strokes of the intellect. We believe he suppressed more sparkling jokes than he ever wrote or uttered; that the fertility of his fancy was great, but that its expression was checked by his taste. There are as many stories of his readiness as of his premeditation. His calling Whitbread's image of the phœnix "a poulterer's description of a phœnix," and his objecting to a tax on mile-stones as unconstitutional, because "they were a race who could not meet to remonstrate," are as happy as any of his most elaborated epigrams.

HIPPOLYTE TAINE
From *History of English Literature*
tr. H. Van Laun
1871, Book 3, Chapter 1

His theatre was in accordance; all was brilliant, but the metal was not all his own, nor was it of the best quality. His comedies were comedies of society, the most amusing ever written, but merely comedies of society. Imagine the exaggerated caricatures artists are wont to improvise, in a drawing-room where they are intimate, about eleven o'clock in the evening. His first play, *The Rivals*, and afterwards his *Duenna*, and *The Critic*, are loaded with these, and scarce anything else. There is Mrs. Malaprop, a silly pretentious woman, who uses grand words higgledy-piggledy, delighted with herself, in "a nice derangement of epitaphs" before her nouns, and declaring that her niece is "as headstrong as an allegory on the banks of the Nile." There is Mr. Acres, who suddenly becomes a hero, gets engaged in a duel, and being led on the ground, calculates the effect of the balls, thinks of his will, burial, embalmment, and wishes he were at home. There is another in the person of a clumsy and cowardly servant, of an irascible and brawling father, of a sentimental and romantic young lady, of a touchy Irish duelist. All this jogs and jostles on, without much order, amid the surprises of a twofold plot, by aid of expedients and rencontres, without the full and regular government of a dominating idea. But in vain one perceives it is a patchwork; the high spirit carries off everything; we laugh heartily; every single scene has its facetious and rapid movement; we forget that the clumsy valet makes remarks as witty as Sheridan himself, [1] and that the irascible gentleman speaks as well as the most elegant of writers. [2] The playwright is also a man of letters; if, through mere animal and social spirit, he wished to amuse others and to amuse himself, he does not forget the interests of his talent and the care for his reputation. He has taste, he appreciates the refinements of style, the worth of a new image, of a striking contrast, of a witty and well-considered insinuation. He has, above all, wit, a wonderful conversational wit, the art of rousing and sustaining the attention, of being sharp, varied, of taking his hearers unawares, of throwing in a repartee, of setting folly in relief, of accumulating one after another witticisms and happy phrases. He brought himself to perfection subsequently to his first play, having acquired theatrical experience, writing and erasing; trying various scenes, recasting, arranging; his desire was that nothing should arrest the interest, no improbability shock the spectator; that his comedy might glide on with the precision, certainty, uniformity of a good machine. He invents jests, replaces them by better ones; he whets his jokes, binds them up like a sheaf of arrows, and writes at the bottom of the last page, "Finished, thank God.—Amen." He is right, for the work costs him some pains; he will not write a second. This kind of writing, artificial and condensed as the satires of La Bruyère, is like a cut phial, into which the author has distilled without reservation all his reflections, his reading, his understanding.

What is there in this celebrated *School for Scandal*? And what is there, that has cast upon English comedy, which day by day was being more and more forgotten, the radiance of a last success? Sheridan took two characters from Fielding, Blifil, and Tom Jones; two plays of Molière, *Le Misanthrope* and *Tartufe*; and from these puissant materials, condensed with admirable cleverness, he has constructed the most brilliant firework imaginable. Molière has only one female slanderer,

Célimène; the other characters serve only to give her a cue: there is quite enough of such a jeering woman; she rails on within certain bounds, without hurry, like a true queen of the drawing-room, who has time to converse, who knows that she is listened to, who listens to herself: she is a woman of society, who preserves the tone of refined conversation; and in order to smooth down the harshness, her slanders are interrupted by the calm reason and sensible discourse of the amiable Eliante. Molière represents the malice of the world without exaggeration; but here they are rather caricatured then depicted. "Ladies, your servant," says Sir Peter; "mercy upon me! the whole set—a character dead at every sentence."[3] In fact, they are ferocious: it is a regular quarry; they even befoul one another, to deepen the outrage. Mrs. Candour remarks: "Yesterday Miss Prim assured me, that Mr. and Mrs. Honeymoon are now become mere man and wife, like the rest of their acquaintance. She likewise hinted, that a certain widow in the next street had got rid of her dropsy, and recovered her shape in a most surprising manner. . . . I was informed, too, that Lord Flimsy caught his wife at a house of no extraordinary fame; and that Tom Saunter and Sir Harry Idle were to measure swords on a similar occasion."[4] Their animosity is so bitter that they descend to the part of buffoons. The most elegant person in the room, Lady Teazle, shows her teeth to ape a ridiculous lady, draws her mouth on one side, and makes faces. There is no pause, no softening; sarcasms fly like pistol shots. The author had laid in a stock, he had to use them up. It is he speaking through the mouth of each of his characters; he gives them all the same wit, that is his own, his irony, his harshness, his picturesque vigor; whatever they are, clowns, fops, old women, girls, no matter, the author's main business is to break out into twenty explosions in a minute. ⟨. . .⟩

Observe also the change which the hypocrite undergoes under his treatment. Doubtless all the grandeur disappears from the part. Joseph Surface does not uphold, like Tartufe, the interest of the comedy; he does not possess, like his ancestor, the nature of a cabman, the boldness of a man of action, the manners of a beadle, the neck and shoulders of a monk. He is merely selfish and cautious; if he is engaged in an intrigue, it is rather against his will; he is only half-hearted in the matter, like a correct young man, well dressed, with a fair income, timorous and fastidious by nature, discreet in manners, and without violent passions; all about him is soft and polished, he takes his tone from the times, he makes no display of religion, though he does of morality; he is a man of measured speech, of lofty sentiments, a disciple of Johnson or of Rousseau, a dealer in set phrases. There is nothing on which to construct a drama in this commonplace person; and the fine situations which Sheridan takes from Molière lose half their force through depending on such pitiful support. But how this insufficiency is covered by the quickness, abundance, naturalness of the incidents! how skill makes up for everything! how it seems capable of supplying everything, even genius! how the spectator laughs to see Joseph caught in his sanctuary like a fox in his hole; obliged to hide the wife, then to conceal the husband; forced to run from one to the other; busy in hiding the one behind his screen, and the other in his closet; reduced in casting himself into his own snares, in justifying those whom he wished to ruin, the husband in the eyes of the wife, the nephew in the eyes of the uncle; to ruin the only man whom he wished to justify, namely, the precious and immaculate Joseph Surface; to turn out in the end ridiculous, odious, baffled, confounded, in spite of his adroitness, even by reason of his adroitness, step by step, without quarter or remedy; to sneak off, poor fox, with his tail between his legs, his skin spoiled, amid hootings and laughter! And how,

at the same time, side by side with this, the naggings of Sir Peter and his wife, the suppers, songs, the picture sale at the spendthrift's house, weave a comedy in a comedy, and renew the interest by renewing the attention! We cease to think of the meagreness of the characters, as we cease to think of the variation from truth; we are willingly carried away by the vivacity of the action, dazzled by the brilliancy of the dialogue; we are charmed, applaud; admit that, after all, next to great inventive faculty, animation and wit are the most agreeable gifts in the world: we appreciate them in their season, and find that they also have their place in the literary banquet; and that if they are not worth as much as the substantial joints, the natural and generous wines of the first course, at least they furnish the dessert.

Notes

1. *Acres.* Odds blades! David, no gentleman will ever risk the loss of his honor.
   David. I say, then, it would be but civil in honor never to risk the loss of a gentleman.—Look ye, master, this honor seems to me to be a marvellous false friend; ay, truly, a very courtier-like servant.—*The Rivals*, iv. 1.
2. *Sir Anthony.*—Nay, but Jack, such eyes! so innocently wild! so bashfully irresolute! Not a glance but speaks and kindles some thought of love! Then, Jack, her cheeks! so deeply blushing at the insinuations of her tell-tale eyes! Then, Jack, her lips! O Jack, lips, smiling at their own discretion! and if not smiling, more sweetly pouting, more lovely in sullenness!—*The Rivals*, iii. 1.
3. *The School for Scandal*, ii. 2.
4. *The School for Scandal*, i. 1.

MARGARET OLIPHANT
From "His First Dramatic Works"
Sheridan
1883, pp. 49–55

The *Rivals*—to the ordinary spectator who, looking on with uncritical pleasure at the progress of that episode of mimic life, in which everybody's remarks are full of such a quintessence of wit as only a very few remarkable persons are able to emulate in actual existence, accepts the piece for the sake of these and other qualities—is so little like a transcript from any actual conditions of humanity that to consider it as studied from the life would be absurd, and we receive these creations of fancy as belonging to a world entirely apart from the real. But the reader who has accompanied Sheridan through the previous chapter of his history will be inclined, on the contrary, to feel that the young dramatist has but selected a few incidents from the still more curious comedy of life in which he himself had so recently been one of the actors, and in which elopements, duels, secret correspondences, and all the rest of the simple-artificial round, were the order of the day. Whether he drew his characters from the life it is needless to inquire, or if there was an actual prototype for Mrs. Malaprop. Nothing, however, in imagination is so highly fantastical as reality; and it is very likely that some two or three ladies of much pretension and gentility flourished upon the parade and frequented the Pump-room, from whose conversation her immortal parts of speech were appropriated; but this is of very little importance in comparison with the delightful success of the result. The *Rivals* is no such picture of life in Bath as that which, half a century later, in altered times, which yet were full of humours of their own, Miss Austen made for us in all the modest flutter of youthful life and hopes. Sheridan's brilliant dramatic sketch is slight in comparison, though far more instantly effective, and with a concentration in its sharp effects which the stage requires. But yet, no doubt, in the bustle and hurry of the successive arrivals, in the eager brushing up of the countryman new-launched on such a scene, and the aspect of the idle yet bustling society, all agog for excitement and pleasure, the brisk little holiday city was delightfully recognisable in the eyes of those to whom "the Bath" represented all those vacation rambles and excursions over the world which amuse our leisure now. Scarcely ever was play so full of liveliness and interest constructed upon a slighter machinery. The Rivals of the title, by means of the most simple yet amusing of mystifications, are one person. The gallant young lover, who is little more than the conventional type of that well-worn character, but a manly and lively one, has introduced himself to the romantic heroine in the character of Ensign Beverley, a poor young subaltern, instead of his own much more eligible personality as the heir of Sir Anthony Absolute, a baronet with four thousand a year, and has gained the heart of the sentimental Lydia, who prefers love in a cottage to the finest settlements, and looks forward to an elopement and the loss of a great part of her fortune with delight: when his plans are suddenly confounded by the arrival of his father on the scene, bent on marrying him forthwith in his own character to the same lady. Thus he is at the same time the romantic and adored Beverley and the detested Captain Absolute in her eyes; and how to reconcile her to marrying peaceably and with the approval of all her belongings, instead of clandestinely and with all the *éclat* of a secret running away, is the problem. This, however, is solved precipitately by the expedient of a duel with the third rival, Bob Acres, which shows the fair Lydia that the safety of her Beverley, even if accompanied by the congratulations of friends and a humdrum marriage, is the one thing to be desired. Thus the whole action of the piece turns upon a mystification, which affords some delightfully comic scenes, but few of those occasions of suspense and uncertainty which give interest to the drama. This we find in the brisk and delightful movement of the piece, in the broad but most amusing sketches of character, and the unfailing wit and sparkle of the dialogue. In fact, we believe that many an audience has enjoyed the play, and, what is more wonderful, many a reader laughed over it in private, without any clear realisation of the story at all, so completely do Sir Anthony's fits of temper, and Mrs. Malaprop's fine language and stately presence, and the swagger of Bob Acres, occupy and amuse us. Even Faulkland, the jealous and doubting, who invents a new misery for himself at every word, and finds an occasion for wretchedness even in the smiles of his mistress, which are always either too cold or too warm for him, is so laughable in his starts aside at every new suggestion of jealous fancy, that we forgive him not only a great deal of fine language, but the still greater drawback of having nothing to do with the action of the piece at all.

Mrs. Malaprop's ingenious "derangement of epitaphs" is her chief distinction to the popular critic; and even though such a great competitor as Dogberry has occupied the ground before her, those delightful absurdities have never been surpassed. But justice has hardly been done to the individual character of this admirable if broad sketch of a personage quite familiar in such scenes as that which Bath presented a century ago, the plausible, well-bred woman, with a great deal of vanity, and no small share of good-nature, whose inversion of phrases is quite representative of the blurred realisation she has of surrounding circumstances, and who is quite sincerely puzzled by the discovery that she is not so well qualified to enact the character of Delia as her niece would be. Mrs.

Malaprop has none of the harshness of Mrs. Hardcastle, in *She Stoops to Conquer*, and we take it unkind of Captain Absolute to call her "a weatherbeaten she-dragon." The complacent nod of her head, the smirk on her face, her delightful self-satisfaction and confidence in her "parts of speech," have nothing repulsive in them. No doubt she imposed upon Bob Acres; and could Catherine Morland and Mrs. Allen have seen her face and heard her talk, these ladies would, we feel sure, have been awed by her presence. And she is not unkind to Lydia, though the minx deserves it, and has no desire to appropriate her fortune. She smiles upon us still in many a watering-place—large, gracious, proud of her conversational powers, always a delightful figure to meet with, and filling the shop-keeping ladies with admiration. Sir Anthony, though so amusing on stage, is more conventional, since we know he must get angry presently whenever we meet him, although his coming round again is equally certain; but Mrs. Malaprop is never quite to be calculated upon, and is always capable of a new simile as captivating as that of the immortal "allegory on the banks of the Nile."

The other characters, though full of brilliant talk, cleverness, and folly, have less originality. The country hobbledehoy, matured into a dandy and braggart by his entrance into the intoxicating excitement of Bath society, is comical in the highest degree; but he is not characteristically human. While Mrs. Malaprop can hold her ground with Dogberry, Bob Acres is not fit to be mentioned in the same breath with the "exquisite reasons" of that delightful knight, Sir Andrew Aguecheek. And thus it becomes at once apparent that Sheridan's eye for a situation, and the details that make up a striking combination on the stage, was far more remarkable than his insight into human motives and action. There is no scene on the stage which retains its power of amusing an ordinary audience more brilliantly than that of the proposed duel, where the wittiest of boobies confesses to feeling his valour ooze out at his finger-ends, and the fire-eating Sir Lucius promises, to console him, that he shall be pickled and sent home to rest with his fathers, if not content with the snug lying in the abbey. The two men are little more than symbols of the slightest description, but their dialogue is instinct with wit, and that fun, the most English of qualities, which does not reach the height of humour, yet overwhelms even gravity itself with a laughter in which there is no sting or bitterness. Molière sometimes attains this effect, but rarely, having too much meaning in him; but with Shakspeare it is frequent amongst higher things. And in Sheridan this gift of innocent ridicule and quick embodiment of the ludicrous without malice or *arrière-pensée* reaches to such heights of excellence as have given his nonsense a sort of immortality.

It is, however, difficult to go far in discussion or analysis of a literary production which attempts no deeper investigation into human nature than this. Sheridan's art, from its very beginning, was theatrical, if we may use the word, rather than dramatic. It aimed at strong situations and highly effective scenes rather than at a finely constructed story, or the working out of either plot or passion. There is nothing to be discovered in it by the student, as in those loftier dramas which deal with the higher qualities and developments of the human spirit. It is possible to excite a very warm controversy in almost any company of ordinarily educated people at any moment upon the character of Hamlet. And criticism will always find another word to say even upon the less profound but delightful mysteries of such a poetical creation as Rosalind, all glowing with ever varied life and love and fancy. But the lighter drama with which we have now to deal hides no depths under its brilliant surface. The pretty, fantastical Lydia, with her romances, her impatience of ordinary life, her hot little spark of temper, was new to the stage, and when she finds a fitting representative can be made delightful upon it; but there is nothing further to find out about her. The art is charming, the figures full of vivacity, the touch that sets them before us exquisite: except, indeed, in the Faulkland scenes, probably intended as a foil for the brilliancy of the others, in which Julia's magnificent phrases are too much for us, and make us deeply grateful to Sheridan for the discrimination which kept him—save in one appalling instance—from the serious drama. But there are no depths to be sounded, and no suggestions to be carried out. While, however, its merits as literature are thus lessened, its attractions as a play are increased. There never was a comedy more dear to actors, as there never was one more popular on the stage. The even balance of its characters, the equality of the parts, scarcely one of them being quite insignificant, and each affording scope enough for a good player to show what is in him, must make it always popular in the profession. It is, from the same reason, the delight of amateurs.

RICHARD GRANT WHITE
From "Introduction"
The Dramatic Works of Richard Brinsley Sheridan
1883, pp. xxxii–xlii

Sheridan's claim upon the attention of the world, now and hereafter, is wholly comprised in two of his dramatic works, *The Rivals* and *The School for Scandal*. *The Duenna* is a pretty thing of the *vaudeville* order, and *The Critic* is little more than a burlesque, and is, moreover, a copy of the Duke of Buckingham's *Rehearsal*. Neither of them rises to the plane of literature; neither has even enough of the dramatic quality to maintain a position upon the stage, where neither will probably ever be seen again. *The Trip to Scarborough* is in no proper sense of the word Sheridan's work. It is merely Farquhar's *Relapse*, from which certain intolerably indecent characters and scenes have been violently torn away. A comparison of the texts discovers that they are in all other respects the same, being word for word alike, with the exception of a few brief passages which have no modifying value whatever upon the literary or dramatic character of the play. This identity exists even in the stage directions, in which a remarkable little verbal peculiarity of *The Relapse* is carried without change into the so-called *Trip to Scarborough*. In the former, certain speeches are directed to be spoken sometimes "aside," as usual, but sometimes "apart." The presence of these words in both plays—if we can apply the word "both" to that which, under two names, is word for word the same—shows that Sheridan did not even rewrite, or even materially rearrange Farquhar's work, but probably, we may say quite surely, did no more than cut up a copy of *The Relapse*, and, excising the objectionable passages, paste the rest together with a few connecting speeches. Such a performance may be dismissed at once without further attention. *Pizarro* professes to be no more than a translation of Kotzebue's *Spaniards in Peru*, and the translation was not made by Sheridan. The translator's style was very bad. It has the form of poetry without its spirit; its very metrical arrangement being often obtained merely by an awkward inversion of the natural succession of thought. Its language is pompous and inflated, and is deformed with a profusion of epithet which is without

any real significance. Possibly Sheridan might have improved it in these respects if he had tried to do so; although I think this is not probable, for reasons hereafter to be given. But he did not try. His indolence led him to accept the translator's language with little modification. The manuscript of the translation which he used was seen by Moore, who says of the whole: "In the plot and arrangement of the scenes it is well known there is but little alteration from the German original. The omission of the comic scenes of Diego, which Kotzebue himself intended to omit, the judicious suppression of Elvira's love for Alonzo,—the introduction, so striking in representation, of Rolla's passage across the bridge, and the re-appearance of Elvira in the habit of a man, form, I believe, the only important points in which the play of Mr. Sheridan differs from the structure of the original drama. With respect to the dialogue, his share in its composition is reducible to a compass not much more considerable. A few speeches and a few short scenes rewritten, constitute almost the whole of the contributions he has furnished to it. Even that scene where Cora describes the 'white buds' and 'crimson blossoms of her infant's teeth,' which I have often heard cited as specimens of Sheridan's false ornament, is indebted to this unknown paraphrast for the whole of its embroidery." But the little that he did write for this play was of no better quality than the much which he did not write, and seems indeed to be of the same substance. *Pizarro* may be dismissed with *The Trip to Scarborough*, and with them must go *The Camp*. This is included in the present publication, in order that it may be an exact reprint of the Murray edition of Sheridan's dramatic works; but it is now known that he had no share whatever in its composition.

Thus Sheridan did no original dramatic work worthy of consideration which is not found in the two comedies already specified, and which are indeed the only plays by which his name is kept before the general public. Of these *The Rivals*, the first written and the less celebrated, is the better in every essential dramatic quality. For it is superior in characterization; it has greater variety; it is subtler; it has more value and interest as a lifelike—we cannot say an idealized—representation of human nature. True, its characterization nearly approaches caricature; but that which it exaggerates is real; it is genuinely human. It is indeed a modern *Every Man in his Humour*, and much more amusing than its prototype, if less vigorous. Sir Anthony Absolute, Sir Lucius O'Trigger, and Mrs. Malaprop are types the truth of which we all recognize; and for poor Bob Acres—a figure almost worthy of Fielding— we have, notwithstanding his pretension and his cowardice, a lurking kindness. Mrs. Malaprop, it is true, is not a wholly original conception. She is Mrs. Quickly raised to the rank of a gentlewoman; but those who regard her "nice distribution of epitaphs" as a gross exaggeration of what could be possible in a woman in her position in life, must be unacquainted with the remains of the epistolary compositions of many ladies of her rank at her period. The same objection might be made with equal force to the language of one of Smollet's well known personages, Mistress Tabitha Bramble. General opinion has condemned, and has justly condemned, the conduct and the substance of the secondary plot, in which Faulkland and Julia weary us with weak platitudes and the melancholy commonplaces of distrustful love-making; and this point of the otherwise delightful comedy reveals a radical defect in Sheridan's nature, and even in his intellect, which must have prevented him from ever rising even to the moderate heights of dramatic power:—he was devoid of sentiment. He not only was wholly without it himself, but he did not know what it was in others.

He was incapable of feeling, incapable of understanding, and as incapable of representing, that union of passion, and tenderness and respect which makes the higher love of the sexes, and without which dramatic life, as without which real life, is devoid of the grace and the glow that give to our existence one of its chiefest charms. He never conceived a deep, absorbing love; he never presented an ardent lover of either sex. What true woman would be content with the love-making of Captain Absolute or of Charles Surface? And without an earnest lover, what drama of society can interest us deeply? We may admire much, but we care little. Sheridan himself seems to have felt his weakness in this respect; and in his second comedy we have even less endeavor thitherward than in his first.

The School for Scandal, although it is so much inferior to *The Rivals* in characterization and in genuine dramatic interest, is greatly its superior in stage effect and in wit. It is the wittiest and the most theatrically effective comedy of society in the English language. But when this is said for it, there is nothing to be added, except in the way of amplification and explanation. A play so weak in characterization is not to be found among those that keep the boards. Only two of its personages have any real individuality, Sir Peter and Lady Teazle. Charles Surface is merely the conventional gay, good-natured, unprincipled young rake of the social comedy of all languages and peoples; Joseph, the equally conventional, worldly, selfish hypocrite. Both are made to talk very cleverly in the style appropriate to their respective positions and purposes; but neither of them utters a phrase or a word, or does an act to show that his soul is his own soul, and that the dramatist to whom he owes his existence conceived him as a creature of flesh and blood, or as in any way radically different from a hundred others of his kind who had gone before him, or another hundred who were to come after him. Sir Oliver is in a like manner cast by a pattern. He is the testy, warm-hearted, vain, rich old nabob of English tale and drama in the eighteenth century. India produced such, or was supposed to produce them, as her jungles produced tigers and fevers; and the men differed no more from each other than the several beasts or the several fits of disease. As to the rest of the people, the Sneerwells, the Candours, the Crabtrees, and the Backbites, they differ in the spelling of their names, and some of them wear petticoats and others breeches; and it is well that it is so; for except for these distinctions the one could not be told from the other. Their talk is never dull, although it is shallow and flippant; but it is wholly devoid of individuality. They might one and all exchange speeches promiscuously, helter-skelter, throughout the play without any violation of dramatic propriety. Their thoughts are as common to them all as their follies and their vices. Sir Peter Teazle and Lady Teazle are somewhat higher in the scale of humanity; but not much. They may be said to be mentally and morally vertebrate; but they do not rise above the lowest line of that limit. In characterization he is little more than the conventional elderly husband of a beautiful young wife,—fond, inclined to dote, deceived with his eyes open, and ready to reward generously the calculating caresses of his wife. She is a somewhat superior sort of social creature. She is not only the gay, handsome girl who has made a match partly of interest, partly to escape the tedium of a rustic home, and who spreads very broad and golden wings, and takes a very roving flight when she emerges from her rural chrysalis. She has wit, penetration, and social tact; and although not intended to be so, is altogether the most impressive figure in the comedy. Yet even Lady Teazle has not the power of exciting sufficient sympathy to cause us to take an interest in her personality, her conduct, or her fate. She is merely a gem of softer tint and milder ray surrounded and set off by sparkling little brilliants.

To what, then, is due the continued favor of this comedy, through which trip and jostle a little crowd of people about whom we do not care a grain of the powder in their hair, or a spangle on one of their bedizened coats? Merely to the wit and the ease of the dialogue, and the dramatic effect of the situations. *The School for Scandal* is a glitter of words from the rise to the fall of the curtain. It may be said that almost every speech is more or less witty, either in spirit, or in form, or in both; that either in itself, or in its relation to what goes before or is to come after it, produces a pleased surprise. But it is to be remarked that this wit is all of one kind. It is mere society raillery and repartee. All the personages speak with one voice and one tongue; the voice and the tongue of the witty, cynical, captivating Richard Brinsley Sheridan. Putting himself thus upon the stage in brilliant monotony, he obtained variety by his stage effects. From beginning to end of this comedy Sheridan showed himself master of what the French call *mise-en-scène*. The situations have all a sort of smart impressiveness; the action is never without a life and spirit that take and hold the attention; and the relations of the characters when Charles Surface throws down the screen produce, however often we may have seen the play, an impression unequalled by that of any situation in any other comedy of social life.

Sheridan's was a brilliant shallow intellect, a shifty selfish nature; his one great quality, his one great element of success as a dramatist, as an orator, and as a man, was mastery of effect. His tact was exquisitely nice and fine. He knew how to say and how to do the right thing, at the right time, in the right way. This was the sum of him; there was no more. Without wisdom, without any real insight into the human heart, without imagination, with a flimsy semblance of fancy, entirely devoid of true poetic feeling, even of the humblest order, incapable of philosophic reflection, never rising morally above the satirizing of the fashionable vices and follies of his day, to him the doors of the great theatre of human life were firmly closed. His mind flitted lightly over the surface of society, now casting a reflection of himself upon it, now making it sparkle and ripple with a touch of his flashing wing. He was a surface man, and the name of the two chief agents in the plot of his principal comedy is so suitable to him as well as to their characters, that the choice of it would seem to have been instinctive and intuitive. He united the qualities of his Charles and Joseph Surface; having the wit, the charming manner, the careless good nature of the one, with at least a capacity of the selfishness, the duplicity, and the crafty design, but without the mischief and the malice, of the other.

It is to be said, however, that nothing came to Sheridan instinctively and intuitively. His wit was thought out and wrought out with a painful elaboration hardly credible were it not for the evidence that remained of it among his papers. *The School for Scandal* was worked over and altered, cast and re-cast, changed in purpose, changed in personages, again and again. Some of the scenes as they were first written are very tame and spiritless, and what is more remarkable, altogether without that easy flow of dialogue, and that air of polished society which pervades the finished comedy. There is reason for believing that Sheridan expended more labor upon Sir Benjamin Backbite than Shakespeare did upon King Lear.

One great deficiency of Sheridan as a dramatist, a deficiency fatal to his fitness to write comedy of the highest order, is yet to be mentioned. The most brilliant of wits among modern English dramatists, he was, or at least he showed himself, almost entirely wanting in humor. In no dramatic writer of his class is the distinction between wit and humor so strikingly exemplified as it is in him. His nearest approach to humor, in creation and in language, is in Bob Acres, and the scenes between him and Sir Lucius O'Trigger. And strange to say, among all the many amusing anecdotes of him which have come down to us, although most of them show him as a wit, and as one who lives by his wits, only one reveals him in any striking manner as a humorist. At the time when William Wilberforce was one of the most prominent figures in London, as a philanthropist and a writer upon religion of the evangelical sort, Sheridan was returning home late one night so tipsy that he fell. On being raised by some passersby, and asked his name and residence, he replied: "Gentlemen, I'm not often this way. My name is Wilberforce." This has the humor and the impudence of the Falstaff of the *Second Part of King Henry the Fourth*. But among Sheridaniana it is alone of its kind. For, in conclusion, it may be said that Sheridan was a Falstaff without fat and without humor. A comparison of the two characters will discover this likeness at every stage, and lead to a thorough understanding of them both.

AUGUSTINE BIRRELL
From "Introduction"
The School for Scandal and The Rivals
1896, pp. xvii–xxii

No criticism of ⟨his⟩ plays seems to be less to the purpose than that which concerns itself with the undeniable use their author made of the methods and manners of his predecessors. Sheridan is only to be judged by the effect he produces, and that effect is his, and nobody else's. Could anybody ever have said that the credit of *The School for Scandal* belonged to him and not to Sheridan? Without the *Rehearsal*, there would have been no *Critic*; without Dogberry and Sir Andrew Aguecheek, there would have been no Mrs. Malaprop and no Bob Acres. Possibly, in the same way, without the Fall of Man there would have been neither comedy nor tragedy. Sheridan by the order of his mind belonged to the race who borrow. Lord Thanet quoted aptly when, in reply to Moore, who was talking foolishly about the use Sheridan made of other men's wit, he called to mind Molière's famous phrase, "*C'est mon bien et je le prends ou je le trouve.*"[1] Stolen goods betray the receiver, who does not know how to get rid of them; but Sheridan had no difficulty in disposing of his appropriations. Were it pretended on Sheridan's behalf that he was an original dramatist, it might be necessary to consider the extent of his pilferings, but as no such claim can be made, the charge of literary theft may be contemptuously dismissed. Landor, in one of his *Imaginary Conversations*,[2] remarks, "Some traveller a little while ago was so witty as to call Venice Rome—not indeed the Rome of the Tiber, but the Rome of the sea. A poet ran instantly to the printers out of breath at so glorious an opportunity of perpetuating his fame and declaring to all Europe that he had called Venice Rome the year before."

Though Sheridan as a dramatist can lay no claim to especial originality, he nevertheless wrought a great change, appearing as he did just when such a change was demanded. He belonged to the school of artificial comedy—to the school of Wycherley, Congreve, Vanbrugh, and Farquhar—where wit predominates and where human nature, happily not altogether absent, is yet condemned to breathe the air of a forcing-house for jests, and risible, because risky, situations.

The elder men were, if one may say so, broader in the beam than Sheridan. There are passages in Congreve far stronger than anything Sheridan ever wrote. For example, the well-known passage in *Love for Love*, when Valentine reminds his obdurate father though the latter could deprive him of the family estate, he could not disinherit him of the hereditary passions and tendencies with which he had endowed him at birth. Nor is there anything in Sheridan's comedies so comical and original as the fancy of Heartfree in Vanbrugh's *Provoked Wife*, which first foreshadows, nay indeed proclaims, the now famous philosophy of Clothes.

But these elder dramatists had already become impossible, not so much by reason of the coarseness of their language, though that was reprehensible enough and made Miss Burney blush, as by the exceeding hardness of their hearts, their downright, vile inhumanity. Well does Lord Macaulay put it, "We are surrounded by foreheads of bronze, hearts like the nether-millstone, and tongues set on fire of hell." What can be more abominable than the words of Valentine (almost his first words) in the fourth scene of the first act of Congreve's *Love for Love?* Who is to be blamed if on encountering them he reads no more Congreve that day or any other day? This is the real offence of these admirable writers and undeniably witty fellows.

These dramatists were followed by a turgid and insipid race of playwrights, who thought to make up for their plentiful lack of wit and finish by copious draughts of bombast, floods of tears, and sentiment false as Belial. They won applause, but of necessity their day was short. It was Sheridan's allotted task to be witty after the fashion of Congreve without inhumanity, and to give mere sentiment the slip.

In *The Rivals* we note the transition, for Julia and her Faulkland are still hopelessly entangled in the thicket of sentiment, and there were those, we know, in the early audiences who preferred the sentiment to the wit, and the speeches of these boring lovers to the humour of Bob Acres and Sir Anthony Absolute. But in *The School for Scandal* the triumph of wit is complete.

The complaint so frequently urged against Sheridan, that his servants are as witty as their masters, appears to me an unreasonable one in artificial comedy. Why should they not be? The wit in question is not that of a Benedict or a Falstaff, but a production quite as likely to flourish in the servants' hall as in the card-room. All that is required is a little additional pertness, and this Sheridan usually supplies. After all, it is not one bit more unlikely that Fag and Trip should talk as they do, than that the empty-headed libertines they serve should always prove themselves so prodigal of epigram and such masters of style.

No! the real risk to which *The School for Scandal* is more and more exposed as the years roll by, is lest it may be found trespassing on the borderlands of truth and reality, and evoking genuine feeling; for as soon as it does this, the surroundings must become incongruous and therefore painful.

Too long ago, when Miss Ellen Terry used to act Lady Teazle at the Vaudeville with a moving charm still happily hers, I remember hearing behind me a youthful voice full of tears and terror (it was of course when Joseph Surface was making his insidious proposals to Lady Teazle) exclaim, "Oh, mother, I hope she won't yield!" and I then became aware of the proximity of some youthful creature to whom all this comic business (for one knew the screen was soon to fall) was sheer tragedy. It made me a little uncomfortable. To Sheridan, nearer to Congreve than we now are to Sheridan, it was all pure comedy. We see this from the boisterous laughter with which Charles Surface greets the *dénouement*. Charles was no doubt a rake, but he was not meant to be a heartless rake after the fashion of the Wildairs of an earlier day. Had he not refused five hundred pounds for a trumpery picture of his uncle, for whose fortune he was waiting? It was all comedy to Sheridan, and if it ever ceases to be all comedy to us, it will be the first blow this triumphant piece has ever received.

We do not go to the play to argue with the players as to the view of life they present to us on their mimic stage. We go to agree, not to quarrel; to laugh or to cry (what passes for crying), not to wrangle or discuss. Sooner than to do these latter things, we will stop away altogether. It is indeed a fierce light that beats upon the stage. Were it as easy for a book to be damned as for a play, there would be many more ugly gaps in our shelves than there are. We can read in our arm-chairs and enjoy with a languid pleasure many a book, which, were its characters and incidents to be presented to us on the boards, would outrage our feelings and evoke our displeasure.

The comedies of Sheridan have already had a long life, and though they are now entering upon a century sure to prove one of critical stir and stress, when old canons of taste, and rules of dialogue and of scenic propriety will be rudely upset, I see no reason why *The Rivals, The School for Scandal, The Duenna*, and *The Critic* should not triumphantly emerge through the ordeal and be received as warmly throughout the twentieth century as they ever have been during the nineteenth. And if so, the Sheridan tradition will be kept alive a good while longer.

Notes

1. Moore's *Diary*.
2. The Abbé Delille and Walter Landor.

G. S. STREET
From "Sheridan and Mr. Shaw"

Blackwood's Magazine, June 1900, pp. 832–36

Nowhere is the authority of tradition more absolute and the acceptance of the new more timid than in the theatre. (On no subject, by the way, is it easier to state a platitude.) It is likely, therefore, that the title of this essay may be regarded as sarcastic, or ironical, or of some other objectionable intention at the expense of Mr Shaw. That is not the case. Seeing *The Rivals* and *You Never Can Tell* on consecutive days has suggested certain comparisons. But they are respectful comparisons. It is possible to say a word against the Sheridan tradition, and the least return one can make for the hearty laughter afforded one by Mr Shaw is to take him seriously. The pleasures one had of the two performances were of course different in kind, and an accurate comparison of them, if it could be made, would be rather an interesting study in æsthetics. At the Haymarket there was the pleasure of old memories and associations, of noting differences in acting, of waiting for familiar scenes and phrases; at the other play the pleasure, a little rare in the theatre, of being stimulated by ideas and points of view and social questions which are more particularly of the times in which one lives. As for comic effects, time and frequency had deprived Sheridan's of their force, as was inevitable, while novelty was on the side of Mr Shaw. The subjective pleasures, then, were different in kind; but reflection disclosed some likeness in the authors. Before coupling them, however, it is convenient to take them apart.

The fact that Sheridan has held the stage, while his far greater predecessor, Congreve, has disappeared from it, is due to an accident of time. Luckily for Sheridan's permanence, he began to write when that wave of squeamishness and reticence in regard to certain things, on which Mr Andrew Lang discoursed the other month in *Maga*, had fairly washed over England. Mr Lang was unable to explain this sudden phenomenon, and it is useless for me to go about to do so. The fact remains that it happened, and that first novelists and then dramatists had to take account of it. The theatre was less completely submerged at first than the library, but it was half under water very soon. Sheridan was able to put a few unnecessary innuendoes into *The School for Scandal*, but he could not leave Sir Peter Teazle the immemorial husband as whose type he must first have conceived him. Tradition dies hard on the stage, as it has been remarked already, and it is notable that Charles Lamb saw *The School for Scandal* played with its sentimentality minimised, and with Joseph, not Charles, for the real hero of the piece: also *Love for Love*, Congreve's best acting play, held the stage into this century. For all that the stage, it was certain, had to be bowdlerised, and Sheridan, who was lucky in most things, contrived to be born at the right time. If he had written a generation earlier, he would have disappeared with Congreve; if Congreve had lived three generations later, he would have remained with Sheridan, and, if merit counted in these matters (a doubtful hypothesis), would have been revived a great deal more often.

No one who knows them both can doubt that Sheridan helped himself from Congreve with a generous hand. It is probable that he consciously "refined" him: it is certain that he unconsciously vulgarised him. If you will admit for a moment that directness of speech is not necessarily a negation of good breeding,—and surely it is not when it does not offend the person addressed,—you must admit that Congreve's characters have a breeding Sheridan's entirely lack. Compare the "fine gentlemen" of the two—Jack Absolute with Mirabel, for example—or the fantastic gentlemen—Sir Benjamin Backbite with Witwoud. Mrs Malaprop and Lady Wishfort have the same dramatic motive (the bowdlerising allowed for), and both are ridiculous in their dialects, but Lady Wishfort is a gentlewoman and Mrs Malaprop is not. And where in Sheridan is there a "lady of fashion" to be compared with the divine Millamant, or even with Lady Froth? Alas! I fear that to many of my readers Mirabel and Witwoud and Lady Froth will suggest nothing: but I must go on with the list. Well, in this matter of breeding Sheridan comes off ill. In the more important matter of intellect he comes off worse. Epigrams and witty remarks apart, in which Congreve can beat the whole of Sheridan with one act of *The Way of the World*, there is a meaning, a thought, in Congreve's characters and oppositions of characters which Sheridan never approaches. In this respect, at least, Sheridan is by far the coarser of the two. How empty and barren, to take a small instance, is the wit of the impossible servant Fag in *The Rivals*, compared with that of the (perhaps also impossible, but far more plausible) servant Jeremy in *Love for Love*. The one is funnily fantastic, and that is all: the other bites, and explains (and here is even a theatrical advantage) his master's character and proceedings. Or, to take a greater instance, it is almost brutal to compare Sir Anthony and Jack Absolute with Sir Sampson and Valentine Legend. There is an angry father in both cases, in both a deceitful son. But the scenes Sheridan got out of his pair are merely funny, theatrical explosions of temper: Congreve put into his all the philosophy of the parental relation, and that without a moment of dulness. It follows from this latter difference that if we are to define comedy and farce—a useless proceeding, it may be—

Congreve's plays are more genuine comedies than Sheridan's. Sheridan had an eye for fantastic accessories and little more in his plays: Congreve was concerned, not primarily perhaps, but because he could not help using his intellect and his knowledge of life, with essentials of character and human relations. Yet he does not lose in gaiety, because his attitude to these essentials and to all human affairs is sceptical, light, and gay: whereas when Sheridan *does* touch on some matter not quite superficial, such as the comparative merits of Charles and Joseph, he becomes heavy at once.

Sheridan, then, is popularly regarded as the great and permanent exemplar of witty old English comedy by an accident. He does not deserve this pre-eminence, which should have been Congreve's. But he does deserve to hold the stage, and to be revived at the expense of contemporary dramatists. His wit is superficial and intellectually coarse, but there is plenty of it. His characters are rather thin and farcical, but they are distinct and act funnily on one another. A few lapses excepted, he is gay and lively. He has a style and a manner. Above all, he is an ingenious and effective craftsman, and therefore a good friend and a stimulus to the players. He is a fair taskmaster to them. If they act well, they are sure of their due effect: he does not stultify them with inconsistencies or negations. It is well he should be played, but it would be better if Congreve were played. ⟨. . .⟩

However, regarded as dramatists, at present Sheridan has over Mr Shaw the advantages I have mentioned—that he wrote plays which are excellent as plays, that he had a distinguished style, and that he encouraged the players. But there is one resemblance which goes very far. The greatest writers of comedy could use normal characters and make them dramatic, entertaining, or what they willed. Sheridan was not one of them, and he was content to exploit eccentricity. Mr Shaw is not one of them (at present), and his eye is for eccentricity exclusively. He thinks it is not, as one of his characters would say, but it is. Even the characters he designs to be normal and a contrast to his eccentrics he makes eccentrically normal. Consequently in this respect—and it is most important—one's amusement in seeing his plays is just the same as one's amusement would have been in seeing Sheridan's, if one had been Sheridan's contemporary. The sentimental schoolgirl in *The Rivals* is on precisely the same plane as the woman in *You Never Can Tell*, who was "advanced" in the sixties and believes herself to be "advanced" still. Only Lydia Languish is gone from real life, and in watching Mrs Clandon my mind strayed to Mr H. A. Jones. That is the added advantage of actuality. Lucky Mr Shaw!

These remarks are on playwrights, not on players, but it would be ungrateful not to add in conclusion that Mr Cyril Maude's Bob Acres, Miss Emery's Lydia, and Mrs Calvert's Mrs Malaprop were the best I have seen, or at least remember. I was especially obliged to Mr Maude for not making Bob a vulgar Cockney, which is Bob's usual fate. With the exception of the delightful twins, Mr Shaw's characters were all uphill work for the actors; but with hardly an exception they got reasonably near the top, and Mr Welch as the sympathetic waiter—the most human of all Mr Shaw's creations—was perfect.

ADDITIONAL READING

ANDREW MARVELL

Birrell, Augustine. *Marvell*. New York: Macmillan, 1905.

Buxton, Travers. "The Correspondence of Andrew Marvell." *Gentleman's Magazine* 281 (1896): 570–79.

Cibber, Theophilus. "Andrew Marvell." In *The Lives of the Poets*. London: R. Griffiths, 1753, Volume 1, pp. 124–45.

Coleridge, Hartley. *Biographia Borealis*. London: Whitaker & Treacher, 1833.

Cooke, Thomas. "Life of Marvell." In *The Works of Andrew Marvell, Esq*. London: E. Curll, 1726.

Disraeli, Isaac. "Parker and Marvell." In *Quarrels of Authors*. London: John Murray, 1814, Volume 2, pp. 171–207.

Dove, John. *The Life of Andrew Marvell, the Celebrated Patriot*. London: Simpkin & Marshall, 1832.

Hood, Edwin Paxton. *Andrew Marvell: The Wit, Statesman, and Poet*. London: Partridge & Oakey, 1853.

Ker, W. P. "Andrew Marvell." In *English Prose*, ed. Henry Craik. New York: Macmillan, 1894, Volume 3, pp. 31–34.

Whittier, John Greenleaf. "Andrew Marvell." In *Old Portraits and Modern Sketches*. Boston: Ticknor & Fields, 1850.

Unsigned. *Mr. Andrew Marvell's Character of Popery*. London: Richard Baldwin, 1689.

––––––. "Andrew Marvell's Works." *Retrospective Review* 10 (1824): 328–43; 11 (1825): 174–95.

JOHN BUNYAN

Brown, John. *John Bunyan: His Life, Times and Work*. London: William Isbister, 1885.

Cheever, G. B. *Lectures on the* Pilgrim's Progress, *and on the Life and Times of John Bunyan*. New York: Wiley & Putnam, 1844.

Dawson, George. "John Bunyan." In *Biographical Lectures*. Ed. George St. Clair. London: Kegan Paul, Trench, 1886, pp. 106–24.

Froude, James Anthony. *Bunyan*. London: Macmillan, 1880.

Ivimey, Joseph. *The Life, Times and Characteristics of John Bunyan*. New York: D. Appleton & Co., 1839.

Royce, Josiah. *Studies of Good and Evil*. New York: D. Appleton & Co., 1898, pp. 29–75.

Smith, Goldwin. "John Bunyan." *Contemporary Review* 50 (1886): 464–80.

Stanley, A. P. "John Bunyan." *Macmillan's Magazine* 30 (1874): 273–79.

Venables, Edmund. *Life of John Bunyan*. London: Walter Scott, 1888.

Wharey, James Blanton. A *Study of the Sources of Bunyan's Allegories*. Baltimore: J. H. Furst, 1904.

Whyte, A. *Bunyan's Characters in the* Pilgrim's Progress. Edinburgh: Oliphants, 1893–97. 2 vols.

Wright, Samuel. *The* Pilgrim's Progress *and Its Lessons*. London: Elliott Stock, 1873.

JOHN DRYDEN

Buckingham, George Villiers, Duke of, et al. *The Rehearsall*. London: Thomas Dring, 1672.

Collins, George Stuart. *Dryden's Dramatic Theory and Praxis*. Leipzig: Oswald Schmidt, 1892.

Dennis, John. "John Dryden." *Fraser's Magazine* 25 (1882): 179–91.

Evans, John Amphlett. "Dryden's Prose Works." *Temple Bar* 89 (1891): 549–58.

Garnett, Richard. *The Age of Dryden*. London: George Bell, 1895.

Hannay, James. *Satire and Satirists*. London: D. Bogue, 1854.

Henneman, John B. "Dryden after Two Centuries (1700–1900)." *Sewanee Review* 9 (1901): 57–72.

Heraud, John A. "Dryden." *Temple Bar* 7 (1863): 77–100.

Milbourne, Luke. *Notes on Dryden's Virgil*. London: R. Cavill, 1698.

Sherwood, Margaret. *Dryden's Dramatic Theory and Practice*. Boston: Lamson, Wolfee, 1898.

Skelton, John. "John Dryden: A Vindication." *Fraser's Magazine* 72 (1865): 160–79.

Swinburne, Algernon Charles. "A Relic of Dryden." *Gentleman's Magazine* 249 (1880): 416–23.

Wilkins, J. W. "The Genius of Dryden." *Edinburgh Review* 102 (1855): 1–40.

Wilson, John. "Dryden and Pope." *Blackwood's Edinburgh Magazine* 57 (1845): 369–400.

DANIEL DEFOE

Chadwick, William. *The Life and Times of Daniel De Foe*. London: J. R. Smith, 1859.

Chalmers, George. *The Life of Daniel De Foe*. London: J. Stockdale, 1790.

Gildon, Charles. *The Life and Strange Surprizing Adventures of D—— D– F——*. London: J. Roberts, 1719.

Hadden, J. Cuthbert. "The Making of *Robinson Crusoe*." *Century Magazine* 58 (1899): 387–95.

Hale, Edward Everett. "*Robinson Crusoe* and Defoe." *Outlook* 55 (1897): 1031–35.

Ireland, M. E. "The Defoe Family in America." *Scribner's Monthly* 12 (1876): 61–64.

Lee, William. *Daniel Defoe: His Life and Recently Discovered Writings*. London: J. C. Hotten, 1869. 2 vols.

Oliphant, Margaret. "The Author of *Robinson Crusoe*." *Century Magazine* 46 (1893): 740–53.

Rannie, D. W. *Daniel Defoe*. Oxford: Blackwell, 1890.

Robinson, E. Forbes. *Defoe in Stoke Newington*. London: W. L. Prewer, 1889.

Smith, Josiah Renick. "New Presentments of Defoe." *Dial* 19 (1895): 14–16.

Tuckerman, Henry T. "De Foe: Writer for the People." In *Essays Biographical and Critical*. Boston: Phillips, Sampson, 1857. pp. 285–303.

Whitten, W. *Daniel Defoe*. London: Kegan Paul, Trench, 1900.

Windsor, Arthur Lloyd. "De Foe and the Rise of Pamphleteering." In *Ethica*. London: Smith, Elder, 1860.

Wright, Thomas. *The Life of Daniel Defoe*. London: Cassell, 1894.

ALEXANDER POPE

Carruthers, Robert. *The Life of Alexander Pope*. London: H. G. Bohn, 1857.

Conington, John. "The Poetry of Pope." In *Oxford Essays*. London: J. W. Parker & Son, 1858.

Dennis, John. *The Age of Pope*. London: George Bell, 1894.

Dilke, Charles Wentworth. "Pope's Writings." In *The Papers of a Critic*. London: John Murray, 1875, Volume 1, pp. 93–342.

Dyce, Alexander. "Memoir of Pope." In *The Poetical Works of Alexander Pope*. Boston: Little, Brown, 1859.

Gosse, Edmund. *From Shakespeare to Pope.* Cambridge: Cambridge University Press, 1885.

McLean, L. Mary. "The Riming System of Pope." *PMLA* 6 (1891): 134–60.

Mason, William. *Musaeus: A Monody to the Memory of Mr. Pope.* London: R. Dodsley, 1747.

Mayor, J. B. "Pope's *Essay on Man*." *Contemporary Review* 14 (1870): 115–24.

Pattison, Mark. "Pope and His Editors." In *Essays.* Ed. Henry Nettleship. Oxford: Clarendon Press, 1889, Volume 2, pp. 350–95.

Ruffhead, Owen. *The Life of Alexander Pope, Esq.* London: C. Bathurst, 1769.

Theobald, Lewis. *Shakespeare Restored.* London: R. Francklin, 1726.

Wakefield, Gilbert. *Observations on Pope.* London: A. Hamilton, 1796.

Ward, Edward. *Durgen; or, A Plain Satyr upon a Pompous Satyrist.* London: T. Warner, 1729.

Williams, A. M. "Pope." *Gentleman's Magazine* 279 (1895): 361–75.

JONATHAN SWIFT

Barrett, J. *An Essay on the Earlier Part of the Life of Swift.* London: J. Johnson, 1808.

Craik, Henry. *The Life of Jonathan Swift.* London: John Murray, 1882.

Dilworth, W. H. *The Life of Dr. Jonathan Swift.* London: G. Wright, 1758.

Dobson, Austin. "The Journal to Stella." In *Eighteenth Century Vignettes.* London: Chatto & Windus, 1894.

Forster, John. *The Life of Jonathan Swift.* London: John Murray, 1875.

Mitford, John. "Life of Swift." In *The Poetical Works of Jonathan Swift.* London: W. Pickering, 1833, Volume 1, pp. ix–cxiv.

Moriarty, Gerald P. *Dean Swift and His Writings.* New York: Scribner's, 1899.

Oliphant, Margaret. "The Author of *Gulliver*." *Century Magazine* 46 (1893): 401–18.

Sheridan, Thomas. *The Life of the Rev. Dr. Jonathan Swift.* London: J. E. & C. Rivington, 1757.

Smith, George Barnett. "Dean Swift." *International Review* 3 (1876): 306–16.

Wilde, W. R. *The Closing Years of Swift's Life.* Dublin: Hodges & Smith, 1849.

HENRY FIELDING

Aitken, G. A. "Henry Fielding." *Athenaeum*, 1 February 1890, p. 149.

Dobson, Austin. "Fresh Facts about Fielding." *Macmillan's Magazine* 2 (1907): 417–22.

Henley, W. E. "An Essay on the Life, Genius and Achievement of Henry Fielding." In *The Complete Works of Henry Fielding, Esq.* London: Heinemann, 1903.

Herbert, David. "Memoir." In *The Writings of Henry Fielding.* Edinburgh: W. P. Nimmo, 1872.

Jeaffreson, John Cordy. *Novels and Novelists.* London: Hurst & Blackett, 1858, Volume 1, pp. 91–117.

Lawrence, Frederick. *The Life of Henry Fielding.* London: A. Hall, Virtue, 1855.

Maynadier, G. H. "Introduction" to *The Works of Henry Fielding.* London: Gay & Bird, 1903.

Moriarty, G. P. "The Political World of Fielding and Smollett." *Macmillan's Magazine* 69 (1894): 215–21.

Patmore, Coventry. "Fielding and Thackeray." *North British Review* 24 (1855): 197–216.

Raleigh, Walter. *The English Novel.* New York: Scribner's, 1894, pp. 162–79.

Smith, George Barnett. "Henry Fielding." In *Poets and Novelists.* London: Simon, Elder, 1875, pp. 252–306.

Watson, William. "The Life of Henry Fielding." In *Select Works of Henry Fielding.* Edinburgh: Mundell, Doig, & Stevenson, 1807, Volume 1, pp. 7–176.

LAURENCE STERNE

Baker, Thomas Stockman. "The Influence of Laurence Sterne upon German Literature." *Americana Germanica* 2, No. 4 (1899): 41–56.

Carey, Mathew. "Remarks on the Charge of Plagiarism Alleged against Sterne." In *Miscellaneous Essays.* Philadelphia: Carey & Hart, 1830, pp. 438–46.

Cross, Wilbur L. *The Life and Times of Sterne.* New York: Macmillan, 1909.

Ferriar, John. *Illustrations of Sterne.* London: Cadell & Davies, 1798.

Fitzgerald, Percy. *The Life of Laurence Sterne.* London: Chapman & Hall, 1864.

Hill, Adams Sherman. "Laurence Sterne." *North American Review* 107 (1868): 1–37.

Howes, Alan B. *Yorick and the Critics: Sterne's Reputation in England, 1760–1868.* New Haven: Yale University Press, 1958.

Jeaffreson, John Cordy. *Novels and Novelists.* London: Hurst & Blackett, 1858, Volume 1, pp. 180–222.

Mudford, William. "Critical Observation upon *Tristram Shandy* and the *Sentimental Journey*." In *The British Novelists.* London: W. Clarke & Goddard, 1811, Volume 3, pp. 1–8.

Traill, H. D. *Sterne.* London: Macmillan, 1882.

Whyte, D. *The Fallacy of French Freedom and Dangerous Tendency of Sterne's Writings.* London: J. Hatchard, 1799.

Woolf, Virginia. "Sterne." *Times Literary Supplement*, 12 August 1909, pp. 289–90.

THOMAS GRAY

Courthope, William John. "Wordsworth and Gray." *Quarterly Review* 141 (1876): 104–36.

Gosse, Edmund. *Gray.* London: Macmillan, 1882.

Lounsbury, Thomas R. "Gray's Works." *Nation*, 5 March 1885, pp. 204–6.

Mason, William. *The Poems of Mr. Gray, To Which Are Prefixed Memoirs of His Life and Writings.* York: A. Ward, 1775.

Mitford, John. "The Life of Thomas Gray, Esq." In *The Poems of Thomas Gray.* London: White, Cochrane, 1814, pp. i–lxxiv.

Perry, Thomas S. "Gray, Collins, and Beattie." *Atlantic* 46 (December 1880): 810–17.

Scott, John. "On Gray's Church-Yard Elegy." In *Critical Essays on Some of the Poems, of Several English Poets.* London: James Phillips, 1785, pp. 185–246.

Shelley, Henry C. "The Birthplace of Gray's *Elegy*." *New England Magazine* 18 (1898): 665–73.

Tindal, W. *Remarks on Dr. Johnson's Life and Critical Observations on the Works of Mr. Gray.* London: J. Fielding, 1782.

Warren, Thomas H. "Gray and Dante." *Monthly Review* 3 (1901): 147–64.

Whitaker, Thomas D. "Thomas Gray." *Quarterly Review* 11 (1814): 304–18.

TOBIAS SMOLLETT

Boucé, Paul Gabriel. "Smollett Criticism, 1770–1924: Corrections and Additions." *Notes and Queries* 14 (1967): 184–87.

Chambers, Robert. *Smollett: His Life and a Selection of His Writings*. London: W. & R. Chambers, 1867.

Cordasco, Francesco. *Smollett Criticism, 1770–1924: A Bibliography Enumerative and Annotative*. Southampton: Long Island University Press, 1948.

Griffiths, Ralph. Review of *The Adventures of Ferdinand Count Fathom*. *Monthly Review* 8 (1753): 203–14.

_____. "Smollett's Translation of *Don Quixote*." *Monthly Review* 13 (1755): 196–202.

Hannay, David. *Life of Tobias George Smollett*. London: Walter Scott, 1887.

Hannay, James. "Tobias Smollett." *Quarterly Review* 103 (1858): 66–108.

Hawkesworth, John. Review of *The History and Adventures of Atom*. *Monthly Review* 40 (1769): 443–55.

Jeaffreson, John Cordy. *Novels and Novelists*. London: Hurst & Blackett, 1858, Volume 1, pp. 148–79.

Moore, John. "The Life of T. Smollett, M.D." In *The Works of Tobias Smollett*. London: B. Law, 1797.

Moriarty, G. P. "The Political World of Fielding and Smollett." *Macmillan's Magazine* 69 (1894): 215–21.

Ruffhead, Owen. "Smollett's *History of England*, Volume 4." *Monthly Review* 18 (1758): 289–305.

Seccombe, Thomas. "Smelfungus Goes South." *Cornhill Magazine* 11 (1901): 192–210.

OLIVER GOLDSMITH

Aikin, John. "A Critical Dissertation." In *The Poetical Works of Oliver Goldsmith*. London, 1796.

De Quincey, Thomas. "Oliver Goldsmith." In *Collected Writings*. Ed. David Masson. London: A. & C. Black, 1890, Volume 4, pp. 288–322.

Dobson, Austin. *Life of Oliver Goldsmith*. London: Walter Scott, 1888.

_____. "Oliver Goldsmith." In *English Prose*, ed. Henry Craik. London: Macmillan, 1895, Volume 4, pp. 345–49.

Forster, John. *The Life and Times of Oliver Goldsmith*. London: Bradbury & Evans, 1854.

Hawes, William. *An Account of the Late Dr. Oliver Goldsmith's Illness*. London: W. Brown & H. Gardner, 1774.

Kirkland, C. M. "Irving's *Life of Goldsmith*." *North American Review* 70 (1850): 265–89.

Mitford, John. "Life of Goldsmith." In *The Poetical Works of Oliver Goldsmith*. London: W. Pickering, 1831, pp. vii–xviii.

Towle, George M. "Oliver Goldsmith." *Appleton's Journal* 11 (1874): 459–62.

DAVID HUME

Albee, Ernest. "Hume's Ethical System." *Philosophical Review* 6 (1897): 337–55.

Bain, Alexander. *Moral Science*. New York: D. Appleton & Co., 1869.

Bisset, Andrew. "Hume." In *Essays on Historical Truth*. London: Longmans, 1871.

Burton, John Hill. *The Life and Correspondence of David Hume*. Edinburgh: W. Tait, 1846. 2 vols.

Calderwood, Henry. *David Hume*. London: Oliphant, Anderson & Ferrier, 1898.

Morris, George S. "David Hume." In *British Thought and Thinkers*. Chicago: S. C. Griggs, 1880.

Orr, J. *David Hume and His Influence on Philosophy and Theology*. Edinburgh: T. & T. Clark, 1903.

Pratt, S. J. *An Apology for the Life and Writings of David Hume, Esq.* London: Fielding & Walker, 1777.

Ritchie, Thomas Edward. *An Account of the Life and Writings of David Hume, Esq.* London: T. Cadell & W. Davies, 1807.

Taylor, W. C. "The Philosophy of David Hume." *Bentley's Miscellany* 19 (1846): 494–502.

Warburton, William, and Richard Hurd. *Remarks on Mr. David Hume's Essay on the Natural History of Religion*. London: W. Cooper, 1757.

SAMUEL JOHNSON

Birrell, Augustine. "Do We Really Know Dr. Johnson?" *Outlook* 69 (1901): 906–15.

Burroughs, John. "Dr. Johnson and Carlyle." *Critic*, 2 January 1886, pp. 1–2.

Chalmers, Alexander. "The Character of Dr. Johnson." *Gentleman's Magazine* 58 (1788): 300–303.

Cooke, William. *The Life of Samuel Johnson*. London: Kearsley, 1785.

Craig, W. H. *Dr. Johnson and the Fair Sex*. London: Sampson Low, Marston, 1895.

Elwin, Whitwell. "The Early Life of Samuel Johnson." *Quarterly Review* 102 (1858): 279–328.

Grant, Frederick Richard Charles. *Samuel Johnson*. London: Walter Scott, 1887.

Hill, George Birkbeck. *Dr. Johnson: His Friends and His Critics*. London: Smith, Elder, 1878.

Mason, Edward T. *Johnson: His Words and His Ways*. New York: Harper & Brothers, 1879.

Massingham, H. W. "Some Johnsonian Characteristics." *Gentleman's Magazine* 268 (1890): 155–64.

Mudford, William. *A Critical Enquiry into the Moral Writings of Dr. Samuel Johnson*. London: Cobbett & Morgan, 1802.

Murphy, Arthur. *An Essay on the Life and Genius of Samuel Johnson*. London: Longmans, 1792.

Sargeaunt, John. "Dr. Johnson's Politics." *Bookman* (New York) 6 (1898): 420–22.

Seccombe, Thomas. *The Age of Johnson*. London: George Bell, 1899.

EDWARD GIBBON

Bailey, J. C. "The Man Gibbon." *Fortnightly Review* 67 (1897): 441–55.

Brougham, Henry, Lord. "Gibbon." In *Lives of Men of Letters and Science Who Flourished in the Time of George III*. London: C. Knight, 1845–46.

Browne, Edward Gaylord. "Autobiography and Letters of Edward Gibbon." *American Historical Review* 2 (1897): 727–29.

Holden, R. "Gibbon as a Soldier." *Macmillan's Magazine* 71 (1895): 31–38.

Howells, W. D. "Edward Gibbon." *Atlantic* 41 (1878): 99–111.

Morison, James Cotter. *Gibbon*. London: Macmillan, 1878.

Paul, Herbert. "Gibbon's Life and Letters." *Nineteenth Century* 41 (1897): 293–310.

Proceedings of the Gibbon Commemoration 1794–1894. London: Longmans, 1895.

Rae, W. F. "Gibbon's Library." *Athenaeum*, 5 June 1897, pp. 744–45.

Whitaker, T. D. "Gibbon's Miscellaneous Works." *Quarterly Review* 12 (1815): 368–91.

ROBERT BURNS

Chambers, Robert. "The Character and Genius of Burns." In *The Life and Works of Robert Burns*. Edinburgh: W. & R. Chambers, 1851–52.

Cunningham, Allan. "Robert Burns and Lord Byron." *London Magazine* 10 (1824): 117–22.

Henderson, Thomas F. *Robert Burns*. London: Methuen, 1904.

Heron, Robert. "A Memoir of the Life of the Late Robert Burns." In *Poems, Chiefly in the Scottish Dialect*. Belfast: W. Magee, 1803.

Hogg, James. "Memoir of Burns." In *The Works of Robert Burns*. Glasgow: A. Fullarton, 1841.

Jeffrey, Francis, Lord. *"Reliques of Burns." Edinburgh Review* 13 (1809): 249–76.

Kingsley, Charles. "Burns and His School." In *Literary and General Lectures and Essays*. London: Macmillan, 1880.

Lockhart, Robert M. "Mr. Henley and Highland Mary." *Westminster Review* 149 (1898): 332–36.

Myers, Willard L. "The Influence of Fergusson on Burns." *Sewanee Review* 13 (1905): 61–70.

Peterkin, Alexander. "Life of Burns, with a Criticism of His Writings." In *The Life and Works of Robert Burns*. Edinburgh: Macredie, Skelly, & Muckersy, 1815.

Ross, John D. *Burnsiana: A Collection of Literary Odds and Ends Relating to Robert Burns*. London: A. Gardner, 1892–95.

———, ed. *Henley and Burns; or, The Critic Censured: Being a Collection of Papers Replying to an Offensive Critique on the Life, Genius, and Achievement of the Scottish Poet*. Stirling, Scotland: E. Mackay, 1901.

Sime, James. "Robert Burns." *English Illustrated Magazine* 4 (1887): 330–39.

Tyler, Samuel. *Robert Burns: As a Poet and as a Man*. Dublin: James McGlashan, 1849.

Walker, Josiah. *An Account of the Life and Character of Robert Burns*. Edinburgh: J. Moir, 1811.

Wilson, John. *Burns and His Poetry: An Essay on His Life and Genius*. Philadelphia: W. P. Hazard, 1854.

RICHARD BRINSLEY SHERIDAN

Brougham, Henry, Lord. *Historical Sketches of Statesmen Who Flourished in the Time of George III*. London: C. Knight, 1839.

Fitzgerald, Percy. *Lives of the Sheridans*. London: Bentley, 1886. 2 vols.

———. *The Real Sheridan*. London: Francis J. Griffiths, 1897.

Green, Emanual. *Linley, Sheridan and Mathews at Bath*. Bath: Privately printed, 1903.

Jerrold, Walter. *Bon-Mots of Sydney Smith and R. Brinsley Sheridan*. London: J. M. Dent, 1893.

Lefanu, Alicia. *Memoirs of Mrs. Frances Sheridan, with Remarks upon a Late Life of R. B. Sheridan*. London: G. & W. B. Whittaker, 1824.

Lytton, Edward Bulwer-Lytton, Lord. *Caxtoniana: A Series of Essays on Life, Literature and Manners*. Edinburgh: William Blackwood, 1863.

Sheridaniana: His Table Talk and Bon-Mots. London: Henry Colburn, 1826.

Sichel, Walter. *Sheridan*. Boston: Houghton Mifflin, 1909. 2 vols.

Smyth, William. *Memoirs of Mr. Sheridan*. Leeds: J. Cross, 1840.